A Concordance to the Poems of
BEN JONSON

THE CORNELL CONCORDANCES

S. M. Parrish, *General Editor*

Supervisory Committee

M. H. Abrams
Donald D. Eddy
Ephim Fogel
Alain Seznec

POEMS OF MATTHEW ARNOLD, *edited by S. M. Parrish* (Out of Print)
POEMS OF W. B. YEATS, *edited by S. M. Parrish*
POEMS OF EMILY DICKINSON, *edited by S. P. Rosenbaum*
WRITINGS OF WILLIAM BLAKE, *edited by David V. Erdman*
BYRON'S *DON JUAN, edited by C. W. Hagelman, Jr., and R. J. Barnes*
THÉÂTRE ET POÉSIES DE JEAN RACINE, *edited by Bryant C. Freeman*
BEOWULF, *edited by J. B. Bessinger, Jr.*
PLAYS OF W. B. YEATS, *edited by Eric Domville*
POEMS OF JONATHAN SWIFT, *edited by Michael Shinagel*
PLAYS OF WILLIAM CONGREVE, *edited by David Mann*
POEMS OF SAMUEL JOHNSON, *edited by Helen Naugle*
FABLES AND TALES OF JEAN DE LA FONTAINE, *edited by J. Allen Tyler*
POEMS OF OSIP MANDELSTAM, *edited by Demetrius J. Koubourlis*
POEMS OF SIR PHILIP SIDNEY, *edited by Herbert S. Donow*
PLAYS AND POEMS OF FEDERICO GARCÍA LORCA, *edited by Alice M. Pollin*
PASCAL'S *PENSÉES, edited by Hugh M. Davidson and Pierre H. Dubé*
COMPLETE WRITINGS OF GEORGE HERBERT, *edited by Mario A. Di Cesare and Rigo Mignani*
THE ANGLO-SAXON POETIC RECORDS, *edited by J. B. Bessinger, Jr.*
POEMS OF BEN JONSON, *edited by Mario A. Di Cesare and Ephim Fogel*

A Concordance to the Poems of

BEN JONSON

Edited by

MARIO A. DI CESARE

and

EPHIM FOGEL

Cornell University Press

ITHACA AND LONDON

First published 1978 by Cornell University Press.
Published in the United Kingdom by Cornell University Press Ltd., 2–4 Brook Street, London W1Y 1AA.

International Standard Book Number 0–8014–1217–X
Library of Congress Catalog Card Number 78–59630
Printed in the United States of America
Librarians: Library of Congress cataloging information appears on the last page of the book.

CONTENTS

Preface   vii

Abbreviations   xvii

Concordance to the Poems of Ben Jonson   1

Appendixes

    Index Words, Ordered by Frequency   835

    Index Words, in Alphabetical Order   859

    Compound Words, in Alphabetical Order   867

        Ordered by Second Element   869

        Ordered by Third Element   871

    Words Containing Apostrophes, in Alphabetical Order   873

        Ordered by Second Element   877

    Homographs   881

PREFACE

Pure and neat language I love,
yet plaine and customary.

—Jonson, *Discoveries*

In the 1580's, notes J. V. Cunningham, English poets developed a "new plain style, modeled on the plain style of Latin Antiquity. In this the innovator was Sidney, [as the] many passages in *Astrophil and Stella* in a fully accomplished plain style" attest. That style, Cunningham continues, "was recognized and imitated by Campian and Donne, and perfected by Jonson. . . . It became the central style of English Poetry."[1] Even those who may not follow Cunningham through all the details of his argument will recognize the centrality of Sidney, Donne, and Jonson in the evolution of one of the major modes of Elizabethan and, later, Anglo-American poetic style. The impact of Jonson's style in particular —lean and sinewy, rugged and vehement, sober and unaffected, unyielding in the integrity of its diction and syntax—may be felt in modern poets as diverse as Yeats, Robinson, Frost, and Auden, not to mention such spare poets as Winters and Cunningham himself. And of course that impact began to be felt in Jonson's own lifetime: witness the reverence of Jacobean and Caroline "Sons of Ben" for the person and poetic example of their master. Through them and through his own fondness for the heroic couplet and the taut, subtly alliterated antithesis ("Or crafty Malice, might pretend this praise,/And thinke to ruine, where it seem'd to raise"), Jonson bequeathed a legacy to Augustan poetry, just as his fondness for "fitting to metrical arrangement a selection of the real language of men" provided one among several examples for those nineteenth-century poets who rebelled against the affected diction of the followers of Dryden, Pope, and Samuel Johnson. Few English poets have had a more enduring or more salutary influence.

There are of course different levels of style in Jonson, with effects different from those implied by such adjectives as "rugged" and "vehement." Jonson is also the master of words for music, of mellifluous melodies and delicate nuances of rhythm. He is the artificer of predications with the sense intricately drawn out from line to line. He sometimes divides a single word between two lines ("twi-/ Lights") or a proper name between two stanzas ("*Ben*/[*The Stand*] *Johnson*"). His linguistic effects and tonalities are indeed as various as genre, occasion, addressee, and emotion require. From panegyric to pasquinade, from epigram to epithalamium and funeral elegy, from the formal and the ceremonial to the famil-

---

1. *The Renaissance in England,* ed. J. V. Cunningham (New York, 1966), pp. xlii–xliii.

vii

iar and heartfelt, he is the commander of the word that suffices and the answerable style. Moreover, Jonson had the distinction—rare among poets of the early periods—of trying to make sure that his words emerged in print in the exact form favored by his theories. Certain about the importance of elision, compounding, and other forms of syntax, he exercised great care over the graphic presentation of his words. Here, then, is a potentially rich harvest for both the makers and the users of concordances.

Of the three major poets mentioned by Cunningham, Donne has had his concordance for almost four decades. Concordance-makers are dependent on scholarly editors: the Donne concordance came first because Sir Herbert Grierson's splendid edition of the poems was published early in the present century,[2] while the Sidney and Jonson concordances had to wait until the magisterial editions of William Ringler and of C. H. Herford and Percy and Evelyn Simpson appeared in the middle of the century.[3] Some observations on the relation of the present concordance to the Herford and Simpson edition are in order.

Scope of the Concordance

With some exceptions explained below, this is a concordance to the poems identified as Jonson's in Volume VIII of Herford and Simpson; specifically, we have followed the text of Volume VIII reprinted lithographically in 1954 from corrected sheets of the first edition of that volume (1947). Accordingly, we have excluded the poems and songs in the plays, masques, and entertainments, printed in earlier volumes of Herford and Simpson. We regret the resulting omission of various familiar lyrics. But Jonson's dramatic and quasi-dramatic works will no doubt have their own concordances in due course, and any other plan—such as selecting the most "memorable" lyrics in those works—would inevitably have been arbitrary and moot. We have not included several poems that appear to us to be authentic although they were rejected by Herford and Simpson, such as those in the appendix to Robert Chester's *Loves Martyr* signed by "Chorus Vatum" but not collected by Jonson in his *Workes* of 1616 or in the posthumous second volume of the *Workes* of 1640. A concordance, after all, is not a forum for advancing new arguments about a canon.

Where previous arguments, however, have defined a consensus tending to reject poems included by Herford and Simpson with Jonson's, we have omitted those poems: "An Elegie" (p. 194), probably written by Donne; "Faire friend, 'tis true, your beauties move" (p. 265), probably by Sidney Godolphin; "On the Kings Birth-day" (p. 267), probably by Sir Henry Wotton; and the dubiously ascribed "Truth is the triall of it selfe" (p. 393). We have omitted also all the "Poems ascribed to Jonson" (pp. 424–452); all non-English material, such as the Latin verses and Latin and Greek tag lines (but not individual words incorporated in text or title); and all prose, such as the prefatory material to the *Epigrams* or

2. *The Poems of John Donne* (2 vols.; Oxford, 1912).
3. Ringler, *The Poems of Sir Philip Sidney* (Oxford, 1962); Herford and Simpson, *Ben Jonson* (11 vols.; Oxford, 1925–1952).

the *Underwood* or the prose incorporated with the "Epitaph" on Cecilia Bulstrode (p. 372) or with the Coryat poems (pp. 374ff.).

Certain texts that Herford and Simpson print in the body of their work we have treated as variants: the Phillips manuscript version of the "Triumph" of Charis (pp. 135f.); the earlier version of Jonson's Horace (pp. 338–355); and the Rawlinson manuscript version of "A Grace" (p. 419). Especially in the *Art of Poetry*, this editorial decision has obviated extensive duplication; most of that long poem is substantially the same in both versions.

Variants

Variant readings in the poems of Ben Jonson present a larger problem to the concordance-maker than do the variants in, say, Sidney or Yeats. Ringler has shown that almost all of the quarto variants in *Astrophil and Stella*, for example, are corruptions. (The text, Mona Wilson quipped, must have been conveyed by the likes of Snug the joiner.) Moreover, Ringler believes that with few exceptions ("What tongue can her perfections tell" is a notable one) Sidney seldom revised a poem once he had arrived at a version for fair copying. A modern example appears in the variants in the printed texts of Yeats's poems. The Allt and Alspach Variorum Edition of the poems facilitates the separation of misprints from genuine authorial variants, and few are likely to quarrel with Stephen Parrish's choices in the Yeats concordance. But the printed variants in the Herford and Simpson *Jonson* are relatively undramatic; we don't recall any printer's error which produced so interesting a transposition as "soldier Aristotle" for the correct "solider Aristotle" in Yeats's "Among School Children." Apart from a limited number of printed variants, chiefly from the Benson quarto and duodecimo editions of miscellaneous works by Jonson (1640), our task has been to separate probably authorial from probably nonauthorial variants in the manuscript versions of Jonson's poems. In this, we have again had to follow the lead of Herford and Simpson. Without the editors' massive collation of manuscript variants, we should not have been able to proceed at all. But in the absence of a genealogy of manuscripts derived from presumed Jonsonian archetypes and of estimated percentages of error in particular manuscripts (such as Ringler provides in his Sidney), we have had to proceed selectively. (The absence of stemmata and related editorial aids is, of course, understandable; the editors were engaged with the Jonson corpus, primarily dramatic, for several decades, and the work on Volume VIII went on during the war years, when manuscripts were dispersed for purposes of preservation and were not available for final consultation and assessment.)

Where Herford and Simpson clearly designate the authority of variants, we have followed them. We have included variants from the following:

—four holograph manuscripts, including original copies of Epigrams xliii and lxiii (in the Cecil Papers at Hatfield); the autograph of Epigram xci (at the British Library); and of Underwood xxv (at Christ Church, Oxford).

—Rawlinson Poetry MS 31 (Bodleian Library) and the Newcastle MS (British Library, Harleian MS 4955), which contain first drafts of numerous poems;

—early published texts;

 —the Drummond texts of Underwood viii and ix;

 —manuscript versions designated by Herford and Simpson as first drafts or early drafts (pp. 8ff.), particularly the early versions of the "Execration upon Vulcan."

For this last poem, we have also included such variants from Benson's quarto and duodecimo editions as clearly indicate another state of the text. (On the other hand, we are fully aware, as W. D. Briggs [*Anglia,* XXXVII] and Herford and Simpson warn, that the antecedents of Benson's two editions are often questionable.)

To go much further would have been hazardous. Herford and Simpson provide only limited information about the manuscripts. Though they list some holographs and name some first drafts or early drafts, and refer (in passing) to some manuscripts as "bad" texts, they do not describe most of the manuscripts at all, nor do they state plainly which of these they regard as preserving authorial variants, which as not. Lacking adequate guidance, we had to conclude that to adopt a latitudinarian attitude toward all manuscript variants would inevitably clog this concordance with many scribal contaminations.

All students of Jonson's text are aware, of course, that Jonson often put a poem into circulation before it had crystallized into final form. He sent his epitaph on Cecilia Bulstrode to his friend George Garrard with the comment that he had written it "streightned with time," and that his invention had "not cooled so much to judge" (VIII, 372); and he made some substantive changes between the earlier holograph version and the later printed version of Epigram xliii. But despite sometimes excited speculations, we could not offer as authentic variants the readings from manuscripts that Herford and Simpson do not characterize at all. To be sure, we were often tempted to include some variants when they made good sense and seemed technically sound: consider the printed version of Epigram v and the manuscript version (from Rawlinson Poetry 160, Bodleian Library, RP 9):

On the Union
When was there contract better driven by *Fate?*
Or celebrated with more truth of state?
The world the temple was, the priest a king,
 The spoused paire two realmes, the sea the ring.

On the Union
Was ever contract driven by better *Fate?*
Or solemnized with more Royall state?
The world the temple is, the priest the king,
 The married paire two realmes, the sea the ring.

The second (manuscript) version could represent an earlier draft by the poet himself, written at the time of the Union (note the present tense in line 3) and later revised (and, we think, improved). Or it could represent unauthorized variations on an original represented by the printed text. Such unauthorized variations occur frequently in transmission, and the RP 9 variants are not beyond the reach of a connoisseur of poetry with a reasonably good ear. Which of these possibilities

is more likely to be fact? We cannot be sure. But we are sure of one thing: in the absence of an analytic description and evaluation of RP 9 or of an editorial statement about the authority of these particular variants, we cannot conclude that the variants are Jonson's. Hence we have excluded them. Readers who disagree with our decision may consider Selden's comment to Jonson, which we here adapt: "Your curious learning and judgement may correct where [we] have erred, and adde where [our] notes and memory have left [us] short."[4]

NOTES FOR USERS

Text

In preparing the text for indexing, we have included complete titles (except, of course, for titles editorially imposed on the inscriptions, pp. 662 and 666). We have expanded the refrain of "A New-yeares-Gift" (p. 265), since *&c* was a typographical device used to save space. We have omitted prose materials, Latin tags, all rubrics, and marginalia. We have ignored the angle brackets that Herford and Simpson used for varying purposes.

Our basic intention has been to adhere to old spelling, with few specific modifications. We have silently adjusted the *v/u* and *i/j* exchanges throughout. Our typography could not accommodate diacritical marks or ligatures; these are omitted. Superscripts—those "*Syllabes* . . . often compendiously and shortly written," as Jonson put it in the *English Grammar* (VIII, 500)—are normalized: S^r becomes *Sir,* y^e = *the,* W^th = *with,* y^t = *that,* etc. The few Greek words in the text are transliterated simply. In several poems among the *Ungathered Verse* which Herford and Simpson transcribed from manuscripts, we have converted initial *ff* to *F* (or, in a few obvious cases, *f*). We have ignored printer's or poet's usage of italics and of presenting some words completely in upper case.

Otherwise, we have not intervened, not even to regularize plain inconsistencies —as, for example, when Jonson, usually so fond of compounding, deliberately and consistently writes "to day," "to morrow," "to night" (see the opening and closing phrases of Epigram ci or lines 9-10 of Epigram cii, or lines 15, 18, and 21 of the Charis poem, "Clayming a second kisse by Desert").

Order, Format

We have followed the order of Herford and Simpson's edition. When an index word occurs more than once in a given line, the line is printed only once. The columns on the right list page number, short title, and line number; for variant readings, the symbol V precedes the line number.

Individual variants follow text order. For the *Art of Poetry,* special considerations apply. When Jonson revised his translation of the *Ars poetica,* he adopted the 1610 Latin text edited by Daniel Heinsius, who had reordered Horace's poem to produce what he regarded as a more logical sequence. Hence there are signif-

---

4. John Selden, *Titles of Honor,* second edition (1631), p. 412, as cited in Herford and Simpson, XI, 57.

icant differences in lineation between the two versions (as William B. Hunter makes clear by printing the texts on facing pages in his 1963 edition). Whenever the lineation of variant lines differs, we have given both line numbers, separated by a slash.

The context is always the line of poetry. In a few instances, however, the indexed word exists on two lines, since Jonson divided the word at the end of a line, for special effects. The instances are: clowd-/Like (straddling lines 60–61 of "Epistle to a Friend," p. 164); Hill-/foot (183–184 of "Vulcan," p. 211); twi-/Lights (92–93 of the "Ode," p. 246); bor-/Dring (20–21 of the *Art of Poetry*, p. 305); ill-/Natur'd (264–265 of the *Art of Poetry*, p. 317). In all these, we have treated the split words as compounds and have provided both preceding and succeeding line contexts.

The short titles of Jonson's poems in his *Epigrams, Forest,* and *Underwood* are prefixed by E, F, or U and the traditional number. Following this preface, an alphabetical list of all short titles is provided, with corresponding full titles or first lines as well as the page numbers to three important editions besides Herford and Simpson's: William B. Hunter, *The Complete Poetry of Ben Jonson* (New York, 1963); George A. E. Parfitt, *Ben Jonson: The Complete Poems* (Harmondsworth, Middlesex, 1975); and Ian Donaldson, *Ben Jonson: Poems* (Oxford, 1975).

The Entries

1. *Alphabetization.* Our alphabet begins, properly, with the letter A, not with the apostrophe. The ampersand *&* is alphabetized as *and.* In most cases, we have adjusted or ignored apostrophes in alphabetizing, so that elided forms or their parts are listed in their proper places. Thus *he's,* indexed three times (as *he', he's,* and *'s*), is alphabetized next to, or as, *he, he's,* and *is.*

2. *Omissions.* In canons of moderate size, such as Jonson's, one need not restrict the usefulness of concordances for many kinds of linguistic study by omitting large numbers of so-called nonsignificant words. Accordingly, we have omitted only three high-frequency words: *a* (1097 occurrences), *and* (2610), and *the* (2581). We have, however, indexed the elided form *th'* and the ampersand *&* (as *and*).

3. *Apostrophes.* Jonson used the apostrophe freely but deliberately. In the *English Grammar* he called it the "Semicircle"—"an affection of words coupled, and joyned together" (VIII, 528), and placed it under "Syntax," as an important element in the "Construction of words," which the "learneder sort" used properly. He pointed out that Latin and Hebrew lack this useful device, and that Greek has only the limited kind in which "a Vowell is cast away" at the end of a word. On the other hand, the usage is frequent in "our common speech" on "which all Precepts are grounded"; such usage he defined as "Natures call," arguing that English has special syntactical advantages not only in the apostrophe and elision but in being able to join two words by apostrophe even without ellipsis of any vowel—as in *Diana'alone* or *too'unwieldie.* In his nondramatic verse, there are over one thousand forms containing apostrophes.

To provide as much scope as possible for the student of Jonson's deliberate syntax, we have treated the apostrophic forms very broadly. Forms that are con-

tractions of two words—*it's, th'Exchange*—we have listed three times, under the full form and under each of the component parts. Where one letter is elided in such a compound form (*'s, 't*), we have alphabetized the form next to the full form (*is, it*). But we have usually not intervened in the cases of contractions that involve more than one letter (except for *th'* as a contraction of *thou* or *they*) or that involve unusual or complex changes like metathesis (*o're*). To signal Jonson's usage, we have included the apostrophe in the separate indexing. Thus, for instance, *I'm* is entered as *I', I'm*, and *'m*. The apparent awkwardness of some of these—*I'* or *he'* or *who'*—is compensated, as inspection of *I'* will show; at a glance, one finds nine different combinations: *I'le, I'have, I'am, I'had, I'ld, I'm, I'ad, I'll, I'me*.

We have listed all forms containing apostrophes in an appendix (p. 873); there, the forms are alphabetized first in the usual fashion, but then in a special list (p. 877) the forms are ordered by the element that follows the apostrophe. This latter list brings together the varieties of *'s* and the words in which silent *e* in preterite forms is elided.

4. *Compound Words.* In the "composition" of compound words, said Jonson, "our *English* tongue is above all other very hardy, and happy; joyning together, after a most eloquent manner, sundry words of every kind of Speech" (VIII, 504). Where compound words are joined by hyphens, we have listed the words several times—under the full compound and under each component element. Since Jonson uses almost five hundred such forms in his poems, we have also listed them all together alphabetically (p. 867) and as ordered by the second element (p. 869) and by the third (p. 871).

There are five special instances of hyphenation, listed above—words Jonson deliberately divided between two lines. We have given special treatment to these words, reuniting them artificially by a slash so that each portion is seen in full context. All are ordinary hyphenated compounds except for "bor-/Dring," which, in Jonson's view, also had an affinity with the action of a compound.

5. *Spelling and Cross References.* Except for the changes noted above (*i/j, u/v, ff/F* or *f*) and expansion of the "Syllabes" which "are often compendiously, and shortly written," we have not normalized orthography. Instead, we have provided cross references from the common modern spelling (or a seventeenth-century form hardly different from it) to the seventeenth-century spellings. The operative rule is usefulness. When the old spelling occurs alphabetically near where the modern spelling would be, and is easily recognizable, we have not made a cross reference. The cross reference is usually to the base or simple form (for example, singular of noun, infinitive of verb); other forms will be found easily enough in the general vicinity. There is no cross reference to *battaile*, for instance: the form is recognizable enough, is very near to where the modern *battle* would be, and is next to Jonson's *Battels*.

6. *Homographs.* Our criterion is the standard one: the two words must be different in both etymology and meaning. We have been accommodating, however, in matters of etymology, since such authorities as C. T. Onions's *Oxford Dictionary of English Etymology* (Oxford, 1966) and Ernest Klein's *A Comprehensive Etymological Dictionary of the English Language*, two volumes (New

York, 1966–1967), are not always clear or consistent in the distinctions they make or the lineage they trace. The decisions we have recorded (p. 881) are deliberate, though we recognize that others might reasonably make other choices.

Homographs are sometimes matters of orthography: *wast* may be the verb form, or it may be a variant spelling of *waste; sent* may mean *scent;* so also with *to/too* and *than/then.* We have searched many haystacks for elusive needles, sometimes in vain—as when we looked for the *if* among all the occurrences of *and,* the *deer* among all the examples of *doe* (= *do*), the *before* among all the *or's,* and the *own* among all the *one's.* Some homographs are concealed by orthography, while possible puns create ambiguities of their own. In "Proludium," line 11, "soules" is obviously a pun, but it is beyond the scope of this book to single out such literary devices. A different case involved deciphering Jonson's intention. In the variant of line 614 of Horace (p. 353), *sound,* Jonson obviously intended the meaning of *swoon*—as his revision demonstrates (p. 333), where he writes *swoune* (and alters the rime word from *ground* to *groun'*). The Latin original is *dicunt:*

> Ut qui conducti plorant in funere, dicunt,
> Et faciunt prope plura. . . .

[431 f.]

> As those that hir'd to weepe at Funeralls, swoune [*variant,* sound]
> Cry, and doe more. . . .

[614 f.]

7. *Variants.* Our guidelines for selecting variants are described above. In indexing variants, we have ignored orthographic changes and such pronominal changes as *ye/you, thy/thine, thy/your;* minor shifts of verbal or auxiliary forms, like *does/doth;* all variants that were originally *a, an, and, the;* interchanges of singular and plural in nouns (and corresponding verbs), but not in pronouns; and finally, changes limited to punctuation or word order. Our variants are mainly of two kinds—lines containing only one or two variant words, and lines that are substantially or completely different from corresponding lines in the final version. Where the variant word or words do not substantially modify the line itself, we have merely substituted the variant word or words and have not printed the entire manuscript version of the line; usually the other variations (of orthography or punctuation) are accidents of copyists rather than specific Jonsonian alternatives. Our method emphasizes the verbal variant while retaining the integral text; it provides, incidentally, that the substantive verbal variants appear every time a nonvariant word in the line is indexed. Finally, it also avoids the enormous clutter that would ensue from the inclusion of numerous divergent spellings and keeps to a minimum the number of false entries that might otherwise occur.

Appendixes

Our appendixes include lists of frequencies for Jonson's total poetic vocabulary and lists of words containing apostrophes, compound words, and homographs. The frequency lists are of two kinds—words listed by frequency (p. 835) and

words listed alphabetically (p. 859); the first is complete, whereas the alphabetical list includes only words of a frequency of three or more; one aim of this alphabetical list is to provide the user in a few pages with a conspectus of Jonson's vocabulary.

The lists of compound words and words containing apostrophes are ordered in several ways, as noted above: in normal alphabetical order; compound words by second element and by third element; words containing apostrophes by second element.

The concordance was programmed on an IBM 360, in COBOL, at the Computer Center, State University of New York at Binghamton. A tape of the complete text of Jonson's nondramatic poems from Volume VIII of Herford and Simpson (including the selected variants) is stored in the Rare Books Room of the Library of the State University of New York at Binghamton. Copies are available at cost to interested users.

ACKNOWLEDGMENTS

We wish to acknowledge with thanks a number of obligations contracted in the course of our work.

We are grateful to the Delegates of Oxford University Press for their kind permission to use the text of the poems provided in Volume VIII of the admirable edition of Jonson's complete works by C. H. Herford and Percy and Evelyn Simpson (1925–1952).

We owe a special debt of gratitude to the General Editor of the Cornell Concordances, Stephen Parrish. It was he who first proposed an old-spelling concordance to Jonson's poems; for a long time, before the pressure of other obligations compelled him to withdraw, he was co-editor with Ephim Fogel of the concordance-in-progress and supervised the key-punching and preliminary printouts of the text. It gives us great pleasure to acknowledge his continuing counsel, his hard work, and his good-humored patience. We are grateful as well for the advice and support of the members of the Supervisory Committee, M. H. Abrams, Donald D. Eddy, and Alain Seznec, and to former members of the Committee, W. R. Keast and the late Stephen Emerson Whicher. We are also indebted to Robert M. Adams and David Novarr. At an early stage, Fredson Bowers was kind enough to share with the Committee some of his thoughts on old-spelling concordances. Matthias Shaaber and Samuel Schoenbaum provided a forum, at the Modern Language Association, for the airing of preliminary thoughts on electronic computers and Elizabethan texts. Needless to say, none of these scholars is responsible for any errors in the present concordance; that responsibility is ours alone.

We are grateful for grants that helped to meet the costs of editing, key-punching, and programming. The National Endowment for the Humanities provided funds at an early important stage; at a later, crucial stage, funds were expeditiously provided by the State University of New York at Binghamton, from monies under the jurisdiction of Sheldon Grebstein, Dean of Arts and Sciences, and Arthur Smith, Provost for Graduate Studies and Research, and by the Humanities

Faculty Research Grants Committee of Cornell University, under the jurisdiction of Harry Levin, Dean of Arts and Sciences.

Our greatest debt is to Lea Ann Boone, our programmer, who brought to our project admirable care, insight, and skill, continually suggesting imaginative ways of eliciting new data from our text. Without her perseverance at tedious tasks and her unstinting dedication, the job would not now be finished.

MARIO A. DI CESARE

State University of New York at Binghamton

EPHIM FOGEL

Cornell University

ABBREVIATIONS

Short Title	Title/*first line*	H&S	WBH	ID	GP
Aleman	On the Author, Worke, and Translator. (*Who tracks this Authors, or Translators Pen,*)	389	370	306	262
Answer	This was Mr. Ben: Johnsons Answer of the suddayne.	418		337	344
Author	In Authorem. (*Thou, that wouldst finde the habit of true passion,*)	362	326	284	256
Author	To the Author. (*In Picture, they which truly understand,*)	370	346	292	257
Author	To his much and worthily esteemed friend the Author. (*Who takes thy volume to his vertuous hand,*)	383	362	301	260
Beaumont	On the honor'd Poems of his honored Friend, Sir John Beaumont, Baronet.	400	384	318	270
Bedford	Author ad Librum. (*Goe little Booke, Goe little Fable*)	662	333		256
Brome	To my old Faithfull Servant: and (by his continu'd Vertue) my loving Friend: the Author of this Work, M. Rich. Brome.	409	398	328	271
Brooke	To his friend the Author upon his Richard.	385	365	303	261
Browne	To my truly-belov'd Freind, Mr. Browne: on his Pastorals.	386	368	304	261
Cavendish	Charles Cavendish to his posteritie.	387	370	305	275
Censure	*Censure, not sharplye then, but mee advise*	421		340	342
Chapman	To my worthy and honour'd Friend, Mr George Chapman, on his Translation of Hesiods Works, & Dayes.	388	369	305	262
Coryat 1	*Here, like Arion, our Coryate doth draw*	374	357	296	343
Coryat 2	To the Right Noble Tom, Tell-Troth of his travailes, the Coryate of Odcombe, and his Booke now going to travell.	378	359	298	258
Coryat 3	Certaine Verses Written Upon Coryats Crudities, Which should Have beene Printed with the other Panegyricke lines, but then were upon some occasions omitted, and now communicated to the World.	379	360	298	258
Detractor	To my Detractor. (*My verses were commended, thou dar'st say.*)	408	397	327	
Door Apollo	Over the Door at the Entrance into the Apollo.	657	376	372	341

Short Title	Title/*first line*	H&S	WBH	ID	GP
Dover	An Epigram To My Joviall Good Freind Mr. Robert Dover, on his great Instauration of his Hunting, and Dauncing At Cotswold.	415	403	334	277
Drayton	The Vision Of Ben. Jonson, On The Muses Of His Friend M. Drayton.	396	379	313	267
E1 Reader	To the Reader.	27	4	7	35
E2 My Booke	To my Booke.	27	4	7	35
E3 Bookseller	To my Booke-seller.	27	5	8	35
E4 James 1	To King James.	28	5	8	36
E5 Union	On the Union.	28	6	9	36
E6 Alchymists	To Alchymists.	29	6	9	36
E7 Hot-house	On the new Hot-house.	29	6	10	36
E8 Robbery	On a robbery.	29	6	10	37
E9 To All	To all, to whom I write.	29	7	10	37
E10 Ignorant	To my lord Ignorant.	29	7	11	37
E11 Something	On Some-thing, that walkes some-where.	30	7	11	37
E12 Shift	On lieutenant Shift.	30	7	11	38
E13 Empirick	To doctor Empirick.	31	8	12	38
E14 Camden	To William Camden.	31	9	13	39
E15 Court-worm	On Court-worme.	31	9	13	39
E16 Brain-hardy	To Brayne-hardie.	32	9	14	39
E17 Critic	To the learned Critick.	32	10	14	40
E18 Censurer	To my meere English Censurer.	32	10	15	40
E19 Cod 1	On Sir Cod the perfumed.	33	11	15	40
E20 Cod 2	To the same Sir Cod.	33	11	15	40
E21 Gam'ster	On reformed Gam'ster.	33	11	16	41
E22 Daughter	On my first Daughter.	33	11	16	41
E23 Donne 1	To John Donne.	34	12	17	41
E24 Parliament	To the Parliament.	34	12	17	42
E25 Beast 1	On Sir Voluptuous Beast.	34	12	17	42
E26 Beast 2	On the same Beast.	35	13	18	42
E27 Roe 1	On Sir John Roe.	35	13	18	42
E28 Surly	On Don Surly.	35	13	19	43
E29 Tilter	To Sir Annual Tilter.	36	14	20	43
E30 Guiltie	To Person Guiltie.	36	14	20	44
E31 Banck	On Banck the Usurer.	36	15	20	44
E32 Roe 2	On Sir John Roe.	37	15	21	44
E33 Roe 3	To the same.	37	15	21	44
E34 Death	Of Death.	37	16	22	45
E35 James 2	To King James.	37	16	22	45
E36 Martial	To the Ghost of Martial.	38	16	22	45
E37 Chev'ril	On Chev'rill the Lawyer.	38	17	23	45
E38 Guiltie 2	To Person Guiltie.	38	17	23	46
E39 Colt	On Old Colt.	39	17	23	46
E40 Ratcliffe	On Margaret Ratcliffe.	39	18	24	46
E41 Gypsee	On Gypsee.	39	18	24	47
E42 Giles	On Giles and Jone.	40	18	25	47
E43 Salisbury 1	To Robert Earle of Salisburie.	40	19	25	47
E44 Chuff	On Chuffe, Bancks the Usurer's Kinsman.	41	20	26	48
E45 First Son	On my First Sonne.	41	20	26	48
E46 Luckless 1	To Sir Lucklesse Woo-all.	42	21	27	48
E47 Luckless 2	To the same.	42	21	27	49

Short Title	Title/*first line*	H&S	WBH	ID	GP
E48 Mungril	On Mungril Esquire.	42	21	28	49
E49 Playwrt 1	To Play-wright.	42	21	28	49
E50 Cod 3	To Sir Cod.	42	22	28	49
E51 James 3	To King James. Upon the happy false rumour of his death, the two and twentieth day of March, 1607.	43	22	29	50
E52 Courtling	To Censorious Courtling.	43	22	29	50
E53 Old-end	To Old-end Gatherer.	43	23	30	50
E54 Chev'ril 2	On Chev'ril.	44	23	30	51
E55 Beaumont	To Francis Beaumont.	44	23	30	51
E56 Poet-Ape	On Poet-Ape.	44	24	31	51
E57 Bawds	On Baudes, and Usurers.	45	24	31	52
E58 Groome	To Groome Ideot.	45	24	32	52
E59 Spies	On Spies.	45	25	32	52
E60 Mounteagle	To William Lord Mounteagle.	46	25	32	52
E61 Foole	To Foole, or Knave.	46	25	33	53
E62 Would-bee	To Fine Lady Would-bee.	46	26	33	53
E63 Salisbury 2	To Robert Earle of Salisburie.	47	26	34	53
E64 Salisbury 3	To the same.	47	27	34	54
E65 Muse	To my Muse.	48	27	35	54
E66 Cary	To Sir Henrie Cary.	48	28	36	55
E67 Suffolk	To Thomas Earle of Suffolke.	49	29	36	55
E68 Playwrt 2	On Play-wright.	49	29	37	56
E69 Cob	To Pertinax Cob.	50	29	37	56
E70 Wm Roe 1	To William Roe.	50	30	38	56
E71 Parrat	On Court-Parrat.	50	30	38	56
E72 Court-ling	To Court-ling.	50	30	38	57
E73 Fine Grand	To Fine Grand.	51	30	39	57
E74 Chancelor	To Thomas Lord Chancelor.	51	31	39	58
E75 Lippe	On Lippe, the Teacher.	52	32	40	58
E76 Bedford 1	On Lucy Countesse of Bedford.	52	32	40	58
E77 Not name	To one that desired me not to name him.	53	33	41	59
E78 Hornet	To Hornet.	53	33	41	59
E79 Rutland	To Elizabeth Countesse of Rutland.	53	33	42	59
E80 Life/Death	Of Life, and Death.	53	34	42	60
E81 Proule	To Proule the Plagiary.	54	34	43	60
E82 Surly	On Cashierd Capt. Surly.	54	34	43	60
E83 Friend	To a Friend.	54	35	43	60
E84 Bedford 2	To Lucy Countesse of Bedford.	54	35	43	61
E85 Goodyere 1	To Sir Henry Goodyere.	55	35	44	61
E86 Goodyere 2	To the same.	55	36	44	61
E87 Hazard	On Captaine Hazard the Cheater.	56	36	45	62
E88 Monsieur	On English Monsieur.	56	37	45	62
E89 Allen	To Edward Allen.	56	37	46	62
E90 Mill	On Mill my Ladies Woman.	57	38	46	63
E91 Vere	To Sir Horace Vere.	58	39	47	64
E92 New Crie	The new Crie.	58	39	48	64
E93 Radcliffe	To Sir John Radcliffe.	60	41	49	65
E94 Bedford 3	To Lucy, Countesse of Bedford, with Mr. Donnes Satyres.	60	42	50	66
E95 Savile	To Sir Henrie Savile.	61	42	51	66
E96 Donne 2	To John Donne.	62	44	52	67
E97 Motion	On the new Motion.	62	44	53	68

Short Title	Title/first line	H&S	WBH	ID	GP
E98 Th Roe 1	To Sir Thomas Roe.	63	45	54	69
E99 Th Roe 2	To the same.	63	45	54	69
E100 Playwrt 3	On Play-wright.	64	46	55	69
E101 Supper	Inviting a friend to supper.	64	46	55	70
E102 Pembroke	To William Earle of Pembroke.	66	48	57	71
E103 L Wroth 1	To Mary Lady Wroth.	66	49	57	71
E104 Montgomery	To Susan Countesse of Montgomery.	67	49	58	72
E105 L Wroth 2	To Mary Lady Wroth.	67	50	59	72
E106 E Herbert	To Sir Edward Herbert.	68	51	60	73
E107 Hungry	To Captayne Hungry.	68	51	60	73
E108 Soldiers	To true Souldiers.	69	53	62	74
E109 Nevil	To Sir Henry Nevil.	70	53	62	75
E110 Edmonds 1	To Clement Edmonds, on his Caesars Commentaries observed, and translated.	71	54	63	75
E111 Edmonds 2	To the same; On the same.	72	55	64	76
E112 Gamster	To a weake Gamster in Poetry.	72	55	64	77
E113 Overbury	To Sir Thomas Overbury.	73	56	65	77
E114 Sydney	To Mrs. Philip Sydney.	73	57	66	78
E115 Honest Man	On the Townes honest Man.	74	57	66	78
E116 Jephson	To Sir William Jephson.	75	58	68	79
E117 Groyne	On Groyne.	75	59	68	80
E118 Gut	On Gut.	76	59	68	80
E119 Shelton	To Sir Raph Shelton.	76	59	69	80
E120 S. P.	Epitaph on S. P. a child of Q. El. Chappel.	77	60	69	81
E121 Rudyerd 1	To Benjamin Rudyerd.	78	61	70	81
E122 Rudyerd 2	To the same.	78	61	71	82
E123 Rudyerd 3	To the same.	78	61	71	82
E124 Elizabeth	Epitaph on Elizabeth, L.H.	79	62	71	82
E125 Uvedale	To Sir William Uvedale.	79	62	72	83
E126 Mrs Cary	To his Lady, then Mrs. Cary.	80	63	73	83
E127 Aubigny	To Esme, Lord 'Aubigny.	80	63	73	83
E128 Wm Roe 2	To William Roe.	80	64	74	84
E129 Mime	To Mime.	81	64	74	84
E130 Ferrab. 1	To Alphonso Ferrabosco, on his Booke.	82	65	75	85
E131 Ferrab. 2	To the same.	82	66	76	85
E132 Sylvester	To Mr. Josuah Sylvester.	83	67	77	86
E133 Voyage	On the famous Voyage.	84	68	77	86
Epitaph	Epitaph. (*Stay, view this stone: And, if thou beest not such.*)	371	356	295	273
F1 Why write not	Why I write not of Love.	93	77	87	95
F2 Penshurst	To Penshurst.	93	77	87	95
F3 Wroth	To Sir Robert Wroth.	96	81	91	98
F4 To the World	To the World. A farewell for a Gentle-woman, vertuous and noble.	100	84	95	101
F5 Celia 1	Song. To Celia.	102	86	97	103
F6 Celia 2	To the same.	103	92	98	103
F7 Women but	Song. That Women are but Mens shad-dowes.	104	93	98	104
F8 Sicknesse	To Sicknesse.	104	93	99	104
F9 Celia 3	Song. To Celia.	106	95	101	106
F10 Proludium	*And must I sing? what subject shall I*	107	96	101	106
F10 Proludium	*An elegie? no, muse. . . .*	108		103	335
F11 Epode	Epode.	109	97	104	107

Short Title	Title/*first line*	H&S	WBH	ID	GP
F12 Rutland	Epistle To Elizabeth Countesse of Rutland.	113	102	107	111
F13 Aubigny	Epistle. To Katherine, Lady Aubigny.	116	106	111	113
F14 Sydney	Ode. To Sir William Sydney, on his Birthday.	120	110	115	117
F15 Heaven	To Heaven.	122	112	117	119
Filmer	To my worthy Friend, Master Edward Filmer, on his Worke published.	401	385	318	270
Fletcher	To the worthy Author M. John Fletcher.	370	347	293	257
Ghyrlond	The Ghyrlond of the blessed Virgin Marie.	412	399	330	350
Gill	*Shall the prosperity of a Pardon still*	410	390	328	
Glover	*To my worthy, and deserving Brother*	666			
Grace	A Grace by Ben: Johnson, extempore. before King James.	418		337	344
Horace	Horace, of the Art of Poetrie.	305	274		354
Husband	To the worthy Author on the Husband.	385	365	304	260
Inigo Jones 1	An Expostulacion with Inigo Jones.	402	391	319	345
Inigo Jones 2	To Inigo Marquess Would be A Corollary.	406	395	325	347
Inigo Jones 3	To a Freind an Epigram Of him.	407	396	326	348
Jane Ogle	To the memorye of that most honoured Ladie Jane, eldest Daughter, to Cuthbert Lord Ogle: and Countesse of Shrewsbury:—	394	377	311	275
Lady Ogle	*T'Is a Record in heaven. You, that were*	399	383	316	276
Lucan	A speech out of Lucane.	422	350	341	353
May	To my chosen Friend, The learned Translator of Lucan, Thomas May, Esquire.	395	378	312	266
Moon	*To the wonders of the Peake,*	416	404	335	334
Murder	Murder.	363	327	285	340
Ode: If Men	Ode: (*Yff Men, and tymes were nowe*)	419	406	338	284
Ode Splendor	Ode ⟨Enthusiastic⟩. (*Splendor! O more then mortall,*)	364	334	286	278
Ode Who saith	Ode. ⟨Allegoric⟩. (*Who saith our Times nor have, nor can*)	366	337	287	279
Palmer	*When late (grave Palmer) these thy graffs and flowers*	361	325	283	255
Peace	Peace.	363	327	285	340
Phoenix	The Phoenix Analysde.	364	333	286	341
Reader	To the Reader. (*This Figure, that thou here seest put.*)	390	371	307	263
Rich	A speach presented unto king James at a tylting in the behalfe of the two noble Brothers sir Robert & sir Henrye Rich, now Earles of warwick and Hollande.	382	364	301	273
Riches	Riches.	363	327	285	340
Rutter	To my deare Sonne, and right-learned Friend, Master Joseph Rutter.	414	402	332	272
Shakespeare	To the memory of my beloved, the Author Mr. William Shakespeare: And what he hath left us.	390	372	307	263
Somerset	To the most noble, and above his Titles, Robert, Earle of Somerset.	384	363	302	274

Short Title	Title/*first line*	H&S	WBH	ID	GP
Sutcliffe	To Mrs. Alice Sutcliffe, on her divine Meditations.	411	399	329	271
U1 Trinitie	1. The Sinners Sacrifice. To the Holy Trinitie.	127	118	125	123
U1 Father	2. A Hymne to God the Father.	129	119	127	124
U1 Nativitie	3. A Hymne On the Nativitie of my Saviour.	130	120	128	125
U2 Excuse	1. His Excuse for loving.	131	121	129	126
U2 How he saw	2. How he saw her.	132	122	130	127
U2 Suffered	3. What hee suffered.	133	123	131	128
U2 Triumph	4. Her Triumph.	134	124	132	129
U2 Cupid	5. His discourse with Cupid.	136	125	133	129
U2 Kisse	6. Clayming a second kisse by Desert.	137	127	135	131
U2 Another	7. Begging another, on colour of mending the former.	139	128	136	132
U2 Promise	8. Urging her of a promise.	139	128	137	133
U2 Her man	9. Her man described by her owne Dictamen.	140	129	138	133
U2 Exception	10. Another Ladyes exception present at the hearing.	142	131	139	135
U3 Musicall	The Musicall Strife: In a Pastorall Dialogue.	143	131	140	135
U4 Song	A Song.	144	132	141	137
U5 Woman-kind	In the person of Woman-kind. A Song Apologetique.	145	133	141	137
U6 Defence	Another. In defence of their Inconstancie. A Song.	146	133	142	138
U7 Nymph	A Nymphs Passion.	147	134	143	138
U8 Houre-glasse	The Houre-glasse.	148	135	144	140
U9 Picture	My Picture left in Scotland.	149	136	145	140
U10 Jealousie	Against Jealousie.	150	136	145	141
U11 Dreame	The Dreame.	150	137	146	141
U12 Corbet	An Epitaph on Master Vincent Corbet.	151	137	146	142
U13 Sacvile	An Epistle to Sir Edward Sacvile, now Earle of Dorset.	153	139	148	143
U14 Selden	An Epistle to Master John Selden.	158	144	152	147
U15 Friend-Wars	An Epistle to a Friend, to perswade him to the Warres.	162	147	155	150
U16 Gray	An Epitaph on Master Philip Gray.	168	154	161	155
U17 Friend-Debt	Epistle To a Friend.	169	154	162	155
U18 Elegy Can	An Elegie.	169	155	162	156
U19 Elegy By	An Elegie.	170	156	163	156
U20 Shrub	A Satyricall Shrub.	171	157	164	157
U21 Ltl Shrub	A Little Shrub growing by.	172	158	165	158
U22 Elegy Tho	An Elegie.	173	158	166	158
U23 Himselfe	An Ode. To himselfe.	174	159	167	160
U24 Frontispice	The mind of the Frontispice to a Booke.	175	161	170	161
U25 Desmond	An Ode to James Earle of Desmond, writ in Queene Elizabeths time, since lost, and recovered.	176	161	170	161
U26 Ode High	An Ode.	180	164	173	163
U27 Ode Helen	An Ode.	180	164	174	164

Short Title	Title/*first line*	H&S	WBH	ID	GP
U28 Worth	A Sonnet, To the noble Lady, the Lady Mary Worth.	182	166	175	165
U29 Fit of Rime	A Fit of Rime against Rime.	183	166	176	166
U30 Burleigh	An Epigram On William Lord Burl: Lo: high Treasurer of England.	185	168	178	168
U31 Elsmere	An Epigram. To Thomas Lo: Elsmere, the last Terme he sate Chancellor.	185	169	179	168
U32 Elsmere	Another to him.	186	170	179	169
U33 Councellour	An Epigram to the Councellour that pleaded, and carried the cause.	186	170	180	169
U34 Small Poxe	An Epigram. To the small Poxe.	188	172	181	171
U35 Chute	An Epitaph.	188	172	182	171
U36 Song	A Song.	189	173	182	171
U37 Friend-Book	An Epistle to a friend.	189	173	183	172
U38 Elegy 'Tis	An Elegie.	191	175	185	173
U40 Elegy That	An Elegie.	197	181	188	177
U41 Elegy Since	An Elegie.	199	182	190	178
U42 Elegy Let	An Elegie.	199	183	190	179
U43 Vulcan	An Execration upon Vulcan.	202	186	193	181
U44 Speach	A speach according to Horace.	213	195	201	187
U45 Squib	An Epistle to Master Arth: Squib.	216	199	205	190
U46 Coke	An Epigram on Sir Edward Coke, when he was Lord chiefe Justice of England.	217	199	206	191
U47 Tribe	An Epistle answering to one that asked to be Sealed of the Tribe of Ben.	218	200	207	191
U48 Bacchus	The Dedication of the Kings new Cellar. To Bacchus.	220	203	210	194
U49 Pucell	An Epigram on The Court Pucell.	222	205	212	195
U50 Countesse	An Epigram. To the honour'd———— Countesse of————.	224	206	214	197
U51 Bacon	Lord Bacons Birth-day.	225	207	215	198
U52 Answer	My Answer. The Poet to the Painter.	226	209	217	199
U53 Newcastle	An Epigram. To William, Earle of New-castle.	228	210	218	200
U54 Squib	Epistle To Mr. Arthur Squib.	229	211	219	200
U55 Burges	To Mr. John Burges.	229	211	220	201
U56 Covell	Epistle. To my Lady Covell.	230	212	220	201
U57 Burges	To Master John Burges.	231	213	221	202
U58 Book-seller	Epigram, to my Book-seller.	232	214	222	203
U59 Newcastle	An Epigram. To William Earle of New-castle.	232	214	223	203
U60 La-ware	An Epitaph, on Henry L. La-ware. To the Passer-by.	233	215	224	204
U61 Epigram	An Epigram.	234	216	225	205
U62 Charles 1	An Epigram. To K. Charles for a 100. pounds he sent me in my sicknesse. 1629.	235	216	226	205
U63 Charles 2	To K. Charles, and Q. Mary. For the losse of their first-borne, An Epigram Consolatorie. 1629.	235	217	226	206
U64 Charles 3	An Epigram. To our great and good K. Charles On his Anniversary Day. 1629.	236	218	227	206
U65 Prince	An Epigram on the Princes birth. 1630.	237	219	228	207

Short Title	Title/*first line*	H&S	WBH	ID	GP
U66 Queene	An Epigram to the Queene, then lying in. 1630.	238	219	229	208
U67 Muses	An Ode, or Song, by all the Muses. In celebration of her Majesties birth-day. 1630.	239	220	229	208
U68 House-hold	An Epigram, To the House-hold. 1630.	241	222	231	210
U69 Friend Son	Epigram. To a Friend, and Sonne.	241	222	232	211
U70 Ode	To the immortall memorie, and friendship of that noble paire, Sir Lucius Cary, and Sir H. Morison.	242	223	233	211
U71 Treasurer	To the Right Honourable, the Lord high Treasurer of England. An Epistle Mendicant. 1631.	248	228	238	215
U72 King	To the King. On his Birth-day. An Epigram Anniversarie. Novemb. 19. 1632.	249	228	239	216
U73 Weston	On the Right Honourable, and vertuous Lord Weston, L. high Treasurer of England, Upon the Day, Hee was made Earle of Portland, 17. Febr. 1632. To the Envious.	250	229	240	217
U74 Weston	To the Right Hon'ble Hierome, L. Weston. An Ode gratulatorie, For his Returne from his Embassie. 1632.	250	230	241	217
U75 Epithalam	Epithalamion; Or, A Song: Celebrating The Nuptials of that Noble Gentleman, Mr. Hierome Weston, Son, and Heire, of the Lord Weston, Lord high Treasurer of England, with the Lady Frances Stuart, Daughter of Esme D. of Lenox deceased, and Sister of the Surviving Duke of the same name.	252	231	242	218
U76 Petition	The humble Petition of poore Ben.	259	237	249	224
U77 Treasurer	To the right Honourable, the Lord Treasurer of England. An Epigram.	260	238	250	225
U78 Digby	An Epigram To my Muse, the Lady Digby, on her Husband, Sir Kenelme Digby.	262	239	251	226
U79 New-yeares	A New-yeares-Gift sung to King Charles, 1635.	263	241	253	227
U82 Christning	To my L. the King, On the Christning His second Sonne James.	268	246	255	231
U83 Pawlet	An Elegie On the Lady Jane Pawlet, Marchion: of Winton.	268	247	256	232
U84 Cradle	1. The Dedication of her Cradle.	272	250	260	235
U84 Descent	2. The Song of her Descent.	274	252	262	236
U84 Body	3. The Picture of the Body.	275	253	263	237
U84 Mind	4. The Mind.	277	254	264	238
U84 Kenelme	To Kenelme, John, George.	281	256	267	240
U84 Muse	9. Elegie on my Muse. The truly honoured Lady, the Lady Venetia Digby; who living, gave me leave to call her so. Being Her Apotheosis, or Relation to the Saints.	282	257	268	241

Short Title	Title/first line	H&S	WBH	ID	GP
U85 Country	The praises of a Countrie life.	289	264	274	247
U86 Hor. 4:1	Ode the first. The fourth Booke. To Venus.	292	267	277	249
U87 Hor. 3:9	Ode IX. 3 Booke, to Lydia. Dialogue of Horace, and Lydia.	293	268	278	250
U88 Petronius	*Doing, a filthy pleasure is, and short;*	294	269	279	251
U89 Mart. 8:77	*Liber, of all thy friends, thou sweetest care,*	294	269	280	252
U90 Mart. 10:47	*The Things that make the happier life, are these,*	295	404	280	352
Welcome	*Fresh as the Day, and new as are the Flowers,*	416	378	334	333

A Concordance to the Poems of
BEN JONSON

		Page	Title	Line

AARONS
how lyke the Carbuncle in Aarons brest . . . . . 361 Palmer 14
AB
Had burst with storme, and downe fell, ab excelsis, . . . 86 E133 Voyage 95
ABANDON'D
Or so my selfe abandon'd, as because . . . . . 117 F13 Aubigny 17
ABATE
The publike, from the private; to abate . . . . . 327 Horace 488
ABBEVILE
Hee's carried 'twixt Montrell and Abbevile. " . . . 374 Coryat 1 13
In a Cart twixt Montrell and Abbevile. " . . . 380 Coryat 3 53
A-BED
A-bed canst heare the loud stag speake, " . . . 97 F3 Wroth 22
ABHORD
Away, and leave me, thou thing most abhord, " . . . 48 E65 Muse 1
ABHORRES
Abhorres low numbers, and the private straine . . . 311 Horace 123
ABIDE
That had no Muse to make their fame abide. " . . . 114 F12 Rutland 48
Among thy Saints elected to abide, " . . . 128 U1 Trinitie 45
ABLE
One was; and he, for brawne, and braine, right able . . . 84 E133 Voyage 23
With all corroding Arts, be able to untie! " . . . 257 U75 Epithalam. 136
Able to talk of Euclide, and correct " . . . 402 Inigo Jones 1 4
Able to eat into his bones & pierce " . . . 407 Inigo Jones 3 4
ABLER
And, than this same, I know no abler way " . . . 80 E127 Aubigny 11
my abler faculties; and thus brake foorth . . . 362 Palmer 29
ABOUND
And that's made up as doth the purse abound. . . . 230 U56 Covell 12
Made up still as the pockett doth abound. . . . 230 U56 Covell V 12
ABOUNDS
Let their spite (which now abounds) " . . . 260 U76 Petition 28
'BOUT
Nor 'bout the beares, nor noyse to make lords sport. . . 63 E97 Motion 12
And the Girdle 'bout her waste, " . . . 137 U2 Cupid 41
Discharge it 'bout the Iland, in an houre, . . . 249 U72 King 3
Discharging 'bout the Iland, in an houre, " . . . 249 U72 King V 3
Were like a ring of Vertues, 'bout her set, . . . 270 U81 Pawlet 41
Of Constellations 'bout her horld; " . . . 277 U84 Body 27
And 'bout the steeming Chimney set! " . . . 291 U85 Country 66
And 'bout the shining Chimney set! " . . . 291 U85 Country V 66
Thrice 'bout thy Altar with their Ivory feet. . . . 292 U86 Hor.4:1 28
And ('bout thy Ivory neck,) no youth did fling . . . 293 U87 Hor.3:9 2
ABOUT
Or then, or since, about our Muses springs, . . . 53 E79 Rutland 3
About his forme. What then so swells each lim? . . . 63 E97 Motion 19
About the towne; and knowne too, at that price. " . . 74 E115 Honest Man 6
About the shore, of farts, but late departed, " . . 87 E133 Voyage 125
There's none, that dwell about them, wish them downe; . 94 F2 Penshurst 47
Livers, round about the towne. " . . . 105 F8 Sicknesse 17
Heare, what the Muses sing about thy roote, " . . 119 F13 Aubigny 100
Every Cloud about thy eye; . . . 132 U2 How he saw 12
Still flie about the Odour of your Name; " . . 186 U31 Elsmere 8
Or goe about to countenance the vice, " . . 191 U38 Elegy 'Tis 24
About in Cloudes, and wrapt in raging weather, " . 193 U38 Elegy 'Tis 75
Or in small Fagots have him blaze about " . . 211 U43 Vulcan 185
Or els^ in penny Fagots blaze about " . . . 211 U43 Vulcan V185
How comes it all things so about thee smile? . . 225 U51 Bacon 2
And as it turnes our joyfull yeare about, " . . 236 U64 Charles 3 5
Thou, looking then about, . . . 242 U70 Ode 5
Have cast a trench about mee, now, five yeares; . . 248 U71 Treasurer 6
If you can cast about your either eye, " . . . 271 U81 Pawlet 85
And see all dead here, or about to dye! " . . 271 U81 Pawlet 86
Whoorles me about, and to blaspheme in fashion! . . 283 U84 Muse 32
These thoughts when Usurer Alphius, now about " . 291 U85 Country 67
These thinges when Usurer Alphius, now about " . 291 U85 Country V 67
Was meant at first. Why, forcing still about . . . 307 Horace 29
The worst of Statuaries, here about " . . . 307 Horace 45
In his train'd Gowne about the Stage: So grew . . 319 Horace 305
In his train'd Gowne about the Stage: thus grew . 346 Horace V305
The Tragedie, and carried it about, " . . . 319 Horace 312
Of an entangling suit; and bring 't about: . . . 333 Horace 604
And stalketh, like a Fowler, round about, " . . 335 Horace 650
Of Fortunes wheele by Lucan driv'n about, . . . 395 May 3
About the towne: this reck'ning I will pay, . . . 396 Drayton 9
Hot from thy trumpet, round, about the world. . . 396 Drayton 14
And flight about the Ile, well neare, by this, . . 397 Drayton 49
Up & about? Dyve into Cellars too " " . . 405 Inigo Jones 1 80
ABOUTE
Aboute this Isle, and Charme the rounde, as when " . 421 Ode:If Men 39
'BOVE
But 'bove the fat of rammes, or bulls, to prize . . 127 U1 Trinitie 11
It were a plague 'bove scorne, " . . . 147 U7 Nymph 12
His new Cassandra, 'bove the old; " . . . 181 U27 Ode Helen 23
'Bove all your standing waters, choak'd with weedes. . 198 U40 Elegy That 28
'Bove all your Fire-workes, had at Ephesus, . . . 211 U43 Vulcan 194
'Bove all our Fire-workes, had at Ephesus, . . . 211 U43 Vulcan V194
'Bove rattling Rime. . . . 273 U84 Cradle 16
With thee 'bove all his Rivals gifts take place, . . 292 U86 Hor.4:1 18
Be nought so'bove him but his sword let claime. . . 313 Horace 174
Be nought so'bove him, but his bold sword claime. . 342 Horace V174
Or are you soe ambitious 'bove your peers! " . . 403 Inigo Jones 1 19

1

	Page	Title	Line

ABOVE
And, now, above the poole, a face right fat   88   E133 Voyage   160
Adde to thy free provisions, farre above   95   F2 Penshurst   58
Above your under-carved ornaments,   115   F12 Rutland   85
Of your blest wombe, made fruitfull from above,   119   F13 Aubigny   95
Just above her sparkling eyes,   136   U2 Cupid   16
And, above her even chin,   136   U2 Cupid   24
That ne're was knowne to last above a fit!   171   U20 Shrub   6
Her upright head, above the reach of Chance,   176   U25 Desmond   6
And (which doth all Atchievements get above)   187   U33 Councellour   38
That to speake well, thinke it above all sinne,   218   U47 Tribe   19
That when King James, above here,   221   U48 Bacchus   37
Of Vertue, got above his name?   234   U60 La-ware   10
Shee showes so farre above   240   U67 Muses   31
Above his fact?   243   U70 Ode   24
Above the rest   253   U75 Epithalam.   38
Made her friends joyes to get above their feares!   270   U81 Pawlet   60
The Serpents head: Gets above Death, and Sinne,   272   U81 Pawlet   99
Whom her Redeemer, honour'd hath above   285   U84 Muse   100
Whose strength is above strength;   367   Ode Who saith   55
To the most noble, and above his Titles, . .   384   Somerset   Ttl
Above th'ill fortune of them, or the need.   391   Shakespeare   16
Above his Reader, or his Prayser, is.   400   Beaumont   2
ABROAD
And, after, swom abroad in ample flakes,   87   E133 Voyage   138
That talke abroad of Womans change,   146   U6 Defence   2
To be abroad chanting some baudie song,   164   U15 Friend-Wars   74
Thy blatant Muse abroad, and teach it rather   411   Gill   11
How are thy gifts, and graces blaz'd abroad!   413   Ghyrlond   36
ABRO'D
How are thy gifts and graces blaz'd abro'd,   414   Ghyrlond   53
ABSENCE
His absence in my verse, is all I aske.   107   F10 Proludium   21
His absence in our verse, is all I aske.   107   F10 Proludium   V. 21
Absence, or Distance, shall not breed decay.   194   U38 Elegy 'Tis   116
Shortly againe: and make our absence sweet.   197   U40 Elegy That   8
We ask your absence here, we all love peace,   212   U43 Vulcan   209
We crave your absence here, we all love peace,   212   U43 Vulcan   V209
ABSENT
On all Soules that are absent; even the dead;   218   U47 Tribe   17
ABSOLUTE
He should those rare, and absolute numbers view,   53   E79 Rutland   11
. . . A Gentleman absolute in all Numbers;   272   U84 Eupheme   Ttl
ABSOLV'D
Before, I thinke my wish absolv'd had beene.   228   U53 Newcastle   14
ABSTAINE
And both from Wine, and Women did abstaine.   333   Horace   590
ABSTAYNE
Though we acknowledge, who can so abstayne,   112   F11 Epode   85
ABSTINENCE
Have fill'd with abstinence: 111   F11 Epode   84
Have grac'd with abstinence: 111   F11 Epode   V 84
ABSTRUSE
Yet, if by chance, in utt'ring things abstruse,   307   Horace   69
ABSURDITY
Discover Vice? Commit Absurdity?   405   Inigo Jones 1   82
ABUSE
And, as thou'hast mine, his houres, and youth abuse.   48   E65 Muse   6
That's, sit, and eate: doe not my eares abuse.   68   E107 Hungry   2
With tales of Troyes just knight, our faiths abuse: 84   E133 Voyage   4
Thou did'st abuse, and then betray;   101   F4 To the World   42
On whom I could take up, and ne're abuse   161   U14 Selden   83
To use the present, then, is not abuse,   171   U19 Elegy By   21
Dar'st not abuse thy wisdome, in the Lawes,   187   U33 Councellour   17
Will unto Licence that faire leave abuse.   190   U37 Friend-Book   24
I will no more abuse my vowes to you,   194   U38 Elegy 'Tis   107
Whilst other soules convert to base abuse   361   Palmer   11
Will unto Lycence, that free Leave Abuse: 422   Censure   17
ABUS'D
And all his followers, that had so abus'd him: 86   E133 Voyage   97
In man, because man hath the flesh abus'd.   192   U38 Elegy 'Tis   66
ABUSED
Tyran Rime hath so abused,   184   U29 Fit of Rime   46
ABUSES
And art a god, if Fame thee not abuses,   85   E133 Voyage   53
He the half of Life abuses,   657   Door Apollo   9
ACADEMIE
The Academie, where the Gallants meet--   215   U44 Speach   89
ACCENTS
Adding her owne glad accents, to this Day,   249   U72 King   7
Adding her owne great accents, to this Day,   249   U72 King   V 7
ACCEPT
But for their powers, accept my pietie.   31   E14 Camden   14
Accept his Muse; and tell, I know you can,   231   U56 Covell   26
Accept this garland, plant it on thy head,   245   U70 Ode   77
ACCEPTABLE
His armes more acceptable free,   293   U87 Hor.3:9   3
ACCEPTABLY
With something that was acceptably new.   321   Horace   327
ACCEPTANCE
It is the faire acceptance, Sir, creates   64   E101 Supper   7
For thy acceptance. O, behold me right,   127   U1 Trinitie   13

2

ACCEPTED
   And that this so accepted summe,   -   -   -   -   259 U76 Petition   14
ACCESSE
   This Fort of so impregnable accesse,   -   -   -   -   401 Beaumont   17
ACCITE
   But in my Deske, what was there to accite - -   -   -   206 U43 Vulcan   85
ACCIUS
   Of Accius, and Ennius, rare appeares: -   -   -   -   323 Horace   382
   Paccuvius, Accius, him of Cordova dead, -   -   -   -   391 Shakespeare   35
ACCOMPLISH
   We must accomplish; 'Tis the last Key-stone - - -   157 U13 Sacvile   136
ACCOMPT
   Upon th'accompt, hers grew the quicker trade. - -   -   56 E87 Hazard   5
   Make accompt, unlesse you can,   -   -   -   -   140 U2 Promise   29
   Are lost upon accompt! And none will know - -   -   -   237 U64 Charles 3   21
   Are lost upon accompt! And none doe know -   -   -   -   237 U64 Charles 3   V 21
ACCOMPTED
   Of race accompted, that no passion have -   -   -   -   201 U42 Elegy Let   49
ACCORDING
   A speach according to Horace.   -   -   -   -   213 U44 Speach   Ttl
   And give her place, according to her blood, - - -   284 U84 Muse   83
   According to the Moone. But, then the boyes - - -   335 Horace   647
ACCOUNT
   (Or Poet, in the court account) then I, -   -   -   -   115 F12 Rutland   69
ACCOUNTED
   These have crimes accounted beene.   -   -   -   -   102 F5 Celia 1   18
   And the Poets' Horse accounted.   -   -   -   -   657 Door Apollo   13
ACCOUNTS   (See 'COUNTS)
ACCUMULATED
   Accumulated on her, by the Lord   -   -   -   -   285 U84 Muse   111
ACCURSED
   And that accursed ground, the Parish-Garden: - - -   209 U43 Vulcan   147
ACCUSATIONS
   That seeming prayses, are, yet accusations. - -   -   75 E115 Honest Man   32
ACCUSE
   T'accuse, or quit all Parties to be heard! - -   -   284 U84 Muse   60
ACHE   (See AKE)
ACHERON
   All, that they boast of Styx, of Acheron, - - - - 84 E133 Voyage   7
   And so they did, from Styx, to Acheron: -   -   -   -   88 E133 Voyage   141
ACHIEVEMENT   (See ATCHIEVEMENTS)
ACHILLES
   Achilles was not first, that valiant was, - -   -   114 F12 Rutland   51
   Honour'd Achilles chance by thee be seiz'd, - - -   313 Horace   171
ACKNOWLEDGE
   Though we acknowledge, who can so abstayne, - -   -   112 F11 Epode   85
   Though I acknowledge, who can so refraine, - -   -   112 F11 Epode   V 85
ACQUAINTANCE
   I lent you, on meere acquaintance, at a feast. - -   51 E73 Fine Grand   6
   And Gossip-got acquaintance, as, to us -   -   -   -   398 Drayton   85
ACQUAINTED
   Nor thumbe, nor finger to the stop acquainted, - - 87 E133 Voyage   134
ACQUIT   (See AQUIT)
ACROSTICHS
   Acrostichs, and Telestichs, on jumpe names, - - -   204 U43 Vulcan   39
   Acrostichs, and Telestichs, or jumpe names, - - -   204 U43 Vulcan   V 39
   Acrostichs, and Telestichs, on fine names, - - -   204 U43 Vulcan   V 39
ACROSTICKS
   Or else Acrosticks, or those finer flammes - - -   204 U43 Vulcan   V 36
ACT
   And that thou seek'st reward of thy each act, - - - 47 E63 Salisbury 2   5
   As others speake, but onely thou dost act. - - -   57 E89 Allen   12
   And did act (what now we mone)   -   -   -   -   77 E120 S. P.   13
   Had power to act, what they to faine had not. - -   84 E133 Voyage   6
   Act a brave worke, call it thy last adventry: - -   85 E133 Voyage   57
   Some act of Love's bound to reherse,   -   -   -   -   93 F1 Why write no   1
   Will prove old Orpheus act no tale to be: - -   -   115 F12 Rutland   77
   And in the Act did so my blush prevent. -   -   -   -   153 U13 Sacvile   11
   Forme, Act or Ensigne, that hath scap'd your sight? - 160 U14 Selden   V 48
   It is an Act of tyrannie, not love,   -   -   -   -   190 U37 Friend-Book   25
   And shewing so weake an Act to vulgar eyes, - - -   218 U47 Tribe   7
   Not only shunning by your act, to doe   -   -   -   -   224 U50 Countesse   5
   Not by the act?   -   -   -   -   -   -   -   -   -   243 U70 Ode   22
   Who the whole Act expresse;   -   -   -   -   255 U75 Epithalam.   87
   And act the businesse, which they paint, or carve. - 261 U77 Treasurer   16
   And act the businesse, which these paint, or carve. - 261 U77 Treasurer   V 16
   Could summe to a perfection, was her Act! - -   -   270 U81 Pawlet   46
   Could heap to a perfection, was her Act! -   -   -   270 U81 Pawlet   V 46
   And, in her last act, taught the Standers-by, - -   270 U81 Pawlet   61
   In that great Act of judgement: which the Father - 288 U84 Muse   215
   Lookes after honours, and bewares to act -   -   -   315 Horace   239
   Those that did sing, and act: their faces dy'd - - 319 Horace   314
   The Poets act! and for his Country's sake - -   -   398 Drayton   63
   It is an Act of Tyranye, not Love,   -   -   -   -   422 Censure   18
ACTED
   Or feats of darknesse acted in Mid-Sun, -   -   -   156 U13 Sacvile   95
   So acted to the life, as Maurice might, -   -   -   -   214 U44 Speach   41
   Or acted told. But, ever, things that run - -   -   317 Horace   256
ACTETH
   the sword, but that it acteth what it list. - - -   423 Lucan   14
ACTION
   Action, or engine, worth a note of thine, - - -   71 E110 Edmonds 1   20
   And that, in action, there is nothing new, - -   -   72 E111 Edmonds 2   5
   If onely love should make the action pris'd: - -   78 E121 Rudyerd 1   6

3

ACTION (cont.)

	Page	Title	Line
But, in the action, greater man then hee:	84	E133 Voyage	26
They tooke 'hem all to witnesse of their action:	89	E133 Voyage	191
That gaspe for action, and would yet revive	162	U15 Friend-Wars	6
In one full Action; nor have you now more	180	U26 Ode High	17
No love of action, and high Arts,	234	U60 La-ware	12
In him all action is beheld in State:	262	U78 Digby	V 6
Witnesse his Action done at Scanderone;	262	U78 Digby	13
And his great Action done at Scanderoone:	262	U78 Digby	V 13
In action, winged as the wind,	280	U84 Mind	65

ACTIONS

	Page	Title	Line
Whose actions so themselves doe celebrate;	40	E43 Salisbury 1	2
What would his serious actions me have learned?	55	E85 Goodyere 1	12
The councells, actions, orders, and events	62	E95 Savile	32
And did not shame it with my actions, then,	70	E108 Soldiers	7
All his actions to be such,	142	U2 Her man	45
And adde his Actions unto these,	152	U12 Corbet	19
That men such reverence to such actions show!	156	U13 Sacvile	98
In all his Actions rarified to spright;	197	U40 Elegy That	20
In at a hole, and see these Actions creepe	201	U42 Elegy Let	60
Not liv'd; for Life doth her great actions spell,	245	U70 Ode	59
In his great Actions: view whom his large hand	250	U73 Weston	3
Have all his actions wondred at, and view'd	284	U84 Muse	77
In all her petite actions, so devote,	287	U84 Muse	177
That Rebells actions, are but valiant crimes!	397	Drayton	44
Just and fit actions Ptolemey (he saith)	422	Lucan	1

ACTIVE

	Page	Title	Line
Active in's braine, and passive in his bones.	49	E68 Playwrt 2	4
For the more countenance to my active Muse?	107	F10 Proludium	3
For the more countenance to our active Muse?	107	F10 Proludium	V 3
As light, and active as the youngest hee	200	U42 Elegy Let	6
See, see our active King	240	U67 Muses	37
And by his Rise, in active men, his Name	256	U75 Epithalam.	116
Keepe him still active, angry, un-appeas'd,	313	Horace	172

ACTORS

	Page	Title	Line
An Actors parts, and Office too, the Quire	317	Horace	276

ACTS

	Page	Title	Line
I leave thy acts, which should I prosequute	58	E91 Vere	9
I leave, then, acts, which should I prosequute	58	E91 Vere	V 9
To have engrav'd these acts, with his owne stile,	71	E110 Edmonds 1	6
Acts old Iniquitie, and in the fit	74	E115 Honest Man	27
For acts of grace.	128	U1 Trinitie	28
Increase those acts, o glorious Trinitie	128	U1 Trinitie	29
All other Acts of Worldlings, are but toyle	162	U15 Friend-Wars	9
All other Acts of Worldlings, are meere toyle	162	U15 Friend-Wars V	9
And comming home, to tell what acts were done	213	U44 Speach	19
To sordid flatteries, acts of strife,	244	U70 Ode	39
Of Homers, forth in acts, then of thine owne,	313	Horace	185
Have more or lesse then just five Acts: nor laid,	317	Horace	272
Betweene the Acts, a quite cleane other thing	317	Horace	278
His farre-admired Acts,	367	Ode Who saith	59

ACTUATE

	Page	Title	Line
Of popular noyses, borne to actuate things.	341	Horace	V120

AD

	Page	Title	Line
Author ad Librum.	662	Bedford	Ttl

ADAM

	Page	Title	Line
Into the Kindred, whence thy Adam drew	274	U84 Descent	15
How would he firke? lyke Adam overdooe	405	Inigo Jones 1	79

ADD

	Page	Title	Line
What can one witnesse, and a weake one, add	385	Brooke	4
I am come to Add, and speake,	416	Moon	2

ADDE

	Page	Title	Line
Unto the cryes of London Ile adde one;	58	E92 New Crie	2
O, would'st thou adde like hand, to all the rest!	61	E95 Savile	13
Adde to thy free provisions, farre above	95	F2 Penshurst	58
Adde a thousand, and so more:	103	F6 Celia 2	11
And adde his Actions unto these,	152	U12 Corbet	19
Profit in ought: each day some little adde,	157	U13 Sacvile	132
I adde that (but) because I understand	169	U17 Friend-Debt	10
That thought can adde, unthankfull, the lay-stall	172	U21 Ltl Shrub	8
He cries, Good boy, thou'lt keepe thine owne. Now, adde	327	Horace	470

ADDED

	Page	Title	Line
You have unto my Store added a booke,	189	U37 Friend-Book	4

ADDING

	Page	Title	Line
Of adding to thy fame; thine may to me,	41	E43 Salisbury 1	8
Of adding to thy prayse; thine may to me,	41	E43 Salisbury 1 V	8
Adding her owne glad accents, to this Day,	249	U72 King	7
Adding her owne greate accents, to this Day,	249	U72 King	V 7

ADJUNCTS

	Page	Title	Line
In fitting proper adjuncts to each day.	317	Horace	254

ADMIRABLE

	Page	Title	Line
An admirable Verse. The great Scurfe take	333	Horace	594
An admirable verse: the great Scab take	353	Horace	V594

ADMIRACION

	Page	Title	Line
I could not but in admiracion stand.	361	Palmer	4

ADMIRATION

	Page	Title	Line
In admiration, stretch'd upon the rack	163	U15 Friend-Wars	50
With admiration, and applause to die!	270	U81 Pawlet	62
And jests; and both to admiration raise	323	Horace	400
And jests; and both to admiration rais'd,	348	Horace	V386/400

ADMIRE

	Page	Title	Line
When thou wert wont t'admire, not censure men.	32	E18 Censurer	8
Tilter, the most may'admire thee, though not I:	36	E29 Tilter	1

		Page	Title	Line

ADMIRE (cont.)
If to admire were to commend, my praise ... ... 83 E132 Sylvester 1
To touch these Mysteries! We may admire ... ... 269 U81 Pawlet 31
To touch those Mysteries! We may admire ... ... 269 U81 Pawlet V 31
Or moathes shall eate, what all these Fooles admire.. ... 371 Fletcher 16
To understand, hee may at length admire. ... ... 383 Author 10
ADMIR'D
In the full floud of her admir'd perfection? ... ... 112 F11 Epode 107
Then I admir'd, the rare and precious use ... ... 361 Palmer 9
ADMIRED
His farre-admired Acts, ... 367 Ode Who saith 59
In thy admired Periegesis, ... 397 Drayton 50
And most to be admired of thy Sexe, ... 414 Ghyrlond 46
ADMIRING
Besides the other Swannes admiring him, ... 366 Ode Who saith 5
ADMIT
For you admit no companie, but good, ... 224 U50 Countesse 25
If Praises, when th'are full, heaping admit, ... 385 Brooke 6
ADMITTED
Admitted to the sight, although his friends, ... 305 Horace 6
ADMYRED
Of her admyred brightnesse, ... 364 Ode Splendor V 3
ADOE
And Goody Sculpture, brought with much adoe ... . 403 Inigo Jones 1 38
ADONIS
The young Adonis courted ... ... 135 U2 Triumph V 40
ADOPT
Adopt us Heires, by grace, who were of those ... . 286 U84 Muse 140
ADORATION
With Modestie so crown'd, and Adoration seene. ... ... 254 U75 Epithalam.. 48
ADORE
I could adore, almost t'idolatrie. ... ... 79 E125 Uvedale 10
Whom I adore so much, should so slight me, ... 149 U9 Picture 4
Yet give me leave t'adore in you ... ... 174 U22 Elegy Tho 35
He did lay up, and would adore the shooe, ... 201 U42 Elegy Let 55
May rather yet adore, then spy.. ... ... 276 U84 Body 20
ADOR'D
Where Nero falls, and Galba is ador'd, ... 61 E95 Savile 8
As if they' ador'd the Head, wheron th'are fixt. ... .. 413 Ghyrlond 28
ADORND
Judgement (adornd with Learning) ... ... 365 Ode Splendor 9
ADORNE
That bloud not mindes, but mindes did bloud adorne: ... .. 75 E116 Jephson 11
Nothing can more adorne it, then the seat ... . 284 U84 Muse 71
ADORNES
Calls for his stoole, adornes the stage: god payes.. ... .. 30 E12 Shift 18
ADRIA
And then rough Adria, angrier, farre; 294 U87 Hor.3:9 23
ADULTERATE
Adulterate moneys, such as might not goe: ... . 204 U43 Vulcan 45
Adulterate maskings, such as might not goe: ... . 204 U43 Vulcan V 45
ADULTERIES
Adulteries, now, are not so hid, or strange, ... 165 U15 Friend-Wars 85
ADULTERS
He'adulters still: his thoughts lye with a whore. ... .. 35 E26 Beast 2 2
ADULT'RERS
Or thought they, Leda's white Adult'rers place ... . 369 Ode Who saith 104
ADVANCE
Which if they misse, they yet should re-advance ... .. 55 E85 Goodyere 1 8
T'advance his doubtfull issue, and ore-flow ... . 117 F13 Aubigny 40
And all doe strive t'advance ... ... 120 F14 Sydney 5
No! he must feele and know, that will advance.. ... .. 156 U13 Sacvile 123
High, as his mind, that doth advance ... . 176 U25 Desmond 5
If that were so, thou rather would'st advance ... . 209 U43 Vulcan 151
Made, or indentur'd, or leas'd out t'advance ... . 246 U70 Ode 100
Yet have all debts forgiven us, and advance ... . 286 U84 Muse 143
Or blinde Affection, which doth ne're advance ... . 391 Shakespeare 9
How they advance true Love, and neighbourhood, ... 416 Dover 7
ADVANC'D
More then advanc'd the houses, and their rites? ... .. 210 U43 Vulcan 164
And had his noble name advanc'd with men: ... . 244 U70 Ode 36
Advanc'd, and made a Constellation there! ... . 392 Shakespeare 76
Upon this obeliske, advanc'd for it, ... 416 Welcome 5
ADVANCED
Or in cleft-sticks, advanced to make calls ... . 28 E3 Bookseller 8
Were you advanced, past those times, to be ... . 67 E104 Montgomery 11
ADVANCES
Or else a health advances, ... 222 U48 Bacchus 49
ADVANTAGE
With th'advantage of her haire, ... 138 U2 Kisse 10
But rather with advantage to be found ... ... 229 U54 Squib 11
I have, with strict advantage of free tyme ... . 421 Censure 6
ADVENTER
Shee brought the Poets forth, but ours th'adventer.. ... .. 84 E133 Voyage 20
ADVENTRY
Act a brave worke, call it thy last adventry: ... . 85 E133 Voyage 57
ADVENTURE
I Sing the brave adventure of two wights, ... 84 E133 Voyage 21
ADVENTURES
With all th'adventures; Three bookes not afraid ... .. 207 U43 Vulcan 95
With all th'adventures; Three bookes not amisse ... .. 207 U43 Vulcan V 95
ADVERSARIES
Thy Adversaries fall, as not a word ... ... 187 U33 Councellour 33

5

		Page	Title	Line

ADVISE
And to conceale your ulcers, did advise,   38   E38 Guiltie 2   2
Shall I advise thee, Pucell? steale away   223   U49 Pucell   35
Censure, not sharplye then, but mee advise   421   Censure   1
ADVISETH
Hee that soe Censureth, or adviseth synns,   421   Censure   4
ADVOCATE
My judge, my witnesse, and my advocate.   122   F15 Heaven   12
AEACUS
A sope-boyler; and Aeacus him nigh,   89   E133 Voyage   188
AELIAN
Translated Aelian tactickes to be read,   214   U44 Speach   35
AEMILIAN
Th'Aemilian Schoole, in brasse can fashion out   307   Horace   46
AEMULATE
And teach your nephewes it to aemulate: 387   Cavendish   10
AEMULATION
Faire Aemulation, and no Envy is;   389   Aleman   22
AENEAS
This is that good Aeneas, past through fire,   81   E128 Wm Roe 2   12
AERIE
As aerie light, and as like wit as those?   222   U49 Pucell   10
Three Kingdomes Mirth, in light, and aerie man,   249   U72 King   11
AESCHILUS   (See also ESCHYLUS)
For names; but call forth thund'ring Aeschilus,   391   Shakespeare   33
AESCULAPE
Of old, they gave a cock to Aesculape;   31   E13 Empirick   2
AESOPE
As skilfull Roscius, and grave Aesope, men,   56   E89 Allen   3
Old Aesope Gundomar: the French can tell,   213   U44 Speach   5
AETERNALL
This second marriage, will aeternall make.   394   Jane Ogle   26
Our great reward, th'aeternall Crown to win.   412   Sutcliffe   19
AETERNITIES
Aeternities great charter; which became   400   Lady Ogle   35
AETNA
Would you had kept your Forge at Aetna still,   212   U43 Vulcan   197
Conceipt, and into burning Aetna leap'd.   335   Horace   663
Were they as strong ram'd up as Aetna gates.   363   Riches   10
AETNEAN
And, after all theyr Aetnean Ire,   179   U25 Desmond   44
A-FARRE
Or was she gracious a-farre off? but neere   169   U18 Elegy Can   5
Or in the bending Vale beholds a-farre   290   U85 Country   13
AFEARD
And make Love or me afeard.   141   U2 Her man   24
You know, I never was of Truth afeard,   414   Rutter   4
AFFAIRES
Publike affaires command me now to goe   194   U38 Elegy 'Tis   114
In Politique, and Militar Affaires.   214   U44 Speach   60
That censure all the Towne, and all th'affaires,   218   U47 Tribe   23
Or were Affaires in tune,   253   U75 Epithalam.   15
AFFEARD
Lash'd by their consciences, to die, affeard.   84   E133 Voyage   18
Touching this cause, where they will be affeard   87   E133 Voyage   106
AFFECT
An hower will come they must affect theyr Ease,   179   U25 Desmond   V 42
Smiles in his Sphaere, to see the rest affect,   366   Ode Who saith   13
AFFECTED
An ill-affected limbe (what e're it aile)   192   U38 Elegy 'Tis   45
Be not affected with these markes too much   193   U38 Elegy 'Tis   83
AFFECTION
And which no' affection praise enough can give!   34   E23 Donne 1   6
That no affection in thy voyce commands;   51   E74 Chancelor   4
What savage, brute affection,   112   F11 Epode   108
Chance that the Friends affection proves Allay   158   U14 Selden   10
On these darke rymes; that my affection   177   U25 Desmond   15
On these darke rymes; that our affection   177   U25 Desmond   V 15
Sooner then my affection from the faire.   200   U42 Elegy Let   13
From all affection! when they urg'd the Cure   270   U81 Pawlet   49
Or blinde Affection, which doth ne're advance   391   Shakespeare   9
AFFECTIONS
In all affections shee concurreth still.   40   E42 Giles   15
A subtle thing, that doth affections win   74   E115 Honest Man   7
To wakeful reason, our affections king: 109   F11 Epode   13
For either our affections doe rebell,   109   F11 Epode   21
This makes, that your affections still be new,   119   F13 Aubigny   118
What my Affections were.   150   U10 Jealousie   11
AFFECTS
But both th'hast so, as who affects the state   78   E123 Rudyerd 3   3
So he that varying still affects to draw   339   Horace   V 42/ 40
AFFOARDS
Vermilion, Lake, or Cinnopar affoards   406   Inigo Jones 1   94
AFFOORD
Court Hieroglyphicks! & all Artes affoord   404   Inigo Jones 1   43
AFFORD
That selfe-divided Belgia did afford;   37   E32 Roe 2   3
I, that's a Charme and halfe! She must afford   163   U15 Friend-Wars   52
Afford? The Mountaines travail'd, and brought forth   315   Horace   198
AFFORDS
Thy noblest spouse affords them welcome grace;   98   F3 Wroth   55
Thy noblest spouse affords them welcome place;   98   F3 Wroth   V 55
'Tis not enough, th'elaborate Muse affords   311   Horace   140

		Page	Title	Line

AFFORDS (cont.)
'Tis not enough, the labouring Muse affords   341   Horace   V140
AFFRAID
That, at thy birth, mad'st the poore Smith affraid,   107   F10 Proludium   14
AFFRICKE
Then Affricke knew, or the full Grecian store!   398   Drayton   88
AFFRIGHT
Shall make us sad next morning: or affright   65   E101 Supper   41
That neither want doe thee affright,   100   F3 Wroth   104
That neither want should thee affright,   100   F3 Wroth   V104
AFFRIGHTED
Upon th'affrighted world: 243   U70 Ode   16
AFFRIGHTS
Is it the paine affrights? that's soone forgot.   46   E62 Would-bee   5
As light breakes from you, that affrights despaire,   191   U38 Elegy 'Tis   10
A-FIRE
A Sparke to set whole worlds a-fire,   189   U36 Song   9
AFORE
Knew I all this afore? had I perceiv'd,   171   U20 Shrub   9
AFRAID
Who saw the light, and were afraid,   130   U1 Nativitie   5
And sleepe so guiltie and afraid,   151   U11 Dreame   13
Then to make falshood blush, and fraud afraid: 186   U32 Elsmere   4
With all th'adventures; Three bookes not afraid   207   U43 Vulcan   95
Thy just defences made th' oppressor afraid.   217   U46 Coke   8
Creepes on the ground; too safe, too afraid of storme.   307   Horace   39
AFRONT
Or in remembrance of thy afront, and scorne,   203   U43 Vulcan   7
AFTER
Doe beg thy care unto thy after-state.   43   E51 James 3   8
He markes not whose 'twas first: and after-times   45   E56 Poet-Ape   11
Shee shall instruct my after-thoughts to write   48   E65 Muse   13
Item, a tale or two, some fortnight after;   51   E73 Fine Grand   7
Thou need'st not shrinke at voyce of after-times;   61   E95 Savile   20
And, after, swom abroad in ample flakes,   87   E133 Voyage   138
And, after mouldie growne, againe were tosted,   88   E133 Voyage   150
Though never after; whiles it gaynes the voyce   113   F12 Rutland   11
Though never after; whiles it gaynes the will   113   F12 Rutland   V 11
And after varyed, as fresh objects goes,   118   F13 Aubigny   66
And almost, all dayes after, while they live;   118   F13 Aubigny   75
Let 'hem waste body, and state; and after all,   118   F13 Aubigny   81
And judge me after: if I dare pretend   122   F15 Heaven   7
And destin'd unto judgement, after all.   122   F15 Heaven   20
After many scornes like these,   133   U2 Suffered   1
After flight; and put new stings   137   U2 Cupid   36
Like Money-brokers, after Names, and hire   155   U13 Sacvile   62
Those thousands on his back, shall after blow   165   U15 Friend-Wars   104
And, after all theyr Aetnean Ire,   179   U25 Desmond   44
And take some sirrup after; so doe I,   197   U40 Elegy That   5
Court every hanging Gowne, and after that,   201   U42 Elegy Let   57
After the Fathers, and those wiser Guides   207   U43 Vulcan   103
To goe out after—till when take this letter   229   U54 Squib   19
In changing. Let our after Nephewes see   238   U65 Prince   V 7
You lik'd, then after, to apply   247   U70 Ode   108
(After the last child borne;) This is our wedding day.   258   U75 Epithalam.   168
Nor after Chloe did his Lydia sound;   293   U87 Hor.3:9   6
After, mens Wishes, crown'd in their events,   309   Horace   108
And tortures us: and, after, by the tongue   311   Horace   156
Speake to me, Muse, the Man, who, after Troy was sack't,   315   Horace   201
Wonders forth after: As Antiphates,   315   Horace   205
Lookes after honours, and bewares to act   315   Horace   239
For the vile Goat, soone after, forth did send   319   Horace   320
Now, after all, let no man   364   Phoenix   1
To make these good, and what comes after, better.   666   Glover   10
AFTERNOONES
A mornings, and at afternoones, to foole   230   U56 Covell   22
AFTER-STATE
Doe beg thy care unto thy after-state.   43   E51 James 3   8
AFTER-THOUGHTS
Shee shall instruct my after-thoughts to write   48   E65 Muse   13
AFTER-TIMES
He markes not whose 'twas first: and after-times   45   E56 Poet-Ape   11
Thou need'st not shrinke at voyce of after-times;   61   E95 Savile   20
AFTERWARDS
Where, afterwards, it grew a butter-flye: 31   E15 Court-worm   3
AGAIN (See also AGEN)
Again, thy Architect to ashes turne!   406   Inigo Jones 1   102
AGAINE
Takes private beatings, and begins againe.   49   E68 Playwrt 2   2
Since when, hee's sober againe, and all play's made.   56   E87 Hazard   6
They murder him againe, that envie thee.   72   E111 Edmonds 2   14
Who prov'st, all these were, and againe may bee.   78   E122 Rudyerd 2   10
And, after mouldie growne, againe were tosted,   88   E133 Voyage   150
With which he fled me: and againe,   93   F1 Why write no   8
Bender his head in there againe?   101   F4 To the World   32
Sunnes, that set, may rise againe: 102   F5 Celia 1   6
Kisse againe: no creature comes.   103   F6 Celia 2   5
For Loves-sake, kisse me once againe,   139   U2 Another   1
To fall againe; at such a feast,   144   U3 Musicall   23
I Love, and he loves me againe,   147   U7 Nymph   1
Of sleepe againe, who was his Aid;   151   U11 Dreame   12
Of Gathering? Bountie' in pouring out againe?   159   U14 Selden   38
Give me but that againe, that I must wast   167   U15 Friend-Wars   152

		Page	Title	Line

AGAINE (cont.)

	Page	Title	Line
Give me but that againe, which I must wast	167	U15 Friend-Wars	V152
But what she gives, thou dar'st give her againe;	168	U15 Friend-Wars	184
To give the world againe:	175	U23 Himselfe	29
Scarce the Hill againe doth flourish,	184	U29 Fit of Rime	37
Phoebus to his Crowne againe;	184	U29 Fit of Rime	40
Could you demand the gifts you gave, againe?	192	U38 Elegy 'Tis	55
But to exact againe what once is given,	192	U38 Elegy 'Tis	63
Shortly againe: and make our absence sweet.	197	U40 Elegy That	8
T' have paid againe a blessing was but lent,	271	U81 Pawlet	80
Or Kid forc't from the Wolfe againe.	291	U85 Country	60
At th'Calends, puts all out againe.	291	U85 Country	70
Venus, againe thou mov'st a warre	292	U86 Hor.4:1	1
And both doe crave, and give againe, this leave.	305	Horace	13
Things in themselves agreeing: If againe	313	Horace	170
Forbids thee forth againe thy foot to draw.	313	Horace	194
Once seene, to be againe call'd for, and plaid,	317	Horace	271
While he was young; he sweat, and freez'd againe:	333	Horace	589
From thence, display thy wing againe	367	Ode Who saith	41
And up againe, in skies, and aire to vent	368	Ode Who saith	77
To life againe, to heare thy Buskin tread,	391	Shakespeare	36
But when againe I veiw the parts so peiz'd,	395	May	7
But that I heare, againe, thy Drum to beate	397	Drayton	55
Againe hath brought the Lillie to the Rose;	401	Filmer	8

'GAINST

	Page	Title	Line
'Tis 'gainst the manners of an Epigram:	29	E9 To All	3
Like aydes 'gainst treasons who hath found before?	38	E35 James 2	7
Still, 'tis his lucke to praise me 'gainst his will.	50	E71 Parrat	2
T'inveigh 'gainst playes: what did he then but play?	52	E75 Lippe	4
Or 'gainst the Bishops, for the Brethren, raile,	59	E92 New Crie	35
Cryes out 'gainst cocking, since he cannot bet,	76	E119 Shelton	3
For what a sinne 'gainst your great fathers spirit,	114	F12 Rutland	31
'Gainst stormes, or pyrats, that might charge your peace;	119	F13 Aubigny	93
Thy gift 'gainst envie. O how I doe count	161	U14 Selden	79
Who 'gainst the Law, weave Calumnies, my——;	187	U33 Councellour	6
I ne're attempted, Vulcan, 'gainst thy life;	202	U43 Vulcan	5
What could their care doe 'gainst the spight	234	U60 La-ware	5
Stiffe! starke! my joynts 'gainst one another knock!	269	U81 Pawlet	9
'Gainst th'Ides, his moneys he gets in with paine,	291	U85 Country	69
'Gainst th'Ides, his gott moneyes he gets in with paine,	291	U85 Country	V 69
There words will never follow 'gainst their will.	349	Horace	V444

AGAINST

	Page	Title	Line
Against thy fortune: when no foe, that day,	49	E66 Cary	9
Against my grave, and time could not forgive.	58	E91 Vere	12
Wherewith, against thy bloud, they'offenders bee.	60	E93 Radcliffe	16
Against the bad, but of, and to the good:	66	E102 Pembroke	3
To make thy lent life, good against the Fates:	70	E109 Nevil	11
Against their breasts. Here, sev'rall ghosts did flit	87	E133 Voyage	124
Against Jealousie.	150	U10 Jealousie	Ttl
Against his will that do's 'hem? that hath weav'd	153	U13 Sacvile	26
A banke against it. Nothing but the round	160	U14 Selden	63
Against his Maker; high alone with weeds,	163	U15 Friend-Wars	33
Against or Faith, or honours lawes.	173	U22 Elegy Tho	12
A Fit of Rime against Rime.	183	U29 Fit of Rime	Ttl
Against a multitude; and (with thy Stile	187	U33 Councellour	31
I ne're attempted ought against thy life;	202	U43 Vulcan	V 5
Squire of the Squibs, against the Pageant day,	208	U43 Vulcan	119
Squire of the Squibs, against the next Maiors day,	208	U43 Vulcan	V119
Against thy furie, when to serve their needs,	208	U43 Vulcan	125
Against the Globe, the Glory of the Banke.	208	U43 Vulcan	132
Against this Vulcan? No Injunction?	210	U43 Vulcan	175
I murmure against God, for having ta'en	283	U84 Muse	33
Who will be there, against that day prepar'd,	284	U84 Muse	59
Against the Nature he would worship. Hee	284	U84 Muse	75
Against the Husband comes home tir'd;	291	U85 Country	44
There words will follow, not against their will.	325	Horace	444
Wilt nothing against nature speake, or doe:	331	Horace	574
Hee that preserves a man, against his will,	335	Horace	665
But thou art proofe against them, and indeed	391	Shakespeare	15
Hanch against Hanch, or raise a riming Club	396	Drayton	8
Drums against Drums, the neighing of the Horse,	397	Drayton	40
A Trench against it, nor a Battry plac't?	401	Beaumont	14
By barking against mee. Thou look'st at least,	408	Detractor	10

AGE

	Page	Title	Line
Then thee the age sees not that thing more grave,	31	E14 Camden	5
And, if no other miserie, yet age?	41	E45 First Son	8
Of love, and what the golden age did hold	47	E64 Salisbury 3	3
A treasure, art: contemn'd in th'age of gold.	47	E64 Salisbury 3	4
If Rome so great, and in her wisest age,	56	E89 Allen	1
And, finding good securitie in his age,	57	E90 Mill	6
Nor could the age have mist thee, in this strife	66	E102 Pembroke	5
Of former age, or glorie of our one,	67	E104 Montgomery	10
I' your selfe, all treasure lost of th'age before.	68	E105 L Wroth 2	20
For, where his person liv'd scarce one just age,	71	E110 Edmonds 1	13
That age, when thou stood'st up the master-braine:	75	E116 Jephson	4
Groyne, come of age, his state sold out of hand	75	E117 Groyne	1
He, that, but living halfe his age, dyes such;	76	E119 Shelton	15
The aged Saturne's age, and rites to know;	78	E122 Rudyerd 2	2
Then let the former age, with this content her,	84	E133 Voyage	19
A fortune, in this age, but rarely knowne.	96	F2 Penshurst	92
Such, and no other was that age, of old,	98	F3 Wroth	63
That they may sleepe with scarres in age.	98	F3 Wroth	70
That houre upon my morne of age,	100	F4 To the World	2

AGE (cont.)
To age, misfortune, sicknesse, griefe: „   „   „   „ 102 F4 To the World   62
And this age will build no more: „   „   „   „   „ 105 F8 Sicknesse   12
Then this, our guilt, nor golden age can deeme, „   „   „   „ 114 F12 Rutland   22
Keepe the middle age at stay,   „   „   „   „   „ 131 U2 Excuse   21
He that no more for Age, Cramps, Palsies, can   „   „   „   „ 166 U15 Friend-Wars 135
And since our Daintie age,   „   „   „   „   „   „   „   „ 175 U23 Himselfe   31
Not a Poet in an Age,   „   „   „   „   „   „   „   „   „ 183 U29 Fit of Rime   26
One beautie in an Age, and free from thee?   „   „   „   „ 188 U34 Small Poxe   2
It is a ryming Age, and Verses swarme   „   „   „   „   „ 200 U42 Elegy Let   27
And so, have kept me dying a whole age,   „   „   „   „ 205 U43 Vulcan   55
And so, have kept them dying a whole age,   „   „   „   „ 205 U43 Vulcan   V 55
This Age would lend no faith to Dorrels Deed;   „   „   „   „ 223 U49 Pucell   42
As though his age imperfect might appeare,   „   „   „   „ 244 U70 Ode   51
To swell thine age;   „   „   „   „   „   „   „   „   „ 244 U70 Ode   56
Hee leap'd the present age,   „   „   „   „   „ 245 U70 Ode   79
In all thy age of Journals thou hast tooke,   „   „   „   „ 254 U75 Epithalam.   75
The customes of each age thou must observe,   „   „   „   „ 315 Horace   223
The parts of age to youth be given; or men   „   „   „   „ 317 Horace   252
I, therefore will begin. Soule of the Age!   „   „   „   „ 391 Shakespeare   17
He was not of an age, but for all time!   „   „   „   „ 391 Shakespeare   43
This is the money-gett, Mechanick Age!   „   „   „   „ 404 Inigo Jones 1   52
Which I, your Master, first did teach the Age.   „   „   „   „ 409 Brome   8
And in this Age, canst hope no other grace.   „   „   „   „ 420 Ode:If Men   27
AGED
The aged Saturne's age, and rites to know;   „   „   „   „   78 E122 Rudyerd 2   2
Fat, aged carps, that runne into thy net.   „   „   „   „   94 F2 Penshurst   33
The first-borne dying; so the aged state   „   „   „   „ 309 Horace   87
The first-borne dying; so the aged Fate   „   „   „   „ 340 Horace   V 87
AGEN
Some have lov'd as old agen.   „   „   „   „   „   „   „   „ 131 U2 Excuse   6
In whom alone Love lives agen?   „   „   „   „ „   „   „   „ 173 U22 Elegy Tho   14
Till I may see both it and you agen.   „   „   „   „   „ 199 U41 Elegy Since   22
That have good places: therefore once agen,   „   „   „   „ 212 U43 Vulcan   212
That have good fortunes: therefore once agen,   „   „   „   „ 212 U43 Vulcan   V212
That have good places: wherefore once agen,   „   „   „   „ 212 U43 Vulcan   V212
AGENTS
Your Arch-Dukes Agents, and your Beringhams,   „   „   „   „   69 E107 Hungry   23
AGES
Then knew the former ages: yet to life,   •   „   „   „   „ 242 U69 Friend Son   23
Which, unto all Ages, for his will be knowne,   „   „   „   „ 379 Coryat 3   11
AGILE
A gentler, and more agile hand, to tend   „   „   „   „ 180 U26 Ode High   4
AGINCOURT
An Agincourt, an Agincourt, or dye.   „   „   „   „   „ 398 Drayton   70
AGREE
I know no couple better can agree!   „   „   „   „   „   40 E42 Giles   18
This peece, my Piso's, and that booke agree,   „   „   „   „ 305 Horace   8
That Book, my Piso's, and this piece agree,   „   „   „   „ 338 Horace   V 8
AGREEING
Things in themselves agreeing: If againe   „   „   „   „ 313 Horace   170
'GREES
Then to the purpose leades, and fitly 'grees.   „   „   „   „ 317 Horace   279
AID   (See also AYDES)
Of sleepe againe, who was his Aid;   „   „   „   „   „ 151 U11 Dreame   12
For houshold aid, and Children sweet;   „   „   „   •   „ 291 U85 Country   40
AIDE
Alwayes at hand, to aide the merry Muses.   „   „   „   „   85 E133 Voyage   54
Thy present Aide: Arise Invention,   „   „   „   „   „ 176 U25 Desmond   2
Thy present Aide: Spirit Invention,   „   „   „   „   „ 176 U25 Desmond   V 2
Without the pompe of Counsell; or more Aide,   „   „   „   „ 186 U32 Elsmere   3
When, being the Strangers helpe, the poore mans aide, „ „ „   „ 217 U46 Coke   7
Needs lend an aide, to thine she had her eyes.   „   „   „   „ 217 U46 Coke   24
Send these suspected helpes, to aide   „   „   „   „   „ 275 U84 Body   5
AIDED
Who aided him, will thee, the issue of Joves braine.   „ „   „ 175 U23 Himselfe   30
Who aided them, will thee, the issue of Joves braine. „ „ „   „ 175 U23 Himselfe   V 30
Whom Fortune aided lesse, or vertue more.   „   „   „   „ 217 U46 Coke   4
None Fortune aided lesse, or Vertue more.   „   „   „   „ 217 U46 Coke   22
AIDES
Of Princes aides, or good mens Charities.   „   „   „   „ 248 U71 Treasurer   3
Great aides to Empire, as they are great care   „   „   „   „ 268 U80 Christning   6
AILE
An ill-affected limbe (what e're it aile)   „   „   „   „   „ 192 U38 Elegy 'Tis   45
AIME   (See also AYME)
No aime at glorie, or, in warre,   „   „   „   „   „ 234 U60 La-ware   13
I durst not aime at that: The dotes were such   „   „   „   „ 269 U81 Pawlet   25
I durst not aime at, the dotes thereof were such „   „   „   „ 269 U81 Pawlet   V 25
Sharpe, and contemning lawes, at him should aime, „   „   „   „ 313 Horace   173
AIRE   (MELODY)
French Aire and English Verse here Wedded lie.   „   •   „   „ 401 Filmer   6
AIRE   (See also AERIE, AYRE)
Marrie the Muse is one, can tread the Aire,   „   „   „   „ 230 U56 Covell   13
Marrie his Muse is one, can tread the Aire,   „   „   „   „ 230 U56 Covell   V 13
Not tost or troubled with light Lady-aire;   „   „   „   „ 287 U84 Muse   164
Or, whilst he shuns the Earth, to catch at Aire   „   „   „   „ 321 Horace   335
But prove the Aire, and saile from Coast to Coast: „ „ „   „ 367 Ode Who saith   37
And up againe, in skies, and aire to vent   -   „   „   „   „ 368 Ode Who saith   77
AIRISING
Airising in that place, through which, who goes, „   „   „   „   87 E133 Voyage   131
A-JAX
My Muse had plough'd with his, that sung A-jax.   „   „   „   „   89 E133 Voyage   196

AJAX
    Ajax, or Idomen, or all the store,   114 F12 Rutland   54
AKE
    T'effect it, feele, thou'ast made thine owne heart ake.   250 U73 Weston   12
AL
    They're dark, bid cleare 'hem; al that's doubtful wrote   354 Horace   V637
ALARMES
    Nor Souldier-like started with rough alarmes,   289 U85 Country   5
    How do his trumpets breath! What loud alarmes!   398 Drayton   66
ALARUM   (See also 'LARUM)
ALAS   (See also 'LASSE)
    But viewing him since (alas, too late)   77 E120 S. P.   19
    Row close then, slaves. Alas, they will beshite us.   86 E133 Voyage   90
    Yes, threaten, doe. Alas I feare   101 F4 To the World   37
    Hercules? alas his bones are yet sore,   107 F10 Proludium   4
    But alas, thou seest the least   137 U2 Cupid   43
    Alas I ha' lost my heat, my blood, my prime,   199 U41 Elegy Since   11
    Alas, but Morison fell young: 244 U70 Ode   43
    Alas, I am all Marble! write the rest   269 U81 Pawlet   13
    And in their numbers; For, alas, what knew   319 Horace   300
    Alas: then whither wade I,   365 Ode Splendor   17
    Alas: then whither trade I,   365 Ode Splendor   V 17
ALBA
    Beneath a Sweet-wood Roofe, neere Alba Lake: 292 U86 Hor.4:1   20
ALBIN'S
    There's Albin's sonne will say, Substract an ounce   327 Horace   467
ALCHIMIST
    Some Alchimist there may be yet, or odde   208 U43 Vulcan   118
ALCHYMISTS
    To Alchymists.   29 E6 Alchymists   Ttl
ALCIDES
    Alcides, be thou succouring to my song.   85 E133 Voyage   50
    Were you Jove's sonnes, or had Alcides might.   89 E133 Voyage   182
ALCORAN
    The Talmud, and the Alcoran had come,   205 U43 Vulcan   65
ALDE
    And tell thou, Alde-Legh, None can tell more true   274 U84 Descent   13
ALDE-LEGH
    And tell thou, Alde-Legh, None can tell more true   274 U84 Descent   13
ALDERMAN
    Doe I reflect. Some alderman has power,   117 F13 Aubigny   38
ALDERMANITIE
    The Battells of thy Aldermanitie;   214 U44 Speach   46
ALE
    Who kept an ale-house; with my little Minos,   89 E133 Voyage   189
    The wit of Ale, and Genius of the Malt   193 U38 Elegy 'Tis   95
    Or Ale! He build a pallace! Thou a shopp   407 Inigo Jones 2   9
    at Pem Wakers good ale Tapp,   417 Moon   39
    or theire Ale, they break the peace,   418 Moon   42
ALE-HOUSE
    Who kept an ale-house; with my little Minos,   89 E133 Voyage   189
ALEXANDER
    Mr. Alexander Glover   666 Glover   2
ALEXANDRIA
    Or Alexandria; and though a Divine   211 U43 Vulcan   195
ALICE
    To Mrs. Alice Sutcliffe, on her divine Meditations.   411 Sutcliffe   Ttl
    Must Celia bee, the Anagram of Alice.   412 Sutcliffe   23
A-LIFE
    If they goe on, and that thou lov'st a-life   232 U58 Book-seller   13
ALIGHT
    Till thou at Tames alight,   368 Ode Who saith   79
ALIKE
    Thy praise, or dispraise is to me alike,   46 E61 Foole   1
    Who did, alike with thee, thy house up-beare,   60 E93 Radcliffe   3
    When Vice alike in time with vertue dur'd.   176 U24 Frontispice   8
    A wise simplicity; freindes alike-stated;   295 U90 Mart.10:47   7
    Alike of kin, to that most blessed Trine,   413 Ghyrlond   34
ALIKE-STATED
    A wise simplicity; freindes alike-stated;   295 U90 Mart.10:47   7
ALIVE   (See also 'LIVE)
    Where merit is not sepulcher'd alive.   47 E64 Salisbury 3   10
    Whose noyse shall keepe thy miming most alive,   81 E129 Mime   10
    It is a call to keepe the spirits alive   162 U15 Friend-Wars   5
    Of putrid flesh alive! of blood, the sinke!   172 U21 Ltl Shrub   9
    Alive yet, in the noise; and still the same;   214 U44 Speach   56
    That scarce you heare a publike voyce alive,   234 U61 Epigram   5
    Alive, which else would die,   257 U75 Epithalam.   151
    Be kept alive those Sweet, and Sacred fires   257 U75 Epithalam.   163
    Their names of being kept alive,   273 U84 Cradle   6
    It would, must be: lest it alive would draw   329 Horace   509
    And art alive still, while thy Booke doth live,   391 Shakespeare   23
    As Love, here studied to keep Grace alive.   412 Ghyrlond   8
    How they doe keepe alive his memorie;   416 Dover   5
ALL'
    All's done in me.   128 U1 Trinitie   24
    Then to your love, and gift. And all's but due.   189 U37 Friend-Book   3
ALL   (See also AL)
    If all you boast of your great art be true;   29 E6 Alchymists   1
    To all, to whom I write.   29 E9 To All   Ttl
    His onely answere is to all, god payes.   31 E12 Shift   20
    All that I am in arts, all that I know,   31 E14 Camden   2
    Which conquers all, be once over-come by thee.   31 E14 Camden   12

ALL (cont.)

	Page	Title	Line
All men are wormes: But this no man. In silke	31	E15 Court-worm	1
Make good what thou dar'st doe in all the rest.	32	E16 Brain-hardy	8
Thy faith is all the knowledge that thou hast.	32	E18 Censurer	10
Yet, all heavens gifts, being heavens due;	33	E22 Daughter	3
Who, to thy one, all other braines refuse;	34	E23 Donne 1	2
All which I meant to praise, and, yet, I would;	34	E23 Donne 1	9
Makes serious use of all great trade he knowes.	35	E28 Surly	3
All braines, at times of triumph, should runne wit.	36	E29 Tilter	4
Could not effect, not all the furies doe,	37	E32 Roe 2	2
Seas, serenes, swords, shot, sicknesse, all are there.	37	E32 Roe 2	10
For all night-sinnes, with others wives, unknowne,	39	E39 Colt	1
All the gazers on the skies	39	E40 Ratcliffe	5
And get more gold, then all the colledge can:	39	E41 Gypsee	2
All this doth Jone. Or that his long yearn'd life	40	E42 Giles	11
In all affections shee concurreth still.	40	E42 Giles	15
And rich in issue to inherit all,	41	E44 Chuff	2
Saw all his race approch the blacker floods:	41	E44 Chuff	4
O, could I loose all father, now. For why	41	E45 First Son	5
For whose sake, hence-forth, all his vowes be such,	41	E45 First Son	11
To Sir Lucklesse Woo-all.	42	E46 Luckless 1	Ttl
He takes up all, makes each mans wit his owne.	45	E56 Poet-Ape	8
Who can behold all envie so declin'd	47	E63 Salisbury 2	7
Without his, thine, and all times injurie?	47	E63 Salisbury 2	10
Make him loose all his friends; and, which is worse,	48	E65 Muse	9
Almost all wayes, to any better course.	48	E65 Muse	10
Most thinke all praises flatteries. But truth brings	49	E67 Suffolk	2
As all thy honors were by them first sought;	49	E67 Suffolk	8
At Madames table, where thou mak'st all wit	50	E72 Court-ling	3
To draw thee custome: but her selfe gets all.	53	E78 Hornet	2
Nature, they thought, in all, that he would faine.	53	E79 Rutland	8
For all thou hear'st, thou swear'st thy selfe didst doo.	54	E81 Proule	5
Since when, hee's sober againe, and all play's made.	56	E87 Hazard	6
By which his damme conceiv'd him, clothes and all?	56	E88 Monsieur	11
Out-stript, then they did all that went before:	57	E89 Allen	10
And present worth in all dost so contract,	57	E89 Allen	11
They all get Porta, for the sundrie wayes	59	E92 New Crie	25
With England. All forbidden bookes they get.	59	E92 New Crie	31
Stand'st thou, to shew the times what you all were?	60	E93 Radcliffe	4
Thou, that art all their valour, all their spirit,	60	E93 Radcliffe	9
Nor could I, had I seene all Natures roule,	60	E93 Radcliffe	12
So hast thou rendred him in all his bounds,	61	E95 Savile	5
And all his numbers, both of sense, and sounds.	61	E95 Savile	6
O, would'st thou adde like hand, to all the rest!	61	E95 Savile	13
But most we need his faith (and all have you)	62	E95 Savile	35
Reade all I send: and, if I find but one	62	E96 Donne 2	7
Are all but Luthers beere, to this I sing.	65	E101 Supper	34
It is an Epigramme, on all man-kind;	66	E102 Pembroke	2
Of vice, and vertue; wherein all great life	66	E102 Pembroke	6
And glorie of them all, but to repeate!	66	E103 L Wroth 1	8
Madame, had all antiquitie beene lost,	67	E105 L Wroth 2	1
All historie seal'd up, and fables crost;	67	E105 L Wroth 2	2
Who could not but create them all, from you?	67	E105 L Wroth 2	6
If dancing, all would cry th'Idalian Queene;	68	E105 L Wroth 2	11
I' your selfe, all treasure lost of th'age before.	68	E105 L Wroth 2	20
All-vertuous Herbert! on whose every part	68	E106 E Herbert	3
Truth might spend all her voyce, Fame all her art.	68	E106 E Herbert	4
And yet, they, all together, lesse then thee.	68	E106 E Herbert	10
And, in some yeere, all these together heap'd,	69	E107 Hungry	15
Where all is faire, beside thy pedigree.	70	E109 Nevil	4
Not Caesars deeds, nor all his honors wonne,	71	E110 Edmonds 1	1
All yeelding to his fortune, nor, the while,	71	E110 Edmonds 1	5
Not all these, Edmonds, or what else put too,	71	E110 Edmonds 1	11
T'all future time, not onely doth restore	71	E110 Edmonds 1	21
Which all, but ignorant Captaynes, will confesse:	72	E111 Edmonds 2	7
Thy all, at all: and what so ere I doe,	72	E112 Gamster	5
But, in your love, made all his servants wise.	74	E114 Sydney	8
Doe all, that longs to the anarchy of drinke,	74	E115 Honest Man	12
Tell's of him, all the tales, it selfe then makes;	74	E115 Honest Man	17
It will deny all; and forsweare it too:	74	E115 Honest Man	19
An inginer, in slanders, of all fashions,	75	E115 Honest Man	31
All gentrie, yet, owe part of their best flame!	75	E116 Jephson	2
Gut eates all day, and lechers all the night,	76	E118 Gut	1
So all his meate he tasteth over, twise:	76	E118 Gut	2
No, Shelton, give me thee, canst want all these,	76	E119 Shelton	7
Weepe with me all you that read	77	E120 S. P.	1
They all consented;	77	E120 S. P.	18
Who prov'st, all these were, and againe may bee.	78	E122 Rudyerd 2	10
If, at all, shee had a fault,	79	E124 Elizabeth	7
Then that it liv'd at all. Farewell.	79	E124 Elizabeth	12
So, all reward, or name, that growes to mee	80	E127 Aubigny	9
T'extract, and choose th- best of all these knowne,	80	E128 Wm Roe 2	3
Attend thee hence; and there, may all thy ends,	81	E128 Wm Roe 2	6
The very call, to make all others come:	81	E129 Mime	8
Including all, were thence call'd harmonie:	82	E130 Ferrab. 1	14
But when I have said, The proofes of all these bee	82	E130 Ferrab. 1	17
For, then, all mouthes will judge, and their owne way:	82	E131 Ferrab. 2	3
And though we could all men, all censures heare,	83	E131 Ferrab. 2	5
And utter stranger to all ayre of France)	83	E132 Sylvester	4
All, that they boast of Styx, of Acheron,	84	E133 Voyage	7
All, that are readers: but, me thinkes 'tis od,	85	E133 Voyage	43
That all this while I have forgot some god,	85	E133 Voyage	44
Thou hast seene hell (some say) and know'st all nookes there,	85	E133 Voyage	51

ALL (cont.)

	Page	Title	Line
Of all your night-tubs, when the carts doe cluster,	85	E133 Voyage	64
Ploughing the mayne. When, see (the worst of all lucks)	86	E133 Voyage	78
And all his followers, that had so abus'd him:	86	E133 Voyage	97
Vanish'd away: as you must all presume	87	E133 Voyage	110
Then all those Atomi ridiculous,	87	E133 Voyage	127
But open, and un-armed encounter'd all:	87	E133 Voyage	135
All was to them the same, they were to passe,	88	E133 Voyage	140
They tooke 'hem all to witnesse of their action:	89	E133 Voyage	191
At his great birth, where all the Muses met.	94	F2 Penshurst	14
But all come in, the farmer, and the clowne:	94	F2 Penshurst	48
With all, that hospitalitie doth know!	95	F2 Penshurst	60
For fire, or lights, or livorie: all is there;	95	F2 Penshurst	73
With all their zeale, to warme their welcome here.	95	F2 Penshurst	81
To have her linnen, plate, and all things nigh,	96	F2 Penshurst	86
These, Penshurst, are thy praise, and yet not all.	96	F2 Penshurst	89
Or with thy friends; the heart of all the yeere,	97	F3 Wroth	25
Or with thy friends: the heate of all the yeere,	97	F3 Wroth	V 25
While all, that follow, their glad eares apply	97	F3 Wroth	31
From all the nets that thou canst spread.	100	F4 To the World	8
And all thy good is to be sold.	100	F4 To the World	16
With all my powers, my selfe to loose?	101	F4 To the World	28
When all the causes were away.	101	F4 To the World	44
That, what to all may happen here,	101	F4 To the World	55
From all my kinde: that, for my sake,	101	F4 To the World	59
All your bounties will betray.	103	F6 Celia 2	4
All the grasse that Rumney yeelds,	103	F6 Celia 2	13
All the sands in Chelsey fields,	103	F6 Celia 2	V 14
Live not we, as, all thy stalls,	104	F8 Sicknesse	9
Them, and all their officers.	105	F8 Sicknesse	35
That, to make all pleasure theirs,	105	F8 Sicknesse	36
His absence in my verse, is all I aske.	107	F10 Proludium	21
His absence in our verse, is all I aske.	107	F10 Proludium	V 21
Nor all the ladies of the Thespian lake,	108	F10 Proludium	25
and Conjures all my faculties t'approve	108	F10 Proludium	14
Not to know vice at all, and keepe true state,	109	F11 Epode	1
The'Elixir of all joyes?	110	F11 Epode	56
Of all his happinesse? But soft: I heare	111	F11 Epode	65
All taste of bitternesse, and makes the ayre	112	F11 Epode	97
All her best symmetrie in that one feature!	112	F11 Epode	101
Whil'st that, for which, all vertue now is sold,	113	F12 Rutland	1
Well, or ill, onely, all the following yeere,	113	F12 Rutland	7
Or perhaps lesse: whil'st gold beares all this sway,	113	F12 Rutland	18
The world hath seene, which all these had in trust,	114	F12 Rutland	39
Ajax, or Idomen, or all the store,	114	F12 Rutland	54
Of all Lucina's traine; Lucy the bright,	115	F12 Rutland	66
Then all, that have but done my Muse least grace,	115	F12 Rutland	79
Then all, that have but done my verse lesse grace,	115	F12 Rutland	V 79
And so doe many more. All which can call	117	F13 Aubigny	31
And, in those outward formes, all fooles are wise.	117	F13 Aubigny	36
Without which, all the rest were sounds, or lost.	118	F13 Aubigny	50
For truthes complexion, where they all weare maskes.	118	F13 Aubigny	70
And almost, all dayes after, while they live;	118	F13 Aubigny	75
Let 'hem waste body, and state; and after all,	118	F13 Aubigny	81
Into your harbor, and all passage shut	119	F13 Aubigny	92
And all doe strive t'advance	120	F14 Sydney	5
When all the noyse	120	F14 Sydney	17
Strive all right wayes it can,	121	F14 Sydney	25
And hearts of all, if I be sad for show,	122	F15 Heaven	6
As thou art all, so be thou all to mee,	122	F15 Heaven	9
And destin'd unto judgement, after all.	122	F15 Heaven	20
As my heart lies in peeces, all confus'd,	127	U1 Trinitie	7
All-gracious God, the Sinners sacrifice,	127	U1 Trinitie	9
This All of nothing, gavest it forme, and fate,	127	U1 Trinitie	18
All coeternall in your Majestie,	128	U1 Trinitie	38
With all since bought.	129	U1 Father	22
That did us all salvation bring,	130	U1 Nativitie	8
To see this Babe, all innocence;	130	U1 Nativitie	22
All the world for love may die.	131	U2 Excuse	24
All the Pride the fields than have:	132	U2 How he saw	4
Mock'd of all: and call'd of one	132	U2 How he saw	28
Looser-like, now, all my wreake	133	U2 Suffered	21
As she goes, all hearts doe duty	134	U2 Triumph	5
All that Loves world compriseth!	134	U2 Triumph	12
All the Gaine, all the Good, of the Elements strife.	134	U2 Triumph	20
I confesse all, I replide,	137	U2 Cupid	39
All is Venus: save unchaste.	137	U2 Cupid	42
Of the Court, to day, then all	138	U2 Kisse	15
As might all the Graces lead,	138	U2 Kisse	26
To have left all sight for you:	138	U2 Kisse	33
And all your bountie wrong:	139	U2 Another	10
All that heard her, with desire.	139	U2 Promise	6
We all feare, she loveth none.	140	U2 Promise	12
All your sweet of life is past,	140	U2 Promise	28
All his blood should be a flame	141	U2 Her man	30
'Twere to long, to speake of all:	141	U2 Her man	33
All his actions to be such,	142	U2 Her man	45
All I wish is understood.	142	U2 Exception	6
And challenge all the Spheares,	143	U3 Musicall	2
And all the world turne Eares.	143	U3 Musicall	4
So going thorow all your straine,	145	U5 Woman-kind	10
Where Love may all his Torches light,	147	U7 Nymph	24
And all my closes meet	149	U9 Picture	V 7

	Page	Title	Line

ALL (cont.)

And all these through her eyes, have stopt her eares.	150	U9 Picture	18
On all mens Fruit, and flowers, as well as mine.	150	U10 Jealousie	8
In all my wild desire,	151	U11 Dreame	11
All order, and Disposure, still.	151	U12 Corbet	14
If, Sackvile, all that have the power to doe	153	U13 Sacvile	1
All this corrupts the thankes; lesse hath he wonne,	154	U13 Sacvile	33
All the Towne-curs take each their snatch at me.	155	U13 Sacvile	72
All as their prize, turne Pyrats here at Land,	155	U13 Sacvile	81
Find you to reckon nothing, me owe all.	158	U13 Sacvile	164
Unto the Censure. Yours all need doth flie	158	U14 Selden	11
Ever at home: yet, have all Countries seene:	159	U14 Selden	30
In sharpnesse of all Search, wisdome of Choise,	160	U14 Selden	59
All that dare rowse: or are not loth to quit	162	U15 Friend-Wars	3
All other Acts of Worldlings, are but toyle	162	U15 Friend-Wars	9
All other Acts of Worldlings, are meere toyle	162	U15 Friend-Wars V	9
For all their spight, be like him if they could:	162	U15 Friend-Wars	26
And impious ranknesse of all Sects and seeds:	163	U15 Friend-Wars	34
And shamefastnesse together! All lawes dead,	163	U15 Friend-Wars	40
And shamefac'dnesse together! All lawes dead,	163	U15 Friend-Wars V	40
All which he makes the servants of the Groine,	163	U15 Friend-Wars	46
That all respect; She must lie downe: Nay more,	163	U15 Friend-Wars	53
Doe all the tricks of a saut Lady Bitch;	164	U15 Friend-Wars	76
Or use all arts, or haunt all Companies	165	U15 Friend-Wars	91
Goe, quit 'hem all. And take along with thee,	167	U15 Friend-Wars	175
That thou dost all things more for truth, then glory,	168	U15 Friend-Wars	179
All that is left of Philip Gray,	168	U16 Gray	4
All is not barren land, doth fallow lie.	169	U17 Friend-Debt	16
A terror? or is all this but my feare?	169	U18 Elegy Can	6
Of all that can be done him; Such a one	171	U19 Elegy By	23
His Issue, and all Circumstance of life,	171	U19 Elegy By	26
Knew I all this afore? had I perceiv'd,	171	U20 Shrub	9
Knew I, that all their Dialogues, and discourse,	172	U20 Shrub	13
Then all Ingredients made into one curse,	172	U20 Shrub	18
Thinke but the Sin of all her sex, 'tis she!	172	U20 Shrub	20
The Divell; and be the damning of us all.	172	U20 Shrub	24
Of all vice hurld together, there he was,	172	U21 Ltl Shrub	6
Proud, false, and trecherous, vindictive, all	172	U21 Ltl Shrub	7
And draw, and conquer all mens love,	173	U22 Elegy Tho	7
To whom all Lovers are design'd,	173	U22 Elegy Tho	26
Are all th'Aonian springs	174	U23 Himselfe	7
And, after all theyr Aetnean Ire,	179	U25 Desmond	44
As farre from all revolt, as you are now from Fortune.	180	U25 Desmond	65
Which all the world then styl'd divine?	181	U27 Ode Helen	20
Which all the Fate of Troy foretold?	181	U27 Ode Helen	24
Have all these done (and yet I misse	182	U27 Ode Helen	29
Come short of all this learned throng,	182	U27 Ode Helen	34
For in your verse all Cupids Armorie,	182	U28 Worth	9
All good Poetrie hence was flowne,	183	U29 Fit of Rime	14
All Parnassus Greene did wither,	183	U29 Fit of Rime	17
All light failed!	183	U29 Fit of Rime	24
Read here in one, what thou in all canst find,	185	U30 Burleigh	2
That in all tempests, never quit the helme,	185	U30 Burleigh	10
Of all the Land. Who now at such a Rate,	185	U30 Burleigh	19
So, justest Lord, may all your Judgements be	185	U31 Elsmere	1
So, from all sickness, may you rise to health,	186	U31 Elsmere	5
All mouthes, that dare entitle them (from hence)	187	U33 Councellour	11
Arm'd at all peeces, as to keepe a Fort	187	U33 Councellour	30
And (which doth all Atchievements get above)	187	U33 Councellour	38
Alone, but all thy ranke a reverend Name.	187	U33 Councellour	40
Make all hereafter, had'st thou ruin'd this?	188	U34 Small Poxe	16
What wonder perfect, all were fil'd,	188	U35 Chute	3
All lights into his one doth run;	189	U36 Song	6
Without which all the world were darke;	189	U36 Song	7
'Tis true, I'm broke! Vowes, Oathes, and all I had	191	U38 Elegy 'Tis	1
We cut not off, till all Cures else doe faile:	192	U38 Elegy 'Tis	46
That were to wither all, and make a Grave	192	U38 Elegy 'Tis	59
He cannot angrie be, but all must quake,	193	U38 Elegy 'Tis	71
It shakes even him, that all things else doth shake.	193	U38 Elegy 'Tis	72
As all with storme and tempest ran together.	193	U38 Elegy 'Tis	76
Streight puts off all his Anger, and doth kisse	193	U38 Elegy 'Tis	88
What Fooles, and all their Parasites can apply;	193	U38 Elegy 'Tis	94
How all my Fibres by your Spirit doe move,	194	U38 Elegy 'Tis	111
Till then 'tis all but darknesse, that I have;	194	U38 Elegy 'Tis	121
To put all relish from my memorie	197	U40 Elegy That	6
In all his Actions rarified to spright;	197	U40 Elegy That	20
And turning all he toucheth into pelfe,	197	U40 Elegy That	22
'Bove all your standing waters, choak'd with weedes.	198	U40 Elegy That	28
In all that is call'd lovely: take my sight	200	U42 Elegy Let	12
And all the originall riots of the place:	202	U42 Elegy Let	80
That since thou tak'st all envious care and paine,	203	U43 Vulcan	13
Th'Esplandians, Arthurs, Palmerins, and all	203	U43 Vulcan	30
Not ravish'd all hence in a minutes rage.	205	U43 Vulcan	56
Thou should'st have cry'd, and all beene proper stuffe.	205	U43 Vulcan	64
Thou should'st have cry'd, and all fine proper stuffe.	205	U43 Vulcan	V 64
All the madde Rolands, and sweet Oliveers;	206	U43 Vulcan	70
The weekly Corrants, with Pauls Seale; and all	206	U43 Vulcan	81
The weekly Corrants, with Poules stall; and all	206	U43 Vulcan	V 81
All the old Venusine, in Poetrie,	207	U43 Vulcan	89
With all th'adventures; Three bookes not afraid	207	U43 Vulcan	95
With all th'adventures; Three bookes not amisse	207	U43 Vulcan	V 95
All soote, and embers! odious, as thy worke!	207	U43 Vulcan	106
O no, cry'd all, Fortune, for being a whore,	209	U43 Vulcan	153

	Page	Title	Line
ALL (cont.)			
In those Records, which, were all Chroniclers gone,	210	U43 Vulcan	171
But say, all sixe good men, what answer yee?	210	U43 Vulcan	173
But I'le conclude all in a civill curse.	211	U43 Vulcan	190
To all as fatall as't hath beene to me,	211	U43 Vulcan	192
To all as chargefull as they have beene to me,	211	U43 Vulcan	V192
'Bove all your Fire-workes, had at Ephesus,	211	U43 Vulcan	194
'Bove all our Fire-workes, had at Ephesus,	211	U43 Vulcan	V194
Make your Petards, and Granats, all your fine	212	U43 Vulcan	206
We aske your absence here, we all love peace,	212	U43 Vulcan	209
We crave your absence here, we all love peace,	212	U43 Vulcan	V209
And all the Evils that flew out of her box	212	U43 Vulcan	214
And all Those ills that flew out of her box	212	U43 Vulcan	V214
All Ensignes of a Warre, are not yet dead,	213	U44 Speach	11
These ten yeares day; As all may sweare that looke	213	U44 Speach	27
All licence in our lives? What need we know,	215	U44 Speach	70
All that they doe at Playes. O, but first here	215	U44 Speach	91
But why are all these Irons i'the fire	215	U44 Speach	93
He that should search all Glories of the Gowne,	217	U46 Coke	1
And steps of all rais'd servants of the Crowne,	217	U46 Coke	2
He could not find, then thee, of all that store	217	U46 Coke	3
No lesse of praise, then readers in all kinds	217	U46 Coke	19
Such is thy All; that (as I sung before)	217	U46 Coke	21
Men that are safe, and sure, in all they doe,	218	U47 Tribe	1
On all Soules that are absent; even the dead;	218	U47 Tribe	17
That to speake well, thinke it above all sinne,	218	U47 Tribe	19
That censure all the Towne, and all th'affaires,	218	U47 Tribe	23
I wish all well, and pray high heaven conspire	219	U47 Tribe	37
Lose all my credit with my Christmas Clay,	219	U47 Tribe	52
With reverence using all the gifts thence given.	219	U47 Tribe	62
But all so cleare, and led by reasons flame,	220	U47 Tribe	69
And free it from all question to preserve.	220	U47 Tribe	72
Of all to the great Master.	220	U48 Bacchus	8
By all the Arts of Gladnesse,	221	U48 Bacchus	19
Pursue thee in all places,	221	U48 Bacchus	34
And set us all on skipping,	222	U48 Bacchus	51
Make State, Religion, Bawdrie, all a theame?	222	U49 Pucell	12
By all oblique Degrees, that killing height	224	U50 Countesse	11
And though all praise bring nothing to your name,	224	U50 Countesse	13
A cheerefull worke to all good eyes, to see	224	U50 Countesse	16
How comes it all things so about thee smile?	225	U51 Bacon	2
For whose returnes, and many, all these pray:	225	U51 Bacon	6
My Superficies: that was all you saw.	227	U52 Answer	9
An Archetype, for all the world to see,	227	U52 Answer	14
To all posteritie; I will write Burlase.	227	U52 Answer	24
To all the uses of the field, and race,	228	U53 Newcastle	3
Run all the Rounds in a soft Ladyes eare,	230	U56 Covell	16
Thou, Friend, wilt heare all censures; unto thee	232	U58 Book-seller	1
All mouthes are open, and all stomacks free:	232	U58 Book-seller	2
As all defence, or offence, were a chime!	232	U59 Newcastle	6
All this (my Lord) is Valour! This is yours!	233	U59 Newcastle	19
And was your Fathers! All your Ancestours!	233	U59 Newcastle	20
Who durst live great, 'mongst all the colds, and heates,	233	U59 Newcastle	21
Of humane life! as all the frosts, and sweates	233	U59 Newcastle	22
And all the games of Fortune, plaid at Court;	234	U61 Epigram	2
I'obtaine of God, what all the Land should aske?	234	U61 Epigram	11
Who dares denie, that all first-fruits are due	235	U63 Charles 2	1
And thinke all still the best, that he will doe.	236	U63 Charles 2	10
When all your life's a president of dayes,	237	U64 Charles 3	13
An Ode, or Song, by all the Muses. . . .	239	U67 Muses	Ttl
Of all her Brothers storie,	240	U67 Muses	29
Of all her Fathers storie,	240	U67 Muses	V 29
Whilst all the ravish'd rout	240	U67 Muses	40
Sweet! happy Mary! All	240	U67 Muses	49
All live dogs from the lane, and his shops sight,	241	U69 Friend Son	12
At a Friends freedome, proves all circling meanes	242	U69 Friend Son	15
To judge; So all men comming neere can spie,	242	U69 Friend Son	20
All is but web, and painting; be the strife	242	U69 Friend Son	24
And all on utmost ruine set;	243	U70 Ode	18
No doubt all Infants would returne like thee.	243	U70 Ode	20
Hee stoop'd in all mens sight	244	U70 Ode	38
All Offices were done	244	U70 Ode	48
And titles, by which all made claimes	247	U70 Ode	114
Repeating all Great Britain's joy, and more,	249	U72 King	6
Made lighter with the Wine. All noises else,	249	U72 King	12
Made loftier by the Winds all noises else,	249	U72 King	V 12
At Bonefires, squibs, and mirth, with all their Shoutes	249	U72 King	V 13
As all the wealth of Season, there was spread;	251	U74 Weston	15
Bring all your friends, (faire Lord) that burne	251	U74 Weston	20
With all the fruit shall follow it,	251	U74 Weston	23
Hath filled, with Caroches, all the way,	252	U75 Epithalam.	11
By all the Spheares consent, so in the heart of June?	253	U75 Epithalam.	16
As they came all to see, and to be seene!	253	U75 Epithalam.	20
In all her bloome, and flower;	253	U75 Epithalam.	23
The Month of youth, which calls all Creatures forth	253	U75 Epithalam.	26
Through which not only we, but all our Species are.	253	U75 Epithalam.	32
And all did ring th'approches of the Bride;	253	U75 Epithalam.	36
Of all the Maidens faire;	253	U75 Epithalam.	39
On all that come her Simplesse to rebuke!	253	U75 Epithalam.	44
The choisest Virgin-troup of all the Land!	254	U75 Epithalam.	50
And all the Ground were Garden, where she led!	254	U75 Epithalam.	68
With all the pompe of Youth, and all our Court beside.	254	U75 Epithalam.	72
Our Court, and all the Grandees; now, Sun, looke,	254	U75 Epithalam.	73

	Page	Title	Line

ALL (cont.)

In all thy age of Journals thou hast tooke,   254 U75 Epithalam. 75
Who, in all they doe,   255 U75 Epithalam. 78
All else we see beside, are Shadowes, and goe lesse.   255 U75 Epithalam. 88
All is a story of the King and Queene!   255 U75 Epithalam. 91
In all the prov'd assayes,   255 U75 Epithalam. 101
That farre-all-seeing Eye   256 U75 Epithalam. 109
With all corroding Arts, be able to untie!   257 U75 Epithalam. 136
All that their Fathers, and their Mothers might   257 U75 Epithalam. 147
The longing Couple, all that elder Lovers know.   258 U75 Epithalam. 192
To make all the Muses debters   259 U76 Petition 8
All the envie of the Rymes,   259 U76 Petition 18
All there envie of the Rymes,   259 U76 Petition V 18
This would all their envie burst: 260 U76 Petition 30
That would all their envie burst: 260 U76 Petition V 30
In honour, courtesie, and all the parts   262 U78 Digby 3
In him all vertue is beheld in State: 262 U78 Digby 6
In him all action is beheld in State: 262 U78 Digby V 6
Where all heroique ample thoughts doe meet: 262 U78 Digby 10
Being sent to one, they will be read of all.   263 U78 Digby 32
Lute, Lyre, Theorbo, all are call'd to day.   263 U79 New-yeares 2
And shuts the old. Haste, haste, all loyall Swaines,   263 U79 New-yeares 10
To him we owe all profits of our grounds.   264 U79 New-yeares 15
Of all that Nature, yet, to life did bring;   264 U79 New-yeares 33
Haste, haste you hither, all you gentler Swaines,   265 U79 New-yeares 46
To whom you owe all duties of your grounds;   265 U79 New-yeares 49
Hee gives all plentie, and encrease,   265 U79 New-yeares 56
Hee gives all plentie, and encrease,   265 U79 New-yeares 68
A horrour in mee! all my blood is steele!   269 U81 Pawlet 8
Alas, I am all Marble! write the rest   269 U81 Pawlet 13
And pietie the Center, where all met.   270 U81 Pawlet 42
From all affection! when they urg'd the Cure   270 U81 Pawlet 49
And I, into the world, all Soule, was sent!   270 U81 Pawlet 56
What the beginnings of all beauties be;   271 U81 Pawlet 74
And all beatitudes, that thence doe flow: 271 U81 Pawlet 75
And see all dead here, or about to dye!   271 U81 Pawlet 86
Whole Nations! nay, Mankind! the World, with all   271 U81 Pawlet 90
When we were all borne, we began to die;   271 U81 Pawlet 94
. . . A Gentleman absolute in all Numbers;   272 U84 Eupheme Ttl
That all Posteritie, as wee,   273 U84 Cradle 13
Of ord'ring all.   273 U84 Cradle 32
Draw first a Cloud: all save her neck;   276 U84 Body 13
And Men may thinke, all light rose there.   276 U84 Body 16
But at such distance, all the eye   276 U84 Body V 19
With all that Youth, or it can bring: 276 U84 Body 22
That all may say, that see the frame,   278 U84 Mind 23
It moveth all; and makes a flight   279 U84 Mind 31
In all the bounds of beautie fit   280 U84 Mind 51
Smooth, soft, and sweet, in all a floud   280 U84 Mind 61
Which all men doe, that urge not their owne deeds   281 U84 Kenelme 17
Hang all your roomes, with one large Pedigree: 282 U84 Kenelme 20
Study illustrious Him, and you have all.   282 U84 Kenelme 23
Who was my Muse, and life of all I sey'd,   282 U84 Muse 2
All that was good, or great in me she weav'd,   282 U84 Muse 4
With all her aydes, to save her from the seize   283 U84 Muse 17
I summe up mine owne breaking, and wish all.   283 U84 Muse 26
T'accuse, or quit all Parties to be heard!   284 U84 Muse 60
To Body, and Soule! where Love is all the guest!   284 U84 Muse 64
All other gladnesse, with the thought is barr'd;   284 U84 Muse 67
Will honour'd be in all simplicitie!   284 U84 Muse 76
Have all his actions wondred at, and view'd   284 U84 Muse 77
Amongst her Peeres, those Princes of all good!   284 U84 Muse 84
By all the wealth of blessings, and the store   285 U84 Muse 110
There, all the happy soules, that ever were,   285 U84 Muse 113
But all of God: They still shall have to say,   286 U84 Muse 119
But make him All in All, their Theme, that Day: 286 U84 Muse 120
Where Hee will be, all Beautie to the Sight;   286 U84 Muse 122
Hee will all Glory, all Perfection be,   286 U84 Muse 127
Yet have all debts forgiven us, and advance   286 U84 Muse 143
Who knowes the hearts of all, and can dissect   286 U84 Muse 150
Find all our Atomes from a point t' a span!   287 U84 Muse 152
Of title in her! All Nobilitie   287 U84 Muse 159
She swaid all bus'nesse in the Familie!   287 U84 Muse 168
He run; and all did strive with diligence   287 U84 Muse 171
In all her petite actions, so devote,   287 U84 Muse 177
Of sorrow, then all pompe of gaudy daies: 287 U84 Muse 182
And hers were all Humilitie! they beat   288 U84 Muse 189
On all the world! She saw him on the Crosse   288 U84 Muse 201
Of raising, judging, and rewarding all   288 U84 Muse 207
All this by Faith she saw, and fram'd a Plea,   288 U84 Muse 209
The last of houres, and shutter up of all;   289 U84 Muse 219
Of all are dead to life! His Wisdome show   289 U84 Muse 221
And giving dues to all Mankinds deserts!   289 U84 Muse 224
Happie is he, that from all Businesse cleere,   289 U85 Country 1
And all invite to easie sleepe.   290 U85 Country 28
At th'Calends, puts all out againe.   291 U85 Country 70
With thee 'bove all his Rivals gifts take place,   292 U86 Hor.4:1 18
In name, I went all names before,   293 U87 Hor.3:9 7
Liber, of all thy friends, thou sweetest care,   294 U89 Mart.8:77 1
Of daring all, hath still beene given; we know it: 305 Horace 12
His matter to his power, in all he makes,   307 Horace 57
Of the Cethegi; And all men will grace,   309 Horace 72
Our selves, and all that's ours, to death we owe: 309 Horace 90

ALL (cont.)

	Page	Title	Line
Being taught a better way. All mortall deeds	309	Horace	98
All the Grammarians strive; and yet in Court	309	Horace	111
To chant the Gods, and all their God-like race,	311	Horace	114
With weightie sorrow hurles us all along,	311	Horace	155
With weightie woes she hurles us all along	342	Horace	V155
Or do's all businesse coldly, and with feare;	317	Horace	244
Yet, to the Stage, at all thou maist not tender	317	Horace	260
Any fourth man, to speake at all, aspire.	317	Horace	275
And so to turne all earnest into jest,	321	Horace	330
Quite from all face of Tragedie to goe,	321	Horace	344
But meere Iambicks all, from first to last.	323	Horace	374
Or rather, thinking all my faults may spie,	323	Horace	392
Within the hope of having all forgiven?	323	Horace	394
Exclude all sober Poets, from their share	325	Horace	421
And better stayes them there, then all fine noise	327	Horace	459
All way of life was shewen; the grace of Kings	329	Horace	497
All which I tell, lest when Apollo's nam'd,	329	Horace	501
Or trundling Wheele, he can sit still, from all;	331	Horace	568
Can; or all toile, without a wealthie veine:	331	Horace	584
Hee'd bid, blot all: and to the anvile bring	333	Horace	627
They're darke, bid cleare this: all that's doubtfull wrote	335	Horace	637
All; So this grievous Writer puts to flight	337	Horace	676
Now, after all, let no man	364	Phoenix	1
For other formes come short all	364	Ode Splendor	2
All Nature of commending.	365	Ode Splendor	16
Hath all beene Harmony:	367	Ode Who saith	51
And conquers all things, yea it selfe, at length.	367	Ode Who saith	56
All which, when they but heare a straine	368	Ode Who saith	89
Conceal'd from all but cleare Propheticke eyes.	369	Ode Who saith	112
With all the race	369	Ode Who saith	118
All which are parts commend the cunning hand;	370	Author	4
And all your Booke (when it is throughly scan'd)	370	Author	5
And wish that all the Muses blood were spilt,	371	Fletcher	12
Or moathes shall eate, what all these Fooles admire.	371	Fletcher	16
With Rites not bound, but conscience. Wouldst thou All?	372	Epitaph	11
All sorts of fish with Musicke of his maw.	374	Coryat 1	11
Who, because his matter in all should be meete,	379	Coryat 3	3
Which, unto all Ages, for his will be knowne,	379	Coryat 3	11
Horse, foote, and all but flying in the ayre:	380	Coryat 3	28
hath armde att all poyntes; charge mee humblye kneele	382	Rich	2
That all, that view you then, and late; may say,	384	Somerset	25
My suffrage brings thee all increase, to crowne	385	Brooke	7
will all turne dust, & may not make me swell.	387	Cavendish	4
Will all be dust, & may not make me swell.	387	Cavendish	V 4
Let such as justly have out-liv'd all prayse,	387	Cavendish	5
If all the vulgar Tongues, that speake this day,	388	Chapman	7
As, now, of all men, it is call'd thy Trade:	389	Chapman	11
Had cloath'd him so. Here's all I can supply	389	Aleman	20
All, that was ever writ in brasse.	390	Reader	8
'Tis true, and all mens suffrage. But these wayes	390	Shakespeare	5
The truth, but gropes, and urgeth all by chance;	391	Shakespeare	10
Of all, that insolent Greece, or haughtie Rome	391	Shakespeare	39
To whom all Scenes of Europe homage owe.	391	Shakespeare	42
He was not of an age, but for all time!	391	Shakespeare	43
And all the Muses still were in their prime,	391	Shakespeare	44
Yet must I not give Nature all: Thy Art,	392	Shakespeare	55
Calme Brutus tenor start; but all along	395	May	11
A Friend at all; or, if at all, to thee:	396	Drayton	2
That all Earth look'd on; and that earth, all Eyes!	396	Drayton	16
Did all so strike me, as I cry'd, who can	397	Drayton	31
Of all that reade thy Poly-Olbyon.	397	Drayton	52
To all thy vertuous, and well chosen Friends,	398	Drayton	90
Code, Digests, Pandects of all faemale glory!	399	Lady Ogle	8
Upon her selfe) to all her sexe!	399	Lady Ogle	10
All Circles had their spring and end	399	Lady Ogle	14
All that was solid, in the name	399	Lady Ogle	17
Of Angells, and all witnesses of light,	400	Lady Ogle	38
And doth deserve all muniments of praise,	400	Beaumont	9
By all your Titles, & whole style at ones	402	Inigo Jones 1	15
And all men eccho you have made a Masque.	403	Inigo Jones 1	30
Court Hieroglyphicks! & all Artes affoord	404	Inigo Jones 1	43
His name is Skeuopoios wee all knowe,	404	Inigo Jones 1	60
All in the Worke! And soe shall still for Ben:	404	Inigo Jones 1	65
Of all the Worthyes hope t'outlast thy one,	406	Inigo Jones 1	99
With all Remonstrance make an honest man.	406	Inigo Jones 1	104
All kings to doe the self same deeds with some!	406	Inigo Jones 2	4
An Earle of show: for all thy worke is showe:	407	Inigo Jones 2	21
An Earle of show: for all thy worth is showe:	407	Inigo Jones 2	V 21
Will well designe thee, to be viewd of all	408	Inigo Jones 3	12
Both learned, and unlearned, all write Playes.	410	Brome	12
All which thou hast incurr'd deservedly:	410	Gill	5
The motives, and true Spurres to all good Nations.	411	Sutcliffe	5
The gladdest ground to all the numbred-five,	412	Ghyrlond	6
But, that which summes all, is the Eglantine,	413	Ghyrlond	21
All, pouring their full showre of graces downe,	413	Ghyrlond	31
Most venerable. Cause of all our joy.	414	Ghyrlond	42
Who mad'st us happy all, in thy reflexe,	414	Ghyrlond	47
Through all the lines of this circumference,	414	Ghyrlond	54
T'imprint in all purg'd hearts this virgin sence,	414	Ghyrlond	55
Or why to like; they found, it all was new,	415	Rutter	9
A Say-master, hath studied all the tricks	415	Rutter	26
Yo'have all the Mysteries of Wits new Mint,	415	Rutter	28

	Page	Title	Line

ALL (cont.)
And I sweare by all the light . . . . . . 416 Moon 5
morts, and mirkins that wagg all, ... 417 Moon 15
God blesse them all, and keepe them safe: . . . 419 Grace 7
God blesse us all, Bedford keepe safe: . . . 419 Grace V 7
And better Blason them, then all their Coates, . . . 419 Ode:If Men 8
Yet ware; thou mayst do all things cruellie: . . . 423 Lucan 15
Welcome all, who lead or follow, ... 657 Door Apollo 1
All his Answers are Divine, ... 657 Door Apollo 5
Hang up all the poor Hop-Drinkers, ... 657 Door Apollo 7
Fly it, and you all are mounted. . . . . 657 Door Apollo 14
Pays all Debts, cures all Diseases, ... 657 Door Apollo 17
Welcome all, who lead or follow, ... 657 Door Apollo 19
ALLAY
Chance that the Friends affection proves Allay . . . 158 U14 Selden 10
A vertue, like Allay, so gone . . . . 173 U22 Elegy Tho 5
There were some pieces of as base allay, . . . 204 U43 Vulcan 42
ALLEDGE
T'alledge, that greatest men were not asham'd, . . . 82 E130 Ferrab. 1 9
ALLEGORIC
Ode. <Allegoric>. . . . . . 366 Ode Who saith Ttl
ALIEN
To Edward Allen. . . . . . 56 E89 Allen Ttl
That, Allen, I should pause to publish thee? . . . 57 E89 Allen 8
ALLEY
Upon th'Exchange, still, out of Popes-head-Alley; . . 206 U43 Vulcan 80
ALL-GRACIOUS
All-gracious God, the Sinners sacrifice, . . . 127 U1 Trinitie 9
ALLIED
Borne, bred, allied? what's he dare tutor us? . . 215 U44 Speach 66
ALLIES
Or your Allies, you make your bookes your friends, . . 224 U50 Countesse 27
Transmitt it to your Nephewes, Freinds, Allies, . . 399 Lady Ogle 3
ALLMIGHTY
Allmighty Architecture? who noe less . . . 406 Inigo Jones 1 92
ALLOTTED
The place allotted it, with decent thewes. . . . 311 Horace 125
The place allotted it, with decent praise. . . . 341 Horace V131/125
ALLOW
Yet dare not, to my thought, lest hope allow . . . 41 E43 Salisbury 1 7
As thou hast best authoritie, t'allow. . . . 62 E96 Donne 2 6
Vertuously practise must at least allow . . . 75 E116 Jephson 14
A Roman to Caecilius will allow, . . . 309 Horace 77
And allow you for each particular mile, . . . 379 Coryat 3 9
ALLOWANCE
So, the allowance from the King to use, . . . 241 U68 House-hold 10
ALLOW'D
Where comes no guest, but is allow'd to eate, . . 95 F2 Penshurst 61
That the Bride (allow'd a Maid) . . . 138 U2 Kisse 8
Great, brave, and fashion'd folke, these are allow'd . . 164 U15 Friend-Wars 84
How well I lov'd Truth: I was scarce allow'd . . 414 Rutter 6
ALLOWED
And the allowed warre: . . . . . 253 U75 Epithalam. 31
ALLOWES
Allowes them? Then, what copies shall be had, . . 263 U78 Digby 29
Allowes them? Then, what copies will be had, . . 263 U78 Digby V 29
ALLOY (See also ALLAY)
Of Finenesse, and alloy: follow his hint, . . . 415 Rutter 27
ALL'S
All's done in me. . . . . 128 U1 Trinitie 24
Then to your love, and gift. And all's but due. . . 189 U37 Friend-Book 3
ALLURES
Such her quaint practise is, so it allures, . . . 39 E41 Gypsee 3
ALL-VERTUOUS
All-vertuous Herbert! on whose every part . . . 68 E106 E Herbert 3
ALMANACKS
And unto whom: They are the almanacks . . . 59 E92 New Crie 13
ALMES
Her solemne houres she spent, or giving Almes, . . 288 U84 Muse 192
ALMIGHTIE
And almost every vice, almightie gold, . . . 113 F12 Rutland 2
ALMIGHTIES
That the Almighties will to you is such: . . . 236 U63 Charles 2 8
ALMOND
The second string is the sweet Almond bloome . . 412 Ghyrlond 9
ALMONDS
The M. the Myrtle, A. the Almonds clame, . . . 412 Ghyrlond 3
ALMOST
Almost all wayes, to any better course. . . . 48 E65 Muse 10
Durst valour make, almost, but not a crime. . . 48 E66 Cary 6
Almost, is exercis'd: and scarse one knowes, . . 66 E102 Pembroke 7
I could adore, almost t'idolatrie. . . . 79 E125 Uvedale 10
And almost every vice, almightie gold, . . . 113 F12 Rutland 2
Almost you have, or may have, when you will? . . 114 F12 Rutland 34
'Tis growne almost a danger to speake true . . . 116 F13 Aubigny 1
And almost, all dayes after, while they live; . . 118 F13 Aubigny 75
And almost deifie the Authors! make . . . 156 U13 Sacvile 99
At fifty yeares, almost, to value it, . . . 171 U20 Shrub 5
Hee's good, as great. I am almost a stone! . . 269 U81 Pawlet 11
ALOFT
Aloft, grow lesse and streightned, full of knot; . . 157 U13 Sacvile 152
ALONE
He doth, at meales, alone, his pheasant eate, . . 35 E28 Surly 12

ALONE (cont.)

	Page	Title	Line
But saver of my countrey thee alone.	46	E60 Mounteagle	10
How like a columne, Radcliffe, left alone	60	E93 Radcliffe	1
That so alone canst judge, so'alone dost make:	62	E96 Donne 2	3
Diana'alone, so hit, and hunted so.	68	E105 L Wroth 2	14
Let her alone, shee will court you.	104	F7 Women but	4
It is the Muse, alone, can raise to heaven,	114	F12 Rutland	41
Of vertue, which you tread? what if alone?	118	F13 Aubigny	55
And he, with his best Genius left alone.	120	F14 Sydney	20
As alone there triumphs to the life	134	U2 Triumph	19
In love, doth not alone help forth	146	U6 Defence	20
Alone in money, but in manners too.	157	U13 Sacvile	134
Against his Maker; high alone with weeds,	163	U15 Friend-Wars	33
As would make himself, to make himselfe alone,	171	U19 Elegy By	24
In whom alone Love lives agen?	173	U22 Elegy Tho	14
Alone, but all thy ranke a reverend Name.	187	U33 Councellour	40
Alone lend succours, and this furie stay,	191	U38 Elegy 'Tis	8
As not alone the Cure, but scarre be faire.	192	U38 Elegy 'Tis	52
'Tis vertue alone, or nothing, that knits friends:	216	U45 Squib	12
'T is not alone the Merchant, but the Clowne,	237	U64 Charles 3	19
Alone, and such a race,	257	U75 Epithalam.	157
So great; his Body now alone projects the shade.	258	U75 Epithalam.	184
This worke I can performe alone;	277	U84 Mind	3
'Tis Vertue alone, is true Nobilitie.	282	U84 Kenelme	21
Plaine phrase, my Piso's, as alone, t'approve	321	Horace	342
Alone, without a rivall, by his will.	335	Horace	632
Alone, without a rivall, at your will.	354	Horace	V632
Thy tunes alone;	367	Ode Who saith	36
When him alone we sing)	368	Ode Who saith	63
That durst be that in Court: a vertu' alone	371	Epitaph	4
Leave thee alone, for the comparison	391	Shakespeare	38
As it, alone, (and onely it) had roome,	412	Ghyrlond	11

ALONG

	Page	Title	Line
Or magick sacrifice, they past along!	85	E133 Voyage	49
Goe, quit 'hem all. And take along with thee,	167	U15 Friend-Wars	175
Who walkes on Earth as May still went along,	264	U79 New-yeares	26
With weightie sorrow hurles us all along,	311	Horace	155
With weightie woes she hurles us all along	342	Horace	V155
Calme Brutus tenor start; but all along	395	May	11

ALONG'ST

	Page	Title	Line
Along'st the curled woods, and painted meades,	97	F3 Wroth	17

ALOOFE

	Page	Title	Line
But sing high and aloofe,	175	U23 Himselfe	35

ALOUD

	Page	Title	Line
He wont was to encounter me, aloud,	62	E97 Motion	7
Him not, aloud, that boasts so good a fame:	74	E115 Honest Man	2
Aloud; and (happ'ly) it may last as long.	261	U77 Treasurer	28
Hide faults, pray to the Gods, and wish aloud	319	Horace	285
Hide faults, and pray to th'gods, and wish aloud	345	Horace	V285
And cry aloud, Helpe, gentle Countrey-men,	335	Horace	653

ALOW'D

	Page	Title	Line
Carryed and wrapt, I only am alow'd	155	U13 Sacvile	88

ALPES

	Page	Title	Line
Here, up the Alpes (not so plaine as to Dunstable)	374	Coryat 1	16

ALPHIUS

	Page	Title	Line
These thoughts when Usurer Alphius, now about	291	U85 Country	67
These thinges when Usurer Alphius, now about	291	U85 Country	V 67

ALPHONSO

	Page	Title	Line
To Alphonso Ferrabosco, on his Booke.	82	E130 Ferrab. 1	Ttl
To urge, my lov'd Alphonso, that bold fame	82	E130 Ferrab. 1	1
When we doe give, Alphonso, to the light,	82	E131 Ferrab. 2	1

ALREADY

	Page	Title	Line
I have already us'd some happy houres,	115	F12 Rutland	74
Who (see) already hath ore-flowne	368	Ode Who saith	65

ALS'

	Page	Title	Line
Is sung: as als' her getting up	274	U84 Cradle	37

ALSO

	Page	Title	Line
That is his Lordships, shall be also mine.	95	F2 Penshurst	64
In using also of new words, to be	307	Horace	65
Were also clos'd: But, who the man should be,	309	Horace	109

ALTAR

	Page	Title	Line
Thrice 'bout thy Altar with their Ivory feet.	292	U86 Hor.4:1	28
Diana's Grove, or Altar, with the bor-/Dring	305	Horace	20
Diana's Grove, or Altar, with the nether	338	Horace	V 20

ALTARS

	Page	Title	Line
To thy altars, by their nights	104	F8 Sicknesse	4
His Altars kept from the Decay,	173	U22 Elegy Tho	19
The holy Altars, when it least presumes.	288	U84 Muse	188

ALTER (NOUN)

	Page	Title	Line
presentes a Royall Alter of fayre peace,	382	Rich	6
hee freely bringes; and on this Alter layes	383	Rich	9

ALTER

	Page	Title	Line
These studies alter now, in one, growne man;	315	Horace	237
Or alter kinde.	367	Ode Who saith	30
Noe velvet Sheath you weare, will alter kynde.	403	Inigo Jones 1	26

ALTER'D

	Page	Title	Line
Of Fortune, have not alter'd yet my looke,	117	F13 Aubigny	16

ALTERNATE

	Page	Title	Line
But fate doth so alternate the designe,	246	U70 Ode	95

ALTHOUGH

	Page	Title	Line
Although to write be lesser then to doo,	61	E95 Savile	25
Although the coldest of the yeere!	97	F3 Wroth	36
Although, perhaps it has, what's that to me,	167	U15 Friend-Wars	149

ALTHOUGH (cont.)

	Page	Title	Line
When he is furious, love, although not lust.	200	U42 Elegy Let	18
Although my Fame, to his, not under-heares,	219	U47 Tribe	49
By this, although you fancie not the man,	231	U56 Covell	25
Although it fall, and die that night;	245	U70 Ode	71
Although that thou, O Sun, at our intreaty stay!	254	U75 Epithalam.	56
Admitted to the sight, although his friends,	305	Horace	6
Into a pit, or hole; although he call,	335	Horace	652
Not thence be sav'd, although indeed he could?	335	Horace	658
Although the gate were hard, the gayne is sweete.	418	Answer	7

ALWAYES

	Page	Title	Line
As is thy conscience, which is alwayes one:	52	E74 Chancelor	8
Be alwayes to thy gather'd selfe the same:	63	E98 Th Roe 1	9
And perfect in a circle alwayes meet.	81	E128 Wm Roe 2	8
Alwayes at hand, to aide the merry Muses.	85	E133 Voyage	54
He alwayes gives what he knowes meet;	99	F3 Wroth	98
He alwayes gives what he thinks meet;	99	F3 Wroth	V 98
And it is not alwayes face,	131	U2 Excuse	7
Thou shrinke or start not, but be alwayes one;	168	U15 Friend-Wars	186
The fairest flowers are alwayes found;	264	U79 New-yeares	37
Be simple quite throughout, and alwayes one.	339	Horace	V 32
To children; we must alwayes dwell, and stay	317	Horace	253
Nor alwayes doth the loosed Bow, hit that	329	Horace	524

'M

	Page	Title	Line
I'm sure my language to her, was as sweet,	149	U9 Picture	6
I'm sure my language to her, is as sweet,	149	U9 Picture	V 6
I feele, I'm rather dead then he!	152	U12 Corbet	36
'Tis true, I'm broke! Vowes, Oathes, and all I had	191	U38 Elegy 'Tis	1
Why not? I'm gentle, and free-borne, doe hate	331	Horace	571
To say, I'm ignorant. Just as a Crier	333	Horace	597

'ME

	Page	Title	Line
Once say I'me ignorant. Just as a Cryer,	353	Horace	V597

AM

	Page	Title	Line
And, I a Poet here, no Herald am.	29	E9 To All	4
Let me give two: that doubly am got free,	31	E13 Empirick	3
All that I am in arts, all that I know,	31	E14 Camden	2
I, not the worst, am covetous of thee.	40	E43 Salisbury 1	6
When I am read, thou fain'st a weake applause,	43	E52 Courtling	3
How I doe feare my selfe, that am not worth	44	E55 Beaumont	3
I, that am glad of thy great chance, here doo!	46	E60 Mounteagle	5
I'am more asham'd to have thee thought my foe.	53	E77 Not name	4
Which, if thou leave not soone (though I am loth)	54	E81 Proule	7
Goodyere, I'am glad, and gratefull to report,	55	E85 Goodyere 1	1
To whom I am so bound, lov'd Aubigny?	80	E127 Aubigny	3
I, that am gratefull for him, have prepar'd	116	F12 Rutland	96
And howsoever; as I am at fewd	116	F13 Aubigny	9
And, in this name, am given out dangerous	117	F13 Aubigny	11
I, Madame, am become your praiser. Where,	117	F13 Aubigny	21
I can rest me where I am.	142	U2 Her man	56
I am undone to night;	150	U11 Dreame	3
Carryed and wrapt, I only am alow'd	155	U13 Sacvile	88
Ride, saile, am coach'd, know I how farre I have gone,	156	U13 Sacvile	121
I Know to whom I write. Here, I am sure,	158	U14 Selden	1
Though I am short, I cannot be obscure:	158	U14 Selden	2
I wonder'd at the richnesse, but am lost,	160	U14 Selden	53
You both are modest. So am I. Farewell.	161	U14 Selden	86
When I am hoarse, with praising his each cast,	167	U15 Friend-Wars	151
No more, I am sorry for so fond cause, say,	171	U20 Shrub	4
How penitent I am, or I should be!	172	U20 Shrub	16
Among which faithfull troope am I.	173	U22 Elegy Tho	28
What I, in her, am griev'd to want.	174	U22 Elegy Tho	36
Since I exscribe your Sonnets, am become	182	U28 Worth	3
Sir, I am thankfull, first, to heaven, for you;	189	U37 Friend-Book	1
Of Credit lost. And I am now run madde:	191	U38 Elegy 'Tis	2
I am regenerate now, become the child	192	U38 Elegy 'Tis	39
Let me be what I am, as Virgil cold;	199	U42 Elegy Let	1
What I am not, and what I faine would be,	216	U45 Squib	1
I neither am, nor art thou one of those	216	U45 Squib	5
Live to that point I will, for which I am man,	219	U47 Tribe	59
I am no States-man, and much lesse Divine,	223	U49 Pucell	25
Farthest I am from the Idolatrie	223	U49 Pucell	27
I am not so voluminous, and vast,	226	U52 Answer	2
With one great blot, yo'had form'd me as I am.	227	U52 Answer	12
With one great blot, you had drawne me as I am.	227	U52 Answer	V 12
I Am to dine, Friend, where I must be weigh'd	229	U54 Squib	1
That day, which I predestin'd am to sing,	262	U78 Digby	V 17
Hee's good, as great. I am almost a stone!	269	U81 Pawlet	11
Alas, I am all Marble! write the rest	269	U81 Pawlet	13
Sure, I am dead, and know it not! I feele	283	U84 Muse	29
Am turned with an others powers. My Passion	283	U84 Muse	31
A new Song to his praise, and great I Am:	285	U84 Muse	90
I am not such, as in the Reigne	292	U86 Hor.4:1	3
'Tis true, I'am Thracian Chloes, I,	293	U87 Hor.3:9	9
And I, am mutually on fire	293	U87 Hor.3:9	13
My selfe for shortnesse labour, and am stil'd	339	Horace	V 36/ 35
Or I am much deceiv'd, shall be to place	307	Horace	60
Or Varius? Why am I now envi'd so,	309	Horace	79
Am I call'd Poet? wherefore with wrong shame,	311	Horace	129
Twice, or thrice good, I wonder: but am more	329	Horace	535
Vice, and, am knowne to have a Knights estate.	331	Horace	572
My selfe am so neare drowning?	365	Ode Splendor	20
I, that am glad, thy Innocence was thy Guilt,	371	Fletcher	11

AM (cont.)

	Page	Title	Line
Am I thus ample to thy Booke, and Fame:	390	Shakespeare	2
Onely my losse is, that I am not there:	398	Drayton	91
And, till I worthy am to wish I were,	398	Drayton	92
I am too fat t'envy him. He too leane	405	Inigo Jones 1	69
I am come to Add, and speake,	416	Moon	2
at my back, I am no spright,	416	Moon	6

AMADIS

	Page	Title	Line
Had I compil'd from Amadis de Gaule,	203	U43 Vulcan	29

AMAZE

	Page	Title	Line
Then like, then love; and now would they amaze?	169	U18 Elegy Can	4

AMAZEMENT

	Page	Title	Line
With silence, and amazement! not with rude,	284	U84 Muse	78
till giddie with amazement I fell downe	361	Palmer	25

AMBASSADOUR

	Page	Title	Line
T'have wak'd, if sleeping, Spaines Ambassadour,	213	U44 Speach	4

AMBER

	Page	Title	Line
Not though that haire grew browne, which once was amber,	57	E90 Mill	9
Lying for the spirit of amber.	105	F8 Sicknesse	32
Lying on the spirit of amber.	105	F8 Sicknesse	V 32

AMBITION

	Page	Title	Line
Of what ambition, faction, pride can raise;	66	E102 Pembroke	15
Who'in such ambition can but follow thee.	73	E113 Overbury	12
Ambition to become a Starre,	234	U60 La-ware	14
Caesar's ambition, Cato's libertie,	395	May	10

AMBITIOUS

	Page	Title	Line
Those proud, ambitious heaps, and nothing else,	96	F2 Penshurst	101
That at great times, art no ambitious guest	96	F3 Wroth	5
Looke on th'ambitious man, and see him nurse	162	U15 Friend-Wars	11
Ambitious, factious, superstitious, lowd	167	U15 Friend-Wars	168
Hee, that's ambitious in the race to touch	333	Horace	587
Or are you soe ambitious 'bove your peers!	403	Inigo Jones 1	19
Thou'rt too ambitious: and dost fear in vaine!	408	Inigo Jones 3	6

AMBITIOUSLY

	Page	Title	Line
To speake my selfe out too ambitiously,	218	U47 Tribe	6

AMBLING

	Page	Title	Line
Those ambling visits, passe in verse, betweene	396	Drayton	4

AMBROSIACK

	Page	Title	Line
Or Constables Ambrosiack Muse	182	U27 Ode Helen	27

AMEN

	Page	Title	Line
The Solemne Quire cryes, Joy; and they returne, Amen.	256	U75 Epithalam.	128

AMEND

	Page	Title	Line
His very Manners taught t'amend,	152	U12 Corbet	22

AMENDS

	Page	Title	Line
To make amends, yo'are thought a wholesome creature.	46	E62 Would-bee	8
Hymens amends, to make it worth his fault.	384	Somerset	14

AMIABLE

	Page	Title	Line
If a Bird so amiable,	364	Phoenix	3
unto the bright, and amiable	662	Bedford	2

AMID'

	Page	Title	Line
A Dolphin, and a Boare amid' the floods.	307	Horace	42

AMIDST (See also MIDST)

	Page	Title	Line
Of which wee'll speake our minds, amidst our meate;	65	E101 Supper	23

AMISSE

	Page	Title	Line
That heaven should make no more; or should amisse,	188	U34 Small Poxe	15
With all th'adventures; Three bookes not amisse	207	U43 Vulcan	V 95
Who nought assaies unaptly, or amisse?	315	Horace	200

AMITIE

	Page	Title	Line
Little know they, that professe Amitie,	190	U37 Friend-Book	19
I envie it the Angels amitie!	283	U84 Muse	36

AMITYE

	Page	Title	Line
Little knowne they that proffesse Amitye	421	Censure	12

AMONG

	Page	Title	Line
Shift, here, in towne, not meanest among squires,	30	E12 Shift	1
Among thy Saints elected to abide,	128	U1 Trinitie	45
Among my commings in, and see it mount,	161	U14 Selden	80
Among which faithfull troope am I.	173	U22 Elegy Tho	28
Shine more, then she, the Stars among?	181	U27 Ode Helen	12
The puritie of Language; and among	207	U43 Vulcan	93
Up among Nations. In the stead of bold	214	U44 Speach	51
Among the daily Ruines that fall foule,	224	U50 Countesse	17
Great Charles, among the holy gifts of grace	235	U62 Charles 1	1
Among these Cates how glad the sight doth come	291	U85 Country	61
Or why, my well-grac'd words among,	293	U86 Hor.4:1	35
Among the starres should be resign'd	369	Ode Who saith	105

AMONGE

	Page	Title	Line
Sonnes, seeke not me amonge these polish'd stones:	387	Cavendish	1

'MONG'ST

	Page	Title	Line
But 'mong'st these Tiberts, who do'you thinke there was?	88	E133 Voyage	155

'MONGST

	Page	Title	Line
Be of the best: and 'mongst those, best are you.	61	E94 Bedford 3	14
'Mongst Hampton shades, and Phoebus grove of bayes,	80	E126 Mrs Cary	2
'Mongst loughing heards, and solide hoofes:	97	F3 Wroth	16
'Mongst my Muses finding me,	136	U2 Cupid	7
Monarch in Letters! 'Mongst thy Titles showne	160	U14 Selden	65
'Mongst which, if I have any friendships sent,	220	U47 Tribe	63
Who durst live great, 'mongst all the colds, and heates,	233	U59 Newcastle	21
But like an Arme of Eminence 'mongst them,	258	U75 Epithalam.	179

AMONGST (See also MONGST)

	Page	Title	Line
Hath plac'd amongst her virgin-traine:	34	E22 Daughter	9
(Because th'are every where amongst Man-kind	167	U15 Friend-Wars	171
Amongst my many other, that I may	171	U20 Shrub	3
Or like a Ghost walke silent amongst men,	199	U41 Elegy Since	21

20

		Page	Title	Line

AMONGST (cont.)
Amongst her Peeres, those Princes of all good!   - - - - 284 U84 Muse 84
Who (amongst these delights) would not forget   - - - - 290 U85 Country 37
AMOROUS
Thy thoughts did never melt in amorous fire,   - - - - 108 F10 Proludium 3
AMPHION
Amphion, too, that built the Theban towres,   - - - - 327 Horace 483
AMPLE
And, after, swom abroad in ample flakes,   - - - - 87 E133 Voyage 138
Front, an ample field of snow;   - - - - 141 U2 Her man 18
By him, so ample, full, and round,   - - - - 244 U70 Ode 49
Where all heroique ample thoughts doe meet: - - - - 262 U78 Digby 10
Am I thus ample to thy Booke, and Fame: - - - - 390 Shakespeare 2
Keepe due proportion in the ample song,   - - - - 395 May 12
AN (See also ANE)
'Tis 'gainst the manners of an Epigram: - - - - 29 E9 To All 3
I sent the cause: Hee wooes with an ill sprite.   - - - - 33 E19 Cod 1 2
It was as if thou printed had'st an oath,   - - - - 43 E53 Old-end 5
An obeliske, or columne to thy name,   - - - - 46 E60 Mounteagle 2
With me thou leav'st an happier Muse then thee,   - - - - 48 E65 Muse 11
Or take an Epigramme so fearefully: - - - - 51 E73 Fine Grand 2
Item, an epitaph on my lords cock,   - - - - 51 E73 Fine Grand 18
An olive, capers, or some better sallade   - - - - 64 E101 Supper 10
It is an Epigramme, on all man-kind;   - - - - 66 E102 Pembroke 2
The name of Pompey for an enemie,   - - - - 71 E110 Edmonds 1 3
An Epick poeme; thou hast the same end.   - - - - 72 E112 Gamster 10
Next morne, an Ode: Thou mak'st a song ere night.   - - - - 72 E112 Gamster 12
Where shall I scape thee? in an Epigramme?   - - - - 73 E112 Gamster 15
An inginer, in slanders, of all fashions,   - - - - 75 E115 Honest Man 31
We ought not give them taste, we had an eare.   - - - - 83 E131 Ferrab. 2 6
Belch'd forth an ayre, as hot, as at the muster   - - - - 85 E133 Voyage 63
Or, that it lay, heap'd like an usurers masse,   - - - - 88 E133 Voyage 139
Who kept an ale-house; with my little Minos,   - - - - 89 E133 Voyage 189
An ancient pur-blinde fletcher, with a high nose;   - - - - 89 E133 Voyage 190
Or stayre, or courts; but stand'st an ancient pile,   - - - - 93 F2 Penshurst 5
An embleme of themselves, in plum, or peare.   - - - - 95 F2 Penshurst 56
And now an Epode to deepe eares I sing.   - - - - 108 F10 Proludium 30
And now an Epode to deepe eares we sing.   - - - - 108 F10 Proludium V 30
An elegie? no, muse; yt askes a straine   - - - - 108 F10 Proludium 1
and now an Epode, to deepe Eares, wee singe.   - - - - 108 F10 Proludium 16
That is an essence, farre more gentle, fine,   - - - - 110 F11 Epode 45
That is an essence, most gentile and fine,   - - - - 110 F11 Epode V 45
A fixed thought, an eye un-taught to glance;   - - - - 111 F11 Epode 61
To the Countesse of Rutland: An Elegie.   - - - - 113 F12 Rutland VTtl
Worth an estate, treble to that you have.   - - - - 114 F12 Rutland 36
Or, in an armies head, that, lockt in brasse,   - - - - 114 F12 Rutland 52
Had not their forme touch'd by an English wit.   - - - - 115 F12 Rutland 82
And keepe an even, and unalter'd gaite;   - - - - 118 F13 Aubigny 61
An offring meet   - - - - 127 U1 Trinitie 12
From your lips, and suck'd an ayre   - - - - 137 U2 Kisse 3
Front, an ample field of snow;   - - - - 141 U2 Her man 18
An Epitaph on Master Vincent Corbet.   - - - - 151 U12 Corbet Ttl
An Epitaph, deserv'd a Tombe: - - - - 152 U12 Corbet 38
An Epistle to Sir Edward Sacvile, now Earle of Dorset.   - - 153 U13 Sacvile Ttl
An Epistle to Master John Selden.   - - - - 158 U14 Selden Ttl
An Epistle to a Friend, to perswade him to the Warres.   - - 162 U15 Friend-Wars Ttl
How they may make some one that day an Asse   - - - - 164 U15 Friend-Wars 64
In this, and like, an itch of Vanitie,   - - - - 166 U15 Friend-Wars 143
An Epitaph on Master Philip Gray.   - - - - 168 U16 Gray Ttl
An Elegie.   - - - - 169 U18 Elegy Can Ttl
An Elegie.   - - - - 170 U19 Elegy By Ttl
An Elegie.   - - - - 173 U22 Elegy Tho Ttl
Who as an off'ring at your shrine,   - - - - 174 U22 Elegy Tho 29
An Ode. To himselfe.   - - - - 174 U23 Himselfe Ttl
An Ode to James Earle of Desmond, writ - - -   - - - 176 U25 Desmond Ttl
An hower will come they must affect theyr Ease,   - - - - 179 U25 Desmond V 42
Oft scape an Imputation, more through luck, then wit.   - - 179 U25 Desmond 52
An Ode.   - - - - 180 U26 Ode High Ttl
An Ode.   - - - - 181 U27 Ode Helen Ttl
Whose fame hath an eternall voice?   - - - - 181 U27 Ode Helen 16
Not a Poet in an Age,   - - - - 183 U29 Fit of Rime 26
An Epigram On William Lord Burl: - - -   - - - 185 U30 Burleigh Ttl
An Epigram. To Thomas Lo: Elsmere, - - -   - - 185 U31 Elsmere Ttl
An Epigram to the Councellour that pleaded, - - -   - 186 U33 Councellour Ttl
Or skill, to carry out an evill cause!   - - - - 187 U33 Councellour 18
An Epigram. To the small Poxe.   - - - - 188 U34 Small Poxe Ttl
One beautie in an Age, and free from thee?   - - - - 188 U34 Small Poxe 2
An Epitaph.   - - - - 188 U35 Chute Ttl
An Epistle to a friend.   - - - - 189 U37 Friend-Book Ttl
It is an Act of tyrannie, not love,   - - - - 190 U37 Friend-Book 25
An Elegie.   - - - - 191 U38 Elegy 'Tis Ttl
An ill-affected limbe (what e're it aile)   - - - - 192 U38 Elegy 'Tis 45
You may so place me, and in such an ayre,   - - - - 192 U38 Elegy 'Tis 51
This looketh like an Execution day?   - - - - 193 U38 Elegy 'Tis 80
An Elegie.   - - - - 197 U40 Elegy That Ttl
But the grave Lover ever was an Asse;   - - - - 198 U40 Elegy That 32
An Elegie.   - - - - 199 U41 Elegy Since Ttl
An Elegie.   - - - - 199 U42 Elegy Let Ttl
An Officer there, did make most solemne love,   - - - - 201 U42 Elegy Let 53
Under that cover; an old Mid-wives hat!   - - - - 202 U42 Elegy Let 83
An Execration upon Vulcan.   - - - - 202 U43 Vulcan Ttl
So many my Yeares-labours in an houre?   - - - - 202 U43 Vulcan 4
So ravenous, and vast an appetite?   - - - - 206 U43 Vulcan 86

	Page	Title	Line

AN (cont.)

Text	Page	Title	Line
There was a Judgement shew'n too in an houre.	210	U43 Vulcan	158
Hill-/foot (out in Sussex) to an iron Mill;	211	U43 Vulcan	184
An Epistle to Master Arth: Squib.	216	U45 Squib	Ttl
An Epigram on Sir Edward Coke, when . . .	217	U46 Coke	Ttl
Needs lend an aide, to thine she had her eyes.	217	U46 Coke	24
An Epistle answering to one that asked . . .	218	U47 Tribe	Ttl
And shewing so weake an Act to vulgar eyes,	218	U47 Tribe	7
An Epigram on The Court Pucell.	222	U49 Pucell	Ttl
And in an Epicoene fury can write newes	222	U49 Pucell	8
An Epigram. To the honour'd ——— Countesse of ———	224	U50 Countesse	Ttl
An Archetype, for all the world to see,	227	U52 Answer	14
An Epigram. To William, Earle of Newcastle.	228	U53 Newcastle	Ttl
An ill commoditie! 'T must make good weight.	229	U54 Squib	6
An Epigram. To William Earle of Newcastle.	232	U59 Newcastle	Ttl
An Epitaph, on Henry L. La-ware. To the Passer-by.	233	U60 La-ware	Ttl
An Epigram.	234	U61 Epigram	Ttl
An Epigram. To K. Charles for a 100. Pounds . . .	235	U62 Charles 1	Ttl
. . . first-borne, An Epigram Consolatorie. 1629.	235	U63 Charles 2	Ttl
An Epigram. To our great and good K. Charles . . .	236	U64 Charles 3	Ttl
An Epigram on the Princes birth. 1630.	237	U65 Prince	Ttl
An Epigram on Prince Charles his Birth: May. 29th. 1630	237	U65 Prince	VTtl
On the Princes Birth-day. An Epigram	237	U65 Prince	VTtl
An Epigram to the Queene, then lying in. 1630.	238	U66 Queene	Ttl
An Epigram to the Queens Health.	238	U66 Queene	VTtl
And by an Angell, to the blessed'st Maid,	238	U66 Queene	2
So generall a gladnesse to an Isle,	238	U66 Queene	9
An Ode, or Song, by all the Muses. . . .	239	U67 Muses	Ttl
Hath brought the Land an Heire!	240	U67 Muses	53
An Epigram, To the House-hold. 1630.	241	U68 House-hold	Ttl
Or standing long an Oake, three hundred yeare,	245	U70 Ode	67
. . . England. An Epistle Mendicant. 1631.	248	U71 Treasurer	Ttl
. . . An Epigram Anniversarie. Novemb. 19. 1632.	249	U72 King	Ttl
Discharge it 'bout the Iland, in an houre,	249	U72 King	3
Discharging 'bout the Iland, in an houre,	249	U72 King	V 3
To the Right Hon'ble Hierome, L. Weston. An Ode . . .	250	U74 Weston	Ttl
Shoot up an Olive fruitfull, faire,	251	U74 Weston	28
But like an Arme of Eminence 'mongst them,	258	U75 Epithalam.	179
. . . An Epigram.	260	U77 Treasurer	Ttl
Which, though I cannot as an Architect	261	U77 Treasurer	25
Which, though I cannot like as an Architect	261	U77 Treasurer	V 25
An Epigram To my Muse, the Lady Digby, . . .	262	U78 Digby	Ttl
To Sir Kenelme Digby. An Epigram	262	U78 Digby	VTtl
An Elegie On the Lady Jane Pawlet, Marchion: of Winton.	268	U81 Pawlet	Ttl
A reverend State she had, an awfull Eye,	270	U81 Pawlet	43
This, utter'd by an antient Bard,	274	U84 Cradle	33
You could make shift to paint an Eye,	278	U84 Mind	9
An Eagle towring in the skye,	278	U84 Mind	10
Still left an Eccho in the sense.	279	U84 Mind	40
Am turned with an others powers. My Passion	283	U84 Muse	31
What 'tis t'enjoy, an everlasting breath!	285	U84 Muse	92
B'imputed right to an inheritance	286	U84 Muse	144
But, kept an even gate, as some streight tree	287	U84 Muse	165
Would sit in an Infirmery, whole dayes	288	U84 Muse	195
Shee saw her Saviour, by an early light,	288	U84 Muse	199
An Ode in Horace in prayse of a Countrye lyfe, Translated.	289	U85 Country	VTtl
With an uncomely silence failes my tongue?	293	U86 Hor.4:1	36
If in th'escape an artlesse path we tread.	339	Horace	V 46/ 44
Or an Heroe; if a ripe old man,	313	Horace	162
An Actors parts, and Office too, the Quire	317	Horace	276
Receive, or give it an applause, the more.	321	Horace	364
Be like a Whet-stone, that an edge can put	325	Horace	433
There's Albin's sonne will say, Substract an ounce	327	Horace	467
An ounce, what makes it then? The halfe pound just;	327	Horace	471
And thus, at first, an honour, and a name	327	Horace	491
May, with some right, upon an Author creepe.	329	Horace	538
An admirable Verse. The great Scurfe take	333	Horace	594
An admirable verse: the great Scab take	353	Horace	V594
Of an entangling suit; and bring 't about:	333	Horace	604
Become an Aristarchus. And, not say,	335	Horace	639
And, there an end of him, reciting makes:	337	Horace	678
And there an end of him with reading makes:	355	Horace	V678
Closde in an orbe of Christall.	365	Ode Splendor	12
To fill an Epitaph. But she had more.	371	Epitaph	5
And as an ever-lasting Sacrifice	382	Rich	7
That an ill man dares not securely looke	389	Aleman	8
He was not of an age, but for all time!	391	Shakespeare	43
And fill'd an Orbe as circular, as heaven!	396	Drayton	19
A wild, and an authoriz'd wickednesse!	397	Drayton	46
An Agincourt, an Agincourt, or dye.	398	Drayton	70
In faire freehould, not an Inmate:	399	Lady Ogle	26
An Expostulacion with Inigo Jones.	402	Inigo Jones 1	Ttl
you are; from them leapt forth an Architect,	402	Inigo Jones 1	3
you would be an Asinigo, by your ears?	403	Inigo Jones 1	20
you'l be as Langley sayd, an Inigo still.	403	Inigo Jones 1	22
In the mere perspective of an Inch board!	404	Inigo Jones 1	44
With all Remonstrance make an honest man.	406	Inigo Jones 1	104
An Earle of show: for all thy worke is showe:	407	Inigo Jones 2	21
An Earle of show: for all thy worth is showe:	407	Inigo Jones 2	V 21
To a Freind an Epigram Of him.	407	Inigo Jones 3	Ttl
An honest Bilbo-Smith would make good blades,	410	Brome	15
An Epigram To My Joviall Good Freind Mr. Robert Dover,	415	Dover	Ttl
Hee dyes with an Ill sent,	420	Ode:If Men	16

22

AN   (cont.)
    It is an Act of Tyranye, not Love, ...   422   Censure   18
ANACREON
    Of which had Horace, or Anacreon tasted,   .   .   .   65   E101 Supper   31
    To Sicknesse. Ode Anacreon: 104   F8 Sicknesse   VTtl
    So, Anacreon drawne the Ayre   136   U2 Cupid   14
    In whom Anacreon once did joy, ...   181   U27 Ode Helen   6
    As Horace fat; or as Anacreon old;   .   .   .   199   U42 Elegy Let   2
ANAGRAM
    Item, your mistris anagram, i' your hilt.   .   .   51   E73 Fine Grand   16
    Must Celia bee, the Anagram of Alice.   .   .   .   412   Sutcliffe   23
ANAGRAMS
    Or pomp'd for those hard trifles, Anagrams,   .   .   204   U43 Vulcan   35
    Or pomp'd for those fine trifles, Anagrams,   .   .   204   U43 Vulcan   V 35
ANALYSDE
    The Phoenix Analysde.   364   Phoenix   Ttl
ANARCHIE
    That live in the wild Anarchie of Drinke,   .   .   218   U47 Tribe   10
ANARCHY
    Doe all, that longs to the anarchy of drinke,   .   .   74   E115 Honest Man   12
ANATOMIE
    When her dead essence (like the Anatomie   .   .   .   179   U25 Desmond   37
ANCESTORS
    With dust of ancestors, in graves but dwell.   .   .   121   F14 Sydney   40
    Our Ancestors impos'd on Prince and State.   .   .   215   U44 Speach   78
    Boast not these Titles of your Ancestors;   .   .   281   U84 Kenelme   10
    Up to their Ancestors; the rivers side,   .   .   .   281   U84 Kenelme   18
    Our Ancestors did Plautus numbers praise,   .   .   323   Horace   399
    Your Ancestors, old Plautus numbers prais'd,   .   .   348   Horace   V385/399
ANCESTOURS
    And was your Fathers! All your Ancestours!   .   .   .   233   U59 Newcastle   20
ANCIENT   (See also ANTIENT)
    An ancient pur-blinde fletcher, with a high nose;   .   89   E133 Voyage   190
    Or stayre, or courts; but stand'st an ancient pile,   .   93   F2 Penshurst   5
    Me thought I read the ancient Art of Thrace,   .   .   228   U53 Newcastle   4
    Then now beneath some ancient Oke he may,   .   .   290   U85 Country   23
&
    Is Banke-rupt turn'd! Cloak, Cassock, Robe, & Gowne,   .   237   U64 Charles 3   V 20
    That thus hath crown'd our hopes, with thee, our Spring & May,   237   U65 Prince   V 2
    A horse neck joyn, & sundry plumes ore-fold   .   .   338   Horace   V 2
    Not one but thrives; in spite of stormes & thunder,   .   361   Palmer   7
    Though, now by Love transform'd, & dayly dying: .   369   Ode Who saith   101
    . . . & sir Henrye Rich, now Earles of warwick and Hollande.   382   Rich   Ttl
    shall looke, & on hyme soe, then arte's a lyer   .   .   383   Rich   15
    will all turne dust, & may not make me swell.   .   .   387   Cavendish   4
    Will all be dust, & may not make me swell.   .   .   387   Cavendish   V 4
    I made my lyfe my monument, & yours: .   .   .   387   Cavendish   7
    . . . on his Translation of Hesiods Works, & Dayes.   .   388   Chapman   Ttl
    Heard the soft ayres, between our Swaynes & thee,   .   397   Drayton   26
    Both him & Archimede; damne Architas   .   .   .   402   Inigo Jones 1   5
    Drawne Aristotle on us! & thence showne   .   .   .   402   Inigo Jones 1   9
    By all your Titles, & whole style at ones   .   .   402   Inigo Jones 1   15
    Of Tyre-man, Mounte-banck & Justice Jones,   .   .   402   Inigo Jones 1   16
    In Towne & Court? Are you growne rich? & proud?   .   403   Inigo Jones 1   24
    That doe cry up the Machine, & the Showes!   .   .   403   Inigo Jones 1   32
    Court Hieroglyphicks! & all Artes affoord   .   .   404   Inigo Jones 1   43
    Of many Coulors! read them! & reveale   .   .   .   404   Inigo Jones 1   47
    Painting & Carpentry are the Soule of Masque.   .   .   404   Inigo Jones 1   50
    Be Inigo, the Whistle, & his men!   405   Inigo Jones 1   66
    Hee's warme on his feet now he sayes, & can   .   .   405   Inigo Jones 1   67
    Up & about? Dyve into Cellars too   405   Inigo Jones 1   80
    He may have skill & judgment to designe   .   .   406   Inigo Jones 2   7
    Cittyes & Temples! thou a Cave for Wyne,   .   .   406   Inigo Jones 2   8
    With slyding windowes, & false Lights a top!   .   .   407   Inigo Jones 2   10
    Able to eat into his bones & pierce   407   Inigo Jones 3   4
    He makes the Camell & dull Ass his prize.   .   .   408   Inigo Jones 3   8
    Most holy, & pure Virgin, blessed Mayd,   .   .   .   413   Ghyrlond   37
ANE
    on a lovers dust, made sand for ane Houre Glasse   .   148   U8 Houre-glasse VTtl
ANENST
    And many a sinke pour'd out her rage anenst 'hem;   .   86   E133 Voyage   75
A-NEW
    But even their names were to be made a-new,   .   .   67   E105 L Wroth 2   5
ANGELL
    And by an Angell, to the blessed'st Maid,   .   .   .   238   U66 Queene   2
ANGELLS
    They say the Angells marke each deed,   .   .   .   144   U3 Musicall   17
    Of Angells, and all witnesses of light,   .   .   .   400   Lady Ogle   38
ANGELO
    Titian, or Raphael, Michael Angelo, ...   260   U77 Treasurer   7
ANGELS
    And with thy Angels, placed side, by side,   .   .   128   U1 Trinitie   46
    The Angels so did sound it, ...   130   U1 Nativitie   3
    Of Angels should be driven   144   U3 Musicall   22
    The Angels from their Spheares: 239   U67 Muses   21
    With Angels, Muse, to speake these: Nothing can   .   255   U75 Epithalam.   84
    Let Angels sing her glories, who did call   .   .   270   U81 Pawlet   63
    I envie it the Angels amitie!   283   U84 Muse   36
    Angels, Arch-angels, Principalities,   .   .   .   285   U84 Muse   86
    Equall with Angels, and Co-heires of it?   .   .   286   U84 Muse   146
ANGER
    Declineth anger, perswades clemencie,   .   .   .   82   E130 Ferrab. 1   5
    Not make a verse; Anger; or laughter would,   .   .   164   U15 Friend-Wars   62

	Page	Title	Line

ANGER (cont.)
Streight puts off all his Anger, and doth kisse - - - 193   U38 Elegy 'Tis   88
Or urgeth us to anger; and anon - - - - 311   Horace   154
ANGLES
To hit in angles, and to clash with time: - - - 232   U59 Newcastle   5
Or without angles, it was shee! - - - 399   Lady Ogle   16
ANGRIE
Come, be not angrie, you are Hungry; eate; - - 69   E107 Hungry   31
He cannot angrie be, but all must quake, - - 193   U38 Elegy 'Tis   71
ANGRIER
And then rough Adria, angrier, farre; - - - 294   U87 Hor.3:9   23
ANGRY
But 's angry for the Captayne, still: is such. - - 70   E108 Soldiers   10
O, be not angry with those fires, - - - 144   U4 Song   5
Her voyce, and angry Chremes chafes out-right - - 311   Horace   133
The angry brow; the sportive, wanton things; - - 311   Horace   150
Keepe him still active, angry, un-appeas'd, - - 313   Horace   172
Soone angry, and soone pleas'd, is sweet, or sowre, - 315   Horace   227
The angry, and love those that feare t'offend. - 317   Horace   282
Angry. Sometimes, I heare good Homer snore. - 329   Horace   536
Angry, if once I heare good Homer snore. - - 351   Horace   V512/536
Under the angry Moon. But then the boys - - 354   Horace   V647
ANIMATED
And animated Porc'lane of the Court, - - - 219   U47 Tribe   53
ANNE
Swim without Corke! Why, thank the good Queen Anne. - 405   Inigo Jones 1   68
ANNEXED
Annexed to thy Person, and thy place, - - - 235   U62 Charles 1   2
ANNIVERSARIE
. . . An Epigram Anniversarie. Novemb. 19. 1632. - - 249   U72 King   Ttl
ANNIVERSARY
. . . On his Anniversary Day. 1629. - - - 236   U64 Charles 3   Ttl
ANNOY'D
The engines, that have them annoy'd; - - - 101   F4 To the World   34
ANNUAL
To Sir Annual Tilter. - - - - - 36   E29 Tilter   Ttl
ANNUITIE
A large hundred Markes annuitie, - - - 259   U76 Petition   11
A full hundred Markes annuitie, - - - 259   U76 Petition   V 11
ANON
Or urgeth us to anger; and anon - - - - 311   Horace   154
ANCNE
Present anone: Medea must not kill - - - 317   Horace   263
ANOTHER
Earth, thou hast not such another. - - - 39   E40 Ratcliffe   17
Then a thousand, then another - - - 103   F6 Celia 2   9
Upon my flesh t'inflict another wound. - - 122   F15 Heaven   22
May not claime another kisse. - - - 138   U2 Kisse   36
7. Begging another, on colour of mending the former. - 139   U2 Another   Ttl
10. Another Ladyes exception present at the hearing. - 142   U2 Exception   Ttl
Another. In defence of their Inconstancie. A Song. - 146   U6 Defence   Ttl
Tilt one upon another, and now beare - - 166   U15 Friend-Wars   125
till one upon another, and now beare - - 166   U15 Friend-Wars   V125
Another to him. - - - - - 186   U32 Elsmere   Ttl
Upon the hope to have another sin - - - 193   U38 Elegy 'Tis   90
Under another Name, I take your health; - - 197   U40 Elegy That   10
Another answers, 'Lasse, those Silkes are none, - 202   U42 Elegy Let   74
Like Eccho playing from another shore. - - 249   U72 King   V 8
See, at another doore, - - - - 254   U75 Epithalam.   69
Doe long to make themselves, so, another way: - 257   U75 Epithalam.   140
Stiffe! starke! my joynts 'gainst one another knock! - 269   U81 Pawlet   9
As it another Nature were, - - - - 279   U84 Mind   30
To another, Move; he went; To a third, Go, - 287   U84 Muse   170
Obscure. Another striving smooth to runne, - 339   Horace   V 37/ 36
Or any thing else that another should hide, - - 380   Coryat 3   51
ANOTHERS
Made from the hazard of anothers shame: - - 27   E2 My Booke   10
He keepes anothers wife, which is a spice - - 36   E28 Surly   15
He that will follow but anothers wife, - - 165   U15 Friend-Wars   87
And each shall know, there, one anothers face, - 285   U84 Muse   115
ANSWER
But say, all sixe good men, what answer yee? - - 210   U43 Vulcan   173
My Answer. The Poet to the Painter. - - 226   U52 Answer   Ttl
This was Mr Ben: Johnsons Answer of the suddayne. - 418   Answer   Ttl
ANSWERE
His onely answere is to all, god payes. - - 31   E12 Shift   20
To answere me. And sure, it was th'intent - 87   E133 Voyage   107
ANSWER'D
I answer'd, Daphne now no paine can prove. - - 80   E126 Mrs Cary   6
Are they not worthy to be answer'd so, - - 154   U13 Sacvile   59
Each syllab'e answer'd, and was form'd, how faire; - 245   U70 Ode   63
ANSWERING
An Epistle answering to one that asked . . . - - 218   U47 Tribe   Ttl
ANSWERS
Another answers, 'Lasse, those Silkes are none, - 202   U42 Elegy Let   74
All his Answers are Divine, - - - - 657   Door Apollo   5
ANTICIRA'S
The head that three Anticira's cannot heale. - - 349   Horace   V428
ANTICKS
Vizors or Anticks? or it comprehend - - - 402   Inigo Jones 1   13
ANTICYRA'S
Their heads, which three Anticyra's cannot heale. - 325   Horace   428

```
                                                      Page      Title       Line
ANTIENT
  Haile, happie Genius of this antient pile!    -   -   -   -   225  U51 Bacon       1
  This, utter'd by an antient Bard,       -   -   -   -   -   274  U84 Cradle      33
  Thus, to his antient Art the Piper lent  -   -   -   -   -   319  Horace         303
ANTIPATHY
  I Cannot thinke there's that antipathy  -   -   -   -   -    52  E75 Lippe        1
ANTIPHATES
  Wonders forth after: As Antiphates,   -   -   -   -   -   -   315  Horace         205
ANTIQUATED
  But antiquated, and deserted lye     -   -   -   -   -   -   392  Shakespeare     53
ANTIQUE
  What sight in searching the most antique springs!   -   -   -    31  E14 Camden       8
  What th'antique souldiers were, the moderne bee?    -   -   -    72  E111 Edmonds 2   2
  Preserved, in her antique bed of Vert,   -   -   -   -   -   413  Ghyrlond        19
ANTIQUITIE
  Madame, had all antiquitie beene lost,   -   -   -   -   -    67  E105 L Wroth 2   1
  Newnesse of Sense, Antiquitie of voyce!   -   -   -   -   -   160  U14 Selden      60
  Times witnesse, herald of Antiquitie,   -   -   -   -   -   176  U24 Frontispice 17
ANTIQUITIES
  Antiquities search'd! Opinions dis-esteem'd!   -   -   -   -   160  U14 Selden      40
ANTWERPE
  Or his to Antwerpe. Therefore, once more, list ho'.   -   -    85  E133 Voyage     40
ANVILE
  Hee'd bid, blot all: and to the anvile bring   -   -   -   -   333  Horace         627
  Upon the Muses anvile: turne the same,   -   -   -   -   -   392  Shakespeare     61
ANY
  If any sword could save from Fates, Roe's could;   -   -   -    35  E27 Roe 1        3
  If any Muse out-live their spight, his can;   -   -   -   -    35  E27 Roe 1        4
  If any friends teares could restore, his would;   -   -   -    35  E27 Roe 1        5
  If any pious life ere lifted man     -   -   -   -   -   -    35  E27 Roe 1        6
  Any man else, you clap your hands, and rore,   -   -   -   -    38  E38 Guiltie 2    4
  Almost all wayes, to any better course.   -   -   -   -   -    48  E65 Muse        10
  That, any way, my booke should speake thy name:   -   -   -    53  E77 Not name     2
  To any one, were envie: which would live   -   -   -   -   -    58  E91 Vere        11
  Of any Madames, hath neadd squires, and must.   -   -   -   -    63  E97 Motion      14
  Nor shall our cups make any guiltie men:   -   -   -   -   -    65  E101 Supper     37
  Need any Muses praise to give it fame?   -   -   -   -   -    66  E103 L Wroth 1   6
  Nor may'any feare, to loose of their degree,   -   -   -   -    73  E113 Overbury   11
  Dar'st breath in any ayre; and with safe skill,   -   -   -    76  E119 Shelton     9
  That scarse the Towne designeth any feast   -   -   -   -   -    81  E129 Mime       5
  By any arte. Then wonder not,   -   -   -   -   -   -   -    93  F1 Why write no 10
  Any paines; yea, thinke it price,   -   -   -   -   -   -   105  F8 Sicknesse    27
  Dare entayle their loves on any,   -   -   -   -   -   -   105  F8 Sicknesse    39
  Dare entayle their loves to any,   -   -   -   -   -   -   105  F8 Sicknesse  V 39
  By many? scarse by any.   -   -   -   -   -   -   -   -   109  F11 Epode       20
  Of any good minde, now: There are so few.   -   -   -   -   116  F13 Aubigny      2
  Nor for any threat, or call,   -   -   -   -   -   -   -   132  U2 How he saw   18
  Whether any would up-braid   -   -   -   -   -   -   -   138  U2 Kisse        30
  Skin as smooth as any rush,   -   -   -   -   -   -   -   141  U2 Her man      27
  In any curious peece you see   -   -   -   -   -   -   -   145  U5 Woman-kind   14
  Where any Deed is forc't, the Grace is mard.   -   -   -   -   153  U13 Sacvile     24
  As farre as any poore Sword i' the Land.   -   -   -   -   -   154  U13 Sacvile     55
  Of any, is a great and generous Deed.   -   -   -   -   -   155  U13 Sacvile     76
  Thy person fit for any charge thou tak'st;   -   -   -   -   168  U15 Friend-Wars 182
  His name in any mettall, it would breake.   -   -   -   -   172  U21 Ltl Shrub    2
  Any beliefe, in Madam Baud-bees bath,   -   -   -   -   -   188  U34 Small Poxe  10
  There is not any punishment, or paine,   -   -   -   -   -   194  U38 Elegy 'Tis 103
  Weaknesse of braine, or any charme of Wine,   -   -   -   -   198  U40 Elegy That  45
  As any Mercer; or the whale-bone man   -   -   -   -   -   200  U42 Elegy Let   31
  He would have done in verse, with any of those   -   -   -   201  U42 Elegy Let   62
  Any Comparison had with his Cheap-side.   -   -   -   -   -   202  U42 Elegy Let   76
  Or a Close-stoole so cas'd; or any fat   -   -   -   -   -   202  U42 Elegy Let   84
  To ruine any issue of the braine?   -   -   -   -   -   -   203  U43 Vulcan      14
  Any, least loose, or scurrile paper, lie   -   -   -   -   203  U43 Vulcan      20
  Scap'd not his Justice any jot the more:   -   -   -   -   210  U43 Vulcan     154
  Scap'd not this Justice any jot the more:   -   -   -   -   210  U43 Vulcan    V154
  Scap'd not thy Justice any whitt the more,   -   -   -   -   210  U43 Vulcan    V154
  Past any need of vertue. Let them care,   -   -   -   -   215  U44 Speach      83
  Of any Companie but that they are in,   -   -   -   -   -   218  U47 Tribe       20
  'Mongst which, if I have any friendships sent,   -   -   -   220  U47 Tribe       63
  From any thought like sadnesse.   -   -   -   -   -   -   221  U48 Bacchus     20
  And that as any are strooke, her breath creates   -   -   -   222  U49 Pucell       5
  I never stood for any place: my wit   -   -   -   -   -   223  U49 Pucell      23
  You were not tied, by any Painters Law,   -   -   -   -   227  U52 Answer       7
  Nor any of their houshold, halfe so well.   -   -   -   -   228  U53 Newcastle   16
  Nor any least fit   -   -   -   -   -   -   -   -   231  U57 Burges       18
  Nor any quick-warming-pan helpe him to bed,   -   -   -   232  U57 Burges       27
  And so disdaining any tryer;   -   -   -   -   -   -   278  U84 Mind        27
  Where it may run to any good;   -   -   -   -   -   -   280  U84 Mind        62
  Into our Seas send any such:   -   -   -   -   -   -   -   291  U85 Country     52
  Thou lighter then the barke of any tree,   -   -   -   -   294  U87 Hor.3:9     22
  Any fourth man, to speake at all, aspire.   -   -   -   -   317  Horace         275
  As neither any God, were brought in there,   -   -   -   321  Horace         331
  As neither any God, be brought in there,   -   -   -   -   346  Horace     V323/331
  Receive, or give it any Crowne the more.   -   -   -   -   347  Horace     V356/364
  Provided, ne're to yeeld, in any case   -   -   -   -   -   323  Horace         379
  If either you, or I know any way   -   -   -   -   -   -   348  Horace     V388/402
  So, any Poeme, fancied, or forth-brought   -   -   -   -   331  Horace         561
  He sayes to the world, let any man mend it,   -   -   -   379  Coryat 3        15
  Or any thing else that another should hide,   -   -   -   380  Coryat 3        51
  No stone in any wall here, but can tell   -   -   -   -   394  Jane Ogle        9
  Will any of these express your place? or witt?   -   -   -   402  Inigo Jones 1   18
  Of any Art, besyde what he calls his!   -   -   -   -   -   404  Inigo Jones 1   58
```

	Page	Title	Line
ANY (cont.)			
Or if any strife bety'de	417	Moon	33
shall never dare do any thing but feare.	423	Lucan	20
if any way she do rewarde thee	662	Bedford	8
AONIAN			
Are all th'Aonian springs	174	U23 Himselfe	7
APART			
To see you set apart, thus, from the rest,	234	U61 Epigram	10
APE			
On Poet-Ape.	44	E56 Poet-Ape	Ttl
Poore Poet-Ape, that would be thought our chiefe,	44	E56 Poet-Ape	1
Or else one that plaid his Ape,	132	U2 How he saw	31
APOLLO'			
All which I tell, lest when Apollo's nam'd,	329	Horace	501
APOLLO			
And why that bird was sacred to Apollo,	55	E85 Goodyere 1	4
Thee still, and leave Apollo,	221	U48 Bacchus	26
Lest of the singer Apollo, and Muses fam'd	353	Horace	V579/501
Whil'st pleas'd Apollo	366	Ode Who saith	12
When like Apollo he came forth to warme	392	Shakespeare	45
Over the Door at the Entrance into the Apollo.	657	Door Apollo	Ttl
To the Oracle of Apollo.	657	Door Apollo	2
To the Oracle of Apollo.	657	Door Apollo	20
APOLLO'S			
Apollo's harpe, and Hermes lyre resound,	98	F3 Wroth	51
That sits in shadow of Apollo's tree.	149	U9 Picture	10
And Apollo's Musique die,	183	U29 Fit of Rime	23
All which I tell, lest when Apollo's nam'd,	329	Horace	501
APOLOGETIQUE			
In the person of Woman-kind. A Song Apologetique.	145	U5 Woman-kind	Ttl
APOSTACIE			
Straines fancie unto foule Apostacie,	363	Riches	15
APOSTLE			
When the Apostle Barnabee the bright	262	U78 Digby	15
APOSTROPHE			
In manner of a daily Apostrophe,	288	U84 Muse	210
APOTHECARY (See 'POTHECARIE)			
APCTHEOSIS			
- - - apotheosis, or Relation to the Saints.	282	U84 Muse	Ttl
APPEARE			
Which shewes, where ever death doth please t'appeare,	37	E32 Roe 2	9
To this, if ought appeare, which I not know of,	65	E101 Supper	25
Crooked appeare; so that doth my conceipt:	170	U18 Elegy Can	8
Appeare, and that to shortest view,	174	U22 Elegy Tho	34
As though his age imperfect might appeare,	244	U70 Ode	51
Whose Majesties appeare,	254	U75 Epithalam.	53
That know the times, and seasons when t'appeare,	263	U79 New-yeares	11
Till, like her face, it doe appeare,	276	U84 Body	15
What love with mercy mixed doth appeare?	286	U84 Muse	138
Where first his Power will appeare, by call	289	U84 Muse	220
The last doth from the midst dis-joyn'd appeare.	315	Horace	218
To see thee in our waters yet appeare,	392	Shakespeare	72
And by their takeinge, lett it once appeare	421	Ode:If Men	44
APPEAR'D			
In the first jawes appear'd that ugly monster,	85	E133 Voyage	61
Of fortune! when, or death appear'd, or bands!	233	U59 Newcastle	23
APPEARES			
When this appeares, just Lord, to your sharp sight,	186	U32 Elsmere	15
Stamp'd to the time. As woods whose change appeares	309	Horace	85
Of Accius, and Ennius, rare appeares:	323	Horace	382
APPEAS'D			
Keepe him still active, angry, un-appeas'd,	313	Horace	172
APPETITE			
At last, ease, appetite, and example wan	57	E90 Mill	4
Or appetite of offending, but a skill,	156	U13 Sacvile	107
So ravenous, and vast an appetite?	206	U43 Vulcan	86
APPLAUD			
That watch, and catch, at what they may applaud,	167	U15 Friend-Wars	157
APPLAUSE			
When I am read, thou fain'st a weake applause,	43	E52 Courtling	3
Though every fortitude deserves applause,	49	E66 Cary	15
'Tis crowne enough to vertue still, her owne applause.	174	U23 Himselfe	18
With admiration, and applause to die!	270	U81 Pawlet	62
If such a ones applause thou dost require,	315	Horace	220
Receive, or give it an applause, the more.	321	Horace	364
The applause! delight! the wonder of our Stage!	391	Shakespeare	18
And you doe them well, with good applause,	409	Brome	5
APPLE			
The apple-harvest, that doth longer last;	98	F3 Wroth	43
The apple-harvest and ploued land up cast;	98	F3 Wroth	V 43
For the Apple, and those three	137	U2 Cupid	47
APPLE-HARVEST			
The apple-harvest, that doth longer last;	98	F3 Wroth	43
The apple-harvest and ploued land up cast;	98	F3 Wroth	V 43
APPLES			
Some nuts, some apples; some that thinke they make	95	F2 Penshurst	52
His head, with mellow Apples crown'd,	290	U85 Country	18
APPLIE			
Cynthius, I applie	176	U25 Desmond	8
Pythius, I applie	176	U25 Desmond	V 8
APPLY			
That to the vulgar canst thy selfe apply,	76	E119 Shelton	11
While all, that follow, their glad eares apply	97	F3 Wroth	31

APPLY (cont.)
    But thou, my Wroth, if I can truth apply, ...   99 F3 Wroth   91
    But thou, my Wroth, if I may truth apply, ...   99 F3 Wroth   V 91
    Still, still, the hunters of false fame apply .   .   .   .   155 U13 Sacvile   65
    Which in the taking if you mis-apply, ...   180 U26 Ode High   11
    But then his Mothers sweets you so apply, ...   182 U28 Worth   12
    That is, if still your Favours you apply, ...   192 U38 Elegy 'Tis 53
    What Fooles, and all their Parasites can apply; . .   .   .   193 U38 Elegy 'Tis 94
    You lik'd, then after, to apply   .   .   .   .   .   .   247 U70 Ode   108
    So swift, so pure, should yet apply   .   .   .   .   .   279 U84 Mind   42
    But he hath every suffrage, can apply   .   .   .   .   .   329 Horace   514
APPREHENSION
    To take Apprehension   .   .   .   .   231 U57 Burges   11
APPROACH
    Laden with Bellie, and doth hardly approach   .   .   .   .   230 U56 Covell   9
    That liking; and approach so one the tother, ...   247 U70 Ode   109
APPROACHES
    This sadnesse makes no approaches, but to kill.   .   .   .   191 U38 Elegy 'Tis   4
    Of making just approaches, how to kill, ...   232 U59 Newcastle   4
    And made those strong approaches, by False braies, .   .   .   248 U71 Treasurer   7
APPROACHing
    Of the fed flocks approaching home!   .   .   .   .   .   291 U85 Country   62
APPROCH
    Saw all his race approch the blacker floods: .   .   .   .   41 E44 Chuff   4
APPROCHES
    And all did ring th'approches of the Bride;   .   .   .   .   253 U75 Epithalam. 36
    Stay, till she make her vaine Approches. Then   .   .   .   401 Beaumont   15
APPROPRIATES
    appropriates still unto that County: .   .   .   .   .   662 Bedford   4
APPROVE
    and Conjures all my faculties t'approve   .   .   .   .   .   108 F10 Proludium   14
    Embrace, and cherish; but he can approve .   .   .   .   .   161 U14 Selden   74
    Plaine phrase, my Piso's, as alone, t'approve .   .   .   .   321 Horace   342
APRICOT
    The blushing apricot, and woolly peach   .   .   .   .   .   94 F2 Penshurst   43
APRIL
    What gentle Ghost, besprent with April deaw, ...   268 U81 Pawlet   1
    What goodly Ghost, besprent with April deaw, ...   268 U81 Pawlet   V 1
APT
    Of historie, and how to apt their places; .   .   .   .   .   61 E95 Savile   28
    (But this more apt .   .   .   .   368 Ode Who saith   62
APTETH
    And some one apteth to be trusted, then, ...   113 F12 Rutland   10
APULIANS
    Some lustie quick Apulians spouse, ...   291 U85 Country   42
AQUIT
    As Love, t'aquit such excellence, ...   173 U22 Elegy Tho   23
ARAR
    Slow Arar, nor swift Rhone; the Loyre, nor Seine, .   .   .   369 Ode Who saith 117
ARCH   (NOUN)
    That makes the Arch. The rest that there were put .   .   .   157 U13 Sacvile   137
ARCH
    Your Arch-Dukes Agents, and your Beringhams, ...   69 E107 Hungry   23
    Angels, Arch-angels, Principalities, ...   285 U84 Muse   86
ARCH-ANGELS
    Angels, Arch-angels, Principalities, ...   285 U84 Muse   86
ARCH-DUKES
    Your Arch-Dukes Agents, and your Beringhams, ...   69 E107 Hungry   23
ARCHED
    And from her arched browes, such a grace .   .   .   .   .   134 U2 Triumph   17
ARCHETYPE
    An Archetype, for all the world to see, ...   227 U52 Answer   14
ARCHILOCHUS
    Th'Iambick arm'd Archilochus to rave, ...   311 Horace   117
ARCHIMEDE
    Both him & Archimede; damne Architas   .   .   .   .   .   402 Inigo Jones 1   5
ARCHITAS
    Both him & Archimede; damne Architas   .   .   .   .   .   402 Inigo Jones 1   5
ARCHITECT
    From friendship, is it's owne fames architect. .   .   .   .   75 E115 Honest Man 30
    Which, though I cannot as an Architect   .   .   .   .   .   261 U77 Treasurer   25
    Which, though I cannot like as an Architect .   .   .   .   261 U77 Treasurer V 25
    you are; from them leapt forth an Architect, ...   402 Inigo Jones 1   3
    Oh wise Surveyor! wyser Architect!   .   .   .   .   .   405 Inigo Jones 1   85
    Again, thy Architect to ashes turne!   .   .   .   .   .   406 Inigo Jones 1 102
ARCHITECTONICE
    How much Architectonice is your owne!   .   .   .   .   .   402 Inigo Jones 1   10
ARCHITECTS
    Terme of the Architects is called Designe! .   .   .   .   404 Inigo Jones 1   56
ARCHITECTURE
    Dame History, Dame Architecture too, ...   403 Inigo Jones 1   37
    Allmighty Architecture? who noe less   .   .   .   .   .   406 Inigo Jones 1   92
ARDEN
    Stunke not so ill; nor, when shee kist, Kate Arden. .   .   .   87 E133 Voyage   118
    Nay, sigh'd a Sister, 'twas the Nun, Kate Arden,   .   .   .   209 U43 Vulcan   148
    Nay, sayth a sister, Venus Nun, Kate Arden, ...   209 U43 Vulcan   V148
ARDOR
    With the Ardor, and the Passion, ...   131 U2 Excuse   11
    Inflam'd with ardor to that mystick Shine, ...   413 Ghyrlond   23
'RE
    But grant us perfect, they're not knowne. .   .   .   .   .   104 F7 Women but   10
    Shall find their depth: they're sounded with a spoone. .   .   198 U40 Elegy That 30
    They're darke, bid cleare this: all that's doubtfull wrote   .   335 Horace   637

'RE (cont.)
| They're dark, bid cleare 'hem; al that's doubtful wrote | - | - | 354 | Horace | V637 |

ARE
Thou are not covetous of least selfe-fame,	-	-	-	-	27	E2 My Booke	9
Thou wert, as chiefe of them are said t'have beene.	-	-	-	28	E4 James 1	6
And still be a whore-house. Th'are Synonima.	-	-	-	29	E7 Hot-house	4
All men are wormes: But this no man. In silke	-	-	31	E15 Court-worm	1
Both which are great. And laugh at ill-made clothes;	-	-	35	E28 Surly	10
Seas, serenes, swords, shot, sicknesse, all are there.	-	-	37	E32 Roe 2	10
You laugh when you are touch'd, and long before	-	-	38	E38 Guiltie 2	3
The children, that he keepes, Giles sweares are none	-	-	40	E42 Giles	13
Chev'ril cryes out, my verses libells are;	-	-	44	E54 Chev'ril 2	1
What are thy petulant pleadings, Chev'ril, then,	-	-	44	E54 Chev'ril 2	3
Whose workes are eene the fripperie of wit,	-	-	44	E56 Poet-Ape	2
Spies, you are lights in state, but of base stuffe,	-	-	45	E59 Spies	1
Stinke, and are throwne away. End faire enough.	-	-	45	E59 Spies	3
To make amends, yo'are thought a wholesome creature.	-	-	46	E62 Would-bee	8
When they cost dearest, and are done most free,	-	-	49	E66 Cary	14
I Grieve not, Courtling, thou are started up	-	-	50	E72 Court-ling	1
That Poets are far rarer births then kings,	-	-	53	E79 Rutland	1
The ports of death are sinnes; of life, good deeds:	-	-	53	E80 Life/Death	1
Humanitie, and pietie, which are	-	-	-	58	E91 Vere	15
As noble in great chiefes, as they are rare.	-	-	58	E91 Vere	16
Ripe are their ruffes, their cuffes, their beards, their gate,	-	58	E92 New Crie	6
And unto whom: They are the almanacks	-	-	59	E92 New Crie	13
Are sure to con the catalogue by hart;	-	-	59	E92 New Crie	22
Though not unprov'd: which shewes, thy fortunes are	-	-	60	E93 Radcliffe	14
Lucy, you brightnesse of our spheare, who are	-	-	60	E94 Bedford 3	1
Be of the best: and 'mongst those, best are you.	-	-	61	E94 Bedford 3	14
Lucy, you brightnesse of our spheare, who are	-	-	61	E94 Bedford 3	15
Nor are the Queenes most honor'd maides by th'eares	-	-	63	E97 Motion	18
From place, or fortune, are made high, or low,	-	-	64	E99 Th Roe 2	9
And, though fowle, now, be scarce, yet there are clarkes,	-	-	65	E101 Supper	15
Are all but Luthers beere, to this I sing.	-	-	65	E101 Supper	34
Both which are ask'd, to have thee understood.	-	-	66	E102 Pembroke	4
And are so good, and bad, just at a price,	-	-	66	E102 Pembroke	11
Forgive me then, if mine but say you are	-	-	67	E103 L Wroth 1	9
So are you Natures Index, and restore,	-	-	68	E105 L Wroth 2	19
And yet are with their Princes: Fill them full	-	-	69	E107 Hungry	7
That are your wordes of credit. Keepe your Names	-	-	69	E107 Hungry	24
For your next meale: this you are sure of. Why	-	-	69	E107 Hungry	27
Come, be not angrie, you are Hungry; eate;	-	-	69	E107 Hungry	31
Such as are misse-call'd Captaynes, and wrong you;	-	-	69	E108 Soldiers	2
Thou are not one, seek'st miseries with hope,	-	-	70	E109 Nevil	5
Wherein thou shew'st, how much the latter are	-	-	72	E111 Edmonds 2	3
That seeming prayses, are, yet accusations.	-	-	75	E115 Honest Man	32
So well in that are his inventions wrought,	-	-	83	E132 Sylvester	11
All, that are readers: but, me thinkes 'tis od,	-	-	85	E133 Voyage	43
With great gray eyes, are lifted up, and mew'd;	-	-	88	E133 Voyage	161
That since, my numbers are so cold,	-	-	93	F1 Why write no	11
Thou hast no lantherne, whereof tales are told;	-	-	93	F2 Penshurst	4
There, in the writhed barke, are cut the names	-	-	94	F2 Penshurst	15
Fresh as the ayre, and new as are the houres.	-	-	94	F2 Penshurst	40
They'are rear'd with no mans ruine, no mans grone,	-	-	94	F2 Penshurst	46
These, Penshurst, are thy praise, and yet not all.	-	-	96	F2 Penshurst	89
They are, and have beene taught religion: Thence	-	-	96	F2 Penshurst	93
Each morne, and even, they are taught to pray,	-	-	96	F2 Penshurst	95
Nor are the Muses strangers found:	-	-	98	F3 Wroth	52
And in their cups, their cares are drown'd;	-	-	98	F3 Wroth	60
I know thy formes are studyed arts,	-	-	100	F4 To the World	9
And what thou call'st thy gifts are baits.	-	-	100	F4 To the World	12
But, what we'are borne for, we must beare:	-	-	101	F4 To the World	53
But make my strengths, such as they are,	-	-	102	F4 To the World	67
Fame, and rumor are but toyes.	-	-	102	F5 Celia 1	10
Song. That Women are but Mens shaddowes.	-	-	104	F7 Women but	Ttl
Say, are not women truely, then,	-	-	104	F7 Women but	5
At morne, and even, shades are longest;	-	-	104	F7 Women but	7
At noone, they are or short, or none:	-	-	104	F7 Women but	8
So men at weakest, they are strongest,	-	-	104	F7 Women but	9
Say, are not women truely, then,	-	-	104	F7 Women but	11
There are those, that, for thy sake,	-	-	105	F8 Sicknesse	25
In decoctions; and are mann'd	-	-	105	F8 Sicknesse	30
Hercules? alas his bones are yet sore,	-	-	107	F10 Proludium	4
Th'are base, and idle feares	-	-	109	F11 Epode	26
Whose linkes are bright, and even,	-	-	110	F11 Epode	48
A forme more fresh, then are the Eden bowers,	-	-	111	F11 Epode	57
Such spirits as are onely continent,	-	-	111	F11 Epode	77
Because lust's meanes are spent:	-	-	111	F11 Epode	78
And, for it, life, conscience, yea, soules are given,	-	-	113	F12 Rutland	4
When his proud patrons favours are asleepe;	-	-	113	F12 Rutland	14
Of any good minde, now: There are so few.	-	-	116	F13 Aubigny	2
The bad, by number, are so fortified,	-	-	116	F13 Aubigny	3
Men are not just, or keepe no holy lawes	-	-	117	F13 Aubigny	18
And, in those outward formes, all fooles are wise.	-	-	117	F13 Aubigny	36
A Princes fortune: These are gifts of chance,	-	-	117	F13 Aubigny	41
Are you engaged to your happy fate,	-	-	118	F13 Aubigny	47
In single paths, dangers with ease are watch'd;	-	-	118	F13 Aubigny	57
For which you worthy are the glad encrease	-	-	119	F13 Aubigny	94
They speake; since you are truly that rare wife,	-	-	119	F13 Aubigny	110
What your try'd manners are, what theirs should bee.	-	-	119	F13 Aubigny	112
You are depending on his word, and will;	-	-	119	F13 Aubigny	114
Are fled and gone,	-	-	120	F14 Sydney	19
Are justly summ'd, that make you man;	-	-	120	F14 Sydney	22

ARE (cont.)

		Page	Title	Line
Whose nephew, whose grand-child you are;	-	121	F14 Sydney	42
Poets, though divine, are men:	-	131	U2 Excuse	5
Noblest Charis, you that are	-	136	U2 Cupid	1
Thence, as sweet, as you are faire,	-	137	U2 Kisse	4
What w'are but once to doe, we should doe long.	-	139	U2 Another	12
No tunes are sweet, nor words have sting,	-	143	U3 Musicall	15
We are no women then, but wives.	-	146	U6 Defence	6
For benefits are ow'd with the same mind	-	153	U13 Sacvile	5
As they are done, and such returnes they find:	-	153	U13 Sacvile	6
They are the Noblest benefits, and sinke	-	153	U13 Sacvile	19
They are so long a comming, and so hard;	-	153	U13 Sacvile	23
Are they not worthy to be answer'd so,	-	154	U13 Sacvile	59
Her ends are honestie, and publike good!	-	156	U13 Sacvile	111
No more are these of us, let them then goe,	-	156	U13 Sacvile	113
Can I discerne how shadowes are decreast,	-	156	U13 Sacvile	118
Are nothing till that comes to bind and shut.	-	157	U13 Sacvile	138
Such Notes are vertuous men! they live as fast	-	157	U13 Sacvile	143
As they are high; are rooted, and will last.	-	157	U13 Sacvile	144
Are Dwarfes of Honour, and have neither weight	-	157	U13 Sacvile	147
Truth, and the Graces best, when naked are.	-	158	U14 Selden	4
Since, naked, best Truth, and the Graces are.	-	158	U14 Selden	V 4
How are Traditions there examin'd: how	-	160	U14 Selden	49
You both are modest. So am I. Farewell.	-	161	U14 Selden	86
All that dare rowse: or are not loth to quit	-	162	U15 Friend-Wars	3
All other Acts of Worldlings, are but toyle	-	162	U15 Friend-Wars	9
All other Acts of Worldlings, are meere toyle	-	162	U15 Friend-Wars	V 9
But there are objects, bid him to be gone	-	163	U15 Friend-Wars	28
Our Delicacies are growne capitall,	-	163	U15 Friend-Wars	37
And even our sports are dangers! what we call	-	163	U15 Friend-Wars	38
As they are made! Pride, and stiffe Clownage mixt	-	163	U15 Friend-Wars	43
Great, brave, and fashion'd folke, these are allow'd	-	164	U15 Friend-Wars	84
Adulteries, now, are not so hid, or strange,	-	165	U15 Friend-Wars	85
Thus they doe talke. And are these objects fit	-	165	U15 Friend-Wars	101
To be beholders, when their powers are spent.	-	166	U15 Friend-Wars	140
(Because th'are every where amongst Man-kind	-	167	U15 Friend-Wars	171
They are not, Sir, worst Owers, that doe pay	-	169	U17 Friend-Debt	1
Some grounds are made the richer, for the Rest;	-	169	U17 Friend-Debt	17
But which shall lead me on? both these are blind:	-	170	U18 Elegy Can	11
And then the best are, still, the blindest friends!	-	170	U18 Elegy Can	14
You blush, but doe not: friends are either none,	-	171	U19 Elegy By	13
And you are he: the Dietie	-	173	U22 Elegy Tho	25
To whom all Lovers are design'd,	-	173	U22 Elegy Tho	26
Are all th'Aonian springs	-	174	U23 Himselfe	7
Minds that are great and free,	-	174	U23 Himselfe	16
But both might know their wayes are understood,	-	176	U24 Frontispice	V 7
Assisted by no strengths, but are her owne,	-	176	U24 Frontispice	14
As farre from all revolt, as you are now from Fortune.	-	180	U25 Desmond	65
And now are out of sight.	-	180	U26 Ode High	8
You are unkind.	-	180	U26 Ode High	12
His very eyes are yours to overthrow.	-	182	U28 Worth	11
Are there for Charitie, and not for fee.	-	186	U32 Elsmere	6
Where mutuall frauds are fought, and no side yeild;	-	186	U33 Councellour	4
Such are his powers, whom time hath stil'd,	-	189	U36 Song	13
Offended Mistris, you are yet so faire,	-	191	U38 Elegy 'Tis	9
How much you are the better part of me;	-	194	U38 Elegy 'Tis	110
That are like cloath'd: must I be of those fooles	-	201	U42 Elegy Let	48
Such Songsters there are store of: witnesse he	-	201	U42 Elegy Let	65
Another answers, 'Lasse, those Silkes are none,	-	202	U42 Elegy Let	74
(Which, some are pleas'd to stile but thy madde pranck)	-	208	U43 Vulcan	131
All Ensignes of a Warre, are not yet dead,	-	213	U44 Speach	11
Us, in our bearing, that are thus, and thus,	-	215	U44 Speach	65
Are we by Booke-wormes to be awde? must we	-	215	U44 Speach	67
Why are we rich, or great, except to show	-	215	U44 Speach	69
That in the Cradle of their Gentrie are;	-	215	U44 Speach	84
But why are all these Irons i'the fire	-	215	U44 Speach	93
Those poore Ties, depend on those false ends,	-	216	U45 Squib	11
For there are many slips, and Counterfeits.	-	216	U45 Squib	17
Men that are safe, and sure, in all they doe,	-	218	U47 Tribe	1
Care not what trials they are put unto;	-	218	U47 Tribe	2
And though Opinion stampe them not, are gold.	-	218	U47 Tribe	4
On all Soules that are absent; even the dead;	-	218	U47 Tribe	17
Of any Companie but that they are in,	-	218	U47 Tribe	20
And are received for the Covey of Witts;	-	218	U47 Tribe	22
Such as are square, wel-tagde, and permanent,	-	220	U47 Tribe	64
As are the Glorious Scenes, at the great sights;	-	220	U47 Tribe	66
Are asked to climbe. First give me faith, who know	-	220	U47 Tribe	75
Sir, you are Sealed of the Tribe of Ben.	-	220	U47 Tribe	78
The narrow Seas are shadie,	-	222	U48 Bacchus	53
And that as any are strooke, her breath creates	-	222	U49 Pucell	5
Are growne so fruitfull, and false pleasures climbe,	-	224	U50 Countesse	10
Are in your selfe rewarded; yet 'twill be	-	224	U50 Countesse	15
As they are hard, for them to make their owne,	-	225	U50 Countesse	33
So are they profitable to be knowne:	-	225	U50 Countesse	34
But there are lines, wherewith I might b'embrac'd.	-	226	U52 Answer	3
But, you are he can paint; I can but write:	-	227	U52 Answer	19
How many verses, Madam, are your Due!	-	231	U56 Covell	27
All mouthes are open, and all stomacks free:	-	232	U58 Book-seller	2
At which there are, would sell the Prince, and State:	-	234	U61 Epigram	4
Yet are got off thence, with cleare mind, and hands	-	234	U61 Epigram	7
He, that in such a flood, as we are in	-	234	U61 Epigram	16
Who dares denie, that all first-fruits are due	-	235	U63 Charles 2	1
When you that raigne, are her Example growne,	-	236	U64 Charles 3	9

ARE (cont.)

	Page	Title	Line
When thou that rul'st, are her Example growne,	236	U64 Charles 3	V 9
And what are bounds to her, you make your owne?	236	U64 Charles 3	10
Are lost upon accompt! And none will know	237	U64 Charles 3	21
Are lost upon accompt! And none doe know	237	U64 Charles 3	V 21
Are they so scanted in their store? or driven	241	U68 House-hold	3
Though now of flattery, as of picture, are	242	U69 Friend Son	21
To light: her measures are, how well	245	U70 Ode	62
And shine as you exalted are;	246	U70 Ode	97
Are faine to seeke for succours, and supplies	248	U71 Treasurer	2
Through which not only we, but all our Species are.	253	U75 Epithalam.	32
They are th'exampled Paire, and mirrour of their kind.	255	U75 Epithalam.	80
All else we see beside, are Shadowes, and goe lesse.	255	U75 Epithalam.	88
In him the times, no lesse then Prince, are prais'd,	256	U75 Epithalam.	115
Their names are not recorded on the File	257	U75 Epithalam.	155
That when you both are old,	258	U75 Epithalam.	165
They both are slip'd to Bed; Shut fast the Doore,	258	U75 Epithalam.	185
What you have studied are the arts of life;	261	U77 Treasurer	17
Lute, Lyre, Theorbo, all are call'd to day.	263	U79 New-yeares	2
The fairest flowers are always found;	264	U79 New-yeares	37
In truth of colours, both are best.	265	U79 New-yeares	45
The better grasse, and flowers are found.	265	U79 New-yeares	59
How much they are belov'd of God, in thee;	268	U80 Christning	4
Would they would understand it! Princes are	268	U80 Christning	5
Great aides to Empire, as they are great care	268	U80 Christning	6
To be describ'd! Fames fingers are too foule	269	U81 Pawlet	30
Which they that have the Crowne are sure to know!	271	U81 Pawlet	76
Which the Elect of God are sure to know!	271	U81 Pawlet	V 76
The Starres, that are the Jewels of the Night,	271	U81 Pawlet	87
Yet, here are no such Trifles brought,	273	U84 Cradle	25
Painter yo' are come, but may be gone,	277	U84 Mind	1
But these are like a Mind, not it.	278	U84 Mind	12
(Brave Youths) th'are their possessions, none of yours:	281	U84 Kenelme	11
For they are strong Supporters: But, till then,	281	U84 Kenelme	14
The greatest are but growing Gentlemen.	281	U84 Kenelme	15
By which yo'are planted, shew's your fruit shall bide.	281	U84 Kenelme	19
For, as there are three Natures, Schoolemen call	284	U84 Muse	51
Of all are dead to life! His Wisdome show	289	U84 Muse	221
The lowing herds there grazing are:	290	U85 Country	14
Are gathering by the Wintry houres;	290	U85 Country	30
The Things that make the happier life, are these,	295	U90 Mart.10:47	1
Whose shapes, like sick-mens dreames, are fain'd so vaine,	305	Horace	9
Whose shapes, like sick-mens dreames, are form'd so vaine,	338	Horace	V 9
Are, with the likenesse of the truth, undone.	307	Horace	34
Are with the likeness of the truth beguil'd:	339	Horace	V 35/ 34
Are, by thy cunning placing, made meere new.	307	Horace	68
That are Spectators, with their miserie,	311	Horace	137
When they are poore, and banish'd, must throw by	311	Horace	138
Mens faces, still, with such as laugh, are prone	311	Horace	143
Mens count'nances, with such as laugh, are prone	342	Horace	V143
From what th'obscene, and petulant Satyres are.	321	Horace	340
And office of a Judge are, what the parts	325	Horace	450
There are yet faults, which we would well forgive,	329	Horace	520
You Sir, the elder brother, though you are	331	Horace	545
Nine yeares kept in, your papers by, yo'are free	331	Horace	578
Nine yeares kept by, your papers in, y'are free	352	Horace	V554/578
(Whether yo'are given to, or giver are.)	333	Horace	608
Rich men are said with many cups to plie,	333	Horace	617
Great men are said with many cups to plye,	354	Horace	V617
Those that are wise, a furious Poet feare,	354	Horace	V643
Are deeper then their Faces:	365	Ode Splendor	22
But these are Mysteries	369	Ode Who saith	111
All which are parts commend the cunning hand;	370	Author	4
And louse-dropping Case, are the Armes of his travell.	375	Coryat 1	27
That sacred to Odcombe are there now suspended,	380	Coryat 3	40
They are not those, are present with theyre face,	384	Somerset	1
Such weare true wedding robes, and are true freindes,	384	Somerset	5
If Praises, when th'are full, heaping admit,	385	Brooke	6
Who are his Test, and what their judgement is:	385	Husband	3
On credit, and are cossen'd; see, that thou	386	Browne	11
These are, as some infamous Baud, or Whore,	391	Shakespeare	13
(Such as thine are) and strike the second heat	392	Shakespeare	60
Are still th'interpreters twixt godds, and men!	395	May	18
That Rebells actions, are but valiant crimes!	397	Drayton	44
That reade it? that are ravish'd! such was I	397	Drayton	53
Brave are the Musters, that the Muse will make.	398	Drayton	64
What charming Peales are these,	401	Filmer	1
They are the Mariage-rites	401	Filmer	3
They are a Schoole to win	402	Filmer	11
you are; from them leapt forth an Architect,	402	Inigo Jones 1	3
I doe salute you! Are you fitted yet?	402	Inigo Jones 1	17
Or are you soe ambitious 'bove your peers!	403	Inigo Jones 1	19
In Towne & Court? Are you growne rich? & proud?	403	Inigo Jones 1	24
You are the Spectacles of State! Tis true	403	Inigo Jones 1	42
Painting & Carpentry are the Soule of Masque.	404	Inigo Jones 1	50
Sense, what they are! which by a specious fyne	404	Inigo Jones 1	55
Now, you are got into a nearer roome,	409	Brome	3
Cropt, branded, slit, neck-stockt; go, you are stript.	411	Gill	16
From fearefull back-slides; And the debt we'are in,	412	Sutcliffe	15
Here, are five letters in this blessed Name,	412	Ghyrlond	1
(Divinest graces) are so entermixt,	413	Ghyrlond	26
As if they' ador'd the Head, wheron th'are fixt.	413	Ghyrlond	28
How are thy gifts, and graces blaz'd abroad!	413	Ghyrlond	36

ARE   (cont.)
```
How are thy gifts and graces blaz'd abro'd,       -    -    -    -    414  Ghyrlond          53
In spite of Hipocrites, who are the worst         -    -    -    -    416  Dover              9
Fresh as the Day, and new as are the Howers,      -    -    -    -    416  Welcome            1
are distant, so is proffitt from just aymes.      -    -    -    -    422  Lucan              8
All his Answers are Divine,       -    -          -    -    -    -    657  Door Apollo        5
Ply it, and you all are mounted.        -         -    -    -    -    657  Door Apollo       14
```
ARGENIS
```
Reveald (if some can judge) of Argenis,           -    -    -    -    207  U43 Vulcan       V 96
Reveald (if some do judge) of Argenis,            -    -    -    -    207  U43 Vulcan       V 96
```
ARGIVE
```
How many equall with the Argive Queene,           -    -    -    -    114  F12 Rutland       49
```
ARGO
```
Who placed Jasons Argo in the skie?       -       -    -    -    -    115  F12 Rutland       59
```
ARGUE
```
He will both argue, and discourse in oathes,      -    -    -    -     35  E28 Surly          9
I will not argue thee, from those, of guilt,      -    -    -    -    210  U43 Vulcan       165
I will not argue thee, from them, of guilt,       -    -    -    -    210  U43 Vulcan       V165
I will not argue thee Iron. Them of guilt         -    -    -    -    210  U43 Vulcan       V165
```
ARGUED
```
Un-argued then, and yet hath fame from those;     -    -    -    -     71  E110 Edmonds 1    10
```
ARGUMENT
```
Of Argument, still drawing forth the best,        -    -    -    -    187  U33 Councellour   27
```
ARGUS
```
Or, with the milke of Thebes; or Argus, fed.      -    -    -    -    313  Horace           168
```
ARIADNES
```
Or set bright Ariadnes crowne so high?       -    -    -    -    -    115  F12 Rutland       60
```
ARIGHT
```
If ever we will love aright.        -    -        -    -    -    -    146  U6 Defence        10
```
ARION
```
Here, like Arion, our Coryate doth draw           -    -    -    -    374  Coryat 1          10
```
ARISE
```
Thy present Aide: Arise Invention,       -        -    -    -    -    176  U25 Desmond        2
```
ARISTARCHUS
```
Become an Aristarchus. And, not say,              -    -    -    -    335  Horace           639
```
ARISTOPHANES
```
The merry Greeke, tart Aristophanes,       -      -    -    -    -    392  Shakespeare       51
```
ARISTOTLE
```
Drawne Aristotle on us! & thence showne           -    -    -    -    402  Inigo Jones 1      9
```
ARMDE
```
hath armde att all poyntes; charge mee humblye kneele   -    -    382  Rich               2
```
ARME
```
But like an Arme of Eminence 'mongst them,        -    -    -    -    258  U75 Epithalam.   179
```
ARM'D
```
Arm'd with bow, shafts, and fire;       -         -    -    -    -    110  F11 Epode         38
Both arm'd with wealth, and slander to oppose,    -    -    -    -    186  U32 Elsmere        8
Arm'd at all peeces, as to keepe a Fort           -    -    -    -    187  U33 Councellour   30
Th'Iambick arm'd Archilochus to rave,             -    -    -    -    311  Horace           117
```
ARMED
```
And, armed to the chase, so bare her bow          -    -    -    -     68  E105 L Wroth 2    13
But open, and un-armed encounter'd all:           -    -    -    -     87  E133 Voyage      135
```
ARMES   (LIMBS)
```
And, at her strong armes end, hold up, and even,  -    -    -    -    114  F12 Rutland       42
And, at her strong armes end, there hold up even, -    -    -    -    114  F12 Rutland      V 42
Breake the knit Circle of her Stonie Armes,       -    -    -    -    177  U25 Desmond       19
Her broken Armes up, to their emptie moulds.      -    -    -    -    216  U44 Speach       102
```
ARMES
```
His bought armes Mung' not lik'd; for his first day   -    -    -     42  E48 Mungril        1
Upbraiding rebells armes, and barbarous pride:    -    -    -    -     60  E93 Radcliffe      6
The mysteries of manners, armes, and arts.        -    -    -    -     96  F2 Penshurst      98
Let others watch in guiltie armes, and stand      -    -    -    -     98  F3 Wroth          67
Her armes when Paris wonne her       -    -        -    -    -    -    135  U2 Triumph       V 34
And there made Swords, Bills, Glaves, and Armes your fill;  -    -    212  U43 Vulcan       198
Of bearing Armes! most civill Soldierie!          -    -    -    -    214  U44 Speach        44
To serve the State by Councels, and by Armes:     -    -    -    -    215  U44 Speach        85
They talke of Fencing, and the use of Armes,      -    -    -    -    232  U59 Newcastle      1
His armes more acceptable free,       -    -       -    -    -    -    293  U87 Hor.3:9        3
In vertue, and renowne of armes, then in          -    -    -    -    325  Horace           412
His armes in Mars his field, he doth refuse;      -    -    -    -    331  Horace           566
And louse-dropping Case, are the Armes of his travell.  -    -    375  Coryat 1          27
And when he ships them where to use their Armes,  -    -    -    -    398  Drayton           65
```
ARMIES
```
Or, in an armies head, that, lockt in brasse,     -    -    -    -    114  F12 Rutland       52
```
ARMORIE
```
For in your verse all Cupids Armorie,       -     -    -    -    -    182  U28 Worth          9
```
ARMOUR
```
No Armour to the mind! he is shot-free            -    -    -    -    179  U25 Desmond       48
That we have Trumpets, Armour, and great Horse,   -    -    -    -    213  U44 Speach         7
```
ARMYES
```
whole armyes fall, swayd by those nyce respects.  -    -    -    -    423  Lucan             11
```
AROMATIQUE
```
In making soft her aromatique bed.        -       -    -    -    -    251  U74 Weston        18
```
ARRAIGN'D
```
Ridway was tane, arraign'd, condemn'd to dye;     -    -    -    -     29  E8 Robbery         2
No, I will stand arraign'd, and cast, to be       -    -    -    -    191  U38 Elegy 'Tis    27
```
ARRAS
```
Not with the Arras, but the Persian Loomes.       -    -    -    -    260  U77 Treasurer      4
Not from the Arras, but the Persian Loomes.       -    -    -    -    260  U77 Treasurer    V 4
```
ARRAYES
```
By that one spell he lives, eates, drinkes, arrayes    -    -    -     30  E12 Shift          5
```
ARRERAGE
```
So, in short time, th'art in arrerage growne      -    -    -    -     32  E16 Brain-hardy    5
```

								Page	Title	Line

ARREST
Betweene thy Tropicks, to arrest thy sight, ... 252 U75 Epithalam. 4
ARRIVE
Object arrive there, but the heart (our spie) . . . 109 F11 Epode 11
'Tis by degrees that men arrive at glad . . . 157 U13 Sacvile 131
Still, still, dost thou arrive with, at our shore, . . 388 Chapman 5
ARROW
Letting Bow and Arrow fall, ... 132 U2 How he saw 17
Both the Arrow he had quit, ... 132 U2 How he saw 21
But the Arrow home did draw . . . . . 133 U2 Suffered 14
ARROWES
His double Bow, and round his Arrowes sends; . . . 170 U19 Elegy By 4
ARSE
Who from the Divels-Arse did Guns beget; . . . 212 U43 Vulcan 202
That from the Divels-Arse did Guns beget; . . . 212 U43 Vulcan V202
ARSENIKE
Arsenike would thee fit for societie make. . . 42 E50 Cod 3 3
ARSES
Arses were heard to croake, in stead of frogs; . . 84 E133 Voyage 13
'RT
To which thou'rt not a weeke, bespoke a guest; . . 81 E129 Mime 6
Thou'rt too ambitious: and dost fear in vaine! . . 408 Inigo Jones 3 6
ART (NOUN)
If all you boast of your great art be true; . . 29 E6 Alchymists 1
What art is thine, that so thy friend deceives? . . 44 E55 Beaumont 8
A treasure, art: contemn'd in th'age of gold. . . 47 E64 Salisbury 3 4
Truth might spend all her voyce, Fame all her art. . . 68 E106 E Herbert 4
Thy learned hand, and true Promethean art . . 71 E110 Edmonds 1 17
By thy great Art: and doth proclaime by mee, . . 72 E111 Edmonds 2 V 13
When these were but the praises of the Art. . . 82 E130 Ferrab. 1 16
And (to gaine her by his Art) . . . . . 133 U2 Suffered 15
In loves art, and yet no sinners. . . . 141 U2 Her man V 32
And having pleas'd our art, wee'll try . . 145 U5 Woman-kind 17
Lesse shall I for the Art or dressing care, . . 158 U14 Selden 3
Forme, Art or Ensigne, that hath scap'd your sight? . . 160 U14 Selden 48
And Art banish'd. . . . . . . 183 U29 Fit of Rime 15
Art, her false servant; Nor, for Sir Hugh Plat, . . 188 U34 Small Poxe 7
The art of kindling the true Coale, by Lungs: . . 206 U43 Vulcan 76
The art of kindling the true Coale, of Lungs: . . 206 U43 Julcan V 76
O happy Art: and wise Epitome . . . 214 U44 Speach 43
Which if in compasse of no Art it came . . 227 U52 Answer 10
Me thought I read the ancient Art of Thrace, . . 228 U53 Newcastle 4
The art of urging, and avoyding harmes, . . 232 U59 Newcastle 2
Not, that your Art I doe refuse: . . . 277 U84 Mind 5
With such a Raritie, and not rowse Art . . 282 U84 Muse 16
Thy table without art, and easy-rated: . . 295 U90 Mart.10:47 8
Horace, His Art of Poetrie Made English . . 303 Horace Ttl
Horace, of The Art of Poetrie. . . . 305 Horace Ttl
. . . the Art of Poetry to the Piso's. . . 338 Horace VTtl
Thus, to his antient Art the Piper lent . . 319 Horace 303
Or a worse Crime, the ignorance of art. . . 323 Horace 386
A Poeme, of no grace, weight, art, in rimes, . . 327 Horace 456
Nature, or Art. My Judgement will not pierce . . 331 Horace 582
So bold, as shewes your Art you can command. . . 370 Author 6
The art of uttring wares, if they were bad; . . 385 Husband 6
Yet must I not give Nature all: Thy Art, . . 392 Shakespeare 55
His Art doth give the fashion. And, that he, . . 392 Shakespeare 58
That Art, or Ingine, on the strength can raise. . . 400 Beaumont 10
Of any Art, besyde what he calls his! . . 404 Inigo Jones 1 58
ART
And such a Prince thou art, wee daily see, . . 28 E4 James 1 7
So, in short time, th'art in arrerage growne . . 32 E16 Brain-hardy 5
Glad-mention'd Roe: thou art but gone before, . . 37 E33 Roe 3 2
Thou art the father, and the witnesse too. . . 44 E53 Old-end 8
And thou design'd to be the same thou art, . . 49 E67 Suffolk 9
Cob, thou nor souldier, thiefe, nor fencer art, . . 50 E69 Cob 1
That still th'art present to the better cause; . . 52 E74 Chancelor 5
Whil'st thou art certaine to thy words, once gone, . . 52 E74 Chancelor 7
Which thou art to thy selfe: whose fame was wonne . . 58 E91 Vere 5
Thou, that art all their valour, all their spirit, . . 60 E93 Radcliffe 9
That art so reverenc'd, as thy comming in, . . 66 E102 Pembroke 17
What man art thou, that art so many men, . . 68 E106 E Herbert 2
To be the same in roote, thou art in height: . . 70 E109 Nevil 13
With thy small stocke, why art thou ventring still, . . 72 E112 Gamster 1
Art still at that, and think'st to blow me'up too? . . 72 E112 Gamster 6
And never art encounter'd, I confesse: . . 73 E112 Gamster 19
Roe (and my joy to name) th'art now, to goe . . 80 E128 Wm Roe 2 1
That still th'art made the suppers flagge, the drum, . . 81 E129 Mime 7
And art a god, if Fame thee not abuses, . . 85 E133 Voyage 53
Thou art not, Penshurst, built to envious show, . . 93 F2 Penshurst 1
And these grudg'd at, art reverenc'd the while. . . 93 F2 Penshurst 6
Of wood, of water: therein thou art faire. . . 93 F2 Penshurst 8
How blest art thou, canst love the countrey, Wroth, . . 96 F3 Wroth 1
Art tane with neithers vice, nor sport: . . 96 F3 Wroth 4
That at great times, art no ambitious guest . . 96 F3 Wroth 5
Which who can use is happy: Such art thou. . . 99 F3 Wroth V 99
Yet art thou both shrunke up, and old, . . 100 F4 To the World 14
I know thou whole art but a shop . . . 100 F4 To the World 17
Yet art thou falser then thy wares. . . 100 F4 To the World 20
Peace, Luxurie, thou art like one of those . . 111 F11 Epode 69
As thou art all, so be thou all to mee, . . 122 F15 Heaven 9
Here's a shaft, thou art to slow! . . . 132 U2 How he saw 10
Thou art jealous of thy Wifes, or Daughters Case: . . 202 U42 Elegy Let 87

32

ARI (cont.)
Where art thou, Genius? l should use   .   "   "   "   .   176   U25 Desmond   1
Genius, where art thou? I should use   "   "   "   "   .   176   U25 Desmond   V 1
Thou art my Cause: whose manners since I knew,   "   .   .   187   U33 Councellour   13
Thou art true Vulcan still! Thou durst not spare   "   .   210   U43 Vulcan   V159
I neither am, nor art thou one of those   "   "   "   .   216   U45 Squib   5
Since, Bacchus, thou art father   "   "   "   "   "   .   220   U48 Bacchus   1
Where now, thou art made Dweller;   "   "   "   "   .   220   U48 Bacchus   4
For, Bacchus, thou art freer   "   "   "   "   .   221   U48 Bacchus   13
And art thou borne, brave Babe? Blest be thy birth,   "   237   U65 Prince   1
And art thou borne, brave Babe? Blest be the day,   "   237   U65 Prince   V 1
The same that thou art promis'd, but be slow,   "   .   237   U65 Prince   6
Though thou art past thy Summer standing, stay   "   .   252   U75 Epithalam.   V 1
That thou art lov'd of God, this worke is done,   "   .   268   U80 Christning   1
Faire Fame, who art ordain'd to crowne   "   "   .   "   272   U84 Cradle   1
Yet know, with what thou art possest,   "   "   "   .   281   U84 Mind   70
(For so thou art with me) now shee is gone.   "   "   .   283   U84 Muse   22
Will to bee, what thou art; and nothing more: "   .   295   U90 Mart.10:47   12
Happier then wretched art, and doth, by it,   "   "   .   325   Horace   420
But thou art proofe against them, and indeed   "   "   .   391   Shakespeare   15
Thou art a Moniment, without a tombe,   "   "   "   .   391   Shakespeare   22
And art alive still, while thy Booke doth live,   "   .   391   Shakespeare   23
There, thou art Homer! Pray thee, use the stile   "   .   398   Drayton   59
With bold Tyrtaeus verse, when thou art nam'd,   "   .   398   Drayton   68
To be knowne what thou art, a blatant beast,   "   .   408   Detractor   9
Thou art not worth it. Who will care to knowe   "   .   409   Detractor   13
And art the spotlesse Mirrour to Mans eyes.   "   .   .   414   Ghyrlond   44
ARTE'
shall looke, & on hyme soe, then arte's a lyer   "   "   .   383   Rich   15
ARTE
By any arte. Then wonder not,   "   "   "   "   "   .   93   F1 Why write no   10
The seaven-fold flower of Arte (more rich then gold)   "   361   Palmer   15
That hath not Countrye impudence enough to laughe att Arte,   420   Ode:If Men   14
ARTE'S
shall looke, & on hyme soe, then arte's a lyer   "   "   .   383   Rich   15
ARTES
Court Hieroglyphicks! & all Artes affoord   "   "   .   404   Inigo Jones 1   43
ARTH
An Epistle to Master Arth: Squib.   "   "   "   "   .   216   U45 Squib   Ttl
ARTHUR
From Guy, or Bevis, Arthur, or from whom   "   "   .   215   U44 Speach   81
My gentle Arthur; that it might be said   "   "   .   216   U45 Squib   3
Epistle To Mr. Arthur Squib.   "   "   "   "   "   .   229   U54 Squib   Ttl
Lend me, deare Arthur, for a weeke five more,   "   .   229   U54 Squib   16
ARTHURS
To have beene stiled of King Arthurs table.   "   "   .   84   E133 Voyage   24
Th'Esplandians, Arthurs, Palmerins, and all   "   "   .   203   U43 Vulcan   30
ARTICHOKES
When every clerke eates artichokes, and peason,   "   .   88   E133 Voyage   166
ARTICLE
That Article, may not become our lover: "   "   .   198   U40 Elegy That   48
ARTILLERIE
Well, I say, thrive, thrive brave Artillerie yard,   "   .   213   U44 Speach   23
ARTLESSE
When in a wrong, and artlesse way we tread.   "   "   .   307   Horace   44
If in th'escape an artlesse path we tread.   "   "   .   339   Horace   V 46/ 44
On artlesse Verse; the hard ones he will blame;   "   .   335   Horace   634
ARTS
If, without these vile arts, it will not sell,   "   "   .   28   E3 Bookseller   11
All that I am in arts, all that I know,   "   "   "   .   31   E14 Camden   2
To it, thy language, letters, arts, best life,   "   "   .   34   E23 Donne 1   7
Surly, use other arts, these only can   "   "   "   .   36   E28 Surly   21
These were thy knowing arts: which who doth now   "   .   75   E116 Jephson   13
I need no other arts, but studie thee: "   "   "   .   78   E122 Rudyerd 2   9
The mysteries of manners, armes, and arts.   "   "   .   96   F2 Penshurst   98
I know thy formes are studyed arts,   "   "   "   .   100   F4 To the World   9
Where envious arts professed be,   "   "   "   "   .   101   F4 To the World 47
Will prove old Orpheus Arts no tale to be: "   "   .   115   F12 Rutland   V 77
By arts, and practise of the vicious,   "   "   "   .   117   F13 Aubigny   12
Or use all arts, or haunt all Companies   "   "   .   165   U15 Friend-Wars   91
Informers, Masters both of Arts and lies;   "   "   .   167   U15 Friend-Wars 164
That eats on wits, and Arts, and destroyes them both.   "   174   U23 Himselfe   6
There were of search, and mastry in the Arts.   "   .   206   U43 Vulcan   88
There were of search, and mastry of the Arts.   "   .   206   U43 Vulcan   V 88
'Cause thou canst halt, with us, in Arts, and Fire!   "   .   208   U43 Vulcan   110
Their Sonnes to studie Arts, the Lawes, the Creed: "   215   U44 Speach   74
By all the Arts of Gladnesse,   "   "   "   "   "   .   221   U48 Bacchus   19
No love of action, and high Arts,   "   "   "   "   .   234   U60 La-ware   12
Got up and thriv'd with honest arts: "   "   "   .   244   U70 Ode   34
Have multipli'd their arts, and powers,   "   "   "   .   251   U74 Weston   17
With all corroding Arts, be able to untie!   "   "   .   257   U75 Epithalam.   136
Catch'd with these Arts, wherein the Judge is wise   "   .   261   U77 Treasurer   11
Caught them these Arts, wherein the Judge is wise   "   .   261   U77 Treasurer V 11
What you have studied are the arts of life;   "   "   .   261   U77 Treasurer   17
Court can call hers, or Man could call his Arts.   "   .   262   U78 Digby   4
Court can call hers, or Man would call the Arts.   "   .   262   U78 Digby   V 4
Child of a hundred Arts, and farre   "   "   "   .   292   U86 Hor.4:1   15
Can tell a States-mans dutie, what the arts   "   "   .   325   Horace   449
A pound, or piece, by their long compting arts: "   .   327   Horace   466
What godds but those of arts, and eloquence?   "   "   .   395   May   16
As it had beene the circle of the Arts!   "   "   "   .   396   Drayton   22
Of Fellowship, professing my old Arts.   "   "   "   .   409   Brome   4

		Page	Title	Line

ARUNDELL
Of bold Sir Bevis, and his Arundell: .   .   .   .   .   .   228 U53 Newcastle   10
AS'
  As't were a challenge, or a borrowers letter?   .   .   .   51 E73 Fine Grand   3
  To all as fatall as't hath beene to me,   .   .   .   211 U43 Vulcan   192
AS
  As mad-men stones: not caring whom they hit.   .   .   27 E2 My Booke   6
  Call'st a booke good, or bad, as it doth sell,   .   .   27 E3 Bookseller   2
  Not offer'd, as it made sute to be bought;   .   .   28 E3 Bookseller   6
  Thou wert, as chiefe of them are said t'have beene.   .   28 E4 James 1   6
  As chiefe of those still promise they will bee.   .   28 E4 James 1   8
  Thou call'st me Poet, as a terme of shame;   .   .   29 E10 Ignorant   1
  To seeme a statesman: as I neere it came,   .   .   30 E11 Something   3
  For I will doe none: and as little ill,   .   .   30 E11 Something   7
  'Twas brought to court first wrapt, and white as milke;   .   31 E15 Court-worm   2
  As guiltie men doe magistrates: glad I,   .   .   32 E17 Critic   2
  As theirs did with thee, mine might credit get: .   32 E18 Censurer   6
  If thou'ldst but use thy faith, as thou didst then,   .   32 E18 Censurer   7
  But leave, because I cannot as I should!   .   .   34 E23 Donne 1   10
  And, that is done, as he saw great men doe.   .   35 E28 Surly   6
  He toyles to be at hell, as soone as they.   .   .   36 E31 Banck   4
  Hast purg'd thy realmes, as we have now no cause   .   38 E35 James 2   5
  But as they come, on both sides he takes fees,   .   38 E37 Chev'ril   2
  Rich, as nature could bequeath thee: .   .   .   39 E40 Ratcliffe   3
  Rare, as wonder, was her wit;   .   .   .   .   39 E40 Ratcliffe   9
  As thou stand'st cleere of the necessitie.   .   .   41 E43 Salisbury 1   12
  As what he loves may never like too much.   .   .   41 E45 First Son   12
  As if thou wert my friend, but lack'dst a cause.   .   43 E52 Courtling   4
  It was as if thou printed had'st an oath,   .   .   43 E53 Old-end   5
  And that, as puritanes at baptisme doo,   .   .   44 E53 Old-end   7
  As we, the rob'd, leave rage, and pittie it.   .   44 E56 Poet-Ape   4
  May judge it to be his, as well as ours.   .   .   45 E56 Poet-Ape   12
  Foole, as if halfe eyes will not know a fleece   .   45 E56 Poet-Ape   13
  If, as their ends, their fruits were so, the same,   .   45 E57 Bawds   1
  Nor glad as those, that old dependents bee,   .   47 E64 Salisbury 3   5
  As her owne conscience, still, the same reward.   .   48 E64 Salisbury 3   14
  And, as thou'hast mine, his houres, and youth abuse.   .   48 E65 Muse   6
  As, to be rais'd by her, is onely fame.   .   .   49 E67 Suffolk   4
  As all thy honors were by them first sought: .   49 E67 Suffolk   8
  Goe high, or low, as thou wilt value it.   .   .   50 E72 Court-ling   4
  As is thy conscience, which is alwayes one: .   52 E74 Chancelor   8
  'Twixt puritanes, and players, as some cry;   .   52 E75 Lippe   2
  To honor, serve, and love; as Poets use.   .   .   52 E76 Bedford 1   4
  As he would burne, or better farre his booke.   .   53 E79 Rutland   12
  So to front death, as men might judge us past it.   .   54 E80 Life/Death   7
  As french-men in his companie, should seeme dutch?   .   56 E88 Monsieur   8
  As skilfull Roscius, and grave Aesope, men,   .   56 E89 Allen   3
  Yet crown'd with honors, as with riches, then;   .   56 E89 Allen   4
  As others speake, but onely thou dost act.   .   57 E89 Allen   12
  Sung by a Horace, or a Muse as free;   .   .   58 E91 Vere   4
  As noble in great chiefes, as they are rare.   .   58 E91 Vere   16
  And grave as ripe, like mellow as their faces.   .   59 E92 New Crie   7
  And understand 'hem, as most chapmen doe.   .   59 E92 New Crie   10
  With ignorance on us, as they have done   .   .   59 E92 New Crie   37
  That know not so much state, wrong, as they doo.   .   59 E92 New Crie   40
  And two, that would have falne as great, as they,   .   60 E93 Radcliffe   7
  The Muses evening, as their morning-starre.   .   61 E94 Bedford 3   16
  As, then, his cause, his glorie emulate.   .   .   61 E95 Savile   24
  As free simplicitie, to dis-avow,   .   .   .   62 E96 Donne 2   5
  As thou hast best authoritie, t'allow.   .   .   62 E96 Donne 2   6
  If time to facts, as unto men would owe?   .   64 E99 Th Roe 2   6
  The selfe-same deeds, as diversly they come,   .   64 E99 Th Roe 2   8
  Their lives, as doe their lines, till now had lasted.   .   65 E101 Supper   32
  But, at our parting, we will be, as when   .   .   65 E101 Supper   38
  As nothing else discernes the vertue' or vice.   .   66 E102 Pembroke   12
  That art so reverenc'd, as thy comming in,   .   66 E102 Pembroke   17
  A Sydney: but in that extend as farre   .   .   67 E103 L Wroth 1   10
  As lowdest praisers, who perhaps would find   .   67 E103 L Wroth 1   11
  Such as are misse-call'd Captaynes, and wrong you;   .   69 E108 Soldiers   2
  And that so strong and deepe, as 't might be thought,   .   71 E110 Edmonds 1   7
  Can so speake Caesar, as thy labours doe.   .   71 E110 Edmonds 1   12
  (As by a new creation) part by part,   .   .   71 E110 Edmonds 1   18
  Caesar stands up, as from his urne late rose,   .   72 E111 Edmonds 2   12
  As but to speake thee, Overbury, is praise: .   73 E113 Overbury   2
  Might be found out as good, and not my Lord.   .   75 E116 Jephson   8
  As Heaven and Nature seem'd to strive   .   .   77 E120 S. P.   7
  as, sooth, the Parcae thought him one,   .   .   77 E120 S. P.   15
  Rudyerd, as lesser dames, to great ones use,   .   78 E121 Rudyerd 1   1
  If I would vertue set, as shee was yong,   .   .   78 E122 Rudyerd 2   5
  But both th'hast so, as who affects the state   .   78 E123 Rudyerd 3   3
  As much beautie, as could dye: .   .   .   .   79 E124 Elizabeth   4
  May windes as soft as breath of kissing friends,   .   81 E128 Wm Roe 2   5
  As the beginnings here, prove purely sweet,   .   81 E128 Wm Roe 2   7
  But, as it is (the Child of Ignorance,   .   .   83 E132 Sylvester   3
  As his will now be the translation thought,   .   83 E132 Sylvester   12
  Belch'd forth an ayre, as hot, as at the muster   .   85 E133 Voyage   63
  Crack did report it selfe, as if a cloud   .   .   86 E133 Voyage   94
  Vanish'd away: as you must all presume   .   .   87 E133 Voyage   110
  Of the hulke touch'd, and, as by Polypheme   .   87 E133 Voyage   112
  Thou hast thy walkes for health, as well as sport: .   93 F2 Penshurst   9
  As loth, the second draught, or cast to stay;   .   94 F2 Penshurst   35
  Fresh as the ayre, and new as are the houres.   .   94 F2 Penshurst   40
  And I not faine to sit (as some, this day,   .   95 F2 Penshurst   65

AS (cont.)

	Page	Title	Line
As if thou, then, wert mine, or I raign'd here:	95	F2 Penshurst	74
Shine bright on every harth as the desires	95	F2 Penshurst	78
As if it had expected such a guest!	96	F2 Penshurst	88
As if in Saturnes raigne it were;	98	F3 Wroth	50
And each where boast it as his merit,	99	F3 Wroth	78
Like such as blow away their lives,	100	F4 To the World	22
As little, as I hope from thee:	101	F4 To the World	38
But, as 'tis rumor'd, so beleev'd:	101	F4 To the World	50
As shall not need thy false reliefe.	102	F4 To the World	64
As wandrers doe, that still doe rome,	102	F4 To the World	66
But make my strengths, such as they are,	102	F4 To the World	67
How to tell' hem, as they flow,	103	F6 Celia 2	20
Live not we, as, all thy stalls,	104	F8 Sicknesse	9
Move it, as their humblest sute,	106	F8 Sicknesse	46
Move it, as their humble sute,	106	F8 Sicknesse	V 46
As giving it a hope, that there	106	F9 Celia 3	11
Such, as in lustes wilde forrest love to rainge,	108	F10 Proludium	9
The first; as prone to move	110	F11 Epode	32
Inconstant, as the sea, of whence 'tis borne,	110	F11 Epode	V 39
And boyles, as if he were	110	F11 Epode	42
And lasting, as her flowers:	111	F11 Epode	58
Richer then Time, and as Time's vertue, rare.	111	F11 Epode	59
Sober, as saddest care:	111	F11 Epode	60
As this chaste love we sing.	111	F11 Epode	68
As this chaste love I sing.	111	F11 Epode	V 68
Such spirits as are onely continent,	111	F11 Epode	77
As sweet, as shee is fayre.	112	F11 Epode	98
As if Nature disclos'd	112	F11 Epode	100
They hold in my strange poems, which, as yet,	115	F12 Rutland	81
But high, and noble matter, such as flies	116	F12 Rutland	89
A vow as new, and ominous as the yeare,	116	F12 Rutland	98
As what th'have lost t'expect, they dare deride.	116	F13 Aubigny	4
And howsoever; as I am at fewd	116	F13 Aubigny	9
Such as suspect them-selves, and thinke it fit	117	F13 Aubigny	13
Or so my selfe abandon'd, as because	117	F13 Aubigny	17
And this shall be no false one, but as much	117	F13 Aubigny	27
Remov'd, as you from need to have it such.	117	F13 Aubigny	28
Not taken up o' th' doctors, but as well	117	F13 Aubigny	33
As I, can say, and see it doth excell.	117	F13 Aubigny	34
As bloud, and match. Wherein, how more then much	117	F13 Aubigny	46
And after varyed, as fresh objects goes,	118	F13 Aubigny	66
Grow, grow, faire tree, and as thy branches shoote,	119	F13 Aubigny	99
And that your soules conspire, as they were gone	119	F13 Aubigny	119
Live that one, still; and as long yeeres doe passe,	120	F13 Aubigny	121
So may you live in honor, as in name,	121	F14 Sydney	51
As with the light	121	F14 Sydney	58
As thou art all, so be thou all to mee,	122	F15 Heaven	9
As my heart lies in peeces, all confus'd,	127	U1 Trinitie	7
As minds ill bent	129	U1 Father	13
As sure to win	130	U1 Father	31
And as that wisedome had decreed,	130	U1 Nativitie	16
Some have lov'd as old agen.	131	U2 Excuse	6
But be glad, as soone with me,	131	U2 Excuse	17
Such a Lightning (as I drew)	132	U2 How he saw	24
As she goes, all hearts doe duty	134	U2 Triumph	5
As Loves starre when it riseth!	134	U2 Triumph	14
As alone there triumphs to the life	134	U2 Triumph	19
As the Bath your verse discloses	136	U2 Cupid	21
Such as oft I wanton in!	136	U2 Cupid	23
Thence, as sweet, as you are faire,	137	U2 Kisse	4
Of th'Assembly, as did you!	138	U2 Kisse	12
So, as those that had your sight,	138	U2 Kisse	17
As might all the Graces lead,	138	U2 Kisse	26
And, if such a verse as this,	138	U2 Kisse	35
I'le taste as lightly as the Bee,	139	U2 Another	5
As, untill she tell her one,	140	U2 Promise	11
Be as good, as was the last:	140	U2 Promise	27
Forehead large, and white as snow;	141	U2 Her man	V 18
Smooth as is the Billiard Ball:	141	U2 Her man	20
Chin, as woolly as the Peach;	141	U2 Her man	21
He would have a hand as soft	141	U2 Her man	25
He should have a hand as soft	141	U2 Her man	V 25
As the Downe, and shew it oft;	141	U2 Her man	26
Skin as smooth as any rush,	141	U2 Her man	27
Quickly fir'd, as in beginners	141	U2 Her man	31
Valiant he should be as fire,	142	U2 Her man	41
Bounteous as the clouds to earth;	142	U2 Her man	43
And as honest as his Birth.	142	U2 Her man	44
As to doe no thing too much.	142	U2 Her man	46
As he durst love Truth and me.	142	U2 Her man	52
Nor spread them as distract with feares,	145	U4 Song	11
And as a cunning Painter takes	145	U5 Woman-kind	13
Such as in valour would excell,	146	U6 Defence	7
But as 'tis often vext and tri'd.	146	U6 Defence	18
The pleasure is as good as none,	147	U7 Nymph	6
Unlesse my heart would as my thought be torne.	147	U7 Nymph	14
As Summers sky, or purged Ayre,	147	U7 Nymph	17
And lookes as Lillies doe,	147	U7 Nymph	18
As make away my doubt,	147	U7 Nymph	23
As it would be to each a fame:	148	U7 Nymph	34
Yes; and in death, as life, unblest,	149	U8 Houre-glasse	9
I'm sure my language to her, was as sweet,	149	U9 Picture	6

AS (cont.)

	Page	Title	Line
I'm sure my language to her, is as sweet,	149	U9 Picture	V 6
In sentence, of as subtile feet,	149	U9 Picture	8
In numbers, of as subtile feet,	149	U9 Picture	V 8
As hath the youngest Hee,	149	U9 Picture	9
As makes the youngest Hee,	149	U9 Picture	V 9
Read so much wast, as she cannot imbrace	150	U9 Picture	16
On all mens Fruit, and flowers, as well as mine.	150	U10 Jealousie	8
As since he dares not come within my sight.	151	U11 Dreame	14
It vent it selfe, but as it would,	151	U12 Corbet	2
Would say as much, as both have done	151	U12 Corbet	3
His Mind as pure, and neatly kept,	151	U12 Corbet	15
As were his Nourceries; and swept	151	U12 Corbet	16
They were as specious as his Trees.	152	U12 Corbet	20
As twice to trespasse in his sight,	152	U12 Corbet	26
Great and good turns, as wel could time them too,	153	U13 Sacvile	2
As they are done, and such returnes they find:	153	U13 Sacvile	6
As I did feele it done, as soone as meant:	153	U13 Sacvile	12
This Good from you, as freely will it owe;	153	U13 Sacvile	14
In that proud manner, as a good so gain'd,	154	U13 Sacvile	37
As I have seene some Infants of the Sword,	154	U13 Sacvile	47
As farre as any poore Sword i' the Land.	154	U13 Sacvile	55
Dam's whom he damn'd to, as the veriest Gull,	154	U13 Sacvile	57
All as their prize, turne Pyrats here at Land,	155	U13 Sacvile	81
Such Notes are vertuous men! they live as fast	157	U13 Sacvile	143
As they are high; are rooted, and will last.	157	U13 Sacvile	144
As if they would belie their stature; those	157	U13 Sacvile	146
That I may love your Person (as I doe)	157	U13 Sacvile	157
(As their true rule or lesson) either men,	158	U13 Sacvile	162
Though I confesse (as every Muse hath err'd,	159	U14 Selden	19
And estimate thy Paines; as having wrought	161	U14 Selden	75
In outward face, but inward, light as Furre,	162	U15 Friend-Wars	20
Be honour is so mixt) by such as would,	162	U15 Friend-Wars	25
As farre as he can flie, or follow day,	163	U15 Friend-Wars	29
As farre as he can flee, or follow day,	163	U15 Friend-Wars	V 29
Honour and honestie, as poore things thought	163	U15 Friend-Wars	42
As they are made! Pride, and stiffe Clownage mixt	163	U15 Friend-Wars	43
O, these so ignorant Monsters! light, as proud,	164	U15 Friend-Wars	59
As if a Brize were gotten i' their tayle;	164	U15 Friend-Wars	71
Whom no great Mistresse hath as yet infam'd,	165	U15 Friend-Wars	97
This way, now that, as if their number were	166	U15 Friend-Wars	126
Runs sweetly, as it had his Lordships Soule;	167	U15 Friend-Wars	148
As a poore single flatterer, without Baud,	167	U15 Friend-Wars	158
For, if such men as he could die,	168	U16 Gray	6
That as the lesser breach: for he that takes	169	U17 Friend-Debt	11
Now so much friend, as you would trust in me,	169	U17 Friend-Debt	14
That as the water makes things, put in't streight,	170	U18 Elegy Can	7
So well as I may tell in verse, 'tis so?	170	U19 Elegy By	12
Others, in time may love, as we doe now.	171	U19 Elegy By	18
Slip no occasion; As time stands not still,	171	U19 Elegy By	19
As would make shift, to make himselfe alone,	171	U19 Elegy By	24
As in his place, because he would not varie,	171	U19 Elegy By	27
were such as I will now relate, or worse?	172	U20 Shrub	14
But she is such, as she might, yet, forestall	172	U20 Shrub	23
As not the World can praise too much,	173	U22 Elegy Tho	3
Throughout your forme; as though that move,	173	U22 Elegy Tho	6
As Love, t'aquit such excellence,	173	U22 Elegy Tho	23
Who as an off'ring at your shrine,	174	U22 Elegy Tho	29
Or droop they as disgrac't,	174	U23 Himselfe	11
As 'tis too just a cause;	174	U23 Himselfe	14
By which as proper titles, she is knowne	176	U24 Frontispice	16
High, as his mind, that doth advance	176	U25 Desmond	5
(As prov'd in you)	177	U25 Desmond	24
Of such as savour	177	U25 Desmond	34
As patience lasteth.	179	U25 Desmond	47
(As my hope tells) that our faire Phoebe's shine,	179	U25 Desmond	58
(As my hope tells) that our drad Cynthia's shine,	179	U25 Desmond	V 58
As farre from all revolt, as you are now from Fortune.	180	U25 Desmond	65
So speake (as yet it is not mute)	181	U27 Ode Helen	4
As he whom Maro did rehearse?	181	U27 Ode Helen	8
Rap't from the Earth, as not to die?	181	U27 Ode Helen	14
Her joyes, her smiles, her loves, as readers take	182	U28 Worth	13
Fastning Vowells, as with fetters	183	U29 Fit of Rime	11
Soone as lazie thou wert knowne,	183	U29 Fit of Rime	13
As before.	184	U29 Fit of Rime	42
As with the safetie, and honour of the Lawes,	186	U31 Elsmere	9
As though the Court pursues them on the sent,	186	U32 Elsmere	13
As if the generall store thou didst command	187	U33 Councellour	26
Arm'd at all peeces, as to keepe a Fort	187	U33 Councellour	30
Thy Adversaries fall, as not a word	187	U33 Councellour	33
But, as a friend, which name your selfe receave,	190	U37 Friend-Book	10
As flatt'ry with friends humours still to move.	190	U37 Friend-Book	27
Forgive it, as my frailtie, and not me.	190	U37 Friend-Book	30
As light breakes from you, that affrights despaire,	191	U38 Elegy 'Tis	10
As I would urge Authoritie for sinne.	191	U38 Elegy 'Tis	26
That as the last of punishments is meant;	192	U38 Elegy 'Tis	43
As not alone the Cure, but scarre be faire.	192	U38 Elegy 'Tis	52
Is natures meere obliquitie! as Heaven	192	U38 Elegy 'Tis	64
As all with storme and tempest ran together.	193	U38 Elegy 'Tis	76
As I the penitents here emulate:	193	U38 Elegy 'Tis	86
He when he sees a sorrow such as this,	193	U38 Elegy 'Tis	87
I number these as being of the Chore	193	U38 Elegy 'Tis	99
A man should flie from, as he would disdaine.	194	U38 Elegy 'Tis	104

AS (cont.)

	Page	Title		Line
And then I taste it. But as men drinke up	197	U40 Elegy That		3
As neither wine doe rack it out, or mirth.	197	U40 Elegy That		18
As if that ex'lent Dulnesse were Loves grace;	198	U40 Elegy That		24
To others, as he will deserve the Trust	198	U40 Elegy That		39
The Jewell of your name, as close as sleepe	198	U40 Elegy That		42
It is as if a night should shade noone-day,	199	U41 Elegy Since		5
As if it were not worthy to be there:	199	U41 Elegy Since		16
Let me be what I am, as Virgil cold;	199	U42 Elegy Let		1
As Horace fat; or as Anacreon old;	199	U42 Elegy Let		2
As light, and active as the youngest hee	200	U42 Elegy Let		6
Where I may handle Silke, as free, and neere,	200	U42 Elegy Let		30
As any Mercer; or the whale-bone man	200	U42 Elegy Let		31
But when thy Wife (as thou conceiv'st) is brave?	201	U42 Elegy Let		50
In smiling L'envoye, as he would deride	202	U42 Elegy Let		75
There were some pieces of as base allay,	204	U43 Vulcan		42
And as false stampe there; parcels of a Play,	204	U43 Vulcan		43
Adulterate moneys, such as might not goe:	204	U43 Vulcan		45
Adulterate maskings, such as might not goe:	204	U43 Vulcan	V	45
All soote, and embers! odious, as thy worke!	207	U43 Vulcan		106
As th'other may his braines with Quicksilver.	208	U43 Vulcan		122
To all as fatall as't hath beene to me,	211	U43 Vulcan		192
To all as chargefull as they have beene to me,	211	U43 Vulcan	V	192
Losse, remaines yet, as unrepair'd as mine.	211	U43 Vulcan		196
Losse, remaines yet, as much despair'd as mine.	211	U43 Vulcan	V	196
And Ord'nance too: so much as from the Tower	213	U44 Speach		3
These ten yeares day; As all may sweare that looke	213	U44 Speach		27
So, in that ground, as soone it grew to be	214	U44 Speach		37
So acted to the life, as Maurice might,	214	U44 Speach		41
As Stiles, Dike, Ditchfield, Millar, Crips, and Fen:	214	U44 Speach		54
And as within your Office, you doe take	216	U45 Squib		13
Such is thy All; that (as I sung before)	217	U46 Coke		21
They meet the fire, the Test, as Martyrs would;	218	U47 Tribe		3
As make it their proficiencie, how much	218	U47 Tribe		12
And dwell as in my Center, as I can,	219	U47 Tribe		60
Such as are square, wel-tagde, and permanent,	220	U47 Tribe		64
As are the Glorious Scenes, at the great sights;	220	U47 Tribe		66
As but to stumble in her sight were shame;	220	U47 Tribe		70
As you have writ your selfe. Now stand, and then,	220	U47 Tribe		77
As shall the feasts faire grounds be.	221	U48 Bacchus		42
And that as any breath creates	222	U49 Pucell		5
As aerie light, and as like wit as those?	222	U49 Pucell		10
And as lip-thirstie, in each words expence,	222	U49 Pucell		13
To Church, as others doe to Feasts and Playes,	222	U49 Pucell		16
As new rewards of her old secrecie?	223	U49 Pucell		20
What though she hath won on Trust, as many doe,	223	U49 Pucell		21
Is of so brave example, as he were	224	U50 Countesse		7
As makes Penelopes old fable true,	224	U50 Countesse		20
As they are hard, for them to make their owne,	225	U50 Countesse		33
Thou stand'st as if some Mysterie thou did'st!	225	U51 Bacon		4
'Tis true, as my wombe swells, so my backe stoupes,	227	U52 Answer		4
With one great blot, yo'had form'd me as I am.	227	U52 Answer		12
With one great blot, you had drawne me as I am.	227	U52 Answer	V	12
As I began to wish my selfe a horse.	228	U53 Newcastle		12
So well! as when I saw the floore, and Roome,	228	U53 Newcastle		17
So well! as when I view'd the floore, and Roome,	228	U53 Newcastle	V	17
And that's made up as doth the purse abound.	230	U56 Covell		12
Made up still as the pockett doth abound.	230	U56 Covell	V	12
As if that part lay for a [ ] most fit!	232	U58 Book-seller		12
As all defence, or offence, were a camel	232	U59 Newcastle		6
As they out-did the lightnihg in the course;	233	U59 Newcastle		12
Of humane life! as all the frosts, and sweates	233	U59 Newcastle		22
He, that in such a flood, as we are in	234	U61 Epigram		16
As thou dost cure our Evill, at thy charge.	235	U62 Charles 1		8
And as it turnes our joyfull yeare about,	236	U64 Charles 3		5
(Without prophanenesse) as, a Poet, cry,	238	U66 Queene	V	4
As in this Prince? Let it be lawfull, so	238	U66 Queene		11
To compare small with great, as still we owe	238	U66 Queene		12
As fearfull to awake	239	U67 Muses		10
The Citie, as to shake	239	U67 Muses	V	11
As here no Venus were;	240	U67 Muses		34
As the old Bard, should no Canary lack.	241	U68 House-hold		11
But as the wretched Painter, who so ill	241	U69 Friend Son		9
For as at distance, few have facultie	242	U69 Friend Son		19
Though now of flattery, as of picture, are	242	U69 Friend Son		21
As, could they but lifes miseries fore-see,	243	U70 Ode		19
So deep, as he did then death's waters sup;	244	U70 Ode		41
As though his age imperfect might appeare,	244	U70 Ode		51
Such truths, as we expect for happy men,	246	U70 Ode		83
And shine as you exalted are;	246	U70 Ode		97
But as a Cary, or a Morison.	247	U70 Ode		116
As they that saw	247	U70 Ode		118
Health, or scarce breath, as she had never bin,	248	U71 Treasurer		12
As lowd as Thunder, and as swift as fire.	249	U72 King		4
Such pleasure as the teeming Earth,	250	U74 Weston		1
As all the wealth of Season, there was spread;	251	U74 Weston		15
As they came all to see, and to be seene!	253	U75 Epithalam.		20
As they had learn'd new changes, for the day,	253	U75 Epithalam.		35
As she did lack	254	U75 Epithalam.		46
As they did lack	254	U75 Epithalam.	V	46
O, now thou smil'st, faire Sun, and shin'st, as thou wouldst stay!	254	U75 Epithalam.		64
As if her ayrie steps did spring the flowers,	254	U75 Epithalam.		67
Weston, their Treasure, as their Treasurer,	255	U75 Epithalam.		97

AS (cont.)

		Page	Title		Line
Yet, as we may, we will, with chast desires,		257	U75 Epithalam.		161
As farre as sense, and onely by the eyes.		261	U77 Treasurer		12
As farre as sense, and onely by his eyes.		261	U77 Treasurer	V	12
Which, though I cannot as an Architect		261	U77 Treasurer		25
Which, though I cannot like as an Architect		261	U77 Treasurer	V	25
Aloud; and (happ'ly) it may last as long.		261	U77 Treasurer		28
As loude; and (happ'ly) it may last as long.		261	U77 Treasurer	V	28
As other soules, to his, dwell in a Lane:		262	U78 Digby		12
Who walkes on Earth as May still went along,		264	U79 New-yeares		26
As if the beauties of the yeare,		264	U79 New-yeares		38
Your teeming Ewes, aswell as mounting Rammes.		265	U79 New-yeares		51
Great aides to Empire, as they are great care		268	U80 Christning		6
As hath thy James; cleans'd from originall drosse,		268	U80 Christning		9
Grow up, sweet Babe, as blessed, in thy Name,		268	U80 Christning		11
As in renewing thy good Grandsires fame;		268	U80 Christning		12
Hee's good, as great. I am almost a stone!		269	U81 Pawlet		11
Had I a thousand Mouthes, as many Tongues,		269	U81 Pawlet		23
Just as she in it liv'd! and so exempt		270	U81 Pawlet		48
Her suffrings, as the body had beene away!		270	U81 Pawlet		51
On Natures secrets, there, as her owne bookes:		271	U81 Pawlet		70
On naturall secret, there, as her owne bookes:		271	U81 Pawlet	V	70
And trusted so, as it deposited lay		271	U81 Pawlet		81
But as he soares at that, he bruiseth then		272	U81 Pawlet		98
That all Posteritie, as wee,		273	U84 Cradle		13
As prop'rest gifts, to Girles, and Boyes,		273	U84 Cradle		19
With Sayles of silke, as the first notes		273	U84 Cradle		23
As coming with his Harpe, prepar'd		274	U84 Cradle		35
Is sung: as als' her getting up		274	U84 Cradle		37
For such as Shee.		274	U84 Cradle		40
Gave two such Houses as Northumberland,		274	U84 Descent		5
Of vertues in her, as, in short, shee grew		274	U84 Descent		11
But at such distance, as the eye		276	U84 Body		19
As you goe on, by what brave way		278	U84 Mind		18
As 'tis not radiant, but divine:		278	U84 Mind		26
As it another Nature were,		279	U84 Mind		30
As circular, as infinite.		279	U84 Mind		32
As what it spoke, it planted there.		279	U84 Mind		36
As some soft chime had stroak'd the ayre;		279	U84 Mind		38
As it slid moulded off from Heaven.		280	U84 Mind		56
But stooping gently, as a Cloud,		280	U84 Mind		58
As smooth as Oyle pour'd forth, and calme		280	U84 Mind		59
As showers; and sweet as drops of Balme.		280	U84 Mind		60
In action, winged as the wind,		280	U84 Mind		65
As spirits had stolne her Spirit, in a kisse,		283	U84 Muse		42
For, as there are three Natures, Schoolemen call		284	U84 Muse		51
This as it guilty is, or guiltlesse found,		284	U84 Muse		56
And white, as that, put on: and in her hand,		285	U84 Muse		95
And to the Touch, a Flower, like soft as Palme.		286	U84 Muse		126
Each line, as it were graphick, in the face!		287	U84 Muse		154
As nature could not more increase the flood		287	U84 Muse		158
She had a mind as calme, as she was faire;		287	U84 Muse		163
But, kept an even gate, as some streight tree		287	U84 Muse		165
As her whole life was now become one note		287	U84 Muse		178
Poring, as on a Map, to find the wayes		288	U84 Muse		196
(As being Redeemer, and Repairer too		288	U84 Muse		213
As being the Sonne of Man) to shew his Power,		288	U84 Muse		217
As the old race of Mankind were,		289	U85 Country		2
As the old stock of Mankind were,		289	U85 Country	V	2
The Fountaines murmure as the streames doe creepe,		290	U85 Country		27
Such as the Sabines, or a Sun-burnt-blowse,		291	U85 Country		41
I am not such, as in the Reigne		292	U86 Hor.4:1		3
As, for her, I'ld not feare to die,		293	U87 Hor.3:9		11
As neither head, nor foot, one forme retaine.		305	Horace		10
Yet, not as therefore wild, and tame should cleave		305	Horace		14
Yet not as therefore cruell things should cleave		338	Horace	V	14
Wants strength, and sinewes, as his spirits were done;		339	Horace	V 38/	37
Stamp'd to the time. As woods whose change appeares		309	Horace		85
As fit t'exchange discourse; a Verse to win		311	Horace		119
Mens faces, still, with such as laugh, are prone		311	Horace		143
Mens count'nances, with such as laugh, are prone		342	Horace		V143
Unto the last, as when he first went forth,		313	Horace		181
Not care, as thou wouldst faithfully translate,		313	Horace		190
Nor so begin, as did that Circler late,		313	Horace		195
Wonders forth after: As Antiphates,		315	Horace		205
(As if he knew it) rapps his hearer to		315	Horace		212
Falshood with truth, as no man can espie		315	Horace		216
Falsehood and truth, as no man can espy		343	Horace		V216
And give their yeares, and natures, as they swerve,		315	Horace		224
To every vice, as hardly to be brought		315	Horace		232
And then as swift to leave what he hath lov'd.		315	Horace		236
As his departing take much thence: lest, then,		317	Horace		251
The Hau'-boy, not as now with latten bound,		319	Horace		287
As loud enough to fill the seates, not yet		319	Horace		291
But, as they conquer'd, and enlarg'd their bound,		319	Horace		295
As neither any God, were brought in there,		321	Horace		331
As neither any God, be brought in there,		346	Horace	V323/331
But, as a Matrone drawne at solemne times		321	Horace		338
Plaine phrase, my Piso's, as alone, t'approve		321	Horace		342
As not make difference, whether Davus speake,		321	Horace		345
And so, as every man may hope the same;		321	Horace		350
Fell into fault so farre, as now they saw		321	Horace		367
So rare, as with some taxe it doth ingage		323	Horace		383

	Page	Title	Line
AS (cont.)			
As doctrine, and delight together go.	329	Horace	516
Will passe the Seas, and long as nature is,	329	Horace	518
How then? Why, as a Scrivener, if h'offend	329	Horace	529
As Painting, so is Poesie. Some mans hand	329	Horace	539
As some the farther off: This loves the darke;	331	Horace	541
As jarring Musique doth, at jolly feasts,	331	Horace	557
As Poppie, and Sardane honey; 'cause without	331	Horace	559
To say, I'm ignorant. Just as a Crier	333	Horace	597
Once say I'me ignorant. Just as a Cryer,	353	Horace	V597
As those that hir'd to weepe at Funeralls, swoune,	333	Horace	614
And shun to touch him, as a man that were	335	Horace	644
And flye to touch him, as a man that were	354	Horace	V644
And, as a Beare, if he the strength but had	337	Horace	674
thus, as a ponderous thinge in water cast	361	Palmer	17
wear spent with wonder as they weare delated,	361	Palmer	24
And thou in them shalt live as longe as Fame.	362	Palmer	31
Not wearing moodes, as gallants doe a fashion,	362	Author	3
If they seeme wry, to such as looke asquint,	362	Author	7
For, as one comming with a laterall viewe,	362	Author	9
His proofe their praise, will meete, as in this line.	362	Author	14
Were they as strong ram'd up as Aetna gates.	363	Riches	10
And makes her supple feete, as swift as winde.	363	Riches	12
As farre as Sinne's from lightnesse.	364	Ode Splendor	4
Her wit as quicke, and sprightfull	365	Ode Splendor	5
As fire; and more delightfull	365	Ode Splendor	6
Cleare as a naked vestall	365	Ode Splendor	11
This change'd his Downe; till this, as white	366	Ode Who saith	25
As the whole heard in sight,	366	Ode Who saith	26
The Vale, that bred thee pure, as her Hills Snow.	367	Ode Who saith	40
But should they know (as I) that this,	369	Ode Who saith	97
So bold, as shewes your Art you can command.	370	Author	8
As fit to have encreas'd the harmony	371	Epitaph	8
Of Spheares, as light of starres; She was earthes Eye:	372	Epitaph	9
Up so much truth, as could I it pursue	372	Epitaph	13
Here, up the Alpes (not so plaine as to Dunstable)	374	Coryat 1	16
As well as from his braines, and claimest thereby	378	Coryat 2	90
To be his Bacchus as his Pallas: bee	378	Coryat 2	91
No: as I first said, who would write a story at	381	Coryat 3	59
And as an ever-lasting Sacrifice	382	Rich	7
As true oblations; his Brothers Embleme sayes,	383	Rich	10
Except your Gratious Eye as through a Glass	383	Rich	11
Yet may as blind men sometimes hit the marke.	383	Author	6
And pray, thy joyes as lasting bee, as great.	384	Somerset	8
So, be your Concord, still, as deepe, as mute;	384	Somerset	17
To such a worke, as could not need theirs? Yet	385	Brooke	5
I know for such, as (if my word will waigh)	386	Husband	11
Upon th'Exchange of Letters, as I wou'd	386	Browne	14
Let such as justly have out-liv'd all prayse,	387	Cavendish	5
As, now, of all men, it is call'd thy Trade:	389	Chapman	11
As in this Spanish Proteus; who, though writ	389	Aleman	5
As a deformed face doth a true glasse.	389	Aleman	10
As was the Genius wherewith they were wrote;	389	Aleman	12
As well in brasse, as he hath hit	390	Reader	6
As neither Man, nor Muse, can praise too much.	390	Shakespeare	4
These are, as some infamous Baud, or Whore,	391	Shakespeare	13
As, since, she will vouchsafe no other Wit.	392	Shakespeare	50
As they were not of Natures family.	392	Shakespeare	54
(Such as thine are) and strike the second heat	392	Shakespeare	60
For a good Poet's made, as well as borne.	392	Shakespeare	64
As brandish't at the eyes of Ignorance.	392	Shakespeare	70
Such things, of every body, and as well.	394	Jane Ogle	10
Then entertaine, and as Deaths Harbinger;	394	Jane Ogle	21
As neither Pompey's popularitie,	395	May	9
As not the smallest joint, or gentlest word	395	May	21
Thy Muse, and mine, as they expect. 'Tis true:	396	Drayton	5
It cast a beame as when the chear-full Sun	396	Drayton	17
And fill'd an Orbe as circular, as heaven!	396	Drayton	19
As it had beene the circle of the Arts!	396	Drayton	22
Did all so strike me, as I cry'd, who can	397	Drayton	31
As, on two flowry Carpets, that did rise,	398	Drayton	81
And Gossip-got acquaintance, as, to us	398	Drayton	85
Such, as the creeping common Pioners use	400	Beaumont	5
But higher power, as spight could not make lesse,	401	Beaumont	18
you'l be as Langley sayd, an Inigo still.	403	Inigo Jones 1	22
Attyre the Persons as noe thought can teach	404	Inigo Jones 1	54
To pitty him, as smiling at his Feat	405	Inigo Jones 1	71
Sir Inigo doth feare it as I heare	407	Inigo Jones 3	1
For thou objectest (as thou hast been told)	408	Detractor	3
If such a Tyke as thou, er'e wer't, or noe?	409	Detractor	14
Nameless, and noysome, as thy infamy!	409	Detractor	16
No man will tarry by thee, as hee goes,	409	Detractor	17
As Love, here studied to keep Grace alive.	412	Ghyrlond	8
As it, alone, (and onely it) had roome,	412	Ghyrlond	11
But lowlie laid, as on the earth asleep,	413	Ghyrlond	18
As if they' ador'd the Head, wheron th'are fixt.	413	Ghyrlond	28
Thou Throne of glory, beauteous as the Moone,	414	Ghyrlond	49
As it were spun by nature, off the fleece:	415	Rutter	18
Fresh as the Day, and new as are the Howers,	416	Welcome	1
We offer as a Circle the most fit	416	Welcome	6
And you, with them, as Father of our spring.	416	Welcome	8
or as some would say to breake	416	Moon	3
And as either newes or mirth	417	Moon	17

	Page	Title	Line

AS (cont.)
as the standerd shall engage hir, ... 417 Moon 27
Though shee chainge as oft as shee, ... 417 Moon 29
and of Circle be as free, ... 417 Moon 30
As when they both were greate, and both knewe howe . . 419 Ode:If Men 3
As shall besides delyght . . . . 420 Ode:If Men 33
Aboute this Isle, and Charme the rounde, as when . . 421 Ode:If Men 39
As Cleare, and distant, as yourselfe from Cryme; . . 421 Censure 8
And though your virtue (as becomes it) still . . 421 Censure 9
Forgive it as my Frayltie, and not mee. . . . 422 Censure 23
whom thou seest happy; wretches flee as foes: . . 422 Lucan 6
whom thou seest happy; wretches shun, as foes: . . 422 Lucan V 6
As the token of my Love . . . . . 666 Glover 3

ASCEND
Shee saw him too, in glory to ascend . . . . 288 U84 Muse 205

ASCENT
Th'ascent of Lady Fame which none could spy . . . 403 Inigo Jones 1 35

ASCRIBE
To thine owne proper I ascribe then more; . . . 61 E95 Savile 9

ASHAM'D
I'am more asham'd to have thee thought my foe. . . 53 E77 Not name 4
T'alledge, that greatest men were not asham'd, . . 82 E130 Ferrab. 1 9
Nor is my Muse, or I asham'd to owe it . . . 182 U28 Worth 5
And let your mercie make me asham'd t'offend. . . 194 U38 Elegy 'Tis 106
Upon the Lyre, thou chance to be asham'd. . . . 353 Horace V580/502
And lesse asham'd; not when I told the crowd . . 414 Rutter 5

ASHAMED
And would (being ask'd the truth) ashamed say, . . 83 E131 Ferrab. 2 11

ASHES
Even ashes of lovers find no rest. . . . . 149 U8 Houre-glasse 11
Sent forth, or since did from their ashes come. . . 391 Shakespeare 40
Again, thy Architect to ashes turne! . . . 406 Inigo Jones 1 102

ASHORE
Fertile of wood, Ashore, and Sydney's copp's, . . 94 F2 Penshurst 26

ASIDE
Lay that aside, the Epicks office is. . . . 307 Horace 64

ASINIGO
you would be an Asinigo, by your ears? . . . 403 Inigo Jones 1 20

ASKE
And, ere I could aske you, I was prevented: . . 54 E84 Bedford 2 3
Nay, aske you, how the day goes, in your eare. . . 59 E92 New Crie 18
Crowne with their owne. Rare poemes aske rare friends. . 60 E94 Bedford 3 6
Dare for these poemes, yet, both aske, and read, . . 60 E94 Bedford 3 12
There's none so dull, that for your stile would aske, . 68 E105 L Wroth 2 15
Doth aske a drinke divine: . . . . . 106 F9 Celia 3 6
His absence in my verse, is all I aske. . . . 107 F10 Proludium 21
His absence in our verse, is all I aske. . . . 107 F10 Proludium V 21
Can he that loves, aske lesse then one? . . . 139 U2 Another 8
To aske it: though in most of workes it be . . . 158 U14 Selden 7
Upon my selfe, and aske to whom? and why? . . . 159 U14 Selden 24
I'le therefore aske no more, but bid you love; . . 171 U19 Elegy By 15
Doe not you aske to know her, she is worse . . . 172 U20 Shrub 17
Aske not to know this Man. If fame should speake . . 172 U21 Ltl Shrub 1
Why was't? did e're the Cloudes aske back their raine? . 192 U38 Elegy 'Tis 56
Should aske the blood, and spirits he hath infus'd . . 192 U38 Elegy 'Tis 65
None of their pleasures! nor will aske thee, why . . 202 U42 Elegy Let 86
We aske your absence here, we all love peace, . . 212 U43 Vulcan 209
T'obtaine of God, what all the Land should aske? . . 234 U61 Epigram 11
But dare not aske our wish in Language fescennine: . . 257 U75 Epithalam. 160
And e're I can aske more of her, shee's gone! . . 269 U81 Pawlet 12
Would aske a Heavens Intelligence; . . . . 278 U84 Mind 14
May aske, what Author would conceale his name? . . 383 Author 4
What is the cause you pompe it soe? I aske, . . . 403 Inigo Jones 1 29
You aske noe more then certeyne politique Eyes, . . 404 Inigo Jones 1 45
To aske thy name, if he have half his Nose! . . . 409 Detractor 18

ASK'D
It made me a great face, I ask'd the name. . . . 30 E11 Something 4
Rest in soft peace, and, ask'd, say here doth lye . . 41 E45 First Son 9
I ask'd a lord a buck, and he denyed me; . . . 54 E84 Bedford 2 2
Both which are ask'd, to have thee understood. . . 66 E102 Pembroke 4
And would (being ask'd the truth) ashamed say, . . 83 E131 Ferrab. 2 11

ASKED
An Epistle answering to one that asked . . . . 218 U47 Tribe Ttl
Are asked to climbe. First give me faith, who know . 220 U47 Tribe 75

ASKES
An elegie? no, muse; yt askes a straine . . . 108 F10 Proludium 1
That askes but to be censur'd by the eyes: . . . 117 F13 Aubigny 35
Your conscience, and not wonder, if none askes . . 118 F13 Aubigny 69
Askes first, Who gives her (I Charles) then he plights . 256 U75 Epithalam. 124

ASKETH
gentlie hee asketh, shee will pay: no suits, . . 258 U75 Epithalam. V188

ASKT
Were askt of thy Discoveries; They must say, . . 388 Chapman 8

ASLEEP
But lowlie laid, as on the earth asleep, . . . 413 Ghyrlond 18

ASLEEPE
When his proud patrons favours are asleepe; . . . 113 F12 Rutland 14

ASPIRE
Don Surly, to aspire the glorious name . . . 35 E28 Surly 1
Nor fashion; if they chance aspire to height, . . 157 U13 Sacvile 148
With Japhets lyne, aspire . . . . . 175 U23 Himselfe 27
Thou woo Minerva! or to wit aspire! . . . 208 U43 Vulcan 109
Not to designe the whole. Should I aspire . . . 307 Horace 49

ASPIRE (cont.)
Any fourth man, to speake at all, aspire. . . . . . 317 Horace 275
ASQUINT
If they seeme wry, to such as looke asquint, . . . 362 Author 7
ASS
He makes the Camell & dull Ass his prize. . . . 408 Inigo Jones 3 8
ASSAIES
Who nought assaies unaptly, or amisse? . . . 315 Horace 200
ASSAY'D
And twice, or thrice assay'd it, but in vain; . . . 354 Horace V626
ASSAYES
In all the prov'd assayes, ... 255 U75 Epithalam. 101
ASSE
How they may make some one that day an Asse . . 164 U15 Friend-Wars 64
But the grave Lover ever was an Asse; . . . . 198 U40 Elegy That 32
ASSEMBLY
Of th'assembly, as did you! . . . . . . 138 U2 Kisse 12
ASSES
And, till they burst, their backs, like asses load: . 62 E96 Donne 2 11
Safe from the wolves black jaw, and the dull Asses hoofe. . 175 U23 Himselfe 36
ASSIDUOUS
When your assiduous practise doth secure . . . 236 U64 Charles 3 11
ASSIGN'D
For every part a character assign'd. . . . . 67 E103 L Wroth 1 12
Beene trusted to thee: not to't selfe assign'd. . . 283 U84 Muse 20
This saying: To some things there is assign'd . . 331 Horace 548
ASSIGNES
That I must send one first, my Choyce assignes, . . 170 U18 Elegy Can 23
ASSIST
And Fortune once, t'assist the spirits that dare. . . 170 U18 Elegy Can 10
ASSISTED
Assisted by no strengths, but are her owne, . . . 176 U24 Frontispice 14
ASSURANCE
To give the world assurance thou wert both; . . 43 E53 Old-end 6
Which in assurance to your brest I tell, . . . 198 U40 Elegy That 49
ASSURE
Of her disease, how did her soule assure . . . 270 U81 Pawlet 50
ASSUR'D
So that my Reader is assur'd, I now . . . 159 U14 Selden 27
And the reward, and punishment assur'd, . . . 176 U24 Frontispice V 8
ASSURED
but being well assured that there . . . . 106 F9 Celia 3 V 11
ASSYRIA (See also 'SYRIAN)
Of Colchis borne; or in Assyria bred; . . . 313 Horace 167
AS'T
As't were a challenge, or a borrowers letter? . . 51 E73 Fine Grand 3
To all as fatall as't hath beene to me, . . . 211 U43 Vulcan 192
ASTERISME
In this bright Asterisme: . . . . . 246 U70 Ode 89
ASTREA
Or put to flight Astrea, when her ingots . . . 114 F12 Rutland 24
ASUNDER
Their guarded gates asunder? . . . . . 239 U67 Muses 12
ASWELL
Which we in love must doe aswell, ... 146 U6 Defence 9
Your teeming Ewes, aswell as mounting Rammes. . 265 U79 New-yeares 51
AT'
To pay at's day of marriage. By my hand . . 42 E46 Luckless 1 4
AT
At court I met it, in clothes brave enough, . . 30 E11 Something 1
At dice his borrow'd money: which, god payes. . . 30 E12 Shift 12
At sixe moneths end, shee parted hence . . . 33 E22 Daughter 5
Both which are great. And laugh at ill-made clothes; . 35 E28 Surly 10
He doth, at meales, alone, his pheasant eate, . . 35 E28 Surly 12
Which is maine greatnesse. And, at his still boord, . 35 E28 Surly 13
Of solemne greatnesse. And he dares, at dice, . . 36 E28 Surly 16
All braines, at times of triumph, should runne wit. . 36 E29 Tilter 4
He toyles to be at hell, as soone as they. . . 36 E31 Banck 4
What could not worke; at home in his repaire . . 37 E32 Roe 2 7
Who sayes that Giles and Jone at discord be? . . 40 E42 Giles 1
Harsh sights at home, Giles wisheth he were blind. . 40 E42 Giles 10
And that, as puritanes at baptisme doo, . . . 44 E53 Old-end 7
That quit'st the cause so oft, and rayl'st at men? . 44 E54 Chev'ril 2 4
At once thou mak'st me happie, and unmak'st; . . 44 E55 Beaumont 5
At first he made low shifts, would picke and gleane, . 45 E56 Poet-Ape 5
So have I seene at Christ-masse sports one lost, . . 45 E58 Groome 7
What should the cause be? Oh, you live at court: . 46 E62 Would-bee 9
Two kindes of valour he doth shew, at ones; . . 49 E68 Playwrt 2 3
At Madames table, where thou mak'st all wit . . 50 E72 Court-ling 3
I lent you, on meere acquaintance, at a feast. . . 51 E73 Fine Grand 6
Item, a gulling imprese for you, at tilt. . . 51 E73 Fine Grand 15
Though Lippe, at Pauls, ranne from his text away, . 52 E75 Lippe 3
At which, shee happily displeas'd, made you: . . 53 E79 Rutland 9
And Phoebus-selfe should be at eating it. . . 55 E84 Bedford 2 8
At last, ease, appetite, and example wan . . . 57 E90 Mill 4
At sixe and twentie, ripe. You shall 'hem meet, . . 58 E92 New Crie 4
They meet in sixes, and at every mart, . . . 59 E92 New Crie 21
Or, every day, some one at Rimee's looks, . . . 59 E92 New Crie 23
At naming the French King, their heads they shake, . 59 E92 New Crie 33
And at the Pope, and Spaine slight faces make. . . 59 E92 New Crie 34
Thou need'st not shrinke at voyce of after-times; . 61 E95 Savile 20
Whose knowledge clayeth at the helme to stand; . . 61 E95 Savile 21
That thou at once, then, nobly maist defend . . 63 E98 Th Roe 1 7

AT (cont.)

	Page	Title	Line
But, at our parting, we will be, as when	65	E101 Supper	38
That shall be utter'd at our mirthfull boord,	65	E101 Supper	40
And are so good, and bad, just at a price,	66	E102 Pembroke	11
What at Ligorne, Rome, Florence you did doe:	69	E107 Hungry	14
Then can a flea at twise skip i'the Map.	69	E107 Hungry	18
At this so subtile sport: and play'st so ill?	72	E112 Gamster	2
Thy all, at all: and what so ere I doe,	72	E112 Gamster	5
Art still at that, and think'st to blow me'up too?	72	E112 Gamster	6
For Cupid, who (at first) tooke vaine delight,	73	E114 Sydney	3
About the towne; and knowne too, at that price.	74	E115 Honest Man	6
At every meale, where it doth dine, or sup,	74	E115 Honest Man	23
And those that lack'd it, to suspect at length,	75	E116 Jephson	6
Vertuously practise must at least allow	75	E116 Jephson	14
At hunting railes, having no guift in othes,	76	E119 Shelton	2
If, at all, shee had a fault,	79	E124 Elizabeth	7
Then that it liv'd at all. Farewell.	79	E124 Elizabeth	12
Men love thee not for this: They laugh at thee.	81	E129 Mime	18
For, if the hum'rous world will talke at large,	83	E131 Ferrab. 2	7
They should be fooles, for me, at their owne charge.	83	E131 Ferrab. 2	8
Who gave, to take at his returne from Hell,	84	E133 Voyage	27
At Bread-streets Mermaid, having din'd, and merry,	85	E133 Voyage	37
Alwayes at hand, to aide the merry Muses.	85	E133 Voyage	54
Belch'd forth an ayre, as hot, as at the muster	85	E133 Voyage	63
Over your heads: Well, row. At this a loud	86	E133 Voyage	93
Thrise did it spit: thrise div'd. At last, it view'd	88	E133 Voyage	162
They laugh't, at his laugh-worthy fate. And past	89	E133 Voyage	185
The tripple head without a sop. At last,	89	E133 Voyage	186
And these grudg'd at, art reverenc'd the while.	93	F2 Penshurst	6
At his great birth, where all the Muses met.	94	F2 Penshurst	14
Officiously, at first, themselves betray:	94	F2 Penshurst	36
At great mens tables) and yet dine away.	95	F2 Penshurst	66
That at great times, art no ambitious guest	96	F3 Wroth	5
But canst, at home, in thy securer rest,	97	F3 Wroth	13
In autumne, at the Partrich makes a flight,	97	F3 Wroth	27
Or hauking at the river, or the bush,	97	F3 Wroth	33
Or shooting at the greedie thrush,	97	F3 Wroth	34
Or shooting at the hungrie thrush,	97	F3 Wroth	V 34
Let this man sweat, and wrangle at the barre,	99	F3 Wroth	73
Here in my bosome, and at home.	102	F4 To the World	68
He, at length, our good will sever.	102	F5 Celia 1	4
He, at length, our blisse will sever.	102	F5 Celia 1	V 4
At morne, and even, shades are longest;	104	F7 Women but	7
At noone, they are or short, or none:	104	F7 Women but	8
So men at weakest, they are strongest,	104	F7 Women but	9
And, for thee, at common game,	105	F8 Sicknesse	41
And, for that, at common game,	105	F8 Sicknesse	V 41
That, at thy birth, mad'st the poore Smith affraid,	107	F10 Proludium	14
Not to know vice at all, and keepe true state,	109	F11 Epode	1
At th'eye and eare (the ports unto the minde)	109	F11 Epode	9
Would, at suggestion of a steepe desire,	111	F11 Epode	63
Who, being at sea, suppose,	111	F11 Epode	70
That, being at sea, suppose,	111	F11 Epode	V 70
And, at her strong armes end, hold up, and even,	114	F12 Rutland	42
And, at her strong armes end, there hold up even,	114	F12 Rutland	V 42
And howsoever; as I am at fewd	116	F13 Aubigny	9
No lady, but, at some time, loves her glasse.	117	F13 Aubigny	26
When their owne Parasites laugh at their fall,	118	F13 Aubigny	82
Other great wives may blush at: when they see	119	F13 Aubigny	111
To ought but grace, or ayme at other end.	122	F15 Heaven	8
Keepe the middle age at stay,	131	U2 Excuse	21
At my face, that tooke my sight,	132	U2 How he saw	25
At her hand, with oath, to make	133	U2 Suffered	10
See the Chariot at hand here of Love,	134	U2 Triumph	1
That at every motion sweld	138	U2 Kisse	24
French to boote, at least in fashion,	141	U2 Her man	7
10. Another Ladyes exception present at the hearing.	142	U2 Exception	Ttl
At such a Call, what beast or fowle,	143	U3 Musicall	5
To fall againe; at such a feast,	144	U3 Musicall	23
Wee shall, at last, of parcells make	145	U5 Woman-kind	11
That others should not warme them at my fire,	150	U10 Jealousie	6
Not at my prayers, but your sense; which laid	153	U13 Sacvile	9
Then turning unto him is next at hand,	154	U13 Sacvile	56
All the Towne-curs take each their snatch at me.	155	U13 Sacvile	72
Feed those, at whom the Table points at still?	155	U13 Sacvile	74
All as their prize, turne Pyrats here at Land,	155	U13 Sacvile	81
Of Valour, but at this Idolatrous rate?	156	U13 Sacvile	104
'Tis by degrees that men arrive at glad	157	U13 Sacvile	131
Ever at home: yet, have all Countries seene:	159	U14 Selden	30
I wonder'd at the richnesse, but am lost,	160	U14 Selden	53
To gaine upon his belly; and at last	162	U15 Friend-Wars	17
Till envie wound, or maime it at a blow!	162	U15 Friend-Wars	22
Honour'd at once, and envi'd (if it can	162	U15 Friend-Wars	24
Be at their Visits, see 'hem squemish, sick,	164	U15 Friend-Wars	68
Ready to cast, at one, whose band sits ill,	164	U15 Friend-Wars	69
From Hide-Parke to the Stage, where at the last	165	U15 Friend-Wars	109
Goe make our selves the Usurers at a cast.	166	U15 Friend-Wars	134
That watch, and catch, at what they may applaud,	167	U15 Friend-Wars	157
Nor should I at this time protested be,	169	U17 Friend-Debt	7
By those bright Eyes, at whose immortall fires	170	U19 Elegy By	1
Where men at once may plant, and gather blisses:	170	U19 Elegy By	10
At fifty yeares, almost, to value it,	171	U20 Shrub	5
Who as an off'ring at your shrine,	174	U22 Elegy Tho	29

42

	Page	Title	Line
AT (cont.)			
Sweat at the forge, their hammers beating;	179	U25 Desmond	41
At the Well no Muse did stay,	183	U29 Fit of Rime	20
Of all the Land. Who now at such a Rate,	185	U30 Burleigh	19
Or the great Hall at Westminster, the field	186	U33 Councellour	3
Of Bookes, of Presidents, hast thou at hand!	187	U33 Councellour	25
Arm'd at all peeces, as to keepe a Fort	187	U33 Councellour	30
God lightens not at mans each fraile offence,	193	U38 Elegy 'Tis	68
They looke at best like Creame-bowles, and you soone	198	U40 Elegy That	29
Out with the other, for hee's still at home;	198	U40 Elegy That	34
At every stall; The Cittie Cap's a charme.	200	U42 Elegy Let	28
In at a hole, and see these Actions creepe	201	U42 Elegy Let	60
When thou wert borne, and that thou look'st at best,	208	U43 Vulcan	113
When thou wert borne, and when thou look'st at best,	208	U43 Vulcan	V113
At Common-Law: me thinkes in his despight	211	U43 Vulcan	177
At Common-Law: me thinkes in this despight	211	U43 Vulcan	V177
'Bove all your Fire-workes, had at Ephesus,	211	U43 Vulcan	194
Beyond your Fire-workes, had at Ephesus,	211	U43 Vulcan	V194
'Bove all our Fire-workes, had at Ephesus,	211	U43 Vulcan	V194
Would you had kept your Forge at Aetna still,	212	U43 Vulcan	197
Maintain'd the trade at Bilbo, or else-where;	212	U43 Vulcan	199
Strooke in at Millan with the Cutlers there;	212	U43 Vulcan	200
Strooke in at Millan with the villors there;	212	U43 Vulcan	V200
To see the Pride at Court, their Wives doe make:	213	U44 Speach	16
And Spinola have blushed at the sight.	214	U44 Speach	42
That turnes us so much moneys, at which rate	215	U44 Speach	77
All that they doe at Playes. O, but first here	215	U44 Speach	91
Shall carry me at Call; and I'le be well,	219	U47 Tribe	45
As are the Glorious Scenes, at the great sights;	220	U47 Tribe	66
But yet the Tun at Heidelberg had houpes.	227	U52 Answer	6
At these Immortall Mangers Virgil fed.	228	U53 Newcastle	20
A mornings, and at afternoones, to foole	230	U56 Covell	22
Will come at the Court,	231	U57 Burges	20
No aime at glorie, or, in warre,	234	U60 La-ware	13
And all the games of Fortune, plaid at Court;	234	U61 Epigram	2
At which there are, would sell the Prince, and State:	234	U61 Epigram	4
As thou dost cure our Evill, at thy charge.	235	U62 Charles 1	8
What (at his liking) he will take away.	236	U63 Charles 2	6
And murmure cannot quarrell at your wayes?	237	U64 Charles 3	14
At a Friends freedome, proves all circling meanes	242	U69 Friend Son	15
For as at distance, few have facultie	242	U69 Friend Son	19
How well at twentie had he falne, or stood!	243	U70 Ode	31
To fall a logge at last, dry, bald, and seare:	245	U70 Ode	68
Of rimes, or ryots, at your feasts,	246	U70 Ode	103
Let Ireland meet it out at Sea, halfe way,	249	U72 King	5
At Bonefires, Rockets, Fire-workes, with the Shoutes	249	U72 King	13
At Bonefires, squibs, and mirth, with all their Shoutes	249	U72 King	V 13
Had they but grace, of thinking, at these routes,	249	U72 King	15
If they had leisure, at these lawfull routs,	249	U72 King	V 15
When look'd the yeare, at best,	253	U75 Epithalam.	13
What Beavie of beauties, and bright youths at charge	253	U75 Epithalam.	17
Doe boast their Loves, and Brav'ries so at large,	253	U75 Epithalam.	19
And celebrate (perfection at the worth)	253	U75 Epithalam.	28
Although that thou, O Sun, at our intreaty stay!	254	U75 Epithalam.	56
See, at another doore,	254	U75 Epithalam.	69
And wonder'd at the bounties of this day:	255	U75 Epithalam.	90
Of Nuptiall Sweets, at such a season, owe,	257	U75 Epithalam.	148
These I looke up at, with a reverent eye,	261	U77 Treasurer	23
These looke you up at, with a measuring eye,	261	U77 Treasurer	V 23
For that to dwell in, and be still at home.	262	U78 Digby	8
For those to dwell in, and be still at home.	262	U78 Digby	V 8
Witnesse his Action done at Scanderone;	262	U78 Digby	13
And his great Action done at Scanderoone;	262	U78 Digby	V 13
Busie, or frowne at first; when he sees thee,	262	U78 Digby	20
When hee shall read them at the Treasurers bord,	263	U78 Digby	27
When hee doth read them at the Treasurers bord,	263	U78 Digby	V 27
At land she triumphs in the triple shade,	268	U80 Christning	15
At least may beare th'inscription to her Tombe.	269	U81 Pawlet	18
I durst not aime at that: The dotes were such	269	U81 Pawlet	25
I durst not aime at, the dotes thereof were such	269	U81 Pawlet	V 25
If you dare grudge at Heaven, and repent	271	U81 Pawlet	79
At pleasure, to be call'd for, every day!	271	U81 Pawlet	82
But as he soares at that, he bruiseth then	272	U81 Pawlet	98
At either Stemme, and know the veines of good	274	U84 Descent	8
But at such distance, as the eye	276	U84 Body	19
But at such distance, all the eye	276	U84 Body	V 19
Thou hast no more blowes, Fate, to drive at one:	283	U84 Muse	27
Have all his actions wondred at, and view'd	284	U84 Muse	77
Or at the Feast of Bounds, the Lambe then slaine,	291	U85 Country	59
At th'Calends, puts all out againe.	291	U85 Country	70
To bend a man, now at his fiftieth yeare	292	U86 Hor.4:1	6
Never at Law; seldome in office gown'd;	295	U90 Mart.10:47	5
Was meant at first. Why, forcing still about	307	Horace	29
If Custome please; at whose disposing will	309	Horace	103
Sharpe, and contemning lawes, at him should aime,	313	Horace	173
In at the eare, doe stirre the mind more slow	317	Horace	257
Yet, to the Stage, at all thou maist not tender	317	Horace	260
Any fourth man, to speake at all, aspire.	317	Horace	275
But soft, and simple, at few holes breath'd time	319	Horace	289
And they uncensur'd might at Feasts, and Playes	319	Horace	297
Or, whilst he shuns the Earth, to catch at Aire	321	Horace	335
But, as a Matrone drawne at solemne times	321	Horace	338
Yet he that offers at it, may sweat much,	321	Horace	351

AT (cont.)

	Page	Title	Line
Be I their Judge, they doe at no time dare	321	Horace	356
Will take offence, at this: Nor, though it strike	321	Horace	361
Take just offence at this: nor, though it strike	347	Horace	V353/361
My Verse at randome, and licentiously?	323	Horace	391
My title, at their rate, I'ad rather, I,	325	Horace	432
First frighted men, that wildly liv'd, at ods,	327	Horace	480
And thus, at first, an honour, and a name	327	Horace	491
Is laugh'd at, that still jarreth on one string:	329	Horace	532
Or Pleader at the Barre, that may come short	331	Horace	551
As jarring Musique doth, at jolly feasts,	331	Horace	557
Or, who's unskilfull at the Coit, or Ball,	331	Horace	567
Or great in money's out at use, command	333	Horace	600
Or wealthy in money's out at use, command	353	Horace	V600
Out at his friendly eyes, leape, beat the groun'.	333	Horace	613
As those that hir'd to weepe at Funeralls, swoune,	333	Horace	614
Alone, without a rivall, at your will.	354	Horace	V632
And conquers all things, yea it selfe, at length.	367	Ode Who saith	56
Who ever sipt at Baphyre river,	367	Ode Who saith	57
Till thou at Tames alight,	368	Ode Who saith	79
At their returne, nor Po,	369	Ode Who saith	114
To lie at Livory, while the Horses did stand.	375	Coryat 1	33
Of travell he discourseth so at large,	378	Coryat 2	82
Marry he sets it out at his owne charge;	378	Coryat 2	83
Who ever he be, would write a Story at	379	Coryat 3	1
He went out at each place, and at what he came in,	380	Coryat 3	25
How long he did stay, at what signe he did Inne.	380	Coryat 3	26
And lay in straw with the horses at Bergamo,	380	Coryat 3	38
Nay more in his wardrobe, if you will laugh at a	380	Coryat 3	47
And being at Flushing enforced to feele	380	Coryat 3	54
No: as I first said, who would write a story at	381	Coryat 3	59
A Speach Presented unto King James at a tylting . . .	382	Rich	Ttl
To understand, hee may at length admire.	383	Author	10
At these thy Nuptials; but, whose heart, and thought	384	Somerset	3
Still, still, thou dost thou arrive with, at our shore,	388	Chapman	5
Which, when it sounds at best, but eccho's right;	390	Shakespeare	8
As brandish't at the eyes of Ignorance.	392	Shakespeare	70
At least so great a Lady. She was wife	394	Jane Ogle	15
So wood at last, that he was wonne to her	394	Jane Ogle	22
At every line some pinn thereof should slacke	395	May	5
At least, if not the generall Engine cracke.	395	May	6
A Friend at all; or, if at all, to thee:	396	Drayton	2
The Fights, the Cryes, and wondring at the Jarres	397	Drayton	41
Yet give mee leave, to wonder at the birth	398	Drayton	83
By all your Titles, & whole style at ones	402	Inigo Jones 1	15
To pitty him, as smiling at his Feat	405	Inigo Jones 1	71
Aymd at in thy omnipotent Designe!	406	Inigo Jones 1	96
Thy Canvas Gyant, at some Channell aymes,	407	Inigo Jones 2	15
By barking against mee. Thou look'st at least,	408	Detractor	10
At libelling? Shall no Star-Chamber Peers,	410	Gill	3
I'll laugh at thee poor wretched Tike, go send	410	Gill	10
. . . and Dauncing At Cotswold.	415	Dover	Ttl
at my back, I am no spright,	416	Moon	6
at Pem Wakers good ale Tapp,	417	Moon	39
Over the Door at the Entrance into the Apollo.	657	Door Apollo	Ttl
And at once three Senses pleases.	657	Door Apollo	18
Till I, at much expense of Time, and Taper	666	Glover	7

ATCHIEVEMENTS

	Page	Title	Line
And (which doth all Atchievements get above)	187	U33 Councellour	38

ATHENIAN

	Page	Title	Line
Pearch'd over head, the wise Athenian Owle:	397	Drayton	34

ATOMES

	Page	Title	Line
By Atomes mov'd;	148	U8 Houre-glasse	3
Find all our Atomes from a point t' a span!	287	U84 Muse	152

ATOMI

	Page	Title	Line
Then all those Atomi ridiculous,	87	E133 Voyage	127

ATREUS

	Page	Title	Line
ill-/Natur'd, and wicked Atreus cooke, to th'eye,	317	Horace	265

AT'S

	Page	Title	Line
To pay at's day of marriage. By my hand	42	E46 Luckless 1	4

ATT

	Page	Title	Line
hath armde att all poyntes; charge mee humblye kneele	382	Rich	2
That hath not Countrye impudence enough to laughe att Arte,	420	Ode:If Men	14

ATTAINE

	Page	Title	Line
Till I attaine the long'd-for mysterie	128	U1 Trinitie	31

ATTEMPT

	Page	Title	Line
By her attempt, shall still be owing thee.	80	E127 Aubigny	10
Whom never yet he durst attempt awake;	151	U11 Dreame	6

ATTEMPTED

	Page	Title	Line
I ne're attempted, Vulcan, 'gainst thy life;	202	U43 Vulcan	5
I ne're attempted ought against thy life;	202	U43 Vulcan	V 5
Attempted by the Muses tunes, and strings;	329	Horace	498

ATTEND

	Page	Title	Line
Attend thee hence; and there, may all thy ends,	81	E128 Wm Roe 2	6
See then thou dost attend him,	221	U48 Bacchus	17

ATTENDING

	Page	Title	Line
Attending such a studie, such a choice.	55	E86 Goodyere 2	6

ATTIRE (See also TIRE, TYRE)

	Page	Title	Line
Of severall makings? helps, helps, t'attire	215	U44 Speach	94

ATTIR'D

	Page	Title	Line
And see a minde attir'd in perfect straines;	362	Author	2

ATTRIBUTES

	Page	Title	Line
And number Attributes unto a flood:	394	Jane Ogle	6

44

ATTYRE
Attyre the Persons as noe thought can teach . . . . 404 Inigo Jones 1 54
ATTYRES
Let who will follow fashions, and attyres, ... 118 F13 Aubigny 71
'AUBIGNY
To Esme, Lord 'Aubigny. . . . . 80 E127 Aubigny Ttl
T'expect the honors of great 'Aubigny: . . . . 119 F13 Aubigny 105
AUBIGNY
To whom I am so bound, lov'd Aubigny? . . . . 80 E127 Aubigny 3
Epistle. To Katherine, Lady Aubigny. . . . . 116 F13 Aubigny Ttl
AUDITOR
The sluggish gaping auditor devoures; . . . . 45 E56 Poet-Ape 10
AUDLEYS
Beauchamps, and Nevills, Cliffords, Audleys old; . . 214 U44 Speach 52
AUGHT (See OUGHT)
AUGURE
Or (by our Turtles Augure) . . . . . . 364 Phoenix 5
AULUS
Or knowes not what Cassellius Aulus can; . . . . 331 Horace 553
AUSPICE
Under the Auspice of young Swynnerton. . . . . 213 U44 Speach 20
AUSPICIOUS
(so well dispos'd by thy auspicious hand) . . . . 361 Palmer 2
AUSPITIOUSLY
If I auspitiously divine, ... 179 U25 Desmond 57
AUSTERE
Rigid, and harsh, which is a Drug austere . . . . 190 U37 Friend-Book 17
AUTHOR
The Author both of Life, and light; . . . . 130 U1 Nativitie 2
Hee is the author of our peace. . . . . . 265 U79 New-yeares 57
Hee is the author of our peace. . . . . . 265 U79 New-yeares 69
With honour make the farre-knowne Author live. . . 329 Horace 519
May, with some right, upon an Author creepe. . . . 329 Horace 538
To the Author. . . . . 370 Author Ttl
To the worthy Author M. John Fletcher. . . . . 370 Fletcher Ttl
Of Tom of Odcombe that odde Joviall Author, . . . 378 Coryat 2 87
To his much and worthily esteemed friend the Author. . 383 Author Ttl
May aske, what Author would conceale his name? . . 383 Author 4
To his friend the Author upon his Richard. . . . 385 Brooke Ttl
To the worthy Author on the Husband. . . . . 385 Husband Ttl
On the Author, Worke, and Translator. . . . . 389 Aleman Ttl
To the memory of my beloved, the Author . . . . 390 Shakespeare Ttl
. . . the Author of this Work, M. Rich. Brome. . . 409 Brome Ttl
Author ad Librum. . . . . 662 Bedford Ttl
AUTHOREM
In Authorem. . . . . 362 Author Ttl
AUTHORITIE
What weight, and what authoritie in thy speech! . . 31 E14 Camden 9
That sound, and that authoritie with her name, . . 49 E67 Suffolk 3
As thou hast best authoritie, t'allow. . . . . 62 E96 Donne 2 6
As I would urge Authoritie for sinne. . . . . 191 U38 Elegy 'Tis 26
And skill in thee, now, grew Authoritie; . . . 217 U46 Coke 10
AUTHORITIES
Impostures branded! And Authorities urg'd! . . . 160 U14 Selden 41
AUTHORIZ'D
A wild, and an authoriz'd wickednesse! . . . . 397 Drayton 46
AUTHORS
Thou wert content the authors name to loose: . . . 43 E53 Old-end 3
If workes (not th'authors) their owne grace should looke, . 60 E94 Bedford 3 3
Both love the cause, and authors of the feast? . . 120 F14 Sydney 10
And almost deifie the Authors! make . . . . 156 U13 Sacvile 99
Records, and Authors of! how rectified . . . . 160 U14 Selden 43
So with this Authors Readers will it thrive: . . . 362 Author 12
And, where the most reade bookes, on Authors fames, . 386 Browne 9
Who tracks this Authors, or Translators Pen, . . 389 Aleman 1
Nor flatt'ry! but secur'd, by the Authors Name, . . 401 Beaumont 19
AUTUMNE
In autumne, at the Partrich makes a flight, . . . 97 F3 Wroth 27
Or when that Autumne, through the fields, lifts round . 290 U85 Country 17
AVAILES
But much it now availes, what's done, of whom: . . 64 E99 Th Roe 2 7
AVERNUS
A Docke there is, that called is Avernus, . . . 85 E133 Voyage 41
AVERT
And doe their penance, to avert Gods rod, . . . 235 U61 Epigram 19
AVOID
Retire themselves, avoid the publike baths; . . . 325 Horace 424
AVOIDED
Their un-avoided subject, fewest see: . . . . 60 E94 Bedford 3 8
AVON
Sweet Swan of Avon! what a sight it were . . . 392 Shakespeare 71
AVOW
As free simplicitie, to dis-avow, ... 62 E96 Donne 2 5
AVOYD
If I could not thy ginnes avoyd. . . . . 101 F4 To the World 36
AVOYDING
The art of urging, and avoyding harmes, . . . 232 U59 Newcastle 2
AWAKE
Whom never yet he durst attempt awake; . . . 151 U11 Dreame 6
Wake, friend, and finde thy self; awake, the Drum . . 162 U15 Friend-Wars V 1
As fearfull to awake . . . . . . 239 U67 Muses 10
In earth, till the last Trumpe awake the Sheepe . . 283 U84 Muse 46
It was no Dreame! I was awake, and saw! . . . 396 Drayton 11

```
AWAY
  Of bearing them in field, he threw 'hem away:        .    .    .    .    42   E48 Mungril        2
  Stinke, and are throwne away.  End faire enough.      .    .    .    45   E59 Spies          3
  Away, and leave me, thou thing most abhord,     .    .    .    .    48   E65 Muse           1
  That vertuous is, when the reward's away.       .    .    .    .    49   E66 Cary          18
  Though Lippe, at Pauls, ranne from his text away,    .    .    .    52   E75 Lippe          3
  The Belgick fever ravished away.            .    .    .    .    60   E93 Radcliffe      8
  Tell them, what parts yo'have tane, whence run away,      .    .    69   E107 Hungry        9
  Vanish'd away: as you must all presume     .    .    .    .    87   E133 Voyage      110
  Tempt not his furie, Pluto is away:        .    .    .    .    89   E133 Voyage      179
  Which when he felt, Away (quoth hee)       .    .    .    .    93   F1 Why write no    3
  At great mens tables) and yet dine away.        .    .    .    95   F2 Penshurst      66
  Like such as blow away their lives,        .    .    .    .   100   F4 To the World   22
  When all the causes were away.     .    .    .    .    .   101   F4 To the World   44
  Play away, health, wealth, and fame.       .    .    .    .   105   F8 Sicknesse      42
  Melt downe their husbands land, to poure away       .    .    .   118   F13 Aubigny       73
  Or his courage; for away      .    .    .    .    .    .   132   U2 How he saw      15
  That doth but touch his flower, and flies away.      .    .    .   139   U2 Another         6
  Take that away, you take our lives,        .    .    .    .   146   U6 Defence         5
  As make away my doubt,           .    .    .    .    .   147   U7 Nymph          23
  A Benefit; or that doth throw't away:       .    .    .    .   154   U13 Sacvile       42
  The withered Garlands tane away;           .    .    .    .   173   U22 Elegy Tho     18
  Pegasus did flie away,      .    .    .    .    .    .   183   U29 Fit of Rime    19
  Out of your eyes, and be awhile away;      .    .    .    .   194   U38 Elegy 'Tis   115
  Or that the Sun was here, but forc't away;      .    .    .   199   U41 Elegy Since    6
  This other for his eye-browes; hence, away,     .    .    .   215   U44 Speach         97
  Shall I advise thee, Pucell? steale away        .    .    .   223   U49 Pucell        35
  And cri'd, Away with the Caesarian bread,       .    .    .   228   U53 Newcastle     19
  Away ill company, and helpe in rime    .    .    .    .   231   U56 Covell         23
  What (at his liking) he will take away.        .    .    .   236   U63 Charles 2      6
  Now, Sun, and post away the rest of day:        .    .    .   257   U75 Epithalam.   138
  Her suffrings, as the body had beene away!      .    .    .   270   U81 Pawlet        51
  Till swept away, th'were cancell'd with a broome!    .    .    282   U84 Muse           8
  Then why should we dispaire? Dispaire, away:    .    .    .   363   Riches            17
AWDE
  Are we by Booke-wormes to be awde? must we      .    .    .   215   U44 Speach        67
AWE
  "Where neither Force can bend, nor Feare can awe.    .    .    367   Ode Who saith    48
AWFULL
  A reverend State she had, an awfull Eye,        .    .    .   270   U81 Pawlet        43
  And by the awfull manage of her Eye        .    .    .    .   287   U84 Muse         167
A-WHILE
  A-while with us bright Sun, and helpe our light;     .    .   252   U75 Epithalam.     2
  A-while with us bright Sun, and mend our light;      .    .   252   U75 Epithalam.  V  2
  Th'Ignoble never liv'd, they were a-while       .    .    .   257   U75 Epithalam.   153
AWHILE
  Out of your eyes, and be awhile away;      .    .    .    .   194   U38 Elegy 'Tis   115
AWL    (See NALL)
AXE
  Who, with his axe, thy fathers mid-wife plaid.       .    .   107   F10 Proludium    15
AYDES
  Like aydes 'gainst treasons who hath found before?       .    .    38   E35 James 2        7
  Wherin (besides the noble aydes were lent,      .    .    .   207   U43 Vulcan     V 99
  Wherin (besides the noble Aydes were spent,     .    .    .   207   U43 Vulcan     V 99
  Wherin (besides the noble aydes were sent,      .    .    .   207   U43 Vulcan     V 99
  With all her aydes, to save her from the seize      .    .    283   U84 Muse         17
  Thy list of aydes, and force, for so it is:     .    .    .   398   Drayton          62
AYE
  To see 'hem aye discoursing with their Glasse,      .    .    164   U15 Friend-Wars   63
AYMD
  Aymd at in thy omnipotent Designe!     .    .    .    .   406   Inigo Jones 1     96
AYME
  To ought but grace, or ayme at other end.       .    .    .   122   F15 Heaven         8
  I, that thy Ayme was; but her fate prevail'd:        .    .   188   U34 Small Poxe    17
  When their pot-guns ayme to hit,           .    .    .    .   259   U76 Petition      21
  Now must we plie our ayme; our Swan's on wing.       .    .   368   Ode Who saith    64
AYMED
  Aymed with that selfe-same shaft.     .    .    .    .   133   U2 Suffered       12
AYMES
  Thy Canvas Gyant, at some Channell aymes,       .    .    .   407   Inigo Jones 2     15
  are distant, so is proffitt from just aymes.        .    .   422   Lucan             8
AYRE    (TUNE)
  Whose ayre will sooner Hell, then their dull senses peirce,   .   420   Ode:If Men        23
AYRE    (MANNER)
  And utter stranger to all ayre of France)       .    .    .    83   E132 Sylvester     4
  Of some grand peere, whose ayre doth make rejoyce    .    .   113   F12 Rutland       12
  So, Anacreon drawne the Ayre       .    .    .    .    .   136   U2 Cupid          14
  No face, no hand, proportion, line, or Ayre     .    .    .   200   U42 Elegy Let     14
AYRE
  The cold of Mosco, and fat Irish ayre,     .    .    .    .    37   E32 Roe 2          5
  Dar'st breath in any ayre; and with safe skill,     .    .    76   E119 Shelton       9
  Belch'd forth an ayre, as hot, as at the muster     .    .    85   E133 Voyage       63
  Thou joy'st in better markes, of soyle, of ayre,    .    .    93   F2 Penshurst       7
  Fresh as the ayre, and new as are the houres.       .    .    94   F2 Penshurst      40
  And tasting ayre, and freedome, wull     .    .    .    .   101   F4 To the World   31
  All taste of bitternesse, and makes the ayre        .    .   112   F11 Epode         97
  From your lips, and suck'd an ayre     .    .    .    .   137   U2 Kisse            3
  As Summers sky, or purged Ayre,    .    .    .    .    .   147   U7 Nymph          17
  Lest Ayre, or Print, but flies it: Such men would       .    .   154   U13 Sacvile       45
  You may so place me, and in such an ayre,       .    .    .   192   U38 Elegy 'Tis    51
  The Sunne his heat, and light, the ayre his dew?    .    .   192   U38 Elegy 'Tis    57
  Your Power of handling shadow, ayre, and spright,   .    .   227   U52 Answer        17
  Of bodies, meet like rarified ayre!    .    .    .    .   233   U59 Newcastle      10
```

```
                                                          Page    Title        Line

AYRE  (cont.)
   Of honour, nor no ayre of good?      .    .    .    .    .   234   U60 La-ware       7
   And cleave both ayre and ground,          .    .    .    .   239   U67 Muses        14
   And shake both ayre and ground,      .    .    .    .    .   239   U67 Muses      V 14
   These make the lines of life, and that's her ayre.    .    .   245   U70 Ode         64
   The rudest Winds obey the calmest Ayre:    .    .    .    .   251   U74 Weston        9
   That ever Nature, or the later Ayre     .    .    .    .   274   U84 Descent        4
   Needs nought to cloath it but the ayre.    .    .    .    .   275   U84 Body          8
   As some soft chime had stroak'd the ayre;    .    .    .   279   U84 Mind         38
   Horse, foote, and all but flying in the ayre:    .    .   380   Coryat 3         28
   For though Spaine gave him his first ayre and Vogue,    .   389   Aleman          15
   Like him, to make the ayre, one volary:    .    .    .   397   Drayton         36
AYRES
   Heard the soft ayres, between our Swaynes & thee,    .    .   397   Drayton         26
AYRIE
   Yet should the Lover still be ayrie and light,    .    .   197   U40 Elegy That    19
   As if her ayrie steps did spring the flowers,    .    .   254   U75 Epithalam.    67
B'
   But there are lines, wherewith I might b'embrac'd.    .    .   226   U52 Answer        3
   B'imputed right to an inheritance      .    .    .    .   286   U84 Muse        144
   Or Muse, upon the Lyre, thou chance b'asham'd.    .    .   329   Horace         502
BAAL
   Th'admir'd discourses of the Prophet Baal:    .    .    .   206   U43 Vulcan     V 82
BABE
   To see this Babe, all innocence;      .    .    .    .   130   U1 Nativitie     22
   And art thou borne, brave Babe? Blest be thy birth,    .   237   U65 Prince        1
   And art thou borne, brave Babe? Blest be the day,    .   237   U65 Prince      V 1
   Grow up, sweet Babe, as blessed, in thy Name,    .    .   268   U80 Christning   11
BABES
   Both for the Mothers, and the Babes of grace,    .    .   223   U49 Pucell       44
BABION
   Out-dance the Babion, or out-boast the Brave;    .    .    81   E129 Mime        12
BABYLONIAN
   Item, the babylonian song you sing;    .    .    .    .    51   E73 Fine Grand    9
BACCHUS
   Where Pan, and Bacchus their high feasts have made,    .    93   F2 Penshurst     11
   The Dedication of the Kings new Cellar. to Bacchus.    .   220   U48 Bacchus     Ttl
   Since, Bacchus, thou art father     .    .    .    .   220   U48 Bacchus       1
   For, Bacchus, thou art freer          .    .    .    .   221   U48 Bacchus      13
   Or old Silenus, Bacchus guard, and Nurse.    .    .    .   321   Horace         348
   To be his Bacchus as his Pallas: bee    .    .    .    .   378   Coryat 2         91
BACK
   Not looking by, or back (like those, that waite    .    .   118   F13 Aubigny      62
   Could be brought once back to looke.    .    .    .    .   132   U2 How he saw    19
   His Lace and Starch; And fall upon her back    .    .   163   U15 Friend-Wars   49
   Those thousands on his back, shall after blow    .    .   165   U15 Friend-Wars  104
   Thou hast the brave scorne, to put back the fee!    .    .   187   U33 Councellour  22
   Why was't? did e're the Cloudes aske back their raine?    .   192   U38 Elegy 'Tis   56
   And force back that, which will not be restor'd,    .    .   219   U47 Tribe        40
   Did wiser Nature draw thee back,      .    .    .    .   243   U70 Ode         11
   Did wisest Nature draw thee back,      .    .    .    .   243   U70 Ode        V 11
   Her tresses trim her back,     .    .    .    .    .   254   U75 Epithalam.    45
   Goe where Youths soft intreaties call thee back.    .    .   292   U86 Hor.4:1       8
   From fearefull back-slides; And the debt we'are in,    .   412   Sutcliffe        15
   at my back, I am no spright,     .    .    .    .    .   416   Moon             6
BACKE
   If I would strive to bring backe times, and trie    .    .    78   E122 Rudyerd 2    3
   Came backe untouch'd. This man hath travail'd well.    .    81   E128 Wm Roe 2    14
   Great Club-fist, though thy backe, and bones be sore,    .    85   E133 Voyage      55
   Backe, cry'd their brace of Charons: they cry'd, no,    .    86   E133 Voyage      87
   No going backe; on still you rogues, and row.    .    .    86   E133 Voyage      88
   Cannot the Plague-bill keepe you backe? nor bells    .    .    88   E133 Voyage     173
   And so went bravely backe, without protraction.    .    .    89   E133 Voyage     192
   And sent'st it backe to mee:     .    .    .    .    .   106   F9 Celia 3       14
   Backe the intelligence, and falsely sweares,    .    .   109   F11 Epode        25
   Of going backe     .    .    .    .    .    .    .   121   F14 Sydney       28
   'Tis true, as my wombe swells, so my backe stoupes,    .   227   U52 Answer        4
   When first, my Lord, I saw you backe your horse,    .   228   U53 Newcastle     1
   Now, bring him backe, he'le be no more a man,    .    .   355   Horace        V668
   A Horse here is sadled, but no Tom him to backe,    .   374   Coryat 1         14
   The Reverse on the backe side.     .    .    .    .   413   Ghyrlond        Ttl
BACKES
   To utmost Thule: whence, he backes the Seas    .    .   368   Ode Who saith    69
BACKS
   And, till they burst, their backs, like asses load:    .    62   E96 Donne 2      11
BACK-SLIDES
   From fearefull back-slides; And the debt we'are in,    .   412   Sutcliffe        15
BACKWARD
   Or him that backward went to Berwicke, or which    .    .    85   E133 Voyage      35
BACON
   Since Bacon, and thy Lord was borne, and here;    .    .   225   U51 Bacon         8
BACONS
   Lord Bacons Birth-day.     .    .    .    .    .    .   225   U51 Bacon        Ttl
BAD  (VERB)
   Guiltie, because I bad you late be wise,    .    .    .    38   E38 Guiltie 2     1
   My Muse bad, Bedford write, and that was shee.    .    .    52   E76 Bedford 1    18
   And bad me lay th'usurped laurell downe:    .    .    .    80   E126 Mrs Cary     4
   And bad her fare-well sough, unto the lurden:    .    .    87   E133 Voyage     115
BAD
   Call'st a booke good, or bad, as it doth sell,    .    .    27   E3 Bookseller     2
   Delay is bad, doubt worse, depending worst;    .    .    50   E70 Wm Roe 1      5
   Against the bad, but of, and to the good:    .    .    .    66   E102 Pembroke     3
   And are so good, and bad, just at a price,    .    .    .    66   E102 Pembroke    11
```

	Page	Title	Line

BAD (cont.)
The bad, by number, are so fortified, ... 116 F13 Aubigny 3
The good, from bad, is not describe, ... 146 U6 Defence 17
Who seldome sleepes! whom bad men only hate! . . . 250 U73 Weston 6
The art of uttring wares, if they were bad; . . . 385 Husband 6

BAG
Or have tasted the bag o'the Bee? . . . . 135 U2 Triumph 29

BAGS
Sweet bags, sweet Powders, nor sweet words will passe . . 165 U15 Friend-Wars 112

BAIES
Not a worke deserving Baies, ... 183 U29 Fit of Rime 28

BAITS (See also BAYTES)
And what thou call'st thy gifts are baits. . . . 100 F4 To the World 12

BAKE
Or fumie clysters, thy moist lungs to bake: . . . 42 E50 Cod 3 2

BALD
Bald, or blinde, or nere so many: . . . . 105 F8 Sicknesse 40
To fall a logge at last, dry, bald, and seare: . . . 245 U70 Ode 68

BALES
Now use the bales, we see doth hire a man . . . 166 U15 Friend-Wars V136

BALL
Smooth as is the Billiard Ball: . . . . 141 U2 Her man 20
Th'admir'd discourses of the Prophet Ball: . . . 206 U43 Vulcan 82
Th'admir'd discourses of the Profit Ball: . . . 206 U43 Vulcan V 82
Or, who's unskilfull at the Coit, or Ball, . . . 331 Horace 567

BALLADRIE
Of worded Balladrie, ... 175 U23 Himselfe 21

BALLADS
A Tune to drown the Ballads of thy Father: . . . 411 Gill 12

BALLANCE
Quarrell with Nature, or in ballance brought . . . 188 U34 Small Poxe 6
Within the ballance; and not want a mite; . . . 229 U54 Squib 10

BALME
Thy Hearers Nectar, and thy Clients Balme, . . . 187 U33 Councellour 36
As showers; and sweet as drops of Balme. . . . 280 U84 Mind 60
Unto the Sent, a Spicerie, or Balme; . . . 286 U84 Muse 125

BALMES
I send nor Balmes, nor Cor'sives to your wound, . . 180 U26 Ode High 2

BANCK
Of Tyre-man, Mounte-banck & Justice Jones, . . . 402 Inigo Jones 1 16

BANCK (NAME)
On Banck the Usurer. . . . . . 36 E31 Banck Ttl
Banck feeles no lamenesse of his knottie gout, . . . 36 E31 Banck 1

BANCK
Makes the poore Banck-side creature wet it' shoone, . . 84 E133 Voyage 30
Bred on the Banck, in time of Poperie, . . . 209 U43 Vulcan 143

BANCKE
Bred by your breath, on this low bancke of ours; . . 416 Welcome 3

BANCKS
On Chuffe, Bancks the Usurer's Kinsman. . . . 41 E44 Chuff Ttl

BANCK-SIDE
Makes the poore Banck-side creature wet it' shoone, . . 84 E133 Voyage 30

BANCKSIDE
Well fare the wise-men yet, on the Banckside, . . . 208 U43 Vulcan 123

BAND
'Tis Lucklesse he, that tooke up one on band . . . 42 E46 Luckless 1 3
And pronounce, which band, or lace, . . . 140 U2 Promise 19
His Clothes rich, and band sit neat, . . . 142 U2 Exception 4
Ready to cast, at one, whose band sits ill, . . . 164 U15 Friend-Wars 69
And their words too; where I but breake my Band. . . 169 U17 Friend-Debt 9
Simply my Band, his trust in me forsakes, . . . 169 U17 Friend-Debt 12
His Lordship. That is for his Band, his haire . . . 215 U44 Speach 95

BANDS
Of fortune! when, or death appear'd, or bands! . . . 233 U59 Newcastle 23
O happy bands! and thou more happy place, . . . 256 U75 Epithalam. 129
And is not in the Usurers bands: . . . . 289 U85 Country 4

BANISH'D
And Art banish'd. . . . . . . 183 U29 Fit of Rime 15
When they are poore, and banish'd, must throw by . . 311 Horace 138

BANKE (DEPOSITORY)
In so much land a yeare, or such a Banke, . . . 215 U44 Speach 76
Is Banke-rupt turn'd! the Cassock, Cloake, and Gowne, . . 237 U64 Charles 3 20
Is Banke-rupt turn'd! Cloak, Cassock, Robe, & Gowne, . . 237 U64 Charles 3 V 20

BANKE
Each banke doth yeeld thee coneyes; and the topps . . 94 F2 Penshurst 25
Have you plac'd the banke of kisses, . . . 136 U2 Cupid 25
A banke against it. Nothing but the round . . . 160 U14 Selden 63
And lastly by your lips, the banke of kisses, . . . 170 U19 Elegy By 9
Against the Globe, the Glory of the Banke. . . . 208 U43 Vulcan 132
Rare Plants from ev'ry banke doe rise, . . . 251 U74 Weston 10
Upon a banke, or field of flowers, . . . 280 U84 Mind 67

BANKE-RUPT
Is Banke-rupt turn'd! the Cassock, Cloake, and Gowne, . . 237 U64 Charles 3 20
Is Banke-rupt turn'd! Cloak, Cassock, Robe, & Gowne, . . 237 U64 Charles 3 V 20

BANKES (NAME)
Old Bankes the juggler, our Pythagoras, . . . 88 E133 Voyage 156
They cry'd out Pusse. He told them he was Bankes, . . 89 E133 Voyage 183

BANKES
The ever-boyling floud. Whose bankes upon . . . 88 E133 Voyage 142
Whilst from the higher Bankes doe slide the floods; . . 290 U85 Country 25
And make those flights upon the bankes of Thames, . . 392 Shakespeare 73

BANQUET
And the whole Banquet is full sight of God! . . . 284 U84 Muse 65

								Page	Title	Line

BAPHYRE
   Who ever sipt at Baphyre river, ... 367 Ode Who saith 57
BAPTISME
   And that, as puritanes at baptisme doo, ... 44 E53 Old-end 7
   This day, by Baptisme, and his Saviours crosse: . . . 268 U80 Christning 10
BAR   (See BARRE)
BARBAROUS
   Upbraiding rebells armes, and barbarous pride; . . . . 60 E93 Radcliffe 6
BARBER
   And from the Barber Licinus conceale . . . . . 325 Horace 427
BARBICAN
   He had so highly set; and, in what Barbican. . . . 256 U75 Epithalam. 112
   He had so highly plac'd; and, in what Barbican. . . . 256 U75 Epithalam. V112
BARD
   As the old Bard, should no Canary lack. . . . . 241 U68 House-hold 11
   This, utter'd by an antient Bard, ... 274 U84 Cradle 33
BARE   (VERB)
   And, armed to the chase, so bare her bow . . . 68 E105 L Wroth 2 13
BARE
   And then of times (besides the bare Conduct . . . 160 U14 Selden 51
   To view the weary Oxen draw, with bare . . . 291 U85 Country 63
   But a bare Type and Figure. . . . . . 364 Phoenix 8
BARKE
   There, in the writhed barke, are cut the names . . . 94 F2 Penshurst 15
   Thou lighter then the barke of any tree, . . . 294 U87 Hor.3:9 22
BARKING
   By barking against mee. Thou look'st at least, . . . 408 Detractor 10
   Keep in thy barking Wit, thou bawling Fool? . . . 410 Gill 8
BARNABEE
   When the Apostle Barnabee the bright . . . . 262 U78 Digby 15
BARONET
   . . . Sir John Beaumont, Baronet. . . . . 400 Beaumont Ttl
BARONS
   I saw, and read, it was thy Barons Warres! . . . 397 Drayton 42
BARRE
   And threatens the starre-chamber, and the barre: . . 44 E54 Chev'ril 2 2
   Let this man sweat, and wrangle at the barre, . . 99 F3 Wroth 73
   That I, hereafter, doe not thinke the Barre, . . 186 U33 Councellour 1
   But flees the Barre and Courts, with the proud bords, . 289 U85 Country 7
   Or Pleader at the Barre, that may come short . . . 331 Horace 551
BARR'D
   All other gladnesse, with the thought is barr'd; . . 284 U84 Muse 67
BARRELL
   Have issue from the Barrell; . . . . . 221 U48 Bacchus 32
BARREN
   The world reputes you barren: but I know . . . 46 E62 Would-bee 3
   All is not barren land, doth fallow lie. . . . 169 U17 Friend-Debt 16
   How is she barren growne of love! or broke! . . 237 U64 Charles 3 15
   How is she barren growne in love! or broke! . . 237 U64 Charles 3 V 15
   A Soyle, not barren; a continewall fire; . . . 295 U90 Mart.10:47 4
   A kingly worke; or that long barren fen . . . 309 Horace 93
BARTAS
   Behold! the reverend shade of Bartas stands . . . 83 E132 Sylvester 7
   Bartas doth wish thy English now were his. . . . 83 E132 Sylvester 10
BASE
   Spies, you are lights in state, but of base stuffe, . . 45 E59 Spies 1
   Th'are base, and idle feares . . . . . 109 F11 Epode 26
   There were some pieces of as base allay, . . . 204 U43 Vulcan 42
   Clowne, Towns-man, base, and noble, mix'd, to judge? . 319 Horace 302
   With poore base termes, through every baser shop: . . 321 Horace 334
   Whilst other soules convert to base abuse . . . 361 Palmer 11
BASENESSE
   And from basenesse to be free, ... 142 U2 Her man 51
BASER
   With poore base termes, through every baser shop: . . 321 Horace 334
BASEST
   Where breathe the basest of thy fooles; . . . 101 F4 To the World 46
B'ASHAM'D
   Or Muse, upon the Lyre, thou chance b'asham'd. . . 329 Horace 502
BASKETS
   This way to husbands; and whose baskets beare . . 95 F2 Penshurst 55
BASTARD
   Will cal't a Bastard, when a Prophet's borne. . . 223 U49 Pucell 46
BASTINADO
   The late tane bastinado. So I thought. . . . 33 E21 Gam'ster 6
   A Rabbin confutes him with the Bastinado. . . . 375 Coryat 1 23
BATH
   As the Bath your verse discloses . . . . 136 U2 Cupid 21
   Any beliefe, in Madam Baud-bees bath, . . . 188 U34 Small Poxe 10
BATHES
   In bathes to steepe him; . . . . . 77 E120 S. P. 22
   By those pure bathes your either cheeke discloses, . . 170 U19 Elegy By 7
BATHS
   Retire themselves, avoid the publike baths; . . . 325 Horace 424
   In secret places, flee the public baths. . . . 349 Horace V424
BATTAILE
   Two bravely in the battaile fell, and dy'd, . . . 60 E93 Radcliffe 5
BATTELLS
   The Battells of thy Aldermanitie; . . . . 214 U44 Speach 46
BATTRY
   A Trench against it, nor a Battry plac't? . . . 401 Beaumont 14
BAUD
   But see! th'old baud hath serv'd him in his trim, . . 31 E12 Shift 23

49

	Page	Title	Line

BAUD (cont.)
Gypsee, new baud, is turn'd physitian,	39	E41 Gypsee	1
For what shee gave, a whore; a baud, shee cures.	39	E41 Gypsee	4
As a poore single flatterer, without Baud,	167	U15 Friend-Wars	158
Any beliefe, in Madam Baud-bees bath,	188	U34 Small Poxe	10
These are, as some infamous Baud, or Whore,	391	Shakespeare	13

BAUD-BEES
| Any beliefe, in Madam Baud-bees bath, | 188 | U34 Small Poxe | 10 |

BAUDES
| On Baudes, and Usurers. | 45 | E57 Bawds | Ttl |

BAUDIE
| Nor baudie stock, that travells for encrease, | 63 | E97 Motion | 10 |
| To be abroad chanting some baudie song, | 164 | U15 Friend-Wars | 74 |

BAUDRIE'
| Baudrie', and usurie were one kind of game. | 45 | E57 Bawds | 2 |

BAUDY
| Talkes loud, and baudy, has a gather'd deale | 74 | E115 Honest Man | 9 |

BAWD
| Bawd, in a Velvet scabberd! I envy | 202 | U42 Elegy Let | 85 |

BAWDIE
| Or crack out bawdie speeches, and uncleane. | 321 | Horace | 359 |

BAWDRIE
| I have no salt: no bawdrie he doth meane. | 42 | E49 Playwrt 1 | 3 |
| Make State, Religion, Bawdrie, all a theame? | 222 | U49 Pucell | 12 |

BAWDRY
| For bawdry, 'tis her language, and not mine. | 223 | U49 Pucell | 26 |

BAWDS
| Till that no usurer, nor his bawds dare lend | 118 | F13 Aubigny | 78 |

BAWLE
| But bawle thou on; I pitty thee, poore Curre, | 408 | Detractor | 7 |

BAWLING
| Keep in thy barking Wit, thou bawling Fool? | 410 | Gill | 8 |

BAYES
And, but a sprigge of bayes, given by thee,	32	E17 Critic	5
So Phoebus makes me worthy of his bayes,	73	E113 Overbury	1
'Mongst Hampton shades, and Phoebus grove of bayes,	80	E126 Mrs Cary	2
Thanke him: if other, hee can give no Bayes.	232	U58 Book-seller	6
And come forth worthie Ivye, or the Bayes,	420	Ode:If Men	26

BAYTES
| Be taken with false Baytes | 175 | U23 Himselfe | 20 |

BB'S
| Thy Wives pox on thee, and B.B.'s too. | 212 | U43 Vulcan | 216 |

BE'
| Or stands to be'n Commission o' the blade? | 155 | U13 Sacvile | 64 |

BE (See also BEE, BE'ST)
It will be look'd for, booke, when some but see	27	E2 My Booke	1
Thou should'st be bold, licentious, full of gall,	27	E2 My Booke	3
To lye upon thy stall, till it be sought;	28	E3 Bookseller	5
Not offer'd, as it made sute to be bought:	28	E3 Bookseller	6
If all you boast of your great art be true;	29	E6 Alchymists	1
And still be a whore-house. Th'are Synonima.	29	E7 Hot-house	4
To be a courtier; and lookes grave enough,	30	E11 Something	2
Which conquers all, be once over-come by thee.	31	E14 Camden	12
Thou saist, that cannot be: for thou hast seene	32	E18 Censurer	3
What doth he else, but say, leave to be chast,	34	E25 Beast 1	7
Of a great man, and to be thought the same,	35	E28 Surly	2
Nay more, for greatnesse sake, he will be one	36	E28 Surly	19
Guiltie, be wise; and though thou know'st the crimes	36	E30 Guiltie	1
Be thine, I taxe; yet doe not owne my rimes:	36	E30 Guiltie	2
He toyles to be at hell, as soone as they.	36	E31 Banck	4
Who wets my grave, can be no friend of mine.	37	E35 Roe 3	6
Who would not be thy subject, James, t'obay	37	E35 James 2	1
Guiltie, because I bad you late be wise,	38	E38 Guiltie 2	1
Who sayes that Giles and Jone at discord be?	40	E42 Giles	1
By his free will, be in Jones company.	40	E42 Giles	5
The selfe-same things, a note of concord be:	40	E42 Giles	17
When he made him executor, might be heire.	41	E44 Chuff	6
For whose sake, hence-forth, all his vowes be such,	41	E45 First Son	11
Poore Poet-Ape, that would be thought our chiefe,	44	E56 Poet-Ape	1
May judge it to be his, as well as ours.	45	E56 Poet-Ape	12
What should the cause be? Oh, you live at court:	46	E62 Would-bee	9
And can to these be silent, Salisburie,	47	E63 Salisbury 2	9
Curst be his Muse, that could lye dumbe, or hid	47	E63 Salisbury 2	11
Curst be my voyce if it lye dumbe, or hid	47	E63 Salisbury 2 V	11
Be thy most masters more unluckie Muse,	48	E65 Muse	5
That neither fame, nor love might wanting be	48	E66 Cary	3
In onely thee, might be both great, and glad.	48	E66 Cary	4
It may be much, or little, in the cause.	49	E66 Cary	16
As, to be rais'd by her, is onely fame.	49	E67 Suffolk	4
And thou design'd to be the same thou art,	49	E67 Suffolk	9
Though life be short, let us not make it so.	50	E70 Wm Roe 1	8
I meant shee should be curteous, facile, sweet,	52	E76 Bedford 1	9
Be safe, nor feare thy selfe so good a fame,	53	E77 Not name	1
And here, it should be one of our first strifes,	54	E80 Life/Death	6
To be the wealthy witnesse of my pen:	54	E81 Proule	4
And Phoebus-selfe should be at eating it.	55	E84 Bedford 2	8
Till they be sure to make the foole their quarrie.	55	E85 Goodyere 1	10
Where, though 't be love, that to thy praise doth move	55	E86 Goodyere 2	7
That he, untravell'd, should be french so much,	56	E88 Monsieur	7
Illustrous Vere, or Horace; fit to be	58	E91 Vere	3
Throughout, might flatt'rie seeme; and to be mute	58	E91 Vere	10
Ere cherries ripe, and straw-berries be gone,	58	E92 New Crie	1
Whose poemes would not wish to be your booke?	60	E94 Bedford 3	4

50

BE (cont.)

	Page	Title	Line
Be of the best: and 'mongst those, best are you.	61	E94 Bedford 3	14
Although to write bee lesser then to doo,	61	E95 Savile	25
By his each glorious parcell to be knowne!	62	E97 Motion	6
Be alwayes to thy gather'd selfe the same:	63	E98 Th Roe 1	9
Though both be good, the latter yet is worst,	63	E98 Th Roe 1	11
And that to write things worthy to be read:	63	E99 Th Roe 2	4
Is not to be despair'd of, for our money;	65	E101 Supper	14
And, though fowle, now, be scarce, yet there are clarkes,	65	E101 Supper	15
May yet be there; and godwit, if we can:	65	E101 Supper	19
Which is the Mermaids, now, but shall be mine:	65	E101 Supper	30
But, at our parting, we will be, as when	65	E101 Supper	38
That shall be utter'd at our mirthfull boord,	65	E101 Supper	40
Know you to be a Sydney, though un-named?	66	E103 L Wroth 1	4
Were you advanced, past those times, to be	67	E104 Montgomery	11
But even their names were to be made a-new,	67	E105 L Wroth 2	5
For which there must more sea, and land be leap'd,	69	E107 Hungry	16
If but to be beleev'd you have the hap,	69	E107 Hungry	17
Come, be not angrie, you are Hungry; eate;	69	E107 Hungry	31
Be nor put on you, nor you take offence.	69	E108 Soldiers	4
To be the same in roote, thou art in height;	70	E109 Nevil	13
And that so strong and deepe, as 't might be thought,	71	E110 Edmonds 1	7
Troth, if it be, I pitty thy ill lucke;	73	E112 Gamster	17
That the wit there, and manners might be sav'd:	73	E113 Overbury	6
And him it layes on; if he be not there.	74	E115 Honest Man	16
But, if it shall be question'd, undertakes,	74	E115 Honest Man	18
Might be found out as good, and not my Lord.	75	E116 Jephson	8
Yet is the office not to be despis'd,	78	E121 Rudyerd 1	5
Nor he, for friendship, to be thought unfit,	78	E121 Rudyerd 1	7
By her attempt, shall still be owing thee.	80	E127 Aubigny	10
Of old, even by her practise, to be fam'd;	82	E130 Ferrab. 1	10
They should be fooles, for me, at their owne charge.	83	E131 Ferrab. 2	8
They were not to be nam'd on the same day.	83	E131 Ferrab. 2	12
As his will now be the translation thought,	83	E132 Sylvester	12
Alcides, be thou succouring to my song.	85	E133 Voyage	50
Great Club-fist, though thy backe, and bones be sore,	85	E133 Voyage	66
But I will speake (and know I shall be heard)	87	E133 Voyage	105
Touching this cause, where they will be affeard	87	E133 Voyage	106
These be the cause of those thicke frequent mists	87	E133 Voyage	130
Into my ri'mes could ne're be got	93	F1 Why write no	9
And, for thy messe, is willing to be kill'd.	94	F2 Penshurst	30
And though thy walls be of the countrey stone,	94	F2 Penshurst	45
That is his Lordships, shall be also mine.	95	F2 Penshurst	64
Strive, Wroth, to be long innocent.	98	F3 Wroth	V 66
Get place, and honor, and be glad to keepe	99	F3 Wroth	87
Get place, and honor, and be proud to keepe	99	F3 Wroth	V 87
Which who can use is happy: Such be thou.	99	F3 Wroth	99
Be thanks to him, and earnest prayer, to finde	99	F3 Wroth	101
Thy subtle wayes, be narrow straits;	100	F4 To the World	10
And all thy good is to be sold.	100	F4 To the World	16
Where envious arts professed be,	101	F4 To the World	47
There should a miracle be wrought.	101	F4 To the World	60
Time will not be ours, for ever:	102	F5 Celia 1	3
To be taken, to be seene,	102	F5 Celia 1	17
What their number is, be pin'd.	103	F6 Celia 2	22
Who could be false to? chiefly, when he knowes	112	F11 Epode	103
Who would be false to? chiefly, when he knowes	112	F11 Epode	V103
Would not be fearefull to offend a dame	112	F11 Epode	109
And some one apteth to be trusted, then,	113	F12 Rutland	10
Will prove old Orpheus act no tale to be:	115	F12 Rutland	77
Will prove old Orpheus Arts no tale to be:	115	F12 Rutland	V 77
Who, wheresoere he be, on what dear coast,	116	F12 Rutland	93
Before his swift and circled race be run,	116	F12 Rutland	99
Before his swift and fethered race be run,	116	F12 Rutland	V 99
And this shall be no false one, but as much	117	F13 Aubigny	27
That askes but to be censur'd by the eyes:	117	F13 Aubigny	35
Whether it be a face they weare, or no.	118	F13 Aubigny	80
And call it their brave sinne. For such there be	119	F13 Aubigny	85
This makes, that your affections still be new,	119	F13 Aubigny	118
Madame, be bold to use this truest glasse:	120	F13 Aubigny	122
'T will be exacted of your name, whose sonne,	121	F14 Sydney	41
Which must be now,	121	F14 Sydney	47
If with this truth you be inspir'd,	121	F14 Sydney	52
Be more, and long desir'd:	121	F14 Sydney	55
Of love be bright,	121	F14 Sydney	57
O, be thou witnesse, that the reynes dost know,	122	F15 Heaven	5
And hearts of all, if I be sad for show,	122	F15 Heaven	6
As thou art all, so be thou all to mee,	122	F15 Heaven	9
With holy Paul, lest it be thought the breath	122	F15 Heaven	24
What odour can be, then a heart contrite,	127	U1 Trinitie	15
First, prepare you to be sorie,	131	U2 Excuse	14
But be glad, as soone with me,	131	U2 Excuse	17
Till she be the reason why,	131	U2 Excuse	23
Could be brought once back to looke.	132	U2 How he saw	19
And would on Conditions, be	133	U2 Suffered	5
This here sung, can be no other	136	U2 Cupid	11
Such my Mothers blushes be,	136	U2 Cupid	20
To be envi'd of the Queene.	138	U2 Kisse	28
Once more, and (faith) I will be gone,	139	U2 Another	7
This could be call'd but halfe a kisse,	139	U2 Another	11
When the worke would be effected:	140	U2 Promise	8
Be as good, as was the last:	140	U2 Promise	27
All his blood should be a flame	141	U2 Her man	30

		Page	Title	Line

BE (cont.)

	Page	Title	Line
In a body, should be there.	141	U2 Her man	35
Valiant he should be as fire,	142	U2 Her man	41
All his actions to be such,	142	U2 Her man	45
And from basenesse to be free,	142	U2 Her man	51
Let his Title be but great,	142	U2 Exception	3
Himselfe young, and face be good,	142	U2 Exception	5
Till each of us be made a Starre,	143	U3 Musicall	3
Of Angels should be driven	144	U3 Musicall	22
Lest I be sick with seeing;	144	U4 Song	2
O, be not angry with those fires,	144	U4 Song	5
Yet if it be not knowne,	147	U7 Nymph	5
I'le tell, that if they be not glad,	147	U7 Nymph	8
And of them pittied be,	147	U7 Nymph	11
And yet it cannot be foreborne,	147	U7 Nymph	13
Unlesse my heart would as my thought be torne.	147	U7 Nymph	14
And feare much more, that more of him be showne.	147	U7 Nymph	21
Will be my Rivall, though she have but eares.	148	U7 Nymph	28
As it would be to each a fame:	148	U7 Nymph	34
For else it could not be,	149	U9 Picture	2
or else it could not be,	149	U9 Picture	V 2
For truly, since he left to be,	152	U12 Corbet	35
Who makes the one, so't be first, makes both.	152	U12 Corbet	40
That puts it in his Debt-booke e're 't be done;	154	U13 Sacvile	34
Are they not worthy to be answer'd so,	154	U13 Sacvile	59
Cannot a man be reck'ned in the State	156	U13 Sacvile	103
But like to be, that every day mends one,	156	U13 Sacvile	116
Who was this Morning such a one, should be	157	U13 Sacvile	126
In time 'twill be a heape; This is not true	157	U13 Sacvile	133
Their difference, cannot choose which you will be.	157	U13 Sacvile	154
For me to be your Indice. Keep you such,	157	U13 Sacvile	156
May grow so great to be example, when	158	U13 Sacvile	161
Though I am short, I cannot be obscure:	158	U14 Selden	2
To aske it: though in most of workes it be	158	U14 Selden	7
A pennance, where a man may not be free,	158	U14 Selden	8
Humanitie enough to be a friend,	161	U14 Selden	77
And strength to be a Champion, and defend	161	U14 Selden	78
Their vitious ease, and be o'rewhelm'd with it.	162	U15 Friend-Wars	4
Be honour is so mixt) by such as would,	162	U15 Friend-Wars	25
For all their spight, be like him if they could:	162	U15 Friend-Wars	26
But there are objects, bid him to be gone	163	U15 Friend-Wars	28
Not to be checkt, or frighted now with fate,	163	U15 Friend-Wars	35
'Tis there civilitie to be a whore;	163	U15 Friend-Wars	54
Be at their Visits, see 'hem squemish, sick,	164	U15 Friend-Wars	68
To be abroad chanting some baudie song,	164	U15 Friend-Wars	74
Nature, that will not let his Wife be a whore;	165	U15 Friend-Wars	90
Lesse must not be thought on then Mistresse: or,	165	U15 Friend-Wars	95
If it be thought kild like her Embrions; for,	165	U15 Friend-Wars	96
To be beholders, when their powers are spent.	166	U15 Friend-Wars	140
And be belov'd, while the Whores last. O times,	167	U15 Friend-Wars	161
Thy true friends wishes, Colby, which shall be,	167	U15 Friend-Wars	176
Thy true friends wishes, which shall ever be,	167	U15 Friend-Wars	V176
That thine be just, and honest; that thy Deeds	167	U15 Friend-Wars	177
And never but for doing wrong be sory;	168	U15 Friend-Wars	180
Thou shrinke or start not, but be alwayes one;	168	U15 Friend-Wars	186
And from that thought strive to be understood.	168	U15 Friend-Wars	188
Is done for gaine: If't be, 'tis not sincere.	169	U17 Friend-Debt	6
Nor should I at this time protested be,	169	U17 Friend-Debt	7
And lookes unto the forfeit. If you be	169	U17 Friend-Debt	13
Except the way be errour to those ends:	170	U18 Elegy Can	13
Be brought by us to meet our Destinie.	170	U18 Elegy Can	20
If it be thus; Come Love, and Fortune goe,	170	U18 Elegy Can	21
Of all that can be done him; Such a one	171	U19 Elegy By	23
Is constant to be extraordinarie.	171	U19 Elegy By	28
How penitent I am, or I should be!	172	U20 Shrub	16
And that pour'd out upon Man-kind can be!	172	U20 Shrub	19
The Divell; and be the damning of us all.	172	U20 Shrub	24
Though Beautie be the Marke of praise,	173	U22 Elegy Tho	1
And yours of whom I sing be such	173	U22 Elegy Tho	2
If hence thy silence be,	174	U23 Himselfe	13
If hence they silent be,	174	U23 Himselfe	V 13
Be taken with false Baytes	175	U23 Himselfe	20
Might be defrauded, nor the great secur'd,	176	U24 Frontispice	6
Though many Gems be in your bosome stor'd,	179	U25 Desmond	55
Must now be rayn'd.	180	U26 Ode High	15
To doe, then be a husband of that store.	180	U26 Ode High	18
Yet sure my tunes will be the best,	182	U27 Ode Helen	35
Words, and sweetnesse, and be scant	184	U29 Fit of Rime	44
And his Title be long foole,	184	U29 Fit of Rime	58
And goe no farther: let this Circle be	185	U30 Burleigh	3
So, justest Lord, may all your Judgements be	185	U31 Elsmere	1
When those good few, that her Defenders be,	186	U32 Elsmere	5
And make the Scarre faire; If that will not be,	187	U33 Councellour	21
Envious and foule Disease, could there not be	188	U34 Small Poxe	1
Though Envie oft his shadow be,	189	U36 Song	3
From each of which I labour to be free,	190	U37 Friend-Book	28
Yet if with eithers vice I teynted be,	190	U37 Friend-Book	29
But shall sometimes be tempted to obey	190	U37 Friend-Book	32
That you should be too noble to destroy.	191	U38 Elegy 'Tis	12
If there be nothing worthy you can see	191	U38 Elegy 'Tis	15
Spare your owne goodnesse yet; and be not great	191	U38 Elegy 'Tis	17
Or in confessing of the Crime be nice,	191	U38 Elegy 'Tis	23
No, I will stand arraign'd, and cast, to be	191	U38 Elegy 'Tis	27

BE (cont.)

	Page	Title	Line
Thinke that I once was yours, or may be now;	192	U38 Elegy 'Tis	35
Your just commands; yet those, not I, be lost.	192	U38 Elegy 'Tis	38
Of your compassion; Parents should be mild:	192	U38 Elegy 'Tis	40
No man inflicts that paine, till hope be spent:	192	U38 Elegy 'Tis	44
As not alone the Cure, but scarre be faire.	192	U38 Elegy 'Tis	52
He cannot angrie be, but all must quake,	193	U38 Elegy 'Tis	71
Be not affected with these markes too much	193	U38 Elegy 'Tis	83
Then I will studie falshood, to be true.	194	U38 Elegy 'Tis	108
You would be then most confident, that tho	194	U38 Elegy 'Tis	113
Out of your eyes, and be awhile away;	194	U38 Elegy 'Tis	115
And must be bred, so to conceale his birth,	197	U40 Elegy That	17
Yet should the Lover still be ayrie and light,	197	U40 Elegy That	19
And never be by time, or folly brought,	198	U40 Elegy That	44
Be idle words, though of a parting Man;	199	U41 Elegy Since	4
As if it were not worthy to be there:	199	U41 Elegy Since	16
O, keepe it still; for it had rather be	199	U41 Elegy Since	17
Let me be what I am, as Virgil cold;	199	U42 Elegy Let	1
(If they be faire and worth it) have their lives	200	U42 Elegy Let	20
So to be sure you doe injoy your selves.	200	U42 Elegy Let	24
That are like cloath'd: must I be of those fooles	201	U42 Elegy Let	48
Conceal'd, or kept there, that was fit to be,	203	U43 Vulcan	21
Or Goddesse, could be patient of thy face.	207	U43 Vulcan	108
Some Alchimist there may be yet, or odde	208	U43 Vulcan	118
For they were burnt, but to be better built.	210	U43 Vulcan	166
Will be remembred by Six Clerkes, to one.	210	U43 Vulcan	172
No order? no Decree? Though we be gone	211	U43 Vulcan	176
Pox on your flameship, Vulcan; if it be	211	U43 Vulcan	191
Pox on your fire workes, Vulcan; if it be	211	U43 Vulcan	V191
Translated Aelian tactickes to be read,	214	U44 Speach	35
So, in that ground, as soone it grew to be	214	U44 Speach	37
That keepe the warre, though now't be growne more tame,	214	U44 Speach	55
Are we by Booke-wormes to be awde? must we	215	U44 Speach	67
Let poore Nobilitie be vertuous: Wee,	215	U44 Speach	79
Descended in a rope of Titles, be	215	U44 Speach	80
What I am not, and what I faine would be,	216	U45 Squib	1
My gentle Arthur; that it might be said	216	U45 Squib	3
Turne him, and see his Threds: looke, if he be	216	U45 Squib	21
Friend to himselfe, that would be friend to thee.	216	U45 Squib	22
For that is first requir'd, A man be his owne.	216	U45 Squib	23
. . . to be Sealed of the Tribe of Ben.	218	U47 Tribe	Ttl
Then these can ever be; or else wish none.	219	U47 Tribe	30
Be, or be not, to get the Val-telline?	219	U47 Tribe	32
Whether the Dispensation yet be sent,	219	U47 Tribe	35
And force back that, which will not be restor'd,	219	U47 Tribe	40
Shall carry me at Call; and I'le be well,	219	U47 Tribe	45
Lest it be justled, crack'd, made nought, or lesse:	219	U47 Tribe	58
And that there be no fev'ry heats, nor colds,	220	U47 Tribe	67
So mayst thou still be younger	221	U48 Bacchus	21
And not a Song be other	221	U48 Bacchus	35
As shall the feasts faire grounds be.	221	U48 Bacchus	42
Be it he hold Communion	221	U48 Bacchus	43
What though her Chamber be the very pit	222	U49 Pucell	3
To shew their Tires? to view, and to be view'd?	222	U49 Pucell	17
What though she be with Velvet gownes indu'd,	222	U49 Pucell	18
No friend to vertue, could be silent here.	224	U50 Countesse	8
Are in your selfe rewarded; yet 'twill be	224	U50 Countesse	15
So are they profitable to be knowne:	225	U50 Countesse	34
It will be shame for them, if they have none.	225	U50 Countesse	36
'Tis a brave cause of joy, let it be knowne,	225	U51 Bacon	17
To be describ'd by a Monogram,	227	U52 Answer	11
But whilst you curious were to have it be	227	U52 Answer	13
I look'd for Hercules to be the Groome:	228	U53 Newcastle	18
I Am to dine, Friend, where I must be weigh'd	229	U54 Squib	1
But rather with advantage to be found	229	U54 Squib	11
And then to be return'd; on protestation	229	U54 Squib	18
If there be no money;	231	U57 Burges	21
If the 'Chequer be emptie, so will be his Head.	232	U57 Burges	28
His judgement is; If he be wise, and praise,	232	U58 Book-seller	5
Will be reward enough: to weare like those,	232	U58 Book-seller	9
To God, denies the God-head to be true:	235	U63 Charles 2	2
That Faith, which she professeth to be pure?	236	U64 Charles 3	12
And art thou borne, brave Babe? Blest be thy birth,	237	U65 Prince	1
And art thou borne, brave Babe? Blest be the day,	237	U65 Prince	V 1
The same that thou art promis'd, but be slow,	237	U65 Prince	6
The same that thou hast promis'd, but be slow,	237	U65 Prince	V 6
As in this Prince? Let it be lawfull, so	238	U66 Queene	11
Be silent, to the people	239	U67 Muses	5
Let every Lyre be strung,	239	U67 Muses	16
What can the cause be, when the K. hath given	241	U68 House-hold	1
All is but web, and painting; be the strife	242	U69 Friend Son	24
You liv'd to be the great surnames,	247	U70 Ode	113
Hath rais'd to be the Port unto his Land!	250	U73 Weston	4
To vertue, and true worth, be ever blind.	250	U73 Weston	10
O how will then our Court be pleas'd,	251	U74 Weston	25
To be a shadow to his Heire,	251	U74 Weston	29
And see, what can be seene,	252	U75 Epithalam.	7
As they came all to see, and to be seene!	253	U75 Epithalam.	20
Be duly done to those	255	U75 Epithalam.	93
With all corroding Arts, be able to untie!	257	U75 Epithalam.	136
The Chappell empties, and thou may'st be 'gone	257	U75 Epithalam.	137
Be kept alive those Sweet, and Sacred fires	257	U75 Epithalam.	163
To be a watchfull Servant for this State;	258	U75 Epithalam.	178

BE   (cont.)

	Page	Title	Line
To be given me in gratuitie	259	U76 Petition	12
For that to dwell in, and be still at home.	262	U78 Digby	8
For those to dwell in, and be still at home.	262	U78 Digby	V 8
Goe, Muse, in, and salute him. Say he be	262	U78 Digby	19
Goe, Muse, in, and salute him thoughe he be	262	U78 Digby	V 19
And praise them too. O! what a fame 't will be?	263	U78 Digby	25
Allowes them? Then, what copies shall be had,	263	U78 Digby	29
Allowes them? Then, what copies will be had,	263	U78 Digby	V 29
Wilt thou be, Muse, when this shall them befall?	263	U78 Digby	31
Wilt thou be, Muse, when this shall then befall?	263	U78 Digby	V 31
Being sent to one, they will be read of all.	263	U78 Digby	32
And the disposure will be something new,	269	U81 Pawlet	16
And the disposure will be somewhat new,	269	U81 Pawlet	V 16
To be describ'd! Fames fingers are too foule	269	U81 Pawlet	30
What the beginnings of all beauties be;	271	U81 Pawlet	74
Goe now, her happy Parents, and be sad,	271	U81 Pawlet	77
At pleasure, to be call'd for, every day!	271	U81 Pawlet	82
With Gold, or Claspes, which might be bought	273	U84 Cradle	27
Who claimes (of reverence) to be heard,	274	U84 Cradle	34
Sitting, and ready to be drawne,	275	U84 Body	1
And let there be a starry Robe	276	U84 Body	26
Painter yo' are come, but may be gone,	277	U84 Mind	1
Hence-forth may every line be you;	278	U84 Mind	22
'Twill be but faire, to leane upon their Fames;	281	U84 Kenelme	13
Those other two; which must be judg'd, or crown'd:	284	U84 Muse	55
Who will be there, against that day prepar'd,	284	U84 Muse	59
T'accuse, or quit all Parties to be heard!	284	U84 Muse	60
Better be dumbe, then superstitious!	284	U84 Muse	73
Will honour'd be in all simplicitie!	284	U84 Muse	76
Where Hee will be, all Beautie to the Sight;	286	U84 Muse	122
Hee will all Glory, all Perfection be,	286	U84 Muse	127
Will there revealed be in Majestie!	286	U84 Muse	130
He that shall be our supreme Judge, should leave	286	U84 Muse	148
To him should be her Judge, true God, true Man,	288	U84 Muse	211
More sweet then Olives, that new gather'd be	291	U85 Country	55
Shall Verse be set to Harpe and Lute,	292	U86 Hor.4:1	23
Though he be fairer then a Starre;	294	U87 Hor.3:9	21
With Doves; or Lambes, with Tygres coupled be.	305	Horace	16
The whole fleet wreck'd? a great jarre to be shap'd,	305	Horace	28
Be simple quite throughout, and wholly one.	307	Horace	32
Be simple quite throughout, and alwayes one.	339	Horace	V 32
To be that Smith; then live, mark'd one of those,	307	Horace	51
To be that fellow, then to be markt out	339	Horace	V 53/ 51
Unto your strength, and long be turning it:	339	Horace	V 56/ 54
Or I am much deceiv'd, shall be to place	307	Horace	60
Much, that mought now be spoke: omitted here	307	Horace	62
In using also of new words, to be	307	Horace	65
Much phrase that now is dead, shall be reviv'd;	309	Horace	101
Were also clos'd: But, who the man should be,	309	Horace	109
The Comick matter will not be exprest	311	Horace	121
Yet Comick matter shunnes to be exprest	341	Horace	V127/121
If thou would'st have me weepe, be thou first drown'd	311	Horace	145
Honour'd Achilles chance by thee be seiz'd,	313	Horace	171
Be nought so'bove him but his sword let claime.	313	Horace	174
Be nought so'bove him, but his bold sword claime.	342	Horace	V174
Still to be like himselfe, and hold his worth.	313	Horace	182
That tarries till the hangings be ta'en downe,	315	Horace	221
I'the open field; is Waxe like to be wrought	315	Horace	231
To every vice, as hardly to be brought	315	Horace	232
The parts of age to youth be given; or men	317	Horace	252
Things worthy to be done within, but take	317	Horace	261
Once seene, to be againe call'd for, and plaid,	317	Horace	271
Must maintaine manly; not be heard to sing,	317	Horace	277
Must manly keep, and not be heard to sing	345	Horace	V277
Be wonne a friend; it must both sway, and bend	317	Horace	281
They might with ease be numbred, being a few	319	Horace	293
Thespis is said to be the first found out	319	Horace	311
Were to be staid with softnesses, and wonne	321	Horace	326
As neither any God, be brought in there,	346	Horace	V323/331
A royall Crowne, and purple, be made hop,	321	Horace	333
A royall Crowne, and Scarlet; be made hop	346	Horace	V325/333
Be I their Judge, they doe at no time dare	321	Horace	356
Her licence fit to be restrain'd by law:	321	Horace	368
Her force was fit to be restrain'd by law:	348	Horace	V402/368
Grow a safe Writer, and be warie-driven	323	Horace	393
Be like a Whet-stone, that an edge can put	325	Horace	433
On steele, though 't selfe be dull, and cannot cut.	325	Horace	434
Is to be wise; thy matter first to know;	325	Horace	441
Thinke wee, or hope, there can be Verses fain'd	327	Horace	474
In juyce of Cedar worthy to be steep'd,	327	Horace	475
And in smooth Cypresse boxes to be keep'd?	327	Horace	476
Upon the Lyre, thou chance to be asham'd.	353	Horace	V580/502
Be briefe, in what thou wouldst command, that so	329	Horace	503
Let what thou fain'st for pleasures sake, be neere	329	Horace	507
It would, must be: lest it alive would draw	329	Horace	509
Will in the light be view'd: This, once, the sight	331	Horace	543
There may a Lawyer be, may not excell;	331	Horace	550
Poets should ever be indifferent.	331	Horace	556
To send it to be judg'd by Metius eare,	331	Horace	576
And, to your Fathers, and to mine; though 't be	331	Horace	577
Him that is last, I scorne to be behind,	353	Horace	V595
Will be a suretie; or can helpe him out	333	Horace	603

BE (cont.)

	Page	Title	Line
If of their friendship he be worthy, or no:	333	Horace	619
Looke through him, and be sure, you take not mocks	333	Horace	621
Reprove; and, what is to be changed, note:	335	Horace	638
Dispute; and what is to be changed, note;	354	Horace	V638
Not thence be sav'd, although indeed he could?	335	Horace	658
Hee, while he labour'd to be thought a God	335	Horace	661
Let Poets perish, that will not be kept.	335	Horace	664
Recall him yet, hee'ld be no more a man:	335	Horace	668
Now, bring him backe, he'le be no more a man,	355	Horace	V668
Be then both Rare, and Good; and long	367	Ode Who saith	33
Be proofe, the glory of his hand,	367	Ode Who saith	49
Among the starres should be resign'd	369	Ode Who saith	105
Or Tames be rap't from us	369	Ode Who saith	107
That durst be that in Court: a vertu' alone	371	Epitaph	4
Here, by a Boore too, hee's like to be beaten	375	Coryat 1	24
Beeing in feare to be robd, he most learnedly begs.	375	Coryat 1	35
To be his Bacchus as his Pallas: bee	378	Coryat 2	91
Who ever he be, would write a Story at	379	Coryat 3	1
Who, because his matter in all should be meete,	379	Coryat 3	3
Which, unto all Ages, for his will be knowne,	379	Coryat 3	11
There nam'd to be travell'd? For this our Tom saith:	380	Coryat 3	21
He was in his travaile, how like to be beaten,	380	Coryat 3	35
Must be intended still to understand:	383	Author	2
So, be there never discontent, or sorrow,	384	Somerset	15
So, be your Concord, still, as deepe, as mute;	384	Somerset	17
And when your yeares rise more, then would be told,	384	Somerset	23
To see his worke be good; but that he looke	385	Husband	2
I find thee write most worthy to be read.	386	Browne	6
It must be thine owne judgment, yet, that sends	386	Browne	7
Will all be dust, & may not make me swell.	387	Cavendish	V 4
it will be matter lowd inoughe to tell	387	Cavendish	11
Whose worke could this be, Chapman, to refine	388	Chapman	1
And this hath met that one, that may be stil'd	389	Aleman	13
He would be call'd, henceforth, the English-Rogue,	389	Aleman	16
While I confesse thy writings to be such,	390	Shakespeare	3
For though the Poets matter, Nature be,	392	Shakespeare	57
To call on Sicknes still, to be her Guest,	394	Jane Ogle	19
With us be call'd, the Naso, but this man?	397	Drayton	32
And will be bought of every Lord, and Knight,	398	Drayton	72
Of tender eyes will more be wept, then seene:	398	Drayton	76
If I can be a Friend, and Friend to thee.	398	Drayton	94
you would be an Asinigo, by your ears?	403	Inigo Jones 1	20
Why much good doo't you! Be what beast you will,	403	Inigo Jones 1	21
you'l be as Langley sayd, an Inigo still.	403	Inigo Jones 1	22
To be the Musick Master! Fabler too!	404	Inigo Jones 1	63
He is, or would be the mayne Dominus doe	404	Inigo Jones 1	64
Be Inigo, the Whistle, & his men!	405	Inigo Jones 1	66
To be worth Envy. Henceforth I doe meane	405	Inigo Jones 1	70
Soe the Materialls be of Purbeck stone!	406	Inigo Jones 1	100
To Inigo Marquess Would Be A Corollary	406	Inigo Jones 2	Ttl
Besydes, his Man may merit it, and be	406	Inigo Jones 2	5
Content thee to be Pancridge Earle the whyle;	407	Inigo Jones 2	20
If thou be soe desyrous to be read,	408	Inigo Jones 3	9
Will well designe thee, to be viewd of all	408	Inigo Jones 3	12
To be knowne what thou art, a blatant beast,	408	Detractor	9
Hee'll be a Pilot, scarce can guide a Plough.	410	Brome	18
To be the Denis of thy Father's School,	410	Gill	7
A Rogue by Statute, censur'd to be whipt,	411	Gill	15
And most to be admired of thy Sexe,	414	Ghyrlond	46
And truely, so I would, could I be heard.	414	Rutter	3
Cry'd up of late: Whereto there must be first	415	Rutter	21
I shall think on't ere't be day.	417	Moon	11
for if there, or peace or warr be,	417	Moon	22
If there be a Coockold Major,	417	Moon	25
and of Circle be as free,	417	Moon	30
Or if't be the Gossipps happ	417	Moon	37
nor cann be of desert,	420	Ode:If Men	13
From each of which, I labor to be free,	422	Censure	21
he that will honest be, may quitt the Court,	423	Lucan	17

BEADLE

	Page	Title	Line
One said, it was bold Briareus, or the beadle,	86	E133 Voyage	81

BEAME

	Page	Title	Line
Rich beame of honour, shed your light	177	U25 Desmond	14
It cast a beame as when the chear-full Sun	396	Drayton	17

BEAMES

	Page	Title	Line
Then let the beames of that, disperse	276	U84 Body	17
From Zephyr's rape would close him with his beames.	366	Ode Who saith	24

BEAMIE

	Page	Title	Line
Which makes that (lighted by the beamie hand	176	U24 Frontispice	9
This makes, that lighted by the beamie hand	176	U24 Frontispice V	9

BEARD

	Page	Title	Line
Cupids Statue with a Beard,	132	U2 How he saw	30
Till he cherish'd too much beard,	141	U2 Her man	23

BEARDS

	Page	Title	Line
Ripe are their ruffes, their cuffes, their beards, their gate,	58	E92 New Crie	6
Their nailes, nor shave their beards, but to by-paths	325	Horace	423
Their nails, nor shave their beards, but seek by-paths	349	Horace	V423
To the merry beards in Hall,	417	Moon	13

BEARE (ANIMAL)

	Page	Title	Line
Like a rung Beare, or Swine: grunting owt wit	232	U58 Book-seller	11
And, as a Beare, if he the strength but had	337	Horace	674

	Page	Title	Line

BEARE (See also BARE)

How, best of Kings, do'st thou a scepter beare! . . . 28 E4 James 1 1
That love to make so well, a child to beare? . . . 46 E62 Would-bee 2
Make it your gift. See whither that will beare mee. . . . 55 E84 Bedford 2 10
First bearing him a calfe, beare him a bull. . . . 57 E90 Mill 18
Who did, alike with thee, thy house up-beare, . . . 60 E93 Radcliffe 3
This way to husbands; and whose baskets beare . . . 95 F2 Penshurst 55
I know thou canst nor shew, nor beare . . . 101 F4 To the World 39
But, what we'are borne for, we must beare: . . . 101 F4 To the World 53
But I will beare these, with that scorne, . . . 102 F4 To the World 63
Just to the waight their this dayes-presents beare; . . . 113 F12 Rutland 8
My best of wishes, may you beare a sonne. . . . 116 F12 Rutland 100
What reputation to beare one Glasse more? . . . 166 U15 Friend-Wars 119
Tilt one upon another, and now beare . . . 166 U15 Friend-Wars 125
till one upon another, and now beare . . . 166 U15 Friend-Wars V125
At least may beare th'inscription to her Tombe. . . . 269 U81 Pawlet 18
Upon your shoulders. Prove what they will beare, . . . 307 Horace 55
Prove what your shoulders will, or will not beare. . . . 339 Horace V 57/ 55
The steadie Spondaees; so themselves to beare . . . 323 Horace 377
The steadie Spondaees; so themselves doe beare . . . 347 Horace V363/377
the Moone will beare it. . . . . 417 Moon 28
That prince that shames a tyrants name to beare, . . . 423 Lucan 19

BEARER

When oft the Bearer, is borne out of dore? . . . 166 U15 Friend-Wars 120

BEARES (NOUN)

Nor 'bout the beares, nor noyse to make lords sport. . . . 63 E97 Motion 12
The meate-boate of Beares colledge, Paris-garden, . . . 87 E133 Voyage 117
And cry'd, it was a threatning to the beares: . . . 209 U43 Vulcan 146
And sayd twas sure a threatning to the beares; . . . 209 U43 Vulcan V146
And cry'd 'Twas verily a threatning to the beares; . . . 209 U43 Vulcan V146
That guides the Motions, and directs the beares. . . . 219 U47 Tribe 50

BEARES

Whose soule heavens Queene, (whose name shee beares) . . . 33 E22 Daughter 7
Which of thy names I take, not onely beares . . . 58 E91 Vere 1
In equall knots: This beares no brands, nor darts, . . . 110 F11 Epode 51
Or perhaps lesse: whil'st gold beares all this sway, . . . 113 F12 Rutland 18
Some note of which each varied Pillar beares, . . . 176 U24 Frontispice 15

BEARING

Of bearing them in field, he threw 'hem away: . . . 42 E48 Mungril 2
First bearing him a calfe, beare him a bull. . . . 57 E90 Mill 18
Of bearing Armes! most civill Soldierie! . . . 214 U44 Speach 44
Us, in our bearing, that are thus, and thus, . . . 215 U44 Speach 65
(Bearing the promise of some better fate) . . . 252 U75 Epithalam. 10

BEAST

On Sir Voluptuous Beast. . . . 34 E25 Beast 1 Ttl
While Beast instructs his faire, and innocent wife, . . . 34 E25 Beast 1 1
On the same Beast. . . . 35 E26 Beast 2 Ttl
Then his chast wife, though Beast now know no more, . . . 35 E26 Beast 2 1
What bird, or beast, is knowne so dull, . . . 101 F4 To the World 29
At such a Call, what beast or fowle, . . . 143 U3 Musicall 5
And feeles it; Else he tarries by the Beast. . . . 156 U13 Sacvile 117
Why much good doo't you! Be what beast you will, . . . 403 Inigo Jones 1 21
To be knowne what thou art, a blatant beast, . . . 408 Detractor 9

BEASTLY

Much lesse with lewd, prophane, and beastly phrase, . . . 27 E2 My Booke 11

BEASTS

Of building townes, and making wilde beasts tame, . . . 82 E130 Ferrab. 1 2
Like lustfull beasts, that onely know to doe it: . . . 294 U88 Petronius 4

BEAT

Blaspheme god, greatly. Or some poore hinde beat, . . . 36 E28 Surly 17
And hers were all Humilitie! they beat . . . 288 U84 Muse 189
Out at his friendly eyes, leape, beat the groun'. . . . 333 Horace 613

BEATE

Urine, and plaisters? when the noise doth beate . . . 88 E133 Voyage 170
But that I heare, againe, thy Drum to beate . . . 397 Drayton 55

BEATEN

Here, by a Boore too, hee's like to be beaten . . . 375 Coryat 1 24
He was in his travaile, how like to be beaten, . . . 380 Coryat 3 35

BEATES

Beates brave, and loude in Europe, and bids come . . . 162 U15 Friend-Wars 2

BEATIFICK

By beatifick vertue of the Place. . . . 285 U84 Muse 116

BEATING

Sweat at the forge, their hammers beating; . . . 179 U25 Desmond 41
With beating of our Drums: . . . 239 U67 Muses 15
With beating of their Drums: . . . 239 U67 Muses V 15

BEATINGS

Takes private beatings, and begins againe. . . . 49 E68 Playwrt 2 2

BEATITUDE

What fulnesse of beatitude is here? . . . 286 U84 Muse 137

BEATITUDES

And all beatitudes, that thence doe flow: . . . 271 U81 Pawlet 75

BEAUCHAMPS

Beauchamps, and Nevills, Cliffords, Audleys old; . . . 214 U44 Speach 52

BEAUMONT

To Francis Beaumont. . . . 44 E55 Beaumont Ttl
How I doe love thee Beaumont, and thy Muse, . . . 44 E55 Beaumont 1
Chaucer, or Spenser, or bid Beaumont lye . . . 391 Shakespeare 20
. . . Sir John Beaumont, Baronet. . . . 400 Beaumont Ttl

BEAUMONTS

Though I confesse a Beaumonts Booke to bee . . . 400 Beaumont 7

BEAUTEOUS

Thou Throne of glory, beauteous as the Moone, . . . 414 Ghyrlond 49

56

BEAUTIE
  A dead beautie under-neath thee, ...   39   E40 Ratcliffe   2
  Where finding so much beautie met with vertue,   .   .   74   E114 Sydney   6
  As much beautie, as could dye: 79   E124 Elizabeth   4
  A beautie of that merit, that should take   .   .   .   108   F10 Proludium   27
  A beautie of that cleere, and sparkling light,   .   .   112   F11 Epode   93
  A beautie of that cleere, and sparkling sight,   .   .   112   F11 Epode   V 93
  Beautie, I know, is good, and bloud is more;   .   .   114   F12 Rutland   37
  Have beautie knowne, yet none so famous seene?   .   .   114   F12 Rutland   50
  Your beautie; for you see that every day: .   .   .   117   F13 Aubigny   30
  Nor that your beautie wanted not a dower,   .   .   .   117   F13 Aubigny   37
  Of whose Beautie it was sung, ...   131   U2 Excuse   19
  Can Beautie that did prompt me first to write,   .   .   169   U18 Elegy Can   1
  I know no beautie, nor no youth that will.   .   .   .   171   U19 Elegy By   20
  Though Beautie be the Marke of praise,   .   .   .   173   U22 Elegy Tho   1
  One beautie in an Age, and free from thee?   .   .   .   188   U34 Small Poxe   2
  Of Beautie, so to nullifie a face, ...   188   U34 Small Poxe   14
  What Beautie would have lovely stilde,   .   .   .   188   U35 Chute   1
  Of beautie; but the Muse hath interest in: .   .   .   200   U42 Elegy Let   15
  This, and that box his Beautie to repaire;   .   .   .   215   U44 Speach   96
  In small proportions, we just beautie see: .   .   .   245   U70 Ode   73
  Of the prime beautie of the yeare, the Spring.   .   .   251   U74 Weston   6
  And both a strength, and Beautie to his Land!   .   .   251   U74 Weston   30
  The bountie of a King, and beautie of his Queene!   .   252   U75 Epithalam.   8
  This beautie without falshood fayre,   .   .   .   275   U84 Body   7
  In all the bounds of beautie fit   280   U84 Mind   51
  Where Hee will be, all Beautie to the Sight;   .   .   286   U84 Muse   122
  Her Poem's beautie, but a sweet delight   .   .   .   311   Horace   141
BEAUTIES
  And takes, and gives the beauties of the mind.   .   .   117   F13 Aubigny   44
  Which the prouder Beauties please,   .   .   .   133   U2 Suffered   2
  Thy beauties, yet could write of thee?   .   .   .   181   U27 Ode Helen   2
  Have eaten with the Beauties, and the wits,   .   .   200   U42 Elegy Let   33
  Nay, so your Seate his beauties did endorse,   .   .   228   U53 Newcastle   11
  What Beavie of beauties, and bright youths at charge   .   253   U75 Epithalam.   17
  As if the beauties of the yeare, ...   264   U79 New-yeares   38
  What the beginnings of all beauties be;   .   .   .   271   U81 Pawlet   74
  And thou hast painted beauties world.   .   .   .   277   U84 Body   28
BEAUTY
  in whom the flame of every beauty raignes,   .   .   .   108   F10 Proludium   8
  Unto her beauty;   134   U2 Triumph   6
  For this Beauty yet doth hide   137   U2 Cupid   49
  The charmed beauty and the inchanted Wharfes;   .   .   205   U43 Vulcan   V 68
  I doe obey you, Beauty! for in death,   .   .   .   269   U81 Pawlet   5
  I saw a Beauty from the Sea to rise,   .   .   .   396   Drayton   15
BEAUTYE
  Beautye, more then mortall, ...   364   Ode Splendor   V   1
BEAVIE
  What Beavie of beauties, and bright youths at charge   .   253   U75 Epithalam.   17
BECAME
  Saw'st thou that Paire, became these Rites so well,   .   254   U75 Epithalam.   76
  Became her Birth-day to Eternitie!   .   .   .   271   U81 Pawlet   68
  She had, and it became her! she was fit   .   .   .   287   U84 Muse   161
  Aeternities great charter; which became   .   .   .   400   Lady Ogle   35
BECAM'ST
  To take our nature; becam'st man, and dyd'st,   .   .   128   U1 Trinitie   22
BECAUSE   (See also BY-CAUSE, 'CAUSE)
  But leave, because I cannot as I should!   .   .   .   34   E23 Donne 1   10
  Guiltie, because I bad you late be wise,   .   .   .   38   E38 Guiltie 2   1
  Or, because some scarce thinke that storie true,   .   .   67   E104 Montgomery   5
  Because they move, the continent doth so: .   .   .   111   F11 Epode   71
  Because lust's meanes are spent: 111   F11 Epode   78
  Because they lack'd the sacred pen, could give   .   .   115   F12 Rutland   56
  Or so my selfe abandon'd, as because   .   .   .   117   F13 Aubigny   17
  Because that studies spectacles, and showes,   .   .   118   F13 Aubigny   65
  Because nor it can change, nor such a minde.   .   .   120   F13 Aubigny   124
  (Because th'are every where amongst Man-kind   .   .   167   U15 Friend-Wars   171
  I adde that (but) because I understand   .   .   .   169   U17 Friend-Debt   10
  Because they would free Justice imitate,   .   .   .   170   U18 Elegy Can   18
  As in his place, because he would not varie,   .   .   171   U19 Elegy By   27
  Wherein you triumph yet: because   173   U22 Elegy Tho   9
  In man, because man hath the flesh abus'd.   .   .   .   192   U38 Elegy 'Tis   66
  Was it because thou wert of old denied   .   .   .   203   U43 Vulcan   11
  Because it durst have noblier dy'd.   .   .   .   234   U60 La-ware   18
  Because the order of the whole is faire!   .   .   .   251   U74 Weston   12
  Is it because it sees us dull, ...   279   U84 Mind   45
  Either because he seekes, and, having found,   .   .   317   Horace   242
  How he could jest, because he mark'd and saw,   .   .   319   Horace   323
  Because Democritus beleeves a wit   .   .   .   325   Horace   419
  Who, because his matter in all should be meete,   .   .   379   Coryat 3   3
  Because, who make the question, have not seene   .   .   396   Drayton   3
BECKNING
  And beckning wooes me, from the fatall tree   .   .   268   U81 Pawlet   3
BECOME
  Become a petulant thing, hurle inke, and wit,   .   .   27   E2 My Booke   5
  The courtier is become the greater thiefe.   .   .   29   E8 Robbery   6
  From brocage is become so bold a thiefe,   .   .   .   44   E56 Poet-Ape   3
  And best become the valiant man to weare,   .   .   .   58   E91 Vere   17
  To become thy sacrifice.   105   F8 Sicknesse   28
  I, Madame, am become your praiser. Where,,   .   .   117   F13 Aubigny   21
  Reader, whose life, and name, did e're become   .   .   152   U12 Corbet   37
  Since I exscribe your Sonnets, am become   .   .   .   182   U28 Worth   3
  I am regenerate now, become the child   .   .   .   192   U38 Elegy 'Tis   39

BECOME (cont.)
That Article, may not become our lover:	198	U40 Elegy That	48
And so I spare it. Come what can become	199	U41 Elegy Since	19
that from the Foot-man, when he was become	201	U42 Elegy Let	52
The Herald will. Our blood is now become	215	U44 Speach	82
Ambition to become a Starre,	234	U60 La-ware	14
When I, who would her Poet have become,	269	U81 Pawlet	17
As her whole life was now become one note	287	U84 Muse	178
Become an Aristarchus. And, not say,	335	Horace	639
Our Charles should make thee such? 'Twill not become	406	Inigo Jones 2	3

BECOMES
Becomes none more then you, who need it least.	67	E103 L Wroth 1	14
So each, that's done, and tane, becomes a Brace.	154	U13 Sacvile	40
Till he becomes both their, and his owne curse!	162	U15 Friend-Wars	14
And where it stayes, it there becomes	280	U84 Mind	63
So he that flaggeth much, becomes to me	329	Horace	533
And though your virtue (as becomes it) still	421	Censure	9

BECOMMETH
| The Poet, what becommeth, and what not: | 325 | Horace | 438 |

BECOMMING
| One un-becomming thought doth move | 148 | U7 Nymph | 31 |

BECUM
| Palmer thy travayles well becum thy name, | 362 | Palmer | 30 |

BED
A-bed canst heare the loud stag speake,	97	F3 Wroth	22
Sydney e're night! or that did goe to bed	157	U13 Sacvile	127
Nor any quick-warming-pan helpe him to bed,	232	U57 Burges	27
The bed of the chast Lilly, and the Rose!	237	U65 Prince	3
Fix'd to the bed, and boords, unlike to win	248	U71 Treasurer	11
Fix'd to the bed, and borde, and like to win	248	U71 Treasurer	V 11
A Bed-rid Wit, then a besieged Towne.	248	U71 Treasurer	15
In making soft her aromatique bed.	251	U74 Weston	18
(The holy perfumes of the Mariage bed.)	257	U75 Epithalam.	162
They both are slip'd to Bed; Shut fast the Doore,	258	U75 Epithalam.	185
From off her pillow, and deluded bed;	283	U84 Muse	43
And heat, with softest love, thy softer bed.	295	U89 Mart.8:77	6
No sowre, or sollen bed-mate, yet a Chast;	295	U90 Mart.10:47	10
Preserved, in her antique bed of Vert,	413	Ghyrlond	19

BEDEW'D
| Have they bedew'd the Earth, where she doth tread, | 254 | U75 Epithalam. | 66 |
| Have they bedew'd the Earth, where she did tread, | 254 | U75 Epithalam. | V 66 |

BEDFORD
On Lucy Countesse of Bedford.	52	E76 Bedford 1	Ttl
My Muse bad, Bedford write, and that was shee.	52	E76 Bedford 1	18
To Lucy Countesse of Bedford.	54	E84 Bedford 2	Ttl
To Lucy, Countesse of Bedford, with Mr. Donnes Satyres.	60	E94 Bedford 3	Ttl
God blesse us all, Bedford keepe safe:	419	Grace	V 7
Lucy of Bedford; she, that Bounty	662	Bedford	3

BED-MATE
| No sowre, or sollen bed-mate, yet a Chast; | 295 | U90 Mart.10:47 | 10 |

BED-RID
| A Bed-rid Wit, then a besieged Towne. | 248 | U71 Treasurer | 15 |

BEDS
| On their beds, most prostitute, | 106 | F8 Sicknesse | 45 |

BEE (NOUN)
| Or have tasted the bag o'the Bee? | 135 | U2 Triumph | 29 |
| I'le taste as lightly as the Bee. | 139 | U2 Another | 5 |

BEE
As chiefe of those still promise they will bee.	28	E4 James 1	8
First thou preserved wert, our king to bee,	38	E35 James 2	9
Thou flattered'st thine, mine cannot flatter'd bee.	38	E36 Martial	4
To Fine Lady Would-bee.	46	E62 Would-bee	Ttl
Fine Madame Would-Bee, wherefore should you feare,	46	E62 Would-bee	1
Nor glad as those, that old dependents bee,	47	E64 Salisbury 3	5
Love honors, which of best example bee,	49	E66 Cary	13
And land on one, whose face durst never bee	56	E88 Monsieur	5
Wherewith, against thy bloud, they'offenders bee.	60	E93 Radcliffe	16
Yet, Satyres, since the most of mankind bee	60	E94 Bedford 3	7
Who shall doubt, Donne, where I a Poet bee,	62	E96 Donne 2	1
Well, though thy name lesse then our great ones bee,	64	E99 Th Roe 2	11
Digestive cheese, and fruit there sure will bee;	65	E101 Supper	27
Even in the dew of grace, what you would bee?	67	E104 Montgomery	2
Their latter praise would still the greatest bee,	68	E106 E Herbert	9
What th'antique souldiers were, the moderne bee?	72	E111 Edmonds 2	2
I Must beleeve some miracles still bee,	73	E114 Sydney	1
Who prov'st, all these were, and againe may bee.	78	E122 Rudyerd 2	10
Is there a hope, that Man would thankefull bee,	80	E127 Aubigny	1
But when I have said, The proofes of all these bee	82	E130 Ferrab. 1	17
It could not withered bee.	106	F9 Celia 3	12
It would not withered bee.	106	F9 Celia 3	V 12
In my character, what your features bee,	117	F13 Aubigny	24
Right, the right way: yet must your comfort bee	118	F13 Aubigny	68
What your try'd manners are, what theirs should bee.	119	F13 Aubigny	112
But it must, straight, my melancholy bee?	122	F15 Heaven	2
Of discontent; or that these prayers bee	122	F15 Heaven	25
Nay, rather both our soules bee strayn'd	144	U3 Musicall	25
May his joynts tormented bee,	184	U29 Fit of Rime	50
And waste still, that they still might bee.	189	U36 Song	12
Who shall forbid me then in Rithme to bee	200	U42 Elegy Let	5
Bee thou my Bookes intelligencer, note	232	U58 Book-seller	3
Thee quickly come the gardens eye to bee,	238	U65 Prince	8
In bulke, doth make man better bee;	245	U70 Ode	66
And in short measures, life may perfect bee.	245	U70 Ode	74

BEE (cont.)
  Who read what the Crepundia bee, ...   273   U84 Cradle   14
  Dare I prophane, so irreligious bee   283   U84 Muse   39
  Whether in Mars his field thou bee, ...   293   U86 Hor.4:1   39
  Will to bee, what thou art; and nothing more: .   .   .   295   U90 Mart.10:47   12
  And ever will, to utter termes that bee   309   Horace   84
  Of some small thankfull land: whether he bee   .   .   .   313   Horace   166
  Much in the Poeme shine, I will not bee   329   Horace   526
  F. shewes what he was, K. what he will bee.   .   .   .   375   Coryat 1   29
  To be his Bacchus as his Pallas: bee   378   Coryat 2   91
  And pray, thy joyes as lasting bee, as great.   .   .   .   384   Somerset   8
  Out-bee that Wife, in worth, thy freind did make: .   .   384   Somerset   12
  Mortality, till you immortall bee.   384   Somerset   22
  And, if thou list thy selfe, what thou canst bee.   .   .   386   Browne   4
  Will bee receiv'd in Court; If not, would I   .   .   .   389   Aleman   19
  It hath beene question'd, Michael, if I bee   .   .   .   396   Drayton   1
  In her! and what could perfect bee, ...   399   Lady Ogle   15
  What was proportion, or could bee   399   Lady Ogle   21
  Untill the dust retorned bee   400   Lady Ogle   31
  Though I confesse a Beaumonts Booke to bee   .   .   .   400   Beaumont   7
  Must Celia bee, the Anagram of Alice.   412   Sutcliffe   23
  or hir quarters lighter bee, ...   417   Moon   31
  Whoe worthie wine, whoe not, to bee wyse Pallas guests.   .   421   Ode:If Men   45
  before, I wryte more verse, to bee more wyse.   .   .   .   421   Censure   2
  yett, yf with eythers vyce, I tainted bee,   .   .   .   422   Censure   22
  But sometymes shall bee tempted to obaye   422   Censure   25
BEECH
  Beneath the broad beech, and the chest-nut shade;   .   .   93   F2 Penshurst   12
BEEING
  Beeing in feare to be robd, he most learnedly begs.   .   .   375   Coryat 1   35
BEEN (See also BIN)
  These, had'st thou been pleas'd either to dine, or sup,   .   206   U43 Vulcan   V 83
  For thou objectest (as thou hast been told)   .   .   .   408   Detractor   3
BEENE
  Thou wert, as chiefe of them are said t'have beene.   .   .   28   E4 James 1   6
  Davis, and Weever, and the best have beene,   .   .   .   32   E18 Censurer   4
  Madame, had all antiquitie beene lost, ...   67   E105 L Wroth 2   1
  Yet three fill'd Zodiackes had he beene   77   E120 S. P.   11
  I, and this Muse had beene, if thou hadst not   .   .   .   80   E127 Aubigny   7
  To have beene stiled of King Arthurs table.   .   .   .   84   E133 Voyage   24
  Had it beene seconded, and not in fume   87   E133 Voyage   109
  Cats there lay divers had beene flead, and rosted,   .   .   88   E133 Voyage   149
  Of the Penates had beene set on flame, ...   95   F2 Penshurst   79
  They are, and have beene taught religion: Thence   .   .   96   F2 Penshurst   93
  These have crimes accounted beene.   102   F5 Celia 1   18
  Where have I beene this while exil'd from thee?   .   .   122   F15 Heaven   13
  Beene sterne to mee, ...   129   U1 Father   8
  I thought that Fortitude had beene a meane   .   .   .   156   U13 Sacvile   105
  Men have beene great, but never good by chance,   .   .   156   U13 Sacvile   124
  Stand forth my Object, then, you that have beene   .   .   159   U14 Selden   29
  I That have beene a lover, and could shew it,   .   .   .   182   U28 Worth   1
  Perhaps, to have beene burned with my bookes.   .   .   .   203   U43 Vulcan   18
  Thou should'st have cry'd, and all beene proper stuffe.   .   205   U43 Vulcan   64
  To all as fatall as't hath beene to me,   .   .   .   211   U43 Vulcan   192
  To all as chargefull as they have beene to me,   .   .   211   U43 Vulcan   V192
  Before, I thinke my wish absolv'd had beene.   .   .   .   228   U53 Newcastle   14
  To mee; or beene the same to you; if show,   .   .   .   241   U69 Friend Son   2
  To shew thou hast beene long, ...   245   U70 Ode   58
  Her suffrings, as the body had beene away!   .   .   .   270   U81 Pawlet   51
  Beene trusted to thee: not to't selfe assign'd.   .   .   283   U84 Muse   20
  Of daring all, hath still beene given; we know it: .   .   305   Horace   12
  Of daring ought, hath still beene given; we know it: .   .   338   Horace   V 12
  New names of things. It hath beene ever free,   .   .   .   309   Horace   83
  These, the free meale might have beene well drawne out: .   331   Horace   560
  Hath all beene Harmony: 367   Ode Who saith   51
  . . . Which should Have beene Printed with the other . . .   379   Coryat 3   Ttl
  It hath beene question'd, Michael, if I bee   .   .   .   396   Drayton   1
  As it had beene the circle of the Arts!   396   Drayton   22
BEERE
  Are all but Luthers beere, to this I sing.   .   .   .   65   E101 Supper   34
  Where the same beere, and bread, and selfe-same wine,   .   95   F2 Penshurst   63
  In Sugar Candide, or in butter'd beere, ...   167   U15 Friend-Wars   153
BEES
  Any beliefe, in Madam Baud-bees bath, ...   188   U34 Small Poxe   10
BEEST
  Stay, view this stone: And, if thou beest not such,   .   .   371   Epitaph   1
BEFALL
  Wilt thou be, Muse, when this shall them befall?   .   .   263   U78 Digby   31
  Wilt thou be, Muse, when this shall then befall?   .   .   263   U78 Digby   V 31
BEFORE (See also 'FORE)
  Glad-mention'd Roe: thou art but gone before,   .   .   .   37   E33 Roe 3   2
  Like aydes 'gainst treasons who hath found before?   .   .   38   E35 James 2   7
  You laugh when you are touch'd, and long before   .   .   38   E38 Guiltie 2   3
  Before thou wert it, in each good mans heart.   .   .   .   49   E67 Suffolk   10
  Your noblest father prov'd: like whom, before,   .   .   .   53   E79 Rutland   2
  Out-stript, then they did all that went before: .   .   57   E89 Allen   10
  And gratulate the breach, I griev'd before: .   .   .   61   E95 Savile   10
  I' your selfe, all treasure lost of th'age before.   .   .   68   E105 L Wroth 2   20
  Before my thought, and (in thy right) commands   .   .   .   83   E132 Sylvester   8
  Before the fisher, or into his hand.   94   F2 Penshurst   38
  Gave killing strokes. There were brave men, before   .   .   114   F12 Rutland   53
  Before his swift and circled race be run,   .   .   .   116   F12 Rutland   99
  Before his swift and fetherd race be run,   .   .   .   116   F12 Rutland   V 99

```
                                                          Page     Title        Line
BEFORE  (cont.)
   Before the moones have fill'd their tripple trine,   .   .   .   119   F13 Aubigny      102
   Before my losse           .   .   .   .   .   .   .   130   U1 Father         29
   Before rude hands have touch'd it?    .   .   .   .   134   U2 Triumph        22
   Before the soyle hath smutch'd it?    .   .   .   .   134   U2 Triumph        24
   (By searching) what before was strange,   .   .   .   146   U6 Defence        15
   Before me here, the Friend and Sonne;    .   .   .   151   U12 Corbet         4
   Pernitious enemie; we see, before     .   .   .   .   158   U14 Selden        14
   Before men get a verse: much lesse a Praise;   .   .   159   U14 Selden        26
   As before.                .   .   .   .   184   U29 Fit of Rime   42
   Rather than meet him: And, before his eyes   .   .   185   U30 Burleigh      16
   Your honour now, then your disgrace before.   .   .   191   U38 Elegy 'Tis    30
   Before you prove a medicine, is unjust.   .   .   .   192   U38 Elegy 'Tis    50
   A cause before; or leave me one behind.   .   .   .   203   U43 Vulcan        28
   Such is thy All; that (as I sung before)   .   .   .   217   U46 Coke          21
   Before his braine doe know it;   .   .   .   .   .   221   U48 Bacchus        30
   Before, I thinke my wish absolv'd had beene.   .   .   228   U53 Newcastle     14
   Dreame thou could'st hurt it; but before thou wake   .   250   U73 Weston        11
   The Clowdes rack cleare before the Sun,   .   .   .   251   U74 Weston         8
   Some houres before it should, that these may know   .   257   U75 Epithalam.   146
   Me thought, Great Britaine in her Sea, before,   .   .   268   U80 Christning    13
   That, planted round, there sing before the Lamb,   .   285   U84 Muse          89
   Much more desir'd, and dearer then before,   .   .   285   U84 Muse         109
   In name, I went all names before,    .   .   .   .   293   U87 Hor.3:9        7
   Before the Judge, it hangs, and waites report.   .   309   Horace           112
   Her Sonnes before the people; nor the ill-/Natur'd   317   Horace           264
   That may judge for his six-pence) had, before   .   .   371   Fletcher           7
   For Grapes he had gather'd before they were eaten.   375   Coryat 1          25
   For grapes he had gather'd, before they were eaten.   380   Coryat 3          36
   That went before, a Husband.  Shee, Ile sweare,   .   386   Husband            9
   Who hadst before wrought in rich Homers Mine?   .   388   Chapman            3
   And I had stil'd thee, Orpheus, but before   .   .   397   Drayton           37
   Before this worke? where Envy hath not cast   .   .   401   Beaumont          13
   And not fall downe before it? and confess   .   .   406   Inigo Jones 1     91
   A Grace by Ben: Johnson. extempore. before King James.   418   Grace            Ttl
   before, I wryte more verse, to bee more wyse.   .   .   421   Censure            2
BEG
   Doe beg thy care unto thy after-state.   .   .   .    43   E51 James 3        8
   Nor will I beg of thee, Lord of the vine,   .   .   .   107   F10 Proludium     10
   Nor will we beg of thee, Lord of the vine,   .   .   107   F10 Proludium   V 10
   I long, and should not beg in vaine,   .   .   .   .   139   U2 Another         2
   Or beg thy Greedie flame, thus to devoure   .   .   202   U43 Vulcan       V  3
BEGAN
   And, in a pittious tune, began.  How dare   .   .    88   E133 Voyage      164
   As I began to wish my selfe a horse.    .   .   .   228   U53 Newcastle     12
   When we were all borne, we began to die;   .   .   271   U81 Pawlet        94
BEGANN
   Mr Surveyor, you that first begann    .   .   .   .   402   Inigo Jones 1      1
BEGAN'ST
   From whose prowde bosome, thou began'st thy flight.   .   368   Ode Who saith     80
BEGAT
   It was a knowledge, that begat that love.   .   .   .    55   E86 Goodyere 2     8
BEG'D
   Beg'd Ridwayes pardon: Duncote, now, doth crye;   .    29   E8 Robbery         4
BEGET
   Made thee beget that cruell Stratagem,   .   .   .   208   U43 Vulcan       130
   Who from the Divels-Arse did Guns beget;   .   .   .   212   U43 Vulcan       202
   That from the Divels-Arse did Guns beget;   .   .   .   212   U43 Vulcan      V202
   Who with the Divell did Ordinance beget;   .   .   .   212   U43 Vulcan      V202
BEGETTING
   Of his begetting.  And so sweares his Jone.   .   .    40   E42 Giles         14
BEGG'D
   His unjust hopes, with praises begg'd, or (worse)   .   162   U15 Friend-Wars   12
   What transcripts begg'd? how cry'd up, and how glad,   263   U78 Digby         30
BEGGING
   7. Begging another, on colour of mending the former.   139   U2 Another       Ttl
BEGIN   (See also BEGYN)
   Then to begin, my Roe: He makes a state   .   .   .    50   E70 Wm Roe 1       2
   I now begin to doubt, if ever Grace,   .   .   .   .   207   U43 Vulcan       107
   Nor so begin, as did that Circler late,   .   .   .   313   Horace           195
   Yet, looking in thy face, they shall begin   .   .   369   Ode Who saith     93
   I, therefore will begin.  Soule of the Age!   .   .   391   Shakespeare       17
   I Could begin with that grave forme, Here lies,   .   394   Jane Ogle          1
   And the world in it, I begin to doubt,   .   .   .   395   May                4
   And, though I now begin, 'tis not to rub   .   .   .   396   Drayton            7
   To Crowne the years, which you begin, great king,   .   416   Welcome            7
BEGINNERS
   Quickly fir'd, as in beginners   .   .   .   .   .   141   U2 Her man        31
BEGINNING
   That ever had beginning there, to'ave end!   .   .   271   U81 Pawlet        91
   Can this decay, but is beginning ever.   .   .   .   294   U88 Petronius     10
BEGINNINGS
   As the beginnings here, prove purely sweet,   .   .    81   E128 Wm Roe 2      7
   And noted the beginnings and decayes!   .   .   .   160   U14 Selden        46
   Such, Coke, were thy beginnings, when thy good   .   217   U46 Coke           5
   What the beginnings of all beauties be;   .   .   .   271   U81 Pawlet        74
   In grave beginnings, and great things profest,   .   305   Horace            17
BEGINNS
   Soe ended your Epistle, myne beginns   .   .   .   .   421   Censure            3
BEGINS
   Takes private beatings, and begins againe.   .   .    49   E68 Playwrt 2      2
   Of Diomede; nor Troyes sad Warre begins   .   .   .   315   Horace           209
```

BEGIN'ST
   And still begin'st the greeting: .   .   .   .   .   221 U48 Bacchus   16
BEGOT
   Lent timely succours, and new life begot: .   .   .   .   80 E127 Aubigny   8
   And so some goodlier monster had begot: .   .   .   204 U43 Vulcan   32
   Freedome, and Truth; with love from those begot: .   241 U69 Friend Son   5
   What nourisheth, what formed, what begot   .   .   .   325 Horace   437
BEGOTTEN
   Begotten by that wind, and showers.   .   .   .   280 U84 Mind   68
BEGS
   Beeing in feare to be robd, he most learnedly begs.   .   .   375 Coryat 1   35
BEGUILE
   Or his easier eares beguile, ...   102 F5 Celia 1   13
   Or hir easier eares beguile, ...   102 F5 Celia 1   V 13
BEGUIL'D
   Are with the likeness of the truth beguil'd: .   .   339 Horace   V 35/ 34
BEGUILES
   Outward Grace weake love beguiles: .   .   .   137 U2 Cupid   51
BEGUN
   Thou hast begun well, Roe, which stand well too,   .   .   63 E98 Th Roe 1   1
   In dreames, begun in hope, and end in spoile.   .   .   162 U15 Friend-Wars   10
   Is fayre got up, and day some houres begun!   .   .   396 Drayton   18
BEGUNNE
   When well begunne: .   .   .   .   .   .   121 F14 Sydney   46
BEGYN
   if it begyn religious thoughts to cherish;   .   .   422 Lucan   10
BEHALFE
   . . . in the Behalfe of the two Noble Brothers sir Robert . .   382 Rich   Ttl
BEHELD
   I Beheld her, on a day, ...   132 U2 How he saw   1
   Which when she beheld to bleed,   .   .   .   133 U2 Suffered   17
   Of your Peeres, you were beheld,   .   .   .   138 U2 Kisse   23
   That you have seene the pride, beheld the sport,   .   234 U61 Epigram   1
   In him all vertue is beheld in State: .   .   262 U78 Digby   6
   In him all action is beheld in State: .   .   262 U78 Digby   V 6
BEHIND
   And cast my love behind: .   .   .   .   149 U9 Picture   5
   And cast my suite behind: .   .   .   .   149 U9 Picture   V 5
   A cause before; or leave me one behind.   .   .   203 U43 Vulcan   28
   And more is behind: .   .   .   .   231 U57 Burges   13
   There is a Feast behind, ...   257 U75 Epithalam. 141
   In rest, like spirits left behind   .   .   .   280 U84 Mind   66
   Him that is last, I scorne to come behind,   .   .   333 Horace   595
   Him that is last, I scorne to be behind,   .   .   353 Horace   V595
BEHOLD
   Who can behold all envie so declin'd   .   .   .   47 E63 Salisbury 2   7
   Whil'st I behold thee live with purest hands;   .   .   51 E74 Chancelor   3
   Then doe I love thee, and behold thy ends   .   .   55 E86 Goodyere 2   3
   Or did our times require it, to behold   .   .   .   67 E104 Montgomery   3
   Behold! the reverend shade of Bartas stands   .   .   83 E132 Sylvester   7
   Behold where Cerberus, rear'd on the wall   .   .   89 E133 Voyage   176
   For thy acceptance. O, behold me right,   .   .   127 U1 Trinitie   13
   Who can behold their Manners, and not clowd-/Like   .   164 U15 Friend-Wars   60
   Behold the royall Mary, ...   240 U67 Muses   25
   Till you behold a race to fill your Hall,   .   .   258 U75 Epithalam. 169
   Next, that which rapt mee, was: I might behold   .   361 Ode Who saith   13
   Behold, where one doth swim;   .   .   .   366 Ode Who saith   3
   When you behold me wish my selfe, the man   .   .   389 Aleman   23
BEHOLDEN
   Beholden, to this master of the warre;   .   .   .   72 E111 Edmonds 2   V 4
BEHOLDER
   And the beholder to himselfe doth render.   .   .   317 Horace   259
BEHOLDERS
   To be beholders, when their powers are spent.   .   .   166 U15 Friend-Wars 140
BEHOLDING
   Beholding, to this master of the warre;   .   .   .   72 E111 Edmonds 2   4
   Beholding one in three, and three in one,   .   .   128 U1 Trinitie   33
BEHOLDS
   When he beholds a graft of his owne hand,   .   .   251 U74 Weston   27
   Beholds her Maker! and, in him, doth see   .   .   271 U81 Pawlet   73
   Or in the bending Vale beholds a-farre   .   .   290 U85 Country   13
   Or in the bending Vale beholds from far   .   .   290 U85 Country   V 13
BEHOULD
   made prospective, behould hym, hee must passe   .   .   383 Rich   12
BEING
   Yet, all heavens gifts, being heavens due,   .   .   33 E22 Daughter   3
   For the great marke of vertue, those being gone   .   60 E93 Radcliffe   2
   And, being nam'd, how little doth that name   .   .   66 E103 L Wroth 1   5
   Being no vitious person, but the vice   .   .   .   74 E115 Honest Man   5
   But, being so much too good for earth,   .   .   .   77 E120 S. P.   23
   And would (being ask'd the truth) ashamed say,   .   83 E131 Ferrab. 2   11
   Being, beyond sea, burned for one witch: .   .   88 E133 Voyage   158
   By being organes to great sinne,   .   .   .   99 F3 Wroth   86
   but being well assured that there   .   .   .   106 F9 Celia 3   V 11
   Who, being at sea, suppose,   .   .   .   111 F11 Epode   70
   That, being at sea, suppose,   .   .   .   111 F11 Epode   V 70
   Unto himselfe, by being so deare to you.   .   .   119 F13 Aubigny 117
   Dwell, dwell here still: O, being every-where,   .   122 F15 Heaven   15
   Farre I was from being stupid,   .   .   .   132 U2 How he saw   5
   And was worthy (being so seene)   .   .   .   138 U2 Kisse   27
   Lest shame destroy their being.   .   .   .   144 U4 Song   4
   From being forsaken, then doth worth: .   .   146 U6 Defence   22
   If it were cleare, but being so in cloud   .   .   155 U13 Sacvile   87

	Page	Title	Line
BEING (cont.)			
But few and faire Divisions: but being got	157	U13 Sacvile	151
Since, being deceiv'd, I turne a sharper eye	159	U14 Selden	23
And being a thing, blowne out of nought, rebells	163	U15 Friend-Wars	32
But being in Motion still (or rather in race)	166	U15 Friend-Wars	124
I could forgive her being proud! a whore!	172	U20 Shrub	21
And not being borrow'd by thee, but possest.	187	U33 Councellour	28
And have their being, their waste to see;	189	U36 Song	11
And which you (being the worthier) gave me leave	190	U37 Friend-Book	11
And lesse they know, who being free to use	190	U37 Friend-Book	22
I number these as being of the Chore	193	U38 Elegy 'Tis	99
Being, the best clothes still to praeoccupie.	201	U42 Elegy Let	42
O no, cry'd all, Fortune, for being a whore,	209	U43 Vulcan	153
When, being the Strangers helpe, the poore mans aide,	217	U46 Coke	7
And you may justly, being a tardie, cold,	230	U56 Covell	7
Valour! to sleight it, being done to you!	233	U59 Newcastle	16
Being sent to one, they will be read of all.	263	U78 Digby	32
Their names of being kept alive,	273	U84 Cradle	6
. . . gave me leave to call her so. Being Her . . .	282	U84 Muse	Ttl
This being thus: why should my tongue, or pen	284	U84 Muse	69
(As being Redeemer, and Repairer too	288	U84 Muse	213
As being the Sonne of Man) to shew his Power,	288	U84 Muse	217
Being over-safe, and fearing of the flaw:	339	Horace V 41/ 39	
And give, being taken modestly, this leave,	309	Horace	73
Being taught a better way. All mortall deeds	309	Horace	98
For, being a Poet, thou maist feigne, create,	313	Horace	189
What he despaires, being handled, might not show.	315	Horace	214
Th'unbearded Youth, his Guardian once being gone,	315	Horace	229
They might with ease be numbred, being a few	319	Horace	293
Having well eat, and drunke (the rites being done)	319	Horace	325
With specious places, and being humour'd right,	327	Horace	457
Being men were covetous of nought, but praise.	327	Horace	463
Why not? being honest, and free-borne, doth hate	352	Horace V547/571	
which thoughts being circumvolvd in gyerlyk mocion	361	Palmer	23
Which being eyed directly, I divine,	362	Author	13
Being tould there, Reason cannot, Sense may erre.	370	Author	14
And being at Flushing enforced to feele	380	Coryat 3	54
Which he not denies. Now being so free,	381	Coryat 3	57
Of being Daughter, Mother, Spouse of God!	414	Ghyrlond	56
And lesse they knowe, that being free to use	422	Censure	15
BELCH'D			
Belch'd forth an ayre, as hot, as at the muster	85	E133 Voyage	63
BELCHETH			
The while he belcheth loftie Verses out,	335	Horace	649
BELEEVE			
Pr'y thee beleeve still, and not judge so fast,	32	E18 Censurer	9
Beleeve it, Guiltie, if you loose your shame,	38	E38 Guiltie 2	7
Would you beleeve, when you this Mounsieur see,	56	E88 Monsieur	1
I should beleeve, the soule of Tacitus	61	E95 Savile	3
And I must now beleeve him: for, to day,	64	E100 Playwrt 3	3
I Must beleeve some miracles still bee,	73	E114 Sydney	1
Could you beleeve, that this,	148	U8 Houre-glasse	4
That, henceforth, I beleeve nor bookes, nor men,	187	U33 Councellour	5
We will beleeve, like men of our owne Ranke,	215	U44 Speach	75
What so is showne, I not beleeve, and hate.	317	Horace	269
But who will beleeve this, that chanceth to looke	379	Coryat 3	17
BELEEV'D			
If but to be beleev'd you have the hap,	69	E107 Hungry	17
But, as 'tis rumor'd, so beleev'd:	101	F4 To the World	50
BELEEVED			
The faithfull mans beleeved Mysterie,	127	U1 Trinitie	3
BELEEVES			
Because Democritus beleeves a wit	325	Horace	419
BELGIA			
That selfe-divided Belgia did afford;	37	E32 Roe 2	3
BELGICK			
The Belgick fever ravished away.	60	E93 Radcliffe	8
BELGICUS			
And the Gazetti, or Gallo-Belgicus:	59	E92 New Crie	16
BELIE (See also BELYE)			
As if they would belie their stature; those	157	U13 Sacvile	146
Farre from the Nest, and so himselfe belie	198	U40 Elegy That	38
BELIEFE			
Any beliefe, in Madam Baud-bees bath,	188	U34 Small Poxe	10
BELIEVE			
Due to that one, that doth believe him just.	198	U40 Elegy That	40
BELIKE			
Or the States Ships sent forth belike to meet	219	U47 Tribe	33
BELL			
Or in the Bell-Mans Lanthorne, like a spie,	211	U43 Vulcan	187
BELLIE			
Laden with Bellie, and doth hardly approach	230	U56 Covell	9
BELL-MANS			
Or in the Bell-Mans Lanthorne, like a spie,	211	U43 Vulcan	187
BELLS			
Cannot the Plague-bill keepe you backe? nor bells	88	E133 Voyage	173
The Poetrie of Steeples, with the Bells,	249	U72 King	10
The Poetrie of Steeples, with their Bells,	249	U72 King	V 10
Harke how the Bells upon the waters play	253	U75 Epithalam.	33
BELLY			
In a great belly. Write, then on thy wombe,	46	E62 Would-bee	11
Thy wit lives by it, Proule, and belly too.	54	E81 Proule	6
Thus, in his belly, can he change a sin,	76	E118 Gut	5

BELLY (cont.)
  My mountaine belly, and my rockie face,   .   .   .   150   U9 Picture   17
  To gaine upon his belly; and at last   162   U15 Friend-Wars   17
  Could not goe downe my belly then   291   U85 Country   54
BELONG   (See LONGS)
BELOV'D
  To my truly-belov'd Freind, Mr Browne: on his Pastorals.   .   .   386   Browne   Ttl
BELOV'D
  And be belov'd, while the Whores last. O times,   .   .   .   167   U15 Friend-Wars   161
  How much they are belov'd of God, in thee;   .   .   .   268   U80 Christning   4
BELOVED
  To the memory of my beloved, the Author   390   Shakespeare   Ttl
BELOW
  He knowes, below, he shall finde plentie of meate,   .   .   .   95   F2 Penshurst   70
  And exercise below, ...   144   U3 Musicall   18
  Wee exercise below, ...   144   U3 Musicall   V 18
BELYE
  With which a learned Madame you belye.   51   E73 Fine Grand   11
B'EMBRAC'D
  But there are lines, wherewith I might b'embrac'd.   .   .   .   226   U52 Answer   3
BE'N
  Or stands to be'n Commission o' the blade?   155   U13 Sacvile   64
BEN
  Ben. Jonson his best piece of poetrie.   41   E45 First Son   10
  Of your Trouble, Ben, to ease me, ...   140   U2 Her man   1
  Ben: Jonson To His Honord Friend Mr John Selden Health.   .   158   U14 Selden   VTtl
  Ben: Jonson upon the burning of his study and bookes   .   .   202   U43 Vulcan   VTtl
  . . . to be Sealed of the Tribe of Ben.   .   .   .   218   U47 Tribe   Ttl
  Sir, you are Sealed of the Tribe of Ben.   .   .   .   220   U47 Tribe   78
  Tell him his Ben   231   U57 Burges   7
  And there he lives with memorie; and Ben   .   .   .   246   U70 Ode   84
  The Humble Petition of Poore Ben.   259   U76 Petition   Ttl
  The Vision Of Ben. Jonson, On The   396   Drayton   Ttl
  All in the Worke! And soe shall still for Ben: .   .   404   Inigo Jones 1   65
  This was Mr Ben: Johnsons Answer of the suddayne.   .   .   418   Answer   Ttl
  Il may Ben Johnson slander so his feete,   .   .   .   418   Answer   5
  A Grace by Ben: Johnson. extempore. before King James.   .   418   Grace   Ttl
BENCH
  The wise, and many-headed Bench, that sits   .   .   .   370   Fletcher   1
BEND
  Where's thy Quiver? bend thy Bow: 132   U2 How he saw   9
  To bend, to breake, provoke, or suffer it!   .   .   .   233   U59 Newcastle   18
  To bend, or breake, provoke, or suffer it!   .   .   .   233   U59 Newcastle   V 18
  To bend a man, now at his fiftieth yeare   .   .   .   292   U86 Hor.4:1   6
  Be wonne a friend; it must both sway, and bend   .   .   317   Horace   281
  "Where neither Force can bend, nor Feare can awe.   .   .   367   Ode Who saith   48
BENDING
  Or in the bending Vale beholds a-farre   290   U85 Country   13
  Or in the bending Vale beholds from far   .   .   .   290   U85 Country   V 13
BENDS
  The lower land, that to the river bends   94   F2 Penshurst   22
  By that faire Stand, your forehead, whence he bends   .   .   170   U19 Elegy By   3
  It bends the hams of Gossip Vigilance, ...   363   Riches   11
BENE
  It should rather have bene Tom that a horse did lack.   .   374   Coryat 1   15
BENEATH
  And farre beneath least pause of such a king,   .   .   .   43   E51 James 3   4
  Beneath the broad beech, and the chest-nut shade;   .   .   93   F2 Penshurst   12
  Sinke not beneath these terrors: 177   U25 Desmond   30
  Then now beneath some ancient Oke he may,   .   .   .   290   U85 Country   23
  Beneath a Sweet-wood Roofe, neere Alba Lake: .   .   .   292   U86 Hor.4:1   20
BENEFIT
  A Benefit; or that doth throw't away: 154   U13 Sacvile   42
BENEFITS
  To thanke thy benefits: which is, to pay.   .   .   .   80   E127 Aubigny   12
  For benefits are ow'd with the same mind   .   .   .   153   U13 Sacvile   5
  They are the Noblest benefits, and sinke   .   .   .   153   U13 Sacvile   19
BENJAMIN
  To Benjamin Rudyerd.   78   E121 Rudyerd 1   Ttl
BENT
  As minds ill bent   129   U1 Father   13
  Both her Browes, bent like my Bow.   136   U2 Cupid   17
  Eye-brows bent like Cupids bow, ...   141   U2 Her man   17
BEQUEATH
  Rich, as nature could bequeath thee: 39   E40 Ratcliffe   3
BEREAVES
  What fate is mine, that so it selfe bereaves?   .   .   .   44   E55 Beaumont   7
BERENICES
  Who made a lampe of Berenices hayre?   115   F12 Rutland   61
BERGAMO
  And lay in straw with the horses at Bergamo,   .   .   .   380   Coryat 3   38
BERGHEN
  The Berghen siege, and taking in Breda, ...   214   U44 Speach   40
BERINGHAMS
  Your Arch-Dukes Agents, and your Beringhams,   .   .   .   69   E107 Hungry   23
BERMUDAS
  Ha' their Bermudas, and their streights i'th' Strand: .   155   U13 Sacvile   82
BERRIES
  Ere cherries ripe, and straw-berries be gone,   .   .   .   58   E92 New Crie   1
BERWICKE
  Or him that backward went to Berwicke, òr which   .   .   85   E133 Voyage   35
BESETT
  besett with statues, shall I reare your head,   .   .   .   115   F12 Rutland   V 84

	Page	Title	Line
BESHITE			
Row close then, slaves. Alas, they will beshite us.	86	E133 Voyage	90
BESIDE (See also BESYDE)			
Where all is faire, beside thy pedigree.	70	E109 Nevil	4
Wherein was oyle, beside the succour spent,	207	U43 Vulcan	99
With all the pompe of Youth, and all our Court beside.	254	U75 Epithalam.	72
All else we see beside, are Shadowes, and goe lesse.	255	U75 Epithalam.	88
Beside, your hand will never hit,	277	U84 Mind	7
BESIDES			
And then of times (besides the bare Conduct	160	U14 Selden	51
Wherin (besides the noble aydes were lent,	207	U43 Vulcan	V 99
Wherin (besides the noble Aydes were spent,	207	U43 Vulcan	V 99
Wherin (besides the noble aydes were sent,	207	U43 Vulcan	V 99
Besides the other Swannes admiring him,	366	Ode Who saith	5
Require (besides the likenesse of the thing)	370	Author	2
Besides he tried Ship, Cart, Waggon, and Chayre,	380	Coryat 3	27
As shall besides delyght	420	Ode:If Men	33
BESIEG'D			
And one true posture, though besieg'd with ill	66	E102 Pembroke	14
BESIEGED			
A Bed-rid Wit, then a besieged Towne.	248	U71 Treasurer	15
BESPOKE			
To which thou'rt not a weeke, bespoke a guest;	81	E129 Mime	6
BESPRENT			
What gentle Ghost, besprent with April deaw,	268	U81 Pawlet	1
What goodly Ghost, besprent with April deaw,	268	U81 Pawlet	V 1
BESS			
Thy Wives pox on thee, and Bess Broughtons too.	212	U43 Vulcan	V216
BESSE			
The Paltzgrave, and the Lady Besse,	418	Grace	2
BE'ST			
If thou be'st wise, with 'Syrian Oyle let shine	294	U89 Mart.8:77	3
BEST			
How, best of Kings, do'st thou a scepter beare!	28	E4 James 1	1
How, best of Poets, do'st thou laurell weare!	28	E4 James 1	2
Whom should my Muse then flie to, but the best	28	E4 James 1	9
Davis, and Weever, and the best have beene,	32	E18 Censurer	4
To it, thy language, letters, arts, best life,	34	E23 Donne 1	7
Ben. Jonson his best piece of poetrie.	41	E45 First Son	10
Love honors, which of best example bee,	49	E66 Cary	13
Each best day of our life escapes us, first.	50	E70 Wm Roe 1	6
And best become the valiant man to weare,	58	E91 Vere	17
Be of the best: and 'mongst those, best are you.	61	E94 Bedford 3	14
As thou hast best authoritie, t'allow.	62	E96 Donne 2	6
All gentrie, yet, owe part of their best flame!	75	E116 Jephson	2
In men, but every bravest was the best:	75	E116 Jephson	10
Till thou canst finde the best, choose the least ill.	76	E119 Shelton	10
Of the best writer, and judge, should emulate.	78	E123 Rudyerd 3	4
T'extract, and choose the best of all these knowne,	80	E128 Wm Roe 2	3
Canst tell me best, how every Furie lookes there,	85	E133 Voyage	52
Ladies? and of them the best?	104	F8 Sicknesse	2
None but them, and leave the best.	106	F8 Sicknesse	V 48
All her best symmetrie in that one feature!	112	F11 Epode	101
My best of wishes, may you beare a sonne.	116	F12 Rutland	100
And he, with his best Genius left alone.	120	F14 Sydney	20
Is my best part:	129	U1 Father	3
Of her good, who is the best	137	U2 Cupid	44
O sing not you then, lest the best	144	U3 Musicall	21
Sing you no more then, lest the best	144	U3 Musicall	V 21
Truth, and the Graces best, when naked are.	158	U14 Selden	4
Since, naked, best Truth, and the Graces are.	158	U14 Selden	v 4
That scratching now's our best Felicitie?	166	U15 Friend-Wars	144
And I will bring a Crop, if not the best,	169	U17 Friend-Debt	18
And then the best are, still, the blindest friends!	170	U18 Elegy Can	14
O then (my best-best lov'd) let me importune,	180	U25 Desmond	63
O then (our best-best lov'd) let me importune,	180	U25 Desmond	V 63
Yet sure my tunes will be the best,	182	U27 Ode Helen	35
Both braines and hearts; and mine now best doe know it:	182	U28 Worth	8
Of Argument, still drawing forth the best,	187	U33 Councellour	27
For Love in shadow best is made.	189	U36 Song	2
They looke at best like Creame-bowles, and you soone	198	U40 Elegy That	29
Being, the best clothes still to praeoccupie.	201	U42 Elegy Let	42
When thou wert borne, and that thou look'st at best,	208	U43 Vulcan	113
When thou wert borne, and when thou look'st at best,	208	U43 Vulcan	V113
In others-evill best was understood:	217	U46 Coke	6
Equall with that, which for the best newes goes,	222	U49 Pucell	9
And thinke all still the best, that he will doe.	236	U63 Charles 2	10
When look'd the yeare, at best,	253	U75 Epithalam.	13
And looking with thy best Inquirie, tell,	254	U75 Epithalam.	74
To Th'Best Of Monarchs, Masters, Men, King Charles	259	U76 Petition	2
We sing the best of Monarchs, Masters, Men;	263	U79 New-yeares	7
Best Kings expect first-fruits of your glad gaines.	263	U79 New-yeares	13
Of Pan wee sing, the best of Hunters, Pan,	264	U79 New-yeares	20
And were shee lost, could best supply her place,	264	U79 New-yeares	34
In truth of colours, both are best.	265	U79 New-yeares	45
And best he knew her noble Character,	287	U84 Muse	155
Of lapsed Nature) best know what to doe,	288	U84 Muse	214
What number best can fit, Homer declares.	309	Horace	106
And so their prating to present was best,	321	Horace	329
And so their pratling to present were best,	346	Horace	V321/329
Which the Socratick writings best can show:	325	Horace	442
What height of love, a Parent will fit best,	325	Horace	447
And that, say Philosophers, is the best modell.	379	Coryat 3	5

BEST (cont.)
Which, when it sounds at best, but eccho's right; . . . 390 Shakespeare 8
The best of Woemen! her whole life . . . . . 399 Lady Ogle 11
BEST-BEST
O then (my best-best lov'd) let me importune, . . . 180 U25 Desmond 63
O then (our best-best lov'd) let me importune, . . . 180 U25 Desmond V 63
BESTOWES
How onely shee bestowes . . . . 112 F11 Epode 104
BESTOWING
Till time, strong by her bestowing, ... 39 E40 Ratcliffe 11
BESTRYDE
He some Colossus to bestryde the Seas, ... 407 Inigo Jones 2 13
BESYDE
Of any Art, besyde what he calls his! . . . . 404 Inigo Jones 1 58
BESYDES
Besydes, his Man may merit it, and be . . . . 406 Inigo Jones 2 5
BET
Cryes out 'gainst cocking, since he cannot bet, . . 76 E119 Shelton 3
BETIDE (See BETYDE)
BETRAY
'Twere madnesse in thee, to betray thy fame, . . . 36 E30 Guiltie 3
Would both thy folly, and thy spite betray. . . . 43 E52 Courtling 6
Could conquer thee, but chance, who did betray. . . 49 E66 Cary 10
Never did bottom more betray her burden; . . . 87 E133 Voyage 116
Officiously, at first, themselves betray. . . . 94 F2 Penshurst 36
Thou did'st abuse, and then betray; . . . . 101 F4 To the World 42
All your bounties will betray. . . . . . 103 F6 Celia 2 4
Mine owne enough betray me. . . . . . 145 U4 Song 12
Her furie, yet no friendship to betray. . . . 190 U37 Friend-Book 33
Doth, while he keepes his watch, betray his stand. . 198 U40 Elegy That 36
Betray it true: . . . . 366 Ode Who saith 6
BETRAYE
hir Furye, though noe Frindshipp hee betraye. . . 422 Censure 26
BETRAY'D
That hast betray'd me to a worthlesse lord; . . . 48 E65 Muse 2
Where every freedome is betray'd, ... 101 F4 To the World 51
BETRAYES
Not his poore cocatrice but he betrayes . . . . 31 E12 Shift 21
BETTER
When was there contract better driven by Fate? . . 28 E5 Union 1
Many of thine this better could, then I, . . . 31 E14 Camden 13
Take better ornaments, my teares, and verse. . . 35 E27 Roe 1 2
I know no couple better can agree! . . . . 40 E42 Giles 18
For writing better, I must envie thee. . . . 44 E55 Beaumont 10
Almost all wayes, to any better course. . . . 48 E65 Muse 10
That still th'art present to the better cause; . . 52 E74 Chancelor 5
As he would burne, or better farre his booke. . . 53 E79 Rutland 12
Or, better worke! were thy glad countrey blest, . . 61 E95 Savile 14
Mark'd by thy hand, and with the better stone, . . 62 E96 Donne 2 8
An olive, capers, or some better sallade . . . 64 E101 Supper 10
Livie, or of some better booke to us, . . . 65 E101 Supper 22
To morrow vice, if shee give better pay: . . . 66 E102 Pembroke 10
And to live great, was better, then great borne. . . 75 E116 Jephson 12
Treading a better path, not contrary; . . . 76 E119 Shelton 12
Whose better studies while shee emulates, . . . 78 E121 Rudyerd 1 3
Thou joy'st in better markes, of soyle, of ayre, . . 93 F2 Penshurst 7
The better cheeses, bring 'hem; or else send . . 95 F2 Penshurst 53
Nor com'st to view the better cloth of state; . . 96 F3 Wroth 7
'Tis better, if he there can dwell. . . . . 99 F3 Wroth 94
'Tis better, if he then can dwell. . . . . 99 F3 Wroth V 94
Were yet unfound, and better plac'd in earth, . . 114 F12 Rutland 25
Were yet unfound, and better plac'd on earth, . . 114 F12 Rutland V 25
Who, though shee have a better verser got, . . . 115 F12 Rutland 68
Wherewith, then, Madame, can you better pay . . . 118 F13 Aubigny 53
Better fits him, then his face; . . . . . 140 U2 Promise 20
For what is better, or to make . . . . . 146 U6 Defence 14
Well, let it goe. Yet this is better, then . . . 166 U15 Friend-Wars 145
That would their better objects find: . . . 173 U22 Elegy Tho 27
A better lover, and much better Poet. . . . 182 U28 Worth 4
How much you are the better part of me; . . . 194 U38 Elegy 'Tis 110
For they were burnt, but to be better built. . . 210 U43 Vulcan 166
Only your time you better entertaine, . . . 224 U50 Countesse 23
For your securitie. I can no better. . . . 229 U54 Squib 20
'T were better spare a Butt, then spill his Muse. . 241 U68 House-hold 12
In bulke, doth make man better bee; . . . . 245 U70 Ode 66
(Bearing the promise of some better fate) . . . 252 U75 Epithalam. 10
To better Pastures then great Pales can: . . . 264 U79 New-yeares 30
The better grasse, and flowers are found. . . . 265 U79 New-yeares 59
Now I have better thought thereon, ... 277 U84 Mind 2
Better be dumbe, then superstitious! . . . . 284 U84 Muse 73
Being taught a better way. All mortall deeds . . 309 Horace 98
And thou maist better bring a Rhapsody . . . 313 Horace 184
A scorned Mouse! O, how much better this, . . . 315 Horace 199
A trifling Mouse! O, how much better this, . . . 343 Horace V199
Out better Poems? But I cannot buy . . . . 325 Horace 431
And better stayes them there, then all fine noise . 327 Horace 459
For hee'll cry, Good, brave, better, excellent! . . 333 Horace 611
If you denied, you had no better straine, . . . 333 Horace 625
With the same looke, or with a better, shine. . . 384 Somerset 10
A better cause, and strike the bravest Meate . . 397 Drayton 56
And better Blason them, then all their Coates, . . 419 Ode:If Men 8
To make these good, and what comes after, better. . 666 Glover 10

65

BETTER'D
   Better'd thy trust to letters; that thy skill; . . . . 63 E99 Th Roe 2   2
   His better'd mind seeks wealth, and friendship: than . . . 315 Horace   238
BETTRING
   To bettring of the mind of man, in ought, ... 331 Horace   562
BETWEEN   (See alsc 'TWEENE)
   Heard the soft ayres, between our Swaynes & thee, . . . 397 Drayton   26
   Is so implexed, and laid in, between, ... 412 Ghyrlond   7
BETWEENE
   Betweene two walls; where, on one side, to scar men, . . 86 E133 Voyage   67
   The well-greas'd wherry now had got betweene, . . . 87 E133 Voyage   114
   Runs betweene man, and man; 'tweene dame, and dame; . . 113 F12 Rutland   16
   And betweene each rising breast, ... 137 U2 Cupid   33
   That flie my thoughts betweene, ... 149 U9 Picture   12
   Betweene thy Tropicks, to arrest thy sight, . . . 252 U75 Epithalam.   4
   Of Love betweene you, and your Lovely-head; . . . 257 U75 Epithalam.   164
   Discerne betweene a Statue, and a Man; . . . 261 U77 Treasurer   14
   Betweene the Acts, a quite cleane other thing . . . 317 Horace   278
   Betweene the doubtfull sway of Reason', and sense; . . 370 Author   12
   Those ambling visits, passe in verse, betweene . . . 396 Drayton   4
BETWIXT   (See also 'TWIXT)
   Of Body and Spirit together, plac'd betwixt . . . 284 U84 Muse   54
BETY'DE
   Or if any strife bety'de . . . . 417 Moon   33
BEVER
   Have you felt the wooll o' the Bever? . . . . 135 U2 Triumph   25
BEVIS
   From Guy, or Bevis, Arthur, or from whom . . . 215 U44 Speach   81
   Of bold Sir Bevis, and his Arundell: . . . . 228 U53 Newcastle   10
BEVY   (See BEAVIE)
BEWAILD
   Ino bewaild; Ixion false, forsworne; . . . . . 313 Horace   176
BEWAIL'D
   But bewail'd . . . . 183 U29 Fit of Rime   21
BEWARE
   But, let the Faunes, drawne from their Groves, beware, . 321 Horace   355
   But you, my Piso, carefully beware, ... 333 Horace   607
BEWARES
   Lookes after honours, and bewares to act . . . 315 Horace   239
BEYOND
   Being, beyond sea, burned for one witch: . . . 88 E133 Voyage   158
   But nought beyond. He thou hast given it to, . . . 161 U14 Selden   71
   Beyond your Fire-workes, had at Ephesus, . . . 211 U43 Vulcan   V194
BID
   But there are objects, bid him to be gone . . . 163 U15 Friend-Wars   28
   I'le bid thee looke no more, but flee, flee friend, . . 166 U15 Friend-Wars   129
   I'le therefore aske no more, but bid you love; . . 171 U19 Elegy By   15
   Since you must goe, and I must bid farewell, . . . 199 U41 Elegy Since   1
   In short; I bid, Let what thou work'st upon, . . 307 Horace   31
   And I still bid the learned Maker looke . . . 325 Horace   453
   Hee'd bid, blot all: and to the anvile bring . . 333 Horace   627
   They're darke, bid cleare this: all that's doubtfull wrote . 335 Horace   637
   They're dark, bid cleare 'hem; al that's doubtful wrote . 354 Horace   V637
   That bid, God give thee joy, and have no endes. . . 384 Somerset   6
   Chaucer, or Spenser, or bid Beaumont lye . . . 391 Shakespeare   20
BIDE
   But in a businesse, that will bide the Touch, . . 187 U33 Councellour   23
   By which yo'are planted, shew's your fruit shall bide. . 281 U84 Kenelme   19
BIDS
   When Nature bids us leave to live, 'tis late . . 50 E70 Wm Roe 1   1
   And hurt seeks Cure, the Surgeon bids take bread, . . 155 U13 Sacvile   68
   Beates brave, and loude in Europe, and bids come . . 162 U15 Friend-Wars   2
   Religiously here he bids, row from the stewes, . . 375 Coryat 1   20
BIG
   'Tis like light Canes, that first rise big and brave, . 157 U13 Sacvile   149
BILBO
   Maintain'd the trade at Bilbo, or else-where; . . 212 U43 Vulcan   199
   Maintain'd the trade of Bilbo, or else-where; . . 212 U43 Vulcan   V199
   An honest Bilbo-Smith would make good blades, . . 410 Brome   15
BILBO-SMITH
   An honest Bilbo-Smith would make good blades, . . 410 Brome   15
BILL
   A purging bill, now fix'd upon the dore, . . . 29 E7 Hot-house   2
   Lookes o're the bill, likes it: and say's, god payes. . 30 E12 Shift   10
   Cannot the Plague-bill keepe you backe? nor bells . 88 E133 Voyage   173
BILLIARD
   Smooth as is the Billiard Ball: . . . . . 141 U2 Her man   20
BILLOW
   Should he heare of billo . wind, and storme, . . 214 U44 Speach   63
BILLS
   And there made Swords, Bills, Glaves, and Armes your fill; . 212 U43 Vulcan   198
BILS
   Or Bils, and there he buyes the names of books. . . 59 E92 New Crie   24
B'IMPUTED
   B'imputed right to an inheritance . . . . 286 U84 Muse   144
BIN
   Had bin fitt meate for Vulcan to lick up. . . . 206 U43 Vulcan   V 84
   And raz'd, e're thought could urge, This might have bin! . 209 U43 Vulcan   136
   What a strong Fort old Pimblicoe had bin! . . . 213 U44 Speach   21
   Health, or scarce breath, as she had never bin, . . 248 U71 Treasurer   12
   Nor had our Italie more glorious bin . . . . 325 Horace   411
   That knew the Crafts they had bin bred in, right: . . 410 Brome   14

	Page	Title	Line
BIND			
Are nothing till that comes to bind and shut. . . .	157	U13 Sacvile	138
That, while they bind the senses, doe so please? . . .	401	Filmer	2
BINDE			
I thought to binde him, in my verse:	93	F1 Why write no	2
BIRD			
And why that bird was sacred to Apollo, ...	55	E85 Goodyere 1	4
What bird, or beast, is knowne so dull, ...	101	F4 To the World	29
Busie to catch a Black-bird; if he fall	335	Horace	651
If a Bird so amiable, ...	364	Phoenix	3
A gentler Bird, then this, ...	366	Ode Who saith	7
So blacke a Bird, so bright a Qualitie.	369	Ode Who saith	96
BIRDS			
The soft birds quarrell in the Woods, ...	290	U85 Country	26
BIRTH			
This grave partakes the fleshly birth.	34	E22 Daughter	11
Of birth, of match, of forme, of chastitie? . . .	67	E104 Montgomery	8
And have sought (to give new birth)	77	E120 S. P.	21
At his great birth, where all the Muses met. . . .	94	F2 Penshurst	14
That, at thy birth, mad'st the poore Smith affraid, . .	107	F10 Proludium	14
Then, here, to give pride fame, and peasants birth. . .	114	F12 Rutland	26
Then, now give pride fame, or peasants birth. . .	114	F12 Rutland	V 26
Of so great title, birth, but vertue most, . . .	118	F13 Aubigny	49
Ode. To Sir William Sydney, on his Birth-day. . .	120	F14 Sydney	Ttl
The Birth-day shines, when logs not burne, but men. . .	121	F14 Sydney	60
I Sing the birth, was borne to night, . . .	130	U1 Nativitie	1
And as honest as his Birth.	142	U2 Her man	44
Where only a mans birth is his offence, . . .	177	U25 Desmond	32
When only a mans birth is his offence, . . .	177	U25 Desmond	V 32
And must be bred, so to conceale his birth, . . .	197	U40 Elegy That	17
Lord Bacons Birth-day.	225	U51 Bacon	Ttl
An Epigram on the Princes birth. 1630. . . .	237	U65 Prince	Ttl
An Epigram on Prince Charles his Birth: May. 29th. 1630 .	237	U65 Prince	VTtl
On the Princes Birth-day. An Epigram . . .	237	U65 Prince	VTtl
And art thou borne, brave Babe? Blest be thy birth, .	237	U65 Prince	1
. . . In celebration of her Majesties birth-day. 1630. .	239	U67 Muses	Ttl
To the Queene on her Birth-day	239	U67 Muses	VTtl
To the King. On his Birth-day	249	U72 King	Ttl
Upon King Charles his Birth-day. . . .	249	U72 King	VTtl
This is King Charles his birth day. Speake it, thou Towre,	249	U72 King	V 1
Doth take in easie Natures birth, ...	250	U74 Weston	2
Of Life, that fall so; Christians know their birth .	257	U75 Epithalam.	156
Upon my Birth-day the eleventh of June; . . .	262	U78 Digby	14
Witnesse my Birth-day the eleventh of June; . . .	262	U78 Digby	V 14
Became her Birth-day to Eternitie!	271	U81 Pawlet	68
The Roman Gentrie, men of birth, and meane, . .	321	Horace	360
Into their birth-right, and for fitnesse sake, . .	323	Horace	376
And ev'ry birth encrease the heate of Love. . .	384	Somerset	20
In blood, in birth, by match, and by her seate; . .	394	Jane Ogle	4
Yet give mee leave, to wonder at the birth . .	398	Drayton	83
she desires of every birth	417	Moon	19
BIRTH-DAY			
Ode. To Sir William Sydney, on his Birth-day. . .	120	F14 Sydney	Ttl
The Birth-day shines, when logs not burne, but men. .	121	F14 Sydney	60
Lord Bacons Birth-day.	225	U51 Bacon	Ttl
On the Princes Birth-day. An Epigram . . .	237	U65 Prince	VTtl
. . . In celebration of her Majesties birth-day. 1630. .	239	U67 Muses	Ttl
To the Queene on her Birth-day	239	U67 Muses	VTtl
To the King. On his Birth-day	249	U72 King	Ttl
Upon King Charles his Birth-day. . . .	249	U72 King	VTtl
Upon my Birth-day the eleventh of June; . . .	262	U78 Digby	14
Witnesse my Birth-day the eleventh of June; . . .	262	U78 Digby	V 14
Became her Birth-day to Eternitie!	271	U81 Pawlet	68
BIRTH-RIGHT			
Into their birth-right, and for fitnesse sake, . .	323	Horace	376
BIRTHS			
That Poets are far rarer births then kings, . . .	53	E79 Rutland	1
BISHOP			
And Bishop stay, to consummate the Rites: . . .	256	U75 Epithalam.	122
And this their chosen Bishop celebrate, . . .	256	U75 Epithalam.	132
BISHOPS			
Or 'gainst the Bishops, for the Brethren, raile, . .	59	E92 New Crie	35
Fit for a Bishops knees! O bow them oft, . . .	234	U61 Epigram	13
BITCH			
Doe all the tricks of a saut Lady Bitch; . . .	164	U15 Friend-Wars	76
BITE			
Then give it to the Hound that did him bite; . .	155	U13 Sacvile	70
BITTEN			
But one is bitten by the Dog he fed, . . .	155	U13 Sacvile	67
BITTER			
That Love's a bitter sweet, I ne're conceive . .	197	U40 Elegy That	1
BITTERNESSE			
All taste of bitternesse, and makes the ayre . .	112	F11 Epode	97
BLACK			
White, black, blew, greene, and in more formes out-started,	87	E133 Voyage	126
Gold, upon a ground of black.	141	U2 Her man	14
Safe from the wolves black jaw, and the dull Asses hoofe.	175	U23 Himselfe	36
Let Brontes, and black Steropes, . . .	179	U25 Desmond	40
A Poet hath no more but black and white, . . .	227	U52 Answer	20
Put black, and mourning on? and say you misse . .	285	U84 Muse	98
With faire black eyes, and haire; and a wry nose. .	307	Horace	52
With faire black eyes, and hair, and some vile snout. .	339	Horace	V 54/ 52
Busie to catch a Black-bird; if he fall . . .	335	Horace	651

	Page	Title	Line

BLACK-BIRD
Busie to catch a Black-bird; if he fall . . . . . 335 Horace 651

BLACKE
And her blacke spight expell. . . . . . 109 F11 Epode 4
Which in a blacke foule fish uncomely ends: . . . 338 Horace V 5
Produce us a blacke Swan? . . . . . . 366 Ode Who saith 2
To Loumond lake, and Twedes blacke-springing fountaine. . . 368 Ode Who saith 72
So blacke a Bird, so bright a Qualitie. . . . . 369 Ode Who saith 96
Jest, he saies. Item one sute of blacke taffata . . 380 Coryat 3 48

BLACKENESSE
And Phoebus love cause of his blackenesse is. . . . 366 Ode Who saith 16

BLACKER
Saw all his race approch the blacker floods: . . . 41 E44 Chuff 4

BLACKE-SPRINGING
To Loumond lake, and Twedes blacke-springing fountaine. . . 368 Ode Who saith 72

BLACKEST
And turne the blackest sorrowes to bright joyes: . . . 112 F11 Epode 95

BLACKS
Ere blacks were bought for his owne funerall, . . . 41 E44 Chuff 3

BLADE
Or stands to be'n Commission o' the blade? . . . 155 U13 Sacvile 64

BLADES
An honest Bilbo-Smith would make good blades, . . . 410 Brome 15

BLAME
But so exempt from blame, ... 148 U7 Nymph 33
'Tis cleare, this way I have got off from blame, . . 323 Horace 395
On artlesse Verse; the hard ones he will blame; . . 335 Horace 634

BLANCH'T
Him that buyes chiches blanch't, or chance to like . . 321 Horace 362

BLASON
And better Blason them, then all their Coates, . . . 419 Ode:If Men 8

BLASPHEME
Blaspheme god, greatly. Or some poore hinde beat, . . 36 E28 Surly 17
And last, blaspheme not, we did never heare . . . 168 U15 Friend-Wars 191
Whoorles me about, and to blaspheme in fashion! . . 283 U84 Muse 32

BLASPHEMIE
Imposture, witchcraft, charmes, or blasphemie, . . . 203 U43 Vulcan 16

BLASPHEMY
Nor dare we under blasphemy conceive . . . . 286 U84 Muse 147

BLAST
When on thy trumpet shee did sound a blast, . . . 58 E91 Vere 7

BLATANT
To be knowne what thou art, a blatant beast, . . . 408 Detractor 9
Thy blatant Muse abroad, and teach it rather . . . 411 Gill 11

BLAZE
Or in small Fagots have him blaze about . . . 211 U43 Vulcan 185
Or else in penny Fagots blaze about . . . . 211 U43 Vulcan V185
That trembles in the blaze, then) mounts higher! . . 233 U59 Newcastle 8
The blaze, and splendor, but not handle fire! . . 269 U81 Pawlet 32
Whilest lyke a blaze of strawe, ... 420 Ode:If Men 15

BLAZ'D
How are thy gifts, and graces blaz'd abroad! . . . 413 Ghyrlond 36
How are thy gifts and graces blaz'd abro'd, . . . 414 Ghyrlond 53

BLAZON
But ever without blazon, or least shade . . . 197 U40 Elegy That 13

BLEED
Which when she beheld to bleed, ... 133 U2 Suffered 17

BLEEDING
Seldome descend but bleeding to their grave. . . . 363 Murder 2

BLEEDS
Not wound thy conscience, when thy body bleeds; . . 168 U15 Friend-Wars 178

BLESSE
To have thy God to blesse, thy King to grace, . . 256 U75 Epithalam. 131
Our King and Queen the Lord-God blesse, . . . 418 Grace 1
Our King and Queen the Prince God blesse, . . . 418 Grace V 1
And God blesse every living thing, ... 418 Grace 3
God blesse the Councell of Estate, ... 419 Grace 5
God blesse the Councell and the State, ... 419 Grace V 5
God blesse them all, and keepe them safe: . . . 419 Grace 7
God blesse us all, Bedford keepe safe: . . . . 419 Grace V 7
And God blesse me, and God blesse Raph. . . . 419 Grace 8

BLESSED
Makes a most blessed gayne. . . . . . 112 F11 Epode 86
O Holy, blessed, glorious Trinitie . . . . 127 U1 Trinitie 1
James the blessed, pleas'd the rather, ... 259 U76 Petition 6
Grow up, sweet Babe, as blessed, in thy Name, . . 268 U80 Christning 11
Her blessed Soule, hence, forth this valley vane . . 283 U84 Muse 34
The Ghyrlond of the blessed Virgin Marie. . . . 412 Ghyrlond Ttl
Here, are five letters in this blessed Name, . . 412 Ghyrlond 1
Alike of kin, to that most blessed Trine, . . . 413 Ghyrlond 34
Most holy, & pure Virgin, blessed Mayd, . . . 413 Ghyrlond 37
Renew the Glories of our blessed Jeames: . . . 415 Dover 4

BLESSED'ST
And by an Angell, to the blessed'st Maid, . . . 238 U66 Queene 2

BLESSING
This blessing of your starres, then by that way . . 118 F13 Aubigny 54
Of divine blessing, would not serve a State? . . 185 U30 Burleigh 20
And by thy blessing, may thy People see . . . 268 U80 Christning 3
T' have paid againe a blessing was but lent, . . 271 U81 Pawlet 80

BLESSINGS
If he but weigh'd the blessings of this day? . . 236 U64 Charles 3 4
What worlds of blessings to good Kings they owe: . . 261 U77 Treasurer 20
By all the wealth of blessings, and the store . . 285 U84 Muse 110

		Page	Title	Line
BLEST				
Was his blest fate, but our hard lot to find.	. . .	37	E32 Roe 2	8
Or, better worke! were thy glad countrey blest,	. . .	61	E95 Savile	14
So, when we, blest with thy returne, shall see	. . .	81	E128 Wm Roe 2	9
How blest art thou, canst love the countrey, Wroth,	. . .	96	F3 Wroth	1
Live, with un-bought provision blest;	. . .	97	F3 Wroth	14
Who (blest with such high chance)	. . .	111	F11 Epode	62
Of your blest wombe, made fruitfull from above,	. . .	119	F13 Aubigny	95
O, then how blest,	. . .	128	U1 Trinitie	44
Upon record, in this blest child.	. . .	188	U35 Chute	4
Your happinesse, and doth not speake you blest,	. . .	234	U61 Epigram	9
With a long, large, and blest posteritie!	. . .	236	U63 Charles 2	12
And art thou borne, brave Babe? Blest be thy birth,	. . .	237	U65 Prince	1
And art thou borne, brave Babe? Blest be the day,	. . .	237	U65 Prince	V 1
Then comforted her Lord! and blest her Sonne!	. . .	270	U81 Pawlet	57
BLEW				
White, black, blew, greene, and in more formes out-started,	.	87	E133 Voyage	126
Would make the very Greene-cloth to looke blew:	. .	241	U68 House-hold	8
BLIND				
Harsh sights at home, Giles wisheth he were blind.	. .	40	E42 Giles	10
How wilfull blind is he then, that would stray,	. .	53	E80 Life/Death	3
I Now thinke, Love is rather deafe, then blind,	. .	149	U9 Picture	1
I Doubt that, Love is rather deafe, then blind,	. .	149	U9 Picture	V 1
But which shall lead me on? both these are blind:	. .	170	U18 Elegy Can	11
Or Love, or Fortune blind, when they but winke	. .	170	U18 Elegy Can	16
To vertue, and true worth, be ever blind.	. .	250	U73 Weston	10
Yet may as blind men sometimes hit the marke.	. .	383	Author	6
BLINDE				
An ancient pur-blinde fletcher, with a high nose;	. .	89	E133 Voyage	190
Bald, or blinde, or nere so many:	. .	105	F8 Sicknesse	40
And strike our reason blinde.	. .	110	F11 Epode	30
The thing, they here call Love, is blinde Desire,	. .	110	F11 Epode	37
And strikes the quickest-sighted Judgement blinde.	. .	363	Riches	16
Or blinde Affection, which doth ne're advance	. .	391	Shakespeare	9
BLINDEST				
And then the best are, still, the blindest friends!	. .	170	U18 Elegy Can	14
BLINDLY				
Let us not then rush blindly on unto it,	. . .	294	U88 Petronius	3
BLISSE				
He, at length, our blisse will sever.	. .	102	F5 Celia 1	V 4
If you can envie your owne Daughters blisse,	. .	271	U81 Pawlet	83
If you can enjoy your owne Daughters blisse,	. .	271	U81 Pawlet	V 83
So sweetly taken to the Court of blisse,	. .	283	U84 Muse	41
BLISSES				
Where, you say, men gather blisses,	. . .	136	U2 Cupid	26
Where men at once may plant, and gather blisses:	. .	170	U19 Elegy By	10
BLOCK				
A Goat in Velvet; or some block could move	. .	202	U42 Elegy Let	82
BLOCK'D				
But lyes block'd up, and straightned, narrow'd in,	. .	248	U71 Treasurer	10
BLOCKS				
These Carkasses of honour; Taylors blocks,	. .	216	U44 Speach	99
BLOCKT				
It is a Darknesse hath blockt up my sense,	. .	191	U38 Elegy 'Tis	5
BLOOD (See also BLOUD)				
A lord, it cryed, buried in flesh, and blood,	. .	30	E11 Something	5
Sleeked limmes, and finest blood?	. .	105	F8 Sicknesse	23
Sleeked limmes, and fyned blood?	. .	105	F8 Sicknesse	V 23
Your blood	. . .	121	F14 Sydney	33
And doe governe more my blood,	. .	136	U2 Cupid	3
Noble; or of greater Blood:	. .	140	U2 Her man	4
Noble; or of greatest Blood:	. .	140	U2 Her man	V 4
All his blood should be a flame	. .	141	U2 Her man	30
And spunge-like with it dry up the blood quite:	. .	155	U13 Sacvile	69
Hee's one of blood, and fashion! and with these	. .	164	U15 Friend-Wars	55
Lewd slanderers, soft whisperers that let blood	. .	167	U15 Friend-Wars	165
Lewd standers, soft whisperers that let blood	. .	167	U15 Friend-Wars	V165
Of putrid flesh alive! of blood, the sinke!	. .	172	U21 Ltl Shrub	9
What is there more that can ennoble blood?	. .	185	U30 Burleigh	6
Should aske the blood, and spirits he hath infus'd	. .	192	U38 Elegy 'Tis	65
Alas I ha' lost my heat, my blood, my prime,	. .	199	U41 Elegy Since	11
Without the hazard of a drop of blood,	. .	214	U44 Speach	47
The Herald will. Our blood is now become	. .	215	U44 Speach	82
And when you want those friends, or neere in blood,	. .	224	U50 Countesse	26
But crept like darknesse through his blood?	. .	234	U60 La-ware	8
That knits brave minds, and manners, more then blood.	. .	246	U70 Ode	106
Which knits brave minds, and manners, more then blood.	. .	246	U70 Ode	V106
To pious parents, who would have their blood	. .	268	U80 Christning	7
A horrour in mee! all my blood is steele!	. .	269	U81 Pawlet	8
From the inherent Graces in her blood!	. .	270	U81 Pawlet	36
The wonder of her Sexe, and of your Blood,	. .	274	U84 Descent	12
And give her place, according to her blood,	. .	284	U84 Muse	83
And to that forme, lent two such veines of blood	. .	287	U84 Muse	157
Till he drop off, a Horse-leech, full of blood.	. .	337	Horace	680
Till, horse-leech-like, he drop off, full of blood.	. .	355	Horace	V680
Those that in blood such violent pleasure have,	. .	363	Murder	1
And wish that all the Muses blood were spilt,	. .	371	Fletcher	12
In blood, in birth, by match, and by her seate;	. .	394	Jane Ogle	4
That ever yet did fire the English blood!	:	397	Drayton	57
BLOOME				
In all her bloome, and flower;	. . .	253	U75 Epithalam.	23
The second string is the sweet Almond bloome	. .	412	Ghyrlond	9

BLOOMED
   Who, e're the first downe bloomed on the chin, ...   247 U70 Ode   127
BLOOMING
   The bus'nesse of your blooming wit, ...   251 U74 Weston   22
BLOT
   With one great blot, yo'had form'd me as I am.   .   .   .   227 U52 Answer   12
   With one great blot, you had drawne me as I am.   .   .   227 U52 Answer V 12
   To taxe that Verse, which many a day, and blot   .   .   325 Horace   416
   Hee'd bid, blot all: and to the anvile bring   .   .   .   333 Horace   627
   Blot out the carelesse, with his turned pen;   .   .   .   335 Horace   635
BLOTS
   What blots and errours, have you watch'd and purg'd   .   .   160 U14 Selden   42
BLOTT
   Breake then thie quills, blott out   .   .   .   .   420 Ode:If Men   19
BLOUD
   High in thy bloud, thy place, but highest then,   .   .   49 E67 Suffolk   6
   Of greatest bloud, and yet more good then great;   .   .   52 E76 Bedford 1   6
   Wherewith, against thy bloud, thee y'offenders bee.   .   60 E93 Radcliffe 16
   That bloud not mindes, but mindes did bloud adorne: .   75 E116 Jephson   11
   And those to turne to bloud, and make thine owne: .   .   80 E128 Wm Roe 2   4
   Beautie, I know, is good, and bloud is more;   .   .   .   114 F12 Rutland   37
   As bloud, and match. Wherein, how more then much   .   117 F13 Aubigny   46
   To Clifton's bloud, that is deny'd their name.   .   .   .   119 F13 Aubigny   98
   Her owne bloud gave her: Shee ne're had, nor hath   .   188 U34 Small Poxe   9
BLOW   (NOUN)
   Till envie wound, or maime it at a blow!   .   .   .   162 U15 Friend-Wars 22
   But that's a blow, by which in time I may   .   .   .   219 U47 Tribe   51
BLOW
   Art still at that, and think'st to blow me'up too?   .   .   72 E112 Gamster   6
   To blow up orphanes, widdowes, and their states;   .   .   99 F3 Wroth   79
   Like such as blow away their lives,   .   .   .   100 F4 To the World 22
   Which thus we over-blow.   .   .   .   .   .   110 F11 Epode   36
   Those thousands on his back, shall after blow   .   .   165 U15 Friend-Wars 104
   (Made to blow up loves secrets) to discover   .   .   .   198 U40 Elegy That 47
   Blow up, and ruine, myne, and countermyne,   .   .   .   212 U43 Vulcan   205
BLOWES
   Thou hast no more blowes, Fate, to drive at one: .   .   283 U84 Muse   27
BLOWNE   (BLOOMED)
   His rosie tyes and garters so ore-blowne,   .   .   .   62 E97 Motion   5
   That were this morning blowne;   .   .   .   .   147 U7 Nymph   19
BLOWNE
   Blowne up; and he (too'unwieldie for that place)   .   .   57 E90 Mill   14
   For fame, with breath soone kindled, soone blowne out.   .   83 E131 Ferrab. 2 14
   like glasse, blowne up, and fashion'd by desire.   .   .   108 F10 Proludium   4
   And being a thing, blowne out of nought, rebells   .   163 U15 Friend-Wars 32
BLOWSE
   Such as the Sabines, or a Sun-burnt-blowse,   .   .   .   291 U85 Country   41
BLUE   (See BLEW)
BLUNTLY
   Who bluntly doth but looke upon the same, ...   383 Author   3
BLURT
   And farre unworthy to blurt out light rimes;   .   .   .   321 Horace   337
BLUSH
   If it may stand with your soft blush to heare   .   .   117 F13 Aubigny   22
   Other great wives may blush at: when they see   .   .   119 F13 Aubigny 111
   And so thin, to see a blush   .   .   .   .   141 U2 Her man   28
   And in the Act did so my blush prevent,   .   .   .   153 U13 Sacvile   11
   You blush, but doe not: friends are either none,   .   .   171 U19 Elegy By   13
   Then to make falshood blush, and fraud afraid: .   .   186 U32 Elsmere   4
   Shee need not blush upon the Mariage-Day.   .   .   386 Husband   12
BLUSHED
   And Spinola have blushed at the sight.   .   .   .   214 U44 Speach   42
BLUSHES
   Such my Mothers blushes be, ...   136 U2 Cupid   20
BLUSHING
   The blushing apricot, and woolly peach   .   .   .   94 F2 Penshurst   43
BOARD
   In the mere perspective of an Inch board!   .   .   .   404 Inigo Jones 1 44
BOARDES
   Oh, to make Boardes to speake! There is a taske   .   404 Inigo Jones 1 49
BOARDS
   A Goddesse is, then paynted Cloth, Deal-boards,   .   .   406 Inigo Jones 1 93
BOARE
   A Dolphin, and a Boare amid' the floods.   .   .   .   307 Horace   42
BOAST
   If all you boast of your great art be true;   .   .   .   29 E6 Alchymists   1
   Fear'd not to boast the glories of her stage,   .   .   56 E89 Allen   2
   Onely to boast thy merit in supply.   .   .   .   61 E95 Savile   12
   Out-dance the Babion, or out-boast the Brave;   .   .   81 E129 Mime   12
   Thine the originall; and France shall boast,   .   .   83 E132 Sylvester 13
   All, that they boast of Styx, of Acheron,   .   .   .   84 E133 Voyage   7
   Of touch, or marble; nor canst boast a row   .   .   .   93 F2 Penshurst   2
   And each where boast it as his merit,   .   .   .   99 F3 Wroth   78
   Shall thronging come, and boast the happy place   .   .   115 F12 Rutland   80
   Boast, but how oft they have gone wrong to man: .   .   119 F13 Aubigny   84
   Thinke, yea and boast, that they have done it so   .   .   186 U32 Elsmere   12
   The sinne of Boast, or other countermine   .   .   .   198 U40 Elegy That 46
   But that's a marke, wherof thy Rites doe boast,   .   .   205 U43 Vulcan   57
   Rather to boast rich hangings, then rare friends.   .   242 U69 Friend Son 26
   Doe boast their Loves, and Brav'ries so at large,   .   253 U75 Epithalam. 19
   Boast not these Titles of your Ancestors;   .   .   .   281 U84 Kenelme   10
   The greater part, that boast the Muses fire,   .   .   339 Horace   V 33
   Nor let one River boast   .   .   .   .   .   367 Ode Who saith 35

		Page	Title	Line

BOASTED
Not boasted in your life, but practis'd true, ... 225 U50 Countesse 32
BOASTERS
Boasters, and perjur'd, with the infinite more . . . 167 U15 Friend-Wars 169
BOASTING
And my selfe most, in some selfe-boasting Rimes? . . 203 U43 Vulcan 26
And my selfe most, in lewd selfe-boasting Rimes? . . 203 U43 Vulcan V 26
BOASTS
Him not, aloud, that boasts so good a fame: . . . 74 E115 Honest Man 2
Which boasts t'have had the head of gold. . . . 98 F3 Wroth 64
BOATE
The meate-boate of Beares colledge, Paris-garden, . . 87 E133 Voyage 117
BOATES
Man out their Boates to th' Temple, and not shift . . 155 U13 Sacvile 83
The charmed Boates, and the inchanted Wharfes; . . . 205 U43 Vulcan 68
And safely trust to dresse, not burne their Boates. . . 208 U43 Vulcan 128
Their painted Maskes, their paper Boates, . . . 273 U84 Cradle 22
BODIES
The bodies stripes, I see, the soule may save. . . . 33 E21 Gam'ster 8
That quilts those bodies, I have leave to span: . . 200 U42 Elegy Let 32
Of bodies, meet like rarified ayre! . . . . 233 U59 Newcastle 10
BODY
That his whole body should speake french, not he? . . 56 E88 Monsieur 2
Mill was the same. Since, both his body and face . . 57 E90 Mill 13
Restored in thy body, and thy minde! . . . . 79 E125 Uvedale 4
Who sees a soule, in such a body set, . . . 79 E125 Uvedale 5
And is t'a body, often, ill inclin'd, . . . 82 E130 Ferrab. 1 7
A body sound, with sounder minde; . . . 99 F3 Wroth 102
A body so harmoniously compos'd, . . . 112 F11 Epode 99
Let 'hem waste body, and state; and after all, . . 118 F13 Aubigny 81
In a body, should be there. . . . . 141 U2 Her man 35
The body was . . . . . 148 U8 Houre-glasse 5
His body to the Counters, or the Fleete? . . 165 U15 Friend-Wars 105
His body to the compters, or the Fleete? . . 165 U15 Friend-Wars V105
And whilst our states, strength, body, and mind we waste, . 166 U15 Friend-Wars 133
Not wound thy conscience, when thy body bleeds; . . 168 U15 Friend-Wars 178
I dare not say a body, but some parts . . . 206 U43 Vulcan 87
I have a body, yet, that spirit drawes . . . 219 U47 Tribe 41
Not he, that should the body have, for Case . . 223 U49 Pucell 33
Of State, of fame, of body, and of soule, . . 224 U50 Countesse 18
That spread his body o're, to kill: . . . 234 U60 La-ware 16
So great; his Body now alone projects the shade. . 258 U75 Epithalam. 184
So large; his Body then, not boughs, project his shade. . 258 U75 Epithalam. V184
Her suffrings, as the body had beene away! . . 270 U81 Pawlet 51
'Tis but a body which you can torment, . . 270 U81 Pawlet 55
For Mind, and Body, the most excellent . . 274 U84 Descent 3
3. The Picture of the Body. . . . 275 U84 Body Ttl
And left her lovely body unthought dead! . . 283 U84 Muse 44
Of Body and Spirit together, plac'd betwixt . . 284 U84 Muse 54
To Body, and Soule! where Love is all the guest! . 284 U84 Muse 64
Out of her noble body, to this Feast: . . 284 U84 Muse 82
A quiet mind; free powers; and body sound; . . 295 U90 Mart.10:47 6
Such things, of every body, and as well. . . 394 Jane Ogle 10
BODYES
(Though they may number bodyes) or but one. . . 171 U19 Elegy By 14
Or Mallowes loosing bodyes ill: . . . 291 U85 Country 58
Or Mallowes good for bodyes ill: . . . 291 U85 Country V 58
BOGG'D
Rather then here so bogg'd in vices stay. . . 163 U15 Friend-Wars 30
BOIL (See BOYLER)
BOLD
Thou should'st be bold, licentious, full of gall, . . 27 E2 My Booke 3
From brocage is become so bold a thiefe, . . 44 E56 Poet-Ape 3
Phoebus replyed. Bold head, it is not shee: . . 80 E126 Mrs Cary 7
To urge, my lov'd Alphonso, that bold fame . . 82 E130 Ferrab. 1 1
One said, it was bold Briareus, or the beadle, . . 86 E133 Voyage 81
Madame, be bold to use this truest glasse: . . 120 F13 Aubigny 122
Supplant bold Panton; and brought there to view . . 214 U44 Speach 34
Up among Nations. In the stead of bold . . 214 U44 Speach 51
Of bold Sir Bevis, and his Arundell: . . 228 U53 Newcastle 10
Speake it, you bold Penates, you that stand . . 274 U84 Descent 7
Be nought so'bove him, but his bold sword claime. . 342 Horace V174
And the bold Pythias, having cheated weake . . 321 Horace 346
So bold, as shewes your Art you can command. . . 370 Author 8
With bold Tyrtaeus verse, when thou art nam'd, . . 398 Drayton 68
BOLDER
No more let Greece her bolder fables tell . . 84 E133 Voyage 1
My bolder numbers to thy golden Lyre: . . 177 U25 Desmond 9
BOLDNESSE
I can helpe that with boldnesse; And Love sware, . . 170 U18 Elegy Can 9
BOMBARD
And with both bombard-stile, and phrase, rehearse . . 85 E133 Voyage 46
Their bombard-phrase, and foot-and-halfe-foot words. . 311 Horace 139
BOMBARD-PHRASE
Their bombard-phrase, and foot-and-halfe-foot words. . 311 Horace 139
BOMBARD-STILE
And with both bombard-stile, and phrase, rehearse . . 85 E133 Voyage 46
BOND
Signes to new bond, forfeits: and cryes, god payes. . . 30 E12 Shift 14
BONDMEN
The wealthy houshold swarme of bondmen met, . . 291 U85 Country 65
BONE
Of bone-fires. Then . . . . 121 F14 Sydney 59

	Page	Title	Line
BONE (cont.)			
As any Mercer; or the whale-bone man	200	U42 Elegy Let	31
BONE-FIRES			
Of bone-fires. Then	121	F14 Sydney	59
BONEFIRES			
At Bonefires, Rockets, Fire-workes, with the Shoutes	249	U72 King	13
At Bonefires, squibs, and mirth, with all their Shoutes	249	U72 King	V 13
BONES			
Active in's braine, and passive in his bones.	49	E68 Playwrt 2	4
Great Club-fist, though thy backe, and bones be sore,	85	E133 Voyage	55
Hercules? alas his bones are yet sore,	107	F10 Proludium	4
Of him whose bones this Grave doth gather:	151	U12 Corbet	6
Now use the bones, we see doth hire a man	166	U15 Friend-Wars	136
these only hide part of my flesh, and bones:	387	Cavendish	2
Able to eat into his bones & pierce	407	Inigo Jones 3	4
BONNIE			
Come forth thou bonnie bouncing booke then, daughter	378	Coryat 2	86
BOOK			
Epigram, to my Book-seller.	232	U58 Book-seller	Ttl
Quintus Horatius Flaccus his book of . . .	338	Horace	VTtl
That Book, my Piso's, and this piece agree,	338	Horace	V 8
BOOKE			
Epigrammes. I. Booke.	23	Epigrammes	Ttl
Pray thee, take care, that tak'st my booke in hand,	27	E1 Reader	1
To my Booke.	27	E2 My Booke	Ttl
It will be look'd for, booke, when some but see	27	E2 My Booke	1
To my Booke-seller.	27	E3 Bookseller	Ttl
Call'st a booke good, or bad, as it doth sell,	27	E3 Bookseller	2
May none, whose scatter'd names honor my booke,	29	E9 To All	1
When, in my booke, men reade but Cecill's name,	41	E43 Salisbury 1	9
In my chast booke: professe them in thine owne.	42	E49 Playwrt 1	6
When having pill'd a booke, which no man buyes,	43	E53 Old-end	2
That, any way, my booke should speake thy name:	53	E77 Not name	2
As he would burne, or better farre his booke.	53	E79 Rutland	12
Throughout my booke. 'Troth put out woman too.	54	E83 Friend	2
Whose poemes would not wish to be your booke?	60	E94 Bedford 3	4
Livie, or of some better booke to us,	65	E101 Supper	22
Who Edmonds, reades thy booke, and doth not see	72	E111 Edmonds 2	1
To Alphonso Ferrabosco, on his Booke.	82	E130 Ferrab. 1	Ttl
That puts it in his Debt-booke e're 't be done;	154	U13 Sacvile	34
Your Booke, my Selden, I have read, and much	158	U14 Selden	5
The mind of the Frontispice to a Booke.	175	U24 Frontispice	Ttl
You have unto my Store added a booke,	189	U37 Friend-Book	4
But on thy practise, and the Posture booke:	213	U44 Speach	28
Are we by Booke-wormes to be awde? must we	215	U44 Speach	67
A booke to a few lynes: but, it was fit	230	U56 Covell	3
Upon them, (next to Spenser's noble booke,)	263	U78 Digby	24
Ode the first. The fourth Booke. To Venus.	292	U86 Hor.4:1	Ttl
Ode IX. 3 Booke, to Lydia. Dialogue of Horace, and Lydia.	293	U87 Hor.3:9	Ttl
This peece, my Piso's, and that booke agree,	305	Horace	8
On life, and manners, and make those his booke,	325	Horace	454
This booke will get the Sosii money; This	329	Horace	517
And all your Booke (when it is throughly scan'd)	370	Author	5
. . . the Coryate of Odcombe, and his Booke now going to travell	378	Coryat 2	Ttl
Come forth thou bonnie bouncing booke then, daughter	378	Coryat 2	86
By the scale of his booke, a yard of his stile?	379	Coryat 3	10
The Mappe of his journey, and sees in his booke,	379	Coryat 3	18
Yes. And thanks God in his Pistle or his Booke	380	Coryat 3	43
It fits not onely him that makes a Booke,	385	Husband	1
And hath the noblest marke of a good Booke,	389	Aleman	7
Not on his Picture, but his Booke.	390	Reader	10
Am I thus ample to thy Booke, and Fame:	390	Shakespeare	2
And art alive still, while thy Booke doth live,	391	Shakespeare	23
This booke! it is a Catechisme to fight,	398	Drayton	71
With pause upon it; make this page your booke;	399	Lady Ogle	6
Your booke? your volume! Nay, the state, and story!	399	Lady Ogle	7
This Booke will live; It hath a Genius: This	400	Beaumont	1
Though I confesse a Beaumonts Booke to bee	400	Beaumont	7
Goe little Booke, Goe little Fable	662	Bedford	1
BOOKES			
Upon thy wel-made choise of friends, and bookes;	55	E86 Goodyere 2	2
In making thy friends bookes, and thy bookes friends:	55	E86 Goodyere 2	4
With England. All forbidden bookes they get.	59	E92 New Crie	31
His deedes too dying, but in bookes (whose good	71	E110 Edmonds 1	15
His deedes too dying, save in bookes (whose good	71	E110 Edmonds 1	V 15
A many of bookes, even good judgements wound	159	U14 Selden	15
That, henceforth, I beleeve nor bookes, nor men,	187	U33 Councellour	5
Of Bookes, of Presidents, hast thou at hand!	187	U33 Councellour	25
Ben: Jonson upon the burning of his study and bookes	202	U43 Vulcan	VTtl
Perhaps, to have beene burned with my bookes.	203	U43 Vulcan	18
With all th'adventures; Three bookes not afraid	207	U43 Vulcan	95
With all th'adventures; Three bookes not amisse	207	U43 Vulcan	V 95
Or your Allies, you make your bookes your friends,	224	U50 Countesse	27
Bee thou my Bookes intelligencer, note	232	U58 Book-seller	3
Or dispenc'd in bookes, or bread,	259	U76 Petition	15
Well dispenc'd in bookes, or bread,	259	U76 Petition	V 15
On Natures secrets, there, as her owne bookes:	271	U81 Pawlet	70
On naturall secret, there, as her owne bookes:	271	U81 Pawlet	V 70
Some men, of Bookes or Freinds not speaking right,	386	Browne	1
And, where the most reade bookes, on Authors fames,	386	Browne	9
Shall finde, that either hath read Bookes, and Men:	389	Aleman	2
Such Bookes deserve Translators, of like coate	389	Aleman	11

		Page	Title	Line

BOOKE-SELLER
  To my Booke-seller. . . . . 27 E3 Bookseller Ttl
BOOKE-WORMES
  Are we by Booke-wormes to be awde? must we . . . 215 U44 Speach 67
BOOKS
  Or Bils, and there he buyes the names of books. . . . 59 E92 New Crie 24
BOOK-SELLER
  Epigram, to my Book-seller. . . . . . . 232 U58 Book-seller Ttl
BOORD
  Which is maine greatnesse. And, at his still boord, . 35 E28 Surly 13
  That shall be utter'd at our mirthfull boord, . . . 65 E101 Supper 40
  The neede of such? whose liberall boord doth flow, . 95 F2 Penshurst 59
BOORDS
  Fix'd to the bed, and boords, unlike to win . . 248 U71 Treasurer 11
BOORE
  Here, by a Boore too, hee's like to be beaten . . 375 Coryat 1 24
BOOT
  But if, to boot with these, a chaste Wife meet . . 291 U85 Country 39
BOOTE
  Cato's to boote, Rome, and her libertie, . . . 71 E110 Edmonds 1 4
  That which, to boote with hell, is thought worth heaven, . 113 F12 Rutland 3
  French to boote, at least in fashion, . . . 141 U2 Her man 7
  But he that's both, and slave to boote, shall live, . 167 U15 Friend-Wars 160
BOR
  Diana's Grove, or Altar, with the bor-/Dring . . 305 Horace 20
  bor-/Dring Circles of swift waters that intwine . . 305 Horace 21
BORD
  When hee shall read them at the Treasurers bord, . 263 U78 Digby 27
  When hee doth read them at the Treasurers bord, . 263 U78 Digby V 27
BORDE
  Fix'd to the bed, and borde, and like to win . . 248 U71 Treasurer V 11
BORDERS
  Or th'other on their borders, that will jeast . . 218 U47 Tribe 16
BOR-DRING
  Diana's Grove, or Altar, with the bor-/Dring . . 305 Horace 20
  bor-/Dring Circles of swift waters that intwine . . 305 Horace 21
BORDS
  But flees the Barre and Courts, with the proud bords, . 289 U85 Country 7
BORES
  Wild Bores into his toyles pitch'd round: . . . 290 U85 Country 32
BORN
  Like men Town-born, and neere the place, reherse . 347 Horace V349/357
BORNE (ENDURED)
  Borne up by statues, shall I reare your head, . . 115 F12 Rutland 84
  When oft the Bearer, is borne out of dore? . . 166 U15 Friend-Wars 120
BORNE
  Of the not borne, yet buried, here's the tombe. . 46 E62 Would-bee 12
  Or, more then borne for the comparison . . . 67 E104 Montgomery 9
  And to live great, was better, then great borne. . 75 E116 Jephson 12
  And brag, that they were therefore borne. . . 99 F3 Wroth 72
  But, what we'are borne for, we must beare: . . 101 F4 To the World 53
  No, I doe know, that I was borne . . . 101 F4 To the World 61
  Inconstant, like the sea, of whence 'tis borne, . 110 F11 Epode 39
  Inconstant, as the sea, of whence 'tis borne, . . 110 F11 Epode V 39
  That bred them, graves: when they were borne, they di'd, . 114 F12 Rutland 47
  Conceiv'd in sinne, and unto labour borne, . . 122 F15 Heaven 18
  I Sing the birth, was borne to night, . . . 130 U1 Nativitie 1
  A Martyr borne in our defence; . . . . 130 U1 Nativitie 23
  And free societie, hee's borne else-where, . . 197 U40 Elegy That 16
  When thou wert borne, and that thou look'st at best, . 208 U43 Vulcan 113
  When thou wert borne, and that thou look'st at best, . 208 U43 Vulcan V113
  Borne, bred, allied? what's he dare tutor us? . . 215 U44 Speach 66
  Will cal't a Bastard, when a Prophet's borne. . . 223 U49 Pucell 46
  Since Bacon, and thy Lord was borne, and here; . 225 U51 Bacon 8
  Or what we heare our home-borne Legend tell, . . 228 U53 Newcastle 9
  . . . first-borne, An Epigram Consolatorie. 1629. . 235 U63 Charles 2 Ttl
  And art thou borne, brave Babe? Blest be thy birth, . 237 U65 Prince 1
  And art thou borne, brave Babe? Blest be the day, . 237 U65 Prince V 1
  (After the last child borne;) This is our wedding day. . 258 U75 Epithalam. 168
  When we were all borne, we began to die; . . 271 U81 Pawlet 94
  The first-borne dying; so the aged state . . 309 Horace 87
  The first-borne dying; so the aged Fate . . . 340 Horace V 87
  Of words decay, and phrases borne but late . . 309 Horace 88
  Of popular noyses, borne to actuate things. . . 341 Horace V120
  Of Colchis borne; or in Assyria bred; . . . 313 Horace 167
  Like men street-borne, and neere the Hall, reherse . 321 Horace 357
  And celebrating our owne home-borne facts; . . 323 Horace 408
  Why not? I'm gentle, and free-borne, doe hate . . 331 Horace 571
  Why not? being honest, and free-borne, doth hate . 352 Horace V547/571
  Yes thou wert borne out of his travelling thigh . 378 Coryat 2 89
  For a good Poet's made, as well as borne. . . 392 Shakespeare 64
BORROW'D
  At dice his borrow'd money: which, god payes. . 30 E12 Shift 12
  His deare and borrow'd Bravery he must cast? . . 165 U15 Friend-Wars 110
  And not being borrow'd by thee, but possest. . . 187 U33 Councellour 28
BORROWERS
  As't were a challenge, or a borrowers letter? . . 51 E73 Fine Grand 3
  Well knowne, and practiz'd borrowers on their word, . 154 U13 Sacvile 48
BORROWING
  Is borrowing; that but stopt, they doe invade . . 155 U13 Sacvile 80
BOSOME
  Fit in that softer bosome to reside. . . . 52 E76 Bedford 1 12
  Here in my bosome, and at home. . . . . 102 F4 To the World 68

73

BOSOME (cont.)

	Page	Title	Line
Though many Gems be in your bosome stor'd,	179	U25 Desmond	55
Sleepe in a Virgins bosome without feare,	230	U56 Covell	15
From whose prowde bosome, thou began'st thy flight.	368	Ode Who saith	80

BOTH

	Page	Title	Line
And gave thee both, to shew they could no more.	28	E4 James 1	4
Rob'd both of money, and the lawes reliefe,	29	E8 Robbery	5
When both it is the old way, and the true.	32	E18 Censurer	2
He will both argue, and discourse in oathes,	35	E28 Surly	9
Both which are great. And laugh at ill-made clothes;	35	E28 Surly	10
But as they come, on both sides he takes fees,	38	E37 Chev'ril	2
And pleaseth both. For while he melts his greace	38	E37 Chev'ril	3
Conquer'd hath both life and it.	39	E40 Ratcliffe	12
Would both thy folly, and thy spite betray.	43	E52 Courtling	6
To give the world assurance thou wert both;	43	E53 Old-end	6
And there's both losse of time, and losse of sport	46	E62 Would-bee	10
In onely thee, might be both great, and glad.	48	E66 Cary	4
I must a libell make, and cosen both.	54	E81 Proule	8
Where I both learn'd, why wise-men hawking follow,	55	E85 Goodyere 1	3
Who both their graces in thy selfe hast more	57	E89 Allen	9
Mill was the same. Since, both his body and face	57	E90 Mill	13
Dare for these poemes, yet, both aske, and read,	60	E94 Bedford 3	12
And all his numbers, both of sense, and sounds.	61	E95 Savile	6
Though both be good, the latter yet is worst,	63	E98 Th Roe 1	11
To night, grave sir, both my poore house, and I	64	E101 Supper	1
Both which are ask'd, to have thee understood,	66	E102 Pembroke	4
Where vertue makes them both, and that's in thee:	70	E109 Nevil	3
That both for wit, and sense, so oft dost plucke,	73	E112 Gamster	18
But both th'hast so, as who affects the state	78	E123 Rudyerd 3	3
Both whose dimensions, lost, the world might finde	79	E125 Uvedale	3
Might then both thee, thy worke and merit raise:	83	E132 Sylvester	2
And with both bombard-stile, and phrase, rehearse	85	E133 Voyage	46
Grave tutor to the learned horse. Both which,	88	E133 Voyage	157
Whether by choice, or fate, or both;	96	F3 Wroth	2
Yet art thou both shrunke up, and old,	100	F4 To the World	14
So both the prais'd, and praisers suffer: Yet,	116	F13 Aubigny	5
(They finde it both so wittie, and safe to give.)	118	F13 Aubigny	76
Both love the cause, and authors of the feast?	120	F14 Sydney	10
I know my state, both full of shame, and scorne,	122	F15 Heaven	17
Eternall Spirit, God from both proceeding,	128	U1 Trinitie	25
The Author both of Life, and light;	130	U1 Nativitie	2
Both wills were in one stature;	130	U1 Nativitie	15
Both the Arrow he had quit,	132	U2 How he saw	21
Both the Bow, and shaft I held,	133	U2 Suffered	8
Both my fortune, and my Starre!	136	U2 Cupid	2
Both her Browes, bent like my Bow.	136	U2 Cupid	17
Nay, rather both our soules bee strayn'd	144	U3 Musicall	25
Wee have both wits, and fancies too,	145	U5 Woman-kind	5
Hath both my heart and me surpriz'd,	151	U11 Dreame	5
Would say as much, as both have done	151	U12 Corbet	3
For I both lost a friend and Father,	151	U12 Corbet	5
Who makes the one, so't be first, makes both.	152	U12 Corbet	40
You both are modest. So am I. Farewell.	161	U14 Selden	86
Till he becomes both their, and his owne curse!	162	U15 Friend-Wars	14
But both fell prest under the load they make.	166	U15 Friend-Wars	128
But he that's both, and slave to boote, shall live,	167	U15 Friend-Wars	160
But he that's both, and slave to both, shall live,	167	U15 Friend-Wars	V160
Informers, Masters both of Arts and lies:	167	U15 Friend-Wars	164
But which shall lead me on? both these are blind:	170	U18 Elegy Can	11
That which we can, who both in you, his Wife,	171	U19 Elegy By	25
That eats on wits, and Arts, and destroyes them both.	174	U23 Himselfe	6
But both might know their wayes were understood,	176	U24 Frontispice	7
But both might know their wayes are understood,	176	U24 Frontispice V	7
Both braines and hearts; and mine now best doe know it:	182	U28 Worth	8
Both arm'd with wealth, and slander to oppose,	186	U32 Elsmere	8
Till I may see both it and you agen.	199	U41 Elegy Since	22
And vouches both the Pageant, and the Day,	202	U42 Elegy Let	77
On both sides doe your mischiefes with delight;	212	U43 Vulcan	204
One lesson we have both learn'd, and well read;	216	U45 Squib	4
That both, their odour take him,	220	U48 Bacchus	11
Both for the Mothers, and the Babes of grace,	223	U49 Pucell	44
So seem'd your horse and you, both of a peece!	228	U53 Newcastle	6
Of so much health, both to our Land, and King.	238	U66 Queene	V 14
And cleave both ayre and ground,	239	U67 Muses	14
And shake both ayre and ground,	239	U67 Muses	V 14
Troubled both foes, and friends;	243	U70 Ode	28
Both to the honour of the King and State.	251	U74 Weston	24
And both a strength, and Beautie to his Land!	251	U74 Weston	30
Both Crownes, and Kingdomes in their either hand;	254	U75 Epithalam.	52
Whilst they both stand,	256	U75 Epithalam.	126
That when you both are old,	258	U75 Epithalam.	165
They are slip'd to Bed; Shut fast the Doore,	258	U75 Epithalam.	185
(For with both the Muse was fed)	259	U76 Petition	16
(For with both the Muse it fed)	259	U76 Petition	V 16
That leades our flocks and us, and calls both forth	264	U79 New-yeares	29
In truth of colours, both are best.	265	U79 New-yeares	45
By Thee, and Conscience, both who thrive	273	U84 Cradle	7
For he's both noble, lovely, young,	292	U86 Hor.4:1	13
And both doe crave, and give againe, this leave.	305	Horace	13
His course so hurtfull both to graine, and seedes,	309	Horace	97
If custome please, with whom both choyse, and will,	341	Horace	V103
Yet sometime both the Comedy doth raise	341	Horace	V132
Complaines in humble phrase. Both Telephus,	311	Horace	135

BOTH (cont.)
In sound, quite from his fortune; both the rout, . . . 313 Horace 159
Be wonne a friend; it must both sway, and bend . . . 317 Horace 281
Both in their tunes, the licence greater grew, . . . 319 Horace 299
And jests; and both to admiration raise . . . 323 Horace 400
And jests; and both to admiration rais'd, . . . 348 Horace V386/400
The wished goale, both did, and suffer'd much . . . 333 Horace 588
And both from Wine, and Women did abstaine. . . . 333 Horace 590
Be then both Rare, and Good; and long . . . 367 Ode Who saith 33
Here France, and Italy both to him shed . . . 375 Coryat 1 30
And see both climing up the slippery staire . . . 395 May 2
Of thy strange Moon-Calfe, both thy straine of mirth, . . . 398 Drayton 84
Both Saints, and Martyrs, by her loved Lord. . . . 400 Lady Ogle 39
Both him & Archimede; damne Architas . . . 402 Inigo Jones 1 5
Both learned, and unlearned, all write Playes. . . . 410 Brome 12
And doe both Church, and Common-wealth the good, . . . 416 Dover 8
As when they both were greate, and both knewe howe . . . 419 Ode:If Men 3
BOTTLE
Or the Tripos, his Tower Bottle: . . . 657 Door Apollo 4
BOTTOM
Never did bottom more betray her burden; . . . 87 E133 Voyage 116
BOTTOME
In hast the bottome of a med'cin'd Cup, . . . 197 U40 Elegy That 4
BOUGH
Sans helpe of Sybil, or a golden bough, . . . 85 E133 Voyage 48
BOUGHES
The trees cut out in log; and those boughes made . . . 98 F3 Wroth 45
BOUGHS
So large; his Body then, not boughs, project his shade. . . . 258 U75 Epithalam. V184
With boughs of Palme, a crowned Victrice stand! . . . 285 U84 Muse 96
BOUGHT
Not offer'd, as it made sute to be bought; . . . 28 E3 Bookseller 6
Ere blacks were bought for his owne funerall, . . . 41 E44 Chuff 3
A knight-hood bought, to goe a wooing in? . . . 42 E46 Luckless 1 2
His bought armes Mung' not lik'd; for his first day . . . 42 E48 Mungril 1
Yet have they seene the maps, and bought 'hem too, . . . 59 E92 New Crie 9
Live, with un-bought provision blest; . . . 97 F3 Wroth 14
With all since bought. . . . 129 U1 Father 22
Bought Flatteries, the issue of his purse, . . . 162 U15 Friend-Wars 13
Thinke but how deare you bought . . . 180 U26 Ode High 19
With Gold, or Claspes, which might be bought . . . 273 U84 Cradle 27
Except a dublet, and bought of the Jewes: . . . 380 Coryat 3 49
Do wayte upon thee: and theyre Love not bought. . . . 384 Somerset 4
And will be bought of every Lord, and Knight, . . . 398 Drayton 72
BOULSTRED
She was 'Sell Boulstred. In which name, I call . . . 372 Epitaph 12
BOUNCING
Come forth thou bonnie bouncing booke then, daughter . . . 378 Coryat 2 86
BOUND (BOUNDARY)
Large claspe of Nature, such a wit can bound. . . . 160 U14 Selden 64
But, as they conquer'd, and enlarg'd their bound, . . . 319 Horace 295
The Bound, and Frontire of our Poetrie; . . . 400 Beaumont 8
BOUND
To whom I am so bound, lov'd Aubigny? . . . 80 E127 Aubigny 3
Is this we heare? of frogs? No, guts wind-bound, . . . 86 E133 Voyage 92
Some act of Love's bound to reherse, . . . 93 F1 Why write no 1
They were bound! . . . 183 U29 Fit of Rime 12
The Hau'-boy, not as now with latten bound, . . . 319 Horace 287
With Rites not bound, but conscience. Wouldst thou All? . . . 372 Epitaph 11
BOUNDS
So hast thou rendred him in all his bounds. . . . 61 E95 Savile 5
And what are bounds to her, you make your owne? . . . 236 U64 Charles 3 10
Pan is the great Preserver of our bounds. . . . 264 U79 New-yeares 14
This is the great Preserver of our bounds, . . . 265 U79 New-yeares 48
In all the bounds of beautie fit . . . 280 U84 Mind 51
Or at the Feast of Bounds, the Lambe then slaine, . . . 291 U85 Country 59
BOUNTEOUS
Bounteous as the clouds to earth; . . . 142 U2 Her man 43
BOUNTIE'
Of Gathering? Bountie' in pouring out againe? . . . 159 U14 Selden 38
BOUNTIE
And all your bountie wrong: . . . 139 U2 Another 10
When by thy sordid bountie she hath on . . . 201 U42 Elegy Let 45
O bountie! so to difference the rates! . . . 235 U62 Charles 1 12
The bountie of a King, and beautie of his Queene! . . . 252 U75 Epithalam. 8
To his bountie; by extension . . . 259 U76 Petition 9
To his bountie; by dimension . . . 259 U76 Petition V 9
BOUNTIES
All your bounties will betray. . . . 103 F6 Celia 2 4
Their bounties forth, to him that last was made, . . . 155 U13 Sacvile 63
And not the bounties you ha' done, deny. . . . 192 U38 Elegy 'Tis 54
And wonder'd at the bounties of this day: . . . 255 U75 Epithalam. 90
BOUNTY
Lucy of Bedford; she, that Bounty . . . 662 Bedford 3
BOUTERSHEIM
Hans-spiegle, Rotteinberg, and Boutersheim, . . . 69 E107 Hungry 26
BOUTS
Bouts of fleet waters, that doe intertwine . . . 338 Horace V 21
BOW (VERB)
Fit for a Bishops knees! O bow them oft, . . . 234 U61 Epigram 13
BOW (NAME)
To Braynford, Hackney, Bow, but thou mak'st one; . . . 81 E129 Mime 4

	Page	Title	Line

BOW

And, armed to the chase, so bare her bow	68	E105 L Wroth 2	13
Arm'd with bow, shafts, and fire;	110	F11 Epode	38
Where's thy Quiver? bend thy Bow:	132	U2 How he saw	9
Letting Bow and Arrow fall,	132	U2 How he saw	17
And the Bow: with thought to hit	132	U2 How he saw	22
Both the Bow, and shaft I held,	133	U2 Suffered	8
Both her Browes, bent like my Bow.	136	U2 Cupid	17
Eye-brows bent like Cupids bow,	141	U2 Her man	17
His double Bow, and round his Arrowes sends;	170	U19 Elegy By	4
His flames, his shafts, his Quiver, and his Bow,	182	U28 Worth	10
Nor alwayes doth the loosed Bow, hit that	329	Horace	524

BOWER

| To welcome home a Paire, and deck the nuptiall bower? | 253 | U75 Epithalam. | 24 |

BOWERS

A forme more fresh, then are the Eden bowers,	111	F11 Epode	57
To see their Seats and Bowers by chattring Pies defac't?	174	U23 Himselfe	12
The Thrones, the Cherube, and Seraphick bowers,	285	U84 Muse	88

BOWLE (GAME)

| To flatter my good Lord, and cry his Bowle | 167 | U15 Friend-Wars | 147 |

BOWLE

| Give me a deep-crown'd-Bowle, that I may sing | 225 | U51 Bacon | 19 |

BOWLES

| They looke at best like Creame-bowles, and you soone | 198 | U40 Elegy That | 29 |

BOX

To take the box up for him; and pursues	166	U15 Friend-Wars	137
And all the Evils that flew out of her box	212	U43 Vulcan	214
And all Those ills that flew out of her box	212	U43 Vulcan	V214
This, and that box his Beautie to repaire;	215	U44 Speach	96

BOXES

| And in smooth Cypresse boxes to be keep'd? | 327 | Horace | 476 |

BOY

My sinne was too much hope of thee, lov'd boy,	41	E45 First Son	2
Let the old boy, your sonne, ply his old taske,	107	F10 Proludium	19
Have you seene the boy from the Chace	135	U2 Triumph	V 39
Of Phaos forme? or doth the Boy	181	U27 Ode Helen	5
Was, t'have a Boy stand with a Club, and fright	241	U69 Friend Son	11
And Phrygian Hau'boy, not without the Flute.	292	U86 Hor.4:1	24
Me now, nor Wench, nor wanton Boy,	293	U86 Hor.4:1	29
So Fates would let the Boy a long thred run.	293	U87 Hor.3:9	16
The Hau'-boy, not as now with latten bound,	319	Horace	287
He cries, Good boy, thou'lt keepe thine owne. Now, adde	327	Horace	470

BOY'D

| But that the Corke of Title boy'd him up. | 244 | U70 Ode | 42 |

BOYES

Of the lesse-Poetique boyes;	259	U76 Petition	20
Of the brave Poetique boyes;	259	U76 Petition	V 20
As prop'rest gifts, to Girles, and Boyes,	273	U84 Cradle	19
According to the Moone. But, then the boyes	335	Horace	647
And stradling shews the Boyes Brown paper fleet,	407	Inigo Jones 2	17

BOYLER

| A sope-boyler; and Aeacus him nigh, | 89 | E133 Voyage | 188 |

BOYLES

| And boyles, as if he were | 110 | F11 Epode | 42 |

BOYLING

| The ever-boyling floud. Whose bankes upon | 88 | E133 Voyage | 142 |

BOYS

| Under the angry Moon. But then the boys | 354 | Horace | V647 |

BRACE

| Backe, cry'd their brace of Charons: they cry'd, no, | 86 | E133 Voyage | 87 |
| So each, that's done, and tane, becomes a Brace. | 154 | U13 Sacvile | 40 |

BRAG

| And brag, that they were therefore borne. | 99 | F3 Wroth | 72 |

BRAID

| Whether any would up-braid | 138 | U2 Kisse | 30 |

BRAIES

| And made those strong approaches, by False braies, | 248 | U71 Treasurer | 7 |

BRAINE

Hardie, thy braine is valiant, 'tis confest,	32	E16 Brain-hardy	1
Active in's braine, and passive in his bones.	49	E68 Playwrt 2	4
(Save that most masculine issue of his braine)	53	E79 Rutland	6
Of what shee had wrought came in, and wak'd his braine,	56	E87 Hazard	4
That age, when thou stood'st up the master-braine:	75	E116 Jephson	4
One was; and he, for brawne, and braine, right able	84	E133 Voyage	23
Sure, said he, if I have Braine,	136	U2 Cupid	10
Who aided him, will thee, the issue of Joves braine.	175	U23 Himselfe	30
Who aided them, will thee, the issue of Joves braine.	175	U23 Himselfe	V 30
Thy Priest in this strange rapture; heat my braine	177	U25 Desmond	11
And the Muses to their braine;	184	U29 Fit of Rime	41
Weaknesse of braine, or any charme of Wine,	198	U40 Elegy That	45
To ruine any issue of the braine?	203	U43 Vulcan	14
To ruine every issue of her braine?	203	U43 Vulcan	V 14
Before his braine doe know it;	221	U48 Bacchus	30
But since the Wine hath steep'd my braine,	230	U55 Burges	5
Into the Profits, what a meere rude braine	331	Horace	583
So in my braine; the stronge impression	361	Palmer	21
Of his foote, or his penne, his braine or his hoofe,	380	Coryat 3	32
That I not mixe thee so, my braine excuses;	391	Shakespeare	25

BRAINES

Who, to thy one, all other braines refuse;	34	E23 Donne 1	2
All braines, at times of triumph, should runne wit.	36	E29 Tilter	4
Then, leave these lighter numbers, to light braines	108	F10 Proludium	7
From braines entranc'd, and fill'd with extasies;	116	F12 Rutland	90

	Page	Title	Line
BRAINES (cont.)			
Both braines and hearts; and mine now best doe know it:	182	U28 Worth	8
As th'other may his braines with Quicksilver.	208	U43 Vulcan	122
In these pide times, only to shewe their braines,	362	Author	4
As well as from his braines, and claimest thereby	378	Coryat 2	90
Ever his thighes Male then, and his braines Shee.	378	Coryat 2	92
Thy Dirty braines, Men smell thy want of worth.	409	Detractor	22
BRAINS			
Clears the Brains, makes Wit the Quicker:	657	Door Apollo	16
BRAKE (NOUN)			
Or were set up in a Brake.	142	U2 Her man	40
Or were pent up in a Brake.	142	U2 Her man	V 40
BRAKE			
my abler faculties; and thus brake foorth	362	Palmer	29
BRAKES			
Crush'd in the snakie brakes, that he had past!	162	U15 Friend-Wars	18
BRANCH			
I pluck'd a branch; the jealous god did frowne,	80	E126 Mrs Cary	3
BRANCHES			
Grow, grow, faire tree, and as thy branches shoote,	119	F13 Aubigny	99
Clos'd to their peace, he saw his branches shoot,	185	U30 Burleigh	17
From fattest branches of the Tree:	291	U85 Country	56
BRANCHING			
Foure Rivers branching forth like Seas,	276	U84 Body	23
BRAND			
Itch to defame the State? or brand the Times?	203	U43 Vulcan	25
Nor from the brand, with which the life did burne	315	Horace	207
Thy Forehead is too narrow for my Brand.	408	Inigo Jones 3	14
BRANDED			
Impostures branded! And Authorities urg'd!	160	U14 Selden	41
Cropt, branded, slit, neck-stockt; go, you are stript.	411	Gill	16
BRANDISH'D			
So brightly brandish'd) wound'st, defend'st! the while	187	U33 Councellour	32
BRANDISH'T			
As brandish't at the eyes of Ignorance.	392	Shakespeare	70
BRANDS			
In equall knots: This beares no brands, nor darts,	110	F11 Epode	51
BRASSE			
Thy fact, in brasse or marble writ the same)	46	E60 Mounteagle	4
Or, in an armies head, that, lockt in brasse,	114	F12 Rutland	52
Th'Aemilian Schoole, in brasse can fashion out	307	Horace	46
As well in brasse, as he hath hit	390	Reader	6
All, that was ever writ in brasse.	390	Reader	8
BRAULES			
Thy selfe into fresh braules: when, call'd upon,	32	E16 Brain-hardy	3
BRAVADO			
And there, while he gives the zealous Bravado,	375	Coryat 1	22
BRAVE			
At court I met it, in clothes brave enough,	30	E11 Something	1
What two brave perills of the private sword	37	E32 Roe 2	1
Out-dance the Babion, or out-boast the Brave;	81	E129 Mime	12
I Sing the brave adventure of two wights,	84	E133 Voyage	21
Act a brave worke, call it thy last adventry:	85	E133 Voyage	57
And, on they went, like Castor brave, and Pollux:	86	E133 Voyage	77
Our brave Heroes with a milder glare,	88	E133 Voyage	163
With his brave sonne, the Prince, they saw thy fires	95	F2 Penshurst	77
Gave killing strokes. There were brave men, before	114	F12 Rutland	53
And your brave friend, and mine so well did love.	116	F12 Rutland	92
And your brave friend, and mine so well did love.	116	F12 Rutland	V 92
And call it their brave sinne. For such there be	119	F13 Aubigny	85
And her dressing did out-brave	132	U2 How he saw	3
'Tis like light Canes, that first rise big and brave,	157	U13 Sacvile	149
Beates brave, and loude in Europe, and bids come	162	U15 Friend-Wars	2
Great, brave, and fashion'd folke, these are allow'd	164	U15 Friend-Wars	84
Thou hast the brave scorne, to put back the fee!	187	U33 Councellour	22
But when thy Wife (as thou conceiv'st) is brave?	201	U42 Elegy Let	50
Well, I say, thrive, thrive brave Artillerie yard,	213	U44 Speach	23
Is of so brave example, as he were	224	U50 Countesse	7
'Tis a brave cause of joy, let it be knowne,	225	U51 Bacon	17
You made it a brave piece, but not like me.	227	U52 Answer	15
Henry, the brave young Lord La-ware,	233	U60 La-ware	3
And art thou borne, brave Babe? Blest be thy birth,	237	U65 Prince	1
And art thou borne, brave Babe? Blest be the day,	237	U65 Prince	V 1
Some brave un-common way:	239	U67 Muses	3
Brave Infant of Saguntum, cleare	242	U70 Ode	1
That knits brave minds, and manners, more then blood.	246	U70 Ode	106
Which knits brave minds, and manners, more then blood.	246	U70 Ode	V106
Of the brave Poetique boyes;	259	U76 Petition	V 20
His brest is a brave Palace, a broad Street,	262	U78 Digby	9
And, but for that Contention, and brave strife	271	U81 Pawlet	95
As you goe on, by what brave way	278	U84 Mind	18
(Brave Youths) th'are their possessions, none of yours:	281	U84 Kenelme	11
Medea make brave with impetuous scorne;	313	Horace	175
Of a brave Chiefe sent to the warres: He can,	325	Horace	451
For hee'll cry, Good, brave, better, excellent!	333	Horace	611
With the shops Foreman, or some such brave sparke,	371	Fletcher	6
Brave are the Musters, that the Muse will make.	398	Drayton	64
BRAVELY			
Two bravely in the battaile fell, and dy'd,	60	E93 Radcliffe	5
And so went bravely backe, without protraction.	89	E133 Voyage	192
BRAVERIE			
Of the short braverie of the night;	96	F3 Wroth	10

	Page	Title	Line
BRAVERIES			
And braveries of Court, and felt their fits	200	U42 Elegy Let	34
DRAVERY			
In bravery, or gluttony, or coyne,	163	U15 Friend-Wars	45
The bravery makes, she can no honour leese:	164	U15 Friend-Wars	56
His deare and borrow'd Bravery he must cast?	165	U15 Friend-Wars	110
BRAVEST			
In men, but every bravest was the best:	75	E116 Jephson	10
A better cause, and strike the bravest heate	397	Drayton	56
BRAV'RIES (See BRAUL)			
Doe boast their Loves, and Brav'ries so at large,	253	U75 Epithalam.	19
BRAWL			
BRAWNE			
One was; and he, for brawne, and braine, right able	84	E133 Voyage	23
BRAY			
What makes your Wretchednes to bray soe loud	403	Inigo Jones 1	23
BRAYES			
To every cause he meets, this voyce he brayes:	31	E12 Shift	19
BRAYNE			
To Brayne-hardie.	32	E16 Brain-hardy	Ttl
BRAYNE-HARDIE			
To Brayne-hardie.	32	E16 Brain-hardy	Ttl
BRAYNFORD			
To Braynford, Hackney, Bow, but thou mak'st one;	81	E129 Mime	4
BRAZEN			
And voyce to raise them from my brazen Lungs,	269	U81 Pawlet	24
And us dis-joyn'd force to her brazen yoke,	294	U87 Hor.3:9	18
BREACH			
And gratulate the breach, I griev'd before:	61	E95 Savile	10
That as the lesser breach: for he that takes	169	U17 Friend-Debt	11
To note in Poemes, breach of harmonie;	323	Horace	388
BREACHES			
Goe enter breaches, meet the cannons rage,	98	F3 Wroth	69
BREAD			
At Bread-streets Mermaid, having din'd, and merry,	85	E133 Voyage	37
Where the same beere, and bread, and selfe-same wine,	95	F2 Penshurst	63
And hurt seeks Cure, the Surgeon bids take bread,	155	U13 Sacvile	68
And cri'd, Away with the Caesarian bread,	228	U53 Newcastle	19
Or dispenc'd in bookes, or bread,	259	U76 Petition	15
Well dispenc'd in bookes, or bread,	259	U76 Petition	V 15
Seek out some hungry painter, that for bread	408	Inigo Jones 3	10
BREAD-STREETS			
At Bread-streets Mermaid, having din'd, and merry,	85	E133 Voyage	37
BREAK			
or theire Ale, they break the peace,	418	Moon	42
BREAKE			
To breake up seales, and close 'hem. And they know,	59	E92 New Crie	29
Or, if thou list the night in watch to breake,	97	F3 Wroth	21
The secrets, that shall breake their sleepe:	99	F3 Wroth	88
Debts when they can: good men may breake their day,	169	U17 Friend-Debt	2
And their words too; where I but breake my Band.	169	U17 Friend-Debt	9
His name in any mettall, it would breake.	172	U21 Ltl Shrub	2
Breake the knit Circle of her Stonie Armes,	177	U25 Desmond	19
The Hawking language? or our Day to breake	215	U44 Speach	72
His friends, but to breake Chaires, or cracke a Coach.	230	U56 Covell	10
To bend, to breake, provoke, or suffer it!	233	U59 Newcastle	18
To bend, or breake, provoke, or suffer it!	233	U59 Newcastle	V 18
Their Carract was! I, or my trump must breake,	269	U81 Pawlet	27
Their Carract was! for my trump must breake,	269	U81 Pawlet	V 27
And, out of that, make Day to breake;	276	U84 Body	14
or as some would say to breake	416	Moon	3
Breake then thie quills, blott out	420	Ode:If Men	19
BREAKES			
Fortune upon him breakes her selfe, if ill,	63	E98 Th Roe 1	5
As light breakes from you, that affrights despaire,	191	U38 Elegy 'Tis	10
BREAKING			
Launces, and men, and some a breaking force.	213	U44 Speach	8
I summe up mine owne breaking, and wish all.	283	U84 Muse	26
BREAST (See also BREST)			
And betweene each rising breast,	137	U2 Cupid	33
Did never dint the breast of Tamisis.	366	Ode Who saith	8
BREASTS			
Against their breasts. Here, sev'rall ghosts did flit	87	E133 Voyage	124
Throughout their generall breasts,	421	Ode:If Men	43
BREATH			
Then Cicero, whose every breath was fame:	57	E89 Allen	6
Dar'st breath in any ayre; and with safe skill,	76	E119 Shelton	9
May windes as soft as breath of kissing friends,	81	E128 Wm Roe 2	5
For fame, with breath soone kindled, soone blowne out.	83	E131 Ferrab. 2	14
And change possessions, oftner with his breath,	99	F3 Wroth	75
While you breath. First give a hundred,	103	F6 Celia 2	8
But thou thereon did'st onely breath,	106	F9 Celia 3	13
Whose od'rous breath destroyes	112	F11 Epode	96
With holy Paul, lest it be thought the breath	122	F15 Heaven	24
Rip'ned with a breath more sweet,	137	U2 Cupid	27
Each suck others breath.	139	U2 Another	16
And that as any are strooke, her breath creates	222	U49 Pucell	5
Health, or scarce breath, as she had never bin,	248	U71 Treasurer	12
You seeme a faire one! O that you had breath,	269	U81 Pawlet	6
You seeme a faire one! O that I had breath,	269	U81 Pawlet	V 6
What 'tis t'enjoy, an everlasting breath!	285	U84 Muse	92
The safetie of our soules, and forfeit breath!	286	U84 Muse	136
To justifie, and quicken us in breath!	288	U84 Muse	204

		Page	Title	Line

BREATH (cont.)
Her breath for sweete exceeding . . . . . 365 Ode Splendor 13
Her breath farre sweete exceeding . . . . 365 Ode Splendor V 13
How do his trumpets breath! What loud alarmes! . . 398 Drayton 66
Bred by your breath, on this low bancke of ours; . . 416 Welcome 3
BREATHE
Breathe to expect my when, and make my how. . . 37 E33 Roe 3 4
Where breathe the basest of thy fooles; . . . 101 F4 To the World 46
BREATH'D
But soft, and simple, at few holes breath'd time . . 319 Horace 289
BREATHES
That breathes in his dogs way: and this is great. . . 36 E28 Surly 18
BREATH'S
That lives, and breath's, and loves the King. . . . 418 Grace 4
BREATH'ST
And breath'st into it, life, and light, with state . . 127 U1 Trinitie 19
BRED
They, then, that living where the matter is bred, . . 60 E94 Bedford 3 11
That bred them, graves: when they were borne, they di'd, . . 114 F12 Rutland 47
We were not bred to sit on stooles, ... 146 U6 Defence 3
To have his Court-bred-fillie there commend . . 163 U15 Friend-Wars 48
And kept, and bred, and brought up true. . . . 173 U22 Elegy Tho 16
And must be bred, so to conceale his birth, . . 197 U40 Elegy That 17
Bred on the Banck, in time of Poperie, . . . 209 U43 Vulcan 143
Borne, bred, allied? what's he dare tutor us? . . 215 U44 Speach 66
O Times! O Manners! Surfet bred of ease, . . . 237 U64 Charles 3 17
Of Colchis borne; or in Assyria bred; . . . 313 Horace 167
The Vale, that bred thee pure, as her Hills Snow. . . 367 Ode Who saith 40
That knew the Crafts they had bin bred in, right: . . 410 Brome 14
Bred by your breath, on this low bancke of ours; . . 416 Welcome 3
BREDA
The Berghen siege, and taking in Breda, ... 214 U44 Speach 40
BREECHES
for the breeches with the bride, ... 417 Moon 34
BREED
The middle grounds thy mares, and horses breed. . . 94 F2 Penshurst 24
Is that which doth perfection breed. . . . . 146 U6 Defence 12
Absence, or Distance, shall not breed decay. . . 194 U38 Elegy 'Tis 116
With Citizens? let Clownes, and Tradesmen breed . . 215 U44 Speach 73
BREEDES
Keepe secret in his Channels what he breedes, . . 198 U40 Elegy That 27
BREEDING
Father and Sonne; the Comforter, in breeding . . 128 U1 Trinitie 26
The Phoenix place of breeding, ... 365 Ode Splendor 14
BREEDS
'Tis not thy judgement breeds the prejudice, . . 50 E72 Court-ling 5
Thy sincere practise, breeds not thee a fame . . 187 U33 Councellour 39
BREST
That hast thy brest so cleere of present crimes, . . 61 E95 Savile 19
Which to effect (since no brest is so sure, . . 109 F11 Epode 5
Which in assurance to your brest I tell, . . 198 U40 Elegy That 49
She durst not kisse, but flung thee from her brest. . . 208 U43 Vulcan 114
His brest is a brave Palace, a broad Street, . . 262 U78 Digby 9
Thou wouldst have written, Fame, upon my brest: . . 269 U81 Pawlet 14
Thou entertaining in thy brest, ... 281 U84 Mind 71
how lyke the Carbuncle in Aarons brest . . . 361 Palmer 14
And still is in the Brest: . . . . . 366 Ode Who saith 27
BRESTS
In our enflamed brests: . . . . . 110 F11 Epode 34
Such a religious horrour in the brests . . . 155 U13 Sacvile 91
But flowes out, that ore-swelleth in full brests. . . 329 Horace 506
BRETHREN
Or 'gainst the Bishops, for the Brethren, raile, . . 59 E92 New Crie 35
Much like those Brethren; thinking to prevaile . . 59 E92 New Crie 36
The Brethren, they streight nois'd it out for Newes, . . 209 U43 Vulcan 139
The brethren they streight ways noisd out for newes, . . 209 U43 Vulcan V139
What brethren, what a stranger, and his guest, . . 325 Horace 448
BRETONS
With Nicholas Bretons Meddle with your match, . . 206 U43 Vulcan V 77
Looke here on Bretons worke, the master print: . . 362 Author 5
BREVITIE
Where brevitie, where splendor, and where height, . . 62 E95 Savile 29
BREW
But to confine him to the Brew-houses, . . . 211 U43 Vulcan 179
BREW-HOUSES
But to confine him to the Brew-houses, . . . 211 U43 Vulcan 179
BRIAREUS
One said, it was bold Briareus, or the beadle, . . 86 E133 Voyage 81
BRICK
Condemne him to the Brick-kills, or some Hill-/foot . . 211 U43 Vulcan 183
Condemne him to some Brick-hills, or some Hill-/foot . . 211 U43 Vulcan V183
Condemne him to the Brick-kills, or a forge . . 211 U43 Vulcan V183
BRICK-HILLS
Condemne him to some Brick-hills, or some Hill-/foot . . 211 U43 Vulcan V183
BRICK-KILLS
Condemne him to the Brick-kills, or some Hill-/foot . . 211 U43 Vulcan 183
Condemne him to the Brick-kills, or a forge . . 211 U43 Vulcan V183
BRIDE
Of some Bride-well, and may, in time, concerne us . . 85 E133 Voyage 42
That the Bride (allow'd a Maid) . . . . 138 U2 Kisse 8
Wisht the Bride were chang'd to night, . . . 138 U2 Kisse 18
By Jove to have Minerva for thy Bride, . . . 203 U43 Vulcan 12
And all did ring th'approches of the Bride; . . 253 U75 Epithalam. 36

79

BRIDE (cont.)
The Bridegroome meets the Bride . . . . . . 254 U75 Epithalam. 71
To lay her here, inclos'd, his second Bride. . . . 394 Jane Ogle 24
for the breeches with the bride, ... 417 Moon 34
BRIDEGROOME
The Bridegroome meets the Bride . . . . . 254 U75 Epithalam. 71
BRIDES
The bright Brides paths, embelish'd more then thine . . 254 U75 Epithalam. 59
BRIDE-WELL
Of some Bride-well, and may, in time, concerne us . . . 85 E133 Voyage 42
BRIEFE
Be briefe, in what thou wouldst command, that so . . 329 Horace 503
BRIER
Or have smelt o'the bud o'the Brier? . . . . 135 U2 Triumph 27
Which, of the field is clep'd the sweetest brier, . . 413 Ghyrlond 22
BRIGHT
Then they might in her bright eyes. . . . . 39 E40 Ratcliffe 8
You were the bright Oenone, Flora, or May? . . . 68 E105 L Wroth 2 10
Bright eeles, that emulate them, and leape on land, . . 94 F2 Penshurst 37
Shine bright on every harth as the desires . . . 95 F2 Penshurst 78
Whose linkes are bright, and even, . . . 110 F11 Epode 48
And turne the blackest sorrowes to bright joyes: . . 112 F11 Epode 95
Or set bright Ariadnes crowne so high? . . . 115 F12 Rutland 60
Of all Lucina's traine; Lucy the bright, . . . 115 F12 Rutland 66
Of love be bright, ... 121 F14 Sydney 57
Doe but looke on her Haire, it is bright . . . 134 U2 Triumph 13
Have you seene but a bright Lillie grow, . . . 134 U2 Triumph 21
But he hath eyes so round, and bright, . . . 147 U7 Nymph 22
By those bright Eyes, at whose immortall fires . . 170 U19 Elegy By 1
(Whose heart in that bright Sphere flames clearest, . . 179 U25 Desmond 54
With bright Lycoris, Gallus choice, . . . 181 U27 Ode Helen 15
Their Jemme of Riches, and bright Stone, that brings . 206 U43 Vulcan 74
To see that bright eternall Day: . . . . 245 U70 Ode 81
In this bright Asterisme: . . . . . 246 U70 Ode 89
A-while with us bright Sun, and helpe our light; . . 252 U75 Epithalam. 2
A-while with us bright Sun, and mend our light; . . 252 U75 Epithalam. V 2
What Beavie of beauties, and bright youths at charge . 253 U75 Epithalam. 17
The bright Brides paths, embelish'd more then thine . . 254 U75 Epithalam. 59
When the Apostle Barnabee the bright . . . 262 U78 Digby 15
Her fellowes, with the oyle of gladnesse, bright . . 285 U84 Muse 101
Incarnate in the Manger, shining bright . . . 288 U84 Muse 200
Nor Turbot, nor bright Golden-eyes: . . . 291 U85 Country 50
If with bright floods, the Winter troubled much, . . 291 U85 Country 51
With thy bright Swans, of Paulus Maximus: . . . 292 U86 Hor.4:1 10
That I bright Chloe off should shake; . . . 294 U87 Hor.3:9 19
But light from smoake; that he may draw his bright . 315 Horace 204
With entheate rage, to publish their bright tracts? . . 368 Ode Who saith 61
So blacke a Bird, so bright a Qualitie. . . . 369 Ode Who saith 96
When, by thy bright Ideas standing by, . . . 397 Drayton 23
Yett: since the bright, and wyse, . . . 420 Ode:If Men 28
unto the bright, and amiable . . . . 662 Bedford 2
BRIGHTER
I meant the day-starre should not brighter rise, . . 52 E76 Bedford 1 7
Where never Star shone brighter yet? . . . 181 U27 Ode Helen 26
BRIGHTEST
Of brightest Mira, doe we raise our Song; . . . 264 U79 New-yeares 24
Of brightest Mira, is our Song; the grace . . . 264 U79 New-yeares 32
BRIGHTLY
So brightly brandish'd) wound'st, defend'st! the while . 187 U33 Councellour 32
Of Shakespeares minde, and manners brightly shines . . 392 Shakespeare 67
BRIGHTNESSE
Lucy, you brightnesse of our spheare, who are . . 60 E94 Bedford 3 1
Lucy, you brightnesse of our spheare, who are . . 61 E94 Bedford 3 15
Of her illustrate brightnesse, ... 364 Ode Splendor 3
Of her admyred brightnesse, ... 364 Ode Splendor V 3
BRILL
Would thinke no more of Vlushing, or the Brill: . . 213 U44 Speach 30
BRING
With thy new place, bring I these early fruits . . 47 E64 Salisbury 3 2
Where good mens vertues them to honors bring, . . 47 E64 Salisbury 3 11
Strength of my Countrey, whilst I bring to view . . 69 E108 Soldiers 1
If I would strive to bring backe times, and trie . . 78 E122 Rudyerd 2 3
Some bring a capon, some a rurall cake, . . . 95 F2 Penshurst 51
The better cheeses, bring 'hem; or else send . . 95 F2 Penshurst 53
My Muse up by commission: No, I bring . . . 108 F10 Proludium 28
Our muse up by commission: No, we bring . . . 108 F10 Proludium V 28
To her remembrance; which when time shall bring . . 115 F12 Rutland 75
That did us all salvation bring, . . . 130 U1 Nativitie 8
Then once to number, or bring forth to hand, . . 167 U15 Friend-Wars 173
And I will bring a Crop, if not the best. . . 169 U17 Friend-Debt 18
And shall not I my Celia bring, . . . 182 U27 Ode Helen 31
Powder, or paper, to bring up the youth . . . 213 U44 Speach 25
Much lesse a name would we bring up, or nurse, . . 216 U45 Squib 9
And though all praise bring nothing to your name, . . 224 U50 Countesse 13
Looke up, thou seed of envie, and still bring . . 250 U73 Weston 1
Bring all your friends, (faire Lord) that burne . . 251 U74 Weston 20
To day, the Fathers service; who could bring . . 256 U75 Epithalam. 107
Of all that Nature, yet, to life did bring; . . 264 U79 New-yeares 33
With all that Youth, or it can bring: . . . 276 U84 Body 22
And thou maist better bring a Rhapsody . . . 313 Horace 184
Mans comming yeares much good with them doe bring: . 317 Horace 250
For choller! If I did not, who could bring . . 325 Horace 430
For Choler! if I did not, none could bring . . 349 Horace V430

BRING (cont.)
 Whether truth may, and whether error bring. 325 Horace 439
 Of an entangling suit; and bring 't about: 333 Horace 604
 You doe not bring, to judge your Verses, one, 333 Horace 609
 Hee'd bid, blot all: and to the anvile bring 333 Horace 627
 Now, bring him backe, he'le be no more a man, 355 Horace V668
 And pray thee Reader, bring thy weepinge Eyes 394 Jane Ogle 2
 I Cannot bring my Muse to dropp her Vies 415 Dover 1
BRINGES
 hee freely bringes; and on this Alter layes 383 Rich 9
BRINGING
 By bringing forth God's onely Son, no other. 414 Ghyrlond 48
BRINGS
 The taylor brings a suite home; he it 'ssayes, 30 E12 Shift 9
 Scarse thy weekes swearing brings thee of, of one. 32 E16 Brain-hardy 4
 Most thinke all praises flatteries. But truth brings 49 E67 Suffolk 2
 Their Jemme of Riches, and bright Stone, that brings 206 U43 Vulcan 74
 And Charles brings home the Ladie. 222 U48 Bacchus 54
 It brings Friends Joy, Foes Griefe, Posteritie Fame; 256 U75 Epithalam. 114
 Of Meleager, brings he the returne 315 Horace 208
 My suffrage brings thee all increase, to crowne 385 Brooke 7
BRING'ST
 He will cleare up his forehead, thinke thou bring'st 263 U78 Digby 21
 He will cheare up his forehead, thinke thou bring'st 263 U78 Digby V 21
BRINGST
 Unto the Scene thou bringst, and dar'st create 313 Horace 179
 Unto the Stage thou bringst, and dar'st create 342 Horace V179
BRISTO'
 A harder tasque, then either his to Bristo', 85 E133 Voyage 39
BRITAINE
 Indeed, when had great Britaine greater cause 236 U64 Charles 3 7
 Me thought, Great Britaine in her Sea, before, 268 U80 Christning 13
 Triumph, my Britaine, thou hast one to showe, 391 Shakespeare 41
BRITAIN'S
 Repeating all Great Britain's joy, and more, 249 U72 King 6
BRITTAINS
 For Brittains honour, and to Charles my King: 262 U78 Digby V 18
BRIZE
 As if a Brize were gotten i' their tayle; 164 U15 Friend-Wars 71
BROAD
 A man should seeke great glorie, and not broad. 62 E96 Donne 2 12
 Beneath the broad beech, and the chest-nut shade; 93 F2 Penshurst 12
 His brest is a brave Palace, a broad Street, 262 U78 Digby 9
 If thou the vile, broad-troden ring forsake. 313 Horace 188
 Or, to so many, and so Broad-seales had, 385 Brooke 3
BROADER
 To brookes, and broader streames, 366 Ode Who saith 23
BROADEST
 And brooding o're it sit, with broadest eyes, 99 F3 Wroth 83
BROAD-SEALES
 Or, to so many, and so Broad-seales had, 385 Brooke 3
BROAD-TRODEN
 If thou the vile, broad-troden ring forsake. 313 Horace 188
BROCAGE
 From brocage is become so bold a thiefe, 44 E56 Poet-Ape 3
BROECK
 To live when Broeck not stands, nor Roor doth runne. 49 E66 Cary 12
BROKE (See also BRAKE)
 That fled his cage, or broke his chaine, 101 F4 To the World 30
 Yet he broke them, e're they could him, 151 U12 Corbet 10
 But that some greater names have broke with me, 169 U17 Friend-Debt 8
 'Tis true, I'm broke! Vowes, Oathes, and all I had 191 U38 Elegy 'Tis 1
 How is she barren growne of love! or broke! 237 U64 Charles 3 15
 How is she barren growne in love! or broke! 237 U64 Charles 3 V 15
BROKEN
 A broken heart thou wert not wont despise, 127 U1 Trinitie 10
 A broken heart, 129 U1 Father 2
 Her broken Armes up, to their emptie moulds. 216 U44 Speach 102
 Her broken sighes did never misse whole sense: 288 U84 Muse 185
 Get broken peeces, and fight well by those. 398 Drayton 74
BROKERS
 Like Money-brokers, after Names, and hire 155 U13 Sacvile 62
 Or, like our Money-Brokers, take up names 386 Browne 10
BROME
 . . . the Author of this Work, M. Rich. Brome. 409 Brome Ttl
 I had you for a Servant, once, Dick Brome; 409 Brome 1
BRONTES
 Let Brontes, and black Steropes, 179 U25 Desmond 40
BROODING
 And brooding o're it sit, with broadest eyes, 99 F3 Wroth 83
 And howrely brooding ore the same, 400 Lady Ogle 29
BROOKES (NOUN)
 To brookes, and broader streames, 366 Ode Who saith 23
BROOKES
 None brookes the Sun-light worse then he. 189 U36 Song 4
BROOME
 Till swept away, th'were cancell'd with a broome! 282 U84 Muse 8
BROTHER
 Fate, in a brother. To conclude, 39 E40 Ratcliffe 15
 The brother trades a sister; and the friend 165 U15 Friend-Wars 93
 To Sir Lucius Carey, on the death of his Brother Morison 242 U70 Ode VTtl
 There shall the Brother, with the Sister walke, 285 U84 Muse 117
 You Sir, the elder brother, though you are 331 Horace 545

	Page	Title	Line
BROTHER (cont.)			
To my worthy, and deserving Brother	666	Glover	1
BROTHERS			
Of all her Brothers storie, ...	240	U67 Muses	29
And of her Brothers prowesse!	240	U67 Muses	V 30
. . . in the Behalfe of the two Noble Brothers sir Robert . .	382	Rich	Ttl
As true oblations; his Brothers Embleme sayes, . . .	383	Rich	10
BROUGHT			
'Twas brought to court first wrapt, and white as milke; .	31	E15 Court-worm	2
Thy selfe, with thy first thoughts, brought home by thee, .	81	E128 Wm Roe 2	10
Shee brought the Poets forth, but ours th'adventer. .	84	E133 Voyage	20
False world, good-night: since thou hast brought .	100	F4 To the World	1
That Homer brought to Troy; yet none so live: .	115	F12 Rutland	55
Could be brought once back to looke. . . .	132	U2 How he saw	19
In the same Mines of knowledge; and thence brought .	161	U14 Selden	76
In the rich Mines of knowledge; and thence brought .	161	U14 Selden	V 76
Brought on us, and will every hour increase. .	166	U15 Friend-Wars	122
Be brought by us to meet our Destinie. . .	170	U18 Elegy Can	20
And kept, and bred, and brought up true. .	173	U22 Elegy Tho	16
Quarrell with Nature, or in ballance brought .	188	U34 Small Poxe	6
And never be by time, or folly brought, .	198	U40 Elegy That	44
Supplant bold Panton; and brought there to view .	214	U44 Speach	34
And spangled Petticotes brought forth to eye, .	223	U49 Pucell	19
(Except the joy that the first Mary brought, .	238	U66 Queene	7
(And leave the joy that the first Mary brought, .	238	U66 Queene	V 7
Hath brought the Land an Heire!	240	U67 Muses	53
In season, and so brought .	245	U70 Ode	61
One to the other, long e're these to light were brought. .	257	U75 Epithalam.	144
Shee, to the Crowne, hath brought encrease. .	264	U79 New-yeares	41
Yet, here are no such Trifles brought, .	273	U84 Cradle	25
And wealth unto our language; and brought forth .	309	Horace	82
Afford? The Mountaines travail'd, and brought forth .	315	Horace	198
To every vice, as hardly to be brought .	315	Horace	232
The rash, and head-long eloquence brought forth .	319	Horace	307
Brought in the Visor, and the robe of State, .	319	Horace	316
As neither any God, were brought in there, .	321	Horace	331
As neither any God, be brought in there, .	346	Horace	V323/331
So, any Poeme, fancied, or forth-brought .	331	Horace	561
What treasure hast thou brought us! and what store .	388	Chapman	4
But who hath them interpreted, and brought .	395	May	19
Thou hadst brought Lapland, or old Cobalus, .	398	Drayton	86
Againe hath brought the Lillie to the Rose; .	401	Filmer	8
And Goody Sculpture, brought with much adoe .	403	Inigo Jones 1	38
BROUGHTONS			
Thy Wives pox on thee, and Bess Broughtons too. .	212	U43 Vulcan	V216
BROUGHT'ST			
And which thou brought'st me, welcome povertie. .	48	E65 Muse	12
BROW			
The angry brow; the sportive, wanton things; .	311	Horace	150
BROWES			
And from her arched browes, such a grace .	134	U2 Triumph	17
Both her Browes, bent like my Bow. .	136	U2 Cupid	17
This other for his eye-browes; hence, away, .	215	U44 Speach	97
BROWN			
And stradling shews the Boyes Brown paper fleet, .	407	Inigo Jones 2	17
BROWNE (NAME)			
To my truly-belov'd Freind, Mr Browne: on his Pastorals. .	386	Browne	Ttl
BROWNE			
Not though that haire grew browne, which once was amber, .	57	E90 Mill	9
BROWS			
Eye-brows bent like Cupids bow, ...	141	U2 Her man	17
BRUIS'D			
My selfe up to thee, harrow'd, torne, and bruis'd .	127	U1 Trinitie	5
BRUISED			
Nor can the bruised heart want eloquence: .	288	U84 Muse	186
BRUISETH			
But as he soares at that, he bruiseth then .	272	U81 Pawlet	98
BRUNSFIELD			
Brunsfield, and Mansfield doe this yeare, my fates .	219	U47 Tribe	44
BRUSH'D			
To ev'ry Petticote he brush'd, and Glove .	201	U42 Elegy Let	54
BRUTE			
What savage, brute affection, . . .	112	F11 Epode	108
BRUTUS			
Calme Brutus tenor start; but all along .	395	May	11
BUCK			
I ask'd a lord a buck, and he denyed me; .	54	E84 Bedford 2	2
BUCKINGHAM			
And Buckingham the fortunate. . . .	419	Grace	6
BUCKLERS			
Send it to Bucklers-bury, there 'twill, well. .	28	E3 Bookseller	12
BUCKLERS-BURY			
Send it to Bucklers-bury, there 'twill, well. .	28	E3 Bookseller	12
BUD			
Or have smelt o'the bud o'the Brier? . .	135	U2 Triumph	27
BUDS			
Like tender buds shoot up, and freshly grow. .	309	Horace	89
BUILD (See also BUYLDING)			
And this age will build no more: .	105	F8 Sicknesse	12
Did not she save from thence, to build a Rome? .	210	U43 Vulcan	162
Build Townes, and carve the Lawes in leaves of wood. .	327	Horace	490
Or Ale! He build a pallace! Thou a shopp .	407	Inigo Jones 2	9

	Page	Title	Line

BUILDERS
Or builders of Story have oft imputation . . . . . 380 Coryat 3 — 30

BUILDING
Of building townes, and making wilde beasts tame, . . . 82 E130 Ferrab. 1 — 2

BUILT
Thou art not, Penshurst, built to envious show, . . . 93 F2 Penshurst — 1
May say, their lords have built, but thy lord dwells. . . 96 F2 Penshurst — 102
For they were burnt, but to be better built. . . . 210 U43 Vulcan — 166
Not built with Canvasse, paper, and false lights, . . . 220 U47 Tribe — 65
Which to this use, wert built and consecrate! . . . 256 U75 Epithalam. — 130
And he is built like some imperiall roome . . . . 262 U78 Digby — 7
Built a small-timbred Stage, and taught them talke . . 319 Horace — 317
Amphion, too, that built the Theban towres, . . . 327 Horace — 483

BULKE
In bulke, doth make man better bee; . . . . 245 U70 Ode — 66

BULL
First bearing him a calfe, beare him a bull. . . . 57 E90 Mill — 18
Of your Moravian horse, Venetian bull. . . . . 69 E107 Hungry — 8

BULLOCKS
Thy sheepe, thy bullocks, kine, and calves doe feed: . . 94 F2 Penshurst — 23

BULLS
But 'bove the fat of rammes, or bulls, to prize . . . 127 U1 Trinitie — 11

BULWARKES
In Bulwarkes, Rav'lins, Ramparts, for defense, . . . 400 Beaumont — 4

BUOY (See BOY'D)

BURDEN (LOAD)
And ever close the burden of the Song, . . . 249 U72 King — 17
And then noyse forth the burden of their Song, . . 249 U72 King — V 17

BURDEN (See also BURTHEN)
Never did bottom more betray her burden; . . . 87 E133 Voyage — 116

BURGES
To Mr. John Burges. . . . . 229 U55 Burges — Ttl
Would God, my Burges, I could thinke . . . 229 U55 Burges — 1
To Master John Burges. . . . . . 231 U57 Burges — Ttl
Father John Burges, ... 231 U57 Burges — 1

BURIED
A lord, it cryed, buried in flesh, and blood, . . . 30 E11 Something — 5
Of the not borne, yet buried, here's the tombe. . . 46 E62 Would-bee — 12
Mans buried honour, in his sleepie life: . . . 162 U15 Friend-Wars — 7
Buried in ease and sloth? . . . . . 174 U23 Himselfe — 2

BURL
An Epigram On William Lord Burl: . . . 185 U30 Burleigh — Ttl

BURLASE
To all posteritie; I will write Burlase. . . . 227 U52 Answer — 24

BURNE
As he would burne, or better farre his booke. . . 53 E79 Rutland — 12
From whence, so lately, I did burne, . . . 101 F4 To the World — 27
The Birth-day shines, when logs not burne, but men. . 121 F14 Sydney — 60
And on them burne so chaste a flame, . . . 173 U22 Elegy Tho — 21
Who more they burne, they more desire, . . . 189 U36 Song — 10
And safely trust to dresse, not burne their Boates. . 208 U43 Vulcan — 128
No Foole would his owne harvest spoile, or burne! . 209 U43 Vulcan — 150
Burne to a snuffe, and then stinke out, and die: . . 211 U43 Vulcan — 188
Bring all your friends, (faire Lord) that burne . . 251 U74 Weston — 20
Your hottest Causticks to, burne, lance, or cut: . . 270 U81 Pawlet — 54
Your hotter Causticks to, burne, lance, or cut: . . 270 U81 Pawlet — V 54
Nor from the brand, with which the life did burne . 315 Horace — 207
Lyve long the Feasting Roome. And ere thou burne . 406 Inigo Jones 1 — 101

BURNED
Being, beyond sea, burned for one witch: . . . 88 E133 Voyage — 158
Perhaps, to have beene burned with my bookes. . . 203 U43 Vulcan — 18

BURNING
Ben: Jonson upon the burning of his study and bookes . 202 U43 Vulcan — VTtl
Conceipt, and into burning Aetna leap'd. . . . 335 Horace — 663
Thus, Love, and Hope, and burning Charitie, . . . 413 Ghyrlond — 25

BURNT
Leave Cod, tabacco-like, burnt gummes to take, . . 42 E50 Cod 3 — 1
Who, when you'have burnt your selves downe to the snuffe, 45 E59 Spies — 2
He burnt that Idoll of the Revels too: . . . 210 U43 Vulcan — 155
For they were burnt, but to be better built. . . 210 U43 Vulcan — 166
Such as the Sabines, or a Sun-burnt-blowse, . . . 291 U85 Country — 41

BURST
And, till they burst, their backs, like asses load: . . 62 E96 Donne 2 — 11
Had burst with storme, and downe fell, ab excelsis, . . 86 E133 Voyage — 95
This would all their envie burst: . . . . 260 U76 Petition — 30
That would all their envie burst: . . . 260 U76 Petition — V 30
A Master-worker call'd, th'old standerd burst . . 415 Rutter — 22
Of Subjects; Let such envie, till they burst. . . 416 Dover — 10

BURTHEN
To crowne the burthen which you goe withall, . . 119 F13 Aubigny — 103

BURY (PLACE)
Send it to Bucklers-bury, there 'twill, well. . . 28 E3 Bookseller — 12

BURY
Which you will bury; but therein, the strife . . 158 U13 Sacvile — 160

BURYED
Leave it buryed in this vault. . . . . 79 E124 Elizabeth — 8

BUSH
Or hauking at the river, or the bush, . . . 97 F3 Wroth — 33
In Moses bush, un-wasted in the fire. . . . 413 Ghyrlond — 24

BUSIE
Busie, or frowne at first; when he sees thee, . . 262 U78 Digby — 20
Have busie search made in his mysteries! . . . 284 U84 Muse — 80
Busie to catch a Black-bird; if he fall . . . 335 Horace — 651

BUSIED
He vexed time, and busied the whole State; . . . . 243 U70 Ode 27

BUSINESSE
H'has tympanies of businesse, in his face, ... 35 E28 Surly 7
But in a businesse, that will bide the Touch, ... 187 U33 Councellour 23
And act the businesse, which they paint, or carve. . . . 261 U77 Treasurer 16
And act the businesse, which these paint, or carve. . . . 261 U77 Treasurer V 16
Happie is he, that from all Businesse cleere, ... 289 U85 Country 1
Fresh Lovers businesse, and the Wines free source. . . . 311 Horace 116
On popular noise with, and doe businesse in. . . . 311 Horace 120
Or do's all businesse coldly, and with feare; . . . . 317 Horace 244
The businesse either on the Stage is done, ... 317 Horace 255

BUSKIN
Loftie, and grave; and in the buskin stalke. . . . . 319 Horace 318
Loftie, and great; and in the buskin walk. . . . . 348 Horace V398/318
To life againe, to heare thy Buskin tread, ... 391 Shakespeare 36

BUSKINS
This foot the socks tooke up, and buskins grave, . . . 311 Horace 118

BUS'NESSE
The bus'nesse of your blooming wit, ... 251 U74 Weston 22
She swaid all bus'nesse in the Familie! . . . . 287 U84 Muse 168

BUT
It will be look'd for, booke, when some but see . . . 27 E2 My Booke 1
Use mine so, too: I give thee leave. But crave . . . 27 E3 Bookseller 3
But two things, rare, the Fates had in their store, . . 28 E4 James 1 3
Whom should my Muse then flie to, but the best . . . 28 E4 James 1 9
But, for this money was a courtier found, ... 29 E8 Robbery 3
But I have my revenge made, in thy name. . . . . 29 E10 Ignorant 2
Not his poore cocatrice but he betrayes . . . . 31 E12 Shift 21
But see! th'old baud hath serv'd him in his trim, . . . 31 E12 Shift 23
Man scarse can make that doubt, but thou canst teach. . . 31 E14 Camden 10
But for their powers, accept my pietie. . . . . 31 E14 Camden 14
All men are wormes: But this no man. In silke . . . 31 E15 Court-worm 1
And, but a sprigge of bayes, given by thee, ... 32 E17 Critic 5
If thou'ldst but use thy faith, as thou didst then, . . . 32 E18 Censurer 7
Forbidd' his side! and nothing, but the word . . . . 33 E21 Gam'ster 4
But leave, because I cannot as I should! . . . . 34 E23 Donne 1 10
What doth he else, but say, leave to be chast, . . . 34 E25 Beast 1 7
May heare my Epigrammes, but like of none. . . . . 36 E28 Surly 20
Stile thee a most great foole, but no great man. . . . 36 E28 Surly 22
But that's put in, thou'lt say. Why, so is thine. . . . 36 E29 Tilter 6
Was his blest fate, but our hard lot to find. . . . . 37 E32 Roe 2 8
Glad-mention'd Roe: thou art but gone before, ... 37 E33 Roe 3 2
Left us of feare, but first our crimes, then lawes. . . . 38 E35 James 2 6
But in my royall subject I passe thee, ... 38 E36 Martial 3
But as they come, on both sides he takes fees, . . . 38 E37 Chev'ril 2
But that his Jone doth too. And Giles would never, . . 40 E42 Giles 4
The like is Jone. But turning home, is sad. . . . . 40 E42 Giles 8
When, in my booke, men reade but Cecill's name, . . . 41 E43 Salisbury 1 9
When, in my Verse, men reade but Sarum's name, . . . 41 E43 Salisbury 1 V 9
Which though it did but panick terror prove, ... 43 E51 James 3 3
Looke not upon thy dangers, but our feares. . . . . 43 E51 James 3 10
As if thou wert my friend, but lack'dst a cause. . . . 43 E52 Courtling 4
This but thy judgement fooles: the other way . . . . 43 E52 Courtling 5
But when (in place) thou didst the patrons choose, . . . 43 E53 Old-end 4
For, but thy selfe, where, out of motly, 's hee . . . . 44 E53 Old-end 9
Ideot, last night, I pray'd thee but forbeare . . . . 45 E58 Groome 1
Spies, you are lights in state, but of base stuffe, . . . 45 E59 Spies 1
Or, if shee would but modestly have prais'd . . . . 46 E60 Mounteagle 3
But thine, for which I doo't, so much exceeds! . . . 46 E60 Mounteagle 8
But saver of my countrey thee alone. . . . . 46 E60 Mounteagle 10
The world reputes you barren: but I know . . . . 46 E62 Would-bee 3
Not from the publike voyce, but private fact; . . . . 47 E63 Salisbury 2 6
But I am glad to see that time survive, ... 47 E64 Salisbury 3 9
That whil'st I meant but thine to gratulate, ... 48 E64 Salisbury 3 17
But I repent me: Stay. Who e're is rais'd, ... 48 E65 Muse 15
Durst valour make, almost, but not a crime. . . . . 48 E66 Cary 6
Could conquer thee, but chance, who did betray. . . . 49 E66 Cary 10
Most thinke all praises flatteries. But truth brings . . 49 E67 Suffolk 2
High in thy bloud, thy place, but highest then, . . . 49 E67 Suffolk 6
T'inveigh 'gainst playes: what did he then but play? . . 52 E75 Lippe 4
To draw thee custome: but her selfe gets all. . . . . 53 E78 Hornet 2
For good men but see death, the wicked tast it. . . . 54 E80 Life/Death 8
And never stoupe, but to strike ignorance: . . . . 55 E85 Goodyere 1 7
Each night, to drowne his cares: But when the gaine . . 56 E87 Hazard 3
As others speake, but onely thou dost act. . . . . 57 E89 Allen 12
Longer a day, but with his Mill will marry. . . . . 57 E90 Mill 16
A romane sound, but romane vertue weares, ... 58 E91 Vere 2
Nor lesse in practice; but lesse mark'd, lesse knowne: . . 58 E91 Vere 14
And have'hem yeeld no savour, but of state. . . . . 58 E92 New Crie 5
Others more modest, but contemne us too, ... 59 E92 New Crie 39
But these, desir'd by you, the makers ends . . . . 60 E94 Bedford 3 5
But, when they heard it tax'd, tooke more offence. . . . 60 E94 Bedford 3 10
But when I read that speciall piece, restor'd, ... 61 E95 Savile 7
But, wisely, thrusts not forth a forward hand, ... 61 E95 Savile 22
But most we need his faith (and all have you) . . . . 62 E95 Savile 35
Reade all I send: and, if I find but one . . . . 62 E96 Donne 2 7
But one more rare, and in the case so new: . . . . 62 E97 Motion 3
But much it now availes, what's done, of whom: . . . 64 E99 Th Roe 2 7
But that your worth will dignifie our feast, ... 64 E101 Supper 4
But that, which most doth take my Muse, and mee, . . . 65 E101 Supper 28
Which is the Mermaids, now, but shall be mine: . . . 65 E101 Supper 30
Are all but Luthers beere, to this I sing. . . . . 65 E101 Supper 34

			Page	Title	Line

BUT (cont.)

	Page	Title	Line
Of this we will sup free, but moderately,	65	E101 Supper	35
But, at our parting, we will be, as when	65	E101 Supper	38
I Doe but name thee Pembroke, and I find	66	E102 Pembroke	1
Against the bad, but of, and to the good:	66	E102 Pembroke	3
But thou, whose noblesse keeps one stature still,	66	E102 Pembroke	13
But in the view, doth interrupt their sinne;	66	E102 Pembroke	18
That but the twi-light of your sprite did see,	66	E103 L Wroth 1	2
And glorie of them all, but to repeate!	66	E103 L Wroth 1	8
Forgive me then, if mine but say you are	67	E103 L Wroth 1	9
A Sydney: but in that extend as farre	67	E103 L Wroth 1	10
But even their names were to be made a-new,	67	E105 L Wroth 2	5
Who could not but create them all, from you?	67	E105 L Wroth 2	6
He, that but saw you weare the wheaten hat,	68	E105 L Wroth 2	7
If but to be beleev'd you have the hap,	69	E107 Hungry	17
But 's angry for the Captayne, still: is such.	70	E108 Soldiers	10
That serves nor fame, nor titles; but doth chuse	70	E109 Nevil	2
His deedes too dying, but in bookes (whose good	71	E110 Edmonds 1	15
His life, but makes, that he can dye no more.	71	E110 Edmonds 1	22
Which all, but ignorant Captaynes, will confesse:	72	E111 Edmonds 2	7
Tragick, or Comick; but thou writ'st the play.	72	E112 Gamster	8
As but to speake thee, Overbury, is praise:	73	E113 Overbury	2
Who'in such ambition can but follow thee.	73	E113 Overbury	12
But, in your love, made all his servants wise.	74	E114 Sydney	8
Naming so many, too! But, this is one,	74	E115 Honest Man	3
Suffers no name, but a description:	74	E115 Honest Man	4
Being no vitious person, but the vice	74	E115 Honest Man	5
But, if it shall be question'd, undertakes,	74	E115 Honest Man	18
Not that it feares, but will not have to doo	74	E115 Honest Man	20
The cloth's no sooner gone, but it gets up	74	E115 Honest Man	24
In men, but every bravest was the best:	75	E116 Jephson	10
That bloud not mindes, but mindes did bloud adorne:	75	E116 Jephson	11
But dost it out of judgement, not disease;	76	E119 Shelton	8
He, that, but living halfe his age, dyes such;	76	E119 Shelton	15
But viewing him since (alas, too late)	77	E120 S. P.	19
But, being so much too good for earth,	77	E120 S. P.	23
I need no other arts, but studie thee:	78	E122 Rudyerd 2	9
But both th'hast so, as who affects the state	78	E123 Rudyerd 3	3
But I, no child, no foole, respect the kinde,	79	E125 Uvedale	7
Cary my love is, Daphne but my tree.	80	E126 Mrs Cary	8
But the first question is, when one saw thee?	81	E129 Mime	2
To Braynford, Hackney, Bow, but thou mak'st one;	81	E129 Mime	4
And thine owne Coriat too. But (would'st thou see)	81	E129 Mime	17
When these were but the praises of the Art.	82	E130 Ferrab. 1	16
But when I have said, The proofes of all these bee	82	E130 Ferrab. 1	17
Shed in thy Songs; 'tis true: but short of thee.	82	E130 Ferrab. 1	18
But, as it is the Child of Ignorance,	83	E132 Sylvester	3
How can I speake of thy great paines, but erre?	83	E132 Sylvester	5
Shee brought the Poets forth, but ours th'adventer.	84	E133 Voyage	20
But, in the action, greater man then hee:	84	E133 Voyage	26
All, that are readers: but, me thinkes 'tis od,	85	E133 Voyage	43
But hold my torch, while I describe the entry	85	E133 Voyage	58
'Tis but light paines: Indeede this Dock's no rose.	85	E133 Voyage	60
But they unfrighted passe, though many a privie	86	E133 Voyage	73
But still their valour, and their vertue fenc't 'hem,	86	E133 Voyage	76
But, comming neere, they found it but a liter,	86	E133 Voyage	85
But many Moones there shall not wane (quoth hee)	87	E133 Voyage	103
But I will speake (and know I shall be heard)	87	E133 Voyage	105
About the shore, of farts, but late departed,	87	E133 Voyage	125
But open, and un-armed encounter'd all:	87	E133 Voyage	135
But still, it seem'd, the ranknesse did convince 'hem.	88	E133 Voyage	152
But 'mong'st these Tiberts, who do'you thinke there was?	88	E133 Voyage	155
But you will visit grisly Pluto's hall?	89	E133 Voyage	175
And stayes but till you come unto the dore!	89	E133 Voyage	178
Or stayre, or courts; but stand'st an ancient pile,	93	F2 Penshurst	5
But all come in, the farmer, and the clowne.	94	F2 Penshurst	48
But what can this (more then expresse their love)	95	F2 Penshurst	57
Where comes no guest, but is allow'd to eate,	95	F2 Penshurst	61
But gives me what I call, and lets me eate,	95	F2 Penshurst	69
What (great, I will not say, but) sodayne cheare	95	F2 Penshurst	82
When shee was farre: and not a roome, but drest,	96	F2 Penshurst	87
A fortune, in this age, but rarely knowne.	96	F2 Penshurst	92
May say, their lords have built, but thy lord dwells.	96	F2 Penshurst	102
But canst, at home, in thy securer rest,	97	F3 Wroth	13
But thou, my Wroth, if I can truth apply,	99	F3 Wroth	91
But thou, my Wroth, if I may truth apply,	99	F3 Wroth	V 91
Nor death; but when thy latest sand is spent,	100	F3 Wroth	105
Thou maist thinke life, a thing but lent.	100	F3 Wroth	106
Thy curtesie but sodaine starts,	100	F4 To the World	11
I know thou whole art but a shop	100	F4 To the World	17
If these, who have but sense, can shun	101	F4 To the World	33
But, as 'tis rumor'd, so beleev'd:	101	F4 To the World	50
But, what we'are borne for, we must beare:	101	F4 To the World	53
But I will beare these, with that scorne,	102	F4 To the World	63
But make my strengths, such as they are,	102	F4 To the World	67
But if once we loose this light,	102	F5 Celia 1	7
But when once wee lose the light,	102	F5 Celia 1	V 7
Fame, and rumor are but toyes.	102	F5 Celia 1	10
But the sweet theft to reveale:	102	F5 Celia 1	16
Song. That Women are but Mens shaddowes.	104	F7 Women but	Ttl
Stil'd but the shaddowes of us men?	104	F7 Women but	6
But grant us perfect, they're not knowne.	104	F7 Women but	10
Stil'd but the shaddowes of us men?	104	F7 Women but	12

	Page	Title	Line

BUT (cont.)

	Page	Title	Line
But, forgive me, with thy crowne	105	F8 Sicknesse	18
None but them, and leave the rest.	106	F8 Sicknesse	48
None but them, and leave the best.	106	F8 Sicknesse	V 48
Or leave a kisse but in the cup,	106	F9 Celia 3	3
Leave but a kisse within the cup,	106	F9 Celia 3	V 3
But might I of Jove's Nectar sup,	106	F9 Celia 3	7
But might I of love's Nectar sipp,	106	F9 Celia 3	V 7
but being well assured that there	106	F9 Celia 3	V 11
But thou thereon did'st onely breath,	106	F9 Celia 3	13
Not of it selfe, but thee.	106	F9 Celia 3	16
Not like it selfe, but thee.	106	F9 Celia 3	V 16
Or safe, but shee'll procure	106	F9 Celia 3	
Object arrive there, but the heart (our spie)	109	F11 Epode	6
But this true course is not embrac'd by many:	109	F11 Epode	11
But this faire course is not embrac'd by many:	109	F11 Epode	19
But this doth from the cloud of error grow,	109	F11 Epode	V 19
But, in a calme, and god-like unitie,	110	F11 Epode	35
Of all his happinesse? But soft: I heare	110	F11 Epode	53
But we propose a person like our Dove,	111	F11 Epode	65
But I Conceive a person like my Dove,	112	F11 Epode	91
Man may securely sinne, but safely never.	112	F11 Epode	V 91
But let this drosse carry what price it will	113	F11 Epode	116
Riches thought most: But, Madame, thinke what store	114	F12 Rutland	27
Or in their windowes; doe but prove the wombs,	114	F12 Rutland	38
But onely Poets, rapt with rage divine?	114	F12 Rutland	46
But holie Poets, rapt with sence divine?	115	F12 Rutland	63
Then all, that have but done my Muse least grace,	115	F12 Rutland	V 63
Then all, that have but done my verse lesse grace,	115	F12 Rutland	79
But high, and noble matter, such as flies	115	F12 Rutland	V 79
Your selfe but told unto your selfe, and see	116	F12 Rutland	89
No lady, but, at some time, loves her glasse.	117	F13 Aubigny	23
And this shall be no false one, but as much	117	F13 Aubigny	26
Not taken up o' th' doctors, but as well	117	F13 Aubigny	27
That askes but to be censur'd by the eyes:	117	F13 Aubigny	33
Of so great title, birth, but vertue most,	117	F13 Aubigny	35
Boast, but how oft they have gone wrong to man:	118	F13 Aubigny	49
But which the Fates forbid me to reveale.	119	F13 Aubigny	84
But to please him, who is the dearer prise	119	F13 Aubigny	107
Give me my cup, but from the Thespian well,	119	F13 Aubigny	116
With dust of ancestors, in graves but dwell.	120	F14 Sydney	11
The Birth-day shines, when logs not burne, but men.	121	F14 Sydney	40
But it must, straight, my melancholy bee?	121	F14 Sydney	60
To ought but grace, or ayme at other end.	122	F15 Heaven	2
And whither rap'd, now thou but stoup'st to mee?	122	F15 Heaven	8
But 'bove the fat of rammes, or bulls, to prize	122	F15 Heaven	14
But left me free,	127	U1 Trinitie	11
But in thy presence, truly glorified,	128	U1 Trinitie	47
But, I'le come in,	129	U1 Father	9
But the Language, and the Truth,	130	U1 Father	28
But be glad, as soone with me,	131	U2 Excuse	10
But, he had not gain'd his sight	131	U2 Excuse	17
This my object. But she threw	132	U2 How he saw	13
But the Arrow home did draw	132	U2 How he saw	23
But the Pittie comes too late.	133	U2 Suffered	14
But enjoy such a sight,	133	U2 Suffered	20
Doe but looke on her eyes, they doe light	134	U2 Triumph	8
Doe but looke on her Haire, it is bright	134	U2 Triumph	11
Doe but marke, her forehead's smoother	134	U2 Triumph	13
Have you seene but a bright Lillie grow,	134	U2 Triumph	15
Have you mark'd but the fall o'the Snow	134	U2 Triumph	21
By description, but my Mother!	134	U2 Triumph	23
But alas, thou seest the least	136	U2 Cupid	12
Of her Sex; But could'st thou, Love,	137	U2 Cupid	43
But shee's Juno, when she walkes,	137	U2 Cupid	45
To no other Grace but you!	137	U2 Cupid	53
That doth but touch his flower, and flies away.	138	U2 Kisse	20
This could be call'd but halfe a kisse.	139	U2 Another	6
What w'are but once to doe, we should doe long.	139	U2 Another	11
I will but mend the last, and tel¹	139	U2 Another	12
But we find that cold delay,	139	U2 Another	13
But of one, if short he come,	140	U2 Promise	9
Let his Title be but great,	142	U2 Her man	55
What man but must lose his?	142	U2 Exception	3
What need of mee? doe you but sing,	143	U3 Musicall	8
But what those lips doe make.	143	U3 Musicall	13
But what your lips doe make.	143	U3 Musicall	16
Nor cast them downe, but let them rise,	143	U3 Musicall	V 16
Nor doe we doubt, but that we can,	144	U4 Song	3
We are no women then, but wives.	145	U5 Woman-kind	7
But as 'tis often vext and tri'd.	146	U6 Defence	6
Our pleasure; but preserves us more	146	U6 Defence	18
For that's a narrow joy is but our owne.	146	U6 Defence	21
But then if I grow jealous madde,	147	U7 Nymph	7
But he hath eyes so round, and bright,	147	U7 Nymph	10
But then t'increase my feares,	147	U7 Nymph	22
What Nymph so e're his voyce but heares,	148	U7 Nymph	26
Will be my Rivall, though she have but eares.	148	U7 Nymph	27
But so exempt from blame,	148	U7 Nymph	28
Doe but consider this small dust,	148	U7 Nymph	33
Oh, but my conscious feares,	148	U8 Houre-glasse	1
But under the Disguise of love,	149	U9 Picture	11
But leaves me to inquire,	150	U10 Jealousie	9
	151	U11 Dreame	10

BUT (cont.)

It vent it selfe, but as it would,	151	U12 Corbet	2
But was by sweetning so his will,	151	U12 Corbet	13
But that I understood him scant.	152	U12 Corbet	31
You then, whose will not only, but desire	153	U13 Sacvile	7
Not at my prayers, but your sense; which laid	153	U13 Sacvile	9
You cannot doubt, but I, who freely know	153	U13 Sacvile	13
But by meere Chance? for interest? or to free	154	U13 Sacvile	30
Nought but in corners; and is loath to leave,	154	U13 Sacvile	44
Lest Ayre, or Print, but flies it: Such men would	154	U13 Sacvile	45
But then, fist-fill'd, to put me off the sent.	154	U13 Sacvile	52
My Sword ('tis but a poore Sword, understand)	154	U13 Sacvile	54
And seeke not wants to succour: but enquire,	155	U13 Sacvile	61
But one is bitten by the Dog he fed,	155	U13 Sacvile	67
I not deny it, but to helpe the need	155	U13 Sacvile	75
But these men ever want: their very trade	155	U13 Sacvile	79
Is borrowing; that but stopt, they doe invade	155	U13 Sacvile	80
Now, but command; make tribute, what was gift;	155	U13 Sacvile	84
If it were cleare, but being so in cloud	155	U13 Sacvile	87
Of Valour, but at this Idolatrous rate?	156	U13 Sacvile	104
Or appetite of offending, but a skill,	156	U13 Sacvile	107
But like to be, that every day mends one,	156	U13 Sacvile	116
Men have beene great, but never good by chance,	156	U13 Sacvile	124
Alone in money, but in manners too.	157	U13 Sacvile	134
But few and faire Divisions: but being got	157	U13 Sacvile	151
Which you will bury; but therein, the strife	158	U13 Sacvile	160
But I on yours farre otherwise shall doe,	159	U14 Selden	17
But I to yours, farre from this fault, shall doo;	159	U14 Selden	V 17
Not flie the Crime, but the Suspition too:	159	U14 Selden	18
But 'twas with purpose to have made them such.	159	U14 Selden	22
I wonder'd at the richnesse, but am lost,	160	U14 Selden	53
But to the Subject, still the Colours fit	160	U14 Selden	58
A banke against it. Nothing but the round	160	U14 Selden	63
But nought beyond. He thou hast given it to,	161	U14 Selden	71
Embrace, and cherish; but he can approve	161	U14 Selden	74
But here's no time, nor place, my wealth to tell,	161	U14 Selden	85
All other Acts of Worldlings, are but toyle	162	U15 Friend-Wars	9
In outward face, but inward, light as Furre,	162	U15 Friend-Wars	20
But there are objects, bid him to be gone	163	U15 Friend-Wars	28
But more licentious made, and desperate!	163	U15 Friend-Wars	36
He that will follow but anothers wife,	165	U15 Friend-Wars	87
Lives to the Lord, but to the Ladies end.	165	U15 Friend-Wars	94
Lives for the Lord, but to the Ladies end.	165	U15 Friend-Wars	V 94
But being in Motion still (or rather in race)	166	U15 Friend-Wars	124
But both fell prest under the load they make.	166	U15 Friend-Wars	128
I'le bid thee looke no more, but flee, flee friend,	166	U15 Friend-Wars	129
Or side, but threatens Ruine. The whole Day	166	U15 Friend-Wars	131
Is not enough now, but the Nights to play:	166	U15 Friend-Wars	132
Is not enough now, but the Nights we play:	166	U15 Friend-Wars	V132
Give me but that againe, that I must wast	167	U15 Friend-Wars	152
Give me but that againe, which I must wast	167	U15 Friend-Wars	V152
But he that's both, and slave to boote, shall live,	167	U15 Friend-Wars	160
But he that's both, and slave to both, shall live,	167	U15 Friend-Wars	V160
And never but for doing wrong be sory;	168	U15 Friend-Wars	180
But what she gives, thou dar'st give her againe;	168	U15 Friend-Wars	184
Thou shrinke or start not, but be alwayes one;	168	U15 Friend-Wars	186
That thou thinke nothing great, but what is good,	168	U15 Friend-Wars	187
But here doth lie, till the last Day,	168	U16 Gray	3
But that some greater names have broke with me,	169	U17 Friend-Debt	8
And their words too; where I but breake my Band.	169	U17 Friend-Debt	9
I adde that (but) because I understand	169	U17 Friend-Debt	10
Or was she gracious a-farre off? but neere	169	U18 Elegy Can	5
A terror? or is all this but my feare?	169	U18 Elegy Can	6
But which shall lead me on? both these are blind:	170	U18 Elegy Can	11
Or Love, or Fortune blind, when they but winke	170	U18 Elegy Can	16
You blush, but doe not: friends are either none,	171	U19 Elegy By	13
(Though they may number bodyes) or but one.	171	U19 Elegy By	14
I'le therefore aske no more, but bid you love;	171	U19 Elegy By	15
Or have the least of Good, but what it must	171	U20 Shrub	7
But their whole inside full of ends, and knots?	171	U20 Shrub	12
Thinke but the Sin of all her sex, 'tis she!	172	U20 Shrub	20
But she is such, as she might, yet, forestall	172	U20 Shrub	23
But who should lesse expect from you,	173	U22 Elegy Tho	13
Which if it kindle not, but scant	174	U22 Elegy Tho	33
But sing high and aloofe,	175	U23 Himselfe	35
But both might know their wayes were understood,	176	U24 Frontispice	7
But both might know their wayes were understood,	176	U24 Frontispice	V 7
Assisted by no strengths, but are her owne,	176	U24 Frontispice	14
But whisper; O glad Innocence,	177	U25 Desmond	31
Nothing, but practise upon honours thrall.	179	U25 Desmond	35
Is but a Statists theame, to read Phlebotomie.	179	U25 Desmond	39
Though but while mettal's heating:	179	U25 Desmond	43
But to your selfe, most loyal Lord,	179	U25 Desmond	53
The Cure of that, which is but corporall,	180	U26 Ode High	5
Thinke but how deare you bought	180	U26 Ode High	19
But charme the Senses, others over-come	182	U28 Worth	7
But then his Mothers sweets you so apply,	182	U28 Worth	12
That expresseth but by fits,	183	U29 Fit of Rime	2
But false weight.	183	U29 Fit of Rime	6
But bewail'd	183	U29 Fit of Rime	21
But rests foiled.	184	U29 Fit of Rime	36
But stood unshaken in his Deeds, and Name,	185	U30 Burleigh	11
But when I read or heare the names so rife	187	U33 Councellour	7

BUT (cont.)

	Page	Title	Line
But first dost vexe, and search it! If not sound,	187	U33 Councellour	19
But in a businesse, that will bide the Touch,	187	U33 Councellour	23
And not being borrow'd by thee, but possest.	187	U33 Councellour	28
They had, but were a Reed unto thy Sword.	187	U33 Councellour	34
Alone, but all thy ranke a reverend Name.	187	U33 Councellour	40
I, that thy Ayme was; but her fate prevail'd:	188	U34 Small Poxe	17
And scorn'd, thou'ast showne thy malice, but hast fail'd.	188	U34 Small Poxe	18
Yet he himselfe is but a sparke.	189	U36 Song	8
Then to your love, and gift. And all's but due.	189	U37 Friend-Book	3
But must confesse from whom what gift I tooke.	189	U37 Friend-Book	6
Which is indeed but friendship of the spit:	190	U37 Friend-Book	9
But, as a friend, which name your selfe receave,	190	U37 Friend-Book	10
In friendship, I confesse: But, deare friend, heare.	190	U37 Friend-Book	18
That friendship which no chance but love did chuse,	190	U37 Friend-Book	23
But shall sometimes be tempted to obey	190	U37 Friend-Book	32
This sadnesse makes no approaches, but to kill.	191	U38 Elegy 'Tis	4
Looke forth, but cannot last in such a forme.	191	U38 Elegy 'Tis	14
As not alone the Cure, but scarre be faire.	192	U38 Elegy 'Tis	52
But to exact againe what once is given,	192	U38 Elegy 'Tis	63
He cannot angrie be, but all must quake,	193	U38 Elegy 'Tis	71
But view the mildnesse of your Makers state,	193	U38 Elegy 'Tis	85
O, that you could but by dissection see	194	U38 Elegy 'Tis	109
And that there is no life in me, but love.	194	U38 Elegy 'Tis	112
I may dilate my selfe, but not depart.	194	U38 Elegy 'Tis	118
Till then 'tis all but darknesse, that I have;	194	U38 Elegy 'Tis	121
And then I taste it. But as men drinke up	197	U40 Elegy That	3
But ever without blazon, or least shade	197	U40 Elegy That	13
But the grave Lover ever was an Asse;	198	U40 Elegy That	32
If I had writ no word, but Deare, farewell.	198	U40 Elegy That	50
Or that the Sun was here, but forc't away;	199	U41 Elegy Since	6
Of beautie; but the Muse hath interest in:	200	U42 Elegy Let	15
But is the Poets matter: And he must,	200	U42 Elegy Let	17
But then consent, your Daughters and your Wives,	200	U42 Elegy Let	19
But I who live, and have liv'd twentie yeare	200	U42 Elegy Let	29
But when thy Wife (as thou conceiv'st) is brave?	201	U42 Elegy Let	50
When not the Shops, but windowes doe display	202	U42 Elegy Let	78
But, on thy malice, tell me, didst thou spie	203	U43 Vulcan	19
On such my serious follies; But, thou'lt say,	204	U43 Vulcan	41
Or such my serious follies; But, thou'lt say,	204	U43 Vulcan	V 41
But that's a marke, wherof thy Rites doe boast,	205	U43 Vulcan	57
Had I fore-knowne but of thy least desire	205	U43 Vulcan	V 59
But in my Deske, what was there to accite	206	U43 Vulcan	85
But in my Deske, what was there to envite	206	U43 Vulcan	V 85
I dare not say a body, but some parts	206	U43 Vulcan	87
She durst not kisse, but flung from her brest.	208	U43 Vulcan	114
For none but Smiths would have made thee a God.	208	U43 Vulcan	117
But, O those Reeds! thy meere disdaine of them,	208	U43 Vulcan	129
But, O those weedes; thy meere disdaine of them,	208	U43 Vulcan	V129
(Which, some are pleas'd to stile but thy madde pranck)	208	U43 Vulcan	131
See the worlds Ruines! nothing but the piles	209	U43 Vulcan	137
But, others fell with that conceipt by the eares,	209	U43 Vulcan	145
But, others fell by that conceipt by the eares,	209	U43 Vulcan	V145
Kindled the fire! But then, did one returne,	209	U43 Vulcan	149
Though but in daunces, it shall know his power;	210	U43 Vulcan	157
Though but in daunces, it shall know high power;	210	U43 Vulcan	V157
Though but in daunger, it shall know thy power;	210	U43 Vulcan	V157
For they were burnt, but to be better built.	210	U43 Vulcan	166
But say, all sixe good men, what answer yee?	210	U43 Vulcan	173
But to confine him to the Brew-houses,	211	U43 Vulcan	179
But I'le conclude all in a civill curse.	211	U43 Vulcan	190
Or stay'd but where the Fryar, and you first met,	212	U43 Vulcan	201
But we have Powder still for the Kings Day,	213	U44 Speach	2
If they stay here, but till Saint Georges Day.	213	U44 Speach	10
But they may see Gold-Chaines, and Pearle worne then,	213	U44 Speach	13
But on thy practise, and the Posture booke:	213	U44 Speach	28
He that but saw thy curious Captaines drill,	213	U44 Speach	29
But give them over to the common eare	214	U44 Speach	31
But he that should perswade, to have this done	214	U44 Speach	61
All that they doe at Playes. O, but first here	215	U44 Speach	91
But why are all these Irons i'the fire	215	U44 Speach	93
That could but claime a kindred from the purse.	216	U45 Squib	10
No piece of money, but you know, or make	216	U45 Squib	14
But these with wearing will themselves unfold:	216	U45 Squib	19
But he that's too-much that, is friend of none.	216	U45 Squib	24
I could say more of such, but that I flie	218	U47 Tribe	5
But for a Sealing: let these men protest.	218	U47 Tribe	15
Of any Companie but that they are in,	218	U47 Tribe	20
But if, for honour, we must draw the Sword,	219	U47 Tribe	39
But that's a blow, by which in time I may	219	U47 Tribe	51
But all so cleare, and led by reasons flame,	220	U47 Tribe	69
As but to stumble in her sight were shame;	220	U47 Tribe	70
But 'tis with a condition,	220	U48 Bacchus	6
But Venus and the Graces	221	U48 Bacchus	33
Ought that is ill, but the suspition too,	224	U50 Countesse	6
For you admit no companie, but good,	224	U50 Countesse	25
Not boasted in your life, but practis'd true,	225	U50 Countesse	32
But there are lines, wherewith I might b'embrac'd.	226	U52 Answer	3
But yet the Tun at Heidelberg had houpes.	227	U52 Answer	6
To square my Circle, I confesse; but draw	227	U52 Answer	8
But whilst you curious were to have it be	227	U52 Answer	13
You made it a brave piece, but not like me.	227	U52 Answer	15
But, you are he can paint; I can but write:	227	U52 Answer	19

BUT (cont.)

Text	Page	Title	Line
A Poet hath no more but black and white,	227	U52 Answer	20
And surely had I but your Stable seene	228	U53 Newcastle	13
But rather with advantage to be found	229	U54 Squib	11
But since the Wine hath steep'd my braine,	230	U55 Burges	5
But Scarlet-like out-lasts the Cloth.	230	U55 Burges	8
A booke to a few lynes: but, it was fit	230	U56 Covell	3
His friends, but to breake Chaires, or cracke a Coach.	230	U56 Covell	10
If his wit reach no higher, but to spring	232	U58 Book-seller	7
That trembles in the blaze, but (then) mounts higher!	233	U59 Newcastle	8
If, Passenger, thou canst but reade:	233	U60 La-ware	1
But crept like darknesse through his blood?	234	U60 La-ware	8
But whisper'd Counsells, and those only thrive;	234	U61 Epigram	6
But thou wilt yet a Kinglier mastrie trie,	235	U62 Charles 1	5
But, that he cure the Peoples Evill too?	235	U62 Charles 1	14
But thanke his greatnesse, and his goodnesse too;	236	U63 Charles 2	9
Cannot but heape that grace, he will requite.	236	U63 Charles 2	14
Most pious King, but his owne good in you!	236	U64 Charles 3	2
If he but weigh'd the blessings of this day?	236	U64 Charles 3	4
'T is not alone the Merchant, but the Clowne,	237	U64 Charles 3	19
The same that thou art promis'd, but be slow,	237	U65 Prince	6
The same that thou hast promis'd, but be slow,	237	U65 Prince	V 6
And threat' the great Eclipse. Two houres but runne,	238	U65 Prince	11
And thereat the great Eclipse. Two houres but runne,	238	U65 Prince	V 11
But, that shee raigning here,	240	U67 Muses	35
Well, they should know him, would the K. but grant	241	U68 House-hold	5
Profit, or Chance had made us: But I know	241	U69 Friend Son	3
But as the wretched Painter, who so ill	241	U69 Friend Son	9
All is but web, and painting; be the strife	242	U69 Friend Son	24
As, could they but lifes miseries fore-see,	243	U70 Ode	19
But ever to no ends:	243	U70 Ode	29
What did this Stirrer, but die late?	243	U70 Ode	30
But weary of that flight,	244	U70 Ode	37
But that the Corke of Title boy'd him up.	244	U70 Ode	42
Alas, but Morison fell young:	244	U70 Ode	43
But most, a vertuous Sonne.	244	U70 Ode	47
But fate doth so alternate the designe,	246	U70 Ode	95
Two names of friendship, but one Starre:	246	U70 Ode	98
But simple love of greatnesse, and of good;	246	U70 Ode	105
But as a Cary, or a Morison.	247	U70 Ode	116
But lyes block'd up, and straightned, narrow'd in,	248	U71 Treasurer	10
Had they but grace, of thinking, at these routes,	249	U72 King	15
Still to have such a Charles, but this Charles long.	249	U72 King	18
The wish is great; but where the Prince is such,	249	U72 King	22
Thou sluggish spawne, that canst, but wilt not see?	250	U73 Weston	8
Dreame thou could'st hurt it; but before thou wake	250	U73 Weston	11
Through which not only we, but all our Species are.	253	U75 Epithalam.	32
Of Sex, to rob the Creature; but from Man	255	U75 Epithalam.	82
Illustrate these, but they	255	U75 Epithalam.	85
But doth his Carract, and just Standard keepe	255	U75 Epithalam.	100
But dare not aske our wish in Language fescennine:	257	U75 Epithalam.	160
There; but, renewed, say,	258	U75 Epithalam.	167
But like an Arme of Eminence 'mongst them,	258	U75 Epithalam.	179
But we last out, still unlay'd.	259	U76 Petition	24
But hee lasteth and unlay'd.	259	U76 Petition	V 24
Not with the Arras, but the Persian Loomes.	260	U77 Treasurer	4
Not from the Arras, but the Persian Loomes.	260	U77 Treasurer	V 4
But you I know, my Lord; and know you can	261	U77 Treasurer	13
Sate safe enough, but now secured more.	268	U80 Christning	14
But rather I, should I of that part speake!	269	U81 Pawlet	28
The blaze, and splendor, but not handle fire!	269	U81 Pawlet	32
The heat, and splendor, but not handle fire!	269	U81 Pawlet	V 32
But a fain'd way, doth rob it of the true.	270	U81 Pawlet	38
But a fain'd way, doth spoyle it of the true.	270	U81 Pawlet	V 38
'Tis but a body which you can torment,	270	U81 Pawlet	55
T' have paid againe a blessing was but lent,	271	U81 Pawlet	80
And, but for that Contention, and brave strife	271	U81 Pawlet	95
But as he soares at that, he bruiseth then	272	U81 Pawlet	98
But, here's a Song of her Descent;	273	U84 Cradle	29
Needs nought to cloath it but the ayre.	275	U84 Body	8
But at such distance, as the eye	276	U84 Body	19
But at such distance, all the eye	276	U84 Body	V 19
But, Painter, see thou doe not sell	277	U84 Body	29
Whose 'tis: but if it favour find,	277	U84 Body	31
Painter yo' are come, but may be gone,	277	U84 Mind	1
But here I may no colours use.	277	U84 Mind	6
But here we may no colours use.	277	U84 Mind	V 6
But these are like a Mind, not it.	278	U84 Mind	12
But what's of kinne to whence it came.	278	U84 Mind	16
This is no Picture, but the same.	278	U84 Mind	24
As 'tis not radiant, but divine:	278	U84 Mind	26
But, that a Mind so rapt, so high,	279	U84 Mind	41
But stooping gently, as a Cloud,	280	U84 Mind	58
But such a Mind, mak'st God thy Guest.	281	U84 Mind	72
'Twill be but faire, to leane upon their Fames;	281	U84 Kenelme	13
For they are strong Supporters: But, till then,	281	U84 Kenelme	14
The greatest are but growing Gentlemen.	281	U84 Kenelme	15
Nothing I doe; but, like a heavie wheele,	283	U84 Muse	30
Indeed, she is not dead! but laid to sleepe ·	283	U84 Muse	45
But all of God; They still shall have to say,	286	U84 Muse	119
But make him All in All, their Theme, that Day:	286	U84 Muse	120
(But pride, that schisme of incivilitie)	287	U84 Muse	160
T' have knowne no envy, but by suffring it!	287	U84 Muse	162

BUT   (cont.)

	Page	Title	Line
But, kept an even gate, as some streight tree	207	U84 Muse	165
But flees the Barre and Courts, with the proud bords,	289	U85 Country	7
But if, to boot with these, a chaste Wife meet	291	U85 Country	39
But, why, oh why, my Ligurine,	293	U86 Hor.4:1	33
I hold thee fast! but fled hence, with the Light,	293	U86 Hor.4:1	38
But, say old Love returne should make,	294	U87 Hor.3:9	17
But thus, thus, keeping endlesse Holy-day,	294	U88 Petronius	6
Can this decay, but is beginning ever.	294	U88 Petronius	10
Hee, that but living halfe his dayes, dies such,	295	U89 Mart.8:77	7
Not labour'd for, but left thee by thy Sire;	295	U90 Mart.10:47	3
Thy night not dronken, but from cares layd wast;	295	U90 Mart.10:47	9
But equall power, to Painter, and to Poet,	305	Horace	11
Or Rainbow is describ'd. But here was now	305	Horace	23
But in the maine worke haplesse: since he knowes	307	Horace	48
Of words decay, and phrases borne but late	309	Horace	88
Once rowable, but now doth nourish men	309	Horace	94
Were also clos'd: But, who the man should be,	309	Horace	109
Her Poem's beautie, but a sweet delight	311	Horace	141
Be nought so'bove him but his sword let claime.	313	Horace	174
Be nought so'bove him, but his bold sword claime.	342	Horace	V174
But light from smoake; that he may draw his bright	315	Horace	204
Or acted told. But, ever, things that run	317	Horace	256
Things worthy to be done within, but take	317	Horace	261
But soft, and simple, at few holes breath'd time	319	Horace	289
So over-thick, but, where the people met,	319	Horace	292
But, as they conquer'd, and enlarg'd their bound,	319	Horace	295
But, as a Matrone drawne at solemne times	321	Horace	338
But, let the Faunes, drawne from their Groves, beware,	321	Horace	355
But meere Iambicks all, from first to last.	323	Horace	374
But every Judge hath not the facultie	323	Horace	387
But, in conclusion, merited no fame.	323	Horace	396
But you, Pompilius off-spring, spare you not	325	Horace	415
Their nailes, nor shave their beards, but to by-paths	325	Horace	423
Their nails, nor shave their beards, but seek by-paths	349	Horace	V423
But fame of Poets, they thinke, if they come forth,	325	Horace	426
Out better Poems? But I cannot buy	325	Horace	431
But a well-compass'd mouth to utter it;	327	Horace	462
Being men were covetous of nought, bear praise.	327	Horace	463
But flowes out, that ore-swelleth in full brests.	329	Horace	506
Our Gallants give them none, but passe them by:	329	Horace	513
But he hath every suffrage, can apply	329	Horace	514
The hand, and mind would, but it will resound	329	Horace	522
A Choerilus, in whom if I but see	329	Horace	534
Twice, or thrice good, I wonder: but am more	329	Horace	535
But, I confesse, that, in a long worke, sleepe	329	Horace	537
But neither, Men, nor Gods, nor Pillars meant,	331	Horace	555
Or thick grosse ointment, but offend the Guests:	331	Horace	558
But, if hereafter thou shalt write, not feare	331	Horace	575
But, now, it is enough to say; I make	333	Horace	593
His flatterers to their gaine. But say, he can	333	Horace	601
His praisers to their gaine: but say he can	353	Horace	V601
But you, my Piso, carefully beware,	333	Horace	607
And twice, or thrice assay'd it, but in vain;	354	Horace	V626
In vaine, but you, and yours, you should love still	335	Horace	631
According to the Moone. But, then the boyes	335	Horace	647
Under the angry Moon. But then the boys	354	Horace	V647
I'le tell you but the death, and the disease	335	Horace	659
Here's one makes verses, but there's none knows why:	355	Horace	V670
(Defiled) touch'd; but certaine he was mad,	337	Horace	673
Polluted, touch't: but certainly he's mad:	355	Horace	V673
And, as a Beare, if he the strength but had	337	Horace	674
I could not but in admiracion stand.	361	Palmer	4
Not one but thrives; in spite of stormes & thunder,	361	Palmer	7
The fault's not in the object, but their eyes.	362	Author	8
Seldome descend but bleeding to their grave.	363	Murder	2
But a bare Type and Figure.	364	Phoenix	8
But mixt with sound, transcending	365	Ode Splendor	15
Marke, marke, but when his wing he takes,	366	Ode Who saith	9
But prove the Aire, and saile from Coast to Coast:	367	Ode Who saith	37
But first to Cluid stoope low,	367	Ode Who saith	39
That heard but Spight deliver	367	Ode Who saith	58
(But this more apt	368	Ode Who saith	62
But over Land to Trent:	368	Ode Who saith	73
All which, when they but heare a straine	368	Ode Who saith	89
But should they know (as I) that this,	369	Ode Who saith	97
But these are Mysteries	369	Ode Who saith	111
Conceal'd from all but cleare Propheticke eyes.	369	Ode Who saith	112
But now, your Worke is done, if they that view	370	Author	9
To fill an Epitaph. But she had more.	371	Epitaph	5
With Rites not bound, but conscience. Wouldst thou All?	372	Epitaph	11
Here, not up Holdborne, but downe a steepe hill,	374	Coryat 1	12
A Horse here is sadled, but no Tom him to backe,	374	Coryat 1	14
For he did but kisse her, and so let her go.	375	Coryat 1	19
But here, neither trusting his hands, nor his legs,	375	Coryat 1	34
Trie and trust Roger, was the word, but now	378	Coryat 2	80
. . . Panegyricke lines, but then were upon some occasions . . .	379	Coryat 3	Ttl
Yet who could have hit on't but the wise noddell	379	Coryat 3	6
To line out no stride, but pas'd by himselfe?	379	Coryat 3	8
Since he treads in no other Mans steps but his owne.	379	Coryat 3	12
But who will beleeve this, that chanceth to looke	379	Coryat 3	17
Horse, foote, and all but flying in the ayre:	380	Coryat 3	28
That he dares to informe you, but somewhat meticulous,	380	Coryat 3	33

	Page	Title	Line
BUT (cont.)			
Doth he once dissemble, but tels he did ride	380	Coryat 3	52
still that same little poynte hee was; but when	383	Rich	13
Who bluntly doth but looke upon the same,	383	Author	3
Who cannot reade, but onely doth desire	383	Author	9
At these thy Nuptials; but, whose heart, and thought	384	Somerset	3
Not only this, but every day of thine,	384	Somerset	9
Sure, this glad payre were married, but this day.	384	Somerset	26
To see his worke be good; but that he looke	385	Husband	2
But I have seene thy worke, and I know thee:	386	Browne	3
For, though but early in these pathes thou tread,	386	Browne	5
With the how much they set forth, but th'how well.	386	Browne	16
nor yet inscription like it. Write but that;	387	Cavendish	9
nor yet inscription like it writt but that	387	Cavendish	V 9
not when I die'd, but how I livd. Farewell.	387	Cavendish	12
Olde Hesiods Ore, and give it us; but thine,	388	Chapman	2
To say but one, were single. Then it chimes,	389	Aleman	3
But in one tongue, was form'd with the worlds wit:	389	Aleman	6
Upon it, but will loath, or let it passe,	389	Aleman	9
But that hee's too well suted, in a cloth,	389	Aleman	17
O, could he but have drawne his wit	390	Reader	5
But, since he cannot, Reader, looke	390	Reader	9
Not on his Picture, but his Booke.	390	Reader	10
'Tis true, and all mens suffrage. But these wayes	390	Shakespeare	5
Which, when it sounds at best, but eccho's right;	390	Shakespeare	8
The truth, but gropes, and urgeth all by chance;	391	Shakespeare	10
But thou art proofe against them, and indeed	391	Shakespeare	15
I meane with great, but disproportion'd Muses:	391	Shakespeare	26
For names; but call forth thund'ring Aeschilus,	391	Shakespeare	33
He was not of an age, but for all time!	391	Shakespeare	43
But antiquated, and deserted lye	392	Shakespeare	53
But stay, I see thee in the Hemisphere	392	Shakespeare	75
And despaires day, but for thy Volumes light.	392	Shakespeare	80
But every Table in this Church can say,	394	Jane Ogle	7
No stone in any wall here, but can tell	394	Jane Ogle	9
But, I would have, thee, to know something new,	394	Jane Ogle	13
But of one Husband; and since he left life,	394	Jane Ogle	16
But Sorrow, she desir'd no other Friend:	394	Jane Ogle	17
But when againe I veiw the parts so peiz'd,	395	May	7
Calme Brutus tenor start; but all along	395	May	11
What godds but those of arts, and eloquence?	395	May	16
But who hath them interpreted, and brought	395	May	19
But then, thy'epistolar Heroick Songs,	397	Drayton	29
With us be call'd, the Naso, but this man?	397	Drayton	32
And I had stil'd thee, Orpheus, but before	397	Drayton	37
That Rebells actions, are but valiant crimes!	397	Drayton	44
Sayst thou so, Lucan? But thou scornst to stay	397	Drayton	47
But that I heare, againe, thy Drum to beate	397	Drayton	55
That can but reade; who cannot, may in prose	398	Drayton	73
But then refreshed, with thy Fayerie Court,	398	Drayton	79
To veiw the truth and owne it. Doe but looke	399	Lady Ogle	5
But higher power, as spight could not make lesse,	401	Beaumont	18
Nor flatt'ry! but secur'd, by the Authors Name,	401	Beaumont	19
But in the practisd truth Destruction is	404	Inigo Jones 1	57
The Scene! the Engyne! but he now is come	404	Inigo Jones 1	62
Should but the king his Justice-hood employ	405	Inigo Jones 1	77
But wisest Inigo! who can reflect	405	Inigo Jones 1	86
But cause thou hearst the mighty k. of Spaine	406	Inigo Jones 2	1
But when thou turnst a Reall Inigo;	407	Inigo Jones 2	22
But bawle thou on; I pitty thee, poore Curre,	408	Detractor	7
But fly thee, like the Pest! Walke not the street	409	Detractor	19
The Cobler kept him to his nall; but, now	410	Brome	17
But Tune and Noise the Eccho of thy Shame.	411	Gill	14
But lowlie laid, as on the earth asleep,	413	Ghyrlond	18
But, that which summes all, is the Eglantine,	413	Ghyrlond	21
Now, for mine owne part, and it is but due,	415	Rutter	12
But I can tell thee, Dover, how thy Games	415	Dover	3
But a very merry wight	416	Moon	7
but have lost it by the way,	417	Moon	10
'tis but the next neighbour ride	417	Moon	35
But unto more dispayre to Imitate their sounde.	420	Ode:If Men	36
Censure, not sharplye then, but mee advise	421	Censure	1
That Frindshipp, which noe Chaunce, but Love did Chuse,	422	Censure	16
But sometymes shall bee tempted to obaye	422	Censure	25
the sword, but that it acteth what it list.	423	Lucan	14
not safe; but when thou dost them thoroughlie:	423	Lucan	16
shall never dare do any thing but feare.	423	Lucan	20
But with a Kisse, (if thou canst dare it)	662	Bedford	9
I send this small, but hearty testimony: and with charge,	666	Glover	5
BUTT			
'T were better spare a Butt, then spill his Muse.	241	U68 House-hold	12
Butt, Clownishe pride hath gott	420	Ode:If Men	10
BUTTER			
Where, afterwards, it grew a butter-flye:	31	E15 Court-worm	3
The Lybian Lion hunts noe butter flyes,	408	Inigo Jones 3	7
BUTTER'D			
In Sugar Candide, or in butter'd beere,	167	U15 Friend-Wars	153
BUTTER-FLYE			
Where, afterwards, it grew a butter-flye:	31	E15 Court-worm	3
BUTTOCK			
Is fill'd with buttock? And the walls doe sweate	88	E133 Voyage	169
BUY			
For vulgar praise, doth it too dearely buy.	27	E2 My Booke	14

		Page	Title	Line
BUY (cont.)				
Buy the reversion of old playes; now growne		45	E56 Poet-Ape	6
To stuffes and Laces, those my Man can buy.		223	U49 Pucell	28
Out better Poems? But I cannot buy		325	Horace	431
BUYER				
That to the sale of Wares calls every Buyer;		333	Horace	598
BUYES				
When having pill'd a booke, which no man buyes,		43	E53 Old-end	2
Or Bils, and there he buyes the names of books.		59	E92 New Crie	24
While thus it buyes great grace, and hunts poore fame;		113	F12 Rutland	15
Him that buyes chiches blanch't, or chance to like		321	Horace	362
Him that buyes Pulse there, or perhaps may like		347	Horace	V354/362
BUYLDING				
Whether the buylding of the Stage or Scene!		402	Inigo Jones 1	11
BY'				
A Prince, that rules by'example, more than sway?		37	E35 James 2	2
BY (BE)				
And newer, then could please them, by-cause trew.		415	Rutter	10
BY				
And by thy wiser temper, let men know		27	E2 My Booke	8
When was there contract better driven by Fate?		28	E5 Union	1
By that one spell he lives, eates, drinkes, arrayes		30	E12 Shift	5
Or else by water goes, and so to playes;		30	E12 Shift	17
Which conquers all, be once over-come by thee.		31	E14 Camden	12
Nor need'st thou: for those few, by oath releast,		32	E16 Brain-hardy	7
And, but a sprigge of bayes, given by thee,		32	E17 Critic	5
Till time, strong by her bestowing,		39	E40 Ratcliffe	11
By his free will, be in Jones company.		40	E42 Giles	5
Exacted by thy fate, on the just day.		41	E45 First Son	4
To pay at's day of marriage. By my hand		42	E46 Luckless 1	4
Sir Lucklesse, troth, for lucks sake passe by one:		42	E47 Luckless 2	1
By constant suffring of thy equall mind;		47	E63 Salisbury 2	8
As, to be rais'd by her, is onely fame.		49	E67 Suffolk	4
As all thy honors were by them first sought:		49	E67 Suffolk	8
Which, by no lesse confirm'd, then thy kings choice,		49	E67 Suffolk	11
Yet by thy weapon liv'st! Th'hast one good part.		50	E69 Cob	2
Or that I'have by, two good sufficient men,		54	E81 Proule	3
Thy wit lives by it, Proule, and belly too.		54	E81 Proule	6
Shee doth instruct men by her gallant flight,		55	E85 Goodyere 1	5
By which his damme conceiv'd him, clothes and all?		56	E88 Monsieur	11
So many Poets life, by one should live.		57	E89 Allen	14
Went on: and proving him still, day by day,		57	E90 Mill	7
Sung by a Horace, or a Muse as free;		58	E91 Vere	4
Are sure to con the catalogue by hart;		59	E92 New Crie	22
But these, desir'd by you, the makers ends		60	E94 Bedford 3	5
Mark'd by thy hand, and with the better stone,		62	E96 Donne 2	8
By his each glorious parcell to be knowne!		62	E97 Motion	6
Nor are the Queenes most honor'd maides by th'eares		63	E97 Motion	18
Play-wright, by chance, hearing some toyes I'had writ,		64	E100 Playwrt 3	1
And we will have no Pooly', or Parrot by;		65	E101 Supper	36
That we have left us, nor by time, nor place,		67	E105 L Wroth 2	3
There Juno sate, and yet no Peacock by.		68	E105 L Wroth 2	18
I sweare by your true friend, my Muse, I love		70	E108 Soldiers	5
And that, midst envy' and parts; then fell by rage:		71	E110 Edmonds 1	14
(As by a new creation) part by part,		71	E110 Edmonds 1	18
By thy great helpe: and doth proclaime by mee,		72	E111 Edmonds 2	13
By thy great Art: and doth proclaime by mee,		72	E111 Edmonds 2	V 13
By speaking well o' the company' it 's in.		74	E115 Honest Man	8
Executes men in picture. By defect,		75	E115 Honest Man	29
So, by error, to his fate		77	E120 S. P.	17
By her attempt, shall still be owing thee.		80	E127 Aubigny	10
Thy selfe, with thy first thoughts, brought home by thee,		81	E128 Wm Roe 2	10
Of old, even by her practise, to be fam'd;		82	E130 Ferrab. 1	10
Mov'd by her order, and the ninth more high,		82	E130 Ferrab. 1	13
Lash'd by their consciences, to die, affeard.		84	E133 Voyage	18
So huge, it seem'd, they could by no meanes quite her.		86	E133 Voyage	86
Their Mercury did now. By this, the stemme		87	E133 Voyage	111
Of the hulke touch'd, and, as by Polypheme		87	E133 Voyage	112
By this time had they reach'd the Stygian poole,		87	E133 Voyage	121
By which the Masters sweare, when, on the stoole		87	E133 Voyage	122
Calling for Radamanthus, that dwelt by,		89	E133 Voyage	187
By any arte. Then wonder not,		93	F1 Why write no	10
By their ripe daughters, whom they would commend		95	F2 Penshurst	54
Here no man tells my cups; nor, standing by,		95	F2 Penshurst	67
Whether by choice, or fate, or both;		96	F3 Wroth	2
Purchas'd by rapine, worse then stealth,		99	F3 Wroth	82
By being organes to great sinne,		99	F3 Wroth	86
So removed by our wile?		102	F5 Celia 1	14
Thus removed by many a mile?		102	F5 Celia 1	V 14
To thy altars, by their nights		104	F8 Sicknesse	4
Will by coach, and water goe,		105	F8 Sicknesse	37
My Muse up by commission: No, I bring		108	F10 Proludium	28
Our muse up by commission: No, we bring		108	F10 Proludium	V 28
like glasse, blowne up, and fashion'd by desire.		108	F10 Proludium	4
But this true course is not embrac'd by many:		109	F11 Epode	19
But this faire course is not embrac'd by many:		109	F11 Epode	V 19
By many? scarse by any.		109	F11 Epode	20
Thus, by these subtle traines,		110	F11 Epode	28
Toyles, by grave custome, up and downe the court,		113	F12 Rutland	5
Had not their forme touch'd by an English wit.		115	F12 Rutland	82
Borne up by statues, shall I reare your head,		115	F12 Rutland	84
The bad, by number, are so fortified.		116	F13 Aubigny	3
By arts, and practise of the vicious,		117	F13 Aubigny	12

BY (cont.)

	Page	Title	Line
That askes but to be censur'd by the eyes:	117	F13 Aubigny	35
This blessing of your starres, then by that way	118	F13 Aubigny	54
Not looking by, or back (like those, that waite	118	F13 Aubigny	62
By me, their priest (if they can ought divine)	119	F13 Aubigny	101
Unto himselfe, by being so deare to you.	119	F13 Aubigny	117
Stand silent by,	120	F14 Sydney	8
By sinne, and Sathan; and my flesh misus'd,	127	U1 Trinitie	6
And with thy Angels, placed side, by side,	128	U1 Trinitie	46
What comfort by him doe wee winne,	130	U1 Nativitie	19
And (to gaine her by his Art)	133	U2 Suffered	15
That they still were to run by her side,	134	U2 Triumph	9
By description, but my Mother!	136	U2 Cupid	12
By her lookes I doe her know,	136	U2 Cupid	18
And the Glasse hangs by her side,	137	U2 Cupid	40
6. Clayming a second kisse by Desert.	137	U2 Kisse	Ttl
If by us, the oddes were laid,	138	U2 Kisse	7
To fetch in the Formes goe by:	140	U2 Promise	18
9. Her man described by her owne Dictamen.	140	U2 Her man	Ttl
To make a new, and hang that by.	145	U5 Woman-kind	18
(By searching) what before was strange,	146	U6 Defence	15
By Atomes mov'd;	148	U8 Houre-glasse	3
Turn'd to cinders by her eye?	149	U8 Houre-glasse	8
Think'st thou that love is help'd by feare?	150	U10 Jealousie	12
But was by sweeting so his will,	151	U12 Corbet	13
Now I conceive him by my want,	152	U12 Corbet	32
But by meere Chance? for interest? or to free	154	U13 Sacvile	30
Give thankes by stealth, and whispering in the eare,	154	U13 Sacvile	49
But one is bitten by the Dog he fed,	155	U13 Sacvile	67
And feeles it; Else he tarries by the Beast.	156	U13 Sacvile	117
Or growne; by height or lowenesse of the Sunne?	156	U13 Sacvile	119
Men have beene great, but never good by chance,	156	U13 Sacvile	124
'Tis by degrees that men arrive at glad	157	U13 Sacvile	131
By thanking thus the curtesie to life,	158	U13 Sacvile	159
Be honour is so mixt) by such as would,	162	U15 Friend-Wars	25
And comes by these Degrees, the Stile t'inherit	164	U15 Friend-Wars	81
Or by Damnation voids it? or by stealth?	166	U15 Friend-Wars	116
That may stand by, and hold my peace? will he,	167	U15 Friend-Wars	150
That by commanding first thy selfe, thou mak'st	168	U15 Friend-Wars	181
Be brought by us to meet our Destinie.	170	U18 Elegy Can	20
By those bright Eyes, at whose immortall fires	170	U19 Elegy By	1
By that faire Stand, your forehead, whence he bends	170	U19 Elegy By	3
By that tall Grove, your haire; whose globy rings	170	U19 Elegy By	5
By those pure bathes your either cheeke discloses,	170	U19 Elegy By	7
And lastly by your lips, the banke of kisses,	170	U19 Elegy By	9
A little Shrub growing by.	172	U21 Ltl Shrub	Ttl
By whom he is restor'd to men:	173	U22 Elegy Tho	15
To see their Seats and Bowers by chattring Pies defac't?	174	U23 Himselfe	12
Which makes that (lighted by the beamie hand	176	U24 Frontispice	9
This makes, that lighted by the beamie hand	176	U24 Frontispice V	9
And guided by Experience, whose straite wand	176	U24 Frontispice	11
Assisted by no strengths, but are her owne,	176	U24 Frontispice	14
By which as proper titles, she is knowne	176	U24 Frontispice	16
Graced by your Reflection!	177	U25 Desmond	17
Was Lesbia sung by learn'd Catullus?	181	U27 Ode Helen	9
Or Delia's Graces, by Tibullus?	181	U27 Ode Helen	10
Or hath Corynna, by the name	181	U27 Ode Helen	17
That expresseth but by fits,	183	U29 Fit of Rime	2
Happy Greeke, by this protection,	184	U29 Fit of Rime	32
A right by the prosperitie of their Crimes;	186	U32 Elsmere	10
Mak'st it religion to grow rich by Crimes!	187	U33 Councellour	16
And not being borrow'd by thee, but possest.	187	U33 Councellour	28
Of those that set by their false faces more	188	U34 Small Poxe	4
Then this did by her true? She never sought	188	U34 Small Poxe	5
By naming in what companie 'twas in,	191	U38 Elegy 'Tis	25
Or winds the Spirit, by which the flower so grew?	192	U38 Elegy 'Tis	58
He pardons slips, goes by a world of ills,	193	U38 Elegy 'Tis	69
O, that you could but by dissection see	194	U38 Elegy 'Tis	109
How all my Fibres by your Spirit doe move,	194	U38 Elegy 'Tis	111
Others by common Stars their courses run,	194	U38 Elegy 'Tis	119
This makes me, Mrs. that sometime by stealth,	197	U40 Elegy That	9
And never be by time, or folly brought,	198	U40 Elegy That	44
Made longer by our praises. Or, if not,	200	U42 Elegy Let	21
Curst in their Cradles, or there chang'd by Elves,	200	U42 Elegy Let	23
When by thy sordid bountie she hath on	201	U42 Elegy Let	45
Wrung on the Withers, by Lord Loves despight,	201	U42 Elegy Let	63
By Jove to have Minerva for thy Bride,	203	U43 Vulcan	12
By thy owne vote, a sacrifice to thee?	203	U43 Vulcan	22
Thou mightst have had me perish, piece, by piece,	205	U43 Vulcan	51
Thou mightst have had them perish, piece, by piece,	205	U43 Vulcan	V 51
The art of kindling the true Coale, by Lungs:	206	U43 Vulcan	76
and lighted by the Stagirite, could spie,	207	U43 Vulcan	90
By Carew, Cotton, Selden, oyle was spent	207	U43 Vulcan	V100
By Carew, Cotton, Seldens oyle was spent	207	U43 Vulcan	V100
But, others fell with that conceipt by the eares,	209	U43 Vulcan	145
But, others fell by that conceipt by the eares,	209	U43 Vulcan	V145
So would'st th'have run upon the Rolls by stealth,	210	U43 Vulcan	169
Will be remembred by Six Clerkes, to one.	210	U43 Vulcan	172
Lent by the London Dames, to the Lords men;	213	U44 Speach	14
Are we by Booke-wormes to be awde? must we	215	U44 Speach	67
Live by their Scale, that dare doe nothing free?	215	U44 Speach	68
To serve the State by Councels, and by Armes:	215	U44 Speach	85
But that's a blow, by which in time I may	219	U47 Tribe	51

BY (cont.)

	Page	Title	Line
But all so cleare, and led by reasons flame,	220	U47 Tribe	69
By all the Arts of Gladnesse,	221	U48 Bacchus	19
Her face there's none can like by Candle light.	223	U49 Pucell	32
Not only shunning by your act, to doe	224	U50 Countesse	5
By all oblique Degrees, that killing height	224	U50 Countesse	11
You were not tied, by any Painters Law,	227	U52 Answer	7
To be describ'd by a Monogram,	227	U52 Answer	11
Of either Suitor, or a Servant by.	230	U56 Covell	18
Of suitor, or of servant standing by.	230	U56 Covell	V 18
By this, although you fancie not the man,	231	U56 Covell	25
By thys Tyme, though you fancie not the man,	231	U56 Covell	V 25
An Epitaph, on Henry L. La-ware. To the Passer-by.	233	U60 La-ware	Ttl
Doth by his doubt, distrust his promise more.	235	U63 Charles 2	4
And by an Angell, to the blessed'st Maid,	238	U66 Queene	2
An Ode, or Song, by all the Muses.	239	U67 Muses	Ttl
What, by that name, wee each to other owe,	241	U69 Friend Son	4
For, what is life, if measur'd by the space,	243	U70 Ode	21
Not by the act?	243	U70 Ode	22
Or masked man, if valu'd by his face,	243	U70 Ode	23
Hee entred well, by vertuous parts,	244	U70 Ode	33
By him, so ample, full, and round,	244	U70 Ode	49
By what was done and wrought	245	U70 Ode	60
Of hearts the union. And those not by chance	246	U70 Ode	99
Each stiled, by his end,	247	U70 Ode	111
And titles, by which all made claimes	247	U70 Ode	114
Poore wretched states, prest by extremities,	248	U71 Treasurer	1
And made those strong approaches, by False braies,	248	U71 Treasurer	7
Made loftier by the Winds all noises else,	249	U72 King	V 12
By all the Spheares consent, so in the heart of June?	253	U75 Epithalam.	16
And by his Rise, in active men, his Name	256	U75 Epithalam.	116
A Richard, and a Hierome, by their names	258	U75 Epithalam.	170
By this Sun's Noone-sted's made	258	U75 Epithalam.	183
To his bountie; by extension	259	U76 Petition	9
To his bountie; by dimension	259	U76 Petition	V 9
As farre as sense, and onely by the eyes.	261	U77 Treasurer	12
As farre as sense, and onely by his eyes.	261	U77 Treasurer	V 12
Of sweets, and safeties, they possesse by Peace.	261	U77 Treasurer	22
Fame and Honour you, they possesse by Peace.	261	U77 Treasurer	V 22
And strike Religion in the standers-by;	261	U77 Treasurer	24
See where he walkes with Mira by his side.	264	U79 New-yeares	18
That they may take it eccho'd by the Floods.	265	U79 New-yeares	53
And by thy blessing, may thy People see	268	U80 Christning	3
This day, by Baptisme, and his Saviours crosse:	268	U80 Christning	10
What she did here, by great example, well,	269	U81 Pawlet	33
What she did by a great example, well,	269	U81 Pawlet	V 33
Else, who doth praise a person by a new,	270	U81 Pawlet	37
And, in her last act, taught the Standers-by,	270	U81 Pawlet	61
By Thee, and Conscience, both who thrive	273	U84 Cradle	7
By the just trade	273	U84 Cradle	8
May something by that twilight see	273	U84 Cradle	15
This, utter'd by an antient Bard,	274	U84 Cradle	33
By Jacobs Ladder, to the top	274	U84 Cradle	38
By Ranulph———	274	U84 Descent	18
As you goe on, by what brave way	278	U84 Mind	18
Us forth, by some Celestiall slight	279	U84 Mind	47
Begotten by that wind, and showers.	280	U84 Mind	68
By which yo'are planted, shew's your fruit shall bide.	281	U84 Kenelme	19
By Death, on Earth, I should have had remorse	282	U84 Muse	12
Must come to take a sentence, by the sense	284	U84 Muse	57
By all the wealth of blessings, and the store	285	U84 Muse	110
Accumulated on her, by the Lord	285	U84 Muse	111
By beatifick vertue of the Place.	285	U84 Muse	116
By light, and comfort of spirituall Grace;	286	U84 Muse	131
To style us Friends, who were, by Nature, Foes?	286	U84 Muse	139
Adopt us Heires, by grace, who were of those	286	U84 Muse	140
T' have knowne no envy, but by suffring it!	287	U84 Muse	162
Mov'd by the wind, so comely moved she.	287	U84 Muse	166
And by the awfull manage of her Eye	287	U84 Muse	167
In frequent speaking by the pious Psalmes	288	U84 Muse	191
By sure Election, and predestin'd grace!	288	U84 Muse	198
Shee saw her Saviour, by an early light,	288	U84 Muse	199
All this by Faith she saw, and fram'd a Plea,	288	U84 Muse	209
Where first his Power will appeare, by call	289	U84 Muse	220
Are gathering by the Wintry houres;	290	U85 Country	30
That penning the glad flock in hurdles by,	291	U85 Country	45
Not labour'd for, but left thee by thy Sire;	295	U90 Mart.10:47	3
To paint him, hath by swimming, hopelesse, scap'd,	305	Horace	27
Professing greatnesse, swells: That, low by lee	307	Horace	38
Downe close by shore, this other creeping steales,	339	Horace	V 40/ 39
Are, by thy cunning placing, made meere new.	307	Horace	68
Yet, if by chance, in utt'ring things abstruse,	307	Horace	69
When they are poore, and banish'd, must throw by	311	Horace	138
And tortures us: and, after, by the tongue	311	Horace	156
Honour'd Achilles chance by thee be seiz'd,	313	Horace	171
Then those the faithfull eyes take in by show,	317	Horace	258
Her licence fit to be restrain'd by law:	321	Horace	368
Her force was fit to be restrain'd by law:	348	Horace	V402/368
A lawfull Verse, by th'eare, or finger scan.	323	Horace	404
Happier then wretched art, and doth, by it,	325	Horace	420
Their nailes, nor shave their beards, but to by-paths	325	Horace	423
Their nails, nor shave their beards, but seek by-paths	349	Horace	V423
A pound, or piece, by their long compting arts:	327	Horace	466

94

	Page	Title	Line
BY (cont.)			
Was said to move the stones, by his Lutes powers,	327	Horace	484
Attempted by the Muses tunes, and strings;	329	Horace	498
Cast out by voyces; want they pleasure, then	329	Horace	512
Our Gallants give them none, but passe them by:	329	Horace	513
Informed rightly, by your Fathers care,	331	Horace	546
To send it to be judg'd by Metius eare,	331	Horace	576
Nine yeares kept in, your papers by, yo'are free	331	Horace	578
Nine yeares kept by, your papers in, y'are free	352	Horace	V554/578
Alone, without a rivall, by his will.	335	Horace	632
Or love of this so famous death lay by.	335	Horace	669
Or love of this his famous death lay by.	355	Horace	V669
(so well dispos'd by thy auspicious hand)	361	Palmer	2
Or (by our Turtles Augure)	364	Phoenix	5
Though, now by Love transform'd, & dayly dying:	369	Ode Who saith	101
Here, by a Boore too, hee's like to be beaten	375	Coryat 1	24
To line out no stride, but pas'd by himselfe?	379	Coryat 3	8
By the scale of his booke, a yard of his stile?	379	Coryat 3	10
By offring not more sureties, then inow,	386	Browne	12
The truth, but gropes, and urgeth all by chance;	391	Shakespeare	10
My Shakespeare, rise; I will not lodge thee by	391	Shakespeare	19
In blood, in birth, by match, and by her seate;	394	Jane Ogle	4
Importune wish; and by her lov'd Lords side	394	Jane Ogle	23
Of Fortunes wheele by Lucan driv'n about,	395	May	3
When, by thy bright Ideas standing by,	397	Drayton	23
And flight about the Ile, well neare, by this,	397	Drayton	49
Get broken peeces, and fight well by those.	398	Drayton	74
I feele it by mine owne, that over flow,	398	Drayton	77
By warrant call'd just Symetry,	399	Lady Ogle	22
Her right, by gift, and purchase of the Lambe:	400	Lady Ogle	36
Both Saints, and Martyrs, by her loved Lord.	400	Lady Ogle	39
Nor flatt'ry! but secur'd, by the Authors Name,	401	Beaumont	19
By all your Titles, & whole style at ones	402	Inigo Jones 1	15
you would be an Asinigo, by your ears?	403	Inigo Jones 1	20
Sense, what they are! which by a specious fyne	404	Inigo Jones 1	55
Whirling his Whymseys, by a subtilty	405	Inigo Jones 1	73
By barking against mee. Thou look'st at least,	408	Detractor	10
No man will tarry by thee, as hee goes,	409	Detractor	17
. . . (by his continu'd Vertue) my loving friend: . . .	409	Brome	Ttl
By observation of those Comick Lawes	409	Brome	7
A Rogue by Statute, censur'd to be whipt,	411	Gill	15
And the deceipt of pleasures, by Consent.	411	Sutcliffe	11
To follow Goodnesse, by our owne discerning	412	Sutcliffe	17
By bringing forth God's onely Son, no other.	414	Ghyrlond	48
By those deepe-grounded, understanding men,	414	Rutter	7
As it were spun by nature, off the fleece:	415	Rutter	18
Bred by your breath, on this low bancke of ours;	416	Welcome	3
Now, in a garland by the graces knit;	416	Welcome	4
And I sweare by all the light	416	Moon	5
but have lost it by the way,	417	Moon	10
to the Peake it is so hard-by,	417	Moon	23
Or by chance if in their grease	418	Moon	41
A Grace by Ben: Johnson. extempore. before King James.	418	Grace	Ttl
By Cherissheinge the Spirrits that gave their greatnesse grace:	419	Ode:If Men	5
And by their takeinge, lett it once appeare	421	Ode:If Men	44
whole armyes fall, swayd by those nyce respects.	423	Lucan	11
BY-CAUSE			
And newer, then could please them, by-cause trew.	415	Rutter	10
BY'EXAMPLE			
A Prince, that rules by'example, more than sway?	37	E35 James 2	2
BY-PATHS			
Their nailes, nor shave their beards, but to by-paths	325	Horace	423
Their nailes, nor shave their beards, but seek by-paths	349	Horace	V423
CABALLS			
To Merlins Marvailes, and his Caballs losse,	206	U43 Vulcan	71
To Martins Marvailes, and his Caballs losse,	206	U43 Vulcan	V 71
CABINET			
Might love the treasure for the cabinet.	79	E125 Uvedale	6
CADMUS			
Into a Swallow there; Nor Cadmus take,	317	Horace	267
CAECILIUS			
A Roman to Caecilius will allow,	309	Horace	77
CAESAR			
Can so speake Caesar, as thy labours doe.	71	E110 Edmonds 1	12
Nor to give Caesar this, makes ours the lesse.	72	E111 Edmonds 2	8
Caesar stands up, as from his urne late rose,	72	E111 Edmonds 2	12
And Madame Caesar, great Proserpina,	89	E133 Voyage	180
CAESARIAN			
And cri'd, Away with the Caesarian bread,	228	U53 Newcastle	19
CAESAR'S			
Caesar's ambition, Cato's libertie,	395	May	10
CAESARS			
To Clement Edmonds, on his Caesars . . .	71	E110 Edmonds 1	Ttl
Not Caesars deeds, nor all his honors wonne,	71	E110 Edmonds 1	1
Of Caesars Daughter, and the line	181	U27 Ode Helen	19
CAESURA (See CEASURE)			
CAGE			
That fled his cage, or broke his chaine,	101	F4 To the World	30
CAKE			
Some bring a capon, some a rurall cake,	95	F2 Penshurst	51
CAL'			
Will cal't a Bastard, when a Prophet's borne.	223	U49 Pucell	46

CALAIS
With gentle Calais, Thurine Orniths Sonne; . . . 293 U87 Hor.3:9 14
CALAMITIE
Of teares, and dungeon of calamitie! . . . . 283 U84 Muse 35
CAL'D
Lyes the Valley, cal'd my nest, ... 137 U2 Cupid 34
Rather his sonne, I should have cal'd thee, why? . . 378 Coryat 2 88
CALEDON
To Caledon, ... 368 Ode Who saith 70
CALENDS
At th'Calends, puts all out againe. . . . . 291 U85 Country 70
CALFE
First bearing him a calfe, beare him a bull. . . 57 E90 Mill 18
Of thy strange Moon-Calfe, both thy straine of mirth, . 398 Drayton 84
CALL
Would call you more then Ceres, if not that: . . 68 E105 L Wroth 2 8
No, I doe, therefore, call Posteritie . . . 80 E127 Aubigny 4
The very call, to make all others come: . . . 81 E129 Mime 8
And pitty 'tis, I cannot call 'hem knights: . . 84 E133 Voyage 22
Act a brave worke, call it thy last adventry: . . 85 E133 Voyage 57
Were seene your ugly Centaures, yee call Car-men, . 86 E133 Voyage 68
But gives me what I call, and lets me eate, . . 95 F2 Penshurst 69
His children thy great lord may call his owne: . . 96 F2 Penshurst 91
Pallas, nor thee I call on, mankinde maid, . . 107 F10 Proludium 13
Pallas, nor thee we call on, mankinde maid, . . 107 F10 Proludium V 13
The thing, they here call Love, is blinde Desire, . 110 F11 Epode 37
And so doe many more. All which can call . . 117 F13 Aubigny 31
And call it their brave sinne. For such there be . 119 F13 Aubigny 85
Nor for any threat, or call, ... 132 U2 How he saw 18
Which you call my Shafts. And see! . . . 136 U2 Cupid 19
Call to mind the formes, that strove . . . 137 U2 Cupid 46
What we harmonie doe call . . . . . 141 U2 Her man 34
What you please, you parts may call, . . . 142 U2 Exception 7
At such a Call, what beast or fowle, . . . 143 U3 Musicall 5
And call the walking woods? . . . . . 143 U3 Musicall 12
Or that doth sound a Trumpet, and doth call . . 154 U13 Sacvile 35
It is a call to keepe the spirits alive . . . 162 U15 Friend-Wars 5
And even our sports are dangers! what we call . . 163 U15 Friend-Wars 38
Did her perfections call me on to gaze, . . . 169 U18 Elegy Can 3
What had I done that might call on thine ire? . . 202 U43 Vulcan 2
What have I done that might call on thine ire? . . 202 U43 Vulcan V 2
Call every night to Supper in these fitts, . . 218 U47 Tribe 21
Shall carry me at Call; and I'le be well, . . 219 U47 Tribe 45
I would call mine, to which not many Staires . . 220 U47 Tribe 74
The People her doe call! . . . . . 240 U67 Muses 50
Call, noble Lucius, then for Wine, . . . 245 U70 Ode 75
Upon a Thomas, or a Francis call; . . . 258 U75 Epithalam. 171
Upon a Thomas, or a Sister call; . . . 258 U75 Epithalam. V171
Court can call hers, or Man could call his Arts. . 262 U78 Digby 4
Court can call hers, or Man would call the Arts. . 262 U78 Digby V 4
Let Angels sing her glories, who did call . . 270 U81 Pawlet 63
And Call to the high Parliament . . . . 273 U84 Cradle 30
I call you Muse; now make it true: . . . 278 U84 Mind 21
. . . gave me leave to call her so. Being Her . . . 282 U84 Muse Ttl
For, as there are three Natures, Schoolemen call . 284 U84 Muse 51
Hee knowes, what worke h'hath done, to call this Guest, . 284 U84 Muse 81
Where first his Power will appeare, by call . . 289 U84 Muse 220
Goe where Youths soft intreaties call thee back. . 292 U86 Hor.4:1 8
Into a pit, or hole; although he call, . . . 335 Horace 652
She was 'Sell Boulstred. In which name, I call . 372 Epitaph 12
Who reads may roave, and call the passage darke, . 383 Author 5
For names; but call forth thund'ring Aeschilus, . 391 Shakespeare 33
To call on Sicknes still, to be her Guest, . . 394 Jane Ogle 19
I call the world, that envies mee, to see . . 398 Drayton 93
CALL'D
Thy selfe into fresh braules: when, call'd upon, . 32 E16 Brain-hardy 3
And he growne youth, was call'd to his ladies chamber. . 57 E90 Mill 10
Such as are misse-call'd Captaynes, and wrong you; . 69 E108 Soldiers 2
Including all, were thence call'd harmonie: . . 82 E130 Ferrab. 1 14
For I ran and call'd on Cupid; . . . . 132 U2 How he saw 6
Mock'd of all: and call'd of one . . . . 132 U2 How he saw 28
This could be call'd but halfe a kisse. . . . 139 U2 Another 11
See him, that's call'd, and thought the happiest man, . 162 U15 Friend-Wars 23
The Husband now's call'd churlish, or a poore . 165 U15 Friend-Wars 89
In all that is call'd lovely: take my sight . . 200 U42 Elegy Let 12
To cure the call'd Kings Evill with thy touch; . 235 U62 Charles 1 4
Sonne, and my Friend, I had not call'd you so . 241 U69 Friend Son 1
Lute, Lyre, Theorbo, all are call'd to day. . . 263 U79 New-yeares 2
At pleasure, to be call'd for, every day! . . 271 U81 Pawlet 82
Am I call'd Poet? wherefore with wrong shame, . 311 Horace 129
Once seene, to be againe call'd for, and plaid, . 317 Horace 271
As, now, of all men, it is call'd thy Trade: . . 389 Chapman 11
He would be call'd, henceforth, the English-Rogue, . 389 Aleman 16
With us be call'd, the Naso, but this man? . . 397 Drayton 32
By warrant call'd just Symetry, ... 399 Lady Ogle 22
A Master-worker call'd, th'old standerd burst . 415 Rutter 22
CALLED
A Docke there is, that called is Avernus, . . 85 E133 Voyage 41
Terme of the Architects is called Designe! . . 404 Inigo Jones 1 56
CALLING
What severall wayes men to their calling have! . 33 E21 Gam'ster 7
Calling for Radamanthus, that dwelt by, . . 89 E133 Voyage 187

	Page	Title	Line
CALLING (cont.)			
Wresting words, from their true calling;	183	U29 Fit of Rime	7
And, calling truth to witnesse, make that good	270	U81 Pawlet	35
And, calling truth to witnesse, make it good	270	U81 Pawlet	V 35
CALL'S			
No cobweb Call's; no Surcoates wrought	273	U84 Cradle	26
CALLS			
Or in cleft-sticks, advanced to make calls	28	E3 Bookseller	8
Calls for his stoole, adornes the stage: god payes.	30	E12 Shift	18
Who now calls on thee, Nevil, is a Muse;	70	E109 Nevil	1
To some coole, courteous shade, which he calls his,	97	F3 Wroth	19
That makes us live, not that which calls to die.	193	U38 Elegy 'Tis	78
The Month of youth, which calls all Creatures forth	253	U75 Epithalam.	26
That leades our flocks and us, and calls both forth	264	U79 New-yeares	29
That to the sale of Wares calls every Buyer;	333	Horace	598
Of any Art, besyde what he calls his!	404	Inigo Jones 1	58
CALL'ST			
Call'st a booke good, or bad, as it doth sell,	27	E3 Bookseller	2
Thou call'st me Poet, as a terme of shame:	29	E10 Ignorant	1
And what thou call'st thy gifts are baits.	100	F4 To the World	12
CALL'T			
Which (would the world not mis-call't flatterie)	79	E125 Uvedale	9
CALME			
But, in a calme, and god-like unitie,	110	F11 Epode	53
In a calme skie, then when the heaven is horl'd	193	U38 Elegy 'Tis	74
As smooth as Oyle pour'd forth, and calme	280	U84 Mind	59
She had a mind as calme, as she was faire;	287	U84 Muse	163
Calme Brutus tenor start; but all along	395	May	11
CALMEST			
The rudest Winds obey the calmest Ayre:	251	U74 Weston	9
CAL'T			
Will cal't a Bastard, when a Prophet's borne.	223	U49 Pucell	46
CALUMNIES			
Who 'gainst the Law, weave Calumnies, my ——;	187	U33 Councellour	6
CALVES			
Thy sheepe, thy bullocks, kine, and calves doe feed:	94	F2 Penshurst	23
CAMDEN			
To William Camden.	31	E14 Camden	Ttl
Camden, most reverend head, to whom I owe	31	E14 Camden	1
CAME			
To seeme a statesman: as I neere it came,	30	E11 Something	3
Came forth example, and remaines so, yet:	34	E23 Donne 1	4
Came not that soule exhausted so their store.	53	E79 Rutland	4
Of what shee had wrought came in, and wak'd his braine,	56	E87 Hazard	4
When Mill first came to court, the unprofiting foole,	57	E90 Mill	1
Came backe untouch'd. This man hath travail'd well.	81	E128 Wm Roe 2	14
To entertayne them; or the countrey came,	95	F2 Penshurst	80
Rising through it e're it came;	141	U2 Her man	29
But of one, if short he came,	142	U2 Her man	55
That never came ill odour thence:	152	U12 Corbet	18
Were the Rack offer'd them, how they came so;	157	U13 Sacvile	130
Ne're came to taste the plenteous Mariage-horne.	165	U15 Friend-Wars	100
Of love, and hate: and came so nigh to know	200	U42 Elegy Let	35
Which if in compasse of no Art it came	227	U52 Answer	10
As they came all to see, and to be seene!	253	U75 Epithalam.	20
But what's of kinne to whence it came.	278	U84 Mind	16
And came forth ever cheered, with the rod	287	U84 Muse	183
Chaste, thriftie, modest folke, that came to view.	319	Horace	294
To divine Poets, and their Verses came.	327	Horace	492
Or, of the things, that ne're came in my mind,	333	Horace	596
And, when they came	366	Ode Who saith	22
With vices, which they look'd for, and came to.	371	Fletcher	10
He went out at each place, and at what he came in,	380	Coryat 3	25
When like Apollo he came forth to warme	392	Shakespeare	45
CAMELL			
He makes the Camell & dull Ass his prize.	408	Inigo Jones 3	8
CAM'ST			
How cam'st thou thus to enter me?	150	U10 Jealousie	2
Thou sai'st, thou only cam'st to prove	150	U10 Jealousie	10
CAN			
Who scarse can spell th'hard names: whose knight lesse can.	28	E3 Bookseller	10
Man scarse can make that doubt, but thou canst teach.	31	E14 Camden	10
That Cod can get no widdow, yet a knight,	33	E19 Cod 1	1
And which no' affection praise enough can give!	34	E23 Donne 1	6
If any Muse out-live their spight, his can;	35	E27 Roe 1	4
And, can forget mens names, with a great grace.	35	E28 Surly	8
Surly, use other arts, these only can	36	E28 Surly	21
Who wets my grave, can be no friend of mine.	37	E33 Roe 3	6
To thy Domitian, than I can my James:	38	E36 Martial	2
And get more gold, then all the colledge can:	39	E41 Gypsee	2
Th'observing neighbours no such mood can see.	40	E42 Giles	2
I know no couple better can agree!	40	E42 Giles	18
That can restore that. Will it hurt your feature?	46	E62 Would-bee	7
Who can consider thy right courses run,	47	E63 Salisbury 2	1
And not thy fortune; who can cleerely see	47	E63 Salisbury 2	3
Who can behold all envie so declin'd	47	E63 Salisbury 2	7
And can to these be silent, Salisburie,	47	E63 Salisbury 2	9
In life, that can employ it; and takes hold	50	E70 Wm Roe 1	3
How can so great example dye in mee,	57	E89 Allen	7
For who can master those great parts like thee,	61	E95 Savile	17
We need a man, can speake of the intents,	62	E95 Savile	31
Can write the things, the causes, and the men.	62	E95 Savile	34
If we can get her, full of egs, and then,	64	E101 Supper	12

CAN (cont.)
```
May yet be there; and godwit, if we can:           .    .    .    65   E101 Supper        19
Of what ambition, faction, pride can raise;        .    .    .    66   E102 Pembroke      15
Judge they, that can: here I have rais'd to show   .    .    .    67   E104 Montgomery    13
Then can a flea at twise skip i'the Map.           .    .    .    69   E107 Hungry        18
Can so speake Caesar, as thy labours doe.          .    .    .    71   E110 Edmonds 1     12
His life, but makes, that he can dye no more.      .    .    .    71   E110 Edmonds 1     22
Think'st thou it is meere fortune, that can win?   .    .    .    72   E112 Gamster        3
There's no vexation, that can make thee prime.     .    .    .    73   E112 Gamster       22
Who'in such ambition can but follow thee.          .    .    .    73   E113 Overbury      12
Can come from Tripoly, leape stooles, and winke,   .    .    .    74   E115 Honest Man    11
Except the duell.  Can sing songs, and catches;    .    .    .    74   E115 Honest Man    13
Thus, in his belly, can he change a sin,           .    .    .    76   E118 Gut            5
With me can merit more, then that good man,        .    .    .    76   E119 Shelton        5
Would'st thou heare, what man can say              .    .    .    79   E124 Elizabeth      1
Made for what Nature could, or Vertue can;         .    .    .    79   E125 Uvedale        2
I answer'd, Daphne now no paine can prove.         .    .    .    80   E126 Mrs Cary       6
How can I speake of thy great paines, but erre?    .    .    .    83   E132 Sylvester      5
Since they can only judge, that can conferre.      .    .    .    83   E132 Sylvester      6
Can Poets hope to fetter mee?                      .    .    .    93   F1 Why write no     4
But what can this (more then expresse their love)  .    .    .    95   F2 Penshurst      57
There's nothing I can wish, for which I stay.      .    .    .    95   F2 Penshurst      75
But thou, my Wroth, if I can truth apply,          .    .    .    99   F3 Wroth          91
'Tis better, if he there can dwell.                .    .    .    99   F3 Wroth          94
'Tis better, if he then can dwell.                 .    .    .    99   F3 Wroth        V 94
Which who can use is happy: Such be thou.          .    .    .    99   F3 Wroth          99
Which who can use is happy: Such art thou.         .    .    .    99   F3 Wroth        V 99
If these, who have but sense, can shun            .    .    .   101   F4 To the World   33
While we can, the sports of love;                 .    .    .   102   F5 Celia 1       V  2
Can your favours keepe, and cover,                .    .    .   103   F6 Celia 2          2
Turtles can chastly dye;                          .    .    .   111   F11 Epode         74
Though we acknowledge, who can so abstayne,        .    .    .   112   F11 Epode         85
Though I acknowledge, who can so refraine,         .    .    .   112   F11 Epode       V 85
To every squire, or groome, that can report       .    .    .   113   F12 Rutland      V  6
Then this, our guilt, nor golden age can deeme,    .    .    .   114   F12 Rutland        22
It is the Muse, alone, can raise to heaven,        .    .    .   114   F12 Rutland        41
And so doe many more.  All which can call          .    .    .   117   F13 Aubigny        31
As I, can say, and see it doth excell.             .    .    .   117   F13 Aubigny        34
'Tis onely that can time, and chance defeat:       .    .    .   118   F13 Aubigny        51
Wherewith, then, Madame, can you better pay        .    .    .   118   F13 Aubigny        53
May they have nothing left, whereof they can       .    .    .   118   F13 Aubigny        83
By me, their priest (if they can ought divine)     .    .    .   119   F13 Aubigny       101
Because nor it can change, nor such a minde.       .    .    .   120   F13 Aubigny       124
Strive all right wayes it can,                     .    .    .   121   F14 Sydney         25
Nor can a little of the common store,              .    .    .   121   F14 Sydney         31
Good, and great God, can I not thinke of thee,     .    .    .   122   F15 Heaven          1
How can I doubt to finde thee ever, here?          .    .    .   122   F15 Heaven         16
What odour can be, then a heart contrite,          .    .    .   127   U1 Trinitie        15
The gladdest light, darke man can thinke upon;     .    .    .   128   U1 Trinitie        35
Who more can crave                                 .    .    .   129   U1 Father          17
Can man forget this Storie?                        .    .    .   130   U1 Nativitie       24
This here sung, can be no other                    .    .    .   136   U2 Cupid          11
Can he that loves, aske lesse then one?            .    .    .   139   U2 Another          8
Make accompt, unlesse you can,                     .    .    .   140   U2 Promise        29
I can rest me where I am.                          .    .    .   142   U2 Her man        56
Nor doe we doubt, but that we can,                 .    .    .   145   U5 Woman-kind      7
He is, if they can find him, faire,               .    .    .   147   U7 Nymph          15
Can I owe thankes, for Curtesies receiv'd         .    .    .   153   U13 Sacvile        25
Can I discerne how shadowes are decreast,          .    .    .   156   U13 Sacvile       118
And can I lesse of substance? When I runne,        .    .    .   156   U13 Sacvile       120
Without your gift, though I can take that too,     .    .    .   157   U13 Sacvile       158
Large claspe of Nature, such a wit can bound.      .    .    .   160   U14 Selden        64
Embrace, and cherish; but he can approve           .    .    .   161   U14 Selden        74
Honour'd at once, and envi'd (if it can            .    .    .   162   U15 Friend-Wars    24
No part or corner man can looke upon,              .    .    .   163   U15 Friend-Wars    27
As farre as he can flie, or follow day,            .    .    .   163   U15 Friend-Wars    29
As farre as he can flee, or follow day,            .    .    .   163   U15 Friend-Wars V 29
The bravery makes, she can no honour leese:        .    .    .   164   U15 Friend-Wars    56
Who can behold their Manners, and not clowd-/Like  .    .    .   164   U15 Friend-Wars    60
He that no more for Age, Cramps, Palsies, can      .    .    .   166   U15 Friend-Wars   135
Can we not leave this worme? or will we not?       .    .    .   166   U15 Friend-Wars   141
Debts when they can: good men may breake their day,.    .    .   169   U17 Friend-Debt    2
Can Beautie that did prompt me first to write,     .    .    .   169   U18 Elegy Can      1
I can helpe that with boldnesse; And Love sware,   .    .    .   170   U18 Elegy Can      9
Of all that can be done him; Such a one            .    .    .   171   U19 Elegy By      23
That which we can, who both in you, his Wife,      .    .    .   171   U19 Elegy By      25
And that pour'd out upon Man-kind can be!          .    .    .   172   U20 Shrub        19
That thought can adde, unthankfull, the lay-stall  .    .    .   172   U21 Ltl Shrub     8
As not the World can praise too much,              .    .    .   173   U22 Elegy Tho      3
What is there more that can ennoble blood?         .    .    .   185   U30 Burleigh       6
If there be nothing worthy you can see             .    .    .   191   U38 Elegy 'Tis    15
Thinke that your selfe like heaven forgive me can: .    .    .   192   U38 Elegy 'Tis    32
What Fooles, and all their Parasites can apply;    .    .    .   193   U38 Elegy 'Tis    94
Can pumpe for; or a Libell without salt            .    .    .   193   U38 Elegy 'Tis    96
Moves like a sprightly River, and yet can          .    .    .   198   U40 Elegy That    26
Can lock the Sense up, or the heart a thought,     .    .    .   198   U40 Elegy That    43
What it is like: And doe not thinke they can       .    .    .   199   U41 Elegy Since    3
And so I spare it. Come what can become            .    .    .   199   U41 Elegy Since   19
Reveald (if some can judge) of Argenis,            .    .    .   207   U43 Vulcan      V 96
Old Aesope Gundomar: the French can tell,          .    .    .   213   U44 Speach        5
Of worthiest knowledge, that can take mens minds.  .    .    .   217   U46 Coke         20
Then these can ever be; or else wish none.         .    .    .   219   U47 Tribe        30
And dwell as in my Center, as I can,               .    .    .   219   U47 Tribe        60
```

	Page	Title	Line

CAN (cont.)

	Page	Title	Line
And in an Epicoene fury can write newes	222	U49 Pucell	8
To stuffes and Laces, those my Man can buy.	223	U49 Pucell	28
In Contract twice, what can shee perjure more?	223	U49 Pucell	30
Her face there's none can like by Candle light.	223	U49 Pucell	32
But, you are he can paint; I can but write:	227	U52 Answer	19
For your securitie. I can no better.	229	U54 Squib	20
I only can the Paper staine;	230	U55 Burges	6
Marrie the Muse is one, can tread the Aire,	230	U56 Covell	13
Marrie his Muse is one, can tread the Aire,	230	U56 Covell	V 13
And can for other Graces her commend,	230	U56 Covell	20
Accept his Muse; and tell, I know you can,	231	U56 Covell	26
I can lose none in tendring these to you.	231	U56 Covell	28
Thanke him: if other, hee can give no Bayes.	232	U58 Book-seller	6
What can the Poet wish his King may doe,	235	U62 Charles 1	13
Who doubts, those fruits God can with gaine restore,	235	U63 Charles 2	3
Hee can, he will, and with large int'rest pay,	236	U63 Charles 2	5
That nothing can her gratitude provoke!	237	U64 Charles 3	16
What can the cause be, when the K. hath given	241	U68 House-hold	1
To judge; So all men comming neere can spie,	242	U69 Friend Son	20
What Drums or Trumpets, or great Ord'nance can,	249	U72 King	9
What prayers (People) can you thinke too much?	249	U72 King	20
And see, what can be seene,	252	U75 Epithalam.	7
This Feast, then can the Day,	254	U75 Epithalam.	7
With Angels, Muse, to speake these: Nothing can	255	U75 Epithalam.	84
But you I know, my Lord; and know you can	261	U77 Treasurer	13
Can doe the things that Statues doe deserve,	261	U77 Treasurer	15
Unto your honour: I can tune in song	261	U77 Treasurer	27
Unto your honour: I can voyce in song	261	U77 Treasurer	V 27
Court can call hers, or Man could call his Arts.	262	U78 Digby	4
Court can call hers, or Man would call the Arts.	262	U78 Digby	V 4
And in the chase, more then Sylvanus can,	264	U79 New-yeares	22
To better Pastures then great Pales can:	264	U79 New-yeares	30
To sweeter Pastures lead hee can,	265	U79 New-yeares	60
And e're I can aske more of her, shee's gone!	269	U81 Pawlet	12
Of Winchester; the Heralds can tell this:	269	U81 Pawlet	20
Thereof, no notion can expresse how much	269	U81 Pawlet	26
No Nation can expresse how much	269	U81 Pawlet	V 26
'Tis but a body which you can torment,	270	U81 Pawlet	55
If you can envie your owne Daughters blisse,	271	U81 Pawlet	83
If you can enjoy your owne Daughters blisse,	271	U81 Pawlet	V 83
If you can cast about your either eye,	271	U81 Pawlet	85
With what injustice can one soule pretend	271	U81 Pawlet	V 92
And tell thou, Alde-Legh, None can tell more true	274	U84 Descent	13
Hee shall, if he can understand,	276	U84 Body	11
With all that Youth, or it can bring:	276	U84 Body	22
This worke I can performe alone;	277	U84 Mind	3
Since nothing can report that flame,	278	U84 Mind	15
Since nothing can report her flame,	278	U84 Mind	V 15
'Tis got where it can try the fire.	278	U84 Mind	28
Nothing, that could remaine, or yet can stirre	282	U84 Muse	9
Nothing can more adorne it, then the seat	284	U84 Muse	71
Who knowes the hearts of all, and can dissect	286	U84 Muse	150
The smallest Fibre of our flesh; he can	286	U84 Muse	151
Our closest Creekes, and Corners, and can trace	287	U84 Muse	153
Nor can the bruised heart want eloquence:	288	U84 Muse	186
Jesus, the onely-gotten Christ! who can	288	U84 Muse	212
Can this decay, but is beginning ever.	294	U88 Petronius	10
Th'Aemilian Schoole, in brasse can fashion out	307	Horace	46
If I can give some small increase? when, loe,	309	Horace	80
What number best can fit, Homer declares.	309	Horace	106
Of Poems here describ'd, I can, nor use,	311	Horace	127
Falshood with truth, as no man can espie	315	Horace	216
Falsehood and truth, as no man can espy	343	Horace	V216
And can tread firme, longs with like lads to play;	315	Horace	226
I can out of knowne geare, a fable frame,	321	Horace	349
I can, out of knowne stuff, a Fable frame,	347	Horace	V341/349
To part scurrilitie from wit: or can	323	Horace	403
Be like a Whet-stone, that an edge can put	325	Horace	433
Which the Socratick writings best can show:	325	Horace	442
Can tell a States-mans dutie, what the arts	325	Horace	449
Of a brave Chiefe sent to the warres: He can,	325	Horace	451
Thinke wee, or hope, there can be Verses fain'd	327	Horace	474
But he hath every suffrage, can apply	329	Horace	514
Or knowes not what Cassellius Aulus can;	331	Horace	553
Or trundling Wheele, he can sit still, from all;	331	Horace	568
Can; or all toile, without a wealthie veine:	331	Horace	584
His flatterers to their gaine. But say, he can	333	Horace	601
His praisers to their gaine: but say he can	353	Horace	V601
Will be a suretie; or can helpe him out	333	Horace	603
Nor did he doe this once; for if you can	335	Horace	667
Nor did he do this, once; if yet you can,	355	Horace	V667
Who saith our Times nor have, nor can	366	Ode Who saith	1
"Where neither Force can bend, nor Feare can awe.	367	Ode Who saith	48
Of Europes waters can	369	Ode Who saith	119
So bold, as shewes your Art you can command.	370	Author	8
What can one witnesse, and a weake one, add	385	Brooke	4
Had cloath'd him so. Here's all I can supply	389	Aleman	20
That would have done, that, which you onely can.	389	Aleman	24
As neither Man, nor Muse, can praise too much.	390	Shakespeare	4
But every Table in this Church can say,	394	Jane Ogle	7
No stone in any wall here, but can tell	394	Jane Ogle	9
Did all so strike me, as I cry'd, who can	397	Drayton	31

CAN (cont.)

That can but reade; who cannot, may in prose . . . . 398 Drayton 73
If I can be a Friend, and Friend to thee. . . . 398 Drayton 94
That Art, or Ingine, on the strength can raise. . . . 400 Beaumont 10
Eyes that can pierce into the Misteryes . . . . 404 Inigo Jones 1 46
To plant the Musick where noe eare can reach! . . . 404 Inigo Jones 1 53
Attyre the Persons as noe thought can teach . . . 404 Inigo Jones 1 54
Hee's warme on his feet now he sayes, & can . . . 405 Inigo Jones 1 67
But wisest Inigo! who can reflect . . . . 405 Inigo Jones 1 86
Whom not ten fyres, nor a Parlyament can . . . 406 Inigo Jones 1 103
Hee'll be a Pilot, scarce can guide a Plough. . . . 410 Brome 18
And know the woofe, and warpe thereof; can tell . . 415 Rutter 15
But I can tell thee, Dover, how thy Games . . . 415 Dover 3
Those dull Girls, no good can mean us, . . . 657 Door Apollo 11
of her white Hand; or she can spare it. . . . 662 Bedford 10

CANARY
Is a pure cup of rich Canary-wine, ... 65 E101 Supper 29
As the old Bard, should no Canary lack. . . . . 241 U68 House-hold 11

CANARY-WINE
Is a pure cup of rich Canary-wine, ... 65 E101 Supper 29

CANCELL'D
Till swept away, th'were cancell'd with a broome! . . 282 U84 Muse 8

CANDIDATES
New in their stead, out of the Candidates? . . . 222 U49 Pucell 6

CANDIDE
In Sugar Candide, or in butter'd beere, . . . 167 U15 Friend-Wars 153

CANDLE
Her face there's none can like by Candle light. . . 223 U49 Pucell 32

CANDOR
I know not which th'hast most, candor, or wit: . . . 78 E123 Rudyerd 3 2

CANES
'Tis like light Canes, that first rise big and brave, . 157 U13 Sacvile 149

CANKER'D
Or canker'd Jealousie, ... 257 U75 Epithalam. 135
Sixe ounces. O, when once the canker'd rust, . . . 327 Horace 472

CANN
nor cann be of desert, ... 420 Ode:If Men 13

CANNONS
Goe enter breaches, meet the cannons rage, . . . 98 F3 Wroth 69

CANNOT
Thou saist, that cannot be: for thou hast seene . . 32 E18 Censurer 3
But leave, because I cannot as I should! . . . 34 E23 Donne 1 10
Thou flattered'st thine, mine cannot flatter'd bee. . . 38 E36 Martial 4
I Cannot thinke there's that antipathy . . . 52 E75 Lippe 1
I cannot for the stage a Drama lay, . . . 72 E112 Gamster 7
Cryes out 'gainst cocking, since he cannot bet, . . 76 E119 Shelton 3
And pitty 'tis, I cannot call 'hem knights: . . . 84 E133 Voyage 22
Cannot the Plague-bill keepe you backe? nor bells . . 88 E133 Voyage 173
Cannot we delude the eyes . . . . . 102 F5 Celia 1 11
Hermes, the cheater, cannot mixe with us, . . . 107 F10 Proludium V 22
Cannot so safely sinne. Their chastitie . . . 111 F11 Epode 81
Giddie with change, and therefore cannot see . . . 118 F13 Aubigny 67
And yet it cannot be foreborne. . . . . 147 U7 Nymph 13
Read so much wast, as she cannot imbrace . . . 150 U9 Picture 16
You cannot doubt, but I, who freely know . . . 153 U13 Sacvile 13
Cannot a man be reck'ned in the State . . . 156 U13 Sacvile 103
Their difference, cannot choose which you will be. . 157 U13 Sacvile 154
Though I am short, I cannot be obscure: . . . 158 U14 Selden 2
Flowes in upon me, and I cannot raise . . . 160 U14 Selden 62
Cannot indure reproofe, ... 175 U23 Himselfe 32
Looke forth, but cannot last in such a forme. . . 191 U38 Elegy 'Tis 14
He cannot angrie be, but all must quake, . . . 193 U38 Elegy 'Tis 71
Why yet, my noble hearts, they cannot say, . . . 213 U44 Speach 1
They cannot last. No lie grew ever old. . . . 216 U45 Squib 20
What though she talke, and cannot once with them, . 222 U49 Pucell 11
Cannot but heape that grace, he will requite. . . 236 U63 Charles 2 14
And murmure cannot quarrell at your wayes? . . . 237 U64 Charles 3 14
Great Say-Master of State, who cannot erre, . . . 255 U75 Epithalam. 99
Which, though I cannot as an Architect . . . 261 U77 Treasurer 25
Which, though I cannot like as an Architect . . . 261 U77 Treasurer V 25
To draw a thing that cannot sit. . . . 277 U84 Mind 8
My wounded mind cannot sustaine this stroke, . . 283 U84 Muse 23
Their heads, which three Anticyra's cannot heale. . 325 Horace 428
The head that three Anticira's cannot heale. . . 349 Horace V428
Out better Poems? But I cannot buy . . . 325 Horace 431
On steele, though 't selfe be dull, and cannot cut. . 325 Horace 434
Being tould there, Reason cannot, Sense may erre. . 370 Author 14
Who cannot reade, but onely doth desire . . . 383 Author 9
But, since he cannot, Reader, looke . . . 390 Reader 9
That can but reade; who cannot, may in prose . . 398 Drayton 73
I Cannot bring my Muse to dropp her Vies . . . 415 Dover 1

CANON
With the just Canon of his life, ... 151 U12 Corbet 11

CANST
Man scarse can make that doubt, but thou canst teach. . 31 E14 Camden 10
That so alone canst judge, so'alone dost make: . . 62 E96 Donne 2 3
No, Shelton, give me thee, canst want all these, . . 76 E119 Shelton 7
Till thou canst finde the best, choose the least ill. . 76 E119 Shelton 10
That to the vulgar canst thy selfe apply, . . . 76 E119 Shelton 11
Canst tell me best, how every Furie lookes there, . . 85 E133 Voyage 52
Of touch, or marble; nor canst boast a row . . . 93 F2 Penshurst 2
How blest art thou, canst love the countrey, Wroth, . 96 F3 Wroth 1
But canst, at home, in thy securer rest, . . . 97 F3 Wroth 13

CANST (cont.)
   A-bed canst heare the loud stag speake,   .   .   .   97   F3 Wroth   22
   Thou canst with some delight the day out-weare, .   .   .   97   F3 Wroth   V 35
   And such since thou canst make thine owne content, .   .   .   98   F3 Wroth   65
   Doe not once hope, that thou canst tempt   .   .   .   100   F4 To the World   5
   From all the nets that thou canst spread.   .   .   .   100   F4 To the World   8
   I know thou canst nor shew, nor beare   .   .   .   101   F4 To the World   39
   Read here in one, what thou in all canst find,   .   .   .   185   U30 Burleigh   2
   'Cause thou canst halt, with us, in Arts, and Fire! . .   .   208   U43 Vulcan   110
   Cause thou canst doe these halting tricks in fire? .   .   .   208   U43 Vulcan   V110
   Thou canst draw forth thy forces, and fight drie   . .   .   214   U44 Speach   45
   If, Passenger, thou canst but reade: .   .   .   233   U60 La-ware   1
   Thou sluggish spawne, that canst, but wilt not see? . .   .   250   U73 Weston   8
   Thou canst not meet more Glory, on the way,   .   .   .   252   U75 Epithalam.   3
   And, if thou list thy selfe, what thou canst bee.   .   .   .   386   Browne   4
   Or canst of truth the least intrenchment pitch,   .   .   .   407   Inigo Jones 2   23
   And in this Age, canst hope no other grace.   .   .   .   420   Ode:If Men   27
   But with a Kisse, (if thou canst dare it)   .   .   .   662   Bedford   9
CANT
   Though gold or Ivory haftes cant make it good.   .   .   .   403   Inigo Jones 1   V 28
CANTILENA
   Cantilena   143   U3 Musicall   VTtl
CANVAS
   Thy Canvas Gyant, at some Channell aymes,   .   .   .   407   Inigo Jones 2   15
CANVASSE
   Not built with Canvasse, paper, and false lights,   .   .   .   220   U47 Tribe   65
CAP
   Velvet, or Taffata cap, rank'd in the darke   .   .   .   371   Fletcher   5
CAPARISON
   A Gowne of that, was the Caparison?   201   U42 Elegy Let   46
CAPERS
   An olive, capers, or some better sallade   .   .   .   64   E101 Supper   10
CAPITALL   (See also CAP'TALI)
   Our Delicacies are growne capitall, ...   163   U15 Friend-Wars   37
CAPON
   Some bring a capon, some a rurall cake,   .   .   .   95   F2 Penshurst   51
CAPONS
   Sindge Capons, or poore Pigges, dropping their eyes;   .   .   205   U43 Vulcan   53
   Sindge capons, or crispe Pigges, dropping their eyes; .   .   205   U43 Vulcan   V 53
CAPP
   each to pawne hir husbands capp, ...   417   Moon   38
CAP'RING
   to loose, and Cap'ring, for thy stricter veyne.   .   .   .   108   F10 Proludium   2
CAP'S
   At every stall; The Cittie Cap's a charme.   .   .   .   200   U42 Elegy Let   28
CAPT
   On Cashierd Capt. Surly.   54   E82 Surly   Ttl
CAPTAINE
   On Captaine Hazard the Cheater.   56   E87 Hazard   Ttl
   Or Captaine Pamphlets horse, and foot, that sallie .   .   .   206   U43 Vulcan   79
   Oure Captaine Pamphlets horse, and foot, that sallie   .   .   206   U43 Vulcan   V 79
   Or Captaine Pamphletts, which on foote doe sally   .   .   .   206   U43 Vulcan   V 79
   Were now the greater Captaine? for they saw   .   .   .   214   U44 Speach   39
   (Compos'd of Gamester, Captaine, Knight, Knight's man, .   .   370   Fletcher   3
CAPTAINES
   He that but saw thy curious Captaines drill,   .   .   .   213   U44 Speach   29
   The gests of Kings, great Captaines, and sad Warres,   .   .   309   Horace   105
   The deeds of Kings, great Captaines, and sad Warres,   .   .   341   Horace   V105
CAP'TALL
   For their owne cap'tall crimes, t'indite my wit;   .   .   .   117   F13 Aubigny   14
CAPTAYNE
   Nor Captayne Pod, nor yet the Eltham-thing;   .   .   .   62   E97 Motion   2
   To Captayne Hungry.   68   E107 Hungry   Ttl
   Doe what you come for, Captayne, with your newes;   .   .   .   68   E107 Hungry   1
   Doe what you come for, Captayne, There's your meate.   .   .   69   E107 Hungry   32
   But 's angry for the Captayne, still: is such.   .   .   .   70   E108 Soldiers   10
CAPTAYNES
   Such as are misse-call'd Captaynes, and wrong you; .   .   .   69   E108 Soldiers   2
   Which all, but ignorant Captaynes, will confesse: .   .   .   72   E111 Edmonds 2   7
CAPTIV'D
   To have her captiv'd spirit freed from flesh,   .   .   .   285   U84 Muse   93
CAR   (See also CARRE)
   Were seene your ugly Centaures, yee call Car-men,   .   .   .   86   E133 Voyage   68
CARBUNCLE
   how lyke the Carbuncle in Aarons brest   .   .   .   361   Palmer   14
'CARE
   And interpose thy selfe, ('care not how soone.)   .   .   .   238   U65 Prince   10
CARE
   Pray thee, take care, that tak'st my booke in hand,   .   .   27   E1 Reader   1
   Doe beg thy care unto thy after-state.   43   E51 James 3   8
   Sober, as saddest care: 111   F11 Epode   60
   For his Mind, I doe not care, ...   142   U2 Exception   1
   If wee would search with care, and paine,   .   .   .   145   U5 Woman-kind   8
   Lesse shall I for the Art or dressing care,   .   .   .   158   U14 Selden   3
   The Care, and wish still of the publike wealth: .   .   .   186   U31 Elsmere   6
   That since thou tak'st all envious care and paine,   .   .   203   U43 Vulcan   13
   Troy, though it were so much his Venus care.   .   .   .   210   U43 Vulcan   160
   Past any need of vertue. Let them care,   .   .   .   215   U44 Speach   83
   Care not what trials they are put unto;   .   .   .   218   U47 Tribe   2
   Minerva's and the Muses care!   233   U60 La-ware   4
   What could their care doe 'gainst the spight   .   .   .   234   U60 La-ware   5
   Great aides to Empire, as they are great care   .   .   .   268   U80 Christning   6
   Nor care I now healths to propound;   293   U86 Hor.4:1   31

		Page	Title	Line

CARE (cont.)
Liber, of all thy friends, thou sweetest care,	. . .	294	U89 Mart.8:77	1
Not care, as thou wouldst faithfully translate,	. . .	313	Horace	190
Her language, if the Stay, and Care t'have mended,	. .	325	Horace	413
And care of getting, thus, our minds hath stain'd,	. .	327	Horace	473
Informed rightly, by your Fathers care,	. . .	331	Horace	546
There's none will take the care, to helpe him then;	. .	335	Horace	654
trust in the tombes, their care-full freinds do rayse;	. .	387	Cavendish	6
Thou art not worth it. Who will care to knowe	. .	409	Detractor	13

CARE-FULL
| trust in the tombes, their care-full freinds do rayse; | . | 387 | Cavendish | 6 |

CAREFULLY
| But you, my Piso, carefully beware, | . . . . . | 333 | Horace | 607 |

CARELESSE
Where do'st thou carelesse lie,	. . .	174	U23 Himselfe	1
For his owne good, a carelesse letter-goe	. . .	315	Horace	234
Blot out the carelesse, with his turned pen;	. .	335	Horace	635
They vexe, and carelesse follow him with noise.	. .	354	Horace	V648

CARES
Each night, to drowne his cares: But when the gaine	. .	56	E87 Hazard	3
That shee removeth cares, sadnesse ejects,	. .	82	E130 Ferrab. 1	4
And in their cups, their cares are drown'd:	. .	98	F3 Wroth	60
Of cares, and over-seer	. . . .	221	U48 Bacchus	14
Loves cares so evill, and so great?	. .	290	U85 Country	38
Thy night not dronken, but from cares layd wast;	. .	295	U90 Mart.10:47	9
Their cares in wine; with sure	. . . .	368	Ode Who saith	87

CAREW
Which noble Carew, Cotton, Selden lent:	. . .	207	U43 Vulcan	100
By Carew, Cotton, Selden, oyle was spent	. . .	207	U43 Vulcan	V100
By Carew, Cotton, Seldens oyle was spent	. . .	207	U43 Vulcan	V100
Of Carew, Cotton, Selden, oyles were spent	. .	207	U43 Vulcan	V100

CAREY
| To Sir Lucius Carey, on the death of his Brother Morison | . | 242 | U70 Ode | VTtl |

CARIED
| And caried, though with shoute, and noyse, confesse | . . | 397 | Drayton | 45 |

CARING
| As mad-men stones: not caring whom they hit. | . . | 27 | E2 My Booke | 6 |

CARKASSE
| To live, or fall a Carkasse in the cause. | . . . | 219 | U47 Tribe | 42 |

CARKASSES
| These Carkasses of honour; Taylors blocks, | . . | 216 | U44 Speach | 99 |

CAR-MEN
| Were seene your ugly Centaures, yee call Car-men, | . . | 86 | E133 Voyage | 68 |

CAROCHES
| Hath filled, with Caroches, all the way, | . . . | 252 | U75 Epithalam. | 11 |

CAROLINE
| And Charles a Caroline! | . . . . . | 240 | U67 Muses | 54 |

CARPENTRY
| Painting & Carpentry are the Soule of Masque. | . . | 404 | Inigo Jones 1 | 50 |

CARPER
| The emptye Carper, scorne, not Creditt wynns. | . . | 421 | Censure | 5 |

CARPETS
| As, on two flowry Carpets, that did rise, | . . | 398 | Drayton | 81 |

CARPS
| Fat, aged carps, that runne into thy net. | . . . | 94 | F2 Penshurst | 33 |

CARRACT
But doth his Carract, and just Standard keepe	. .	255	U75 Epithalam.	100
doth his prime Carract, and just Standard keepe	. .	255	U75 Epithalam.	V100
Their Carract was! I, or my trump must breake,	. .	269	U81 Pawlet	27
Their Carract was! for my trump must breake,	. .	269	U81 Pawlet	V 27
Concluded from a Carract to a dramme.	. .	415	Rutter	30

CARRE
| And well the Carre Love guideth. | . . . . | 134 | U2 Triumph | 4 |

CARRIAGE
| Carriage, and dressing. There is up of late | . . | 215 | U44 Speach | 88 |

CARRIED
. . . and carried the Cause.	. . .	186	U33 Councellour	Ttl
The Tragedie, and carried it about,	. . .	319	Horace	312
Hee's carried 'twixt Montrell and Abbevile.	. .	374	Coryat 1	13
Hee's carried like a Cripple, from Constable to Constable.	.	374	Coryat 1	17

CARRIES
| It carries Palme with it, (where e're it goes) | . . | 363 | Riches | 6 |

CARRY
They carry in their pockets Tacitus,	. .	59	E92 New Crie	15
But let this drosse carry what price it will	. .	114	F12 Rutland	27
Or skill, to carry out an evill cause!	. .	187	U33 Councellour	18
To carry noble danger in the face:	. .	194	U38 Elegy 'Tis	102
Shall carry me at Call; and I'le be well,	. .	219	U47 Tribe	45
To carry, and conduct the Complement	. .	270	U81 Pawlet	66

CARRYED
| Carryed and wrapt, I only am alow'd | . . . | 155 | U13 Sacvile | 88 |

CART
Phoebus. No? tend thy cart still. Envious day	. .	107	F10 Proludium	7
Besides he tried Ship, Cart, Waggon, and Chayre,	. .	380	Coryat 3	27
In a Cart twixt Montrell and Abbevile.	. .	380	Coryat 3	53

CARTS
| Of all your night-tubs, when the carts doe cluster, | . . | 85 | E133 Voyage | 64 |
| Till then unknowne, in Carts, wherein did ride | . . | 319 | Horace | 313 |

CARVE
And act the businesse, which they paint, or carve.	. .	261	U77 Treasurer	16
And act the businesse, which these paint, or carve.	. .	261	U77 Treasurer	V 16
Build Townes, and carve the Lawes in leaves of wood.	. .	327	Horace	490

		Page	Title	Line

CARV'D
Painted, or carv'd upon our great-mens tombs, ... 114   F12 Rutland   45
CARVED
Above your under-carved ornaments, ... 115   F12 Rutland   85
CARY
To Sir Henrie Cary.   48   E66 Cary   Ttl
To greatnesse, Cary, I sing that, and thee.   .   .   . 48   E66 Cary   2
To his Lady, then Mrs. Cary.   80   E126 Mrs Cary   Ttl
Cary my love is, Daphne but my tree.   80   E126 Mrs Cary   8
Cary to passe her melancholie time.   .   .   . 231   U56 Covell   V 24
. . . paire, Sir Lucius Cary, and Sir H. Morison.   .   . 242   U70 Ode   Ttl
But as a Cary, or a Morison.   247   U70 Ode   116
CASE (ENCLOSURE)
Not he, that should the body have, for Case   .   . 223   U49 Pucell   33
And louse-dropping Case, are the Armes of his travell.   .   . 375   Coryat 1   27
CASE
But one more rare, and in the case so new: .   .   . 62   E97 Motion   3
Thou art jealous of thy Wifes, or Daughters Case: .   . 202   U42 Elegy Let   87
Provided, ne're to yeeld, in any case   .   .   . 323   Horace   379
CAS'D
Or a Close-stoole so cas'd; or any fat   .   .   . 202   U42 Elegy Let   84
CASHIERD
On Cashierd Capt. Surly.   54   E82 Surly   Ttl
CASKE
That saw you put on Pallas plumed caske: .   .   . 68   E105 L Wroth 2   16
CASSANDRA
His new Cassandra, 'bove the old;   .   .   . 181   U27 Ode Helen   23
CASSELLIUS
Or knowes not what Cassellius Aulus can;   .   .   . 331   Horace   553
CASSIOPEA
Or lifted Cassiopea in her chayre?   115   F12 Rutland   62
CASSOCK
Is Banke-rupt turn'd! the Cassock, Cloake, and Gowne,   .   . 237   U64 Charles 3   20
Is Banke-rupt turn'd! Cloak, Cassock, Robe, & Gowne,   .   . 237   U64 Charles 3   V 20
CAST
He cast, yet keeps her well! No, shee keeps him.   .   . 54   E82 Surly   2
As loth, the second draught, or cast to stay,   .   . 94   F2 Penshurst   35
The apple-harvest and ploued land up cast;   .   . 98   F3 Wroth   V 43
Cast himselfe from the spire   111   F11 Epode   64
Cast in thousand snares, and rings   .   .   . 141   U2 Her man   11
Nor cast them downe, but let them rise,   .   .   . 144   U4 Song   3
And cast my love behind: 149   U9 Picture   5
And cast my suite behind: 149   U9 Picture   V 5
Ready to cast, at one, whose band sits ill,   .   .   . 164   U15 Friend-Wars   69
His deare and borrow'd Bravery he must cast?   .   . 165   U15 Friend-Wars   110
Goe make our selves the Usurers at a cast.   .   . 166   U15 Friend-Wars   134
When I am hoarse, with praising his each cast,   .   . 167   U15 Friend-Wars   151
No, I will stand arraign'd, and cast, to be   .   . 191   U38 Elegy 'Tis   27
'Twas Jupiter that cast thee headlong downe,   .   . 203   U43 Vulcan   V 9
From whence they fall, cast downe with their owne weight.   .   . 224   U50 Countesse   12
Have cast a trench about mee, now, five yeares;   .   . 248   U71 Treasurer   6
If you can cast about your either eye,   .   .   . 271   U81 Pawlet   85
Cast out by voyces; want they pleasure, then   .   . 329   Horace   512
To let it downe, who knowes, if he did cast   .   . 335   Horace   656
thus, as a ponderous thinge in water cast   .   . 361   Palmer   17
It cast a beame as when the chear-full Sun   .   . 396   Drayton   17
Before this worke? where Envy hath not cast   .   . 401   Beaumont   13
Uppon soe humbled earth to cast hir eyes: .   . 420   Ode:If Men   30
CASTOR
And, on they went, like Castor brave, and Pollux: .   . 86   E133 Voyage   77
Or Castor mounted on his Cyllarus: .   .   . 228   U53 Newcastle   8
CASTS
Who casts to write a living line, must sweat,   .   . 392   Shakespeare   59
CAT
Their spirits transmigrated to a cat: .   .   . 88   E133 Voyage   159
CATALOGUE
Are sure to con the catalogue by hart;   .   .   . 59   E92 New Crie   22
Thy Catalogue of Ships, exceeding his,   .   .   . 398   Drayton   61
CATAPLASMES
Suppositories, cataplasmes, and lotions.   .   .   . 86   E133 Voyage   102
CATCH
To catch the worlds loose laughter, or vaine gaze.   .   . 27   E2 My Booke   12
To catch the flesh in, and to pound a Prick.   .   . 164   U15 Friend-Wars   67
That watch, and catch, at what they may applaud,   .   . 167   U15 Friend-Wars   157
And the strong lines, that so the time doe catch: .   . 206   U43 Vulcan   78
And the strong lines, which so the time doe catch: .   . 206   U43 Vulcan   V 78
Or, whilst he shuns the Earth, to catch at Aire   .   . 321   Horace   335
Busie to catch a Black-bird; if he fall   .   .   . 335   Horace   651
CATCH'D
Contagion in the prease is soonest catch'd.   .   . 118   F13 Aubigny   58
Catch'd with these Arts, wherein the Judge is wise   .   . 261   U77 Treasurer   11
CATCHES
Except the duell. Can sing songs, and catches;   .   . 74   E115 Honest Man   13
CATECHISME
This booke! it is a Catechisme to fight,   .   .   . 398   Drayton   71
CATER
Which was a cater-piller. So 'twill dye.   .   .   . 31   E15 Court-worm   4
CATER-PILLER
Which was a cater-piller. So 'twill dye.   .   .   . 31   E15 Court-worm   4
CATES
The entertaynment perfect: not the cates.   .   .   . 64   E101 Supper   8
Among these Cates how glad the sight doth come   .   . 291   U85 Country   61

CATO'S
  Cato's to boote, Rome, and her libertie, ... 71 E110 Edmonds 1 4
  Cato's and Ennius tongues have lent much worth, . . 309 Horace 81
  Caesar's ambition, Cato's libertie, ... 395 May 10
CATS
  Cats there lay divers had beene flead, and rosted, . . 88 E133 Voyage 149
CATTELL
  Like Swine, or other Cattell here on earth: . . . 257 U75 Epithalam. 154
CATULLUS
  Was Lesbia sung by learn'd Catullus? . . . 181 U27 Ode Helen 9
CAUGHT
  This same which you have caught, . . . 180 U26 Ode High 20
  Caught them these Arts, wherein the Judge is wise . . 261 U77 Treasurer V 11
'CAUSE
  Or feare to draw true lines, 'cause others paint: . . 117 F13 Aubigny 20
  Man thought the valianter, 'cause he durst sweare, . . 168 U15 Friend-Wars 192
  More honour in him, 'cause we'ave knowne him mad: . . 168 U15 Friend-Wars 194
  'Cause thou canst halt, with us, in Arts, and Fire! . . 208 U43 Vulcan 110
  As Poppie, and Sardane honey: 'cause without . . 331 Horace 559
  Poppy, with hony of Sardus; 'cause without . . . 351 Horace V535/559
CAUSE
  To every cause he meets, this voyce he brayes: . . 31 E12 Shift 19
  I sent the cause: Hee wooes with an ill sprite. . . 33 E19 Cod 1 2
  Hast purg'd thy realmes, as we have now no cause . . 38 E35 James 2 5
  No cause, nor client fat, will Chev'rill leese, . . 38 E37 Chev'ril 1
  As if thou wert my friend, but lack'dst a cause. . . 43 E52 Courtling 4
  That quit'st the cause so oft, and rayl'st at men? . . 44 E54 Chev'ril 2 4
  What should the cause be? Oh, you live at court: . . 46 E62 Would-bee 9
  It may be much, or little, in the cause. . . . 49 E66 Cary 16
  That still th'art present to the better cause; . . 52 E74 Chancelor 5
  As, then, his cause, his glorie emulate. . . . 61 E95 Savile 24
  Know you the cause? H'has neither land, nor lease, . . 63 E97 Motion 9
  Touching this cause, where they will be affeard . . 87 E133 Voyage 106
  These be the cause of those thicke frequent mists . . 87 E133 Voyage 130
  They thinke not, then, which side the cause shall leese, . 98 F3 Wroth 61
  Close, the close cause of it. . . . 109 F11 Epode 16
  Both love the cause, and authors of the feast? . . 120 F14 Sydney 10
  No more, I am sorry for so fond cause, say, . . 171 U20 Shrub 4
  As 'tis too just a cause; . . . . 174 U23 Himselfe 14
  You favour Truth, and me, in this mans Cause. . . 186 U31 Elsmere 10
  When a good Cause is destitute of friends, . . 186 U32 Elsmere 2
  . . . and carried the Cause. . . . 186 U33 Councellour Ttl
  Thou art my Cause: whose manners since I knew, . . 187 U33 Councellour 13
  Or skill, to carry out an evill cause! . . . 187 U33 Councellour 18
  What was the cause then? Thought'st thou in disgrace . . 188 U34 Small Poxe 13
  A cause before; or leave me one behind. . . . 203 U43 Vulcan 28
  Cause thou canst doe these halting tricks in fire? . . 208 U43 Vulcan V110
  More for thy Patronage, then for their Cause, . . 217 U46 Coke 12
  To live, or fall a Carkasse in the cause. . . . 219 U47 Tribe 42
  'Tis a brave cause of joy, let it be knowne, . . 225 U51 Bacon 17
  Indeed, when had great Britaine greater cause . . 236 U64 Charles 3 7
  What can the cause be, when the K. hath given . . 241 U68 House-hold 1
  Peace, and the open ports, that peace doth cause. . . 317 Horace 284
  The open ports, and sports that peace doth cause, . . 345 Horace V284
  His cause of making Verses none knowes why: . . 335 Horace 670
  And Phoebus love cause of his blackenesse is. . . 366 Ode Who saith 16
  Poore Tom have we cause to suspect just thee? . . 381 Coryat 3 58
  A better cause, and strike the bravest heate . . 397 Drayton 56
  What is the cause you pompe it soe? I aske, . . 403 Inigo Jones 1 29
  But cause thou hearst the mighty k. of Spaine . . 406 Inigo Jones 2 1
  Most venerable. Cause of all our joy. . . . 414 Ghyrlond 42
  And newer, then could please them, by-cause trew. . . 415 Rutter 10
  Give cause to some of wonnder, some despite, . . 420 Ode:If Men 35
  Cause Reverence, yf not Feare, ... 421 Ode:If Men 42
CAUS'D
  Which Fate (it seemes) caus'd in the historie, . . 61 E95 Savile 11
CAUSES
  On the true causes, ere they grow too old. . . 50 E70 Wm Roe 1 4
  Can write the things, the causes, and the men. . . 62 E95 Savile 34
  Shuns prease, for two maine causes, poxe, and debt, . . 76 E119 Shelton 4
  When all the causes were away. . . . 101 F4 To the World 44
  The causes and the Guests too, . . . 221 U48 Bacchus 39
CAUSTICKS
  Your hottest Causticks to, burne, lance, or cut: . . 270 U81 Pawlet 54
  Your hotter Causticks to, burne, lance, or cut: . . 270 U81 Pawlet V 54
CAVE
  Cittyes & Temples! thou a Cave for Wyne, . . . 406 Inigo Jones 2 8
CAVENDISH
  Charles Cavendish to his posteritie. . . . 387 Cavendish Ttl
CEASE
  His power of foulely hurting made to cease. . . 323 Horace 370
CEASURE
  Other ceasure. . . . . . . 184 U29 Fit of Rime 48
CECIL
  These (noblest Cecil) labour'd in my thought, . . 48 E64 Salisbury 3 15
CECILIA (See 'SELL)
CECILL
  Cecill, the grave, the wise, the great, the good, . . 185 U30 Burleigh 5
CECILL'S
  When, in my booke, men reade but Cecill's name, . . 41 E43 Salisbury 1 9
CEDAR (See also CAEDAR)
  In juyce of Cedar worthy to be steep'd, . . . 327 Horace 475

CELEBRATE
Whose actions so themselves doe celebrate; . . . . 40 E43 Salisbury 1 2
And celebrate (perfection at the worth) . . . . 253 U75 Epithalam. 28
And this their chosen Bishop celebrate, ... 256 U75 Epithalam. 132
CELEBRATED
Or celebrated with more truth of state? . . . . 28 E5 Union 2
CELEBRATING
Epithalamion; Or, A Song: Celebrating The nuptials of . . . 252 U75 Epithalam. Ttl
And celebrating our owne home-borne facts; . . . . 323 Horace 408
CELEBRATION
A Celebration of Charis in ten Lyrick Peeces. . . . 131 U2 Charis Ttl
. . . In celebration of her Majesties birth-day. 1630. . . 239 U67 Muses Ttl
CELESTIALL
Us forth, by some Celestiall slight . . . . 279 U84 Mind 47
CELIA   (See also COELIA)
Song. To Celia. . . . . . . 102 F5 Celia 1 Ttl
Come my Celia, let us prove, ... 102 F5 Celia 1 1
Come sweet Celia, let us prove, ... 102 F5 Celia 1 V 1
Song. To Celia. . . . . . . 106 F9 Celia 3 Ttl
And shall not I my Celia bring, ... 182 U27 Ode Helen 31
Must Celia bee, the Anagram of Alice. . . . 412 Sutcliffe 23
CELLAR
The Dedication of the Kings new Cellar. to Bacchus. . . 220 U48 Bacchus Ttl
We dedicate this Cellar, ... 220 U48 Bacchus 3
CELLARS
Up & about? Dyve into Cellars too . . . . 405 Inigo Jones 1 80
CENSORIOUS
To Censorious Courtling. . . . . . 43 E52 Courtling Ttl
CENSURE
Charge them, for crowne, to thy sole censure hye. . . 32 E17 Critic 4
When thou wert wont t'admire, not censure men. . . 32 E18 Censurer 8
Of state, and censure them: we need his pen . . . 62 E95 Savile 33
Unto the Censure. Yours all need doth flie . . . 158 U14 Selden 11
That censure all the Towne, and all th'affaires, . . 218 U47 Tribe 23
Do's the Court-Pucell then so censure me, . . . 222 U49 Pucell 1
Wants facultie to make a censure true: . . . 362 Author 11
That sit to censure Playes, yet know not when, . . 414 Rutter 8
This is my censure. Now there is a new . . . 415 Rutter 19
Censure, not sharplye then, but mee advise . . . 421 Censure 1
CENSUR'D
That askes but to be censur'd by the eyes: . . . 117 F13 Aubigny 35
A Rogue by Statute, censur'd to be whipt, . . . 411 Gill 15
CENSURER
To my meere English Censurer. . . . . 32 E18 Censurer Ttl
CENSURES
And, in thy censures, evenly, dost take . . . 62 E96 Donne 2 4
And though we could all men, all censures heare, . . 83 E131 Ferrab. 2 5
Thou, Friend, wilt heare all censures; unto thee . . 232 U58 Book-seller 1
CENSURETH
Hee that soe Censureth, or adviseth synns, . . . 421 Censure 4
CENSURING
And still correcting youth, and censuring. . . . 317 Horace 249
CENTAURE
And saw a Centaure, past those tales of Greece; . . 228 U53 Newcastle 5
CENTAURES
Were seene your ugly Centaures, yee call Car-men, . . 86 E133 Voyage 68
CENTER
Upon your Center, doe your Circle fill . . . 159 U14 Selden 32
And dwell as in my Center, as I can, . . . 219 U47 Tribe 60
Of deepest lore, could we the Center find! . . . 243 U70 Ode 10
And pietie the Center, where all met. . . . 270 U81 Pawlet 42
did sparcle foorth in Center of the rest: . . . 361 Palmer 16
CERBERUS
And for one Cerberus, the whole coast was dogs. . . 84 E133 Voyage 14
Behold where Cerberus, rear'd on the wall . . . 89 E133 Voyage 176
CEREMONIES
And turne the Ceremonies of those Nights . . . 197 U40 Elegy That 11
CERES
Would call you more then Ceres, if not that: . . 68 E105 L Wroth 2 8
CERTAINE
Whil'st thou art certaine to thy words, once gone, . . 52 E74 Chancelor 7
Unto their praise, in certaine swearing rites! . . 156 U13 Sacvile 102
(Defiled) touch'd; but certaine he was mad, . . 337 Horace 673
Certaine Verses Written Upon Coryats Crudities, . . . 379 Coryat 3 Ttl
CERTAINLY
Polluted, touch't: but certainly he's mad: . . . 355 Horace V673
CERTEYNE
You aske noe more then certeyne politique Eyes, . . 404 Inigo Jones 1 45
CESTON
For Venus Ceston, every line you make. . . . 182 U28 Worth 14
Had got the Ceston on! . . . . . 240 U67 Muses 36
Had put the Ceston on! . . . . . 240 U67 Muses V 36
CESTRIAN
Meschines honour with the Cestrian fame . . . 274 U84 Descent 16
CETHEGI
Of the Cethegi; And all men will grace, . . . 309 Horace 72
CHACE
Have you seene the boy from the Chace . . . 135 U2 Triumph V 39
CHAFES
Her voyce, and angry Chremes chafes out-right . . 311 Horace 133
CHAINE
Twirle the poore chaine you run a feasting in. . . 69 E107 Hungry 30
That fled his cage, or broke his chaine, . . . 101 F4 To the World 30

CHAINE (cont.)
It is a golden chaine let downe from heaven,   .   .   .   110 F11 Epode   47
Lovers, made into a Chaine!   .   .   .   .   137 U2 Cupid   32
CHAINED
And, with their Chained dance,   .   .   .   401 Filmer   9
CHAINES
But they may see Gold-Chaines, and Pearle worne then,   .   213 U44 Speach   13
CHAINGE
only pursewinge Constancy, in Chainge;   .   .   108 F10 Proludium   10
Though shee chainge as oft as shee,   .   .   417 Moon   29
CHAIRE (See also CHAYRE)
Hath got the stewards chaire; he will not tarry   .   57 E90 Mill   15
For there the wicked in the Chaire of scorne,   .   223 U49 Pucell   45
In his soft Cradle to his Fathers Chaire,   .   .   225 U51 Bacon   14
CHAIRES
So I might dote upon thy Chaires and Stooles   .   201 U42 Elegy Let   47
His friends, but to breake Chaires, or cracke a Coach.   .   230 U56 Covell   10
CHALICE
I sayd, who'had supp'd so deepe of this sweet Chalice,   .   412 Sutcliffe   21
CHALK
With rotten chalk, or Cole upon a wall,   .   .   .   408 Inigo Jones 3   11
CHALKE
Produce; though threatning with a coale, or chalke   .   193 U38 Elegy 'Tis   97
CHALLENGE
As't were a challenge, or a borrowers letter?   .   51 E73 Fine Grand   3
And challenge all the Spheares,   .   .   143 U3 Musicall   2
CHAMBER
That lost, he keepes his chamber, reades Essayes,   .   30 E12 Shift   15
And threatens the starre-chamber, and the barre: .   44 E54 Chev'ril 2   2
A chamber-critick, and dost dine, and sup   .   50 E72 Court-ling   2
And he growne youth, was call'd to his ladies chamber.   .   57 E90 Mill   10
Keepe a starre-chamber sentence close, twelve dayes: .   59 E92 New Crie   19
With ten Emp'ricks, in their chamber,   .   .   105 F8 Sicknesse   31
Thy learned Chamber-fellow, knowes to doe   .   161 U14 Selden   72
What though her Chamber be the very pit   .   222 U49 Pucell   3
At libelling? Shall no Star-Chamber Peers,   .   410 Gill   3
CHAMBER-CRITICK
A chamber-critick, and dost dine, and sup   .   50 E72 Court-ling   2
CHAMBER-FELLOW
Thy learned Chamber-fellow, knowes to doe   .   161 U14 Selden   72
CHAMBERS
I saw with two poore Chambers taken in,   .   .   209 U43 Vulcan   135
And waiting Chambers of great Lords.   .   .   289 U85 Country   8
CHAMPION
And strength to be a Champion, and defend   .   161 U14 Selden   78
The conqu'ring Champion, the prime Horse in course,   .   311 Horace   115
CHANCE (See also CHAUNCE)
I, that am glad of thy great chance, here doo!   .   46 E60 Mounteagle   5
Could conquer thee, but chance, who did betray.   .   49 E66 Cary   10
Play-wright, by chance, hearing some toyes I'had writ,   .   64 E100 Playwrt 3   1
If't chance to me, I must not grutch.   .   .   101 F4 To the World   56
Who (blest with such high chance)   .   .   111 F11 Epode   62
A Princes fortune: These are gifts of chance,   .   117 F13 Aubigny   41
'Tis onely that can time, and chance defeat: .   118 F13 Aubigny   51
But by meere Chance? for interest? or to free   .   154 U13 Sacvile   30
Men have beene great, but never good by chance,   .   156 U13 Sacvile   124
Nor fashion; if they chance aspire to height,   .   157 U13 Sacvile   148
Chance that the Friends affection proves Allay   .   158 U14 Selden   10
Her upright head, above the reach of Chance,   .   176 U25 Desmond   6
That friendship which no chance but love did chuse,   .   190 U37 Friend-Book   23
Or if Chance must, to each man that doth rise,   .   217 U46 Coke   23
Profit, or Chance had made us: But I know   .   241 U69 Friend Son   3
Of hearts the union. And those not by chance   .   246 U70 Ode   99
Yet, if by chance, in utt'ring things abstruse,   .   307 Horace   69
Honour'd Achilles chance by thee be seiz'd,   .   313 Horace   171
Him that buyes chiches blanch't, or chance to like   .   321 Horace   362
Or Muse, upon the Lyre, thou chance b'asham'd.   .   329 Horace   502
Upon the Lyre, thou chance to be asham'd.   .   353 Horace   V580/502
The truth, but gropes, and urgeth all by chance;   .   391 Shakespeare   10
Or by chance if in their grease   .   .   .   .   418 Moon   41
CHANC'D
That chanc'd the lace, laid on a Smock, to see,   .   201 U42 Elegy Let   66
CHANCELLOR
- - . the last Terme he sate Chancellor.   .   .   185 U31 Elsmere   Ttl
Englands high Chancellor: the destin'd heire   .   225 U51 Bacon   13
CHANCELOR
To Thomas Lord Chancelor.   .   .   .   .   51 E74 Chancelor   Ttl
CHANCERIE
Lyes there no Writ, out of the Chancerie   .   .   210 U43 Vulcan   174
CHANCETH
But who will beleeve this, that chanceth to looke   .   379 Coryat 3   17
CHANC'T
Where he chanc't your name to see   .   .   .   136 U2 Cupid   8
CHANGE
Just wife, and, to change me, make womans hast?   .   34 E25 Beast 1   8
His often change of clime (though not of mind)   .   37 E32 Roe 2   6
Thus, in his belly, can he change a sin,   .   .   76 E118 Gut   5
And change possessions, oftner with his breath,   .   99 F3 Wroth   75
I would not change for thine.   .   .   .   .   106 F9 Celia 3   8
Giddie with change, and therefore cannot see   .   118 F13 Aubigny   67
Because nor it can change, nor such a minde.   .   120 F13 Aubigny   124
That talke abroad of Womans change,   .   .   146 U6 Defence   2
Doe change, though man, and often fight,   .   146 U6 Defence   8

CHANGE   (cont.)

Nor is't inconstancie to change   146   U6 Defence   13
Lawes; and no change e're come to one decree: .   .   185   U31 Elsmere   2
What fate is this, to change mens dayes and houres,   .   .   199   U41 Elegy Since   9
With some more change, and tast of tyranny: .   .   .   205   U43 Vulcan   V 50
Your change of Notes, the flat, the meane, the sharpe,   .   263   U79 New-yeares   3
Stamp'd to the time. As woods whose change appeares .   .   309   Horace   85
To change, and mend, what you not forth doe set.   .   .   331   Horace   579
Then change; no word, or worke, more would he spend   .   335   Horace   630
your Trappings will not change you. Change your mynd.   .   403   Inigo Jones 1   25

CHANG'D

Lord, how is Gam'ster chang'd! his haire close cut!   .   33   E21 Gam'ster   1
Hath chang'd his soule, and made his object you: .   .   74   E114 Sydney   5
And would faine have chang'd the fate,   .   .   .   133   U2 Suffered   19
Wisht the Bride were chang'd to night,   .   .   .   138   U2 Kisse   18
Coach'd, or on foot-cloth, thrice chang'd every day,   .   165   U15 Friend-Wars   107
Curst in their Cradles, or there chang'd by Elves,   .   .   200   U42 Elegy Let   23
Which, chang'd, a five-fold mysterie designe,   .   .   .   412   Ghyrlond   2

CHANGED

Or the wilde river, who hath changed now   .   .   .   309   Horace   96
Reprove; and, what is to be changed, note: .   .   335   Horace   638
Dispute; and what is to be changed, note;   .   .   .   354   Horace   V638

CHANGE'D

This change'd his Downe; till this, as white   .   .   366   Ode Who saith   25

CHANGES

As they had learn'd new changes, for the day,   .   .   253   U75 Epithalam.   35
If now the changes, and the severall hues   .   .   341   Horace   V121/126

CHANGETH

He knowes not why, and changeth every houre.   .   .   .   315   Horace   228

CHANGING

And long in changing. Let our Nephewes see   .   .   238   U65 Prince   7
In changing, let our Nephewes joyfull see   .   .   238   U65 Prince   V 7
In changing. Let our after Nephewes see   .   .   238   U65 Prince   V 7

CHANNELL

Thy Canvas Gyant, at some Channell aymes,   .   .   407   Inigo Jones 2   15

CHANNELS

Keepe secret in his Channels what he breedes,   .   .   198   U40 Elegy That   27

CHANT

To chant her 'gree, ...   274   U84 Cradle   36
To chant the Gods, and all their God-like race,   .   .   311   Horace   114

CHANTING

To be abroad chanting some baudie song,   .   .   164   U15 Friend-Wars   74

CHAPLAINES

They may say Grace, and for Loves Chaplaines passe;   .   198   U40 Elegy That   31

CHAPMAN

To my worthy and honour'd Friend, Mr George Chapman, . . .   388   Chapman   Ttl
Whose worke could this be, Chapman, to refine   .   .   388   Chapman   1

CHAPMEN

And understand 'hem, as most chapmen doe.   .   .   59   E92 New Crie   10

CHAPPEL

Epitaph on S. P. a Child of Q. El. Chappel.   .   .   77   E120 S. P.   Ttl

CHAPPELL

See, now the Chappell opens; where the King   .   .   256   U75 Epithalam.   121
The Chappell empties, and thou may'st be gone   .   .   257   U75 Epithalam.   137

CHARACTER

To ope' the character. They'have found the sleight   .   59   E92 New Crie   27
For every part a character assign'd.   .   .   .   67   E103 L Wroth 1   12
In my character, what your features bee,   .   .   117   F13 Aubigny   24
So short you read my Character, and theirs   .   .   220   U47 Tribe   73
And best he knew her noble Character,   .   .   .   287   U84 Muse   155

CHARACTERS

Their Seales, their Characters, Hermetique rings,   .   .   206   U43 Vulcan   73
Their Charmes, their Characters, Hermetique rings,   .   .   206   U43 Vulcan   V 73

CHARGE

The charge of that state, with this charme, god payes.   .   30   E12 Shift   4
Charge them, for crowne, to thy sole censure hye.   .   32   E17 Critic   4
They should be fooles, for me, at their owne charge.   .   83   E131 Ferrab. 2   8
'Gainst stormes, or pyrats, that might charge your peace;   .   119   F13 Aubigny   93
Thy person fit for any charge thou tak'st;   .   .   168   U15 Friend-Wars   182
For that unnecessarie Charge they were.   .   .   214   U44 Speach   32
As thou dost cure our Evill, at thy charge.   .   .   235   U62 Charles 1   8
What Bevie of beauties, and bright youths at charge   .   253   U75 Epithalam.   17
Hearing their charge, and then   256   U75 Epithalam.   127
Their Charge, and Office, whence their wealth to fet,   .   325   Horace   436
Marry he sets it out at his owne charge;   .   .   378   Coryat 2   83
hath armde att all poyntes; charge mee humblye kneele   .   382   Rich   2
I send this small, but hearty testimony: and with charge,   .   666   Glover   5

CHARG'D

Or have charg'd his sight of Crime,   .   .   .   138   U2 Kisse   32

CHARGEFULL

To all as chargefull as they have beene to me,   .   .   211   U43 Vulcan   V192

CHARIOT

See the Chariot at hand here of Love,   .   .   .   134   U2 Triumph   1
Sols Chariot for new fire, ...   175   U23 Himselfe   28

CHARIS

A Celebration of Charis in ten Lyrick Peeces.   .   .   131   U2 Charis   Ttl
Noblest Charis, you that are   136   U2 Cupid   1
Charis, guesse, and doe not misse,   .   .   .   137   U2 Kisse   1
Charis one day in discourse   139   U2 Promise   1
Therefore, Charis, you must do't,   .   .   .   140   U2 Promise   13

CHARITABLE

So charitable, to religious end, ...   287   U84 Muse   176

CHARITIE
Are there for Charitie, and not for fee. . . . . 186 U32 Elsmere 6
Or doing other deeds of Charitie, ... 288 U84 Muse 193
Thus, Love, and Hope, and burning Charitie, . . . 413 Ghyrlond 25
CHARITIES
Of Princes aides, or good mens Charities. . . . 248 U71 Treasurer 3
CHARLES
And Charles brings home the Ladie. . . . 222 U48 Bacchus 54
An Epigram. To K. Charles for a 100. Pounds . . . 235 U62 Charles 1 Ttl
Great Charles, among the holy gifts of grace . . 235 U62 Charles 1 1
To K. Charles, and Q. Mary. For the losse of their . . . 235 U63 Charles 2 Ttl
Then, Royall Charles, and Mary, doe not grutch . . 236 U63 Charles 2 7
An Epigram. To our great and good K. Charles . . . 236 U64 Charles 3 Ttl
To the great and Gratious King Charles. . . . . 236 U64 Charles 3 VTtl
How many times, Live long, Charles, would he say, . 236 U64 Charles 3 3
How much to heaven for thee, great Charles, they owe! . 237 U64 Charles 3 22
An Epigram on Prince Charles his Birth: May. 29th. 1630 . 237 U65 Prince VTtl
Sol will re-shine. If not, Charles hath a Sonne. . 238 U65 Prince 12
And Sol will shine. If not, Charles hath a Sonne. . 238 U65 Prince V 12
And Charles a Caroline! . . . . . 240 U67 Muses 54
Upon King Charles his Birth-day. . . . 249 U72 King VTtl
This is King Charles his Day. Speake it, thou Towre, . 249 U72 King 1
This is King Charles his birth day. Speake it, thou Towre, . 249 U72 King V 1
Still to have such a Charles, but this Charles long. . 249 U72 King 18
To see great Charles of Travaile eas'd, . . . 251 U74 Weston 26
Askes first, Who gives her (I Charles) then he plights . 256 U75 Epithalam. 124
To Th'Best Of Monarchs, Masters, Men, King Charles . 259 U76 Petition 2
For Brittains honour, and to Charles my King: . . 262 U78 Digby V 18
A New-yeares gift Sung to King Charles, 1635. . 263 U79 New-yeares Ttl
(Charles Montjoy) whose command . . . 367 Ode Who saith 50
Charles Cavendish to his posteritie. . . . 387 Cavendish Ttl
Our Charles should make thee such? 'Twill not become . 406 Inigo Jones 2 3
CHARME
The charge of that state, with this charme, god payes. . 30 E12 Shift 4
Item, a charme surrounding fearefully . . 51 E73 Fine Grand 12
I, that's a Charme and halfe! She must afford . . 163 U15 Friend-Wars 52
But charme the Senses, others over-come . . 182 U28 Worth 7
Weaknesse of braine, or any charme of Wine, . . 198 U40 Elegy That 45
At every stall; The Cittie Cap's a charme. . . 200 U42 Elegy Let 28
There charme the rout . . . . . 367 Ode Who saith 44
Our eares, or like a Mercury to charme! . . 392 Shakespeare 46
Aboute this Isle, and Charme the rounde, as when . 421 Ode:If Men 39
CHARMED
The charmed Boates, and the inchanted Wharfes; . . 205 U43 Vulcan 68
The charmed beauty and the inchanted Wharfes; . . 205 U43 Vulcan V 68
CHARMES
Then shall my Verses, like strong Charmes, . . 177 U25 Desmond 18
Then shall our Verses, like strong Charmes, . . 177 U25 Desmond V 18
Imposture, witchcraft, charmes, or blasphemie, . . 203 U43 Vulcan 16
Their Charmes, their Characters, Hermetique rings, . 206 U43 Vulcan V 73
CHARMING
What charming Peales are these, ... 401 Filmer 1
CHARON
And in it, two more horride knaves, then Charon. . . 84 E133 Voyage 12
CHARONS
Backe, cry'd their brace of Charons: they cry'd, no, . 86 E133 Voyage 87
CHARTER
Aeternities great charter; which became . . . 400 Lady Ogle 35
CHARYBDIS
Scylla, Charybdis, Polypheme, with these. . . . 315 Horace 206
CHASE (See also CHACE)
And, armed to the chase, so bare her bow . . . 68 E105 L Wroth 2 13
And in the chase, more then Sylvanus can, . . 264 U79 New-yeares 22
CHAST
Shall out-live gyrlands, stolne from the chast tree. . 32 E17 Critic 6
What doth he else, but say, leave to be chast, . . 34 E25 Beast 1 7
Then his chast wife, though Beast now know no more, . 35 E26 Beast 2 1
In my chast booke: professe them in thine owne. . 42 E49 Playwrt 1 6
To pay your lord the pledges of chast love: . . 119 F13 Aubigny 96
O so yong o so streight O so chast so chast is shee . 136 U2 Triumph V 46
And stroke the water, nimble, chast, and faire, . . 230 U56 Covell 14
The bed of the chast Lilly, and the Rose! . . . 237 U65 Prince 3
Yet, as we may, we will, with chast desires, . . 257 U75 Epithalam. 161
No sowre, or sollen bed-mate, yet a Chast; . . 295 U90 Mart.10:47 10
Religious, wise, chast, loving, gratious, good, . . 394 Jane Ogle 5
CHASTE
Thy lady's noble, fruitfull, chaste withall. . . 96 F2 Penshurst 90
As this chaste love we sing. . . . . 111 F11 Epode 68
As this chaste love I sing. . . . . 111 F11 Epode V 68
And on them burne so chaste a flame, . . . 173 U22 Elegy Tho 21
But if, to boot with these, a chaste Wife meet . . 291 U85 Country 39
Chaste, thriftie, modest folke, that came to view. . 319 Horace 294
CHASTETYE
Could ne'er make prize of thy white Chastetye. . . 108 F10 Proludium 6
CHASTITIE
Of birth, of match, of forme, of chastitie? . . 67 E104 Montgomery 8
Cannot so safely sinne. Their chastitie . . 111 F11 Epode 81
CHASTLY
Turtles can chastly dye; . . . . 111 F11 Epode 74
Turtles will chastly dye; . . . . 111 F11 Epode V 74
CHATTELL
Unprofitable Chattell, fat and old, . . . 230 U56 Covell 8

                                                 Page   Title   Line

CHATTELS
  Chuffe, lately rich in name, in chattels, goods,   .   .   .   41   E44 Chuff   1
CHATTRING
  To see their Seats and Bowers by chattring Pies defac't?   . .   174   U23 Himselfe   12
CHAUCER
  Chaucer, or Spenser, or bid Beaumont lye   391   Shakespeare   20
CHAUNCE
  That Frindshipp, which noe Chaunce, but Love did Chuse,   .   422   Censure   16
CHAYRE
  Or lifted Cassiopea in her chayre?   .   .   .   115   F12 Rutland   62
  Besides he tried Ship, Cart, Waggon, and Chayre,   .   .   380   Coryat 3   27
CHEAP
  Any Comparison had with his Cheap-side.   .   .   .   202   U42 Elegy Let   76
CHEAPE
  Pardon his Lordship. Flattry's growne so cheape   .   167   U15 Friend-Wars 155
  Is to make cheape, the Lord, the lines, the price.   .   .   408   Detractor   6
CHEAP-SIDE
  Any Comparison had with his Cheap-side.   .   .   .   202   U42 Elegy Let   76
CHEAR
  It cast a beame as when the chear-full Sun   .   .   396   Drayton   17
CHEARE
  What (great, I will not say, but) sodayne cheare   .   95   F2 Penshurst   82
  For though Love thrive, and may grow up with cheare,   .   197   U40 Elegy That 15
  And neither good Cheare, -   231   U57 Burges   16
  He will cheare up his forehead, thinke thou bring'st   .   263   U78 Digby   V 21
CHEAR'D
  Chear'd her faire Sisters in her race to runne!   .   .   270   U81 Pawlet   58
CHEAR-FULL
  It cast a beame as when the chear-full Sun   .   .   396   Drayton   17
CHEARFULL
  Whose chearfull look our sadnesse doth destroy,   .   .   414   Ghyrlond   43
CHEARFULLY
  Shee chearfully supporteth what she reares,   .   .   176   U24 Frontispice 13
CHEATED
  The knight-wright's cheated then: Hee'll never pay.   .   42   E46 Luckless 1   5
  And the bold Pythias, having cheated weake   .   .   321   Horace   346
CHEATER
  On Captaine Hazard the Cheater.   56   E87 Hazard   Ttl
  Hermes, the cheater, shall not mixe with us,   .   .   107   F10 Proludium 22
  Hermes, the cheater, cannot mixe with us,   .   .   .   107   F10 Proludium V 22
CHECKT
  Not to be checkt, or frighted now with fate,   .   .   163   U15 Friend-Wars 35
CHEEKE
  Even nose, and cheeke (withall)   141   U2 Her man   19
  By those pure bathes your either cheeke discloses,   .   170   U19 Elegy By   7
CHEEKES
  In her cheekes, of Milke, and Roses;   .   .   .   136   U2 Cupid   22
CHEEKS
  Flow my thin teares, downe these pale cheeks of mine?   .   293   U86 Hor.4:1   34
CHEERE
  And fills thy open hall with mirth, and cheere,   .   98   F3 Wroth   49
  Or influence, chide, or cheere the drooping Stage;   .   392   Shakespeare   78
CHEERED
  And came forth ever cheered, with the rod   .   .   287   U84 Muse   183
CHEEREFULL
  No! Gifts and thankes should have one cheerefull face,   .   154   U13 Sacvile   39
  A cheerefull worke to all good eyes, to see   .   .   224   U50 Countesse   16
CHEESE
  Digestive cheese, and fruit there sure will bee;   .   65   E101 Supper   27
CHEESES
  The better cheeses, bring 'hem; or else send   .   .   95   F2 Penshurst   53
CHEIFEST
  In cheifest glory Sunne-her   135   U2 Triumph   V 32
CHELSEY
  Or the sands in Chelsey fields, ...   103   F6 Celia 2   14
  All the sands in Chelsey fields, ...   103   F6 Celia 2 V 14
'CHEQUER
  If the 'Chequer be emptie, so will be his Head.   .   232   U57 Burges   28
CHEQUER
  With Chequer Inke, upon his guift, my paper,   -   .   666   Glover   8
CHERISH
  Embrace, and cherish; but he can approve   .   .   161   U14 Selden   74
  Her order is to cherish, and preserve,   .   .   .   192   U38 Elegy 'Tis 61
  if it begyn religious thoughts to cherish;   .   .   422   Lucan   10
CHERISH'D
  Till he cherish'd too much beard, ...   141   U2 Her man   23
CHERISHING
  With grace, with love, with cherishing intire: .   128   U1 Trinitie   43
CHERISSHEINGE
  By Cherissheinge the Spirrits that gave their greatnesse grace: 419   Ode:If Men   5
CHERRIES
  Ere cherries ripe, and straw-berries be gone,   .   .   58   E92 New Crie   1
CHERRY
  The earely cherry, with the later plum,   .   .   94   F2 Penshurst   41
CHERUBE
  The Thrones, the Cherube, and Seraphick bowers,   .   .   285   U84 Muse   88
CHEST
  Beneath the broad beech, and the chest-nut shade;   .   .   93   F2 Penshurst   12
CHEST-NUT
  Beneath the broad beech, and the chest-nut shade;   .   .   93   F2 Penshurst   12
CHESTNUT
  Chestnut colour, or more slack   141   U2 Her man   13

CHEV'RIL
  On Chev'ril.   44   E54 Chev'ril 2   Tt]
  Chev'ril cryes out, my verses libells are;   .   .   .   44   E54 Chev'ril 2
  What are thy petulant pleadings, Chev'ril, then,   .   .   44   E54 Chev'ril 2   3
CHEV'RILL
  On Chev'rill the Lawyer.   38   E37 Chev'ril   Tt]
  No cause, nor client fat, will Chev'rill leese,   .   .   38   E37 Chev'ril
CHICHES
  Him that buyes chiches blanch't, or chance to like   .   321   Horace   36:
CHID
  It chid the vice, yet not the Men.   152   U12 Corbet   2
CHIDE
  Or influence, chide, or cheere the drooping Stage;   .   392   Shakespeare   78
CHIEFE
  Thou wert, as chiefe of them are said t'have beene.   .   28   E4 James 1
  As chiefe of those still promise they will bee.   .   .   28   E4 James 1   8
  Poore Poet-Ape, that would be thought our chiefe,   .   44   E56 Poet-Ape
  So comm'st thou like a Chiefe into the Court,   .   .   187   U33 Councellour   29
  . . . he was Lord chiefe Justice of England.   .   .   217   U46 Coke   Tt]
  Of Pan wee sing, the Chiefe of Leaders, Pan,   .   .   264   U79 New-yeares   28
  Of a brave Chiefe sent to the warres: He can,   .   .   325   Horace   45
CHIEFES
  As noble in great chiefes, as they are rare.   .   .   58   E91 Vere   10
CHIEFLY
  Who could be false to? chiefly, when he knowes   .   .   112   F11 Epode   10:
  Who would be false to? chiefly, when he knowes   .   .   112   F11 Epode   V10:
CHILD
  Farewell, thou child of my right hand, and joy;   .   .   41   E45 First Son
  That love to make so well, a child to beare?   .   .   46   E62 Would-bee   2
  Epitaph on S. P. a Child of Q. El. Chappel.   .   .   77   E120 S. P.   Tt]
  'Twas a child, that so did thrive   77   E120 S. P.
  But I, no child, no foole, respect the kinde,   .   .   79   E125 Uvedale   7
  But, as it is (the Child of Ignorance,   .   .   .   83   E132 Sylvester   3
  Hang on thy walls, that every child may reach.   .   .   94   F2 Penshurst   40
  Whose nephew, whose grand-child you are;   .   .   121   F14 Sydney   42
  Upon record, in this blest child.   188   U35 Chute   0
  The eldest God, yet still a Child.   189   U36 Song   10
  I am regenerate now, become the child   .   .   .   192   U38 Elegy 'Tis   39
  Wise child, did'st hastily returne, ...   242   U70 Ode
  (After the last child borne;) This is our wedding day.   .   258   U75 Epithalam.   168
  Earle Rivers Grand-Child--serve not formes, good Fame,   .   269   U81 Pawlet   2
  Earle Rivers Grand-Child--serve not titles Fame,   .   269   U81 Pawlet   V 2
  If you not understand, what Child you had.   .   .   271   U81 Pawlet   78
  Child of a hundred Arts, and farre   292   U86 Hor.4:1   1
  Fit rites. The Child, that now knowes how to say,   .   315   Horace   22:
  Fit dues. The Child, that now knowes how to say,   .   .   344   Horace   V22:
  The Child, when Lamia'has din'd, out of her maw.   .   329   Horace   51(
  More then the Foster-father of this Child;   .   .   389   Aleman   1(
CHILDREN
  The children, that he keepes, Giles sweares are none   .   40   E42 Giles   13
  His children thy great lord may call his owne: .   .   96   F2 Penshurst   9
  For houshold aid, and Children sweet;   .   .   .   291   U85 Country   40
  To children; we must alwayes dwell, and stay   .   .   317   Horace   253
  Her Children, and Grand-children, reed it heere!   .   399   Lady Ogle   2
CHIMAERA
  Man, that had never heard of a Chimaera.   .   .   86   E133 Voyage   8(
  With the Chimaera of the Rosie-Crosse,   .   .   .   206   U43 Vulcan   7:
CHIME   (See also CHYME)
  As all defence, or offence, were a chime!   .   .   232   U59 Newcastle   (
  No pleasures vaine did chime, ...   246   U70 Ode   102
  To doe their Offices in Natures Chime,   .   .   .   253   U75 Epithalam.   27
  As some soft chime had stroak'd the ayre;   .   .   279   U84 Mind   38
CHIMES
  To say but one, were single. Then it chimes,   .   .   389   Aleman   3
CHIMNEY
  And 'bout the steeming Chimney set!   .   .   .   291   U85 Country   66
  And 'bout the shining Chimney set!   .   .   .   291   U85 Country   V 66
CHIN
  Nay, now you puffe, tuske, and draw up your chin,   .   69   E107 Hungry   29
  And, above her even chin, ...   136   U2 Cupid   24
  Chin, as woolly as the Peach;   141   U2 Her man   2
  Who, e're the first downe bloomed on the chin,   .   247   U70 Ode   127
CHINCKE
  May shine (through every chincke) to every sight   .   177   U25 Desmond   1(
CHINNES
  Of worship, they their nodding chinnes doe hit   .   87   E133 Voyage   123
CHLOE
  Nor after Chloe did his Lydia sound;   .   .   .   293   U87 Hor.3:9   (
  That I bright Chloe off should shake;   .   .   .   294   U87 Hor.3:9   19
CHLOES
  'Tis true, I'am Thracian Chloes, I,   .   .   .   293   U87 Hor.3:9   9
CHOAKE
  Or lest that vapour might the Citie choake,   .   .   211   U43 Vulcan   182
  Or lest that vapour should the Citie choake,   .   .   211   U43 Vulcan   V182
CHOAK'D
  'Bove all your standing waters, choak'd with weedes.   .   198   U40 Elegy That   28
CHOERILUS
  A Choerilus, in whom if I but see   329   Horace   534
CHOICE   (See also CHOYCE)
  Which, by no lesse confirm'd, then thy kings choice,   .   49   E67 Suffolk   1:
  Attending such a studie, such a choice.   .   .   .   55   E86 Goodyere 2   (
  Whether by choice, or fate, or both;   .   .   .   96   F3 Wroth   2
  With bright Lycoris, Gallus choice,   .   .   .   181   U27 Ode Helen   15

		Page	Title	Line
CHOICE (cont.)				
And what they will not. Him, whose choice doth reare	. .	307	Horace	56
CHOICEST				
Of two, the choicest Paire of Mans delights,	. . .	401	Filmer	4
CHOIR (See QUIRE)				
CHOISE				
Upon thy wel-made choise of friends, and bookes;	. .	55	E86 Goodyere 2	2
In sharpnesse of all Search, wisdome of Choise,	. .	160	U14 Selden	59
His choise, who's matter to his power doth reare,	. .	339	Horace V 58/	56
The choise of Europes pride;	. . .	368	Ode Who saith	83
Your true freind in Judgement and Choise	. . .	395	May	25
CHOISEST				
The choisest Virgin-troup of all the Land!	. . .	254	U75 Epithalam.	50
CHOLER				
For Choler! if I did not, none could bring	. .	349	Horace	V430
CHOLLER				
For choller! If I did not, who could bring	. .	325	Horace	430
CHOOSE (See also CHUSE)				
But when (in place) thou didst the patrons choose,	. .	43	E53 Old-end	4
Till thou canst finde the best, choose the least ill.	.	76	E119 Shelton	10
T'extract, and choose the best of all these knowne,	. .	80	E128 Wm Roe 2	3
Their difference, cannot choose which you will be.	. .	157	U13 Sacvile	154
CHORE				
I number these as being of the Chore	. . .	193	U38 Elegy 'Tis	99
CHORUS				
And tune too, fitted to the Chorus rime,	. .	319	Horace	290
Which law receiv'd, the Chorus held his peace,	. .	323	Horace	369
CHOSE				
Whom they have chose,	. . . . .	255	U75 Epithalam.	94
CHOSEN				
And this their chosen Bishop celebrate,	. .	256	U75 Epithalam.	132
To my chosen Friend, the learned Translator of Lucan, . . .		395	May	Ttl
To all thy vertuous, and well chosen Friends,	. . .	398	Drayton	90
CHOYCE				
Yet choyce from whom I take them; and would shame	. .	153	U13 Sacvile	17
That I must send one first, my Choyce assignes,	. .	170	U18 Elegy Can	23
CHOYSE				
If custome please, with whom both choyse, and will,	. .	341	Horace	V103
CHOYSEST				
Out of their Choysest, and their whitest wooll.	. .	225	U51 Bacon	16
CHREMES				
her voyce, and angry Chremes chafes out-right	. .	311	Horace	133
CHRIST				
So have I seene at Christ-masse sports one lost,	. .	45	E58 Groome	7
Jesus, the onely-gotten Christ! who can	. . .	288	U84 Muse	212
CHRISTALL				
Closde in an orbe of Christall.	. . . .	365	Ode Splendor	12
CHRISTENDOME				
They know the states of Christendome, not the places:	. .	59	E92 New Crie	8
Of Christendome! And neither of these know,	. .	157	U13 Sacvile	129
CHRISTIAN				
The Christian hath t'enjoy the future life,	. .	271	U81 Pawlet	96
And Christian name too, with a Heralds witt.	. .	394	Jane Ogle	12
CHRISTIANS				
Of Life, that fall so; Christians know their birth	. .	257	U75 Epithalam.	156
The comfort of weake Christians, with their warning,	. .	411	Sutcliffe	13
CHRISTMAS				
Lose all my credit with my Christmas Clay,	. .	219	U47 Tribe	52
Christmas is neere;	. . . . .	231	U57 Burges	15
CHRIST-MASSE				
So have I seene at Christ-masse sports one lost,	. .	45	E58 Groome	7
CHRISTMASSE				
Their vice of loving for a Christmasse fit;	. . .	190	U37 Friend-Book	8
CHRISTNING				
To My L. the King, On the Christning His second Sonne James.	.	268	U80 Christning	Ttl
CHRONICLERS				
In those Records, which, were all Chroniclers gone,	. .	210	U43 Vulcan	171
In those Records, which, were our Chroniclers gone,	. .	210	U43 Vulcan	V171
CHRYSTALL				
Thie Chrystall sheild	. . . . . .	421	Ode:If Men	38
CHUFFE				
On Chuffe, Bancks the Usurer's Kinsman.	. .	41	E44 Chuff	Ttl
Chuffe, lately rich in name, in chattels, goods,	. .	41	E44 Chuff	1
CHURCH				
Or taxe the Glories of the Church, and Gowne?	. .	203	U43 Vulcan	24
Or taxe the Glories of the Church, or Gowne?	. .	203	U43 Vulcan	V 24
To Church, as others doe to Feasts and Playes,	. .	222	U49 Pucell	16
These two, now holy Church hath made them one,	. .	257	U75 Epithalam.	139
Shewes he dares more then Paules Church-yard durst do.	. .	378	Coryat 2	85
But every Table in this Church can say,	. .	394	Jane Ogle	7
And doe both Church, and Common-wealth the good,	. .	416	Dover	8
CHURCH-YARD				
Shewes he dares more then Paules Church-yard durst do.	. .	378	Coryat 2	85
CHURLISH				
The Husband now's call'd churlish, or a poore	. .	165	U15 Friend-Wars	89
CHUSE				
That serves nor fame, nor titles; but doth chuse	. .	70	E109 Nevil	2
And must I sing? what subject shall I chuse?	. .	107	F10 Proludium	1
We must sing too? what subject shall we chuse?	. .	107	F10 Proludium	V 1
The noblest freedome, not to chuse	. . .	173	U22 Elegy Tho	11
That friendship which no chance but love did chuse,	. .	190	U37 Friend-Book	23
That Frindshipp, which noe Chaunce, but Love did Chuse,	. .	422	Censure	16

	Page	Title	Line

CHYME
I chyme that too: And I have mett with those . . . . . 403 Inigo Jones 1 31

CICERO
Then Cicero, whose every breath was fame: . . . . . 57 E89 Allen 6

CINDERS
Turn'd to cinders by her eye? . . . . 149 U8 Houre-glasse 8

CINNAMON
Have you tasted the Cinnamon-tree . . . . . 135 U2 Triumph V 37

CINNAMON-TREE
Have you tasted the Cinnamon-tree . . . . . 135 U2 Triumph V 37

CINNOPAR
Vermilion, Lake, or Cinnopar affoards . . . . . 406 Inigo Jones 1 94

CIPRESSE
Know'st only well to paint a Cipresse tree. . . . . 305 Horace 25

CIRCLE
To former height, and there in circle tarrie, ... 55 E85 Goodyere 1 9
And perfect in a circle alwayes meet. . . . . 81 E128 Wm Roe 2 8
In the greene circle of thy Ivy twine. . . . . 107 F10 Proludium 12
Upon your Center, doe your Circle fill . . . . 159 U14 Selden 32
Breake the knit Circle of her Stonie Armes, ... 177 U25 Desmond 19
And goe no farther: let this Circle be . . . . 185 U30 Burleigh 3
To square my Circle, I confesse: but draw . . . . 227 U52 Answer 8
How summ'd a circle didst thou leave man-kind . . . . 243 U70 Ode 9
Of joy the Circle, and sole Period! . . . . 284 U84 Muse 66
As it had beene the circle of the Arts! . . . . 396 Drayton 22
We offer as a Circle the most fit . . . . 416 Welcome 6
and of Circle be as free, ... 417 Moon 30

CIRCLED
Before his swift and circled race be run, ... 116 F12 Rutland 99

CIRCLER
Nor so begin, as did that Circler late, ... 313 Horace 195

CIRCLES
Last, draw the circles of this Globe, ... 276 U84 Body 25
bor-/Dring Circles of swift waters that intwine . . . . 305 Horace 21
extendeth circles into infinits, ... 361 Palmer 18
All Circles had their spring and end . . . . 399 Lady Ogle 14

CIRCLING
At a Friends freedome, proves all circling meanes . . . . 242 U69 Friend Son 15
On the reverse of this your circling crowne, ... 413 Ghyrlond 30

CIRCUITS
Thy Circuits, and thy Rounds free, ... 221 U48 Bacchus 41

CIRCULAR
As circular, as infinite. . . . . . 279 U84 Mind 32
And fill'd an Orbe as circular, as heaven! . . . . 396 Drayton 19

CIRCUMDUCTION
Or universall circumduction . . . . . 397 Drayton 51

CIRCUMFERENCE
Through all the lines of this circumference, ... 414 Ghyrlond 54

CIRCUMFUSED
And now, through circumfused light, she lookes . . . . 271 U81 Pawlet 69

CIRCUMSTANCE
His Issue, and all Circumstance of life, ... 171 U19 Elegy By 26

CIRCUMVOLVD
which thoughts being circumvolvd in gyerlyk mocion . . . . 361 Palmer 23

CITIE
The citie since hath rais'd a Pyramide. . . . . 89 E133 Voyage 194
And, though so neere the citie, and the court, ... 96 F3 Wroth 3
Or lest that vapour might the Citie choake, ... 211 U43 Vulcan 182
Or lest that vapour should the Citie choake, ... 211 U43 Vulcan V182
This Citie, or to shake . . . . . 239 U67 Muses 11
The Citie, as to shake . . . . 239 U67 Muses V 11
That wider Walls embrac'd their Citie round, ... 319 Horace 296

CITIZENS
More then citizens dare lend . . . . 105 F8 Sicknesse 34
Withall, the dirtie paines those Citizens take, ... 213 U44 Speach 15
With Citizens? let Clownes, and Tradesmen breed . . . . 215 U44 Speach 38
Of froward Citizens; make the Nations know . . . . 261 U77 Treasurer V 19

CITTIE
At every stall; The Cittie Cap's a charme. . . . . 200 U42 Elegy Let 28
The Cittie-Question, whether Tilly, or he, ... 214 U44 Speach 38

CITTIE-QUESTION
The Cittie-Question, whether Tilly, or he, ... 214 U44 Speach 38

CITTYES
Cittyes & Temples! thou a Cave for Wyne, ... 406 Inigo Jones 2 8

CIVILITIE
'Tis there civilitie to be a whore; . . . . 163 U15 Friend-Wars 54

CIVILL
The Seat made of a more then civill warre; . . . . 186 U33 Councellour 2
But I'le conclude all in a civill curse. . . . . 211 U43 Vulcan 190
Of bearing Armes! most civill Soldierie! . . . . 214 U44 Speach 44
Of Civill virtue, that hee now is not . . . . 420 Ode:If Men 12

CLAIME
May not claime another kisse. . . . . 138 U2 Kisse 36
Fathers, and Husbands, I doe claime a right . . . . 200 U42 Elegy Let 11
That could but claime a kindred from the purse. . . . . 216 U45 Squib 10
Be nought so'bove him but his sword let claime. . . . . 313 Horace 174
Be nought so'bove him, but his bold sword claime. . . . . 342 Horace V174

CLAIMES
And titles, by which all made claimes . . . . 247 U70 Ode 114
Who claimes (of reverence) to be heard, ... 274 U84 Cradle 34

CLAIMEST
As well as from his braines, and claimest thereby . . . . 378 Coryat 2 90

112

		Page	Title	Line
CLAME				
The M. the Myrtle, A. the Almonds clame, ...	.	412	Ghyrlond	3
CLAP				
Any man else, you clap your hands, and rore, . .	.	38	E38 Guiltie 2	4
And sits, till th'Epilogue saies Clap, or Crowne: .	.	315	Horace	222
CLAPS				
My title's seal'd. Those that for claps doe write, .	.	62	E96 Donne 2	9
CLARIUS				
Doth Clarius Harp want strings, ...	.	174	U23 Himselfe	9
CLARKE				
For termers, or some clarke-like serving-man, .	.	28	E3 Bookseller	9
CLARKE-LIKE				
For termers, or some clarke-like serving-man, .	.	28	E3 Bookseller	9
CLARKES				
And, though fowle, now, be scarce, yet there are clarkes,	.	65	E101 Supper	15
CLASH				
To hit in angles, and to clash with time: . .	.	232	U59 Newcastle	5
CLASPE				
Large claspe of Nature, such a wit can bound. .	.	160	U14 Selden	64
CLASPES				
With Gold, or Claspes, which might be bought .	.	273	U84 Cradle	27
CLAW (See CLEIES)				
CLAY				
Lose all my credit with my Christmas Clay, .	.	219	U47 Tribe	52
And stuck in clay here, it would pull . .	.	279	U84 Mind	46
CLAYM'D				
She might have claym'd t'have made the Graces foure;	.	371	Epitaph	6
CLAYMETH				
Whose knowledge claymeth at the helme to stand;	.	61	E95 Savile	21
CLAYMING				
6. Clayming a second kisse by Desert. .	.	137	U2 Kisse	Ttl
CLEANE				
Betweene the Acts, a quite cleane other thing	.	317	Horace	278
CLEANS'D				
As hath thy James; cleans'd from originall drosse,	.	268	U80 Christning	9
Simo, and of a talent cleans'd his purse; .	.	346	Horace	V339/347
CLEARE				
And yet (in this t'expresse our selves more cleare)	.	111	F11 Epode	75
And yet (in this t'expresse my self more cleare)	.	111	F11 Epode	V 75
If it were cleare, but being so in cloud .	.	155	U13 Sacvile	87
But all so cleare, and led by reasons flame, .	.	220	U47 Tribe	69
Yet are got off thence, with cleare mind, and hands	.	234	U61 Epigram	7
Brave Infant of Saguntum, cleare . .	.	242	U70 Ode	1
The Clowdes rack cleare before the Sun, .	.	251	U74 Weston	8
To make more cleare . .	.	254	U75 Epithalam.	54
He will cleare up his forehead, thinke thou bring'st	.	263	U78 Digby	21
Darke thy cleare glasse with old Falernian Wine;	.	295	U89 Mart.8:77	5
'Tis cleare, this way I have got off from blame,	.	323	Horace	395
They're darke, bid cleare this: all that's doubtfull wrote	.	335	Horace	637
They're dark, bid cleare 'hem; al that's doubtful wrote	.	354	Horace	V637
Cleare as a naked vestall . . .	.	365	Ode Splendor	11
The cleare Dircaean Fount .	.	366	Ode Who saith	19
Conceal'd from all but cleare Propheticke eyes.	.	369	Ode Who saith	112
As Cleare, and distant, as yourselfe from Cryme;	.	421	Censure	8
CLEAREST				
(Whose heart in that bright Sphere flames clearest,	.	179	U25 Desmond	54
CLEARNESSE				
Muffles the clearnesse of Election, . . .	.	363	Riches	14
CLEARS				
Clears the Brains, makes Wit the Quicker: . .	.	657	Door Apollo	16
CLEAVE				
And cleave both ayre and ground, . . .	.	239	U67 Muses	14
Yet, not as therefore wild, and tame should cleave	.	305	Horace	14
Yet not as therefore cruell things should cleave	.	338	Horace	V 14
CLEERE				
As thou stand'st cleere of the necessitie. .	.	41	E43 Salisbury 1	12
That hast thy brest so cleere of present crimes,	.	61	E95 Savile	19
A beautie of that cleere, and sparkling light,	.	112	F11 Epode	93
A beautie of that cleere, and sparkling sight,	.	112	F11 Epode	V 93
My mirror is more subtile, cleere, refin'd,	.	117	F13 Aubigny	43
Happie is he, that from all Businesse cleere,	.	289	U85 Country	1
Nor language, nor cleere order ere forsakes.	.	307	Horace	58
Nor language, nor cleere order will forsake.	.	339	Horace	V 59/ 58
CLEERELY				
And not thy fortune; who can cleerely see	.	47	E63 Salisbury 2	3
CLEFT				
Or in cleft-sticks, advanced to make calls	.	28	E3 Bookseller	8
He shew'd him first the hoofe-cleft Spring,	.	366	Ode Who saith	17
CLEFT-STICKS				
Or in cleft-sticks, advanced to make calls	.	28	E3 Bookseller	8
CLEIES				
Of Vulture death, and those relentlesse cleies?	.	283	U84 Muse	18
CLEMENCIE				
Declineth anger, perswades clemencie, . .	.	82	E130 Ferrab. 1	5
CLEMENT				
To Clement Edmonds, on his Caesars . . .	.	71	E110 Edmonds 1	Ttl
CLENSE				
Thou prov'st the gentler wayes, to clense the wound,	.	187	U33 Councellour	20
CLEP'D				
Which, of the field is clep'd the sweetest brier,	.	413	Ghyrlond	22
CLERKE				
When every clerke eates artichokes, and peason,	.	88	E133 Voyage	166
Well did thy craftie Clerke, and Knight, Sir Hugh,	.	214	U44 Speach	33

		Page	Title	Line
CLERKES				
Will be remembred by Six Clerkes, to one.	. . . . .	210	U43 Vulcan	172
CLIENT (See also CLYENT)				
No cause, nor client fat, will Chev'rill leese,	. .	38	E37 Chev'ril	1
CLIENTS				
Eate on her clients, and some one devoure.	. .	119	F13 Aubigny	88
Thy Hearers Nectar, and thy Clients Balme,	. .	187	U33 Councellour	36
That Clients strove, in Question of the Lawes,	. .	217	U46 Coke	11
CLIFFORDS				
Beauchamps, and Nevills, Cliffords, Audleys old;	. .	214	U44 Speach	52
CLIFTON'S				
To Clifton's bloud, that is deny'd their name.	. .	119	F13 Aubigny	98
CLIMBE				
Are asked to climbe. First give me faith, who know	. .	220	U47 Tribe	75
Are growne so fruitfull, and false pleasures climbe,	. .	224	U50 Countesse	10
CLIME				
His often change of clime (though not of mind)	. .	37	E32 Roe 2	6
CLIMES				
Countries, and climes, manners, and men to know,	. .	80	E128 Wm Roe 2	2
Countries, and Climes, manners, and men to know.	. .	224	U50 Countesse	22
CLIMING				
And see both climing up the slippery staire	. .	395	May	2
CLING				
You cling to Lords, and Lords, if them you leave	. .	223	U49 Pucell	38
CLOAK				
Is Banke-rupt turn'd! Cloak, Cassock, Robe, & Gowne,	.	237	U64 Charles 3	V 20
CLOAKE				
Is Banke-rupt turn'd! the Cassock, Cloake, and Gowne,	.	237	U64 Charles 3	20
CLOATH				
Needs nought to cloath it but the ayre.	. . .	275	U84 Body	8
To cloath the naked, feed the hungry. Shee	. .	288	U84 Muse	194
CLOATH'D				
That are like cloath'd: must I be of those fooles	. .	201	U42 Elegy Let	48
Had cloath'd him so. Here's all I can supply	. .	389	Aleman	20
CLOCKE				
The truth of his heart there, and tell's what a clocke	. .	380	Coryat 3	24
CLOKE				
His cloke with orient velvet quite lin'd through,	. .	62	E97 Motion	4
CLOSDE				
Closde in an orbe of Christall.	.	365	Ode Splendor	12
CLOSE				
Lord, how is Gam'ster chang'd! his haire close cut!	.	33	E21 Gam'ster	1
Keepe a starre-chamber sentence close, twelve dayes:	.	59	E92 New Crie	19
To breake up seales, and close 'hem. And they know,	.	59	E92 New Crie	29
Row close then, slaves. Alas, they will beshite us.	.	86	E133 Voyage	90
Close, the close cause of it.	.	109	F11 Epode	16
On the close groome, and page, on new-yeeres day,	.	118	F13 Aubigny	74
And every close did meet	.	149	U9 Picture	7
The Jewell of your name, as close as sleepe	. .	198	U40 Elegy That	42
Or a Close-stoole so cas'd; or any fat	. . .	202	U42 Elegy Let	84
And hold me to it close; to stand upright	. .	229	U54 Squib	9
Reducts, Halfe-moones, Horne-workes, and such close wayes,	.	248	U71 Treasurer	8
And ever close the burden of the Song,	. . .	249	U72 King	17
Downe close by shore, this other creeping steales,	. .	339	Horace V 40/	39
From Zephyr's rape would close him with his beames.	.	366	Ode Who saith	24
CLOS'D				
Clos'd to their peace, he saw his branches shoot,	. .	185	U30 Burleigh	17
With Clownes, and Tradesmen, kept thee clos'd in horne.	.	203	U43 Vulcan	8
Were also clos'd: But, who the man should be,	. .	309	Horace	109
CLOSELY				
Let us together closely lie, and kisse,	. . .	294	U88 Petronius	7
CLOSER				
And then lye with you, closer, then a punque,	. .	69	E107 Hungry	20
CLOSES				
And all my closes meet	.	149	U9 Picture	V 7
CLOSEST				
Our closest Creekes, and Corners, and can trace	. .	287	U84 Muse	153
CLOSE-STOOLE				
Or a Close-stoole so cas'd; or any fat	. . .	202	U42 Elegy Let	84
CLOTH'				
The cloth's no sooner gone, but it gets up	. .	74	E115 Honest Man	24
CLOTH				
Nor com'st to view the better cloth of state;	. .	96	F3 Wroth	7
To do't with Cloth, or Stuffes, lusts name might merit;	.	164	U15 Friend-Wars	57
Coach'd, or on foot-cloth, thrice chang'd every day,	.	165	U15 Friend-Wars	107
Cloth Spices, or guard sweet meates from the flies;	.	205	U43 Vulcan	V 53
But Scarlet-like out-lasts the Cloth.	. . .	230	U55 Burges	8
Would make the very Greene-cloth to looke blew:	.	241	U68 House-hold	8
But that hee's too well suted, in a cloth,	. .	389	Aleman	17
A Goddesse is, then paynted Cloth, Deal-boards,	.	406	Inigo Jones 1	93
CLOTHES				
At court I met it, in clothes brave enough,	. .	30	E11 Something	1
His clothes two fashions of, and poore! his sword	.	33	E21 Gam'ster	3
Both which are great. And laugh at ill-made clothes;	.	35	E28 Surly	10
By which his damme conceiv'd him, clothes and all?	.	56	E88 Monsieur	11
Onely his clothes have over-leaven'd him. .	. .	63	E97 Motion	20
Not he that flies the court for want of clothes,	.	76	E119 Shelton	1
Clothes, or Fortune gives the grace; . . .	.	131	U2 Excuse	8
Well he should his clothes to weare:	. . .	141	U2 Her man	36
His Clothes rich, and band sit neat, . . .	.	142	U2 Exception	4
Being, the best clothes still to praeoccupie.	. .	201	U42 Elegy Let	42
And clothes, and guifts, that only do thee grace	. .	384	Somerset	2

	Page	Title	Line
CLOTH'S			
The cloth's no sooner gone, but it gets up	74	E115 Honest Man	24
CLOUD			
Crack did report it selfe, as if a cloud	86	E133 Voyage	94
But this doth from the cloud of error grow,	110	F11 Epode	35
Every Cloud about his eye;	132	U2 How he saw	12
If it were cleare, but being so in cloud	155	U13 Sacvile	87
Draw first a Cloud: all save her neck;	276	U84 Body	13
The Cloud, and show the Universe;	276	U84 Body	18
But stooping gently, as a Cloud,	280	U84 Mind	58
CLOUDES			
Why was't? did e're the Cloudes aske back their raine?	192	U38 Elegy 'Tis	56
About in Cloudes, and wrapt in raging weather,	193	U38 Elegy 'Tis	75
The majesty of Juno in the Cloudes,	403	Inigo Jones 1	33
CLOUDS			
Bounteous as the clouds to earth;	142	U2 Her man	43
CLOWD			
Who can behold their Manners, and not clowd-/Like	164	U15 Friend-Wars	60
clowd-/Like upon them lighten? If nature could	164	U15 Friend-Wars	61
CLOWDES			
The Clowdes rack cleare before the Sun,	251	U74 Weston	8
And emptie Clowdes. For Tragedie is faire,	321	Horace	336
CLOWD-LIKE			
Who can behold their Manners, and not clowd-/Like	164	U15 Friend-Wars	60
clowd-/Like upon them lighten? If nature could	164	U15 Friend-Wars	61
CLOWNAGE			
As they are made! Pride, and stiffe Clownage mixt	163	U15 Friend-Wars	43
CLOWNE			
But all come in, the farmer, and the clowne:	94	F2 Penshurst	48
'T is not alone the Merchant, but the Clowne,	237	U64 Charles 3	19
Clowne, Towns-man, base, and noble, mix'd, to judge?	319	Horace	302
CLOWNES			
My wonder, why the taking a Clownes purse,	155	U13 Sacvile	89
With Clownes, and Tradesmen, kept thee clos'd in horne.	203	U43 Vulcan	8
No mar'le the Clownes of Lemnos tooke thee up,	208	U43 Vulcan	116
With Citizens? let Clownes, and Tradesmen breed	215	U44 Speach	73
CLOWNISHE			
Butt, Clownishe pride hath gott	420	Ode:If Men	10
CLUB			
Great Club-fist, though thy backe, and bones be sore,	85	E133 Voyage	55
Was, t'have a Boy stand with a Club, and fright	241	U69 Friend Son	11
Hanch against Hanch, or raise a riming Club	396	Drayton	8
CLUBB			
Thy Noddle, with his clubb; and dashing forth	409	Detractor	21
CLUB-FIST			
Great Club-fist, though thy backe, and bones be sore,	85	E133 Voyage	55
CLUID			
But first to Cluid stoope low,	367	Ode Who saith	39
CLUSTER			
Of all your night-tubs, when the carts doe cluster,	85	E133 Voyage	64
CLYENT			
And for the troubled Clyent fyl's his tongue,	292	U86 Hor.4:1	14
CLYSTERS			
Or fumie clysters, thy moist lungs to bake:	42	E50 Cod 3	2
CO			
And Stanley, to the which shee was Co-heire.	274	U84 Descent	6
Equall with Angels, and Co-heires of it?	286	U84 Muse	146
COACH			
Will by coach, and water goe,	105	F8 Sicknesse	37
And firke, and jerke, and for the Coach-man raile,	164	U15 Friend-Wars	72
Put a Coach-mare in Tissue, must I horse	201	U42 Elegy Let	43
His friends, but to breake Chaires, or cracke a Coach.	230	U56 Covell	10
COACH'D			
Ride, saile, am coach'd, know I how farre I have gone,	156	U13 Sacvile	121
Coach'd, or on foot-cloth, thrice chang'd every day,	165	U15 Friend-Wars	107
COACH-MAN			
And firke, and jerke, and for the Coach-man raile,	164	U15 Friend-Wars	72
COACH-MARE			
Put a Coach-mare in Tissue, must I horse	201	U42 Elegy Let	43
COALE (See also COLE)			
Produce; though threatning with a coale, or chalke	193	U38 Elegy 'Tis	97
The art of kindling the true Coale, by Lungs:	206	U43 Vulcan	76
The art of kindling the true Coale, of Lungs:	206	U43 Vulcan	V 76
To live in Sea-coale, and goe forth in smoake;	211	U43 Vulcan	181
To live in Sea-coale, and goe out in smoake;	211	U43 Vulcan	V181
COARSE (See COURSE)			
COAST			
And for one Cerberus, the whole coast was dogs.	84	E133 Voyage	14
Who, wheresoere he be, on what dear coast,	116	F12 Rutland	93
But prove the Aire, and saile from Coast to Coast:	367	Ode Who saith	37
To the Greeke coast thine onely knew the way.	388	Chapman	9
COAT (See also COTES)			
What each man sayes of it, and of what coat	232	U58 Book-seller	4
COATE			
Such Bookes deserve Translators, of like coate	389	Aleman	11
COATES			
Whom they durst handle in their holy-day coates,	208	U43 Vulcan	127
Whom they durst handle in their high day coates,	208	U43 Vulcan	V127
Their Corrals, Whistles, and prime Coates,	273	U84 Cradle	21
And better Blason them, then all their Coates,	419	Ode:If Men	8
COB (NAME)			
To Pertinax Cob.	50	E69 Cob	Ttl
Cob, thou nor souldier, thiefe, nor fencer art,	50	E69 Cob	1

COB
In solemne cypres, the other cob-web-lawne. . . . . 51 E73 Fine Grand 14
COBALUS
Thou hadst brought Lapland, or old Cobalus, ... 398 Drayton 86
COBLED
From Venice to Flushing, were not they well cobled? . . 380 Coryat 3 42
COBLER
The Cobler kept him to his nall; but, now . . . . 410 Brome 17
COBWEB
No cobweb Call's; no Surcoates wrought . . . . 273 U84 Cradle 26
COB-WEB-LAWNE
In solemne cypres, the other cob-web-lawne. . . . . 51 E73 Fine Grand 14
COBWEBS
And set it forth; the rest were Cobwebs fine, . . . 282 U84 Muse 5
COCATRICE
Not his poore cocatrice but he betrayes . . . . 31 E12 Shift 21
COCK
Of old, they gave a cock to Aesculape; . . . . 31 E13 Empirick 2
Item, an epitaph on my lords cock, ... 51 E73 Fine Grand 18
Of partrich, pheasant, wood-cock, of which some . . 65 E101 Supper 18
COCKING
Cryes out 'gainst cocking, since he cannot bet, . . . 76 E119 Shelton 3
COCKS
Where fight the prime Cocks of the Game, for wit? . . 222 U49 Pucell 4
COCYTUS
Cocytus, Phlegeton, our have prov'd in one; . . . 84 E133 Voyage 8
How hight the place? a voyce was heard, Cocytus. . . 86 E133 Voyage 89
COD
On Sir Cod the perfumed. . . . . . . 33 E19 Cod 1 Ttl
That Cod can get no widdow, yet a knight, . . . 33 E19 Cod 1 1
To the same Sir Cod. . . . . . 33 E20 Cod 2 Ttl
Except thou could'st, Sir Cod, weare them within. . 33 E20 Cod 2 2
To Sir Cod. . . . . 42 E50 Cod 3 Ttl
Leave Cod, tabacco-like, burnt gummes to take, . . 42 E50 Cod 3 1
CODE
Code, Digests, Pandects of all faemale glory! . . . 399 Lady Ogle 8
COELIA
Drinke to me, Coelia, with thine eyes, . . . 106 F9 Celia 3 V 1
COETERNALL
All coeternall in your Majestie, ... 128 U1 Trinitie 38
CO-HEIRE
And Stanley, to the which shee was Co-heire. . . . 274 U84 Descent 6
CO-HEIRES
Equall with Angels, and Co-heires of it? . . . 286 U84 Muse 146
COIN (See COYNE)
COIT
Or, who's unskilfull at the Coit, or Ball, . . . 331 Horace 567
COKE
An Epigram on Sir Edward Coke, when . . . . 217 U46 Coke Ttl
Such, Coke, were thy beginnings, when thy good . . 217 U46 Coke 5
COKELY
Thou dost out-zany Cokely, Pod; nay, Gue: . . . 81 E129 Mime 16
COLBY
Thy true friends wishes, Colby, which shall be, . . 167 U15 Friend-Wars 176
COLCHIS
Of Colchis borne; or in Assyria bred; . . . 313 Horace 167
COLD
The cold of Mosco, and fat Irish ayre, . . . 37 E32 Roe 2 5
That since, my numbers are so cold, . . . 93 F1 Why write no 11
But we find that cold delay, . . . 140 U2 Promise 9
Lock't in her cold embraces, from the view . . 177 U25 Desmond 22
The cold tumor in his feet, ... 184 U29 Fit of Rime 56
Now hot, now cold, now fierce, now mild. . . 189 U36 Song 15
Let me be what I am, as Virgil cold; . . . 199 U42 Elegy Let 1
And you may justly, being a tardie, cold, . . 230 U56 Covell 7
You find no cold . . . . . 258 U75 Epithalam. 166
You feele no cold . . . . . 258 U75 Epithalam. V166
COLDEST
Although the coldest of the yeere! . . . 97 F3 Wroth 36
COLDLY
Or do's all businesse coldly, and with feare; . . . 317 Horace 244
COLDS
And that there be no fev'ry heats, nor colds, . . . 220 U47 Tribe 67
Who durst live great, 'mongst all the colds, and heates, . 233 U59 Newcastle 21
COLE
With rotten chalk, or Cole upon a wall, . . . 408 Inigo Jones 3 11
COLLEDGE
And get more gold, then all the colledge can: . . . 39 E41 Gypsee 2
The meate-boate of Beares colledge, Paris-garden, . . 87 E133 Voyage 117
COLOSSUS
He some Colossus to bestryde the Seas, . . . 407 Inigo Jones 2 13
COLOUR (See also COULORS, CULLORS)
Nor scarce dost colour for it, which is lesse. . . 73 E112 Gamster 20
7. Begging another, on colour of mending the former. . 139 U2 Another Ttl
Chestnut colour, or more slack . . . 141 U2 Her man 13
Thou then hadst had some colour for thy flames, . . 204 U43 Vulcan 40
COLOURS
But to the Subject, still the Colours fit . . . 160 U14 Selden 58
Of many Colours; outward fresh, from spots, . . 171 U20 Shrub 11
Ne knowes he flatt'ring Colours, or false light. . . 227 U52 Answer 21
In truth of colours, both are best. . . . 265 U79 New-yeares 45
But here I may no colours use. . . . 277 U84 Mind 6
But here we may no colours use. . . . 277 U84 Mind V 6

								Page	Title		Line

COLOURS (cont.)
If now the turnes, the colours, and right hues . . . . 311 Horace 126
COLT
On Old Colt. . . . . 39 E39 Colt Ttl
Colt, now, doth daily penance in his owne. . . . 39 E39 Colt 2
COLUMNE
An obeliske, or columne to thy name, ... 46 E60 Mounteagle 2
How like a columne, Radcliffe, left alone . . . 60 E93 Radcliffe 1
COMAUND
The mayne comaund of scepters, soone doth perishe . . . 422 Lucan 9
COMBE
A paire of Scisars, and a Combe in verse; . . . . 204 U43 Vulcan 38
COMBES
When not his Combes, his Curling-irons, his Glasse, . . 165 U15 Friend-Wars 111
COMBINES
That falls like sleepe on lovers, and combines . . . 110 F11 Epode 49
COME
The quarter day is come; the hostesse sayes, . . . 30 E12 Shift 7
Which conquers all, be once over-come by thee. . . 31 E14 Camden 12
And mine come nothing like. I hope so. Yet, . . 32 E18 Censurer 5
But as they come, on both sides he takes fees, . . 38 E37 Chev'ril 2
And shooe, and tye, and garter should come hether, . . 56 E88 Monsieur 4
For twelve yeeres yet to come, what each state lacks. . . 59 E92 New Crie 14
The selfe-same deeds, as diversly they come, . . 64 E99 Th Roe 2 8
With those that come; whose grace may make that seeme . 64 E101 Supper 5
Ile tell you of more, and lye, so you will come: . . 65 E101 Supper 17
Doe what you come for, Captayne, with your newes; . . 68 E107 Hungry 1
Come, be not angrie, you are Hungry; eate; . . 69 E107 Hungry 31
Doe what you come for, Captayne, There's your meate. . . 69 E107 Hungry 32
Can come from Tripoly, leape stooles, and winke, . . 74 E115 Honest Man 11
Groyne, come of age, his state sold out of hand . . 75 E117 Groyne 1
The very call, to make all others come: . . . 81 E129 Mime 8
And stayes but till you come unto the dore! . . 89 E133 Voyage 178
Fig, grape, and quince, each in his time doth come: . . 94 F2 Penshurst 42
But all come in, the farmer, and the clowne: . . 94 F2 Penshurst 48
The rout of rurall folke come thronging in, . . 98 F3 Wroth 53
Come my Celia, let us prove, ... 102 F5 Celia 1 1
Come sweet Celia, let us prove, ... 102 F5 Celia 1 V 1
Shall thronging come, and boast the happy place . . 115 F12 Rutland 80
But, I'le come in, ... 130 U1 Father 28
Marke of glorie, come with me; . . . . 132 U2 How he saw 8
Come, with our Voyces, let us warre, . . . 143 U3 Musicall 1
As since he dares not come within my sight. . . 151 U11 Dreame 14
Beates brave, and loude in Europe, and bids come . . 162 U15 Friend-Wars 2
If it be thus; Come Love, and Fortune goe, . . 170 U18 Elegy Can 21
Pyracmon's houre will come to give them ease, . . 179 U25 Desmond 42
An hower will come they must affect theyr Ease, . . 179 U25 Desmond V 42
Come short of all this learned throng, . . . 182 U27 Ode Helen 34
But charme the Senses, others over-come . . . 182 U28 Worth 7
Lawes; and no change e're come to one decree: . . 185 U31 Elsmere 2
They will come of, and scape the Punishment. . . 186 U32 Elsmere 14
Come, let us here enjoy the shade; . . . 189 U36 Song 1
Is fix'd upon one leg, and dares not come . . 198 U40 Elegy That 33
Like the dull wearied Crane that (come on land) . . 198 U40 Elegy That 35
Winter is come a Quarter e're his Time, . . . 199 U41 Elegy Since 12
And so I spare it. Come what can become . . 199 U41 Elegy Since 19
The Talmud, and the Alcoran had come, . . . 205 U43 Vulcan 65
Foole, wilt thou let that in example come? . . 210 U43 Vulcan 161
Come to their Schooles,) show 'hem the use of Guns; . . 214 U44 Speach 58
It doe not come: One piece I have in store, . . 229 U54 Squib 15
Will come at the Court, ... 231 U57 Burges 20
Will come to the Table, ... 232 U57 Burges 23
Thee quickly come the gardens eye to bee, . . . 238 U65 Prince 8
Nor dares he come in the comparison. . . . 241 U69 Friend Son 8
Some of his formes, he lets him not come neere . . 242 U69 Friend Son 17
On all that come her Simplesse to rebuke! . . . 253 U75 Epithalam. 44
For done service, and to come: . . . . 259 U76 Petition 13
For done service, or to come: . . . . 259 U76 Petition V 13
Painter yo' are come, but may be gone, . . . 277 U84 Mind 1
It selfe to us, and come so nigh . . . . 279 U84 Mind 43
And Goates together, whither they must come . . 283 U84 Muse 47
Must come to take a sentence, by the sense . . 284 U84 Muse 57
Thither, you hope to come; and there to find . . 285 U84 Muse 103
And snares the fearfull Hare, and new-come Crane, . . 290 U85 Country 35
Among these Cates how glad the sight doth come . . 291 U85 Country 61
And come not too much wrested. What's that thing, . . 309 Horace 76
With sloth, yet greedy still of what's to come: . . 317 Horace 246
To have a God come in; except a knot . . . 317 Horace 273
More slow, and come more weightie to the eare: . . 323 Horace 378
But fame of Poets, they thinke, if they come forth, . . 325 Horace 426
Or Pleader at the Barre, that may come short . . 331 Horace 551
Him that is last, I scorne to come behind, . . 333 Horace 595
For other formes come short all . . . . 364 Ode Splendor 2
Come forth thou bonnie bouncing booke then, daughter . 378 Coryat 2 86
Sent forth, or since did from their ashes come. . . 391 Shakespeare 40
Or Rurall Virgil come, to pipe to us! . . . 397 Drayton 28
If, maymed, she come off, 'tis not of men . . 401 Beaumont 16
The Scene! the Engyne! but he now is come . . 404 Inigo Jones 1 62
I am come to Add, and speake, ... 416 Moon 2
And come forth worthie Ivye, or the Bayes, . . 420 Ode:If Men 26
whom fortune hath deprest; come nere the fates . . 422 Lucan 4
whom, yf fortune hath deprest; come nere the fates . . 422 Lucan V 4

		Page	Title	Line

COMEDIE (See also COMOEDIE)
Yet, sometime, doth the Comedie excite . . . . . 311 Horace 132

COMELIE
And seeke to scant her comelie libertie, ... 190 U37 Friend-Book 2(

COMELY
Shoot forth in smooth and comely spaces; have . . . 157 U13 Sacvile 15(
Mov'd by the wind, so comely moved she. . . . 287 U84 Muse 166

COMELYE
and seeke to scant her comelye Libertye, ... 421 Censure 13

COMENDS
The Moone comends hir . . . . 417 Moon 12

COMES
Lust it comes out, that gluttony went in. . . . 76 E118 Gut 6
My lighter comes, to kisse thy learned Muse; . . . 78 E121 Rudyerd 1 2
Where comes no guest, but is allow'd to eate, . . . 95 F2 Penshurst 61
Kisse againe: no creature comes. . . . . 103 F6 Celia 2 9
But the Pittie comes too late. . . . . . 133 U2 Suffered 2(
Are nothing till that comes to bind and shut. . . . 157 U13 Sacvile 138
And comes by these Degrees, the Stile t'inherit . . . 164 U15 Friend-Wars 81
Till the sower Minute comes of taking leave, . . . 197 U40 Elegy That 2
How comes it all things so about thee smile? . . . 225 U51 Bacon 2
Comes in the pompe, and glorie . . . . . 240 U67 Muses 28
Against the Husband comes home tir'd; . . . . 291 U85 Country 44
Thy labouring wheele, comes scarce a Pitcher out? . . 307 Horace 3(
There comes sometimes to things of meanest place. . . 321 Horace 354
To make these good, and what comes after, better. . . 666 Glover 1(

COMFORT
In comfort of her mothers teares, ... 33 E22 Daughter 8
Right, the right way: nor must your comfort bee . . . 118 F13 Aubigny 68
What comfort by him doe wee winne, ... 130 U1 Nativitie 19
By light, and comfort of spirituall Grace; . . . 286 U84 Muse 131
Of divine Comfort, when sh' had talk'd with God. . . 287 U84 Muse 184
The comfort of weake Christians, with their warning, . 411 Sutcliffe 13

COMFORTED
Then comforted her Lord! and blest her Sonne! . . . 270 U81 Pawlet 57

COMFORTER
Father and Sonne; the Comforter, in breeding . . . 128 U1 Trinitie 2(

COMFORTS
So, may those Mariage-Pledges, comforts prove: . . . 384 Somerset 19

COMICK
Tragick, or Comick; but thou writ'st the play. . . . 72 E112 Gamster 8
The Comick matter will not be exprest . . . . 311 Horace 12
Yet Comick matter shunnes to be exprest . . . . 341 Horace V127/121
By observation of those Comick Lawes . . . . 409 Brome 7

COMMAND (See also COMAUND)
The furie of a rash command, ... 98 F3 Wroth 68
The furie of some rash command, ... 98 F3 Wroth V 68
Now dam'mee, Sir, if you shall not command . . . 154 U13 Sacvile 53
Now, but command; make tribute, what was gift; . . 155 U13 Sacvile 84
Doth now command; . . . . 180 U25 Desmond 62
True valour doth her owne renowne command . . . 180 U26 Ode High 16
As if the generall store thou didst command . . . 187 U33 Councellour 26
Publike affaires command me now to goe . . . . 194 U38 Elegy 'Tis 114
Provoke his mettall, and command his force . . . 228 U53 Newcastle 2
Be briefe, in what thou wouldst command, that so . . 329 Horace 50:
Or great in money's out at use, command . . . 333 Horace 60(
Or wealthy in money's out at use, command . . . 353 Horace V60(
(Charles Montjoy) whose command . . . . 367 Ode Who saith 5(
So bold, as shewes your Art you can command. . . . 370 Author 8

COMMANDEMENTS
T'obey, and serve her sweet Commandements. . . . 287 U84 Muse 172

COMMANDING
That by commanding first thy selfe, thou mak'st . . 168 U15 Friend-Wars 181

COMMANDS
That no affection in thy voyce commands; . . . 51 E74 Chancelor 4
Before my thought, and (in thy right) commands . . 83 E132 Sylvester 8
Your just commands; yet those, not I, be lost. . . 192 U38 Elegy 'Tis 38
Too stubborne for Commands so slack: 292 U86 Hor.4:1 7

COMMEND
If to admire were to commend, my praise . . . 83 E132 Sylvester 1
By their ripe daughters, whom they would commend . . 95 F2 Penshurst 54
To have his Court-bred-fillie there commend . . . 163 U15 Friend-Wars 48
And can for other Graces her commend, ... 230 U56 Covell 20
All which are parts commend the cunning hand; . . . 370 Author 4
And therefore I commend unto the Wife, . . . 386 Husband 8

COMMENDED
Commended the French-hood, and Scarlet gowne . . . 201 U42 Elegy Let 69
My verses were commended, thou dar'st say, . . . 408 Detractor 1

COMMENDER
Froward, complaining, a commender glad . . . . 317 Horace 247

COMMENDING
All Nature of commending. . . . . . . 365 Ode Splendor 16

COMMENDS
This thy worke forth: that judgment mine commends. . 386 Browne 8

COMMENTARIES
- - - Commentaries observed, and translated. . . . 71 E110 Edmonds 1 Ttl

COMMING
That art so reverenc'd, as thy comming in, . . . 66 E102 Pembroke 17
I thinke, the Fate of court thy comming crav'd, . . 73 E113 Overbury 5
But, comming neere, they found it but a liter, . . . 86 E133 Voyage 85
They are so long a comming, and so hard, . . . 153 U13 Sacvile 23
And, till the comming of the Soule, ... 188 U35 Chute 5
And comming home, to tell what acts were done . . . 213 U44 Speach 19

118

	Page	Title	Line

COMMING (cont.)
To judge; So all men comming neere can spie, — 242 U69 Friend Son 20
Thy comming forth in that great yeare, — 242 U70 Ode 2
On th'often comming of this Holy-day: — 249 U72 King 16
As comming with his Harpe, prepar'd — 274 U84 Cradle 35
Mans comming yeares much good with them doe bring: — 317 Horace 250
For, as one comming with a laterall viewe, — 362 Author 9
Here, finer then comming from his Punke you him see, — 375 Coryat 1 28

COMMINGS
Among my commings in, and see it mount, — 161 U14 Selden 80

COMMISSION
My Muse up by commission: No, I bring — 108 F10 Proludium 28
Our muse up by commission: No, we bring — 108 F10 Proludium V 28
Or stands to be'n Commission o' the blade? — 155 U13 Sacvile 64
And seale thee thy Commission: — 220 U48 Bacchus 5

COMMIT
Made me commit most fierce idolatrie — 48 E65 Muse 3
Them in, if not, from thee; or must commit — 75 E116 Jephson 15
Will quickly taste the treason, and commit — 109 F11 Epode 15
Not like your Countrie-neighbours, that commit — 190 U37 Friend-Book 7
I should commit thee surely with thy peeres, — 391 Shakespeare 28
Discover Vice? Commit Absurdity? — 405 Inigo Jones 1 82

COMMIXT
Like single; so, there is a third, commixt, — 284 U84 Muse 53

COMMODITIE
Then takes up fresh commoditie, for dayes; — 30 E12 Shift 13
They're growne Commoditie upon Exchange; — 165 U15 Friend-Wars 86
An ill commoditie! 'T must make good weight. — 229 U54 Squib 6
His is more safe commoditie, or none: — 241 U69 Friend Son 7

COMMON
From servile flatterie (common Poets shame) — 41 E43 Salisbury 1 11
And proud, my worke shall out-last common deeds, — 46 E60 Mounteagle 6
The common-wealth still safe, must studie thee. — 66 E102 Pembroke 20
When the common courting jay — 103 F6 Celia 2 3
And, for thee, at common game, — 105 F8 Sicknesse 41
And, for that, at common game, — 105 F8 Sicknesse V 41
Or those, who doubt the common mouth of fame, — 111 F11 Epode 79
Or those, which doubt the common mouth of fame, — 111 F11 Epode V 79
Or common places, filch'd, that take these times, — 116 F12 Rutland 88
Nor can a little of the common store, — 121 F14 Sydney 31
It is the common Moath, — 174 U23 Himselfe 5
Others by common Stars their courses run, — 194 U38 Elegy 'Tis 119
And didst invade part of the Common-wealth, — 210 U43 Vulcan 170
At Common-Law: me thinkes in his despight — 211 U43 Vulcan 177
At Common-Law: me thinkes in this despight — 211 U43 Vulcan V177
But give them over to the common eare — 214 U44 Speach 31
Some brave un-common way: — 239 U67 Muses 3
T'escape this common knowne necessitie, — 271 U81 Pawlet 93
Most worthie praise, when words that common grew, — 307 Horace 67
'Tis hard, to speake things common, properly: — 313 Horace 183
Yet common matter thou thine owne maist make, — 313 Horace 187
Such, as the creeping common Pioners use — 400 Beaumont 5
And doe both Church, and Common-wealth the good, — 416 Dover 8

COMMON-LAW
At Common-Law: me thinkes in his despight — 211 U43 Vulcan 177
At Common-Law: me thinkes in this despight — 211 U43 Vulcan V177

COMMON-WEALTH
The common-wealth still safe, must studie thee. — 66 E102 Pembroke 20
And didst invade part of the Common-wealth, — 210 U43 Vulcan 170
And doe both Church, and Common-wealth the good, — 416 Dover 8

COMM'ST
So comm'st thou like a Chiefe into the Court, — 187 U33 Councellour 29

COMMUNICATED
. . . omitted, and now communicated to the World — 379 Coryat 3 Ttl

COMMUNION
Be it he hold Communion — 221 U48 Bacchus 43

COMMUNITIE
Preserves communitie. — 110 F11 Epode 54

COMOEDIE
To these succeeded the old Comoedie, — 321 Horace 365

COMOEDY
Yet sometime both the Comoedy doth raise — 341 Horace V132
Or 'twere the gowned Comoedy they taught. — 323 Horace 410

COMON
That sit upon the Comon Draught: or Strand! — 408 Inigo Jones 3 13

COMPANIE
As french-men in his companie, should seeme dutch? — 56 E88 Monsieur 8
Doe equally desire your companie: — 64 E101 Supper 2
For these with her young Companie shee'll enter, — 164 U15 Friend-Wars 79
By naming in what companie 'twas in, — 191 U38 Elegy 'Tis 25
Of any Companie but that they are in, — 218 U47 Tribe 20
For you admit no companie, but good, — 224 U50 Countesse 25

COMPANIES
Or use all arts, or haunt all Companies — 165 U15 Friend-Wars 91

COMPANIONS
Without companions? 'Tis safe to have none. — 118 F13 Aubigny 56

COMPANY'
By speaking well o' the company' it 's in. — 74 E115 Honest Man 8

COMPANY
By his free will, be in Jones company. — 40 E42 Giles 5
Away ill company, and helpe in rime — 231 U56 Covell 23

COMPARE
To compare small with great, as still we owe — 238 U66 Queene 12

119

		Page	Title	Line

COMPARE (cont.)
That might compare with thee? what story shall . . . . 406 Inigo Jones 1 9
COMPAR'D
Compar'd unto that long eternitie, ... 285 U84 Muse 10
COMPARISON
Or, more then borne for the comparison . . . . 67 E104 Montgomery 9
Any Comparison had with his Cheap-side. . . . 202 U42 Elegy Let 7
Nor dares he come in the comparison. . . . 241 U69 Friend Son 8
Leave thee alone, for the comparison . . . . 391 Shakespeare 3
COMPASS'D
But a well-compass'd mouth to utter it; . . . . 327 Horace 46
COMPASSE
And like a Compasse keeping one foot still . . . 159 U14 Selden 3
Which if in compasse of no Art it came . . . 227 U52 Answer 1
To Compasse men, and manners; stint the strife . . 261 U77 Treasurer V 1
COMPASSION
And take compassion on my grievous plight. . . 127 U1 Trinitie 1
Of your compassion; Parents should be mild: . . 192 U38 Elegy 'Tis 4
COMPEERES
Want, with the rest of his conceal'd compeeres, . . 248 U71 Treasurer 9
COMPIL'D
Had I compil'd from Amadis de Gaule, . . . 203 U43 Vulcan 29
COMPLAINE
Yet dare I not complaine, or wish for death . . 122 F15 Heaven 23
That fortune never make thee to complaine, . . 168 U15 Friend-Wars 183
COMPLAINES
Whereof the loyall conscience so complaines. . . 110 F11 Epode 27
Complaines in humble phrase. Both Telephus, . . 311 Horace 135
COMPLAINING
Froward, complaining, a commender glad . . 317 Horace 247
COMPLEAT
That she is in, or, make it more compleat? . . 284 U84 Muse 72
COMPLEMENT
To carry, and conduct the Complement . . . 270 U81 Pawlet 66
COMPLEXION
For truthes complexion, where they all weare maskes. . 118 F13 Aubigny 70
COMPLEXIONS
Or your complexions losse? you have a pot, . . 46 E62 Would-bee 6
COMPOSE
To compose men, and manners; stint the strife . . 261 U77 Treasurer 18
Who did this Knot compose, . . . 401 Filmer 7
COMPOS'D
A body so harmoniously compos'd, . . . 112 F11 Epode 99
(Compos'd of Gamester, Captaine, Knight, Knight's man, . 370 Fletcher 3
COMPREHEND
Vizors or Anticks? or it comprehend . . . 402 Inigo Jones 1 13
COMPRISETH
All that Loves world compriseth! . . . 134 U2 Triumph 13
COMPROMISE
Put conscience and my right to compromise. . . 218 U47 Tribe 8
COMPTERS
His body to the compters, or the Fleete? . . . 165 U15 Friend-Wars V105
COMPTING
A pound, or piece, by their long compting arts: . . 327 Horace 46
COMPTROLLER
And a Comptroller, two most rigid men . . . 415 Rutter 2
COM'ST
Nor com'st to view the better cloth of state; . . 96 F3 Wroth 7
Then com'st thou off with Victorie and Palme, . . 187 U33 Councellour 3
COMUS
Comus puts in, for new delights; . . . 98 F3 Wroth 48
CON
Are sure to con the catalogue by hart; . . . 59 E92 New Crie 22
CONCEALE
And to conceale your ulcers, did advise, . . . 38 E38 Guiltie 2 2
And must be bred, so to conceale his birth, . . 197 U40 Elegy That 17
And from the Barber Licinus conceale . . 325 Horace 427
May aske, what Author would conceale his name? . . 383 Author 8
CONCEAL'D
Conceal'd, or kept there, that was fit to be, . . 203 U43 Vulcan 21
Want, with the rest of his conceal'd compeeres, . . 248 U71 Treasurer 9
Conceal'd from all but cleare Propheticke eyes. . . 369 Ode Who saith 112
CONCEALES
For praises, where the mind conceales a foxe. . . 333 Horace 622
CONCEIPT
Crooked appeare; so that doth my conceipt: . . 170 U18 Elegy Can 8
True Conceipt, . . . 183 U29 Fit of Rime 3
But, others fell with that conceipt by the eares, . . 209 U43 Vulcan 145
But, others fell by that conceipt by the eares, . . 209 U43 Vulcan V145
Conceipt, and into burning Aetna leap'd. . . 335 Horace 663
CONCEITS
They die with their conceits, . . . 175 U23 Himselfe 23
They drincke with their conceits, . . . 175 U23 Himselfe V 23
CONCEIVE
But I Conceive a person like my Dove, . . . 112 F11 Epode V 9
Now I conceive him by my want, . . . 152 U12 Corbet 32
Have made me to conceive a Lawyer new. . . 187 U33 Councellour 14
That Love's a bitter sweet, I ne're conceive . . 197 U40 Elegy That 7
Nor dare we under blasphemy conceive . . . 286 U84 Muse 147
CONCEIV'D
By which his damme conceiv'd him, clothes and all? . 56 E88 Monsieur 11
Conceiv'd in sinne, and unto labour borne, . . 122 F15 Heaven 18
With lust conceiv'd thee; Father thou hadst none. . 208 U43 Vulcan 112

		Page	Title	Line
CONCEIV'D (cont.)				
The Spirit that I wrote with, and conceiv'd;	. . .	282	U84 Muse	3
CONCEIV'ST				
But when thy Wife (as thou conceiv'st) is brave?	. . .	201	U42 Elegy Let	50
CONCERNE				
Of some Bride-well, and may, in time, concerne us	. .	85	E133 Voyage	42
CONCEYVD				
Thy twice conceyvd, thrice payd for Imagery?	. . .	405	Inigo Jones 1	90
CONCLUDE				
Fate, in a brother. To conclude,	. . .	39	E40 Ratcliffe	15
Who would with judgement search, searching conclude	. .	177	U25 Desmond	25
But I'le conclude all in a civill curse.	. . .	211	U43 Vulcan	190
Heare me conclude; let what thou workst upon	. .	339	Horace	V 31
CONCLUDED				
Who, when shee heard the match, concluded streight,	. .	229	U54 Squib	5
Concluded from a Carract to a dramme.	. . .	415	Rutter	30
CONCLUSION				
But, in conclusion, merited no fame.	. . .	323	Horace	396
CONCORD				
The selfe-same things, a note of concord be:	. .	40	E42 Giles	17
So, be your Concord, still, as deepe, as mute;	. .	384	Somerset	17
CONCURRETH				
In all affections shee concurreth still.	. . .	40	E42 Giles	15
CONDEMNE				
Nor o're-praise, nor yet condemne;	. .	142	U2 Her man	47
Nor out-praise, nor yet condemne;	. .	142	U2 Her man	V 47
Condemne him to the Brick-kills, or some Hill-/foot	. .	211	U43 Vulcan	183
Condemne him to some Brick-hills, or some Hill-/foot	. .	211	U43 Vulcan	V183
Condemne him to the Brick-kills, or a forge	. .	211	U43 Vulcan	V183
CONDEMN'D				
Ridway was tane, arraign'd, condemn'd to dye;	. .	29	E8 Robbery	2
Condemn'd me to the Ovens with the pies;	. .	205	U43 Vulcan	54
Condemn'd them to the Ovens with the pies;	. .	205	U43 Vulcan	V 54
CONDITION				
Our fraile condition it is such,	. .	101	F4 To the World	54
But 'tis with a condition,	. .	220	U48 Bacchus	6
CONDITIONS				
And would on Conditions, be	. .	133	U2 Suffered	5
CONDUCT				
And then of times (besides the bare Conduct	. .	160	U14 Selden	51
To carry, and conduct the Complement	. .	270	U81 Pawlet	66
CONDUITS				
For then, our water-conduits doe runne wine;	. .	36	E29 Tilter	5
CONEY				
Limons, and wine for sauce: to these, a coney	. .	65	E101 Supper	13
No Plover, or Coney	. .	231	U57 Burges	22
CONEYES				
Each banke doth yeeld thee coneyes; and the topps	. .	94	F2 Penshurst	25
CONFERRE				
Since they can only judge, that can conferre.	. .	83	E132 Sylvester	6
CONFERRING				
Without conferring symboles. This's my day.	. .	396	Drayton	10
CONFESS				
And not fall downe before it? and confess	. .	406	Inigo Jones 1	91
CONFESSE				
Which all, but ignorant Captaynes, will confesse:	. .	72	E111 Edmonds 2	7
And never art encounter'd, I confesse:	. .	73	E112 Gamster	19
I confesse all, I replide,	. .	137	U2 Cupid	39
Titles, I confesse, doe take me;	. .	140	U2 Her man	5
Though I confesse (as every Muse hath err'd,	. .	159	U14 Selden	19
But must confesse from whom what gift I tooke.	. .	189	U37 Friend-Book	6
In friendship, I confesse: But, deare friend, heare.	. .	190	U37 Friend-Book	18
To square my Circle, I confesse: but draw	. .	227	U52 Answer	8
But, I confesse, that, in a long worke, sleepe	. .	329	Horace	537
Though I confesse, that, in a long worke, sleepe	. .	351	Horace	V513/537
Will well confesse; presenting, limiting,	. .	370	Author	6
While I confesse thy writings to be such,	. .	390	Shakespeare	3
And caried, though with shoute, and noyse, confesse	. .	397	Drayton	45
Though I confesse a Beaumonts Booke to bee	. .	400	Beaumont	7
CONFESSING				
Or in confessing of the Crime be nice,	. .	191	U38 Elegy 'Tis	23
CONFEST				
Hardie, thy braine is valiant, 'tis confest,	. .	32	E16 Brain-hardy	1
CONFIDENT				
You would be then most confident, that tho	. .	194	U38 Elegy 'Tis	113
CONFINE				
But to confine him to the Brew-houses,	. .	211	U43 Vulcan	179
CONFINING				
And Paradise confining these.	. .	276	U84 Body	24
CONFIRM'D				
Which, by no lesse confirm'd, then thy kings choice,	. .	49	E67 Suffolk	11
CONFUS'D				
As my heart lies in peeces, all confus'd,	. .	127	U1 Trinitie	7
CONFUSED				
Subtly distinguish'd, was confused here.	. .	84	E133 Voyage	10
CONFUTES				
A Rabbin confutes him with the Bastinado.	. .	375	Coryat 1	23
CONJECTURES				
Conjectures retriv'd! And a Storie now	. .	160	U14 Selden	50
CONJURES				
and Conjures all my faculties t'approve	. .	108	F10 Proludium	14
CONJURING				
To raise my spirits with thy conjuring wine,	. .	107	F10 Proludium	11

	Page	Title	Line

CONJURING (cont.)
  To raise our spirits with thy conjuring wine,   107 F10 Proludium V 11
CONNEXION
  Of Order, and Connexion; so much grace   321 Horace   353
CONQUER
  Could conquer thee, but chance, who did betray.   49 E66 Cary   10
  And draw, and conquer all mens love,   173 U22 Elegy Tho   7
  To conquer rumour, and triumph on spight;   224 U50 Countesse   4
CONQUER'D
  Conquer'd hath both life and it.   39 E40 Ratcliffe 12
  But, as they conquer'd, and enlarg'd their bound,   319 Horace   295
CONQUERS
  Which conquers all, be once over-come by thee.   31 E14 Camden   12
  And conquers all things, yea it selfe, at length.   367 Ode Who saith 56
CONQU'RING
  The conqu'ring Champion, the prime Horse in course,   311 Horace   115
CONSCIENCE
  As her owne conscience, still, the same reward.   48 E64 Salisbury 3 14
  As is thy conscience, which is alwayes one: 52 E74 Chancelor   8
  And studie conscience, more then thou would'st fame.   63 E98 Th Roe 1   10
  Which is to live to conscience, not to show.   76 E119 Shelton   14
  Whereof the loyall conscience so complaines.   110 F11 Epode   27
  Nor meane we those, whom vowes and conscience   110 F11 Epode   83
  Nor meane I those, whose vowes and conscience   111 F11 Epode   V 83
  And, for it, life, conscience, yea, soules are given, 113 F12 Rutland   4
  Your conscience, and not wonder, if none askes   118 F13 Aubigny   69
  Run from the Conscience of it, if they could.   154 U13 Sacvile   46
  Not wound thy conscience, when thy body bleeds;   168 U15 Friend-Wars 178
  So, may the King proclaime your Conscience is   185 U31 Elsmere   3
  Put conscience and my right to compromise.   218 U47 Tribe   8
  Who (herein studying conscience, and not fame)   224 U50 Countesse 14
  By Thee, and Conscience, both who thrive   273 U84 Cradle   7
  Of that great Evidence, the Conscience!   284 U84 Muse   58
  In the discerning of each conscience, so!   289 U84 Muse   222
  With Rites not bound, but conscience. Wouldst thou All? 372 Epitaph   11
  The Peace of Conscience, and the Godly's strife.   411 Sutcliffe   7
CONSCIENCES
  Lash'd by their consciences, to die, affeard.   84 E133 Voyage   18
CONSCIOUS
  Oh, but my conscious feares,   149 U9 Picture   11
CONSECRATE
  Which to this use, wert built and consecrate!   256 U75 Epithalam. 130
CONSENT
  But then consent, your Daughters and your Wives,   200 U42 Elegy Let 19
  By all the Spheares consent, so in the heart of June? 253 U75 Epithalam. 16
  And the deceipt of pleasures, by Consent.   411 Sutcliffe   11
CONSENTED
  They all consented;   77 E120 S. P.   18
CONSIDER
  Who can consider thy right courses run,   47 E63 Salisbury 2 1
  Doe but consider this small dust,   148 U8 Houre-glasse 1
CONSISTING
  Under-woods. Consisting Of Divers Poems.   125 Under-wood   Ttl
CONSISTS
  One said, the other swore, the world consists.   87 E133 Voyage   129
CONSOLATORIE
  . . . first-borne, An Epigram Consolatorie. 1629.   235 U63 Charles 2 Ttl
CONSORT
  Virtue, and Soveraigntie, they not consort.   423 Lucan   18
CONSPIRE
  And that your soules conspire, as they were gone   119 F13 Aubigny   119
  I wish all well, and pray high heaven conspire   219 U47 Tribe   37
  And friendly should unto one end conspire.   333 Horace   586
  And friendly should unto their end conspire.   353 Horace   V586
CONSTABLE
  Hee's carried like a Cripple, from Constable to Constable. 374 Coryat 1   17
CONSTABLES
  Or Constables Ambrosiack Muse   182 U27 Ode Helen 27
CONSTANCY
  only pursewinge Constancy, in Chainge;   108 F10 Proludium 10
CONSTANT
  By constant suffring of thy equall mind;   47 E63 Salisbury 2 8
  Is constant to be extraordinarie.   171 U19 Elegy By   28
CONSTELLATION
  Advanc'd, and made a Constellation there!   392 Shakespeare   76
CONSTELLATIONS
  Of Constellations 'bout her horld;   277 U84 Body   27
CONSTRAINE
  Whose manners draw, more than thy powers constraine.   37 E35 James 2   3
CONSULT
  To consult, if Fucus this   140 U2 Promise   26
CONSUMING
  I had deserv'd, then, thy consuming lookes,   203 U43 Vulcan   17
CONSUMMATE
  And Bishop stay, to consummate the Rites: 256 U75 Epithalam. 122
CONSUMPTION
  To make consumption, ever, where thou go'st;   205 U43 Vulcan   58
  To make consumption, every where thou go'st;   205 U43 Vulcan   V 58
  To sow consumption, every where thou go'st;   205 U43 Vulcan   V 58
  Of riot, and consumption, knowes the way   235 U61 Epigram   17
CONSUMPTIONS
  Consumptions nature to destroy, and sterve.   192 U38 Elegy 'Tis 62

		Page	Title	Line

CONTAGION
Contagion in the prease is soonest catch'd. . . . . 118 F13 Aubigny 58
CONTAINE
Could you contain your laughter? Credit mee, ... 305 Horace 7
CONTEMNE
Others more modest, but contemne us too, ... 59 E92 New Crie 39
Nor out-valew, nor contemne; . . . . . . 142 U2 Her man 48
CONTEMN'D
A treasure, art: contemn'd in th'age of gold. . . . 47 E64 Salisbury 3 4
CONTEMNING
Sharpe, and contemning lawes, at him should aime, . . . 313 Horace 173
CONTEMPT
How did she leave the world? with what contempt? . . . 270 U81 Pawlet 47
CONTEND
Hee too, that did in Tragick Verse contend . . . . 319 Horace 319
CONTENDS
Contends t'have worth enjoy, from his regard, ... 48 E64 Salisbury 3 13
CONTENT
Thou wert content the authors name to loose: . . . . 43 E53 Old-end 3
Then let the former age, with this content her, . . . 84 E133 Voyage 19
And such since thou canst make thine owne content, . . . 98 F3 Wroth 65
She content was to restore . . . . . . 133 U2 Suffered 3
Of what he throwes: Like letchers growne content . . . 166 U15 Friend-Wars 139
Content thee to be Pancridge Earle the whyle; . . . 407 Inigo Jones 2 20
CONTENTED
'Pray thee, feed contented, then, ... 105 F8 Sicknesse 13
CONTENTION
And, but for that Contention, and brave strife . . . 271 U81 Pawlet 95
CONTINENT
Because they move, the continent doth so: . . . . 111 F11 Epode 71
Such spirits as are onely continent, ... 111 F11 Epode 77
CONTINEWALL
A Soyle, not barren; a continewall fire; 295 U90 Mart.10:47 4
CONTINUALL
In a continuall tempest. Now, true Love . . . . 110 F11 Epode 43
CONTINUE
Continue thy sweete Song. . . . . . . 367 Ode Who saith 34
CONTINU'D
Still Mill continu'd: Nay, his face growing worse, . . . 57 E90 Mill 11
. . . (by his continu'd Vertue) my loving friend: . . . 409 Brome Ttl
CONTRACT
When was there contract better driven by Fate? . . . 28 E5 Union 1
And present worth in all dost so contract, ... 57 E89 Allen 11
In Contract twice, what can shee perjure more? . . . 223 U49 Pucell 30
CONTRARY
Treading a better path, not contrary; . . . . . 76 E119 Shelton 12
CONTRITE
What odour can be, then a heart contrite, ... 127 U1 Trinitie 15
The contrite Soule, who hath no thought to win . . . 193 U38 Elegy 'Tis 89
CONTROLL
Controll Ctesibius: overbearing us . . . . . 402 Inigo Jones 1 7
CONTROULE
The rock, the spindle, and the sheeres controule . . . 52 E76 Bedford 1 15
CONTROULES
A farther fury my ray'sd spirit Controules, ... 108 F10 Proludium 12
CONTUMELIE
Of Contumelie, and urge a good man more . . . . 193 U38 Elegy 'Tis 100
CONVERT
Whilst other soules convert to base abuse . . . . 361 Palmer 11
CONVERTED
First, midst, and last, converted one, and three; . . . 122 F15 Heaven 10
CONVERTING
He will expiate this sinne with converting the Jewes. . . 375 Coryat 1 21
CONVICT
Play-wright convict of publike wrongs to men, . . . 49 E68 Playwrt 2 1
CONVINCE
But still, it seem'd, the ranknesse did convince 'hem. . . 88 E133 Voyage 152
COOCKOLD
If there be a Coockold Major, ... 417 Moon 25
COOKE
ill-/Natur'd, and wicked Atreus cooke, to th'eye, . . . 317 Horace 265
COOKES
Your Fleet-lane Furies; and hot cookes doe dwell, . . . 88 E133 Voyage 143
COOLE
To some coole, courteous shade, which he calls his, . . . 97 F3 Wroth 19
There coole thy Plumes, ... 368 Ode Who saith 76
COP'CES
Of flowrie fields, of cop'ces greene, ... 97 F3 Wroth 38
COPIE
The Copie of his friend. . . . . . . 247 U70 Ode 112
A Copie of this peece; nor tell . . . . . 277 U84 Body 30
COPIES
Allowes them? Then, what copies shall be had, . . . 263 U78 Digby 29
Allowes them? Then, what copies will be had, . . . 263 U78 Digby V 29
COPPIE
And this a coppie is of the Record. . . . . 400 Lady Ogle 40
COPP'S
Thy copp's, too, nam'd of Gamage, thou hast there, . . . 94 F2 Penshurst 19
Fertile of wood, Ashore, and Sydney's copp's, . . . 94 F2 Penshurst 26
CORBET
An Epitaph on Master Vincent Corbet. . . . . 151 U12 Corbet Ttl
Deare Vincent Corbet who so long . . . . . 151 U12 Corbet 7

		Page	Title	Line

CORDOVA
    Paccuvius, Accius, him of Cordova dead, ...   391   Shakespeare   35
CORIAT
    And thine owne Coriat too. But (would'st thou see)   .   .   81   E129 Mime   17
    Coriat, should rise the most sufficient head   .   .   .   157   U13 Sacvile   128
CORKE
    But that the Corke of Title boy'd him up.   244   U70 Ode   42
    Swim without Corke! Why, thank the good Queen Anne.   .   .   405   Inigo Jones 1   68
CORNER
    No part or corner man can looke upon, ...   163   U15 Friend-Wars 27
CORNERS
    Nought but in corners; and is loath to leave,   .   .   .   154   U13 Sacvile   44
    Our closest Creekes, and Corners, and can trace   .   .   .   287   U84 Muse   153
COROLLARY
    To Inigo Marquess Would Be A Corollary   406   Inigo Jones 2   Ttl
CORPORALL
    The Cure of that, which is but corporall, ...   180   U26 Ode High   5
    So that upon the point, my corporall feare   .   .   .   229   U54 Squib   7
    One corporall, only; th'other spirituall, ...   284   U84 Muse   52
CORRALS
    Their Corrals, Whistles, and prime Coates, ...   273   U84 Cradle   21
CORRANTS
    The weekly Corrants, with Pauls Seale; and all   .   .   .   206   U43 Vulcan   81
    The weekly Corrants, with Poules stall; and all   .   .   .   206   U43 Vulcan   V 81
CORRECT
    His lookes would so correct it, when   152   U12 Corbet   27
    Able to talk of Euclide, and correct   402   Inigo Jones 1   4
CORRECTED
    Not, ten times o're, corrected to the naile.   .   .   .   325   Horace   418
CORRECTING
    And still correcting youth, and censuring.   317   Horace   249
CORRODING   (See also COR'SIVE)
    With all corroding Arts, be able to untie!   .   .   .   257   U75 Epithalam. 136
CORRUPT
    That may corrupt her, even in his eyes.   165   U15 Friend-Wars 92
    Like flies, or wormes, with mans corrupt parts fed: .   .   218   U47 Tribe   18
CORRUPTS
    All this corrupts the thankes; lesse hath he wonne,   .   .   154   U13 Sacvile   33
CORSE
    O! had I seene her laid out a faire Corse,   .   .   .   282   U84 Muse   11
COR'SIVES
    I send nor Balmes, nor Cor'sives to your wound,   .   .   .   180   U26 Ode High   2
CORYATE
    Here, like Arion, our Coryate doth draw   374   Coryat 1   10
    - - - the Coryate of Odcombe, and his Booke now going to travell   378   Coryat 2   Ttl
    The height, let him learne of Mr. Tom. Coryate;   .   .   379   Coryat 3   2
    The height, let him learne of Mr. Tom Coryate. .   .   .   381   Coryat 3   60
CORYATS
    Certaine Verses Written Upon Coryats Crudities, ...   379   Coryat 3   Ttl
CORYNNA
    Or hath Corynna, by the name   181   U27 Ode Helen   17
COSEN   (NOUN)
    The least of which was to the plague a cosen.   .   .   .   86   E133 Voyage   72
COSEN
    I must a libell make, and cosen both.   54   E81 Proule   8
COSENING
    Cosening Judgement with a measure, ...   183   U29 Fit of Rime 5
COS'NING
    Or cos'ning farmer of the customes so, ...   117   F13 Aubigny   39
COSSEN'D
    On credit, and are cossen'd; see, that thou   .   .   .   386   Browne   11
COST
    When they cost dearest, and are done most free,   .   .   .   49   E66 Cary   14
    In most vile verses, and cost me more paine,   .   .   .   51   E73 Fine Grand   19
    To see the workmanship so'xceed the cost!   .   .   .   160   U14 Selden   54
COTES
    Inscrib'd in touch or marble, or the cotes   .   .   .   114   F12 Rutland   44
COTSWOLD
    - - - and Dauncing At Cotswold.   415   Dover   Ttl
    Twixt Cotswold, and the Olimpicke exercise: .   .   .   415   Dover   2
COTTON
    Which noble Carew, Cotton, Selden lent: 207   U43 Vulcan   100
    By Carew, Cotton, Selden, oyle was spent   .   .   .   207   U43 Vulcan   V100
    By Carew, Cotton, Seldens oyle was spent   .   .   .   207   U43 Vulcan   V100
    Of Carew, Cotton, Selden, oyles were spent   .   .   .   207   U43 Vulcan   V100
COULD
    Deceive their malice, who could wish it so.   .   .   .   27   E2 My Booke   7
    And gave thee both, to shew they could no more.   .   .   .   28   E4 James 1   4
    Many of thine this better could, then I, ...   31   E14 Camden   13
    If any sword could save from Fates, Roe's could;   .   .   .   35   E27 Roe 1   3
    If any friends teares could restore, his would;   .   .   .   35   E27 Roe 1   5
    Could not effect, not all the furies doe,   .   .   .   37   E32 Roe 2   2
    What could not worke; at home in his repaire   .   .   .   37   E32 Roe 2   7
    And than in them, how could we know god more?   .   .   .   38   E35 James 2   8
    Rich, as nature could bequeath thee: 39   E40 Ratcliffe   3
    O, could I loose all father, now. For why   .   .   .   41   E45 First Son   5
    Could save that line to dedicate to thee?   .   .   .   44   E53 Old-end   10
    Curst be his Muse, that could lye dumbe, or hid   .   .   .   47   E63 Salisbury 2 11
    Could conquer thee, but chance, who did betray.   .   .   .   49   E66 Cary   10
    What kinde of creature I could most desire,   .   .   .   52   E76 Bedford 1   3
    No male unto him: who could so exceed   53   E79 Rutland   7
    And, ere I could aske you, I was prevented: .   .   .   54   E84 Bedford 2   3
    Against my grave, and time could not forgive.   .   .   .   58   E91 Vere   12

COULD (cont.)

	Page	Title	Line
Nor could I, had I seene all Natures roule,	60	E93 Radcliffe	12
Something, which, else, could hope for no esteeme	64	E101 Supper	6
Nor could the age have mist thee, in this strife	66	E102 Pembroke	5
Who could not but create them all, from you?	67	E105 L Wroth 2	6
Could make such men, and such a place repent:	73	E113 Overbury	10
Parts, then th'Italian could doe, with his dore.	74	E115 Honest Man	26
As much beautie, as could dye:	79	E124 Elizabeth	4
Made for what Nature could, or Vertue can;	79	E125 Uvedale	2
I could adore, almost t'idolatrie.	79	E125 Uvedale	10
And though we could all men, all censures heare,	83	E131 Ferrab. 2	5
So huge, it seem'd, they could by no meanes quite her.	86	E133 Voyage	86
And I could wish for their eterniz'd sakes,	89	E133 Voyage	195
Into my ri'mes could ne're be got	93	F1 Why write no	9
If I could not thy ginnes avoyd.	101	F4 To the World	36
It could not withered bee.	106	F9 Celia 3	12
(Though they were crusht into one forme) could make	108	F10 Proludium	26
Could ne'er make prize of thy white Chastetye.	108	F10 Proludium	6
Who could be false to? chiefly, when he knowes	112	F11 Epode	103
Because they lack'd the sacred pen, could give	115	F12 Rutland	56
Hee whom the whole world could not take,	130	U1 Nativitie	10
Could be brought once back to looke.	132	U2 How he saw	19
This could be call'd but halfe a kisse.	139	U2 Another	11
What a man she could love well:	139	U2 Promise	4
I would have him, if I could,	140	U2 Her man	3
I could give my very heart;	142	U2 Her man	54
That's a Toy, that I could spare:	142	U2 Exception	2
Could you beleeve, that this,	148	U8 Houre-glasse	4
For else it could not be,	149	U9 Picture	2
or else it could not be,	149	U9 Picture	V 2
I Have my Pietie too, which could	151	U12 Corbet	1
Yet he broke them, e're they could him,	151	U12 Corbet	10
'Tis true, he could not reprehend;	152	U12 Corbet	21
Great and good turns, as wel could time them too,	153	U13 Sacvile	2
Run from the Conscience of it, if they could.	154	U13 Sacvile	46
On whom I could take up, and ne're abuse	161	U14 Selden	83
For all their spight, be like him if they could:	162	U15 Friend-Wars	26
clowd-/Like upon them lighten? If nature could	164	U15 Friend-Wars	61
More then themselves, or then our lives could take,	166	U15 Friend-Wars	127
For, if such men as he could die,	168	U16 Gray	6
I could forgive her being proud! a whore!	172	U20 Shrub	21
Thy beauties, yet could write of thee?	181	U27 Ode Helen	2
I That have beene a lover, and could shew it,	182	U28 Worth	1
Envious and foule Disease, could there not be	188	U34 Small Poxe	1
Would live his glory that could keepe it on:	192	U38 Elegy 'Tis	48
Could you demand the gifts you gave, againe?	192	U38 Elegy 'Tis	55
O, that you could by dissection see	194	U38 Elegy 'Tis	109
A Goat in Velvet; or some block could move	202	U42 Elegy Let	82
and lighted by the Stagirite, could spie,	207	U43 Vulcan	90
To teach some that, their Nurses could not doe,	207	U43 Vulcan	92
To teach some what, their Nurses could not doe,	207	U43 Vulcan	V 92
Or Goddesse, could be patient of thy face.	207	U43 Vulcan	108
My friends, the Watermen! They could provide	208	U43 Vulcan	124
Our friends, the Watermen! They could provide	208	U43 Vulcan	V124
And raz'd, e're thought could urge, This might have bin!	209	U43 Vulcan	136
I could invent a sentence, yet were worse;	211	U43 Vulcan	189
I could invent a sentence, yet more worse;	211	U43 Vulcan	V189
And could (if our great men would let their Sonnes	214	U44 Speach	57
That could but claime a kindred from the purse.	216	U45 Squib	10
He could not find, then thee, of all that store	217	U46 Coke	3
I could say more of such, but that I flie	218	U47 Tribe	5
No friend to vertue, could be silent here.	224	U50 Countesse	8
Then the great Homers wit, for her, could faine;	224	U50 Countesse	24
Would God, my Burges, I could thinke	229	U55 Burges	1
What could their care doe 'gainst the spight	234	U60 La-ware	5
Could stop the malice of this ill,	234	U60 La-ware	15
Of deepest lore, could we the Center find!	243	U70 Ode	10
As, could they but lifes miseries fore-see,	243	U70 Ode	19
To day, the Fathers service; who could bring	256	U75 Epithalam.	107
Could soone espie	256	U75 Epithalam.	110
I would, if price, or prayer could them get,	260	U77 Treasurer	5
This I would doe, could I know Weston, one	260	U77 Treasurer	10
This I would doe, if I could thinke you one	260	U77 Treasurer	V 10
Court can call hers, or Man could call his Arts.	262	U78 Digby	4
And were shee lost, could best supply her place,	264	U79 New-yeares	34
Then ever Pales could, or Pan;	265	U79 New-yeares	61
Of Winchester; the Heralds could tell this:	269	U81 Pawlet	V 20
Could summe to a perfection, was her Act!	270	U81 Pawlet	46
Could heap to a perfection, was her Act!	270	U81 Pawlet	V 46
You could make shift to paint an Eye,	278	U84 Mind	9
Nothing, that could remaine, or yet can stirre	282	U84 Muse	9
As nature could not more increase the flood	287	U84 Muse	158
Not Lucrine Oysters I could then more prize,	291	U85 Country	49
Could not goe downe my belly then	291	U85 Country	54
Could you contaune your laughter? Credit mee,	305	Horace	7
Saw many Townes, and Men, and could their manners tract.	315	Horace	202
How he could jest, because he mark'd and saw,	319	Horace	323
For choller! If I did not, who could bring	325	Horace	430
For Choler! if I did not, none could bring	349	Horace	V430
Not thence be sav'd, although indeed he could?	335	Horace	658
I could not but in admiracion stand.	361	Palmer	4
Nor Sunne could make to vary from the rest,	367	Ode Who saith	29
Up so much truth, as could I it pursue	372	Epitaph	13

COULD (cont.)

	Page	Title	Line
Yet who could have hit on't but the wise noddell	379	Coryat 3	6
To such a worke, as could not need theirs? Yet	385	Brooke	5
Whose worke could this be, Chapman, to refine	388	Chapman	1
O, could he but have drawne his wit	390	Reader	5
Should praise a Matron. What could hurt her more?	391	Shakespeare	14
I Could begin with that grave forme, Here lies,	394	Jane Ogle	1
My lippes could forme the voyce, I heard that Rore,	397	Drayton	38
In her! and what could perfect bee,	399	Lady Ogle	15
What was proportion, or could bee	399	Lady Ogle	21
But higher power, as spight could not make lesse,	401	Beaumont	18
Th'ascent of Lady Fame which none could spy	403	Inigo Jones 1	35
And truely, so I would, could I be heard.	414	Rutter	3
And newer, then could please them, by-cause trew.	415	Rutter	10
I then could rayse my notes	419	Ode:If Men	6

COULD'ST

	Page	Title	Line
Except thou could'st, Sir Cod, weare them within.	33	E20 Cod 2	2
Of her Sex; But could'st thou, Love,	137	U2 Cupid	45
Dreame thou could'st hurt it; but before thou wake	250	U73 Weston	11

COULDST

	Page	Title	Line
Sleepie, or stupid Nature, couldst thou part	282	U84 Muse	15

COULORS

	Page	Title	Line
Of many Coulors! read them! & reveale	404	Inigo Jones 1	47
Reviving with fresh coulors the pale Ghosts	405	Inigo Jones 1	88

COUNCELL

	Page	Title	Line
God blesse the Councell of Estate,	419	Grace	5
God blesse the Councell and the State,	419	Grace	V 5

COUNCELLOUR

	Page	Title	Line
An Epigram to the Councellour that pleaded, ...	186	U33 Councellour	Ttl

COUNCELLS

	Page	Title	Line
The councells, actions, orders, and events	62	E95 Savile	32

COUNCELS

	Page	Title	Line
The councels, projects, practises they know,	59	E92 New Crie	11
To serve the State by Councels, and by Armes:	215	U44 Speach	85

COUNSELL

	Page	Title	Line
In every counsell, stratageme, designe,	71	E110 Edmonds 1	19
Without the pompe of Counsell; or more Aide,	186	U32 Elsmere	3
To endure counsell: a Provider slow	315	Horace	233

COUNSELLS

	Page	Title	Line
But whisper'd Counsells, and those only thrive;	234	U61 Epigram	6
That Mine of Wisdome, and of Counsells deep,	255	U75 Epithalam.	98

COUNT

	Page	Title	Line
Thy gift 'gainst envie. O how I doe count	161	U14 Selden	79

COUNTENANCE

	Page	Title	Line
For the more countenance to my active Muse?	107	F10 Proludium	3
For the more countenance to our active Muse?	107	F10 Proludium	V 3
Or goe about to countenance the vice,	191	U38 Elegy 'Tis	24

COUNTERFEITS

	Page	Title	Line
For there are many slips, and Counterfeits.	216	U45 Squib	17

COUNTERMINE

	Page	Title	Line
The sinne of Boast, or other countermine	198	U40 Elegy That	46

COUNTERMYNE

	Page	Title	Line
Blow up, and ruine, myne, and countermyne,	212	U43 Vulcan	205

COUNTERS

	Page	Title	Line
His body to the Counters, or the Fleete?	165	U15 Friend-Wars	105

COUNTESSE

	Page	Title	Line
On Lucy Countesse of Bedford.	52	E76 Bedford 1	Ttl
To Elizabeth Countesse of Rutland.	53	E79 Rutland	Ttl
To Lucy Countesse of Bedford.	54	E84 Bedford 2	Ttl
To Lucy, Countesse of Bedford, with Mr. Donnes Satyres.	60	E94 Bedford 3	Ttl
To Susan Countesse of Montgomery.	67	E104 Montgomery	Ttl
Epistle To Elizabeth Countesse of Rutland.	113	F12 Rutland	Ttl
To the Countesse of Rutland: An Elegie.	113	F12 Rutland	VTtl
An Epigram. To the honour'd————Countesse of————	224	U50 Countesse	Ttl
. . . and Countesse of Shrewsbury:—	394	Jane Ogle	Ttl
To see (who'it is?) A noble Countesse, greate,	394	Jane Ogle	3

COUNTING   (See COMPTING)

COUNT'NANCES

	Page	Title	Line
Mens count'nances, with such as laugh, are prone	342	Horace	V143

COUNTREY

	Page	Title	Line
(How nothing's that?) to whom my countrey owes	31	E14 Camden	3
Loe, what my countrey should have done (have rais'd	46	E60 Mounteagle	1
But saver of my countrey thee alone.	46	E60 Mounteagle	10
Or, better worke! were thy glad countrey blest,	61	E95 Savile	14
Strength of my Countrey, whilst I bring to view	69	E108 Soldiers	1
And though thy walls be of the countrey stone,	94	F2 Penshurst	45
To entertayne them; or the countrey came,	95	F2 Penshurst	80
How blest art thou, canst love the countrey, Wroth,	96	F3 Wroth	1
To doe thy countrey service, thy selfe right;	100	F3 Wroth	103
What to his Countrey, what his friends he owes,	325	Horace	446
And cry aloud, Helpe, gentle Countrey-men,	335	Horace	653
With the Glad Countrey, and Posteritie:	416	Dover	6

COUNTREY-MEN

	Page	Title	Line
And cry aloud, Helpe, gentle Countrey-men,	335	Horace	653

COUNTREY'S

	Page	Title	Line
Or fixt in the Low-Countrey's, where you might	212	U43 Vulcan	203

COUNTRIE

	Page	Title	Line
Not like your Countrie-neighbours, that commit	190	U37 Friend-Book	7
The praises of a Countrie life.	289	U85 Country	Ttl

COUNTRIE-NEIGHBOURS

	Page	Title	Line
Not like your Countrie-neighbours, that commit	190	U37 Friend-Book	7

COUNTRIES

	Page	Title	Line
Which should thy countries love to speake refuse,	40	E43 Salisbury 1	3

	Page	Title	Line

COUNTRIES (cont.)
My countries parents I have many knowne; . . . . . 46 E60 Mounteagle 9
Countries, and climes, manners, and men to know, . . 80 E128 Wm Roe 2 2
Ever at home: yet, have all Countries seene: . . . 159 U14 Selden 30
Countries, and Climes, manners, and men to know. . . 224 U50 Countesse 22
The Low-countries, Germany and Rhetia . . . . 379 Coryat 3 20
COUNTRY
To Sir Robert Wroth in praise of a Country life. Epode. . . 96 F3 Wroth VTtl
COUNTRYE
An Ode in Horace in prayse of a Countrye lyfe, Translated. . 289 U85 Country VTtl
That hath not Countrye impudence enough to laughe att Arte, . 420 Ode:If Men 14
COUNTRY'S
The Poets act! and for his Country's sake . . . . 398 Drayton 63
'COUNTS
And 'counts them sweet rewards so ta'en: . . . 290 U85 Country 36
COUNTY
appropriates still unto that County. . . . . 662 Bedford 4
COUPLE
I know no couple better can agree! . . . . 40 E42 Giles 18
The longing Couple, all that elder Lovers know. . . 258 U75 Epithalam. 192
COUPLED
With Doves; or Lambes, with Tygres coupled be. . . . 305 Horace 16
COURAGE
Or his courage; for away . . . . . . 132 U2 How he saw 15
COURSE   (ADJECTIVE)
A fellow of course Letcherie, is nam'd, . . . 165 U15 Friend-Wars 98
COURSE
Almost all wayes, to any better course. . . . 48 E65 Muse 10
With thine owne course the judgement of thy friend, . . 63 E98 Th Roe 1 8
But this true course is not embrac'd by many: . . 109 F11 Epode 19
But this faire course is not embrac'd by many: . . 109 F11 Epode V 19
And, keeping a just course, have earely put . . 119 F13 Aubigny 91
As they out-did the lightning in the course; . . . 233 U59 Newcastle 12
His course so hurtfull both to graine, and seedes, . . 309 Horace 97
The conqu'ring Champion, the prime Horse in course, . . 311 Horace 115
Or some hot youth, yet in his flourishing course; . . 313 Horace 163
Or sweet, or various, in the course! . . . . 399 Lady Ogle 20
Who like a Giant hasts his course to run, . . 414 Ghyrlond 51
in Course of Frindshipp, wholie to reprove: . . 422 Censure 19
COURSER
I, and for this neglect, the courser sort . . . . 219 U47 Tribe 54
COURSES
Who can consider thy right courses run, . . . 47 E63 Salisbury 2 1
Others by common Stars their courses run, . . . 194 U38 Elegy 'Tis 119
COURT
At court I met it, in clothes brave enough, . . . 30 E11 Something 1
On Court-worme. . . . . 31 E15 Court-worm Ttl
'Twas brought to court first wrapt, and white as milke; . . 31 E15 Court-worm 2
What should the cause be? Oh, you live at court: . . 46 E62 Would-bee 9
On Court-Parrat. . . . . 50 E71 Parrat Ttl
To Court-ling. . . . . 50 E72 Court-ling Ttl
When Mill first came to court, the unprofiting foole, . . 57 E90 Mill 1
Nor office in the towne, nor place in court, . . . 63 E97 Motion 11
I thinke, the Fate of court thy comming crav'd, . . 73 E113 Overbury 5
Not he that flies the court for want of clothes, . . 76 E119 Shelton 1
And, though so neere the citie, and the court, . . 96 F3 Wroth 3
Who, for it, makes thy house his court; . . . 97 F3 Wroth 24
Who, for it, makes thy lodge his court; . . . 97 F3 Wroth V 24
So court a mistris, shee denyes you; . . . 104 F7 Women but 3
Let her alone, shee will court you. . . . 104 F7 Women but 4
Toyles, by grave custome, up and downe the court, . . 113 F12 Rutland 5
(Or Poet, in the court account) then I, . . 115 F12 Rutland 69
Not fashion'd for the court, or strangers eyes; . . 119 F13 Aubigny 115
Of the Court, to day, then all . . . . 138 U2 Kisse 15
To have his Court-bred-fillie there commend . . 163 U15 Friend-Wars 48
A parcell of Court-durt, a heape, and masse . . 172 U21 Ltl Shrub 5
As though the Court pursues them on the sent, . . 186 U32 Elsmere 13
So comm'st thou like a Chiefe into the Court, . . 187 U33 Councellour 29
And braveries of Court, and felt their fits . . 200 U42 Elegy Let 34
Court every hanging Gowne, and after that, . . 201 U42 Elegy Let 57
A Court of Equitie should doe us right, . . . 211 U43 Vulcan 178
To see the Pride at Court, their Wives doe make: . . 213 U44 Speach 16
And animated Porc'lane of the Court, . . . 219 U47 Tribe 53
To put his Court in dances, ... 222 U48 Bacchus 50
An Epigram on The Court Pucell. . . . 222 U49 Pucell Ttl
Do's the Court-Pucell then so censure me, . . 222 U49 Pucell 1
From Court, while yet thy fame hath some small day; . . 223 U49 Pucell 36
Or if it would, the Court is the worst place, . . 223 U49 Pucell 43
Will come at the Court, ... 231 U57 Burges 20
And all the games of Fortune, plaid at Court; . . 234 U61 Epigram 2
This day the Court doth measure . . . 240 U67 Muses 43
O how will then our Court be pleas'd, . . . 251 U74 Weston 25
With all the pompe of Youth, and all our Court beside. . 254 U75 Epithalam. 72
Our Court, and all the Grandees; now, Sun, looke, . . 254 U75 Epithalam. 73
Court can call hers, or Man could call his Arts. . . 262 U78 Digby 4
Court can call hers, or Man would call the Arts. . . 262 U78 Digby V 4
So sweetly taken to the Court of blisse, . . 283 U84 Muse 41
All the Grammarians strive; and yet in Court . . 309 Horace 111
Of eloquent Messalla's power in Court, . . . 331 Horace 552
That durst be that in Court: a vertu' alone . . 371 Epitaph 4
Will bee receiv'd in Court: If not, would I . . 389 Aleman 19
But then refreshed, with thy Fayerie Court, . . 398 Drayton 79
In Towne & Court? Are you growne rich? & proud? . . 403 Inigo Jones 1 24

127

		Page	Title	Line
COURT (cont.)				
Court Hieroglyphicks! & all Artes affoord	. . . .	404	Inigo Jones 1	43
Now each Court-Hobby-horse will wince in rime;	. . .	410	Brome	11
he that will honest be, may quitt the Court,	. . .	423	Lucan	17
COURT-BRED-FILLIE				
To have his Court-bred-fillie there commend	. . .	163	U15 Friend-Wars	48
COURT-DURT				
A parcell of Court-durt, a heape, and masse	. .	172	U21 Ltl Shrub	5
COURTED				
The young Adonis courted	. . . .	135	U2 Triumph	V 40
COURTEOUS				
To some coole, courteous shade, which he calls his,	. .	97	F3 Wroth	19
COURTESIE (See also CURTESIE)				
In honour, courtesie, and all the parts	. . .	262	U78 Digby	3
Her Sweetnesse, Softnesse, her faire Courtesie,	. .	270	U81 Pawlet	39
COURTESIES				
The smallest courtesies with thankes, I make	. .	153	U13 Sacvile	16
COURT-HOBBY-HORSE				
Now each Court-Hobby-horse will wince in rime;	. . .	410	Brome	11
COURTIER				
But, for this money was a courtier found,	. . .	29	E8 Robbery	3
The courtier is become the greater thiefe.	. . .	29	E8 Robbery	6
To be a courtier; and lookes grave enough,	. . .	30	E11 Something	2
COURTIERS				
And the returne those thankfull Courtiers yeeld,	. .	213	U44 Speach	17
COURTING				
When the common courting jay	. . . .	103	F6 Celia 2	3
COURT-LING				
To Court-ling.	. . . .	50	E72 Court-ling	Ttl
COURTLING				
To Censorious Courtling.	. . . .	43	E52 Courtling	Ttl
Courtling, I rather thou should'st utterly	. .	43	E52 Courtling	1
I Grieve not, Courtling, thou are started up	. .	50	E72 Court-ling	1
Thy person only, Courtling, is the vice.	. .	50	E72 Court-ling	6
COURT-PARRAT				
On Court-Parrat.	. . . .	50	E71 Parrat	Ttl
COURT-PUCELL				
Do's the Court-Pucell then so censure me,	. . .	222	U49 Pucell	1
COURTS				
Get him the times long grudge, the courts ill will;	. .	48	E65 Muse	7
Or stayre, or courts; but stand'st an ancient pile,	. .	93	F2 Penshurst	5
The Courts just honour, and thy Judges love.	. .	187	U33 Councellour	37
But flees the Barre and Courts, with the proud bords,	. .	289	U85 Country	7
COURT-WORME				
On Court-worme.	. . . .	31	E15 Court-worm	Ttl
COUSIN (See COSEN)				
COVELL				
Epistle. To my Lady Covell.	. . . .	230	U56 Covell	Ttl
COVER				
Which cover lightly, gentle earth.	. . .	34	E22 Daughter	12
Marble, weepe, for thou dost cover	. . .	39	E40 Ratcliffe	1
Can your favours keepe, and cover,	. . .	103	F6 Celia 2	2
Under that cover; an old Mid-wives hat!	. .	202	U42 Elegy Let	83
Left! and wit since to cover it with Tiles.	. .	209	U43 Vulcan	138
COVER'D				
Cover'd with Tissue, whose prosperitie mocks	. .	216	U44 Speach	100
COVERS				
When night their meeting covers.	. . .	365	Ode Splendor	8
It covers, first, a Virgin; and then, one	. .	371	Epitaph	3
COVETOUS				
Thou are not covetous of least selfe-fame,	. .	27	E2 My Booke	9
I, not the worst, am covetous of thee.	. .	40	E43 Salisbury 1	6
Your covetous hand,	. . . .	180	U26 Ode High	13
Being men were covetous of nought, but praise.	. .	327	Horace	463
COVEY				
And are received for the Covey of Witts;	. . .	218	U47 Tribe	22
COYN'D				
And those thy new, and late-coyn'd words receive,	. .	309	Horace	74
COYNE				
I oft looke on false coyne, to know't from true:	. .	68	E107 Hungry	3
In bravery, or gluttony, or coyne,	. . .	163	U15 Friend-Wars	45
CRACK				
Crack did report it selfe, as if a cloud	. .	86	E133 Voyage	94
Or crack out bawdie speeches, and uncleane.	. .	321	Horace	359
CRACKE				
His friends, but to breake Chaires, or cracke a Coach.	. .	230	U56 Covell	10
Or cracke out shamefull speeches, or uncleane.	. . .	347	Horace	V351/359
At least, if not the generall Engine cracke.	. .	395	May	6
CRACK'D				
Lest it be justled, crack'd, made nought, or lesse:	. .	219	U47 Tribe	58
CRACKERS				
The nut-crackers throughout, will they therefore	. .	321	Horace	363
CRACKT				
Solders crackt friendship; makes love last a day;	. .	113	F12 Rutland	17
CRADLE				
Of that wise Nature would a Cradle have.	. . .	192	U38 Elegy 'Tis	60
That in the Cradle of their Gentrie are;	. . .	215	U44 Speach	84
In his soft Cradle to his Fathers Chaire,	. . .	225	U51 Bacon	14
1. The Dedication of her Cradle.	. . .	272	U84 Cradle	Ttl
This Cradle, and for Goodnesse sake,	. . .	273	U84 Cradle	10
CRADLES				
Curst in their Cradles, or there chang'd by Elves,	. .	200	U42 Elegy Let	23
Of Egges, and Halberds, Cradles, and a Herse,	. .	204	U43 Vulcan	37

	Page	Title	Line
CRAFTIE			
Well did thy craftie Clerke, and Knight, Sir Hugh,	214	U44 Speach	33
CRAFTS			
Wise-crafts, on which the flatterer ventures not.	241	U69 Friend Son	6
That knew the Crafts they had bin bred in, right:	410	Brome	14
CRAFTY			
Or crafty Malice, might pretend this praise,	391	Shakespeare	11
CRAMP			
Thy Wife a fit of laughter; a Cramp-ring	232	U58 Book-seller	8
CRAMPE			
Goe, crampe dull Mars, light Venus, when he snorts,	107	F10 Proludium	16
CRAMP'D			
Cramp'd for ever;	184	U29 Fit of Rime	51
CRAMP-RING			
Thy Wife a fit of laughter; a Cramp-ring	232	U58 Book-seller	8
CRAMPS			
He that no more for Age, Cramps, Palsies, can	166	U15 Friend-Wars	135
CRANCK			
Every Cranck in towne to know;	105	F8 Sicknesse	V 38
CRANE			
Like the dull wearied Crane that (come on land)	198	U40 Elegy That	35
And snares the fearfull Hare, and new-come Crane,	290	U85 Country	35
CRAVE			
Use mine so, too: I give thee leave. But crave	27	E3 Bookseller	3
More high, more holy, that shee more would crave.	31	E14 Camden	6
Who more can crave	129	U1 Father	17
We crave your absence here, we all love peace,	212	U43 Vulcan	V209
And both doe crave, and give againe, this leave.	305	Horace	13
Some want, they say in a sort he did crave:	380	Coryat 3	55
CRAV'D			
I thinke, the Fate of court thy comming crav'd,	73	E113 Overbury	5
CRAVES			
He do's you wrong, that craves you to doe right.	186	U32 Elsmere	16
CREAME			
They looke at best like Creame-bowles, and you soone	198	U40 Elegy That	29
CREAME-BOWLES			
They looke at best like Creame-bowles, and you soone	198	U40 Elegy That	29
CREATE			
Who could not but create them all, from you?	67	E105 L Wroth 2	6
Eternall Father, God, who did'st create	127	U1 Trinitie	17
Unto the Scene thou bringst, and dar'st create	313	Horace	179
Unto the Stage thou bringst, and dar'st create	342	Horace	V179
For, being a Poet, thou maist feigne, create,	313	Horace	189
CREATED			
of thy rich labors worlds of thoughts created,	361	Palmer	22
CREATES			
It is the faire acceptance, Sir, creates	64	E101 Supper	7
And that as any are strooke, her breath creates	222	U49 Pucell	5
your Royal Eye which still creates new men	383	Rich	14
CREATION			
(As by a new creation) part by part,	71	E110 Edmonds 1	18
CREATURE			
To make amends, yo'are thought a wholesome creature.	46	E62 Would-bee	8
What kinde of creature I could most desire,	52	E76 Bedford 1	3
Which own'd the creature.	77	E120 S. P.	8
Makes the poore Banck-side creature wet it' shoone,	84	E133 Voyage	30
Kisse againe: no creature comes.	103	F6 Celia 2	5
O, so divine a creature	112	F11 Epode	102
And (stil'd your mercies Creature) will live more	191	U38 Elegy 'Tis	29
Of Sex, to rob the Creature; but from Man	255	U75 Epithalam.	82
On every limbe, ta'en from a severall creature,	305	Horace	3
That Natures fairest Creature,	364	Phoenix	6
CREATURES			
The Month of youth, which calls all Creatures forth	253	U75 Epithalam.	26
The king of Creatures, take his paritie	255	U75 Epithalam.	83
CREDIT			
As theirs did with thee, mine might credit get:	32	E18 Censurer	6
To'a little wealth, and credit in the scene,	45	E56 Poet-Ape	7
That are your wordes of credit. Keepe your Names	69	E107 Hungry	24
The Credit, what would furnish a tenth Muse!	161	U14 Selden	84
Of Credit lost. And I am now run madde:	191	U38 Elegy 'Tis	2
Lose all my credit with my Christmas Clay,	219	U47 Tribe	52
Stinketh my credit, if into the Pocket	229	U54 Squib	14
Could you containe your laughter? Credit mee,	305	Horace	7
On credit, and are cossen'd; see, that thou	386	Browne	11
CREDITT			
The emptie Carper, scorne, not Creditt wynns.	421	Censure	5
CREDULOUS			
Delights, nor credulous hope of mutuall Joy,	293	U86 Hor.4:1	30
CREED			
Their Sonnes to studie Arts, the Lawes, the Creed:	215	U44 Speach	74
CREEKES			
Sought out the Fountaines, Sources, Creekes, paths, wayes,	160	U14 Selden	45
Our closest Creekes, and Corners, and can trace	287	U84 Muse	153
CREEP			
No faith's more firme, or flat, then where't doth creep.	413	Ghyrlond	20
CREEPE			
In at a hole, and see these Actions creepe	201	U42 Elegy Let	60
The Fountaines murmure as the streames doe creepe,	290	U85 Country	27
May, with some right, upon an Author creepe.	329	Horace	538
CREEPES			
Creepes on the ground; too safe, too afraid of storme.	307	Horace	39

				Page	Title	Line

CREEPING
Downe close by shore, this other creeping steales, . . . 339 Horace V 40/ 3
Such, as the creeping common Pioners use . . . 400 Beaumont

CREPT
What furie of late is crept into our Feasts? . . . 166 U15 Friend-Wars 11
But crept like darknesse through his blood? . . . 234 U60 La-ware

CREPUNDIA
Who read what the Crepundia bee, . . . 273 U84 Cradle 1

CREST
Ymounted high upon Selinis crest: . . . 412 Ghyrlond 1

CRIE
That's greater, yet: to crie his owne up neate. . . . 35 E28 Surly 1
And crie good! good! This quite perverts my sense, . . . 38 E38 Guiltie 2
The new Crie. . . . 58 E92 New Crie Tt
My wofull crie, . . . 231 U57 Burges
How faine for his venery he was to crie (Tergum o) . . . 380 Coryat 3 3

CRI'D
And cri'd, Away with the Caesarian bread, . . . 228 U53 Newcastle 1

CRIER
To say, I'm ignorant. Just as a Crier . . . 333 Horace 59

CRIES
The cries, the gladnesse, which their hearts would pay, . . . 249 U72 King V 1
He cries, Good boy, thou'lt keepe thine owne. Now, adde . . . 327 Horace 47
Cries Old Sym, the King of Skinkers; . . . 657 Door Apollo

CRIME (See also CRYME)
Durst valour make, almost, but not a crime. . . . 48 E66 Cary
Or have charg'd his sight of Crime, . . . 138 U2 Kisse 3
Not flie the Crime, but the Suspition too: . . . 159 U14 Selden 1
'Tis then a crime, when the Usurer is Judge. . . . 169 U17 Friend-Debt
Or in confessing of the Crime be nice, . . . 191 U38 Elegy 'Tis 2
Or a worse Crime, the ignorance of art. . . . 323 Horace 38

CRIMES
Guiltie, be wise; and though thou know'st the crimes . . . 36 E30 Guiltie
Left us of feare, but first our crimes, then lawes. . . . 38 E35 James 2
And, told of this, he slights it. Tut, such crimes . . . 45 E56 Poet-Ape
That hast thy brest so cleere of present crimes, . . . 61 E95 Savile 1
These have crimes accounted beene. . . . 102 F5 Celia 1 1
For their owne cap'tall crimes, t'indite my wit; . . . 117 F13 Aubigny 1
A right by the prosperitie of their Crimes; . . . 186 U32 Elsmere 1
Mak'st it religion to grow rich by Crimes! . . . 187 U33 Councellour 1
That Rebells actions, are but valiant crimes! . . . 397 Drayton 4

CRINGE
And stoupe, and cringe. O then, it needs must prove . . . 56 E88 Monsieur 1

CRIPPLE
Hee's carried like a Cripple, from Constable to Constable. . . 374 Coryat 1 1

CRIPS
As Stiles, Dike, Ditchfield, Millar, Crips, and Fen: . . . 214 U44 Speach 5

CRISPE
Sindge capons, or crispe Pigges, dropping their eyes; . . . 205 U43 Vulcan V 5

CRISPED
Yet a man; with crisped haire . . . 141 U2 Her man 1

CRISPETH
He flying curles, and crispeth, with his wings; . . . 170 U19 Elegy By

CRITICALL
And doubtfull Dayes (which were nam'd Criticall,) . . . 180 U26 Ode High

CRITICK
To the learned Critick. . . . 32 E17 Critic Tt
A chamber-critick, and dost dine, and sup . . . 50 E72 Court-ling

CROAKE
Arses were heard to croake, in stead of frogs; . . . 84 E133 Voyage 1

CROAKING
No matter, stinkards, row. What croaking sound . . . 86 E133 Voyage 9

CROOKED
Crooked appeare; so that doth my conceipt: . . . 170 U18 Elegy Can

CROP
And I will bring a Crop, if not the best. . . . 169 U17 Friend-Debt 1

CROPT
Cropt, branded, slit, neck-stockt; go, you are stript. . . 411 Gill 1

CROSSE (ADJECTIVE)
Defies, what's crosse to Piety, or good Fame. . . . 401 Beaumont 2

CROSSE
To pay our debts, upon thy Crosse, and cryd'st, . . . 128 U1 Trinitie 2
Under his Crosse. . . . 130 U1 Father 3
With the Chimaera of the Rosie-Crosse, . . . 206 U43 Vulcan 7
This day, by Baptisme, and his Saviours crosse: . . . 268 U80 Christning 1
On all the world! She saw him on the Crosse . . . 288 U84 Muse 20

CROST
All historie seal'd up, and fables crost; . . . 67 E105 L Wroth 2
Errour and folly in me may have crost . . . 192 U38 Elegy 'Tis 3

CROWD
And lesse asham'd; not when I told the crowd . . . 414 Rutter

CROWN
Our great reward, th'aeternall Crown to win. . . . 412 Sutcliffe 1

CROWN'D
Give me a deep-crown'd-Bowle, that I may sing . . . 225 U51 Bacon 1

CROWNE
Charge them, for crowne, to thy sole censure hye. . . . 32 E17 Critic
Crowne with their owne. Rare poemes aske rare friends. . . 60 E94 Bedford 3
How well, faire crowne of your faire sexe, might hee, . . . 66 E103 L Wroth 1
To crowne thy open table, doth provide . . . 94 F2 Penshurst 2
The richer hangings, or crowne-plate; . . . 96 F3 Wroth
But, forgive me, with thy crowne . . . 105 F8 Sicknesse 1
Is more crowne-worthy still, . . . 112 F11 Epode 8

ROWNE (cont.)
Or set bright Ariadnes crowne so high?   115 F12 Rutland   60
To crowne the burthen which you goe withall,   119 F13 Aubigny   103
'Tis crowne enough to vertue still, her owne applause.   174 U23 Himselfe   18
Phoebus to his Crowne againe;   184 U29 Fit of Rime   40
And Mars, that gave thee a Lanthorne for a Crowne.   203 U43 Vulcan   10
Did I there wound the honours of the Crowne?   203 U43 Vulcan   23
And steps of all rais'd servants of the Crowne,   217 U46 Coke   2
When the Prodigious Hannibal did crowne   242 U70 Ode   3
Unlesse some saving-Honour of the Crowne,   248 U71 Treasurer   13
Mens Loves unto the Lawes, and Lawes to love the Crowne.   255 U75 Epithalam.   104
Shee, to the Crowne, hath brought encrease.   264 U79 New-yeares   41
Which they that have the Crowne are sure to know!   271 U81 Pawlet   76
Faire Fame, who art ordain'd to crowne   272 U84 Cradle   1
The joy of Saints! the Crowne for which it lives,   283 U84 Muse   37
Thy locks, and rosie garlands crowne thy head;   294 U89 Mart.8:77   4
And sits, till th'Epilogue saies Clap, or Crowne: 315 Horace   222
A royall Crowne, and purple, be made hop,   321 Horace   333
A royall Crowne, and Scarlet; be made hop   346 Horace   V325/333
Receive, or give it any Crowne the more.   347 Horace   V356/364
Nor did they merit the lesse Crowne to weare,   323 Horace   406
Playes were found out; and rest, the end, and crowne   329 Horace   499
* * * *   When loe to crowne thy worth   361 Palmer   27
Do crowne thy murdred Poeme: which shall rise   371 Fletcher   14
My suffrage brings thee all increase, to crowne   385 Brooke   7
To gaine the Crowne of immortalitye,   400 Lady Ogle   34
To knit thy Crowne, and glorifie the rest.   412 Ghyrlond   12
On the reverse of this your circling crowne,   413 Ghyrlond   30
To Crowne the years, which you begin, great king,   416 Welcome   7
ROWN'D
Yet crown'd with honors, as with riches, then;   56 E89 Allen   4
Now that the harth is crown'd with smiling fire,   120 F14 Sydney   1
That so hath crown'd our hopes, our spring, and earth,   237 U65 Prince   2
which thus hast crown'd our hopes, our spring, and earth,   237 U65 Prince   V 2
That so hath crown'd our hopes, our spring, our earth,   237 U65 Prince   V 2
That thus hath crown'd our hopes, with thee, our Spring & May, 237 U65 Prince   V 2
With Modestie so crown'd, and Adoration seene.   254 U75 Epithalam.   48
Those other two; which must be judg'd, or crown'd: 284 U84 Muse   55
His head, with mellow Apples crown'd,   290 U85 Country   18
After, mens Wishes, crown'd in their events,   309 Horace   108
ROWNED
Summe up this crowned day,   240 U67 Muses   47
Make up this crowned day,   240 U67 Muses   V 47
With boughs of Palme, a crowned Victrice stand!   285 U84 Muse   96
ROWNE-PLATE
The richer hangings, or crowne-plate;   96 F3 Wroth   8
ROWNES
Stood up thy Nations fame, her Crownes defence.   217 U46 Coke   14
Both Crownes, and Kingdomes in their either hand;   254 U75 Epithalam.   52
ROWNE-WORTHY
Is more crowne-worthy still,   112 F11 Epode   88
ROWNING
Worth a crowning.   183 U29 Fit of Rime   27
RUDITIES
Certaine Verses Written Upon Coryats Crudities, . . .   379 Coryat 3   Ttl
RUELL
When Fates turn'd cruell,   77 E120 S. P.   10
The name of Cruell weather, storme, and raine?   193 U38 Elegy 'Tis   82
Made thee beget that cruell Stratagem,   208 U43 Vulcan   130
Yet not as therefore cruell things should cleave   338 Horace   V 14
RUELLIE
Yet ware; thou mayst do all things cruellie: 423 Lucan   15
RUELTIE
Of crueltie, lest they doe make you such.   193 U38 Elegy 'Tis   84
Thou mightst have yet enjoy'd thy crueltie   204 U43 Vulcan   49
RUSH'D
Crush'd in the snakie brakes, that he had past!   162 U15 Friend-Wars   18
RUSHT
(Though they were crusht into one forme) could make   108 F10 Proludium   26
RY   (See also CRIE)
'Twixt puritanes, and players, as some cry;   52 E75 Lippe   2
If dancing, all would cry th'Idalian Queene,   68 E105 L Wroth 2   11
Or, keeping your due state, that would not cry,   68 E105 L Wroth 2   17
To the full greatnesse of the cry: 97 F3 Wroth   32
Their thoughts and meanes to making loude the cry;   155 U13 Sacvile   66
To flatter my good Lord, and cry his Bowle   167 U15 Friend-Wars   147
For safetie of such Majestie, cry out?   236 U64 Charles 3   6
(Without prophanenesse) yet, a Poet, cry,   238 U66 Queene   4
(Without prophanenesse) as, a Poet, cry,   238 U66 Queene   V 4
That cry that gladnesse, which their hearts would pray,   249 U72 King   14
For hee'll cry, Good, brave, better, excellent!   333 Horace   611
Cry, and doe more then the true Mourners: so   333 Horace   615
A wise, and honest man will cry out shame   335 Horace   633
And cry aloud, Helpe, gentle Countrey-men,   335 Horace   653
It makes me ravish'd with just wonder, cry   395 May   13
So shall our English Youth urge on, and cry   398 Drayton   69
That doe cry up the Machine, & the Showes!   403 Inigo Jones 1   32
RYD'ST
To pay our debts, upon thy Crosse, and cryd'st,   128 U1 Trinitie   23
RYE
Beg'd Ridwayes pardon: Duncote, now, doth crye;   29 E8 Robbery   4
A good and wise man will crye open shame   354 Horace   V633

CRY'D
Cry'd to my face, they were th'elixir of wit: . . . 64 E100 Playwrt 3
Backe, cry'd their brace of Charons: they cry'd, no, . . 86 E133 Voyage 8
They cry'd out Pusse. He told them he was Bankes, . . 89 E133 Voyage 18
Thou should'st have cry'd, and all beene proper stuffe. . 205 U43 Vulcan 6
Thou should'st have cry'd, and all fine proper stuffe. . 205 U43 Vulcan V 6
And cry'd, it was a threatning to the beares; . . 209 U43 Vulcan 14
And cry'd 'Twas verily a threatning to the beares; . 209 U43 Vulcan V14
O no, cry'd all, Fortune, for being a whore, . . 209 U43 Vulcan 15
What transcripts begg'd? how cry'd up, and how glad, . 263 U78 Digby 3
What transcripts made? how cry'd up, and how glad, . 263 U78 Digby V 3
Did all so strike me, as I cry'd, who can . . . 397 Drayton 3
Cry'd up of late: Whereto there must be first . . . 415 Rutter 2
CRYED
A lord, it cryed, buried in flesh, and blood, . . . 30 E11 Something
CRYER
Once say I'me ignorant. Just as a Cryer, . . . 353 Horace V59
CRYES
Signes to new bond, forfeits: and cryes, god payes. . . 30 E12 Shift 1
Chev'ril cryes out, my verses libells are; . . . 44 E54 Chev'ril 2
Unto the cryes of London Ile adde one; . . . 58 E92 New Crie
Cryes out 'gainst cocking, since he cannot bet, . . . 76 E119 Shelton
And, for the cryes of Ghosts, women, and men, . . . 84 E133 Voyage 1
And out-cryes of the damned in the Fleet? . . . 88 E133 Voyage 17
That cryes, we dreame, and sweares, there's no such thing, . 111 F11 Epode 6
That cryes, I dreame, and sweares, there's no such thing, . 111 F11 Epode V 6
The Solemne Quire cryes, Joy; and they returne, Amen. . 256 U75 Epithalam. 12
The Fights, the Cryes, and wondring at the Jarres . . 397 Drayton 4
CRYING
Poore Mercury, crying out on Paracelsus, . . . 86 E133 Voyage 9
CRYME
As Cleare, and distant, as yourselfe from Cryme; . . 421 Censure
CRY'ST
O, (thou cry'st out) that is thy proper game. . . . 73 E112 Gamster 1
CRYSTAL (See CHRISTALL)
CTESIBIUS
Controll Ctesibius: overbearing us . . . 402 Inigo Jones 1
CUCKOLD (See COOCKOLD)
CUCQUEANE
And now, her (hourely) her owne cucqueane makes, . . 34 E25 Beast 1
CUFFES
Ripe are their ruffes, their cuffes, their beards, their gate, 58 E92 New Crie
CULL'D
The third, is from the garden cull'd, the Rose, . . 413 Ghyrlond 1
CULLORING
Light, Posture, Height'ning, Shadow, Culloring, . . 370 Author
CULLORS
And shew their feathers shot, and cullors torne, . . 98 F3 Wroth 7
CUNNING
And as a cunning Painter takes . . . 145 U5 Woman-kind 1
Looke on the false, and cunning man, that loves . . 162 U15 Friend-Wars 1
So doth the flatt'rer with faire cunning strike . . 242 U69 Friend Son 1
Who sings so sweet, and with such cunning plaies, . . 293 U87 Hor.3:9 1
Are, by thy cunning placing, made meere new. . . 307 Horace 6
Unto a cunning piece wrought perspective, . . . 362 Author 1
All which are parts commend the cunning hand; . . 370 Author
CUNNINGE
And Cunninge of their grownde . . . 420 Ode:If Men 3
CUNNINGLY
And so well faines, so mixeth cunningly . . . 315 Horace 21
CUP
Is a pure cup of rich Canary-wine, . . . 65 E101 Supper 2
Or leave a kisse but in the cup, . . . 106 F9 Celia 3
Leave but a kisse within the cup, . . . 106 F9 Celia 3
Give me my cup, but from the Thespian well, . . . 120 F14 Sydney 1
In hast the bottome of a med'cin'd Cup, . . . 197 U40 Elegy That
And so did Jove, who ne're meant thee his Cup: . . 208 U43 Vulcan 11
CUPID
For Cupid, who (at first) tooke vaine delight, . . 73 E114 Sydney
For I ran and call'd on Cupid; . . . 132 U2 How he saw
5. His discourse with Cupid. . . . 136 U2 Cupid Tt
Then Cupid, and his Mother. . . . 221 U48 Bacchus 3
CUPIDS
Cupids Statue with a Beard, . . . 132 U2 How he saw 3
Eye-brows bent like Cupids bow, . . . 141 U2 Her man 1
For in your verse all Cupids Armorie, . . . 182 U28 Worth
With Cupids wing; . . . 369 Ode Who saith 10
CUPPING
Stick on your Cupping-glasses, fear not, put . . 270 U81 Pawlet 5
CUPPING-GLASSES
Stick on your Cupping-glasses, fear not, put . . 270 U81 Pawlet 5
CUPS
Nor shall our cups make any guiltie men: . . . 65 E101 Supper 3
Here no man tells my cups; nor, standing by, . . . 95 F2 Penshurst 6
And in their cups, their cares are drown'd: . . . 98 F3 Wroth 6
Rich men are said with many cups to plie, . . . 333 Horace 61
Great men are said with many cups to plye, . . . 354 Horace V61
CURBES
That curbes your spirit: . . . 177 U25 Desmond V 2
CURE
No lesse a sov'raigne cure, then to the mind: . . 82 E130 Ferrab. 1
And hurt seeks Cure, the Surgeon bids take bread, . . 155 U13 Sacvile 6
Looke to and cure; Hee's not a man hath none, . . 156 U13 Sacvile 11

CURE   (cont.)
    The Cure of that, which is but corporall,   .   .   .   180 U26 Ode High   5
    As not alone the Cure, but scarre be faire.   .   .   .   192 U38 Elegy 'Tis   52
    And cure the Worlds diseases: .   .   .   .   .   221 U48 Bacchus   24
    To cure the call'd Kings Evill with thy touch;   .   .   .   235 U62 Charles 1   4
    To cure the Poets Evill, Povertie: .   .   .   .   235 U62 Charles 1   6
    As thou dost cure our Evill, at thy charge.   .   .   .   235 U62 Charles 1   8
    But, that he cure the Peoples Evill too?   .   ..   .   .   235 U62 Charles 1   14
    From all affection! when they urg'd the Cure   .   .   .   270 U81 Pawlet   49
    For thou hast nought in thee to cure his Fame,   .   .   . 411 Gill   13
CURES
    For what shee gave, a whore; a baud, shee cures.   .   .   .   39 E41 Gypsee   4
    We cut not off, till all Cures else doe faile: .   .   .   192 U38 Elegy 'Tis   46
    And, in these Cures, do'st so thy selfe enlarge,   .   .   . 235 U62 Charles 1   7
    Pays all Debts, cures all Diseases, ... 657 Door Apollo   17
CURIOUS
    That the curious may not know   .   .   .   .   .   . 103 F6 Celia 2   19
    To curious light, the notes, I then shall sing,   .   .   .   115 F12 Rutland   76
    To curious light, to notes, I then shall sing,   .   .   .   115 F12 Rutland   V 76
    In any curious peece you see   .   .   .   .   .   . 145 U5 Woman-kind   14
    Of Logogriphes, and curious Palindromes, ... 204 U43 Vulcan   34
    He that but saw thy curious Captaines drill,   .   .   .   213 U44 Speach   29
    But whilst you curious were to have it be   .   .   .   . 227 U52 Answer   13
    I would present you now with curious plate   .   .   .   .   260 U77 Treasurer   2
    I would present you with some curious plate   .   .   .   . 260 U77 Treasurer   V 2
CURLE
    There; or to reforme a curle;   .   .   .   .   .   . 140 U2 Promise   24
CURLED
    Along'st the curled woods, and painted meades,   .   .   .   97 F3 Wroth   17
    The nailes, and every curled haire disclose;   .   .   .   307 Horace   47
CURLES
    Planting their Purles, and Curles spread forth like Net,   .   164 U15 Friend-Wars 65
    He flying curles, and crispeth, with his wings;   .   .   . 170 U19 Elegy By   6
CURLING
    When not his Combes, his Curling-irons, his Glasse,   .   .   165 U15 Friend-Wars 111
CURLING-IRONS
    When not his Combes, his Curling-irons, his Glasse,   .   .   165 U15 Friend-Wars 111
CURRE
    But bawle thou on; I pitty thee, poore Curre,   .   .   .   408 Detractor   7
    A Mungrel Curre? Thou should'st stinck forth, and dye   .   . 409 Detractor   15
CURS
    All the Towne-curs take each their snatch at me.   .   .   . 155 U13 Sacvile   72
CURSE
    Till he becomes both their, and his owne curse!   .   .   . 162 U15 Friend-Wars 14
    Then all Ingredients made into one curse, ... 172 U20 Shrub   18
    But I'le conclude all in a civill curse.   .   .   .   . 211 U43 Vulcan   190
CURST
    Curst be his Muse, that could lye dumbe, or hid   .   .   . 47 E63 Salisbury 2 11
    Curst be my voyce if it lye dumbe, or hid   .   .   .   . 47 E63 Salisbury 2 V 11
    For were the worthiest woman curst   .   .   .   .   . 146 U6 Defence   23
    Curst in their Cradles, or there chang'd by Elves,   .   .   200 U42 Elegy Let   23
CURTEOUS
    I meant shee should be curteous, facile, sweet,   .   .   . 52 E76 Bedford 1   9
CURTESIE
    Thy curtesie but sodaine starts, ...   100 F4 To the World 11
    By thanking thus the curtesie to life, ...   158 U13 Sacvile   159
CURTESIES
    Can I owe thankes, for Curtesies receiv'd   .   .   .   . 153 U13 Sacvile   25
CUSTOME
    To draw thee custome: but her selfe gets all.   .   .   .   53 E78 Hornet   2
    Toyles, by grave custome, up and downe the court,   .   .   113 F12 Rutland   5
    Farre from the maze of custome, error, strife,   .   .   . 118 F13 Aubigny   60
    If Custome please; at whose disposing will   .   .   .   309 Horace   103
    If custome please, with whom both choyse, and will,   .   .   341 Horace   V103
CUSTOMER
    Home to the Customer: his Letcherie   .   .   .   .   . 201 U42 Elegy Let   41
CUSTOMES
    Or cos'ning farmer of the customes so, ...   117 F13 Aubigny   39
    Times, manners, customes! Innovations spide!   .   .   .   160 U14 Selden   44
    The customes of each age thou must observe,   .   .   .   315 Horace   223
CUT
    Lord, how is Gam'ster chang'd! his haire close cut!   .   .   33 E21 Gam'ster   1
    Made of the trull, that cut her fathers lock: .   .   .   86 E133 Voyage   84
    There, in the writhed barke, are cut the names   .   .   . 94 F2 Penshurst   15
    The eares cut downe in their most height, ... 98 F3 Wroth   V 41
    The trees cut out in log; and those boughes made   .   .   . 98 F3 Wroth   45
    When gold was made no weapon to cut throtes,   .   .   .   114 F12 Rutland   23
    We cut not off, till all Cures else doe faile: .   .   .   192 U38 Elegy 'Tis   46
    Your hottest Causticks to, burne, lance, or cut: .   .   270 U81 Pawlet   54
    Your hotter Causticks to, burne, lance, or cut: .   .   270 U81 Pawlet   V 54
    On steele, though 't selfe be dull, and cannot cut.   .   .   325 Horace   434
    Cut off superfluous ornaments; and when   .   .   .   . 335 Horace   636
    It was for gentle Shakespeare cut;   .   .   .   .   . 390 Reader   2
    The Orbe was cut forth into Regions seaven.   .   .   .   396 Drayton   20
    To cut a Dike? or sticke a Stake up, here,   .   .   .   401 Beaumont   12
CUTHBERT
    . . . eldest Daughter, to Cuthbert Lord Ogle: . . .   .   . 394 Jane Ogle   Ttl
CUTLERS
    Strooke in at Millan with the Cutlers there;   .   .   .   212 U43 Vulcan   200
CYCNUS
    Were Cycnus, once high flying   .   .   .   .   .   . 369 Ode Who saith   99
CYLLARUS
    Or Castor mounted on his Cyllarus: .   .   .   .   . 228 U53 Newcastle   8

CYNARA
   Of the good Cynara I was: Refraine, ... 292   U86 Hor.4:1   4
CYNTHIA
   Doth Cynthia, in Propertius song 181   U27 Ode Helen   11
   Taught Pallas language; Cynthia modesty; . . . 371   Epitaph   7
   I looke on Cynthia, and Sirenas sport, . . . 398   Drayton   80
CYNTHIA'S
   (As my hope tells) that our drad Cynthia's shine, . . 179   U25 Desmond   V 58
CYNTHIAS
   to Cynthias fayrest Nymph hath sent thee, ... 662   Bedford   6
CYNTHIUS
   Cynthius, I applie 176   U25 Desmond   8
CYPHER
   To write in cypher, and the severall keyes, . . . 59   E92 New Crie   26
CYPRES   (See also CIPRESSE)
   In solemne cypres, the other cob-web-lawne. . . . 51   E73 Fine Grand   14
CYPRESSE
   And in smooth Cypresse boxes to be keep'd? . . . 327   Horace   476
D
. . . Esme D. of Lenox deceased, and Sister of the 252   U75 Epithalam.   Ttl
'D
   To love one man, hee'd leave her first. 146   U6 Defence   24
   I feare they'd love him too; 147   U7 Nymph   4
   Hee'd say, Mend this, good friend, and this; 'tis naught. . 333   horace   624
   He'd say, mend this my friend, and this, 'tis nought. . 354   Horace   V624
   Hee'd bid, blot all: and to the anvile bring . . 333   Horace   627
DAGGER
   A wodden Dagger, is a Dagger of wood 403   Inigo Jones 1   27
DAIES
   Of sorrow, then all pompe of gaudy daies: . . . 287   U84 Muse   182
   So Fate would give her life, and longer daies. . . 293   U87 Hor.3:9   12
   Out in the Dog-daies, least the killer meete . . 409   Detractor   20
DAILY   (See also DAYLY)
   And such a Prince thou art, wee daily see, . . . 28   E4 James 1   7
   Colt, now, doth daily penance in his owne. . . . 39   E39 Colt   2
   Daily to turne in Pauls, and helpe the trade. . . 56   E88 Monsieur   16
   Among the daily Ruines that fall foule, . . . 224   U50 Countesse   17
   In manner of a daily Apostrophe, ... 288   U84 Muse   210
DAINTIE
   Your daintie nostrills (in so hot a season, . . . 88   E133 Voyage   165
   And since our Daintie age, ... 175   U23 Himselfe   31
   With touch of daintie thum's! 239   U67 Muses   18
DAINTINESSE
   Daintinesse, and softer ease, ... 105   F8 Sicknesse   22
DAINTY
   There shall thy dainty Nostrill take 292   U86 Hor.4:1   21
DALE
   To the Eugenian dale; 367   Ode Who saith   43
DAM'
   Now dam'mee, Sir, if you shall not command . . . 154   U13 Sacvile   53
DAMASKE
   Have you seene a faire Damaske-rose 135   U2 Triumph   V 31
DAMASKE-ROSE
   Have you seene a faire Damaske-rose 135   U2 Triumph   V 31
DAMD
   They saw it halfe, damd thy whole play, and more; . . 371   Fletcher   8
DAME
   Would not be fearefull to offend a dame . . . 112   F11 Epode   109
   Runs betweene man, and man; 'tweene dame, and dame; . 113   F12 Rutland   16
   That payes, or what he will: The Dame is steele. . . 164   U15 Friend-Wars   78
   Is, she will play Dame Justice, too severe; . . 229   U54 Squib   8
   Of Dame Venetia Digby, styl'd The Faire: . . . 274   U84 Descent   2
   Not they that sided her, Dame Poetry, . . . 403   Inigo Jones 1   36
   Dame History, Dame Architecture too, ... 403   Inigo Jones 1   37
DAMES
   Rudyerd, as lesser dames, to great ones use, . . 78   E121 Rudyerd 1   1
   Of errant Knight-hood, with the Dames, and Dwarfes; . 205   U43 Vulcan   67
   Lent by the London Dames, to the Lords men; . . 213   U44 Speach   14
   A Kate, a Frank, to honour their Grand-dames, . . 258   U75 Epithalam.   172
DAMME
   By which his damme conceiv'd him, clothes and all? . . 56   E88 Monsieur   11
DAM'MEE
   Now dam'mee, Sir, if you shall not command . . . 154   U13 Sacvile   53
DAMNATION
   Or by Damnation voids it? or by stealth? . . . 166   U15 Friend-Wars   116
DAMNE
   He that dares damne himselfe, dares more then fight. . 32   E16 Brain-hardy   10
   Both him & Archimede; damne Architas . . . 402   Inigo Jones 1   5
DAMN'D
   Dam's whom he damn'd to, as the veriest Gull, . . 154   U13 Sacvile   57
DAMNED
   And out-cryes of the damned in the Fleet? . . . 88   E133 Voyage   172
DAMNES
   Play-wright me reades, and still my verses damnes, . 42   E49 Playwrt 1   1
DAMNING
   The Divell; and be the damning of us all. . . . 172   U20 Shrub   24
DAM'S
   Dam's whom he damn'd to, as the veriest Gull, . . 154   U13 Sacvile   57
DANCE   (See also DAUNCE)
   Out-dance the Babion, or out-boast the Brave; . . 81   E129 Mime   12
   Did dance the famous Morrisse, unto Norwich) . . 85   E133 Voyage   36
   And some doe drinke, and some doe dance, . . . 120   F14 Sydney   2
   To Dance, so she should, shamefac'd, differ farre . 321   Horace   339
   And, with their Chained dance, ... 401   Filmer   9

	Page	Title	Line

DANCES
To put his Court in dances,   222   U48 Bacchus   50

DANCING
If dancing, all would cry th'Idalian Queene,   68   E105 L Wroth 2   11

DANES
The Danes that drench   368   Ode Who saith   86

DANGER   (See also DAUNGER)
From my diseases danger, and from thee.   31   E13 Empirick   4
'Tis growne almost a danger to speake true   116   F13 Aubigny   1
And freed the soule from danger;   130   U1 Nativitie   9
Shewing danger more then ire.   142   U2 Her man   42
To carry noble danger in the face: 194   U38 Elegy 'Tis   102
To know the heads of danger! where 'tis fit   233   U59 Newcastle   17
The Danger of delaying to Repent,   411   Sutcliffe   9

DANGEROUS
When men a dangerous disease did scape,   31   E13 Empirick   1
And, in this name, am given out dangerous   117   F13 Aubigny   11

DANGERS
Looke not upon thy dangers, but our feares.   43   E51 James 3   10
And not to dangers. When so wise a king   47   E64 Salisbury 3   12
In single paths, dangers with ease are watch'd: 118   F13 Aubigny   57
And even our sports are dangers! what we call   163   U15 Friend-Wars   38

DAPHNE
I answer'd, Daphne now no paine can prove.   80   E126 Mrs Cary   6
Cary my love is, Daphne but my tree.   80   E126 Mrs Cary   8

DAPPER
That first sent forth the dapper Elegie,   309   Horace   110

DARBY
Specially the newes of Darby;   417   Moon   21

DARE
For I will dare none. Good Lord, walke dead still.   30   E11 Something   8
Yet dare not, to my thought, lest hope allow   41   E43 Salisbury 1   7
Dare for these poemes, yet, both aske, and read,   60   E94 Bedford 3   12
When I dare send my Epigrammes to thee?   62   E96 Donne 2   2
No more, then I dare now doe, with my pen.   70   E108 Soldiers   8
And, in a pittious tune, began. How dare   88   E133 Voyage   164
That for th'oyle of Talke, dare spend   105   F8 Sicknesse   33
More then citizens dare lend   105   F8 Sicknesse   34
Dare entayle their loves on any,   105   F8 Sicknesse   39
Dare entayle their loves to any,   105   F8 Sicknesse   V 39
As what th'have lost t'expect, they dare deride.   116   F13 Aubigny   4
Till that no usurer, nor his bawds dare lend   118   F13 Aubigny   78
And judge me after: if I dare pretend   122   F15 Heaven   7
Yet dare I not complaine, or wish for death   122   F15 Heaven   23
Yet dare I not tell who;   147   U7 Nymph   2
And superstition I dare scarce reveale,   155   U13 Sacvile   86
All that dare rowse: or are not loth to quit   162   U15 Friend-Wars   3
And Fortune once, t'assist the spirits that dare.   170   U18 Elegy Can   10
All mouthes, that dare entitle them (from hence)   187   U33 Councellour   11
I dare not say a body, but some parts   206   U43 Vulcan   87
Borne, bred, allied? what's he dare tutor us?   215   U44 Speach   66
Live by their Scale, that dare doe nothing free?   215   U44 Speach   68
And thinkes I dare not her? let the world see.   222   U49 Pucell   2
Dare thinke it, to relieve, no lesse renowne,   248   U71 Treasurer   14
But dare not aske our wish in Language fescennine: 257   U75 Epithalam.   160
If you dare grudge at Heaven, and repent   271   U81 Pawlet   79
If you dare Quarrell Heaven, and repent   271   U81 Pawlet   V 79
Dare I prophane, so irreligious bee   283   U84 Muse   39
Nor dare we under blasphemy conceive   286   U84 Muse   147
Be I their Judge, they doe at no time dare   321   Horace   356
shall never dare do any thing but feare.   423   Lucan   20
But with a Kisse, (if thou canst dare it)   662   Bedford   9

DARES
He that dares damne himselfe, dares more then fight.   32   E16 Brain-hardy   10
Of solemne greatnesse. And he dares, at dice,   36   E28 Surly   16
Hee's valiant'st, that dares fight, and not for pay;   49   E66 Cary   17
That dares nor write things false, nor hide things true.   62   E95 Savile   36
As since he dares not come within my sight.   151   U11 Dreame   14
Is fix'd upon one leg, and dares not come   198   U40 Elegy That   33
Who dares denie, that all first-fruits are due   235   U63 Charles 2   1
Nor dares he come in the comparison.   241   U69 Friend Son   8
Yet who's most ignorant, dares Verses make.   331   Horace   570
Shewes he dares more then Paules Church-yard durst do.   378   Coryat 2   85
That he dares to informe you, but somewhat meticulous,   380   Coryat 3   33
That an ill man dares not securely looke   389   Aleman   8
Yet, who dares offer a redoubt to reare?   401   Beaumont   11

DARING
Of daring, not to doe a wrong, is true   233   U59 Newcastle   15
Of daring all, hath still beene given; we know it: 305   Horace   12
Of daring ought, hath still beene given; we know it: 338   Horace   V 12
In daring to forsake the Grecian tracts,   323   Horace   407

DARK
Keepe in reserv'd in his Dark-lanterne face, '   198   U40 Elegy That   23
They're dark, bid cleare 'hem; al that's doubtful wrote   354   Horace   V637

DARKE
The gladdest light, darke man can thinke upon;   128   U1 Trinitie   35
From Death, and darke oblivion, neere the same,   175   U24 Frontispice   1
On these darke rymes; that my affection   177   U25 Desmond   15
On these darke rymes; that our affection   177   U25 Desmond   V 15
Without which all the world were darke;   189   U36 Song   7
In darke, and sullen mornes, doe we not say,   193   U38 Elegy 'Tis   79
Where we must feele it Darke for halfe a yeare.   199   U41 Elegy Since   8
To hang a window, or make darke the roome,   282   U84 Muse   7

	Page	Title	Line
DARKE (cont.)			
Darke thy cleare glasse with old Falernian Wine;	295	U89 Mart.8:77	5
As some the farther off: This loves the darke;	331	Horace	541
They're darke, bid cleare this: all that's doubtfull wrote	335	Horace	637
Velvet, or Taffata cap, rank'd in the darke	371	Fletcher	5
Who reads may roave, and call the passage darke,	383	Author	5
DARKEST			
Sleepe, that will make the darkest howres swift-pac't;	295	U90 Mart.10:47	11
DARK-LANTERNE			
Keepe in reserv'd in his Dark-lanterne face,	198	U40 Elegy That	23
DARKNESSE			
Or feats of darknesse acted in Mid-Sun,	156	U13 Sacvile	95
Where darknesse with her gloomie-sceptred hand,	180	U25 Desmond	61
It is a Darknesse hath blockt up my sense,	191	U38 Elegy 'Tis	5
Till then 'tis all but darknesse, that I have;	194	U38 Elegy 'Tis	121
But crept like darknesse through his blood?	234	U60 La-ware	8
Of Death, and Darknesse; and deprive	273	U84 Cradle	5
DARLING			
A darling, yet inviting, Majestie:	270	U81 Pawlet	V 44
DAR'ST			
Thou more; that with it every day, dar'st jest	32	E16 Brain-hardy	2
Make good what thou dar'st doe in all the rest.	32	E16 Brain-hardy	8
Or thy ranke setting? that thou dar'st put in	72	E112 Gamster	4
Dar'st breath in any ayre; and with safe skill,	76	E119 Shelton	9
But what she gives, thou dar'st give her againe;	168	U15 Friend-Wars	184
Dar'st not abuse thy wisdome, in the Lawes,	187	U33 Councellour	17
Unto the Scene thou bringst, and dar'st create	313	Horace	179
Unto the Stage thou bringst, and dar'st create	342	Horace	V179
My verses were commended, thou dar'st say,	408	Detractor	1
DARTED			
Their weapons darted, with that flame, and force,	233	U59 Newcastle	V 11
DARTING			
And Sister: darting forth a dazling light	253	U75 Epithalam.	43
DARTS			
In equall knots: This beares no brands, nor darts,	110	F11 Epode	51
DASHING			
Thy Noddle, with his clubb; and dashing forth	409	Detractor	21
DATE			
Or grace of speech, should hope a lasting date.	309	Horace	100
DAUGHTER			
On my first Daughter.	33	E22 Daughter	Ttl
Mary, the daughter of their youth:	33	E22 Daughter	2
Of Caesars Daughter, and the line	181	U27 Ode Helen	19
The Daughter of great Harry!	240	U67 Muses	26
. . . England, with the Lady Frances Stuart, Daughter of . . .	252	U75 Epithalam.	Ttl
Like what she is, the Daughter of a Duke,	253	U75 Epithalam.	42
Whose Daughter? ha? Great Savage of the Rock?	269	U81 Pawlet	10
Come forth thou bonnie bouncing booke then, daughter	378	Coryat 2	86
. . . eldest Daughter, to Cuthbert Lord Oglc: . . .	394	Jane Ogle	Ttl
The faire French Daughter to learne English in;	402	Filmer	12
Daughter, and Mother, and the Spouse of God,	413	Ghyrlond	33
Of being Daughter, Mother, Spouse of God!	414	Ghyrlond	56
DAUGHTERS			
By their ripe daughters, whom they would commend	95	F2 Penshurst	54
But then consent, your Daughters and your Wives,	200	U42 Elegy Let	19
Thou art jealous of thy Wifes, or Daughters Case:	202	U42 Elegy Let	87
If you can envie your owne Daughters blisse,	271	U81 Pawlet	83
If you can enjoy your owne Daughters blisse,	271	U81 Pawlet	V 83
And Sons, and Daughters, with their Parents talke;	285	U84 Muse	118
DAUNCE			
Let these in wanton feete daunce out their soules.	108	F10 Proludium	11
DAUNCES			
In the Daunces, with what spight	138	U2 Kisse	22
Though but in daunces, it shall know his power;	210	U43 Vulcan	157
Though but in daunces, it shall know high power;	210	U43 Vulcan	V157
DAUNCING			
. . . and Dauncing At Cotswold.	415	Dover	Ttl
DAUNGER			
Though but in daunger, it shall know thy power;	210	U43 Vulcan	V157
DAVIDS			
Sweet Tree of Life, King Davids Strength and Tower,	413	Ghyrlond	38
DAVIS			
Davis, and Weever, and the best have beene,	32	E18 Censurer	4
DAVUS			
As not make difference, whether Davus speake,	321	Horace	345
DAY (See also DAIES)			
The quarter day is come; the hostesse sayes,	30	E12 Shift	7
Thou more; that with it every day, dar'st jest	32	E16 Brain-hardy	2
And though the soundest legs goe every day,	36	E31 Banck	3
Exacted by thy fate, on the just day.	41	E45 First Son	4
To pay at's day of marriage. By my hand	42	E46 Luckless 1	4
Yes, now he weares his knight-hood every day.	42	E46 Luckless 1	6
His bought armes Mung' not lik'd; for his first day	42	E48 Mungril	1
. . . the two and twentieth day of March, 1607.	43	E51 James 3	Ttl
Against thy fortune: when no foe, that day,	49	E66 Cary	9
Each best day of our life escapes us, first.	50	E70 Wm Roe 1	6
I meant the day-starre should not brighter rise,	52	E76 Bedford 1	7
Went on: and proving him still, day by day,	57	E90 Mill	7
Longer a day, but with his Mill will marry.	57	E90 Mill	16
Nay, aske you, how the day goes, in your eare.	59	E92 New Crie	18
Or, every day, some one at Rimee's looks,	59	E92 New Crie	23
Life of the Muses day, their morning-starre!	60	E94 Bedford 3	2
And I must now beleeve him: for, to day,	64	E100 Playwrt 3	3

DAY (cont.)

	Page	Title	Line
They follow vertue, for reward, to day;	66	E102 Pembroke	9
Gut eates all day, and lechers all the night,	76	E118 Gut	1
They were not to be nam'd on the same day.	83	E131 Ferrab. 2	12
It was the day, what time the powerfull Moone	84	E133 Voyage	29
Yet, one day in the yeere, for sweet 'tis voyc't,	87	E133 Voyage	119
And I not faine to sit (as some, this day,	95	F2 Penshurst	65
Thy tables hoord not up for the next day,	95	F2 Penshurst	71
With the whole houshold, and may, every day,	96	F2 Penshurst	96
Thou dost with some delight the day out-weare,	97	F3 Wroth	35
Thou canst with some delight the day out-weare,	97	F3 Wroth	V 35
And never will redeeme a day,	100	F4 To the World	23
Phoebus. No? tend thy cart still. Envious day	107	F10 Proludium	7
Would make a day of night,	112	F11 Epode	94
Solders crackt friendship; makes love last a day;	113	F12 Rutland	17
Your beautie; for you see that every day:	117	F13 Aubigny	30
On the close groome, and page, on new-yeeres day,	118	F13 Aubigny	74
Ode. To Sir William Sydney, on his Birth-day.	120	F14 Sydney	Ttl
This day	120	F14 Sydney	13
This day sayes, then, the number of glad yeeres	120	F14 Sydney	21
This day	121	F14 Sydney	54
The Birth-day shines, when logs not burne, but men.	121	F14 Sydney	60
I Beheld her, on a day,	132	U2 How he saw	1
Of the Court, to day, then all	138	U2 Kisse	15
Charis one day in discourse	139	U2 Promise	1
And excuse spun every day,	140	U2 Promise	10
But like to be, that every day mends one,	156	U13 Sacvile	116
Profit in ought: each day some little adde,	157	U13 Sacvile	132
As farre as he can flie, or follow day,	163	U15 Friend-Wars	29
As farre as he can flee, or follow day,	163	U15 Friend-Wars	V 29
How they may make some one that day an Asse	164	U15 Friend-Wars	64
Coach'd, or on foot-cloth, thrice chang'd every day,	165	U15 Friend-Wars	107
Or side, but threatens Ruine. The whole Day	166	U15 Friend-Wars	131
But here doth lie, till the last Day,	168	U16 Gray	3
Debts when they can: good men may breake their day,	169	U17 Friend-Debt	2
Such shall you heare to day, and find great foes,	186	U32 Elsmere	7
This looketh like an Execution day?	193	U38 Elegy 'Tis	80
It is as if a night should shade noone-day,	199	U41 Elegy Since	5
And vouches both the Pageant, and the Day,	202	U42 Elegy Let	77
Fitter to see the fire-light, then the day;	204	U43 Vulcan	44
Squire of the Squibs, against the Pageant day,	208	U43 Vulcan	119
Squire of the Squibs, upon the Pageant day,	208	U43 Vulcan	V119
Squire of the Squibs, against the next Maiors day,	208	U43 Vulcan	V119
Whom they durst handle in their holy-day coates,	208	U43 Vulcan	127
Whom they durst handle in their high day coates,	208	U43 Vulcan	V127
But we have Powder still for the Kings Day,	213	U44 Speach	2
If they stay here, but till Saint Georges Day.	213	U44 Speach	10
These ten yeares day; As all may sweare that looke	213	U44 Speach	27
More then the surfets, in thee, that day stood.	214	U44 Speach	48
The Hawking language? or our Day to breake	215	U44 Speach	72
From Court, while yet thy fame hath some small day;	223	U49 Pucell	36
Lord Bacons Birth-day.	225	U51 Bacon	Ttl
Pardon, I read it in thy face, the day	225	U51 Bacon	5
I gaine, in having leave to keepe my Day,	231	U56 Covell	29
. . . On the Universary day of his Raigne. 1629.	236	U64 Charles 3	VTtl
. . . On his Anniversary Day. 1629.	236	U64 Charles 3	Ttl
If he but weigh'd the blessings of this day?	236	U64 Charles 3	4
On the Princes Birth-day. An Epigram	237	U65 Prince	VTtl
And art thou borne, brave Babe? Blest be the day,	237	U65 Prince	V 1
. . . In celebration of her Majesties birth-day. 1630.	239	U67 Muses	Ttl
To the Queene on her Birth-day	239	U67 Muses	VTtl
Ring thou it Holy-day.	239	U67 Muses	6
This day the Court doth measure	240	U67 Muses	43
Summe up this crowned day,	240	U67 Muses	47
Make up this crowned day,	240	U67 Muses	V 47
A Lillie of a Day,	245	U70 Ode	69
To see that bright eternall Day:	245	U70 Ode	81
To the King. On his Birth-day . . .	249	U72 King	Ttl
Upon King Charles his Birth-day.	249	U72 King	VTtl
This is King Charles his Day. Speake it, thou Towre,	249	U72 King	1
This is King Charles his birth day. Speake it, thou Towre,	249	U72 King	V 1
Adding her owne glad accents, to this Day,	249	U72 King	7
Adding her owne greate accents, to this Day,	249	U72 King	V 7
On th'often comming of this Holy-day:	249	U72 King	16
. . . high Treasurer of England, Upon the Day, Hee was . . .	250	U73 Weston	Ttl
Then thou shalt see to day:	252	U75 Epithalam.	5
See, the Procession! what a Holy day	252	U75 Epithalam.	9
As they had learn'd new changes, for the day,	253	U75 Epithalam.	35
This Feast, then can the Day,	254	U75 Epithalam.	55
Themselves to day,	255	U75 Epithalam.	86
And wonder'd at the bounties of this day:	255	U75 Epithalam.	90
To day, the Fathers service; who could bring	256	U75 Epithalam.	107
Now, Sun, and post away the rest of day:	257	U75 Epithalam.	138
(After the last child borne;) This is our wedding day.	258	U75 Epithalam.	168
Will last till day;	258	U75 Epithalam.	190
Upon my Birth-day the eleventh of June;	262	U78 Digby	14
Witnesse my Birth-day the eleventh of June;	262	U78 Digby	V 14
That day, which I predestin'd am to sing,	262	U78 Digby	V 17
Lute, Lyre, Theorbo, all are call'd to day.	263	U79 New-yeares	2
To day old Janus opens the new yeare,	263	U79 New-yeares	9
This day, by Baptisme, and his Saviours crosse:	268	U80 Christning	10
Became her Birth-day to Eternitie!	271	U81 Pawlet	68
At pleasure, to be call'd for, every day!	271	U81 Pawlet	82

DAY (cont.)
And Day, deceasing! with the Prince of light, ... 271 U81 Pawlet 88
And, out of that, make Day to breake; . . . . 276 U84 Body 14
Who will be there, against that day prepar'd, ... 284 U84 Muse 59
O Day of joy, and suretie to the just! . . . . 284 U84 Muse 61
That great eternall Holy-day of rest, ... 284 U84 Muse 63
But make him All in All, their Theme, that Day: . . . . 286 U84 Muse 120
That happy Day, that never shall see night! . . . . 286 U84 Muse 121
There twice a day in sacred Laies, ... 292 U86 Hor.4:1 25
But thus, thus, keeping endlesse Holy-day, ... 294 U88 Petronius 6
Nor feare thy latest day, nor wish therfore. 295 U90 Mart.10:47 13
In fitting proper adjuncts to each day. . . . . 317 Horace 254
The Idiot, keeping holy-day, or drudge, ... 319 Horace 301
In hand, and turne them over, day, and night. . . . . 323 Horace 398
To taxe that Verse, which many a day, and blot . . . . 325 Horace 416
Not only this, but every day of thine, ... 384 Somerset 9
May she, whome thou for spouse, to day, dost take, ... 384 Somerset 11
Sure, this glad payre were married, but this day. . . . . 384 Somerset 26
Shee need not blush upon the Mariage-Day. . . . . 386 Husband 12
If all the vulgar Tongues, that speake this day, ... 388 Chapman 7
And despaires day, but for thy Volumes light. . . . . 392 Shakespeare 80
Without conferring symboles. This's my day. . . . . 396 Drayton 10
Is fayre got up, and day some houres begun! . . . . 396 Drayton 18
And when the flesh, here, shut up day, ... 400 Lady Ogle 27
Fresh as the Day, and new as are the Howers, ... 416 Welcome 1
I shall think on't ere't be day. . . . . 417 Moon 11
DAYES
For such a Poet, while thy dayes were greene, ... 28 E4 James 1 5
Then takes up fresh commoditie, for dayes; . . . . 30 E12 Shift 13
My selfe a witnesse of thy few dayes sport; . . . . 55 E85 Goodyere 1 2
Keepe a starre-chamber sentence close, twelve dayes: . . . . 59 E92 New Crie 19
Spent in surfets: and their dayes, ... 104 F8 Sicknesse 5
Just to the waight their this dayes-presents beare; . . . . 113 F12 Rutland 8
And almost, all dayes after, while they live; . . . . 118 F13 Aubigny 75
To live untill to morrow' hath lost two dayes. . . . . 121 F14 Sydney 50
And what I write? and vexe it many dayes . . . . 159 U14 Selden 25
And doubtfull Dayes (which were nam'd Criticall,) . . . . 180 U26 Ode High 6
What fate is this, to change mens dayes and houres, ... 199 U41 Elegy Since 9
What though she ride two mile on Holy-dayes . . . . 222 U49 Pucell 15
When all your life's a president of dayes, ... 237 U64 Charles 3 13
Goe now, and tell out dayes summ'd up with feares, ... 244 U70 Ode 53
The Muse not peepes out, one of hundred dayes; . . . . 248 U71 Treasurer 9
Would sit in an Infirmery, whole dayes . . . . 288 U84 Muse 195
Hee, that but living halfe his dayes, dies such, ... 295 U89 Mart.8:77 7
Steepe the glad Genius in the Wine, whole dayes, ... 319 Horace 298
. . . on his Translation of Hesiods Works, & Dayes. . . . . 388 Chapman Ttl
A Prentise-ship: which few doe now a dayes. . . . . 410 Brome 10
Thou that doest spend thie dayes . . . . 420 Ode:If Men 24
DAYES-PRESENTS
Just to the waight their this dayes-presents beare; . . . . 113 F12 Rutland 8
DAYLY
Though, now by Love transform'd, & dayly dying: . . . . 369 Ode Who saith 101
DAY-STARRE
I meant the day-starre should not brighter rise, ... 52 E76 Bedford 1 7
DAZELING
A quick, and dazeling motion! when a paire . . . . 233 U59 Newcastle 9
Offended with the dazeling flame . . . . 234 U60 La-ware 9
DAZLING
And Sister: darting forth a dazling light . . . . 253 U75 Epithalam. 43
A dazling, yet inviting, Majestie: . . . . 270 U81 Pawlet 44
DE
Had I compil'd from Amadis de Gaule, ... 203 U43 Vulcan 29
DEAD
For I will dare none. Good Lord, walke dead still. . . . . 30 E11 Something 8
A dead beautie under-neath thee, ... 39 E40 Ratcliffe 2
How full of want, how swallow'd up, how dead . . . . 80 E127 Aubigny 6
Let who will thinke us dead, or wish our death. . . . . 139 U2 Another 18
I feele, I'm rather dead then he! . . . . 152 U12 Corbet 36
Quickning dead Nature, to her noblest strife. . . . . 162 U15 Friend-Wars 8
And shamefastnesse together! All lawes dead, ... 163 U15 Friend-Wars 40
And shamefac'dnesse together! All lawes dead, ... 163 U15 Friend-Wars V 40
So, 'live or dead, thou wilt preserve a fame . . . . 168 U15 Friend-Wars 189
When her dead essence (like the Anatomie . . . . 179 U25 Desmond 37
All Ensignes of a Warre, are not yet dead, ... 213 U44 Speach 11
On all Soules that are absent; even the dead; . . . . 218 U47 Tribe 17
Stay, drop a teare for him that's dead, ... 233 U60 La-ware 2
And sunke in that dead sea of life . . . . 244 U70 Ode 40
And thinke, nay know, thy Morison's not dead. . . . . 245 U70 Ode 78
And see all dead here, or about to dye! . . . . 271 U81 Pawlet 86
'Twere time that I dy'd too, now shee is dead, ... 282 U84 Muse 1
Sure, I am dead, and know it not! I feele . . . . 283 U84 Muse 29
And left her lovely body unthought dead! . . . . 283 U84 Muse 44
Indeed, she is not dead! but laid to sleepe . . . . 283 U84 Muse 45
Of all are dead to life! His Wisdome show . . . . 289 U84 Muse 221
Much phrase that now is dead, shall be reviv'd; . . . . 309 Horace 101
Paccuvius, Accius, him of Cordova dead, ... 391 Shakespeare 35
Of thy dead Standards: or (with miracle) see . . . . 405 Inigo Jones 1 89
DEADLY
Forgive me this one foolish deadly sin, ... 171 U20 Shrub 2
DEAFE
I Now thinke, Love is rather deafe, then blind, ... 149 U9 Picture 1
I Doubt that, Love is rather deafe, then blind, ... 149 U9 Picture V 1

		Page	Title	Line
DEAL				
A Goddess is, then paynted Cloth, Deal-boards,	. . . .	406	Inigo Jones 1	93
DEAL-BOARDS				
A Goddess is, then paynted Cloth, Deal-boards,	. . . .	406	Inigo Jones 1	93
DEALE (WOOD)				
Mythology there painted on slit deale!	. . . .	404	Inigo Jones 1	48
DEALE				
Talkes loud, and baudy, has a gather'd deale	. .	74	E115 Honest Man	9
And now such is thy stand; while thou dost deale	. .	217	U46 Coke	15
I have no portion in them, nor their deale	. .	218	U47 Tribe	27
DEAR				
Who, wheresoere he be, on what dear coast,	. . .	116	F12 Rutland	93
DEARE				
Fortie things more, deare Grand, which you know true,	. .	51	E73 Fine Grand	21
He is no favourites favourite, no deare trust	. . .	63	E97 Motion	13
Unto himselfe, by being so deare to you.	. . .	119	F13 Aubigny	117
Deare Vincent Corbet who so long	. . .	151	U12 Corbet	7
His deare and borrow'd Bravery he must cast?	. .	165	U15 Friend-Wars	110
Thinke but how deare you bought	. . .	180	U26 Ode High	19
In friendship, I confesse: But, deare friend, heare.	.	190	U37 Friend-Book	18
If I had writ no word, but Deare, farewell.	. .	198	U40 Elegy That	50
Lend me, deare Arthur, for a weeke five more,	. .	229	U54 Squib	16
That shall re-joyne yee. Was she, then, so deare,	. .	285	U84 Muse	107
To my Deare Sonne, and right-learned Friend, . . .	.	414	Rutter	Ttl
DEARELY				
For vulgar praise, doth it too dearely buy.	. .	27	E2 My Booke	14
DEARER				
To him, man's dearer, then t'himselfe.	. . .	99	F3 Wroth	96
But to please him, who is the dearer prise	. . .	119	F13 Aubigny	116
Much more desir'd, and dearer then before,	. . .	285	U84 Muse	109
DEAREST				
When they cost dearest, and are done most free,	. .	49	E66 Cary	14
Unknowne which is the Dearest)	. . .	179	U25 Desmond	56
DEATH				
Which shewes, where ever death doth please t'appeare,	. .	37	E32 Roe 2	9
Of Death.	. . .	37	E34 Death	Ttl
He that feares death, or mournes it, in the just,	. .	37	E34 Death	1
To King James. Upon the happy false rumour of his death, . . .		43	E51 James 3	Ttl
Of Life, and Death.	.	53	E80 Life/Death	Ttl
The ports of death are sinnes; of life, good deeds:	. .	53	E80 Life/Death	1
So to front death, as men might judge us past it.	. .	54	E80 Life/Death	7
For good men but see death, the wicked tast it.	. .	54	E80 Life/Death	8
Th'other let it sleepe with death:	. . .	79	E124 Elizabeth	10
Then either money, warre, or death:	. . .	99	F3 Wroth	76
Nor death; but when thy latest sand is spent,	. . .	100	F3 Wroth	105
Yet dare I not complaine, or wish for death	. . .	122	F15 Heaven	23
Sinne, Death, and Hell,	. . .	129	U1 Father	23
Let who will thinke us dead, or wish our death.	. .	139	U2 Another	18
Yes; and in death, as life, unblest,	. . .	149	U8 Houre-glasse	9
From Death, and darke oblivion, neere the same,	. .	175	U24 Frontispice	1
Of fortune! when, or death appear'd, or bands!	. .	233	U59 Newcastle	23
To Sir Lucius Carey, on the death of his Brother Morison	.	242	U70 Ode	VTtl
Lay trampled on; the deeds of death, and night,	. .	243	U70 Ode	14
I doe obey you, Beauty! for in death,	. . .	269	U81 Pawlet	5
'Twixt death and life! Where her mortalitie	. .	271	U81 Pawlet	67
The Serpents head: Gets above Death, and Sinne,	. .	272	U81 Pawlet	99
Of Death, and Darknesse; and deprive	. . .	273	U84 Cradle	5
By Death, on Earth, I should have had remorse	. .	282	U84 Muse	12
Of Vulture death, and those relentlesse cleies?	. .	283	U84 Muse	18
And she doth know, out of the shade of Death,	. .	285	U84 Muse	91
Through his inherent righteousnesse, in death,	. .	286	U84 Muse	135
Shee saw him rise, triumphing over Death	. . .	288	U84 Muse	203
Our selves, and all that's ours, to death we owe:	. .	309	Horace	90
I'le tell you but the death, and the disease	. .	335	Horace	659
Or love of this so famous death lay by.	. . .	335	Horace	669
Or love of this his famous death lay by.	. . .	355	Horace	V669
Upon the Life, and Death of Playes, and Wits,	. .	370	Fletcher	2
Where spight of Death, next Life, for her Loves sake	.	394	Jane Ogle	25
DEATH'S				
Death's selfe is sorry.	. . .	77	E120 S. P.	4
So deep, as he did then death's waters sup;	. .	244	U70 Ode	41
DEATHS				
This world deaths region is, the other lifes:	. .	54	E80 Life/Death	5
Then entertaine, and as Deaths Harbinger;	. .	394	Jane Ogle	21
DEAW				
What gentle Ghost, besprent with April deaw,	. .	268	U81 Pawlet	1
What goodly Ghost, besprent with April deaw,	. .	268	U81 Pawlet	V 1
DEBENTUR				
To send my Debentur.	. . .	231	U57 Burges	6
DEBT				
Shuns prease, for two maine causes, poxe, and debt,	. .	76	E119 Shelton	4
Into the debt; and reckon on her head,	. .	80	E127 Aubigny	5
That puts it in his Debt-booke e're 't be done;	. .	154	U13 Sacvile	34
Hee, that hath studied well the debt, and knowes	. .	325	Horace	445
From fearefull back-slides; And the debt we'are in,	. .	412	Sutcliffe	15
DEBT-BOOKE				
That puts it in his Debt-booke e're 't be done;	. .	154	U13 Sacvile	34
DEBTER				
The world must know your greatnesse is my debter.	. .	51	E73 Fine Grand	4
DEBTERS				
To make all the Muses debters	. . .	259	U76 Petition	8
DEBTS				
To pay our debts, upon thy Crosse, and cryd'st,	. .	128	U1 Trinitie	23

		Page	Title	Line
DEBTS (cont.)				
Debts when they can: good men may breake their day,	· · ·	169	U17 Friend-Debt	2
Yet have all debts forgiven us, and advance	· · ·	286	U84 Muse	143
Pays all Debts, cures all Diseases,	· · · · ·	657	Door Apollo	17
DECAY				
And let nothing high decay,	· · · · ·	131	U2 Excuse	22
His Altars kept from the Decay,	· · · ·	173	U22 Elegy Tho	19
Absence, or Distance, shall not breed decay.	· · ·	194	U38 Elegy 'Tis	116
For lust will languish, and that heat decay.	· · ·	294	U88 Petronius	5
Can this decay, but is beginning ever.	· · ·	294	U88 Petronius	10
Of words decay, and phrases borne but late	· ·	309	Horace	88
DECAY'D				
Parts of me (they judg'd) decay'd,	· · ·	259	U76 Petition	23
Parts of him, the Judge decay'd,	· · ·	259	U76 Petition	V 23
Some Forme defective, or decay'd;	· · ·	275	U84 Body	6
DECAYES				
And noted the beginnings and decayes!	· · · ·	160	U14 Selden	46
DECEASED				
. . . Esme D. of Lenox deceased, and Sister of the . . .		252	U75 Epithalam.	Ttl
DECEASING				
And Day, deceasing! with the Prince of light,	· · ·	271	U81 Pawlet	88
DECEAST				
On what's deceast.	· · · · · · ·	121	F14 Sydney	38
DECEIPT				
And the deceipt of pleasures, by Consent.	· · ·	411	Sutcliffe	11
DECEIT				
Deceit is fruitfull. Men have Masques and nets,	· ·	216	U45 Squib	18
DECEIVE				
Deceive their malice, who could wish it so.	· · ·	27	E2 My Booke	7
DECEIV'D				
Since, being deceiv'd, I turne a sharper eye	· · ·	159	U14 Selden	23
Or I am much deceiv'd, shall be to place	· · ·	307	Horace	60
DECEIVES				
What art is thine, that so thy friend deceives?	· ·	44	E55 Beaumont	8
DECENT				
The place allotted it, with decent thewes.	· · ·	311	Horace	125
The place allotted it, with decent praise.	· · ·	341	Horace	V131/125
DECK				
With the Lace that doth it deck,	· · ·	137	U2 Cupid	30
To welcome home a Paire, and deck the nuptiall bower?	·	253	U75 Epithalam.	24
To deck the hallow'd Harth with old wood fir'd	· ·	291	U85 Country	43
DECKE				
In place of scutcheons, that should decke thy herse,	· ·	35	E27 Roe 1	1
DECLARES				
What number best can fit, Homer declares.	· · ·	309	Horace	106
DECLINE				
This makes, that wisely you decline your life,	· ·	118	F13 Aubigny	59
Humber, or Owse, decline;	· · · · ·	368	Ode Who saith	74
DECLIN'D				
Who can behold all envie so declin'd	· · · ·	47	E63 Salisbury 2	7
DECLINETH				
Declineth anger, perswades clemencie,	· · · ·	82	E130 Ferrab. 1	5
DECOCTIONS				
In decoctions; and are mann'd	· · · · ·	105	F8 Sicknesse	30
DECREAST				
Can I discerne how shadowes are decreast,	· ·	156	U13 Sacvile	118
DECREE				
Lawes; and no change e're come to one decree:	· ·	185	U31 Elsmere	2
No order? no Decree? Though we be gone	· · ·	211	U43 Vulcan	176
DECREED				
Hence was it, that the destinies decreed	· · ·	53	E79 Rutland	5
And as that wisedome had decreed,	· · ·	130	U1 Nativitie	16
I have decreed; keepe it from waves, and presse;	· ·	219	U47 Tribe	57
DEDICATE				
Could save that line to dedicate to thee?	· · ·	44	E53 Old-end	10
We dedicate this Cellar,	· · · · ·	220	U48 Bacchus	3
DEDICATED				
A dedicated Ensigne make	· · · · ·	273	U84 Cradle	11
DEDICATION				
The Dedication of the Kings new Cellar. to Bacchus.	·	220	U48 Bacchus	Ttl
1. The Dedication of her Cradle.	· · ·	272	U84 Cradle	Ttl
DEED				
Which deed I know not, whether were more high,	· ·	49	E66 Cary	7
Now, I must give thy life, and deed, the voice	· ·	55	E86 Goodyere 2	5
It is the next deed, and a great one too.	· ·	61	E95 Savile	26
In memorie of which most liquid deed,	· ·	89	E133 Voyage	193
She repented of the deed,	· · ·	133	U2 Suffered	18
They say the Angells marke each deed,	· ·	144	U3 Musicall	17
The frequent varying of the deed,	· ·	146	U6 Defence	11
Where any Deed is forc't, the Grace is mard.	· ·	153	U13 Sacvile	24
Of any, is a great and generous Deed:	· ·	155	U13 Sacvile	76
This Age would lend no faith to Dorrels Deed;	· ·	223	U49 Pucell	42
Friendship, in deed, was written, not in words:	· ·	247	U70 Ode	123
DEEDES				
Thy deedes, unto thy name, will prove new wombes,	· ·	70	E109 Nevil	17
His deedes too dying, but in bookes (whose good	· ·	71	E110 Edmonds 1	15
His deedes too dying, save in bookes (whose good	· ·	71	E110 Edmonds 1	V 15
DEEDS				
And proud, my worke shall out-last common deeds,	· ·	46	E60 Mounteagle	6
The ports of death are sinnes; of life, good deeds:	· ·	53	E80 Life/Death	1
In th'eye of Europe, where thy deeds were done,	· ·	58	E91 Vere	6
The selfe-same deeds, as diversly they come,	· ·	64	E99 Th Roe 2	8
Not Caesars deeds, nor all his honors wonne,	· ·	71	E110 Edmonds 1	1

			Page	Title	Line

DEEDS (cont.)
That thine be just, and honest; that thy Deeds . . . . 167 U15 Friend-Wars 177
But stood unshaken in his Deeds, and Name, ... 185 U30 Burleigh 11
Lay trampled on; the deeds of death, and night, ... 243 U70 Ode 14
Which all men doe, that urge not their owne deeds . . . 281 U84 Kenelme 17
Or doing other deeds of Charitie, ... 288 U84 Muse 193
Being taught a better way. All mortall deeds . . . . 309 Horace 98
The deeds of Kings, great Captaines, and sad Warres, . . 341 Horace V105
All kings to doe the self same deeds with some! . . . 406 Inigo Jones 2 4
DEEME
Then this, our guilt, nor golden age can deeme, . . . 114 F12 Rutland 22
DEEP
Give me a deep-crown'd-Bowle, that I may sing . . . 225 U51 Bacon 19
So deep, as he did then death's waters sup; . . . 244 U70 Ode 41
That Mine of Wisdome, and of Counsells deep, . . . 255 U75 Epithalam. 98
DEEP-CROWN'D-BOWLE
Give me a deep-crown'd-Bowle, that I may sing . . . 225 U51 Bacon 19
DEEPE
And that so strong and deepe, as 't might be thought, . . 71 E110 Edmonds 1 7
And now an Epode to deepe eares I sing. . . . . 108 F10 Proludium 30
And now an Epode to deepe eares we sing. . . . . 108 F10 Proludium V 30
and now an Epode, to deepe Eares, wee singe. . . . 108 F10 Proludium 16
in a deepe trance; * * * * * . . . . 361 Palmer 26
So, be your Concord, still, as deepe, as mute; . . . 384 Somerset 17
I sayd, who'had supp'd so deepe of this sweet Chalice, . . 412 Sutcliffe 21
By those deepe-grounded, understanding men, . . . 414 Rutter 7
DEEPE-GROUNDED
By those deepe-grounded, understanding men, . . . 414 Rutter 7
DEEPER
Are deeper then their Faces: . . . . . . 365 Ode Splendor 22
DEEPEST
Deepest in Man, of which when he doth thinke, . . . 153 U13 Sacvile 20
Of deepest lore, could we the Center find! . . . 243 U70 Ode 10
DEERE
That never failes to serve thee season'd deere, . . . 94 F2 Penshurst 20
Divid'st, upon the lesser Deere; . . . . . 97 F3 Wroth 26
Dispend'st, upon the lesser Deere; . . . . . 97 F3 Wroth V 26
DEFAC'T
To see their Seats and Bowers by chattring Pies defac't? . . 174 U23 Himselfe 12
DEFAME
Itch to defame the State? or brand the Times? . . . 203 U43 Vulcan 25
DEFEAT
'Tis onely that can time, and chance defeat: . . . 118 F13 Aubigny 51
In will and power, only to defeat. . . . . 191 U38 Elegy 'Tis 18
DEFECT
Executes men in picture. By defect, ... 75 E115 Honest Man 29
DEFECTIVE
Some Forme defective, or decay'd; . . . . . 275 U84 Body 6
DEFENCE
A Martyr borne in our defence; . . . . . 130 U1 Nativitie 23
Another. In defence of their Inconstancie. A Song. . . 146 U6 Defence Ttl
Stood up thy Nations fame, her Crownes defence. . . . 217 U46 Coke 14
As all defence, or offence, were a chime! . . . 232 U59 Newcastle 6
DEFENCES
Thy just defences made th' oppressor afraid. . . . 217 U46 Coke 8
DEFEND
That thou at once, then, nobly maist defend . . . 63 E98 Th Roe 1 7
And strength to be a Champion, and defend . . . 161 U14 Selden 78
Lyaeus, and defend him, ... 221 U48 Bacchus 18
Then: If your fault you rather had defend . . . 335 Horace 629
DEFENDERS
When those good few, that her Defenders be, . . . 186 U32 Elsmere 5
DEFEND'ST
So brightly brandish'd) wound'st, defend'st! the while . . 187 U33 Councellour 32
DEFENSE
In Bulwarkes, Rav'lins, Ramparts, for defense, . . . 400 Beaumont 4
DEFERRE
Why should we deferre our joyes? . . . . . 102 F5 Celia 1 9
DEFERRER
A great deferrer, long in hope, growne numbe . . . 317 Horace 245
DEFIES
Defies, what's crosse to Piety, or good Fame. . . . 401 Beaumont 20
DEFILED
(Defiled) touch'd; but certaine he was mad, . . . 337 Horace 673
DEFIN'D
Describ'd, it 's thus: Defin'd would you it have? . . 75 E115 Honest Man 33
DEFORM'D
And the whole lumpe growes round, deform'd, and droupes, . 227 U52 Answer 5
DEFORMED
Wish, you had fowle ones, and deformed got; . . . 200 U42 Elegy Let 22
As a deformed face doth a true glasse. . . . . 389 Aleman 10
DEFRAUDED
Might be defrauded, nor the great secur'd, . . . 176 U24 Frontispice 6
DEFRAYES
Keepes himselfe, with halfe a man, and defrayes . . 30 E12 Shift 3
DEGENERATE
"For stile of rarenesse, to degenerate. . . . . 367 Ode Who saith 32
DEGRADATION
Nor Degradation from the Ministry, ... 410 Gill 6
DEGREE
Nor may'any feare, to loose of their degree, . . . 73 E113 Overbury 11
The other was a squire, of faire degree; . . . 84 E133 Voyage 25
Freedome doth with degree dispense. . . . . 98 F3 Wroth 58

<table>
<thead>
<tr><th></th><th>Page</th><th>Title</th><th>Line</th></tr>
</thead>
<tbody>
</tbody>
</table>

DEGREE (cont.)
Now with a Title more to the Degree; · · · · · 225 U51 Bacon 12
In number, measure, or degree · · · 399 Lady Ogle 23
DEGREES
For strict degrees of ranke, or title looke: · · · 29 E9 To All 2
'Tis by degrees that men arrive at glad · · · 157 U13 Sacvile 131
And comes by these Degrees, the Stile t'inherit · · 164 U15 Friend-Wars 81
By all oblique Degrees, that killing height · · · 224 U50 Countesse 11
DEIFIE
And almost deifie the Authors! make · · · 156 U13 Sacvile 99
DEIGNES
Mynerva deignes · · · · 420 Ode:If Men 29
deignes myne the power to find, yett want I will · · 421 Censure 10
DEITY (See DIETIE)
DELATED
wear spent with wonder as they weare delated, · · · 361 Palmer 24
DELAY
Delay is bad, doubt worse, depending worst; · · · 50 E70 Wm Roe 1 5
But we find that cold delay, · · · · · 140 U2 Promise 9
He neither gives, or do's, that doth delay · · · 154 U13 Sacvile 41
Strifes, murmures, or delay, · · · · · 258 U75 Epithalam. 189
DELAYES
Excuses, or Delayes? or done 'hem scant, · · · 153 U13 Sacvile 27
DELAYING
The Danger of delaying to Repent, · · · · 411 Sutcliffe 9
DELIA'S
Or Delia's Graces, by Tibullus? · · · · 181 U27 Ode Helen 10
DELICACIES
Our Delicacies are growne capitall, · · · 163 U15 Friend-Wars 37
DELICIOUS
Wine, or delicious fruits, unto the Taste; · · · 286 U84 Muse 123
DELIGHT
Donne, the delight of Phoebus, and each Muse, · · · 34 E23 Donne 1 1
Let pui'nees, porters, players praise delight, · · · 62 E96 Donne 2 10
For Cupid, who (at first) tooke vaine delight, · · · 73 E114 Sydney 3
And, striving so to double his delight, · · · 76 E118 Gut 3
Thou dost with some delight the day out-weare, · · · 97 F3 Wroth 35
Thou canst with some delight the day out-weare, · · · 97 F3 Wroth V 35
He did me the Delight, · · · 151 U11 Dreame 8
On both sides doe your mischiefes with delight; · · · 212 U43 Vulcan 204
Indeed, her Dressing some man might delight, · · · 223 U49 Pucell 31
How I would draw, and take hold and delight. · · · 227 U52 Answer 18
Her Poem's beautie, but a sweet delight · · · 311 Horace 141
More strongly takes the people with delight, · · · 327 Horace 458
Poets would either profit, or delight, · · · 327 Horace 477
As doctrine, and delight together go. · · · 329 Horace 516
Doth please; this, ten times over, will delight. · · 331 Horace 544
With more delight, and grace) · · · · 369 Ode Who saith 103
The applause! delight! the wonder of our Stage! · · 391 Shakespeare 18
DELIGHTFULL
As fire; and more delightfull · · · · · 365 Ode Splendor 6
DELIGHTS
Comus puts in, for new delights; · · · · 98 F3 Wroth 48
When youths ply their stolne delights. · · · 103 F6 Celia 2 18
The memorie delights him more, from whom · · · 153 U13 Sacvile 21
Who (amongst these delights) would not forget · · · 290 U85 Country 37
Delights, nor credulous hope of mutuall Joy, · · · 293 U86 Hor.4:1 30
Of two, the choicest Paire of Mans delights, · · · 401 Filmer 4
DELIVER
That heard but Spight deliver · · · · · 367 Ode Who saith 58
DELIVER'D
Shee lies deliver'd, without paine, · · · 251 U74 Weston 5
Seal'd and deliver'd to her, in the sight · · · 400 Lady Ogle 37
DELPHICK
With Delphick fire: · · · · · 177 U25 Desmond 12
Now differ'd not from Delphick riddling. · · · 319 Horace 310
DELUDE
Cannot we delude the eyes · · · · 102 F5 Celia 1 11
DELUDED
From off her pillow, and deluded bed; · · · 283 U84 Muse 43
DELYGHT
As shall besides delyght · · · · · 420 Ode:If Men 33
DEMAND
Could you demand the gifts you gave, againe? · · · 192 U38 Elegy 'Tis 55
DEMERIT
There is no Father that for one demerit, · · · 192 U38 Elegy 'Tis 41
DEMOCRITE
Whereof old Democrite, and Hill Nicholas, · · · 87 E133 Voyage 128
DEMOCRITUS
Because Democritus beleeves a wit · · · · 325 Horace 419
DENIE
Who dares denie, that all first-fruits are due · · 235 U63 Charles 2 1
The Kings fame lives. Go now, denie his Teirce. · · 241 U68 House-hold 14
DENIED
Was it because thou wert of old denied · · · 203 U43 Vulcan 11
Wast not hee: thou wert of old denied · · · 203 U43 Vulcan V 11
If you denied, you had no better straine, · · · 333 Horace 625
DENIES
To God, denies the God-head to be true: · · · 235 U63 Charles 2 2
Which he not denies. Now being so free, · · · 381 Coryat 3 57
DENIS
To be the Denis of thy Father's School, · · · 410 Gill 7

	Page	Title	Line
DENMARKE			
Nor did the king of Denmarke him salute,	63	E97 Motion	15
DENY			
It will deny all; and forsweare it too:	74	E115 Honest Man	19
I not deny it, but to helpe the need	155	U13 Sacvile	75
And not the bounties you ha' done, deny.	192	U38 Elegy 'Tis	54
DENYD'ST			
Eternall God the Sonne, who not denyd'st	128	U1 Trinitie	21
DENY'D			
To Clifton's bloud, that is deny'd their name.	119	F13 Aubigny	98
DENYED			
I ask'd a lord a buck, and he denyed me;	54	E84 Bedford 2	2
DENYES			
So court a mistris, shee denyes you;	104	F7 Women but	3
DEPART			
I may dilate my selfe, but not depart.	194	U38 Elegy 'Tis	118
My health will leave me; and when you depart,	199	U41 Elegy Since	13
If ne're so little it depart the first,	331	Horace	563
DEPARTED			
About the shore, of farts, but late departed,	87	E133 Voyage	125
When shee departed? you will meet her there,	285	U84 Muse	108
DEPARTING			
Heare, Mistris, your departing servant tell	199	U41 Elegy Since	2
As his departing take much thence: lest, then,	317	Horace	251
DEPARTS			
He that departs with his owne honesty	27	E2 My Booke	13
DEPEND			
Those are poore Ties, depend on those false ends,	216	U45 Squib	11
DEPENDENTS			
Nor glad as those, that old dependents bee,	47	E64 Salisbury 3	5
DEPENDING			
Delay is bad, doubt worse, depending worst;	50	E70 Wm Roe 1	5
You are depending on his word, and will;	119	F13 Aubigny	114
DEPOSITED			
And trusted so, as it deposited lay	271	U81 Pawlet	81
DEPRAVE			
And thence, deprave thee, and thy worke. To those	72	E111 Edmonds 2	11
DEPREST			
whom fortune hath deprest; come nere the fates	422	Lucan	4
whom, yf fortune hath deprest; come nere the fates	422	Lucan	V 4
DEPRIVE			
Of Death, and Darknesse; and deprive	273	U84 Cradle	5
DEPTH			
Doth mete, whose lyne doth sound the depth of things:)	176	U24 Frontispice	12
Shall find their depth: they're sounded with a spoone.	198	U40 Elegy That	30
DERIDE			
As what th'have lost t'expect, they dare deride.	116	F13 Aubigny	4
In smiling L'envoye, as he would deride	202	U42 Elegy Let	75
DESCEND			
Seldome descend but bleeding to their grave.	363	Murder	2
DESCENDED			
Descended in a rope of Titles, be	215	U44 Speach	80
DESCENT			
But, here's a Song of her Descent;	273	U84 Cradle	29
2. The Song of her Descent.	274	U84 Descent	Ttl
I Sing the just, and uncontrol'd Descent	274	U84 Descent	1
Nay they will venter ones Descent to hitt,	394	Jane Ogle	11
DESCRIBE			
But hold my torch, while I describe the entry	85	E133 Voyage	58
DESCRIB'D			
Describ'd, it 's thus: Defin'd would you it have?	75	E115 Honest Man	33
To be describ'd by a Monogram,	227	U52 Answer	11
To be describ'd! Fames fingers are too foule	269	U81 Pawlet	30
Or Rainbow is describ'd. But here was now	305	Horace	23
Of Poems here describ'd, I can, nor use,	311	Horace	127
DESCRIBED			
9. Her man described by her owne Dictamen.	140	U2 Her man	Ttl
DESCRIDE			
The good, from bad, is not descride,	146	U6 Defence	17
DESCRIPTION			
Suffers no name, but a description:	74	E115 Honest Man	4
By description, but my Mother!	136	U2 Cupid	12
DESERT			
6. Clayming a second kisse by Desert.	137	U2 Kisse	Ttl
To your desert, who'have done it, Friend. And this	389	Aleman	21
nor cann be of desert,	420	Ode:If Men	13
DESERTED			
But antiquated, and deserted lye	392	Shakespeare	53
DESERTS			
And giving dues to all Mankinds deserts!	289	U84 Muse	224
DESERVE			
These, disease, will thee deserve:	106	F8 Sicknesse	43
These, disease, will they deserve:	106	F8 Sicknesse	V 43
To others, as he will deserve the Trust	198	U40 Elegy That	39
Can doe the things that Statues doe deserve,	261	U77 Treasurer	15
Such Bookes deserve Translators, of like coate	389	Aleman	11
And doth deserve all muniments of praise,	400	Beaumont	9
DESERV'D			
An Epitaph, deserv'd a Tombe:	152	U12 Corbet	38
I had deserv'd, then, thy consuming lookes,	203	U43 Vulcan	17
Thou hast deserv'd: And let me reade the while	398	Drayton	60
(You have deserv'd it from me) I have read,	415	Rutter	13

	Page	Title	Line

DESERVEDLY
All which thou hast incurr'd deservedly: · · · · · 410 Gill 5
DESERVES
Though every fortitude deserves applause, · · · · 49 E66 Cary 15
Deserves no pardon; or who'd play, and sing · · · 329 Horace 531
DESERVING
Not a worke deserving Baies, · · · · · 183 U29 Fit of Rime 28
Nor a lyne deserving praise, · · · · · 183 U29 Fit of Rime 29
To my worthy, and deserving Brother · · · · · 666 Glover 1
DESIGNE
In every counsell, stratageme, designe, · · · · 71 E110 Edmonds 1 19
What is't to me whether the French Designe · · · 219 U47 Tribe 31
But fate doth so alternate the designe, · · · · 246 U70 Ode 95
Not to designe the whole. Should I aspire · · · 307 Horace 49
Terme of the Architects is called Designe! · · · 404 Inigo Jones 1 56
Aymd at in thy omnipotent Designe! · · · · 406 Inigo Jones 1 96
He may have skill & judgment to designe · · · 406 Inigo Jones 2 7
Will well designe thee, to be viewd of all · · · 408 Inigo Jones 3 12
Which, chang'd, a five-fold mysterie designe, · · · 412 Ghyrlond 2
DESIGN'D
And thou design'd to be the same thou art, · · · 49 E67 Suffolk 9
To whom all Lovers are design'd, · · · · 173 U22 Elegy Tho 26
The Heaven design'd, draw next a Spring, · · · 276 U84 Body 21
DESIGNED
For his designed worke, the perfect end · · · · 288 U84 Muse 206
DESIGNES
Nature her selfe was proud of his designes, · · · 392 Shakespeare 47
DESIGNETH
That scarse the Towne designeth any feast · · · 81 E129 Mime 5
DESIRE
What kinde of creature I could most desire, · · · 52 E76 Bedford 1 3
Doe equally desire your companie: · · · · 64 E101 Supper 2
And your high names: I doe desire, that thence · · · 69 E108 Soldiers 3
like glasse, blowne up, and fashion'd by desire. · · 108 F10 Proludium 4
The thing, they here call Love, is blinde Desire, · · 110 F11 Epode 37
Would, at suggestion of a steepe desire, · · · 111 F11 Epode 63
To heare, to mediate, sweeten my desire, · · · 128 U1 Trinitie 42
All that heard her, with desire. · · · · 139 U2 Promise 6
To meet their high desire; · · · · · 144 U3 Musicall 26
To vent that poore desire, · · · · · 150 U10 Jealousie 5
In all my wild desire, · · · · · 151 U11 Dreame 11
You then, whose will not only, but desire · · · 153 U13 Sacvile 7
Who more they burne, they more desire, · · · 189 U36 Song 10
Had I fore-knowne of this thy least desire · · · 205 U43 Vulcan 59
Had I fore-knowne but of thy least desire · · · 205 U43 Vulcan V 59
My Princes safetie, and my Kings desire; · · · 219 U47 Tribe 38
To forme a worke, I would no more desire · · · 307 Horace 50
To frame a worke, I would no more desire · · · 339 Horace V 52/ 50
Heare, what it is the People, and I desire: · · · 315 Horace 219
Of money, haughtie, to desire soon mov'd, · · · 315 Horace 235
Two noble knightes, whome true desire and zeale, · 382 Rich 1
Who cannot reade, but onely doth desire · · · 383 Author 9
DESIR'D
But these, desir'd by you, the makers ends · · · 60 E94 Bedford 3 5
Be more, and long desir'd: · · · · · 121 F14 Sydney 55
Much more desir'd, and dearer then before, · · · 285 U84 Muse 109
But Sorrow, she desir'd no other Friend: · · · 394 Jane Ogle 17
DESIRED
To one that desired me not to name him. · · · 53 E77 Not name Ttl
Desired Justice to the publique Weale, · · · 217 U46 Coke 16
DESIRES
Shine bright on every harth as the desires · · · 95 F2 Penshurst 78
Nor looke too kind on my desires, · · · · 144 U4 Song 7
Love lights his torches to inflame desires; · · · 170 U19 Elegy By 2
Yet, as we may, we will, with chast desires, · · · 257 U75 Epithalam. 161
she desires of every birth · · · · · 417 Moon 19
DESKE
But in my Deske, what was there to accite · · · 206 U43 Vulcan 85
But in my Deske, what was there to envite · · · 206 U43 Vulcan V 85
DESMOND
An Ode to James Earle of Desmond, writ . . . · · · 176 U25 Desmond Ttl
DESPAIRE (See also DISPAIRE)
As light breakes from you, that affrights despaire, · 191 U38 Elegy 'Tis 10
Doe not despaire my mending; to distrust · · · 192 U38 Elegy 'Tis 49
DESPAIR'D
Is not to be despair'd of, for our money; · · · 65 E101 Supper 14
Losse, remaines yet, as much despair'd as mine. · · 211 U43 Vulcan V196
DESPAIRES
What he despaires, being handled, might not show. · 315 Horace 214
And despaires day, but for thy Volumes light. · · 392 Shakespeare 80
DESPERATE
A desperate soloecisme in truth and wit. · · · 75 E116 Jephson 16
But more licentious made, and desperate! · · · 163 U15 Friend-Wars 36
Or doe upon my selfe some desperate ill; · · · 191 U38 Elegy 'Tis 3
DESPIGHT
Wrung on the Withers, by Lord Loves despight, · · 201 U42 Elegy Let 63
At Common-Law: me thinkes in his despight · · 211 U43 Vulcan 177
At Common-Law: me thinkes in this despight · · 211 U43 Vulcan V177
DESPISE (See also DISPISED)
A broken heart thou wert not wont despise, · · · 127 U1 Trinitie 10
DESPIS'D
Yet is the office not to be despis'd, · · · · 78 E121 Rudyerd 1 5

DESPITE
  Give cause to some of wonnder, some despite,   •   •   •   420   Ode:If Men   35
DESTIN'D
  And destin'd unto judgement, after all.   •   •   •   122   F15 Heaven   20
  Englands high Chancellor: the destin'd heire   •   •   225   U51 Bacon   13
DESTINIE
  Of destinie, and spin her owne free houres.   •   •   52   E76 Bedford 1   16
  Be brought by us to meet our Destinie.   •   •   •   170   U18 Elegy Can   20
DESTINIES
  Hence was it, that the destinies decreed   •   •   •   53   E79 Rutland   5
DESTITUTE
  When a good Cause is destitute of friends,   •   •   186   U32 Elsmere   2
DESTROY
  Lest shame destroy their being.   •   •   •   •   144   U4 Song   4
  That you should be too noble to destroy.   •   •   •   191   U38 Elegy 'Tis   12
  Consumptions nature to destroy, and sterve.   •   •   192   U38 Elegy 'Tis   62
  To shift their seasons, and destroy their powers!   •   199   U41 Elegy Since   10
  Whose chearfull look our sadnesse doth destroy,   •   414   Ghyrlond   43
DESTROY'D
  'Tis true, that in thy wish they were destroy'd,   •   210   U43 Vulcan   167
DESTROYES
  Whose od'rous breath destroyes   •   •   •   112   F11 Epode   96
  That eats on wits, and Arts, and destroyes them both.   •   174   U23 Himselfe   6
DESTRUCTION
  But in the practisd truth Destruction is   •   •   404   Inigo Jones 1   57
DESYROUS
  If thou be soe desyrous to be read,   •   •   •   408   Inigo Jones 3   9
DETRACTOR
  To my Detractor.   •   •   •   •   •   408   Detractor   Ttl
DEVICE
  For thy late sharpe device. I say 'tis fit   •   •   36   E29 Tilter   3
DEVIL   (See DIVELL)
DEVOTE
  In all her petite actions, so devote,   •   •   •   287   U84 Muse   177
DEVOTION
  I. Poems Of Devotion.   •   •   •   •   127   Under-wood   Ttl
DEVOTIONS
  For her devotions, and those sad essayes   •   •   287   U84 Muse   181
DEVOURE
  Woman-kinde; devoure the wast   •   •   •   105   F8 Sicknesse   16
  Eate on her clients, and some one devoure.   •   119   F13 Aubigny   88
  Or urge thy Greedie flame, thus to devoure   •   202   U43 Vulcan   3
  Or beg thy Greedie flame, thus to devoure   •   202   U43 Vulcan   V 3
DEVOURES
  The sluggish gaping auditor devoures;   •   •   45   E56 Poet-Ape   10
DEVOUT
  No lesse than if from perill; and devout,   •   •   43   E51 James 3   7
DEW   (See also DEAW)
  Even in the dew of grace, what you would bee?   •   67   E104 Montgomery   2
  The Sunne his heat, and light, the ayre his dew?   •   192   U38 Elegy 'Tis   57
  And in a dew of sweetest Raine,   •   •   •   251   U74 Weston   4
  Look pale, distill a dew was never meant   •   •   353   Horace   V612
DEXTEROUSLY
  Which how Dexterously I doe,   •   •   •   133   U2 Suffered   25
DIALOGUE
  The Musicall Strife; In a Pastorall Dialogue.   •   •   143   U3 Musicall   Ttl
  Ode IX. 3 Booke, to Lydia. Dialogue of Horace, and Lydia.   293   U87 Hor.3:9   Ttl
DIALOGUES
  Knew I, that all their Dialogues, and discourse,   •   172   U20 Shrub   13
DIAN
  Made Dian, not his notes refuse?   •   •   •   182   U27 Ode Helen   28
DIANA'
  Diana'alone, so hit, and hunted so.   •   •   •   68   E105 L Wroth 2   14
DIANA'ALONE
  Diana'alone, so hit, and hunted so.   •   •   •   68   E105 L Wroth 2   14
DIANA'S
  Diana's Grove, or Altar, with the bor-/Dring   •   •   305   Horace   20
  Diana's Grove, or Altar, with the nether   •   •   338   Horace   V 20
DICE
  At dice his borrow'd money: which, god payes.   •   30   E12 Shift   12
  Of solemne greatnesse. And he dares, at dice,   •   36   E28 Surly   16
  Whose dice not doing well, to'a pulpit ran.   •   •   76   E119 Shelton   6
  The Dice with glassen eyes, to the glad viewes   •   166   U15 Friend-Wars   138
  The Dice with glassen eyes, to the glad Viewers   •   166   U15 Friend-Wars   V138
DICK
  I had you for a Servant, once, Dick Brome;   •   •   409   Brome   1
DICTAMEN
  9. Her man described by her owne Dictamen.   •   •   140   U2 Her man   Ttl
DID
  When men a dangerous disease did scape,   •   •   31   E13 Empirick   1
  As theirs did with thee, mine might credit get: •   32   E18 Censurer   6
  That selfe-divided Belgia did afford;   •   •   37   E32 Roe 2   3
  And to conceale your ulcers, did advise,   •   •   38   E38 Guiltie 2   2
  Great heav'n did well, to give ill fame free wing;   •   43   E51 James 3   2
  Which though it did but panick terror prove,   •   43   E51 James 3   3
  Long-gathering Old-end, I did feare thee wise,   •   43   E53 Old-end   1
  Of love, and what the golden age did hold   •   •   47   E64 Salisbury 3   3
  Could conquer thee, but chance, who did betray.   •   49   E66 Cary   10
  T'inveigh 'gainst playes: what did he then but play?   •   52   E75 Lippe   4
  O Madame, if your grant did thus transferre mee,   •   55   E84 Bedford 2   9
  Or had his father, when he did him get,   •   •   56   E88 Monsieur   9
  Out-stript, then they did all that went before: •   57   E89 Allen   10
  Weare this renowne. 'Tis just, that who did give   •   57   E89 Allen   13

DID (cont.)

						Page	Title	Line

When on thy trumpet shee did sound a blast, ... 58 E91 Vere 7
Who did, alike with thee, thy house up-beare, . . . 60 E93 Radcliffe 3
Nor did the king of Denmarke him salute, ... 63 E97 Motion 15
That but the twi-light of your sprite did see, . . . 66 E103 L Wroth 1 2
Were they that nam'd you, prophets? Did they see, . . 67 E104 Montgomery 1
Or did our times require it, to behold . . . . 67 E104 Montgomery 3
To make those faithfull, did the Fates send you? . . 67 E104 Montgomery 6
What at Ligorne, Rome, Florence you did doe: . . . 69 E107 Hungry 14
Your great profession; which I once, did prove: . . 70 E108 Soldiers 6
And did not shame it with my actions, then, . . . 70 E108 Soldiers 7
So did thy vertue'enforme, thy wit sustaine . . . 75 E116 Jephson 3
That bloud not mindes, but mindes did bloud adorne: . . 75 E116 Jephson 11
'Twas a child, that so did thrive . . . . 77 E120 S. P. 5
And did act (what now we mone) . . . . 77 E120 S. P. 13
Which in life did harbour give . . . . 79 E124 Elizabeth 5
I pluck'd a branch; the jealous god did frowne, . . 80 E126 Mrs Cary 3
Did dance the famous Morrisse, unto Norwich) . . . 85 E133 Voyage 36
Ycleped Mud, which, when their oares did once stirre, . 85 E133 Voyage 62
Crack did report it selfe, as if a cloud . . . 86 E133 Voyage 94
Their Mercury did now. By this, the stemme . . . 87 E133 Voyage 111
Never did bottom more betray her burden: . . . 87 E133 Voyage 116
Against their breasts. Here, sev'rall ghosts did flit . 87 E133 Voyage 124
And that ours did. For, yet, no nare was tainted, . . 87 E133 Voyage 133
And so they did, from Styx, to Acheron: . . . 88 E133 Voyage 141
But still, it seem'd, the ranknesse did convince 'hem. . 88 E133 Voyage 152
Thrise did it spit: thrise div'd. At last, it view'd . 88 E133 Voyage 162
It is enough, they once did get . . . . 93 F1 Why write no 5
The milke, nor oyle, did ever flowe soe free . . . 98 F3 Wroth V 60
From whence, so lately, I did burne, ... 101 F4 To the World 27
Thy thoughts did never melt in amorous fire, . . . 108 F10 Proludium 3
Moodes, which the god-like Sydney oft did prove, . . 116 F12 Rutland 91
And your brave friend, and mine so well did love. . . 116 F12 Rutland 92
And your brave friend, and mine to well did love. . . 116 F12 Rutland V 92
The Angels so did sound it, ... 130 U1 Nativitie 3
That did us all salvation bring, ... 130 U1 Nativitie 8
The Word, which heaven, and earth did make; . . . 130 U1 Nativitie 11
And her dressing did out-brave . . . . 132 U2 How he saw 3
And (withall) I did untie . . . . 132 U2 How he saw 11
But the Arrow home did draw . . . . 133 U2 Suffered 14
Of th'Assembly, as did you! . . . . 138 U2 Kisse 12
Or, that did you sit, or walke, ... 138 U2 Kisse 13
And did think, such Rites were due . . . . 138 U2 Kisse 19
Or, if you did move to night . . . . 138 U2 Kisse 21
And a woman God did make me: . . . . 140 U2 Her man 6
And every close did meet . . . . 149 U9 Picture 7
He did me the Delight, ... 151 U11 Dreame 8
That though they did possesse each limbe, . . . 151 U12 Corbet 9
Reader, whose life, and name, did e're become . . . 152 U12 Corbet 37
And in the Act did so my blush prevent, . . . 153 U13 Sacvile 11
As I did feele it done, as soone as meant: . . . 153 U13 Sacvile 12
Or if he did it not to succour me, ... 154 U13 Sacvile 29
Then give it to the Hound that did him bite; . . . 155 U13 Sacvile 70
Sydney e're night! or that did goe to bed . . . 157 U13 Sacvile 127
Thither it flowes. How much did Stallion spend . . 163 U15 Friend-Wars 47
And last, blaspheme not, we did never heare . . . 168 U15 Friend-Wars 191
Can Beautie that did prompt me first to write, . . . 169 U18 Elegy Can 1
Now threaten, with those meanes she did invite? . . 169 U18 Elegy Can 2
Did her perfections call me on to gaze, . . . 169 U18 Elegy Can 3
Helen, did Homer never see . . . . 181 U27 Ode Helen 1
Did Sappho on her seven-tongu'd Lute, . . . 181 U27 Ode Helen 3
In whom Anacreon once did joy, ... 181 U27 Ode Helen 6
As he whom Maro did rehearse? . . . . 181 U27 Ode Helen 8
All Parnassus Greene did wither, ... 183 U29 Fit of Rime 17
Pegasus did flie away, ... 183 U29 Fit of Rime 19
At the Well no Muse did stay, ... 183 U29 Fit of Rime 20
Starveling rimes did fill the Stage, ... 183 U29 Fit of Rime 25
Whose Offices, and honours did surprize, . . . 185 U30 Burleigh 15
What did she worth thy spight? were there not store . . 188 U34 Small Poxe 3
Then this did by her true? She never sought . . . 188 U34 Small Poxe 5
That friendship which no chance but love did chuse, . . 190 U37 Friend-Book 23
Why was't? did e're the Cloudes aske back their raine? . 192 U38 Elegy 'Tis 56
No Poets verses yet did ever move, ... 199 U42 Elegy Let 3
Whose Readers did not thinke he was in love. . . . 199 U42 Elegy Let 4
An Officer there, did make most solemne love, . . . 201 U42 Elegy Let 53
He did lay up, and would adore the shooe, . . . 201 U42 Elegy Let 55
Did I there wound the honours of the Crowne? . . . 203 U43 Vulcan 23
And so did Jove, who ne're meant thee his Cup: . . 208 U43 Vulcan 115
There were, that streight did nose it out for newes, . . 209 U43 Vulcan V139
Kindled the fire! But then, did one returne, . . . 209 U43 Vulcan 149
Hee is true Vulcan still! He did not spare . . . 210 U43 Vulcan 159
He was right Vulcan still! He did not spare . . . 210 U43 Vulcan V159
Did not she save from thence, to build a Rome? . . 210 U43 Vulcan 162
Who from the Divels-Arse did Guns beget; . . . 212 U43 Vulcan 202
That from the Divels-Arse did Guns beget; . . . 212 U43 Vulcan V202
Who with the Divell did Ordinance beget; . . . 212 U43 Vulcan V202
For they did see it the last tilting well, . . . 213 U44 Speach 6
Well did thy craftie Clerke, and Knight, Sir Hugh, . . 214 U44 Speach 33
That never yet did friend, or friendship seeke . . . 218 U47 Tribe 14
Nay, so your Seate his beauties did endorse, . . . 228 U53 Newcastle 11
You won them too, your oddes did merit it. . . . 230 U56 Covell 4
As they out-did the lightning in the course; . . . 233 U59 Newcastle 12
When the Prodigious Hannibal did crowne . . . 242 U70 Ode 3

	Page	Title	Line
DID (cont.)			
Did wiser Nature draw thee back,	243	U70 Ode	11
Did wisest Nature draw thee back,	243	U70 Ode	V 11
What did this Stirrer, but die late?	243	U70 Ode	30
For three of his foure-score, he did no good.	243	U70 Ode	32
So deep, as he did then death's waters sup;	244	U70 Ode	41
No pleasures vaine did chime,	246	U70 Ode	102
Or so did shine,	253	U75 Epithalam.	22
And all did ring th'approches of the Bride;	253	U75 Epithalam.	36
As she did lack	254	U75 Epithalam.	46
As they did lack	254	U75 Epithalam.	V 46
Have they bedew'd the Earth, where she did tread,	254	U75 Epithalam.	V 66
As if her ayrie steps did spring the flowers,	254	U75 Epithalam.	67
Of all that Nature, yet, to life did bring;	264	U79 New-yeares	33
What she did here, by great example, well,	269	U81 Pawlet	33
What she did by a great example, well,	269	U81 Pawlet	V 33
How did she leave the world? with what contempt?	270	U81 Pawlet	47
Of her disease, how did her soule assure	270	U81 Pawlet	50
Let Angels sing her glories, who did call	270	U81 Pawlet	63
On Nature, for her: who did let her lie,	282	U84 Muse	13
To one she said, Doe this, he did it; So	287	U84 Muse	169
He run; and all did strive with diligence	287	U84 Muse	171
Her broken sighes did never misse whole sense:	288	U84 Muse	185
And ('bout thy Ivory neck,) no youth did fling	293	U87 Hor.3:9	2
Nor after Chloe did his Lydia sound;	293	U87 Hor.3:9	6
Nor so begin, as did that Circler late,	313	Horace	195
Nor from the brand, with which the life did burne	315	Horace	207
From the two Egges, that did disclose the twins.	315	Horace	210
Till then unknowne, in Carts, wherein did ride	319	Horace	313
Those that did sing, and act: their faces dy'd	319	Horace	314
Hee too, that did in Tragick Verse contend	319	Horace	319
For the vile Goat, soone after, forth did send	319	Horace	320
Nor is't long since, they did with patience take	323	Horace	375
Our Ancestors did Plautus numbers praise,	323	Horace	399
Nor did they merit the lesse Crowne to weare,	323	Horace	406
For choller! If I did not, who could bring	325	Horace	430
For Choler! if I did not, none could bring	349	Horace	V430
On edge the Masculine spirits, and did whet	327	Horace	494
Their minds to Warres, with rimes they did rehearse;	329	Horace	495
The wished goale, both did, and suffer'd much	333	Horace	588
And both from Wine, and Women did abstaine.	333	Horace	590
Did learne them first, and once a Master fear'd.	333	Horace	592
To let it downe, who knowes, if he did cast	335	Horace	656
Nor did he doe this once; for if you can	335	Horace	667
Nor did he do this, once; if yet you can	355	Horace	V667
First: thy successe did strike my sence with wonder;	361	Palmer	5
did sparcle foorth in Center of the rest:	361	Palmer	16
I struggled with this passion that did drowne	362	Palmer	28
Did never dint the breast of Tamisis.	366	Ode Who saith	8
It should rather have bene Tom that a horse did lack.	374	Coryat 1	15
For he did but kisse her, and so let her go.	375	Coryat 1	19
To lie at Livory, while the Horses did stand.	375	Coryat 1	33
How long he did stay, at what signe he did Inne.	380	Coryat 3	26
Doth he once dissemble, but tels he did ride	380	Coryat 3	52
Some want, they say in a sort he did crave:	380	Coryat 3	55
I writ he onely his taile there did wave;	380	Coryat 3	56
Out-bee that Wife, in worth, thy freind did make:	384	Somerset	12
which, did they neere so neate, or proudly dwell,	387	Cavendish	3
Sent forth, or since did from their ashes come.	391	Shakespeare	40
That so did take Eliza, and our James!	392	Shakespeare	74
Whom shee, with Sorrow first did lodge, then feast,	394	Jane Ogle	20
Did all so strike me, as I cry'd, who can	397	Drayton	31
That ever yet did fire the English blood!	397	Drayton	57
As, on two flowry Carpets, that did rise,	398	Drayton	81
Fames heate upon the grave did stay;	400	Lady Ogle	28
For this did Katherine, Ladie Ogle, die	400	Lady Ogle	33
Who did this Knot compose,	401	Filmer	7
Which I, your Master, first did teach the Age.	409	Brome	8
That Frindshipp, which noe Chaunce, but Love did Chuse,	422	Censure	16
Tell her, his Muse that did invent thee	662	Bedford	5
DID'ST			
Then thou did'st late my sense, loosing my points.	45	E58 Groome	6
Did'st thou, then, make 'hem! and what praise was heap'd	95	F2 Penshurst	83
Thou did'st abuse, and then betray;	101	F4 To the World	42
But thou thereon did'st onely breath,	106	F9 Celia 3	13
Eternall Father, God, who did'st create	127	U1 Trinitie	17
Thou stand'st as if some Mysterie thou did'st!	225	U51 Bacon	4
Wise child, did'st hastily returne,	242	U70 Ode	7
DIDST			
If thou'ldst but use thy faith, as thou didst then,	32	E18 Censurer	7
But when (in place) thou didst the patrons choose,	43	E53 Old-end	4
For all thou hear'st, thou swear'st thy selfe didst doo.	54	E81 Proule	5
As if the generall store thou didst command	187	U33 Councellour	26
Thou didst tell me; and wert o're-joy'd to peepe	201	U42 Elegy Let	59
But, on thy malice, tell me, didst thou spie	203	U43 Vulcan	19
And didst invade part of the Common-wealth,	210	U43 Vulcan	170
How summ'd a circle didst thou leave man-kind	243	U70 Ode	9
And tell, how farre thou didst our Lily out-shine,	391	Shakespeare	29
DIE (See also DYE)			
Lash'd by their consciences, to die, affeard.	84	E133 Voyage	18
All the world for love may die.	131	U2 Excuse	24
For, if such men as he could die,	168	U16 Gray	6
Knowledge, that sleepes, doth die;	174	U23 Himselfe	3

DIE (cont.)
  They die with their conceits, ...   175   U23 Himselfe   23
  Rap't from the Earth, as not to die?   181   U27 Ode Helen   14
  And Apollo's Musique die, ...   183   U29 Fit of Rime   23
  That makes us live, not that which calls to die.   .   193   U38 Elegy 'Tis   78
  Rather then once displease you more, to die,   .   .   193   U38 Elegy 'Tis   92
  Burne to a snuffe, and then stinke out, and die: .   211   U43 Vulcan   188
  wast to a snuffe, and then stinke out, and die: .   211   U43 Vulcan   V188
  What did this Stirrer, but die late?   .   .   .   243   U70 Ode   30
  Although it fall, and die that night;   .   .   .   245   U70 Ode   71
  Alive, which else would die, ...   257   U75 Epithalam.   151
  With admiration, and applause to die!   .   .   .   270   U81 Pawlet   62
  When we were all borne, we began to die;   .   .   271   U81 Pawlet   94
  And saw that portion of her selfe to die.   .   .   282   U84 Muse   14
  As, for her, I'ld not feare to die,   .   .   .   293   U87 Hor.3:9   11
  Yet would I wish to love, live, die with thee.   .   294   U87 Hor.3:9   24
  For this did Katherine, Ladie Ogle, die   .   .   400   Lady Ogle   33
DI'D
  That bred them, graves: when they were borne, they di'd,   .   114   F12 Rutland   47
DIE'D
  not when I die'd, but how I livd. Farewell.   .   .   387   Cavendish   12
DIES
  Hee, that but living halfe his dayes, dies such,   .   .   295   U89 Mart.8:77   7
DIET (See also DYET)
  Praise the spare diet, wholsome justice, lawes,   .   .   317   Horace   283
DIETIE
  And you are he: the Dietie   173   U22 Elegy Tho   25
DIFFER
  Invention. Now, to speake; and then differ   .   .   307   Horace   61
  Is now to speak, and even now to differ   .   .   .   339   Horace   V 61
  It much will differ, if a God speake, than,   .   .   313   Horace   161
  To Dance, so she should, shamefac'd, differ farre   .   321   Horace   339
DIFFER'D
  Now differ'd not from Delphick riddling.   .   .   .   319   Horace   310
DIFFERENCE
  Discern'd no difference of his yeeres, or play,   .   .   57   E90 Mill   8
  That Nature no such difference had imprest   .   .   75   E116 Jephson   9
  Shee learnes to know long difference of their states.   .   78   E121 Rudyerd 1   4
  Their difference, cannot choose which you will be.   .   157   U13 Sacvile   154
  O bountie! so to difference the rates!   .   .   .   235   U62 Charles 1   12
  As not make difference, whether Davus speake,   .   .   321   Horace   345
DIFFERENT
  To murther different hearts, ...   110   F11 Epode   52
DIFFERING
  your workes thus differing, troth let soe your style: .   .   407   Inigo Jones 2   19
DIFFERS
  Where the midst differs from the first: or where   .   .   315   Horace   217
DIGBY
  An Epigram To my Muse, the Lady Digby, ...   262   U78 Digby   Ttl
  To Sir Kenelme Digby. An Epigram   262   U78 Digby   VTtl
  - - - on her Husband, Sir Kenelme Digby.   .   .   .   262   U78 Digby   Ttl
  Tho', happy Muse, thou know my Digby well;   .   .   262   U78 Digby   1
  - - - Of that truly-noble Lady, the Lady Venetia Digby, . . .   272   U84 Eupheme   Ttl
  Of Dame Venetia Digby, styl'd The Faire: .   .   .   274   U84 Descent   2
  - - - the Lady Venetia Digby; who living, ...   282   U84 Muse   Ttl
DIGESTIVE
  Digestive cheese, and fruit there sure will bee;   .   .   65   E101 Supper   27
DIGESTS
  Code, Digests, Pandects of all faemale glory!   .   .   399   Lady Ogle   8
DIGNIFIE
  But that your worth will dignifie our feast,   .   .   64   E101 Supper   4
DIGNITIE
  And to your Scene lent no lesse dignitie   .   .   .   67   E104 Montgomery   7
  And what of Dignitie, and Honour may   .   .   .   255   U75 Epithalam.   92
DIGNITIES
  Wrestlest with dignities, or fain'st a scope   .   .   70   E109 Nevil   6
  To lose the formes, and dignities of men,   .   .   166   U15 Friend-Wars 146
DIKE
  As Stiles, Dike, Ditchfield, Millar, Crips, and Fen: .   214   U44 Speach   54
  To cut a Dike? or sticke a Stake up, here,   .   .   401   Beaumont   12
DILATE
  I may dilate my selfe, but not depart.   .   .   .   194   U38 Elegy 'Tis   118
DILIGENCE
  He run; and all did strive with diligence   .   .   287   U84 Muse   171
DILIGENT
  Where some great Lady, or her diligent Nourse;   .   .   313   Horace   164
DIMENSION
  To his bountie; by dimension   259   U76 Petition   V 9
DIMENSIONS
  Both whose dimensions, lost, the world might finde   .   79   E125 Uvedale   3
DIMME
  To dimme and drowne   369   Ode Who saith   108
DIMN'D
  Her Ovid gave her, dimn'd the fame   181   U27 Ode Helen   18
DINE
  A chamber-critick, and dost dine, and sup   .   .   .   50   E72 Court-ling   2
  At every meale, where it doth dine, or sup,   .   .   74   E115 Honest Man   23
  At great mens tables) and yet dine away.   .   .   .   95   F2 Penshurst   66
  These, had'st thou pleas'd either to dine, or sup,   .   206   U43 Vulcan   83
  These, had'st thou pleas'd either to dine, or sup,   .   206   U43 Vulcan   V 83
  I Am to dine, Friend, where I must be weigh'd   .   .   229   U54 Squib   1
DIN'D
  At Bread-streets Mermaid, having din'd, and merry,   .   .   85   E133 Voyage   37

		Page	Title	Line

DIN'D (cont.)
The Child, when Lamia'has din'd, out of her maw. . . . 329 Horace 510
DING
See you yond' Motion? Not the old Fa-ding, . . . 62 E97 Motion 1
DINNER
Of Sheriffes dinner, or Majors feast. . . . . 96 F3 Wroth 6
Of Sergeants dinner, or sheriffes feast. . . . . 96 F3 Wroth V 6
DINT
Did never dint the breast of Tamisis. . . . 366 Ode Who saith 8
DIOMEDE
Of Diomede; nor Troyes sad Warre begins . . . 315 Horace 209
DIOSCURI
twi-/Lights, the Dioscuri; . . . . . 246 U70 Ode 93
DIRCAEAN
The cleare Dircaean Fount . . . . . 366 Ode Who saith 19
DIRE
To this dire passage. Say, thou stop thy nose: . . 85 E133 Voyage 59
DIRECT
How upward, and direct! . . . . . 366 Ode Who saith 11
DIRECTLY
Which being eyed directly, I divine, ... 362 Author 13
DIRECTS
That guides the Motions, and directs the beares. . . 219 U47 Tribe 50
DIRTIE
Withall, the dirtie paines those Citizens take, . . 213 U44 Speach 15
DIRTY
Thy Dirty braines, Men smell thy want of worth. . . 409 Detractor 22
DIS
And so my sharpnesse thou no lesse dis-joynts, . . . 45 E58 Groome 5
As free simplicitie, to dis-avow, ... 62 E96 Donne 2 5
Which though the turning world may dis-esteeme, . . 118 F13 Aubigny 64
Antiquities search'd! Opinions dis-esteem'd! . . . 160 U14 Selden 40
Or the dis-favour . . . . . 177 U25 Desmond 33
Or two, or three, a Sonne will dis-inherit, . . . 192 U38 Elegy 'Tis 42
And us dis-joyn'd force to her brazen yoke, . . . 294 U87 Hor.3:9 18
The last doth from the midst dis-joyn'd appeare. . . 315 Horace 218
DIS-AVOW
As free simplicitie, to dis-avow, ... 62 E96 Donne 2 5
DISAVOW
Or Plautus, and in Virgil disavow, ... 309 Horace 78
DISCARD
And sworne, that he will quite discard thee . . . 662 Bedford 7
DISCERNE
Can I discerne how shadowes are decreast, . . . 156 U13 Sacvile 118
Discerne betweene a Statue, and a Man; . . . 261 U77 Treasurer 14
DISCERN'D
Discern'd no difference of his yeeres, or play, . . 57 E90 Mill 8
DISCERNED
Now, in whose pleasures I have this discerned, . . 55 E85 Goodyere 1 11
DISCERNES
As nothing else discernes the vertue' or vice. . . 66 E102 Pembroke 12
DISCERNING
Or Science of discerning Good and Ill. . . 156 U13 Sacvile 108
In the discerning of each conscience, so! . . . 289 U84 Muse 222
Doth shine in her discerning, . . . 365 Ode Splendor 10
To follow Goodnesse, by our owne discerning . . . 412 Sutcliffe 17
DISCHARGE
Who shall discharge first his merd-urinous load: . . 85 E133 Voyage 65
Discharge it 'bout the Iland, in an houre, . . . 249 U72 King 3
DISCHARGING
Discharging 'bout the Iland, in an houre, . . . 249 U72 King V 3
DISCIPLINE
And the Greeke Discipline (with the moderne) shed . . 214 U44 Speach 36
DISCLOSE
Have you seene faire Helen disclose . . . 135 U2 Triumph V 33
What Month then May, was fitter to disclose . . . 237 U65 Prince 4
The nailes, and every curled haire disclose; . . 307 Horace 47
The nailes, and every gentle haire disclose; . . 339 Horace V 49/ 47
From the two Egges, that did disclose the twins. . . 315 Horace 210
DISCLOS'D
As if Nature disclos'd . . . . 112 F11 Epode 100
DISCLOSES
As the Bath your verse discloses . . . 136 U2 Cupid 21
By those pure bathes your either cheeke discloses, . . 170 U19 Elegy By 7
DISCONTENT
Of discontent; or that these prayers bee . . . 122 F15 Heaven 25
So, be there never discontent, or sorrow, . . . 384 Somerset 15
DISCORD
Who sayes that Giles and Jone at discord be? . . 40 E42 Giles 1
DISCORDS
Upon your eares, of discords so un-sweet? . . . 88 E133 Voyage 171
DISCOURSE
He will both argue, and discourse in oathes, . . . 35 E28 Surly 9
5. His discourse with Cupid. . . . 136 U2 Cupid Ttl
Heare, what late Discourse of you, . . . 136 U2 Cupid 5
Charis one day in discourse . . . 139 U2 Promise 1
Knew I, that all their Dialogues, and discourse, . . 172 U20 Shrub 13
As fit t'exchange discourse; a Verse to win . . . 311 Horace 119
DISCOURSES
Th'admir'd discourses of the Prophet Ball: . . . 206 U43 Vulcan 82
Th'admir'd discourses of the Profit Ball: . . . 206 U43 Vulcan V 82
Th'admir'd discourses of the Prophet Baal: . . . 206 U43 Vulcan V 82

	Page	Title	Line

DISCOURSETH
Speakes Heavens Language! and discourseth free . . . . 271 U81 Pawlet 71
Of travell he discourseth so at large, ... 378 Coryat 2 82
DISCOURSING
To see 'hem aye discoursing with their Glasse, . . . 164 U15 Friend-Wars 63
DISCOVER
(Made to blow up loves secrets) to discover . . . . 198 U40 Elegy That 47
Discover Vice? Commit Absurdity? . . . . 405 Inigo Jones 1 82
DISCOVERETH
Speakes Heavens Language! and discovereth free . . . 271 U81 Pawlet V 71
DISCOVERIES
Were askt of thy Discoveries; They must say, . . . 388 Chapman 8
DISCREETER
A tender Mother, a discreeter Wife, ... 287 U84 Muse 174
DISDAINE
A man should flie from, as he would disdaine. . . . 194 U38 Elegy 'Tis 104
But, O those Reeds! thy meere disdaine of them, . . . 208 U43 Vulcan 129
But, O those weedes; thy meere disdaine of them, . . . 208 U43 Vulcan V129
It thawes the frostiest, and most stiffe disdaine: . . . 363 Riches 13
DISDAINED
And here he disdained not, in a forraine land . . . 375 Coryat 1 32
DISDAINING
And so disdaining any tryer; . . . . . . 278 U84 Mind 27
DISEASE
When men a dangerous disease did scape, ... 31 E13 Empirick 1
The french disease, with which he labours yet? . . . 56 E88 Monsieur 10
But dost it out of judgement, not disease; . . . . 76 E119 Shelton 8
Why, Disease, dost thou molest . . . . . 104 F8 Sicknesse 1
These, disease, will thee deserve: . . . . . 106 F8 Sicknesse 43
These, disease, will they deserve: . . . . . 106 F8 Sicknesse V 43
Is it interpreted in me disease, ... 122 F15 Heaven 3
I ne're will owe my health to a disease. . . . . 150 U10 Jealousie 16
Is it that man pulls on himselfe Disease? . . . . 165 U15 Friend-Wars 114
Envious and foule Disease, could there not be . . . 188 U34 Small Poxe 1
Of a Disease, that lov'd no light . . . . . 234 U60 La-ware 6
The truly Epidemicall disease! . . . . . 237 U64 Charles 3 18
Disease, the Enemie, and his Ingineeres, ... 248 U71 Treasurer 4
Of her disease, how did her soule assure . . . . 270 U81 Pawlet 50
I'le tell you but the death, and the disease . . . 335 Horace 659
DISEASES
From my diseases danger, and from thee. . . . . 31 E13 Empirick 4
Hung stench, diseases, and old filth, their mother, . . 86 E133 Voyage 70
And have more diseases made. . . . . . 105 F8 Sicknesse 20
Had wrestled with Diseases strong, ... 151 U12 Corbet 8
And cure the Worlds diseases: . . . . . 221 U48 Bacchus 24
Hee drives diseases from our Folds, ... 265 U79 New-yeares 62
Pays all Debts, cures all Diseases, ... 657 Door Apollo 17
DIS-ESTEEME
Which though the turning world may dis-esteeme, . . . 118 F13 Aubigny 64
DIS-ESTEEM'D
Antiquities search'd! Opinions dis-esteem'd! . . . 160 U14 Selden 40
DIS-FAVOUR
Or the dis-favour . . . . . . 177 U25 Desmond 33
DISGORGE
some 4 myles hence and have him there disgorge . . . 211 U43 Vulcan V184
DISGRACE
What was the cause then? Thought'st thou in disgrace . . 188 U34 Small Poxe 13
Your honour now, then your disgrace before. . . . 191 U38 Elegy 'Tis 30
DISGRAC'T
Or droop they as disgrac't, ... 174 U23 Himselfe 11
DISGUISD
Disguisd? and thence drag forth Enormity? . . . . 405 Inigo Jones 1 81
DISGUISE
But under the Disguise of love, ... 150 U10 Jealousie 9
DISGUIS'D
Love in a subtile Dreame disguis'd, ... 151 U11 Dreame 4
DISH
Then, selling not, a dish was tane to mince 'hem, . . 88 E133 Voyage 151
And if the high-swolne Medway faile thy dish, . . . 94 F2 Penshurst 31
DISHERRIT
Then hardest let him more disherrit, ... 99 F3 Wroth V 77
DIS-INHERIT
Or two, or three, a Sonne will dis-inherit, . . . 192 U38 Elegy 'Tis 42
DISINHERIT
Let him, then hardest sires, more disinherit, . . . 99 F3 Wroth 77
DIS-JOYN'D
And us dis-joyn'd force to her brazen yoke, . . . 294 U87 Hor.3:9 18
The last doth from the midst dis-joyn'd appeare. . . 315 Horace 218
DIS-JOYNTS
And so my sharpnesse thou no lesse dis-joynts, . . . 45 E58 Groome 5
DISPAIRE
Then why should we dispaire? Dispaire, away: . . . 363 Riches 17
DISPAYRE
But unto more dispayre to Imitate their sounde. . . . 420 Ode:If Men 36
DISPENC'D
Or dispenc'd in bookes, or bread, ... 259 U76 Petition 15
Well dispenc'd in bookes, or bread, ... 259 U76 Petition V 15
DISPEND'ST
Dispend'st, upon the lesser Deere; . . . . . 97 F3 Wroth V 26
DISPENSATION
Whether the Dispensation yet be sent, ... 219 U47 Tribe 35
DISPENSE
And subtiltie of mettalls) they dispense . . . . 86 E133 Voyage 100

	Page	Title	Line
DISPENSE (cont.)			
Freedome doth with degree dispense.	98	F3 Wroth	58
DISPERSE			
Then let the beames of that, disperse	276	U84 Body	17
DISPISED			
Thy skill hath made of ranck dispised weedes;	361	Palmer	10
DISPLAY			
When not the Shops, but windowes doe display	202	U42 Elegy Let	78
Will he display the Ensignes of thy warre.	292	U86 Hor.4:1	16
From thence, display thy wing againe	367	Ode Who saith	41
DISPLEASE			
Rather then once displease you more, to die,	193	U38 Elegy 'Tis	92
DISPLEAS'D			
At which, shee happily displeas'd, made you:	53	E79 Rutland	9
DISPOS'D			
(so well dispos'd by thy auspicious hand)	361	Palmer	2
DISPOSING			
If Custome please; at whose disposing will	309	Horace	103
DISPOSURE			
All order, and Disposure, still.	151	U12 Corbet	14
And the disposure will be something new,	269	U81 Pawlet	16
And the disposure will be somewhat new,	269	U81 Pawlet	V 16
DISPRAISE			
Dispraise my worke, then praise it frostily:	43	E52 Courtling	2
Thy praise, or dispraise is to me alike,	46	E61 Foole	1
DISPROPORTION'D			
I meane with great, but disproportion'd Muses:	391	Shakespeare	26
DISPUTE			
Dispute; and what is to be changed, note;	354	Horace	V638
DISSECT			
Who knowes the hearts of all, and can dissect	286	U84 Muse	150
DISSECTION			
O, that you could but by dissection see	194	U38 Elegy 'Tis	109
DISSEMBLE			
Doth he once dissemble, but tels he did ride	380	Coryat 3	52
DISTANCE			
Absence, or Distance, shall not breed decay.	194	U38 Elegy 'Tis	116
For as at distance, few have facultie	242	U69 Friend Son	19
But at such distance, as the eye	276	U84 Body	19
But at such distance, all the eye	276	U84 Body	V 19
DISTANT			
As Cleare, and distant, as yourselfe from Cryme;	421	Censure	8
are distant, so is proffitt from just aymes.	422	Lucan	8
DISTILL			
That distill their husbands land	105	F8 Sicknesse	29
Looke pale, distill a showre (was never meant)	333	Horace	612
Look pale, distill a dew was never meant	353	Horace	V612
DISTINCT			
Distinct in persons, yet in Unitie	128	U1 Trinitie	39
DISTINCTIONS			
Where he would fixe, for the distinctions feare.	242	U69 Friend Son	18
DISTINGUISH'D			
Subtly distinguish'd, was confused here.	84	E133 Voyage	10
DISTRACT			
Nor spread them as distract with feares,	145	U4 Song	11
DISTRUST			
Doe not despaire my mending; to distrust	192	U38 Elegy 'Tis	49
Doth by his doubt, distrust his promise more.	235	U63 Charles 2	4
DITCH			
Flanck'd with a Ditch, and forc'd out of a Marish,	209	U43 Vulcan	134
Fenced with a Ditch, and forc'd out of a Marish,	209	U43 Vulcan	V134
Wee'll have thee styld the Marquess of New-Ditch.	407	Inigo Jones 2	24
Wee'll have thee styld the Marquess of Town-Ditch.	407	Inigo Jones 2	V 24
DITCHFIELD			
As Stiles, Dike, Ditchfield, Millar, Crips, and Fen:	214	U44 Speach	54
DITTIE			
Whilst it the Dittie heares.	239	U67 Muses	24
DITTIES			
Hee'ld frame such ditties of their store, and want,	241	U68 House-hold	7
DIV'D			
Thrise did it spit: thrise div'd. At last, it view'd	88	E133 Voyage	162
DIVELL			
The Divell; and be the damning of us all.	172	U20 Shrub	24
Who with the Divell did Ordinance beget;	212	U43 Vulcan	V202
DIVELS			
Who from the Divels-Arse did Guns beget;	212	U43 Vulcan	202
That from the Divels-Arse did Guns beget;	212	U43 Vulcan	V202
DIVELS-ARSE			
Who from the Divels-Arse did Guns beget;	212	U43 Vulcan	202
That from the Divels-Arse did Guns beget;	212	U43 Vulcan	V202
DIVERS			
Cats there lay divers had beene flead, and rosted,	88	E133 Voyage	149
Under-woods. Consisting Of Divers Poems.	125	Under-wood	Ttl
Set a Horse-neck, and divers feathers fold	305	Horace	2
DIVERSLY			
The selfe-same deeds, as diversly they come,	64	E99 Th Roe 2	8
DIVIDE			
Sound, sound his praises loud, and with his, hers divide.	264	U79 New-yeares	19
How to divide, into a hundred parts,	327	Horace	465
The Dutch whom Wealth (not Hatred) doth divide;	368	Ode Who saith	85
DIVIDED			
That selfe-divided Belgia did afford;	37	E32 Roe 2	3
To harbour a divided thought	101	F4 To the World	58

	Page	Title	Line
DIVID'ST			
Divid'st, upon the lesser Deere;	97	F3 Wroth	26
DIVINE (See also DEVINE)			
Doth aske a drinke divine:	106	F9 Celia 3	6
Pure, perfect, nay divine;	110	F11 Epode	46
O, so divine a creature	112	F11 Epode	102
But onely Poets, rapt with rage divine?	115	F12 Rutland	63
But holie Poets, rapt with sence divine?	115	F12 Rutland	V 63
By me, their priest (if they can ought divine)	119	F13 Aubigny	101
Poets, though divine, are men:	131	U2 Excuse	5
If I auspitiously divine,	179	U25 Desmond	57
Which all the world then styl'd divine?	181	U27 Ode Helen	20
Of divine blessing, would not serve a State?	185	U30 Burleigh	20
Or Alexandria; and though a Divine	211	U43 Vulcan	195
I am no States-man, and much lesse Divine,	223	U49 Pucell	25
And this the wombe divine.	240	U67 Muses	51
As 'tis not radiant, but divine:	278	U84 Mind	26
Of divine Comfort, when sh' had talk'd with God.	287	U84 Muse	184
To divine Poets, and their Verses came.	327	Horace	492
Which being eyed directly, I divine,	362	Author	13
To Mrs. Alice Sutcliffe, on her divine Meditations.	411	Sutcliffe	Ttl
Of Persons, yet in Union (One) divine.	413	Ghyrlond	35
All his Answers are Divine,	657	Door Apollo	5
DIVINER			
One sparke of your Diviner heat	174	U22 Elegy Tho	31
DIVINEST			
(Divinest graces) are so entermixt,	413	Ghyrlond	26
DIVINITIE			
With humble Gleanings in Divinitie,	207	U43 Vulcan	102
DIVISION (See DEVISION)			
DIVISIONS			
But few and faire Divisions: but being got	157	U13 Sacvile	151
DO'			
But 'mong'st these Tiberts, who do'you thinke there was?	88	E133 Voyage	155
Therefore, Charis, you must do't,	140	U2 Promise	13
To do't with Cloth, or Stuffes, lusts name might merit;	164	U15 Friend-Wars	57
DO (See also DOE, DOO)			
Reveald (if some do judge) of Argenis,	207	U43 Vulcan	V 96
When you write Verses, with your judge do so:	333	Horace	620
Nor did he do this, once; if yet you can,	355	Horace	V667
Do turne into a Woman.	355	Horace	V667
Their motives were, since it had not to do	364	Phoenix	4
Do crowne thy murdred Poeme: which shall rise	371	Fletcher	9
Shewes he dares more then Paules Church-yard durst do.	371	Fletcher	14
And clothes, and guifts, that only do thee grace	378	Coryat 2	85
Do wayte upon thee: and theyre Love not bought.	384	Somerset	2
Which I do, early, vertuous Somerset;	384	Somerset	4
Least a false praise do make theyr dotage his.	384	Somerset	7
I do not feele that ever yet I had	385	Husband	4
trust in the tombes, their care-full freinds do rayse;	385	Husband	5
How do his trumpets breath! What loud alarmes!	387	Cavendish	6
These Mysteries do point to three more great,	398	Drayton	66
Yet ware; thou mayst do all things cruellie:	413	Ghyrlond	29
shall never dare do any thing but feare.	423	Lucan	15
if any way she do rewarde thee	423	Lucan	20
DOCILE	662	Bedford	8
The docile mind may soone thy precepts know,	329	Horace	504
DOCK'			
'Tis but light paines: Indeede this Dock's no rose.	85	E133 Voyage	60
DOCKE			
A Docke there is, that called is Avernus,	85	E133 Voyage	41
DOCK'S			
'Tis but light paines: Indeede this Dock's no rose.	85	E133 Voyage	60
DOCTOR			
To doctor Empirick.	31	E13 Empirick	Ttl
DOCTORS			
Not taken up o' th' doctors, but as well	117	F13 Aubigny	33
And to the Torturers (her Doctors) say,	270	U81 Pawlet	52
DOCTRINE			
That stranger doctrine of Pythagoras,	61	E95 Savile	2
As doctrine, and delight together go.	329	Horace	516
DOE			
For I will doe none: and as little ill,	30	E11 Something	7
Make good what thou dar'st doe in all the rest.	32	E16 Brain-hardy	8
As guiltie men doe magistrats: glad I,	32	E17 Critic	2
Longer a knowing, then most wits doe live.	34	E23 Donne 1	5
And, that is done, as he saw great men doe.	35	E28 Surly	6
For then, our water-conduits doe runne wine;	36	E29 Tilter	5
Be thine, I taxe, yet doe not owne my rimes:	36	E30 Guiltie	2
Could not effect, not all the furies doe,	37	E32 Roe 2	2
Whose actions so themselves doe celebrate;	40	E43 Salisbury 1	2
Doe beg thy care unto thy after-state.	43	E51 James 3	8
How I doe love thee Beaumont, and thy Muse,	44	E55 Beaumont	1
How I doe feare my selfe, that am not worth	44	E55 Beaumont	3
Since men have left to doe praise-worthy things,	49	E67 Suffolk	1
Then doe I love thee, and behold thy ends	55	E86 Goodyere 2	3
And understand 'hem, as most chapmen doe.	59	E92 New Crie	10
On them: And therefore doe not onely shunne	59	E92 New Crie	38
Then whose I doe not know a whiter soule,	60	E93 Radcliffe	11
My title's seal'd. Those that for claps doe write,	62	E96 Donne 2	9
Doe equally desire your companie:	64	E101 Supper	2
Their lives, as doe their lines, till now had lasted.	65	E101 Supper	32
I Doe but name thee Pembroke, and I find	66	E102 Pembroke	1

DOE (cont.)

	Page	Title	Line
Doe what you come for, Captayne, with your newes;	68	E107 Hungry	1
That's, sit, and eate: doe not my eares abuse.	68	E107 Hungry	2
What at Ligorne, Rome, Florence you did doe:	69	E107 Hungry	14
Doe what you come for, Captayne, There's your meate.	69	E107 Hungry	32
And your high names: I doe desire, that thence	69	E108 Soldiers	3
No more, then I dare now doe, with my pen.	70	E108 Soldiers	8
Can so speake Caesar, as thy labours doe.	71	E110 Edmonds 1	12
Thy all, at all: and what so ere I doe,	72	E112 Gamster	5
Doe all, that longs to the anarchy of drinke,	74	E115 Honest Man	12
Parts, then th'Italian could doe, with his dore.	74	E115 Honest Man	26
No, I doe, therefore, call Posteritie	80	E127 Aubigny	4
When we doe give, Alphonso, to the light,	82	E131 Ferrab. 2	1
Even those for whom they doe this, know they erre:	83	E131 Ferrab. 2	10
Of all your night-tubs, when the carts doe cluster,	85	E133 Voyage	64
Of worship, they their nodding chinnes doe hit	87	E133 Voyage	123
Your Fleet-lane Furies; and hot cookes doe dwell,	88	E133 Voyage	143
Is fill'd with buttock? And the walls doe sweate	88	E133 Voyage	169
Thy Mount, to which the Dryads doe resort,	93	F2 Penshurst	10
Thy sheepe, thy bullocks, kine, and calves doe feed:	94	F2 Penshurst	23
To doe thy countrey service, thy selfe right;	100	F3 Wroth	103
That neither want doe thee affright,	100	F3 Wroth	104
Doe not once hope, that thou canst tempt	100	F4 To the World	5
Yes, threaten, doe. Alas I feare	101	F4 To the World	37
No, I doe know, that I was borne	101	F4 To the World	61
As wandrers doe, that still doe rome,	102	F4 To the World	66
Doe not men, ynow of rites	104	F8 Sicknesse	3
Take heed, Sicknesse, what you doe,	104	F8 Sicknesse	7
I doe feare, you'll surfet too.	104	F8 Sicknesse	V 8
Doe enough; and who would take	105	F8 Sicknesse	26
For either our affections doe rebell,	109	F11 Epode	21
Doe severall passions invade the minde,	110	F11 Epode	29
Though thy wild thoughts with sparrowes wings doe flye,	111	F11 Epode	73
We doe not number, here,	111	F11 Epode	76
I doe not number, here,	111	F11 Epode	V 76
Or in their windowes; doe but prove the wombs,	114	F12 Rutland	46
And so doe many more. All which can call	117	F13 Aubigny	31
Doe I reflect. Some alderman has power,	117	F13 Aubigny	38
That doe sinne onely for the infamie:	119	F13 Aubigny	86
Live that one, still; and as long yeeres doe passe,	120	F13 Aubigny	121
And some doe drinke, and some doe dance,	120	F14 Sydney	2
And all doe strive t'advance	120	F14 Sydney	5
Which I doe tell:	120	F14 Sydney	16
What comfort by him doe wee winne,	130	U1 Nativitie	19
Which how Dexterously I doe,	133	U2 Suffered	25
As she goes, all hearts doe duty	134	U2 Triumph	5
And enamour'd, doe wish, so they might	134	U2 Triumph	7
Doe but looke on her eyes, they doe light	134	U2 Triumph	11
Doe but looke on her Haire, it is bright	134	U2 Triumph	13
Doe but marke, her forehead's smoother	134	U2 Triumph	15
And doe governe more my blood,	136	U2 Cupid	3
By her lookes I doe her know,	136	U2 Cupid	18
Charis, guesse, and doe not misse,	137	U2 Kisse	1
Why doe you doubt, or stay?	139	U2 Another	4
What w'are but once to doe, we should doe long.	139	U2 Another	12
Titles, I confesse, doe take me;	140	U2 Her man	5
What we harmonie doe call	141	U2 Her man	34
As to doe no thing too much.	142	U2 Her man	46
Nor doe wrongs, nor wrongs receave;	142	U2 Her man	49
For his Mind, I doe not care,	142	U2 Exception	1
What need of mee? doe you but sing,	143	U3 Musicall	13
But what those lips doe make.	143	U3 Musicall	16
But what your lips doe make.	143	U3 Musicall	V 16
Oh doe not wanton with those eyes,	144	U4 Song	1
O, doe not steepe them in thy Teares,	145	U4 Song	9
Nor doe we doubt, but that we can,	145	U5 Woman-kind	7
Doe change, though man, and often fight,	146	U6 Defence	8
Which we in love must doe aswell,	146	U6 Defence	9
And lookes as Lillies doe,	147	U7 Nymph	18
Doe but consider this small dust,	148	U8 Houre-glasse	1
If, Sackvile, all that have the power to doe	153	U13 Sacvile	1
To have such doe me good, I durst not name:	153	U13 Sacvile	18
Is borrowing; that but stopt, they doe invade	155	U13 Sacvile	80
That I may love your Person (as I doe)	157	U13 Sacvile	157
But I on yours farre otherwise shall doe,	159	U14 Selden	17
Upon your Center, doe your Circle fill	159	U14 Selden	32
Heard what times past have said, seene what ours doe:	159	U14 Selden	34
Thy learned Chamber-fellow, knowes to doe	161	U14 Selden	72
Thy gift 'gainst envie. O how I doe count	161	U14 Selden	79
Doe all the tricks of a saut Lady Bitch!	164	U15 Friend-Wars	76
Thus they doe talke. And are these objects fit	165	U15 Friend-Wars	101
Our vices doe not tarry in a place,	166	U15 Friend-Wars	123
They are not, Sir, worst Owers, that doe pay	169	U17 Friend-Debt	1
Tell me (my lov'd Friend) doe you love, or no,	170	U19 Elegy By	11
You blush, but doe not: friends are either none,	171	U19 Elegy By	13
Others, in time may love, as we doe now.	171	U19 Elegy By	18
Knew I this Woman? yes; And you doe see,	172	U20 Shrub	15
Doe not you aske to know her, she is worse	172	U20 Shrub	17
To doe, then be a husband of that store.	180	U26 Ode High	18
Where men may see whom I doe sing?	182	U27 Ode Helen	32
Both braines and hearts; and mine now best doe know it:	182	U28 Worth	8
He do's me wrong, that craves you to doe right.	186	U32 Elsmere	16
That I, hereafter, doe not thinke the Barre,	186	U33 Councellour	1

DOE (cont.)

Upon the reverend Pleaders; doe now shut . . . . 187 U33 Councellour 10
Or doe upon my selfe some desperate ill; . . . . 191 U38 Elegy 'Tis 3
We cut not off, till all Cures else doe faile: . . . 192 U38 Elegy 'Tis 46
Doe not despaire my mending; to distrust . . . 192 U38 Elegy 'Tis 49
In darke, and sullen mornes, doe we not say, . . 193 U38 Elegy 'Tis 79
Of crueltie, lest they doe make you such. . . . 193 U38 Elegy 'Tis 84
How all my Fibres by your Spirit doe move, . . 194 U38 Elegy 'Tis 111
When I see you, then I doe see my Sun, . . 194 U38 Elegy 'Tis 120
And take some sirrup after; so doe I, . . . 197 U40 Elegy That 5
As neither wine doe rack it out, or mirth. . . 197 U40 Elegy That 18
What it is like: And doe not thinke they can . . 199 U41 Elegy Since 3
How shall I doe, sweet Mistris, for my heart? . . 199 U41 Elegy Since 14
Fathers, and Husbands, I doe claime a right . . 200 U42 Elegy Let 11
So to be sure you doe injoy your selves. . . 200 U42 Elegy Let 24
To doe her Husbands rites in, e're 'twere gone . . 201 U42 Elegy Let 40
Lift up some one, and doe, I tell not what. . . 201 U42 Elegy Let 58
When not the Shops, but windowes doe display . . 202 U42 Elegy Let 78
But that's a marke, wherof thy Rites doe boast, . . 205 U43 Vulcan 57
And the strong lines, that so the time doe catch: . . 206 U43 Vulcan 78
And the strong lines, which so the time doe catch: . . 206 U43 Vulcan V 78
Or Captaine Pamphletts, which on foote doe sally . . 206 U43 Vulcan V 79
To teach some that, their Nurses could not doe, . . 207 U43 Vulcan 92
To teach some what, their Nurses could not doe, . . 207 U43 Vulcan V 92
Cause thou canst doe these halting tricks in fire? . . 208 U43 Vulcan V110
Nay, let White-Hall with Revels have to doe, . . 210 U43 Vulcan 156
Scarce let White-Hall with Revels have to doe, . . 210 U43 Vulcan V156
A Court of Equitie should doe us right, . . 211 U43 Vulcan 178
On both sides doe your mischiefes with delight; . . 212 U43 Vulcan 204
To see the Pride at Court, their Wives doe make: . . 213 U44 Speach 16
Live by their Scale, that dare doe nothing free? . . 215 U44 Speach 68
All that they doe at Playes. O, but first here . . 215 U44 Speach 91
And as within your Office, you doe take . . 216 U45 Squib 13
Inquirie of the worth: So must we doe, . . 216 U45 Squib 15
Men that are safe, and sure, in all they doe, . . 218 U47 Tribe 1
Brunsfield, and Mansfield doe this yeare, my fates . . 219 U47 Tribe 44
Though I doe neither heare these newes, nor tell . . 219 U47 Tribe 46
Well, with mine owne fraile Pitcher, what to doe . . 219 U47 Tribe 56
Before his braine doe know it; . . . . 221 U48 Bacchus 30
To Church, as others doe to Feasts and Playes, . . 222 U49 Pucell 16
What though she hath won on Trust, as many doe, . . 223 U49 Pucell 21
Not only shunning by your act, to doe . . 224 U50 Countesse 5
And so doe I. This is the sixtieth yeare . . 225 U51 Bacon 7
If I doe lose it: And, without a Tale, . . 229 U54 Squib 3
It doe not come: One piece I have in store, . . 229 U54 Squib 15
Such, (if her manners like you) I doe send: . . 230 U56 Covell 19
Of daring, not to doe a wrong, is true . . 233 U59 Newcastle 15
What could their care doe 'gainst the spight . . 234 U60 La-ware 5
And wee doe weepe, to water, for our sinne. . . 234 U61 Epigram 15
And doe their penance, to avert Gods rod, . . 235 U61 Epigram 19
What can the Poet wish his King may doe, . . 235 U62 Charles 1 13
Then, Royall Charles, and Mary, doe not grutch . . 236 U63 Charles 2 7
And thinke all still the best, that he will doe. . . 236 U63 Charles 2 10
Are lost upon accompt! And none doe know . . 237 U64 Charles 3 V 21
Doe mingle in a shout, ... 240 U67 Muses 41
The People her doe call! . . . . 240 U67 Muses 50
Why doe I irritate, or stirre up thee, . . 250 U73 Weston 7
The Rivers in their shores doe run, . . 251 U74 Weston 7
Rare Plants from ev'ry banke doe rise, . . 251 U74 Weston 10
Doe boast their Loves, and Brav'ries so at large, . . 253 U75 Epithalam. 19
To doe their Offices in Natures Chime, . . 253 U75 Epithalam. 27
Stay, thou wilt see what rites the Virgins doe! . . 254 U75 Epithalam. 49
Who, in all they doe, ... 255 U75 Epithalam. 78
Him up, to doe the same himselfe had done. . . 256 U75 Epithalam. 108
Doe long to make themselves, so, another way: . . 257 U75 Epithalam. 140
Then goe on, and doe its worst; . . . 260 U76 Petition 29
This I would doe, could I know Weston, one . . 260 U77 Treasurer 10
This I would doe, if I could thinke you one . . 260 U77 Treasurer V 10
Can doe the things that Statues doe deserve, . . 261 U77 Treasurer 15
Where all heroique ample thoughts doe meet: . . 262 U78 Digby 10
Of brightest Mira, doe we raise our Song, . . 264 U79 New-yeares 24
I doe obey you, Beauty! for in death, . . 269 U81 Pawlet 5
And all beatitudes, that thence doe flow: . . 271 U81 Pawlet 75
Till, like her face, it doe appeare, . . 276 U84 Body 15
But, Painter, see thou doe not sell . . 277 U84 Body 29
Not, that your Art I doe refuse: . . 277 U84 Mind 5
Our sense you doe with knowledge fill, . . 278 U84 Mind 19
Which all men doe, that urge not their owne deeds . . 281 U84 Kenelme 17
Nothing I doe; but, like a heavie wheele, . . 283 U84 Muse 30
To one she said, Doe this, he did it; So . . 287 U84 Muse 169
Of lapsed Nature) best know what to doe, . . 288 U84 Muse 214
Whilst from the higher Bankes doe slide the floods; . . 290 U85 Country 25
The Fountaines murmure as the streames doe creepe, . . 290 U85 Country 27
Like lustfull beasts, that onely know to doe it; . . 294 U88 Petronius 4
And both doe crave, and give againe, this leave. . . 305 Horace 13
Bouts of fleet waters, that doe intertwine . . 338 Horace V 21
On popular noise with, and doe businesse in. . . 311 Horace 120
The old man many evils doe girt round; . . 315 Horace 241
Mans comming yeares much good with them doe bring: . . 317 Horace 250
In at the eare, doe stirre the mind more slow . . 317 Horace 257
Be I their Judge, they doe at no time dare . . 321 Horace 356
The steadie Spondaees; so themselves doe beare . . 347 Horace V363/377
Why not? I'm gentle, and free-borne, doe hate . . 331 Horace 571

DOE   (cont.)
    Wilt nothing against nature speake, or doe: .   .   .   331 Horace   574
    To change, and mend, what you not forth doe set.   .   .   .   331 Horace   579
    You doe not bring, to judge your Verses, one,   .   .   .   333 Horace   609
    Cry, and doe more then the true Mourners: so   .   .   .   333 Horace   615
    When you make verses, with your judge doe so: .   .   .   354 Horace   V620
    Nor did he doe this once; for if you can   .   .   .   335 Horace   667
    Not wearing moodes, as gallants doe a fashion, ...   362 Author   3
    Where, such perfections to the life doe rise.   .   .   .   362 Author   6
    When the old words doe strike on the new times,   .   .   .   389 Aleman   4
    To veiw the truth and owne it. Doe but looke   .   .   .   399 Lady Ogle   5
    When they doe sweat to fortifie a Muse.   .   .   .   400 Beaumont   6
    That, while they bind the senses, doe so please?   .   .   .   401 Filmer   2
    I doe salute you! Are you fitted yet?   .   .   .   402 Inigo Jones 1 17
    That doe cry up the Machine, & the Showes!   .   .   .   403 Inigo Jones 1 32
    He is, or would be the mayne Dominus doe   .   .   .   404 Inigo Jones 1 64
    To be worth Envy. Henceforth I doe meane   .   .   .   405 Inigo Jones 1 70
    What would he doe now, gi'ng his mynde that waye   .   .   .   405 Inigo Jones 1 75
    All kings to doe the self same deeds with some!   .   .   .   406 Inigo Jones 2   4
    Foole, doe not rate my Rymes; I'have found thy Vice .   .   .   408 Detractor   5
    And you doe doe them well, with good applause,   .   .   .   409 Brome   5
    A Prentise-ship: which few doe now a dayes.   .   .   .   410 Brome   10
    How they doe keepe alive his memorie;   .   .   .   416 Dover   5
    And doe both Church, and Common-wealth the good,   .   .   .   416 Dover   8
    yet doe not feare it.   .   .   .   .   417 Moon   32
    It is a lycense to doe ill, protectes,   .   .   .   423 Lucan   12
DOES
    A meane, and toleration, which does well: .   .   .   331 Horace   549
DOEST
    Thou that doest spend thie dayes   .   .   .   420 Ode:If Men   24
DOG
    But one is bitten by the Dog he fed,   .   .   .   155 U13 Sacvile   67
    More then to praise a Dog? or Horse? or speake   .   .   .   215 U44 Speach   71
    Painted a Dog, that now his subtler skill   .   .   .   241 U69 Friend Son 10
    Out in the Dog-daies, least the killer meete .   .   .   409 Detractor   20
DOG-DAIES
    Out in the Dog-daies, least the killer meete .   .   .   409 Detractor   20
DOGGES
    Loves Dogges, and Horses; and is ever one   .   .   .   315 Horace   230
DOGS
    That breathes in his dogs way: and this is great. .   .   .   36 E28 Surly   18
    And for one Cerberus, the whole coast was dogs.   .   .   .   84 E133 Voyage   14
    The heads, houghs, entrailes, and the hides of dogs: . .   .   88 E133 Voyage   146
    To the Wolves studie, or Dogs eloquence;   .   .   .   187 U33 Councellour 12
    All live dogs from the lane, and his shops sight, .   .   .   241 U69 Friend Son 12
DOING
    Whose dice not doing well, to'a pulpit ran.   .   .   .   76 E119 Shelton   6
    Not doing good, scarce when he dyes.   .   .   .   99 F3 Wroth   84
    And never but for doing wrong be sory;   .   .   .   168 U15 Friend-Wars 180
    Or doing other deeds of Charitie,   .   .   .   288 U84 Muse   193
    Doing, a filthy pleasure is, and short;   .   .   .   294 U88 Petronius   1
DOLPHIN
    A Dolphin, and a Boare amid' the floods.   .   .   .   307 Horace   42
DOMINATIONS
    The Dominations, Vertues, and the Powers,   .   .   .   285 U84 Muse   87
DOMINUS
    He is, or would be the mayne Dominus doe   .   .   .   404 Inigo Jones 1 64
DOMITIAN
    To thy Domitian, than I can my James: .   .   .   38 E36 Martial   2
DON
    On Don Surly.   .   .   .   .   35 E28 Surly   Ttl
    Don Surly, to aspire the glorious name   .   .   .   35 E28 Surly   1
    The learned Librarie of Don Quixote;   .   .   .   204 U43 Vulcan   31
DONE
    And, that is done, as he saw great men doe.   .   .   .   35 E28 Surly   6
    Loe, what my countrey should have done (have rais'd . .   .   46 E60 Mounteagle 1
    When they cost dearest, and are done most free,   .   .   .   49 E66 Cary   14
    In th'eye of Europe, where thy deeds were done,   .   .   .   58 E91 Vere   6
    With ignorance on us, as they have done   .   .   .   59 E92 New Crie   37
    But much it now availes, what's done, of whom: .   .   .   64 E99 Th Roe 2   7
    In these west-parts, nor when that warre was done, .   .   .   71 E110 Edmonds 1 2
    Little, for me, had reason done,   .   .   .   101 F4 To the World 35
    Yet, for the timely favours shee hath done,   .   .   .   115 F12 Rutland   71
    Then all, that have but done my Muse least grace, .   .   .   115 F12 Rutland   79
    Then all, that have but done my verse lesse grace, .   .   .   115 F12 Rutland V 79
    All's done in me.   .   .   .   .   128 U1 Trinitie   24
    Then thou hast done?   .   .   .   .   129 U1 Father   18
    What my Muse and I have done: .   .   .   138 U2 Kisse   5
    Would say as much, as both have done   .   .   .   151 U12 Corbet   3
    And more, and more, I should have done,   .   .   .   152 U12 Corbet   30
    As they are done, and such returnes they find: .   .   .   153 U13 Sacvile   6
    As I did feele it done, as soone as meant, ,   .   .   .   153 U13 Sacvile   12
    Excuses, or Delayes? or done 'hem scant, ,   .   .   .   153 U13 Sacvile   27
    That puts it in his Debt-booke e're 't be done;   .   .   .   154 U13 Sacvile   34
    So each, that's done, and tane, becomes a Brace.   .   .   .   154 U13 Sacvile   40
    And told of with more License then th'were done!   .   .   .   156 U13 Sacvile   96
    Is done for gaine: If't be, 'tis not sincere.   .   .   .   169 U17 Friend-Debt 6
    Of all that can be done him; Such a one   .   .   .   171 U19 Elegy By   23
    Have all these done (and yet I misse   .   .   .   182 U27 Ode Helen   29
    Thinke, yea and boast, that they have done it so   .   .   .   186 U32 Elsmere   12
    And not the bounties they ha' done, deny.   .   .   .   192 U38 Elegy 'Tis 54
    He would have done in verse, with any of those   .   .   .   201 U42 Elegy Let 62
    What had I done that might call on thine ire?   .   .   .   202 U43 Vulcan   2

	Page	Title	Line
DONE (cont.)			
What have I done that might call on thine ire?	202	U43 Vulcan	V 2
And what hast thou done in these pettie spights,	210	U43 Vulcan	163
And comming home, to tell what acts were done	213	U44 Speach	19
But he that should perswade, to have this done	214	U44 Speach	61
Valour! to sleight it, being done to you!	233	U59 Newcastle	16
All Offices were done	244	U70 Ode	48
By what was done and wrought	245	U70 Ode	60
Unto the Vertue. Nothing perfect done,	247	U70 Ode	115
Be duly done to those	255	U75 Epithalam.	93
Him up, to doe the same himselfe had done.	256	U75 Epithalam.	108
For done service, and to come:	259	U76 Petition	13
For done service, or to come:	259	U76 Petition	13
Witnesse his Action done at Scanderone;	262	U78 Digby	13
And his great Action done at Scanderoone;	262	U78 Digby	V 13
That thou art lov'd of God, this worke is done,	268	U80 Christning	1
Hee knowes, what worke h'hath done, to call this Guest,	284	U84 Muse	81
And done, we straight repent us of the sport:	294	U88 Petronius	2
Wants strength, and sinewes, as his spirits were done;	339	Horace V 38/ 37
The businesse either on the Stage is done,	317	Horace	255
Things worthy to be done within, but take	317	Horace	261
Having well eat, and drunke (the rites being done)	319	Horace	325
But now, your Worke is done, if they that view	370	Author	9
To your desert, who'have done it, Friend. And this	389	Aleman	21
That would have done, that, which you onely can.	389	Aleman	24
DONNE (VERB)			
Then Time hath donne,	367	Ode Who saith	54
DONNE			
To John Donne.	34	E23 Donne 1	Ttl
Donne, the delight of Phoebus, and each Muse,	34	E23 Donne 1	1
To John Donne.	62	E96 Donne 2	Ttl
Who shall doubt, Donne, where I a Poet bee,	62	E96 Donne 2	1
DONNEE'S			
Donnor's or Donnee's, to their practise shall	158	U13 Sacvile	163
DONNES			
To Lucy, Countesse of Bedford, with Mr. Donnes Satyres.	60	E94 Bedford 3	Ttl
DONNOR'S			
Donnor's or Donnee's, to their practise shall	158	U13 Sacvile	163
DOO'			
But thine, for which I doo't, so much exceeds!	46	E60 Mounteagle	8
Why much good doo't you! Be what beast you will,	403	Inigo Jones 1	21
DOO			
And that, as puritanes at baptisme doo,	44	E53 Old-end	7
I, that am glad of thy great chance, here doo!	46	E60 Mounteagle	5
For all thou hear'st, thou swear'st thy selfe didst doo.	54	E81 Proule	5
That know not so much state, wrong, as they doo.	59	E92 New Crie	40
Although to write be lesser then to doo,	61	E95 Savile	25
And I know nothing more thou hast to doo.	63	E98 Th Roe 1	2
Not that it feares, but will not have to doo	74	E115 Honest Man	20
But I to yours, farre from this fault, shall doo;	159	U14 Selden	V 17
Light on thee: Or if those plagues will not doo,	212	U43 Vulcan	215
Light upon thee: Or if those plagues will not doo,	212	U43 Vulcan	V215
With Nature, to out-doo the life:	390	Reader	4
DOOME			
To heare their Judge, and his eternall doome;	283	U84 Muse	48
The kind of Man, on whom his doome should fall!	288	U84 Muse	208
DOOR			
Over the Door at the Entrance into the Apollo.	657	Door Apollo	Ttl
DOORE			
See, at another doore,	254	U75 Epithalam.	69
They both are slip'd to Bed; Shut fast the Doore,	258	U75 Epithalam.	185
The doore of Grace, and found the Mercy-Seat.	288	U84 Muse	190
DOORES			
And having got him out of doores is glad.	40	E42 Giles	7
Enforcing yron doores to yeeld it way,	363	Riches	9
DOO'T			
But thine, for which I doo't, so much exceeds!	46	E60 Mounteagle	8
Why much good doo't you! Be what beast you will,	403	Inigo Jones 1	21
DORE			
A purging bill, now fix'd upon the dore,	29	E7 Hot-house	2
Parts, then th'Italian could doe, with his dore.	74	E115 Honest Man	26
And stayes but till you come unto the dore!	89	E133 Voyage	178
When oft the Bearer, is borne out of dore?	166	U15 Friend-Wars	120
DORRELS			
This Age would lend no faith to Dorrels Deed;	223	U49 Pucell	42
DORSET			
An Epistle to Sir Edward Sacvile, now Earle of Dorset.	153	U13 Sacvile	Ttl
DO'S			
Against his will that do's 'hem? that hath weav'd	153	U13 Sacvile	26
He neither gives, or do's, that doth delay	154	U13 Sacvile	41
He do's you wrong, that craves you to doe right.	186	U32 Elsmere	16
Do's the Court-Pucell then so censure me,	222	U49 Pucell	1
Or do's all businesse coldly, and with feare;	317	Horace	244
DOSE			
Give every one his dose of mirth: and watches	74	E115 Honest Man	14
DOSEN			
With famine, wants, and sorrowes many a dosen,	86	E133 Voyage	71
DO'ST			
How, best of Kings, do'st thou a scepter beare!	28	E4 James 1	1
How, best of Poets, do'st thou laurell weare!	28	E4 James 1	2
To put out the word, whore, thou do'st me woo,	54	E83 Friend	1
Where do'st thou carelesse lie,	174	U23 Himselfe	1
And, in these Cures, do'st so thy selfe enlarge,	235	U62 Charles 1	7

156

DOST
	Page	Title	Line
Some hundred quarrels, yet dost thou fight none;	32	E16 Brain-hardy	6
Marble, weepe, for thou dost cover	39	E40 Ratcliffe	1
That unto me dost such religion use!	44	E55 Beaumont	2
A chamber-critick, and dost dine, and sup	50	E72 Court-ling	2
And present worth in all dost so contract,	57	E89 Allen	11
As others speake, but onely thou dost act.	57	E89 Allen	12
That so alone canst judge, so'alone dost make:	62	E96 Donne 2	3
And, in thy censures, evenly, dost take	62	E96 Donne 2	4
To Satyres; and thou dost pursue me. Where,	73	E112 Gamster	14
That both for wit, and sense, so oft dost plucke,	73	E112 Gamster	18
Nor scarce dost colour for it, which is lesse.	73	E112 Gamster	20
But dost it out of judgement, not disease;	76	E119 Shelton	8
Whil'st thou dost rayse some Player, from the grave,	81	E129 Mime	11
Thou dost out-zany Cokely, Pod; nay, Gue:	81	E129 Mime	16
Thou dost with some delight the day out-weare,	97	F3 Wroth	35
Why, Disease, dost thou molest	104	F8 Sicknesse	1
O, be thou witnesse, that the reynes dost know,	122	F15 Heaven	5
That thou dost all things more for truth, then glory,	168	U15 Friend-Wars	179
So dost thou studie matter, men, and times,	187	U33 Councellour	15
But first dost vexe, and search it! If not sound,	187	U33 Councellour	19
How in these ruines, Vulcan, thou dost lurke,	207	U43 Vulcan	105
And now such is thy stand; while thou dost deale	217	U46 Coke	15
See then thou dost attend him,	221	U48 Bacchus	17
As thou dost cure our Evill, at thy charge.	235	U62 Charles 1	8
If a fit livor thou dost seeke to toast;	292	U86 Hor.4:1	12
Or follow fame, thou that dost write, or faine	313	Horace	169
If such a ones applause thou dost require,	315	Horace	220
May she, whome thou for spouse, to day, dost take,	384	Somerset	11
Still, still, dost thou arrive with, at our shore,	388	Chapman	5
O, how in those, dost thou instruct these times,	397	Drayton	43
Thou'rt too ambitious: and dost fear in vaine!	408	Inigo Jones 3	6
not safe; but when thou dost them thoroughlie:	423	Lucan	16

DO'T
	Page	Title	Line
Therefore, Charis, you must do't,	140	U2 Promise	13
To do't with Cloth, or Stuffes, lusts name might merit;	164	U15 Friend-Wars	57

DOTAGE
	Page	Title	Line
Least a false praise do make theyr dotage his.	385	Husband	4

DOTE
	Page	Title	Line
So I might dote upon thy Chaires and Stooles	201	U42 Elegy Let	47

DOTES
	Page	Title	Line
I durst not aime at that: The dotes were such	269	U81 Pawlet	25
I durst not aime at, the dotes thereof were such	269	U81 Pawlet	V 25

DOTH
	Page	Title	Line
For vulgar praise, doth it too dearely buy.	27	E2 My Booke	14
Call'st a booke good, or bad, as it doth sell,	27	E3 Bookseller	2
Beg'd Ridwayes pardon: Duncote, now, doth crye;	29	E8 Robbery	4
Where, while that sever'd doth remaine,	34	E22 Daughter	10
What doth he else, but say, leave to be chast,	34	E25 Beast 1	7
He doth, at meales, alone, his pheasant eate,	35	E28 Surly	12
Which shewes, where ever death doth please t'appeare,	37	E32 Roe 2	9
Colt, now, doth daily penance in his owne.	39	E39 Colt	2
But that his Jone doth too. And Giles would never,	40	E42 Giles	4
And so is Jone. Oft-times, when Giles doth find	40	E42 Giles	9
All this doth Jone. Or that his long yearn'd life	40	E42 Giles	11
Rest in soft peace, and, ask'd, say here doth lye	41	E45 First Son	9
I have no salt: no bawdrie he doth meane.	42	E49 Playwrt 1	3
One doth not stroke me, nor the other strike.	46	E61 Foole	2
To live when Broeck not stands, nor Roor doth runne.	49	E66 Cary	12
Two kindes of valour he doth shew, at ones;	49	E68 Playwrt 2	3
Surly's old whore in her new silkes doth swim:	54	E82 Surly	1
Shee doth instruct men by her gallant flight,	55	E85 Goodyere 1	5
Where, though 't be love, that to thy praise doth move	55	E86 Goodyere 2	7
Or is it some french statue? No: 'T doth move,	56	E88 Monsieur	13
And what each prince doth for intelligence owe,	59	E92 New Crie	12
But that, which most doth take my Muse, and mee,	65	E101 Supper	28
But in the view, doth interrupt their sinne;	66	E102 Pembroke	18
And, being nam'd, how little doth that name	66	E103 L Wroth 1	5
That serves nor fame, nor titles; but doth chuse	70	E109 Nevil	2
T'all future time, not onely doth restore	71	E110 Edmonds 1	21
Who Edmonds, reades thy booke, and doth not see	72	E111 Edmonds 2	1
By thy great helpe: and doth proclaime by mee,	72	E111 Edmonds 2	13
By thy great Art: and doth proclaime by mee,	72	E111 Edmonds 2	V 13
Where, what makes others great, doth keepe thee good!	73	E113 Overbury	4
A subtle thing, that both affections win	74	E115 Honest Man	7
At every meale, where it doth dine, or sup,	74	E115 Honest Man	23
And, shifting of it's faces, doth play more	74	E115 Honest Man	25
These were thy knowing arts: which who doth now	75	E116 Jephson	13
For'his whore: Groyne doth still occupy his land.	75	E117 Groyne	2
Under-neath this stone doth lye	79	E124 Elizabeth	3
To more vertue, then doth live.	79	E124 Elizabeth	6
Or (mounted on a stoole) thy face doth hit	81	E129 Mime	13
Doth sweeten mirth, and heighten pietie;	82	E130 Ferrab. 1	6
Bartas doth wish thy English now were his.	83	E132 Sylvester	10
(Who hath the hundred hands when he doth meddle)	86	E133 Voyage	82
Urine, and plaisters? when the noise doth beate	88	E133 Voyage	170
Each banke doth yeeld thee coneyes; and the topps	94	F2 Penshurst	25
To crowne thy open table, doth provide	94	F2 Penshurst	27
Fig, grape, and quince, each in his time doth come:	94	F2 Penshurst	42
The neede of such? whose liberall boord doth flow,	95	F2 Penshurst	59
With all, that hospitalitie doth know!	95	F2 Penshurst	60
A waiter, doth my gluttony envy:	95	F2 Penshurst	68
The apple-harvest, that doth longer last;	98	F3 Wroth	43

DOTH (cont.)
  Freedome doth with degree dispense.   98   F3 Wroth   58
  And thinke his power doth equall Fates.   99   F3 Wroth   80
  The thirst, that from the soule doth rise, ...   106   F9 Celia 3   5
  Doth aske a drinke divine: 106   F9 Celia 3   6
  (That should ring larum to the heart) doth sleepe,   .   .   .   109   F11 Epode   23
  (That shal ring larum to the heart) doth sleepe,   .   .   .   109   F11 Epode   V 23
  Or some great thought doth keepe   109   F11 Epode   24
  But this doth from the cloud of error grow, ...   110   F11 Epode   35
  No such effects doth prove: 110   F11 Epode   44
  Because they move, the continent doth so: 111   F11 Epode   71
  Of some grand peere, whose ayre doth make rejoyce   .   .   .   113   F12 Rutland   12
  And, who doth me (though I not him) envy, ...   115   F12 Rutland   70
  As I, can say, and see it doth excell.   117   F13 Aubigny   34
  And never thinke, how vice doth every houre, ...   119   F13 Aubigny   87
  Doth say, ...   120   F14 Sydney   14
  Since he doth lacke   121   F14 Sydney   27
  Doth urge him to runne wrong, or to stand still.   121   F14 Sydney   30
  With the Lace that doth it deck, ...   137   U2 Cupid   30
  For this Beauty yet doth hide   137   U2 Cupid   49
  That doth but touch his flower, and flies away.   139   U2 Another   6
  What Tree or stone doth want a soule?   143   U3 Musicall   7
  Is that which doth perfection breed.   146   U6 Defence   12
  In love, doth not alone help forth   146   U6 Defence   20
  From being forsaken, then doth worth: 146   U6 Defence   22
  One un-becomming thought doth move   148   U7 Nymph   31
  Of him whose bones this Grave doth gather: 151   U12 Corbet   6
  Deepest in Man, of which when he doth thinke, ...   153   U13 Sacvile   20
  Or that doth sound a Trumpet, and doth call   154   U13 Sacvile   35
  He neither gives, or do's, that doth delay   154   U13 Sacvile   41
  A Benefit; or that doth throw't away: 154   U13 Sacvile   42
  No more then he doth thanke, that will receive   154   U13 Sacvile   43
  Rather then Office, when it doth or may   158   U14 Selden   9
  Unto the Censure. Yours all need doth flie   158   U14 Selden   11
  Now use the bones, we see doth hire a man   166   U15 Friend-Wars   136
  Now use the bales, we see doth hire a man   166   U15 Friend-Wars   V136
  But here doth lie, till the last Day, ...   168   U16 Gray   3
  All is not barren land, doth fallow lie.   169   U17 Friend-Debt   16
  Crooked appeare; so that doth my conceipt: 170   U18 Elegy Can   8
  Where he doth steepe himselfe in Milke and Roses;   .   .   .   170   U19 Elegy By   8
  Knowledge, that sleepes, doth die;   174   U23 Himselfe   3
  Doth Clarius Harp want strings, ...   174   U23 Himselfe   9
  Doth vindicate it to eternitie.   175   U24 Frontispice   4
  Doth mete, whose lyne doth sound the depth of things:) .   .   .   176   U24 Frontispice   12
  High, as his mind, that doth advance   176   U25 Desmond   5
  Doth now command;   180   U25 Desmond   62
  Yet doth some wholsome Physick for the mind, ...   180   U26 Ode High   9
  True valour doth her owne renowne command   180   U26 Ode High   16
  Of Phaos forme? or doth the Boy   181   U27 Ode Helen   5
  Doth Cynthia, in Propertius song   181   U27 Ode Helen   11
  Scarce the Hill againe doth flourish, ...   184   U29 Fit of Rime   37
  Scarce the world a Wit doth nourish, ...   184   U29 Fit of Rime   38
  And (which doth all Atchievements get above)   187   U33 Councellour   38
  Where Love doth shine, there needs no Sunne, ...   189   U36 Song   5
  All lights into his one doth run;   189   U36 Song   6
  Where weaknesse doth offend, and vertue grieve, ...   192   U38 Elegy 'Tis   33
  It shakes even him, that all things else doth shake.   .   .   .   193   U38 Elegy 'Tis   72
  And with the vulgar doth it not obtaine   193   U38 Elegy 'Tis   81
  Streight puts off all his Anger, and doth kisse   193   U38 Elegy 'Tis   88
  Doth, while he keepes his watch, betray his stand.   .   .   .   198   U40 Elegy That   36
  Due to that one, that doth believe him just.   198   U40 Elegy That   40
  That from the Muses fountaines doth indorse   200   U42 Elegy Let   7
  So doth the King, and most of the Kings men   212   U43 Vulcan   211
  Or if Chance must, to each man that doth rise, ...   217   U46 Coke   23
  Doth labour with the Phrase more then the sense?   222   U49 Pucell   14
  Laden with Bellie, and doth hardly approach   230   U56 Covell   9
  And that's made up as doth the purse abound.   230   U56 Covell   12
  Made up still as the pockett doth abound.   230   U56 Covell   V 12
  Your happinesse, and doth not speake you blest, ...   234   U61 Epigram   9
  Doth by his doubt, distrust his promise more.   235   U63 Charles 2   4
  When your assiduous practise doth secure   236   U64 Charles 3   11
  This day the Court doth measure   240   U67 Muses   43
  So doth the flatt'rer with faire cunning strike   242   U69 Friend Son   14
  Not liv'd; for Life doth her great actions spell,   .   .   .   245   U70 Ode   59
  In bulke, doth make man better bee;   245   U70 Ode   66
  But fate doth so alternate the designe, ...   246   U70 Ode   95
  Doth take in easie Natures birth, ...   250   U74 Weston   2
  Doth show, the Graces, and the Houres   251   U74 Weston   16
  Such joyes, such sweet's doth your Returne   251   U74 Weston   19
  With light of love, this Paire doth intertexe!   254   U75 Epithalam.   60
  Have they bedew'd the Earth, where she doth tread,   .   .   .   254   U75 Epithalam.   66
  But doth his Carract, and just Standard keepe   255   U75 Epithalam.   100
  doth his prime Carract, and just Standard keepe   255   U75 Epithalam.   V100
  Doth Emulation stirre;   256   U75 Epithalam.   117
  —Doth most humbly show it, ...   259   U76 Petition   3
  Yet read him in these lines: He doth excell   262   U78 Digby   2
  Yet take him in these lines: He doth excell   262   U78 Digby   V 2
  Unto our yeare doth give the longest light.   262   U78 Digby   16
  For hee doth love my Verses, and will looke   263   U78 Digby   23
  When hee doth read them at the Treasurers bord, ...   263   U78 Digby   V 27
  Else, who doth praise a person by a new, ...   270   U81 Pawlet   37
  But a fain'd way, doth rob it of the true.   270   U81 Pawlet   38
  But a fain'd way, doth spoyle it of the true.   270   U81 Pawlet   V 38

		Page	Title	Line

DOTH (cont.)

Beholds her Maker! and, in him, doth see	271	U81 Pawlet	73
And she doth know, out of the shade of Death,	285	U84 Muse	91
What love with mercy mixed doth appeare?	286	U84 Muse	138
The Poplar tall, he then doth marrying twine	290	U85 Country	9
There, or the tall witch-hazill hee doth twine	290	U85 Country	V 9
Or the prest honey in pure pots doth keepe	290	U85 Country	15
Their swelling udders doth draw dry:	291	U85 Country	46
Among these Cates how glad the sight doth come	291	U85 Country	61
This hath pleas'd, doth please, and long will please; never	294	U88 Petronius	9
So, shunning faults, to greater fault doth lead,	307	Horace	43
The shunning vice, to greater vice doth lead,	339	Horace	V 45/ 43
And what they will not. Him, whose choice doth reare	307	Horace	56
His choise, who's matter to his power doth reare,	339	Horace	V 58/ 56
That from the North, the Navie safe doth store,	309	Horace	92
Once rowable, but now doth nourish men	309	Horace	94
Yet, sometime, doth the Comedie excite	311	Horace	132
Yet sometime both the Comoedy doth raise	341	Horace	V132
For Nature, first, within doth fashion us	311	Horace	152
What doth this Promiser such gaping worth	313	Horace	197
What doth this Promiser such great gaping worth	343	Horace	V197
The last doth from the midst dis-joyn'd appeare.	315	Horace	218
Doth wretchedly the use of things forbeare,	317	Horace	243
And the beholder to himselfe doth render.	317	Horace	259
Peace, and the open ports, that peace doth cause.	317	Horace	284
The open ports, and sports that peace doth cause,	345	Horace	V284
So rare, as with some taxe it doth ingage	323	Horace	383
Happier then wretched art, and doth, by it,	325	Horace	420
For, neither doth the String still yeeld that sound	329	Horace	521
Nor alwayes doth the loosed Bow, hit that	329	Horace	524
Which it doth threaten. Therefore, where I see	329	Horace	525
Doth please; this, ten times over, will delight.	331	Horace	544
As jarring Musique doth, at jolly feasts,	331	Horace	557
His armes in Mars his field, he doth refuse;	331	Horace	566
Why not? being honest, and free-borne, doth hate	352	Horace	V547/571
So doth the one, the others helpe require,	333	Horace	585
So doth the Poet, who is rich in land,	333	Horace	599
So doth the Poet, that is rich in Land,	353	Horace	V599
The Scoffer, the true Praiser doth out-goe.	333	Horace	616
Doth the same thing with him, that would him kill.	335	Horace	666
Doth shine in her discerning,	365	Ode Splendor	10
Behold, where one doth swim;	366	Ode Who saith	3
"So much doth Virtue hate,	367	Ode Who saith	31
The Dutch whom Wealth (not Hatred) doth divide;	368	Ode Who saith	85
Here, like Arion, our Coryate doth draw	374	Coryat 1	10
Each leafe of his journall, and line doth unlocke	380	Coryat 3	23
He there doth protest he saw of the eleven.	380	Coryat 3	46
Doth he once dissemble, but tels he did ride	380	Coryat 3	52
Who bluntly doth but looke upon the same,	383	Author	3
Who cannot reade, but onely doth desire	383	Author	9
As a deformed face doth a true glasse.	389	Aleman	10
Or blinde Affection, which doth ne're advance	391	Shakespeare	9
And art alive still, while thy Booke doth live,	391	Shakespeare	23
His Art doth give the fashion. And, that he,	392	Shakespeare	58
And doth deserve all muniments of praise,	400	Beaumont	9
Something your Surship doth not yet intend!	402	Inigo Jones 1	14
Sir Inigo doth feare it as I heare	407	Inigo Jones 3	1
No faith's more firme, or flat, then where't doth creep.	413	Ghyrlond	20
Whose chearfull look our sadnesse doth destroy,	414	Ghyrlond	43
for when the profitt with the payne doth meete,	418	Answer	6
The mayne comaund of scepters, soone doth perishe	422	Lucan	9
Truth itself doth flow in Wine.	657	Door Apollo	6

DOUBLE

| And, striving so to double his delight, | 76 | E118 Gut | 3 |
| His double Bow, and round his Arrowes sends; | 170 | U19 Elegy By | 4 |

DOUBLY

| Let me give two: that doubly am got free, | 31 | E13 Empirick | 3 |
| For whom I doubly would expire, | 293 | U87 Hor.3:9 | 15 |

DOUBT

Man scarse can make that doubt, but thou canst teach.	31	E14 Camden	10
Yet give thy jealous subjects leave to doubt:	43	E51 James 3	5
Delay is bad, doubt worse, depending worst;	50	E70 Wm Roe 1	5
Who shall doubt, Donne, where I a Poet bee,	62	E96 Donne 2	1
Goe on, and doubt not, what posteritie,	70	E109 Nevil	15
Or those, who doubt the common mouth of fame,	111	F11 Epode	79
Or those, which doubt the common mouth of fame,	111	F11 Epode	V 79
How can I doubt to finde thee ever, here?	122	F15 Heaven	16
Why doe you doubt, or stay?	139	U2 Another	4
Nor doe we doubt, but that we can,	145	U5 Woman-kind	7
Yet, yet I doubt he is not knowne,	147	U7 Nymph	20
As make away my doubt,	147	U7 Nymph	23
I Doubt that, Love is rather deafe, then blind,	149	U9 Picture	V 1
You cannot doubt, but I, who freely know	153	U13 Sacvile	13
I now begin to doubt, if ever Grace,	207	U43 Vulcan	107
The first of which, I doubt, you will refuse;	230	U56 Covell	V 6
Doth by his doubt, distrust his promise more.	235	U63 Charles 2	4
No doubt all Infants would returne like thee.	243	U70 Ode	20
And the world in it, I begin to doubt,	395	May	4

DOUBTFUL

| They're dark, bid cleare 'hem; al that's doubtful wrote | 354 | Horace | V637 |

DOUBTFULL

| T'advance his doubtfull issue, and ore-flow | 117 | F13 Aubigny | 40 |
| And doubtfull Dayes (which were nam'd Criticall,) | 180 | U26 Ode High | 6 |

159

	Page	Title	Line

DOUBTFULL (cont.)
They're darke, bid cleare this: all that's doubtfull wrote . 335 Horace 637
Betweene the doubtfull sway of Reason', and sense; . . . 370 Author 12
DOUBTING
Seeke doubting Men to please, ... 150 U10 Jealousie 15
DOUBTS
Who doubts, those fruits God can with gaine restore, . 235 U63 Charles 2 3
DOVE
But we propose a person like our Dove, . . . 112 F11 Epode 91
But I Conceive a person like my Dove, . . . 112 F11 Epode V 91
Each that drawes, is a Swan, or a Dove, . . . 134 U2 Triumph 3
DOVER
An Epigram To My Joviall Good Freind Mr. Robert Dover, . . 415 Dover Ttl
But I can tell thee, Dover, how thy Games . . . 415 Dover 3
DOVES
With Doves; or Lambes, with Tygres coupled be. . . 305 Horace 16
DOWER
Nor that your beautie wanted not a dower, . . . 117 F13 Aubigny 37
DOWGATE
Or Dowgate Torrent falling into Thames, . . . 407 Inigo Jones 2 16
DOWNE (NOUN)
Or Swans Downe ever? . . . . . . 135 U2 Triumph 26
As the Downe, and shew it oft; . . . . 141 U2 Her man 26
Who, e're the first downe bloomed on the chin, . . 247 U70 Ode 127
This change'd his Downe; till this, as white . . 366 Ode Who saith 25
DOWNE
Who, when you'have burnt your selves downe to the snuffe, . 45 E59 Spies 2
To plucke downe mine, Poll sets up new wits still, . 50 E71 Parrat 1
And bad me lay th'usurped laurell downe: . . 80 E126 Mrs Cary 4
Had burst with storme, and downe fell, ab excelsis, . 86 E133 Voyage 95
Or were precipitated downe the jakes, . . . 87 E133 Voyage 137
There's none, that dwell about them, wish them downe; . 94 F2 Penshurst 47
The eares cut downe in their most height, . . 98 F3 Wroth V 41
It is a golden chaine let downe from heaven, . . 110 F11 Epode 47
Toyles, by grave custome, up and downe the court, . 113 F12 Rutland 5
Melt downe their husbands land, to poure away . . 118 F13 Aubigny 73
Nor cast them downe, but let them rise, . . 144 U4 Song 3
That all respect; She must lie downe: Nay more, . 163 U15 Friend-Wars 53
It is not likely I should now looke downe . . 200 U42 Elegy Let 37
'Twas Jupiter that hurl'd thee headlong downe, . . 203 U43 Vulcan 9
'Twas Jupiter that cast thee headlong downe, . . 203 U43 Vulcan V 9
Of Spaine or France; or were not prick'd downe one . 219 U47 Tribe 47
From whence they fall, cast downe with their owne weight. . 224 U50 Countesse 12
Of Tryals, to worke downe . . . . 255 U75 Epithalam. 103
Their Heads, that Envy would hold downe . . 272 U84 Cradle 3
Could not goe downe my belly then . . . 291 U85 Country 54
Flow my thin teares, downe these pale cheeks of mine? . 293 U86 Hor.4:1 34
Downe close by shore, this other creeping steales, . 339 Horace V 40/ 39
That tarries till the hangings be ta'en downe, . . 315 Horace 221
Of their long labours, was in Verse set downe: . . 329 Horace 500
To let it downe, who knowes, if he did cast . . 335 Horace 656
till giddie with amazement I fell downe . . 361 Palmer 25
Here, not up Holdborne, but downe a steepe hill, . 374 Coryat 1 12
Honest Tom Tell-Troth puts downe Roger, How? . . 378 Coryat 2 81
Thy Richard, rais'd in song, past pulling downe. . 385 Brooke 8
And not fall downe before it? and confess . . 406 Inigo Jones's 1 91
yearly set out there, to sayle downe the Street, . 407 Inigo Jones 2 18
All, pouring their full showre of graces downe, . . 413 Ghyrlond 31
DOWRIE
Wherein wise Nature you a dowrie gave, . . . 114 F12 Rutland 35
DO'YOU
But 'mong'st these Tiberts, who do'you thinke there was? . 88 E133 Voyage 155
DOZEN (See DOSEN)
DRAD
(As my hope tells) that our drad Cynthia's shine, . . 179 U25 Desmond V 58
DRAG
Disguisd? and thence drag forth Enormity? . . . 405 Inigo Jones 1 81
DRAMA
I cannot for the stage a Drama lay, . . . 72 E112 Gamster 7
DRAMME
Concluded from a Carract to a dramme. . . . 415 Rutter 30
DRAUGHT
As loth, the second draught, or cast to stay, . . 94 F2 Penshurst 35
Mee, the scope of his next draught, . . . 133 U2 Suffered 11
That sit upon the Comon Draught: or Strand! . . 408 Inigo Jones 3 13
DRAW
Whose manners draw, more than thy powers constraine. . 37 E35 James 2 3
To draw the custome: but her selfe gets all. . . 53 E78 Hornet 2
Thou must draw more: and they, that hope to see . 66 E102 Pembroke 19
Nay, now you puffe, tuske, and draw up your chin, . 69 E107 Hungry 29
Some vicious foole draw neare, ... 111 F11 Epode 66
Or feare to draw true lines, 'cause others paint: . 117 F13 Aubigny 20
But the Arrow home did draw . . . . 133 U2 Suffered 14
And draw, and conquer all mens love, . . . 173 U22 Elegy Tho 7
For Silke will draw some sneaking Songster thither. . 200 U42 Elegy Let 26
Thou canst draw forth thy forces, and fight drie . 214 U44 Speach 45
But if, for honour, we must draw the Sword, . . 219 U47 Tribe 39
To square my Circle, I confesse; but draw . . 227 U52 Answer 8
How I would draw, and take hold and delight. . . 227 U52 Answer 18
Yet when of friendship I would draw the face, . . 227 U52 Answer 22
This were a spectacle! A sight to draw . . 233 U59 Newcastle 13
Did wiser Nature draw thee back, . . . 243 U70 Ode 11
Did wisest Nature draw thee back, . . . 243 U70 Ode V 11

160

	Page	Title	Line
DRAW (cont.)			
Draw first a Cloud: all save her neck;	276	U84 Body	13
The Heaven design'd, draw next a Spring,	276	U84 Body	21
Last, draw the circles of this Globe,	276	U84 Body	25
Next sitting we will draw her mind.	277	U84 Body	32
To draw a thing that cannot sit.	277	U84 Mind	8
Their swelling udders doth draw dry:	291	U85 Country	46
To view the weary Oxen draw, with bare	291	U85 Country	63
So he that varying still affects to draw	339	Horace V 42/	40
Forbids thee forth againe thy foot to draw.	313	Horace	194
But light from smoake; that he may draw his bright	315	Horace	204
Thence draw forth true expressions. For, sometimes,	327	Horace	455
It would, must be: lest it alive would draw	329	Horace	509
"Musicke hath power to draw,	367	Ode Who saith	47
Here, like Arion, our Coryate doth draw	374	Coryat 1	10
To draw no envy (Shakespeare) on thy name,	390	Shakespeare	1
Lend me thy voyce, O Fame, that I may draw	396	Drayton	12
He draw a Forum, with quadriviall Streets!	407	Inigo Jones 2	11
DRAWER			
Or swaggering with the Watch, or Drawer, drunke;	156	U13 Sacvile	94
DRAWES			
Each that drawes, is a Swan, or a Dove,	134	U2 Triumph	3
With endlesse labours, whilst thy learning drawes	217	U46 Coke	18
I have a body, yet, that spirit drawes	219	U47 Tribe	41
Not letting goe his hold, where he drawes food,	337	Horace	679
Not letting goe the skin, where he drawes food,	355	Horace	V679
DRAWING			
Of Argument, still drawing forth the best,	187	U33 Councellour	27
DRAWNE			
Your partie-per-pale picture, one halfe drawne	51	E73 Fine Grand	13
So, Anacreon drawne the Ayre	136	U2 Cupid	14
Lie drawne to life, in his soft Verse,	181	U27 Ode Helen	7
Was drawne to practise other hue, then that	188	U34 Small Poxe	8
Whom Faction had not drawne to studie sides.	207	U43 Vulcan	104
Whom fashion had not drawne to studie sides.	207	U43 Vulcan	V104
To have their Husbands drawne forth to the field,	213	U44 Speach	18
With one great blot, you had drawne me as I am.	227	U52 Answer	V 12
Till he had sold his Piece, drawne so unlike:	242	U69 Friend Son	13
Hath drawne on me, from the times,	259	U76 Petition	17
Hath drawne on him, from the times,	259	U76 Petition	V 17
Sitting, and ready to be drawne,	275	U84 Body	1
But, as a Matrone drawne at solemne times	321	Horace	338
But, let the Faunes, drawne from their Groves, beware,	321	Horace	355
These, the free meale might have beene well drawne out:	331	Horace	560
How many learned men he have drawne with his hooke	380	Coryat 3	44
O, could he but have drawne his wit	390	Reader	5
Drawne Aristotle on us! & thence showne	402	Inigo Jones 1	9
DRAYTON			
. . . Muses Of His Friend M. Drayton.	396	Drayton	Ttl
DREADS			
Nor dreads the Seas inraged harmes:	289	U85 Country	6
DREAME			
That cryes, we dreame, and sweares, there's no such thing,	111	F11 Epode	67
That cryes, I dreame, and sweares, there's no such thing,	111	F11 Epode	V 67
The Dreame.	150	U11 Dreame	Ttl
Love in a subtile Dreame disguis'd,	151	U11 Dreame	4
Dreame thou could'st hurt it; but before thou wake	250	U73 Weston	11
Hard-hearted, I dreame every Night	293	U86 Hor.4:1	37
It was no Dreame! I was awake, and saw!	396	Drayton	11
DREAMES			
In dreames, begun in hope, and end in spoile.	162	U15 Friend-Wars	10
Whose shapes, like sick-mens dreames, are fain'd so vaine,	305	Horace	9
Whose shapes, like sick-mens dreames, are form'd so vaine,	338	Horace	V 9
DRENCH			
The Danes that drench	368	Ode Who saith	86
DRESSE			
And elements of honor, then the dresse;	70	E109 Nevil	10
And safely trust to dresse, not burne their Boates.	208	U43 Vulcan	128
She spent more time in teares her selfe to dresse	287	U84 Muse	180
DRESSING			
And her dressing did out-brave	132	U2 How he saw	3
Lesse shall I for the Art or dressing care,	158	U14 Selden	3
And every Dressing for a Pitfall set	164	U15 Friend-Wars	66
Carriage, and dressing. There is up of late	215	U44 Speach	88
Indeed, her Dressing some man might delight,	223	U49 Pucell	31
To make you merry on the Dressing stoole	230	U56 Covell	21
And joy'd to weare the dressing of his lines!	392	Shakespeare	48
DREST			
Hornet, thou hast thy wife drest, for the stall,	53	E78 Hornet	1
And, drest in shepheards tyre, who would not say:	68	E105 L Wroth 2	9
When shee was farre: and not a roome, but drest,	96	F2 Penshurst	87
Drest, you still for man should take him;	141	U2 Her man	38
Wherein she sits so richly drest,	251	U74 Weston	14
The Lady Frances, drest	253	U75 Epithalam.	37
Our great, our good. Where one's so drest	265	U79 New-yeares	44
DREW			
Such a Lightning (as I drew)	132	U2 How he saw	24
Since I drew a Morning kisse	137	U2 Kisse	2
Into the Kindred, whence thy Adam drew	274	U84 Descent	15
DRIE			
So to see the Fountaine drie,	183	U29 Fit of Rime	22
Thou canst draw forth thy forces, and fight drie	214	U44 Speach	45

	Page	Title	Line

DRI'D
Dri'd up? lyes Thespia wast? . . . . . . 174 U23 Himselfe 8
DRILL
He that but saw thy curious Captaines drill, . . . 213 U44 Speach 29
DRINCKE
They drincke with their conceits, ... 175 U23 Himselfe V 23
DRING
Diana's Grove, or Altar, with the bor-/Dring . . 305 Horace 20
bor-/Dring Circles of swift waters that intwine . . 305 Horace 21
DRINKE
Doe all, that longs to the anarchy of drinke, . . 74 E115 Honest Man 12
Drinke to me, onely, with thine eyes, . . . 106 F9 Celia 3 1
Drinke to me, Coelia, with thine eyes, . . . 106 F9 Celia 3 V 1
Doth aske a drinke divine: . . . 106 F9 Celia 3 6
And some doe drinke, and some doe dance, . . 120 F14 Sydney 2
Lowd sacrifice of drinke, for their health-sake! . . 156 U13 Sacvile 100
Is nothing, such scarce meat and drinke he'le give, . 167 U15 Friend-Wars 159
And then I taste it. But as men drinke up . . 197 U40 Elegy That 3
That live in the wild Anarchie of Drinke, . . . 218 U47 Tribe 10
Orgies of drinke, or fain'd protests: . . . 246 U70 Ode 104
DRINKERS
Hang up all the poor Hop-Drinkers, ... 657 Door Apollo 7
DRINKES
By that one spell he lives, eates, drinkes, arrayes . . 30 E12 Shift 5
He drinkes to no man: that's, too, like a lord. . . 35 E28 Surly 14
Surfet? and Quarrel? drinkes the tother health? . . 166 U15 Friend-Wars 115
DRINKING
forfeitinge their drinking lease, ... 418 Moon 43
DRIVE
Thou hast no more blowes, Fate, to drive at one: . . 283 U84 Muse 27
DRIVEN
When was there contract better driven by Fate? . . 28 E5 Union 1
Of Angels should be driven . . . 144 U3 Musicall 22
Are they so scanted in their store? or driven . . 241 U68 House-hold 3
Grow a safe Writer, and be warie-driven . . 323 Horace 393
DRIVES
And drives it in to eat on my offence, . . . 191 U38 Elegy 'Tis 6
That drives the Hart to seeke unused wayes, . . 264 U79 New-yeares 21
Hee drives diseases from our Folds, . . . 265 U79 New-yeares 62
Or hence, or thence, he drives with many a Hound . . 290 U85 Country 31
DRIV'N
Of Fortunes wheele by Lucan driv'n about, . . . 395 May 3
DRONKEN
Thy night not dronken, but from cares layd wast; . . 295 U90 Mart.10:47 9
DROOP
Or droop they as disgrac't, ... 174 U23 Himselfe 11
DROOPING
Or influence, chide, or cheere the drooping Stage; . . 392 Shakespeare 78
DROP
Without the hazard of a drop of blood, . . . 214 U44 Speach 47
Stay, drop a teare for him that's dead, . . . 233 U60 La-ware 2
Till he drop off, a Horse-leech, full of blood. . . 337 Horace 680
Till, horse-leech-like, he drop off, full of blood. . . 355 Horace V680
Shall powre forth many a line, drop many a letter, . . 666 Glover 9
DROPP
I Cannot bring my Muse to dropp her Vies . . . 415 Dover 1
DROPPING
Sindge Capons, or poore Pigges, dropping their eyes; . 205 U43 Vulcan 53
Sindge capons, or crispe Pigges, dropping their eyes; . 205 U43 Vulcan V 53
And louse-dropping Case, are the Armes of his travell. . 375 Coryat 1 27
DROPS
The least indulgent thought thy pen drops forth! . . 44 E55 Beaumont 4
Or the drops in silver Thames, . . . 103 F6 Celia 2 15
As showers; and sweet as drops of Balme. . . . 280 U84 Mind 60
DROSSE
But let this drosse carry what price it will . . 114 F12 Rutland 27
As hath thy James; cleans'd from originall drosse, . . 268 U80 Christning 9
DROUPES
And the whole lumpe growes round, deform'd, and droupes, . 227 U52 Answer 5
DROWN
A Tune to drown the Ballads of thy Father: . . . 411 Gill 12
DROWND
till th'one hath drownd the other in our sightes, . . 361 Palmer 20
DROWNE
Each night, to drowne his cares: But when the gaine . . 56 E87 Hazard 3
Of parting, drowne it in the hope to meet . . . 197 U40 Elegy That 7
I struggled with this passion that did drowne . . 362 Palmer 28
To dimme and drowne . . . . . 369 Ode Who saith 108
DROWN'D
Yet drown'd they not. They had five lives in future. . . 88 E133 Voyage 154
And in their cups, their cares are drown'd: . . . 98 F3 Wroth 60
If thou would'st have me weepe, be thou first drown'd . . 311 Horace 145
DROWNES
So much my Subject drownes the rest. . . . 182 U27 Ode Helen 36
DROWNING
Joynting Syllabes, drowning Letters, . . . 183 U29 Fit of Rime 10
My selfe am so neare drowning? . . . . 365 Ode Splendor 20
DRUDGE
The Idiot, keeping holy-day, or drudge, . . . 319 Horace 301
DRUG
Your 'pothecarie, and his drug sayes no. . . . 46 E62 Would-bee 4
Rigid, and harsh, which is a Drug austere . . . 190 U37 Friend-Book 17

DRUM
That still th'art made the suppers flagge, the drum,   .   .   81   E129 Mime   7
Wake, friend, from forth thy Lethargie: the Drum   .   .   .   162   U15 Friend-Wars   1
Wake, friend, and finde thy self: awake, the Drum   .   .   162   U15 Friend-Wars V   1
But that I heare, againe, thy Drum to beate   .   .   .   397   Drayton   55
DRUMS
With beating of our Drums: 239   U67 Muses   15
With beating of their Drums: 239   U67 Muses   V 15
What Drums or Trumpets, or great Ord'nance can,   .   .   249   U72 King   9
Drums against Drums, the neighing of the Horse,   .   .   397   Drayton   40
DRUNKARDS
Vile Tavernes, and the Drunkards pisse him out;   .   .   211   U43 Vulcan   186
Vile Tavernes, and have Drunkards pisse him out;   .   .   211   U43 Vulcan   V186
DRUNKE   (See also DRONKEN)
Hazard a month forsware his; and grew drunke,   .   .   56   E87 Hazard   2
Give your yong States-men, (that first make you drunke,   .   69   E107 Hungry   19
Or swaggering with the Watch, or Drawer, drunke;   .   .   156   U13 Sacvile   94
Having well eat, and drunke (the rites being done)   .   319   Horace   325
DRUNKENNEST
What honour given to the drunkennest Guests?   .   .   166   U15 Friend-Wars   118
DRY   (See also DRIE)
And spunge-like with it dry up the blood quite: .   .   155   U13 Sacvile   69
To fall a logge at last, dry, bald, and seare: .   .   245   U70 Ode   68
Their swelling udders doth draw dry: 291   U85 Country   46
DRYADS
Thy Mount, to which the Dryads doe resort,   .   .   .   93   F2 Penshurst   10
DUBLET
Except a dublet, and bought of the Jewes: .   .   .   380   Coryat 3   49
DUE
Yet, all heavens gifts, being heavens due,   .   .   .   33   E22 Daughter   3
Or, keeping your due state, that would not cry,   .   .   68   E105 L Wroth 2   17
O, runne not proud of this. Yet, take thy due.   .   .   81   E129 Mime   15
And did think, such Rites were due   .   .   .   138   U2 Kisse   19
Such worship due to kicking of a Punck!   .   .   .   155   U13 Sacvile   93
Then to your love, and gift. And all's but due.   .   189   U37 Friend-Book   3
Due to that one, that doth believe him just.   .   .   198   U40 Elegy That   40
How many verses, Madam, are your Due!   .   .   231   U56 Covell   27
Who dares denie, that all first-fruits are due   .   .   235   U63 Charles 2   1
Keepe due proportion in the ample song,   .   .   .   395   May   12
Now, for mine owne part, and it is but due,   .   .   415   Rutter   12
DUELL
Except the duell. Can sing songs, and catches;   .   .   74   E115 Honest Man   13
DUE'LLISTS
And hath no honor lost, our Due'llists say.   .   .   42   E48 Mungril   3
DUELY
Old men so duely, ...   77   E120 S. P.   14
DUES
And giving dues to all Mankinds deserts!   .   .   289   U84 Muse   224
Fit dues. The Child, that now knowes how to say,   .   344   Horace   V225
Indeed, give fitting dues to every man.   .   .   .   325   Horace   452
DUKE
. . . Surviving Duke of the same name.   .   .   252   U75 Epithalam.   Ttl
Like what she is, the Daughter of a Duke,   .   .   253   U75 Epithalam.   42
DUKES
Your Arch-Dukes Agents, and your Beringhams,   .   .   69   E107 Hungry   23
DULL
Was dull, and long, ere shee would goe to man: .   57   E90 Mill   3
There's none so dull, that for your stile would aske,   .   68   E105 L Wroth 2   15
What bird, or beast, is knowne so dull,   .   .   101   F4 To the World   29
Of his dull god-head, were sinne. Ile implore   .   107   F10 Proludium   6
Of his dull god-head, were sinne. Lets implore   .   107   F10 Proludium   V 6
Goe, crampe dull Mars, light Venus, when he snorts,   .   107   F10 Proludium   16
Hang up those dull, and envious fooles,   .   .   .   146   U6 Defence   1
Safe from the wolves black jaw, and the dull Asses hoofe.   175   U23 Himselfe   36
Like the dull wearied Crane that (come on land)   .   198   U40 Elegy That   35
To th' dull, a Spur   256   U75 Epithalam.   118
Is it because it sees us dull, ...   279   U84 Mind   45
Dull, and prophane, weake, and imperfect eyes,   .   284   U84 Muse   79
On steele, though 't selfe be dull, and cannot cut.   .   325   Horace   434
He makes the Camell & dull Ass his prize.   .   .   408   Inigo Jones 3   8
Whose ayre will sooner Hell, then their dull senses peirce,   420   Ode:If Men   23
Those dull Girls, no good can mean us,   .   .   .   657   Door Apollo   11
DULNESSE
As if that ex'lent Dulnesse were Loves grace;   .   198   U40 Elegy That   24
DULY
Be duly done to those   255   U75 Epithalam.   93
DUMBE
Curst be his Muse, that could lye dumbe, or hid   .   47   E63 Salisbury 2   11
Curst be my voyce if it lye dumbe, or hid   .   .   47   E63 Salisbury 2 V   11
Where ere he met me; now hee's dumbe, or proud.   .   62   E97 Motion   8
Though not in these, in rithmes not wholly dumbe,   .   182   U28 Worth   2
Better be dumbe, then superstitious!   .   .   .   284   U84 Muse   73
DUNCOTE
Ridway rob'd Duncote of three hundred pound,   .   29   E8 Robbery   1
Beg'd Ridwayes pardon: Duncote, now, doth crye;   .   29   E8 Robbery   4
DUNGEON
Of teares, and dungeon of calamitie!   .   .   .   283   U84 Muse   35
DUNSTABLE
Here, up the Alpes (not so plaine as to Dunstable)   .   374   Coryat 1   16
DUR'D
When Vice alike in time with vertue dur'd.   .   .   176   U24 Frontispice   8
DURST
Durst thinke it great, and worthy wonder too,   .   46   E60 Mounteagle   7

DURST (cont.)

	Page	Title	Line
Durst valour make, almost, but not a crime.	48	E66 Cary	6
And land on one, whose face durst never bee	56	E88 Monsieur	5
If, my religion safe, I durst embrace	61	E95 Savile	1
Strait hee ran, and durst not stay,	132	U2 How he saw	16
As he durst love Truth and me.	142	U2 Her man	52
Whom never yet he durst attempt awake;	151	U11 Dreame	6
To have such doe me good, I durst not name:	153	U13 Sacvile	18
Man thought the valianter, 'cause he durst sweare,	168	U15 Friend-Wars	192
How in these ruines, Vulcan, durst thou lurke,	207	U43 Vulcan	V105
She durst not kisse, but flung thee from her brest.	208	U43 Vulcan	114
Whom they durst handle in their holy-day coates,	208	U43 Vulcan	127
Whom they durst handle in their high day coates,	208	U43 Vulcan	V127
Thou art true Vulcan still! Thou durst not spare	210	U43 Vulcan	V159
Who durst live great, 'mongst all the colds, and heates,	233	U59 Newcastle	21
Because it durst have noblier dy'd.	234	U60 La-ware	18
The good, and durst not practise it, were glad	247	U70 Ode	119
I durst not aime at that: The dotes were such	269	U81 Pawlet	25
I durst not aime at, the dotes thereof were such	269	U81 Pawlet	V 25
That durst be that in Court: a vertu' alone	371	Epitaph	4
Shewes he dares more then Paules Church-yard durst do.	378	Coryat 2	85

DURT

	Page	Title	Line
A parcell of Court-durt, a heape, and masse	172	U21 Ltl Shrub	5

DURTIE

	Page	Title	Line
Oylie Expansions, or shrunke durtie folds,	220	U47 Tribe	68

DUST

	Page	Title	Line
And now lye lost in their forgotten dust.	114	F12 Rutland	40
With dust of ancestors, in graves but dwell.	121	F14 Sydney	40
on a lovers dust, made sand for ane Houre Glasse	148	U8 Houre-glasse	VTtl
Doe but consider this small dust,	148	U8 Houre-glasse	1
will all turne dust, & may not make me swell.	387	Cavendish	4
Will all be dust, & may not make me swell.	387	Cavendish	V 4
Untill the dust retorned bee	400	Lady Ogle	31

DUTCH

	Page	Title	Line
As french-men in his companie, should seeme dutch?	56	E88 Monsieur	8
Tell the grosse Dutch those grosser tales of yours,	68	E107 Hungry	5
The Dutch whom Wealth (not Hatred) doth divide;	368	Ode Who saith	85

DUTIE

	Page	Title	Line
Can tell a States-mans dutie, what the arts	325	Horace	449

DUTIES

	Page	Title	Line
To whom you owe all duties of your grounds;	265	U79 New-yeares	49

DUTY

	Page	Title	Line
As she goes, all hearts doe duty	134	U2 Triumph	5

DWARFES

	Page	Title	Line
Are Dwarfes of Honour, and have neither weight	157	U13 Sacvile	147
Of errant Knight-hood, with the Dames, and Dwarfes?	205	U43 Vulcan	67

DWELL

	Page	Title	Line
Your Fleet-lane Furies; and hot cookes doe dwell,	88	E133 Voyage	143
There's none, that dwell about them, wish them downe;	94	F2 Penshurst	47
'Tis better, if he there can dwell.	99	F3 Wroth	94
'Tis better, if he then can dwell.	99	F3 Wroth	V 94
With dust of ancestors, in graves but dwell.	121	F14 Sydney	40
Dwell, dwell here still: O, being every-where,	122	F15 Heaven	15
And dwell as in my Center, as I can,	219	U47 Tribe	60
For never saw I yet the Muses dwell,	228	U53 Newcastle	15
For that to dwell in, and be still at home.	262	U78 Digby	8
For those to dwell in, and be still at home.	262	U78 Digby	V 8
As other soules, to his, dwell in a Lane:	262	U78 Digby	12
To children; we must alwayes dwell, and stay	317	Horace	253
which, did they neere so neate, or proudly dwell,	387	Cavendish	3

DWELLER

	Page	Title	Line
Where now, thou art made Dweller;	220	U48 Bacchus	4

DWELLS

	Page	Title	Line
May say, their lords have built, but thy lord dwells.	96	F2 Penshurst	102

DWELT

	Page	Title	Line
Calling for Radamanthus, that dwelt by,	89	E133 Voyage	187

DYD'ST

	Page	Title	Line
To take our nature; becam'st man, and dyd'st,	128	U1 Trinitie	22

DYE (NOUN)

	Page	Title	Line
The Glasse-house, Dye-fats, and their Fornaces;	211	U43 Vulcan	180
Yet with a Dye, that feares no Moth,	230	U55 Burges	7

DYE

	Page	Title	Line
Ridway was tane, arraign'd, condemn'd to dye;	29	E8 Robbery	2
Which was a cater-piller. So 'twill dye.	31	E15 Court-worm	4
How can so great example dye in mee,	57	E89 Allen	7
His life, but makes, that he can dye no more.	71	E110 Edmonds 1	22
As much beautie, as could dye:	79	E124 Elizabeth	4
Turtles can chastly dye;	111	F11 Epode	74
Turtles will chastly dye;	111	F11 Epode	V 74
And see all dead here, or about to dye!	271	U81 Pawlet	86
And much shall dye, that now is nobly liv'd,	309	Horace	102
With every song, I sweare, and so would dye:	397	Drayton	54
An Agincourt, an Agincourt, or dye.	398	Drayton	70
A Mungrel Curre? Thou should'st stinck forth, and dye	409	Detractor	15

DY'D

	Page	Title	Line
Two bravely in the battaile fell, and dy'd,	60	E93 Radcliffe	5
Because it durst have noblier dy'd.	234	U60 La-ware	18
'Twere time that I dy'd too, now shee is dead,	282	U84 Muse	1

DY'D (COLORED)

	Page	Title	Line
Those that did sing, and act: their faces dy'd	319	Horace	314

DYED

	Page	Title	Line
Fitter, where it dyed, to tell,	79	E124 Elizabeth	11

	Page	Title	Line
DYE-FATS			
The Glasse-house, Dye-fats, and their Fornaces;	211	U43 Vulcan	180
DYERS			
the Dyers, Glasshouse and the furnaces;	211	U43 Vulcan	V180
DYES			
He, that, but living halfe his age, dyes such;	76	E119 Shelton	15
Not doing good, scarce when he dyes.	99	F3 Wroth	84
his life, his love, his honour, which ne'r dyes,	382	Rich	8
Hee dyes with an Ill sent,	420	Ode:If Men	16
DYING			
His deedes too dying, but in bookes (whose good	71	E110 Edmonds 1	15
His deedes too dying, save in bookes (whose good	71	E110 Edmonds 1	V 15
And so, have kept me dying a whole age,	205	U43 Vulcan	55
And so, have kept them dying a whole age,	205	U43 Vulcan	V 55
Suffring, and dying to redeeme our losse!	288	U84 Muse	202
The first-borne dying; so the aged state	309	Horace	87
The first-borne dying; so the aged Fate	340	Horace	V 87
Though, now by Love transform'd, & dayly dying:	369	Ode Who saith	101
DYVE			
Up & about? Dyve into Cellars too	405	Inigo Jones 1	80
E			
R. Rose, I. Ivy, E. sweet Eglantine.	412	Ghyrlond	4
EACH			
Here lyes to each her parents ruth,	33	E22 Daughter	1
Donne, the delight of Phoebus, and each Muse,	34	E23 Donne 1	1
Telling the motions of each petticote,	34	E25 Beast 1	3
He takes up all, makes each mans wit his owne.	45	E56 Poet-Ape	8
And that thou seek'st reward of thy each act,	47	E63 Salisbury 2	5
Before thou wert it, in each good mans heart.	49	E67 Suffolk	10
Each best day of our life escapes us, first.	50	E70 Wm Roe 1	6
I meant each softest vertue, there should meet,	52	E76 Bedford 1	11
Each night, to drowne his cares: But when the gaine	56	E87 Hazard	3
And what each prince doth for intelligence owe,	59	E92 New Crie	12
For twelve yeeres yet to come, what each state lacks.	59	E92 New Crie	14
By his each glorious parcell to be knowne!	62	E97 Motion	6
About his forme. What then so swells each lim?	63	E97 Motion	19
We each to other may this voyce enspire;	81	E128 Wm Roe 2	11
That, not a paire of friends each other see,	81	E129 Mime	1
Furies there wanted not: each scold was ten.	84	E133 Voyage	15
Tempte such a passage? when each privies seate	88	E133 Voyage	168
Each banke doth yeeld thee coneyes; and the topps	94	F2 Penshurst	25
Fig, grape, and quince, each in his time doth come:	94	F2 Penshurst	42
Each morne, and even, they are taught to pray,	96	F2 Penshurst	95
And each where boast it as his merit,	99	F3 Wroth	78
Each into other, and had now made one.	120	F13 Aubigny	120
Each that drawes, is a Swan, or a Dove,	134	U2 Triumph	3
And betweene each rising breast,	137	U2 Cupid	33
Each suck others breath.	139	U2 Another	16
Till each of us be made a Starre,	143	U3 Musicall	3
Till each of us is made a Starre,	143	U3 Musicall	V 3
They say the Angells marke each deed,	144	U3 Musicall	17
As it would be to each a fame:	148	U7 Nymph	34
That though they did possesse each limbe,	151	U12 Corbet	9
So each, that's done, and tane, becomes a Brace.	154	U13 Sacvile	40
All the Towne-curs take each their snatch at me.	155	U13 Sacvile	72
Profit in ought: each day some little adde,	157	U13 Sacvile	132
And jealous each of other, yet thinke long	164	U15 Friend-Wars	73
To teach each suit he has, the ready way	165	U15 Friend-Wars	108
When I am hoarse, with praising his each cast,	167	U15 Friend-Wars	151
Some note of which each varied Pillar beares,	176	U24 Frontispice	15
Is Horace his each love so high	181	U27 Ode Helen	13
From each of which I labour to be free,	190	U37 Friend-Book	28
God lightens not at mans each fraile offence,	193	U38 Elegy 'Tis	68
Or if Chance must, to each man that doth rise,	217	U46 Coke	23
And as lip-thirstie, in each words expence,	222	U49 Pucell	13
What each man sayes of it, and of what coat	232	U58 Book-seller	4
And each intelligence	239	U67 Muses	22
What, by that name, wee each to other owe,	241	U69 Friend Son	4
Each syllab'e answer'd, and was form'd, how faire;	245	U70 Ode	63
Each stiled, by his end,	247	U70 Ode	111
How each one playes his part, of the large Pedigree.	258	U75 Epithalam.	176
And each shall know, there, one anothers face,	285	U84 Muse	115
Each line, as it were graphick, in the face!	287	U84 Muse	154
In the discerning of each conscience, so!	289	U84 Muse	222
Fit for the sock: Each subject should retaine	311	Horace	124
Her truch-man, she reports the minds each throw.	313	Horace	157
The customes of each age thou must observe,	315	Horace	223
In fitting proper adjuncts to each day.	317	Horace	254
That found out profit, and foretold each thing,	319	Horace	309
Each subt'lest Passion, with her source, and spring,	370	Author	7
Each subject Passion, with her source, and spring,	370	Author	V 7
And allow you for each particular mile,	379	Coryat 3	9
Each leafe of his journall, and line doth unlocke	380	Coryat 3	23
He went out at each place, and at what he came in,	380	Coryat 3	25
In each of which, he seemes to shake a Lance,	392	Shakespeare	69
Now each Court-Hobby-horse will wince in rime;	410	Brome	11
each to pawne hir husbands capp,	417	Moon	38
From each of which, I labor to be free,	422	Censure	21
EAGLE			
An Eagle towring in the skye,	278	U84 Mind	10
EARE			
Nay, aske you, how the day goes, in your eare.	59	E92 New Crie	18
Whose name's un-welcome to the present eare,	74	E115 Honest Man	15

EARE (cont.)

	Page	Title	Line
We ought not give them taste, we had an eare.	83	E131 Ferrab. 2	6
At th'eye and eare (the ports unto the minde)	109	F11 Epode	9
Give thankes by stealth, and whispering in the eare,	154	U13 Sacvile	49
Out of his Grave, and poyson every eare.	172	U21 Ltl Shrub	4
But give them over to the common eare	214	U44 Speach	31
Run all the Rounds in a soft Ladyes eare,	230	U56 Covell	16
Of grace, and Musique to the eare,	279	U84 Mind	35
In at the eare, doe stirre the mind more slow	317	Horace	257
More slow, and come more weightie to the eare:	323	Horace	378
A lawfull Verse, by th'eare, or finger scan.	323	Horace	404
To send it to be judg'd by Metius eare,	331	Horace	576
To plant the Musick where noe eare can reach!	404	Inigo Jones 1	53
And once more stryke the eare of tyme with those fresh straynes:	420	Ode:If Men	32

EARELY

Whose every worke, of thy most earely wit,	34	E23 Donne 1	3
The earely cherry, with the later plum,	94	F2 Penshurst	41
And, keeping a just course, have earely put	119	F13 Aubigny	91

EARES (GRAIN)

The ripened eares, yet humble in their height,	98	F3 Wroth	41
The eares cut downe in their most height,	98	F3 Wroth	V 41

EARES

For we, that have our eyes still in our eares,	43	E51 James 3	9
Nor are the Queenes most honor'd maides by th'eares	63	E97 Motion	18
That's, sit, and eate: doe not my eares abuse.	68	E107 Hungry	2
Upon your eares, of discords so un-sweet?	88	E133 Voyage	171
While all, that follow, their glad eares apply	97	F3 Wroth	31
Or his easier eares beguile,	102	F5 Celia 1	13
Or hir easier eares beguile,	102	F5 Celia 1	V 13
And now an Epode to deepe eares I sing.	108	F10 Proludium	30
And now an Epode to deepe eares we sing.	108	F10 Proludium	V 30
and now an Epode, to deepe Eares, wee singe.	108	F10 Proludium	16
And all the world turne Eares.	143	U3 Musicall	4
Will be my Rivall, though she have but eares.	148	U7 Nymph	28
And all these through her eyes, have stopt her eares.	150	U9 Picture	18
But, others fell with that conceipt by the eares,	209	U43 Vulcan	145
But, others fell by that conceipt by the eares,	209	U43 Vulcan	V145
A Musique in the Eares, will ever last;	286	U84 Muse	124
In many a Gumme, and for thy soft eares sake	292	U86 Hor.4:1	22
Our eares, or like a Mercury to charme!	392	Shakespeare	46

EARLE

To Robert Earle of Salisburie.	40	E43 Salisbury 1	Ttl
. . . Earle of Salisbury. Epigramme.	40	E43 Salisbury 1	VTtl
To Robert Earle of Salisburie.	47	E63 Salisbury 2	Ttl
To Thomas Earle of Suffolke.	49	E67 Suffolk	Ttl
To William Earle of Pembroke.	66	E102 Pembroke	Ttl
An Epistle to Sir Edward Sacvile, now Earle of Dorset.	153	U13 Sacvile	Ttl
An Ode to James Earle of Desmond, writ . . .	176	U25 Desmond	Ttl
An Epigram. To William, Earle of Newcastle.	228	U53 Newcastle	Ttl
An Epigram. To William Earle of Newcastle.	232	U59 Newcastle	Ttl
To the Right Honorable William Earle of Newcastle.	232	U59 Newcastle	VTtl
. . . made Earle of Portland. 17. Febr. 1632. To the Envious.	250	U73 Weston	Ttl
Earle Rivers Grand-Child--serve not formes, good Fame,	269	U81 Pawlet	21
Earle Rivers Grand-Child--serve not titles Fame,	269	U81 Pawlet	V 21
. . . Robert, Earle of Somerset.	384	Somerset	Ttl
Content thee to be Pancridge Earle the whyle;	407	Inigo Jones 2	20
An Earle of show: for all thy worke is showe:	407	Inigo Jones 2	21
An Earle of show: for all thy worth is showe:	407	Inigo Jones 2	V 21

EARLES

. . . & sir Henrye Rich, now Earles of warwick and Hollande.	382	Rich	Ttl

EARLY

No more would Jone he should. Giles riseth early,	40	E42 Giles	6
With thy new place, bring I these early fruits	47	E64 Salisbury 3	2
Of two so early men,	247	U70 Ode	125
Extend a reaching vertue, early and late:	258	U75 Epithalam.	180
Shee saw her Saviour, by an early light,	288	U84 Muse	199
Which I do, early, vertuous Somerset,	384	Somerset	7
For, though but early in these pathes thou tread,	386	Browne	5

EARNEST

Be thankes to him, and earnest prayer, to finde	99	F3 Wroth	101
Is thankes to him, and earnest prayer, to finde	99	F3 Wroth	V101
And so to turne all earnest into jest,	321	Horace	330
And so to turne our earnest into jest,	346	Horace	V322/330

EARS

you would be an Asinigo, by your ears?	403	Inigo Jones 1	20
Pillory nor Whip, nor want of Ears,	410	Gill	4

EARTH

Which cover lightly, gentle earth.	34	E22 Daughter	12
Earth, thou hast not such another.	39	E40 Ratcliffe	17
The Virgin, long-since fled from earth, I see,	52	E74 Chancelor	9
But, being so much too good for earth,	77	E120 S. P.	23
Were yet unfound, and better plac'd in earth,	114	F12 Rutland	25
Were yet unfound, and better plac'd on earth,	114	F12 Rutland	V 25
The Word, which heaven, and earth did make;	130	U1 Nativitie	11
Bounteous as the clouds to earth;	142	U2 Her man	43
Mistaking earth for heaven.	144	U3 Musicall	24
Light thee from hell on earth: where flatterers, spies,	167	U15 Friend-Wars	163
Rap't from the Earth, as not to die?	181	U27 Ode Helen	14
That so hath crown'd our hopes, our spring, and earth,	237	U65 Prince	2
which thus hast crown'd our hopes, our spring, and earth,	237	U65 Prince	V 2
That so hath crown'd our hopes, our spring, our earth,	237	U65 Prince	V 2
Whilst that in heav'n, this light on earth must shine.	246	U70 Ode	96
Such pleasure as the teeming Earth,	250	U74 Weston	1

EARTH (cont.)
  When look'd the Earth so fine,   .   .   . 253 U75 Epithalam.   21
  Have they bedew'd the Earth, where she doth tread, . . 254 U75 Epithalam.   66
  Have they bedew'd the Earth, where she did tread, . . 254 U75 Epithalam. V 66
  Like Swine, or other Cattell here on earth: . . 257 U75 Epithalam.   154
  Who walkes on Earth as May still went along,   . . 264 U79 New-yeares   26
  By Death, on Earth, I should have had remorse   . . 282 U84 Muse   12
  In earth, till the last Trumpe awake the Sheepe . . 283 U84 Muse   46
  Of Earth, and sheares the tender Sheepe   . . 290 U85 Country   16
  Or, whilst he shuns the Earth, to catch at Aire . . 321 Horace   335
  That all Earth look'd on; and that earth, all Eyes! . 396 Drayton   16
  But lowlie laid, as on the earth asleep,   . . 413 Ghyrlond   18
  rise or fall uppon the earth, ... 417 Moon   18
  Uppon soe humbled earth to cast hir eyes: . . 420 Ode:If Men   30
  Looke how the starres from earth, or seas from flames . 422 Lucan   7
EARTHEN
  Of earthen Jarres, there may molest me too: .   . 219 U47 Tribe   55
EARTHES
  Of Spheares, as light of starres; She was earthes Eye: . 372 Epitaph   9
EARTHLY
  With his old earthly labours. T'exact more,   .   . 107 F10 Proludium   5
EARTHS
  Earths grossnesse; There's the how, and why.   .   . 279 U84 Mind   44
EASE
  At last, ease, appetite, and example wan   .   .   .   57 E90 Mill   4
  Daintinesse, and softer ease, ... 105 F8 Sicknesse   22
  In single paths, dangers with ease are watch'd: . . 118 F13 Aubigny   57
  That, laden with my sinnes, I seeke for ease?   . . 122 F15 Heaven   4
  Of your Trouble, Ben, to ease me, ... 140 U2 Her man   1
  Their vitious ease, and be o'rewhelm'd with it. . . 162 U15 Friend-Wars   4
  Buried in ease and sloth?   .   .   .   . . 174 U23 Himselfe   2
  Pyracmon's houre will come to give them ease,   . . 179 U25 Desmond   42
  An hower will come they must affect theyr Ease, . . 179 U25 Desmond   V 42
  O Times! O Manners! Surfet bred of ease,   . . 237 U64 Charles 3   17
  Most pleasant Martial; Substance got with ease, . . 295 U90 Mart.10:47   2
  They might with ease be numbred, being a few   . . 319 Horace   293
EAS'D
  To see great Charles of Travaile eas'd,   .   . . 251 U74 Weston   26
EASED
  hir minde is eased.   .   .   .   .   . . 417 Moon   40
EASES
  To give mankind their eases, ... 221 U48 Bacchus   23
EASIE
  Doth take in easie Natures birth, ... 250 U74 Weston   2
  And all invite to easie sleepe.   .   .   . . 290 U85 Country   28
EASIER
  Or his easier eares beguile, ... 102 F5 Celia 1   13
  Or hir easier eares beguile, ... 102 F5 Celia 1   V 13
  Spread through the World) is easier farre to find, . 167 U15 Friend-Wars   172
EAST
  If with East floods, the Winter troubled much, .   . 291 U85 Country   V 51
EASY
  Thy table without art, and easy-rated: .   . . 295 U90 Mart.10:47   8
EASY-RATED
  Thy table without art, and easy-rated: .   . . 295 U90 Mart.10:47   8
EAT
  And pikes, now weary their owne kinde to eat,   . .   94 F2 Penshurst   34
  You shall neither eat, nor sleepe, ... 140 U2 Promise   15
  And not thinke h'had eat a stake, ... 142 U2 Her man   39
  And drives it in to eat on my offence,   .   . . 191 U38 Elegy 'Tis   6
  Having well eat, and drunke (the rites being done) . 319 Horace   325
  Able to eat into his bones & pierce   .   .   . . 407 Inigo Jones 3   4
EATE
  He doth, at meales, alone, his pheasant eate,   . .   35 E28 Surly   12
  That's, sit, and eate: doe not my eares abuse. . .   68 E107 Hungry   2
  Come, be not angrie, you are Hungry; eate;   . .   69 E107 Hungry   31
  Where comes no guest, but is allow'd to eate,   . .   95 F2 Penshurst   61
  But gives me what I call, and lets me eate,   . .   95 F2 Penshurst   69
  And, so they ride in purple, eate in plate,   . .   99 F3 Wroth   89
  Eate on her clients, and some one devoure.   . . 119 F13 Aubigny   88
  To eate a Snake, in his next Song.   .   .   . . 260 U76 Petition   V 32
  Or moathes shall eate, what all these Fooles admire. . 371 Fletcher   16
EATEN
  Have eaten with the Beauties, and the wits,   . . 200 U42 Elegy Let   33
  For Grapes he had gather'd before they were eaten. . 375 Coryat 1   25
  For grapes he had gather'd, before they were eaten. . 380 Coryat 3   36
EATES
  By that one spell he lives, eates, drinkes, arrayes .   30 E12 Shift   5
  Gut eates all day, and lechers all the night,   . .   76 E118 Gut   1
  When every clerke eates artichokes, and peason, . .   88 E133 Voyage   166
EATING
  And Phoebus-selfe should be at eating it. .   . .   55 E84 Bedford 2   8
  For th'eating Thrush, or Pit-falls sets: .   . . 290 U85 Country   34
EATS
  That eats on wits, and Arts, and destroyes them both. . 174 U23 Himselfe   6
ECCHO
  Like Eccho playing from the other shore.   .   . . 249 U72 King   8
  Like Eccho playing from another shore.   .   . . 249 U72 King   V 8
  Rivers, and Vallies, Eccho what wee sing. .   . . 264 U79 New-yeares   27
  Rivers, and Valleys, Eccho what wee sing. .   . . 264 U79 New-yeares   35
  Still left an Eccho in the sense.   .   .   . . 279 U84 Mind   40
  And all men eccho you have made a Masque. .   . . 403 Inigo Jones 1   30
  But Tune and Noise the Eccho of thy Shame. .   . . 411 Gill   14

		Page	Title	Line

ECCHO'D
That they may take it eccho'd by the Floods.   .   .   .   265 U79 New-yeares   53
ECCHO'S
Which, when it sounds at best, but eccho's right;   .   .   .   390 Shakespeare   8
ECLIPSE
And threat' the great Eclipse. Two houres but runne,   .   .   238 U65 Prince   11
And thereat the great Eclipse. Two houres but runne,   .   .   238 U65 Prince   V 11
ECSTASY   (See EXTASIE)
EDEN
A forme more fresh, then are the Eden bowers,   .   .   .   111 F11 Epode   57
EDGE
Be like a Whet-stone, that an edge can put   .   .   .   325 Horace   433
On edge the Masculine spirits, and did whet   .   .   .   327 Horace   494
EDIFICES
With other edifices, when they see   .   .   .   .   96 F2 Penshurst   100
EDMONDS
To Clement Edmonds, on his Caesars . . .   .   .   .   71 E110 Edmonds 1   Ttl
Not all these, Edmonds, or what else put too,   .   .   .   71 E110 Edmonds 1   11
Who Edmonds, reades thy booke, and doth not see   .   .   72 E111 Edmonds 2   1
EDUCATION
For education of our Lordings; Soone   .   .   .   .   214 U44 Speach   62
EDWARD
To Edward Allen.   .   .   .   .   56 E89 Allen   Ttl
To Sir Edward Herbert.   .   .   .   .   .   68 E106 E Herbert   Ttl
An Epistle to Sir Edward Sacvile, now Earle of Dorset.   .   153 U13 Sacvile   Ttl
An Epigram on Sir Edward Coke, when . . .   .   .   217 U46 Coke   Ttl
To my worthy Friend, Master Edward Filmer, ...   401 Filmer   Ttl
EEKE
His spirits, now, in pills, and eeke in potions,   .   .   86 E133 Voyage   101
EELES
Bright eeles, that emulate them, and leape on land,   .   .   94 F2 Penshurst   37
EENE
Whose workes are eene the fripperie of wit,   .   .   .   44 E56 Poet-Ape   2
EFFECT
Could not effect, not all the furies doe,   .   .   .   37 E32 Roe 2   2
Which to effect (since no brest is so sure,   .   .   .   109 F11 Epode   5
T'effect it, feele, thou'ast made thine owne heart ake.   .   250 U73 Weston   12
EFFECTED
When the worke would be effected: .   .   .   .   140 U2 Promise   8
EFFECTS
Which Musick had; or speake her knowne effects,   .   .   82 E130 Ferrab. 1   3
No such effects doth prove;   .   .   .   .   110 F11 Epode   44
EGERTON
Whil'st thy weigh'd judgements, Egerton, I heare,   .   .   51 E74 Chancelor   1
EGGES
Of Egges, and Halberds, Cradles, and a Herse,   .   .   204 U43 Vulcan   37
From the two Egges, that did disclose the twins.   .   .   315 Horace   210
EGLANTINE
R. Rose, I. Ivy, E. sweet Eglantine.   .   .   .   412 Ghyrlond   4
But, that which summes all, is the Eglantine,   .   .   413 Ghyrlond   21
EGS
If we can get her, full of egs, and then,   .   .   .   64 E101 Supper   12
A Punke here pelts him with egs. How so?   .   .   375 Coryat 1   18
EIGHT
That the eight sphaere, no lesse, then planets seaven,   .   82 E130 Ferrab. 1   12
Of our fift Henry, eight of his nine yeare;   .   .   207 U43 Vulcan   98
EITHER   (See also EYTHER)
A harder tasgue, then either his to Bristo',   .   .   85 E133 Voyage   39
And feasts, that either shearers keepe;   .   .   .   97 F3 Wroth   40
And feasts, which either shearers keepe;   .   .   .   97 F3 Wroth   V 40
Then either money, warre, or death: .   .   .   99 F3 Wroth   76
For either our affections doe rebell,   .   .   .   109 F11 Epode   21
Either whom to love, or how: .   .   .   .   131 U2 Excuse   16
And in either Prose, or Song, ...   133 U2 Suffered   23
From either heart, I know;   .   .   .   .   148 U7 Nymph   32
(As their true rule or lesson) either men,   .   .   158 U13 Sacvile   162
By those pure bathes your either cheeke discloses,   .   170 U19 Elegy By   7
You blush, but doe not: friends are either none,   .   171 U19 Elegy By   13
And so that either may example prove   .   .   .   171 U19 Elegy By   16
These, had'st thou pleas'd either to dine, or sup,   .   206 U43 Vulcan   83
These, had'st thou been pleas'd either to dine, or sup,   .   206 U43 Vulcan   V 83
Of either Suitor, or a Servant by.   .   .   .   230 U56 Covell   18
Till either grew a portion of the other: .   .   247 U70 Ode   110
Their Sister-tunes, from Thames his either side,   .   253 U75 Epithalam.   34
Both Crownes, and Kingdomes in their either hand;   .   254 U75 Epithalam.   52
(Lillies and Roses, Flowers of either Sexe)   .   .   254 U75 Epithalam.   58
If you can cast about your either eye,   .   .   .   271 U81 Pawlet   85
At either Stemme, and know the veines of good   .   .   274 U84 Descent   8
A purple piece, or two stitch'd in: when either   .   338 Horace   V 19
Most Writers, noble Sire, and either Sonne,   .   .   307 Horace   33
To ignorance still, then either learne, or know?   .   311 Horace   131
Either because he seekes, and, having found,   .   317 Horace   242
The businesse either on the Stage is done,   .   .   317 Horace   255
If either you, or I, know the right way   .   .   323 Horace   402
If either you, or I know any way   .   .   .   348 Horace   V388/402
Poets would either profit, or delight,   .   .   .   327 Horace   477
Shall finde, that either hath read Bookes, and Men: .   389 Aleman   2
And as either newes or mirth   .   .   .   .   417 Moon   17
EITHERS
Yet if with eithers vice I teynted be,   .   .   .   190 U37 Friend-Book   29
More then of eithers manners, wit, or face!   .   .   202 U42 Elegy Let   88
EJECTS
That shee removeth cares, sadnesse ejects,   .   .   82 E130 Ferrab. 1   4

	Page	Title	Line

EL
Epitaph on S. P. a Child of Q. El. Chappel. . . . . 77 E120 S. P. Ttl

ELABORATE
'Tis not enough, th'elaborate Muse affords . . . . 311 Horace 140

ELDER
A present, which (if elder writs reherse . . . . 113 F12 Rutland 20
The longing Couple, all that elder Lovers know. . 258 U75 Epithalam. 192
You Sir, the elder brother, though you are . . . . 331 Horace 545
The elder of these two, riche hopes Increase, . . . 382 Rich 5

ELDERS
More, then to varie what our elders knew: . . . . 72 E111 Edmonds 2 6

ELDEST
The eldest God, yet still a Child. . . . . 189 U36 Song 16
. . . eldest Daughter, to Cuthbert Lord Ogle: . . . 394 Jane Ogle Ttl

ELECT
Which the Elect of God are sure to know! . . . . 271 U81 Pawlet V 76
Himselfe so un-inform'd of his elect, ... 286 U84 Muse 149

ELECTED
Among thy Saints elected to abide, ... 128 U1 Trinitie 45

ELECTION
By sure Election, and predestin'd grace! . . . . 288 U84 Muse 198
Muffles the clearnesse of Election, ... 363 Riches 14

ELEGIE
An elegie? no, muse; yt askes a straine . . . 108 F10 Proludium 1
To the Countesse of Rutland: An Elegie. . . . 113 F12 Rutland VTtl
An Elegie. . . . . 169 U18 Elegy Can Ttl
An Elegie. . . . . 170 U19 Elegy By Ttl
An Elegie. . . . . 173 U22 Elegy Tho Ttl
An Elegie. . . . . 191 U38 Elegy 'Tis Ttl
An Elegie. . . . . 197 U40 Elegy That Ttl
An Elegie. . . . . 199 U41 Elegy Since Ttl
An Elegie. . . . . 199 U42 Elegy Let Ttl
An Elegie On the Lady Jane Pawlet, Marchion: of Winton. . 268 U81 Pawlet Ttl
9. Elegie on my Muse. The truly honoured Lady, . . . 282 U84 Muse Ttl
That first sent forth the dapper Elegie, ... 309 Horace 110

ELEGIES
I passe to Elegies; Thou meet'st me there: . . . 73 E112 Gamster 13

ELEMENTS
And elements of honor, then the dresse; . . . 70 E109 Nevil 10
All the Gaine, all the Good, of the Elements strife. . 134 U2 Triumph 20

ELEVEN
He there doth protest he saw of the eleven. . . . 380 Coryat 3 46

ELEVENTH
Upon my Birth-day the eleventh of June; . . . . 262 U78 Digby 14
Witnesse my Birth-day the eleventh of June; . . . . 262 U78 Digby V 14

ELFE
Of our Odcombian, that literate Elfe? . . . . 379 Coryat 3 7

ELIXIR
Cry'd to my face, they were th'elixir of wit: . . . 64 E100 Playwrt 3 2
The'Elixir of all joyes? . . . . 110 F11 Epode 56

ELIZA
That so did take Eliza, and our James! . . . . 392 Shakespeare 74

ELIZABETH
To Elizabeth Countesse of Rutland. . . . . 53 E79 Rutland Ttl
Epitaph on Elizabeth, L. H. . . . . . 79 E124 Elizabeth Ttl
One name was Elizabeth, ... 79 E124 Elizabeth 9
Epistle To Elizabeth Countesse of Rutland. . . . 113 F12 Rutland Ttl

ELIZABETHS
. . . in Queene Elizabeths Time, since lost, and recovered. . 176 U25 Desmond Ttl

ELOCUTION
And manly elocution, not one while . . . . 160 U14 Selden 56
And masculine elocution, not one while . . . . 160 U14 Selden V 56

ELOQUENCE
For (where he was the god of eloquence, ... 86 E133 Voyage 99
To the Wolves studie, or Dogs eloquence; . . . . 187 U33 Councellour 12
And that thy strong and manly Eloquence . . . . 217 U46 Coke 13
Nor can the bruised heart want eloquence: . . . . 288 U84 Muse 186
The rash, and head-long eloquence brought forth . . . 319 Horace 307
What godds but those of arts, and eloquence? . . . 395 May 16
The Eloquence of Masques! What need of prose . . . 403 Inigo Jones 1 40

ELOQUENT
Of eloquent Messalla's power in Court, ... 331 Horace 552

ELSE
Or else by water goes, and so to playes; . . . 30 E12 Shift 17
What doth he else, but say, leave to be chast, . . . 34 E25 Beast 1 7
Any man else, you clap your hands, and rore, . . . 38 E38 Guiltie 2 4
Something, which, else, could hope for no esteeme. . 64 E101 Supper 6
As nothing else discernes the vertue' or vice. . . 66 E102 Pembroke 12
Not all these, Edmonds, or what else put too, . . . 71 E110 Edmonds 1 11
The better cheeses, bring 'hem; or else send . . . 95 F2 Penshurst 53
Those proud, ambitious heaps, and nothing else, . . . 96 F2 Penshurst 101
Else, I my state should much mistake, . . . 101 F4 To the World 57
Or else the sentinell . . . . . 109 F11 Epode 22
Or else one that plaid his Ape, ... 132 U2 How he saw 31
Else that glister'd in White-hall; . . . . 138 U2 Kisse 16
For else it could not be, ... 149 U9 Picture 2
or else it could not be, ... 149 U9 Picture V 2
His Groomes to witnesse; or else lets it fall . . . 154 U13 Sacvile 36
And feeles it; Else he tarries by the Beast. . . . 156 U13 Sacvile 117
To see men feare: or else for truth, and State, . . . 170 U18 Elegy Can 17
We cut not off, till his Cures being doe faile: . . . 192 U38 Elegy 'Tis 46
It shakes even him, that all things else doth shake. . 193 U38 Elegy 'Tis 72
And free societie, hee's borne else-where, . . . 197 U40 Elegy That 16

		Page	Title	Line
ELSE (cont.)				
Or else Acrosticks, or those finer flammes		204	U43 Vulcan	V 36
Or else in penny Fagots blaze about	• •	211	U43 Vulcan	V185
Maintain'd the trade at Bilbo, or else-where;		212	U43 Vulcan	199
Maintain'd the trade of Bilbo, or else-where;		212	U43 Vulcan	V199
Subject to quarrell only; or else such	•	218	U47 Tribe	11
Then these can ever be; or else wish none.		219	U47 Tribe	30
Or else a health advances,	• •	222	U48 Bacchus	49
Made lighter with the Wine. All noises else,		249	U72 King	12
Made loftier by the Winds all noises else,		249	U72 King	V 12
All else we see beside, are Shadowes, and goe lesse.		255	U75 Epithalam.	88
Alive, which else would die,		257	U75 Epithalam.	151
Else, who doth praise a person by a new,	•	270	U81 Pawlet	37
Or any thing else that another should hide,		380	Coryat 3	51
And who make thither else, rob, or invade.		389	Chapman	12
Or else Magnetique in the force,	• •	399	Lady Ogle	19
I had somwhat else to say,	•	417	Moon	9
ELSE-WHERE				
And free societie, hee's borne else-where,		197	U40 Elegy That	16
Maintain'd the trade at Bilbo, or else-where;		212	U43 Vulcan	199
Maintain'd the trade of Bilbo, or else-where;		212	U43 Vulcan	V199
ELSMERE				
An Epigram. To Thomas Lo: Elsmere, . . .	•	185	U31 Elsmere	Ttl
ELTHAM				
Nor Captayne Pod, nor yet the Eltham-thing;		62	E97 Motion	2
ELTHAM-THING				
Nor Captayne Pod, nor yet the Eltham-thing;		62	E97 Motion	2
ELVES				
Curst in their Cradles, or there chang'd by Elves,		200	U42 Elegy Let	23
EMBARK (See IMBARQU'D)				
EMBASSAGE				
Of sixe times to, and fro, without embassage,		85	E133 Voyage	34
Of some wel-wrought Embassage:	• •	221	U48 Bacchus	46
EMBASSIE				
• • • gratulatorie For his Returne from his Embassie. 1632.		250	U74 Weston	Ttl
EMBASSIES				
Give them your services, and embassies	•	69	E107 Hungry	11
EMBELISH'D				
The bright Brides paths, embelish'd more then thine		254	U75 Epithalam.	59
EMBERS				
All soote, and embers! odious, as thy worke!		207	U43 Vulcan	106
EMBLEME				
An embleme of themselves, in plum, or peare.		95	F2 Penshurst	56
As true oblations; his Brothers Embleme sayes,		383	Rich	10
EMBLEMES				
The Emblemes of their way.	• •	254	U75 Epithalam.	63
EMBRACE (See also IMBRACE)				
And, hood-wink'd, for a man, embrace a post.		45	E58 Groome	8
If, my religion safe, I durst embrace		61	E95 Savile	1
Embrace, and cherish; but he can approve	•	161	U14 Selden	74
These I will honour, love, embrace, and serve:		220	U47 Tribe	71
EMBRAC'D				
But this true course is not embrac'd by many:		109	F11 Epode	19
But this faire course is not embrac'd by many:		109	F11 Epode	V 19
That wider Walls embrac'd their Citie round,		319	Horace	296
EMBRACES				
Have you seene Love-Queenes embraces	• •	135	U2 Triumph	V 35
Lock't in her cold embraces, from the view		177	U25 Desmond	22
EMBRIONS				
If it be thought kild like her Embrions; for,		165	U15 Friend-Wars	96
EMBRODERIES				
Embroderies, Feathers, Fringes, Lace,	• •	275	U84 Body	3
EMINENCE				
But like an Arme of Eminence 'mongst them,		258	U75 Epithalam.	179
EMISSARIE				
With your emissarie eye,	• •	140	U2 Promise	17
EMPEDOCLES				
Of the Sicilian Poet Empedocles,	• •	335	Horace	660
EMPEROURS				
How great you were with their two Emperours;		68	E107 Hungry	6
EMPIRE				
Great aides to Empire, as they are great care		268	U80 Christning	6
EMPIRICK				
To doctor Empirick.	• • •	31	E13 Empirick	Ttl
EMPLOY				
In life, that can employ it; and takes hold		50	E70 Wm Roe 1	3
Should but the king his Justice-hood employ		405	Inigo Jones 1	77
EMPLOYD				
When these, and such, their voices have employd;		385	Brooke	1
EMP'RICKS				
With ten Emp'ricks, in their chamber,	•	105	F8 Sicknesse	31
EMPTIE				
Of reason emptie is?!	• • •	143	U3 Musicall	6
Her broken Armes up, to their emptie moulds.		216	U44 Speach	102
If the 'Chequer be emptie, so will be his Head.		232	U57 Burges	28
And emptie Clowdes. For Tragedie is faire,		321	Horace	336
EMPTIES				
The Chappell empties, and thou may'st be gone		257	U75 Epithalam.	137
EMPTY				
And no one empty-handed, to salute	•	95	F2 Penshurst	49
EMPTYE				
The emptye Carper, scorne, not Creditt wynns.		421	Censure	5

```
                                                       Page      Title        Line
EMPTY-HANDED
   And no one empty-handed, to salute   .   .   .   .   .    95   F2 Penshurst      49
EMPUSA
   Empusa, Lamia, or some Monster, more   .   .   .   .     398   Drayton           87
EMPYRE
   In heaven Empyre, and with a robe of light?   .   .   .  285   U84 Muse         102
EMULATE   (See also AEMULATE)
   As, then, his cause, his glorie emulate.   .   .   .   .   61   E95 Savile        24
   Of the best writer, and judge, should emulate.   .   .    78   E123 Rudyerd 3     4
   Bright eeles, that emulate them, and leape on land,   .   94   F2 Penshurst      37
   As I the penitents here emulate:   .   .   .   .   .      193   U38 Elegy 'Tis    86
EMULATES
   Whose better studies while shee emulates,   .   .   .     78   E121 Rudyerd 1     3
EMULATION
   Doth Emulation stirre;   .   .   .   .   .   .   .        256   U75 Epithalam.   117
ENABLE
   Or Wine to enable   .   .   .   .   .   .   .   .         232   U57 Burges        24
ENAMOR'D
   Enamor'd of their golden gyves?   .   .   .   .   .       100   F4 To the World   24
ENAMOUR'D
   And enamour'd, doe wish, so they might   .   .   .        134   U2 Triumph         7
ENCHANT   (See INCHANTED)
ENCLOSE   (See INCLOS'D)
ENCOUNTER
   He wont was to encounter me, aloud,   .   .   .   .        62   E97 Motion         7
ENCOUNTER'D
   And never art encounter'd, I confesse:   .   .   .   .     73   E112 Gamster      19
   But open, and un-armed encounter'd all:   .   .   .   .    87   E133 Voyage      135
ENCOURAGE
   Thy fact is more: let truth encourage thee.   .   .   .    64   E99 Th Roe 2      12
ENCREASE
   And thine owne goodnesse to encrease thy merit,   .   .    60   E93 Radcliffe     10
   Nor baudie stock, that travells for encrease,   .   .   . 63   E97 Motion        10
   For which you worthy are the glad encrease   .   .   .    119   F13 Aubigny       94
   Shee, to the Crowne, hath brought encrease.   .   .   .   264   U79 New-yeares    41
   Hee gives all plentie, and encrease,   .   .   .   .      265   U79 New-yeares    56
   Hee gives all plentie, and encrease,   .   .   .   .      265   U79 New-yeares    68
   And ev'ry birth encrease the heate of Love.   .   .   .   384   Somerset          20
ENCREAS'D
   As fit to have encreas'd the harmony   .   .   .   .      371   Epitaph            8
ENCREAST
   That thou hast kept thy love, encreast thy will,   .   .   63   E99 Th Roe 2       1
END
   Thou, that mak'st gaine thy end, and wisely well,   .   .  27   E3 Bookseller      1
   At sixe moneths end, shee parted hence   .   .   .   .     33   E22 Daughter       5
   To Old-end Gatherer.   .   .   .   .   .   .   .   .       43   E53 Old-end      Ttl
   Long-gathering Old-end, I did feare thee wise,   .   .     43   E53 Old-end        1
   Stinke, and are throwne away. End faire enough.   .   .    45   E59 Spies          3
   Of service to the publique, when the end   .   .   .   .   70   E109 Nevil         7
   An Epick poeme; thou hast the same end.   .   .   .   .    72   E112 Gamster      10
   And, at her strong armes end, hold up, and even,   .   .  114   F12 Rutland       42
   And, at her strong armes end, there hold up even,   .   . 114   F12 Rutland    V 42
   To ought but grace, or ayme at other end.   .   .   .     122   F15 Heaven         8
   In dreames, begun in hope, and end in spoile.   .   .     162   U15 Friend-Wars   10
   Lives to the Lord, but to the Ladies end.   .   .   .     165   U15 Friend-Wars   94
   Lives for the Lord, but to the Ladies end.   .   .   .    165   U15 Friend-Wars V 94
   This Praecipice, and Rocks that have no end,   .   .   .  166   U15 Friend-Wars  130
   Then Mistris, here here let your rigour end,   .   .   .  194   U38 Elegy 'Tis   105
   Hee stood, a Souldier to the last right end,   .   .   .  244   U70 Ode           45
   Each stiled, by his end,   .   .   .   .   .   .   .      247   U70 Ode          111
   Mariage, the end of life,   .   .   .   .   .   .   .     253   U75 Epithalam.    29
   That ever had beginning there, to'ave end!   .   .   .    271   U81 Pawlet        91
   Hope, hath her end! and Faith hath her reward!   .   .    284   U84 Muse          68
   So charitable, to religious end,   .   .   .   .   .      287   U84 Muse         176
   For his designed worke, the perfect end   .   .   .   .   288   U84 Muse         206
   He ever hastens to the end, and so   .   .   .   .   .    315   Horace           211
   Playes were found out; and rest, the end, and crowne  .  329   Horace           499
   And friendly should unto one end conspire.   .   .   .    333   Horace           586
   And friendly should unto their end conspire.   .   .   .  353   Horace          V586
   And, there an end of him, reciting makes:   .   .   .     337   Horace           678
   And there an end of him with reading makes:   .   .   .   355   Horace          V678
   And her, she made her Inmate, to the End,   .   .   .     394   Jane Ogle         18
   All Circles had their spring and end   .   .   .   .      399   Lady Ogle         14
   Thinking to stir me, thou hast lost thy End,   .   .   .  410   Gill               9
ENDED
   My part is ended on thy stage.   .   .   .   .   .   .    100   F4 To the World    4
   Soe ended your Epistle, myne beginns   .   .   .   .      421   Censure            3
ENDES
   That bid, God give thee joy, and have no endes.   .   .   384   Somerset           6
ENDEW'D
   With sinne and vice, though with a throne endew'd;   .   . 116   F13 Aubigny      10
ENDLESSE
   With endlesse labours, whilst thy learning drawes   .   . 217   U46 Coke         18
   But thus, thus, keeping endlesse Holy-day,   .   .   .    294   U88 Petronius      6
ENDORSE
   Nay, so your Seate his beauties did endorse,   .   .   .  228   U53 Newcastle    11
ENDS
   If, as their ends, their fruits were so, the same,   .   . 45   E57 Bawds         1
   Then doe I love thee, and behold thy ends   .   .   .      55   E86 Goodyere 2    3
   But these, desir'd by you, the makers ends   .   .   .     60   E94 Bedford 3     5
   Thy standing upright to thy selfe, thy ends   .   .   .    68   E106 E Herbert    7
   Attend thee hence; and there, may all thy ends,   .   .    81   E128 Wm Roe 2     6
   Our owne false praises, for your ends:   .   .   .   .    145   U5 Woman-kind      4
```

ENDS (cont.)
Her ends are honestie, and publike good! . . . . 156 U13 Sacvile 111
Except the way be errour to those ends: . . . . 170 U18 Elegy Can 13
But their whole inside full of ends, and knots? . . . 171 U20 Shrub 12
Those are poore Ties, depend on those false ends, . . 216 U45 Squib 11
And studie them unto the noblest ends, ... 224 U50 Countesse 28
Never so great to get them: and the ends, . . . 242 U69 Friend Son 25
But ever to no ends: . . . . 243 U70 Ode 29
Which in some swarthie fish uncomely ends: . . . 305 Horace 5
Which in a blacke foule fish uncomely ends: . . . 338 Horace V 5
I gratulate it to thee, and thy Ends, ... 398 Drayton 89
ENDURE (See also DUR'D)
To endure counsell: a Provider slow . . . . 315 Horace 233
ENDURES
to which there's no materiall that endures; . . . 387 Cavendish 8
ENEMIE
The name of Pompey for an enemie, ... 71 E110 Edmonds 1 3
Pernitious enemie; we see, before . . . . 158 U14 Selden 14
Disease, the Enemie, and his Ingineeres, . . . 248 U71 Treasurer 4
ENEMIES
Law, to his Law; and thinke your enemies his: . . 185 U31 Elsmere 4
ENFLAMED
In our enflamed brests: . . . . . . 110 F11 Epode 34
ENFORCE
or if thou wouldst enforce the power from her, . . 204 U43 Vulcan V 48
ENFORCED
And being at Flushing enforced to feele . . . 380 Coryat 3 54
ENFORCING
Enforcing yron doores to yeeld it way, . . . 363 Riches 9
ENFORME
So did thy vertue'enforme, thy wit sustaine . . 75 E116 Jephson 3
ENGAGE (See also INGAGE)
as the standerd shall engage hir, ... 417 Moon 27
ENGAGED
Are you engaged to your happy fate, ... 118 F13 Aubigny 47
ENGINE (See also INGINE, ENGYNE)
Action, or engine, worth a note of thine, . . . 71 E110 Edmonds 1 20
At least, if not the generall Engine cracke. . . 395 May 6
ENGINES
The engines, that have them annoy'd; . . . . 101 F4 To the World 34
Engines of Murder, and receive the praise . . . 212 U43 Vulcan 207
Engines of Murder, and enjoy with praise . . . 212 U43 Vulcan V207
ENGLAND
With England. All forbidden bookes they get. . . 59 E92 New Crie 31
Now thincking on you, though to England lost, . . 116 F12 Rutland 94
. . . Lo: high Treasurer of England. . . . 185 U30 Burleigh Ttl
. . . he was Lord chiefe Justice of England. . . 217 U46 Coke Ttl
. . . England. An Epistle Mendicant. 1631. . . 248 U71 Treasurer Ttl
. . . high Treasurer of England, Upon the Day, Hee was . . . 250 U73 Weston Ttl
. . . England, with the Lady Frances Stuart, Daughter of . . . 252 U75 Epithalam. Ttl
To the right Honourable, the Lord Treasurer of England. . . . 260 U77 Treasurer Ttl
ENGLANDS
Englands high Chancellor: the destin'd heire . . . 225 U51 Bacon 13
ENGLISH
To my meere English Censurer. . . . . 32 E18 Censurer Ttl
On English Mounsieur. . . . . . 56 E88 Monsieur Ttl
Bartas doth wish thy English now were his. . . 83 E132 Sylvester 10
Had not their forme touch'd by an English wit. . . 115 F12 Rutland 82
Was there made English: with the Grammar too, . . 207 U43 Vulcan 91
And keepe the Glorie of the English name, . . . 214 U44 Speach 50
And there instruct the noble English heires . . 214 U44 Speach 59
Fame, and foundation of the English Weale. . . 225 U51 Bacon 10
Horace, His Art of Poetrie Made English . . . 303 Horace Ttl
He would be call'd, henceforth, the English-Rogue, . 389 Aleman 16
That ever yet did fire the English blood! . . 397 Drayton 57
So shall our English Youth urge on, and cry . . 398 Drayton 69
French Aire and English Verse here Wedded lie. . . 401 Filmer 6
The faire French Daughter to learne English in; . . 402 Filmer 12
ENGLISH-ROGUE
He would be call'd, henceforth, the English-Rogue, . 389 Aleman 16
ENGRAV'D
To have engrav'd these acts, with his owne stile, . . 71 E110 Edmonds 1 6
ENGYNE
The Scene! the Engyne! but he now is come . . 404 Inigo Jones 1 62
ENHANCE
And raise not vertue; they may vice enhance. . . 117 F13 Aubigny 42
ENJOY (See also INJOY)
Contends t'have worth enjoy, from his regard, . . 48 E64 Salisbury 3 13
The libertie, that wee'll enjoy to night. . . . 65 E101 Supper 42
But enjoy such a sight, ... 134 U2 Triumph 8
Of others honours, thus, enjoy thine owne. . . 160 U14 Selden 66
Of others honours, thus, enjoy their owne. . . 160 U14 Selden V 66
Come, let us here enjoy the shade; . . . 189 U36 Song 1
Let the poore fooles enjoy their follies, love . . 202 U42 Elegy Let 81
Engines of Murder, and enjoy with praise . . . 212 U43 Vulcan V207
If you can enjoy your owne Daughters blisse, . . 271 U81 Pawlet V 83
The Christian hath t'enjoy the future life, . . 271 U81 Pawlet 96
What 'tis t'enjoy, an everlasting breath! . . 285 U84 Muse 92
My gentle Shakespeare, must enjoy a part. . . 392 Shakespeare 56
ENJOY'D
Thou mightst have yet enjoy'd thy crueltie . . 204 U43 Vulcan 49
Which thou hast only vented, not enjoy'd. . . 210 U43 Vulcan 168
You once enjoy'd: A short space severs yee, . . 285 U84 Muse 105

ENJOYES
  O, who is he, that (in this peace) enjoyes   .   .   .   . 110 F11 Epode   55
ENLARGE   (See also INLARG'D)
  And, in these Cures, do'st so thy selfe enlarge,   .   .   . 235 U62 Charles 1   7
ENLARG'D
  But, as they conquer'd, and enlarg'd their bound, .   .   . 319 Horace   295
ENLIVEN   (See INLIVE)
ENNIUS
  Cato's and Ennius tongues have lent much worth,   .   .   . 309 Horace   81
  Of Accius, and Ennius, rare appeares: .   .   .   .   . 323 Horace   382
ENNOBLE
  What is there more that can ennoble blood?   .   .   .   . 185 U30 Burleigh   6
ENORMITY
  Disguisd? and thence drag forth Enormity?   .   .   .   . 405 Inigo Jones 1   81
ENOUGH   (See also INOUGH, INOW, YNOW)
  At court I met it, in clothes brave enough, ...   30 E11 Something   1
  To be a courtier; and lookes grave enough, ...   30 E11 Something   2
  And which no' affection praise enough can give!   .   .   .   34 E23 Donne 1   6
  Her foes enough would fame thee in their hate.   .   .   .   40 E43 Salisbury 1   4
  Stinke, and are throwne away. End faire enough.   .   .   .   45 E59 Spies   3
  It is enough, they once did get   .   .   .   .   .   .   93 F1 Why write no   5
  Doe enough; and who would take   .   .   .   .   .   . 105 F8 Sicknesse   26
  Mine owne enough betray me.   .   .   .   . 145 U4 Song   12
  One good reason for a songs sake.   .   .   .   .   .   . 145 U5 Woman-kind   12
  Humanitie enough to be a friend, ... 161 U14 Selden   77
  Is not enough now, but the Nights to play: .   .   .   . 166 U15 Friend-Wars 132
  Is not enough now, but the Nights we play: .   .   .   . 166 U15 Friend-Wars V132
  Two letters were enough the plague to teare   .   .   .   . 172 U21 Ltl Shrub   3
  'Tis crowne enough to vertue still, her owne applause. .   . 174 U23 Himselfe   18
  To redeeme mine, I had sent in; Enough, ... 205 U43 Vulcan   63
  Will be reward enough: to weare like those, ... 232 U58 Book-seller   9
  'T is not enough (thy pietie is such)   .   .   .   .   . 235 U62 Charles 1   3
  Sate safe enough, but now secured more.   .   .   .   .   . 268 U80 Christning   14
  'Tis not enough, th'elaborate Muse affords   .   .   .   . 311 Horace   140
  'Tis not enough, the labouring Muse affords   .   .   .   . 341 Horace   V140
  As loud enough to fill the seates, not yet   .   .   .   . 319 Horace   291
  But, now, it is enough to say; I make   .   .   .   .   . 333 Horace   593
  That hath not Countrye impudence enough to laughe att Arte,   . 420 Ode:If Men   14
ENQUIRE   (See also INQUIRE)
  And seeke not wants to succour: but enquire, ... 155 U13 Sacvile   61
ENRAGE   (See INRAGED)
ENSHRIN'D
  The full, the flowing graces there enshrin'd;   .   .   .   .   79 E125 Uvedale   8
ENSIGNE
  Forme, Art or Ensigne, that hath scap'd your sight?   .   .   . 160 U14 Selden   48
  Forme, Act or Ensigne, that hath scap'd your sight?   .   .   . 160 U14 Selden   V 48
  A dedicated Ensigne make   .   .   .   . 273 U84 Cradle   11
ENSIGNES
  All Ensigns of a Warre, are not yet dead, ... 213 U44 Speach   11
  Porting the Ensignes of united Two, ... 254 U75 Epithalam.   51
  Will he display the Ensignes of thy warre. 292 U86 Hor.4:1   16
ENSPIRE
  We each to other may this voyce enspire;   .   .   .   .   .   81 E128 Wm Roe 2   11
ENTANGLING
  Of an entangling suit; and bring 't about: .   .   .   .   . 333 Horace   604
ENTAYLE
  Dare entayle their loves on any, ... 105 F8 Sicknesse   39
  Dare entayle their loves to any, ... 105 F8 Sicknesse   V 39
ENTAYL'D
  'Twas not entayl'd on title. That some word   .   .   .   .   75 E116 Jephson   7
ENTEND
  I leave thee there, and giving way, entend   .   .   .   .   .   72 E112 Gamster   9
ENTER
  Goe enter breaches, meet the cannons rage, ...   98 F3 Wroth   69
  How cam'st thou thus to enter me?   .   .   .   . 150 U10 Jealousie   2
  For these with her young Companie shee'll enter, ... 164 U15 Friend-Wars   79
ENTERMIXT
  (Divinest graces) are so entermixt, ... 413 Ghyrlond   26
ENTERTAINE
  Only your time you better entertaine, ... 224 U50 Countesse   23
  Then entertaine, and as Deaths Harbinger;   .   .   .   .   . 394 Jane Ogle   21
ENTERTAINING
  Thou entertaining in thy brest, ... 281 U84 Mind   71
  In entertaining late   .   .   .   . 368 Ode Who saith   82
ENTERTAYNE
  To entertayne them; or the countrey came, ...   95 F2 Penshurst   80
ENTERTAYNMENT
  The entertaynment perfect: not the cates.   .   .   .   .   .   64 E101 Supper   8
ENTHEATE
  With entheate rage, to publish their bright tracts?   .   .   . 368 Ode Who saith   61
ENTHUSIASTIC
  Ode <Enthusiastic>.   .   .   .   . 364 Ode Splendor   Ttl
ENTIRE   (See INTIRE)
ENTITLE
  All mouthes, that dare entitle them (from hence)   .   .   .   . 187 U33 Councellour   11
ENTRAILES   (See also INTRAILES)
  The heads, houghs, entrailes, and the hides of dogs: .   .   .   88 E133 Voyage   146
  His Nephews entrailes; nor must Progne flie   .   .   .   .   . 317 Horace   266
ENTRANCE
  Some way of entrance) we must plant a guard   .   .   .   .   . 109 F11 Epode   7
  Over the Door at the Entrance into the Apollo.   .   .   .   . 657 Door Apollo   Ttl
ENTRANC'D
  From braines entranc'd, and fill'd with extasies;   .   .   .   . 116 F12 Rutland   90

	Page	Title	Line

ENTREAT   (See INTREAT)
ENTRED
    Hee entred well, by vertuous parts,   244 U70 Ode   33
ENTRY
    But hold my torch, while I describe the entry   85 E133 Voyage   58
ENTWINE   (See INTWINE)
ENVIE
    What not the envie of the seas reach'd too,   37 E32 Roe 2   4
    Will man lament the state he should envie?   41 E45 First Son   6
    For writing better, I must envie thee.   44 E55 Beaumont   10
    Who can behold all envie so declin'd   47 E63 Salisbury 2   7
    To any one, were envie: which would live   58 E91 Vere   11
    Whose life, ev'n they, that envie it, must praise; 66 E102 Pembroke 16
    They murder him againe, that envie thee.   72 E111 Edmonds 2   14
    They yet may envie me: 147 U7 Nymph   9
    Thy gift 'gainst envie. O how I doe count   161 U14 Selden   79
    Till envie wound, or maime it at a blow!   162 U15 Friend-Wars 22
    That envie wish'd, and Nature fear'd.   173 U22 Elegy Tho   20
    Or the times envie: 176 U25 Desmond   7
    Though Envie oft his shadow be,   189 U36 Song   3
    Looke up, thou seed of envie, and still bring 250 U73 Weston   1
    All the envie of the Rymes,   259 U76 Petition   18
    All there envie of the Rymes,   259 U76 Petition   V 18
    This would all their envie burst: 260 U76 Petition   30
    That would all their envie burst: 260 U76 Petition   V 30
    If you can envie your owne Daughters blisse,   271 U81 Pawlet   83
    I envie it the Angels amitie!   283 U84 Muse   36
    And (in the place) envie   369 Ode Who saith   95
    Of Subjects; Let such envie, till they burst. 416 Dover   10
ENVI'D
    To be envi'd of the Queene.   138 U2 Kisse   28
    Honour'd at once, and envi'd (if it can   162 U15 Friend-Wars 24
    Or Varius? Why am I now envi'd so,   309 Horace   79
ENVIES
    I call the world, that envies mee, to see   398 Drayton   93
ENVIOUS   (See also ENVYOUS)
    Thou art not, Penshurst, built to envious show, 93 F2 Penshurst   1
    Where envious arts professed be,   101 F4 To the World 47
    And the envious, when they find   103 F6 Celia 2   21
    Phoebus. No? tend thy cart still. Envious day 107 F10 Proludium   7
    Hang up those dull, and envious fooles,   146 U6 Defence   1
    Of the poore sufferers) where the envious, proud, 167 U15 Friend-Wars 167
    Envious and foule Disease, could there not be 188 U34 Small Poxe   1
    That since thou tak'st all envious care and paine, 203 U43 Vulcan   13
    And there to stand so. Hast now envious Moone, 238 U65 Prince   9
    And still to stand so. Hast thou envious Moone, 238 U65 Prince   V 9
    . . . made Earle of Portland. 17. Febr. 1632. To the Envious. 250 U73 Weston Ttl
    It is: to th' envious meant,   256 U75 Epithalam.   119
ENVITE
    But in my Deske, what was there to envite   206 U43 Vulcan   V 85
ENVOYE
    In smiling L'envoye, as he would deride   202 U42 Elegy Let   75
ENVY'
    And that, midst envy' and parts; then fell by rage: 71 E110 Edmonds 1 14
ENVY
    If not, 'tis fit for you, some should envy.   67 E104 Montgomery 16
    A waiter, doth my gluttony envy: 95 F2 Penshurst   68
    Shalt neither that, nor this envy: 99 F3 Wroth   92
    And, who doth me (though I not him) envy,   115 F12 Rutland   70
    Bawd, in a Velvet scabberd! I envy   202 U42 Elegy Let   85
    Their Heads, that Envy would hold downe   272 U84 Cradle   3
    T' have knowne no envy, but by suffring it!   287 U84 Muse   162
    Faire Aemulation, and no Envy is;   389 Aleman   22
    To draw no envy (Shakespeare) on thy name,   390 Shakespeare   1
    Before this worke? where Envy hath not cast   401 Beaumont   13
    I am too fat t'envy him. He too leane   405 Inigo Jones 1   69
    To be worth Envy. Henceforth I doe meane   405 Inigo Jones 1   70
ENVYE
    The Rebell Gyants stoope, and Gorgon Envye yeild, 421 Ode:If Men   41
ENVY'D
    And only, his great Soule envy'd,   234 U60 La-ware   17
ENVYOUS
    Unseason'd frostes, or the most envyous weather. 361 Palmer   8
EPHESUS
    'Bove all your Fire-workes, had at Ephesus,   211 U43 Vulcan   194
    Beyond your Fire-workes, had at Ephesus,   211 U43 Vulcan   V194
    'Bove all our Fire-workes, had at Ephesus,   211 U43 Vulcan   V194
EPICK
    An Epick poeme; thou hast the same end.   72 E112 Gamster   10
EPICKS
    Lay that aside, the Epicks office is.   307 Horace   64
EPICOENE
    And in an Epicoene fury can write newes   222 U49 Pucell   8
EPIDEMICALL
    The truly Epidemicall disease!   237 U64 Charles 3   18
EPIGRAM
    'Tis 'gainst the manners of an Epigram: 29 E9 To All   3
    An Epigram On William Lord Burl: . . .   185 U30 Burleigh   Ttl
    An Epigram. To Thomas Lo: Elsmere, . . .   185 U31 Elsmere   Ttl
    An Epigram to the Councellour that pleaded, . . . 186 U33 Councellour Ttl
    An Epigram. To the small Poxe.   188 U34 Small Poxe Ttl
    An Epigram on Sir Edward Coke, when . . .   217 U46 Coke   Ttl
    An Epigram on The Court Pucell.   222 U49 Pucell   Ttl

	Page	Title	Line

EPIGRAM (cont.)
Entry	Page	Title	Line
An Epigram. To the honour'd —— Countesse of ——	224	U50 Countesse	Ttl
An Epigram. To William, Earle of Newcastle.	228	U53 Newcastle	Ttl
Epigram, to my Book-seller.	232	U58 Book-seller	Ttl
An Epigram. To William Earle of Newcastle.	232	U59 Newcastle	Ttl
An Epigram.	234	U61 Epigram	Ttl
An Epigram. To K. Charles for a 100. Pounds . . .	235	U62 Charles 1	Ttl
. . . first-borne, An Epigram Consolatorie. 1629.	235	U63 Charles 2	Ttl
An Epigram. To our great and good K. Charles . . .	236	U64 Charles 3	Ttl
An Epigram on the Princes birth. 1630.	237	U65 Prince	Ttl
An Epigram on Prince Charles his Birth: May. 29th. 1630	237	U65 Prince	VTtl
On the Princes Birth-day. An Epigram	237	U65 Prince	VTtl
An Epigram to the Queene, then lying in. 1630.	238	U66 Queene	Ttl
An Epigram to the Queens Health.	238	U66 Queene	VTtl
An Epigram, To the House-hold. 1630.	241	U68 House-hold	Ttl
Epigram. To a Friend, and Sonne.	241	U69 Friend Son	Ttl
. . . An Epigram Anniversarie. Novemb. 19. 1632.	249	U72 King	Ttl
. . . An Epigram.	260	U77 Treasurer	Ttl
An Epigram To my Muse, the Lady Digby, . . .	262	U78 Digby	Ttl
To Sir Kenelme Digby. An Epigram	262	U78 Digby	VTtl
To a Freind an Epigram Of him.	407	Inigo Jones 3	Ttl
An Epigram To My Joviall Good Freind Mr. Robert Dover,	415	Dover	Ttl

EPIGRAMME
Entry	Page	Title	Line
. . . Earle of Salisbury. Epigramme.	40	E43 Salisbury 1	VTtl
Or take an Epigramme so fearefully:	51	E73 Fine Grand	2
It is an Epigramme, on all man-kind;	66	E102 Pembroke	2
Where shall I scape thee? in an Epigramme?	73	E112 Gamster	15

EPIGRAMMES
Entry	Page	Title	Line
Epigrammes. I. Booke.	23	Epigrammes	Ttl
Thy title, Epigrammes, and nam'd of mee,	27	E2 My Booke	2
To thee, my way in Epigrammes seemes new,	32	E18 Censurer	1
May heare my Epigrammes, but like of none.	36	E28 Surly	20
Martial, thou gav'st farre nobler Epigrammes	38	E36 Martial	1
He sayes, I want the tongue of Epigrammes;	42	E49 Playwrt 1	2
When I dare send my Epigrammes to thee?	62	E96 Donne 2	2

EPILOGUE
Entry	Page	Title	Line
And sits, till th'Epilogue saies Clap, or Crowne:	315	Horace	222

EPISTLE (See also PISTLE)
Entry	Page	Title	Line
Epistle To Elizabeth Countesse of Rutland.	113	F12 Rutland	Ttl
Epistle. To Katherine, Lady Aubigny.	116	F13 Aubigny	Ttl
An Epistle to Sir Edward Sacvile, now Earle of Dorset.	153	U13 Sacvile	Ttl
An Epistle to Master John Selden.	158	U14 Selden	Ttl
An Epistle to a Friend, to perswade him to the Warres.	162	U15 Friend-Wars	Ttl
Epistle To a Friend.	169	U17 Friend-Debt	Ttl
An Epistle to a friend.	189	U37 Friend-Book	Ttl
An Epistle to Master Arth: Squib.	216	U45 Squib	Ttl
An Epistle answering to one that asked . . .	218	U47 Tribe	Ttl
Epistle To Mr. Arthur Squib.	229	U54 Squib	Ttl
Epistle. To my Lady Covell.	230	U56 Covell	Ttl
. . . England. An Epistle Mendicant. 1631.	248	U71 Treasurer	Ttl
Soe ended your Epistle, myne beginns	421	Censure	3

EPISTOLAR
Entry	Page	Title	Line
But then, thy'epistolar Heroick Songs,	397	Drayton	29

EPITAPH
Entry	Page	Title	Line
Item, an epitaph on my lords cock,	51	E73 Fine Grand	18
Epitaph on S. P. a Child of Q. El. Chappel.	77	E120 S. P.	Ttl
Epitaph on Elizabeth, L. H.	79	E124 Elizabeth	Ttl
An Epitaph on Master Vincent Corbet.	151	U12 Corbet	Ttl
An Epitaph, deserv'd a Tombe:	152	U12 Corbet	38
An Epitaph on Master Philip Gray.	168	U16 Gray	Ttl
An Epitaph.	188	U35 Chute	Ttl
An Epitaph, on Henry L. La-ware. To the Passer-by.	233	U60 La-ware	Ttl
Epitaph.	371	Epitaph	Ttl
To fill an Epitaph. But she had more.	371	Epitaph	5

EPITHALAMION
Entry	Page	Title	Line
Epithalamion; Or, A Song: Celebrating The nuptials of . . .	252	U75 Epithalam.	Ttl

EPITHITES
Entry	Page	Title	Line
A list of Epithites: And prayse this way.	394	Jane Ogle	8

EPITOME
Entry	Page	Title	Line
Thy Universe, though his Epitome.	185	U30 Burleigh	4
O happy Art! and wise Epitome	214	U44 Speach	43

EPODE
Entry	Page	Title	Line
To Sir Robert Wroth in praise of a Country life. Epode.	96	F3 Wroth	VTtl
And now an Epode to deepe eares I sing.	108	F10 Proludium	30
And now an Epode to deepe eares we sing.	108	F10 Proludium	V 30
and now an Epode, to deepe Eares, wee singe.	108	F10 Proludium	16
Epode.	109	F11 Epode	Ttl

EQUALL
Entry	Page	Title	Line
By constant suffring of thy equall mind;	47	E63 Salisbury 2	8
A new Susanna, equall to that old?	67	E104 Montgomery	4
And thinke his power doth equall Fates.	99	F3 Wroth	80
Till you equall with the store,	103	F6 Celia 2	12
In equall knots: This beares no brands, nor darts,	110	F11 Epode	51
How many equall with the Argive Queene,	114	F12 Rutland	49
Equall with her? or Ronsart prais'd	181	U27 Ode Helen	22
Equall with that, which for the best newes goes,	222	U49 Pucell	9
Have left in fame to equall, or out-goe	260	U77 Treasurer	8
Equall with Angels, and Co-heires of it?	286	U84 Muse	146
But equall power, to Painter, and to Poet,	305	Horace	11

EQUALL'D
Entry	Page	Title	Line
When your owne Vertues, equall'd have their Names,	281	U84 Kenelme	12

EQUALLY
Entry	Page	Title	Line
Doe equally desire your companie:	64	E101 Supper	2

EQUALLY (cont.)
          And like it too; if they looke equally: 67   E104 Montgomery   15
EQUITIE
          A Court of Equitie should doe us right, ...   211   U43 Vulcan   178
E'RE
          But I repent me: Stay. Who e're is rais'd, ...   48   E65 Muse   15
          Rising through it e're it came;   141   U2 Her man   29
          What Nymph so e're his voyce but heares, ...   148   U7 Nymph   27
          Yet he broke them, e're they could him, ...   151   U12 Corbet   10
          Reader, whose life, and name, did e're become   .   .   .   152   U12 Corbet   37
          That puts it in his Debt-booke e're 't be done;   .   .   .   154   U13 Sacvile   34
          Sydney e're night! or that did goe to bed   157   U13 Sacvile   127
          Lawes; and no change e're come to one decree: .   .   .   185   U31 Elsmere   2
          An ill-affected limbe (what e're it aile)   192   U38 Elegy 'Tis   45
          Why was't? did e're the Cloudes aske back their raine?   .   .   192   U38 Elegy 'Tis   56
          On every wall, and sung where e're I walke.   193   U38 Elegy 'Tis   98
          Winter is come a Quarter e're his Time, ...   199   U41 Elegy Since 12
          To doe her Husbands rites in, e're 'twere gone   .   .   .   201   U42 Elegy Let   40
          And raz'd, e're thought could urge, This might have bin!   .   .   209   U43 Vulcan   136
          E're thou wert halfe got out, ...   242   U70 Ode   6
          Jonson, who sung this of him, e're he went   246   U70 Ode   85
          Who, e're the first downe bloomed on the chin,   .   .   .   247   U70 Ode   127
          One to the other, long e're these to light were brought.   .   .   257   U75 Epithalam. 144
          Where e're he goes upon the ground, ...   265   U79 New-yeares   58
          And e're I can aske more of her, shee's gone!   .   .   .   269   U81 Pawlet   12
          The truth; nor let thy Fable thinke, what e're   .   .   .   329   Horace   508
          It carries Palme with it, (where e're it goes)   .   .   .   363   Riches   6
          If such a Tyke as thou, er'e wer't, or noe?   409   Detractor   14
          I shall think on't ere't be day.   417   Moon   11
ERE
          If any pious life ere lifted man   35   E27 Roe 1   6
          And person to the world; ere I thy name.   36   E30 Guiltie   4
          Ere blacks were bought for his owne funerall,   .   .   .   41   E44 Chuff   3
          On the true causes, ere they grow too old.   50   E70 Wm Roe 1   4
          And, ere I could aske you, I was prevented: 54   E84 Bedford 2   3
          Was dull, and long, ere shee would goe to man: .   .   .   57   E90 Mill   3
          Ere cherries ripe, and straw-berries be gone,   .   .   .   58   E92 New Crie   1
          For none ere tooke that pleasure in sinnes sense,   .   .   60   E94 Bedford 3   9
          Where ere he met me; now hee's dumbe, or proud.   .   .   .   62   E97 Motion   8
          Knat, raile, and ruffe too. How so ere, my man   .   .   .   65   E101 Supper   20
          My praise is plaine, and where so ere profest,   .   .   .   67   E103 L Wroth 1   13
          Thy all, at all: and what so ere I doe, ...   72   E112 Gamster   5
          Next morne, an Ode: Thou mak'st a song ere night.   .   .   72   E112 Gamster   12
          'Twill see it's sister naked, ere a sword.   74   E115 Honest Man 22
          And will, long ere thou should'st starve, ...   106   F8 Sicknesse   44
          To keepe him off; and how-so-e're he gleanes   .   .   .   242   U69 Friend Son   16
          Where ere they tread th'enamour'd ground, ...   264   U79 New-yeares   36
          Nor language, nor cleere order ere forsakes.   .   .   .   307   Horace   58
          What Poesy ere was painted on a wall   406   Inigo Jones 1   97
          Lyve long the Feasting Roome. And ere thou burne   .   .   406   Inigo Jones 1   101
ERECT
          In glorious Piles, or Pyramids erect   261   U77 Treasurer   26
          In stately Piles, and Pyramids erect   261   U77 Treasurer V 26
ERECTED
          It was erected; and still walking under   157   U13 Sacvile   141
ERE'T
          I shall think on't ere't be day.   417   Moon   11
ERIDANUS
          In heav'n the Signe of old Eridanus: 369   Ode Who saith   109
ERRANT
          Of errant Knight-hood, with the Dames, and Dwarfes;   .   .   205   U43 Vulcan   67
ERRANT'ST
          Then, The townes honest Man's her errant'st knave.   .   .   75   E115 Honest Man 34
ERRE
          Even those for whom they doe this, know they erre: .   .   83   E131 Ferrab. 2   10
          How can I speake of thy great paines, but erre?   .   .   .   83   E132 Sylvester   5
          Nay, you may erre in this, ...   139   U2 Another   9
          Great Say-Master of State, who cannot erre, ...   255   U75 Epithalam.   99
          Great Say-Master of State, who not to erre, ...   255   U75 Epithalam. V 99
          Being tould there, Reason cannot, Sense may erre.   .   .   370   Author   14
ERR'D
          Though I confesse (as every Muse hath err'd,   .   .   .   159   U14 Selden   19
ERROR
          So, by error, to his fate   77   E120 S. P.   17
          But this doth from the cloud of error grow, ...   110   F11 Epode   35
          Farre from the maze of custome, error, strife,   .   .   .   118   F13 Aubigny   60
          Whether truth may, and whether error bring.   325   Horace   439
ERRORS
          And, in their errors maze, thine owne way know: .   .   .   76   E119 Shelton   13
          If subject to the jealous errors   177   U25 Desmond   28
ERROUR
          Except the way be errour to those ends: 170   U18 Elegy Can   13
          Errour and folly in me may have crost   192   U38 Elegy 'Tis   37
ERROURS
          What blots and errours, have you watch'd and purg'd   .   .   160   U14 Selden   42
ESCAPE
          T'escape this common knowne necessitie, ...   271   U81 Pawlet   93
          If in th'escape an artlesse path we tread.   339   Horace   V 46/ 44
ESCAPES (See also SCAPE)
          Each best day of our life escapes us, first.   .   .   .   50   E70 Wm Roe 1   6
ESCHYLUS
          With lees of Wine. Next Eschylus, more late,   .   .   .   319   Horace   315

ESME
To Esme, Lord 'Aubigny. . . . . 80 E127 Aubigny Ttl
. . . Esme D. of Lenox deceased, and Sister of the . . . . 252 U75 Epithalam. Ttl
ESPECIALLY
Especially in paper; that, that steame . . . . 205 U43 Vulcan 61
Especially in paper; many a Reame . . . . 205 U43 Vulcan V 61
ESPIE
Could soone espie . . . . 256 U75 Epithalam. 110
Falshood with truth, as no man can espie . . . . 315 Horace 216
ESPLANDIANS
Th'Esplandians, Arthurs, Palmerins, and all . . . 203 U43 Vulcan 30
ESPY
Falsehood and truth, as no man can espy . . . . 343 Horace V216
ESQUIRE
On Mungril Esquire. . . . . 42 E48 Mungril Ttl
. . . Thomas May, Esquire. . . . . 395 May Ttl
ESSAY (See ASSAY'D, SAY-MASTER, 'SSAYD)
ESSAYES
That lost, he keepes his chamber, reades Essayes, . . 30 E12 Shift 15
For her devotions, and those sad essayes . . . 287 U84 Muse 181
ESSENCE
That is an essence, farre more gentle, fine, . . . 110 F11 Epode 45
That is an essence, most gentile and fine, . . . 110 F11 Epode V 45
When her dead essence (like the Anatomie . . . 179 U25 Desmond 37
For God, whose essence is so infinite, . . . 236 U63 Charles 2 13
ESTATE
Worth an estate, treble to that you have. . . . 114 F12 Rutland 36
Vice, and, am knowne to have a Knights estate. . . 331 Horace 572
Vice, and is knowne to have a Knights estate. . . 352 Horace V548/572
God blesse the Councell of Estate, ... 419 Grace 5
ESTATES
O pietie! so to weigh the poores estates! . . . 235 U62 Charles 1 11
ESTEEM'D
Antiquities search'd! Opinions dis-esteem'd! . . . 160 U14 Selden 40
ESTEEME
Something, which, else, could hope for no esteeme, . . 64 E101 Supper 6
The truth of times) was once of more esteeme, . . . 114 F12 Rutland 21
Which though the turning world may dis-esteeme, . . 118 F13 Aubigny 64
ESTEEMED
To his much and worthily esteemed friend the Author. . . 383 Author Ttl
ESTIMATE
And estimate thy Paines; as having wrought . . . 161 U14 Selden 75
ETEOSTICHS
Or Eteostichs, or those finer flammes . . . 204 U43 Vulcan 36
ETERNALL
Eternall Father, God, who did'st create . . . 127 U1 Trinitie 17
Eternall God the Sonne, who not denyd'st . . . 128 U1 Trinitie 21
Eternall Spirit, God from both proceeding, . . . 128 U1 Trinitie 25
The Sonne of God, th'Eternall King, . . . 130 U1 Nativitie 7
Whose fame hath an eternall voice? . . . 181 U27 Ode Helen 16
To see that bright eternall Day: . . . 245 U70 Ode 81
Of that eternall Port kept ope' . . . 274 U84 Cradle 39
To heare their Judge, and his eternall doome; . . 283 U84 Muse 48
That great eternall Holy-day of rest, . . . 284 U84 Muse 63
In his eternall Kingdome, where we sit . . . 286 U84 Muse 145
To that eternall Rest, where now sh'hath place . . 288 U84 Muse 197
Thou worthy in eternall Flower to fare, . . . 294 U89 Mart.8:77 2
ETERNITIE (See also AETERNITIES)
Whose rellish to eternitie shall last. . . . 58 E91 Vere 8
Whose rellish to eternitie will last. . . . 58 E91 Vere V 8
Doth vindicate it to eternitie. . . . . 175 U24 Frontispice 4
Became her Birth-day to Eternitie! . . . 271 U81 Pawlet 68
Compar'd unto that long eternitie, . . . 285 U84 Muse 106
ETERNIZ'D
And I could wish for their eterniz'd sakes, . . . 89 E133 Voyage 195
ETHNICISME
Of Ethnicisme, makes his Muse a Saint. . . . 401 Beaumont 22
EUCLIDE
Able to talk of Euclide, and correct . . . 402 Inigo Jones 1 4
EUGENIAN
To the Eugenian dale; . . . . . . 367 Ode Who saith 43
EUPHEME
Eupheme; Or, The Faire Fame Left To Posteritie . . . 272 U84 Eupheme Ttl
EURIPIDES
Euripides, and Sophocles to us, ... 391 Shakespeare 34
EUROPE
In th'eye of Europe, where thy deeds were done, . . 58 E91 Vere 6
Beates brave, and loude in Europe, and bids come . . 162 U15 Friend-Wars 2
The wished Peace of Europe: . . . . 222 U48 Bacchus 48
To whom all Scenes of Europe homage owe. . . . 391 Shakespeare 42
EUROPES
The choise of Europes pride; . . . . 368 Ode Who saith 83
Of Europes waters can . . . . . . 369 Ode Who saith 119
EUTHANASEE
To 'greet, or grieve her soft Euthanasee? . . . 283 U84 Muse 40
EVEN (NOUN)
Each morne, and even, they are taught to pray, . . 96 F2 Penshurst 95
At morne, and even, shades are longest; . . . 104 F7 Women but 7
EVEN (See also EENE)
When even there, where most thou praysest mee, . . 44 E55 Beaumont 9
I purpos'd her; that should, with even powers, . . 52 E76 Bedford 1 14
And even the praisers judgement suffers so. . . 64 E99 Th Roe 2 10
Even in the dew of grace, what you would bee? . . 67 E104 Montgomery 2

	Page	Title	Line

EVEN (cont.)

	Page	Title	Line
But even their names were to be made a-new,	67	E105 L Wroth 2	5
Of old, even by her practise, to be fam'd;	82	E130 Ferrab. 1	10
Even those for whom they doe this, know they erre:	83	E131 Ferrab. 2	10
Whose linkes are bright, and even,	110	F11 Epode	48
And, at her strong armes end, hold up, and even,	114	F12 Rutland	42
And, at her strong armes end, there hold up even,	114	F12 Rutland	V 42
And keepe an even, and unalter'd gaite;	118	F13 Aubigny	61
And, above her even chin,	136	U2 Cupid	24
Even nose, and cheeke (withall)	141	U2 Her man	19
Even ashes of lovers find no rest.	149	U8 Houre-glasse	11
They were so even, grave, and holy;	152	U12 Corbet	23
A many of bookes, even good judgements wound	159	U14 Selden	15
And even our sports are dangers! what we call	163	U15 Friend-Wars	38
That may corrupt her, even in his eyes.	165	U15 Friend-Wars	92
Even in youth.	181	U26 Ode High	24
It shakes even him, that all things else doth shake.	193	U38 Elegy 'Tis	72
On all Soules that are absent; even the dead;	218	U47 Tribe	17
Whose even Thred the Fates spinne round, and full,	225	U51 Bacon	15
So polish't, perfect, round, and even,	280	U84 Mind	55
But, kept an even gate, as some streight tree	287	U84 Muse	165
Is now to speak, and even now to differ	339	Horace	V 61
Lives in his issue, even so, the race	392	Shakespeare	66
Where it runs round, and even: where so well,	415	Rutter	16
Even states most hated, when no lawes resist	423	Lucan	13

EVENING

	Page	Title	Line
The Muses evening, as their morning-starre.	61	E94 Bedford 3	16
Whose morning, and whose evening vow	99	F3 Wroth	V100

EVENING'S

	Page	Title	Line
Thy morning's, and thy evening's vow	99	F3 Wroth	100

EVENLY

	Page	Title	Line
And, in thy censures, evenly, dost take	62	E96 Donne 2	4

EVENTS

	Page	Title	Line
The councells, actions, orders, and events	62	E95 Savile	32
After, mens Wishes, crown'd in their events,	309	Horace	108

EVER (See also ERE)

	Page	Title	Line
Which shewes, where ever death doth please t'appeare,	37	E32 Roe 2	9
And like Nectar ever flowing:	39	E40 Ratcliffe	10
Indeed, poore Giles repents he married ever.	40	E42 Giles	3
And ever is ill got without the first.	63	E98 Th Roe 1	12
I would restore, and keepe it ever such;	78	E122 Rudyerd 2	8
The ever-boyling floud. Whose bankes upon	88	E133 Voyage	142
The milke, nor oyle, did ever flowe soe free	98	F3 Wroth	V 60
Time will not be ours, for ever:	102	F5 Celia 1	3
And to his sense object this sentence ever,	113	F11 Epode	115
For he, that once is good, is ever great.	118	F13 Aubigny	52
How can I doubt to finde thee ever, here?	122	F15 Heaven	16
Love, if thou wilt ever see	132	U2 How he saw	7
Or Swans Downe ever?	135	U2 Triumph	26
If ever we will love aright.	146	U6 Defence	10
To license ever was so light,	152	U12 Corbet	25
But these men ever want: their very trade	155	U13 Sacvile	79
Ever at home: yet, have all Countries seene:	159	U14 Selden	30
Thy true friends wishes, which shall ever be,	167	U15 Friend-Wars	V176
Cramp'd for ever;	184	U29 Fit of Rime	51
Or Turners oyle of Talck. Nor ever got	188	U34 Small Poxe	11
Which, how most sacred I will ever keepe,	190	U37 Friend-Book	13
But ever without blazon, or least shade	197	U40 Elegy That	13
But the grave Lover ever was an Asse:	198	U40 Elegy That	32
No Poets verses yet did ever move,	199	U42 Elegy Let	3
To make consumption, ever, where thou go'st;	205	U43 Vulcan	58
To make propter viam, ever, where thou go'st;	205	U43 Vulcan	V 58
I now begin to doubt, if ever Grace,	207	U43 Vulcan	107
Nor ever trusted to that friendship yet,	216	U45 Squib	7
They cannot last. No lie grew ever old.	216	U45 Squib	20
Then these can ever be; or else wish none.	219	U47 Tribe	30
Or that the Match from Spaine was ever meant?	219	U47 Tribe	36
Still looking to, and ever loving heaven;	219	U47 Tribe	61
But ever to no ends:	243	U70 Ode	29
And ever close the burden of the Song,	249	U72 King	17
To vertue, and true worth, be ever blind.	250	U73 Weston	10
Then ever Pales could, or Pan;	265	U79 New-yeares	61
That ever had beginning there, to'ave end!	271	U81 Pawlet	91
With ever-greene, and great renowne,	272	U84 Cradle	2
That ever Nature, or the later Ayre	274	U84 Descent	4
There, all the happy soules, that ever were,	285	U84 Muse	113
A Musique in the Eares, will ever last;	286	U84 Muse	124
And came forth ever cheered, with the rod	287	U84 Muse	183
Can this decay, but is beginning ever.	294	U88 Petronius	10
New names of things. It hath beene ever free,	309	Horace	83
And ever will, to utter termes that bee	309	Horace	84
And the severe, speech ever serious.	311	Horace	151
He ever hastens to the end, and so	315	Horace	211
Loves Dogges, and Horses; and is ever one	315	Horace	230
Or acted told. But, ever, things that run	317	Horace	256
Poets should ever be indifferent.	331	Horace	556
Who ever sipt at Baphyre river,	367	Ode Who saith	57
Ever his thighes Male then, and his braines Shee.	378	Coryat 2	92
Who ever he be, would write a Story at	379	Coryat 3	1
And therefore how ever the travelling nation,	380	Coryat 3	29
And as an ever-lasting Sacrifice	382	Rich	7
I do not feele that ever yet I had	385	Husband	5
All, that was ever writ in brasse.	390	Reader	8

	Page	Title	Line

EVER (cont.)

	Page	Title	Line
That ever yet did fire the English blood!	397	Drayton	57
The noblest Ingenyre that ever was!	402	Inigo Jones 1	6

EVER-BOYLING

	Page	Title	Line
The ever-boyling floud. Whose bankes upon	88	E133 Voyage	142

EVER-GREENE

	Page	Title	Line
With ever-greene, and great renowne,	272	U84 Cradle	2

EVER-LASTING

	Page	Title	Line
And as an ever-lasting Sacrifice	382	Rich	7

EVERLASTING

	Page	Title	Line
What 'tis t'enjoy, an everlasting breath!	285	U84 Muse	92

EVE'RY

	Page	Title	Line
And eve'ry joy, in mariage, turne a fruite.	384	Somerset	18

EVERY (See also EV'RY)

	Page	Title	Line
To every cause he meets, this voyce he brayes:	31	E12 Shift	19
Thou more; that with it every day, dar'st jest	32	E16 Brain-hardy	2
Whose every worke, of thy most earely wit,	34	E23 Donne 1	3
And though the soundest legs goe every day,	36	E31 Banck	3
Yes, now he weares his knight-hood every day.	42	E46 Luckless 1	6
Hee that wooes every widdow, will get none.	42	E47 Luckless 2	2
Though every fortitude deserves applause,	49	E66 Cary	15
I would have spent: how every Muse should know it,	55	E84 Bedford 2	7
Then Cicero, whose every breath was fame:	57	E89 Allen	6
Ripe statesmen, ripe: They grow in every street.	58	E92 New Crie	3
They meet in sixes, and at every mart,	59	E92 New Crie	21
Or, every day, some one at Rimee's looks,	59	E92 New Crie	23
For every part a character assign'd.	67	E103 L Wroth 1	12
All-vertuous Herbert! on whose every part	68	E106 E Herbert	3
In every counsell, stratageme, designe,	71	E110 Edmonds 1	19
Give every one his dose of mirth: and watches	74	E115 Honest Man	14
At every meale, where it doth dine, or sup,	74	E115 Honest Man	23
In men, but every bravest was the best:	75	E116 Jephson	10
Canst tell me best, how every Furie lookes there,	85	E133 Voyage	52
When every clerke eates artichokes, and peason,	88	E133 Voyage	166
The painted partrich lyes in every field,	94	F2 Penshurst	29
Hang on thy walls, that every child may reach.	94	F2 Penshurst	44
Shine bright on every harth as the desires	95	F2 Penshurst	78
With the whole houshold, and may, every day,	96	F2 Penshurst	96
For every price, in every jarre,	99	F3 Wroth	74
Where every freedome is betray'd,	101	F4 To the World	51
And every goodnesse tax'd, or griev'd.	101	F4 To the World	52
Every stew in towne to know;	105	F8 Sicknesse	38
Every Cranck in towne to know;	105	F8 Sicknesse	V 38
in whom the flame of every beauty raignes,	108	F10 Proludium	8
And almost every vice, almightie gold,	113	F12 Rutland	2
To every squire, or groome, that will report	113	F12 Rutland	6
To every squire, or groome, that can report	113	F12 Rutland	V 6
With every vertue, wheresoere it move,	116	F13 Aubigny	8
Your beautie; for you see that every day:	117	F13 Aubigny	30
And never thinke, how vice doth every houre,	119	F13 Aubigny	87
Dwell, dwell here still: O, being every-where,	122	F15 Heaven	15
Every Cloud about his eye;	132	U2 How he saw	12
That at every motion sweld	138	U2 Kisse	24
And excuse spun every day,	140	U2 Promise	10
To say over every purle	140	U2 Promise	23
Such a man, with every part,	142	U2 Her man	53
And every close did meet	149	U9 Picture	7
But like to be, that every day mends one,	156	U13 Sacvile	116
Though I confesse (as every Muse hath err'd,	159	U14 Selden	19
And every Dressing for a Pitfall set	164	U15 Friend-Wars	66
Coach'd, or on foot-cloth, thrice chang'd every day,	165	U15 Friend-Wars	107
Brought on us, and will every hour increase.	166	U15 Friend-Wars	122
(Because th'are every where amongst Man-kind	167	U15 Friend-Wars	171
Out of his Grave, and poyson every eare.	172	U21 Ltl Shrub	4
May shine .(through every chincke) to every sight	177	U25 Desmond	16
For Venus Ceston, every line you make.	182	U28 Worth	14
On every wall, and sung where e're I walke.	193	U38 Elegy 'Tis	98
At every stall; The Cittie Cap's a charme.	200	U42 Elegy Let	28
Court every hanging Gowne, and after that,	201	U42 Elegy Let	57
To ruine every issue of her braine?	203	U43 Vulcan	V 14
To make consumption, every where thou go'st;	205	U43 Vulcan	V 58
To sow consumption, every where thou go'st;	205	U43 Vulcan	V 58
Call every night to Supper in these fitts,	218	U47 Tribe	21
Let every Lyre be strung,	239	U67 Muses	16
To every Order, ev'ry Hierarchie!	271	U81 Pawlet	72
At pleasure, to be call'd for, every day!	271	U81 Pawlet	82
On every Stall.	273	U84 Cradle	28
Where every lim takes like a face?	275	U84 Body	4
Hence-forth may every line be you;	278	U84 Mind	22
Hard-hearted, I dreame every Night	293	U86 Hor.4:1	37
On every limbe, ta'en from a severall creature,	305	Horace	3
The nailes, and every curled haire disclose;	307	Horace	47
The nailes, and every gentle haire disclose:	339	Horace	V 49/ 47
To every state of fortune; she helpes on,	311	Horace	153
To every Fortunes habit; she helps on,	342	Horace	V153
He knowes not why, and changeth every houre.	315	Horace	228
To every vice, as hardly to be brought	315	Horace	232
With poore base termes, through every baser shop:	321	Horace	334
And so, as every man may hope the same;	321	Horace	350
But every Judge hath not the facultie	323	Horace	387
Had not our every Poet like offended.	325	Horace	414
O I left-witted, that purge every spring	325	Horace	429
Indeed, give fitting dues to every man.	325	Horace	452

	Page	Title	Line
EVERY (cont.)			
But he hath every suffrage, can apply	329	Horace	514
That to the sale of Wares calls every Buyer;	333	Horace	598
Not only this, but every day of thine,	384	Somerset	9
But every Table in this Church can say,	394	Jane Ogle	7
Such things, of every body, and as well.	394	Jane Ogle	10
At every line some pinn thereof should slacke	395	May	5
With every song, I sweare, and so would dye:	397	Drayton	54
And will be bought of every Lord, and Knight,	398	Drayton	72
And stop my sight, in every line I goe.	398	Drayton	78
she desires of every birth	417	Moon	19
And God blesse every living thing,	418	Grace	3
To every sence, and scorne to those that sawe	420	Ode:If Men	17
EVERY~WHERE			
Dwell, dwell here still: O, being every~where,	122	F15 Heaven	15
EVIDENCE			
Of that great Evidence, the Conscience!	284	U84 Muse	58
EVILL			
Raising the World to good or evill fame,	175	U24 Frontispice	3
Or skill, to carry out an evill cause!	187	U33 Councellour	18
In others-evill best was understood:	217	U46 Coke	6
To cure the call'd Kings Evill with thy touch;	235	U62 Charles 1	4
To cure the Poets Evill, Povertie:	235	U62 Charles 1	6
As thou dost cure our Evill, at thy charge.	235	U62 Charles 1	8
But, that he cure the Peoples Evill too?	235	U62 Charles 1	14
Loves cares so evill, and so great?	290	U85 Country	38
EVILS			
And all the Evils that flew out of her box	212	U43 Vulcan	214
The old man many evils doe girt round;	315	Horace	241
EV'N			
Whose life, ev'n they, that envie it, must praise;	66	E102 Pembroke	16
EV'RY			
To ev'ry Petticote he brush'd, and Glove	201	U42 Elegy Let	54
When shee puts forth the life of ev'ry thing:	250	U74 Weston	3
Rare Plants from ev'ry banke doe rise,	251	U74 Weston	10
And ev'ry Plant the sense surprize,	251	U74 Weston	11
To every Order, ev'ry Hierarchie!	271	U81 Pawlet	72
And ev'ry birth encrease the heate of Love.	384	Somerset	20
And weigh'd your Play: untwisted ev'ry thread,	415	Rutter	14
EWES			
Our teeming Ewes, and lustie-mounting Rammes.	264	U79 New-yeares	17
Your teeming Ewes, aswell as mounting Rammes.	265	U79 New-yeares	51
EXACT			
With his old earthly labours. T'exact more,	107	F10 Proludium	5
But to exact againe what once is given,	192	U38 Elegy 'Tis	63
EXACTED			
Exacted by thy fate, on the just day.	41	E45 First Son	4
'T will be exacted of your name, whose sonne,	121	F14 Sydney	41
EXACTS			
Exacts then she is pleas'd to pay: no suits,	258	U75 Epithalam.	188
EXALT			
And thou to her, that Husband, may exalt	384	Somerset	13
EXALTED			
And shine as you exalted are;	246	U70 Ode	97
There, high exalted in the Spheare,	279	U84 Mind	29
That pure, that pretious, and exalted mind	285	U84 Muse	104
EXAMINE			
Unto your strength, and long examine it,	307	Horace	54
EXAMIN'D			
Where nothing is examin'd, weigh'd,	101	F4 To the World	49
How are Traditions there examin'd: how	160	U14 Selden	49
O're read, examin'd, try'd, and prov'd your Ryme	421	Censure	7
EXAMINING			
Who (in th'examining)	109	F11 Epode	14
EXAMPLE			
Came forth example, and remaines so, yet:	34	E23 Donne 1	4
A Prince, that rules by'example, more than sway?	37	E35 James 2	2
Love honors, which of best example bee,	49	E66 Cary	13
How can so great example dye in mee,	57	E89 Mill	7
At last, ease, appetite, and example wan	57	E90 Roe	4
How much of great example wert thou, Roe,	64	E99 Th Roe 2	5
Heare and make Example too.	133	U2 Suffered	26
May grow so great to be example, when	158	U13 Sacvile	161
And so that either may example prove	171	U19 Elegy By	16
O may your wisdome take example hence,	193	U38 Elegy 'Tis	67
Foole, wilt thou let that in example come?	210	U43 Vulcan	161
Is of so brave example, as he were	224	U50 Countesse	7
When you that raigne, are her Example growne,	236	U64 Charles 3	9
When thou that rul'st, are her Example growne,	236	U64 Charles 3	V 9
And such a force the faire example had,	247	U70 Ode	117
What she did here, by great example, well,	269	U81 Pawlet	33
What she did by a great example, well,	269	U81 Pawlet	V 33
Was the example of a wife!	399	Lady Ogle	12
EXAMPLED			
They are th'exampled Paire, and mirrour of their kind.	255	U75 Epithalam.	80
EXAMPLES			
Take you the Greeke Examples, for your light,	323	Horace	397
EXCEED (See also 'XCEED)			
No male unto him: who could so exceed	53	E79 Rutland	7
EXCEEDETH			
And hunting, Pan, exceedeth thee.	265	U79 New-yeares	55
And hunting, Pan, exceedeth thee.	265	U79 New-yeares	67

EXCEEDING
  Her breath for sweete exceeding   .   .   .   . 365 Ode Splendor   13
  Her breath farre sweete exceeding   .   .   .   . 365 Ode Splendor   V 13
  Thy Catalogue of Ships, exceeding his, ... 398 Drayton   61
EXCEEDS
  But thine, for which I doo't, so much exceeds!   .   .   .   .   46 E60 Mounteagle   8
EXCELL
  As I, can say, and see it doth excell.   .   .   .   .   .   . 117 F13 Aubigny   34
  Such as in valour would excell, ... 146 U6 Defence   7
  Yet read him in these lines: He doth excell   .   .   .   . 262 U78 Digby   2
  Yet take him in these lines: He doth excell   .   .   .   . 262 U78 Digby   V 2
  There may a Lawyer be, may not excell;   .   .   .`.   .   . 331 Horace   550
EXCELLENCE
  As Love, t'aquit such excellence, ... 173 U22 Elegy Tho   23
  And toile in vaine: the excellence is such   .   .   .   . 321 Horace   352
EXCELLENT   (See also EX'LENT)
  To marke the excellent seas'ning of your Stile!   .   .   . 160 U14 Selden   55
  To the Kings Most Excellent Majesty   .   .   .   .   . 259 U76 Petition   VTtl
  For Mind, and Body, the most excellent   .   .   .   .   . 274 U84 Descent   3
  For hee'll cry, Good, brave, better, excellent!   .   .   . 333 Horace   611
EXCELLING
  Of this excelling frame?   .   .   .   . 112 F11 Epode   110
EXCELSIS
  Had burst with storme, and downe fell, ab excelsis,   .   .   .   86 E133 Voyage   95
EXCEPT
  Except thou could'st, Sir Cod, weare them within.   .   .   .   33 E20 Cod 2   2
  Except the duell. Can sing songs, and catches;   .   .   .   74 E115 Honest Man   13
  Except the way be errour to those ends: .   .   .   . 170 U18 Elegy Can   13
  Why are we rich, or great, except to show   .   .   .   . 215 U44 Speach   69
  (Except the joy that the first Mary brought, ... 238 U66 Queene   7
  To have a God come in; except a knot   .   .   .   .   . 317 Horace   273
  Except a dublet, and bought of the Jewes: .   .   .   . 380 Coryat 3   49
  Except your Gratious Eye as through a Glass   .   .   .   . 383 Rich   11
EXCEPTION
  10. Another Ladyes exception present at the hearing.   .   . 142 U2 Exception   Ttl
EXCESSE
  In speech; it is with that excesse   .   .   .   .   . 279 U84 Mind   34
EXCHANGE
  They're growne Commoditie upon Exchange;   .   .   .   . 165 U15 Friend-Wars   86
  Varietie of Silkes were on th'Exchange!   .   .   .   . 202 U42 Elegy Let   72
  Upon th'Exchange, still, out of Popes-head-Alley;   .   .   . 206 U43 Vulcan   80
  As fit t'exchange discourse; a Verse to win   .   .   . 311 Horace   119
  Upon th'Exchange of Letters, as I wou'd   .   .   .   . 386 Browne   14
EXCHEQUER   (See 'CHEQUER)
EXCITE   (See also ACCITE)
  Yet, sometime, doth the Comedie excite   .   .   .   . 311 Horace   132
EXCLUDE
  Exclude all sober Poets, from their share   .   .   .   . 325 Horace   421
EXCUSE
  1. His Excuse for loving.   .   .   .   .   .   . 131 U2 Excuse   Ttl
  And excuse spun every day, ... 140 U2 Promise   10
  Is that the truer excuse? or have we got   .   .   .   . 166 U15 Friend-Wars 142
  You have a Husband is the just excuse   .   .   .   . 171 U19 Elegy By   22
  Or lay the excuse upon the Vintners vault;   .   .   . 191 U38 Elegy 'Tis   22
  Thou need new termes; thou maist, without excuse,   .   .   . 307 Horace   70
EXCUSES
  Excuses, or Delayes? or done 'hem scant, ... 153 U13 Sacvile   27
  That I not mixe thee so, my braine excuses;   .   .   . 391 Shakespeare   25
EXECRATION
  An Execration upon Vulcan.   .   .   .   .   .   . 202 U43 Vulcan   Ttl
EXECUTES
  Executes men in picture. By defect, ...   75 E115 Honest Man   29
EXECUTION
  This looketh like an Execution day?   .   .   .   . 193 U38 Elegy 'Tis   80
EXECUTIONER
  Shee is the Judge, Thou Executioner: .   .   .   . 204 U43 Vulcan   47
EXECUTOR
  When he made him executor, might be heire.   .   .   .   41 E44 Chuff   6
EXEMPT
  Upon thy throate, and live exempt   .   .   .   . 100 F4 To the World   7
  But so exempt from blame, ... 148 U7 Nymph   33
  Just as she in it liv'd! and so exempt   .   .   .   . 270 U81 Pawlet   48
EXERCISE
  When thou would'st feast, or exercise thy friends.   .   .   .   94 F2 Penshurst   21
  More for thy exercise, then fare;   .   .   .   .   .   97 F3 Wroth   30
  And exercise below, ... 144 U3 Musicall   18
  Wee exercise below, ... 144 U3 Musicall   V 18
  Twixt Cotswold, and the Olimpicke exercise: .   .   . 415 Dover   2
EXERCIS'D
  Almost, is exercis'd: and scarse one knowes,   .   .   .   66 E102 Pembroke   7
EXHAUSTED
  Came not that soule exhausted so their store.   .   .   .   53 E79 Rutland   4
EXIL'D
  Where have I beene this while exil'd from thee?   .   .   . 122 F15 Heaven   13
EX'LENT
  As if that ex'lent Dulnesse were Loves grace;   .   .   . 198 U40 Elegy That   24
EXPANSIONS
  Oylie Expansions, or shrunke durtie folds,   .   .   . 220 U47 Tribe   68
EXPECT
  Breathe to expect my when, and make my how.   .   .   .   37 E33 Roe 3   4
  And Ile expect no wine.   .   .   .   .   .   . 106 F9 Celia 3   V 4
  As what th'have lost t'expect, they dare deride.   .   .   . 116 F13 Aubigny   4
  T'expect the honors of great 'Aubigny: .   .   .   . 119 F13 Aubigny   105

		Page	Title	Line
EXPECT (cont.)				
But who should lesse expect from you,		173	U22 Elegy Tho	13
Such truths, as we expect for happy men,		246	U70 Ode	83
New yeares, expect new gifts: Sister, your Harpe,		263	U79 New-yeares	1
Best Kings expect first-fruits of your glad gaines.		263	U79 New-yeares	13
Thy Muse, and mine, as they expect. 'Tis true:		396	Drayton	5
EXPECTED				
As if it had expected such a guest!		96	F2 Penshurst	88
With the rest, I long expected,		140	U2 Promise	7
Expected with the fleshes restitution.		283	U84 Muse	50
EXPELL				
And her blacke spight expell.		109	F11 Epode	4
EXPENCE				
Th'expence in odours is a most vaine sinne,		33	E20 Cod 2	1
With so much Loyalties expence,		173	U22 Elegy Tho	22
And as lip-thirstie, in each words expence,		222	U49 Pucell	13
And rather wish, in their expence of Sack,		241	U68 House-hold	9
Of light expence;		273	U84 Cradle	20
EXPENSE				
Hence, then, prophane: Here needs no words expense		400	Beaumont	3
Till I, at much expense of Time, and Taper		666	Glover	7
EXPERIENCE				
And guided by Experience, whose straite wand		176	U24 Frontispice	11
EXPIATE				
Willing to expiate the fault in thee,		60	E93 Radcliffe	15
He will expiate this sinne with converting the Jewes.		375	Coryat 1	21
EXPIRE				
For whom I doubly would expire,		293	U87 Hor.3:9	15
EXPLAT'ST				
Like Solons selfe; explat'st the knottie Lawes		217	U46 Coke	17
EXPOSTULACION				
An Expostulacion with Inigo Jones.		402	Inigo Jones 1	Ttl
EXPRESS				
Will any of these express your place? or witt?		402	Inigo Jones 1	18
Or Verse, or Sense t'express Immortall you?		403	Inigo Jones 1	41
EXPRESSE				
But what can this (more then expresse their love)		95	F2 Penshurst	57
And yet (in this t'expresse our selves more cleare)		111	F11 Epode	75
And yet (in this t'expresse my self more cleare)		111	F11 Epode	V 75
Who the whole Act expresse:		255	U75 Epithalam.	87
Thereof, no notion can expresse how much		269	U81 Pawlet	26
No Nation can expresse how much		269	U81 Pawlet	V 26
No, to expresse a Mind to sense,		278	U84 Mind	13
No, to expresse this Mind to sense,		278	U84 Mind	V 13
Whose Notions when it will expresse		279	U84 Mind	33
EXPRESSER				
Expresser truth, or truer glorie,		39	E40 Ratcliffe	7
EXPRESSETH				
That expresseth but by fits,		183	U29 Fit of Rime	2
EXPRESSION				
Expression for! with that unbounded lyne		406	Inigo Jones 1	95
EXPRESSIONS				
Thence draw forth true expressions. For, sometimes,		327	Horace	455
EXPREST				
To have't exprest,		149	U8 Houre-glasse	10
To have exprest,		246	U70 Ode	88
The Comick matter will not be exprest		311	Horace	121
Yet Comick matter shunnes to be exprest		341	Horace	V 127/121
EXSCRIBE				
Since I exscribe your Sonnets, am become		182	U28 Worth	3
EXTASIE				
In this sweet Extasie, she was rapt hence.		289	U84 Muse	225
EXTASIES				
From braines entranc'd, and fill'd with extasies;		116	F12 Rutland	90
EXTEMPORE				
A Grace by Ben: Johnson. extempore. before King James.		418	Grace	Ttl
EXTEND				
A Sydney: but in that extend as farre		67	E103 L Wroth 1	10
Extend a reaching vertue, early and late:		258	U75 Epithalam.	180
EXTENDETH				
extendeth circles into infinits,		361	Palmer	18
EXTENDS				
The Judge his favour timely then extends,		186	U32 Elsmere	1
EXTENSION				
To his bountie; by extension		259	U76 Petition	9
EXTRACT				
T'extract, and choose the best of all these knowne,		80	E128 Wm Roe 2	3
EXTRAORDINARIE				
Is constant to be extraordinarie.		171	U19 Elegy By	28
EXTREMITIES				
Poore wretched states, prest by extremities,		248	U71 Treasurer	1
EYE				
In th'eye of Europe, where thy deeds were done,		58	E91 Vere	6
The skilfull mischife of a rovinge Eye		108	F10 Proludium	5
At th'eye and eare (the ports unto the minde)		109	F11 Epode	9
A fixed thought, an eye un-taught to glance;		111	F11 Epode	61
Every Cloud about his eye;		132	U2 How he saw	12
You were more the eye, and talke		138	U2 Kisse	14
With your emissarie eye,		140	U2 Promise	17
Eye-brows bent like Cupids bow,		141	U2 Her man	17
Turn'd to cinders by her eye?		149	U8 Houre-glasse	8
Since, being deceiv'd, I turne a sharper eye		159	U14 Selden	23
This other for his eye-browes; hence, away,		215	U44 Speach	97

	Page	Title	Line
EYE (cont.)			
And spangled Petticotes brought forth to eye,	223	U49 Pucell	19
Thee quickly come the gardens eye to bee,	238	U65 Prince	8
Weston! That waking man! that Eye of State!	250	U73 Weston	5
That farre-all-seeing Eye	256	U75 Epithalam.	109
These I looke up at, with a reverent eye,	261	U77 Treasurer	23
These looke you up at, with a measuring eye,	261	U77 Treasurer V	23
A reverend State she had, an awfull Eye,	270	U81 Pawlet	43
If you can cast about your either eye,	271	U81 Pawlet	85
But at such distance, as the eye	276	U84 Body	19
But at such distance, all the eye	276	U84 Body V	19
You could make shift to paint an Eye,	278	U84 Mind	9
And by the awfull manage of her Eye	287	U84 Muse	167
ill-/Natur'd, and wicked Atreus cooke, to th'eye,	317	Horace	265
Of Spheares, as light of starres; She was earthes Eye:	372	Epitaph	9
Except your Gratious Eye as through a Glass	383	Rich	11
your Royal Eye which still creates new men	383	Rich	14
The Eye of flowers, worthy, for his scent,	413	Ghyrlond	14
EYE-BROWES			
This other for his eye-browes; hence, away,	215	U44 Speach	97
EYE-BROWS			
Eye-brows bent like Cupids bow,	141	U2 Her man	17
EYED			
Which being eyed directly, I divine,	362	Author	13
EYES			
His neck fenc'd round with ruffe! his eyes halfe shut!	33	E21 Gam'ster	2
Then they might in her bright eyes.	39	E40 Ratcliffe	8
For we, that have our eyes still in our eares,	43	E51 James 3	9
Foole, as if halfe eyes will not know a fleece	45	E56 Poet-Ape	13
Stand high, then, Howard, high in eyes of men,	49	E67 Suffolk	5
He hath not onely gain'd himselfe his eyes,	74	E114 Sydney	7
With great gray eyes, are lifted up, and mew'd;	88	E133 Voyage	161
And brooding o're it sit, with broadest eyes,	99	F3 Wroth	83
Cannot we delude the eyes	102	F5 Celia 1	11
Drinke to me, onely, with thine eyes,	106	F9 Celia 3	1
Drinke to me, Coelia, with thine eyes,	106	F9 Celia 3 V	1
That askes but to be censur'd by the eyes:	117	F13 Aubigny	35
Not fashion'd for the court, or strangers eyes;	119	F13 Aubigny	115
Eyes and limbes; to hurt me more.	133	U2 Suffered	4
Doe but looke on her eyes, they doe light	134	U2 Triumph	11
Just above her sparkling eyes,	136	U2 Cupid	16
Venus, and Minerva's eyes,	141	U2 Her man	15
Oh doe not wanton with those eyes,	144	U4 Song	1
But he hath eyes so round, and bright,	147	U7 Nymph	22
And all these through her eyes, have stopt her eares.	150	U9 Picture	18
That may corrupt her, even in his eyes.	165	U15 Friend-Wars	92
The Dice with glassen eyes, to the glad viewes	166	U15 Friend-Wars	138
The Dice with glassen eyes, to the glad Viewers	166	U15 Friend-Wars V	138
Vaile their owne eyes, and would impartially	170	U18 Elegy Can	19
By those bright Eyes, at whose immortall fires	170	U19 Elegy By	1
Of eyes more true,	177	U25 Desmond	23
His very eyes are yours to overthrow.	182	U28 Worth	11
Rather than meet him: And, before his eyes	185	U30 Burleigh	16
Out of your eyes, and be awhile away;	194	U38 Elegy 'Tis	115
Sindge Capons, or poore Pigges, dropping their eyes;	205	U43 Vulcan	53
Sindge capons, or crispe Pigges, dropping their eyes;	205	U43 Vulcan V	53
And for it lose his eyes with Gun-powder,	208	U43 Vulcan	121
Needs lend an aide, to thine she had her eyes.	217	U46 Coke	24
And shewing so weake an Act to vulgar eyes,	218	U47 Tribe	7
A cheerefull worke to all good eyes, to see	224	U50 Countesse	16
Thy faint, and narrow eyes, to reade the King	250	U73 Weston	2
As farre as sense, and onely by the eyes.	261	U77 Treasurer	12
As farre as sense, and onely by his eyes.	261	U77 Treasurer V	12
Dull, and prophane, weake, and imperfect eyes,	284	U84 Muse	79
Nor Turbot, nor bright Golden-eyes:	291	U85 Country	50
With faire black eyes, and haire; and a wry nose.	307	Horace	52
With faire black eyes, and hair, and some vile snout.	339	Horace V 54/	52
Then those the faithfull eyes take in by show,	317	Horace	258
Out at his friendly eyes, leape, beat the groun'.	333	Horace	613
The fault's not in the object, but their eyes.	362	Author	8
Conceal'd from all but cleare Propheticke eyes.	369	Ode Who saith	112
In such a Martirdome; To vexe their eyes,	371	Fletcher	13
As brandish't at the eyes of Ignorance.	392	Shakespeare	70
And pray thee Reader, bring thy weepinge Eyes	394	Jane Ogle	2
That all Earth look'd on; and that earth, all Eyes!	396	Drayton	16
Of tender eyes will more be wept, then seene:	398	Drayton	76
And with their grassie greene restor'd mine eyes.	398	Drayton	82
Tenants, and Servants, have they harts, and eyes,	399	Lady Ogle	4
You aske noe more then certeyne politique Eyes,	404	Inigo Jones 1	45
Eyes that can pierce into the Misteryes	404	Inigo Jones 1	46
And art the spotlesse Mirrour to Mans eyes.	414	Ghyrlond	44
Uppon soe humbled earth to cast hir eyes:	420	Ode:If Men	30
EYTHER			
To rise with eyther of you, on the morrow.	384	Somerset	16
EYTHERS			
yett, yf with eythers vyce, I tainted bee,	422	Censure	22
F			
F. shewes what he was, K. what he will bee.	375	Coryat 1	29
FA			
See you yond' Motion? Not the old Fa-ding,	62	E97 Motion	1
FABLE			
As makes Penelopes old fable true,	224	U50 Countesse	20
Nor must the Fable, that would hope the Fate,	317	Horace	270

	Page	Title	Line
FABLE (cont.)			
I can out of knowne geare, a fable frame,	321	Horace	349
I can, out of knowne stuff, a Fable frame,	347	Horace	V341/349
The truth; nor let thy Fable thinke, what e're	329	Horace	508
Receive it for a Fable,	364	Phoenix	2
Might make the Fable of Good Women true.	372	Epitaph	14
Goe little Booke, Goe little Fable	662	Bedford	1
FABLER			
To be the Musick Master! Fabler too!	404	Inigo Jones 1	63
FABLES			
All historie seal'd up, and fables crost;	67	E105 L Wroth 2	2
No more let Greece her bolder fables tell	84	E133 Voyage	1
What fables have you vext! what truth redeem'd!	159	U14 Selden	39
FACE			
It made me a great face, I ask'd the name.	30	E11 Something	4
H'has tympanies of businesse, in his face,	35	E28 Surly	7
And land on one, whose face durst never bee	56	E88 Monsieur	5
Still Mill continu'd: Nay, his face growing worse,	57	E90 Mill	11
Mill was the same. Since, both his body and face	57	E90 Mill	13
Cry'd to my face, they were th'elixir of wit;	64	E100 Playwrt 3	2
When Sydneys name I heare, or face I see:	73	E114 Sydney	2
Or (mounted on a stoole) thy face doth hit	81	E129 Mime	13
And, now, above the poole, a face right fat	88	E133 Voyage	160
Turne, upon scorned verse, their quarter-face:	114	F12 Rutland	29
Whether it be a face they weare, or no.	118	F13 Aubigny	80
of seeing your face.	128	U1 Trinitie	32
And it is not alwayes face,	131	U2 Excuse	7
At my face, that tooke my sight,	132	U2 How he saw	25
Sheds it selfe through the face,	134	U2 Triumph	18
Have you seene faire Ledas face	135	U2 Triumph	V 41
Of her face, and made to rise,	136	U2 Cupid	15
Better fits him, then his face;	140	U2 Promise	20
Himselfe young, and face be good,	142	U2 Exception	5
My mountaine belly, and my rockie face,	150	U9 Picture	17
No! Gifts and thankes should have one cheerefull face,	154	U13 Sacvile	39
In outward face, but inward, light as Furre,	162	U15 Friend-Wars	20
That whatsoever face thy fate puts on,	168	U15 Friend-Wars	185
Of Beautie, so to nullifie a face,	188	U34 Small Poxe	14
There may some face or menace of a storme	191	U38 Elegy 'Tis	13
To carry noble danger in the face:	194	U38 Elegy 'Tis	102
Keepe in reserv'd in his Dark-lanterne face,	198	U40 Elegy That	23
No face, no hand, proportion, line, or Ayre	200	U42 Elegy Let	14
More then of eithers manners, wit, or face!	202	U42 Elegy Let	88
Or Goddesse, could be patient of thy face.	207	U43 Vulcan	108
Her face there's none can like by Candle light.	223	U49 Pucell	32
Pardon, I read it in thy face, the day	225	U51 Answer	5
Yet when of friendship I would draw the face,	227	U52 Answer	22
Or masked man, if valu'd by his face,	243	U70 Ode	23
Where every lim takes like a face?	275	U84 Body	4
Till, like her face, it doe appeare,	276	U84 Body	15
And each shall know, there, one anothers face,	285	U84 Muse	115
The vision of our Saviour, face to face,	286	U84 Muse	132
Each line, as it were graphick, in the face!	287	U84 Muse	154
Quite from all face of Tragedie to goe,	321	Horace	344
Yet, looking in thy face, they shall begin	369	Ode Who saith	93
They are not those, are present with theyre face,	384	Somerset	1
As a deformed face doth a true glasse.	389	Aleman	10
His face; the Print would then surpasse	390	Reader	7
And such wert thou. Looke how the fathers face	392	Shakespeare	65
Of that true Face	419	Ode:If Men	2
to gett thee a leane Face,	420	Ode:If Men	25
FACES			
And grave as ripe, like mellow as their faces.	59	E92 New Crie	7
And at the Pope, and Spaine slight faces make.	59	E92 New Crie	34
And, shifting of it's faces, doth play more	74	E115 Honest Man	25
Of those that set by their false faces more	188	U34 Small Poxe	4
Whether their faces were their owne, or no:	200	U42 Elegy Let	36
And looke unto their faces,	220	U48 Bacchus	9
Mens faces, still, with such as laugh, are prone	311	Horace	143
Those that did sing, and act: their faces dy'd	319	Horace	314
Are deeper then their Faces:	365	Ode Splendor	22
FACILE			
I meant shee should be curteous, facile, sweet,	52	E76 Bedford 1	9
FACT			
Thy fact, in brasse or marble writ the same)	46	E60 Mounteagle	4
Not from the publike voyce, but private fact;	47	E63 Salisbury 2	6
Thy fact is more: let truth encourage thee.	64	E99 Th Roe 2	12
Above his fact?	243	U70 Ode	24
What Nature, Fortune, Institution, Fact	270	U81 Pawlet	45
FACTION			
That liv'st from hope, from feare, from faction free;	61	E95 Savile	18
Of what ambition, faction, pride can raise;	66	E102 Pembroke	15
Whom Faction had not drawne to studie sides.	207	U43 Vulcan	104
Whom Faction had not taught to studie sides.	207	U43 Vulcan	V104
FACTIOUS			
Ambitious, factious, superstitious, lowd	167	U15 Friend-Wars	168
FACTS			
If time to facts, as unto men would owe?	64	E99 Th Roe 2	6
And celebrating our owne home-borne facts;	323	Horace	408
FACULTIE			
Had he had the facultie to reade, and write!	201	U42 Elegy Let	64
For as at distance, few have facultie	242	U69 Friend Son	19
But every Judge hath not the facultie	323	Horace	387

FACULTIE (cont.)
Wants facultie to make a censure true: . . . . . 362 Author 11
FACULTIES
and Conjures all my faculties t'approve . . . . 108 F10 Proludium 14
my abler faculties; and thus brake foorth . . . . 362 Palmer 29
FA-DING
See you yond' Motion? Not the old Fa-ding, . . . 62 E97 Motion 1
FAEMALE
Code, Digests, Pandects of all faemale glory! . . . 399 Lady Ogle 8
FAGOTS
Or in small Fagots have him blaze about . . . . 211 U43 Vulcan 185
Or else in penny Fagots blaze about . . . . . 211 U43 Vulcan V185
FAILE
If I should faile, in gratitude, to thee, . . . 80 E127 Aubigny 2
And if the high-swolne Medway faile thy dish, . . 94 F2 Penshurst 31
And such, or my hopes faile, shall make you shine. . 115 F12 Rutland 64
We cut not off, till all Cures else doe faile: . . 192 U38 Elegy 'Tis 46
Have not kept in; and (lest perfection faile) . . 325 Horace 417
FAIL'D
And scorn'd, thou'ast showne thy malice, but hast fail'd. . 188 U34 Small Poxe 18
FAILED
All light failed! . . . . 183 U29 Fit of Rime 24
FAILES
That never failes to serve thee season'd deere, . . 94 F2 Penshurst 20
With an uncomely silence failes my tongue? . . . 293 U86 Hor.4:1 36
FAINE (VERB)
Such when I meant to faine, and wish'd to see, . . 52 E76 Bedford 1 17
Nature, they thought, in all, that he would faine. . 53 E79 Rutland 8
Had power to act, what they to faine had not. . . 84 E133 Voyage 6
Then the great Homers wit, for her, could faine; . . 224 U50 Countesse 24
Faine words, unheard of to the well-truss'd race . . 309 Horace 71
Faine words, unheard of to the girded race . . . 340 Horace V 71
Or follow fame, thou that dost write, or faine . . 313 Horace 169
FAINE
And I not faine to sit (as some, this day, . . . 95 F2 Penshurst 65
And would faine have chang'd the fate, . . . 133 U2 Suffered 19
What I am not, and what I faine would be, . . . 216 U45 Squib 1
Are faine to seeke for succours, and supplies . . 248 U71 Treasurer 2
How faine for his venery he was to crie (Tergum o) . 380 Coryat 3 37
FAIN'D
Orgies of drinke, or fain'd protests: . . . 246 U70 Ode 104
But a fain'd way, doth rob it of the true. . . . 270 U81 Pawlet 38
But a fain'd way, doth spoyle it of the true. . . 270 U81 Pawlet V 38
Whose shapes, like sick-mens dreames, are fain'd so vaine, . 305 Horace 9
Thinke wee, or hope, there can be Verses fain'd . . 327 Horace 474
FAINED
The fained Queene of Love, ... 240 U67 Muses 32
FAINES
And so well faines, so mixeth cunningly . . . 315 Horace 215
FAIN'ST
When I am read, thou fain'st a weake applause, . . 43 E52 Courtling 3
Wrestlest with dignities, or fain'st a scope . . . 70 E109 Nevil 6
Let what thou fain'st for pleasures sake, be neere . 329 Horace 507
FAINT
Of nature, and societie, I should faint; . . . 117 F13 Aubigny 19
Thy faint, and narrow eyes, to reade the King . . 250 U73 Weston 2
FAINTING
And fainting necks, the turned Share! . . . 291 U85 Country 64
FAIRE (See also FAYRE)
While Beast instructs his faire, and innocent wife, . 34 E25 Beast 1 1
Read not in faire heavens storie, ... 39 E40 Ratcliffe 6
Stinke, and are throwne away. End faire enough. . . 45 E59 Spies 3
Item, a faire greeke poesie for a ring: . . . 51 E73 Fine Grand 10
I meant to make her faire, and free, and wise, . . 52 E76 Bedford 1 5
It is the faire acceptance, Sir, creates . . . 64 E101 Supper 7
How well, faire crowne of your faire sexe, might hee, . 66 E103 L Wroth 1 1
Where all is faire, beside thy pedigree. . . . 70 E109 Nevil 4
Repent thee not of thy faire precedent, . . . 73 E113 Overbury 9
Retyr'd, with purpose your faire worth to praise, . 80 E126 Mrs Cary 1
The other was a squire, of faire degree; . . . 84 E133 Voyage 25
Of wood, of water: therein thou art faire. . . . 93 F2 Penshurst 8
But this faire course is not embrac'd by many: . . 109 F11 Epode V 19
Grow, grow, faire tree, and as thy branches shoote, . 119 F13 Aubigny 99
O so faire! O so soft! O so sweet is she! . . . 135 U2 Triumph V 30
Have you seene a faire Damaske-rose . . . . 135 U2 Triumph V 31
Have you seene faire Helen disclose . . . . 135 U2 Triumph V 33
O so faire O so kind o so sweet so sweet is shee . . 135 U2 Triumph V 38
Have you seene faire Ledas face . . . . . 135 U2 Triumph V 41
Thence, as sweet, as you are faire, ... 137 U2 Kisse 4
Look'd not halfe so fresh, and faire, . . . 138 U2 Kisse 9
Young Il'd have him to, and faire, ... 141 U2 Her man 9
He is, if they can find him, faire, ... 147 U7 Nymph 15
But few and faire Divisions: but being got . . . 157 U13 Sacvile 151
By that faire Stand, your forehead, whence he bends . 170 U19 Elegy By 3
(As my hope tells) that our faire Phoebe's shine, . 179 U25 Desmond 58
Happy in that faire honour it hath gain'd, . . . 180 U26 Ode High 14
And make the Scarre faire; If that will not be, . . 187 U33 Councellour 21
Will unto Licence that faire leave abuse. . . . 190 U37 Friend-Book 24
Offended Mistris, you are yet so faire, . . . 191 U38 Elegy 'Tis 9
As not alone the Cure, but scarre be faire. . . . 192 U38 Elegy 'Tis 52
And how more faire, and lovely lookes the world . . 193 U38 Elegy 'Tis 73
Sooner then my affection from the faire. . . . 200 U42 Elegy Let 13
(If they be faire and worth it) have their lives . . 200 U42 Elegy Let 20

FAIRE   (cont.)

As shall the feasts faire grounds be.   •   •   •   221 U48 Bacchus   42
And stroke the water, nimble, chast, and faire,   •   •   230 U56 Covell   14
So fruitfull, and so faire,   •   •   •   •   240 U67 Muses   52
So doth the flatt'rer with faire cunning strike   •   242 U69 Friend Son   14
Each syllab'e answer'd, and was form'd, how faire;   245 U70 Ode   63
And such a force the faire example had,   •   •   247 U70 Ode   117
Because the order of the whole is faire!   •   •   251 U74 Weston   12
Bring all your friends, (faire Lord) that burne   •   251 U74 Weston   20
Shoot up an Olive fruitfull, faire,   •   •   251 U74 Weston   28
Of all the Maidens faire;   •   •   •   •   253 U75 Epithalam.   39
O, now thou smil'st, faire Sun, and shin'st, as thou wouldst stay!   254 U75 Epithalam.   64
You seeme a faire one! O that you had breath,   •   269 U81 Pawlet   6
You seeme a faire one! O that I had breath,   •   269 U81 Pawlet   V 6
It is a large faire table, and a true,   •   •   269 U81 Pawlet   15
Her Sweetnesse, Softnesse, her faire Courtesie,   •   270 U81 Pawlet   39
Chear'd her faire Sisters in her race to runne!   •   270 U81 Pawlet   58
Eupheme; Or, The Faire Fame Left To Posteritie . . .   272 U84 Eupheme   Ttl
Faire Fame, who art ordain'd to crowne   •   •   272 U84 Cradle   9
Of Dame Venetia Digby, styl'd The Faire: •   274 U84 Descent   2
The Voyce so sweet, the words so faire,   •   •   279 U84 Mind   37
In thee, faire Mansion, let it rest,   •   •   281 U84 Mind   69
'Twill be but faire, to leane upon their Fames;   •   281 U84 Kenelme   13
O! had I seene her laid out a faire Corse,   •   282 U84 Muse   11
She had a mind as calme, as she was faire;   •   287 U84 Muse   163
Presenting upwards, a faire female feature,   •   305 Horace   4
With faire black eyes, and haire; and a wry nose.   307 Horace   52
With faire black eyes, and hair, and some vile snout.   339 Horace   V 54/ 52
Much from the sight, which faire report will make   317 Horace   262
And emptie Clowdes. For Tragedie is faire,   •   321 Horace   336
How faire a flight he makes!   •   •   •   •   366 Ode Who saith   10
Faire Aemulation, and no Envy is;   •   •   389 Aleman   22
In faire freehould, not an Inmate: •   •   399 Lady Ogle   26
The faire French Daughter to learne English in;   •   402 Filmer   12

FAIRER

Is fairer farre, in May,   •   •   •   •   245 U70 Ode   70
Though he be fairer then a Starre;   •   •   294 U87 Hor.3:9   21

FAIREST

Have made their fairest flight,   •   •   •   180 U26 Ode High   7
The fairest flowers are alwayes found;   •   •   264 U79 New-yeares   37
That Natures fairest Creature,   •   •   •   364 Phoenix   6
To top the fairest Lillie, now, that growes,   •   413 Ghyrlond   15

FAIRY   (See FAYERIE)

FAITH'

No faith's more firme, or flat, then where't doth creep.   •   413 Ghyrlond   20

FAITH

What name, what skill, what faith hast thou in things!   31 E14 Camden   7
If thou'ldst but use thy faith, as thou didst then,   •   32 E18 Censurer   7
Thy faith is all the knowledge that thou hast.   •   32 E18 Censurer   10
But most we need his faith (and all have you)   •   62 E95 Savile   35
My faith, my hope, my love: and in this state,   •   122 F15 Heaven   11
Once more, and (faith) I will be gone,   •   •   139 U2 Another   7
Or faith in things? or is't your wealth and will   •   159 U14 Selden   36
Against or Faith, or honours lawes.   •   •   173 U22 Elegy Tho   12
Are asked to climbe. First give me faith, who know   220 U47 Tribe   75
This Age would lend no faith to Dorrels Deed;   •   223 U49 Pucell   42
That Faith, which she professeth to be pure?   •   236 U64 Charles 3   12
Where shame, faith, honour, and regard of right   •   243 U70 Ode   13
Hope, hath her end! and Faith hath her reward!   •   284 U84 Muse   68
All this by Faith she saw, and fram'd a Plea,   •   288 U84 Muse   209
Pies on't, you have his historicall faith.   •   380 Coryat 3   22
make many, hurt themselves; a praysed faith   •   422 Lucan   2
make many, hurt himselfe; a praysed faith   •   422 Lucan   V 2

FAITHFULL

To make those faithfull, did the Fates send you?   •   67 E104 Montgomery   6
The faithfull mans beleeved Mysterie,   •   •   127 U1 Trinitie   3
Among which faithfull troope am I.   •   •   173 U22 Elegy Tho   28
The only faithfull Watchman for the Realme,   •   185 U30 Burleigh   9
Then those the faithfull eyes take in by show,   •   317 Horace   258
To my old Faithfull Servant: And . . .   •   409 Brome   Ttl
And you perform'd a Servants faithfull parts: •   409 Brome   2

FAITHFULLY

Not care, as thou wouldst faithfully translate,   •   313 Horace   190
And hold them faithfully; For nothing rests,   •   329 Horace   505

FAITH'S

No faith's more firme, or flat, then where't doth creep.   •   413 Ghyrlond   20

FAITHS

With tales of Troyes just knight, our faiths abuse: •   84 E133 Voyage   4

FAL

The Morning-star, whose light our Fal hath stay'd.   •   413 Ghyrlond   40

FALERNIAN

Darke thy cleare glasse with old Falernian Wine;   •   295 U89 Mart.8:77   5

FALL   (See also FALNE)

When their owne Parasites laugh at their fall,   •   118 F13 Aubigny   82
It shall a ripe and timely issue fall,   •   •   119 F13 Aubigny   104
Standing with feare, and must with horror fall,   •   122 F15 Heaven   19
Letting Bow and Arrow fall,   •   •   •   132 U2 How he saw   17
Have you mark'd but the fall o'the Snow   •   •   134 U2 Triumph   23
Have you seene the fall o'the Snow   •   •   135 U2 Triumph   V 23
To fall againe; at such a feast,   •   •   144 U3 Musicall   23
His Groomes to witnesse; or else lets it fall   •   154 U13 Sacvile   36
His Lace and Starch; And fall upon her back   •   163 U15 Friend-Wars   49
O vertues fall,   •   •   •   •   •   •   179 U25 Desmond   36

FALL (cont.)

	Page	Title	Line
Thy Adversaries fall, as not a word	187	U33 Councellour	33
To live, or fall a Carkasse in the cause.	219	U47 Tribe	42
From whence they fall, cast downe with their owne weight.	224	U50 Countesse	12
Among the daily Ruines that fall foule,	224	U50 Countesse	17
To fall a logge at last, dry, bald, and seare:	245	U70 Ode	68
Although it fall, and die that night;	245	U70 Ode	71
Of Life, that fall so; Christians know their birth	257	U75 Epithalam.	156
The Sunne! great Kings, and mightiest Kingdomes fall!	271	U81 Pawlet	89
The Sunne! great Kings, and mighty Kingdomes fall!	271	U81 Pawlet	V 89
Which Vertue from your Father, ripe, will fall;	282	U84 Kenelme	22
The world to ruine with it; in her Fall,	283	U84 Muse	25
The kind of Man, on whom his doome should fall!	288	U84 Muse	208
So they fall gently from the Grecian spring,	309	Horace	75
Busie to catch a Black-bird; if he fall	335	Horace	651
And not fall downe before it? and confess	406	Inigo Jones 1	91
those turnd up, and those that fall,	417	Moon	14
rise or fall uppon the earth,	417	Moon	18
whole armyes fall, swayd by those nyce respects.	423	Lucan	11

FALLING

	Page	Title	Line
The skie not falling, thinke we may have larkes.	65	E101 Supper	16
His falling Temples you have rear'd,	173	U22 Elegy Tho	17
Propping Verse, for feare of falling	183	U29 Fit of Rime	8
Or Dowgate Torrent falling into Thames,	407	Inigo Jones 2	16

FALLOW

	Page	Title	Line
All is not barren land, doth fallow lie.	169	U17 Friend-Debt	16

FALLS

	Page	Title	Line
Where Nero falls, and Galba is ador'd,	61	E95 Savile	8
That falls like sleepe on lovers, and combines	110	F11 Epode	49
Who falls for love of God, shall rise a Starre.	168	U15 Friend-Wars	196
For th'eating Thrush, or Pit-falls sets:	290	U85 Country	34

FALL'ST

	Page	Title	Line
Hee never fell, thou fall'st, my tongue.	244	U70 Ode	44

FALNE

	Page	Title	Line
And two, that would have falne as great, as they,	60	E93 Radcliffe	7
How well at twentie had he falne, or stood!	243	U70 Ode	31

FALSE

	Page	Title	Line
To King James. Upon the happy false rumour of his death,	43	E51 James 3	Ttl
Touch'd with the sinne of false play, in his pungue,	56	E87 Hazard	1
That dares nor write things false, nor hide things true.	62	E95 Savile	36
I oft looke on false coyne, to know't from true:	68	E107 Hungry	3
False world, good-night: since thou hast brought	100	F4 To the World	1
As shall not need thy false reliefe.	102	F4 To the World	64
Who could be false to? chiefly, when he knowes	112	F11 Epode	103
Who would be false to? chiefly, when he knowes	112	F11 Epode	V103
And this shall be no false one, but as much	117	F13 Aubigny	27
Our owne false praises, for your ends:	145	U5 Woman-kind	4
Still, still, the hunters of false fame apply	155	U13 Sacvile	65
Looke on the false, and cunning man, that loves	162	U15 Friend-Wars	15
Proud, false, and trecherous, vindictive, all	172	U21 Ltl Shrub	7
Be taken with false Baytes	175	U23 Himselfe	20
But false weight.	183	U29 Fit of Rime	6
Of those that set by their false faces more\	188	U34 Small Poxe	4
Art, her false servant; Nor, for Sir Hugh Plat,	188	U34 Small Poxe	7
And as false stampe there; parcels of a Play,	204	U43 Vulcan	43
Those are poore Ties, depend on those false ends,	216	U45 Squib	11
Not built with Canvasse, paper, and false lights,	220	U47 Tribe	65
Are growne so fruitfull, and false pleasures climbe,	224	U50 Countesse	10
Ne knowes he flatt'ring Colours, or false light.	227	U52 Answer	21
And made those strong approaches, by False braies,	248	U71 Treasurer	7
Ino bewaild; Ixion false, forsworne;	313	Horace	176
To judge which Passion's false, and which is true,	370	Author	11
Least a false praise do make theyr dotage his.	385	Husband	4
With slyding windowes, & false Lights a top!	407	Inigo Jones 2	10

FALSEHOOD

	Page	Title	Line
Falsehood and truth, as no man can espy	343	Horace	V216

FALSELY

	Page	Title	Line
Backe the intelligence, and falsely sweares,	109	F11 Epode	25

FALSER

	Page	Title	Line
Yet art thou falser then thy wares.	100	F4 To the World	20

FALSHOOD

	Page	Title	Line
Then to make falshood blush, and fraud afraid:	186	U32 Elsmere	4
Then I will studie falshood, to be true.	194	U38 Elegy 'Tis	108
This beautie without falshood fayre,	275	U84 Body	7
Falshood with truth, as no man can espie	315	Horace	216

FAME

	Page	Title	Line
Thou are not covetous of least selfe-fame,	27	E2 My Booke	9
That wish my poemes a legitimate fame,	32	E17 Critic	3
'Twere madnesse in thee, to betray thy fame,	36	E30 Guiltie	3
Her foes enough would fame thee in their hate.	40	E43 Salisbury 1	4
Of adding to thy fame; thine may to me,	41	E43 Salisbury 1	8
Great heav'n did well, to give ill fame free wing;	43	E51 James 3	2
That neither fame, nor love might wanting be	48	E66 Cary	1
As, to be rais'd by her, is onely fame.	49	E67 Suffolk	4
Be safe, nor feare thy selfe so good a fame,	53	E77 Not name	1
Then Cicero, whose every breath was fame:	57	E89 Allen	6
Which thou art to thy selfe: whose fame was wonne	58	E91 Vere	5
And studie conscience, more then thou would'st fame.	63	E98 Th Roe 1	10
Need any Muses praise to give it fame?	66	E103 L Wroth 1	6
Truth might spend all her voyce, Fame all her art.	68	E106 E Herbert	4
That serves nor fame, nor titles; but doth chuse	70	E109 Nevil	2
Un-argued then, and yet hath fame from those;	71	E110 Edmonds 1	10
Him not, aloud, that boasts so good a fame:	74	E115 Honest Man	2

FAME (cont.)
  To urge, my lov'd Alphonso, that bold fame   .   .   .   82   E130 Ferrab. 1   1
  For fame, with breath soone kindled, soone blowne out.   .   .   83   E131 Ferrab. 2   14
  And art a god, if Fame thee not abuses,   .   .   .   85   E133 Voyage   53
  Fame, and rumor are but toyes.   102   F5 Celia 1   10
  Play away, health, wealth, and fame.   105   F8 Sicknesse   42
  Or those, who doubt the common mouth of fame,   .   .   .   111   F11 Epode   79
  Or those, which doubt the common mouth of fame,   .   .   .   111   F11 Epode   V 79
  While thus it buyes great grace, and hunts poore fame;   .   .   113   F12 Rutland   15
  While thus it gets grace, and hunts poore fame;   .   .   .   113   F12 Rutland   V 15
  Then, here, to give pride fame, and peasants birth.   .   .   114   F12 Rutland   26
  Then, now give pride fame, or peasants birth.   .   .   .   114   F12 Rutland   V 26
  That had no Muse to make their fame abide.   .   .   .   114   F12 Rutland   48
  And raise a noble stemme, to give the fame,   .   .   .   119   F13 Aubigny   97
  As it would be to each a fame: 148   U7 Nymph   34
  Still, still, the hunters of false fame apply   .   .   .   155   U13 Sacvile   65
  The life, and fame-vaynes (yet not understood   .   .   .   167   U15 Friend-Wars   166
  So, 'live or dead, thou wilt preserve a fame   .   .   .   168   U15 Friend-Wars   189
  Aske not to know this Man. If fame should speake   .   .   172   U21 Ltl Shrub   1
  Raising the World to good or evill fame,   .   .   .   175   U24 Frontispice   3
  Whose fame hath an eternall voice?   181   U27 Ode Helen   16
  Her Ovid gave her, dimm'd the fame   .   .   .   181   U27 Ode Helen   18
  And labour'd in the worke; not with the fame: .   .   .   185   U30 Burleigh   12
  So may the gentler Muses, and good fame   .   .   .   186   U31 Elsmere   7
  Thy sincere practise, breeds not thee a fame   .   .   .   187   U33 Councellour   39
  And Fame wake for me, when I yeeld to sleepe.   .   .   .   190   U37 Friend-Book   15
  Thou should'st have stay'd, till publike fame said so.   .   204   U43 Vulcan   46
  Goe on, increase in vertue; and in fame: 214   U44 Speach   49
  Stood up thy Nations fame, her Crownes defence.   .   .   .   217   U46 Coke   14
  Although my Fame, to his, not under-heares,   .   .   .   219   U47 Tribe   49
  From Court, while yet thy fame hath some small day;   .   .   223   U49 Pucell   36
  Who (herein studying conscience, and not fame)   .   .   .   224   U50 Countesse   14
  Of State, of fame, of body, and of soule,   .   .   .   224   U50 Countesse   18
  Fame, and foundation of the English Weale.   .   .   .   225   U51 Bacon   10
  The Kings fame lives. Go now, denie his Teirce.   .   .   .   241   U68 House-hold   14
  He purchas'd friends, and fame, and honours then,   .   .   244   U70 Ode   35
  It brings Friends Joy, Foes Griefe, Posteritie Fame;   .   .   256   U75 Epithalam.   114
  For Fame keepes Vertue up, and it Posteritie.   .   .   .   257   U75 Epithalam.   152
  Have left in fame to equall, or out-goe   260   U77 Treasurer   8
  Fame and Honour too, they possesse by Peace.   .   .   .   261   U77 Treasurer   V 22
  And praise them too. O! what a fame 't will be?   .   .   .   263   U78 Digby   25
  As in renewing thy good Grandsires fame;   .   .   .   268   U80 Christning   12
  Thou wouldst have written, Fame, upon my brest: .   .   .   269   U81 Pawlet   14
  Earle Rivers Grand-Child--serve not formes, good Fame,   .   269   U81 Pawlet   21
  Earle Rivers Grand-Child--serve not titles Fame,   .   .   269   U81 Pawlet   V 21
  T' inlive posteritie, her Fame may tell!   269   U81 Pawlet   34
  Eupheme; Or, The Faire Fame Left To Posteritie . . .   272   U84 Eupheme   Ttl
  Faire Fame, who art ordain'd to crowne   .   .   .   272   U84 Cradle   1
  Meschines honour with the Cestrian fame   .   .   .   274   U84 Descent   16
  Or follow fame, thou that dost write, or faine   .   .   .   313   Horace   169
  But, in conclusion, merited no fame.   323   Horace   396
  But fame of Poets, they thinke, if they come forth,   .   .   325   Horace   426
  And thou in them shalt live as longe as Fame.   .   .   .   362   Palmer   31
  Am I thus ample to thy Booke, and Fame: 390   Shakespeare   2
  Lend me thy voyce, O Fame, that I may draw   .   .   .   396   Drayton   12
  Defies, what's crosse to Piety, or good Fame.   .   .   .   401   Beaumont   20
  Th'ascent of Lady Fame which none could spy   .   .   .   403   Inigo Jones 1   35
  Shall not worke out unto it, such a fame.   409   Detractor   12
  For thou hast nought in thee to cure his Fame,   .   .   .   411   Gill   13
FAM'D
  Of old, even by her practise, to be fam'd;   .   .   .   82   E130 Ferrab. 1   10
  Lest of the singer Apollo, and Muses fam'd   .   .   .   353   Horace   V579/501
  From the fam'd pillars of old Hercules!   407   Inigo Jones 2   14
FAMES
  From friendship, is it's owne fames architect.   .   .   .   75   E115 Honest Man   30
  And keepe their Fames   257   U75 Epithalam.   150
  To be describ'd! Fames fingers are too foule   .   .   .   269   U81 Pawlet   30
  'Twill be but faire, to leane upon their Fames;   .   .   .   281   U84 Kenelme   13
  And, where the most reade bookes, on Authors fames,   .   .   386   Browne   9
  Fames heate upon the grave did stay;   400   Lady Ogle   28
FAME-VAYNES
  The life, and fame-vaynes (yet not understood   .   .   .   167   U15 Friend-Wars   166
FAMILIAR
  Familiar, for the uses sake;   146   U6 Defence   16
FAMILIE
  Of the first Lupus, to the Familie   274   U84 Descent   17
  She swaid all bus'nesse in the Familie!   287   U84 Muse   168
FAMILIES
  And in the noblest Families tooke root   185   U30 Burleigh   18
FAMILY
  As they were not of Natures family.   392   Shakespeare   54
FAMINE
  With famine, wants, and sorrowes many a dosen,   .   .   .   86   E133 Voyage   71
  Sword, fire, and famine, with fell fury met;   .   .   .   243   U70 Ode   17
FAMOUS
  Where lately harbour'd many a famous whore,   .   .   .   29   E7 Hot-house   1
  On the famous Voyage.   84   E133 Voyage   Ttl
  Did dance the famous Morrisse, unto Norwich)   .   .   .   85   E133 Voyage   36
  Thorough her wombe they make their famous road,   .   .   .   85   E133 Voyage   66
  Have beautie knowne, yet none so famous seene?   .   .   .   114   F12 Rutland   50
  Send in, what Romans famous, Tintoret, ...   260   U77 Treasurer   V 6
  This foot yet, in the famous Trimeters   323   Horace   381
  Or love of this so famous death lay by.   335   Horace   669

	Page	Title	Line
FAMOUS (cont.)			
Or love of this his famous death lay by.	355	Horace	V669
FAN			
Lady, or Pusil, that weares maske, or fan,	370	Fletcher	4
FANCIE			
By this, although you fancie not the man,	231	U56 Covell	25
By thys Tyme, though you fancie not the man,	231	U56 Covell	V 25
Worke with my fancie, his owne hand.	276	U84 Body	12
Straines fancie unto foule Apostacie,	363	Riches	15
FANCIED			
I fancied to my selfe, what wine, what wit	55	E84 Bedford 2	6
So, any Poeme, fancied, or forth-brought	331	Horace	561
FANCIES			
Wee have both wits, and fancies too,	145	U5 Woman-kind	5
FAR			
That Poets are far rarer births then kings,	53	E79 Rutland	1
Or in the bending Vale beholds from far	290	U85 Country	V 13
FARE			
He makes himselfe a thorough-fare of vice.	76	E118 Gut	4
And bad her fare-well sough, unto the lurden:	87	E133 Voyage	115
More for thy exercise, then fare;	97	F3 Wroth	30
Well fare the wise-men yet, on the Banckside,	208	U43 Vulcan	123
Thou worthy in eternall Flower to fare,	294	U89 Mart.8:77	2
FARE-WELL			
And bad her fare-well sough, unto the lurden:	87	E133 Voyage	115
FAREWELL			
Farewell, thou child of my right hand, and joy;	41	E45 First Son	1
Then that it liv'd at all. Farewell.	79	E124 Elizabeth	12
To the World. A farewell for a Gentle-woman, . . .	100	F4 To the World	Ttl
You both are modest. So am I. Farewell.	161	U14 Selden	86
If I had writ no word, but Deare, farewell.	198	U40 Elegy That	50
Since you must goe, and I must bid farewell,	199	U41 Elegy Since	1
not when I die'd, but how I livd. Farewell.	387	Cavendish	12
FARMER			
But all come in, the farmer, and the clowne:	94	F2 Penshurst	48
Or cos'ning farmer of the customes so,	117	F13 Aubigny	39
To turne mere farmer, had spoke out,	291	U85 Country	68
A ventring Merchant, or the Farmer free	313	Horace	165
FARRE			
Martial, thou gav'st farre nobler Epigrammes	38	E36 Martial	1
And lyes so farre from wit, 'tis impudence.	38	E38 Guiltie 2	6
And what I write thereof find farre, and free	41	E43 Salisbury 1	10
And farre beneath least pause of such a king,	43	E51 James 3	4
As he would burne, or better farre his booke.	53	E79 Rutland	12
A Sydney: but in that extend as farre	67	E103 L Wroth 1	10
Adde to thy free provisions, farre above	95	F2 Penshurst	58
When shee was farre: and not a roome, but drest,	96	F2 Penshurst	87
Nor for my peace will I goe farre,	102	F4 To the World	65
That is an essence, farre more gentle, fine,	110	F11 Epode	45
Farre from the maze of custome, error, strife,	118	F13 Aubigny	60
Say you have follow'd farre,	121	F14 Sydney	45
Farre I was from being stupid,	132	U2 How he saw	5
As farre as any poore Sword i' the Land.	154	U13 Sacvile	55
Ride, saile, am coach'd, know I how farre I have gone,	156	U13 Sacvile	121
But I on yours farre otherwise shall doe,	159	U14 Selden	17
But I to yours, farre from this fault, shall doo;	159	U14 Selden	V 17
As farre as he can flie, or follow day,	163	U15 Friend-Wars	29
As farre as he can flee, or follow day,	163	U15 Friend-Wars	V 29
Spread through the World) is easier farre to find,	167	U15 Friend-Wars	172
Or was she gracious a-farre off? but neere	169	U18 Elegy Can	5
As farre from all revolt, as you are now from Fortune.	180	U25 Desmond	65
Farre from the Nest, and so himselfe belie	198	U40 Elegy That	38
So farre without inquirie what the States,	219	U47 Tribe	43
Shee showes so farre above	240	U67 Muses	31
More subtle workes, and finer pieces farre,	242	U69 Friend Son	22
Is fairer farre, in May,	245	U70 Ode	70
That farre-all-seeing Eye	256	U75 Epithalam.	109
As farre as sense, and onely by the eyes.	261	U77 Treasurer	12
As farre as sense, and onely by his eyes.	261	U77 Treasurer	V 12
Or in the bending Vale beholds a-farre	290	U85 Country	13
Child of a hundred Arts, and farre	292	U86 Hor.4:1	15
And then rough Adria, angrier, farre;	294	U87 Hor.3:9	23
Shall perish: so farre off it is, the state,	309	Horace	99
And farre unworthy to blurt out light rimes;	321	Horace	337
To Dance, so she should, shamefac'd, differ farre	321	Horace	339
Fell into fault so farre, as now they saw	321	Horace	367
With honour make the farre-knowne Author live.	329	Horace	519
As farre as Sinne's from lightnesse.	364	Ode Splendor	4
Her breath farre sweete exceeding	365	Ode Splendor	V 13
His farre-admired Acts,	367	Ode Who saith	59
And tell, how farre thou didst our Lily out-shine,	391	Shakespeare	29
FARRE-ADMIRED			
His farre-admired Acts,	367	Ode Who saith	59
FARRE-ALL-SEEING			
That farre-all-seeing Eye	256	U75 Epithalam.	109
FARRE-KNOWNE			
With honour make the farre-knowne Author live.	329	Horace	519
FART			
Of the grave fart, late let in parliament,	87	E133 Voyage	108
FARTHER			
Toward the sea, farther then halfe-way tree?	56	E88 Monsieur	6
A farther fury my ray'sd spirit Controules,	108	F10 Proludium	12
Me farther tosse,	130	U1 Father	30

	Page	Title	Line

FARTHER (cont.)

Himselfe of farther trouble, or the weight	154	U13 Sacvile	31
And goe no farther: let this Circle be	185	U30 Burleigh	3
As some the farther off: This loves the darke;	331	Horace	541

FARTHEST

Farthest I am from the Idolatrie	223	U49 Pucell	27

FARTS

About the shore, of farts, but late departed,	87	E133 Voyage	125

FASHION

Life, whose griefe was out of fashion,	39	E40 Ratcliffe	13
Nor glad for fashion. Nor to shew a fit	47	E64 Salisbury 3	7
Gives the Lover weight, and fashion.	131	U2 Excuse	12
French to boote, at least in fashion,	141	U2 Her man	7
Nor fashion; if they chance aspire to height,	157	U13 Sacvile	148
Hee's one of blood, and fashion! and with these	164	U15 Friend-Wars	55
Of woman of fashion, and a Lady of spirit:	164	U15 Friend-Wars	82
Put on for fashion, and take up on trust:	171	U20 Shrub	8
Whom fashion had not drawne to studie sides.	207	U43 Vulcan	V104
And you shall make me good, in weight, and fashion,	229	U54 Squib	17
Whoorles me about, and to blaspheme in fashion!	283	U84 Muse	32
Th'Aemilian Schoole, in brasse can fashion out	307	Horace	46
For Nature, first, within doth fashion us	311	Horace	152
Not wearing moodes, as gallants doe a fashion,	362	Author	3
His Art doth give the fashion. And, that he,	392	Shakespeare	58
Of weight, or fashion, it was shee.	399	Lady Ogle	24

FASHION'D

like glasse, blowne up, and fashion'd by desire.	108	F10 Proludium	4
Not fashion'd for the court, or strangers eyes;	119	F13 Aubigny	115
Great, brave, and fashion'd folke, these are allow'd	164	U15 Friend-Wars	84

FASHIONS

His clothes two fashions of, and poore! his sword	33	E21 Gam'ster	3
An inginer, in slanders, of all fashions,	75	E115 Honest Man	31
Let who will follow fashions, and attyres,	118	F13 Aubigny	71

FAST (VERB)

To teach the people, how to fast, and pray,	235	U61 Epigram	18

FAST

Pr'y thee beleeve still, and not judge so fast,	32	E18 Censurer	9
Such Notes are vertuous men! they live as fast	157	U13 Sacvile	143
They both are slip'd to Bed; Shut fast the Doore,	258	U75 Epithalam.	185
I hold thee fast! but fled hence, with the Light,	293	U86 Hor.4:1	38

FASTNING

Fastning Vowells, as with fetters	183	U29 Fit of Rime	11

FAT

The cold of Mosco, and fat Irish ayre,	37	E32 Roe 2	5
No cause, nor client fat, will Chev'rill leese,	38	E37 Chev'ril	1
And, now, above the poole, a face right fat	88	E133 Voyage	160
Fat, aged carps, that runne into thy net.	94	F2 Penshurst	33
The hogs return'd home fat from mast;	98	F3 Wroth	44
The hogs return'd home fat with mast;	98	F3 Wroth	V 44
But 'bove the fat of rammes, or bulls, to prize	127	U1 Trinitie	11
As Horace fat; or as Anacreon old;	199	U42 Elegy Let	2
Or a Close-stoole so cas'd; or any fat	202	U42 Elegy Let	84
Unprofitable Chattell, fat and old,	230	U56 Covell	8
I am too fat t'envy him. He too leane	405	Inigo Jones 1	69

FATALL

To all as fatall as't hath beene to me,	211	U43 Vulcan	192
And beckning wooes me, from the fatall tree	268	U81 Pawlet	3

FATE

When was there contract better driven by Fate?	28	E5 Union	1
Was his blest fate, but our hard lot to find.	37	E32 Roe 2	8
Fate, in a brother. To conclude,	39	E40 Ratcliffe	15
Exacted by thy fate, on the just day.	41	E45 First Son	4
What fate is mine, that so it selfe bereaves?	44	E55 Beaumont	7
Which Fate (it seemes) caus'd in the historie,	61	E95 Savile	11
I thinke, the Fate of court thy comming crav'd,	73	E113 Overbury	5
So, by error, to his fate	77	E120 S. P.	17
They laugh't, at his laugh-worthy fate. And past	89	E133 Voyage	185
Whether by choice, or fate, or both;	96	F3 Wroth	2
Though poyson, thinke it a great fate.	99	F3 Wroth	90
Is vertue, and not Fate:	109	F11 Epode	2
Are you engaged to your happy fate,	118	F13 Aubigny	47
This All of nothing, gavest it forme, and fate,	127	U1 Trinitie	18
And would faine have chang'd the fate,	133	U2 Suffered	19
Not to be checkt, or frighted now with fate,	163	U15 Friend-Wars	35
That whatsoever face thy fate puts on,	168	U15 Friend-Wars	185
I'le lead you on; or if my fate will so,	170	U18 Elegy Can	22
Your fate hath found,	180	U26 Ode High	3
Which all the Fate of Troy foretold?	181	U27 Ode Helen	24
I, that thy Ayme was; but her fate prevail'd:	188	U34 Small Poxe	17
What fate is this, to change mens dayes and houres,	199	U41 Elegy Since	9
To speake the fate of the Sicilian Maid	207	U43 Vulcan	96
The fate of things: whilst totter'd vertue holds	216	U44 Speach	101
But fate doth so alternate the designe,	246	U70 Ode	95
(Bearing the promise of some better fate)	252	U75 Epithalam.	10
Thou hast no more blowes, Fate, to drive at one:	283	U84 Muse	27
So Fate would give her life, and longer daies.	293	U87 Hor.3:9	12
The first-borne dying; so the aged Fate	340	Horace	V 87
I sing a noble Warre, and Priam's Fate.	313	Horace	196
Nor must the Fable, that would hope the Fate,	317	Horace	270
Tames, prowde of thee, and of his Fate	368	Ode Who saith	81

FATES

But two things, rare, the Fates had in their store,	28	E4 James 1	3
If any sword could save from Fates, Roe's could;	35	E27 Roe 1	3

	Page	Title	Line
FATES (cont.)			
To make those faithfull, did the Fates send you?	67	E104 Montgomery	6
To make thy lent life, good against the Fates:	70	E109 Nevil	11
When Fates turn'd cruell,	77	E120 S. P.	10
And thinke his power doth equall Fates.	99	F3 Wroth	80
But which the Fates forbid me to reveale.	119	F13 Aubigny	107
Brunsfield, and Mansfield doe this yeare, my fates	219	U47 Tribe	44
Whose even Thred the Fates spinne round, and full,	225	U51 Bacon	15
So Fates would let the Boy a long thred run.	293	U87 Hor.3:9	16
whom fortune hath deprest; come nere the fates	422	Lucan	4
whom, yf fortune hath deprest; come nere the fates	422	Lucan	V 4
FATHER			
It makes the father, lesse, to rue.	33	E22 Daughter	4
O, could I loose all father, now. For why	41	E45 First Son	5
Thou art the father, and the witnesse too.	44	E53 Old-end	8
Your noblest father prov'd: like whom, before,	53	E79 Rutland	2
Or had his father, when he did him get,	56	E88 Monsieur	9
Eternall Father, God, who did'st create	127	U1 Trinitie	17
Father and Sonne; the Comforter, in breeding	128	U1 Trinitie	26
Father, and Sonne, and Holy Ghost, you three	128	U1 Trinitie	37
2. A Hymne to God the Father.	129	U1 Father	Ttl
For I both lost a friend and Father,	151	U12 Corbet	5
There is no Father that for one demerit,	192	U38 Elegy 'Tis	41
With lust conceiv'd thee; Father thou hadst none.	208	U43 Vulcan	112
Since, Bacchus, thou art father	220	U48 Bacchus	1
What then his Father was, that since is hee,	225	U51 Bacon	11
Father John Burges,	231	U57 Burges	1
That whereas your royall Father	259	U76 Petition	5
Whereas late your royall Father	259	U76 Petition	V 5
Hee is the Father of our peace;	264	U79 New-yeares	40
Which Vertue from your Father, ripe, will fall;	282	U84 Kenelme	22
In that great Act of judgement: which the Father	288	U84 Muse	215
Father, and sons right worthy of your Sire,	339	Horace	V 34
More then the Foster-father of this Child;	389	Aleman	14
A Tune to drown the Ballads of thy Father:	411	Gill	12
And you, with them, as Father of our spring.	416	Welcome	8
FATHER'S			
To be the Denis of thy Father's School,	410	Gill	7
FATHERS			
To see thy fathers rites new laid on thee.	47	E64 Salisbury 3	6
Made of the trull, that cut her fathers lock:	86	E133 Voyage	84
Who, with his axe, thy fathers mid-wife plaid.	107	F10 Proludium	15
For what a sinne 'gainst your great fathers spirit,	114	F12 Rutland	31
The Fathers wisedome will'd it so,	130	U1 Nativitie	13
Fathers, and Husbands, I doe claime a right	200	U42 Elegy Let	11
After the Fathers, and those wiser Guides	207	U43 Vulcan	103
In his soft Cradle to his Fathers Chaire,	225	U51 Bacon	14
And was your Fathers! All your Ancestours!	233	U59 Newcastle	20
Of all her Fathers storie,	240	U67 Muses	V 29
And of her Fathers prowesse!	240	U67 Muses	30
To day, the Fathers service; who could bring	256	U75 Epithalam.	107
All that their Fathers, and their Mothers might	257	U75 Epithalam.	147
Those your Fathers Markes, your Pounds;	260	U76 Petition	27
Informed rightly, by your Fathers care,	331	Horace	546
And, to your Fathers, and to mine; though 't be	331	Horace	577
Whether he piss'd upon his Fathers grave;	335	Horace	671
And such wert thou. Looke how the fathers face	392	Shakespeare	65
FATS			
The Glasse-house, Dye-fats, and their Fornaces;	211	U43 Vulcan	180
FATTEST			
From fattest branches of the Tree:	291	U85 Country	56
FAULT'			
The fault's not in the object, but their eyes.	362	Author	8
FAULT			
Willing to expiate the fault in thee,	60	E93 Radcliffe	15
If, at all, shee had a fault,	79	E124 Elizabeth	7
But I to yours, farre from this fault, shall doo;	159	U14 Selden	V 17
I will not stand to justifie my fault,	191	U38 Elegy 'Tis	21
So, shunning faults, to greater fault doth lead,	307	Horace	43
Fell into fault so farre, as now they saw	321	Horace	367
Then: If your fault you rather had defend	335	Horace	629
'Tis not your fault, if they shall sense preferre,	370	Author	13
Hymens amends, to make it worth his fault.	384	Somerset	14
FAULTES			
or Malyce to make Faultes, which nowe is skill.	421	Censure	11
FAULT'S			
The fault's not in the object, but their eyes.	362	Author	8
FAULTS			
I have the lyst of mine owne faults to know,	156	U13 Sacvile	114
So, shunning faults, to greater fault doth lead,	307	Horace	43
Hide faults, pray to the Gods, and wish aloud	319	Horace	285
Hide faults, and pray to th'gods, and wish aloud	345	Horace	V285
Or rather, thinking all my faults may spie,	323	Horace	392
There are yet faults, which we would well forgive,	329	Horace	520
FAUNES			
The lighter Faunes, to reach thy Ladies oke.	94	F2 Penshurst	18
But, let the Faunes, drawne from their Groves, beware,	321	Horace	355
FAVORITE			
He is the Man, and Favorite of God.	235	U61 Epigram	20
FAVOUR			
For the lucks sake, it thus much favour have,	27	E3 Bookseller	4
Or the dis-favour	177	U25 Desmond	33
You favour Truth, and me, in this mans Cause.	186	U31 Elsmere	10

		Page	Title	Line

FAVOUR (cont.)

The Judge his favour timely then extends,		186	U32 Elsmere	1
It is their Grace, and favour, that makes seene,		255	U75 Epithalam.	89
Whose 'tis: but if it favour find,		277	U84 Body	31
It still must favour good men, and to these		317	Horace	280

FAVOURING

| Themselves through favouring what is there not found: | | 159 | U14 Selden | 16 |
| Themselves through favouring that is there not found: | | 159 | U14 Selden | V 16 |

FAVOURITE

| He is no favourites favourite, no deare trust | | 63 | E97 Motion | 13 |

FAVOURITES

| He is no favourites favourite, no deare trust | | 63 | E97 Motion | 13 |

FAVOURS

Can your favours keepe, and cover,		103	F6 Celia 2	2
When his proud patrons favours are asleepe;		113	F12 Rutland	14
Yet, for the timely favours shee hath done,		115	F12 Rutland	71
That is, if still your Favours you apply,		192	U38 Elegy 'Tis	53

FAYERIE

| But then refreshed, with thy Fayerie Court, | | 398 | Drayton | 79 |

FAYNE

| Hath made his Inigo Marquess, wouldst thou fayne | | 406 | Inigo Jones 2 | 2 |

FAYRE

As sweet, as shee is fayre.		112	F11 Epode	98
This beautie without falshood fayre,		275	U84 Body	7
presentes a Royall Alter of fayre peace,		382	Rich	6
Is fayre got up, and day some houres begun!		396	Drayton	18

FAYREST

| to Cynthias fayrest Nymph hath sent thee, | | 662 | Bedford | 6 |

FEAR

| Stick on your Cupping-glasses, fear not, put | | 270 | U81 Pawlet | 53 |
| Thou'rt too ambitious: and dost fear in vaine! | | 408 | Inigo Jones 3 | 6 |

FEARE

May others feare, flie, and traduce thy name,		32	E17 Critic	1
Left us of feare, but first our crimes, then lawes.		38	E35 James 2	6
Long-gathering Old-end, I did feare thee wise,		43	E53 Old-end	1
How I doe feare my selfe, that am not worth		44	E55 Beaumont	3
Fine Madame Would-Bee, wherefore should you feare,		46	E62 Would-bee	1
Be safe, nor feare thy selfe so good a fame,		53	E77 Not name	1
Who more should seeke mens reverence, then feare.		58	E91 Vere	18
And talke reserv'd, lock'd up, and full of feare,		59	E92 New Crie	17
That liv'st from hope, from feare, from faction free;		61	E95 Savile	18
Nor may'any feare, to loose of their degree,		73	E113 Overbury	11
They met the second Prodigie, would feare a		86	E133 Voyage	79
Without his feare, and of thy lords owne meate:		95	F2 Penshurst	62
Yes, threaten, doe. Alas I feare		101	F4 To the World	37
I shall feare, you'll surfet too.		104	F8 Sicknesse	8
I doe feare, you'll surfet too.		104	F8 Sicknesse	V 8
With whom who sailes, rides on the surge of feare,		110	F11 Epode	41
Or feare to draw true lines, 'cause others paint:		117	F13 Aubigny	20
Standing with feare, and must with horror fall,		122	F15 Heaven	19
We all feare, she loveth none.		140	U2 Promise	12
I feare they'd love him too;		147	U7 Nymph	4
And feare much more, that more of him be showne.		147	U7 Nymph	21
If Love, or feare, would let me tell his name.		148	U7 Nymph	35
Think'st thou that love is help'd by feare?		150	U10 Jealousie	12
'Twixt feare and rashnesse: not a lust obscene,		156	U13 Sacvile.	106
A terror? or is all this but my feare?		169	U18 Elegy Can	6
To see men feare: or else for truth, and State,		170	U18 Elegy Can	17
Propping Verse, for feare of falling		183	U29 Fit of Rime	8
You would restore it? No, that's worth a feare,		199	U41 Elegy Since	15
So that upon the point, my corporall feare		229	U54 Squib	7
The first of which, I feare, you will refuse;		230	U56 Covell	6
Sleepe in a Virgins bosome without feare,		230	U56 Covell	15
And with a reverend feare,		240	U67 Muses	45
Where he would fixe, for the distinctions feare.		242	U69 Friend Son	18
As, for her, I'ld not feare to die,		293	U87 Hor.3:9	11
Nor feare thy latest day, nor wish therfore.		295	U90 Mart.10:47	13
Or do's all businesse coldly, and with feare;		317	Horace	244
The angry, and love those that feare t'offend.		317	Horace	282
But, if hereafter thou shalt write, not feare		331	Horace	575
Wise, sober folke, a frantick Poet feare,		335	Horace	643
Those that are wise, a furious Poet feare,		335	Horace	V643
"Where neither Force can bend, nor Feare can awe.		354	Horace	
To loose that feare;		367	Ode Who saith	48
Beeing in feare to be robd, he most learnedly begs.		369	Ode Who saith	94
Sir Inigo doth feare it as I heare		375	Coryat 1	35
(And labours to seem worthy of that feare)		407	Inigo Jones 3	1
yet doe not feare it.		407	Inigo Jones 3	2
Cause Reverence, yf not Feare,		417	Moon	32
shall never dare do any thing but feare.		421	Ode:If Men	42
		423	Lucan	20

FEAR'D

Fear'd not to boast the glories of her stage,		56	E89 Allen	2
That envie wish'd, and Nature fear'd.		173	U22 Elegy Tho	20
Did learne them first, and once a Master fear'd.		333	Horace	592

FEAREFULL

| Would not be fearefull to offend a dame | | 112 | F11 Epode | 109 |
| From fearefull back-slides; And the debt we'are in, | | 412 | Sutcliffe | 15 |

FEAREFULLY

| Or take an Epigramme so fearefully: | | 51 | E73 Fine Grand | 2 |
| Item, a charme surrounding fearefully | | 51 | E73 Fine Grand | 12 |

FEARES

| He that feares death, or mournes it, in the just, | | 37 | E34 Death | 1 |
| Looke not upon thy dangers, but our feares. | | 43 | E51 James 3 | 10 |

FEARES (cont.)
Not that it feares, but will not have to doo . . . . 74 E115 Honest Man 20
Since stird'st up jealousies and feares, . . . 101 F4 To the World 43
Th'are base, and idle feares . . . . . 109 F11 Epode 26
His heart sinnes, though he feares. . . . . 112 F11 Epode 90
Nor spread them as distract with feares, ... 145 U4 Song 11
But then t'increase my feares, ... 148 U7 Nymph 26
Oh, but my conscious feares, ... 149 U9 Picture 11
And that her truster feares her? Must I too? . . . 223 U49 Pucell 22
Yet with a Dye, that feares no Moth, ... 230 U55 Burges 7
Goe now, and tell out dayes summ'd up with feares, . . 244 U70 Ode 53
Made her friends joyes to get above their feares! . . 270 U81 Pawlet 60
Of lying, he feares so much the reproofe . . . . 380 Coryat 3 31
FEARFULL
As fearfull to awake . . . . 239 U67 Muses 10
And snares the fearfull Hare, and new-come Crane, . . . 290 U85 Country 35
FEARING
Being over-safe, and fearing of the flaw: . . . . 339 Horace   V 41/ 39
This, fearing not the subtlest Judges marke, . . . 331 Horace 542
FEAST
I lent you, on meere acquaintance, at a feast. . . . 51 E73 Fine Grand 6
But that your worth will dignifie our feast, . . . 64 E101 Supper 4
That scarse the Towne designeth any feast . . . 81 E129 Mime 5
When thou would'st feast, or exercise thy friends. . . 94 F2 Penshurst 21
Of Sheriffes dinner, or Majors feast. . . . . 96 F3 Wroth 6
Of Sergeants dinner, or sheriffes feast. . . . 96 F3 Wroth   V 6
Both love the cause, and authors of the feast? . . . 120 F14 Sydney 10
To fall againe; at such a feast, . . . 144 U3 Musicall 23
T'have held a Triumph, or a feast of fire, . . . 205 U43 Vulcan 60
Of feast, and merry meeting, ... 221 U48 Bacchus 15
Shall feast it, thou maist love there . . . 221 U48 Bacchus 38
So like a feast? . . . . . 253 U75 Epithalam. 14
This Feast, then can the Day, ... 254 U75 Epithalam. 55
There is a Feast behind, ... 257 U75 Epithalam. 141
Who in that feast of Resurrection trust! . . . 284 U84 Muse 62
Out of her noble body, to this Feast: . . . 284 U84 Muse 82
Or at the Feast of Bounds, the Lambe then slaine, . . 291 U85 Country 59
There jest, and feast, make him thine host, . . . 292 U86 Hor.4:1 11
In tragick Verse; no lesse Thyestes feast . . . 311 Horace 122
Whom shee, with Sorrow first did lodge, then feast, . . 394 Jane Ogle 20
FEASTING
Twirle the poore chaine you run a feasting in. . . . 69 E107 Hungry 30
Lyve long the Feasting Roome. And ere thou burne . . 406 Inigo Jones 1 101
FEASTS
Where Pan, and Bacchus their high feasts have made, . . 93 F2 Penshurst 11
And feasts, that either shearers keepe; . . . 97 F3 Wroth 40
And feasts, which either shearers keepe; . . . 97 F3 Wroth   V 40
What furie of late is crept into our Feasts? . . . 166 U15 Friend-Wars 117
As shall the feasts faire grounds be. . . . 221 U48 Bacchus 42
To Church, as others doe to Feasts and Playes, . . 222 U49 Pucell 16
Of rimes, or ryots, at your feasts, ... 246 U70 Ode 103
And they uncensur'd might at Feasts, and Playes . . 319 Horace 297
As jarring Musique doth, at jolly feasts, . . . 331 Horace 557
FEAT
To pitty him, as smiling at his Feat . . . . 405 Inigo Jones 1 71
FEATHERS
And shew their feathers shot, and cullors torne, . . 98 F3 Wroth 71
Ha's Feathers, and will serve a man to pull. . . . 154 U13 Sacvile 58
Or Feathers: lay his fortune out to show, . . . 162 U15 Friend-Wars 21
They saw too store of feathers, and more may, . . 213 U44 Speach 9
Embroderies, Feathers, Fringes, Lace, . . . 275 U84 Body 3
Set a Horse-neck, and divers feathers fold . . . 305 Horace 2
FEATS
Or feats of darknesse acted in Mid-Sun, . . . 156 U13 Sacvile 95
FEATURE
For wit, feature, and true passion, . . . 39 E40 Ratcliffe 16
That can restore that. Will it hurt your feature? . . 46 E62 Would-bee 7
In grace, and feature, ... 77 E120 S. P. 6
All her best symmetrie in that one feature! . . . 112 F11 Epode 101
Or the feature, or the youth: . . . . 131 U2 Excuse 9
Presenting upwards, a faire female feature, . . . 305 Horace 4
Prove of his Mistris Feature, ... 364 Phoenix 7
FEATURES
In my character, what your features bee, . . . 117 F13 Aubigny 24
FEBR
. . . made Earle of Portland. 17. Febr. 1632. To the Envious. . 250 U73 Weston Ttl
FED
But one is bitten by the Dog he fed, . . . 155 U13 Sacvile 67
Like flies, or wormes, with mans corrupt parts fed: . . 218 U47 Tribe 18
At these Immortall Mangers Virgil fed. . . . 228 U53 Newcastle 20
(For with both the Muse was fed) . . . 259 U76 Petition 16
(For with both the Muse it fed) . . . 259 U76 Petition   V 16
Of the fed flocks approaching home! . . . 291 U85 Country 62
Or, with the milke of Thebes; or Argus, fed. . . 313 Horace 168
FEE
Are there for Charitie, and not for fee. . . . 186 U32 Elsmere 6
Thou hast the brave scorne, to put back the fee! . . 187 U33 Councellour 22
FEED
Thy sheepe, thy bullocks, kine, and calves doe feed: . . 94 F2 Penshurst 23
'Pray thee, feed contented, then, . . . 105 F8 Sicknesse 13
And out of inward pleasure feed . . . 144 U3 Musicall 19
And out of inward passion feed . . . 144 U3 Musicall   V 19
Feed those, at whom the Table points at still? . . 155 U13 Sacvile 74

	Page	Title	Line
FEED (cont.)			
Feed on thy selfe for spight, and shew thy Kind:	250	U73 Weston	9
To cloath the naked, feed the hungry. Shee	288	U84 Muse	194
FEEDING			
Pure thoughts in man: with fiery zeale them feeding	128	U1 Trinitie	27
FEELE			
I feele my griefes too, and there scarce is ground,	122	F15 Heaven	21
I feele, I'm rather dead then he!	152	U12 Corbet	36
As I did feele it done, as soone as meant:	153	U13 Sacvile	123
No! he must feele and know, that will advance.	156	U13 Sacvile	123
For t'other pound of sweet-meats, he shall feele	164	U15 Friend-Wars	77
Where we must feele it Darke for halfe a yeare.	199	U41 Elegy Since	8
T'effect it, feele, thou'ast made thine owne heart ake.	250	U73 Weston	12
You feele no cold	258	U75 Epithalam.	V166
And mightiest Monarchs feele what large increase	261	U77 Treasurer	21
To give your shade a name! Stay, stay, I feele	269	U81 Pawlet	7
To give your shade a lasting name! Stay, stay, I feele	269	U81 Pawlet	V 7
Sure, I am dead, and know it not! I feele	283	U84 Muse	29
And being at Flushing enforced to feele	380	Coryat 3	54
I do not feele that ever yet I had	385	Husband	5
I feele it by mine owne, that over flow,	398	Drayton	77
FEELES			
Banck feeles no lamenesse of his knottie gout,	36	E31 Banck	1
And feeles it; Else he tarries by the Beast.	156	U13 Sacvile	117
In neighbour-townes, and feeles the weightie plough:	309	Horace	95
FEES			
But as they come, on both sides he takes fees,	38	E37 Chev'ril	2
Nor how to get the lawyer fees.	98	F3 Wroth	62
FEET			
In sentence, of as subtile feet,	149	U9 Picture	8
In numbers, of as subtile feet,	149	U9 Picture	V 8
The cold tumor in his feet,	184	U29 Fit of Rime	56
Thrice 'bout thy Altar with their Ivory feet.	292	U86 Hor.4:1	28
To his strength, hath measur'd it out with his feet.	379	Coryat 3	4
Hee's warme on his feet now he sayes, & can	405	Inigo Jones 1	67
FEETE			
Let these in wanton feete daunce out their soules.	108	F10 Proludium	11
And makes her supple feete, as swift as winde.	363	Riches	12
Il may Ben Johnson slander so his feete,	418	Answer	5
FEIGNE (See also FAINE, FAYNE)			
For, being a Poet, thou maist feigne, create,	313	Horace	189
FEILD			
Thou mad'st in open Feild	421	Ode:If Men	40
FELICITIE			
That scratching now's our best Felicitie?	166	U15 Friend-Wars	144
FELL (ADJECTIVE)			
Sword, fire, and famine, with fell fury met;	243	U70 Ode	17
FELL			
Two bravely in the battaile fell, and dy'd,	60	E93 Radcliffe	5
And that, midst envy' and parts; then fell by rage:	71	E110 Edmonds 1	14
Had burst with storme, and downe fell, ab excelsis,	86	E133 Voyage	95
But both fell prest under the load they make.	166	U15 Friend-Wars	128
But, others fell with that conceipt by the eares,	209	U43 Vulcan	145
But, others fell by that conceipt by the eares,	209	U43 Vulcan	V145
Alas, but Morison fell young:	244	U70 Ode	43
Hee never fell, thou fall'st, my tongue.	244	U70 Ode	44
Hee never fell, thou tripst, my tongue.	244	U70 Ode	V 44
Fell into fault so farre, as now they saw	321	Horace	367
till giddie with amazement I fell downe	361	Palmer	25
FELLOW			
Thy learned Chamber-fellow, knowes to doe	161	U14 Selden	72
A fellow of course Letcherie, is nam'd,	165	U15 Friend-Wars	98
To be that fellow, then to be markt out	339	Horace	V 53/ 51
FELLOWES			
Her fellowes, with the oyle of gladnesse, bright	285	U84 Muse	101
FELLOWSHIP			
Of fellowship, the fourth, or second place.	323	Horace	380
Of Fellowship, professing my old Arts.	409	Brome	4
FELLS			
Our milke. Our fells. Our fleeces. and first Lambs.	264	U79 New-yeares	16
Your Milkes, your Fells, your Fleeces, and first Lambes,	265	U79 New-yeares	50
FELT			
Which when he felt, Away (quoth hee)	93	F1 Why write no	3
Have you felt the wooll o' the Bever?	135	U2 Triumph	25
And braveries of Court, and felt their fits	200	U42 Elegy Let	34
My Lord, till felt griefe make our stone hearts soft,	234	U61 Epigram	14
FEMALE (See also FAEMALE)			
Presenting upwards, a faire female feature,	305	Horace	4
FEN			
As Stiles, Dike, Ditchfield, Millar, Crips, and Fen:	214	U44 Speach	54
A kingly worke; or that long barren fen	309	Horace	93
FENC'D			
His neck fenc'd round with ruffe! his eyes halfe shut!	33	E21 Gam'ster	2
FENCED			
Fenced with a Ditch, and forc'd out of a Marish,	209	U43 Vulcan	V134
FENCER			
Cob, thou nor souldier, thiefe, nor fencer art,	50	E69 Cob	1
FENCING			
They talke of Fencing, and the use of Armes,	232	U59 Newcastle	1
FENC'T			
But still their valour, and their vertue fenc't 'hem,	86	E133 Voyage	76
FERRABOSCO			
To Alphonso Ferrabosco, on his Booke.	82	E130 Ferrab. 1	Ttl

FERTILE
   Fertile of wood, Ashore, and Sydney's copp's,   • • • • 94 F2 Penshurst   26

FESCENNINE
   But dare not aske our wish in Language fescennine: • • • 257 U75 Epithalam. 160

FET
   Their Charge, and Office, whence their wealth to fet,   • • 325 Horace   436

FETCH
   To fetch in the Formes goe by: • • • • • 140 U2 Promise   18
   To fetch the flesh, we keepe the Rowle.   • • • 188 U35 Chute   6

FETHER
   That so much skarfe of France, and hat, and fether,   • • 56 E88 Monsieur   3

FETHERD
   Before his swift and fetherd race be run,   • • • 116 F12 Rutland V 99

FETTER
   Can Poets hope to fetter mee?   • • • • 93 F1 Why write no   4

FETTERS
   Fastning Vowells, as with fetters   • • • 183 U29 Fit of Rime 11

FEVER
   The Belgick fever ravished away.   • • • • 60 E93 Radcliffe   8

FEV'RY
   And that there be no fev'ry heats, nor colds,   • • • 220 U47 Tribe   67

FEW
   Nor need'st thou: for those few, by oath releast,   • • • 32 E16 Brain-hardy   7
   In these times. Few so have ru'de   • • • 39 E40 Ratcliffe 14
   My selfe a witnesse of thy few dayes sport: • • 55 E85 Goodyere 1   2
   And like them too; must needfully, though few,   • • 61 E94 Bedford 3 13
   How few have read! how fewer understood!)   • • • 71 E110 Edmonds 1 16
   Of a few poore houshold spyes?   • • • • 102 F5 Celia 1 12
   Of any good minde, now: There are so few.   • • 116 F13 Aubigny   2
   But few and faire Divisions: but being got   • • 157 U13 Sacvile 151
   When those good few, that her Defenders be,   • • 186 U32 Elsmere   5
   A booke to a few lynes: but, it was fit   • • 230 U56 Covell   3
   For as at distance, few have facultie   • • • 242 U69 Friend Son 19
   But soft, and simple, at few holes breath'd time   • 319 Horace 289
   They might with ease be numbred, being a few   • • 319 Horace 293
   Offended with few spots, which negligence   • • 329 Horace 527
   A Prentise-ship: which few doe now a dayes.   • • 410 Brome 10

FEWD
   And howsoever; as I am at fewd   • • • 116 F13 Aubigny   9

FEWER
   How few have read! how fewer understood!)   • • 71 E110 Edmonds 1 16

FEWEST
   Their un-avoided subject, fewest see: • • • 60 E94 Bedford 3   8

FIBRE
   The smallest Fibre of our flesh; he can   • • • 286 U84 Muse 151

FIBRES
   How all my Fibres by your Spirit doe move,   • • 194 U38 Elegy 'Tis 111

FIELD
   Of bearing them in field, he threw 'hem away: • • 42 E48 Mungril   2
   The painted partrich lyes in every field,   • • 94 F2 Penshurst 29
   Front, an ample field of snow;   • • • 141 U2 Her man 18
   The poores full Store-house, and just servants field.   • 185 U30 Burleigh   8
   Or the great Hall at Westminster, the field   • • 186 U33 Councellour   3
   To have their Husbands drawne forth to the field,   • 213 U44 Speach 18
   To all the uses of the field, and race,   • • • 228 U53 Newcastle   3
   Upon a banke, or field of flowers,   • • • 280 U84 Mind 67
   Whether in Mars his field thou bee,   • • • 293 U86 Hor.4:1 39
   I'the open field; is Waxe like to be wrought   • • 315 Horace 231
   His armes in Mars his field, he doth refuse;   • • 331 Horace 566
   Which, of the field is clep'd the sweetest brier,   • 413 Ghyrlond 22

FIELDS
   Of flowrie fields, of cop'ces greene,   • • • 97 F3 Wroth 38
   Or the sands in Chelsey fields,   • • • • 103 F6 Celia 2 14
   All the sands in Chelsey fields,   • • • 103 F6 Celia 2 V 14
   All the Pride the fields than have: • • • 132 U2 How he saw   4
   Or in Moore-fields, this other night! sings one,   • 202 U42 Elegy Let 73
   Or when that Autumne, through the fields, lifts round   290 U85 Country 17

FIER
   yf from a little sparke hee rise not fier.   • • • 383 Rich 16

FIERCE
   Made me commit most fierce idolatrie   • • • 48 E65 Muse   3
   Now hot, now cold, now fierce, now mild.   • • 189 U36 Song 15
   Medea make wild, fierce, impetuous;   • • • 342 Horace V175
   Was Tigers, said, and Lyons fierce, to tame.   • 327 Horace 482

FIERY
   Pure thoughts in man: with fiery zeale them feeding   • 128 U1 Trinitie 27

FIFT
   Of our fift Henry, eight of his nine yeare;   • • 207 U43 Vulcan 98
   Of our fift Henry, right of his nine yeare;   • • 207 U43 Vulcan V 98

FIFTIE
   Though I now write fiftie yeares,   • • • 131 U2 Excuse   3
   Or spun out Riddles, and weav'd fiftie tomes   • 204 U43 Vulcan 33

FIFTIETH
   To bend a man, now at his fiftieth yeare   • • 292 U86 Hor.4:1   6

FIFTY
   At fifty yeares, almost, to value it,   • • • 171 U20 Shrub   5

FIG
   Fig, grape, and quince, each in his time doth come: • 94 F2 Penshurst 42

FIGHT
   Some hundred quarrells, yet dost thou fight none;   • 32 E16 Brain-hardy   6
   He that dares damne himselfe, dares more then fight.   32 E16 Brain-hardy 10
   Hee's valiant'st, that dares fight, and not for pay;   • 49 E66 Cary 17

FIGHT (cont.)

Doe change, though man, and often fight, . . . 146 U6 Defence 8
Thou canst draw forth thy forces, and fight drie . . 214 U44 Speach 45
Where fight the prime Cocks of the Game, for wit? . . 222 U49 Pucell 4
This booke! it is a Catechisme to fight, . . . 398 Drayton 71
Get broken peeces, and fight well by those. . . . 398 Drayton 74

FIGHTS

The Fights, the Cryes, and wondring at the Jarres . . 397 Drayton 41

FIGURE

Upon the Stage, the figure of a Snake. . . . 317 Horace 268
But a bare Type and Figure. . . . . 364 Phoenix 8
This Figure, that thou here seest put, . . . 390 Reader 1

FIGURES

The severall figures, languish in suspence, . . . 370 Author 10

FILCH'D

Or common places, filch'd, that take these times, . 116 F12 Rutland 88

FILE   (See also FYL'S)

Their names are not recorded on the File . . . 257 U75 Epithalam. 155

FIL'D

What wonder perfect, all were fil'd, ... 188 U35 Chute 3

FILED

In his well torned, and true-filed lines: . . . 392 Shakespeare 68

FILL

And yet are with their Princes: Fill them full . . 69 E107 Hungry 7
Upon your Center, doe your Circle fill . . . 159 U14 Selden 32
Starveling rimes did fill the Stage, . . . 183 U29 Fit of Rime 25
And there made Swords, Bills, Glaves, and Armes your fill; 212 U43 Vulcan 198
Till you behold a race to fill your Hall, . . . 258 U75 Epithalam. 169
Our sense you doe with knowledge fill, . . . 278 U84 Mind 19
As loud enough to fill the seates, not yet . . 319 Horace 291
To fill an Epitaph. But she had more. . . . 371 Epitaph 5

FILL'D

But then, fist-fill'd, to put me off the sent. . . 154 U13 Sacvile 52

FILL'D

Yet three fill'd Zodiackes had he beene . . . 77 E120 S. P. 11
Is fill'd with buttock? And the walls doe sweate . . 88 E133 Voyage 169
Have fill'd with abstinence: . . . . 111 F11 Epode 84
From braines entranc'd, and fill'd with extasies; . 116 F12 Rutland 90
Before the moones have fill'd their tripple trine, . 119 F13 Aubigny 102
And fill'd an Orbe as circular, as heaven! . . 396 Drayton 19

FILLED

Had filled your large nostrills with the steame: . . 205 U43 Vulcan V 62
Hath filled, with Caroches, all the way, . . . 252 U75 Epithalam. 11

FILLIE

To have his Court-bred-fillie there commend . . 163 U15 Friend-Wars 48

FILLS

And fills thy open hall with mirth, and cheere, . . 98 F3 Wroth 49
And fills my powers with perswading joy, . . . 191 U38 Elegy 'Tis 11

FILMER

To my worthy Friend, Master Edward Filmer, . . . 401 Filmer Ttl

FILTH

The filth, stench, noyse: save only what was there . 84 E133 Voyage 9
Hung stench, diseases, and old filth, their mother, . 86 E133 Voyage 70

FILTHY

Doing, a filthy pleasure is, and short; . . . 294 U88 Petronius 1

FINALL

To have that finall retribution, ... 283 U84 Muse 49

FIND

Was his blest fate, but our hard lot to find. . . 37 E32 Roe 2 8
And so is Jone. Oft-times, when Giles doth find . . 40 E42 Giles 9
And what I write thereof find farre, and free . . 41 E43 Salisbury 1 10
Reade all I send: and, if I find but one . . . 62 E96 Donne 2 7
I Doe but name thee Pembroke, and I find . . . 66 E102 Pembroke 1
As lowdest praisers, who perhaps would find . . 67 E103 L Wroth 1 11
And the envious, when they find . . . . 103 F6 Celia 2 21
With you, I know, my offring will find grace. . . 114 F12 Rutland 30
But we find that cold delay, ... 140 U2 Promise 9
Find some one good, in some one man; . . . 145 U5 Woman-kind 9
He is, if they can find him, faire, . . . 147 U7 Nymph 15
Even ashes of lovers find no rest. . . . 149 U8 Houre-glasse 11
As they are done, and such returnes they find: . . 153 U13 Sacvile 6
Find you to reckon nothing, me owe all. . . . 158 U13 Sacvile 164
Spread through the World) is easier farre to find, . 167 U15 Friend-Wars 172
Such Guides men use not, who their way would find, . 170 U18 Elegy Can 12
That would their better objects find: . . . 173 U22 Elegy Tho 27
Read here in one, what thou in all canst find, . . 185 U30 Burleigh 2
Such shall you heare to day, and find great foes, . 186 U32 Elsmere 7
Shall find their depth: they're sounded with a spoone. 198 U40 Elegy That 30
If none of these, then why this fire? Or find . . 203 U43 Vulcan 27
He could not find, then thee, of all that store . . 217 U46 Coke 3
For when they find so many meet in one, . . . 225 U50 Countesse 35
Of deepest lore, could we the Center find! . . . 243 U70 Ode 10
Where they might read, and find . . . 247 U70 Ode 122
Search, Sun, and thou wilt find, . . . 255 U75 Epithalam. 79
Search, Sun, and thou shalt find, . . . 255 U75 Epithalam. V 79
You find no cold . . . . . 258 U75 Epithalam. 166
Whose 'tis: but if it favour find, . . . 277 U84 Body 31
Thither, you hope to come; and there to find . . 285 U84 Muse 103
Find all our Atomes from a point t' a span! . . 287 U84 Muse 152
Poring, as on a Map, to find the wayes . . . 288 U84 Muse 196
I find thee write most worthy to be read. . . . 386 Browne 6
deignes myne the power to find, yett want I will . . 421 Censure 10

	Page	Title	Line

FINDE

Till thou canst finde the best, choose the least ill.	76	E119 Shelton	10
Both whose dimensions, lost, the world might finde	79	E125 Uvedale	3
He knowes, below, he shall finde plentie of meate,	95	F2 Penshurst	70
Be thankes to him, and earnest prayer, to finde	99	F3 Wroth	101
Is thankes to him, and earnest prayer, to finde	99	F3 Wroth	V101
(They finde it both so wittie, and safe to give.)	118	F13 Aubigny	76
Wherein, your forme, you still the same shall finde;	120	F13 Aubigny	123
How can I doubt to finde thee ever, here?	122	F15 Heaven	16
Wake, friend, and finde thy self; awake, the Drum	162	U15 Friend-Wars V	1
Thou, that wouldst finde the habit of true passion,	362	Author	1
Shall finde, that either hath read Bookes, and Men:	389	Aleman	2

FINDING

And, finding good securitie in his age,	57	E90 Mill	6
Where finding so much beautie met with vertue,	74	E114 Sydney	6
'Mongst my Muses finding me,	136	U2 Cupid	7

FINDS

And when he smiling finds his Grace	292	U86 Hor.4:1	17

FINE   (See also FYNE)

To Fine Lady Would-bee.	46	E62 Would-bee	Ttl
Fine Madame Would-Bee, wherefore should you feare,	46	E62 Would-bee	1
To Fine Grand.	51	E73 Fine Grand	Ttl
What is't, fine Grand, makes thee my friendship flye,	51	E73 Fine Grand	1
That is an essence, farre more gentle, fine,	110	F11 Epode	45
That is an essence, most gentile and fine,	110	F11 Epode	V 45
Is it for these that Fine-man meets the street	165	U15 Friend-Wars	106
Or pomp'd for those fine trifles, Anagrams,	204	U43 Vulcan	V 35
Acrostichs, and Telestichs, on fine names,	204	U43 Vulcan	V 39
Thou should'st have cry'd, and all fine proper stuffe.	205	U43 Vulcan	V 64
Make your Petards, and Granats, all your fine	212	U43 Vulcan	206
When look'd the Earth so fine,	253	U75 Epithalam.	21
A Mind so pure, so perfect fine,	278	U84 Mind	25
And set it forth; the rest were Cobwebs fine,	282	U84 Muse	5
And better stayes them there, then all fine noise	327	Horace	459

FINE-MAN

Is it for these that Fine-man meets the street	165	U15 Friend-Wars	106

FINENESSE

Of Finenesse, and alloy: follow his hint,	415	Rutter	27

FINER

Or Eteostichs, or those finer flammes	204	U43 Vulcan	36
Or else Acrosticks, or those finer flammes	204	U43 Vulcan	V 36
More subtle workes, and finer pieces farre,	242	U69 Friend Son	22
Here, finer then comming from his Punke you him see,	375	Coryat 1	28
Finer then was his Spanish, if my Oath	389	Aleman	18

FINEST

Sleeked limmes, and finest blood?	105	F8 Sicknesse	23
Rime, the rack of finest wits,	183	U29 Fit of Rime	1

FINGER

Nor thumbe, nor finger to the stop acquainted,	87	E133 Voyage	134
A lawfull Verse, by th'eare, or finger scan.	323	Horace	404

FINGERS

For Loves fingers, and his wings:	141	U2 Her man	12
To be describ'd! Fames fingers are too foule	269	U81 Pawlet	30

FIRE   (See also FIER, FYER)

This morning, timely rapt with holy fire,	52	E76 Bedford 1	1
This is that good Aeneas, past through fire,	81	E128 Wm Roe 2	12
For lights, or livorie: all is there;	95	F2 Penshurst	73
A fire now, that lent a shade!	98	F3 Wroth	46
My owne true fire. Now my thought takes wing,	108	F10 Proludium	29
Our owne true fire. Now our thought takes wing,	108	F10 Proludium	V 29
Thy thoughts did never melt in amorous fire,	108	F10 Proludium	3
Arm'd with bow, shafts, and fire;	110	F11 Epode	38
Now that the harth is crown'd with smiling fire,	120	F14 Sydney	1
Or the Nard i' the fire?	135	U2 Triumph	28
And that promise set on fire	139	U2 Promise	5
Valiant he should be as fire,	142	U2 Her man	41
That others should not warme them at my fire,	150	U10 Jealousie	6
To succour my necessities, tooke fire,	153	U13 Sacvile	8
Sols Chariot for new fire,	175	U23 Himselfe	28
With Delphick fire:	177	U25 Desmond	12
Gold, that is perfect, will out-live the fire.	179	U25 Desmond	45
A Sparke to set whole worlds a-fire,	189	U36 Song	9
Then sword, or fire, or what is of the race	193	U38 Elegy 'Tis	101
And why to me this, thou lame Lord of fire,	202	U43 Vulcan	1
And why to me this, thou lame god of fire,	202	U43 Vulcan	V 1
If none of these, then why this fire? Or find	203	U43 Vulcan	27
Fitter to see the fire-light, then the day;	204	U43 Vulcan	44
T'have held a Triumph, or a feast of fire,	205	U43 Vulcan	60
'Cause thou canst halt, with us, in Arts, and Fire!	208	U43 Vulcan	110
Cause thou canst doe these halting tricks in fire?	208	U43 Vulcan	V110
And this a Sparkle of that fire let loose	209	U43 Vulcan	141
That this sparke of the same fire let loose	209	U43 Vulcan	V141
Kindled the fire! But then, did one returne,	209	U43 Vulcan	149
Pox on your fire workes, Vulcan; if it be	211	U43 Vulcan	V191
'Bove all your Fire-workes, had at Ephesus,	211	U43 Vulcan	194
Beyond your Fire-workes, had at Ephesus,	211	U43 Vulcan	V194
'Bove all our Fire-workes, had at Ephesus,	211	U43 Vulcan	V194
But why are all these Irons i'the fire	215	U44 Speach	93
They meet the fire, the Test, as Martyrs would;	218	U47 Tribe	3
The fire, the wine, the men! and in the midst,	225	U51 Bacon	3
I hate such measur'd, give me mettall'd fire	233	U59 Newcastle	7
Sword, fire, and famine, with fell fury met;	243	U70 Ode	17
As lowd as Thunder, and as swift as fire.	249	U72 King	4

	Page	Title	Line
FIRE (cont.)			
At Bonefires, Rockets, Fire-workes, with the Shoutes	249	U72 King	13
The blaze, and splendor, but not handle fire!	269	U81 Pawlet	32
The heat, and splendor, but not handle fire!	269	U81 Pawlet	V 32
'Tis got where it can try the fire.	278	U84 Mind	28
And I, am mutually on fire	293	U87 Hor.3:9	13
A Soyle, not barren; a continewall fire;	295	U90 Mart.10:47	4
The greater part, that boast the Muses fire,	339	Horace	V 33
As fire; and more delightfull	365	Ode Splendor	6
A glorified worke to Time, when Fire,	371	Fletcher	15
That ever yet did fire the English blood!	397	Drayton	57
In Moses bush, un-wasted in the fire.	413	Ghyrlond	24
FIR'D			
Quickly fir'd, as in beginners	141	U2 Her man	31
To deck the hallow'd Harth with old wood fir'd	291	U85 Country	43
FIRE-LIGHT			
Fitter to see the fire-light, then the day;	204	U43 Vulcan	44
FIRES			
With his brave sonne, the Prince, they saw thy fires	95	F2 Penshurst	77
Of bone-fires. Then	121	F14 Sydney	59
O, be not angry with those fires,	144	U4 Song	5
By those bright Eyes, at whose immortall fires	170	U19 Elegy By	1
Be kept alive those Sweet, and Sacred fires	257	U75 Epithalam.	163
FIRE-WORKES			
'Bove all your Fire-workes, had at Ephesus,	211	U43 Vulcan	194
Beyond your Fire-workes, had at Ephesus,	211	U43 Vulcan	V194
'Bove all our Fire-workes, had at Ephesus,	211	U43 Vulcan	V194
At Bonefires, Rockets, Fire-workes, with the Shoutes	249	U72 King	13
FIRKE			
And firke, and jerke, and for the Coach-man raile,	164	U15 Friend-Wars	72
How would he firke? lyke Adam overdooe	405	Inigo Jones 1	79
FIRME			
For that firme grace he holdes in your regard,	116	F12 Rutland	95
And can tread firme, longs with like lads to play;	315	Horace	226
No faith's more firme, or flat, then where't doth creep.	413	Ghyrlond	20
FIRST			
'Twas brought to court first wrapt, and white as milke;	31	E15 Court-worm	2
On my first Daughter.	33	E22 Daughter	Ttl
Left us of feare, but first our crimes, then lawes.	38	E35 James 2	6
First thou preserved wert, our king to bee,	38	E35 James 2	9
On my First Sonne.	41	E45 First Son	Ttl
His bought armes Mung' not lik'd; for his first day	42	E48 Mungril	1
At first he made low shifts, would picke and gleane,	45	E56 Poet-Ape	5
He markes not whose 'twas first: and after-times	45	E56 Poet-Ape	11
As all thy honors were by them first sought:	49	E67 Suffolk	8
Each best day of our life escapes us, first.	50	E70 Wm Roe 1	6
And here, it should be one of our first strifes,	54	E80 Life/Death	6
When Mill first came to court, the unprofiting foole,	57	E90 Mill	1
First bearing him a calfe, beare him a bull.	57	E90 Mill	18
And ever is ill got without the first.	63	E98 Th Roe 1	12
Give your yong States-men, (that first make you drunke,	69	E107 Hungry	19
And first to know thine owne state, then the States.	70	E109 Nevil	12
For Cupid, who (at first) tooke vaine delight,	73	E114 Sydney	3
Thou wert the first, mad'st merit know her strength,	75	E116 Jephson	5
And heare her speake with one, and her first tongue;	78	E122 Rudyerd 2	6
Uv'dale, thou piece of the first times, a man	79	E125 Uvedale	1
Thy selfe, with thy first thoughts, brought home by thee,	81	E128 Wm Roe 2	10
But the first question is, when one saw thee?	81	E129 Mime	2
In the first jawes appear'd that ugly monster,	85	E133 Voyage	61
Who shall discharge first his merd-urinous load:	85	E133 Voyage	65
Officiously, at first, themselves betray.	94	F2 Penshurst	36
My tender, first, and simple yeeres	101	F4 To the World	41
While you breath. First give a hundred,	103	F6 Celia 2	8
The first; as prone to move	110	F11 Epode	32
Achilles was not first, that valiant was,	114	F12 Rutland	51
First, midst, and last, converted one, and three;	122	F15 Heaven	10
First made of nought,	129	U1 Father	21
First, prepare you to be sorie,	131	U2 Excuse	14
First, that I must kneeling yeeld	133	U2 Suffered	7
To love one man, hee'd leave her first.	146	U6 Defence	24
Who makes the one, so't be first, makes both.	152	U12 Corbet	40
'Tis like light Canes, that first rise big and brave,	157	U13 Sacvile	149
Which Grace shall I make love to first? your skill,	159	U14 Selden	35
I first salute thee so; and gratulate,	161	U14 Selden	67
That by commanding first thy selfe, thou mak'st	168	U15 Friend-Wars	181
Can Beautie that did prompt me first to write,	169	U18 Elegy Can	1
That I must send one first, my Choyce assignes,	170	U18 Elegy Can	23
He that first invented thee,	184	U29 Fit of Rime	49
But first dost vexe, and search it! If not sound,	187	U33 Councellour	19
Sir, I am thankfull, first, to heaven, for you;	189	U37 Friend-Book	1
Or stay'd but where the Fryar, and you first met,	212	U43 Vulcan	201
All that they doe at Playes. O, but first here	215	U44 Speach	91
First weigh a friend, then touch, and trie him too:	216	U45 Squib	16
For that is first requir'd, A man be his owne.	216	U45 Squib	23
Are asked to climbe. First give me faith, who know	220	U47 Tribe	75
When first, my Lord, I saw you backe your horse,	228	U53 Newcastle	1
The first of which, I feare, you will refuse;	230	U56 Covell	6
The first of which, I doubt, you will refuse;	230	U56 Covell	V 6
. . . first-borne, An Epigram Consolatorie. 1629.	235	U63 Charles 2	Ttl
Who dares denie, that all first-fruits are due	235	U63 Charles 2	6
(Except the joy that the first Mary brought,	238	U66 Queene	7
(And leave the joy that the first Mary brought,	238	U66 Queene	V 7
This made you first to know the Why	247	U70 Ode	107

FIRST (cont.)
```
Who, e're the first downe bloomed on the chin,          .    .    .    .    247   U70 Ode            127
Askes first, Who gives her (I Charles) then he plights .    .    .    256   U75 Epithalam.     124
And let him freely gather Loves First-fruits,          .    .    .    258   U75 Epithalam.     186
Busie, or frowne at first; when he sees thee,          .    .    .    262   U78 Digby           20
Best Kings expect first-fruits of your glad gaines.    .    .    .    263   U79 New-yeares      13
Our milke.  Our fells.  Our fleeces.  and first Lambs. .    .    .    264   U79 New-yeares      16
Your Milkes, your Fells, your Fleeces, and first Lambes,    .    .    265   U79 New-yeares      50
Should take first Seisin of the publique good,         .    .    .    268   U80 Christning       8
With Sayles of silke, as the first notes               .    .    .    273   U84 Cradle          23
Of the first Lupus, to the Familie       .             .    .    .    274   U84 Descent         17
Draw first a Cloud: all save her neck;                 .    .    .    276   U84 Body            13
Where first his Power will appeare, by call            .    .    .    289   U84 Muse           220
Ode the first.  The fourth Booke.  To Venus.           .    .    .    292   U86 Hor.4:1         Ttl
Was meant at first.  Why, forcing still about          .    .    .    307   Horace              29
The first-borne dying; so the aged state               .    .    .    309   Horace              87
The first-borne dying; so the aged Fate                .    .    .    340   Horace            V 87
In Verse unequall match'd; first sowre Laments,        .    .    .    309   Horace             107
That first sent forth the dapper Elegie,               .    .    .    309   Horace             110
If thou would'st have me weepe, be thou first drown'd  .    .    .    311   Horace             145
For Nature, first, within doth fashion us              .    .    .    311   Horace             152
Unto the last, as when he first went forth,            .    .    .    313   Horace             181
First publish things unspoken, and unknowne.           .    .    .    313   Horace             186
Where the midst differs from the first: or where       .    .    .    315   Horace             217
Thespis is said to be the first found out              .    .    .    319   Horace             311
But meere Iambicks all, from first to last.            .    .    .    323   Horace             374
Is to be wise; thy matter first to know;               .    .    .    325   Horace             441
First frighted men, that wildly liv'd, at ods,         .    .    .    327   Horace             480
And thus, at first, an honour, and a name              .    .    .    327   Horace             491
If ne're so little it depart the first,                .    .    .    331   Horace             563
Did learne them first, and once a Master fear'd.       .    .    .    333   Horace             592
First: thy successe did strike my sence with wonder;   .    .    .    361   Palmer               5
He shew'd him first the hoofe-cleft Spring,            .    .    .    366   Ode Who saith       17
But first to Cluid stoope low,     .                   .    .    .    367   Ode Who saith       39
It covers, first, a Virgin; and then, one              .    .    .    371   Epitaph              3
No: as I first said, who would write a story at        .    .    .    381   Coryat 3            59
For though Spaine gave him his first ayre and Vogue,   .    .    .    389   Aleman              15
Whom shee, with Sorrow first did lodge, then feast,    .    .    .    394   Jane Ogle           20
Mr Surveyor, you that first began.       .             .    .    .    402   Inigo Jones 1        1
Which I, your Master, first did teach the Age.         .    .    .    409   Brome                8
Unto the world, in praise of your first Play:          .    .    .    414   Rutter               2
Cry'd up of late: Whereto there must be first          .    .    .    415   Rutter              21
Our first of fruits, that is the prime of flowers      .    .    .    416   Welcome              2
FIRST-BORNE
 . . . first-borne, An Epigram Consolatorie. 1629.     .    .    .    235   U63 Charles 2       Ttl
The first-borne dying; so the aged state               .    .    .    309   Horace              87
The first-borne dying; so the aged Fate                .    .    .    340   Horace            V 87
FIRST-FRUITS
Who dares denie, that all first-fruits are due         .    .    .    235   U63 Charles 2        1
And let him freely gather Loves First-fruits,          .    .    .    258   U75 Epithalam.     186
Best Kings expect first-fruits of your glad gaines.    .    .    .    263   U79 New-yeares      13
FISH
Thou hast thy ponds, that pay thee tribute fish,       .    .    .     94   F2 Penshurst        32
Which in some swarthie fish uncomely ends:             .    .    .    305   Horace               5
Which in a blacke foule fish uncomely ends:            .    .    .    338   Horace            V  5
All sorts of fish with Musicke of his maw.             .    .    .    374   Coryat 1            11
FISHER
Before the fisher, or into his hand.    .    .    .    .    .    .     94   F2 Penshurst        38
FIST
Great Club-fist, though thy backe, and bones be sore,  .    .    .     85   E133 Voyage         55
But then, fist-fill'd, to put me off the sent.         .    .    .    154   U13 Sacvile         52
FIST-FILL'D
But then, fist-fill'd, to put me off the sent.         .    .    .    154   U13 Sacvile         52
FIT   (NOUN)
Nor glad for fashion.  Nor to shew a fit     .         .    .    .     47   E64 Salisbury 3      7
Acts old Iniquitie, and in the fit      .             .    .    .     74   E115 Honest Man     27
That ne're was knowne to last above a fit!             .    .    .    171   U20 Shrub            6
A Fit of Rime against Rime.                            .    .    .    183   U29 Fit of Rime    Ttl
Thy Wife a fit of laughter; a Cramp-ring               .    .    .    232   U58 Book-seller      8
FIT
For thy late sharpe device.  I say 'tis fit            .    .    .     36   E29 Tilter           3
Arsenike would thee fit for societie make.             .    .    .     42   E50 Cod 3            3
Then had I made 'hem good, to fit your vaine.          .    .    .     51   E73 Fine Grand      20
Fit in that softer bosome to reside.     .             .    .    .     52   E76 Bedford 1       12
Illustrous Vere, or Horace; fit to be                  .    .    .     58   E91 Vere             3
If not, 'tis fit for you, some should envy.            .    .    .     67   E104 Montgomery     16
Such as suspect them-selves, and thinke it fit         .    .    .    117   F13 Aubigny         13
But to the Subject, still the Colours fit              .    .    .    160   U14 Selden          58
Thus they doe talke.  And are these objects fit        .    .    .    165   U15 Friend-Wars    101
Thy person fit for any charge thou tak'st;             .    .    .    168   U15 Friend-Wars    182
Their vice of loving for a Christmasse fit;            .    .    .    190   U37 Friend-Book      8
Conceal'd, or kept there, that was fit to be,          .    .    .    203   U43 Vulcan          21
A booke to a few lynes: but, it was fit                .    .    .    230   U56 Covell           3
Nor any least fit    .    .    .    .                  .    .    .    231   U57 Burges          18
As if that part lay for a <     > most fit!            .    .    .    232   U58 Book-seller     12
To know the heads of danger! where 'tis fit            .    .    .    233   U59 Newcastle       17
Fit for a Bishops knees! O bow them oft,               .    .    .    234   U61 Epigram         13
To fit the softnesse of our Yeares-gift: when          .    .    .    263   U79 New-yeares       6
In all the bounds of beautie fit     .    .    .      .    .    .    280   U84 Mind            51
A sorrow in me, fit to wait on her!     .             .    .    .    282   U84 Muse            10
She had, and it became her! she was fit                .    .    .    287   U84 Muse           161
If a fit livor thou dost seeke to toast;               .    .    .    292   U86 Hor.4:1         12
Take, therefore, you that write, still, matter fit     .    .    .    307   Horace              53
```

	Page	Title	Line

FIT (cont.)
Take therefore, you that write, a subject fit · · · 339 Horace V 55/ 53
What number best can fit, Homer declares. · · · 309 Horace 106
As fit t'exchange discourse; a Verse to win · · · 311 Horace 119
Fit for the sock: Each subject should retaine · · · 311 Horace 124
Fit rites. The Child, that now knowes how to say, · · · 315 Horace 225
Fit dues. The Child, that now knowes how to say, · · · 344 Horace V225
Her licence fit to be restrain'd by law: · · · 321 Horace 368
Her force was fit to be restrain'd by law: · · · 348 Horace V402/368
What height of love, a Parent will fit best, · · · 325 Horace 447
Or mixing sweet, and fit, teach life the right. · · · 327 Horace 478
As fit to have encreas'd the harmony · · · 371 Epitaph 8
Which were so richly spun, and woven so fit, · · · 392 Shakespeare 49
We offer as a Circle the most fit · · · 416 Welcome 6
Just and fit actions Ptolemey (he saith) · · · 422 Lucan 1

FITLY
Were fitly interpos'd; so new: · · · 275 U84 Body 10
Then to the purpose leades, and fitly 'grees. · · · 317 Horace 279

FITNESSE
Into their birth-right, and for fitnesse sake, · · · 323 Horace 376

FITS (NOUN)
That expresseth but by fits, · · · 183 U29 Fit of Rime 2
And braveries of Court, and felt their fits · · · 200 U42 Elegy Let 34
They say you weekly invite with fits o'th' Mother, · · · 223 U49 Pucell 40

FITS
Better fits him, then his face; · · · 140 U2 Promise 20
Sad language fits sad lookes; stuff'd menacings, · · · 311 Horace 149
It fits not onely him that makes a Booke, · · · 385 Husband 1

FITT
Had bin fitt meate for Vulcan to lick up. · · · 206 U43 Vulcan V 84
When their pot-guns thinke to fitt, · · · 259 U76 Petition V 21

FITTED
And tune too, fitted to the Chorus rime, · · · 319 Horace 290
I doe salute you! Are you fitted yet? · · · 402 Inigo Jones 1 17

FITTER
Fitter, where it dyed, to tell, · · · 79 E124 Elizabeth 11
Fitter to see the fire-light, then the day; · · · 204 U43 Vulcan 44
What Month then May, was fitter to disclose · · · 237 U65 Prince 4
Till fitter season. Now, to like of this, · · · 307 Horace 63

FITTING
And most his Justice, in the fitting parts, · · · 289 U84 Muse 223
In fitting proper adjuncts to each day. · · · 317 Horace 254
Indeed, give fitting dues to every man. · · · 325 Horace 452

FITTS
Call every night to Supper in these fitts, · · · 218 U47 Tribe 21

FIVE
Five of my jests, then stolne, past him a play. · · · 64 E100 Playwrt 3 4
Yet drown'd they not. They had five lives in future. · · · 88 E133 Voyage 154
Lend me, deare Arthur, for a weeke five more, · · · 229 U54 Squib 16
Have cast a trench about mee, now, five yeares; · · · 248 U71 Treasurer 6
Have more or lesse then just five Acts: nor laid, · · · 317 Horace 272
From the five ounces; what remaines? pronounce · · · 327 Horace 468
In five monthes he went it, in five monthes he pend it. · · · 379 Coryat 3 16
Here, are five letters in this blessed Name, · · · 412 Ghyrlond 1
Which, chang'd, a five-fold mysterie designe, · · · 412 Ghyrlond 2
The gladdest ground to all the numbred-five, · · · 412 Ghyrlond 6

FIVE-FOLD
Which, chang'd, a five-fold mysterie designe, · · · 412 Ghyrlond 2

FIXE
Where he would fixe, for the distinctions feare. · · · 242 U69 Friend Son 18

FIX'D
A purging bill, now fix'd upon the dore, · · · 29 E7 Hot-house 2
To make up Greatnesse! and mans whole good fix'd · · · 163 U15 Friend-Wars 44
Is fix'd upon one leg, and dares not come · · · 198 U40 Elegy That 33
Fix'd to the bed, and boords, unlike to win · · · 248 U71 Treasurer 11
Fix'd to the bed, and borde, and like to win · · · 248 U71 Treasurer V 11

FIXED
A fixed thought, an eye un-taught to glance; · · · 111 F11 Epode 61
Your forme shines here, here fixed in my heart: · · · 194 U38 Elegy 'Tis 117

FIXT
Or fixt in the Low-Countrey's, where you might · · · 212 U43 Vulcan 203
As if they' ador'd the Head, wheron th'are fixt. · · · 413 Ghyrlond 28

FLACCUS
Quintus Horatius Flaccus his book of . . . · · · 338 Horace VTtl

FLAGGE
That still th'art made the suppers flagge, the drum, · · · 81 E129 Mime 7

FLAGGETH
So he that flaggeth much, becomes to me · · · 329 Horace 533

FLAKES
And, after, swom abroad in ample flakes, · · · 87 E133 Voyage 138

FLAME
All gentrie, yet, owe part of their best flame! · · · 75 E116 Jephson 2
Of thy Penates had beene set on flame, · · · 95 F2 Penshurst 79
in whom the flame of every beauty raignes, · · · 108 F10 Proludium 8
And with the flame · · · 121 F14 Sydney 56
All his blood should be a flame · · · 141 U2 Her man 30
And in his Mrs. flame, playing like a flye, · · · 149 U8 Houre-glasse 7
And on them burne so chaste a flame, · · · 173 U22 Elegy Tho 21
Or urge thy Greedie flame, thus to devoure · · · 202 U43 Vulcan 3
Or beg thy Greedie flame, thus to devoure · · · 202 U43 Vulcan V 3
But all so cleare, and led by reasons flame, · · · 220 U47 Tribe 69
Their weapons shot out, with that flame, and force, · · · 233 U59 Newcastle 11
Their weapons darted, with that flame, and force, · · · 233 U59 Newcastle V 11

FLAME (cont.)
  Offended with the dazeling flame . . . . . . 234 U60 La-ware 9
  Since nothing can report that flame, ... 278 U84 Mind 15
  Since nothing can report her flame, ... 278 U84 Mind V 15
FLAMES
  Of many a Sylvane, taken with his flames. . . . 94 F2 Penshurst 16
  (Whose heart in that bright Sphere flames clearest, . . 179 U25 Desmond 54
  His shafts, his Quiver, and his Bow, . . 182 U28 Worth 10
  Thou then hadst had some colour for thy flames, . . 204 U43 Vulcan 40
  Looke how the starres from earth, or seas from flames . . 422 Lucan 7
FLAMESHIP
  Pox on your flameship, Vulcan; if it be . . . 211 U43 Vulcan 191
FLAMING
  And in his Mrs. flaming, playing like a flye, . . 149 U8 Houre-glasse V 7
FLAMMES
  Or Eteostichs, or those finer flammes . . . 204 U43 Vulcan 36
  Or else Acrosticks, or those finer flammes . . 204 U43 Vulcan V 36
FLANCK'D
  Flanck'd with a Ditch, and forc'd out of a Marish, . . 209 U43 Vulcan 134
FLAT
  Your change of Notes, the flat, the meane, the sharpe, . . 263 U79 New-yeares 3
  Oft-times a Sharpe, when we require a Flat: . . 329 Horace 523
  No faith's more firme, or flat, then where't doth creep. . 413 Ghyrlond 20
FLATTER
  Let thousands more goe flatter vice, and winne, . . 99 F3 Wroth 85
  To flatter my good Lord, and cry his Bowle . . 167 U15 Friend-Wars 147
FLATTER'D
  Thou flattered'st thine, mine cannot flatter'd bee. . . 38 E36 Martial 4
FLATTERED'ST
  Thou flattered'st thine, mine cannot flatter'd bee. . . 38 E36 Martial 4
FLATTERER
  As a poore single flatterer, without Baud, . . 167 U15 Friend-Wars 158
  Wise-crafts, on which the flatterer ventures not. . . 241 U69 Friend Son 6
FLATTERERS
  Light thee from hell on earth: where flatterers, spies, . . 167 U15 Friend-Wars 163
  His flatterers to their gaine. But say, he can . . 333 Horace 601
FLATTERIE
  From servile flatterie (common Poets shame) . . 41 E43 Salisbury 1 11
  Of flatterie to thy titles. Nor of wit. . . . 47 E64 Salisbury 3 8
  Which (would the world not mis-call't flatterie) . 79 E125 Uvedale 9
FLATTERIES
  Most thinke all praises flatteries. But truth brings . 49 E67 Suffolk 2
  Bought Flatteries, the issue of his purse, . . 162 U15 Friend-Wars 13
  To sordid flatteries, acts of strife, . . . 244 U70 Ode 39
FLATTERY
  Though now of flattery, as of picture, are . . 242 U69 Friend Son 21
FLATTERYE
  And Flatterye, with Frindes humors: still to move. . . 422 Censure 20
FLATT'RER
  So doth the flatt'rer with faire cunning strike . . 242 U69 Friend Son 14
FLATT'RIE
  Throughout, might flatt'rie seeme; and to be mute . 58 E91 Vere 10
FLATT'RING
  You know (without my flatt'ring you) too much . . 157 U13 Sacvile 155
  Ne knowes he flatt'ring Colours, or false light. . . 227 U52 Answer 21
FLATTRY'
  Pardon his Lordship. Flattry's growne so cheape . . 167 U15 Friend-Wars 155
  As flatt'ry with friends humours still to move. . . 190 U37 Friend-Book 27
  Nor flatt'ry! but secur'd, by the Authors Name, . . 401 Beaumont 19
FLATTRY'S
  Pardon his Lordship. Flattry's growne so cheape . . 167 U15 Friend-Wars 155
FLAW
  Being over-safe, and fearing of the flaw: . . . 339 Horace V 41/ 39
FLEA
  Then can a flea at twise skip i'the Map. . . . 69 E107 Hungry 18
FLEAD
  Cats there lay divers had beene flead, and rosted, . . 88 E133 Voyage 149
FLED
  The Virgin, long-since fled from earth, I see, . . 52 E74 Chancelor 9
  For since, what ignorance, what pride is fled! . . 73 E113 Overbury 7
  With which he fled me: and againe, . . . 93 F1 Why write no 8
  When Love is fled, and I grow old. . . 93 F1 Why write no 12
  That fled his cage, or broke his chaine, . . 101 F4 To the World 30
  Are fled and gone, . . . 120 F14 Sydney 19
  Friendship is now mask'd Hatred! Justice fled, . . 163 U15 Friend-Wars 39
  Nor markes of wealth so from our Nation fled, . . 213 U44 Speach 12
  I hold thee fast! but fled hence, with the Light, . . 293 U86 Hor.4:1 38
FLEE
  As farre as he can flee, or follow day, . . . 163 U15 Friend-Wars V 29
  I'le bid thee looke no more, but flee, flee friend, . . 166 U15 Friend-Wars 129
  In secret places, flee the public baths. . . 349 Horace V424
  whom thou seest happy; wretches flee as foes: . . 422 Lucan 6
FLEECE
  Foole, as if halfe eyes will not know a fleece . . 45 E56 Poet-Ape 13
  As it were spun by nature, off the fleece: . . 415 Rutter 18
FLEECED
  The mowed meddowes, with the fleeced sheepe. . . 97 F3 Wroth 39
FLEECES
  Our milke. Our fells. Our fleeces. and first Lambs. . 264 U79 New-yeares 16
  Your Milkes, your Fells, your Fleeces, and first Lambes, . 265 U79 New-yeares 50
FLEES
  But flees the Barre and Courts, with the proud bords, . . 289 U85 Country 7

FLEET (SWIFT)
Bouts of fleet waters, that doe intertwine · · · · 338 Horace V 21
FLEET (NAME)
Your Fleet-lane Furies; and hot cookes doe dwell, · · · 88 E133 Voyage 143
And out-cryes of the damned in the Fleet? · · · · 88 E133 Voyage 172
FLEET
Some hopes of Spaine in their West-Indian Fleet? · · · 219 U47 Tribe 34
The whole fleet wreck'd? a great jarre to be shap'd, · · 305 Horace 28
And stradling shews the Boyes Brown paper fleet, · · · 407 Inigo Jones 2 17
FLEETE
His body to the Counters, or the Fleete? · · · · 165 U15 Friend-Wars 105
His body to the compters, or the Fleete? · · · · 165 U15 Friend-Wars V105
FLEET-LANE
Your Fleet-lane Furies; and hot cookes doe dwell, · · · 88 E133 Voyage 143
FLESH
A lord, it cryed, buried in flesh, and blood, · · · 30 E11 Something 5
And noted for what flesh such soules were fram'd, · · · 66 E103 L Wroth 1 3
And that thy soule should give thy flesh her weight. · · 70 E109 Nevil 14
Upon my flesh t'inflict another wound. · · · · 122 F15 Heaven 22
By sinne, and Sathan; and my flesh misus'd, · · · 127 U1 Trinitie 6
The Word was now made Flesh indeed, · · · · 130 U1 Nativitie 17
To catch the flesh in, and to pound a Prick. · · · 164 U15 Friend-Wars 67
Of putrid flesh alive! of blood, the sinke! · · · 172 U21 Ltl Shrub 9
To fetch the flesh, we keepe the Rowle. · · · · 188 U35 Chute 6
In man, because man hath the flesh abus'd. · · · 192 U38 Elegy 'Tis 66
To have her captiv'd spirit freed from flesh, · · · 285 U84 Muse 93
The smallest Fibre of our flesh; he can · · · · 286 U84 Muse 151
these only hide part of my flesh, and bones: · · · 387 Cavendish 2
And when the flesh, here, shut up day, · · · · 400 Lady Ogle 27
FLESHES
To have so soone scap'd worlds, and fleshes rage, · · · 41 E45 First Son 7
Expected with the fleshes restitution. · · · · 283 U84 Muse 50
Her soule possest her fleshes state · · · · 399 Lady Ogle 25
FLESHLY
This grave partakes the fleshly birth. · · · · 34 E22 Daughter 11
FLETCHER
An ancient pur-blinde fletcher, with a high nose; · · 89 E133 Voyage 190
To the worthy Author M. John Fletcher. · · · · 370 Fletcher Ttl
FLEW
And all the Evils that flew out of her box · · · 212 U43 Vulcan 214
And all Those ills that flew out of her box · · · 212 U43 Vulcan V214
FLIE
Whom should my Muse then flie to, but the best · · · 28 E4 James 1 9
May others feare, flie, and traduce thy name, · · · 32 E17 Critic 1
That flie my thoughts betweene, · · · · 149 U9 Picture 12
Unto the Censure. Yours all need doth flie · · · 158 U14 Selden 11
Not flie the Crime, but the Suspition too: · · · 159 U14 Selden 18
As farre as he can flie, or follow day, · · · · 163 U15 Friend-Wars 29
Friend, flie from hence; and let these kindled rimes · · 167 U15 Friend-Wars 162
Pegasus did flie away, · · · · 183 U29 Fit of Rime 19
Still flie about the Odour of your Name; · · · · 186 U31 Elsmere 8
A man should flie from, as he would disdaine. · · · 194 U38 Elegy 'Tis 104
Where he that knowes will, like a Lapwing, flie · · 198 U40 Elegy That 37
I could say more of such, but that I flie · · · · 218 U47 Tribe 5
His Nephews entrailes; nor must Progne flie · · · 317 Horace 266
FLIES (NOUN)
Cloth Spices, or guard sweet meates from the flies; · · 205 U43 Vulcan V 53
Like flies, or wormes, with mans corrupt parts fed: · · 218 U47 Tribe 18
FLIES
Not he that flies the court for want of clothes, · · · 76 E119 Shelton 1
Follow a shaddow, it still flies you; · · · · 104 F7 Women but 1
But high, and noble matter, such as flies · · · · 116 F12 Rutland 89
That doth but touch his flower, and flies away. · · · 139 U2 Another 6
Lest Ayre, or Print, but flies it: Such men would · · 154 U13 Sacvile 45
It rages, runs, flies, stands, and would provoke · · 283 U84 Muse 24
FLIGHT
Shee doth instruct men by her gallant flight, · · · 55 E85 Goodyere 1 5
In autumne, at the Partrich makes a flight, · · · 97 F3 Wroth 27
Or put to flight Astrea, when her ingots · · · · 114 F12 Rutland 24
After flight; and put new stings · · · · 137 U2 Cupid 36
Have made their fairest flight, · · · · 180 U26 Ode High 7
But weary of that flight, · · · · 244 U70 Ode 37
It moveth all; and makes a flight · · · · 279 U84 Mind 31
All; So this grievous Writer puts to flight · · · 337 Horace 676
How faire a flight he makes! · · · · 366 Ode Who saith 10
From whose prowde bosome, thou began'st thy flight. · · 368 Ode Who saith 80
Which, since thy flight from hence, hath mourn'd like night, · 392 Shakespeare 79
And flight about the Ile, well neare, by this, · · 397 Drayton 49
FLIGHTS
And make those flights upon the bankes of Thames, · · 392 Shakespeare 73
FLING
And ('bout thy Ivory neck,) no youth did fling · · · 293 U87 Hor.3:9 2
FLIT
Against their breasts. Here, sev'rall ghosts did flit · · 87 E133 Voyage 124
FLOCK
That have a Flock, or Herd, upon these plaines; · · · 265 U79 New-yeares 47
That penning the glad flock in hurdles by, · · · 291 U85 Country 45
FLOCKS
That leades our flocks and us, and calls both forth · · 264 U79 New-yeares 29
Of the fed flocks approaching home! · · · · 291 U85 Country 62
FLOOD
Then the various Moone the flood! · · · · 136 U2 Cupid 4
He, that in such a flood, as we are in · · · · 234 U61 Epigram 16

			Page	Title	Line

FLOOD (cont.)
Meeting of Graces, that so swell'd the flood . . . 274 U84 Descent 10
As nature could not more increase the flood . . . 287 U84 Muse 158
And number Attributes unto a flood: . . . . 394 Jane Ogle 6

FLOODS
Saw all his race approch the blacker floods: . . . 41 E44 Chuff 4
To stay the running floods, . . . 143 U3 Musicall 10
That they may take it eccho'd by the Floods. . . . 265 U79 New-yeares 53
Whilst from the higher Bankes doe slide the floods; . . 290 U85 Country 25
If with bright floods, the Winter troubled much, . . 291 U85 Country 51
If with East floods, the Winter troubled much, . . 291 U85 Country V 51
A Dolphin, and a Boare amid' the floods. . . . 307 Horace 42

FLOORE
So well! as when I saw the floore, and Roome, . . 228 U53 Newcastle 17
So well! as when I view'd the floore, and Roome, . . 228 U53 Newcastle V 17
On the same floore, ... 254 U75 Epithalam. 70

FLORA
You were the bright Oenone, Flora, or May? . . 68 E105 L Wroth 2 10

FLORENCE
What at Ligorne, Rome, Florence you did doe: . . . 69 E107 Hungry 14

FLOUD
The ever-boyling floud. Whose bankes upon . . . 88 E133 Voyage 142
In the full floud of her admir'd perfection? . . . 112 F11 Epode 107
Smooth, soft, and sweet, in all a floud . . . 280 U84 Mind 61

FLOURISH
Scarce the Hill againe doth flourish, . . . 184 U29 Fit of Rime 37

FLOURISHING
Or some hot youth, yet in his flourishing course; . . 313 Horace 163

FLOURISHT
When her looke out-flourisht May: . . . . 132 U2 How he saw 2

FLOW
The neede of such? whose liberall boord doth flow, . . 95 F2 Penshurst 59
How to tell' hem, as they flow, . . . 103 F6 Celia 2 20
T'advance his doubtfull issue, and ore-flow . . 117 F13 Aubigny 40
That to such Natures let their full hands flow, . . 154 U13 Sacvile 60
And all beatitudes, that thence doe flow: . . . 271 U81 Pawlet 75
Flow my thin teares, downe these pale cheeks of mine? . 293 U86 Hor.4:1 34
Obscure. This, striving to run smooth, and flow, . . 307 Horace 36
If now the phrase of him that speakes, shall flow, . . 313 Horace 158
I feele it by mine owne, that over flow, . . . 398 Drayton 77
Truth itself doth flow in Wine. . . . . 657 Door Apollo 6

FLOWE
The milke, nor oyle, did ever flowe soe free . . . 98 F3 Wroth V 60

FLOWER
That doth but touch his flower, and flies away. . . 139 U2 Another 6
Or winds the Spirit, by which the flower so grew? . . 192 U38 Elegy 'Tis 58
In all her bloome, and flower; . . . 253 U75 Epithalam. 23
And to the Touch, a Flower, like soft as Palme. . . 286 U84 Muse 126
Thou worthy in eternall Flower to fare, . . . 294 U89 Mart.8:77 ' 2
The seaven-fold flower of Arte (more rich then gold) . 361 Palmer 15

FLOWERS
Then hath thy orchard fruit, thy garden flowers, . . 94 F2 Penshurst 39
And lasting, as her flowers: . . . 111 F11 Epode 58
Then when flowers, and West-winds meet, . . . 137 U2 Cupid 28
On all mens Fruit, and flowers, as well as mine. . . 150 U10 Jealousie 8
This Prince of flowers? Soone shoot thou up, and grow 237 U65 Prince 5
(Lillies and Roses, Flowers of either Sexe) . . 254 U75 Epithalam. 58
As if her ayrie steps did spring the flowers, . . 254 U75 Epithalam. 67
The fairest flowers are alwayes found; . . . 264 U79 New-yeares 37
The better grasse, and flowers are found. . . . 265 U79 New-yeares 59
Upon a banke, or field of flowers, . . . 280 U84 Mind 67
Or with fresh flowers to girt my temple round. . . 293 U86 Hor.4:1 32
When late (grave Palmer) these thy graffs and flowers 361 Palmer 1
The Eye of flowers, worthy, for his scent, . . 413 Ghyrlond 14
Our first of fruits, that is the prime of flowers . 416 Welcome 2

FLOWES
Flowes in upon me, and I cannot raise . . . 160 U14 Selden 62
Thither it flowes. How much did Stallion spend . . 163 U15 Friend-Wars 47
But flowes out, that ore-swelleth in full brests. . . 329 Horace 506
Flowes from the surfets which we take in peace. . . 363 Peace 4

FLOWING
And like Nectar ever flowing: . . . 39 E40 Ratcliffe 10
The full, the flowing graces there enshrin'd; . . . 79 E125 Uvedale 8
My flowing numbers to thy golden Lyre: . . . 177 U25 Desmond V 9

FLOWNE
All good Poetrie hence was flowne, . . . 183 U29 Fit of Rime 14
Who (see) already hath ore-flowne . . . 368 Ode Who saith 65

FLOWRE
Hay! for the flowre of France! . . . 240 U67 Muses 42
It was the Plant, and flowre of light. . . . 245 U70 Ode 72

FLOWRIE
Of flowrie fields, of cop'ces greene, . . . 97 F3 Wroth 38

FLOWRY
As, on two flowry Carpets, that did rise, . . . 398 Drayton 81

FLUNG
She durst not kisse, but flung thee from her brest. . 208 U43 Vulcan 114

FLUSHING (See also VLUSHING)
From Venice to Flushing, were not they well cobled? . 380 Coryat 3 42
And being at Flushing enforced to feele . . 380 Coryat 3 54

FLUTE
And Phrygian Hau'boy, not without the Flute. . . 292 U86 Hor.4:1 24

FLY (See also FLIE)
But fly thee, like the Pest! Walke not the street . . 409 Detractor 19

		Page	Title	Line
FLYE (NOUN)				
Where, afterwards, it grew a butter-flye:	• • • •	31	E15 Court-worm	3
And in his Mrs. flame, playing like a flye,	• • • •	149	U8 Houre-glasse	7
And in his Mrs. flaming, playing like a flye,	• • • •	149	U8 Houre-glasse V	7
FLYE				
What is't, fine Grand, makes thee my friendship flye,	• •	51	E73 Fine Grand	1
Seeme to flye it, it will pursue:	• • •	104	F7 Women but	2
Though thy wild thoughts with sparrowes wings doe flye,	•	111	F11 Epode	73
And flye to touch him, as a man that were	• • •	354	Horace	V644
FLYES				
The Lybian Lion hunts noe butter flyes,	• • •	408	Inigo Jones 3	7
FLYING				
And, in the winter, hunt'st the flying hare,	• • •	97	F3 Wroth	29
Or in the winter, hunt'st the flying hare,	• • •	97	F3 Wroth V	29
He flying curles, and crispeth, with his wings;	• •	170	U19 Elegy By	6
Were Cycnus, once high flying	• • •	369	Ode Who saith	99
Horse, foote, and all but flying in the ayre:	• • •	380	Coryat 3	28
FOAME				
That thou hast lost thy noyse, thy foame, thy stirre,	•	408	Detractor	8
FOE				
Against thy fortune: when no foe, that day,	• •	49	E66 Cary	9
I'am more asham'd to have thee thought my foe.	• •	53	E77 Not name	4
FOES				
Her foes enough would fame thee in their hate.	• •	40	E43 Salisbury 1	4
Nor that his worke liv'd in the hands of foes,	• •	71	E110 Edmonds 1	9
Such shall you heare to day, and find great foes,	• •	186	U32 Elsmere	7
Troubled both foes, and friends:	• • •	243	U70 Ode	28
It brings Friends Joy, Foes Griefe, Posteritie Fame;	•	256	U75 Epithalam.	114
To style us Friends, who were, by Nature, Foes?	•	256	U75 Epithalam.	114
May hurt them more with praise, then Foes with spight.	•	286	U84 Muse	139
whom thou seest happy; wretches flee as foes:	•	386	Browne	2
whom thou seest happy; wretches, shun, as foes:	•	422	Lucan	6
FOILED				V 6
But rests foiled.	• • • • •	184	U29 Fit of Rime	36
FOIST				
And that is when it is the Lord Maiors foist.	• •	87	E133 Voyage	120
FOLD				
Set a Horse-neck, and divers feathers fold	• •	305	Horace	2
A horse neck joyn, & sundry plumes ore-fold	• •	338	Horace V	2
The seaven-fold flower of Arte (more rich then gold)	•	361	Palmer	15
Which, chang'd, a five-fold mysterie designe,	• •	412	Ghyrlond	2
Till he hath reach'd his two-fold point of Noone.	• •	414	Ghyrlond	52
FOLDS				
Oylie Expansions, or shrunke durtie folds,	• •	220	U47 Tribe	68
Hee drives diseases from our Folds,	• • •	265	U79 New-yeares	62
FOLKE				
The rout of rurall folke come thronging in,	• •	98	F3 Wroth	53
Great, brave, and fashion'd folke, these are allow'd	•	164	U15 Friend-Wars	84
One Poet, then of other folke ten score.	• •	235	U62 Charles 1	10
Chaste, thriftie, modest folke, that came to view.	•	319	Horace	294
Wise, sober folke, a franick Poet feare,	• •	335	Horace	643
FOLKES				
Or robbing the poore Market-folkes should nurse	•	155	U13 Sacvile	90
FOLLIES				
Let the poore fooles enjoy their follies, love	• •	202	U42 Elegy Let	81
On such my serious follies; But, thou'lt say,	• •	204	U43 Vulcan	41
Or such my serious follies; But, thou'lt say,	• •	204	U43 Vulcan V	41
FOLLOW				
Whither the world must follow. And I, now,	• •	37	E33 Roe 3	3
Where I both learn'd, why wise-men hawking follow,	•	55	E85 Goodyere 1	3
They follow vertue, for reward, to day;	• •	66	E102 Pembroke	9
Who'in such ambition can but follow thee.	• •	73	E113 Overbury	12
While all, that follow, their glad eares apply	• •	97	F3 Wroth	31
Follow a shadow, it still flies you;	• • •	104	F7 Women but	1
Let who will follow fashions, and attyres,	• •	118	F13 Aubigny	71
As farre as he can flie, or follow day,	• •	163	U15 Friend-Wars	29
As farre as he can flee, or follow day,	• •	163	U15 Friend-Wars V	29
He that will follow but anothers wife,	• •	165	U15 Friend-Wars	87
So may the Muses follow	• • •	221	U48 Bacchus	25
With all the fruit shall follow it,	• • •	251	U74 Weston	23
Or Tybers winding streames, I follow thee.	• •	293	U86 Hor.4:1	40
Or follow fame, thou that dost write, or faine	• •	313	Horace	169
There words will follow, not against their will.	• •	325	Horace	444
There words will never follow 'gainst their will.	• •	349	Horace	V444
They vexe, and follow him with shouts, and noise,	•	335	Horace	648
They vexe, and carelesse follow him with noise.	•	354	Horace	V648
In vaine to follow:	• • • •	366	Ode Who saith	14
To follow Goodnesse, by our owne discerning	• •	412	Sutcliffe	17
Of Finenesse, and alloy: follow his hint,	• •	415	Rutter	27
Welcome all, who lead or follow,	• • •	657	Door Apollo	1
Welcome all, who lead or follow,	• • •	657	Door Apollo	19
FOLLOW'D				
Say you have follow'd farre,	• • •	121	F14 Sydney	45
With him, for he is follow'd with that heape	• •	167	U15 Friend-Wars	156
FOLLOWERS				
And all his followers, that had so abus'd him:	• •	86	E133 Voyage	97
FOLLOWING				
Well, or ill, onely, all the following yeere,	• •	113	F12 Rutland	7
FOLLY				
Would both thy folly, and thy spite betray.	• •	43	E52 Courtling	6
No stubbornnesse so stiffe, nor folly	• •	152	U12 Corbet	24
And only pitious scorne, upon their folly waites.	•	175	U23 Himselfe	24
Errour and folly in me may have crost	• •	192	U38 Elegy 'Tis	37

	Page	Title	Line

FOLLY (cont.)
And never be by time, or folly brought, ... 198 U40 Elegy That 44
FOND
No more, I am sorry for so fond cause, say, . . . 171 U20 Shrub 4
FONDLY
Too patiently, that I not fondly say; . . . . 323 Horace 401
FOOD
If thy leanenesse love such food, . . . 105 F8 Sicknesse 24
Not letting goe his hold, where he drawes food, . . . 337 Horace 679
Not letting goe the skin, where he drawes food, . . . 355 Horace V679
FOOL
Keep in thy barking Wit, thou bawling Fool? . . . 410 Gill 8
FOOLE
Stile thee a most great foole, but no great man. . 36 E28 Surly 22
Foole, as if halfe eyes will not know a fleece . . 45 E56 Poet-Ape 13
To Foole, or Knave. . . . . . . 46 E61 Foole Ttl
Till they be sure to make the foole their quarrie. . . 55 E85 Goodyere 1 10
When Mill first came to court, the unprofiting foole, . 57 E90 Mill 1
But I, no child, no foole, respect the kinde, . . 79 E125 Uvedale 7
Some vicious foole draw neare, . . . 111 F11 Epode 66
The foole that gave it; who will want, and weepe, . . 113 F12 Rutland 13
The foole that gave it; that will want, and weepe, . . 113 F12 Rutland V 13
I foole-hardie, there up-tooke . . . . 132 U2 How he saw 20
And his Title be long foole, . . . 184 U29 Fit of Rime 58
No Foole would his owne harvest spoile, or burne! . . 209 U43 Vulcan 150
Foole, wilt thou let that in example come? . . 210 U43 Vulcan 161
A mornings, and at afternoones, to foole . . 230 U56 Covell 22
Foole, doe not rate my Rymes; I'have found thy Vice . . 408 Detractor 5
FOOLE-HARDIE
I foole-hardie, there up-tooke . . . . 132 U2 How he saw 20
FOOLES
This but thy judgement fooles: the other way . . . 43 E52 Courtling 5
They should be fooles, for me, at their owne charge. . . 83 E131 Ferrab. 2 8
That onely fooles make thee a saint, . . . 100 F4 To the World 15
Where breathe the basest of thy fooles; . . . 101 F4 To the World 46
And, in those outward formes, all fooles are wise. . . 117 F13 Aubigny 36
The fooles, or Tyrants with your friends, . . . 145 U5 Woman-kind 2
Hang up those dull, and envious fooles, . . . 146 U6 Defence 1
So fooles, we see, . . . 179 U25 Desmond 51
The ignorant, and fooles, no pittie have. . . 191 U38 Elegy 'Tis 20
What Fooles, and all their Parasites can apply; . . 193 U38 Elegy 'Tis 94
That are like cloath'd: must I be of those fooles . 201 U42 Elegy Let 48
Let the poore fooles enjoy their follies, love . . 202 U42 Elegy Let 81
Or moathes shall eate, what all these Fooles admire. . . 371 Fletcher 16
FOOLING
Mirth, fooling, nor wit, ... 231 U57 Burges 17
FOOLISH
Wretched and foolish Jealousie, ... 150 U10 Jealousie 1
Forgive me this one foolish deadly sin, . . . 171 U20 Shrub 2
FOORTH
did sparcle foorth in Center of the rest: . . . . 361 Palmer 16
my abler faculties; and thus brake foorth . . 362 Palmer 29
FOOT
And like a Compasse keeping one foot still . . 159 U14 Selden 31
Coach'd, or on foot-cloth, thrice chang'd every day, . 165 U15 Friend-Wars 107
that from the Foot-man, when he was become . . 201 U42 Elegy Let 52
Or Captaine Pamphlets horse, and foot, that sallie . 206 U43 Vulcan 79
Oure Captaine Pamphlets horse, and foot, that sallie . 206 U43 Vulcan V 79
Condemne him to the Brick-kills, or some Hill-/foot . . 211 U43 Vulcan 183
Condemne him to some Brick-hills, or some Hill-/foot . . 211 U43 Vulcan V183
Hill-/foot (out in Sussex) to an iron Mill; . . 211 U43 Vulcan 184
Hill-/foot (out in Sussex) to some iron Mill; . . 211 U43 Vulcan V184
As neither head, nor foot, one forme retaine. . . 305 Horace 10
This foot the socks tooke up, and buskins grave, . . 311 Horace 118
Their bombard-phrase, and foot-and-halfe-foot words. . . 311 Horace 139
Forbids thee forth againe thy foot to draw. . . 313 Horace 194
A foot, whose swiftnesse gave the Verse the name . . 323 Horace 372
This foot yet, in the famous Trimeters . . . 323 Horace 381
FOOT-AND-HALFE-FOOT
Their bombard-phrase, and foot-and-halfe-foot words. . . 311 Horace 139
FOOT-CLOTH
Coach'd, or on foot-cloth, thrice chang'd every day, . . 165 U15 Friend-Wars 107
FOOTE
Or Captaine Pamphletts, which on foote doe sally . . . 206 U43 Vulcan V 79
Horse, foote, and all but flying in the ayre: . . 380 Coryat 3 28
Of his foote, or his penne, his braine or his hoofe, . . 380 Coryat 3 32
FOOT-MAN
that from the Foot-man, when he was become . . 201 U42 Elegy Let 52
FOR'
For'his whore: Groyne doth still occupy his land. . . 75 E117 Groyne 2
FOR
It will be look'd for, booke, when some but see . . . 27 E2 My Booke 1
For vulgar praise, doth it too dearely buy. . . 27 E2 My Booke 14
For the lucks sake, it thus much favour have, . . 27 E3 Bookseller 4
For termers, or some clarke-like serving-man, . . 28 E3 Bookseller 9
For such a Poet, while thy dayes were greene, . . 28 E4 James 1 5
Of Kings for grace; of Poets for my test? . . . 28 E4 James 1 10
But, for this money was a courtier found, . . 29 E8 Robbery 3
For strict degrees of ranke, or title looke: . . 29 E9 To All 2
For I will doe none: and as little ill, . . . 30 E11 Something 7
For I will dare none. Good Lord, walke dead still. . . 30 E11 Something 8
Then takes up fresh commoditie, for dayes; . . 30 E12 Shift 13
Calls for his stoole, adornes the stage: god payes. . . 30 E12 Shift 18

FOR (cont.)

	Page	Title	Line
Thus: and for his letcherie, scores, god payes.	31	E12 Shift	22
But for their powers, accept my pietie.	31	E14 Camden	14
Nor need'st thou: for those few, by oath releast,	32	E16 Brain-hardy	7
Charge them, for crowne, to thy sole censure hye.	32	E17 Critic	4
Thou saist, that cannot be: for thou hast seene	32	E18 Censurer	3
Mens manners ne're were viler, for your sake.	34	E24 Parliament	2
In varied shapes, which for his lust shee takes:	34	E25 Beast 1	6
Wee, sad for him, may glorie, and not sinne.	35	E27 Roe 1	8
Nay more, for greatnesse sake, he will be one	36	E28 Surly	19
For thy late sharpe device. I say 'tis fit	36	E29 Tilter	3
For then, our water-conduits doe runne wine;	36	E29 Tilter	5
His monyes travaile for him, in and out;	36	E31 Banck	2
And since, the whole land was preserv'd for thee.	38	E35 James 2	10
And pleaseth both. For while he melts his greace	38	E37 Chev'ril	3
For this: that winnes, for whom he holds his peace.	38	E37 Chev'ril	4
For all night-sinnes, with others wives, unknowne,	39	E39 Colt	1
Marble, weepe, for thou dost cover	39	E40 Ratcliffe	1
For wit, feature, and true passion,	39	E40 Ratcliffe	16
For what shee gave, a whore; a baud, shee cures.	39	E41 Gypsee	4
Ere blacks were bought for his owne funerall,	41	E44 Chuff	3
O, could I loose all father, now. For why	41	E45 First Son	5
For whose sake, hence-forth, all his vowes be such,	41	E45 First Son	11
Sir Lucklesse, troth, for lucks sake passe by one:	42	E47 Luckless 2	1
His bought armes Mung' not lik'd; for his first day	42	E48 Mungril	1
For wittie, in his language, is obscene.	42	E49 Playwrt 1	4
Arsenike would thee fit for societie make.	42	E50 Cod 3	3
For we, that have our eyes still in our eares,	43	E51 James 3	9
For, but thy selfe, where, out of motly, 's hee	44	E53 Old-end	9
For writing better, I must envie thee.	44	E55 Beaumont	10
For offring, with thy smiles, my wit to grace,	45	E58 Groome	3
And, hood-wink'd, for a man, embrace a post.	45	E58 Groome	8
But thine, for which I doo't, so much exceeds!	46	E60 Mounteagle	8
Nor glad for fashion. Nor to shew a fit	47	E64 Salisbury 3	7
For worth he has not, He is tax'd, not prais'd.	48	E65 Muse	16
Hee's valiant'st, that dares fight, and not for pay;	49	E66 Cary	17
In-primis, Grand, you owe me for a jest,	51	E73 Fine Grand	5
Item, a faire greeke poesie for a ring;	51	E73 Fine Grand	10
Item, a gulling imprese for you, at tilt.	51	E73 Fine Grand	15
For which, or pay me quickly', or Ile pay you.	51	E73 Fine Grand	22
For, if thou shame, ranck'd with my friends, to goe,	53	E77 Not name	3
Hornet, thou hast thy wife drest, for the stall,	53	E78 Hornet	1
For good men but see death, the wicked tast it.	54	E80 Life/Death	8
For all thou hear'st, thou swear'st thy selfe didst doo.	54	E81 Proule	5
For your most noble offer had supply'd me.	54	E84 Bedford 2	4
Blowne up; and he (too'unwieldie for that place)	57	E90 Mill	14
And what each prince doth for intelligence owe,	59	E92 New Crie	12
For twelve yeeres yet to come, what each state lacks.	59	E92 New Crie	14
They all get Porta, for the sundrie wayes	59	E92 New Crie	25
Or 'gainst the Bishops, for the Brethren, raile,	59	E92 New Crie	35
For the great marke of vertue, those being gone	60	E93 Radcliffe	2
For none ere tooke that pleasure in sinnes sense,	60	E94 Bedford 3	9
Dare for these poemes, yet, both aske, and read,	60	E94 Bedford 3	12
For who can master those great parts like thee,	61	E95 Savile	17
My title's seal'd. Those that for claps doe write,	62	E96 Donne 2	9
Nor baudie stock, that travells for encrease,	63	E97 Motion	10
And I must now beleeve him: for, to day,	64	E100 Playwrt 3	3
Something, which, else, could hope for no esteeme.	64	E101 Supper	6
Limons, and wine for sauce: to these, a coney	65	E101 Supper	13
Is not to be despair'd of, for our money;	65	E101 Supper	14
They follow vertue, for reward, to day;	66	E102 Pembroke	1
And noted for what flesh such soules were fram'd,	66	E103 L Wroth 1	3
For every part a character assign'd.	67	E103 L Wroth 1	12
Or, more then borne for the comparison	67	E104 Montgomery	9
A picture, which the world for yours must know,	67	E104 Montgomery	14
If not, 'tis fit for you, some should envy.	67	E104 Montgomery	14
There's none so dull, that for your stile would aske,	68	E105 L Wroth 2	15
If men get name, for some one vertue: Then,	68	E106 E Herbert	1
Doe what you come for, Captayne, with your newes;	68	E107 Hungry	1
For which there must more sea, and land be leap'd,	69	E107 Hungry	16
For newes) your Ville-royes, and Silleries,	69	E107 Hungry	21
For your next meale: this you are sure of. Why	69	E107 Hungry	27
Doe what you come for, Captayne, There's your meate.	69	E107 Hungry	32
But 's angry for the Captayne, still: is such.	70	E108 Soldiers	10
Whil'st others toyle for titles to their tombes.	70	E109 Nevil	18
The name of Pompey for an enemie,	71	E110 Edmonds 1	3
For, where his person liv'd scarce one just age,	71	E110 Edmonds 1	13
I cannot for the stage a Drama lay,	72	E112 Gamster	7
That both for wit, and sense, so oft dost plucke,	73	E112 Gamster	18
Nor scarce dost colour for it, which is lesse.	73	E112 Gamster	20
For since, what ignorance, what pride is fled!	73	E113 Overbury	7
For Cupid, who (at first) tooke vaine delight,	73	E114 Sydney	3
Not he that flies the court for want of clothes,	76	E119 Shelton	1
Shuns prease, for two maine causes, poxe, and debt,	76	E119 Shelton	4
And know, for whom a teare you shed,	77	E120 S. P.	3
But, being so much too good for earth,	77	E120 S. P.	23
Nor he, for friendship, to be thought unfit,	78	E121 Rudyerd 1	7
If I would wish, for truth, and not for show,	78	E122 Rudyerd 2	1
Made for what Nature could, or Vertue can;	79	E125 Uvedale	2
Might love the treasure for the cabinet;	79	E125 Uvedale	6
Through seas, stormes, tempests: and imbarqu'd for hell,	81	E128 Wm Roe 2	13
Men love thee not for this: They laugh at thee.	81	E129 Mime	18
For, then, all mouthes will judge, and their owne way:	82	E131 Ferrab. 2	3

FOR (cont.)

For, if the hum'rous world will talke at large,	83	E131 Ferrab. 2	7
They should be fooles, for me, at their owne charge.	83	E131 Ferrab. 2	8
Even those for whom they doe this, know they erre:	83	E131 Ferrab. 2	10
For fame, with breath soone kindled, soone blowne out.	83	E131 Ferrab. 2	14
That to the world I publish, for him, this;	83	E132 Sylvester	9
And for one Cerberus, the whole coast was dogs.	84	E133 Voyage	14
And, for the cryes of Ghosts, women, and men,	84	E133 Voyage	16
One was; and he, for brawne, and braine, right able	84	E133 Voyage	23
His three for one. Now, lordings, listen well.	84	E133 Voyage	28
For (where he was the god of eloquence,	86	E133 Voyage	99
Yet, one day in the yeere, for sweet 'tis voyc't,	87	E133 Voyage	119
And that ours did. For, yet, no nare was tainted,	87	E133 Voyage	133
For, to say truth, what scullion is so nastie,	88	E133 Voyage	147
For, here they were throwne in wi'the melted pewter,	88	E133 Voyage	153
Being, beyond sea, burned for one witch:	88	E133 Voyage	158
Calling for Radamanthus, that dwelt by,	89	E133 Voyage	187
And I could wish for their eterniz'd sakes,	89	E133 Voyage	195
Thou hast thy walkes for health, as well as sport:	93	F2 Penshurst	9
And, for thy messe, is willing to be kill'd.	94	F2 Penshurst	30
Thy tables hoord not up for the next day,	95	F2 Penshurst	71
For fire, or lights, or livorie: all is there;	95	F2 Penshurst	73
There's nothing I can wish, for which I stay.	95	F2 Penshurst	75
There wasted, some not paid for yet!	97	F3 Wroth	12
In spring, oft roused for thy masters sport,	97	F3 Wroth	23
In spring tyme roused for their masters sport,	97	F3 Wroth	V 23
Who, for it, makes thy house his court;	97	F3 Wroth	24
Who, for it, makes thy lodge his court;	97	F3 Wroth	V 24
More for thy exercise, then fare;	97	F3 Wroth	30
Comus puts in, for new delights;	98	F3 Wroth	48
For every price, in every jarre,	99	F3 Wroth	74
To the World. A farewell for a Gentle-woman,	100	F4 To the World	Ttl
Little, for me, had reason done,	101	F4 To the World	35
But, what we'are borne for, we must beare:	101	F4 To the World	53
From all my kinde: that, for my sake,	101	F4 To the World	59
Nor for my peace will I goe farre,	102	F4 To the World	65
Time will not be ours, for ever:	102	F5 Celia 1	3
There are those, that, for thy sake,	105	F8 Sicknesse	25
Lying for the spirit of amber.	105	F8 Sicknesse	32
That for th'oyle of Talke, dare spend	105	F8 Sicknesse	33
And, for thee, at common game,	105	F8 Sicknesse	41
And, for that, at common game,	105	F8 Sicknesse	V 41
And Ile not looke for wine.	106	F9 Celia 3	4
I would not change for thine.	106	F9 Celia 3	8
For the more countenance to my active Muse?	107	F10 Proludium	3
For the more countenance to our active Muse?	107	F10 Proludium	V 3
to loose, and Cap'ring, for thy stricter veyne.	108	F10 Proludium	2
For either our affections doe rebell,	109	F11 Epode	21
And for their place, and name,	111	F11 Epode	80
He that for love of goodnesse hateth ill,	112	F11 Epode	87
Then he, which for sinnes penaltie forbeares.	112	F11 Epode	89
Then he, that for sinnes penaltie forbeares.	112	F11 Epode	V 89
Whil'st that, for which, all vertue now is sold,	113	F12 Rutland	1
And, for it, life, conscience, yea, soules are given,	113	F12 Rutland	4
For what a sinne 'gainst your great fathers spirit,	114	F12 Rutland	31
Yet, for the timely favours shee hath done,	115	F12 Rutland	71
For I shall move stocks, stones, no lesse then he.	115	F12 Rutland	78
For that firme grace he holdes in your regard,	116	F12 Rutland	95
I, that am gratefull for him, have prepar'd	116	F12 Rutland	96
For others ill, ought none their good forget.	116	F13 Aubigny	6
For their owne cap'tall crimes, t'indite my wit;	117	F13 Aubigny	14
Your beautie; for you see that every day:	117	F13 Aubigny	30
For such a lot! that mixt you with a state	118	F13 Aubigny	48
For he, that once is good, is ever great.	118	F13 Aubigny	52
For truthes complexion, where they all weare maskes.	118	F13 Aubigny	70
Maintayne their liedgers forth, for forraine wyres,	118	F13 Aubigny	72
And call it their brave sinne. For such there be	119	F13 Aubigny	85
That doe sinne onely for the infamie:	119	F13 Aubigny	86
For which you worthy are the glad encrease	119	F13 Aubigny	94
Not fashion'd for the court, or strangers eyes;	119	F13 Aubigny	115
And great, must seeke for new,	121	F14 Sydney	35
For they, that swell	121	F14 Sydney	39
That, laden with my sinnes, I seeke for ease?	122	F15 Heaven	4
And hearts of all, if I be sad for show,	122	F15 Heaven	6
Yet dare I not complaine, or wish for death	122	F15 Heaven	23
For wearinesse of life, not love of thee.	122	F15 Heaven	26
For thy acceptance. O, behold me right,	127	U1 Trinitie	13
For acts of grace.	128	U1 Trinitie	28
Till I attaine the long'd-for mysterie	128	U1 Trinitie	31
For, sin's so sweet,	129	U1 Father	12
1. His Excuse for loving.	131	U2 Excuse	Ttl
All the world for love may die.	131	U2 Excuse	24
For I ran and call'd on Cupid;	132	U2 How he saw	6
Or his courage; for away	132	U2 How he saw	15
Nor for any threat, or call,	132	U2 How he saw	18
For the Apple, and those three	137	U2 Cupid	47
For this Beauty yet doth hide	137	U2 Cupid	49
To have left all sight for you:	138	U2 Kisse	33
For Loves-sake, kisse me once againe,	139	U2 Another	1
For I will so urge you to't,	140	U2 Promise	14
For Loves fingers, and his wings:	141	U2 Her man	12
For he must looke wanton-wise.	141	U2 Her man	16
Drest, you still for man should take him;	141	U2 Her man	38

FOR (cont.)

	Page	Title	Line
For his Mind, I doe not care,	142	U2 Exception	1
Mistaking earth for heaven.	144	U3 Musicall	24
For then their threats will kill me;	144	U4 Song	6
For then my hopes will spill me.	144	U4 Song	8
For so will sorrow slay me;	145	U4 Song	10
Our owne false praises, for your ends:	145	U5 Woman-kind	4
One good enough for a songs sake.	145	U5 Woman-kind	12
For what is better, or to make	146	U6 Defence	14
Familiar, for the uses sake;	146	U6 Defence	16
For were the worthiest woman curst	146	U6 Defence	23
For if the Nymphs should know my Swaine,	147	U7 Nymph	3
For that's a narrow joy is but our owne.	147	U7 Nymph	7
on a lovers dust, made sand for ane Houre Glasse	148	U8 Houre-glasse VTtl	
For else it could not be,	149	U9 Picture	2
Nor will he tell me for whose sake	151	U11 Dreame	7
For I both lost a friend and Father,	151	U12 Corbet	5
That they for me their teares will shed;	152	U12 Corbet	34
For truly, since he left to be,	152	U12 Corbet	35
For benefits are ow'd with the same mind	153	U13 Sacvile	5
Can I owe thankes, for Curtesies receiv'd	153	U13 Sacvile	25
But by meere Chance? for interest? or to free	154	U13 Sacvile	30
Must make me sad for what I have obtain'd.	154	U13 Sacvile	38
For what they streight would to the world forsweare;	154	U13 Sacvile	50
Lowd sacrifice of drinke, for their health-sake!	156	U13 Sacvile	100
For me to be your Indice. Keep you such,	157	U13 Sacvile	156
Lesse shall I for the Art or dressing care,	158	U14 Selden	3
That gaspe for action, and would yet revive	162	U15 Friend-Wars	6
For all their spight, be like him if they could:	162	U15 Friend-Wars	26
And every Dressing for a Pitfall set	164	U15 Friend-Wars	66
And firke, and jerke, and for the Coach-man raile,	164	U15 Friend-Wars	72
For t'other pound of sweet-meats, he shall feele	164	U15 Friend-Wars	77
For these with her young Companie shee'll enter,	164	U15 Friend-Wars	79
Is lov'd, though he let out his owne for life:	165	U15 Friend-Wars	88
Lives for the Lord, but to the Ladies end.	165	U15 Friend-Wars V 94	
If it be thought kild like her Embrions; for,	165	U15 Friend-Wars	96
For man to spend his money on? his wit?	165	U15 Friend-Wars	102
His time? health? soule? will he for these goe throw	165	U15 Friend-Wars	103
Is it for these that Pine-man meets the street	165	U15 Friend-Wars	106
For lesse Securitie? O for these	165	U15 Friend-Wars	113
For less Securitie? O Freind, for these	165	U15 Friend-Wars V113	
He that no more for Age, Cramps, Palsies, can	166	U15 Friend-Wars	135
To take the box up for him; and pursues	166	U15 Friend-Wars	137
For the recovery of my voyce? No, there	167	U15 Friend-Wars	154
With him, for he is follow'd with that heape	167	U15 Friend-Wars	156
That thou dost all things more for truth, then glory,	168	U15 Friend-Wars	179
And never but for doing wrong be sory;	168	U15 Friend-Wars	180
Thy person fit for any charge thou tak'st;	168	U15 Friend-Wars	182
Who falls for love of God, shall rise a Starre.	168	U15 Friend-Wars	196
For, if such men as he could die,	168	U16 Gray	6
Is done for gaine: If't be, 'tis not sincere.	169	U17 Friend-Debt	6
That as the lesser breach: for he that takes	169	U17 Friend-Debt	11
Some grounds are made the richer, for the Rest;	169	U17 Friend-Debt	17
To see men feare: or else for truth, and State,	170	U18 Elegy Can	17
No more, I am sorry for so fond cause, say,	171	U20 Shrub	4
Put on for fashion, and take up on trust:	171	U20 Shrub	8
Sols Chariot for new fire,	175	U23 Himselfe	28
For fury wasteth,	179	U25 Desmond	46
Yet doth some wholsome Physick for the mind,	180	U26 Ode High	9
For men to use their fortune reverently,	181	U26 Ode High	23
For in your verse all Cupids Armorie,	182	U28 Worth	9
for Venus Ceston, every line you make.	182	U28 Worth	14
Propping Verse, for feare of falling	183	U29 Fit of Rime	8
For a thousand yeares together,	183	U29 Fit of Rime	16
Cramp'd for ever;	184	U29 Fit of Rime	51
The only faithfull Watchman for the Realme,	185	U30 Burleigh	9
That still was good for goodnesse sake, nor thought	185	U30 Burleigh	13
Are there for Charitie, and not for fee.	186	U32 Elsmere	6
Art, her false servant; Nor, for Sir Hugh Plat,	188	U34 Small Poxe	7
For Love in shadow best is made.	189	U36 Song	2
Sir, I am thankfull, first, to heaven, for you;	189	U37 Friend-Book	1
Next to your selfe, for making your love true:	189	U37 Friend-Book	2
Their vice of loving for a Christmasse fit;	190	U37 Friend-Book	8
And Fame wake for me, when I yeeld to sleepe.	190	U37 Friend-Book	15
For no man lives so out of passions sway,	190	U37 Friend-Book	31
As I would urge Authoritie for sinne.	191	U38 Elegy 'Tis	26
There is no Father that for one demerit,	192	U38 Elegy 'Tis	41
And then with pause; for sever'd once, that's gone,	192	U38 Elegy 'Tis	47
Can pumpe for; or a Libell without salt	193	U38 Elegy 'Tis	96
For though Love thrive, and may grow up with cheare,	197	U40 Elegy That	15
They may say Grace, and for Loves Chaplaines passe;	198	U40 Elegy That	31
Out with the other, for hee's still at home;	198	U40 Elegy That	34
Where we must feele it Darke for halfe a yeare.	199	U41 Elegy Since	8
How shall I doe, sweet Mistris, for my heart?	199	U41 Elegy Since	14
O, keepe it still; for it had rather be	199	U41 Elegy Since	17
For Silke will draw some sneaking Songster thither.	200	U42 Elegy Let	26
And Mars, that gave thee a Lanthorne for a Crowne.	203	U43 Vulcan	10
By Jove to have Minerva for thy Bride,	203	U43 Vulcan	12
Or pomp'd for those hard trifles, Anagrams,	204	U43 Vulcan	35
Or pomp'd for those fine trifles, Anagrams,	204	U43 Vulcan V 35	
Thou then hadst had some colour for thy flames,	204	U43 Vulcan	40
Had made a meale for Vulcan to lick up.	206	U43 Vulcan	84
Had bin fitt meate for Vulcan to lick up.	206	U43 Vulcan V 84	

FOR (cont.)

for our owne Ladyes; and in storie there	207	U43 Vulcan	V 97
Sonne of the Wind! for so thy mother gone	208	U43 Vulcan	111
For none but Smiths would have made thee a God.	208	U43 Vulcan	117
And for it lose his eyes with Gun-powder,	208	U43 Vulcan	121
The Brethren, they streight nois'd it out for Newes,	209	U43 Vulcan	139
There were, that streight did nose it out for newes,	209	U43 Vulcan	V139
The brethren they streight ways noisd out for newes,	209	U43 Vulcan	V139
O no, cry'd all, Fortune, for being a whore,	209	U43 Vulcan	153
For they were burnt, but to be better built.	210	U43 Vulcan	166
But we have Powder still for the Kings Day,	213	U44 Speach	2
For they did see it the last tilting well,	213	U44 Speach	6
For that unnecessarie Charge they were.	214	U44 Speach	32
Were now the greater Captaine? for they saw	214	U44 Speach	39
For education of our Lordings; Soone	214	U44 Speach	62
His Lordship. That is for his Band, his haire	215	U44 Speach	95
This other for his eye-browes; hence, away,	215	U44 Speach	97
For there are many slips, and Counterfeits.	216	U45 Squib	17
For that is first requir'd, A man be his owne.	216	U45 Squib	23
More for thy Patronage, then for their Cause,	217	U46 Coke	12
But for a Sealing: let these men protest.	218	U47 Tribe	15
And are received for the Covey of Witts;	218	U47 Tribe	22
But if, for honour, we must draw the Sword,	219	U47 Tribe	39
I, and for this neglect, the courser sort	219	U47 Tribe	54
Live to that point I will, for which I am man,	219	U47 Tribe	59
For, Bacchus, thou art freer	221	U48 Bacchus	13
Where fight the prime Cocks of the Game, for wit?	222	U49 Pucell	4
Equall with that, which for the best newes goes,	222	U49 Pucell	9
I never stood for any place: my wit	223	U49 Pucell	23
For bawdry, 'tis her language, and not mine.	223	U49 Pucell	26
Not he, that should the body have, for Case	223	U49 Pucell	33
For Sermoneeres: of which now one, now other,	223	U49 Pucell	39
And practise for a Miracle; take heed,	223	U49 Pucell	41
Both for the Mothers, and the Babes of grace,	223	U49 Pucell	44
For there the wicked in the Chaire of scorne,	223	U49 Pucell	45
Then the great Homers wit, for her, could faine;	224	U50 Countesse	24
For you admit no companie, but good,	224	U50 Countesse	25
Searching for knowledge, and to keepe your mind	225	U50 Countesse	29
As they are hard, for them to make their owne,	225	U50 Countesse	33
For when they find so many meet in one,	225	U50 Countesse	35
It will be shame for them, if they have none.	225	U50 Countesse	36
For whose returnes, and many, all these pray:	225	U51 Bacon	6
For 't were a narrow gladnesse, kept thine owne.	225	U51 Bacon	18
An Archetype, for all the world to see,	227	U52 Answer	14
For never saw I yet the Muses dwell,	228	U53 Newcastle	15
I look'd for Hercules to be the Groome:	228	U53 Newcastle	18
For a just wager, and that wager paid	229	U54 Squib	2
Lend me, deare Arthur, for a weeke five more,	229	U54 Squib	16
For your securitie. I can no better.	229	U54 Squib	20
And can for other Graces her commend,	230	U56 Covell	20
As if that part lay for a < > most fit!	232	U58 Book-seller	12
Stay, drop a teare for him that's dead,	233	U60 La-ware	2
Fit for a Bishops knees! O bow them oft,	234	U61 Epigram	13
And wee doe weepe, to water, for our sinne.	234	U61 Epigram	15
An Epigram. To K. Charles for a 100. Pounds . . .	235	U62 Charles 1	Ttl
To K. Charles, and Q. Mary. For the losse of their . . .	235	U63 Charles 2	Ttl
For God, whose essence is so infinite,	236	U63 Charles 2	13
For safetie of such Majestie, cry out?	236	U64 Charles 3	6
How much to heaven for thee, great Charles, they owe!	237	U64 Charles 3	22
Hay! for the flowre of France!	240	U67 Muses	42
For want of knowing the Poet, to say him nay?	241	U68 House-hold	4
For in the Genius of a Poets Verse,	241	U68 House-hold	13
Where he would fixe, for the distinctions feare.	242	U69 Friend Son	18
For as at distance, few have facultie	242	U69 Friend Son	19
For, what is life, if measur'd by the space,	243	U70 Ode	21
For three of his foure-score, he did no good.	243	U70 Ode	32
Not liv'd; for Life doth her great actions spell,	245	U70 Ode	59
Call, noble Lucius, then for Wine,	245	U70 Ode	75
Such truths, as we expect for happy men,	246	U70 Ode	83
The profits for a time.	246	U70 Ode	101
Are faine to seeke for succours, and supplies	248	U71 Treasurer	2
Feed on thy selfe for spight, and shew thy Kind:	250	U73 Weston	9
. . . gratulatorie For his Returne from his Embassie. 1632.	250	U74 Weston	Ttl
As they had learn'd new changes, for the day,	253	U75 Epithalam.	35
Stand there; for when a noble Nature's rais'd,	256	U75 Epithalam.	113
For Fame keepes Vertue up, and it Posteritie.	257	U75 Epithalam.	152
To be a watchfull Servant for this State;	258	U75 Epithalam.	178
For done service, and to come:	259	U76 Petition	13
For done service, or to come:	259	U76 Petition	V 13
(For with both the Muse was fed)	259	U76 Petition	16
(For with both the Muse it fed)	259	U76 Petition	V 16
Of your grace, for goodnesse sake,	260	U76 Petition	26
For that to dwell in, and be still at home.	262	U78 Digby	8
For those to dwell in, and be still at home.	262	U78 Digby	V 8
For Brittains honour, and to Charles my King:	262	U78 Digby	V 18
For he doth love my Verses, and will looke	263	U78 Digby	23
For, had we here said lesse, we had sung nothing then.	263	U79 New-yeares	8
To pluck a Garland, for her selfe, or mee?	268	U81 Pawlet	4
I doe obey you, Beauty! for in death,	269	U81 Pawlet	5
Their Carract was! for my trump must breake,	269	U81 Pawlet	V 27
At pleasure, to be call'd for, every day!	271	U81 Pawlet	82
And, but for that Contention, and brave strife	271	U81 Pawlet	95
This Cradle, and for Goodnesse sake,	273	U84 Cradle	10

	Page	Title	Line

FOR (cont.)

For, though that Rattles, Timbrels, Toyes, ... 273 U84 Cradle 17
For such as Shee. . . . . 274 U84 Cradle 40
For Mind, and Body, the most excellent . . . . 274 U84 Descent 3
For her t'inhabit? There is it. . . . . 280 U84 Mind 52
For this so loftie forme, so streight; . . . . 280 U84 Mind 54
For they are strong Supporters: But, till then, ... 281 U84 Kenelme 14
On Nature, for her: who did let her lie, ... 282 U84 Muse 13
(For so thou art with me) now shee is gone. . . . . 283 U84 Muse 22
I murmure against God, for having ta'en . . . . 283 U84 Muse 33
The joy of Saints! the Crowne for which it lives, ... 283 U84 Muse 37
For, as there are three Natures, Schoolemen call . . . . 284 U84 Muse 51
For 'twas himselfe who form'd, and gave it her. . . . . 287 U84 Muse 156
For her devotions, and those sad essayes . . . . 287 U84 Muse 181
For, Prayer is the Incense most perfumes . . . . 288 U84 Muse 187
For his designed worke, the perfect end . . . . 288 U84 Muse 206
For th'eating Thrush, or Pit-falls sets: . . . . 290 U85 Country 34
For houshold aid, and Children sweet; . . . . 291 U85 Country 40
Or Mallowes good for bodyes ill: . . . . 291 U85 Country V 58
Too stubborne for Commands so slack: 292 U86 Hor.4:1 7
For he's both noble, lovely, young, ... 292 U86 Hor.4:1 13
And for the troubled Clyent fyl's his tongue, ... 292 U86 Hor.4:1 14
In many a Gumme, and for thy soft eares sake 292 U86 Hor.4:1 22
As, for her, I'ld not feare to die, ... 293 U87 Hor.3:9 11
For whom I doubly would expire, ... 293 U87 Hor.3:9 15
For lust will languish, and that heat decay. . . . . 294 U88 Petronius 5
Not labour'd for, but left thee by thy Sire; 295 U90 Mart.10:47 3
No place for these. And, Painter, hap'ly, thou . . . . 305 Horace 24
My selfe for shortnesse labour; and I grow . . . . 307 Horace 35
My selfe for shortnesse labour, and am stil'd . . . . 339 Horace V 36/ 35
Fit for the sock: Each subject should retaine . . . . 311 Horace 124
For Nature, first, within doth fashion us . . . . 311 Horace 152
For, being a Poet, thou maist feigne, create, ... 313 Horace 189
To render word for word: nor with thy sleight . . . . 313 Horace 191
For his owne good, a carelesse letter-goe . . . . 315 Horace 234
Once seene, to be againe call'd for, and plaid, ... 317 Horace 271
And rivall with the Trumpet for his sound, ... 319 Horace 288
And in their numbers; For, alas, what knew . . . . 319 Horace 300
For the vile Goat, soone after, forth did send . . . . 319 Horace 320
And emptie Clowdes. For Tragedie is faire, ... 321 Horace 336
Into their birth-right, and for fitnesse sake, ... 323 Horace 376
Take you the Greeke Examples, for your light, ... 323 Horace 397
For so, they shall not only gaine the worth, ... 325 Horace 425
For choller! If I did not, who could bring . . . . 325 Horace 430
For Choler! if I did not, none could bring . . . . 349 Horace V430
Thence draw forth true expressions. For, sometimes, ... 327 Horace 455
Orpheus, a priest, and speaker for the Gods . . . . 327 Horace 479
From slaughters, and foule life; and for the same . . . . 327 Horace 481
And hold them faithfully; For nothing rests, ... 329 Horace 505
Let what thou fain'st for pleasures sake, be neere . . . . 329 Horace 507
For, neither doth the String still yeeld that sound . . . . 329 Horace 521
Make a great Supper; or for some poore man . . . . 333 Horace 602
For hee'll cry, Good, brave, better, excellent! . . . . 333 Horace 611
For praises, where the mind conceales a foxe. . . . . 333 Horace 622
For praises, where the mind harbours a foxe. . . . . 354 Horace V622
For, if one should, and with a rope make haste . . . . 335 Horace 655
Nor did he doe this once; for if you can . . . . 335 Horace 667
For, as one comming with a laterall viewe, ... 362 Author 9
Receive it for a Fable, ... 364 Phoenix 2
For other formes come short all . . . . 364 Ode Splendor 2
Her breath for sweete exceeding . . . . 365 Ode Splendor 13
"For stile of rarenesse, to degenerate. . . . . 367 Ode Who saith 32
That may judge for his six-pence) had, before . . . . 371 Fletcher 7
With vices, which they look'd for, and came to. . . . . 371 Fletcher 10
For he did but kisse her, and so let her go. . . . . 375 Coryat 1 19
For Grapes he had gather'd before they were eaten. . . . . 375 Coryat 1 25
And allow you for each particular mile, ... 379 Coryat 3 9
Which, unto all Ages, for his will be knowne, ... 379 Coryat 3 11
There nam'd to be travell'd? For this our Tom saith: . . . . 380 Coryat 3 21
For grapes he had gather'd, before they were eaten. . . . . 380 Coryat 3 36
How faine for his venery he was to crie (Tergum o) . . . . 380 Coryat 3 37
May she, whome thou for spouse, to day, dost take, ... 384 Somerset 11
What place is for my testimony void? . . . . 385 Brooke 2
I know for such, as (if my word will waigh) . . . . 386 Husband 11
For, though but early in these pathes thou tread, ... 386 Browne 5
For though Spaine gave him his first ayre and Vogue, ... 389 Aleman 15
It was for gentle Shakespeare cut; . . . . 390 Reader 2
For seeliest Ignorance on these may light, ... 390 Shakespeare 7
For, if I thought my judgement were of yeeres, ... 391 Shakespeare 27
For names; but call forth thund'ring Aeschilus, ... 391 Shakespeare 33
Leave thee alone, for the comparison . . . . 391 Shakespeare 38
He was not of an age, but for all time! . . . . 391 Shakespeare 43
For though the Poets matter, Nature be, ... 392 Shakespeare 57
Or for the lawrell, he may gaine a scorne, ... 392 Shakespeare 63
For a good Poet's made, as well as borne. . . . . 392 Shakespeare 64
And despaires day, but for thy Volumes light. . . . . 392 Shakespeare 80
Where spight of Death, next Life, for her Loves sake . . . . 394 Jane Ogle 25
Thy list of aydes, and force, for so it is: . . . . 398 Drayton 62
The Poets act! and for his Country's sake . . . . 398 Drayton 63
For this did Katherine, Ladie Ogle, die . . . . 400 Lady Ogle 33
In Bulwarkes, Rav'lins, Ramparts, for defense, ... 400 Beaumont 4
All in the Worke! And soe shall still for Ben: . . . . 404 Inigo Jones 1 65
Thy twice conceyvd, thrice payd for Imagery? . . . . 405 Inigo Jones 1 90

	Page	Title	Line

FOR (cont.)
- Expression for! with that unbounded lyne · · · · 406 Inigo Jones 1 95
- Cittyes & Temples! thou a Cave for Wyne, · · · · 406 Inigo Jones 2 8
- An Earle of show: for all thy worke is showe: · · · · 407 Inigo Jones 2 21
- An Earle of show: for all thy worth is showe: · · · · 407 Inigo Jones 2 V 21
- Seek out some hungry painter, that for bread · · · · 408 Inigo Jones 3 10
- Thy Forehead is too narrow for my Brand. · · · · 408 Inigo Jones 3 14
- For thou objectest (as thou hast been told) · · · · 408 Detractor 3
- I had you for a Servant, once, Dick Brome; · · · · 409 Brome 1
- You learn'd it well; and for it, serv'd your time · · · · 410 Brome 9
- For thou hast nought in thee to cure his Fame, · · · · 411 Gill 13
- The Eye of flowers, worthy, for his scent, · · · · 413 Ghyrlond 14
- Now, for mine owne part, and it is but due, · · · · 415 Rutter 12
- For order, and for governing the pixe, · · · · 415 Rutter 25
- Upon this obeliske, advanc'd for it, · · · · 416 Welcome 5
- for if there, or peace or warr be, · · · · 417 Moon 22
- that the wife heades for a wager · · · · 417 Moon 26
- for the breeches with the bride, · · · · 417 Moon 34
- for when the profitt with the payne doth meete, · · · · 418 Answer 6
- For noe Man Lyves, soe out of passions swaye, · · · · 422 Censure 24

FORBEARE
- Ideot, last night, I pray'd thee but forbeare · · · · 45 E58 Groome 1
- Forbeare to tempt me, Proule, I will not show · · · · 54 E81 Proule 1
- Sower Mother of sweet Loves, forbeare · · · · 292 U86 Hor.4:1 5
- Doth wretchedly the use of things forbeare, · · · · 317 Horace 243

FORBEARES
- Then he, which for sinnes penaltie forbeares. · · · · 112 F11 Epode 89
- Then he, that for sinnes penaltie forbeares. · · · · 112 F11 Epode V 89

FORBID
- To so true worth, though thou thy selfe forbid. · · · · 47 E63 Salisbury 2 12
- To such true worth, though thou thy selfe forbid. · · · · 47 E63 Salisbury 2 V 12
- But which the Fates forbid me to reveale. · · · · 119 F13 Aubigny 107
- Who shall forbid me then in Rithme to bee · · · · 200 U42 Elegy Let 5

FORBIDD'
- Forbidd' his side! and nothing, but the word · · · · 33 E21 Gam'ster 4

FORBIDDEN
- With England. All forbidden bookes they get. · · · · 59 E92 New Crie 31

FORBIDS
- Forbids thee forth againe thy foot to draw. · · · · 313 Horace 194

FORCE
- Had of Love, and of his force, · · · · 139 U2 Promise 2
- Her presently? Or leape thy Wife of force, · · · · 201 U42 Elegy Let 44
- Launces, and men, and some a breaking force. · · · · 213 U44 Speach 8
- And force back that, which will not be restor'd, · · · · 219 U47 Tribe 40
- What though with Tribade lust she force a Muse, · · · · 222 U49 Pucell 7
- Provoke his mettall, and command his force · · · · 228 U53 Newcastle 2
- Their weapons shot out, with that flame, and force, · · · · 233 U59 Newcastle 11
- Their weapons darted, with that flame, and force, · · · · 233 U59 Newcastle V 11
- And such a force the faire example had, · · · · 247 U70 Ode 117
- Force from the Phoenix, then, no raritie · · · · 255 U75 Epithalam. 81
- And us dis-joyn'd force to her brazen yoke, · · · · 294 U87 Hor.3:9 18
- Her force was fit to be restrain'd by law: · · · · 348 Horace V402/368
- To force the grates, that hold him in, would fright · · · · 337 Horace 675
- "Where neither Force can bend, nor Feare can awe." · · · · 367 Ode Who saith 48
- And Rouze, the Marching of a mighty force, · · · · 397 Drayton 39
- Thy list of aydes, and force, for so it is: · · · · 398 Drayton 62
- Or else Magnetique in the force, · · · · 399 Lady Ogle 19

FORC'D
- Of these forc'd joyes, · · · · 120 F14 Sydney 18
- Flanck'd with a Ditch, and forc'd out of a Marish, · · · · 209 U43 Vulcan 134
- Fenced with a Ditch, and forc'd out of a Marish, · · · · 209 U43 Vulcan V134

FORCES
- Thou canst draw forth thy forces, and fight drie · · · · 214 U44 Speach 45

FORCING
- Was meant at first. Why, forcing still about · · · · 307 Horace 29

FORC'T
- Where any Deed is forc't, the Grace is mard. · · · · 153 U13 Sacvile 24
- Or that the Sun was here, but forc't away; · · · · 199 U41 Elegy Since 6
- Or Kid forc't from the Wolfe againe. · · · · 291 U85 Country 60

'FORE
- 'Fore your Idoll Glasse a whit, · · · · 140 U2 Promise 22

FORE
- Had I fore-knowne of this thy least desire · · · · 205 U43 Vulcan 59
- Had I fore-knowne but of thy least desire · · · · 205 U43 Vulcan V 59
- As, could they but lifes miseries fore-see, · · · · 243 U70 Ode 19

FOREBORNE
- And yet it cannot be foreborne, · · · · 147 U7 Nymph 13

FOREHEAD'
- Doe but marke, her forehead's smoother · · · · 134 U2 Triumph 15

FOREHEAD
- Forehead large, and white as snow; · · · · 141 U2 Her man V 18
- By that faire Stand, your forehead, whence he bends · · · · 170 U19 Elegy By 3
- He will cleare up his forehead, thinke thou bring'st · · · · 263 U78 Digby 21
- He will cheare up his forehead, thinke thou bring'st · · · · 263 U78 Digby V 21
- Thy Forehead is too narrow for my Brand. · · · · 408 Inigo Jones 3 14

FOREHEAD'S
- Doe but marke, her forehead's smoother · · · · 134 U2 Triumph 15

FORE-KNOWNE
- Had I fore-knowne of this thy least desire · · · · 205 U43 Vulcan 59
- Had I fore-knowne but of thy least desire · · · · 205 U43 Vulcan V 59

FOREMAN
- With the shops Foreman, or some such brave sparke, · · · · 371 Fletcher 6

		Page	Title	Line
FORE-SEE				
As, could they but lifes miseries fore-see,	. . . .	243	U70 Ode	19
FORESTALL				
But she is such, as she might, yet, forestall	. . .	172	U20 Shrub	23
FORETOLD				
Which all the Fate of Troy foretold?	. .	181	U27 Ode Helen	24
That found out profit, and foretold each thing,	. . .	319	Horace	309
FORFEIT				
And lookes unto the forfeit. If you be	. . .	169	U17 Friend-Debt	13
The safetie of our soules, and forfeit breath!	. . .	286	U84 Muse	136
FORFEITINGE				
forfeitinge their drinking lease,	. . . .	418	Moon	43
FORFEITS				
Signes to new bond, forfeits: and cryes, god payes.	. . .	30	E12 Shift	14
FORGE				
Sweat at the forge, their hammers beating;	. . .	179	U25 Desmond	41
Condemne him to the Brick-kills, or a forge	. . .	211	U43 Vulcan	V183
Would you had kept your Forge at Aetna still,	. . .	212	U43 Vulcan	197
FORGET				
And, can forget mens names, with a great grace.	. .	35	E28 Surly	8
For others ill, ought none their good forget.	. .	116	F13 Aubigny	6
Can man forget this Storie?	. .	130	U1 Nativitie	24
Who (amongst these delights) would not forget	. .	290	U85 Country	37
FORGIVE				
Against my grave, and time could not forgive.	. . .	58	E91 Vere	12
Forgive me then, if mine but say you are	. . .	67	E103 L Wroth 1	9
But, forgive me, with thy crowne	. . .	105	F8 Sicknesse	18
Forgive me this one foolish deadly sin,	. . .	171	U20 Shrub	2
I could forgive her being proud! a whore!	. . .	172	U20 Shrub	21
Forgive it, as my frailtie, and not me.	. . .	190	U37 Friend-Book	30
God, and the good, know to forgive, and save.	. . .	191	U38 Elegy 'Tis	19
Thinke that your selfe like heaven forgive me can:	. . .	192	U38 Elegy 'Tis	32
There are yet faults, which we would well forgive,	. . .	329	Horace	520
Forgive it as my Frayltie, and not mee.	. . .	422	Censure	23
FORGIVEN				
Forgiven him; And in that lyne stand I,	. . .	193	U38 Elegy 'Tis	91
Yet have all debts forgiven us, and advance	. . .	286	U84 Muse	143
Within the hope of having all forgiven?	. . .	323	Horace	394
FORGOT				
Is it the paine affrights? that's soone forgot.	. . .	46	E62 Would-bee	5
That all this while I have forgot some god,	. . .	85	E133 Voyage	44
I had forgot	. . . . . .	129	U1 Father	10
FORGOTTEN				
And now lye lost in their forgotten dust.	. . .	114	F12 Rutland	40
FOR'HIS				
For'his whore: Groyne doth still occupy his land.	. . .	75	E117 Groyne	2
FORKE				
Or straines on his small forke his subtill nets	. . .	290	U85 Country	33
Or straines on his small forke his subtler nets	. . .	290	U85 Country	V 33
FORKED				
The pale Pyrene, and the forked Mount:	. . .	366	Ode Who saith	21
FORME				
I thought to forme unto my zealous Muse,	. . .	52	E76 Bedford 1	2
About his forme. What then so swells each lim?	. . .	63	E97 Motion	19
Of birth, of match, of forme, of chastitie?	. . .	67	E104 Montgomery	8
(Though they were crusht into one forme) could make	. . .	108	F10 Proludium	26
A forme more fresh, then are the Eden bowers,	. . .	111	F11 Epode	57
Had not their forme touch'd by an English wit.	. . .	115	F12 Rutland	82
Your forme imprest there: not with tickling rimes,	. . .	116	F12 Rutland	87
Your forme imprest there: not with tinckling rimes,	. . .	116	F12 Rutland	V 87
Wherein, your forme, you still the same shall finde;	. . .	120	F13 Aubigny	123
This All of nothing, gavest it forme, and fate,	. . .	127	U1 Trinitie	18
Forme, Art or Ensigne, that hath scap'd your sight?	. . .	160	U14 Selden	48
Forme, Act or Ensigne, that hath scap'd your sight?	. . .	160	U14 Selden	V 48
Throughout your forme; as though that move,	. . .	173	U22 Elegy Tho	6
Of Phaos forme? or doth the Boy	. . .	181	U27 Ode Helen	5
Looke forth, but cannot last in such a forme.	. . .	191	U38 Elegy 'Tis	14
Your forme shines here, here fixed in my heart:	. . .	194	U38 Elegy 'Tis	117
Some Forme defective, or decay'd;	. . .	275	U84 Body	6
For this so loftie forme, so streight,	. . .	280	U84 Mind	54
And to that forme, lent two such veines of blood	. . .	287	U84 Muse	157
As neither head, nor foot, one forme retaine.	. . .	305	Horace	10
This, seeking, in a various kind, to forme	. . .	307	Horace	40
To forme a worke, I would no more desire	. . .	307	Horace	50
I Could begin with that grave forme, Here lies,	. . .	394	Jane Ogle	1
My lippes could forme the voyce, I heard that Rore,	. . .	397	Drayton	38
These forme thy Ghyrlond. Wherof Myrtle green,	. . .	412	Ghyrlond	5
FORM'D				
With one great blot, yo'had form'd me as I am.	. . .	227	U52 Answer	12
Each syllab'e answer'd, and was form'd, how faire;	. . .	245	U70 Ode	63
For 'twas himselfe who form'd, and gave it her.	. . .	287	U84 Muse	156
Whose shapes, like sick-mens dreames, are form'd so vaine,	. .	338	Horace	V 9
But in one tongue, was form'd with the worlds wit:	. . .	389	Aleman	6
FORMED				
What nourisheth, what formed, what begot	. . .	325	Horace	437
FORMER				
To former height, and there in circle tarrie,	. . .	55	E85 Goodyere 1	9
Of former age, or glorie of our one,	. . .	67	E104 Montgomery	10
Then let the former age, with this content her,	. . .	84	E133 Voyage	19
Still, with thy former labours; yet, once more,	. . .	85	E133 Voyage	56
7. Begging another, on colour of mending the former.	. . .	139	U2 Another	Ttl
Then knew the former ages: yet to life,	. . .	242	U69 Friend Son	23

		Page	Title	Line

FORMES
In meere out-formes, untill he lost his sight, ... 73 E114 Sydney 4
White, black, blew, greene, and in more formes out-started, . 87 E133 Voyage 126
I know thy formes are studyed arts, ... 100 F4 To the World 9
And, in those outward formes, all fooles are wise. . . 117 F13 Aubigny 36
Call to mind the formes, that strove . . . . 137 U2 Cupid 46
To fetch in the Formes goe by: . . . . . 140 U2 Promise 18
To lose the formes, and dignities of men, . . . 166 U15 Friend-Wars 146
Some of his formes, he lets him not come neere . . 242 U69 Friend Son 17
Earle Rivers Grand-Child--serve not formes, good Fame, . 269 U81 Pawlet 21
For other formes come short all . . . . . 364 Ode Splendor 2
FORNACES
The Glasse-house, Dye-fats, and their Fornaces; . . 211 U43 Vulcan 180
FORRAINE
Maintayne their liedgers forth, for forraine wyres, . . 118 F13 Aubigny 72
And here he disdained not, in a forraine land . . 375 Coryat 1 32
FORREST (See also FOREST)
The Forrest. . . . . 93 The Forrest Ttl
Such, as in lustes wilde forrest love to rainge, . . 108 F10 Proludium 9
FORSAKE
Nor language, nor cleere order will forsake. . . 339 Horace V 59/ 58
If thou the vile, broad-troden ring forsake. . . 313 Horace 188
In daring to forsake the Grecian tracts, . . . 323 Horace 407
FORSAKEN
From being forsaken, then doth worth: . . . 146 U6 Defence 22
FORSAKES
Simply my Band, his trust in me forsakes, . . . 169 U17 Friend-Debt 12
Nor language, nor cleere order ere forsakes. . . 307 Horace 58
FORSOOKE
I, that have suffer'd this; and, though forsooke . . 117 F13 Aubigny 15
FORSWARE
Hazard a month forsware his; and grew drunke, . . 56 E87 Hazard 2
FORSWEARE
It will deny all; and forsweare it too: . . . 74 E115 Honest Man 19
For what they streight would to the world forsweare; . 154 U13 Sacvile 50
FORSWORE
And trust her I would least, that hath forswore . . 223 U49 Pucell 29
FORSWORNE
Ino bewaild; Ixion false, forsworne; . . . . 313 Horace 176
FORT
Arm'd at all peeces, as to keepe a Fort . . . 187 U33 Councellour 30
Which, though it were the Fort of the whole Parish, . . 209 U43 Vulcan 133
What a strong Fort old Pimblicoe had bin! . . . 213 U44 Speach 21
This Fort of so impregnable accesse, ... 401 Beaumont 17
FORTH (See also FOORTH)
Came forth example, and remaines so, yet: . . . 34 E23 Donne 1 4
For whose sake, hence-forth, all his vowes be such, . . 41 E45 First Son 11
The least indulgent thought thy pen drops forth! . . 44 E55 Beaumont 4
But, wisely, thrusts not forth a forward hand, . . 61 E95 Savile 22
Were leading forth the Graces on the greene: . . 68 E105 L Wroth 2 12
Shee brought the Poets forth, but ours th'adventer. . 84 E133 Voyage 20
Belch'd forth an ayre, as hot, as at the muster . . 85 E133 Voyage 63
Hence-forth I quit thee from my thought, . . . 100 F4 To the World 3
Times, and occasions, to start forth, and seeme) . . 118 F13 Aubigny 63
Maintayne their liedgers forth, for forraine wyres, . . 118 F13 Aubigny 72
No, nor forth your window peepe, ... 140 U2 Promise 16
In love, doth not alone help forth . . . . 146 U6 Defence 20
Goe, get thee quickly forth, ... 150 U10 Jealousie 13
Their bounties forth, to him that last was made, . . 155 U13 Sacvile 63
Yea, of th'ingratefull: and he forth must tell . . 155 U13 Sacvile 77
Shoot forth in smooth and comely spaces; have . . 157 U13 Sacvile 150
Stand forth my Object, then, you that have beene . . 159 U14 Selden 29
Wake, friend, from forth thy Lethargie: the Drum . 162 U15 Friend-Wars 1
Planting their Purles, and Curles spread forth like Net, . 164 U15 Friend-Wars 65
Then once to number, or bring forth to hand, . . 167 U15 Friend-Wars 173
Of Argument, still drawing forth the best, . . . 187 U33 Councellour 27
Looke forth, but cannot last in such a forme. . . 191 U38 Elegy 'Tis 14
To live in Sea-coale, and goe forth in smoake; . . 211 U43 Vulcan 181
To have their Husbands drawne forth to the field, . . 213 U44 Speach 18
Thou canst draw forth thy forces, and fight drie . . 214 U44 Speach 45
Or the States Ships sent forth belike to meet . . 219 U47 Tribe 33
And spangled Petticotes brought forth to eye, . . 223 U49 Pucell 19
Their noises forth in Thunder: . . . . 239 U67 Muses 9
Thy comming forth in that great yeare, . . . 242 U70 Ode 2
Urg'd, hurried forth, and horld . . . . 243 U70 Ode 15
And told forth fourescore yeares; . . . . 243 U70 Ode 26
And then noyse forth the burden of their Song, . . 249 U72 King V 17
When shee puts forth the life of ev'ry thing: . . 250 U74 Weston 3
The Month of youth, which calls all Creatures forth . 253 U75 Epithalam. 26
See, how she paceth forth in Virgin-white, . . 253 U75 Epithalam. 41
And Sister: darting forth a dazling light . . . 253 U75 Epithalam. 43
Peepe forth a Gemme; to see . . . . 258 U75 Epithalam. 175
To shew the rites, and t'usher forth the way . . 263 U79 New-yeares 4
That leades our flocks and us, and calls both forth . 264 U79 New-yeares 29
Foure Rivers branching forth like Seas, . . . 276 U84 Body 23
Hence-forth may every line be you; . . . . 278 U84 Mind 22
Us forth, by some Celestiall slight . . . . 279 U84 Mind 47
As smooth as Oyle pour'd forth, and calme . . . 280 U84 Mind 59
And set it forth; the rest were Cobwebs fine, . . 282 U84 Muse 5
Her blessed Soule, hence, forth this valley vane . 283 U84 Muse 34
And came forth ever cheered, with the rod . . . 287 U84 Muse 183
And wealth unto our language; and brought forth . . 309 Horace 82
That first sent forth the dapper Elegie, . . . 309 Horace 110

FORTH (cont.)
   Unto the last, as when he first went forth, ... 313   Horace   181
   Of Homers, forth in acts, then of thine owne, ... 313   Horace   185
   Forbids thee forth againe thy foot to draw.   313   Horace   194
   Afford? The Mountaines travail'd, and brought forth   .   .   . 315   Horace   198
   Wonders forth after: As Antiphates, ... 315   Horace   205
   The rash, and head-long eloquence brought forth   319   Horace   307
   For the vile Goat, soone after, forth did send   319   Horace   320
   But fame of Poets, they thinke, if they come forth,   .   .   . 325   Horace   426
   Thence draw forth true expressions. For, sometimes,   .   .   . 327   Horace   455
   So, any Poeme, fancied, or forth-brought   331   Horace   561
   To change, and mend, what you not forth doe set. 331   Horace   579
   Come forth thou bonnie bouncing booke then, daughter   .   .   . 378   Coryat 2   86
   This thy worke forth: that judgment mine commends.   .   .   . 386   Browne   8
   With the how much they set forth, but th'how well.   .   .   . 386   Browne   V 6
   For names; but call forth thund'ring Aeschilus, ... 391   Shakespeare   33
   Sent forth, or since did from their ashes come.   391   Shakespeare   40
   When like Apollo he came forth to warme   392   Shakespeare   45
   Shine forth, thou Starre of Poets, and with rage,   .   .   . 392   Shakespeare   77
   The Orbe was cut forth into Regions seaven.   396   Drayton   20
   you are; from them leapt forth an Architect, ... 402   Inigo Jones 1   3
   And peering forth of Iris in the Shrowdes!   403   Inigo Jones 1   34
   In setting forth of such a solemne Toye!   405   Inigo Jones 1   78
   In setting forth of such a serious Toye!   405   Inigo Jones 1   V 78
   Disguisd? and thence drag forth Enormity?   405   Inigo Jones 1   81
   A Mungrel Curre? Thou should'st stinck forth, and dye .   .   . 409   Detractor   15
   Thy Noddle, with his clubb; and dashing forth   409   Detractor   21
   By bringing forth God's onely Son, no other.   414   Ghyrlond   48
   And come forth worthie Ivye, or the Bayes, ... 420   Ode:If Men   26
   Shall powre forth many a line, drop many a letter,   .   .   . 666   Glover   9
FORTH-BROUGHT
   So, any Poeme, fancied, or forth-brought   331   Horace   561
FORTIE
   Fortie things more, deare Grand, which you know true, .   .   . 51   E73 Fine Grand   21
   Told seven and fortie yeares, ... 150   U9 Picture   15
   Told six and fortie yeares, ... 150   U9 Picture   V 15
FORTIFIE
   When they doe sweat to fortifie a Muse.   400   Beaumont   6
FORTIFIED
   The bad, by number, are so fortified, ... 116   F13 Aubigny   3
FORTITUDE
   Though every fortitude deserves applause, ... 49   E66 Cary   15
   I thought that Fortitude had beene a meane   156   U13 Sacvile   105
FORTNIGHT
   Item, a tale or two, some fortnight after;   51   E73 Fine Grand   7
FORTUNATE
   And Buckingham the fortunate.   419   Grace   6
FORTUNE
   And not thy fortune; who can cleerely see   47   E63 Salisbury 2   3
   Against thy fortune: when no foe, that day, ... 49   E66 Cary   9
   Fortune upon him breakes her selfe, if ill, ... 63   E98 Th Roe 1   5
   From place, or fortune, are made high, or low, ... 64   E99 Th Roe 2   9
   All yeelding to his fortune, nor, the while, ... 71   E110 Edmonds 1   5
   Think'st thou it is meere fortune, that can win? 72   E112 Gamster   3
   A fortune, in this age, but rarely knowne.   96   F2 Penshurst   92
   Of Fortune, have not alter'd yet my looke, ... 117   F13 Aubigny   16
   A Princes fortune: These are gifts of chance, ... 117   F13 Aubigny   41
   Though it reject not those of Fortune: such   117   F13 Aubigny   45
   Clothes, or Fortune gives the grace;   131   U2 Excuse   8
   Both my fortune, and my Starre!   136   U2 Cupid   2
   And though my fortune humble me, to take   153   U13 Sacvile   15
   Or Feathers: lay his fortune out to show, ... 162   U15 Friend-Wars   21
   That fortune never make thee to complaine.   168   U15 Friend-Wars   183
   And Fortune once, t'assist the spirits that dare. 170   U18 Elegy Can   10
   Or Love, or Fortune blind, when they but winke   170   U18 Elegy Can   16
   If it be thus; Come Love, and Fortune goe, ... 170   U18 Elegy Can   21
   Love to my heart, and Fortune to my lines.   170   U18 Elegy Can   24
   Should not on fortune pause, ... 174   U23 Himselfe   17
   As farre from all revolt, as you are now from Fortune. .   .   . 180   U25 Desmond   65
   For men to use their fortune reverently, ... 181   U26 Ode High   23
   O no, cry'd all, Fortune, for being a whore, ... 209   U43 Vulcan   153
   Whom Fortune aided lesse, or vertue more.   217   U46 Coke   4
   None Fortune aided lesse, or Vertue more.   217   U46 Coke   22
   Of fortune! when, or death appear'd, or bands!   233   U59 Newcastle   23
   And all the games of Fortune, plaid at Court;   234   U61 Epigram   2
   Good fortune to him, in the note thou sing'st, ... 263   U78 Digby   V 22
   What Nature, Fortune, Institution, Fact   270   U81 Pawlet   45
   To every state of fortune; she helpes on, ... 311   Horace   153
   In sound, quite from his fortune; both the rout, ... 313   Horace   159
   Fortune would love the poore, and leave the proud.   .   .   . 319   Horace   286
   Above th'ill fortune of them, or the need.   391   Shakespeare   16
   that Fortune to imbrace, ... 419   Ode:If Men   4
   whom fortune hath deprest; come nere the fates   422   Lucan   4
   whom, yf fortune hath deprest; come nere the fates   .   .   . 422   Lucan   V 4
FORTUNES
   I'have sung the greater fortunes of our state.   48   E64 Salisbury 3   18
   Though not unprov'd: which shewes, thy fortunes are   .   .   . 60   E93 Radcliffe   14
   Making his fortunes swim   112   F11 Epode   106
   That have good fortunes: therefore once agen, ... 212   U43 Vulcan   V212
   To every Fortunes habit; she helps on, ... 342   Horace   V153
   Of Fortunes wheele by Lucan driv'n about, ... 395   May   3
FORTY
   Th'envy'd returne, of forty pound in gold.   408   Detractor   4

		Page	Title	Line

FORUM
He draw a Forum, with quadriviall Streets! . . . 407 Inigo Jones 2 11
FORWARD
But, wisely, thrusts not forth a forward hand, . . . 61 E95 Savile 22
FOSTER
More then the Foster-father of this Child; . . . 389 Aleman 14
FOSTER-FATHER
More then the Foster-father of this Child; . . . 389 Aleman 14
FOUGHT
He wrote, with the same spirit that he fought, . . . 71 E110 Edmonds 1 8
Where mutuall frauds are fought, and no side yeild; . . 186 U33 Councellour 4
FOULE (See also FOWLE)
Envious and foule Disease, could there not be . . . 188 U34 Small Poxe 1
Among the daily Ruines that fall foule, . . . 224 U50 Countesse 17
To be describ'd! Fames fingers are too foule . . . 269 U81 Pawlet 30
Which in a blacke foule fish uncomely enðs: . . . 338 Horace V 5
From slaughters, and foule life; and for the same . . 327 Horace 481
Straines fancie unto foule Apostacie, . . . 363 Riches 15
Tough, foule, or Tender. . . . . . . 417 Moon 16
FOULELY
His power of foulely hurting made to cease. . . . 323 Horace 370
FOUND
But, for this money was a courtier found, . . . 29 E8 Robbery 3
Like aydes 'gainst treasons who hath found before? . . 38 E35 James 2 7
To ope' the character. They'have found the sleight . . 59 E92 New Crie 27
Might be found out as good, and not my Lord. . . . 75 E116 Jephson 8
But, comming neere, they found it but a liter, . . . 86 E133 Voyage 85
That found King James, when hunting late, this way, . . 95 F2 Penshurst 76
Nor are the Muses strangers found: . . . 98 F3 Wroth 52
Yet search'd, and true they found it. . . . 130 U1 Nativitie 6
Themselves through favouring what is there not found: . 159 U14 Selden 16
Themselves through favouring that is there not found: . 159 U14 Selden V 16
Your fate hath found, ... 180 U26 Ode High 3
But rather with advantage to be found . . . 229 U54 Squib 11
Whilst the maine tree, still found . . . 258 U75 Epithalam. 181
The fairest flowers are alwayes found; . . . 264 U79 New-yeares 37
The better grasse, and flowers are found. . . . 265 U79 New-yeares 59
Some Paradise, or Palace found . . . 280 U84 Mind 50
This as it guilty is, or guiltlesse found, . . . 284 U84 Muse 56
The doore of Grace, and found the Mercy-Seat. . . 288 U84 Muse 190
Either because he seekes, and, having found, . . 317 Horace 242
That found out profit, and foretold each thing, . . 319 Horace 309
Thespis is said to be the first found out . . . 319 Horace 311
Playes were found out; and rest, the end, and crowne . 329 Horace 499
Such Passage hast thou found, such Returnes made, . . 389 Chapman 10
I found it pure, and perfect Poesy, . . . 397 Drayton 24
Foole, doe not rate my Rymes; I'have found thy Vice . 408 Detractor 5
Or why to like; they found, it all was new, . . . 415 Rutter 9
FOUNDATION
Fame, and foundation of the English Weale. . . . 225 U51 Bacon 10
FOUNDER
Was the founder. . . . . . . 184 U29 Fit of Rime 60
FOUNDRED
And foundred thy hot teame, to tune my lay. . . . 107 F10 Proludium 9
And foundred thy hot teame, to tune our lay. . . . 107 F10 Proludium V 9
FOUNT
The cleare Dircaean Fount . . . . . 366 Ode Who saith 19
FOUNTAINE
So to see the Fountaine drie, . . . 183 U29 Fit of Rime 22
To Loumond lake, and Twedes blacke-springing fountaine. . 368 Ode Who saith 72
FOUNTAINES
Sought out the Fountaines, Sources, Creekes, paths, wayes, . 160 U14 Selden 45
That from the Muses fountaines doth indorse . . 200 U42 Elegy Let 7
The Fountaines murmure as the streames doe creepe, . . 290 U85 Country 27
FOURE
For three of his foure-score, he did no good. . . 243 U70 Ode 32
Foure Rivers branching forth like Seas, . . . 276 U84 Body 23
A third of twelve, you may: foure ounces. Glad, . . 327 Horace 469
She might have claym'd t'have made the Graces foure; . 371 Epitaph 6
FOURE-SCORE
For three of his foure-score, he did no good. . . 243 U70 Ode 32
FOURESCORE
And told forth fourescore yeares; . . . 243 U70 Ode 26
FOURTH
Ode the first. The fourth Booke. To Venus. . . 292 U86 Hor.4:1 Ttl
Any fourth man, to speake at all, aspire. . . . 317 Horace 275
Of fellowship, the fourth, or second place. . . 323 Horace 380
The fourth is humble Ivy, intersert, . . . 413 Ghyrlond 17
FOWLE (ADJECTIVE)
Wish, you had fowle ones, and deformed got; . . 200 U42 Elegy Let 22
FOWLE
And, though fowle, now, be scarce, yet there are clarkes, . 65 E101 Supper 15
At such a Call, what beast or fowle, . . . 143 U3 Musicall 5
And looking up, I saw Minervas fowle, . . . 397 Drayton 33
FOWLER
And stalketh, like a Fowler, round about, . . . 335 Horace 650
FOXE
For praises, where the mind conceales a foxe. . . 333 Horace 622
For praises, where the mind harbours a foxe. . . 354 Horace V622
FRAGRANT
And fresh and fragrant too, . . . 147 U7 Nymph 16
FRAILE
Our fraile condition it is such, . . . 101 F4 To the World 54

```
                                                        Page    Title          Line

FRAILE  (cont.)
    God lightens not at mans each fraile offence,     .  .  .  193  U38 Elegy 'Tis   68
    Well, with mine owne fraile Pitcher, what to doe  .  .  .  219  U47 Tribe        56
FRAILTIE
    Forgive it, as my frailtie, and not me.           .  .  .  190  U37 Friend-Book  30
    Thinke it was frailtie, Mistris, thinke me man,   .  .  .  192  U38 Elegy 'Tis   31
    Hath shed, or humane frailtie not kept thence.    .  .  .  329  Horace          528
FRAME
    Of this excelling frame?          .      .  .  .  .  .  .  112  F11 Epode       110
    Hee'ld frame such ditties of their store, and want,  .  .  241  U68 House-hold    7
    That all may say, that see the frame,     .  .  .  .  .  278  U84 Mind         23
    To frame a worke, I would no more desire  .  .  .  .  .  339  Horace   V 52/ 50
    I can out of knowne geare, a fable frame,  .  .  .  .  .  321  Horace          349
    I can, out of knowne stuff, a Fable frame,  .  .  .  .  347  Horace   V341/349
    Two rests, a short and long, th'Iambick frame;  .  .  .  323  Horace          371
    (And himselfe with it) that he thinkes to frame;  .  .  392  Shakespeare      62
    Lucans whole frame unto us, and so wrought,  .  .  .  .  395  May             20
    Of vertue, pretious in the frame:     .  .  .  .  .  .  399  Lady Ogle        18
FRAM'D
    And noted for what flesh such soules were fram'd,  .  .  66  E103 L Wroth 1    3
    All this by Faith she saw, and fram'd a Plea,  .  .  .  288  U84 Muse        209
FRANCE
    That so much skarfe of France, and hat, and fether,  .  56  E88 Monsieur      3
    And utter stranger to all ayre of France)  .  .  .  .  83  E132 Sylvester    4
    Thine the originall; and France shall boast,  .  .  .  83  E132 Sylvester   13
    Of Spaine or France; or were not prick'd downe one  .  219  U47 Tribe        47
    Hay! for the flowre of France!    .  .  .  .  .  .  .  240  U67 Muses        42
    Here France, and Italy both to him shed  .  .  .  .  375  Coryat 1         30
    France, Savoy, Italy, and Helvetia,    .  .  .  .  .  379  Coryat 3         19
    Our right in France! if ritely understood.  .  .  .  397  Drayton          58
    Recelebrates the joyfull Match with France.  .  .  .  401  Filmer           10
FRANCES
    . . . England, with the Lady Frances Stuart, Daughter of . . .  252  U75 Epithalam.  Ttl
    The Lady Frances, drest    .  .  .  .  .  .  .  .  .  253  U75 Epithalam.   37
FRANCIS
    To Francis Beaumont.      .  .  .  .  .  .  .  .  .  44  E55 Beaumont      Ttl
    Upon a Thomas, or a Francis call;  .  .  .  .  .  .  258  U75 Epithalam.  171
FRANK
    A Kate, a Frank, to honour their Grand-dames,  .  .  .  258  U75 Epithalam.  172
FRANTICK
    Wise, sober folke, a frantick Poet feare,  .  .  .  .  335  Horace          643
FRAUD
    Then to make falshood blush, and fraud afraid:  .  .  .  186  U32 Elsmere       4
FRAUDS
    Where mutuall frauds are fought, and no side yeild;  .  186  U33 Councellour   4
FRAYLTIE
    Forgive it as my Frayltie, and not mee.  .  .  .  .  422  Censure          23
FREE
    Let me give two: that doubly am got free,  .  .  .  .  31  E13 Empirick      3
    Pardon free truth, and let thy modestie,  .  .  .  .  31  E14 Camden       11
    By his free will, be in Jones company.    .  .  .  .  40  E42 Giles         5
    And what I write thereof find farre, and free  .  .  .  41  E43 Salisbury 1  10
    Great heav'n did well, to give ill fame free wing;  .  .  43  E51 James 3      2
    When they cost dearest, and are done most free,  .  .  49  E66 Cary         14
    I meant to make her faire, and free, and wise,  .  .  52  E76 Bedford 1     5
    Of destinie, and spin her owne free houres.  .  .  .  52  E76 Bedford 1    16
    Sung by a Horace, or a Muse as free:    .  .  .  .  58  E91 Vere          4
    That liv'st from hope, from feare, from faction free;  .  61  E95 Savile       18
    As free simplicitie, to dis-avow,     .  .  .  .  .  62  E96 Donne 2        5
    Of this we will sup free, but moderately,  .  .  .  .  65  E101 Supper      35
    Adde to thy free provisions, farre above  .  .  .  .  95  F2 Penshurst     58
    Free from proud porches, or their guilded roofes,  .  .  97  F3 Wroth         15
    The milke, nor oyle, did ever flowe soe free  .  .  .  98  F3 Wroth       V 60
    But left me free,      .      .  .  .  .  .  .  .  129  U1 Father         9
    To free a slave,      .      .  .  .  .  .  .  .  129  U1 Father        20
    And from basenesse to be free,      .  .  .  .  .  .  142  U2 Her man       51
    But by meere Chance? for interest? or to free  .  .  .  154  U13 Sacvile      30
    A pennance, where a man may not be free,  .  .  .  .  158  U14 Selden        8
    Because they would free Justice imitate,  .  .  .  .  170  U18 Elegy Can    18
    Minds that are great and free,      .  .  .  .  .  .  174  U23 Himselfe      16
    No Armour to the mind! he is shot-free    .  .  .  .  179  U25 Desmond       48
    Greeke was free from Rimes infection,    .  .  .  .  184  U29 Fit of Rime   31
    Is not yet free from Rimes wrongs,      .  .  .  .  184  U29 Fit of Rime   35
    One beautie in an Age, and free from thee?  .  .  .  .  188  U34 Small Poxe    2
    And lesse they know, who being free to use  .  .  .  190  U37 Friend-Book  22
    From each of which I labour to be free,  .  .  .  .  190  U37 Friend-Book  28
    And free societie, hee's borne else-where,  .  .  .  197  U40 Elegy That    16
    Where I may handle Silke, as free, and neere,  .  .  .  200  U42 Elegy Let    30
    Live by their Scale, that dare doe nothing free?  .  .  215  U44 Speach       68
    And free it from all question to preserve.  .  .  .  220  U47 Tribe        72
    Thy Circuits, and thy Rounds free,    .  .  .  .  .  221  U48 Bacchus       41
    When you would play so nobly, and so free.  .  .  .  230  U56 Covell         2
    All mouthes are open, and all stomacks free:  .  .  .  232  U58 Book-seller   2
    Of a free Poetique Pension,      .  .  .  .  .  .  259  U76 Petition       10
    Speakes Heavens Language! and discourseth free  .  .  271  U81 Pawlet       71
    Speakes Heavens Language! and discovereth free  .  .  271  U81 Pawlet     V 71
    His armes more acceptable free,      .  .  .  .  .  293  U87 Hor.3:9        3
    A quiet mind; free powers; and body sound:  .  .  .  295  U90 Mart.10:47    6
    New names of things.  It hath beene ever free,  .  .  309  Horace           83
    Fresh Lovers businesse, and the Wines free source.  .  311  Horace          116
    A ventring Merchant, or the Farmer free  .  .  .  .  313  Horace          165
    A ventring Merchant, or the husband free  .  .  .  .  342  Horace       V165
    The free spectators, subject to no Law,  .  .  .  .  319  Horace          324
```

216

	Page	Title	Line
FREE (cont.)			
These, the free meale might have beene well drawne out: . .	331	Horace	560
Lest the throng'd rings should a free laughter take: . .	352	Horace	V545/569
Why not? I'm gentle, and free-borne, doe hate . . .	331	Horace	571
Why not? being honest, and free-borne, doth hate . .	352	Horace	V547/571
Nine yeares kept in, your papers by, yo'are free . .	331	Horace	578
Nine yeares kept by, your papers in, y'are free . .	352	Horace	V554/578
Which he not denies. Now being so free, ...	381	Coryat 3	57
And like a hallow'd Temple, free from taint . . .	401	Beaumont	21
and of Circle be as free, ...	417	Moon	30
I have, with strict advantage of free tyme . . .	421	Censure	6
And lesse they knowe, that being free to use . .	422	Censure	15
Will unto Lycence, that free Leave Abuse: . . .	422	Censure	17
From each of which, I labor to be free, . . .	422	Censure	21
FREE-BORNE			
Why not? I'm gentle, and free-borne, doe hate . .	331	Horace	571
Why not? being honest, and free-borne, doth hate . .	352	Horace	V547/571
FREED			
And freed the soule from danger;	130	U1 Nativitie	9
To have her captiv'd spirit freed from flesh, . .	285	U84 Muse	93
FREEDOME			
Freedome doth with degree dispense.	98	F3 Wroth	58
And tasting ayre, and freedome, wull . . .	101	F4 To the World	31
Where every freedome is betray'd, ...	101	F4 To the World	51
This hath our ill-us'd freedome, and soft peace . .	166	U15 Friend-Wars	121
The noblest freedome, not to chuse . . .	173	U22 Elegy Tho	11
Freedome, and Truth; with love from those begot, .	241	U69 Friend Son	5
At a Friends freedome, proves all circling meanes .	242	U69 Friend Son	15
FREEHOULD			
In faire freehould, not an Inmate:	399	Lady Ogle	26
FREELY			
You cannot doubt, but I, who freely know . .	153	U13 Sacvile	13
This Good from you, as freely will it owe; . .	153	U13 Sacvile	14
And let him freely gather Loves First-fruits, . .	258	U75 Epithalam.	186
hee freely bringes; and on this Alter layes . .	383	Rich	9
FREER			
For, Bacchus, thou art freer	221	U48 Bacchus	13
FREEZ'D			
While he was young; he sweat; and freez'd againe: .	333	Horace	589
FREIND			
For less Securitie? O Freind, for these . .	165	U15 Friend-Wars	V113
Out-bee that Wife, in worth, thy freind did make: .	384	Somerset	12
To my truly-belov'd Freind, Mr Browne: on his Pastorals. .	386	Browne	Ttl
Your true freind in Judgement and Choise . .	395	May	25
Or of a parent! or a freind!	399	Lady Ogle	13
To a Freind an Epigram Of him. . . .	407	Inigo Jones 3	Ttl
An Epigram To My Joviall Good Freind Mr. Robert Dover, .	415	Dover	Ttl
FREINDES			
A wise simplicity; freindes alike-stated; . .	295	U90 Mart.10:47	7
Such weare true wedding robes, and are true freindes, .	384	Somerset	5
FREINDS			
Some men, of Bookes or Freinds not speaking right, .	386	Browne	1
trust in the tombes, their care-full freinds do rayse; .	387	Cavendish	6
Transmitt it to your Nephewes, Freinds, Allies, .	399	Lady Ogle	3
FREINDSHIP			
And to the perpetuating of our freindship . .	666	Glover	4
FRENCH			
That his whole body should speake french, not he? .	56	E88 Monsieur	2
That he, untravell'd, should be french so much, .	56	E88 Monsieur	7
As french-men in his companie, should seeme dutch? .	56	E88 Monsieur	8
The french disease, with which he labours yet? .	56	E88 Monsieur	10
Or is it some french statue? No: 'T doth move, .	56	E88 Monsieur	13
The new french-taylors motion, monthly made, .	56	E88 Monsieur	15
At naming the French King, their heads they shake, .	59	E92 New Crie	33
French to boote, at least in fashion, . .	141	U2 Her man	7
Commended the French-hood, and Scarlet gowne .	201	U42 Elegy Let	69
Old Aesope Gundomar: the French can tell, . .	213	U44 Speach	5
What is't to me whether the French Designe .	219	U47 Tribe	31
The nimble French;	368	Ode Who saith	84
French Aire and English Verse here wedded lie. .	401	Filmer	6
The faire French Daughter to learne English in; .	402	Filmer	12
FRENCH-HOOD			
Commended the French-hood, and Scarlet gowne .	201	U42 Elegy Let	69
FRENCH-MEN			
As french-men in his companie, should seeme dutch? .	56	E88 Monsieur	8
FRENCH-TAYLORS			
The new french-taylors motion, monthly made, .	56	E88 Monsieur	15
FREQUENT			
These be the :ause of those thicke frequent mists .	87	E133 Voyage	130
Most frequent tumults, horrors, and unrests, .	110	F11 Epode	33
The frequent varying of the deed, . . .	146	U6 Defence	11
In frequent speaking by the pious Psalmes . .	288	U84 Muse	191
FRESH			
Then takes up fresh commoditie, for dayes; .	30	E12 Shift	13
Thy selfe into fresh braules: when, call'd upon, .	32	E16 Brain-hardy	3
Fresh as the ayre, and new as are the houres. .	94	F2 Penshurst	40
A forme more fresh, then are the Eden bowers, .	111	F11 Epode	57
And after varyed, as fresh objects goes, . .	118	F13 Aubigny	66
Look'd not halfe so fresh, and faire, . .	138	U2 Kisse	9
And fresh and fragrant too, ...	147	U7 Nymph	16
Of many Colours; outward fresh, from spots, .	171	U20 Shrub	11
And on her Innocence, a garment fresh . .	285	U84 Muse	94
Or with fresh flowers to girt my temple round. .	293	U86 Hor.4:1	32

		Page	Title	Line

FRESH (cont.)
Fresh Lovers businesse, and the Wines free source. . . 311 Horace 116
If something fresh, that never yet was had . . 342 Horace V178
Reviving with fresh coulors the pale Ghosts . . 405 Inigo Jones 1 88
Fresh as the Day, and new as are the Howers, . . . 416 Welcome 1
And once more stryke the eare of tyme with those fresh straynes: 420 Ode:If Men 32
FRESHLY
Like tender buds shoot up, and freshly grow. . . . 309 Horace 89
FRIAR (See FRYAR)
FRIE
What though the greedie Frie . . . 175 U23 Himselfe 19
FRIEND (See also FREIND)
Who wets my grave, can be no friend of mine. . . 37 E33 Roe 3 6
As if thou wert my friend, but lack'dst a cause. . . 43 E52 Courtling 4
What art is thine, that so thy friend deceives? . . 44 E55 Beaumont 8
To a Friend. . . . . 54 E83 Friend Ttl
With thine owne course the judgement of thy friend, . 63 E98 Th Roe 1 8
Inviting a friend to supper. . . 64 E101 Supper Ttl
I sweare by your true friend, my Muse, I love . 70 E108 Soldiers 5
Is private gaine, which hath long guilt to friend. . 70 E109 Nevil 8
If holiest friend-ship, naked to the touch, . 78 E122 Rudyerd 2 7
And your brave friend, and mine so well did love. . 116 F12 Rutland 92
And your brave friend, and mine to well did love. . 116 F12 Rutland V 92
Before me here, the Friend and Sonne; . . 151 U12 Corbet 4
For I both lost a friend and Father, . . 151 U12 Corbet 5
Ben: Jonson To His Honord Friend Mr John Selden Health. 158 U14 Selden VTtl
Humanitie enough to be a friend, . . 161 U14 Selden 77
An Epistle to a Friend, to perswade him to the Warres. 162 U15 Friend-Wars Ttl
Wake, friend, from forth thy Lethargie: the Drum . 162 U15 Friend-Wars 1
Wake, friend, and finde thy self; awake, the Drum . 162 U15 Friend-Wars V 1
The brother trades a sister; and the friend . 165 U15 Friend-Wars 93
I'le bid thee looke no more, but flee, flee friend, . 166 U15 Friend-Wars 129
Friend, flie from hence; and let these kindled rimes 167 U15 Friend-Wars 162
Epistle To a Friend. . . . . 169 U17 Friend-Debt Ttl
Now so much friend, as you would trust in me, . 169 U17 Friend-Debt 14
Tell me (my lov'd Friend) doe you love, or no, . 170 U19 Elegy By 11
High-spirited friend, . . . 180 U26 Ode High 1
An Epistle to a friend. . . . 189 U37 Friend-Book Ttl
But, as a friend, which name your selfe receave, . 190 U37 Friend-Book 10
In friendship, I confesse: But, deare friend, heare. 190 U37 Friend-Book 18
First weigh a friend, then touch, and trie him too: . 216 U45 Squib 16
Friend to himselfe, that would be friend to thee. . 216 U45 Squib 22
But he that's too-much that, is friend of none. . 216 U45 Squib 24
That never yet did friend, or friendship seeke . 218 U47 Tribe 14
No friend to vertue, could be silent here. . 224 U50 Countesse 8
I Am to dine, Friend, where I must be weigh'd . 229 U54 Squib 1
Thou, Friend, wilt heare all censures; unto thee . 232 U58 Book-seller 1
Epigram. To a Friend, and Sonne. . . 241 U69 Friend Son Ttl
Sonne, and my Friend, I had not call'd you so . 241 U69 Friend Son 1
A perfect Patriot, and a noble friend, . . 244 U70 Ode 46
The Copie of his friend. . . . 247 U70 Ode 112
A Wife, a Friend, a Lady, or a Love; . . 285 U84 Muse 99
A solemne Mistresse, and so good a Friend, . 287 U84 Muse 175
Be wonne a friend; it must both sway, and bend . 317 Horace 281
Whether his soothing friend speake truth, or no. . 333 Horace 606
Hee'd say, Mend this, good friend, and this; 'tis naught. 333 Horace 624
He'd say, mend this my friend, and this, 'tis nought. 354 Horace V624
Why should I grieve my friend, this trifling way? . 335 Horace 640
To his much and worthily esteemed friend the Author. 383 Author Ttl
To his friend the Author upon his Richard. . 385 Brooke Ttl
To my worthy and honour'd Friend, Mr George Chapman, . . . 388 Chapman Ttl
To your desert, who'have done it, Friend. And this . 389 Aleman 21
But Sorrow, she desir'd no other Friend: . . 394 Jane Ogle 17
To my chosen Friend, the learned Translator of Lucan, . . . 395 May Ttl
. . . Muses Of His Friend M. Drayton. . . 396 Drayton Ttl
A Friend at all; or, if at all, to thee: . . 396 Drayton 2
If I can be a Friend, and Friend to thee. . . 398 Drayton 94
On the honor'd Poems of his honored Friend, . . . 400 Beaumont Ttl
To my worthy Friend, Master Edward Filmer, . . 401 Filmer Ttl
. . . (by his continu'd Vertue) my loving friend: . . . 409 Brome Ttl
To my Deare Sonne, and right-learned Friend, . . . 414 Rutter Ttl
FRIENDLY
And friendly should unto one end conspire. . . 333 Horace 586
And friendly should unto their end conspire. . 353 Horace V586
Out at his friendly eyes, leape, beat the groun'. . 333 Horace 613
FRIENDS
If any friends teares could restore, his would; . 35 E27 Roe 1 5
Make him loose all his friends; and, which is worse, 48 E65 Muse 9
For, if thou shame, ranck'd with my friends, to goe, 53 E77 Not name 3
Upon thy wel-made choise of friends, and bookes; . 55 E86 Goodyere 2 2
In making thy friends bookes, and thy bookes friends: 55 E86 Goodyere 2 4
Crowne with their owne. Rare poemes aske rare friends. 60 E94 Bedford 3 6
Like straight, thy pietie to God, and friends: . 68 E106 E Herbert 8
May windes as soft as breath of kissing friends, . 81 E128 Wm Roe 2 5
That, not a paire of friends each other see, . 81 E129 Mime 1
When thou would'st feast, or exercise thy friends. . 94 F2 Penshurst 21
Or with thy friends; the heart of all the yeere, . 97 F3 Wroth 25
Or with thy friends; the heate of all the yeere, . 97 F3 Wroth V 25
The fooles, or Tyrants with your friends, . . 145 U5 Woman-kind 2
Chance that the Friends affection proves Allay . 158 U14 Selden 10
Thy true friends wishes, Colby, which shall be, . 167 U15 Friend-Wars 176
Thy true friends wishes, which shall ever be, . 167 U15 Friend-Wars V176
And then the best are, still, the blindest friends! . 170 U18 Elegy Can 14

	Page	Title	Line
FRIENDS (cont.)			
You blush, but doe not: friends are either none,	171	U19 Elegy By	13
When a good Cause is destitute of friends,	186	U32 Elsmere	2
As flatt'ry with friends humours still to move.	190	U37 Friend-Book	27
I give, or owe my friends, into your Rites,	197	U40 Elegy That	12
My friends, the Watermen! They could provide	208	U43 Vulcan	124
Our friends, the Watermen! They could provide	208	U43 Vulcan	V124
'Tis vertue alone, or nothing, that knits friends:	216	U45 Squib	12
Then rest, and a friends value understand,	216	U45 Squib	25
And when you want those friends, or neere in blood,	224	U50 Countesse	26
Or your Allies, you make your bookes your friends,	224	U50 Countesse	27
His friends, but to breake Chaires, or cracke a Coach.	230	U56 Covell	10
At a Friends freedome, proves all circling meanes	242	U69 Friend Son	15
Rather to boast rich hangings, then rare friends.	242	U69 Friend Son	26
Troubled both foes, and friends;	243	U70 Ode	28
He purchas'd friends, and fame, and honours then,	244	U70 Ode	35
Bring all your friends, (faire Lord) that burne	251	U74 Weston	20
It brings Friends Joy, Foes Griefe, Posteritie Fame;	256	U75 Epithalam.	114
Made her friends joyes to get above their feares!	270	U81 Pawlet	60
To style us Friends, who were, by Nature, Foes?	286	U84 Muse	139
Liber, of all thy friends, thou sweetest care,	294	U89 Mart.8:77	1
Admitted to the sight, although his friends,	305	Horace	6
What to his Countrey, what his friends he owes,	325	Horace	446
To all thy vertuous, and well chosen Friends,	398	Drayton	90
FRIEND-SHIP			
If holiest friend-ship, naked to the touch,	78	E122 Rudyerd 2	7
FRIENDSHIP			
What is't, fine Grand, makes thee my friendship flye,	51	E73 Fine Grand	1
From friendship, is it's owne fames architect.	75	E115 Honest Man	30
Nor he, for friendship, to be thought unfit,	78	E121 Rudyerd 1	7
Solders crackt friendship; makes love last a day;	113	F12 Rutland	17
Friendship is now mask'd Hatred! Justice fled,	163	U15 Friend-Wars	39
And he is not in friendship. Nothing there	169	U17 Friend-Debt	5
A Womans friendship! God whom I trust in,	171	U20 Shrub	1
Which is indeed but friendship of the spit:	190	U37 Friend-Book	9
In friendship, I confesse: But, deare friend, heare.	190	U37 Friend-Book	18
That friendship which no chance but love did chuse,	190	U37 Friend-Book	23
In practiz'd friendship wholly to reprove,	190	U37 Friend-Book	26
Her furie, yet no friendship to betray.	190	U37 Friend-Book	33
Nor ever trusted to that friendship yet,	216	U45 Squib	7
That never yet did friend, or friendship seeke	218	U47 Tribe	14
Yet when of friendship I would draw the face,	227	U52 Answer	22
To the immortall memorie, and friendship of that noble	242	U70 Ode	Ttl
Two names of friendship, but one Starre:	246	U70 Ode	98
Friendship, in deed, was written, not in words:	247	U70 Ode	123
His better'd mind seekes wealth, and friendship: than	315	Horace	238
If of their friendship he be worthy, or no:	333	Horace	619
Of Latine and Greeke, to his friendship. And seven	380	Coryat 3	45
FRIENDSHIPS			
The Gaine of your two friendships! Hayward and	161	U14 Selden	81
The Graine of your two friendships! Hayward and	161	U14 Selden	V 81
I studie other friendships, and more one,	219	U47 Tribe	29
'Mongst which, if I have any friendships sent,	220	U47 Tribe	63
Where it were friendships schisme,	246	U70 Ode	90
FRIGHT			
Was, t'have a Boy stand with a Club, and fright	241	U69 Friend Son	11
To force the grates, that hold him in, would fright	337	Horace	675
FRIGHTED			
Not to be checkt, or frighted now with fate,	163	U15 Friend-Wars	35
First frighted men, that wildly liv'd, at ods,	327	Horace	480
FRIGHTS			
And then his thunder frights more, then it kills.	193	U38 Elegy 'Tis	70
FRINDES			
And Flatterye, with Frindes humors: still to move.	422	Censure	20
FRINDSHIPP			
That Frindshipp, which noe Chaunce, but Love did Chuse,	422	Censure	16
in Course of Frindshipp, wholie to reprove:	422	Censure	19
hir Furye, though noe Frindshipp hee betraye.	422	Censure	26
FRINGES			
The Stuffes, the Velvets, Plushes, Fringes, Lace,	202	U42 Elegy Let	79
Embroideries, Feathers, Fringes, Lace,	275	U84 Body	3
FRIPPERIE			
Whose workes are eene the fripperie of wit,	44	E56 Poet-Ape	2
FRO			
Of sixe times to, and fro, without embassage,	85	E133 Voyage	34
FROGS			
Arses were heard to croake, in stead of frogs;	84	E133 Voyage	13
Is this we heare? of frogs? No, guts wind-bound,	86	E133 Voyage	92
FROM			
Made from the hazard of anothers shame:	27	E2 My Booke	10
And such from whom let no man hope least good,	30	E11 Something	6
From my diseases danger, and from thee.	31	E13 Empirick	4
Shall out-live gyrlands, stolne from the chast tree.	32	E17 Critic	6
If any sword could save from Fates, Roe's could;	35	E27 Roe 1	3
And lyes so farre from wit, 'tis impudence.	38	E38 Guiltie 2	6
From servile flatterie (common Poets shame)	41	E43 Salisbury 1	11
Who this thy scape from rumour gratulate,	43	E51 James 3	6
No lesse than if from perill; and devout,	43	E51 James 3	7
From brocage is become so bold a thiefe,	44	E56 Poet-Ape	3
From locks of wooll, or shreds from the whole peece?	45	E56 Poet-Ape	14
Not from the publike voyce, but private fact;	47	E63 Salisbury 2	6
Contends t'have worth enjoy, from his regard,	48	E64 Salisbury 3	13
The Virgin, long-since fled from earth, I see,	52	E74 Chancelor	9

FROM (cont.)

	Page	Title	Line
Though Lippe, at Pauls, ranne from his text away,	52	E75 Lippe	3
Nor lend like influence from his lucent seat.	52	E76 Bedford 1	8
That liv'st from hope, from feare, from faction free;	61	E95 Savile	18
From place, or fortune, are made high, or low,	64	E99 Th Roe 2	9
Who could not but create them all, from you?	67	E105 L Wroth 2	6
I oft looke on false coyne, to know't from true:	68	E107 Hungry	3
Un-argued then, and yet hath fame from those;	71	E110 Edmonds 1	10
Caesar stands up, as from his urne late rose,	72	E111 Edmonds 2	12
Can come from Tripoly, leape stooles, and winke,	74	E115 Honest Man	11
From friendship, is it's owne fames architect.	75	E115 Honest Man	30
Them in, if not, from thee; or must commit	75	E116 Jephson	15
Whil'st thou dost rayse some Player, from the grave,	81	E129 Mime	11
Who gave, to take at his returne from Hell,	84	E133 Voyage	27
From Venice, Paris, or some in-land passage	85	E133 Voyage	33
And so they did, from Styx, to Acheron:	88	E133 Voyage	141
Is now from home. You lose your labours quite,	89	E133 Voyage	181
Free from proud porches, or their guilded roofes,	97	F3 Wroth	15
The hogs return'd home fat from mast;	98	F3 Wroth	44
Nor yellow honie from the tree	98	F3 Wroth	V 60
Hence-forth I quit thee from my thought,	100	F4 To the World	3
From all the nets that thou canst spread.	100	F4 To the World	8
From whence, so lately, I did burne,	101	F4 To the World	27
As little, as I hope from thee:	101	F4 To the World	38
From all my kinde: that, for my sake,	101	F4 To the World	59
The thirst, that from the soule doth rise,	106	F9 Celia 3	5
The thirst, that from the soule proceedes,	106	F9 Celia 3	V 5
But this doth from the cloud of error grow,	110	F11 Epode	35
It is a golden chaine let downe from heaven,	110	F11 Epode	47
Cast himselfe from the spire	111	F11 Epode	64
From thoughts of such a straine.	111	F11 Epode	114
From braines entranc'd, and fill'd with extasies;	112	F11 Epode	90
You will not from the paper slightly passe:	116	F12 Rutland	90
Remov'd, as you from need to have it such.	117	F13 Aubigny	25
Farre from the maze of custome, error, strife,	117	F13 Aubigny	28
Of your blest wombe, made fruitfull from above,	118	F13 Aubigny	60
Give me my cup, but from the Thespian well,	119	F13 Aubigny	95
Where have I beene this while exil'd from thee?	120	F14 Sydney	11
Eternall Spirit, God from both proceeding,	122	F15 Heaven	13
And freed the soule from danger;	128	U1 Trinitie	25
Farre I was from being stupid,	130	U1 Nativitie	9
And my motion from me quite;	132	U2 How he saw	5
And from her arched browes, such a grace	132	U2 How he saw	26
Have you seene the boy from the Chace	134	U2 Triumph	17
From your lips, and suck'd an ayre	135	U2 Triumph	V 39
And from basenesse to be free,	137	U2 Kisse	3
The good, from bad, is not descride,	142	U2 Her man	51
From being forsaken, then doth worth:	146	U6 Defence	17
From either heart, I know;	146	U6 Defence	22
But so exempt from blame,	148	U7 Nymph	32
Much from him I professe I wonne,	148	U7 Nymph	33
This Good from you, as freely will it owe;	152	U12 Corbet	29
Yet choyce from whom I take them; and would shame	153	U13 Sacvile	14
The memorie delights him more, from whom	153	U13 Sacvile	17
Then what he hath receiv'd. Gifts stinke from some,	153	U13 Sacvile	21
Run from the Conscience of it, if they could.	153	U13 Sacvile	22
And speaking worst of those, from whom they went	154	U13 Sacvile	46
But I to yours, farre from this fault, shall doo;	154	U13 Sacvile	51
Wake, friend, from forth thy Lethargie: the Drum	159	U14 Selden	V 17
From Hide-Parke to the Stage, where at the last	162	U15 Friend-Wars	1
Friend, flie from hence; and let these kindled rimes	165	U15 Friend-Wars	109
Light thee from hell on earth: where flatterers, spies,	167	U15 Friend-Wars	162
And from that thought strive to be understood.	167	U15 Friend-Wars	163
Of many Colours; outward fresh, from spots,	168	U15 Friend-Wars	188
But who should lesse expect from you,	171	U20 Shrub	11
His Altars kept from the Decay,	173	U22 Elegy Tho	13
Safe from the wolves black jaw, and the dull Asses hoofe.	173	U22 Elegy Tho	19
From Death, and darke oblivion, neere the same,	175	U23 Himselfe	36
Lock't in her cold embraces, from the view	175	U24 Frontispice	1
From injurie,	177	U25 Desmond	22
As farre from all revolt, as you are now from Fortune.	179	U25 Desmond	49
Rap't from the Earth, as not to die?	180	U25 Desmond	65
Wresting words, from their true calling;	181	U27 Ode Helen	14
Greeke was free from Rimes infection,	183	U29 Fit of Rime	7
Is not yet free from Rimes wrongs,	184	U29 Fit of Rime	31
So, from all sicknesse, may you rise to health,	184	U29 Fit of Rime	35
All mouthes, that dare entitle them (from hence)	186	U31 Elsmere	5
One beautie in an Age, and free from thee?	187	U33 Councellour	11
But must confesse from whom what gift I tooke.	188	U34 Small Poxe	2
From each of which I labour to be free,	189	U37 Friend-Book	6
As light breakes from you, that affrights despaire,	190	U37 Friend-Book	28
A man should flie from, as he would disdaine.	191	U38 Elegy 'Tis	10
To put all relish from my memorie	194	U38 Elegy 'Tis	104
Farre from the Nest, and so himselfe belie	197	U40 Elegy That	6
That from the Muses fountaines doth indorse	198	U40 Elegy That	38
Sooner then my affection from the faire.	200	U42 Elegy Let	7
that from the Foot-man, when he was become	200	U42 Elegy Let	13
From the poore wretch, which though he play'd in prose,	201	U42 Elegy Let	52
Had I compil'd from Amadis de Gaule,	201	U42 Elegy Let	61
or if thou wouldst enforce the power from her,	203	U43 Vulcan	29
Cloth Spices, or guard sweet meates from the flies,	204	U43 Vulcan	V 48
She durst not kisse, but flung thee from her brest.	205	U43 Vulcan	V 53
Did not she save from thence, to build a Rome?	208	U43 Vulcan	114
	210	U43 Vulcan	162

220

		Page	Title	Line
FROM (cont.)				
I will not argue thee, from those, of guilt,	. . . .	210	U43 Vulcan	165
I will not argue thee, from them, of guilt,	. . . .	210	U43 Vulcan	V165
Who from the Divels-Arse did Guns beget;	. . . .	212	U43 Vulcan	202
That from the Divels-Arse did Guns beget;	. . . .	212	U43 Vulcan	V202
And Ord'nance too: so much as from the Tower	. . .	213	U44 Speach	3
Nor markes of wealth so from our Nation fled,	. . .	213	U44 Speach	12
From the Tempestuous Grandlings, Who'll informe	. .	215	U44 Speach	64
From Guy, or Bevis, Arthur, or from whom	. . .	215	U44 Speach	81
That could but claime a kindred from the purse.	. .	216	U45 Squib	10
Or that the Match from Spaine was ever meant?	. . .	219	U47 Tribe	36
I have decreed; keepe it from waves, and presse;	. .	219	U47 Tribe	57
And free it from all question to preserve.	. . .	220	U47 Tribe	72
From any thought like sadnesse.	. . . .	221	U48 Bacchus	20
Have issue from the Barrell;	. . . .	221	U48 Bacchus	32
Farthest I am from the Idolatrie	. . . .	223	U49 Pucell	27
From Court, while yet thy fame hath some small day;	.	223	U49 Pucell	36
From whence they fall, cast downe with their owne weight.	.	224	U50 Countesse	12
To see you set apart, thus, from the rest,	. . .	234	U61 Epigram	10
The Angels from their Spheares:	. . . .	239	U67 Muses	21
So, the allowance from the King to use,	. . .	241	U68 House-hold	10
Freedome, and Truth; with love from those begot:	. .	241	U69 Friend Son	5
All live dogs from the lane, and his shops sight,	. .	241	U69 Friend Son	12
From out the horrour of that sack?	. . . .	243	U70 Ode	12
And keepe the one halfe from his Harry.	. . .	246	U70 Ode	94
Unto the Ships, and they from tier, to tier,	. . .	249	U72 King	2
Like Eccho playing from the other shore.	. . .	249	U72 King	8
Like Eccho playing from another shore.	. . .	249	U72 King	V 8
. . . gratulatorie For his Returne from his Embassie. 1632.	.	250	U74 Weston	Ttl
Rare Plants from ev'ry banke doe rise,	. . .	251	U74 Weston	10
From Greenwich, hither, to Row-hampton gate!	. . .	252	U75 Epithalam.	12
Their Sister-tunes, from Thames his either side,	. .	253	U75 Epithalam.	34
Force from the Phoenix, then, no raritie	. . .	255	U75 Epithalam.	81
Of Sex, to rob the Creature; but from Man	. . .	255	U75 Epithalam.	82
Hath drawne on me, from the times,	. . .	259	U76 Petition	17
Hath drawne on him, from the times,	. . .	259	U76 Petition	V 17
Not from the Arras, but the Persian Loomes.	. . .	260	U77 Treasurer	V 4
Hee drives diseases from our Folds,	. . .	265	U79 New-yeares	62
The theefe from spoyle, his presence holds.	. . .	265	U79 New-yeares	63
As hath thy James; cleans'd from originall drosse,	. .	268	U80 Christning	9
And beckning wooes me, from the fatall tree	. . .	268	U81 Pawlet	3
And voyce to raise them from my brazen Lungs,	. . .	269	U81 Pawlet	24
From the inherent Graces in her blood!	. . .	270	U81 Pawlet	36
From all affection! when they urg'd the Cure	. . .	270	U81 Pawlet	49
Run from your rootes; Tell, testifie the grand	. .	274	U84 Descent	9
As it slid moulded off from Heaven.	. . .	280	U84 Mind	56
Which Vertue from your Father, ripe, will fall;	. .	282	U84 Kenelme	22
With all her aydes, to save her from the seize	. .	283	U84 Muse	17
From off her pillow, and deluded bed;	. . .	283	U84 Muse	43
To have her captiv'd spirit freed from flesh,	. .	285	U84 Muse	93
Find all our Atomes from a point t' a span!	. . .	287	U84 Muse	152
Happie is he, that from all Businesse cleere,	. . .	289	U85 Country	1
Or in the bending Vale beholds from far	. . .	290	U85 Country	V 13
Whilst from the higher Bankes doe slide the floods;	. .	290	U85 Country	25
And from the sweet Tub Wine of this yeare takes,	. .	291	U85 Country	47
From fattest branches of the Tree:	. . .	291	U85 Country	56
Or Kid forc't from the Wolfe againe.	. . .	291	U85 Country	60
Thy night not dronken, but from cares layd wast;	. .	295	U90 Mart.10:47	9
On every limbe, ta'en from a severall creature,	. .	305	Horace	3
So they fall gently from the Grecian spring,	. . .	309	Horace	75
That from the North, the Navie safe doth store,	. .	309	Horace	92
In sound, quite from his fortune; both the rout,	. .	313	Horace	159
From whence thy Modestie, or Poemes law	. . .	313	Horace	193
Hee thinkes not, how to give you smoake from light,	. .	315	Horace	203
But light from smoake; that he may draw his bright	. .	315	Horace	204
Nor from the brand, with which the life did burne	. .	315	Horace	207
From the two Egges, that did disclose the twins.	. .	315	Horace	210
Where the midst differs from the first: or where	. .	315	Horace	217
The last doth from the midst dis-joyn'd appeare.	. .	315	Horace	218
Much from the sight, which faire report will make	. .	317	Horace	262
Now differ'd not from Delphick riddling.	. . .	319	Horace	310
From what th'obscene, and petulant Satyres are.	. .	321	Horace	340
Quite from all face of Tragedie to goe,	. . .	321	Horace	344
But, let the Faunes, drawne from their Groves, beware,	.	321	Horace	355
But meere Iambicks all, from first to last.	. . .	323	Horace	374
'Tis cleare, this way I have got off from blame,	. .	323	Horace	395
To part scurrilitie from wit: or can	. . .	323	Horace	403
Exclude all sober Poets, from their share	. . .	325	Horace	421
And from the Barber Licinus conceale	. . .	325	Horace	427
From the five ounces; what remaines? pronounce	. .	327	Horace	468
From slaughters, and foule life; and for the same	. .	327	Horace	481
Things sacred, from profane to separate;	. . .	327	Horace	487
The publike, from the private; to abate	. . .	327	Horace	488
Or trundling Wheele, he can sit still, from all;	. .	331	Horace	568
And both from Wine, and Women did abstaine.	. . .	333	Horace	590
Flowes from the surfets which we take in peace.	. .	363	Peace	4
As farre as Sinne's from lightnesse.	. . .	364	Ode Splendor	4
From Zephyr's rape would close him with his beames.	. .	366	Ode Who saith	24
Nor Sunne could make to vary from the rest,	. . .	367	Ode Who saith	29
But prove the Aire, and saile from Coast to Coast:	. .	367	Ode Who saith	37
From thence, display thy wing againe	. . .	367	Ode Who saith	41
From thence is gon	. . . .	368	Ode Who saith	68
From whose prowde bosome, thou began'st thy flight.	. .	368	Ode Who saith	80

		Page	Title	Line

FROM (cont.)
Or Tames be rap't from us . . . . 369 Ode Who saith 107
Conceal'd from all but cleare Propheticke eyes. . . . 369 Ode Who saith 112
Hee's carried like a Cripple, from Constable to Constable. . 374 Coryat 1 17
Religiously here he bids, row from the stewes, . . . 375 Coryat 1 20
Here, finer then comming from his Punke you him see, . . 375 Coryat 1 28
As well as from his braines, and claimest thereby . . 378 Coryat 2 90
From Venice to Flushing, were not they well cobled? . . 380 Coryat 3 42
yf from a little sparke hee rise not fier. . . . 383 Rich 16
From thence to honour thee, I would not seeke . . . 391 Shakespeare 32
Sent forth, or since did from their ashes come. . . . 391 Shakespeare 40
Which, since thy flight from hence, hath mourn'd like night, . 392 Shakespeare 79
Hot from thy trumpet, round, about the world. . . . 396 Drayton 14
I saw a Beauty from the Sea to rise, ... 396 Drayton 15
And like a hallow'd Temple, free from taint . . . 401 Beaumont 21
From thirty pound in pipkins, to the Man . . . 402 Inigo Jones 1 2
you are; from them leapt forth an Architect, . . . 402 Inigo Jones 1 3
Suckt from the Veynes of shop-philosophy. . . . 405 Inigo Jones 1 74
From the fam'd pillars of old Hercules! . . . . 407 Inigo Jones 2 14
Which you have justly gained from the Stage, . . . 409 Brome 6
Nor Degradation from the Ministry, ... 410 Gill 6
From fearefull back-slides; And the debt we'are in, . . 412 Sutcliffe 15
The third, is from the garden cull'd, the Rose, . . . 413 Ghyrlond 13
(You have deserv'd it from me) I have read, . . . 415 Rutter 13
Concluded from a Carract to a dramme. . . . 415 Rutter 30
As Cleare, and distant, as yourselfe from Cryme; . . 421 Censure 8
From each of which, I labor to be free, . . . 422 Censure 21
Looke how the starres from earth, or seas from flames . 422 Lucan 7
are distant, so is proffitt from just aymes. . . . 422 Lucan 8
FRONT
So to front death, as men might judge us past it. . . 54 E80 Life/Death 7
Front, an ample field of snow; . . . . . 141 U2 Her man 18
The Minde of the Front . . . . . . 175 U24 Frontispice VTtl
FRONTIRE
The Bound, and Frontire of our Poetrie; . . . . 400 Beaumont 8
FRONTISPICE
The mind of the Frontispice to a Booke. . . . 175 U24 Frontispice Ttl
FROSTES
Unseason'd frostes, or the most envyous weather. . . 361 Palmer 8
FROSTIEST
It thawes the frostiest, and most stiffe disdaine: . . 363 Riches 13
FROSTILY
Dispraise my worke, then praise it frostily: . . . 43 E52 Courtling 2
FROSTS
Of humane life! as all the frosts, and sweates . . 233 U59 Newcastle 22
FROWARD
Of froward Citizens; make the Nations know . . . 261 U77 Treasurer V 19
Froward, complaining, a commender glad . . . 317 Horace 247
FROWNE
I pluck'd a branch; the jealous god did frowne, . . 80 E126 Mrs Cary 3
Busie, or frowne at first; when he sees thee, . . . 262 U78 Digby 20
How they would frowne! . . . . . . 369 Ode Who saith 110
FROWNES
Who frownes, who jealous is, who taxeth me. . . . 200 U42 Elegy Let 10
FROWNING
Pallas frowning. . . . . 183 U29 Fit of Rime 30
FRUIT
Digestive cheese, and fruit there sure will bee; . . 65 E101 Supper 27
Then hath thy orchard fruit, thy garden flowers, . . 94 F2 Penshurst 39
'Tis no sinne, loves fruit to steale, ... 102 F5 Celia 1 15
On all mens Fruit, and flowers, as well as mine. . . 150 U10 Jealousie 8
With all the fruit shall follow it, ... 251 U74 Weston 23
By which yo'are planted, shew's your fruit shall bide. . 281 U84 Kenelme 19
FRUITE
And eve'ry joy, in mariage, turne a fruite. . . . 384 Somerset 18
FRUITES
And pray the fruites thereof, and the increase; . . 212 U43 Vulcan 210
FRUITFULL
Thy lady's noble, fruitfull, chaste withall. . . . 96 F2 Penshurst 90
Of your blest wombe, made fruitfull from above, . . 119 F13 Aubigny 95
So may the fruitfull Vine my temples steepe, . . . 190 U37 Friend-Book 14
Deceit is fruitfull. Men have Masques and nets, . . 216 U45 Squib 18
Are growne so fruitfull, and false pleasures climbe, . . 224 U50 Countesse 10
So fruitfull, and so faire, ... 240 U67 Muses 52
Shoot up an Olive fruitfull, faire, ... 251 U74 Weston 28
Your fruitfull spreading Vine, ... 257 U75 Epithalam. 159
FRUITLESSE
And with his hooke lops off the fruitlesse race, . . 290 U85 Country 11
FRUITS
If, as their ends, their fruits were so, the same, . . 45 E57 Bawds 1
With thy new place, bring I these early fruits . . 47 E64 Salisbury 3 2
Who dares denie, that all first-fruits are due . . 235 U63 Charles 2 1
Who doubts, those fruits God can with gaine restore, . . 235 U63 Charles 2 3
Had sow'd these fruits, and got the harvest in. . . 247 U70 Ode 128
And let him freely gather Loves First-fruits, . . . 258 U75 Epithalam. 186
Best Kings expect first-fruits of your glad gaines. . . 263 U79 New-yeares 13
Wine, or delicious fruits, unto the Taste; . . . 286 U84 Muse 123
Our first of fruits, that is the prime of flowers . . 416 Welcome 2
FRY   (See FRIE)
FRYAR
Or stay'd but where the Fryar, and you first met, . . 212 U43 Vulcan 201
FRYERS
That haunt Pickt-hatch, Mersh-Lambeth, and White-fryers, . 30 E12 Shift 2

			Page	Title	Line

FUCUS
To consult, if Fucus this . . . . 140 U2 Promise 26
FULIGINOUS
Of Lanterne-lerry: with fuliginous heat . . . . 405 Inigo Jones 1 72
FULL
Thou should'st be bold, licentious, full of gall, . . . 27 E2 My Booke 3
And talke reserv'd, lock'd up, and full of feare, . . 59 E92 New Crie 17
If we can get her, full of egs, and then, ... 64 E101 Supper 12
And yet are with their Princes: Fill them full . . 69 E107 Hungry 7
The full, the flowing graces there enshrin'd; . . . 79 E125 Uvedale 8
How full of want, how swallow'd up, how dead . . . 80 E127 Aubigny 6
To the full greatnesse of the cry: . . . . . 97 F3 Wroth 32
In the full floud of her admir'd perfection? . . . 112 F11 Epode 107
I know my state, both full of shame, and scorne, . . 122 F15 Heaven 17
That to such Natures let their full hands flow, . . 154 U13 Sacvile 60
Aloft, grow lesse and streightned, full of knot; . . 157 U13 Sacvile 152
But their whole inside full of ends, and knots? . . 171 U20 Shrub 12
In one full Action; nor have you now more . . . 180 U26 Ode High 17
The poores full Store-house, and just servants field. . 185 U30 Burleigh 8
Whose even Thred the Fates spinne round, and full, . 225 U51 Bacon 15
Full twentie stone; of which I lack two pound: . . 229 U54 Squib 12
Haile Mary, full of grace, it once was said, . . . 238 U66 Queene 1
Haile Mary, full of honours, to my Queene, . . . 238 U66 Queene 5
That when the Quire is full, ... 239 U67 Muses 19
By him, so ample, full, and round, ... 244 U70 Ode 49
Or taste a part of that full joy he meant . . . 246 U70 Ode 87
With what full hands, and in how plenteous showers . 254 U75 Epithalam. 65
A full hundred Markes annuitie, ... 259 U76 Petition V 11
And the whole Banquet is full sight of God! . . . 284 U84 Muse 65
But flowes out, that ore-swelleth in full brests. . . 329 Horace 506
Till he drop off, a Horse-leech, full of blood. . . 337 Horace 680
Till, horse-leech-like, he drop off, full of blood. . 355 Horace V680
Old Hat here, torne Hose, with Shoes full of gravell, . 375 Coryat 1 26
If Praises, when th'are full, heaping admit, . . . 385 Brooke 6
trust in the tombes, their care-full freinds do rayse; . 387 Cavendish 6
It cast a beame as when the chear-full Sun . . . 396 Drayton 17
Then Affricke knew, or the full Grecian store! . . 398 Drayton 88
All, pouring their full showre of graces downe, . . 413 Ghyrlond 31
FULNESSE
Presume to interpell that fulnesse, when . . . . 284 U84 Muse 70
What fulnesse of beatitude is here? . . . . . 286 U84 Muse 137
FUME
Had it beene seconded, and not in fume . . . . 87 E133 Voyage 109
FUMES
Their reeking fumes; . . . . 368 Ode Who saith 78
FUMIE
Or fumie clysters, thy moist lungs to bake: . . . 42 E50 Cod 3 2
FUNERALL
Ere blacks were bought for his owne funerall, . . . 41 E44 Chuff 3
FUNERALLS
As those that hir'd to weepe at Funeralls, swoune, . 333 Horace 614
FURIE
Canst tell me best, how every Furie lookes there, . 85 E133 Voyage 52
Tempt not his furie, Pluto is away: . . . . . 89 E133 Voyage 179
The furie of a rash command, ... 98 F3 Wroth 68
The furie of some rash command, ... 98 F3 Wroth V 68
What furie of late is crept into our Feasts? . . . 166 U15 Friend-Wars 117
Her furie, yet no friendship to betray. . . . . 190 U37 Friend-Book 33
Alone lend succours, and this furie stay, ... 191 U38 Elegy 'Tis 8
Against thy furie, when to serve their needs, . . . 208 U43 Vulcan 125
FURIES
Could not effect, not all the furies doe, ... 37 E32 Roe 2 2
Furies there wanted not: each scold was ten. . . . 84 E133 Voyage 15
Your Fleet-lane Furies; and hot cookes doe dwell, . 88 E133 Voyage 143
FURIOUS
When he is furious, love, although not lust. . . . 200 U42 Elegy Let 18
Those that are wise, a furious Poet feare, . . . 354 Horace V643
The yellow Jaundies, or were furious mad . . . . 335 Horace 646
FURNACE (See FORNACE)
FURNACES
the Dyers, Glasshouse and the furnaces; . . . . 211 U43 Vulcan V180
FURNISH
The Credit, what would furnish a tenth Muse! . . 161 U14 Selden 84
FURNITURE
No noble furniture of parts, ... 234 U60 La-ware 11
FURRE
In outward face, but inward, light as Furre, . . . 162 U15 Friend-Wars 20
FURROWES
And furrowes laden with their weight; . . . . 98 F3 Wroth 42
FURTHER
A little further, to make thee a roome: . . . . 391 Shakespeare 21
FURY
A farther fury my ray'sd spirit Controules, . . . 108 F10 Proludium 12
For fury wasteth, ... 179 U25 Desmond 46
And in an Epicoene fury can write newes . . . . 222 U49 Pucell 8
Sword, fire, and famine, with fell fury met; . . . 243 U70 Ode 17
FURYE
hir Furye, though noe Frindshipp hee betraye. . . . 422 Censure 26
FUTURE
T'all future time, not onely doth restore . . . . 71 E110 Edmonds 1 21
Yet drown'd they not. They had five lives in future. . 88 E133 Voyage 154
The Christian hath t'enjoy the future life, ... 271 U81 Pawlet 96

	Page	Title	Line

FYL'S
And for the troubled Clyent fyl's his tongue, . . . 292 U86 Hor.4:1 14
FYNE
Sense, what they are! which by a specious fyne . . . 404 Inigo Jones 1 55
FYNED
Sleeked limmes, and fyned blood? . . . 105 F8 Sicknesse V 23
FYRE
And rather to the Fyre, then to the Rowte . . . 420 Ode:If Men 21
FYRES
Whom not ten fyres, nor a Parlyament can . . . 406 Inigo Jones 1 103
GAINE   (See also GAYNE)
Thou, that mak'st gaine thy end, and wisely well, . . . 27 E3 Bookseller 1
Each night, to drowne his cares: But when the gaine . . . 56 E87 Hazard 3
Is private gaine, which hath long guilt to friend. . . . 70 E109 Nevil 8
And (to gaine her by his Art) . . . 133 U2 Suffered 15
All the Gaine, all the Good, of the Elements strife. . . . 134 U2 Triumph 20
The Gaine of your two friendships! Hayward and . . . 161 U14 Selden 81
To gaine upon his belly; and at last . . . 162 U15 Friend-Wars 17
Is done for gaine: If't be, 'tis not sincere. . . . 169 U17 Friend-Debt 6
Who thus long safe, would gaine upon the times . . . 186 U32 Elsmere 9
I gaine, in having leave to keepe my Day, . . . 231 U56 Covell 29
Who doubts, those fruits God can with gaine restore, . . . 235 U63 Charles 2 3
The glorie, and gaine of rest, which the place gives! . . . 283 U84 Muse 38
For so, they shall not onely gaine the worth, . . . 325 Horace 425
His flatterers to their gaine. But say, he can . . . 333 Horace 601
His praisers to their gaine: but say he can . . . 353 Horace V601
Or for the lawrell, he may gaine a scorne, . . . 392 Shakespeare 63
To gaine the Crowne of immortalitye, . . . 400 Lady Ogle 34
GAIN'D
He hath not onely gain'd himselfe his eyes, . . . 74 E114 Sydney 7
But, he had not gain'd his sight . . . 132 U2 How he saw 13
In that proud manner, as a good so gain'd, . . . 154 U13 Sacvile 37
Happy in that faire honour it hath gain'd, . . . 180 U26 Ode High 14
So have you gain'd a Servant, and a Muse: . . . 230 U56 Covell 5
GAINED
Which you have justly gained from the Stage, . . . 409 Brome 6
GAINES
Best Kings expect first-fruits of your glad gaines. . . . 263 U79 New-yeares 13
GAITE   (See also GATE)
And keepe an even, and unalter'd gaite; . . . 118 F13 Aubigny 61
GALBA
Where Nero falls, and Galba is ador'd, . . . 61 E95 Savile 8
GALL
Thou should'st be bold, licentious, full of gall, . . . 27 E2 My Booke 3
GALLANT
Shee doth instruct men by her gallant flight, . . . 55 E85 Goodyere 1 5
GALLANTRY
Of our Towne Gallantry! or why there rests . . . 155 U13 Sacvile 92
GALLANTS
The Academie, where the Gallants meet-- . . . 215 U44 Speach 89
Our Gallants give them none, but passe them by: . . . 329 Horace 513
Not wearing moodes, as gallants doe a fashion, . . . 362 Author 3
GALLO
And the Gazetti, or Gallo-Belgicus: . . . 59 E92 New Crie 16
GALLO-BELGICUS
And the Gazetti, or Gallo-Belgicus: . . . 59 E92 New Crie 16
GALLUS
With bright Lycoris, Gallus choice, . . . 181 U27 Ode Helen 15
GAMAGE
Thy copp's, too, nam'd of Gamage, thou hast there, . . . 94 F2 Penshurst 19
GAMBOL
Of gambol, or sport . . . 231 U57 Burges 19
GAME
Baudrie', and usurie were one kind of game. . . . 45 E57 Bawds 2
O, (thou cry'st out) that is thy proper game. . . . 73 E112 Gamster 16
And, for thee, at common game, . . . 105 F8 Sicknesse 41
And, for that, at common game, . . . 105 F8 Sicknesse V 41
Where fight the prime Cocks of the Game, for wit? . . . 222 U49 Pucell 4
GAMES
And all the games of Fortune, plaid at Court; . . . 234 U61 Epigram 2
Hee, that not knowes the games, nor how to use . . . 331 Horace 565
But I can tell thee, Dover, how thy Games . . . 415 Dover 3
GAMESTER
(Compos'd of Gamester, Captaine, Knight, Knight's man, . . . 370 Fletcher 3
GAM'STER
On reformed Gam'ster. . . . 33 E21 Gam'ster Ttl
Lord, how is Gam'ster chang'd! his haire close cut! . . . 33 E21 Gam'ster 1
GAMSTER
To a weake Gamster in Poetry. . . . 72 E112 Gamster Ttl
GANIMEDE
And how his Ganimede mov'd, and how his goate, . . . 34 E25 Beast 1 4
GAPING
The sluggish gaping auditor devoures; . . . 45 E56 Poet-Ape 10
What doth this Promiser such gaping worth . . . 313 Horace 197
What doth this Promiser such great gaping worth . . . 343 Horace V197
GARDEN
The meate-boate of Beares colledge, Paris-garden, . . . 87 E133 Voyage 117
Then hath thy orchard fruit, thy garden flowers, . . . 94 F2 Penshurst 39
And that accursed ground, the Parish-Garden: . . . 209 U43 Vulcan 147
And that prophaner ground, the Parish-Garden: . . . 209 U43 Vulcan V147
And all the Ground were Garden, where she led! . . . 254 U75 Epithalam. 68
The third, is from the garden cull'd, the Rose, . . . 413 Ghyrlond 13

GARDENS
Thee quickly come the gardens eye to bee, ... 238 U65 Prince 8
GARLAND (See also GHYRLOND, GYRLAND)
Put on my Ivy Garland, let me see . . . . . 200 U42 Elegy Let 9
Accept this garland, plant it on thy head, . . . 245 U70 Ode 77
In gracefull Ornament of Garland, Gemmes, and Haire. . . 253 U75 Epithalam. 40
To pluck a Garland, for her selfe, or mee? . . . . 268 U81 Pawlet 4
Now, in a garland by the graces knit: . . . . 416 Welcome 4
GARLANDS
The withered Garlands tane away; . . . . . 173 U22 Elegy Tho 18
Thy locks, and rosie garlands crowne thy head; . . . 294 U89 Mart.8:77 4
GARMENT
And on her Innocence, a garment fresh . . . . 285 U84 Muse 94
GARTER
And shooe, and tye, and garter should come hether, . . . 56 E88 Monsieur 4
GARTERS
His rosie tyes and garters so ore-blowne, ... 62 E97 Motion 5
GASPE
That gaspe for action, and would yet revive . . . 162 U15 Friend-Wars 6
GATE (ENTRY)
And to left-Lydia, now the gate stood ope. . . . 294 U87 Hor.3:9 20
The House of gold, the Gate of heavens power, . . . 413 Ghyrlond 39
GATE
Ripe are their ruffes, their cuffes, their beards, their gate, 58 E92 New Crie 6
Or Saturnias gate . . . . 136 U2 Triumph V 44
What love you then? your whore. what study? gate, . . 215 U44 Speach 87
From Greenwich, hither, to Row-hampton gate! . . . 252 U75 Epithalam. 12
But, kept an even gate, as some streight tree . . . 287 U84 Muse 165
Although the gate were hard, the gayne is sweete. . . . 418 Answer 7
GATES
Their guarded gates asunder? . . . . . 239 U67 Muses 12
Were they as strong ram'd up as Aetna gates. . . . 363 Riches 10
GATHER
Where, you say, men gather blisses, ... 136 U2 Cupid 26
Of him whose bones this Grave doth gather: . . . 151 U12 Corbet 6
Where men at once may plant, and gather blisses: . . 170 U19 Elegy By 10
And let him freely gather Loves First-fruits, . . . 258 U75 Epithalam. 186
GATHER'D
Be alwayes to thy gather'd selfe the same: . . . 63 E98 Th Roe 1 9
Talkes loud, and baudy, has a gather'd deale . . . 74 E115 Honest Man 9
More sweet then Olives, that new gather'd be . . . 291 U85 Country 55
For grapes he had gather'd before they were eaten. . . 375 Coryat 1 25
For grapes he had gather'd, before they were eaten. . . 380 Coryat 3 36
GATHERER
To Old-end Gatherer. . . . . . . 43 E53 Old-end Ttl
GATHERING
Long-gathering Old-end, I did feare thee wise, . . . 43 E53 Old-end 1
Of Gathering? Bountie' in pouring out againe? . . . 159 U14 Selden 38
Are gathering by the Wintry houres; . . . . 290 U85 Country 30
GAUDY
Of sorrow, then all pompe of gaudy daies: . . . 287 U84 Muse 182
GAULE
Had I compil'd from Amadis de Gaule, ... 203 U43 Vulcan 29
GAVE
And gave thee both, to shew they could no more. . . 28 E4 James 1 4
Of old, they gave a cock to Aesculape; . . . 31 E13 Empirick 2
For what shee gave, a whore; a baud, shee cures. . . 39 E41 Gypsee 4
Who gave, to take at his returne from Hell, . . . 84 E133 Voyage 27
The foole that gave it; who will want, and weepe, . . 113 F12 Rutland 13
The foole that gave it; that will want, and weepe, . . 113 F12 Rutland V 13
Wherein wise Nature you a dowrie gave, . . . 114 F12 Rutland 35
Gave killing strokes. There were brave men, before . . 114 F12 Rutland 53
Her Ovid gave her, dimm'd the fame . . . . 181 U27 Ode Helen 18
Her owne bloud gave her: Shee ne're had, nor hath . . 188 U34 Small Poxe 9
And which you (being the worthier) gave me leave . . 190 U37 Friend-Book 11
Could you demand the gifts you gave, againe? . . . 192 U38 Elegy 'Tis 55
And Mars, that gave thee a Lanthorne for a Crowne. . . 203 U43 Vulcan 10
Gave two such Houses as Northumberland, . . . 274 U84 Descent 5
. . . gave me leave to call her so. Being Her . . . 282 U84 Muse Ttl
For 'twas himselfe who form'd, and gave it her. . . 287 U84 Muse 156
Unto the Lyrick Strings, the Muse gave grace . . . 309 Horace 113
A foot, whose swiftnesse gave the Verse the name . . 323 Horace 372
The Muse not only gave the Greek's a wit, . . . 327 Horace 461
For though Spaine gave him his first ayre and Vogue, . . 389 Aleman 15
By Cherissheinge the Spirrits that gave their greatnesse grace: 419 Ode:If Men 5
GAVEST
This All of nothing, gavest it forme, and fate, . . . 127 U1 Trinitie 18
GAV'ST
Martial, thou gav'st farre nobler Epigrammes . . . 38 E36 Martial 1
That gav'st a Sonne, ... 129 U1 Father 19
Thy Neeces line, then thou that gav'st thy Name . . 274 U84 Descent 14
GAYNE
Makes a most blessed gayne. . . . . . 112 F11 Epode 86
Although the gate were hard, the gayne is sweete. . . 418 Answer 7
GAYNES
Though never after; whiles it gaynes the voyce . . . 113 F12 Rutland 11
Though never after; whiles it gaynes the will . . . 113 F12 Rutland V 11
GAZE
To catch the worlds loose laughter, or vaine gaze. . . 27 E2 My Booke 12
Did her perfections call me on to gaze, . . . 169 U18 Elegy Can 3
GAZERS
All the gazers on the skies . . . . . 39 E40 Ratcliffe 5

		Page	Title	Line

GAZETTI
   And the Gazetti, or Gallo-Belgicus: 59   E92 New Crie   16
GEARE
   I can out of knowne geare, a fable frame,   321   Horace   349
GEESE
   To light Tobacco, or save roasted Geese,   205   U43 Vulcan   52
   To light Tobacco, or have roasted Geese,   205   U43 Vulcan   V 52
GEFFRY
   Thou paint a Lane, where Thumb with Geffry meets!   407   Inigo Jones 2   V 12
GEMME   (See also JEMME)
   Peepe forth a Gemme; to see   258   U75 Epithalam.   175
GEMMES
   In gracefull Ornament of Garland, Gemmes, and Haire.   253   U75 Epithalam.   40
GEMS
   Though many Gems be in your bosome stor'd,   179   U25 Desmond   55
GENERALL
   Of generall knowledge; watch'd men, manners too,   159   U14 Selden   33
   As if the generall store thou didst command   187   U33 Councellour   26
   So generall a gladnesse to an Isle,   238   U66 Queene   9
   At least, if not the generall Engine cracke.   395   May   6
   Throughout their generall breasts,   421   Ode:If Men   43
GENEROUS
   Much more a noble, and right generous mind   112   F11 Epode   111
   Much more a noble, or a generous mind   112   F11 Epode   V111
   Of any, is a great and generous Deed: 155   U13 Sacvile   76
GENIUS
   And he, with his best Genius left alone.   120   F14 Sydney   20
   Where art thou, Genius? I should use   176   U25 Desmond   1
   Genius, where art thou? I should use   176   U25 Desmond   V 1
   The wit of Ale, and Genius of the Malt   193   U38 Elegy 'Tis   95
   Haile, happie Genius of this antient pile!   225   U51 Bacon   1
   For in the Genius of a Poets Verse,   241   U68 House-hold   13
   Steepe the glad Genius in the Wine, whole dayes,   319   Horace   298
   As was the Genius wherewith they were wrote;   389   Aleman   12
   The selfe same Genius! so the worke will say.   395   May   23
   This Booke will live; It hath a Genius: This   400   Beaumont   1
GENTILE
   That is an essence, most gentile and fine,   110   F11 Epode   V 45
GENTLE
   Which cover lightly, gentle earth.   34   E22 Daughter   12
   To the World. A farewell for a Gentle-woman, ...   100   F4 To the World   Ttl
   That is an essence, farre more gentle, fine,   110   F11 Epode   45
   My gentle Arthur; that it might be said   216   U45 Squib   3
   What gentle Ghost, besprent with April deaw,   268   U81 Pawlet   1
   With gentle Calais, Thurine Orniths Sonne;   293   U87 Hor.3:9   14
   To gentle: not that we should Serpents see   338   Horace   V 15
   The nailes, and every gentle haire disclose;   339   Horace   V 49/ 47
   Why not? I'm gentle, and free-borne, doe hate   331   Horace   571
   And cry aloud, Helpe, gentle Countrey-men,   335   Horace   653
   It was for gentle Shakespeare cut;   390   Reader   2
   My gentle Shakespeare, must enjoy a part.   392   Shakespeare   56
GENTLEMAN
   ... that Noble Gentleman, Mr. Hierome Weston, Son, and ...   252   U75 Epithalam.   Ttl
   ... A Gentleman absolute in all Numbers;   272   U84 Eupheme   Ttl
GENTLEMEN
   The greatest are but growing Gentlemen.   281   U84 Kenelme   15
GENTLER
   Their gentler spirits have suck'd innocence.   96   F2 Penshurst   94
   A gentler, and more agile hand, to tend   180   U26 Ode High   4
   So may the gentler Muses, and good fame   186   U31 Elsmere   7
   Thou prov'st the gentler wayes, to clense the wound,   187   U33 Councellour   20
   Haste, haste you hither, all you gentler Swaines,   265   U79 New-yeares   46
   A gentler Bird, then this,   366   Ode Who saith   7
GENTLEST
   As not the smallest joint, or gentlest word   395   May   21
GENTLE-WOMAN
   To the World. A farewell for a Gentle-woman, ...   100   F4 To the World   Ttl
GENTLIE
   gentlie hee asketh, shee will pay: no suits,   258   U75 Epithalam.   V188
GENTLY
   But stooping gently, as a Cloud,   280   U84 Mind   58
   So they fall gently from the Grecian spring,   309   Horace   75
GENT'MAN
   And he remov'd to gent'man of the horse,   57   E90 Mill   12
GENTRIE
   All gentrie, yet, owe part of their best flame!   75   E116 Jephson   2
   That in the Cradle of their Gentrie are;   215   U44 Speach   84
   And Roman Gentrie, jearing, will laugh out.   313   Horace   160
   And Roman Gentrie, will with laughter shout.   342   Horace   V160
   The Roman Gentrie, men of birth, and meane,   321   Horace   360
GEORGE
   To Kenelme, John, George.   281   U84 Kenelme   Ttl
   To my worthy and honour'd Friend, Mr George Chapman, ...   388   Chapman   Ttl
GEORGES
   If they stay here, but till Saint Georges Day.   213   U44 Speach   10
   In great Saint Georges Union;   221   U48 Bacchus   44
GERMANY
   Their hornes, and Germany pukes on his head.   375   Coryat 1   31
   The Low-countries, Germany and Rhetia   379   Coryat 3   20
GESTS
   The gests of Kings, great Captaines, and sad Warres,   309   Horace   105
GESTURE
   On some new gesture, that's imputed wit?   81   E129 Mime   14

GESTURE (cont.)
Gesture, and riot, whilst he swooping went . . . . 319 Horace 304
Gesture, and riot, whilst he wandring went . . . . 346 Horace V304
GET
As theirs did with thee, mine might credit get: . . . 32 E18 Censurer 6
That Cod can get no widdow, yet a knight, . . . 33 E19 Cod 1 1
And get more gold, then all the colledge can: . . . 39 E41 Gypsee 2
Hee that wooes every widdow, will get none. . . . 42 E47 Luckless 2 2
Get him the times long grudge, the courts ill will; . . . 48 E65 Muse 7
Or had his father, when he did him get, ... 56 E88 Monsieur 9
They all get Porta, for the sundrie wayes . . . 59 E92 New Crie 25
With England. All forbidden bookes they get. . . . 59 E92 New Crie 31
If we can get her, full of egs, and then, . . . 64 E101 Supper 12
If men get name, for some one vertue: Then, . . . 68 E106 E Herbert 1
It is enough, they once did get . . . . 93 F1 Why write no 5
Nor how to get the lawyer fees. . . . 98 F3 Wroth 62
Get place, and honor, and be glad to keepe . . . 99 F3 Wroth 87
Get place, and honor, and be proud to keepe . . . 99 F3 Wroth V 87
Goe, get thee quickly forth, ... 150 U10 Jealousie 13
Before men get a verse: much lesse a Praise; . . . 159 U14 Selden 26
And (which doth all Atchievements get above) . . . 187 U33 Councellour 38
Of newes they get, to strew out the long meale, . . . 218 U47 Tribe 28
Be, or be not, to get the Val-telline? . . . 219 U47 Tribe 32
Never so great to get them: and the ends, . . . 242 U69 Friend Son 25
I would, if price, or prayer could them get, . . . 260 U77 Treasurer 5
Made her friends joyes to get above their feares! . . . 270 U81 Pawlet 60
This booke will get the Sosii money; This . . . 329 Horace 517
Get broken peeces, and fight well by those. . . . 398 Drayton 74
GETS
To draw thee custome: but her selfe gets all. . . . 53 E78 Hornet 2
The cloth's no sooner gone, but it gets up . . . 74 E115 Honest Man 24
Of miming, gets th'opinion of a wit. . . . 74 E115 Honest Man 28
While thus it gets grace, and hunts poore fame; . . . 113 F12 Rutland V 15
The Serpents head: Gets above Death, and Sinne, . . . 272 U81 Pawlet 99
'Gainst th'Ides, his moneys he gets in with paine, . . . 291 U85 Country 69
'Gainst th'Ides, his gott moneyes he gets in with paine, . . . 291 U85 Country V 69
GETT
This is the money-gett, Mechanick Age! . . . 404 Inigo Jones 1 52
to gett thee a leane Face, ... 420 Ode:If Men 25
GETTING
Is sung: as als' her getting up . . . 274 U84 Cradle 37
And care of getting, thus, our minds hath stain'd, . . . 327 Horace 473
GHEST
Not that we thinke us worthy such a ghest, . . . 64 E101 Supper 3
GHOST
To the Ghost of Martial. . . . . 38 E36 Martial Ttl
Father, and Sonne, and Holy Ghost, you three . . . 128 U1 Trinitie 37
Or like a Ghost walke silent amongst men, . . . 199 U41 Elegy Since 21
What gentle Ghost, besprent with April deaw, . . . 268 U81 Pawlet 1
What goodly Ghost, besprent with April deaw, . . . 268 U81 Pawlet V 1
GHOSTS
And, for the cryes of Ghosts, women, and men, . . . 84 E133 Voyage 16
Against their breasts. Here, sev'rall ghosts did flit . . . 87 E133 Voyage 124
Reviving with fresh coulors the pale Ghosts . . . 405 Inigo Jones 1 88
GHYRLOND
The Ghyrlond of the blessed Virgin Marie. . . . 412 Ghyrlond Ttl
These forme thy Ghyrlond. Wherof Myrtle green, . . . 412 Ghyrlond 5
GIANT (See also GYANT)
Who like a Giant hasts his course to run, . . . 414 Ghyrlond 51
GIDDIE
Giddie with change, and therefore cannot see . . . 118 F13 Aubigny 67
till giddie with amazement I fell downe . . . 361 Palmer 25
GIFT (See also GUIFT)
Make it your gift. See whither that will beare mee. . . . 55 E84 Bedford 2 10
O take my gift. . . . . 127 U1 Trinitie 8
Now, but command; make tribute, what was gift; . . . 155 U13 Sacvile 84
Without your gift, though I can rate that too, . . . 157 U13 Sacvile 158
Thy gift 'gainst envie. O how I doe count . . . 161 U14 Selden 79
Then to your love, and gift. And all's but due. . . . 189 U37 Friend-Book 5
But must confesse from whom what gift I tooke. . . . 189 U37 Friend-Book 6
Thoughts worthy of thy gift, this Inke, . . . 229 U55 Burges 2
A New-yeares gift Sung to King Charles, 1635. . . . 263 U79 New-yeares Ttl
To fit the softnesse of our Yeares-gift: when . . . 263 U79 New-yeares 6
Her right, by gift, and purchase of the Lambe: . . . 400 Lady Ogle 36
GIFTS
Yet, all heavens gifts, being heavens due, . . . 33 E22 Daughter 3
And what thou call'st thy gifts are baits. . . . 100 F4 To the World 12
A Princes fortune: These are gifts of chance, . . . 117 F13 Aubigny 41
Then what he hath receiv'd. Gifts stinke from some, . . . 153 U13 Sacvile 22
No! Gifts and thankes should have one cheerefull face, . . . 154 U13 Sacvile 39
Could you demand the gifts you gave, againe? . . . 192 U38 Elegy 'Tis 55
With reverence using all the gifts thence given. . . . 219 U47 Tribe 62
Great Charles, among the holy gifts of grace . . . 235 U62 Charles 1 1
New yeares, expect new gifts: Sister, your Harpe, . . . 263 U79 New-yeares 1
As prop'rest gifts, to Girles, and Boyes, . . . 273 U84 Cradle 19
With thee 'bove all his Rivals gifts take place, . . . 292 U86 Hor.4:1 18
How are thy gifts, and graces blaz'd abroad! . . . 413 Ghyrlond 36
How are thy gifts and graces blaz'd abro'd, . . . 414 Ghyrlond 53
GILD (See GUILD, GUILT)
GILES
On Giles and Jone. . . . . 40 E42 Giles Ttl
Who sayes that Giles and Jone at discord be? . . . 40 E42 Giles 1
Indeed, poore Giles repents he married ever. . . . 40 E42 Giles 3

GILES (cont.)
But that his Jone doth too. And Giles would never,   .   .   . 40 E42 Giles 4
No more would Jone he should. Giles riseth early,   .   .   . 40 E42 Giles 6
And so is Jone. Oft-times, when Giles doth find   .   .   . 40 E42 Giles 9
Harsh sights at home, Giles wisheth he were blind.   .   . 40 E42 Giles 10
The children, that he keepes, Giles sweares are none   .   . 40 E42 Giles 13
GILL
Secure thy railing Rhymes, infamous Gill, ... 410 Gill 2
GI'NG
What would he doe now, gi'ng his mynde that waye   .   . 405 Inigo Jones 1 75
GINNES
If I could not thy ginnes avoyd.   .   .   .   .   . 101 F4 To the World 36
GINNY
Th'Ionian God-wit, nor the Ginny hen   .   .   .   . 291 U85 Country 53
GIRDED
Faine words, unheard of to the girded race   .   .   . 340 Horace V 71
GIRDLE
And the Girdle 'bout her waste, ... 137 U2 Cupid 41
GIRLES
As prop'rest gifts, to Girles, and Boyes,   .   .   . 273 U84 Cradle 19
GIRLS
Those dull Girls, no good can mean us,   .   .   . 657 Door Apollo 11
GIRT
This sea-girt Isle upon: .   .   .   .   . 240 U67 Muses 33
This sea-girt ground upon: .   .   .   .   . 240 U67 Muses V 33
Or with fresh flowers to girt my temple round.   .   . 293 U86 Hor.4:1 32
The old man many evils doe girt round;   .   .   . 315 Horace 241
GIVE
Use mine so, too: I give thee leave. But crave   .   . 27 E3 Bookseller 3
Let me give two: that doubly am got free,   .   .   . 31 E13 Empirick 3
And which no' affection praise enough can give!   .   . 34 E23 Donne 1 6
Great heav'n did well, to give ill fame free wing;   .   . 43 E51 James 3 2
Yet give thy jealous subjects leave to doubt: .   .   . 43 E51 James 3 5
To give the world assurance thou wert both;   .   .   . 43 E53 Old-end 6
Now, I must give thy life, and deed, the voice   .   . 55 E86 Goodyere 2 5
Weare this renowne. 'Tis just, that who did give   .   . 57 E89 Allen 13
To morrow vice, if shee give better pay: .   .   . 66 E102 Pembroke 10
Need any Muses praise to give it fame?   .   .   . 66 E103 L Wroth 1 6
Give them your services, and embassies   .   .   . 69 E107 Hungry 11
Give your yong States-men, (that first make you drunke,   . 69 E107 Hungry 19
And that thy soule should give thy flesh her weight.   . 70 E109 Nevil 14
Nor to give Caesar this, makes ours the lesse.   .   . 72 E111 Edmonds 2 8
Pr'y thee, yet save thy rest; give ore in time: .   . 73 E112 Gamster 21
Give every one his dose of mirth: and watches   .   . 74 E115 Honest Man 14
No, Shelton, give me thee, canst want all these,   .   . 76 E119 Shelton 7
And have sought (to give new birth)   .   .   .   . 77 E120 S. P. 21
Which in life did harbour give   .   .   .   .   . 79 E124 Elizabeth 5
When we doe give, Alphonso, to the light,   .   .   . 82 E131 Ferrab. 2 1
We ought not give them taste, we had an eare.   .   . 83 E131 Ferrab. 2 6
While you breath. First give a hundred,   .   .   . 103 F6 Celia 2 8
Shall not give out, that I have made thee stay,   .   . 107 F10 Proludium 8
Shall not give out, that we have made thee stay,   .   . 107 F10 Proludium V 8
Give knowledge instantly, ... 109 F11 Epode 12
Then, here, to give pride fame, and peasants birth.   . 114 F12 Rutland 26
Then, now give pride fame, or peasants birth.   .   . 114 F12 Rutland V 26
Because they lack'd the sacred pen, could give   .   . 115 F12 Rutland 56
(They finde it both so wittie, and safe to give.)   .   . 118 F13 Aubigny 76
And raise a noble stemme, to give the fame,   .   .   . 119 F13 Aubigny 97
Give me my cup, but from the Thespian well,   .   . 120 F14 Sydney 11
I could give my very heart;   .   .   .   .   . 142 U2 Her man 54
Give thankes by stealth, and whispering in the eare,   . 154 U13 Sacvile 49
Then give it to the Hound that did him bite;   .   . 155 U13 Sacvile 70
Give me but that againe, that I must wast   .   .   . 167 U15 Friend-Wars 152
Give me but that againe, which I must wast   .   .   . 167 U15 Friend-Wars V152
Is nothing, such scarce meat and drinke he'le give,   . 167 U15 Friend-Wars 159
But what she gives, thou dar'st give her againe;   .   . 168 U15 Friend-Wars 184
Yet give me leave t'adore in you   .   .   .   . 174 U22 Elegy Tho 35
To give the world againe: .   .   .   .   . 175 U23 Himselfe 29
Pyracmon's houre will come to give them ease,   .   . 179 U25 Desmond 42
I give, or owe my friends, into your Rites,   .   .   . 197 U40 Elegy That 12
But give them over to the common eare   .   .   . 214 U44 Speach 31
Are asked to climbe. First give me faith, who know   . 220 U47 Tribe 75
To give mankind their eases, ... 221 U48 Bacchus 23
Give me a deep-crown'd-Bowle, that I may sing   .   . 225 U51 Bacon 19
Then would I promise here to give   .   .   .   . 229 U55 Burges 3
Thanke him: if other, hee can give no Bayes.   .   . 232 U58 Book-seller 6
I hate such measur'd, give me mettall'd fire   .   . 233 U59 Newcastle 7
To give a greater Name, and Title to! Their owne!   . 255 U75 Epithalam. 96
Unto our yeare doth give the longest light.   .   . 262 U78 Digby 16
Which I have vow'd posteritie to give.   .   .   . 262 U78 Digby 18
To give your shade a name! Stay, stay, I feele   .   . 269 U81 Pawlet 7
To give your shade a lasting name! Stay, stay, I feele   . 269 U81 Pawlet V 7
Sound thou her Vertues, give her soule a Name.   .   . 269 U81 Pawlet 22
And give you reasons more then one.   .   .   . 277 U84 Mind 4
Looke on thy sloth, and give thy selfe undone,   .   . 283 U84 Muse 21
And give her place, according to her blood,   .   . 284 U84 Muse 83
So Fate would give her life, and longer daies.   .   . 293 U87 Hor.3:9 12
And both doe crave, and give againe, this leave.   .   . 305 Horace 13
And give, being taken modestly, this leave,   .   .   . 309 Horace 73
If I can give some small increase? when, loe,   .   . 309 Horace 80
Hee thinks not, how to give you smoake from light,   . 315 Horace 203
And give their yeares, and natures, as they swerve,   . 315 Horace 224
Receive, or give it an applause, the more.   .   .   . 321 Horace 364

GIVE (cont.)

Receive, or give it any Crowne the more.   .   .   .   347 Horace   V356/364
Indeed, give fitting dues to every man.   .   .   .   325 Horace   452
Our Gallants give them none, but passe them by: .   329 Horace   513
That bid, God give thee joy, and have no endes.   .   384 Somerset   6
Olde Hesiods Ore, and give it us; but thine,   .   .   388 Chapman   2
And we have wits to read, and praise to give.   .   391 Shakespeare   24
Yet must I not give Nature all: Thy Art.   .   .   392 Shakespeare   55
His Art doth give the fashion. And, that he,   .   392 Shakespeare   58
Yet give mee leave, to wonder at the birth   .   398 Drayton   83
Give cause to some of wonnder, some despite,   .   420 Ode:If Men   35

GIVEN

And, but a sprigge of bayes, given by thee,   .   32 E17 Critic   5
Makes, the whole longer, then 'twas given him, much.   .   76 E119 Shelton   16
And, for it, life, conscience, yea, soules are given,   .   113 F12 Rutland   4
And, in this name, am given out dangerous   .   117 F13 Aubigny   11
But nought beyond. He thou hast given it to,   .   161 U14 Selden   71
What honour given to the drunkennest Guests?   .   166 U15 Friend-Wars   118
But to exact againe what once is given,   .   .   192 U38 Elegy 'Tis   63
With reverence using all the gifts thence given.   .   219 U47 Tribe   62
What can the cause be, when the K. hath given   .   241 U68 House-hold   1
To be given me in gratuitie   .   .   .   259 U76 Petition   12
Hath given wholly to the Sonne (the rather   .   288 U84 Muse   216
Makes his life longer then 'twas given him, much.   .   295 U89 Mart.8:77   8
Of daring all, hath still beene given; we know it: .   305 Horace   12
Of daring ought, hath still beene given; we know it: .   338 Horace   V 12
The parts of age to youth be given; or men   .   317 Horace   252
And there is given too unworthy leave   .   .   323 Horace   389
The Oracles, too, were given out in Verse;   .   329 Horace   496
Yet, there's a value given to this man.   .   .   331 Horace   554
(Whether yo'are given to, or giver are.)   .   .   333 Horace   608
With joy of what is given him, over-gone: .   333 Horace   610

GIVER

(Whether yo'are given to, or giver are.)   .   .   333 Horace   608

GIVES

But gives me what I call, and lets me eate,   .   95 F2 Penshurst   69
He alwayes gives what he knowes meet;   .   .   99 F3 Wroth   98
He alwayes gives what he thinks meet;   .   .   99 F3 Wroth   V 98
And takes, and gives the beauties of the mind.   .   117 F13 Aubigny   44
Clothes, or Fortune gives the grace;   .   .   131 U2 Excuse   8
Gives the Lover weight, and fashion.   .   .   131 U2 Excuse   12
He neither gives, or do's, that doth delay   .   154 U13 Sacvile   41
But what she gives, thou dar'st give her againe;   .   168 U15 Friend-Wars   184
Askes first, Who gives her (I Charles) then he plights   256 U75 Epithalam.   124
Hee gives all plentie, and encrease,   .   .   265 U79 New-yeares   56
Hee gives all plentie, and encrease,   .   .   265 U79 New-yeares   68
The glorie, and gaine of rest, which the place gives!   283 U84 Muse   38
And there, while he gives the zealous Bravado,   .   375 Coryat 1   22

GIVING

And giving largely to me, more thou tak'st.   .   44 E55 Beaumont   6
I leave thee there, and giving way, entend   .   72 E112 Gamster   9
As giving it a hope, that there   .   .   .   106 F9 Celia 3   11
Her solemne houres she spent, or giving Almes,   .   288 U84 Muse   192
And giving dues to all Mankinds deserts!   .   .   289 U84 Muse   224

GIV'ST

And giv'st thy gladder guests the sight;   .   .   97 F3 Wroth   28
And giv'st thy welcome guests the right;   .   .   97 F3 Wroth   V 28

GLAD

As guiltie men doe magistrates: glad I,   .   .   32 E17 Critic   2
Glad-mention'd Roe: thou art but gone before,   .   37 E33 Roe 3   2
And having got him out of doores is glad.   .   .   40 E42 Giles   7
'Tofore, great men were glad of Poets: Now,   .   40 E43 Salisbury 1   5
I, that am glad of thy great chance, here doo!   .   46 E60 Mounteagle   5
Not glad, like those that have new hopes, or sutes,   .   47 E64 Salisbury 3   1
Nor glad as those, that old dependents bee,   .   47 E64 Salisbury 3   5
Nor glad for fashion. Nor to shew a fit   .   47 E64 Salisbury 3   7
But I am glad to see that time survive,   .   .   47 E64 Salisbury 3   9
In onely thee, might be both great, and glad.   .   48 E66 Cary   4
Goodyere, I'am glad, and gratefull to report,   .   55 E85 Goodyere 1   1
Or, better worke! were thy glad countrey blest,   .   61 E95 Savile   14
While all, that follow, their glad eares apply   .   97 F3 Wroth   31
Get place, and honor, and be glad to keepe   .   99 F3 Wroth   87
For which you worthy are the glad encrease   .   119 F13 Aubigny   94
This day sayes, then, the number of glad yeeres   .   120 F14 Sydney   21
But be glad, as soone with me,   .   .   .   131 U2 Excuse   17
I'le tell, that if they be not glad,   .   .   147 U7 Nymph   8
'Tis by degrees that men arrive at glad   .   157 U13 Sacvile   131
The Dice with glassen eyes, to the glad viewes   .   166 U15 Friend-Wars   138
The Dice with glassen eyes, to the glad Viewers   .   166 U15 Friend-Wars V138
But whisper; O glad Innocence,   .   .   177 U25 Desmond   31
The good, and durst not practise it, were glad   .   247 U70 Ode   119
Adding her owne glad accents, to this Day,   .   249 U72 King   7
Which their glad Parents taught   .   .   257 U75 Epithalam.   143
What transcripts begg'd? how cry'd up, and how glad,   263 U78 Digby   30
What transcripts made? how cry'd up, and how glad,   263 U78 Digby   V 30
Best Kings expect first-fruits of your glad gaines.   263 U79 New-yeares   13
And purple-matching Grapes, hee's glad!   .   290 U85 Country   20
That penning the glad flock in hurdles by,   .   291 U85 Country   45
Among these Cates how glad the sight doth come   .   291 U85 Country   61
Froward, complaining, a commender glad   .   317 Horace   247
Steepe the glad Genius in the Wine, whole dayes,   .   319 Horace   298
A third of twelve, you may: foure ounces. Glad,   .   327 Horace   469
I, that am glad, thy Innocence was thy Guilt,   .   371 Fletcher   11

	Page	Title	Line

GLAD (cont.)
Sure, this glad payre were married, but this day. · · 384 Somerset 26
With the Glad Countrey, and Posteritie: · · 416 Dover 6

GLADDER
And giv'st thy gladder guests the sight; · 97 F3 Wroth 28

GLADDEST
The gladdest light, darke man can thinke upon; · · 128 U1 Trinitie 35
The gladdest ground to all the numbred-five, · · 412 Ghyrlond 6

GLADDING
Of Summers Liveries, and gladding greene; · · 253 U75 Epithalam. 18

GLAD-MENTION'D
Glad-mention'd Roe: thou art but gone before, · 37 E33 Roe 3 2

GLADNESSE
The gladnesse higher: · · · 120 F14 Sydney 6
By all the Arts of Gladnesse, · · 221 U48 Bacchus 19
For 't were a narrow gladnesse, kept thine owne. · 225 U51 Bacon 18
So generall a gladnesse to an Isle, · · 238 U66 Queene 9
And let thy lookes with gladnesse shine: · · 245 U70 Ode 76
That cry that gladnesse, which their hearts would pray, · 249 U72 King 14
The cries, the gladnesse, which their hearts would pay, · 249 U72 King V 14
With gladnesse temper'd her sad Parents teares! · 270 U81 Pawlet 59
Which gladnesse temper'd her sad Parents teares! · 270 U81 Pawlet V 59
All other gladnesse, with the thought is barr'd; · 284 U84 Muse 67
Her fellowes, with the oyle of gladnesse, bright · 285 U84 Muse 101
Shall meet with gladnesse in one Theatre; · · 285 U84 Muse 114

GLANCE
A fixed thought, an eye un-taught to glance; · · 111 F11 Epode 61

GLARE
Our brave Heroes with a milder glare, · · 88 E133 Voyage 163

GLASS
Except your Gratious Eye as through a Glass · 383 Rich 11

GLASSE
like glasse, blowne up, and fashion'd by desire. · 108 F10 Proludium 4
No lady, but, at some time, loves her glasse. · 117 F13 Aubigny 26
Madame, be bold to use this truest glasse: · 120 F13 Aubigny 122
And the Glasse hangs by her side, · · 137 U2 Cupid 40
'Fore your Idoll Glasse a whit, · · 140 U2 Promise 22
The Houre-glasse. · 148 U8 Houre-glasse Ttl
on a lovers dust, made sand for ane Houre Glasse · 148 U8 Houre-glasse VTtl
Here running in the Glasse, · · 148 U8 Houre-glasse 2
To see 'hem aye discoursing with their Glasse, · 164 U15 Friend-Wars 63
When not his Combes, his Curling-irons, his Glasse, · 165 U15 Friend-Wars 111
What reputation to beare one Glasse more? · 166 U15 Friend-Wars 119
The Glasse-house, Dye-fats, and their Fornaces. · 211 U43 Vulcan 180
Darke thy cleare glasse with old Falernian Wine; · 295 U89 Mart.8:77 5
As a deformed face doth a true glasse. · · 389 Aleman 10

GLASSE-HOUSE
The Glasse-house, Dye-fats, and their Fornaces; · 211 U43 Vulcan 180

GLASSEN
The Dice with glassen eyes, to the glad viewes · 166 U15 Friend-Wars 138
The Dice with glassen eyes, to the glad Viewers · 166 U15 Friend-Wars V138

GLASSES
Stick on your Cupping-glasses, fear not, put · 270 U81 Pawlet 53

GLASSHOUSE
the Dyers, Glasshouse and the furnaces; · · 211 U43 Vulcan V180

GLAVES
And there made Swords, Bills, Glaves, and Armes your fill; · 212 U43 Vulcan 198

GLEANE
At first he made low shifts, would picke and gleane, · 45 E56 Poet-Ape 5

GLEANES
To keepe him off; and how-so-e're he gleanes · 242 U69 Friend Son 16

GLEANINGS
With humble Gleanings in Divinitie, · · 207 U43 Vulcan 102

GLISTER'D
Else that glister'd in White-hall; · · 138 U2 Kisse 16

GLOBE
Against the Globe, the Glory of the Banke. · 208 U43 Vulcan 132
Last, draw the circles of this Globe, · · 276 U84 Body 25

GLOBY
By that tall Grove, your haire; whose globy rings · 170 U19 Elegy By 5

GLOOMIE
Where darknesse with her gloomie-sceptred hand, · 180 U25 Desmond 61

GLOOMIE-SCEPTRED
Where darknesse with her gloomie-sceptred hand, · 180 U25 Desmond 61

GLORIE
Wee, sad for him, may glorie, and not sinne. · · 35 E27 Roe 1 8
Expresser truth, or truer glorie, · · 39 E40 Ratcliffe 7
As, then, his cause, his glorie emulate. · · 61 E95 Savile 24
A man should seeke great glorie, and not broad. · 62 E96 Donne 2 12
And glorie of them all, but to repeate! · · 66 E103 L Wroth 1 8
Of former age, or glorie of our one, · · 67 E104 Montgomery 10
Marke of glorie, come with me; · · 132 U2 How he saw 1
There greatnesse takes a glorie to relieve. · 192 U38 Elegy 'Tis 34
And keepe the Glorie of the English name, · 214 U44 Speach 50
No aime at glorie, or, in warre, · · 234 U60 La-ware 13
Glorie to God. Then, Haile to Mary! spring · 238 U66 Queene 13
Comes in the pompe, and glorie · · 240 U67 Muses 28
The glorie, and gaine of rest, which the place gives! · 283 U84 Muse 38

GLORIES
Fear'd not to boast the glories of her stage, · 56 E89 Allen 2
No more, those mayden glories shee hath lost. · 83 E132 Sylvester 14
the glories of yt. Now our muse takes winge, · 108 F10 Proludium 15
Or taxe the Glories of the Church, and Gowne? · 203 U43 Vulcan 24

```
                                                       Page    Title        Line

GLORIES  (cont.)
  Or taxe the Glories of the Church, or Gowne?       .   .   203   U43 Vulcan     V 24
  He that should search all Glories of the Gowne,    .   .   217   U46 Coke         1
  Let Angels sing her glories, who did call    .   .   .   .   270   U81 Pawlet      63
  Renew the Glories of our blessed Jeames:           .   .   415   Dover            4
GLORIFIE
  To knit thy Crowne, and glorifie the rest.     .   .   .   412   Ghyrlond        12
GLORIFIED
  But in thy presence, truly glorified,          .   .   .   128   U1 Trinitie     47
  A glorified worke to Time, when Fire,          .   .   .   371   Fletcher        15
GLORIOUS
  Don Surly, to aspire the glorious name         .   .   .    35   E28 Surly        1
  By his each glorious parcell to be knowne!     .   .   .    62   E97 Motion       6
  The soules, shee loves.  Those other glorious notes,  .   114   F12 Rutland     43
  O Holy, blessed, glorious Trinitie   .   .   .   .   .   127   U1 Trinitie      1
  Increase those acts, o glorious Trinitie       .   .   .   128   U1 Trinitie     29
  His glorious Name                              .   .   .   129   U1 Father       24
  As are the Glorious Scenes, at the great sights;   .   .   220   U47 Tribe       66
  In glorious Piles, or Pyramids erect    .   .   .   .   261   U77 Treasurer     26
  That holy, great, and glorious Mysterie,       .   .   .   286   U84 Muse        129
  Nor had our Italie more glorious bin   .   .   .   .   325   Horace          411
  The glorious Trinity in Union met.             .   .   .   413   Ghyrlond        32
GLORY
  To make us heires of glory!        .   .   .   .   .   130   U1 Nativitie     21
  In cheifest glory Sunne-her        .   .   .   .   .   135   U2 Triumph     V 32
  That thou dost all things more for truth, then glory,  .   168   U15 Friend-Wars 179
  Would live his glory that could keepe it on;   .   .   .   192   U38 Elegy 'Tis   48
  Against the Globe, the Glory of the Banke.     .   .   .   208   U43 Vulcan      132
  Thou canst not meet more Glory, on the way,    .   .   .   252   U75 Epithalam.    3
  Sister of Pan, and glory of the Spring:        .   .   .   264   U79 New-yeares   25
  Hee will all Glory, all Perfection be,         .   .   .   286   U84 Muse        127
  Shee saw him too, in glory to ascend     .   .   .   .   288   U84 Muse        205
  Be proofe, the glory of his hand,        .   .   .   .   367   Ode Who saith    49
  Code, Digests, Pandects of all faemale glory!  .   .   .   399   Lady Ogle        8
  Thou Throne of glory, beauteous as the Moone,  .   .   .   414   Ghyrlond        49
GLOVE
  To ev'ry Petticote he brush'd, and Glove       .   .   .   201   U42 Elegy Let    54
GLOVER
  Mr. Alexander Glover   .   .   .   .   .   .   .   666   Glover           2
GLUTTED
  They'ave glutted in, and letcher'd out that weeke,  .   .   218   U47 Tribe       13
GLUTTONY
  Lust it comes out, that gluttony went in.      .   .   .    76   E118 Gut         6
  A waiter, doth my gluttony envy:         .   .   .   .    95   F2 Penshurst     68
  In bravery, or gluttony, or coyne,       .   .   .   .   163   U15 Friend-Wars  45
GNAT  (See KNAT)
GO  (See also GOE)
  The Kings fame lives.  Go now, denie his Teirce.   .   .   241   U68 House-hold   14
  To another, Move; he went; To a third, Go,    .   .   .   287   U84 Muse        170
  As doctrine, and delight together go.    .   .   .   .   329   Horace          516
  For he did but kisse her, and so let her go.   .   .   .   375   Coryat 1        19
  I'll laugh at thee poor wretched Tike, go send  .   .   .   410   Gill            10
  Cropt, branded, slit, neck-stockt; go, you are stript. .   411   Gill            16
GOALE
  The wished goale, both did, and suffer'd much   .   .   .   333   Horace          588
GOAT
  A Goat in Velvet; or some block could move     .   .   .   202   U42 Elegy Let    82
  For the vile Goat, soone after, forth did send  .   .   .   319   Horace          320
GOATE
  And how his Ganimede mov'd, and how his goate,  .   .   .    34   E25 Beast 1      4
GOATES
  And Goates together, whither they must come    .   .   .   283   U84 Muse        47
GOD
  The charge of that state, with this charme, god payes.  .    30   E12 Shift        4
  Himselfe: his whole revennue is, god payes.    .   .   .    30   E12 Shift        6
  Shee must have money: he returnes, god payes.  .   .   .    30   E12 Shift        8
  Lookes o're the bill, likes it: and say's, god payes.  .    30   E12 Shift       10
  At dice his borrow'd money: which, god payes.  .   .   .    30   E12 Shift       12
  Signes to new bond, forfeits: and cryes, god payes.  .    30   E12 Shift       14
  Takes physick, teares the papers: still god payes.  .   .    30   E12 Shift       16
  Calls for his stoole, adornes the stage: god payes.  .    30   E12 Shift       18
  His onely answere is to all, god payes.  .   .   .   .    31   E12 Shift       20
  Thus: and for his letcherie, scores, god payes.  .   .   .    31   E12 Shift       22
  Blaspheme god, greatly.  Or some poore hinde beat,  .    36   E28 Surly       17
  And than in them, how could we know god more?  .   .   .    38   E35 James 2      8
  Like straight, thy pietie to God, and friends:  .   .   .    68   E106 E Herbert   8
  I pluck'd a branch; the jealous god did frowne,  .   .   .    80   E126 Mrs Cary    3
  That all this while I have forgot some god,    .   .   .    85   E133 Voyage     44
  And art a god, if Fame thee not abuses,        .   .   .    85   E133 Voyage     53
  For (where he was the god of eloquence,        .   .   .    86   E133 Voyage     99
  God wisheth, none should wracke on a strange shelfe.  .    99   F3 Wroth        95
  Of his dull god-head, were sinne.  Ile implore  .   .   .   107   F10 Proludium    6
  Of his dull god-head, were sinne.  Lets implore  .   .   .   107   F10 Proludium  V 6
  But, in a calme, and god-like unitie,          .   .   .   110   F11 Epode       53
  Moodes, which the god-like Sydney oft did prove,  .   .   116   F12 Rutland     91
  Good, and great God, can I not thinke of thee,  .   .   .   122   F15 Heaven       1
  Of persons, still one God, in Unitie,          .   .   .   127   U1 Trinitie      2
  All-gracious God, the Sinners sacrifice,       .   .   .   127   U1 Trinitie      9
  Eternall Father, God, who did'st create        .   .   .   127   U1 Trinitie     17
  Eternall God the Sonne, who not denyd'st       .   .   .   128   U1 Trinitie     21
  Eternall Spirit, God from both proceeding,     .   .   .   128   U1 Trinitie     25
  Of persons, still one God in Unitie;           .   .   .   128   U1 Trinitie     30
  One God to see,   .   .   .   .   .   .   .   .   128   U1 Trinitie     40
```

	Page	Title	Line
GOD (cont.)			
2. A Hymne to God the Father.	129	U1 Father	Ttl
Heare mee, O God!	129	U1 Father	1
The Sonne of God, th'Eternall King,	130	U1 Nativitie	7
And a woman God did make me:	140	U2 Her man	6
Who falls for love of God, shall rise a Starre.	168	U15 Friend-Wars	196
A Womans friendship! God whom I trust in,	171	U20 Shrub	1
The eldest God, yet still a Child.	189	U36 Song	16
God, and the good, know to forgive, and save.	191	U38 Elegy 'Tis	19
God lightens not at mans each fraile offence,	193	U38 Elegy 'Tis	68
And why to me this, thou lame god of fire,	202	U43 Vulcan	V 1
For none but Smiths would have made thee a God.	208	U43 Vulcan	117
Would God, my Burges, I could thinke	229	U55 Burges	1
T'obtaine of God, what all the Land should aske?	234	U61 Epigram	11
He is the Man, and Favorite of God.	235	U61 Epigram	20
To God, denies the God-head to be true:	235	U63 Charles 2	2
Who doubts, those fruits God can with gaine restore,	235	U63 Charles 2	3
For God, whose essence is so infinite,	236	U63 Charles 2	13
Glorie to God. Then, Haile to Mary! spring	238	U66 Queene	13
Our thanks to God. Then, Haile to Mary! spring	238	U66 Queene	V 13
To have thy God to blesse, thy King to grace,	256	U75 Epithalam.	131
That thou art lov'd of God, this worke is done,	268	U80 Christning	1
How much they are belov'd of God, in thee:	268	U80 Christning	4
It is too neere of kin to God, the Soule,	269	U81 Pawlet	V 29
Which the Elect of God are sure to know!	271	U81 Pawlet	V 76
But such a Mind, mak'st God thy Guest.	281	U84 Mind	72
I murmure against God, for having ta'en	283	U84 Muse	33
And the whole Banquet is full sight of God!	284	U84 Muse	65
Who violates the God-head, is most vitious	284	U84 Muse	74
Of life, and light, the Sonne of God, the Word!	285	U84 Muse	112
But all of God; They still shall have to say,	286	U84 Muse	119
God, in the Union, and the Trinitie!	286	U84 Muse	128
Of divine Comfort, when sh' had talk'd with God.	287	U84 Muse	184
To him should be her Judge, true God, true Man,	288	U84 Muse	211
Th'Ionian God-wit, nor the Ginny hen	291	U85 Country	53
To chant the Gods, and all their God-like race,	311	Horace	114
It much will differ, if a God speake, than,	313	Horace	161
It much will sway whether a god speak, than:	342	Horace	V161
To have a God come in; except a knot	317	Horace	273
As neither any God, were brought in there,	321	Horace	331
As neither any God, be brought in there,	346	Horace	V323/331
Or Semi-god, that late was seene to weare	321	Horace	332
Hee, while he labour'd to be thought a God	335	Horace	661
Yes. And thanks God in his Pistle or his Booke	380	Coryat 3	43
That bid, God give thee joy, and have no endes.	384	Somerset	6
What Muse, or rather God of harmony	395	May	14
Daughter, and Mother, and the Spouse of God,	413	Ghyrlond	33
Of being Daughter, Mother, Spouse of God!	414	Ghyrlond	56
Our King and Queen the Lord-God blesse,	418	Grace	1
Our King and Queen the Prince God blesse,	418	Grace	V 1
And God blesse every living thing,	418	Grace	3
God blesse the Councell of Estate,	419	Grace	5
God blesse the Councell and the State,	419	Grace	V 5
God blesse them all, and keepe them safe:	419	Grace	7
God blesse us all, Bedford keepe safe:	419	Grace	V 7
And God blesse me, and God blesse Raph.	419	Grace	8
GODDESS			
A Goddess is, then paynted Cloth, Deal-boards,	406	Inigo Jones 1	93
GODDESSE			
Or goddesse to invoke, to stuffe my verse;	85	E133 Voyage	45
Or Goddesse, could be patient of thy face.	207	U43 Vulcan	108
GODDS			
What godds but those of arts, and eloquence?	395	May	16
Are still th'interpreters twixt godds, and men!	395	May	18
GOD-HEAD			
Of his dull god-head, were sinne. Ile implore	107	F10 Proludium	6
Of his dull god-head, were sinne. Lets implore	107	F10 Proludium	V 6
To God, denies the God-head to be true:	235	U63 Charles 2	2
Who violates the God-head, is most vitious	284	U84 Muse	74
GOD-LIKE			
But, in a calme, and god-like unitie,	110	F11 Epode	53
Moodes, which the god-like Sydney oft did prove,	116	F12 Rutland	91
To chant the Gods, and all their God-like race,	311	Horace	114
GODLY'S			
The Peace of Conscience, and the Godly's strife,	411	Sutcliffe	7
GOD'S			
By bringing forth God's onely Son, no other.	414	Ghyrlond	48
GODS			
Proves, that is gods, which was the peoples voice.	49	E67 Suffolk	12
And doe their penance, to avert Gods rod,	235	U61 Epigram	19
To chant the Gods, and all their God-like race,	311	Horace	114
Hide faults, pray to the Gods, and wish aloud	319	Horace	285
Hide faults, and pray to th'gods, and wish aloud	345	Horace	V285
Orpheus, a priest, and speaker for the Gods	327	Horace	479
But neither, Men, nor Gods, nor Pillars meant,	331	Horace	555
and the immortall gods; love only those	422	Lucan	5
GOD-WIT			
Th'Ionian God-wit, nor the Ginny hen	291	U85 Country	53
GODWIT			
May yet be there; and godwit, if we can:	65	E101 Supper	19
GOE			
And though the soundest legs goe every day,	36	E31 Banck	3
A knight-hood bought, to goe a wooing in?	42	E46 Luckless 1	2

232

GOE (cont.)
  Goe high, or low, as thou wilt value it.   50   E72 Court-ling   4
  For, if thou shame, ranck'd with my friends, to goe,   .   .   .   53   E77 Not name   3
  Was dull, and long, ere shee would goe to man: .   .   .   57   E90 Mill   3
  If the States make peace, how it will goe   59   E92 New Crie   30
  Goe on, and doubt not, what posteritie: 70   E109 Nevil   15
  Roe (and my joy to name) th'art now, to goe   80   E128 Wm Roe 2   1
  Propos'd to goe to Hol'borne in a wherry: 85   E133 Voyage   38
  Goe enter breaches, meet the cannons rage, ...   98   F3 Wroth   69
  Let that goe heape a masse of wretched wealth,   .   .   .   99   F3 Wroth   81
  Let thousands more goe flatter vice, and winne,   .   .   .   99   F3 Wroth   85
  Nor for my peace will I goe farre, ...   102   F4 To the World   65
  Will by coach, and water goe, ...   105   F8 Sicknesse   37
  Goe, crampe dull Mars, light Venus, when he snorts,   .   .   107   F10 Proludium   16
  To crowne the burthen which you goe withall,   .   .   .   119   F13 Aubigny   103
  To fetch in the Formes goe by: 140   U2 Promise   18
  Goe, get thee quickly forth, ...   150   U10 Jealousie   13
  No more are these of us, let them then goe,   .   .   .   156   U13 Sacvile   113
  Sydney e're night! or that did goe to bed   157   U13 Sacvile   127
  Yet we must more then move still, or goe on,   .   .   .   157   U13 Sacvile   135
  And last, goe out in nothing: You that see   .   .   .   157   U13 Sacvile   153
  His time? health? soule? will he for these goe throw   .   165   U15 Friend-Wars 103
  Goe make our selves the Usurers at a cast.   .   .   .   166   U15 Friend-Wars 134
  Well, let it goe. Yet this is better, then   .   .   .   166   U15 Friend-Wars 145
  Goe, quit 'hem all. And take along with thee,   .   .   .   167   U15 Friend-Wars 175
  These take, and now goe seeke thy peace in Warre,   .   .   168   U15 Friend-Wars 195
  If it be thus; Come Love, and Fortune goe,   .   .   .   170   U18 Elegy Can   21
  And goe no farther: let this Circle be   185   U30 Burleigh   3
  Or goe about to countenance the vice, ...   191   U38 Elegy 'Tis   24
  Publike affaires command me now to goe   194   U38 Elegy 'Tis   114
  Since you must goe, and I must bid farewell,   .   .   .   199   U41 Elegy Since   1
  Adulterate moneys, such as might not goe: .   .   .   204   U43 Vulcan   45
  Adulterate maskings, such as might not goe: .   .   .   204   U43 Vulcan   V 45
  To live in Sea-coale, and goe forth in smoake;   .   .   .   211   U43 Vulcan   181
  To live in Sea-coale, and goe out in smoake;   .   .   .   211   U43 Vulcan   V181
  Goe on, increase in vertue; and in fame: 214   U44 Speach   49
  Whilst your Ulisses hath ta'ne leave to goe,   .   .   .   224   U50 Countesse   21
  To goe out after—till when take this letter   .   .   .   229   U58 Squib   19
  If they goe on, and that thou lov'st a-life   .   .   .   232   U58 Book-seller   13
  Goe now, and tell out dayes summ'd up with feares,   .   .   244   U70 Ode   53
  (Where she shall goe)   254   U75 Epithalam.   62
  All else we see beside, are Shadowes, and goe lesse.   .   255   U75 Epithalam.   88
  Then goe on, and doe its worst;   260   U76 Petition   29
  Have left in fame to equall, or out-goe   260   U77 Treasurer   8
  Goe, Muse, in, and salute him. Say he be   .   .   .   262   U78 Digby   19
  Goe, Muse, in, and salute him thoughe he be   .   .   .   262   U78 Digby   V 19
  Goe now, her happy Parents, and be sad, ...   271   U81 Pawlet   77
  As you goe on, by what brave way   278   U84 Mind   18
  Could not goe downe my belly then   291   U85 Country   54
  Goe where Youths soft intreaties call thee back.   .   .   292   U86 Hor.4:1   8
  The middle of his matter: letting goe   315   Horace   213
  For his owne good, a carelesse letter-goe   .   .   .   315   Horace   234
  Quite from all face of Tragedie to goe, ...   321   Horace   344
  The Scoffer, the true Praiser doth out-goe.   .   .   .   333   Horace   616
  Not letting goe his hold, where he drawes food,   .   .   337   Horace   679
  Not letting goe the skin, where he drawes food,   .   .   355   Horace   V679
  And stop my sight, in every line I goe.   398   Drayton   78
  Goe little Booke, Goe little Fable   662   Bedford   1
GOES
  Or else by water goes, and so to playes;   30   E12 Shift   17
  The great renowne, and name wherewith shee goes.   .   .   31   E14 Camden   4
  Nay, aske you, how the day goes, in your eare.   .   .   .   59   E92 New Crie   18
  Airising in that place, through which, who goes,   .   .   87   E133 Voyage   131
  And after varyed, as fresh objects goes, ...   118   F13 Aubigny   66
  As she goes, all hearts doe duty   134   U2 Triumph   5
  He pardons slips, goes by a world of ills,   .   .   .   193   U38 Elegy 'Tis   69
  That hearkens to a Jacks-pulse, when it goes.   .   .   .   216   U45 Squib   6
  Equall with that, which for the best newes goes,   .   .   222   U49 Pucell   9
  Where e're he goes upon the ground, ...   265   U79 New-yeares   58
  It carries Palme with it, (where e're it goes)   .   .   .   363   Riches   6
  No man will tarry by thee, as hee goes, ...   409   Detractor   17
GOING
  Of Hercules, or Theseus going to hell, ...   84   E133 Voyage   2
  No going backe; on still you rogues, and row.   .   .   .   86   E133 Voyage   88
  Of going backe   121   F14 Sydney   28
  So going thorow all your straine, ...   145   U5 Woman-kind   10
  . . . the Coryate of Odcombe, and his Booke now going to travell   378   Coryat 2   Ttl
GOLD'
  Where Gold's the Motive, women have no Nay.   .   .   .   363   Riches   18
GOLD
  And get more gold, then all the colledge can: .   .   .   39   E41 Gypsee   2
  A treasure, art: contemn'd in th'age of gold.   .   .   .   47   E64 Salisbury 3   4
  The world's pure gold, and wise simplicitie;   .   .   .   78   E122 Rudyerd 2   4
  Of polish'd pillars, or a roofe of gold: 93   F2 Penshurst   3
  Which boasts t'have had the head of gold.   98   F3 Wroth   64
  And almost every vice, almightie gold, ...   113   F12 Rutland   2
  Or perhaps lesse: whil'st gold beares all this sway,   .   113   F12 Rutland   18
  When gold was made no weapon to cut throtes,   .   .   .   114   F12 Rutland   23
  Gold, upon a ground of black.   141   U2 Her man   14
  Gold, that is perfect, will out-live the fire.   .   .   .   179   U25 Desmond   45
  But they may see Gold-Chaines, and Pearle worne then,   .   213   U44 Speach   13
  And though Opinion stampe them not, are gold.   .   .   .   218   U47 Tribe   4
  With Gold, or Claspes, which might be bought   .   .   .   273   U84 Cradle   27

	Page	Title	Line
GOLD (cont.)			
The seaven-fold flower of Arte (more rich then gold)	361	Palmer	15
Gold is a sutor, never tooke repulse,	363	Riches	5
Though gold or Ivory haftes would make it good.	403	Inigo Jones 1	28
Though gold or Ivory haftes cant make it good.	403	Inigo Jones 1	V 28
Th'envy'd returne, of forty pound in gold.	408	Detractor	4
The House of gold, the Gate of heavens power,	413	Ghyrlond	39
GOLD-CHAINES			
But they may see Gold-Chaines, and Pearle worne then,	213	U44 Speach	13
GOLDEN			
Of love, and what the golden age did hold	47	E64 Salisbury 3	3
Sans helpe of Sybil, or a golden bough,	85	E133 Voyage	48
Enamor'd of their golden gyves?	100	F4 To the World	24
It is a golden chaine let downe from heaven,	110	F11 Epode	47
Then this, our guilt, nor golden age can deeme,	114	F12 Rutland	22
There like a rich, and golden pyramede,	115	F12 Rutland	83
My bolder numbers to thy golden Lyre:	177	U25 Desmond	9
My flowing numbers to thy golden Lyre:	177	U25 Desmond	V 9
Nor Turbot, nor bright Golden-eyes:	291	U85 Country	50
GOLDEN-EYES			
Nor Turbot, nor bright Golden-eyes:	291	U85 Country	50
GOLD'S			
Where Gold's the Motive, women have no Nay.	363	Riches	18
GON			
From thence is gon	368	Ode Who saith	68
GONE			
Glad-mention'd Roe: thou art but gone before,	37	E33 Roe 3	2
Whil'st thou art certaine to thy words, once gone,	52	E74 Chancelor	7
Ere cherries ripe, and straw-berries be gone,	58	E92 New Crie	1
For the great marke of vertue, those being gone	60	E93 Radcliffe	2
Since he was gone, more then the one he weares.	63	E97 Motion	17
The cloth's no sooner gone, but it gets up	74	E115 Honest Man	24
Boast, but how oft they have gone wrong to man:	119	F13 Aubigny	84
And that your soules conspire, as they were gone	119	F13 Aubigny	119
Are fled and gone,	120	F14 Sydney	19
Once more, and (faith) I will be gone,	139	U2 Another	7
Ride, saile, an coach'd, know I how farre I have gone,	156	U13 Sacvile	121
But there are objects, bid him to be gone	163	U15 Friend-Wars	28
A vertue, like Allay, so gone	173	U22 Elegy Tho	5
Is gone himselfe into your Name.	173	U22 Elegy Tho	24
And then with pause; for sever'd once, that's gone,	192	U38 Elegy 'Tis	47
To doe her Husbands rites in, e're 'twere gone	201	U42 Elegy Let	40
Sonne of the Wind! for so thy mother gone	208	U43 Vulcan	111
In those Records, which, were all Chroniclers gone,	210	U43 Vulcan	171
In those Records, which, were our Chroniclers gone,	210	U43 Vulcan	V171
No order? no Decree? Though we be gone	211	U43 Vulcan	176
The Chappell empties, and thou may'st be gone	257	U75 Epithalam.	137
And e're I can aske more of her, shee's gone!	269	U81 Pawlet	12
Painter yo' are come, but may be gone,	277	U84 Mind	1
(For so thou art with me) now shee is gone.	283	U84 Muse	22
What's left a Poet, when his Muse is gone?	283	U84 Muse	28
To publish her a Saint. My Muse is gone.	289	U84 Muse	228
Th'unbearded Youth, his Guardian once being gone,	315	Horace	229
With joy of what is given him, over-gone:	333	Horace	610
GOOD			
Call'st a booke good, or bad, as it doth sell,	27	E3 Bookseller	2
And such from whom let no man hope least good,	30	E11 Something	6
For I will dare none. Good Lord, walke dead still.	30	E11 Something	8
Make good what thou dar'st doe in all the rest.	32	E16 Brain-hardy	8
There's reason good, that you good lawes should make:	34	E24 Parliament	1
And crie good! good! This quite perverts my sense,	38	E38 Guiltie 2	5
Where good mens vertues them to honors bring,	47	E64 Salisbury 3	11
Before thou wert it, in each good mans heart.	49	E67 Suffolk	10
Yet by thy weapon liv'st! Th'hast one good part.	50	E69 Cob	2
Then had I made 'hem good, to fit your vaine.	51	E73 Fine Grand	20
Of greatest bloud, and yet more good then great;	52	E76 Bedford 1	6
Be safe, nor feare thy selfe so good a fame,	53	E77 Not name	1
The ports of death are sinnes: of life, good deeds:	53	E80 Life/Death	1
For good men but see death, the wicked tast it.	54	E80 Life/Death	8
Or that I'have by, two good sufficient men,	54	E81 Proule	3
And, finding good securitie in his age,	57	E90 Mill	6
Though both be good, the latter yet is worst,	63	E98 Th Roe 1	11
Against the bad, but of, and to the good;	66	E102 Pembroke	3
And are so good, and bad, just at a price,	66	E102 Pembroke	11
To make thy lent life, good against the Fates:	70	E109 Nevil	11
His deedes too dying, but in bookes (whose good	71	E110 Edmonds 1	15
His deedes too dying, save in bookes (whose good	71	E110 Edmonds 1	V 15
Where, what makes others great, doth keepe thee good!	73	E113 Overbury	4
Him not, aloud, that boasts so good a fame:	74	E115 Honest Man	2
Might be found out as good, and not my Lord.	75	E116 Jephson	8
With me can merit more, then that good man,	76	E119 Shelton	5
But, being so much too good for earth,	77	E120 S. P.	23
This is that good Aeneas, past through fire,	81	E128 Wm Roe 2	12
On thy good lady, then! who, therein, reap'd	95	F2 Penshurst	84
Not doing good, scarce when he dyes.	99	F3 Wroth	84
False world, good-night: since thou hast brought	100	F4 To the World	1
And all thy good is to be sold.	100	F4 To the World	16
He, at length, our good will sever.	102	F5 Celia 1	4
Beautie, I know, is good, and bloud is more;	114	F12 Rutland	37
Of any good minde, now: There are so few.	116	F13 Aubigny	2
For others ill, ought none their good forget.	116	F13 Aubigny	6
For he, that once is good, is ever great.	118	F13 Aubigny	52
So good	121	F14 Sydney	34

	Page	Title	Line
GOOD (cont.)			
Good, and great God, can I not thinke of thee,	122	F15 Heaven	1
All the Gaine, all the Good, of the Elements strife.	134	U2 Triumph	20
Of her good, who is the best	137	U2 Cupid	44
Be as good, as was the last:	140	U2 Promise	27
Himselfe young, and face be good,	142	U2 Exception	5
'Tis one good part I'ld lie withall.	142	U2 Exception	8
Find some one good, in some one man;	145	U5 Woman-kind	9
One good enough for a songs sake.	145	U5 Woman-kind	12
The good, from bad, is not describe,	146	U6 Defence	17
The pleasure is as good as none,	147	U7 Nymph	6
Great and good turns, as wel could time them too,	153	U13 Sacvile	2
This Good from you, as freely will it owe;	153	U13 Sacvile	14
To have such doe me good, I durst not name:	153	U13 Sacvile	18
In that proud manner, as a good so gain'd,	154	U13 Sacvile	37
Or Science of discerning Good and Ill.	156	U13 Sacvile	108
Her ends are honestie, and publike good!	156	U13 Sacvile	111
Men have beene great, but never good by chance,	156	U13 Sacvile	124
A many of bookes, even good judgements wound	159	U14 Selden	15
To make up Greatnesse! and mans whole good fix'd	163	U15 Friend-Wars	44
To flatter my good Lord, and cry his Bowle	167	U15 Friend-Wars	147
That thou thinke nothing great, but what is good,	168	U15 Friend-Wars	187
Debts when they can: good men may breake their day,	169	U17 Friend-Debt	2
Or have the Least of Good, but what it must	171	U20 Shrub	7
Raising the World to good or evill fame,	175	U24 Frontispice	3
Wise Providence would so; that nor the good	176	U24 Frontispice	5
high Providence would so; that nor the good	176	U24 Frontispice V	5
All good Poetrie hence was flowne,	183	U29 Fit of Rime	14
Cecill, the grave, the wise, the great, the good,	185	U30 Burleigh	5
That still was good for goodnesse sake, nor thought	185	U30 Burleigh	13
So may the gentler Muses, and good fame	186	U31 Elsmere	7
When a good Cause is destitute of friends,	186	U32 Elsmere	2
When those good few, that her Defenders be,	186	U32 Elsmere	5
God, and the good, know to forgive, and save.	191	U38 Elegy 'Tis	19
Of Contumelie, and urge a good man more	193	U38 Elegy 'Tis	100
But say, all sixe good men, what answer yee?	210	U43 Vulcan	173
That have good places: therefore once agen,	212	U43 Vulcan	212
That have good fortunes: therefore once agen,	212	U43 Vulcan	V212
That have good places: wherefore once agen,	212	U43 Vulcan	V212
Such, Coke, were thy beginnings, when thy good	217	U46 Coke	5
A cheerefull worke to all good eyes, to see	224	U50 Countesse	16
For you admit no companie, but good,	224	U50 Countesse	25
An ill commoditie! 'T must make good weight.	229	U54 Squib	6
And you shall make me good, in weight, and fashion,	229	U54 Squib	17
And neither good Cheare,	231	U57 Burges	16
Of honour, nor no ayre of good?	234	U60 La-ware	7
An Epigram. To our great and good K. Charles	236	U64 Charles 3	Ttl
Most pious King, but his owne good in you!	236	U64 Charles 3	2
For three of his foure-score, he did no good.	243	U70 Ode	32
But simple love of greatnesse, and of good;	246	U70 Ode	105
The good, and durst not practise it, were glad	247	U70 Ode	119
Of Princes aides, or good mens Charities.	248	U71 Treasurer	3
What worlds of blessings to good Kings they owe:	261	U77 Treasurer	20
Good Omen to him, in the note thou sing'st,	263	U78 Digby	22
Good fortune to him, in the note thou sing'st,	263	U78 Digby	V 22
Our great, our good. Where one's so drest	265	U79 New-yeares	44
Should take first Seisin of the publique good,	268	U80 Christning	8
As in renewing thy good Grandsires fame;	268	U80 Christning	12
Hee's good, as great. I am almost a stone!	269	U81 Pawlet	11
Earle Rivers Grand-Child--serve not formes, good Fame,	269	U81 Pawlet	21
And, calling truth to witnesse, make that good	270	U81 Pawlet	35
And, calling truth to witnesse, make it good	270	U81 Pawlet	V 35
At either Stemme, and know the veines of good	274	U84 Descent	8
Where it may run to any good;	280	U84 Mind	62
All that was good, or great in me she weav'd,	282	U84 Muse	4
Amongst her Peeres, those Princes of all good!	284	U84 Muse	84
A solemne Mistresse, and so good a Friend,	287	U84 Muse	175
Or Mallowes good for bodyes ill:	291	U85 Country	V 58
Of the good Cynara I was: Refraine,	292	U86 Hor.4:1	4
For his owne good, a carelesse letter-goe	315	Horace	234
Mans comming yeares much good with them doe bring:	317	Horace	250
It still must favour good men, and to these	317	Horace	280
He cries, Good boy, thou'lt keepe thine owne. Now, adde	327	Horace	470
Wild raging lusts; prescribe the mariage good;	327	Horace	489
Twice, or thrice good, I wonder: but am more	329	Horace	535
Angry. Sometimes, I heare good Homer snore.	329	Horace	536
Angry, if once I heare good Homer snore.	351	Horace	V512/536
For hee'll cry, Good, brave, better, excellent!	333	Horace	611
Hee'd say, Mend this, good friend, and this; 'tis naught.	333	Horace	624
A good and wise man will crye open shame	354	Horace	V633
Be then both Rare, and Good; and long	367	Ode Who saith	33
Might make the Fable of Good Women true.	372	Epitaph	14
To see his worke be good; but that he looke	385	Husband	2
Was worthy of a Good one; And this, here,	386	Husband	10
Hold thyne owne worth unbroke: which is so good	386	Browne	13
And hath the noblest marke of a good Booke,	389	Aleman	7
For a good Poet's made, as well as borne.	392	Shakespeare	64
Religious, wise, chast, loving, gratious, good,	394	Jane Ogle	5
Keeps warme the spice of her good name,	400	Lady Ogle	30
Defies, what's crosse to Piety, or good Fame.	401	Beaumont	20
Why much good doo't you! Be what beast you will,	403	Inigo Jones 1	21
Though gold or Ivory haftes would make it good.	403	Inigo Jones 1	28
Though gold or Ivory haftes cant make it good.	403	Inigo Jones 1	V 28

	Page	Title	Line

GOOD (cont.)
Swim without Corke! Why, thank the good Queen Anne.   .   .   .   405   Inigo Jones 1   68
And they were very good: yet thou think'st nay.   .   .   .   408   Detractor   2
And you doe doe them well, with good applause,   .   .   .   409   Brome   5
An honest Bilbo-Smith would make good blades,   .   .   .   410   Brome   15
The motives, and true Spurres to all good Nations.   .   .   .   411   Sutcliffe   5
An Epigram To My Joviall Good Freind Mr. Robert Dover,   .   .   .   415   Dover   Ttl
And doe both Church, and Common-wealth the good,   .   .   .   416   Dover   8
at Pem Wakers good ale Tapp, ...   417   Moon   39
Those dull Girls, no good can mean us,   .   .   .   657   Door Apollo   11
To make these good, and what comes after, better.   .   .   .   666   Glover   10
GOODLIER
And so some goodlier monster had begot: .   .   .   204   U43 Vulcan   32
GOODLY
What goodly Ghost, besprent with April deaw,   .   .   .   268   U81 Pawlet   V 1
GOODNESSE
And thine owne goodnesse to encrease thy merit,   .   .   .   60   E93 Radcliffe   10
And every goodnesse tax'd, or griev'd.   .   .   .   101   F4 To the World   52
He that for love of goodnesse hateth ill,   .   .   .   112   F11 Epode   87
Unto your name, and goodnesse of your life,   .   .   .   119   F13 Aubigny   109
That still was good for goodnesse sake, nor thought   .   .   .   185   U30 Burleigh   13
Spare your owne goodnesse yet; and be not great   .   .   .   191   U38 Elegy 'Tis   17
But thanke his greatnesse, and his goodnesse too;   .   .   .   236   U63 Charles 2   9
Of your grace, for goodnesse sake,   .   .   .   260   U76 Petition   26
Of Goodnesse still: Vouchsafe to take   .   .   .   273   U84 Cradle   9
This Cradle, and for Goodnesse sake,   .   .   .   273   U84 Cradle   10
To follow Goodnesse, by our owne discerning   .   .   .   412   Sutcliffe   17
GOOD-NIGHT
False world, good-night: since thou hast brought   .   .   .   100   F4 To the World   1
GOODS
Chuffe, lately rich in name, in chattels, goods,   .   .   .   41   E44 Chuff   1
GOODY
And Goody Sculpture, brought with much adoe   .   .   .   403   Inigo Jones 1   38
GOODYERE
To Sir Henry Goodyere.   55   E85 Goodyere 1   Ttl
Goodyere, I'am glad, and gratefull to report,   .   .   .   55   E85 Goodyere 1   1
When I would know thee Goodyere, my thought lookes   .   .   .   55   E86 Goodyere 2   1
GOOSE
That was rak'd up in the Winchestrian Goose   .   .   .   209   U43 Vulcan   142
Which was rak'd up in the Winchestrian Goose   .   .   .   209   U43 Vulcan   V142
That was lock'd up in the Winchestrian Goose   .   .   .   209   U43 Vulcan   V142
GORGON
The Rebell Gyants stoope, and Gorgon Envye yeild,   .   .   .   421   Ode:If Men   41
GORGONIAN
Gorgonian scolds, and Harpyes: on the other   .   .   .   86   E133 Voyage   69
GOSSIP
It bends the hams of Gossip Vigilance,   .   .   .   363   Riches   11
And Gossip-got acquaintance, as, to us   .   .   .   398   Drayton   85
GOSSIP-GOT
And Gossip-got acquaintance, as, to us   .   .   .   398   Drayton   85
GOSSIPPS
Or if't be the Gossipps happ   .   .   .   417   Moon   37
GO'ST
To make consumption, ever, where thou go'st;   .   .   .   205   U43 Vulcan   58
To make consumption, every where thou go'st;   .   .   .   205   U43 Vulcan   58
To sow consumption, every where thou go'st;   .   .   .   205   U43 Vulcan   V 58
To make propter viam, ever, where thou go'st;   .   .   .   205   U43 Vulcan   V 58
GOT
Let me give two: that doubly am got free,   .   .   .   31   E13 Empirick   3
And having got him out of doores is glad.   .   .   .   40   E42 Giles   7
Hath got the stewards chaire; he will not tarry   .   .   .   57   E90 Mill   15
When he was here. Nor hath he got a sute,   .   .   .   63   E97 Motion   16
And ever is ill got without the first.   .   .   .   63   E98 Th Roe 1   12
We have a Shelton, and a Heyden got,   .   .   .   84   E133 Voyage   5
The well-greas'd wherry now had got betweene,   .   .   .   87   E133 Voyage   114
Into my ri'mes could ne're be got   .   .   .   93   F1 Why write no   9
Who, though shee have a better verser got,   .   .   .   115   F12 Rutland   68
But few and faire Divisions: but being got   .   .   .   157   U13 Sacvile   151
Is that the truer excuse? or have we got   .   .   .   166   U15 Friend-Wars   142
Or Turners oyle of Talck. Nor ever got   .   .   .   188   U34 Small Poxe   11
Wish, you had fowle ones, and deformed got;   .   .   .   200   U42 Elegy Let   22
Of Vertue, got above his name?   234   U60 La-ware   10
Yet are got off thence, with cleare mind, and hands   .   .   .   234   U61 Epigram   7
A Nations sinne got pardon'd! 'twere a taske   .   .   .   234   U61 Epigram   12
Had got the Ceston on!   240   U67 Muses   36
E're thou wert halfe got out,   .   .   .   242   U70 Ode   6
Got up and thriv'd with honest arts: .   .   .   244   U70 Ode   34
Had sow'd these fruits, and got the harvest in.   .   .   .   247   U70 Ode   128
'Tis got where it can try the fire.   .   .   .   278   U84 Mind   28
Most pleasant Martial; Substance got with ease,   .   .   .   295   U90 Mart.10:47   2
'Tis cleare, this way I have got off from blame,   .   .   .   323   Horace   395
Is fayre got up, and day some houres begun!   .   .   .   396   Drayton   18
And Gossip-got acquaintance, as, to us   .   .   .   398   Drayton   85
Now, you are got into a nearer roome,   .   .   .   409   Brome   3
GOTT
'Gainst th'Ides, his gott moneyes he gets in with paine,   .   .   .   291   U85 Country   V 69
Butt, Clownishe pride hath gott   420   Ode:If Men   10
GOTTEN
As if a Brize were gotten i' their tayle;   .   .   .   164   U15 Friend-Wars   71
Jesus, the onely-gotten Christ! who can   .   .   .   288   U84 Muse   212
GOUT
Banck feeles no lamenesse of his knottie gout,   .   .   .   36   E31 Banck   1

		Page	Title	Line

GOVERNE
And doe governe more my blood, ... 136 U2 Cupid 3
GOVERNING
For order, and for governing the pixe, ... 415 Rutter 25
GOWNE
Upon a Velvet Petticote, or a Gowne, ... 200 U42 Elegy Let 38
A Gowne of that, was the Caparison? . . . . . 201 U42 Elegy Let 46
Court every hanging Gowne, and after that, . . . 201 U42 Elegy Let 57
Commended the French-hood, and Scarlet gowne . . . 201 U42 Elegy Let 69
Or taxe the Glories of the Church, and Gowne? . . . 203 U43 Vulcan 24
Or taxe the Glories of the Church, or Gowne? . . . 203 U43 Vulcan V 24
He that should search all Glories of the Gowne, . . 217 U46 Coke 1
Is Banke-rupt turn'd! the Cassock, Cloake, and Gowne, . 237 U64 Charles 3 20
Is Banke-rupt turn'd! Cloak, Cassock, Robe, & Gowne, . 237 U64 Charles 3 V 20
In his train'd Gowne about the Stage: So grew . . . 319 Horace 305
In his train'd Gowne about the Stage: thus grew . . 346 Horace V305
GOWN'D
Never at Law; seldome in office gown'd; 295 U90 Mart.10:47 5
GOWNED
Hook-handed Harpies, gowned Vultures, put . . . . 187 U33 Councellour 9
Or 'twere the gowned Comoedy they taught. . . . . 323 Horace 410
GOWNES
What though she be with Velvet gownes indu'd, . . . 222 U49 Pucell 18
GRAC'D
Or why, my well-grac'd words among, ... 293 U86 Hor.4:1 35
GRACE
Of Kings for grace; of Poets for my test? . . . . 28 E4 James 1 10
And, can forget mens names, with a great grace. . . 35 E28 Surly 8
For offring, with thy smiles, my wit to grace, . . 45 E58 Groome 3
If workes (not th'authors) their owne grace should looke, . 60 E94 Bedford 3 3
With those that come; whose grace may make that seeme . 64 E101 Supper 5
Even in the dew of grace, what you would bee? . . . 67 E104 Montgomery 2
Least mention of a Nymph, a Muse, a Grace, . . . 67 E105 L Wroth 2 4
In grace, and feature, ... 77 E120 S. P. 6
Thy noblest spouse affords them welcome grace; . . 98 F3 Wroth 55
While thus it buyes great grace, and hunts poore fame; . 113 F12 Rutland 15
While thus it gets grace, and hunts poore fame; . . 113 F12 Rutland V 15
With you, I know, my offring will find grace. . . . 114 F12 Rutland 30
Then all, that have but done my Muse least grace, . . 115 F12 Rutland 79
Then all, that have but done my verse least grace, . . 115 F12 Rutland V 79
For that firme grace he holdes in your regard, . . 116 F12 Rutland 95
To ought but grace, or ayme at other end. . . . 122 F15 Heaven 8
For acts of grace. . . . . 128 U1 Trinitie 28
With grace, with love, with cherishing intire: . . 128 U1 Trinitie 43
Clothes, or Fortune gives the grace; . . . . 131 U2 Excuse 8
And from her arched browes, such a grace . . . . 134 U2 Triumph 17
Outward Grace weake love beguiles: . . . . . 137 U2 Cupid 51
To no other Grace but you! . . . . . . 138 U2 Kisse 20
So they in state of Grace retain'd, ... 144 U3 Musicall 27
Where any Deed is forc't, the Grace is mard. . . . 153 U13 Sacvile 24
Which Grace shall I make love to first? your skill, . . 159 U14 Selden 35
The Subject of your Grace in pardoning me, . . . 191 U38 Elegy 'Tis 28
As if that ex'lent Dulnesse were Loves grace; . . . 198 U40 Elegy That 24
They may say Grace, and for Loves Chaplaines passe; . . 198 U40 Elegy That 31
I now begin to doubt, if ever Grace, ... 207 U43 Vulcan 107
To his poore Instrument, now out of grace. . . . 223 U49 Pucell 34
Both for the Mothers, and the Babes of grace, . . . 223 U49 Pucell 44
Great Charles, among the holy gifts of grace . . . 235 U62 Charles 1 1
Cannot but heape that grace, he will requite. . . . 236 U63 Charles 2 14
Haile Mary, full of grace, it once was said, . . . 238 U66 Queene 1
Had they but grace, of thinking, at these routes, . . 249 U72 King 15
It is their Grace, and favour, that makes seene, . . 255 U75 Epithalam. 89
To have thy God to blesse, thy King to grace, . . . 256 U75 Epithalam. 131
We pray may grace . . . . 257 U75 Epithalam. 158
Of his speciall grace to Letters, ... 259 U76 Petition 7
Of your grace, for goodnesse sake, ... 260 U76 Petition 26
Of brightest Mira, is our Song; the grace . . . 264 U79 New-yeares 32
Of grace, and Musique to the eare, ... 279 U84 Mind 35
By light, and comfort of spirituall Grace; . . . 286 U84 Muse 131
Adopt us Heires, by grace, who were of those . . . 286 U84 Muse 140
The doore of Grace, and found the Mercy-Seat. . . . 288 U84 Muse 190
By sure Election, and predestin'd grace! . . . . 288 U84 Muse 198
And when he smiling finds his Grace 292 U86 Hor.4:1 17
The vertue of which order, and true grace, . . . 307 Horace 59
The vertue and grace of which, or I mistake, . . . 339 Horace V 60/ 59
Of the Cethegi; And all men will grace, ... 309 Horace 72
Or grace of speech, should hope a lasting date. . . 309 Horace 100
Unto the Lyrick Strings, the Muse gave grace . . . 309 Horace 113
Of Order, and Connexion; so much grace . . . . 321 Horace 353
A Poeme, of no grace, weight, art, in rimes, . . . 327 Horace 456
All way of life was shewen; the grace of Kings . . 329 Horace 497
With more delight, and grace) . . . . . . 369 Ode Who saith 103
And clothes, and guifts, that only do thee grace . . 384 Somerset 2
As Love, here studied to keep Grace alive. . . . 412 Ghyrlond 8
A Grace by Ben: Johnson. extempore. before King James. . 418 Grace Ttl
By Cherissheinge the Spirrits that gave their greatnesse grace: . 419 Ode:If Men 5
And in this Age, canst hope no other grace. . . . 420 Ode:If Men 27
GRAC'D
Have grac'd with abstinence; . . . . . . 111 F11 Epode V 84
Grac'd with a Phoenix love; . . . . . . 112 F11 Epode 92
GRACED
Graced by your Reflection! . . . . . . 177 U25 Desmond 17
And, graced with her song, ... 402 Filmer 13

		Page	Title	Line
GRACEFULL				
In gracefull Ornament of Garland, Gemmes, and Haire.	· ·	253	U75 Epithalam.	40
GRACES (MYTH)				
Were leading forth the Graces on the greene:	· · ·	68	E105 L Wroth 2	12
As might all the Graces lead,	· · · ·	138	U2 Kisse	26
Truth, and the Graces best, when naked are.	· · ·	158	U14 Selden	4
Since, naked, best Truth, and the Graces are.	· ·	158	U14 Selden	V 4
But Venus and the Graces	· · · ·	221	U48 Bacchus	33
Doth show, the Graces, and the Houres	· ·	251	U74 Weston	16
She might have claym'd t'have made the Graces foure;	· ·	371	Epitaph	6
Now, in a garland by the graces knit:	· · ·	416	Welcome	4
GRACES				
Who both their graces in thy selfe hast more	· ·	57	E89 Allen	9
I speake thy other graces, not lesse showne,	· ·	58	E91 Vere	13
We need a man that knowes the severall graces	· ·	61	E95 Savile	27
The full, the flowing graces there enshrin'd;	· ·	79	E125 Uvedale	8
With lovely Graces	· · · · ·	135	U2 Triumph	V 36
With lustrous Graces,	· · · · ·	179	U25 Desmond	60
Or Delia's Graces, by Tibullus?	· · ·	181	U27 Ode Helen	10
To those true numerous Graces; whereof some,	· ·	182	U28 Worth	6
Of Graces, or your mercie here in mee,	· ·	191	U38 Elegy 'Tis	16
These Graces, when the rest of Ladyes view	· ·	225	U50 Countesse	31
And can for other Graces her commend,	· ·	230	U56 Covell	20
From the inherent Graces in her blood!	· ·	270	U81 Pawlet	36
Meeting of Graces, that so swell'd the flood	· ·	274	U84 Descent	10
Retire, and say; Her Graces	· · · ·	365	Ode Splendor	21
(Divinest graces) are so entermixt,	· ·	413	Ghyrlond	26
All, pouring their full showre of graces downe,	· ·	413	Ghyrlond	31
How are thy gifts, and graces blaz'd abroad!	·	413	Ghyrlond	36
How are thy gifts and graces blaz'd abro'd,	·	414	Ghyrlond	53
GRACIOUS (See also GRATIOUS)				
Which if most gracious heaven grant like thine,	· ·	37	E33 Roe 3	5
All-gracious God, the Sinners sacrifice,	· ·	127	U1 Trinitie	9
Or was she gracious a-farre off? but neere	· ·	169	U18 Elegy Can	5
GRAFFS				
When late (grave Palmer) these thy graffs and flowers	· ·	361	Palmer	1
GRAFT				
When he beholds a graft of his owne hand,	· · ·	251	U74 Weston	27
GRAFTED				
How plucking Peares, his owne hand grafted had,	· ·	290	U85 Country	19
GRAFTES				
And graftes more happy in the place:	· · ·	290	U85 Country	V 12
GRAINE				
The Graine of your two friendships! Hayward and	· ·	161	U14 Selden	V 81
His course so hurtfull both to graine, and seedes,	· ·	309	Horace	97
GRAMMAR				
Was there made English: with the Grammar too,	· · ·	207	U43 Vulcan	91
GRAMMARIANS				
All the Grammarians strive; and yet in Court	· ·	309	Horace	111
GRAMPIUS				
And over Grampius mountaine,	· · · ·	368	Ode Who saith	71
GRANATS				
Make your Petards, and Granats, all your fine	· ·	212	U43 Vulcan	206
GRAND				
To Fine Grand.	· · · · ·	51	E73 Fine Grand	Ttl
What is't, fine Grand, makes thee my friendship flye,	· ·	51	E73 Fine Grand	1
In-primis, Grand, you owe me for a jest,	· ·	51	E73 Fine Grand	5
Fortie things more, deare Grand, which you know true,	· ·	51	E73 Fine Grand	21
Of some grand peere, whose ayre doth make rejoyce	· ·	113	F12 Rutland	12
Whose nephew, whose grand-child you are;	· ·	121	F14 Sydney	42
A Kate, a Frank, to honour their Grand-dames,	· ·	258	U75 Epithalam.	172
Earle Rivers Grand-Child--serve not formes, good Fame,	· ·	269	U81 Pawlet	21
Earle Rivers Grand-Child--serve not titles Fame,	· ·	269	U81 Pawlet	V 21
Run from your rootes; Tell, testifie the grand	· ·	274	U84 Descent	9
Her Children, and Grand-children, reed it heere!	· ·	399	Lady Ogle	2
GRAND-CHILD				
Whose nephew, whose grand-child you are;	· ·	121	F14 Sydney	42
Earle Rivers Grand-Child--serve not formes, good Fame,	· ·	269	U81 Pawlet	21
Earle Rivers Grand-Child--serve not titles Fame,	· ·	269	U81 Pawlet	V 21
GRAND-CHILDREN				
Her Children, and Grand-children, reed it heere!	· ·	399	Lady Ogle	2
GRAND-DAMES				
A Kate, a Frank, to honour their Grand-dames,	· ·	258	U75 Epithalam.	172
GRANDEES				
Our Court, and all the Grandees; now, Sun, looke,	· ·	254	U75 Epithalam.	73
GRANDLINGS				
From the Tempestuous Grandlings, Who'll informe	· ·	215	U44 Speach	64
GRANDSIRES				
And 'tweene their Grandsires thighes,	· ·	258	U75 Epithalam.	173
As in renewing thy good Grandsires fame;	· ·	268	U80 Christning	12
GRANT				
Which if most gracious heaven grant like thine,	· ·	37	E33 Roe 3	5
Grant then, no rude hand remove her.	· · ·	39	E40 Ratcliffe	4
O Madame, if your grant did thus transferre mee,	· ·	55	E84 Bedford 2	9
But grant us perfect, they're not knowne.	· ·	104	F7 Women but	10
O grant it me!	· · · ·	128	U1 Trinitie	36
Well, they should know him, would the K. but grant	· ·	241	U68 House-hold	5
GRAPE				
Fig, grape, and quince, each in his time doth come:	· ·	94	F2 Penshurst	42
GRAPES				
And purple-matching Grapes, hee's glad!	· ·	290	U85 Country	20
For Grapes he had gather'd before they were eaten.	· ·	375	Coryat 1	25
For grapes he had gather'd, before they were eaten.	· ·	380	Coryat 3	36

		Page	Title	Line

GRAPHICK
    Each line, as it were graphick, in the face!   . . . 287 U84 Muse   154
GRASSE
    All the grasse that Rumney yeelds, ... 103 F6 Celia 2   13
    The better grasse, and flowers are found.   . . . 265 U79 New-yeares   59
    Now in the rooted Grasse him lay, ... 290 U85 Country   24
GRASSIE
    And with their grassie greene restor'd mine eyes.   . . . 398 Drayton   82
GRATEFULL
    Goodyere, I'am glad, and gratefull to report,   . . . 55 E85 Goodyere 1   1
    My gratefull soule, the subject of her powers,   . . . 115 F12 Rutland   73
    I, that am gratefull for him, have prepar'd   . . . 116 F12 Rutland   96
GRATES
    To force the grates, that hold him in, would fright   . . 337 Horace   675
GRATIOUS
    To the great and Gratious King Charles. . . .   . . 236 U64 Charles 3 VTtl
    Except your Gratious Eye as through a Glass   . . . 383 Rich   11
    Religious, wise, chast, loving, gratious, good,   . . . 394 Jane Ogle   5
GRATITUDE
    If I should faile, in gratitude, to thee,   . . . 80 E127 Aubigny   2
    That nothing can her gratitude provoke!   . . . 237 U64 Charles 3   16
    That nothing will her gratitude provoke!   . . . 237 U64 Charles 3 V 16
GRATUITIE
    To be given me in gratuitie   . . . . 259 U76 Petition   12
GRATULATE
    Who this thy scape from rumour gratulate,   . . . 43 E51 James 3   6
    That whil'st I meant but thine to gratulate,   . . . 48 E64 Salisbury 3 17
    And gratulate the breach, I griev'd before: . . . 61 E95 Savile   10
    I first salute thee so; and gratulate,   . . . 161 U14 Selden   67
    I gratulate it to thee, and thy Ends,   . . . 398 Drayton   89
GRATULATES
    Or gratulates the passage   . . . . 221 U48 Bacchus   45
GRATULATORIE
    . . . gratulatorie For his Returne from his Embassie. 1632.   . 250 U74 Weston Ttl
GRAVE   (ADJECTIVE)
    To be a courtier; and lookes grave enough,   . . . 30 E11 Something   2
    Then thee the age sees not that thing more grave,   . . 31 E14 Camden   5
    As skilfull Roscius, and grave Aesope, men,   . . . 56 E89 Allen   3
    And grave as ripe, like mellow as their faces.   . . . 59 E92 New Crie   7
    To night, grave sir, both my poore house, and I   . . . 64 E101 Supper   1
    Of the grave fart, late let in parliament,   . . . 87 E133 Voyage   108
    Grave tutor to the learned horse. Both which,   . . . 88 E133 Voyage   157
    Toyles, by grave custome, up and downe the court,   . . 113 F12 Rutland   5
    They were so even, grave, and holy;   . . . . 152 U12 Corbet   23
    See the grave, sower, and supercilious Sir   . . . 162 U15 Friend-Wars 19
    The Mistresse of Mans life, grave Historie,   . . . 175 U24 Frontispice   2
    Cecill, the grave, the wise, the great, the good,   . . 185 U30 Burleigh   5
    But the grave Lover ever was an Asse;   . . . 198 U40 Elegy That 32
    Sonne to the grave wise Keeper of the Seale,   . . . 225 U51 Bacon   9
    In grave beginnings, and great things profest,   . . . 305 Horace   17
    This foot the socks tooke up, and buskins grave,   . . 311 Horace   118
    To the grave Harp, and Violl voyces new;   . . . 346 Horace V306
    Loftie, and grave; and in the buskin stalke.   . . . 319 Horace   318
    The Poems void of profit, our grave men   . . . 329 Horace   511
    When late (grave Palmer) these thy graffs and flowers   . 361 Palmer   1
    I Could begin with that grave forme, Here lies,   . . 394 Jane Ogle   1
GRAVE
    This grave partakes the fleshly birth.   . . . . 34 E22 Daughter   11
    Who wets my grave, can be no friend of mine.   . . . 37 E33 Roe 3   6
    Against my grave, and time could not forgive.   . . . 58 E91 Vere   12
    Whil'st thou dost rayse some Player, from the grave,   . 81 E129 Mime   11
    Sleepe, and the Grave will wake.   . . . . 143 U3 Musicall   14
    Of him whose bones this Grave doth gather: . . . 151 U12 Corbet   6
    Out of his Grave, and poyson every eare.   . . . 172 U21 Ltl Shrub   4
    That were to wither all, and make a Grave   . . . 192 U38 Elegy 'Tis 59
    Rather then want your light, I wish a grave.   . . . 194 U38 Elegy 'Tis 122
    Whether he piss'd upon his Fathers grave;   . . . 335 Horace   671
    Seldome descend but bleeding to their grave.   . . . 363 Murder   2
    Fames heate upon the grave did stay;   . . . . 400 Lady Ogle   28
GRAVELL
    Old Hat here, torne Hose, with Shoes full of gravell,   . 375 Coryat 1   26
GRAVER
    Wherein the Graver had a strife   . . . . . 390 Reader   3
GRAVES
    That bred them, graves: when they were borne, they di'd,   . 114 F12 Rutland   47
    With dust of ancestors, in graves but dwell.   . . . 121 F14 Sydney   40
GRAVITIE
    Though sower, with safetie of his gravitie,   . . . 319 Horace   322
GRAY   (NAME)
    An Epitaph on Master Philip Gray.   . . . . 168 U16 Gray Ttl
    All that is left of Philip Gray, ... 168 U16 Gray   4
GRAY
    With great gray eyes, are lifted up, and mew'd;   . . 88 E133 Voyage 161
    My hundred of gray haires, ... 150 U9 Picture   14
GRAZING
    The lowing herds there grazing are: . . . . 290 U85 Country   14
GREACE
    And pleaseth both. For while he melts his greace   . . 38 E37 Chev'ril   3
GREAS'D
    The well-greas'd wherry now had got betweene,   . . . 87 E133 Voyage 114
GREASE
    The sinkes ran grease, and haire of meazled hogs,   . . 88 E133 Voyage 145
    Or by chance if in their grease   . . . . . 418 Moon   41

GREAT

	Page	Title	Line
If all you boast of your great art be true;	29	E6 Alchymists	1
It made me a great face, I ask'd the name.	30	E11 Something	4
The great renowne, and name wherewith shee goes.	31	E14 Camden	4
Of a great man, and to be thought the same,	35	E28 Surly	2
Makes serious use of all great trade he knowes.	35	E28 Surly	3
Which hee thinkes great; and so reades verses, too:	35	E28 Surly	5
And, that is done, as he saw great men doe.	35	E28 Surly	6
And, can forget mens names, with a great grace.	35	E28 Surly	8
Both which are great. And laugh at ill-made clothes;	35	E28 Surly	10
That breathes in his dogs way: and this is great.	36	E28 Surly	18
Stile thee a most great foole, but no great man.	36	E28 Surly	22
'Tofore, great men were glad of Poets: Now,	40	E43 Salisbury 1	5
Great heav'n did well, to give ill fame free wing;	43	E51 James 3	2
I, that am glad of thy great chance, here doo!	46	E60 Mounteagle	5
Durst thinke it great, and worthy wonder too,	46	E60 Mounteagle	7
In a great belly. Write, then on thy wombe,	46	E62 Would-bee	11
To a great image through thy luxurie.	48	E65 Muse	4
In onely thee, might be both great, and glad.	48	E66 Cary	4
Love thy great losse, which a renowne hath wonne,	49	E66 Cary	11
Of greatest bloud, and yet more good then great;	52	E76 Bedford 1	6
If Rome so great, and in her wisest age,	56	E89 Allen	1
How can so great example dye in mee,	57	E89 Allen	7
As noble in great chiefes, as they are rare.	58	E91 Vere	16
For the great marke of vertue, those being gone	60	E93 Radcliffe	2
And two, that would have falne as great, as they,	60	E93 Radcliffe	5
For who can master those great parts like thee,	61	E95 Savile	17
It is the next deed, and a great one too.	61	E95 Savile	26
A man should seeke great glorie, and not broad.	62	E96 Donne 2	12
How much of great example wert thou, Roe,	64	E99 Th Roe 2	5
Well, though thy name lesse then our great ones bee,	64	E99 Th Roe 2	11
Of vice, and vertue; wherein all great life	66	E102 Pembroke	6
Which is, it selfe, the imprese of the great,	66	E103 L Wroth 1	7
How great ye were with their two Emperours;	68	E107 Hungry	6
Your great profession; which I once, did prove:	70	E108 Soldiers	6
By thy great helpe: and doth proclaime by mee,	72	E111 Edmonds 2	13
By thy great Art: and doth proclaime by mee,	72	E111 Edmonds 2 V 13
Where, what makes others great, doth keepe thee good!	73	E113 Overbury	4
And to live great, was better, then great borne.	75	E116 Jephson	12
Rudyerd, as lesser dames, to great ones use,	78	E121 Rudyerd 1	1
Think'st thou, Mime, this is great? or, that they strive	81	E129 Mime	9
How can I speake of thy great paines, but erre?	83	E132 Sylvester	5
Great Club-fist, though thy backe, and bones be sore,	85	E133 Voyage	55
With great gray eyes, are lifted up, and mew'd;	88	E133 Voyage	161
And Madame Caesar, great Proserpina,	89	E133 Voyage	180
At his great birth, where all the Muses met.	94	F2 Penshurst	14
At great mens tables) and yet dine away.	95	F2 Penshurst	66
What (great, l will not say, but) sodayne cheare	95	F2 Penshurst	82
His children thy great lord may call his owne:	96	F2 Penshurst	91
That at great times, art no ambitious guest	96	F3 Wroth	5
And the great Heroes, of her race,	98	F3 Wroth	56
By being organes to great sinne,	99	F3 Wroth	86
Though poyson, thinke it a great fate.	99	F3 Wroth	90
Or whose great name in Poets heaven use,	107	F10 Proludium	2
Or some great thought doth keepe	109	F11 Epode	24
While thus it buyes great grace, and hunts poore fame;	113	F12 Rutland	15
For what a sinne 'gainst your great fathers spirit,	114	F12 Rutland	31
Painted, or carv'd upon our great-mens tombs,	114	F12 Rutland	45
Of so great title, birth, but vertue most,	118	F13 Aubigny	49
For he, that once is good, is ever great.	118	F13 Aubigny	52
T'expect the honors of great 'Aubigny:	119	F13 Aubigny	105
Other great wives may blush at: when they see	119	F13 Aubigny	111
And great, must seeke for new,	121	F14 Sydney	35
Good, and great God, can I not thinke of thee,	122	F15 Heaven	1
Let his Title be but great,	142	U2 Exception	3
Great and good turns, as wel could time them too,	153	U13 Sacvile	2
Of any, is a great and generous Deed:	155	U13 Sacvile	76
Men have beene great, but never good by chance,	156	U13 Sacvile	124
May grow so great to be example, when	158	U13 Sacvile	161
In offering this thy worke to no great Name,	161	U14 Selden	69
Great, brave, and fashion'd folke, these are allow'd	164	U15 Friend-Wars	84
Whom no great Mistresse hath as yet infam'd,	165	U15 Friend-Wars	97
That thou thinke nothing great, but what is good,	168	U15 Friend-Wars	187
Minds that are great and free,	174	U23 Himselfe	16
Might be defrauded, nor the great secur'd,	176	U24 Frontispice	6
Hath our great Sidney, Stella set,	181	U27 Ode Helen	25
Cecill, the grave, the wise, the great, the good,	185	U30 Burleigh	5
Such shall you heare to day, and find great foes,	186	U32 Elsmere	7
Or the great Hall at Westminster, the field	186	U33 Councellour	3
Spare your owne goodnesse yet; and be not great	191	U38 Elegy 'Tis	17
That we have Trumpets, Armour, and great Horse,	213	U44 Speach	7
And could (if our great men would let their Sonnes	214	U44 Speach	57
Why are we rich, or great, except to show	215	U44 Speach	69
As are the Glorious Scenes, at the great sights;	220	U47 Tribe	66
Of all to the great Master.	220	U48 Bacchus	8
In great Saint Georges Union;	221	U48 Bacchus	44
So great a Vertue stand upright to view,	224	U50 Countesse	19
Then the great Homers wit, for her, could faine;	224	U50 Countesse	24
With one great blot, yo'had form'd me as I am.	227	U52 Answer	12
With one great blot, you had drawne me as I am.	227	U52 Answer	V 12
Who durst live great, 'mongst all the colds, and heates,	233	U59 Newcastle	21
And only, his great Soule envy'd,	234	U60 La-ware	17
Great Charles, among the holy gifts of grace	235	U62 Charles 1	1

	Page	Title		Line
GREAT (cont.)				
An Epigram. To our great and good K. Charles . . .	236	U64	Charles 3	Ttl
To the great and Gratious King Charles. . . .	236	U64	Charles 3	VTtl
Indeed, when had great Britaine greater cause	236	U64	Charles 3	7
How much to heaven for thee, great Charles, they owe!	237	U64	Charles 3	22
And threat' the great Eclipse. Two houres but runne,	238	U65	Prince	11
And thereat the great Eclipse. Two houres but runne,	238	U65	Prince	V 11
To compare small with great, as still we owe	238	U66	Queene	12
The Daughter of great Harry!	240	U67	Muses	26
Never so great to get them: and the ends,	242	U69	Friend Son	25
Thy coming forth in that great yeare,	242	U70	Ode	2
Not liv'd; for Life doth her great actions spell,	245	U70	Ode	59
You liv'd to be the great surnames,	247	U70	Ode	113
Repeating all Great Britain's joy, and more,	249	U72	King	6
What Drums or Trumpets, or great Ord'nance can,	249	U72	King	9
The wish is great; but where the Prince is such,	249	U72	King	19
In his great Actions: view whom his large hand	250	U73	Weston	3
To see great Charles of Travaile eas'd,	251	U74	Weston	26
Great Say-Master of State, who cannot erre,	255	U75	Epithalam.	99
Great Say-Master of State, who not to erre,	255	U75	Epithalam.	V 99
So great; his Body now alone projects the shade.	258	U75	Epithalam.	184
If to my mind, great Lord, I had a state,	260	U77	Treasurer	1
And his great Action done at Scanderoone;	262	U78	Digby	V 13
Pan is the great Preserver of our bounds.	264	U79	New-yeares	14
To better Pastures then great Pales can:	264	U79	New-yeares	30
Pan only our great Shep'ard is,	265	U79	New-yeares	43
Our great, our good. Where one's so drest	265	U79	New-yeares	44
This is the great Preserver of our bounds,	265	U79	New-yeares	48
This only the great Shep'ard is.	265	U79	New-yeares	65
Great King, thy having of a second Sonne:	268	U80	Christning	2
Great aides to Empire, as they are great care	268	U80	Christning	6
Me thought, Great Britaine in her Sea, before,	268	U80	Christning	13
Whose Daughter? ha? Great Savage of the Rock?	269	U81	Pawlet	10
Hee's good, as great. I am almost a stone!	269	U81	Pawlet	11
What she did here, by great example, well,	269	U81	Pawlet	33
What she did by a great example, well,	269	U81	Pawlet	V 33
The Sunne! great Kings, and mightiest Kingdomes fall!	271	U81	Pawlet	89
The Sunne! great Kings, and mighty Kingdomes fall!	271	U81	Pawlet	V 89
With ever-greene, and great renowne,	272	U84	Cradle	2
All that was good, or great in me she weav'd,	282	U84	Muse	4
Of that great Evidence, the Conscience!	284	U84	Muse	58
That great eternall Holy-day of rest,	284	U84	Muse	63
A new Song to his praise, and great I Am:	285	U84	Muse	90
That holy, great, and glorious Mysterie,	286	U84	Muse	129
In that great Act of judgement: which the Father	288	U84	Muse	215
And waiting Chambers of great Lords.	289	U85	Country	8
Loves cares so evill, and so great?	290	U85	Country	38
In grave beginnings, and great things profest,	305	Horace		17
The whole fleet wreck'd? a great jarre to be shap'd,	305	Horace		28
The gests of Kings, great Captaines, and sad Warres,	309	Horace		105
The deeds of Kings, great Captaines, and sad Warres,	341	Horace		V105
Where some great Lady, or her diligent Nourse;	313	Horace		164
What doth this Promiser such great gaping worth	343	Horace		V197
A great deferrer, long in hope, growne numbe	317	Horace		245
Loftie, and great; and in the buskin walk.	348	Horace		V398/318
In Helicon; a great sort will not pare	325	Horace		422
Next these great Homer and Tyrtaeus set	327	Horace		493
An admirable Verse. The great Scurfe take	333	Horace		594
An admirable verse: the great Scab take	353	Horace		V594
Or great in money's out at use, command	333	Horace		600
Make a great Supper; or for some poore man	333	Horace		602
Great men are said with many cups to plye,	354	Horace		V617
And pray, thy joyes as lasting bee, as great.	384	Somerset		8
I meane with great, but disproportion'd Muses:	391	Shakespeare		26
At least so great a Lady. She was wife	394	Jane Ogle		15
In the great masse, or machine there is stirr'd?	395	May		22
Aeternities great charter; which became	400	Lady Ogle		35
Our great reward, th'aeternall Crown to win.	412	Sutcliffe		19
These Mysteries do point to three more great,	413	Ghyrlond		29
Great Queen of Queens, most mild, most meek, most wise,	414	Ghyrlond		41
. . . on his great Instauration of his Hunting, . . .	415	Dover		Ttl
To Crowne the years, which you begin, great king,	416	Welcome		7
GREATE				
Adding her owne great accents, to this Day,	249	U72	King	V 7
To see (who'it is?) A noble Countesse, greate,	394	Jane Ogle		3
As when they both were greate, and both knewe howe	419	Ode:If Men		3
GREATER				
The courtier is become the greater thiefe.	29	E8	Robbery	6
That's greater, yet: to crie his owne up neate.	35	E28	Surly	11
I'have sung the greater fortunes of our state.	48	E64	Salisbury 3	18
But, in the action, greater man then hee:	84	E133	Voyage	26
And greater rites, yet writ in mysterie,	119	F13	Aubigny	106
Noble; or of greater Blood:	140	U2	Her man	4
But that some greater names have broke with me,	169	U17	Friend-Debt	8
Were now the greater Captaine? for they saw	214	U44	Speach	39
Indeed, when had great Britaine greater cause	236	U64	Charles 3	7
To give a greater Name, and Title to! Their owne!	255	U75	Epithalam.	96
The greater part, that boast the Muses fire,	339	Horace		V 33
So, shunning faults, to greater fault doth lead,	307	Horace		43
The shunning vice, to greater vice doth lead,	339	Horace		V 45/ 43
Both in their tunes, the licence greater grew,	319	Horace		299
GREATEST				
Of greatest bloud, and yet more good then great;	52	E76	Bedford 1	6

GREATEST (cont.)
```
Their latter praise would still the greatest bee,      .    .    .   68   E106 E Herbert      9
T'alledge, that greatest men were not asham'd,         .    .    .   82   E130 Ferrab. 1      9
Noble; or of greatest Blood:                           .    .    .  140   U2 Her man       V  4
The greatest are but growing Gentlemen.                .    .    .  281   U84 Kenelme        15
still making that the greatest that is last            .    .    .  361   Palmer             19
Warres greatest woes, and miseries increase,           .    .    .  363   Peace               3
```
GREATLY
```
Blaspheme god, greatly.  Or some poore hinde beat,     .    .    .   36   E28 Surly          17
```
GREAT-MENS
```
Painted, or carv'd upon our great-mens tombs,          .    .    .  114   F12 Rutland        45
```
GREATNESSE
```
Which is maine greatnesse.  And, at his still boord,   .    .    .   35   E28 Surly          13
Of solemne greatnesse.  And he dares, at dice,         .    .    .   36   E28 Surly          16
Nay more, for greatnesse sake, he will be one          .    .    .   36   E28 Surly          19
To greatnesse, Cary, I sing that, and thee.            .    .    .   48   E66 Cary            2
The world must know your greatnesse is my debter.      .    .    .   51   E73 Fine Grand      4
Hating that solemne vice of greatnesse, pride;         .    .    .   52   E76 Bedford 1      10
To the full greatnesse of the cry:                     .    .    .   97   F3 Wroth           32
To make up Greatnesse! and mans whole good fix'd       .    .    .  163   U15 Friend-Wars    44
There greatnesse takes a glorie to relieve.            .    .    .  192   U38 Elegy 'Tis     34
But thanke his greatnesse, and his goodnesse too;      .    .    .  236   U63 Charles 2       9
But simple love of greatnesse, and of good;            .    .    .  246   U70 Ode           105
Professing greatnesse, swells: That, low by lee        .    .    .  307   Horace             38
His Muse professing height, and greatnesse, swells;    .    .    .  339   Horace         V 39/ 38
By Cherissheinge the Spirrits that gave their greatnesse grace:    .  419   Ode:If Men          5
```
GRECIAN   (See also GRAECIAN)
```
So they fall gently from the Grecian spring,           .    .    .  309   Horace             75
In daring to forsake the Grecian tracts,               .    .    .  323   Horace            407
Then Affricke knew, or the full Grecian store!         .    .    .  398   Drayton            88
```
'GREE
```
To chant her 'gree,                                    .    .    .  274   U84 Cradle         36
```
GREECE
```
No more let Greece her bolder fables tell              .    .    .   84   E133 Voyage         1
And saw a Centaure, past those tales of Greece;        .    .    .  228   U53 Newcastle       5
Of all, that insolent Greece, or haughtie Rome         .    .    .  391   Shakespeare        39
```
GREEDIE
```
Or shooting at the greedie thrush,                     .    .    .   97   F3 Wroth           34
What though the greedie Frie                           .    .    .  175   U23 Himselfe       19
Or urge thy Greedie flame, thus to devoure             .    .    .  202   U43 Vulcan          3
Or beg thy Greedie flame, thus to devoure              .    .    .  202   U43 Vulcan       V  3
```
GREEDY
```
With sloth, yet greedy still of what's to come:        .    .    .  317   Horace            246
```
GREEK
```
The old Greek-hands in picture, or in stone.           .    .    .  260   U77 Treasurer       9
```
GREEKE
```
Item, a faire greeke poesie for a ring:                .    .    .   51   E73 Fine Grand     10
Greeke was free from Rimes infection,                  .    .    .  184   U29 Fit of Rime    31
Happy Greeke, by this protection,                      .    .    .  184   U29 Fit of Rime    32
And the Greeke Discipline (with the moderne) shed      .    .    .  214   U44 Speach         36
Take you the Greeke Examples, for your light,          .    .    .  323   Horace            397
Of Latine and Greeke, to his friendship.  And seven    .    .    .  380   Coryat 3           45
To the Greeke coast thine onely knew the way.          .    .    .  388   Chapman             9
And though thou hadst small Latine, and lesse Greeke,  .    .    .  391   Shakespeare        31
The merry Greeke, tart Aristophanes,                   .    .    .  392   Shakespeare        51
```
GREEK-HANDS
```
The old Greek-hands in picture, or in stone.           .    .    .  260   U77 Treasurer       9
```
GREEK'S
```
The Muse not only gave the Greek's a wit,              .    .    .  327   Horace            461
```
GREEN
```
These forme thy Ghyrlond.  Wherof Myrtle green,        .    .    .  412   Ghyrlond            5
```
GREENE
```
For such a Poet, while thy dayes were greene,          .    .    .   28   E4 James 1          5
Were leading forth the Graces on the greene:           .    .    .   68   E105 L Wroth 2     12
White, black, blew, greene, and in more formes out-started,  .    .   87   E133 Voyage       126
Of flowrie fields, of cop'ces greene,                  .    .    .   97   F3 Wroth           38
In the greene circle of thy Ivy twine.                 .    .    .  107   F10 Proludium      12
All Parnassus Greene did wither,                       .    .    .  183   U29 Fit of Rime    17
Would make the very Greene-cloth to looke blew:        .    .    .  241   U68 House-hold      8
Of Summers Liveries, and gladding greene;              .    .    .  253   U75 Epithalam.     18
With ever-greene, and great renowne,                   .    .    .  272   U84 Cradle          2
And with their grassie greene restor'd mine eyes.      .    .    .  398   Drayton            82
```
GREENE-CLOTH
```
Would make the very Greene-cloth to looke blew:        .    .    .  241   U68 House-hold      8
```
GREENWICH
```
From Greenwich, hither, to Row-hampton gate!           .    .    .  252   U75 Epithalam.     12
```
'GREET
```
To 'greet, or grieve her soft Euthanasee?              .    .    .  283   U84 Muse           40
```
GREET
```
With which, Priapus, he may greet thy hands,           .    .    .  290   U85 Country     V 21
```
GREETING
```
And still begin'st the greeting:                       .    .    .  221   U48 Bacchus        16
```
GREW
```
Where, afterwards, it grew a butter-flye:              .    .    .   31   E15 Court-worm      3
Hazard a month forsware his; and grew drunke,          .    .    .   56   E87 Hazard          2
Upon th'accompt, hers grew the quicker trade.          .    .    .   56   E87 Hazard          5
Not though that haire grew browne, which once was amber,  .    .    57   E90 Mill            9
Or winds the Spirit, by which the flower so grew?      .    .    .  192   U38 Elegy 'Tis     58
So, in that ground, as soone it grew to be             .    .    .  214   U44 Speach         37
They cannot last.  No lie grew ever old.               .    .    .  216   U45 Squib          20
And skill in thee, now, grew Authoritie;               .    .    .  217   U46 Coke           10
Till either grew a portion of the other:               .    .    .  247   U70 Ode           110
Of vertues in her, as, in short, shee grew             .    .    .  274   U84 Descent        11
```

GREW (cont.)
   Most worthie praise, when words that common grew,   .   .   .   307   Horace   67
   Most worthie praise, when words that vulgar grew,   .   .   .   340   Horace   V 67
   Both in their tunes, the licence greater grew,   .   .   .   319   Horace   299
   In his train'd Gowne about the Stage: So grew   .   .   .   319   Horace   305
   In his train'd Gowne about the Stage: thus grew   .   .   346   Horace   V305
GRIEFE
   Life, whose griefe was out of fashion, ...   39   E40 Ratcliffe   13
   To age, misfortune, sicknesse, griefe: .   .   .   102   F4 To the World   62
   (Which with griefe and wrath I heard)   .   .   .   132   U2 How he saw   29
   My Lord, till felt griefe make our stone hearts soft,   .   234   U61 Epigram   14
   It brings Friends Joy, Foes Griefe, Posteritie Fame;   .   256   U75 Epithalam.   114
   A meere upbraiding Griefe, and tort'ring punishment.   .   256   U75 Epithalam.   120
   It is inough, their griefe shall know   .   .   .   369   Ode Who saith   113
GRIEFES
   I feele my griefes too, and there scarce is ground,   .   .   122   F15 Heaven   21
GRIEVE
   I Grieve not, Courtling, thou are started up   .   .   .   50   E72 Court-ling   1
   Where weaknesse doth offend, and vertue grieve,   .   .   192   U38 Elegy 'Tis   33
   To 'greet, or grieve her soft Euthanasee?   .   .   .   283   U84 Muse   40
   To laughter; so they grieve with those that mone.   .   311   Horace   144
   Why should I grieve my friend, this trifling way?   .   335   Horace   640
GRIEV'D
   And gratulate the breach, I griev'd before: .   .   .   61   E95 Savile   10
   And every goodnesse tax'd, or griev'd.   .   .   .   101   F4 To the World   52
   What I, in her, am griev'd to want.   .   .   .   174   U22 Elegy Tho   36
   Io still wandring; griev'd Orestes sad: .   .   .   342   Horace   V177
GRIEVOUS
   And take compassion on my grievous plight.   .   .   127   U1 Trinitie   14
   All; So this grievous Writer puts to flight   .   .   337   Horace   676
GRISLY
   But you will visit grisly Pluto's hall?   .   .   .   89   E133 Voyage   175
GROINE
   All which he makes the servants of the Groine,   .   .   163   U15 Friend-Wars   46
GRONE
   They'are rear'd with no mans ruine, no mans grone,   .   .   94   F2 Penshurst   46
GROOME
   To Groome Ideot.   45   E58 Groome   Ttl
   To every squire, or groome, that will report   .   .   113   F12 Rutland   6
   To every squire, or groome, that can report   .   .   113   F12 Rutland   V 6
   On the close groome, and page, on new-yeeres day,   .   118   F13 Aubigny   74
   Then ope thy wardrobe, thinke me that poore Groome   .   201   U42 Elegy Let   51
   I look'd for Hercules to be the Groome: .   .   .   228   U53 Newcastle   18
GROOMES
   His Groomes to witnesse; or else lets it fall   .   .   154   U13 Sacvile   36
   The knottie heads of the most surly Groomes,   .   .   363   Riches   8
GROPES
   The truth, but gropes, and urgeth all by chance;   .   .   391   Shakespeare   10
GROSSE
   Tell the grosse Dutch those grosser tales of yours,   .   .   68   E107 Hungry   5
   Or thick grosse ointment, but offend the Guests: .   .   331   Horace   558
GROSSER
   Tell the grosse Dutch those grosser tales of yours,   .   .   68   E107 Hungry   5
GROSSNESSE
   Earths grossnesse; There's the how, and why.   .   .   279   U84 Mind   44
   our grossnesse; There's the how, and why.   .   .   .   279   U84 Mind   V 44
GROUN'
   Out at his friendly eyes, leape, beat the groun'.   .   .   333   Horace   613
GROUND
   I feele my griefes too, and there scarce is ground,   .   .   122   F15 Heaven   21
   Gold, upon a ground of black.   141   U2 Her man   14
   To the ground.   183   U29 Fit of Rime   9
   And that accursed ground, the Parish-Garden: .   .   209   U43 Vulcan   147
   And that prophaner ground, the Parish-Garden: .   .   209   U43 Vulcan   V147
   So, in that ground, as soone it grew to be   .   .   214   U44 Speach   37
   And cleave both ayre and ground, ...   239   U67 Muses   14
   And shake both ayre and ground, ...   239   U67 Muses   V 14
   This sea-girt ground upon: 240   U67 Muses   V 33
   And all the Ground were Garden, where she led!   .   .   254   U75 Epithalam.   68
   Where ere they tread th'enamour'd ground,   .   .   264   U79 New-yeares   36
   Where e're he goes upon the ground,   .   .   .   265   U79 New-yeares   58
   Or hath she here, upon the ground,   .   .   .   280   U84 Mind   49
   Creepes on the ground; too safe, too afraid of storme.   .   307   Horace   39
   The gladdest ground to all the numbred-five,   .   .   412   Ghyrlond   6
GROUNDED
   By those deepe-grounded, understanding men,   .   .   414   Rutter   7
GROUNDS
   The middle grounds thy mares, and horses breed.   .   .   94   F2 Penshurst   24
   Some grounds are made the richer, for the Rest;   .   .   169   U17 Friend-Debt   17
   As shall the feasts faire grounds be.   .   .   .   221   U48 Bacchus   42
   To him we owe all profits of our grounds.   .   .   264   U79 New-yeares   15
   To whom you owe all duties of your grounds;   .   .   265   U79 New-yeares   49
   The pleasant grounds, or when the River Rhine,   .   .   305   Horace   22
GROVE
   'Mongst Hampton shades, and Phoebus grove of bayes,   .   80   E126 Mrs Cary   2
   By that tall Grove, your haire; whose globy rings   .   170   U19 Elegy By   5
   Diana's Grove, or Altar, with the bor-/Dring   .   .   305   Horace   20
   Diana's Grove, or Altar, with the nether   .   .   .   338   Horace   V 20
GROVES
   Heare, o you Groves, and, Hills, resound his praise.   .   264   U79 New-yeares   23
   Heare, O you Groves, and, Hills, resound his worth.   .   264   U79 New-yeares   31
   But, let the Faunes, drawne from their Groves, beware,   .   321   Horace   355

```
                                                              Page      Title      Line
GROW
  On the true causes, ere they grow too old.       .    .    .    50   E70 Wm Roe 1      4
  Ripe statesmen, ripe: They grow in every street.     .    .    58   E92 New Crie      3
  When Love is fled, and I grow old.      .    .    .    .    93   F1 Why write no     12
  But this doth from the cloud of error grow,      .    .    110   F11 Epode         35
  Grow, grow, faire tree, and as thy branches shoote,  .    119   F13 Aubigny       99
  Have you seene but a bright Lillie grow,    .    .    .    134   U2 Triumph        21
  Have you seene the white Lillie grow,       .    .    .    134   U2 Triumph     V 21
  But then if I grow jealous madde,    .    .    .    .    147   U7 Nymph          10
  Aloft, grow lesse and streightned, full of knot;    .    157   U13 Sacvile      152
  May grow so great to be example, when      .    .    158   U13 Sacvile      161
  Grow unsounder,    .    .    .    .    .    .    .    184   U29 Fit of Rime   57
  Mak'st it religion to grow rich by Crimes!      .    .    187   U33 Councellour   16
  For though Love thrive, and may grow up with cheare, .   197   U40 Elegy That    15
  And should grow rich, had I much more to pay.    .    231   U56 Covell        30
  And should grow rich, if I had more to pay.      .    231   U56 Covell     V 30
  This Prince of flowers? Soone shoot thou up, and grow    237   U65 Prince         5
  Grow up, sweet Babe, as blessed, in thy Name,    .    268   U80 Christning    11
  My selfe for shortnesse labour; and I grow     .    .    307   Horace            35
  Like tender buds shoot up, and freshly grow.     .    309   Horace            89
  Grow a safe Writer, and be warie-driven     .    .    323   Horace           393
GROWE
  Whither? oh whither will this Tire-man growe?    .    .    404   Inigo Jones 1     59
GROWES
  So, all reward, or name, that growes to mee     .    .    80   E127 Aubigny       9
  Since when it growes, and smells, I sweare,     .    .    106   F9 Celia 3        15
  True noblesse. Palme growes straight, though handled ne're so rude. 177   U25 Desmond   26
  And the whole lumpe growes round, deform'd, and droupes,  .   227   U52 Answer         5
  To top the fairest Lillie, now, that growes,    .    .    413   Ghyrlond          15
GROWING
  Still Mill continu'd: Nay, his face growing worse,   .    57   E90 Mill          11
  A little Shrub growing by.    .    .    .    .    .    172   U21 Ltl Shrub     Ttl
  It is not growing like a tree    .    .    .    .    245   U70 Ode           65
  The greatest are but growing Gentlemen.     .    .    281   U84 Kenelme       15
GROWNDE
  And Cunninge of their grownde    .    .    .    .    420   Ode:If Men        34
GROWNE
  So, in short time, th'art in arrerage growne    .    .    32   E16 Brain-hardy    5
  Buy the reversion of old playes; now growne     .    45   E56 Poet-Ape       6
  And he growne youth, was call'd to his ladies chamber.  .   57   E90 Mill          10
  And, after mouldie growne, againe were tosted,   .    88   E133 Voyage      150
  'Tis growne almost a danger to speake true      .    116   F13 Aubigny        1
  Or growne; by height or lowenesse of the Sunne?      156   U13 Sacvile      119
  Our Delicacies are growne capitall,     .    .    .    163   U15 Friend-Wars   37
  They're growne Commoditie upon Exchange;    .    .    165   U15 Friend-Wars   86
  Of what he throwes: Like letchers growne content    166   U15 Friend-Wars  139
  Pardon his Lordship.  Flattry's growne so cheape     167   U15 Friend-Wars  155
  That keepe the warre, though now't be growne more tame, .   214   U44 Speach        55
  Are growne so fruitfull, and false pleasures climbe, .   224   U50 Countesse     10
  When you that raigne, are her Example growne,    .    236   U64 Charles 3      9
  When thou that rul'st, are her Example growne,   .    236   U64 Charles 3   V  9
  How is she barren growne of love! or broke!     .    237   U64 Charles 3     15
  How is she barren growne in love! or broke!     .    237   U64 Charles 3   V 15
  With the growne issue of the Vine;      .    .    .    290   U85 Country       10
  These studies alter now, in one, growne man;    .    315   Horace           237
  A great deferrer, long in hope, growne numbe    .    317   Horace           245
  In Towne & Court? Are you growne rich? & proud?      403   Inigo Jones 1     24
GROYNE
  On Groyne.    .    .    .    .    .    .    .    .    75   E117 Groyne      Ttl
  Groyne, come of age, his state sold out of hand     .    75   E117 Groyne        1
  For'his whore: Groyne doth still occupy his land.    75   E117 Groyne        2
GRUDGE
  Get him the times long grudge, the courts ill will;  .    48   E65 Muse           7
  And yet the noble Nature never grudge;      .    .    169   U17 Friend-Debt    3
  If you dare grudge at Heaven, and repent    .    .    271   U81 Pawlet        79
GRUDG'D
  And these grudg'd at, art reverenc'd the while.  .    93   F2 Penshurst       6
GRUNTING
  Like a rung Beare, or Swine: grunting out wit    .    232   U58 Book-seller   11
GRUTCH
  Yet thou, perhaps, shalt meet some tongues will grutch,  .   72   E111 Edmonds 2     9
  If't chance to me, I must not grutch.       .    .    101   F4 To the World   56
  Then, Royall Charles, and Mary, doe not grutch   .    236   U63 Charles 2      7
GUARD
  Some way of entrance) we must plant a guard      .    109   F11 Epode         47
  Cloth Spices, or guard sweet meates from the flies;  .   205   U43 Vulcan     V 53
  Or old Silenus, Bacchus guard, and Nurse.   .    .    321   Horace           348
GUARDED
  Their guarded gates asunder?    .    .    .    .    239   U67 Muses         12
  Whether the guarded Tragedie they wrought,      .    323   Horace           409
GUARDES
  Her wary guardes, her wise simplicitie,     .    .    270   U81 Pawlet        40
GUARDIAN
  Th'unbearded Youth, his Guardian once being gone,    315   Horace           229
GUE
  Thou dost out-zany Cokely, Pod; nay, Gue:   .    .    81   E129 Mime         16
GUESSE
  Charis, guesse, and doe not misse,      .    .    .    137   U2 Kisse           1
  Guesse of these, which is the true;     .    .    .    138   U2 Kisse          34
GUEST   (See also GHEST)
  To which thou'rt not a weeke, bespoke a guest;   .    81   E129 Mime          6
  Where comes no guest, but is allow'd to eate,    .    95   F2 Penshurst      61
  As if it had expected such a guest!     .    .    .    96   F2 Penshurst      88
```

		Page	Title	Line

GUEST (cont.)
That at great times, art no ambitious guest · · · · 96 F3 Wroth 5
But such a Mind, mak'st God thy Guest. · · · 281 U84 Mind 72
To Body, and Soule! where Love is all the guest! · · 284 U84 Muse 64
Hee knowes, what worke h'hath done, to call this Guest, · 284 U84 Muse 81
What brethren, what a stranger, and his guest, · · 325 Horace 448
To call on Sicknes still, to be her Guest, · · · 394 Jane Ogle 19
GUESTS
And giv'st thy gladder guests the sight; · · · 97 F3 Wroth 28
And giv'st thy welcome guests the right; · · · 97 F3 Wroth V 28
What honour given to the drunkennest Guests? · · 166 U15 Friend-Wars 118
The causes and the Guests too, · · · · 221 U48 Bacchus 39
Or thick grosse ointment, but offend the Guests: · · 331 Horace 558
Whoe worthie wine, whoe not, to bee wyse Pallas guests. · 421 Ode:If Men 45
GUIDE
Hee'll be a Pilot, scarce can guide a Plough. · · · 410 Brome 18
GUIDED
And guided by Experience, whose straite wand · · 176 U24 Frontispice 11
GUIDES
Such Guides men use not, who their way would find, · · 170 U18 Elegy Can 12
After the Fathers, and those wiser Guides · · · 207 U43 Vulcan 103
That guides the Motions, and directs the beares. · · 219 U47 Tribe 50
GUIDETH
And well the Carre Love guideth. · · · · 134 U2 Triumph 4
GUIFT
At hunting railes, having no guift in othes, · · · 76 E119 Shelton 2
With Chequer Inke, upon his guift, my paper, · · 666 Glover 8
GUIFTS
Spend not then his guifts in vaine. · · · 102 F5 Celia 1 5
And clothes, and guifts, that only do thee grace · · 384 Somerset 2
GUILD
Or the starres, that guild his streames, · · · 103 F6 Celia 2 16
GUILDED
Free from proud porches, or their guilded roofes, · · 97 F3 Wroth 15
GUILT (GILT)
Then this, our guilt, nor golden age can deeme, · · 114 F12 Rutland 22
GUILT
Is private gaine, which hath long guilt to friend. · · 70 E109 Nevil 8
That knowes the waight of guilt: He will refraine · · 112 F11 Epode 113
Who, though their guilt, and perjurie they know, · · 186 U32 Elsmere 11
I will not argue thee, from those, of guilt, · · · 210 U43 Vulcan 165
I will not argue thee, from them, of guilt, · · · 210 U43 Vulcan V165
I will not argue thee Iron. Them of guilt · · · 210 U43 Vulcan V165
I, that am glad, thy Innocence was thy Guilt, · · 371 Fletcher 11
GUILTIE
As guiltie men doe magistrates: glad I, · · · 32 E17 Critic 2
To Person Guiltie. · · · · · · 36 E30 Guiltie Ttl
Guiltie, be wise; and though thou know'st the crimes · 36 E30 Guiltie 1
To Person Guiltie. · · · · · 38 E38 Guiltie 2 Ttl
Guiltie, because I bad you late be wise, · · · 38 E38 Guiltie 2 1
Beleeve it, Guiltie, if you loose your shame, · · · 38 E38 Guiltie 2 7
Nor shall our cups make any guiltie men: · · · 65 E101 Supper 37
Let others watch in guiltie armes, and stand · · 98 F3 Wroth 67
And sleepe so guiltie and afraid, · · · · 151 U11 Dreame 13
GUILTLESSE
And thou, right guiltlesse, may'st plead to it, why? · · 36 E29 Tilter 2
This as it guilty is, or guiltlesse found, · · · 284 U84 Muse 56
GUILTY
This as it guilty is, or guiltlesse found, · · · 284 U84 Muse 56
GULL
Dam's whom he damn'd to, as the veriest Gull, · · 154 U13 Sacvile 57
GULL'D
What States yo'have gull'd, and which yet keepes yo'in pay. · 69 E107 Hungry 10
GULLING
Item, a gulling imprese for you, at tilt. · · · 51 E73 Fine Grand 15
GUMME
In many a Gumme, and for thy soft eares sake · · 292 U86 Hor.4:1 22
GUMMES
Leave Cod, tabacco-like, burnt gummes to take, · · 42 E50 Cod 3 1
A nest of odorous spice, and gummes. · · · 280 U84 Mind 64
A nest of Spices, Odors, Gummes. · · · 280 U84 Mind V 64
GUN
And for it lose his eyes with Gun-powder, · · · 208 U43 Vulcan 121
GUNDOMAR
Old Aesope Gundomar: the French can tell, · · 213 U44 Speach 5
GUNNES
And Gunnes there, spare to poure · · · 239 U67 Muses 8
GUN-POWDER
And for it lose his eyes with Gun-powder, · · · 208 U43 Vulcan 121
GUNS
Who from the Divels-Arse did Guns beget; · · 212 U43 Vulcan 202
That from the Divels-Arse did Guns beget; · · 212 U43 Vulcan V202
Come to their Schooles,) show 'hem the use of Guns; · 214 U44 Speach 58
When their pot-guns ayme to hit, · · · · 259 U76 Petition 21
When their pot-guns thinke to fitt, · · · 259 U76 Petition V 21
GUT
On Gut. · · · · · · · · 76 E118 Gut Ttl
Gut eates all day, and lechers all the night, · · · 76 E118 Gut 1
GUTS
Is this we heare? of frogs? No, guts wind-bound, · · 86 E133 Voyage 92
GUY
From Guy, or Bevis, Arthur, or from whom · · · 215 U44 Speach 81

		Page	Title	Line
GYANT				
Thy Canvas Gyant, at some Channell aymes,	· · ·	407	Inigo Jones 2	15
GYANTS				
The Rebell Gyants stoope, and Gorgon Envye yeild,	·	421	Ode:If Men	41
GYERLYK				
which thoughts being circumvolvd in gyerlyk mocion		361	Palmer	23
GYPSEE				
On Gypsee. · · · · · ·		39	E41 Gypsee	Ttl
Gypsee, new baud, is turn'd physitian,	· · ·	39	E41 Gypsee	1
GYRLANDS				
Shall out-live gyrlands, stolne from the chast tree.	·	32	E17 Critic	6
GYVES				
Enamor'd of their golden gyves? · · · ·		100	F4 To the World	24
H				
Epitaph on Elizabeth, L. H. · · · ·		79	E124 Elizabeth	Ttl
- - · paire, Sir Lucius Cary, and Sir H. Morison.	·	242	U70 Ode	Ttl
HA				
Whose Daughter? ha? Great Savage of the Rock?	·	269	U81 Pawlet	10
HABIT				
To every Fortunes habit; she helps on,	· ·	342	Horace	V153
Thou, that wouldst finde the habit of true passion,	·	362	Author	1
HACKNEY				
To Braynford, Hackney, Bow, but thou mak'st one;	·	81	E129 Mime	4
'AD				
My title, at their rate, I'ad rather, I, · · ·		325	Horace	432
HAD				
But two things, rare, the Fates had in their store,	·	28	E4 James 1	3
Whose house, if it no other honor had,	·	48	E66 Cary	3
Then had I made 'hem good, to fit your vaine.	·	51	E73 Fine Grand	20
For your most noble offer had supply'd me.	·	54	E84 Bedford 2	4
Of what shee had wrought came in, and wak'd his braine,		56	E87 Hazard	4
Or had his father, when he did him get,	·	56	E88 Monsieur	9
Who had no lesse a trumpet of their name,	·	57	E89 Allen	5
Nor could I, had I seene all Natures roule,	·	60	E93 Radcliffe	12
Play-wright, by chance, hearing some toyes I'had writ,		64	E100 Playwrt 3	1
Of which had Horace, or Anacreon tasted,	·	65	E101 Supper	31
Their lives, as doe their lines, till now had lasted.	·	65	E101 Supper	32
Madame, had all antiquitie beene lost,	·	67	E105 L Wroth 2	1
That we had left us, nor by time, nor place,	·	67	E105 L Wroth 2	3
That Nature no such difference had imprest	·	75	E116 Jephson	9
Yet three fill'd Zodiackes had he beene	·	77	E120 S. P.	11
If, at all, shee had a fault,	·	79	E124 Elizabeth	7
I, and this Muse had beene, if thou hadst not	·	80	E127 Aubigny	7
Which Musick had; or speake her knowne effects,	·	82	E130 Ferrab. 1	3
I, yet, had utter'd nothing on thy part,	·	82	E130 Ferrab. 1	15
We ought not give them taste, we had an eare.	·	83	E131 Ferrab. 2	6
Had power to act, what they to faine had not.	·	84	E133 Voyage	6
Their wherry had no saile, too; ours had none:	·	84	E133 Voyage	11
Man, that had never heard of a Chimaera.	·	86	E133 Voyage	80
Had burst with storme, and downe fell, ab excelsis,	·	86	E133 Voyage	95
And all his followers, that had so abus'd him:	·	86	E133 Voyage	97
And, in so shitten sort, so long had us'd him:	·	86	E133 Voyage	98
Had it beene seconded, and not in fume	·	87	E133 Voyage	109
The well-greas'd wherry now had got betweene,	·	87	E133 Voyage	114
By this time had they reach'd the Stygian poole,	·	87	E133 Voyage	121
Cats there lay divers had beene flead, and rosted,	·	88	E133 Voyage	149
Yet drown'd they not. They had five lives in future.	·	88	E133 Voyage	154
Were you Jove's sonnes, or had Alcides might.	·	89	E133 Voyage	182
That had, so often, shew'd 'hem merry prankes.	·	89	E133 Voyage	184
My Muse had plough'd with his, that sung A-jax.	·	89	E133 Voyage	196
Of thy Penates had beene set on flame,	·	95	F2 Penshurst	79
As if it had expected such a guest!	·	96	F2 Penshurst	88
Thus Pan, and Sylvane, having had their rites,	·	98	F3 Wroth	47
When Pan, and Sylvane, having had their rites,	·	98	F3 Wroth	V 47
Which boasts t'have had the head of gold.	·	98	F3 Wroth	64
Little, for me, had reason done,	·	101	F4 To the World	35
The world hath seene, which all these had in trust,	·	114	F12 Rutland	39
That had no Muse to make their fame abide.	·	114	F12 Rutland	48
Had not their forme touch'd by an English wit.	·	115	F12 Rutland	82
Each into other, and had now made one.	·	120	F13 Aubigny	120
I had forgot · · · · ·		129	U1 Father	10
And as that wisedome had decreed,	·	130	U1 Nativitie	16
I have had, and have my Peeres:	·	131	U2 Excuse	4
But, he had not gain'd his sight	·	132	U2 How he saw	13
Both the Arrow he had quit,	·	132	U2 How he saw	21
Love, and I have had; and true.	·	136	U2 Cupid	6
So, as those that had your sight,	·	138	U2 Kisse	17
Had of Love, and of his force,	·	139	U2 Promise	2
And not thinke h'had eat a stake,	·	142	U2 Her man	39
Though hate had put them out;	·	147	U7 Nymph	25
Had wrestled with Diseases strong,	·	151	U12 Corbet	8
I thought that Fortitude had beene a meane	·	156	U13 Sacvile	105
Crush'd in the snakie brakes, that he had past!	·	162	U15 Friend-Wars	18
Runs sweetly, as it had his Lordships Soule;	·	167	U15 Friend-Wars	148
No more, then we should thinke a Lord had had	·	168	U15 Friend-Wars	193
And if I had no more to say,	·	168	U16 Gray	2
Knew I all this afore? had I perceiv'd,	·	171	U20 Shrub	9
They had, but were a Reed unto thy Sword.	·	187	U33 Councellour	34
Her owne bloud gave her: Shee ne're had, nor hath	·	188	U34 Small Poxe	9
'Tis true, I'm broke! Vowes, Oathes, and all I had	·	191	U38 Elegy 'Tis	1
If I had writ no word, but Deare, farewell.	·	198	U40 Elegy That	50
O, keepe it still; for it had rather be	·	199	U41 Elegy Since	17
Wish, you had fowle ones, and deformed got;	·	200	U42 Elegy Let	22

HAD (cont.)

	Page	Title	Line
Had he had the facultie to reade, and write!	201	U42 Elegy Let	64
Any Comparison had with his Cheap-side.	202	U42 Elegy Let	76
What had I done that might call on thine ire?	202	U43 Vulcan	2
had I wrote treason there, or heresie,	203	U43 Vulcan	15
I had deserv'd, then, thy consuming lookes,	203	U43 Vulcan	17
Had I compil'd from Amadis de Gaule,	203	U43 Vulcan	29
And so some goodlier monster had begot:	204	U43 Vulcan	32
Thou then hadst had some colour for thy flames,	204	U43 Vulcan	40
Thou mightst have had me perish, piece, by piece,	205	U43 Vulcan	51
Thou mightst have had them perish, piece, by piece,	205	U43 Vulcan	V 51
Had I fore-knowne of this thy least desire	205	U43 Vulcan	59
Had I fore-knowne but of thy least desire	205	U43 Vulcan	V 59
Had tickled your large Nosthrill: many a Reame	205	U43 Vulcan	62
Had filled your large nostrills with the steame:	205	U43 Vulcan	V 62
To redeeme mine, I had sent in; Enough,	205	U43 Vulcan	63
The Talmud, and the Alcoran had come,	205	U43 Vulcan	65
Had made a meale for Vulcan to lick up.	206	U43 Vulcan	84
Had bin fitt meate for Vulcan to lick up.	206	U43 Vulcan	V 84
Whom Faction had not drawne to studie sides.	207	U43 Vulcan	104
Whom fashion had not drawne to studie sides.	207	U43 Vulcan	V104
Whom Faction had not taught to studie sides.	207	U43 Vulcan	V104
'Bove all your Fire-workes, had at Ephesus,	211	U43 Vulcan	194
Beyond your Fire-workes, had at Ephesus,	211	U43 Vulcan	V194
'Bove all our Fire-workes, had at Ephesus,	211	U43 Vulcan	V194
Would you had kept your Forge at Aetna still,	212	U43 Vulcan	197
What a strong Fort old Pimblicoe had bin!	213	U44 Speach	21
Needs lend an aide, to thine she had her eyes.	217	U46 Coke	24
But yet the Tun at Heidelberg had houpes.	227	U52 Answer	6
With one great blot, yo'had form'd me as I am.	227	U52 Answer	12
With one great blot, you had drawne me as I am.	227	U52 Answer	V 12
O, had I now your manner, maistry, might,	227	U52 Answer	16
And surely had I but your Stable seene	228	U53 Newcastle	13
Before, I thinke my wish absolv'd had beene.	228	U53 Newcastle	14
And should grow rich, had I much more to pay.	231	U56 Covell	30
And should grow rich, if I had more to pay.	231	U56 Covell	V 30
Indeed, when had great Britaine greater cause	236	U64 Charles 3	7
Had got the Ceston on!	240	U67 Muses	36
Had put the Ceston on!	240	U67 Muses	V 36
Sonne, and my Friend, I had not call'd you so	241	U69 Friend Son	1
Profit, or Chance had made us: But I know	241	U69 Friend Son	3
Till he had sold his Piece, drawne so unlike:	242	U69 Friend Son	13
How well at twentie had he falne, or stood!	243	U70 Ode	31
And had his noble name advanc'd with men:	244	U70 Ode	36
And such a force the faire example had,	247	U70 Ode	117
Had sow'd these fruits, and got the harvest in.	247	U70 Ode	128
health, or scarce breath, as she had never bin,	248	U71 Treasurer	12
Had they but grace, of thinking, at these routes,	249	U72 King	15
If they had leisure, at these lawfull routs,	249	U72 King	V 15
As they had learn'd new changes, for the day,	253	U75 Epithalam.	35
Him up, to doe the same himselfe had done.	256	U75 Epithalam.	108
He had so highly set; and, in what Barbican.	256	U75 Epithalam.	112
He had so highly plac'd; and, in what Barbican.	256	U75 Epithalam.	V112
If to my mind, great Lord, I had a state,	260	U77 Treasurer	1
Allowes them? Then, what copies shall be had,	263	U78 Digby	29
Allowes them? Then, what copies will be had,	263	U78 Digby	V 29
For, had we here said lesse, we had sung nothing then.	263	U79 New-yeares	8
You seeme a faire one! O that you had breath,	269	U81 Pawlet	6
You seeme a faire one! O that I had breath,	269	U81 Pawlet	V 6
Had I a thousand Mouthes, as many Tongues,	269	U81 Pawlet	23
A reverend State she had, an awfull Eye,	270	U81 Pawlet	43
Her suffrings, as the body had beene away!	270	U81 Pawlet	51
If you not understand, what Child you had.	271	U81 Pawlet	78
That ever had beginning there, to'ave end!	271	U81 Pawlet	91
As some soft chime had stroak'd the ayre;	279	U84 Mind	38
O! had I seene her laid out a faire Corse,	282	U84 Muse	11
By Death, on Earth, I should have had remorse,	282	U84 Muse	12
Thou wouldst have lost the Phoenix, had the kind	283	U84 Muse	19
As spirits had stolne her Spirit, in a kisse,	283	U84 Muse	42
Had lost our selves? and prodigally spent	286	U84 Muse	141
She had, and it became her! she was fit	287	U84 Muse	161
She had a mind as calme, as she was faire;	287	U84 Muse	163
Of divine Comfort, when sh' had talk'd with God.	287	U84 Muse	184
How plucking Peares, his owne hand grafted had,	290	U85 Country	19
To turne mere farmer, had spoke out,	291	U85 Country	68
Perversly modest, had I rather owe	311	Horace	130
If something strange, that never yet was had	313	Horace	178
If something fresh, that never yet was had	342	Horace	V178
Nor had our Italie more glorious bin	325	Horace	411
Had not our every Poet like offended.	325	Horace	414
This was the wisdome, that they had of old,	327	Horace	486
If you denied, you had no better straine,	333	Horace	625
And twice, or thrice had 'ssayd it, still in vaine:	333	Horace	626
Then: If your fault you rather had defend	335	Horace	629
Infected with the leprosie, or had	335	Horace	645
And, as a Beare, if he the strength but had	337	Horace	674
That may judge for his six-pence) had, before	371	Fletcher	7
Their motives were, since it had not to do	371	Fletcher	9
To fill an Epitaph. But she had more.	371	Epitaph	5
For Grapes he had gather'd before they were eaten.	375	Coryat 1	25
For grapes he had gather'd, before they were eaten.	380	Coryat 3	36
Or, to so many, and so Broad-seales had,	385	Brooke	3
I do not feele that ever yet I had	385	Husband	5

247

	Page	Title	Line
HAD (cont.)			
Had cloath'd him so. Here's all I can supply	389	Aleman	20
Wherein the Graver had a strife	390	Reader	3
As it had beene the circle of the Arts!	396	Drayton	22
And I had stil'd thee, Orpheus, but before	397	Drayton	37
All Circles had their spring and end	399	Lady Ogle	14
Under the Morall? shewe he had a pate	405	Inigo Jones 1	83
I had you for a Servant, once, Dick Brome;	409	Brome	1
That knew the Crafts they had bin bred in, right:	410	Brome	14
When I had read your holy Meditations,	411	Sutcliffe	1
I sayd, who'had supp'd so deepe of this sweet Chalice,	412	Sutcliffe	21
As it, alone, (and onely it) had roome,	412	Ghyrlond	11
I had somwhat else to say,	417	Moon	9
HAD'ST			
It was as if thou printed had'st an oath,	43	E53 Old-end	5
Make all hereafter, had'st thou ruin'd this?	188	U34 Small Poxe	16
These, had'st thou pleas'd either to dine, or sup,	206	U43 Vulcan	83
These, had'st thou been pleas'd either to dine, or sup,	206	U43 Vulcan	V 83
HADST			
I, and this Muse had beene, if thou hadst not	80	E127 Aubigny	7
If thou hadst not	129	U1 Father	7
Thou then hadst had some colour for thy flames,	204	U43 Vulcan	40
With lust conceiv'd thee; Father thou hadst none.	208	U43 Vulcan	112
Who hadst before wrought in rich Homers Mine?	388	Chapman	3
And though thou hadst small Latine, and lesse Greeke,	391	Shakespeare	31
Thou hadst brought Lapland, or old Cobalus,	398	Drayton	86
HAFTES			
Though gold or Ivory haftes would make it good.	403	Inigo Jones 1	28
Though gold or Ivory haftes cant make it good.	403	Inigo Jones 1	V 28
HAILE			
Haile, happie Genius of this antient pile!	225	U51 Bacon	1
Haile Mary, full of grace, it once was said,	238	U66 Queene	1
Haile Mary, full of honours, to my Queene,	238	U66 Queene	5
Glorie to God. Then, Haile to Mary! spring	238	U66 Queene	13
Our thanks to God. Then, Haile to Mary! spring	238	U66 Queene	V 13
HAIR (See also HAYRE)			
With faire black eyes, and hair, and some vile snout.	339	Horace	V 54/ 52
HAIRE			
Lord, how is Gam'ster chang'd! his haire close cut!	33	E21 Gam'ster	1
Not though that haire grew browne, which once was amber,	57	E90 Mill	9
The sinkes ran grease, and haire of meazled hogs,	88	E133 Voyage	145
Doe but looke on her Haire, it is bright	134	U2 Triumph	13
So hath Homer prais'd her haire;	136	U2 Cupid	13
With th'advantage of her haire,	138	U2 Kisse	10
Yet a man; with crisped haire	141	U2 Her man	10
By that tall Grove, your haire; whose globy rings	170	U19 Elegy By	5
His Lordship. That is for his Band, his haire	215	U44 Speach	95
In gracefull Ornament of Garland, Gemmes, and Haire.	253	U75 Epithalam.	40
The nailes, and every curled haire disclose;	307	Horace	47
The nailes, and every gentle haire disclose;	339	Horace	V 49/ 47
With faire black eyes, and haire; and a wry nose.	307	Horace	52
HAIRES			
My hundred of gray haires,	150	U9 Picture	14
HALBERDS			
Of Egges, and Halberds, Cradles, and a Herse,	204	U43 Vulcan	37
HALF			
To aske thy name, if he have half his Nose!	409	Detractor	18
He the half of Life abuses,	657	Door Apollo	9
HALFE			
Keepes himselfe, with halfe a man, and defrayes	30	E12 Shift	3
His neck fenc'd round with ruffe! his eyes halfe shut!	33	E21 Gam'ster	2
Which might with halfe mankind maintayne a strife.	34	E23 Donne 1	8
Foole, as if halfe eyes will not know a fleece	45	E56 Poet-Ape	13
Your partie-per-pale picture, one halfe drawne	51	E73 Fine Grand	13
Toward the sea, farther then halfe-way tree?	56	E88 Monsieur	6
He, that, but living halfe his age, dyes such;	76	E119 Shelton	15
Look'd not halfe so fresh, and faire,	138	U2 Kisse	9
This could be call'd but halfe a kisse.	139	U2 Another	11
I, that's a Charme and halfe! She must afford	163	U15 Friend-Wars	52
Where we must feele it Darke for halfe a yeare.	199	U41 Elegy Since	8
Nor any of their houshold, halfe so well.	228	U53 Newcastle	16
E're thou wert halfe got out,	242	U70 Ode	6
And keepe the one halfe from his Harry.	246	U70 Ode	94
Reduicts, Halfe-moones, Horne-workes, and such close wayes,	248	U71 Treasurer	8
Let Ireland meet it out at Sea, halfe way,	249	U72 King	5
Hee, that but living halfe his dayes, dies such,	295	U89 Mart.8:77	7
Their bombard-phrase, and foot-and-halfe-foot words.	311	Horace	139
An ounce, what makes it then? The halfe pound just;	327	Horace	471
They saw it halfe, damd thy whole play, and more;	371	Fletcher	8
HALFE-MOONES			
Reduicts, Halfe-moones, Horne-workes, and such close wayes,	248	U71 Treasurer	8
HALFE-WAY			
Toward the sea, farther then halfe-way tree?	56	E88 Monsieur	6
HALL			
In it' owne hall; when these (in worthy scorne	85	E133 Voyage	31
But you will visit grisly Pluto's hall?	89	E133 Voyage	175
And fills thy open hall with mirth, and cheere,	98	F3 Wroth	49
Else that glister'd in White-hall;	138	U2 Kisse	16
In Surgeons hall)	179	U25 Desmond	38
Or the great Hall at Westminster, the field	186	U33 Councellour	3
Nay, let White-Hall with Revels have to doe,	210	U43 Vulcan	156
Scarce let White-Hall with Revels have to doe,	210	U43 Vulcan	V156
Till you behold a race to fill your Hall,	258	U75 Epithalam.	169

		Page	Title	Line

HALL (cont.)
| Like men street-borne, and neere the Hall, reherse | . . . | 321 | Horace | 357 |
| To the merry beards in Hall, | . . . . | 417 | Moon | 13 |

HALLOW'D
| To deck the hallow'd Harth with old wood fir'd | . . | 291 | U85 Country | 43 |
| And like a hallow'd Temple, free from taint | . . | 401 | Beaumont | 21 |

HALT
| 'Cause thou canst halt, with us, in Arts, and Fire! | . . | 208 | U43 Vulcan | 110 |

HALTING
| Cause thou canst doe these halting tricks in fire? | . . | 208 | U43 Vulcan | V110 |

HAMMERING
| Those ill-torn'd Verses, to new hammering. | . . . | 333 | Horace | 628 |

HAMMERS
| Sweat at the forge, their hammers beating; | . . | 179 | U25 Desmond | 41 |

HAMPTON
| 'Mongst Hampton shades, and Phoebus grove of bayes, | . . | 80 | E126 Mrs Cary | 2 |
| From Greenwich, hither, to Row-hampton gate! | . . | 252 | U75 Epithalam. | 12 |

HAMS
| It bends the hams of Gossip Vigilance, | . . . | 363 | Riches | 11 |

HANCH
| Hanch against Hanch, or raise a riming Club | . . | 396 | Drayton | 8 |

HAND
Pray thee, take care, that tak'st my booke in hand,	. .	27	E1 Reader	1
Grant then, no rude hand remove her. . .	. .	39	E40 Ratcliffe	4
Farewell, thou child of my right hand, and joy;	. .	41	E45 First Son	1
To pay at's day of marriage. By my hand	. .	42	E46 Luckless 1	4
O, would'st thou adde like hand, to all the rest!	. .	61	E95 Savile	13
But, wisely, thrusts not forth a forward hand,	. .	61	E95 Savile	22
Mark'd by thy hand, and with the better stone,	. .	62	E96 Donne 2	8
Thy learned hand, and true Promethean art	. .	71	E110 Edmonds 1	17
Groyne, come of age, his state sold out of hand	. .	75	E117 Groyne	1
Alwayes at hand, to aide the merry Muses.	. .	85	E133 Voyage	54
Before the fisher, or into his hand.	. .	94	F2 Penshurst	38
At her hand, with oath, to make .	. .	133	U2 Suffered	10
See the Chariot at hand here of Love,	. .	134	U2 Triumph	1
He would have a hand as soft	. .	141	U2 Her man	25
He should have a hand as soft	. .	141	U2 Her man	V 25
Then turning unto him is next at hand,	. .	154	U13 Sacvile	56
Then once to number, or bring forth to hand,	. .	167	U15 Friend-Wars	173
Then take in hand thy Lyre,	. .	175	U23 Himselfe	25
Which makes that (lighted by the beamie hand	. .	176	U24 Frontispice	9
This makes, that lighted by the beamie hand	. .	176	U24 Frontispice V	9
Where darknesse with her gloomie-sceptred hand,	. .	180	U25 Desmond	61
A gentler, and more agile hand, to tend	. .	180	U26 Ode High	4
Your covetous hand, . . .	. .	180	U26 Ode High	13
Of Bookes, of Presidents, hast thou at hand!	. .	187	U33 Councellour	25
No face, no hand, proportion, line, or Ayre	. .	200	U42 Elegy Let	14
In his great Actions: view whom his large hand	. .	250	U73 Weston	3
When he beholds a graft of his owne hand,	. .	251	U74 Weston	27
Both Crownes, and Kingdomes in their either hand;	. .	254	U75 Epithalam.	52
One in the others hand,	. .	256	U75 Epithalam.	125
Worke with my fancie, his owne hand. .	. .	276	U84 Body	12
Beside, your hand will never hit,	. .	277	U84 Mind	7
And white, as that, put on: and in her hand,	. .	285	U84 Muse	95
How plucking Peares, his owne hand grafted had,	. .	290	U85 Country	19
In hand, and turne them over, day, and night.	. .	323	Horace	398
The hand, and mind would, but it will resound	. .	329	Horace	522
As Painting, so is Poesie. Some mans hand	. .	329	Horace	539
(so well dispos'd by thy auspicious hand)	. .	361	Palmer	2
Be proofe, the glory of his hand, .	. .	367	Ode Who saith	49
All which are parts commend the cunning hand;	. .	370	Author	4
Who takes thy volume to his vertuous hand,	. .	383	Author	1
May take thy volume to his vertuous hand.	. .	383	Author	8
of her white Hand; or she can spare it.	. .	662	Bedford	10

HANDED
| And no one empty-handed, to salute | . . | 95 | F2 Penshurst | 49 |
| Hook-handed Harpies, gowned Vultures, put | . . | 187 | U33 Councellour | 9 |

HANDLE
Where I may handle Silke, as free, and neere,	. .	200	U42 Elegy Let	30
Whom they durst handle in their holy-day coates,	. .	208	U43 Vulcan	127
Whom they durst handle in their high day coates,	. .	208	U43 Vulcan	V127
The blaze, and splendor, but not handle fire!	. .	269	U81 Pawlet	32
The heat, and splendor, but not handle fire!	. .	269	U81 Pawlet	V 32

HANDLED
| True noblesse. Palme growes straight, though handled ne're so rude. | . . | 177 | U25 Desmond | 26 |
| What he despaires, being handled, might not show. | . . | 315 | Horace | 214 |

HANDLES
| So soft, and smooth it handles, the whole piece, | . . | 415 | Rutter | 17 |

HANDLING
| Your Power of handling shadow, ayre, and spright, | . . | 227 | U52 Answer | 17 |

HANDS
Any man else, you clap your hands, and rore,	. .	38	E38 Guiltie 2	4
Whil'st I behold thee live with purest hands;	. .	51	E74 Chancelor	3
Nor that his worke liv'd in the hands of foes,	. .	71	E110 Edmonds 1	9
(Who hath the hundred hands when he doth meddle)	. .	86	E133 Voyage	82
Before rude hands have touch'd it?	. .	134	U2 Triumph	22
That to such Natures let their full hands flow,	. .	154	U13 Sacvile	60
And valiant were, with, or without their hands.	. .	233	U59 Newcastle	24
Yet are got off thence, with cleare mind, and hands	. .	234	U61 Epigram	7
With what full hands, and in how plenteous showers	. .	254	U75 Epithalam.	65
The old Greek-hands in picture, or in stone.	. .	260	U77 Treasurer	9
With which, Priapus, he may thanke thy hands,	. .	290	U85 Country	21
With which, Priapus, he may greet thy hands,	. .	290	U85 Country	V 21

	Page	Title	Line

HANDS (cont.)
But here, neither trusting his hands, nor his legs, . . . 375 Coryat 1 34
HANG
Hang on thy walls, that every child may reach. . . . 94 F2 Penshurst 44
To make a new, and hang that by. . . . 145 U5 Woman-kind 18
Hang up those dull, and envious fooles, . . . 146 U6 Defence 1
That hang their richest jewells i'their nose; . . . 232 U58 Book-seller 10
Of Noremberg, or Turkie; hang your roomes . . . 260 U77 Treasurer 3
Hang all your roomes, with one large Pedigree: . . . 282 U84 Kenelme 20
To hang a window, or make darke the roome, . . . 282 U84 Muse 7
Hang up all the poor Hop-Drinkers, . . . 657 Door Apollo 7
HANGING
Court every hanging Gowne, and after that, . . . 201 U42 Elegy Let 57
HANGINGS
The richer hangings, or crowne-plate; . . . 96 F3 Wroth 8
Rather to boast rich hangings, then rare friends. . . . 242 U69 Friend Son 26
That tarries till the hangings be ta'en downe, . . . 315 Horace 221
HANGS
And the Glasse hangs by her side, . . . 137 U2 Cupid 40
Before the Judge, it hangs, and waites report. . . . 309 Horace 112
HANNIBAL
When the Prodigious Hannibal did crowne . . . 242 U70 Ode 3
HANNOW
Of Hannow, Shieter-huissen, Popenheim, . . . 69 E107 Hungry 25
HANS
Hans-spiegle, Rotteinberg, and Boutersheim, . . . 69 E107 Hungry 26
HANS-SPIEGLE
Hans-spiegle, Rotteinberg, and Boutersheim, . . . 69 E107 Hungry 26
HAP
If but to be beleev'd you have the hap, . . . 69 E107 Hungry 17
HAPLESSE
But in the maine worke haplesse: since he knowes . . . 307 Horace 48
HAP'LY
No place for these. And, Painter, hap'ly, thou . . . 305 Horace 24
HAPP
Or if't be the Gossipps happ . . . 417 Moon 37
HAPPEN
That, what to all may happen here, . . . 101 F4 To the World 55
Worth his untying happen there: And not . . . 317 Horace 274
HAPPIE
At once thou mak'st me happie, and unmak'st; . . . 44 E55 Beaumont 5
Or thou more happie, it to justifie . . . 49 E66 Cary 8
Haile, happie Genius of this antient pile! . . . 225 U51 Bacon 1
And wish her state lesse happie then it is! . . . 271 U81 Pawlet 84
Happie is he, that from all Businesse cleere, . . . 289 U85 Country 1
I wonder how this happie man should know, . . . 333 Horace 605
That were the happie subject of my songe. . . . 419 Ode:If Men 9
HAPPIER
With me thou leav'st an happier Muse then thee, . . . 48 E65 Muse 11
The Things that make the happier life, are these, . . . 295 U90 Mart.10:47 1
Happier then wretched art, and doth, by it, . . . 325 Horace 420
HAPPIEST
And in this short time of thy happiest raigne, . . . 37 E35 James 2 4
See him, that's call'd, and thought the happiest man, . . . 162 U15 Friend-Wars 23
HAPPILY
At which, shee happily displeas'd, made you: . . . 53 E79 Rutland 9
HAPPINESSE
Of all his happinesse? But soft: I heare . . . 111 F11 Epode 65
Your happinesse, and doth not speake you blest, . . . 234 U61 Epigram 9
HAPP'LY
Aloud; and (happ'ly) it may last as long. . . . 261 U77 Treasurer 28
As loude; and (happ'ly) it may last as long. . . . 261 U77 Treasurer V 28
HAPPY
To heaven; his hath: O happy state! wherein . . . 35 E27 Roe 1 7
To King James. Upon the happy false rumour of his death, . . . 43 E51 James 3 Ttl
Which who can use is happy: Such be thou. . . . 99 F3 Wroth 99
Which who can use is happy: Such art thou. . . . 99 F3 Wroth V 99
I have already us'd some happy houres, . . . 115 F12 Rutland 74
Shall thronging come, and boast the happy place . . . 115 F12 Rutland 80
Are you engaged to your happy fate, . . . 118 F13 Aubigny 47
Happy in that faire honour it hath gain'd, . . . 180 U26 Ode High 14
Happy Greeke, by this protection, . . . 184 U29 Fit of Rime 32
O happy Art! and wise Epitome . . . 214 U44 Speach 43
How happy were the Subject, if he knew . . . 236 U64 Charles 3 1
Sweet! happy Mary! All . . . 240 U67 Muses 49
Such truths, as we expect for happy men, . . . 246 U70 Ode 83
O happy bands! and thou more happy place, . . . 256 U75 Epithalam. 129
Tho', happy Muse, thou know my Digby well; . . . 262 U78 Digby 1
Goe now, her happy Parents, and be sad, . . . 271 U81 Pawlet 77
Thrice happy house, that hast receipt . . . 280 U84 Mind 53
There, all the happy soules, that ever were, . . . 285 U84 Muse 113
That happy Day, that never shall see night! . . . 286 U84 Muse 121
And sets more happy in the place: . . . 290 U85 Country 12
And graftes more happy in the place: . . . 290 U85 Country V 12
Who mad'st us happy all, in thy reflexe, . . . 414 Ghyrlond 47
whom thou seest happy; wretches flee as foes: . . . 422 Lucan 6
whom thou seest happy; wretches, shun, as foes: . . . 422 Lucan V 6
HARBINGER
Then entertaine, and as Deaths Harbinger; . . . 394 Jane Ogle 21
HARBOR
Into your harbor, and all passage shut . . . 119 F13 Aubigny 92
HARBOUR
Which in life did harbour give . . . 79 E124 Elizabeth 5

HARBOUR (cont.)
  To harbour a divided thought · · · · · · · 101 F4 To the World 58
HARBOUR'D
  Where lately harbour'd many a famous whore, · · · 29 E7 Hot-house 1
HARBOURS
  For praises, where the mind harbours a foxe. · · · 354 Horace V622
HARD
  Who scarse can spell th'hard names: whose knight lesse can. · 28 E3 Bookseller 10
  Was his blest fate, but our hard lot to find. · · · 37 E32 Roe 2 8
  Lesse list of proud, hard, or ingratefull Men. · · 153 U13 Sacvile 4
  They are so long a comming, and so hard; · · · 153 U13 Sacvile 23
  Or pomp'd for those hard trifles, Anagrams, · · 204 U43 Vulcan 35
  As they are hard, for them to make their owne, · · 225 U50 Countesse 33
  Hard-hearted, I dreame every Night · · · 293 U86 Hor.4:1 37
  'Tis hard, to speake things common, properly: · · 313 Horace 183
  On artlesse Verse; the hard ones he will blame; · · 335 Horace 634
  to the Peake it is so hard-by, · · · · · 417 Moon 23
  Although the gate were hard, the gayne is sweete. · · 418 Answer 7
HARD-BY
  to the Peake it is so hard-by, · · · · · 417 Moon 23
HARDER
  A harder tasque, then either his to Bristo', · · 85 E133 Voyage 39
HARDEST
  Let him, then hardest sires, more disinherit, · · 99 F3 Wroth 77
  Then hardest let him more disherrit, · · · 99 F3 Wroth V 77
HARD-HEARTED
  Hard-hearted, I dreame every Night · · · 293 U86 Hor.4:1 37
HARDIE (NAME)
  To Brayne-hardie. · · · · · · · 32 E16 Brain-hardy Ttl
  Hardie, thy braine is valiant, 'tis confest, · · 32 E16 Brain-hardy 1
HARDIE
  I foole-hardie, there up-tooke · · · · 132 U2 How he saw 20
HARDLY
  On my lips, thus hardly sundred, · · · · 103 F6 Celia 2 7
  Laden with Bellie, and doth hardly approach · · 230 U56 Covell 9
  To every vice, as hardly to be brought · · 315 Horace 232
HARE
  And, in the winter, hunt'st the flying hare, · · 97 F3 Wroth 29
  Or in the winter, hunt'st the flying hare, · · 97 F3 Wroth V 29
  And snares the fearfull Hare, and new-come Crane, · 290 U85 Country 35
HARKE
  Harke how the Bells upon the waters play · · 253 U75 Epithalam. 33
HARMES
  We neither love the Troubles, nor the harmes. · · 215 U44 Speach 86
  The art of urging, and avoyding harmes, · · 232 U59 Newcastle 2
  Nor dreads the Seas inraged harmes: · · · 289 U85 Country 6
  Nor treades the Seas inraged harmes: · · 289 U85 Country V 6
HARMONIE
  Including all, were thence call'd harmonie: · · 82 E130 Ferrab. 1 14
  What we harmonie doe call · · · · · 141 U2 Her man 34
  To note in Poemes, breach of harmonie; · · 323 Horace 388
HARMONIOUSLY
  A body so harmoniously compos'd, · · · 112 F11 Epode 99
HARMONY
  The Harmony may pull · · · · · 239 U67 Muses 20
  Hath all beene Harmony: · · · · · 367 Ode Who saith 51
  As fit to have encreas'd the harmony · · 371 Epitaph 8
  What Muse, or rather God of harmony · · 395 May 14
HARMS
  Thy selfe in tears, then me thy harms will wound, · 342 Horace V146
HARP
  Doth Clarius Harp want strings, · · · 174 U23 Himselfe 9
  To the grave Harp, and Violl voyces new; · · 346 Horace V306
HARPE
  Apollo's harpe, and Hermes lyre resound, · · 98 F3 Wroth 51
  Harpe, Lute, Theorbo sprung, · · · · 239 U67 Muses 17
  New yeares, expect new gifts: Sister, your Harpe, · 263 U79 New-yeares 1
  As comming with his Harpe, prepar'd · · 274 U84 Cradle 35
  Shall Verse be set to Harpe and Lute, · · 292 U86 Hor.4:1 23
HARPIES
  Hook-handed Harpies, gowned Vultures, put · · 187 U33 Councellour 9
HARPYES
  Gorgonian scolds, and Harpyes: on the other · · 86 E133 Voyage 69
HARROW'D
  My selfe up to thee, harrow'd, torne, and bruis'd · 127 U1 Trinitie 5
HARRY
  The Daughter of great Harry! · · · · 240 U67 Muses 26
  And keepe the one halfe from his Harry. · · 246 U70 Ode 94
HARSH
  Harsh sights at home, Giles wisheth he were blind. · 40 E42 Giles 10
  Rigid, and harsh, which is a Drug austere · · 190 U37 Friend-Book 17
HART (HEART)
  Are sure to con the catalogue by hart; · · 59 E92 New Crie 22
HART
  That drives the Hart to seeke unused wayes, · · 264 U79 New-yeares 21
HARTES
  to tender thus, their lives, their loves, their hartes! · 382 Rich 4
HARTH
  Shine bright on every harth as the desires · · 95 F2 Penshurst 78
  Now that the harth is crown'd with smiling fire, · 120 F14 Sydney 1
  To deck the hallow'd Harth with old wood fir'd · 291 U85 Country 43
HARTS
  Tenants, and Servants, have they harts, and eyes, · 399 Lady Ogle 4

		Page	Title	Line

HARVEST
The apple-harvest, that doth longer last,   • • • • 98 F3 Wroth   43
The apple-harvest and ploued land up cast;   • • 98 F3 Wroth   V 43
No Foole would his owne harvest spoile, or burne!   • 209 U43 Vulcan   150
Had sow'd these fruits, and got the harvest in.   • 247 U70 Ode   128

HA'S
Ha's Feathers, and will serve a man to pull.   • • 154 U13 Sacvile   58

HAS
H'has tympanies of businesse, in his face,   • 35 E28 Surly   7
For worth he has not, He is tax'd, not prais'd.   • 48 E65 Muse   16
Know you the cause? H'has neither land, nor lease,   • 63 E97 Motion   9
Talkes loud, and baudy, has a gather'd deale   • 74 E115 Honest Man   9
Doe I reflect. Some alderman has power,   • 117 F13 Aubigny   38
To teach each suit he has, the ready way   • 165 U15 Friend-Wars   108
Although, perhaps it has, what's that to me,   • 167 U15 Friend-Wars   149
The Child, when Lamia'has din'd, out of her maw.   • 329 Horace   510

'AST
And scorn'd, thou'ast showne thy malice, but hast fail'd.   188 U34 Small Poxe   18
T'effect it, feele, thou'ast made thine owne heart ake.   250 U73 Weston   12

HAST (HASTE)
Just wife, and, to change me, make womans hast?   • 34 E25 Beast 1   8
In hast the bottome of a med'cin'd Cup,   • 197 U40 Elegy That   4
And there to stand so. Hast now envious Moone,   • 238 U65 Prince   9

HAST
What name, what skill, what faith hast thou in things!   • 31 E14 Camden   7
Thou saist, that cannot be: for thou hast seene   • 32 E18 Censurer   3
Thy faith is all the knowledge that thou hast.   • 32 E18 Censurer   10
Hast purg'd thy realmes, as we have now no cause   • 38 E35 James 2   5
Earth, thou hast not such another.   • 39 E40 Ratcliffe   17
What need hast thou of me? or of my Muse?   • 40 E43 Salisbury 1   1
That hast betray'd me to a worthlesse lord;   • 48 E65 Muse   2
And, as thou'hast mine, his houres, and youth abuse.   • 48 E65 Muse   6
Yet by thy weapon liv'st! Th'hast one good part.   • 50 E69 Cob   2
Hornet, thou hast thy wife drest, for the stall,   • 53 E78 Hornet   1
Who both their graces in thy selfe hast more   • 57 E89 Allen   9
So hast thou rendred him in all his bounds,   • 61 E95 Savile   5
That hast thy brest so cleere of present crimes,   • 61 E95 Savile   19
As thou hast best authoritie, t'allow.   • 62 E96 Donne 2   6
Thou hast begun well, Roe, which stand well too,   • 63 E98 Th Roe 1   1
And I know nothing more thou hast to doo.   • 63 E98 Th Roe 1   2
That thou hast kept thy love, encrease thy will,   • 63 E99 Th Roe 2   1
Hast taught thy selfe worthy thy pen to tread,   • 63 E99 Th Roe 2   3
An Epick poeme; thou hast the same end.   • 72 E112 Gamster   10
I know not which th'hast most, candor, or wit: • 78 E123 Rudyerd 3   2
But both th'hast so, as who affects the state   • 78 E123 Rudyerd 3   3
Thou hast seene hell (some say) and know'st all nookes there,   85 E133 Voyage   51
Thou hast no lantherne, whereof tales are told;   • 93 F2 Penshurst   4
Thou hast thy walkes for health, as well as sport: • 93 F2 Penshurst   9
Thy copp's, too, nam'd of Gamage, thou hast there,   • 94 F2 Penshurst   19
Thou hast thy ponds, that pay thee tribute fish,   • 94 F2 Penshurst   32
The whil'st, the severall seasons thou hast seene   • 97 F3 Wroth   37
False world, good-night: since thou hast brought   • 100 F4 To the World   1
More hatred, then thou hast to mee.   • • 101 F4 To the World   40
Then, in a soile hast planted me,   • 101 F4 To the World   45
Then thou hast done?   • • • 129 U1 Father   18
Something more then thou hast spi'd.   • 137 U2 Cupid   50
But nought beyond. He thou hast given it to,   • 161 U14 Selden   71
Thou hast the brave scorne, to put back the fee!   • 187 U33 Councellour   22
Of Bookes, of Presidents, hast thou at hand!   • 187 U33 Councellour   25
And scorn'd, thou'ast showne thy malice, but hast fail'd.   188 U34 Small Poxe   18
And what hast thou done in these pettie spights,   • 210 U43 Vulcan   163
Which thou hast only vented, not enjoy'd.   • 210 U43 Vulcan   168
Thou Seed-plot of the warre, that hast not spar'd   213 U44 Speach   24
which thus hast crown'd our hopes, our spring, and earth,   237 U65 Prince   V 2
The same that thou hast promis'd, but be slow,   • 237 U65 Prince   V 6
And still to stand so. Hast thou envious Moone,   • 238 U65 Prince   V 9
To shew thou hast beene long,   • • 245 U70 Ode   58
Though thou hast past thy Summer standing, stay   • 252 U75 Epithalam.   1
In all thy age of Journals thou hast tooke,   • 254 U75 Epithalam.   75
And thou hast painted beauties world.   • 277 U84 Body   28
Thrice happy house, that hast receipt   • 280 U84 Mind   53
Thou hast no more blowes, Fate, to drive at one: • 283 U84 Muse   27
What treasure hast thou brought us! and what store   388 Chapman   4
Such Passage hast thou found, such Returnes made,   • 389 Chapman   10
Triumph, my Britaine, thou hast one to showe,   • 391 Shakespeare   41
Under one title. Thou hast made thy way   • 397 Drayton   48
Thou hast deserv'd: And let me reade the while   398 Drayton   60
For thou objectest (as thou hast been told)   • 408 Detractor   3
That thou hast lost thy noyse, thy foame, thy stirre,   408 Detractor   8
All which thou hast incurr'd deservedly: • 410 Gill   5
Thinking to stir me, thou hast lost thy End,   • 410 Gill   9
For thou hast nought in thee to cure his Fame,   • 411 Gill   13

HASTE (See also HAST)
Haste, haste, officious Sun, and send them Night   257 U75 Epithalam.   145
And shuts the old. Haste, haste, all loyall Swaines,   263 U79 New-yeares   10
Haste, haste you hither, all you gentler Swaines,   265 U79 New-yeares   46
Of too much haste, and negligence in part,   • 323 Horace   385
For, if one should, and with a rope make haste   • 335 Horace   655
Haste, Haste, sweete Singer: Nor to Tine,   • 368 Ode Who saith   73

HASTENS
He ever hastens to the end, and so   • • 315 Horace   211

HASTILY
Wise child, did'st hastily returne,   • • 242 U70 Ode   7

HASTS
    Who like a Giant hasts his course to run, ... 414   Ghyrlond   51
HASTY
    This hasty sacrifice, wherein I reare   116   F12 Rutland   97
HAT
    That so much skarfe of France, and hat, and fether,   .   .   . 56   E88 Monsieur   3
    He, that but saw you weare the wheaten hat,   .   .   . 68   E105 L Wroth 2   7
    Under that cover; an old Mid-wives hat!   .   .   . 202   U42 Elegy Let   33
    Old Hat here, torne Hose, with Shoes full of gravell,   .   . 375   Coryat 1   26
HATCH
    That haunt Pickt-hatch, Mersh-Lambeth, and White-fryers,   .   . 30   E12 Shift   2
HATE
    Her foes enough would fame thee in their hate.   .   .   . 40   E43 Salisbury 1   4
    Though hate had put them out;   147   U7 Nymph   25
    Of love, and hate: and came so nigh to know   .   .   . 200   U42 Elegy Let   35
    I hate such measur'd, give me mettall'd fire   .   .   . 233   U59 Newcastle   7
    Who seldome sleepes! whom bad men only hate!   .   .   . 250   U73 Weston   6
    What so is showne, I not beleeve, and hate.   .   .   . 317   Horace   269
    Why not? I'm gentle, and free-borne, doe hate   .   .   . 331   Horace   571
    Why not? being honest, and free-borne, doth hate   .   . 352   Horace   V547/571
    "So much doth Virtue hate, ... 367   Ode Who saith   31
HATED
    Even states most hated, when no lawes resist   .   .   . 423   Lucan   13
HATETH
    He that for love of goodnesse hateth ill, ... 112   F11 Epode   87
HATH
    But see! th'old baud hath serv'd him in his trim,   .   .   . 31   E12 Shift   23
    Lent him a pockie whore. Shee hath paid him.   .   .   . 31   E12 Shift   24
    Quick in his lips! who hath this wonder wrought?   .   .   . 33   E21 Gam'ster   5
    Hath plac'd amongst her virgin-traine: 34   E22 Daughter   9
    To heaven; his hath: O happy state! wherein   .   .   . 35   E27 Roe 1   7
    Like aydes 'gainst treasons who hath found before?   .   . 38   E35 James 2   7
    Conquer'd hath both life and it.   39   E40 Ratcliffe   12
    Were quite out-spun. The like wish hath his wife.   .   . 40   E42 Giles   12
    And hath no honor lost, our Due'llists say.   .   .   . 42   E48 Mungril   3
    With what thy vertue on the times hath won,   .   .   . 47   E63 Salisbury 2   2
    Wherein what wonder see thy name hath wrought?   .   .   . 48   E64 Salisbury 3   16
    Love thy great losse, which a renowne hath wonne,   .   . 49   E66 Cary   11
    T'our times return'd, hath made her heaven in thee.   .   . 52   E74 Chancelor   10
    And hath it, in his powers, to make his way!   .   .   . 53   E80 Life/Death   4
    Hath got the stewards chaire; he will not tarry   .   .   . 57   E90 Mill   15
    Of any Madames, hath neadd squires, and must.   .   .   . 63   E97 Motion   14
    When he was here. Nor hath he got a sute,   .   .   . 63   E97 Motion   16
    Is private gaine, which hath long guilt to friend.   .   . 70   E109 Nevil   8
    Un-argued then, and yet hath fame from those;   .   .   . 71   E110 Edmonds 1   10
    Hath chang'd his soule, and made his object you: .   .   . 74   E114 Sydney   5
    He hath not onely gain'd himselfe his eyes,   .   .   . 74   E114 Sydney   7
    Came backe untouch'd. This man hath travail'd well.   .   . 81   E128 Wm Roe 2   14
    No more, those mayden glories shee hath lost.   .   .   . 83   E132 Sylvester   14
    (Who hath the hundred hands when he doth meddle)   .   .   . 86   E133 Voyage   82
    The citie since hath rais'd a Pyramide.   89   E133 Voyage   194
    Then hath thy orchard fruit, thy garden flowers,   .   .   . 94   F2 Penshurst   39
    The world hath seene, which all these had in trust,   .   . 114   F12 Rutland   39
    Yet, for the timely favours shee hath done,   .   .   . 115   F12 Rutland   71
    To my lesse sanguine Muse, wherein she'hath wonne,   .   . 115   F12 Rutland   72
    To live untill to morrow' hath lost two dayes.   .   .   . 121   F14 Sydney   50
    Before the soyle hath smutch'd it?   134   U2 Triumph   24
    So hath Homer prais'd her haire;   136   U2 Cupid   13
    But he hath eyes so round, and bright, ... 147   U7 Nymph   22
    As hath the youngest Hee, ... 149   U9 Picture   9
    Tell me that she hath seene   149   U9 Picture   13
    prompt me that she hath seene   149   U9 Picture   V 13
    Hath both my heart and me surpriz'd, ... 151   U11 Dreame   5
    Then what he hath receiv'd. Gifts stinke from some,   .   . 153   U13 Sacvile   22
    Against his will that do's 'hem? that hath weav'd   .   . 153   U13 Sacvile   26
    All this corrupts the thankes; lesse hath he wonne,   .   . 154   U13 Sacvile   33
    Looke to and cure; Hee's not a man hath none,   .   .   . 156   U13 Sacvile   115
    Though I confesse (as every Muse hath err'd,   .   .   . 159   U14 Selden   19
    Forme, Art or Ensigne, that hath scap'd your sight?   .   . 160   U14 Selden   48
    Forme, Act or Ensigne, that hath scap'd your sight?   .   . 160   U14 Selden   V 48
    Whom no great Mistresse hath as yet infam'd,   .   .   . 165   U15 Friend-Wars   97
    This hath our ill-us'd freedome, and soft peace   .   . 166   U15 Friend-Wars   121
    Your fate hath found, ... 180   U26 Ode High   3
    Happy in that faire honour it hath gain'd,   .   .   . 180   U26 Ode High   14
    Whose fame hath an eternall voice?   181   U27 Ode Helen   16
    Or hath Corynna, by the name   181   U27 Ode Helen   17
    Hath Petrarch since his Laura rais'd   181   U27 Ode Helen   21
    Hath our great Sidney, Stella set, ... 181   U27 Ode Helen   25
    Tyran Rime hath so abused, ... 184   U29 Fit of Rime   46
    Her owne bloud gave her: Shee ne're had, nor hath   .   . 188   U34 Small Poxe   9
    Such are his powers, whom time hath stil'd,   .   .   . 189   U36 Song   13
    It is a Darknesse hath blockt up my sense,   .   .   . 191   U38 Elegy 'Tis   5
    Should aske the blood, and spirits he hath infus'd   .   . 192   U38 Elegy 'Tis   65
    In man, because man hath the flesh abus'd.   .   .   . 192   U38 Elegy 'Tis   66
    The contrite Soule, who hath no thought to win   .   . 193   U38 Elegy 'Tis   89
    Of beautie; but the Muse hath interest in: .   .   . 200   U42 Elegy Let   15
    When by thy sordid bountie she hath on   201   U42 Elegy Let   45
    To all as fatall as't hath beene to me, ... 211   U43 Vulcan   192
    What though she hath won on Trust, as many doe,   .   . 223   U49 Pucell   21
    And trust her I would least, that hath forswore   .   . 223   U49 Pucell   29
    From Court, while yet thy fame hath some small day;   .   . 223   U49 Pucell   36
    Whilst your Ulisses hath ta'ne leave to goe,   .   .   . 224   U50 Countesse   21
    A Poet hath no more but black and white,   .   .   . 227   U52 Answer   20

		Page	Title	Line

HATH (cont.)
```
But since the Wine hath steep'd my braine,          .     .     .   230  U55 Burges        5
That so hath crown'd our hopes, our spring, and earth,   .     .   237  U65 Prince         2
That so hath crown'd our hopes, our spring, our earth,   .     .   237  U65 Prince      V  2
That thus hath crown'd our hopes, with thee, our Spring & May,     237  U65 Prince      V  2
Sol will re-shine. If not, Charles hath a Sonne.   .     .     .   238  U65 Prince        12
And Sol will shine. If not, Charles hath a Sonne.  .     .     .   238  U65 Prince     V 12
Hath taken twice the Ring    .     .     .     .     .     .     .  240  U67 Muses        38
Hath brought the Land an Heire!    .     .     .     .     .     .  240  U67 Muses        53
What can the cause be, when the K. hath given   .     .     .   .  241  U68 House-hold    1
Hath rais'd to be the Port unto his Land!    .     .     .     .   250  U73 Weston        4
Hath filled, with Caroches, all the way,   .     .     .     .   . 252  U75 Epithalam.   11
These two, now holy Church hath made them one,   .     .     .   . 257  U75 Epithalam.  139
Hath drawne on me, from the times,    .     .     .     .     .   . 259  U76 Petition     17
Hath drawne on him, from the times,   .     .     .     .     .   . 259  U76 Petition  V 17
Where Nature such a large survey hath ta'en,    .     .     .   .  262  U78 Digby        11
Shee, to the Crowne, hath brought encrease.   .     .     .     .  264  U79 New-yeares   41
As hath thy James; cleans'd from originall drosse,    .     .   .  268  U80 Christning    9
The Christian hath t'enjoy the future life,    .     .     .     . 271  U81 Pawlet       96
Or hath she here, upon the ground,   .     .     .     .     .   .  280  U84 Mind        49
Hope, hath her end! and Faith hath her reward!   .     .     .   . 284  U84 Muse        68
Hee knowes, what worke h'hath done, to call this Guest,   .     .  284  U84 Muse        81
Whom her Redeemer, honour'd hath above    .     .     .     .   .  285  U84 Muse       100
To that eternall Rest, where now sh'hath place    .     .     .   288  U84 Muse       197
Hath given wholly to the Sonne (the rather   .     .     .     .   288  U84 Muse       216
This hath pleas'd, doth please, and long will please; never   .   294  U88 Petronius    9
Of daring all, hath still beene given; we know it:    .     .   .  305  Horace         12
Of daring ought, hath still beene given; we know it:    .     .   338  Horace      V  12
To paint him, hath by swimming, hopelesse, scap'd,    .     .   .  305  Horace         27
Hath neither soule, nor sinewes.  Loftie he    .     .     .     . 307  Horace         37
New names of things.  It hath beene ever free,    .     .     .   309  Horace         83
Or the wilde river, who hath changed now    .     .     .     .   . 309 Horace         96
And then as swift to leave what he hath lov'd.   .     .     .   . 315  Horace        236
But every Judge hath not the facultie    .     .     .     .     . 323  Horace        387
Hee, that studied well the debt, and knowes   .     .     .     .  325  Horace        445
And care of getting, thus, our minds hath stain'd,    .     .   .  327  Horace        473
But he hath every suffrage, can apply    .     .     .     .     . 329  Horace        514
Hath shed, or humane frailtie not kept thence.   .     .     .   . 329 Horace         528
Thy skill hath made of ranck dispised weedes;    .     .     .   . 361 Palmer         10
till th'one hath drownd the other in our sightes,   .     .     .  361  Palmer         20
"Musicke hath power to draw,   .     .     .     .     .     .   .  367  Ode Who saith   47
Hath all beene Harmony:    .     .     .     .     .     .     .   367  Ode Who saith   51
And more hath wonne    .     .     .     .     .     .     .     .  367  Ode Who saith   52
Then Time hath donne,    .     .     .     .     .     .     .   .  367  Ode Who saith   54
Who (see) already hath ore-flowne    .     .     .     .     .   .  368  Ode Who saith   65
Hath sent her Mermaides in,    .     .     .     .     .     .   .  368  Ode Who saith   91
To his strength, hath measur'd it out with his feet.   .     .   . 379  Coryat 3        4
hath armde att all poyntes; charge mee humblye kneele   .     .   382  Rich            2
Shall finde, that either hath read Bookes, and Men:   .     .   .  389  Aleman          2
And hath the noblest marke of a good Booke,   .     .     .     .  389  Aleman          4
And this hath met that one, that may be stil'd    .     .     .   389  Aleman         13
As well in brasse, as he hath hit    .     .     .     .     .   .  390  Reader          6
. . . Mr. William Shakespeare: And what he hath left us.    .   .  390  Shakespeare   Ttl
Which, since thy flight from hence, hath mourn'd like night,   .   392  Shakespeare    79
But who hath them interpreted, and brought    .     .     .     .  395  May            19
It hath beene question'd, Michael, if I bee   .     .     .     .  396  Drayton         1
This Booke will live; It is a Genius: This    .     .     .     .  400  Beaumont        1
Before this worke? where Envy hath not cast   .     .     .     .  401  Beaumont       13
Againe hath brought the Lillie to the Rose;   .     .     .     .  401  Filmer          8
Hath made his Inigo Marquess, wouldst thou fayne   .     .     .  406  Inigo Jones 2   2
The Morning-star, whose light our Fal hath stay'd.    .     .   .  413  Ghyrlond       40
Till he hath reach'd his two-fold point of Noone.   .     .     .  414  Ghyrlond       52
A Say-master, hath studied all the tricks    .     .     .     .   415  Rutter         26
Butt, Clownishe pride hath gott    .     .     .     .     .     .  420  Ode:If Men     10
That hath not Countrye impudence enough to laughe att Arte,   .   420  Ode:If Men     14
whom fortune hath deprest; come nere the fates    .     .     .   422  Lucan           4
whom, yf fortune hath deprest; come nere the fates    .     .   .  422  Lucan       V  4
to Cynthias fayrest Nymph hath sent thee,    .     .     .     .   662  Bedford         6
```
HATING
```
Hating that solemne vice of greatnesse, pride;   .     .     .   .  52  E76 Bedford 1   10
```
HATRED
```
More hatred, then thou hast to mee.   .     .     .     .     .   . 101  F4 To the World 40
Friendship is now mask'd Hatred! Justice fled,   .     .     .   . 163  U15 Friend-Wars 39
The Dutch whom Wealth (not Hatred) doth divide;    .     .     .  368  Ode Who saith   85
```
HAU'
```
And Phrygian Hau'boy, not without the Flute.   .     .     .     . 292  U86 Hor.4:1     24
```
HAU'
```
The Hau'-boy, not as now with latten bound,   .     .     .     .  319  Horace        287
```
HAU'-BOY
```
The Hau'-boy, not as now with latten bound,   .     .     .     .  319  Horace        287
```
HAU'BOY
```
And Phrygian Hau'boy, not without the Flute.   .     .     .     . 292  U86 Hor.4:1     24
```
HAUGHTIE
```
Of money, haughtie, to desire soon mov'd,    .     .     .     .   315  Horace        235
Of all, that insolent Greece, or haughtie Rome    .     .     .   391  Shakespeare    39
```
HAUKING
```
Or hauking at the river, or the bush,    .     .     .     .     .  97  F3 Wroth        33
```
HAUNCH   (See HANCH)
HAUNT
```
That haunt Pickt-hatch, Mersh-Lambeth, and White-fryers,   .   .   30  E12 Shift        2
Or use all arts, or haunt all Companies    .     .     .     .   . 165  U15 Friend-Wars 91
```
'AVE
```
More honour in him, 'cause we'ave knowne him mad:   .     .     . 168  U15 Friend-Wars 194
```

	Page	Title	Line
'AVE (cont.)			
They'ave glutted in, and letcher'd out that weeke,	218	U47 Tribe	13
That ever had beginning there, to'ave end!	271	U81 Pawlet	91
HA'			
Ha' their Bermudas, and their streights i'th' Strand:	155	U13 Sacvile	82
And not the bounties you ha' done, deny.	192	U38 Elegy 'Tis	54
Alas I ha' lost my heat, my blood, my prime,	199	U41 Elegy Since	11
HAVE'			
And have'hem yeeld no savour, but of state.	58	E92 New Crie	5
To have't exprest,	149	U8 Houre-glasse	10
HAVE			
For the lucks sake, it thus much favour have,	27	E3 Bookseller	4
Nor have my title-leafe on posts, or walls,	28	E3 Bookseller	7
Thou wert, as chiefe of them are said t'have beene.	28	E4 James 1	6
But I have my revenge made, in thy name.	29	E10 Ignorant	2
Shee must have money: he returnes, god payes.	30	E12 Shift	8
Davis, and Weever, and the best have beene,	32	E18 Censurer	4
What severall wayes men to their calling have!	33	E21 Gam'ster	7
Hast purg'd thy realmes, as we have now no cause	38	E35 James 2	5
In these times. Few so have ru'de	39	E40 Ratcliffe	14
To have so soone scap'd worlds, and fleshes rage,	41	E45 First Son	7
I have no salt: no bawdrie he doth meane.	42	E49 Playwrt 1	3
Play-wright, I loath to have thy manners knowne	42	E49 Playwrt 1	5
For we, that have our eyes still in our eares,	43	E51 James 3	9
So have I seene at Christ-masse sports one lost,	45	E58 Groome	7
Who, when you'have burnt your selves downe to the snuffe,	45	E59 Spies	2
Loe, what my countrey should have done (have rais'd	46	E60 Mounteagle	1
Or, if shee would but modestly have prais'd	46	E60 Mounteagle	3
My countries parents I have many knowne;	46	E60 Mounteagle	9
Or your complexions losse? you have a pot,	46	E62 Would-bee	6
Not glad, like those that have new hopes, or sutes,	47	E64 Salisbury 3	1
Contends t'have worth enjoy, from his regard,	48	E64 Salisbury 3	13
I'have sung the greater fortunes of our state.	48	E64 Salisbury 3	18
Since men have left to doe praise-worthy things,	49	E67 Suffolk	1
I'am more asham'd to have thee thought my foe.	53	E77 Not name	4
Or that I'have by, two good sufficient men,	54	E81 Proule	3
I would have spent: how every Muse should know it,	55	E84 Bedford 2	7
Now, in whose bosome I have this discerned,	55	E85 Goodyere 1	11
What would his serious actions me have learned?	55	E85 Goodyere 1	12
Yet have they seene the maps, and bought 'hem too,	59	E92 New Crie	9
To ope' the Character. They'have found the sleight	59	E92 New Crie	27
With ignorance on us, as they have done	59	E92 New Crie	37
And we, that would have falne as great, as they,	60	E93 Radcliffe	7
To have her storie woven in thy thred;	61	E95 Savile	15
But most we need his faith (and all have you)	62	E95 Savile	35
Onely his clothes have over-leaven'd him.	63	E97 Motion	20
Yet shall you have, to rectifie your palate,	64	E101 Supper	9
The skie not falling, thinke we may have larkes.	65	E101 Supper	16
And we will have no Pooly', or Parrot by;	65	E101 Supper	36
Both which are ask'd, to have thee understood.	66	E102 Pembroke	4
Nor could the age have mist thee, in this strife	66	E102 Pembroke	5
Judge then, that can: here I have rais'd to show	67	E104 Montgomery	13
Tell them, what parts yo'have tane, whence run away,	69	E107 Hungry	9
What States yo'have gull'd, and which yet keepes yo'in pay.	69	E107 Hungry	10
If but to be beleev'd you have the hap,	69	E107 Hungry	17
Now I have sung thee thus, shall judge of thee.	70	E109 Nevil	16
To have engrav'd these acts, with his owne stile,	71	E110 Edmonds 1	6
How few have read! how fewer understood!)	71	E110 Edmonds 1	16
Not that it feares, but will not have to doo	74	E115 Honest Man	20
Describ'd, it 's thus: Defin'd would you it have?	75	E115 Honest Man	33
They have repented.	77	E120 S. P.	20
And have sought (to give new birth)	77	E120 S. P.	21
But when I have said, The proofes of all these bee	82	E130 Ferrab. 1	17
The learn'd have no more priviledge, then the lay.	82	E131 Ferrab. 2	4
We have a Shelton, and a Heyden got,	84	E133 Voyage	5
Cocytus, Phlegeton, our have prov'd in one;	84	E133 Voyage	8
To have beene stiled of King Arthurs table.	84	E133 Voyage	24
That all this while I have forgot some god,	85	E133 Voyage	44
Where Pan, and Bacchus their high feasts have made,	93	F2 Penshurst	11
Thy lord, and lady, though they have no sute.	95	F2 Penshurst	50
To have her linnen, plate, and all things nigh,	96	F2 Penshurst	86
They are, and have beene taught religion: Thence	96	F2 Penshurst	93
Their gentler spirits have suck'd innocence.	96	F2 Penshurst	94
May say, their lords have built, but thy lord dwells.	96	F2 Penshurst	102
Nor throng'st (when masquing is) to have a sight	96	F3 Wroth	9
Nor throng'st (where masquing is) to have a sight	96	F3 Wroth	V 9
Which boasts t'have had the head of gold.	98	F3 Wroth	64
If these, who have but sense, can shun	101	F4 To the World	33
The engines, that have them annoy'd;	101	F4 To the World	34
These have crimes accounted beene.	102	F5 Celia 1	18
And have more diseases made.	105	F8 Sicknesse	20
Shall not give out, that I have made thee stay,	107	F10 Proludium	8
Shall not give out, that we have made thee stay,	107	F10 Proludium	V 8
'Tis the securest policie we have,	109	F11 Epode	17
Of which usurping rancke, some have thought love	110	F11 Epode	31
Have fill'd with abstinence:	111	F11 Epode	84
Have grac'd with abstinence:	111	F11 Epode	V 84
I, that have none (to send you) send you verse.	113	F12 Rutland	19
Almost you have, or may have, when you will?	114	F12 Rutland	34
Worth an estate, treble to that you have.	114	F12 Rutland	36
Have beautie knowne, yet none so famous seene?	114	F12 Rutland	50
Who, though shee have a better verser got,	115	F12 Rutland	68
I have already us'd some happy houres,	115	F12 Rutland	74

255

HAVE (cont.)

	Page	Title	Line
Then all, that have but done my Muse least grace,	115	F12 Rutland	79
Then all, that have but done my verse lesse grace,	115	F12 Rutland	V 79
I, that am gratefull for him, have prepar'd	116	F12 Rutland	96
As what th'have lost t'expect, they dare deride.	116	F13 Aubgny	4
I, that have suffer'd this; and, though forsooke	117	F13 Aubigny	15
Of Fortune, have not alter'd yet my looke,	117	F13 Aubigny	16
Remov'd, as you from need to have it such.	117	F13 Aubigny	28
Without companions? 'Tis safe to have none.	118	F13 Aubigny	56
May they have nothing left, whereof they can	118	F13 Aubigny	83
Boast, but how oft they have gone wrong to man:	119	F13 Aubigny	84
You, Madame, yong have learn'd to shunne these shelves,	119	F13 Aubigny	89
And, keeping a just course, have earely put	119	F13 Aubigny	91
Before the moones have fill'd their tripple trine,	119	F13 Aubigny	102
Say you have follow'd farre,	121	F14 Sydney	45
Where have I beene this while exil'd from thee?	122	F15 Heaven	13
I have had, and have my Peeres:	131	U2 Excuse	4
Some have lov'd as old agen.	131	U2 Excuse	6
All the Pride the fields than have:	132	U2 How he saw	4
And would faine have chang'd the fate,	133	U2 Suffered	19
Is, that I have leave to speake,	133	U2 Suffered	22
Have you seene but a bright Lillie grow,	134	U2 Triumph	21
Have you seene the white Lillie grow,	134	U2 Triumph	V 21
Before rude hands have touch'd it?	134	U2 Triumph	22
Have you mark'd but the fall o'the Snow	134	U2 Triumph	23
Have you seene the fall o'the Snow	135	U2 Triumph	V 23
Have you felt the wooll o' the Bever?	135	U2 Triumph	25
Or have smelt o'the bud o'the Brier?	135	U2 Triumph	27
Or have tasted the bag o'the Bee?	135	U2 Triumph	29
Have you seene a faire Damaske-rose	135	U2 Triumph	V 31
Have you seene faire Helen disclose	135	U2 Triumph	V 33
Have you seene Love-Queenes embraces	135	U2 Triumph	V 35
Have you tasted the Cinnamon-tree	135	U2 Triumph	V 37
Have you seene the boy from the Chace	135	U2 Triumph	V 39
Have you seene faire Ledas face	135	U2 Triumph	V 41
Have you seen the Palme-trees state	136	U2 Triumph	V 43
Have you tasted virginitye	136	U2 Triumph	V 45
Love, and I have had; and true.	136	U2 Cupid	6
Sure, said he, if I have Braine,	136	U2 Cupid	10
Have you plac'd the banke of kisses,	136	U2 Cupid	25
What my Muse and I have done:	138	U2 Kisse	5
Whether we have lost, or wonne,	138	U2 Kisse	6
Or if you would yet have stay'd,	138	U2 Kisse	29
Or have charg'd his sight of Crime,	138	U2 Kisse	32
To have left all sight for you:	138	U2 Kisse	33
Where, how it would have relish'd well;	139	U2 Another	14
I would have him, if I could,	140	U2 Her man	3
Young Il'd have him to, and faire,	141	U2 Her man	9
He would have a hand as soft	141	U2 Her man	25
He should have a hand as soft	141	U2 Her man	V 25
No tunes are sweet, nor words have sting,	143	U3 Musicall	15
No voice so sweet, nor words have sting,	143	U3 Musicall	V 15
Wee have both wits, and fancies too,	145	U5 Woman-kind	5
Will be his Rivall, though shee have but eares.	148	U7 Nymph	28
And all these through her eyes, have stopt her eares.	150	U9 Picture	18
Nor have I yet the narrow mind	150	U10 Jealousie	4
I Have my Pietie too, which could	151	U12 Corbet	1
Would say as much, as both have done	151	U12 Corbet	3
And more, and more, I should have done,	152	U12 Corbet	30
If, Sackvile, all that have the power to doe	153	U13 Sacvile	1
And knew their how, and where: we should have, then,	153	U13 Sacvile	3
To have such doe me good, I durst not name:	153	U13 Sacvile	18
That they have more opprest me, then my want?	153	U13 Sacvile	28
Must make me sad for what I have obtain'd.	154	U13 Sacvile	38
No! Gifts and thankes should have one cheerefull face,	154	U13 Sacvile	39
As I have seene some Infants of the Sword,	154	U13 Sacvile	47
I have the lyst of mine owne faults to know,	156	U13 Sacvile	114
Ride, saile, am coach'd, know I how farre I have gone,	156	U13 Sacvile	121
And my minds motion not? or have I none?	156	U13 Sacvile	122
Men have beene great, but never good by chance,	156	U13 Sacvile	124
Are Dwarfes of Honour, and have neither weight	157	U13 Sacvile	147
Shoot forth in smooth and comely spaces; have	157	U13 Sacvile	150
Your Booke, my Selden, I have read, and much	158	U14 Selden	5
And mine not least) I have too oft prefer'd	159	U14 Selden	20
But 'twas with purpose to have made them such.	159	U14 Selden	22
Stand forth my Object, then, you that have beene	159	U14 Selden	29
Ever at home: yet, have all Countries seene:	159	U14 Selden	30
Heard what times past have said, seene what ours doe:	159	U14 Selden	34
What fables have you vext! what truth redeem'd!	159	U14 Selden	39
What blots and errours, have you watch'd and purg'd	160	U14 Selden	42
That would, perhaps, have prais'd, and thank'd the same,	161	U14 Selden	70
To have his Court-bred-fillie there commend	163	U15 Friend-Wars	48
This Praecipice, and Rocks that have no end,	166	U15 Friend-Wars	130
Is that the truer excuse? or have we got	166	U15 Friend-Wars	142
What suretie of life have thou, and I?	168	U16 Gray	7
But that some greater names have broke with me,	169	U17 Friend-Debt	8
You have a Husband is the just excuse	171	U19 Elegy By	22
Or have the least of Good, but what it must	171	U20 Shrub	7
His falling Temples you have rear'd,	173	U22 Elegy Tho	17
Have sung this Hymne, and here intreat	174	U22 Elegy Tho	30
Have made their fairest flight,	180	U26 Ode High	7
In one full Action; nor have you now more	180	U26 Ode High	17
This same which you have caught,	180	U26 Ode High	20

HAVE (cont.)

	Page	Title	Line
Have all these done (and yet I misse	182	U27 Ode Helen	29
I That have beene a lover, and could shew it,	182	U28 Worth	1
That they long since have refused	184	U29 Fit of Rime	47
Thinke, yea and boast, that they have done it so	186	U32 Elsmere	12
Have made me to conceive a Lawyer new.	187	U33 Councellour	14
What Beautie would have lovely stilde,	188	U35 Chute	1
And have their being, their waste to see;	189	U36 Song	11
You have unto my Store added a booke,	189	U37 Friend-Book	4
The ignorant, and fooles, no pittie have.	191	U38 Elegy 'Tis	20
Errour and folly in me may have crost	192	U38 Elegy 'Tis	37
Of that wise Nature would a Cradle have.	192	U38 Elegy 'Tis	60
Upon the hope to have another sin	193	U38 Elegy 'Tis	90
Till then 'tis all but darknesse, that I have;	194	U38 Elegy 'Tis	121
(If they be faire and worth it) have their lives	200	U42 Elegy Let	20
But I who live, and have liv'd twentie yeare	200	U42 Elegy Let	29
That quilts those bodies, I have leave to span:	200	U42 Elegy Let	32
Have eaten with the Beauties, and the wits,	200	U42 Elegy Let	33
Whose like I have knowne the Taylors Wife put on	201	U42 Elegy Let	39
Of race accompted, that no passion have	201	U42 Elegy Let	49
He would have done in verse, with any of those	201	U42 Elegy Let	62
What have I done that might call on thine ire?	202	U43 Vulcan	V 2
By Jove to have Minerva for thy Bride,	203	U43 Vulcan	12
Perhaps, to have beene burned with my bookes.	203	U43 Vulcan	18
Thou should'st have stay'd, till publike fame said so.	204	U43 Vulcan	46
Thou migatst have yet enjoy'd thy crueltie	204	U43 Vulcan	49
Thou mightst have had me perish, piece, by piece,	205	U43 Vulcan	51
Thou mightst have had them perish, piece, by piece,	205	U43 Vulcan	V 51
To light Tobacco, or have roasted Geese,	205	U43 Vulcan	V 52
And so, have kept me dying a whole age,	205	U43 Vulcan	55
And so, have kept them dying a whole age,	205	U43 Vulcan	V 55
T'have held a Triumph, or a feast of fire,	205	U43 Vulcan	60
Thou should'st have cry'd, and all beene proper stuffe.	205	U43 Vulcan	64
Thou should'st have cry'd, and all fine proper stuffe.	205	U43 Vulcan	V 64
For none but Smiths would have made thee a God.	208	U43 Vulcan	117
And raz'd, e're thought could urge, This might have bin!	209	U43 Vulcan	136
Nay, let White-Hall with Revels have to doe,	210	U43 Vulcan	156
Scarce let White-Hall with Revels have to doe,	210	U43 Vulcan	V156
So would'st th'have run upon the Rolls by stealth,	210	U43 Vulcan	169
some 4 myles hence and have him there disgorge	211	U43 Vulcan	V184
Or in small Fagots have him blaze about	211	U43 Vulcan	185
Vile Tavernes, and have Drunkards pisse him out;	211	U43 Vulcan	V186
To all as chargefull as they have beene to me,	211	U43 Vulcan	V192
That have good places: therefore once agen,	212	U43 Vulcan	212
That have good fortunes: therefore once agen,	212	U43 Vulcan	V212
That have good places: wherefore once agen,	212	U43 Vulcan	V212
But we have Powder still for the Kings Day,	213	U44 Speach	2
T'have wak'd, if sleeping, Spaines Ambassadour,	213	U44 Speach	4
That we have Trumpets, Armour, and great Horse,	213	U44 Speach	7
To have their Husbands drawne forth to the field,	213	U44 Speach	18
And Spinola have blushed at the sight.	214	U44 Speach	42
But he that should perswade, to have this done	214	U44 Speach	61
One lesson we have both learn'd, and well read;	216	U45 Squib	4
Deceit is fruitfull. Men have Masques and nets,	216	U45 Squib	18
Let these men have their wayes, and take their times	218	U47 Tribe	25
I have no portion in them, nor their deale	218	U47 Tribe	27
I have a body, yet, that spirit drawes	219	U47 Tribe	41
I have decreed; keepe it from waves, and presse;	219	U47 Tribe	57
'Mongst which, if I have any friendships sent,	220	U47 Tribe	63
As you have writ your selfe. Now stand, and then,	220	U47 Tribe	77
Have issue from the Barrell;	221	U48 Bacchus	32
And have thy tales and jests too,	221	U48 Bacchus	40
Not he, that should the body have, for Case	223	U49 Pucell	33
It will be shame for them, if they have none.	225	U50 Countesse	36
But whilst you curious were to have it be	227	U52 Answer	13
It doe not come: One piece I have in store,	229	U54 Squib	15
So have you gain'd a Servant, and a Muse:	230	U56 Covell	5
Because it durst have nobler dy'd.	234	U60 La-ware	18
That you have seene the pride, beheld the sport,	234	U61 Epigram	1
Was, t'have a Boy stand with a Club, and fright	241	U69 Friend Son	11
For as at distance, few have facultie	242	U69 Friend Son	19
To have exprest,	246	U70 Ode	88
Have cast a trench about mee, now, five yeares;	248	U71 Treasurer	6
Still to have such a Charles, but this Charles long.	249	U72 King	18
Have multipli'd their arts, and powers,	251	U74 Weston	17
Have they bedew'd the Earth, where she doth tread,	254	U75 Epithalam.	66
Have they bedew'd the Earth, where she did tread,	254	U75 Epithalam.	V 66
Whom they have chose,	255	U75 Epithalam.	94
To have thy God to blesse, thy King to grace,	256	U75 Epithalam.	131
Have left in fame to equall, or out-goe	260	U77 Treasurer	8
What you have studied are the arts of life;	261	U77 Treasurer	17
Which I have vow'd posteritie to give.	262	U78 Digby	18
That have a Flock, or Herd, upon these plaines;	265	U79 New-yeares	47
To pious parents, who would have their blood	268	U80 Christning	7
Her Rose, and Lilly, intertwind, have made.	268	U80 Christning	16
Thou wouldst have written, Fame, upon my brest:	269	U81 Pawlet	14
When I, who would her Poet have become,	269	U81 Pawlet	17
Which they that have the Crowne are sure to know!	271	U81 Pawlet	76
T' have paid againe a blessing was but lent,	271	U81 Pawlet	80
Now I have better thought thereon,	277	U84 Mind	2
When your owne Vertues, equall'd have their Names,	281	U84 Kenelme	12
Study illustrious Him, and you have all.	282	U84 Kenelme	23
By Death, on Earth, I should have had remorse	282	U84 Muse	12

HAVE (cont.)

Thou wouldst have lost the Phoenix, had the kind	. . .	283	U84 Muse	19
To have that finall retribution,	. . .	283	U84 Muse	49
Have all his actions wondred at, and view'd	. . .	284	U84 Muse	77
Have busie search made in his mysteries!	. . .	284	U84 Muse	80
To have her captiv'd spirit freed from flesh,	. . .	285	U84 Muse	93
But all of God; They still shall have to say,	. . .	286	U84 Muse	119
Yet have all debts forgiven us, and advance	. . .	286	U84 Muse	143
T' have knowne no envy, but by suffring it!	. . .	287	U84 Muse	162
That thus have ventur'd these true straines upon;	. . .	289	U84 Muse	227
Ye have oft-times, that may ore-shine the rest,	. . .	305	Horace	18
Ye have oft-times, that may out-shine the rest,	. . .	338	Horace	V 18
Cato's and Ennius tongues have lent much worth,	. . .	309	Horace	81
If thou would'st have me weepe, be thou first drown'd	. . .	311	Horace	145
Have more or lesse then just five Acts: nor laid,	. . .	317	Horace	272
To have a God come in; except a knot	. . .	317	Horace	273
'Tis cleare, this way I have got off from blame,	. . .	323	Horace	395
Her language, if the Stay, and Care t'have mended,	. . .	325	Horace	413
Have not kept in; and (lest perfection faile)	. . .	325	Horace	417
These, the free meale might have beene well drawne out:	. . .	331	Horace	560
Vice, and, am knowne to have a Knights estate.	. . .	331	Horace	572
Vice, and is knowne to have a Knights estate.	. . .	352	Horace	V548/572
Or the sad thunder-stroken thing he have	. . .	335	Horace	672
Those that in blood such violent pleasure have,	. . .	363	Murder	1
Where Gold's the Motive, women have no Nay.	. . .	363	Riches	18
Who saith our Times nor have, nor can	. . .	366	Ode Who saith	1
She might have claym'd t'have made the Graces foure;	. . .	371	Epitaph	6
As fit to have encreas'd the harmony	. . .	371	Epitaph	8
It should rather have bene Tom that a horse did lack.	. . .	374	Coryat 1	15
Father his sonne, I should have cal'd thee, why?	. . .	378	Coryat 2	88
. . . Which should Have beene Printed with the other . . .	. . .	379	Coryat 3	Ttl
Yet who could have hit on't but the wise noddell	. . .	379	Coryat 3	6
Pies on't, you have his historicall faith.	. . .	380	Coryat 3	22
Or builders of Story have oft imputation	. . .	380	Coryat 3	30
How many learned men he have drawne with his hooke	. . .	380	Coryat 3	44
Poore Tom have we cause to suspect just thee?	. . .	381	Coryat 3	58
That bid, God give thee joy, and have no endes.	. . .	384	Somerset	6
When these, and such, their voices have employd;	. . .	385	Brooke	1
But I have seene thy worke, and I know thee:	. . .	386	Browne	3
Let such as justly have out-liv'd all prayse,	. . .	387	Cavendish	5
To your desert, who'have done it, Friend. And this	. . .	389	Aleman	21
That would have done, that, which you onely can.	. . .	389	Aleman	24
O, could he but have drawne his wit	. . .	390	Reader	5
And we have wits to read, and praise to give.	. . .	391	Shakespeare	24
But, I would have, thee, to know something new,	. . .	394	Jane Ogle	13
Because, who make the question, have not seene	. . .	396	Drayton	3
You have not writ to me, nor I to you;	. . .	396	Drayton	6
Wonder to truth! and have my Vision hoorld,	. . .	396	Drayton	13
Tenants, and Servants, have they harts, and eyes,	. . .	399	Lady Ogle	4
And all men eccho you have made a Masque.	. . .	403	Inigo Jones 1	30
I chyme that too: And I have mett with those	. . .	403	Inigo Jones 1	31
He may have skill & judgment to designe	. . .	406	Inigo Jones 2	7
Wee'll have thee styld the Marquess of New-Ditch.	. . .	407	Inigo Jones 2	24
Wee'll have thee styld the Marquess of Town-Ditch.	. . .	407	Inigo Jones 2	V 24
Foole, doe not rate my Rymes; I'have found thy Vice	. . .	408	Detractor	5
To aske thy Name, if he have half his Nose!	. . .	409	Detractor	18
Which you have justly gained from the Stage,	. . .	409	Brome	6
Such men I met withall, and so have you.	. . .	415	Rutter	11
(You have deserv'd it from me) I have read,	. . .	415	Rutter	13
Yo'have all the Mysteries of Wits new Mint,	. . .	415	Rutter	28
but have lost it by the way,	. . .	417	Moon	10
I have, with strict advantage of free tyme	. . .	421	Censure	6
HAVE'HEM				
And have'hem yeeld no savour, but of state.	. . .	58	E92 New Crie	5
HAVE'T				
To have't exprest,	. . . . . .	149	U8 Houre-glasse	10
HAVING				
And having got him out of doores is glad.	. . .	40	E42 Giles	7
When having pill'd a booke, which no man buyes,	. . .	43	E53 Old-end	2
He that not trusts me, having vow'd thus much,	. . .	70	E108 Soldiers	9
At hunting railes, having no guift in othes,	. . .	76	E119 Shelton	2
At Bread-streets Mermaid, having din'd, and merry,	. . .	85	E133 Voyage	37
Thus Pan, and Sylvane, having had their rites,	. . .	98	F3 Wroth	47
When Pan, and Sylvane, having had their rites,	. . .	98	F3 Wroth	V 47
Or, having scap'd, shall I returne,	. . .	101	F4 To the World	25
And having pleas'd our art, wee'll try	. . .	145	U5 Woman-kind	17
And estimate thy Paines; as having wrought	. . .	161	U14 Selden	75
I gaine, in having leave to keepe my Day,	. . .	231	U56 Covell	29
Great King, thy having of a second Sonne:	. . .	268	U80 Christning	2
I murmure against God, for having ta'en	. . .	283	U84 Muse	33
Either because he seekes, and, having found,	. . .	317	Horace	242
Having well eat, and drunke (the rites being done)	. . .	319	Horace	325
And the bold Pythias, having cheated weake	. . .	321	Horace	346
Within the hope of having all forgiven?	. . .	323	Horace	394
HAWKING (See also HAUKING)				
Where I both learn'd, why wise-men hawking follow,	. . .	55	E85 Goodyere 1	3
The Hawking language? or our Day to breake	. . .	215	U44 Speach	72
HAY				
Hay! for the flowre of France!	. . . . .	240	U67 Muses	42
HAYLES				
Hayles me, so solemnly, to yonder Yewgh?	. . .	268	U81 Pawlet	2
HAYRE				
Who made a lampe of Berenices hayre?	. . .	115	F12 Rutland	61

	Page	Title	Line
HAYWARD			
The Gaine of your two friendships! Hayward and . . .	161	U14 Selden	81
The Graine of your two friendships! Hayward and . . .	161	U14 Selden	V 81
HAZARD			
Made from the hazard of anothers shame: . . .	27	E2 My Booke	10
On Captaine Hazard the Cheater.	56	E87 Hazard	Ttl
Hazard a month forsware his; and grew drunke, . .	56	E87 Hazard	2
Without the hazard of a drop of blood, . . .	214	U44 Speach	47
HAZILL			
There, or the tall witch-hazill hee doth twine . .	290	U85 Country	V 9
H'			
H'has tympanies of businesse, in his face, . .	35	E28 Surly	7
Know you the cause? H'has neither land, nor lease, .	63	E97 Motion	9
And not thinke h'had eat a stake, . . .	142	U2 Her man	39
Hee knowes, what worke h'hath done, to call this Guest, .	284	U84 Muse	81
How then? Why, as a Scrivener, if h'offend . .	329	Horace	529
HE'			
He'adulters still: his thoughts lye with a whore. .	35	E26 Beast 2	2
Is nothing, such scarce meat and drinke he'le give, .	167	U15 Friend-Wars	159
For he's both noble, lovely, young, . . .	292	U86 Hor.4:1	13
He'll thee a Marble Statue make . . .	292	U86 Hor.4:1	19
He'd say, mend this my friend, and this, 'tis nought. .	354	Horace	V624
Now, bring him backe, he'le be no more a man, .	355	Horace	V668
Polluted, touch't: but certainly he's mad: . .	355	Horace	V673
HE (See also H', HEE)			
He that departs with his owne honesty . .	27	E2 My Booke	13
By that one spell he lives, eates, drinkes, arrayes .	30	E12 Shift	5
Shee must have money: he returnes, god payes. .	30	E12 Shift	8
The taylor brings a suite home; he it 'ssayes, .	30	E12 Shift	9
He steales to ordinaries; there he playes .	30	E12 Shift	11
That lost, he keepes his chamber, reades Essayes, .	30	E12 Shift	15
To every cause he meets, this voyce he brayes: .	31	E12 Shift	19
Not his poore cocatrice but he betrayes .	31	E12 Shift	21
He that dares damne himselfe, dares more then fight. .	32	E16 Brain-hardy	10
What doth he else, but say, leave to be chast, .	34	E25 Beast 1	7
Makes serious use of all great trade he knowes. .	35	E28 Surly	3
He speakes to men with a Rhinocerotes nose, .	35	E28 Surly	4
And, that is done, as he saw great men doe. .	35	E28 Surly	6
He will both argue, and discourse in oathes, .	35	E28 Surly	9
He doth, at meales, alone, his pheasant eate, .	35	E28 Surly	12
He drinkes to no man: that's, too, like a lord. .	35	E28 Surly	14
He keepes anothers wife, which is a spice .	36	E28 Surly	15
Of solemne greatnesse. And he dares, at dice, .	36	E28 Surly	16
Nay more, for greatnesse sake, he will bo one .	36	E28 Surly	19
He toyles to be at hell, as soone as they. .	36	E31 Banck	4
He that feares death, or mournes it, in the just, .	37	E34 Death	1
But as they come, on both sides he takes fees, .	38	E37 Chev'ril	2
And pleaseth both. For while he melts his greace .	38	E37 Chev'ril	3
For this: that winnes, for whom he holds his peace. .	38	E37 Chev'ril	4
Indeed, poore Giles repents he married ever. .	40	E42 Giles	3
No more would Jone he should. Giles riseth early, .	40	E42 Giles	6
Harsh sights at home, Giles wisheth he were blind. .	40	E42 Giles	10
The children, that he keepes, Giles sweares are none .	40	E42 Giles	13
He meant they thither should make swift repaire, .	41	E44 Chuff	5
When he made him executor, might be heire. .	41	E44 Chuff	6
Will man lament the state he should envie? .	41	E45 First Son	6
As what he loves may never like too much. .	41	E45 First Son	12
'Tis Lucklesse he, that tooke up one on band .	42	E46 Luckless 1	2
Yes, now he weares his knight-hood every day. .	42	E46 Luckless 1	6
Of bearing them in field, he threw 'hem away: .	42	E48 Mungril	2
He sayes, I want the tongue of Epigrammes; .	42	E49 Playwrt 1	2
I have no salt: no bawdrie he doth meane. .	42	E49 Playwrt 1	3
At first he made low shifts, would picke and gleane, .	45	E56 Poet-Ape	5
He takes up all, makes each mans wit his owne. .	45	E56 Poet-Ape	8
And, told of this, he slights it. Tut, such crimes .	45	E56 Poet-Ape	9
He markes not whose 'twas first: and after-times .	45	E56 Poet-Ape	11
For worth he has not, He is tax'd, and not prais'd. .	48	E65 Muse	16
Two kindes of valour he doth shew, at ones; .	49	E68 Playwrt 2	3
Then to begin, my Roe: He makes a state .	50	E70 Wm Roe 1	2
T'inveigh 'gainst playes: what did he then but play? .	52	E75 Lippe	4
Nature, they thought, in all, that he would faine. .	53	E79 Rutland	8
On whom, if he were living now, to looke, .	53	E79 Rutland	10
He should those rare, and absolute numbers view, .	53	E79 Rutland	11
As he would burne, or better farre his booke. .	53	E79 Rutland	12
How wilfull blind is he then, that would stray, .	53	E80 Life/Death	3
He cast, yet keeps her well! No, shee keeps him. .	54	E82 Surly	2
I ask'd a lord a buck, and he denyed me; .	54	E84 Bedford 2	2
That his whole body should speake french, not he? .	56	E88 Monsieur	2
That he, untravell'd, should be french so much, .	56	E88 Monsieur	7
Or had his father, when he did him get, .	56	E88 Monsieur	9
The french disease, with which he labours yet? .	56	E88 Monsieur	10
And he growne youth, was call'd to his ladies chamber. .	57	E90 Mill	10
And he remov'd to gent'man of the horse, .	57	E90 Mill	12
Blowne up; and he (too'unwieldie for that place) .	57	E90 Mill	14
Hath got the stewards chaire; he will not tarry .	57	E90 Mill	15
Or Bils, and there he buyes the names of books. .	59	E92 New Crie	24
He wont was to encounter me, aloud, .	62	E97 Motion	7
Where ere he met me; now hee's dumbe, or proud. .	62	E97 Motion	8
He is no favourites favourite, no deare trust .	62	E97 Motion	13
When he was here. Nor hath he got a sute, .	63	E97 Motion	16
Since he was gone, more then the one he weares. .	63	E97 Motion	17
He that is round within himselfe, and streight, .	63	E98 Th Roe 1	3
To which, yet, of the sides himselfe he owes. .	66	E102 Pembroke	8

HE (cont.)

	Page	Title	Line
He, that but saw you weare the wheaten hat,	68	E105 L Wroth 2	7
He that not trusts me, having vow'd thus much,	70	E108 Soldiers	9
He wrote, with the same spirit that he fought,	71	E110 Edmonds 1	8
His life, but makes, that he can dye no more.	71	E110 Edmonds 1	22
In meere out-formes, untill he lost his sight,	73	E114 Sydney	4
He hath not onely gain'd himselfe his eyes,	74	E114 Sydney	7
And him it layes on; if he be not there.	74	E115 Honest Man	16
So all his meate he tasteth over, twise:	76	E118 Gut	2
He makes himselfe a thorough-fare of vice.	76	E118 Gut	4
Thus, in his belly, can he change a sin,	76	E118 Gut	5
Not he that flies the court for want of clothes,	76	E119 Shelton	1
Cryes out 'gainst cocking, since he cannot bet,	76	E119 Shelton	3
He, that, but living halfe his age, dyes such;	76	E119 Shelton	15
Yeeres he numbred scarse thirteene	77	E120 S. P.	9
Yet three fill'd Zodiackes had he beene	77	E120 S. P.	11
He plai'd so truely.	77	E120 S. P.	16
Nor he, for friendship, to be thought unfit,	78	E121 Rudyerd 1	7
One was; and he, for brawne, and braine, right able	84	E133 Voyage	23
(Who hath the hundred hands when he doth meddle)	86	E133 Voyage	82
For (where he was the god of eloquence,	86	E133 Voyage	99
They cry'd out Pusse. He told them he was Bankes,	89	E133 Voyage	183
Which when he felt, Away (quoth hee)	93	F1 Why write no	3
With which he fled me: and againe,	93	F1 Why write no	8
He knowes, below, he shall finde plentie of meate,	95	F2 Penshurst	70
To some coole, courteous shade, which he calls his,	97	F3 Wroth	19
Not doing good, scarce when he dyes.	99	F3 Wroth	84
'Tis better, if he there can dwell.	99	F3 Wroth	94
'Tis better, if he then can dwell.	99	F3 Wroth	V 94
He alwayes gives what he knowes meet;	99	F3 Wroth	98
He alwayes gives what he thinks meet;	99	F3 Wroth	V 98
He, at length, our good will sever.	102	F5 Celia 1	4
He, at length, our blisse will sever.	102	F5 Celia 1	V 4
Goe, crampe dull Mars, light Venus, when he snorts,	107	F10 Proludium	16
Though he would steale his sisters Pegasus,	107	F10 Proludium	23
And boyles, as if he were	110	F11 Epode	42
O, who is he, that (in this peace) enjoyes	110	F11 Epode	55
He that for love of goodnesse hateth ill,	112	F11 Epode	87
Then he, which for sinnes penaltie forbeares.	112	F11 Epode	89
Then he, that for sinnes penaltie forbeares.	112	F11 Epode	V 89
His heart sinnes, though he feares.	112	F11 Epode	90
Who could be false to? chiefly, when he knowes	112	F11 Epode	103
Who would be false to? chiefly, when he knowes	112	F11 Epode	V103
That knowes the waight of guilt: He will refraine	112	F11 Epode	113
For I shall move stocks, stones, no lesse then he.	115	F12 Rutland	78
Who, wheresoere he be, on what dear coast,	116	F12 Rutland	93
For that firme grace he holdes in your regard,	116	F12 Rutland	95
For he, that once is good, is ever great.	118	F13 Aubigny	52
And he may thinke on that	120	F14 Sydney	15
And he, with his best Genius left alone.	120	F14 Sydney	20
Since he doth lacke	121	F14 Sydney	27
And he that stayes	121	F14 Sydney	49
2. How he saw her.	132	U2 How he saw	Ttl
But, he had not gain'd his sight	132	U2 How he saw	13
Sooner, then he lost his might,	132	U2 How he saw	14
Both the Arrow he had quit,	132	U2 How he saw	21
He no sooner heard the Law,	133	U2 Suffered	13
Where he chanc't your name to see	136	U2 Cupid	8
Sure, said he, if I have Braine,	136	U2 Cupid	10
Can he that loves, aske lesse then one?	139	U2 Another	8
For he must looke wanton-wise.	141	U2 Her man	16
Till he cherish'd too much beard,	141	U2 Her man	23
He would have a hand as soft	141	U2 Her man	25
He should have a hand as soft	141	U2 Her man	V 25
Well he should his clothes to weare;	141	U2 Her man	36
Valiant he should be as fire,	142	U2 Her man	41
As he durst love Truth and me.	142	U2 Her man	52
But of one, if short he came,	142	U2 Her man	55
More pleasure while the thing he makes	145	U5 Woman-kind	15
I Love, and he loves me againe,	147	U7 Nymph	1
He is, if they can find him, faire,	147	U7 Nymph	15
Yet, yet I doubt he is not knowne,	147	U7 Nymph	20
But he hath eyes so round, and bright,	147	U7 Nymph	22
And he loves me; yet no	148	U7 Nymph	30
Whom never yet he durst attempt awake;	151	U11 Dreame	6
Nor will he tell me for whose sake	151	U11 Dreame	7
He did me the Delight,	151	U11 Dreame	8
As since he dares not come within my sight.	151	U11 Dreame	14
Yet he broke them, e're they could him,	151	U12 Corbet	10
'Tis true, he could not reprehend;	152	U12 Corbet	21
For truly, since he left to be,	152	U12 Corbet	35
I feele, I'm rather dead then he!	152	U12 Corbet	36
Deepest in Man, of which when he doth thinke,	153	U13 Sacvile	20
Then what he hath receiv'd. Gifts stinke from some,	153	U13 Sacvile	22
Or if he did it not to succour me,	154	U13 Sacvile	29
All this corrupts the thankes, lesse hath he wonne,	154	U13 Sacvile	33
He neither gives, or do's, that doth delay	154	U13 Sacvile	41
No more then he doth thanke, that will receive	154	U13 Sacvile	43
Dam's whom he damn'd to, as the veriest Gull,	154	U13 Sacvile	57
But one is bitten by the Dog he fed,	155	U13 Sacvile	67
Pardon, sayes he, that were a way to see	155	U13 Sacvile	71
O, is it so? knowes he so much? and will	155	U13 Sacvile	73
Yea, of th'ingratefull: and he forth must tell	155	U13 Sacvile	77

	Page	Title	Line

HE (cont.)

And feeles it; Else he tarries by the Beast.	.	.	.	.	156	U13	Sacvile	117
No! he must feele and know, that will advance.	.	.	.	.	156	U13	Sacvile	123
Or on the sudden. It were strange that he	.	.	.	.	156	U13	Sacvile	125
But nought beyond. He thou hast given it to,	.	.	.	.	161	U14	Selden	71
It true respects. He will not only love,	.	.	.	.	161	U14	Selden	73
Embrace, and cherish; but he can approve	.	.	.	.	161	U14	Selden	74
Till he becomes both their, and his owne curse!	.	.	.	.	162	U15	Friend-Wars	14
No person, nor is lov'd: what wayes he proves	.	.	.	.	162	U15	Friend-Wars	16
Crush'd in the snakie brakes, that he had past!	.	.	.	.	162	U15	Friend-Wars	18
As farre as he can flie, or follow day,	.	.	.	.	163	U15	Friend-Wars	29
As farre as he can flee, or follow day,	.	.	.	.	163	U15	Friend-Wars V	29
All which he makes the servants of the Groine,	.	.	.	.	163	U15	Friend-Wars	46
For t'other pound of sweet-meats, he shall feele	.	.	.	.	164	U15	Friend-Wars	77
That payes, or what he will: The Dame is steele.	.	.	.	.	164	U15	Friend-Wars	78
He that will follow but anothers wife,	.	.	.	.	165	U15	Friend-Wars	87
Is lov'd, though he let out his owne for life:	.	.	.	.	165	U15	Friend-Wars	88
His time? health? soule? will he for these goe throw	.	.	.	165	U15	Friend-Wars	103
To teach each suit he has, the ready way	.	.	.	.	165	U15	Friend-Wars	108
His deare and borrow'd Bravery he must cast?	.	.	.	.	165	U15	Friend-Wars	110
He that no more for Age, Cramps, Palsies, can	.	.	.	.	166	U15	Friend-Wars	135
Of what he throwes: Like letchers growne content	.	.	.	.	166	U15	Friend-Wars	139
That may stand by, and hold my peace? will he,	.	.	.	.	167	U15	Friend-Wars	150
With him, for he is follow'd with that heape	.	.	.	.	167	U15	Friend-Wars	156
But he that's both, and slave to boote, shall live,	.	.	.	167	U15	Friend-Wars	160
But he that's both, and slave to both, shall live,	.	.	.	167	U15	Friend-Wars V	160
Man thought the valianter, 'cause he durst sweare,	.	.	.	168	U15	Friend-Wars	192
For, if such men as he could die,	.	.	.	.	168	U16	Gray	6
And he is not in friendship. Nothing there	.	.	.	.	169	U17	Friend-Debt	5
That as the lesser breach: for he that takes	.	.	.	.	169	U17	Friend-Debt	11
By that faire Stand, your forehead, whence he bends	.	.	.	170	U19	Elegy By	3
He flying curles, and crispeth, with his wings;	.	.	.	.	170	U19	Elegy By	6
Where he doth steepe himselfe in Milke and Roses;	.	.	.	170	U19	Elegy By	8
As in his place, because he would not varie,	.	.	.	.	171	U19	Elegy By	27
Of all vice hurld together, there he was,	.	.	.	.	172	U21	Ltl Shrub	6
And so I leave to stirre him, lest he stinke.	.	.	.	.	172	U21	Ltl Shrub	10
By whom he is restor'd to men:	.	.	.	.	173	U22	Elegy Tho	15
And you are he: the Dietie	.	.	.	.	173	U22	Elegy Tho	25
No Armour to the mind! he is shot-free	.	.	.	.	179	U25	Desmond	48
That is not hurt; not he, that is not hit;	.	.	.	.	179	U25	Desmond	50
As he whom Maro did rehearse?	.	.	.	.	181	U27	Ode Helen	8
He that first invented thee,	.	.	.	.	184	U29	Fit of Rime	49
Clos'd to their peace, he saw his branches shoot,	.	.	.	185	U30	Burleigh	17
. . . the last Terme he sate Chancellor.	.	.	.	.	185	U31	Elsmere	Ttl
He do's you wrong, that craves you to doe right.	.	.	.	.	186	U32	Elsmere	16
None brookes the Sun-light worse then he.	.	.	.	.	189	U36	Song	4
Yet he himselfe is but a sparke.	.	.	.	.	189	U36	Song	8
Should aske the blood, and spirits he hath infus'd	.	.	.	192	U38	Elegy 'Tis	65
He pardons slips, goes by a world of ills,	.	.	.	.	193	U38	Elegy 'Tis	69
He cannot angrie be, but all must quake,	.	.	.	.	193	U38	Elegy 'Tis	71
He when he sees a sorrow such as this,	.	.	.	.	193	U38	Elegy 'Tis	87
A man should flie from, as he would disdaine.	.	.	.	.	194	U38	Elegy 'Tis	104
And turning all he toucheth into pelfe,	.	.	.	.	197	U40	Elegy That	22
Keepe secret in his Channels what he breedes,	.	.	.	.	198	U40	Elegy That	27
Doth, while he keepes his watch, betray his stand.	.	.	.	198	U40	Elegy That	36
Where he that knowes will, like a Lapwing, flie	.	.	.	198	U40	Elegy That	37
To others, as he will deserve the Trust	.	.	.	.	198	U40	Elegy That	39
Whose Readers did not thinke he was in love.	.	.	.	.	199	U42	Elegy Let	4
But is the Poets matter: And he must,	.	.	.	.	200	U42	Elegy Let	17
When he is furious, love, although not lust.	.	.	.	.	200	U42	Elegy Let	18
that from the Foot-man, when he was become	.	.	.	.	201	U42	Elegy Let	52
To ev'ry Petticote he brush'd, and Glove	.	.	.	.	201	U42	Elegy Let	54
He did lay up, and would adore the shooe,	.	.	.	.	201	U42	Elegy Let	55
From the poore wretch, which though he play'd in prose,	.	.	201	U42	Elegy Let	61
He would have done in verse, with any of those	.	.	.	201	U42	Elegy Let	62
Had he had the facultie to reade, and write!	.	.	.	.	201	U42	Elegy Let	64
Such Songsters there are store of: witnesse he	.	.	.	.	201	U42	Elegy Let	65
In smiling L'envoye, as he would deride	.	.	.	.	202	U42	Elegy Let	75
He burnt that Idoll of the Revels too:	.	.	.	.	210	U43	Vulcan	155
Hee is true Vulcan still! He did not spare	.	.	.	.	210	U43	Vulcan	159
He was right Vulcan still! He did not spare	.	.	.	.	210	U43	Vulcan V	159
He that but saw thy curious Captaines drill,	.	.	.	.	213	U44	Speach	29
The Cittie-Question, whether Tilly, or he,	.	.	.	.	214	U44	Speach	38
But he that should perswade, to have this done	.	.	.	214	U44	Speach	61
Should he heare of billow, wind, and storme,	.	.	.	.	214	U44	Speach	63
Borne, bred, allied? what's he dare tutor us?	.	.	.	.	215	U44	Speach	66
Turne him, and see his Threds: looke, if he be	.	.	.	.	216	U45	Squib	21
But he that's too-much that, is friend of none.	.	.	.	216	U45	Squib	24
. . . he was Lord chiefe Justice of England.	.	.	.	.	217	U46	Coke	Ttl
He that should search all Glories of the Gowne,	.	.	.	217	U46	Coke	1
He could not find, then thee, of all that store	.	.	.	.	217	U46	Coke	3
Be it he hold Communion	.	.	.	.	221	U48	Bacchus	43
Whereby he may knit sure up	.	.	.	.	222	U48	Bacchus	47
Not he, that should the body have, for Case	.	.	.	.	223	U49	Pucell	33
Is of so brave example, as he were	.	.	.	.	224	U50	Countesse	7
But, you are he can paint; I can but write:	.	.	.	.	227	U52	Answer	19
Ne knowes he flatt'ring Colours, or false light.	.	.	.	227	U52	Answer	21
And that he will venter	.	.	.	.	231	U57	Burges	5
He lov'd the Muses;	.	.	.	.	231	U57	Burges	9
Though now he refuses,	.	.	.	.	231	U57	Burges	10
His judgement is; If he be wise, and praise,	.	.	.	.	232	U58	Book-seller	5
He, that in such a flood, as we are in	.	.	.	.	234	U61	Epigram	16
He is the Man, and Favorite of God.	.	.	.	.	235	U61	Epigram	20

261

HE (cont.)

	Page	Title	Line
. . . he sent me in my Sicknesse. 1629.	235	U62 Charles 1	Ttl
But, that he cure the Peoples Evill too?	235	U62 Charles 1	14
Hee can, he will, and with large int'rest pay,	236	U63 Charles 2	5
What (at his liking) he will take away.	236	U63 Charles 2	6
And thinke all still the best, that he will doe.	236	U63 Charles 2	10
That thought shall make, he will this losse supply	236	U63 Charles 2	11
Cannot but heape that grace, he will requite.	236	U63 Charles 2	14
How happy were the Subject, if he knew	236	U64 Charles 3	1
How many times, Live long, Charles, would he say,	236	U64 Charles 3	3
If he but weigh'd the blessings of this day?	236	U64 Charles 3	4
Nor dares he come in the comparison.	241	U69 Friend Son	8
Till he had sold his Piece, drawne so unlike:	242	U69 Friend Son	13
To keepe him off; and how-so-e're he gleanes	242	U69 Friend Son	16
Some of his formes, he lets him not come neere	242	U69 Friend Son	17
Where he would fixe, for the distinctions feare.	242	U69 Friend Son	18
He vexed time, and busied the whole State;	243	U70 Ode	27
How well at twentie had he falne, or stood!	243	U70 Ode	31
For three of his foure-score, he did no good.	243	U70 Ode	32
He purchas'd friends, and fame, and honours then,	244	U70 Ode	35
So deep, as he did then death's waters sup;	244	U70 Ode	41
And there he lives with memorie; and Ben	246	U70 Ode	84
Jonson, who sung this of him, e're he went	246	U70 Ode	85
Or taste a part of that full joy he meant	246	U70 Ode	87
When he beholds a graft of his owne hand,	251	U74 Weston	27
He had so highly set; and, in what Barbican.	256	U75 Epithalam.	112
He had so highly plac'd; and, in what Barbican.	256	U75 Epithalam.	V112
Askes first, Who gives her (I Charles) then he plights	256	U75 Epithalam.	124
Yet read him in these lines: He doth excell	262	U78 Digby	2
Yet take him in these lines: He doth excell	262	U78 Digby	V 2
And he is built like some imperiall roome	262	U78 Digby	7
Goe, Muse, in, and salute him. Say he be	262	U78 Digby	19
Goe, Muse, in, and salute him thoughe he be	262	U78 Digby	V 19
Busie, or frowne at first; when he sees thee,	262	U78 Digby	20
He will cleare up his forehead, thinke thou bring'st	263	U78 Digby	21
He will cheare up his forehead, thinke thou bring'st	263	U78 Digby	V 21
For he doth love my Verses, and will looke	263	U78 Digby	23
See where he walkes with Mira by his side.	264	U79 New-yeares	18
Where e're he goes upon the ground,	265	U79 New-yeares	58
But as he soares at that, he bruiseth then	272	U81 Pawlet	98
Hee shall, if he can understand,	276	U84 Body	11
Against the Nature he would worship. Hee	284	U84 Muse	75
He that shall be our supreme Judge, should leave	286	U84 Muse	148
The smallest Fibre of our flesh; he can	286	U84 Muse	151
And best he knew her noble Character,	287	U84 Muse	155
To one she said, Doe this, he did it; So	287	U84 Muse	169
To another, Move; he went; To a third, Go,	287	U84 Muse	170
He run; and all did strive with diligence	287	U84 Muse	171
Happie is he, that from all Businesse cleere,	289	U85 Country	1
The Poplar tall, he then doth marrying twine	290	U85 Country	9
With which, Priapus, he may thanke thy hands,	290	U85 Country	21
With which, Priapus, he may greet thy hands,	290	U85 Country	V 21
Then now beneath some ancient Oke he may,	290	U85 Country	23
Or hence, or thence, he drives with many a Hound	290	U85 Country	31
'Gainst th'Ides, his moneys he gets in with paine,	291	U85 Country	69
'Gainst th'Ides, his gott moneyes he gets in with paine,	291	U85 Country	V 69
Will he display the Ensignes of thy warre	292	U86 Hor.4:1	16
And when he smiling finds his Grace	292	U86 Hor.4:1	17
Though he be fairer then a Starre;	294	U87 Hor.3:9	21
What's this? if he whose money hireth thee	305	Horace	26
Hath neither soule, nor sinewes. Loftie he	307	Horace	37
So he that varying still affects to draw	339	Horace	V 42/ 40
But in the maine worke haplesse: since he knowes	307	Horace	48
His matter to his power, in all he makes,	307	Horace	57
Of some small thankfull land: whether he bee	313	Horace	166
A meere new person, looke he keepe his state	313	Horace	180
Unto the last, as when he first went forth,	313	Horace	181
But light from smoake; that he may draw his bright	315	Horace	204
Of Meleager, brings he the returne	315	Horace	208
He ever hastens to the end, and so	315	Horace	211
(As if he knew it) rapps his hearer to	315	Horace	212
What he despaires, being handled, might not show.	315	Horace	214
He knowes not why, and changeth every houre.	315	Horace	228
And then as swift to leave what he hath lov'd.	315	Horace	236
What straight-way he must labour to retract.	315	Horace	240
Either because he seekes, and, having found,	317	Horace	242
Of the times past, when he was a young lad;	317	Horace	248
Gesture, and riot, whilst he swooping went	319	Horace	304
Gesture, and riot, whilst he wandring went	346	Horace	V304
How he could jest, because he mark'd and saw,	319	Horace	323
Or, whilst he shuns the Earth, to catch at Aire	321	Horace	335
Yet he that offers at it, may sweat much,	321	Horace	351
What to his Countrey, what his friends he owes,	325	Horace	446
Of a brave Chiefe sent to the warres: He can,	325	Horace	451
He cries, Good boy, thou'lt keepe thine owne. Now, adde	327	Horace	470
And lead them with soft songs, where that he would.	327	Horace	485
But he hath every suffrage, can apply	329	Horace	514
So he that flaggeth much, becomes to mee	329	Horace	533
His armes in Mars his field, he doth refuse:	331	Horace	566
Or trundling Wheele, he can sit still, from all;	331	Horace	568
While he was young; he sweat; and freez'd againe:	333	Horace	589
His flatterers to their gaine. But say, he can	333	Horace	601
His praisers to their gaine: but say he can	353	Horace	V601

HE (cont.)

	Page	Title	Line
If of their friendship he be worthy, or no:	333	Horace	619
Then change; no word, or worke, more would he spend	335	Horace	630
On artlesse Verse; the hard ones he will blame;	335	Horace	634
The while he belcheth loftie Verses out,	335	Horace	649
Busie to catch a Black-bird; if he fall	335	Horace	651
Into a pit, or hole; although he call,	335	Horace	652
To let it downe, who knowes, if he did cast	335	Horace	656
Not thence be sav'd, although indeed he could?	335	Horace	658
Hee, while he labour'd to be thought a God	335	Horace	661
Nor did he doe this once; for if you can	335	Horace	667
Nor did he do this, once; if yet you can,	355	Horace	V667
Whether he piss'd upon his Fathers grave;	335	Horace	671
Or the sad thunder-stroken thing he have	335	Horace	672
(Defiled) touch'd; but certaine he was mad,	337	Horace	673
And, as a Beare, if he the strength but had	337	Horace	674
Learn'd and unlearn'd; holding, whom once he takes;	337	Horace	677
Learn'd, and unlearn'd; holdeth whom once he takes;	355	Horace	V677
Not letting goe his hold, where he drawes food,	337	Horace	679
Not letting goe the skin, where he drawes food,	355	Horace	V679
Till he drop off, a Horse-leech, full of blood.	337	Horace	680
Till, horse-leech-like, he drop off, full of blood.	355	Horace	V680
Marke, marke, but when his wing he takes,	366	Ode Who saith	9
How faire a flight he makes!	366	Ode Who saith	10
He shew'd him first the hoofe-cleft Spring,	366	Ode Who saith	17
To utmost Thule: whence, he backes the Seas	368	Ode Who saith	69
To him, and he there shrin'd;	369	Ode Who saith	106
For he did but kisse her, and so let her go.	375	Coryat 1	19
Religiously here he bids, row from the stewes,	375	Coryat 1	20
He will expiate this sinne with converting the Jewes.	375	Coryat 1	21
And there, while he gives the zealous Bravado,	375	Coryat 1	22
For Grapes he had gather'd before they were eaten.	375	Coryat 1	25
F. shewes what he was, K. what he will bee.	375	Coryat 1	29
And here he disdained not, in a forraine land	375	Coryat 1	32
Beeing in feare to be robd, he most learnedly begs.	375	Coryat 1	35
Of travell he discourseth so at large,	378	Coryat 2	82
Marry he sets it out at his owne charge;	378	Coryat 2	83
Shewes he dares more then Paules Church-yard durst do.	378	Coryat 2	85
Who ever he be, would write a Story and	379	Coryat 3	1
Since he treads in no other Mans steps but his owne.	379	Coryat 3	12
And that you may see he most luckily ment	379	Coryat 3	13
To write it with the selfe same spirit he went,	379	Coryat 3	14
He sayes to the world, let any man mend it,	379	Coryat 3	15
In five monthes he went it, in five monthes he pend it.	379	Coryat 3	16
He went out at each place, and at what he came in,	380	Coryat 3	25
How long he did stay, at what signe he did Inne.	380	Coryat 3	26
Besides he tried Ship, Cart, Waggon, and Chayre,	380	Coryat 3	27
Of lying, he feares so much the reproofe	380	Coryat 3	31
That he dares to informe you, but somewhat meticulous,	380	Coryat 3	33
He was in his travaile, how like to be beaten,	380	Coryat 3	35
For grapes he had gather'd, before they were eaten	380	Coryat 3	36
How faine for his venery he was to crie (Tergum o)	380	Coryat 3	37
I meane that one paire, wherewith he so hobled	380	Coryat 3	41
How many learned men he have drawne with his hooke	380	Coryat 3	44
He there doth protest he saw of the eleven.	380	Coryat 3	46
Jest, he saies. Item one sute of blacke taffata	380	Coryat 3	48
Doth he once dissemble, but tels he did ride	380	Coryat 3	52
Some want, they say in a sort he did crave:	380	Coryat 3	55
I writ he onely his taile there did wave;	380	Coryat 3	56
Which he not denies. Now being so free,	381	Coryat 3	57
To see his worke be good; but that he looke	385	Husband	2
He would be call'd, henceforth, the English-Rogue,	389	Aleman	16
O, could he but have drawne his wit	390	Reader	5
As well in brasse, as he hath hit	390	Reader	6
But, since he cannot, Reader, looke	390	Reader	9
. . . Mr. William Shakespeare: And what he hath left us.	390	Shakespeare	Ttl
He was not of an age, but for all time!	391	Shakespeare	43
When like Apollo he came forth to warme	392	Shakespeare	45
His Art doth give the fashion. And, that he,	392	Shakespeare	58
(And himselfe with it) that he thinkes to frame;	392	Shakespeare	62
Or for the lawrell, he may gaine a scorne,	392	Shakespeare	63
In each of which, he seemes to shake a Lance,	392	Shakespeare	69
But of one Husband; and since he left life,	394	Jane Ogle	16
So wood at last, that he was wonne to her	394	Jane Ogle	22
And when he ships them where to use their Armes,	398	Drayton	65
Of any Art, besyde what he calls his!	404	Inigo Jones 1	58
The Scene! the Engyne! but he now is come	404	Inigo Jones 1	62
He is, or would be the mayne Dominus doe	404	Inigo Jones 1	64
Hee's warme on his feet now he sayes, & can	405	Inigo Jones 1	67
I am too fat t'envy him. He too leane	405	Inigo Jones 1	69
What would he doe now, gi'ng his mynde that waye	405	Inigo Jones 1	75
How would he firke? lyke Adam overdooe	405	Inigo Jones 1	79
Under the Morall? shewe he had a pate	405	Inigo Jones 1	83
He may have skill & judgment to designe	406	Inigo Jones 2	7
Or Ale! He build a pallace! Thou a shopp	407	Inigo Jones 2	9
He draw a Forum, with quadriviall Streets!	407	Inigo Jones 2	11
He some Colossus to bestryde the Seas,	407	Inigo Jones 2	13
He makes the Camell & dull Ass his prize.	408	Inigo Jones 3	8
To aske thy name, if he have half his Nose!	409	Detractor	18
Till he hath reach'd his two-fold point of Noone.	414	Ghyrlond	52
Just and fit actions Ptolemey (he saith)	422	Lucan	1
he that will honest be, may quitt the Court,	423	Lucan	17
Here he speaks out of his Pottle,	657	Door Apollo	3

HE (cont.)
```
He the half of Life abuses,                                      657  Door Apollo       9
And sworne, that he will quite discard thee                      662  Bedford           7
HEAD
Camden, most reverend head, to whom I owe                         31  E14 Camden        1
Phoebus replyed. Bold head, it is not shee:                       80  E126 Mrs Cary     7
Into the debt; and reckon on her head,                            80  E127 Aubigny      5
The tripple head without a sop. At last,                          89  E133 Voyage     186
Which boasts t'have had the head of gold.                         98  F3 Wroth         64
Render his head in there againe?                                 101  F4 To the World  32
Of his dull god-head, were sinne. Ile implore                    107  F10 Proludium     6
Of his dull god-head, were sinne. Lets implore                   107  F10 Proludium   V 6
Or, in an armies head, that, lockt in brasse,                    114  F12 Rutland      52
Borne up by statues, shall I reare your head,                    115  F12 Rutland      84
besett with statues, shall I reare your head,                    115  F12 Rutland    V 84
Coriat, should rise the most sufficient head                     157  U13 Sacvile     128
Her upright head, above the reach of Chance,                     176  U25 Desmond       6
Upon th'Exchange, still, out of Popes-head-Alley;                206  U43 Vulcan       80
If the 'Chequer be emptie, so will be his Head.                  232  U57 Burges       28
To God, denies the God-head to be true:                          235  U63 Charles 2     2
Accept this garland, plant it on thy head,                       245  U70 Ode          77
Of Love betweene you, and your Lovely-head:                      257  U75 Epithalam.  164
The Serpents head: Gets above Death, and Sinne,                  272  U81 Pawlet       99
Who violates the God-head, is most vitious                       284  U84 Muse         74
His head, with mellow Apples crown'd,                            290  U85 Country      18
Thy locks, and rosie garlands crowne thy head;                   294  U89 Mart.3:77     4
If to a Womans head a Painter would                              305  Horace           1
As neither head, nor foot, one forme retaine.                    305  Horace          10
The rash, and head-long eloquence brought forth                  319  Horace         307
The head that three Anticira's cannot heale.                     349  Horace        V428
Their hornes, and Germany pukes on his head.                     375  Coryat 1        31
Pearch'd over head, the wise Athenian Owle:                      397  Drayton         34
As if they' ador'd the Head, wheron th'are fixt.                 413  Ghyrlond        28
HEADED
The wise, and many-headed Bench, that sits                       370  Fletcher         1
HEADES
that the wife heades for a wager                                 417  Moon            26
HEAD-LONG
The rash, and head-long eloquence brought forth                  319  Horace         307
HEADLONG
'Twas Jupiter that hurl'd thee headlong downe,                   203  U43 Vulcan       9
'Twas Jupiter that cast thee headlong downe,                     203  U43 Vulcan     V 9
HEADS
At naming the French King, their heads they shake,                59  E92 New Crie    33
Over your heads: Well, row. At this a loud                        86  E133 Voyage     93
The heads, houghs, entrailes, and the hides of dogs:              88  E133 Voyage    146
Of Hol'borne (three sergeants heads) lookes ore,                  89  E133 Voyage    177
To know the heads of danger! where 'tis fit                      233  U59 Newcastle   17
Their Heads, that Envy would hold downe                          272  U84 Cradle       3
Their heads, which three Anticyra's cannot heale.                325  Horace         428
The knottie heads of the most surly Groomes,                     363  Riches           8
HE'ADULTERS
He'adulters still: his thoughts lye with a whore.                 35  E26 Beast 2      2
HEALE
Their heads, which three Anticyra's cannot heale.                325  Horace         428
The head that three Anticira's cannot heale.                     349  Horace        V428
HEALTH
Thou hast thy walkes for health, as well as sport:                93  F2 Penshurst     9
Play away, health, wealth, and fame.                             105  F8 Sicknesse    42
I ne're will owe my health to a disease.                         150  U10 Jealousie   16
Lowd sacrifice of drinke, for their health-sake!                 156  U13 Sacvile    100
Ben: Jonson To His Honord Friend Mr John Selden Health.          158  U14 Selden    VTtl
His time? health? soule? will he for these goe throw             165  U15 Friend-Wars 103
Surfet? and Quarrel? drinkes the tother health?                  166  U15 Friend-Wars 115
So, from all sicknesse, may you rise to health,                  186  U31 Elsmere      5
Under another Name, I take your health;                          197  U40 Elegy That  10
My health will leave me; and when you depart,                    199  U41 Elegy Since  13
Or else a health advances,                                       222  U48 Bacchus     49
An Epigram to the Queens Health.                                 238  U66 Queene    VTtl
Of so much health, both to our Land, and King.                   238  U66 Queene     V 14
Health, or scarce breath, as she had never bin,                  248  U71 Treasurer   12
HEALTHS
Nor care I now healths to propound;                              293  U86 Hor.4:1     31
HEALTH-SAKE
Lowd sacrifice of drinke, for their health-sake!                 156  U13 Sacvile    100
HEAP
Could heap to a perfection, was her Act!                         270  U81 Pawlet    V 46
HEAPE
Let that goe heape a masse of wretched wealth,                    99  F3 Wroth        81
In time 'twill be a heape; This is not true                      157  U13 Sacvile    133
With him, for he is follow'd with that heape                     167  U15 Friend-Wars 156
A parcell of Court-durt, a heape, and masse                      172  U21 Ltl Shrub    5
Cannot but heape that grace, he will requite.                    236  U63 Charles 2   14
HEAP'D
And, in some yeere, all these together heap'd,                    69  E107 Hungry    15
Or, that it lay, heap'd like an usurers masse,                    88  E133 Voyage    139
Did'st thou, then, make 'hem! and what praise was heap'd          95  F2 Penshurst   83
HEAPES
Lest the throng'd heapes should on a laughter take:              331  Horace         569
HEAPING
If Praises, when th'are full, heaping admit,                     385  Brooke           6
HEAPS
Those proud, ambitious heaps, and nothing else,                   96  F2 Penshurst  101
```

HEARD   (NOUN)
| As the whole heard in sight, | . . . . . | 366 | Ode Who saith | 26 |

HEARD
But, when they heard it tax'd, tooke more offence.	. .	60	E94 Bedford 3	10
Arses were heard to croake, in stead of frogs;	.	84	E133 Voyage	13
Laden with plague-sores, and their sinnes, were heard,	.	84	E133 Voyage	17
Man, that had never heard of a Chimaera.	. .	86	E133 Voyage	80
How hight the place? a voyce was heard, Cocytus.	.	86	E133 Voyage	89
But I will speake (and know I shall be heard)	.	87	E133 Voyage	105
(Which with griefe and wrath I heard)	. . .	132	U2 How he saw	29
He no sooner heard the Law,	. . . .	133	U2 Suffered	13
All that heard her, with desire.	. . .	139	U2 Promise	6
Heard what times past have said, seene what ours doe:	.	159	U14 Selden	34
Who, when shee heard the match, concluded streight,	.	229	U54 Squib	5
Who claimes (of reverence) to be heard,	.	274	U84 Cradle	34
T'accuse, or quit all Parties to be heard!	.	284	U84 Muse	60
Must maintaine manly; not be heard to sing,	.	317	Horace	277
Must manly keep, and not be heard to sing	.	345	Horace	V277
Who, since, to sing the Pythian Rites is heard,	.	333	Horace	591
Who now to sing the Pythian Rites is heard,	.	353	Horace	V591
That heard but Spight deliver	. .	367	Ode Who saith	58
Heard the soft ayres, between our Swaynes & thee,	.	397	Drayton	26
My lippes could forme the voyce, I heard that Rore,	.	397	Drayton	38
And truely, so I would, could I be heard.	. .	414	Rutter	3

HEARDS
| 'Mongst loughing heards, and solide hoofes: | . . | 97 | F3 Wroth | 16 |

HEARE
May heare my Epigrammes, but like of none.	.	36	E28 Surly	20
To reade my verses; now I must to heare:	.	45	E58 Groome	2
Whil'st thy weigh'd judgements, Egerton, I heare,	.	51	E74 Chancelor	1
When Sydnyes name I heare, or face I see:	.	73	E114 Sydney	2
And heare her speake with one, and her first tongue;	.	78	E122 Rudyerd 2	6
Would'st thou heare, what man can say	.	79	E124 Elizabeth	1
And though we could all men, all censures heare,	.	83	E131 Ferrab. 2	5
Is this we heare? of frogs? No, guts wind-bound,	.	86	E133 Voyage	92
A-bed canst heare the loud stag speake,	.	97	F3 Wroth	22
Of all his happinesse? But soft: I heare	.	111	F11 Epode	65
If it may stand with your soft blush to heare	.	117	F13 Aubigny	22
Heare, what the Muses sing about thy roote,	.	119	F13 Aubigny	100
To heare, to mediate, sweeten my desire,	.	128	U1 Trinitie	42
Heare mee, O God!	. . .	129	U1 Father	1
Heare and make Example too.	. . .	133	U2 Suffered	26
Heare, what late Discourse of you,	.	136	U2 Cupid	5
And last, blaspheme not, we did never heare	.	168	U15 Friend-Wars	191
Such shall you heare to day, and find great foes,	.	186	U32 Elsmere	7
But when I read or heare the names so rife	.	187	U33 Councellour	7
In friendship, I confesse: But, deare friend, heare.	.	190	U37 Friend-Book	18
Heare, Mistris, your departing servant tell	.	193	U41 Elegy Since	2
Should he heare of billow, wind, and storme,	.	214	U44 Speach	63
Though I doe neither heare these newes, nor tell	.	219	U47 Tribe	46
Or what we heare our home-borne Legend tell,	.	228	U53 Newcastle	9
Thou, Friend, wilt heare all censures; unto thee	.	232	U58 Book-seller	1
That scarce you heare a publike voyce alive,	.	234	U61 Epigram	5
With love, to heare your modestie relate,	.	251	U74 Weston	21
Heare, o you Groves, and, Hills, resound his praise.	.	264	U79 New-yeares	23
Heare, O you Groves, and, Hills, resound his worth.	.	264	U79 New-yeares	31
To heare their Judge, and his eternall doome;	.	283	U84 Muse	48
In his humanitie! To heare him preach	.	286	U84 Muse	133
heare me conclude; let what thou workst upon	.	339	Horace	V 31
Heare, what it is the People, and I desire:	.	315	Horace	219
Angry. Sometimes, I heare good Homer snore.	.	329	Horace	536
Angry, if once I heare good Homer snore.	.	351	Horace	V512/536
All which, when they but heare a straine	.	368	Ode Who saith	89
To life againe, to heare thy Buskin tread,	.	391	Shakespeare	36
But that I heare, againe, thy Drum to beate	.	397	Drayton	55
Sir Inigo doth feare it as I heare	.	407	Inigo Jones 3	1
shee soone will heare it.	. . .	417	Moon	24

HEARER
| (As if he knew it) rapps his hearer to | . | 315 | Horace | 212 |

HEARERS
| Thy Hearers Nectar, and thy Clients Balme, | . | 187 | U33 Councellour | 36 |
| To worke the hearers minds, still, to their plight. | . | 311 | Horace | 142 |

HEARES
What Nymph so e're his voyce but heares,	.	148	U7 Nymph	27
Although my Fame, to his, not under-heares,	.	219	U47 Tribe	49
Whilst it the Dittie heares.	.	239	U67 Muses	24

HEARING
Play-wright, by chance, hearing some toyes I'had writ,	.	64	E100 Playwrt 3	1
10. Another Ladyes exception present at the hearing.	.	142	U2 Exception	Ttl
Hearing their charge, and then	. .	256	U75 Epithalam.	127

HEARKENS
| That hearkens to a Jacks-pulse, when it goes. | . | 216 | U45 Squib | 6 |

HEARSE   (See HERSE)

HEAR'ST
| For all thou hear'st, thou swear'st thy selfe didst doo. | . | 54 | E81 Proule | 5 |

HEARST
| But cause thou hearst the mighty k. of Spaine | . | 406 | Inigo Jones 2 | 1 |

HEART   (See also HART)
Before thou wert it, in each good mans heart.	.	49	E67 Suffolk	10
Or with thy friends; the heart of all the yeere,	.	97	F3 Wroth	25
Object arrive there, but the heart (our spie)	.	109	F11 Epode	11
(That should ring larum to the heart) doth sleepe,	.	109	F11 Epode	23
(That shal ring larum to the heart) doth sleepe,	.	109	F11 Epode	V 23

		Page	Title	Line

HEART (cont.)
His heart sinnes, though he feares. . . . . 112 F11 Epode 90
As my heart lies in peeces, all confus'd, . . . 127 U1 Trinitie 7
A broken heart thou wert not wont despise, . . . 127 U1 Trinitie 10
What odour can be, then a heart contrite, . . . 127 U1 Trinitie 15
A broken heart, ... 129 U1 Father 2
Left it sticking in my heart: . . . . 133 U2 Suffered 16
I could give my very heart; . . . . 142 U2 Her man 54
Unlesse my heart would as my thought be torne. . . 147 U7 Nymph 14
From either heart, I know; . . . . 148 U7 Nymph 32
Hath both my heart and me surpriz'd, . . . 151 U11 Dreame 5
Love to my heart, and Fortune to my lines. . . 170 U18 Elegy Can 24
(Whose heart in that bright Sphere flames clearest, . 179 U25 Desmond 54
Your forme shines here, here fixed in my heart: . . 194 U38 Elegy That 117
Can lock the Sense up, or the heart a thought; . . 198 U40 Elegy That 43
How shall I doe, sweet Mistris, for my heart? . . 199 U41 Elegy Since 14
A letter'd mind, and a large heart would place . . 227 U52 Answer 23
And with the heart, not pen, . . . 247 U70 Ode 124
T'effect it, feele, thou'ast made thine owne heart ake. . 250 U73 Weston 12
By all the Spheares consent, so in the heart of June? . 253 U75 Epithalam. 16
Nor can the bruised heart want eloquence: . . 288 U84 Muse 186
And Peleus, if they seeke to heart-strike us . . 311 Horace 136
The truth of his heart there, and tell's what a clocke . 380 Coryat 3 24
At these thy Nuptials; but, whose heart, and thought . 384 Somerset 3
HEARTED
Hard-hearted, I dreame every Night . . . 293 U86 Hor.4:1 37
HEARTH (See HARTH)
HEARTS
To murther different hearts, . . . 110 F11 Epode 52
And hearts of all, if I be sad for show, . . . 122 F15 Heaven 6
As she goes, all hearts doe duty . . . 134 U2 Triumph 5
Is my Mothers! Hearts of slaine . . . 137 U2 Cupid 31
Both braines and hearts; and mine now best doe know it: 182 U28 Worth 8
Why yet, my noble hearts, they cannot say, . . 213 U44 Speach 1
My Lord, till felt griefe make our stone hearts soft, . 234 U61 Epigram 14
To make the hearts of a whole Nation smile, . . 238 U66 Queene 10
Of hearts the union. And those not by chance . . 246 U70 Ode 99
That cry that gladnesse, which their hearts would pray, . 249 U72 King 2
The cries, the gladnesse, which their hearts would pay, . 249 U72 King 2
Who knowes the hearts of all, and can dissect . . 249 U72 King V 14
T'imprint in all purg'd hearts this virgin sence, . . 286 U84 Muse 150
HEART-STRIKE . . . 414 Ghyrlond 55
And Peleus, if they seeke to heart-strike us . . 311 Horace 136
HEARTY
I send this small, but hearty testimony: and with charge, 666 Glover 5
HEAT
One sparke of your Diviner heat . . . 174 U22 Elegy Tho 31
Thy Priest in this strange rapture; heat my braine . 177 U25 Desmond 11
The Sunne his heat, and light, the ayre his dew? . 192 U38 Elegy 'Tis 57
Alas I ha' lost my heat, my blood, my prime, . . 199 U41 Elegy Since 11
The heat, and splendor, but not handle fire! . . 269 U81 Pawlet V 32
For lust will languish, and that heat decay. . . 294 U88 Petronius 5
And heat, with softest love, thy softer bed. . . 295 U89 Mart.8:77 6
(Such as thine are) and strike the second heat . . 392 Shakespeare 60
Of Lanterne-lerry: with fuliginous heat . . 405 Inigo Jones 1 72
HEATE
Or with thy friends; the heate of all the yeere, . . 97 F3 Wroth V 25
And ev'ry birth encrease the heate of Love. . . 384 Somerset 20
A better cause, and strike the bravest heate . . 397 Drayton 56
Fames heate upon the grave did stay; . . . 400 Lady Ogle 28
HEATES
Who durst live great, 'mongst all the colds, and heates, 233 U59 Newcastle 21
HEATING
Though but while mettal's heating: . . . 179 U25 Desmond 43
HEATS
And that there be no fev'ry heats, nor colds, . . 220 U47 Tribe 67
HEAV'D
Like life unto 'hem. Who heav'd Hercules . . 115 F12 Rutland 57
HEAV'EN
which rap's mee up to the true heav'en of love; . . 108 F10 Proludium 13
HEAVEN
To heaven; his hath: O happy state! wherein . . 35 E27 Roe 1 7
Which if most gracious heaven grant like thine, . . 37 E33 Roe 3 5
T'our times return'd, hath made her heaven in thee. . 52 E74 Chancelor 10
As Heaven and Nature seem'd to strive . . . 77 E120 S. P. 7
Heaven vowes to keepe him. . . . 77 E120 S. P. 24
To say, indeed, shee were the soule of heaven, . . 82 E130 Ferrab. 1 11
Or whose great name in Poets heaven use, . . 107 F10 Proludium 2
It is a golden chaine let downe from heaven, . . 110 F11 Epode 47
That which, to boote with hell, is thought worth heaven, 113 F12 Rutland 3
It is the Muse, alone, can raise to heaven, . . 114 F12 Rutland 41
Then which, a nobler heaven it selfe knowes not. . 115 F12 Rutland 67
To Heaven. . . . . 122 F15 Heaven Ttl
The Word, which heaven, and earth did make; . . 130 U1 Nativitie 11
Mistaking earth for heaven. . . . 144 U3 Musicall 24
That heaven should make no more; or should amisse, . 188 U34 Small Poxe 15
Sir, I am thankfull, first, to heaven, for you; . . 189 U37 Friend-Book 1
Thinke that your selfe like heaven forgive me can: . 192 U38 Elegy 'Tis 32
Is natures meere obliquitie! as Heaven . . 192 U38 Elegy 'Tis 64
In a calme skie, then when the heaven is horl'd . . 193 U38 Elegy 'Tis 74
I wish all well, and pray high heaven conspire . . 219 U47 Tribe 37
Still looking to, and ever loving heaven; . . 219 U47 Tribe 61
To lift to heaven: who is't not understands . . 234 U61 Epigram 8

		Page	Title	Line

HEAVEN (cont.)

How much to heaven for thee, great Charles, they owe!   237 U64 Charles 3   22
It is too neere of kin to Heaven, the Soule,   269 U81 Pawlet   29
If you dare grudge at Heaven, and repent   271 U81 Pawlet   79
If you dare Quarrell Heaven, and repent   271 U81 Pawlet   V 79
And, sure of Heaven, rides triumphing in.   272 U81 Pawlet   100
Of Heaven; where Seraphim take tent   273 U84 Cradle   31
The Heaven design'd, draw next a Spring,   276 U84 Body   21
As it slid moulded off from Heaven.   280 U84 Mind   56
In heaven Empyre, and with a robe of light?   285 U84 Muse   102
And fill'd an Orbe as circular, as heaven!   396 Drayton   19
T'Is a Record in heaven. You, that were   399 Lady Ogle   1

HEAVENS

Yet, all heavens gifts, being heavens due,   33 E22 Daughter   3
Whose soule heavens Queene, (whose name shee beares)   33 E22 Daughter   7
Read not in faire heavens storie,   39 E40 Ratcliffe   6
Speakes Heavens Language! and discourseth free   271 U81 Pawlet   71
Speakes Heavens Language! and discovereth free   271 U81 Pawlet   V 71
Would aske a Heavens Intelligence?   278 U84 Mind   14
The House of gold, the Gate of heavens power,   413 Ghyrlond   39

HEAVIE

Nothing I doe; but, like a heavie wheele,   283 U84 Muse   30
Those heavie Verses, sent so to the Stage,   323 Horace   384

HEAV'N

Great heav'n did well, to give ill fame free wing;   43 E51 James 3   2
Whilst that in heav'n, this light on earth must shine.   246 U70 Ode   96
In heav'n the Signe of old Eridanus: 369 Ode Who saith   109

HEBRID

The Hebrid Isles, and knowne   368 Ode Who saith   66

HE'D

He'd say, mend this my friend, and this, 'tis nought.   354 Horace   V624

HEE'

The knight-wright's cheated then: Hee'll never pay.   42 E46 Luckless 1   5
Hee's valiant'st, that dares fight, and not for pay;   49 E66 Cary   17
Since when, hee's sober againe, and all play's made.   56 E87 Hazard   6
Where ere he met me; now hee's dumbe, or proud.   62 E97 Motion   8
To love one man, hee'd leave her first.   146 U6 Defence   24
Looke to and cure; Hee's not a man hath none,   156 U13 Sacvile   115
Hee's one of blood, and fashion! and with these   164 U15 Friend-Wars   55
And free societie, hee's borne else-where,   197 U40 Elegy That   16
Out with the other, for hee's still at home;   198 U40 Elegy That   34
Hee'ld frame such ditties of their store, and want,   241 U68 House-hold   7
Hee's Master of the Office; yet no more   258 U75 Epithalam.   187
Hee's prudent, valiant, just, and temperate;   262 U78 Digby   5
Hee's good, as great. I am almost a stone!   269 U81 Pawlet   11
And purple-matching Grapes, hee's glad!   290 U85 Country   20
For hee'll cry, Good, brave, better, excellent!   333 Horace   611
Hee'd say, Mend this, good friend, and this; 'tis naught.   333 Horace   624
Hee'd bid, blot all: and to the anvile bring   333 Horace   627
Recall him yet, hee'ld be no more a man: 335 Horace   668
Hee's carried 'twixt Montrell and Abbevile.   374 Coryat 1   13
Hee's carried like a Cripple, from Constable to Constable.   374 Coryat 1   17
Here, by a Boore too, hee's like to be beaten   375 Coryat 1   24
But that hee's too well suted, in a cloth,   389 Aleman   17
Hee's warme on his feet now he sayes, & can   405 Inigo Jones 1   67
Hee'll be a Pilot, scarce can guide a Plough.   410 Brome   18

HEE

I sent the cause: Hee wooes with an ill sprite.   33 E19 Cod 1   2
Which hee thinkes great; and so reades verses, too: 35 E28 Surly   5
Hee that wooes every widdow, will get none.   42 E47 Luckless 2   2
For, but thy selfe, where, out of motly, 's hee   44 E53 Old-end   9
How well, faire crowne of your faire sexe, might hee,   66 E103 L Wroth 1   1
But, in the action, greater man then hee: 84 E133 Voyage   26
But many Moones there shall not wane (quoth hee)   87 E133 Voyage   103
Which when he felt, Away (quoth hee)   93 F1 Why write no   3
Hee whom the whole world could not take,   130 U1 Nativitie   10
Strait hee ran, and durst not stay,   132 U2 How he saw   16
3. What hee suffered.   133 U2 Suffered   Ttl
As hath the youngest Hee,   149 U9 Picture   9
As makes the youngest Hee,   149 U9 Picture   V 9
As light, and active as the youngest hee   200 U42 Elegy Let   6
Wast not hee: thou wert of old denied   203 U43 Vulcan   V 11
Hee is true Vulcan still! He did not spare   210 U43 Vulcan   159
What then his Father was, that since is hee,   225 U51 Bacon   11
Thanke him: if other, hee can give no Bayes.   232 U58 Book-seller   6
Hee can, he will, and with large int'rest pay,   236 U63 Charles 2   5
Hee entred well, by vertuous parts,   244 U70 Ode   33
Hee stoop'd in all mens sight   244 U70 Ode   38
Hee never fell, thou fall'st, my tongue.   244 U70 Ode   44
Hee never fell, thou tripst, my tongue.   244 U70 Ode   V 44
Hee stood, a Souldier to the last right end,   244 U70 Ode   45
Hee leap'd the present age,   245 U70 Ode   79
. . . high Treasurer of England, Upon the Day, Hee was . . .   250 U73 Weston   Ttl
gentlie hee asketh, shee will pay: no suits,   258 U75 Epithalam.   V188
But hee lasteth and unlay'd.   259 U76 Petition   V 24
When hee shall read them at the Treasurers bord,   263 U78 Digby   27
When hee doth read them at the Treasurers bord,   263 U78 Digby   V 27
Hee is the Father of our peace;   264 U79 New-yeares   40
'Tis hee, 'tis hee, in singing hee.   265 U79 New-yeares   54
Hee gives all plentie, and encrease,   265 U79 New-yeares   56
Hee is the author of our peace.   265 U79 New-yeares   57
To sweeter Pastures lead hee can,   265 U79 New-yeares   60
Hee drives diseases from our Folds,   265 U79 New-yeares   62

	Page	Title	Line
HEE (cont.)			
'Tis hee, 'tis hee, in singing hee,	265	U79 New-yeares	66
Hee gives all plentie, and encrease,	265	U79 New-yeares	68
Hee is the author of our peace.	265	U79 New-yeares	69
Hee were the wretched'st of the race of men:	272	U81 Pawlet	97
Hee shall, if he can understand,	276	U84 Body	11
Against the Nature he would worship. Hee	284	U84 Muse	75
Hee knowes, what worke h'hath done, to call this Guest,	284	U84 Muse	81
Where Hee will be, all Beautie to the Sight;	286	U84 Muse	122
Hee will all Glory, all Perfection be,	286	U84 Muse	127
There, or the tall witch-hazill hee doth twine	290	U85 Country	V 9
Hee, that but living halfe his dayes, dies such,	295	U89 Mart.8:77	7
Hee thinkes not, how to give you smoake from light,	315	Horace	203
Hee too, that did in Tragick Verse contend	319	Horace	319
Hee, that hath studied well the debt, and knowes	325	Horace	445
Hee, that not knowes the games, nor how to use	331	Horace	565
Hee, that's ambitious in the race to touch	333	Horace	587
Hee, while he labour'd to be thought a God	335	Horace	661
Hee that preserves a man, against his will,	335	Horace	665
hee freely bringes; and on this Alter layes	383	Rich	9
made prospective, behould hym, hee must passe	383	Rich	12
still that same little poynte hee was; but when	383	Rich	13
yf from a little sparke hee rise not fier.	383	Rich	16
To understand, hee may at length admire.	383	Author	10
No man will tarry by thee, as hee goes,	409	Detractor	17
Of Civill virtue, that hee now is not	420	Ode:If Men	12
Hee dyes with an Ill sent,	420	Ode:If Men	16
howe soone with a selfe ticklinge hee was spent.	420	Ode:If Men	18
Hee that soe Censureth, or adviseth synns,	421	Censure	4
hir Furye, though noe Frindshipp hee betraye.	422	Censure	26
HEE'D			
To love one man, hee'd leave her first.	146	U6 Defence	24
Hee'd say, Mend this, good friend, and this; 'tis naught.	333	Horace	624
Hee'd bid, blot all: and to the anvile bring	333	Horace	627
HEED			
Take heed, Sicknesse, what you doe,	104	F8 Sicknesse	7
And practise for a Miracle; take heed,	223	U49 Pucell	41
HEE'LD			
Hee'ld frame such ditties of their store, and want,	241	U68 House-hold	7
Recall him yet, hee'ld be no more a man:	335	Horace	668
HEE'LL			
The knight-wright's cheated then: Hee'll never pay.	42	E46 Luckless 1	5
For hee'll cry, Good, brave, better, excellent!	333	Horace	611
Hee'll be a Pilot, scarce can guide a Plough.	410	Brome	18
HEERE (See also HERE)			
Her Children, and Grand-children, reed it heere!	399	Lady Ogle	2
HEE'S			
Hee's valiant'st, that dares fight, and not for pay;	49	E66 Cary	17
Since when, hee's sober againe, and all play's made.	56	E87 Hazard	6
Where ere he met me; now hee's dumbe, or proud.	62	E97 Motion	8
Looke to and cure; Hee's not a man hath none,	156	U13 Sacvile	115
Hee's one of blood, and fashion! and with these	164	U15 Friend-Wars	55
And free societie, hee's borne else-where,	197	U40 Elegy That	16
Out with the other, for hee's still at home;	198	U40 Elegy That	34
Hee's Master of the Office; yet no more	258	U75 Epithalam.	187
Hee's prudent, valiant, just, and temperate;	262	U78 Digby	5
Hee's good, as great. I am almost a stone!	269	U81 Pawlet	11
And purple-matching Grapes, hee's glad!	290	U85 Country	20
Hee's carried 'twixt Montrell and Abbevile.	374	Coryat 1	13
Hee's carried like a Cripple, from Constable to Constable.	374	Coryat 1	17
Here, by a Boore too, hee's like to be beaten	375	Coryat 1	24
But that hee's too well suted, in a cloth,	389	Aleman	17
Hee's warme on his feet now he sayes, & can	405	Inigo Jones 1	67
HEIDELBERG			
But yet the Tun at Heidelberg had houpes.	227	U52 Answer	6
HEIGHT (See also HIGHT)			
To former height, and there in circle tarrie,	55	E85 Goodyere 1	9
Where brevitie, where splendor, and where height,	62	E95 Savile	29
Need seeke no other strength, no other height;	63	E98 Th Roe 1	4
To be the same in roote, thou art in height;	70	E109 Nevil	13
The ripened eares, yet humble in their height,	98	F3 Wroth	41
The eares cut downe in their most height,	98	F3 Wroth	V 41
Or growne; by height or lowenesse of the Sunne?	156	U13 Sacvile	119
Observe the strength, the height, the why, and when,	157	U13 Sacvile	140
Nor fashion; if they chance aspire to height,	157	U13 Sacvile	148
By all oblique Degrees, that killing height	224	U50 Countesse	11
His Muse professing height, and greatnesse, swells;	339	Horace	V 39/ 38
What height of love, a Parent will fit best,	325	Horace	447
The height, let him learne of Mr. Tom. Coryate;	379	Coryat 3	2
The height, let him learne of Mr. Tom Coryate.	381	Coryat 3	60
HEIGHTEN			
Doth sweeten mirth, and heighten pietie,	82	E130 Ferrab. 1	6
HEIGHT'NING			
Light, Posture, Height'ning, Shadow, Culloring,	370	Author	3
HEIRE			
When he made him executor, might be heire.	41	E44 Chuff	6
Englands high Chancellor: the destin'd heire	225	U51 Bacon	13
Hath brought the Land an Heire!	240	U67 Muses	33
To be a shadow to his Heire,	251	U75 Epithalam.	29
. . . Heire, of the Lord Weston, Lord high Treasurer of . . .	252	U75 Epithalam.	Ttl
And Stanley, to the which shee was Co-heire.	274	U84 Descent	6
HEIRES			
To make us heires of glory!	130	U1 Nativitie	21

HEIRES (cont.)
    And there instruct the noble English heires . . . . 214 U44 Speach 59
    Adopt us Heires, by grace, who were of those . . . 286 U84 Muse 140
    Equall with Angels, and Co-heires of it? . . . 286 U84 Muse 146
HELD
    Both the Bow, and shaft I held, ... 133 U2 Suffered 8
    I'have held a Triumph, or a feast of fire, . . . 205 U43 Vulcan 60
    How it held out! how (last) 'twas taken in! . . . 213 U44 Speach 22
    Which law receiv'd, the Chorus held his peace, . . . 323 Horace 369
HE'LE
    Is nothing, such scarce meat and drinke he'le give, . . 167 U15 Friend-Wars 159
    Now, bring him backe, he'le be no more a man, . . . 355 Horace V668
HELEN
    Have you seene faire Helen disclose . . . . 135 U2 Triumph V 33
    Helen, did Homer never see . . . . . 181 U27 Ode Helen 1
HELICON
    In Helicon; a great sort will not pare . . . 325 Horace 422
HE'LL
    He'll thee a Marble Statue make 292 U86 Hor.4:1 19
HELL
    He toyles to be at hell, as soone as they. . . . 36 E31 Banck 4
    Through seas, stormes, tempests: and imbarqu'd for hell, . . 81 E128 Wm Roe 2 13
    Of Hercules, or Theseus going to hell, . . . 84 E133 Voyage 2
    Who gave, to take at his returne from Hell, . . . 84 E133 Voyage 27
    Thou hast seene hell (some say) and know'st all nookes there, . 85 E133 Voyage 51
    That, with still-scalding steemes, make the place hell. . . 88 E133 Voyage 144
    That which, to boote with hell, is thought worth heaven, . 113 F12 Rutland 3
    Sinne, Death, and Hell, ... 129 U1 Father 23
    Light thee from hell on earth: where flatterers, spies, . . 167 U15 Friend-Wars 163
    Whose ayre will sooner Hell, then their dull senses peirce, . 420 Ode:If Men 23
HELME
    Whose knowledge claymeth at the helme to stand; . . 61 E95 Savile 21
    That in all tempests, never quit the helme, . . . 185 U30 Burleigh 10
HELP
    Yet no Taylor help to make him; . . . . 141 U2 Her man 37
    In love, doth not alone help forth . . . . 146 U6 Defence 20
HELPE
    Daily to turne in Pauls, and helpe the trade. . . . 56 E88 Monsieur 16
    By thy great helpe: and doth proclaime by mee, . . 72 E111 Edmonds 2 13
    Sans helpe of Sybil, or a golden bough, . . . 85 E133 Voyage 48
    Helpe, helpe to lift . . . . . 127 U1 Trinitie 4
    I not deny it, but to helpe the need . . . 155 U13 Sacvile 75
    I can helpe that with boldnesse; And Love sware, . . 170 U18 Elegy Can 9
    Or there to sterve it. Helpe, O you that may . . 191 U38 Elegy 'Tis 7
    When, being the Strangers helpe, the poore mans aide, . . 217 U46 Coke 7
    Away ill company, and helpe in rime . . . 231 U56 Covell 23
    Nor any quick-warming-pan helpe him to bed, . . . 232 U57 Burges 27
    A-while with us bright Sun, and helpe our light; . . 252 U75 Epithalam. 2
    So doth the one, the others helpe require, . . . 333 Horace 585
    Will be a suretie; or can helpe him out . . . 333 Horace 603
    And cry aloud, Helpe, gentle Countrey-men, . . . 335 Horace 653
    There's none will take the care, to helpe him then; . . 335 Horace 654
HELP'D
    Think'st thou that love is help'd by feare? . . . 150 U10 Jealousie 12
HELPES
    Send these suspected helpes, to aide . . . . 275 U84 Body 5
    To every state of fortune; she helpes on, . . . 311 Horace 153
HELPS
    Of severall makings? helps, helps, t'attire . . . 215 U44 Speach 94
    To every Fortunes habit; she helps on, . . . 342 Horace V153
HELVETIA
    France, Savoy, Italy, and Helvetia, ... 379 Coryat 3 19
HEMISPHERE
    And we were left under that Hemisphere, . . . 199 U41 Elegy Since 7
    But stay, I see thee in the Hemisphere . . . 392 Shakespeare 75
HEN
    Ushring the mutton; with a short-leg'd hen, . . . 64 E101 Supper 11
    Th'Ionian God-wit, nor the Ginny hen . . . 291 U85 Country 53
HENCE
    At sixe moneths end, shee parted hence . . . 33 E22 Daughter 5
    For whose sake, hence-forth, all his vowes be such, . . 41 E45 First Son 11
    Hence was it, that the destinies decreed . . . 53 E79 Rutland 5
    Attend thence; and there, may all thy ends, . . . 81 E128 Wm Roe 2 6
    Hence-forth I quit thee from my thought, . . . 100 F4 To the World 3
    Friend, flie from hence; and let these kindled rimes . . 167 U15 Friend-Wars 162
    If hence thy silence be, ... 174 U23 Himselfe 13
    If hence they silent be, ... 174 U23 Himselfe V 13
    All good Poetrie hence was flowne, ... 183 U29 Fit of Rime 14
    All mouthes, that dare entitle them (from hence) . . 187 U33 Councellour 11
    O may your wisdome take example hence, . . . 193 U38 Elegy 'Tis 67
    Not ravish'd all hence in a minutes rage. . . . 205 U43 Vulcan 56
    Not snatch them hence in one poor minutes rage. . . 205 U43 Vulcan V 56
    some 4 myles hence and have him there disgorge . . 211 U43 Vulcan V184
    This other for his eye-browes; hence, away, . . . 215 U44 Speach 97
    Hence-forth may every line be you; . . . . 278 U84 Mind 22
    Her blessed Soule, hence, forth this valley vane . . 283 U84 Muse 34
    In this sweet Extasie, she was rapt hence. . . . 289 U84 Muse 225
    Or hence, or thence, he drives with many a Hound . . 290 U85 Country 31
    I hold thee fast! but fled hence, with the Light, . . 293 U86 Hor.4:1 38
    Which, since thy flight from hence, hath mourn'd like night, . 392 Shakespeare 79
    Hence, then, prophane: Here needs no words expense . . 400 Beaumont 3
HENCE-FORTH
    For whose sake, hence-forth, all his vowes be such, . . 41 E45 First Son 11

	Page	Title	Line
HENCE-FORTH (cont.)			
Hence-forth I quit thee from my thought,	100	F4 To the World	3
Hence-forth may every line be you;	278	U84 Mind	22
HENCEFORTH			
That, henceforth, I beleeve nor bookes, nor men,	187	U33 Councellour	5
He would be call'd, henceforth, the English-Rogue,	389	Aleman	16
To be worth Envy. Henceforth I doe meane	405	Inigo Jones 1	70
HENRIE			
To Sir Henrie Cary.	48	E66 Cary	Ttl
To Sir Henrie Savile.	61	E95 Savile	Ttl
HENRY			
To Sir Henry Goodyere.	55	E85 Goodyere 1	Ttl
To Sir Henry Nevil.	70	E109 Nevil	Ttl
Of our fift Henry, eight of his nine yeare:	207	U43 Vulcan	98
Of our fift Henry, right of his nine yeare;	207	U43 Vulcan	V 98
An Epitaph, on Henry L. La-ware. To the Passer-by.	233	U60 La-ware	Ttl
Henry, the brave young Lord La-ware,	233	U60 La-ware	3
HENRYE			
- - . & sir Henrye Rich, now Earles of warwick and Hollande.	382	Rich	Ttl
HER (See also HIR)			
Here lyes to each her parents ruth,	33	E22 Daughter	1
With safetie of her innocence;	33	E22 Daughter	6
In comfort of her mothers teares,	33	E22 Daughter	8
Hath plac'd amongst her virgin-traine:	34	E22 Daughter	9
And now, her (hourely) her owne cucqueane makes,	34	E25 Beast 1	5
Grant then, no rude hand remove her.	39	E40 Ratcliffe	4
Then they might in her bright eyes.	39	E40 Ratcliffe	8
Rare, as wonder, was her wit;	39	E40 Ratcliffe	9
Till time, strong by her bestowing,	39	E40 Ratcliffe	11
Such her quaint practise is, so it allures,	39	E41 Gypsee	3
Her foes enough would fame thee in their hate.	40	E43 Salisbury 1	4
As her owne conscience, still, the same reward.	48	E64 Salisbury 3	14
That sound, and that authoritie with her name,	49	E67 Suffolk	3
As, to be rais'd by her, is onely fame.	49	E67 Suffolk	4
T'our times return'd, hath made her heaven in thee.	52	E74 Chancelor	10
I meant to make her faire, and free, and wise,	52	E76 Bedford 1	5
I purpos'd her; that should, with even powers,	52	E76 Bedford 1	14
Of destinie, and spin her owne free houres.	52	E76 Bedford 1	16
To draw thee custome: but her selfe gets all.	53	E78 Hornet	2
Surly's old whore in her new silkes doth swim:	54	E82 Surly	1
He cast, yet keeps her well! No, shee keeps him.	54	E82 Surly	5
Shee doth instruct men by her gallant flight,	55	E85 Goodyere 1	5
If Rome so great, and in her wisest age,	56	E89 Allen	1
Fear'd not to boast the glories of her stage,	56	E89 Allen	2
The nicer thing to tast her ladies page;	57	E90 Mill	5
To have her storie woven in thy thred;	61	E95 Savile	15
Fortune upon him breakes her selfe, if ill,	63	E98 Th Roe 1	5
If we can get her, full of egs, and then,	64	E101 Supper	12
And, armed to the chase, so bare her bow	68	E105 L Wroth 2	13
Truth might spend all her voyce, Fame all her art.	68	E106 E Herbert	4
And that thy soule should give thy flesh her weight.	70	E109 Nevil	14
Cato's to boote, Rome, and her libertie,	71	E110 Edmonds 1	4
Then, The townes honest Man's her errant'st knave.	75	E115 Honest Man	34
Thou wert the first, mad'st merit know her strength,	75	E116 Jephson	5
And heare her speake with one, and her first tongue;	78	E122 Rudyerd 2	6
Into the debt; and reckon on her head,	80	E127 Aubigny	5
By her attempt, shall still be owing thee.	80	E127 Aubigny	10
Which Musick had; or speake her knowne effects,	82	E130 Ferrab. 1	3
Of old, even by her practise, to be fam'd;	82	E130 Ferrab. 1	10
Mov'd by her order, and the ninth more high,	82	E130 Ferrab. 1	13
No more let Greece her bolder fables tell	84	E133 Voyage	1
Then let the former age, with this content her,	84	E133 Voyage	19
Thorough her wombe they make their famous road,	85	E133 Voyage	66
And many a sinke pour'd out her rage anenst 'hem;	86	E133 Voyage	75
Made of the trull, that cut her fathers lock:	86	E133 Voyage	84
So huge, it seem'd, they could by no meanes quite her.	86	E133 Voyage	86
And bad her fare-well sough, unto the lurden:	87	E133 Voyage	115
Never did bottom more betray her burden;	87	E133 Voyage	116
The just reward of her high huswifery;	96	F2 Penshurst	85
To have her linnen, plate, and all things nigh,	96	F2 Penshurst	86
And the great Heroes, of her race,	98	F3 Wroth	56
Let her alone, shee will court you.	104	F7 Women but	4
And her blacke spight expell.	109	F11 Epode	4
And lasting, as her flowers:	111	F11 Epode	58
All her best symmetrie in that one feature!	112	F11 Epode	101
The wealthy treasure of her love on him;	112	F11 Epode	105
The wealthy treasure of her love in him;	112	F11 Epode	V105
In the full floud of her admir'd perfection?	112	F11 Epode	107
Or put to flight Astrea, when her ingots	114	F12 Rutland	24
And, at her strong armes end, hold up, and even,	114	F12 Rutland	42
And, at her strong armes end, there hold up even,	114	F12 Rutland	V 42
Or lifted Cassiopea in her chayre?	115	F12 Rutland	62
My gratefull soule, the subject of her powers,	115	F12 Rutland	73
To her remembrance; which when time shall bring	115	F12 Rutland	75
No lady, but, at some time, loves her glasse.	117	F13 Aubigny	26
Eate on her clients, and some one devoure.	119	F13 Aubigny	88
2. How he saw her.	132	U2 How he saw	Ttl
I Beheld her, on a day,	132	U2 How he saw	1
When her looke out-flourisht May:	132	U2 How he saw	2
And her dressing did out-brave	132	U2 How he saw	3
Unto her; which Love might take	133	U2 Suffered	9
At her hand, with oath, to make	133	U2 Suffered	10
And (to gaine her by his Art)	133	U2 Suffered	15

HER (cont.)

	Page	Title	Line
4. Her Triumph.	134	U2 Triumph	Ttl
Unto her beauty;	134	U2 Triumph	6
That they still were to run by her side,	134	U2 Triumph	9
Doe but looke on her eyes, they doe light	134	U2 Triumph	11
Doe but looke on her Haire, it is bright	134	U2 Triumph	13
Doe but marke, her forehead's smoother	134	U2 Triumph	15
Then words that sooth her!	134	U2 Triumph	16
And from her arched browes, such a grace	134	U2 Triumph	17
In cheifest glory Sunne-her	135	U2 Triumph	V 32
Her armes when Paris wonne her	135	U2 Triumph	V 34
So hath Homer prais'd her haire;	136	U2 Cupid	13
Of her face, and made to rise,	136	U2 Cupid	15
Just above her sparkling eyes,	136	U2 Cupid	16
Both her Browes, bent like my Bow.	136	U2 Cupid	17
By her lookes I doe her know,	136	U2 Cupid	18
In her cheekes, of Milke, and Roses;	136	U2 Cupid	22
And, above her even chin,	136	U2 Cupid	24
Nay, her white and polish'd neck,	137	U2 Cupid	29
To my shafts! Her very Name,	137	U2 Cupid	37
And the Glasse hangs by her side,	137	U2 Cupid	40
And the Girdle 'bout her waste,	137	U2 Cupid	41
Of her good, who is the best	137	U2 Cupid	44
Of her Sex; But could'st thou, Love,	137	U2 Cupid	45
With th'advantage of her haire,	138	U2 Kisse	10
And her Jewels, to the view	138	U2 Kisse	11
8. Urging her of a promise.	139	U2 Promise	Ttl
All that heard her, with desire.	139	U2 Promise	6
As, untill she tell her one,	140	U2 Promise	11
9. Her man described by her owne Dictamen.	140	U2 Her man	Ttl
To love one man, hee'd leave her first.	146	U6 Defence	24
Turn'd to cinders by her eye?	149	U8 Houre-glasse	8
I'm sure my language to her, was as sweet,	149	U9 Picture	6
I'm sure my language to her, is as sweet,	149	U9 Picture	V 6
And all these through her eyes, have stopt her eares.	150	U9 Picture	18
That with these mixtures we put out her light.	156	U13 Sacvile	110
Her ends are honestie, and publike good!	156	U13 Sacvile	111
Quickning dead Nature, to her noblest strife.	162	U15 Friend-Wars	8
His Lace and Starch; And fall upon her back	163	U15 Friend-Wars	49
For these with her young Companie shee'll enter,	164	U15 Friend-Wars	79
That may corrupt her, even in his eyes.	165	U15 Friend-Wars	92
If it be thought kild like her Embrions; for,	165	U15 Friend-Wars	96
But what she gives, thou dar'st give her againe;	168	U15 Friend-Wars	184
Did her perfections call me on to gaze,	169	U18 Elegy Can	3
Doe not you aske to know her, she is worse	172	U20 Shrub	17
Thinke but the Sin of all her sex, 'tis she!	172	U20 Shrub	20
I could forgive her being proud! a whore!	172	U20 Shrub	21
What I, in her, am griev'd to want.	174	U22 Elegy Tho	36
'Tis crowne enough to vertue still, her owne applause.	174	U23 Himselfe	18
Assisted by no strengths, but are her owne,	176	U24 Frontispice	14
Her upright head, above the reach of Chance,	176	U25 Desmond	6
Breake the knit Circle of her Stonie Armes,	177	U25 Desmond	19
Lock't in her cold embraces, from the view	177	U25 Desmond	22
When her dead essence (like the Anatomie	179	U25 Desmond	37
Where darknesse with her gloomie-sceptred hand,	180	U25 Desmond	61
True valour doth her owne renowne command	180	U26 Ode High	16
Did Sappho on her seven-tongu'd Lute,	181	U27 Ode Helen	3
Her Ovid gave her, dimn'd the fame	181	U27 Ode Helen	18
Equall with her? or Ronsart prais'd	181	U27 Ode Helen	22
Her joyes, her smiles, her loves, as readers take	182	U28 Worth	13
When those good few, that her Defenders be,	186	U32 Elsmere	5
Then this did by her true? She never sought	188	U34 Small Poxe	5
Art, her false servant; Nor, for Sir Hugh Plat,	188	U34 Small Poxe	7
Her owne bloud gave her: Shee ne're had, nor hath	188	U34 Small Poxe	9
Spanish receipt, to make her teeth to rot.	188	U34 Small Poxe	12
I, that thy Ayme was; but her fate prevail'd:	188	U34 Small Poxe	17
And seeke to scant her comelie libertie,	190	U37 Friend-Book	20
How much they lame her in her propertie.	190	U37 Friend-Book	21
Her furie, yet no friendship to betray.	190	U37 Friend-Book	33
Her order is to cherish, and preserve,	192	U38 Elegy 'Tis	61
To doe her Husbands rites in, e're 'twere gone	201	U42 Elegy Let	40
Her presently? Or leape thy Wife of force,	201	U42 Elegy Let	44
To ruine every issue of her braine?	203	U43 Vulcan	V 14
Or if thou needs would'st trench upon her power,	204	U43 Vulcan	48
or if thou wouldst enforce the power from her,	204	U43 Vulcan	V 48
She durst not kisse, but flung thee from her brest.	208	U43 Vulcan	114
And all the Evils that flew out of her box	212	U43 Vulcan	214
And all Those ills that flew out of her box	212	U43 Vulcan	V214
Her broken Armes up, to their emptie moulds.	216	U44 Speach	102
Stood up thy Nations fame, her Crownes defence.	217	U46 Coke	14
Needs lend an aide, to thine she had her eyes.	217	U46 Coke	24
As but to stumble in her sight some shame;	220	U47 Tribe	70
And thinkes I dare not her? let the world see.	222	U49 Pucell	2
What though her Chamber be the very pit	222	U49 Pucell	3
And that as any are strooke, her breath creates	222	U49 Pucell	5
As new rewards of her old secrecie?	223	U49 Pucell	20
And that her truster feares her? Must I too?	223	U49 Pucell	22
For bawdry, 'tis her language, and not mine.	223	U49 Pucell	26
And trust her I would least, that hath forswore	223	U49 Pucell	29
Indeed, her Dressing some man might delight,	223	U49 Pucell	31
Her face there's none can like by Candle light.	223	U49 Pucell	32
Then the great Homers wit, for her, could faine;	224	U50 Countesse	24
Such, (if her manners like you) I doe send:	230	U56 Covell	19

HER (cont.)

	Page	Title	Line
And can for other Graces her commend,	230	U56 Covell	20
Your Joane to passe her melancholie time.	231	U56 Covell	24
Cary to passe her melancholie time.	231	U56 Covell	V 24
When you that raigne, are her Example growne,	236	U64 Charles 3	9
When thou that rul'st, are her Example growne,	236	U64 Charles 3	V 9
And what are bounds to her, you make your owne?	236	U64 Charles 3	10
That nothing can her gratitude provoke!	237	U64 Charles 3	16
That nothing will her gratitude provoke!	237	U64 Charles 3	V 16
. . . In celebration of her Majesties birth-day. 1630.	239	U67 Muses	Ttl
To the Queene on her Birth-day	239	U67 Muses	VTtl
Of all her Brothers storie,	240	U67 Muses	29
Of all her Fathers storie,	240	U67 Muses	V 29
And of her Fathers prowesse!	240	U67 Muses	30
And of her Brothers prowesse!	240	U67 Muses	V 30
Her joy in state, and pleasure;	240	U67 Muses	44
Her two and twenti'th yeare!	240	U67 Muses	48
Her oné and twenty yeare!	240	U67 Muses	V 48
The People her doe call!	240	U67 Muses	50
Not liv'd; for Life doth her great actions spell,	245	U70 Ode	59
To light: her measures are, how well	245	U70 Ode	62
These make the lines of life, and that's her ayre.	245	U70 Ode	64
Whose lines her rowles were, and records.	247	U70 Ode	126
Whose lives her rowles were, and records.	247	U70 Ode	V126
Adding her owne glad accents, to this Day,	249	U72 King	7
Adding her owne greate accents, to this Day,	249	U72 King	V 7
The very verdure of her nest,	251	U74 Weston	13
In making soft her aromatique bed.	251	U74 Weston	18
In all her bloome, and flower;	253	U75 Epithalam.	23
On all that come her Simplesse to rebuke!	253	U75 Epithalam.	44
Her tresses trim her back,	254	U75 Epithalam.	45
As if her ayrie steps did spring the flowers,	254	U75 Epithalam.	67
Askes first, Who gives her (I Charles) then he plights	256	U75 Epithalam.	124
. . . on her Husband, Sir Kenelme Digby.	262	U78 Digby	Ttl
And were shee lost, could best supply her place,	264	U79 New-yeares	34
Me thought, Great Britaine in her Sea, before,	268	U80 Christning	13
Her Rose, and Lilly, intertwind, have made.	268	U80 Christning	16
To pluck a Garland, for her selfe, or mee?	268	U81 Pawlet	4
And e're I can aske more of her, shee's gone!	269	U81 Pawlet	12
When I, who would her Poet have become,	269	U81 Pawlet	17
At least may beare th'inscription to her Tombe.	269	U81 Pawlet	18
Sound thou her Vertues, give her soule a Name.	269	U81 Pawlet	22
T' inlive posteritie, her Fame may tell!	269	U81 Pawlet	34
From the inherent Graces in her blood!	270	U81 Pawlet	36
Her Sweetnesse, Softnesse, her faire Courtesie,	270	U81 Pawlet	39
Her wary guardes, her wise simplicitie,	270	U81 Pawlet	40
Were like a ring of Vertues, 'bout her set,	270	U81 Pawlet	41
Could summe to a perfection, was her Act!	270	U81 Pawlet	46
Could heap to a perfection, was her Act!	270	U81 Pawlet	V 46
Of her disease, how did her soule assure	270	U81 Pawlet	50
Her suffrings, as the body had beene away!	270	U81 Pawlet	51
And to the Torturers (her Doctors) say,	270	U81 Pawlet	52
Then comforted her Lord! and blest her Sonne!	270	U81 Pawlet	57
Chear'd her faire Sisters in her race to runne!	270	U81 Pawlet	58
With gladnesse temper'd her sad Parents teares!	270	U81 Pawlet	59
Which gladnesse temper'd her sad Parents teares!	270	U81 Pawlet	V 59
Made her friends joyes to get above their feares!	270	U81 Pawlet	60
And, in her last act, taught the Standers-by,	270	U81 Pawlet	61
Let Angels sing her glories, who did call	270	U81 Pawlet	63
Her spirit home, to her originall!	270	U81 Pawlet	64
'Twixt death and life! Where her mortalitie	271	U81 Pawlet	67
Became her Birth-day to Eternitie!	271	U81 Pawlet	68
On Natures secrets, there, as her owne bookes:	271	U81 Pawlet	70
On naturall secret, there, as her owne bookes:	271	U81 Pawlet	V 70
Beholds her Maker! and, in him, doth see	271	U81 Pawlet	73
Goe now, her happy Parents, and be sad,	271	U81 Pawlet	77
And wish her state lesse happie then it is!	271	U81 Pawlet	84
1. The Dedication of her Cradle.	272	U84 Cradle	Ttl
With her, in shade	272	U84 Cradle	4
But, here's a Song of her Descent;	273	U84 Cradle	29
To chant her 'gree,	274	U84 Cradle	36
Is sung: as als' her getting up	274	U84 Cradle	37
2. The Song of her Descent.	274	U84 Descent	Ttl
Of vertues in her, as, in short, shee grew	274	U84 Descent	11
The wonder of her Sexe, and of your Blood.	274	U84 Descent	12
Draw first a Cloud: all save her neck;	276	U84 Body	13
Till, like her face, it doe appeare,	276	U84 Body	15
Of Constellations 'bout her horld;	277	U84 Body	27
Next sitting we will draw her mind.	277	U84 Body	32
Since nothing can report her flame,	278	U84 Mind	V 15
Up to her owne sublimed hight?	279	U84 Mind	48
For her t'inhabit? There is it.	280	U84 Mind	52
. . . gave me leave to call her so. Being Her . . .	282	U84 Muse	Ttl
A sorrow in me, fit to wait to her!	282	U84 Muse	10
O! had I seene her laid out a faire Corse,	282	U84 Muse	11
On Nature, for her: who did let her lie,	282	U84 Muse	13
And saw that portion of her selfe to die.	282	U84 Muse	14
With all her aydes, to save her from the seize	283	U84 Muse	17
The world to ruine with it; in her Fall,	283	U84 Muse	25
Her blessed Soule, hence, forth this valley vane	283	U84 Muse	34
To 'greet, or grieve her soft Euthanasee?	283	U84 Muse	40
As spirits had stolne her Spirit, in a kisse,	283	U84 Muse	42
From off her pillow, and deluded bed;	283	U84 Muse	43

	Page	Title	Line
HER (cont.)			
And left her lovely body unthought dead!	283	U84 Muse	44
Hope, hath her end! and Faith hath her reward!	284	U84 Muse	68
Out of her noble body, to this Feast:	284	U84 Muse	82
And give her place, according to her blood,	284	U84 Muse	83
Amongst her Peeres, those Princes of all good!	284	U84 Muse	84
To have her captiv'd spirit freed from flesh,	285	U84 Muse	93
And on her Innocence, a garment fresh	285	U84 Muse	94
And white, as that, put on: and in her hand,	285	U84 Muse	95
Whom her Redeemer, honour'd hath above	285	U84 Muse	100
Her fellowes, with the oyle of gladnesse, bright	285	U84 Muse	101
When shee departed? you will meet her there,	285	U84 Muse	108
Accumulated on her, by the Lord	285	U84 Muse	111
And best he knew her noble Character,	287	U84 Muse	155
For 'twas himselfe who form'd, and gave it her.	287	U84 Muse	156
Of title in her! All Nobilitie	287	U84 Muse	159
She had, and it became her! she was fit	287	U84 Muse	161
And by the awfull manage of her Eye	287	U84 Muse	167
T'obey, and serve her sweet Commandements.	287	U84 Muse	172
In all her petite actions, so devote,	287	U84 Muse	177
As her whole life was now become one note	287	U84 Muse	178
She spent more time in teares her selfe to dresse	287	U84 Muse	180
For her devotions, and those sad essayes	287	U84 Muse	181
Her broken sighes did never misse whole sense:	288	U84 Muse	185
Her solemne houres she spent, or giving Almes,	288	U84 Muse	192
Shee saw her Saviour, by an early light,	288	U84 Muse	199
To him should be her Judge, true God, true Man,	288	U84 Muse	211
To publish her a Saint. My Muse is gone.	289	U84 Muse	228
As, for her, I'ld not feare to die,	293	U87 Hor.3:9	11
So Fate would give her life, and longer daies.	293	U87 Hor.3:9	12
And us dis-joyn'd force to her brazen yoke,	294	U87 Hor.3:9	18
Her voyce, and angry Chremes chafes out-right	311	Horace	133
Her Poem's beautie, but a sweet delight	311	Horace	141
Her truch-man, she reports the minds each throw.	313	Horace	157
Where some great Lady, or her diligent Nourse;	313	Horace	164
Her Sonnes before the people; nor the ill-/Natur'd	317	Horace	264
Her licence fit to be restrain'd by law:	321	Horace	368
Her force was fit to be restrain'd by law:	348	Horace	V402/368
Her language, if the Stay, and Care t'have mended,	325	Horace	413
The Child, when Lamia'has din'd, out of her maw.	329	Horace	510
And makes her supple feete, as swift as winde.	363	Riches	12
Of her illustrate brightnesse,	364	Ode Splendor	3
Of her admyred brightnesse,	364	Ode Splendor	V 3
Her wit as quicke, and sprightfull	365	Ode Splendor	5
Doth shine in her discerning,	365	Ode Splendor	10
Her breath for sweete exceeding	365	Ode Splendor	13
Her breath farre sweete exceeding	365	Ode Splendor	V 13
When seeking her renowning,	365	Ode Splendor	19
Retire, and say; Her Graces	365	Ode Splendor	21
The Vale, that bred thee pure, as her Hills Snow.	367	Ode Who saith	40
Hath sent her Mermaides in,	368	Ode Who saith	91
Each subt'lest Passion, with her source, and spring,	370	Author	7
Each subject Passion, with her source, and spring,	370	Author	V 7
For he did but kisse her, and so let her go.	375	Coryat 1	19
And thou to her, that Husband, may exalt	384	Somerset	13
Should praise a Matron. What could hurt her more?	391	Shakespeare	14
Nature her selfe was proud of his designes,	392	Shakespeare	47
In blood, in birth, by match, and by her seate;	394	Jane Ogle	4
And her, she made her Inmate, to the End,	394	Jane Ogle	18
To call on Sicknes still, to be her Guest,	394	Jane Ogle	19
So wood at last, that he was wonne to her	394	Jane Ogle	22
Importuno wish; and by her lov'd Lords side	394	Jane Ogle	23
To lay her here, inclos'd, his second Bride.	394	Jane Ogle	24
Where spight of Death, next Life, for her Loves sake	394	Jane Ogle	25
Her Children, and Grand-children, reed it heere!	399	Lady Ogle	2
Upon her selfe) to all her sexe!	399	Lady Ogle	10
The best of Woemen! her whole life	399	Lady Ogle	11
In her! and what could perfect bee,	399	Lady Ogle	15
Her soule possest her fleshes state	399	Lady Ogle	25
Keeps warme the spice of her good name,	400	Lady Ogle	30
Her right, by gift, and purchase of the Lambe:	400	Lady Ogle	36
Seal'd and deliver'd to her, in the sight	400	Lady Ogle	37
Both Saints, and Martyrs, by her loved Lord.	400	Lady Ogle	39
Stay, till she make her vaine Approches. Then	401	Beaumont	15
And, graced with her song,	402	Filmer	13
To make the Language sweet upon her tongue.	402	Inigo Jones 1	14
Not they that sided her, Dame Poetry,	403	Inigo Jones 1	36
To hold her up. O Showes! Showes! Mighty Showes!	403	Inigo Jones 1	39
To Mrs. Alice Sutcliffe, on her divine Meditations.	411	Sutcliffe	Ttl
Preserved, in her antique bed of Vert,	413	Ghyrlond	19
I Cannot bring my Muse to dropp her Vies	415	Dover	1
and seeke to scant her comelye Libertye,	421	Censure	13
Is her owne scourge, when it sustaines their states	422	Lucan	3
Tell her, his Muse that did invent thee	662	Bedford	5
of her white Hand; or she can spare it.	662	Bedford	10
HERALD			
And, I a Poet here, no Herald am.	29	E9 To All	4
Times witnesse, herald of Antiquitie,	176	U24 Frontispice	17
The Herald will. Our blood is now become	215	U44 Speach	82
HERALDS			
Of Winchester; the Heralds can tell this:	269	U81 Pawlet	20
Of Winchester; the Heralds could tell this:	269	U81 Pawlet	V 20
And Christian name too, with a Heralds witt.	394	Jane Ogle	12

273

		Page	Title	Line
HERB				
Or the herb Sorrell, that lóves Meadows still, · · · ·		291	U85 Country	57
HERBERT				
To Sir Edward Herbert. · · · · · ·		68	E106 E Herbert	Ttl
All-vertuous Herbert! on whose every part · · ·		68	E106 E Herbert	3
HERCULES				
Of Hercules, or Theseus going to hell, · · ·		84	E133 Voyage	2
Hercules? alas his bones are yet sore, · · ·		107	F10 Proludium	4
Like life unto 'hem. Who heav'd Hercules · · ·		115	F12 Rutland	57
In a Hercules-his shape. · · · · ·		132	U2 How he saw	32
I look'd for Hercules to be the Groome: · · ·		228	U53 Newcastle	18
From the fam'd pillars of old Hercules! · · ·		407	Inigo Jones 2	14
HERCULES-HIS				
In a Hercules-his shape. · · · · ·		132	U2 How he saw	32
HERD (See also HEARD)				
That have a Flock, or Herd, upon these plaines; · ·		265	U79 New-yeares	47
HERDS				
The lowing herds there grazing are: · · ·		290	U85 Country	14
HERE'				
Of the not borne, yet buried, here's the tombe. · ·		46	E62 Would-bee	12
Here's a shaft, thou art to slow! · · ·		132	U2 How he saw	10
Here's none to spie, or see; · · · ·		139	U2 Another	3
But here's no time, nor place, my wealth to tell, · ·		161	U14 Selden	85
Here's one out-liv'd his Peeres, · · ·		243	U70 Ode	25
But, here's a Song of her Descent; · · ·		273	U84 Cradle	29
Here's one makes verses, but there's none knows why: ·		355	Horace	V670
Had cloath'd him so. Here's all I can supply · ·		389	Aleman	20
HERE				
And, I a Poet here, no Herald am. · · ·		29	E9 To All	4
Shift, here, in towne, not meanest among squires, · ·		30	E12 Shift	1
Here lyes to each her parents ruth, · · ·		33	E22 Daughter	1
Rest in soft peace, and, ask'd, say here doth lye · ·		41	E45 First Son	9
I, that am glad of thy great chance, here doo! · ·		46	E60 Mounteagle	5
And here, it should be one of our first strifes, · ·		54	E80 Life/Death	6
When he was here. Nor hath he got a sute, · ·		63	E97 Motion	16
Judge they, that can: here I have rais'd to show · ·		67	E104 Montgomery	13
Will you part with them, here, unthriftely? · ·		69	E107 Hungry	28
As the beginnings here, prove purely sweet, · ·		81	E128 Wm Roe 2	7
Subtly distinguish'd, was confused here. · · ·		84	E133 Voyage	10
Against their breasts. Here, sev'rall ghosts did flit		87	E133 Voyage	124
For, here they were throwne in wi'the melted pewter, ·		88	E133 Voyage	153
Here no man tells my cups; nor, standing by, · ·		95	F2 Penshurst	67
As if thou, then, wert mine, or I raign'd here: · ·		95	F2 Penshurst	74
With all their zeale, to warme their welcome here. ·		95	F2 Penshurst	81
That, what to all may happen here, · · ·		101	F4 To the World	55
Here in my bosome, and at home. · · ·		102	F4 To the World	68
The thing, they here call Love, is blinde Desire, · ·		110	F11 Epode	37
We doe not number, here, · · · ·		111	F11 Epode	76
I doe not number, here, · · · ·		111	F11 Epode	V 76
Then, here, to give pride fame, and peasants birth. ·		114	F12 Rutland	26
Dwell, dwell here still: O, being every-where, · ·		122	F15 Heaven	15
How can I doubt to finde thee ever, here? · ·		122	F15 Heaven	16
See the Chariot at hand here of Love, · · ·		134	U2 Triumph	1
This here sung, can be no other · · ·		136	U2 Cupid	11
Here running in the Glasse, · · ·		148	U8 Houre-glasse	2
Before me here, the Friend and Sonne, · · ·		151	U12 Corbet	4
Nor wants it here through penurie, or sloth, · ·		152	U12 Corbet	39
All as their prize, turne Pyrats here at Land, · ·		155	U13 Sacvile	81
I Know to whom I write. Here, I am sure, · ·		158	U14 Selden	1
Rather then here so bogg'd in vices stay. · ·		163	U15 Friend-Wars	30
The whole world here leaven'd with madnesse swells; ·		163	U15 Friend-Wars	31
But here doth lie, till the last Day, · · ·		168	U16 Gray	3
Have sung this Hymne, and here intreat · ·		174	U22 Elegy Tho	30
Read here in one, what thou in all canst find, · ·		185	U30 Burleigh	2
Come, let us here enjoy the shade; · · ·		189	U36 Song	1
Of Graces, or your mercie here in me, · · ·		191	U38 Elegy 'Tis	16
As I the penitents here emulate: · · ·		193	U38 Elegy 'Tis	86
Then Mistris, here, here let your rigour end, · ·		194	U38 Elegy 'Tis	105
Your forme shines here, here fixed in my heart: · ·		194	U38 Elegy 'Tis	117
Or that the Sun was here, but forc't away; · ·		199	U41 Elegy Since	6
Your sacrifice, then here remaine with me. · ·		199	U41 Elegy Since	18
We aske your absence here, we all love peace, · ·		212	U43 Vulcan	209
We crave your absence here, we all love peace, · ·		212	U43 Vulcan	V209
If they stay here, but till Saint Georges Day. · ·		213	U44 Speach	10
All that they doe at Playes. O, but first here · ·		215	U44 Speach	91
That thou remaine here taster · · ·		220	U48 Bacchus	7
That when King James, above here, · · ·		221	U48 Bacchus	37
No friend to vertue, could be silent here. · ·		224	U50 Countesse	8
Since Bacon, and thy Lord was borne, and here; · ·		225	U51 Bacon	8
Then would I promise here to give · · ·		229	U55 Burges	3
As here no Venus were; · · · ·		240	U67 Muses	34
But, that shee raigning here, · · ·		240	U67 Muses	35
Like Swine, or other Cattell here on earth: · ·		257	U75 Epithalam.	154
For, had we here said lesse, we had sung nothing then.		263	U79 New-yeares	8
What she did here, by great example, well, · ·		269	U81 Pawlet	33
And see all dead here, or about to dye! · ·		271	U81 Pawlet	86
Yet, here are no such Trifles brought, · · ·		273	U84 Cradle	25
But here I may no colours use. · · ·		277	U84 Mind	6
But here we may no colours use. · · ·		277	U84 Mind	V 6
And stuck in clay here, it would pull · · ·		279	U84 Mind	46
Or hath she here, upon the ground, · · ·		280	U84 Mind	49
What fulnesse of beatitude is here? · · ·		286	U84 Muse	137
Or Rainbow is describ'd. But here was now · ·		305	Horace	23

	Page	Title	Line

HERE (cont.)
The worst of Statuaries, here about . . . . . 307 Horace 45
Much, that mought now be spoke: omitted here . . . 307 Horace 62
Of Poems here describ'd, I can, nor use, . . . 311 Horace 127
Our Poets, too, left nought unproved here; . . . 323 Horace 405
Looke here on Bretons worke, the master print: . . . 362 Author 5
To hold them here: . . . 368 Ode Who saith 92
Read here a little, that thou mayst know much. . . . 371 Epitaph 2
Here, like Arion, our Coryate doth draw . . . 374 Coryat 1 10
Here, not up Holdborne, but downe a steepe hill, . . . 374 Coryat 1 12
A Horse here is sadled, but no Tom him to backe, . . . 374 Coryat 1 14
Here, up the Alpes (not so plaine as to Dunstable) . . 374 Coryat 1 16
A Punke here pelts him with egs. How so? . . . 375 Coryat 1 18
Religiously here he bids, row from the stewes, . . . 375 Coryat 1 20
Here, by a Boore too, hee's like to be beaten . . . 375 Coryat 1 24
Old Hat here, torne Hose, with Shoes full of gravell, . . 375 Coryat 1 26
Here, finer then comming from his Punke you him see, . . 375 Coryat 1 28
Here France, and Italy both to him shed . . . 375 Coryat 1 30
And here he disdained not, in a forraine land . . . 375 Coryat 1 32
But here, neither trusting his hands, nor his legs, . . 375 Coryat 1 34
Was worthy of a Good one; And this, here, . . . 386 Husband 10
This Figure, that thou here seest put, . . . 390 Reader 1
I Could begin with that grave forme, Here lies, . . . 394 Jane Ogle 1
No stone in any wall here, but can tell . . . 394 Jane Ogle 9
To lay her here, inclos'd, his second Bride. . . . 394 Jane Ogle 24
And when the flesh, here, shut up day, . . . 400 Lady Ogle 27
Hence, then, prophane: Here needs no words expense . . 400 Beaumont 3
To cut a Dike? or sticke a Stake up, here, . . . 401 Beaumont 12
French Aire and English Verse here Wedded lie. . . . 401 Filmer 6
Here, are five letters in this blessed Name, . . . 412 Ghyrlond 1
As Love, here studied to keep Grace alive. . . . 412 Ghyrlond 8
Here he speaks out of his Pottle, . . . 657 Door Apollo 3
HEREAFTER
That I, hereafter, doe not thinke the Barre, . . . 186 U33 Councellour 1
Make all hereafter, had'st thou ruin'd this? . . . 188 U34 Small Poxe 16
But, if hereafter thou shalt write, not feare . . . 331 Horace 575
HEREIN
Who (herein studying conscience, and not fame) . . . 224 U50 Countesse 14
HERE'S
Of the not borne, yet buried, here's the tombe. . . . 46 E62 Would-bee 12
Here's a shaft, thou art to slow! . . . 132 U2 How he saw 10
Here's none to spie, or see; . . . 139 U2 Another 3
But here's no time, nor place, my wealth to tell, . . . 161 U14 Selden 85
Here's one out-liv'd his Peeres, . . . 243 U70 Ode 25
But, here's a Song of her Descent; . . . 273 U84 Cradle 29
Here's one makes verses, but there's none knows why: . . 355 Horace V670
Had cloath'd him so. Here's all I can supply . . . 389 Aleman 20
HERESIE
Had I wrote treason there, or heresie, . . . 203 U43 Vulcan 15
HERETOFORE (See 'TOFORE)
HERMES
Apollo's harpe, and Hermes lyre resound, . . . 98 F3 Wroth 51
Hermes, the cheater, shall not mixe with us, . . . 107 F10 Proludium 22
Hermes, the cheater, cannot mixe with us, . . . 107 F10 Proludium V 22
Phoebus, and Hermes? They whose tongue, or pen . . . 395 May 17
HERMETIQUE
Their Seales, their Characters, Hermetique rings, . . . 206 U43 Vulcan 73
Their Charmes, their Characters, Hermetique rings, . . 206 U43 Vulcan V 73
HEROE
Or an Heroe; if a ripe old man, ... 313 Horace 162
HEROES
Our brave Heroes with a milder glare, . . . 88 E133 Voyage 163
And the great Heroes, of her race, . . . 98 F3 Wroth 56
HEROICK
But then, thy'epistolar Heroick Songs, . . . 397 Drayton 29
HEROIQUE
Where all heroique ample thoughts doe meet: . . . 262 U78 Digby 10
HERS
Upon th'accompt, hers grew the quicker trade. . . . 56 E87 Hazard 5
Court can call hers, or Man could call his Arts. . . . 262 U78 Digby 4
Court can call hers, or Man would call the Arts. . . . 262 U78 Digby V 4
Sound, sound his praises loud, and with his, hers divide. . 264 U79 New-yeares 19
And hers were all Humilitie! they beat . . . 288 U84 Muse 189
HERSE
In place of scutcheons, that should decke thy herse, . . 35 E27 Roe 1 1
Of Egges, and Halberds, Cradles, and a Herse, . . . 204 U43 Vulcan 37
HE'S
For he's both noble, lovely, young, . . . 292 U86 Hor.4:1 13
Polluted, touch't: but certainly he's mad: . . . 355 Horace V673
HESIODS
. . . on his Translation of Hesiods Works, & Dayes. . . 388 Chapman Ttl
Olde Hesiods Ore, and give it us; but thine, . . . 388 Chapman 2
HETHER
And shooe, and tye, and garter should come hether, . . 56 E88 Monsieur 4
that mongst so manie plants transplanted hether, . . . 361 Palmer 6
HEYDEN
We have a Shelton, and a Heyden got, . . . 84 E133 Voyage 5
H'HAD
And not thinke h'had eat a stake, . . . 142 U2 Her man 39
H'HAS
H'has tympanies of businesse, in his face, . . . 35 E28 Surly 7
Know you the cause? H'has neither land, nor lease, . . 63 E97 Motion 9

	Page	Title	Line
H'HATH			
Hee knowes, what worke h'hath done, to call this Guest,	284	U84 Muse	81
HID			
Curst be his Muse, that could lye dumbe, or hid	47	E63 Salisbury 2	11
Curst be my voyce if it lye dumbe, or hid	47	E63 Salisbury 2 V	11
Adulteries, now, are not so hid, or strange,	165	U15 Friend-Wars	85
HIDDEN			
Of Truth that searcheth the most hidden Springs,	176	U24 Frontispice	10
Of Truth which searcheth the most hidden Springs,	176	U24 Frontispice V	10
HIDE (NAME)			
From Hide-Parke to the Stage, where at the last	165	U15 Friend-Wars	109
HIDE			
That dares nor write things false, nor hide things true.	62	E95 Savile	36
For this Beauty yet doth hide	137	U2 Cupid	49
Hide faults, pray to the Gods, and wish aloud	319	Horace	285
Hide faults, and pray to th'gods, and wish aloud	345	Horace	V285
Or any thing else that another should hide,	380	Coryat 3	51
these only hide part of my flesh, and bones:	387	Cavendish	2
HIDE-PARKE			
From Hide-Parke to the Stage, where at the last	165	U15 Friend-Wars	109
HIDES			
The heads, houghs, entrailes, and the hides of dogs:	88	E133 Voyage	146
HIE			
More timely hie thee to the house,	292	U86 Hor.4:1	9
HIERARCHIE			
To every Order, ev'ry Hierarchie!	271	U81 Pawlet	72
HIERARCHIES			
Saints, Martyrs, Prophets, with those Hierarchies,	285	U84 Muse	85
HIEROGLYPHICKS			
Court Hieroglyphicks! & all Artes affoord	404	Inigo Jones 1	43
HIEROME			
To the Right Hon'ble Hierome, L. Weston. An Ode . . .	250	U74 Weston	Ttl
. . . that Noble Gentleman, Mr. Hierome Weston, Son, and . . .	252	U75 Epithalam.	Ttl
A Richard, and a Hierome, by their names	258	U75 Epithalam.	170
HIGH (See also HYE)			
More high, more holy, that shee more would crave.	31	E14 Camden	6
Which deed I know not, whether were more high,	49	E66 Cary	7
Stand high, then, Howard, high in eyes of men,	49	E67 Suffolk	5
High in thy bloud, thy place, but highest then,	49	E67 Suffolk	6
Goe high, or low, as thou wilt value it.	50	E72 Court-ling	4
From place, or fortune, are made high, or low,	64	E99 Th Roe 2	9
And your high names: I doe desire, that thence	69	E108 Soldiers	3
Mov'd by her order, and the ninth more high,	82	E130 Ferrab. 1	13
An ancient pur-blinde fletcher, with a high nose;	89	E133 Voyage	190
Where Pan, and Bacchus their high feasts have made,	93	F2 Penshurst	11
And if the high-swolne Medway faile thy dish,	94	F2 Penshurst	31
The just reward of her high huswifery;	96	F2 Penshurst	85
Who (blest with such high chance)	111	F11 Epode	62
Or set bright Ariadnes crowne so high?	115	F12 Rutland	60
But high, and noble matter, such as flies	116	F12 Rutland	89
And let nothing high decay,	131	U2 Excuse	22
To meet their high desire;	144	U3 Musicall	26
As they are high; are rooted, and will last.	157	U13 Sacvile	144
Against his Maker; high alone with weeds,	163	U15 Friend-Wars	33
But sing high and aloofe,	175	U23 Himselfe	35
high Providence would so; that nor the good	176	U24 Frontispice V	5
High, as his mind, that doth advance	176	U25 Desmond	5
High-spirited friend,	180	U26 Ode High	1
'Tis wisdome, and that high,	181	U26 Ode High	22
Is Horace his each love so high	181	U27 Ode Helen	13
. . . Lo: high Treasurer of England.	185	U30 Burleigh	Ttl
Whom they durst handle in their high day coates,	208	U43 Vulcan	V127
Though but in daunces, it shall know high power;	210	U43 Vulcan	V157
I wish all well, and pray high heaven conspire	219	U47 Tribe	37
Englands high Chancellor: the destin'd heire	225	U51 Bacon	13
No love of action, and high Arts,	234	U60 La-ware	12
To the Right Honourable, the Lord high Treasurer of . . .	248	U71 Treasurer	Ttl
. . . high Treasurer of England, Upon the Day, Hee was . . .	250	U73 Weston	Ttl
. . . Heire, of the Lord Weston, Lord high Treasurer of . . .	252	U75 Epithalam.	Ttl
And Call to the high Parliament	273	U84 Cradle	30
There, high exalted in the Spheare,	279	U84 Mind	29
But, that a Mind so rapt, so high,	279	U84 Mind	41
Were Cycnus, once high flying	369	Ode Who saith	99
Ymounted high upon Selinis crest:	412	Ghyrlond	10
HIGHER			
The gladnesse higher:	120	F14 Sydney	6
If his wit reach no higher, but to spring	232	U58 Book-seller	7
That trembles in the blaze, but (then) mounts higher!	233	U59 Newcastle	8
Whilst from the higher Bankes doe slide the floods;	290	U85 Country	25
But higher power, as spight could not make lesse,	401	Beaumont	18
HIGHEST			
High in thy bloud, thy place, but highest then,	49	E67 Suffolk	6
And highest; sinketh to the lowest, and worst.	331	Horace	564
HIGHLY			
He had so highly set; and, in what Barbican.	256	U75 Epithalam.	112
He had so highly plac'd; and, in what Barbican.	256	U75 Epithalam.	V112
HIGH-SPIRITED			
High-spirited friend,	180	U26 Ode High	1
HIGH-SWOLNE			
And if the high-swolne Medway faile thy dish,	94	F2 Penshurst	31
HIGHT (VERB)			
How hight the place? a voyce was heard, Cocytus.	86	E133 Voyage	89

	Page	Title	Line

HIGHT
Up to her owne sublimed hight?   279 U84 Mind   48
HILL
Whereof old Democrite, and Hill Nicholas,   87 E133 Voyage   128
Scarce the Hill againe doth flourish,   184 U29 Fit of Rime   37
Condemne him to the Brick-kills, or some Hill-/foot   211 U43 Vulcan   183
Condemne him to some Brick-hills, or some Hill-/foot   211 U43 Vulcan   V183
Hill-/foot (out in Sussex) to an iron Mill;   211 U43 Vulcan   184
Hill-/foot (out in Sussex) to some iron Mill;   211 U43 Vulcan   V184
Here, not up Holdborne, but downe a steepe hill,   374 Coryat 1   12
HILL-FOOT
Condemne him to the Brick-kills, or some Hill-/foot   211 U43 Vulcan   183
Condemne him to some Brick-hills, or some Hill-/foot   211 U43 Vulcan   V183
Hill-/foot (out in Sussex) to an iron Mill;   211 U43 Vulcan   184
Hill-/foot (out in Sussex) to some iron Mill;   211 U43 Vulcan   V184
HILLS
Condemne him to some Brick-hills, or some Hill-/foot   211 U43 Vulcan   V183
Heare, o you Groves, and, Hills, resound his praise.   264 U79 New-yeares   23
Heare, O you Groves, and, Hills, resound his worth.   264 U79 New-yeares   31
The Vale, that bred thee pure, as her Hills Snow.   367 Ode Who saith   40
HILT
Item, your mistris anagram, i' your hilt.   51   E73 Fine Grand   16
HIM   (See also HYM)
But see! th'old baud hath serv'd him in his trim,   31   E12 Shift   23
Lent him a pockie whore. Shee hath paid him.   31   E12 Shift   24
Wee, sad for him, may glorie, and not sinne.   35   E27 Roe 1   8
His monyes travaile for him, in and out: 36   E31 Banck   2
And having got him out of doores is glad.   40   E42 Giles   7
When he made him executor, might be heire.   41   E44 Chuff   6
Get him the times long grudge, the courts ill will;   48   E65 Muse   7
And, reconcil'd, keepe him suspected still.   48   E65 Muse   8
Make him loose all his friends; and, which is worse,   48   E65 Muse   9
To one that desired me not to name him.   53   E77 Not name   Ttl
No male unto him: who could so exceed   53   E79 Rutland   7
He cast, yet keeps her well! No, shee keeps him.   54   E82 Surly   2
Or had his father, when he did him get,   56   E88 Monsieur   9
By which damme conceiv'd him, clothes and all?   56   E88 Monsieur   11
Went on: and proving him still, day by day,   57   E90 Mill   7
First bearing him a calfe, beare him a bull.   57   E90 Mill   18
So hast thou rendred him in all his bounds,   61   E95 Savile   5
Nor did the king of Denmarke him salute,   63   E97 Motion   15
Onely his clothes have over-leaven'd him.   63   E97 Motion   20
Fortune upon him breakes her selfe, if ill,   63   E98 Th Roe 1   5
And I must now beleeve him: for, to day,   64   E100 Playwrt 3   3
Five of my jests, then stolne, past him a play.   64   E100 Playwrt 3   4
They murder him againe, that envie thee.   72   E111 Edmonds 2   14
Him not, aloud, that boasts so good a fame: 74   E115 Honest Man   2
And him it layes on; if he be not there.   74   E115 Honest Man   16
Tell's of him, all the tales, it selfe then makes;   74   E115 Honest Man   17
Makes, the whole longer, then 'twas given him, much.   76   E119 Shelton   16
As, sooth, the Parcae thought him one,   77   E120 S. P.   15
But viewing him since (alas, too late)   77   E120 S. P.   19
In bathes to steepe him;   77   E120 S. P.   22
Heaven vowes to keepe him.   77   E120 S. P.   24
Said I wrong'd him, and (which was more) his love.   80   E126 Mrs Cary   5
That to the world I publish, for him, this;   83   E132 Sylvester   9
Or him that backward went to Berwicke, or which   85   E133 Voyage   35
And all his followers, that had so abus'd him: 86   E133 Voyage   97
And, in so shitten sort, so long had us'd him;   86   E133 Voyage   98
A sope-boyler; and Aeacus him nigh,   89   E133 Voyage   188
I thought to binde him, in my verse: 93   F1 Why write no   2
Let him, then hardest sires, more disinherit,   99   F3 Wroth   77
Then hardest let him more disherrit,   99   F3 Wroth   V 77
To him, man's dearer, then t'himselfe.   99   F3 Wroth   96
Be thankes to him, and earnest prayer, to finde   99   F3 Wroth   101
Is thankes to him, and earnest prayer, to finde   99   F3 Wroth   V101
And riffle him: or pawne his Petasus.   107 F10 Proludium   24
The wealthy treasure of her love on him;   112 F11 Epode   105
The wealthy treasure of her love in him;   112 F11 Epode   V105
And, who doth me (though I not him) envy,   115 F12 Rutland   70
I, that am gratefull for him, have prepar'd   116 F12 Rutland   96
How you love one, and him you should; how still   119 F13 Aubigny   113
But to please him, who is the dearer prise   119 F13 Aubigny   116
Doth urge him to runne wrong, or to stand still.   121 F14 Sydney   30
And tooke on him our Nature.   130 U1 Nativitie   18
What comfort by him doe wee winne,   130 U1 Nativitie   19
Better fits him, then his face;   140 U2 Promise   20
I would have him, if I could,   140 U2 Her man   3
Young Il'd have him to, and faire,   141 U2 Her man   9
Yet no Taylor help to make him;   141 U2 Her man   37
Drest, you still for man should take him;   141 U2 Her man   38
I feare they'd love him too;   147 U7 Nymph   4
He is, if they can find him, faire,   147 U7 Nymph   15
And feare much more, that more of him be showne.   147 U7 Nymph   21
Of him whose bones this Grave doth gather: 151 U12 Corbet   6
Yet he broke them, e're they could him,   151 U12 Corbet   10
Much from him I professe I wonne,   152 U12 Corbet   29
But that I understood him scant.   152 U12 Corbet   31
Now I conceive him by my want,   152 U12 Corbet   32
The memorie delights him more, from whom   153 U13 Sacvile   21
Then turning unto him is next at hand,   154 U13 Sacvile   56
Their bounties forth, to him that last was made,   155 U13 Sacvile   63
Then give it to the Hound that did him bite;   155 U13 Sacvile   70

HIM (cont.)

Text	Page	Title	Line
An Epistle to a Friend, to perswade him to the Warres.	162	U15 Friend-Wars	Ttl
Looke on th'ambitious man, and see him nurse	162	U15 Friend-Wars	11
See him, that's call'd, and thought the happiest man,	162	U15 Friend-Wars	23
For all their spight, be like him if they could:	162	U15 Friend-Wars	26
But there are objects, bid him to be gone	163	U15 Friend-Wars	28
To take the box up for him; and pursues	166	U15 Friend-Wars	137
With him, for he is follow'd with that heape	167	U15 Friend-Wars	156
More honour in him, 'cause we'ave knowne him mad:	168	U15 Friend-Wars	194
Of all that can be done him; Such a one	171	U19 Elegy By	23
And so I leave to stirre him, lest he stinke.	172	U21 Ltl Shrub	10
stryke him in thy proper straine,	175	U23 Himselfe	V 26
Who aided him, will thee, the issue of Joves braine.	175	U23 Himselfe	30
Upon reward, till the reward him sought.	185	U30 Burleigh	14
Rather than meet him: And, before his eyes	185	U30 Burleigh	16
Another to him.	186	U32 Elsmere	Ttl
It shakes even him, that all things else doth shake.	193	U38 Elegy 'Tis	72
Forgiven him; And in that lyne stand I,	193	U38 Elegy 'Tis	91
Due to that one, that doth believe him just.	198	U40 Elegy That	40
But to confine him to the Brew-houses,	211	U43 Vulcan	179
Condemne him to the Brick-kills, or some Hill-/foot	211	U43 Vulcan	183
Condemne him to some Brick-hills, or some Hill-/foot	211	U43 Vulcan	V183
Condemne him to the Brick-kills, or a forge	211	U43 Vulcan	V183
some 4 myles hence and have him there disgorge	211	U43 Vulcan	V184
Or in small Fagots have him blaze about	211	U43 Vulcan	185
Vile Tavernes, and the Drunkards pisse him out;	211	U43 Vulcan	186
Vile Tavernes, and have Drunkards pisse him out;	211	U43 Vulcan	V186
First weigh a friend, then touch, and trie him too:	216	U45 Squib	16
Turne him, and see his Threds: looke, if he be	216	U45 Squib	21
That both, their odour take him,	220	U48 Bacchus	11
And relish merry make him.	220	U48 Bacchus	12
See then thou dost attend him,	221	U48 Bacchus	17
Lyaeus, and defend him,	221	U48 Bacchus	18
In raysing him the wisdome of my King.	225	U51 Bacon	20
Tell him his Ben	231	U57 Burges	7
Put him in mind	231	U57 Burges	14
Nor any quick-warming-pan helpe him to bed,	232	U57 Burges	27
Thanke him: if other, hee can give no Bayes.	232	U58 Book-seller	6
Stay, drop a teare for him that's dead,	233	U60 La-ware	2
For want of knowing the Poet, to say him nay?	241	U68 House-hold	4
Well, they should know him, would the K. but grant	241	U68 House-hold	5
To keepe him off; and how-so-e're he gleanes	242	U69 Friend Son	16
Some of his formes, he lets him not come neere	242	U69 Friend Son	17
But that the Corke of Title boy'd him up.	244	U70 Ode	42
By him, so ample, full, and round,	244	U70 Ode	49
Jonson, who sung this of him, e're he went	246	U70 Ode	85
Him up, to doe the same himselfe had done.	256	U75 Epithalam.	108
In him the times, no lesse then Prince, are prais'd,	256	U75 Epithalam.	115
And let him freely gather Loves First-fruits,	258	U75 Epithalam.	186
Hath drawne on him, from the times,	259	U76 Petition	V 17
Parts of him, the Judge decay'd,	259	U76 Petition	V 23
Yet read him in these lines: He doth excell	262	U78 Digby	2
Yet take him in these lines: He doth excell	262	U78 Digby	V 2
In him all vertue is beheld in State:	262	U78 Digby	6
In him all action is beheld in State:	262	U78 Digby	V 6
Goe, Muse, in, and salute him. Say he be	262	U78 Digby	19
Goe, Muse, in, and salute him thoughe he be	262	U78 Digby	V 19
Good Omen to him, in the note thou sing'st,	263	U78 Digby	22
Good fortune to him, in the note thou sing'st,	263	U78 Digby	V 22
To him we owe all profits of our grounds.	264	U79 New-yeares	15
Beholds her Maker! and, in him, doth see	271	U81 Pawlet	73
Study illustrious Him, and you have all.	282	U84 Kenelme	23
But make him All in All, their Theme, that Day:	286	U84 Muse	120
In his humanitie! To heare him preach	286	U84 Muse	133
On all the world! She saw him on the Crosse	288	U84 Muse	201
Shee saw him rise, triumphing over Death	288	U84 Muse	203
Shee saw him too, in glory to ascend	288	U84 Muse	205
To him should be her Judge, true God, true Man,	288	U84 Muse	211
Now in the rooted Grasse him lay,	290	U85 Country	24
There jest, and feast, make him thine host,	292	U86 Hor.4:1	11
Makes his life longer then 'twas given him, much.	295	U89 Mart.8:77	8
To paint him, hath by swimming, hopelesse, scap'd,	305	Horace	27
And what they will not. Him, whose choice doth reare	307	Horace	56
If now the phrase of him that speakes, shall flow,	313	Horace	158
Keepe him still active, angry, un-appeas'd,	313	Horace	172
Sharpe, and contemning lawes, at him should aime,	313	Horace	173
Be nought so'bove him but his sword let claime.	313	Horace	174
Be nought so'bove him, but his bold sword claime.	342	Horace	V174
Him that buyes chiches blanch't, or chance to like	321	Horace	362
Him that buyes Pulse there, or perhaps may like	347	Horace	V354/362
Him that is last, I scorne to come behind,	333	Horace	595
Him that is last, I scorne to be behind,	353	Horace	V595
Will be a suretie; or can helpe him out	333	Horace	603
With joy of what is given him, over-gone:	333	Horace	610
Looke through him, and be sure, you take not mocks	333	Horace	621
And shun to touch him, as a man that were	335	Horace	644
And flye to touch him, as a man that were	354	Horace	V644
They vexe, and follow him with shouts, and noise,	335	Horace	648
They vexe, and carelesse follow him with noise.	354	Horace	V648
There's none will take the care, to helpe him then;	335	Horace	654
Doth the same thing with him, that would him kill.	335	Horace	666
Recall him yet, hee'ld be no more a man:	335	Horace	668
Now, bring him backe, he'le be no more a man,	355	Horace	V668

				Page	Title	Line

HIM (cont.)

	Page	Title	Line
To force the grates, that hold him in, would fright	337	Horace	675
And, there an end of him, reciting makes:	337	Horace	678
And there an end of him with reading makes:	355	Horace	V678
Besides the other Swannes admiring him,	366	Ode Who saith	5
He shew'd him first the hoofe-cleft Spring,	366	Ode Who saith	17
From Zephyr's rape would close him with his beames.	366	Ode Who saith	24
When him alone we sing)	368	Ode Who saith	63
(Which makes him sing	369	Ode Who saith	102
To him, and he there shrin'd;	369	Ode Who saith	106
A Horse here is sadled, but no Tom him to backe,	374	Coryat 1	14
A Punke here pelts him with egs. How so?	375	Coryat 1	18
A Rabbin confutes him with the Bastinado.	375	Coryat 1	23
Here, finer then comming from his Punke you him see,	375	Coryat 1	28
Here France, and Italy both to him shed	375	Coryat 1	30
The height, let him learne of Mr. Tom. Coryate;	379	Coryat 3	2
The height, let him learne of Mr. Tom Coryate.	381	Coryat 3	60
It fits not onely him that makes a Booke,	385	Husband	1
For though Spaine gave him his first ayre and Vogue,	389	Aleman	15
Had cloath'd him so. Here's all I can supply	389	Aleman	20
Paccuvius, Accius, him of Cordova dead,	391	Shakespeare	35
Like him, to make the ayre, one volary:	397	Drayton	36
Both him & Archimede; damne Architas	402	Inigo Jones 1	5
I am too fat t'envy him. He too leane	405	Inigo Jones 1	69
To pitty him, as smiling at his Feat	405	Inigo Jones 1	71
To a Freind an Epigram Of him.	407	Inigo Jones 3	Ttl
That I should wryte upon him some sharp verse,	407	Inigo Jones 3	3
The Cobler kept him to his nall; but, now	410	Brome	17
that it remayne with him	666	Glover	6

HIMSELFE

	Page	Title	Line
Keepes himselfe, with halfe a man, and defrayes	30	E12 Shift	3
Himselfe: his whole revennue is, god payes.	30	E12 Shift	6
He that dares damne himselfe, dares more then fight.	32	E16 Brain-hardy	10
He that is round within himselfe, and streight,	63	E98 Th Roe 1	3
To which, yet, of the sides himselfe he owes.	66	E102 Pembroke	8
He hath not onely gain'd himselfe his eyes,	74	E114 Sydney	7
He makes himselfe a thorough-fare of vice.	76	E118 Gut	4
To him, man's dearer, then t'himselfe.	99	F3 Wroth	96
Cast himselfe from the spire	111	F11 Epode	64
Unto himselfe, by being so deare to you.	119	F13 Aubigny	117
Who made himselfe the price of sinne,	130	U1 Nativitie	20
To himselfe his losse of Time;	138	U2 Kisse	31
Himselfe young, and face be good,	142	U2 Exception	5
Himselfe of farther trouble, or the weight	154	U13 Sacvile	31
Is it that man pulls on himselfe Disease?	165	U15 Friend-Wars	114
Where he doth steepe himselfe in Milke and Roses;	170	U19 Elegy By	8
As would make shift, to make himselfe alone,	171	U19 Elegy By	24
Is gone himselfe into your Name.	173	U22 Elegy Tho	24
An Ode. To himselfe.	174	U23 Himselfe	Ttl
Yet he himselfe is but a sparke.	189	U36 Song	8
Not, like a Midas, shut up in himselfe,	197	U40 Elegy That	21
Farre from the Nest, and so himselfe belie	198	U40 Elegy That	38
Friend to himselfe, that would be friend to thee.	216	U45 Squib	22
Himselfe to rest,	246	U70 Ode	86
Him up, to doe the same himselfe had done.	256	U75 Epithalam.	108
Himselfe so un-inform'd of his elect,	286	U84 Muse	149
For 'twas himselfe who form'd, and gave it her.	287	U84 Muse	156
Still to be like himselfe, and hold his worth.	313	Horace	182
And the beholder to himselfe doth render.	317	Horace	259
Himselfe there purposely, or no; and would	335	Horace	657
To line out no stride, but pas'd by himselfe?	379	Coryat 3	8
(And himselfe with it) that he thinkes to frame;	392	Shakespeare	62
make many, hurt himselfe; a praysed faith	422	Lucan	V 2

HINDE

	Page	Title	Line
Blaspheme god, greatly. Or some poore hinde beat,	36	E28 Surly	17

HINT

	Page	Title	Line
Of Finenesse, and alloy: follow his hint,	415	Rutter	27

HIPOCRITES

	Page	Title	Line
In spite of Hipocrites, who are the worst	416	Dover	9

HIPPOCRENES

	Page	Title	Line
Then Hippocrenes liquor:	221	U48 Bacchus	28

HIR

	Page	Title	Line
Or hir easier eares beguile,	102	F5 Celia 1	V 13
The Moone comends hir	417	Moon	12
some tast to send hir.	417	Moon	20
as the standerd shall engage hir,	417	Moon	27
or hir quarters lighter bee,	417	Moon	31
each to pawne hir husbands capp,	417	Moon	38
hir minde is eased.	417	Moon	40
Uppon soe humbled earth to cast hir eyes:	420	Ode:If Men	30
Howe much they lame hir, in hir propertye:	421	Censure	14
hir Furye, though noe Frindshipp hee betraye.	422	Censure	26

HIRE

	Page	Title	Line
Like Money-brokers, after Names, and hire	155	U13 Sacvile	62
Now use the bones, we see doth hire a man	166	U15 Friend-Wars	136
Now use the bales, we see doth hire a man	166	U15 Friend-Wars	V136

HIR'D

	Page	Title	Line
As those that hir'd to weepe at Funeralls, swoune,	333	Horace	614

HIRELINGS

	Page	Title	Line
Of hirelings, wranglers, stitchers-to of strife,	187	U33 Councellour	8

HIRETH

	Page	Title	Line
What's this? if he whose money hireth thee	305	Horace	26

'S
   To pay at's day of marriage. By my hand   .   .   . 42 E46 Luckless 1   4
   Active in's braine, and passive in his bones.   .   .   49 E68 Playwrt 2   4
HIS
   He that departs with his owne honesty   .   .   27 E2 My Booke   13
   Himselfe: his whole revennue is, god payes.   .   30 E12 Shift   6
   At dice his borrow'd money: which, god payes.   .   30 E12 Shift   12
   That lost, he keepes his chamber, reades Essayes,   .   30 E12 Shift   15
   Calls for his stoole, adornes the stage: god payes.   .   30 E12 Shift   18
   His onely answere is to all, god payes.   .   .   31 E12 Shift   20
   Not his poore cocatrice but he betrayes   .   .   31 E12 Shift   21
   Thus: and for his letcherie, scores, god payes.   .   31 E12 Shift   22
   But see! th'old baud hath serv'd him in his trim,   .   31 E12 Shift   23
   Lord, how is Gam'ster chang'd! his haire close cut!   .   33 E21 Gam'ster   1
   His neck fenc'd round with ruffe! his eyes halfe shut!   .   33 E21 Gam'ster   2
   His clothes two fashions of, and poore! his sword   .   33 E21 Gam'ster   3
   Forbidd' his side! and nothing, but the word   .   33 E21 Gam'ster   4
   Quick in his lips! who hath this wonder wrought?   .   33 E21 Gam'ster   5
   While Beast instructs his faire, and innocent wife,   .   34 E25 Beast 1   1
   In the past pleasures of his sensuall life,   .   34 E25 Beast 1   2
   And how his Ganimede mov'd, and how his goate,   .   34 E25 Beast 1   4
   In varied shapes, which for his lust shee takes: .   34 E25 Beast 1   6
   Then his chast wife, though Beast now know no more,   .   35 E26 Beast 2   1
   He'adulters still: his thoughts lye with a whore.   .   35 E26 Beast 2   2
   If any Muse out-live their spight, his can;   .   35 E27 Roe 1   4
   If any friends teares could restore, his would;   .   35 E27 Roe 1   5
   To heaven; his hath: O happy state! wherein   .   35 E27 Roe 1   7
   H'has tympanies of businesse, in his face,   .   35 E28 Surly   7
   That's greater, yet: to crie his owne up neate.   .   35 E28 Surly   11
   He doth, at meales, alone, his pheasant eate,   .   35 E28 Surly   12
   Which is maine greatnesse. And, at his still boord,   .   35 E28 Surly   13
   That breathes in his dogs way: and this is great.   .   36 E28 Surly   18
   Banck feeles no lamenesse of his knottie gout,   .   36 E31 Banck   1
   His monyes travaile for him, in and out: .   36 E31 Banck   2
   His often change of clime (though not of mind)   .   37 E32 Roe 2   6
   What could not worke; at home in his repaire   .   37 E32 Roe 2   7
   Was his blest fate, but our hard lot to find.   .   37 E32 Roe 2   8
   And pleaseth both. For while he melts his greace   .   38 E37 Chev'ril   3
   For this: that winnes, for whom he holds his peace.   .   38 E37 Chev'ril   4
   Colt, now, doth daily penance in his owne.   .   39 E39 Colt   2
   But this his Jone doth too. And Giles would never,   .   40 E42 Giles   4
   By his free will, be in Jones company.   .   40 E42 Giles   5
   All this doth Jone. Or that his long yearn'd life   .   40 E42 Giles   11
   Were quite out-spun. The like wish hath his wife.   .   40 E42 Giles   12
   Of his begetting. And so sweares his Jone.   .   40 E42 Giles   14
   To the most Worthy of his Honors. Robert, . . .   40 E43 Salisbury 1 VTtl
   Ere blacks were bought for his owne funerall,   .   41 E44 Chuff   3
   Saw all his race approch the blacker floods: .   41 E44 Chuff   4
   Ben. Jonson his best piece of poetrie.   .   41 E45 First Son   10
   For whose sake, hence-forth, all his vowes be such,   .   41 E45 First Son   11
   Yes, now he weares his knight-hood every day.   .   42 E46 Luckless 1   6
   His bought armes Mung' not lik'd; for his first day   .   42 E48 Mungril   1
   For wittie, in his language, is obscene.   .   42 E49 Playwrt 1   4
   To King James. Upon the happy false rumour of his death, . . .   43 E51 James 3   Ttl
   He takes up all, makes each mans wit his owne.   .   45 E56 Poet-Ape   8
   May judge it to be his, as well as ours.   .   45 E56 Poet-Ape   12
   Your 'pothecarie, and his drug sayes no.   .   46 E62 Would-bee   4
   Without his, thine, and all times injurie?   .   47 E63 Salisbury 2   10
   Curst be his Muse, that could lye dumbe, or hid   .   47 E63 Salisbury 2   11
   Contends t'have worth enjoy, from his regard,   .   48 E64 Salisbury 3   13
   And, as thou'hast mine, his houres, and youth abuse.   .   48 E65 Muse   6
   Make him loose all his friends; and, which is worse,   .   48 E65 Muse   9
   Active in's braine, and passive in his bones.   .   49 E68 Playwrt 2   4
   Still, 'tis his lucke to praise me 'gainst his will.   .   50 E71 Parrat   2
   Though Lippe, at Pauls, ranne from his text away,   .   52 E75 Lippe   3
   Nor lend like influence from his lucent seat.   .   52 E76 Bedford 1   8
   (Save that most masculine issue of his braine)   .   53 E79 Rutland   6
   As he would burne, or better farre his booke.   .   53 E79 Rutland   12
   And hath it, in his powers, to make his way!   .   53 E80 Life/Death   4
   What would his serious actions me have learned?   .   55 E85 Goodyere 1   12
   Touch'd with the sinne of false play, in his punque,   .   56 E87 Hazard   1
   Hazard a month forsware his; and grew drunke,   .   56 E87 Hazard   2
   Each night, to drowne his cares: But when the gaine   .   56 E87 Hazard   3
   Of what shee had wrought came in, and wak'd his braine,   .   56 E87 Hazard   4
   That his whole body should speake french, not he?   .   56 E88 Monsieur   2
   As french-men in his companie, should seeme dutch?   .   56 E88 Monsieur   8
   Or had his father, when he did him get,   .   56 E88 Monsieur   9
   By which his damme conceiv'd him, clothes and all?   .   56 E88 Monsieur   11
   And, finding good securitie in his age,   .   57 E90 Mill   6
   Discern'd no difference of his yeeres, or play,   .   57 E90 Mill   8
   And he growne youth, was call'd to his ladies chamber.   .   57 E90 Mill   10
   Still Mill continu'd: Nay, his face growing worse,   .   57 E90 Mill   11
   Mill was the same. Since, both his body and face   .   57 E90 Mill   13
   Longer a day, but with his Mill will marry.   .   57 E90 Mill   16
   So hast thou rendred him in all his bounds,   .   61 E95 Savile   5
   And all his numbers, both of sense, and sounds.   .   61 E95 Savile   6
   As, then, his cause, his glorie emulate.   .   61 E95 Savile   24
   Of state, and censure them: we need his pen   .   62 E95 Savile   33
   But most we need his faith (and all have you)   .   62 E95 Savile   35
   His cloke with orient velvet quite lin'd through,   .   62 E97 Motion   4
   His rosie tyes and garters so ore-blowne,   .   62 E97 Motion   5
   By his each glorious parcell to be knowne!   .   62 E97 Motion   6
   About his forme. What then so swells each lim?   .   63 E97 Motion   19

		Page	Title	Line
HIS (cont.)				
Onely his clothes have over-leaven'd him.		63	E97 Motion	20
And what would hurt his vertue makes it still.		63	E98 Th Roe 1	6
To Clement Edmonds, on his Caesars . . .		71	E110 Edmonds 1	Ttl
Not Caesars deeds, nor all his honors wonne,		71	E110 Edmonds 1	1
All yeelding to his fortune, nor, the while,		71	E110 Edmonds 1	5
To have engrav'd these acts, with his owne stile,		71	E110 Edmonds 1	6
Nor that his worke liv'd in the hands of foes,		71	E110 Edmonds 1	9
For, where his person liv'd scarce one just age,		71	E110 Edmonds 1	13
His deedes too dying, but in bookes (whose good		71	E110 Edmonds 1	15
His deedes too dying, save in bookes (whose good		71	E110 Edmonds 1	V 15
His life, but makes, that he can dye no more.		71	E110 Edmonds 1	22
Caesar stands up, as from his urne late rose,		72	E111 Edmonds 2	12
So Phoebus makes me worthy of his bayes,		73	E113 Overbury	1
In meere out-formes, untill he lost his sight,		73	E114 Sydney	4
Hath chang'd his soule, and made his object you:		74	E114 Sydney	5
He hath not onely gain'd himselfe his eyes,		74	E114 Sydney	7
But, in your love, made all his servants wise.		74	E114 Sydney	8
Give every one his dose of mirth: and watches		74	E115 Honest Man	14
Parts, then th'Italian could doe, with his dore.		74	E115 Honest Man	26
Groyne, come of age, his state sold out of hand		75	E117 Groyne	1
For'his whore: Groyne doth still occupy his land.		75	E117 Groyne	2
So all his meate he tasteth over, twise:		76	E118 Gut	2
And, striving so to double his delight,		76	E118 Gut	3
Thus, in his belly, can he change a sin,		76	E118 Gut	5
He, that, but living halfe his age, dyes such;		76	E119 Shelton	15
So, by error, to his fate		77	E120 S. P.	17
That strives, his manners should precede his wit.		78	E121 Rudyerd 1	8
To his Lady, then Mrs. Cary.		80	E126 Mrs Cary	Ttl
Said I wrong'd him, and (which was more) his love.		80	E126 Mrs Cary	5
To Alphonso Ferrabosco, on his Booke.		82	E130 Ferrab. 1	Ttl
Bartas doth wish thy English now were his.		83	E132 Sylvester	10
So well in that are his inventions wrought,		83	E132 Sylvester	11
As his will now be the translation thought,		83	E132 Sylvester	12
Who gave, to take at his returne from Hell,		84	E133 Voyage	27
His three for one. Now, lordings, listen well.		84	E133 Voyage	28
A harder tasque, then either his to Bristo',		85	E133 Voyage	39
Or his to Antwerpe. Therefore, once more, list ho'.		85	E133 Voyage	40
Who shall discharge first his merd-urinous load:		85	E133 Voyage	65
And all his followers, that had so abus'd him:		86	E133 Voyage	97
His spirits, now, in pills, and eeke in potions,		86	E133 Voyage	101
Tempt not his furie, Pluto is away:		89	E133 Voyage	179
They laugh't, at his laugh-worthy fate. And past		89	E133 Voyage	185
My Muse had plough'd with his, that sung A-jax.		89	E133 Voyage	196
At his great birth, where all the Muses met.		94	F2 Penshurst	14
Of many a Sylvane, taken with his flames.		94	F2 Penshurst	16
Before the fisher, or into his hand.		94	F2 Penshurst	38
Fig, grape, and quince, each in his time doth come:		94	F2 Penshurst	42
Without his feare, and of thy lords owne meate:		95	F2 Penshurst	62
That is his Lordships, shall be also mine.		95	F2 Penshurst	64
With his brave sonne, the Prince, they saw thy fires		95	F2 Penshurst	77
His children thy great lord may call his owne:		96	F2 Penshurst	91
To some coole, courteous shade, which he calls his,		97	F3 Wroth	19
Who, for it, makes thy house his court;		97	F3 Wroth	24
Who, for it, makes thy lodge his court;		97	F3 Wroth	V 24
And change possessions, oftner with his breath,		99	F3 Wroth	75
And each where boast it as his merit,		99	F3 Wroth	78
And thinke his power doth equall Fates.		99	F3 Wroth	80
That fled his cage, or broke his chaine,		101	F4 To the World	30
Render his head in there againe?		101	F4 To the World	32
Spend not then his guifts in vaine.		102	F5 Celia 1	5
Or his easier eares beguile,		102	F5 Celia 1	13
Or the starres, that guild his streames,		103	F6 Celia 2	16
To his Mistresse		106	F9 Celia 3	VTtl
Hercules? alas his bones are yet sore,		107	F10 Proludium	4
With his old earthly labours. T'exact more,		107	F10 Proludium	5
Of his dull god-head, were sinne. Ile implore		107	F10 Proludium	6
Of his dull god-head, were sinne. Lets implore		107	F10 Proludium	V 6
Who, with his axe, thy fathers mid-wife plaid.		107	F10 Proludium	15
Let the old boy, your sonne, ply his old taske,		107	F10 Proludium	19
His absence in my verse, is all I aske.		107	F10 Proludium	21
His absence in our verse, is all I aske.		107	F10 Proludium	V 21
Though he would steale his sisters Pegasus,		107	F10 Proludium	23
And riffle him: or pawne his Petasus.		107	F10 Proludium	24
Of all his happinesse? But soft: I heare		111	F11 Epode	65
His heart sinnes, though he feares.		112	F11 Epode	90
Making his fortunes swim		112	F11 Epode	106
And to his sense object this sentence ever,		113	F11 Epode	115
When his proud patrons favours are asleepe;		113	F12 Rutland	14
His love unto the Muses, when his skill		114	F12 Rutland	33
Before his swift and circled race be run,		116	F12 Rutland	99
Before his swift and fetherd race be run,		116	F12 Rutland	V 99
T'advance his doubtfull issue, and ore-flow		117	F13 Aubigny	40
Till that no usurer, nor his bawds dare lend		118	F13 Aubigny	78
You are depending on his word, and will;		119	F13 Aubigny	114
Ode. To Sir William Sydney, on his Birth-day.		120	F14 Sydney	Ttl
And he, with his best Genius left alone.		120	F14 Sydney	20
His glorious Name		129	U1 Father	24
Under his Crosse.		130	U1 Father	32
1. His Excuse for loving.		131	U2 Excuse	Ttl
Every Cloud about his eye;		132	U2 How he saw	12
But, he had not gain'd his sight		132	U2 How he saw	13
Sooner, then he lost his might,		132	U2 How he saw	14

HIS (cont.)

Entry	Page	Title	Line
Or his courage; for away	132	U2 How he saw	15
Or else one that plaid his Ape,	132	U2 How he saw	31
In a Hercules-his shape.	132	U2 How he saw	32
Mee, the scope of his next draught,	133	U2 Suffered	11
And (to gaine her by his Art)	133	U2 Suffered	15
5. His discourse with Cupid.	136	U2 Cupid	Ttl
To himselfe his losse of Time;	138	U2 Kisse	31
Or have charg'd his sight of Crime,	138	U2 Kisse	32
That doth but touch his flower, and flies away.	139	U2 Another	6
Had of Love, and of his force,	139	U2 Promise	2
Better fits him, then his face;	140	U2 Promise	20
And his Manners of that Nation.	141	U2 Her man	8
For Loves fingers, and his wings:	141	U2 Her man	12
And his lip should kissing teach,	141	U2 Her man	22
All his blood should be a flame	141	U2 Her man	30
Well he should his clothes to weare;	141	U2 Her man	36
And as honest as his Birth.	142	U2 Her man	44
All his actions to be such,	142	U2 Her man	45
For his Mind, I doe not care,	142	U2 Exception	1
Let his Title be but great,	142	U2 Exception	3
His Clothes rich, and band sit neat,	142	U2 Exception	4
What man but must lose his?	143	U3 Musicall	8
Where Love may all his Torches light,	147	U7 Nymph	24
What Nymph so e're his voyce but heares,	148	U7 Nymph	27
If Love, or feare, would let me tell his name.	148	U7 Nymph	35
And in his Mrs. flame, playing like a flye,	149	U8 Houre-glasse	7
And in his Mrs. flaming, playing like a flye,	149	U8 Houre-glasse V	7
Verses on his Picture	149	U9 Picture	VTtl
Loves sicknesse, and his noted want of worth,	150	U10 Jealousie	14
Of sleepe againe, who was his Aid;	151	U11 Dreame	12
With the just Canon of his life,	151	U12 Corbet	11
But was by sweetning so his will,	151	U12 Corbet	13
His Mind as pure, and neatly kept,	151	U12 Corbet	15
As were his Nourceries; and swept	151	U12 Corbet	16
And adde his Actions unto these,	152	U12 Corbet	19
They were as specious as his Trees.	152	U12 Corbet	20
His very Manners taught t'amend,	152	U12 Corbet	22
As twice to trespasse in his sight,	152	U12 Corbet	26
His lookes would so correct it, when	152	U12 Corbet	27
Against his will that do's 'hem? that hath weav'd	153	U13 Sacvile	26
That puts it in his Debt-booke e're 't be done;	154	U13 Sacvile	34
His Groomes to witnesse; or else lets it fall	154	U13 Sacvile	36
Ben: Jonson To His Honord Friend Mr John Selden Health.	158	U14 Selden	VTtl
Mans buried honour, in his sleepie life:	162	U15 Friend-Wars	7
His unjust hopes, with praises begg'd, or (worse)	162	U15 Friend-Wars	12
Bought Flatteries, the issue of his purse,	162	U15 Friend-Wars	13
Till he becomes both their, and his owne curse!	162	U15 Friend-Wars	14
To gaine upon his belly; and at last	162	U15 Friend-Wars	17
Or Feathers: lay his fortune out to show,	162	U15 Friend-Wars	21
Against his Maker; high alone with weeds,	163	U15 Friend-Wars	33
To have his Court-bred-fillie there commend	163	U15 Friend-Wars	48
His Lace and Starch; And fall upon her back	163	U15 Friend-Wars	49
Of lust, to his rich Suit and Title, Lord?	163	U15 Friend-Wars	51
Is lov'd, though he let out his owne for life:	165	U15 Friend-Wars	88
Nature, that will not let his Wife be a whore;	165	U15 Friend-Wars	90
That may corrupt her, even in his eyes.	165	U15 Friend-Wars	92
For man to spend his money on? his wit?	165	U15 Friend-Wars	102
His time? health? soule? will he for these goe throw	165	U15 Friend-Wars	103
Those thousands on his back, shall after blow	165	U15 Friend-Wars	104
His body to the Counters, or the Fleete?	165	U15 Friend-Wars	105
His body to the compters, or the Fleete?	165	U15 Friend-Wars	V105
His deare and borrow'd Bravery he must cast?	165	U15 Friend-Wars	110
When not his Combes, his Curling-irons, his Glasse,	165	U15 Friend-Wars	111
To flatter my good Lord, and cry his Bowle	167	U15 Friend-Wars	147
Runs sweetly, as it had his Lordships Soule;	167	U15 Friend-Wars	148
When I am hoarse, with praising his each cast,	167	U15 Friend-Wars	151
Pardon his Lordship. Flattry's growne so cheape	167	U15 Friend-Wars	155
Simply my Band, his trust in me forsakes,	169	U17 Friend-Debt	12
Love lights his torches to inflame desires;	170	U19 Elegy By	2
His double Bow, and round his Arrowes sends;	170	U19 Elegy By	4
He flying curles, and crispeth, with his wings;	170	U19 Elegy By	6
That which we can, who both in you, his Wife,	171	U19 Elegy By	25
His Issue, and all Circumstance of life,	171	U19 Elegy By	26
As in his place, because he would not varie,	171	U19 Elegy By	27
His name in any mettall, it would breake.	172	U21 Ltl Shrub	2
Out of his Grave, and poyson every eare.	172	U21 Ltl Shrub	4
His falling Temples you have rear'd,	173	U22 Elegy Tho	17
His Altars kept from the Decay,	173	U22 Elegy Tho	19
High, as his mind, that doth advance	176	U25 Desmond	5
Where only a mans birth is his offence,	177	U25 Desmond	32
When only a mans birth is his offence,	177	U25 Desmond	V 32
Lie drawne to life, in his soft Verse,	181	U27 Ode Helen	7
Is Horace his each love so high	181	U27 Ode Helen	13
Hath Petrarch since his Laura rais'd	181	U27 Ode Helen	21
His new Cassandra, 'bove the old;	181	U27 Ode Helen	23
Made Dian, not his notes refuse?	182	U27 Ode Helen	28
His flames, his shafts, his Quiver, and his Bow,	182	U28 Worth	10
His very eyes are yours to overthrow.	182	U28 Worth	11
But then his Mothers sweets you so apply,	182	U28 Worth	12
Phoebus to his Crowne againe.	184	U29 Fit of Rime	40
May his joynts tormented bee,	184	U29 Fit of Rime	50
May his Sense, when it would meet	184	U29 Fit of Rime	55

HIS (cont.)

	Page	Title	Line
The cold tumor in his feet,	184	U29 Fit of Rime	56
And his Title be long foole,	184	U29 Fit of Rime	58
Thy Universe, though his Epitome.	185	U30 Burleigh	4
But stood unshaken in his Deeds, and Name,	185	U30 Burleigh	11
Rather than meet him: And, before his eyes	185	U30 Burleigh	16
Clos'd to their peace, he saw his branches shoot,	185	U30 Burleigh	17
Law, to his Law; and thinke your enemies his:	185	U31 Elsmere	4
The Judge his favour timely then extends,	186	U32 Elsmere	1
Though Envie oft his shadow be,	189	U36 Song	3
All lights into his one doth run;	189	U36 Song	6
Such are his powers, whom time hath stil'd,	189	U36 Song	13
Would live his glory that could keepe it on;	192	U38 Elegy 'Tis	48
The Sunne his heat, and light, the ayre his dew?	192	U38 Elegy 'Tis	57
And then his thunder frights more, then it kills.	193	U38 Elegy 'Tis	70
Streight puts off all his Anger, and doth kisse	193	U38 Elegy 'Tis	88
And must be bred, so to conceale his birth,	197	U40 Elegy That	17
In all his Actions rarified to spright;	197	U40 Elegy That	20
Keepe in reserv'd in his Dark-lanterne face,	198	U40 Elegy That	23
Keepe secret in his Channels what he breedes,	198	U40 Elegy That	27
Doth, while he keepes his watch, betray his stand.	198	U40 Elegy That	36
Winter is come a Quarter e're his Time,	199	U41 Elegy Since	12
His lynes, and hourely sits the Poets horse?	200	U42 Elegy Let	8
Home to the Customer: his Letcherie	201	U42 Elegy Let	41
That (in pure Madrigall) unto his Mother	201	U42 Elegy Let	68
Any Comparison had with his Cheap-side.	202	U42 Elegy Let	76
Ben: Jonson upon the burning of his study and bookes	202	U43 Vulcan	VTtl
To Merlins Marvailes, and his Caballs losse,	206	U43 Vulcan	71
To Martins Marvailes, and his Caballs losse,	206	U43 Vulcan	V 71
With Merlins Marvailes, and his tables losse,	206	U43 Vulcan	V 71
Of our fift Henry, eight of his nine yeare;	207	U43 Vulcan	98
Of our fift Henry, right of his nine yeare;	207	U43 Vulcan	V 98
And so did Jove, who ne're meant thee his Cup:	208	U43 Vulcan	115
And for it lose his eyes with Gun-powder,	208	U43 Vulcan	121
As th'other may his braines with Quicksilver.	208	U43 Vulcan	122
No Foole would his owne harvest spoile, or burne!	209	U43 Vulcan	150
Scap'd not his Justice any jot the more:	210	U43 Vulcan	154
Though but in daunces, it shall know his power;	210	U43 Vulcan	157
Troy, though it were so much his Venus care.	210	U43 Vulcan	160
At Common-Law: me thinkes in his despight	211	U43 Vulcan	177
His Lordship. That is for his Band, his haire	215	U44 Speach	95
This, and that box his Beautie to repaire;	215	U44 Speach	96
This other for his eye-browes; hence, away,	215	U44 Speach	97
Turne him, and see his Threds: looke, if he be	216	U45 Squib	21
For that is first requir'd, A man be his owne.	216	U45 Squib	23
Although my Fame, to his, not under-heares,	219	U47 Tribe	49
Before his braine doe know it;	221	U48 Bacchus	30
Then Cupid, and his Mother.	221	U48 Bacchus	36
To put his Court in dances,	222	U48 Bacchus	50
When with his royall shipping	222	U48 Bacchus	52
To his poore Instrument, now out of grace.	223	U49 Pucell	34
What then his Father was, that since is hee,	225	U51 Bacon	11
In his soft Cradle to his Fathers Chaire,	225	U51 Bacon	11
. . . On his Horsemanship, and Stable.	228	U53 Newcastle	VTtl
Provoke his mettall, and command his force	228	U53 Newcastle	2
Or Castor mounted on his Cyllarus:	228	U53 Newcastle	8
Of bold Sir Bevis, and his Arundell:	228	U53 Newcastle	10
Nay, so your Seate his beauties did endorse,	228	U53 Newcastle	11
His friends, but to breake Chaires, or cracke a Coach.	230	U56 Covell	10
His weight is twenty Stone within two pound;	230	U56 Covell	11
Marrie his Muse is one, can tread the Aire,	230	U56 Covell	V 13
Accept his Muse; and tell, I know you can,	231	U56 Covell	26
Tell him his Ben	231	U57 Burges	7
if the 'Chequer be emptie, so will be his Head.	232	U57 Burges	28
His judgement is: If he be wise, and praise,	232	U58 Book-seller	5
If his wit reach no higher, but to spring	232	U58 Book-seller	7
But crept like darknesse through his blood?	234	U60 La-ware	8
Of Vertue, got above his name?	234	U60 La-ware	10
That spread his body o're, to kill:	234	U60 La-ware	16
And only, his great Soule envy'd,	234	U60 La-ware	17
What can the Poet wish his King may doe,	235	U62 Charles 1	13
Doth by his doubt, distrust his promise more.	235	U63 Charles 2	4
What (at his liking) he will take away.	236	U63 Charles 2	6
But thanke his greatnesse, and his goodnesse too;	236	U63 Charles 2	9
. . . On the Universary day of his Raigne. 1629.	236	U64 Charles 3	VTtl
. . . On his Anniversary Day. 1629.	236	U64 Charles 3	Ttl
Most pious King, but his owne good in you!	236	U64 Charles 3	2
Then now, to love the Soveraigne, or his Lawes?	236	U64 Charles 3	V 8
An Epigram on Prince Charles his Birth: May. 29th. 1630	237	U65 Prince	VTtl
Upon his pointed Lance:	240	U67 Muses	39
His Poet Sack, the House-hold will not pay?	241	U68 House-hold	2
His Poet leave to sing his House-hold true;	241	U68 House-hold	6
'T were better spare a Butt, then spill his Muse.	241	U68 House-hold	12
The Kings fame lives. Go now, denie his Teirce.	241	U68 House-hold	14
His is more safe commoditie, or none:	241	U69 Friend Son	7
Painted a Dog, that now his subtler skill	241	U69 Friend Son	10
All live dogs from the lane, and his shops sight,	241	U69 Friend Son	12
Till he had sold his Piece, drawne so unlike:	242	U69 Friend Son	13
Some of his formes, he lets him not come neere	242	U69 Friend Son	17
To Sir Lucius Carey, on the death of his Brother Morison	242	U70 Ode	VTtl
His rage, with razing your immortall Towne.	242	U70 Ode	4
Or masked man, if valu'd by his face,	243	U70 Ode	23
Above his fact?	243	U70 Ode	24

HIS (cont.)

	Page	Title	Line
Here's one out-liv'd his Peeres,	243	U70 Ode	25
For three of his foure-score, he did no good.	243	U70 Ode	32
And had his noble name advanc'd with men:	244	U70 Ode	36
As though his age imperfect might appeare,	244	U70 Ode	51
His life was of Humanitie the Sphaere.	244	U70 Ode	52
(Were not his Lucius long with us to tarry)	246	U70 Ode	91
And keepe the one halfe from his Harry.	246	U70 Ode	94
Each stiled, by his end,	247	U70 Ode	111
The Copie of his friend.	247	U70 Ode	112
Disease, the Enemie, and his Ingineeres,	248	U71 Treasurer	4
Want, with the rest of his conceal'd compeeres,	248	U71 Treasurer	5
To the King. On his Birth-day . . .	249	U72 King	Ttl
Upon King Charles his Birth-day.	249	U72 King	VTtl
This is King Charles his Day. Speake it, thou Towre,	249	U72 King	1
This is King Charles his birth day. Speake it, thou Towre,	249	U72 King	V 1
In his great Actions: view whom his large hand	250	U73 Weston	3
Hath rais'd to be the Port unto his Land!	250	U73 Weston	4
. . . gratulatorie For his Returne from his Embassie. 1632.	250	U74 Weston	Ttl
When he beholds a graft of his owne hand,	251	U74 Weston	27
To be a shadow to his Heire,	251	U74 Weston	29
And both a strength, and Beautie to his Land!	251	U74 Weston	30
The bountie of a King, and beautie of his Queene!	252	U75 Epithalam.	8
Their Sister-tunes, from Thames his either side,	253	U75 Epithalam.	34
The king of Creatures, take his paritie	255	U75 Epithalam.	83
But doth his Carract, and just Standard keepe	255	U75 Epithalam.	100
doth his prime Carract, and just Standard keepe	255	U75 Epithalam.	V100
To pay, with honours, to his noble Sonne	256	U75 Epithalam.	106
And by his Rise, in active men, his Name	256	U75 Epithalam.	116
How each one playes his part, of the large Pedigree.	258	U75 Epithalam.	176
So great; his Body now alone projects the shade.	258	U75 Epithalam.	184
So large; his Body then, not boughs, project his shade.	258	U75 Epithalam.	V184
Of his speciall grace to Letters,	259	U76 Petition	7
To his bountie; by extension	259	U76 Petition	9
To his bountie; by dimension	259	U76 Petition	V 9
To his Poet of a Pension,	259	U76 Petition	V 10
You'ld reade a Snake, in his next Song.	260	U76 Petition	32
To eate a Snake, in his next Song.	260	U76 Petition	V 32
As farre as sense, and onely by his eyes.	261	U77 Treasurer	V 12
Court can call hers, or Man could call his Arts.	262	U78 Digby	4
His brest is a brave Palace, a broad Street,	262	U78 Digby	9
As other soules, to his, dwell in a Lane:	262	U78 Digby	12
Witnesse his Action done at Scanderone;	262	U78 Digby	13
And his great Action done at Scanderone.	262	U78 Digby	V 13
He will cleare up his forehead, thinke thou bring'st	263	U78 Digby	21
He will cheare up his forehead, thinke thou bring'st	263	U78 Digby	V 21
See where he walkes with Mira by his side.	263	U78 Digby	
Sound, sound his praises loud, and with his, hers divide.	264	U79 New-yeares	18
Heare, o you Groves, and, Hills, resound his praise.	264	U79 New-yeares	19
Heare, O you Groves, and, Hills, resound his worth.	264	U79 New-yeares	23
Wee know no other power then his,	264	U79 New-yeares	31
The theefe from spoyle, his presence holds.	265	U79 New-yeares	42
Pan knowes no other power then his,	265	U79 New-yeares	63
To My L. the King, On the Christning His second Sonne James.	265	U79 New-yeares	64
This day, by Baptisme, and his Saviours crosse:	268	U80 Christning	Ttl
As comming with his Harpe, prepar'd	268	U80 Christning	10
Worke with my fancie, his owne hand.	274	U84 Cradle	35
What's left a Poet, when his Muse is gone?	276	U84 Body	12
To heare their Judge, and his eternall doome;	283	U84 Muse	28
Have all his actions wondred at, and view'd	283	U84 Muse	48
Have busie search made in his mysteries!	284	U84 Muse	77
A new Song to his praise, and great I Am:	284	U84 Muse	80
In his humanitie! To heare him preach	285	U84 Muse	90
Through his inherent righteousnesse, in death,	286	U84 Muse	133
In his eternall Kingdome, where we sit	286	U84 Muse	135
Himselfe so un-inform'd of his elect,	286	U84 Muse	145
For his designed worke, the perfect end	286	U84 Muse	149
The kind of Man, on whom his doome should fall!	288	U84 Muse	206
As being the Sonne of Man) to shew his Power,	288	U84 Muse	208
His Wisdome, and his Justice, in that houre,	288	U84 Muse	217
Where first his Power will appeare, by call	288	U84 Muse	218
Of all are dead to life! His Wisdome show	289	U84 Muse	220
And most his Justice, in the fitting parts,	289	U84 Muse	221
With his owne Oxen tills his Sires left lands,	289	U84 Muse	223
And with his hooke lops off the fruitlesse race,	289	U85 Country	3
His head, with mellow Apples crown'd,	290	U85 Country	11
How plucking Peares, his owne hand grafted had,	290	U85 Country	18
And, Sylvane, thine that keptst his Lands!	290	U85 Country	19
And, Sylvane, thine that keep'st his Lands!	290	U85 Country	22
Then when the thundring Jove his Snow and showres	290	U85 Country	V 22
Wild Bores into his toyles pitch'd round:	290	U85 Country	29
Or straines on his small forke his subtill nets	290	U85 Country	32
Or straines on his small forke his subtler nets	290	U85 Country	33
'Gainst th'Ides, his moneys he gets in with paine,	290	U85 Country	V 33
'Gainst th'Ides, his gott moneyes he gets in with paine,	291	U85 Country	69
To bend a man, now at his fiftieth yeare	291	U85 Country	V 69
And for the troubled Clyent fyl's his tongue,	292	U86 Hor.4:1	6
And when he smiling finds his Grace	292	U86 Hor.4:1	14
With thee 'bove all his Rivals gifts take place,	292	U86 Hor.4:1	17
Whether in Mars his field thou bee,	292	U86 Hor.4:1	18
His armes more acceptable free,	293	U86 Hor.4:1	39
Nor after Chloe did his Lydia sound;	293	U87 Hor.3:9	3
Hee, that but living halfe his dayes, dies such,	293	U87 Hor.3:9	6
	295	U89 Mart.8:77	7

284

HIS (cont.)
    Makes his life longer then 'twas given him, much.   .   .   .   295   U89 Mart.8:77   8
    Horace, His Art of Poetrie Made English   303   Horace   Ttl
    Quintus Horatius Flaccus his book of   338   Horace   VTtl
    Admitted to the sight, although his friends,   .   .   .   305   Horace   6
    Wants strength, and sinewes, as his spirits were done;   .   .   339   Horace   V 38/ 37
    His Muse professing height, and greatnesse, swells;   .   .   339   Horace   V 39/ 38
    His choise, who's matter to his power doth reare,   .   .   .   339   Horace   V 58/ 56
    His matter to his power, in all he makes,   .   .   .   307   Horace   57
    His course so hurtfull both to graine, and seedes,   .   .   .   309   Horace   97
    In sound, quite from his fortune; both the rout,   .   .   .   313   Horace   159
    Or some hot youth, yet in his flourishing course;   .   .   .   313   Horace   163
    Be nought so'bove him but his sword let claime.   .   .   .   313   Horace   174
    Be nought so'bove him, but his bold sword claime.   .   .   342   Horace   V174
    A meere new person, looke he keepe his state   .   .   .   313   Horace   180
    Still to be like himselfe, and hold his worth.   .   .   .   313   Horace   182
    But light from smoake; that he may draw his bright   .   .   315   Horace   204
    (As if he knew it) rapps his hearer to   .   .   .   315   Horace   212
    The middle of his matter: letting goe   .   .   .   315   Horace   213
    Th'unbearded Youth, his Guardian once being gone,   .   .   315   Horace   229
    For his owne good, a carelesse letter-goe   .   .   .   315   Horace   234
    His better'd mind seekes wealth, and friendship: than   .   .   315   Horace   238
    As his departing take much thence: lest, then,   .   .   .   317   Horace   251
    His Nephews entrailes; nor must Progne flie   .   .   .   317   Horace   266
    Worth his untying happen there: And not   317   Horace   274
    And rivall with the Trumpet for his sound,   .   .   .   319   Horace   288
    Thus, to his antient Art the Piper lent   319   Horace   303
    In his train'd Gowne about the Stage: So grew   .   .   .   319   Horace   305
    In his train'd Gowne about the Stage: thus grew   .   .   346   Horace   V305
    Though sower, with safetie of his gravitie,   .   .   .   319   Horace   322
    Simo; and, of a talent wip'd his purse;   321   Horace   347
    Simo, and of a talent cleans'd his purse;   .   .   .   346   Horace   V339/347
    Which law receiv'd, the Chorus held his peace,   .   .   .   323   Horace   369
    His power of foulely hurting made to cease.   .   .   .   323   Horace   370
    What to his Countrey, what his friends he owes,   .   .   .   325   Horace   446
    What brethren, what a stranger, and his guest,   .   .   .   325   Horace   448
    On life, and manners, and make those his meanes,   .   .   325   Horace   454
    Was said to move the stones, by his Lutes powers,   .   .   327   Horace   484
    Sweet mix'd with sowre, to his Reader, so   .   .   .   329   Horace   515
    His armes in Mars his field, he doth refuse;   .   .   .   331   Horace   566
    His flatterers to their gaine. But say, he can   .   .   .   333   Horace   601
    His praisers to their gaine: but say he can   .   .   .   353   Horace   V601
    Whether his soothing friend speake truth, or no.   .   .   .   333   Horace   606
    Out at his friendly eyes, leape, beat the groun'.   .   .   333   Horace   613
    Alone, without a rivall, by his will.   335   Horace   632
    Blot out the carelesse, with his turned pen;   .   .   .   335   Horace   635
    Hee that preserves a man, against his will,   .   .   .   335   Horace   665
    Or love of this his famous death lay by.   .   .   .   355   Horace   V669
    His cause of making Verses none knowes why: .   .   .   335   Horace   670
    Whether he piss'd upon his Fathers grave;   .   .   .   335   Horace   671
    Not letting goe his hold, where he drawes food,   .   .   .   337   Horace   679
    His proofe their praise, will meete, as in this line.   .   .   362   Author   14
    Prove of his Mistris Feature, ...   364   Phoenix   7
    Marke, marke, but when his wing he takes,   .   .   .   366   Ode Who saith   9
    Smiles in his Sphaere, to see the rest affect,   .   .   .   366   Ode Who saith   13
    This Swanne is onely his, ...   366   Ode Who saith   15
    And Phoebus love cause of his blackenesse is.   .   .   .   366   Ode Who saith   16
    From Zephyr's rape would close him with his beames.   .   .   366   Ode Who saith   24
    This change'd his Downe; till this, as white   .   .   .   366   Ode Who saith   25
    Be proofe, the glory of his hand, ...   367   Ode Who saith   49
    His farre-admired Acts, ...   367   Ode Who saith   59
    Tames, prowde of thee, and of his Fate   368   Ode Who saith   81
    That may judge for his six-pence) had, before   .   .   .   371   Fletcher   7
    All sorts of fish with Musicke of his maw.   .   .   .   374   Coryat 1   11
    And louse-dropping Case, are the Armes of his travell.   .   .   375   Coryat 1   27
    Here, finer then comming from his Punke you him see,   .   .   375   Coryat 1   28
    Their hornes, and Germany pukes on his head.   .   .   .   375   Coryat 1   31
    But here, neither trusting his hands, nor his legs,   .   .   375   Coryat 1   34
    To the Right Noble Tom, Tell-Troth of his travailes, ...   378   Coryat 2   Ttl
    Marry he sets it out at his owne charge;   .   .   .   378   Coryat 2   83
    And therein (which is worth his valour too)   .   .   .   378   Coryat 2   84
    Rather his sonne, I should have cal'd thee, why?   .   .   378   Coryat 2   88
    Yes thou wert borne out of his travelling thigh   .   .   .   378   Coryat 2   89
    As well as from his braines, and claimest thereby   .   .   378   Coryat 2   90
    To be his Bacchus as his Pallas: bee   378   Coryat 2   91
    Ever his thighes Male then, and his braines Shee.   .   .   378   Coryat 2   92
    Who, because his matter in all should be meete,   .   .   379   Coryat 3   3
    To his strength, hath measur'd it out with his feet.   .   .   379   Coryat 3   4
    By the scale of his booke, a yard of his stile?   .   .   379   Coryat 3   10
    Which, unto all Ages, for his will be knowne,   .   .   379   Coryat 3   11
    Since he treads in no other Mans steps but his owne.   .   .   379   Coryat 3   12
    The Mappe of his journey, and sees in his booke,   .   .   379   Coryat 3   18
    Pies on't, you have his historicall faith.   .   .   .   380   Coryat 3   22
    Each leafe of his journall, and line doth unlocke   .   .   380   Coryat 3   23
    The truth of his heart there, and tell's what a clocke   .   .   380   Coryat 3   24
    Of his foote, or his penne, his braine or his hoofe,   .   .   380   Coryat 3   32
    He was in his travaile, how like to be beaten,   .   .   380   Coryat 3   35
    How faine for his venery he was to crie (Tergum o)   .   .   380   Coryat 3   37
    How well, and how often his shoes too were mended,   .   .   380   Coryat 3   39
    Yes. And thanks God in his Pistle or his Booke   .   .   380   Coryat 3   43
    How many learned men he have drawne with his hooke   .   .   380   Coryat 3   44
    Of Latine and Greeke, to his friendship. And seven   .   .   380   Coryat 3   45
    Nay more in his wardrobe, if you will laugh at a   .   .   380   Coryat 3   47

HIS (cont.)

	Page	Title	Line
So that not them, his scabbes, lice, or the stewes,	380	Coryat 3	50
I writ he onely his taile there did wave;	380	Coryat 3	56
his life, his love, his honour, which ne'r dyes,	382	Rich	8
As true oblations; his Brothers Embleme sayes,	383	Rich	10
To his much and worthily esteemed friend the Author.	383	Author	Ttl
Who takes thy volume to his vertuous hand,	383	Author	1
May aske, what Author would conceale his name?	383	Author	4
May take thy volume to his vertuous hand.	383	Author	8
To the most noble, and above his Titles, . . .	384	Somerset	Ttl
Hymens amends, to make it worth his fault.	384	Somerset	14
To his friend the Author upon his Richard.	385	Brooke	Ttl
To see his worke be good; but that he looke	385	Husband	2
Who are his Test, and what their judgement is:	385	Husband	3
Least a false praise do make theyr dotage his.	385	Husband	4
To my truly-belov'd Freind, Mr Browne: on his Pastorals.	386	Browne	Ttl
Charles Cavendish to his posteritie.	387	Cavendish	Ttl
. . . on his Translation of Hesiods Works, & Dayes.	388	Chapman	Ttl
For though Spaine gave him his first ayre and Vogue,	389	Aleman	15
Finer then was his Spanish, if my Oath	389	Aleman	18
O, could he but have drawne his wit	390	Reader	5
His face; the Print would then surpasse	390	Reader	7
Not on his Picture, but his Booke.	390	Reader	10
Nature her selfe was proud of his designes,	392	Shakespeare	47
And joy'd to weare the dressing of his lines!	392	Shakespeare	48
His Art doth give the fashion. And, that he,	392	Shakespeare	58
Lives in his issue, even so, the race	392	Shakespeare	66
In his well torned, and true-filed lines:	392	Shakespeare	68
To lay her here, inclos'd, his second Bride.	394	Jane Ogle	24
. . . Muses Of His Friend M. Drayton.	396	Drayton	Ttl
Thy Catalogue of Ships, exceeding his,	398	Drayton	61
The Poets act! and for his Country's sake	398	Drayton	63
How do his trumpets breath! What loud alarmes!	398	Drayton	66
On the honor'd Poems of his honored Friend, . . .	400	Beaumont	Ttl
Above his Reader, or his Prayser, is.	400	Beaumont	2
Of Ethnicisme, makes his Muse a Saint.	401	Beaumont	22
. . . on his Worke published.	401	Filmer	Ttl
Of any Art, besyde what he calls his!	404	Inigo Jones 1	58
His name is Skeuopoios wee all knowe,	404	Inigo Jones 1	60
Be Inigo, the Whistle, & his men!	405	Inigo Jones 1	66
Hee's warme on his feet now he sayes, & can	405	Inigo Jones 1	67
To pitty him, as smiling at his Feat	405	Inigo Jones 1	71
Whirling his Whymseys, by a subtilty	405	Inigo Jones 1	73
What would he doe now, gi'ng his mynde that waye	405	Inigo Jones 1	75
Should but the king his Justice-hood employ	405	Inigo Jones 1	77
Hath made his Inigo Marquess, wouldst thou fayne	406	Inigo Jones 2	2
Besydes, his Man may merit it, and be	406	Inigo Jones 2	5
Able to eat into his bones & pierce	407	Inigo Jones 3	4
He makes the Camell & dull Ass his prize.	408	Inigo Jones 3	8
To aske thy name, if he have half his Nose!	409	Detractor	18
Thy Noddle, with his clubb; and dashing forth	409	Detractor	21
. . . (by his continu'd Vertue) my loving friend: . . .	409	Brome	Ttl
The Cobler kept him to his nall; but, now	410	Brome	17
For thou hast nought in thee to cure his Fame,	411	Gill	13
The Eye of flowers, worthy, for his scent,	413	Ghyrlond	14
Who like a Giant hasts his course to run,	414	Ghyrlond	51
Till he hath reach'd his two-fold point of Noone.	414	Ghyrlond	52
Of Finenesse, and alloy: follow his hint,	415	Rutter	27
. . . on his great Instauration of his Hunting, . . .	415	Dover	Ttl
How they doe keepe alive his memorie;	416	Dover	5
Il may Ben Johnson slander his feete,	418	Answer	5
Here he speaks out of his Pottle,	657	Door Apollo	3
Or the Tripos, his Tower Bottle:	657	Door Apollo	4
All his Answers are Divine,	657	Door Apollo	5
Tell her, his Muse that did invent thee	662	Bedford	5
With Chequer Inke, upon his guift, my paper,	666	Glover	8

HISTORICALL

	Page	Title	Line
Pies on't, you have his historicall faith.	380	Coryat 3	22

HISTORIE

	Page	Title	Line
Which Fate (it seemes) caus'd in the historie,	61	E95 Savile	11
Of historie, and how to apt their places;	61	E95 Savile	28
All historie seal'd up, and fables crost;	67	E105 L Wroth 2	2
The Mistresse of Mans life, grave Historie,	175	U24 Frontispice	2

HISTORY

	Page	Title	Line
Dame History, Dame Architecture too,	403	Inigo Jones 1	37

HIT

	Page	Title	Line
As mad-men stones: not caring whom they hit.	27	E2 My Booke	6
Diana'alone, so hit, and hunted so.	68	E105 L Wroth 2	14
Or (mounted on a stoole) thy face doth hit	81	E129 Mime	13
Of worship, they their nodding chinnes doe hit	87	E133 Voyage	123
And the Bow: with thought to hit	132	U2 How he saw	22
That is not hurt; not he, that is not hit;	179	U25 Desmond	50
To hit in angles, and to clash with time:	232	U59 Newcastle	5
When their pot-guns ayme to hit,	259	U76 Petition	21
Beside, your hand will never hit,	277	U84 Mind	7
Nor alwayes doth the loosed Bow, hit that	329	Horace	524
Yet who could have hit on't but the wise noddell	379	Coryat 3	6
Yet may as blind men sometimes hit the marke.	383	Author	6
As well in brasse, as he hath hit	390	Reader	6

HITHER (See also HETHER)

	Page	Title	Line
From Greenwich, hither, to Row-hampton gate!	252	U75 Epithalam.	12
Haste, haste you hither, all you gentler Swaines,	265	U79 New-yeares	46

HITT
    Nay they will venter ones Descent to hitt, ... 394   Jane Ogle   11
HO'
    Or his to Antwerpe. Therefore, once more, list ho'.   .   . 85   E133 Voyage   40
HOARD   (See HOORD)
HOARSE
    When I am hoarse, with praising his each cast,   .   .   . 167   U15 Friend-Wars 151
HOBBY
    Now each Court-Hobby-horse will wince in rime;   .   .   . 410   Brome   11
HOBLED
    I meane that one paire, wherewith he so hobled   .   .   . 380   Coryat 3   41
HODGES
    Insert thy Hodges, and those newer men, ... 214   U44 Speach   53
H'OFFEND
    How then? Why, as a Scrivener, if h'offend   .   .   .   329   Horace   529
HOGS
    The sinkes ran grease, and haire of meazled hogs,   .   . 88   E133 Voyage   145
    The hogs return'd home fat from mast;   98   F3 Wroth   44
    The hogs return'd home fat with mast;   98   F3 Wroth   V 44
HOL'BORNE
    Propos'd to goe to Hol'borne in a wherry: .   .   .   85   E133 Voyage   38
    Of Hol'borne (three sergeants heads) looks ore,   .   .   89   E133 Voyage   177
HOLD
    Of love, and what the golden age did hold   .   .   .   47   E64 Salisbury 3   3
    In life, that can employ it; and takes hold   .   .   .   50   E70 Wm Roe 1   3
    But hold my torch, while I describe the entry   .   .   . 85   E133 Voyage   58
    And, at her strong armes end, hold up, and even,   .   .   114   F12 Rutland   42
    And, at her strong armes end, there hold up even,   .   .   114   F12 Rutland   V 42
    They hold in my strange poems, which, as yet,   .   .   . 115   F12 Rutland   81
    That may stand by, and hold my peace? will he,   .   .   . 167   U15 Friend-Wars 150
    That hold your spirit: 177   U25 Desmond   20
    Be it he hold Communion   221   U48 Bacchus   43
    How I would draw, and take hold and delight.   .   .   . 227   U52 Answer   18
    And hold me to it close; to stand upright   .   .   .   229   U54 Squib   9
    An Epigram, To the House-hold. 1630.   241   U68 House-hold   Ttl
    His Poet Sack, the House-hold will not pay?   .   .   . 241   U68 House-hold   2
    His Poet leave to sing his House-hold true;   .   .   . 241   U68 House-hold   6
    Their Heads, that Envy would hold downe   .   .   .   272   U84 Cradle   3
    I hold thee fast! but fled hence, with the Light,   .   .   293   U86 Hor.4:1   38
    Still to be like himselfe, and hold his worth.   .   .   . 313   Horace   182
    And hold them faithfully; For nothing rests,   .   .   . 329   Horace   505
    To force the grates, that hold him in, would fright   . 337   Horace   675
    Not letting goe his hold, where he drawes food,   .   . 337   Horace   679
    With thy soft notes, and hold them within Pale   .   .   367   Ode Who saith   45
    To hold them here: 368   Ode Who saith   92
    Hold thyne owne worth unbroke: which is so good   .   .   386   Browne   13
    To hold her up. O Showes! Showes! Mighty Showes!   .   403   Inigo Jones 1   39
HOLDBORNE
    Here, not up Holdborne, but downe a steepe hill,   .   .   374   Coryat 1   12
HOLDES
    For that firme grace he holdes in your regard,   .   .   116   F12 Rutland   95
HOLDETH
    Learn'd, and unlearn'd; holdeth whom once he takes;   . 355   Horace   V677
HOLDING
    Learn'd and unlearn'd; holding, whom once he takes;   . 337   Horace   677
HOLDS
    For this: that winnes, for whom he holds his peace.   . 38   E37 Chev'ril   4
    The fate of things: whilst totter'd vertue holds   .   . 216   U44 Speach   101
    The theefe from spoyle, his presence holds.   .   .   . 265   U79 New-yeares   63
HOLE
    In at a hole, and see these Actions creepe   .   .   . 201   U42 Elegy Let   60
    Into a pit, or hole; although he call, ... 335   Horace   652
HOLES
    But soft, and simple, at few holes breath'd time   .   . 319   Horace   289
HOLIE
    But holie Poets, rapt with sence divine?   .   .   .   115   F12 Rutland   V 63
HOLIEST
    If holiest friend-ship, naked to the touch,   .   .   . 78   E122 Rudyerd 2   7
HOLINESSE
    Of Pietie, and private holinesse.   287   U84 Muse   179
HOLLAND
    In Ireland, Holland, Sweden, pompous lies,   .   .   . 69   E107 Hungry   12
HOLLANDE
    . . . & sir Henrye Rich, now Earles of warwick and Hollande.   . 382   Rich   Ttl
HOLY
    More high, more holy, that shee more would crave.   .   . 31   E14 Camden   6
    This morning, timely rapt with holy fire,   .   .   .   52   E76 Bedford 1   1
    Men are not just, or keepe no holy lawes   .   .   .   117   F13 Aubigny   18
    With holy Paul, lest it be thought the breath   .   .   122   F15 Heaven   24
    1. The Sinners Sacrifice. To the Holy Trinitie.   .   . 127   U1 Trinitie   Ttl
    O Holy, blessed, glorious Trinitie   127   U1 Trinitie   1
    Father, and Sonne, and Holy Ghost, you three   .   .   128   U1 Trinitie   37
    They were so even, grave, and holy;   152   U12 Corbet   23
    Whom they durst handle in their holy-day coates,   .   . 208   U43 Vulcan   127
    What though she ride two mile on Holy-dayes   .   .   . 222   U49 Pucell   15
    Great Charles, among the holy gifts of grace   .   .   . 235   U62 Charles 1   1
    Ring thou it Holy-day.   239   U67 Muses   6
    Possest with holy rage, ... 245   U70 Ode   80
    On th'often comming of this Holy-day: 249   U72 King   16
    See, the Procession! what a Holy day   252   U75 Epithalam.   9
    That holy strife, ... 253   U75 Epithalam.   30
    The holy Prelate prayes, then takes the Ring,   .   .   . 256   U75 Epithalam.   123
    These two, now holy Church hath made them one,   .   . 257   U75 Epithalam.   139

		Page	Title	Line
HOLY (cont.)				
(The holy perfumes of the Mariage bed.)		257	U75 Epithalam.	162
That great eternall Holy-day of rest,		284	U84 Muse	63
That holy, great, and glorious Mysterie,		286	U84 Muse	129
The holy Altars, when it least presumes.		288	U84 Muse	188
But thus, thus, keeping endlesse Holy-day,		294	U88 Petronius	5
The Idiot, keeping holy-day, or drudge,		319	Horace	301
When I had read your holy Meditations,		411	Sutcliffe	1
Most holy, & pure Virgin, blessed Mayd,		413	Ghyrlond	37
HOLY-DAY				
Whom they durst handle in their holy-day coates,		208	U43 Vulcan	127
Ring thou it Holy-day.		239	U67 Muses	6
On th'often comming of this Holy-day:		249	U72 King	16
That great eternall Holy-day of rest,		284	U84 Muse	63
But thus, thus, keeping endlesse Holy-day,		294	U88 Petronius	6
The Idiot, keeping holy-day, or drudge,		319	Horace	301
HOLY-DAYES				
What though she ride two mile on Holy-dayes		222	U49 Pucell	15
HOLYE				
Throwe, Holye Virgin, then		421	Ode:If Men	37
HOMAGE				
To whom all Scenes of Europe homage owe.		391	Shakespeare	42
HOME				
The taylor brings a suite home; he it 'ssayes,		30	E12 Shift	9
What could not worke; at home in his repaire		37	E32 Roe 2	7
The like is Jone. But turning home, is sad.		40	E42 Giles	8
Harsh sights at home, Giles wisheth he were blind.		40	E42 Giles	10
Straight went I home; and there most like a Poet,		55	E84 Redford 2	5
Thy selfe, with thy first thoughts, brought home by thee,		81	E128 Wm Roe 2	10
Is now from home. You lose your labours quite,		89	E133 Voyage	181
But canst, at home, in thy securer rest,		97	F3 Wroth	13
The hogs return'd home fat from mast;		98	F3 Wroth	44
The hogs return'd home fat with mast;		98	F3 Wroth	V 44
Here in my bosome, and at home.		102	F4 To the World	68
But the Arrow home did draw		133	U2 Suffered	14
Ever at home: yet, have all Countries seene:		159	U14 Selden	30
Out with the other, for hee's still at home;		198	U40 Elegy That	34
Home to the Customer: his Letcherie		201	U42 Elegy Let	41
And comming home, to tell what acts were done		213	U44 Speach	19
And Charles brings home the Ladie.		222	U48 Bacchus	54
Or what we heare our home-borne Legend tell,		228	U53 Newcastle	9
To welcome home a Paire, and deck the nuptiall bower?		253	U75 Epithalam.	24
For that to dwell in, and be still at home.		262	U78 Digby	8
For those to dwell in, and be still at home.		262	U78 Digby	V 8
Her spirit home, to her originall!		270	U81 Pawlet	64
Against the Husband comes home tir'd;		291	U85 Country	44
Of the fed flocks approaching home!		291	U85 Country	62
And celebrating our owne home-borne facts;		323	Horace	408
HOME-BORNE				
Or what we heare our home-borne Legend tell,		228	U53 Newcastle	9
And celebrating our owne home-borne facts;		323	Horace	408
HOMER				
That Homer brought to Troy; yet none so live:		115	F12 Rutland	55
So hath Homer prais'd her haire;		136	U2 Cupid	13
Helen, did Homer never see		181	U27 Ode Helen	1
What number best can fit, Homer declares.		309	Horace	106
Next these great Homer and Tyrtaeus set		327	Horace	493
Angry. Sometimes, I heare good Homer snore.		329	Horace	536
Angry, if once I heare good Homer snore.		351	Horace	V512/536
There, thou art Homer! Pray thee, use the stile		398	Drayton	59
HOMERS				
Then the great Homers wit, for her, could faine;		224	U50 Countesse	24
Of Homers, forth in acts, then of thine owne,		313	Horace	185
Who hadst before wrought in rich Homers Mine?		388	Chapman	3
HON'BLE				
To the Right Hon'ble Hierome, L. Weston. An Ode		250	U74 Weston	Ttl
HONEST				
On the Townes honest Man.		74	E115 Honest Man	Ttl
Then, The townes honest Man's her errant'st knave.		75	E115 Honest Man	34
And as honest as his Birth.		142	U2 Her man	44
That thine be just, and honest; that thy Deeds		167	U15 Friend-Wars	177
Got up and thriv'd with honest arts:		244	U70 Ode	34
Why not? being honest, and free-borne, doth hate		352	Horace	V547/571
A wise, and honest man will cry out shame		335	Horace	633
Honest Tom Tell-Troth puts downe Roger, How?		378	Coryat 2	81
With all Remonstrance make an honest man.		406	Inigo Jones 1	104
A Noble honest Soule! what's this to thee?		406	Inigo Jones 2	6
An honest Bilbo-Smith would make good blades,		410	Brome	15
he that will honest be, may quitt the Court,		423	Lucan	17
HONESTIE				
Her ends are honestie, and publike good!		156	U13 Sacvile	111
Honour and honestie, as poore things thought		163	U15 Friend-Wars	42
HONESTY				
He that departs with his owne honesty		27	E2 My Booke	13
HONEY (See also HONY)				
Or the prest honey in pure pots doth keepe		290	U85 Country	15
As Poppie, and Sardane honey; 'cause without		331	Horace	559
HONIE				
Nor yellow honie from the tree		98	F3 Wroth	V 60
HONOR				
May none, whose scatter'd names honor my booke,		29	E9 To All	1
And hath no honor lost, our Due'llists say.		42	E48 Mungril	3
Whose house, if it no other honor had,		48	E66 Cary	3

HONOR (cont.)
  To honor, serve, and love; as Poets use.   52   E76 Bedford 1   4
  And elements of honor, then the dresse;   .   .   .   70   E109 Nevil   10
  Get place, and honor, and be glad to keepe   .   .   99   F3 Wroth   87
  Get place, and honor, and be proud to keepe   .   .   99   F3 Wroth   V 87
  Not so to honor thee, ...   106   F9 Celia 3   V 10
  So may you live in honor, as in name,   .   .   .   121   F14 Sydney   51
HONORABLE
  To the Right Honorable William Viscount Mansfield: . . .   228   U53 Newcastle   VTtl
  To the Right Honorable William Earle of Newcastle.   .   232   U59 Newcastle   VTtl
HONORD
  Ben: Jonson To His Honord Friend Mr John Selden Health.   .   158   U14 Selden   VTtl
HONOR'D
  Nor are the Queenes most honor'd maides by th'eares   .   63   E97 Motion   18
  On the honor'd Poems of his honored Friend, ...   400   Beaumont   Ttl
HONORED
  On the honor'd Poems of his honored Friend, ...   400   Beaumont   Ttl
HONORING
  Not so much honoring thee, ...   106   F9 Celia 3   10
HONORS
  To the most Worthy of his Honors. Robert, ...   40   E43 Salisbury 1 VTtl
  Where good mens vertues them to honors bring,   .   .   47   E64 Salisbury 3   11
  Love honors, which of best example bee,   .   .   .   49   E66 Cary   13
  As all thy honors were by them first sought: .   .   49   E67 Suffolk   8
  Yet crown'd with honors, as with riches, then;   .   56   E89 Allen   4
  Not Caesars deeds, nor all his honors wonne,   .   .   71   E110 Edmonds 1   1
  T'expect the honors of great 'Aubigny: .   .   .   119   F13 Aubigny   105
HONOUR
  Are Dwarfes of Honour, and have neither weight   .   .   157   U13 Sacvile   147
  Mans buried honour, in his sleepie life: .   .   162   U15 Friend-Wars   7
  Be honour is so mixt) by such as would,   .   .   162   U15 Friend-Wars   25
  Honour and honestie, as poore things thought   .   163   U15 Friend-Wars   42
  The bravery makes, she can no honour leese: .   164   U15 Friend-Wars   56
  What honour given to the drunkennest Guests?   .   166   U15 Friend-Wars   118
  More honour in him, 'cause we'ave knowne him mad: .   168   U15 Friend-Wars   194
  Rich beame of honour, shed your light   .   .   177   U25 Desmond   14
  Happy in that faire honour it hath gain'd,   .   180   U26 Ode High   14
  As with the safetie, and honour of the Lawes,   .   186   U31 Elsmere   9
  The Courts just honour, and thy Judges love.   .   187   U33 Councellour   37
  Your honour now, then your disgrace before.   .   191   U38 Elegy 'Tis   30
  These Carkasses of honour; Taylors blocks,   .   216   U44 Speach   99
  But if, for honour, we must draw the Sword,   .   219   U47 Tribe   39
  These I will honour, love, embrace, and serve: .   220   U47 Tribe   71
  Of honour, nor no ayre of good? .   .   .   234   U60 La-ware   7
  Where shame, faith, honour, and regard of right   .   243   U70 Ode   13
  Unlesse some saving-Honour of the Crowne,   .   .   248   U71 Treasurer   13
  Both to the honour of the King and State.   .   251   U74 Weston   24
  And what of Dignitie, and Honour may   .   .   255   U75 Epithalam.   92
  A Kate, a Frank, to honour their Grand-dames,   .   258   U75 Epithalam.   172
  Fame and Honour you, they possesse by Peace.   .   261   U77 Treasurer   V 22
  Unto your honour: I can tune in song   .   .   261   U77 Treasurer   27
  Unto your honour: I can voyce in song   .   261   U77 Treasurer   V 27
  In honour, courtesie, and all the parts   .   262   U78 Digby   3
  For Brittains honour, and to Charles my King: .   262   U78 Digby   V 18
  Meschines honour with the Cestrian fame   .   274   U84 Descent   16
  And thus, at first, an honour, and a name   .   327   Horace   491
  With honour make the farre-knowne Author live.   .   329   Horace   519
  his life, his love, his honour, which ne'r dyes,   .   382   Rich   8
  To make thy honour, and our wealth the more!   .   388   Chapman   6
  From thence to honour thee, I would not seeke   .   391   Shakespeare   32
HONOURABLE
  To the Right Honourable, the Lord high Treasurer of . . .   248   U71 Treasurer   Ttl
  On the Right Honourable, and vertuous Lord Weston, L.   250   U73 Weston   Ttl
  To the right Honourable, the Lord Treasurer of England.   260   U77 Treasurer   Ttl
HONOUR'D
  Honour'd at once, and envi'd (if it can   .   .   162   U15 Friend-Wars   24
  An Epigram. To the honour'd ——— Countesse of ———   .   224   U50 Countesse   Ttl
  Will honour'd be in all simplicitie!   .   .   .   284   U84 Muse   76
  Whom her Redeemer, honour'd hath above   .   .   285   U84 Muse   100
  Honour'd Achilles chance by thee be seiz'd,   .   313   Horace   171
  To my worthy and honour'd Friend, Mr George Chapman, . . .   388   Chapman   Ttl
HONOURED
  9. Elegie on my Muse. The truly honoured Lady, . . .   282   U84 Muse   Ttl
  To the memorye of that most Honoured Ladie Jane, . . .   394   Jane Ogle   Ttl
HONOURS
  Of others honours, thus, enjoy thine owne.   .   .   160   U14 Selden   66
  Of others honours, thus, enjoy their owne.   .   .   160   U14 Selden   V 66
  Against or Faith, or honours lawes. .   .   .   173   U22 Elegy Tho   12
  Nothing, but practise upon honours thrall.   .   179   U25 Desmond   35
  Whose Offices, and honours did surprize,   .   185   U30 Burleigh   15
  Did I there wound the honours of the Crowne?   .   203   U43 Vulcan   23
  Haile Mary, full of honours, to my Queene,   .   238   U66 Queene   5
  He purchas'd friends, and fame, and honours then,   .   244   U70 Ode   35
  To pay, with honours, to his noble Sonne   .   256   U75 Epithalam.   106
  Lookes after honours, and bewares to act   .   315   Horace   239
HONY
  Poppy, with hony of Sardus; 'cause without   .   351   Horace   V535/559
HOOD (NOUN)
  And, hood-wink'd, for a man, embrace a post.   .   45   E58 Groome   8
HOOD
  A knight-hood bought, to goe a wooing in?   .   42   E46 Luckless 1   2
  Yes, now he weares his knight-hood every day.   .   42   E46 Luckless 1   6
  Commended the French-hood, and Scarlet gowne   .   201   U42 Elegy Let   69

		Page	Title	Line
HOOD (cont.)				
Of errant Knight-hood, with the Dames, and Dwarfes;	•	205	U43 Vulcan	67
Should but the king his Justice-hood employ	•	405	Inigo Jones 1	77
HOOD-WINK'D				
And, hood-wink'd, for a man, embrace a post.		45	E58 Groome	8
HOOFE				
Safe from the wolves black jaw, and the dull Asses hoofe.	•	175	U23 Himselfe	36
He shew'd him first the hoofe-cleft Spring,	•	366	Ode Who saith	17
Of his foote, or his penne, his braine or his hoofe,	•	380	Coryat 3	32
HOOFE-CLEFT				
He shew'd him first the hoofe-cleft Spring,	•	366	Ode Who saith	17
HOOFES				
'Mongst loughing heards, and solide hoofes:	•	97	F3 Wroth	16
HOOK				
Hook-handed Harpies, gowned Vultures, put	•	187	U33 Councellour	9
HOOKE				
And with his hooke lops off the fruitlesse race,	•	290	U85 Country	11
How many learned men he have drawne with his hooke	•	380	Coryat 3	44
HOOK-HANDED				
Hook-handed Harpies, gowned Vultures, put	•	187	U33 Councellour	9
HOOP (See HOUPES)				
HOORD				
Thy tables hoord not up for the next day,	•	95	F2 Penshurst	71
HOORLD				
Wonder to truth! and have my Vision hoorld,	•	396	Drayton	13
HOP				
A royall Crowne, and purple, be made hop,	•	321	Horace	333
A royall Crowne, and Scarlet; be made hop	•	346	Horace	V325/333
Hang up all the poor Hop-Drinkers,	•	657	Door Apollo	7
HOP-DRINKERS				
Hang up all the poor Hop-Drinkers,	•	657	Door Apollo	7
HOPE				
And such from whom let no man hope least good,	•	30	E11 Something	6
And mine come nothing like. I hope so. Yet,	•	32	E18 Censurer	5
Yet dare not, to my thought, lest hope allow	•	41	E43 Salisbury 1	7
My sinne was too much hope of thee, lov'd boy,	•	41	E45 First Son	2
That liv'st from hope, from feare, from faction free;	•	61	E95 Savile	18
Something, which, else, could hope for no esteeme.	•	64	E101 Supper	6
Thou must draw more: and they, that hope to see	•	66	E102 Pembroke	19
Thou are not one, seek'st miseries with hope,	•	70	E109 Nevil	5
Is there a hope, that Man would thankefull bee,	•	80	E127 Aubigny	1
Can Poets hope to fetter mee?	•	93	F1 Why write no	4
Doe not once hope, that thou canst tempt	•	100	F4 To the World	5
As little, as I hope from thee:	•	101	F4 To the World	38
As giving it a hope, that there	•	106	F9 Celia 3	11
My faith, my hope, my love: and in this state,	•	122	F15 Heaven	11
In dreames, begun in hope, and end in spoile.	•	162	U15 Friend-Wars	10
(As my hope tells) that our faire Phoebe's shine,	•	179	U25 Desmond	58
(As my hope tells) that our drad Cynthia's shine,	•	179	U25 Desmond	V 58
No man inflicts that paine, till hope be spent:	•	192	U38 Elegy 'Tis	44
Upon the hope to have another sin	•	193	U38 Elegy 'Tis	90
Of parting, drowne it in the hope to meet	•	197	U40 Elegy That	7
Hope, hath her end! and Faith hath her reward!	•	284	U84 Muse	68
Thither, you hope to come; and there to find	•	285	U84 Muse	103
Delights, nor credulous hope of mutuall Joy,	•	293	U86 Hor.4:1	30
Or grace of speech, should hope a lasting date.	•	309	Horace	100
A great deferrer, long in hope, growne numbe	•	317	Horace	245
Nor must the Fable, that would hope the Fate,	•	317	Horace	270
And so, as every man may hope the same;	•	321	Horace	350
Within the hope of having all forgiven?	•	323	Horace	394
Thinke wee, or hope, there can be Verses fain'd	•	327	Horace	474
Of all the Worthyes hope t'outlast thy one,	•	406	Inigo Jones 1	99
Thus, Love, and Hope, and burning Charitie;	•	413	Ghyrlond	25
And in this Age, canst hope no other grace.	•	420	Ode:If Men	27
HOP'D				
And it is hop'd, that shee, like Milo, wull	•	57	E90 Mill	17
HOPELESSE				
To paint him, hath by swimming, hopelesse, scap'd,	•	305	Horace	27
HOPES				
Not glad, like those that have new hopes, or sutes,	•	47	E64 Salisbury 3	1
And such, or my hopes faile, shall make you shine.	•	115	F12 Rutland	64
For then my hopes will spill me.	•	144	U4 Song	8
His unjust hopes, with praises begg'd, or (worse)	•	162	U15 Friend-Wars	12
Some hopes of Spaine in their West-Indian Fleet?	•	219	U47 Tribe	34
That so hath crown'd our hopes, our spring, and earth,	•	237	U65 Prince	2
which thus hast crown'd our hopes, our spring, and earth,	•	237	U65 Prince	V 2
That so hath crown'd our hopes, our spring, our earth,	•	237	U65 Prince	V 2
That thus hath crown'd our hopes, with thee, our Spring & May,	•	237	U65 Prince	V 2
The elder of these two, riche hopes Increase,	•	382	Rich	5
Who reads, who roaves, who hopes to understand,	•	383	Author	7
HORACE				
To Sir Horace Vere.	•	58	E91 Vere	Ttl
To the worthy Sir Horace Vere.	•	58	E91 Vere	VTtl
Illustrous Vere, or Horace; fit to be	•	58	E91 Vere	3
Sung by a Horace, or a Muse as free;	•	58	E91 Vere	4
Of which had Horace, or Anacreon tasted,	•	65	E101 Supper	31
Is Horace his each love so high	•	181	U27 Ode Helen	13
As Horace fat; or as Anacreon old;	•	199	U42 Elegy Let	2
A speech according to Horace.	•	213	U44 Speech	Ttl
An Ode in Horace in prayse of a Countrye lyfe, Translated.	•	289	U85 Country	VTtl
Ode IX. 3 Booke, to Lydia. Dialogue of Horace, and Lydia.	•	293	U87 Hor.3:9	Ttl
Whilst Horace lov'd no Mistres more,	•	293	U87 Hor.3:9	5
Horace, His Art of Poetrie Made English	•	303	Horace	Ttl

	Page	Title	Line

HORACE (cont.)
    Horace, of The Art of Poetrie. .   .   .   .   305 Horace   Ttl
HORATIUS
    Quintus Horatius Flaccus his book of . . .   .   338 Horace   VTtl
HORLD
    Urg'd, hurried forth, and horld   .   .   .   .   .   .   243 U70 Ode   15
    Of Constellations 'bout her horld;   .   .   .   .   .   277 U84 Body   27
HORL'D
    In a calme skie, then when the heaven is horl'd   .   .   193 U38 Elegy 'Tis   74
HORNE
    Ne're came to taste the plenteous Mariage-horne.   .   .   165 U15 Friend-Wars   100
    With Clownes, and Tradesmen, kept thee clos'd in horne. .   203 U43 Vulcan   8
    Reduicts, Halfe-moones, Horne-workes, and such close wayes, 248 U71 Treasurer   8
HORNES
    Their hornes, and Germany pukes on his head.   .   .   .   375 Coryat 1   31
HORNET
    To Hornet. .   .   .   .   53 E78 Hornet   Ttl
    Hornet, thou hast thy wife drest, for the stall,   .   .   53 E78 Hornet   1
HORNE-WORKES
    Reduicts, Halfe-moones, Horne-workes, and such close wayes, 248 U71 Treasurer   8
HORRIDE
    And in it, two more horride knaves, then Charon.   .   .   84 E133 Voyage   12
HORROR
    Standing with feare, and must with horror fall,   .   .   122 F15 Heaven   19
HORRORS
    Most frequent tumults, horrors, and unrests,   .   .   .   110 F11 Epode   33
HORROUR
    Such a religious horrour in the brests   .   .   .   .   155 U13 Sacvile   91
    With horrour rough, then rioting with wit!   .   .   .   160 U14 Selden   57
    From out the horrour of that sack?   .   .   .   .   .   243 U70 Ode   12
    A horrour in mee! all my blood is steele!   .   .   .   269 U81 Pawlet   8
HORSE
    And he remov'd to gent'man of the horse,   .   .   .   57 E90 Mill   12
    Of your Moravian horse, Venetian bull.   .   .   .   .   69 E107 Hungry   8
    Grave tutor to the learned horse. Both which,   .   .   88 E133 Voyage   157
    His lynes, and hourely sits the Poets horse?   .   .   200 U42 Elegy Let   8
    Put a Coach-mare in Tissue, must I horse   .   .   .   201 U42 Elegy Let   43
    Or Captaine Pamphlets horse, and foot, that sallie   .   206 U43 Vulcan   79
    Oure Captaine Pamphlets horse, and foot, that sallie   206 U43 Vulcan   V 79
    That we have Trumpets, Armour, and great Horse,   .   213 U44 Speach   7
    More then to praise a Dog? or Horse? or speake   .   215 U44 Speach   71
    When first, my Lord, I saw you backe your horse,   .   228 U53 Newcastle   1
    So seem'd your horse and you, both of a peece!   .   228 U53 Newcastle   6
    As I began to wish my selfe a horse.   .   .   .   .   228 U53 Newcastle   12
    Set a Horse-neck, and divers feathers fold   .   .   305 Horace   2
    A horse neck joyn, & sundry plumes ore-fold   .   .   338 Horace   7 2
    The conqu'ring Champion, the prime Horse in course,   311 Horace   115
    Till he drop off, a Horse-leech, full of blood.   .   337 Horace   680
    Till, horse-leech-like, he drop off, full of blood.   355 Horace   V680
    A Horse here is sadled, but no Tom him to backe,   .   374 Coryat 1   14
    It should rather have bene Tom that a horse did lack. 374 Coryat 1   15
    Horse, foote, and all but flying in the ayre: .   380 Coryat 3   28
    Drums against Drums, the neighing of the Horse,   .   397 Drayton   40
    Now each Court-Hobby-horse will wince in rime;   .   410 Brome   11
    And the Poets' Horse accounted. .   .   .   .   .   657 Door Apollo   13
HORSE-LEECH
    Till he drop off, a Horse-leech, full of blood.   .   .   337 Horace   680
HORSE-LEECH-LIKE
    Till, horse-leech-like, he drop off, full of blood.   .   355 Horace   V680
HORSEMANSHIP
    . . . On his Horsemanship, and Stable.   .   .   .   228 U53 Newcastle   VTtl
HORSE-NECK
    Set a Horse-neck, and divers feathers fold   .   .   305 Horace   2
HORSES
    The middle grounds thy mares, and horses breed.   .   94 F2 Penshurst   24
    Loves Dogges, and Horses; and is ever one   .   .   315 Horace   230
    To lie at Livory, while the Horses did stand.   .   .   375 Coryat 1   33
    And lay in straw with the horses at Bergamo,   .   380 Coryat 3   38
HOSE
    Old Hat here, torne Hose, with Shoes full of gravell, .   375 Coryat 1   26
HOSPITALITIE
    With all, that hospitalitie doth know!   .   .   .   95 F2 Penshurst   60
HOSPITALLS
    Spittles, pest-house, hospitalls, ...   104 F8 Sicknesse   10
HOST
    There jest, and feast, make him thine host,   .   .   292 U86 Hor.4:1   11
HOSTESSE
    The quarter day is come; the hostesse sayes,   .   .   30 E12 Shift   7
HOT
    On the new Hot-house. .   .   .   .   29 E7 Hot-house   Ttl
    Tells you it is a hot-house: So it ma',   .   .   .   29 E7 Hot-house   3
    Belch'd forth an ayre, as hot, as at the muster   .   85 E133 Voyage   63
    Your Fleet-lane Furies; and hot cookes doe dwell,   88 E133 Voyage   143
    Your daintie nostrills (in so hot a season,   .   .   88 E133 Voyage   165
    And foundred thy hot teame, to tune my lay.   .   .   107 F10 Proludium   9
    And foundred thy hot teame, to tune our lay.   .   107 F10 Proludium   V 9
    Now hot, now cold, now fierce, now mild.   .   .   189 U36 Song   15
    Or some hot youth, yet in his flourishing course;   .   313 Horace   163
    Hot from thy trumpet, round, about the world.   .   396 Drayton   14
HOT-HOUSE
    On the new Hot-house. .   .   .   .   29 E7 Hot-house   Ttl
    Tells you it is a hot-house: So it ma', ...   29 E7 Hot-house   3

		Page	Title	Line

HOTTER
   Your hotter Causticks to, burne, lance, or cut: .   .   270 U81 Pawlet   V 54
HOTTEST
   Your hottest Causticks to, burne, lance, or cut: .   .   270 U81 Pawlet   54
HOUGHS
   The heads, houghs, entrailes, and the hides of dogs: .   88 E133 Voyage   146
HOUND
   Then give it to the Hound that did him bite;   .   .   155 U13 Sacvile   70
   Or hence, or thence, he drives with many a Hound   .   290 U85 Country   31
HOUPES
   But yet the Tun at Heidelberg had houpes.   .   .   227 U52 Answer   6
HOUR   (See also HOWER)
   Brought on us, and will every hour increase.   .   .   166 U15 Friend-Wars   122
HOURE
   That houre upon my morne of age,   .   .   .   100 F4 To the World   2
   And never thinke, how vice doth every houre,   .   .   119 F13 Aubigny   87
   The Houre-glasse.   .   .   .   .   148 U8 Houre-glasse   Ttl
   on a lovers dust, made sand for ane Houre Glasse   .   148 U8 Houre-glasse   VTtl
   Pyracmon's houre will come to give them ease,   .   179 U25 Desmond   42
   So many my Yeares-labours in an houre?   .   .   202 U43 Vulcan   4
   There was a Judgement shew'n too in an houre.   .   210 U43 Vulcan   158
   Discharge it 'bout the Iland, in an houre,   .   .   249 U72 King   3
   Discharging 'bout the Iland, in an houre,   .   .   249 U72 King   V 3
   His Wisdome, and his Justice, in that houre,   .   288 U84 Muse   218
   He knowes not why, and changeth every houre.   .   315 Horace   228
HOURE-GLASSE
   The Houre-glasse.   .   .   .   .   148 U8 Houre-glasse   Ttl
HOURELY
   And now, her (hourely) her owne cucqueane makes,   .   34 E25 Beast 1   5
   Of loud Sepulchres with their hourely knells,   .   89 E133 Voyage   174
   His lynes, and hourely sits the Poets horse?   .   200 U42 Elegy Let   8
HOURES
   And, as thou'hast mine, his houres, and youth abuse.   .   48 E65 Muse   6
   Of destinie, and spin her owne free houres.   .   52 E76 Bedford 1   16
   Fresh as the ayre, and new as are the houres.   .   94 F2 Penshurst   40
   I have already us'd some happy houres,   .   .   115 F12 Rutland   74
   What fate is this, to change mens dayes and houres,   .   199 U41 Elegy Since   9
   And threat' the great Eclipse. Two houres but runne,   .   238 U65 Prince   11
   And thereat the great Eclipse. Two houres but runne,   .   238 U65 Prince   V 11
   Doth show, the Graces, and the Houres   .   .   251 U74 Weston   16
   Some houres before it should, that these may know   .   257 U75 Epithalam.   146
   Her solemne houres she spent, or giving Almes,   .   288 U84 Muse   192
   The last of houres, and shutter up of all;   .   289 U84 Muse   219
   Are gathering by the Wintry houres;   .   .   290 U85 Country   30
   Is fayre got up, and day some houres begun!   .   396 Drayton   18
HOUSE
   On the new Hot-house.   .   .   .   29 E7 Hot-house   Ttl
   Tells you it is a hot-house: So it ma',   .   .   29 E7 Hot-house   3
   And still be a whore-house. Th'are Synonima.   .   29 E7 Hot-house   4
   Whose house, if it no other honor had,   .   .   48 E66 Cary   3
   That yet maintaynes you, and your house in laughter.   .   51 E73 Fine Grand   8
   Who did, alike with thee, thy house up-beare,   .   60 E93 Radcliffe   3
   To night, grave sir, both my poore house, and I   .   64 E101 Supper   1
   Who kept an ale-house; with my little Minos,   .   89 E133 Voyage   189
   Who, for it, makes thy house his court;   .   .   97 F3 Wroth   24
   Spittles, pest-house, hospitalls,   .   .   104 F8 Sicknesse   10
   The poores full Store-house, and just servants field.   .   185 U30 Burleigh   8
   The Glasse-house, Dye-fats, and their Fornaces;   .   211 U43 Vulcan   180
   An Epigram, To the House-hold. 1630.   .   .   241 U68 House-hold   Ttl
   His Poet Sack, the House-hold will not pay?   .   241 U68 House-hold   2
   His Poet leave to sing his House-hold true;   .   241 U68 House-hold   6
   Thrice happy house, that hast receipt   .   .   280 U84 Mind   53
   More timely hie thee to the house,   .   .   292 U86 Hor.4:1   9
   The sole Religious house, and Votary,   .   .   372 Epitaph   10
   The House of gold, the Gate of heavens power,   .   413 Ghyrlond   39
HOUSE-HOLD
   An Epigram, To the House-hold. 1630.   .   .   241 U68 House-hold   Ttl
   His Poet Sack, the House-hold will not pay?   .   241 U68 House-hold   2
   His Poet leave to sing his House-hold true;   .   241 U68 House-hold   6
HOUSES
   More then advanc'd the houses, and their rites?   .   210 U43 Vulcan   164
   But to confine him to the Brew-houses,   .   .   211 U43 Vulcan   179
   Gave two such Houses as Northumberland,   .   .   274 U84 Descent   5
HOUSHOLD
   With the whole houshold, and may, every day,   .   96 F2 Penshurst   96
   Of a few poore houshold spyes?   .   .   .   102 F5 Celia 1   12
   Nor any of their houshold, halfe so well.   .   .   228 U53 Newcastle   16
   For houshold aid, and Children sweet;   .   .   291 U85 Country   40
   The wealthy houshold swarme of bondmen met,   .   291 U85 Country   65
HOW
   How, best of Kings, do'st thou a scepter beare!   .   28 E4 James 1   1
   How, best of Poets, do'st thou laurell weare!   .   28 E4 James 1   2
   (How nothing's that?) to whom my countrey owes   .   31 E14 Camden   3
   Lord, how is Gam'ster chang'd! his haire close cut!   .   33 E21 Gam'ster   1
   And how his Ganimede mov'd, and how his goate,   .   34 E25 Beast 1   4
   Breathe to expect my when, and make my how.   .   37 E33 Roe 3   4
   And than in them, how could we know god more?   .   38 E35 James 2   8
   How I doe love thee Beaumont, and thy Muse,   .   44 E55 Beaumont   1
   How I doe feare my selfe, that am not worth   .   44 E55 Beaumont   3
   How wilfull blind is he then, that would stray,   .   53 E80 Life/Death   3
   Madame, I told you late how I repented,   .   .   54 E84 Bedford 2   1
   I would have spent: how every Muse should know it,   .   55 E84 Bedford 2   7
   How can so great example dye in mee,   .   .   57 E89 Allen   7

	Page	Title	Line
HOW (cont.)			
Nay, aske you, how the day goes, in your eare.	59	E92 New Crie	18
If the States make peace, how it will goe	59	E92 New Crie	30
How like a columne, Radcliffe, left alone	60	E93 Radcliffe	1
Of historie, and how to apt their places;	61	E95 Savile	28
How much of great example wert thou, Roe,	64	E99 Th Roe 2	5
Knat, raile, and ruffe too. How so ere, my man	65	E101 Supper	20
How well, faire crowne of your faire sexe, might hee,	66	E103 L Wroth 1	1
And, being nam'd, how little doth that name	66	E103 L Wroth 1	5
How great you were with their two Emperours;	68	E107 Hungry	6
How few have read! how fewer understood!)	71	E110 Edmonds 1	16
Wherein thou shew'st, how much the latter are	72	E111 Edmonds 2	3
How full of want, how swallow'd up, how dead	80	E127 Aubigny	6
How can I speake of thy great paines, but erre?	83	E132 Sylvester	5
The many perills of this Port, and how	85	E133 Voyage	47
Canst tell me best, how every Furie lookes there,	85	E133 Voyage	52
How hight the place? a voyce was heard, Cocytus.	86	E133 Voyage	89
And, in a pittious tune, began. How dare	88	E133 Voyage	164
How blest art thou, canst love the countrey, Wroth,	96	F3 Wroth	1
Nor how to get the lawyer fees.	98	F3 Wroth	62
How to tell' hem, as they flow,	103	F6 Celia 2	20
How onely shee bestowes	112	F11 Epode	104
How many equall with the Argive Queene,	114	F12 Rutland	49
And show, how, to the life, my soule presents	115	F12 Rutland	86
As bloud, and match. Wherein, how more then much	117	F13 Aubigny	46
Boast, but how oft they have gone wrong to man:	119	F13 Aubigny	84
And never thinke, am coach'd, how vice doth every houre,	119	F13 Aubigny	87
How you love one, and him you should; how still	119	F13 Aubigny	113
They teach you, how.	121	F14 Sydney	48
How can I doubt to finde thee ever, here?	122	F15 Heaven	16
O, then how blest,	128	U1 Trinitie	44
Either whom to love, or how:	131	U2 Excuse	16
2. How he saw her.	132	U2 How he saw	Ttl
Which how Dexterously I doe,	133	U2 Suffered	25
Where, how it would have relish'd well;	139	U2 Another	14
How cam'st thou thus to enter me?	150	U10 Jealousie	2
And knew their how, and where: we should have, then,	153	U13 Sacvile	3
Can I discerne how shadowes are decreast,	156	U13 Sacvile	118
Ride, saile, am coach'd, know I how farre I have gone,	156	U13 Sacvile	121
Were the Rack offer'd them, how they came so;	157	U13 Sacvile	130
Records, and Authors of! how rectified	160	U14 Selden	43
How are Traditions there examin'd: how	160	U14 Selden	49
Thy gift 'gainst envie. O how I doe count	161	U14 Selden	79
Thither it flowes. How much did Stallion spend	163	U15 Friend-Wars	47
How they may make some one that day an Asse	164	U15 Friend-Wars	64
Oh how a Lover may mistake! to thinke,	170	U18 Elegy Can	15
Unto the other; and live patterns, how	171	U19 Elegy By	17
How penitent I am, or I should be!	172	U20 Shrub	16
Thinke but how deare you bought	180	U26 Ode High	19
What use, what strength of reason! and how much	187	U33 Councellour	24
Which, how most sacred I will ever keepe,	190	U37 Friend-Book	13
how much they lame her in her propertie.	190	U37 Friend-Book	21
And how more faire, and lovely lookes the world	193	U38 Elegy 'Tis	73
How much you are the better part of me;	194	U38 Elegy 'Tis	110
How all my Fibres by your Spirit doe move	194	U38 Elegy 'Tis	111
How shall I doe, sweet Mistris, for my heart?	199	U41 Elegy Since	14
How in these ruines, Vulcan, thou dost lurke,	207	U43 Vulcan	105
How in these ruines, Vulcan, durst thou lurke,	207	U43 Vulcan	V105
How it held out! how (last) 'twas taken in!	213	U44 Speach	22
As make it their proficiencie, how much	218	U47 Tribe	12
How comes it all things so about thee smile?	225	U51 Bacon	2
How I would draw, and take hold and delight.	227	U52 Answer	18
How many verses, Madam, are your Due!	231	U56 Covell	27
Of making just approaches, how to kill,	232	U59 Newcastle	4
To teach the people, how to fast, and pray,	235	U61 Epigram	18
How happy were the Subject, if he knew	236	U64 Charles 3	1
How many times, Live long, Charles, would he say,	236	U64 Charles 3	3
How is she barren growne of love! or broke!	237	U64 Charles 3	15
How is she barren growne in love! or broke!	237	U64 Charles 3	V 15
How much to heaven for thee, great Charles, they owe!	237	U64 Charles 3	22
And interpose thy selfe, ('care not how soone.)	238	U65 Prince	10
To keepe him off; and how-so-e're he gleanes	242	U69 Friend Son	16
How summ'd a circle didst thou leave man-kind	243	U70 Ode	9
How well at twentie had he falne, or stood!	243	U70 Ode	31
To light: her measures are, how well	245	U70 Ode	62
Each syllab'e answer'd, and was form'd, how faire;	245	U70 Ode	63
O how will then our Court be pleas'd,	251	U74 Weston	25
Harke how the Bells upon the waters play	253	U75 Epithalam.	33
See, how she paceth forth in Virgin-white,	253	U75 Epithalam.	41
See, how with Roses, and with Lillies shine,	254	U75 Epithalam.	57
With what full hands, and in how plenteous showers	254	U75 Epithalam.	65
How each one playes his part, of the large Pedigree.	258	U75 Epithalam.	176
What transcripts begg'd? how cry'd up, and how glad,	263	U78 Digby	30
What transcripts made? how cry'd up, and how glad,	263	U78 Digby	V 30
How much they are belov'd of God, in thee;	268	U80 Christning	4
Thereof, no notion can expresse how much	269	U81 Pawlet	26
No Nation can expresse how much	269	U81 Pawlet	V 26
How did she leave the world? with what contempt?	270	U81 Pawlet	47
Of her disease, how did her soule assure	270	U81 Pawlet	50
Earths grossnesse; There's the how, and why.	279	U84 Mind	44
our grossnesse; There's the how, and why.	279	U84 Mind	V 44
How plucking Peares, his owne hand grafted had,	290	U85 Country	19
Among these Cates how glad the sight doth come	291	U85 Country	61

	Page	Title	Line
HOW (cont.)			
A scorned Mouse! O, how much better this,	315	Horace	199
A trifling Mouse! O, how much better this,	343	Horace	'199
Hee thinkes not, how to give you smoake from light,	315	Horace	203
Fit rites. The Child, that now knowes how to say,	315	Horace	225
Fit dues. The Child, that now knowes how to say,	344	Horace	V225
How he could jest, because he mark'd and saw,	319	Horace	323
How to divide, into a hundred parts,	327	Horace	465
How then? Why, as a Scrivener, if h'offend	329	Horace	529
Hee, that not knowes the games, nor how to use	331	Horace	565
I wonder how this happie man should know,	333	Horace	605
how lyke the Carbuncle in Aarons brest	361	Palmer	14
How faire a flight he makes!	366	Ode Who saith	10
How upward, and direct!	366	Ode who saith	11
How they would frowne!	369	Ode Who saith	110
A Punke here pelts him with egs. How so?	375	Coryat 1	18
Honest Tom Tell-Troth puts downe Roger, How?	378	Coryat 2	81
How long he did stay, at what signe he did Inne.	380	Coryat 3	26
And therefore how ever the travelling nation,	380	Coryat 3	29
How scabbed, how ragged, and how pediculous	380	Coryat 3	34
He was in his travaile, how like to be beaten,	380	Coryat 3	35
How faine for his venery he was to crie (Tergum o)	380	Coryat 3	37
How well, and how often his shoes too were mended,	380	Coryat 3	39
How many learned men he have drawne with his hooke	380	Coryat 3	44
With the how much they set forth, but th'how well.	386	Browne	16
not when I di'd, but how I livd. Farewell.	387	Cavendish	12
And tell, how farre thou didst our Lily out-shine,	391	Shakespeare	29
And such wert thou. Looke how the fathers face	392	Shakespeare	65
O, how in those, dost thou instruct these times,	397	Drayton	43
How do his trumpets breath! What loud alarmes!	398	Drayton	66
Looke, how we read the Spartans were inflam'd	398	Drayton	67
How much Architectonice is your owne!	402	Inigo Jones 1	10
How would he firke? lyke Adam overdooe	405	Inigo Jones 1	79
How are thy gifts, and graces blaz'd abroad!	413	Ghyrlond	36
How are thy gifts and graces blaz'd abro'd,	414	Ghyrlond	53
How well I lov'd Truth: I was scarce allow'd	414	Rutter	6
But I can tell thee, Dover, how thy Games	415	Dover	3
How they doe keepe alive his memorie;	416	Dover	5
How they advance true Love, and neighbourhood,	416	Dover	7
Looke how the starres from earth, or seas from flames	422	Lucan	7
HOWARD			
Stand high, then, Howard, high in eyes of men,	49	E67 Suffolk	5
HOWE			
As when they both were greate, and both knewe howe	419	Ode:If Men	3
howe soone with a selfe ticklinge hee was spent.	420	Ode:If Men	18
Howe much they lame hir, in hir propertye:	421	Censure	14
HOWER			
An hower will come they must affect theyr Ease,	179	U25 Desmond	V 42
HOWERS			
Fresh as the Day, and new as are the Howers,	416	Welcome	1
HOWRELY			
And howrely brooding ore the same,	400	Lady Ogle	29
HOWRES			
Sleepe, that will make the darkest howres swift-pac't;	295	U90 Mart.10:47	11
HOW-SO-E'RE			
To keepe him off; and how-so-e're he gleanes	242	U69 Friend Son	16
HOWSOEVER			
And, howsoever we may thinke things sweet,	99	F3 Wroth	97
And howsoever; as I am at fewd	116	F13 Aubigny	9
HUE			
Was drawne to practise other hue, then that	188	U34 Small Poxe	8
Whose Note, and Hue,	366	Ode Who saith	4
HUES			
If now the turnes, the colours, and right hues	311	Horace	126
If now the changes, and the severall hues	341	Horace	V121/126
HUGE			
So huge, it seem'd, they could by no meanes quite her.	86	E133 Voyage	86
HUGH			
Art, her false servant; Nor, for Sir Hugh Plat,	188	U34 Small Poxe	7
Well did thy craftie Clerke, and Knight, Sir Hugh,	214	U44 Speach	33
HUISHERS			
While it makes huishers serviceable men,	113	F12 Rutland	9
HUISSEN			
Of Hannow, Shieter-huissen, Popenheim,	69	E107 Hungry	25
HULKE			
Of the hulke touch'd, and, as by Polypheme	87	E133 Voyage	112
HUMANE			
Of humane life! as all the frosts, and sweates	233	U59 Newcastle	22
Hath shed, or humane frailtie not kept thence.	329	Horace	528
HUMANITIE			
Humanitie, and pietie, which are	58	E91 Vere	15
And letters, and humanitie in the stead!	73	E113 Overbury	8
Of this so vitious Humanitie.	158	U14 Selden	12
Humanitie enough to be a friend,	161	U14 Selden	77
And twice-twelve-yeares stor'd up humanitie,	207	U43 Vulcan	101
With twice-twelve-yeares stor'd up humanitie,	207	U43 Vulcan	V101
His life was of Humanitie the Sphaere.	244	U70 Ode	52
In his humanitie! To heare him preach	286	U84 Muse	133
HUMBER			
Humber, or Owse, decline;	368	Ode Who saith	74
HUMBLE			
The ripened eares, yet humble in their height,	98	F3 Wroth	41
Move it, as their humble sute,	106	F8 Sicknesse	V 46

		Page	Title	Line

HUMBLE (cont.)
And though my fortune humble me, to take . . . . . 153 U13 Sacvile 15
With humble Gleanings in Divinitie, ... 207 U43 Vulcan 102
The Humble Petition of Poore Ben. . . . . . 259 U76 Petition Ttl
Complaines in humble phrase. Both Telephus, . . . 311 Horace 135
The fourth is humble Ivy, intersert, ... 413 Ghyrlond 17
HUMBLED
Uppon soe humbled earth to cast hir eyes: . . . . 420 Ode:If Men 30
HUMBLEST
Move it, as their humblest sute, ... 106 F8 Sicknesse 46
HUMBLY
—Doth most humbly show it, ... 259 U76 Petition 3
HUMBLYE
hath armde att all poyntes; charge mee humblye kneele . . 382 Rich 2
HUMILITIE
And hers were all Humilitie! they beat . . . . 288 U84 Muse 189
With od'rous sweets and soft humilitie, ... 413 Ghyrlond 27
HUMORS
And Flatterye, with Frindes humors: still to move. . . 422 Censure 20
HUMOUR'D
With specious places, and being humour'd right, . . . 327 Horace 457
HUMOURS
As flatt'ry with friends humours still to move. . . . 190 U37 Friend-Book 27
HUM'ROUS
For, if the hum'rous world will talke at large, . . . 83 E131 Ferrab. 2 7
HUNDRED
Ridway rob'd Duncote of three hundred pound, . . . 29 E8 Robbery 1
Some hundred quarrells, yet dost thou fight none; . . 32 E16 Brain-hardy 6
(Who hath the hundred hands when he doth meddle) . . 86 E133 Voyage 82
While you breath. First give a hundred, . . . 103 F6 Celia 2 8
Hundred, then unto the tother . . . . . 103 F6 Celia 2 10
My hundred of gray haires, ... 150 U9 Picture 14
Or standing long an Oake, three hundred yeare, . . 245 U70 Ode 67
The Muse not peepes out, one of hundred dayes; . . 248 U71 Treasurer 9
A large hundred Markes annuitie, ... 259 U76 Petition 11
A full hundred Markes annuitie, ... 259 U76 Petition V 11
Child of a hundred Arts, and farre 292 U86 Hor.4:1 15
How to divide, into a hundred parts, ... 327 Horace 465
HUNG
Or hung some Mounsieurs picture on the wall, . . . 56 E88 Monsieur 12
Hung stench, diseases, and old filth, their mother, . . 86 E133 Voyage 70
HUNGARY
In Hungary, and Poland, Turkie too; . . . . 69 E107 Hungry 13
HUNGRIE
Or shooting at the hungrie thrush, ... 97 F3 Wroth V 34
HUNGRY
To Captayne Hungry. . . . . . . 68 E107 Hungry Ttl
Come, be not angrie, you are Hungry; eate; . . . 69 E107 Hungry 31
To cloath the naked, feed the hungry. Shee . . . 288 U84 Muse 194
Seek out some hungry painter, that for bread . . . 408 Inigo Jones 3 10
HUNTED
Diana'alone, so hit, and hunted so. . . . . 68 E105 L Wroth 2 14
HUNTERS
Still, still, the hunters of false fame apply . . . 155 U13 Sacvile 65
Of Pan wee sing, the best of Hunters, Pan, . . . 264 U79 New-yeares 20
HUNTING
At hunting railes, having no guift in othes, . . . 76 E119 Shelton 2
That found King James, when hunting late, this way, . . 95 F2 Penshurst 76
And hunting, Pan, exceedeth thee. . . . . 265 U79 New-yeares 55
And hunting, Pan, exceedeth thee. . . . . 265 U79 New-yeares 67
. . . on his great Instauration of his Hunting, . . . 415 Dover Ttl
HUNTS
While thus it buyes great grace, and hunts poore fame; . 113 F12 Rutland 15
While thus it gets grace, and hunts poore fame; . . 113 F12 Rutland V 15
The Lybian Lion hunts noe butter flyes, . . . 408 Inigo Jones 3 7
HUNT'ST
And, in the winter, hunt'st the flying hare, . . . 97 F3 Wroth 29
Or in the winter, hunt'st the flying hare, . . . 97 F3 Wroth V 29
HURDLES
That penning the glad flock in hurdles by, . . . 291 U85 Country 45
HURLD
Of all vice hurld together, there he was, . . . 172 U21 Ltl Shrub 6
HURLE
Become a petulant thing, hurle inke, and wit, . . . 27 E2 My Booke 5
HURLED (See HORL'D)
HURL'D
'Twas Jupiter that hurl'd thee headlong downe, . . . 203 U43 Vulcan 9
HURLES
With weightie sorrow hurles us all along, . . . 311 Horace 155
With weightie woes she hurles us all along . . . 342 Horace V155
HURRIED
Urg'd, hurried forth, and horld . . . . . 243 U70 Ode 15
HURT
That can restore that. Will it hurt your feature? . . 46 E62 Would-bee 7
Thou yet remayn'st, un-hurt in peace, or warre, . . 60 E93 Radcliffe 13
And what would hurt his vertue makes it still. . . 63 E98 Th Roe 1 6
Eyes and limbes; to hurt me more. . . . . 133 U2 Suffered 4
And hurt seeks Cure, the Surgeon bids take bread, . . 155 U13 Sacvile 68
That is not hurt; not he, that is not hit; . . . 179 U25 Desmond 50
Dreame thou could'st hurt it; but before thou wake . . 250 U73 Weston 11
May hurt them more with praise, then Foes with spight. . 386 Browne 2
Should praise a Matron. What could hurt her more? . . 391 Shakespeare 14
make many, hurt themselves; a praysed faith . . . 422 Lucan 2

HURT (cont.)
make many, hurt himselfe; a praysed faith . . . . 422 Lucan V 2
HURTFULL
His course so hurtfull both to graine, and seedes, . . 309 Horace 97
HURTING
His power of foulely hurting made to cease. . . . 323 Horace 370
HUSBAND
The Husband now's call'd churlish, or a poore . . 165 U15 Friend-Wars 89
You have a Husband is the just excuse . . . 171 U19 Elegy By 22
To doe, then be a husband of that store. . . . 180 U26 Ode High 18
. . . on her Husband, Sir Kenelme Digby. . . . 262 U78 Digby Ttl
Against the Husband comes home tir'd; . . . 291 U85 Country 44
A ventring Merchant, or the husband free . . . 342 Horace V165
And thou to her, that Husband, may exalt . . . 384 Somerset 13
To the worthy Author on the Husband. . . . 385 Husband Ttl
That went before, a Husband. Shee, Ile sweare, . . 386 Husband 9
But of one Husband; and since he left life, . . . 394 Jane Ogle 16
HUSBANDS
This way to husbands; and whose baskets beare . . 95 F2 Penshurst 55
That distill their husbands land . . . . 105 F8 Sicknesse 29
Melt downe their husbands land, to poure away . . 118 F13 Aubigny 73
Fathers, and Husbands, I doe claime a right . . 200 U42 Elegy Let 11
To doe her Husbands rites in, e're 'twere gone . . 201 U42 Elegy Let 40
To have their Husbands drawne forth to the field, . 213 U44 Speach 18
each to pawne hir husbands capp, ... 417 Moon 38
HUSWIFERY
The just reward of her high huswifery; . . . . 96 F2 Penshurst 85
HYDRA
The other thought it Hydra, or the rock . . . 86 E133 Voyage 83
HYE
Charge them, for crowne, to thy sole censure hye. . 32 E17 Critic 4
HYM
made prospective, behould hym, hee must passe . . 383 Rich 12
HYME
shall looke, & on hyme soe, then arte's a lyer . . 383 Rich 15
HYMENS
Hymens amends, to make it worth his fault. . . . 384 Somerset 14
HYMNE
2. A Hymne to God the Father. . . . . 129 U1 Father Ttl
3. A Hymne On the Nativitie of my Saviour. . . 130 U1 Nativitie Ttl
Have sung this Hymne, and here intreat . . . 174 U22 Elegy Tho 30
HYPOCRITE (See HIPOCRITES)
I'
I'le loose my modestie, and tell your name. . . 38 E38 Guiltie 2 8
I'have sung the greater fortunes of our state. . . 48 E64 Salisbury 3 18
I'am more asham'd to have thee thought my foe. . . 53 E77 Not name 4
Or that I'have by, two good sufficient men, . . 54 E81 Proule 3
Goodyere, I'am glad, and gratefull to report, . . 55 E85 Goodyere 1 1
Play-wright, by chance, hearing some toyes I'had writ, . 64 E100 Playwrt 3 1
But, I'le come in, ... 130 U1 Father 28
I'le taste as lightly as the Bee, . . . 139 U2 Another 5
'Tis one good part I'ld lie withall. . . . 142 U2 Exception 8
I'le tell, that if they be not glad, . . . 147 U7 Nymph 8
I'le tell no more, and yet I love, . . . 148 U7 Nymph 29
I'm sure my language to her, was as sweet, . . 149 U9 Picture 6
I'm sure my language to her, is as sweet, . . 149 U9 Picture V 6
I feele, I'm rather dead then he! . . . 152 U12 Corbet 36
I'le bid thee looke no more, but flee, flee friend, . 166 U15 Friend-Wars 129
I'le lead you on; or if my fate will so, . . 170 U18 Elegy Can 22
I'le therefore aske no more, but bid you love; . . 171 U19 Elegy By 15
'Tis true, I'm broke! Vowes, Oathes, and all I had . 191 U38 Elegy 'Tis 1
Of me, I'le softly tread unto my Tombe; . . . 199 U41 Elegy Since 20
But I'le conclude all in a civill curse. . . . 211 U43 Vulcan 190
Shall carry me at Call; and I'le be well, . . 219 U47 Tribe 45
'Tis true, I'am Thracian Chloes, I, . . . 293 U87 Hor.3:9 9
As, for her, I'ld not feare to die, . . . 293 U87 Hor.3:9 11
My title, at their rate, I'ad rather, I, . . . 325 Horace 432
Why not? I'm gentle, and free-borne, doe hate . . 331 Horace 571
To say, I'm ignorant. Just as a Crier . . . 333 Horace 597
Once say I'me ignorant. Just as a Cryer, . . 353 Horace V597
I'le tell you but the death, and the disease . . 335 Horace 659
Foole, doe not rate my Rymes; I'have found thy Vice . 408 Detractor 5
I'll laugh at thee poor wretched Tike, go send . . 410 Gill 10
I (AYE)
I, that's a Charme and halfe! She must afford . . 163 U15 Friend-Wars 52
I, that thy Ayme was; but her fate prevail'd: . . 188 U34 Small Poxe 17
I, and for this neglect, the courser sort . . . 219 U47 Tribe 54
I
Use mine so, too: I give thee leave. But crave . . 27 E3 Bookseller 3
To all, to whom I write. . . . . 29 E9 To All Ttl
And, I a Poet here, no Herald am. . . . 29 E9 To All 4
But I have my revenge now, in thy name. . . . 29 E10 Ignorant 2
At court I met it, in clothes brave enough, . . 30 E11 Something 1
To seeme a statesman: as I neere it came, . . 30 E11 Something 3
It made me a great face, I ask'd the name. . . 30 E11 Something 4
For I will doe none: and as little ill, . . . 30 E11 Something 7
For I will dare none. Good Lord, walke dead still. . 30 E11 Something 8
Camden, most reverend head, to whom I owe . . 31 E14 Camden 1
All that I am in arts, all that I know, . . . 31 E14 Camden 2
Many of thine this better could, then I, . . . 31 E14 Camden 13
As guiltie men doe magistrates: glad I, . . . 32 E17 Critic 2
And mine come nothing like. I hope so. Yet, . . 32 E18 Censurer 5

I (cont.)

	Page	Title	Line
I sent the cause: Hee wooes with an ill sprite.	33	E19 Cod 1	2
The late tane bastinado. So I thought.	33	E21 Gam'ster	6
The bodies stripes, I see, the soule may save.	33	E21 Gam'ster	8
All which I meant to praise, and, yet, I would;	34	E23 Donne 1	9
But leave, because I cannot as I should!	34	E23 Donne 1	10
Tilter, the most may'admire thee, though not I:	36	E29 Tilter	1
For thy late sharpe device. I say 'tis fit	36	E29 Tilter	3
Be thine, I taxe, yet doe not owne my rimes:	36	E30 Guiltie	2
And person to the world; ere I thy name.	36	E30 Guiltie	4
Whither the world must follow. And I, now,	37	E33 Roe 3	3
To thy Domitian, than I can my James:	38	E36 Martial	2
But in my royall subject I passe thee,	38	E36 Martial	3
Guiltie, because I bad you late be wise,	38	E38 Guiltie 2	1
I know no couple better can agree!	40	E42 Giles	18
I, not the worst, am covetous of thee.	40	E43 Salisbury 1	6
And what I write thereof find farre, and free	41	E43 Salisbury 1	10
Seven yeeres tho'wert lent to me, and I thee pay,	41	E45 First Son	3
O, could I loose all father, now. For why	41	E45 First Son	5
He sayes, I want the tongue of Epigrammes;	42	E49 Playwrt 1	2
I have no salt: no bawdrie he doth meane.	42	E49 Playwrt 1	3
Play-wright, I loath to have thy manners knowne	42	E49 Playwrt 1	5
Courtling, I rather thou should'st utterly	43	E52 Courtling	1
When I am read, thou fain'st a weake applause,	43	E52 Courtling	3
Long-gathering Old-end, I did feare thee wise,	43	E53 Old-end	1
How I doe love thee Beaumont, and thy Muse,	44	E55 Beaumont	1
How I doe feare my selfe, that am not worth	44	E55 Beaumont	3
For writing better, I must envie thee.	44	E55 Beaumont	10
Ideot, last night, I pray'd thee but forbeare	45	E58 Groome	1
To reade my verses; now I must to heare:	45	E58 Groome	2
So have I seene at Christ-masse sports one lost,	45	E58 Groome	7
I, that am glad of thy great chance, here doo!	46	E60 Mounteagle	5
But thine, for which I doo't, so much exceeds!	46	E60 Mounteagle	8
My countries parents I have many knowne;	46	E60 Mounteagle	9
The world reputes you barren: but I know	46	E62 Would-bee	3
With thy new place, bring I these early fruits	47	E64 Salisbury 3	2
But I am glad to see that time survive,	47	E64 Salisbury 3	9
That whil'st I meant but thine to gratulate,	48	E64 Salisbury 3	17
But I repent me: Stay. Who e're is rais'd,	48	E65 Muse	15
To greatnesse, Cary, I sing that, and thee.	48	E66 Cary	2
Which deed I know not, whether were more high,	49	E66 Cary	7
I Grieve not, Courtling, thou are started up	50	E72 Court-ling	1
I lent you, on meere acquaintance, at a feast.	51	E73 Fine Grand	6
Then had I made 'hem good, to fit your vaine.	51	E73 Fine Grand	20
Whil'st thy weigh'd judgements, Egerton, I heare,	51	E74 Chancelor	1
Whil'st I behold thee live with purest hands;	51	E74 Chancelor	3
The Virgin, long-since fled from earth, I see,	52	E74 Chancelor	9
I Cannot thinke there's that antipathy	52	E75 Lippe	1
I thought to forme unto my zealous Muse,	52	E76 Bedford 1	2
What kinde of creature I could most desire,	52	E76 Bedford 1	3
I meant to make her faire, and free, and wise,	52	E76 Bedford 1	5
I meant the day-starre should not brighter rise,	52	E76 Bedford 1	7
I meant shee should be curteous, facile, sweet,	52	E76 Bedford 1	9
I meant each softest vertue, there should meet,	52	E76 Bedford 1	11
I purpos'd her; that should, with even powers,	52	E76 Bedford 1	14
Such when I meant to faine, and wish'd to see,	52	E76 Bedford 1	17
Forbeare to tempt me, Proule, I will not show	54	E81 Proule	1
Which, if thou leave not soone (though I am loth)	54	E81 Proule	7
I must a libell make, and cosen both.	54	E81 Proule	8
Madame, I told you late how I repented,	54	E84 Bedford 2	1
I ask'd a lord a buck, and he denyed me;	54	E84 Bedford 2	2
And, ere I could aske you, I was prevented:	54	E84 Bedford 2	3
Straight went I home; and there most like a Poet,	55	E84 Bedford 2	5
I fancied to my selfe, what wine, what wit	55	E84 Bedford 2	6
I would have spent: how every Muse should know it,	55	E84 Bedford 2	7
Where I both learn'd, why wise-men hawking follow,	55	E85 Goodyere 1	3
Now, in whose pleasures I have this discerned,	55	E85 Goodyere 1	11
When I would know thee Goodyere, my thought lookes	55	E86 Goodyere 2	1
Then doe I love thee, and behold thy ends	55	E86 Goodyere 2	3
Now, I must give thy life, and deed, the voice	55	E86 Goodyere 2	5
That, Allen, I should pause to publish thee?	57	E89 Allen	8
Which of thy names I take, not onely beares	58	E91 Vere	1
I leave thy acts, which should I prosequute	58	E91 Vere	9
I leave, then, acts, which should I prosequute	58	E91 Vere V	9
I speake thy other graces, not lesse showne,	58	E91 Vere	13
Then whose I doe not know a whiter soule,	60	E93 Radcliffe	11
Nor could I, had I seene all Natures roule,	60	E93 Radcliffe	12
If, my religion safe, I durst embrace	61	E95 Savile	1
I should beleeve, the soule of Tacitus	61	E95 Savile	3
But when I read that speciall piece, restor'd,	61	E95 Savile	7
To thine owne proper I ascribe then more;	61	E95 Savile	9
And gratulate the breach, I griev'd before:	61	E95 Savile	10
Who shall doubt, Donne, where I a Poet bee,	62	E96 Donne 2	1
When I dare send my Epigrammes to thee?	62	E96 Donne 2	2
Reade all I send: and, if I find but one	62	E96 Donne 2	7
And I know nothing more thou hast to doo.	63	E98 Th Roe 1	2
And I must now beleeve him: for, to day,	64	E100 Playwrt 3	3
To night, grave sir, both my poore house, and I	64	E101 Supper	1
To this, if ought appeare, which I not know of,	65	E101 Supper	25
Are all but Luthers beere, to this I sing.	65	E101 Supper	34
I Doe but name thee Pembroke, and I find	66	E102 Pembroke	1
Judge they, that can: here I have rais'd to show	67	E104 Montgomery	13
I oft looke on false coyne, to know't from true:	68	E107 Hungry	3

I (cont.)

	Page	Title		Line
Not that I love it, more, then I will you.	68	E107 Hungry		4
Strength of my Countrey, whilst I bring to view	69	E108 Soldiers		1
And your high names: I doe desire, that thence	69	E108 Soldiers		3
I sweare by your true friend, my Muse, I love	70	E108 Soldiers		5
Your great profession; which I once, did prove:	70	E108 Soldiers		6
No more, then I dare now doe, with my pen.	70	E108 Soldiers		8
Now I have sung thee thus, shall judge of thee.	70	E109 Nevil		16
Thy all, at all: and what so ere I doe,	72	E112 Gamster		5
I cannot for the stage a Drama lay,	72	E112 Gamster		7
I leave thee there, and giving way, entend	72	E112 Gamster		9
I modestly quit that, and thinke to write,	72	E112 Gamster		11
I passe to Elegies; Thou meet'st me there:	73	E112 Gamster		13
Where shall I scape thee? in an Epigramme?	73	E112 Gamster		15
Troth, if it be, I pitty thy ill lucke:	73	E112 Gamster		17
And never art encounter'd, I confesse:	73	E112 Gamster		19
I thinke, the Fate of court thy comming crav'd,	73	E113 Overbury		5
I Must beleeve some miracles still bee,	73	E114 Sydney		1
When Sydnyes name I heare, or face I see:	73	E114 Sydney		2
You wonder, who this is! and, why I name	74	E115 Honest Man		1
If I would wish, for truth, and not for show,	78	E122 Rudyerd 2		1
If I would strive to bring backe times, and trie	78	E122 Rudyerd 2		3
If I would vertue set, as shee was yong,	78	E122 Rudyerd 2		5
I would restore, and keepe it ever such:	78	E122 Rudyerd 2		8
I need no other arts, but studie thee:	78	E122 Rudyerd 2		9
I know not which th'hast most, candor, or wit:	78	E123 Rudyerd 3		2
But I, no child, no foole, respect the kinde,	79	E125 Uvedale		7
I could adore, almost t'idolatrie.	79	E125 Uvedale		10
I pluck'd a branch; the jealous god did frowne,	80	E126 Mrs Cary		3
Said I wrong'd him, and (which was more) his love.	80	E126 Mrs Cary		5
I answer'd, Daphne now no paine can prove.	80	E126 Mrs Cary		6
If I should faile, in gratitude, to thee,	80	E127 Aubigny		2
To whom I am so bound, lov'd Aubigny?	80	E127 Aubigny		3
No, I doe, therefore, call Posteritie	80	E127 Aubigny		4
I, and this Muse had beene, if thou hadst not	80	E127 Aubigny		7
And, than this same, I know no abler way	80	E127 Aubigny		11
I, yet, had utter'd nothing on thy part,	82	E130 Ferrab. 1		15
But when I have said, The proofes of all these bee	82	E130 Ferrab. 1		17
How can I speake of thy great paines, but erre?	83	E132 Sylvester		5
That to the world I publish, for him, this:	83	E132 Sylvester		9
I Sing the brave adventure of two wights,	84	E133 Voyage		21
And pitty 'tis, I cannot call 'hem knights:	84	E133 Voyage		22
That all this while I have forgot some god,	85	E133 Voyage		44
But hold my torch, while I describe the entry	85	E133 Voyage		58
But I will speake (and know I shall be heard)	87	E133 Voyage		105
And I could wish for their eterniz'd sakes,	89	E133 Voyage		195
Why I write not of Love.	93	F1 Why write no		Ttl
I thought to binde him, in my verse:	93	F1 Why write no		2
I weare not these my wings in vaine.	93	F1 Why write no		7
When Love is fled, and I grow old.	93	F1 Why write no		12
And I not faine to sit (as some, this day,	95	F2 Penshurst		65
But gives me what I call, and lets me eate,	95	F2 Penshurst		69
Nor, when I take my lodging, need I pray	95	F2 Penshurst		72
As if thou, then, wert mine, or I raign'd here:	95	F2 Penshurst		74
There's nothing I can wish, for which I stay.	95	F2 Penshurst		75
What (great, I will not say, but) sodayne cheare	95	F2 Penshurst		82
But thou, my Wroth, if I can truth apply,	99	F3 Wroth		91
But thou, my Wroth, if I may truth apply,	99	F3 Wroth	V	91
Hence-forth I quit thee from my thought,	100	F4 To the World		3
I know thy formes are studyed arts,	100	F4 To the World		9
I know too, though thou strut, and paint,	100	F4 To the World		13
I know thou whole art but a shop	100	F4 To the World		17
And, knowing this, should I yet stay,	100	F4 To the World		21
Or, having scap'd, shall I returne,	101	F4 To the World		25
From whence, so lately, I did burne,	101	F4 To the World		27
If I could not thy ginnes avoyd.	101	F4 To the World		36
Yes, threaten, doe. Alas I feare	101	F4 To the World		37
As little, as I hope from thee:	101	F4 To the World		38
I know thou canst nor shew, nor beare	101	F4 To the World		39
If't chance to me, I must not grutch.	101	F4 To the World		56
Else, I my state should much mistake,	101	F4 To the World		57
No, I doe know, that I was borne	101	F4 To the World		61
But I will beare these, with that scorne	102	F4 To the World		63
Nor for my peace will I goe farre,	102	F4 To the World		65
I shall feare, you'll surfet too.	104	F8 Sicknesse		8
I doe feare, you'll surfet too.	104	F8 Sicknesse	V	8
And I will pledge with mine;	106	F9 Celia 3		2
But might I of Jove's Nectar sup,	106	F9 Celia 3		7
But might I of love's Nectar sipp,	106	F9 Celia 3	V	7
I would not change for thine.	106	F9 Celia 3		8
I sent thee, late, a rosie wreath,	106	F9 Celia 3		9
I sent to thee a rosie wreath,	106	F9 Celia 3	V	9
Since when it growes, and smells, I sweare,	106	F9 Celia 3		15
Since when it lives, and smells, I sweare,	106	F9 Celia 3	V	15
And must I sing? what subject shall I chuse?	107	F10 Proludium		1
Shall not give out, that I have made thee stay,	107	F10 Proludium		8
Nor will I beg of thee, Lord of the vine,	107	F10 Proludium		10
Pallas, nor thee I call on, mankinde maid,	107	F10 Proludium		13
His absence in my verse, is all I aske.	107	F10 Proludium		21
His absence in our verse, is all I aske.	107	F10 Proludium	V	21
My Muse up by commission: No, I bring	108	F10 Proludium		28
And now an Epode to deepe eares I sing.	108	F10 Proludium		30
Of all his happinesse? But soft: I heare	111	F11 Epode		65

I (cont.)

		Page	Title		Line
That cryes, I dreame, and sweares, there's no such thing,		111	F11	Epode	V 67
As this chaste love I sing.		111	F11	Epode	V 68
No, vice, I let thee know,		111	F11	Epode	V 72
I doe not number, here,		111	F11	Epode	V 76
Nor meane I those, whose vowes and conscience		111	F11	Epode	V 83
Though I acknowledge, who can so refraine,		112	F11	Epode	V 85
But I Conceive a person like my Dove,		112	F11	Epode	V 91
I, that have none (to send you) send you verse.		113	F12	Rutland	19
With you, I know, my offring will find grace.		114	F12	Rutland	30
Beautie, I know, is good, and bloud is more;		114	F12	Rutland	37
(Or Poet, in the court account) then I,		115	F12	Rutland	69
And, who doth me (though I not him) envy,		115	F12	Rutland	70
I have already us'd some happy houres,		115	F12	Rutland	74
To curious light, the notes, I then shall sing,		115	F12	Rutland	76
To curious light, to notes, I then shall sing,		115	F12	Rutland	V 76
For I shall move stocks, stones, no lesse then he.		115	F12	Rutland	78
Borne up by statues, shall I reare your head,		115	F12	Rutland	84
besett with statues, shall I reare your head,		115	F12	Rutland	V 84
I, that am gratefull for him, have prepar'd		116	F12	Rutland	96
This hasty sacrifice, wherein I reare		116	F12	Rutland	97
I, therefore, who professe my selfe in love		116	F13	Aubigny	7
And howsoever; as I am at fewd		116	F13	Aubigny	9
I, that have suffer'd this; and, though forsooke		117	F13	Aubigny	15
Of nature, and societie, I should faint;		117	F13	Aubigny	19
I, Madame, am become your praiser. Where,		117	F13	Aubigny	21
Looke then, and see your selfe. I will not say		117	F13	Aubigny	29
As I, can say, and see it doth excell.		117	F13	Aubigny	34
Doe I reflect. Some alderman has power,		117	F13	Aubigny	38
Wherefore should I		120	F14	Sydney	7
That I may tell to Sydney, what		120	F14	Sydney	12
Which I doe tell:		120	F14	Sydney	16
Good, and great God, can I not thinke of thee,		122	F15	Heaven	1
That, laden with my sinnes, I seeke for ease?		122	F15	Heaven	4
And hearts of all, if I be sad for show,		122	F15	Heaven	6
And judge me after: if I dare pretend		122	F15	Heaven	7
Where have I beene this while exil'd from thee?		122	F15	Heaven	13
How can I doubt to finde thee ever, here?		122	F15	Heaven	16
I know my state, both full of shame, and scorne,		122	F15	Heaven	17
I feele my griefes too, and there scarce is ground,		122	F15	Heaven	21
Yet dare I not complaine, or wish for death		122	F15	Heaven	23
Till I attaine the long'd-for mysterie		128	U1	Trinitie	31
Shall I there rest!		128	U1	Trinitie	48
That I may prove		129	U1	Father	5
I had forgot		129	U1	Father	10
Yet I rebell,		129	U1	Father	26
I Sing the birth, was borne to night,		130	U1	Nativitie	1
Lesse your laughter; that I love.		131	U2	Excuse	2
Though I now write fiftie yeares,		131	U2	Excuse	3
I have had, and have my Peeres;		131	U2	Excuse	4
I Beheld her, on a day,		132	U2	How he saw	1
Farre I was from being stupid,		132	U2	How he saw	5
For I ran and call'd on Cupid;		132	U2	How he saw	6
And (withall) I did untie		132	U2	How he saw	11
I foole-hardie, there up-tooke		132	U2	How he saw	20
Such a Lightning (as I drew)		132	U2	How he saw	24
So that, there, I stood a stone,		132	U2	How he saw	27
(Which with griefe and wrath I heard)		132	U2	How he saw	29
First, that I must kneeling yeeld		133	U2	Suffered	7
Both the Bow, and shaft I held,		133	U2	Suffered	8
Is, that I have leave to speake,		133	U2	Suffered	22
Which how Dexterously I doe,		133	U2	Suffered	25
Love, and I have had; and true.		136	U2	Cupid	6
Sure, said he, if I have Braine,		136	U2	Cupid	10
By her lookes I doe her know,		136	U2	Cupid	18
Such as oft I wanton in!		136	U2	Cupid	23
Where I sit and proyne my wings		137	U2	Cupid	35
I confesse all, I replide,		137	U2	Cupid	39
Since I drew a Morning kisse		137	U2	Kisse	2
What my Muse and I have done:		138	U2	Kisse	5
I long, and should not beg in vaine,		139	U2	Another	2
Once more, and (faith) I will be gone,		139	U2	Another	7
I will but mend the last, and tell		139	U2	Another	13
With the rest, I long expected,		140	U2	Promise	7
For I will so urge you to't,		140	U2	Promise	14
Nay, I will not let you sit		140	U2	Promise	21
I will tell what Man would please me.		140	U2	Her man	2
I would have him, if I could,		140	U2	Her man	3
Titles, I confesse, doe take me;		140	U2	Her man	5
I could give my very heart;		142	U2	Her man	54
I can rest me where I am.		142	U2	Her man	56
For his Mind, I doe not care,		142	U2	Exception	1
That's a Toy, that I could spare:		142	U2	Exception	2
All I wish is understood.		142	U2	Exception	6
Lest I be sick with seeing;		144	U4	Song	2
I Love, and he loves me againe,		147	U7	Nymph	1
Yet dare I not tell who;		147	U7	Nymph	2
I feare they'd love him too;		147	U7	Nymph	4
But then if I grow jealous madde,		147	U7	Nymph	10
Yet, yet I doubt he is not knowne,		147	U7	Nymph	20
I'le tell no more, and yet I love,		148	U7	Nymph	29
From either heart, I know;		148	U7	Nymph	32
I Now thinke, Love is rather deafe, then blind,		149	U9	Picture	1

299

I (cont.)

	Page	Title	Line
I Doubt that, Love is rather deafe, then blind,	149	U9 Picture	V 1
Whom I adore so much, should so slight me,	149	U9 Picture	4
I ne're was of thy kind;	150	U10 Jealousie	3
Nor have I yet the narrow mind	150	U10 Jealousie	4
I wish the Sun should shine	150	U10 Jealousie	7
I ne're will owe my health to a disease.	150	U10 Jealousie	16
I must the true Relation make,	150	U11 Dreame	2
I am undone to night;	150	U11 Dreame	3
I Have my Pietie too, which could	151	U12 Corbet	1
For I both lost a friend and Father,	151	U12 Corbet	5
Much from him I professe I wonne,	152	U12 Corbet	29
And more, and more, I should have done,	152	U12 Corbet	30
But that I understood him scant.	152	U12 Corbet	31
Now I conceive him by my want,	152	U12 Corbet	32
I feele, I'm rather dead then he!	152	U12 Corbet	36
As I did feele it done, as soone as meant:	153	U13 Sacvile	12
You cannot doubt, but I, who freely know	153	U13 Sacvile	13
The smallest courtesies with thanks, I make	153	U13 Sacvile	16
Yet choyce from whom I take them; and would shame	153	U13 Sacvile	17
To have such doe me good, I durst not name:	153	U13 Sacvile	18
Can I owe thankes, for Curtesies receiv'd	153	U13 Sacvile	25
Must make me sad for what I have obtain'd	154	U13 Sacvile	38
As I have seene some Infants of the Sword,	154	U13 Sacvile	47
I not deny it, but to helpe the need	155	U13 Sacvile	75
And superstition I dare scarce reveale,	155	U13 Sacvile	86
Carryed and wrapt, I only am alow'd	155	U13 Sacvile	88
Sure there is Misterie in it, I not know,	156	U13 Sacvile	97
I thought that Fortitude had beene a meane	156	U13 Sacvile	105
And you, Sir, know it well, to whom I write,	156	U13 Sacvile	109
I have the lyst of mine owne faults to know,	156	U13 Sacvile	114
Can I discerne how shadowes are decreast,	156	U13 Sacvile	118
And can I lesse of substance? When I runne,	156	U13 Sacvile	120
Ride, saile, am coach'd, know I how farre I have gone,	156	U13 Sacvile	121
And my minds motion not? or have I none?	156	U13 Sacvile	122
That I may love your Person (as I doe)	157	U13 Sacvile	157
Without your gift, though I can rate that too,	157	U13 Sacvile	158
I Know to whom I write. Here, I am sure,	158	U14 Selden	1
Though I am short, I cannot be obscure:	158	U14 Selden	2
Lesse shall I for the Art or dressing care,	158	U14 Selden	3
Your Booke, my Selden, I have read, and much	158	U14 Selden	5
But I on yours farre otherwise shall doe,	159	U14 Selden	17
But I to yours, farre from this fault, shall doo;	159	U14 Selden	V 17
Though I confesse (as every Muse hath err'd,	159	U14 Selden	19
And mine not least) I have too oft preferr'd	159	U14 Selden	20
Since, being deceiv'd, I turne a sharper eye	159	U14 Selden	23
And what I write? and vexe it many dayes	159	U14 Selden	25
So that my Reader is assur'd, I now	159	U14 Selden	27
Meane what I speake: and still will keepe that Vow.	159	U14 Selden	28
Which Grace shall I make love to first? your skill,	159	U14 Selden	35
I wonder'd at the richnesse, but am lost,	160	U14 Selden	53
I yeeld, I yeeld, the matter of your praise	160	U14 Selden	61
Flowes in upon me, and I cannot raise	160	U14 Selden	62
I first salute thee so; and gratulate,	161	U14 Selden	67
Thy gift 'gainst envie. O how I doe count	161	U14 Selden	79
On whom I could take up, and ne're abuse	161	U14 Selden	83
You both are modest. So am I. Farewell.	161	U14 Selden	86
When I am hoarse, with praising his each cast,	167	U15 Friend-Wars	151
Give me but that againe, that I must wast	167	U15 Friend-Wars	152
Give me but that againe, which I must wast	167	U15 Friend-Wars	V152
And if I had no more to say,	168	U16 Gray	2
What suretie of life have thou, and I?	168	U16 Gray	7
Nor should I at this time protested be,	169	U17 Friend-Debt	7
And their words too; where I but breake my Band.	169	U17 Friend-Debt	9
I adde that (but) because I understand	169	U17 Friend-Debt	10
And I will bring a Crop, if not the best.	169	U17 Friend-Debt	18
I can helpe that with boldnesse; And Love sware,	170	U18 Elegy Can	9
That I must send one first, my Choyce assignes,	170	U18 Elegy Can	23
So well as I may tell in verse, 'tis so?	170	U19 Elegy By	12
I know no beautie, nor no youth that will.	170	U19 Elegy By	20
A Womans friendship! God whom I trust in,	171	U20 Shrub	1
Amongst my many other, that I may	171	U20 Shrub	3
No more, I am sorry for so fond cause, say,	171	U20 Shrub	4
Knew I had this afore? had I perceiv'd,	171	U20 Shrub	9
Knew I, that all their Dialogues, and discourse,	172	U20 Shrub	13
were such as I will now relate, or worse?	172	U20 Shrub	14
Knew I this Woman? yes; And you doe see,	172	U20 Shrub	15
How penitent I am, or I should be!	172	U20 Shrub	16
I could forgive her being proud! a whore!	172	U20 Shrub	21
And so I leave to stirre him, lest he stinke.	172	U21 Ltl Shrub	10
And yours of whom I sing be such	173	U22 Elegy Tho	2
Yet is't your vertue now I raise.	173	U22 Elegy Tho	4
Among which faithfull troope am I.	173	U22 Elegy Tho	28
What I, in her, am griev'd to want.	174	U22 Elegy Tho	36
Where art thou, Genius? I should use	176	U25 Desmond	1
Genius, where art thou? I should use	176	U25 Desmond	V 1
Cynthius, I applie	176	U25 Desmond	8
Pythius, I applie	176	U25 Desmond	V 8
That I may sing my thoughts, in some unvulgar straine.	177	U25 Desmond	13
If I auspiciously divine,	179	U25 Desmond	57
I send nor Balmes, nor Cor'sives to your wound,	180	U26 Ode High	2
Have all these done (and yet I misse	182	U27 Ode Helen	29
And shall not I my Celia bring,	182	U27 Ode Helen	31

300

I (cont.)

	Page	Title	Line
Where men may see whom I doe sing?	182	U27 Ode Helen	32
Though I, in working of my song,	182	U27 Ode Helen	33
I That have beene a lover, and could shew it,	182	U28 Worth	1
Since I exscribe your Sonnets, am become	182	U28 Worth	3
Nor is my Muse, or I asham'd to owe it:	182	U28 Worth	5
That I, hereafter, doe not thinke the Barre,	186	U33 Councellour	1
That, henceforth, I beleeve nor bookes, nor men,	187	U33 Councellour	5
But when I read or heare the names so rife	187	U33 Councellour	7
Thou art my Cause: whose manners since I knew,	187	U33 Councellour	13
Sir, I am thankfull, first, to heaven, for you;	189	U37 Friend-Book	1
On which with profit, I shall never looke,	189	U37 Friend-Book	5
But must confesse from whom what gift I tooke.	189	U37 Friend-Book	6
Which, how most sacred I will ever keepe,	190	U37 Friend-Book	13
And Fame wake for me, when I yeeld to sleepe.	190	U37 Friend-Book	15
In friendship, I confesse: But, deare friend, heare.	190	U37 Friend-Book	18
From each of which I labour to be free,	190	U37 Friend-Book	28
Yet if with eithers vice I teynted be,	190	U37 Friend-Book	29
'Tis true, I'm broke! Vowes, Oathes, and all I had	191	U38 Elegy 'Tis	1
Of Credit lost. And I am now run madde:	191	U38 Elegy 'Tis	2
I will not stand to justifie my fault,	191	U38 Elegy 'Tis	21
As I would urge Authoritie for sinne.	191	U38 Elegy 'Tis	26
No, I will stand arraign'd, and cast, to be	191	U38 Elegy 'Tis	27
Thinke that I once was yours, or may be now;	192	U38 Elegy 'Tis	35
Your just commands; yet those, not I, be lost.	192	U38 Elegy 'Tis	38
I am regenerate now, become the child	192	U38 Elegy 'Tis	39
As I the penitents here emulate:	193	U38 Elegy 'Tis	86
Forgiven him; And in that lyne stand I,	193	U38 Elegy 'Tis	91
On every wall, and sung where e're I walke.	193	U38 Elegy 'Tis	98
I number these as being of the Chore	193	U38 Elegy 'Tis	99
I will no more abuse my vowes to you,	194	U38 Elegy 'Tis	107
Then I will studie falshood, to be true.	194	U38 Elegy 'Tis	108
I may dilate my selfe, but not depart.	194	U38 Elegy 'Tis	118
When I see you, then I doe see my Sun,	194	U38 Elegy 'Tis	120
Till then 'tis all but darknesse, that I have;	194	U38 Elegy 'Tis	121
Rather then want your light, I wish a grave.	194	U38 Elegy 'Tis	122
That Love's a bitter sweet, I ne're conceive	197	U40 Elegy That	1
And then I taste it. But as men drinke up	197	U40 Elegy That	3
And take some sirrup after; so doe I,	197	U40 Elegy That	5
Under another Name, I take your health;	197	U40 Elegy That	10
I give, or owe my friends, into your Rites,	197	U40 Elegy That	12
Which in assurance to your brest I tell,	198	U40 Elegy That	49
If I had writ no word, but Deare, farewell.	198	U40 Elegy That	50
Since you must goe, and I must bid farewell,	199	U41 Elegy Since	1
Alas I ha' lost my heat, my blood, my prime,	199	U41 Elegy Since	11
How shall I doe, sweet Mistris, for my heart?	199	U41 Elegy Since	14
And so I spare it. Come what can become	199	U41 Elegy Since	19
Till I may see both it and you agen.	199	U41 Elegy Since	22
Let me be what I am, as Virgil cold;	199	U42 Elegy Let	1
Fathers, and Husbands, I doe claime a right	200	U42 Elegy Let	11
But I who live, and have liv'd twentie yeare	200	U42 Elegy Let	29
Where I may handle Silke, as free, and neare	200	U42 Elegy Let	30
That quilts those bodies, I have leave to span:	200	U42 Elegy Let	32
It is not likely I should now looke downe	200	U42 Elegy Let	37
Whose like I have knowne the Taylors Wife put on	201	U42 Elegy Let	39
Put a Coach-mare in Tissue, must I horse	201	U42 Elegy Let	43
So I might dote upon thy Chaires and Stooles	201	U42 Elegy Let	47
That are like cloath'd: must I be of those fooles	201	U42 Elegy Let	48
Lift up some one, and doe, I tell not what.	201	U42 Elegy Let	58
Bawd, in a Velvet scabberd! I envy	202	U42 Elegy Let	85
What had I done that might call on thine ire?	202	U43 Vulcan	2
What have I done that might call on thine ire?	202	U43 Vulcan	V 2
I ne're attempted, Vulcan, 'gainst thy life;	202	U43 Vulcan	5
I ne're attempted ought against thy life;	202	U43 Vulcan	V 5
Had I wrote treason there, or heresie,	203	U43 Vulcan	15
I had deserv'd, then, thy consuming lookes,	203	U43 Vulcan	17
Did I there wound the honours of the Crowne?	203	U43 Vulcan	23
Had I compil'd from Amadis de Gaule,	203	U43 Vulcan	29
Had I fore-knowne of this thy least desire	205	U43 Vulcan	59
Had I fore-knowne but of thy least desire	205	U43 Vulcan	V 59
To redeeme mine, I had sent in; Enough,	205	U43 Vulcan	63
I dare not say a body, but some parts	206	U43 Vulcan	87
I now begin to doubt, if ever Grace,	207	U43 Vulcan	107
I saw with two poore Chambers taken in,	209	U43 Vulcan	135
I will not argue thee, from those, of guilt,	210	U43 Vulcan	165
I will not argue thee, from them, of guilt,	210	U43 Vulcan	V165
I will not argue thee Iron. Them of guilt	210	U43 Vulcan	V165
I could invent a sentence, yet were worse;	211	U43 Vulcan	189
I could invent a sentence, yet more worse;	211	U43 Vulcan	V189
Well, I say, thrive, thrive brave Artillerie yard,	213	U44 Speach	23
I may no longer on these pictures stay,	216	U44 Speach	98
What I am not, and what I faine would be,	216	U45 Squib	1
Whilst I informe my selfe, I would teach thee,	216	U45 Squib	2
I neither am, nor art thou one of those	216	U45 Squib	5
Such is the All; that (as I sung before)	217	U46 Coke	21
I could say more of such, but that I flie	218	U47 Tribe	5
I have no portion in them, nor their deale	218	U47 Tribe	27
I studie other friendships, and more one,	219	U47 Tribe	29
I wish all well, and pray high heaven conspire	219	U47 Tribe	37
I have a body, yet, that spirit drawes	219	U47 Tribe	41
Though I doe neither heare these newes, nor tell	219	U47 Tribe	46
But that's a blow, by which in time I may	219	U47 Tribe	51
I have decreed; keepe it from waves, and presse;	219	U47 Tribe	57

I (cont.)

	Page	Title		Line
Live to that point I will, for which I am man,	219	U47	Tribe	59
And dwell in my Center, as I can,	219	U47	Tribe	60
'Mongst which, if I have any friendships sent,	220	U47	Tribe	63
These I will honour, love, embrace, and serve:	220	U47	Tribe	71
I would call mine, to which not many Staires	220	U47	Tribe	74
My selfe a little. I will take you so,	220	U47	Tribe	76
And thinkes I dare not her? let the world see.	222	U49	Pucell	2
And that her truster feares her? Must I too?	223	U49	Pucell	22
I never stood for any place: my wit	223	U49	Pucell	23
I am no States-man, and much lesse Divine,	223	U49	Pucell	25
Farthest I am from the Idolatrie	223	U49	Pucell	27
And trust her I would least, that hath forswore	223	U49	Pucell	29
Shall I advise thee, Pucell? steale away	223	U49	Pucell	35
Pardon, I read it in thy face, the day	225	U51	Bacon	5
And so doe I. This is the sixtieth yeare	225	U51	Bacon	7
Give me a deep-crown'd-Bowle, that I may sing	225	U51	Bacon	19
Why? though I seeme of a prodigious wast,	226	U52	Answer	1
I am not so voluminous, and vast,	226	U52	Answer	2
But there are lines, wherewith I might b'embrac'd.	226	U52	Answer	3
To square my Circle, I confesse; but draw	227	U52	Answer	8
With one great blot, yo'had form'd me as I am.	227	U52	Answer	12
With one great blot, you had drawne me as I am.	227	U52	Answer	V 12
O, had I now your manner, maistry, might,	227	U52	Answer	16
How I would draw, and take hold and delight.	227	U52	Answer	18
But, you are he can paint; I can but write:	227	U52	Answer	19
Yet when of friendship I would draw the face,	227	U52	Answer	22
To all posteritie; I will write Burlase.	227	U52	Answer	24
When first, my Lord, I saw you backe your horse,	228	U53	Newcastle	1
Me thought I read the ancient Art of Thrace,	228	U53	Newcastle	4
As I began to wish my selfe a horse.	228	U53	Newcastle	12
And surely had I but your Stable seene	228	U53	Newcastle	13
Before, I thinke my wish absolv'd had beene.	228	U53	Newcastle	14
For never saw I yet the Muses dwell,	228	U53	Newcastle	15
So well! as when I saw the floore, and Roome,	228	U53	Newcastle	17
So well! as when I view'd the floore, and Roome,	228	U53	Newcastle	V 17
I look'd for Hercules to be the Groome:	228	U53	Newcastle	18
I Am to dine, Friend, where I must be weigh'd	229	U54	Squib	1
If I doe lose it: And, without a Tale,	229	U54	Squib	3
Full twentie stone; of which I lack two pound:	229	U54	Squib	12
It doe not come: One piece I have in store,	229	U54	Squib	15
For your securitie. I can no better.	229	U54	Squib	20
Would God, my Burges, I could thinke	229	U55	Burges	1
Then would I promise here to give	229	U55	Burges	3
I only can the Paper staine.	230	U55	Burges	6
The first of which, I feare, you will refuse;	230	U56	Covell	6
The first of which, I doubt, you will refuse;	230	U56	Covell	V 6
Such, (if her manners like you) I doe send:	230	U56	Covell	19
Accept his Muse; and tell, I know you can,	231	U56	Covell	26
I can lose none in tendring these to you.	231	U56	Covell	28
I gaine, in having leave to keepe my Day,	231	U56	Covell	29
And should grow rich, had I much more to pay.	231	U56	Covell	30
And should grow rich, if I had more to pay.	231	U56	Covell	V 30
I hate such measur'd, give mee mettall'd fire	233	U59	Newcastle	7
The Mother of our Lord: why may not I	238	U66	Queene	3
Sonne, and my Friend, I had not call'd you so	241	U69	Friend Son	1
Profit, or Chance had made us: But I know	241	U69	Friend Son	3
Why doe I irritate, or stirre up thee,	250	U73	Weston	7
Askes first, Who gives her (I Charles) then he plights	256	U75	Epithalam.	124
If to my mind, great Lord, I had a state,	260	U77	Treasurer	1
I would present you now with curious plate	260	U77	Treasurer	2
I would present you with some curious plate	260	U77	Treasurer	V 2
I would, if price, or prayer could them get,	260	U77	Treasurer	5
This I would doe, could I know Weston, one	260	U77	Treasurer	10
This I would doe, if I could thinke you one	260	U77	Treasurer	V 10
But I know, my Lord; and know you can	261	U77	Treasurer	13
These I looke up at, with a reverent eye,	261	U77	Treasurer	23
Which, though I cannot as an Architect	261	U77	Treasurer	25
Which, though I cannot like as an Architect	261	U77	Treasurer	V 25
Unto your honour: I can tune in song	261	U77	Treasurer	27
Unto your honour: I can voyce in song	261	U77	Treasurer	V 27
That day, which I predestin'd am to sing,	262	U78	Digby	V 17
Which I have vow'd posteritie to give.	262	U78	Digby	18
I doe obey you, Beauty! for in death,	269	U81	Pawlet	5
You seeme a faire one! O that I had breath,	269	U81	Pawlet	V 6
To give your shade a name! Stay, stay, I feele	269	U81	Pawlet	7
To give your shade a lasting name! Stay, stay, I feele	269	U81	Pawlet	V 7
Hee's good, as great. I am almost a stone!	269	U81	Pawlet	11
And e're I can aske more of her, shee's gone!	269	U81	Pawlet	12
Alas, I am all Marble! write the rest	269	U81	Pawlet	13
When I, who would her Poet have become,	269	U81	Pawlet	17
Had I a thousand Mouthes, as many Tongues,	269	U81	Pawlet	23
I durst not aime at that: The dotes were such	269	U81	Pawlet	25
I durst not aime at, the dotes thereof were such	269	U81	Pawlet	V 25
Their Carract was! I, or my trump must breake,	269	U81	Pawlet	27
But rather I, should I of that part speake!	269	U81	Pawlet	28
And I, into the world, all Soule, was sent!	270	U81	Pawlet	56
And I, into the world with my Soule, was sent!	270	U81	Pawlet	V 56
I Sing the just, and uncontrol'd Descent	274	U84	Descent	1
Now I have better thought thereon,	277	U84	Mind	2
This worke I can performe alone;	277	U84	Mind	3
Not, that your Art I doe refuse:	277	U84	Mind	5
But here I may no colours use.	277	U84	Mind	6

	Page	Title	Line

I (cont.)

	Page	Title	Line
I call you Muse; now make it true:	278	U84 Mind	21
'Twere time that I dy'd too, now shee is dead,	282	U84 Muse	1
Who was my Muse, and life of all I sey'd,	282	U84 Muse	2
The Spirit that I wrote with, and conceiv'd;	282	U84 Muse	3
O! had I seene her laid out a faire Corse,	282	U84 Muse	11
By Death, on Earth, I should have had remorse	282	U84 Muse	12
I summe up mine owne breaking, and wish all.	283	U84 Muse	26
Sure, I am dead, and know it not! I feele	283	U84 Muse	29
Nothing I doe; but, like a heavie wheele,	283	U84 Muse	30
I murmure against God, for having ta'en	283	U84 Muse	33
I envie it the Angels amitie!	283	U84 Muse	36
Dare I prophane, so irreligious bee	283	U84 Muse	39
A new Song to his praise, and great I Am:	285	U84 Muse	90
Not Lucrine Oysters I could then more prize,	291	U85 Country	49
I am not such, as in the Reigne	292	U86 Hor.4:1	3
Of the good Cynara I was: Refraine,	292	U86 Hor.4:1	4
Nor care I now healths to propound;	293	U86 Hor.4:1	31
Hard-hearted, I dreame every Night	293	U86 Hor.4:1	37
I hold thee fast! but fled hence, with the Light,	293	U86 Hor.4:1	38
Or Tybers winding streames, I follow thee.	293	U86 Hor.4:1	40
Whilst, Lydia, I was lov'd of thee,	293	U87 Hor.3:9	1
I thought me richer then the Persian King.	293	U87 Hor.3:9	4
In name, I went all names before,	293	U87 Hor.3:9	7
'Tis true, I'am Thracian Chloes, I,	293	U87 Hor.3:9	9
And I, am mutually on fire	293	U87 Hor.3:9	13
For whom I doubly would expire,	293	U87 Hor.3:9	15
That I bright Chloe off should shake;	294	U87 Hor.3:9	19
Yet would I wish to love, live, die with thee.	294	U87 Hor.3:9	24
In short; I bid, Let what thou work'st upon,	307	Horace	31
My selfe for shortnesse labour; and I grow	307	Horace	35
Not to designe the whole. Should I aspire	307	Horace	49
To forme a worke, I would no more desire	307	Horace	50
To frame a worke, I would no more desire	339	Horace	V 52/ 50
The vertue and grace of which, or I mistake,	339	Horace	V 60/ 59
Or I am much deceiv'd, shall be to place	307	Horace	60
Or Varius? Why am I now envi'd so,	309	Horace	79
If I can give some small increase? when, loe,	309	Horace	80
Of Poems here describ'd, I can, nor use,	311	Horace	127
Am I call'd Poet? wherefore with wrong shame,	311	Horace	129
Perversly modest, had I rather owe	311	Horace	130
And ill-penn'd things, I shall, or sleepe, or smile.	311	Horace	148
I sing a noble Warre, and Priam's Fate.	313	Horace	196
Heare, what it is the People, and I desire:	315	Horace	219
What so is showne, I not beleeve, and hate.	317	Horace	269
Nor I, when I write Satyres, will so love	321	Horace	341
Meere raigning words: nor will I labour so	321	Horace	343
I can out of knowne geare, a fable frame,	321	Horace	349
I can, out of knowne stuff, a Fable frame,	347	Horace	V341/349
Be I their Judge, they doe at no time dare	321	Horace	356
To Roman Poets. Shall I therefore weave	323	Horace	390
'Tis cleare, this way I have got off from blame,	323	Horace	395
Too patiently, that I not fondly say;	323	Horace	401
If either you, or I, know the right way	323	Horace	402
If either you, or I know any way	348	Horace	V388/402
O I left-witted, that purge every spring	325	Horace	429
For choller! If I did not, who could bring	325	Horace	430
For Choler! if I did not, none could bring	349	Horace	V430
Out better Poems? But I cannot buy	325	Horace	431
My title, at their rate, I'ad rather, I,	325	Horace	432
I, writing nought my selfe, will teach them yet	325	Horace	435
And I still bid the learned Maker looke	325	Horace	453
All which I tell, lest when Apollo's nam'd,	329	Horace	501
Which it doth threaten. Therefore, where I see	329	Horace	525
Much in the Poeme shine, I will not bee	329	Horace	526
A Choerilus, in whom if I but see	329	Horace	534
Twice, or thrice good, I wonder: but am more	329	Horace	535
Angry. Sometimes, I heare good Homer snore.	329	Horace	536
Angry, if once I heare good Homer snore.	351	Horace	V512/536
But, I confesse, that, in a long worke, sleepe	329	Horace	537
Though I confesse, that, in a long worke, sleepe	351	Horace	V513/537
But, now, it is enough to say; I make	333	Horace	593
Him that is last, I scorne to come behind,	333	Horace	595
Him that is last, I scorne to be behind,	353	Horace	V595
I wonder how this happie man should know,	333	Horace	605
Why should I grieve my friend, this trifling way?	335	Horace	640
I could not but in admiracion stand.	361	Palmer	4
Then I admir'd, the rare and prescious use	361	Palmer	9
Next, that which rapt mee, was: I might behold	361	Palmer	13
till giddie with amazement I fell downe	361	Palmer	25
I struggled with this passion that did drowne	362	Palmer	28
Which being eyed directly, I divine,	362	Author	13
Alas: then whither wade I,	365	Ode Splendor	17
Alas: then whither trade I,	365	Ode Splendor	V 17
But should they know (as I) that this,	369	Ode Who saith	97
I, that am glad, thy Innocence was thy Guilt,	371	Fletcher	11
She was 'Sell Boulstred. In which name, I call	372	Epitaph	12
Up so much truth, as could I it pursue	372	Epitaph	13
Rather his sonne, I should have cal'd thee, why?	378	Coryat 2	88
I meane that one paire, wherewith he so hobled	380	Coryat 3	41
I writ he onely his taile there did wave;	380	Coryat 3	56
No: as I first said, who would write a story at	381	Coryat 3	59
Which I do, early, vertuous Somerset,	384	Somerset	7

303

I (cont.)

	Page	Title	Line
I do not feele that ever yet I had	385	Husband	5
And therefore I commend unto the Wife,	386	Husband	8
I know for such, as (if my word will waigh)	386	Husband	11
But I have seene thy worke, and I know thee:	386	Browne	3
I find thee write most worthy to be read.	386	Browne	6
Upon th'Exchange of Letters, as I wou'd	386	Browne	14
I made my lyfe my monument, & yours:	387	Cavendish	7
not when I die'd, but how I livd. Farewell.	387	Cavendish	12
Will bee receiv'd in Court; If not, would I	389	Aleman	19
Had cloath'd him so. Here's all I can supply	389	Aleman	20
Am I thus ample to thy Booke, and Fame:	390	Shakespeare	2
While I confesse thy writings to be such,	390	Shakespeare	3
Were not the paths I meant unto thy praise:	390	Shakespeare	6
I, therefore will begin. Soule of the Age!	390	Shakespeare	17
My Shakespeare, rise; I will not lodge thee by	391	Shakespeare	17
That I not mixe thee so, my braine excuses;	391	Shakespeare	19
I meane with great, but disproportion'd Muses:	391	Shakespeare	25
For, if I thought my judgement were of yeeres,	391	Shakespeare	26
I should commit thee surely with thy peeres,	391	Shakespeare	27
From thence to honour thee, I would not seeke	391	Shakespeare	28
Yet must I not give Nature all: Thy Art,	391	Shakespeare	32
But stay, I see thee in the Hemisphere	392	Shakespeare	55
I Could begin with that grave forme, Here lies,	392	Shakespeare	75
But, I would have, thee, to know something new,	394	Jane Ogle	1
When, Rome, I reade thee in thy mighty paire,	394	Jane Ogle	13
And the world in it, I begin to doubt,	395	May	1
It hath beene question'd, Michael, if I bee	395	May	4
You have not writ to me, nor I to you;	395	May	7
And, though I now begin, 'tis not to rub	396	Drayton	1
About the towne: this reck'ning I will pay,	396	Drayton	6
It was no Dreame! I was awake, and saw!	396	Drayton	7
Lend me thy voyce, O Fame, that I may draw	396	Drayton	9
I saw a Beauty from the Sea to rise,	396	Drayton	11
I found it pure, and perfect Poesy,	396	Drayton	12
There read I, streight, thy learned Legends three,	396	Drayton	15
Did all so strike me, as I cry'd, who can	397	Drayton	24
And looking up, I saw Minervas fowle,	397	Drayton	25
I thought thee then our Orpheus, that wouldst try	397	Drayton	31
And I had stil'd thee, Orpheus, but before	397	Drayton	33
My lippes could forme the voyce, I heard that Rore,	397	Drayton	35
I saw, and read, it was thy Barons Warres!	397	Drayton	37
That reade it? that are ravish'd! such was I	397	Drayton	38
With every song, I sweare, and so would dye:	397	Drayton	42
But that I heare, againe, thy Drum to beate	397	Drayton	53
I feele it by mine owne, that over flow,	397	Drayton	54
And stop my sight, in every line I goe.	397	Drayton	55
I looke on Cynthia, and Sirenas sport,	398	Drayton	77
I gratulate it to thee, and thy Ends,	398	Drayton	78
Onely my losse is, that I am not there:	398	Drayton	80
And, till I worthy am to wish I were,	398	Drayton	89
I call the world, that envies mee, to see	398	Drayton	91
If I can be a Friend, and Friend to thee.	398	Drayton	92
	398	Drayton	93
	398	Drayton	94
Though I confesse a Beaumonts Booke to bee	400	Beaumont	7
I doe salute you! Are you fitted yet?	402	Inigo Jones 1	17
What is the cause you pompe it soe? I aske,	403	Inigo Jones 1	29
I chyme that too: And I have mett with those	403	Inigo Jones 1	31
I am too fat t'envy him. He too leane	405	Inigo Jones 1	69
To be worth Envy. Henceforth I doe meane	405	Inigo Jones 1	70
Sir Inigo doth feare it as I heare	407	Inigo Jones 3	1
That I should wryte upon him some sharp verse,	407	Inigo Jones 3	3
The Marrow! Wretch, I quitt thee of thy paine	408	Inigo Jones 3	5
But bawle thou on; I pitty thee, poore Curre,	408	Detractor	7
I now would write on thee? No, wretch; thy name	409	Detractor	11
I had you for a Servant, once, Dick Brome;	409	Brome	1
Which I, your Master, first did teach the Age.	409	Brome	8
When I had read your holy Meditations,	411	Sutcliffe	1
I sayd, who'had supp'd so deepe of this sweet Chalice,	412	Sutcliffe	21
R. Rose, I. Ivy, E. sweet Eglantine.	412	Ghyrlond	4
You looke, my Joseph, I should something say	414	Rutter	1
And truely, so I would, could I be heard.	414	Rutter	3
You know, I never was of Truth afeard,	414	Rutter	4
And lesse asham'd; not when I told the crowd	414	Rutter	7
How well I lov'd Truth: I was scarce allow'd	414	Rutter	11
Such men I met withall, and so have you.	415	Rutter	13
(You have deserv'd it from me) I have read,	415	Dover	1
I Cannot bring my Muse to dropp her Vies	415	Dover	3
But I can tell thee, Dover, how thy Games	416	Moon	2
I am come to Add, and speake,	416	Moon	5
And I sweare by all the light	416	Moon	6
at my back, I am no spright,	417	Moon	9
I had somwhat else to say,	417	Moon	11
I shall think on't ere't be day.	419	Ode:If Men	6
I then could rayse my notes	421	Censure	2
before, I wryte more verse, to bee more wyse.	421	Censure	6
I have, with strict advantage of free tyme	421	Censure	10
deignes myne the power to find, yett want I will	422	Censure	21
From each of which, I labor to be free,	422	Censure	22
yett, yf with eythers vyce, I tainted bee,	666	Glover	5
I send this small, but hearty testimony: and with charge,	666	Glover	7
Till I, at much expense of Time, and Taper			

		Page	Title	Line
I'AD				
My title, at their rate, I'ad rather, I,	. . . .	325	Horace	432
I'AM				
I'am more asham'd to have thee thought my foe.		53	E77 Not name	4
Goodyere, I'am glad, and gratefull to report,	. . .	55	E85 Goodyere 1	1
'Tis true, I'am Thracian Chloes, I,	. . . .	293	U87 Hor.3:9	9
IAMBICK				
Th'Iambick arm'd Archilochus to rave,	. . .	311	Horace	117
Two rests, a short and long, th'Iambick frame;	. .	323	Horace	371
IAMBICKS				
But meere Iambicks all, from first to last.	. . .	323	Horace	374
IBERUS				
Iberus, Tagus, Rheine,	. . . . . .	369	Ode Who saith	115
IDALIAN				
If dancing, all would cry th'Idalian Queene,	. . .	68	E105 L Wroth 2	11
IDEAS				
When, by thy bright Ideas standing by,	. . . .	397	Drayton	23
IDEOT				
To Groome Ideot.	. . . .	45	E58 Groome	Ttl
Ideot, last night, I pray'd thee but forbeare	. . .	45	E58 Groome	1
IDES				
'Gainst th'Ides, his moneys he gets in with paine,	. .	291	U85 Country	69
'Gainst th'Ides, his gott moneyes he gets in with paine,	.	291	U85 Country	V 69
IDIOT				
The Idiot, keeping holy-day, or drudge,	. . . .	319	Horace	301
IDLE				
Th'are base, and idle feares	. . . . .	109	F11 Epode	26
Be idle words, though of a parting Man;	. . . .	199	U41 Elegy Since	4
IDOLATRIE				
Made me commit most fierce idolatrie	. . . .	48	E65 Muse	3
I could adore, almost t'idolatrie.	. . . .	79	E125 Uvedale	10
Farthest I am from the Idolatrie	. . . .	223	U49 Pucell	27
IDOLATROUS				
Of Valour, but at this Idolatrous rate?	. . .	156	U13 Sacvile	104
IDOLL				
'Fore your Idoll Glasse a whit,	. . . .	140	U2 Promise	22
He burnt that Idoll of the Revels too:	. . . .	210	U43 Vulcan	155
IDOMEN				
Ajax, or Idomen, or all the store,	. . . .	114	F12 Rutland	54
IERNA				
Over Ierna maine,	. . . . . .	367	Ode Who saith	42
IF'				
If't chance to me, I must not grutch.	. . .	101	F4 To the World	56
Is done for gaine: If't be, 'tis not sincere.	. .	169	U17 Friend-Debt	6
Or if't be the Gossipps happ	. . . .	417	Moon	37
IF (See also YF)				
If, without these vile arts, it will not sell,	. .	28	E3 Bookseller	11
If all you boast of your great art be true;	. .	29	E6 Alchymists	1
If thou'ldst but use thy faith, as thou didst then,	. .	32	E18 Censurer	7
If any sword could save from Fates, Roe's could;	. .	35	E27 Roe 1	3
If any Muse out-live their spight, his can;	. .	35	E27 Roe 1	4
If any friends teares could restore, his would;	. .	35	E27 Roe 1	5
If any pious life ere lifted man	. . .	35	E27 Roe 1	6
Which if most gracious heaven grant like thine,	. .	37	E33 Roe 3	5
Beleeve it, Guiltie, if you loose your shame,	. .	38	E38 Guiltie 2	7
If, now, with man and wife, to will, and nill	. .	40	E42 Giles	16
And, if no other miserie, yet age?	. . .	41	E45 First Son	8
No lesse than if from perill; and devout,	. .	43	E51 James 3	7
As if thou wert my friend, but lack'dst a cause.	. .	43	E52 Courtling	4
It was as if thou printed had'st an oath,	. .	43	E53 Old-end	5
Foole, as if halfe eyes will not know a fleece	. .	45	E56 Poet-Ape	13
If, as their ends, their fruits were so, the same,	. .	45	E57 Bawds	1
Or, if shee would but modestly have prais'd	. .	46	E60 Mounteagle	3
Curst be my voyce if it lye dumbe, or hid	. .	47	E63 Salisbury 2	V 11
Whose house, if it no other honor had,	. .	48	E66 Cary	3
For, if thou shame, ranck'd with my friends, to goe,	. .	53	E77 Not name	3
On whom, if he were living now, to looke,	. .	53	E79 Rutland	10
Which, if thou leave not soone (though I am loth)	. .	54	E81 Proule	7
O Madame, if your grant did thus transferre mee,	. .	55	E84 Bedford 2	9
Which if they misse, they yet should re-advance	. .	55	E85 Goodyere 1	8
If Rome so great, and in her wisest age,	. .	56	E89 Allen	1
If the States make peace, how it will goe	. .	59	E92 New Crie	30
If workes (not th'authors) their owne grace should looke,	.	60	E94 Bedford 3	3
If, my religion safe, I durst embrace	. . .	61	E95 Savile	1
Reade all I send: and, if I find but one	. .	62	E96 Donne 2	7
Fortune upon him breakes her selfe, if ill,	. .	63	E98 Th Roe 1	5
If time to facts, as unto men would owe?	. .	64	E99 Th Roe 2	6
If we can get her, full of egs, and then,	. .	64	E101 Supper	12
May yet be there; and godwit, if we can:	. .	65	E101 Supper	19
To this, if ought appeare, which I not know of,	. .	65	E101 Supper	25
To morrow vice, if shee give better pay:	. .	66	E102 Pembroke	10
Forgive me then, if mine but say you are	. .	67	E103 L Wroth 1	9
And like it too; if they looke equally:	. .	67	E104 Montgomery	15
If not, 'tis fit for you, some should envy.	. .	67	E104 Montgomery	16
Would call you more then Ceres, if not that:	. .	68	E105 L Wroth 2	8
If dancing, all would cry th'Idalian Queene,	. .	68	E105 L Wroth 2	11
If men get name, for some one vertue: Then,	. .	68	E106 E Herbert	1
If but to be beleev'd you have the hap,	. .	69	E107 Hungry	17
Troth, if it be, I pitty thy ill lucke;	. .	73	E112 Gamster	17
And him it layes on; if he be not there.	. .	74	E115 Honest Man	16
But, if it shall be question'd, undertakes,	. .	74	E115 Honest Man	18
Them in, if not, from thee; or must commit	. .	75	E116 Jephson	15
If onely love should make the action pris'd:	. .	78	E121 Rudyerd 1	6

305

IF (cont.)

	Page	Title	Line
If I would wish, for truth, and not for show,	78	E122 Rudyerd 2	1
If I would strive to bring backe times, and trie	78	E122 Rudyerd 2	3
If I would vertue set, as shee was yong,	78	E122 Rudyerd 2	5
If holiest friend-ship, naked to the touch,	78	E122 Rudyerd 2	7
If, at all, shee had a fault,	78	E122 Rudyerd 2	7
If I should faile, in gratitude, to thee,	79	E124 Elizabeth	7
I, and this Muse had beene, if thou hadst not	80	E127 Aubigny	2
For, if the hum'rous world will talke at large,	80	E127 Aubigny	7
If to admire were to commend, my praise	83	E131 Ferrab. 2	7
And art a god, if Fame thee not abuses,	83	E132 Sylvester	1
Crack did report it selfe, as if a cloud	85	E133 Voyage	53
And if the high-swolne Medway faile thy dish,	86	E133 Voyage	94
As if thou, then, wert mine, or I raign'd here:	94	F2 Penshurst	31
As if it had expected such a guest!	95	F2 Penshurst	74
Or, if thou list the night in watch to breake,	96	F2 Penshurst	88
As if in Saturnes raigne it were;	97	F3 Wroth	21
But thou, my Wroth, if I can truth apply,	98	F3 Wroth	50
But thou, my Wroth, if I may truth apply,	99	F3 Wroth	91
'Tis better, if he there can dwell.	99	F3 Wroth	V 91
'Tis better, if he then can dwell.	99	F3 Wroth	94
If these, who have but sense, can shun	99	F3 Wroth	V 94
If I could not thy ginnes avoyd.	101	F4 To the World	33
But if once we loose this light,	101	F4 To the World	36
Or if needs thy lust will tast	102	F5 Celia 1	7
If thy leanenesse love such food,	105	F8 Sicknesse	15
And boyles, as if he were	105	F8 Sicknesse	24
As if Nature disclos'd	110	F11 Epode	42
A present, which (if elder writs reherse	112	F11 Epode	100
If it may stand with your soft blush to heare	113	F12 Rutland	20
Of vertue, which you tread? what if alone?	117	F13 Aubigny	22
Your conscience, and not wonder, if none askes	118	F13 Aubigny	55
By me, their priest (if they can ought divine)	118	F13 Aubigny	69
If with this truth you be inspir'd,	119	F13 Aubigny	101
And hearts of all, if I be sad for show,	121	F14 Sydney	52
And judge me after: if I dare pretend	122	F15 Heaven	6
If thou hadst not	122	F15 Heaven	7
If you then will read the Storie,	129	U1 Father	7
Love, if thou wilt ever see	131	U2 Excuse	13
Sure, said he, if I have Braine,	132	U2 How he saw	7
If by us, the oddes were laid,	136	U2 Cupid	10
Or, if you did move to night	138	U2 Kisse	7
Or if you would yet have stay'd,	138	U2 Kisse	21
And, if such a verse as this,	138	U2 Kisse	29
To consult, if Fucus this	138	U2 Kisse	35
I would have him, if I could,	140	U2 Promise	26
But of one, if short he came,	140	U2 Her man	3
Men, if you love us, play no more	142	U2 Her man	55
And if wee must, let's sing of you.	145	U5 Woman-kind	1
If wee would search with care, and paine,	145	U5 Woman-kind	6
If ever we will love aright.	145	U5 Woman-kind	8
For if the Nymphs should know my Swaine,	146	U6 Defence	10
Yet if it be not knowne,	147	U7 Nymph	3
I'le tell, that if they be not glad,	147	U7 Nymph	5
But then if I grow jealous madde,	147	U7 Nymph	8
He is, if they can find him, faire,	147	U7 Nymph	10
If Love, or feare, would let me tell his name.	147	U7 Nymph	15
If, Sackvile, all that have the power to doe	148	U7 Nymph	35
Or if he did it not to succour me,	153	U13 Sacvile	1
Run from the Conscience of it, if they could.	154	U13 Sacvile	29
Now dam'mee, Sir, if you shall not command	154	U13 Sacvile	46
If it were cleare, but being so in cloud	154	U13 Sacvile	53
As if they would belie their stature; those	155	U13 Sacvile	87
Nor fashion; if they chance aspire to height,	157	U13 Sacvile	146
Honour'd at once, and envi'd (if it can	157	U13 Sacvile	148
For all their spight, be like him if they could:	162	U15 Friend-Wars	24
clowd-/Like upon them lighten? If nature could	162	U15 Friend-Wars	26
As if a Brize were gotten i' their tayle;	164	U15 Friend-Wars	61
If it be thought kild like her Embrions; for,	164	U15 Friend-Wars	71
This way, now that, as if their number were	165	U15 Friend-Wars	96
And if I had no more to say,	166	U15 Friend-Wars	126
For, if such men as he could die,	168	U16 Gray	2
And lookes unto the forfeit. If you be	168	U16 Gray	6
And I will bring a Crop, if not the best.	169	U17 Friend-Debt	13
If it be thus; Come Love, and Fortune goe,	169	U17 Friend-Debt	18
I'le lead you on; or if my fate will so,	170	U18 Elegy Can	21
Perjur'd! and painted! if she were no more--,	170	U18 Elegy Can	22
Aske not to know this Man. If fame should speake	172	U20 Shrub	22
Which if it kindle not, but scant	172	U21 Ltl Shrub	1
If hence thy silence be,	174	U22 Elegy Tho	33
If hence they silent be,	174	U23 Himselfe	13
If subject to the jealous errors	174	U23 Himselfe	V 13
If I auspitiously divine,	177	U25 Desmond	28
Which in the taking if you mis-apply,	179	U25 Desmond	57
If thou wouldst know the vertues of Man-kind,	180	U26 Ode High	11
But first dost vexe, and search it! If not sound,	185	U30 Burleigh	1
And make the Scarre faire; If that will not be,	187	U33 Councellour	19
As if the generall store thou didst command	187	U33 Councellour	21
Yet if with eithers vice ty teynted be,	187	U33 Councellour	26
If there be nothing worthy you can see	190	U37 Friend-Book	29
That is, if still your Favours you apply,	191	U38 Elegy 'Tis	15
As if that ex'lent Dulnesse were Loves grace;	192	U38 Elegy 'Tis	53
If I had writ no word, but Deare, farewell.	198	U40 Elegy That	24
	198	U40 Elegy That	50

IF (cont.)

	Page	Title	Line
It is as if a night should shade noone-day,	199	U41 Elegy Since	5
As if it were not worthy to be there:	199	U41 Elegy Since	16
(If they be faire and worth it) have their lives	200	U42 Elegy Let	20
Made longer by our praises. Or, if not,	200	U42 Elegy Let	21
If none of these, then why this fire? Or find	203	U43 Vulcan	27
Or if thou needs would'st trench upon her power,	204	U43 Vulcan	48
or if thou wouldst enforce the power from her,	204	U43 Vulcan	V 48
Reveald (if some can judge) of Argenis,	207	U43 Vulcan	V 96
Reveald (if some do judge) of Argenis,	207	U43 Vulcan	V 96
I now begin to doubt, if ever Grace,	207	U43 Vulcan	107
If that were so, thou rather would'st advance	209	U43 Vulcan	151
Pox on your flameship, Vulcan; if it be	211	U43 Vulcan	191
Pox on your fire workes, Vulcan; if it be	211	U43 Vulcan	V191
Light on thee: Or if those plagues will not doo,	212	U43 Vulcan	215
Light upon thee: Or if those plagues will not doo,	212	U43 Vulcan	V215
T'have wak'd, if sleeping, Spaines Ambassadour,	213	U44 Speach	4
If they stay here, but till Saint Georges Day.	213	U44 Speach	10
And could (if our great men would let their Sonnes	214	U44 Speach	57
Turne him, and see his Threds: looke, if he be	216	U45 Squib	21
Or if Chance must, to each man that doth rise,	217	U46 Coke	23
But if, for honour, we must draw the Sword,	219	U47 Tribe	39
'Mongst which, if I have any friendships sent,	220	U47 Tribe	63
The wits will leave you, if they once perceive	223	U49 Pucell	37
You cling to Lords, and Lords, if them you leave	223	U49 Pucell	38
Or if it would, the Court is the worst place,	223	U49 Pucell	43
It will be shame for them, if they have none.	225	U50 Countesse	36
Thou stand'st as if some Mysterie thou did'st!	225	U51 Bacon	4
Which if in compasse of no Art it came	227	U52 Answer	10
If I doe lose it: And, without a Tale,	229	U54 Squib	3
Stinketh my credit, if into the Pocket	229	U54 Squib	14
Such, (if her manners like you) I doe send:	230	U56 Covell	19
And should grow rich, if I had more to pay.	231	U56 Covell	V 30
If there be no money;	231	U57 Burges	21
If the 'Chequer be emptie, so will be his Head.	232	U57 Burges	28
His judgement is; If he be wise, and praise,	232	U58 Book-seller	5
Thanke him: if other, hee can give no Bayes.	232	U58 Book-seller	6
If his wit reach no higher, but to spring	232	U58 Book-seller	7
As if that part lay for a [ ] most fit!	232	U58 Book-seller	12
If they goe on, and that thou lov'st a-life	232	U58 Book-seller	13
If, Passenger, thou canst but reade:	233	U60 La-ware	1
How happy were the Subject, if he knew	236	U64 Charles 3	1
If he but weigh'd the blessings of this day?	236	U64 Charles 3	4
Sol will re-shine. If not, Charles hath a Sonne.	238	U65 Prince	12
And Sol will shine. If not, Charles hath a Sonne.	238	U65 Prince	V 12
To mee; or beene the same to you; if show,	241	U69 Friend Son	2
For, what is life, if measur'd by the space,	243	U70 Ode	21
Or masked man, if valu'd by his face,	243	U70 Ode	23
If they had leisure, at these lawfull routs,	249	U72 King	V 15
As if her ayrie steps did spring the flowers,	254	U75 Epithalam.	67
If to my mind, great Lord, I had a state,	260	U77 Treasurer	1
I would, if price, or prayer could them get,	260	U77 Treasurer	5
This I would doe, if I could thinke you one	260	U77 Treasurer	V 10
As if the beauties of the yeare,	264	U79 New-yeares	38
If you not understand, what Child you had.	271	U81 Pawlet	78
If you dare grudge at Heaven, and repent	271	U81 Pawlet	79
If you dare Quarrell Heaven, and repent	271	U81 Pawlet	V 79
If you can envie your owne Daughters blisse,	271	U81 Pawlet	83
If you can enjoy your owne Daughters blisse,	271	U81 Pawlet	V 83
If you can cast about your either eye,	271	U81 Pawlet	85
Hee shall, if he can understand,	276	U84 Body	11
Whose 'tis: but if it favour find,	277	U84 Body	31
But if, to boot with these, a chaste Wife meet	291	U85 Country	39
If with bright floods, the Winter troubled much,	291	U85 Country	51
If with East floods, the Winter troubled much,	291	U85 Country	V 51
If a fit livor thou dost seeke to toast;	292	U86 Hor.4:1	12
If thou be'st wise, with 'Syrian Oyle let shine	294	U89 Mart.8:77	3
If to a Womans head a Painter would	305	Horace	1
What's this? if he whose money hireth thee	305	Horace	26
If in th'escape an artlesse path we tread.	339	Horace	V 46/ 44
Yet, if by chance, in utt'ring things abstruse,	307	Horace	69
If I can give some small increase? when, loe,	309	Horace	80
If Custome please; at whose disposing will	309	Horace	103
If custome please, with whom both choyse, and will,	341	Horace	V103
If now the turnes, the colours, and right hues	311	Horace	126
If now the changes, and the severall hues	341	Horace	V121/126
And Peleus, if they seeke to heart-strike us	311	Horace	136
If thou would'st have me weepe, be thou first drown'd	311	Horace	145
Peleus, or Telephus. If you speake vile	311	Horace	147
If now the phrase of him that speakes, shall flow,	313	Horace	158
It much will differ, if a God speake, than,	313	Horace	161
Or an Heroe; if a ripe old man,	313	Horace	162
Things in themselves agreeing: If againe	313	Horace	170
If something strange, that never yet was had	313	Horace	178
If something fresh, that never yet was had	342	Horace	V178
If thou the vile, broad-troden ring forsake.	313	Horace	188
(As if he knew it) rapps his hearer to	315	Horace	212
If such a ones applause thou dost require,	315	Horace	220
If either you, or I, know the right way	323	Horace	402
If either you, or I know any way	348	Horace	V388/402
Her language, if the Stay, and Care t'have mended,	325	Horace	413
But fame of Poets, they thinke, if they come forth,	325	Horace	426
For choller! If I did not, who could bring	325	Horace	430

		Page	Title	Line
IF (cont.)				
For Choler! if I did not, none could bring	. . .	349	Horace	V430
How then? Why, as a Scrivener, if h'offend	. .	329	Horace	529
A Choerilus, in whom if I but see	. . .	329	Horace	534
Angry, if once I heare good Homer snore.	. . .	351	Horace	V512/536
If ne're so little it depart the first,	. . .	331	Horace	563
But, if hereafter thou shalt write, not feare	. .	331	Horace	575
If of their friendship he be worthy, or no:	. .	331	Horace	575
If to Quintilius, you recited ought:	. .	333	Horace	619
If you denied, you had no better straine.	. .	333	Horace	623
Then: If your fault you rather had defend	. .	333	Horace	625
Busie to catch a Black-bird; if he fall	. .	335	Horace	629
For, if one should, and with a rope make haste	. .	335	Horace	651
To let it downe, who knowes, if he did cast	. .	335	Horace	655
Nor did he doe this once; for if you can	. .	335	Horace	656
Nor did he do this, once; if yet you can,	. .	335	Horace	667
And, as a Beare, if he the strength but had	. .	355	Horace	V667
If they seeme wry, to such as looke asquint,	. .	337	Horace	674
If a Bird so amiable,	. . .	362	Author	7
But now, your Worke is done, if they that view	. .	364	Phoenix	3
'Tis not your fault, if they shall sense preferre,	. .	370	Author	9
Stay, view this stone: And, if thou beest not such,	. .	370	Author	13
Nay more in his wardrobe, if you will laugh at a	. .	371	Epitaph	1
If Praises, when th'are full, heaping admit,	. .	380	Coryat 3	47
The art of uttring wares, if they were bad;	. .	385	Brooke	6
I know for such, as (if my word will waigh)	. .	385	Husband	6
And, if thou list thy selfe, what thou canst bee.	. .	386	Husband	11
If all the vulgar Tongues, that speake this day,	. .	386	Browne	4
Finer then was his Spanish, if my Oath	. .	388	Chapman	7
Will bee receiv'd in Court; If not, would I	. .	389	Aleman	18
For, if I thought my judgement were of yeeres,	. .	389	Aleman	19
At least, if not the generall Engine cracke.	. .	391	Shakespeare	27
It hath beene question'd, Michael, if I bee	. .	395	May	6
A Friend at all; or, if at all, to thee:	. .	396	Drayton	1
Our right in France! if ritely understood.	. .	396	Drayton	2
If I can be a Friend, and Friend to thee.	. .	397	Drayton	58
If, maymed, she come off, 'tis not of men	. .	398	Drayton	94
If thou be soe desyrous to be read,	. .	401	Beaumont	16
If such a Tyke as thou, er'e wer't, or noe?	. .	408	Inigo Jones 3	9
To aske thy name, if he have half his Nose!	. .	409	Detractor	14
As if they' ador'd the Head, wheron th'are fixt.	. .	409	Detractor	18
for if there, or peace or warr be,	. . .	413	Ghyrlond	28
If there be a Coockold Major,	. . .	417	Moon	22
Or if any strife bety'de	. . .	417	Moon	25
Or by chance if in their grease	. . .	417	Moon	33
if it begyn religious thoughts to cherish;	. .	418	Moon	41
if any way she do rewarde thee	. .	422	Lucan	10
But with a Kisse, (if thou canst dare it)	. .	662	Bedford	8
IF'T		662	Bedford	9
If't chance to me, I must not grutch.	. . .	101	F4 To the World	56
Is done for gaine: if be, 'tis not sincere.	. .	169	U17 Friend-Debt	6
Or if't be the Gossipps happ	. .	417	Moon	37
IGNOBLE				
Th'Ignoble never liv'd, they were a-while	. .	257	U75 Epithalam.	153
IGNORANCE				
Thy ignorance still laughs in the wrong place.	. .	45	E58 Groome	4
And never stoupe, but to strike ignorance:	. .	55	E85 Goodyere 1	7
With ignorance on us, as they have done	. .	59	E92 New Crie	37
For since, what ignorance, what pride is fled!	. .	73	E113 Overbury	7
But, as it is (the Child of Ignorance,	. .	83	E132 Sylvester	3
And pride, and ignorance the schooles,	. .	101	F4 To the World	48
And know whose ignorance is more then theirs;	. .	218	U47 Tribe	24
To ignorance still, then either learne, or know?	. .	311	Horace	131
To ignorance still, then yet to learne, or know?	. .	341	Horace	V126/131
Or a worse Crime, the ignorance of art.	. .	323	Horace	386
For seeliest Ignorance on these may light,	. .	390	Shakespeare	7
As brandish't at the eyes of Ignorance.	. .	392	Shakespeare	70
IGNORANT				
To my lord Ignorant.	. . .	29	E10 Ignorant	Ttl
Which all, but ignorant Captaynes, will confesse:	. .	72	E111 Edmonds 2	7
O, these so ignorant Monsters! light, as proud,	. .	164	U15 Friend-Wars	59
The ignorant, and fooles, no pittie have.	. .	191	U38 Elegy 'Tis	20
Yet who's most ignorant, dares Verses make.	. .	331	Horace	570
To say, I'm ignorant. Just as a Crier	. .	333	Horace	597
Once say I'me ignorant. Just as a Cryer,	. .	353	Horace	V597
IGNORANTS				
With noble ignorants, and let them still,	. .	114	F12 Rutland	28
I'HAD				
Play-wright, by chance, hearing some toyes I'had writ,	.	64	E100 Playwrt 3	1
I'HAVE				
I'have sung the greater fortunes of our state.	. .	48	E64 Salisbury 3	18
Or that I'have by, two good sufficient men,	. .	54	E81 Proule	3
Foole, doe not rate my Rymes; I'have found thy Vice	. .	408	Detractor	5
IL				
Il may Ben Johnson slander so his feete,	. .	418	Answer	5
ILAND				
Discharge it 'bout the Iland, in an houre,	. .	249	U72 King	3
Discharging 'bout the Iland, in an houre,	. .	249	U72 King	V 3
I'LD				
'Tis one good part I'ld lie withall.	. .	142	U2 Exception	8
As, for her, I'ld not feare to die,	. .	293	U87 Hor.3:9	11
I'LE				
I'le loose my modestie, and tell your name.	. .	38	E38 Guiltie 2	8

I'LE (cont.)
But, I'le come in, ...	130	U1 Father	28
I'le taste as lightly as the Bee, . . .	139	U2 Another	5
I'le tell, that if they be not glad, . . .	147	U7 Nymph	8
I'le tell no more, and yet I love, . . .	148	U7 Nymph	29
I'le bid thee looke no more, but flee, flee friend,	166	U15 Friend-Wars	129
I'le lead you on; or if my fate will so, . .	170	U18 Elegy Can	22
I'le therefore aske no more, but bid you love;	171	U19 Elegy By	15
Of me, I'le softly tread unto my Tombe; .	199	U41 Elegy Since	20
But I'le conclude all in a civill curse. .	211	U43 Vulcan	190
Shall carry me at Call: and I'le be well, .	219	U47 Tribe	45
I'le tell you but the death, and the disease	335	Horace	659
ILE   (ISLE)
And flight about the Ile, well neare, by this, .	397	Drayton	49
ILE
Ile not offend thee with a vaine teare more, .	37	E33 Roe 3	1
For which, or pay me quickly', or Ile pay you.	51	E73 Fine Grand	22
Unto the cryes of London Ile adde one; .	58	E92 New Crie	2
Ile tell you of more, and lye, so you will come:	65	E101 Supper	17
And Ile professe no verses to repeate: .	65	E101 Supper	24
And Ile not looke for wine. . . .	106	F9 Celia 3	4
And Ile expect no wine.	106	F9 Celia 3	V 4
Of his dull god-head, were sinne. Ile implore	107	F10 Proludium	6
That went before, a Husband. Shee, Ile sweare,	386	Husband	9
IL'D
Young Il'd have him to, and faire, . .	141	U2 Her man	9
ILIA
The Roman Ilia was not more renown'd. .	293	U87 Hor.3:9	8
I'LL
I'll laugh at thee poor wretched Tike, go send .	410	Gill	10
ILL
For I will doe none: and as little ill, .	30	E11 Something	7
I sent the cause: Hee wooes with an ill sprite.	33	E19 Cod 1	2
Both which are great. And laugh at ill-made clothes;	35	E28 Surly	10
Great heav'n did well, to give ill fame free wing;	43	E51 James 3	2
Get him the times long grudge, the courts ill will;	48	E65 Muse	7
Fortune upon him breakes her selfe, if ill, .	63	E98 Th Roe 1	5
And ever is ill got without the first. .	63	E98 Th Roe 1	12
And one true posture, though besieg'd with ill	66	E102 Pembroke	14
At this so subtile sport: and play'st so ill?	72	E112 Gamster	2
Troth, if it be, I pitty thy ill lucke; .	73	E112 Gamster	17
Till thou canst finde the best, choose the least ill.	76	E119 Shelton	10
And is t'a body, often, ill inclin'd, .	82	E130 Ferrab. 1	7
Stunke not so ill; nor, when shee kist, Kate Arden.	87	E133 Voyage	118
He that for love of goodnesse hateth ill, .	112	F11 Epode	87
Well, or ill, onely, all the following yeere,	113	F12 Rutland	7
For others ill, ought none their good forget.	116	F13 Aubigny	6
As minds ill bent	129	U1 Father	13
That never came ill odour thence: . .	152	U12 Corbet	18
Or Science of discerning Good and Ill. .	156	U13 Sacvile	108
Ready to cast, at one, whose band sits ill,	164	U15 Friend-Wars	69
This hath our ill-us'd freedome, and soft peace	166	U15 Friend-Wars	121
Or doe upon my selfe some desperate ill; .	191	U38 Elegy 'Tis	3
An ill-affected limbe (what e're it aile) .	192	U38 Elegy 'Tis	45
Ought that is ill, but the suspition too, .	224	U50 Countesse	6
An ill commoditie! 'T must make good weight.	229	U54 Squib	6
Away ill company, and helpe in rime .	231	U56 Covell	23
Could stop the malice of this ill, . .	234	U60 La-ware	15
But as the wretched Painter, who so ill .	241	U69 Friend Son	9
Or Mallowes loosing bodyes ill: . .	291	U85 Country	58
Or Mallowes good for bodyes ill: . .	291	U85 Country	V 58
And ill-penn'd things, I shall, or sleepe, or smile.	311	Horace	148
Her Sonnes before the people; nor the ill-/Natur'd	317	Horace	264
ill-/Natur'd, and wicked Atreus cooke, to th'eye,	317	Horace	265
Those ill-torn'd Verses, to new hammering.	333	Horace	628
That an ill man dares not securely looke .	389	Aleman	8
Above th'ill fortune of them, or the need.	391	Shakespeare	16
Hee dyes with an Ill sent, . . .	420	Ode:If Men	16
It is a lycense to doe ill, protectes, .	423	Lucan	12
ILL-AFFECTED
An ill-affected limbe (what e're it aile) .	192	U38 Elegy 'Tis	45
ILL-MADE
Both which are great. And laugh at ill-made clothes;	35	E28 Surly	10
ILL-NATUR'D
Her Sonnes before the people; nor the ill-/Natur'd	317	Horace	264
ill-/Natur'd, and wicked Atreus cooke, to th'eye,	317	Horace	265
ILL-PENN'D
And ill-penn'd things, I shall, or sleepe, or smile.	311	Horace	148
ILLS
He pardons slips, goes by a world of ills, .	193	U38 Elegy 'Tis	69
And all Those ills that flew out of her box .	212	U43 Vulcan	V214
ILL-TORN'D
Those ill-torn'd Verses, to new hammering.	333	Horace	628
ILL-US'D
This hath our ill-us'd freedome, and soft peace	166	U15 Friend-Wars	121
ILLUSTRATE
Illustrate these, but they . . .	255	U75 Epithalam.	85
Of her illustrate brightnesse, . . .	364	Ode Splendor	3
ILLUSTRIOUS
Study illustrious Him, and you have all. .	282	U84 Kenelme	23
ILLUSTROUS
Illustrous Vere, or Horace; fit to be .	58	E91 Vere	3

		Page	Title	Line

I'M
I'm sure my language to her, was as sweet, . . . 149 U9 Picture 6
I'm sure my language to her, is as sweet, . . . 149 U9 Picture V 6
I feele, I'm rather dead then he! . . . 152 U12 Corbet 36
'Tis true, I'm broke! Vowes, Oathes, and all I had . . 191 U38 Elegy 'Tis 1
Why not? I'm gentle, and free-borne, doe hate . . 331 Horace 571
To say, I'm ignorant. Just as a Crier . . . 333 Horace 597

IMAGE
To a great image through thy luxurie. . . . 48 E65 Muse 4

IMAGERY
Thy twice conceyvd, thrice payd for Imagery? . . . 405 Inigo Jones 1 90

IMBARQU'D
Through seas, stormes, tempests: and imbarqu'd for hell, . 81 E128 Wm Roe 2 13

IMBRACE
Read so much wast, as she cannot imbrace . . . 150 U9 Picture 16
that Fortune to imbrace, ... 419 Ode:If Men 4

I'ME
Once say I'me ignorant. Just as a Cryer, . . . 353 Horace V597

IMITATE (See also YMITATE)
Because they would free Justice imitate, . . . 170 U18 Elegy Can 18
O imitate that sweet Serenitie . . . . 193 U38 Elegy 'Tis 77
But unto more dispayre to Imitate their sounde. . . 420 Ode:If Men 36

IMITATION
Of imitation, leape into a streight, . . . 313 Horace 192

IMMORTALITYE
To gaine the Crowne of immortalitye, . . . 400 Lady Ogle 34

IMMORTALL
By those bright Eyes, at whose immortall fires . . 170 U19 Elegy By 1
At these Immortall Mangers Virgil fed. . . . 228 U53 Newcastle 20
To the immortall memorie, and friendship of that noble . . . 242 U70 Ode Ttl
His rage, with razing your immortall Towne. . . 242 U70 Ode 4
Immortall, tooke a melancholique, odde . . . 335 Horace 662
Mortality, till you immortall bee. . . . 384 Somerset 22
Or Verse, or Sense t'express Immortall you? . . 403 Inigo Jones 1 41
and the immortall gods; love only those . . . 422 Lucan 5

IMPARTIALLY
Vaile their owne eyes, and would impartially . . 170 U18 Elegy Can 19

IMPERFECT
As though his age imperfect might appeare, . . 244 U70 Ode 51
Dull, and prophane, weake, and imperfect eyes, . . 284 U84 Muse 79

IMPERIALL
And he is built like some imperiall roome . . 262 U78 Digby 7

IMPETUOUS
Medea make brave with impetuous scorne; . . . 313 Horace 175
Medea make wild, fierce, impetuous; . . . 342 Horace V175

IMPIOUS
And impious ranknesse of all Sects and seeds: . . 163 U15 Friend-Wars 34

IMPLEXED
Is so implexed, and laid in, between, . . . 412 Ghyrlond 7

IMPLORE
Of his dull god-head, were sinne. Ile implore . . 107 F10 Proludium 6
Of his dull god-head, were sinne. Lets implore . . 107 F10 Proludium V 6

IMPORTUNE
O then (my best-best lov'd) let me importune, . . 180 U25 Desmond 63
O then (our best-best lov'd) let me importune, . . 180 U25 Desmond V 63
Importune wish; and by her lov'd Lords side . . 394 Jane Ogle 23

IMPOS'D
Our Ancestors impos'd on Prince and State. . . 215 U44 Speach 78

IMPOSTURE
Imposture, witchcraft, charmes, or blasphemie, . . 203 U43 Vulcan 16

IMPOSTURES
Impostures branded! And Authorities urg'd! . . 160 U14 Selden 41

IMPREGNABLE
This Fort of so impregnable accesse, . . . 401 Beaumont 17

IMPRESE
Item, a gulling imprese for you, at tilt. . . . 51 E73 Fine Grand 15
Which is, it selfe, the imprese of the great, . . 66 E103 L Wroth 1 7

IMPRESSION
So in my braine; the stronge impression . . . 361 Palmer 21

IMPREST
That Nature no such difference had imprest . . 75 E116 Jephson 9
Your forme imprest there: not with tickling rimes, . . 116 F12 Rutland 87
Your forme imprest there: not with tinckling rimes, . . 116 F12 Rutland V 87

IMPRINT
T'imprint in all purg'd hearts this virgin sence, . . 414 Ghyrlond 55

IMPRISON
(In the meane time, let 'hem imprison mee) . . . 87 E133 Voyage 104

IMPUDENCE
And lyes so farre from wit, 'tis impudence. . . 38 E38 Guiltie 2 6
That hath not Countrye impudence enough to laughe att Arte, . 420 Ode:If Men 14

IMPUTATION
Oft scape an Imputation, more through luck, then wit. . 179 U25 Desmond 52
Oft scape theyr Imputation, more through luck, then wit. . 179 U25 Desmond V 52
Or builders of Story have oft imputation . . . 380 Coryat 3 30

IMPUTED
On some new gesture, that's imputed wit? . . 81 E129 Mime 14
B'imputed right to an inheritance . . . 286 U84 Muse 144

I'
Item, your mistris anagram, i' your hilt. . . . 51 E73 Fine Grand 16
I' your selfe, all treasure lost of th'age before. . . 68 E105 L Wroth 2 20
Then can a flea at twise skip i'the Map. . . . 69 E107 Hungry 18
Or the Nard i' the fire? . . . . 135 U2 Triumph 28
As farre as any poore Sword i' the Land. . . 154 U13 Sacvile 55
As if a Brize were gotten i' their tayle; . . . 164 U15 Friend-Wars 71

I' (cont.)
But why are all these Irons i'the fire . . . . 215 U44 Speach 93
That hang their richest jewells i'their nose; . . . 232 U58 Book-seller 10
Nor know t'observe: why (i'the Muses name) . . . . 311 Horace 128
I'the open field; is Waxe like to be wrought . . . 315 Horace 231
'N
Or stands to be'n Commission o' the blade? . . . 155 U13 Sacvile 64
IN'
Active in's braine, and passive in his bones. . . . 49 E68 Playwrt 2 4
That as the water makes things, put in't streight, . . 170 U18 Elegy Can 7
IN
Pray thee, take care, that tak'st my booke in hand, . . . 27 E1 Reader 1
Or in cleft-sticks, advanced to make calls . . . 28 E3 Bookseller 8
But two things, rare, the Fates had in their store, . . 28 E4 James 1 3
Sure, willing povertie lives most in you. . . . 29 E6 Alchymists 2
But I have my revenge made, in thy name. . . . 29 E10 Ignorant 2
At court I met it, in clothes brave enough, . . . 30 E11 Something 1
A lord, it cryed, buried in flesh, and blood, . . . 30 E11 Something 5
Shift, here, in towne, not meanest among squires, . . 30 E12 Shift 1
But see! th'old baud hath serv'd him in his trim, . . 31 E12 Shift 23
All that I am in arts, all that I know, . . . 31 E14 Camden 2
What name, what skill, what faith hast thou in things! . . 31 E14 Camden 7
What sight in searching the most antique springs! . . 31 E14 Camden 8
What weight, and what authoritie in thy speech! . . 31 E14 Camden 9
All men are wormes: But this no man. In silke . . 31 E15 Court-worm 1
So, in short time, th'art in arrerage growne . . . 32 E16 Brain-hardy 5
Make good what thou dar'st doe in all the rest. . . 32 E16 Brain-hardy 8
To thee, my way in Epigrammes seemes new, . . . 32 E18 Censurer 1
Th'expence in odours is a most vaine sinne, . . . 33 E20 Cod 2 1
Quick in his lips! who hath this wonder wrought? . . 33 E21 Gam'ster 5
In comfort of her mothers teares, . . . 33 E22 Daughter 8
In the past pleasures of his sensuall life, . . . 34 E25 Beast 1 2
In varied shapes, which for his lust shee takes: . . 34 E25 Beast 1 6
In place of scutcheons, that should decke thy herse, . . 35 E27 Roe 1 1
H'has tympanies of businesse, in his face, . . . 35 E28 Surly 7
He will both argue, and discourse in oathes, . . . 35 E28 Surly 9
That breathes in his dogs way: and this is great. . . 36 E28 Surly 18
But that's put in, thou'lt say. Why, so is thine. . . 36 E29 Tilter 6
'Twere madnesse in thee, to betray thy fame, . . . 36 E30 Guiltie 3
His monyes travaile for him, in and out: . . . 36 E31 Banck 2
What could not worke; at home in his repaire . . . 37 E32 Roe 2 7
He that feares death, or mournes it, in the just, . . 37 E34 Death 1
And in this short time of thy happiest raigne, . . 37 E35 James 2 4
And than in them, how could we know god more? . . 38 E35 James 2 8
But in my royall subject I passe thee, . . . 38 E36 Martial 3
Colt, now, doth daily penance in his owne. . . . 39 E39 Colt 2
Read not in faire heavens storie, . . . 39 E40 Ratcliffe 6
Then they might in her bright eyes. . . . 39 E40 Ratcliffe 8
In these times. Few so have ru'de . . . 39 E40 Ratcliffe 14
Fate, in a brother. To conclude, . . . 39 E40 Ratcliffe 15
By his free will, be in Jones company. . . . 40 E42 Giles 5
In all affections shee concurreth still. . . . 40 E42 Giles 15
Her foes enough would fame thee in their hate. . . 40 E43 Salisbury 1 4
When, in my booke, men reade but Cecill's name, . . 41 E43 Salisbury 1 9
When, in my Verse, men reade but Sarum's name, . . 41 E43 Salisbury 1 V 9
Chuffe, lately rich in name, in chattels, goods, . . 41 E44 Chuff 1
And rich in issue to inherit all, . . . 41 E44 Chuff 2
Rest in soft peace, and, ask'd, say here doth lye . . 41 E45 First Son 9
A knight-hood bought, to goe a wooing in? . . . 42 E46 Luckless 1 2
Of bearing them in field, he threw 'hem away: . . 42 E48 Mungril 2
For wittie, in his language, is obscene. . . . 42 E49 Playwrt 1 4
In my chast booke: professe them in thine owne. . . 42 E49 Playwrt 1 6
For we, that have our eyes still in our eares, . . 43 E51 James 3 9
But when (in place) thou didst the patrons choose, . . 43 E53 Old-end 4
To'a little wealth, and credit in the scene, . . . 45 E56 Poet-Ape 7
Thy ignorance still laughs in the wrong place. . . 45 E58 Groome 4
Spies, you are lights in state, but of base stuffe, . . 45 E59 Spies 1
Thy fact, in brasse or marble writ the same) . . 46 E60 Mounteagle 4
In a great belly. Write, then on thy wombe, . . 46 E62 Would-bee 11
The judgement of the king so shine in thee; . . 47 E63 Salisbury 2 4
A treasure, art: contemn'd in th'age of gold. . . 47 E64 Salisbury 3 4
These (noblest Cecil) labour'd in my thought, . . 48 E64 Salisbury 3 15
In onely thee, might be both great, and glad. . . 48 E66 Cary 4
It may be much, or little, in the cause. . . . 49 E66 Cary 16
Stand high, then, Howard, high in eyes of men, . . 49 E67 Suffolk 5
High in thy bloud, thy place, but highest then, . . 49 E67 Suffolk 6
When, in mens wishes, so thy vertues wrought, . . 49 E67 Suffolk 7
Before thou wert it, in each good mans heart. . . 49 E67 Suffolk 10
Active in's braine, and passive in his bones. . . 49 E68 Playwrt 2 4
In life, that can employ it; and takes hold . . 50 E70 Wm Roe 1 3
In-primis, Grand, you owe me for a jest, . . . 51 E73 Fine Grand 5
That yet maintaynes you, and your house in laughter. . 51 E73 Fine Grand 8
In solemne cypres, the other cob-web-lawne. . . 51 E73 Fine Grand 14
Item, your owne, sew'd in your mistris smock. . . 51 E73 Fine Grand 17
In most vile verses, and cost me more paine, . . 51 E73 Fine Grand 19
That no affection in thy voyce commands. . . . 51 E74 Chancelor 4
And no lesse wise, then skilfull in the lawes; . . 52 E74 Chancelor 6
T'our times return'd, hath made her heaven in thee. . 52 E74 Chancelor 10
Fit in that softer bosome to reside. . . . 52 E76 Bedford 1 12
Nature, they thought, in all, that he would faine. . 53 E79 Rutland 8
And hath it, in his powers, to make his way! . . 53 E80 Life/Death 4
Surly's old whore in her new silkes doth swim: . . 54 E82 Surly 1
To former height, and there in circle tarrie, . . 55 E85 Goodyere 1 9

			Page	Title	Line

IN (cont.)

	Page	Title	Line
Now, in whose pleasures I have this discerned,	55	E85 Goodyere 1	11
In making thy friends bookes, and thy bookes friends:	55	E86 Goodyere 2	4
Touch'd with the sinne of false play, in his pungue,	56	E87 Hazard	1
Of what shee had wrought came in, and wak'd his braine,	56	E87 Hazard	4
As french-men in his companie, should seeme dutch?	56	E88 Monsieur	8
Daily to turne in Pauls, and helpe the trade.	56	E88 Monsieur	16
If Rome so great, and in her wisest age,	56	E89 Allen	1
How can so great example dye in mee,	57	E89 Allen	7
Who both their graces in thy selfe hast more	57	E89 Allen	9
And present worth in all dost so contract,	57	E89 Allen	11
And, finding good securitie in his age,	57	E90 Mill	6
In th'eye of Europe, where thy deeds were done,	58	E91 Vere	6
Nor lesse in practice; but lesse mark'd, lesse knowne:	58	E91 Vere	14
As noble in great chiefes, as they are rare.	58	E91 Vere	16
Ripe statesmen, ripe: They grow in every street.	58	E92 New Crie	3
They carry in their pockets Tacitus,	59	E92 New Crie	15
Nay, aske you, how the day goes, in your eare.	59	E92 New Crie	18
They meet in sixes, and at every mart,	59	E92 New Crie	21
To write in cypher, and the severall keyes,	59	E92 New Crie	26
Two bravely in the battaile fell, and dy'd,	60	E93 Radcliffe	5
Thou yet remayn'st, un-hurt in peace, or warre,	60	E93 Radcliffe	13
Willing to expiate the fault in thee,	60	E93 Radcliffe	15
For none ere tooke that pleasure in sinnes sense,	60	E94 Bedford 3	9
In thee, most weighty Savile, liv'd to us:	61	E95 Savile	4
So hast thou rendred him in all his bounds,	61	E95 Savile	5
Which Fate (it seemes) caus'd in the historie,	61	E95 Savile	11
Onely to boast thy merit in supply.	61	E95 Savile	12
To have her storie woven in thy thred;	61	E95 Savile	15
No more then Salust in the Romane state!	61	E95 Savile	23
And, in thy censures, evenly, dost take	62	E96 Donne 2	4
But one more rare, and in the case so new:	62	E97 Motion	3
Nor office in the towne, nor place in court,	63	E97 Motion	11
Nor could the age have mist thee, in this strife	66	E102 Pembroke	5
That art so reverenc'd, as thy comming in,	66	E102 Pembroke	17
But in the view, doth interrupt their sinne;	66	E102 Pembroke	18
A Sydney: but in that extend as farre	67	E103 L Wroth 1	10
Even in the dew of grace, what you would bee?	67	E104 Montgomery	2
And, drest in shepheards tyre, who would not say:	68	E105 L Wroth 2	9
What States yo'have gull'd, and which yet keepes yo'in pay.	69	E107 Hungry	10
In Ireland, Holland, Sweden, pompous lies,	69	E107 Hungry	12
In Hungary, and Poland, Turkie too;	69	E107 Hungry	13
And, in some yeere, all these together heap'd,	69	E107 Hungry	15
Twirle the poore chaine you run a feasting in.	69	E107 Hungry	30
Where vertue makes them both, and that's in thee:	70	E109 Nevil	3
To be the same in roote, thou art in height;	70	E109 Nevil	13
In these west-parts, nor when that warre was done,	71	E110 Edmonds 1	2
Nor that his worke liv'd in the hands of foes,	71	E110 Edmonds 1	9
His deedes too dying, but in bookes (whose good	71	E110 Edmonds 1	11
His deedes too dying, save in bookes (whose good	71	E110 Edmonds 1	V 15
In every counsell, stratageme, designe,	71	E110 Edmonds 1	19
And that, in action, there is nothing new,	72	E111 Edmonds 2	5
To a weake Gamster in Poetry.	72	E112 Gamster	Ttl
Or thy ranke setting? that thou dar'st put in	72	E112 Gamster	4
Where shall I scape thee? in an Epigramme?	73	E112 Gamster	15
Pr'y thee, yet save thy rest; give ore in time:	73	E112 Gamster	21
And letters, and humanitie in the stead!	73	E113 Overbury	8
Who'in such ambition can but follow thee.	73	E113 Overbury	12
In meere out-formes, untill he lost his sight,	73	E114 Sydney	4
But, in your love, made all his servants wise.	74	E114 Sydney	8
By speaking well o' the company' it 's in.	74	E115 Honest Man	8
Acts old Iniquitie, and in the fit	74	E115 Honest Man	27
Executes men in picture. By defect,	75	E115 Honest Man	29
An inginer, in slanders, of all fashions,	75	E115 Honest Man	31
In men, but every bravest was the best:	75	E116 Jephson	10
Them in, if not, from thee; or must commit	75	E116 Jephson	15
A desperate soloecisme in truth and wit.	75	E116 Jephson	16
Thus, in his belly, can he change a sin,	76	E118 Gut	5
Lust it comes out, that gluttony went in.	76	E118 Gut	6
At hunting railes, having no guift in othes,	76	E119 Shelton	2
Dar'st breath in any ayre; and with safe skill,	76	E119 Shelton	9
And, in their errors maze, thine owne way know:	76	E119 Shelton	13
In grace, and feature,	77	E120 S. P.	6
In bathes to steepe him;	77	E120 S. P.	22
In a little? Reader, stay.	79	E124 Elizabeth	2
Which in life did harbour give	79	E124 Elizabeth	5
Leave it buryed in this vault.	79	E124 Elizabeth	8
Restored in thy body, and thy minde!	79	E125 Uvedale	4
Who sees a soule, in such a body set,	79	E125 Uvedale	5
If I should faile, in gratitude, to thee,	80	E127 Aubigny	2
And perfect in a circle alwayes meet.	81	E128 Wm Roe 2	8
Shed in thy Songs; 'tis true: but short of thee.	82	E130 Ferrab. 1	18
Before my thought, and (in thy right) commands	83	E132 Sylvester	8
So well in that are his inventions wrought,	83	E132 Sylvester	11
Cocytus, Phlegeton, our have prov'd in one;	84	E133 Voyage	8
And in it, two more horride knaves, then Charon.	84	E133 Voyage	12
Arses were heard to croake, in stead of frogs,	84	E133 Voyage	13
But, in the action, greater man then hee:	84	E133 Voyage	26
In it' owne hall; when these in worthy scorne	85	E133 Voyage	31
From Venice, Paris, or some in-land passage	85	E133 Voyage	33
Propos'd to goe to Hol'borne in a wherry:	85	E133 Voyage	38
Of some Bride-well, and may, in time, concerne us	85	E133 Voyage	42
In the first jawes appear'd that ugly monster,	85	E133 Voyage	61

		Page	Title		Line
IN (cont.)					
Spake to 'hem louder, then the oxe in Livie:	. . . .	86	E133 Voyage		74
And, in so shitten sort, so long had us'd him:	. . . .	86	E133 Voyage		98
His spirits, now, in pills, and eeke in potions,	. . . .	86	E133 Voyage		101
(In the meane time, let 'hem imprison mee)	. . . .	87	E133 Voyage		104
Of the grave fart, late let in parliament,	. . . .	87	E133 Voyage		108
Had it beene seconded, and not in fume	. . . .	87	E133 Voyage		109
The slie Ulysses stole in a sheepes-skin,	. . . .	87	E133 Voyage		113
Yet, one day in the yeere, for sweet 'tis voyc't,	. . . .	87	E133 Voyage		119
White, black, blew, greene, and in more formes out-started,	. .	87	E133 Voyage		126
Airising in that place, through which, who goes,	. . . .	87	E133 Voyage		131
And, after, swom abroad in ample flakes,	. . . .	87	E133 Voyage		138
To put the skins, and offall in a pastie?	. . . .	88	E133 Voyage		148
For, here they were throwne in wi'the melted pewter,	. .	88	E133 Voyage		153
Yet drown'd they not. They had five lives in future.	. .	88	E133 Voyage		154
And, in a pittious tune, began. How dare	. . . .	88	E133 Voyage		164
Your daintie nostrills (in so hot a season,	. . . .	88	E133 Voyage		165
And out-cryes of the damned in the Fleet?	. . . .	88	E133 Voyage		172
In memorie of which most liquid deed,	. . . .	89	E133 Voyage		193
I thought to binde him, in my verse:	. . . .	93	F1 Why write no		2
Mars, and my Mother, in their net:	. . . .	93	F1 Why write no		6
I weare not these my wings in vaine.	. . . .	93	F1 Why write no		7
Thou joy'st in better markes, of soyle, of ayre,	. . . .	93	F2 Penshurst		7
There, in the writhed barke, are cut the names	. . . .	94	F2 Penshurst		15
The painted partrich lyes in every field,	. . . .	94	F2 Penshurst		29
Fig, grape, and quince, each in his time doth come:	. .	94	F2 Penshurst		42
But all come in, the farmer, and the clowne:	. . . .	94	F2 Penshurst		48
An emblene of themselves, in plum, or peare.	. . . .	95	F2 Penshurst		56
A fortune, in this age, but rarely knowne.	. . . .	96	F2 Penshurst		92
Reade, in their vertuous parents noble parts,	. . . .	96	F2 Penshurst		97
To Sir Robert Wroth in praise of a Country life. Epode.	. .	96	F3 Wroth		VTtl
But canst, at home, in thy securer rest,	. . . .	97	F3 Wroth		13
Or, if thou list the night in watch to breake,	. . . .	97	F3 Wroth		21
In spring, oft roused for thy masters sport,	. . . .	97	F3 Wroth		23
In spring tyme roused for their masters sport,	. . . .	97	F3 Wroth	V	23
In autumne, at the Partrich makes a flight,	. . . .	97	F3 Wroth		27
And, in the winter, hunt'st the flying hare,	. . . .	97	F3 Wroth		29
Or in the winter, hunt'st the flying hare	. . . .	97	F3 Wroth	V	29
The ripened eares, yet humble in their height,	. . . .	98	F3 Wroth		41
The eares cut downe in their most height,	. . . .	98	F3 Wroth	V	41
The trees cut out in log; and those boughes made	. .	98	F3 Wroth		45
Comus puts in, for new delights;	. . . .	98	F3 Wroth		48
As if in Saturnes raigne it were;	. . . .	98	F3 Wroth		50
The rout of rurall folke come thronging in,	. . . .	98	F3 Wroth		53
And in their cups, their cares are drown'd:	. . . .	98	F3 Wroth		60
Let others watch in guiltie armes, and stand	. . . .	98	F3 Wroth		67
That they may sleepe with scarres in age.	. . . .	98	F3 Wroth		70
For every price, in every jarre,	. . . .	99	F3 Wroth		74
And, so they ride in purple, eate in plate,	. . . .	99	F3 Wroth		89
Render his head in there againe?	. . . .	101	F4 To the World		32
Then, in a soile hast planted me,	. . . .	101	F4 To the World		45
Here in my bosome, and at home.	. . . .	102	F4 To the World		68
Spend not then his quifts in vaine.	. . . .	102	F5 Celia 1		5
Or the sands in Chelsey fields,	. . . .	103	F6 Celia 2		14
All the sands in Chelsey fields,	. . . .	103	F6 Celia 2	V	14
Or the drops in silver Thames,	. . . .	103	F6 Celia 2		15
In the silent sommer-nights,	. . . .	103	F6 Celia 2		17
Spent in surfets: and their dayes,	. . . .	104	F8 Sicknesse		5
And nights too, in worser wayes?	. . . .	104	F8 Sicknesse		6
In decoctions; and are mann'd	. . . .	105	F8 Sicknesse		30
With ten Emp'ricks, in their chamber,	. . . .	105	F8 Sicknesse		31
Every stew in towne to know;	. . . .	105	F8 Sicknesse		38
Every Cranck in towne to know;	. . . .	105	F8 Sicknesse	V	38
In thy justice to molest	. . . .	106	F8 Sicknesse		47
Or leave a kisse but in the cup,	. . . .	106	F9 Celia 3		3
Or whose great name in Poets heaven use,	. . . .	107	F10 Proludium		2
In the greene circle of thy Ivy twine.	. . . .	107	F10 Proludium		12
His absence in my verse, is all I aske.	. . . .	107	F10 Proludium		21
His absence in our verse, is all I aske.	. . . .	107	F10 Proludium	V	21
Thy thoughts did never melt in amorous fire,	. . . .	108	F10 Proludium		3
in whom the flame of every beauty raignes,	. . . .	108	F10 Proludium		8
Such, as in lustes wilde forrest love to rainge,	. . . .	108	F10 Proludium		9
only pursewinge Constancy, in Chainge;	. . . .	108	F10 Proludium		10
Let these in wanton feete daunce out their soules.	. .	108	F10 Proludium		11
Who (in th'examining)	. . . .	109	F11 Epode		14
In our enflamed brests:	. . . .	110	F11 Epode		34
In a continuall tempest. Now, true Love	. . . .	110	F11 Epode		43
In equall knots: This beares no brands, nor darts,	. .	110	F11 Epode		51
But, in a calme, and god-like unitie,	. . . .	110	F11 Epode		53
O, who is he, that (in this peace) enjoyes	. . . .	110	F11 Epode		55
And yet (in this t'expresse our selves more cleare)	. .	111	F11 Epode		75
And yet (in this t'expresse my self more cleare)	. .	111	F11 Epode	V	75
All her best symmetrie in that one feature!	. . . .	112	F11 Epode		101
The wealthy treasure of her love in him;	. . . .	112	F11 Epode	V	105
In the full floud of her admir'd perfection?	. . . .	112	F11 Epode		107
Were yet unfound, and better plac'd in earth,	. . . .	114	F12 Rutland		25
The world hath seene, which all these had in trust,	. .	114	F12 Rutland		39
And now lye lost in their forgotten dust.	. . . .	114	F12 Rutland		40
Inscrib'd in touch or marble, or the cotes	. . . .	114	F12 Rutland		44
Or in their windowes; doe but prove the wombs,	. . . .	114	F12 Rutland		46
Or, in an armies head, that, lockt in brasse,	. . . .	114	F12 Rutland		52
Who placed Jasons Argo in the skie?	. . . .	115	F12 Rutland		59
Or lifted Cassiopea in her chayre?	. . . .	115	F12 Rutland		62

IN (cont.)

	Page	Title		Line
(Or Poet, in the court account) then I,	115	F12	Rutland	69
They hold in my strange poems, which, as yet,	115	F12	Rutland	81
For that firme grace he holdes in your regard,	116	F12	Rutland	95
I, therefore, who professe my selfe in love	116	F13	Aubigny	7
And, in this name, am given out dangerous	117	F13	Aubigny	11
In my character, what your features bee,	117	F13	Aubigny	24
And, in those outward formes, all fooles are wise.	117	F13	Aubigny	36
In single paths, dangers with ease are watch'd:	118	F13	Aubigny	57
Contagion in the prease is soonest catch'd,	118	F13	Aubigny	58
And greater rites, yet writ in mysterie,	119	F13	Aubigny	106
Of nobles vertue, shew in you;	121	F14	Sydney	32
With dust of ancestors, in graves but dwell.	121	F14	Sydney	40
So may you live in honor, as in name,	121	F14	Sydney	51
Is it interpreted in me disease,	122	F15	Heaven	3
My faith, my hope, my love: and in this state,	122	F15	Heaven	11
Conceiv'd in sinne, and unto labour borne,	122	F15	Heaven	18
Of persons, still one God, in Unitie.	127	U1	Trinitie	2
As my heart lies in peeces, all confus'd,	127	U1	Trinitie	7
All's done in me.	128	U1	Trinitie	24
Father and Sonne; the Comforter, in breeding	128	U1	Trinitie	26
Pure thoughts in man: with fiery zeale them feeding	128	U1	Trinitie	27
Of persons, still one God in Unitie;	128	U1	Trinitie	30
Beholding one in three, and three in one,	128	U1	Trinitie	33
A Trinitie, to shine in Union;	128	U1	Trinitie	34
All coeternall in your Majestie,	128	U1	Trinitie	38
Distinct in persons, yet in Unitie	128	U1	Trinitie	39
But in thy presence, truly glorified,	128	U1	Trinitie	47
But, I'le come in,	130	U1	Father	28
Was now laid in a Manger.	130	U1	Nativitie	12
Both wills were in one stature;	130	U1	Nativitie	15
A Martyr borne in our defence;	130	U1	Nativitie	23
A Celebration of Charis in ten Lyrick Peeces.	131	U2	Charis	Ttl
In a Hercules-his shape.	132	U2	How he saw	32
Left it sticking in my heart:	133	U2	Suffered	16
And in either Prose, or Song,	133	U2	Suffered	23
In cheifest glory Sunne-her	135	U2	Triumph	V 32
In her cheekes, of Milke, and Roses;	136	U2	Cupid	22
Such as oft I wanton in!	136	U2	Cupid	23
Make in one, the same were shee.	137	U2	Cupid	48
Else that glister'd in White-hall;	138	U2	Kisse	16
In the Daunces, with what spight	138	U2	Kisse	22
I long, and should not beg in vaine,	139	U2	Another	2
Nay, you may erre in this,	139	U2	Another	9
Charis one day in discourse	139	U2	Promise	1
To fetch in the Formes goe by:	140	U2	Promise	18
French to boote, at least in fashion,	141	U2	Her man	7
Cast in thousand snares, and rings	141	U2	Her man	11
Quickly fir'd, as in beginners	141	U2	Her man	31
In loves schoole, and yet no sinners.	141	U2	Her man	32
In loves art, and yet no sinners.	141	U2	Her man	V 32
In a body, should be there.	141	U2	Her man	35
Or were set up in a Brake.	142	U2	Her man	40
Or were pent up in a Brake.	142	U2	Her man	V 40
The Musicall Strife; In a Pastorall Dialogue.	143	U3	Musicall	Ttl
So they in state of Grace retain'd,	144	U3	Musicall	27
O, doe not steepe them in thy Teares,	145	U4	Song	9
In the person of Woman-kind. A Song Apologetique.	145	U5	Woman-kind	Ttl
Find some one good, in some one man;	145	U5	Woman-kind	9
In any curious peece you see	145	U5	Woman-kind	14
Another. In defence of their Inconstancie. A Song.	146	U6	Defence	Ttl
Such as in valour would excell,	146	U6	Defence	7
Which we in love must doe aswell,	146	U6	Defence	9
In love, doth not alone help forth	146	U6	Defence	20
Here running in the Glasse,	148	U8	Houre-glasse	2
And in his Mrs. flame, playing like a flye,	149	U8	Houre-glasse	7
And in his Mrs. flaming, playing like a flye,	149	U8	Houre-glasse	V 7
Yes; and in death, as life, unblest,	149	U8	Houre-glasse	9
My Picture left in Scotland.	149	U9	Picture	Ttl
In sentence, of as subtile feet,	149	U9	Picture	8
In numbers, of as subtile feet,	149	U9	Picture	V 8
That sits in shadow of Apollo's tree.	149	U9	Picture	10
Love in a subtile Dreame disguis'd,	151	U11	Dreame	4
In all my wild desire,	151	U11	Dreame	11
As twice to trespasse in his sight,	152	U12	Corbet	26
And in the Act did so my blush prevent,	153	U13	Sacvile	11
Deepest in Man, of which when he doth thinke,	153	U13	Sacvile	20
Of pressure, like one taken in a streight?	154	U13	Sacvile	32
That puts it in his Debt-booke e're 't be done;	154	U13	Sacvile	34
In that proud manner, as a good so gain'd,	154	U13	Sacvile	37
Nought but in corners; and is loath to leave,	154	U13	Sacvile	44
Give thankes by stealth, and whispering in the eare,	154	U13	Sacvile	49
If it were cleare, but being so in cloud	155	U13	Sacvile	87
Such a religious horrour in the brests	155	U13	Sacvile	91
Or feats of darknesse acted in Mid-Sun,	156	U13	Sacvile	95
Sure there is Misterie in it, I not know,	156	U13	Sacvile	97
Reare-Suppers in their Names! and spend whole nights	156	U13	Sacvile	101
Unto their praise, in certaine swearing rites!	156	U13	Sacvile	102
Cannot a man be reck'ned in the State	156	U13	Sacvile	103
Profit in ought: each day some little adde,	157	U13	Sacvile	132
In time 'twill be a heape; This is not true	157	U13	Sacvile	133
Alone in money, but in manners too.	157	U13	Sacvile	134
Shoot forth in smooth and comely spaces; have	157	U13	Sacvile	150

314

	Page	Title	Line
	Page	Title	Line

IN (cont.)

Text	Page	Title	Line
And last, goe out in nothing: You that see	157	U13 Sacvile	153
To aske it: though in most of workes it be	158	U14 Selden	7
Or faith in things? or is't your wealth and will	159	U14 Selden	36
Of Gathering? Bountie' in pouring out againe?	159	U14 Selden	38
Of what it tells us) weav'd in to instruct.	160	U14 Selden	52
In sharpnesse of all Search, wisdome of Choise,	160	U14 Selden	59
Flowes in upon me, and I cannot raise	160	U14 Selden	62
Monarch in Letters! 'Mongst thy Titles showne	160	U14 Selden	65
In offering this thy worke to no great Name,	161	U14 Selden	69
In the same Mines of knowledge; and thence brought	161	U14 Selden	76
In the rich Mines of knowledge; and thence brought	161	U14 Selden	V 76
Among my commings in, and see it mount,	161	U14 Selden	80
Beates brave, and loude in Europe, and bids come	162	U15 Friend-Wars	2
Mans buried honour, in his sleepie life:	162	U15 Friend-Wars	7
In dreames, begun in hope, and end in spoile.	162	U15 Friend-Wars	10
Crush'd in the snakie brakes, that he had past!	162	U15 Friend-Wars	18
In outward face, but inward, light as Furre,	162	U15 Friend-Wars	20
Rather then here so bogg'd in vices stay.	163	U15 Friend-Wars	30
In bravery, or gluttony, or coyne,	163	U15 Friend-Wars	45
In admiration, stretch'd upon the rack	163	U15 Friend-Wars	50
To catch the flesh in, and to pound a Prick.	164	U15 Friend-Wars	67
That may corrupt her, even in his eyes.	165	U15 Friend-Wars	92
The Servant of the Serving-woman, in scorne,	165	U15 Friend-Wars	99
Our vices doe not tarry in a place,	166	U15 Friend-Wars	123
But being in Motion still (or rather in race)	166	U15 Friend-Wars	124
In this, and like, an itch of Vanitie,	166	U15 Friend-Wars	143
In Sugar Candide, or in butter'd beere,	167	U15 Friend-Wars	153
More honour in him, 'cause we'ave knowne him mad:	168	U15 Friend-Wars	194
These take, and now goe seeke thy peace in Warre,	168	U15 Friend-Wars	195
And he is not in friendship. Nothing there	169	U17 Friend-Debt	5
Simply my Band, his trust in me forsakes,	169	U17 Friend-Debt	12
Now so much friend, as you would trust in me,	169	U17 Friend-Debt	14
Where he doth steepe himselfe in Milke and Roses;	170	U19 Elegy By	8
So well as I may tell in verse, 'tis so?	170	U19 Elegy By	12
Others, in time may love, as we doe now.	171	U19 Elegy By	18
That which we can, who both in you, his Wife,	171	U19 Elegy By	25
As in his place, because he would not varie,	171	U19 Elegy By	27
A Womans friendship! God whom I trust in,	171	U20 Shrub	1
His name in any mettall, it would breake.	172	U21 Ltl Shrub	2
In whom alone Love lives agen?	173	U22 Elegy Tho	14
Yet give me leave t'adore in you	174	U22 Elegy Tho	35
What I, in her, am griev'd to want.	174	U22 Elegy Tho	36
Buried in ease and sloth?	174	U23 Himselfe	2
Then take in hand thy Lyre,	175	U23 Himselfe	25
Strike in thy proper straine,	175	U23 Himselfe	26
stryke him in thy proper straine,	175	U23 Himselfe	V 26
When Vice alike in time with vertue dur'd.	176	U24 Frontispice	8
. . . in Queene Elizabeths Time, since lost, and recovered.	176	U25 Desmond	Ttl
Thy Priest in this strange rapture; heat my braine	177	U25 Desmond	11
That I may sing my thoughts, in some unvulgar straine.	177	U25 Desmond	13
Lock't in her cold embraces, from the view	177	U25 Desmond	22
(As prov'd in you)	177	U25 Desmond	24
In Surgeons hall)	179	U25 Desmond	38
(Whose heart in that bright Sphere flames clearest,	179	U25 Desmond	54
Though many Gems be in your bosome stor'd,	179	U25 Desmond	55
Wrapt in this paper lie,	180	U26 Ode High	10
Which in the taking if you mis-apply,	180	U26 Ode High	11
Happy in that faire honour it hath gain'd,	180	U26 Ode High	14
In one full Action; nor have you now more	180	U26 Ode High	17
Such thoughts wil make you more in love with truth.	181	U26 Ode High	21
Even in youth.	181	U26 Ode High	24
In whom Anacreon once did joy,	181	U27 Ode Helen	6
Lie drawne to life, in his soft Verse,	181	U27 Ode Helen	7
Doth Cynthia, in Propertius song	181	U27 Ode Helen	11
Though I, in working of my song,	182	U27 Ode Helen	33
Though not in these, in rithmes not wholly dumbe,	182	U28 Worth	2
For in your verse all Cupids Armorie,	182	U28 Worth	9
Not a Poet in an Age,	183	U29 Fit of Rime	26
The cold tumor in his feet,	184	U29 Fit of Rime	56
That in rearing such a Schoole,	184	U29 Fit of Rime	59
Read here in one, what thou in all canst find,	185	U30 Burleigh	2
That in all tempests, never quit the helme,	185	U30 Burleigh	10
But stood unshaken in his Deeds, and Name,	185	U30 Burleigh	11
And labour'd in the worke; not with the fame:	185	U30 Burleigh	12
And in the noblest Families tooke root	185	U30 Burleigh	18
You favour Truth, and me, in this mans Cause.	186	U31 Elsmere	10
Dar'st not abuse thy wisdome, in the Lawes,	187	U33 Councellour	17
But in a businesse, that will bide the Touch,	187	U33 Councellour	23
One beautie in an Age, and free from thee?	188	U34 Small Poxe	2
Quarrell with Nature, or in ballance brought	188	U34 Small Poxe	6
Any beliefe, in Madam Baud-bees paints,	188	U34 Small Poxe	10
What was the cause then? Thought'st thou in disgrace	188	U34 Small Poxe	13
Upon record, in this blest child.	188	U35 Chute	4
For Love in shadow best is made.	189	U36 Song	2
In letters, that mixe spirits, thus to weave.	190	U37 Friend-Book	12
In friendship, I confesse: But, deare friend, heare.	190	U37 Friend-Book	18
How much they lame her in her propertie.	190	U37 Friend-Book	21
In practiz'd friendship wholly to reprove,	190	U37 Friend-Book	26
And drives it in to eat on my offence,	191	U38 Elegy 'Tis	6
Looke forth, but cannot last in such a forme.	191	U38 Elegy 'Tis	14
Of Graces, or your mercie here in me,	191	U38 Elegy 'Tis	16
In will and power, only to defeat.	191	U38 Elegy 'Tis	18

315

	Page	Title	Line

IN (cont.)

```
Or in confessing of the Crime be nice,                 191  U38 Elegy 'Tis   23
By naming in what companie 'twas in,                   191  U38 Elegy 'Tis   25
The Subject of your Grace in pardoning me,             191  U38 Elegy 'Tis   28
Errour and folly in me may have crost                  191  U38 Elegy 'Tis   37
You may so place me, and in such an ayre,              192  U38 Elegy 'Tis   51
In man, because man hath the flesh abus'd.             192  U38 Elegy 'Tis   66
In a calme skie, then when the heaven is horl'd        193  U38 Elegy 'Tis   74
About in Cloudes, and wrapt in raging weather,         193  U38 Elegy 'Tis   75
In darke, and sullen mornes, doe we not say,           193  U38 Elegy 'Tis   79
Forgiven him; And in that lyne stand I,                193  U38 Elegy 'Tis   91
To carry noble danger in the face:                     194  U38 Elegy 'Tis  102
And that there is no life in me, but love.             194  U38 Elegy 'Tis  112
Your forme shines here, here fixed in my heart:        194  U38 Elegy 'Tis  117
In hast the bottome of a med'cin'd Cup,                197  U40 Elegy That    4
Of parting, drowne it in the hope to meet              197  U40 Elegy That    7
Of vowes so sacred, and in silence made;               197  U40 Elegy That   14
In all his Actions rarified to spright;                197  U40 Elegy That   20
Not, like a Midas, shut up in himselfe,                197  U40 Elegy That   21
Keepe in reserv'd in his Dark-lanterne face,           198  U40 Elegy That   23
Keepe secret in his Channels what he breedes,          198  U40 Elegy That   27
Which in assurance to your brest I tell,               198  U40 Elegy That   49
Whose Readers did not thinke he was in love.           199  U42 Elegy Let     4
Who shall forbid me then in Rithme to bee              200  U42 Elegy Let     5
In all that is call'd lovely: take my sight            200  U42 Elegy Let    12
Of beautie; but the Muse hath interest in:             200  U42 Elegy Let    15
Curst in their Cradles, or there chang'd by Elves,     200  U42 Elegy Let    23
Yet keepe those up in sackcloth too, or lether,        200  U42 Elegy Let    25
To doe her Husbands rites in, e're 'twere gone         201  U42 Elegy Let    40
Put a Coach-mare in Tissue, must I horse               201  U42 Elegy Let    43
In at a hole, and see these Actions creepe             201  U42 Elegy Let    60
From the poore wretch, which though he play'd in prose, 201  U42 Elegy Let   61
He would have done in verse, with any of those         201  U42 Elegy Let    62
That (in pure Madrigall) unto his Mother               201  U42 Elegy Let    68
Or in Moore-fields, this other night! sings one,       202  U42 Elegy Let    73
In smiling L'envoye, as he would deride                202  U42 Elegy Let    75
A Goat in Velvet; or some block could move             202  U42 Elegy Let    82
Bawd, in a Velvet scabberd! I envy                     202  U42 Elegy Let    85
So many my Yeares-labours in an houre?                 202  U43 Vulcan       4
Or in remembrance of thy afront, and scorne,           203  U43 Vulcan       7
With Clownes, and Tradesmen, kept thee clos'd in horne. 203  U43 Vulcan       8
And my selfe most, in some selfe-boasting Rimes?       203  U43 Vulcan      26
And my selfe most, in lewd selfe-boasting Rimes?       203  U43 Vulcan    V 26
Or spun or weav'd in Riddles 50 tomes                  204  U43 Vulcan    V 33
in weaving Riddles in more wretched ryme,              204  U43 Vulcan    V 34
A paire of Scisars, and a Combe in verse;              204  U43 Vulcan      38
Not ravish'd all hence in a minutes rage.              205  U43 Vulcan      56
Not snatcht them hence in one poor minutes rage.       205  U43 Vulcan    V 56
Especially in paper; that, that steame                 205  U43 Vulcan      61
Especially in paper; many a Reame                      205  U43 Vulcan    V 61
To redeeme mine, I had sent in; Enough,                205  U43 Vulcan      63
But in my Deske, what was there to accite              206  U43 Vulcan      85
But in my Deske, what was there to envite              206  U43 Vulcan    V 85
There were of search, and mastry in the Arts.          206  U43 Vulcan      88
All the old Venusine, in Poetrie,                      207  U43 Vulcan      89
What the old Venusine, in Poetrie,                     207  U43 Vulcan    V 89
With the old Venusine, in Poetrie,                     207  U43 Vulcan    V 89
To our owne Ladyes; and in storie there                207  U43 Vulcan      97
for our owne Ladyes; and in storie there               207  U43 Vulcan    V 97
With humble Gleanings in Divinitie,                    207  U43 Vulcan     102
How in these ruines, Vulcan, thou dost lurke,          207  U43 Vulcan     105
How in these ruines, Vulcan, durst thou lurke,         207  U43 Vulcan    V105
'Cause thou canst halt, with us, in Arts, and Fire!    208  U43 Vulcan     110
Cause thou canst doe these halting tricks in fire?     208  U43 Vulcan    V110
Whom they durst handle in their holy-day coates,       208  U43 Vulcan     127
Whom they durst handle in their high day coates,       208  U43 Vulcan    V127
I saw with two poore Chambers taken in,                209  U43 Vulcan     135
That was rak'd up in the Winchestrian Goose            209  U43 Vulcan     142
Which was rak'd up in the Winchestrian Goose           209  U43 Vulcan    V142
That was lock'd up in the Winchestrian Goose           209  U43 Vulcan    V142
Bred on the Banck, in time of Poperie,                 209  U43 Vulcan     143
Though but in daunces, it shall know his power;        210  U43 Vulcan     157
Though but in daunces, it shall know high power;       210  U43 Vulcan    V157
Though but in daunger, it shall know thy power;        210  U43 Vulcan    V157
There was a Judgement shew'n too in an houre.          210  U43 Vulcan     158
Foole, wilt thou let that in example come?             210  U43 Vulcan     161
And what hast thou done in these pettie spights,       210  U43 Vulcan     163
'Tis true, that in thy wish they were destroy'd,       210  U43 Vulcan     167
In those Records, which, were all Chroniclers gone,    210  U43 Vulcan     171
In those Records, which, were our Chroniclers gone,    210  U43 Vulcan    V171
At Common-Law: me thinkes in his despight              211  U43 Vulcan     177
At Common-Law: me thinkes in this despight             211  U43 Vulcan    V177
To live in Sea-coale, and goe forth in smoake;         211  U43 Vulcan     181
To live in Sea-coale, and goe out in smoake;           211  U43 Vulcan    V181
Hill-/foot (out in Sussex) to an iron Mill;            211  U43 Vulcan     184
Hill-/foot (out in Sussex) to some iron Mill;          211  U43 Vulcan    V184
Or in small Fagots have him blaze about                211  U43 Vulcan     185
Or else in penny Fagots blaze about                    211  U43 Vulcan    V185
Or in the Bell-Mans Lanthorne, like a spie,            211  U43 Vulcan     187
But I'le conclude all in a civill curse.               211  U43 Vulcan     190
Strooke in at Millan with the Cutlers there;           212  U43 Vulcan     200
Strooke in at Millan with the villors there;           212  U43 Vulcan    V200
Or fixt in the Low-Countrey's, where you might         212  U43 Vulcan     203
```

316

IN (cont.)

	Page	Title	Line
How it held out! how (last) 'twas taken in!	213	U44 Speach	22
Of London, in the Militarie truth,	213	U44 Speach	26
So, in that ground, as soone it grew to be	214	U44 Speach	37
The Berghen siege, and taking in Breda,	214	U44 Speach	40
More then the surfets, in thee, that day stood.	214	U44 Speach	48
Goe on, increase in vertue; and in fame:	214	U44 Speach	49
Up among Nations. In the stead of bold	214	U44 Speach	51
Alive yet, in the noise; and still the same;	214	U44 Speach	56
In Politique, and Militar Affaires.	214	U44 Speach	60
Us, in our bearing, that are thus, and thus,	215	U44 Speach	65
All licence in our lives? What need we know,	215	U44 Speach	70
In so much land a yeare, or such a Banke,	215	U44 Speach	76
Descended in a rope of Titles, be	215	U44 Speach	80
That in the Cradle of their Gentrie are;	215	U44 Speach	84
In others-evill best was understood:	217	U46 Coke	6
And skill in thee, now, grew Authoritie;	217	U46 Coke	10
That Clients strove, in Question of the Lawes,	217	U46 Coke	11
No lesse of praise, then readers in all kinds	217	U46 Coke	19
Men that are safe, and sure, in all they doe,	218	U47 Tribe	1
That live in the wild Anarchie of Drinke,	218	U47 Tribe	10
They'ave glutted in, and letcher'd out that weeke,	218	U47 Tribe	13
Of any Companie but that they are in,	218	U47 Tribe	20
Call every night to Supper in these fitts,	218	U47 Tribe	21
I have no portion in them, nor their deale	218	U47 Tribe	27
Some hopes of Spaine in their West-Indian Fleet?	219	U47 Tribe	34
To live, or fall a Carkasse in the cause.	219	U47 Tribe	42
But that's a blow, by which in time I may	219	U47 Tribe	51
And dwell as in my Center, as I can,	219	U47 Tribe	60
As but to stumble in her sight were shame;	220	U47 Tribe	70
Pursue thee in all places,	221	U48 Bacchus	34
In great Saint Georges Union;	221	U48 Bacchus	44
To put his Court in dances,	222	U48 Bacchus	50
New in their stead, out of the Candidates?	222	U49 Pucell	6
And in an Epicoene fury can write newes	222	U49 Pucell	8
And as lip-thirstie, in each words expence,	222	U49 Pucell	13
In Contract twice, what can shee perjure more?	223	U49 Pucell	30
For there the wicked in the Chaire of scorne,	223	U49 Pucell	45
Are in your selfe rewarded; yet 'twill be	224	U50 Countesse	15
And when you want those friends, or neere in blood,	224	U50 Countesse	26
Not boasted in your life, but practis'd true,	225	U50 Countesse	32
For when they find so many meet in one,	225	U50 Countesse	35
The fire, the wine, the men! and in the midst,	225	U51 Bacon	3
Pardon, I read it in thy face, the day	225	U51 Bacon	5
In his soft Cradle to his Fathers Chaire,	225	U51 Bacon	14
In raysing him the wisdome of my King.	225	U51 Bacon	20
Which if in compasse of no Art it came	227	U52 Answer	10
That's six in silver; now within the Socket	229	U54 Squib	13
It doe not come: One piece I have in store,	229	U54 Squib	15
And you shall make me good, in weight, and fashion,	229	U54 Squib	17
Sleepe in a Virgins bosome without feare,	230	U56 Covell	15
Run all the Rounds in a soft Ladyes eare,	230	U56 Covell	16
Away ill company, and helpe in rime	231	U56 Covell	23
I can lose none in tendring these to you.	231	U56 Covell	28
I gaine, in having leave to keepe my Day,	231	U56 Covell	29
Put him in mind	231	U57 Burges	14
To hit in angles, and to clash with time:	232	U59 Newcastle	5
That trembles in the blaze, but (then) mounts higher!	233	U59 Newcastle	8
As they out-did the lightning in the course;	233	U59 Newcastle	12
No aime at glorie, or, in warre,	234	U60 La-ware	13
He, that in such a flood, as we are in	234	U61 Epigram	16
. . . he sent me in my Sicknesse. 1629.	235	U62 Charles 1	Ttl
And, in these Cures, do'st so thy selfe enlarge,	235	U62 Charles 1	7
Nay, and in this, thou show'st to value more	235	U62 Charles 1	9
Most pious King, but his owne good in you!	236	U64 Charles 3	2
How is she barren growne in love! or broke!	237	U64 Charles 3	V 15
And long in changing. Let our Nephewes see	238	U65 Prince	7
In changing, let our Nephewes joyfull see	238	U65 Prince	V 7
In changing. Let our after Nephewes see	238	U65 Prince	V 7
An Epigram to the Queene, then lying in. 1630.	238	U66 Queene	Ttl
As in this Prince? Let it be lawfull, so	238	U66 Queene	11
. . . in celebration of her Majesties birth-day. 1630.	239	U67 Muses	Ttl
Their noises forth in Thunder:	239	U67 Muses	9
Their noises out in Thunder:	239	U67 Muses	V 9
Comes in the pompe, and glorie	240	U67 Muses	28
Doe mingle in a shout,	240	U67 Muses	41
Her joy in state, and pleasure;	240	U67 Muses	44
Are they so scanted in their store? or driven	241	U68 House-hold	3
And rather wish, in their expence of Sack,	241	U68 House-hold	9
For in the Genius of a Poets Verse,	241	U68 House-hold	13
Nor dares he come in the comparison.	241	U69 Friend Son	8
Thy comming forth in that great yeare,	242	U70 Ode	2
Hee stoop'd in all mens sight	244	U70 Ode	38
And sunke in that dead sea of life	244	U70 Ode	40
In weight, in measure, number, sound,	244	U70 Ode	50
In season, and so brought	245	U70 Ode	61
In bulke, doth make man better bee;	245	U70 Ode	66
Is fairer farre, in May,	245	U70 Ode	70
In small proportions, we just beautie see:	245	U70 Ode	73
And in short measures, life may perfect bee.	245	U70 Ode	74
In this bright Asterisme:	246	U70 Ode	89
Whilst that in heav'n, this light on earth must shine.	246	U70 Ode	96
Friendship, in deed, was written, not in words:	247	U70 Ode	123

	Page	Title	Line

IN (cont.)

Had sow'd these fruits, and got the harvest in.	247	U70 Ode	128
But lyes block'd up, and straightned, narrow'd in,	248	U71 Treasurer	10
Discharge it 'bout the Iland, in an houre,	249	U72 King	3
Discharging 'bout the Iland, in an houre,	249	U72 King	V 3
Three Kingdomes Mirth, in light, and aerie man,	249	U72 King	11
In his great Actions: view whom his large hand	250	U73 Weston	3
Doth take in easie Natures birth,	250	U74 Weston	2
And in a dew of sweetest Raine,	251	U74 Weston	4
The Rivers in their shores doe run,	251	U74 Weston	7
In making soft her aromatique bed.	251	U74 Weston	18
Or were Affaires in tune,	253	U75 Epithalam.	15
By all the Spheares consent, so in the heart of June?	253	U75 Epithalam.	16
In all her bloome, and flower;	253	U75 Epithalam.	23
To doe their Offices in Natures Chime,	253	U75 Epithalam.	27
In gracefull Ornament of Garland, Gemmes, and Haire.	253	U75 Epithalam.	40
See, how she paceth forth in Virgin-white,	253	U75 Epithalam.	41
Both Crownes, and Kingdomes in their either hand;	254	U75 Epithalam.	52
With what full hands, and in how plenteous showers	254	U75 Epithalam.	65
In all thy age of Journals thou hast tooke,	254	U75 Epithalam.	75
Who, in all they doe,	255	U75 Epithalam.	78
In all the prov'd assayes,	255	U75 Epithalam.	101
He had so highly set; and, in what Barbican.	256	U75 Epithalam.	112
He had so highly plac'd; and, in what Barbican.	256	U75 Epithalam.	V112
In him the times, no lesse then Prince, are prais'd,	256	U75 Epithalam.	115
And by his Rise, in active men, his Name	256	U75 Epithalam.	116
One in the others hand,	256	U75 Epithalam.	125
But dare not aske our wish in Language fescennine:	257	U75 Epithalam.	160
To be given me in gratuitie	259	U76 Petition	12
Or dispenc'd in bookes, or bread,	259	U76 Petition	15
Well dispenc'd in bookes, or bread,	259	U76 Petition	V 15
You'ld reade a Snake, in his next Song.	260	U76 Petition	32
To eate a Snake, in his next Song.	260	U76 Petition	V 32
Send in, what or Romano, Tintoret,	260	U77 Treasurer	6
Send in, what Romans famous, Tintoret,	260	U77 Treasurer	V 6
Have left in fame to equall, or out-goe	260	U77 Treasurer	8
The old Greek-hands in picture, or in stone.	260	U77 Treasurer	9
And strike Religion in the standers-by;	261	U77 Treasurer	24
In glorious Piles, or Pyramids erect	261	U77 Treasurer	26
In stately Piles, and Pyramids erect	261	U77 Treasurer	V 26
Unto your honour: I can tune in song	261	U77 Treasurer	27
Unto your honour: I can voyce in song	261	U77 Treasurer	V 27
Yet read him in these lines: He doth excell	262	U78 Digby	2
Yet take him in these lines: He doth excell	262	U78 Digby	V 2
In honour, courtesie, and all the parts	262	U78 Digby	3
In him all vertue is beheld in State:	262	U78 Digby	6
In him all action is beheld in State:	262	U78 Digby	V 6
For that to dwell in, and be still at home.	262	U78 Digby	8
For those to dwell in, and be still at home.	262	U78 Digby	V 8
As other soules, to his, dwell in a Lane:	262	U78 Digby	12
In signe the Subject, and the Song will live,	262	U78 Digby	17
Goe, Muse, in, and salute him. Say he be	262	U78 Digby	19
Goe, Muse, in, and salute him thoughe he be	262	U78 Digby	V 19
Good Omen to him, in the note thou sing'st,	263	U78 Digby	22
Good fortune to him, in the note thou sing'st,	263	U78 Digby	V 22
Of the New Yeare, in a new silken warpe,	263	U79 New-yeares	5
And in the chase, more then Sylvanus can,	264	U79 New-yeares	22
In truth of colours, both are best.	265	U79 New-yeares	45
'Tis hee, 'tis hee, in singing hee,	265	U79 New-yeares	54
'Tis hee, 'tis hee, in singing hee,	265	U79 New-yeares	66
How much they are belov'd of God, in thee;	268	U80 Christning	4
Grow up, sweet Babe, as blessed, in thy Name,	268	U80 Christning	11
As in renewing thy good Grandsires fame;	268	U80 Christning	12
Me thought, Great Britaine in her Sea, before,	268	U80 Christning	13
At land she triumphs in the triple shade,	268	U80 Christning	15
I doe obey you, Beauty! for in death,	269	U81 Pawlet	5
A horrour in mee! all my blood is steele!	269	U81 Pawlet	8
From the inherent Graces in her blood!	270	U81 Pawlet	36
Just as she in it liv'd! and so exempt	270	U81 Pawlet	48
Chear'd her faire Sisters in her race to runne!	270	U81 Pawlet	58
And, in her last act, taught the Standers-by,	270	U81 Pawlet	61
Beholds her Maker! and, in him, doth see	271	U81 Pawlet	73
And, sure of Heaven, rides triumphing in.	272	U81 Pawlet	100
. . . A Gentleman absolute in all Numbers;	272	U84 Eupheme	Tt1
With her, in shade	272	U84 Cradle	4
Of vertues in her, as, in short, shee grew	274	U84 Descent	11
An Eagle towring in the skye,	278	U84 Mind	10
There, high exalted in the Spheare,	279	U84 Mind	29
In speech; it is with that excesse	279	U84 Mind	34
Still left an Eccho in the sense.	279	U84 Mind	40
And stuck in clay here, it would pull	279	U84 Mind	46
In all the bounds of beautie fit	280	U84 Mind	51
Smooth, soft, and sweet, in all a floud	280	U84 Mind	61
In action, winged as the wind,	280	U84 Mind	65
In rest, like spirits left behind	280	U84 Mind	66
In thee, faire Mansion, let it rest,	281	U84 Mind	69
Thou entertaining in thy brest,	281	U84 Mind	71
All that was good, or great in me she weav'd,	282	U84 Muse	4
Spun out in name of some of the old Nine!	282	U84 Muse	6
A sorrow in me, fit to wait to her!	282	U84 Muse	10
The world to ruine with it; in her Fall,	283	U84 Muse	25
Whoorles me about, and to blaspheme in fashion!	283	U84 Muse	32
As spirits had stolne her Spirit, in a kisse,	283	U84 Muse	42

IN (cont.)

	Page	Title	Line
In earth, till the last Trumpe awake the Sheepe	283	U84 Muse	46
Who in that feast of Resurrection trust!	284	U84 Muse	62
That she is in, or, make it more compleat?	284	U84 Muse	72
Will honour'd be in all simplicitie!	284	U84 Muse	76
Have busie search made in his mysteries!	284	U84 Muse	80
And white, as that, put on: and in her hand,	285	U84 Muse	95
In heaven Empyre, and with a robe of light?	285	U84 Muse	102
Shall meet with gladnesse in one Theatre;	285	U84 Muse	114
But make him All in All, their Theme, that Day:	286	U84 Muse	120
A Musique in the Eares, will ever last;	286	U84 Muse	124
God, in the Union, and the Trinitie!	286	U84 Muse	128
Will there revealed be in Majestie!	286	U84 Muse	130
In his humanitie! To heare him preach	286	U84 Muse	133
Through his inherent righteousnesse, in death,	286	U84 Muse	135
In his eternall Kingdome, where we sit	286	U84 Muse	145
Each line, as it were graphick, in the face!	287	U84 Muse	154
Of title in her! All Nobilitie	287	U84 Muse	159
She swaid all bus'nesse in the Familie!	287	U84 Muse	168
She was, in one, a many parts of life;	287	U84 Muse	173
In all her petite actions, so devote,	287	U84 Muse	177
She spent more time in teares her selfe to dresse	287	U84 Muse	180
In frequent speaking by the pious Psalmes	288	U84 Muse	191
Would sit in an Infirmery, whole dayes	288	U84 Muse	195
Incarnate in the Manger, shining bright	288	U84 Muse	200
To justifie, and quicken us in breath!	288	U84 Muse	204
Shee saw him too, in glory to ascend	288	U84 Muse	205
In manner of a daily Apostrophe,	288	U84 Muse	210
In that great Act of judgement: which the Father	288	U84 Muse	215
His Wisdome, and his Justice, in that houre,	288	U84 Muse	218
In the discerning of each conscience, so!	289	U84 Muse	222
And most his Justice, in the fitting parts,	289	U84 Muse	223
In this sweet Extasie, she was rapt hence.	289	U84 Muse	225
An Ode in Horace in prayse of a Countrye lyfe, Translated.	289	U85 Country	VTtl
And is not in the Usurers bands:	289	U85 Country	4
And sets more happy in the place:	290	U85 Country	12
And graftes more happy in the place:	290	U85 Country	V 12
Or in the bending Vale beholds a-farre	290	U85 Country	13
Or in the bending Vale beholds from far	290	U85 Country	V 13
Or the prest honey in pure pots doth keepe	290	U85 Country	15
Now in the rooted Grasse him lay,	290	U85 Country	24
The soft birds quarrell in the Woods,	290	U85 Country	26
That penning the glad flock in hurdles by,	291	U85 Country	45
'Gainst th'Ides, his moneys he gets in with paine,	291	U85 Country	69
'Gainst th'Ides, his gott moneys he gets in with paine,	291	U85 Country	V 69
I am not such, as in the Reigne	292	U86 Hor.4:1	3
In many a Gumme, and for thy soft eares sake	292	U86 Hor.4:1	22
There twice a day in sacred Laies,	292	U86 Hor.4:1	25
And in the Salian manner meet	292	U86 Hor.4:1	27
Whether in Mars his field thou bee,	293	U86 Hor.4:1	39
In name, I went all names before,	293	U87 Hor.3:9	7
There is no labour, nor no shame in this;	294	U88 Petronius	8
Thou worthy in eternall Flower to fare,	294	U89 Mart.8:77	2
Never at Law; seldome in office gown'd:	295	U90 Mart.10:47	5
Which in some swarthie fish uncomely ends:	305	Horace	5
Which in a blacke foule fish uncomely ends:	338	Horace	V 5
In grave beginnings, and great things profest,	305	Horace	17
A Scarlet peece, or two, stitch'd in: when or	305	Horace	19
A purple piece, or two stitch'd in: when either	338	Horace	V 19
In short; I bid, Let what thou work'st upon,	307	Horace	31
This, seeking, in a various kind, to forme	307	Horace	40
One thing prodigiously, paints in the woods,	307	Horace	41
When in a wrong, and artlesse way we tread.	307	Horace	44
If in th'escape an artlesse path we tread.	339	Horace	V 46/ 44
Th'Aemilian Schoole, in brasse can fashion out	307	Horace	46
But in the maine worke haplesse: since he knowes	307	Horace	48
His matter to his power, in all he makes,	307	Horace	57
In using also of new words, to be	307	Horace	65
Yet, if by chance, in utt'ring things abstruse,	307	Horace	69
Or Plautus, and in Virgil disavow,	309	Horace	78
Still in their leaves, throughout the sliding yeares,	309	Horace	86
In neighbour-townes, and feeles the weightie plough:	309	Horace	95
In Verse unequall match'd, first sowre Laments,	309	Horace	107
After, mens Wishes, crown'd in their events,	309	Horace	108
All the Grammarians strive; and yet in Court	309	Horace	111
The conqu'ring Champion, the prime Horse in course,	311	Horace	115
On popular noise with, and doe businesse in.	311	Horace	120
In tragick Verse; no lesse Thyestes feast	311	Horace	122
Complaines in humble phrase. Both Telephus,	311	Horace	135
Thy selfe in teares, then thy losse will wound,	311	Horace	146
Thy selfe in tears, then me thy harms will wound,	342	Horace	V146
In sound, quite from his fortune: both the rout,	313	Horace	159
Or some hot youth, yet in his flourishing course;	313	Horace	163
Of Colchis borne; or in Assyria bred;	313	Horace	167
Things in themselves agreeing: If againe	313	Horace	170
Of Homers, forth in acts, then of thine owne,	313	Horace	185
These studies alter now, in one, growne man;	315	Horace	237
A great deferrer, long in hope, growne numbe	317	Horace	245
In fitting proper adjuncts to each day.	317	Horace	254
In at the eare, doe stirre the mind more slow	317	Horace	257
Then those the faithfull eyes take in by show,	317	Horace	258
To have a God come in; except a knot	317	Horace	273
Steepe the glad Genius in the Wine, whole dayes,	319	Horace	298

					Page	Title	Line

IN (cont.)

	Page	Title	Line
Both in their tunes, the licence greater grew, ...	319	Horace	299
And in their numbers; For, alas, what knew	319	Horace	300
In his train'd Gowne about the Stage: So grew . . .	319	Horace	305
In his train'd Gowne about the Stage: thus grew . .	346	Horace	V305
In time to Tragedie, a Musicke new.	319	Horace	306
Till then unknowne, in Carts, wherein did ride . . .	319	Horace	313
Brought in the Visor, and the robe of State, . . .	319	Horace	316
Loftie, and grave; and in the buskin stalke. . . .	319	Horace	318
Loftie, and great; and in the buskin walk. . . .	348	Horace	V398/318
Hee too, that did in Tragick Verse contend . . .	319	Horace	319
As neither any God, were brought in there, . . .	321	Horace	331
As neither any God, be brought in there, ...	346	Horace	V323/331
And toile in vaine: the excellence is such . . .	321	Horace	352
Their youthfull tricks in over-wanton verse: . . .	321	Horace	358
Or play young tricks in over-wanton verse; . . .	347	Horace	V350/358
Provided, ne're to yeeld, in any case	323	Horace	379
This foot yet, in the famous Trimeters	323	Horace	381
Of too much haste, and negligence in part, . . .	323	Horace	385
To note in Poemes, breach of harmonie;	323	Horace	388
But, in conclusion, merited no fame.	323	Horace	396
In hand, and turne them over, day, and night. . .	323	Horace	398
In daring to forsake the Grecian tracts, ...	323	Horace	407
In vertue, and renowne of armes, then in . . .	325	Horace	412
Have not kept in; and (lest perfection faile) . . .	325	Horace	417
In Helicon; a great sort will not pare	325	Horace	422
In secret places, flee the public baths. . . .	349	Horace	V424
A Poeme, of no grace, weight, art, in rimes, . . .	327	Horace	456
In juyce of Cedar worthy to be steep'd, ...	327	Horace	475
And in smooth Cypresse boxes to be keep'd? . . .	327	Horace	476
Build Townes, and carve the Lawes in leaves of wood. . .	327	Horace	490
The Oracles, too, were given out in Verse; . . .	329	Horace	496
Of their long labours, was in Verse set downe: . . .	329	Horace	500
Be briefe, in what thou wouldst command, that so . .	329	Horace	503
But flowes out, that ore-swelleth in full brests. . .	329	Horace	506
Much in the Poeme shine, I will not bee	329	Horace	526
Still in the same, and warned will not mend, . . .	329	Horace	530
A Choerilus, in whom if I but see	329	Horace	534
But, I confesse, that, in a long worke, sleepe . .	329	Horace	537
Though I confesse, that, in a long worke, sleepe . .	351	Horace	V513/537
Will in the light be view'd: This, once, the sight . .	331	Horace	543
Of eloquent Messalla's power in Court, ...	331	Horace	552
To bettring of the mind of man, in ought, . . .	331	Horace	562
His armes in Mars his field, he doth refuse; . . .	331	Horace	566
Nine yeares kept in, your papers by, yo'are free . .	331	Horace	578
Nine yeares kept by, your papers in, y'are free . .	352	Horace	V554/578
Hee, that's ambitious in the race to touch . . .	333	Horace	587
Or, of the things, that ne're came in my mind, . . .	333	Horace	596
So doth the Poet, who is rich in land, ...	333	Horace	599
So doth the Poet, that is rich in Land, ...	353	Horace	V599
Or great in money's out at use, command . . .	333	Horace	600
Or wealthy in money's out at use, command . . .	353	Horace	V600
And twice, or thrice had 'ssayd it, still in vaine: . .	333	Horace	626
And twice, or thrice assay'd it, but in vain; . .	354	Horace	V626
In vaine, but you, and yours, you should love still . .	335	Horace	631
To force the grates, that hold him in, would fright . .	337	Horace	675
I could not but in admiracion stand. . . .	361	Palmer	4
Not one but thrives; in spite of stormes & thunder, . .	361	Palmer	7
how lyke the Carbuncle in Aarons brest . . .	361	Palmer	14
did sparcle foorth in Center of the rest: . . .	361	Palmer	16
thus, as a ponderous thinge in water cast . . .	361	Palmer	17
till th'one hath drownd the other in our sightes, . .	361	Palmer	20
So in my braine; the stronge impression . . .	361	Palmer	21
which thoughts being circumvolvd in gyerlyk mocion . .	361	Palmer	23
in a deepe trance; * * * * * . . .	361	Palmer	26
And thou in them shalt live as longe as Fame. . .	362	Palmer	31
In Authorem.	362	Author	Ttl
And see a minde attir'd in perfect straines; . . .	362	Author	2
In these pide times, only to shewe their braines, . .	362	Author	4
The fault's not in the object, but their eyes. . . .	362	Author	8
His proofe their praise, will meete, as in this line. .	362	Author	14
Those that in blood such violent pleasure have, . .	363	Murder	1
Flowes from the surfets which we take in peace. . .	363	Peace	4
Doth shine in her discerning, ...	365	Ode Splendor	10
Closde in an orbe of Christall.	365	Ode Splendor	12
In thought to praise this Ladie;	365	Ode Splendor	18
Smiles in his Sphaere, to see the rest affect, . . .	366	Ode Who saith	13
In vaine to follow:	366	Ode Who saith	14
As the whole heard in sight, ...	366	Ode Who saith	26
And still is in the Brest:	366	Ode Who saith	27
And up againe, in skies, and aire to vent . . .	368	Ode Who saith	77
In entertaining late	368	Ode Who saith	82
Their cares in wine; with sure	368	Ode Who saith	87
Hath sent her Mermaides in, ...	368	Ode Who saith	91
Yet, looking in thy face, they shall begin . . .	369	Ode Who saith	93
And (in the place) envie	369	Ode Who saith	95
In heav'n the Signe of old Eridanus:	369	Ode Who saith	109
In Picture, they which truly understand, . . .	370	Author	1
The severall figures, languish in suspence, . . .	370	Author	10
Velvet, or Taffata cap, rank'd in the darke . . .	371	Fletcher	5
In such a Martirdome; To vexe their eyes, . . .	371	Fletcher	13
That durst be that in Court: a vertu' alone . . .	371	Epitaph	4
She was 'Sell Boulstred. In which name, I call	372	Epitaph	12

	Page	Title	Line
IN (cont.)			
And here he disdained not, in a forraine land	375	Coryat 1	32
Beeing in feare to be robd, he most learnedly begs.	375	Coryat 1	35
Who, because his matter in all should be meete,	379	Coryat 3	3
Since he treads in no other Mans steps but his owne.	379	Coryat 3	12
In five monthes he went it, in five monthes he pend it.	379	Coryat 3	16
The Mappe of his journey, and sees in his booke,	379	Coryat 3	18
He went out at each place, and at what he came in,	380	Coryat 3	25
Horse, foote, and all but flying in the ayre:	380	Coryat 3	28
He was in his travaile, how like to be beaten,	380	Coryat 3	35
And lay in straw with the horses at Bergamo,	380	Coryat 3	38
Yes. And thanks God in his Pistle or his Booke	380	Coryat 3	43
Nay more in his wardrobe, if you will laugh at a	380	Coryat 3	47
In a Cart twixt Montrell and Abbevile.	380	Coryat 3	53
Some want, they say in a sort he did crave:	380	Coryat 3	55
. . . in the Behalfe of the two Noble Brothers sir Robert . .	382	Rich	Ttl
Out-bee that Wife, in worth, thy freind did make:	384	Somerset	12
And eve'ry joy, in mariage, turne a fruite.	384	Somerset	18
So, in theyr number, may you never see	384	Somerset	21
Thy Richard, rais'd in song, past pulling downe.	385	Brooke	8
Or skill of making matches in my life:	386	Husband	7
For, though but early in these pathes thou tread,	386	Browne	5
trust in the tombes, their care-full freinds do rayse;	387	Cavendish	6
Who hadst before wrought in rich Homers Mine?	388	Chapman	3
As in this Spanish Proteus; who, though writ	389	Aleman	5
But in one tongue, was form'd with the worlds wit:	389	Aleman	6
But that hee's too well suted, in a cloth,	389	Aleman	17
Will bee receiv'd in Court; If not, would I	389	Aleman	19
As well in brasse, as he hath hit	390	Reader	6
All, that was ever writ in brasse.	390	Reader	8
And all the Muses still were in their prime,	391	Shakespeare	44
Lives in his issue, even so, the race	392	Shakespeare	66
In his well torned, and true-filed lines:	392	Shakespeare	68
In each of which, he seemes to shake a Lance,	392	Shakespeare	69
To see thee in our waters yet appeare,	392	Shakespeare	72
But stay, I see thee in the Hemisphere	392	Shakespeare	75
In blood, in birth, by match, and by her seate;	394	Jane Ogle	4
But every Table in this Church can say,	394	Jane Ogle	7
No stone in any wall here, but can tell	394	Jane Ogle	9
Not usuall in a Lady; and yet true:	394	Jane Ogle	14
When, Rome, I reade thee in thy mighty paire,	395	May	1
And the world in it, I begin to doubt,	395	May	4
And those in number so, and measure rais'd,	395	May	8
Keepe due proportion in the ample song,	395	May	12
In the great masse, or machine there is stirr'd?	395	May	22
Your true freind in Judgement and Choise	395	May	25
Those ambling visits, passe in verse, betweene	396	Drayton	4
O, how in those, dost thou instruct these times,	397	Drayton	43
In thy admired Periegesis,	397	Drayton	50
Our right in France! if ritely understood.	397	Drayton	58
That can but reade; who cannot, may in prose	398	Drayton	73
And stop my sight, in every line I goe.	398	Drayton	78
T'Is a Record in heaven. You, that were	399	Lady Ogle	1
In her! and what could perfect bee,	399	Lady Ogle	15
All that was solid, in the name	399	Lady Ogle	17
Of vertue, pretious in the frame:	399	Lady Ogle	18
Or else Magnetique in the force,	399	Lady Ogle	19
Or sweet, or various, in the course!	399	Lady Ogle	20
In number, measure, or degree	399	Lady Ogle	23
In faire freehould, not an Inmate:	399	Lady Ogle	26
Seal'd and deliver'd to her, in the sight	400	Lady Ogle	37
In Bulwarkes, Rav'lins, Ramparts, for defense,	400	Beaumont	4
The faire French Daughter to learne English in;	402	Filmer	12
From thirty pound in pipkins, to the Man	402	Inigo Jones 1	2
In Towne & Court? Are you growne rich? & proud?	403	Inigo Jones 1	24
The majesty of Juno in the Cloudes,	403	Inigo Jones 1	33
And peering forth of Iris in the Shrowdes!	403	Inigo Jones 1	34
In the mere perspective of an Inch board!	404	Inigo Jones 1	44
But in the practisd truth Destruction is	404	Inigo Jones 1	57
The maker of the Propertyes! in summe	404	Inigo Jones 1	61
All in the Worke! And soe shall still for Ben:	404	Inigo Jones 1	65
In presentacion of some puppet play!	405	Inigo Jones 1	76
In setting forth of such a solemne Toye!	405	Inigo Jones 1	78
In setting forth of such a serious Toye!	405	Inigo Jones 1	V 78
Aymd at in thy omnipotent Designe!	406	Inigo Jones 1	96
Thou'rt too ambitious: and dost fear in vaine!	408	Inigo Jones 3	6
Th'envy'd returne, of forty pound in gold.	408	Detractor	4
Out in the Dog-daies, least the killer meete	409	Detractor	20
Now each Court-Hobby-horse will wince in rime;	410	Brome	11
That knew the Crafts they had bin bred in, right:	410	Brome	14
Keep in thy barking Wit, thou bawling Fool?	410	Gill	8
For thou hast nought in thee to cure his Fame,	411	Gill	13
And in them view'd th'uncertainty of Life,	411	Sutcliffe	3
From fearefull back-slides; And the debt we'are in,	412	Sutcliffe	15
Here, are five letters in this blessed Name,	412	Ghyrlond	1
Is so implexed, and laid in, between,	412	Ghyrlond	7
Preserved, in her antique bed of Vert,	413	Ghyrlond	19
In Moses bush, un-wasted in the fire.	413	Ghyrlond	24
The glorious Trinity in Union met.	413	Ghyrlond	32
Of Persons, yet in Union (One) divine.	413	Ghyrlond	35
Who mad'st us happy all, in thy reflexe,	414	Ghyrlond	47
T'imprint in all purg'd hearts this virgin sence,	414	Ghyrlond	55
Unto the world, in praise of your first Play:	414	Rutter	2

321

	Page	Title	Line
IN (cont.)			
In spite of Hipocrites, who are the worst	416	Dover	9
Now, in a garland by the graces knit:	416	Welcome	4
prest in to se you.	416	Moon	8
To the merry beards in Hall,	417	Moon	13
Or by chance if in their grease	418	Moon	41
And in this Age, canst hope no other grace.	420	Ode:If Men	27
Thou mad'st in open Feild	421	Ode:If Men	40
Howe much they lame hir, in hir propertye:	421	Censure	14
in Course of Frindshipp, wholie to reprove:	422	Censure	19
Truth itself doth flow in Wine.	657	Door Apollo	6
INCARNATE			
Incarnate in the Manger, shining bright	288	U84 Muse	200
INCENSE			
For, Prayer is the Incense most perfumes	288	U84 Muse	187
INCH			
In the mere perspective of an Inch board!	404	Inigo Jones 1	44
INCHANTED			
The charmed Boates, and the inchanted Wharfes;	205	U43 Vulcan	68
The charmed beauty and the inchanted Wharfes;	205	U43 Vulcan	V 68
INCIVILITIE			
(But pride, that schisme of incivilitie)	287	U84 Muse	160
INCLIN'D			
And is t'a body, often, ill inclin'd,	82	E130 Ferrab. 1	7
(To vertuous moods inclin'd)	112	F11 Epode	112
INCLOS'D			
To lay her here, inclos'd, his second Bride.	394	Jane Ogle	24
INCLUDING			
Including all, were thence call'd harmonie:	82	E130 Ferrab. 1	14
INCONSTANCIE			
Another. In defence of their Inconstancie. A Song.	146	U6 Defence	Ttl
Nor is't inconstancie to change	146	U6 Defence	13
INCONSTANT			
Inconstant, like the sea, of whence 'tis borne,	110	F11 Epode	39
Inconstant, as the sea, of whence 'tis borne,	110	F11 Epode	V 39
INCREASE (See also ENCREASE)			
Increase those acts, o glorious Trinitie	128	U1 Trinitie	29
But then t'increase my feares,	148	U7 Nymph	26
Brought on us, and will every hour increase.	166	U15 Friend-Wars	122
And pray the fruites thereof, and the increase;	212	U43 Vulcan	210
Goe on, increase in vertue; and in fame:	214	U44 Speach	49
And mightiest Monarchs feele what large increase	261	U77 Treasurer	21
As nature could not more increase the flood	287	U84 Muse	158
If I can give some small increase? when, loe,	309	Horace	80
Warres greatest woes, and miseries increase,	363	Peace	3
The elder of these two, riche hopes Increase,	382	Rich	5
My suffrage brings thee all increase, to crowne	385	Brooke	7
INCURR'D			
All which thou hast incurr'd deservedly:	410	Gill	5
INDEED			
Indeed, poore Giles repents he married ever.	40	E42 Giles	3
To say, indeed, shee were the soule of heaven,	82	E130 Ferrab. 1	11
The Word was now made Flesh indeed,	130	U1 Nativitie	17
Which is indeed but friendship of the spit:	190	U37 Friend-Book	9
Indeed, her Dressing some man might delight,	223	U49 Pucell	31
Indeed, when had great Britaine greater cause	236	U64 Charles 3	7
Indeed, she is not dead! but laid to sleepe	283	U84 Muse	45
Indeed, give fitting dues to every man.	325	Horace	452
Not thence be sav'd, although indeed he could?	335	Horace	658
But thou art proofe against them, and indeed	391	Shakespeare	15
INDEEDE			
'Tis but light paines: Indeede this Dock's no rose.	85	E133 Voyage	60
INDENTUR'D			
Made, or indentur'd, or leas'd out t'advance	246	U70 Ode	100
INDEX			
So are you Natures Index, and restore,	68	E105 L Wroth 2	19
INDIAN			
Some hopes of Spaine in their West-Indian Fleet?	219	U47 Tribe	34
INDICE			
For me to be your Indice. Keep you such,	157	U13 Sacvile	156
INDIFFERENT			
Poets should ever be indifferent.	331	Horace	556
INDITE			
For their owne cap'tall crimes, t'indite my wit;	117	F13 Aubigny	14
INDORSE			
That from the Muses fountaines doth indorse	200	U42 Elegy Let	7
INDU'D			
What though she be with Velvet gownes indu'd,	222	U49 Pucell	18
INDULGENT			
The least indulgent thought thy pen drops forth!	44	E55 Beaumont	4
INDURE			
Cannot indure reproofe,	175	U23 Himselfe	32
INFAM'D			
Whom no great Mistresse hath as yet infam'd,	165	U15 Friend-Wars	97
INFAMIE			
That doe sinne onely for the infamie:	119	F13 Aubigny	86
To suffer tortures, scorne, and Infamie,	193	U38 Elegy 'Tis	93
INFAMOUS			
These are, as some infamous Baud, or Whore,	391	Shakespeare	13
Secure thy railing Rhymes, infamous Gill,	410	Gill	2
INFAMY			
Nameless, and noysome, as thy infamy!	409	Detractor	16

INFANT
Brave Infant of Saguntum, cleare . . . . . 242 U70 Ode 1
INFANTS
As I have seene some Infants of the Sword, . . . 154 U13 Sacvile 47
No doubt all Infants would returne like thee. . . 243 U70 Ode 20
Take little Infants with their noyse, ... 273 U84 Cradle 18
INFECTED
Infected with the leprosie, or had . . . . 335 Horace 645
INFECTION
Greeke was free from Rimes infection, ... 184 U29 Fit of Rime 31
INFINITE
Boasters, and perjur'd, with the infinite more . . . 167 U15 Friend-Wars 169
For God, whose essence is so infinite, . . . 236 U63 Charles 2 13
As circular, as infinite. . . . . 279 U84 Mind 32
INFINITS
extendeth circles into infinits, ... 361 Palmer 18
INFIRMERY
Would sit in an Infirmery, whole dayes . . . 288 U84 Muse 195
INFLAME (See also ENFLAMED)
Love lights his torches to inflame desires; . . . 170 U19 Elegy By 2
INFLAM'D
Looke, how we read the Spartans were inflam'd . . 398 Drayton 67
Inflam'd with ardor to that mystick Shine, . . . 413 Ghyrlond 23
INFLICT
Upon my flesh t'inflict another wound. . . . 122 F15 Heaven 22
INFLICTS
No man inflicts that paine, till hope be spent: . . 192 U38 Elegy 'Tis 44
INFLUENCE
Nor lend like influence from his lucent seat. . . . 52 E76 Bedford 1 8
Or influence, chide, or cheere the drooping Stage; . . 392 Shakespeare 78
INFORM'D
Himselfe so un-inform'd of his elect, ... 286 U84 Muse 149
INFORME (See also ENFORME)
To informe and teach? or your unweary'd paine . . 159 U14 Selden V 37
From the Tempestuous Grandlings, Who'll informe . . 215 U44 Speach 64
Whilst I informe my selfe, I would teach thee, . . 216 U45 Squib 2
That he dares to informe you, but somewhat meticulous, . 380 Coryat 3 33
INFORMED
Informed rightly, by your Fathers care, . . . 331 Horace 546
INFORMERS
Informers, Masters both of Arts and lies; . . . 167 U15 Friend-Wars 164
INFUS'D
Should aske the blood, and spirits he hath infus'd . . 192 U38 Elegy 'Tis 65
INGAGE
So rare, as with some taxe it doth ingage . . . 323 Horace 383
INGENYRE
The noblest Ingenyre that ever was! . . . . 402 Inigo Jones 1 6
INGINE
That Art, or Ingine, on the strength can raise. . . 400 Beaumont 10
INGINEERES
Disease, the Enemie, and his Ingineeres, . . . 248 U71 Treasurer 4
INGINER
An inginer, in slanders, of all fashions, . . . 75 E115 Honest Man 31
INGOTS
Or put to flight Astrea, when her ingots . . . 114 F12 Rutland 24
INGRATEFULL
Lesse list of proud, hard, or ingratefull Men. . . 153 U13 Sacvile 4
Yea, of th'ingratefull: and he forth must tell . . 155 U13 Sacvile 77
INGREDIENTS
Then all Ingredients made into one curse, . . . 172 U20 Shrub 18
INHABIT
For her t'inhabit? There is it. . . . . 280 U84 Mind 52
INHERENT
From the inherent Graces in her blood! . . . 270 U81 Pawlet 36
Through his inherent righteousnesse, in death, . . 286 U84 Muse 135
INHERIT
And rich in issue to inherit all, ... 41 E44 Chuff 2
Were it to thinke, that you should not inherit . . 114 F12 Rutland 32
And comes by these Degrees, the Stile t'inherit . . 164 U15 Friend-Wars 81
Or two, or three, a Sonne will dis-inherit . . . 192 U38 Elegy 'Tis 42
INHERITANCE
The place, that was thy Wives inheritance. . . . 209 U43 Vulcan 152
The Plot, that was thy Wives inheritance. . . . 209 U43 Vulcan V152
B'imputed right to an inheritance . . . . 286 U84 Muse 144
INIGO
An Expostulacion with Inigo Jones. . . . . 402 Inigo Jones 1 Ttl
you'l be as Langley sayd, an Inigo still. . . . 403 Inigo Jones 1 22
Be Inigo, the Whistle, & his men! . . . . 405 Inigo Jones 1 66
But wisest Inigo! who can reflect . . . . 405 Inigo Jones 1 86
To Inigo Marquess Would Be A Corollary . . . 406 Inigo Jones 2 Ttl
Hath made his Inigo Marquess, wouldst thou fayne . . 406 Inigo Jones 2 2
But when thou turnst a Reall Inigo; . . . . 407 Inigo Jones 2 22
Sir Inigo doth feare it as I heare . . . . 407 Inigo Jones 3 1
INIQUITIE
Acts old Iniquitie, and in the fit . . . . 74 E115 Honest Man 27
INJOY
So to be sure you doe injoy your selves. . . . 200 U42 Elegy Let 24
INJUNCTION
Against this Vulcan? No Injunction? . . . . 210 U43 Vulcan 175
INJURIE
Without his, thine, and all times injurie? . . . 47 E63 Salisbury 2 10
From injurie, ... 179 U25 Desmond 49

```
                                                        Page      Title        Line
INJUSTICE
   With what injustice should one soule pretend    .    .    .    .  271   U81 Pawlet      92
   With what injustice can one soule pretend       .    .    .    .  271   U81 Pawlet    V 92
INKE
   Become a petulant thing, hurle inke, and wit,   .    .    .    .   27   E2 My Booke      5
   Thoughts worthy of thy gift, this Inke,         .    .    .    .  229   U55 Burges       2
   With Chequer Inke, upon his guift, my paper,    .    .    .    .  666   Glover           8
IN-LAND
   From Venice, Paris, or some in-land passage     .    .    .    .   85   E133 Voyage     33
INLIVE
   T' inlive posteritie, her Fame may tell!        .    .    .    .  269   U81 Pawlet      34
INMATE
   And her, she made her Inmate, to the End,       .    .    .    .  394   Jane Ogle       18
   In faire freehould, not an Inmate:              .    .    .    .  399   Lady Ogle       26
INNE
   How long he did stay, at what signe he did Inne. .   .    .    .  380   Coryat 3        26
INNOCENCE
   With safetie of her innocence;                  .    .    .    .   33   E22 Daughter     6
   Their gentler spirits have suck'd innocence.    .    .    .    .   96   F2 Penshurst    94
   To see this Babe, all innocence;                .    .    .    .  130   U1 Nativitie    22
   But whisper; O glad Innocence,                  .    .    .    .  177   U25 Desmond     31
   And on her Innocence, a garment fresh           .    .    .    .  285   U84 Muse        94
   I, that am glad, thy Innocence was thy Guilt,   .    .    .    .  371   Fletcher        11
INNOCENT
   While Beast instructs his faire, and innocent wife,  .    .    .   34   E25 Beast 1      1
   Strive, Wroth, to live long innocent.           .    .    .    .   98   F3 Wroth        66
   Strive, Wroth, to be long innocent.             .    .    .    .   98   F3 Wroth      V 66
INNOCENTLY
   We innocently met.  No simple word,             .    .    .    .   65   E101 Supper     39
INNOVATIONS
   Times, manners, customes! Innovations spide!    .    .    .    .  160   U14 Selden      44
INO
   Ino bewaild; Ixion false, forsworne;            .    .    .    .  313   Horace         176
INOUGH
   It is inough, their griefe shall know           .    .    .    .  369   Ode Who saith  113
INOUGHE
   it will be matter lowd inoughe to tell          .    .    .    .  387   Cavendish       11
INOW
   By offring not more sureties, then inow,        .    .    .    .  386   Browne          12
IN-PRIMIS
   In-primis, Grand, you owe me for a jest,        .    .    .    .   51   E73 Fine Grand   5
INQUIRE   (See also ENQUIRE)
   But leaves me to inquire,                       .    .    .    .  151   U11 Dreame      10
INQUIR'D
   'Tis now inquir'd, which makes the nobler Verse, .   .    .    .  331   Horace         581
INQUIRIE
   Inquirie of the worth: So must we doe,          .    .    .    .  216   U45 Squib       15
   So farre without inquirie what the States,      .    .    .    .  219   U47 Tribe       43
   And looking with thy best Inquirie, tell,       .    .    .    .  254   U75 Epithalam.  74
INRAGED
   Nor dreads the Seas inraged harmes:             .    .    .    .  289   U85 Country      6
   Nor treades the Seas inraged harmes:            .    .    .    .  289   U85 Country    V 6
IN'S
   Active in's braine, and passive in his bones.   .    .    .    .   49   E68 Playwrt 2    4
INSCRIB'D
   Inscrib'd in touch or marble, or the cotes      .    .    .    .  114   F12 Rutland     44
INSCRIPTION
   At least may beare th'inscription to her Tombe. .    .    .    .  269   U81 Pawlet      18
   nor yet inscription like it.  Write but that;   .    .    .    .  387   Cavendish        9
   nor yet inscription like it writt but that      .    .    .    .  387   Cavendish     V 9
INSERT
   Insert thy Hodges, and those newer men,         .    .    .    .  214   U44 Speach      53
INSIDE
   But their whole inside full of ends, and knots? .    .    .    .  171   U20 Shrub       12
INSOLENT
   Of all, that insolent Greece, or haughtie Rome  .    .    .    .  391   Shakespeare     39
INSPIRE   (See also ENSPIRE)
   O, then inspire                                 .    .    .    .  177   U25 Desmond     10
   O, thou inspire                                 .    .    .    .  177   U25 Desmond   V 10
INSPIR'D
   If with this truth you be inspir'd,             .    .    .    .  121   F14 Sydney      52
   The same it was inspir'd, rich, and refin'd.    .    .    .    .  225   U50 Countesse   30
INSTANTLY
   Give knowledge instantly,                       .    .    .    .  109   F11 Epode       12
INSTAURATION
   . . . on his great Instauration of his Hunting, . . . .    .    .  415   Dover          Ttl
INSTITUTION
   What Nature, Fortune, Institution, Fact         .    .    .    .  270   U81 Pawlet      45
INSTRUCT
   Shee shall instruct my after-thoughts to write  .    .    .    .   48   E65 Muse        13
   Shee doth instruct men by her gallant flight,   .    .    .    .   55   E85 Goodyere 1   5
   T'instruct and teach? or your unweary'd paine   .    .    .    .  159   U14 Selden      37
   Of what it tells us) weav'd in to instruct.     .    .    .    .  160   U14 Selden      52
   And there instruct the noble English heires     .    .    .    .  214   U44 Speach      59
   O, how in those, dost thou instruct these times, .   .    .    .  397   Drayton         43
INSTRUCTS
   While Beast instructs his faire, and innocent wife,  .    .    .   34   E25 Beast 1      1
INSTRUMENT
   To his poore Instrument, now out of grace.      .    .    .    .  223   U49 Pucell      34
IN'T
   That as the water makes things, put in't streight, . .    .    .  170   U18 Elegy Can    7
INTEGRITIE
   Such was thy Processe, when Integritie,         .    .    .    .  217   U46 Coke         9
```

	Page	Title	Line
INTELLIGENCE			
And what each prince doth for intelligence owe,	59	E92 New Crie	12
Backe the intelligence, and falsely sweares,	109	F11 Epode	25
And each intelligence	239	U67 Muses	22
Would aske a Heavens Intelligence;	278	U84 Mind	14
Who reades, will pardon my Intelligence,	289	U84 Muse	226
INTELLIGENCER			
Bee thou my Bookes intelligencer, note	232	U58 Book-seller	3
INTEND (See also EXTEND)			
Something your Surship doth not yet intend!	402	Inigo Jones 1	14
INTENDED			
Must be intended still to understand:	383	Author	2
INTENT			
To answere me. And sure, it was th'intent	87	E133 Voyage	107
INTENTION			
To towre with my intention	176	U25 Desmond	4
INTENTS			
We need a man, can speake of the intents,	62	E95 Savile	31
INTEREST			
But by meere Chance? for interest? or to free	154	U13 Sacvile	30
Of beautie; but the Muse hath interest in:	200	U42 Elegy Let	15
INTERMITTED			
Long intermitted, pray thee, pray thee spare:	292	U86 Hor.4:1	2
INTERMIX (See ENTERMIXT)			
INTERPELL			
Presume to interpell that fulnesse, when	284	U84 Muse	70
INTERPOSE			
And interpose thy selfe, ('care not how soone.)	238	U65 Prince	10
INTERPOS'D			
Were fitly interpos'd; so new:	275	U84 Body	10
INTERPRETED			
Is it interpreted in me disease,	122	F15 Heaven	3
But who hath them interpreted, and brought	395	May	19
INTERPRETERS			
Are still th'interpreters twixt godds, and men!	395	May	18
INTERRUPT			
But in the view, doth interrupt their sinne;	66	E102 Pembroke	18
INTERSERT			
The fourth is humble Ivy, intersert,	413	Ghyrlond	17
INTERTEXE			
With light of love, this Paire doth intertexe!	254	U75 Epithalam.	60
INTERTWIND			
Her Rose, and Lilly, intertwind, have made.	268	U80 Christning	16
INTERTWINE			
Bouts of fleet waters, that doe intertwine	338	Horace	V 21
INTIRE			
With grace, with love, with cherishing intire:	128	U1 Trinitie	43
INTO			
Thy selfe into fresh braules: when, call'd upon,	32	E16 Brain-hardy	3
Into the debt; and reckon on her head,	80	E127 Aubigny	5
Into my ri'mes could ne're be got	93	F1 Why write no	9
Fat, aged carps, that runne into thy net.	94	F2 Penshurst	33
Before the fisher, or into his hand.	94	F2 Penshurst	38
And thrust my necke into the noose,	101	F4 To the World	26
(Though they were crusht into one forme) could make	108	F10 Proludium	26
Into your harbor, and all passage shut	119	F13 Aubigny	92
Each into other, and had now made one.	120	F13 Aubigny	120
And breath'st into it, life, and light, with state	127	U1 Trinitie	19
Lovers, made into a Chaine!	137	U2 Cupid	32
What furie of late is crept into our Feasts?	166	U15 Friend-Wars	117
Then all Ingredients made into one curse,	172	U20 Shrub	18
Is gone himselfe into your Name.	173	U22 Elegy Tho	24
So comm'st thou like a Chiefe into the Court,	187	U33 Councellour	29
All lights into his one doth run;	189	U36 Song	6
I give, or owe my friends, into your Rites,	197	U40 Elegy That	12
And turning all he toucheth into pelfe,	197	U40 Elegy That	22
The rest, my journey into Scotland song,	207	U43 Vulcan	94
The rest, my journey into Scotland sung	207	U43 Vulcan	V 94
Stinketh my credit, if into the Pocket	229	U54 Squib	14
And I, into the world, all Soule, was sent!	270	U81 Pawlet	56
And I, into the world with my Soule, was sent!	270	U81 Pawlet	V 56
Into the Kindred, whence thy Adam drew	274	U84 Descent	15
Wild Bores into his toyles pitch'd round:	290	U85 Country	32
Into our Seas send any such:	291	U85 Country	52
Whether the Sea receiv'd into the shore,	309	Horace	91
Of imitation, leape into a streight,	313	Horace	192
Into a Swallow there; Nor Cadmus take,	317	Horace	267
And so to turne all earnest into jest,	321	Horace	330
And so to turne our earnest into jest,	346	Horace	V322/330
Fell into fault so farre, as now they saw	321	Horace	367
Into their birth-right, and for fitnesse sake,	323	Horace	376
How to divide, into a hundred parts,	327	Horace	465
Into the Profits, what a meere rude braine	331	Horace	583
These trifles into serious mischiefes lead	335	Horace	641
Into a pit, or hole; although he call,	335	Horace	652
Conceipt, and into burning Aetna leap'd.	335	Horace	663
extendeth circles into infinits,	361	Palmer	18
Do turne into a Woman.	364	Phoenix	4
The Orbe was cut forth into Regions seaven.	396	Drayton	20
Into a Phoenix, which is shee.	400	Lady Ogle	32
Eyes that can pierce into the Misteryes	404	Inigo Jones 1	46
Up & about? Dyve into Cellars too	405	Inigo Jones 1	80
Or Dowgate Torrent falling into Thames,	407	Inigo Jones 2	16

325

	Page	Title	Line
INTO (cont.)			
Able to eat into his bones & pierce	407	Inigo Jones 3	4
Now, you are got into a nearer roome,	409	Brome	3
Over the Door at the Entrance into the Apollo.	657	Door Apollo	Ttl
INTREAT			
Have sung this Hymne, and here intreat	174	U22 Elegy Tho	30
INTREATIES			
Goe where Youths soft intreaties call thee back.	292	U86 Hor.4:1	8
INTREATY			
Although that thou, O Sun, at our intreaty stay!	254	U75 Epithalam.	56
INTRENCHMENT			
Or canst of truth the least intrenchment pitch,	407	Inigo Jones 2	23
INT'REST			
Hee can, he will, and with large int'rest pay,	236	U63 Charles 2	5
INTWINE			
bor-/Dring Circles of swift waters that intwine	305	Horace	21
INVADE			
Doe severall passions invade the minde,	110	F11 Epode	29
Is borrowing; that but stopt, they doe invade	155	U13 Sacvile	80
And didst invade part of the Common-wealth,	210	U43 Vulcan	170
And who make thither else, rob, or invade.	389	Chapman	12
INVEIGH			
T'inveigh 'gainst playes: what did he then but play?	52	E75 Lippe	4
INVENT			
Or, with thy Tribade trine, invent new sports,	107	F10 Proludium	17
I could invent a sentence, yet were worse;	211	U43 Vulcan	189
I could invent a sentence, yet more worse;	211	U43 Vulcan	V189
Tell her, his Muse that did invent thee	662	Bedford	5
INVENTED			
He that first invented thee,	184	U29 Fit of Rime	49
INVENTION			
Thy present Aide: Arise Invention,	176	U25 Desmond	2
Thy present Aide: Spirit Invention,	176	U25 Desmond	V 2
Invention. Now, to speake; and then differ	307	Horace	61
INVENTIONS			
So well in that are his inventions wrought,	83	E132 Sylvester	11
INVISIBILITIE			
Invisibilitie, and strength, and tongues:	206	U43 Vulcan	75
INVITE (See also ENVITE)			
Now threaten, with those meanes she did invite?	169	U18 Elegy Can	2
They say you weekly invite with fits o'th' Mother,	223	U49 Pucell	40
And all invite to easie sleepe.	290	U85 Country	28
INVITING			
Inviting a friend to supper.	64	E101 Supper	Ttl
A dazling, yet inviting, Majestie:	270	U81 Pawlet	44
A darling, yet inviting, Majestie:	270	U81 Pawlet	V 44
INVOKE			
Or goddesse to invoke, to stuffe my verse;	85	E133 Voyage	45
INWARD			
And out of inward pleasure feed	144	U3 Musicall	19
And out of inward passion feed	144	U3 Musicall	V 19
In outward face, but inward, light as Furre,	162	U15 Friend-Wars	20
IO			
Poore Io wandring; wild Orestes mad:	313	Horace	177
Io still wandring; griev'd Orestes sad:	342	Horace	V177
IONIAN			
Th'Ionian God-wit, nor the Ginny hen	291	U85 Country	53
IRE			
Shewing danger more then ire.	142	U2 Her man	42
And, after all theyr Aetnean Ire,	179	U25 Desmond	44
What had I done that might call on thine ire?	202	U43 Vulcan	2
What have I done that might call on thine ire?	202	U43 Vulcan	V 2
IRELAND			
In Ireland, Holland, Sweden, pompous lies,	69	E107 Hungry	12
Let Ireland meet it out at Sea, halfe way,	249	U72 King	5
IRIS			
And peering forth of Iris in the Shrowdes!	403	Inigo Jones 1	34
IRISH			
The cold of Mosco, and fat Irish ayre,	37	E32 Roe 2	5
IRISHRY			
Upon the Kerne, and wildest Irishry,	367	Ode Who saith	53
IRON (See also YRON)			
I will not argue thee Iron. Them of guilt	210	U43 Vulcan	V165
Hill-/foot (out in Sussex) to an iron Mill;	211	U43 Vulcan	184
Hill-/foot (out in Sussex) to some iron Mill;	211	U43 Vulcan	V184
IRONS			
When not his Combes, his Curling-irons, his Glasse,	165	U15 Friend-Wars	111
But why are all these Irons i'the fire	215	U44 Speach	93
IRRELIGIOUS			
Dare I prophane, so irreligious bee	283	U84 Muse	39
IRRITATE			
Why doe I irritate, or stirre up thee,	250	U73 Weston	7
'S			
(How nothing's that?) to whom my countrey owes	31	E14 Camden	3
There's reason good, that you good lawes should make:	34	E24 Parliament	1
That's greater, yet: to crie his owne up neate.	35	E28 Surly	11
He drinkes to no man: that's, too, like a lord.	35	E28 Surly	14
But that's put in, thou'lt say. Why, so is thine.	36	E29 Tilter	6
The knight-wright's cheated then: Hee'll never pay.	42	E46 Luckless 1	5
For, but thy selfe, where, out of motly, 's hee	44	E53 Old-end	9
Is it the paine affrights? that's soone forgot.	46	E62 Would-bee	5
And there's both losse of time, and losse of sport	46	E62 Would-bee	10
Of the not borne, yet buried, here's the tombe.	46	E62 Would-bee	12

326

	Page	Title	Line
'S (cont.)			
Hee's valiant'st, that dares fight, and not for pay;	49	E66 Cary	17
That vertuous is, when the reward's away.	49	E66 Cary	18
I Cannot thinke there's that antipathy	52	E75 Lippe	1
Since when, hee's sober againe, and all play's made.	56	E87 Hazard	6
My title's seal'd. Those that for claps doe write,	62	E96 Donne 2	9
Where ere he met me; now hee's dumbe, or proud.	62	E97 Motion	8
But much it now availes, what's done, of whom:	64	E99 Th Roe 2	7
There's none so dull, that for your stile would aske,	68	E105 L Wroth 2	15
That's, sit, and eate: doe not my eares abuse.	68	E107 Hungry	2
Doe what you come for, Captayne, There's your meate.	69	E107 Hungry	32
But 's angry for the Captayne, still: is such.	70	E108 Soldiers	10
Where vertue makes them both, and that's in thee:	70	E109 Nevil	3
There's no vexation, that can make thee prime.	73	E112 Gamster	22
By speaking well o' the company' it 's in.	74	E115 Honest Man	8
Whose name's un-welcome to the present eare,	74	E115 Honest Man	15
The cloth's no sooner gone, but it gets up	74	E115 Honest Man	24
Describ'd, it 's thus: Defin'd would you it have?	75	E115 Honest Man	33
Then, The townes honest Man's her errant'st knave.	75	E115 Honest Man	34
That there's no journey set, or thought upon,	81	E129 Mime	3
On some new gesture, that's imputed wit?	81	E129 Mime	14
'Tis but light paines: Indeede this Dock's no rose.	85	E133 Voyage	60
There's none, that dwell about them, wish them downe;	94	F2 Penshurst	47
There's nothing I can wish, for which I stay.	95	F2 Penshurst	75
Thy lady's noble, fruitfull, chaste withall.	96	F2 Penshurst	90
To him, man's dearer, then t'himselfe.	99	F3 Wroth	96
That cryes, we dreame, and sweares, there's no such thing,	111	F11 Epode	67
That cryes, I dreame, and sweares, there's no such thing,	111	F11 Epode	V 67
On what's deceast.	121	F14 Sydney	38
All's done in me.	128	U1 Trinitie	24
For, sin's so sweet,	129	U1 Father	12
Where's thy Quiver? bend thy Bow:	132	U2 How he saw	9
Here's a shaft, thou art to slow!	132	U2 How he saw	10
Doe but marke, her forehead's smoother	134	U2 Triumph	15
But shee's Juno, when she walkes,	137	U2 Cupid	53
Here's none to spie, or see;	139	U2 Another	3
That's a Toy, that I could spare:	142	U2 Exception	2
For that's a narrow joy is but our owne.	147	U7 Nymph	7
So each, that's done, and tane, becomes a Brace.	154	U13 Sacvile	40
Looke to and cure; Hee's not a man hath none,	156	U13 Sacvile	115
But here's no time, nor place, my wealth to tell,	161	U14 Selden	85
See him, that's call'd, and thought the happiest man,	162	U15 Friend-Wars	23
I, that's a Charme and halfe! She must afford	163	U15 Friend-Wars	52
Hee's one of blood, and fashion! and with these	164	U15 Friend-Wars	55
The Husband now's call'd churlish, or a poore	165	U15 Friend-Wars	89
That scratching now's our best Felicitie?	166	U15 Friend-Wars	144
Although, perhaps it has, what's that to me,	167	U15 Friend-Wars	149
Pardon his Lordship. Flattry's growne so cheape	167	U15 Friend-Wars	155
But he that's both, and slave to boote, shall live,	167	U15 Friend-Wars	160
But he that's both, and slave to both, shall live,	167	U15 Friend-Wars	V160
Though but while mettal's heating:	179	U25 Desmond	43
Then to your love, and gift. And all's but due.	189	U37 Friend-Book	3
And then with pause; for sever'd once, that's gone,	192	U38 Elegy 'Tis	47
That Love's a bitter sweet, I ne're conceive	197	U40 Elegy That	1
And free societie, hee's borne else-where,	197	U40 Elegy That	16
Out with the other, for he's still at home;	198	U40 Elegy That	34
You would restore it? No, that's worth a feare,	199	U41 Elegy Since	15
But that's a marke, wherof thy Rites doe boast,	205	U43 Vulcan	57
Borne, bred, allied? what's he dare tutor us?	215	U44 Speach	66
But he that's too-much that, is friend of none.	216	U45 Squib	24
But that's a blow, by which in time I may	219	U47 Tribe	51
Her face there's none can like by Candle light.	223	U49 Pucell	32
Will cal't a Bastard, when a Prophet's borne.	223	U49 Pucell	46
That's six in silver; now within the Socket	229	U54 Squib	13
And that's made up as doth the purse abound.	230	U56 Covell	12
Stay, drop a teare for him that's dead,	233	U60 La-ware	2
When all your life's a president of dayes,	237	U64 Charles 3	13
Here's one out-liv'd his Peeres,	243	U70 Ode	25
These make the lines of life, and that's her ayre.	245	U70 Ode	64
And thinke, nay know, thy Morison's not dead.	245	U70 Ode	78
Stand there; for when a noble Nature's rais'd,	256	U75 Epithalam.	113
By this Sun's Noone-sted's made	258	U75 Epithalam.	183
Hee's Master of the Office; yet no more	258	U75 Epithalam.	187
Hee's prudent, valiant, just, and temperate;	262	U78 Digby	5
Our great, our good. Where one's so drest	265	U79 New-yeares	44
Hee's good, as great. I am almost a stone!	269	U81 Pawlet	11
And e're I can aske more of her, shee's gone!	269	U81 Pawlet	12
But, here's a Song of her Descent:	273	U84 Cradle	29
But what's of kinne to whence it came.	278	U84 Mind	16
Earths grossnesse; There's the how, and why.	279	U84 Mind	44
our grossnesse; There's the how, and why.	279	U84 Mind	V 44
What's left a Poet, when his Muse is gone?	283	U84 Muse	28
And purple-matching Grapes, hee's glad!	290	U85 Country	20
For he's both noble, lovely, young,	292	U86 Hor.4:1	13
What's this? if he whose money hireth thee	305	Horace	26
And come not too much wrested. What's that thing,	309	Horace	76
Our selves, and all that's ours, to death we owe:	309	Horace	90
With sloth, yet greedy still of what's to come:	317	Horace	246
There's Albin's sonne will say, Substract an ounce	327	Horace	467
All which I tell, lest when Apollo's nam'd,	329	Horace	501
Yet, there's a value given to this man.	331	Horace	554
Or, who's unskilfull at the Coit, or Ball,	331	Horace	567
Yet who's most ignorant, dares Verses make.	331	Horace	570

327

	Page	Title	Line

'S (cont.)

Hee, that's ambitious in the race to touch	333	Horace	587
They're darke, bid cleare this: all that's doubtfull wrote	335	Horace	637
They're dark, bid cleare 'hem; al that's doubtful wrote	354	Horace	V637
There's none will take the care, to helpe him then;	335	Horace	654
Here's one makes verses, but there's none knows why:	355	Horace	V670
Polluted, touch't: but certainly he's mad:	355	Horace	V673
The fault's not in the object, but their eyes.	362	Author	8
Where Gold's the Motive, women have no Nay.	363	Riches	18
As farre as Sinne's from lightnesse.	364	Ode Splendor	4
Yet shee's nor nice to shew them,	365	Ode Splendor	23
Now must we plie our ayme; our Swan's on wing.	368	Ode Who saith	64
Hee's carried 'twixt Montrell and Abbevile.	374	Coryat 1	13
Hee's carried like a Cripple, from Constable to Constable.	374	Coryat 1	17
Here, by a Boore too, hee's like to be beaten	375	Coryat 1	24
shall looke, & on hyme soe, then arte's a lyer	383	Rich	15
to which there's no materiall that endures;	387	Cavendish	8
But that hee's too well suted, in a cloth,	389	Aleman	17
Had cloath'd him so. Here's all I can supply	389	Aleman	20
For a good Poet's made, as well as borne.	392	Shakespeare	64
Without conferring symboles. This's my day.	396	Drayton	10
Defies, what's crosse to Piety, or good Fame.	401	Beaumont	20
Hee's warme on his feet now he sayes, & can	405	Inigo Jones 1	67
A Noble honest Soule! what's this to thee?	406	Inigo Jones 2	6
No faith's more firme, or flat, then where't doth creep.	413	Ghyrlond	20

IS'

What is't, fine Grand, makes thee my friendship flye,	51	E73 Fine Grand	1
Nor is't inconstancie to change	146	U6 Defence	13
Or faith in things? or is't your wealth and will	159	U14 Selden	36
Yet is't your vertue now I raise.	173	U22 Elegy Tho	4
What is't to me whether the French Designe	219	U47 Tribe	31
To lift to heaven: who is't not understands	234	U61 Epigram	8
Nor is't long since, they did with patience take	323	Horace	375

IS (See also 'TIS)

To reade it well: that is, to understand.	27	E1 Reader	2
Tells you it is a hot-house: So it ma',	29	E7 Hot-house	3
The courtier is become the greater thiefe.	29	E8 Robbery	6
Himselfe: his whole revennue is, god payes.	30	E12 Shift	6
The quarter day is come; the hostesse sayes,	30	E12 Shift	7
His onely answere is to all, god payes.	31	E12 Shift	20
Hardie, thy braine is valiant, 'tis confest,	32	E16 Brain-hardy	1
When both it is the old way, and the true.	32	E18 Censurer	2
Thy faith is all the knowledge that thou hast.	32	E18 Censurer	10
Th'expence in odours is a most vaine sinne,	33	E20 Cod 2	1
Lord, how is Gam'ster chang'd! his haire close cut!	33	E21 Gam'ster	1
And, that is done, as he saw great men doe.	35	E28 Surly	6
Which is maine greatnesse. And, at his still boord,	35	E28 Surly	13
He keepes anothers wife, which is a spice	36	E28 Surly	15
That breathes in his dogs way: and this is great.	36	E28 Surly	18
But that's put in, thou'lt say. Why, so is thine.	36	E29 Tilter	6
Gypsee, new baud, is turn'd physitian,	39	E41 Gypsee	1
Such her quaint practise is, so it allures,	39	E41 Gypsee	3
And having got him out of doores is glad.	40	E42 Giles	7
The like is Jone. But turning home, is sad.	40	E42 Giles	8
And so is Jone. Oft-times, when Giles doth find	40	E42 Giles	9
Is this the Sir, who, some wast wife to winne,	42	E46 Luckless 1	1
For wittie, in his language, is obscene.	42	E49 Playwrt 1	4
What fate is mine, that so it selfe bereaves?	44	E55 Beaumont	7
What art is thine, that so thy friend deceives?	44	E55 Beaumont	8
From brocage is become so bold a thiefe,	44	E56 Poet-Ape	3
Thy praise, or dispraise is to me alike,	46	E61 Foole	1
Is it the paine affrights? that's soone forgot.	46	E62 Would-bee	5
Where merit is not sepulcher'd alive.	47	E64 Salisbury 3	10
Make him loose all his friends; and, which is worse,	48	E65 Muse	9
But I repent me: Stay. Who e're is rais'd,	48	E65 Muse	15
For worth he has not, He is tax'd, not prais'd.	48	E65 Muse	16
That vertuous is, when the reward's away.	49	E66 Cary	18
As, to be rais'd by her, is onely fame.	49	E67 Suffolk	4
Proves, that is gods, which was the peoples voice.	49	E67 Suffolk	12
Delay is bad, doubt worse, depending worst;	50	E70 Wm Roe 1	5
Thy person only, Courtling, is the vice.	50	E72 Court-ling	6
The world must know your greatnesse is my debter.	51	E73 Fine Grand	4
As is thy conscience, which is alwayes one:	52	E74 Chancelor	8
How wilfull blind is he then, that would stray,	53	E80 Life/Death	3
This world deaths region is, the other lifes:	54	E80 Life/Death	5
Or is it some french statue? No: 'T doth move,	56	E88 Monsieur	13
And it is hop'd, that shee, like Milo, wull	57	E90 Mill	17
They, then, that living where the matter is bred,	60	E94 Bedford 3	11
Where Nero falls, and Galba is ador'd,	61	E95 Savile	8
It is the next deed, and a great one too.	61	E95 Savile	26
Where sweetnesse is requir'd, and where weight;	62	E95 Savile	30
He is no favourites favourite, no deare trust	63	E97 Motion	13
He that is round within himselfe, and streight,	63	E98 Th Roe 1	3
Though both be good, the latter yet is worst,	63	E98 Th Roe 1	11
And ever is ill got without the first.	63	E98 Th Roe 1	12
Thy fact is more: let truth encourage thee.	64	E99 Th Roe 2	12
It is the faire acceptance, Sir, creates	64	E101 Supper	7
Is not to be despair'd of, for our money;	65	E101 Supper	14
Is a pure cup of rich Canary-wine,	65	E101 Supper	29
Which is the Mermaids, now, but shall be mine:	65	E101 Supper	30
It is an Epigramme, on all man-kind;	66	E102 Pembroke	2
Almost, is exercis'd: and scarse one knowes,	66	E102 Pembroke	7
Which is, it selfe, the imprese of the great,	66	E103 L Wroth 1	7

IS (cont.)

My praise is plaine, and where so ere profest,	67	E103 L Wroth 1	13
But 's angry for the Captayne, still: is such.	70	E108 Soldiers	10
Who now calls on thee, Nevil, is a Muse,	70	E109 Nevil	1
Where all is faire, beside thy pedigree.	70	E109 Nevil	4
Is private gaine, which hath long guilt to friend.	70	E109 Nevil	8
And that, in action, there is nothing new,	72	E111 Edmonds 2	5
Think'st thou it is meere fortune, that can win?	72	E112 Gamster	3
O, (thou cry'st out) that is thy proper game.	73	E112 Gamster	16
Nor scarce dost colour for it, which is lesse.	73	E112 Gamster	20
As but to speake thee, Overbury, is praise:	73	E113 Overbury	2
For since, what ignorance, what pride is fled!	73	E113 Overbury	7
You wonder, who this is! and, why I name	74	E115 Honest Man	1
Naming so many, too! But, this is one,	74	E115 Honest Man	3
From friendship, is it's owne fames architect.	75	E115 Honest Man	30
Which is to live to conscience, not to show.	76	E119 Shelton	14
Death's selfe is sorry.	77	E120 S. P.	4
Yet is the office not to be despis'd,	78	E121 Rudyerd 1	5
Phoebus replyed. Bold head, it is not shee:	80	E126 Mrs Cary	7
Cary my love is, Daphne but my tree.	80	E126 Mrs Cary	8
Is there a hope, that Man would thankefull bee,	80	E127 Aubigny	1
To thanke thy benefits: which is, to pay.	80	E127 Aubigny	12
This is that good Aeneas, past through fire,	81	E128 Wm Roe 2	12
But the first question is, when one saw thee?	81	E129 Mime	2
Think'st thou, Mime, this is great? or, that they strive	81	E129 Mime	9
And is t'a body, often, ill inclin'd,	82	E130 Ferrab. 1	7
But, as it is (the Child of Ignorance,	83	E132 Sylvester	3
A Docke there is, that called is Avernus,	85	E133 Voyage	41
Is this we heare? of frogs? No, guts wind-bound,	86	E133 Voyage	92
And that is when it is the Lord Maiors foist.	87	E133 Voyage	120
For, to say truth, what scullion is so nastie,	88	E133 Voyage	147
Is fill'd with buttock? And the walls doe sweate	88	E133 Voyage	169
Tempt not his furie, Pluto is away:	89	E133 Voyage	179
Is now from home. You lose your labours quite,	89	E133 Voyage	181
It is enough, they once did get	93	F1 Why write no	5
When Love is fled, and I grow old.	93	F1 Why write no	12
And, for thy messe, is willing to be kill'd.	94	F2 Penshurst	30
Where comes no guest, but is allow'd to eate,	95	F2 Penshurst	61
That is his Lordships, shall be also mine.	95	F2 Penshurst	64
For fire, or lights, or livorie: all is there;	95	F2 Penshurst	73
Nor throng'st (when masquing is) to have a sight	96	F3 Wroth	9
Nor throng'st (where masquing is) to have a sight	96	F3 Wroth	V 9
And makes sleepe softer then it is!	97	F3 Wroth	20
(Their rudenesse then is thought no sinne)	98	F3 Wroth	54
Thy peace is made; and, when man's state is well,	99	F3 Wroth	93
Which who can use is happy: Such be thou.	99	F3 Wroth	99
Which who can use is happy: Such art thou.	99	F3 Wroth	V 99
Is thankes to him, and earnest prayer, to finde	99	F3 Wroth	V101
Nor death; but when thy latest sand is spent,	100	F3 Wroth	105
My part is ended on thy stage.	100	F4 To the World	4
And all thy good is to be sold.	100	F4 To the World	16
What bird, or beast, is knowne so dull,	101	F4 To the World	29
Where nothing is examin'd, weigh'd,	101	F4 To the World	49
Where every freedome is betray'd,	101	F4 To the World	51
Our fraile condition it is such,	101	F4 To the World	54
What their number is, be pin'd.	103	F6 Celia 2	22
His absence in my verse, is all I aske.	107	F10 Proludium	21
His absence in our verse, is all I aske.	107	F10 Proludium	V 21
Is vertue, and not Fate:	109	F11 Epode	2
Next, to that vertue, is to know vice well,	109	F11 Epode	3
Which to effect (since no brest is so sure,	109	F11 Epode	5
But this true course is not embrac'd by many:	109	F11 Epode	19
But this faire course is not embrac'd by many:	109	F11 Epode	V 19
The thing, they here call Love, is blinde Desire,	110	F11 Epode	37
That is an essence, farre more gentle, fine,	110	F11 Epode	45
That is an essence, most gentile and fine,	110	F11 Epode	V 45
It is a golden chaine let downe from heaven,	110	F11 Epode	47
O, who is he, that (in this peace) enjoyes	110	F11 Epode	55
Is meere necessitie.	111	F11 Epode	82
Is more crowne-worthy still,	112	F11 Epode	88
Is more praiseworthy still,	112	F11 E:ode	V 88
As sweet, as shee is fayre.	112	F11 Epode	98
Whil'st that, for which, all vertue now is sold,	113	F12 Rutland	1
That which, to boote with hell, is thought worth heaven,	113	F12 Rutland	3
Beautie, I know, is good, and bloud is more;	114	F12 Rutland	37
It is the Muse, alone, can raise to heaven,	114	F12 Rutland	41
My mirror is more subtile, cleere, refin'd,	117	F13 Aubigny	43
For he, that once is good, is ever great.	118	F13 Aubigny	52
Contagion in the prease is soonest catch'd.	118	F13 Aubigny	58
To Clifton's bloud, that is deny'd their name.	119	F13 Aubigny	98
But to please him, who is the dearer prise ,	119	F13 Aubigny	116
Now that the harth is crown'd with smiling fire,	120	F14 Sydney	1
Is it interpreted in me disease,	122	F15 Heaven	3
I feele my griefes too, and there scarce is ground,	122	F15 Heaven	21
Is my best part:	129	U1 Father	3
And it is not alwayes face,	131	U2 Excuse	7
When you know, that this is she,	131	U2 Excuse	18
Is, that I have leave to speake,	133	U2 Suffered	22
Each that drawes, is a Swan, or a Dove,	134	U2 Triumph	3
Doe but looke on her Haire, it is bright	134	U2 Triumph	13
O so white! O so soft! O so sweet is she!	135	U2 Triumph	30
O so faire! O so soft! O so sweet is she!	135	U2 Triumph	V 30
O so faire O so kind o so sweet so sweet is shee	135	U2 Triumph	V 38

IS (cont.)

	Page		Title	Line
O so yong o so streight O so chast so chast is shee	136	U2	Triumph	V 46
Is my Mothers! Hearts of slaine	137	U2	Cupid	31
With my Mothers is the same.	137	U2	Cupid	38
All is Venus: save unchaste.	137	U2	Cupid	42
Of her good, who is the best	137	U2	Cupid	44
Shee is Venus, when she smiles,	137	U2	Cupid	52
Guesse of these, which is the true;	138	U2	Kisse	34
All your sweet of life is past,	140	U2	Promise	28
Smooth as is the Billiard Ball:	141	U2	Her man	20
All I wish is understood.	142	U2	Exception	6
Till each of us is made a Starre,	143	U3	Musicall	V 3
Of reason emptie is?!	143	U3	Musicall	6
Our proper vertue is to range:	146	U6	Defence	4
Is that which doth perfection breed.	146	U6	Defence	12
For what is better, or to make	146	U6	Defence	14
The good, from bad, is not describe,	146	U6	Defence	17
The pleasure is as good as none,	147	U7	Nymph	6
For that's a narrow joy is but our owne.	147	U7	Nymph	7
He is, if they can find him, faire,	147	U7	Nymph	15
Yet, yet I doubt he is not knowne,	147	U7	Nymph	20
I Now thinke, Love is rather deafe, then blind,	149	U9	Picture	1
I Doubt that, Love is rather deafe, then blind,	149	U9	Picture	V 1
I'm sure my language to her, is as sweet,	149	U9	Picture	V 6
Think'st thou that love is help'd by feare?	150	U10	Jealousie	12
Where any Deed is forc't, the Grace is mard.	153	U13	Sacvile	24
Nought but in corners; and is loath to leave,	154	U13	Sacvile	44
Then turning unto him is next at hand,	154	U13	Sacvile	56
But one is bitten by the Dog he fed,	155	U13	Sacvile	67
O, is it so? knowes he so much? and will	155	U13	Sacvile	73
Of any, is a great and generous Deed:	155	U13	Sacvile	76
Is borrowing; that but stopt, they doe invade	155	U13	Sacvile	80
And it is paid 'hem with a trembling zeale,	155	U13	Sacvile	85
Sure there is Misterie in it, I not know,	156	U13	Sacvile	97
And where they want, she is not understood.	156	U13	Sacvile	112
In time 'twill be a heape; This is not true	157	U13	Sacvile	133
Then which there is not unto Studie'a more	158	U14	Selden	13
Themselves through favouring what is there not found:	159	U14	Selden	16
Themselves through favouring that is there not found:	159	U14	Selden	V 16
So that my Reader is assur'd, I now	159	U14	Selden	27
Where is that nominall marke, or reall rite,	160	U14	Selden	47
It is a call to keepe the spirits alive	162	U15	Friend-Wars	5
No person, nor is lov'd: what wayes he proves	162	U15	Friend-Wars	16
Be honour is so mixt) by such as would,	162	U15	Friend-Wars	25
Friendship is now mask'd Hatred! Justice fled,	163	U15	Friend-Wars	39
With Velvet, Plush, and Tissues, it is spirit.	164	U15	Friend-Wars	58
That payes, or what he will: The Dame is steele.	164	U15	Friend-Wars	78
Nor is the title question'd with our proud,	164	U15	Friend-Wars	83
Is lov'd, though he let out his owne for life:	164	U15	Friend-Wars	88
A fellow of course Letcherie, is nam'd,	165	U15	Friend-Wars	98
Is it for these that Fine-man meets the street	165	U15	Friend-Wars	106
Is it that man pulls on himselfe Disease?	165	U15	Friend-Wars	114
What furie of late is crept into our Feasts?	166	U15	Friend-Wars	117
When oft the Bearer, is borne out of dore?	166	U15	Friend-Wars	120
Is not enough now, but the Nights to play:	166	U15	Friend-Wars	132
Is not enough now, but the Nights we play:	166	U15	Friend-Wars	V132
Is that the truer excuse? or have we got	166	U15	Friend-Wars	142
Well, let it goe. Yet this is better, then	166	U15	Friend-Wars	145
With him, for he is follow'd with that heape	167	U15	Friend-Wars	156
Is nothing, such scarce meat and drinke he'le give,	167	U15	Friend-Wars	159
Spread through the World) is easier farre to find,	167	U15	Friend-Wars	172
That thou thinke nothing great, but what is good,	168	U15	Friend-Wars	187
All that is left of Philip Gray,	168	U16	Gray	4
'Tis then a crime, when the Usurer is Judge.	169	U17	Friend-Debt	4
And he is not in friendship. Nothing there	169	U17	Friend-Debt	5
Is done for gaine: If't be, 'tis not sincere.	169	U17	Friend-Debt	6
All is not barren land, doth fallow lie.	169	U17	Friend-Debt	16
A terror? or is all this but my feare?	169	U18	Elegy Can	6
To use the present, then, is not abuse,	171	U19	Elegy By	21
You have a Husband is the just excuse	171	U19	Elegy By	22
Is constant to be extraordinarie.	171	U19	Elegy By	28
Doe not you aske to know her, she is worse	172	U20	Shrub	17
But she is such, as she might, yet, forestall	172	U20	Shrub	23
By whom he is restor'd to men:	173	U22	Elegy Tho	15
Is gone himselfe into your Name.	173	U22	Elegy Tho	24
It is the common Moath,	174	U23	Himselfe	5
By which as proper titles, she is knowne	176	U24	Frontispice	16
Where only a mans birth is his offence,	177	U25	Desmond	32
When only a mans birth is his offence,	177	U25	Desmond	V 32
Is but a Statists theame, to read Phlebotomie.	179	U25	Desmond	39
Gold, that is perfect, will out-live the fire.	179	U25	Desmond	45
No Armour to the mind! he is shot-free	179	U25	Desmond	48
That is not hurt; not he, that is not hit;	179	U25	Desmond	50
Unknowne which is the Dearest)	179	U25	Desmond	56
The Cure of that, which is but corporall,	180	U26	Ode High	5
So speake (as yet it is not mute)	181	U27	Ode Helen	4
Is Horace his each love so high	181	U27	Ode Helen	13
Nor is my Muse, or I asham'd to owe it	182	U28	Worth	5
Is not yet free from Rimes wrongs,	184	U29	Fit of Rime	35
What is there more that can ennoble blood?	185	U30	Burleigh	6
So, may the King proclaime your Conscience is	185	U31	Elsmere	3
When a good Cause is destitute of friends,	186	U32	Elsmere	2
For Love in shadow best is made.	189	U36	Song	2

IS (cont.)

	Page	Title	Line
Yet he himselfe is but a sparke.	189	U36 Song	8
Which is indeed but friendship of the spit:	190	U37 Friend-Book	9
Rigid, and harsh, which is a Drug austere	190	U37 Friend-Book	17
It is an Act of tyrannie, not love,	190	U37 Friend-Book	25
It is a Darknesse hath blockt up my sense,	191	U38 Elegy 'Tis	5
Nothing is vile, that is a part of you:	192	U38 Elegy 'Tis	36
There is no Father that for one demerit,	192	U38 Elegy 'Tis	41
That as the last of punishments is meant;	192	U38 Elegy 'Tis	43
Before you prove a medicine, is unjust.	192	U38 Elegy 'Tis	50
That is, if still your Favours you apply,	192	U38 Elegy 'Tis	53
Her order is to cherish, and preserve,	192	U38 Elegy 'Tis	61
But to exact againe what once is given,	192	U38 Elegy 'Tis	63
Is natures meere obliquitie! as Heaven	192	U38 Elegy 'Tis	64
In a calme skie, then when the heaven is horl'd	193	U38 Elegy 'Tis	74
Then sword, or fire, or what is of the race	193	U38 Elegy 'Tis	101
There is not any punishment, or paine,	194	U38 Elegy 'Tis	103
And that there is no life in me, but love.	194	U38 Elegy 'Tis	112
Is fix'd upon one leg, and dares not come	198	U40 Elegy That	33
And such your Servant is, who vowes to keepe	198	U40 Elegy That	41
What it is like: And doe not thinke they can	199	U41 Elegy Since	3
It is as if a night should shade noone-day,	199	U41 Elegy Since	5
What fate is this, to change mens dayes and houres,	199	U41 Elegy Since	9
Winter is come a Quarter e're his Time,	199	U41 Elegy Since	12
Who frownes, who jealous is, who taxeth me.	200	U42 Elegy Let	10
In all that is call'd lovely: take my sight	200	U42 Elegy Let	12
There is not worne that lace, purle, knot or pin,	200	U42 Elegy Let	16
But is the Poets matter: And he must,	200	U42 Elegy Let	17
When he is furious, love, although not lust.	200	U42 Elegy Let	18
It is a ryming Age, and Verses swarme	200	U42 Elegy Let	27
It is not likely I should now looke downe	200	U42 Elegy Let	37
But when thy Wife (as thou conceiv'st) is brave?	201	U42 Elegy Let	50
Shee is the Judge, Thou Executioner:	204	U43 Vulcan	47
Hee is true Vulcan still! He did not spare	210	U43 Vulcan	159
The Herald will. Our blood is now become	215	U44 Speach	82
Carriage, and dressing. There is up of late	215	U44 Speach	88
His Lordship. That is for his Band, his haire	215	U44 Speach	95
Deceit is fruitfull. Men have Masques and nets,	216	U45 Squib	18
For that is first requir'd, A man be his owne.	216	U45 Squib	23
But he that's too-much that, is friend of none.	216	U45 Squib	24
It is a richer Purchase then of land.	216	U45 Squib	26
And now such is thy stand; while thou dost deale	217	U46 Coke	15
Such is thy All; that (as I sung before)	217	U46 Coke	21
And know whose ignorance is more then theirs;	218	U47 Tribe	24
Or if it would, the Court is the worst place,	223	U49 Pucell	43
Ought that is ill, but the suspition too,	224	U50 Countesse	6
Is of so brave example, as he were	224	U50 Countesse	7
And so doe I. This is the sixtieth yeare	225	U51 Bacon	7
What then his Father was, that since is hee,	225	U51 Bacon	11
A Merchants Wife is Regent of the Scale.	229	U54 Squib	4
Is, she will play Dame Justice, too severe;	229	U54 Squib	8
His weight is twenty Stone within two pound;	230	U56 Covell	11
Marrie the Muse is one, can tread the Aire,	230	U56 Covell	13
Marrie his Muse is one, can tread the Aire,	230	U56 Covell	V 13
And more is behind:	231	U57 Burges	13
Christmas is neere;	231	U57 Burges	15
His judgement is; If he be wise, and praise,	232	U58 Book-seller	5
Wonder to Valour! No, it is the Law	233	U59 Newcastle	14
Of daring, not to doe a wrong, is true	233	U59 Newcastle	15
All this (my Lord) is Valour! This is yours!	233	U59 Newcastle	19
He is the Man, and Favorite of God.	235	U61 Epigram	20
'T is not enough (thy pietie is such)	235	U62 Charles 1	3
That the Almighties will to you is such:	236	U63 Charles 2	8
For God, whose essence is so infinite,	236	U63 Charles 2	13
How is she barren growne of love! or broke!	237	U64 Charles 3	15
How is she barren growne in love! or broke!	237	U64 Charles 3	V 15
'T is not alone the Merchant, but the Clowne,	237	U64 Charles 3	19
Is Banke-rupt turn'd! the Cassock, Cloake, and Gowne,	237	U64 Charles 3	20
Is Banke-rupt turn'd! Cloak, Cassock, Robe, & Gowne,	237	U64 Charles 3	V 20
That when the Quire is full,	239	U67 Muses	19
His is more safe commoditie, or none:	241	U69 Friend Son	7
All is but web, and painting; be the strife	242	U69 Friend Son	24
For, what is life, if measur'd by the space,	243	U70 Ode	21
It is not growing like a tree	245	U70 Ode	65
Is fairer farre, in May,	245	U70 Ode	70
This is King Charles his Day. Speake it, thou Towre,	249	U72 King	1
This is King Charles his birth day. Speake it, thou Towre,	249	U72 King	V 1
The wish is great; but where the Prince is such,	249	U72 King	19
Because the order of the whole is faire!	251	U74 Weston	12
It is the kindly Season of the time,	253	U75 Epithalam.	25
Like what she is, the Daughter of a Duke,	253	U75 Epithalam.	42
It is their Grace, and favour, that makes seene,	255	U75 Epithalam.	89
All is a story of the King and Queene!	255	U75 Epithalam.	91
It is: to th' envious meant,	256	U75 Epithalam.	119
There is a Feast behind,	257	U75 Epithalam.	141
(After the last child borne;) This is our wedding day.	258	U75 Epithalam.	168
Exacts then she is pleas'd to pay: no suits,	258	U75 Epithalam.	188
Catch'd with these Arts, wherein the Judge is wise	261	U77 Treasurer	11
Caught them these Arts, wherein the Judge is wise	261	U77 Treasurer	V 11
In him all vertue is beheld in State:	262	U78 Digby	6
In him all action is beheld in State:	262	U78 Digby	V 6
And he is built like some imperiall roome	262	U78 Digby	7
His brest is a brave Palace, a broad Street,	262	U78 Digby	9

```
IS  (cont.)                                             Page    Title        Line
```

	Page	Title	Line
Pan is the great Preserver of our bounds.	264	U79 New-yeares	14
Of brightest Mira, is our Song; the grace	264	U79 New-yeares	32
Hee is the Father of our peace;	264	U79 New-yeares	40
Pan only our great Shep'ard is,	265	U79 New-yeares	43
This is the great Preserver of our bounds,	265	U79 New-yeares	48
Hee is the author of our peace.	265	U79 New-yeares	57
This only the great Shep'ard is.	265	U79 New-yeares	65
Hee is the author of our peace.	265	U79 New-yeares	69
That thou art lov'd of God, this worke is done,	268	U80 Christning	1
A horrour in mee! all my blood is steele!	269	U81 Pawlet	8
It is a large faire table, and a true,	269	U81 Pawlet	15
It is too neere of kin to Heaven, the Soule,	269	U81 Pawlet	29
It is too neere of kin to God, the Soule,	269	U81 Pawlet	V 29
And wish her state lesse happie then it is!	271	U81 Pawlet	84
Is sung: as als' her getting up	274	U84 Cradle	37
This is no Picture, but the same.	278	U84 Mind	24
In speech; it is with that excesse	279	U84 Mind	34
Is it because it sees us dull,	279	U84 Mind	45
For her t'inhabit? There is it.	280	U84 Mind	52
It is a wretched thing to trust to reedes;	281	U84 Kenelme	16
'Tis Vertue alone, is true Nobilitie.	282	U84 Kenelme	21
'Twere time that I dy'd too, now shee is dead,	282	U84 Muse	1
(For so thou art with me) now shee is gone.	283	U84 Muse	22
What's left a Poet, when his Muse is gone?	283	U84 Muse	28
Indeed, she is not dead! but laid to sleepe	283	U84 Muse	45
Like single; so, there is a third, commixt,	284	U84 Muse	53
This as it guilty is, or guiltlesse found,	284	U84 Muse	56
To Body, and Soule! where Love is all the guest!	284	U84 Muse	64
And the whole Banquet is full sight of God!	284	U84 Muse	65
All other gladnesse, with the thought is barr'd;	284	U84 Muse	67
That she is in, or, make it more compleat?	284	U84 Muse	72
Who violates the God-head, is most vitious	284	U84 Muse	74
What fulnesse of beatitude is here?	286	U84 Muse	137
For, Prayer is the Incense most perfumes	288	U84 Muse	187
To publish her a Saint. My Muse is gone.	289	U84 Muse	228
Happie is he, that from all Businesse cleere,	289	U85 Country	1
And is not in the Usurers bands:	289	U85 Country	4
Doing, a filthy pleasure is, and short;	294	U88 Petronius	1
There is no labour, nor no shame in this;	294	U88 Petronius	8
Can this decay, but is beginning ever.	294	U88 Petronius	10
Or Rainbow is describ'd. But here was now	305	Horace	23
Is now to speak, and even now to differ	339	Horace	V 61
Lay that aside, the Epicks office is.	307	Horace	64
Shall perish: so farre off it is, the state,	309	Horace	99
Much phrase that now is dead, shall be reviv'd;	309	Horace	101
And much shall dye, that now is nobly liv'd,	309	Horace	102
Heare, what it is the People, and I desire:	315	Horace	219
Soone angry, and soone pleas'd, is sweet, or sowre,	315	Horace	227
Loves Dogges, and Horses; and is ever one	315	Horace	230
I'the open field; is Waxe like to be wrought	315	Horace	231
The businesse either on the Stage is done,	317	Horace	255
What so is showne, I not beleeve, and hate.	317	Horace	269
Thespis is said to be the first found out	319	Horace	311
And emptie Clowdes. For Tragedie is faire,	321	Horace	336
And toile in vaine: the excellence is such	321	Horace	352
And there is given too unworthy leave	323	Horace	389
Is to be wise; thy matter first to know;	325	Horace	441
And, where the matter is provided still,	325	Horace	443
Will passe the Seas, and long as nature is,	329	Horace	518
Is laugh'd at, that still jarreth on one string:	329	Horace	532
As Painting, so is Poesie. Some mans hand	329	Horace	539
This saying: To some things there is assign'd	331	Horace	548
Vice, and is knowne to have a Knights estate.	352	Horace	V548/572
Thou, such thy judgement is, thy knowledge too,	331	Horace	573
Who, since, to sing the Pythian rites is heard,	333	Horace	591
Who now to sing the Pythian Rites is heard,	353	Horace	V591
But, now, it is enough to say; I make	333	Horace	593
Him that is last, I scorne to come behind,	333	Horace	595
Him that is last, I scorne to be behind,	353	Horace	V595
So doth the Poet, who is rich in land,	333	Horace	599
So doth the Poet, that is rich in Land,	353	Horace	V599
With joy of what is given him, over-gone:	333	Horace	610
Reprove; and, what is to be changed, note:	335	Horace	638
Dispute; and what is to be changed, note;	354	Horace	V638
still making that the greatest that is last	361	Palmer	19
Gold is a sutor, never tooke repulse,	363	Riches	5
This Swanne is onely his,	366	Ode Who saith	15
And Phoebus love cause of his blackenesse is.	366	Ode Who saith	16
And still is in the Brest:	366	Ode Who saith	27
Whose strength is above strength;	367	Ode Who saith	55
And is not rap't	367	Ode Who saith	60
From thence is gon	368	Ode Who saith	68
It is inough, their griefe shall know	369	Ode Who saith	113
And all your Booke (when it is throughly scan'd)	370	Author	5
But now, your Worke is done, if they that view	370	Author	9
To judge which Passion's false, and which is true,	370	Author	11
A Horse here is sadled, but no Tom him to backe,	374	Coryat 1	14
And therein (which is worth his valour too)	378	Coryat 2	84
And that, say Philosophers, is the best modell.	379	Coryat 3	5
What place is for my testimony void?	385	Brooke	2
Who are his Test, and what their judgement is:	385	Husband	3
Hold thyne owne worth unbroke: which is so good	386	Browne	13

332

	Page	Title	Line
IS (cont.)			
As, now, of all men, it is call'd thy Trade:	389	Chapman	11
Faire Aemulation, and no Envy is;	389	Aleman	22
To see (who'it is?) A noble Countesse, greate,	394	Jane Ogle	3
In the great masse, or machine there is stirr'd?	395	May	22
Is fayre got up, and day some houres begun!	396	Drayton	18
Thy list of aydes, and force, for so it is:	398	Drayton	62
This booke! it is a Catechisme to fight,	398	Drayton	71
Onely my losse is, that I am not there:	398	Drayton	91
Into a Phoenix, which is shee.	400	Lady Ogle	32
And this a coppie is of the Record.	400	Lady Ogle	40
Above his Reader, or his Prayser, is.	400	Beaumont	2
How much Architectonice is your owne!	402	Inigo Jones 1	10
A wodden Dagger, is a Dagger of wood	403	Inigo Jones 1	27
What is the cause you pompe it soe? I aske,	403	Inigo Jones 1	29
Oh, to make Boardes to speake! There is a taske	404	Inigo Jones 1	49
This is the money-gett, Mechanick Age!	404	Inigo Jones 1	52
Terme of the Architects is called Designe!	404	Inigo Jones 1	56
But in the practisd truth Destruction is	404	Inigo Jones 1	57
His name is Skeuopoios wee all knowe,	404	Inigo Jones 1	60
The Scene! the Engyne! but he now is come	404	Inigo Jones 1	62
He is, or would be the mayne Dominus doe	404	Inigo Jones 1	64
A Goddess is, then paynted Cloth, Deal-boards,	406	Inigo Jones 1	93
An Earle of show: for all thy worke is showe:	407	Inigo Jones 2	21
An Earle of show: for all thy worth is showe:	407	Inigo Jones 2	V 21
Thy Forehead is too narrow for my Brand.	408	Inigo Jones 3	14
Is to make cheape, the Lord, the lines, the price.	408	Detractor	6
Is so implexed, and laid in, between,	412	Ghyrlond	7
The second string is the sweet Almond bloome	412	Ghyrlond	9
The third, is from the garden cull'd, the Rose,	413	Ghyrlond	13
The fourth is humble Ivy, intersert,	413	Ghyrlond	17
But, that which summes all, is the Eglantine,	413	Ghyrlond	21
Which, of the field is clep'd the sweetest brier,	413	Ghyrlond	22
Now, for mine owne part, and it is but due,	415	Rutter	12
This is my censure. Now there is a new	415	Rutter	19
Office of Wit, a Mint, and (this is true)	415	Rutter	20
Our first of fruits, that is the prime of flowers	416	Welcome	2
to the Peake it is so hard-by,	417	Moon	23
and she is pleased.	417	Moon	36
hir minde is eased.	417	Moon	40
Although the gate were hard, the gayne is sweete.	418	Answer	7
Of Civill virtue, that hee now is not	420	Ode:If Men	12
or Malyce to make Faultes, which nowe is skill.	421	Censure	11
It is an Act of Tyranye, not Love,	422	Censure	18
Is her owne scourge, when it sustaines their states	422	Lucan	3
are distant, so is proffitt from just aymes.	422	Lucan	8
It is a lycense to doe ill, protectes,	423	Lucan	12
Wine it is the Milk of Venus,	657	Door Apollo	12
ISLE (See also ILE)			
So generall a gladnesse to an Isle,	238	U66 Queene	9
This sea-girt Isle upon:	240	U67 Muses	33
Aboute this Isle, and Charme the rounde, as when	421	Ode:If Men	39
ISLES			
The Hebrid Isles, and knowne	368	Ode Who saith	66
ISSUE			
And rich in issue to inherit all,	41	E44 Chuff	2
(Save that most masculine issue of his braine)	53	E79 Rutland	6
T'advance his doubtfull issue, and ore-flow	117	F13 Aubigny	40
It shall a ripe and timely issue fall,	119	F13 Aubigny	104
Bought Flatteries, the issue of his purse,	162	U15 Friend-Wars	13
His Issue, and all Circumstance of life,	171	U19 Elegy By	26
Who aided him, will thee, the issue of Joves braine.	175	U23 Himselfe	30
Who aided them, will thee, the issue of Joves braine.	175	U23 Himselfe	V 30
To ruine any issue of the braine?	203	U43 Vulcan	14
To ruine every issue of her braine?	203	U43 Vulcan	V 14
Was issue of the Taverne, or the Spit:	216	U45 Squib	8
To vent their Libels, and to issue rimes,	218	U47 Tribe	26
Have issue from the Barrell;	221	U48 Bacchus	32
With the growne issue of the Vine;	290	U85 Country	10
Lives in his issue, even so, the race	392	Shakespeare	66
IS'T			
What is't, fine Grand, makes thee my friendship flye,	51	E73 Fine Grand	1
Nor is't inconstancie to change	146	U6 Defence	13
Or faith in things? or is't your wealth and will	159	U14 Selden	36
Yet is't your vertue now I raise.	173	U22 Elegy Tho	4
What is't to me whether the French Designe	219	U47 Tribe	31
To lift to heaven: who is't not understands	234	U61 Epigram	8
Nor is't long since, they did with patience take	323	Horace	375
'T			
But thine, for which I doo't, so much exceeds!	46	E60 Mounteagle	8
What is't, fine Grand, makes thee my friendship flye,	51	E73 Fine Grand	1
As't were a challenge, or a borrowers letter?	51	E73 Fine Grand	3
Where, though 't be love, that to thy praise doth move	55	E86 Goodyere 2	7
Or is it some french statue? No: 'T doth move,	56	E88 Monsieur	13
I oft looke on false coyne, to know't from true:	68	E107 Hungry	3
And that so strong and deepe, as 't might be thought,	71	E110 Edmonds 1	7
Which (would the world not mis-call't flatterie)	79	E125 Uvedale	9
If't chance to me, I must not grutch.	101	F4 To the World	56
'T will be exacted of your name, whose sonne,	121	F14 Sydney	41
Therefore, Charis, you must do't,	140	U2 Promise	13
For I will so urge you to't,	140	U2 Promise	14
Nor is't inconstancie to change	146	U6 Defence	13
To have't exprest,	149	U8 Houre-glasse	10

```
                                                      Page      Title       Line
'T   (cont.)
    Who makes the one, so't be first, makes both.    .    .    .    .   152   U12 Corbet       40
    That puts it in his Debt-booke e're 't be done;  .    .    .    .   154   U13 Sacvile      34
    A Benefit; or that doth throw't away:            .    .    .    .   154   U13 Sacvile      42
    Or faith in things? or is't your wealth and will .    .    .    .   159   U14 Selden       36
    To do't with Cloth, or Stuffes, lusts name might merit;   .   .   164   U15 Friend-Wars  57
    Is done for gaine: If't be, 'tis not sincere.    .    .    .    .   169   U17 Friend-Debt   6
    That as the water makes things, put in't streight,   .   .   .   170   U18 Elegy Can     7
    Yet is't your vertue now I raise.                .    .    .    .   173   U22 Elegy Tho     4
    Why was't? did e're the Cloudes aske back their raine?   .   .   192   U38 Elegy 'Tis   56
    To all as fatall as't hath beene to me,          .    .    .    .   211   U43 Vulcan      192
    That keepe the warre, though now't be growne more tame,   .   .   214   U44 Speach       55
    What is't to me whether the French Designe       .    .    .    .   219   U47 Tribe        31
    Will cal't a Bastard, when a Prophet's borne.    .    .    .    .   223   U49 Pucell       46
    For 't were a narrow gladnesse, kept thine owne. .    .    .    .   225   U51 Bacon        18
    An ill commoditie! 'T must make good weight.     .    .    .    .   229   U54 Squib         6
    To lift to heaven: who is't not understands      .    .    .    .   234   U61 Epigram      8
    'T is not enough (thy pietie is such)            .    .    .    .   235   U62 Charles 1     3
    'T is not alone the Merchant, but the Clowne,    .    .    .    .   237   U64 Charles 3    19
    'T were better spare a Butt, then spill his Muse. .   .    .    .   241   U68 House-hold   12
    And praise them too.  O! what a fame 't will be? .    .    .    .   263   U78 Digby        25
    Beene trusted to thee: not to't selfe assign'd.  .    .    .    .   283   U84 Muse         20
    Nor is't long since, they did with patience take .    .    .    .   323   Horace         375
    On steele, though 't selfe be dull, and cannot cut.  .    .    .   325   Horace         434
    And, to your Fathers, and to mine; though 't be  .    .    .    .   331   Horace         577
    Of an entangling suit; and bring 't about:       .    .    .    .   333   Horace         604
    Yet who could have hit on't but the wise noddell .    .    .    .   379   Coryat 3         6
    Pies on't, you have his historicall faith.       .    .    .    .   380   Coryat 3        22
    Why much good doo't you! Be what beast you will,  .    .    .    .   403   Inigo Jones 1   21
    No faith's more firme, or flat, then where't doth creep.  .   .   413   Ghyrlond        20
    I shall think on't ere't be day.    .    .    .    .    .    .    .   417   Moon            11
    Or if't be the Gossipps happ    .    .    .    .    .    .    .   417   Moon            37
IT'
    Makes the poore Banck-side creature wet it' shoone,  .    .    .    84   E133 Voyage      30
    In it' owne hall; when these (in worthy scorne   .    .    .    .    85   E133 Voyage      31
IT   (See also YT, 'TIS, 'TWAS)
    To reade it well: that is, to understand.    .    .    .    .    .    27   E1 Reader        2
    It will be look'd for, booke, when some but see  .    .    .    .    27   E2 My Booke       1
    Deceive their malice, who could wish it so.      .    .    .    .    27   E2 My Booke       7
    For vulgar praise, doth it too dearely buy.      .    .    .    .    27   E2 My Booke      14
    Call'st a booke good, or bad, as it doth sell,   .    .    .    .    27   E3 Bookseller     2
    For the lucks sake, it thus much favour have,    .    .    .    .    27   E3 Bookseller     4
    To lye upon thy stall, till it be sought;        .    .    .    .    28   E3 Bookseller     5
    Not offer'd, as it made sute to be bought;       .    .    .    .    28   E3 Bookseller     6
    If, without these vile arts, it will not sell,   .    .    .    .    28   E3 Bookseller    11
    Send it to Bucklers-bury, there 'twill, well.    .    .    .    .    28   E3 Bookseller    12
    Tells you it is a hot-house: So it ma',    .    .    .    .    .    29   E7 Hot-house      3
    At court I met it, in clothes brave enough,      .    .    .    .    30   E11 Something     1
    To seeme a statesman: as I neere it came,    .    .    .    .    .    30   E11 Something     3
    It made me a great face, I ask'd the name.       .    .    .    .    30   E11 Something     4
    A lord, it cryed, buried in flesh, and blood,    .    .    .    .    30   E11 Something     5
    The taylor brings a suite home; he it 'ssayes,   .    .    .    .    30   E12 Shift         9
    Lookes o're the bill, likes it: and say's, god payes.    .    .    30   E12 Shift        10
    Where, afterwards, it grew a butter-flye:    .    .    .    .    .    31   E15 Court-worm    3
    Thou more; that with it every day, dar'st jest   .    .    .    .    32   E16 Brain-hardy   2
    When both it is the old way, and the true.    .    .    .    .    .    32   E18 Censurer      2
    It makes the father, lesse, to rue.     .    .    .    .    .    .    33   E22 Daughter      4
    To it, thy language, letters, arts, best life,   .    .    .    .    34   E23 Donne 1       7
    And thou, right guiltlesse, may'st plead to it, why?    .    .    36   E29 Tilter        2
    He that feares death, or mournes it, in the just,    .    .    .    37   E34 Death         1
    Beleeve it, Guiltie, if you loose your shame,    .    .    .    .    38   E38 Guiltie 2     7
    Conquer'd hath both life and it.     .    .    .    .    .    .    .    39   E40 Ratcliffe    12
    Such her quaint practise is, so it allures,      .    .    .    .    39   E41 Gypsee        3
    Which though it did but panick terror prove,     .    .    .    .    43   E51 James 3       3
    Dispraise my worke, then praise it frostily:     .    .    .    .    43   E52 Courtling     2
    It was as if thou printed had'st an oath,    .    .    .    .    .    43   E53 Old-end       5
    What fate is mine, that so it selfe bereaves?    .    .    .    .    44   E55 Beaumont      7
    As we, the rob'd, leave rage, and pittie it.     .    .    .    .    44   E56 Poet-Ape      4
    And, told of this, he slights it. Tut, such crimes   .    .    .    45   E56 Poet-Ape      9
    May judge it to be his, as well as ours.     .    .    .    .    .    45   E56 Poet-Ape     12
    Durst thinke it great, and worthy wonder too,    .    .    .    .    46   E60 Mounteagle    7
    Is it the paine affrights? that's soone forgot.  .    .    .    .    46   E62 Would-bee     5
    That can restore that.  Will it hurt your feature?   .    .    .    46   E62 Would-bee     7
    Curst be my voyce if it lye dumbe, or hid    .    .    .    .    .    47   E63 Salisbury 2 V 11
    Whose house, if it no other honor had,    .    .    .    .    .    48   E66 Cary           3
    Or thou more happie, it to justifie    .    .    .    .    .    .    49   E66 Cary           8
    It may be much, or little, in the cause.     .    .    .    .    .    49   E66 Cary          16
    Before thou wert it, in each good mans heart.    .    .    .    .    49   E67 Suffolk       10
    In life, that can employ it; and takes hold      .    .    .    .    50   E70 Wm Roe 1      3
    Though life be short, let us not make it so.     .    .    .    .    50   E70 Wm Roe 1      8
    Goe high, or low, as thou wilt value it.     .    .    .    .    .    50   E72 Court-ling    4
    Hence was it, that the destinies decreed     .    .    .    .    .    53   E79 Rutland       5
    And hath it, in his powers, to make his way!     .    .    .    .    53   E80 Life/Death    4
    And here, it should be one of our first strifes, .    .    .    .    54   E80 Life/Death    6
    So to front death, as men might judge us past it.    .    .    .    54   E80 Life/Death    7
    For good men but see death, the wicked tast it.  .    .    .    .    54   E80 Life/Death    8
    A line unto thee, till the world it know;    .    .    .    .    .    54   E81 Proule        2
    Thy wit lives by it, Proule, and belly too.      .    .    .    .    54   E81 Proule        6
    I would have spent: how every Muse should know it,   .    .    .    55   E84 Bedford 2     7
    And Phoebus-selfe should be at eating it.    .    .    .    .    .    55   E84 Bedford 2     8
    Make it your gift. See whither that will beare mee.  .    .    .    55   E84 Bedford 2    10
    It was a knowledge, that begat that love.    .    .    .    .    .    55   E86 Goodyere 2    8
    Or is it some french statue? No: 'T doth move,   .    .    .    .    56   E88 Monsieur      13
```

IT (cont.)

	Page	Title	Line
And stoupe, and cringe. O then, it needs must prove	56	E88 Monsieur	14
And it is hop'd, that shee, like Milo, wull	57	E90 Mill	17
If the States make peace, how it will goe	59	E92 New Crie	30
But, when they heard it tax'd, tooke more offence.	60	E94 Bedford 3	10
Which Fate (it seemes) caus'd in the historie,	61	E95 Savile	11
It is the next deed, and a great one too.	61	E95 Savile	26
And what would hurt his vertue makes it still.	63	E98 Th Roe 1	6
But much it now availes, what's done, of whom:	64	E99 Th Roe 2	7
It is the faire acceptance, Sir, creates	64	E101 Supper	7
It is an Epigramme, on all man-kind;	66	E102 Pembroke	2
Whose life, ev'n they, that envie it, must praise;	66	E102 Pembroke	16
Need any Muses praise to give it fame?	66	E103 L Wroth 1	6
Which is, it selfe, the imprese of the great,	66	E103 L Wroth 1	7
Becomes none more then you, who need it least.	67	E103 L Wroth 1	14
Or did our times require it, to behold	67	E104 Montgomery	3
And like it too; if they looke equally:	67	E104 Montgomery	15
Or valour, or thy judgement seasoning it,	68	E106 E Herbert	6
Not that I love it, more, then I will you.	68	E107 Hungry	4
And did not shame it with my actions, then,	70	E108 Soldiers	7
Think'st thou it is meere fortune, that can win?	72	E112 Gamster	3
Troth, if it be, I pitty thy ill lucke;	73	E112 Gamster	17
Nor scarce dost colour for it, which is lesse.	73	E112 Gamster	20
By speaking well o' the company' it 's in.	74	E115 Honest Man	8
And him it layes on; if he be not there.	74	E115 Honest Man	16
Tell's of him, all the tales, it selfe then makes;	74	E115 Honest Man	17
But, if it shall be question'd, undertakes,	74	E115 Honest Man	18
It will deny all; and forsweare it too:	74	E115 Honest Man	19
Not that it feares, but will not have to doo	74	E115 Honest Man	20
At every meale, where it doth dine, or sup,	74	E115 Honest Man	23
The cloth's no sooner gone, but it gets up	74	E115 Honest Man	24
Describ'd, it 's thus: Defin'd would you it have?	75	E115 Honest Man	33
And those that lack'd it, to suspect at length,	75	E116 Jephson	6
Lust it comes out, that gluttony went in.	76	E118 Gut	6
But dost it out of judgement, not disease;	76	E119 Shelton	8
I would restore, and keepe it ever such;	78	E122 Rudyerd 2	8
Leave it buryed in this vault.	79	E124 Elizabeth	8
Th'other let it sleepe with death:	79	E124 Elizabeth	10
Fitter, where it dyed, to tell,	79	E124 Elizabeth	11
Then that it liv'd at all. Farewell.	79	E124 Elizabeth	12
Phoebus replyed. Bold head, it is not shee:	80	E126 Mrs Cary	7
But, as it is (the Child of Ignorance,	83	E132 Sylvester	3
And in it, two more horride knaves, then Charon.	84	E133 Voyage	12
It was the day, what time the powerfull Moone	84	E133 Voyage	29
Act a brave worke, call it thy last adventry:	85	E133 Voyage	57
One said, it was bold Briareus, or the beadle,	86	E133 Voyage	81
The other thought it Hydra, or the rock	86	E133 Voyage	83
But, comming neere, they found it but a liter,	86	E133 Voyage	85
So huge, it seem'd, they could by no meanes quite her.	86	E133 Voyage	86
Crack did report it selfe, as if a cloud	86	E133 Voyage	94
To answere me. And sure, it was th'intent	87	E133 Voyage	107
Had it beene seconded, and not in fume	87	E133 Voyage	109
And that is when it is the Lord Maiors foist.	87	E133 Voyage	120
Whether it languishing stucke upon the wall,	87	E133 Voyage	136
Or, that it lay, heap'd like an usurers masse,	88	E133 Voyage	139
But still, it seem'd, the ranknesse did convince 'hem.	88	E133 Voyage	152
Thrise did it spit: thrise div'd. At last, it view'd	88	E133 Voyage	162
The Voyage it selfe.	84	E134 Voyage	Ttl
It is enough, they once did get	93	F1 Why write no	5
As if it had expected such a guest!	96	F2 Penshurst	88
And makes sleepe softer then it is!	97	F3 Wroth	20
Who, for it, makes thy house his court;	97	F3 Wroth	24
Who, for it, makes thy lodge his court;	97	F3 Wroth	V 24
As if in Saturnes raigne it were;	98	F3 Wroth	50
And each where boast it as his merit,	99	F3 Wroth	78
And brooding o're it sit, with broadest eyes,	99	F3 Wroth	83
Though poyson, thinke it a great fate.	99	F3 Wroth	90
Our fraile condition it is such,	101	F4 To the World	54
Follow a shaddow, it still flies you;	104	F7 Women but	1
Seeme to flye it, it will pursue:	104	F7 Women but	2
Any paines; yea, thinke it price,	105	F8 Sicknesse	27
Move it, as their humblest sute,	106	F8 Sicknesse	46
Move it, as their humble sute,	106	F8 Sicknesse	V 46
As giving it a hope, that there	106	F9 Celia 3	11
It could not withered bee.	106	F9 Celia 3	12
It would not withered bee.	106	F9 Celia 3	V 12
And sent'st it backe to mee:	106	F9 Celia 3	14
Since when it growes, and smells, I sweare,	106	F9 Celia 3	15
Since when it lives, and smells, I sweare,	106	F9 Celia 3	V 15
Not of it selfe, but thee.	106	F9 Celia 3	16
Not like it selfe, but thee.	106	F9 Celia 3	V 16
Close, the close cause of it.	109	F11 Epode	16
It is a golden chaine let downe from heaven,	110	F11 Epode	47
And, for it, life, conscience, yea, soules are given,	113	F12 Rutland	4
While it makes huishers serviceable men,	113	F12 Rutland	9
Though never after; whiles it gaynes the voyce	113	F12 Rutland	11
Though never after; whiles it gaynes the will	113	F12 Rutland	V 11
The foole that gave it; who will want, and weepe,	113	F12 Rutland	13
The foole that gave it; that will want, and weepe,	113	F12 Rutland	V 13
While thus it buyes great grace, and hunts poore fame;	113	F12 Rutland	15
While thus it gets grace, and hunts poore fame;	113	F12 Rutland	V 15
But let this drosse carry what price it will	114	F12 Rutland	27
Were it to thinke, that you should not inherit	114	F12 Rutland	32

IT (cont.)

	Page	Title	Line
It is the Muse, alone, can raise to heaven,	114	F12 Rutland	41
Then which, a nobler heaven it selfe knowes not.	115	F12 Rutland	67
With every vertue, wheresoere it move,	116	F13 Aubigny	8
Such as suspect them-selves, and thinke it fit	117	F13 Aubigny	13
If it may stand with your soft blush to heare	117	F13 Aubigny	22
Remov'd, as you from need to have it such.	117	F13 Aubigny	28
It perfect, proper, pure, and naturall,	117	F13 Aubigny	32
As I, can say, and see it doth excell.	117	F13 Aubigny	34
Though it reject not those of Fortune: such	117	F13 Aubigny	45
(They finde it both so wittie, and safe to give.)	118	F13 Aubigny	76
Whether it be a face they weare, or no.	118	F13 Aubigny	80
And call it their brave sinne. For such there be	119	F13 Aubigny	85
It shall a ripe and timely issue fall,	119	F13 Aubigny	104
Because nor it can change, nor such a minde.	120	F13 Aubigny	124
Strive all right wayes it can,	121	F14 Sydney	25
But it must, straight, my melancholy bee?	122	F15 Heaven	2
Is it interpreted in me disease,	122	F15 Heaven	3
With holy Paul, lest it be thought the breath	122	F15 Heaven	24
This All of nothing, gavest it forme, and fate,	127	U1 Trinitie	18
And breath'st into it, life, and light, with state	127	U1 Trinitie	19
O grant it me!	128	U1 Trinitie	36
The Angels so did sound it,	130	U1 Nativitie	3
Yet search'd, and true they found it.	130	U1 Nativitie	6
The Fathers wisedome will'd it so,	130	U1 Nativitie	13
Let it not your wonder move,	131	U2 Excuse	1
And it is not alwayes face,	131	U2 Excuse	7
Of whose Beautie it was sung,	131	U2 Excuse	19
Left it sticking in my heart:	133	U2 Suffered	16
Doe but looke on her Haire, it is bright	134	U2 Triumph	13
As Loves starre when it riseth!	134	U2 Triumph	14
Sheds it selfe through the face,	134	U2 Triumph	18
Before rude hands have touch'd it?	134	U2 Triumph	22
Before the soyle hath smutch'd it?	134	U2 Triumph	24
With the Lace that doth it deck,	137	U2 Cupid	30
Where, how it would have relish'd well;	139	U2 Another	14
As the Downe, and shew it oft;	141	U2 Her man	26
Rising through it e're it came;	141	U2 Her man	29
Yet if it be not knowne,	147	U7 Nymph	5
It were a plague 'bove scorne,	147	U7 Nymph	12
And yet it cannot be foreborne,	147	U7 Nymph	13
As it would be to each a fame:	148	U7 Nymph	34
For else it could not be,	149	U9 Picture	2
or else it could not be,	149	U9 Picture	V 2
It vent it selfe, but as it would,	151	U12 Corbet	2
His lookes would so correct it, when	152	U12 Corbet	27
It chid the vice, yet not the Men.	152	U12 Corbet	28
Nor wants it here through penurie, or sloth,	152	U12 Corbet	39
As I did feele it done, as soone as meant:	153	U13 Sacvile	12
This Good from you, as freely will it owe;	153	U13 Sacvile	14
Or if he did it not to succour me,	154	U13 Sacvile	29
That puts it in his Debt-booke e're 't be done;	154	U13 Sacvile	34
His Groomes to witnesse; or else lets it fall	154	U13 Sacvile	36
Lest Ayre, or Print, but flies it: Such men would	154	U13 Sacvile	45
Run from the Conscience of it, if they could.	154	U13 Sacvile	46
And spunge-like with it dry up the blood quite:	155	U13 Sacvile	69
Then give it to the Hound that did him bite;	155	U13 Sacvile	70
O, is it so? knowes he so much? and will	155	U13 Sacvile	73
I not deny it, but to helpe the need	155	U13 Sacvile	75
And it is paid 'hem with a trembling zeale,	155	U13 Sacvile	85
If it were cleare, but being so in cloud	155	U13 Sacvile	87
Sure there is Misterie in it, I not know,	156	U13 Sacvile	97
And you, Sir, know it well, to whom I write,	156	U13 Sacvile	109
And feeles it; Else he tarries by the Beast.	156	U13 Sacvile	117
Or on the sudden. It were strange that he	156	U13 Sacvile	125
Then stands it a triumphall marke! then Men	157	U13 Sacvile	139
It was erected; and still walking under	157	U13 Sacvile	141
To aske it: though in most of workes it be	158	U14 Selden	7
Rather then Office, when it doth or may	158	U14 Selden	9
And what I write? and vexe it many dayes	159	U14 Selden	25
Of what it tells us) weav'd in to instruct.	160	U14 Selden	52
A banke against it. Nothing but the round	160	U14 Selden	63
But nought beyond. He thou hast given it to,	161	U14 Selden	71
It true respects. He will not only love,	161	U14 Selden	73
Among my commings in, and see it mount,	161	U14 Selden	80
Their vitious ease, and be o'rewhelm'd with it.	162	U15 Friend-Wars	4
It is a call to keepe the spirits alive	162	U15 Friend-Wars	5
Till envie wound, or maime it at a blow!	162	U15 Friend-Wars	22
Honour'd at once, and envi'd (if it can	162	U15 Friend-Wars	24
Thither it flowes. How much did Stallion spend	163	U15 Friend-Wars	47
With Velvet, Plush, and Tissues, it is spirit.	164	U15 Friend-Wars	58
If it be thought kild like her Embrions; for,	165	U15 Friend-Wars	96
Is it for these that Fine-man meets the street	165	U15 Friend-Wars	106
Is it that man pulls on himselfe Disease?	165	U15 Friend-Wars	114
Or by Damnation voids it? or by stealth?	166	U15 Friend-Wars	116
Well, let it goe. Yet this is better, then	166	U15 Friend-Wars	145
Runs sweetly, as it had his Lordships Soule;	167	U15 Friend-Wars	148
Although, perhaps it has, what's that to me,	167	U15 Friend-Wars	149
It might thy patience richly pay:	168	U16 Gray	
If it be thus; Come Love, and Fortune goe,	170	U18 Elegy Can	21
At fifty yeares, almost, to value it,	171	U20 Shrub	5
Or have the least of Good, but what it must	171	U20 Shrub	7
His name in any mettall, it would breake.	172	U21 Ltl Shrub	2

IT (cont.)

	Page	Title	Line
Which if it kindle not, but scant	174	U22 Elegy Tho	33
It is the common Moath,	174	U23 Himselfe	5
And thinke it Poesie?	175	U23 Himselfe	22
Doth vindicate it to eternitie.	175	U24 Frontispice	4
Happy in that faire honour it hath gain'd,	180	U26 Ode High	14
So speake (as yet it is not mute)	181	U27 Ode Helen	4
I That have beene a lover, and could shew it,	182	U28 Worth	1
Nor is my Muse, or I asham'd to owe it	182	U28 Worth	5
Both braines and hearts; and mine now best doe know it:	182	U28 Worth	8
May his Sense, when it would meet	184	U29 Fit of Rime	55
Thinke, yea and boast, that they have done it so	186	U32 Elsmere	12
Mak'st it religion to grow rich by Crimes!	187	U33 Councellour	16
But first dost vexe, and search it! If not sound,	187	U33 Councellour	19
It is an Act of tyrannie, not love,	190	U37 Friend-Book	25
Forgive it, as my frailtie, and not me.	190	U37 Friend-Book	30
It is a Darknesse hath blockt up my sense,	191	U38 Elegy 'Tis	5
And drives it in to eat on my offence,	191	U38 Elegy 'Tis	6
Or there to sterve it. Helpe, O you that may	191	U38 Elegy 'Tis	7
Thinke it was frailtie, Mistris, thinke me man,	192	U38 Elegy 'Tis	31
An ill-affected limbe (what e're it aile)	192	U38 Elegy 'Tis	45
Would live his glory that could keepe it on;	192	U38 Elegy 'Tis	48
And then his thunder frights more, then it kills.	193	U38 Elegy 'Tis	70
It shakes even him, that all things else doth shake.	193	U38 Elegy 'Tis	72
And with the vulgar doth it not obtaine	193	U38 Elegy 'Tis	81
And then I taste it. But as men drinke up	197	U40 Elegy That	3
Of parting, drowne it in the hope to meet	197	U40 Elegy That	7
As neither wine doe rack it out, or mirth.	197	U40 Elegy That	18
What it is like: And doe not thinke they can	199	U41 Elegy Since	3
It is as if a night should shade noone-day,	199	U41 Elegy Since	5
Where we must feele it Darke for halfe a yeare.	199	U41 Elegy Since	8
You would restore it? No, that's worth a feare,	199	U41 Elegy Since	15
As if it were not worthy to be there:	199	U41 Elegy Since	16
O, keepe it still; for it had rather be	199	U41 Elegy Since	17
And so I spare it. Come what can become	199	U41 Elegy Since	19
Till I may see both it and you agen.	199	U41 Elegy Since	22
(If they be faire and worth it) have their lives	200	U42 Elegy Let	20
It is a ryming Age, and Verses swarme	200	U42 Elegy Let	27
It is not likely I should now looke downe	200	U42 Elegy Let	37
Or slipper was left off, and kisse it too,	201	U42 Elegy Let	56
Was it because thou wert of old denied	203	U43 Vulcan	11
And for it lose his eyes with Gun-powder,	208	U43 Vulcan	121
Which, though it were the Fort of the whole Parish,	209	U43 Vulcan	133
Left! and wit since to cover it with Tiles.	209	U43 Vulcan	138
The Brethren, they streight nois'd it out for Newes,	209	U43 Vulcan	139
There were, that streight did nose it out for newes,	209	U43 Vulcan	V139
And cry'd, it was a threatning to the beares;	209	U43 Vulcan	146
Though but in daunces, it shall know his power;	210	U43 Vulcan	157
Though but in daunces, it shall know high power;	210	U43 Vulcan	V157
Though but in daunger, it shall know thy power;	210	U43 Vulcan	V157
Troy, though it were so much his Venus care.	210	U43 Vulcan	160
Troy, though it were so much thy Venus joycare.	210	U43 Vulcan	V160
Pox on your flameship, Vulcan; if it be	211	U43 Vulcan	191
Pox on your fire workes, Vulcan; if it be	211	U43 Vulcan	V191
For they did see it the last tilting well,	213	U44 Speach	6
How it held out! how (last) 'twas taken in!	213	U44 Speach	22
So, in that ground, as soone it grew to be	214	U44 Speach	37
My gentle Arthur; that it might be said	216	U45 Squib	3
That hearkens to a Jacks-pulse, when it goes.	216	U45 Squib	6
It is a richer Purchase then of land.	216	U45 Squib	26
As make it their proficiencie, how much	218	U47 Tribe	12
That to speake well, thinke it above all sinne,	218	U47 Tribe	19
I have decreed; keepe it from waves, and presse;	219	U47 Tribe	57
Lest it be justled, crack'd, made nought, or lesse:	219	U47 Tribe	58
And free it from all question to preserve.	220	U47 Tribe	72
Before his braine doe know it;	221	U48 Bacchus	30
Shall feast it, thou maist love there	221	U48 Bacchus	38
Be it he hold Communion	221	U48 Bacchus	43
Thinkes it selfe nought, though she should valew it.	223	U49 Pucell	24
Or if it would, the Court is the worst place,	223	U49 Pucell	43
The same it was inspir'd, rich, and refin'd.	225	U50 Countesse	30
It will be shame for them, if they have none.	225	U50 Countesse	36
How comes it all things so about thee smile?	225	U51 Bacon	2
Pardon, I read it in thy face, the day	225	U51 Bacon	5
'Tis a brave cause of joy, let it be knowne,	225	U51 Bacon	17
Which if in compasse of no Art it came	227	U52 Answer	10
But whilst you curious were to have it be	227	U52 Answer	13
You made it a brave piece, but not like me.	227	U52 Answer	15
If I doe lose it: And, without a Tale,	229	U54 Squib	3
And hold me to it close; to stand upright	229	U54 Squib	9
It doe not come: One piece I have in store,	229	U54 Squib	15
A booke to a few lynes: but, it was fit	230	U56 Covell	3
You won them too, your oddes did merit it.	230	U56 Covell	4
The Parish will know it.	232	U57 Burges	26
What each man sayes of it, and of what coat	232	U58 Book-seller	4
Wonder to Valour! No, it is the Law	233	U59 Newcastle	14
Valour! to sleight it, being done to you!	233	U59 Newcastle	16
To bend, to breake, provoke, or suffer it!	233	U59 Newcastle	18
To bend, or breake, provoke, or suffer it!	233	U59 Newcastle	V 18
Because it durst have noblier dy'd.	234	U60 La-ware	18
And as it turnes our joyfull yeare about,	236	U64 Charles 3	5
Haile Mary, full of grace, it once was said,	238	U66 Queene	1
As in this Prince? Let it be lawfull, so	238	U66 Queene	11

```
                                                    Page    Title       Line
IT  (cont.)
    Ring thou it Holy-day.                      .    239    U67 Muses      6
    May wish it selfe a sense,      .    .    .     239    U67 Muses     23
    Whilst it the Dittie heares.         .    .     239    U67 Muses     24
    It is not growing like a tree   .    .          245    U70 Ode       65
    Although it fall, and die that night;      .    245    U70 Ode       71
    It was the Plant, and flowre of light.     .    245    U70 Ode       72
    Accept this garland, plant it on thy head,      245    U70 Ode       77
    Where it were friendships schisme,    .    .    246    U70 Ode       90
    The good, and durst not practise it, were glad  247    U70 Ode      119
    Dare thinke it, to relieve, no lesse renowne,   248    U71 Treasurer  14
    This is King Charles his Day. Speake it, thou Towre,  249  U72 King    1
    This is King Charles his birth day. Speake it, thou Towre,  249  U72 King  V  1
    Discharge it 'bout the Iland, in an houre,      249    U72 King       3
    Let Ireland meet it out at Sea, halfe way,      249    U72 King       5
    Dreame thou could'st hurt it; but before thou wake  250  U73 Weston   11
    T'effect it, feele, thou'ast made thine owne heart ake.  250  U73 Weston  12
    With all the fruit shall follow it,       .    251    U74 Weston     23
    It is the kindly Season of the time,     .    253    U75 Epithalam.  25
    It is their Grace, and favour, that makes seene,  255  U75 Epithalam.  89
    It brings Friends Joy, Foes Griefe, Posteritie Fame;  256  U75 Epithalam.  114
    It is: to th' envious meant,          .    .    256    U75 Epithalam.  119
    Some houres before it should, that these may know  256  U75 Epithalam.  146
    For Fame keepes Vertue up, and it Posteritie.   257    U75 Epithalam.  152
    —Doth most humbly show it,         .    .    .    259    U76 Petition    3
    (For with both the Muse it fed)        .    .    259    U76 Petition   V 16
    Aloud; and (happ'ly) it may last as long.       261    U77 Treasurer   28
    As loude; and (happ'ly) it may last as long.    261    U77 Treasurer  V 28
    That they may take it eccho'd by the Floods.    265    U79 New-yeares  53
    Would they would understand it! Princes are     268    U80 Christning   5
    It is a large faire table, and a true,    .    269    U81 Pawlet      15
    It is too neere of kin to Heaven, the Soule,    269    U81 Pawlet      29
    It is too neere of kin to God, the Soule,  .    269    U81 Pawlet     V 29
    And, calling truth to witnesse, make it good    270    U81 Pawlet     V 35
    But a fain'd way, doth rob it of the true.      270    U81 Pawlet      38
    But a fain'd way, doth spoyle it of the true.   270    U81 Pawlet     V 38
    Just as she in it liv'd! and so exempt     .    270    U81 Pawlet      48
    Who saw the way was made it! and were sent      270    U81 Pawlet      65
    That saw the way was made it! and were sent     270    U81 Pawlet     V 65
    And trusted so, as it deposited lay    .    .    271    U81 Pawlet      81
    And wish her state lesse happie then it is!     271    U81 Pawlet      84
    Speake it, you bold Penates, you that stand     274    U84 Descent      7
    Needs nought to cloath it but the ayre.         275    U84 Body         8
    Till, like her face, it doe appeare,      .    276    U84 Body        15
    With all that Youth, or it can bring:     .    276    U84 Body        22
    Whose 'tis: but if it favour find,     .    .    277    U84 Body        31
    But these are like a Mind, not it.         .    278    U84 Mind        12
    But what's of kinne to whence it came.          278    U84 Mind        16
    I call you Muse; now make it true:        .    278    U84 Mind        21
    'Tis got where it can try the fire.       .    278    U84 Mind        28
    As it another Nature were,        .    .    .    279    U84 Mind        30
    It moveth all; and makes a flight      .    .    279    U84 Mind        31
    Whose Notions when it will expresse    .    .    279    U84 Mind        33
    In speech; it is with that excesse        .    279    U84 Mind        34
    As what it spoke, it planted there.       .    279    U84 Mind        36
    It selfe to us, and come so nigh       .    .    279    U84 Mind        43
    Is it because it sees us dull,            .    279    U84 Mind        45
    And stuck in clay here, it would pull     .    279    U84 Mind        46
    For her t'inhabit? There is it.        .    .    280    U84 Mind        52
    As it slid moulded off from Heaven.       .    280    U84 Mind        56
    Where it may run to any good;          .    .    280    U84 Mind        62
    And where it stayes, it there becomes     .    280    U84 Mind        63
    In thee, faire Mansion, let it rest,      .    281    U84 Mind        69
    It is a wretched thing to trust to reedes;      281    U84 Kenelme     16
    And set it forth; the rest were Cobwebs fine,   282    U84 Muse         5
    It rages, runs, flies, stands, and would provoke  283  U84 Muse       24
    The world to ruine with it; in her Fall,   .    283    U84 Muse        25
    Sure, I am dead, and know it not! I feele       283    U84 Muse        29
    I envie it the Angels amitie!          .    .    283    U84 Muse        36
    The joy of Saints! the Crowne for which it lives,  283  U84 Muse       37
    This as it guilty is, or guiltlesse found,      284    U84 Muse        56
    Nothing can more adorne it, then the seat       284    U84 Muse        71
    That she is in, or, make it more compleat?      284    U84 Muse        72
    Equall with Angels, and Co-heires of it?        286    U84 Muse       146
    Each line, as it were graphick, in the face!    287    U84 Muse       154
    For 'twas himselfe who form'd, and gave it her.  287   U84 Muse       156
    She had, and it became her! she was fit         287    U84 Muse       161
    T' have knowne no envy, but by suffring it!     287    U84 Muse       162
    To one she said, Doe this, he did it; So        287    U84 Muse       169
    The holy Altars, when it least presumes.        288    U84 Muse       188
    Let us not then rush blindly on unto it,        294    U88 Petronius    3
    Like lustfull beasts, that onely know to doe it:  294  U88 Petronius    4
    Of daring all, hath still beene given; we know it:  305  Horace        12
    Of daring ought, hath still beene given; we know it:  338  Horace     V 12
    Unto your strength, and long examine it,        307    Horace          54
    Unto your strength, and long be turning it:     339    Horace        V 56/ 54
    New names of things.  It hath beene ever free,  309    Horace          83
    Shall perish: so farre off it is, the state,    309    Horace          99
    Before the Judge, it hangs, and waites report.  309    Horace         112
    The place allotted it, with decent thewes.      311    Horace         125
    The place allotted it, with decent praise.      341    Horace       V131/125
    It much will differ, if a God speake, than,     313    Horace         161
    It much will sway whether a god speak, than;    342    Horace        V161
```

	Page	Title	Line

IT (cont.)

(As if he knew it) rapps his hearer to	315	Horace	212
Heare, what it is the People, and I desire:	315	Horace	219
It still must favour good men, and to these	317	Horace	280
Be wonne a friend; it must both sway, and bend	317	Horace	281
The Tragedie, and carried it about,	319	Horace	312
Yet he that offers at it, may sweat much,	321	Horace	351
Will take offence, at this: Nor, though it strike	321	Horace	361
Take just offence at this: nor, though it strike	347	Horace	V353/361
Receive, or give it an applause, the more.	321	Horace	364
Receive, or give it any Crowne the more.	347	Horace	V356/364
Of Trimeter, when yet it was sixe-pac'd,	323	Horace	373
So rare, as with some taxe it doth ingage	323	Horace	383
Happier then wretched art, and doth, by it,	325	Horace	420
But a well-compass'd mouth to utter it;	327	Horace	462
An ounce, what makes it then? The halfe pound just;	327	Horace	471
It would, must be: lest it alive would draw	329	Horace	509
The hand, and mind would, but it will resound	329	Horace	522
Which it doth threaten. Therefore, where I see	329	Horace	525
If ne're so little it depart the first,	331	Horace	563
To send it to be judg'd by Metius eare,	331	Horace	576
But, now, it is enough to say; I make	333	Horace	593
And twice, or thrice had 'ssayd it, still in vaine:	333	Horace	626
And twice, or thrice assay'd it, but in vain:	354	Horace	V626
To let it downe, who knowes, if he did cast	335	Horace	656
So with this Authors Readers will it thrive:	362	Author	12
It carries Palme with it, (where e're it goes)	363	Riches	6
Respect, and observation; it uncovers	363	Riches	7
Enforcing yron doores to yeeld it way,	363	Riches	9
It bends the hams of Gossip Vigilance,	363	Riches	11
It thawes the frostiest, and most stiffe disdaine:	363	Riches	13
Receive it for a Fable,	364	Phoenix	2
Betray it true:	366	Ode Who saith	6
And conquers all things, yea it selfe, at length.	367	Ode Who saith	56
It is inough, their griefe shall know	369	Ode Who saith	113
And all your Booke (when it is throughly scan'd)	370	Author	5
They saw it halfe, damd thy whole play, and more;	371	Fletcher	8
Their motives were, since it had not to do	371	Fletcher	9
It covers, first, a Virgin; and then, one	371	Epitaph	3
Up so much truth, as could I it pursue	372	Epitaph	13
It should rather have bene Tom that a horse did lack.	374	Coryat 1	15
Marry he sets it out at his owne charge;	378	Coryat 2	83
To his strength, hath measur'd it out with his feet.	379	Coryat 3	4
To write it with the selfe same spirit he went,	379	Coryat 3	14
He sayes to the world, let any man mend it,	379	Coryat 3	15
In five monthes he went it, in five monthes he pend it.	379	Coryat 3	16
Hymens amends, to make it worth his fault.	384	Somerset	14
It fits not onely him that makes a Booke,	385	Husband	1
It must be thine owne judgment, yet, that sends	386	Browne	7
nor yet inscription like it. Write but that;	387	Cavendish	9
nor yet inscription like it writt but that	387	Cavendish	V 9
And teach your nephewes it to aemulate:	387	Cavendish	10
it will be matter lowd inoughe to tell	387	Cavendish	11
Olde Hesiods Ore, and give it us; but thine,	388	Chapman	2
As, now, of all men, it is call'd thy Trade:	389	Chapman	11
To say but one, were single. Then it chimes,	389	Aleman	3
Upon it, but will loath, or let it passe,	389	Aleman	9
To your desert, who'have done it, Friend. And this	389	Aleman	21
It was for gentle Shakespeare cut;	390	Reader	2
Which, when it sounds at best, but eccho's right;	390	Shakespeare	8
And thinke to ruine, where it seem'd to raise.	391	Shakespeare	12
(And himselfe with it) that he thinkes to frame;	392	Shakespeare	62
Sweet Swan of Avon! what a sight it were	392	Shakespeare	71
To see (who'it is?) A noble Countesse, greate,	394	Jane Ogle	3
And the world in it, I begin to doubt,	395	May	4
It makes me ravish'd with just wonder, cry	395	May	13
It hath beene question'd, Michael, if I bee	396	Drayton	1
It was no Dreame! I was awake, and saw!	396	Drayton	11
It cast a beame as when the chear-full Sun	396	Drayton	17
As it had beene the circle of the Arts!	396	Drayton	22
I found it pure, and perfect Poesy,	397	Drayton	24
I saw, and read, it was thy Barons Warres!	397	Drayton	42
That reade it? that are ravish'd! such was I	397	Drayton	53
Thy list of aydes, and force, for so it is:	398	Drayton	62
This booke! it is a Catechisme to fight,	398	Drayton	71
I feele it by mine owne, that over flow,	398	Drayton	77
I gratulate it to thee, and thy Ends,	398	Drayton	89
Her Children, and Grand-children, reed it heere!	399	Lady Ogle	2
Transmitt it to your Nephewes, Freinds, Allies,	399	Lady Ogle	3
To veiw the truth and owne it. Doe but looke	399	Lady Ogle	5
With pause upon it; make this page your booke;	399	Lady Ogle	6
Or without angles, it was shee!	399	Lady Ogle	16
Of weight, or fashion, it was shee.	399	Lady Ogle	24
This Booke will live; It hath a Genius: This	400	Beaumont	1
A Trench against it, nor a Battry plac't?	401	Beaumont	14
Or making of the Propertyes it meane?	402	Inigo Jones 1	12
Vizors or Anticks? or it comprehend	402	Inigo Jones 1	13
Though gold or Ivory haftes would make it good.	403	Inigo Jones 1	28
Though gold or Ivory haftes cant make it good.	403	Inigo Jones 1	V 28
What is the cause you pompe it soe? I aske,	403	Inigo Jones 1	29
And not fall downe before it? and confess	406	Inigo Jones 1	91
Besydes, his Man may merit it, and be	406	Inigo Jones 2	5
Sir Inigo doth feare it as I heare	407	Inigo Jones 3	1

IT   (cont.)
Shall not worke out unto it, such a fame.   409   Detractor   12
Thou art not worth it. Who will care to knowe   .   .   .   409   Detractor   13
You learn'd it well; and for it, serv'd your time   .   .   410   Brome   9
It was not so of old: Men tooke up trades   .   .   .   410   Brome   13
Thy blatant Muse abroad, and teach it rather   .   .   411   Gill   11
As it, alone, (and onely it) had roome,   .   .   .   412   Ghyrlond   11
Or why to like; they found, it all was new,   .   .   415   Rutter   9
Now, for mine owne part, and it is but due,   .   .   415   Rutter   12
(You have deserv'd it from me) I have read,   .   .   415   Rutter   13
Where it runs round, and even: where so well,   .   .   415   Rutter   16
So soft, and smooth it handles, the whole piece,   .   .   415   Rutter   17
As it were spun by nature, off the fleece: .   .   415   Rutter   18
Upon this obeliske, advanc'd for it, ...   416   Welcome   5
but have lost it by the way, ...   417   Moon   10
to the Peake it is so hard-by, ...   417   Moon   23
shee soone will heare it.   417   Moon   24
the Moone will beare it.   417   Moon   28
yet doe not feare it.   417   Moon   32
shee will not seise it.   417   Moon   44
And by their takeinge, lett it once appeare   .   .   418   Moon   44
And though your virtue (as becomes it) still   .   .   421   Ode:If Men   44
It is an Act of Tyranye, not Love,   .   .   .   421   Censure   9
Forgive it as my Frayltie, and not mee.   .   .   .   422   Censure   18
Is her owne scourge, when it sustaines their states   .   422   Censure   23
if it begyn religious thoughts to cherish;   .   .   .   422   Lucan   3
It is a lycense to doe ill, protectes,   .   .   .   422   Lucan   10
the sword, but that it acteth what it list.   .   .   423   Lucan   12
Wine it is the Milk of Venus, ...   423   Lucan   14
Ply it, and you all are mounted.   657   Door Apollo   12
But with a Kisse, (if thou canst dare it)   .   .   657   Door Apollo   14
of her white Hand; or she can spare it.   .   .   .   662   Bedford   9
that it remayne with him   662   Bedford   10
ITALIAN   666   Glover   6
Parts, then th'Italian could doe, with his dore.   .   .   74   E115 Honest Man   26
ITALIE
Nor had our Italie more glorious bin   325   Horace   411
ITALY
Though slower Spaine; and Italy mature.   .   .   .   368   Ode Who saith   88
Here France, and Italy both to him shed   .   .   .   375   Coryat 1   30
France, Savoy, Italy, and Helvetia, ...   379   Coryat 3   19
ITCH
And laugh, and measure thighes, then squeake, spring, itch,   .   164   U15 Friend-Wars   75
In this, and like, an itch of Vanitie,   .   .   .   166   U15 Friend-Wars   143
Itch to defame the State? or brand the Times?   .   .   203   U43 Vulcan   25
ITEM
Item, a tale or two, some fortnight after;   .   .   51   E73 Fine Grand   7
Item, the babylonian song you sing;   .   .   .   51   E73 Fine Grand   9
Item, a faire greeke poesie for a ring: .   .   .   51   E73 Fine Grand   10
Item, a charme surrounding fearefully   .   .   .   51   E73 Fine Grand   12
Item, a gulling imprese for you, at tilt.   .   .   .   51   E73 Fine Grand   15
Item, your mistris anagram, i' your hilt.   .   .   51   E73 Fine Grand   16
Item, your owne, sew'd in your mistris smock.   .   .   51   E73 Fine Grand   17
Item, an epitaph on my lords cock,   .   .   .   51   E73 Fine Grand   18
Jest, he saies. Item one sute of blacke taffata   .   .   380   Coryat 3   48
I'TH'
Ha' their Bermudas, and their streights i'th' Strand: .   155   U13 Sacvile   82
I'THE
Then can a flea at twise skip i'the Map.   .   .   69   E107 Hungry   18
But why are all these Irons i'the fire   .   .   .   215   U44 Speach   93
Nor know t'observe: why (i'the Muses name)   .   .   311   Horace   128
I'the open field; is Waxe like to be wrought   .   .   315   Horace   231
I'THEIR
That hang their richest jewells i'their nose;   .   .   232   U58 Book-seller   10
IT'S
With such a one. And therein keepes it's word.   .   .   74   E115 Honest Man   21
'Twill see it's sister naked, ere a sword.   .   .   74   E115 Honest Man   22
And, shifting of it's faces, doth play more   .   .   74   E115 Honest Man   25
From friendship, is it's owne fames architect.   .   .   75   E115 Honest Man   30
ITS
Then goe on, and doe its worst;   260   U76 Petition   29
ITSELF
Truth itself doth flow in Wine.   657   Door Apollo   6
IVORY
Thrice 'bout thy Altar with their Ivory feet.   .   .   292   U86 Hor.4:1   28
And ('bout thy Ivory neck,) no youth did fling   .   293   U87 Hor.3:9   2
Though gold or Ivory haftes would make it good.   .   403   Inigo Jones 1   28
Though gold or Ivory haftes cant make it good.   .   403   Inigo Jones 1   V 28
IVY
In the greene circle of thy Ivy twine.   .   .   .   107   F10 Proludium   12
Put on my Ivy Garland, let me see   .   .   .   200   U42 Elegy Let   9
R. Rose, I. Ivy, E. sweet Eglantine.   .   .   .   412   Ghyrlond   4
The fourth is humble Ivy, intersert,   .   .   .   413   Ghyrlond   17
IVYE
And come forth worthie Ivye, or the Bayes,   .   .   420   Ode:If Men   26
IXION
Ino bewaild; Ixion false, forsworne;   .   .   .   313   Horace   176
JACKS
That hearkens to a Jacks-pulse, when it goes.   .   .   216   U45 Squib   6
JACKS-PULSE
That hearkens to a Jacks-pulse, when it goes,   .   .   216   U45 Squib   6
JACOBS
By Jacobs Ladder, to the top   274   U84 Cradle   38

JAKES
Or were precipitated downe the jakes, ... 87 E133 Voyage 137

JAMES (See also JEAMES)
To King James. . . . . 28 E4 James 1 Ttl
To King James. . . . . 37 E35 James 2 Ttl
Who would not be thy subject, James, t'obay . . . 37 E35 James 2 1
To thy Domitian, than I can my James: . . . . 38 E36 Martial 2
To King James. Upon the happy false rumour of his death, . . . 43 E51 James 3 Ttl
That found King James, when hunting late, this way, . . . 95 F2 Penshurst 76
An Ode to James Earle of Desmond, writ . . . . 176 U25 Desmond Ttl
That when King James, above here, ... 221 U48 Bacchus 37
James the blessed, pleas'd the rather, ... 259 U76 Petition 6
To My L. the King, On the Christning His second Sonne James. . 268 U80 Christning Ttl
As hath thy James; cleans'd from originall drosse, . . 268 U80 Christning 9
A Speach Presented unto King James at a tilting . . . 382 Rich Ttl
That so did take Eliza, and our James! . . . . 392 Shakespeare 74
A Grace by Ben: Johnson. extempore. before King James. . 418 Grace Ttl

JANE
An Elegie On the Lady Jane Pawlet, Marchion: of Winton. . 268 U81 Pawlet Ttl
Shee was the Lady Jane, and Marchionisse . . . 269 U81 Pawlet 19
To the memorye of that most Honoured Ladie Jane, . . . 394 Jane Ogle Ttl

JANIN'S
Janin's, your Nuncio's, and your Tuilleries, . . . 69 E107 Hungry 22

JANUS
To day old Janus opens the new yeare, . . . 263 U79 New-yeares 9

JAPHETS
With Japhets lyne, aspire . . . . . 175 U23 Himselfe 27

JARRE (DISCORD)
Still may Syllabes jarre with time, ... 184 U29 Fit of Rime 52

JARRE
For every price, in every jarre, ... 99 F3 Wroth 74
The whole fleet wreck'd? a great jarre to be shap'd, . . 305 Horace 28

JARRES (DISCORD)
The Fights, the Cryes, and wondring at the Jarres . . 397 Drayton 41

JARRES
Of earthen Jarres, there may molest me too: . . . 219 U47 Tribe 55

JARRETH
Is laugh'd at, that still jarreth on one string: . . . 329 Horace 532

JARRING
As jarring Musique doth, at jolly feasts, . . . 331 Horace 557

JASONS
Who placed Jasons Argo in the skie? . . . . 115 F12 Rutland 59

JAUNDIES
The yellow Jaundies, or were furious mad . . . 335 Horace 646

JAUNDIS
The yellow jaundis, or were truely mad, ... 354 Horace V646

JAW
Safe from the wolves black jaw, and the dull Asses hoofe. . 175 U23 Himselfe 36

JAWES
In the first jawes appear'd that ugly monster, . . . 85 E133 Voyage 61

JAX
My Muse had plough'd with his, that sung A-jax. . . 89 E133 Voyage 196

JAY
When the common courting jay . . . . . 103 F6 Celia 2 3

JEALOUS
Yet give thy jealous subjects leave to doubt: . . . 43 E51 James 3 5
I pluck'd a branch; the jealous god did frowne, . . 80 E126 Mrs Cary 3
But then if I grow jealous madde, ... 147 U7 Nymph 10
And jealous each of other, yet thinke long . . . 164 U15 Friend-Wars 73
If subject to the jealous errors . . . . 177 U25 Desmond 28
Who frownes, who jealous is, who taxeth me. . . 200 U42 Elegy Let 10
Thou art jealous of thy Wifes, or Daughters Case: . . 202 U42 Elegy Let 87

JEALOUSIE
Against Jealousie. . . . . . . 150 U10 Jealousie Ttl
Wretched and foolish Jealousie, ... 150 U10 Jealousie 1
Widow or Wife, without the jealousie . . . . 230 U56 Covell 17
Or canker'd Jealousie, ... 257 U75 Epithalam. 135

JEALOUSIES
Since stird'st up jealousies and feares, . . . 101 F4 To the World 43
Their loves, their quarrels, jealousies, and wrongs, . . 397 Drayton 30

JEAMES
Renew the Glories of our blessed Jeames: . . . 415 Dover 4

JEARING
And Roman Gentrie, jearing, will laugh out. . . 313 Horace 160

JEAST
Or th'other on their borders, that will jeast . . . 218 U47 Tribe 16

JEMME
Their Jemme of Riches, and bright Stone, that brings . 206 U43 Vulcan 74

JEPHSON
To Sir William Jephson. . . . . . 75 E116 Jephson Ttl
Jephson, thou man of men, to whose lov'd name . . 75 E116 Jephson 1

JERKE
And firke, and jerke, and for the Coach-man raile, . . 164 U15 Friend-Wars 72

JEST
Thou more; that with it every day, dar'st jest . . 32 E16 Brain-hardy 2
In-primis, Grand, you owe me for a jest, . . . 51 E73 Fine Grand 5
There jest, and feast, make him thine host, . . . 292 U86 Hor.4:1 11
How he could jest, because he mark'd and saw, . . 319 Horace 323
And so to turne all earnest into jest, . . . 321 Horace 330
And so to turne our earnest into jest, . . . 346 Horace V322/330
Jest, he saies. Item one sute of blacke taffata . . 380 Coryat 3 48

JESTS
Five of my jests, then stolne, past him a play. . . 64 E100 Playwrt 3 4

JESTS (cont.)
And have thy tales and jests too, ... 221 U48 Bacchus 40
And jests; and both to admiration raise . . . . 323 Horace 400
And jests; and both to admiration rais'd, ... 348 Horace V386/400
JESUS
Jesus, the onely-gotten Christ! who can . . . . 288 U84 Muse 212
JEWELL
The stages jewell; . . . . . . 77 E120 S. P. 12
The Jewell of your name, as close as sleepe . . . 198 U40 Elegy That 42
JEWELLS
To view the jewells, stuffes, the paines, the wit . . 97 F3 Wroth 11
That hang their richest jewells i'their nose; . . . 232 U58 Book-seller 10
JEWELS
And her Jewels, to the view . . . . 138 U2 Kisse 11
The Starres, that are the Jewels of the Night, . . 271 U81 Pawlet 87
JEWES
He will expiate this sinne with converting the Jewes. . 375 Coryat 1 21
Except a dublet, and bought of the Jewes: . . . 380 Coryat 3 49
JOANE
Your Joane to passe her melancholie time. . . . 231 U56 Covell 24
JOHN
To John Donne. . . . . 34 E23 Donne 1 Ttl
On Sir John Roe. . . . . 35 E27 Roe 1 Ttl
On Sir John Roe. . . . . 37 E32 Roe 2 Ttl
To Sir John Radcliffe. . . . . 60 E93 Radcliffe Ttl
To John Donne. . . . . 62 E96 Donne 2 Ttl
An Epistle to Master John Selden. . . . . . 158 U14 Selden Ttl
Ben: Jonson To His Honord Friend Mr John Selden Health. . 158 U14 Selden VTtl
To Mr. John Burges. . . . . 229 U55 Burges Ttl
To Master John Burges. . . . . . . 231 U57 Burges Ttl
Father John Burges, ... 231 U57 Burges 1
To Kenelme, John, George. . . . . . . 281 U84 Kenelme Ttl
To the worthy Author M. John Fletcher. . . . . 370 Fletcher Ttl
. . . Sir John Beaumont, Baronet. . . . . 400 Beaumont Ttl
JOHNSON
Il may Ben Johnson slander so his feete, . . . 418 Answer 5
A Grace by Ben: Johnson. extempore. before King James. . 418 Grace Ttl
JOHNSONS
This was Mr Ben: Johnsons Answer of the suddayne. . . 418 Answer Ttl
JOIN (See JOYN)
JOINT (See also JOYNTS)
As not the smallest joint, or gentlest word . . . 395 May 21
JOLLY
The jolly wassall walkes the often round, . . . 98 F3 Wroth 59
As jarring Musique doth, at jolly feasts, . . . 331 Horace 557
JONE
On Giles and Jone. . . . . 40 E42 Giles Ttl
Who sayes that Giles and Jone at discord be? . . 40 E42 Giles 1
But that his Jone doth too. And Giles would never, . 40 E42 Giles 4
No more would Jone he should. Giles riseth early, . 40 E42 Giles 6
The like is Jone. But turning home, is sad. . . 40 E42 Giles 8
And so is Jone. Oft-times, when Giles doth find . 40 E42 Giles 9
All this doth Jone. Or that his long yearn'd life . 40 E42 Giles 11
Of his begetting. And so sweares his Jone. . . 40 E42 Giles 14
JONES
By his free will, be in Jones company. . . . 40 E42 Giles 5
An Expostulacion with Inigo Jones. . . . . 402 Inigo Jones 1 Ttl
Of Tyre-man, Mounte-banck & Justice Jones, . . . 402 Inigo Jones 1 16
JONSON
Ben. Jonson his best piece of poetrie. . . . 41 E45 First Son 10
Ben: Jonson To His Honord Friend Mr John Selden Health. . 158 U14 Selden VTtl
Ben: Jonson upon the burning of his study and bookes . 202 U43 Vulcan VTtl
Jonson, who sung this of him, e're he went . . . 246 U70 Ode 85
The Vision Of Ben. Jonson, On The . . . . . 396 Drayton Ttl
JOSEPH
. . . Master Joseph Rutter. . . . . . 414 Rutter Ttl
You looke, my Joseph, I should something say . . 414 Rutter 1
JOSUAH
To Mr. Josuah Sylvester. . . . . . . 83 E132 Sylvester Ttl
JOT
Scap'd not his Justice any jot the more: . . . 210 U43 Vulcan 154
Scap'd not this Justice any jot the more: . . . 210 U43 Vulcan V154
JOURNALL
Each leafe of his journall, and line doth unlocke . . 380 Coryat 3 23
JOURNALS
In all thy age of Journals thou hast tooke, . . . 254 U75 Epithalam. 75
JOURNEY
That there's no journey set, or thought upon, . . 81 E129 Mime 3
The rest, my journey into Scotland song, . . . 207 U43 Vulcan 94
The rest, my journey into Scotland sung . . . 207 U43 Vulcan V 94
The Lippe of his journey, and sees in his booke, . . 379 Coryat 3 18
JOVE
By Jove to have Minerva for thy Bride, . . . 203 U43 Vulcan 12
And so did Jove, who ne're meant thee his Cup: . . 208 U43 Vulcan 115
Then when the thundring Jove his Snow and showres . 290 U85 Country 29
JOVE'S
Were you Jove's sonnes, or had Alcides might. . . 89 E133 Voyage 182
But might I of Jove's Nectar sup, ... 106 F9 Celia 3 7
JOVES
When with Joves swans she sported . . . . 135 U2 Triumph V 42
Who aided him, will thee, the issue of Joves braine. . 175 U23 Himselfe 30
Who aided them, will thee, the issue of Joves braine. . 175 U23 Himselfe V 30

	Page	Title	Line
JOVIALL			
Of Tom of Odcombe that odde Joviall Author, • • • •	378	Coryat 2	87
An Epigram To My Joviall Good Freind Mr. Robert Dover, • •	415	Dover	Ttl
JOY			
Farewell, thou child of my right hand, and joy; • • •	41	E45 First Son	1
Roe (and my joy to name) th'art now, to goe • • •	80	E128 Wm Roe 2	1
For that's a narrow joy is but our owne. • • • •	147	U7 Nymph	7
In whom Anacreon once did joy, • • • •	181	U27 Ode Helen	6
And fills my powers with perswading joy, • • •	191	U38 Elegy 'Tis	11
'Tis a brave cause of joy, let it be knowne, • •	225	U51 Bacon	17
(Except the joy that the first Mary brought, • •	238	U66 Queene	7
(And leave the joy that the first Mary brought, •	238	U66 Queene	V 7
Up publike joy, remember • • • •	239	U67 Muses	1
Her joy in state, and pleasure; • • • •	240	U67 Muses	44
Or taste a part of that full joy he meant • •	246	U70 Ode	87
Repeating all Great Britain's joy, and more, • •	249	U72 King	6
It brings Friends Joy, Foes Griefe, Posteritie Fame; •	256	U75 Epithalam.	114
The Solemne Quire cryes, Joy; and they returne, Amen. •	256	U75 Epithalam.	128
The joy of Saints! the Crowne for which it lives, •	283	U84 Muse	37
O Day of joy, and suretie to the just! • • •	284	U84 Muse	61
Of joy the Circle, and sole Period! • • • •	284	U84 Muse	66
Delights, nor credulous hope of mutuall Joy, •	293	U86 Hor.4:1	30
With joy of what is given him, over-gone: • •	333	Horace	610
That bid, God give thee joy, and have no endes. •	384	Somerset	6
And eve'ry joy, in mariage, turne a fruite. • •	384	Somerset	18
Most venerable. Cause of all our joy. • • •	414	Ghyrlond	42
JOYCARE			
Troy, though it were so much thy Venus joycare. •	210	U43 Vulcan	V160
JOY'D			
Thou didst tell me; and wert o're-joy'd to peepe •	201	U42 Elegy Let	59
JOY'D			
And joy'd to weare the dressing of his lines! • • •	392	Shakespeare	48
JOYES			
Why should we deferre our joyes? • • • •	102	F5 Celia 1	9
The'Elixir of all joyes? • • • • •	110	F11 Epode	56
And turne the blackest sorrowes to bright joyes: •	112	F11 Epode	95
Of these forc'd joyes, • • • • •	120	F14 Sydney	18
Her joyes, her smiles, her loves, as readers take •	182	U28 Worth	13
Such joyes, such sweet's doth your Returne • •	251	U74 Weston	19
Made her friends joyes to get above their feares! •	270	U81 Pawlet	60
And pray, thy joyes as lasting bee, as great. • •	384	Somerset	8
JOYFULL			
And as it turnes our joyfull yeare about, • • •	236	U64 Charles 3	5
In changing, let our Nephewes joyfull see • •	238	U65 Prince	V 7
Recelebrates the joyfull Match with France. •	401	Filmer	10
JOYN			
A horse neck joyn, & sundry plumes ore-fold •	338	Horace	V 2
JOYN'D			
And us dis-joyn'd force to her brazen yoke, • •	294	U87 Hor.3:9	18
The last doth from the midst dis-joyn'd appeare. •	315	Horace	218
JOYNE			
Joyne lip to lip, and try: • • • • •	139	U2 Another	15
That shall re-joyne yee. Was she, then, so deare, •	285	U84 Muse	107
JOYNTING			
Joynting Syllabes, drowning Letters, • • •	183	U29 Fit of Rime	10
JOYNTS			
And so my sharpnesse thou no lesse dis-joynts, •	45	E58 Groome	5
May his joynts tormented bee, • • • •	184	U29 Fit of Rime	50
Stiffe! starke! my joynts 'gainst one another knock! •	269	U81 Pawlet	9
JOY'ST			
Thou joy'st in better markes, of soyle, of ayre, •	93	F2 Penshurst	7
JUDGE			
Pr'y thee beleeve still, and not judge so fast, •	32	E18 Censurer	9
May judge it to be his, as well as ours. • •	45	E56 Poet-Ape	12
And know thee, then, a judge, not of one yeare; •	51	E74 Chancelor	2
So to front death, as men might judge us past it. •	54	E80 Life/Death	7
That so alone canst judge, so'alone dost make: •	62	E96 Donne 2	3
Judge they, that can: here I have rais'd to show •	67	E104 Montgomery	13
Now I have sung thee thus, shall judge of thee. :	70	E109 Nevil	16
Of the best writer, and judge, should emulate. •	78	E123 Rudyerd 3	4
For, then, all mouthes will judge, and their owne way: •	82	E131 Ferrab. 2	3
Since they can only judge, that can conferre. •	83	E132 Sylvester	6
And judge me after: if I dare pretend • •	122	F15 Heaven	7
My judge, my witnesse, and my advocate. • •	122	F15 Heaven	12
'Tis then a crime, when the Usurer is Judge. •	169	U17 Friend-Debt	4
The Judge his favour timely then extends, • •	186	U32 Elsmere	1
Shee is the Judge, Thou Executioner: • • •	204	U43 Vulcan	47
Reveald (if some can judge) of Argenis, • •	207	U43 Vulcan	V 96
Reveald (if some do judge) of Argenis, • •	207	U43 Vulcan	V 96
To judge; So all men comming neere can spie, •	242	U69 Friend Son	20
Parts of him, the Judge decay'd. • • •	259	U76 Petition	V 23
Catch'd with these Arts, wherein the Judge is wise •	261	U77 Treasurer	11
Caught them these Arts, wherein the Judge is wise •	261	U77 Treasurer	V 11
To heare their Judge, and his eternall doome; •	283	U84 Muse	48
He that shall be our supreme Judge, should leave •	286	U84 Muse	148
To him should be her Judge, true God, true Man, •	288	U84 Muse	211
Before the Judge, it hangs, and waites report. •	309	Horace	112
Clowne, Towns-man, base, and noble, mix'd, to judge? •	319	Horace	302
Be I their Judge, they doe at no time dare •	321	Horace	356
But every Judge hath not the facultie • •	323	Horace	387
And office of a Judge are, what the parts • •	325	Horace	450
You doe not bring, to judge your Verses, one, •	333	Horace	609
When you write Verses, with your judge do so: •	333	Horace	620

343

	Page	Title	Line

JUDGE (cont.)

When you make verses, with your judge doe so:	354	Horace	V620
To judge which Passion's false, and which is true,	370	Author	11
That may judge for his six-pence) had, before	371	Fletcher	7

JUDG'D

Parts of me (they judg'd) decay'd,	259	U76 Petition	23
Those other two; which must be judg'd, or crown'd:	284	U84 Muse	55
To send it to be judg'd by Metius eare,	331	Horace	576

JUDGEMENT

This but thy judgement fooles: the other way	43	E52 Courtling	5
The judgement of the king so shine in thee;	47	E63 Salisbury 2	4
'Tis not thy judgement breeds the prejudice,	50	E72 Court-ling	5
With thine owne course the judgement of thy friend,	63	E98 Th Roe 1	8
And even the praisers judgement suffers so.	64	E99 Th Roe 2	10
Or valour, or thy judgement seasoning it,	68	E106 E Herbert	6
But dost it out of judgement, not disease;	76	E119 Shelton	8
And destin'd unto judgement, after all.	122	F15 Heaven	20
Was trusted, that you thought my judgement such	158	U14 Selden	6
Who would with judgement search, searching conclude	177	U25 Desmond	25
Cosening Judgement with a measure,	183	U29 Fit of Rime	5
There was a Judgement shew'n too in an houre.	210	U43 Vulcan	158
His judgement is; If he be wise, and praise,	232	U58 Book-seller	5
And this well mov'd the Judgement of the King	256	U75 Epithalam.	105
In that great Act of judgement: which the Father	288	U84 Muse	215
Thou, such thy judgement is, thy knowledge too,	331	Horace	573
Nature, or Art. My Judgement will not pierce	331	Horace	582
And strikes the quickest-sighted Judgement blinde.	363	Riches	16
Judgement (adorn'd with Learning)	365	Ode Splendor	9
Who are his Test, and what their judgement is:	385	Husband	3
For, if I thought my judgement were of yeeres,	391	Shakespeare	27
Your true freind in Judgement and Choise	395	May	25

JUDGEMENTS

Whil'st thy weigh'd judgements, Egerton, I heare,	51	E74 Chancelor	1
A many of bookes, even good judgements wound	159	U14 Selden	15
So, justest Lord, may all your Judgements be	185	U31 Elsmere	1
Their perfum'd judgements, let them kisse thy Wife.	232	U58 Book-seller	14

JUDGES

| The Courts just honour, and thy Judges love. | 187 | U33 Councellour | 37 |
| This, fearing not the subtlest Judges marke, | 331 | Horace | 542 |

JUDGING

| Writing thy selfe, or judging others writ, | 78 | E123 Rudyerd 3 | 1 |
| Of raising, judging, and rewarding all | 288 | U84 Muse | 207 |

JUDGMENT

It must be thine owne judgment, yet, that sends	386	Browne	7
This thy worke forth: that judgment mine commends.	386	Browne	8
He may have skill & judgment to designe	406	Inigo Jones 2	7

JUGGLER

| Old Bankes the juggler, our Pythagoras, | 88 | E133 Voyage | 156 |

JUICE (See JUYCE)

JUMPE

| Acrostichs, and Telestichs, on jumpe names, | 204 | U43 Vulcan | 39 |
| Acrostichs, and Telestichs, or jumpe names, | 204 | U43 Vulcan | V 39 |

JUNE

By all the Spheares consent, so in the heart of June?	253	U75 Epithalam.	16
Upon my Birth-day the eleventh of June;	262	U78 Digby	14
Witnesse my Birth-day the eleventh of June;	262	U78 Digby	V 14

JUNO

There Juno sate, and yet no Peacock by.	68	E105 L Wroth 2	18
But shee's Juno, when she walkes,	137	U2 Cupid	53
The majesty of Juno in the Cloudes,	403	Inigo Jones 1	33

JUPITER

| 'Twas Jupiter that hurl'd thee headlong downe, | 203 | U43 Vulcan | 9 |
| 'Twas Jupiter that cast thee headlong downe, | 203 | U43 Vulcan | V 9 |

JUST

Just wife, and, to change me, make womans hast?	34	E25 Beast 1	8
He that feares death, or mournes it, in the just,	37	E34 Death	1
Exacted by thy fate, on the just day.	41	E45 First Son	4
Weare this renowne. 'Tis just, that who did give	57	E89 Allen	13
And are so good, and bad, just at a price,	66	E102 Pembroke	11
For, where his person liv'd scarce one just age,	71	E110 Edmonds 1	13
With tales of Troyes just knight, our faiths abuse:	84	E133 Voyage	4
The just reward of her high huswifery;	96	F2 Penshurst	85
Just to the waight their this dayes-presents beare;	113	F12 Rutland	8
Men are not just, or keepe no holy lawes	117	F13 Aubigny	18
And, keeping a just course, have earely put	119	F13 Aubigny	91
Just above her sparkling eyes,	136	U2 Cupid	16
With the just Canon of his life,	151	U12 Corbet	11
That thine be just, and honest; that thy Deeds	167	U15 Friend-Wars	177
You have a Husband is the just excuse	171	U19 Elegy By	22
As 'tis too just a cause;	174	U23 Himselfe	14
The poores full Store-house, and just servants field.	185	U30 Burleigh	8
When this appeares, just Lord, to your sharp sight,	186	U32 Elsmere	15
The Courts just honour, and thy Judges love.	187	U33 Councellour	37
Your just commands: yet those, not I, be lost.	192	U38 Elegy 'Tis	38
Due to that one, that doth believe him just.	198	U40 Elegy That	40
Thy just defences made th' oppressor afraid.	217	U46 Coke	8
For a just wager, and that wager paid	229	U54 Squib	2
Of making just approaches, how to kill,	232	U59 Newcastle	4
And Sister to just Lewis!	240	U67 Muses	27
In small proportions, we just beautie see:	245	U70 Ode	73
But doth his Carract, and just Standard keepe	255	U75 Epithalam.	100
doth his prime Carract, and just Standard keepe	255	U75 Epithalam.	V100
Hee's prudent, valiant, just, and temperate;	262	U78 Digby	5

	Page	Title	Line
JUST (cont.)			
And offer your just service on these plaines;	263	U79 New-yeares	12
Just as she in it liv'd! and so exempt	270	U81 Pawlet	48
By the just trade	273	U84 Cradle	8
I Sing the just, and uncontrol'd Descent	274	U84 Descent	1
O Day of joy, and suretie to the just!	284	U84 Muse	61
Have more or lesse then just five Acts: nor laid,	317	Horace	272
Take just offence at this: nor, though it strike	347	Horace	V353/361
An ounce, what makes it then? The halfe pound just;	327	Horace	471
To say, I'm ignorant. Just as a Crier	333	Horace	597
Once say I'me ignorant. Just as a Cryer,	353	Horace	V597
Poore Tom have we cause to suspect just thee?	381	Coryat 3	58
It makes me ravish'd with just wonder, cry	395	May	13
By warrant call'd just Symetry,	399	Lady Ogle	22
Just and fit actions Ptolemey (he saith)	422	Lucan	1
are distant, so is proffitt from just aymes.	422	Lucan	8
JUSTEST			
So, justest Lord, may all your Judgements be	185	U31 Elsmere	1
JUSTICE			
In thy justice to molest	106	F8 Sicknesse	47
Friendship is now mask'd Hatred! Justice fled,	163	U15 Friend-Wars	39
Because they would free Justice imitate,	170	U18 Elegy Can	18
Scap'd not his Justice any jot the more:	210	U43 Vulcan	154
Scap'd not this Justice any jot the more:	210	U43 Vulcan	V154
Scap'd not thy Justice any whitt the more:	210	U43 Vulcan	V154
. . . he was Lord chiefe Justice of England.	217	U46 Coke	Ttl
Desired Justice to the publique Weale,	217	U46 Coke	16
Is, she will play Dame Justice, too severe;	229	U54 Squib	8
His Wisdome, and his Justice, in that houre,	288	U84 Muse	218
And most his Justice, in the fitting parts,	289	U84 Muse	223
Praise the spare diet, wholsome justice, lawes,	317	Horace	283
Of Tyre-man, Mounte-banck & Justice Jones,	402	Inigo Jones 1	16
Should but the king his Justice-hood employ	405	Inigo Jones 1	77
JUSTICE-HOOD			
Should but the king his Justice-hood employ	405	Inigo Jones 1	77
JUSTIFIE			
Or thou more happie, it to justifie	49	E66 Cary	8
I will not stand to justifie my fault,	191	U38 Elegy 'Tis	21
To justifie, and quicken us in breath!	288	U84 Muse	204
JUSTLED			
Lest it be justled, crack'd, made nought, or lesse:	219	U47 Tribe	58
JUSTLY			
Are justly summ'd, that make you man;	120	F14 Sydney	22
And you may justly, being a tardie, cold,	230	U56 Covell	7
Let such as justly have out-liv'd all prayse,	387	Cavendish	5
Which you have justly gained from the Stage,	409	Brome	6
JUYCE			
With juyce of limons, onions, pisse, to write.	59	E92 New Crie	28
In juyce of Cedar worthy to be steep'd,	327	Horace	475
K			
An Epigram. To K. Charles for a 100. Pounds . . .	235	U62 Charles 1	Ttl
To K. Charles, and Q. Mary. For the losse of their . . .	235	U63 Charles 2	Ttl
An Epigram. To our great and good K. Charles . . .	236	U64 Charles 3	Ttl
What can the cause be, when the K. hath given	241	U68 House-hold	1
Well, they should know him, would the K. but grant	241	U68 House-hold	5
F. shewes what he was, K. what he will bee.	375	Coryat 1	29
But cause thou hearst the mighty k. of Spaine	406	Inigo Jones 2	1
KATE			
Stunke not so ill; nor, when shee kist, Kate Arden.	87	E133 Voyage	118
Nay, sigh'd a Sister, 'twas the Nun, Kate Arden,	209	U43 Vulcan	148
Nay, sayth a sister, Venus Nun, Kate Arden,	209	U43 Vulcan	V148
A Kate, a Frank, to honour their Grand-dames,	258	U75 Epithalam.	172
KATHERINE			
Epistle. To Katherine, Lady Aubigny.	116	F13 Aubigny	Ttl
For this did Katherine, Ladie Ogle, die	400	Lady Ogle	33
KEEP			
For me to be your Indice. Keep you such,	157	U13 Sacvile	156
Must manly keep, and not be heard to sing	345	Horace	V277
Keep in thy barking Wit, thou bawling Fool?	410	Gill	8
As Love, here studied to keep Grace alive.	412	Ghyrlond	8
KEEPE			
Keepe thy selfe there, and thinke thy valure right,	32	E16 Brain-hardy	9
And, reconcil'd, keepe him suspected still.	48	E65 Muse	8
Keepe a starre-chamber sentence close, twelve dayes:	59	E92 New Crie	19
That are your wordes of credit. Keepe your Names	69	E107 Hungry	24
Where, what makes others great, doth keepe thee good!	73	E113 Overbury	4
Heaven vowes to keepe him.	77	E120 S. P.	24
I would restore, and keepe it ever such;	78	E122 Rudyerd 2	8
Whose noyse shall keepe thy miming most alive,	81	E129 Mime	10
Cannot the Plague-bill keepe you backe? nor bells	88	E133 Voyage	173
And feasts, that either shearers keepe;	97	F3 Wroth	40
And feasts, which either shearers keepe;	97	F3 Wroth	V 40
Get place, and honor, and be glad to keepe	99	F3 Wroth	87
Get place, and honor, and be proud to keepe	99	F3 Wroth	V 87
Can your favours keepe, and cover,	103	F6 Celia 2	2
Not to know vice at all, and keepe true state,	109	F11 Epode	1
Or some great thought doth keepe	109	F11 Epode	24
Men are not just, or keepe no holy lawes	117	F13 Aubigny	18
And keepe an even, and unalter'd gaite;	118	F13 Aubigny	61
Keepe the middle age at stay,	131	U2 Excuse	21
Meane what I speake: and still will keepe that Vow.	159	U14 Selden	28
It is a call to keepe the spirits alive	162	U15 Friend-Wars	5
Arm'd at all peeces, as to keepe a Fort	187	U33 Councellour	30

		Page	Title	Line
KEEPE (cont.)				
To fetch the flesh, we keepe the Rowle.		188	U35 Chute	6
Which, how most sacred I will ever keepe,		190	U37 Friend-Book	13
Would live his glory that could keepe it on;		192	U38 Elegy 'Tis	48
Keepe in reserv'd in his Dark-lanterne face,		198	U40 Elegy That	23
Keepe secret in his Channels what he breedes,		198	U40 Elegy That	27
And such your Servant is, who vowes to keepe		198	U40 Elegy That	41
O, keepe it still; for it had rather be		199	U41 Elegy Since	17
Yet keepe those up in sackcloth too, or lether,		200	U42 Elegy Let	25
And keepe the Glorie of the English name,		214	U44 Speach	50
That keepe the warre, though now't be growne more tame,		214	U44 Speach	55
I have decreed; keepe it from waves, and presse;		219	U47 Tribe	57
Searching for knowledge, and to keepe your mind		225	U50 Countesse	29
I gaine, in having leave to keepe my Day,		231	U56 Covell	29
To keepe him off; and how-so-e're he gleanes		242	U69 Friend Son	16
And keepe the one halfe from his Harry.		246	U70 Ode	94
But doth his Carract, and just Standard keepe		255	U75 Epithalam.	100
doth his prime Carract, and just Standard keepe		255	U75 Epithalam.	V100
And keepe their Fames		257	U75 Epithalam.	150
Or the prest honey in pure pots doth keepe		257	U75 Epithalam.	150
Keepe him still active, angry, un-appeas'd,		290	U85 Country	15
A meere new person, looke he keepe his state		313	Horace	172
He cries, Good boy, thou'lt keepe thine owne. Now, adde		313	Horace	180
Keepe due proportion in the ample song,		327	Horace	470
How they doe keepe alive his memorie;		395	May	12
God blesse them all, and keepe them safe:		416	Dover	5
God blesse us all, Bedford keepe safe:		419	Grace	7
		419	Grace	V 7
KEEP'D				
And in smooth Cypresse boxes to be keep'd?		327	Horace	476
KEEPER				
Sonne to the grave wise Keeper of the Seale,		225	U51 Bacon	9
KEEPES				
Keepes himselfe, with halfe a man, and defrayes		30	E12 Shift	3
That lost, he keepes his chamber, reades Essayes,		30	E12 Shift	15
He keepes anothers wife, which is a spice		36	E28 Surly	15
The children, that he keepes, Giles sweares are none		40	E42 Giles	13
What States yo'have gull'd, and which yet keepes yo'in pay.		69	E107 Hungry	10
With such a one. And therein keepes it's word.		74	E115 Honest Man	21
And keepes your merit		177	U25 Desmond	21
Doth, while he keepes his watch, betray his stand.		198	U40 Elegy That	36
For Fame keepes Vertue up, and it Posteritie.		257	U75 Epithalam.	152
KEEPING				
Or, keeping your due state, that would not cry,		68	E105 L Wroth 2	17
And, keeping a just course, have earely put		119	F13 Aubigny	91
And like a Compasse keeping one foot still		159	U14 Selden	31
With that thy Stile, thy keeping of thy State,		161	U14 Selden	68
But thus, thus, keeping endlesse Holy-day,		294	U88 Petronius	6
The Idiot, keeping holy-day, or drudge,		319	Horace	301
KEEPS				
He cast, yet keeps her well! No, shee keeps him.		54	E82 Surly	2
But thou, whose noblesse keeps one stature still,		66	E102 Pembroke	13
Keeps warme the spice of her good name,		400	Lady Ogle	30
KEEP'ST				
And, Sylvane, thine that keep'st his Lands!		290	U85 Country	V 22
KENELME				
To Sir Kenelme Digby. An Epigram		262	U78 Digby	VTtl
- - - on her Husband, Sir Kenelme Digby.		262	U78 Digby	Ttl
- - - late Wife of Sir Kenelme Digby, Knight: - - -		272	U84 Eupheme	Ttl
To Kenelme, John, George.		281	U84 Kenelme	Ttl
KEPT				
That thou hast kept thy love, encreast thy will,		63	E99 Th Roe 2	1
Who kept an ale-house; with my little Minos,		89	E133 Voyage	189
His Mind as pure, and neatly kept,		151	U12 Corbet	15
That kept man living! Pleasures only sought!		163	U15 Friend-Wars	41
And kept, and bred, and brought up true.		173	U22 Elegy Tho	16
His Altars kept from the Decay,		173	U22 Elegy Tho	19
With Clownes, and Tradesmen, kept thee clos'd in horne.		203	U43 Vulcan	8
Conceal'd, or kept there, that was fit to be,		203	U43 Vulcan	21
And so, have kept me dying a whole age,		205	U43 Vulcan	55
And so, have kept them dying a whole age,		205	U43 Vulcan	V 55
Would you had kept your Forge at Aetna still,		212	U43 Vulcan	197
For 't were a narrow gladnesse, kept thine owne.		225	U51 Bacon	18
Be kept alive those Sweet, and Sacred fires		257	U75 Epithalam.	163
Their names of being kept alive,		273	U84 Cradle	6
Of that eternall Port kept ope'		274	U84 Cradle	39
But, kept an even gate, as some streight tree		287	U84 Muse	165
Have not kept in; and (lest perfection faile)		325	Horace	417
Hath shed, or humane frailtie not kept thence.		329	Horace	528
Nine yeares kept in, your papers by, yo'are free		331	Horace	578
Nine yeares kept by, your papers in, y'are free		352	Horace	V554/578
Let Poets perish, that will not be kept.		335	Horace	664
The Cobler kept him to his nall; but, now		410	Brome	17
KEPTST				
And, Sylvane, thine that keptst his Lands!		290	U85 Country	22
KERNE				
Upon the Kerne, and wildest Irishry,		367	Ode Who saith	53
KEY				
We must accomplish; 'Tis the last Key-stone		157	U13 Sacvile	136
KEYES				
To write in cypher, and the severall keyes,		59	E92 New Crie	26
KEY-STONE				
We must accomplish; 'Tis the last Key-stone		157	U13 Sacvile	136

	Page	Title	Line
KICKING			
Such worship due to kicking of a Punck!	155	U13 Sacvile	93
KID (KYD)			
Or sporting Kid, or Marlowes mighty line.	391	Shakespeare	30
KID			
Or Kid forc't from the Wolfe againe.	291	U85 Country	60
KILD			
If it be thought kild like her Embrions; for,	165	U15 Friend-Wars	96
KILL			
For then their threats will kill me;	144	U4 Song	6
This sadnesse makes no approaches, but to kill.	191	U38 Elegy 'Tis	4
Of making just approaches, how to kill,	232	U59 Newcastle	4
That spread his body o're, to kill:	234	U60 La-ware	16
Present anone: Medea must not kill	317	Horace	263
Doth the same thing with him, that would him kill.	335	Horace	666
KILL'D			
And, for thy messe, is willing to be kill'd.	94	F2 Penshurst	30
KILLER			
Out in the Dog-daies, least the killer meete	409	Detractor	20
KILLING			
Gave killing strokes. There were brave men, before	114	F12 Rutland	53
By all oblique Degrees, that killing height	224	U50 Countesse	11
KILLS (KILNS)			
Condemne him to the Brick-kills, or some Hill-/foot	211	U43 Vulcan	183
Condemne him to the Brick-kills, or a forge	211	U43 Vulcan	V183
KILLS			
And then his thunder frights more, then it kills.	193	U38 Elegy 'Tis	70
KILN (See KILLS)			
KIN			
It is too neere of kin to Heaven, the Soule,	269	U81 Pawlet	29
It is too neere of kin to God, the Soule,	269	U81 Pawlet	V 29
Alike of kin, to that most blessed Trine,	413	Ghyrlond	34
KIND (See also KYNDE)			
Baudrie', and usurie were one kind of game.	45	E57 Bawds	2
It is an Epigramme, on all man-kind;	66	E102 Pembroke	2
O so faire O so kind o so sweet so sweet is shee	135	U2 Triumph	V 38
Nor looke too kind on my desires,	144	U4 Song	7
In the person of Woman-kind. A Song Apologetique.	145	U5 Woman-kind	Ttl
I ne're was of thy kind;	150	U10 Jealousie	3
(Because th'are every where amongst Man-kind	167	U15 Friend-Wars	171
And that pour'd out upon Man-kind can be!	172	U20 Shrub	19
If thou wouldst know the vertues of Man-kind,	185	U30 Burleigh	1
Of massacring Man-kind so many wayes.	212	U43 Vulcan	208
Whereby the safetie of Man-kind was wrought)	238	U66 Queene	8
How summ'd a circle didst thou leave man-kind	243	U70 Ode	9
Was left yet to Man-kind;	247	U70 Ode	121
Feed on thy selfe for spight, and shew thy Kind:	250	U73 Weston	9
They are th'exampled Paire, and mirrour of their kind.	255	U75 Epithalam.	80
What kind of waking Man	256	U75 Epithalam.	111
To them of kind,	257	U75 Epithalam.	142
Thou wouldst have lost the Phoenix, had the kind	283	U84 Muse	19
The kind of Man, on whom his doome should fall!	288	U84 Muse	208
This, seeking, in a various kind, to forme	307	Horace	40
KINDE			
What kinde of creature I could most desire,	52	E76 Bedford 1	3
But I, no child, no foole, respect the kinde,	79	E125 Uvedale	7
And pikes, now weary their owne kinde to eat,	94	F2 Penshurst	34
From all my kinde: that, for my sake,	101	F4 To the World	59
Woman-kinde; devoure the wast	105	F8 Sicknesse	16
Or alter kinde.	367	Ode Who saith	30
KINDES			
Two kindes of valour he doth shew, at ones;	49	E68 Playwrt 2	3
KINDLE			
Which if it kindle not, but scant	174	U22 Elegy Tho	33
KINDLED			
For fame, with breath soone kindled, soone blowne out.	83	E131 Ferrab. 2	14
Friend, flie from hence; and let these kindled rimes	167	U15 Friend-Wars	162
Kindled the fire! But then, did one returne,	209	U43 Vulcan	149
KINDLING			
The art of kindling the true Coale, by Lungs:	206	U43 Vulcan	76
The art of kindling the true Coale, of Lungs:	206	U43 Vulcan	V 76
KINDLY			
It is the kindly Season of the time,	253	U75 Epithalam.	25
KINDRED			
That could but claime a kindred from the purse.	216	U45 Squib	10
Into the Kindred, whence thy Adam drew	274	U84 Descent	15
KINDS			
No lesse of praise, then readers in all kinds	217	U46 Coke	19
KINE			
Thy sheepe, thy bullocks, kine, and calves doe feed:	94	F2 Penshurst	23
KING			
To King James.	28	E4 James 1	Ttl
The world the temple was, the priest a king,	28	E5 Union	3
To King James.	37	E35 James 2	Ttl
First thou preserved wert, our king to bee,	38	E35 James 2	9
To King James. Upon the happy false rumour of his death,	43	E51 James 3	Ttl
And farre beneath least pause of such a king,	43	E51 James 3	4
The judgement of the king so shine in thee;	47	E63 Salisbury 2	4
And not to dangers. When so wise a king	47	E64 Salisbury 3	12
At naming the French King, their heads they shake,	59	E92 New Crie	33
Nor did the king of Denmarke him salute,	63	E97 Motion	15
To have beene stiled of King Arthurs table.	84	E133 Voyage	24
That found King James, when hunting late, this way,	95	F2 Penshurst	76

347

	Page	Title	Line
KING (cont.)			
To wakefull reason, our affections king:	109	F11 Epode	13
The Sonne of God, th'Eternall King,	130	U1 Nativitie	7
So, may the King proclaime your Conscience is	185	U31 Elsmere	3
So doth the King, and most of the Kings men	212	U43 Vulcan	211
That when King James, above here,	221	U48 Bacchus	37
In raysing him the wisdome of my King.	225	U51 Bacon	20
What can the Poet wish his King may doe,	235	U62 Charles 1	13
To the great and Gratious King Charles. . . .	236	U64 Charles 3	VTtl
Most pious King, but his owne good in you!	236	U64 Charles 3	1
Of so much safetie to the Realme, and King.	238	U66 Queene	14
Of so much health, both to our Land, and King.	238	U66 Queene	V 14
See, see our active King	240	U67 Muses	37
So, the allowance from the King to use,	241	U68 House-hold	10
Upon King Charles his Birth-day . . .	249	U72 King	Ttl
This is King Charles his Day. Speake it, thou Towre,	249	U72 King	VTtl
This is King Charles his Day. Speake it, thou Towre,	249	U72 King	1
This is King Charles his birth day. Speake it, thou Towre,	249	U72 King	V 1
Thy faint, and narrow eyes, to reade the King	250	U73 Weston	2
Both to the honour of the King and State.	251	U74 Weston	24
The bountie of a King, and beautie of his Queene!	252	U75 Epithalam.	8
The king of Creatures, take his paritie	255	U75 Epithalam.	83
All is a story of the King and Queene!	255	U75 Epithalam.	91
And this well mov'd the Judgement of the King	256	U75 Epithalam.	105
See, now the Chappell opens; where the King	256	U75 Epithalam.	121
To have thy God to blesse, thy King to grace,	256	U75 Epithalam.	131
To Th'Best Of Monarchs, Masters, Men, King Charles	259	U76 Petition	2
For Brittans honour, and to Charles my King:	262	U78 Digby	V 18
A New-yeares gift Sung to King Charles, 1635.	263	U79 New-yeares	Ttl
To My L. the King, On the Christning His second Sonne James.	268	U80 Christning	Ttl
Great King, thy having of a second Sonne:	268	U80 Christning	2
I thought me richer then the Persian King.	293	U87 Hor.3:9	4
A Speach Presented unto King James at a tylting . . .	382	Rich	Ttl
unto thee, king of men; their noblest partes	382	Rich	3
Should but the king his Justice-hood employ	405	Inigo Jones 1	77
Sweet Tree of Life, King Davids Strength and Tower,	413	Ghyrlond	38
To Crowne the years, which you begin, great king,	416	Welcome	7
A Grace by Ben: Johnson. extempore. before King James.	418	Grace	Ttl
Our King and Queen the Lord-God blesse,	418	Grace	1
Our King and Queen the Prince God blesse,	418	Grace	V 1
That lives, and breath's, and loves the King.	418	Grace	4
That the King loves, and loves the King.	418	Grace	V 4
Cries Old Sym, the King of Skinkers;	657	Door Apollo	8
KINGDOME			
In his eternall Kingdome, where we sit	286	U84 Muse	145
KINGDOMES			
Three Kingdomes Mirth, in light, and aerie man,	249	U72 King	11
Both Crownes, and Kingdomes in their either hand;	254	U75 Epithalam.	52
The Sunne! great Kings, and mightiest Kingdomes fall!	271	U81 Pawlet	89
The Sunne! great Kings, and mighty Kingdomes fall!	271	U81 Pawlet	V 89
KINGLIER			
But thou wilt yet a Kinglier mastrie trie,	235	U62 Charles 1	5
KINGLY			
A kingly worke; or that long barren fen	309	Horace	93
KINGS			
How, best of Kings, do'st thou a scepter beare!	28	E4 James 1	1
Of Kings for grace; of Poets for my test?	28	E4 James 1	10
Which, by no lesse confirm'd, then thy kings choice,	49	E67 Suffolk	11
That Poets are far rarer births then kings,	53	E79 Rutland	1
So doth the King, and most of the Kings men	212	U43 Vulcan	211
But we have Powder still for the Kings Day,	213	U44 Speach	2
My Princes safetie, and my Kings desire,	219	U47 Tribe	38
The Dedication of the Kings new Cellar. to Bacchus.	220	U48 Bacchus	Ttl
To cure the call'd Kings Evill with thy touch;	235	U62 Charles 1	4
The Kings fame lives. Go now, denie his Teirce.	241	U68 House-hold	14
To the Kings Most Excellent Majesty	259	U76 Petition	VTtl
What worlds of blessings to good Kings they owe:	261	U77 Treasurer	20
Best Kings expect first-fruits of your glad gaines.	263	U79 New-yeares	13
The Sunne! great Kings, and mightiest Kingdomes fall!	271	U81 Pawlet	89
The Sunne! great Kings, and mighty Kingdomes fall!	271	U81 Pawlet	V 89
The gests of Kings, great Captaines, and sad Warres,	309	Horace	105
The deeds of Kings, great Captaines, and sad Warres,	341	Horace	V105
All way of life was shewen; the grace of Kings	329	Horace	497
All kings to doe the self same deeds with some!	406	Inigo Jones 2	4
KINNE			
But what's of kinne to whence it came.	278	U84 Mind	16
KINSMAN			
On Chuffe, Bancks the Usurer's Kinsman.	41	E44 Chuff	Ttl
KISSE			
My lighter comes, to kisse thy learned Muse;	78	E121 Rudyerd 1	2
Kisse me, sweet: The warie lover	103	F6 Celia 2	1
Kisse againe: no creature comes.	103	F6 Celia 2	5
Kisse, and score up wealthy summes.	103	F6 Celia 2	6
Or leave a kisse but in the cup,	106	F9 Celia 3	3
Leave but a kisse within the cup,	106	F9 Celia 3	V 3
6. Clayming a second kisse by Desert.	137	U2 Kisse	Ttl
Since I drew a Morning kisse	137	U2 Kisse	2
May not claime another kisse.	138	U2 Kisse	36
For Loves-sake, kisse me once againe,	139	U2 Another	1
This could be call'd but halfe a kisse.	139	U2 Another	11
Streight puts off all his Anger, and doth kisse	193	U38 Elegy 'Tis	88
Or slipper was left off, and kisse it too,	201	U42 Elegy Let	56
She durst not kisse, but flung thee from her brest.	208	U43 Vulcan	114

```
                                                   Page      Title       Line

KISSE  (cont.)
  Their perfum'd judgements, let them kisse thy Wife.   .    .    .   232   U58 Book-seller    14
  As spirits had stolne her Spirit, in a kisse,      .    .    .   283   U84 Muse           42
  Let us together closely lie, and kisse,     .      .    .    .   294   U88 Petronius       7
  For he did but kisse her, and so let her go.       .    .    .   375   Coryat 1           19
  But with a Kisse, (if thou canst dare it)  .       .    .    .   662   Bedford             9
KISSES
  Have you plac'd the banke of kisses,     .    .    .    .    .   136   U2 Cupid           25
  And lastly by your lips, the banke of kisses,      .    .    .   170   U19 Elegy By        9
KISSING
  May windes as soft as breath of kissing friends,   .    .    .    81   E128 Wm Roe 2       5
  And his lip should kissing teach,     .    .    .    .    .   141   U2 Her man         22
KIST
  Stunke not so ill; nor, when shee kist, Kate Arden.     .    .    87   E133 Voyage       118
KNAT
  Knat, raile, and ruffe too.  How so ere, my man         .    .    65   E101 Supper        20
KNAVE
  To Foole, or Knave.     .    .    .    .    .    .    .    .    46   E61 Foole         Ttl
  Then, The townes honest Man's her errant'st knave.      .    .    75   E115 Honest Man    34
KNAVES
  And in it, two more horride knaves, then Charon.        .    .    84   E133 Voyage        12
KNEELE
  hath armde att all poyntes; charge mee humblye kneele      .   382   Rich                2
KNEELING
  First, that I must kneeling yeeld     .    .    .    .    .   133   U2 Suffered         7
KNEES
  Fit for a Bishops knees! O bow them oft,      .    .    .    .   234   U61 Epigram        13
KNELLS
  Of loud Sepulchres with their hourely knells,      .    .    .    89   E133 Voyage       174
KNEW
  More, then to varie what our elders knew:     .    .    .    .    72   E111 Edmonds 2      6
  The Sonnes obedience knew no No,     .    .    .    .    .   130   U1 Nativitie       14
  That you never knew till now,     .    .    .    .    .    .   131   U2 Excuse          15
  A life that knew nor noise, nor strife:    .    .    .    .   151   U12 Corbet         12
  And knew their how, and where: we should have, then,    .    .   153   U13 Sacvile         3
  Knew I all this afore? had I perceiv'd,    .    .    .    .   171   U20 Shrub           9
  Knew I, that all their Dialogues, and discourse,      .    .   172   U20 Shrub          13
  Knew I this Woman? yes; And you doe see,      .    .    .    .   172   U20 Shrub          15
  Thou art my Cause: whose manners since I knew,     .    .    .   187   U33 Councellour    13
  Knew the time, when      .    .    .    .    .    .    .    .   231   U57 Burges          8
  How happy were the Subject,  if he knew    .    .    .    .   236   U64 Charles 3       1
  Then knew the former ages: yet to life,    .    .    .    .   242   U69 Friend Son     23
  And best he knew her noble Character,      .    .    .    .   287   U84 Muse          155
  (As if he knew it) rapps his hearer to     .    .    .    .   315   Horace            212
  And in their numbers; For, alas, what knew     .    .    .    .   319   Horace            300
  To the Greeke coast thine onely knew the way.      .    .    .   388   Chapman             9
  Then Affricke knew, or the full Grecian store!     .    .    .   398   Drayton            88
  That knew the Crafts they had bin bred in, right:       .    .   410   Brome              14
KNEWE
  As when they both were greate, and both knewe howe      .    .   419   Ode:If Men          3
KNIGHT
  Who scarse can spell th'hard names: whose knight lesse can.   .    28   E3 Bookseller      10
  That Cod can get no widdow, yet a knight,     .    .    .    .    33   E19 Cod 1           1
  A knight-hood bought, to goe a wooing in?     .    .    .    .    42   E46 Luckless 1      2
  The knight-wright's cheated then: Hee'll never pay.     .    .    42   E46 Luckless 1      5
  Yes, now he weares his knight-hood every day.      .    .    .    42   E46 Luckless 1      6
  With tales of Troyes just knight, our faiths abuse:     .    .    84   E133 Voyage         4
  Of errant Knight-hood, with the Dames, and Dwarfes;     .    .   205   U43 Vulcan         67
  Well did thy craftie Clerke, and Knight, Sir Hugh,      .    .   214   U44 Speach         33
  . . . late Wife of Sir Kenelme Digby, Knight: . . .     .    .   272   U84 Eupheme       Ttl
  (Compos'd of Gamester, Captaine, Knight, Knight's man,     .   370   Fletcher            3
  And will be bought of every Lord, and Knight,      .    .    .   398   Drayton            72
KNIGHTES
  Two noble knightes, whome true desire and zeale,     .    .    .   382   Rich                1
KNIGHT-HOOD
  A knight-hood bought, to goe a wooing in?     .    .    .    .    42   E46 Luckless 1      2
  Yes, now he weares his knight-hood every day.      .    .    .    42   E46 Luckless 1      6
  Of errant Knight-hood, with the Dames, and Dwarfes;     .    .   205   U43 Vulcan         67
KNIGHT'S
  (Compos'd of Gamester, Captaine, Knight, Knight's man,     .   370   Fletcher            3
KNIGHTS
  And pitty 'tis, I cannot call 'hem knights:     .    .    .    84   E133 Voyage        22
  Vice, and, am knowne to have a Knights estate.     .    .    .   331   Horace            572
  Vice, and is knowne to have a Knights estate.      .    .    .   352   Horace       V548/572
KNIGHT-WRIGHT'
  The knight-wright's cheated then: Hee'll never pay.     .    .    42   E46 Luckless 1      5
KNIGHT-WRIGHT'S
  The knight-wright's cheated then: Hee'll never pay.     .    .    42   E46 Luckless 1      5
KNIT
  Breake the knit Circle of her Stonie Armes,     .    .    .   177   U25 Desmond        19
  Whereby he may knit sure up     .    .    .    .    .    .   222   U48 Bacchus        47
  And knit the Nuptiall knot,     .    .    .    .    .    .   257   U75 Epithalam.    133
  To knit thy Crowne, and glorifie the rest.      .    .    .   412   Ghyrlond           12
  Now, in a garland by the graces knit:      .    .    .    .   416   Welcome             4
KNITS
  'Tis vertue alone, or nothing, that knits friends:      .    .   216   U45 Squib          12
  That knits brave minds, and manners, more then blood.   .    .   246   U70 Ode           106
  Which knits brave minds, and manners, more then blood.   .    .   246   U70 Ode          V106
KNOCK
  Stiffe! starke! my joynts 'gainst one another knock!    .    .   269   U81 Pawlet          9
KNOT
  Aloft, grow lesse and streightned, full of knot;   .    .    .   157   U13 Sacvile       152
  There is not worne that lace, purle, knot or pin,       .    .   200   U42 Elegy Let      16
```

349

	Page	Title	Line

KNOT (cont.)

		Page	Title	Line
And knit the Nuptiall knot,	. . . . .	257	U75 Epithalam.	133
To have a God come in; except a knot	. . .	317	Horace	273
Who did this Knot compose,	. . . . .	401	Filmer	7

KNOTS

In equall knots: This beares no brands, nor darts,	. .	110	F11 Epode	51
Nor tie knots, nor knots unweave;	. .	142	U2 Her man	50
But their whole inside full of ends, and knots?	.	171	U20 Shrub	12

KNOTTIE

Banck feeles no lamenesse of his knottie gout,	.	36	E31 Banck	1
Like Solons selfe; explat'st the knottie Lawes	.	217	U46 Coke	17
The knottie heads of the most surly Groomes,	.	363	Riches	8

KNOW'

I oft looke on false coyne, to know't from true:	.	68	E107 Hungry	3

KNOW

And by thy wiser temper, let men know	.	27	E2 My Booke	8
All that I am in arts, all that I know,	.	31	E14 Camden	2
Then his chast wife, though Beast now know no more,	.	35	E26 Beast 2	1
And than in them, how could we know god more?	.	38	E35 James 2	8
I know no couple better can agree!	. . .	40	E42 Giles	18
That we thy losse might know, and thou our love,	.	43	E51 James 3	1
Foole, as if halfe eyes will not know a fleece	.	45	E56 Poet-Ape	13
The world reputes you barren: but I know	.	46	E62 Would-bee	3
Which deed I know not, whether were more high,	.	49	E66 Cary	7
Then, since we (more then many) these truths know:	.	50	E70 Wm Roe 1	7
The world must know your greatnesse is my debter.	.	51	E73 Fine Grand	4
Fortie things more, deare Grand, which you know true,	.	51	E73 Fine Grand	21
And know thee, then, a judge, not of one yeare;	.	51	E74 Chancelor	2
A line unto thee, till the world it know;	.	54	E81 Proule	2
I would have spent: how every Muse should know it,	.	55	E84 Bedford 2	7
When I would know thee Goodyere, my thought lookes	.	55	E86 Goodyere 2	1
They know the states of Christendome, not the places:	.	59	E92 New Crie	8
The councels, projects, practises they know,	.	59	E92 New Crie	11
To breake up seales, and close 'hem. And they know,	.	59	E92 New Crie	29
That know not so much state, wrong, as they doo.	.	59	E92 New Crie	40
Then whose I doe not know a whiter soule,	.	60	E93 Radcliffe	11
Know you the cause? H'has neither land, nor lease,	.	63	E97 Motion	9
And I know nothing more thou hast to doo.	.	63	E98 Th Roe 1	2
To this, if ought appeare, which I not know of,	.	65	E101 Supper	25
Know you to be a Sydney, though un-named?	.	66	E103 L Wroth 1	4
A picture, which the world for yours must know,	.	67	E104 Montgomery	14
And first to know thine owne state, then the States.	.	70	E109 Nevil	12
Thou wert the first, mad'st merit know her strength,	.	75	E116 Jephson	5
And, in their errors maze, thine owne way know:	.	76	E119 Shelton	13
And know, for whom a teare you shed,	.	77	E120 S. P.	3
Shee learnes to know long difference of their states.	.	78	E121 Rudyerd 1	4
The aged Saturne's age, and rites to know;	.	78	E122 Rudyerd 2	2
I know not which th'hast most, candor, or wit:	.	78	E123 Rudyerd 3	2
And, than this same, I know no abler way	.	80	E127 Aubigny	11
Countries, and climes, manners, and men to know,	.	80	E128 Wm Roe 2	2
Even those for whom they doe this, know they erre:	.	83	E131 Ferrab. 2	10
But I will speake (and know I shall be heard)	.	87	E133 Voyage	105
With all, that hospitalitie doth know!	.	95	F2 Penshurst	60
I know thy formes are studyed arts,	.	100	F4 To the World	9
I know too, though thou strut, and paint,	.	100	F4 To the World	13
I know thou whole art but a shop	.	100	F4 To the World	17
I know thou canst nor shew, nor beare	.	101	F4 To the World	39
No, I doe know, that I was borne	.	101	F4 To the World	61
That the curious may not know	.	103	F6 Celia 2	19
Every stew in towne to know;	.	105	F8 Sicknesse	38
Every Cranck in towne to know;	.	105	F8 Sicknesse	V 38
Not to know vice at all, and keepe true state,	.	109	F11 Epode	1
Next, to that vertue, is to know vice well,	.	109	F11 Epode	3
No, vice, we let thee know,	.	111	F11 Epode	72
No, vice, I let thee know,	.	111	F11 Epode	V 72
With you, I know, my offring will find grace.	.	114	F12 Rutland	30
Beautie, I know, is good, and bloud is more;	.	114	F12 Rutland	37
Them, or their officers: and no man know,	.	118	F13 Aubigny	79
O, be thou witnesse, that the reynes dost know,	.	122	F15 Heaven	5
I know my state, both full of shame, and scorne,	.	122	F15 Heaven	17
When you know, that this is she,	.	131	U2 Excuse	18
By her lookes I doe her know,	.	136	U2 Cupid	18
On what they viewing know.	.	144	U3 Musicall	20
On which they see or know.	.	144	U3 Musicall	V 20
For if the Nymphs should know my Swaine,	.	147	U7 Nymph	3
From either heart, I know;	.	148	U7 Nymph	32
You cannot doubt, but I, who freely know	.	153	U13 Sacvile	13
Sure there is Misterie in it, I not know,	.	156	U13 Sacvile	97
And you, Sir, know it well, to whom I write,	.	156	U13 Sacvile	109
I have the lyst of mine owne faults to know,	.	156	U13 Sacvile	114
Ride, saile, am coach'd, know I how farre I have gone,	.	156	U13 Sacvile	121
No! he must feele and know, that will advance.	.	156	U13 Sacvile	123
Of Christendome! And neither of these know,	.	157	U13 Sacvile	129
You know (without my flatt'ring you) too much	.	157	U13 Sacvile	155
I Know to whom I write. Here, I am sure,	.	158	U14 Selden	1
I know no beautie, nor no youth that will.	.	171	U19 Elegy By	20
Doe not you aske to know her, she is worse	.	172	U20 Shrub	17
Aske not to know this Man. If fame should speake	.	172	U21 Ltl Shrub	1
But both might know their wayes were understood,	.	176	U24 Frontispice	7
But both might know their wayes are understood,	.	176	U24 Frontispice	V 7
Both braines and hearts, and mine now best doe know it:	.	182	U28 Worth	8
If thou wouldst know the vertues of Man-kind,	.	185	U30 Burleigh	1
Who, though their guilt, and perjurie they know,	.	186	U32 Elsmere	11

	Page	Title	Line
KNOW (cont.)			
Little know they, that professe Amitie,	190	U37 Friend-Book	19
And lesse they know, who being free to use	190	U37 Friend-Book	22
God, and the good, know to forgive, and save.	191	U38 Elegy 'Tis	19
Of love, and hate: and came so nigh to know	200	U42 Elegy Let	35
Though but in daunces, it shall know his power;	210	U43 Vulcan	157
Though but in daunces, it shall know high power;	210	U43 Vulcan	V157
Though but in daunger, it shall know thy power;	210	U43 Vulcan	V157
All licence in our lives? What need we know,	215	U44 Speach	70
No piece of money, but you know, or make	216	U45 Squib	14
And know whose ignorance is more then theirs;	218	U47 Trite	24
Are asked to climbe. First give me faith, who know	220	U47 Tribe	75
Before his braine doe know it;	221	U48 Bacchus	30
Countries, and Climes, manners, and men to know.	224	U50 Countesse	22
Accept his Muse; and tell, I know you can,	231	U56 Covell	26
The Parish will know it.	232	U57 Burges	26
To know the heads of danger! where 'tis fit	233	U59 Newcastle	17
Are lost upon accompt! And none will know	237	U64 Charles 3	21
Are lost upon accompt! And none doe know	237	U64 Charles 3	V 21
Well, they should know him, would the K. but grant	241	U68 House-hold	5
Profit, or Chance had made us: But I know	241	U69 Friend Son	3
And thinke, nay know, thy Morison's not dead.	245	U70 Ode	78
This made you first to know the Why	247	U70 Ode	107
Some houres before it should, that these may know	257	U75 Epithalam.	146
Of Life, that fall so; Christians know their birth	257	U75 Epithalam.	156
The longing Couple, all that elder Lovers know.	258	U75 Epithalam.	192
This I would doe, could I know Weston, one	260	U77 Treasurer	10
But you I know, my Lord; and know you can	261	U77 Treasurer	13
Of murmuring Subjects; make the Nations know	261	U77 Treasurer	19
Of froward Citizens; make the Nations know	261	U77 Treasurer	V 19
Tho', happy Muse, thou know my Digby well;	262	U78 Digby	1
That know the times, and seasons when t'appeare,	263	U79 New-yeares	11
Wee know no other power then his,	265	U79 New-yeares	42
Which they that have the Crowne are sure to know!	271	U81 Pawlet	76
Which the Elect of God are sure to know!	271	U81 Pawlet	V 76
At either Stemme, and know the veines of good	274	U84 Descent	8
Yet know, with what thou art possest,	281	U84 Mind	70
Sure, I am dead, and know it not! I feele	283	U84 Muse	29
And she doth know, out of the shade of Death,	285	U84 Muse	91
And each shall know, there, one anothers face,	285	U84 Muse	115
Of lapsed Nature) best know what to doe,	288	U84 Muse	214
Like lustfull beasts, that onely know to doe it:	294	U88 Petronius	4
Of daring all, hath still beene given; we know it:	305	Horace	12
Of daring ought, hath still beene given; we know it:	338	Horace	V 12
Nor know t'observe: why (i'the Muses name)	311	Horace	128
To ignorance still, then either learne, or know?	311	Horace	131
To ignorance still, then yet to learne, or know?	341	Horace	V126/131
If either you, or I, know the right way	323	Horace	402
If either you, or I know any way	348	Horace	V388/402
Is to be wise; thy matter first to know;	325	Horace	441
The docile mind may soone thy precepts know,	329	Horace	504
I wonder how this happie man should know,	333	Horace	605
Nor takes she pride to know them.	365	Ode Splendor	24
But should they know (as I) that this,	369	Ode Who saith	97
It is inough, their griefe shall know	369	Ode Who saith	113
Read here a little, that thou mayst know much.	371	Epitaph	2
I know for such, as (if my word will waigh)	386	Husband	11
But I have seene thy worke, and I know thee:	386	Browne	3
But, I would have, thee, to know something new,	394	Jane Ogle	13
You know, I never was of Truth afeard,	414	Rutter	4
That sit to censure Playes, yet know not when,	414	Rutter	8
And know the woofe, and warpe thereof; can tell	415	Rutter	15
KNOWE			
His name is Skeuopoios wee all knowe,	404	Inigo Jones 1	60
Thou art not worth it. Who will care to knowe	409	Detractor	13
And lesse they knowe, that being free to use	422	Censure	15
KNOWES			
Makes serious use of all great trade he knowes.	35	E28 Surly	3
We need a man that knowes the severall graces	61	E95 Savile	27
Almost, is exercis'd: and scarse one knowes,	66	E102 Pembroke	7
He knowes, below, he shall finde plentie of meate,	95	F2 Penshurst	70
He alwayes gives what he knowes meet;	99	F3 Wroth	98
Who could be false to? chiefly, when he knowes	112	F11 Epode	103
Who would be false to? chiefly, when he knowes	112	F11 Epode	V103
That knowes the waight of guilt: He will refraine	112	F11 Epode	113
Then which, a nobler heaven it selfe knowes not.	115	F12 Rutland	67
O, is it so? knowes he so much? and will	155	U13 Sacvile	73
Thy learned Chamber-fellow, knowes to doe	161	U14 Selden	72
Where he that knowes will, like a Lapwing, flie	198	U40 Elegy That	37
Ne knowes he flatt'ring Colours, or false light.	227	U52 Answer	21
Of riot, and consumption, knowes the way	235	U61 Epigram	17
Pan knowes no other power then his,	265	U79 New-yeares	64
Hee knowes, what worke h'hath done, to call this Guest,	284	U84 Muse	81
Who knowes the hearts of all, and can dissect	286	U84 Muse	150
But in the maine worke haplesse: since he knowes	307	Horace	48
Fit rites. The Child, that now knowes how to say,	315	Horace	225
Fit dues. The Child, that now knowes how to say,	344	Horace	V225
He knowes not why, and changeth every houre.	315	Horace	228
Hee, that hath studied well the debt, and knowes	325	Horace	445
Or knowes not what Cassellius Aulus can;	331	Horace	553
Hee, that not knowes the games, nor how to use	331	Horace	565
To let it downe, who knowes, if he did cast	335	Horace	656
His cause of making Verses none knowes why:	335	Horace	670

		Page	Title	Line

KNOWING

Longer a knowing, then most wits doe live.	· · ·	34	E23 Donne 1	5
These were thy knowing arts: which who doth now	· · ·	75	E116 Jephson	13
And, knowing this, should I yet stay, ·	· · ·	100	F4 To the World	21
For want of knowing the Poet, to say him nay?	· · ·	241	U68 House-hold	4
The knowing Weston, and that learned Lord	· · ·	263	U78 Digby	28
And will you, worthy Sonne, Sir, knowing this,	· · ·	285	U84 Muse	97

KNOWLEDGE

Thy faith is all the knowledge that thou hast.	· · ·	32	E18 Censurer	10
That they to knowledge so should toure upright,	· · ·	55	E85 Goodyere 1	6
It was a knowledge, that begat that love. ·	· · ·	55	E86 Goodyere 2	8
Whose knowledge claymeth at the helme to stand:	· · ·	61	E95 Savile	21
Give knowledge instantly, · ·	· · ·	109	F11 Epode	12
Of generall knowledge; watch'd men, manners too,	· · ·	159	U14 Selden	33
In the same Mines of knowledge; and thence brought	· ·	161	U14 Selden	76
In the rich Mines of knowledge; and thence brought	· ·	161	U14 Selden	V 76
Knowledge, that sleepes, doth die; · ·	· · ·	174	U23 Himselfe	3
Of worthiest knowledge, that can take mens minds.	· · ·	217	U46 Coke	20
Searching for knowledge, and to keepe your mind	· ·	225	U50 Countesse	29
Our sense you doe with knowledge fill, ·	· · ·	278	U84 Mind	19
Thou, such thy judgement is, thy knowledge too,	· · ·	331	Horace	573

KNOWNE

Play-wright, I loath to have thy manners knowne	· · ·	42	E49 Playwrt 1	5
My countries parents I have many knowne; ·	· · ·	46	E60 Mounteagle	9
Nor lesse in practice; but lesse mark'd, lesse knowne:	· ·	58	E91 Vere	14
By his each glorious parcell to be knowne!	· · ·	62	E97 Motion	6
About the towne; and knowne too, at that price.	· · ·	74	E115 Honest Man	6
T'extract, and choose the best of all these knowne,	· ·	80	E128 Wm Roe 2	3
Which Musick had; or speake her knowne effects,	· ·	82	E130 Ferrab. 1	3
A fortune, in this age, but rarely knowne. ·	· · ·	96	F2 Penshurst	92
What bird, or beast, is knowne so dull, ·	· · ·	101	F4 To the World	29
But grant us perfect, they're not knowne. ·	· · ·	104	F7 Women but	10
Have beautie knowne, yet none so famous seene?	· · ·	114	F12 Rutland	50
Yet if it be not knowne, · · ·	· · ·	147	U7 Nymph	5
Yet, yet I doubt he is not knowne, · ·	· · ·	147	U7 Nymph	20
Well knowne, and practiz'd borrowers on their word,	· ·	154	U13 Sacvile	48
More honour in him, 'cause we'ave knowne him mad:	· ·	168	U15 Friend-Wars	194
That ne're was knowne to last above a fit!	· · ·	171	U20 Shrub	6
By which as proper titles, she is knowne ·	· · ·	176	U24 Frontispice	16
Soone as lazie thou wert knowne, · ·	· · ·	183	U29 Fit of Rime	13
Whose like I have knowne the Taylors Wife put on	· ·	201	U42 Elegy Let	39
Had I fore-knowne of this thy least desire ·	· ·	205	U43 Vulcan	59
Had I fore-knowne but of thy least desire ·	· · ·	205	U43 Vulcan	V 59
So are they profitable to be knowne: · ·	· · ·	225	U50 Countesse	34
'Tis a brave cause of joy, let it be knowne,	· · ·	225	U51 Bacon	17
T'escape this common knowne necessitie, ·	· · ·	271	U81 Pawlet	93
T' have knowne no envy, but by suffring it!	· · ·	287	U84 Muse	162
I can out of knowne geare, a fable frame, ·	· · ·	321	Horace	349
I can, out of knowne stuff, a Fable frame, ·	· ·	347	Horace	V341/349
With honour make the farre-knowne Author live.	· · ·	329	Horace	519
Vice, and, am knowne to have a Knights estate.	· · ·	331	Horace	572
Vice, and is knowne to have a Knights estate.	· · ·	352	Horace	V548/572
The Hebrid Isles, and knowne · ·	· · ·	368	Ode Who saith	66
Which, unto all Ages, for his will be knowne,	· · ·	379	Coryat 3	11
To be knowne what thou art, a blatant beast,	· · ·	408	Detractor	9
Little knowne they that proffesse Amitye ·	· · ·	421	Censure	12

KNOWS

| Here's one makes verses, but there's none knows why: | · · | 355 | Horace | V670 |

KNOW'ST

Guiltie, be wise; and though thou know'st the crimes	· ·	36	E30 Guiltie	1
Thou hast seene hell (some say) and know'st all nookes there,	·	85	E133 Voyage	51
Know'st only well to paint a Cipresse tree. ·	· ·	305	Horace	25

KNOW'T

| I oft looke on false coyne, to know't from true: | · · | 68 | E107 Hungry | 3 |

KYD   (See KID)

KYNDE

| Noe velvet Sheath you weare, will alter kynde. | · · · | 403 | Inigo Jones 1 | 26 |

L'

| In smiling L'envoye, as he would deride · | · · | 202 | U42 Elegy Let | 75 |

L

Epitaph on Elizabeth, L. H. · · ·	· ·	79	E124 Elizabeth	Ttl
An Epitaph, on Henry L. La-ware. To the Passer-by.	·	233	U60 La-ware	Ttl
On the Right Honourable, and vertuous Lord Weston, L. · · ·		250	U73 Weston	Ttl
To the Right Hon'ble Hierome, L. Weston. An Ode · · ·	·	250	U74 Weston	Ttl
To My L. the King, On the Christning His second Sonne James.	·	268	U80 Christning	Ttl

LA

| An Epitaph, on Henry L. La-ware. To the Passer-by. | · · | 233 | U60 La-ware | Ttl |
| Henry, the brave young Lord La-ware, · · | · · | 233 | U60 La-ware | 3 |

LABOR

| From each of which, I labor to be free, · | · · · | 422 | Censure | 21 |

LABORS

| of thy rich labors worlds of thoughts created, · | · · | 361 | Palmer | 22 |

LABOUR

Conceiv'd in sinne, and unto labour borne, ·	· ·	122	F15 Heaven	18
From each of which I labour to be free, ·	· · ·	190	U37 Friend-Book	28
Doth labour with the Phrase more then the sense?	· · ·	222	U49 Pucell	14
There is no labour, nor no shame in this: ·	· ·	294	U88 Petronius	8
My selfe for shortnesse labour; and I grow ·	· · ·	307	Horace	35
My selfe for shortnesse labour, and am stil'd ·	· ·	339	Horace	V 36/ 35
What straight-way he must labour to retract. ·	· ·	315	Horace	240
Meere raigning words: nor will I labour so ·	· ·	321	Horace	343

LABOUR'D

| These (noblest Cecil) labour'd in my thought, · | · · | 48 | E64 Salisbury 3 | 15 |

352

		Page	Title	Line

LABOUR'D (cont.)
And labour'd in the worke; not with the fame:	. . . .	185	U30 Burleigh	12
Not labour'd for, but left thee by thy Sire;	. . . .	295	U90 Mart.10:47	3
Hee, while he labour'd to be thought a God	. . . .	335	Horace	661
Their labour'd tunes reherse,	. . . .	420	Ode:If Men	22

LABOURING
| Thy labouring wheele, comes scarce a Pitcher out? | . . . | 307 | Horace | 30 |
| 'Tis not enough, the labouring Muse affords | . . . | 341 | Horace | V140 |

LABOURS
The french disease, with which he labours yet?	. . .	56	E88 Monsieur	10
Can so speake Caesar, as thy labours doe. .	. . .	71	E110 Edmonds 1	12
Still, with thy former labours; yet, once more,	. . .	85	E133 Voyage	56
Is now from home. You lose your labours quite,	. . .	89	E133 Voyage	181
With his old earthly labours. T'exact more,	. . .	107	F10 Proludium	5
So many my Yeares-labours in an houre? .	. . .	202	U43 Vulcan	4
With endlesse labours, whilst thy learning drawes	. . .	217	U46 Coke	18
Of their long labours, was in Verse set downe:	. . .	329	Horace	500
(And labours to seem worthy of that feare)	. . .	407	Inigo Jones 3	2

LACE
With the Lace that doth it deck, .	. . .	137	U2 Cupid	30
And pronounce, which band, or lace, .	. . .	140	U2 Promise	19
His Lace and Starch; And fall upon her back	. . .	163	U15 Friend-Wars	49
There is not worne that lace, purle, knot or pin,	. . .	200	U42 Elegy Let	16
That chanc'd the lace, laid on a Smock, to see,	. . .	201	U42 Elegy Let	66
The Stuffes, the Velvets, Plushes, Fringes, Lace,	. . .	202	U42 Elegy Let	79
Embroideries, Feathers, Fringes, Lace, .	. . .	275	U84 Body	3

LACES
| To stuffes and Laces, those my Man can buy. | . . . | 223 | U49 Pucell | 28 |

LACK
Full twentie stone; of which I lack two pound:	. . .	229	U54 Squib	12
As the old Bard, should no Canary lack. .	. . .	241	U68 House-hold	11
As she did lack	. . .	254	U75 Epithalam.	46
As they did lack	. . .	254	U75 Epithalam.	V 46
It should rather have bene Tom that a horse did lack.	. . .	374	Coryat 1	15

LACKE
| Since he doth lacke . . . | . . . | 121 | F14 Sydney | 27 |

LACK'D
| And those that lack'd it, to suspect at length, | . . | 75 | E116 Jephson | 6 |
| Because they lack'd the sacred pen, could give | . . | 115 | F12 Rutland | 56 |

LACK'DST
| As if thou wert my friend, but lack'dst a cause. | . . . | 43 | E52 Courtling | 4 |

LACKS
| For twelve yeeres yet to come, what each state lacks. | . . | 59 | E92 New Crie | 14 |

LAD
| Of the times past, when he was a young lad; | . . . | 317 | Horace | 248 |

LADDER
| By Jacobs Ladder, to the top . . | . . . | 274 | U84 Cradle | 38 |

LADEN
Laden with plague-sores, and their sinnes, were heard,	. .	84	E133 Voyage	17
And furrowes laden with their weight; .	. . .	98	F3 Wroth	42
That, laden with my sinnes, I seeke for ease?	. . .	122	F15 Heaven	4
Laden with Bellie, and doth hardly approach	. . .	230	U56 Covell	9

LADIE
And Charles brings home the Ladie. .	. . .	222	U48 Bacchus	54
In thought to praise this Ladie; . .	. . .	365	Ode Splendor	18
To the memorye of that most Honoured Ladie Jane, . . .	.	394	Jane Ogle	Ttl
For this did Katherine, Ladie Ogle, die .	. . .	400	Lady Ogle	33

LADIES
On Mill my Ladies Woman. .	. . .	57	E90 Mill	Ttl
The nicer thing to tast her ladies page;	. . .	57	E90 Mill	5
And he growne youth, was call'd to his ladies chamber.	. . .	57	E90 Mill	10
The lighter Faunes, to reach thy Ladies oke.	. . .	94	F2 Penshurst	18
Ladies? and of them the best? .	. . .	104	F8 Sicknesse	2
Nor all the ladies of the Thespian lake,	. . .	108	F10 Proludium	25
Lives to the Lord, but to the Ladies end. .	. . .	165	U15 Friend-Wars	94
Lives for the Lord, but to the Ladies end. .	. . .	165	U15 Friend-Wars	V 94

LADS
| And can tread firme, longs with like lads to play; | . . | 315 | Horace | 226 |

LADY'
| Thy lady's noble, fruitfull, chaste withall. | . . . | 96 | F2 Penshurst | 90 |

LADY
To Fine Lady Would-bee. . . .	. . .	46	E62 Would-bee	Ttl
To Mary Lady Wroth. . . .	. . .	66	E103 L Wroth 1	Ttl
To Mary Lady Wroth. . . .	. . .	67	E105 L Wroth 2	Ttl
To his Lady, then Mrs. Cary. . .	. . .	80	E126 Mrs Cary	Ttl
Thy lord, and lady, though they have no sute.	. . .	95	F2 Penshurst	50
On thy good lady, then! who, therein, reap'd	. . .	95	F2 Penshurst	84
Epistle. To Katherine, Lady Aubigny. .	. . .	116	F13 Aubigny	Ttl
No lady, but, at some time, loves her glasse. .	. . .	117	F13 Aubigny	26
Wherein my Lady rideth! .	. . .	134	U2 Triumph	2
So to see a Lady tread, .	. . .	138	U2 Kisse	25
Doe all the tricks of a saut Lady Bitch; .	. . .	164	U15 Friend-Wars	76
Of woman of fashion, and a Lady of spirit:'	. . .	164	U15 Friend-Wars	82
A Sonnet, to the noble Lady, the Lady Mary Worth.	. .	182	U28 Worth	Ttl
The Lady Mayresse pass'd through the Towne,	. . .	201	U42 Elegy Let	70
Epistle. To my Lady Covell. . .	. . .	230	U56 Covell	Ttl
. . . England, with the Lady Frances Stuart, Daughter of . . .	252	U75 Epithalam.	Ttl
The Lady Frances, drest . .	. . .	253	U75 Epithalam.	37
An Epigram To my Muse, the Lady Digby, . .	.	262	U78 Digby	Ttl
An Elegie On the Lady Jane Pawlet, Marchion: of Winton.	.	268	U81 Pawlet	Ttl
Shee was the Lady Jane, and Marchionisse .	.	269	U81 Pawlet	19
. . Of that truly-noble Lady, the Lady Venetia Digby, . . .		272	U84 Eupheme	Ttl
9. Elegie on my Muse. The truly honoured Lady, . . .		282	U84 Muse	Ttl

		Page	Title	Line

LADY (cont.)
A Wife, a Friend, a Lady, or a Love; . . . . . 285 U84 Muse 99
Not tost or troubled with light Lady-aire; . . . . 287 U84 Muse 164
Where some great Lady, or her diligent Nourse; . . . 313 Horace 164
Lady, or Pusil, that weares maske, or fan, . . . 370 Fletcher 4
Not usuall in a Lady; and yet true: . . . . . 394 Jane Ogle 14
At least so great a Lady. She was wife . . . . 394 Jane Ogle 15
Th'ascent of Lady Fame which none could spy . . . 403 Inigo Jones 1 35
The Paltzgrave, and the Lady Besse, ... 418 Grace 2
LADY-AIRE
Not tost or troubled with light Lady-aire; . . . . 287 U84 Muse 164
LADYES
10. Another Ladyes exception present at the hearing. . . 142 U2 Exception Ttl
To our owne Ladyes; and in storie there . . . . 207 U43 Vulcan 97
for our owne Ladyes; and in storie there . . . . 207 U43 Vulcan V 97
These Graces, when the rest of Ladyes view . . . 225 U50 Countesse 31
Run all the Rounds in a soft Ladyes eare, ... 230 U56 Covell 16
LADY'S
Thy lady's noble, fruitfull, chaste withall. . . . 96 F2 Penshurst 90
LAID
To see thy fathers rites new laid on thee. . . . 47 E64 Salisbury 3 6
Was now laid in a Manger. . . . . . 130 U1 Nativitie 12
If by us, the oddes were laid, ... 138 U2 Kisse 7
Not at my prayers, but your sense; which laid . . . 153 U13 Sacvile 9
That chanc'd the lace, laid on a Smock, to see, . . . 201 U42 Elegy Let 66
O! had I seene her laid out a faire Corse, . . . 282 U84 Muse 11
Indeed, she is not dead! but laid to sleepe . . . 283 U84 Muse 45
Have more or lesse then just five Acts: nor laid, . . 317 Horace 272
Is so implexed, and laid in, between, ... 412 Ghyrlond 7
But lowlie laid, as on the earth asleep, ... 413 Ghyrlond 18
LAIES
There twice a day in sacred Laies, ... 292 U86 Hor.4:1 25
LAKE
Nor all the ladies of the Thespian lake, ... 108 F10 Proludium 25
Beneath a Sweet-wood Roofe, neere Alba Lake: . . . 292 U86 Hor.4:1 20
To Loumond lake, and Twedes blacke-springing fountaine. . 368 Ode Who saith 72
Vermilion, Lake, or Cinnopar affoards . . . . 406 Inigo Jones 1 94
LAMB
That, planted round, there sing before the Lamb, . . 285 U84 Muse 89
LAMBE
Or at the Feast of Bounds, the Lambe then slaine, . . 291 U85 Country 59
Her right, by gift, and purchase of the Lambe: . . . 400 Lady Ogle 36
LAMBES
Your Milkes, your Fells, your Fleeces, and first Lambes, . 265 U79 New-yeares 50
With Doves; or Lambes, with Tygres coupled be. . . . 305 Horace 16
LAMBETH
That haunt Pickt-hatch, Mersh-Lambeth, and White-fryers, . 30 E12 Shift 2
LAMBS
Our milke. Our fells. Our fleeces. and first Lambs. . 264 U79 New-yeares 16
LAME
How much they lame her in her propertie. . . . 190 U37 Friend-Book 21
And why to me this, thou lame Lord of fire, . . . 202 U43 Vulcan 1
And why to me this, thou lame god of fire, . . . 202 U43 Vulcan V 1
Howe much they lame hir, in hir propertye: . . . 421 Censure 14
LAMENESSE
Banck feeles no lamenesse of his knottie gout, . . . 36 E31 Banck 1
LAMENT
Will man lament the state he should envie? . . . 41 E45 First Son 6
LAMENTS
In Verse unequall match'd, first sowre Laments, . . 309 Horace 107
LAMIA'
The Child, when Lamia'has din'd, out of her maw. . . 329 Horace 510
LAMIA
Empusa, Lamia, or some Monster, more . . . . 398 Drayton 87
LAMIA'HAS
The Child, when Lamia'has din'd, out of her maw. . . 329 Horace 510
LAMPE
Who made a lampe of Berenices hayre? . . . . 115 F12 Rutland 61
LANCE (See also LAUNCES)
Upon his pointed Lance: . . . . . . 240 U67 Muses 39
Your hottest Causticks to, burne, lance, or cut: . . 270 U81 Pawlet 54
Your hotter Causticks to, burne, lance, or cut: . . 270 U81 Pawlet V 54
In each of which, he seemes to shake a Lance, . . . 392 Shakespeare 69
LANC'LOTS
The Tristrams, Lanc'lots, Turpins, and the Peers, . . 206 U43 Vulcan 69
LAND
And since, the whole land was preserv'd for thee. . . 38 E35 James 2 10
And land on one, whose face durst never bee . . . 56 E88 Monsieur 5
Know you the cause? H'has neither land, nor lease, . . 63 E97 Motion 9
For which there must more sea, and land be leap'd, . . 69 E107 Hungry 16
For'his whore: Groyne doth still occupy his land. . . 75 E117 Groyne 2
From Venice, Paris, or some in-land passage . . . 85 E133 Voyage 33
The lower land, that to the river bends, ... 94 F2 Penshurst 22
Bright eeles, that emulate them, and leape on land, . . 94 F2 Penshurst 37
The apple-harvest and ploued land up cast; . . . 98 F3 Wroth V 43
That distill their husbands land . . . . . 105 F8 Sicknesse 29
Melt downe their husbands land, to poure away . . . 118 F13 Aubigny 73
As farre as any poore Sword i' the Land. . . . 154 U13 Sacvile 55
All as their prize, turne Pyrats here at Land, . . . 155 U13 Sacvile 81
Though thou wert Muster-master of the Land. . . . 167 U15 Friend-Wars 174
All is not barren land, doth fallow lie. . . . 169 U17 Friend-Debt 16
Of all the Land. Who now at such a Rate, . . . 185 U30 Burleigh 19
Like the dull wearied Crane that (come on land) . . 198 U40 Elegy That 35

		Page	Title	Line

LAND (cont.)
In so much land a yeare, or such a Banke,	215	U44 Speach	76
It is a richer Purchase then of land.	216	U45 Squib	26
T'obtaine of God, what all the Land should aske?	234	U61 Epigram	11
Of so much health, both to our Land, and King.	238	U66 Queene	V 14
Hath brought the Land an Heire!	240	U67 Muses	53
Hath rais'd to be the Port unto his Land!	250	U73 Weston	4
And both a strength, and Beautie to his Land!	251	U74 Weston	30
The choisest Virgin-troup of all the Land!	254	U75 Epithalam.	50
At land she triumphs in the triple shade,	268	U80 Christning	15
Of some small thankfull land: whether he bee	313	Horace	166
So doth the Poet, who is rich in land,	333	Horace	599
So doth the Poet, that is rich in Land,	353	Horace	V599
But over Land to Trent:	368	Ode Who saith	75
And here he disdained not, in a forraine land	375	Coryat 1	32

LANDS
With his owne Oxen tills his Sires left lands,	289	U85 Country	3
And, Sylvane, thine that keptst his Lands!	290	U85 Country	22
And, Sylvane, thine that keep'st his Lands!	290	U85 Country	V 22

LANE
Your Fleet-lane Furies; and hot cookes doe dwell,	88	E133 Voyage	143
All live dogs from the lane, and his shops sight,	241	U69 Friend Son	12
As other soules, to his, dwell in a Lane:	262	U78 Digby	12
Thou paint a Lane, where Thumb the Pygmy meets!	407	Inigo Jones 2	12
Thou paint a Lane, where Thumb with Geffry meets!	407	Inigo Jones 2	V 12

LANGLEY
| you'l be as Langley sayd, an Inigo still. | 403 | Inigo Jones 1 | 22 |

LANGUAGE
To it, thy language, letters, arts, best life,	34	E23 Donne 1	7
For wittie, in his language, is obscene.	42	E49 Playwrt 1	4
But the Language, and the Truth,	131	U2 Excuse	10
I'm sure my language to her, was as sweet,	149	U9 Picture	6
I'm sure my language to her, is as sweet,	149	U9 Picture	V 6
The puritie of Language; and among	207	U43 Vulcan	93
The Hawking language? or our Day to breake	215	U44 Speach	72
For bawdry, 'tis her language, and not mine.	223	U49 Pucell	26
But dare not aske our wish in Language fescennine:	257	U75 Epithalam.	160
Speakes Heavens Language! and discourseth free	271	U81 Pawlet	71
Speakes Heavens Language! and discovereth free	271	U81 Pawlet	V 71
Nor language, nor cleere order ere forsakes.	307	Horace	58
Nor language, nor cleere order will forsake.	339	Horace	V 59/ 58
And wealth unto our language; and brought forth	309	Horace	82
Sad language fits sad lookes; stuff'd menacings,	311	Horace	149
Unwonted language; and that sense of worth	319	Horace	308
Her language, if the Stay, and Care t'have mended,	325	Horace	413
Taught Pallas language; Cynthia modesty;	371	Epitaph	7
To make the Language sweet upon her tongue.	402	Inigo Jones 1	14

LANGUAGES
| Vulgar Languages that want | 184 | U29 Fit of Rime | 43 |

LANGUISH
| For lust will languish, and that heat decay. | 294 | U88 Petronius | 5 |
| The severall figures, languish in suspence, | 370 | Author | 10 |

LANGUISHING
| Whether it languishing stucke upon the wall, | 87 | E133 Voyage | 136 |

LANTERNE
| Keepe in reserv'd in his Dark-lanterne face, | 198 | U40 Elegy That | 23 |
| Of Lanterne-lerry: with fuliginous heat | 405 | Inigo Jones 1 | 72 |

LANTERNE-LERRY
| Of Lanterne-lerry: with fuliginous heat | 405 | Inigo Jones 1 | 72 |

LANTHERNE
| Thou hast no lanthorne, whereof tales are told; | 93 | F2 Penshurst | 4 |

LANTHORNE
| And Mars, that gave thee a Lanthorne for a Crowne. | 203 | U43 Vulcan | 10 |
| Or in the Bell-Mans Lanthorne, like a spie, | 211 | U43 Vulcan | 187 |

LAPLAND
| Thou hadst brought Lapland, or old Cobalus, | 398 | Drayton | 86 |

LAPSED
| Of lapsed Nature) best know what to doe, | 288 | U84 Muse | 214 |

LAPWING
| Where he that knowes will, like a Lapwing, flie | 198 | U40 Elegy That | 37 |

LARGE
For, if the hum'rous world will talke at large,	83	E131 Ferrab. 2	7
Forehead large, and white as snow;	141	U2 Her man	V 18
Large claspe of Nature, such a wit can bound.	160	U14 Selden	64
Had tickled your large Nosthrill: many a Reame	205	U43 Vulcan	62
Had filled your large nostrills with the steame:	205	U43 Vulcan	V 62
A letter'd mind, and a large heart would place	227	U52 Answer	23
Hee can, he will, and with large int'rest pay,	236	U63 Charles 2	5
With a long, large, and blest posteritie!	236	U63 Charles 2	12
In his great Actions: view whom his large hand	250	U73 Weston	3
Doe boast their Loves, and Brav'ries so at large,	253	U75 Epithalam.	19
How each one playes his part, of the large Pedigree.	258	U75 Epithalam.	176
So large; his Body then, not boughs, project his shade.	258	U75 Epithalam.	V184
A large hundred Markes annuitie,	259	U76 Petition	11
And mightiest Monarchs feele what large increase	261	U77 Treasurer	21
Where Nature such a large survey hath ta'en,	262	U78 Digby	11
It is a large faire table, and a true,	269	U81 Pawlet	15
Hang all your roomes, with one large Pedigree:	282	U84 Kenelme	20
Of travell he discourseth so at large,	378	Coryat 2	82

LARGELY
| And giving largely to me, more thou tak'st. | 44 | E55 Beaumont | 6 |

LARKES
| The skie not falling, thinke we may have larkes. | 65 | E101 Supper | 16 |

			Page	Title	Line
LARUM					
(That should ring larum to the heart) doth sleepe,	.	.	109	F11 Epode	23
(That shal ring larum to the heart) doth sleepe,	.	.	109	F11 Epode	V 23
LASH'D					
Lash'd by their consciences, to die, affeard.	.	.	84	E133 Voyage	18
'LASSE					
Another answers, 'Lasse, those Silkes are none,	.	.	202	U42 Elegy Let	74
LAST (ENDURE)					
And proud, my worke shall out-last common deeds,	.	.	46	E60 Mounteagle	6
Whose rellish to eternitie shall last.	.	.	58	E91 Vere	8
Whose rellish to eternitie will last.	.	.	58	E91 Vere	V 8
The apple-harvest, that doth longer last;	.	.	98	F3 Wroth	43
Solders crackt friendship; makes love last a day;	.	.	113	F12 Rutland	17
As they are high; are rooted, and will last.	.	.	157	U13 Sacvile	144
And be belov'd, while the Whores last. O times,	.	.	167	U15 Friend-Wars	161
That ne're was knowne to last above a fit!	.	.	171	U20 Shrub	6
Looke forth, but cannot last in such a forme.	.	.	191	U38 Elegy 'Tis	14
They cannot last. No lie grew ever old.	.	.	216	U45 Squib	20
Will last till day;	.	.	258	U75 Epithalam.	190
But we last out, still unlay'd.	.	.	259	U76 Petition	24
Aloud; and (happ'ly) it may last as long.	.	.	261	U77 Treasurer	28
As loude; and (happ'ly) it may last as long.	.	.	261	U77 Treasurer	V 28
A Musique in the Eares, will ever last;	.	.	286	U84 Muse	124
LAST					
Ideot, last night, I pray'd thee but forbeare	.	.	45	E58 Groome	1
At last, ease, appetite, and example wan	.	.	57	E90 Mill	4
Act a brave worke, call it thy last adventry:	.	.	85	E133 Voyage	57
Thrise did it spit: thrise div'd. At last, it view'd	.	.	88	E133 Voyage	162
The tripple head without a sop. At last,	.	.	89	E133 Voyage	186
First, midst, and last, converted one, and three;	.	.	122	F15 Heaven	10
I will but mend the last, and tell	.	.	139	U2 Another	13
Be as good, as was the last:	.	.	140	U2 Promise	27
Wee shall, at last, of parcells make	.	.	145	U5 Woman-kind	11
Their bounties forth, to him that last was made,	.	.	155	U13 Sacvile	63
We must accomplish; 'Tis the last Key-stone	.	.	157	U13 Sacvile	136
And last, goe out in nothing: You that see	.	.	157	U13 Sacvile	153
To gaine upon his belly; and at last	.	.	162	U15 Friend-Wars	17
From Hide-Parke to the Stage, where at the last	.	.	165	U15 Friend-Wars	109
And last, blaspheme not, we did never heare	.	.	168	U15 Friend-Wars	191
But here doth lie, till the last Day,	.	.	168	U16 Gray	3
. . . the last Terme he sate Chancellor.	.	.	185	U31 Elsmere	Ttl
That as the last of punishments is meant;	.	.	192	U38 Elegy 'Tis	43
For they did see it the last tilting well,	.	.	213	U44 Speach	6
How it held out! how (last) 'twas taken in!	.	.	213	U44 Speach	22
Hee stood, a Souldier to the last right end,	.	.	244	U70 Ode	45
To fall a logge at last, dry, bald, and seare:	.	.	245	U70 Ode	68
(After the last child borne;) This is our wedding day.	.	.	258	U75 Epithalam.	168
And, in her last act, taught the Standers-by,	.	.	270	U81 Pawlet	61
Last, draw the circles of this Globe,	.	.	276	U84 Body	25
In earth, till the last Trumpe awake the Sheepe	.	.	283	U84 Muse	46
The last of houres, and shutter up of all;	.	.	289	U84 Muse	219
Unto the last, as when he first went forth,	.	.	313	Horace	181
The last doth from the midst dis-joyn'd appeare.	.	.	315	Horace	218
But meere Iambicks all, from first to last.	.	.	323	Horace	374
Him that is last, I scorne to come behind,	.	.	333	Horace	595
Him that is last, I scorne to be behind,	.	.	353	Horace	V595
still making that the greatest that is last	.	.	361	Palmer	19
So wood at last, that he was wonne to her	.	.	394	Jane Ogle	22
LASTED					
Their lives, as doe their lines, till now had lasted.	.	.	65	E101 Supper	32
LASTETH					
As patience lasteth.	.	.	179	U25 Desmond	47
But hee lasteth and unlay'd.	.	.	259	U76 Petition	V 24
LASTING					
And lasting, as her flowers:	.	.	111	F11 Epode	58
To give your shade a lasting name! Stay, stay, I feele	.	.	269	U81 Pawlet	V 7
Or grace of speech, should hope a lasting date.	.	.	309	Horace	100
And as an ever-lasting Sacrifice	.	.	382	Rich	7
And pray, thy joyes as lasting bee, as great.	.	.	384	Somerset	8
LASTLY					
And lastly by your lips, the banke of kisses,	.	.	170	U19 Elegy By	9
LASTS					
But Scarlet-like out-lasts the Cloth.	.	.	230	U55 Burges	8
LATE					
The late tane bastinado. So I thought.	.	.	33	E21 Gam'ster	6
For thy late sharpe device. I say 'tis fit	.	.	36	E29 Tilter	3
Guiltie, because I bad you late be wise,	.	.	38	E38 Guiltie 2	1
Then thou did'st late my sense, loosing my points.	.	.	45	E58 Groome	6
When Nature bids us leave to live, 'tis late	.	.	50	E70 Wm Roe 1	1
Madame, I told you late how I repented,	.	.	54	E84 Bedford 2	1
Caesar stands up, as from his urne late rose,	.	.	72	E111 Edmonds 2	12
But viewing him since (alas, too late)	.	.	77	E120 S. P.	19
Of the grave fart, late let in parliament,	.	.	87	E133 Voyage	108
About the shore, of farts, but late departed,	.	.	87	E133 Voyage	125
That found King James, when hunting late, this way,	.	.	95	F2 Penshurst	76
I sent thee, late, a rosie wreath,	.	.	106	F9 Celia 3	9
But the Pittie comes too late.	.	.	133	U2 Suffered	20
Heare, what late Discourse of you,	.	.	136	U2 Cupid	5
What furie of late is crept into our Feasts?	.	.	166	U15 Friend-Wars	117
Carriage, and dressing. There is up of late	.	.	215	U44 Speach	88
Of the late Mysterie of reception,	.	.	219	U47 Tribe	48
What did this Stirrer, but die late?	.	.	243	U70 Ode	30
Extend a reaching vertue, early and late:	.	.	258	U75 Epithalam.	180

LATE (cont.)
Whereas late your royall Father . . . . 259 U76 Petition V 5
. . . late Wife of Sir Kenelme Digby, Knight: . . . . . 272 U84 Eupheme Ttl
And those thy new, and late-coyn'd words receive, . . 309 Horace 74
Of words decay, and phrases borne but late . . 309 Horace 88
Nor so begin, as did that Circler late, . . . 313 Horace 195
With lees of Wine. Next Eschylus, more late, . . 319 Horace 315
Or Semi-god, that late was seene to weare . . . 321 Horace 332
When late (grave Palmer) these thy graffs and flowers . 361 Palmer 1
That late were out. . . . . 367 Ode Who saith 46
In entertaining late . . . 368 Ode Who saith 82
That all, that view you then, and late; may say, . . 384 Somerset 25
Cry'd up of late: Whereto there must be first . . 415 Rutter 21
LATE-COYN'D
And those thy new, and late-coyn'd words receive, . . 309 Horace 74
LATELY
Where lately harbour'd many a famous whore, . . . 29 E7 Hot-house 1
Chuffe, lately rich in name, in chattels, goods, . . 41 E44 Chuff 1
From whence, so lately, I did burne, ... 101 F4 To the World 27
LATER
The earely cherry, with the later plum, . . . 94 F2 Penshurst 41
That ever Nature, or the later Ayre . . . . 274 U84 Descent 4
LATERALL
For, as one comming with a laterall viewe, . . . 362 Author 9
LATEST
Nor death; but when thy latest sand is spent, . . 100 F3 Wroth 105
Nor feare thy latest day, nor wish therfore. . . 295 U90 Mart.10:47 13
LATIN
Whilst the Latin, Queene of Tongues, ... 184 U29 Fit of Rime 34
LATINE
Orpheus, Ulysses: or the Latine Muse, . . . 84 E133 Voyage 3
Of Latine and Greeke, to his friendship. And seven . 380 Coryat 3 45
And though thou hadst small Latine, and lesse Greeke, . 391 Shakespeare 31
LATTEN
The Hau'-boy, not as now with latten bound, . . 319 Horace 287
LATTER
Though both be good, the latter yet is worst, . . 63 E98 Th Roe 1 11
Their latter praise would still the greatest bee, . . 68 E106 E Herbert 9
Wherein thou shew'st, how much the latter are . . 72 E111 Edmonds 2 3
LAUGH
Both which are great. And laugh at ill-made clothes; . 35 E28 Surly 10
You laugh when you are touch'd, and long before . . 38 E38 Guiltie 2 3
Men love thee not for this: They laugh at thee. . . 81 E129 Mime 18
They laugh't, at his laugh-worthy fate. And past . 89 E133 Voyage 185
When their owne Parasites laugh at their fall, . . 118 F13 Aubigny 82
And laugh, and measure thighes, then squeake, spring, itch, . 164 U15 Friend-Wars 75
Mens faces, still, with such as laugh, are prone . 311 Horace 143
Mens count'nances, with such as laugh, are prone . . 342 Horace V143
And Roman Gentrie, jearing, will laugh out. . . 313 Horace 160
Nay more in his wardrobe, if you will laugh at a . 380 Coryat 3 47
I'll laugh at thee poor wretched Tike, go send . . 410 Gill 10
LAUGHE
That hath not Countrye impudence enough to laughe att Arte, . 420 Ode:If Men 14
LAUGH'D
Is laugh'd at, that still jarreth on one string: . . 329 Horace 532
LAUGHS
Thy ignorance still laughs in the wrong place. . . 45 E58 Groome 4
LAUGH'T
They laugh't, at his laugh-worthy fate. And past . . 89 E133 Voyage 185
LAUGHTER
To catch the worlds loose laughter, or vaine gaze. . . 27 E2 My Booke 12
That yet maintaynes you, and your house in laughter. . 51 E73 Fine Grand 8
Lesse your laughter; that I love. . . . . 131 U2 Excuse 2
Not make a verse; Anger; or laughter would, . . 164 U15 Friend-Wars 62
Thy Wife a fit of laughter; a Cramp-ring . . . 232 U58 Book-seller 8
Could you containe your laughter? Credit mee, . . 305 Horace 7
To laughter; so they grieve with those that mone. . 311 Horace 144
And Roman Gentrie, will with laughter shout. . . 342 Horace V160
Lest the throng'd heapes should on a laughter take: . 331 Horace 569
Lest the throng'd rings should a free laughter take: . 352 Horace V545/569
LAUGH-WORTHY
They laugh't, at his laugh-worthy fate. And past . 89 E133 Voyage 185
LAUNCES
Launces, and men, and some a breaking force. . . 213 U44 Speach 8
LAURA
Hath Petrarch since his Laura rais'd . . . . 181 U27 Ode Helen 21
LAURELL
How, best of Poets, do'st thou laurell weare! . . 28 E4 James 1 2
And bad me lay th'usurped laurell downe: . . . 80 E126 Mrs Cary 4
LAW
He no sooner heard the Law, ... 133 U2 Suffered 13
Law, to his Law; and thinke your enemies his: . . 185 U31 Elsmere 4
Who 'gainst the Law, weave Calumnies, my ——; . . 187 U33 Councellour 6
At Common-Law: me thinkes in his despight . . 211 U43 Vulcan 177
At Common-Law: me thinkes in this despight . . 211 U43 Vulcan V177
You were not tied, by any Painters Law, . . . 227 U52 Answer 7
Wonder to Valour! No, it is the Law . . . 233 U59 Newcastle 14
That such a Law . . . . . . 247 U70 Ode 120
Never at Law; seldome in office gown'd; . . . 295 U90 Mart.10:47 5
From whence thy Modestie, or Poemes law . . 313 Horace 193
The free spectators, subject to no Law, . . . 319 Horace 324
Her licence fit to be restrain'd by law: . . . 321 Horace 368
Her force was fit to be restrain'd by law: . . 348 Horace V402/368

LAW (cont.)

Which law receiv'd, the Chorus held his peace,   323   Horace   369

LA-WARE

An Epitaph, on Henry L. La-ware. To the Passer-by.   233   U60 La-ware   Ttl
Henry, the brave young Lord La-ware,   233   U60 La-ware   3

LAWES

Rob'd both of money, and the lawes reliefe,   29   E8 Robbery   5
There's reason good, that you good lawes should make: 34   E24 Parliament   1
Left us of feare, but first our crimes, then lawes.   38   E35 James 2   6
And no lesse wise, then skilfull in the lawes;   52   E74 Chancelor   6
Men are not just, or keepe no holy lawes   117   F13 Aubigny   18
And shamefastnesse together! All lawes dead,   163   U15 Friend-Wars   40
And shamefac'dnesse together! All lawes dead,   163   U15 Friend-Wars V 40
Against or Faith, or honours lawes.   173   U22 Elegy Tho   12
Lawes; and no change e're come to one decree: 185   U31 Elsmere   2
As with the safetie, and honour of the Lawes,   186   U31 Elsmere   9
Dar'st not abuse thy wisdome, in the Lawes,   187   U33 Councellour   17
Their Sonnes to studie Arts, the Lawes, the Creed: 215   U44 Speach   74
That Clients strove, in Question of the Lawes,   217   U46 Coke   11
Like Solons selfe; explat'st the knottie Lawes   217   U46 Coke   17
Then now, to love the Soveraigne, and the Lawes?   236   U64 Charles 3   8
Then now, to love the Soveraigne, or his Lawes?   236   U64 Charles 3 V 8
Mens Loves unto the Lawes, and Lawes to love the Crowne.   255   U75 Epithalam.   104
Sharpe, and contemning lawes, at him should aime,   313   Horace   173
Praise the spare diet, wholsome justice, lawes,   317   Horace   283
Build Townes, and carve the Lawes in leaves of wood.   327   Horace   490
By observation of those Comick Lawes   409   Brome   7
Even states most hated, when no lawes resist   423   Lucan   13

LAWFULL

As in this Prince? Let it be lawfull, so   238   U66 Queene   11
If they had leisure, at these lawfull routs,   249   U72 King   V 15
A lawfull Verse, by th'eare, or finger scan.   323   Horace   404

LAWNE

In solemne cypres, the other cob-web-lawne.   51   E73 Fine Grand   14
What makes these Velvets, Silkes, and Lawne,   275   U84 Body   2

LAWRELL

Or for the lawrell, he may gaine a scorne,   392   Shakespeare   63

LAWYER

On Chev'rill the Lawyer.   38   E37 Chev'ril   Ttl
Nor how to get the lawyer fees.   98   F3 Wroth   62
Have made me to conceive a Lawyer new.   187   U33 Councellour   14
There may a Lawyer be, may not excell;   331   Horace   550

LAXATIVE

Laxative lettuce, and such windie meate)   88   E133 Voyage   167

LAY (LAITY)

The learn'd have no more priviledge, then the lay.   82   E131 Ferrab. 2   4

LAY (SONG; see also LAIES)

And foundred thy hot teame, to tune my lay.   107   F10 Proludium   9
And foundred thy hot teame, to tune our lay.   107   F10 Proludium   V 9

LAY

I cannot for the stage a Drama lay,   72   E112 Gamster   7
And bad me lay th'usurped laurell downe: 80   E126 Mrs Cary   4
Or, that it lay, heap'd like an usurers masse,   88   E133 Voyage   139
Cats there lay divers had beene flead, and rosted,   88   E133 Voyage   149
Or Feathers: lay his fortune out to show,   162   U15 Friend-Wars   21
That thought can adde, unthankfull, the lay-stall   172   U21 Ltl Shrub   8
Or lay the excuse upon the Vintners vault;   191   U38 Elegy 'Tis   22
He did lay up, and would adore the shooe,   201   U42 Elegy Let   55
As if that part lay for a [   ] most fit!   232   U58 Book-seller   12
Lay trampled on; the deeds of death, and night,   243   U70 Ode   14
Now in the rooted Grasse him lay,   271   U81 Pawlet   81
Lay that aside, the Epicks office is.   290   U85 Country   24
Or love of this so famous death lay by.   307   Horace   64
Or love of this his famous death lay by.   335   Horace   669
And lay in straw with the horses at Bergamo,   355   Horace   V669
To lay her here, inclos'd, his second Bride.   380   Coryat 3   38
   394   Jane Ogle   24

LAYD

Thy night not dronken, but from cares layd wast;   295   U90 Mart.10:47   9

LAYES

And him it layes on; if he be not there.   74   E115 Honest Man   16
hee freely bringes; and on this Alter layes   383   Rich   9

LAY-STALL

That thought can adde, unthankfull, the lay-stall   172   U21 Ltl Shrub   8

LAZIE

Soone as lazie thou wert knowne,   183   U29 Fit of Rime   13

'LD

'Tis one good part I'ld lie withall.   142   U2 Exception   8
Hee'ld frame such ditties of their store, and want,   241   U68 House-hold   7
You'ld reade a Snake, in his next Song.   260   U76 Petition   32
As, for her, I'ld not feare to die,   293   U87 Hor.3:9   11
Recall him yet, hee'ld be no more a man: 335   Horace   668

'LDST

If thou'ldst but use thy faith, as thou didst then,   32   E18 Censurer   7

'LE

I'le loose my modestie, and tell your name.   38   E38 Guiltie 2   1
But, I'le come in,   130   U1 Father   28
I'le taste as lightly as the Bee,   139   U2 Another   5
I'le tell, that if they be not glad,   147   U7 Nymph   8
I'le tell no more, and yet I love,   148   U7 Nymph   29
I'le bid thee looke no more, but flee, flee friend.   166   U15 Friend-Wars   129
Is nothing, such scarce meat and drinke he'le give,   167   U15 Friend-Wars   159
I'le lead you on; or if my fate will so,   170   U18 Elegy Can   22

	Page	Title	Line

'LE   (cont.)
I'le therefore aske no more, but bid you love; . . . . 171 U19 Elegy By   15
Of me, I'le softly tread unto my Tombe; . . . . 199 U41 Elegy Since   20
But I'le conclude all in a civill curse. . . . . 211 U43 Vulcan   190
Shall carry me at Call; and I'le be well, ... 219 U47 Tribe   45
I'le tell you but the death, and the disease . . . . 335 Horace   659
Now, bring him backe, he'le be no more a man, ... 355 Horace   V668

LEAD
As might all the Graces lead, ... 138 U2 Kisse   26
But which shall lead me on? both these are blind: . . . 170 U18 Elegy Can   11
I'le lead you on; or if my fate will so, ... 170 U18 Elegy Can   22
To sweeter Pastures lead hee can. . . . . 265 U79 New-yeares   60
So, shunning faults, to greater fault doth lead, . . . 307 Horace   43
The shunning vice, to greater vice doth lead, . . . 339 Horace   V 45/ 43
And lead them with soft songs, where that he would. . . 327 Horace   485
These trifles into serious mischiefes lead . . . . 335 Horace   641
Welcome all, who lead or follow, ... 657 Door Apollo   1
Welcome all, who lead or follow, ... 657 Door Apollo   19

LEADERS
Of Pan wee sing, the Chiefe of Leaders, Pan, . . . 264 U79 New-yeares   28

LEADES
Through which a serpent river leades . . . . 97 F3 Wroth   18
That leades our flocks and us, and calls both forth . . 264 U79 New-yeares   29
Then to the purpose leades, and fitly 'grees. . . . 317 Horace   279

LEADING
Were leading forth the Graces on the greene: . . . 68 E105 L Wroth 2   12

LEADS
Through which, our merit leads us to our meeds. . . . 53 E80 Life/Death   2

LEAFE
Nor have my title-leafe on posts, or walls, ... 28 E3 Bookseller   7
Each leafe of his journall, and line doth unlocke . . 380 Coryat 3   23

LEANE   (VERB)
'Twill be but faire, to leane upon their Fames; . . . 281 U84 Kenelme   13

LEANE
I am too fat t'envy him. He too leane . . . . 405 Inigo Jones 1   69
to gett thee a leane Face, ... 420 Ode:If Men   25

LEANENESSE
If thy leanenesse love such food, ... 105 F8 Sicknesse   24

LEAPE
Can come from Tripoly, leape stooles, and winke, . . 74 E115 Honest Man   11
Bright eeles, that emulate them, and leape on land, . . 94 F2 Penshurst   37
And then, leape mad on a neat Pickardill, ... 164 U15 Friend-Wars   70
Her presently? Or leape thy Wife of force, . . . 201 U42 Elegy Let   44
Of imitation, leape into a streight, ... 313 Horace   192
Out at his friendly eyes, leape, beat the groun'. . . 333 Horace   613

LEAP'D
For which there must more sea, and land be leap'd, . . 69 E107 Hungry   16
Hee leap'd the present age, ... 245 U70 Ode   79
Conceipt, and into burning Aetna leap'd. . . . . 335 Horace   663

LEAPT
you are; from them leapt forth an Architect, . . . 402 Inigo Jones 1   3

LEARNE
They learne and studie; and then practise there. . . 215 U44 Speach   92
To ignorance still, then either learne, or know? . . 311 Horace   131
To ignorance still, then yet to learne, or know? . . 341 Horace   V126/131
Our Roman Youths they learne the subtle wayes . . . 327 Horace   464
Our Roman Youths they learne more thriving wayes . . 350 Horace   V464
Did learne them first, and once a Master fear'd. . . 333 Horace   592
The height, let him learne of Mr. Tom. Coryate: . . 379 Coryat 3   2
The height, let him learne of Mr. Tom Coryate. . . 381 Coryat 3   60
The faire French Daughter to learne English in; . . 402 Filmer   12

LEARN'D
Where I both learn'd, why wise-men hawking follow, . . 55 E85 Goodyere 1   3
The learn'd have no more priviledge, then the lay. . . 82 E131 Ferrab. 2   4
You, Madame, yong have learn'd to shunne these shelves, . 119 F13 Aubigny   89
Was Lesbia sung by learn'd Catullus? . . . . 181 U27 Ode Helen   9
One lesson we have both learn'd, and well read; . . 216 U45 Squib   4
As they had learn'd new changes, for the day, . . 253 U75 Epithalam.   35
Learn'd and unlearn'd; holding, whom once he takes; . . 337 Horace   677
Learn'd, and unlearn'd; holdeth whom once he takes; . . 355 Horace   V677
You learn'd it well; and for it, serv'd your time . . 410 Brome   9

LEARNED
To the learned Critick. . . . . . 32 E17 Critic   Ttl
With which a learned Madame you belye. . . . . 51 E73 Fine Grand   11
Onely a learned, and a manly soule . . . . 52 E76 Bedford 1   13
What would his serious actions mē have learned? . . 55 E85 Goodyere 1   12
Thy learned hand, and true Promethean art . . . 71 E110 Edmonds 1   17
My lighter comes, to kisse thy learned Muse; . . . 78 E121 Rudyerd 1   2
Grave tutor to the learned horse. Both which, . . 88 E133 Voyage   157
Thy learned Chamber-fellow, knowes to doe . . . 161 U14 Selden   72
Come short of all this learned throng, ... 182 U27 Ode Helen   34
The learned Librarie of Don Quixote; . . . . 204 U43 Vulcan   31
With touch of learned thum's! . . . . 239 U67 Muses   18
The knowing Weston, and that learned Lord . . . 263 U78 Digby   28
And I still bid the learned Maker looke . . . . 325 Horace   453
How many learned men he have drawne with his hooke . . 380 Coryat 3   44
To my chosen Friend, the learned Translator of Lucan, . . . 395 May   Ttl
There read I, streight, thy learned Legends three, . . 397 Drayton   25
Both learned, and unlearned, all write Playes. . . . 410 Brome   12
To my Deare Sonne, and right-learned Friend, ... 414 Rutter   Ttl

LEARNEDLY
Beeing in feare to be robd, he most learnedly begs. . . 375 Coryat 1   35

	Page	Title	Line

LEARNES
Shee learnes to know long difference of their states. 78 E121 Rudyerd 1 4

LEARNING
Whether thy learning they would take, or wit, 68 E106 E Herbert 5
With endlesse labours, whilst thy learning drawes 217 U46 Coke 18
Judgement (adornd with Learning) 365 Ode Splendor 9

LEASE (See also LEESE)
Know you the cause? H'has neither land, nor lease, 63 E97 Motion 9
forfeitinge their drinking lease, 418 Moon 43

LEAS'D
Made, or indentur'd, or leas'd out t'advance 246 U70 Ode 100

LEAST (LEST)
Least a false praise do make theyr dotage his. 385 Husband 4
Out in the Dog-daies, least the killer meete 409 Detractor 20

LEAST (See also LEST)
Thou are not covetous of least selfe-fame, 27 E2 My Booke 9
And such from whom let no man hope least good, 30 E11 Something 6
And farre beneath least pause of such a king, 43 E51 James 3 4
The least indulgent thought thy pen drops forth! 44 E55 Beaumont 4
Becomes none more then you, who need it least. 67 E103 L Wroth 1 14
Least mention of a Nymph, a Muse, a Grace, 67 E105 L Wroth 2 4
Vertuously practise must at least allow 75 E116 Jephson 14
Till thou canst finde the best, choose the least ill. 76 E119 Shelton 10
The least of which was to the plague a cosen. 86 E133 Voyage 72
Then all, that have but done my Muse least grace, 115 F12 Rutland 79
Who not the least, 120 F14 Sydney 9
But alas, thou seest the least 137 U2 Cupid 43
French to boote, at least in fashion, 141 U2 Her man 7
And mine not least) I have too oft preferr'd 159 U14 Selden 20
Or have the least of Good, but what it must 171 U20 Shrub 7
But ever without blazon, or least shade 197 U40 Elegy That 13
Nor made least line of love to thy loose Wife; 203 U43 Vulcan 6
Any, least loose, or scurrile paper, lie 203 U43 Vulcan 20
Had I fore-knowne of this thy least desire 205 U43 Vulcan 59
Had I fore-knowne but of thy least desire 205 U43 Vulcan V 59
And trust her I would least, that hath forswore 223 U49 Pucell 29
Nor any least fit 231 U57 Burges 18
At least may beare th'inscription to her Tombe. 269 U81 Pawlet 18
The holy Altars, when it least presumes. 288 U84 Muse 188
At least so great a Lady. She was wife 394 Jane Ogle 15
At least, if not the generall Engine cracke. 395 May 6
Or canst of truth the least intrenchment pitch, 407 Inigo Jones 2 23
By barking against mee. Thou look'st at least, 408 Detractor 10

LEATHER (See LETHER)

LEAVE (NOUN)
Use mine so, too: I give thee leave. But crave 27 E3 Bookseller 3
Yet give thy jealous subjects leave to doubt: 43 E51 James 3 5
Is, that I have leave to speake, 133 U2 Suffered 22
Yet give me leave t'adore in you 174 U22 Elegy Tho 35
And which you (being the worthier) gave me leave 190 U37 Friend-Book 11
Will unto Licence that faire leave abuse. 190 U37 Friend-Book 24
Till the sower Minute comes of taking leave, 197 U40 Elegy That 2
That quilts those bodies, I have leave to span: 200 U42 Elegy Let 32
Whilst your Ulisses hath ta'ne leave to goe, 224 U50 Countesse 21
I gaine, in having leave to keepe my Day, 231 U56 Covell 29
(And leave the joy that the first Mary brought, 238 U66 Queene V 7
. . . gave me leave to call her so. Being Her . . . 282 U84 Muse Ttl
And both doe crave, and give againe, this leave. 305 Horace 13
And give, being taken modestly, this leave, 309 Horace 73
And there is given too unworthy leave 323 Horace 389
Yet give mee leave, to wonder at the birth 398 Drayton 83
Will unto Lycence, that free Leave Abuse: 422 Censure 17

LEAVE
But leave, because I cannot as I should! 34 E23 Donne 1 10
What doth he else, but say, leave to be chast, 34 E25 Beast 1 7
Leave Cod, tabacco-like, burnt gummes to take, 42 E50 Cod 3 1
As we, the rob'd, leave rage, and pittie it. 44 E56 Poet-Ape 4
Away, and leave me, thou thing most abhord, 48 E65 Muse 1
When Nature bids us leave to live, 'tis late 50 E70 Wm Roe 1 1
Which, if thou leave not soone (though I am loth) 54 E81 Proule 7
I leave thy acts, which should I prosequute 58 E91 Vere 9
I leave, then, acts, which should I prosequute 58 E91 Vere V 9
I leave thee there, and giving way, entend 72 E112 Gamster 9
Leave it buryed in this vault. 79 E124 Elizabeth 8
None but them, and leave the rest. 106 F8 Sicknesse 48
None but them, and leave the best. 106 F8 Sicknesse V 48
Or leave a kisse but in the cup, 106 F9 Celia 3 3
Leave but a kisse within the cup, 106 F9 Celia 3 V 3
Then, leave these lighter numbers, to light braines 108 F10 Proludium 7
To love one man, hee'd leave her first. 146 U6 Defence 24
Nought but in corners; and is loath to leave, 154 U13 Sacvile 44
Can we not leave this worme? or will we not? 166 U15 Friend-Wars 141
And so I leave to stirre him, lest he stinke. 172 U21 Ltl Shrub 10
My health will leave me; and when you depart, 199 U41 Elegy Since 13
A cause before; or leave me one behind. 203 U43 Vulcan 28
Thee still, and leave Apollo, 221 U48 Bacchus 26
The wits will leave you, if they once perceive 223 U49 Pucell 37
You cling to Lords, and Lords, if them you leave 223 U49 Pucell 38
His Poet leave to sing his House-hold true; 241 U68 House-hold 6
How summ'd a circle didst thou leave man-kind 243 U70 Ode 9
How did she leave the world? with what contempt? 270 U81 Pawlet 47
He that shall be our supreme Judge, should leave 286 U84 Muse 148
And then as swift to leave what he hath lov'd. 315 Horace 236
Fortune would love the poore, and leave the proud. 319 Horace 286

LEAVE (cont.)
Leave thee alone, for the comparison . . . . . . 391 Shakespeare 38
LEAVEN'D
Onely his clothes have over-leaven'd him. . . . . 63 E97 Motion 20
LEAVEN'D
The whole world here leaven'd with madnesse swells; . . 163 U15 Friend-Wars 31
LEAVES (VERB)
But leaves me to inquire, ... 151 U11 Dreame 10
LEAVES
Still in their leaves, throughout the sliding yeares, . 309 Horace 86
Build Townes, and carve the Lawes in leaves of wood. . 327 Horace 490
LEAV'ST
With me thou leav'st an happier Muse then thee, . . 48 E65 Muse 11
LECHERS (See also LETCHERIE)
Gut eates all day, and lechers all the night, . . 76 E118 Gut 1
LED
But all so cleare, and led by reasons flame, . . . 220 U47 Tribe 69
And all the Ground were Garden, where she led! . . 254 U75 Epithalam. 68
LEDA'S
Or thought they, Leda's white Adult'rers place . . 369 Ode Who saith 104
LEDAS
Have you seene faire Ledas face . . . . . 135 U2 Triumph V 41
LEDGER (See LIEDGERS)
LEE
Professing greatnesse, swells: That, low by lee . . 307 Horace 38
LEECH
Till he drop off, a Horse-leech, full of blood. . . 337 Horace 680
Till, horse-leech-like, he drop off, full of blood. . 355 Horace V680
LEES
With lees of Wine. Next Eschylus, more late, . . 319 Horace 315
LEESE
No cause, nor client fat, will Chev'rill leese, . . 38 E37 Chev'ril 1
They thinke not, then, which side the cause shall leese, . 98 F3 Wroth 61
The bravery makes, she can no honour leese: . . 164 U15 Friend-Wars 56
LEFT (ADJECTIVE)
O I left-witted, that purge every spring . . 325 Horace 429
LEFT
Left us of feare, but first our crimes, then lawes. . 38 E35 James 2 6
Since men have left to doe praise-worthy things, . . 49 E67 Suffolk 1
How like a columne, Radcliffe, left alone . . . 60 E93 Radcliffe 1
That we had left us, nor by time, nor place, . . 67 E105 L Wroth 2 3
May they have nothing left, whereof they can . . 118 F13 Aubigny 83
And he, with his best Genius left alone. . . . 120 F14 Sydney 20
But left me free, ... 129 U1 Father 9
Left it sticking in my heart: . . . . 133 U2 Suffered 16
To have left all sight for you: . . . 138 U2 Kisse 33
My Picture left in Scotland. . . . 149 U9 Picture Ttl
For truly, since he left to be, . . . 152 U12 Corbet 35
All that is left of Philip Gray, . . . 168 U16 Gray 4
And we were left under that Hemisphere, . . . 199 U41 Elegy Since 7
Or slipper was left off, and kisse it too, . . . 201 U42 Elegy Let 56
Left! and wit since to cover it with Tiles. . . 209 U43 Vulcan 138
Was left yet to Man-kind; . . . . 247 U70 Ode 121
Have left in fame to equall, or out-goe . . 260 U77 Treasurer 8
Eupheme; Or, The Faire Fame Left To Posteritie . . . 272 U84 Eupheme Ttl
Still left an Eccho in the sense. . . . 279 U84 Mind 40
In rest, like spirits left behind . . . 280 U84 Mind 66
What's left a Poet, when his Muse is gone? . . 283 U84 Muse 28
And left her lovely body unthought dead! . . . 283 U84 Muse 44
With his owne Oxen tills his Sires left lands, . . 289 U85 Country 3
And to left-Lydia, now the gate stood ope. . . 294 U87 Hor.3:9 20
Not labour'd for, but left thee by thy Sire; . . 295 U90 Mart.10:47 3
Our Poets, too, left nought unproved here; . . 323 Horace 405
. . . Mr. William Shakespeare: And what he hath left us. . 390 Shakespeare Ttl
But of one Husband; and since he left life, . . 394 Jane Ogle 16
LEFT-LYDIA
And to left-Lydia, now the gate stood ope. . . 294 U87 Hor.3:9 20
LEFT-WITTED
O I left-witted, that purge every spring . . . 325 Horace 429
LEG
Is fix'd upon one leg, and dares not come . . . 198 U40 Elegy That 33
LEGALL
And legall wayes . . . . . . 255 U75 Epithalam. 102
LEG'D
Ushring the mutton; with a short-leg'd hen, . . 64 E101 Supper 11
LEGEND
With pieces of the Legend; The whole summe . . 205 U43 Vulcan 66
Or what we heare our home-borne Legend tell, . . 228 U53 Newcastle 9
LEGENDS
There read I, streight, thy learned Legends three, . . 397 Drayton 25
LEGH
And tell thou, Alde-Legh, None can tell more true . . 274 U84 Descent 13
LEGITIMATE
That wish my poemes a legitimate fame, . . . 32 E17 Critic 3
LEGS
And though the soundest legs goe every day, . . 36 E31 Banck 3
What, to make legs? yes, and to smell most sweet, . . 215 U44 Speach 90
But here, neither trusting his hands, nor his legs, . . 375 Coryat 1 34
LEISURE
If they had leisure, at these lawfull routs, . . 249 U72 King V 15
LEMNOS
No mar'le the Clownes of Lemnos tooke thee up, . . 208 U43 Vulcan 116

LEMON   (See LIMONS)
LEND
  Nor lend like influence from his lucent seat.   .   52   E76 Bedford 1   8
  More then citizens dare lend   105   F8 Sicknesse   34
  Till that no usurer, nor his bawds dare lend   .   .   118   F13 Aubigny   78
  Alone lend succours, and this furie stay,   .   .   191   U38 Elegy 'Tis   8
  Needs lend an aide, to thine she had her eyes.   .   .   217   U46 Coke   24
  This Age would lend no faith to Dorrels Deed;   .   .   223   U49 Pucell   42
  Lend me, deare Arthur, for a weeke five more,   .   .   229   U54 Squib   16
  Lend me thy voyce, O Fame, that I may draw   .   .   .   396   Drayton   12
LENGTH
  And those that lack'd it, to suspect at length,   .   75   E116 Jephson   6
  He, at length, our good will sever.   .   .   .   102   F5 Celia 1   4
  He, at length, our blisse will sever.   .   .   .   102   F5 Celia 1   V 4
  And conquers all things, yea it selfe, at length.   .   367   Ode Who saith   56
  To understand, hee may at length admire.   .   .   383   Author   10
LENOX
  . . . Esme D. of Lenox deceased, and Sister of the . . .   252   U75 Epithalam.   Ttl
LENT
  Lent him a pockie whore. Shee hath paid him.   .   .   31   E12 Shift   24
  Seven yeeres tho'wert lent to me, and I thee pay,   .   41   E45 First Son   3
  I lent you, on meere acquaintance, at a feast.   .   .   51   E73 Fine Grand   6
  And to your Scene lent no lesse dignitie   .   .   67   E104 Montgomery   7
  To make thy lent life, good against the Fates: .   .   67   E104 Montgomery   7
  Lent timely succours, and new life begot: .   .   70   E109 Nevil   11
  A fire now, that lent a shade!   .   .   .   80   E127 Aubigny   8
  Thou maist thinke life, a thing but lent.   .   .   98   F3 Wroth   46
  Wherin (besides the noble aydes were lent,   .   .   100   F3 Wroth   106
  Which noble Carew, Cotton, Selden lent: .   .   207   U43 Vulcan   V 99
  Lent by the London Dames, to the Lords men;   .   .   207   U43 Vulcan   100
  T' have paid againe a blessing was but lent,   .   .   213   U44 Speach   14
  And to that forme, lent two such veines of blood   .   271   U81 Pawlet   80
  Cato's and Ennius tongues have lent much worth,   . .   287   U84 Muse   157
  Thus, to his antient Art the Piper lent   .   .   309   Horace   81
L'ENVOYE
  In smiling L'envoye, as he would deride   .   .   319   Horace   303
  In smiling L'envoye, as he would deride   .   .   202   U42 Elegy Let   75
LEPROSIE
  Infected with the leprosie, or had   .   .   .   335   Horace   645
LERRY
  Of Lanterne-lerry: with fuliginous heat   .   .   405   Inigo Jones 1   72
LESBIA
  Was Lesbia sung by learn'd Catullus?   .   .   .   181   U27 Ode Helen   9
LESS
  For less Securitie? O Freind, for these   .   .   165   U15 Friend-Wars V113
  Allmighty Architecture? who noe less   .   .   .   406   Inigo Jones 1   92
LESSE
  Much lesse with lewd, prophane, and beastly phrase,   .   27   E2 My Booke   11
  Who scarse can spell th'hard names: whose knight lesse can. 28   E3 Bookseller   10
  It makes the father, lesse, to rue.   .   .   .   33   E22 Daughter   4
  No lesse than if from perill; and devout,   .   .   43   E51 James 3   7
  And so my sharpnesse thou no lesse dis-joynts,   .   .   45   E58 Groome   5
  Which, by no lesse confirm'd, then thy kings choice, .   49   E67 Suffolk   11
  And no lesse wise, then skilfull in the lawes;   .   .   52   E74 Chancelor   6
  Who had no lesse a trumpet of their name,   .   .   57   E89 Allen   5
  I speake thy other graces, not lesse showne,   .   .   58   E91 Vere   13
  Nor lesse in practice; but lesse mark'd, lesse knowne: 58   E91 Vere   14
  Well, though thy name lesse then our great ones bee, .   64   E99 Th Roe 2   11
  And to your Scene lent no lesse dignitie   .   .   67   E104 Montgomery   7
  And yet, they, all together, lesse then thee.   .   .   68   E106 E Herbert   10
  Nor to give Caesar this, makes ours the lesse.   .   .   72   E111 Edmonds 2   8
  Nor scarce dost colour for it, which is lesse.   .   .   73   E112 Gamster   20
  No lesse a sov'raigne cure, then to the mind;   .   .   82   E130 Ferrab. 1   8
  That the eight spheare, no lesse, then planets seaven,   82   E130 Ferrab. 1   12
  Or perhaps lesse: whil'st gold beares all this sway, .   113   F12 Rutland   18
  To my lesse sanguine Muse, wherein she'hath wonne   .   115   F12 Rutland   72
  For I shall move stocks, stones, no lesse then he.   .   115   F12 Rutland   78
  Then all, that have but done my verse lesse grace,   .   115   F12 Rutland   V 79
  Lesse your laughter; that I love.   .   .   .   131   U2 Excuse   2
  Can he that loves, aske lesse then one?   .   .   139   U2 Another   8
  Lesse list of proud, hard, or ingratefull Men.   .   .   153   U13 Sacvile   4
  All this corrupts the thankes: lesse hath he wonne,   .   154   U13 Sacvile   33
  And can I lesse of substance? When I runne,   .   .   156   U13 Sacvile   120
  Aloft, grow lesse and streightned, full of knot;   .   157   U13 Sacvile   152
  Lesse shall I for the Art or dressing care,   .   .   158   U14 Selden   3
  Before men get a verse: much lesse a Praise;   .   .   159   U14 Selden   26
  Lesse must not be thought on then Mistresse: or,   .   165   U15 Friend-Wars   95
  For lesse Securitie? O **for these** .   .   .   165   U15 Friend-Wars 113
  But who should lesse expect from you,   .   .   .   173   U22 Elegy Tho   13
  And lesse they know, who being free to use   .   .   190   U37 Friend-Book   22
  Much lesse a name would we bring up, or nurse,   .   .   216   U45 Squib   9
  Whom Fortune aided lesse, or vertue more.   .   .   217   U46 Coke   4
  No lesse of praise, then readers in all kinds   .   .   217   U46 Coke   19
  None Fortune aided lesse, or Vertue more.   .   .   217   U46 Coke   22
  Lest it be justled, crack'd, made nought, or lesse: .   219   U47 Tribe   58
  I am no States-man, and much lesse Divine,   .   .   223   U49 Pucell   25
  Dare thinke it, to relieve, no lesse renowne,   .   .   248   U71 Treasurer   14
  All else we see beside, are Shadowes, and goe lesse.   255   U75 Epithalam.   88
  In him the times, no lesse then Prince, are prais'd, .   256   U75 Epithalam.   115
  Of the lesse-Poetique boyes;   259   U76 Petition   20
  For, had we here said lesse, we had sung nothing then.   263   U79 New-yeares   8
  And wish her state lesse happie then it is!   .   .   271   U81 Pawlet   84
  In tragick Verse; no lesse Thyestes feast   .   .   311   Horace   122
  Have more or lesse then just five Acts: nor laid,   .   317   Horace   272

	Page	Title	Line
LESSE (cont.)			
Nor did they merit the lesse Crowne to weare, · · ·	323	Horace	406
Of verse meere-matter-lesse, and tinckling toies. · · ·	327	Horace	460
And though thou hadst small Latine, and lesse Greeke, · ·	391	Shakespeare	31
But higher power, as spight could not make lesse, · · ·	401	Beaumont	18
And lesse asham'd; not when I told the crowd · · ·	414	Rutter	5
And lesse they knowe, that being free to use · · ·	422	Censure	15
LESSE-POETIQUE			
Of the lesse-Poetique boyes; · · · · · ·	259	U76 Petition	20
LESSER			
Although to write be lesser then to doo, · · ·	61	E95 Savile	25
Rudyerd, as lesser dames, to great ones use, · · ·	78	E121 Rudyerd 1	1
Divid'st, upon the lesser Deere; · · · ·	97	F3 Wroth	26
Dispend'st, upon the lesser Deere; · · · ·	97	F3 Wroth	V 26
That as the lesser breach: for he that takes · · ·	169	U17 Friend-Debt	11
LESSON			
(As their true rule or lesson) either men, · · ·	158	U13 Sacvile	162
One lesson we have both learn'd, and well read; · ·	216	U45 Squib	4
LEST **(LEAST)**			
Yet dare not, to my thought, lest hope allow · · ·	41	E43 Salisbury 1	7
Lest Ayre, or Print, but flies it: Such men would · ·	154	U13 Sacvile	45
LEST			
With holy Paul, lest it be thought the breath · · ·	122	F15 Heaven	24
O sing not you then, lest the best · · · ·	144	U3 Musicall	21
Sing you no more then, lest the best · · ·	144	U3 Musicall	V 21
Lest I be sick with seeing; · · · · ·	144	U4 Song	2
Lest shame destroy their being. · · · ·	144	U4 Song	4
And so I leave to stirre him, lest he stinke. · · ·	172	U21 Ltl Shrub	10
Of crueltie, lest they doe make you such. · · ·	193	U38 Elegy 'Tis	84
Or lest that vapour might the Citie choake, · · ·	211	U43 Vulcan	182
Or lest that vapour should the Citie choake, · ·	211	U43 Vulcan	V182
Lest it be justled, crack'd, made nought, or lesse: · ·	219	U47 Tribe	58
As his departing take much thence: lest, then, · · ·	317	Horace	251
Have not kept in; and (lest perfection faile) · · ·	325	Horace	417
All which I tell, lest when Apollo's nam'd, · · ·	329	Horace	501
Lest of the singer Apollo, and Muses fam'd · ·	353	Horace	V579/501
It would, must be: lest it alive would draw · · ·	329	Horace	509
Lest the throng'd heapes should on a laughter take: ·	331	Horace	569
Lest the throng'd rings should a free laughter take: ·	352	Horace	V545/569
LET'			
And if wee must, let's sing of you. · · ·	145	U5 Woman-kind	6
Whose praises let's report unto the Woods, · · ·	265	U79 New-yeares	52
LET			
And by thy wiser temper, let men know · · ·	27	E2 My Booke	8
And such from whom let no man hope least good, · ·	30	E11 Something	6
Let me give two: that doubly am got free, · · ·	31	E13 Empirick	3
Pardon free truth, and let thy modestie, · · ·	31	E14 Camden	11
Though life be short, let us not make it so. · · ·	50	E70 Wm Roe 1	8
Let pui'nees, porters, players praise delight, · · ·	62	E96 Donne 2	10
Thy fact is more: let truth encourage thee. · · ·	64	E99 Th Roe 2	12
Th'other let it sleepe with death: · · · ·	79	E124 Elizabeth	10
No more let Greece her bolder fables tell · · ·	84	E133 Voyage	1
Then let the former age, with this content her, · ·	84	E133 Voyage	19
(In the meane time, let 'hem imprison mee) · · ·	87	E133 Voyage	104
Of the grave fart, late let in parliament, · · ·	87	E133 Voyage	108
Let others watch in guiltie armes, and stand · · ·	98	F3 Wroth	67
Let this man sweat, and wrangle at the barre, · ·	99	F3 Wroth	73
Let him, then hardest sires, more disinherit, · · ·	99	F3 Wroth	77
Then hardest let him more disherrit, · · ·	99	F3 Wroth	V 77
Let that goe heape a masse of wretched wealth, · ·	99	F3 Wroth	81
Let thousands more goe flatter vice, and winne, · ·	99	F3 Wroth	85
Come my Celia, let us prove, · · · ·	102	F5 Celia 1	1
Come sweet Celia, let us prove, · · · ·	102	F5 Celia 1	V 1
Let her alone, shee will court you. · · · ·	104	F7 Women but	4
Let the old boy, your sonne, ply his old taske, · ·	107	F10 Proludium	19
Let these in wanton feete daunce out their soules. ·	108	F10 Proludium	11
It is a golden chaine let downe from heaven, · · ·	110	F11 Epode	47
No, vice, we let thee know, · · · ·	111	F11 Epode	72
No, vice, I let thee know, · · · ·	111	F11 Epode	V 72
But let this drosse carry what price it will · · ·	114	F12 Rutland	27
With noble ignorants, and let them still, · · ·	114	F12 Rutland	28
Let who will follow fashions, and attyres, · · ·	118	F13 Aubigny	71
Let 'hem on poulders, oyles, and paintings, spend, ·	118	F13 Aubigny	77
Let 'hem waste body, and state; and after all, · ·	118	F13 Aubigny	81
Let it not your wonder move, · · · ·	131	U2 Excuse	1
And let nothing high decay, · · · ·	131	U2 Excuse	22
Let who will thinke us dead, or wish our death. · ·	139	U2 Another	18
Nay, I will not let you sit · · · ·	140	U2 Promise	21
Let his Title be but great, · · · ·	142	U2 Exception	3
Come, with our Voyces, let us warre, · · ·	143	U3 Musicall	1
Nor cast them downe, but let them rise, · · ·	144	U4 Song	3
If Love, or feare, would let me tell his name. · ·	148	U7 Nymph	35
That to such Natures let their full hands flow, · ·	154	U13 Sacvile	60
No more are these of us, let them then goe, · ·	156	U13 Sacvile	113
Is lov'd, though he let out his owne for life: · ·	165	U15 Friend-Wars	88
Nature, that will not let his Wife be a whore; · ·	165	U15 Friend-Wars	90
Well, let it goe. Yet this is better, then · · ·	166	U15 Friend-Wars	145
Friend, flie from hence; and let these kindled rimes	167	U15 Friend-Wars	162
Lewd slanderers, soft whisperers that let blood · ·	167	U15 Friend-Wars	165
Lewd standers, soft whisperers that let blood · ·	167	U15 Friend-Wars	V165
Let this thought quicken thee, · · · ·	174	U23 Himselfe	15
Let Brontes, and black Steropes, · · ·	179	U25 Desmond	40
O then (my best-best lov'd) let me importune, · ·	180	U25 Desmond	63

LET (cont.)

O then (our best-best lov'd) let me importune, ...   180   U25 Desmond   V 63
And goe no farther: let this Circle be   185   U30 Burleigh   3
Come, let us here enjoy the shade;   189   U36 Song   1
Then Mistris, here, here let your rigour end, ...   194   U38 Elegy 'Tis 105
And let your mercie make me asham'd t'offend.   194   U38 Elegy 'Tis 106
Let me be what I am, as Virgil cold;   199   U42 Elegy Let   1
Put on my Ivy Garland, let me see   200   U42 Elegy Let   9
Let the poore fooles enjoy their follies, love   202   U42 Elegy Let   81
And this a Sparkle of that fire let loose   209   U43 Vulcan   141
That this sparke of the same fire let loose   209   U43 Vulcan   V141
Nay, let White-Hall with Revels have to doe, ...   210   U43 Vulcan   156
Scarce let White-Hall with Revels have to doe, ...   210   U43 Vulcan   V156
Foole, wilt thou let that in example come?   210   U43 Vulcan   161
And could (if our great men would let their Sonnes   214   U44 Speach   57
With Citizens? let Clownes, and Tradesmen breed   215   U44 Speach   73
Let poore Nobilitie be vertuous: Wee, ...   215   U44 Speach   79
Past any need of vertue. Let them care, ...   215   U44 Speach   83
Let those that meerely talke, and never thinke, ...   218   U47 Tribe   9
But for a Sealing: let these men protest.   218   U47 Tribe   15
Let these men have their wayes, and take their times   218   U47 Tribe   25
And thinkes I dare not her? let the world see.   222   U49 Pucell   2
'Tis a brave cause of joy, let it be knowne, ...   225   U51 Bacon   17
Their perfum'd judgements, let them kisse thy Wife.   232   U58 Book-seller 14
And long in changing. Let our Nephewes see   238   U65 Prince   7
In changing, let our Nephewes joyfull see   238   U65 Prince   V 7
In changing. Let our after Nephewes see   238   U65 Prince   V 7
As in this Prince? Let it be lawfull, so   238   U66 Queene   11
Yet, let our Trumpets sound;   238   U66 Queene   11
Let every Lyre be strung, ...   239   U67 Muses   13
And let thy lookes with gladnesse shine: 239   U67 Muses   16
Let Ireland meet it out at Sea, halfe way, ...   245   U70 Ode   76
And let him freely gather Loves First-fruits, ...   249   U72 King   5
Let their spite (which now abounds)   258   U75 Epithalam.   186
Let Angels sing her glories, who did call   260   U76 Petition   28
Then let the beames of that, disperse   270   U81 Pawlet   63
And let there be a starry Robe   276   U84 Body   17
In thee, faire Mansion, let it rest, ...   276   U84 Body   26
On Nature, for her: who did let her lie, ...   281   U84 Mind   69
So Fates would let the Boy a long thred run.   282   U84 Muse   13
Let us not then rush blindly on unto it, ...   293   U87 Hor.3:9   16
Let us together closely lie, and kisse, ...   294   U88 Petronius   3
If thou be'st wise, with 'Syrian Oyle let shine   294   U88 Petronius   7
In short; I bid, Let what thou work'st upon, ...   294   U89 Mart.8:77   3
Heare me conclude; let what thou workst upon   307   Horace   31
Be nought so'bove him but his sword let claime.   339   Horace   V 31
But, let the Faunes, drawne from their Groves, beware, ...   313   Horace   174
Let what thou fain'st for pleasures sake, be neere   321   Horace   355
The truth; nor let thy Fable thinke, what e're   329   Horace   507
To let it downe, who knowes, if he did cast   329   Horace   508
Let Poets perish, that will not be kept.   335   Horace   656
Now, after all, let no man   335   Horace   664
Nor let one River boast   364   Phoenix   1
For he did but kisse her, and so let her go.   367   Ode Who saith   35
The height, let him learne of Mr. Tom. Coryate;   375   Coryat 1   19
He sayes to the world, let any man mend it, ...   379   Coryat 3   2
The height, let him learne of Mr. Tom Coryate.   379   Coryat 3   15
Let such as justly have out-liv'd all prayse, ...   381   Coryat 3   60
Upon it, but will loath, or let it passe, ...   387   Cavendish   5
Thou hast deserv'd: And let me reade the while   389   Aleman   9
your workes thus differing, troth let soe your style: 398   Drayton   60
Of Subjects; Let such envie, till they burst.   407   Inigo Jones 2   19
LETCHER'D   416   Dover   10
They've glutted in, and letcher'd out that weeke, ...   218   U47 Tribe   13
LETCHERIE
Thus: and for his letcherie, scores, god payes.   31   E12 Shift   22
A fellow of course Letcherie, is nam'd, ...   165   U15 Friend-Wars   98
Home to the Customer: his Letcherie   201   U42 Elegy Let   41
LETCHERS
Of what he throwes: Like letchers growne content   166   U15 Friend-Wars   139
LETHARGIE
Wake, friend, from forth thy Lethargie: the Drum   162   U15 Friend-Wars   1
LETHER
Yet keepe those up in sackcloth too, or lether, ...   200   U42 Elegy Let   25
LET'S
And if wee must, let's sing of you.   145   U5 Woman-kind   6
Whose praises let's report unto the Woods, ...   265   U79 New-yeares   52
LETS
But gives me what I call, and lets me eate, ...   95   F2 Penshurst   69
Of his dull god-head, were sinne. Lets implore   107   F10 Proludium   V 6
His Groomes to witnesse; or else lets it fall   154   U13 Sacvile   36
Some of his formes, he lets him not come neere   242   U69 Friend Son   17
LETT
And by their takeinge, lett it once appeare   421   Ode:If Men   44
LETTER
As't were a challenge, or a borrowers letter?   51   E73 Fine Grand   3
To goe out after—till when take this letter   229   U54 Squib   19
To my Lord Weston, Lo: Treasurer. A Letter   248   U71 Treasurer   VTtl
For his owne good, a carelesse letter-goe   315   Horace   234
Shall powre forth many a line, drop many a letter, ...   666   Glover   9
LETTER'D
A letter'd mind, and a large heart would place   227   U52 Answer   23

LETTER-GOE
    For his owne good, a carelesse letter-goe   · · · · · 315 Horace   234
LETTERS
    To it, thy language, letters, arts, best life, · · · 34 E23 Donne 1   7
    Better'd thy trust to letters; that thy skill; · · 63 E99 Th Roe 2 2
    And letters, and humanitie in the stead!   · · · 73 E113 Overbury 8
    Monarch in Letters! 'Mongst thy Titles showne   · 160 U14 Selden 65
    Two letters were enough the plague to teare   · · 172 U21 Ltl Shrub 3
    Joynting Syllabes, drowning Letters, · · · 183 U29 Fit of Rime 10
    In letters, that mixe spirits, thus to weave. · · 190 U37 Friend-Book 12
    Of his speciall grace to Letters, · · · 259 U76 Petition 7
    Upon th'Exchange of Letters, as I wou'd · · 386 Browne 14
    Here, are five letters in this blessed Name, · · 412 Ghyrlond 1
LETTING
    Letting Bow and Arrow fall, · · · · 132 U2 How he saw 17
    The middle of his matter: letting goe · · 315 Horace 213
    Not letting goe his hold, where he drawes food, · 337 Horace 679
    Not letting goe the skin, where he drawes food, · 355 Horace V679
LETTUCE
    Laxative lettuce, and such windie meate) · · · 88 E133 Voyage 167
LEWD
    Much lesse with lewd, prophane, and beastly phrase, · 27 E2 My Booke 11
    Lewd slanderers, soft whisperers that let blood · 167 U15 Friend-Wars 165
    Lewd standers, soft whisperers that let blood · 167 U15 Friend-Wars V165
    And my selfe most, in lewd selfe-boasting Rimes? · 203 U43 Vulcan V 26
LEWIS
    And Sister to just Lewis! · · · · · 240 U67 Muses 27
LIBELL
    I must a libell make, and cosen both. · · · 54 E81 Proule 8
    Can pumpe for; or a Libell without salt · · 193 U38 Elegy 'Tis 96
LIBELLING
    At libelling? Shall no Star-Chamber Peers, · · 410 Gill 3
LIBELLS
    Chev'ril cryes out, my verses libells are; · · 44 E54 Chev'ril 2 1
LIBELS
    To vent their Libels, and to issue rimes, · · 218 U47 Tribe 26
LIBER
    Liber, of all thy friends, thou sweetest care, · · 294 U89 Mart.8:77 1
LIBERALL
    The neede of such? whose liberall boord doth flow, · 95 F2 Penshurst 59
LIBERTIE
    The libertie, that wee'll enjoy to night. · · 65 E101 Supper 42
    Cato's to boote, Rome, and her libertie, · · 71 E110 Edmonds 1 4
    And seeke to scant her comelie libertie, · · 190 U37 Friend-Book 20
    And not without much praise; till libertie · · 321 Horace 366
    Caesar's ambition, Cato's libertie, · · · 395 May 10
LIBERTYE
    and seeke to scant her comelye Libertye, · · 421 Censure 13
LIBRARIE
    The learned Librarie of Don Quixote; · · · 204 U43 Vulcan 31
LIBRUM
    Author ad Librum. · · · · · · 662 Bedford Ttl
LICE
    So that not them, his scabbes, lice, or the stewes, · · 380 Coryat 3 50
LICENCE
    Will unto Licence that faire leave abuse. · · 190 U37 Friend-Book 24
    All licence in our lives? What need we know, · 215 U44 Speach 70
    Both in their tunes, the licence greater grew, · 319 Horace 299
    Her licence fit to be restrain'd by law: · · 321 Horace 368
LICENSE   (See also LYCENCE)
    To license ever was so light, · · · · 152 U12 Corbet 25
    And told of with more License then th'were done! · 156 U13 Sacvile 96
LICENTIOUS
    Thou should'st be bold, licentious, full of gall, · · 27 E2 My Booke 3
    But more licentious made, and desperate! · · 163 U15 Friend-Wars 36
LICENTIOUSLY
    My Verse at randome, and licentiously? · · · 323 Horace 391
LICINUS
    And from the Barber Licinus conceale · · · 325 Horace 427
LICK
    Had made a meale for Vulcan to lick up. · · 206 U43 Vulcan 84
    Had bin fitt meate for Vulcan to lick up. · · 206 U43 Vulcan V 84
LIE   (NOUN)
    They cannot last. No lie grew ever old. · · · 216 U45 Squib 20
LIE   (See also LYE)
    And whilst our tongues perplexed lie, · · · 139 U2 Another 17
    'Tis one good part I'ld lie withall. · · · 142 U2 Exception 8
    That all respect; She must lie downe: Nay more, · 163 U15 Friend-Wars 53
    But here doth lie, till the last Day, · · 168 U16 Gray 3
    All is not barren land, doth fallow lie. · · 169 U17 Friend-Debt 16
    Where do'st thou carelesse lie, · · · 174 U23 Himselfe 1
    Wrapt in this paper lie, · · · · 180 U26 Ode High 10
    Lie drawne to life, in his soft Verse, , · 181 U27 Ode Helen 7
    Any, least loose, or scurrile paper, lie · · 203 U43 Vulcan 20
    On Nature, for her: who did let her lie, · · 282 U84 Muse 13
    Let us together closely lie, and kisse, · · 294 U88 Petronius 7
    To lie at Livory, while the Horses did stand. · 375 Coryat 1 33
    French Aire and English Verse here Wedded lie. · 401 Filmer 6
LIEDGERS
    Maintayne their liedgers forth, for forraine wyres, · 118 F13 Aubigny 72
LIES   (NOUN)
    In Ireland, Holland, Sweden, pompous lies, · · 69 E107 Hungry 12
    Informers, Masters both of Arts and lies; · · 167 U15 Friend-Wars 164

	Page	Title	Line
LIES			
As my heart lies in peeces, all confus'd,	127	U1 Trinitie	7
Shee lies deliver'd, without paine,	251	U74 Weston	5
I Could begin with that grave forme, Here lies,	394	Jane Ogle	1
LIEUTENANT			
On lieutenant Shift.	30	E12 Shift	Ttl
LIFE'			
When all your life's a president of dayes,	237	U64 Charles 3	13
LIFE (See also LYFE)			
To it, thy language, letters, arts, best life,	34	E23 Donne 1	7
In the past pleasures of his sensuall life,	34	E25 Beast 1	2
If any pious life ere lifted man	35	E27 Roe 1	6
Conquer'd hath both life and it.	39	E40 Ratcliffe	12
Life, whose griefe was out of fashion,	39	E40 Ratcliffe	13
All this doth Jone. Or that his long yearn'd life	40	E42 Giles	11
In life, that can employ it; and takes hold	50	E70 Wm Roe 1	3
Each best day of our life escapes us, first.	50	E70 Wm Roe 1	6
Though life be short, let us not make it so.	50	E70 Wm Roe 1	8
Of Life, and Death.	53	E80 Life/Death	Ttl
The ports of death are sinnes; of life, good deeds:	53	E80 Life/Death	1
Now, I must give thy life, and deed, the voice	55	E86 Goodyere 2	5
So many Poets life, by one should live.	57	E89 Allen	14
Life of the Muses day, their morning-starre!	60	E94 Bedford 3	2
Of vice, and vertue; wherein all great life	66	E102 Pembroke	6
Whose life, ev'n they, that envie it, must praise;	66	E102 Pembroke	16
To make thy lent life, good against the Fates:	70	E109 Nevil	11
His life, but makes, that he can dye no more.	71	E110 Edmonds 1	22
So, where thou liv'st, thou mak'st life understood!	73	E113 Overbury	3
Which in life did harbour give	79	E124 Elizabeth	5
Lent timely succours, and new life begot:	80	E127 Aubigny	8
To Sir Robert Wroth in praise of a Country life. Epode.	96	F3 Wroth	VTtl
Thou maist thinke life, a thing but lent.	100	F3 Wroth	106
And, for it, life, conscience, yea, soules are given,	113	F12 Rutland	4
Like life unto 'hem. Who heav'd Hercules	115	F12 Rutland	57
And show, how, to the life, my soule presents	115	F12 Rutland	86
This makes, that wisely you decline your life,	118	F13 Aubigny	59
Unto your name, and goodnesse of your life,	119	F13 Aubigny	109
For wearinesse of life, not love of thee.	122	F15 Heaven	26
And breath'st into it, life, and light, with state	127	U1 Trinitie	19
The Author both of Life, and light;	130	U1 Nativitie	2
As alone there triumphs to the life	134	U2 Triumph	19
All your sweet of life is past,	140	U2 Promise	28
Yes; and in death, as life, unblest,	149	U8 Houre-glasse	9
With the just Canon of his life,	151	U12 Corbet	11
A life that knew nor noise, nor strife:	151	U12 Corbet	12
Reader, whose life, and name, did e're become	152	U12 Corbet	37
By thanking thus the curtesie to life,	158	U13 Sacvile	159
Mans buried honour, in his sleepie life:	162	U15 Friend-Wars	7
Is lov'd, though he let out his owne for life:	165	U15 Friend-Wars	88
The life, and fame-vaynes (yet not understood	167	U15 Friend-Wars	166
What suretie of life have thou, and I?	168	U16 Gray	7
His Issue, and all Circumstance of life,	171	U19 Elegy By	26
That their whole life was wickednesse, though weav'd	171	U20 Shrub	10
The Mistresse of Mans life, grave Historie,	175	U24 Frontispice	2
The light of Truth, and life of Memorie.	176	U24 Frontispice	18
Lie drawne to life, in his soft Verse,	181	U27 Ode Helen	7
And that there is no life in me, but love.	194	U38 Elegy 'Tis	112
I ne're attempted, Vulcan, 'gainst thy life;	202	U43 Vulcan	5
I ne're attempted ought against thy life;	202	U43 Vulcan	V 5
So acted to the life, as Maurice might,	214	U44 Speach	41
The Wisdome, Madam, of your private Life,	224	U50 Countesse	1
Not boasted in your life, but practis'd true,	225	U50 Countesse	32
If they goe on, and that thou lov'st a-life	232	U58 Book-seller	13
Of humane life! as all the frosts, and sweates	233	U59 Newcastle	22
Then knew the former ages: yet to life,	242	U69 Friend Son	23
For, what is life, if measur'd by the space,	243	U70 Ode	21
And sunke in that dead sea of life	244	U70 Ode	40
His life was of Humanitie the Spheare.	244	U70 Ode	52
Not liv'd; for Life doth her great actions spell,	245	U70 Ode	59
These makes the lines of life, and that's her ayre.	245	U70 Ode	64
And in short measures, life may perfect bee.	245	U70 Ode	74
When shee puts forth the life of ev'ry thing:	250	U74 Weston	3
Mariage, the end of life,	253	U75 Epithalam.	29
Of Life, that fall so; Christians know their birth	257	U75 Epithalam.	156
What you have studied are the arts of life;	261	U77 Treasurer	17
Of all that Nature, yet, to life did bring;	264	U79 New-yeares	33
'Twixt death and life! Where her mortalitie	271	U81 Pawlet	67
The Christian hath t'enjoy the future life,	271	U81 Pawlet	96
Who was my Muse, and life of all I sey'd,	282	U84 Muse	2
Of life, and light, the Sonne of God, the Word!	285	U84 Muse	112
She was, in one, a many parts of life;	287	U84 Muse	173
As her whole life was now become one note	287	U84 Muse	178
Of all are dead to life! His Wisdome show	289	U84 Muse	221
The praises of a Countrie life.	289	U85 Country	Ttl
So Fate would give her life, and longer daies.	293	U87 Hor.3:9	12
Makes his life longer then 'twas given him, much.	295	U89 Mart.8:77	8
The Things that make the happier life, are these,	295	U90 Mart.10:47	1
Nor from the brand, with which the life did burne	315	Horace	207
On life, and manners, and make those his booke,	325	Horace	454
Or mixing sweet, and fit, teach life the right.	327	Horace	478
From slaughters, and foule life; and for the same	327	Horace	481
All way of life was shewen; the grace of Kings	329	Horace	497
Where, such perfections to the life doe rise.	362	Author	6

		Page	Title	Line

LIFE (cont.)
Upon the Life, and Death of Playes, and Wits,		370	Fletcher	2
his life, his love, his honour, which ne'r dyes,		382	Rich	8
Or skill of making matches in my life:		386	Husband	7
With Nature, to out-doo the life:		390	Reader	4
To life againe, to heare thy Buskin tread,		391	Shakespeare	36
But of one Husband; and since he left life,		394	Jane Ogle	16
Where spight of Death, next Life, for her Loves sake		394	Jane Ogle	25
The best of Woemen! her whole life		399	Lady Ogle	11
And in them view'd th'uncertainty of Life,		411	Sutcliffe	3
Sweet Tree of Life, King Davids Strength and Tower,		413	Ghyrlond	38
He the half of Life abuses,		657	Door Apollo	9

LIFE'S
| When all your life's a president of dayes, | | 237 | U64 Charles 3 | 13 |

LIFES
| This world deaths region is, the other lifes: | | 54 | E80 Life/Death | 5 |
| As, could they but lifes miseries fore-see, | | 243 | U70 Ode | 19 |

LIFT
Helpe, helpe to lift		127	U1 Trinitie	4
Lift up some one, and doe, I tell not what.		201	U42 Elegy Let	58
To lift to heaven: who is't not understands		234	U61 Epigram	8

LIFTED
If any pious life ere lifted man		35	E27 Roe 1	6
With great gray eyes, are lifted up, and mew'd;		88	E133 Voyage	161
Or lifted Cassiopea in her chayre?		115	F12 Rutland	62

LIFTS
| Or when that Autumne, through the fields, lifts round | | 290 | U85 Country | 17 |

LIGHT (DESCEND)
To light upon a Love of mine.		174	U22 Elegy Tho	32
Light on thee: Or if those plagues will not doo,		212	U43 Vulcan	215
Light upon thee: Or if those plagues will not doo,		212	U43 Vulcan	V215
For seeliest Ignorance on these may light,		390	Shakespeare	7

LIGHT (ADJECTIVE)
'Tis but light paines: Indeede this Dock's no rose.		85	E133 Voyage	60
Goe, crampe dull Mars, light Venus, when he snorts,		107	F10 Proludium	16
Then, leave these lighter numbers, to light braines		108	F10 Proludium	7
To license ever was so light,		152	U12 Corbet	25
'Tis like light Canes, that first rise big and brave,		157	U13 Sacvile	149
In outward face, but inward, light as Furre,		162	U15 Friend-Wars	20
O, these so ignorant Monsters! light, as proud,		164	U15 Friend-Wars	59
Yet should the Lover still be ayrie and light,		197	U40 Elegy That	19
As light, and active as the youngest hee		200	U42 Elegy Let	6
As aerie light, and as like wit as those?		222	U49 Pucell	10
Three Kingdomes Mirth, in light, and aerie man,		249	U72 King	11
Of light expence;		273	U84 Cradle	20
Not tost or troubled with light Lady-aire;		287	U84 Muse	164
And farre unworthy to blurt out light rimes;		321	Horace	337

LIGHT
That but the twi-light of your sprite did see,		66	E103 L Wroth 1	2
The light, and marke unto posteritie?		67	E104 Montgomery	12
When we doe give, Alphonso, to the light,		82	E131 Ferrab. 2	1
But if once we loose this light,		102	F5 Celia 1	7
But when once wee lose the light,		102	F5 Celia 1	V 7
A beautie of that cleere, and sparkling light,		112	F11 Epode	93
You, and that other starre, that purest light,		115	F12 Rutland	65
To curious light, the notes, I then shall sing,		115	F12 Rutland	76
To curious light, to notes, I then shall sing,		115	F12 Rutland	V 76
As with the light		121	F14 Sydney	58
And breath'st into it, life, and light, with state		127	U1 Trinitie	19
The gladdest light, darke man can thinke upon;		128	U1 Trinitie	35
The Author both of Life, and light;		130	U1 Nativitie	2
Who saw the light, and were afraid,		130	U1 Nativitie	5
Doe but looke on her eyes, they doe light		134	U2 Triumph	11
Where Love may all his Torches light,		147	U7 Nymph	24
That with these mixtures we put out her light.		156	U13 Sacvile	110
Light thee from hell on earth: where flatterers, spies,		167	U15 Friend-Wars	163
The light of Truth, and life of Memorie.		176	U24 Frontispice	18
Rich beame of honour, shed your light		177	U25 Desmond	14
Shall light those places		179	U25 Desmond	59
All light failed!		183	U29 Fit of Rime	24
None brookes the Sun-light worse then he.		189	U36 Song	4
As light breakes from you, that affrights despaire,		191	U38 Elegy 'Tis	10
The Sunne his heat, and light, the ayre his dew?		192	U38 Elegy 'Tis	57
Rather then want your light, I wish a grave.		194	U38 Elegy 'Tis	122
Fitter to see the fire-light, then the day;		204	U43 Vulcan	44
To light Tobacco, or save roasted Geese,		205	U43 Vulcan	52
To light Tobacco, or have roasted Geese,		205	U43 Vulcan	V 52
Her face there's none can like by Candle light.		223	U49 Pucell	32
Ne knowes he flatt'ring Colours, or false light.		227	U52 Answer	21
Of a Disease, that lov'd no light		234	U60 La-ware	6
To light: her measures are, how well		245	U70 Ode	62
It was the Plant, and flowre of light.		245	U70 Ode	72
Whilst that in heav'n, this light on earth must shine.		246	U70 Ode	96
A-while with us bright Sun, and helpe our light;		252	U75 Epithalam.	2
A-while with us bright Sun, and mend our light;		252	U75 Epithalam.	V 2
And Sister: darting forth a dazling light		253	U75 Epithalam.	43
With light of love, this Paire doth intertexe!		254	U75 Epithalam.	60
One to the other, long e're these to light were brought.		257	U75 Epithalam.	144
Unto our yeare doth give the longest light.		262	U78 Digby	16
And now, through circumfused light, she lookes		271	U81 Pawlet	69
And Day, deceasing! with the Prince of light,		271	U81 Pawlet	88
And Men may thinke, all light rose there.		276	U84 Body	16
In heaven Empyre, and with a robe of light?		285	U84 Muse	102

LIGHT (cont.)

	Page	Title	Line
Of life, and light, the Sonne of God, the Word!	285	U84 Muse	112
By light, and comfort of spirituall Grace;	286	U84 Muse	131
Shee saw her Saviour, by an early light,	288	U84 Muse	199
I hold thee fast! but fled hence, with the Light,	293	U86 Hor.4:1	38
Hee thinkes not, how to give you smoake from light,	315	Horace	203
But light from smoake; that he may draw his bright	315	Horace	204
Take you the Greeke Examples, for your light,	323	Horace	397
Will in the light be view'd: This, once, the sight	331	Horace	543
Light, Posture, Height'ning, Shadow, Culloring,	370	Author	3
Of Spheares, as light of starres; She was earthes Eye:	372	Epitaph	9
And despaires day, but for thy Volumes light.	392	Shakespeare	80
Shee was the light (without reflexe	399	Lady Ogle	9
Of Angells, and all witnesses of light,	400	Lady Ogle	38
The Morning-star, whose light our Fal hath stay'd.	413	Ghyrlond	40
And I sweare by all the light	416	Moon	5

LIGHTED

	Page	Title	Line
Which makes that (lighted by the beamie hand	176	U24 Frontispice	9
This makes, that lighted by the beamie hand	176	U24 Frontispice V	9
and lighted by the Stagirite, could spie,	207	U43 Vulcan	90

LIGHTEN

	Page	Title	Line
clowd-/Like upon them lighten? If nature could	164	U15 Friend-Wars	61

LIGHTENS

	Page	Title	Line
God lightens not at mans each fraile offence,	193	U38 Elegy 'Tis	68

LIGHTER

	Page	Title	Line
My lighter comes, to kisse thy learned Muse;	78	E121 Rudyerd 1	2
The lighter Faunes, to reach thy Ladies oke.	94	F2 Penshurst	18
Then, leave these lighter numbers, to light braines	108	F10 Proludium	7
Made lighter with the Wine. All noises else,	249	U72 King	12
Thou lighter then the barke of any tree,	294	U87 Hor.3:9	22
or hir quarters lighter bee,	417	Moon	31

LIGHTLY

	Page	Title	Line
Which cover lightly, gentle earth.	34	E22 Daughter	12
I'le taste as lightly as the Bee,	139	U2 Another	5
Lightly promis'd, she would tell	139	U2 Promise	3

LIGHTNESSE

	Page	Title	Line
As farre as Sinne's from lightnesse.	364	Ode Splendor	4

LIGHTNING

	Page	Title	Line
Such a Lightning (as I drew)	132	U2 How he saw	24
As they out-did the lightning in the course;	233	U59 Newcastle	12

LIGHTS

	Page	Title	Line
Spies, you are lights in state, but of base stuffe,	45	E59 Spies	1
For fire, or lights, or livorie: all is there;	95	F2 Penshurst	73
Love lights his torches to inflame desires;	170	U19 Elegy By	2
All lights into his one doth run;	189	U36 Song	6
Not built with Canvasse, paper, and false lights,	220	U47 Tribe	65
To separate these twi-/Lights	246	U70 Ode	92
twi-/Lights, the Dioscuri;	246	U70 Ode	93
With slyding windowes, & false Lights a top!	407	Inigo Jones 2	10

LIGORNE

	Page	Title	Line
What at Ligorne, Rome, Florence you did doe:	69	E107 Hungry	14

LIGURINE

	Page	Title	Line
But, why, oh why, my Ligurine,	293	U86 Hor.4:1	33

LIKE (VERB)

	Page	Title	Line
May heare my Epigrammes, but like of none.	36	E28 Surly	20
As what he loves may never like too much.	41	E45 First Son	12
And like them too; must needfully, though few,	61	E94 Bedford '3	13
And like it too; if they looke equally:	67	E104 Montgomery	15
Then like, then love; and now would they amaze?	169	U18 Elegy Can	4
Her face there's none can like by Candle light.	223	U49 Pucell	32
Which, though I cannot like as an Architect	261	U77 Treasurer V 25	
Till fitter season. Now, to like of this,	307	Horace	63
Him that buyes chiches blanch't, or chance to like	321	Horace	362
Him that buyes Pulse there, or perhaps may like	347	Horace	V354/362
Or why to like; they found, it all was new,	415	Rutter	9

LIKE (See also LYKE)

	Page	Title	Line
For termers, or some clarke-like serving-man,	28	E3 Bookseller	9
And mine come nothing like. I hope so. Yet,	32	E18 Censurer	5
He drinkes to no man: that's, too, like a lord.	35	E28 Surly	14
Which if most gracious heaven grant like thine,	37	E33 Roe 3	5
Like aydes 'gainst treasons who hath found before?	38	E35 James 2	7
And like Nectar ever flowing:	39	E40 Ratcliffe	10
The like is Jone. But turning home, is sad.	40	E42 Giles	8
Were quite out-spun. The like wish hath his wife.	40	E42 Giles	12
Leave Cod, tabacco-like, burnt gummes to take,	42	E50 Cod 3	1
Not glad, like those that have new hopes, or sutes,	47	E64 Salisbury 3	1
Nor lend like influence from his lucent seat.	52	E76 Bedford 1	8
Your noblest father prov'd: like whom, before,	53	E79 Rutland	2
Straight went I home; and there most like a Poet,	55	E84 Bedford 2	5
And it is hop'd, that shee, like Milo, wull	57	E90 Mill	17
And grave as ripe, like mellow as their faces.	59	E92 New Crie	7
Much like those Brethren; thinking to prevaile	59	E92 New Crie	36
How like a columne, Radcliffe, left alone	60	E93 Radcliffe	1
O, would'st thou adde like hand, to all the rest!	61	E95 Savile	13
For who can master those great parts like thee,	61	E95 Savile	17
And, till they burst, their backs, like asses load:	62	E96 Donne 2	11
Like straight, thy pietie to God, and friends:	68	E106 E Herbert	8
And, on they went, like Castor brave, and Pollux:	86	E133 Voyage	77
Or, that it lay, heap'd like an usurers masse,	88	E133 Voyage	139
Like such as blow away their lives,	100	F4 To the World	22
Not like it selfe, but thee.	106	F9 Celia 3	V 16
like glasse, blowne up, and fashion'd by desire.	108	F10 Proludium	4
Inconstant, like the sea, of whence 'tis borne,	110	F11 Epode	39

LIKE (cont.)

	Page	Title	Line
Rough, swelling, like a storme:	110	F11 Epode	40
That falls like sleepe on lovers, and combines	110	F11 Epode	49
But, in a calme, and god-like unitie,	110	F11 Epode	53
Peace, Luxurie, thou art like one of those	111	F11 Epode	69
But we propose a person like our Dove,	112	F11 Epode	91
But I Conceive a person like my Dove,	112	F11 Epode V	91
Like life unto 'hem. Who heav'd Hercules	115	F12 Rutland	57
There like a rich, and golden pyramede,	115	F12 Rutland	83
Moodes, which the god-like Sydney oft did prove,	116	F12 Rutland	91
Not looking by, or back (like those, that waite	118	F13 Aubigny	62
And like the ravish'd Sheep'erds said,	130	U1 Nativitie	4
After many scornes like these,	133	U2 Suffered	1
Looser-like, now, all my wreake	133	U2 Suffered	21
Both her Browes, bent like my Bow.	136	U2 Cupid	17
Eye-brows bent like Cupids bow,	141	U2 Her man	17
And in his Mrs. flame, playing like a flye,	149	U8 Houre-glasse	7
And in his Mrs. flaming, playing like a flye,	149	U8 Houre-glasse V	7
Of pressure, like one taken in a streight?	154	U13 Sacvile	32
Like Money-brokers, after Names, and hire	155	U13 Sacvile	62
And spunge-like with it dry up the blood quite:	155	U13 Sacvile	69
But like to be, that every day mends one,	156	U13 Sacvile	116
'Tis like light Canes, that first rise big and brave,	157	U13 Sacvile	149
And like a Compasse keeping one foot still	159	U14 Selden	31
For all their spight, be like him if they could:	162	U15 Friend-Wars	26
Who can behold their Manners, and not clowd-/Like	164	U15 Friend-Wars	60
clowd-/Like upon them lighten? If nature could	164	U15 Friend-Wars	61
Planting their Purles, and Curles spread forth like Net,	164	U15 Friend-Wars	65
If it be thought kild like her Embrions; for,	165	U15 Friend-Wars	96
Of what he throwes: Like letchers growne content	166	U15 Friend-Wars	139
In this, and like, an itch of Vanitie,	166	U15 Friend-Wars	143
A vertue, like Allay, so gone	173	U22 Elegy Tho	5
Then shall my Verses, like strong Charmes,	177	U25 Desmond	18
Then shall our Verses, like strong Charmes,	177	U25 Desmond V	18
When her dead essence (like the Anatomie	179	U25 Desmond	37
So comm'st thou like a Chiefe into the Court,	187	U33 Councellour	29
Not like your Countrie-neighbours, that commit	190	U37 Friend-Book	7
Thinke that your selfe like heaven forgive me can:	192	U38 Elegy 'Tis	32
This looketh like an Execution day?	193	U38 Elegy 'Tis	80
Not, like a Midas, shut up in himselfe,	197	U40 Elegy That	21
Moves like a sprightly River, and yet can	198	U40 Elegy That	26
They looke at best like Creame-bowles, and you soone	198	U40 Elegy That	29
Like the dull wearied Crane that (come on land)	198	U40 Elegy That	35
Where he that knowes will, like a Lapwing, flie	198	U40 Elegy That	37
What it is like: And doe not thinke they can	199	U41 Elegy Since	3
Or like a Ghost walke silent amongst men,	199	U41 Elegy Since	21
Whose like I have knowne the Taylors Wife put on	201	U42 Elegy Let	39
That are like cloath'd: must I be of those fooles	201	U42 Elegy Let	48
Or in the Bell-Mans Lanthorne, like a spie,	211	U43 Vulcan	187
We will beleeve, like men of our owne Ranke,	215	U44 Speach	75
Like Solons selfe; explat'st the knottie Lawes	217	U46 Coke	17
Like flies, or wormes, with mans corrupt parts fed:	218	U47 Tribe	18
From any thought like sadnesse.	221	U48 Bacchus	20
As aerie light, and as like wit as those?	222	U49 Pucell	10
You made it a brave piece, but not like me.	227	U52 Answer	15
You shew'd like Perseus upon Pegasus;	228	U53 Newcastle	7
But Scarlet-like out-lasts the Cloth.	230	U55 Burges	8
Such, (if her manners like you) I doe send:	230	U56 Covell	19
Will be reward enough: to weare like those,	232	U58 Book-seller	9
Like a rung Beare, or Swine: grunting out wit	232	U58 Book-seller	11
Of bodies, meet like rarified ayre!	233	U59 Newcastle	10
But crept like darknesse through his blood?	234	U60 La-ware	8
No doubt all Infants would returne like thee.	243	U70 Ode	20
It is not growing like a tree	245	U70 Ode	65
Fix'd to the bed, and borde, and like to win	248	U71 Treasurer V	11
Like Eccho playing from the other shore.	249	U72 King	8
Like Eccho playing from another shore.	249	U72 King V	8
So like a feast?	253	U75 Epithalam.	14
Like what she is, the Daughter of a Duke,	253	U75 Epithalam.	42
Like Swine, or other Cattell here on earth:	257	U75 Epithalam.	154
Like pretty Spies,	258	U75 Epithalam.	174
But like an Arme of Eminence 'mongst them,	258	U75 Epithalam.	179
And he is built like some imperiall roome,	262	U78 Digby	7
Were like a ring of Vertues, 'bout her set,	270	U81 Pawlet	41
Where every lim takes like a face?	275	U84 Body	4
Till, like her face, it doe appeare,	276	U84 Body	15
Foure Rivers branching forth like Seas,	276	U84 Body	23
But these are like a Mind, not it.	278	U84 Mind	12
Not swelling like the Ocean proud,	280	U84 Mind	57
In rest, like spirits left behind	280	U84 Mind	66
Nothing I doe; but, like a heavie wheele,	283	U84 Muse	30
Like single; so, there is a third, commixt,	284	U84 Muse	53
And to the Touch, a Flower, like soft as Palme.	286	U84 Muse	126
Nor Souldier-like started with rough alarmes,	289	U85 Country	5
Like lustfull beasts, that onely know to doe it:	294	U88 Petronius	4
Whose shapes, like sick-mens dreames, are fain'd so vaine,	305	Horace	9
Whose shapes, like sick-mens dreames, are form'd so vaine,	338	Horace V	9
Like tender buds shoot up, and freshly grow.	309	Horace	89
To chant the Gods, and all their God-like race,	311	Horace	114
Still to be like himselfe, and hold his worth.	313	Horace	182
And can tread firme, longs with like lads to play;	315	Horace	226
I'the open field; is Waxe like to be wrought	315	Horace	231
Like men street-borne, and neere the Hall, reherse	321	Horace	357

		Page	Title	Line

LIKE   (cont.)
Like men Town-born, and neere the place, reherse   .   .   . 347 Horace   V349/357
Had not our every Poet like offended.   .   .   .   . 325 Horace   414
Be like a Whet-stone, that an edge can put   .   .   . 325 Horace   433
And stalketh, like a Fowler, round about,   .   .   . 335 Horace   650
Till, horse-leech-like, he drop off, full of blood.   .   . 355 Horace   V680
Set out a like, or second to our Swan.   .   .   . 369 Ode Who saith   120
Here, like Arion, our Coryate doth draw   .   .   . 374 Coryat 1   10
Hee's carried like a Cripple, from Constable to Constable.   . 374 Coryat 1   17
Here, by a Boore too, hee's like to be beaten   .   . 375 Coryat 1   24
He was in his travaile, how like to be beaten,   .   . 380 Coryat 3   35
Or, like our Money-Brokers, take up names   .   .   . 386 Browne   10
More of our writers would like thee, not swell   .   . 386 Browne   15
nor yet inscription like it. Write but that;   .   .   . 387 Cavendish   9
nor yet inscription like it writt but that   .   .   . 387 Cavendish   V 9
Such Bookes deserve Translators, of like coate   .   . 389 Aleman   11
When like Apollo he came forth to warme   .   .   . 392 Shakespeare   45
Our eares, or like a Mercury to charme!   .   .   . 392 Shakespeare   46
Which, since thy flight from hence, hath mourn'd like night,   . 392 Shakespeare   79
Like him, to make the ayre, one volary: .   .   . 392 Shakespeare   79
And like a hallow'd Temple, free from taint   .   .   . 397 Drayton   36
But fly thee, like the Pest! Walke not the street   .   . 401 Beaumont   21
Who like a Giant hasts his course to run,   .   .   . 409 Detractor   19
LIK'D   414 Ghyrlond   51
His bought armes Mung' not lik'd; for his first day   .   . 42 E48 Mungril   1
You lik'd, then after, to apply   .   .   .   .   . 247 U70 Ode   108
LIKELY
It is not likely I should now looke downe   .   .   . 200 U42 Elegy Let   37
LIKENESS
Are with the likeness of the truth beguil'd: .   .   . 339 Horace   V 35/ 34
LIKENESSE
Are, with the likenesse of the truth, undone.   .   .   . 307 Horace   34
Require (besides the likenesse of the thing)   .   .   . 370 Author   2
LIKES
Lookes o're the bill, likes it: and say's, god payes.   .   . 30 E12 Shift   10
LIKING
What (at his liking) he will take away.   .   .   . 236 U63 Charles 2   6
That liking; and approach so one the tother,   .   .   . 247 U70 Ode   109
LILLIE
Have you seene but a bright Lillie grow,   .   .   . 134 U2 Triumph   21
Have you seene the white Lillie grow,   .   .   . 134 U2 Triumph   V 21
A Lillie of a Day, ... 245 U70 Ode   69
Againe hath brought the Lillie to the Rose;   .   .   . 401 Filmer   8
To top the fairest Lillie, now, that growes,   .   .   . 413 Ghyrlond   15
LILLIES
And lookes as Lillies doe, ... 147 U7 Nymph   18
See, how with Roses, and with Lillies shine,   .   .   . 254 U75 Epithalam. 57
(Lillies and Roses, Flowers of either Sexe)   .   .   . 254 U75 Epithalam. 58
LILLY
The bed of the chast Lilly, and the Rose!   .   .   . 237 U65 Prince   3
Her Rose, and Lilly, intertwind, have made.   .   .   . 268 U80 Christning 16
LILY
And tell, how farre thou didst our Lily out-shine,   .   . 391 Shakespeare   29
LIM
About his forme. What then so swells each lim?   .   . 63 E97 Motion   19
Where every lim takes like a face?   .   .   .   . 275 U84 Body   4
LIMBE
That though they did possesse each limbe,   .   .   . 151 U12 Corbet   9
An ill-affected limbe (what e're it aile)   .   .   . 192 U38 Elegy 'Tis   45
On every limbe, ta'en from a severall creature,   .   . 305 Horace   3
LIMBES
Eyes and limbes; to hurt me more.   .   .   .   . 133 U2 Suffered   4
LIMITING
Will well confesse; presenting, limiting,   .   .   . 370 Author   6
LIMMES
Sleeked limmes, and finest blood?   .   .   .   . 105 F8 Sicknesse   23
Sleeked limmes, and fyned blood?   .   .   .   . 105 F8 Sicknesse   V 23
LIMONS
With juyce of limons, onions, pisse, to write.   .   .   . 59 E92 New Crie   28
Limons, and wine for sauce: to these, a coney   .   . 65 E101 Supper   13
LINE   (See also LYNE)
Could save that line to dedicate to thee?   .   .   . 44 E53 Old-end   10
A line unto thee, till the world it know;   .   .   . 54 E81 Proule   2
Of Caesars Daughter, and the line   .   .   .   . 181 U27 Ode Helen   19
For Venus Ceston, every line you make.   .   .   . 182 U28 Worth   14
No face, no hand, proportion, line, or Ayre   .   .   . 200 U42 Elegy Let   14
Nor made least line of love to thy loose Wife;   .   . 203 U43 Vulcan   6
Thy Neeces line, then thou that gav'st thy Name   .   . 274 U84 Descent   14
Hence-forth may every line be you;   .   .   .   . 278 U84 Mind   22
Each line, as it were graphick, in the face!   .   .   . 287 U84 Muse   154
His proofe their praise, will meete, as in this line.   .   . 362 Author   14
To line out no stride, but pas'd by himselfe?   .   .   . 379 Coryat 3   8
Each leafe of his journall, and line doth unlocke   .   . 380 Coryat 3   23
Or sporting Kid, or Marlowes mighty line.   .   .   . 391 Shakespeare   30
Who casts to write a living line, must sweat,   .   .   . 392 Shakespeare   59
At every line some pinn thereof should slacke   .   . 395 May   5
And stop my sight, in every line I goe.   .   .   . 398 Drayton   78
Shall powre forth many a line, drop many a letter,   .   . 666 Glover   9
LIN'D
His cloke with orient velvet quite lin'd through,   .   . 62 E97 Motion   4
LINES
Their lives, as doe their lines, till now had lasted.   .   . 65 E101 Supper   32
Or feare to draw true lines, 'cause others paint: .   . 117 F13 Aubigny   20

LINES (cont.)
   Love to my heart, and Fortune to my lines.   .   .   .   170   U18 Elegy Can   24
   And the strong lines, that so the time doe catch: .   .   206   U43 Vulcan   78
   And the strong lines, which so the time doe catch: .   .   206   U43 Vulcan   V 78
   But there are lines, wherewith I might b'embrac'd.   .   .   226   U52 Answer   3
   These make the lines of life, and that's her ayre.   .   .   245   U70 Ode   64
   Whose lines her rowles were, and records.   .   .   .   247   U70 Ode   126
   Yet read him in these lines: He doth excell   .   .   262   U78 Digby   2
   Yet take him in these lines: He doth excell   .   .   262   U78 Digby   V 2
   What reputation to my lines, and me, ...   263   U78 Digby   26
   . . . Panegyricke lines, but then were upon some occasions . . .   379   Coryat 3   Ttl
   And joy'd to weare the dressing of his lines!   .   .   .   392   Shakespeare   48
   In his well torned, and true-filed lines: .   .   .   392   Shakespeare   68
   Is to make cheape, the Lord, the lines, the price.   .   .   408   Detractor   6
   Through all the lines of this circumference,   .   .   .   414   Ghyrlond   54
LING
   To Court-ling.   50   E72 Court-ling   Ttl
LINKES
   Whose linkes are bright, and even, ...   110   F11 Epode   48
LINNEN
   To have her linnen, plate, and all things nigh,   .   .   96   F2 Penshurst   86
LION   (See also LYONS)
   The Lybian Lion hunts noe butter flyes, ...   408   Inigo Jones 3   7
LIP
   Joyne lip to lip, and try: 139   U2 Another   15
   And his lip should kissing teach, ...   141   U2 Her man   22
   And as lip-thirstie, in each words expence,   .   .   .   222   U49 Pucell   13
LIPPE
   On Lippe, the Teacher.   52   E75 Lippe   Ttl
   Though Lippe, at Pauls, ranne from his text away,   .   .   52   E75 Lippe   3
LIPPES
   My lippes could forme the voyce, I heard that Rore,   .   .   397   Drayton   38
LIPS
   Quick in his lips! who hath this wonder wrought?   .   .   33   E21 Gam'ster   5
   On my lips, thus hardly sundred, ...   103   F6 Celia 2   7
   From your lips, and suck'd an ayre   137   U2 Kisse   3
   But what those lips doe make.   143   U3 Musicall   16
   But what your lips doe make.   143   U3 Musicall   V 16
   And lastly by your lips, the banke of kisses,   .   .   .   170   U19 Elegy By   9
LIP-THIRSTIE
   And as lip-thirstie, in each words expence,   .   .   .   222   U49 Pucell   13
LIQUID
   In memorie of which most liquid deed, ...   89   E133 Voyage   193
LIQUOR
   Then Hippocrenes liquor: 221   U48 Bacchus   28
   Tis the true Phoebeian Liquor, ...   657   Door Apollo   15
LIST   (NAUTICAL)
   Or his to Antwerpe. Therefore, once more, list ho'.   .   .   85   E133 Voyage   40
LIST   (NOUN)
   Lesse list of proud, hard, or ingratefull Men.   .   .   153   U13 Sacvile   4
   A list of Epithites: And prayse this way.   .   .   .   394   Jane Ogle   8
   Thy list of aydes, and force, for so it is: .   .   .   398   Drayton   62
LIST
   Or, if thou list the night in watch to breake,   .   .   .   97   F3 Wroth   21
   And, if thou list thy selfe, what thou canst bee.   .   .   386   Browne   4
   the sword, but that it acteth what it list.   .   .   .   423   Lucan   14
LISTEN
   His three for one. Now, lordings, listen well.   .   .   84   E133 Voyage   28
LITER
   But, comming neere, they found it but a liter,   .   .   .   86   E133 Voyage   85
LITERATE
   Of our Odcombian, that literate Elfe?   379   Coryat 3   7
LITTLE
   For I will doe none: and as little ill, ...   30   E11 Something   7
   Shewes of the resurrection little trust.   .   .   .   37   E34 Death   2
   To'a little wealth, and credit in the scene,   .   .   .   45   E56 Poet-Ape   7
   It may be much, or little, in the cause.   .   .   .   49   E66 Cary   16
   And, being nam'd, how little doth that name   .   .   .   66   E103 L Wroth 1   5
   This little storie: 77   E120 S. P.   2
   In a little? Reader, stay.   79   E124 Elizabeth   2
   Who kept an ale-house; with my little Minos,   .   .   .   89   E133 Voyage   189
   Little, for me, had reason done, ...   101   F4 To the World 35
   As little, as I hope from thee: 101   F4 To the World 38
   Little, whose will   121   F14 Sydney   29
   Nor can a little of the common store, ...   121   F14 Sydney   31
   Profit in ought: each day some little adde,   .   .   .   157   U13 Sacvile   132
   A little Shrub growing by.   172   U21 Ltl Shrub   Ttl
   Little know they, that professe Amitie,   .   .   .   190   U37 Friend-Book 19
   My selfe a little. I will take you so,   .   .   .   220   U47 Tribe   76
   Take little Infants with their noyse, ...   273   U84 Cradle   18
   If ne're so little it depart the first,   .   .   .   331   Horace   563
   Read here a little, that thou mayst know much.   .   .   371   Epitaph   2
   still that same little poynte hee was; but when   .   .   383   Rich   13
   yf from a little sparke hee rise not fier.   .   .   .   383   Rich   16
   A little further, to make thee a roome: .   .   .   391   Shakespeare   21
   Little knowne they that proffesse Amitye   .   .   .   421   Censure   12
   Goe little Booke, Goe little Fable   662   Bedford   1
LIV'D
   Here's one out-liv'd his Peeres, ...   243   U70 Ode   25
   Let such as justly have out-liv'd all prayse,   .   .   387   Cavendish   5
   not when I die'd, but how I livd. Farewell.   .   .   .   387   Cavendish   12
'LIVE
   So, 'live or dead, thou wilt preserve a fame   .   .   .   168   U15 Friend-Wars 189

	Page	Title	Line

LIVE

Shall out-live gyrlands, stolne from the chast tree.	32	E17 Critic	6
Longer a knowing, then most wits doe live.	34	E23 Donne 1	5
If any Muse out-live their spight, his can;	35	E27 Roe 1	4
What should the cause be? Oh, you live at court:	46	E62 Would-bee	9
To live when Broeck not stands, nor Roor doth runne.	49	E66 Cary	12
When Nature bids us leave to live, 'tis late	50	E70 Wm Roe 1	1
Whil'st I behold thee live with purest hands;	51	E74 Chancelor	3
So many Poets life, by one should live.	57	E89 Allen	14
To any one, were envie: which would live	58	E91 Vere	11
And to live great, was better, then great borne.	75	E116 Jephson	12
Which is to live to conscience, not to show.	76	E119 Shelton	14
To more vertue, then doth live.	79	E124 Elizabeth	6
Live, with un-bought provision blest;	97	F3 Wroth	14
Strive, Wroth, to live long innocent.	98	F3 Wroth	66
Upon thy throate, and live exempt	100	F4 To the World	7
Live not we, as, all thy stalls.	104	F8 Sicknesse	9
That Homer brought to Troy; yet none so live:	115	F12 Rutland	55
And almost, all dayes after, while they live;	118	F13 Aubigny	75
Live that one, still; and as long yeeres doe passe,	120	F13 Aubigny	121
To live untill to morrow' hath lost two dayes.	121	F14 Sydney	50
So may you live in honor, as in name,	121	F14 Sydney	51
Such Notes are vertuous men! they live as fast	157	U13 Sacvile	143
But he that's both, and slave to boote, shall live,	167	U15 Friend-Wars	160
But he that's both, and slave to both, shall live,	167	U15 Friend-Wars	V160
Unto the other; and live patterns, how	171	U19 Elegy By	17
Gold, that is perfect, will out-live the fire.	179	U25 Desmond	45
And (stil'd your mercies Creature) will live more	191	U38 Elegy 'Tis	29
Would live his glory that could keepe it on;	192	U38 Elegy 'Tis	48
That makes us live, not that which calls to die.	193	U38 Elegy 'Tis	78
But I who live, and have liv'd twentie yeare	200	U42 Elegy Let	29
To live in Sea-coale, and goe forth in smoake;	211	U43 Vulcan	181
To live in Sea-coale, and goe out in smoake;	211	U43 Vulcan	V181
Live by their Scale, that dare doe nothing free?	215	U44 Speach	68
That live in the wild Anarchie of Drinke,	218	U47 Tribe	10
To live, or fall a Carkasse in the cause.	219	U47 Tribe	42
Live to that point I will, for which I am man,	219	U47 Tribe	59
Wherewith this while you live a widow'd wife,	224	U50 Countesse	2
Verse, that should thee, and me out-live.	229	U55 Burges	4
Who durst live great, 'mongst all the colds, and heates,	233	U59 Newcastle	21
How many times, Live long, Charles, would he say,	236	U64 Charles 3	3
All live dogs from the lane, and his shops sight,	241	U69 Friend Son	12
In signe the Subject, and the Song will live,	262	U78 Digby	17
Yet would I wish to love, live, die with thee.	294	U87 Hor.3:9	24
To be that Smith; then live, mark'd one of those,	307	Horace	51
With honour make the farre-knowne Author live.	329	Horace	519
And thou in them shalt live as longe as Fame.	362	Palmer	31
And art alive still, while thy Booke doth live,	391	Shakespeare	23
This Booke will live; It hath a Genius: This	400	Beaumont	1

LIV'D

In thee, most weighty Savile, liv'd to us:	61	E95 Savile	4
Nor that his worke liv'd in the hands of foes,	71	E110 Edmonds 1	9
For, where his person liv'd scarce one just age,	71	E110 Edmonds 1	13
Then that it liv'd at all. Farewell.	79	E124 Elizabeth	12
But I who live, and have liv'd twentie yeare	200	U42 Elegy Let	29
Not liv'd; for Life doth her great actions spell,	245	U70 Ode	59
You liv'd to be the great surnames,	247	U70 Ode	113
Th'Ignoble never liv'd, they were a-while	257	U75 Epithalam.	153
Just as she in it liv'd! and so exempt	270	U81 Pawlet	48
And much shall dye, that now is nobly liv'd,	309	Horace	102
First frighted men, that wildly liv'd, at ods,	327	Horace	480

LIVERIES

Of Summers Liveries, and gladding greene;	253	U75 Epithalam.	18

LIVERS

Livers, round about the towne.	105	F8 Sicknesse	17

LIVES

Sure, willing povertie lives most in you.	29	E6 Alchymists	2
By that one spell he lives, eates, drinkes, arrayes	30	E12 Shift	5
Thy wit lives by it, Proule, and belly too.	54	E81 Proule	6
Their lives, as doe their lines, till now had lasted.	65	E101 Supper	32
Yet drown'd they not. They had five lives in future.	88	E133 Voyage	154
Like such as blow away their lives,	100	F4 To the World	22
Since when it lives, and smells, I sweare,	106	F9 Celia 3	V 15
Take that away, you take our lives,	146	U6 Defence	5
Lives to the Lord, but to the Ladies end.	165	U15 Friend-Wars	94
Lives for the Lord, but to the Ladies end.	165	U15 Friend-Wars	V 94
More then themselves, or then our lives could take,	166	U15 Friend-Wars	127
In whom alone Love lives agen?	173	U22 Elegy Tho	14
For no man lives so out of passions sway,	190	U37 Friend-Book	31
(If they be faire and worth it) have their lives	200	U42 Elegy Let	20
All licence in our lives? What need we know,	215	U44 Speach	70
The Kings fame lives. Go now, denie his Teirce.	241	U68 House-hold	14
And there he lives with memorie; and Ben	246	U70 Ode	84
Whose lives her rowles were, and records.	247	U70 Ode	V126
The joy of Saints! the Crowne for which it lives,	283	U84 Muse	37
to tender thus, their lives, their loves, their hartes!	382	Rich	4
Lives in his issue, even so, the race	392	Shakespeare	66
That lives, and breath's, and loves the King.	418	Grace	4

LIVIE

Livie, or of some better booke to us,	65	E101 Supper	22
Spake to 'hem louder, then the oxe in Livie:	86	E133 Voyage	74

LIVING

On whom, if he were living now, to looke,	53	E79 Rutland	10

LIVING   (cont.)

	Page	Title	Line
They, then, that living where the matter is bred,	60	E94 Bedford 3	11
He, that, but living halfe his age, dyes such;	76	E119 Shelton	15
That kept man living! Pleasures only sought!	163	U15 Friend-Wars	41
. . . the Lady Venetia Digby; who living, . . .	282	U84 Muse	Ttl
Hee, that but living halfe his dayes, dies such,	295	U89 Mart.8:77	7
Who casts to write a living line, must sweat,	392	Shakespeare	59
And God blesse every living thing,	418	Grace	3

LIVOR

| If a fit livor thou dost seeke to toast; | 292 | U86 Hor.4:1 | 12 |

LIVORIE

| For fire, or lights, or livorie: all is there; | 95 | F2 Penshurst | 73 |

LIVORY

| To lie at Livory, while the Horses did stand. | 375 | Coryat 1 | 33 |

LIV'ST

Yet by thy weapon liv'st! Th'hast one good part.	50	E69 Cob	2
That liv'st from hope, from feare, from faction free;	61	E95 Savile	18
So, where thou liv'st, thou mak'st life understood!	73	E113 Overbury	3

'LL

The knight-wright's cheated then: Hee'll never pay.	42	E46 Luckless 1	5
Of which wee'll speake our minds, amidst our meate;	65	E101 Supper	23
The libertie, that wee'll enjoy to night.	65	E101 Supper	42
I shall feare, you'll surfet too.	104	F8 Sicknesse	8
I doe feare, you'll surfet too.	104	F8 Sicknesse	V 8
Or safe, but shee'll procure	109	F11 Epode	6
And having pleas'd our art, wee'll try	145	U5 Woman-kind	17
For these with her young Companie shee'll enter,	164	U15 Friend-Wars	79
From the Tempestuous Grandlings, Who'll informe	215	U44 Speach	64
He'll thee a Marble Statue make	292	U86 Hor.4:1	19
For hee'll cry, Good, brave, better, excellent!	333	Horace	611
Wee'll have thee styld the Marquess of New-Ditch.	407	Inigo Jones 2	24
Wee'll have thee styld the Marquess of Town-Ditch.	407	Inigo Jones 2	V 24
Hee'll be a Pilot, scarce can guide a Plough.	410	Brome	18
I'll laugh at thee poor wretched Tike, go send	410	Gill	10

LO

. . . Lo: high Treasurer of England.	185	U30 Burleigh	Ttl
An Epigram. To Thomas Lo: Elsmere, . . .	185	U31 Elsmere	Ttl
To my Lord Weston, Lo: Treasurer. A Letter	248	U71 Treasurer	VTtl

LOAD

And, till they burst, their backs, like asses load:	62	E96 Donne 2	11
Who shall discharge first his merd-urinous load:	85	E133 Voyage	65
But both fell prest under the load they make.	166	U15 Friend-Wars	128

LOATH

Play-wright, I loath to have thy manners knowne	42	E49 Playwrt 1	5
Nought but in corners; and is loath to leave,	154	U13 Sacvile	44
Upon it, but will loath, or let it passe,	389	Aleman	9

LOCK   (HAIR)

| Made of the trull, that cut her fathers lock: | 86 | E133 Voyage | 84 |

LOCK

| Can lock the Sense up, or the heart a thought, | 198 | U40 Elegy That | 43 |

LOCK'D

| And talke reserv'd, lock'd up, and full of feare, | 59 | E92 New Crie | 17 |
| That was lock'd up in the Winchestrian Goose | 209 | U43 Vulcan | V142 |

LOCKS

| From locks of wooll, or shreds from the whole peece? | 45 | E56 Poet-Ape | 14 |
| Thy locks, and rosie garlands crowne thy head; | 294 | U89 Mart.8:77 | 4 |

LOCK'T

| Lock't in her cold embraces, from the view | 177 | U25 Desmond | 22 |

LOCKT

| Or, in an armies head, that, lockt in brasse, | 114 | F12 Rutland | 52 |

LODGE

Who, for it, makes thy lodge his court;	97	F3 Wroth	V 24
My Shakespeare, rise; I will not lodge thee by	391	Shakespeare	19
Whom shee, with Sorrow first did lodge, then feast,	394	Jane Ogle	20

LODGING

| Nor, when I take my lodging, need I pray | 95 | F2 Penshurst | 72 |

LOE

Loe, what my countrey should have done (have rais'd	46	E60 Mounteagle	1
If I can give some small increase? when, loe,	309	Horace	80
* * * * * When loe to crowne thy worth	361	Palmer	27

LOFTIE

For this so loftie forme, so streight,	280	U84 Mind	54
Hath neither soule, nor sinewes. Loftie he	307	Horace	37
Loftie, and grave; and in the buskin stalke.	319	Horace	318
Loftie, and great; and in the buskin walk.	348	Horace	V398/318
The while he belcheth loftie Verses out,	335	Horace	649

LOFTIER

| Made loftier by the Winds all noises else, | 249 | U72 King | V 12 |

LOG

| The trees cut out in log; and those boughes made | 98 | F3 Wroth | 45 |

LOGGE

| To fall a logge at last, dry, bald, and seare: | 245 | U70 Ode | 68 |

LOGOGRIPHES

| Of Logogriphes, and curious Palindromes, | 204 | U43 Vulcan | 34 |

LOGS

| The Birth-day shines, when logs not burne, but men. | 121 | F14 Sydney | 60 |

LOIRE   (See LOYRE)

LONDON

Unto the cryes of London Ile adde one;	58	E92 New Crie	2
Lent by the London Dames, to the Lords men;	213	U44 Speach	14
Of London, in the Militarie truth,	213	U44 Speach	26

LONG   (VERB)

| I long, and should not beg in vaine, | 139 | U2 Another | 2 |

	Page	Title	Line
LONG (cont.)			
Doe long to make themselves, so, another way:	257	U75 Epithalam.	140
LONG			
You laugh when you are touch'd, and long before	38	E38 Guiltie 2	3
All this doth Jone. Or that his long yearn'd life	40	E42 Giles	11
Long-gathering Old-end, I did feare thee wise,	43	E53 Old-end	1
Get him the times long grudge, the courts ill will:	48	E65 Muse	7
The Virgin, long-since fled from earth, I see,	52	E74 Chancelor	9
Was dull, and long, ere shee would goe to man:	57	E90 Mill	3
Is private gaine, which hath long guilt to friend.	70	E109 Nevil	8
Of newes, and noyse, to strow out a long meale.	74	E115 Honest Man	10
Of newes, and noyse, to sow out a long meale.	74	E115 Honest Man V	10
Shee learnes to know long difference of their states.	78	E121 Rudyerd 1	4
And, in so shitten sort, so long had us'd him:	86	E133 Voyage	98
Strive, Wroth, to live long innocent.	98	F3 Wroth	66
Strive, Wroth, to be long innocent.	98	F3 Wroth V	66
And will, long ere thou should'st starve,	106	F8 Sicknesse	44
Live that one, still; and as long yeeres doe passe,	120	F13 Aubigny	121
Be more, and long desir'd:	121	F14 Sydney	55
What w'are but once to doe, we should doe long.	139	U2 Another	12
With the rest, I long expected,	140	U2 Promise	7
'Twere to long, to speake of all:	141	U2 Her man	33
Deare Vincent Corbet who so long	151	U12 Corbet	7
They are so long a comming, and so hard;	153	U13 Sacvile	23
And jealous each of other, yet thinke long	164	U15 Friend-Wars	73
That they long since have refused	184	U29 Fit of Rime	47
And his Title be long foole,	184	U29 Fit of Rime	58
Who thus long safe, would gaine upon the times	186	U32 Elsmere	9
Of newes they get, to strew out the long meale,	218	U47 Tribe	28
With a long, large, and blest posteritie!	236	U63 Charles 2	12
How many times, Live long, Charles, would he say,	236	U64 Charles 3	3
And long in changing. Let our Nephewes see	238	U65 Prince	7
To shew thou hast beene long,	245	U70 Ode	58
Or standing long an Oake, three hundred yeare,	245	U70 Ode	67
(Were not his Lucius long with us to tarry)	246	U70 Ode	91
Still to have such a Charles, but this Charles long.	249	U72 King	18
One to the other, long e're these to light were brought.	257	U75 Epithalam.	144
Aloud; and (happ'ly) it may last as long.	261	U77 Treasurer	28
As loude; and (happ'ly) it may last as long.	261	U77 Treasurer V	28
Compar'd unto that long eternitie,	285	U84 Muse	106
Long intermitted, pray thee, pray thee spare:	292	U86 Hor.4:1	2
So Fates would let the Boy a long thred run.	293	U87 Hor.3:9	16
This hath pleas'd, doth please, and long will please; never	294	U88 Petronius	9
Unto your strength, and long examine it,	307	Horace	54
Unto your strength, and long be turning it:	307	Horace V 56/	54
A kingly worke; or that long barren fen	339	Horace	93
A great deferrer, long in hope, growne numbe	309	Horace	245
The rash, and head-long eloquence brought forth	317	Horace	307
Two rests, a short and long, th'Iambick frame;	319	Horace	371
Nor is't long since, they did with patience take	323	Horace	375
A pound, or piece, by their long compting arts:	323	Horace	466
Of their long labours, was in Verse set downe:	327	Horace	500
Will passe the Seas, and long as nature is,	329	Horace	518
But, I confesse, that, in a long worke, sleepe	329	Horace	537
Though I confesse, that, in a long worke, sleepe	329	Horace V513/	537
Be then both Rare, and Good; and long	351	Horace	33
How long he did stay, at what signe he did Inne.	367	Ode Who saith	26
Lyve long the Feasting Roome. And ere thou burne	380	Coryat 3	101
Thie long watch'd verse	406	Inigo Jones 1	20
LONG'D	420	Ode:If Men	
Till I attaine the long'd-for mysterie	128	U1 Trinitie	31
LONGE			
And thou in them shalt live as longe as Fame.	362	Palmer	31
LONG'D-FOR			
Till I attaine the long'd-for mysterie	128	U1 Trinitie	31
LONGER			
Longer a knowing, then most wits doe live.	34	E23 Donne 1	5
Longer a day, but with his Mill will marry.	57	E90 Mill	16
Makes, the whole longer, then 'twas given him, much.	76	E119 Shelton	16
The apple-harvest, that doth longer last;	98	F3 Wroth	43
Venter a longer time, and willingly:	169	U17 Friend-Debt	15
Made longer by our praises. Or, if not,	200	U42 Elegy Let	21
I may no longer on these pictures stay,	216	U44 Speach	98
So Fate would give her life, and longer daies.	293	U87 Hor.3:9	12
Makes his life longer then 'twas given him, much.	295	U89 Mart.8:77	8
LONGEST			
At morne, and even, shades are longest;	104	F7 Women but	7
Unto our yeare doth give the longest light.	262	U78 Digby	16
LONG-GATHERING			
Long-gathering Old-end, I did feare thee wise,	43	E53 Old-end	1
LONGING			
The longing Couple, all that elder Lovers know.	258	U75 Epithalam.	192
LONGS (BELONGS)			
Doe all, that longs to the anarchy of drinke,	74	E115 Honest Man	12
LONGS			
And can tread firme, longs with like lads to play;	315	Horace	226
LONG-SINCE			
The Virgin, long-since fled from earth, I see,	52	E74 Chancelor	9
LOOK			
Look pale, distill a dew was never meant	353	Horace	V612
Whose chearfull look our sadnesse doth destroy,	414	Ghyrlond	43
LOOKE			
For strict degrees of ranke, or title looke:	29	E9 To All	2

	Page	Title	Line

LOOKE (cont.)

	Page	Title	Line
Looke not upon thy dangers, but our feares.	43	E51 James 3	10
On whom, if he were living now, to looke,	53	E79 Rutland	10
If workes (not th'authors) their owne grace should looke,	60	E94 Bedford 3	3
And like it too; if they looke equally:	67	E104 Montgomery	15
I oft looke on false coyne, to know't from true:	68	E107 Hungry	3
And Ile not looke for wine.	106	F9 Celia 3	4
Of Fortune, have not alter'd yet my looke,	117	F13 Aubigny	16
Looke then, and see your selfe. I will not say	117	F13 Aubigny	29
When her looke out-flourisht May:	132	U2 How he saw	2
Could be brought once back to looke.	132	U2 How he saw	19
Doe but looke on her eyes, they doe light	134	U2 Triumph	11
Doe but looke on her Haire, it is bright	134	U2 Triumph	13
For he must looke wanton-wise.	141	U2 Her man	16
Nor looke too kind on my desires,	144	U4 Song	7
Looke to and cure; Hee's not a man hath none,	156	U13 Sacvile	115
Meet some new matter to looke up and wonder!	157	U13 Sacvile	142
Looke on th'ambitious man, and see him nurse	162	U15 Friend-Wars	11
Looke on the false, and cunning man, that loves	162	U15 Friend-Wars	15
No part or corner man can looke upon,	163	U15 Friend-Wars	27
I'le bid thee looke no more, but flee, flee friend,	166	U15 Friend-Wars	129
On which with profit, I shall never looke,	189	U37 Friend-Book	5
Looke forth, but cannot last in such a forme.	191	U38 Elegy 'Tis	14
They looke at best like Creame-bowles, and you soone	198	U40 Elegy That	29
It is not likely I should now looke downe	200	U42 Elegy Let	37
These ten yeares day; As all may sweare that looke	213	U44 Speach	27
Turne him, and see his Threds: looke, if he be	216	U45 Squib	21
And looke unto their faces,	220	U48 Bacchus	9
Would make the very Greene-cloth to looke blew:	241	U68 House-hold	8
Looke up, thou seed of envie, and still bring	250	U73 Weston	1
Our Court, and all the Grandees; now, Sun, looke,	254	U75 Epithalam.	73
These I looke up at, with a reverent eye,	261	U77 Treasurer	23
These looke you up at, with a measuring eye,	261	U77 Treasurer	V 23
For he doth love my Verses, and will looke	263	U78 Digby	23
Looke on thy sloth, and give thy selfe undone,	283	U84 Muse	21
A meere new person, looke he keepe his state	313	Horace	180
And I still bid the learned Maker looke	325	Horace	453
Looke pale, distill a showre (was never meant)	333	Horace	612
Looke through him, and be sure, you take not mocks	333	Horace	621
Looke here on Bretons worke, the master print:	362	Author	5
If they seeme wry, to such as looke asquint,	362	Author	7
But who will beleeve this, that chanceth to looke	379	Coryat 3	17
shall looke, & on hyme soe, then arte's a lyer	383	Rich	15
Who bluntly doth but looke upon the same,	383	Author	3
With the same looke, or with a better, shine.	384	Somerset	10
To see his worke be good; but that he looke	385	Husband	2
That an ill man dares not securely looke	389	Aleman	8
But, since he cannot, Reader, looke	390	Reader	9
And such wert thou. Looke how the fathers face	392	Shakespeare	65
Looke, how we read the Spartans were inflam'd	398	Drayton	67
I looke on Cynthia, and Sirenas sport,	398	Drayton	80
To veiw the truth and owne it. Doe but looke	399	Lady Ogle	5
You looke, my Joseph, I should something say	414	Rutter	1
Looke how the starres from earth, or seas from flames	422	Lucan	7

LOOK'D

	Page	Title	Line
It will be look'd for, booke, when some but see	27	E2 My Booke	1
Look'd not halfe so fresh, and faire,	138	U2 Kisse	9
I look'd for Hercules to be the Groome:	228	U53 Newcastle	18
When look'd the yeare, at best,	253	U75 Epithalam.	13
When look'd the Earth so fine,	253	U75 Epithalam.	21
With vices, which they look'd for, and came to.	371	Fletcher	10
That all Earth look'd on; and that earth, all Eyes!	396	Drayton	16

LOOKES

	Page	Title	Line
To be a courtier; and lookes grave enough,	30	E11 Something	2
Lookes o're the bill, likes it: and say's, god payes.	30	E12 Shift	10
When I would know thee Goodyere, my thought lookes	55	E86 Goodyere 2	1
Canst tell me best, how every Furie lookes there,	85	E133 Voyage	52
Of Hol'borne (three sergeants heads) lookes ore,	89	E133 Voyage	177
By her lookes I doe her know,	136	U2 Cupid	18
And lookes as Lillies doe,	147	U7 Nymph	18
His lookes would so correct it, when	152	U12 Corbet	27
And lookes unto the forfeit. If you be	169	U17 Friend-Debt	13
And how more faire, and lovely lookes the world	193	U38 Elegy 'Tis	73
I had deserv'd, then, thy consuming lookes,	203	U43 Vulcan	17
And let thy lookes with gladnesse shine:	245	U70 Ode	76
And now, through circumfused light, she lookes	271	U81 Pawlet	69
Sad language fits sad lookes; stuff'd menacings,	311	Horace	149
Lookes after honours, and bewares to act	315	Horace	239

LOOKETH

	Page	Title	Line
This looketh like an Execution day?	193	U38 Elegy 'Tis	80

LOOKING

	Page	Title	Line
Not looking by, or back (like those, that waite	118	F13 Aubigny	62
Still looking to, and ever loving heaven;	219	U47 Tribe	61
Thou, looking then about,	242	U70 Ode	5
And looking with thy best Inquirie, tell,	254	U75 Epithalam.	74
Yet, looking in thy face, they shall begin	369	Ode Who saith	93
And looking up, I saw Minervas fowle,	397	Drayton	33

LOOKS

	Page	Title	Line
Or, every day, some one at Rimee's looks,	59	E92 New Crie	23

LOOK'ST

	Page	Title	Line
When thou wert borne, and that thou look'st at best,	208	U43 Vulcan	113
When thou wert borne, and when thou look'st at best,	208	U43 Vulcan	V113
By barking against mee. Thou look'st at least,	408	Detractor	10

	Page	Title	Line

LOOME
Minervaes loome was never richer spred. . . . . 61 E95 Savile 16

LOOMES
Not with the Arras, but the Persian Loomes. . . . 260 U77 Treasurer 4
Not from the Arras, but the Persian Loomes. . . . 260 U77 Treasurer V 4

LOOSE (ADJECTIVE)
To catch the worlds loose laughter, or vaine gaze. . . 27 E2 My Booke 12
to loose, and Cap'ring, for thy stricter veyne. . . 108 F10 Proludium 2
Nor made least line of love to thy loose Wife; . . 203 U43 Vulcan 6
Any, least loose, or scurrile paper, lie . . . 203 U43 Vulcan 20
And this a Sparkle of that fire let loose . . . 209 U43 Vulcan 141
That this sparke of the same fire let loose . . . 209 U43 Vulcan V141

LOOSE
Beleeve it, Guiltie, if you loose your shame, . . 38 E38 Guiltie 2 7
I'le loose my modestie, and tell your name. . . 38 E38 Guiltie 2 8
O, could I loose all father, now. For why . . 41 E45 First Son 5
Thou wert content the authors name to loose: . . 43 E53 Old-end 3
Make him loose all his friends; and, which is worse, . . 48 E65 Muse 9
Nor may'any feare, to loose of their degree, . . 73 E113 Overbury 11
With all my powers, my selfe to loose? . . . 101 F4 To the World 28
But if once we loose this light, . . . 102 F5 Celia 1 7
To loose that feare; . . . . . 369 Ode Who saith 94

LOOSED
Nor alwayes doth the loosed Bow, hit that . . . 329 Horace 524

LOOSENESSE
Thou, nor thy loosenesse with my making sorts. . . 107 F10 Proludium 18
Thou, nor their loosenesse with our making sorts. . . 107 F10 Proludium V 18

LOOSER
Looser-like, now, all my wreake . . . . 133 U2 Suffered 21

LOOSER-LIKE
Looser-like, now, all my wreake . . . . 133 U2 Suffered 21

LOOSING
Then thou did'st late my sense, loosing my points. . . 45 E58 Groome 6
Or Mallowes loosing bodyes ill: . . . . 291 U85 Country 58

LOPS
And with his hooke lops off the fruitlesse race, . . 290 U85 Country 11

LORD (See also LO)
To my lord Ignorant. . . . . . 29 E10 Ignorant Ttl
A lord, it cryed, buried in flesh, and blood, . . 30 E11 Something 5
For I will dare none. Good Lord, walke dead still. . 30 E11 Something 8
Lord, how is Gam'ster chang'd! his haire close cut! . 33 E21 Gam'ster 1
He drinkes to no man: that's, too, like a lord. . 35 E28 Surly 14
To William Lord Mounteagle. . . . . 46 E60 Mounteagle Ttl
That hast betray'd me to a worthlesse lord; . . 48 E65 Muse 2
To Thomas Lord Chancelor. . . . . 51 E74 Chancelor Ttl
I ask'd a lord a buck, and he denyed me; . . 54 E84 Bedford 2 2
Might be found out as good, and not my Lord. . . 75 E116 Jephson 8
To Esme, Lord 'Aubigny. . . . . 80 E127 Aubigny Ttl
And that is when it is the Lord Maiors foist. . . 87 E133 Voyage 120
Thy lord, and lady, though they have no sute. . . 95 F2 Penshurst 50
His children thy great lord may call his owne: . . 96 F2 Penshurst 91
May say, their lords have built, but thy lord dwells. . 96 F2 Penshurst 102
Nor will I beg of thee, Lord of the vine, . . 107 F10 Proludium 10
Nor will we beg of thee, Lord of the vine, . . 107 F10 Proludium V 10
To pay your lord the pledges of chast love: . . 119 F13 Aubigny 96
Of lust, to his rich Suit and Title, Lord? . . 163 U15 Friend-Wars 51
Lives to the Lord, but to the Ladies end. . . 165 U15 Friend-Wars 94
Lives for the Lord, but to the Ladies end. . . 165 U15 Friend-Wars V 94
To flatter my good Lord, and cry his Bowle . . 167 U15 Friend-Wars 147
No more, then we should thinke a Lord had had . . 168 U15 Friend-Wars 193
But to your selfe, most loyal Lord, . . . 179 U25 Desmond 53
An Epigram On William Lord Burl: . . . . 185 U30 Burleigh Ttl
So, justest Lord, may all your Judgements be . . 185 U31 Elsmere 1
When this appeares, just Lord, to your sharp sight, . 186 U32 Elsmere 15
Wrung on the Withers, by Lord Loves despight, . . 201 U42 Elegy Let 63
And why to me this, thou lame Lord of fire, . . 202 U43 Vulcan 1
. . . he was Lord chiefe Justice of England. . . 217 U46 Coke Ttl
Lord Bacons Birth-day. . . . . 225 U51 Bacon Ttl
Since Bacon, and thy Lord was borne, and here; . . 225 U51 Bacon 8
When first, my Lord, I saw you backe your horse, . . 228 U53 Newcastle 1
All this (my Lord) is Valour! This is yours! . . 233 U59 Newcastle 19
Henry, the brave young Lord La-ware, . . . 233 U60 La-ware 3
My Lord, till felt griefe make our stone hearts soft, . 234 U61 Epigram 14
The Mother of our Lord: why may not I . . . 238 U66 Queene 3
To the Right Honourable, the Lord high Treasurer of . . . 248 U71 Treasurer Ttl
To my Lord Weston, Lo: Treasurer. A Letter . . 248 U71 Treasurer VTtl
On the Right Honourable, and vertuous Lord Weston, L. . . . 250 U73 Weston Ttl
Bring all your friends, (faire Lord) that burne . . 251 U74 Weston 20
. . . Heire, of the Lord Weston, Lord high Treasurer of . . . 252 U75 Epithalam. Ttl
To the right Honourable, the Lord Treasurer of England. . . . 260 U77 Treasurer Ttl
If to my mind, great Lord, I had a state, . . 260 U77 Treasurer 1
But you I know, my Lord; and know you can . . 261 U77 Treasurer 13
The knowing Weston, and that learned Lord . . 263 U78 Digby 28
Then comforted her Lord! and blest her Sonne! . . 270 U81 Pawlet 57
Accumulated on her, by the Lord . . . 285 U84 Muse 111
. . . eldest Daughter, to Cuthbert Lord Ogle: . . . 394 Jane Ogle Ttl
And will be bought of every Lord, and Knight, . . 398 Drayton 72
Both Saints, and Martyrs, by her loved Lord. . . 400 Lady Ogle 39
Is to make cheape, the Lord, the lines, the price. . 408 Detractor 6
Our King and Queen the Lord-God blesse, . . 418 Grace 1

LORD-GOD
Our King and Queen the Lord-God blesse, . . . 418 Grace 1

		Page	Title	Line

LORDINGS
His three for one. Now, lordings, listen well.   .   .   .   84 E133 Voyage   28
For education of our Lordings; Soone   .   .   .   .   .   214 U44 Speach   62
LORDS
Item, an epitaph on my lords cock, ...   51 E73 Fine Grand   18
Nor 'bout the beares, nor noyse to make lords sport.   .   .   63 E97 Motion   12
Without his feare, and of thy lords owne meate: .   .   95 F2 Penshurst   62
May say, their lords have built, but thy lord dwells.   .   96 F2 Penshurst   102
Lent by the London Dames, to the Lords men;   .   .   213 U44 Speach   14
You cling to Lords, and Lords, if them you leave   .   .   223 U49 Pucell   38
And waiting Chambers of great Lords.   .   .   .   .   289 U85 Country   8
Importune wish; and by her lov'd Lords side   .   .   .   394 Jane Ogle   23
LORDSHIP
Pardon his Lordship. Flattry's growne so cheape   .   .   167 U15 Friend-Wars   155
His Lordship. That is for his Band, his haire   .   .   215 U44 Speach   95
LORDSHIPS
That is his Lordships, shall be also mine.   .   .   .   95 F2 Penshurst   64
Runs sweetly, as it had his Lordships Soule;   .   .   .   167 U15 Friend-Wars   148
LORE
Of deepest lore, could we the Center find!   .   .   .   243 U70 Ode   10
LOSE   (See also LOOSE, LEESE)
Is now from home. You lose your labours quite,   .   .   89 E133 Voyage   181
But when once wee lose the light, ...   102 F5 Celia 1   V 7
What man but must lose his?   .   .   .   .   .   .   143 U3 Musicall   8
To lose the formes, and dignities of men,   .   .   .   166 U15 Friend-Wars   146
And for it lose his eyes with Gun-powder,   .   .   .   208 U43 Vulcan   121
Lose all my credit with my Christmas Clay,   .   .   .   219 U47 Tribe   52
If I doe lose it: And, without a Tale, ...   229 U54 Squib   3
I can lose none in tendring these to you.   .   .   .   231 U56 Covell   28
LOSSE
That we thy losse might know, and thou our love,   .   .   43 E51 James 3   1
Or your complexions losse? you have a pot,   .   .   .   46 E62 Would-bee   6
And there's both losse of time, and losse of sport   .   .   46 E62 Would-bee   10
Love thy great losse, which a renowne hath wonne,   .   49 E66 Cary   11
Sit mixt with losse of state, or reverence.   .   .   .   98 F3 Wroth   57
Before my losse .   .   .   .   130 U1 Father   29
To himselfe his losse of Time;   .   .   .   .   .   138 U2 Kisse   31
To Merlins Marvailes, and his Caballs losse,   .   .   .   206 U43 Vulcan   71
To Martins Marvailes, and his Caballs losse,   .   .   .   206 U43 Vulcan   V 71
With Merlins Marvailes, and his tables losse,   .   .   .   206 U43 Vulcan   V 71
Losse, remaines yet, as unrepair'd as mine.   .   .   .   211 U43 Vulcan   196
Losse, remaines yet, as much despair'd as mine.   .   .   211 U43 Vulcan   V196
To K. Charles, and Q. Mary. For the losse of their . . .   235 U63 Charles 2   Ttl
That thought shall make, he will this losse supply   .   236 U63 Charles 2   11
Suffring, and dying to redeeme our losse!   .   .   .   288 U84 Muse   202
Thy selfe in teares, then me thy losse will wound,   .   311 Horace   146
Onely my losse is, that I am not there: .   .   .   .   398 Drayton   91
LOST
That lost, he keepes his chamber, reades Essayes,   .   30 E12 Shift   15
And hath no honor lost, our Due'llists say.   .   .   .   42 E48 Mungril   3
So have I seene at Christ-masse sports one lost,   .   .   45 E58 Groome   7
Madame, had all antiquitie beene lost, ...   67 E105 L Wroth 2   1
I' your selfe, all treasure lost of th'age before.   .   .   68 E105 L Wroth 2   20
In meere out-formes, untill he lost his sight,   .   .   73 E114 Sydney   4
Both whose dimensions, lost, the world might finde   .   79 E125 Uvedale   3
No more, those mayden glories shee hath lost.   .   .   83 E132 Sylvester   14
And now lye lost in their forgotten dust.   .   .   .   114 F12 Rutland   40
Now thinking on you, though to England lost,   .   .   116 F12 Rutland   94
As what th'have lost t'expect, they dare deride.   .   116 F13 Aubigny   4
Without which, all the rest were sounds, or lost.   .   118 F13 Aubigny   50
To live untill to morrow' hath lost two dayes.   .   .   121 F14 Sydney   50
Sooner, then he lost his might, ...   132 U2 How he saw   14
Whether we have lost, or wonne, ...   138 U2 Kisse   6
For I both lost a friend and Father, ...   151 U12 Corbet   5
I wonder'd at the richnesse, but am lost,   .   .   .   160 U14 Selden   53
. . . in Queene Elizabeths Time, since lost, and recovered.   .   176 U25 Desmond   Ttl
Of Credit lost. And I am now run madde: .   .   .   191 U38 Elegy 'Tis   2
Your just commands; yet those, not I, be lost.   .   .   192 U38 Elegy 'Tis   38
Alas I ha' lost my heat, my blood, my prime,   .   .   199 U41 Elegy Since   11
Are lost upon accompt! And none will know   .   .   .   237 U64 Charles 3   21
Are lost upon accompt! And none doe know   .   .   .   237 U64 Charles 3   V 21
And were shee lost, could best supply her place,   .   .   264 U79 New-yeares   34
Thou wouldst have lost the Phoenix, had the kind   .   283 U84 Muse   19
Had lost our selves? and prodigally spent   .   .   .   286 U84 Muse   141
That thou hast lost thy noyse, thy foame, thy stirre,   .   408 Detractor   8
Thinking to stir me, thou hast lost thy End,   .   .   410 Gill   9
but have lost it by the way, ...   417 Moon   10
LOT
Was his blest fate, but our hard lot to find.   .   .   37 E32 Roe 2   8
For such a lot! that mixt you with a state   .   .   .   118 F13 Aubigny   48
LOTH
Which, if thou leave not soone (though I am loth)   .   .   54 E81 Proule   7
As loth, the second draught, or cast to stay,   .   .   94 F2 Penshurst   35
All that dare rowse: or are not loth to quit   .   .   162 U15 Friend-Wars   3
LOTIONS
Suppositories, cataplasmes, and lotions.   .   .   .   86 E133 Voyage   102
LOUD   (See also LOWD)
Talkes loud, and baudy, has a gather'd deale   .   .   74 E115 Honest Man   9
Over your heads: Well, row. At this a loud   .   .   86 E133 Voyage   93
Of loud Sepulchres with their hourely knells,   .   .   89 E133 Voyage   174
A-bed canst heare the loud stag speake,   .   .   .   97 F3 Wroth   22
Sound, sound his praises loud, and with his, hers divide.   264 U79 New-yeares   19
As loud enough to fill the seates, not yet   .   .   .   319 Horace   291

LOUD (cont.)

How do his trumpets breath! What loud alarmes! . . . 398 Drayton 66
What makes your Wretchednes to bray soe loud . . 403 Inigo Jones 1 23

LOUDE

Their thoughts and meanes to making loude the cry; . . 155 U13 Sacvile 66
Beates brave, and loude in Europe, and bids come . . 162 U15 Friend-Wars 2
As loude; and (happ'ly) it may last as long. . . 261 U77 Treasurer V 28

LOUDER

Spake to 'hem louder, then the oxe in Livie: . . 86 E133 Voyage 74

LOUGHING

'Mongst loughing heards, and solide hoofes: . . 97 F3 Wroth 16

LOUMOND

To Loumond lake, and Twedes blacke-springing fountaine. . 368 Ode Who saith 72

LOUSE

And louse-dropping Case, are the Armes of his travell. . 375 Coryat 1 27

LOUSE-DROPPING

And louse-dropping Case, are the Armes of his travell. . 375 Coryat 1 27

LOVE'

That Love's a bitter sweet, I ne're conceive . . 197 U40 Elegy That 1

LOVE

Which should thy countries love to speake refuse, . . 40 E43 Salisbury 1 3
That we thy losse might know, and thou our love, . . 43 E51 James 3 1
How I doe love thee Beaumont, and thy Muse, . . 44 E55 Beaumont 1
That love to make so well, a child to beare? . . 46 E62 Would-bee 2
Of love, and what the golden age did hold . . 47 E64 Salisbury 3 3
That neither fame, nor love might wanting be . . 48 E66 Cary 1
Love thy great losse, which a renowne hath wonne, . . 49 E66 Cary 11
Love honors, which of best example bee, . . 49 E66 Cary 13
To honor, serve, and love: as Poets use. . . 52 E76 Bedford 1 4
Then doe I love thee, and behold thy ends . . 55 E86 Goodyere 2 3
Where, though 't be love, that to thy praise doth move . 55 E86 Goodyere 2 7
It was a knowledge, that begat that love. . . 55 E86 Goodyere 2 8
That thou hast kept thy love, encreast thy will, . . 63 E99 Th Roe 2 4
Not that I love it, more, then I will you. . . 68 E107 Hungry 1
I sweare by your true friend, my Muse, I love . . 70 E108 Soldiers 5
But, in your love, made all his servants wise. . . 74 E114 Sydney 8
If onely love should make the action pris'd: . . 78 E121 Rudyerd 1 6
Might love the treasure for the cabinet. . . 79 E125 Uvedale 6
Said I wrong'd him, and (which was more) his love. . 80 E126 Mrs Cary 5
Cary my love is, Daphne but my tree. . . 80 E126 Mrs Cary 8
Men love thee not for this: They laugh at thee. . . 81 E129 Mime 18
Why I write not of Love. . . 93 F1 Why write no Ttl
When Love is fled, and I grow old. . . 93 F1 Why write no 12
But what can this (more then expresse their love) . 95 F2 Penshurst 57
How blest art thou, canst love the countrey, Wroth, . 96 F3 Wroth 1
While we may, the sports of love; . . 102 F5 Celia 1 2
While we can, the sports of love; . . 102 F5 Celia 1 V 2
If thy leanenesse love such food, . . 105 F8 Sicknesse 24
Such, as in lustes wilde forrest love to rainge, . 108 F10 Proludium 9
which rap's mee up to the true heav'en of love; . 108 F10 Proludium 13
Of which usurping rancke, some have thought love . 110 F11 Epode 31
The thing, they here call Love, is blinde Desire, . 110 F11 Epode 37
In a continuall tempest. Now, true Love . . 110 F11 Epode 43
As this chaste love we sing. . . 111 F11 Epode 68
As this chaste love I sing. . . 111 F11 Epode V 68
He that for love of goodnesse hateth ill, . . 112 F11 Epode 87
Grac'd with a Phoenix love; . . 112 F11 Epode 92
The wealthy treasure of her love on him; . . 112 F11 Epode 105
The wealthy treasure of her love in him; . . 112 F11 Epode V105
Solders crackt friendship; makes love last a day; . 113 F12 Rutland 17
His love unto the Muses, when his skill . . 114 F12 Rutland 33
And your brave friend, and mine so well did love. . 116 F12 Rutland 92
And your brave friend, and mine to well did love. . 116 F12 Rutland V 92
I, therefore, who professe my selfe in love . . 116 F13 Aubigny 7
To pay your lord the pledges of chast love: . . 119 F13 Aubigny 96
How you love one, and him you should; how still . 119 F13 Aubigny 113
Both love the cause, and authors of the feast? . 120 F14 Sydney 10
Of love be bright, . . 121 F14 Sydney 57
My faith, my hope, my love: and in this state, . 122 F15 Heaven 11
For wearinesse of life, not love of thee. . . 122 F15 Heaven 26
With grace, with love, with cherishing intire: . 128 U1 Trinitie 43
Therein, thy Love. . . 129 U1 Father 6
Lesse your laughter; that I love. . . 131 U2 Excuse 2
Either whom to love, or die. . . 131 U2 Excuse 16
All the world for love may die. . . 131 U2 Excuse 24
Love, if thou wilt ever see . . 132 U2 How he saw 7
Reconcil'd to Love, and me. . . 133 U2 Suffered 6
Unto her; which Love might take . . 133 U2 Suffered 9
See the Chariot at hand here of Love, . . 134 U2 Triumph 1
And well the Carre Love guideth. . . 134 U2 Triumph 4
Have you seene Love-Queenes embraces . . 135 U2 Triumph V 35
Love, and I have had; and true. . . 136 U2 Cupid 6
Of her Sex; But could'st thou, Love, . . 137 U2 Cupid 45
Outward Grace weake love beguiles: . . 137 U2 Cupid 51
Had of Love, and of his force, . . 139 U2 Promise 2
What a man she could love well: . . 139 U2 Promise 4
And make Love or me afeard. . . 141 U2 Her man 24
As he durst love Truth and me. . . 142 U2 Her man 52
Men, if you love us, play no more . . 145 U5 Woman-kind 1
Which we in love must doe aswell, . . 146 U6 Defence 9
If ever we will love aright. . . 146 U6 Defence 10
In love, doth not alone help forth . . 146 U6 Defence 20
To love one man, hee'd leave her first. . . 146 U6 Defence 24

	Page	Title	Line
LOVE (cont.)			
I Love, and he loves me againe,	147	U7 Nymph	1
I feare they'd love him too;	147	U7 Nymph	4
Where Love may all his Torches light,	147	U7 Nymph	24
I'le tell no more, and yet I love,	148	U7 Nymph	29
If Love, or feare, would let me tell his name.	148	U7 Nymph	35
I Now thinke, Love is rather deafe, then blind,	149	U9 Picture	1
I Doubt that, Love is rather deafe, then blind,	149	U9 Picture	V 1
And cast my love behind:	149	U9 Picture	5
But under the Disguise of love,	150	U10 Jealousie	9
Think'st thou that love is help'd by feare?	150	U10 Jealousie	12
Love in a subtile Dreame disguis'd,	151	U11 Dreame	4
That I may love your Person (as I doe)	157	U13 Sacvile	157
Which Grace shall I make love to first? your skill,	159	U14 Selden	35
It true respects. He will not only love,	161	U14 Selden	73
Who falls for love of God, shall rise a Starre.	168	U15 Friend-Wars	196
Then like, then love; and now would they amaze?	169	U18 Elegy Can	4
I can helpe that with boldnesse; And Love sware,	170	U18 Elegy Can	9
Or Love, or Fortune blind, when they but winke	170	U18 Elegy Can	16
If it be thus; Come Love, and Fortune goe,	170	U18 Elegy Can	21
Love to my heart, and Fortune to my lines.	170	U18 Elegy Can	24
Love lights his torches to inflame desires;	170	U19 Elegy By	2
Tell me (my lov'd Friend) doe you love, or no,	170	U19 Elegy By	11
I'le therefore aske no more, but bid you love;	171	U19 Elegy By	15
Others, in time may love, as we doe now.	171	U19 Elegy By	18
And draw, and conquer all mens love,	173	U22 Elegy Tho	7
This subjects you to love of one.	173	U22 Elegy Tho	8
In whom alone Love lives agen?	173	U22 Elegy Tho	14
As Love, t'aquit such excellence,	173	U22 Elegy Tho	23
To light upon a Love of mine.	174	U22 Elegy Tho	32
Such thoughts wil make you more in love with truth.	181	U26 Ode High	21
Is Horace his each love so high	181	U27 Ode Helen	13
The Courts just honour, and thy Judges love.	187	U33 Councellour	37
For Love in shadow best is made.	189	U36 Song	2
Where Love doth shine, there needs no Sunne,	189	U36 Song	5
Next to your selfe, for making your love true:	189	U37 Friend-Book	2
Then to your love, and gift. And all's but due.	189	U37 Friend-Book	3
That friendship which no chance but love did chuse,	190	U37 Friend-Book	23
It is an Act of tyrannie, not love,	190	U37 Friend-Book	25
And that there is no life in me, but love.	194	U38 Elegy 'Tis	112
For though Love thrive, and may grow up with cheare,	197	U40 Elegy That	15
Whose Readers did not thinke he was in love.	199	U42 Elegy Let	4
When he is furious, love, although not lust.	200	U42 Elegy Let	18
Of love, and hate: and came so nigh to know	200	U42 Elegy Let	35
An Officer there, did make most solemne love,	201	U42 Elegy Let	53
Let the poore fooles enjoy their follies, love	202	U42 Elegy Let	81
Nor made least line of love to thy loose Wife;	203	U43 Vulcan	6
We aske your absence here, we all love peace,	212	U43 Vulcan	209
We crave your absence here, we all love peace,	212	U43 Vulcan	V209
We neither love the Troubles, nor the harmes.	215	U44 Speach	86
What love you then? your whore. what study? gate,	215	U44 Speach	87
These I will honour, love, embrace, and serve:	220	U47 Tribe	71
Shall feast it, thou maist love there	221	U48 Bacchus	38
No love of action, and high Arts,	234	U60 La-ware	12
Then now, to love the Soveraigne, and the Lawes?	236	U64 Charles 3	8
Then now, to love the Soveraigne, or his Lawes?	236	U64 Charles 3	V 8
How is she barren growne of love! or broke!	237	U64 Charles 3	15
How is she barren growne in love! or broke!	237	U64 Charles 3	V 15
The fained Queene of Love,	240	U67 Muses	32
Freedome, and Truth; with love from those begot:	241	U69 Friend Son	5
But simple love of greatnesse, and of good;	246	U70 Ode	105
With love, to heare your modestie relate,	251	U74 Weston	21
With light of love, this Paire doth intertexe!	254	U75 Epithalam.	60
Mens Loves unto the Lawes, and Lawes to love the Crowne.	255	U75 Epithalam.	104
Of Love betweene you, and your Lovely-head:	257	U75 Epithalam.	164
For he doth love my Verses, and will looke	263	U78 Digby	23
To Body, and Soule! where Love is all the guest!	284	U84 Muse	64
A Wife, a Friend, a Lady, or a Love;	285	U84 Muse	99
What love with mercy mixed doth appeare?	286	U84 Muse	138
But, say old Love returne should make,	294	U87 Hor.3:9	17
Yet would I wish to love, live, die with thee.	294	U87 Hor.3:9	24
And heat, with softest love, thy softer bed.	295	U89 Mart.8:77	6
The angry, and love those that feare t'offend.	317	Horace	282
Fortune would love the poore, and leave the proud.	319	Horace	286
Nor I, when I write Satyres, will so love	321	Horace	341
What height of love, a Parent will fit best,	325	Horace	447
In vaine, but you, and yours, you should love still	335	Horace	631
Or love of this so famous death lay by.	335	Horace	669
Or love of this his famous death lay by.	355	Horace .	V669
And Phoebus love cause of his blackenesse is.	366	Ode Who saith	16
Though, now by Love transform'd, & dayly dying:	369	Ode Who saith	101
his life, his love, his honour, which ne'r dyes,	382	Rich	8
Do wayte upon thee: and theyre Love not bought.	384	Somerset	4
And ev'ry birth encrease the heate of Love.	384	Somerset	20
As Love, here studied to keep Grace alive.	412	Ghyrlond	8
Thus, Love, and Hope, and burning Charitie,	413	Ghyrlond	25
How they advance true Love, and neighbourhood,	416	Dover	7
That Frindshipp, which noe Chaunce, but Love did Chuse,	422	Censure	16
It is an Act of Tyranye, not Love,	422	Censure	18
and the immortall gods; love only those	422	Lucan	5
As the token of my Love	666	Glover	3
LOV'D			
My sinne was too much hope of thee, lov'd boy,	41	E45 First Son	2

LOV'D (cont.)

Entry	Page	Title	Line
Jephson, thou man of men, to whose lov'd name	75	E116 Jephson	1
To whom I am so bound, lov'd Aubigny?	80	E127 Aubigny	3
To urge, my lov'd Alphonso, that bold fame	82	E130 Ferrab. 1	1
Some have lov'd as old agen.	131	U2 Excuse	6
Of one that lov'd?	148	U8 Houre-glasse	6
No person, nor is lov'd: what wayes he proves	162	U15 Friend-Wars	16
Is lov'd, though he let out his owne for life:	165	U15 Friend-Wars	88
Tell me (my lov'd Friend) doe you love, or no,	170	U19 Elegy By	11
O then (my best-best lov'd) let me importune,	180	U25 Desmond	63
O then (our best-best lov'd) let me importune,	180	U25 Desmond	V 63
He lov'd the Muses;	231	U57 Burges	9
Of a Disease, that lov'd no light	234	U60 La-ware	6
That thou art lov'd of God, this worke is done,	268	U80 Christning	1
Whilst, Lydia, I was lov'd of thee,	293	U87 Hor.3:9	1
Whilst Horace lov'd no Mistres more,	293	U87 Hor.3:9	5
And then as swift to leave what he hath lov'd.	315	Horace	236
Importune wish; and by her lov'd Lords side	394	Jane Ogle	23
How well I lov'd Truth: I was scarce allow'd	414	Rutter	6

LOVED

Entry	Page	Title	Line
Both Saints, and Martyrs, by her loved Lord.	400	Lady Ogle	39

LOVELY

Entry	Page	Title	Line
With lovely Graces	135	U2 Triumph	V 36
What Beautie would have lovely stilde,	188	U35 Chute	1
And how more faire, and lovely lookes the world	193	U38 Elegy 'Tis	73
In all that is call'd lovely: take my sight	200	U42 Elegy Let	12
Of Love betweene you, and your Lovely-head:	257	U75 Epithalam.	164
And left her lovely body unthought dead!	283	U84 Muse	44
For he's both noble, lovely, young,	292	U86 Hor.4:1	13
The Seat of Sapience, the most lovely Mother,	414	Ghyrlond	45

LOVELY-HEAD

Entry	Page	Title	Line
Of Love betweene you, and your Lovely-head:	257	U75 Epithalam.	164

LOVE-QUEENES

Entry	Page	Title	Line
Have you seene Love-Queenes embraces	135	U2 Triumph	V 35

LOVER

Entry	Page	Title	Line
Kisse me, sweet: The warie lover	103	F6 Celia 2	1
Gives the Lover weight, and fashion.	131	U2 Excuse	12
Oh how a Lover may mistake! to thinke,	170	U18 Elegy Can	15
I That have beene a lover, and could shew it,	182	U28 Worth	1
A better lover, and much better Poet.	182	U28 Worth	4
Yet should the Lover still be ayrie and light,	197	U40 Elegy That	19
But the grave Lover ever was an Asse;	198	U40 Elegy That	32
That Article, may not become our lover:	198	U40 Elegy That	48

LOVERS

Entry	Page	Title	Line
That falls like sleepe on lovers, and combines	110	F11 Epode	49
Lovers, made into a Chaine!	137	U2 Cupid	32
on a lovers dust, made sand for ane Houre Glasse	148	U8 Houre-glasse	VTtl
Even ashes of lovers find no rest.	149	U8 Houre-glasse	11
To whom all Lovers are design'd,	173	U22 Elegy Tho	26
The longing Couple, all that elder Lovers know.	258	U75 Epithalam.	192
Fresh Lovers businesse, and the Wines free source.	311	Horace	116
Then the stolne sports of Lovers,	365	Ode Splendor	7

LOVE'S

Entry	Page	Title	Line
Some act of Love's bound to reherse,	93	F1 Why write no	1
But might I of love's Nectar sipp,	106	F9 Celia 3	V 7
That Love's a bitter sweet, I ne're conceive	197	U40 Elegy That	1

LOVES

Entry	Page	Title	Line
As what he loves may never like too much.	41	E45 First Son	12
'Tis no sinne, loves fruit to steale,	102	F5 Celia 1	15
Dare entayle their loves on any,	105	F8 Sicknesse	39
Dare entayle their loves to any,	105	F8 Sicknesse	V 39
The soules, shee loves. Those other glorious notes,	114	F12 Rutland	43
No lady, but, at some time, loves her glasse.	117	F13 Aubigny	26
All that Loves world compriseth!	134	U2 Triumph	12
As Loves starre when it riseth!	134	U2 Triumph	14
For Loves-sake, kisse me once againe,	139	U2 Another	1
Can he that loves, aske lesse then one?	139	U2 Another	8
For Loves fingers, and his wings:	141	U2 Her man	12
In loves schoole, and yet no sinners.	141	U2 Her man	32
In loves art, and yet no sinners.	141	U2 Her man	V 32
I Love, and he loves me againe,	147	U7 Nymph	1
And he loves me; yet no	148	U7 Nymph	30
Loves sicknesse, and his noted want of worth,	150	U10 Jealousie	14
Looke on the false, and cunning man, that loves	162	U15 Friend-Wars	15
Her joyes, her smiles, her loves, as readers take	182	U28 Worth	13
As if that ex'lent Dulnesse were Loves grace;	198	U40 Elegy That	24
They may say Grace, and for Loves Chaplaines passe;	198	U40 Elegy That	31
(Made to blow up loves secrets) to discover	198	U40 Elegy That	47
Wrung on the Withers, by Lord Loves despight,	201	U42 Elegy Let	63
Doe boast their Loves, and Brav'ries so at large,	253	U75 Epithalam.	19
Mens Loves unto the Lawes, and Lawes to love the Crowne.	255	U75 Epithalam.	104
And let him freely gather Loves First-fruits,	258	U75 Epithalam.	186
Loves cares so evill, and so great?	290	U85 Country	38
Or the herb Sorrell, that loves Meadows still,	291	U85 Country	57
Sower Mother of sweet Loves, forbeare	292	U86 Hor.4:1	5
Loves Dogges, and Horses; and is ever one	315	Horace	230
As some the farther off: This loves the darke;	331	Horace	541
to tender thus, their lives, their loves, their hartes!	382	Rich	4
Where spight of Death, next Life, for her Loves sake	394	Jane Ogle	25
Their loves, their quarrels, jealousies, and wrongs,	397	Drayton	30
That lives, and breath's, and loves the King.	418	Grace	4
That the King loves, and loves the King.	418	Grace	V 4

	Page	Title	Line

LOVES-SAKE
For Loves-sake, kisse me once againe, ... 139 U2 Another 1

LOVETH
We all feare, she loveth none. . . . . . . 140 U2 Promise 12

LOVING
1. His Excuse for loving. . . . . . . 131 U2 Excuse Ttl
Their vice of loving for a Christmasse fit; . . . 190 U37 Friend-Book 8
Still looking to, and ever loving heaven; . . . 219 U47 Tribe 61
Religious, wise, chast, loving, gratious, good, . . 394 Jane Ogle 5
. . . (by his continu'd Vertue) my loving friend: . . . 409 Brome Ttl

LOV'ST
If they goe on, and that thou lov'st a-life . . 232 U58 Book-seller 13

LOW
At first he made low shifts, would picke and gleane, . 45 E56 Poet-Ape 5
Goe high, or low, as thou wilt value it. . . . 50 E72 Court-ling 4
From place, or fortune, are made high, or low, . . 64 E99 Th Roe 2 9
Or fixt in the Low-Countrey's, where you might . . 212 U43 Vulcan 203
Professing greatnesse, swells: That, low by lee . 307 Horace 38
Abhorres low numbers, and the private straine . . 311 Horace 123
But first to Cluid stoope low, ... 367 Ode Who saith 39
The Low-countries, Germany and Rhetia · . . 379 Coryat 3 20
Bred by your breath, on this low bancke of ours; . . 416 Welcome 3

LOW-COUNTREY'S
Or fixt in the Low-Countrey's, where you might . 212 U43 Vulcan 203

LOW-COUNTRIES
The Low-countries, Germany and Rhetia . . . 379 Coryat 3 20

LOWD
Lowd sacrifice of drinke, for their health-sake! . . 156 U13 Sacvile 100
Ambitious, factious, superstitious, lowd . . . 167 U15 Friend-Wars 168
As lowd as Thunder, and as swift as fire. . . . 249 U72 King 4
it will be matter lowd inoughe to tell . . . 387 Cavendish 11
Lowd to the wondringe thronge . . . . 419 Ode:If Men 7

LOWDEST
As lowdest praisers, who perhaps would find . . . 67 E103 L Wroth 1 11

LOWENESSE
Or growne; by height or lowenesse of the Sunne? . . 156 U13 Sacvile 119

LOWER
The lower land, that to the river bends, . . . 94 F2 Penshurst 22

LOWEST
And highest; sinketh to the lowest, and worst. . . 331 Horace 564

LOWING
The lowing herds there grazing are: . . . 290 U85 Country 14

LOWLIE
But lowlie laid, as on the earth asleep, . . . 413 Ghyrlond 18

LOYAL
But to your selfe, most loyal Lord, ... 179 U25 Desmond 53

LOYALL
Whereof the loyall conscience so complaines. . . 110 F11 Epode 27
And shuts the old. Haste, haste, all loyall Swaines, . 263 U79 New-yeares 10

LOYALTIES
With so much Loyalties expence, ... 173 U22 Elegy Tho 22

LOYRE
Slow Arar, nor swift Rhone; the Loyre, nor Seine, . . 369 Ode Who saith 117

'LT
But that's put in, thou'lt say. Why, so is thine. . 36 E29 Tilter 6
On such my serious follies; But, thou'lt say, . . 204 U43 Vulcan 41
Or such my serious follies; But, thou'lt say, . . 204 U43 Vulcan V 41
He cries, Good boy, thou'lt keepe thine owne. Now, adde . 327 Horace 470

LUCAN
To my chosen Friend, the learned Translator of Lucan, . . . 395 May Ttl
Of Fortunes wheele by Lucan driv'n about, . . 395 May 3
Taught Lucan these true moodes! Replyes my sence . 395 May 15
Sayst thou so, Lucan? But thou scornst to stay . 397 Drayton 47

LUCANE
A speech out of Lucane. . . . . . 422 Lucan Ttl

LUCANS
Lucans whole frame unto us, and so wrought, . . 395 May 20

LUCENT
Nor lend like influence from his lucent seat. . . 52 E76 Bedford 1 8

LUCINA'S
Of all Lucina's traine; Lucy the bright, . . . 115 F12 Rutland 66

LUCIUS
To Sir Lucius Carey, on the death of his Brother Morison . 242 U70 Ode VTtl
. . . paire, Sir Lucius Cary, and Sir H. Morison. . 242 U70 Ode Ttl
Call, noble Lucius, then for Wine, . . . 245 U70 Ode 75
(Were not his Lucius long with us to tarry) . . 246 U70 Ode 91

LUCK
Oft scape an Imputation, more through luck, then wit. . 179 U25 Desmond 52
Oft scape theyr Imputation, more through luck, then wit. . 179 U25 Desmond V 52

LUCKE
Still, 'tis his lucke to praise me 'gainst his will. . 50 E71 Parrat 2
Troth, if it be, I pitty thy ill lucke; . . 73 E112 Gamster 17

LUCKILY
And that you may see he most luckily ment . . . 379 Coryat 3 13

LUCKLESSE
To Sir Lucklesse Woo-all. . . . . 42 E46 Luckless 1 Ttl
'Tis Luckless he, that tooke up one on band . . 42 E46 Luckless 1 3
Sir Luckless, troth, for lucks sake passe by one: . 42 E47 Luckless 2 1

LUCKS
For the lucks sake, it thus much favour have, . . 27 E3 Bookseller 4
Sir Luckless, troth, for lucks sake passe by one: . 42 E47 Luckless 2 1
Ploughing the mayne. When, see (the worst of all lucks) . 86 E133 Voyage 78

			Page	Title	Line
LUCRINE					
Not Lucrine Oysters I could then more prize,	. . .	.	291	U85 Country	49
LUCY					
On Lucy Countesse of Bedford.	. . . . .	.	52	E76 Bedford 1	Ttl
To Lucy Countesse of Bedford.	. . . . .	.	54	E84 Bedford 2	Ttl
To Lucy, Countesse of Bedford, with Mr. Donnes Satyres.	.	60	E94 Bedford 3	Ttl
Lucy, you brightnesse of our spheare, who are	. .	.	60	E94 Bedford 3	1
Lucy, you brightnesse of our spheare, who are	. .	.	61	E94 Bedford 3	15
Of all Lucina's traine: Lucy the bright,	.	.	115	F12 Rutland	66
Lucy of Bedford; she, that Bounty	.	.	662	Bedford	3
LUMPE					
And the whole lumpe growes round, deform'd, and droupes,	.	227	U52 Answer	5
LUNGS					
Or fumie clysters, thy moist lungs to bake:	. .	.	42	E50 Cod 3	2
The art of kindling the true Coale, by Lungs:	. .	.	206	U43 Vulcan	76
The art of kindling the true Coale, of Lungs:	. .	.	206	U43 Vulcan	V 76
And voyce to raise them from my brazen Lungs,	. .	.	269	U81 Pawlet	24
LUPUS					
Of the first Lupus, to the Familie	. . .	.	274	U84 Descent	17
LURDEN					
And bad her fare-well sough, unto the lurden:	. .	.	87	E133 Voyage	115
LURKE					
How in these ruines, Vulcan, thou dost lurke,	. .	.	207	U43 Vulcan	105
How in these ruines, Vulcan, durst thou lurke,	. .	.	207	U43 Vulcan	V105
LUST					
In varied shapes, which for his lust shee takes:	.	.	34	E25 Beast 1	6
Lust it comes out, that gluttony went in.	. .	.	76	E118 Gut	6
Or if needs thy lust will tast	. .	.	105	F8 Sicknesse	15
'Twixt feare and rashnesse: not a lust obscene,	.	.	156	U13 Sacvile	106
Of lust, to his rich Suit and Title, Lord?	.	.	163	U15 Friend-Wars	51
When he is furious, love, although not lust.	.	.	200	U42 Elegy Let	18
With lust conceiv'd thee; Father thou hadst none.	.	.	208	U43 Vulcan	112
What though with Tribade lust she force a Muse,	.	.	222	U49 Pucell	7
For lust will languish, and that heat decay.	.	.	294	U88 Petronius	5
LUSTES					
Such, as in lustes wilde forrest love to rainge,	. .	.	108	F10 Proludium	9
LUSTFULL					
Like lustfull beasts, that onely know to doe it:	. .	.	294	U88 Petronius	4
LUSTIE					
Our teeming Ewes, and lustie-mounting Rammes.	.	.	264	U79 New-yeares	17
Some lustie quick Apulians spouse,	. . .	.	291	U85 Country	42
LUSTIE-MOUNTING					
Our teeming Ewes, and lustie-mounting Rammes.	.	.	264	U79 New-yeares	17
LUSTROUS					
With lustrous Graces,	. . . . .	.	179	U25 Desmond	60
LUST'S					
Because lust's meanes are spent:	. . . .	.	111	F11 Epode	78
LUSTS					
To do't with Cloth, or Stuffes, lusts name might merit;	.	164	U15 Friend-Wars	57
Wild raging lusts; prescribe the mariage good;	. .	.	327	Horace	489
LUTE					
Did Sappho on her seven-tongu'd Lute,	. .	.	181	U27 Ode Helen	3
Harpe, Lute, Theorbo sprung,	. .	.	239	U67 Muses	17
Lute, Lyre, Theorbo, all are call'd to day.	. .	.	263	U79 New-yeares	2
Shall Verse be set to Harpe and Lute,	. .	.	292	U86 Hor.4:1	23
LUTES					
Was said to move the stones, by his Lutes powers,	. .	.	327	Horace	484
LUTHERS					
Are all but Luthers beere, to this I sing.	. .	.	65	E101 Supper	34
LUXURIE					
To a great image through thy luxurie.	.	.	48	E65 Muse	4
Peace, Luxurie, thou art like one of those	. .	.	111	F11 Epode	69
LYAEUS					
Lyaeus, and defend him,	. . . .	.	221	U48 Bacchus	18
LYBIAN					
The Lybian Lion hunts noe butter flyes,	. .	.	408	Inigo Jones 3	7
LYCENCE					
Will unto Lycence, that free Leave Abuse:	. .	.	422	Censure	17
LYCENSE					
It is a lycense to doe ill, protectes,	. . .	.	423	Lucan	12
LYCORIS					
With bright Lycoris, Gallus choice,	. . . .	.	181	U27 Ode Helen	15
LYDIA					
Ode IX. 3 Booke, to Lydia. Dialogue of Horace, and Lydia.	.	293	U87 Hor.3:9	Ttl
Whilst, Lydia, I was lov'd of thee,	. . . .	.	293	U87 Hor.3:9	1
Nor after Chloe did his Lydia sound;	. . .	.	293	U87 Hor.3:9	6
And to left-Lydia, now the gate stood ope.	. .	.	294	U87 Hor.3:9	20
LYE (DECEIVE)					
Ile tell you of more, and lye, so you will come:	.	.	65	E101 Supper	17
LYE					
To lye upon thy stall, till it be sought;	. .	.	28	E3 Bookseller	5
He'adulters still: his thoughts lye with a whore.	.	.	35	E26 Beast 2	2
Rest in soft peace, and, ask'd, say here doth lye	.	.	41	E45 First Son	9
Curst be his Muse, that could lye dumbe, or hid	.	.	47	E63 Salisbury 2	11
Curst be my voyce if it lye dumbe, or hid	.	.	47	E63 Salisbury 2 V 11
And then lye with you, closer, then a punque,	.	.	69	E107 Hungry	20
Under-neath this stone doth lye	. .	.	79	E124 Elizabeth	3
And now lye lost in their forgotten dust.	. .	.	114	F12 Rutland	40
Chaucer, or Spenser, or bid Beaumont lye	. .	.	391	Shakespeare	20
But antiquated, and deserted lye	. .	.	392	Shakespeare	53
LYER					
shall looke, & on hyme soe, then arte's a lyer	. .	.	383	Rich	15

		Page	Title	Line

LYES
Here lyes to each her parents ruth, ... 33 E22 Daughter 1
And lyes so farre from wit, 'tis impudence. . . . 38 E38 Guiltie 2 6
The painted partrich lyes in every field, ... 94 F2 Penshurst 29
Lyes the Valley, cal'd my nest, ... 137 U2 Cupid 34
Dri'd up? lyes Thespia wast? . . . . 174 U23 Himselfe 8
Lyes there no Writ, out of the Chancerie . . . 210 U43 Vulcan 174
But lyes block'd up, and straightned, narrow'd in, . . 248 U71 Treasurer 10

LYFE
An Ode in Horace in prayse of a Countrye lyfe, Translated. . 289 U85 Country VTtl
I made my lyfe my monument, & yours: . . . 387 Cavendish 7

LYING (DECEIVING)
Of lying, he feares so much the reproofe . . . . 380 Coryat 3 31

LYING
Lying for the spirit of amber. . . . . . 105 F8 Sicknesse 32
Lying on the spirit of amber. . . . . . 105 F8 Sicknesse V 32
An Epigram to the Queene, then lying in. 1630. . . 238 U66 Queene Ttl

LYKE
how lyke the Carbuncle in Aarons brest . . . . 361 Palmer 14
How would he firke? lyke Adam overdooe . . . 405 Inigo Jones 1 79
Whilest lyke a blaze of strawe, ... 420 Ode:If Men 15

LYNE
With Japhets lyne, aspire . . . . . 175 U23 Himselfe 27
Doth mete, whose lyne doth sound the depth of things:) . 176 U24 Frontispice 12
Nor a lyne deserving praise, ... 183 U29 Fit of Rime 29
Forgiven him; And in that lyne stand I, . . . 193 U38 Elegy 'Tis 91
Expression for! with that unbounded lyne . . . 406 Inigo Jones 1 95

LYNES
His lynes, and hourely sits the Poets horse? . . . 200 U42 Elegy Let 8
A booke to a few lynes: but, it was fit . . . 230 U56 Covell 3

LYONS
Was Tigers, said, and Lyons fierce, to tame. . . . 327 Horace 482

LYRE
Apollo's harpe, and Hermes lyre resound, . . . 98 F3 Wroth 51
Then take in hand thy Lyre, ... 175 U23 Himselfe 25
My bolder numbers to thy golden Lyre; . . . 177 U25 Desmond 9
My flowing numbers to thy golden Lyre: . . . 177 U25 Desmond V 9
Let every Lyre be strung, ... 239 U67 Muses 16
Lute, Lyre, Theorbo, all are call'd to day. . . . 263 U79 New-yeares 2
Or Muse, upon the Lyre, thou chance b'asham'd. . . 329 Horace 502
Upon the Lyre, thou chance to be asham'd. . . . 353 Horace V580/502

LYRICK
A Celebration of Charis in ten Lyrick Peeces. . . . 131 U2 Charis Ttl
Unto the Lyrick Strings, the Muse gave grace . . 309 Horace 113

LYST
I have the lyst of mine owne faults to know, . . . 156 U13 Sacvile 114

LYVE
Lyve long the Feasting Roome. And ere thou burne . . 406 Inigo Jones 1 101

LYVES
For noe Man Lyves, soe out of passions swaye, . . 422 Censure 24

M
To the worthy Author M. John Fletcher. . . . 370 Fletcher Ttl
. . . Muses Of His Friend M. Drayton. . . . 396 Drayton Ttl
. . . the Author of this Work, M. Rich. Brome. . . 409 Brome Ttl
The M. the Myrtle, A. the Almonds clame, . . . 412 Ghyrlond 3

MAAS
Scheldt, nor the Maas, ... 369 Ode Who saith 116

MACHINE
In the great masse, or machine there is stirr'd? . . 395 May 22
That doe cry up the Machine, & the Showes! . . 403 Inigo Jones 1 32

MAD
As mad-men stones: not caring whom they hit. . . 27 E2 My Booke 6
And then, leape mad on a neat Pickardill, . . . 164 U15 Friend-Wars 70
More honour in him, 'cause we'ave knowne him mad: . 168 U15 Friend-Wars 194
Poore Io wandring; wild Orestes mad: . . . 313 Horace 177
The yellow Jaundies, or were furious mad . . . 335 Horace 646
The yellow jaundis, or were truely mad, . . . 354 Horace V646
(Defiled) touch'd; but certaine he was mad, . . 337 Horace 673
Polluted, touch't: but certainly he's mad: . . . 355 Horace V673

MADAM
Any beliefe, in Madam Baud-bees bath, . . . 188 U34 Small Poxe 10
The Wisdome, Madam, of your private Life, . . . 224 U50 Countesse 1
You won not Verses, Madam, you won mee, . . . 230 U56 Covell 1
How many verses, Madam, are your Due! . . . 231 U56 Covell 27

MADAME
Fine Madame Would-Bee, wherefore should you feare, . 46 E62 Would-bee 1
With which a learned Madame you belye. . . . 51 E73 Fine Grand 11
Madame, I told you late how I repented, . . . 54 E84 Bedford 2 1
O Madame, if your grant did thus transferre mee, . 55 E84 Bedford 2 9
Madame, had all antiquitie beene lost, . . . 67 E105 L Wroth 2 1
And Madame Caesar, great Proserpina, . . . 89 E133 Voyage 180
Riches thought most: But, Madame, thinke what store . 114 F12 Rutland 38
I, Madame, am become your praiser. Where, . . 117 F13 Aubigny 21
Wherewith, then, Madame, can you better pay . . 118 F13 Aubigny 53
You, Madame, yong have learn'd to shunne these shelves, . 119 F13 Aubigny 89
Madame, be bold to use this truest glasse: . . 120 F13 Aubigny 122

MADAMES
At Madames table, where thou mak'st all wit . . 50 E72 Court-ling 3
Of any Madames, hath neadd squires, and must. . . 63 E97 Motion 14

MADDE
But then if I grow jealous madde, ... 147 U7 Nymph 10
Of Credit lost. And I am now run madde: . . . 191 U38 Elegy 'Tis 2
All the madde Rolands, and sweet Oliveers; . . 206 U43 Vulcan 70

MADDE (cont.)
  (Which, some are pleas'd to stile but thy madde pranck) . . 208 U43 Vulcan 131
MADE
  Made from the hazard of anothers shame: . . 27 E2 My Booke 10
  Not offer'd, as it made sute to be bought; . . . . 28 E3 Bookseller 6
  But I have my revenge made, in thy name. . . 29 E10 Ignorant 2
  It made me a great face, I ask'd the name. . . 30 E11 Something 4
  Both which are great. And laugh at ill-made clothes; . . 35 E28 Surly 10
  When he made him executor, might be heire. . . 41 E44 Chuff 6
  At first he made low shifts, would picke and gleane, . . 45 E56 Poet-Ape 5
  Made me commit most fierce idolatrie . . . 48 E65 Muse 3
  Then had I made 'hem good, to fit your vaine. . . 51 E73 Fine Grand 20
  T'our times return'd, hath made her heaven in thee. . . 52 E74 Chancelor 10
  At which, shee happily displeas'd, made you: . . 53 E79 Rutland 9
  Upon thy wel-made choise of friends, and bookes; . . 55 E86 Goodyere 2 2
  Since when, hee's sober againe, and all play's made. . . 56 E87 Hazard 6
  The new french-taylors motion, monthly made, . . 56 E88 Monsieur 15
  From place, or fortune, are made high, or low, . . 64 E99 Th Roe 2 9
  But even their names were to be made a-new, . . 67 E105 L Wroth 2 5
  Hath chang'd his soule, and made his object you: . . 74 E114 Sydney 5
  But, in your love, made all his servants wise. . . 74 E114 Sydney 8
  Made for what Nature could, or Vertue can; . . 79 E125 Uvedale 2
  That still th'art made the suppers flagge, the drum, . . 81 E129 Mime 7
  Made of the trull, that cut her fathers lock: . . 86 E133 Voyage 84
  Where Pan, and Bacchus their high feasts have made, . . 93 F2 Penshurst 11
  The trees cut out in log; and those boughes made . . 98 F3 Wroth 45
  Thy peace is made; and, when man's state is well, . . 99 F3 Wroth 93
  And have more diseases made. . . . . . 105 F8 Sicknesse 20
  Shall not give out, that I have made thee stay, . . 107 F10 Proludium 8
  Shall not give out, that we have made thee stay, . . 107 F10 Proludium V 8
  When gold was made no weapon to cut throtes, . . 114 F12 Rutland 23
  Who made a lampe of Berenices hayre? . . 115 F12 Rutland 61
  Of your blest wombe, made fruitfull from above, . . 119 F13 Aubigny 95
  Each into other, and had now made one. . . 120 F13 Aubigny 120
  First made of nought, ... 129 U1 Father 21
  The Word was now made Flesh indeed, . . 130 U1 Nativitie 17
  Who made himselfe the price of sinne, . . 130 U1 Nativitie 20
  Of her face, and made to rise, . . 136 U2 Cupid 15
  Lovers, made into a Chaine! . . 137 U2 Cupid 32
  Till each of us be made a Starre, . . 143 U3 Musicall 3
  Till each of us is made a Starre, . . 143 U3 Musicall V 3
  Then when 'tis made, why so will wee. . . 145 U5 Woman-kind 16
  on a lovers dust, made sand for ane Houre Glasse . . 148 U8 Houre-glasse VTtl
  Their bounties forth, to him that last was made, . . 155 U13 Sacvile 63
  But 'twas with purpose to have made them such. . . 159 U14 Selden 22
  But more licentious made, and desperate! . . 163 U15 Friend-Wars 36
  As they are made! Pride, and stiffe Clownage mixt . . 163 U15 Friend-Wars 43
  Some grounds are made the richer, for the Rest; . . 169 U17 Friend-Debt 17
  Then all Ingredients made into one curse, . . 172 U20 Shrub 18
  Have made their fairest flight, . . . 180 U26 Ode High 7
  Made Dian, not his notes refuse? . . 182 U27 Ode Helen 28
  The Seat made of a more then civill warre; . . 186 U33 Councellour 2
  Have made me to conceive a Lawyer new. . . 187 U33 Councellour 14
  For Love in shadow best is made. . . 189 U36 Song 2
  Of vowes so sacred, and in silence made; . . 197 U40 Elegy That 14
  (Made to blow up loves secrets) to discover . . 198 U40 Elegy That 47
  Made longer by our praises. Or, if not, . . 200 U42 Elegy Let 21
  Nor made least line of love to thy loose Wife; . . 203 U43 Vulcan 6
  Had made a meale for Vulcan to lick up. . . 206 U43 Vulcan 84
  Was there made English: with the Grammar too, . . 207 U43 Vulcan 91
  For none but Smiths would have made thee a God. . . 208 U43 Vulcan 117
  They made a Vulcan of a sheafe of Reedes, . . 208 U43 Vulcan 126
  Made thee beget that cruell Stratagem, . . 208 U43 Vulcan 130
  And there made Swords, Bills, Glaves, and Armes your fill; . . 212 U43 Vulcan 198
  Thy just defences made th' oppressor afraid. . . 217 U46 Coke 8
  Lest it be justled, crack'd, made nought, or lesse: . . 219 U47 Tribe 58
  Where now, thou art made Dweller; . . 220 U48 Bacchus 4
  You made it a brave piece, but not like me. . . 227 U52 Answer 15
  And that's made up as doth the purse abound. . . 230 U56 Covell 12
  Made up still as the pockett doth abound. . . 230 U56 Covell V 12
  Profit, or Chance had made us: But I know . . 241 U69 Friend Son 3
  Made, or indentur'd, or leas'd out t'advance . . 246 U70 Ode 100
  This made you first to know the Why . . 247 U70 Ode 107
  And titles, by which all made claimes . . 247 U70 Ode 114
  And made those strong approaches, by False braies, . . 248 U71 Treasurer 7
  Made lighter with the Wine. All noises else, . . 249 U72 King 12
  Made loftier by the Winds all noises else, . . 249 U72 King V 12
  . . . made Earle of Portland. 17. Febr. 1632. To the Envious. . 250 U73 Weston Ttl
  T'effect it, feele, thou'ast made thine owne heart ake. . 250 U73 Weston 12
  These two, now holy Church hath made them one, . . 257 U75 Epithalam. 139
  By this Sun's Noone-sted's made . . 258 U75 Epithalam. 183
  What transcripts made? how cry'd up, and how glad, . . 263 U78 Digby V 30
  Her Rose, and Lilly, intertwind, have made. . . 268 U80 Christning 16
  Made her friends joyes to get above their feares! . . 270 U81 Pawlet 60
  Who saw the way was made it! and were sent . . 270 U81 Pawlet 65
  That saw the way was made it! and were sent . . 270 U81 Pawlet V 65
  Have busie search made in his mysteries! . . 284 U84 Muse 80
  Horace, His Art of Poetrie Made English . . 303 Horace Ttl
  Are, by thy cunning placing, made meere new. . . 307 Horace 68
  A royall Crowne, and purple, be made hop, . . 321 Horace 333
  A royall Crowne, and Scarlet; be made hop . . 346 Horace V325/333
  His power of fouley hurting made to cease. . . 323 Horace 370
  weare made the objects to my weaker powers; . . 361 Palmer 3

MADE (cont.)

Thy skill hath made of ranck dispised weedes;	361	Palmer	10
She might have claym'd t'have made the Graces foure;	371	Epitaph	6
made prospective, behould hym, hee must passe	383	Rich	12
I made my lyfe my monument, & yours:	387	Cavendish	7
Such Passage hast thou found, such Returnes made,	389	Chapman	10
For a good Poet's made, as well as borne.	392	Shakespeare	64
Advanc'd, and made a Constellation there!	392	Shakespeare	76
And her, she made her Inmate, to the End,	394	Jane Ogle	18
Which made me thinke, the old Theocritus,	397	Drayton	27
Under one title. Thou hast made thy way	397	Drayton	48
And all men eccho you have made a Masque.	403	Inigo Jones 1	30
Hath made his Inigo Marquess, wouldst thou fayne	406	Inigo Jones 2	2
Of wit, and a new made: a Warden then,	415	Rutter	23

MAD-MEN

| As mad-men stones: not caring whom they hit. | 27 | E2 My Booke | 6 |

MADNESSE

| 'Twere madnesse in thee, to betray thy fame, | 36 | E30 Guiltie | 3 |
| The whole world here leaven'd with madnesse swells; | 163 | U15 Friend-Wars | 31 |

MADRIGALL

| That (in pure Madrigall) unto his Mother | 201 | U42 Elegy Let | 68 |

MAD'ST

Thou wert the first, mad'st merit know her strength,	75	E116 Jephson	5
That, at thy birth, mad'st the poore Smith affraid,	107	F10 Proludium	14
And mad'st thy Mothers wombe thine urne.	242	U70 Ode	8
Who mad'st us happy all, in thy reflexe,	414	Ghyrlond	47
Thou mad'st in open Feild	421	Ode:If Men	40

MAGICK

| Or magick sacrifice, they past along! | 85 | E133 Voyage | 49 |

MAGISTRATES

| As guiltie men doe magistrates: glad I, | 32 | E17 Critic | 2 |

MAGNETIQUE

| Or else Magnetique in the force, | 399 | Lady Ogle | 19 |

MAID   (See also MAYD)

Pallas, nor thee I call on, mankinde maid,	107	F10 Proludium	13
Pallas, nor thee we call on, mankinde maid,	107	F10 Proludium	V 13
That the Bride (allow'd a Maid)	138	U2 Kisse	8
To speake the fate of the Sicilian Maid	207	U43 Vulcan	96
And by an Angell, to the blessed'st Maid,	238	U66 Queene	2

MAIDEN

| Nought of a Maiden Queene, | 254 | U75 Epithalam. | 47 |

MAIDENS

| Of all the Maidens faire; | 253 | U75 Epithalam. | 39 |

MAIDES

| Nor are the Queenes most honor'd maides by th'eares | 63 | E97 Motion | 18 |

MAIDS

| The Youths and tender Maids shall sing thy praise: | 292 | U86 Hor.4:1 | 26 |

MAIME   (See also MAYME)

| Till envie wound, or maime it at a blow! | 162 | U15 Friend-Wars | 22 |

MAINE

Which is maine greatnesse. And, at his still boord,	35	E28 Surly	13
Shuns prease, for two maine causes, poxe, and debt,	76	E119 Shelton	4
Whilst the maine tree, still found	258	U75 Epithalam.	181
But in the maine worke haplesse: since he knowes	307	Horace	48
Over Ierna maine,	367	Ode Who saith	42
Of thine, shall thinke the Maine	368	Ode Who saith	90

MAINTAINE

| Must maintaine manly; not be heard to sing, | 317 | Horace | 277 |

MAINTAIN'D

When Venus there maintain'd the Misterie.	209	U43 Vulcan	144
Maintain'd the trade at Bilbo, or else-where;	212	U43 Vulcan	199
Maintain'd the trade of Bilbo, or else-where;	212	U43 Vulcan	V199

MAINTAYNE

Which might with halfe mankind maintayne a strife.	34	E23 Donne 1	8
They maintayne the truest trade,	105	F8 Sicknesse	19
Maintayne their liedgers forth, for forraine wyres,	118	F13 Aubigny	72

MAINTAYNES

| That yet maintaynes you, and your house in laughter. | 51 | E73 Fine Grand | 8 |

MAIORS

| And that is when it is the Lord Maiors foist. | 87 | E133 Voyage | 120 |
| Squire of the Squibs, against the next Maiors day, | 208 | U43 Vulcan | V119 |

MAIST

That thou at once, then, nobly maist defend	63	E98 Th Roe 1	7
Thou maist thinke life, a thing but lent.	100	F3 Wroth	106
Shall feast it, thou maist love there	221	U48 Bacchus	38
Thou need new termes; thou maist, without excuse,	307	Horace	70
And thou maist better bring a Rhapsody	313	Horace	184
Yet common matter thou thine owne maist make,	313	Horace	187
For, being a Poet, thou maist feigne, create,	313	Horace	189
Yet, to the Stage, at all thou maist not tender	317	Horace	260

MAISTRING

| The noble Science, and the maistring skill | 232 | U59 Newcastle | 3 |

MAISTRY

| O, had I now your manner, maistry, might, | 227 | U52 Answer | 16 |

MAJESTIE

All coeternall in your Majestie,	128	U1 Trinitie	38
For safetie of such Majestie, cry out?	236	U64 Charles 3	6
To your Majestie your Poet:	259	U76 Petition	4
Please your Majestie to make	260	U76 Petition	25
A dazling, yet inviting, Majestie:	270	U81 Pawlet	44
A darling, yet inviting, Majestie:	270	U81 Pawlet	V 44
Will there revealed be in Majestie!	286	U84 Muse	130

	Page	Title	Line

MAJESTIES

. . . In celebration of her Majesties birth-day. 1630.   239 U67 Muses   Ttl
Whose Majesties appeare,   254 U75 Epithalam.   53

MAJESTY

To the Kings Most Excellent Majesty   259 U76 Petition   VTtl
The majesty of Juno in the Cloudes,   403 Inigo Jones 1   33

MAJOR

If there be a Coockold Major,   417 Moon   25

MAJORS

Of Sheriffes dinner, or Majors feast.   96 F3 Wroth   6

MAKE

Or in cleft-sticks, advanced to make calls   28 E3 Bookseller   8
Man scarse can make that doubt, but thou canst teach.   31 E14 Camden   10
Make good what thou dar'st doe in all the rest.   32 E16 Brain-hardy   8
There's reason good, that you good lawes should make: 34 E24 Parliament   1
Just wife, and, to change me, make womans hast?   34 E25 Beast 1   8
Breathe to expect my when, and make my how.   37 E33 Roe 3   4
He meant they thither should make swift repaire,   41 E44 Chuff   5
Arsenike would thee fit for societie make.   42 E50 Cod 3   3
That love to make so well, a child to beare?   46 E62 Would-bee   2
To make amends, yo'are thought a wholesome creature.   46 E62 Would-bee   8
Make him loose all his friends; and, which is worse,   48 E65 Muse   9
Durst valour make, almost, but not a crime.   48 E66 Cary   6
Though life be short, let us not make it so.   50 E70 Wm Roe 1   8
I meant to make her faire, and free, and wise,   52 E76 Bedford 1   5
And hath it, in his powers, to make his way!   53 E80 Life/Death   4
I must a libell make, and cosen both.   54 E81 Proule   8
Make it your gift. See whither that will beare mee.   55 E84 Bedford 2   10
Till they be sure to make the foole their quarrie.   55 E85 Goodyere 1   10
If the States make peace, how it will goe   59 E92 New Crie   30
And at the Pope, and Spaine slight faces make.   59 E92 New Crie   34
That so alone canst judge, so'alone dost make: 62 E96 Donne 2   3
Nor 'bout the beares, nor noyse to make lords sport.   63 E97 Motion   12
With those that come; whose grace may make that seeme   64 E101 Supper   5
Nor shall our cups make any guiltie men: 65 E101 Supper   37
Shall make us sad next morning: or affright   65 E101 Supper   41
To make those faithfull, did the Fates send you?   67 E104 Montgomery   6
Give your yong States-men, (that first make you drunke,   69 E107 Hungry   19
To make thy lent life, good against the Fates: 70 E109 Nevil   11
There's no vexation, that can make thee prime.   73 E112 Gamster   22
Could make such men, and such a place repent: 73 E113 Overbury   10
If onely love should make the action pris'd: 78 E121 Rudyerd 1   6
And those to turne to bloud, and make thine owne: 80 E128 Wm Roe 2   4
The very call, to make all others come: 81 E129 Mime   8
Thorough her wombe they make their famous road,   85 E133 Voyage   66
That, with still-scalding steemes, make the place hell.   88 E133 Voyage   144
Some nuts, some apples; some that thinke they make   95 F2 Penshurst   52
Did'st thou, then, make 'hem! and what praise was heap'd   95 F2 Penshurst   83
And such since thou canst make thine owne content,   98 F3 Wroth   65
That onely fooles make thee a saint,   100 F4 To the World   15
To take the weake, or make them stop: 100 F4 To the World   19
But make my strengths, such as they are,   102 F4 To the World   67
That, to make all pleasure theirs,   105 F8 Sicknesse   36
(Though they were crusht into one forme) could make   108 F10 Proludium   26
Could ne'er make prize of thy white Chastetye.   108 F10 Proludium   6
To make our sense our slave.   109 F11 Epode   18
Would make a day of night,   112 F11 Epode   94
Of some grand peere, whose ayre doth make rejoyce   113 F12 Rutland   12
That had no Muse to make their fame abide.   114 F12 Rutland   48
And such, or my hopes faile, shall make you shine.   115 F12 Rutland   64
Are justly summ'd, that make you man;   120 F14 Sydney   22
The Word, which heaven, and earth did make;   130 U1 Nativitie   11
To make us heires of glory!   130 U1 Nativitie   21
She shall make the old man young,   131 U2 Excuse   20
At her hand, with oath, to make   133 U2 Suffered   10
Heare and make Example too.   133 U2 Suffered   26
Make in one, the same were shee.   137 U2 Cupid   48
Make accompt, unlesse you can,   140 U2 Promise   29
And a woman God did make me: 140 U2 Her man   6
And make Love or me afeard.   141 U2 Her man   24
Yet no Taylor help to make him;   141 U2 Her man   37
To make the Mountaine Quarries move,   143 U3 Musicall   11
But what those lips doe make.   143 U3 Musicall   16
But what your lips doe make.   143 U3 Musicall   V 16
To make us still sing o're, and o're,   145 U5 Woman-kind   3
Wee shall, at last, of parcells make   145 U5 Woman-kind   11
To make a new, and hang that by.   145 U5 Woman-kind   18
For what is better, or to make   146 U6 Defence   14
As make away my doubt,   147 U7 Nymph   23
I must the true Relation make,   150 U11 Dreame   2
The smallest courtesies with thankes, I make   153 U13 Sacvile   16
Must make me sad for what I have obtain'd.   154 U13 Sacvile   38
Now, but command; make tribute, what was gift;   155 U13 Sacvile   84
And almost deifie the Authors! make   156 U13 Sacvile   99
Which Grace shall I make love to first? your skill,   159 U14 Selden   35
To make up Greatnesse! and mans whole good fix'd   163 U15 Friend-Wars   44
Not make a verse; Anger; or laughter would,   164 U15 Friend-Wars   62
How they may make some one that day an Asse   164 U15 Friend-Wars   64
But both fell prest under the load they make.   166 U15 Friend-Wars   128
Goe make our selves the Usurers at a cast.   166 U15 Friend-Wars   134
That fortune never make thee to complaine,   168 U15 Friend-Wars   183
As would make shift, to make himselfe alone,   171 U19 Elegy By   24
Make not thy selfe a Page,   175 U23 Himselfe   33

MAKE (cont.)

	Page	Title	Line
Such thoughts wil make you more in love with truth.	181	U26 Ode High	21
For Venus Ceston, every line you make.	182	U28 Worth	14
Then to make falshood blush, and fraud afraid:	186	U32 Elsmere	4
And make the Scarre faire; If that will not be,	187	U33 Councellour	21
Spanish receipt, to make her teeth to rot.	188	U34 Small Poxe	12
That heaven should make no more; or should amisse,	188	U34 Small Poxe	15
Make all hereafter, had'st thou ruin'd this?	188	U34 Small Poxe	16
That were to wither all, and make a Grave	192	U38 Elegy 'Tis	59
Of crueltie, lest they doe make you such.	193	U38 Elegy 'Tis	84
And let your mercie make me asham'd t'offend.	194	U38 Elegy 'Tis	106
Shortly againe: and make our absence sweet.	197	U40 Elegy That	8
An Officer there, did make most solemne love,	201	U42 Elegy Let	53
To make consumption, ever, where thou go'st;	205	U43 Vulcan	58
To make consumption, every where thou go'st;	205	U43 Vulcan	58
To make propter viam, ever, where thou go'st;	205	U43 Vulcan	V 58
Make your Petards, and Granats, all your fine	212	U43 Vulcan	206
To see the Pride at Court, their Wives doe make:	213	U44 Speach	16
What, to make legs? yes, and to smell most sweet,	215	U44 Speach	90
No piece of money, but you know, or make	216	U45 Squib	14
As make it their proficiencie, how much	218	U47 Tribe	12
And relish merry make him.	220	U48 Bacchus	12
And thou make many a Poet,	221	U48 Bacchus	29
Make State, Religion, Bawdrie, all a theame?	222	U49 Pucell	12
Or your Allies, you make your bookes your friends,	224	U50 Countesse	27
As they are hard, for them to make their owne,	225	U50 Countesse	33
An ill commoditie! 'T must make good weight.	229	U54 Squib	6
And you shall make me good, in weight, and fashion,	229	U54 Squib	17
To make you merry on the Dressing stoole	230	U56 Covell	21
My Lord, till felt griefe make our stone hearts soft,	234	U61 Epigram	14
That thought shall make, he will this losse supply	236	U63 Charles 2	11
And what are bounds to her, you make your owne?	236	U64 Charles 3	10
To make the hearts of a whole Nation smile,	238	U66 Queene	10
Make up this crowned day,	240	U67 Muses	V 47
Would make the very Greene-cloth to looke blew:	241	U68 House-hold	8
And make them yeares:	244	U70 Ode	54
These make the lines of life, and that's her ayre.	245	U70 Ode	64
In bulke, doth make man better bee;	245	U70 Ode	66
To make more cleare	254	U75 Epithalam.	54
Doe long to make themselves, so, another way:	257	U75 Epithalam.	140
To make all the Muses debters	259	U76 Petition	8
Please your Majestie to make	260	U76 Petition	25
Of murmuring Subjects; make the Nations know	261	U77 Treasurer	19
Of froward Citizens; make the Nations know	261	U77 Treasurer	V 19
And, calling truth to witnesse, make that good	270	U81 Pawlet	35
And, calling truth to witnesse, make it good	270	U81 Pawlet	V 35
A dedicated Ensigne make	273	U84 Cradle	11
And, out of that, make Day to breake;	276	U84 Body	14
You could make shift to paint an Eye,	278	U84 Mind	9
I call you Muse; now make it true:	278	U84 Mind	21
To hang a window, or make darke the roome,	282	U84 Muse	7
That she is in, or, make it more compleat?	284	U84 Muse	72
But make him All in All, their Theme, that Day:	286	U84 Muse	120
There jest, and feast, make him thine host,	292	U86 Hor.4:1	11
He'll thee a Marble Statue make	292	U86 Hor.4:1	19
But, say old Love returne should make,	294	U87 Hor.3:9	17
The Things that make the happier life, are these,	295	U90 Mart.10:47	1
Sleepe, that will make the darkest howres swift-pac't;	295	U90 Mart.10:47	11
Medea make brave with impetuous scorne;	313	Horace	175
Medea make wild, fierce, impetuous;	342	Horace	V175
Yet common matter thou thine owne maist make,	313	Horace	187
Much from the sight, which faire report will make	317	Horace	262
As not make difference, whether Davus speake,	321	Horace	345
On life, and manners, and make those his booke,	325	Horace	454
With honour make the farre-knowne Author live.	329	Horace	519
Yet who's most ignorant, dares Verses make.	331	Horace	570
But, now, it is enough to say; I make	333	Horace	593
Make a great Supper; or for some poore man	333	Horace	602
When you make verses, with your judge doe so:	354	Horace	V620
For, if one should, and with a rope haste	335	Horace	655
Wants facultie to make a censure true:	362	Author	11
Nor Sunne could make to vary from the rest,	367	Ode Who saith	29
Might make the Fable of Good Women true.	372	Epitaph	14
Out-bee that Wife, in worth, thy freind did make:	384	Somerset	12
Hymens amends, to make it worth his fault.	384	Somerset	14
Least a false praise do make theyr dotage his.	385	Husband	4
will all turne dust, & may not make me swell.	387	Cavendish	4
Will all be dust, & may not make me swell.	387	Cavendish.	V 4
To make thy honour, and our wealth the more!	388	Chapman	6
And who make thither else, rob, or invade.	389	Chapman	12
A little further, to make thee a roome:	391	Shakespeare	21
And make those flights upon the bankes of Thames,	392	Shakespeare	73
This second marriage, will aeternall make.	394	Jane Ogle	26
Because, who make the question, have not seene	396	Drayton	3
Like him, to make the ayre, one volary:	397	Drayton	36
Brave are the Musters, that the Muse will make.	398	Drayton	64
With pause upon it; make this page your booke;	399	Lady Ogle	6
Stay, till she make her vaine Approches. Then	401	Beaumont	15
But higher power, as spight could not make lesse,	401	Beaumont	18
To make the Language sweet upon her tongue.	402	Inigo Jones 1	14
Though gold or Ivory haftes would make it good.	403	Inigo Jones 1	28
Though gold or Ivory haftes cant make it good.	403	Inigo Jones 1	V 28
Oh, to make Boardes to speake! There is a taske	404	Inigo Jones 1	49

MAKE (cont.)
With all Remonstrance make an honest man. . . . 406 Inigo Jones 1 104
Our Charles should make thee such? 'Twill not become . . 406 Inigo Jones 2 3
Is to make cheape, the Lord, the lines, the price. . . 408 Detractor 6
An honest Bilbo-Smith would make good blades, . . . 410 Brome 15
or Malyce to make Faultes, which nowe is skill. . . . 421 Censure 11
make many, hurt themselves; a praysed faith . . . 422 Lucan 2
make many, hurt himselfe; a praysed faith . . . 422 Lucan V 2
To make these good, and what comes after, better. . . 666 Glover 10

MAKER
My Maker, Saviour, and my Sanctifier: . . . . 128 U1 Trinitie 41
Against his Maker; high alone with weeds, ... 163 U15 Friend-Wars 33
Beholds her Maker! and, in him, doth see . . . . 271 U81 Pawlet 73
And I still bid the learned Maker looke . . . . 325 Horace 453
The maker of the Propertyes! in summe . . . . 404 Inigo Jones 1 61

MAKERS
But these, desir'd by you, the makers ends . . . . 60 E94 Bedford 3 5
But view the mildnesse of your Makers state, . . . 193 U38 Elegy 'Tis 85

MAKES
It makes the father, lesse, to rue. . . . . 33 E22 Daughter 4
And now, her (hourely) her owne cucqueane makes, . . 34 E25 Beast 1 5
Makes serious use of all great trade he knowes. . . 35 E28 Surly 3
He takes up all, makes each mans wit his owne. . . 45 E56 Poet-Ape 8
Then to begin, my Roe: He makes a state . . . . 50 E70 Wm Roe 1 2
What is't, fine Grand, makes thee my friendship flye, . . 51 E73 Fine Grand 1
And what would hurt his vertue makes it still. . . . 63 E98 Th Roe 1 6
Where vertue makes them both, and that's in thee: . . 70 E109 Nevil 3
His life, but makes, that he can dye no more. . . . 71 E110 Edmonds 1 22
Nor to give Caesar this, makes ours the lesse. . . . 72 E111 Edmonds 2 8
So Phoebus makes me worthy of his bayes, ... 73 E113 Overbury 1
Where, what makes others great, doth keepe thee good! . 73 E113 Overbury 4
Tell's of him, all the tales, it selfe then makes; . . 74 E115 Honest Man 17
He makes himselfe a thorough-fare of vice. . . . 76 E118 Gut 4
Makes, the whole longer, then 'twas given him, much. . . 76 E119 Shelton 16
Makes the poore Banck-side creature wet it' shoone, . . 84 E133 Voyage 30
And makes sleepe softer then it is! . . . . 97 F3 Wroth 20
Who, for it, makes thy house his court; . . . . 97 F3 Wroth 24
Who, for it, makes thy lodge his court; . . . . 97 F3 Wroth V 24
In autumne, at the Partrich makes a flight, . . . 97 F3 Wroth 27
Makes a most blessed gayne. . . . . . 112 F11 Epode 86
All taste of bitternesse, and makes the ayre . . . 112 F11 Epode 97
While it makes huishers serviceable men, ... 113 F12 Rutland 9
Solders crackt friendship; makes love last a day; . . 113 F12 Rutland 17
This makes, that wisely you decline your life, . . . 118 F13 Aubigny 59
This makes, that your affections still be new, . . . 119 F13 Aubigny 118
More pleasure while the thing he makes . . . . 145 U5 Woman-kind 15
As makes the youngest Hee, ... 149 U9 Picture V 9
Who makes the one, so't be first, makes both. . . . 152 U12 Corbet 40
That makes the Arch. The rest that there were put . . 157 U13 Sacvile 137
All which he makes the servants of the Groine, . . 163 U15 Friend-Wars 46
The bravery makes, she can no honour leese: . . . 164 U15 Friend-Wars 56
That as the water makes things, put in't streight, . . 170 U18 Elegy Can 7
Which makes that (lighted by the beamie hand . . . 176 U24 Frontispice 9
This makes, that lighted by the beamie hand . . . 176 U24 Frontispice V 9
This sadnesse makes no approaches, but to kill. . . 191 U38 Elegy 'Tis 4
That makes us live, not that which calls to die. . . 193 U38 Elegy 'Tis 78
This makes me, Mrs. that sometime by stealth, . . . 197 U40 Elegy That 9
As makes Penelopes old fable true, ... 224 U50 Countesse 20
It is their Grace, and favour, that makes seene, . . 255 U75 Epithalam. 89
What makes these Velvets, Silkes, and Lawne, . . . 275 U84 Body 2
It moveth all; and makes a flight . . . . . 279 U84 Mind 31
And unbought viands ready makes: . . . . . 291 U85 Country 48
Makes his life longer then 'twas given him, much. . . 295 U89 Mart.8:77 8
His matter to his power, in all he makes, ... 307 Horace 57
An ounce, what makes it then? The halfe pound just; . . 327 Horace 471
'Tis now inquir'd, which makes the nobler Verse, . . 331 Horace 581
Here's one makes verses, but there's none knows why: . 355 Horace V670
And, there an end of him, reciting makes: . . . 337 Horace 678
And there an end of him with reading makes: . . . 355 Horace V678
And makes her supple feete, as swift as winde. . . 363 Riches 12
How faire a flight he makes! . . . . . 366 Ode Who saith 10
(Which makes him sing . . . . . . 369 Ode Who saith 102
It fits not onely him that makes a Booke, . . . 385 Husband 1
It makes me ravish'd with just wonder, cry . . . 395 May 13
Of Ethnicisme, makes his Muse a Saint. . . . . 401 Beaumont 22
What makes your Wretchednes to bray soe loud . . . 403 Inigo Jones 1 23
He makes the Camell & dull Ass his prize. . . . 408 Inigo Jones 3 8
Clears the Brains, makes Wit the Quicker: . . . 657 Door Apollo 16

MAKING
In making thy friends bookes, and thy bookes friends: . . 55 E86 Goodyere 2 4
Of building townes, and making wilde beasts tame, . . 82 E130 Ferrab. 1 2
Thou, nor thy loosenesse with thy making sorts. . . 107 F10 Proludium 18
Thou, nor their loosenesse with our making sorts. . . 107 F10 Proludium V 18
Making his fortunes swim . . . . . . 112 F11 Epode 106
Their thoughts and meanes to making loude the cry; . . 155 U13 Sacvile 66
Next to your selfe, for making your love true: . . . 189 U37 Friend-Book 2
Of making just approaches, how to kill, ... 232 U59 Newcastle 4
In making soft her aromatique bed. . . . . 251 U74 Weston 18
His cause of making Verses none knowes why: . . . 335 Horace 670
still making that the greatest that is last . . . 361 Palmer 19
Or skill of making matches in my life: . . . . 386 Husband 7
Or making of the Propertyes it meane? . . . . 402 Inigo Jones 1 12

		Page	Title	Line

MAKINGS
Of severall makings? helps, helps, t'attire . . . . 215 U44 Speach 94

MAK'ST
Thou, that mak'st gaine thy end, and wisely well, . . . 27 E3 Bookseller 1
At once thou mak'st me happie, and unmak'st; . . . 44 E55 Beaumont 5
At Madames table, where thou mak'st all wit . . . 50 E72 Court-ling 3
Next morne, an Ode: Thou mak'st a song ere night. . . . 72 E112 Gamster 12
So, where thou liv'st, thou mak'st life understood! . . . 73 E113 Overbury 3
To Braynford, Hackney, Bow, but thou mak'st one; . . . 81 E129 Mime 4
That by commanding first thy selfe, thou mak'st . . . 168 U15 Friend-Wars 181
Mak'st it religion to grow rich by Crimes! . . . 187 U33 Councellour 16
But such a Mind, mak'st God thy Guest. . . . . 281 U84 Mind 72

MALE
No male unto him: who could so exceed . . . 53 E79 Rutland 7
Ever his thighes Male then, and his braines Shee. . . . 378 Coryat 2 92

MALICE
Deceive their malice, who could wish it so. . . . 27 E2 My Booke 7
And scorn'd, thou'ast showne thy malice, but hast fail'd. . . 188 U34 Small Poxe 18
But, on thy malice, tell me, didst thou spie . . . 203 U43 Vulcan 19
Could stop the malice of this ill, ... 234 U60 La-ware 15
Or crafty Malice, might pretend this praise, . . . 391 Shakespeare 11

MALLOWES
Or Mallowes loosing bodyes ill: . . . . 291 U85 Country 58
Or Mallowes good for bodyes ill: . . . . 291 U85 Country V 58

MALT
The wit of Ale, and Genius of the Malt . . . . 193 U38 Elegy 'Tis 95

MALYCE
or Malyce to make Faultes, which nowe is skill. . . 421 Censure 11

MAN'
Then, The townes honest Man's her errant'st knave. . . 75 E115 Honest Man 34
To him, man's dearer, then t'himselfe. . . . . 99 F3 Wroth 96

MAN
For termers, or some clarke-like serving-man, . . . 28 E3 Bookseller 9
And such from whom let no man hope least good, . . . 30 E11 Something 6
Keepes himselfe, with halfe a man, and defrayes . . . 30 E12 Shift 3
Man scarse can make that doubt, but thou canst teach. . . 31 E14 Camden 10
All men are wormes: But this no man. In silke . . 31 E15 Court-worm 1
If any pious life ere lifted man . . . 35 E27 Roe 1 6
Of a great man, and to be thought the same, . . . 35 E28 Surly 2
He drinkes to no man: that's, too, like a lord. . . . 35 E28 Surly 14
Stile thee a most great foole, but no great man. . . . 36 E28 Surly 22
Any man else, you clap your hands, and rore, . . . 38 E38 Guiltie 2 4
If, now, with man and wife, to will, and nill . . . 40 E42 Giles 16
Will man lament the state he should envie? . . . 41 E45 First Son 6
When having pill'd a booke, which no man buyes, . . . 43 E53 Old-end 2
And, hood-wink'd, for a man, embrace a post. . . . 45 E58 Groome 8
Was dull, and long, ere shee would goe to man: . . . 57 E90 Mill 3
And best become the valiant man to weare, . . . 58 E91 Vere 17
We need a man that knowes the severall graces . . . 61 E95 Savile 27
We need a man, can speake of the intents, . . . 62 E95 Savile 31
A man should seeke great glorie, and not broad. . . . 62 E96 Donne 2 12
Knat, raile, and ruffe too. How so ere, my man . . . 65 E101 Supper 20
It is an Epigramme, on all man-kind; . . . . 66 E102 Pembroke 2
What man art thou, that art so many men, . . . 68 E106 E Herbert 2
On the Townes honest Man. . . . 74 E115 Honest Man Ttl
Jephson, thou man of men, to whose lov'd name . . . 75 E116 Jephson 1
With me can merit more, then that good man, . . . 76 E119 Shelton 5
Would'st thou heare, what man can say . . . 79 E124 Elizabeth 1
Uv'dale, thou piece of the first times, a man . . . 79 E125 Uvedale 1
Is there a hope, that Man would thankefull bee, . . . 80 E127 Aubigny 1
Came backe untouch'd. This man hath travail'd well. . . 81 E128 Wm Roe 2 14
Say, this, or that man they to thee preferre; . . . 83 E131 Ferrab. 2 9
But, in the action, greater man then hee: . . . 84 E133 Voyage 26
Man, that had never heard of a Chimaera. . . . 86 E133 Voyage 80
Here no man tells my cups; nor, standing by, . . . 95 F2 Penshurst 67
Let this man sweat, and wrangle at the barre, . . . 99 F3 Wroth 73
Man may securely sinne, but safely never. . . . 113 F11 Epode 116
A man may safely sinne, securely never. . . . 113 F11 Epode V116
Runs betweene man, and man; 'tweene dame, and dame; . . 113 F12 Rutland 16
Them, or their officers: and no man know, . . . 118 F13 Aubigny 79
Boast, but how oft they have gone wrong to man: . . 119 F13 Aubigny 84
Are justly summ'd, that make you man; . . . 120 F14 Sydney 22
To take our nature; becam'st man, and dyd'st, . . . 128 U1 Trinitie 22
Pure thoughts in man: with fiery zeale them feeding . . 128 U1 Trinitie 27
The gladdest light, darke man can thinke upon; . . . 128 U1 Trinitie 35
Can man forget this Storie? . . . . 130 U1 Nativitie 24
She shall make the old man young, . . . 131 U2 Excuse 20
What a man she could love well: . . . . 139 U2 Promise- 4
(And that quickly) speake your Man. . . . 140 U2 Promise 30
9. Her man described by her owne Dictamen. . . . 140 U2 Her man Ttl
I will tell what Man would please me. . . . 140 U2 Her man 2
Yet a man; with crisped haire . . . 141 U2 Her man 10
Drest, you still for man should take him; . . . 141 U2 Her man 38
Such a man, with every part, ... 142 U2 Her man 53
What man but must lose his? . . . . 143 U3 Musicall 8
Find some one good, in some one man; . . . 145 U5 Woman-kind 9
Doe change, though man, and often fight, . . . 146 U6 Defence 8
To love one man, hee'd leave her first. . . . 146 U6 Defence 24
Deepest in Man, of which when he doth thinke, . . . 153 U13 Sacvile 20
Ha's Feathers, and will serve a man to pull. . . . 154 U13 Sacvile 58
Man out their Boates to th' Temple, and not shift . . 155 U13 Sacvile 83
Cannot a man be reck'ned in the State . . . 156 U13 Sacvile 103
Looke to and cure; Hee's not a man hath none, . . . 156 U13 Sacvile 115

MAN (cont.)

	Page	Title	Line
A pennance, where a man may not be free,	158	U14 Selden	8
Looke on th'ambitious man, and see him nurse	162	U15 Friend-Wars	11
Looke on the false, and cunning man, that loves	162	U15 Friend-Wars	15
See him, that's call'd, and thought the happiest man,	162	U15 Friend-Wars	23
No part or corner man can looke upon,	163	U15 Friend-Wars	27
That kept man living! Pleasures only sought!	163	U15 Friend-Wars	41
And firke, and jerke, and for the Coach-man raile,	164	U15 Friend-Wars	72
For man to spend his money on? his wit?	165	U15 Friend-Wars	102
Is it for these that Fine-man meets the street	165	U15 Friend-Wars	106
Is it that man pulls on himselfe Disease?	165	U15 Friend-Wars	114
Now use the bones, we see doth hire a man	166	U15 Friend-Wars	136
Now use the bales, we see doth hire a man	166	U15 Friend-Wars	V136
(Because th'are every where amongst Man-kind	167	U15 Friend-Wars	171
Man thought the valianter, 'cause he durst sweare,	168	U15 Friend-Wars	192
And that pour'd out upon Man-kind can be!	172	U20 Shrub	19
Aske not to know this Man. If fame should speake	172	U21 Ltl Shrub	1
If thou wouldst know the vertues of Man-kind,	185	U30 Burleigh	1
For no man lives so out of passions sway,	190	U37 Friend-Book	31
Thinke it was frailtie, Mistris, thinke me man,	192	U38 Elegy 'Tis	31
No man inflicts that paine, till hope be spent:	192	U38 Elegy 'Tis	44
In man, because man hath the flesh abus'd.	192	U38 Elegy 'Tis	66
Of Contumelie, and urge a good man more	193	U38 Elegy 'Tis	100
A man should flie from, as he would disdaine.	194	U38 Elegy 'Tis	104
No, Mistris, no, the open merrie Man	198	U40 Elegy That	25
Be idle words, though of a parting Man;	199	U41 Elegy Since	4
As any Mercer; or the whale-bone man	200	U42 Elegy Let	31
that from the Foot-man, when he was become	201	U42 Elegy Let	52
Of massacring Man-kind so many wayes.	212	U43 Vulcan	208
For that is first requir'd, A man be his owne.	216	U45 Squib	23
Or if Chance must, to each man that doth rise,	217	U46 Coke	23
Live to that point I will, for which I am man,	219	U47 Tribe	59
I am no States-man, and much lesse Divine,	223	U49 Pucell	25
To stuffes and Laces, those my Man can buy.	223	U49 Pucell	28
Indeed, her Dressing some man might delight,	223	U49 Pucell	31
By this, although you fancie not the man,	231	U56 Covell	25
By thys Tyme, though you fancie not the man,	231	U56 Covell	V 25
What each man sayes of it, and of what coat	232	U58 Book-seller	4
He is the Man, and Favorite of God.	235	U61 Epigram	20
Whereby the safetie of Man-kind was wrought)	238	U66 Queene	8
How summ'd a circle didst thou leave man-kind	243	U70 Ode	9
Or masked man, if valu'd by his face,	243	U70 Ode	23
In bulke, doth make man better bee;	245	U70 Ode	66
Was left yet to Man-kind;	247	U70 Ode	121
Three Kingdomes Mirth, in light, and aerie man,	249	U72 King	11
Weston! That waking man! that Eye of State!	250	U73 Weston	5
Of Sex, to rob the Creature; but from Man	255	U75 Epithalam.	82
What kind of waking Man	256	U75 Epithalam.	111
Discerne betweene a Statue, and a Man;	261	U77 Treasurer	14
Court can call hers, or Man could call his Arts.	262	U78 Digby	4
Court can call hers, or Man would call the Arts.	262	U78 Digby	V 4
The kind of Man, on whom his doome should fall!	288	U84 Muse	208
To him should be her Judge, true God, true Man,	288	U84 Muse	211
As being the Sonne of Man) to shew his Power,	288	U84 Muse	217
To bend a man, now at his fiftieth yeare	292	U86 Hor.4:1	6
Were also clos'd: But, who the man should be,	309	Horace	109
Her truch-man, she reports the minds each throw.	313	Horace	157
Or an Heroe; if a ripe old man,	313	Horace	162
Speake to me, Muse, the Man, who, after Troy was sack't,	315	Horace	201
Falshood with truth, as no man can espie	315	Horace	216
Falsehood and truth, as no man can espy	343	Horace	V216
These studies alter now, in one, growne man;	315	Horace	237
The old man many evils doe girt round;	315	Horace	241
Any fourth man, to speake at all, aspire.	317	Horace	275
Clowne, Towns-man, base, and noble, mix'd, to judge?	319	Horace	302
And so, as every man may hope the same;	321	Horace	350
Indeed, give fitting dues to every man.	325	Horace	452
Yet, there's a value given to this man.	331	Horace	554
To bettring of the mind of man, in ought,	331	Horace	562
Make a great Supper; or for some poore man	333	Horace	602
I wonder how this happie man should know,	333	Horace	605
And rack, with Wine, the man whom they would try,	333	Horace	618
A wise, and honest man will cry out shame	335	Horace	633
A good and wise man will crye open shame	354	Horace	V633
The man once mock'd, and suffer'd wrong to tread.	335	Horace	642
And shun to touch him, as a man that were	335	Horace	644
And flye to touch him, as a man that were	354	Horace	V644
Hee that preserves a man, against his will,	335	Horace	665
Recall him yet, hee'ld be no more a man:	335	Horace	668
Now, bring him backe, he'le be no more a man,	355	Horace	V668
Now, after all, let no man	364	Phoenix	1
(Compos'd of Gamester, Captaine, Knight, Knight's man,	370	Fletcher	3
He sayes to the world, let any man mend it,	379	Coryat 3	15
That an ill man dares not securely looke	389	Aleman	8
When you behold me wish my selfe, the man	389	Aleman	23
As neither Man, nor Muse, can praise too much.	390	Shakespeare	4
With us be call'd, the Naso, but this man?	397	Drayton	32
From thirty pound in pipkins, to the Man	402	Inigo Jones 1	2
Of Tyre-man, Mounte-banck & Justice Jones,	402	Inigo Jones 1	16
Whither? oh whither will this Tire-man growe?	404	Inigo Jones 1	59
With all Remonstrance make an honest man.	406	Inigo Jones 1	104
Besydes, his Man may merit it, and be	406	Inigo Jones 2	5
No man will tarry by thee, as hee goes,	409	Detractor	17

	Page	Title	Line
MAN (cont.)			
For noe Man Lyves, soe out of passions swaye,	422	Censure	24
MANAGE			
And by the awfull manage of her Eye	287	U84 Muse	167
MANGER			
Was now laid in a Manger.	130	U1 Nativitie	12
Incarnate in the Manger, shining bright	288	U84 Muse	200
MANGERS			
At these Immortall Mangers Virgil fed.	228	U53 Newcastle	20
MANIE			
that mongst so manie plants transplanted hether,	361	Palmer	6
MAN-KIND			
It is an Epigramme, on all man-kind;	66	E102 Pembroke	2
(Because th'are every where amongst Man-kind	167	U15 Friend-Wars	171
And that pour'd out upon Man-kind can be!	172	U20 Shrub	19
If thou wouldst know the vertues of Man-kind,	185	U30 Burleigh	1
Of massacring Man-kind so many wayes.	212	U43 Vulcan	208
Whereby the safetie of Man-kind was wrought)	238	U66 Queene	8
How summ'd a circle didst thou leave man-kind	243	U70 Ode	9
Was left yet to Man-kind;	247	U70 Ode	121
MANKIND			
Which might with halfe mankind maintayne a strife.	34	E23 Donne 1	8
Yet, Satyres, since the most of mankind bee	60	E94 Bedford 3	7
Of murthering of mankind many wayes.	212	U43 Vulcan	V208
To give mankind their eases,	221	U48 Bacchus	23
Whole Nations! nay, Mankind! the World, with all	271	U81 Pawlet	90
As the old race of Mankind were,	289	U85 Country	2
As the old stock of Mankind were,	289	U85 Country	V 2
MANKINDE			
Pallas, nor thee I call on, mankinde maid,	107	F10 Proludium	13
Pallas, nor thee we call on, mankinde maid,	107	F10 Proludium	V 13
Whereon the most of mankinde wracke themselves,	119	F13 Aubigny	90
MANKINDS			
And giving dues to all Mankinds deserts!	289	U84 Muse	224
MANLY			
Things manly, and not smelling parasite.	48	E65 Muse	14
Onely a learned, and a manly soule	52	E76 Bedford 1	13
And manly elocution, not one while	160	U14 Selden	56
And that thy strong and manly Eloquence	217	U46 Coke	13
Must maintaine manly; not be heard to sing,	317	Horace	277
Must manly keep, and not be heard to sing	345	Horace	V277
MANN'D			
In decoctions; and are mann'd	105	F8 Sicknesse	30
MANNER			
In that proud manner, as a good so gain'd,	154	U13 Sacvile	37
O, had I now your manner, maistry, might,	227	U52 Answer	16
In manner of a daily Apostrophe,	288	U84 Muse	210
And in the Salian manner meet	292	U86 Hor.4:1	27
MANNERS			
'Tis 'gainst the manners of an Epigram:	29	E9 To All	3
Mens manners ne're were viler, for your sake.	34	E24 Parliament	2
Whose manners draw, more than thy powers constraine.	37	E35 James 2	3
Play-wright, I loath to have thy manners knowne	42	E49 Playwrt 1	5
That the wit there, and manners might be sav'd:	73	E113 Overbury	6
That strives, his manners should precede his wit.	78	E121 Rudyerd 1	8
Countries, and climes, manners, and men to know,	80	E128 Wm Roe 2	2
The mysteries of manners, armes, and arts.	96	F2 Penshurst	98
What your try'd manners are, what theirs should bee.	119	F13 Aubigny	112
And his Manners of that Nation.	141	U2 Her man	8
His very Manners taught t'amend,	152	U12 Corbet	22
Alone in money, but in manners too.	157	U13 Sacvile	134
Of generall knowledge; watch'd men, manners too,	159	U14 Selden	33
Times, manners, customes! Innovations spide!	160	U14 Selden	44
Who can behold their Manners, and not clowd-/Like	164	U15 Friend-Wars	60
Thou art my Cause: whose manners since I knew,	187	U33 Councellour	13
What manners prettie, Nature milde,	188	U35 Chute	2
More then of eithers manners, wit, or face!	202	U42 Elegy Let	88
Countries, and Climes, manners, and men to know.	224	U50 Countesse	22
Such, (if her manners like you) I doe send:	230	U56 Covell	19
O Times! O Manners! Surfet bred of ease,	237	U64 Charles 3	17
That knits brave minds, and manners, more then blood.	246	U70 Ode	106
Which knits brave minds, and manners, more then blood.	246	U70 Ode	V106
To compose men, and manners; stint the strife	261	U77 Treasurer	18
To Compasse men, and manners; stint the strife	261	U77 Treasurer	V 18
Saw many Townes, and Men, and could their manners tract.	315	Horace	202
On life, and manners, and make those his booke,	325	Horace	454
Of Shakespeares minde, and manners brightly shines	392	Shakespeare	67
MAN'S			
Then, The townes honest Man's her errant'st knave.	75	E115 Honest Man	34
Thy peace is made; and, when man's state is well,	99	F3 Wroth	93
To him, man's dearer, then t'himselfe.	99	F3 Wroth	96
MANS			
He takes up all, makes each mans wit his owne.	45	E56 Poet-Ape	8
Before thou wert it, in each good mans heart.	49	E67 Suffolk	10
They'are rear'd with no mans ruine, no mans grone,	94	F2 Penshurst	46
The faithfull mans beleeved Mysterie,	127	U1 Trinitie	3
Mans buried honour, in his sleepie life:	162	U15 Friend-Wars	7
To make up Greatnesse! and mans whole good fix'd	163	U15 Friend-Wars	44
The Mistresse of Mans life, grave Historie,	175	U24 Frontispice	2
Where only a mans birth is his offence,	177	U25 Desmond	32
When only a mans birth is his offence,	177	U25 Desmond	V 32
You favour Truth, and me, in this mans Cause.	186	U31 Elsmere	10
God lightens not at mans each fraile offence,	193	U38 Elegy 'Tis	68

		Page	Title	Line

MANS (cont.)
```
Or in the Bell-Mans Lanthorne, like a spie,          211   U43 Vulcan        187
When, being the Strangers helpe, the poore mans aide, 217   U46 Coke           7
Like flies, or wormes, with mans corrupt parts fed:   218   U47 Tribe         18
Mans comming yeares much good with them doe bring:    317   Horace           250
Can tell a States-mans dutie, what the arts           325   Horace           449
As Painting, so is Poesie.  Some mans hand            329   Horace           539
Since he treads in no other Mans steps but his owne.  379   Coryat 3          12
Of two, the choicest Paire of Mans delights,          401   Filmer            4
And art the spotlesse Mirrour to Mans eyes.           414   Ghyrlond         44
```
MANSFIELD
```
Brunsfield, and Mansfield doe this yeare, my fates    219   U47 Tribe         44
To the Right Honorable William Viscount Mansfield: ... 228  U53 Newcastle    VTtl
```
MANSION
```
In thee, faire Mansion, let it rest,                  281   U84 Mind          69
```
MANY (See also MANIE)
```
Where lately harbour'd many a famous whore,            29   E7 Hot-house       1
Many of thine this better could, then I,               31   E14 Camden        13
My countries parents I have many knowne;               46   E60 Mounteagle     9
Then, since we (more then many) these truths know:     50   E70 Wm Roe 1       7
So many Poets life, by one should live.                57   E89 Allen         14
What man art thou, that art so many men,               68   E106 E Herbert     2
Naming so many, too! But, this is one,                 74   E115 Honest Man    3
The many perills of this Port, and how                 85   E133 Voyage       47
With famine, wants, and sorrowes many a dosen,         86   E133 Voyage       71
But they unfrighted passe, though many a privie        86   E133 Voyage       73
And many a sinke pour'd out her rage anenst 'hem;      86   E133 Voyage       75
But many Moones there shall not wane (quoth hee)       87   E133 Voyage      103
Of many a Sylvane, taken with his flames.              94   F2 Penshurst      16
Thus removed by many a mile?                          102   F5 Celia 1       V 14
Bald, or blinde, or nere so many:                     105   F8 Sicknesse      40
But this true course is not embrac'd by many:         109   F11 Epode         19
But this faire course is not embrac'd by many:        109   F11 Epode        V 19
By many? scarse by any.                               109   F11 Epode         20
How many equall with the Argive Queene,               114   F12 Rutland       49
And so doe many more.  All which can call             117   F13 Aubigny       31
After many scornes like these,                        133   U2 Suffered        1
Many a pound, and piece, will place one well;         155   U13 Sacvile       78
A many of bookes, even good judgements wound          159   U14 Selden        15
And what I write? and vexe it many dayes              159   U14 Selden        25
Amongst my many other, that I may                     171   U20 Shrub          3
Of many Colours; outward fresh, from spots,           171   U20 Shrub         11
Though many Gems be in your bosome stor'd,            179   U25 Desmond       55
So many my Yeares-labours in an houre?                202   U43 Vulcan         4
Especially in paper; many a Reame                     205   U43 Vulcan       V 61
Had tickled your large Nosthrill: many a Reame        205   U43 Vulcan        62
Of massacring Man-kind so many wayes.                 212   U43 Vulcan       208
Of murthering of mankind many wayes.                  212   U43 Vulcan      V208
For there are many slips, and Counterfeits.           216   U45 Squib         17
I would call mine, to which not many Staires          220   U47 Tribe         74
And thou make many a Poet,                            221   U48 Bacchus       29
What though she hath won on Trust, as many doe,       223   U49 Pucell        21
For when they find so many meet in one,               225   U50 Countesse     35
For whose returnes, and many, all these pray:         225   U51 Bacon          6
How many verses, Madam, are your Due!                 231   U56 Covell        27
How many times, Live long, Charles, would he say,     236   U64 Charles 3      3
Had I a thousand Mouthes, as many Tongues,            269   U81 Pawlet        23
She was, in one, a many parts of life;                287   U84 Muse         173
Or hence, or thence, he drives with many a Hound      290   U85 Country       31
In many a Gumme, and for thy soft eares sake          292   U86 Hor.4:1       22
Saw many Townes, and Men, and could their manners tract. 315 Horace          202
The old man many evils doe girt round;                315   Horace           241
To taxe that Verse, which many a day, and blot        325   Horace           416
Rich men are said with many cups to plie,             333   Horace           617
Great men are said with many cups to plye,            354   Horace          V617
The wise, and many-headed Bench, that sits            370   Fletcher           1
How many learned men he have drawne with his hooke    380   Coryat 3          44
Or, to so many, and so Broad-seales had,              385   Brooke             3
Of many Coulors! read them! & reveale                 404   Inigo Jones 1     47
make many, hurt themselves; a praysed faith           422   Lucan              2
make many, hurt himselfe; a praysed faith             422   Lucan            V 2
Shall powre forth many a line, drop many a letter,    666   Glover             9
```
MANY-HEADED
```
The wise, and many-headed Bench, that sits            370   Fletcher           1
```
MAP
```
Then can a flea at twise skip i'the Map.               69   E107 Hungry       18
Poring, as on a Map, to find the wayes                288   U84 Muse         196
```
MAPPE
```
The Mappe of his journey, and sees in his booke,      379   Coryat 3          18
```
MAPS
```
Yet have they seene the maps, and bought 'hem too,     59   E92 New Crie       9
```
MARBLE
```
Marble, weepe, for thou dost cover                     39   E40 Ratcliffe      1
Thy fact, in brasse or marble writ the same)           46   E60 Mounteagle     4
Of touch, or marble: nor canst boast a row             93   F2 Penshurst       2
Inscrib'd in touch or marble, or the cotes            114   F12 Rutland       44
Alas, I am all Marble! write the rest                 269   U81 Pawlet        13
He'll thee a Marble Statue make                       292   U86 Hor.4:1       19
```
MARCH
```
- - - the two and twentieth day of March, 1607.        43   E51 James 3      Ttl
```
MARCHING
```
And Rouze, the Marching of a mighty force,            397   Drayton           39
```

	Page	Title	Line

MARCHION
  An Elegie On the Lady Jane Pawlet, Marchion: of Winton.   .   268   U81 Pawlet   Ttl
MARCHIONISSE
  Shee was the Lady Jane, and Marchionisse   269   U81 Pawlet   19
MARD
  Where any Deed is forc't, the Grace is mard.   . . .   153   U13 Sacvile   24
MARE
  Put a Coach-mare in Tissue, must I horse   . . .   201   U42 Elegy Let   43
MARES
  The middle grounds thy mares, and horses breed.   .   94   F2 Penshurst   24
MARGARET
  On Margaret Ratcliffe.   39   E40 Ratcliffe   Ttl
  The miseries of Margaret the Queene   398   Drayton   75
MARIAGE
  Ne're came to taste the plenteous Mariage-horne.   .   165   U15 Friend-Wars   100
  Mariage, the end of life, ...   253   U75 Epithalam.   29
  (The holy perfumes of the Mariage bed.) . .   257   U75 Epithalam.   162
  Wild raging lusts; prescribe the mariage good; .   327   Horace   489
  And eve'ry joy, in mariage, turne a fruite. . .   384   Somerset   18
  So, may those Mariage-Pledges, comforts prove: .   384   Somerset   19
  Shee need not blush upon the Mariage-Day. . .   386   Husband   12
  They are the Mariage-rites   401   Filmer   3
MARIAGE-DAY
  Shee need not blush upon the Mariage-Day. . .   386   Husband   12
MARIAGE-HORNE
  Ne're came to taste the plenteous Mariage-horne.   .   165   U15 Friend-Wars   100
MARIAGE-PLEDGES
  So, may those Mariage-Pledges, comforts prove: .   384   Somerset   19
MARIAGE-RITES
  They are the Mariage-rites   401   Filmer   3
MARIE
  The Ghyrlond of the blessed Virgin Marie. . .   412   Ghyrlond   Ttl
MARISH
  Flanck'd with a Ditch, and forc'd out of a Marish, . .   209   U43 Vulcan   134
  Fenced with a Ditch, and forc'd out of a Marish, . .   209   U43 Vulcan   V134
MARKE
  For the great marke of vertue, those being gone . .   60   E93 Radcliffe   2
  The light, and marke unto posteritie? . . .   67   E104 Montgomery   12
  Marke of glorie, come with me;   132   U2 How he saw   8
  Doe but marke, her forehead's smoother . . .   134   U2 Triumph   15
  They say the Angells marke each deed, . . .   144   U3 Musicall   17
  Then stands it a triumphall marke! then Men . .   157   U13 Sacvile   139
  Where is that nominall marke, or reall rite, . .   160   U14 Selden   47
  To marke the excellent seas'ning of your Stile! . .   160   U14 Selden   55
  Though Beautie be the Marke of praise, . . .   173   U22 Elegy Tho   1
  But that's a marke, wherof thy Rites doe boast, . .   205   U43 Vulcan   57
  And set the marke upon, ...   255   U75 Epithalam.   95
  And set their marke upon, ...   255   U75 Epithalam.   V 95
  This, fearing not the subtlest Judges marke, . .   331   Horace   542
  Marke, marke, but when his wing he takes, . .   366   Ode Who saith   9
  Yet may as blind men sometimes hit the marke. . .   383   Author   6
  And hath the noblest Character of a good Booke, . .   389   Aleman   7
MARK'D
  Nor lesse in practice; but lesse mark'd, lesse knowne: . .   58   E91 Vere   14
  Mark'd by thy hand, and with the better stone, . .   62   E96 Donne 2   8
  Have you mark'd but the fall o'the Snow . . .   134   U2 Triumph   23
  To be that Smith; then live, mark'd one of those, . .   307   Horace   51
  How he could jest, because he mark'd and saw, . .   319   Horace   323
MARKES   (MONEY)
  A large hundred Markes annuitie, . . .   259   U76 Petition   11
  A full hundred Markes annuitie, . . .   259   U76 Petition   V 11
  Those your Fathers Markes, your Pounds; . .   260   U76 Petition   27
MARKES
  He markes not whose 'twas first: and after-times .   45   E56 Poet-Ape   11
  Thou joy'st in better markes, of soyle, of ayre, . .   93   F2 Penshurst   7
  Be not affected with these markes too much . .   193   U38 Elegy 'Tis   83
  Nor markes of wealth so from our Nation fled, .   213   U44 Speach   12
MARKET
  Or robbing the poore Market-folkes should nurse . .   155   U13 Sacvile   90
MARKET-FOLKES
  Or robbing the poore Market-folkes should nurse . .   155   U13 Sacvile   90
MARKT
  To be that fellow, then to be markt out . .   339   Horace   V 53/ 51
MAR'LE
  No mar'le the Clownes of Lemnos tooke thee up, . .   208   U43 Vulcan   116
MARLOWES
  Or sporting Kid, or Marlowes mighty line. . .   391   Shakespeare   30
MARO
  As he whom Maro did rehearse?   181   U27 Ode Helen   8
MARQUESS
  To Inigo Marquess Would Be A Corollary . .   406   Inigo Jones 2   Ttl
  Hath made his Inigo Marquess, wouldst thou fayne .   406   Inigo Jones 2   2
  Wee'll have thee styld the Marquess of New-Ditch. .   407   Inigo Jones 2   24
  Wee'll have thee styld the Marquess of Town-Ditch. .   407   Inigo Jones 2   V 24
MARRIAGE
  To pay at's day of marriage. By my hand . .   42   E46 Luckless 1   4
  This second marriage, will aeternall make. . .   394   Jane Ogle   26
MARRIE
  Marrie the Muse is one, can tread the Aire, . .   230   U56 Covell   13
  Marrie his Muse is one, can tread the Aire, . .   230   U56 Covell   V 13
MARRIED
  Indeed, poore Giles repents he married ever. . .   40   E42 Giles   3
  Sure, this glad payre were married, but this day. . .   384   Somerset   26

			Page	Title	Line
MARROW					
The Marrow! Wretch, I quitt thee of thy paine	.	.	.	. 408	Inigo Jones 3	5
MARRY (VERB)					
Longer a day, but with his Mill will marry.	.	.	.	. 57	E90 Mill	16
MARRY					
Marry he sets it out at his owne charge;	.	.	.	. 378	Coryat 2	83
MARRYING					
The Poplar tall, he then doth marrying twine	.	.	.	. 290	U85 Country	9
MARS					
Mars, and my Mother, in their net:	.	.	.	. 93	F1 Why write no	6
Goe, crampe dull Mars, light Venus, when he snorts,	.	.	. 107	F10 Proludium	16
And Mars, that gave thee a Lanthorne for a Crowne.	.	.	. 203	U43 Vulcan	10
Whether in Mars his field thou bee,	.	.	.	. 293	U86 Hor.4:1	39
His armes in Mars his field, he doth refuse;	.	.	. 331	Horace	566
MART					
They meet in sixes, and at every mart,	.	.	.	. 59	E92 New Crie	21
MARTIAL					
To the Ghost of Martial.	.	.	.	. 38	E36 Martial	Ttl
Martial, thou gav'st farre nobler Epigrammes	.	.	. 38	E36 Martial	1
Martial.	.	.	.	. 295	U90 Mart.10:47	Ttl
Most pleasant Martial; Substance got with ease,	.	.	. 295	U90 Mart.10:47	2
MARTINS					
To Martins Marvailes, and his Caballs losse,	.	.	.	. 206	U43 Vulcan	V 71
MARTIRDOME					
In such a Martirdome; To vexe their eyes,	.	.	.	. 371	Fletcher	13
MARTYR					
A Martyr borne in our defence;	.	.	.	. 130	U1 Nativitie	23
MARTYRS					
They meet the fire, the Test, as Martyrs would;	.	.	. 218	U47 Tribe	3
Saints, Martyrs, Prophets, with those Hierarchies,	.	.	. 285	U84 Muse	85
Both Saints, and Martyrs, by her loved Lord.	.	.	. 400	Lady Ogle	39
MARVAILES (See also MAR'LE)					
To Merlins Marvailes, and his Caballs losse,	.	.	.	. 206	U43 Vulcan	71
To Martins Marvailes, and his Caballs losse,	.	.	. 206	U43 Vulcan	V 71
With Merlins Marvailes, and his tables losse,	.	.	. 206	U43 Vulcan	V 71
MARY					
Mary, the daughter of their youth:	.	.	.	. 33	E22 Daughter	2
To Mary Lady Wroth.	.	.	.	. 66	E103 L Wroth 1	Ttl
To Mary Lady Wroth.	.	.	.	. 67	E105 L Wroth 2	Ttl
A Sonnet, to the noble Lady, the Lady Mary Worth.	.	.	. 182	U28 Worth	Ttl
To K. Charles, and Q. Mary. For the losse of their	. . .		235	U63 Charles 2	Ttl
Then, Royall Charles, and Mary, doe not grutch	.	.	. 236	U63 Charles 2	7
Haile Mary, full of grace, it once was said,	.	.	. 238	U66 Queene	1
Haile Mary, full of honours, to my Queene,	.	.	. 238	U66 Queene	5
(Except the joy that the first Mary brought,	.	.	. 238	U66 Queene	7
(And leave the joy that the first Mary brought,	.	.	. 238	U66 Queene	V 7
Glorie to God. Then, Haile to Mary! spring	.	.	. 238	U66 Queene	13
Our thanks to God. Then, Haile to Mary! spring	.	.	. 238	U66 Queene	V 13
Behold the royall Mary,	.	.	.	. 240	U67 Muses	25
Sweet! happy Mary! All	.	.	.	. 240	U67 Muses	49
MASCULINE					
(Save that most masculine issue of his braine)	.	.	. 53	E79 Rutland	6
And masculine elocution, not one while	.	.	.	. 160	U14 Selden	V 56
On edge the Masculine spirits, and did whet	.	.	. 327	Horace	494
MASKE					
Turne the stale prologue to some painted maske,	.	.	. 107	F10 Proludium	20
Lady, or Pusil, that weares maske, or fan,	.	.	. 370	Fletcher	4
MASK'D					
Friendship is now mask'd Hatred! Justice fled,	.	.	. 163	U15 Friend-Wars	39
MASKED					
Or masked man, if valu'd by his face,	.	.	.	. 243	U70 Ode	23
MASKES					
For truthes complexion, where they all weare maskes.	.	.	. 118	F13 Aubigny	70
Their painted Maskes, their paper Boates,	.	.	. 273	U84 Cradle	22
MASKINGS					
Adulterate maskings, such as might not goe:	.	.	. 204	U43 Vulcan	V 45
MASQUE					
And all men eccho you have made a Masque.	.	.	. 403	Inigo Jones 1	30
Painting & Carpentry are the Soule of Masque.	.	.	. 404	Inigo Jones 1	50
MASQUES					
Deceit is fruitfull. Men have Masques and nets,	.	.	. 216	U45 Squib	18
The Eloquence of Masques! What need of prose	.	.	. 403	Inigo Jones 1	40
MASQUING					
Nor throng'st (when masquing is) to have a sight	.	.	. 96	F3 Wroth	9
Nor throng'st (where masquing is) to have a sight	.	.	. 96	F3 Wroth	V 9
MASSACRING					
Of massacring Man-kind so many wayes.	.	.	.	. 212	U43 Vulcan	208
MASSE (FEAST)					
So have I seene at Christ-masse sports one lost,	.	.	. 45	E58 Groome	7
MASSE					
Or, that it lay, heap'd like an usurers masse,	.	.	. 88	E133 Voyage	139
Let that goe heape a masse of wretched wealth,	.	.	. 99	F3 Wroth	81
A parcell of Court-durt, a heape, and masse	.	.	. 172	U21 Ltl Shrub	5
Produce thy masse of miseries on the Stage,	.	.	. 244	U70 Ode	55
In the great masse, or machine there is stirr'd?	.	.	. 395	May	22
MAST					
The hogs return'd home fat from mast;	.	.	.	. 98	F3 Wroth	44
The hogs return'd home fat with mast;	.	.	. 98	F3 Wroth	V 44
MASTER (See also MAISTRY)					
For who can master those great parts like thee,	.	.	. 61	E95 Savile	17
Beholding, to this master of the warre;	.	.	. 72	E111 Edmonds 2	4
Beholden, to this master of the warre;	.	.	. 72	E111 Edmonds 2	V 4
That age, when thou stood'st up the master-braine:	.	.	. 75	E116 Jephson	4

MASTER (cont.)
  An Epitaph on Master Vincent Corbet. . . . . . . 151 U12 Corbet   Ttl
  An Epistle to Master John Selden. . . . . . . 158 U14 Selden   Ttl
  Though thou wert Muster-master of the Land. . . . 167 U15 Friend-Wars   174
  An Epitaph on Master Philip Gray. . . . . . . 168 U16 Gray   Ttl
  An Epistle to Master Arth: Squib. . . . . . . 216 U45 Squib   Ttl
  Of all to the great Master. . . . . 220 U48 Bacchus   8
  To Master John Burges. . . . . 231 U57 Burges   Ttl
  Great Say-Master of State, who cannot erre, . . . 255 U75 Epithalam.   99
  Great Say-Master of State, who not to erre, . . . 255 U75 Epithalam.   V 99
  Hee's Master of the Office; yet no more . . . . 258 U75 Epithalam.   187
  Did learne them first, and once a Master fear'd. . 333 Horace   592
  Looke here on Bretons worke, the master print: . . 362 Author   5
  To my worthy Friend, Master Edward Filmer, ... 401 Filmer   Ttl
  To be the Musick Master! Fabler too! . . . . . 404 Inigo Jones 1   63
  Which I, your Master, first did teach the Age. . . 409 Brome   8
  . . . Master Joseph Rutter. . . . . 414 Rutter   Ttl
  A Master-worker call'd, th'old standerd burst . . 415 Rutter   22
  A Say-master, hath studied all the tricks . . . 415 Rutter   26
MASTER-BRAINE
  That age, when thou stood'st up the master-braine: . 75 E116 Jephson   4
MASTERS
  Be thy next masters more unluckie Muse: . . . . 48 E65 Muse   5
  By which the Masters sweare, when, on the stoole . 87 E133 Voyage   122
  In spring, oft roused for thy masters sport, . . 97 F3 Wroth   23
  In spring tyme roused for their masters sport, . 97 F3 Wroth   V 23
  Informers, Masters both of Arts and lies; . . . 167 U15 Friend-Wars   164
  To Th'Best Of Monarchs, Masters, Men, King Charles 259 U76 Petition   2
  We sing the best of Monarchs, Masters, Men; . . 263 U79 New-yeares   7
MASTER-WORKER
  A Master-worker call'd, th'old standerd burst . . 415 Rutter   22
MASTRIE
  But thou wilt yet a Kinglier mastrie trie, . . . 235 U62 Charles 1   5
MASTRY
  There were of search, and mastry in the Arts. . . 206 U43 Vulcan   88
  There were of search, and mastry of the Arts. . . 206 U43 Vulcan   V 88
MATCH
  Of birth, of match, of forme, of chastitie? . . 67 E104 Montgomery   8
  As bloud, and match. Wherein, how more then much 117 F13 Aubigny   46
  With Nicholas Pasquill's, Meddle with your match, 206 U43 Vulcan   77
  With Nicholas Bretons Meddle with your match, . 206 U43 Vulcan   V 77
  Or that the Match from Spaine was ever meant? . 219 U47 Tribe   36
  Who, when shee heard the match, concluded streight, 229 U54 Squib   5
  In blood, in birth, by match, and by her seate; . 394 Jane Ogle   4
  Recelebrates the joyfull Match with France. . . 401 Filmer   10
MATCH'D
  In Verse unequall match'd, first sowre Laments, . 309 Horace   107
MATCHES
  Or skill of making matches in my life: . . . . 386 Husband   7
MATCHING
  And purple-matching Grapes, hee's glad! . . . . 290 U85 Country   20
MATE
  No sowre, or sollen bed-mate, yet a Chast; . . . 295 U90 Mart.10:47   10
MATERIALL
  to which there's no materiall that endures; . . 387 Cavendish   8
MATERIALLS
  Soe the Materialls be of Purbeck stone! . . . . 406 Inigo Jones 1   100
MATRON
  Should praise a Matron. What could hurt her more? 391 Shakespeare   14
MATRONE
  But, as a Matrone drawne at solemne times . . . 321 Horace   338
MATTER
  They, then, that living where the matter is bred, . 60 E94 Bedford 3   11
  Thou rather striv'st the matter to possesse, . . 70 E109 Nevil   9
  No matter, stinkards, row. What croaking sound . 86 E133 Voyage   91
  But high, and noble matter, such as flies . . 116 F12 Rutland   89
  Meet some new matter to looke up and wonder! . . 157 U13 Sacvile   142
  I yeeld, I yeeld, the matter of your praise . . 160 U14 Selden   61
  So dost thou studie matter, men, and times, . . 187 U33 Councellour   15
  But is the Poets matter: And he must, ... 200 U42 Elegy Let   17
  Take, therefore, you that write, still, matter fit 307 Horace   53
  His choise, who's matter to his power doth reare, 339 Horace   V 58/ 56
  His matter to his power, in all he makes, . . 307 Horace   57
  The Comick matter will not be exprest . . . . 311 Horace   121
  Yet Comick matter shunnes to be 'exprest . . . 341 Horace   V127/121
  Yet common matter thou thine owne maist make, . 313 Horace   187
  The middle of his matter: letting goe . . . . 315 Horace   213
  Is to be wise; thy matter first to know; . . . 325 Horace   441
  And, where the matter is provided still, . . . 325 Horace   443
  Of verse meere-matter-lesse, and tinckling toies. 327 Horace   460
  Who, because his matter in all should be meete, . 379 Coryat 3   3
  it will be matter lowd inoughe to tell . . . 387 Cavendish   11
  For though the Poets matter, Nature be, . . . 392 Shakespeare   57
MATURE
  Though slower Spaine; and Italy mature. . . . 368 Ode Who saith   88
MAURICE
  So acted to the life, as Maurice might, . . . 214 U44 Speach   41
MAW
  The Child, when Lamia'has din'd, out of her maw. 329 Horace   510
  All sorts of fish with Musicke of his maw. . . 374 Coryat 1   11
MAXIMUS
  With thy bright Swans, of Paulus Maximus: . . 292 U86 Hor.4:1   10

	Page	Title	Line
MA'			
Tells you it is a hot-house: So it ma',	29	E7 Hot-house	3
MAY'			
Tilter, the most may'admire thee, though not I:	36	E29 Tilter	1
Nor may'any feare, to loose of their degree,	73	E113 Overbury	11
MAY (NAME)			
You were the bright Oenone, Flora, or May?	68	E105 L Wroth 2	10
When her looke out-flourish May:	132	U2 How he saw	2
An Epigram on Prince Charles his Birth: May. 29th. 1630	237	U65 Prince	VTtl
That thus hath crown'd our hopes, with thee, our Spring & May,	237	U65 Prince	V 2
What Month then May, was fitter to disclose	237	U65 Prince	V 4
Is fairer farre, in May,	245	U70 Ode	70
Who walkes on Earth as May still went along,	264	U79 New-yeares	26
. . . Thomas May, Esquire.	395	May	Ttl
The Sunne translated, or the Sonne of May.	395	May	24
MAY (See also MAIST)			
May none, whose scatter'd names honor my booke,	29	E9 To All	1
May others feare, flie, and traduce thy name,	32	E17 Critic	1
The bodies stripes, I see, the soule may save.	33	E21 Gam'ster	8
Wee, sad for him, may glorie, and not sinne.	35	E27 Roe 1	8
May heare my Epigrammes, but like of none.	36	E28 Surly	20
Of adding to thy fame; thine may to me,	41	E43 Salisbury 1	8
Of adding to thy prayse; thine may to me,	41	E43 Salisbury 1 V	8
As what he loves may never like too much.	41	E45 First Son	12
May judge it to be his, as well as ours.	45	E56 Poet-Ape	12
It may be much, or little, in the cause.	49	E66 Cary	16
With those that come; whose grace may make that seeme	64	E101 Supper	5
The skie not falling, thinke we may have larkes.	65	E101 Supper	16
May yet be there; and godwit, if we can:	65	E101 Supper	19
Who prov'st, all these were, and againe may bee.	78	E122 Rudyerd 2	10
May windes as soft as breath of kissing friends,	81	E128 Wm Roe 2	5
Attend thee hence; and there, may all thy ends,	81	E128 Wm Roe 2	6
We each to other may this voyce enspire;	81	E128 Wm Roe 2	11
Of some Bride-well, and may, in time, concerne us	85	E133 Voyage	42
Hang on thy walls, that every child may reach.	94	F2 Penshurst	44
His children thy great lord may call his owne:	96	F2 Penshurst	91
With the whole houshold, and may, every day,	96	F2 Penshurst	96
May say, their lords have built, but thy lord dwells.	96	F2 Penshurst	102
That they may sleepe with scarres in age.	98	F3 Wroth	70
But thou, my Wroth, if I may truth apply,	99	F3 Wroth	V 91
And, howsoever we may thinke things sweet,	99	F3 Wroth	97
That, what to all may happen here,	101	F4 To the World	55
While we may, the sports of love;	102	F5 Celia 1	2
Sunnes, that set, may rise againe:	102	F5 Celia 1	6
That the curious may not know	103	F6 Celia 2	19
Man may securely sinne, but safely never.	113	F11 Epode	116
A man may safely sinne, securely never.	113	F11 Epode	V116
Almost you have, or may have, when you will?	114	F12 Rutland	34
My best of wishes, may you beare a sonne.	116	F12 Rutland	100
If it may stand with your soft blush to heare	117	F13 Aubigny	22
And raise not vertue; they may vice enhance.	117	F13 Aubigny	42
Which though the turning world may dis-esteeme,	118	F13 Aubigny	64
May they have nothing left, whereof they can	118	F13 Aubigny	83
Other great wives may blush at: when they see	119	F13 Aubigny	111
That I may tell to Sydney, what	120	F14 Sydney	12
And he may thinke on that	120	F14 Sydney	15
So may you live in honor, as in name,	121	F14 Sydney	51
So may	121	F14 Sydney	53
That I may prove	129	U1 Father	5
All the world for love may die.	131	U2 Excuse	24
May not claime another kisse.	138	U2 Kisse	36
Nay, you may erre in this,	139	U2 Another	9
What you please, you parts may call,	142	U2 Exception	7
Mixe then your Notes, that we may prove	143	U3 Musicall	9
May wish us of their Quire.	144	U3 Musicall	28
They yet may envie me:	147	U7 Nymph	9
Where Love may all his Torches light,	147	U7 Nymph	24
That I may love your Person (as I doe)	157	U13 Sacvile	157
May grow so great to be example, when	158	U13 Sacvile	161
A pennance, where a man may not be free,	158	U14 Selden	8
Rather then Office, when it doth or may	158	U14 Selden	9
How they may make some one that day an Asse	164	U15 Friend-Wars	64
That may corrupt her, even in his eyes.	165	U15 Friend-Wars	92
That may stand by, and hold my peace? will he,	167	U15 Friend-Wars	150
That watch, and catch, at what they may applaud,	167	U15 Friend-Wars	157
Debts when they can: good men may breake their day,	169	U17 Friend-Debt	2
Oh how a Lover may mistake! to thinke,	170	U18 Elegy Can	15
Where men at once may plant, and gather blisses:	170	U19 Elegy By	10
So well as I may tell in verse, 'tis so?	170	U19 Elegy By	12
(Though they may number bodyes) or but one.	171	U19 Elegy By	14
And so that either may example prove	171	U19 Elegy By	16
Others, in time may love, as we doe now.	171	U19 Elegy By	18
Amongst my many other, that I may	171	U20 Shrub	3
That I may sing my thoughts, in some unvulgar straine.	177	U25 Desmond	13
May shine (through every chincke) to every sight	177	U25 Desmond	16
Where men may see whom I doe sing?	182	U27 Ode Helen	32
May his joynts tormented bee,	184	U29 Fit of Rime	50
Still may Syllabes jarre with time,	184	U29 Fit of Rime	52
Stil may reason warre with rime,	184	U29 Fit of Rime	53
May his Sense, when it would meet	184	U29 Fit of Rime	55
So, justest Lord, may all your Judgements be	185	U31 Elsmere	1
So, may the King proclaime your Conscience is	185	U31 Elsmere	3
So, from all sicknesse, may you rise to health,	186	U31 Elsmere	5

MAY (cont.)

	Page	Title	Line
So may the gentler Muses, and good fame	186	U31 Elsmere	7
So may the fruitfull Vine my temples steepe,	190	U37 Friend-Book	14
Or there to sterve it. Helpe, O you that may	191	U38 Elegy 'Tis	7
There may some face or menace of a storme	191	U38 Elegy 'Tis	13
Thinke that I once was yours, or may be now;	192	U38 Elegy 'Tis	35
Errour and folly in me may have crost	192	U38 Elegy 'Tis	37
You may so place me, and in such an ayre,	192	U38 Elegy 'Tis	51
O may your wisdome take example hence,	193	U38 Elegy 'Tis	67
I may dilate my selfe, but not depart.	194	U38 Elegy 'Tis	118
For though Love thrive, and may grow up with cheare,	197	U40 Elegy That	15
They may say Grace, and for Loves Chaplaines passe;	198	U40 Elegy That	31
That Article, may not become our lover:	198	U40 Elegy That	48
Till I may see both it and you agen.	199	U41 Elegy Since	22
Where I may handle Silke, as free, and neere,	200	U42 Elegy Let	30
Some Alchimist there may be yet, or odde	208	U43 Vulcan	118
May to thy name a Vulcanale say;	208	U43 Vulcan	120
May to thy name a Pagan prayer say;	208	U43 Vulcan	V120
As th'other may his braines with Quicksilver.	208	U43 Vulcan	122
They saw too store of feathers, and more may,	213	U44 Speach	9
But they may see Gold-Chaines, and Pearle worne then,	213	U44 Speach	13
These ten yeares day; As all may sweare that looke	213	U44 Speach	27
I may no longer on these pictures stay,	216	U44 Speach	98
But that's a blow, by which in time I may	219	U47 Tribe	51
Of earthen Jarres, there may molest me too:	219	U47 Tribe	55
So may the Muses follow	221	U48 Bacchus	25
So may there never Quarrell	221	U48 Bacchus	31
Whereby he may knit sure up	222	U48 Bacchus	47
Give me a deep-crown'd-Bowle, that I may sing	225	U51 Bacon	19
And you may justly, being a tardie, cold,	230	U56 Covell	7
What can the Poet wish his King may doe,	235	U62 Charles 1	13
The Mother of our Lord: why may not I	238	U66 Queene	3
The Harmony may pull	239	U67 Muses	20
May wish it selfe a sense,	239	U67 Muses	23
And in short measures, life may perfect bee.	245	U70 Ode	74
And what of Dignitie, and Honour may	255	U75 Epithalam.	92
Some houres before it should, that these may know	257	U75 Epithalam.	146
We pray may grace	257	U75 Epithalam.	158
Yet, as we may, we will, with chast desires,	257	U75 Epithalam.	161
And never may there want one of the Stem,	258	U75 Epithalam.	177
Aloud; and (happ'ly) it may last as long.	261	U77 Treasurer	28
As loude; and (happ'ly) it may last as long.	261	U77 Treasurer	V 28
That they may take it eccho'd by the Floods.	265	U79 New-yeares	53
And by thy blessing, may thy People see	268	U80 Christning	3
At least may beare th'inscription to her Tombe.	269	U81 Pawlet	18
To touch these Mysteries! We may admire	269	U81 Pawlet	31
To touch those Mysteries! We may admire	269	U81 Pawlet	V 31
T' inlive posteritie, her Fame may tell!	269	U81 Pawlet	34
May something by that twilight see	273	U84 Cradle	15
And Men may thinke, all light rose there.	276	U84 Body	16
May rather yet adore, then spy.	276	U84 Body	20
Painter yo' are come, but may be gone,	277	U84 Mind	1
But here I may no colours use.	277	U84 Mind	6
But here we may no colours use.	277	U84 Mind	V 6
Hence-forth may every line be you;	278	U84 Mind	22
That all may say, that see the frame,	278	U84 Mind	23
Where it may run to any good;	280	U84 Mind	62
With which, Priapus, he may thanke thy hands,	290	U85 Country	21
With which, Priapus, he may greet thy hands,	290	U85 Country	V 21
Then now beneath some ancient Oke he may,	290	U85 Country	23
Ye have oft-times, that may ore-shine the rest,	305	Horace	18
Ye have oft-times, that may out-shine the rest,	338	Horace	V 18
But light from smoake; that he may draw his bright	315	Horace	204
And so, as every man may hope the same;	321	Horace	350
Yet he that offers at it, may sweat much,	321	Horace	351
Him that buyes Pulse there, or perhaps may like	347	Horace	V354/362
Or rather, thinking all my faults may spie,	323	Horace	392
Whether truth may, and whether error bring.	325	Horace	439
A third of twelve, you may: foure ounces. Glad,	327	Horace	469
The docile mind may soone thy precepts know,	329	Horace	504
May, with some right, upon an Author creepe.	329	Horace	538
There may a Lawyer be, may not excell;	331	Horace	550
Or Pleader at the Barre, that may come short	331	Horace	551
Being tould there, Reason cannot, Sense may erre.	370	Author	14
That may judge for his six-pence) had, before	371	Fletcher	7
And that you may see he most luckily ment	379	Coryat 3	13
May aske, what Author would conceale his name?	383	Author	4
Who reads may roave, and call the passage darke,	383	Author	5
Yet may as blind men sometimes hit the marke.	383	Author	6
May take thy volume to his vertuous hand.	383	Author	8
To understand, hee may at length admire.	383	Author	10
May she, whome thou for spouse, to day, dost take,	384	Somerset	11
And thou to her, that Husband, may exalt	384	Somerset	13
So, may those Mariage-Pledges, comforts prove:	384	Somerset	19
So, in theyr number, may you never see	384	Somerset	21
That all, that view you then, and late; may say,	384	Somerset	25
May hurt them more with praise, then Foes with spight.	386	Browne	2
will all turne dust, & may not make me swell.	387	Cavendish	4
Will all be dust, & may not make me swell.	387	Cavendish	V 4
And this hath met that one, that may be stil'd	389	Aleman	13
For seeliest Ignorance on these may light,	390	Shakespeare	7
Or for the lawrell, he may gaine a scorne,	392	Shakespeare	63
Lend me thy voyce, O Fame, that I may draw	396	Drayton	12

	Page	Title	Line
MAY (cont.)			
That can but reade; who cannot, may in prose	398	Drayton	73
Besydes, his Man may merit it, and be	406	Inigo Jones 2	5
He may have skill & judgment to designe	406	Inigo Jones 2	7
Il may Ben Johnson slander so his feete,	418	Answer	5
he that will honest be, may quitt the Court,	423	Lucan	17
MAY'ADMIRE			
Tilter, the most may'admire thee, though not I:	36	E29 Tilter	1
MAY'ANY			
Nor may'any feare, to loose of their degree,	73	E113 Overbury	11
MAYD			
Most holy, & pure Virgin, blessed Mayd,	413	Ghyrlond	37
MAYDEN			
No more, those mayden glories shee hath lost.	83	E132 Sylvester	14
MAYMED			
If, maymed, she come off, 'tis not of men	401	Beaumont	16
MAYNE			
Ploughing the mayne. When, see (the worst of all lucks)	86	E133 Voyage	78
He is, or would be the mayne Dominus doe	404	Inigo Jones 1	64
The mayne comaund of scepters, soone doth perishe	422	Lucan	9
MAYOR (See MAIORS)			
MAYRESSE			
The Lady Mayresse pass'd through the Towne,	201	U42 Elegy Let	70
MAY'ST			
And thou, right guiltlesse, may'st plead to it, why?	36	E29 Tilter	2
The Chappell empties, and thou may'st be gone	257	U75 Epithalam.	137
MAYST			
So mayst thou still be younger	221	U48 Bacchus	21
Read here a little, that thou mayst know much.	371	Epitaph	2
Yet ware; thou mayst do all things cruellie:	423	Lucan	15
MAZE			
And, in their errors maze, thine owne way know:	76	E119 Shelton	13
Farre from the maze of custome, error, strife,	118	F13 Aubigny	60
ME'			
Art still at that, and think'st to blow me'up too?	72	E112 Gamster	6
ME (See also MEE)			
Thou call'st me Poet, as a terme of shame:	29	E10 Ignorant	1
It made me a great face, I ask'd the name.	30	E11 Something	4
Let me give two: that doubly am got free,	31	E13 Empirick	3
Just wife, and, to change me, make womans hast?	34	E25 Beast 1	1
What need hast thou of me? or of my Muse?	40	E43 Salisbury 1	1
Of adding to thy fame; thine may to me,	41	E43 Salisbury 1	8
Of adding to thy prayse; thine may to me,	41	E43 Salisbury 1 V	8
Seven yeeres tho'wert lent to me, and I thee pay,	41	E45 First Son	3
Play-wright me reades, and still my verses damnes,	42	E49 Playwrt 1	1
That unto me dost such religion use!	44	E55 Beaumont	2
At once thou mak'st me happie, and unmak'st;	44	E55 Beaumont	5
And giving largely to me, more thou tak'st.	44	E55 Beaumont	6
Thy praise, or dispraise is to me alike,	46	E61 Foole	1
One doth not stroke me, nor the other strike.	46	E61 Foole	2
Away, and leave me, thou thing most abhord,	48	E65 Muse	1
That hast betray'd me to a worthlesse lord;	48	E65 Muse	2
Made me commit most fierce idolatrie	48	E65 Muse	3
With me thou leav'st an happier Muse then thee,	48	E65 Muse	11
And which thou brought'st me, welcome povertie.	48	E65 Muse	12
But I repent me: Stay. Who e're is rais'd,	48	E65 Muse	15
Still, 'tis his lucke to praise me 'gainst his will.	50	E71 Parrat	2
In-primis, Grand, you owe me for a jest,	51	E73 Fine Grand	5
In most vile verses, and cost me more paine,	51	E73 Fine Grand	19
For which, or pay me quickly', or Ile pay you.	51	E73 Fine Grand	22
To one that desired me not to name him.	53	E77 Not name	Ttl
Forbeare to tempt me, Proule, I will not show	54	E81 Proule	1
To put out the word, whore, thou do'st me woo,	54	E83 Friend	1
I ask'd a lord a buck, and he denyed me;	54	E84 Bedford 2	2
For your most noble offer had supply'd me.	54	E84 Bedford 2	4
What would his serious actions me have learned?	55	E85 Goodyere 1	12
He wont was to encounter me, aloud,	62	E97 Motion	7
Where ere he met me; now hee's dumbe, or proud.	62	E97 Motion	8
Forgive me then, if mine but say you are	67	E103 L Wroth 1	9
He that not trusts me, having vow'd thus much,	70	E108 Soldiers	9
I passe to Elegies; Thou meet'st me there:	73	E112 Gamster	13
To Satyres; and thou dost pursue me. Where,	73	E112 Gamster	14
So Phoebus makes me worthy of his bayes,	73	E113 Overbury	1
With me can merit more, then that good man,	76	E119 Shelton	5
No, Shelton, give me thee, canst want all these,	76	E119 Shelton	7
Weepe with me all you that read	77	E120 S. P.	1
And bad me lay th'usurped laurell downe:	80	E126 Mrs Cary	4
They should be fooles, for me, at their owne charge.	83	E131 Ferrab. 2	8
All, that are readers: but, me thinkes 'tis od,	85	E133 Voyage	43
Canst tell me best, how every Furie lookes there,	85	E133 Voyage	52
To answere me. And sure, it was th'intent	87	E133 Voyage	107
With which he fled me: and againe,	93	F1 Why write no	8
But gives me what I call, and lets me eate,	95	F2 Penshurst	69
Little, for me, had reason done,	101	F4 To the World	35
Then, in a soile hast planted me,	101	F4 To the World	45
If't chance to me, I must not grutch.	101	F4 To the World	56
Kisse me, sweet: The warie lover	103	F6 Celia 2	1
But, forgive me, with thy crowne	105	F8 Sicknesse	18
Drinke to me, onely, with thine eyes,	106	F9 Celia 3	1
Drinke to me, Coelia, with thine eyes,	106	F9 Celia 3	V 1
And, who doth me (though I not him) envy,	115	F12 Rutland	70
By me, their priest (if they can ought divine)	119	F13 Aubigny	101
But which the Fates forbid me to reveale.	119	F13 Aubigny	107

		Page	Title		Line

ME (cont.)

	Page	Title		Line
Give me my cup, but from the Thespian well,	120	F14	Sydney	11
Is it interpreted in me disease,	122	F15	Heaven	3
And judge me after: if I dare pretend	122	F15	Heaven	7
For thy acceptance. O, behold me right,	127	U1	Trinitie	13
All's done in me.	128	U1	Trinitie	24
O grant it me!	128	U1	Trinitie	36
But left me free,	129	U1	Father	9
Me farther tosse,	130	U1	Father	30
But be glad, as soone with me,	131	U2	Excuse	17
Marke of glorie, come with me;	132	U2	How he saw	8
And my motion from me quite;	132	U2	How he saw	26
Eyes and limbes; to hurt me more.	133	U2	Suffered	4
Reconcil'd to Love, and me.	133	U2	Suffered	6
To revenge me with my Tongue,	133	U2	Suffered	24
'Mongst my Muses finding me,	136	U2	Cupid	7
For Loves-sake, kisse me once againe,	139	U2	Another	1
Of your Trouble, Ben, to ease me,	140	U2	Her man	1
I will tell what Man would please me.	140	U2	Her man	2
Titles, I confesse, doe take me;	140	U2	Her man	5
And a woman God did make me:	140	U2	Her man	6
And make Love or me afeard.	141	U2	Her man	24
As he durst love Truth and me.	142	U2	Her man	52
I can rest me where I am.	142	U2	Her man	56
For then their threats will kill me;	144	U4	Song	6
For then my hopes will spill me.	144	U4	Song	8
For so will sorrow slay me;	145	U4	Song	10
Mine owne enough betray me.	145	U4	Song	12
I Love, and he loves me againe,	147	U7	Nymph	1
They yet may envie me:	147	U7	Nymph	9
And he loves me; yet no	148	U7	Nymph	30
If Love, or feare, would let me tell his name.	148	U7	Nymph	35
Whom I adore so much, should so slight me,	149	J9	Picture	4
Tell me that she hath seene	149	U9	Picture	13
prompt me that she hath seene	149	U9	Picture	V 13
How cam'st thou thus to enter me?	150	U10	Jealousie	2
Or Scorne, or pittie on me take,	150	U11	Dreame	1
Hath both my heart and me surpriz'd,	151	U11	Dreame	5
Nor will he tell me for whose sake	151	U11	Dreame	7
He did me the Delight,	151	U11	Dreame	8
But leaves me to inquire,	151	U11	Dreame	10
Before me here, the Friend and Sonne;	151	U12	Corbet	4
That they for me their teares will shed;	152	U12	Corbet	34
And though my fortune humble me, to take	153	U13	Sacvile	15
To have such doe me good, I durst not name:	153	U13	Sacvile	18
That they have more opprest me, then my want?	153	U13	Sacvile	28
Or if he did it not to succour me,	154	U13	Sacvile	29
Must make me sad for what I have obtain'd.	154	U13	Sacvile	38
But then, fist-fill'd, to put me off the sent.	154	U13	Sacvile	52
All the Towne-curs take each their snatch at me.	155	U13	Sacvile	72
For me to be your Indice. Keep you such,	157	U13	Sacvile	156
Find you to reckon nothing, me owe all.	158	U13	Sacvile	164
Flowes in upon me, and I cannot raise	160	U14	Selden	62
Although, perhaps it has, what's that to me,	167	U15	Friend-Wars	149
Give me but that againe, that I must wast	167	U15	Friend-Wars	152
Give me but that againe, which I must wast	167	U15	Friend-Wars	V152
But that some greater names have broke with me,	169	U17	Friend-Debt	8
Simply my Band, his trust in me forsakes,	169	U17	Friend-Debt	12
Now so much friend, as you would trust in me,	169	U17	Friend-Debt	14
Can Beautie that did prompt me first to write,	169	U18	Elegy Can	1
Did her perfections call me on to gaze,	169	U18	Elegy Can	3
But which shall lead me on? both these are blind:	170	U18	Elegy Can	11
Tell me (my lov'd Friend) doe you love, or no,	170	U19	Elegy By	11
Forgive me this one foolish deadly sin,	171	U20	Shrub	2
Yet give me leave t'adore in you	174	U22	Elegy Tho	35
O then (my best-best lov'd) let me importune,	180	U25	Desmond	63
O then (our best-best lov'd) let me importune,	180	U25	Desmond	V 63
You favour Truth, and me, in this mans Cause.	186	U31	Elsmere	10
Have made me to conceive a Lawyer new.	187	U33	Councellour	14
And which you (being the worthier) gave me leave	190	U37	Friend-Book	11
And Fame wake for me, when I yeeld to sleepe.	190	U37	Friend-Book	15
Though you sometimes proclaime me too severe,	190	U37	Friend-Book	16
Forgive it, as my frailtie, and not me.	190	U37	Friend-Book	30
Of Graces, or your mercie here in me,	191	U38	Elegy 'Tis	16
The Subject of your Grace in pardoning me,	191	U38	Elegy 'Tis	28
Thinke it was frailtie, Mistris, thinke me man,	192	U38	Elegy 'Tis	31
Thinke that your selfe like heaven forgive me can:	192	U38	Elegy 'Tis	32
Errour and folly in me may have crost	192	U38	Elegy 'Tis	37
You may so place me, and in such an ayre,	192	U38	Elegy 'Tis	51
And let your mercie make me asham'd t'offend.	194	U38	Elegy 'Tis	106
How much you are the better part of me;	194	U38	Elegy 'Tis	110
And that there is no life in me, but love.	194	U38	Elegy 'Tis	112
Publike affaires command me now to goe	194	U38	Elegy 'Tis	114
This makes me, Mrs. that sometime by stealth,	197	U40	Elegy That	9
My health will leave me; and when you depart,	199	U41	Elegy Since	13
Your sacrifice, then here remaine with me.	199	U41	Elegy Since	18
Of me, I'le softly tread unto my Tombe.	199	U41	Elegy Since	20
Let me be what I am, as Virgil cold;	199	U42	Elegy Let	1
Who shall forbid me then in Rithme to bee	200	U42	Elegy Let	5
Put on my Ivy Garland, let me see	200	U42	Elegy Let	9
Who frownes, who jealous is, who taxeth me.	200	U42	Elegy Let	10
Then ope thy wardrobe, thinke me that poore Groome	201	U42	Elegy Let	51
Thou didst tell me; and wert o're-joy'd to peepe	201	U42	Elegy Let	59

	Page	Title	Line

ME (cont.)

And why to me this, thou lame Lord of fire, ... 202 U43 Vulcan 1
And why to me this, thou lame god of fire, ... 202 U43 Vulcan V 1
But, on thy malice, tell me, didst thou spie . . . 203 U43 Vulcan 19
A cause before; or leave me one behind. . . . . 203 U43 Vulcan 28
Thou mightst have had me perish, piece, by piece, . . 205 U43 Vulcan 51
Condemn'd me to the Ovens with the pies; . . . . 205 U43 Vulcan 54
And so, have kept me dying a whole age, ... 205 U43 Vulcan 55
At Common-Law: me thinkes in his despight . . . 211 U43 Vulcan 177
At Common-Law: me thinkes in this despight . . . 211 U43 Vulcan V177
To all as fatall as't hath beene to me, ... 211 U43 Vulcan 192
To all as chargefull as they have beene to me, . . 211 U43 Vulcan V192
What is't to me whether the French Designe . . . 219 U47 Tribe 31
Shall carry me at Call; and I'le be well, ... 219 U47 Tribe 45
Of earthen Jarres, there may molest me too: . . . 219 U47 Tribe 55
Are asked to climbe. First give me faith, who know . 220 U47 Tribe 75
Do's the Court-Pucell then so censure me, . . . 222 U49 Pucell 1
Give me a deep-crown'd-Bowle, that I may sing . . 225 U51 Bacon 19
With one great blot, yo'had form'd me as I am. . . 227 U52 Answer 12
With one great blot, you had drawne me as I am. . . 227 U52 Answer V 12
You made it a brave piece, but not like me. . . . 227 U52 Answer 15
Me thought I read the ancient Art of Thrace, . . . 228 U53 Newcastle 4
And hold me to it close; to stand upright . . . 229 U54 Squib 9
Lend me, deare Arthur, for a weeke five more, . . 229 U54 Squib 16
And you shall make me good, in weight, and fashion, . 229 U54 Squib 17
Verse, that should thee, and me out-live. . . . . 229 U55 Burges 4
I hate such measur'd, give me mettall'd fire . . . 233 U59 Newcastle 7
. . . he sent me in my Sicknesse. 1629. . . . 235 U62 Charles 1 Ttl
To be given me in gratuitie . . . . . . 259 U76 Petition 12
Hath drawne on me, from the times, ... 259 U76 Petition 17
Parts of me (they judg'd) decay'd, ... 259 U76 Petition 23
What reputation to my lines, and me, ... 263 U78 Digby 26
Me thought, Great Britaine in her Sea, before, . . 268 U80 Christning 13
Hayles me, so solemnly, to yonder Yewgh? . . . 268 U81 Pawlet 2
And beckning wooes me, from the fatall tree . . . 268 U81 Pawlet 3
. . . gave me leave to call her so. Being Her . . . 282 U84 Muse Ttl
All that was good, or great in me she weav'd, . . 282 U84 Muse 4
A sorrow in me, fit to wait to her! . . . . 282 U84 Muse 10
(For so thou art with me) now shee is gone. . . . 283 U84 Muse 22
Whoorles me about, and to blaspheme in fashion! . . 283 U84 Muse 32
Me now, nor Wench, nor wanton Boy, ... 293 U86 Hor.4:1 29
I thought me richer then the Persian King. . . . 293 U87 Hor.3:9 4
Heare me conclude; let what thou workst upon . . 339 Horace V 31
If thou would'st have me weepe, be thou first drown'd . 311 Horace 145
Thy selfe in teares, then me thy losse will wound, . 311 Horace 146
Thy selfe in tears, then me thy harms will wound, . . 342 Horace V146
Speake to me, Muse, the Man, who, after Troy was sack't, . 315 Horace 201
So he that flaggeth much, becomes to me . . . 329 Horace 533
Sonnes, seeke not me amonge these polish'd stones: . . 387 Cavendish 1
will all turne dust, & may not make me swell. . . 387 Cavendish 4
Will all be dust, & may not make me swell. . . . 387 Cavendish V 4
When you behold me wish my selfe, the man . . . 389 Aleman 23
It makes me ravish'd with just wonder, cry . . . 395 May 13
You have not writ to me, nor I to you: . . . . 396 Drayton 6
Lend me thy voyce, O Fame, that I may draw . . . 396 Drayton 12
Which made me thinke, the old Theocritus, . . . 397 Drayton 27
Did all so strike me, as I cry'd, who can . . . 397 Drayton 31
Thou hast deserv'd: And let me reade the while . . 398 Drayton 60
Thinking to stir me, thou hast lost thy End, . . . 410 Gill 9
(You have deserv'd it from me) I have read, . . . 415 Rutter 13
And God blesse me, and God blesse Raph. . . . 419 Grace 8

MEADES
Along'st the curled woods, and painted meades, . . 97 F3 Wroth 17

MEADOWS
Or the herb Sorrell, that loves Meadows still, . . 291 U85 Country 57

MEALE
For your next meale: this you are sure of. Why . . 69 E107 Hungry 27
Of newes, and noyse, to strow out a long meale. . . 74 E115 Honest Man 10
Of newes, and noyse, to sow out a long meale. . . 74 E115 Honest Man V 10
At every meale, where it doth dine, or sup, . . . 74 E115 Honest Man 23
Had made a meale for Vulcan to lick up. . . . 206 U43 Vulcan 84
Of newes they get, to strew out the long meale, . . 218 U47 Tribe 28
These, the free meale might have beene well drawne out: . 331 Horace 560

MEALES
He doth, at meales, alone, his pheasant eate, . . . 35 E28 Surly 12

MEAN
Those dull Girls, no good can mean us, ... 657 Door Apollo 11

MEANE (WEALTH)
The Roman Gentrie, men of birth, and meane, . . . 321 Horace 360

MEANE (MIDDLE)
(In the meane time, let 'hem imprison mee) . . . 87 E133 Voyage 104
I thought that Fortitude had beene a meane . . . 156 U13 Sacvile 105
Your change of Notes, the flat, the meane, the sharpe, . 263 U79 New-yeares 3
A meane, and toleration, which does well: . . . 331 Horace 549

MEANE
I have no salt: no bawdrie he doth meane. . . . 42 E49 Playwrt 1 3
Nor meane we those, whom vowes and conscience . . 111 F11 Epode 83
Nor meane I those, whose vowes and conscience . . 111 F11 Epode V 83
Meane what I speake: and still will keepe that Vow. . 159 U14 Selden 28
I meane that one paire, wherewith he so hobled . . 380 Coryat 3 41
I meane with great, but disproportion'd Muses: . . 391 Shakespeare 26
Or making of the Propertyes it meane? . . . . 402 Inigo Jones 1 12
To be worth Envy. Henceforth I doe meane . . . 405 Inigo Jones 1 70

		Page	Title	Line

MEANES
So huge, it seem'd, they could by no meanes quite her. . . . 86 E133 Voyage 86
Because lust's meanes are spent: . . . 111 F11 Epode 78
Their thoughts and meanes to making loude the cry; . . . 155 U13 Sacvile 66
Now threaten, with those meanes she did invite? . . . 169 U18 Elegy Can 2
At a Friends freedome, proves all circling meanes . . . 242 U69 Friend Son 15

MEANEST
Shift, here, in towne, not meanest among squires, . . . 30 E12 Shift 1
There comes sometimes to things of meanest place. . . . 321 Horace 354

MEANT   (See also MENT)
All which I meant to praise, and, yet, I would; . . . 34 E23 Donne 1 9
He meant they thither should make swift repaire, . . . 41 E44 Chuff 5
That whil'st I meant but thine to gratulate, . . . 48 E64 Salisbury 3 17
I meant to make her faire, and free, and wise, . . . 52 E76 Bedford 1 5
I meant the day-starre should not brighter rise, . . . 52 E76 Bedford 1 7
I meant shee should be curteous, facile, sweet, . . . 52 E76 Bedford 1 9
I meant each softest vertue, there should meet, . . . 52 E76 Bedford 1 11
Such when I meant to faine, and wish'd to see, . . . 52 E76 Bedford 1 17
As I did feele it done, as soone as meant: . . . 153 U13 Sacvile 12
That as the last of punishments is meant; . . . 192 U38 Elegy 'Tis 43
And so did Jove, who ne're meant thee his Cup: . . . 208 U44 Vulcan 115
Or that the Match from Spaine was ever meant? . . . 219 U47 Tribe 36
Or taste a part of that full joy he meant . . . 246 U70 Ode 87
It is: to th' envious meant, . . . 256 U75 Epithalam. 119
Was meant at first. Why, forcing still about . . . 307 Horace 29
But neither, Men, nor Gods, nor Pillars meant, . . . 331 Horace 555
Looke paie, distill a showre (was never meant) . . . 333 Horace 612
Look pale, distill a dew was never meant . . . 353 Horace V612
Were not the paths I meant unto thy praise: . . . 390 Shakespeare 6

MEASURE
And laugh, and measure thighes, then squeake, spring, itch, . . . 164 U15 Friend-Wars 75
Cosening Judgement with a measure, . . . 183 U29 Fit of Rime 5
Of true measure, . . . 184 U29 Fit of Rime 45
This day the Court doth measure . . . 240 U67 Muses 43
In weight, in measure, number, sound, . . . 244 U70 Ode 50
And those in number so, and measure rais'd, . . . 395 May 8
In number, measure, or degree . . . 399 Lady Ogle 23

MEASUR'D
I hate such measur'd, give me mettall'd fire . . . 233 U59 Newcastle 7
For, what is life, if measur'd by the space, . . . 243 U70 Ode 21
To his strength, hath measur'd it out with his feet. . . . 379 Coryat 3 4

MEASURES
To light: her measures are, how well . . . 245 U70 Ode 62
And in short measures, life may perfect bee. . . . 245 U70 Ode 74

MEASURING
These looke you up at, with a measuring eye, . . . 261 U77 Treasurer V 23

MEAT
Is nothing, such scarce meat and drinke he'le give, . . . 167 U15 Friend-Wars 159

MEATE
Of which wee'll speake our minds, amidst our meate; . . . 65 E101 Supper 23
Doe what you come for, Captayne, There's your meate. . . . 69 E107 Hungry 32
So all his meate he tasteth over, twise: . . . 76 E118 Gut 2
The meate-boate of Beares colledge, Paris-garden, . . . 87 E133 Voyage 117
Laxative lettuce, and such windie meate) . . . 88 E133 Voyage 167
Without his feare, and of thy lords owne meate: . . . 95 F2 Penshurst 62
He knowes, below, he shall finde plentie of meate, . . . 95 F2 Penshurst 70
Had bin fitt meate for Vulcan to lick up. . . . 206 U43 Vulcan V 84

MEATE-BOATE
The meate-boate of Beares colledge, Paris-garden, . . . 87 E133 Voyage 117

MEATES
Cloth Spices, or guard sweet meates from the flies; . . . 205 U43 Vulcan V 53

MEATS
For t'other pound of sweet-meats, he shall feele . . . 164 U15 Friend-Wars 77

MEAZLED
The sinkes ran grease, and haire of meazled hogs, . . . 88 F133 Voyage 145

MECHANICK
This is the money-gett, Mechanick Age! . . . 404 Inigo Jones 1 52

MED'CIN'D
In hast the bottome of a med'cin'd Cup, . . . 197 U40 Elegy That 4

MEDDLE
(Who hath the hundred hands when he doth meddle) . . . 86 E133 Voyage 82
With Nicholas Pasquill's, Meddle with your match, . . . 206 U43 Vulcan 77
With Nicholas Bretons Meddle with your match, . . . 206 U43 Vulcan V 77

MEDDOWES
The mowed meddowes, with the fleeced sheepe, . . . 97 F3 Wroth 39

MEDEA
Medea make brave with impetuous scorne; . . . 313 Horace 175
Medea make wild, fierce, impetuous; . . . 342 Horace V175
Present anone: Medea must not kill . . . 317 Horace 263

MEDIATE
To heare, to mediate, sweeten my desire, . . . 128 U1 Trinitie 42

MEDICINE
Before you prove a medicine, is unjust. . . . 192 U38 Elegy 'Tis 50

MEDITATIONS
To Mrs. Alice Sutcliffe, on her divine Meditations. . . . 411 Sutcliffe Ttl
When I had read your holy Meditations, . . . 411 Sutcliffe 1

MEDWAY
And if the high-swolne Medway faile thy dish, . . . 94 F2 Penshurst 31

MEE
Thy title, Epigrammes, and nam'd of mee, . . . 27 E2 My Booke 2
When even there, where most thou praysest mee, . . . 44 E55 Beaumont 9
O Madame, if your grant did thus transferre mee, . . . 55 E84 Bedford 2 9
Make it your gift. See whither that will beare mee. . . . 55 E84 Bedford 2 10

401

	Page	Title	Line
MEE (cont.)			
How can so great example dye in mee,	57	E89 Allen	7
But that, which most doth take my Muse, and mee,	65	E101 Supper	28
By thy great helpe: and doth proclaime by mee,	72	E111 Edmonds 2	13
By thy great Art: and doth proclaime by mee,	72	E111 Edmonds 2	V 13
So, all reward, or name, that growes to mee	80	E127 Aubigny	9
(In the meane time, let 'hem imprison mee)	87	E133 Voyage	104
Can Poets hope to fetter mee?	93	F1 Why write no	4
More hatred, then thou hast to mee.	101	F4 To the World	40
And sent'st it backe to mee:	106	F9 Celia 3	14
which rap's mee up to the true heav'en of love;	108	F10 Proludium	13
As thou art all, so be thou all to mee,	122	F15 Heaven	9
And whither rap'd, now thou but stoup'st to mee?	122	F15 Heaven	14
Heare mee, O God!	129	U1 Father	1
Beene sterne to mee,	129	U1 Father	8
Mee, the scope of his next draught,	133	U2 Suffered	11
What need of mee? doe you but sing,	143	U3 Musicall	13
Now dam'mee, Sir, if you shall not command	154	U13 Sacvile	53
You won not Verses, Madam, you won mee,	230	U56 Covell	1
To mee; or beene the same to you; if show,	241	U69 Friend Son	2
Have cast a trench about mee, now, five yeares;	248	U71 Treasurer	6
To pluck a Garland, for her selfe, or mee?	268	U81 Pawlet	4
A horrour in mee! all my blood is steele!	269	U81 Pawlet	8
Could you containe your laughter? Credit mee,	305	Horace	7
Right spare, and warie: then thou speak'st to mee	307	Horace	66
Next, that which rapt mee, was: I might behold	361	Palmer	13
hath armde att all poyntes; charge mee humblye kneele	382	Rich	2
Yet give mee leave, to wonder at the birth	398	Drayton	83
I call the world, that envies mee, to see	398	Drayton	93
By barking against mee. Thou look'st at least,	408	Detractor	10
Censure, not sharplye then, but mee advise	421	Censure	1
Forgive it as my Frayltie, and not mee.	422	Censure	23
MEEDS			
Through which, our merit leads us to our meeds.	53	E80 Life/Death	2
MEEK			
Great Queen of Queens, most mild, most meek, most wise,	414	Ghyrlond	41
MEERE			
To my meere English Censurer.	32	E18 Censurer	Ttl
I lent you, on meere acquaintance, at a feast.	51	E73 Fine Grand	6
Think'st thou it is meere fortune, that can win?	72	E112 Gamster	3
In meere out-formes, untill he lost his sight,	73	E114 Sydney	4
Is meere necessitie.	111	F11 Epode	82
But by meere Chance? for interest? or to free	154	U13 Sacvile	30
All other Acts of Worldlings, are meere toyle	162	U15 Friend-Wars	V 9
Is natures meere obliquitie! as Heaven	192	U38 Elegy 'Tis	64
But, O those Reeds! thy meere disdaine of them,	208	U43 Vulcan	129
But, O those weedes: thy meere disdaine of them,	208	U43 Vulcan	V129
A meere upbraiding Griefe, and tort'ring punishment.	256	U75 Epithalam.	120
Are, by thy cunning placing, made meere new.	307	Horace	68
A meere new person, looke he keepe his state	313	Horace	180
Meere raigning words: nor will I labour so	321	Horace	343
But meere Iambicks all, from first to last.	323	Horace	374
Of verse meere-matter-lesse, and tinckling toies.	327	Horace	460
Into the Profits, what a meere rude braine	331	Horace	583
MEERELY			
Let those that meerely talke, and never thinke,	218	U47 Tribe	9
MEERE-MATTER-LESSE			
Of verse meere-matter-lesse, and tinckling toies.	327	Horace	460
MEET (PROPER)			
He always gives what he knowes meet;	99	F3 Wroth	98
He always gives what he thinks meet;	99	F3 Wroth	V 98
An offring meet	127	U1 Trinitie	12
MEET			
I meant each softest vertue, there should meet,	52	E76 Bedford 1	11
At sixe and twentie, ripe. You shall 'hem meet,	58	E92 New Crie	4
They meet in sixes, and at every mart,	59	E92 New Crie	21
Yet thou, perhaps, shalt meet some tongues will grutch,	72	E111 Edmonds 2	9
And perfect in a circle alwayes meet.	81	E128 Wm Roe 2	8
Goe enter breaches, meet the cannons rage,	98	F3 Wroth	69
Untill they meet	129	U1 Father	15
Then when flowers, and West-winds meet,	137	U2 Cupid	28
To meet their high desire;	144	U3 Musicall	26
And every close did meet	149	U9 Picture	7
And all my closes meet	149	U9 Picture	V 7
The way to meet, what others would upbraid;	153	U13 Sacvile	10
Meet some new matter to looke up and wonder!	157	U13 Sacvile	142
Be brought by us to meet our Destinie.	170	U18 Elegy Can	20
May his Sense, when it would meet	184	U29 Fit of Rime	55
Rather than meet him: And, before his eyes	185	U30 Burleigh	16
Of parting, drowne it in the hope to meet	197	U40 Elegy That	7
The Academie, where the Gallants meet--	215	U44 Speach	89
They meet the fire, the Test, as Martyrs would;	218	U47 Tribe	3
Or the States Ships sent forth belike to meet	219	U47 Tribe	33
For when they find so many meet in one,	225	U50 Countesse	35
Of bodies, meet like rarified ayre!	233	U59 Newcastle	10
Let Ireland meet it out at Sea, halfe way,	249	U72 King	5
Thou canst not meet more Glory, on the way,	252	U75 Epithalam.	3
Where all heroique ample thoughts doe meet:	262	U78 Digby	10
When shee departed? you will meet her there,	285	U84 Muse	108
Shall meet with gladnesse in one Theatre;	285	U84 Muse	114
But if, to boot with these, a chaste Wife meet	291	U85 Country	39
And in the Salian manner meet	292	U86 Hor.4:1	27

MEETE   (PROPER)
  Who, because his matter in all should be meete,   .   .   .   379   Coryat 3   3
MEETE
  His proofe their praise, will meete, as in this line.   .   .   362   Author   14
  Out in the Dog-daies, least the killer meete   .   .   .   409   Detractor   20
  for when the profitt with the payne doth meete,   .   .   418   Answer   6
MEETING
  Of feast, and merry meeting, ...   221   U48 Bacchus   15
  Meeting of Graces, that so swell'd the flood   .   .   .   274   U84 Descent   10
  When night their meeting covers.   365   Ode Splendor   8
MEETS
  To every cause he meets, this voyce he brayes: .   .   31   E12 Shift   19
  Is it for these that Fine-man meets the street   .   .   .   165   U15 Friend-Wars 106
  The Bridegroome meets the Bride   254   U75 Epithalam.   71
  Thou paint a Lane, where Thumb the Pygmy meets!   .   .   407   Inigo Jones 2   12
  Thou paint a Lane, where Thumb with Geffry meets!   .   .   407   Inigo Jones 2 V 12
MEET'ST
  I passe to Elegies; Thou meet'st me there: .   .   .   73   E112 Gamster   13
MELANCHOLIE
  Your Joane to passe her melancholie time.   .   .   .   231   U56 Covell   24
  Cary to passe her melancholie time.   231   U56 Covell   V 24
MELANCHOLIQUE
  Immortall, tooke a melancholique, odde   335   Horace   662
MELANCHOLY
  But it must, straight, my melancholy bee?   .   .   .   122   F15 Heaven   2
MELEAGER
  Of Meleager, brings he the returne   315   Horace   208
MELLOW
  And grave as ripe, like mellow as their faces.   .   .   59   E92 New Crie   7
  His head, with mellow Apples crown'd, ...   290   U85 Country   18
MELT
  Thy thoughts did never melt in amorous fire,   .   .   .   108   F10 Proludium   3
  Melt downe their husbands land, to poure away   .   .   118   F13 Aubigny   73
MELTED
  For, here they were throwne in wi'the melted pewter,   .   88   E133 Voyage   153
MELTS
  And pleaseth both. For while he melts his greace   .   .   38   E37 Chev'ril   3
MEMORIE
  In memorie of which most liquid deed, ...   89   E133 Voyage   193
  The memorie delights him more, from whom   .   .   .   153   U13 Sacvile   21
  The light of Truth, and life of Memorie.   .   .   .   176   U24 Frontispice 18
  To put all relish from my memorie   197   U40 Elegy That   6
  To the immortall memorie, and friendship of that noble . . .   242   U70 Ode   Ttl
  And there he lives with memorie; and Ben   .   .   .   246   U70 Ode   84
  How they doe keepe alive his memorie;   416   Dover   5
MEMORY
  To the memory of my beloved, the Author   390   Shakespeare   Ttl
MEMORYE
  To the memorye of that most Honoured Ladie Jane, . . .   394   Jane Ogle   Ttl
MEN
  As mad-men stones: not caring whom they hit.   .   .   27   E2 My Booke   6
  And by thy wiser temper, let men know   27   E2 My Booke   8
  When men a dangerous disease did scape,   .   .   .   31   E13 Empirick   1
  All men are wormes: But this no man.   In silke   .   .   31   E15 Court-worm   1
  As guiltie men doe magistrates: glad I,   .   .   .   32   E17 Critic   2
  When thou wert wont t'admire, not censure men.   .   .   32   E18 Censurer   8
  What severall wayes men to their calling have!   .   .   33   E21 Gam'ster   7
  He speakes to men with a Rhinocerotes nose,   .   .   35   E28 Surly   4
  And, that is done, as he saw great men doe.   .   .   .   35   E28 Surly   6
  'Tofore, great men were glad of Poets: Now,   .   .   40   E43 Salisbury 1   5
  When, in my booke, men reade but Cecill's name,   .   .   41   E43 Salisbury 1   9
  When, in my Verse, men reade but Sarum's name,   .   .   41   E43 Salisbury 1 V 9
  That quit'st the cause so oft, and rayl'st at men?   .   .   44   E54 Chev'ril 2   4
  Since men have left to doe praise-worthy things,   .   .   49   E67 Suffolk   1
  Stand high, then, Howard, high in eyes of men,   .   .   49   E67 Suffolk   5
  Play-wright convict of publike wrongs to men,   .   .   49   E68 Playwrt 2   1
  So to front death, as men might judge us past it.   .   .   54   E80 Life/Death   7
  For good men but see death, the wicked tast it.   .   .   54   E80 Life/Death   8
  Or that I'have by, two good sufficient men,   .   .   .   54   E81 Proule   3
  Where I both learn'd, why wise-men hawking follow,   .   55   E85 Goodyere 1   3
  Shee doth instruct men by her gallant flight,   .   .   55   E85 Goodyere 1   5
  As french-men in his companie, should seeme dutch?   .   56   E88 Monsieur   8
  As skilfull Roscius, and grave Aesope, men,   .   .   .   56   E89 Allen   3
  Can write the things, the causes, and the men.   .   .   62   E95 Savile   34
  If time to facts, as unto men would owe?   .   .   .   64   E99 Th Foe 2   6
  Nor shall our cups make any guiltie men: .   .   .   65   E101 Supper   37
  If men get name, for some one vertue: Then,   .   .   .   68   E106 E Herbert   1
  What man art thou, that art so many men,   .   .   .   68   E106 E Herbert   2
  Give your yong States-men, (that first make you drunke,   .   69   E107 Hungry   19
  Could make such men, and such a place repent: .   .   73   E113 Overbury   10
  Executes men in picture. By defect, ...   75   E115 Honest Man   29
  Jephson, thou man of men, to whose lov'd name   .   .   75   E116 Jephson   1
  In men, but every bravest was the best: .   .   .   75   E116 Jephson   10
  Old men so duely, ...   77   E120 S. P.   14
  Countries, and climes, manners, and men to know,   .   .   80   E128 Wm Roe 2   2
  Men love thee not for this: They laugh at thee.   .   .   81   E129 Mime   18
  T'alledge, that greatest men were not asham'd,   .   .   82   E130 Ferrab. 1   9
  And though we could all men, all censures heare,   .   .   83   E131 Ferrab. 2   5
  And, for the cryes of Ghosts, women, and men,   .   .   84   E133 Voyage   16
  Betweene two walls; where, on one side, to scar men,   .   86   E133 Voyage   67
  Were seene your ugly Centaures, yee call Car-men,   .   .   86   E133 Voyage   68
  Stil'd but the shaddowes of us men?   104   F7 Women but   6
  So men at weakest, they are strongest,   .   .   .   104   F7 Women but   9

MEN (cont.)

	Page	Title	Line
Stil'd but the shaddowes of us men?	104	F7 Women but	12
Doe not men, ynow of rites	104	F8 Sicknesse	3
Sicknesse; onely on us men.	105	F8 Sicknesse	14
While it makes huishers serviceable men,	113	F12 Rutland	9
Gave killing strokes. There were brave men, before	114	F12 Rutland	53
Men are not just, or keepe no holy lawes	117	F13 Aubigny	18
And men	121	F14 Sydney	43
The Birth-day shines, when logs not burne, but men.	121	F14 Sydney	60
Poets, though divine, are men:	131	U2 Excuse	5
Where, you say, men gather blisses,	136	U2 Cupid	26
Men, if you love us, play no more	145	U5 Woman-kind	1
Seeke doubting Men to please,	150	U10 Jealousie	15
It chid the vice, yet not the Men.	152	U12 Corbet	28
Lesse list of proud, hard, or ingratefull Men.	153	U13 Sacvile	4
Lest Ayre, or Print, but flies it: Such men would	154	U13 Sacvile	45
But these men ever want: their very trade	155	U13 Sacvile	79
That men such reverence to such actions show!	156	U13 Sacvile	98
Men have beene great, but never good by chance,	156	U13 Sacvile	124
'Tis by degrees that men arrive at glad	157	U13 Sacvile	131
Then stands it a triumphall marke! then Men	157	U13 Sacvile	139
Such Notes are vertuous men! they live as fast	157	U13 Sacvile	143
(As their true rule or lesson) either men,	158	U13 Sacvile	162
Men past their termes, and prais'd some names too much,	159	U14 Selden	21
Before men get a verse: much lesse a Praise;	159	U14 Selden	26
Of generall knowledge; watch'd men, manners too,	159	U14 Selden	33
To lose the formes, and dignities of men,	166	U15 Friend-Wars	146
For, if such men as he could die,	168	U16 Gray	6
Debts when they can: good men may breake their day,	169	U17 Friend-Debt	2
Such Guides men use not, who their way would find,	170	U18 Elegy Can	12
To see men feare: or else for truth, and State,	170	U18 Elegy Can	17
Where men at once may plant, and gather blisses:	170	U19 Elegy By	10
By whom he is restor'd to men:	173	U22 Elegy-Tho	15
For men to use their fortune reverently,	181	U26 Ode High	23
Where men may see whom I doe sing?	182	U27 Ode Helen	32
That, henceforth, I beleeve nor bookes, nor men,	187	U33 Councellour	5
So dost thou studie matter, men, and times,	187	U33 Councellour	15
And then I taste it. But as men drinke up	197	U40 Elegy That	3
Or like a Ghost walke silent amongst men,	199	U41 Elegy Since	21
Well fare the wise-men yet, on the Banckside,	208	U43 Vulcan	123
But say, all sixe good men, what answer yee?	210	U43 Vulcan	173
So doth the King, and most of the Kings men	212	U43 Vulcan	211
Launces, and men, and some a breaking force.	213	U44 Speach	8
Lent by the London Dames, to the Lords men;	213	U44 Speach	14
Insert thy Hodges, and those newer men,	214	U44 Speach	53
And could (if our great men would, let their Sonnes	214	U44 Speach	57
We will beleeve, like men of our owne Ranke,	215	U44 Speach	75
Deceit is fruitfull. Men have Masques and nets,	216	U45 Squib	18
Men that are safe, and sure, in all they doe,	218	U47 Tribe	1
But for a Sealing: let these men protest.	218	U47 Tribe	15
Let these men have their wayes, and take their times	218	U47 Tribe	25
Countries, and Climes, manners, and men to know.	224	U50 Countesse	22
The fire, the wine, the men! and in the midst,	225	U51 Bacon	3
To judge; So all men comming neere can spie,	242	U69 Friend Son	20
And had his noble name advanc'd with men:	244	U70 Ode	36
Such truths, as we expect for happy men,	246	U70 Ode	83
Of two so early men,	247	U70 Ode	125
Who seldome sleepes! whom bad men only hate!	250	U73 Weston	6
And by his Rise, in active men, his Name	256	U75 Epithalam.	116
To Th'Best Of Monarchs, Masters, Men, King Charles	259	U76 Petition	2
To compose men, and manners; stint the strife	261	U77 Treasurer	18
To Compasse men, and manners; stint the strife	261	U77 Treasurer V	18
We sing the best of Monarchs, Masters, Men;	263	U79 New-yeares	7
Hee were the wretched'st of the race of men:	272	U81 Pawlet	97
And Men may thinke, all light rose there.	276	U84 Body	16
Which all men doe, that urge not their owne deeds	281	U84 Kenelme	17
Of the Cethegi; And all men will grace,	309	Horace	72
Once rowable, but now doth nourish men	309	Horace	94
Saw many Townes, and Men, and could their manners tract.	315	Horace	202
The parts of age to youth be given; or men	317	Horace	252
It still must favour good men, and to these	317	Horace	280
Like men street-borne, and neere the Hall, reherse	321	Horace	357
Like men Town-born, and neere the place, reherse	347	Horace	V349/357
The Roman Gentrie, men of birth, and meane,	321	Horace	360
Being men were covetous of nought, but praise.	327	Horace	463
First frighted men, that wildly liv'd, at ods,	327	Horace	480
The Poems void of profit, our grave men	329	Horace	511
But neither, Men, nor Gods, nor Pillars meant,	331	Horace	555
Rich men are said with many cups to plie,	333	Horace	617
Great men are said with many cups to plye,	354	Horace	V617
And cry aloud, Helpe, gentle Countrey-men,	335	Horace	653
How many learned men he have drawne with his hooke	380	Coryat 3	44
unto thee, king of men; their noblest partes	382	Rich	3
your Royal Eye which still creates new men	383	Rich	14
Yet may as blind men sometimes hit the marke.	383	Author	6
Some men, of Bookes or Freinds not speaking right,	386	Browne	1
As, now, of all men, it is call'd thy Trade:	389	Chapman	11
Shall finde, that either hath read Bookes, and Men:	389	Aleman	2
Are still th'interpreters twixt godds, and men!	395	May	18
If, maymed, she come off, 'tis not of men	401	Beaumont	16
And all men eccho you have made a Masque.	403	Inigo Jones 1	30
Be Inigo, the Whistle, & his men!	405	Inigo Jones 1	66
Thy Dirty braines, Men smell thy want of worth.	409	Detractor	22

MEN (cont.)
    It was not so of old: Men tooke up trades . . . . . 410 Brome 13
    And the Physician teach men spue, or shite; . . . . 410 Brome 16
    By those deepe-grounded, understanding men, ... 414 Rutter 7
    Such men I met withall, and so have you. . . . . . 415 Rutter 11
    And a Comptroller, two most rigid men . . . . . 415 Rutter 24
    Yff Men, and tymes were nowe . . . . . . 419 Ode:If Men 1
MENACE
    There may some face or menace of a storme . . . . 191 U38 Elegy 'Tis 13
MENACINGS
    Sad language fits sad lookes; stuff'd menacings, . . . 311 Horace 149
MEND
    I will but mend the last, and tell . . . . . 139 U2 Another 13
    A-while with us bright Sun, and mend our light; . . . 252 U75 Epithalam. V 2
    Still in the same, and warned will not mend, . . . 329 Horace 530
    To change, and mend, what you not forth doe set. . . 331 Horace 579
    Hee'd say, Mend this, good friend, and this: 'tis naught. . 333 Horace 624
    He'd say, mend this my friend, and this, 'tis nought. . 354 Horace V624
    He sayes to the world, let any man mend it, . . . 379 Coryat 3 15
MENDED
    Her language, if the Stay, and Care t'have mended, . . 325 Horace 413
    How well, and how often his shoes too were mended, . . 380 Coryat 3 39
MENDICANT
    . . . England. An Epistle Mendicant. 1631. . . . 248 U71 Treasurer Ttl
MENDING
    7. Begging another, on colour of mending the former. . . 139 U2 Another Ttl
    Doe not despaire my mending; to distrust . . . 192 U38 Elegy 'Tis 49
MENDS
    But like to be, that every day mends one, ... 156 U13 Sacvile 116
MENS
    Mens manners ne're were viler, for your sake. . . . 34 E24 Parliament 2
    And, can forget mens names, with a great grace. . . 35 E28 Surly 8
    Where good mens vertues them to honors bring, . . . 47 E64 Salisbury 3 11
    When, in mens wishes, so thy vertues wrought, . . . 49 E67 Suffolk 7
    Who more should seeke mens reverence, then feare. . . 58 E91 Vere 18
    At great mens tables) and yet dine away. . . . . 95 F2 Penshurst 66
    Song. That Women are but Mens shaddowes. . . . . 104 F7 Women but Ttl
    Painted, or carv'd upon our great-mens tombs, . . . 114 F12 Rutland 45
    On all mens Fruit, and flowers, as well as mine. . . 150 U10 Jealousie 8
    And draw, and conquer all mens love, ... 173 U22 Elegy Tho 7
    What fate is this, to change mens dayes and houres, . . 199 U41 Elegy Since 9
    Of worthiest knowledge, that can take mens minds. . . 217 U46 Coke 20
    Hee stoop'd in all mens sight . . . . . 244 U70 Ode 38
    Of Princes aides, or good mens Charities. . . . 248 U71 Treasurer 3
    Mens Loves unto the Lawes, and Lawes to love the Crowne. . 255 U75 Epithalam. 104
    Whose shapes, like sick-mens dreames, are fain'd so vaine, . 305 Horace 9
    Whose shapes, like sick-mens dreames, are form'd so vaine, . 338 Horace V 9
    After, mens Wishes, crown'd in their events, . . . 309 Horace 108
    Mens faces, still, with such as laugh, are prone . . 311 Horace 143
    Mens count'nances, with such as laugh, are prone . . 342 Horace V143
    Yet so the scoffing Satyres to mens view, . . . 321 Horace 328
    'Tis true, and all mens suffrage. But these wayes . . 390 Shakespeare 5
MENT
    And that you may see he most luckily ment . . . 379 Coryat 3 13
MENTION
    Least mention of a Nymph, a Muse, a Grace, . . . 67 E105 L Wroth 2 4
MENTION'D
    Glad-mention'd Roe: thou art but gone before, . . . 37 E33 Roe 3 2
MERCAT
    View'd there the mercat, read the wretched rate . . . 234 U61 Epigram 3
MERCER
    As any Mercer; or the whale-bone man . . . . 200 U42 Elegy Let 31
MERCHANT
    'T is not alone the Merchant, but the Clowne, . . . 237 U64 Charles 3 19
    A ventring Merchant, or the Farmer free . . . 313 Horace 165
    A ventring Merchant, or the husband free . . . 342 Horace V165
MERCHANTS
    A Merchants Wife is Regent of the Scale. . . . . 229 U54 Squib 4
MERCIE
    Of Graces, or your mercie here in me, ... 191 U38 Elegy 'Tis 16
    And let your mercie make me asham'd t'offend. . . . 194 U38 Elegy 'Tis 106
MERCIES
    And (stil'd your mercies Creature) will live more . . 191 U38 Elegy 'Tis 29
MERCURY
    Poore Mercury, crying out on Paracelsus, ... 86 E133 Voyage 96
    Their Mercury did now. By this, the stemme . . . 87 E133 Voyage 111
    Our eares, or like a Mercury to charme! . . . . 392 Shakespeare 46
MERCY
    What love with mercy mixed doth appeare? . . . . 286 U84 Muse 138
    The doore of Grace, and found the Mercy-Seat. . . . 288 U84 Muse 190
MERCY-SEAT
    The doore of Grace, and found the Mercy-Seat. . . . 288 U84 Muse 190
MERD
    Who shall discharge first his merd-urinous load: . . . 85 E133 Voyage 65
MERD-URINOUS
    Who shall discharge first his merd-urinous load: . . . 85 E133 Voyage 65
MERE (See also MEERE)
    To turne mere farmer, had spoke out, ... 291 U85 Country 68
    In the mere perspective of an Inch board! . . . . 404 Inigo Jones 1 44
MERIT
    Where merit is not sepulcher'd alive. . . . . 47 E64 Salisbury 3 10
    Through which, our merit leads us to our meeds. . . 53 E80 Life/Death 2
    And thine owne goodnesse to encrease thy merit, . . . 60 E93 Radcliffe 10

```
                                                              Page      Title       Line
MERIT  (cont.)
    Onely to boast thy merit in supply.        .    .    .    .    61   E95 Savile       12
    Thou wert the first, mad'st merit know her strength,    .    .    75   E116 Jephson      5
    With me can merit more, then that good man,    .    .    .    76   E119 Shelton      5
    Might then both thee, thy worke and merit raise:    .    .    83   E132 Sylvester    2
    And each where boast it as his merit,    .    .    .    .    99   F3 Wroth         78
    A beautie of that merit, that should take    .    .    .    108   F10 Proludium    27
    To do't with Cloth, or Stuffes, lusts name might merit;    .    164   U15 Friend-Wars   57
    And keepes your merit        .    .    .    .    .    .    177   U25 Desmond      21
    You won them too, your oddes did merit it.    .    .    .    230   U56 Covell        4
    Nor did they merit the lesse Crowne to weare,    .    .    323   Horace          406
    Besydes, his Man may merit it, and be    .    .    .    406   Inigo Jones 2     5
MERITED
    But, in conclusion, merited no fame.    .    .    .    .    323   Horace          396
MERLINS
    To Merlins Marvailes, and his Caballs losse,    .    .    206   U43 Vulcan       71
    With Merlins Marvailes, and his tables losse,    .    .    206   U43 Vulcan     V 71
MERMAID
    At Bread-streets Mermaid, having din'd, and merry,    .    85   E133 Voyage      37
MERMAIDES
    Hath sent her Mermaides in,    .    .    .    .    .    368   Ode Who saith    91
MERMAIDS
    Which is the Mermaids, now, but shall be mine:    .    .    65   E101 Supper      30
MERRIE
    No, Mistris, no, the open merrie Man    .    .    .    .    198   U40 Elegy That   25
MERRY
    At Bread-streets Mermaid, having din'd, and merry,    .    85   E133 Voyage      37
    Alwayes at hand, to aide the merry Muses.    .    .    .    85   E133 Voyage      54
    That had, so often, shew'd 'hem merry prankes.    .    .    89   E133 Voyage     184
    And relish merry make him.        .    .    .    .    .    220   U48 Bacchus      12
    Of feast, and merry meeting,    .    .    .    .    .    221   U48 Bacchus      15
    To make you merry on the Dressing stoole    .    .    .    230   U56 Covell       21
    The merry Greeke, tart Aristophanes,    .    .    .    .    392   Shakespeare      51
    But a very merry wight        .    .    .    .    .    416   Moon              7
    To the merry beards in Hall,    .    .    .    .    .    417   Moon             13
MERSH
    That haunt Pickt-hatch, Mersh-Lambeth, and White-fryers,    .    30   E12 Shift         2
MERSH-LAMBETH
    That haunt Pickt-hatch, Mersh-Lambeth, and White-fryers,    .    30   E12 Shift         2
MESCHINES
    Meschines honour with the Cestrian fame    .    .    .    274   U84 Descent      16
MESSALLA'S
    Of eloquent Messalla's power in Court,    .    .    .    331   Horace          552
MESSE
    And, for thy messe, is willing to be kill'd.    .    .    94   F2 Penshurst     30
MET
    At court I met it, in clothes brave enough,    .    .    30   E11 Something     1
    Where ere he met me; now hee's dumbe, or proud.    .    62   E97 Motion        8
    We innocently met.  No simple word,    .    .    .    .    65   E101 Supper      39
    Where finding so much beautie met with vertue,    .    .    74   E114 Sydney       6
    They met the second Prodigie, would feare a    .    .    86   E133 Voyage      79
    At his great birth, where all the Muses met.    .    .    94   F2 Penshurst     14
    Or stay'd but where the Fryar, and you first met,    .    212   U43 Vulcan      201
    Sword, fire, and famine, with fell fury met;    .    .    243   U70 Ode          17
    And pietie the Center, where all met.    .    .    .    270   U81 Pawlet       42
    The wealthy houshold swarme of bondmen met,    .    .    291   U85 Country      65
    So over-thick, but, where the people met,    .    .    319   Horace          292
    And this hath met that one, that may be stil'd    .    .    389   Aleman           13
    The glorious Trinity in Union met.    .    .    .    .    413   Ghyrlond         32
    Such men I met withall, and so have you.    .    .    .    415   Rutter           11
METE
    Doth mete, whose lyne doth sound the depth of things:)    .    176   U24 Frontispice  12
METICULOUS
    That he dares to informe you, but somewhat meticulous,    .    380   Coryat 3         33
METIUS
    To send it to be judg'd by Metius eare,    .    .    .    331   Horace          576
METT
    I chyme that too: And I have mett with those    .    .    403   Inigo Jones 1    31
METTAL'
    Though but while mettal's heating:    .    .    .    .    179   U25 Desmond      43
METTAL  (SPIRIT)
    Provoke his mettal, and command his force    .    .    228   U53 Newcastle     2
METTALL
    His name in any mettall, it would breake.    .    .    .    172   U21 Ltl Shrub     2
METTALL'D
    I hate such measur'd, give me mettall'd fire    .    .    233   U59 Newcastle     7
METTALLS
    And subtiltie of mettalls) they dispense    .    .    .    86   E133 Voyage     100
METTAL'S
    Though but while mettal's heating:    .    .    .    .    179   U25 Desmond      43
ME'UP
    Art still at that, and think'st to blow me'up too?    .    72   E112 Gamster      6
MEW'D
    With great gray eyes, are lifted up, and mew'd;    .    .    88   E133 Voyage     161
MICHAEL
    Titian, or Raphael, Michael Angelo,    .    .    .    .    260   U77 Treasurer     7
    It hath beene question'd, Michael, if I bee    .    .    396   Drayton           1
MID
    Who, with his axe, thy fathers mid-wife plaid.    .    107   F10 Proludium    15
    Or feats of darknesse acted in Mid-Sun,    .    .    .    156   U13 Sacvile      95
    Under that cover; an old Mid-wives hat!    .    .    .    202   U42 Elegy Let    83
MIDAS
    Not, like a Midas, shut up in himselfe,    .    .    .    197   U40 Elegy That   21
```

		Page	Title	Line
MIDDLE				
The middle grounds thy mares, and horses breed.		94	F2 Penshurst	24
Keepe the middle age at stay,		131	U2 Excuse	21
The middle of his matter: letting goe		315	Horace	213
MIDST				
And that, midst envy' and parts; then fell by rage:		71	E110 Edmonds 1	14
First, midst, and last, converted one, and three;		122	F15 Heaven	10
The fire, the wine, the men! and in the midst,		225	U51 Bacon	3
Where the midst differs from the first: or where		315	Horace	217
The last doth from the midst dis-joyn'd appeare.		315	Horace	218
MID-SUN				
Or feats of darknesse acted in Mid-Sun,		156	U13 Sacvile	95
MID-WIFE				
Who, with his axe, thy fathers mid-wife plaid.		107	F10 Proludium	15
MID-WIVES				
Under that cover; an old Mid-wives hat!		202	U42 Elegy Let	83
MIGHT (NOUN)				
Were you Jove's sonnes, or had Alcides might.		89	E133 Voyage	182
MIGHT				
As theirs did with thee, mine might credit get:		32	E18 Censurer	6
Which might with halfe mankind maintayne a strife.		34	E23 Donne 1	8
Then they might in her bright eyes.		39	E40 Ratcliffe	8
When he made him executor, might be heire.		41	E44 Chuff	6
That we thy losse might know, and thou our love,		43	E51 James 3	1
That neither fame, nor love might wanting be		48	E66 Cary	1
In onely thee, might be both great, and glad.		48	E66 Cary	4
So to front death, as men might judge us past it.		54	E80 Life/Death	7
Throughout, might flatt'rie seeme; and to be mute		58	E91 Vere	10
How well, faire crowne of your faire sexe, might hee,		66	E103 L Wroth 1	1
Truth might spend all her voyce, Fame all her art.		68	E106 E Herbert	4
And that so strong and deepe, as 't might be thought,		71	E110 Edmonds 1	7
That the wit there, and manners might be sav'd:		73	E113 Overbury	6
Might be found out as good, and not my Lord.		75	E116 Jephson	8
Both whose dimensions, lost, the world might finde		79	E125 Uvedale	3
Might love the treasure for the cabinet.		79	E125 Uvedale	6
Might then both thee, thy worke and merit raise:		83	E132 Sylvester	2
But might I of Jove's Nectar sup,		106	F9 Celia 3	7
But might I of love's Nectar sipp,		106	F9 Celia 3	V 7
'Gainst stormes, or pyrats, that might charge your peace;		119	F13 Aubigny	93
Sooner, then he lost his might,		132	U2 How he saw	14
Unto her; which Love might take		133	U2 Suffered	9
And enamour'd, doe wish, so they might		134	U2 Triumph	7
As might all the Graces lead,		138	U2 Kisse	26
To do't with Cloth, or Stuffes, lusts name might merit;		164	U15 Friend-Wars	57
It might thy patience richly pay:		168	U16 Gray	5
But she is such, as she might, yet, forestall		172	U20 Shrub	23
Might be defrauded, nor the great secur'd,		176	U24 Frontispice	6
But both might know their wayes were understood,		176	U24 Frontispice	7
But both might know their wayes are understood,		176	U24 Frontispice V	7
And waste still, that they still might bee.		189	U36 Song	12
So I might dote upon thy Chaires and Stooles		201	U42 Elegy Let	47
What had I done that might call on thine ire?		202	U43 Vulcan	2
What have I done that might call on thine ire?		202	U43 Vulcan	V 2
Adulterate moneys, such as might not goe:		204	U43 Vulcan	45
Adulterate maskings, such as might not goe:		204	U43 Vulcan	V 45
And raz'd, e're thought could urge, This might have bin!		209	U43 Vulcan	136
Or lest that vapour might the Citie choake,		211	U43 Vulcan	182
Or fixt in the Low-Countrey's, where you might		212	U43 Vulcan	203
So acted to the life, as Maurice might,		214	U44 Speach	41
My gentle Arthur; that it might be said		216	U45 Squib	3
Indeed, her Dressing some man might delight,		223	U49 Pucell	31
But there are lines, wherewith I might b'embrac'd.		226	U52 Answer	3
O, had I now your manner, maistry, might,		227	U52 Answer	16
As though his age imperfect might appeare,		244	U70 Ode	51
Where they might read, and find		247	U70 Ode	122
All that their Fathers, and their Mothers might		257	U75 Epithalam.	147
With Gold, or Claspes, which might be bought		273	U84 Cradle	27
What he despaires, being handled, might not show.		315	Horace	214
They might with ease be numbred, being a few		319	Horace	293
And they uncensur'd might at Feasts, and Playes		319	Horace	297
These, the free meale might have beene well drawne out:		331	Horace	560
Next, that which rapt mee, was: I might behold		361	Palmer	13
She might have claym'd t'have made the Graces foure;		371	Epitaph	6
Might make the Fable of Good Women true.		372	Epitaph	14
Or crafty Malice, might pretend this praise,		391	Shakespeare	11
That might compare with thee? what story shall		406	Inigo Jones 1	98
MIGHTIEST				
And mightiest Monarchs feele what large increase		261	U77 Treasurer	21
The Sunne! great Kings, and mightiest Kingdomes fall!		271	U81 Pawlet	89
MIGHTST				
Thou mightst have yet enjoy'd thy crueltie		204	U43 Vulcan	49
Thou mightst have had me perish, piece, by piece,		205	U43 Vulcan	51
Thou mightst have had them perish, piece, by piece,		205	U43 Vulcan	V 51
MIGHTY				
The Sunne! great Kings, and mighty Kingdomes fall!		271	U81 Pawlet	V 89
Or sporting Kid, or Marlowes mighty line.		391	Shakespeare	30
When, Rome, I reade thee in thy mighty paire,		395	May	1
And Rouze, the Marching of a mighty force,		397	Drayton	39
To hold her up. O Showes! Showes! Mighty Showes!		403	Inigo Jones 1	39
But cause thou hearst the mighty k. of Spaine		406	Inigo Jones 2	1
MILD				
Now hot, now cold, now fierce, now mild.		189	U36 Song	15
Of your compassion; Parents should be mild:		192	U38 Elegy 'Tis	40

MILD (cont.)
Great Queen of Queens, most mild, most meek, most wise, . . 414 Ghyrlond 41
MILDE
What manners prettie, Nature milde, ... 188 U35 Chute 2
MILDER
Our brave Heroes with a milder glare, . . . 88 E133 Voyage 163
MILDNESSE
But view the mildnesse of your Makers state, . . . 193 U38 Elegy 'Tis 85
MILE (See also MYLES)
Thus removed by many a mile? . . . . 102 F5 Celia 1 V 14
What though she ride two mile on Holy-dayes . . . 222 U49 Pucell 15
And allow you for each particular mile, . . . 379 Coryat 3 9
MILITAR
In Politique, and Militar Affaires. . . . 214 U44 Speach 60
MILITARIE
Of London, in the Militarie truth, . . . 213 U44 Speach 26
MILK
Wine it is the Milk of Venus, ... 657 Door Apollo 12
MILKE
'Twas brought to court first wrapt, and white as milke; . . 31 E15 Court-worm 2
The milke, nor oyle, did ever flowe soe free . . 98 F3 Wroth V 60
In her cheekes, of Milke, and Roses; . . . 136 U2 Cupid 22
Where he doth steepe himselfe in Milke and Roses; . 170 U19 Elegy By 8
Our milke. Our fells. Our fleeces. and first Lambs. . 264 U79 New-yeares 16
Or, with the milke of Thebes; or Argus, fed. . . 313 Horace 168
MILKES
Your Milkes, your Fells, your Fleeces, and first Lambes, . 265 U79 New-yeares 50
MILL (NAME)
On Mill my Ladies Woman. . . . . 57 E90 Mill Ttl
When Mill first came to court, the unprofiting foole, . 57 E90 Mill 1
Still Mill continu'd: Nay, his face growing worse, . 57 E90 Mill 11
Mill was the same. Since, both his body and face . 57 E90 Mill 13
Longer a day, but with his Mill will marry. . . 57 E90 Mill 16
MILL
Hill-/foot (out in Sussex) to an iron Mill; . . 211 U43 Vulcan 184
Hill-/foot (out in Sussex) to some iron Mill; . . 211 U43 Vulcan V184
MILLAN
Strooke in at Millan with the Cutlers there; . . 212 U43 Vulcan 200
Strooke in at Millan with the villors there; . . 212 U43 Vulcan V200
MILLAR
As Stiles, Dike, Ditchfield, Millar, Crips, and Fen: . 214 U44 Speach 54
MILO
And it is hop'd, that shee, like Milo, wull . . 57 E90 Mill 17
MIME
To Mime. . . . . 81 E129 Mime Ttl
Think'st thou, Mime, this is great? or, that they strive . 81 E129 Mime 9
MIMING
Of miming, gets th'opinion of a wit. . . . 74 E115 Honest Man 28
Whose noyse shall keepe thy miming most alive, . . 81 E129 Mime 10
MINCE
Then, selling not, a dish was tane to mince 'hem, . 88 E133 Voyage 151
MIND (See also MYND)
His often change of clime (though not of mind) . . 37 E32 Roe 2 6
By constant suffring of thy equall mind; . . . 47 E63 Salisbury 2 8
No lesse a sov'raigne cure, then to the mind; . . 82 E130 Ferrab. 1 8
Much more a noble, and right generous mind . . 112 F11 Epode 111
Much more a noble, or a generous mind . . . 112 F11 Epode V111
And takes, and gives the beauties of the mind. . . 117 F13 Aubigny 44
Call to mind the formes, that strove . . . 137 U2 Cupid 46
For his Mind, I doe not care, ... 142 U2 Exception 1
Nor have I yet the narrow mind . . . . 150 U10 Jealousie 4
His Mind as pure, and neatly kept, . . . 151 U12 Corbet 15
For benefits are ow'd with the same mind . . . 153 U13 Sacvile 5
And whilst our states, strength, body, and mind we waste, . 166 U15 Friend-Wars 133
The mind of the Frontispice to a Booke. . . . 175 U24 Frontispice Ttl
High, as his mind, that doth advance . . . 176 U25 Desmond 5
No Armour to his mind! he is shot-free . . . 179 U25 Desmond 48
Yet doth some wholsome Physick for the mind, . . 180 U26 Ode High 9
Searching for knowledge, and to keepe your mind . . 225 U50 Countesse 29
A letter'd mind, and a large heart would place . . 227 U52 Answer 23
Put him in mind . . . . . . 231 U57 Burges 14
Yet are got off thence, with cleare mind, and hands . 234 U61 Epigram 7
If to my mind, great Lord, I had a state, . . 260 U77 Treasurer 1
For Mind, and Body, the most excellent . . . 274 U84 Descent 3
Next sitting we will draw her mind. . . . 277 U84 Body 32
4. The Mind. . . . . . . 277 U84 Mind Ttl
But these are like a Mind, not it. . . . 278 U84 Mind 12
No, to expresse a Mind to sense, ... 278 U84 Mind 13
No, to expresse this Mind to sense, . . . 278 U84 Mind V 13
Sweet Mind, then speake your selfe, and say, . . 278 U84 Mind 17
A Mind so pure, so perfect fine, ... 278 U84 Mind 25
But, that a Mind so rapt, so high, . . . 279 U84 Mind 41
But such a Mind, mak'st God thy Guest. . . . 281 U84 Mind 72
My wounded mind cannot sustaine this stroke, . . 283 U84 Muse 23
That pure, that pretious, and exalted mind . . 285 U84 Muse 104
She had a mind as calme, as she was faire. . . 287 U84 Muse 163
A quiet mind; free powers; and body sound; . . 295 U90 Mart.10:47 6
His better'd mind seekes wealth, and friendship: than . 315 Horace 238
In at the eare, doe stirre the mind more slow . . 317 Horace 257
The docile mind may soone thy precepts know, . . 329 Horace 504
The hand, and mind would, but it will resound . . 329 Horace 522
And, of your selfe too, understand; yet mind . . 331 Horace 547
To bettring of the mind of man, in ought, . . 331 Horace 562

		Page	Title	Line

MIND (cont.)
Or, of the things, that ne're came in my mind,	. . . .	333	Horace	596
For praises, where the mind conceales a foxe.	. . .	333	Horace	622
For praises, where the mind harbours a foxe.	. . .	354	Horace	V622
my mind unto you, ...	. .	416	Moon	4

MINDE
Restored in thy body, and thy minde!	. . . .	79	E125 Uvedale	4
A body sound, with sounder minde;	. . .	99	F3 Wroth	102
At th'eye and eare (the ports unto the minde)	. .	109	F11 Epode	9
Doe severall passions invade the minde,	. .	110	F11 Epode	29
Of any good minde, now: There are so few.	. .	116	F13 Aubigny	2
Because nor it can change, nor such a minde.	. .	120	F13 Aubigny	124
The Minde of the Front	. . .	175	U24 Frontispice	VTtl
And see a minde attir'd in perfect straines;	. .	362	Author	2
Of Shakespeares minde, and manners brightly shines	. .	392	Shakespeare	67
hir minde is eased.	. .	417	Moon	40

MINDES
| That bloud not mindes, but mindes did bloud adorne: | . . | 75 | E116 Jephson | 11 |
| The soft, and sweetest mindes | . . | 110 | F11 Epode | 50 |

MINDS
Of which wee'll speake our minds, amidst our meate;	. .	65	E101 Supper	23
As minds ill bent	. .	129	U1 Father	13
And my minds motion not? or have I none?	. . .	156	U13 Sacvile	122
Minds that are great and free,	. .	174	U23 Himselfe	16
Of worthiest knowledge, that can take mens minds.	. .	217	U46 Coke	20
That knits brave minds, and manners, more then blood.	.	246	U70 Ode	106
Which knits brave minds, and manners, more then blood.	.	246	U70 Ode	V106
To worke the hearers minds, still, to their plight.	.	311	Horace	142
Her truch-man, she reports the minds each throw.	.	313	Horace	157
And care of getting, thus, our minds hath stain'd,	.	327	Horace	473
Their minds to Warres, with rimes they did rehearse;	.	329	Horace	495

MINE (NOUN)
| That Mine of Wisdome, and of Counsells deep, | . . | 255 | U75 Epithalam. | 98 |
| Who hadst before wrought in rich Homers Mine? | . . | 388 | Chapman | 3 |

MINE (See also MYNE)
Use mine so, too: I give thee leave. But crave	. .	27	E3 Bookseller	3
And mine come nothing like. I hope so. Yet,	. .	32	E18 Censurer	5
As theirs did with thee, mine might credit get:	. .	32	E18 Censurer	6
Who wets my grave, can be no friend of mine.	. .	37	E33 Roe 3	6
Thou flatter'st thine, mine cannot flatter'd bee.	.	38	E36 Martial	4
What fate is mine, that so it selfe bereaves?	.	44	E55 Beaumont	7
And, as thou'hast mine, his houres, and youth abuse.	.	48	E65 Muse	6
To plucke downe mine, Poll sets up new wits still,	.	50	E71 Parrat	1
Which is the Mermaids, now, but shall be mine:	.	65	E101 Supper	30
Forgive me then, if mine but say you are	. .	67	E103 L Wroth 1	9
That is his Lordships, shall be also mine.	. .	95	F2 Penshurst	64
As if thou, then, wert mine, or I raign'd here:	. .	95	F2 Penshurst	74
And I will pledge with mine;	. .	106	F9 Celia 3	2
And your brave friend, and mine so well did love.	.	116	F12 Rutland	92
And your brave friend, and mine to well did love.	.	116	F12 Rutland	V 92
Mine owne enough betray me.	. .	145	U4 Song	12
On all mens Fruit, and flowers, as well as mine.	.	150	U10 Jealousie	8
I have the lyst of mine owne faults to know,	.	156	U13 Sacvile	114
And mine not least) I have too oft preferr'd	.	159	U14 Selden	20
To light upon a Love of mine.	. .	174	U22 Elegy Tho	32
Both braines and hearts; and mine now best doe know it:	.	182	U28 Worth	8
To redeeme mine, I had sent in; Enough,	. .	205	U43 Vulcan	63
Losse, remaines yet, as unrepair'd as mine.	. .	211	U43 Vulcan	196
Losse, remaines yet, as much despair'd as mine.	.	211	U43 Vulcan	V196
Well, with mine owne fraile Pitcher, what to doe	.	219	U47 Tribe	56
I would call mine, to which not many Staires	.	220	U47 Tribe	74
For bawdry, 'tis her language, and not mine.	.	223	U49 Pucell	26
I summe up mine owne breaking, and wish all.	.	283	U84 Muse	26
Flow my thin teares, downe these pale cheeks of mine?	.	293	U86 Hor.4:1	34
And, to your Fathers, and to mine; though 't be	.	331	Horace	577
This thy worke forth: that judgment mine commends.	.	386	Browne	8
Thy Muse, and mine, as they expect. 'Tis true:	.	396	Drayton	5
I feele it by mine owne, that over flow,	.	398	Drayton	77
And with their grassie greene restor'd mine eyes.	.	398	Drayton	82
Now, for mine owne part, and it is but due,	.	415	Rutter	12

MINERVA (See also MYNERVA)
And Minerva, when she talkes.	. .	137	U2 Cupid	54
By Jove to have Minerva for thy Bride,	. .	203	U43 Vulcan	12
Thou woo Minerva! or to wit aspire!	. .	208	U43 Vulcan	109

MINERVAES
| Minervaes loome was never richer spred. | . . | 61 | E95 Savile | 16 |

MINERVA'S
| Venus, and Minerva's eyes, | . . | 141 | U2 Her man | 15 |
| Minerva's and the Muses care! | . . | 233 | U60 La-ware | 4 |

MINERVAS
| And looking up, I saw Minervas fowle, | . . | 397 | Drayton | 33 |

MINES
| In the same Mines of knowledge; and thence brought | . | 161 | U14 Selden | 76 |
| In the rich Mines of knowledge; and thence brought | . | 161 | U14 Selden | V 76 |

MINGLE
| Doe mingle in a shout, | . . | 240 | U67 Muses | 41 |

MINISTRY
| Nor Degradation from the Ministry, | . . | 410 | Gill | 6 |

MINOS
| Who kept an ale-house; with my little Minos, | . | 89 | E133 Voyage | 189 |

MINT
| Office of Wit, a Mint, and (this is true) | . . | 415 | Rutter | 20 |
| Yo'have all the Mysteries of Wits new Mint, | . | 415 | Rutter | 28 |

MINUTE
Till the sower Minute comes of taking leave, . . . 197 U40 Elegy That 2
MINUTES
Not ravish'd all hence in a minutes rage. . . . 205 U43 Vulcan 56
Not snatcht them hence in one poor minutes rage. . . . 205 U43 Vulcan V 56
MIRA
See where he walkes with Mira by his side. . . . 264 U79 New-yeares 18
Of brightest Mira, doe we raise. our Song, ... 264 U79 New-yeares 24
Of brightest Mira, is our Song; the grace . . . 264 U79 New-yeares 32
MIRACLE
There should a miracle be wrought. . . . 101 F4 To the World 60
And practise for a Miracle; take heed, . . . 223 U49 Pucell 41
Of thy dead Standards: or (with miracle) see . . . 405 Inigo Jones 1 89
MIRACLES
I Must beleeve some miracles still bee, ... 73 E114 Sydney 1
MIRKINS
morts, and mirkins that wagg all, ... 417 Moon 15
MIRROR
My mirror is more subtile, cleere, refin'd, . . . 117 F13 Aubigny 43
MIRROUR
They are th'exampled Paire, and mirrour of their kind. . . 255 U75 Epithalam. 80
And art the spotlesse Mirrour to Mans eyes. . . . 414 Ghyrlond 44
MIRTH
Give every one his dose of mirth: and watches . . . 74 E115 Honest Man 14
Doth sweeten mirth, and heighten pietie, . . . 82 E130 Ferrab. 1 6
And fills thy open hall with mirth, and cheere, . . . 98 F3 Wroth 49
As neither wine doe rack it out, or mirth. . . . 197 U40 Elegy That 18
Mirth, fooling, nor wit, ... 231 U57 Burges 17
Three Kingdomes Mirth, in light, and aerie man, . . 249 U72 King 11
At Bonefires, squibs, and mirth, with all their Shoutes . 249 U72 King V 13
Of thy strange Moon-Calfe, both thy straine of mirth, . . 398 Drayton 84
And as either newes or mirth . . . . . 417 Moon 17
MIRTHFULL
That shall be utter'd at our mirthfull boord, . . . 65 E101 Supper 40
MIS
Which (would the world not mis-call't flatterie) . . . 79 E125 Uvedale 9
Which in the taking if you mis-apply, ... 180 U26 Ode High 11
MIS-APPLY
Which in the taking if you mis-apply, ... 180 U26 Ode High 11
MIS-CALL'
Which (would the world not mis-call't flatterie) . . . 79 E125 Uvedale 9
MIS-CALL'T
Which (would the world not mis-call't flatterie) . . . 79 E125 Uvedale 9
MISCHIEFES
On both sides doe your mischiefes with delight; . . . 212 U43 Vulcan 204
These trifles into serious mischiefes lead . . . 335 Horace 641
MISCHIFE
The skilfull mischife of a rovinge Eye . . . 108 F10 Proludium 5
MISERIE
And, if no other miserie, yet age? . . . . 41 E45 First Son 8
That are Spectators, with their miserie, . . . 311 Horace 137
MISERIES
Thou are not one, seek'st miseries with hope, . . . 70 E109 Nevil 5
As, could they but lifes miseries fore-see, . . . 243 U70 Ode 19
Produce thy masse of miseries on the Stage, . . . 244 U70 Ode 55
Warres greatest woes, and miseries increase, . . . 363 Peace 3
The miseries of Margaret the Queene . . . 398 Drayton 75
MISFORTUNE
To age, misfortune, sicknesse, griefe: . . . 102 F4 To the World 62
MISSE
Which if they misse, they yet should re-advance . . . 55 E85 Goodyere 1 8
Such as are misse-call'd Captaynes, and wrong you; . . 69 E108 Soldiers 2
Charis, guesse, and doe not misse, . . . 137 U2 Kisse 1
Have all these done (and yet I misse . . . 182 U27 Ode Helen 29
Put black, and mourning on? and say you misse . . 285 U84 Muse 98
Her broken sighes did never misse whole sense: . . 288 U84 Muse 185
MISSE-CALL'D
Such as are misse-call'd Captaynes, and wrong you; . . 69 E108 Soldiers 2
MIST
Nor could the age have mist thee, in this strife . . . 66 E102 Pembroke 5
MISTAKE
Else, I my state should much mistake, . . . 101 F4 To the World 57
Oh how a Lover may mistake! to thinke, . . . 170 U18 Elegy Can 15
The vertue and grace of which, or I mistake, . . 339 Horace V 60/ 59
MISTAKING
Mistaking earth for heaven. . . . . 144 U3 Musicall 24
MISTERIE
Sure there is Misterie in it, I not know, . . . 156 U13 Sacvile 97
When Venus there maintain'd the Misterie. . . . 209 U43 Vulcan 144
MISTERYES
Eyes that can pierce into the Misteryes . . . 404 Inigo Jones 1 46
MISTOOKE
With mistooke Names out of Vitruvius! . . . 402 Inigo Jones 1 8
MISTRES
Whilst Horace lov'd no Mistres more, . . . 293 U87 Hor.3:9 5
MISTRESS
To his Mistress . . . . . 106 F9 Celia 3 VTtl
MISTRESSE
Lesse must not be thought on then Mistresse: or, . . 165 U15 Friend-Wars 95
Whom no great Mistresse hath as yet infam'd, . . 165 U15 Friend-Wars 97
The Mistresse of Mans life, grave Historie, . . 175 U24 Frontispice 2
A solemne Mistresse, and so good a Friend, . . 287 U84 Muse 175

MISTRIS
Item, your mistris anagram, i' your hilt. . . . . . 51 E73 Fine Grand 16
Item, your owne, sew'd in your mistris smock. . . . . 51 E73 Fine Grand 17
Unworthy such a mistris, such a schoole, ... 57 E90 Mill 2
So court a mistris, shee denyes you; . . . . 104 F7 Women but 9
Offended Mistris, you are yet so faire, ... 191 U38 Elegy 'Tis 9
Thinke it was frailtie, Mistris, thinke me man, . . . 192 U38 Elegy 'Tis 31
Then Mistris, here, here let your rigour end, . . . 194 U38 Elegy 'Tis 105
No, Mistris, no, the open merrie Man . . . . . 198 U40 Elegy That 25
Heare, Mistris, your departing servant tell . . . 199 U41 Elegy Since 2
How shall I doe, sweet Mistris, for my heart? . . . 199 U41 Elegy Since 14
Prove of his Mistris Feature, ... 364 Phoenix 7
MISTS
These be the cause of those thicke frequent mists . . . 87 E133 Voyage 130
MISUS'D
By sinne, and Sathan; and my flesh misus'd, ... 127 U1 Trinitie 6
MITE
Within the ballance; and not want a mite; . . . . 229 U54 Squib 10
MIXE
Hermes, the cheater, shall not mixe with us, ... 107 F10 Proludium 22
Hermes, the cheater, cannot mixe with us, ... 107 F10 Proludium V 22
Mixe then your Notes, that we may prove . . . . 143 U3 Musicall 9
In letters, that mixe spirits, thus to weave. . . . 190 U37 Friend-Book 12
That I not mixe thee so, my braine excuses; . . . 391 Shakespeare 25
MIX'D
Clowne, Towns-man, base, and noble, mix'd, to judge? . . 319 Horace 302
Sweet mix'd with sowre, to his Reader, so . . . 329 Horace 515
MIXED
What love with mercy mixed doth appeare? . . . . 286 U84 Muse 138
MIXETH
And so well faines, so mixeth cunningly . . . . . 315 Horace 215
MIXING
Or mixing sweet, and fit, teach life the right. . . . 327 Horace 478
MIXT
Sit mixt with losse of state, or reverence. . . . . 98 F3 Wroth 57
For such a lot! that mixt you with a state . . . 118 F13 Aubigny 48
Be honour is so mixt) by such as would, . . . 162 U15 Friend-Wars 25
As they are made! Pride, and stiffe Clownage mixt . . 163 U15 Friend-Wars 43
But mixt with sound, transcending . . . . . 365 Ode Splendor 15
MIXTURES
That with these mixtures we put out her light. . . . 156 U13 Sacvile 110
The valuations, mixtures, and the same . . . . 415 Rutter 29
MOAN   (See MONE)
MOATH
It is the common Moath, ... 174 U23 Himselfe 5
MOATHES
Or moathes shall eate, what all these Fooles admire. . . 371 Fletcher 16
MOCION
which thoughts being circumvolvd in gyerlyk mocion . . 361 Palmer 23
MOCK'D
Mock'd of all: and call'd of one . . . . . 132 U2 How he saw 28
The man once mock'd, and suffer'd wrong to tread. . . 335 Horace 642
MOCKS
Cover'd with Tissue, whose prosperitie mocks . . . 216 U44 Speach 100
Looke through him, and be sure, you take not mocks . . 333 Horace 621
MODELL
And that, say Philosophers, is the best modell. . . 379 Coryat 3 5
MODERATELY
Of this we will sup free, but moderately, . . . 65 E101 Supper 35
MODERNE
What th'antique souldiers were, the moderne bee? . . 72 E111 Edmonds 2 2
And the Greeke Discipline (with the moderne) shed . . 214 U44 Speach 36
MODEST
Others more modest, but contemne us too, . . . 59 E92 New Crie 39
You both are modest. So am I. Farewell. . . . 161 U14 Selden 86
Perversly modest, had I rather owe . . . . . 311 Horace 130
Chaste, thriftie, modest folke, that came to view. . . 319 Horace 294
MODESTIE
Pardon free truth, and let thy modestie, ... 31 E14 Camden 11
I'le loose my modestie, and tell your name. . . . 38 E38 Guiltie 2 8
With love, to heare your modestie relate, . . . 251 U74 Weston 21
With Modestie so crown'd, and Adoration seene. . . . 254 U75 Epithalam. 48
From whence thy Modestie, or Poemes law . . . 313 Horace 193
MODESTLY
Or, if shee would but modestly have prais'd . . . 46 E60 Mounteagle 3
I modestly quit that, and thinke to write, . . . 72 E112 Gamster 11
And give, being taken modestly, this leave, . . . 309 Horace 73
MODESTY
Taught Pallas language; Cynthia modesty; . . . 371 Epitaph 7
MODET
Where Pittes, or Wright, or Modet would not venter, . . 164 U15 Friend-Wars 80
MOIST
Or fumie clysters, thy moist lungs to bake: . . . 42 E50 Cod 3 2
MOLEST
Why, Disease, dost thou molest . . . . 104 F8 Sicknesse 1
In thy justice to molest . . . . . 106 F8 Sicknesse 47
Of earthen Jarres, there may molest me too: . . . 219 U47 Tribe 55
MONARCH
Monarch in Letters! 'Mongst thy Titles showne . . . 160 U14 Selden 65
MONARCHS
To Th'Best Of Monarchs, Masters, Men, King Charles . . 259 U76 Petition 2
And mightiest Monarchs feele what large increase . . 261 U77 Treasurer 21
We sing the best of Monarchs, Masters, Men; . . . 263 U79 New-yeares 7

411

		Page	Title	Line

MONE (NAME)
Salute old Mone, ... 367 Ode Who saith 38

MONE
And did act (what now we mone) . . . . . 77 E120 S. P. 13
To laughter; so they grieve with those that mone. . . 311 Horace 144

MONETHS
At sixe moneths end, shee parted hence . . . 33 E22 Daughter 5

MONEY
But, for this money was a courtier found, . . 29 E8 Robbery 3
Rob'd both of money, and the lawes reliefe, . 29 E8 Robbery 5
Shee must have money: he returnes, god payes. . 30 E12 Shift 8
At dice his borrow'd money: which, god payes. . 30 E12 Shift 12
Is not to be despair'd of, for our money; . . 65 E101 Supper 14
Then either money, warre, or death: . . . 99 F3 Wroth 76
Like Money-brokers, after Names, and hire . . 155 U13 Sacvile 62
Alone in money, but in manners too. . . . 157 U13 Sacvile 134
For man to spend his money on? his wit? . . 165 U15 Friend-Wars 102
No piece of money, but you know, or make . . 216 U45 Squib 14
If there be no money; . . . . . . 231 U57 Burges 21
What's this? if he whose money hireth thee . 305 Horace 26
Of money, haughtie, to desire soon mov'd, . . 315 Horace 235
This booke will get the Sosii money; This . . 329 Horace 517
Or, like our Money-Brokers, take up names . . 386 Browne 10
This is the money-gett, Mechanick Age! . . 404 Inigo Jones 1 52

MONEY-BROKERS
Like Money-brokers, after Names, and hire . . 155 U13 Sacvile 62
Or, like our Money-Brokers, take up names . . 386 Browne 10

MONEYES
Of those, that put out moneyes, on returne . . 85 E133 Voyage 32
'Gainst th'Ides, his gott moneyes he gets in with paine, . 291 U85 Country V 69

MONEY-GETT
This is the money-gett, Mechanick Age! . . 404 Inigo Jones 1 52

MONEY'S
Or great in money's out at use, command . . 333 Horace 600
Or wealthy in money's out at use, command . . 353 Horace V600

MONEYS
Adulterate moneys, such as might not goe: . . 204 U43 Vulcan 45
That turnes us so much moneys, at which rate . 215 U44 Speach 77
'Gainst th'Ides, his moneys he gets in with paine, . 291 U85 Country 69

MONGST
that mongst so manie plants transplanted hether, . 361 Palmer 6

MONIMENT
Thou art a Moniment, without a tombe, . . . 391 Shakespeare 22

MONOGRAM
To be describ'd by a Monogram, ... 227 U52 Answer 11

MONSIEUR (See MOUNSIEUR, MUNSIEUR)

MONSTER
In the first jawes appear'd that ugly monster, . 85 E133 Voyage 61
And so some goodlier monster had begot: . . 204 U43 Vulcan 32
Empusa, Lamia, or some Monster, more . . . 398 Drayton 87

MONSTERS
O, these so ignorant Monsters! light, as proud, . 164 U15 Friend-Wars 59

MONTGOMERY
To Susan Countesse of Montgomery. . . . 67 E104 Montgomery Ttl

MONTH
Hazard a month forsware his; and grew drunke, . 56 E87 Hazard 2
What Month then May, was fitter to disclose . 237 U65 Prince 4
The Month of youth, which calls all Creatures forth . 253 U75 Epithalam. 26

MONTHES
In five monthes he went it, in five monthes he pend it. . 379 Coryat 3 16

MONTHLY
The new french-taylors motion, monthly made, . 56 E88 Monsieur 15

MONTJOY
(Charles Montjoy) whose command . . . . 367 Ode Who saith 50

MONTRELL
Hee's carried 'twixt Montrell and Abbevile. . . 374 Coryat 1 13
In a Cart twixt Montrell and Abbevile. . . 380 Coryat 3 53

MONUMENT
I made my lyfe my monument, & yours: . . . 387 Cavendish 7

MONYES
His monyes travaile for him, in and out: . . 36 E31 Banck 2

MOOD
Th'observing neighbours no such mood can see. . 40 E42 Giles 2

MOODES
Moodes, which the god-like Sydney oft did prove, . 116 F12 Rutland 91
Not wearing moodes, as gallants doe a fashion, . 362 Author 3
Taught Lucan these true moodes! Replyes my sence . 395 May 15

MOODS
(To vertuous moods inclin'd) . . . . . 112 F11 Epode 112

MOON
Under the angry Moon. But then the boys . . 354 Horace V647
Of thy strange Moon-Calfe, both thy straine of mirth, . 398 Drayton 84

MOON-CALFE
Of thy strange Moon-Calfe, both thy straine of mirth, . 398 Drayton 84

MOONE
It was the day, what time the powerfull Moone . 84 E133 Voyage 29
Then the various Moone the flood! . . . 136 U2 Cupid 4
And there to stand so. Hast now envious Moone, . 238 U65 Prince 9
And still to stand so. Hast thou envious Moone, . 238 U65 Prince V 9
According to the Moone. But, then the boyes . 335 Horace 647
Thou Throne of glory, beauteous as the Moone, . 414 Ghyrlond 49
The Moone comends hir . . . . . . 417 Moon 12
the Moone will beare it. . . . . . 417 Moon 28

		Page	Title	Line
MOONES				
But many Moones there shall not wane (quoth hee)	. . .	87	E133 Voyage	103
Before the moones have fill'd their tripple trine,	. .	119	F13 Aubigny	102
Reducts, Halfe-moones, Horne-workes, and such close wayes,	.	248	U71 Treasurer	8
MOORE				
Or in Moore-fields, this other night! sings one,	. . .	202	U42 Elegy Let	73
MOORE-FIELDS				
Or in Moore-fields, this other night! sings one,	. . .	202	U42 Elegy Let	73
MORALL				
Under the Morall? shewe he had a pate	. . . .	405	Inigo Jones 1	83
MORAVIAN				
Of your Moravian horse, Venetian bull.	. . .	69	E107 Hungry	8
MORE				
And gave thee both, to shew they could no more.	. . .	28	E4 James 1	4
Or celebrated with more truth of state?	. . .	28	E5 Union	2
Then thee the age sees not that thing more grave,	. . .	31	E14 Camden	5
More high, more holy, that shee more would crave.	. . .	31	E14 Camden	6
Thou more; that with it every day, dar'st jest	. . .	32	E16 Brain-hardy	2
He that dares damne himselfe, dares more then fight.	. .	32	E16 Brain-hardy	10
Then his chast wife, though Beast now know no more,	. .	35	E26 Beast 2	1
Nay more, for greatnesse sake, he will be one	. . .	36	E28 Surly	19
Ile not offend thee with a vaine teare more,	. . .	37	E33 Roe 3	1
A Prince, that rules by'example, more than sway?	. . .	37	E35 James 2	2
Whose manners draw, more than thy powers constraine.	. .	37	E35 James 2	3
And than in them, how could we know god more?	. . .	38	E35 James 2	8
And get more gold, then all the colledge can:	. . .	39	E41 Gypsee	2
No more would Jone he should. Giles riseth early,	. .	40	E42 Giles	6
And giving largely to me, more thou tak'st.	. . .	44	E55 Beaumont	6
Be thy next masters more unluckie Muse,	. . .	48	E65 Muse	5
Which deed I know not, whether were more high,	. . .	49	E66 Cary	7
Or thou more happie, it to justifie	. . .	49	E66 Cary	8
Then, since we (more then many) these truths know:	. .	50	E70 Wm Roe 1	7
In most vile verses, and cost me more paine,	. . .	51	E73 Fine Grand	19
Fortie things more, deare Grand, which you know true,	. .	51	E73 Fine Grand	21
Of greatest bloud, and yet more good then great;	. . .	52	E76 Bedford 1	6
I'am more asham'd to have thee thought my foe.	. . .	53	E77 Not name	4
Who both their graces in thy selfe hast more	. . .	57	E89 Allen	9
Who more should seeke mens reverence, then feare.	. .	58	E91 Vere	18
Others more modest, but contemne us too,	. . .	59	E92 New Crie	39
But, when they heard it tax'd, tooke once offence.	. .	60	E94 Bedford 3	10
To thine owne proper I ascribe then more;	. . .	61	E95 Savile	9
No more then Salust in the Romane state!	. . .	61	E95 Savile	23
But one more rare, and in the case so new:	. . .	62	E97 Motion	3
Since he was gone, more then the one he weares.	. . .	63	E97 Motion	17
And I know nothing more thou hast to doo.	. . .	63	E98 Th Roe 1	2
And studie conscience, more then thou would'st fame.	. .	63	E98 Th Roe 1	10
Thy fact is more: let truth encourage thee.	. . .	64	E99 Th Roe 2	12
Ile tell you of more, and lye, so you will come:	. .	65	E101 Supper	17
Thou must draw more: and they, that hope to see	. . .	66	E102 Pembroke	19
Becomes none more then you, who need it least.	. . .	67	E103 L Wroth 1	14
Or, more then borne for the comparison	. . .	67	E104 Montgomery	9
Would call you more then Ceres, if not that:	. . .	68	E105 L Wroth 2	8
Not that I love it, more, then I will you.	. . .	68	E107 Hungry	4
For which there must more sea, and land be leap'd,	. .	69	E107 Hungry	16
No more, then I dare now doe, with my pen.	. . .	70	E108 Soldiers	8
His life, but makes, that he can dye no more.	. . .	71	E110 Edmonds 1	22
More, then to varie what our elders knew:	. . .	72	E111 Edmonds 2	6
And, shifting of it's faces, doth play more	. . .	74	E115 Honest Man	25
With me can merit more, then that good man,	. . .	76	E119 Shelton	5
To more vertue, then doth live.	. . .	79	E124 Elizabeth	6
Said I wrong'd him, and (which was more) his love.	. .	80	E126 Mrs Cary	5
Mov'd by her order, and the ninth more high,	. . .	82	E130 Ferrab. 1	13
The learn'd have no more priviledge, then the lay.	. .	82	E131 Ferrab. 2	4
No more, those mayden glories shee hath lost.	. . .	83	E132 Sylvester	14
No more let Greece her bolder fables tell	. . .	84	E133 Voyage	1
And in it, two more horride knaves, then Charon.	. .	84	E133 Voyage	12
Or his to Antwerpe. Therefore, once more, list ho'.	.	85	E133 Voyage	40
Still, with thy former labours; yet, once more,	. .	85	E133 Voyage	56
Never did bottom more betray her burden;	. . .	87	E133 Voyage	116
White, black, blew, greene, and in more formes out-started,	.	87	E133 Voyage	126
But what can this (more then expresse their love)	. .	95	F2 Penshurst	57
More for thy exercise, then fare;	. . .	97	F3 Wroth	30
Let him, then hardest sires, more disinherit,	. . .	99	F3 Wroth	77
Then hardest let him more disherrit,	. . .	99	F3 Wroth	V 77
Let thousands more goe flatter vice, and winne,	. . .	99	F3 Wroth	85
More hatred, then thou hast to mee.	. . .	101	F4 To the World	40
Adde a thousand, and so more:	. . . .	103	F6 Celia 2	11
And this age will build no more:	. . .	105	F8 Sicknesse	12
And have more diseases made.	. . . .	105	F8 Sicknesse	20
More then citizens dare lend	. . . .	105	F8 Sicknesse	34
For the more countenance to my active Muse?	. . .	107	F10 Proludium	3
For the more countenance to our active Muse?	. . .	107	F10 Proludium	V 3
With his old earthly labours. T'exact more,	. . .	107	F10 Proludium	5
That is an essence, farre more gentle, fine,	. . .	110	F11 Epode	45
A forme more fresh, then are the Eden bowers,	. . .	111	F11 Epode	57
And yet (in this t'expresse our selves more cleare)	. .	111	F11 Epode	75
And yet (in this t'expresse my self more cleare)	. . .	111	F11 Epode	V 75
Is more crowne-worthy still,	. . .	112	F11 Epode	88
Is more praiseworthy still,	. . .	112	F11 Epode	V 88
Much more a noble, and right generous mind	. . .	112	F11 Epode	111
Much more a noble, or a generous mind	. . .	112	F11 Epode	V111
The truth of times) was once of more esteeme,	. . .	114	F12 Rutland	21
Beautie, I know, is good, and bloud is more;	. . .	114	F12 Rutland	37

413

	Page	Title		Line
MORE (cont.)				
And so doe many more. All which can call	117	F13	Aubigny	31
My mirror is more subtile, cleere, refin'd,	117	F13	Aubigny	43
As bloud, and match. Wherein, how more then much	117	F13	Aubigny	46
And studie more:	121	F14	Sydney	36
Be more, and long desir'd:	121	F14	Sydney	55
To thee more sweet?	127	U1	Trinitie	16
Who more can crave	129	U1	Father	17
Eyes and limbes; to hurt me more.	133	U2	Suffered	4
And doe governe more my blood,	136	U2	Cupid	3
Rip'ned with a breath more sweet,	137	U2	Cupid	27
Something more then thou hast spi'd.	137	U2	Cupid	50
You were more the eye, and talke	138	U2	Kisse	14
Once more, and (faith) I will be gone,	139	U2	Another	7
Chestnut colour, or more slack	141	U2	Her man	13
Shewing danger more then ire.	142	U2	Her man	42
Sing you no more then, lest the best	144	U3	Musicall	V 21
Men, if you love us, play no more	145	U5	Woman-kind	1
More pleasure while the thing he makes	145	U5	Woman-kind	15
Our pleasure; but preserves us more	146	U6	Defence	21
And feare much more, that more of him be showne.	147	U7	Nymph	21
I'le tell no more, and yet I love,	148	U7	Nymph	29
And more, and more, I should have done,	152	U12	Corbet	30
The memorie delights him more, from whom	153	U13	Sacvile	21
That they have more opprest me, then my want?	153	U13	Sacvile	28
No more then he doth thanke, that will receive	154	U13	Sacvile	43
And told of with more License then th'were done!	156	U13	Sacvile	96
No more are these of us, let them then goe,	156	U13	Sacvile	113
Yet we must more then move still, or goe on,	157	U13	Sacvile	135
Then which there is not unto Studie'a more	158	U14	Selden	13
But more licentious made, and desperate!	163	U15	Friend-Wars	36
That all respect; She must lie downe: Nay more,	163	U15	Friend-Wars	53
What reputation to beare one Glasse more?	166	U15	Friend-Wars	119
More then themselves, or then our lives could take,	166	U15	Friend-Wars	127
I'le bid thee looke no more, but flee, flee friend,	166	U15	Friend-Wars	129
He that no more for Age, Cramps, Palsies, can	166	U15	Friend-Wars	135
Boasters, and perjur'd, with the infinite more	167	U15	Friend-Wars	169
That thou dost all things more for truth, then glory,	168	U15	Friend-Wars	179
No more, then we should thinke a Lord had had	168	U15	Friend-Wars	193
More honour in him, 'cause we'ave knowne him mad:	168	U15	Friend-Wars	194
And if I had no more to say,	168	U16	Gray	2
I'le therefore aske no more, but bid you love;	171	U19	Elegy By	15
No more, I am sorry for so fond cause, say,	171	U20	Shrub	4
Perjur'd! and painted! if she were no more--,	172	U20	Shrub	22
Of eyes more true,	177	U25	Desmond	23
Oft scape an Imputation, more through luck, then wit.	179	U25	Desmond	52
Oft scape theyr Imputation, more through luck, then wit.	179	U25	Desmond	V 52
A gentler, and more agile hand, to tend	180	U26	Ode High	4
In one full Action; nor have you now more	180	U26	Ode High	17
Such thoughts wil make you more in love with truth.	181	U26	Ode High	21
Shine more, then she, the Stars among?	181	U27	Ode Helen	12
What is there more that can ennoble blood?	185	U30	Burleigh	6
Without the pompe of Counsell; or more Aide,	186	U32	Elsmere	3
The Seat made of a more then civill warre;	186	U33	Councellour	2
Of those that set by their false faces more	188	U34	Small Poxe	4
That heaven should make no more; or should amisse,	188	U34	Small Poxe	15
Who more they burne, they more desire,	189	U36	Song	10
And (stil'd your mercies Creature) will live more	191	U38	Elegy 'Tis	29
And then his thunder frights more, then it kills.	193	U38	Elegy 'Tis	70
And how more faire, and lovely lookes the world	193	U38	Elegy 'Tis	73
Rather then once displease you more, to die,	193	U38	Elegy 'Tis	92
Of Contumelie, and urge a good man more	193	U38	Elegy 'Tis	100
I will no more abuse my vowes to you,	194	U38	Elegy 'Tis	107
More then of eithers manners, wit, or face!	202	U42	Elegy Let	88
in weaving Riddles in more wretched ryme,	204	U43	Vulcan	V 34
With some more thrift, and more varietie:	205	U43	Vulcan	50
With some more change, and tast of tyranny:	205	U43	Vulcan	V 50
With some more thrift, and yet varietie:	205	U43	Vulcan	V 50
Scap'd not his Justice any jot the more:	210	U43	Vulcan	154
Scap'd not this Justice any jot the more:	210	U43	Vulcan	V154
Scap'd not thy Justice any whitt the more:	210	U43	Vulcan	V154
More then advanc'd the houses, and their rites?	210	U43	Vulcan	164
I could invent a sentence, yet more worse;	211	U43	Vulcan	V189
They saw too store of feathers, and more may,	213	U44	Speach	9
Would thinke no more of Vlushing, or the Brill:	213	U44	Speach	30
More then the surfets, in thee, that day stood.	214	U44	Speach	48
That keepe the warre, though now't be growne more tame,	214	U44	Speach	55
More then to praise a Dog? or Horse? or speake	215	U44	Speach	71
Whom Fortune aided lesse, or vertue more.	217	U46	Coke	4
More for thy Patronage, then for their Cause,	217	U46	Coke	12
None Fortune aided lesse, or Vertue more.	217	U46	Coke	22
I could say more of such, but that I flie	218	U47	Tribe	5
And know whose ignorance is more then theirs;	218	U47	Tribe	24
I studie other friendships, and more one,	219	U47	Tribe	29
And thinke thy streame more quicker	221	U48	Bacchus	27
Doth labour with the Phrase more then the sense?	222	U49	Pucell	14
In Contract twice, what can shee perjure more?	223	U49	Pucell	30
Now with a Title more to the Degree;	225	U51	Bacon	12
A Poet hath no more but black and white,	227	U52	Answer	20
Lend me, deare Arthur, for a weeke five more,	229	U54	Squib	16
And should grow rich, had I much more to pay.	231	U56	Covell	30
And should grow rich, if I had more to pay.	231	U56	Covell	V 30
And more is behind:	231	U57	Burges	13

414

	Page	Title	Line

MORE (cont.)
Nay, and in this, thou show'st to value more	235	U62 Charles 1	9
Doth by his doubt, distrust his promise more.	235	U63 Charles 2	4
His is more safe commoditie, or none:	241	U69 Friend Son	7
More subtle workes, and finer pieces farre,	242	U69 Friend Son	22
That knits brave minds, and manners, more then blood.	246	U70 Ode	106
Which knits brave minds, and manners, more then blood.	246	U70 Ode	V106
Repeating all Great Britain's joy, and more,	249	U72 King	6
Thou canst not meet more Glory, on the way,	252	U75 Epithalam.	3
To make more cleare	254	U75 Epithalam.	54
The bright Brides paths, embelish'd more then thine	254	U75 Epithalam.	59
O happy bands! and thou more happy place,	256	U75 Epithalam.	129
Hee's Master of the Office; yet no more	258	U75 Epithalam.	187
And in the chase, more then Sylvanus can,	264	U79 New-yeares	22
Sate safe enough, but now secured more.	268	U80 Christning	14
And e're I can aske more of her, shee's gone!	269	U81 Pawlet	12
And tell thou, Alde-Legh, None can tell more true	274	U84 Descent	13
And give you reasons more then one.	277	U84 Mind	4
Thou hast no more blowes, Fate, to drive at one:	283	U84 Muse	27
Nothing can more adorne it, then the seat	284	U84 Muse	71
That she is in, or, make it more compleat?	284	U84 Muse	72
Much more desir'd, and dearer then before,	285	U84 Muse	109
As nature could not more increase the flood	287	U84 Muse	158
She spent more time in teares her selfe to dresse	287	U84 Muse	180
And sets more happy in the place:	290	U85 Country	12
And graftes more happy in the place:	290	U85 Country	V 12
Not Lucrine Oysters I could then more prize,	291	U85 Country	49
More sweet then Olives, that new gather'd be	291	U85 Country	55
More timely hie thee to the house,	292	U86 Hor.4:1	9
His armes more acceptable free,	293	U87 Hor.3:9	3
Whilst Horace lov'd no Mistres more,	293	U87 Hor.3:9	5
The Roman Ilia was not more renown'd.	293	U87 Hor.3:9	8
Will to bee, what thou art; and nothing more:	295	U90 Mart.10:47	12
To forme a worke, I would no more desire	307	Horace	50
To frame a worke, I would no more desire	339	Horace	V 52/ 50
In at the eare, doe stirre the mind more slow	317	Horace	257
Have more or lesse then just five Acts: nor laid,	317	Horace	272
With lees of Wine. Next Eschylus, more late,	319	Horace	315
Receive, or give it an applause, the more.	321	Horace	364
Receive, or give it any Crowne the more.	347	Horace	V356/364
More slow, and come more weightie to the eare:	323	Horace	378
Nor had our Italie more glorious bin	325	Horace	411
More strongly takes the people with delight,	327	Horace	458
Our Roman Youths they learne more thriving wayes	350	Horace	V464
Twice, or thrice good, I wonder: but am more	329	Horace	535
Will take you more, the neerer that you stand;	331	Horace	540
Cry, and doe more then the true Mourners: so	333	Horace	615
Then change; no word, or worke, more would he spend	335	Horace	630
Recall him yet, hee'ld be no more a man:	335	Horace	668
Now, bring him backe, he'le be no more a man.	355	Horace	V668
The seaven-fold flower of Arte (more rich then gold)	361	Palmer	15
Splendor! O more then mortall,	364	Ode Splendor	1
Beautye, more then mortall,	364	Ode Splendor	V 1
As fire; and more delightfull	365	Ode Splendor	6
And more hath wonne	367	Ode Who saith	52
(But this more apt	368	Ode Who saith	62
With more delight, and grace)	369	Ode Who saith	103
They saw it halfe, damd thy whole play, and more;	371	Fletcher	8
To fill an Epitaph. But she had more.	371	Epitaph	5
Shewes he dares more then Paules Church-yard durst do.	378	Coryat 2	85
Nay more in his wardrobe, if you will laugh at a	380	Coryat 3	47
And when your yeares rise more, then would be told,	384	Somerset	23
May hurt them more with praise, then Foes with spight.	386	Browne	2
By offring not more sureties, then inow,	386	Browne	12
More of our writers would like thee, not swell	386	Browne	15
To make thy honour, and our wealth the more!	388	Chapman	6
More then the Foster-father of this Child;	389	Aleman	14
Should praise a Matron. What could hurt her more?	391	Shakespeare	14
Of tender eyes will more be wept, then seene:	398	Drayton	76
Empusa, Lamia, or some Monster, more	398	Drayton	87
You aske noe more then certeyne politique Eyes,	404	Inigo Jones 1	45
No faith's more firme, or flat, then where't doth creep.	413	Ghyrlond	20
These Mysteries do point to three more great,	413	Ghyrlond	29
And once more stryke the eare of tyme with those fresh straynes:	420	Ode:If Men	32
But unto more dispayre to Imitate their sounde.	420	Ode:If Men	36
before, I wryte more verse, to bee more wyse.	421	Censure	2

MORISON'
| And thinke, nay know, thy Morison's not dead. | 245 | U70 Ode | 78 |

MORISON
To Sir Lucius Carey, on the death of his Brother Morison	242	U70 Ode	VTtl
. . . paire, Sir Lucius Cary, and Sir H. Morison.	242	U70 Ode	Ttl
Alas, but Morison fell young:	244	U70 Ode	43
But as a Cary, or a Morison.	247	U70 Ode	116

MORISON'S
| And thinke, nay know, thy Morison's not dead. | 245 | U70 Ode | 78 |

MORNE
Next morne, an Ode: Thou mak'st a song ere night.	72	E112 Gamster	12
Each morne, and even, they are taught to pray,	96	F2 Penshurst	95
That houre upon my morne of age,	100	F4 To the World	2
At morne, and even, shades are longest;	104	F7 Women but	7

MORNES
| In darke, and sullen mornes, doe we not say, | 193 | U38 Elegy 'Tis | 79 |

MORNING
This morning, timely rapt with holy fire, ... 52 E76 Bedford 1 1
Life of the Muses day, their morning-starre! . . . . 60 E94 Bedford 3 2
The Muses evening, as their morning-starre. . . . . 61 E94 Bedford 3 16
Shall make us sad next morning: or affright . . . . 65 E101 Supper 41
Whose morning, and whose evening vow . . . . . 99 F3 Wroth V100
Since I drew a Morning kisse . . . . . . 137 U2 Kisse 2
That were this morning blowne; . . . . . . 147 U7 Nymph 19
Who was this Morning such a one, should be . . . 157 U13 Sacvile 126
The Morning-star, whose light our Fal hath stay'd. . 413 Ghyrlond 40
The rosie Morning, or the rising Sun, ... 414 Ghyrlond 50
MORNING'S
Thy morning's, and thy evening's vow . . . . . 99 F3 Wroth 100
MORNINGS
A mornings, and at afternoones, to foole . . . . 230 U56 Covell 22
MORNING-STAR
The Morning-star, whose light our Fal hath stay'd. . 413 Ghyrlond 40
MORNING-STARRE
Life of the Muses day, their morning-starre! . . . 60 E94 Bedford 3 2
The Muses evening, as their morning-starre. . . . 61 E94 Bedford 3 16
MORRISSE
Did dance the famous Morrisse, unto Norwich) . . . 85 E133 Voyage 36
MORROW'
To live untill to morrow' hath lost two dayes. . . 121 F14 Sydney 50
MORROW
To morrow vice, if shee give better pay: . . . 66 E102 Pembroke 10
To rise with eyther of you, on the morrow. . . . 384 Somerset 16
MORTALITIE
'Twixt death and life! Where her mortalitie . . . 271 U81 Pawlet 67
MORTALITY
Mortality, till you immortall bee. . . . . . 384 Somerset 22
MORTALL
Being taught a better way. All mortall deeds . . . 309 Horace 98
Splendor! O more then mortall, ... 364 Ode Splendor 1
Beautye, more then mortall, ... 364 Ode Splendor V 1
MORTS
morts, and mirkins that wagg all, ... 417 Moon 15
MOSCO
The cold of Mosco, and fat Irish ayre, ... 37 E32 Roe 2 5
MOSES
In Moses bush, un-wasted in the fire. . . . . 413 Ghyrlond 24
MOST
Sure, willing povertie lives most in you. . . . 29 E6 Alchymists 2
Camden, most reverend head, to whom I owe . . . 31 E14 Camden 1
What sight in searching the most antique springs! . 31 E14 Camden 8
Th'expence in odours is a most vaine sinne, . . . 33 E20 Cod 2 1
Whose every worke, of thy most earely wit, . . . 34 E23 Donne 1 3
Longer a knowing, then most wits doe live. . . . 34 E23 Donne 1 5
Stile thee a most great foole, but no great man. . 36 E28 Surly 22
Tilter, the most may'admire thee, though not I: . . 36 E29 Tilter 1
Which if most gracious heaven grant like thine, . . 37 E33 Roe 3 5
To the most Worthy of his Honors. Robert, . . . 40 E43 Salisbury 1 VTtl
When even there, where most thou praysest mee, . . 44 E55 Beaumont 9
Away, and leave me, thou thing most abhord, . . . 48 E65 Muse 1
Made me commit most fierce idolatrie . . . . 48 E65 Muse 3
When they cost dearest, and are done most free, . . 49 E66 Cary 14
Most thinke all praises flatteries. But truth brings 49 E67 Suffolk 2
In most vile verses, and cost me more paine, . . . 51 E73 Fine Grand 19
What kinde of creature I could most desire, . . . 52 E76 Bedford 1 3
(Save that most masculine issue of his braine) . . 53 E79 Rutland 6
For your most noble offer had supply'd me. . . . 54 E84 Bedford 2 4
Straight went I home; and there most like a Poet, . 55 E84 Bedford 2 5
And understand 'hem, as most chapmen doe. . . . 59 E92 New Crie 10
Yet, Satyres, since the most of mankind bee . . . 60 E94 Bedford 3 7
In thee, most weighty Savile, liv'd to us: . . . 61 E95 Savile 4
But most we need his faith (and all have you) . . 62 E95 Savile 35
Nor are the Queenes most honor'd maides by th'eares 63 E97 Motion 18
But that, which most doth take my Muse, and mee, . 65 E101 Supper 28
I know not which th'hast most, candor, or wit: . . 78 E123 Rudyerd 3 2
Whose noyse shall keepe thy miming most alive, . . 81 E129 Mime 10
In memorie of which most liquid deed, ... 89 E133 Voyage 193
The eares cut downe in their most height, . . . 98 F3 Wroth V 41
On their beds, most prostitute, ... 106 F8 Sicknesse 45
Most frequent tumults, horrors, and unrests, . . . 110 F11 Epode 33
That is an essence, most gentile and fine, . . . 110 F11 Epode V 45
Makes a most blessed gayne. . . . . . . 112 F11 Epode 86
Riches thought most: But, Madame, thinke what store 114 F12 Rutland 38
Of so great title, birth, but vertue most, . . . 118 F13 Aubigny 49
Whereon the most of mankinde wracke themselves, . . 119 F13 Aubigny 90
Coriat, should rise the most sufficient head . . . 157 U13 Sacvile 128
To aske it: though in most of workes it be . . . 158 U14 Selden 7
Of Truth that searcheth the most hidden Springs, . 176 U24 Frontispice 10
Of Truth which searcheth the most hidden Springs, . 176 U24 Frontispice V 10
But to your selfe, most loyal Lord, ... 179 U25 Desmond 53
Which, how most sacred I will ever keepe, . . . 190 U37 Friend-Book 13
You would be then most confident, that tho . . . 194 U38 Elegy 'Tis 113
An Officer there, did make most solemne love, . . 201 U42 Elegy Let 53
And my selfe most, in some selfe-boasting Rimes? . 203 U43 Vulcan 26
And my selfe most, in lewd selfe-boasting Rimes? . 203 U43 Vulcan V 26
So doth the King, and most of the Kings men . . . 212 U43 Vulcan 211
Of bearing Armes! most civill Soldierie! . . . 214 U44 Speach 44
What, to make legs? yes, and to smell most sweet, . 215 U44 Speach 90
As if that part lay for a [   ] most fit! . . . 232 U58 Book-seller 12

416

	Page	Title	Line
MOST (cont.)			
Most pious King, but his owne good in you!	236	U64 Charles 3	2
But most, a vertuous Sonne.	244	U70 Ode	47
To the Kings Most Excellent Majesty	259	U76 Petition	VTtl
—Doth most humbly show it,	259	U76 Petition	3
For Mind, and Body, the most excellent	274	U84 Descent	3
Who violates the God-head, is most vitious	284	U84 Muse	74
For, Prayer is the Incense most perfumes	288	U84 Muse	187
And most his Justice, in the fitting parts,	289	U84 Muse	223
Most pleasant Martial; Substance got with ease,	295	U90 Mart.10:47	2
Most Writers, noble Sire, and either Sonne,	307	Horace	33
Most worthie praise, when words that common grew,	307	Horace	67
Most worthie praise, when words that vulgar grew,	340	Horace	V 67
Yet who's most ignorant, dares Verses make.	331	Horace	570
Unseason'd frostes, or the most envyous weather.	361	Palmer	8
the sweetest simples, and most soveraigne seedes.	361	Palmer	12
The knottie heads of the most surly Groomes,	363	Riches	8
It thawes the frostiest, and most stiffe disdaine:	363	Riches	13
Beeing in feare to be robd, he most learnedly begs.	375	Coryat 1	35
And that you may see he most luckily ment	379	Coryat 3	13
To the most noble, and above his Titles, . . .	384	Somerset	Ttl
I find thee write most worthy to be read.	386	Browne	6
And, where the most reade bookes, on Authors fames,	386	Browne	9
To the memorye of that most Honoured Ladie Jane, . . .	394	Jane Ogle	Ttl
Alike of kin, to that most blessed Trine,	413	Ghyrlond	34
Most holy, & pure Virgin, blessed Mayd,	413	Ghyrlond	37
Great Queen of Queens, most mild, most meek, most wise,	414	Ghyrlond	41
Most venerable. Cause of all our joy.	414	Ghyrlond	42
The Seat of Sapience, the most lovely Mother,	414	Ghyrlond	45
And most to be admired of thy Sexe,	414	Ghyrlond	46
And a Comptroller, two most rigid men	415	Rutter	24
We offer as a Circle the most fit	416	Welcome	6
Even states most hated, when no lawes resist	423	Lucan	13
MOTH (See also MOATH)			
Yet with a Dye, that feares no Moth,	230	U55 Burges	7
MOTHER			
Hung stench, diseases, and old filth, their mother,	86	E133 Voyage	70
Mars, and my Mother, in their net:	93	F1 Why write no	6
By description, but my Mother!	136	U2 Cupid	12
That (in pure Madrigall) unto his Mother	201	U42 Elegy Let	68
Sonne of the Wind! for so thy mother gone	208	U43 Vulcan	111
Then Cupid, and his Mother.	221	U48 Bacchus	36
They say you weekly invite with fits o'th' Mother,	223	U49 Pucell	40
The Mother of our Lord: why may not I	238	U66 Queene	3
The Mother of our Prince? When was there seene	238	U66 Queene	6
A tender Mother, a discreeter Wife,	287	U84 Muse	174
Sower Mother of sweet Loves, forbeare	292	U86 Hor.4:1	5
Daughter, and Mother, and the Spouse of God,	413	Ghyrlond	33
The Seat of Sapience, the most lovely Mother,	414	Ghyrlond	45
Of being Daughter, Mother, Spouse of God!	414	Ghyrlond	56
MOTHERS			
In comfort of her mothers teares,	33	E22 Daughter	8
Such my Mothers blushes be,	136	U2 Cupid	20
Is my Mothers! hearts of slaine	137	U2 Cupid	31
With my Mothers is the same.	137	U2 Cupid	38
But then his Mothers sweets you so apply,	182	U28 Worth	12
Both for the Mothers, and the Babes of grace,	223	U49 Pucell	44
And mad'st thy Mothers wombe thine urne.	242	U70 Ode	8
All that their Fathers, and their Mothers might	257	U75 Epithalam.	147
MOTION (See also MOCION)			
The new french-taylors motion, monthly made,	56	E88 Monsieur	15
On the new Motion.	62	E97 Motion	Ttl
See you yond' Motion? Not the old Fa-ding,	62	E97 Motion	1
And my motion from me quite;	132	U2 How he saw	26
That at every motion sweld	138	U2 Kisse	24
And my minds motion not? or have I none?	156	U13 Sacvile	122
But being in Motion still (or rather in race)	166	U15 Friend-Wars	124
A quick, and dazeling motion! when a paire	233	U59 Newcastle	9
MOTIONS			
Telling the motions of each petticote,	34	E25 Beast 1	3
That guides the Motions, and directs the beares.	219	U47 Tribe	50
MOTIVE			
Where Gold's the Motive, women have no Nay.	363	Riches	18
MOTIVES			
Their motives were, since it had not to do	371	Fletcher	9
The motives, and true Spurres to all good Nations.	411	Sutcliffe	5
MOTLY			
For, but thy selfe, where, out of motly, 's hee	44	E53 Old-end	9
MOUGHT			
Much, that mought now be spoke: omitted here	307	Horace	62
MOULDED			
As it slid moulded off from Heaven.	280	U84 Mind	56
Moulded or stroakt up to survey a State!	405	Inigo Jones 1	84
MOULDIE			
And, after mouldie growne, againe were tosted,	88	E133 Voyage	150
MOULDS			
Her broken Armes up, to their emptie moulds.	216	U44 Speach	102
MOUNSIEUR			
On English Mounsieur.	56	E88 Monsieur	Ttl
Would you beleeve, when you this Mounsieur see,	56	E88 Monsieur	1
MOUNSIEURS			
Or hung some Mounsieurs picture on the wall,	56	E88 Monsieur	12

417

	Page	Title	Line
MOUNT (VERB)			
Among my commings in, and see it mount,	161	U14 Selden	80
MOUNT (See also YMOUNTED)			
Thy Mount, to which the Dryads doe resort,	93	F2 Penshurst	10
The pale Pyrene, and the forked Mount:	366	Ode Who saith	21
MOUNTAINE			
To make the Mountaine Quarries move,	143	U3 Musicall	11
My mountaine belly, and my rockie face,	150	U9 Picture	17
And over Grampius mountaine,	368	Ode Who saith	71
MOUNTAINES			
Afford? The Mountaines travail'd, and brought forth	315	Horace	198
MOUNTE			
Of Tyre-man, Mounte-banck & Justice Jones,	402	Inigo Jones 1	16
MOUNTEAGLE			
To William Lord Mounteagle.	46	E60 Mounteagle	Ttl
MOUNTE-BANCK			
Of Tyre-man, Mounte-banck & Justice Jones,	402	Inigo Jones 1	16
MOUNTED			
Or (mounted on a stoole) thy face doth hit	81	E129 Mime	13
Or Castor mounted on his Cyllarus:	228	U53 Newcastle	8
Ply it, and you all are mounted.	657	Door Apollo	14
MOUNTING			
Our teeming Ewes, and lustie-mounting Rammes.	264	U79 New-yeares	17
Your teeming Ewes, aswell as mounting Rammes.	265	U79 New-yeares	51
MOUNTS			
That trembles in the blaze, but (then) mounts higher!	233	U59 Newcastle	8
MOURN'D			
Which, since thy flight from hence, hath mourn'd like night,	392	Shakespeare	79
MOURNERS			
Cry, and doe more then the true Mourners: so	333	Horace	615
MOURNES			
He that feares death, or mournes it, in the just,	37	E34 Death	1
MOURNING			
Put black, and mourning on? and say you misse	285	U84 Muse	98
MOUSE			
A scorned Mouse! O, how much better this,	315	Horace	199
A trifling Mouse! O, how much better this,	343	Horace	V199
MOUTH			
Or those, who doubt the common mouth of fame,	111	F11 Epode	79
Or those, which doubt the common mouth of fame,	111	F11 Epode	V 79
But a well-compass'd mouth to utter it;	327	Horace	462
MOUTHES			
For, then, all mouthes will judge, and their owne way:	82	E131 Ferrab. 2	3
All mouthes, that dare entitle them (from hence)	187	U33 Councellour	11
All mouthes are open, and all stomacks free:	232	U58 Book-seller	2
Had I a thousand Mouthes, as many Tongues,	269	U81 Pawlet	23
MOVE			
Where, though 't be love, that to thy praise doth move	55	E86 Goodyere 2	7
Or is it some french statue? No: 'T doth move,	56	E88 Monsieur	13
Move it, as their humblest sute,	106	F8 Sicknesse	46
Move it, as their humble sute,	106	F8 Sicknesse	V 46
The first; as prone to move	110	F11 Epode	32
Because they move, the continent doth so:	111	F11 Epode	71
For I shall move stocks, stones, no lesse then he.	115	F12 Rutland	78
With every vertue, wheresoere it move,	116	F13 Aubigny	8
Let it not your wonder move,	131	U2 Excuse	1
Or, if you did move to night	138	U2 Kisse	21
To make the Mountaine Quarries move,	143	U3 Musicall	11
One un-becomming thought doth move	148	U7 Nymph	31
Yet we must more then move still, or goe on,	157	U13 Sacvile	135
Throughout your forme; as though that move,	173	U22 Flegy Tho	6
As flatt'ry with friends humours still to move.	190	U37 Friend-Book	27
How all my Fibres by your Spirit doe move,	194	U38 Elegy 'Tis	111
No Poets verses yet did ever move,	199	U42 Elegy Let	3
A Goat in Velvet; or some block could move	202	U42 Elegy Let	82
To another, Move; he went; To a third, Go,	287	U84 Muse	170
Was said to move the stones, by his Lutes powers,	327	Horace	484
And Flatterye, with Frindes humors: still to move.	422	Censure	20
MOV'D			
And how his Ganimede mov'd, and how his goate,	34	E25 Beast 1	4
Mov'd by her order, and the ninth more high,	82	E130 Ferrab. 1	13
By Atomes mov'd;	148	U8 Houre-glasse	3
And this well mov'd the Judgement of the King	256	U75 Epithalam.	105
Mov'd by the wind, so comely moved she.	287	U84 Muse	166
Of money, haughtie, to desire soon mov'd,	315	Horace	235
MOVED			
Mov'd by the wind, so comely moved she.	287	U84 Muse	166
MOVES			
Moves like a sprightly River, and yet can	198	U40 Elegy That	26
MOVETH			
It moveth all; and makes a flight	279	U84 Mind	31
MOV'ST			
Venus, againe thou mov'st a warre	292	U86 Hor.4:1	1
MOWED			
The mowed meddowes, with the fleeced sheepe,	97	F3 Wroth	39
MR			
To Lucy, Countesse of Bedford, with Mr. Donnes Satyres.	60	E94 Bedford 3	Ttl
To Mr. Josuah Sylvester.	83	E132 Sylvester	Ttl
Ben: Jonson To His Honord Friend Mr John Selden Health.	158	U14 Selden	VTtl
Epistle To Mr. Arthur Squib.	229	U54 Squib	Ttl
To Mr. John Burges.	229	U55 Burges	Ttl
. . . that Noble Gentleman, Mr. Hierome Weston, Son, and . . .	252	U75 Epithalam.	Ttl
The height, let him learne of Mr. Tom. Coryate;	379	Coryat 3	2

MR (cont.)

The height, let him learne of Mr. Tom Coryate.	381	Coryat 3	60
To my truly-belov'd Freind, Mr Browne: on his Pastorals.	386	Browne	Ttl
To my worthy and honour'd Friend, Mr George Chapman,	388	Chapman	Ttl
. . . Mr. William Shakespeare: And what he hath left us.	390	Shakespeare	Ttl
Mr Surveyor, you that first begann	402	Inigo Jones 1	1
An Epigram To My Joviall Good Freind Mr. Robert Dover,	415	Dover	Ttl
This was Mr Ben: Johnsons Answer of the suddayne.	418	Answer	Ttl
Mr. Alexander Glover	666	Glover	2

MRS

To Mrs. Philip Sydney.	73	E114 Sydney	Ttl
To his Lady, then Mrs. Cary.	80	E126 Mrs Cary	Ttl
And in his Mrs. flame, playing like a flye,	149	U8 Houre-glasse	7
And in his Mrs. flaming, playing like a flye,	149	U8 Houre-glasse V	7
This makes me, Mrs. that sometime by stealth,	197	U40 Elegy That	9
To Mrs. Alice Sutcliffe, on her divine Meditations.	411	Sutcliffe	Ttl

MUCH

Much lesse with lewd, prophane, and beastly phrase,	27	E2 My Booke	11
For the lucks sake, it thus much favour have,	27	E3 Bookseller	4
My sinne was too much hope of thee, lov'd boy,	41	E45 First Son	2
As what he loves may never like too much.	41	E45 First Son	12
But thine, for which I doo't, so much exceeds!	46	E60 Mounteagle	8
It may be much, or little, in the cause.	49	E66 Cary	16
That so much skarfe of France, and hat, and fether,	56	E88 Monsieur	3
That he, untravell'd, should be french so much,	56	E88 Monsieur	7
Much like those Brethren; thinking to prevaile	59	E92 New Crie	36
That know not so much state, wrong, as they doo.	59	E92 New Crie	40
How much of great example wert thou, Roe,	64	E99 Th Roe 2	5
But much it now availes, what's done, of whom:	64	E99 Th Roe 2	7
He that not trusts me, having vow'd thus much,	70	E108 Soldiers	9
Wherein thou shew'st, how much the latter are	72	E111 Edmonds 2	3
That to the world thou should'st reveale so much,	72	E111 Edmonds 2	10
Where finding so much beautie met with vertue,	74	E114 Sydney	6
Makes, the whole longer, then 'twas given him, much.	76	E119 Shelton	16
But, being so much too good for earth,	77	E120 S. P.	23
As much beautie, as could dye:	79	E124 Elizabeth	4
Else, I my state should much mistake,	101	F4 To the World	57
Not so much honoring thee,	106	F9 Celia 3	10
Much more a noble, and right generous mind	112	F11 Epode	111
Much more a noble, or a generous mind	112	F11 Epode	V111
And this shall be no false one, but as much	117	F13 Aubigny	27
As bloud, and match. Wherein, how more then much	117	F13 Aubigny	46
Onely, thus much, out of a ravish'd zeale,	119	F13 Aubigny	108
Till he cherish'd too much beard,	141	U2 Her man	23
As to doe no thing too much.	142	U2 Her man	46
And feare much more, that more of him be showne!	147	U7 Nymph	21
Whom I adore so much, should so slight me,	149	U9 Picture	4
Read so much wast, as she cannot imbrace	150	U9 Picture	16
Would say as much, as both have done	151	U12 Corbet	3
Much from him I professe I wonne,	152	U12 Corbet	29
O, is it so? knowes he so much? and will	155	U13 Sacvile	73
You know (without my flatt'ring you) too much	157	U13 Sacvile	155
Your Booke, my Selden, I have read, and much	158	U14 Selden	5
Men past their termes, and prais'd some names too much,	159	U14 Selden	21
Before men get a verse: much lesse a Praise;	159	U14 Selden	26
Selden! two Names that so much understand!	161	U14 Selden	82
Thither it flowes. How much did Stallion spend	163	U15 Friend-Wars	47
Now so much friend, as you would trust in me,	169	U17 Friend-Debt	14
As not the World can praise too much,	173	U22 Elegy Tho	3
With so much Loyalties expence,	173	U22 Elegy Tho	22
So much my Subject drownes the rest.	182	U27 Ode Helen	36
A better lover, and much better Poet.	182	U28 Worth	4
What use, what strength of reason! and how much	187	U33 Councellour	24
How much they lame her in her propertie.	190	U37 Friend-Book	21
Be not affected with these markes too much	193	U38 Elegy 'Tis	83
How much you are the better part of me;	194	U38 Elegy 'Tis	110
Troy, though it were so much his Venus care.	210	U43 Vulcan	160
Troy, though it were so much thy Venus joycare.	210	U43 Vulcan	V160
Losse, remaines yet, as much despair'd as mine.	211	U43 Vulcan	V196
And Ord'nance too: so much as from the Tower	213	U44 Speach	3
In so much land a yeare, or such a Banke,	215	U44 Speach	76
That turnes us so much moneys, at which rate	215	U44 Speach	77
Much lesse a name would we bring up, or nurse,	216	U45 Squib	9
But he that's too-much that, is friend of none.	216	U45 Squib	24
As make it their proficiencie, how much	218	U47 Tribe	12
Then Phoebus; and much stronger	221	U48 Bacchus	22
I am no States-man, and much lesse Divine,	223	U49 Pucell	25
And should grow rich, had I much more to pay.	231	U56 Covell	30
How much to heaven for thee, great Charles, they owe!	237	U64 Charles 3	22
Of so much safetie to the Realme, and King.	238	U66 Queene	14
Of so much health, both to our Land, and King.	238	U66 Queene	V 14
What prayers (People) can you thinke too much?	249	U72 King	20
How much they are belov'd of God, in thee;	268	U80 Christning	4
Thereof, no notion can expresse how much	269	U81 Pawlet	26
No Nation can expresse how much	269	U81 Pawlet	V 26
Much more desir'd, and dearer then before,	285	U84 Muse	109
If with bright floods, the Winter troubled much,	291	U85 Country	51
If with East floods, the Winter troubled much,	291	U85 Country	V 51
Makes his life longer then 'twas given him, much.	295	U89 Mart.8:77	8
Or I am much deceiv'd, shall be to place	307	Horace	60
Much, that mought now be spoke: omitted here	307	Horace	62
And come not too much wrested. What's that thing,	309	Horace	76
Cato's and Ennius tongues have lent much worth,	309	Horace	81

		Page	Title	Line
MUCH (cont.)				
Much phrase that now is dead, shall be reviv'd;		309	Horace	101
And much shall dye, that now is nobly liv'd,		309	Horace	102
It much will differ, if a God speake, than,		313	Horace	161
It much will sway whether a god speak, than;		313	Horace	V161
A scorned Mouse! O, how much better this,		342	Horace	199
A trifling Mouse! O, how much better this,		315	Horace	V199
Mans comming yeares much good with them doe bring:		343	Horace	250
As his departing take much thence: lest, then,		317	Horace	251
Much from the sight, which faire report will make		317	Horace	262
Yet he that offers at it, may sweat much,		321	Horace	351
Of Order, and Connexion; so much grace		321	Horace	353
And not without much praise; till libertie		321	Horace	366
Of too much haste, and negligence in part,		321	Horace	385
Much in the Poeme shine, I will not bee		323	Horace	385
So he that flaggeth much, becomes to me		329	Horace	526
The wished goale, both did, and suffer'd much		329	Horace	533
"So much doth Virtue hate,		333	Horace	588
Read here a little, that thou mayst know much.		367	Ode Who saith	31
Up so much truth, as could I it pursue		371	Epitaph	2
Of lying, he feares so much the reproofe		372	Epitaph	13
To his much and worthily esteemed friend the Author.		380	Coryat 3	31
With the how much they set forth, but th'how well.		383	Author	Ttl
As neither Man, nor Muse, can praise too much.		386	Browne	16
How much Architectonice is your owne!		390	Shakespeare	4
Why much good doo't you! Be what beast you will,		402	Inigo Jones 1	10
And Goody Sculpture, brought with much adoe		403	Inigo Jones 1	21
soe much the starte		403	Inigo Jones 1	38
Howe much they lame hir, in hir propertye:		420	Ode:If Men	11
Till I, at much expense of Time, and Taper		421	Censure	14
MUD		666	Glover	7
Ycleped Mud, which, when their oares did once stirre,		85	E133 Voyage	62
MUFFLES				
Muffles the clearnesse of Election,		363	Riches	14
MULTIPLI'D				
Have multipli'd their arts, and powers,		251	U74 Weston	17
MULTITUDE				
Against a multitude; and (with thy Stile		187	U33 Councellour	31
MUNG'				
His bought armes Mung' not lik'd; for his first day		42	E48 Mungril	1
MUNGREL				
A Mungrel Curre? Thou should'st stinck forth, and dye		409	Detractor	15
MUNGRIL				
On Mungril Esquire.		42	E48 Mungril	Ttl
MUNIMENTS				
And doth deserve all muniments of praise,		400	Beaumont	9
MURDER (See also MURTHER)				
They murder him againe, that envie thee.		72	E111 Edmonds 2	14
Engines of Murder, and receive the praise		212	U43 Vulcan	207
Engines of Murder, and enjoy with praise		212	U43 Vulcan	V207
Murder.		363	Murder	Ttl
MURDRED				
Do crowne thy murdred Poeme: which shall rise		371	Fletcher	14
MURMURE				
And murmure cannot quarrell at your wayes?		237	U64 Charles 3	14
I murmure against God, for having ta'en		283	U84 Muse	33
The Fountaines murmure as the streames doe creepe,		290	U85 Country	27
MURMURES				
Strifes, murmures, or delay,		258	U75 Epithalam.	189
MURMURING				
Of murmuring Subjects; make the Nations know		261	U77 Treasurer	19
MURTHER				
To murther different hearts,		110	F11 Epode	52
MURTHERING				
Of murthering of mankind many wayes.		212	U43 Vulcan	V208
MUSE				
Whom should my Muse then flie to, but the best		28	E4 James 1	9
Donne, the delight of Phoebus, and each Muse,		34	E23 Donne 1	1
If any Muse out-live their spight, his can;		35	E27 Roe 1	4
What need hast thou of me? or of my Muse?		40	E43 Salisbury 1	1
How I doe love thee Beaumont, and thy Muse,		44	E55 Beaumont	1
Curst be his Muse, that could lye dumbe, or hid		47	E63 Salisbury 2	11
To my Muse.		48	E65 Muse	Ttl
Be thy next masters more unluckie Muse,		48	E65 Muse	5
With me thou leav'st an happier Muse then thee,		48	E65 Muse	11
I thought to forme unto my zealous Muse,		52	E76 Bedford 1	2
My Muse bad, Bedford write, and that was shee.		52	E76 Bedford 1	18
I would have spent: how every Muse should know it,		55	E84 Bedford 2	7
Sung by a Horace, or a Muse as free;		58	E91 Vere	4
But that, which most doth take my Muse, and mee,		65	E101 Supper	28
Least mention of a Nymph, a Muse, a Grace,		67	E105 L Wroth 2	4
I sweare by your true friend, my Muse, I love		70	E108 Soldiers	5
Who now calls on thee, Nevil, is a Muse,		70	E109 Nevil	1
My lighter comes, to kisse thy learned Muse;		78	E121 Rudyerd 1	2
I, and this Muse had beene, if thou hadst not		80	E127 Aubigny	7
Orpheus, Ulysses: or the Latine Muse,		84	E133 Voyage	3
My Muse had plough'd with his, that sung A-jax.		89	E133 Voyage	196
For the more countenance to my active Muse?		107	F10 Proludium	3
For the more countenance to our active Muse?		107	F10 Proludium	V 3
My Muse up by commission: No, I bring		108	F10 Proludium	28
Our muse up by commission: No, we bring		108	F10 Proludium	V 28
An elegie? no, muse; yt askes a straine		108	F10 Proludium	1
the glories of yt. Now our muse takes winge,		108	F10 Proludium	15

		Page	Title	Line
MUSE (cont.)				
It is the Muse, alone, can raise to heaven,	. . . .	114	F12 Rutland	41
That had no Muse to make their fame abide.	. . . .	114	F12 Rutland	48
To my lesse sanguine Muse, wherein she'hath wonne	. . .	115	F12 Rutland	72
Then all, that have but done my Muse least grace,	. . .	115	F12 Rutland	79
What my Muse and I have done:	. . .	138	U2 Kisse	5
Though I confesse (as every Muse hath err'd,	. . .	159	U14 Selden	19
The Credit, what would furnish a tenth Muse!	. . .	161	U14 Selden	84
Wake, and put on the wings of·Pindars Muse,	. . .	176	U25 Desmond	3
Or Constables Ambrosiack Muse	. . . .	182	U27 Ode Helen	27
Nor is my Muse, or I asham'd to owe it	. . .	182	U28 Worth	5
At the Well no Muse did stay,	. . . .	183	U29 Fit of Rime	20
Of beautie; but the Muse hath interest in:	. . .	200	U42 Elegy Let	15
What though with Tribade lust she force a Muse,	. . .	222	U49 Pucell	7
So have you gain'd a Servant, and a Muse:	. . . .	230	U56 Covell	5
Marrie the Muse is one, can tread the Aire,	. . .	230	U56 Covell	13
Marrie his Muse is one, can tread the Aire,	. . .	230	U56 Covell	V 13
Accept his Muse; and tell, I know you can,	. . .	231	U56 Covell	26
The Muse, or the Poet,	. . . .	232	U57 Burges	25
'T were better spare a Butt, then spill his Muse.	. . .	241	U68 House-hold	12
The Muse not peepes out, one of hundred dayes;	. . .	248	U71 Treasurer	9
With Angels, Muse, to speake these: Nothing can	. . .	255	U75 Epithalam.	84
(For with both the Muse was fed)	. . . .	259	U76 Petition	16
(For with both the Muse it fed)	. . . .	259	U76 Petition	V 16
An Epigram To my Muse, the Lady Digby, . . .	. . .	262	U78 Digby	Ttl
Tho', happy Muse, thou know my Digby well;	. . .	262	U78 Digby	1
Goe, Muse, in, and salute him. Say he be	. . .	262	U78 Digby	19
Goe, Muse, in, and salute him thoughe he be	. . .	262	U78 Digby	V 19
Wilt thou be, Muse, when this shall them befall?	. . .	263	U78 Digby	31
Wilt thou be, Muse, when this shall then befall?	. . .	263	U78 Digby	V 31
I call you Muse; now make it true:	. . . .	278	U84 Mind	21
9. Elegie on my Muse. The truly honoured Lady, . . .	. .	282	U84 Muse	Ttl
Who was my Muse, and life of all I sey'd,	. . . .	282	U84 Muse	2
What's left a Poet, when his Muse is gone?	. . .	283	U84 Muse	28
To publish her a Saint. My Muse is gone.	. . .	289	U84 Muse	228
His Muse professing height, and greatnesse, swells;	. .	339	Horace	V 39/ 38
Unto the Lyrick Strings, the Muse gave grace	. . .	309	Horace	113
'Tis not enough, th'elaborate Muse affords	. . .	311	Horace	140
'Tis not enough, the labouring Muse affords	. . .	341	Horace	V140
Speake to me, Muse, the Man, who, after Troy was sack't,	.	315	Horace	201
The Muse not only gave the Greek's a wit,	. . .	327	Horace	461
Or Muse, upon the Lyre, thou chance b'asham'd.	. . .	329	Horace	502
As neither Man, nor Muse, can praise too much.	. . .	390	Shakespeare	4
What Muse, or rather God of harmony	. . .	395	May	14
Thy Muse, and mine, as they expect. 'Tis true:	. . .	396	Drayton	5
Brave are the Musters, that the Muse will make.	. . .	398	Drayton	64
When they doe sweat to fortifie a Muse.	. . .	400	Beaumont	6
Of Ethnicisme, makes his Muse a Saint.	. . .	401	Beaumont	22
Thy blatant Muse abroad, and teach it rather	. . .	411	Gill	11
I Cannot bring my Muse to dropp her Vies	. . .	415	Dover	1
Tell her, his Muse that did invent thee	. . .	662	Bedford	5
MUSES				
Or then, or since, about our Muses springs,	. . .	53	E79 Rutland	3
Life of the Muses day, their morning-starre!	. . .	60	E94 Bedford 3	2
The Muses evening, as their morning-starre.	. . .	61	E94 Bedford 3	16
Need any Muses praise to give it fame?	. . .	66	E103 L Wroth 1	6
Alwayes at hand, to aide the merry Muses.	. . .	85	E133 Voyage	54
At his great birth, where all the Muses met.	. . .	94	F2 Penshurst	14
Nor are the Muses strangers found:	. . .	98	F3 Wroth	52
His love unto the Muses, when his skill	. . .	114	F12 Rutland	33
Heare, what the Muses sing about thy roote,	. . .	119	F13 Aubigny	100
'Mongst my Muses finding me,	. . .	136	U2 Cupid	7
And the Muses to their braine;	. . .	184	U29 Fit of Rime	41
So may the gentler Muses, and good fame	. . .	186	U31 Elsmere	7
That from the Muses fountaines doth indorse	. . .	200	U42 Elegy Let	7
So may the Muses follow	. . . .	221	U48 Bacchus	25
For never saw I yet the Muses dwell,	. . .	228	U53 Newcastle	15
He lov'd the Muses;	. . . .	231	U57 Burges	9
Minerva's and the Muses care!	. . .	233	U60 La-ware	4
An Ode, or Song, by all the Muses. . . .	. . .	239	U67 Muses	Ttl
To make all the Muses debters	. . .	259	U76 Petition	8
The greater part, that boast the Muses fire,	. . .	339	Horace	V 33
Nor know t'observe: why (i'the Muses name)	. . .	311	Horace	128
Attempted by the Muses tunes, and strings;	. . .	329	Horace	498
Lest of the singer Apollo, and Muses fam'd	. . .	353	Horace	V579/501
And wish that all the Muses blood were spilt,	. . .	371	Fletcher	12
I meane with great, but disproportion'd Muses:	. . .	391	Shakespeare	26
And all the Muses still were in their prime,	. . .	391	Shakespeare	44
Upon the Muses anvile: turne the same,	. . .	392	Shakespeare	61
. . . Muses Of His Friend M. Drayton.	. . .	396	Drayton	Ttl
That sits watering with the Muses.	. . . .	657	Door Apollo	10
MUSICALL				
The Musicall Strife; In a Pastorall Dialogue.	. . .	143	U3 Musicall	Ttl
MUSICK				
Which Musick had; or speake her knowne effects,	. . .	82	E130 Ferrab. 1	3
To plant the Musick where noe eare can reach!	. . .	404	Inigo Jones 1	53
To be the Musick Master! Fabler too!	. . .	404	Inigo Jones 1	63
MUSICKE				
In time to Tragedie, a Musicke new.	. . .	319	Horace	306
"Musicke hath power to draw,	. . .	367	Ode Who saith	47
All sorts of fish with Musicke of his maw.	. . .	374	Coryat 1	11
MUSIQUE				
And Apollo's Musique die,	. . . . .	183	U29 Fit of Rime	23

```
                                                   Page      Title      Line

MUSIQUE (cont.)
  Of grace, and Musique to the eare,        .    .    .    279   U84 Mind        35
  A Musique in the Eares, will ever last;   .    .    .    286   U84 Muse       124
  As jarring Musique doth, at jolly feasts, .    .    .    331   Horace        557
  Musique and Poesie:               .    .    .    .    401   Filmer          5
MUST
  Shee must have money: he returnes, god payes.  .    .    30   E12 Shift        8
  Whither the world must follow.  And I, now,   .    .    37   E33 Roe 3        3
  For writing better, I must envie thee.    .    .    .    44   E55 Beaumont    10
  To reade my verses; now I must to heare:   .    .    .    45   E58 Groome       2
  The world must know your greatnesse is my debter.  .    51   E73 Fine Grand   4
  I must a libell make, and cosen both.     .    .    .    54   E81 Proule       8
  Now, I must give thy life, and deed, the voice  .    .    55   E86 Goodyere 2   5
  And stoupe, and cringe.  O then, it needs must prove   .    56   E88 Monsieur    14
  And like them too; must needfully, though few,  .    .    61   E94 Bedford 3   13
  Of any Madames, hath neadd squires, and must.  .    .    63   E97 Motion      14
  And I must now beleeve him: for, to day,   .    .    .    64   E100 Playwrt 3   3
  Whose life, ev'n they, that envie it, must praise;  .    66   E102 Pembroke   16
  Thou must draw more: and they, that hope to see  .    66   E102 Pembroke   19
  The common-wealth still safe, must studie thee.  .    66   E102 Pembroke   20
  A picture, which the world for yours must know,  .    67   E104 Montgomery  14
  For which there must more sea, and land be leap'd,  .    69   F107 Hungry     16
  I Must beleeve some miracles still bee,   .    .    .    73   E114 Sydney      1
  Vertuously practise must at least allow   .    .    .    75   E116 Jephson    14
  Them in, if not, from thee; or must commit   .    .    75   E116 Jephson    15
  Vanish'd away: as you must all presume    .    .    .    87   E133 Voyage    110
  Must trie the'un-used valour of a nose:   .    .    .    87   E133 Voyage    132
  But, what we'are borne for, we must beare:   .    .    101   F4 To the World  53
  If't chance to me, I must not grutch.     .    .    .   101   F4 To the World  56
  And must I sing? what subject shall I chuse?  .    .   107   F10 Proludium    1
  We must sing too? what subject shall we chuse?  .    107   F10 Proludium   V 1
  Some way of entrance) we must plant a guard   .    .   109   F11 Epode        7
  Right, the right way: yet must your comfort bee  .   118   F13 Aubigny     68
  Must now                   .    .    .    .    .    .   120   F14 Sydney      24
  And great, must seeke for new,       .    .    .    .   121   F14 Sydney      35
  Which must be now,             .    .    .    .    .   121   F14 Sydney      47
  But it must, straight, my melancholy bee?   .    .   122   F15 Heaven       2
  Standing with feare, and must with horror fall,  .   122   F15 Heaven      19
  First, that I must kneeling yeeld     .    .    .    133   U2 Suffered      7
  Therefore, Charis, you must do't,      .    .    .    140   U2 Promise      13
  For he must looke wanton-wise.        .    .    .    .   141   U2 Her man      16
  What man but must lose his?          .    .    .    .   143   U3 Musicall       8
  And if wee must, let's sing of you.    .    .    .    145   U5 Woman-kind    6
  Which we in love must doe aswell,      .    .    .    146   U6 Defence        9
  I must the true Relation make,        .    .    .    .   150   U11 Dreame       2
  Must make me sad for what I have obtain'd.   .    .   154   U13 Sacvile     38
  Yea, of th'ingratefull: and he forth must tell  .   155   U13 Sacvile     77
  No! he must feele and know, that will advance.  .   156   U13 Sacvile    123
  Yet we must more then move still, or goe on,   .    157   U13 Sacvile    135
  We must accomplish; 'Tis the last Key-stone   .    157   U13 Sacvile    136
  I, that's a Charme and halfe! She must afford  .   163   U15 Friend-Wars  52
  That all respect; She must lie downe: Nay more,  .  163   U15 Friend-Wars  53
  Lesse must not be thought on then Mistresse: or,  .  165   U15 Friend-Wars  95
  His deare and borrow'd Bravery he must cast?   .   165   U15 Friend-Wars 110
  Give me but that againe, that I must wast   .    .   167   U15 Friend-Wars 152
  Give me but that againe, which I must wast   .    .   167   U15 Friend-Wars V152
  That I must send one first, my Choyce assignes,  .   170   U18 Elegy Can   23
  Or have the least of Good, but what it must   .    171   U20 Shrub         7
  An hower will come they must affect theyr Ease,  .   179   U25 Desmond    V 42
  Must now be rayn'd.              .    .    .    .    180   U26 Ode High     15
  But must confesse from whom what gift I tooke.  .   189   U37 Friend-Book   6
  He cannot angrie be, but all must quake,   .    .   193   U38 Elegy 'Tis   71
  And must be bred, so to conceale his birth,   .    197   U40 Elegy That   17
  Since you must goe, and I must bid farewell,   .   199   U41 Elegy Since   1
  Where we must feele it Darke for halfe a yeare.  .  199   U41 Elegy Since   8
  But is the Poets matter: And he must,     .    .   200   U42 Elegy Let    17
  Put a Coach-mare in Tissue, must I horse   .    .   201   U42 Elegy Let    43
  That are like cloath'd: must I be of those fooles  .  201   U42 Elegy Let    48
  Are we by Booke-wormes to be awde? must we   .    215   U44 Speach       67
  Inquirie of the worth: So must we doe,    .    .   216   U45 Squib        15
  Or if Chance must, to each man that doth rise,  .   217   U46 Coke         23
  But if, for honour, we must draw the Sword,   .    219   U47 Trite        39
  And that her truster feares her? Must I too?   .   223   U49 Pucell       22
  I Am to dine, Friend, where I must be weigh'd  .   229   U54 Squib         1
  An ill commoditie! 'T must make good weight.   .   229   U54 Squib         6
  Whilst that in heav'n, this light on earth must shine.  246  U70 Ode       96
  Their Carract was! I, or my trump must breake,  .   269   U81 Pawlet       27
  Their Carract was! for my trump must breake,   .   269   U81 Pawlet     V 27
  And Goates together, whither they must come   .    283   U84 Muse         47
  Those other two; which must be judg'd, or crown'd:  .  284  U84 Muse        55
  Must come to take a sentence, by the sense   .    284   U84 Muse         57
  When they are poore, and banish'd, must throw by,  .  311  Horace        138
  The customes of each age thou must observe,   .    315   Horace        223
  What straight-way he must labour to retract.   .   315   Horace        240
  To children; we must alwayes dwell, and stay   .   317   Horace        253
  Present anone: Medea must not kill      .    .    317   Horace        263
  His Nephews entrailes; nor must Progne flie   .    317   Horace        266
  Nor must the Fable, that would hope the Fate,   .   317   Horace        270
  Must maintaine manly; not be heard to sing   .    317   Horace        277
  Must manly keep, and not be heard to sing   .    .   345   Horace       V277
  It still must favour good men, and to these   .    317   Horace        280
  Be wonne a friend; it must both sway, and bend   .   317   Horace        281
  It would, must be: lest it alive would draw   .    329   Horace        509
```

	Page	Title	Line
MUST (cont.)			
Now must we plie our ayme; our Swan's on wing.	368	Ode Who saith	64
made prospective, behould hym, hee must passe	383	Rich	12
Must be intended still to understand:	383	Author	2
It must be thine owne judgment, yet, that sends	386	Browne	7
Were askt of thy Discoveries; They must say,	388	Chapman	8
Yet must I not give Nature all: Thy Art,	392	Shakespeare	55
My gentle Shakespeare, must enjoy a part.	392	Shakespeare	56
Who casts to write a living line, must sweat,	392	Shakespeare	59
Must Celia bee, the Anagram of Alice.	412	Sutcliffe	23
Cry'd up of late: Whereto there must be first	415	Rutter	21
MUSTER			
Belch'd forth an ayre, as hot, as at the muster	85	E133 Voyage	63
Though thou wert Muster-master of the Land.	167	U15 Friend-Wars	174
MUSTER-MASTER			
Though thou wert Muster-master of the Land.	167	U15 Friend-Wars	174
MUSTERS			
Brave are the Musters, that the Muse will make.	398	Drayton	64
MUTE			
Throughout, might flatt'rie seeme; and to be mute	58	E91 Vere	10
So speake (as yet it is not mute)	181	U27 Ode Helen	4
So, be your Concord, still, as deepe, as mute;	384	Somerset	17
MUTTON			
Ushring the mutton; with a short-leg'd hen,	64	E101 Supper	11
MUTUALL			
Where mutuall frauds are fought, and no side yeild;	186	U33 Councellour	4
Delights, nor credulous hope of mutuall Joy,	293	U86 Hor.4:1	30
MUTUALLY			
And I, am mutually on fire	293	U87 Hor.3:9	13
MY			
Pray thee, take care, that tak'st my booke in hand,	27	E1 Reader	1
To my Booke.	27	E2 My Booke	Ttl
To my Booke-seller.	27	E3 Bookseller	Ttl
Nor have my title-leafe on posts, or walls,	28	E3 Bookseller	7
Whom should my Muse then flie to, but the best	28	E4 James 1	9
Of Kings for grace; of Poets for my test?	28	E4 James 1	10
May none, whose scatter'd names honor my booke,	29	E9 To All	1
To my lord Ignorant.	29	E10 Ignorant	Ttl
But I have my revenge made, in thy name.	29	E10 Ignorant	2
From my diseases danger, and from thee.	31	E13 Empirick	4
(How nothing's that?) to whom my countrey owes	31	E14 Camden	3
But for their powers, accept my pietie.	31	E14 Camden	14
That wish my poemes a legitimate fame,	32	E17 Critic	3
To my meere English Censurer.	32	E18 Censurer	Ttl
To thee, my way in Epigrammes seemes new,	32	E18 Censurer	1
On my first Daughter.	33	E22 Daughter	Ttl
Take better ornaments, my teares, and verse.	35	E27 Roe 1	2
May heare my Epigrammes, but like of none.	36	E28 Surly	20
Be thine, I taxe, yet doe not owne my rimes:	36	E30 Guiltie	2
Breathe to expect my when, and make my how.	37	E33 Roe 3	4
Who wets my grave, can be no friend of mine.	37	E33 Roe 3	6
To thy Domitian, than I can my James:	38	E36 Martial	2
But in my royall subject I passe thee,	38	E36 Martial	3
And crie good! good! This quite perverts my sense,	38	E38 Guiltie 2	5
I'le loose my modestie, and tell your name.	38	E38 Guiltie 2	8
What heast hast thou of me? or of my Muse?	40	E43 Salisbury 1	1
Yet dare not, to my thought, lest hope allow	41	E43 Salisbury 1	7
When, in my booke, men reade but Cecill's name,	41	E43 Salisbury 1	9
When, in my Verse, men reade but Sarum's name,	41	E43 Salisbury 1 V	9
On my First Sonne.	41	E45 First Son	Ttl
Farewell, thou child of my right hand, and joy;	41	E45 First Son	1
My sinne was too much hope of thee, lov'd boy,	41	E45 First Son	2
To pay at's day of marriage. By my hand	42	E46 Luckless 1	4
Play-wright me reades, and still my verses damnes,	42	E49 Playwrt 1	1
In my chast booke: professe them in thine owne.	42	E49 Playwrt 1	6
Disprause my worke, then praise it frostily:	43	E52 Courtling	2
As if thou wert my friend, but lack'dst a cause.	43	E52 Courtling	4
Chev'ril cryes out, my verses libells are;	44	E54 Chev'ril 2	1
How I doe feare my selfe, that am not worth	44	E55 Beaumont	3
To reade my verses; now I must to heare:	45	E58 Groome	2
For offring, with thy smiles, my wit to grace,	45	E58 Groome	3
And so my sharpnesse thou no lesse dis-joynts,	45	E58 Groome	5
Then thou did'st late my sense, loosing my points.	45	E58 Groome	6
Loe, what my countrey should have done (have rais'd	46	E60 Mounteagle	1
And proud, my worke shall out-last common deeds,	46	E60 Mounteagle	6
My countries parents I have many knowne;	46	E60 Mounteagle	9
But saver of my countrey thee alone.	46	E60 Mounteagle	10
Curst be my voyce if it lye dumbe, or hid	47	E63 Salisbury 2 V	11
These (noblest Cecil) labour'd in my thought,	48	E64 Salisbury 3	15
To my Muse.	48	E65 Muse	Ttl
Shee shall instruct my after-thoughts to write	48	E65 Muse	13
Then to begin, my Roe: He makes a state	50	E70 Wm Roe 1	2
What is't, fine Grand, makes thee my friendship flye,	51	E73 Fine Grand	1
The world must know your greatnesse is my debter.	51	E73 Fine Grand	4
Item, an epitaph on my lords cock,	51	E73 Fine Grand	18
I thought to forme unto my zealous Muse,	52	E76 Bedford 1	2
My Muse bad, Bedford write, and that was shee.	52	E76 Bedford 1	18
That, any way, my booke should speake thy name:	53	E77 Not name	2
For, if thou shame, ranck'd with my friends, to goe,	53	E77 Not name	3
I'am more asham'd to have thee thought my foe.	53	E77 Not name	4
To be the wealthy witnesse of my pen:	54	E81 Proule	4
Throughout my booke. 'Troth put out woman too.	54	E83 Friend	2
I fancied to my selfe, what wine, what wit	55	E84 Bedford 2	6

MY (cont.)

	Page	Title	Line
My selfe a witnesse of thy few dayes sport:	55	E85 Goodyere 1	2
When I would know thee Goodyere, my thought lookes	55	E86 Goodyere 2	1
On Mill my Ladies Woman.	57	E90 Mill	Ttl
Against my grave, and time could not forgive.	58	E91 Vere	12
If, my religion safe, I durst embrace	61	E95 Savile	1
When I dare send my Epigrammes to thee?	62	E96 Donne 2	2
My title's seal'd. Those that for claps doe write,	62	E96 Donne 2	9
Cry'd to my face, they were th'elixir of wit:	64	E100 Playwrt 3	2
Five of my jests, then stolne, past him a play.	64	E100 Playwrt 3	4
To night, grave sir, both my poore house, and I	64	E101 Supper	1
Knat, raile, and ruffe too. How so ere, my man	65	E101 Supper	20
That will the pastrie, not my paper, show of.	65	E101 Supper	26
But that, which most doth take my Muse, and mee,	65	E101 Supper	28
My praise is plaine, and where so ere profest,	67	E103 L Wroth 1	13
That's, sit, and eate: doe not my eares abuse.	68	E107 Hungry	2
Strength of my Countrey, whilst I bring to view	69	E108 Soldiers	1
I sweare by your true friend, my Muse, I love	70	E108 Soldiers	5
And did not shame it with my actions, then,	70	E108 Soldiers	7
No more, then I dare now doe, with my pen.	70	E108 Soldiers	8
Might be found out as good, and not my Lord.	75	E116 Jephson	8
My lighter comes, to kisse thy learned Muse;	78	E121 Rudyerd 1	2
Cary my love is, Daphne but my tree.	80	E126 Mrs Cary	8
Roe (and my joy to name) th'art now, to goe	80	E128 Wm Roe 2	1
To urge, my lov'd Alphonso, that bold fame	82	E130 Ferrab. 1	1
If to admire were to commend, my praise	83	E132 Sylvester	1
Before my thought, and (in thy right) commands	83	E132 Sylvester	8
Or goddesse to invoke, to stuffe my verse;	85	E133 Voyage	45
Alcides, be thou succouring to my song.	85	E133 Voyage	50
But hold my torch, while I describe the entry	85	E133 Voyage	58
Who kept an ale-house; with my little Minos,	89	E133 Voyage	189
My Muse had plough'd with his, that sung A-jax.	89	E133 Voyage	196
I thought to binde him, in my verse:	93	F1 Why write no	2
Mars, and my Mother, in their net:	93	F1 Why write no	6
I weare not these my wings in vaine.	93	F1 Why write no	7
Into my ri'mes could ne're be got	93	F1 Why write no	9
That since, my numbers are so cold,	93	F1 Why write no	11
Here no man tells my cups; nor, standing by,	95	F2 Penshurst	67
A waiter, doth my gluttony envy:	95	F2 Penshurst	68
Nor, when I take my lodging, need I pray	95	F2 Penshurst	72
But thou, my Wroth, if I can truth apply,	99	F3 Wroth	91
But thou, my Wroth, if I may truth apply,	99	F3 Wroth	V 91
That houre upon my morne of age,	100	F4 To the World	2
Hence-forth I quit thee from my thought,	100	F4 To the World	3
My part is ended on thy stage.	100	F4 To the World	4
And thrust my necke into the noose,	101	F4 To the World	26
With all my powers, my selfe to loose?	101	F4 To the World	28
My tender, first, and simple yeeres	101	F4 To the World	41
Else, I my state should much mistake,	101	F4 To the World	57
From all my kinde: that, for my sake,	101	F4 To the World	59
Nor for my peace will I goe farre,	102	F4 To the World	65
But make my strengths, such as they are,	102	F4 To the World	67
Here in my bosome, and at home.	102	F4 To the World	68
Come my Celia, let us prove,	102	F5 Celia 1	1
On my lips, thus hardly sundred,	103	F6 Celia 2	7
For the more countenance to my active Muse?	107	F10 Proludium	3
And foundred thy hot teame, to tune my lay.	107	F10 Proludium	9
To raise my spirits with thy conjuring wine,	107	F10 Proludium	11
Thou, nor thy loosenesse with my making sorts.	107	F10 Proludium	18
His absence in my verse, is all I aske.	107	F10 Proludium	21
My Muse up by commission: No, I bring	108	F10 Proludium	28
My owne true fire. Now my thought takes wing,	108	F10 Proludium	29
A farther fury my ray'sd spirit Controules,	108	F10 Proludium	12
and Conjures all my faculties t'approve	108	F10 Proludium	14
And yet (in this t'expresse my self more cleare)	111	F11 Epode	V 75
But I Conceive a person like my Dove,	112	F11 Epode	V 91
With you, I know, my offring will find grace.	114	F12 Rutland	30
And such, or my hopes faile, shall make you shine.	115	F12 Rutland	64
To my lesse sanguine Muse, wherein she'hath wonne	115	F12 Rutland	72
My gratefull soule, the subject of her powers,	115	F12 Rutland	73
Then all, that have but done my Muse least grace,	115	F12 Rutland	79
Then all, that have but done my verse lesse grace,	115	F12 Rutland	V 79
They hold in my strange poems, which, as yet,	115	F12 Rutland	81
And show, how, to the life, my soule presents	115	F12 Rutland	86
My best of wishes, may you beare a sonne.	116	F12 Rutland	100
I, therefore, who professe my selfe in love	116	F13 Aubigny	7
For their owne cap'tall crimes, t'indite my wit;	117	F13 Aubigny	14
Of Fortune, have not alter'd yet my looke,	117	F13 Aubigny	16
Or so my selfe abandon'd, as because	117	F13 Aubigny	17
In my character, what your features bee,	117	F13 Aubigny	24
My mirror is more subtile, cleere, refin'd,	117	F13 Aubigny	43
Give me my cup, but from the Thespian well,	120	F14 Sydney	11
But it must, straight, my melancholy bee?	122	F15 Heaven	2
That, laden with my sinnes, I seeke for ease?	122	F15 Heaven	4
My faith, my hope, my love: and in this state,	122	F15 Heaven	11
My judge, my witnesse, and my advocate.	122	F15 Heaven	12
I know my state, both full of shame, and scorne,	122	F15 Heaven	17
I feele my griefes too, and there scarce is ground,	122	F15 Heaven	21
Upon my flesh t'inflict another wound.	122	F15 Heaven	22
My selfe up to thee, harrow'd, torne, and bruis'd	127	U1 Trinitie	5
By sinne, and Sathan; and my flesh misus'd,	127	U1 Trinitie	6
As my heart lies in peeces, all confus'd,	127	U1 Trinitie	7
O take my gift.	127	U1 Trinitie	8

MY (cont.)

	Page	Title	Line
And take compassion on my grievous plight.	127	U1 Trinitie	14
My Maker, Saviour, and my Sanctifier:	128	U1 Trinitie	41
To heare, to mediate, sweeten my desire,	128	U1 Trinitie	42
Is my best part:	129	U1 Father	3
My selfe and thee.	129	U1 Father	11
Before my losse	130	U1 Father	29
3. A Hymne On the Nativitie of my Saviour.	130	U1 Nativitie	Ttl
I have had, and have my Peeres;	131	U2 Excuse	4
This my object. But she threw	132	U2 How he saw	23
At my face, that tooke my sight,	132	U2 How he saw	25
And my motion from me quite;	132	U2 How he saw	26
Left it sticking in my heart:	133	U2 Suffered	16
Looser-like, now, all my wreake	133	U2 Suffered	21
To revenge me with my Tongue,	133	U2 Suffered	24
Wherein my Lady rideth!	134	U2 Triumph	2
Both my fortune, and my Starre!	136	U2 Cupid	2
And doe governe more my blood,	136	U2 Cupid	3
'Mongst my Muses finding me,	136	U2 Cupid	7
By description, but my Mother!	136	U2 Cupid	12
Both her Browes, bent like my Bow.	136	U2 Cupid	17
Which you call my Shafts. And see!	136	U2 Cupid	19
Such my Mothers blushes be,	136	U2 Cupid	20
Is my Mothers! Hearts of slaine	137	U2 Cupid	31
Lyes the Valley, cal'd my nest,	137	U2 Cupid	34
Where I sit and proyne my wings	137	U2 Cupid	35
To my shafts! Her very Name,	137	U2 Cupid	37
With my Mothers is the same.	137	U2 Cupid	38
What my Muse and I have done:	138	U2 Kisse	5
I could give my very heart;	142	U2 Her man	54
Nor looke too kind on my desires,	144	U4 Song	7
For then my hopes will spill me.	144	U4 Song	8
For if the Nymphs should know my Swaine,	147	U7 Nymph	3
Unlesse my heart would as my thought be torne.	147	U7 Nymph	14
As make away my doubt,	147	U7 Nymph	23
But then t'increase my feares,	148	U7 Nymph	26
Will be my Rivall, though she have but eares.	148	U7 Nymph	28
My Picture left in Scotland.	149	U9 Picture	Ttl
And cast my love behind:	149	U9 Picture	5
And cast my suite behind:	149	U9 Picture	V 5
I'm sure my language to her, was as sweet,	149	U9 Picture	6
I'm sure my language to her, is as sweet,	149	U9 Picture	V 6
And all my closes meet	149	U9 Picture	V 7
Oh, but my conscious feares,	149	U9 Picture	11
That flie my thoughts betweene,	149	U9 Picture	12
My hundred of gray haires,	150	U9 Picture	14
My mountaine belly, and my rockie face,	150	U9 Picture	17
That others should not warme them at my fire,	150	U10 Jealousie	6
What my Affections were.	150	U10 Jealousie	11
I ne're will owe my health to a disease.	150	U10 Jealousie	16
Hath both my heart and me surpriz'd,	151	U11 Dreame	5
In all my wild desire,	151	U11 Dreame	11
As since he dares not come within my sight.	151	U11 Dreame	14
I Have my Pietie too, which could	151	U12 Corbet	1
Now I conceive him by my want,	152	U12 Corbet	32
And pray who shall my sorrowes read,	152	U12 Corbet	33
To succour my necessities, tooke fire,	153	U13 Sacvile	8
Not at my prayers, but your sense; which laid	153	U13 Sacvile	9
And in the Act did so my blush prevent,	153	U13 Sacvile	11
And though my fortune humble me, to take	153	U13 Sacvile	15
That they have more opprest me, then my want?	153	U13 Sacvile	28
My Sword ('tis but a poore Sword, understand)	154	U13 Sacvile	54
My wonder, why the taking a Clownes purse,	155	U13 Sacvile	89
And my minds motion not? or have I none?	156	U13 Sacvile	122
You know (without my flatt'ring you) too much	157	U13 Sacvile	155
Your Booke, my Selden, I have read, and much	158	U14 Selden	5
Was trusted, that you thought my judgement such	158	U14 Selden	6
Upon my selfe, and aske to whom? and why?	159	U14 Selden	24
So that my Reader is assur'd, I now	159	U14 Selden	27
Stand forth my Object, then, you that have beene	159	U14 Selden	29
Among my commings in, and see it mount,	161	U14 Selden	80
But here's no time, nor place, my wealth to tell,	161	U14 Selden	85
To flatter my good Lord, and cry his Bowle	167	U15 Friend-Wars	147
That may stand by, and hold my peace? will he,	167	U15 Friend-Wars	150
For the recovery of my voyce? No, there	167	U15 Friend-Wars	154
And their words too; where I but breake my Band.	169	U17 Friend-Debt	9
Simply my Band, his trust in me forsakes,	169	U17 Friend-Debt	12
A terror? or is all this but my feare?	169	U18 Elegy Can	6
Crooked appeare; so that doth my conceipt:	170	U18 Elegy Can	8
I'le lead you on; or if my fate will so,	170	U18 Elegy Can	22
That I must send one first, my Choyce assignes,	170	U18 Elegy Can	23
Love to my heart, and Fortune to my lines.	170	U18 Elegy Can	24
Tell me (my lov'd Friend) doe you love, or no,	170	U19 Elegy By	11
Amongst my many other, that I may	171	U20 Shrub	3
To towre with my intention	176	U25 Desmond	4
My bolder numbers to thy golden Lyre:	177	U25 Desmond	9
My flowing numbers to thy golden Lyre:	177	U25 Desmond	V 9
Thy Priest in this strange rapture; heat my braine	177	U25 Desmond	11
That I may sing my thoughts, in some unvulgar straine.	177	U25 Desmond	13
On these darke rymes; that my affection	177	U25 Desmond	15
Then shall my Verses, like strong Charmes,	177	U25 Desmond	18
(As my hope tells) that our faire Phoebe's shine,	179	U25 Desmond	58
(As my hope tells) that our drad Cynthia's shine,	179	U25 Desmond	V 58

MY (cont.)

	Page	Title	Line
O then (my best-best lov'd) let me importune,	180	U25 Desmond	63
And shall not I my Celia bring,	182	U27 Ode Helen	31
Though I, in working of my song,	182	U27 Ode Helen	33
Yet sure my tunes will be the best,	182	U27 Ode Helen	35
So much my Subject drownes the rest.	182	U27 Ode Helen	36
Nor in my Muse, or I asham'd to owe it	182	U28 Worth	5
Who 'gainst the Law, weave Calumnies, my ——;	187	U33 Councellour	6
Thou art my Cause: whose manners since I knew,	187	U33 Councellour	13
You have unto my Store added a booke,	189	U37 Friend-Book	4
So may the fruitfull Vine my temples steepe,	190	U37 Friend-Book	14
Forgive it, as my frailtie, and not me.	190	U37 Friend-Book	30
Or doe upon my selfe some desperate ill;	191	U38 Elegy 'Tis	3
It is a Darknesse hath blockt up my sense,	191	U38 Elegy 'Tis	5
And drives it in to eat on my offence,	191	U38 Elegy 'Tis	6
And fills my powers with perswading joy,	191	U38 Elegy 'Tis	11
I will not stand to justifie my fault,	191	U38 Elegy 'Tis	21
Doe not despaire my mending; to distrust	192	U38 Elegy 'Tis	49
I will no more abuse my vowes to you,	194	U38 Elegy 'Tis	107
How all my Fibres by your Spirit doe move,	194	U38 Elegy 'Tis	111
Your forme shines here, in my heart:	194	U38 Elegy 'Tis	117
I may dilate my selfe, but not depart.	194	U38 Elegy 'Tis	118
When I see you, then I doe see my Sun,	194	U38 Elegy 'Tis	120
To put all relish from my memorie	197	U40 Elegy That	6
I give, or owe my friends, into your Rites,	197	U40 Elegy That	12
Alas I ha' lost my heat, my blood, my prime,	199	U41 Elegy Since	11
My health will leave me; and when you depart,	199	U41 Elegy Since	13
How shall I doe, sweet Mistris, for my heart?	199	U41 Elegy Since	14
Of me, I'le softly tread unto my Tombe;	199	U41 Elegy Since	20
Put on my Ivy Garland, let me see	200	U42 Elegy Let	9
In all that is call'd lovely: take my sight	200	U42 Elegy Let	12
Sooner then my affection from the faire.	200	U42 Elegy Let	13
So many my Yeares-labours in an houre?	202	U43 Vulcan	4
Perhaps, to have beene burned with my bookes.	203	U43 Vulcan	18
And my selfe most, in some selfe-boasting Rimes?	203	U43 Vulcan	26
And my selfe most, in lewd selfe-boasting Rimes?	203	U43 Vulcan	V 26
or spent my wretched paper or my tyme	204	U43 Vulcan	V 33
On such my serious follies: But, thou'lt say,	204	U43 Vulcan	41
Or such my serious follies: But, thou'lt say,	204	U43 Vulcan	V 41
But in my Deske, what was there to accite	206	U43 Vulcan	85
But in my Deske, what was there to envite	206	U43 Vulcan	V 85
The rest, my journey into Scotland song,	207	U43 Vulcan	94
The rest, my journey into Scotland sung,	207	U43 Vulcan	V 94
My friends, the Watermen! They could provide	208	U43 Vulcan	124
Why yet, my noble hearts, they cannot say,	213	U44 Speach	1
Whilst I informe my selfe, I would teach thee,	216	U45 Squib	2
My gentle Arthur; that it might be said	216	U45 Squib	3
To speake my selfe out too ambitiously,	218	U47 Tribe	6
Put conscience and my right to compromise.	218	U47 Tribe	8
My Princes safetie, and my Kings desire,	219	U47 Tribe	38
Brunsfield, and Mansfield doe this yeare, my fates	219	U47 Tribe	44
Although my Fame, to his, not under-heares,	219	U47 Tribe	49
Lose all my credit with my Christmas Clay,	219	U47 Tribe	52
And dwell as in my Center, as I can,	219	U47 Tribe	60
So short you read my Character, and theirs	220	U47 Tribe	73
My selfe a little. I will take you so,	220	U47 Tribe	76
I never stood for any place: my wit	223	U49 Pucell	23
To stuffes and Laces, those my Man can buy.	223	U49 Pucell	28
In raysing him the wisdome of my King.	225	U51 Bacon	20
My Answer. The Poet to the Painter.	226	U52 Answer	Ttl
'Tis true, as my wombe swells, so my backe stoupes,	227	U52 Answer	4
To square my Circle, I confesse; but draw	227	U52 Answer	8
My Superficies: that was all you saw.	227	U52 Answer	9
When first, my Lord, I saw you backe your horse,	228	U53 Newcastle	1
As I began to wish my selfe a horse.	228	U53 Newcastle	12
Before, I thinke my wish absolv'd had beene.	228	U53 Newcastle	14
So that upon the point, my corporall feare	229	U54 Squib	7
Stinketh my credit, if into the Pocket	229	U54 Squib	14
Would God, my Burges, I could thinke	229	U55 Burges	1
But since the Wine hath steep'd my braine,	230	U55 Burges	5
Epistle. To my Lady Covell.	230	U56 Covell	Ttl
I gaine, in having leave to keepe my Day,	231	U56 Covell	29
My wofull crie,	231	U57 Burges	3
To send my Debentur.	231	U57 Burges	6
Epigram, to my Book-seller.	232	U58 Book-seller	Ttl
Bee thou my Bookes intelligencer, note	232	U58 Book-seller	3
All this (my Lord) is Valour! This is yours!	233	U59 Newcastle	19
My Lord, till felt griefe make our stone hearts soft,	234	U61 Epigram	14
. . . he sent me in my Sicknesse. 1629.	235	U62 Charles 1	Ttl
Haile Mary, full of honours, to my Queene,	238	U66 Queene	5
Sonne, and my Friend, I had not call'd you so	241	U69 Friend Son	1
Hee never fell, thou fall'st, my tongue.	244	U70 Ode	44
Hee never fell, thou tripst, my tongue.	244	U70 Ode	V 44
To my Lord Weston, Lo: Treasurer. A Letter	248	U71 Treasurer	VTtl
If to my mind, great Lord, I had a state,	260	U77 Treasurer	1
But you I know, my Lord; and know you can	261	U77 Treasurer	13
An Epigram To my Muse, the Lady Digby,	262	U78 Digby	Ttl
Tho', happy Muse, thou know my Digby well;	262	U78 Digby	1
Upon my Birth-day the eleventh of June;	262	U78 Digby	14
Witnesse my Birth-day the eleventh of June;	262	U78 Digby	V 14
For Brittains honour, and to Charles my King:	262	U78 Digby	V 18
For he doth love my Verses, and will looke	263	U78 Digby	23
What reputation to my lines, and me,	263	U78 Digby	26

	Page	Title	Line

MY (cont.)

	Page	Title	Line
To My L. the King, On the Christning His second Sonne James.	268	U80 Christning	Ttl
A horrour in mee! all my blood is steele!	269	U81 Pawlet	8
Stiffe! starke! my joynts 'gainst one another knock!	269	U81 Pawlet	9
Thou wouldst have written, Fame, upon my brest:	269	U81 Pawlet	14
And voyce to raise them from my brazen Lungs,	269	U81 Pawlet	24
Their Carract was! I, or my trump must breake,	269	U81 Pawlet	27
Their Carract was! for my trump must breake,	269	U81 Pawlet	V 27
And I, into the world with my Soule, was sent!	270	U81 Pawlet	V 56
Worke with my fancie, his owne hand.	276	U84 Body	12
9. Elegie on my Muse. The truly honoured Lady,	282	U84 Muse	Ttl
Who was my Muse, and life of all I sey'd,	282	U84 Muse	2
My wounded mind cannot sustaine this stroke,	283	U84 Muse	23
Am turned with an others powers. My Passion	283	U84 Muse	31
This being thus: why should my tongue, or pen	284	U84 Muse	69
Who reades, will pardon my Intelligence,	289	U84 Muse	226
To publish her a Saint. My Muse is gone.	289	U84 Muse	228
Could not goe downe my belly then	291	U85 Country	54
Or with fresh flowers to girt my temple round.	293	U86 Hor.4:1	32
But, why, oh why, my Ligurine,	293	U86 Hor.4:1	33
Flow my thin teares, downe these pale cheeks of mine?	293	U86 Hor.4:1	34
Or why, my well-grac'd words among,	293	U86 Hor.4:1	35
With an uncomely silence failes my tongue?	293	U86 Hor.4:1	36
This peece, my Piso's, and that booke agree,	305	Horace	8
That Book, my Piso's, and this piece agree,	338	Horace	V 8
My selfe for shortnesse labour; and I grow	307	Horace	35
My selfe for shortnesse labour, and am stil'd	339	Horace	V 36/ 35
Plaine phrase, my Piso's, as alone, t'approve	321	Horace	342
My Verse at randome, and licentiously?	323	Horace	391
Or rather, thinking all my faults may spie,	323	Horace	392
My title, at their rate, I'ad rather, I,	325	Horace	432
I, writing nought my selfe, will teach them yet	325	Horace	435
Nature, or Art. My Judgement will not pierce	331	Horace	582
Or, of the things, that ne're came in my mind,	333	Horace	596
But you, my Piso, carefully beware,	333	Horace	607
He'd say, mend this my friend, and this, 'tis nought.	354	Horace	V624
Why should I grieve my friend, this trifling way?	335	Horace	640
weare made the objects to my weaker powers;	361	Palmer	3
First: thy successe did strike my sence with wonder;	361	Palmer	5
So in my braine; the stronge impression	361	Palmer	21
my abler faculties; and thus brake foorth	362	Palmer	29
My selfe am so neare drowning?	365	Ode Splendor	20
What place is for my testimony void?	385	Brooke	2
My suffrage brings thee all increase, to crowne	385	Brooke	7
Or skill of making matches in my life:	386	Husband	7
I know for such, as (if my word will waigh)	386	Husband	11
To my truly-belov'd Freind, Mr Browne: on his Pastorals.	386	Browne	Ttl
these only hide part of my flesh, and bones:	387	Cavendish	2
I made my lyfe my monument, & yours:	387	Cavendish	7
To my worthy and honour'd Friend, Mr George Chapman,	388	Chapman	Ttl
Finer then was his Spanish, if my Oath	389	Aleman	18
When you behold me wish my selfe, the man	389	Aleman	23
To the memory of my beloved, the Author	390	Shakespeare	Ttl
My Shakespeare, rise; I will not lodge thee by	391	Shakespeare	19
That I not mixe thee so, my braine excuses;	391	Shakespeare	25
For, if I thought my judgement were of yeeres,	391	Shakespeare	27
Triumph, my Britaine, thou hast one to showe,	391	Shakespeare	41
My gentle Shakespeare, must enjoy a part.	392	Shakespeare	56
To my chosen Friend, the learned Translator of Lucan,	395	May	Ttl
Taught Lucan these true moodes! Replyes my sence	395	May	15
Without conferring symboles. This's my day.	396	Drayton	10
Wonder to truth! and have my Vision hoorld,	396	Drayton	13
My lippes could forme the voyce, I heard that Rore,	397	Drayton	38
And stop my sight, in every line I goe.	398	Drayton	78
Onely my losse is, that I am not there:	398	Drayton	91
To my worthy Friend, Master Edward Filmer,	401	Filmer	Ttl
Thy Forehead is too narrow for my Brand.	408	Inigo Jones 3	14
To my Detractor.	408	Detractor	Ttl
My verses were commended, thou dar'st say,	408	Detractor	1
Foole, doe not rate my Rymes; I'have found thy Vice	408	Detractor	5
To my old Faithfull Servant: And	409	Brome	Ttl
Of Fellowship, professing my old Arts.	409	Brome	4
To my Deare Sonne, and right-learned Friend,	414	Rutter	Ttl
You looke, my Joseph, I should something say	414	Rutter	1
This is my censure. Now there is a new	415	Rutter	19
An Epigram To My Joviall Good Freind Mr. Robert Dover,	415	Dover	Ttl
I Cannot bring my Muse to dropp her Vies	415	Dover	1
my mind unto you,	416	Moon	4
at my back, I am no spright,	416	Moon	6
I then could rayse my notes	419	Ode:If Men	6
That were the happie subject of my songe.	419	Ode:If Men	9
Forgive it as my Frayltie, and not mee.	422	Censure	23
To my worthy, and deserving Brother	666	Glover	1
As the token of my Love	666	Glover	3
With Chequer Inke, upon his guift, my paper,	666	Glover	8

MYLES

	Page	Title	Line
some 4 myles hence and have him there disgorge	211	U43 Vulcan	V184

MYND

	Page	Title	Line
your Trappings will not change you. Change your mynd.	403	Inigo Jones 1	25

MYNDE

	Page	Title	Line
What would he doe now, gi'ng his mynde that waye	405	Inigo Jones 1	75

MYNE (PRONOUN)

	Page	Title	Line
Soe ended your Epistle, myne beginns	421	Censure	3

	Page	Title	Line
MYNE (cont.)			
deignes myne the power to find, yett want I will	421	Censure	10
MYNE			
Blow up, and ruine, myne, and countermyne,	212	U43 Vulcan	205
MYNERVA			
Mynerva deignes	420	Ode:If Men	29
MYRTLE			
The M. the Myrtle, A. the Almonds clame,	412	Ghyrlond	3
These forme thy Ghyrlond. Wherof Myrtle green,	412	Ghyrlond	5
MYSTERIE (See also MISTERIE)			
And greater rites, yet writ in mysterie,	119	F13 Aubigny	106
The faithfull mans beleeved Mysterie,	127	U1 Trinitie	3
Till I attaine the long'd-for mysterie	128	U1 Trinitie	31
Of the late Mysterie of reception,	219	U47 Tribe	48
Thou stand'st as if some Mysterie thou did'st!	225	U51 Bacon	4
That holy, great, and glorious Mysterie,	286	U84 Muse	129
Which, chang'd, a five-fold mysterie designe,	412	Ghyrlond	2
MYSTERIES			
The mysteries of manners, armes, and arts.	96	F2 Penshurst	98
To touch these Mysteries! We may admire	269	U81 Pawlet	31
To touch those Mysteries! We may admire	269	U81 Pawlet	V 31
Have busie search made in his mysteries!	284	U84 Muse	80
But these are Mysteries	369	Ode Who saith	111
These Mysteries do point to three more great,	413	Ghyrlond	29
Yo'have all the Mysteries of Wits new Mint,	415	Rutter	28
MYSTICK			
Inflam'd with ardor to that mystick Shine,	413	Ghyrlond	23
MYTHOLOGY			
Mythology there painted on slit deale!	404	Inigo Jones 1	48
NAILE			
Not, ten times o're, corrected to the naile.	325	Horace	418
NAILES			
The nailes, and every curled haire disclose;	307	Horace	47
The nailes, and every gentle haire disclose;	339	Horace	V 49/ 47
Their nailes, nor shave their beards, but to by-paths	325	Horace	423
NAILS			
Their nails, nor shave their beards, but seek by-paths	349	Horace	V423
NAKED			
'Twill see it's sister naked, ere a sword.	74	E115 Honest Man	22
If holiest friend-ship, naked to the touch,	78	E122 Rudyerd 2	7
Truth, and the Graces best, when naked are.	158	U14 Selden	4
Since, naked, best Truth, and the Graces are.	158	U14 Selden	V 4
To cloath the naked, feed the hungry. Shee	288	U84 Muse	194
The rough rude Satyres naked; and would try,	319	Horace	321
Cleare as a naked vestall	365	Ode Splendor	11
NALL			
The Cobler kept him to his nall; but, now	410	Brome	17
NAME'			
Whose name's un-welcome to the present eare,	74	E115 Honest Man	15
NAME			
But I have my revenge made, in thy name.	29	E10 Ignorant	2
It made me a great face, I ask'd the name.	30	E11 Something	4
The great renowne, and name wherewith shee goes.	31	E14 Camden	4
What name, what skill, what faith hast thou in things!	31	E14 Camden	7
May others feare, flie, and traduce thy name,	32	E17 Critic	1
Whose soule heavens Queene, (whose name shee beares)	33	E22 Daughter	7
Don Surly, to aspire the glorious name	35	E28 Surly	1
And person to the world; ere I thy name.	36	E30 Guiltie	4
I'le loose my modestie, and tell your name.	38	E38 Guiltie 2	8
When, in my booke, men reade but Cecill's name,	41	E43 Salisbury 1	9
When, in my Verse, men reade but Sarum's name,	41	E43 Salisbury 1 V	9
Chuffe, lately rich in name, in chattels, goods,	41	E44 Chuff	1
Thou wert content the authors name to loose:	43	E53 Old-end	3
An obeliske, or columne to thy name,	46	E60 Mounteagle	2
Wherein what wonder see thy name hath wrought?	48	E64 Salisbury 3	16
That sound, and that authoritie with her name,	49	E67 Suffolk	3
To one that desired me not to name him.	53	E77 Not name	Ttl
That, any way, my booke should speake thy name:	53	E77 Not name	2
Who had no lesse a trumpet of their name,	57	E89 Allen	5
Well, though thy name lesse then our great ones bee,	64	E99 Th Roe 2	11
I Doe but name thee Pembroke, and I find	66	E102 Pembroke	1
And, being nam'd, how little doth that name	66	E103 L Wroth 1	5
If men get name, for some one vertue: Then,	68	E106 E Herbert	1
Thy deedes, unto thy name, will prove new wombes,	70	E109 Nevil	17
The name of Pompey for an enemie,	71	E110 Edmonds 1	3
When Sydnyes name I heare, or face I see:	73	E114 Sydney	2
You wonder, who this is! and, why I name	74	E115 Honest Man	1
Suffers no name, but a description:	74	E115 Honest Man	4
Jephson, thou man of men, to whose lov'd name	75	E116 Jephson	1
One name was Elizabeth,	79	E124 Elizabeth	9
So, all reward, or name, that growes to mee	80	E127 Aubigny	9
Roe (and my joy to name) th'art now, to goe	80	E128 Wm Roe 2	1
Or whose great name in Poets heaven use,	107	F10 Proludium	2
And for their place, and name,	111	F11 Epode	80
And, in this name, am given out dangerous	117	F13 Aubigny	11
To Clifton's bloud, that is deny'd their name.	119	F13 Aubigny	98
Unto your name, and goodnesse of your life,	119	F13 Aubigny	109
'T will be exacted of your name, whose sonne,	121	F14 Sydney	41
So may you live in honor, as in name,	121	F14 Sydney	51
His glorious Name	129	U1 Father	24
Where he chanc't your name to see	136	U2 Cupid	8
To my shafts! Her very Name,	137	U2 Cupid	37
If Love, or feare, would let me tell his name.	148	U7 Nymph	35

	Page	Title	Line

NAME (cont.)

	Page	Title	Line
Reader, whose life, and name, did e're become	152	U12 Corbet	37
To have such doe me good, I durst not name:	153	U13 Sacvile	18
In offering this thy worke to no great Name,	161	U14 Selden	69
To do't with Cloth, or Stuffes, lusts name might merit;	164	U15 Friend-Wars	57
Still pretious, with the odour of thy name.	168	U15 Friend-Wars	190
His name in any mettall, it would breake.	172	U21 Ltl Shrub	2
Is gone himselfe into your Name.	173	U22 Elegy Tho	24
Or hath Corynna, by the name	181	U27 Ode Helen	17
But stood unshaken in his Deeds, and Name,	185	U30 Burleigh	11
Still flie about the Odour of your Name;	186	U31 Elsmere	8
Alone, but all thy ranke a reverend Name:	187	U33 Councellour	40
But, as a friend, which name your selfe receave,	190	U37 Friend-Book	10
The name of Cruell weather, storme, and raine?	193	U38 Elegy 'Tis	82
Under another Name, I take your health;	197	U40 Elegy That	10
The Jewell of your name, as close as sleepe	198	U40 Elegy That	42
May to thy name a Vulcanale say;	208	U43 Vulcan	120
May to thy name a Pagan prayer say;	208	U43 Vulcan	V120
And keepe the Glorie of the English name,	214	U44 Speach	50
Much lesse a name would we bring up, or nurse,	216	U45 Squib	9
And though all praise bring nothing to your name,	224	U50 Countesse	13
Of Vertue, got above his name?	234	U60 La-ware	10
What, by that name, wee each to other owe,	241	U69 Friend Son	4
And had his noble name advanc'd with men:	244	U70 Ode	36
. . . Surviving Duke of the same name.	252	U75 Epithalam.	Ttl
To give a greater Name, and Title to! Their owne!	255	U75 Epithalam.	96
And by his Rise, in active men, his Name	256	U75 Epithalam.	116
Grow up, sweet Babe, as blessed, in thy Name,	268	U80 Christning	11
To give your shade a lasting name! Stay, stay, I feele	269	U81 Pawlet	7
To give your shade a lasting name! Stay, stay, I feele	269	U81 Pawlet	V 7
Sound thou her Vertues, give her soule a name.	269	U81 Pawlet	22
Thy Neeces line, then thou that gav'st thy Name	274	U84 Descent	14
Spun out in name of some of the old Nine!	282	U84 Muse	6
In name, I went all names before,	293	U87 Hor.3:9	7
Nor know t'observe: why (i'the Muses name)	311	Horace	128
A foot, whose swiftnesse gave the Verse the name	323	Horace	372
And thus, at first, an honour, and a name	327	Horace	491
Palmer thy travayles well becum thy name,	362	Palmer	30
She was 'Sell Boulstred. In which name, I call	372	Epitaph	12
May aske, what Author would conceale his name?	383	Author	4
To draw no envy (Shakespeare) on thy name,	390	Shakespeare	1
And Christian name too, with a Heralds witt.	394	Jane Ogle	12
All that was solid, in the name	399	Lady Ogle	17
Keeps warme the spice of her good name,	400	Lady Ogle	30
Nor flatt'ry! but secur'd, by the Authors Name,	401	Beaumont	19
His name is Skeuopoios wee all knowe,	404	Inigo Jones 1	60
I now would write on thee? No, wretch; thy name	409	Detractor	11
To aske thy name, if he have half his Nose!	409	Detractor	18
Here, are five letters in this blessed Name,	412	Ghyrlond	1
That prince that shames a tyrants name to beare,	423	Lucan	19

NAM'D

	Page	Title	Line
Thy title, Epigrammes, and nam'd of mee,	27	E2 My Booke	2
And, being nam'd, how little doth that name	66	E103 L Wroth 1	5
Were they that nam'd you, prophets? Did they see,	67	E104 Montgomery	1
They were not to be nam'd on the same day.	83	E131 Ferrab. 2	12
Thy copp's, too, nam'd of Gamage, thou hast there,	94	F2 Penshurst	19
A fellow of course Letcherie, is nam'd,	165	U15 Friend-Wars	98
And doubtfull Dayes (which were nam'd Criticall,)	180	U26 Ode High	6
All which I tell, lest when Apollo's nam'd,	329	Horace	501
There nam'd to be travell'd? For this our Tom saith:	380	Coryat 3	21
With bold Tyrtaeus verse, when thou art nam'd,	398	Drayton	68

NAMED

	Page	Title	Line
Know you to be a Sydney, though un-named?	66	E103 L Wroth 1	4

NAMELESS

	Page	Title	Line
Nameless, and noysome, as thy infamy!	409	Detractor	16

NAME'S

	Page	Title	Line
Whose name's un-welcome to the present eare,	74	E115 Honest Man	15

NAMES

	Page	Title	Line
Who scarse can spell th'hard names: whose knight lesse can.	28	E3 Bookseller	10
May none, whose scatter'd names honor my booke,	29	E9 To All	1
And, can forget mens names, with a great grace.	35	E28 Surly	8
Which of thy names I take, not onely beares	58	E91 Vere	1
Or Bils, and there he buyes the names of books.	59	E92 New Crie	24
But even their names were to be made a-new,	67	E105 L Wroth 1	5
That are your wordes of credit. Keepe your Names	69	E107 Hungry	24
And your high names: I doe desire, that thence	69	E108 Soldiers	3
There, in the writhed barke, are cut the names	94	F2 Penshurst	15
Like Money-brokers, after Names, and hire	155	U13 Sacvile	62
Reare-Suppers in their Names! and spend whole nights	156	U13 Sacvile	101
Men past their termes, and prais'd some names too much,	159	U14 Selden	21
Selden! two Names that so much understand!	161	U14 Selden	82
But that some greater names have broke with me,	169	U17 Friend-Debt	8
But when I read or heare the names so rife	187	U33 Councellour	7
Acrostichs, and Telestichs, on jumpe names,	204	U43 Vulcan	39
Acrostichs, and Telestichs, or jumpe names,	204	U43 Vulcan	V 39
Acrostichs, and Telestichs, on fine names,	204	U43 Vulcan	V 39
Two names of friendship, but one Starre:	246	U70 Ode	98
To propagate their Names,	257	U75 Epithalam.	149
Their names are not recorded on the File	257	U75 Epithalam.	155
A Richard, and a Hierome, by their names	258	U75 Epithalam.	170
Their names of being kept alive,	273	U84 Cradle	6
When your owne Vertues, equall'd have their Names,	281	U84 Kenelme	12
In name, I went all names before,	293	U87 Hor.3:9	7

					Page	Title	Line

NAMES (cont.)

New names of things. It hath beene ever free, · · · 309 Horace 83
Or, like our Money-Brokers, take up names · · · 386 Browne 10
For names; but call forth thund'ring Aeschilus, · · · 391 Shakespeare 33
With mistooke Names out of Vitruvius! · · · · 402 Inigo Jones 1 8

NAMING

At naming the French King, their heads they shake, · · 59 E92 New Crie 33
Naming so many, too! But, this is one, · · · · 74 E115 Honest Man 3
By naming in what companie 'twas in, · · · · 191 U38 Elegy 'Tis 25

NARD

Or the Nard i' the fire? · · · · · · 135 U2 Triumph 28

NARE

And that ours did. For, yet, no nare was tainted, · · 87 E133 Voyage 133

NARROW

Thy subtle wayes, be narrow straits; · · · · 100 F4 To the World 10
For that's a narrow joy is but our owne. · · · 147 U7 Nymph 7
Nor have I yet the narrow mind · · · · · 150 U10 Jealousie 4
The narrow Seas are shadie, · · · · · 222 U48 Bacchus 53
For 't were a narrow gladnesse, kept thine owne. · · 225 U51 Bacon 18
Thy faint, and narrow eyes, to reade the King · · 250 U73 Weston 2
Thy Forehead is too narrow for my Brand. · · · 408 Inigo Jones 3 14

NARROW'D

But lyes block'd up, and straightned, narrow'd in, · · 248 U71 Treasurer 10

NASO

With us be call'd, the Naso, but this man? · · · 397 Drayton 32

NASTIE

For, to say truth, what scullion is so nastie, · · 88 E133 Voyage 147

NATION

And his Manners of that Nation. · · · · 141 U2 Her man 8
Nor markes of wealth so from our Nation fled, · · 213 U44 Speach 12
To make the hearts of a whole Nation smile, · · 238 U66 Queene 10
No Nation can expresse how much · · · · 269 U81 Pawlet V 26
And therefore how ever the travelling nation, · · 380 Coryat 3 29

NATIONS

Up among Nations. In the stead of bold · · · 214 U44 Speach 51
Stood up thy Nations fame, her Crownes defence. · · 217 U46 Coke 14
A Nations sinne got pardon'd! 'twere a taske · · 234 U61 Epigram 12
Of murmuring Subjects; make the Nations know · · 261 U77 Treasurer 19
Of froward Citizens; make the Nations know · · 261 U77 Treasurer V 19
Whole Nations! nay, Mankind! the World, with all · 271 U81 Pawlet 90
The motives, and true Spurres to all good Nations. · 411 Sutcliffe 5

NATIVE

Our native portions, and possessed rent; · · · 286 U84 Muse 142

NATIVITIE

3. A Hymne On the Nativitie of my Saviour. · · 130 U1 Nativitie Ttl

NATURALL

It perfect, proper, pure, and naturall, · · 117 F13 Aubigny 32
On naturall secret, there, as her owne bookes: · · 271 U81 Pawlet V 70

NATUR'D

Her Sonnes before the people; nor the ill-/Natur'd · 317 Horace 264
ill-/Natur'd, and wicked Atreus cooke, to th'eye, · 317 Horace 265

NATURE'

Stand there; for when a noble Nature's rais'd, · · 256 U75 Epithalam. 113

NATURE

Rich, as nature could bequeath thee: · · · 39 E40 Ratcliffe 3
When Nature bids us leave to live, 'tis late · · 50 E70 Wm Roe 1 1
Nature, they thought, in all, that he would faine. · 53 E79 Rutland 8
That Nature no such difference had imprest · · 75 E116 Jephson 9
As Heaven and Nature seem'd to strive · · · 77 E120 S. P. 7
Made for what Nature could, or Vertue can; · · 79 E125 Uvedale 2
As if Nature disclos'd · · · · · 112 F11 Epode 100
Wherein wise Nature you a dowrie gave, · · · 114 F12 Rutland 35
Of nature, and societie, I should faint; · · · 117 F13 Aubigny 19
To take our nature; becam'st man, and dyd'st, · · 128 U1 Trinitie 22
And tooke on him our Nature. · · · · 130 U1 Nativitie 18
Large claspe of Nature, such a wit can bound. · · 160 U14 Selden 64
Quickning dead Nature, to her noblest strife. · · 162 U15 Friend-Wars 8
clowd-/Like upon them lighten? If nature could · · 164 U15 Friend-Wars 61
Nature, that will not let his Wife be a whore; · · 165 U15 Friend-Wars 90
And yet the noble Nature never grudge; · · · 169 U17 Friend-Debt 3
That envie wish'd, and Nature fear'd. · · · 173 U22 Elegy Tho 20
Quarrell with Nature, or in ballance brought · · 188 U34 Small Poxe 6
What manners prettie, Nature milde, · · · 188 U35 Chute 2
Of that wise Nature would a Cradle have. · · 192 U38 Elegy 'Tis 60
Consumptions nature to destroy, and sterve. · · 192 U38 Elegy 'Tis 62
Did wiser Nature draw thee back, · · · · 243 U70 Ode 11
Did wisest Nature draw thee back, · · · · 243 U70 Ode V 11
Where Nature such a large survey hath ta'en, · · 262 U78 Digby 11
Of all that Nature, yet, to life did bring; · · 264 U79 New-yeares 33
What Nature, Fortune, Institution, Fact · · · 270 U81 Pawlet 45
That ever Nature, or the later Ayre · · · 274 U84 Descent 4
As it another Nature were, · · · · · 279 U84 Mind 30
On Nature, for her: who did let her lie, · · · 282 U84 Muse 13
Sleepie, or stupid Nature, couldst thou part · · 282 U84 Muse 15
Against the Nature he would worship. Hee · · 284 U84 Muse 75
To style us Friends, who were, by Nature, Foes? · · 286 U84 Muse 139
As nature could not more increase the flood · · 287 U84 Muse 158
Of lapsed Nature) best know what to doe, · · · 288 U84 Muse 214
For Nature, first, within doth fashion us · · 311 Horace 152
Will passe the Seas, and long as nature is, · · 329 Horace 518
Wilt nothing against nature speake, or doe: · · 331 Horace 574
Nature, or Art. My Judgement will not pierce · · 331 Horace 582
All Nature of commending. · · · · · 365 Ode Splendor 16

NATURE (cont.)
With Nature, to out-doo the life: . . . . 390 Reader 4
Nature her selfe was proud of his designes, . . . 392 Shakespeare 47
Yet must I not give Nature all: Thy Art, . . . 392 Shakespeare 55
For though the Poets matter, Nature be, . . . 392 Shakespeare 57
As it were spun by nature, off the fleece: . . . 415 Rutter 18
NATURE'S
Stand there; for when a noble Nature's rais'd, . . . 256 U75 Epithalam. 113
NATURES
Nor could I, had I seene all Natures roule, . . . 60 E93 Radcliffe 12
So are you Natures Index, and restore, . . . 68 E105 L Wroth 2 19
That to such Natures let their full hands flow, . . . 154 U13 Sacvile 60
Is natures meere obliquitie! as Heaven . . . 192 U38 Elegy 'Tis 64
Doth take in easie Natures birth, . . . 250 U74 Weston 2
To doe their Offices in Natures Chime, . . . 253 U75 Epithalam. 27
On Natures secrets, there, as her owne bookes: . . . 271 U81 Pawlet 70
For, as there are three Natures, Schoolemen call . . . 284 U84 Muse 51
And give their yeares, and natures, as they swerve, . . . 315 Horace 224
That Natures fairest Creature, ... 364 Phoenix 6
As they were not of Natures family. . . . . 392 Shakespeare 54
NAUGHT
Hee'd say, Mend this, good friend, and this; 'tis naught. . 333 Horace 624
NAVIE
That from the North, the Navie safe doth store, . . . 309 Horace 92
NAY
Nay more, for greatnesse sake, he will be one . . . 36 E28 Surly 19
Still Mill continu'd: Nay, his face growing worse, . . . 57 E90 Mill 11
Nay, aske you, how the day goes, in your eare. . . . 59 E92 New Crie 18
Nay, now you puffe, tuske, and draw up your chin, . . . 69 E107 Hungry 29
Thou dost out-zany Cokely, Pod; nay, Gue: . . . 81 E129 Mime 16
Pure, perfect, nay divine: . . . . 110 F11 Epode 46
Nay, her white and polish'd neck, ... 137 U2 Cupid 29
Nay, you may erre in this, ... 139 U2 Another 9
Nay, I will not let you sit . . . . 140 U2 Promise 21
Nay, rather both our soules bee strayn'd . . . 144 U3 Musicall 25
That all respect; She must lie downe: Nay more, . . . 163 U15 Friend-Wars 53
Nay, sigh'd a Sister, 'twas the Nun, Kate Arden, . . . 209 U43 Vulcan 148
Nay, sayth a sister, Venus Nun, Kate Arden, . . . 209 U43 Vulcan V148
Nay, let White-Hall with Revels have to doe, . . . 210 U43 Vulcan 156
Nay, so your Seate his beauties did endorse, . . . 228 U53 Newcastle 11
Nay, and in this, thou show'st to value more . . . 235 U62 Charles 1 9
For want of knowing the Poet, to say him nay? . . . 241 U68 House-hold 4
And thinke, nay know, thy Morison's not dead. . . . 245 U70 Ode 78
Whole Nations! nay, Mankind! the World, with all . . . 271 U81 Pawlet 90
Where Gold's the Motive, women have no Nay. . . . 363 Riches 18
Nay more in his wardrobe, if you will laugh at a . . . 380 Coryat 3 47
Nay they will venter ones Descent to hitt, . . . 394 Jane Ogle 11
Your booke? your volume! Nay, the state, and story! . . . 399 Lady Ogle 7
And they were very good: yet thou think'st nay. . . . 408 Detractor 2
NE
Ne knowes he flatt'ring Colours, or false light. . . . 227 U52 Answer 21
NEADD
Of any Madames, hath neadd squires, and must. . . . 63 E97 Motion 14
NEARE
Some vicious foole draw neare, ... 111 F11 Epode 66
My selfe am so neare drowning? . . . . 365 Ode Splendor 20
And flight about the Ile, well neare, by this, . . . 397 Drayton 49
NEARER
Now, you are got into a nearer roome, ... 409 Brome 3
NEAT
His Clothes rich, and band sit neat, ... 142 U2 Exception 4
And then, leape mad on a neat Pickardill, . . . 164 U15 Friend-Wars 70
Neat Terence, witty Plautus, now not please; . . . 392 Shakespeare 52
NEATE
That's greater, yet: to crie his owne up neate. . . . 35 E28 Surly 11
which, did they neere so neate, or proudly dwell, . . . 387 Cavendish 3
NEATH
A dead beautie under-neath thee, ... 39 E40 Ratcliffe 2
Under-neath this stone doth lye . . . . 79 E124 Elizabeth 3
NEATLY
His Mind as pure, and neatly kept, ... 151 U12 Corbet 15
NECESSITIE
As thou stand'st cleere of the necessitie. . . . 41 E43 Salisbury 1 12
Is meere necessitie. . . . . 111 F11 Epode 82
Necessitie urges . . . . 231 U57 Burges 2
T'escape this common knowne necessitie, . . . 271 U81 Pawlet 93
NECESSITIES
To succour my necessities, tooke fire, ... 153 U13 Sacvile 8
NECK
His neck fenc'd round with ruffe! his eyes halfe shut! . . 33 E21 Gam'ster 2
Nay, her white and polish'd neck, ... 137 U2 Cupid 29
Draw first a Cloud: all save her neck; . . . 276 U84 Body 13
And ('bout thy Ivory neck,) no youth did fling . . . 293 U87 Hor.3:9 2
Set a Horse-neck, and divers feathers fold . . . 305 Horace 2
A horse neck joyn, & sundry plumes ore-fold . . . 338 Horace V 2
Cropt, branded, slit, neck-stockt; go, you are stript. . . 411 Gill 16
NECKE
And thrust my necke into the noose, ... 101 F4 To the World 26
NECKS
And fainting necks, the turned Share! . . . . 291 U85 Country 64
NECK-STOCKT
Cropt, branded, slit, neck-stockt; go, you are stript. . . 411 Gill 16

		Page	Title	Line
NECTAR				
And like Nectar ever flowing:		39	E40 Ratcliffe	10
Tabacco, Nectar, or the Thespian spring,		65	E101 Supper	33
But might I of Jove's Nectar sup,		106	F9 Celia 3	7
But might I of love's Nectar sipp,		106	F9 Celia 3	V 7
Thy Hearers Nectar, and thy Clients Balme,		187	U33 Councellour	36
NEECES				
Thy Neeces line, then thou that gav'st thy Name		274	U84 Descent	14
NEED				
What need hast thou of me? or of my Muse?		40	E43 Salisbury 1	1
We need a man that knowes the severall graces		61	E95 Savile	27
We need a man, can speake of the intents,		62	E95 Savile	31
Of state, and censure them: we need his pen		62	E95 Savile	33
But most we need his faith (and all have you)		62	E95 Savile	35
Need seeke no other strength, no other height;		63	E98 Th Roe 1	4
Need any Muses praise to give it fame?		66	E103 L Wroth 1	6
Becomes none more then you, who need it least.		67	E103 L Wroth 1	14
I need no other arts, but studie thee:		78	E122 Rudyerd 2	9
Nor, when I take my lodging, need I pray		95	F2 Penshurst	72
As shall not need thy false reliefe.		102	F4 To the World	64
Remov'd, as you from need to have it such.		117	F13 Aubigny	28
What need of mee? doe you but sing,		143	U3 Musicall	13
I not deny it, but to helpe the need		155	U13 Sacvile	75
They need no stilts, nor rise upon their toes,		157	U13 Sacvile	145
Unto the Censure. Yours all need doth flie		158	U14 Selden	11
All licence in our lives? What need we know,		215	U44 Speach	70
Past any need of vertue. Let them care,		215	U44 Speach	83
Thou need new termes; thou maist, without excuse,		307	Horace	70
To such a worke, as could not need theirs? Yet		385	Brooke	5
Shee need not blush upon the Mariage-Day.		386	Husband	12
Above th'ill fortune of them, or the need.		391	Shakespeare	16
The Eloquence of Masques! What need of prose		403	Inigo Jones 1	40
NEEDE				
The neede of such? whose liberall boord doth flow,		95	F2 Penshurst	59
NEEDFULLY				
And like them too; must needfully, though few,		61	E94 Bedford 3	13
NEEDS				
And stoupe, and cringe. O then, it needs must prove		56	E88 Monsieur	14
Or if needs thy lust will tast		105	F8 Sicknesse	15
Where Love doth shine, there needs no Sunne,		189	U36 Song	5
Or if thou needs would'st trench upon her power,		204	U43 Vulcan	48
Against thy furie, when to serve their needs,		208	U43 Vulcan	125
Needs lend an aide, to thine she had her eyes.		217	U46 Coke	24
Needs nought to cloath it but the ayre.		275	U84 Body	8
Hence, then, prophane: Here needs no words expense		400	Beaumont	3
NEED'ST				
Nor need'st thou: for those few, by oath releast,		32	E16 Brain-hardy	7
Thou need'st not shrinke at voyce of after-times;		61	E95 Savile	20
NE'ER				
Could ne'er make prize of thy white Chastetye.		108	F10 Proludium	6
NEERE (NEVER)				
which, did they neere so neate, or proudly dwell,		387	Cavendish	3
NEERE				
To seeme a statesman: as I neere it came,		30	E11 Something	3
But, comming neere, they found it but a liter,		86	E133 Voyage	85
And, though so neere the citie, and the court,		96	F3 Wroth	3
Or was she gracious a-farre off? but neere		169	U18 Elegy Can	5
From Death, and darke oblivion, neere the same,		175	U24 Frontispice	1
Where I may handle Silke, as free, and neere,		200	U42 Elegy Let	30
And when you want those friends, or neere in blood,		224	U50 Countesse	26
Christmas is neere;		231	U57 Burges	15
Some of his formes, he lets him not come neere		242	U69 Friend Son	17
To judge; So all men comming neere can spie,		242	U69 Friend Son	20
It is too neere of kin to Heaven, the Soule,		269	U81 Pawlet	29
It is too neere of kin to God, the Soule,		269	U81 Pawlet	V 29
Beneath a Sweet-wood Roofe, neere Alba Lake:		292	U86 Hor.4:1	20
Like men street-borne, and neere the Hall, reherse		321	Horace	357
Like men Town-borne, and neere the place, reherse		347	Horace	V349/357
Let what thou fain'st for pleasures sake, be neere		329	Horace	507
Neere which, the Thespiad's sing;		366	Ode Who saith	18
NEERER				
Will take you more, the neerer that you stand;		331	Horace	540
NEGLECT				
I, and for this neglect, the courser sort		219	U47 Tribe	54
NEGLIGENCE				
Of too much haste, and negligence in part,		323	Horace	385
Offended with few spots, which negligence		329	Horace	527
NEIGHBOUR				
In neighbour-townes, and feeles the weightie plough:		309	Horace	95
'tis but the next neighbour ride		417	Moon	35
NEIGHBOURHOOD				
How they advance true Love, and neighbourhood,		416	Dover	7
NEIGHBOURS				
Th'observing neighbours no such mood can see.		40	E42 Giles	2
Not like your Countrie-neighbours, that commit		190	U37 Friend-Book	7
NEIGHBOUR-TOWNES				
In neighbour-townes, and feeles the weightie plough:		309	Horace	95
NEIGHING				
Drums against Drums, the neighing of the Horse,		397	Drayton	40
NEITHER (See also NEYTHER)				
That neither fame, nor love might wanting be		48	E66 Cary	1
Know you the cause? H'has neither land, nor lease,		63	E97 Motion	9
Shalt neither that, nor this envy:		99	F3 Wroth	92

432

	Page	Title	Line
NEITHER (cont.)			
That neither want doe thee affright,	100	F3 Wroth	104
That neither want should thee affright,	100	F3 Wroth	V104
You shall neither eat, nor sleepe,	140	U2 Promise	15
He neither gives, or do's, that doth delay	154	U13 Sacvile	41
Of Christendome! And neither of these know,	157	U13 Sacvile	129
Are Dwarfes of Honour, and have neither weight	157	U13 Sacvile	147
As neither wine doe rack it out, or mirth.	197	U40 Elegy That	18
We neither love the Troubles, nor the harmes.	215	U44 Speach	86
I neither am, nor art thou one of those	216	U45 Squib	5
Though I doe neither heare these newes, nor tell	219	U47 Tribe	46
And neither good Cheare,	231	U57 Burges	16
As neither head, nor foot, one forme retaine.	305	Horace	10
Hath neither soule, nor sinewes. Loftie he	307	Horace	37
As neither any God, were brought in there,	321	Horace	331
As neither any God, be brought in there,	346	Horace	V323/331
For, neither doth the String still yeeld that sound	329	Horace	521
But neither, Men, nor Gods, nor Pillars meant,	331	Horace	555
"Where neither Force can bend, nor Feare can awe.	367	Ode Who saith	48
But here, neither trusting his hands, nor his legs,	375	Coryat 1	34
As neither Man, nor Muse, can praise too much.	390	Shakespeare	4
As neither Pompey's popularitie,	395	May	9
NEITHERS			
Art tane with neithers vice, nor sport:	96	F3 Wroth	4
NEPHEW			
Whose nephew, whose grand-child you are;	121	F14 Sydney	42
NEPHEWES			
And long in changing. Let our Nephewes see	238	U65 Prince	7
In changing, let our Nephewes joyfull see	238	U65 Prince	V 7
In changing. Let our after Nephewes see	238	U65 Prince	V 7
And teach your nephewes it to aemulate:	387	Cavendish	10
Transmitt it to your Nephewes, Freinds, Allies,	399	Lady Ogle	3
NEPHEWS			
His Nephews entrailes; nor must Progne flie	317	Horace	266
NE'R			
his life, his love, his honour, which ne'r dyes,	382	Rich	8
NE'RE			
Mens manners ne're were viler, for your sake.	34	E24 Parliament	2
Into my ri'mes could ne're be got	93	F1 Why write no	9
I ne're was of thy kind;	150	U10 Jealousie	3
I ne're will owe my health to a disease.	150	U10 Jealousie	16
On whom I could take up, and ne're abuse	161	U14 Selden	83
Ne're came to taste the plenteous Mariage-horne.	165	U15 Friend-Wars	100
That ne're was knowne to last above a fit!	171	U20 Shrub	6
True noblesse. Palme growes straight, though handled ne're so rude.	177	U25 Desmond	26
Her owne bloud gave her: Shee ne're had, nor hath	188	U34 Small Poxe	9
That Love's a bitter sweet, I ne're conceive	197	U40 Elegy That	1
I ne're attempted, Vulcan, 'gainst thy life;	202	U43 Vulcan	5
I ne're attempted ought against thy life;	202	U43 Vulcan	V 5
And so did Jove, who ne're meant thee his Cup:	208	U43 Vulcan	115
Provided, ne're to yeeld, in any case	323	Horace	379
If ne're so little it depart the first,	331	Horace	563
Or, of the things, that ne're came in my mind,	333	Horace	596
Or blinde Affection, which doth ne're advance	391	Shakespeare	9
NERE (NEAR)			
Bald, or blinde, or nere so many:	105	F8 Sicknesse	40
NERE			
whom fortune hath deprest; come nere the fates	422	Lucan	4
whom, yf fortune hath deprest; come nere the fates	422	Lucan	V 4
NERO			
Where Nero falls, and Galba is ador'd,	61	E95 Savile	8
NEST			
Lyes the Valley, cal'd my nest,	137	U2 Cupid	34
Farre from the Nest, and so himselfe belie	198	U40 Elegy That	38
The very verdure of her nest,	251	U74 Weston	13
A nest of odorous spice, and gummes.	280	U84 Mind	64
A nest of Spices, Odors, Gummes.	280	U84 Mind	V 64
NET			
Mars, and my Mother, in their net:	93	F1 Why write no	6
Fat, aged carps, that runne into thy net.	94	F2 Penshurst	33
Planting their Purles, and Curles spread forth like Net,	164	U15 Friend-Wars	65
NETHER			
Diana's Grove, or Altar, with the nether	338	Horace	V 20
NETS			
From all the nets that thou canst spread.	100	F4 To the World	8
Deceit is fruitfull. Men have Masques and nets,	216	U45 Squib	18
Or straines on his small forke his subtill nets	290	U85 Country	33
Or straines on his small forke his subtler nets	290	U85 Country	V 33
NEVER (See also NEERE, NERE)			
But that his Jone doth too. And Giles would never,	40	E42 Giles	4
As what he loves may never like too much.	41	E45 First Son	12
The knight-wright's cheated then: Hee'll never pay.	42	E46 Luckless 1	5
And never stoupe, but to strike ignorance:	55	E85 Goodyere 1	7
And land on one, whose face durst never bee	56	E88 Monsieur	5
Minervaes loome was never richer spred.	61	E95 Savile	16
And never art encounter'd, 1 confesse:	73	E112 Gamster	19
Man, that had never heard of a Chimaera.	86	E133 Voyage	80
Never did bottom more betray her burden;	87	E133 Voyage	116
That never failes to serve thee season'd deere,	94	F2 Penshurst	20
And never will redeeme a day,	100	F4 To the World	23
Thy thoughts did never melt in amorous fire,	108	F10 Proludium	3
Man may securely sinne, but safely never.	113	F11 Epode	116
A man may safely sinne, securely never.	113	F11 Epode	V116

NEVER (cont.)

	Page	Title	Line
Though never after; whiles it gaynes the voyce	113	F12 Rutland	11
Though never after; whiles it gaynes the will	113	F12 Rutland	V 11
And never thinke, how vice doth every houre,	113	F12 Rutland	V 11
That you never knew till now,	119	F13 Aubigny	87
Whom never yet he durst attempt awake;	131	U2 Excuse	15
That never came ill odour thence:	151	U11 Dreame	6
Men have beene great, but never good by chance,	152	U12 Corbet	18
And never but for doing wrong be sory;	156	U13 Sacvile	124
That fortune never make thee to complaine,	168	U15 Friend-Wars	180
And last, blaspheme not, we did never heare	168	U15 Friend-Wars	183
And yet the noble Nature never grudge;	168	U15 Friend-Wars	191
Helen, did Homer never see	169	U17 Friend-Debt	3
Where never Star shone brighter yet?	181	U27 Ode Helen	1
Resting never.	181	U27 Ode Helen	26
That in all tempests, never quit the helme,	184	U29 Fit of Rime	54
Then this did by her true? She never sought	185	U30 Burleigh	10
On which with profit, I shall never looke,	188	U34 Small Poxe	5
And never be by time, or folly brought,	189	U37 Friend-Book	5
Let those that meerely talke, and never thinke,	198	U40 Elegy That	44
That never yet did friend, or friendship seeke	218	U47 Tribe	9
So may there never Quarrell	218	U47 Tribe	14
I never stood for any place: my wit	221	U48 Bacchus	31
For never saw I yet the Muses dwell,	223	U49 Pucell	23
Never so great to get them: and the ends,	228	U53 Newcastle	15
Hee never fell, thou fall'st, my tongue.	242	U69 Friend Son	25
Hee never fell, thou tripst, my tongue.	244	U70 Ode	44
Health, or scarce breath, as she had never bin,	244	U70 Ode	V 44
Th'Ignoble never liv'd, they were a-while	248	U71 Treasurer	12
And never may there want one of the'Stem,	257	U75 Epithalam.	153
Beside, your hand will never hit,	258	U75 Epithalam.	177
That happy Day, that never shall see night!	277	U84 Mind	7
Her broken sighes did never misse whole sense:	286	U84 Muse	121
This hath pleas'd, doth please, and long will please; never	288	U84 Muse	185
Never at Law; seldome in office gown'd;	294	U88 Petronius	9
If something strange, that never yet was had	295	U90 Mart.10:47	5
If something strange, that never yet was had	313	Horace	178
If something fresh, that never yet was had	342	Horace	V178
There words will never follow 'gainst their will.	349	Horace	V444
The Writ, once out, never returned yet.	331	Horace	580
The word, once out, never returned yet.	352	Horace	V556/580
Locke pale, distill a showre (was never meant)	333	Horace	612
Look pale, distill a dew was never meant	353	Horace	V612
Gold is a sutor, never tooke repulse,	363	Riches	5
Did never dint the breast of Tamisis.	366	Ode Who saith	8
So, be there never discontent, or sorrow,	384	Somerset	15
So, in theyr number, may you never see	384	Somerset	21
You know, I never was of Truth afeard,	414	Rutter	4
shall never dare do any thing but feare.	423	Lucan	20

NEVIL

	Page	Title	Line
To Sir Henry Nevil.	70	E109 Nevil	Ttl
Who now calls on thee, Nevil, is a Muse,	70	E109 Nevil	1

NEVILLS

	Page	Title	Line
Beauchamps, and Nevills, Cliffords, Audleys old;	214	U44 Speach	52

NEW

	Page	Title	Line
On the new Hot-house.	29	E7 Hot-house	Ttl
Signes to new bond, forfeits: and cryes, god payes.	30	E12 Shift	14
To thee, my way in Epigrammes seemes new,	32	E18 Censurer	1
Gypsey, new baud, is turn'd physitian,	39	E41 Gypsee	1
Not glad, like those that have new hopes, or sutes,	47	E64 Salisbury 3	1
With thy new place, bring I these early fruits	47	E64 Salisbury 3	2
To see thy fathers rites new laid on thee.	47	E64 Salisbury 3	6
To plucke downe mine, Poll sets up new wits still,	50	E71 Parrat	1
Surly's old whore in her new silkes doth swim:	54	E82 Surly	1
The new french-taylors motion, monthly made,	56	E88 Monsieur	15
The new Crie.	58	E92 New Crie	Ttl
On the new Motion.	62	E97 Motion	Ttl
But one more rare, and in the case so new:	62	E97 Motion	3
A new Susanna, equall to that old?	67	E104 Montgomery	4
But even their names were to be made a-new,	67	E105 L Wroth 2	5
Thy deedes, unto thy name, will prove new wombes,	70	E109 Nevil	17
(As by a new creation) part by part,	71	E110 Edmonds 1	18
And that, in action, there is nothing new,	72	E111 Edmonds 2	5
And have sought (to give new birth)	77	E120 S. P.	21
Lent timely succours, and new life begot:	80	E127 Aubigny	8
On some new gesture, that's imputed wit?	81	E129 Mime	14
Fresh as the ayre, and new as are the houres.	94	F2 Penshurst	40
Comus puts in, for new delights;	98	F3 Wroth	48
Or, with thy Tribade trine, invent new sports,	107	F10 Proludium	17
A vow as new, and ominous as the yeare,	116	F12 Rutland	98
On the close groome, and page, on new-yeeres day,	118	F13 Aubigny	74
This makes, that your affections still be new,	119	F13 Aubigny	118
And great, must seeke for new,	121	F14 Sydney	35
After flight; and put new stings	137	U2 Cupid	36
To make a new, and hang that by.	145	U5 Woman-kind	18
Meet some new matter to looke up and wonder!	157	U13 Sacvile	142
Sols Chariot for new fire,	175	U23 Himselfe	28
His new Cassandra, 'bove the old;	181	U27 Ode Helen	23
Have made me to conceive a Lawyer new.	187	U33 Councellour	14
The Dedication of the Kings new Cellar. to Bacchus.	220	U48 Bacchus	Ttl
New in their stead, out of the Candidates?	222	U49 Pucell	6
As new rewards of her old secrecie?	223	U49 Pucell	20
As they had learn'd new changes, for the day,	253	U75 Epithalam.	35
A New-yeares gift Sung to King Charles, 1635.	263	U79 New-yeares	Ttl

NEW (cont.)
New yeares, expect new gifts: Sister, your Harpe, . . . 263 U79 New-yeares   1
Of the New Yeare, in a new silken warpe, . . . 263 U79 New-yeares   5
To day old Janus opens the new yeare, . . . 263 U79 New-yeares   9
And the disposure will be something new, . . . 269 U81 Pawlet   16
And the disposure will be somewhat new, . . . 269 U81 Pawlet   V 16
Else, who doth praise a person by a new, ... 270 U81 Pawlet   37
Were fitly interpos'd; so new: . . . 275 U84 Body   10
A new Song to his praise, and great I Am: . . . 285 U84 Muse   90
And snares the fearfull Hare, and new-come Crane, . . . 290 U85 Country   35
More sweet then Olives, that new gather'd be . . . 291 U85 Country   55
In using also of new words, to be . . . 307 Horace   65
Are, by thy cunning placing, made meere new. . . . 307 Horace   68
Thou need new termes; thou maist, without excuse, . . . 307 Horace   70
And those thy new, and late-coyn'd words receive, . . . 309 Horace   74
New names of things. It hath beene ever free, . . . 309 Horace   83
A meere new person, looke he keepe his state .. . . 313 Horace   180
In time to Tragedie, a Musicke new. . . . 319 Horace   306
To the grave Harp, and Violl voyces new; . . . 346 Horace   V306
With something that was acceptably new. . . . 321 Horace   327
Those ill-torn'd Verses, to new hammering. . . . 333 Horace   628
your Royal Eye which still creates new men . . . 383 Rich   14
When the old words doe strike on the new times, . . . 389 Aleman   4
But, I would have, thee, to know something new, . . . 394 Jane Ogle   13
On the new priming of thy old Signe postes . . . 405 Inigo Jones 1 87
Wee'll have thee styld the Marquess of New-Ditch. . . . 407 Inigo Jones 2 24
Or why to like; they found, it all was new, . . . 415 Rutter   9
This is my censure. Now there is a new . . . 415 Rutter   19
Of wit, and a new made: a Warden then, . . . 415 Rutter   23
Yo'have all the Mysteries of Wits new Mint, . . . 415 Rutter   28
Fresh as the Day, and new as are the Howers, . . . 416 Welcome   1
NEWCASTLE
An Epigram. To William, Earle of Newcastle. . . . 228 U53 Newcastle Ttl
An Epigram. To William Earle of Newcastle. . . . 232 U59 Newcastle Ttl
To the Right Honorable William Earle of Newcastle. . . . 232 U59 Newcastle VTtl
NEW-COME
And snares the fearfull Hare, and new-come Crane, . . . 290 U85 Country   35
NEW-DITCH
Wee'll have thee styld the Marquess of New-Ditch. . . . 407 Inigo Jones 2 24
NEWER
Insert thy Hodges, and those newer men, ... 214 U44 Speach   53
And newer, then could please them, by-cause trew. . . . 415 Rutter   10
NEWES
Doe what you come for, Captayne, with your newes; . . . 68 E107 Hungry   1
For newes) your Ville-royes, and Silleries, . . . 69 E107 Hungry   21
Of newes, and noyse, to strow out a long meale. . . . 74 E115 Honest Man 10
Of newes, and noyse, to sow out a long meale. . . . 74 E115 Honest Man V 10
The Brethren, they streight nois'd it out for Newes, . . . 209 U43 Vulcan   139
There were, that streight did nose it out for newes, . . . 209 U43 Vulcan   V139
The brethren they streight ways noisd out for newes, . . . 209 U43 Vulcan   V139
Of newes they get, to strew out the long meale, . . . 218 U47 Tribe   28
Though I doe neither heare these newes, nor tell . . . 219 U47 Tribe   46
And in an Epicoene fury can write newes . . . 222 U49 Pucell   8
Equall with that, which for the best newes goes, . . . 222 U49 Pucell   9
And as either newes or mirth . . . 417 Moon   17
Specially the newes of Darby; . . . . 417 Moon   21
NEWNESSE
Newnesse of Sense, Antiquitie of voyce! . . . 160 U14 Selden   60
NEW-YEARES
A New-yeares gift Sung to King Charles, 1635. . . . 263 U79 New-yeares Ttl
NEW-YEERES
On the close groome, and page, on new-yeeres day, . . . 118 F13 Aubigny   74
NEXT
Be thy next masters more unluckie Muse, ... 48 E65 Muse   5
It is the next deed, and a great one too. . . . . 61 E95 Savile   26
Shall make us sad next morning: or affright . . . . 65 E101 Supper   41
For your next meale: this you are sure of. Why . . . 69 E107 Hungry   27
Next morne, an Ode: Thou mak'st a song ere night. . . . 72 E112 Gamster   12
Thy tables hoord not up for the next day, ... 95 F2 Penshurst   71
Next, to that vertue, is to know vice well, . . . 109 F11 Epode   3
Mee, the scope of his next draught, . . . 133 U2 Suffered   11
Then turning unto him is next at hand, . . . 154 U13 Sacvile   56
Next to your selfe, for making your love true: . . . 189 U37 Friend-Book 2
Squire of the Squibs, against the next Maiors day, . . . 208 U43 Vulcan   V119
You'ld reade a Snake, in his next Song. . . . 260 U76 Petition   32
To eate a Snake, in his next Song. . . . 260 U76 Petition   V 32
Upon them, (next to Spenser's noble booke,) . . . 263 U78 Digby   24
The Heaven design'd, draw next a Spring, . . . 276 U84 Body   21
Next sitting we will draw her mind. . . . 277 U84 Body   32
With lees of Wine. Next Eschylus, more late, . . . 319 Horace   315
Next these great Homer and Tyrtaeus set . . . 327 Horace   493
Next, that which rapt mee, was: I might behold . . . 361 Palmer   13
Where spight of Death, next Life, for her Loves sake . . . 394 Jane Ogle   25
'tis but the next neighbour ride . . . . 417 Moon   35
NEYTHER
Yet neyther of you seeme to th'other old. . . . . 384 Somerset   24
NICE (See also NYCE)
Or in confessing of the Crime be nice, . . . 191 U38 Elegy 'Tis   23
Yet shee's nor nice to shew them, . . . 365 Ode Splendor   23
NICER
The nicer thing to tast her ladies page; . . . . 57 E90 Mill   5
NICHOLAS
Whereof old Democrite, and Hill Nicholas, ... 87 E133 Voyage   128

	Page	Title	Line
NICHOLAS (cont.)			
With Nicholas Pasquill's, Meddle with your match,	206	U43 Vulcan	77
With Nicholas Bretons Meddle with your match,	206	U43 Vulcan	V 77
NIECE (See NEECES)			
NIGH			
A sope-boyler; and Aeacus him nigh,	89	E133 Voyage	188
To have her linnen, plate, and all things nigh,	96	F2 Penshurst	86
Of love, and hate: and came so nigh to know	200	U42 Elegy Let	35
It selfe to us, and come so nigh	279	U84 Mind	43
NIGHT			
For all night-sinnes, with others wives, unknowne,	39	E39 Colt	1
Ideot, last night, I pray'd thee but forbeare	45	E58 Groome	1
Each night, to drowne his cares: But when the gaine	56	E87 Hazard	3
To night, grave sir, both my poore house, and I	64	E101 Supper	1
The libertie, that wee'll enjoy to night.	65	E101 Supper	42
Next morne, an Ode: Thou mak'st a song ere night.	72	E112 Gamster	12
Gut eates all day, and lechers all the night,	76	E118 Gut	1
Of all your night-tubs, when the carts doe cluster,	85	E133 Voyage	64
Of the short braverie of the night;	96	F3 Wroth	10
Or, if thou list the night in watch to breake,	97	F3 Wroth	21
False world, good-night: since thou hast brought	100	F4 To the World	1
'Tis, with us, perpetuall night.	102	F5 Celia 1	8
Would make a day of night,	112	F11 Epode	94
I Sing the birth, was borne to night,	130	U1 Nativitie	1
Wisht the Bride were chang'd to night,	138	U2 Kisse	18
Or, if you did move to night	138	U2 Kisse	21
I am undone to night;	150	U11 Dreame	3
Sydney e're night! or that did goe to bed	157	U13 Sacvile	127
It is as if a night should shade noone-day,	199	U41 Elegy Since	5
Or in Moore-fields, this other night! sings one,	202	U42 Elegy Let	73
Call every night to Supper in these fitts,	218	U47 Tribe	21
Lay trampled on; the deeds of death, and night,	243	U70 Ode	14
Although it fall, and die that night;	245	U70 Ode	71
Haste, haste, officious Sun, and send them Night	257	U75 Epithalam.	145
Night, and the sheetes will show	258	U75 Epithalam.	191
The Starres, that are the Jewels of the Night,	271	U81 Pawlet	87
That happy Day, that never shall see night!	286	U84 Muse	121
Hard-hearted, I dreame every Night	293	U86 Hor.4:1	37
Thy night not dronken, but from cares layd wast;	295	U90 Mart.10:47	9
In hand, and, turne them over, day, and night.	323	Horace	398
When night their meeting covers.	365	Ode Splendor	8
Which, since thy flight from hence, hath mourn'd like night,	392	Shakespeare	79
NIGHTS			
In the silent sommer-nights,	103	F6 Celia 2	17
To thy altars, by their nights	104	F8 Sicknesse	4
And nights too, in worser wayes?	104	F8 Sicknesse	6
Reare-Suppers in their Names! and spend whole nights	156	U13 Sacvile	101
Is not enough now, but the Nights to play:	166	U15 Friend-Wars	132
Is not enough now, but the Nights we play:	166	U15 Friend-Wars	V132
And turne the Ceremonies of those Nights	197	U40 Elegy That	11
NIGHT-SINNES			
For all night-sinnes, with others wives, unknowne,	39	E39 Colt	1
NIGHT-TUBS			
Of all your night-tubs, when the carts doe cluster,	85	E133 Voyage	64
NILL			
If, now, with man and wife, to will, and nill	40	E42 Giles	16
NIMBLE			
And stroke the water, nimble, chast, and faire,	230	U56 Covell	14
The nimble French;	368	Ode Who saith	84
NINE			
Of our fift Henry, eight of his nine yeare;	207	U43 Vulcan	98
Of our fift Henry, right of his nine yeare;	207	U43 Vulcan	V 98
Spun out in name of some of the old Nine!	282	U84 Muse	6
Nine yeares kept in, your papers by, yo'are free	331	Horace	578
Nine yeares kept by, your papers in, y'are free	352	Horace	V554/578
NINTH			
Mov'd by her order, and the ninth more high,	82	E130 Ferrab. 1	13
NO'			
And which no' affection praise enough can give!	34	E23 Donne 1	6
NO (See also NOE)			
And gave thee both, to shew they could no more.	28	E4 James 1	4
And, I a Poet here, no Herald am.	29	E9 To All	4
And such from whom let no man hope least good,	30	E11 Something	6
All men are wormes: But this no man. In silke	31	E15 Court-worm	1
That Cod can get no widdow, yet a knight,	33	E19 Cod 1	1
Then his chast wife, though Beast now know no more,	35	E26 Beast 2	1
He drinkes to no man: that's, too, like a lord.	35	E28 Surly	14
Stile thee a most great foole, but no great man.	36	E28 Surly	22
Banck feeles no lamenesse of his knottie gout,	36	E31 Banck	1
Who wets my grave, can be no friend of mine.	37	E33 Roe 3	6
Hast purg'd thy realmes, as we have now no cause	38	E35 James 2	5
No cause, nor client fat, will Chev'rill leese,	38	E37 Chev'ril	1
Grant then, no rude hand remove her.	39	E40 Ratcliffe	4
Th'observing neighbours no such mood can see.	40	E42 Giles	2
No more would Jone he should. Giles riseth early,	40	E42 Giles	6
I know no couple better can agree!	40	E42 Giles	18
And, if no other miserie, yet age?	41	E45 First Son	8
And hath no honor lost, our Due'llists say.	42	E48 Mungril	3
I have no salt: no bawdrie he doth meane.	42	E49 Playwrt 1	3
No lesse than if from perill; and devout,	43	E51 James 3	7
When having pill'd a booke, which no man buyes,	43	E53 Old-end	2
And so my sharpnesse thou no lesse dis-joynts,	45	E58 Groome	5
Your 'pothecarie, and his drug sayes no.	46	E62 Would-bee	4

NO (cont.)

	Page	Title	Line
Whose house, if it no other honor had,	48	E66 Cary	3
Against thy fortune: when no foe, that day,	49	E66 Cary	9
Which, by no lesse confirm'd, then thy kings choice,	49	E67 Suffolk	11
That no affection in thy voyce commands;	51	E74 Chancelor	4
And no lesse wise, then skilfull in the lawes;	52	E74 Chancelor	6
No male unto him: who could so exceed	53	E79 Rutland	7
He cast, yet keeps her well! No, shee keeps him.	54	E82 Surly	2
Or is it some french statue? No: 'T doth move,	56	E88 Monsieur	13
Who had no lesse a trumpet of their name,	57	E89 Allen	5
Discern'd no difference of his yeeres, or play,	57	E90 Mill	8
And have'hem yeeld no savour, but of state.	58	E92 New Crie	5
No more then Salust in the Romane state!	61	E95 Savile	23
He is no favourites favourite, no deare trust	63	E97 Motion	13
Need seeke no other strength, no other height;	63	E98 Th Roe 1	4
Something, which, else, could hope for no esteeme.	64	E101 Supper	6
And Ile professe no verses to repeate:	65	E101 Supper	24
And we will have no Pooly', or Parrot by;	65	E101 Supper	36
We innocently met. No simple word,	65	E101 Supper	39
And to your Scene lent no lesse dignitie	67	E104 Montgomery	7
There Juno sate, and yet no Peacock by.	68	E105 L Wroth 2	18
No more, then I dare now doe, with my pen.	70	E108 Soldiers	8
His life, but makes, that he can dye no more.	71	E110 Edmonds 1	22
There's no vexation, that can make thee prime.	73	E112 Gamster	22
Suffers no name, but a description:	74	E115 Honest Man	4
Being no vitious person, but the vice	74	E115 Honest Man	5
The cloth's no sooner gone, but it gets up	74	E115 Honest Man	24
That Nature no such difference had imprest	75	E116 Jephson	9
At hunting railes, having no guift in othes,	76	E119 Shelton	2
No, Shelton, give me thee, canst want all these,	76	E119 Shelton	7
I need no other arts, but studie thee:	78	E122 Rudyerd 2	9
But I, no child, no foole, respect the kinde,	79	E125 Uvedale	7
I answer'd, Daphne now no paine can prove.	80	E126 Mrs Cary	6
No, I doe, therefore, call Posteritie	80	E127 Aubigny	4
And, than this same, I know no abler way	80	E127 Aubigny	11
That there's no journey set, or thought upon,	81	E129 Mime	3
No lesse a sov'raigne cure, then to the mind;	82	E130 Ferrab. 1	8
That the eight sphaere, no lesse, then planets seaven,	82	E130 Ferrab. 1	12
The learn'd have no more priviledge, then the lay.	82	E131 Ferrab. 2	4
No more, those mayden glories shee hath lost.	83	E132 Sylvester	14
No more let Greece her bolder fables tell	84	E133 Voyage	1
Their wherry had no saile, too; ours had none:	84	E133 Voyage	11
'Tis but light paines: Indeede this Dock's no rose.	85	E133 Voyage	60
So huge, it seem'd, they could by no meanes quite her.	86	E133 Voyage	86
Backe, cry'd their brace of Charons: they cry'd, no,	86	E133 Voyage	87
No going backe; on still you rogues, and row.	86	E133 Voyage	88
No matter, stinkards, row. What cheare? wind-bound,	86	E133 Voyage	91
Is this we heare? of frogs? No, guts wind-bound,	86	E133 Voyage	92
And that ours did. For, yet, no nare was tainted,	87	E133 Voyage	133
Thou hast no lanterne, whereof tales are told;	93	F2 Penshurst	4
They'are rear'd with no mans ruine, no mans grone,	94	F2 Penshurst	46
And no one empty-handed, to salute	95	F2 Penshurst	49
Thy lord, and lady, though they have no sute.	95	F2 Penshurst	50
Where comes no guest, but is allow'd to eate,	95	F2 Penshurst	61
Here no man tells my cups; nor, standing by,	95	F2 Penshurst	67
That at great times, art no ambitious guest	96	F3 Wroth	5
(Their rudenesse then is thought no sinne)	98	F3 Wroth	54
Such, and no other was that age, of old,	98	F3 Wroth	63
No, I doe know, that I was borne	101	F4 To the World	61
'Tis no sinne, loves fruit to steale,	102	F5 Celia 1	15
Kisse againe: no creature comes.	103	F6 Celia 2	5
And this age will build no more:	105	F8 Sicknesse	12
And Ile expect no wine.	106	F9 Celia 3	V 4
Phoebus. No? tend thy cart still. Envious day	107	F10 Proludium	7
My Muse up by commission: No, I bring	108	F10 Proludium	28
Our muse up by commission: No, we bring	108	F10 Proludium	V 28
An elegie? no, muse; yt askes a straine	108	F10 Proludium	1
Which to effect (since no brest is so sure,	109	F11 Epode	5
That no strange, or unkinde	109	F11 Epode	10
No such effects doth prove;	110	F11 Epode	44
In equall knots: This beares no brands, nor darts,	110	F11 Epode	51
That cryes, we dreame, and sweares, there's no such thing,	111	F11 Epode	67
That cryes, I dreame, and sweares, there's no such thing,	111	F11 Epode	V 67
No, vice, we let thee know,	111	F11 Epode	72
No, vice, I let thee know,	111	F11 Epode	V 72
When gold was made no weapon to cut throtes,	114	F12 Rutland	23
That had no Muse to make their fame abide.	114	F12 Rutland	48
Will prove old Orpheus act no tale to be:	115	F12 Rutland	77
Will prove old Orpheus Arts no tale to be:	115	F12 Rutland	V 77
For I shall move stocks, stones, no lesse then he.	115	F12 Rutland	78
Men are not just, or keepe no holy lawes	117	F13 Aubigny	18
No lady, but, at some time, loves her glasse.	117	F13 Aubigny	26
And this shall be no false one, but as much	117	F13 Aubigny	27
Till that no usurer, nor his bawds dare lend	118	F13 Aubigny	78
Them, or their officers: and no man know,	118	F13 Aubigny	79
Whether it be a face they weare, or no.	118	F13 Aubigny	80
The Sonnes obedience knew no No,	130	U1 Nativitie	14
He no sooner heard the Law,	133	U2 Suffered	13
This here sung, can be no other	136	U2 Cupid	11
To no other Grace but you!	138	U2 Kisse	20
No, nor forth your window peepe,	140	U2 Promise	16
In loves schoole, and yet no sinners.	141	U2 Her man	32
In loves art, and yet no sinners.	141	U2 Her man	V 32

NO (cont.)

	Page	Title	Line
Yet no Taylor help to make him;	141	U2 Her man	37
As to doe no thing too much.	142	U2 Her man	46
No tunes are sweet, nor words have sting,	143	U3 Musicall	15
No voice so sweet, nor words have sting,	143	U3 Musicall	V 15
Sing you no more then, lest the best	144	U3 Musicall	V 21
Men, if you love us, play no more	145	U5 Woman-kind	1
We are no women then, but wives.	146	U6 Defence	6
I'le tell no more, and yet I love,	148	U7 Nymph	29
And he loves me; yet no	148	U7 Nymph	30
Even ashes of lovers find no rest.	149	U8 Houre-glasse	11
No stubbornnesse so stiffe, nor folly	152	U12 Corbet	24
No! Gifts and thankes should have one cheerefull face,	154	U13 Sacvile	39
No more then he doth thanke, that will receive	154	U13 Sacvile	43
No more are these of us, let them then goe,	156	U13 Sacvile	113
No! he must feele and know, that will advance.	156	U13 Sacvile	123
They need no stilts, nor rise upon their toes,	157	U13 Sacvile	145
In offering this thy worke to no great Name,	161	U14 Selden	69
But here's no time, nor place, my wealth to tell,	161	U14 Selden	85
No person, nor is lov'd: what wayes he proves	162	U15 Friend-Wars	16
No part or corner man can looke upon,	163	U15 Friend-Wars	27
The bravery makes, she can no honour leese:	164	U15 Friend-Wars	56
Whom no great Mistresse hath as yet infam'd,	165	U15 Friend-Wars	97
I'le bid thee looke no more, but flee, flee friend,	166	U15 Friend-Wars	129
This Praecipice, and Rocks that have no end,	166	U15 Friend-Wars	130
He that no more for Age, Cramps, Palsies, can	166	U15 Friend-Wars	135
For the recovery of my voyce? No, there	167	U15 Friend-Wars	154
No more, then we should thinke a Lord had had	168	U15 Friend-Wars	193
And if I had no more to say,	168	U16 Gray	2
Tell me (my lov'd Friend) doe you love, or no,	170	U19 Elegy By	11
I'le therefore aske no more, but bid you love;	171	U19 Elegy By	15
Slip no occasion; As time stands not still,	171	U19 Elegy By	19
I know no beautie, nor no youth that will.	171	U19 Elegy By	20
No more, I am sorry for so fond cause, say,	171	U20 Shrub	4
Perjur'd! and painted! if she were no more--,	172	U20 Shrub	22
Assisted by no strengths, but are her owne,	176	U24 Frontispice	14
No Armour to the mind! he is shot-free	179	U25 Desmond	48
At the Well no Muse did stay,	183	U29 Fit of Rime	20
And goe no farther: let this Circle be	185	U30 Burleigh	3
Lawes; and no change e're come to one decree:	185	U31 Elsmere	2
Where mutuall frauds are fought, and no side yeild;	186	U33 Councellour	4
That heaven should make no more; or should amisse,	188	U34 Small Poxe	15
Where Love doth shine, there needs no Sunne,	189	U36 Song	5
That friendship which no chance but love did chuse,	190	U37 Friend-Book	23
For no man lives so out of passions sway,	190	U37 Friend-Book	31
Her furie, yet no friendship to betray.	190	U37 Friend-Book	33
This sadnesse makes no approaches, but to kill.	191	U38 Elegy 'Tis	4
The ignorant, and fooles, no pittie have.	191	U38 Elegy 'Tis	20
No, I will stand arraign'd, and cast, to be	191	U38 Elegy 'Tis	27
There is no Father that for one demerit,	192	U38 Elegy 'Tis	41
No man inflicts that paine, till hope be spent:	192	U38 Elegy 'Tis	44
The contrite Soule, who hath no thought to win	193	U38 Elegy 'Tis	89
I will no more abuse my vowes to you,	194	U38 Elegy 'Tis	107
And that there is no life in me, but love.	194	U38 Elegy 'Tis	112
No, Mistris, no, the open merrie Man	198	U40 Elegy That	25
If I had writ no word, but Deare, farewell.	198	U40 Elegy That	50
You would restore it? No, that's worth a feare,	199	U41 Elegy Since	15
No Poets verses yet did ever move,	199	U42 Elegy Let	3
No face, no hand, proportion, line, or Ayre	200	U42 Elegy Let	14
Whether their faces were their owne, or no:	200	U42 Elegy Let	36
Of race accompted, that no passion have	201	U42 Elegy Let	49
No mar'le the Clownes of Lemnos tooke thee up,	208	U43 Vulcan	116
No Foole would his owne harvest spoile, or burne!	209	U43 Vulcan	150
O no, cry'd all, Fortune, for being a whore,	209	U43 Vulcan	153
Lyes there no Writ, out of the Chancerie	210	U43 Vulcan	174
Against this Vulcan? No Injunction?	210	U43 Vulcan	175
No order? no Decree? Though we be gone	211	U43 Vulcan	176
Would thinke no more of Vlushing, or the Brill:	213	U44 Speach	30
I may no longer on these pictures stay,	216	U44 Speach	98
No piece of money, but you know, or make	216	U45 Squib	14
They cannot last. No lie grew ever old.	216	U45 Squib	20
No lesse of praise, then readers in all kinds	217	U46 Coke	19
I have no portion in them, nor their deale	218	U47 Tribe	27
And that there be no fev'ry heats, nor colds,	220	U47 Tribe	67
I am no States-man, and much lesse Divine,	223	U49 Pucell	25
This Age would lend no faith to Dorrels Deed;	223	U49 Pucell	42
No friend to vertue, could be silent here.	224	U50 Countesse	8
For you admit no companie, but good,	224	U50 Countesse	25
Which if in compasse of no Art it came	227	U52 Answer	10
A Poet hath no more but black and white,	227	U52 Answer	20
For your securitie. I can no better.	229	U54 Squib	20
Yet with a Dye, that feares no Moth,	230	U55 Burges	7
If there be no money;	231	U57 Burges	21
No Plover, or Coney	231	U57 Burges	22
Thanke him: if other, hee can give no Bayes.	232	U58 Book-seller	6
If his wit reach no higher, but to spring	232	U58 Book-seller	7
Wonder to Valour! No, it is the Law	233	U59 Newcastle	14
Of a Disease, that lov'd no light	234	U60 La-ware	6
Of honour, nor no ayre of good?	234	U60 La-ware	7
No noble furniture of parts,	234	U60 La-ware	11
No love of action, and high Arts,	234	U60 La-ware	12
No aime at glorie, or, in warre,	234	U60 La-ware	13
As here no Venus were;	240	U67 Muses	34

438

NO (cont.)

	Page	Title	Line
As the old Bard, should no Canary lack.	241	U68 House-hold	11
No doubt all Infants would returne like thee.	243	U70 Ode	20
But ever to no ends:	243	U70 Ode	29
For three of his foure-score, he did no good.	243	U70 Ode	32
No pleasures vaine did chime,	246	U70 Ode	102
Dare thinke it, to relieve, no lesse renowne,	248	U71 Treasurer	14
Force from the Phoenix, then, no raritie	255	U75 Epithalam.	81
In him the times, no lesse then Prince, are prais'd,	256	U75 Epithalam.	115
You find no cold	258	U75 Epithalam.	166
You feele no cold	258	U75 Epithalam.	V166
Hee's Master of the Office; yet no more	258	U75 Epithalam.	187
Exacts then she is pleas'd to pay: no suits,	258	U75 Epithalam.	188
gentlie hee asketh, shee will pay: no suits,	258	U75 Epithalam.	V188
Wee know no other power then his,	265	U79 New-yeares	42
Pan knowes no other power then his,	265	U79 New-yeares	64
Thereof, no notion can expresse how much	269	U81 Pawlet	26
No Nation can expresse how much	269	U81 Pawlet	V 26
Yet, here are no such Trifles brought,	273	U84 Cradle	25
No cobweb Call's; no Surcoates wrought	273	U84 Cradle	26
But here I may no colours use.	277	U84 Mind	6
But here we may no colours use.	277	U84 Mind	V 6
No, to expresse a Mind to sense,	278	U84 Mind	13
No, to expresse this Mind to sense,	278	U84 Mind	V 13
This is no Picture, but the same.	278	U84 Mind	24
Thou hast no more blowes, Fate, to drive at one:	283	U84 Muse	27
T' have knowne no envy, but by suffring it!	287	U84 Muse	162
And ('bout thy Ivory neck,) no youth did fling	293	U87 Hor.3:9	2
Whilst Horace lov'd no Mistres more,	293	U87 Hor.3:9	5
There is no labour, nor no shame in this:	294	U88 Petronius	8
No sowre, or sollen bed-mate, yet a Chast;	295	U90 Mart.10:47	10
No place for these. And, Painter, hap'ly, thou	305	Horace	24
To forme a worke, I would no more desire	307	Horace	50
To frame a worke, I would no more desire	339	Horace	V 52/ 50
In tragick Verse; no lesse Thyestes feast	311	Horace	122
Falshood with truth, as no man can espie	315	Horace	216
Falshood and truth, as no man can espy	343	Horace	V216
The free spectators, subject to no Law,	319	Horace	324
Be I their Judge, they doe at no time dare	321	Horace	356
But, in conclusion, merited no fame.	323	Horace	396
A Poeme, of no grace, weight, art, in rimes,	327	Horace	456
Deserves no pardon; or who'd play, and sing	329	Horace	531
Whether his soothing friend speake truth, or no.	333	Horace	606
If of their friendship he be worthy, or no:	333	Horace	619
If you denied, you had no better straine,	333	Horace	625
Then change; no word, or worke, more would he spend	335	Horace	630
Himselfe there purposely, or no; and would	335	Horace	657
Recall him yet, hee'ld be no more a man:	335	Horace	668
Now, bring him backe, he'le be no more a man,	355	Horace	V668
Where Gold's the Motive, women have no Nay.	363	Riches	18
Now, after all, let no man	364	Phoenix	1
A Horse here is sadled, but no Tom him to backe,	374	Coryat 1	14
To line out no stride, but pas'd by himselfe?	379	Coryat 3	8
Since he treads in no other Mans steps but his owne.	379	Coryat 3	12
No: as I first said, who would write a story at	381	Coryat 3	59
That bid, God give thee joy, and have no endes.	384	Somerset	6
to which there's no materiall that endures;	387	Cavendish	8
Faire Aemulation, and no Envy is;	389	Aleman	22
To draw no envy (Shakespeare) on thy name,	390	Shakespeare	1
As, since, she will vouchsafe no other Wit.	392	Shakespeare	50
No stone in any wall here, but can tell	394	Jane Ogle	9
But Sorrow, she desir'd no other Friend:	394	Jane Ogle	17
It was no Dreame! I was awake, and saw!	396	Drayton	11
Hence, then, prophane: Here needs no words expense	400	Beaumont	3
I now would write on thee? No, wretch; thy name	409	Detractor	11
No man will tarry by thee, as hee goes,	409	Detractor	17
At libelling? Shall no Star-Chamber Peers,	410	Gill	3
No faith's more firme, or flat, then where't doth creep.	413	Ghyrlond	20
By bringing forth God's onely Son, no other.	414	Ghyrlond	48
at my back, I am no spright,	416	Moon	6
And in this Age, canst hope no other grace.	420	Ode:If Men	27
Even states most hated, when no lawes resist	423	Lucan	13
Those dull Girls, no good can mean us,	657	Door Apollo	11

NOBILITIE

	Page	Title	Line
Let poore Nobilitie be vertuous: Wee,	215	U44 Speach	79
'Tis Vertue alone, is true Nobilitie.	282	U84 Kenelme	21
Of title in her! All Nobilitie	287	U84 Muse	159

NOBLE

	Page	Title	Line
For your most noble offer had supply'd me.	54	E84 Bedford 2	4
As noble in great chiefes, as they are rare.	58	E91 Vere	16
Thy lady's noble, fruitfull, chaste withall.	96	F2 Penshurst	90
Reade, in their vertuous parents noble parts,	96	F2 Penshurst	97
. . . vertuous and Noble.	100	F4 To the World	Ttl
Much more a noble, and right generous mind	112	F11 Epode	111
Much more a noble, or a generous mind	112	F11 Epode	V111
With noble ignorants, and let them still,	114	F12 Rutland	28
But high, and noble matter, such as flies	116	F12 Rutland	89
And raise a noble stemme, to give the fame,	119	F13 Aubigny	97
Noble; or of greater Blood:	140	U2 Her man	4
Noble; or of greatest Blood:	140	U2 Her man	V 4
And yet the noble Nature never grudge;	169	U17 Friend-Debt	3
A Sonnet, to the noble Lady, the Lady Mary Worth.	182	U28 Worth	Ttl
That you should be too noble to destroy.	191	U38 Elegy 'Tis	12

	Page	Title	Line
NOBLE (cont.)			
To carry noble danger in the face:	194	U38 Elegy 'Tis	102
Wherin (besides the noble aydes were lent,	207	U43 Vulcan	V 99
Wherin (besides the noble Aydes were spent,	207	U43 Vulcan	V 99
Wherin (besides the noble aydes were sent,	207	U43 Vulcan	V 99
Which noble Carew, Cotton, Selden lent:	207	U43 Vulcan	100
Why yet, my noble hearts, they cannot say,	213	U44 Speach	1
And there instruct the noble English heires	214	U44 Speach	59
The noble Science, and the maistring skill	232	U59 Newcastle	3
No noble furniture of parts,	234	U60 La-ware	11
To the immortall memorie, and friendship of that noble	242	U70 Ode	Ttl
And had his noble name advanc'd with men:	244	U70 Ode	36
A perfect Patriot, and a noble friend,	244	U70 Ode	46
Call, noble Lucius, then for Wine,	245	U70 Ode	75
. . . that Noble Gentleman, Mr. Hierome Weston, Son, and . . .	252	U75 Epithalam.	Ttl
To pay, with honours, to his noble Sonne	256	U75 Epithalam.	106
Stand there; for when a noble Nature's rais'd,	256	U75 Epithalam.	113
Upon them, (next to Spenser's noble booke,)	263	U78 Digby	24
. . . Of that truly-noble Lady, the Lady Venetia Digby, . . .	272	U84 Eupheme	Ttl
Out of her noble body, to this Feast:	284	U84 Muse	82
And best he knew her noble Character,	287	U84 Muse	155
For he's both noble, lovely, young,	292	U86 Hor.4:1	13
Most Writers, noble Sire, and either Sonne,	307	Horace	33
I sing a noble Warre, and Priam's Fate.	313	Horace	196
Clowne, Towns-man, base, and noble, mix'd, to judge?	319	Horace	302
To the Right Noble Tom, Tell-Troth of his travailes. . . .	378	Coryat 2	Ttl
. . . in the Behalfe of the two Noble Brothers sir Robert . .	382	Rich	Ttl
Two noble knightes, whome true desire and zeale,	382	Rich	Ttl
To the most noble, and above his Titles, . . .	384	Somerset	Ttl
To see (who'it is?) A noble Countesse, greate,	394	Jane Ogle	3
A Noble honest Soule! what's this to thee?	406	Inigo Jones 2	6
NOBLER			
Martial, thou gav'st farre nobler Epigrammes	38	E36 Martial	1
Then which, a nobler heaven it selfe knowes not.	115	F12 Rutland	67
'Tis now inquir'd, which makes the nobler Verse,	331	Horace	581
NOBLES			
Of nobles vertue, shew in you;	121	F14 Sydney	32
NOBLESSE			
But thou, whose noblesse keeps one stature still,	66	E102 Pembroke	13
True noblesse. Palme growes straight, though handled ne're so rude.	177	U25 Desmond	26
NOBLEST			
These (noblest Cecil) labour'd in my thought,	48	E64 Salisbury 3	15
Your noblest father prov'd: like whom, before,	53	E79 Rutland	2
Thy noblest spouse affords them welcome grace;	98	F3 Wroth	55
Thy noblest spouse affords them welcome place;	98	F3 Wroth	V 55
Noblest Charis, you that are	136	U2 Cupid	1
They are the Noblest benefits, and'sinke	153	U13 Sacvile	19
Quickning dead Nature, to her noblest strife.	162	U15 Friend-Wars	8
The noblest freedome, not to chuse	173	U22 Elegy Tho	11
And in the noblest Families tooke root	185	U30 Burleigh	18
And studie them unto the noblest ends,	224	U50 Countesse	28
unto thee, king of men; their noblest partes	382	Rich	3
And hath the noblest marke of a good Booke,	389	Aleman	7
The noblest Ingenyre that ever was!	402	Inigo Jones 1	6
NOBLIER			
Because it durst have noblier dy'd.	234	U60 La-ware	18
NOBLY			
That thou at once, then, nobly maist defend	63	E98 Th Roe 1	7
When you would play so nobly, and so free.	230	U56 Covell	2
And much shall dye, that now is nobly liv'd,	309	Horace	102
NODDELL			
Yet who could have hit on't but the wise noddell	379	Coryat 3	6
NODDING			
Of worship, they their nodding chinnes doe hit	87	E133 Voyage	123
NODDLE			
Thy Noddle, with his clubb; and dashing forth	409	Detractor	21
NOE			
Noe velvet Sheath you weare, will alter kynde.	403	Inigo Jones 1	26
You aske noe more then certeyne politique Eyes,	404	Inigo Jones 1	45
To plant the Musick where noe eare can reach!	404	Inigo Jones 1	53
Attyre the Persons as noe thought can teach	404	Inigo Jones 1	54
Allmighty Architecture? who noe less	406	Inigo Jones 1	92
The Lybian Lion hunts noe butter flyes,	408	Inigo Jones 3	7
If such a Tyke as thou, er'e wer't, or noe?	409	Detractor	14
That Frindshipp, which noe Chaunce, but Love did Chuse,	422	Censure	16
For noe Man Lyves, soe out of passions swaye,	422	Censure	24
hir Furye, though noe Frindshipp hee betraye.	422	Censure	26
NOISD			
The brethren they streight ways noisd out for newes,	209	U43 Vulcan	V139
NOISE (See also NOYSE)			
Urine, and plaisters? when the noise doth beate	88	E133 Voyage	170
A life that knew nor noise, nor strife:	151	U12 Corbet	12
Alive yet, in the noise; and still the same;	214	U44 Speach	56
On popular noise with, and doe businesse in.	311	Horace	120
And better stayes them there, then all fine noise	327	Horace	459
They vexe, and follow him with shouts, and noise,	335	Horace	648
They vexe, and carelesse follow him with noise.	354	Horace	V648
But Tune and Noise the Eccho of thy Shame.	411	Gill	14
NOIS'D			
The Brethren, they streight nois'd it out for Newes,	209	U43 Vulcan	139
NOISES			
Their noises forth in Thunder:	239	U67 Muses	9
Their noises out in Thunder:	239	U67 Muses	V 9

NOISES (cont.)
Made lighter with the Wine. All noises else, . . . 249 U72 King   12
Made loftier by the Winds all noises else, . . 249 U72 King   V 12
NOISOME (See NOYSOME)
NOMINALL
Where is that nominall marke, or reall rite, . . . 160 U14 Selden   47
NONE
May none, whose scatter'd names honor my booke, . . 29 E9 To All   1
For I will doe none: and as little ill, . . 30 E11 Something   7
For I will dare none. Good Lord, walke dead still. . 30 E11 Something   8
Some hundred quarrels, yet dost thou fight none; . . 32 E16 Brain-hardy 6
May heare my Epigrammes, but like of none. . . 36 E28 Surly   20
The children, that he keepes, Giles sweares are none . 40 E42 Giles   13
Hee that wooes every widdow, will get none. . . 42 E47 Luckless 2   2
For none ere tooke that pleasure in sinnes sense, . 60 E94 Bedford 3   9
Becomes none more then you, who need it least. . . 67 E103 L Wroth 1   14
There's none so dull, that for your stile would aske, . 68 E105 L Wroth 2   15
Their wherry had no saile, too; ours had none: . . 84 E133 Voyage   11
There's none, that dwell about them, wish them downe; . 94 F2 Penshurst   47
God wisheth, none should wracke on a strange shelfe. . 99 F3 Wroth   95
At noone, they are or short, or none: . . . 104 F7 Women but   8
None but them, and leave the rest. . . . 106 F8 Sicknesse   48
None but them, and leave the best. . . . 106 F8 Sicknesse V 48
I, that have none (to send you) send you verse. . . 113 F12 Rutland   19
Have beautie knowne, yet none so famous seene? . . 114 F12 Rutland   50
That Homer brought to Troy; yet none so live: . . 115 F12 Rutland   55
For others ill, ought none their good forget. . . 116 F13 Aubigny   6
Without companions? 'Tis safe to have none. . . 118 F13 Aubigny   56
Your conscience, and not wonder, if none askes . . 118 F13 Aubigny   69
Here's none to spie, or see; . . . 139 U2 Another   3
We all feare, she loveth none. . . . 140 U2 Promise   12
The pleasure is as good as none, . . . 147 U7 Nymph   6
Looke to and cure; Hee's not a man hath none, . 156 U13 Sacvile   115
And my minds motion not? or have I none? . . 156 U13 Sacvile   122
You blush, but doe not: friends are either none, . 171 U19 Elegy By   13
None brookes the Sun-light worse then he. . . 189 U36 Song   4
Another answers, 'Lasse, those Silkes are none, . 202 U42 Elegy Let   74
None of their pleasures! nor will aske thee, why . 202 U42 Elegy Let   86
If none of these, then why this fire? Or find . 203 U43 Vulcan   27
With lust conceiv'd thee; Father thou hadst none. . 208 U43 Vulcan   112
For none but Smiths would have made thee a God. . 208 U43 Vulcan   117
But he that's too-much that, is friend of none. . 216 U45 Squib   24
None Fortune aided lesse, or Vertue more. . . 217 U46 Coke   22
Then these can ever be; or else wish none. . . 219 U47 Tribe   30
Her face there's none can like by Candle light. . 223 U49 Pucell   32
It will be shame for them, if they have none. . 225 U50 Countesse   36
I can lose none in tendring these to you. . . 231 U56 Covell   28
Are lost upon accompt! And none will know . . 237 U64 Charles 3   21
Are lost upon accompt! And none doe know . . 237 U64 Charles 3 V 21
His is more safe commoditie, or none: . . . 241 U69 Friend Son   7
And tell thou, Alde-Legh, None can tell more true . 274 U84 Descent   13
(Brave Youths) th'are their possessions, none of yours: . 281 U84 Kenelme   11
For Choler! if I did not, none could bring . . 349 Horace   V430
Our Gallants give them none, but passe them by: . 329 Horace   513
There's none will take the care, to helpe him then; . 335 Horace   654
His cause of making Verses none knowes why: . . 335 Horace   670
Here's one makes verses, but there's none knows why: . 355 Horace   V670
Th'ascent of Lady Fame which none could spy . . 403 Inigo Jones 1   35
NOOKES
Thou hast seene hell (some say) and know'st all nookes there, . 85 E133 Voyage   51
NOONE
At noone, they are or short, or none: . . . 104 F7 Women but   8
It is as if a night should shade noone-day, . . 199 U41 Elegy Since   5
By this Sun's Noone-sted's made . . . 258 U75 Epithalam. 183
Till he hath reach'd his two-fold point of Noone. . . 414 Ghyrlond   52
NOONE-DAY
It is as if a night should shade noone-day, . . 199 U41 Elegy Since   5
NOONE-STED'
By this Sun's Noone-sted's made . . . . 258 U75 Epithalam. 183
NOONE-STED'S
By this Sun's Noone-sted's made . . . . 258 U75 Epithalam. 183
NOOSE
And thrust my necke into the noose, . . . 101 F4 To the World   26
NOR
Nor have my title-leafe on posts, or walls, . . 28 E3 Bookseller   7
Nor need'st thou: for those few, by oath releast, . 32 E16 Brain-hardy 7
No cause, nor client fat, will Chev'rill leese, . 38 E37 Chev'ril   1
One doth not stroke me, nor the other strike. . 46 E61 Foole   2
Nor glad as those, that old dependents bee, . 47 E64 Salisbury 3   5
Nor glad for fashion. Nor to shew a fit . 47 E64 Salisbury 3   7
Of flatterie to thy titles. Nor of wit. . . 47 E64 Salisbury 3   8
That neither fame, nor love might wanting be . 48 E66 Cary   1
To live when Broeck not stands, nor Roor doth runne. . 49 E66 Cary   12
Cob, thou nor souldier, thiefe, nor fencer art, . 50 E69 Cob   1
Nor lend like influence from his lucent seat. . 52 E76 Bedford 1   8
Be safe, nor feare thy selfe so good a fame, . 53 E77 Not name   1
Nor lesse in practice; but lesse mark'd, lesse knowne: . 58 E91 Vere   14
Nor could I, had I seene all Natures roule, . 60 E93 Radcliffe   12
That dares nor write things false, nor hide things true. . 62 E95 Savile   36
Nor Captayne Pod, nor yet the Eltham-thing; . . 62 E97 Motion   2
Know you the cause? H'has neither land, nor lease, . 63 E97 Motion   9
Nor baudie stock, that travells for encrease, . . 63 E97 Motion   10
Nor office in the towne, nor place in court, . . 63 E97 Motion   11

NOR (cont.)

		Page	Title	Line
Nor 'bout the beares, nor noyse to make lords sport.		63	E97 Motion	12
Nor did the king of Denmarke him salute,		63	E97 Motion	15
When he was here. Nor hath he got a sute,		63	E97 Motion	16
Nor are the Queenes most honor'd maides by th'eares		63	E97 Motion	18
Nor shall our cups make any guiltie men:		65	E101 Supper	37
Nor could the age have mist thee, in this strife		66	E102 Pembroke	5
That we had left us, nor by time, nor place,		67	E105 L Wroth 2	3
Be nor put on you, nor you take offence.		69	E108 Soldiers	4
That serves nor fame, nor titles; but doth chuse		70	E109 Nevil	2
Not Caesars deeds, nor all his honors wonne,		71	E110 Edmonds 1	1
In these west-parts, nor when that warre was done,		71	E110 Edmonds 1	2
All yeelding to his fortune, nor, the while,		71	E110 Edmonds 1	5
Nor that his worke liv'd in the hands of foes,		71	E110 Edmonds 1	9
Nor to give Caesar this, makes ours the lesse.		72	E111 Edmonds 2	8
Nor scarce dost colour for it, which is lesse.		73	E112 Gamster	20
Nor may'any feare, to loose of their degree,		73	E113 Overbury	11
Nor he, for friendship, to be thought unfit,		78	E121 Rudyerd 1	7
Stunke not so ill; nor, when shee kist, Kate Arden.		87	E133 Voyage	118
Nor thumbe, nor finger to the stop acquainted,		87	E133 Voyage	134
Cannot the Plague-bill keepe you backe? nor bells		88	E133 Voyage	173
Of touch, or marble; nor canst boast a row		93	F2 Penshurst	2
Here no man tells my cups; nor, standing by,		95	F2 Penshurst	67
Nor, when I take my lodging, need I pray		95	F2 Penshurst	72
Art tane with neithers vice, nor sport:		96	F3 Wroth	4
Nor com'st to view the better cloth of state;		96	F3 Wroth	7
Nor throng'st (when masquing is) to have a sight		96	F3 Wroth	9
Nor throng'st (where masquing is) to have a sight		96	F3 Wroth	V 9
Nor are the Muses strangers found:		96	F3 Wroth	52
The milke, nor oyle, did ever flowe soe free		98	F3 Wroth	V 60
Nor yellow honie from the tree		98	F3 Wroth	V 60
Nor how to get the lawyer fees.		98	F3 Wroth	62
Shalt neither that, nor this envy:		99	F3 Wroth	92
Nor death; but when thy latest sand is spent,		100	F3 Wroth	105
I know thou canst nor shew, nor beare		101	F4 To the World	39
Nor for my peace will I goe farre,		102	F4 To the World	65
Nor will I beg of thee, Lord of the vine,		107	F10 Proludium	10
Nor will we beg of thee, Lord of the vine,		107	F10 Proludium	V 10
Pallas, nor thee I call on, mankinde maid,		107	F10 Proludium	13
Pallas, nor thee we call on, mankinde maid,		107	F10 Proludium	V 13
Thou, nor thy loosenesse with my making sorts.		107	F10 Proludium	18
Thou, nor their loosenesse with our making sorts.		107	F10 Proludium	V 18
Nor all the ladies of the Thespian lake,		108	F10 Proludium	25
In equall knots: This beares no brands, nor darts,		110	F11 Epode	51
Nor meane we those, whom vowes and conscience		111	F11 Epode	83
Nor meane I those, whose vowes and conscience		111	F11 Epode	V 83
Then this, our guilt, nor golden age can deeme,		114	F12 Rutland	22
Nor that your beautie wanted not a dower,		117	F13 Aubigny	37
Till that no usurer, nor his bawds dare lend		118	F13 Aubigny	78
Because nor it can change, nor such a minde.		120	F13 Aubigny	124
Nor can a little of the common store,		121	F14 Sydney	31
Nor for any threat, or call,		132	U2 How he saw	18
You shall neither eat, nor sleepe,		140	U2 Promise	15
No, nor forth your window peepe,		140	U2 Promise	16
Nor o're-praise, nor yet condemne:		142	U2 Her man	47
Nor out-praise, nor yet condemne;		142	U2 Her man	V 47
Nor out-valew, nor contemne;		142	U2 Her man	48
Nor doe wrongs, nor wrongs receave;		142	U2 Her man	49
Nor tie knots, nor knots unweave;		142	U2 Her man	50
No tunes are sweet, nor words have sting,		143	U3 Musicall	15
No voice so sweet, nor words have sting,		143	U3 Musicall	V 15
Nor cast them downe, but let them rise,		144	U4 Song	3
Nor looke too kind on my desires,		144	U4 Song	7
Nor spread them as distract with feares,		145	U4 Song	11
Nor doe we doubt, but that we can,		145	U5 Woman-kind	7
Nor is't inconstancie to change		146	U6 Defence	13
Nor have I yet the narrow mind		150	U10 Jealousie	4
Nor will he tell me for whose sake		151	U11 Dreame	7
A life that knew nor noise, nor strife:		151	U12 Corbet	12
No stubbornnesse so stiffe, nor folly		152	U12 Corbet	24
Nor wants it here through penurie, or sloth,		152	U12 Corbet	39
They need no stilts, nor rise upon their toes,		157	U13 Sacvile	145
Nor fashion; if they chance aspire to height,		157	U13 Sacvile	148
But here's no time, nor place, my wealth to tell,		161	U14 Selden	85
No person, nor is lov'd: what wayes he proves		162	U15 Friend-Wars	16
Nor is the title question'd with our proud,		164	U15 Friend-Wars	83
Sweet bags, sweet Powders, nor sweet words will passe		165	U15 Friend-Wars	112
Nor should I at this time protested be,		169	U17 Friend-Debt	7
I know no beautie, nor no youth that will.		171	U19 Elegy By	20
Wise Providence would so; that nor the good		176	U24 Frontispice	5
high Providence would so; that nor the good		176	U24 Frontispice V	5
Might be defrauded, nor the great secur'd,		176	U24 Frontispice	6
Nor thinke your selfe unfortunate,		177	U25 Desmond	27
I send nor Balmes, nor Cor'sives to your wound,		180	U26 Ode High	2
In one full Action; nor have you now more		180	U26 Ode High	17
Nor is my Muse, or I asham'd to owe it		182	U28 Worth	5
Nor a lyne deserving praise,		183	U29 Fit of Rime	29
That still was good for goodnesse sake, nor thought		185	U30 Burleigh	13
That, henceforth, I beleeve nor bookes, nor men,		187	U33 Councellour	5
Art, her false servant; Nor, for Sir Hugh Plat,		188	U34 Small Poxe	7
Her owne bloud gave her: Shee ne're had, nor hath		188	U34 Small Poxe	9
Or Turners oyle of Talck. Nor ever got		188	U34 Small Poxe	11
None of their pleasures! nor will aske thee, why		202	U42 Elegy Let	86

	Page	Title	Line
NOR (cont.)			
Nor made least line of love to thy loose Wife;	203	U43 Vulcan	6
Nor markes of wealth so from our Nation fled,	213	U44 Speach	12
We neither love the Troubles, nor the harmes.	215	U44 Speach	86
I neither am, nor art thou one of those	216	U45 Squib	5
Nor ever trusted to that friendship yet,	216	U45 Squib	7
I have no portion in them, nor their deale	218	U47 Tribe	27
Though I doe neither heare these newes, nor tell	219	U47 Tribe	46
And that there be no fev'ry heats, nor colds,	220	U47 Tribe	67
Nor any of their houshold, halfe so well.	228	U53 Newcastle	16
Mirth, fooling, nor wit,	231	U57 Burges	17
Nor any least fit	231	U57 Burges	18
Nor any quick-warming-pan helpe him to bed,	232	U57 Burges	27
Of honour, nor no ayre of good?	234	U60 La-ware	7
Nor dares he come in the comparison.	241	U69 Friend Son	8
A Copie of this peece; nor tell	277	U84 Body	30
Nor dare we under blasphemy conceive	286	U84 Muse	147
Nor can the bruised heart want eloquence:	288	U84 Muse	186
Nor Souldier-like stárted with rough alarmes,	289	U85 Country	5
Nor dreads the Seas inraged harmes:	289	U85 Country	6
Nor treades the Seas inraged harmes:	289	U85 Country	V 6
Nor Turbot, nor bright Golden-eyes:	291	U85 Country	50
Th'Ionian God-wit, nor the Ginny hen	291	U85 Country	53
Me now, nor Wench, nor wanton Boy,	293	U86 Hor.4:1	29
Delights, nor credulous hope of mutuall Joy,	293	U86 Hor.4:1	30
Nor care I now healths to propound;	293	U86 Hor.4:1	31
Nor after Chloe did his Lydia sound;	293	U87 Hor.3:9	6
There is no labour, nor no shame in this;	294	U88 Petronius	8
Nor feare thy latest day, nor wish therfore.	295	U90 Mart.10:47	13
As neither head, nor foot, one forme retaine.	305	Horace	10
Hath neither soule, nor sinewes. Loftie he	307	Horace	37
Nor language, nor cleere order ere forsakes.	307	Horace	58
Nor language, nor cleere order will forsake.	339	Horace	V 59/ 58
Of Poems here describ'd, I can, nor use,	311	Horace	127
Nor know t'observe: why (i'the Muses name)	311	Horace	128
To render word for word: nor with thy sleight	313	Horace	191
Nor so begin, as did that Circler late,	313	Horace	195
Nor from the brand, with which the life did burne	315	Horace	207
Of Diomede; nor Troyes sad Warre begins	315	Horace	209
Her Sonnes before the people; nor the ill-/Natur'd	317	Horace	264
His Nephews entrailes; nor must Progne flie	317	Horace	266
Into a Swallow there; Nor Cadmus take,	317	Horace	267
Nor must the Fable, that would hope the Fate,	317	Horace	270
Have more or lesse then just five Acts: nor laid,	317	Horace	272
Nor I, when I write Satyres, will so love	321	Horace	341
Meere raigning words: nor will I labour so	321	Horace	343
Will take offence, at this: Nor, though it strike	321	Horace	361
Take just offence at this: nor, though it strike	347	Horace	V353/361
Nor is't long since, they did with patience take	323	Horace	375
Nor did they merit the lesse Crowne to weare,	323	Horace	406
Nor had our Italie more glorious bin	325	Horace	411
Their nailes, nor shave their beards, but to by-paths	325	Horace	423
Their nails, nor shave their beards, but seek by-paths	349	Horace	V423
The truth; nor let thy Fable thinke, what e're	329	Horace	508
Nor alwayes doth the loosed Bow, hit that	329	Horace	524
But neither, Men, nor Gods, nor Pillars meant,	331	Horace	555
Hee, that not knowes the games, nor how to use	331	Horace	565
Nor did he doe this once; for if you can	335	Horace	667
Nor did he do this, once; if yet you can,	355	Horace	V667
Yet shee's nor nice to shew them,	365	Ode Splendor	23
Nor takes she pride to know them.	365	Ode Splendor	24
Who saith our Times nor have, nor can	366	Ode Who saith	1
That part nor Winde,	366	Ode Who saith	28
Nor Sunne could make to vary from the rest,	367	Ode Who saith	29
Nor let one River boast	367	Ode Who saith	35
"Where neither Force can bend, nor Feare can awe.	367	Ode Who saith	48
Haste, Haste, sweete Singer: Nor to Tine,	368	Ode Who saith	73
At their returne, nor Po,	369	Ode Who saith	114
Scheldt, nor the Maas,	369	Ode Who saith	116
Slow Arar, nor swift Rhone; the Loyre, nor Seine,	369	Ode Who saith	117
But here, neither trusting his hands, nor his legs,	375	Coryat	34
nor yet inscription like it. Write but that;	387	Cavendish	9
nor yet inscription like it writt but that	387	Cavendish	V 9
As neither Man, nor Muse, can praise too much.	390	Shakespeare	4
You have not writ to me, nor I to you;	396	Drayton	6
A Trench against it, nor a Battry plac't?	401	Beaumont	14
Nor flatt'ry! but secur'd, by the Authors Name,	401	Beaumont	19
Whom not ten fyres, nor a Parlyament can	406	Inigo Jones 1	103
Pillory nor Whip, nor want of Ears,	410	Gill	4
Nor Degradation from the Ministry,	410	Gill	6
nor cann be of desert,	420	Ode:If Men	13
NOREMBERG			
Of Noremberg, or Turkie; hang your roomes	260	U77 Treasurer	3
NORTH			
That from the North, the Navie safe doth store,	309	Horace	92
NORTHUMBERLAND			
Gave two such Houses as Northumberland,	274	U84 Descent	5
NORWICH			
Did dance the famous Morrisse, unto Norwich)	85	E133 Voyage	36
NOSE			
He speakes to men with a Rhinocerotes nose,	35	E28 Surly	4
To this dire passage. Say, thou stop thy nose:	85	E133 Voyage	59
Must trie the'un-used valour of a nose:	87	E133 Voyage	132

	Page	Title	Line

NOSE (cont.)
An ancient pur-blinde fletcher, with a high nose; · · · 89 E133 Voyage 190
Even nose, and cheeke (withall) · · · 141 U2 Her man 19
There were, that streight did nose it out for newes, · · · 209 U43 Vulcan V139
That hang their richest jewells i'their nose; · · · 232 U58 Book-seller 10
With faire black eyes, and haire; and a wry nose. · · · 307 Horace 52
To aske thy name, if he have half his Nose! · · · 409 Detractor 18

NOSTHRILL
Had tickled your large Nosthrill: many a Reame · · · 205 U43 Vulcan 62

NOSTRILL
There shall thy dainty Nostrill take · · · 292 U86 Hor.4:1 21

NOSTRILLS
Your daintie nostrills (in so hot a season, · · · 88 E133 Voyage 165
Had filled your large nostrills with the steame: · · · 205 U43 Vulcan V 62

NOT
As mad-men stones: not caring whom they hit. · · · 27 E2 My Booke 6
Thou are not covetous of least selfe-fame, · · · 27 E2 My Booke 9
Not offer'd, as it made sute to be bought; · · · 28 E3 Bookseller 6
If, without these vile arts, it will not sell, · · · 28 E3 Bookseller 11
Shift, here, in towne, not meanest among squires, · · · 30 E12 Shift 1
Not his poore cocatrice but he betrayes. · · · 31 E12 Shift 21
Then thee the age sees not that thing more grave, · · · 31 E14 Camden 5
When thou wert wont t'admire, not censure men. · · · 32 E18 Censurer 8
Pr'y thee beleeve still, and not judge so fast, · · · 32 E18 Censurer 9
Wee, sad for him, may glorie, and not sinne. · · · 35 E27 Roe 1 8
Tilter, the most may'admire thee, though not I: · · · 36 E29 Tilter 1
Be thine, I taxe, yet doe not owne my rimes: · · · 36 E30 Guiltie 2
Could not effect, not all the furies doe, · · · 37 E32 Roe 2 2
What not the envie of the seas reach'd too, · · · 37 E32 Roe 2 4
His often change of clime (though not of mind) · · · 37 E32 Roe 2 6
What could not worke; at home in his repaire · · · 37 E32 Roe 2 7
Ile not offend thee with a vaine teare more, · · · 37 E33 Roe 3 1
Who would not be thy subject, James, t'obay · · · 37 E35 James 2 1
Read not in faire heavens storie, · · · 39 E40 Ratcliffe 6
Earth, thou hast not such another. · · · 39 E40 Ratcliffe 17
I, not the worst, am covetous of thee. · · · 40 E43 Salisbury 1 6
Yet dare not, to my thought, lest hope allow · · · 41 E43 Salisbury 1 7
His bought armes Mung' not lik'd; for his first day · · · 42 E48 Mungril 1
Looke not upon thy dangers, but our feares. · · · 43 E51 James 3 10
How I doe feare my selfe, that am not worth · · · 44 E55 Beaumont 3
He markes not whose 'twas first: and after-times · · · 45 E56 Poet-Ape 11
Foole, as if halfe eyes will not know a fleece · · · 45 E56 Poet-Ape 13
One doth not stroke me, nor the other strike. · · · 46 E61 Foole 2
Of the not borne, yet buried, here's the tombe. · · · 46 E62 Would-bee 12
And not thy fortune; who can cleerely see · · · 47 E63 Salisbury 2 2
Not from the publike voyce, but private fact; · · · 47 E63 Salisbury 2 6
Not glad, like those that have new hopes, or sutes, · · · 47 E64 Salisbury 3 1
Where merit is not sepulcher'd alive. · · · 47 E64 Salisbury 3 10
And not to dangers. When so wise a king · · · 47 E64 Salisbury 3 12
Things manly, and not smelling parasite. · · · 48 E65 Muse 14
For worth he has not, He is tax'd, not prais'd. · · · 48 E65 Muse 16
Durst valour make, almost, but not a crime. · · · 48 E66 Cary 6
Which deed I know not, whether were more high, · · · 49 E66 Cary 7
To live when Broeck not stands, nor Roor doth runne. · · · 49 E66 Cary 12
Hee's valiant'st, that dares fight, and not for pay; · · · 49 E66 Cary 17
Though life be short, let us not make it so. · · · 50 E70 Wm Roe 1 8
I Grieve not, Courtling, thou are started up · · · 50 E72 Court-ling 1
'Tis not thy judgement breeds the prejudice. · · · 50 E72 Court-ling 5
And know thee, then, a judge, not of one yeare; · · · 51 E74 Chancelor 2
I meant the day-starre should not brighter rise, · · · 52 E76 Bedford 1 7
To one that desired me not to name him. · · · 53 E77 Not name Ttl
Came not that soule exhausted so their store. · · · 53 E79 Rutland 4
Forbeare to tempt me, Proule, I will not show · · · 54 E81 Proule 1
Which, if thou leave not soone (though I am loth) · · · 54 E81 Proule 7
That his whole body should speake french, not he? · · · 56 E88 Monsieur 2
Fear'd not to boast the glories of her stage, · · · 56 E89 Allen 2
Not though that haire grew browne, which once was amber, · · · 57 E90 Mill 9
Hath got the stewards chaire; he will not tarry · · · 57 E90 Mill 15
Which of thy names I take, not onely beares · · · 58 E91 Vere 1
Against my grave, and time could not forgive. · · · 58 E91 Vere 12
I speake thy other graces, not lesse showne, · · · 58 E91 Vere 13
They know the states of Christendome, not the places: · · · 59 E92 New Crie 8
On them: And therefore doe not onely shunne · · · 59 E92 New Crie 38
That know not so much state, wrong, as they doo. · · · 59 E92 New Crie 40
Then whose I doe not know a whiter soule, · · · 60 E93 Radcliffe 11
Though not unprov'd: which shewes, thy fortunes are · · · 60 E93 Radcliffe 14
If workes (not th'authors) their owne grace should looke, · · · 60 E94 Bedford 3 3
Whose poemes would not wish to be your booke? · · · 60 E94 Bedford 3 4
Thou need'st not shrinke at voyce of after-times; · · · 61 E95 Savile 20
But, wisely, thrusts not forth a forward hand, · · · 61 E95 Savile 22
A man should seeke great glorie, and not broad. · · · 62 E96 Donne 2 12
See you yond' Motion? Not the old Fa-ding, · · · 62 E97 Motion 1
Not that we thinke us worthy such a ghest, · · · 64 E101 Supper 3
The entertaynment perfect: not the cates. · · · 64 E101 Supper 8
Is not to be despair'd of, for our money; · · · 65 E101 Supper 14
The skie not falling, thinke we may have larkes. · · · 65 E101 Supper 16
To this, if ought appeare, which I not know of, · · · 65 E101 Supper 25
That will the pastrie, not my paper, show of. · · · 65 E101 Supper 26
If not, 'tis fit for you, some should envy. · · · 67 E104 Montgomery 16
Who could not but create them all, from you? · · · 67 E105 L Wroth 2 6
Would call you more then Ceres, if not that: · · · 68 E105 L Wroth 2 8
And, drest in shepheards tyre, who would not say: · · · 68 E105 L Wroth 2 9
Or, keeping your due state, that would not cry, · · · 68 E105 L Wroth 2 17

NOT (cont.)

	Page	Title	Line
That's, sit, and eate: doe not my eares abuse.	68	E107 Hungry	2
Not that I love it, more, then I will you.	68	E107 Hungry	4
Come, be not angrie, you are Hungry; eate;	69	E107 Hungry	31
And did not shame it with my actions, then,	70	E108 Soldiers	7
He that not trusts me, having vow'd thus much,	70	E108 Soldiers	9
Thou are not one, seek'st miseries with hope,	70	E109 Nevil	5
Goe on, and doubt not, what posteritie,	70	E109 Nevil	15
Not Caesars deeds, nor all his honors wonne,	71	E110 Edmonds 1	1
Not all these, Edmonds, or what else put too,	71	E110 Edmonds 1	11
T'all future time, not onely doth restore	71	E110 Edmonds 1	21
Who Edmonds, reades thy booke, and doth not see	72	E111 Edmonds 2	1
Repent thee not of thy faire precedent,	73	E113 Overbury	9
He hath not onely gain'd himselfe his eyes,	74	E114 Sydney	7
Him not, aloud, that boasts so good a fame:	74	E115 Honest Man	2
And him it layes on; if he be not there.	74	E115 Honest Man	16
Not that it feares, but will not have to doo	74	E115 Honest Man	20
'Twas not entayl'd on title. That some word	75	E116 Jephson	7
Might be found out as good, and not my Lord.	75	E116 Jephson	8
That bloud not mindes, but mindes did bloud adorne:	75	E116 Jephson	11
Them in, if not, from thee; or must commit	75	E116 Jephson	15
Not he that flies the court for want of clothes,	76	E119 Shelton	1
Whose dice not doing well, to'a pulpit ran.	76	E119 Shelton	6
But dost it out of judgement, not disease;	76	E119 Shelton	8
Treading a better path, not contrary;	76	E119 Shelton	12
Which is to live to conscience, not to show.	76	E119 Shelton	14
Yet is the office not to be despis'd,	78	E121 Rudyerd 1	5
If I would wish, for truth, and not for show,	78	E122 Rudyerd 2	1
I know not which th'hast most, candor, or wit:	78	E123 Rudyerd 3	2
Which (would the world not mis-call't flatterie)	79	E125 Uvedale	9
Phoebus replyed. Bold head, it is not shee:	80	E126 Mrs Cary	7
I, and this Muse hath beene, if thou hadst not	80	E127 Aubigny	7
That, not a paire of friends each other see,	81	E129 Mime	1
To which thou'rt not a weeke, bespoke a guest;	81	E129 Mime	6
O, runne not proud of this. Yet, take thy due.	81	E129 Mime	15
Men love thee not for this: They laugh at thee.	81	E129 Mime	18
T'alledge, that greatest men were not asham'd,	82	E130 Ferrab. 1	9
We ought not give them taste, we had an eare.	83	E131 Ferrab. 2	6
They were not to be nam'd on the same day.	83	E131 Ferrab. 2	12
Then stand unto thy selfe, not seeke without	83	E131 Ferrab. 2	13
Had power to act, what they to faine had not.	84	E133 Voyage	6
Furies there wanted not: each scold was ten.	84	E133 Voyage	15
And art a god, if Fame thee not abuses,	85	E133 Voyage	53
But many Moones there shall we wane (quoth hee)	87	E133 Voyage	103
Had it beene seconded, and not in fume	87	E133 Voyage	109
Stunke not so ill; nor, when shee kist, Kate Arden.	87	E133 Voyage	118
Then, selling not, a dish was tane to mince 'hem,	88	E133 Voyage	151
Yet drown'd they not. They had five lives in future.	88	E133 Voyage	154
Tempt not his furie, Pluto is away:	89	E133 Voyage	179
Why I write not of Love.	93	F1 Why write no	Ttl
I weare not these my wings in vaine.	93	F1 Why write no	7
By any arte. Then wonder not,	93	F1 Why write no	10
Thou art not, Penshurst, built to envious show,	93	F2 Penshurst	1
And I not faine to sit (as some, this day,	95	F2 Penshurst	65
Thy tables hoord not up for the next day,	95	F2 Penshurst	71
What (great, I will not say, but) sodayne cheare	95	F2 Penshurst	82
When shee was farre: and not a roome, but drest,	96	F2 Penshurst	87
These, Penshurst, are thy praise, and yet not all.	96	F2 Penshurst	89
There wasted, some not paid for yet!	97	F3 Wroth	12
They thinke not, then, which side the cause shall leese,	98	F3 Wroth	61
Not doing good, scarce when he dyes.	99	F3 Wroth	84
Doe not once hope, that thou canst tempt	100	F4 To the World	5
If I could not thy ginnes avoyd.	101	F4 To the World	36
If't chance to me, I must not grutch.	101	F4 To the World	56
As shall not need thy false reliefe.	102	F4 To the World	64
Time will not be ours, for ever:	102	F5 Celia 1	3
Spend not then his guifts in vaine.	102	F5 Celia 1	5
That the curious may not know	103	F6 Celia 2	19
Say, are not women truely, then,	104	F7 Women but	5
But grant us perfect, they're not knowne.	104	F7 Women but	10
Say, are not women truely, then,	104	F7 Women but	11
Doe not men, ynow of rites	104	F8 Sicknesse	3
Live not we, as, all thy stalls,	104	F8 Sicknesse	9
And Ile not looke for wine.	106	F9 Celia 3	4
I would not change for thine.	106	F9 Celia 3	8
Not so much honoring thee,	106	F9 Celia 3	10
Not so to honor thee,	106	F9 Celia 3	V 10
It could not withered bee.	106	F9 Celia 3	12
It would not withered bee.	106	F9 Celia 3	V 12
Not of it selfe, but thee.	106	F9 Celia 3	16
Not like it selfe, but thee.	106	F9 Celia 3	V 16
Shall not give out, that I have made thee stay,	107	F10 Proludium	8
Shall not give out, that we have made thee stay,	107	F10 Proludium	V 8
Hermes, the cheater, shall not mixe with us,	107	F10 Proludium	'22
Not to know vice at all, and keepe true state,	109	F11 Epode	1
Is vertue, and not Fate:	109	F11 Epode	2
But this true course is not embrac'd by many:	109	F11 Epode	19
But this faire course is not embrac'd by many:	109	F11 Epode	V 19
We doe not number, here,	111	F11 Epode	76
I doe not number, here,	111	F11 Epode	V 76
Would not be fearefull to offend a dame	112	F11 Epode	109
Were it to thinke, that you should not inherit	114	F12 Rutland	32
Achilles was not first, that valiant was,	114	F12 Rutland	51

NOT (cont.)

	Page	Title	Line
Then which, a nobler heaven it selfe knowes not.	115	F12 Rutland	67
And, who doth me (though I not him) envy,	115	F12 Rutland	70
Had not their forme touch'd by an English wit.	115	F12 Rutland	82
Your forme imprest there: not with tickling rimes,	116	F12 Rutland	87
Your forme imprest there: not with tinckling rimes,	116	F12 Rutland	V 87
Of Fortune, have not alter'd yet my looke,	116	F12 Rutland	V 87
Men are not just, or keepe no holy lawes	117	F13 Aubigny	16
You will not from the paper slightly passe:	117	F13 Aubigny	18
Looke then, and see your selfe. I will not say	117	F13 Aubigny	25
Not taken up o' th' doctors, but as well	117	F13 Aubigny	29
Nor that your beautie wanted not a dower,	117	F13 Aubigny	33
And raise not vertue; they may vice enhance.	117	F13 Aubigny	37
Though it reject not those of Fortune: such	117	F13 Aubigny	42
Not looking by, or back (like those, that waite	117	F13 Aubigny	45
Your conscience, and not wonder, if none askes	118	F13 Aubigny	62
Not fashion'd for the court, or strangers eyes;	118	F13 Aubigny	69
Who not the least,	119	F13 Aubigny	115
Not weary, rest	120	F14 Sydney	9
The Birth-day shines, when logs not burne, but men.	121	F14 Sydney	37
Good, and great God, can I not thinke of thee,	121	F14 Sydney	60
Yet dare I not complaine, or wish for death	122	F15 Heaven	1
For wearinesse of life, not love of thee.	122	F15 Heaven	23
A broken heart thou wert not wont despise,	122	F15 Heaven	26
Eternall God the Sonne, who not denyd'st	127	U1 Trinitie	10
If thou hadst not	128	U1 Trinitie	21
Hee whom the whole world could not take,	129	U1 Father	7
Let it not your wonder move,	130	U1 Nativitie	10
And it is not alwayes face,	131	U2 Excuse	1
But, he had not gain'd his sight	131	U2 Excuse	7
Strait hee ran, and durst not stay,	132	U2 How he saw	13
Charis, guesse, and doe not misse.	132	U2 How he saw	16
Look'd not halfe so fresh, and faire,	137	U2 Kisse	1
May not claime another kisse.	138	U2 Kisse	9
I long, and should not beg in vaine,	138	U2 Kisse	36
Nay, I will not let you sit	139	U2 Another	2
And not thinke h'had eat a stake,	140	U2 Promise	21
For his Mind, I doe not care,	142	U2 Her man	39
O sing not you then, lest the best	142	U2 Exception	1
Oh doe not wanton with those eyes,	144	U3 Musicall	21
O, be not angry with those fires,	144	U4 Song	1
O, doe not steepe them in thy Teares,	144	U4 Song	5
We were not bred to sit on stooles,	145	U4 Song	9
The good, from bad, is not describe,	146	U6 Defence	3
In love, doth not alone help forth	146	U6 Defence	17
Yet dare I not tell who;	146	U6 Defence	20
Yet if it be not knowne,	147	U7 Nymph	2
I'le tell, that if they be not glad,	147	U7 Nymph	5
Yet, yet I doubt he is not knowne,	147	U7 Nymph	8
For else it could not be,	147	U7 Nymph	20
or else it could not be,	149	U9 Picture	2
That others should not warme them at my fire,	149	U9 Picture	V 2
As since he dares not come within my sight.	150	U10 Jealousie	6
'Tis true, he could not reprehend;	151	U11 Dreame	14
It chid the vice, yet not the Men.	152	U12 Corbet	21
You then, whose will not only, but desire	152	U12 Corbet	28
Not at my prayers, but your sense; which laid	153	U13 Sacvile	7
To have such doe me good, I durst not name:	153	U13 Sacvile	9
Or if he did it not to succour me,	153	U13 Sacvile	18
Now dam'mee, Sir, if you shall not command	154	U13 Sacvile	29
Are they not worthy to be answer'd so,	154	U13 Sacvile	53
And seeke not wants to succour: but enquire,	154	U13 Sacvile	59
I not deny it, but to helpe the need	155	U13 Sacvile	61
Man out their Boates to th' Temple, and not shift	155	U13 Sacvile	75
Sure there is Misterie in it, I not know,	155	U13 Sacvile	83
'Twixt feare and rashnesse: not a lust obscene,	156	U13 Sacvile	97
And where they want, she is not understood.	156	U13 Sacvile	106
Looke to and cure; Hee's not a man hath none,	156	U13 Sacvile	112
And my minds motion not? or have I none?	156	U13 Sacvile	115
In time 'twill be a heape; This is not true	156	U13 Sacvile	122
A pennance, where a man may not be free,	157	U13 Sacvile	133
Then which there is not unto Studie'a more	158	U14 Selden	8
Themselves through favouring what is there not found:	158	U14 Selden	13
Themselves through favouring what is there not found:	159	U14 Selden	16
Not flie the Crime, but the Suspition too:	159	U14 Selden	V 16
And mine not least) I have too oft preferr'd	159	U14 Selden	18
And manly elocution, not one while	159	U14 Selden	20
And masculine elocution, not one while	160	U14 Selden	56
It true respects. He will not only love,	160	U14 Selden	V 56
All that dare rowse: or are not loth to quit	161	U14 Selden	73
Not to be checkt, or frighted now with fate,	162	U15 Friend-Wars	3
Who can behold their Manners, and not clowd-/Like	163	U15 Friend-Wars	35
Not make a verse; Anger; or laughter would,	164	U15 Friend-Wars	60
Where Pittes, or Wright, or Modet would not venter,	164	U15 Friend-Wars	62
Adulteries, now, are not so hid, or strange,	164	U15 Friend-Wars	80
Nature, that will not let his Wife be a whore,	165	U15 Friend-Wars	85
Lesse must not be thought on then Mistresse: or,	165	U15 Friend-Wars	90
When not his Combes, his Curling-irons, his Glasse,	165	U15 Friend-Wars	95
Our vices doe not tarry in a place,	165	U15 Friend-Wars	111
Is not enough now, but the Nights to play:	166	U15 Friend-Wars	123
Is not enough now, but the Nights we play:	166	U15 Friend-Wars	132
Can we not leave this worme? or will we not?	166	U15 Friend-Wars	V132
The life, and fame-vaynes (yet not understood	166	U15 Friend-Wars	141
	167	U15 Friend-Wars	166

NOT (cont.)

	Page	Title	Line
Not wound thy conscience, when thy body bleeds;	168	U15 Friend-Wars	178
Thou shrinke or start not, but be alwayes one;	168	U15 Friend-Wars	186
And last, blaspheme not, we did never heare	168	U15 Friend-Wars	191
They are not, Sir, worst Owers, that doe pay	169	U17 Friend-Debt	1
And he is not in friendship. Nothing there	169	U17 Friend-Debt	5
Is done for gaine: If't be, 'tis not sincere.	169	U17 Friend-Debt	6
All is not barren land, doth fallow lie.	169	U17 Friend-Debt	16
And I will bring a Crop, if not the best.	169	U17 Friend-Debt	18
Such Guides men use not, who their way would find,	170	U18 Elegy Can	12
You blush, but doe not: friends are either none,	171	U19 Elegy By	13
Slip no occasion; As time stands not still,	171	U19 Elegy By	19
To use the present, then, is not abuse,	171	U19 Elegy By	21
As in his place, because he would not varie,	171	U19 Elegy By	27
Doe not you aske to know her, she is worse	172	U20 Shrub	17
Aske not to know this Man. If fame should speake	172	U21 Ltl Shrub	1
As not the World can praise too much,	173	U22 Elegy Tho	3
The noblest freedome, not to chuse	173	U22 Elegy Tho	11
Which if it kindle not, but scant	174	U22 Elegy Tho	33
That not a Nymph now sings?	174	U23 Himselfe	10
Should not on fortune pause,	174	U23 Himselfe	17
Make not thy selfe a Page,	175	U23 Himselfe	33
Sinke not beneath these terrors:	177	U25 Desmond	30
That is not hurt; not he, that is not hit;	179	U25 Desmond	50
So speake (as yet it is not mute)	181	U27 Ode Helen	4
Rap't from the Earth, as not to die?	181	U27 Ode Helen	14
Made Dian, not his notes refuse?	182	U27 Ode Helen	28
And shall not I my Celia bring,	182	U27 Ode Helen	31
Though not in these, in rithmes not wholly dumbe,	182	U28 Worth	2
Not a Poet in an Age,	183	U29 Fit of Rime	26
Not a worke deserving Baies,	183	U29 Fit of Rime	28
Was not spoyled.	184	U29 Fit of Rime	33
Is not yet free from Rimes wrongs,	184	U29 Fit of Rime	35
And labour'd in the worke; not with the fame:	185	U30 Burleigh	12
Of divine blessing, would not serve a State?	185	U30 Burleigh	20
Are there for Charitie, and not for fee.	186	U32 Elsmere	6
That I, hereafter, doe not thinke the Barre,	186	U33 Councellour	1
Dar'st not abuse thy wisdome, in the Lawes,	187	U33 Councellour	17
But first dost vexe, and search it! If not sound,	187	U33 Councellour	19
And make the Scarre faire; If that will not be,	187	U33 Councellour	21
And not being borrow'd by thee, but possest.	187	U33 Councellour	28
Thy Adversaries fall, as not a word	187	U33 Councellour	33
Thy sincere practise, breeds not thee a fame	187	U33 Councellour	39
Envious and foule Disease, could there not be	188	U34 Small Poxe	1
What did she worth thy spight? were there not store	188	U34 Small Poxe	3
Not like your Countrie-neighbours, that commit	190	U37 Friend-Book	7
It is an Act of tyrannie, not love,	190	U37 Friend-Book	25
Forgive it, as my frailtie, and not me.	190	U37 Friend-Book	30
Spare your owne goodnesse yet; and be not great	191	U38 Elegy 'Tis	17
I will not stand to justifie my fault,	191	U38 Elegy 'Tis	21
Your just commands; yet those, not I, be lost.	192	U38 Elegy 'Tis	38
We cut not off, till all Cures else doe faile:	192	U38 Elegy 'Tis	46
Doe not despaire my mending; to distrust	192	U38 Elegy 'Tis	49
As not alone the Cure, but scarre be faire.	192	U38 Elegy 'Tis	52
And not the bounties you ha' done, deny.	192	U38 Elegy 'Tis	54
God lightens not at mans each fraile offence,	193	U38 Elegy 'Tis	68
That makes us live, not that which calls to die.	193	U38 Elegy 'Tis	78
In darke, and sullen mornes, doe we not say,	193	U38 Elegy 'Tis	79
And with the vulgar doth it not obtaine	193	U38 Elegy 'Tis	81
Be not affected with these markes too much	193	U38 Elegy 'Tis	83
There is not any punishment, or paine,	194	U38 Elegy 'Tis	103
Absence, or Distance, shall not breed decay.	194	U38 Elegy 'Tis	116
I may dilate my selfe, but not depart.	194	U38 Elegy 'Tis	118
Not, like a Midas, shut up in himselfe,	197	U40 Elegy That	21
Is fix'd upon one leg, and dares not come	198	U40 Elegy That	33
That Article, may not become our lover:	198	U40 Elegy That	48
What it is like: And doe not thinke they can	199	U41 Elegy Since	3
As if it were not worthy to be there:	199	U41 Elegy Since	16
Whose Readers did not thinke he was in love.	199	U42 Elegy Let	4
There is not worne that lace, purle, knot or pin,	200	U42 Elegy Let	16
When he is furious, love, although not lust.	200	U42 Elegy Let	18
Made longer by our praises. Or, if not,	200	U42 Elegy Let	21
It is not likely I should now looke downe	200	U42 Elegy Let	37
Lift up some one, and doe, I tell not what.	201	U42 Elegy Let	58
When not the Shops, but windowes doe display	202	U42 Elegy Let	78
Wast not hee: thou wert of old denied	203	U43 Vulcan	V 11
Adulterate moneys, such as might not goe:	204	U43 Vulcan	45
Adulterate maskings, such as might not goe:	204	U43 Vulcan	V 45
Not ravish'd all hence in a minutes rage.	205	U43 Vulcan	56
Not snatcht them hence in one poor minutes rage.	205	U43 Vulcan	V 56
I dare not say a body, but some parts	206	U43 Vulcan	87
To teach some that, their Nurses could not doe,	207	U43 Vulcan	92
To teach some what, their Nurses could not doe,	207	U43 Vulcan	V 92
With all th'adventures; Three bookes not afraid	207	U43 Vulcan	95
With all th'adventures; Three bookes not amisse	207	U43 Vulcan	V 95
Whom Faction had not drawne to studie sides.	207	U43 Vulcan	104
Whom fashion had not drawne to studie sides.	207	U43 Vulcan	V104
Whom Faction had not taught to studie sides.	207	U43 Vulcan	V104
She durst not kisse, but flung thee from her brest.	208	U43 Vulcan	114
And safely trust to dresse, not burne their Boates.	208	U43 Vulcan	128
Scap'd not his Justice any jot the more:	210	U43 Vulcan	154
Scap'd not this Justice any jot the more:	210	U43 Vulcan	V154
Scap'd not thy Justice any whitt the more:	210	U43 Vulcan	V154

NOT (cont.)

	Page	Title	Line
Hee is true Vulcan still! He did not spare	210	U43 Vulcan	159
Thou art true Vulcan still! Thou durst not spare	210	U43 Vulcan	V159
He was right Vulcan still! He did not spare	210	U43 Vulcan	V159
Did not she save from thence, to build a Rome?	210	U43 Vulcan	162
I will not argue thee, from those, of guilt	210	U43 Vulcan	165
I will not argue thee, from them, of guilt,	210	U43 Vulcan	V165
I will not argue thee Iron. Them of guilt	210	U43 Vulcan	V165
Which thou hast only vented, not enjoy'd.	210	U43 Vulcan	168
Light on thee: Or if those plagues will not doo,	212	U43 Vulcan	215
Light upon thee: Or if those plagues will not doo,	212	U43 Vulcan	V215
All Ensignes of a Warre, are not yet dead,	213	U44 Speach	11
Thou Seed-plot of the warre, that hast not spar'd	213	U44 Speach	24
What I am not, and what I faine would be,	216	U45 Squib	1
He could not find, then thee, of all that store	217	U46 Coke	3
Care not what trials they are put unto;	218	U47 Tribe	2
And though Opinion stampe them not, are gold.	218	U47 Tribe	4
Be, or be not, to get the Val-telline?	219	U47 Tribe	32
And force back that, which will not be restor'd,	219	U47 Tribe	40
Of Spaine or France; or were not prick'd downe one	219	U47 Tribe	47
Although my Fame, to his, not under-heares,	219	U47 Tribe	49
Not built with Canvasse, paper, and false lights,	220	U47 Tribe	65
I would call mine, to which not many Staires	220	U47 Tribe	74
And not a Song be other	221	U48 Bacchus	35
And thinkes I dare not her? let the world see.	222	U49 Pucell	2
For bawdry, 'tis her language, and not mine.	223	U49 Pucell	26
Not he, that should the body have, for Case	223	U49 Pucell	33
Not only shunning by your act, to doe	224	U50 Countesse	5
Who (herein studying conscience, and not fame)	224	U50 Countesse	14
Not boasted in your life, but practis'd true,	225	U50 Countesse	32
I am not so voluminous, and vast,	226	U52 Answer	1
You were not tied, by any Painters Law,	227	U52 Answer	7
You made it a brave piece, but not like me.	227	U52 Answer	15
Within the ballance; and not want a mite;	229	U54 Squib	10
It doe not come: One piece I have in store,	229	U54 Squib	15
You won not Verses, Madam, you won mee,	230	U56 Covell	1
By this, although you fancie not the man,	231	U56 Covell	25
By thys Tyme, though you fancie not the man,	231	U56 Covell	V 25
Of daring, not to doe a wrong, is true	233	U59 Newcastle	15
To lift to heaven: who is't not understands	234	U61 Epigram	8
Your happinesse, and doth not speake you blest,	234	U61 Epigram	9
'T is not enough (thy pietie is such)	235	U62 Charles 1	3
Then, Royall Charles, and Mary, doe not grutch	236	U63 Charles 2	7
'T is not alone the Merchant, but the, Clowne,	237	U64 Charles 3	19
And interpose thy selfe, ('care not how soone.)	238	U65 Prince	10
Sol will re-shine. If not, Charles hath a Sonne.	238	U65 Prince	12
And Sol will shine. If not, Charles hath a Sonne.	238	U65 Prince	V 12
The Mother of our Lord: why may not I	238	U66 Queene	3
His Poet Sack, the House-hold will not pay?	241	U68 House-hold	2
Sonne, and my Friend, I had not call'd you so	241	U69 Friend Son	1
Wise-crafts, on which the flatterer ventures not.	241	U69 Friend Son	6
Some of his formes, he lets him not come neere	242	U69 Friend Son	17
Not by the act?	243	U70 Ode	22
Not liv'd; for Life doth her great actions spell,	245	U70 Ode	59
It is not growing like a tree	245	U70 Ode	65
And thinke, nay know, thy Morison's not dead.	245	U70 Ode	78
(Were not his Lucius long with us to tarry)	246	U70 Ode	91
Of hearts the union. And those not by chance	246	U70 Ode	99
The good, and durst not practise it, were glad	247	U70 Ode	119
Friendship, in deed, was written, not in words:	247	U70 Ode	123
And with the heart, not pen,	247	U70 Ode	124
The Muse not peepes out, one of hundred dayes;	248	U71 Treasurer	9
Thou sluggish spawne, that canst, but wilt not see?	250	U73 Weston	8
Thou canst not meet more Glory, on the way,	252	U75 Epithalam.	3
Through which not only we, but all our Species are.	253	U75 Epithalam.	32
Great Say-Master of State, who not to erre,	255	U75 Epithalam.	V 99
Which Time shall not,	257	U75 Epithalam.	134
Their names are not recorded on the File	257	U75 Epithalam.	155
But dare not aske our wish in Language fescennine:	257	U75 Epithalam.	160
So large; his Body then, not boughs, project his shade.	258	U75 Epithalam.	V184
Not with the Arras, but the Persian Loomes.	260	U77 Treasurer	4
Not from the Arras, but the Persian Loomes.	260	U77 Treasurer	V 4
Earle Rivers Grand-Child--serve not formes, good Fame,	269	U81 Pawlet	21
Earle Rivers Grand-Child--serve not titles Fame,	269	U81 Pawlet	V 21
I durst not aime at that: The dotes were such	269	U81 Pawlet	25
I durst not aime at, the dotes thereof were such	269	U81 Pawlet	V 25
The blaze, and splendor, but not handle fire!	269	U81 Pawlet	32
The heat, and splendor, but not handle fire!	269	U81 Pawlet	V 32
Stick on your Cupping-glasses, fear not, put	270	U81 Pawlet	53
If you not understand, what Child you had.	271	U81 Pawlet	78
But, Painter, see thou doe not sell	277	U84 Body	29
Not, that your Art I doe refuse:	277	U84 Mind	5
But these are like a Mind, not it.	278	U84 Mind	12
As 'tis not radiant, but divine:	278	U84 Mind	26
Not swelling like the Ocean proud,	280	U84 Mind	57
Boast not these Titles of your Ancestors;	281	U84 Kenelme	10
Which all men doe, that urge not their owne deeds	281	U84 Kenelme	17
With such a Raritie, and not rowse Art	282	U84 Muse	16
Beene trusted to thee: not to't selfe assign'd.	283	U84 Muse	20
Sure, I am dead, and know it not! I feele	283	U84 Muse	29
Indeed, she is not dead! but laid to sleepe	283	U84 Muse	45
With silence, and amazement! not with rude,	284	U84 Muse	78
As nature could not more increase the flood	287	U84 Muse	158

	Page	Title	Line
NOT (cont.)			
Not tost or troubled with light Lady-aire;	287	U84 Muse	164
And is not in the Usurers bands:	289	U85 Country	4
Who (amongst these delights) would not forget	290	U85 Country	37
Not Lucrine Oysters I could then more prize,	291	U85 Country	49
Could not goe downe my belly then	291	U85 Country	54
I am not such, as in the Reigne	292	U86 Hor.4:1	3
And Phrygian Hau'boy, not without the Flute.	292	U86 Hor.4:1	24
The Roman Ilia was not more renown'd.	293	U87 Hor.3:9	8
As, for her, I'ld not feare to die,	293	U87 Hor.3:9	11
Let us not then rush blindly on unto it,	294	U88 Petronius	3
Not labour'd for, but left thee by thy Sire;	295	U90 Mart.10:47	3
A Soyle, not barren; a continewall fire;	295	U90 Mart.10:47	4
Thy night not dronken, but from cares layd wast;	295	U90 Mart.10:47	9
Yet, not as therefore wild, and tame should cleave	305	Horace	14
Yet not as therefore cruell things should cleave	338	Horace	V 14
Together: not that we should Serpents see	305	Horace	15
To gentle: not that we should Serpents see	338	Horace	V 15
Not to designe the whole. Should I aspire	307	Horace	49
Prove what your shoulders will, or will not beare.	339	Horace	V 57/ 55
And what they will not. Him, whose choice doth reare	307	Horace	56
And come not too much wrested. What's that thing,	309	Horace	76
The Comick matter will not be exprest	311	Horace	121
'Tis not enough, th'elaborate Muse affords	311	Horace	140
'Tis not enough, the labouring Muse affords	341	Horace	V140
Not care, as thou wouldst faithfully translate,	313	Horace	190
Hee thinkes not, how to give you smoake from light,	315	Horace	203
What he despaires, being handled, might not show.	315	Horace	214
He knowes not why, and changeth every houre.	315	Horace	228
Yet, to the Stage, at all thou maist not tender	317	Horace	260
Present anone: Medea must not kill	317	Horace	263
What so is showne, I not beleeve, and hate.	317	Horace	269
Worth his untying happen there: And not	317	Horace	274
Must maintaine manly; not be heard to sing,	317	Horace	277
Must manly keep, and not be heard to sing	345	Horace	V277
The Hau'-boy, not as now with latten bound,	319	Horace	287
As loud enough to fill the seates, not yet	319	Horace	291
Now differ'd not from Delphick riddling.	319	Horace	310
As not make difference, whether Davus speake,	321	Horace	345
And not without much praise; till libertie	321	Horace	366
But every Judge hath not the facultie	323	Horace	387
Too patiently, that I not fondly say;	323	Horace	401
Had not our every Poet like offended.	325	Horace	414
But you, Pompilius off-spring, spare you not	325	Horace	415
Have not kept in; and (lest perfection faile)	325	Horace	417
Not, ten times o're, corrected to the naile.	325	Horace	418
In Helicon; a great sort will not pare	325	Horace	422
For so, they shall not only gaine the worth,	325	Horace	425
For choller! If I did not, who could bring	325	Horace	430
For Choler! if I did not, none could bring	349	Horace	V430
The Poet, what becommeth, and what not:	325	Horace	438
There words will follow, not against their will.	325	Horace	444
The Muse not only gave the Greek's a wit,	327	Horace	461
Much in the Poeme shine, I will not bee	329	Horace	526
Hath shed, or humane frailtie not kept thence.	329	Horace	528
Still in the same, and warned will not mend,	329	Horace	530
This, fearing not the subtlest Judges marke,	331	Horace	542
There may a Lawyer be, may not excell;	331	Horace	550
Or knowes not what Cassellius Aulus can;	331	Horace	553
Hee, that not knowes the games, nor how to use	331	Horace	565
Why not? I'm gentle, and free-borne, doe hate	331	Horace	571
Why not? being honest, and free-borne, doth hate	352	Horace	V547/571
But, if hereafter thou shalt write, not feare	331	Horace	575
To change, and mend, what you not forth doe set.	331	Horace	579
Nature, or Art. My Judgement will not pierce	331	Horace	582
You doe not bring, to judge your Verses, one,	333	Horace	609
Looke through him, and be sure, you take not mocks	333	Horace	621
Become an Aristarchus. And, not say,	335	Horace	639
Not thence be sav'd, although indeed he could?	335	Horace	658
Let Poets perish, that will not be kept.	335	Horace	664
Not letting goe his hold, where he drawes food,	337	Horace	679
Not letting goe the skin, where he drawes food,	355	Horace	V679
I could not but in admiracion stand.	361	Palmer	4
Not one but thrives; in spite of stormes & thunder,	361	Palmer	7
Not wearing moodes, as gallants doe a fashion,	362	Author	3
The fault's not in the object, but their eyes.	362	Author	8
And is not rap't	367	Ode Who saith	60
The Dutch whom Wealth (not Hatred) doth divide;	368	Ode Who saith	85
'Tis not your fault, if they shall sense preferre,	370	Author	13
Their motives were, since it had not to do	371	Fletcher	9
Stay, view this stone: And, if thou beest not such,	371	Epitaph	1
With Rites not bound, but conscience. Wouldst thou All?	372	Epitaph	11
Here, not up Holdborne, but downe a steepe hill,	374	Coryat 1	12
Here, up the Alpes (not so plaine as to Dunstable)	374	Coryat 1	16
And here he disdained not, in a forraine land	375	Coryat 1	32
From Venice to Flushing, were not they well cobled?	380	Coryat 3	42
So that not them, his scabbes, lice, or the stewes,	380	Coryat 3	50
Which he not denies. Now being so free,	381	Coryat 3	57
yf from a little sparke hee rise not fier.	383	Rich	16
They are not those, are present with theyre face,	384	Somerset	1
Do wayte upon thee: and theyre Love not bought.	384	Somerset	4
Not only this, but every day of thine,	384	Somerset	9
To such a worke, as could not need theirs? Yet	385	Brooke	5

	Page	Title	Line

NOT (cont.)

It fits not onely him that makes a Booke,	385	Husband	1
I do not feele that ever yet I had	385	Husband	5
Shee need not blush upon the Mariage-Day.	386	Husband	12
Some men, of Bookes or Freinds not speaking right,	386	Browne	1
By offring not more sureties, then inow,	386	Browne	12
More of our writers would like thee, not swell	386	Browne	15
Sonnes, seeke not me amonge these polish'd stones:	387	Cavendish	1
will all turne dust, & may not make me swell.	387	Cavendish	4
Will all be dust, & may not make me swell.	387	Cavendish	V 4
not when I die'd, but how I livd. Farewell.	387	Cavendish	12
That an ill man dares not securely looke	389	Aleman	8
Will bee receiv'd in Court; If not, would I	389	Aleman	19
Not on his Picture, but his Booke.	390	Reader	10
Were not the paths I meant unto thy praise:	390	Shakespeare	6
My Shakespeare, rise; I will not lodge thee by	391	Shakespeare	19
That I not mixe thee so, my braine excuses;	391	Shakespeare	25
From thence to honour thee, I would not seeke	391	Shakespeare	32
He was not of an age, but for all time!	391	Shakespeare	43
Neat Terence, witty Plautus, now not please;	392	Shakespeare	52
As they were not of Natures family.	392	Shakespeare	54
Yet must I not give Nature all: Thy Art,	392	Shakespeare	55
Not usuall in a Lady; and yet true:	394	Jane Ogle	14
At least, if not the generall Engine cracke.	395	May	6
As not the smallest joint, or gentlest word	395	May	21
Because, who make the question, have not seene	396	Drayton	3
You have not writ to me, nor I to you;	396	Drayton	6
And, though I now begin, 'tis not to rub	396	Drayton	7
Onely my losse is, that I am not there:	398	Drayton	91
In faire freehould, not an Inmate:	399	Lady Ogle	26
Before this worke? where Envy hath not cast	401	Beaumont	13
If, maymed, she come off, 'tis not of men	401	Beaumont	16
But higher power, as spight could not make lesse,	401	Beaumont	18
Something your Surship doth not yet intend!	402	Inigo Jones 1	14
your Trappings will not change you. Change your mynd.	403	Inigo Jones 1	25
Not they that sided her, Dame Poetry,	403	Inigo Jones 1	36
And not fall downe before it? and confess	406	Inigo Jones 1	91
Whom not ten fyres, nor a Parlyament can	406	Inigo Jones 1	103
Our Charles should make thee such? 'Twill not become	406	Inigo Jones 2	3
Foole, doe not rate my Rymes; I'have found thy Vice	408	Detractor	5
Shall not worke out unto it, such a fame.	409	Detractor	12
Thou art not worth it. Who will care to knowe	409	Detractor	13
But fly thee, like the Pest! Walke not the street	409	Detractor	19
It was not so of old: Men tooke up trades	410	Brome	13
And lesse asham'd; not when I told the crowd	414	Rutter	5
That sit to censure Playes, yet know not when,	414	Rutter	8
yet doe not feare it.	417	Moon	32
shee will not seise it.	418	Moon	44
Of Civill virtue, that hee now is not	420	Ode:If Men	12
That hath not Countrye impudence enough to laughe att Arte,	420	Ode:If Men	14
Cause Reverence, yf not Feare,	421	Ode:If Men	42
Whoe worthie wine, whoe not, to bee wyse Pallas guests.	421	Ode:If Men	45
Censure, not sharplye then, but mee advise	421	Censure	1
The emptye Carper, scorne, not Creditt wynns.	421	Censure	5
It is an Act of Tyranye, not Love,	422	Censure	18
Forgive it as my Frayltie, and not mee.	422	Censure	23
not safe; but when thou dost them thoroughlie:	423	Lucan	16
Virtue, and Soveraigntie, they not consort.	423	Lucan	18

NOTE

The selfe-same things, a note of concord be:	40	E42 Giles	17
Action, or engine, worth a note of thine,	71	E110 Edmonds 1	20
Some note of which each varied Pillar beares,	176	U24 Frontispice	15
Bee thou my Bookes intelligencer, note	232	U58 Book-seller	3
Good Omen to him, in the note thou sing'st,	263	U78 Digby	22
Good fortune to him, in the note thou sing'st,	263	U78 Digby	V 22
As her whole life was now become one note	287	U84 Muse	178
To note in Poemes, breach of harmonie;	323	Horace	388
Reprove; and, what is to be changed, note:	335	Horace	638
Dispute; and what is to be changed, note;	354	Horace	V638
Whose Note, and Hue,	366	Ode Who saith	4

NOTED

And noted for what flesh such soules were fram'd,	66	E103 L Wroth 1	3
Loves sicknesse, and his noted want of worth,	150	U10 Jealousie	14
And noted the beginnings and decayes!	160	U14 Selden	46

NOTES

The soules, shee loves. Those other glorious notes,	114	F12 Rutland	43
To curious light, the notes, I then shall sing,	115	F12 Rutland	76
To curious light, to notes, I then shall sing,	115	F12 Rutland	V 76
Mixe then your Notes, that we may prove	143	U3 Musicall	9
Such Notes are vertuous men! they live as fast	157	U13 Sacvile	143
Made Dian, not his notes refuse?	182	U27 Ode Helen	28
Your change of Notes, the flat, the meane, the sharpe,	263	U79 New-yeares	3
With Sayles of silke, as the first notes	273	U84 Cradle	23
With thy soft notes, and hold them within Pale	367	Ode Who saith	45
I then could rayse my notes	419	Ode:If Men	6

NOTHING'

| (How nothing's that?) to whom my countrey owes | 31 | E14 Camden | 3 |

NOTHING

And mine come nothing like. I hope so. Yet,	32	E18 Censurer	5
Forbidd' his side! and nothing, but the word	33	E21 Gam'ster	4
And I know nothing more thou hast to doo.	63	E98 Th Roe 1	11
As nothing else discernes the vertue' or vice.	66	E102 Pembroke	12
And that, in action, there is nothing new,	72	E111 Edmonds 2	5

NOTHING (cont.)
I, yet, had utter'd nothing on thy part,   .   .   .   82   E130 Ferrab. 1   15
There's nothing I can wish, for which I stay.   .   .   .   95   F2 Penshurst   75
Those proud, ambitious heaps, and nothing else,   .   .   .   96   F2 Penshurst   101
Where nothing is examin'd, weigh'd, ...   101   F4 To the World   49
May they have nothing left, whereof they can   .   .   .   118   F13 Aubigny   83
This All of nothing, gavest it forme, and fate,   .   .   .   127   U1 Trinitie   18
And let nothing high decay, ...   131   U2 Excuse   22
Are nothing till that comes to bind and shut.   .   .   .   157   U13 Sacvile   138
And last, goe out in nothing: You that see   .   .   .   157   U13 Sacvile   153
Find you to reckon nothing, me owe all.   158   U13 Sacvile   164
A banke against it. Nothing but the round   .   .   .   160   U14 Selden   63
Is nothing, such scarce meat and drinke he'le give, .   .   .   167   U15 Friend-Wars 159
That thou thinke nothing great, but what is good, .   .   .   168   U15 Friend-Wars 187
And he is not in friendship. Nothing there   .   .   .   169   U17 Friend-Debt   5
Nothing, but practise upon honours thrall.   .   .   .   179   U25 Desmond   35
If there be nothing worthy you can see   191   U38 Elegy 'Tis   15
Nothing is vile, that is a part of you: 192   U38 Elegy 'Tis   36
See the worlds Ruines! nothing but the piles   .   .   .   209   U43 Vulcan   137
Live by their Scale, that dare doe nothing free?   .   .   .   215   U44 Speach   68
'Tis vertue alone, or nothing, that knits friends: .   .   .   216   U45 Squib   12
And though all praise bring nothing to your name, .   .   .   224   U50 Countesse   13
That nothing can her gratitude provoke!   237   U64 Charles 3   16
That nothing will her gratitude provoke!   237   U64 Charles 3   V 16
Unto the Vertue. Nothing perfect done, ...   247   U70 Ode   115
With Angels, Muse, to speake these: Nothing can   .   .   .   255   U75 Epithalam.   84
For, had we here said lesse, we had sung nothing then. .   .   .   263   U79 New-yeares   8
Since nothing can report that flame, ...   278   U84 Mind   15
Since nothing can report her flame, ...   278   U84 Mind   V 15
Nothing, that could remaine, or yet can stirre   .   .   .   282   U84 Muse   9
Nothing I doe; but, like a heavie wheele, ...   283   U84 Muse   30
Nothing can more adorne it, then the seat   284   U84 Muse   71
Will to bee, what thou art; and nothing more: .   .   .   295   U90 Mart.10:47   12
And hold them faithfully; For nothing rests,   .   .   .   329   Horace   505
Wilt nothing against nature speake, or doe: .   .   .   331   Horace   574
NOTHING'S
(How nothing's that?) to whom my countrey owes   .   .   .   31   E14 Camden   3
NOTION
Thereof, no notion can expresse how much   269   U81 Pawlet   26
NOTIONS
Whose Notions when it will expresse   279   U84 Mind   33
NOUGHT
First made of nought, ...   129   U1 Father   21
Nought but in corners; and is loath to leave,   .   .   .   154   U13 Sacvile   44
But nought beyond. He thou hast given it to,   .   .   .   161   U14 Selden   71
And being a thing, blowne out of nought, rebells   .   .   .   163   U15 Friend-Wars   32
Lest it be justled, crack'd, made nought, or lesse: .   .   .   219   U47 Tribe   58
Thinkes it selfe nought, though she should valew it. .   .   .   223   U49 Pucell   24
Nought of a Maiden Queene, ...   254   U75 Epithalam.   47
Needs nought to cloath it but the ayre.   275   U84 Body   8
Be nought so'bove him but his sword let claime.   .   .   .   313   Horace   174
Be nought so'bove him, but his bold sword claime. .   .   .   342   Horace   V174
Who nought assaies unaptly, or amisse?   315   Horace   200
Our Poets, too, left nought unproved here;   .   .   .   323   Horace   405
I, writing nought my selfe, will teach them yet   .   .   .   325   Horace   435
Being men were covetous of nought, but praise.   .   .   .   327   Horace   463
He'd say, mend this my friend, and this, 'tis nought. .   .   .   354   Horace   V624
For thou hast nought in thee to cure his Fame,   .   .   .   411   Gill   13
NOURCERIES
As were his Nourceries; and swept   151   U12 Corbet   16
NOURISH
Scarce the world a Wit doth nourish, ...   184   U29 Fit of Rime   38
Once rowable, but now doth nourish men   309   Horace   94
NOURISHETH
What nourisheth, what formed, what begot   325   Horace   437
NOURSE
Where some great Lady, or her diligent Nourse;   .   .   .   313   Horace   164
NOVEMB
. . . An Epigram Anniversarie. Novemb. 19. 1632.   .   .   .   249   U72 King   Ttl
NOVEMBER
This sixteenth of November, ...   239   U67 Muses   2
NOW'
The Husband now's call'd churlish, or a poore   .   .   .   165   U15 Friend-Wars   89
That scratching now's our best Felicitie?   166   U15 Friend-Wars 144
That keepe the warre, though now't be growne more tame, . .   .   214   U44 Speach   55
NOW
A purging bill, now fix'd upon the dore, ...   29   E7 Hot-house   2
Beg'd Ridwayes pardon: Duncote, now, doth crye;   .   .   .   29   E8 Robbery   4
And now, her (hourely) her owne cucqueane makes,   .   .   .   34   E25 Beast 1   5
Then his chast wife, though Beast now know no more, .   .   .   35   E26 Beast 2   1
Whither the world must follow. And I, now,   .   .   .   37   E33 Roe 3   3
Hast purg'd thy realmes, as we have now no cause   .   .   .   38   E35 James 2   5
Colt, now, doth daily penance in his owne.   .   .   .   39   E39 Colt   2
If, now, with man and wife, to will, and nill   .   .   .   40   E42 Giles   16
'Tofore, great men were glad of Poets: Now,   .   .   .   40   E43 Salisbury 1   5
O, could I loose all father, now. For why   .   .   .   41   E45 First Son   5
Yes, now he weares his knight-hood every day.   .   .   .   42   E46 Luckless 1   6
Buy the reversion of old playes; now growne   .   .   .   45   E56 Poet-Ape   6
To reade my verses; now I must to heare: 45   E58 Groome   2
On whom, if he were living now, to looke, ...   53   E79 Rutland   10
Now, in whose pleasures I have this discerned,   .   .   .   55   E85 Goodyere 1   11
Now, I must give thy life, and deed, the voice   .   .   .   55   E86 Goodyere 2   5
Where ere he met me; now hee's dumbe, or proud.   .   .   .   62   E97 Motion   8

NOW (cont.)

Line	Page	Title	Line
But much it now availes, what's done, of whom:	64	E99 Th Roe 2	7
And I must now beleeve him: for, to day,	64	E100 Playwrt 3	3
And, though fowle, now, be scarce, yet there are clarkes,	65	E101 Supper	15
Which is the Mermaids, now, but shall be mine:	65	E101 Supper	30
Their lives, as doe their lines, till now had lasted.	65	E101 Supper	32
Nay, now you puffe, tuske, and draw up your chin,	69	E107 Hungry	29
No more, then I dare now doe, with my pen.	70	E108 Soldiers	8
Who now calls on thee, Nevil, is a Muse,	70	E109 Nevil	1
Now I have sung thee thus, shall judge of thee.	70	E109 Nevil	16
These were thy knowing arts: which who doth now	75	E116 Jephson	13
And did act (what now we mone)	77	E120 S. P.	13
I answer'd, Daphne now no paine can prove.	80	E126 Mrs Cary	6
Roe (and my joy to name) th'art now, to goe	80	E128 Wm Roe 2	1
Bartas doth wish thy English now were his.	83	E132 Sylvester	10
As his will now be the translation thought,	83	E132 Sylvester	12
His three for one. Now, lordings, listen well.	84	E133 Voyage	28
His spirits, now, in pills, and eeke in potions,	86	E133 Voyage	101
Their Mercury did now. By this, the stemme	87	E133 Voyage	111
The well-greas'd wherry now had got betweene,	87	E133 Voyage	114
And, now, above the poole, a face right fat	88	E133 Voyage	160
Is now from home. You lose your labours quite,	89	E133 Voyage	181
And pikes, now weary their owne kinde to eat,	94	F2 Penshurst	34
Now, Penshurst, they that will proportion thee	96	F2 Penshurst	99
A fire now, that lent a shade!	98	F3 Wroth	46
My owne true fire. Now my thought takes wing,	108	F10 Proludium	29
Our owne true fire. Now our thought takes wing,	108	F10 Proludium	29
And now an Epode to deepe eares I sing.	108	F10 Proludium	30
And now an Epode to deepe eares we sing.	108	F10 Proludium	30
the glories of yt. Now our muse takes winge,	108	F10 Proludium	15
and now an Epode, to deepe Eares, wee singe.	108	F10 Proludium	16
In a continuall tempest. Now, true Love	110	F11 Epode	43
Whil'st that, for which, all vertue now is sold,	113	F12 Rutland	1
Then, now give pride fame, or peasants birth.	114	F12 Rutland	26
And now lye lost in their forgotten dust.	114	F12 Rutland	40
Now thinking on you, though to England lost,	116	F12 Rutland	94
Of any good minde, now: There are so few.	116	F13 Aubigny	2
Each into other, and had now made one.	120	F13 Aubigny	120
Now that the harth is crown'd with smiling fire,	120	F14 Sydney	1
Must now	120	F14 Sydney	24
Which must be now,	121	F14 Sydney	47
And whither rap'd, now thou but stoup'st to mee?	122	F15 Heaven	14
Was now laid in a Manger.	130	U1 Nativitie	12
The Word was now made Flesh indeed,	130	U1 Nativitie	17
Though I now write fiftie yeares,	131	U2 Excuse	3
That you never knew till now,	131	U2 Excuse	15
Looser-like, now, all my wreake	133	U2 Suffered	21
I Now thinke, Love is rather deafe, then blind,	149	U9 Picture	1
Now I conceive him by my want,	152	U12 Corbet	32
An Epistle to Sir Edward Sacvile, now Earle of Dorset.	153	U13 Sacvile	Ttl
Now dam'mee, Sir, if you shall not command	154	U13 Sacvile	53
Now, but command; make tribute, what was gift;	155	U13 Sacvile	84
So that my Reader is assur'd, I now	159	U14 Selden	27
Conjectures retriv'd! And a Storie now	160	U14 Selden	50
Not to be checkt, or frighted now with fate,	163	U15 Friend-Wars	35
Friendship is now mask'd Hatred! Justice fled,	163	U15 Friend-Wars	39
Adulteries, now, are not so hid, or strange,	165	U15 Friend-Wars	85
Tilt one upon another, and now beare	166	U15 Friend-Wars	125
till one upon another, and now beare	166	U15 Friend-Wars	V125
This way, now that, as if their number were	166	U15 Friend-Wars	126
Is not enough now, but the Nights to play:	166	U15 Friend-Wars	132
Is not enough now, but the Nights we play:	166	U15 Friend-Wars	V132
Now use the bones, we see doth hire a man	166	U15 Friend-Wars	136
Now use the bales, we see doth hire a man	166	U15 Friend-Wars	V136
These take, and now goe seeke thy peace in Warre,	168	U15 Friend-Wars	195
Now so much friend, as you would trust in me,	169	U17 Friend-Debt	14
Now threaten, with those meanes she did invite?	169	U18 Elegy Can	2
Then like, then love; and now would they amaze?	169	U18 Elegy Can	4
Others, in time may love, as we doe now.	171	U19 Elegy By	18
were such as I will now relate, or worse?	172	U20 Shrub	14
Yet is't your vertue now I raise.	173	U22 Elegy Tho	4
That not a Nymph now sings?	174	U23 Himselfe	10
Doth now command;	180	U25 Desmond	62
As farre from all revolt, as you are now from Fortune.	180	U25 Desmond	65
And now out of sight.	180	U26 Ode High	8
Must now be rayn'd.	180	U26 Ode High	15
In one full Action; nor have you now more	180	U26 Ode High	17
Both braines and hearts; and mine now best doe know it:	182	U28 Worth	8
Of all the Land. Who now at such a Rate,	185	U30 Burleigh	19
Upon the reverend Pleaders; doe now shut	187	U33 Councellour	10
Now swift, now slow, now tame, now wild;	189	U36 Song	14
Now hot, now cold, now fierce, now mild.	189	U36 Song	15
Of Credit lost. And I am now run madde:	191	U38 Elegy 'Tis	2
Your honour now, then your disgrace before.	191	U38 Elegy 'Tis	30
Thinke that I once was yours, or may be now;	192	U38 Elegy 'Tis	35
I am regenerate now, become the child	192	U38 Elegy 'Tis	39
Publike affaires command me now to goe	194	U38 Elegy 'Tis	114
It is not likely I should now looke downe	200	U42 Elegy Let	37
I now begin to doubt, if ever Grace,	207	U43 Vulcan	107
Were now the greater Captaine? for they saw	214	U44 Speach	39
The Herald will. Our blood is now become	215	U44 Speach	82
And skill in thee, now, grew Authoritie;	217	U46 Coke	10
And now such is thy stand; while thou dost deale	217	U46 Coke	15

	Page	Title	Line
NOW (cont.)			
As you have writ your selfe. Now stand, and then,	220	U47 Tribe	77
Where now, thou art made Dweller;	220	U48 Bacchus	4
To his poore Instrument, now out of grace.	223	U49 Pucell	34
For Sermoneeres: of which now one, now other,	223	U49 Pucell	39
Now with a Title more to the Degree;	225	U51 Bacon	12
O, had I now your manner, maistry, might,	227	U52 Answer	16
That's six in silver; now within the Socket	229	U54 Squib	13
Though now he refuses,	231	U57 Burges	10
Then now, to love the Soveraigne, and the Lawes?	236	U64 Charles 3	8
Then now, to love the Soveraigne, or his Lawes?	236	U64 Charles 3	V 8
And there to stand so. Hast now envious Moone,	238	U65 Prince	9
The Kings fame lives. Go now, denie his Teirce.	241	U68 House-hold	14
Painted a Dog, that now his subtler skill	241	U69 Friend Son	10
Though now of flattery, as of picture, are	242	U69 Friend Son	21
Goe now, and tell out dayes summ'd up with feares,	244	U70 Ode	53
Have cast a trench about mee, now, five yeares;	248	U71 Treasurer	6
O, now thou smil'st, faire Sun, and shin'st, as thou wouldst stay!	254	U75 Epithalam.	64
Our Court, and all the Grandees; now, Sun, looke,	254	U75 Epithalam.	73
See, now the Chappell opens; where the King	256	U75 Epithalam.	121
Now, Sun, and post away the rest of day:	257	U75 Epithalam.	138
These two, now holy Church hath made them one,	257	U75 Epithalam.	139
So great; his Body now alone projects the shade.	258	U75 Epithalam.	184
Let their spite (which now abounds)	260	U76 Petition	28
I would present you now with curious plate	260	U77 Treasurer	2
Sate safe enough, but now secured more.	268	U80 Christning	14
And now, through circumfused light, she lookes	271	U81 Pawlet	69
Goe now, her happy Parents, and be sad,	271	U81 Pawlet	77
Now I have better thought thereon,	277	U84 Mind	2
I call you Muse; now make it true:	278	U84 Mind	21
'Twere time that I dy'd too, now shee is dead,	282	U84 Muse	1
(For so thou art with me) now shee is gone.	283	U84 Muse	22
As her whole life was now become one note	287	U84 Muse	178
To that eternall Rest, where now sh'hath place	288	U84 Muse	197
Then now beneath some ancient Oke he may,	290	U85 Country	23
Now in the rooted Grasse him lay,	290	U85 Country	24
These thoughts when Usurer Alphius, now about	291	U85 Country	67
These thinges when Usurer Alphius, now about	291	U85 Country	V 67
To bend a man, now at his fiftieth yeare	292	U86 Hor.4:1	6
Me now, nor Wench, nor wanton Boy,	293	U86 Hor.4:1	29
Nor care I now healths to propound;	293	U86 Hor.4:1	31
And to left-Lydia, now the gate stood ope.	294	U87 Hor.3:9	20
Or Rainbow is describ'd. But here was now	305	Horace	23
Invention. Now, to speake; and then differ	307	Horace	61
Is now to speak, and even now to differ	339	Horace	V 61
Much, that mought now be spoke: omitted here	307	Horace	62
Till fitter season. Now, to like of this,	307	Horace	63
Or Varius? Why am I now envi'd so,	309	Horace	79
Once rowable, but now doth nourish men	309	Horace	94
Or the wilde river, who hath changed now	309	Horace	96
Much phrase that now is dead, shall be reviv'd;	309	Horace	101
And much shall dye, that now is nobly liv'd,	309	Horace	102
If now the turnes, the colours, and right hues	311	Horace	126
If now the changes, and the severall hues	341	Horace	V121/126
If now the phrase of him that speakes, shall flow,	313	Horace	158
Fit rites. The Child, that now knowes how to say,	315	Horace	225
Fit dues. The Child. that now knowes how to say,	344	Horace	V225
These studies alter now, in one, growne man;	315	Horace	237
The Hau'-boy, not as now with latten bound,	319	Horace	287
Now differ'd not from Delphick riddling.	319	Horace	310
Fell into fault so farre, as now they saw	321	Horace	367
He cries, Good boy, thou'lt keepe thine owne. Now, adde	327	Horace	470
'Tis now inquir'd, which makes the nobler Verse,	331	Horace	581
Who now to sing the Pythian Rites is heard,	353	Horace	V591
But, now, it is enough to say; I make	333	Horace	593
Now, bring him backe, he'le be no more a man,	355	Horace	V668
Now, after all, let no man	364	Phoenix	1
Now must we plie our ayme; our Swan's on wing.	368	Ode Who saith	64
Though, now by Love transform'd, & dayly dying:	369	Ode Who saith	101
But now, your Worke is done, if they that view	370	Author	9
. . . the Coryate of Odcombe, and his Booke now going to travell	378	Coryat 2	Ttl
Trie and trust Roger, was the word, but now	378	Coryat 2	80
. . . omitted, and now communicated to the World	379	Coryat 3	Ttl
That sacred to Odcombe are there now suspended;	380	Coryat 3	40
Which he not denies. Now being so free,	381	Coryat 3	57
. . . & sir Henrye Rich, now Earles of Warwick and Hollande.	382	Rich	Ttl
As, now, of all men, it is call'd thy Trade:	389	Chapman	11
Neat Terence, witty Plautus, now not please;	392	Shakespeare	52
And, though I now begin, 'tis not to rub	396	Drayton	7
The Scene! the Engyne! but he now is come	404	Inigo Jones 1	62
Hee's warme on his feet now he sayes, & can	405	Inigo Jones 1	67
What would he doe now, gi'ng his mynde that waye	405	Inigo Jones 1	75
I now would write on thee? No, wretch; thy name	409	Detractor	11
Now, you are got into a nearer roome,	409	Brome	3
A Prentise-ship: which few doe now a dayes.	410	Brome	10
Now each Court-Hobby-horse will wince in rime;	410	Brome	11
The Cobler kept him to his nall; but, now	410	Brome	17
To top the fairest Lillie, now, that growes;	413	Ghyrlond	15
Now, for mine owne part, and it is but due,	415	Rutter	12
This is my censure. Now there is a new	415	Rutter	19
Now, in a garland by the graces knit:	416	Welcome	4
Of Civill virtue, that hee now is not	420	Ode:If Men	12

NOWE
    Yff Men, and tymes were nowe   419   Ode:If Men   1
    or Malyce to make Faultes, which nowe is skill. .   .   .   421   Censure   11
NOW'S
    The Husband now's call'd churlish, or a poore   .   .   .   165   U15 Friend-Wars 89
    That scratching now's our best Felicitie?   166   U15 Friend-Wars 144
NOW'T
    That keepe the warre, though now't be growne more tame,   .   214   U44 Speach   55
NOYSE
    Nor 'bout the beares, nor noyse to make lords sport.   .   .   63   E97 Motion   12
    Of newes, and noyse, to strow out a long meale.   .   .   .   74   E115 Honest Man 10
    Of newes, and noyse, to sow out a long meale.   .   .   .   74   E115 Honest Man V 10
    Whose noyse shall keepe thy miming most alive,   .   .   .   81   E129 Mime   10
    The filth, stench, noyse: save only what was there   .   .   84   E133 Voyage   9
    When all the noyse   120   F14 Sydney   17
    And then noyse forth the burden of their Song,   .   .   .   120   F14 Sydney   17
    And the ratling pit-pat-noyse, ...   249   U72 King   V 17
    Take little Infants with their noyse, ...   259   U76 Petition   19
    And caried, though with shoute, and noyse, confesse   .   .   273   U84 Cradle   18
    That thou hast lost thy noyse, thy foame, thy stirre,   .   397   Drayton   45
NOYSES   8
    Of popular noyses, borne to actuate things.   .   .   .   341   Horace   V120
NOYSOME
    Nameless, and noysome, as thy infamy!   409   Detractor   16
NULLIFIE
    Of Beautie, so to nullifie a face, ...   188   U34 Small Poxe   14
NUMBE
    A great deferrer, long in hope, growne numbe   .   .   .   317   Horace   245
NUMBER
    What their number is, be pin'd.   103   F6 Celia 2   22
    We doe not number, here, ...   111   F11 Epode   76
    I doe not number, here, ...   111   F11 Epode   V 76
    The bad, by number, are so fortified, ...   116   F13 Aubigny   3
    This day sayes, then, the number of glad yeeres   .   .   120   F14 Sydney   21
    This way, now that, as if their number were   .   .   .   166   U15 Friend-Wars 126
    Then once to number, or bring forth to hand,   .   .   .   167   U15 Friend-Wars 173
    (Though they may number bodyes) or but one.   .   .   .   171   U19 Elegy By   14
    I number these as being of the Chore   193   U38 Elegy 'Tis   99
    In weight, in measure, number, sound, ...   244   U70 Ode   50
    What number best can fit, Homer declares.   .   .   .   309   Horace   106
    So, in theyr number, may you never see   384   Somerset   21
    And number Attributes unto a flood: 394   Jane Ogle   6
    And those in number so, and measure rais'd,   .   .   .   395   May   8
    In number, measure, or degree   399   Lady Ogle   23
NUMBERS
    He should those rare, and absolute numbers view,   .   .   53   E79 Rutland   11
    And all his numbers, both of sense, and sounds.   .   .   61   E95 Savile   6
    That since, my numbers are so cold, ...   93   F1 Why write no 11
    Then, leave these lighter numbers, to light braines   .   108   F10 Proludium   7
    In numbers, of as subtile feet, ...   149   U9 Picture   V 8
    My bolder numbers to thy golden Lyre: 177   U25 Desmond   9
    My flowing numbers to thy golden Lyre: 177   U25 Desmond   V 9
    . . . A Gentleman absolute in all Numbers;   .   .   .   272   U84 Eupheme   Ttl
    Abhorres low numbers, and the private straine   .   .   .   311   Horace   123
    And in their numbers; For, alas, what knew   .   .   .   319   Horace   300
    Our Ancestors did Plautus numbers praise,   .   .   .   323   Horace   399
    Your Ancestors, old Plautus numbers prais'd,   .   .   .   348   Horace   V385/399
NUMBRED
    Yeeres he numbred scarse thirteene   77   E120 S. P.   9
    They might with ease be numbred, being a few   .   .   .   319   Horace   293
    The gladdest ground to all the numbred-five,   .   .   .   412   Ghyrlond   6
NUMBRED-FIVE
    The gladdest ground to all the numbred-five,   .   .   .   412   Ghyrlond   6
NUMEROUS
    To those true numerous Graces; whereof some,   .   .   .   182   U28 Worth   6
NUN
    Nay, sigh'd a Sister, 'twas the Nun, Kate Arden,   .   .   209   U43 Vulcan   148
    Nay, sayth a sister, Venus Nun, Kate Arden,   .   .   .   209   U43 Vulcan   V148
NUNCIO'S
    Janin's, your Nuncio's, and your Tuilleries,   .   .   .   69   E107 Hungry   22
NUPTIALL
    To welcome home a Paire, and deck the nuptiall bower?   .   253   U75 Epithalam.   24
    And knit the Nuptiall knot, ...   257   U75 Epithalam. 133
    Of Nuptiall Sweets, at such a season, owe,   .   .   .   257   U75 Epithalam. 148
NUPTIALS
    Epithalamion; Or, A Song: Celebrating The nuptials of . . .   252   U75 Epithalam. Ttl
    At these thy Nuptials; but, whose heart, and thought   .   384   Somerset   3
NURSE   (See also NOURSE)
    Or robbing the poore Market-folkes should nurse   .   .   155   U13 Sacvile   90
    Looke on th'ambitious man, and see him nurse   .   .   .   162   U15 Friend-Wars 11
    Much lesse a name would we bring up, or nurse,   .   .   216   U45 Squib   9
    Or old Silenus, Bacchus guard, and Nurse.   .   .   .   321   Horace   348
NURSERY   (See NOURCERIES)
NURSES
    To teach some that, their Nurses could not doe,   .   .   207   U43 Vulcan   92
    To teach some what, their Nurses could not doe,   .   .   207   U43 Vulcan   V 92
NUT
    Beneath the broad beech, and the chest-nut shade;   .   .   93   F2 Penshurst   12
    That taller tree, which of a nut was set,   .   .   .   94   F2 Penshurst   13
    The nut-crackers throughout, will they therefore   .   .   321   Horace   363
NUT-CRACKERS
    The nut-crackers throughout, will they therefore   .   .   321   Horace   363

	Page	Title	Line

NUTS
Some nuts, some apples; some that thinke they make · · · 95 F2 Penshurst 52
NYCE
whole armyes fall, swayd by those nyce respects. · · · 423 Lucan 11
NYMPH
Least mention of a Nymph, a Muse, a Grace, · · · 67 E105 L Wroth 2 4
What Nymph so e're his voyce but heares, · · · 148 U7 Nymph 27
That not a Nymph now sings? · · · 174 U23 Himselfe 10
to Cynthias fayrest Nymph hath sent thee, · · · 662 Bedford 6
NYMPHS
A Nymphs Passion. · · · 147 U7 Nymph Ttl
For if the Nymphs should know my Swaine, · · · 147 U7 Nymph 3
O
To heaven; his hath: O happy state! wherein · · · 35 E27 Roe 1 7
O, could I loose all father, now. For why · · · 41 E45 First Son 5
O Madame, if your grant did thus transferre mee, · · · 55 E84 Bedford 2 9
And stoupe, and cringe. O then, it needs must prove · · · 56 E88 Monsieur 14
O, would'st thou adde like hand, to all the rest! · · · 61 E95 Savile 13
O, (thou cry'st out) that is thy proper game. · · · 73 E112 Gamster 16
O, runne not proud of this. Yet, take thy due. · · · 81 E129 Mime 15
O, who is he, that (in this peace) enjoyes · · · 110 F11 Epode 55
O, so divine a creature · · · 112 F11 Epode 102
O, be thou witnesse, that the reynes dost know, · · · 122 F15 Heaven 5
Dwell, dwell here still: O, being every-where, · · · 122 F15 Heaven 15
O Holy, blessed, glorious Trinitie · · · 127 U1 Trinitie 1
O take my gift. · · · 127 U1 Trinitie 8
For thy acceptance. O, behold me right, · · · 127 U1 Trinitie 13
Increase those acts, o glorious Trinitie · · · 128 U1 Trinitie 29
O grant it me! · · · 128 U1 Trinitie 36
O, then how blest, · · · 128 U1 Trinitie 44
Heare mee, O God! · · · 129 U1 Father 1
O so white! O so soft! O so sweet is she! · · · 135 U2 Triumph 30
O so faire! O so soft! O so sweet is she! · · · 135 U2 Triumph V 30
O so faire O so kind o so sweet so sweet is shee · · · 135 U2 Triumph V 38
O so yong o so streight O so chast so chast is shee · · · 136 U2 Triumph V 46
O sing not you then, lest the best · · · 144 U3 Musicall 21
O, be not angry with those fires, · · · 144 U4 Song 5
O, doe not steepe them in thy Teares, · · · 145 U4 Song 9
O, is it so? knowes he so much? and will · · · 155 U13 Sacvile 73
Thy gift 'gainst envie. O how I doe count · · · 161 U14 Selden 79
O, these so ignorant Monsters! light, as proud, · · · 164 U15 Friend-Wars 59
For lesse Securitie? O · · · 165 U15 Friend-Wars 113
For less Securitie? O Freind, for these · · · 165 U15 Friend-Wars V113
And belov'd, while the Whores last. O times, · · · 167 U15 Friend-Wars 161
O, then inspire · · · 177 U25 Desmond 10
O, thou inspire · · · 177 U25 Desmond V 10
But whisper; O glad Innocence, · · · 177 U25 Desmond 31
O vertues fall, · · · 179 U25 Desmond 36
O then (my best-best lov'd) let me importune, · · · 180 U25 Desmond 63
O then (our best-best lov'd) let me importune, · · · 180 U25 Desmond V 63
Or there to sterve it. Helpe, O you that may · · · 191 U38 Elegy 'Tis 7
O may your wisdome take example hence, · · · 193 U38 Elegy 'Tis 67
O imitate that sweet Serenitie · · · 193 U38 Elegy 'Tis 77
O, that you could but by dissection see · · · 194 U38 Elegy 'Tis 109
O, keepe it still; for it had rather be · · · 199 U41 Elegy Since 17
Unto the Spittle Sermon. O, what strange · · · 201 U42 Elegy Let 71
But, O those Reeds! thy meere disdaine of them, · · · 208 U43 Vulcan 129
But, O those weedes; thy meere disdaine of them, · · · 208 U43 Vulcan V129
O no, cry'd all, Fortune, for being a whore, · · · 209 U43 Vulcan 153
O happy Art! and wise Epitome · · · 214 U44 Speach 43
All that they doe at Playes. O, but first here · · · 215 U44 Speach 91
O, had I now your manner, maistry, might, · · · 227 U52 Answer 16
Fit for a Bishops knees! O bow them oft, · · · 234 U61 Epigram 13
O pietie! so to weigh the poores estates! · · · 235 U62 Charles 1 11
O bountie! so to difference the rates! · · · 235 U62 Charles 1 12
O Times! O Manners! Surfet bred of ease, · · · 237 U64 Charles 3 17
O how will then our Court be pleas'd, · · · 251 U74 Weston 25
Although that thou, O Sun, at our intreaty stay! · · · 254 U75 Epithalam. 56
O, now thou smil'st, faire Sun, and shin'st, as thou wouldst stay! · · · 254 U75 Epithalam. 64
O happy bands! and thou more happy place, · · · 256 U75 Epithalam. 129
And praise them too. O! what a fame 't will be? · · · 263 U78 Digby 25
Heare, o you Groves, and, Hills, resound his praise. · · · 264 U79 New-yeares 23
Heare, o you Groves, and, Hills, resound his worth. · · · 264 U79 New-yeares 31
You seeme a faire one! O that you had breath, · · · 269 U81 Pawlet 6
You seeme a faire one! O that I had breath, · · · 269 U81 Pawlet V 6
O! had I seene her laid out a faire Corse, · · · 282 U84 Muse 11
O Day of joy, and suretie to the just! · · · 284 U84 Muse 61
A scorned Mouse! O, how much better this, · · · 315 Horace 199
A trifling Mouse! O, how much better this, · · · 343 Horace V199
O I left-witted, that purge every spring · · · 325 Horace 429
Sixe ounces. O, when once the canker'd rust, · · · 327 Horace 472
Splendor! O more then mortall, · · · 364 Ode Splendor 1
How faine for his venery he was to crie (Tergum o) · · · 380 Coryat 3 37
O, could he but have drawne his wit · · · 390 Reader 5
Lend me thy voyce, O Fame, that I may draw · · · 396 Drayton 12
O, how in those, dost thou instruct these times, · · · 397 Drayton 43
To hold her up. O Showes! Showes! Mighty Showes! · · · 403 Inigo Jones 1 39
OAKE
Or standing long an Oake, three hundred yeare, · · · 245 U70 Ode 67
OARES
Ycleped Mud, which, when their oares did once stirre, · · · 85 E133 Voyage 62
OATH (See also OTHES)
Nor need'st thou: for those few, by oath release, · · · 32 E16 Brain-hardy 7

OATH (cont.)
   It was as if thou printed had'st an oath, ... 43 E53 Old-end 5
   At her hand, with oath, to make . . . . . 133 U2 Suffered 10
   Finer then was his Spanish, if my Oath . . . . . 389 Aleman 18
OATHES
   He will both argue, and discourse in oathes, . . . 35 E28 Surly 9
   'Tis true, I'm broke! Vowes, Oathes, and all I had . . 191 U38 Elegy 'Tis 1
OBAY
   Who would not be thy subject, James, t'obay . . . 37 E35 James 2 1
OBAYE
   But sometymes shall bee tempted to obaye . . . . 422 Censure 25
OBEDIENCE
   The Sonnes obedience knew no No, ... 130 U1 Nativitie 14
OBELISKE
   An obeliske, or columne to thy name, ... 46 E60 Mounteagle 2
   Upon this obeliske, advanc'd for it, ... 416 Welcome 5
OBEY
   But shall sometimes be tempted to obey . . . . 190 U37 Friend-Book 32
   The rudest Winds obey the calmest Ayre: . . . . 251 U74 Weston 9
   I doe obey you, Beauty! for in death, ... 269 U81 Pawlet 5
   T'obey, and serve her sweet Commandements. . . . 287 U84 Muse 172
OBJECT
   Hath chang'd his soule, and made his object you: . . 74 E114 Sydney 5
   Object arrive there, but the heart (our spie) . . . 109 F11 Epode 11
   And to his sense object this sentence ever, . . . 113 F11 Epode 115
   This my object. But she threw . . . . . 132 U2 How he saw 23
   Stand forth my Object, then, you that have beene . . 159 U14 Selden 29
   The fault's not in the object, but their eyes. . . 362 Author 8
OBJECTEST
   For thou objectest (as thou hast been told) . . . 408 Detractor 3
OBJECTS
   And after varyed, as fresh objects goes, . . . 118 F13 Aubigny 56
   But there are objects, bid him to be gone . . . 163 U15 Friend-Wars 28
   Thus they doe talke. And are these objects fit . . 165 U15 Friend-Wars 101
   That would their better objects find: . . . . 173 U22 Elegy Tho 27
   weare made the objects to my weaker powers; . . . 361 Palmer 3
OBLATIONS
   As true oblations; his Brothers Embleme sayes, . . 383 Rich 10
OBLIQUE
   By all oblique Degrees, that killing height . . . 224 U50 Countesse 11
OBLIQUITIE
   Is natures meere obliquitie! as Heaven . . . . 192 U38 Elegy 'Tis 64
OBLIVION
   From Death, and darke oblivion, neere the same, . . 175 U24 Frontispice 1
OBSCENE
   For wittie, in his language, is obscene. . . . 42 E49 Playwrt 1 4
   'Twixt feare and rashnesse: not a lust obscene, . . 156 U13 Sacvile 106
   From what th'obscene, and petulant Satyres are. . . 321 Horace 340
OBSCURE
   Though I am short, I cannot be obscure: . . . 158 U14 Selden 2
   Obscure. This, striving to run smooth, and flow, . . 307 Horace 36
   Obscure. Another striving smooth to runne, . . . 339 Horace V 37/ 36
OBSERVATION
   Respect, and observation; it uncovers . . . . 363 Riches 7
   By observation of those Comick Lawes . . . . 409 Brome 7
OBSERVE
   Observe the strength, the height, the why, and when, . 157 U13 Sacvile 140
   Nor know t'observe: why (i'the Muses name) . . . 311 Horace 128
   The customes of each age thou must observe, . . . 315 Horace 223
OBSERVED
   . . . Commentaries observed, and translated. . . 71 E110 Edmonds 1 Ttl
OBSERVING
   Th'observing neighbours no such mood can see. . . 40 E42 Giles 2
OBTAINE
   And with the vulgar doth it not obtaine . . . 193 U38 Elegy 'Tis 81
   T'obtaine of God, what all the Land should aske? . . 234 U61 Epigram 11
OBTAIN'D
   Must make me sad for what I have obtain'd. . . . 154 U13 Sacvile 38
OCCASION
   Slip no occasion; As time stands not still, . . . 171 U19 Elegy By 19
OCCASIONS
   Times, and occasions, to start forth, and seeme) . . 118 F13 Aubigny 63
   . . . Panegyricke lines, but then were upon some occasions . . . 379 Coryat 3 Ttl
OCCUPY
   For'his whore: Groyne doth still occupy his land. . . 75 E117 Groyne 2
OCEAN
   Not swelling like the Ocean proud, ... 280 U84 Mind 57
OD
   All, that are readers: but, me thinkes 'tis od, . . 85 E133 Voyage 43
ODCOMBE
   . . . the Coryate of Odcombe, and his Booke now going to travell 378 Coryat 2 Ttl
   Of Tom of Odcombe that odde Joviall Author, . . . 378 Coryat 2 87
   That sacred to Odcombe are there now suspended, . . 380 Coryat 3 40
ODCOMBIAN
   Of our Odcombian, that literate Elfe? . . . . 379 Coryat 3 7
ODDE
   Some Alchimist there may be yet, or odde . . . 208 U43 Vulcan 118
   Immortall, tooke a melancholique, odde . . . . 335 Horace 662
   Of Tom of Odcombe that odde Joviall Author, . . . 378 Coryat 2 87
ODDES
   If by us, the oddes were laid, ... 138 U2 Kisse 7
   You won them too, your oddes did merit it. . . . 230 U56 Covell 4

```
                                                              Page      Title       Line

ODE
   Next morne, an Ode: Thou mak'st a song ere night.    .    .    .     72    E112 Gamster      12
   To Sicknesse. Ode Anacreon.                               .    .    .    104    F8 Sicknesse     VTtl
   Ode. To Sir William Sydney, on his Birth-day.             .    .    .    120    F14 Sydney        Ttl
   An Ode. To himselfe.                                 .    .    .    .    174    U23 Himselfe      Ttl
   An Ode to James Earle of Desmond, writ . . .         .    .    .    .    176    U25 Desmond       Ttl
   An Ode.                             .    .    .    .    .    .    .    180    U26 Ode High      Ttl
   An Ode.                        .    .    .    .    .    .    .    .    181    U27 Ode Helen     Ttl
   An Ode, or Song, by all the Muses. . . .        .    .    .    .    .    239    U67 Muses         Ttl
   To the Right Hon'ble Hierome, L. Weston.   An Ode . . .    .    .    250    U74 Weston        Ttl
   An Ode in Horace in prayse of a Countrye lyfe, Translated.      .    289    U85 Country       VTtl
   Ode the first.   The fourth Booke.   To Venus.       .    .    .    292    U86 Hor.4:1       Ttl
   Ode IX. 3 Booke, to Lydia.  Dialogue of Horace, and Lydia.      .    293    U87 Hor.3:9       Ttl
   Ode <Enthusiastic>.    .    .    .    .    .    .    .    .    364    Ode Splendor      Ttl
   Ode.  <Allegoric>.    .    .    .    .    .    .    .    .    366    Ode Who saith     Ttl
   Ode:    .    .    .    .    .    .    .    .    .    .    .    419    Ode:If Men        Ttl
ODIOUS
   All soote, and embers! odious, as thy worke!    .    .    .    .    207    U43 Vulcan        106
ODOROUS
   A nest of odorous spice, and gummes.       .    .    .    .    .    280    U84 Mind           64
ODORS
   A nest of Spices, Odors, Gummes.       .    .    .    .    .    .    280    U84 Mind         V 64
ODOUR
   What odour can be, then a heart contrite,    .    .    .    .    127    U1 Trinitie        15
   That never came ill odour thence:    .    .    .    .    .    .    152    U12 Corbet         18
   Still pretious, with the odour of thy name.    .    .    .    .    168    U15 Friend-Wars   190
   Still flie about the Odour of your Name;    .    .    .    .    186    U31 Elsmere         8
   That both, their odour take him,    .    .    .    .    .    220    U48 Bacchus        11
ODOURS
   Th'expence in odours is a most vaine sinne,    .    .    .    .    33    E20 Cod 2           1
OD'ROUS
   Whose od'rous breath destroyes    .    .    .    .    .    .    112    F11 Epode          96
   With od'rous sweets and soft humilitie,    .    .    .    .    413    Ghyrlond           27
ODS
   First frighted men, that wildly liv'd, at ods,    .    .    .    327    Horace            480
OENONE
   You were the bright Oenone, Flora, or May?    .    .    .    .    68    E105 L Wroth 2     10
O'
   By speaking well o' the company' it 's in.    .    .    .    .    74    E115 Honest Man     8
   Not taken up o' th' doctors, but as well    .    .    .    .    117    F13 Aubigny        33
   Have you mark'd but the fall o'the Snow    .    .    .    .    134    U2 Triumph         23
   Have you seene the fall o'the Snow    .    .    .    .    .    135    U2 Triumph       V 23
   Have you felt the wooll o' the Bever?    .    .    .    .    135    U2 Triumph         25
   Or have smelt o'the bud o'the Brier?    .    .    .    .    135    U2 Triumph         27
   Or have tasted the bag o'the Bee?    .    .    .    .    .    135    U2 Triumph         29
   Or stands to be'n Commission o' the blade?    .    .    .    .    155    U13 Sacvile        64
OF    (See also ON)
   Thy title, Epigrammes, and nam'd of mee,    .    .    .    .    27    E2 My Booke         2
   Thou should'st be bold, licentious, full of gall,    .    .    .    27    E2 My Booke         3
   Thou are not covetous of least selfe-fame,    .    .    .    .    27    E2 My Booke         9
   Made from the hazard of anothers shame:    .    .    .    .    27    E2 My Booke        10
   How, best of Kings, do'st thou a scepter beare!    .    .    .    28    E4 James 1          1
   How, best of Poets, do'st thou laurell weare!    .    .    .    28    E4 James 1          2
   Thou wert, as chiefe of them are said t'have beene.    .    .    28    E4 James 1          6
   As chiefe of those still promise they will bee.    .    .    .    28    E4 James 1          8
   Of Kings for grace; of Poets for my test?    .    .    .    .    28    E4 James 1         10
   Or celebrated with more truth of state?    .    .    .    .    28    E5 Union            2
   If all you boast of your great art be true;    .    .    .    .    29    E6 Alchymists       1
   Ridway rob'd Duncote of three hundred pound,    .    .    .    29    E8 Robbery          1
   Rob'd both of money, and the lawes reliefe;    .    .    .    29    E8 Robbery          5
   For strict degrees of ranke, or title looke:    .    .    .    29    E9 To All           2
   'Tis 'gainst the manners of an Epigram:    .    .    .    .    29    E9 To All           3
   Thou call'st me Poet, as a terme of shame:    .    .    .    29    E10 Ignorant        1
   The charge of that state, with this charme, god payes.    .    30    E12 Shift           4
   Of old, they gave a cock to Aesculape;    .    .    .    .    31    E13 Empirick        2
   Many of thine this better could, then I,    .    .    .    .    31    E14 Camden         13
   Scarse thy weekes swearing brings thee of, of one.    .    .    32    E16 Brain-hardy     4
   And, but a sprigge of bayes, given by thee,    .    .    .    32    E17 Critic          5
   His clothes two fashions of, and poore! his sword    .    .    33    E21 Gam'ster        3
   Mary, the daughter of their youth:    .    .    .    .    .    33    E22 Daughter        2
   With safetie of her innocence;    .    .    .    .    .    .    33    E22 Daughter        6
   In comfort of her mothers teares,    .    .    .    .    .    33    E22 Daughter        8
   Donne, the delight of Phoebus, and each Muse,    .    .    .    34    E23 Donne 1         1
   Whose every worke, of thy most earely wit,    .    .    .    34    E23 Donne 1         3
   In the past pleasures of his sensuall life,    .    .    .    34    E25 Beast 1         2
   Telling the motions of each petticote,    .    .    .    .    34    E25 Beast 1         3
   In place of scutcheons, that should decke thy herse,    .    35    E27 Roe 1           1
   Of a great man, and to be thought the same,    .    .    .    35    E28 Surly           2
   Makes serious use of all great trade he knowes.    .    .    35    E28 Surly           3
   H'has tympanies of businesse, in his face,    .    .    .    35    E28 Surly           7
   Of solemne greatnesse.  And he dares, at dice,    .    .    .    36    E28 Surly          16
   May heare my Epigrammes, but like of none.    .    .    .    36    E28 Surly          20
   All braines, at times of triumph, should runne wit.    .    36    E29 Tilter          4
   Banck feeles no lamenesse of his knottie gout,    .    .    36    E31 Banck           1
   What two brave perills of the private sword    .    .    .    37    E32 Roe 2           1
   What not the envie of the seas reach'd too,    .    .    .    37    E32 Roe 2           4
   The cold of Mosco, and fat Irish ayre,    .    .    .    .    37    E32 Roe 2           5
   His often change of clime (though not of mind)    .    .    37    E32 Roe 2           6
   Who wets my grave, can be no friend of mine.    .    .    37    E33 Roe 3           6
   Of Death.    .    .    .    .    .    .    .    .    .    37    E34 Death         Ttl
   Shewes of the resurrection little trust.    .    .    .    .    37    E34 Death           2
   And in this short time of thy happiest raigne,    .    .    38    E35 James 2         4
   Left us of feare, but first our crimes, then lawes.    .    .    38    E35 James 2         6
```

OF (cont.)

	Page	Title	Line
To the Ghost of Martial.	38	E36 Martial	Ttl
Life, whose griefe was out of fashion,	39	E40 Ratcliffe	13
And having got him out of doores is glad.	40	E42 Giles	7
Of his begetting. And so sweares his Jone.	40	E42 Giles	14
The selfe-same things, a note of concord be:	40	E42 Giles	17
To Robert Earle of Salisburie.	40	E43 Salisbury 1	Ttl
To the most Worthy of his Honors. Robert, . . .	40	E43 Salisbury 1	VTtl
What need hast thou of me? or of my Muse?	40	E43 Salisbury 1	1
'Tofore, great men were glad of Poets: Now,	40	E43 Salisbury 1	5
I, not the worst, am covetous of thee.	40	E43 Salisbury 1	6
Of adding to thy fame; thine may to me,	41	E43 Salisbury 1	8
Of adding to thy prayse; thine may to me,	41	E43 Salisbury 1	V 8
As thou stand'st cleere of the necessitie.	41	E43 Salisbury 1	12
Farewell, thou child of my right hand, and joy;	41	E45 First Son	1
My sinne was too much hope of thee, lov'd boy,	41	E45 First Son	2
Ben. Jonson his best piece of poetrie.	41	E45 First Son	10
To pay at's day of marriage. By my hand	42	E46 Luckless 1	4
Of bearing them in field, he threw 'hem away:	42	E48 Mungril	2
He sayes, I want the tongue of Epigrammes;	42	E49 Playwrt 1	2
To King James. Upon the happy false rumour of his death, . . .	43	E51 James 3	Ttl
And farre beneath least pause of such a king,	43	E51 James 3	4
For, but thy selfe, where, out of motly, 's hee	44	E53 Old-end	9
Whose workes are eene the fripperie of wit,	44	E56 Poet-Ape	2
Buy the reversion of old playes; now growne	45	E56 Poet-Ape	6
And, told of this, he slights it. Tut, such crimes	45	E56 Poet-Ape	9
From locks of wooll, or shreds from the whole peece?	45	E56 Poet-Ape	14
Baudrie', and usurie were one kind of game.	45	E57 Bawds	2
Spies, you are lights in state, but of base stuffe,	45	E59 Spies	1
I, that am glad of thy great chance, here doo!	46	E60 Mounteagle	5
But saver of my countrey thee alone.	46	E60 Mounteagle	10
And there's both losse of time, and losse of sport	46	E62 Would-bee	10
Of the not borne, yet buried, here's the tombe.	46	E62 Would-bee	12
To Robert Earle of Salisburie.	47	E63 Salisbury 2	Ttl
The judgement of the king so shine in thee;	47	E63 Salisbury 2	4
And that thou seek'st reward of thy each act,	47	E63 Salisbury 2	5
By constant suffring of thy equall mind;	47	E63 Salisbury 2	8
Of love, and what the golden age did hold	47	E64 Salisbury 3	3
A treasure, art: contemn'd in th'age of gold.	47	E64 Salisbury 3	4
Of flatterie to thy titles. Nor of wit.	47	E64 Salisbury 3	8
I'have sung the greater fortunes of our state.	48	E64 Salisbury 3	18
Who, to upbraid the sloth of this our time,	48	E66 Cary	5
Love honors, which of best example bee,	49	E66 Cary	13
To Thomas Earle of Suffolke.	49	E67 Suffolk	Ttl
Stand high, then, Howard, high in eyes of men,	49	E67 Suffolk	5
Play-wright convict of publike wrongs to men,	49	E68 Playwrt 2	1
Two kindes of valour he doth shew, at ones;	49	E68 Playwrt 2	3
Each best day of our life escapes us, first.	50	E70 Wm Roe 1	6
And know thee, then, a judge, not of one yeare;	51	E74 Chancelor	2
On Lucy Countesse of Bedford.	52	E76 Bedford 1	Ttl
What kinde of creature I could most desire,	52	E76 Bedford 1	3
Of greatest bloud, and yet more good then great;	52	E76 Bedford 1	6
Hating that solemne vice of greatnesse, pride;	52	E76 Bedford 1	10
Of destinie, and spin her owne free houres.	52	E76 Bedford 1	16
To Elizabeth Countesse of Rutland.	53	E79 Rutland	Ttl
(Save that most masculine issue of his braine)	53	E79 Rutland	6
Of Life, and Death.	53	E80 Life/Death	Ttl
The ports of death are sinnes; of life, good deeds:	53	E80 Life/Death	1
And here, it should be one of our first strifes,	54	E80 Life/Death	6
To be the wealthy witnesse of my pen:	54	E81 Proule	4
To Lucy Countesse of Bedford.	54	E84 Bedford 2	Ttl
My selfe a witnesse of thy few dayes sport:	55	E85 Goodyere 1	2
Upon thy wel-made choise of friends, and bookes:	55	E86 Goodyere 2	2
Touch'd with the sinne of false play, in his punque,	56	E87 Hazard	1
Of what shee had wrought came in, and wak'd his braine,	56	E87 Hazard	4
That so much skarfe of France, and hat, and fether,	56	E88 Monsieur	3
Fear'd not to boast the glories of her stage,	56	E89 Allen	2
Who had no lesse a trumpet of their name,	57	E89 Allen	5
Discern'd no difference of his yeeres, or play,	57	E90 Mill	7
And he remov'd to gent'man of the horse,	57	E90 Mill	12
Which of thy names I take, not onely beares	58	E91 Vere	1
In th'eye of Europe, where thy deeds were done,	58	E91 Vere	6
Unto the cryes of London Ile adde one;	58	E92 New Crie	2
And have'hem yeeld no savour, but of state.	58	E92 New Crie	5
They know the states of Christendome, not the places:	59	E92 New Crie	8
And talke reserv'd, lock'd up, and full of feare,	59	E92 New Crie	17
Or Bils, and there he buyes the names of books.	59	E92 New Crie	24
With juyce of limons, onions, pisse, to write.	59	E92 New Crie	28
And of the poulder-plot, they will talke yet.	59	E92 New Crie	32
For the great marke of vertue, those being gone	60	E93 Radcliffe	2
To Lucy, Countesse of Bedford, with Mr. Donnes Satyres.	60	E94 Bedford 3	Ttl
Lucy, you brightnesse of our spheare, who are	60	E94 Bedford 3	1
Life of the Muses day, their morning-starre!	60	E94 Bedford 3	2
Yet, Satyres, since the most of mankind bee	60	E94 Bedford 3	7
Be of the best: and 'mongst those, best are you.	61	E94 Bedford 3	14
Lucy, you brightnesse of our spheare, who are	61	E94 Bedford 3	15
That stranger doctrine of Pythagoras,	61	E95 Savile	2
I should beleeve, the soule of Tacitus	61	E95 Savile	3
And all his numbers, both of sense, and sounds.	61	E95 Savile	6
That hast thy brest so cleere of present crimes,	61	E95 Savile	19
Thou need'st not shrinke at voyce of after-times;	61	E95 Savile	20
Of historie, and how to apt their places;	61	E95 Savile	28
We need a man, can speake of the intents,	62	E95 Savile	31

	Page	Title	Line
OF (cont.)			
Of state, and censure them: we need his pen	62	E95 Savile	33
Of any Madames, hath neadd squires, and must.	63	E97 Motion	14
Nor did the king of Denmarke him salute,	63	E97 Motion	15
With thine owne course the judgement of thy friend,	63	E98 Th Roe 1	8
How much of great example wert thou, Roe,	64	E99 Th Roe 2	5
But much it now availes, what's done, of whom:	64	E99 Th Roe 2	7
Cry'd to my face, they were th'elixir of wit:	64	E100 Playwrt 3	2
Five of my jests, then stolne, past him a play.	64	E100 Playwrt 3	4
If we can get her, full of egs, and then,	64	E101 Supper	12
Is not to be despair'd of, for our money;	65	E101 Supper	14
Ile tell you of more, and lye, so you will come:	65	E101 Supper	17
Of partrich, pheasant, wood-cock, of which some	65	E101 Supper	18
Shall reade a piece of Virgil, Tacitus,	65	E101 Supper	21
Livie, or of some better booke to us,	65	E101 Supper	22
Of which wee'll speake our minds, amidst our meate;	65	E101 Supper	23
To this, if ought appeare, which I not know of,	65	E101 Supper	25
That will the pastrie, not my paper, show of.	65	E101 Supper	26
Is a pure cup of rich Canary-wine,	65	E101 Supper	29
Of which had Horace, or Anacreon tasted,	65	E101 Supper	31
Of this we will sup free, but moderately,	65	E101 Supper	35
To William Earle of Pembroke.	66	E102 Pembroke	Ttl
Against the bad, but of, and to the good:	66	E102 Pembroke	3
Of vice, and vertue; wherein all great life	66	E102 Pembroke	6
To which, yet, of the sides himselfe he owes.	66	E102 Pembroke	8
Of what ambition, faction, pride can raise;	66	E102 Pembroke	15
How well, faire crowne of your faire sexe, might hee,	66	E103 L Wroth 1	1
That but the twi-light of your sprite did see,	66	E103 L Wroth 1	2
Which is, it selfe, the imprese of the great,	66	E103 L Wroth 1	7
And glorie of them all, but to repeate!	66	E103 L Wroth 1	8
To Susan Countesse of Montgomery.	67	E104 Montgomery	Ttl
Even in the dew of grace, what you would bee?	67	E104 Montgomery	2
Of birth, of match, of forme, of chastitie?	67	E104 Montgomery	8
Of former age, or glorie of our one,	67	E104 Montgomery	10
Least mention of a Nymph, a Muse, a Grace,	67	E105 L Wroth 2	4
I' your selfe, all treasure lost of th'age before.	68	E105 L Wroth 2	20
Tell the grosse Dutch those grosser tales of yours,	68	E107 Hungry	5
Of your Moravian horse, Venetian bull.	69	E107 Hungry	8
That are your wordes of credit. Keepe your Names	69	E107 Hungry	24
Of Hannow, Shieter-huissen, Popenheim,	69	E107 Hungry	25
For your next meale: this you are sure of. Why	69	E107 Hungry	27
Strength of my Countrey, whilst I bring to view	69	E108 Soldiers	1
Of service to the publique, when the end	70	E109 Nevil	7
And elements of honor, then the dresse;	70	E109 Nevil	10
Now I have sung thee thus, shall judge of thee.	70	E109 Nevil	16
The name of Pompey for an enemie,	71	E110 Edmonds 1	3
Nor that his worke liv'd in the hands of foes,	71	E110 Edmonds 1	9
Action, or engine, worth a note of thine,	71	E110 Edmonds 1	20
Beholding, to this master of the warre;	72	E111 Edmonds 2	4
Beholden, to this master of the warre;	72	E111 Edmonds 2 V	4
So Phoebus makes me worthy of his bayes,	73	E113 Overbury	1
I thinke, the Fate of court thy comming crav'd,	73	E113 Overbury	5
Repent thee not of thy faire precedent,	73	E113 Overbury	9
Nor may'any feare, to loose of their degree,	73	E113 Overbury	11
Of newes, and noyse, to strow out a long meale.	74	E115 Honest Man	10
Of newes, and noyse, to sow out a long meale.	74	E115 Honest Man V	10
Doe all, that longs to the anarchy of drinke,	74	E115 Honest Man	12
Give every one his dose of mirth: and watches	74	E115 Honest Man	14
Tell's of him, all the tales, it selfe then makes;	74	E115 Honest Man	17
And, shifting of it's faces, doth play more	74	E115 Honest Man	25
Of miming, gets th'opinion of a wit.	74	E115 Honest Man	28
An inginer, in slanders, of all fashions,	75	E115 Honest Man	31
Jephson, thou man of men, to whose lov'd name	75	E116 Jephson	1
All gentrie, yet, owe part of their best flame!	75	E116 Jephson	2
Groyne, come of age, his state sold out of hand	75	E117 Groyne	1
He makes himselfe a thorough-fare of vice.	76	E118 Gut	4
Not he that flies the court for want of clothes,	76	E119 Shelton	1
But dost it out of judgement, not disease;	76	E119 Shelton	8
Epitaph on S. P. a Child of Q. El. Chappel.	77	E120 S. P.	Ttl
Shee learnes to know long difference of their states.	78	E121 Rudyerd 1	4
Of the best writer, and judge, should emulate.	78	E123 Rudyerd 3	4
Uv'dale, thou piece of the first times, a man	79	E125 Uvedale	1
'Mongst Hampton shades, and Phoebus grove of bayes,	80	E126 Mrs Cary	2
How full of want, how swallow'd up, how dead	80	E127 Aubigny	6
T'extract, and choose the best of all these knowne,	80	E128 Wm Roe 2	3
May windes as soft as breath of kissing friends,	81	E128 Wm Roe 2	5
That, not a paire of friends each other see,	81	E129 Mime	1
O, runne not proud of this. Yet, take thy due.	81	E129 Mime	15
Of building townes, and making wilde beasts tame,	82	E130 Ferrab. 1	2
Of old, even by her practise, to be fam'd;	82	E130 Ferrab. 1	10
To say, indeed, shee were but praises of heaven,	82	E130 Ferrab. 1	11
When these were but the praises of the Art.	82	E130 Ferrab. 1	16
But when I have said, The proofes of all these bee	82	E130 Ferrab. 1	17
Shed in thy Songs; 'tis true: but short of thee.	82	E130 Ferrab. 1	18
A worke of ours, we part with our owne right;	82	E131 Ferrab. 2	2
But, as it is (the Child of Ignorance,	83	E132 Sylvester	3
And utter stranger to all ayre of France)	83	E132 Sylvester	4
How can I speake of thy great paines, but erre?	83	E132 Sylvester	5
Behold! the reverend shade of Bartas stands	83	E132 Sylvester	7
Of Hercules, or Theseus going to hell,	84	E133 Voyage	2
With tales of Troyes just knight, our faiths abuse:	84	E133 Voyage	4
All, that they boast of Styx, of Acheron,	84	E133 Voyage	7
Arses were heard to croake, in stead of frogs;	84	E133 Voyage	13

459

OF (cont.)

	Page	Title	Line
And, for the cryes of Ghosts, women, and men,	84	E133 Voyage	16
I Sing the brave adventure of two wights,	84	E133 Voyage	21
To have beene stiled of King Arthurs table.	84	E133 Voyage	24
The other was a squire, of faire degree;	84	E133 Voyage	25
Of those, that put out moneyes, on returne	85	E133 Voyage	32
Of sixe times to, and fro, without embassage,	85	E133 Voyage	34
Of some Bride-well, and may, in time, concerne us	85	E133 Voyage	42
The many perills of this Port, and how	85	E133 Voyage	47
Sans helpe of Sybil, or a golden bough,	85	E133 Voyage	48
Of all your night-tubs, when the carts doe cluster,	85	E133 Voyage	64
The least of which was to the plague a cosen.	86	E133 Voyage	72
Ploughing the mayne. When, see (the worst of all lucks)	86	E133 Voyage	78
Man, that had never heard of a Chimaera.	86	E133 Voyage	80
Made of the trull, that cut her fathers lock:	86	E133 Voyage	84
Backe, cry'd their brace of Charons: they cry'd, no,	86	E133 Voyage	87
Is this we heare? of frogs? No, guts wind-bound,	86	E133 Voyage	92
For (where he was the god of eloquence,	86	E133 Voyage	99
And subtiltie of mettalls) they dispense	86	E133 Voyage	100
Of the grave fart, late let in parliament,	87	E133 Voyage	108
Of the hulke touch'd, and, as by Polypheme	87	E133 Voyage	112
The meate-boate of Beares colledge, Paris-garden,	87	E133 Voyage	117
Of worship, they their nodding chinnes doe hit	87	E133 Voyage	123
About the shore, of farts, but late departed,	87	E133 Voyage	125
These be the cause of those thicke frequent mists	87	E133 Voyage	130
Must trie the'un-used valour of a nose:	87	E133 Voyage	132
The sinkes ran grease, and haire of meazled hogs,	88	E133 Voyage	145
The heads, houghs, entrailes, and the hides of dogs:	88	E133 Voyage	146
Upon your eares, of discords so un-sweet?	88	E133 Voyage	171
And out-cryes of the damned in the Fleet?	88	E133 Voyage	172
Of loud Sepulchres with their hourely knells,	88	E133 Voyage	174
Of Hol'borne (three sergeants heads) lookes ore,	89	E133 Voyage	177
They tooke 'hem all to witnesse of their action:	89	E133 Voyage	191
In memorie of which most liquid deed,	89	E133 Voyage	193
Why I write not of Love.	93	F1 Why write no	Ttl
Some act of Love's bound to reherse,	93	F1 Why write no	1
Of touch, or marble; nor canst boast a row	93	F2 Penshurst	2
Of polish'd pillars, or a roofe of gold:	93	F2 Penshurst	3
Thou joy'st in better markes, of soyle, of ayre,	93	F2 Penshurst	7
Of wood, of water: therein thou art faire.	93	F2 Penshurst	8
That taller tree, which of a nut was set,	94	F2 Penshurst	13
Of many a Sylvane, taken with his flames,	94	F2 Penshurst	16
Thy copp's, too, nam'd of Gamage, thou hast there,	94	F2 Penshurst	19
Fertile of wood, Ashore, and Sydney's copp's,	94	F2 Penshurst	26
And though thy walls be of the countrey stone,	94	F2 Penshurst	45
An embleme of themselves, in plum, br peare.	95	F2 Penshurst	56
The neede of such? whose liberall boord doth flow,	95	F2 Penshurst	59
Without his feare, and of thy lords owne meate:	95	F2 Penshurst	62
He knowes, below, he shall finde plentie of meate,	95	F2 Penshurst	70
Of thy Penates had beene set on flame,	95	F2 Penshurst	79
The just reward of her high huswifery;	96	F2 Penshurst	85
The mysteries of manners, armes, and arts.	96	F2 Penshurst	98
To Sir Robert Wroth in praise of a Country life. Epode.	96	F3 Wroth	VTtl
Of Sheriffes dinner, or Majors feast.	96	F3 Wroth	6
Of Sergeants dinner, or sheriffes feast.	96	F3 Wroth	V 6
Nor com'st to view the better cloth of state;	96	F3 Wroth	7
Of the short braverie of the night;	96	F3 Wroth	10
Or with thy friends; the heart of all the yeere,	97	F3 Wroth	25
Or with thy friends; the heate of all the yeere,	97	F3 Wroth	V 25
To the full greatnesse of the cry:	97	F3 Wroth	32
Although the coldest of the yeere!	97	F3 Wroth	36
Of flowrie fields, of cop'ces greene,	97	F3 Wroth	38
The rout of rurall folke come thronging in,	98	F3 Wroth	53
And the great Heroes, of her race,	98	F3 Wroth	56
Sit mixt with losse of state, or reverence.	98	F3 Wroth	57
Such, and no other was that age, of old,	98	F3 Wroth	63
Which boasts t'have had the head of gold.	98	F3 Wroth	64
The furie of a rash command,	98	F3 Wroth	68
The furie of some rash command,	98	F3 Wroth	V 68
Let that goe heape a masse of wretched wealth,	99	F3 Wroth	81
That houre upon my morne of age,	100	F4 To the World	2
Of toyes, and trifles, traps, and snares,	100	F4 To the World	18
Enamor'd of their golden gyves?	100	F4 To the World	24
Where breathe the basest of thy fooles;	101	F4 To the World	46
While we may, the sports of love;	102	F5 Celia 1	2
While we can, the sports of love;	102	F5 Celia 1	V 2
Of a few poore houshold spyes?	102	F5 Celia 1	12
Stil'd but the shaddowes of us men?	104	F7 Women but	6
Stil'd but the shaddowes of us men?	104	F7 Women but	12
Ladies? and of them the best?	104	F8 Sicknesse	2
Doe not men, ynow of rites	104	F8 Sicknesse	3
Lying for the spirit of amber.	104	F8 Sicknesse	32
Lying on the spirit of amber.	105	F8 Sicknesse	V 32
That for th'oyle of Talke, dare spend	105	F8 Sicknesse	33
But might I of Jove's Nectar sup,	106	F9 Celia 3	7
But might I of love's Nectar sipp,	106	F9 Celia 3	V 7
Not of it selfe, but thee.	106	F9 Celia 3	16
Of his dull god-head, were sinne. Ile implore	107	F10 Proludium	6
Of his dull god-head, were sinne. Lets implore	107	F10 Proludium	V 6
Nor will I beg of thee, Lord of the vine,	107	F10 Proludium	10
Nor will we beg of thee, Lord of the vine,	107	F10 Proludium	V 10
In the greene circle of thy Ivy twine.	107	F10 Proludium	12
Nor all the ladies of the Thespian lake,	108	F10 Proludium	25

	Page	Title	Line

OF (cont.)

	Page	Title	Line
A beautie of that merit, that should take	108	F10 Proludium	27
The skilfull mischife of a rovinge Eye	108	F10 Proludium	5
Could ne'er make prize of thy white Chastetye.	108	F10 Proludium	6
in whom the flame of every beauty raignes,	108	F10 Proludium	8
which rap's mee up to the true heav'en of love;	108	F10 Proludium	13
the glories of yt. Now our muse takes winge,	108	F10 Proludium	15
Some way of entrance) we must plant a guard	109	F11 Epode	7
Of thoughts to watch, and ward	109	F11 Epode	8
Close, the close cause of it.	109	F11 Epode	16
Of which usurping rancke, some have thought love	110	F11 Epode	31
But this doth from the cloud of error grow,	110	F11 Epode	35
Inconstant, like the sea, of whence 'tis borne,	110	F11 Epode	39
Inconstant, as the sea, of whence 'tis borne,	110	F11 Epode	V 39
With whom who sailes, rides on the surge of feare,	110	F11 Epode	41
The'Elixir of all joyes?	110	F11 Epode	56
Would, at suggestion of a steepe desire,	111	F11 Epode	63
Of all his happinesse? But soft: I heare	111	F11 Epode	65
Peace, Luxurie, thou art like one of those	111	F11 Epode	69
Or those, who doubt the common mouth of fame,	111	F11 Epode	79
Or those, which doubt the common mouth of fame,	111	F11 Epode	V 79
He that for love of goodnesse hateth ill,	112	F11 Epode	87
A beautie of that cleere, and sparkling light,	112	F11 Epode	93
A beautie of that cleere, and sparkling sight,	112	F11 Epode	V 93
Would make a day of night,	112	F11 Epode	94
All taste of bitternesse, and makes the ayre	112	F11 Epode	97
The wealthy treasure of her love on him;	112	F11 Epode	105
The wealthy treasure of her love in him;	112	F11 Epode	V105
In the full floud of her admir'd perfection?	112	F11 Epode	107
Of this excelling frame?	112	F11 Epode	110
That knowes the waight of guilt: He will refraine	112	F11 Epode	113
From thoughts of such a straine.	112	F11 Epode	114
Epistle To Elizabeth Countesse of Rutland.	113	F12 Rutland	Ttl
To the Countesse of Rutland: An Elegie.	113	F12 Rutland	VTtl
Of some grand peere, whose ayre doth make rejoyce	113	F12 Rutland	12
The truth of times) was once of more esteeme,	114	F12 Rutland	21
Who made a lampe of Berenices hayre?	115	F12 Rutland	61
Of all Lucina's traine; Lucy the bright,	115	F12 Rutland	66
My gratefull soule, the subject of her powers,	115	F12 Rutland	73
My best of wishes, may you beare a sonne.	116	F12 Rutland	100
Of any good minde, now: There are so few.	116	F13 Aubigny	2
By arts, and practise of the vicious,	117	F13 Aubigny	12
Of Fortune, have not alter'd yet my looke,	117	F13 Aubigny	16
Of nature, and societie, I should faint;	117	F13 Aubigny	19
Or cos'ning farmer of the customes so,	117	F13 Aubigny	39
A Princes fortune: These are gifts of chance,	117	F13 Aubigny	41
And takes, and gives the beauties of the mind.	117	F13 Aubigny	44
Though it reject not those of Fortune: such	117	F13 Aubigny	45
Of so great title, birth, but vertue most,	118	F13 Aubigny	49
This blessing of your starres, then by that way	118	F13 Aubigny	54
Of vertue, which you tread? what if alone?	118	F13 Aubigny	55
Farre from the maze of custome, error, strife,	118	F13 Aubigny	60
Whereon the most of mankinde wracke themselves,	119	F13 Aubigny	90
Of your blest wombe, made fruitfull from above,	119	F13 Aubigny	95
To pay your lord the pledges of chast love;	119	F13 Aubigny	96
T'expect the honors of great 'Aubigny:	119	F13 Aubigny	105
Onely, thus much, out of a ravish'd zeale,	119	F13 Aubigny	108
Unto your name, and goodnesse of your life,	119	F13 Aubigny	109
Both love the cause, and authors of the feast?	120	F14 Sydney	10
Of these forc'd joyes,	120	F14 Sydney	18
This day sayes, then, the number of glad yeeres	120	F14 Sydney	21
Of going backe	121	F14 Sydney	28
Nor can a little of the common store,	121	F14 Sydney	31
Of nobles vertue, shew in you;	121	F14 Sydney	32
With dust of ancestors, in graves but dwell.	121	F14 Sydney	40
'T will be exacted of your name, whose sonne,	121	F14 Sydney	41
Of love be bright,	121	F14 Sydney	57
Of bone-fires. Then	121	F14 Sydney	59
Good, and great God, can I not thinke of thee,	122	F15 Heaven	1
And hearts of all, if I be sad for show,	122	F15 Heaven	6
I know my state, both full of shame, and scorne,	122	F15 Heaven	17
Of discontent; or that these prayers bee	122	F15 Heaven	25
For wearinesse of life, not love of thee.	122	F15 Heaven	26
Under-woods. Consisting Of Divers Poems.	125	Under-wood	Ttl
I. Poems Of Devotion.	127	Under-wood	Ttl
Of persons, still one God, in Unitie,	127	U1 Trinitie	2
But 'bove the fat of rammes, or bulls, to prize	127	U1 Trinitie	11
This All of nothing, gavest it forme, and fate,	127	U1 Trinitie	18
For acts of grace.	128	U1 Trinitie	28
Of persons, still one God in Unitie;	128	U1 Trinitie	30
of seeing your face.	128	U1 Trinitie	32
First made of nought,	129	U1 Father	21
3. A Hymne On the Nativitie of my Saviour.	130	U1 Nativitie	Ttl
The Author both of Life, and light;	130	U1 Nativitie	2
The Sonne of God, th'Eternall King,	130	U1 Nativitie	7
Who made himselfe the price of sinne,	130	U1 Nativitie	20
To make us heires of glory!	130	U1 Nativitie	21
A Celebration of Charis in ten Lyrick Peeces.	131	U2 Charis	Ttl
Of whose Beautie it was sung,	131	U2 Excuse	19
Marke of glorie, come with me;	131	U2 How he saw	8
Mock'd of all: and call'd of one	132	U2 How he saw	28
Mee, the scope of his next draught,	132	U2 Suffered	11
She repented of the deed,	133	U2 Suffered	18

	Page	Title	Line

OF (cont.)

	Page	Title	Line
See the Chariot at hand here of Love,	134	U2 Triumph	1
All the Gaine, all the Good, of the Elements strife.	134	U2 Triumph	20
Heare, what late Discourse of you,	136	U2 Cupid	5
Of her face, and made to rise,	136	U2 Cupid	15
In her cheekes, of Milke, and Roses;	136	U2 Cupid	22
Have you plac'd the banke of kisses,	136	U2 Cupid	25
Is my Mothers! Hearts of slaine	137	U2 Cupid	31
Of her good, who is the best	137	U2 Cupid	44
Of her Sex; But could'st thou, Love,	137	U2 Cupid	45
With th'advantage of her haire,	138	U2 Kisse	10
Of th'Assembly, as did you!	138	U2 Kisse	12
Of the Court, to day, then all	138	U2 Kisse	15
Of your Peeres, you were beheld,	138	U2 Kisse	23
To be envi'd of the Queene.	138	U2 Kisse	28
To himselfe his losse of Time;	138	U2 Kisse	31
Or have charg'd his sight of Crime,	138	U2 Kisse	32
Guesse of these, which is the true;	138	U2 Kisse	34
7. Begging another, on colour of mending the former.	139	U2 Another	Ttl
8. Urging her of a promise.	139	U2 Promise	Ttl
Had of Love, and of his force,	139	U2 Promise	2
All your sweet of life is past,	140	U2 Promise	28
Of your Trouble, Ben, to ease me,	140	U2 Her man	1
Noble; or of greater Blood:	140	U2 Her man	4
Noble; or of greatest Blood:	140	U2 Her man	V 4
And his Manners of that Nation.	141	U2 Her man	8
Gold, upon a ground of black.	141	U2 Her man	14
Front, an ample field of snow:	141	U2 Her man	18
'Twere to long, to speake of all:	141	U2 Her man	33
But of one, if short he came,	142	U2 Her man	55
Till each of us be made a Starre,	143	U3 Musicall	3
Till each of us is made a Starre,	143	U3 Musicall	V 3
Of reason emptie is?!	143	U3 Musicall	6
What need of mee? doe you but sing,	143	U3 Musicall	13
And out of inward pleasure feed	144	U3 Musicall	19
And out of inward passion feed	144	U3 Musicall	V 19
Of Angels should be driven	144	U3 Musicall	22
So they in state of Grace retain'd,	144	U3 Musicall	27
May wish us of their Quire.	144	U3 Musicall	28
In the person of Woman-kind. A Song Apologetique.	145	U5 Woman-kind	Ttl
And if wee must, let's sing of you.	145	U5 Woman-kind	6
Wee shall, at last, of parcells make	145	U5 Woman-kind	11
Another. In defence of their Inconstancie. A Song.	146	U6 Defence	Ttl
That talke abroad of Womans change,	146	U6 Defence	2
The frequent varying of the deed,	146	U6 Defence	11
And this profession of a store	146	U6 Defence	19
And of them pittied be,	147	U7 Nymph	11
And feare much more, that more of him be showne.	147	U7 Nymph	21
Of one that lov'd?	148	U8 Houre-glasse	6
Even ashes of lovers find no rest.	149	U8 Houre-glasse	11
In sentence, of as subtile feet,	149	U9 Picture	8
In numbers, of as subtile feet,	149	U9 Picture	V 8
That sits in shadow of Apollo's tree.	149	U9 Picture	10
My hundred of gray haires,	150	U9 Picture	14
I ne're was of thy kind;	150	U10 Jealousie	3
But under the Disguise of love,	150	U10 Jealousie	9
Loves sicknesse, and his noted want of worth,	150	U10 Jealousie	14
Of sleepe againe, who was his Aid;	151	U11 Dreame	12
Of him whose bones this Grave doth gather:	151	U12 Corbet	6
With the just Canon of his life,	151	U12 Corbet	11
So of uncleannesse, or offence,	152	U12 Corbet	17
An Epistle to Sir Edward Sacvile, now Earle of Dorset.	153	U13 Sacvile	Ttl
Lesse list of proud, hard, or ingratefull Men.	153	U13 Sacvile	4
Deepest in Man, of which when he doth thinke,	153	U13 Sacvile	20
Himselfe of farther trouble, or the weight	154	U13 Sacvile	31
Of pressure, like one taken in a streight?	154	U13 Sacvile	32
Run from the Conscience of it, if they could.	154	U13 Sacvile	46
As I have seene some Infants of the Sword,	154	U13 Sacvile	47
And speaking worst of those, from whom they went	154	U13 Sacvile	51
Still, still, the hunters of false fame apply	155	U13 Sacvile	65
Of any, is a great and generous Deed:	155	U13 Sacvile	76
Yea, of th'ingratefull: and he forth must tell	155	U13 Sacvile	77
Of our Towne Gallantry! or why there rests	155	U13 Sacvile	92
Such worship due to kicking of a Punck!	155	U13 Sacvile	93
Or feats of darknesse acted in Mid-Sun,	156	U13 Sacvile	95
And told of with more License then th'were done!	156	U13 Sacvile	96
Lowd sacrifice of drinke, for their health-sake!	156	U13 Sacvile	100
Of Valour, but at this Idolatrous rate?	156	U13 Sacvile	104
Or appetite of offending, but a skill,	156	U13 Sacvile	107
Or Science of discerning Good and Ill.	156	U13 Sacvile	108
No more are these of us, let them then goe,	156	U13 Sacvile	113
I have the lyst of mine owne faults to know,	156	U13 Sacvile	114
Or growne; by height or lowenesse of the Sunne?	156	U13 Sacvile	119
And can I lesse of substance? When I runne,	156	U13 Sacvile	120
Of Christendome! And neither of these know,	157	U13 Sacvile	129
Are Dwarfes of Honour, and have neither weight	157	U13 Sacvile	147
Aloft, grow lesse and streightned, full of knot;	157	U13 Sacvile	152
To aske it: though in most of workes it be	158	U14 Selden	7
Of this so vitious Humanitie.	158	U14 Selden	12
A many of bookes, even good judgements wound	159	U14 Selden	15
Of generall knowledge; watch'd men, manners too,	159	U14 Selden	33
Of Gathering? Bountie' in pouring out againe?	159	U14 Selden	38
Records, and Authors of! how rectified	160	U14 Selden	43

462

OF (cont.)

	Page	Title	Line
And then of times (besides the bare Conduct	160	U14 Selden	51
Of what it tells us) weav'd in to instruct.	160	U14 Selden	52
To marke the excellent seas'ning of your Stile!	160	U14 Selden	55
In sharpnesse of all Search, wisdome of Choise,	160	U14 Selden	59
Newnesse of Sense, Antiquitie of voyce!	160	U14 Selden	60
I yeeld, I yeeld, the matter of your praise	160	U14 Selden	61
Large claspe of Nature, such a wit can bound.	160	U14 Selden	64
Of others honours, thus, enjoy thine owne.	160	U14 Selden	66
Of others honours, thus, enjoy their owne.	160	U14 Selden	V 66
With that thy Stile, thy keeping of thy State,	161	U14 Selden	68
In the same Mines of knowledge; and thence brought	161	U14 Selden	76
In the rich Mines of knowledge; and thence brought	161	U14 Selden	V 76
The Gaine of your two friendships! Hayward and	161	U14 Selden	81
The Graine of your two friendships! Hayward and	161	U14 Selden	V 81
All other Acts of Worldlings, are but toyle	162	U15 Friend-Wars	9
All other Acts of Worldlings, are meere toyle	162	U15 Friend-Wars	V 9
Bought Flatteries, the issue of his purse,	162	U15 Friend-Wars	13
And being a thing, blowne out of nought, rebells	163	U15 Friend-Wars	32
And impious ranknesse of all Sects and seeds:	163	U15 Friend-Wars	34
All which he makes the servants of the Groine,	163	U15 Friend-Wars	46
Of lust, to his rich Suit and Title, Lord?	163	U15 Friend-Wars	51
Hee's one of blood, and fashion! and with these	164	U15 Friend-Wars	55
And jealous each of other, yet thinke long	164	U15 Friend-Wars	73
Doe all the tricks of a saut Lady Bitch;	164	U15 Friend-Wars	76
For t'other pound of sweet-meats, he shall feele	164	U15 Friend-Wars	77
Of woman of fashion, and a Lady of spirit:	164	U15 Friend-Wars	82
A fellow of course Letcherie, is nam'd,	165	U15 Friend-Wars	98
The Servant of the Serving-woman, in scorne,	165	U15 Friend-Wars	99
What furie of late is crept into our Feasts?	166	U15 Friend-Wars	117
When oft the Bearer, is borne out of dore?	166	U15 Friend-Wars	120
Of what he throwes: Like letchers growne content	166	U15 Friend-Wars	139
In this, and like, an itch of Vanitie,	166	U15 Friend-Wars	143
To lose the formes, and dignities of men,	166	U15 Friend-Wars	146
For the recovery of my voyce? No, there	167	U15 Friend-Wars	154
Informers, Masters both of Arts and lies;	167	U15 Friend-Wars	164
Of the poore sufferers) where the envious, proud,	167	U15 Friend-Wars	167
Praevaricators swarme. Of which the store,	167	U15 Friend-Wars	170
Though thou wert Muster-master of the Land.	167	U15 Friend-Wars	174
Still pretious, with the odour of thy name.	168	U15 Friend-Wars	190
Who falls for love of God, shall rise a Starre.	168	U15 Friend-Wars	196
All that is left of Philip Gray,	168	U16 Gray	4
What suretie of life have thou, and I?	168	U16 Gray	7
And lastly by your lips, the banke of kisses,	170	U19 Elegy By	9
Of all that can be done him; Such a one	171	U19 Elegy By	23
His Issue, and all Circumstance of life,	171	U19 Elegy By	26
Or have the least of Good, but what it must	171	U20 Shrub	7
Of many Colours; outward fresh, from spots,	171	U20 Shrub	11
But their whole inside full of ends, and knots?	171	U20 Shrub	12
Thinke but the Sin of all her sex, 'tis she!	172	U20 Shrub	20
The Divell; and be the damning of us all.	172	U20 Shrub	24
Out of his Grave, and poyson every eare.	172	U21 Ltl Shrub	4
A parcell of Court-durt, a heape, and masse	172	U21 Ltl Shrub	5
Of all vice hurld together, there he was,	172	U21 Ltl Shrub	6
Of putrid flesh alive! of blood, the sinke!	172	U21 Ltl Shrub	9
Though Beautie be the Marke of praise,	173	U22 Elegy Tho	1
And yours of whom I sing be such	173	U22 Elegy Tho	2
This subjects you to love of one.	173	U22 Elegy Tho	8
'Tis of your selfe, and that you use	173	U22 Elegy Tho	10
One sparke of your Diviner heat	174	U22 Elegy Tho	31
To light upon a Love of mine.	174	U22 Elegy Tho	32
Of worded Balladrie,	175	U23 Himselfe	21
Who aided him, will thee, the issue of Joves braine.	175	U23 Himselfe	30
Who aided them, will thee, the issue of Joves braine.	175	U23 Himselfe	V 30
The mind of the Frontispice to a Booke.	175	U24 Frontispice	Ttl
The Minde of the Front	175	U24 Frontispice	VTtl
The Mistresse of Mans life, grave Historie.	175	U24 Frontispice	2
Of Truth that searcheth the most hidden Springs,	176	U24 Frontispice	10
Of Truth which searcheth the most hidden Springs,	176	U24 Frontispice	V 10
Doth mete, whose lyne doth sound the depth of things:)	176	U24 Frontispice	12
Some note of which each varied Pillar beares,	176	U24 Frontispice	15
Times witnesse, herald of Antiquitie,	176	U24 Frontispice	17
The light of Truth, and life of Memorie.	176	U24 Frontispice	18
An Ode to James Earle of Desmond, writ . . .	176	U25 Desmond	Ttl
Wake, and put on the wings of Pindars Muse,	176	U25 Desmond	3
Her upright head, above the reach of Chance,	176	U25 Desmond	6
Rich beame of honour, shed your light	177	U25 Desmond	14
Breake the knit Circle of her Stonie Armes,	177	U25 Desmond	19
Of eyes more true,	177	U25 Desmond	23
Of politique pretext, that wryes a State,	177	U25 Desmond	29
Of politique pretext, that swayes a State,	177	U25 Desmond	V 29
Of such as savour	177	U25 Desmond	34
The Cure of that, which is but corporall,	180	U26 Ode High	5
And now are out of sight.	180	U26 Ode High	8
To doe, then be a husband of that store.	180	U26 Ode High	18
Thy beauties, yet could write of thee?	181	U27 Ode Helen	2
Of Phaos forme? or doth the Boy	181	U27 Ode Helen	5
Of Caesars Daughter, and the line	181	U27 Ode Helen	19
Which all the Fate of Troy foretold?	181	U27 Ode Helen	24
Though I, in working of my song,	182	U27 Ode Helen	33
Come short of all this learned throng,	182	U27 Ode Helen	34
A Fit of Rime against Rime.	183	U29 Fit of Rime	Ttl
Rime, the rack of finest wits,	183	U29 Fit of Rime	1

OF (cont.)

	Page	Title	Line
Spoyling Senses of their Treasure,	183	U29 Fit of Rime	4
Propping Verse, for feare of falling	183	U29 Fit of Rime	8
Whilst the Latin, Queene of Tongues,	184	U29 Fit of Rime	34
Of true measure,	184	U29 Fit of Rime	45
. . . Lo: high Treasurer of England.	185	U30 Burleigh	Ttl
If thou wouldst know the vertues of Man-kind,	185	U30 Burleigh	1
Of all the Land. Who now at such a Rate,	185	U30 Burleigh	19
Of divine blessing, would not serve a State?	185	U30 Burleigh	20
The Care, and wish still of the publike wealth:	186	U31 Elsmere	6
Still flie about the Odour of your Name;	186	U31 Elsmere	8
As with the safetie, and honour of the Lawes,	186	U31 Elsmere	9
When a good Cause is destitute of friends,	186	U32 Elsmere	2
Without the pompe of Counsell; or more Aide,	186	U32 Elsmere	3
A right by the prosperitie of their Crimes;	186	U32 Elsmere	10
They will come of, and scape the Punishment.	186	U32 Elsmere	14
The Seat made of a more then civill warre;	186	U33 Councellour	2
Of hirelings, wranglers, stitchers-to of strife,	187	U33 Councellour	8
What use, what strength of reason! and how much	187	U33 Councellour	24
Of Bookes, of Presidents, hast thou at hand!	187	U33 Councellour	25
Of Argument, still drawing forth the best,	187	U33 Councellour	27
Of those that set by their false faces more	188	U34 Small Poxe	4
Or Turners oyle of Talck. Nor ever got	188	U34 Small Poxe	11
Of Beautie, so to nullifie a face,	188	U34 Small Poxe	14
And, till the coming of the Soule	188	U35 Chute	5
Their vice of loving for a Christmasse fit;	190	U37 Friend-Book	8
Which is indeed but friendship of the spit:	190	U37 Friend-Book	9
It is an Act of tyrannie, not love,	190	U37 Friend-Book	25
From each of which I labour to be free,	190	U37 Friend-Book	28
For no man lives so out of passions sway,	190	U37 Friend-Book	31
Of Credit lost. And I am now run madde:	191	U38 Elegy 'Tis	2
There may some face or menace of a storme	191	U38 Elegy 'Tis	13
Of Graces, or your mercie here in me,	191	U38 Elegy 'Tis	16
Or in confessing of the Crime be nice,	191	U38 Elegy 'Tis	23
The Subject of your Grace in pardoning me,	191	U38 Elegy 'Tis	28
Nothing is vile, that is a part of you:	192	U38 Elegy 'Tis	36
Of your compassion; Parents should be mild:	192	U38 Elegy 'Tis	40
That as the last of punishments is meant;	192	U38 Elegy 'Tis	43
Of that wise Nature would a Cradle have.	192	U38 Elegy 'Tis	60
He pardons slips, goes by a world of ills,	193	U38 Elegy 'Tis	69
The name of Cruell weather, storme, and raine?	193	U38 Elegy 'Tis	82
Of crueltie, lest they doe make you such.	193	U38 Elegy 'Tis	84
But view the mildnesse of your Makers state,	193	U38 Elegy 'Tis	85
The wit of Ale, and Genius of the Malt	193	U38 Elegy 'Tis	95
I number these as being of the Chore	193	U38 Elegy 'Tis	99
Of Contumelie, and urge a good man more	193	U38 Elegy 'Tis	100
Then sword, or fire, or what is of the race	193	U38 Elegy 'Tis	101
How much you are the better part of me;	194	U38 Elegy 'Tis	110
Out of your eyes, and be awhile away;	194	U38 Elegy 'Tis	115
Till the sower Minute comes of taking leave,	197	U40 Elegy That	2
In hast the bottome of a med'cin'd Cup,	197	U40 Elegy That	4
Of parting, drowne it in the hope to meet	197	U40 Elegy That	7
And turne the Ceremonies of those Nights	197	U40 Elegy That	11
Of vowes so sacred, and in silence made;	197	U40 Elegy That	14
The Jewell of your name, as close as sleepe	198	U40 Elegy That	42
Weaknesse of braine, or any charme of Wine,	198	U40 Elegy That	45
The sinne of Boast, or other countermine	198	U40 Elegy That	46
Be idle words, though of a parting Man;	199	U41 Elegy Since	4
Of me, I'le softly tread unto my Tombe;	199	U41 Elegy Since	20
Of beautie; but the Muse hath interest in:	200	U42 Elegy Let	15
And braveries of Court, and felt their fits	200	U42 Elegy Let	34
Of love, and hate: and came so nigh to know	200	U42 Elegy Let	35
Her presently? Or leape thy Wife of force,	201	U42 Elegy Let	44
A Gowne of that, was the Caparison?	201	U42 Elegy Let	46
That are like cloath'd: must I be of those fooles	201	U42 Elegy Let	48
Of race accompted, that no passion have	201	U42 Elegy Let	49
He would have done in some, with any of those	201	U42 Elegy Let	62
Such Songsters there are store of; witnesse he	201	U42 Elegy Let	65
Varietie of Silkes were on th'Exchange!	202	U42 Elegy Let	72
And all the originall riots of the place:	202	U42 Elegy Let	80
None of their pleasures! nor will aske thee, why	202	U42 Elegy Let	86
Thou art jealous of thy Wifes, or Daughters Case:	202	U42 Elegy Let	87
More then of eithers manners, wit, or face!	202	U42 Elegy Let	88
Ben: Jonson upon the burning of his study and bookes	202	U43 Vulcan	VTtl
And why to me this, thou lame Lord of fire,	202	U43 Vulcan	V 1
And why to me this, thou lame god of fire,	202	U43 Vulcan	1
Nor made least line of love to thy loose Wife;	203	U43 Vulcan	6
Or in remembrance of thy afront, and scorne,	203	U43 Vulcan	7
Was it because thou wert of old denied	203	U43 Vulcan	11
Wast not hee: thou wert of old denied	203	U43 Vulcan	V 11
To ruine any issue of the braine?	203	U43 Vulcan	14
To ruine every issue of her braine?	203	U43 Vulcan	V 14
Did I there wound the honours of the Crowne?	203	U43 Vulcan	23
Or taxe the Glories of the Church, and Gowne?	203	U43 Vulcan	24
Or taxe the Glories of the Church, or Gowne?	203	U43 Vulcan	V 24
If none of these, then why this fire? Or find	203	U43 Vulcan	27
The learned Librarie of Don Quixote;	204	U43 Vulcan	31
Of Logographes, and curious Palindromes,	204	U43 Vulcan	34
Of Egges, and Halberds, Cradles, and a Herse,	204	U43 Vulcan	37
A paire of Scisars, and a Combe in verse;	204	U43 Vulcan	38
There were some pieces of as base allay,	204	U43 Vulcan	42
And as false stampe there; parcels of a Play,	204	U43 Vulcan	43
With some more change, and tast of tyranny:	205	U43 Vulcan	V 50

OF (cont.)

Had I fore-knowne of this thy least desire	205	U43 Vulcan	59
Had I fore-knowne but of thy least desire	205	U43 Vulcan	V 59
T'have held a Triumph, or a feast of fire,	205	U43 Vulcan	60
With pieces of the Legend; The whole summe	205	U43 Vulcan	66
Of errant Knight-hood, with the Dames, and Dwarfes;	205	U43 Vulcan	67
With the Chimaera of the Rosie-Crosse,	206	U43 Vulcan	72
Their Jemme of Riches, and bright Stone, that brings	206	U43 Vulcan	74
The art of kindling the true Coale, by Lungs:	206	U43 Vulcan	76
The art of kindling the true Coale, of Lungs:	206	U43 Vulcan	V 76
Upon th'Exchange, still, out of Popes-head-Alley;	206	U43 Vulcan	80
Th'admir'd discourses of the Prophet Ball:	206	U43 Vulcan	82
Th'admir'd discourses of the Profit Ball:	206	U43 Vulcan	V 82
Th'admir'd discourses of the Prophet Baal:	206	U43 Vulcan	V 82
There were of search, and mastry in the Arts.	206	U43 Vulcan	88
There were of search, and mastry of the Arts.	206	U43 Vulcan	V 88
The puritie of Language; and among	207	U43 Vulcan	93
To speake the fate of the Sicilian Maid	207	U43 Vulcan	96
Reveald (if some can judge) of Argenis,	207	U43 Vulcan	V 96
Reveald (if some do judge) of Argenis,	207	U43 Vulcan	V 96
Of our fift Henry, eight of his nine yeare;	207	U43 Vulcan	98
Of our fift Henry, right of his nine yeare;	207	U43 Vulcan	V 98
Of Carew, Cotton, Selden, oyles were spent	207	U43 Vulcan	V100
Or Goddesse, could be patient of thy face.	207	U43 Vulcan	108
Sonne of the Wind! for so thy mother gone	208	U43 Vulcan	111
No mar'le the Clownes of Lemnos tooke thee up,	208	U43 Vulcan	116
Squire of the Squibs, against the Pageant day,	208	U43 Vulcan	119
Squire of the Squibs, upon the Pageant day,	208	U43 Vulcan	V119
Squire of the Squibs, against the next Maiors day,	208	U43 Vulcan	V119
They made a Vulcan of a sheafe of Reedes,	208	U43 Vulcan	126
But, O those Reeds! thy meere disdaine of them,	208	U43 Vulcan	129
But, O those weedes; thy meere disdaine of them,	208	U43 Vulcan	V129
Against the Globe, the Glory of the Banke.	208	U43 Vulcan	132
Which, though it were the Fort of the whole Parish,	209	U43 Vulcan	133
Flanck'd with a Ditch, and forc'd out of a Marish,	209	U43 Vulcan	134
Fenced with a Ditch, and forc'd out of a Marish,	209	U43 Vulcan	V134
'Twas verily some Relique of the Stewes:	209	U43 Vulcan	140
And this a Sparkle of that fire let loose	209	U43 Vulcan	141
That this sparke of the same fire let loose	209	U43 Vulcan	V141
Bred on the Banck, in time of Poperie.	209	U43 Vulcan	143
He burnt that Idoll of the Revels too:	210	U43 Vulcan	155
I will not argue thee, from those, of guilt,	210	U43 Vulcan	165
I will not argue thee, from them, of guilt,	210	U43 Vulcan	V165
I will not argue thee Iron. Them of guilt	210	U43 Vulcan	V165
And didst invade part of the Common-wealth,	210	U43 Vulcan	170
Lyes there no Writ, out of the Chancerie	210	U43 Vulcan	174
A Court of Equitie should doe us right,	211	U43 Vulcan	178
Maintain'd the trade of Bilbo, or else-where;	212	U43 Vulcan	V199
Engines of Murder, and receive the praise	212	U43 Vulcan	207
Engines of Murder, and enjoy with praise	212	U43 Vulcan	V207
Of massacring Man-kind so many wayes.	212	U43 Vulcan	208
Of murthering of mankind many wayes.	212	U43 Vulcan	V208
So doth the King, and most of the Kings men	212	U43 Vulcan	211
And all the Evils that flew out of her box	212	U43 Vulcan	214
And all Those ills that flew out of her box	212	U43 Vulcan	V214
They saw too store of feathers, and more may,	213	U44 Speach	9
All Ensignes of a Warre, are not yet dead,	213	U44 Speach	11
Nor markes of wealth so from our Nation fled,	213	U44 Speach	12
Under the Auspice of young Swynnerton.	213	U44 Speach	20
Thou Seed-plot of the warre, that hast not spar'd	213	U44 Speach	24
Of London, in the Militarie truth,	213	U44 Speach	26
Would thinke no more of Vlushing, or the Brill:	213	U44 Speach	30
Of bearing Armes! most civill Soldierie!	214	U44 Speach	44
The Battells of thy Aldermanitie;	214	U44 Speach	46
Without the hazard of a drop of blood,	214	U44 Speach	47
And keepe the Glorie of the English name,	214	U44 Speach	50
Up among Nations. In the stead of bold	214	U44 Speach	51
Come to their Schooles,) show 'hem the use of Guns;	214	U44 Speach	58
For education of our Lordings; Soone	214	U44 Speach	62
Should he heare of billow, wind, and storme,	214	U44 Speach	63
We will beleeve, like men of our owne Ranke,	215	U44 Speach	75
Descended in a rope of Titles, be	215	U44 Speach	80
Past any need of vertue. Let them care,	215	U44 Speach	83
That in the Cradle of their Gentrie are;	215	U44 Speach	84
Carriage, and dressing. There is up of late	215	U44 Speach	88
Of severall makings? helps, t'attire	215	U44 Speach	94
These Carkasses of honour; Taylors blocks,	216	U44 Speach	99
The fate of things: whilst totter'd vertue holds	216	U44 Speach	101
I neither am, nor art thou one of those	216	U45 Squib	5
Was issue of the Taverne, or the Spit:	216	U45 Squib	8
No piece of money, but you know, or make	216	U45 Squib	14
Inquirie of the worth: So must we doe,	216	U45 Squib	15
But he that's too-much that, is friend of none.	216	U45 Squib	24
It is a richer Purchase then of land.	216	U45 Squib	26
. . . he was Lord chiefe Justice of England.	217	U46 Coke	Ttl
He that should search all Glories of the Gowne,	217	U46 Coke	1
And steps of all rais'd servants of the Crowne,	217	U46 Coke	2
He could not find, then thee, of all that store	217	U46 Coke	3
That Clients strove, in Question of the Lawes,	217	U46 Coke	11
No lesse of praise, then readers in all kinds	217	U46 Coke	19
Of worthiest knowledge, that can take mens minds.	217	U46 Coke	20
. . . to be Sealed of the Tribe of Ben.	218	U47 Tribe	Ttl
I could say more of such, but that I flie	218	U47 Tribe	5

OF (cont.)

	Page	Title		Line
That live in the wild Anarchie of Drinke,	218	U47 Tribe		10
Of any Companie but that they are in,	218	U47 Tribe		20
And are received for the Covey of Witts;	218	U47 Tribe		22
Of newes they get, to strew out the long meale,	218	U47 Tribe		28
Some hopes of Spaine in their West-Indian Fleet?	219	U47 Tribe		34
Of Spaine or France; or were not prick'd downe one	219	U47 Tribe		47
Of the late Mysterie of reception,	219	U47 Tribe		48
And animated Porc'lane of the Court,	219	U47 Tribe		53
Of earthen Jarres, there may molest me too:	219	U47 Tribe		55
Sir, you are Sealed of the Tribe of Ben.	220	U47 Tribe		78
The Dedication of the Kings new Cellar. to Bacchus.	220	U48 Bacchus		Ttl
Of Wines, to thee the rather	220	U48 Bacchus		2
Of all to the great Master.	220	U48 Bacchus		8
Of cares, and over-seer	220	U48 Bacchus		8
Of feast, and merry meeting,	221	U48 Bacchus		14
By all the Arts of Gladnesse,	221	U48 Bacchus		15
Of some wel-wrought Embassage:	221	U48 Bacchus		19
The wished Peace of Europe:	221	U48 Bacchus		46
Where fight the prime Cocks of the Game, for wit?	222	U48 Bacchus		48
New in their stead, out of the Candidates?	222	U49 Pucell		4
As new rewards of her old secrecie?	222	U49 Pucell		6
To his poore Instrument, now out of grace.	223	U49 Pucell		20
For Sermoneeres: of which now one, now other,	223	U49 Pucell		34
Both for the Mothers, and the Babes of grace,	223	U49 Pucell		39
For there the wicked in the Chaire of scorne,	223	U49 Pucell		44
An Epigram. To the honour'd ———— Countesse of ——	223	U49 Pucell		45
The Wisdome, Madam, of your private Life,	224	U50 Countesse		Ttl
Is of so brave example, as he were	224	U50 Countesse		1
The rather when the vices of the Time	224	U50 Countesse		7
Of State, of fame, of body, and of soule,	224	U50 Countesse		9
These Graces, when the rest of Ladyes view	224	U50 Countesse		18
Haile, happie Genius of this antient pile!	225	U50 Countesse		31
Sonne to the grave wise Keeper of the Seale,	225	U51 Bacon		1
Fame, and foundation of the English Weale.	225	U51 Bacon		9
Out of their Choysest, and their whitest wooll.	225	U51 Bacon		10
'Tis a brave cause of joy, let it be knowne,	225	U51 Bacon		16
In raysing him the wisdome of my King.	225	U51 Bacon		17
Why? though I seeme of a prodigious wast,	226	U51 Bacon		20
Which if in compasse of no Art it came	227	U52 Answer		1
Your Power of handling shadow, ayre, and spright,	227	U52 Answer		10
Yet when of friendship I would draw the face,	227	U52 Answer		17
An Epigram. To William, Earle of Newcastle.	227	U52 Answer		22
To all the uses of the field, and race,	228	U53 Newcastle		Ttl
Me thought I read the ancient Art of Thrace,	228	U53 Newcastle		3
And saw a Centaure, past those tales of Greece;	228	U53 Newcastle		4
So seem'd your horse and you, both of a peece!	228	U53 Newcastle		5
Of bold Sir Bevis, and his Arundell:	228	U53 Newcastle		6
Nor any of their houshold, halfe so well.	228	U53 Newcastle		10
A Merchants Wife is Regent of the Scale.	229	U53 Newcastle		16
Full twentie stone; of which I lack two pound:	229	U54 Squib		4
Thoughts worthy of thy gift, this Inke,	229	U54 Squib		12
The first of which, I feare, you will refuse;	230	U55 Burges		2
The first of which, I doubt, you will refuse;	230	U56 Covell		6
Of either Suitor, or a Servant by.	230	U56 Covell	V	6
Of suitor, or of servant standing by.	230	U56 Covell		18
Of a yeares Pension,	230	U56 Covell	V	18
Of gambol, or sport	231	U57 Burges		12
What each man sayes of it, and of what coat	231	U57 Burges		19
Thy Wife a fit of laughter; a Cramp-ring	232	U58 Book-seller		4
An Epigram. To William Earle of Newcastle.	232	U58 Book-seller		8
To the Right Honorable William Earle of Newcastle.	232	U59 Newcastle		Ttl
They talke of Fencing, and the use of Armes,	232	U59 Newcastle		VTtl
The art of urging, and avoyding harmes,	232	U59 Newcastle		1
Of making just approaches, how to kill,	232	U59 Newcastle		2
Of bodies, meet like rarified ayre!	232	U59 Newcastle		4
Of daring, not to doe a wrong, is true	233	U59 Newcastle		10
To know the heads of danger! where 'tis fit	233	U59 Newcastle		15
Of humane life! as all the frosts, and sweates	233	U59 Newcastle		17
Of fortune! when, or death appear'd, or bands!	233	U59 Newcastle		22
Of a Disease, that lov'd no light	233	U59 Newcastle		23
Of honour, nor no ayre of good?	234	U60 La-ware		6
Of Vertue, got above his name?	234	U60 La-ware		7
No noble furniture of parts,	234	U60 La-ware		10
No love of action, and high Arts,	234	U60 La-ware		11
Could stop the malice of this ill,	234	U60 La-ware		12
And all the games of Fortune, plaid at Court;	234	U60 La-ware		15
I'obtaine of God, what all the Land should aske?	234	U61 Epigram		2
Of riot, and consumption, knowes the way	234	U61 Epigram		11
He is the Man, and Favorite of God.	235	U61 Epigram		17
Great Charles, among the holy gifts of grace	235	U61 Epigram		20
One Poet, then of other folke ten score.	235	U62 Charles 1		1
To K. Charles, and Q. Mary. For the losse of their . . .	235	U62 Charles 1		10
. . . On the Universary day of his Raigne. 1629.	235	U63 Charles 2		Ttl
If he but weigh'd the blessings of this day?	236	U64 Charles 3		VTtl
For safetie of such Majestie, cry out?	236	U64 Charles 3		4
When all your life's a president of dayes,	236	U64 Charles 3		6
How is she barren growne of love! or broke!	237	U64 Charles 3		13
O Times! O Manners! Surfet bred of ease,	237	U64 Charles 3		15
The bed of the chast Lilly, and the Rose!	237	U64 Charles 3		17
This Prince of flowers? Soone shoot thou up, and grow	237	U65 Prince		3
Haile Mary, full of grace, it once was said,	237	U65 Prince		5
The Mother of our Lord: why may not I	238	U66 Queene		1
	238	U66 Queene		3

	Page	Title	Line

OF (cont.)

Haile Mary, full of honours, to my Queene,	238	U66 Queene	5
The Mother of our Prince? When was there seene	238	U66 Queene	6
Whereby the safetie of Man-kind was wrought)	238	U66 Queene	8
Whereby the safetie of the world was wrought)	238	U66 Queene	V 8
To make the hearts of a whole Nation smile,	238	U66 Queene	10
Of so much safetie to the Realme, and King.	238	U66 Queene	14
Of so much health, both to our Land, and King.	238	U66 Queene	V 14
. . . In celebration of her Majesties birth-day. 1630.	239	U67 Muses	Ttl
This sixteenth of November,	239	U67 Muses	2
With beating of our Drums:	239	U67 Muses	15
With beating of their Drums:	239	U67 Muses	V 15
With touch of daintie thum's!	239	U67 Muses	18
The Daughter of great Harry!	240	U67 Muses	26
Of all her Brothers storie,	240	U67 Muses	29
Of all her Fathers storie,	240	U67 Muses	V 29
And of her Fathers prowesse!	240	U67 Muses	30
And of her Brothers prowesse!	240	U67 Muses	V 30
The fained Queene of Love,	240	U67 Muses	32
Hay! for the flowre of France!	240	U67 Muses	42
For want of knowing the Poet, to say him nay?	241	U68 House-hold	4
Hee'ld frame such ditties of their store, and want,	241	U68 House-hold	7
And rather wish, in their expence of Sack,	241	U68 House-hold	9
For in the Genius of a Poets Verse,	241	U68 House-hold	13
Some of his formes, he lets him not come neere	242	U69 Friend Son	17
Though now of flattery, as of picture, are	242	U69 Friend Son	21
To the immortall memorie, and friendship of that noble . . .	242	U70 Ode	Ttl
To Sir Lucius Carey, on the death of his Brother Morison	242	U70 Ode	VTtl
Brave Infant of Saguntum, cleare	242	U70 Ode	1
Of deepest lore, could we the Center find!	243	U70 Ode	10
From out the horrour of that sack?	243	U70 Ode	12
Where shame, faith, honour, and regard of right	243	U70 Ode	13
Lay trampled on; the deeds of death, and night,	243	U70 Ode	14
For three of his foure-score, he did no good.	243	U70 Ode	32
But weary of that flight,	244	U70 Ode	37
To sordid flatteries, acts of strife,	244	U70 Ode	39
And sunke in that dead sea of life	244	U70 Ode	40
But that the Corke of Title boy'd him up.	244	U70 Ode	42
His life was of Humanitie the Spheare.	244	U70 Ode	52
Produce thy masse of miseries on the Stage,	244	U70 Ode	55
Repeat of things a throng,	245	U70 Ode	57
These make the lines of life, and that's her ayre.	245	U70 Ode	64
A Lillie of a Day,	245	U70 Ode	69
It was the Plant, and flowre of light.	245	U70 Ode	72
Of which we Priests, and Poets say	245	U70 Ode	82
Jonson, who sung this of him, e're he went	246	U70 Ode	85
Or taste a part of that full joy he meant	246	U70 Ode	87
Two names of friendship, but one Starre:	246	U70 Ode	98
Of hearts the union. And those not by chance	246	U70 Ode	99
Of rimes, or ryots, at your feasts,	246	U70 Ode	103
Orgies of drinke, or fain'd protests:	246	U70 Ode	104
But simple love of greatnesse, and of good;	246	U70 Ode	105
Till either grew a portion of the other:	247	U70 Ode	110
The Copie of his friend.	247	U70 Ode	112
Of two so early men,	247	U70 Ode	125
To the Right Honourable, the Lord high Treasurer of . . .	248	U71 Treasurer	Ttl
Of Princes aides, or good mens Charities.	248	U71 Treasurer	3
Want, with the rest of his conceal'd compeeres,	248	U71 Treasurer	5
The Muse not peepes out, one of hundred dayes;	248	U71 Treasurer	9
Unlesse some saving-Honour of the Crowne,	248	U71 Treasurer	13
The Poetrie of Steeples, with the Bells,	249	U72 King	10
The Poetrie of Steeples, with their Bells,	249	U72 King	V 10
Had they but grace, of thinking, at these routes,	249	U72 King	15
On th'often comming of this Holy-day:	249	U72 King	16
And ever close the burden of the Song,	249	U72 King	17
And then noyse forth the burden of their Song,	249	U72 King	V 17
. . . high Treasurer of England, Upon the Day, Hee was . . .	250	U73 Weston	Ttl
Looke up, thou seed of envie, and still bring	250	U73 Weston	1
Weston! That waking man! that Eye of State!	250	U73 Weston	5
When shee puts forth the life of ev'ry thing:	250	U74 Weston	3
And in a dew of sweetest Raine,	251	U74 Weston	4
Of the prime beautie of the yeare, the Spring.	251	U74 Weston	6
Because the order of the whole is faire!	251	U74 Weston	12
The very verdure of her nest,	251	U74 Weston	13
As all the wealth of Season, there was spread;	251	U74 Weston	15
The bus'nesse of your blooming wit,	251	U74 Weston	22
Both to the honour of the King and State.	251	U74 Weston	24
To see great Charles of Travaile eas'd,	251	U74 Weston	26
When he beholds a graft of his owne hand,	251	U74 Weston	27
Epithalamion; Or, A Song: Celebrating The nuptials of . . .	252	U75 Epithalam.	Ttl
The bountie of a King, and beautie of his Queene!	252	U75 Epithalam.	8
(Bearing the promise of some better fate)	252	U75 Epithalam.	10
By all the Spheares consent, so in the heart of June?	253	U75 Epithalam.	16
What Beavie of beauties, and bright youths at charge	253	U75 Epithalam.	17
Of Summers Liveries, and gladding greene;	253	U75 Epithalam.	18
It is the kindly Season of the time,	253	U75 Epithalam.	25
The Month of youth, which calls all Creatures forth	253	U75 Epithalam.	26
Mariage, the end of life,	253	U75 Epithalam.	29
And all did ring th'approches of the Bride;	253	U75 Epithalam.	36
Of all the Maidens faire;	253	U75 Epithalam.	39
In gracefull Ornament of Garland, Gemmes, and Haire.	253	U75 Epithalam.	40
Like what she is, the Daughter of a Duke,	253	U75 Epithalam.	42
Nought of a Maiden Queene,	254	U75 Epithalam.	47

	Page	Title		Line
OF (cont.)				
The choisest Virgin-troup of all the Land!	254	U75	Epithalam.	50
Porting the Ensignes of united Two,	254	U75	Epithalam.	51
(Lillies and Roses, Flowers of either Sexe)	254	U75	Epithalam.	58
With light of love, this Paire doth intertexe!	254	U75	Epithalam.	60
The Emblemes of their way.	254	U75	Epithalam.	63
With all the pompe of Youth, and all our Court beside.	254	U75	Epithalam.	72
In all thy age of Journals thou hast tooke,	254	U75	Epithalam.	75
They are th'exampled Paire, and mirrour of their kind.	255	U75	Epithalam.	80
Of Sex, to rob the Creature; but from Man	255	U75	Epithalam.	82
The king of Creatures, take his paritie	255	U75	Epithalam.	83
And wonder'd at the bounties of this day:	255	U75	Epithalam.	90
All is a story of the King and Queene!	255	U75	Epithalam.	91
And what of Dignitie, and Honour may	255	U75	Epithalam.	92
That Mine of Wisdome, and of Counsells deep,	255	U75	Epithalam.	98
Great Say-Master of State, who cannot erre,	255	U75	Epithalam.	99
Great Say-Master of State, who not to erre,	255	U75	Epithalam.	V 99
Of Tryals, to worke downe	255	U75	Epithalam.	103
And this well mov'd the Judgement of the King	256	U75	Epithalam.	105
What kind of waking Man	256	U75	Epithalam.	111
Now, Sun, and post away the rest of day:	257	U75	Epithalam.	138
To them of kind,	257	U75	Epithalam.	142
Of Nuptiall Sweets, at such a season, owe,	257	U75	Epithalam.	148
Of Life, that fall so; Christians know their birth	257	U75	Epithalam.	156
(The holy perfumes of the Mariage bed.)	257	U75	Epithalam.	162
Of Love betweene you, and your Lovely-head:	257	U75	Epithalam.	164
How each one playes his part, of the large Pedigree.	258	U75	Epithalam.	176
And never may there want one of the Stem,	258	U75	Epithalam.	177
But like an Arme of Eminence 'mongst them,	258	U75	Epithalam.	179
Hee's Master of the Office; yet no more	258	U75	Epithalam.	187
The Humble Petition of Poore Ben.	259	U76	Petition	Ttl
To Th'Best Of Monarchs, Masters, Men, King Charles	259	U76	Petition	2
Of his speciall grace to Letters,	259	U76	Petition	7
Of a free Poetique Pension,	259	U76	Petition	10
To his Poet of a Pension,	259	U76	Petition	10
All the envie of the Rymes,	259	U76	Petition	V 10
All there envie of the Rymes,	259	U76	Petition	18
Of the lesse-Poetique boyes;	259	U76	Petition	V 18
Of the brave Poetique boyes;	259	U76	Petition	20
With their pellets of small wit,	259	U76	Petition	V 20
Parts of me (they judg'd) decay'd,	259	U76	Petition	22
Parts of him, the Judge decay'd,	259	U76	Petition	23
Of your grace, for goodnesse sake,	259	U76	Petition	V 23
To the right Honourable, the Lord Treasurer of England.	260	U76	Petition	26
Of Noremberg, or Turkie; hang your roomes	260	U77	Treasurer	Ttl
What you have studied are the arts of life;	260	U77	Treasurer	3
Of murmuring Subjects; make the Nations know	261	U77	Treasurer	17
Of froward Citizens; make the Nations know	261	U77	Treasurer	19
What worlds of blessings to good Kings they owe:	261	U77	Treasurer	V 19
Of sweets, and safeties, they possesse by Peace.	261	U77	Treasurer	20
Upon my Birth-day the eleventh of June;	261	U77	Treasurer	22
Witnesse my Birth-day the eleventh of June;	262	U78	Digby	14
Being sent to one, they will be read of all.	262	U78	Digby	V 14
Your change of Notes, the flat, the meane, the sharpe,	263	U78	Digby	32
Of the New Yeare, in a new silken warpe,	263	U79	New-yeares	3
To fit the softnesse of our Yeares-gift: when	263	U79	New-yeares	5
We sing the best of Monarchs, Masters, Men;	263	U79	New-yeares	6
Best Kings expect first-fruits of your glad gaines.	263	U79	New-yeares	7
Pan is the great Preserver of our bounds.	263	U79	New-yeares	13
To him we owe all profits of our grounds.	264	U79	New-yeares	14
Of Pan wee sing, the best of Hunters, Pan,	264	U79	New-yeares	15
Of brightest Mira, doe we raise our Song,	264	U79	New-yeares	20
Sister of Pan, and glory of the Spring:	264	U79	New-yeares	24
Of Pan wee sing, the Chiefe of Leaders, Pan,	264	U79	New-yeares	25
Of brightest Mira, is our Song; the grace	264	U79	New-yeares	28
Of all that Nature, yet, to life did bring;	264	U79	New-yeares	32
As if the beauties of the yeare,	264	U79	New-yeares	33
Hee is the Father of our peace.	264	U79	New-yeares	38
In truth of colours, both are best.	264	U79	New-yeares	40
This is the great Preserver of our bounds,	265	U79	New-yeares	45
To whom you owe all duties of your grounds;	265	U79	New-yeares	48
Hee is the author of our peace.	265	U79	New-yeares	49
Hee is the author of our peace.	265	U79	New-yeares	57
That thou art lov'd of God, this worke is done,	265	U79	New-yeares	69
Great King, thy having of a second Sonne:	268	U80	Christning	1
How much they are belov'd of God, in thee;	268	U80	Christning	2
Should take first Seisin of the publique good,	268	U80	Christning	4
An Elegie On the Lady Jane Pawlet, Marchion: of Winton.	268	U80	Christning	8
Whose Daughter? ha? Great Savage of the Rock?	268	U81	Pawlet	Ttl
And e're I can aske more of her, shee's gone!	269	U81	Pawlet	10
Of Winchester; the Heralds can tell this:	269	U81	Pawlet	12
Of Winchester; the Heralds could tell this:	269	U81	Pawlet	20
But rather I, should I of that part speake!	269	U81	Pawlet	V 20
It is too neere of kin to Heaven, the Soule,	269	U81	Pawlet	28
It is too neere of kin to God, the Soule,	269	U81	Pawlet	29
But a fain'd way, doth rob it of the true.	269	U81	Pawlet	V 29
But a fain'd way, doth spoyle it of the true.	270	U81	Pawlet	38
Were like a ring of Vertues, 'bout her set,	270	U81	Pawlet	V 38
Of her disease, how did her soule assure	270	U81	Pawlet	41
What the beginnings of all beauties be;	270	U81	Pawlet	50
Which the Elect of God are sure to know!	271	U81	Pawlet	74
The Starres, that are the Jewels of the Night,	271	U81	Pawlet	V 76
And Day, deceasing! with the Prince of light,	271	U81	Pawlet	87
	271	U81	Pawlet	88

OF (cont.)

	Page	Title	Line
Hee were the wretched'st of the race of men:	272	U81 Pawlet	97
And, sure of Heaven, rides triumphing in.	272	U81 Pawlet	100
. . . Of that truly-noble Lady, the Lady Venetia Digby, . . .	272	U84 Eupheme	Ttl
1. The Dedication of her Cradle.	272	U84 Cradle	Ttl
Of Death, and Darknesse; and deprive	273	U84 Cradle	5
Their names of being kept alive,	273	U84 Cradle	6
Of Goodnesse still: Vouchsafe to take	273	U84 Cradle	9
Of light expence;	273	U84 Cradle	20
With Sayles of silke, as the first notes	273	U84 Cradle	23
But, here's a Song of her Descent;	273	U84 Cradle	29
Of Heaven; where Seraphim take tent	273	U84 Cradle	31
Of ord'ring all.	273	U84 Cradle	32
Who claimes (of reverence) to be heard,	274	U84 Cradle	34
Of that eternall Port kept ope'	274	U84 Cradle	39
2. The Song of her Descent.	274	U84 Descent	Ttl
Of Dame Venetia Digby, styl'd The Faire:	274	U84 Descent	2
At either Stemme, and know the veines of good	274	U84 Descent	8
Meeting of Graces, that so swell'd the flood	274	U84 Descent	10
Of vertues in her, as, in short, shee grew	274	U84 Descent	11
The wonder of her Sexe, and of your Blood.	274	U84 Descent	12
Of the first Lupus, to the Familie	274	U84 Descent	17
3. The Picture of the Body.	275	U84 Body	Ttl
And, out of that, make Day to breake;	276	U84 Body	14
Then let the beames of that, disperse	276	U84 Body	17
Last, draw the circles of this Globe,	276	U84 Body	25
Of Constellations 'bout her horld;	277	U84 Body	27
A Copie of this peece; nor tell	277	U84 Body	30
But what's of kinne to whence it came.	278	U84 Mind	16
Of grace, and Musique to the eare,	279	U84 Mind	35
In all the bounds of beautie fit	280	U84 Mind	51
As showers; and sweet as drops of Balme.	280	U84 Mind	60
A nest of odorous spice, and gummes.	280	U84 Mind	64
A nest of Spices, Odors, Gummes.	280	U84 Mind	V 64
Upon a banke, or field of flowers,	280	U84 Mind	67
Boast not these Titles of your Ancestors;	281	U84 Kenelme	10
(Brave Youths) th'are their possessions, none of yours:	281	U84 Kenelme	11
Who was my Muse, and life of all I sey'd,	282	U84 Muse	2
Spun out in name of some of the old Nine!	282	U84 Muse	6
And saw that portion of her selfe to die.	282	U84 Muse	14
Of Vulture death, and those relentlesse cleies?	283	U84 Muse	18
Of teares, and dungeon of calamitie!	283	U84 Muse	35
The joy of Saints! the Crowne for which it lives,	283	U84 Muse	37
The glorie, and gaine of rest, which the place gives!	283	U84 Muse	38
So sweetly taken to the Court of blisse,	283	U84 Muse	41
Of Body and Spirit together, plac'd betwixt	284	U84 Muse	54
Of that great Evidence, the Conscience!	284	U84 Muse	58
O Day of joy, and suretie to the just!	284	U84 Muse	61
Who in that feast of Resurrection trust!	284	U84 Muse	62
That great eternall Holy-day of rest,	284	U84 Muse	63
And the whole Banquet is full sight of God!	284	U84 Muse	65
Of joy the Circle, and sole Period!	284	U84 Muse	66
Out of her noble body, to this Feast:	284	U84 Muse	82
Amongst her Peeres, those Princes of all good!	284	U84 Muse	84
And she doth know, out of the shade of Death,	285	U84 Muse	91
With boughs of Palme, a crowned Victrice stand!	285	U84 Muse	96
Her fellowes, with the oyle of gladnesse, bright	285	U84 Muse	101
In heaven Empyre, and with a robe of light?	285	U84 Muse	102
By all the wealth of blessings, and the store	285	U84 Muse	110
Of life, and light, the Sonne of God, the Word!	285	U84 Muse	112
By beatifick vertue of the Place.	285	U84 Muse	116
But all of God; They still shall have to say,	286	U84 Muse	119
By light, and comfort of spirituall Grace;	286	U84 Muse	131
The vision of our Saviour, face to face,	286	U84 Muse	132
The price of our Redemption, and to teach	286	U84 Muse	134
The safetie of our soules, and forfeit breath!	286	U84 Muse	136
What fulnesse of beatitude is here?	286	U84 Muse	137
Adopt us Heires, by grace, who were of those	286	U84 Muse	140
Equall with Angels, and Co-heires of it?	286	U84 Muse	146
Himselfe so un-inform'd of his elect,	286	U84 Muse	149
Who knowes the hearts of all, and can dissect	286	U84 Muse	150
The smallest Fibre of our flesh; he can	286	U84 Muse	151
And to that forme, lent two such veines of blood	287	U84 Muse	157
Of title in her! All Nobilitie	287	U84 Muse	159
(But pride, that schisme of incivilitie)	287	U84 Muse	160
And by the awfull manage of her Eye	287	U84 Muse	167
She was, in one, a many parts of life;	287	U84 Muse	173
Of Pietie, and private holinesse.	287	U84 Muse	179
Of sorrow, then all pompe of gaudy daies:	287	U84 Muse	182
Of divine Comfort, when sh' had talk'd with God.	287	U84 Muse	184
The doore of Grace, and found the Mercy-Seat.	288	U84 Muse	190
Or doing other deeds of Charitie,	288	U84 Muse	193
Of raising, judging, and rewarding all	288	U84 Muse	207
The kind of Man, on whom his doome should fall!	288	U84 Muse	208
In manner of a daily Apostrophe,	288	U84 Muse	210
Of lapsed Nature) best know what to doe,	288	U84 Muse	214
In that great Act of judgement: which the Father	288	U84 Muse	215
As being the Sonne of Man) to shew his Power,	288	U84 Muse	217
The last of houres, and shutter up of all;	289	U84 Muse	219
Of all are dead to life! His Wisdome show	289	U84 Muse	221
In the discerning of each conscience, so!	289	U84 Muse	222
The praises of a Countrie life.	289	U85 Country	Ttl
An Ode in Horace in prayse of a Countrye lyfe, Translated.	289	U85 Country	VTtl

OF (cont.)

	Page	Title	Line
As the old race of Mankind were,	289	U85 Country	2
As the old stock of Mankind were,	289	U85 Country	V 2
And waiting Chambers of great Lords.	289	U85 Country	8
With the growne issue of the Vine;	290	U85 Country	10
With sproutinge tendrells of the Vine;	290	U85 Country	V 10
Of Earth, and sheares the tender Sheepe:	290	U85 Country	16
And from the sweet Tub Wine of this yeare takes,	291	U85 Country	47
From fattest branches of the Tree:	291	U85 Country	56
Or at the Feast of Bounds, the Lambe then slaine,	291	U85 Country	59
Of the fed flocks approaching home!	291	U85 Country	62
The wealthy houshold swarme of bondmen met,	291	U85 Country	65
Of the good Cynara I was: Refraine,	292	U86 Hor.4:1	4
Sower Mother of sweet Loves, forbeare	292	U86 Hor.4:1	5
With thy bright Swans, of Paulus Maximus:	292	U86 Hor.4:1	10
Child of a hundred Arts, and farre	292	U86 Hor.4:1	15
Will he display the Ensignes of thy warre.	292	U86 Hor.4:1	16
Delights, nor credulous hope of mutuall Joy,	293	U86 Hor.4:1	30
Flow my thin teares, downe these pale cheeks of mine?	293	U86 Hor.4:1	34
Ode IX. 3 Booke, to Lydia. Dialogue of Horace, and Lydia.	293	U87 Hor.3:9	Ttl
Whilst, Lydia, I was lov'd of thee,	293	U87 Hor.3:9	1
Thou lighter then the barke of any tree,	294	U87 Hor.3:9	22
And done, we straight repent us of the sport:	294	U88 Petronius	2
Liber, of all thy friends, thou sweetest care,	294	U89 Mart.8:77	1
Horace, His Art of Poetrie Made English	303	Horace	Ttl
Horace, of The Art of Poetrie.	305	Horace	Ttl
Quintus Horatius Flaccus his book of . . .	338	Horace	VTtl
Of daring all, hath still beene given; we know it:	305	Horace	12
Of daring ought, hath still beene given; we know it:	338	Horace	V 12
bor-/Dring Circles of swift waters that intwine	305	Horace	21
Bouts of fleet waters, that doe intertwine	338	Horace	V 21
Are, with the likenesse of the truth, undone.	307	Horace	34
Are with the likeness of the truth beguil'd:	339	Horace	V 35/ 34
Father, and sons right worthy of your Sire,	339	Horace	V 34
Creepes on the ground; too safe, too afraid of storme.	307	Horace	39
Being over-safe, and fearing of the flaw:	339	Horace	V 41/ 39
The worst of Statuaries, here about	307	Horace	45
To be that Smith; then live, mark'd one of those,	307	Horace	51
The vertue of which order, and true grace,	307	Horace	59
The vertue and grace of which, or I mistake,	339	Horace	V 60/ 59
Till fitter season. Now, to like of this,	307	Horace	63
In using also of new words, to be	307	Horace	65
Faine words, unheard of to the well-truss'd race	309	Horace	71
Faine words, unheard of to the girded race	340	Horace	V 71
Of the Cethegi; And all men will grace,	309	Horace	72
New names of things. It hath beene ever free,	309	Horace	83
Of words decay, and phrases borne but late	309	Horace	88
Or grace of speech, should hope a lasting date.	309	Horace	100
The power, and rule of speaking resteth still.	309	Horace	104
The gests of Kings, great Captaines, and sad Warres,	309	Horace	105
The deeds of Kings, great Captaines, and sad Warres,	341	Horace	V105
Of popular noyses, borne to actuate things.	341	Horace	V120
Of Poems here describ'd, I can, nor use,	311	Horace	127
To every state of fortune; she helpes on,	311	Horace	153
If now the phrase of him that speakes, shall flow,	313	Horace	158
Of some small thankfull land: whether he bee	313	Horace	166
Of Colchis borne; or in Assyria bred:	313	Horace	167
Or, with the milke of Thebes; or Argus, fed.	313	Horace	168
Of Homers, forth in acts, then of thine owne,	313	Horace	185
Of imitation, leape into a streight,	313	Horace	192
Of Meleager, brings he the returne	315	Horace	208
Of Diomede; nor Troyes sad Warre begins	315	Horace	209
The middle of his matter: letting goe	315	Horace	213
The customes of each age thou must observe,	315	Horace	223
Of money, haughtie, to desire soon mov'd,	315	Horace	235
Doth wretchedly the use of things forbeare,	317	Horace	243
With sloth, yet greedy still of what's to come:	317	Horace	246
Of the times past, when he was a young lad;	317	Horace	248
The parts of age to youth be given; or men	317	Horace	252
Upon the Stage, the figure of a Snake.	317	Horace	268
Unwonted language; and that sense of worth	319	Horace	308
With lees of Wine. Next Eschylus, more late,	319	Horace	315
Brought in the Visor, and the robe of State,	319	Horace	316
Though sower, with safetie of his gravitie,	319	Horace	322
Quite from all face of Tragedie to goe,	321	Horace	344
Simo; and, of a talent wip'd his purse;	321	Horace	347
Simo, and of a talent cleans'd his purse;	346	Horace	V339/347
I can out of knowne geare, a fable frame,	321	Horace	349
I can, out of knowne stuff, a Fable frame,	347	Horace	V341/349
Of Order, and Connexion; so much grace	321	Horace	353
There comes sometimes to things of meanest place.	321	Horace	354
The Roman Gentrie, men of birth, and meane,	321	Horace	360
His power of foulely hurting made to cease.	323	Horace	370
Of Trimeter, when yet it was sixe-pac'd,	323	Horace	373
Of fellowship, the fourth, or second place.	323	Horace	380
Of Accius, and Ennius, rare appeares:	323	Horace	382
Of too much haste, and negligence in part,	323	Horace	385
Or a worse Crime, the ignorance of art.	323	Horace	386
To note in Poemes, breach of harmonie;	323	Horace	388
Within the hope of having all forgiven?	323	Horace	394
In vertue, and renowne of armes, then in	325	Horace	412
But fame of Poets, they thinke, if they come forth,	325	Horace	426
The very root of writing well, and spring	325	Horace	440

OF (cont.)

	Page	Title	Line
What height of love, a Parent will fit best,	325	Horace	447
And office of a Judge are, what the parts	325	Horace	450
Of a brave Chiefe sent to the warres: He can,	325	Horace	451
A Poeme, of no grace, weight, art, in rimes,	327	Horace	456
Of verse meere-matter-lesse, and tinckling toies.	327	Horace	460
Being men were covetous of nought, but praise.	327	Horace	463
A third of twelve, you may: foure ounces. Glad,	327	Horace	469
And care of getting, thus, our minds hath stain'd,	327	Horace	473
In juyce of Cedar worthy to be steep'd,	327	Horace	475
This was the wisdome, that they had of old,	327	Horace	486
Build Townes, and carve the Lawes in leaves of wood.	327	Horace	490
All way of life was shewen; the grace of Kings	329	Horace	497
Of their long labours, was in Verse set downe:	329	Horace	500
Lest of the singer Apollo, and Muses fam'd	353	Horace	V579/501
The Child, when Lamia'has din'd, out of her maw.	329	Horace	510
The Poems void of profit, our grave men	329	Horace	511
And, of your selfe too, understand; yet mind	331	Horace	547
Of eloquent Messalla's power in Court,	331	Horace	552
Poppy, with hony of Sardus; 'cause without	351	Horace	V535/559
To bettring of the mind of man, in ought,	331	Horace	562
Or, of the things, that ne're came in my mind,	333	Horace	596
That to the sale of Wares calls every Buyer;	333	Horace	598
Of an entangling suit; and bring 't about:	333	Horace	604
With joy of what is given him, over-gone:	333	Horace	610
If of their friendship he be worthy, or no:	333	Horace	619
Of the Sicilian Poet Empedocles,	335	Horace	660
Or love of this so famous death lay by.	335	Horace	669
Or love of this his famous death lay by.	355	Horace	V669
His cause of making Verses none knowes why:	335	Horace	670
And, there an end of him, reciting makes:	337	Horace	678
And there an end of him with reading makes:	355	Horace	V678
Till he drop off, a Horse-leech, full of blood.	337	Horace	680
Till, horse-leech-like, he drop off, full of blood.	355	Horace	V680
Not one but thrives; in spite of stormes & thunder,	361	Palmer	7
Thy skill hath made of ranck dispised weedes;	361	Palmer	10
The seaven-fold flower of Arte (more rich then gold)	361	Palmer	15
did sparcle foorth in Center of the rest:	361	Palmer	16
of thy rich labors worlds of thoughts created,	361	Palmer	22
Thou, that wouldst finde the habit of true passion,	362	Author	1
The knottie heads of the most surly Groomes,	363	Riches	8
It bends the hams of Gossip Vigilance,	363	Riches	11
Muffles the clearnesse of Election,	363	Riches	14
Prove of his Mistris Feature,	364	Phoenix	7
Of her illustrate brightnesse,	364	Ode Splendor	3
Of her admyred brightnesse,	364	Ode Splendor	V 3
Then the stolne sports of Lovers,	365	Ode Splendor	7
Closde in an orbe of Christall.	365	Ode Splendor	12
The Phoenix place of breeding,	365	Ode Splendor	14
All Nature of commending.	365	Ode Splendor	16
Did never dint the breast of Tamisis.	366	Ode Who saith	8
And Phoebus love cause of his blackenesse is.	366	Ode Who saith	16
"For stile of rarenesse, to degenerate.	367	Ode Who saith	32
Be proofe, the glory of his hand,	367	Ode Who saith	49
Tames, prowde of thee, and of his Fate	368	Ode Who saith	81
The choise of Europes pride;	368	Ode Who saith	83
Of thine, shall thinke the Maine	368	Ode Who saith	90
In heav'n the Signe of old Eridanus:	369	Ode Who saith	109
Of Europes waters can	369	Ode Who saith	119
Require (besides the likenesse of the thing)	370	Author	2
Betweene the doubtfull sway of Reason', and sense;	370	Author	12
Upon the Life, and Death of Playes, and Wits,	370	Fletcher	2
(Compos'd of Gamester, Captaine, Knight, Knight's man,	370	Fletcher	3
Of Spheares, as light of starres; She was earthes Eye:	372	Epitaph	9
Might make the Fable of Good Women true.	372	Epitaph	14
All sorts of fish with Musicke of his maw.	374	Coryat 1	11
Old Hat here, torne Hose, with Shoes full of gravell,	375	Coryat 1	26
And louse-dropping Case, are the Armes of his travell.	375	Coryat 1	27
To the Right Noble Tom, Tell-Troth of his travailes, . . .	378	Coryat 2	Ttl
Of travell he discourseth so at large,	378	Coryat 2	82
Of Tom of Odcombe that odde Joviall Author,	378	Coryat 2	87
Yes thou wert borne out of his travelling thigh	378	Coryat 2	89
The height, let him learne of Mr. Tom. Coryate;	379	Coryat 3	2
Of our Odcombian, that literate Elfe?	379	Coryat 3	7
By the scale of his booke, a yard of his stile?	379	Coryat 3	10
The Mappe of his journey, and sees in his booke,	379	Coryat 3	18
Each leafe of his journall, and line doth unlocke	380	Coryat 3	23
The truth of his heart there, and tell's what a clocke	380	Coryat 3	24
Or builders of Story have oft imputation	380	Coryat 3	30
Of lying, he feares so much the reproofe	380	Coryat 3	31
Of his foote, and his penne, his braine or his hoofe,	380	Coryat 3	32
Of Latine and Greeke, to his friendship. And seven	380	Coryat 3	45
He there doth protest he saw of the eleven.	380	Coryat 3	46
Jest, he saies. Item one sute of blacke taffata	380	Coryat 3	48
Except a dublet, and bought of the Jewes:	380	Coryat 3	49
The height, let him learne of Mr. Tom Coryate.	381	Coryat 3	60
. . . in the Behalfe of the two Noble Brothers sir Robert . .	382	Rich	Ttl
unto thee, king of men; their noblest partes	382	Rich	3
The elder of these two, riche hopes Increase,	382	Rich	5
presentes a Royall Alter of fayre peace,	382	Rich	6
. . . Robert, Earle of Somerset.	384	Somerset	Ttl
Not only this, but every day of thine,	384	Somerset	9
To rise with eyther of you, on the morrow.	384	Somerset	16

	Page	Title	Line
OF (cont.)			
And ev'ry birth encrease the heate of Love.	384	Somerset	20
Yet neyther of you seeme to th'other old.	384	Somerset	24
The art of uttring wares, if they were bad:	385	Husband	6
Or skill of making matches in my life:	386	Husband	7
Was worthy of a Good one; And this, here,	386	Husband	10
Some men, of Bookes or Freinds not speaking right,	386	Browne	1
Upon th'Exchange of Letters, as I wou'd	386	Browne	14
More of our writers would like thee, not swell	386	Browne	15
these only hide part of my flesh, and bones:	387	Cavendish	2
. . . on his Translation of Hesiods Works, & Dayes.	388	Chapman	Ttl
Were askt of thy Discoveries; They must say,	388	Chapman	8
As, now, of all men, it is call'd thy Trade:	389	Chapman	11
And hath the noblest marke of a good Booke,	389	Aleman	7
Such Bookes deserve Translators, of like coate	389	Aleman	11
More then the Foster-father of this Child;	389	Aleman	14
To the memory of my beloved, the Author . . .	390	Shakespeare	Ttl
Above th'ill fortune of them, or the need.	391	Shakespeare	16
I, therefore will begin. Soule of the Age!	391	Shakespeare	17
The applause! delight! the wonder of our Stage!	391	Shakespeare	18
For, if I thought my judgement were of yeeres,	391	Shakespeare	27
Paccuvius, Accius, him of Cordova dead,	391	Shakespeare	35
Of all, that insolent Greece, or haughtie Rome	391	Shakespeare	39
To whom all Scenes of Europe homage owe.	391	Shakespeare	42
He was not of an age, but for all time!	391	Shakespeare	43
Nature her selfe was proud of his designes,	392	Shakespeare	47
And joy'd to weare the dressing of his lines!	392	Shakespeare	48
As they were not of Natures family.	392	Shakespeare	54
Of Shakespeares minde, and manners brightly shines	392	Shakespeare	67
In each of which, he seemes to shake a Lance,	392	Shakespeare	69
As brandish't at the eyes of Ignorance.	392	Shakespeare	70
Sweet Swan of Avon! what a sight it were	392	Shakespeare	71
And make those flights upon the bankes of Thames,	392	Shakespeare	73
Shine forth, thou Starre of Poets, and with rage,	392	Shakespeare	77
To the memorye of that most Honoured Ladie Jane, . . .	394	Jane Ogle	Ttl
A list of Epithites: And prayse this way.	394	Jane Ogle	8
Such things, of every body, and as well.	394	Jane Ogle	10
But of one Husband; and since he left life,	394	Jane Ogle	16
Where spight of Death, next Life, for her Loves sake	394	Jane Ogle	25
To my chosen Friend, the learned Translator of Lucan, . . .	395	May	Ttl
Of Fortunes wheele by Lucan driv'n about,	395	May	3
What Muse, or rather God of harmony	395	May	14
What godds but those of arts, and eloquence?	395	May	16
The Sunne translated, or the Sonne of May.	395	May	24
The Vision Of Ben. Jonson, On The . . .	396	Drayton	Ttl
As it had beene the circle of the Arts!	396	Drayton	22
And Rouze, the Marching of a mighty force,	397	Drayton	39
Drums against Drums, the neighing of the Horse,	397	Drayton	40
Of all that reade thy Poly-Olbyon.	397	Drayton	52
Thy Catalogue of Ships, exceeding his,	398	Drayton	61
Thy list of aydes, and force, for so it is:	398	Drayton	62
And will be bought of every Lord, and Knight,	398	Drayton	72
The miseries of Margaret the Queene	398	Drayton	75
Of tender eyes will more be wept, then seene:	398	Drayton	76
Of thy strange Moon-Calfe, both thy straine of mirth,	398	Drayton	84
Code, Digests, Pandects of all faemale glory!	399	Lady Ogle	8
The best of Woemen! her whole life	399	Lady Ogle	11
Was the example of a wife!	399	Lady Ogle	12
Or of a parent! or a freind!	399	Lady Ogle	13
Of vertue, pretious in the frame:	399	Lady Ogle	18
Of weight, or fashion, it was shee.	399	Lady Ogle	24
Keeps warme the spice of her good name,	400	Lady Ogle	30
To gaine the Crowne of immortalitye,	400	Lady Ogle	34
Her right, by gift, and purchase of the Lambe:	400	Lady Ogle	36
Of Angells, and all witnesses of light,	400	Lady Ogle	38
And this a coppie is of the Record.	400	Lady Ogle	40
On the honor'd Poems of his honored Friend, . . .	400	Beaumont	Ttl
The Bound, and Frontire of our Poetrie;	400	Beaumont	8
And doth deserve all muniments of praise,	400	Beaumont	9
If, maymed, she come off, 'tis not of men	401	Beaumont	16
This Fort of so impregnable accesse,	401	Beaumont	17
Of Ethnicisme, makes his Muse a Saint.	401	Beaumont	22
Of two, the choicest Paire of Mans delights,	401	Filmer	4
Able to talk of Euclide, and correct	402	Inigo Jones 1	4
With mistooke Names out of Vitruvius!	402	Inigo Jones 1	8
Whether the buylding of the Stage or Scene!	402	Inigo Jones 1	11
Or making of the Propertyes it meane?	402	Inigo Jones 1	12
Of Tyre-man, Mounte-banck & Justice Jones,	402	Inigo Jones 1	16
Will any of these express your place? or witt?	402	Inigo Jones 1	18
A wodden Dagger, is a Dagger of wood	403	Inigo Jones 1	27
The majesty of Juno in the Cloudes,	403	Inigo Jones 1	33
And peering forth of Iris in the Shrowdes!	403	Inigo Jones 1	34
Th'ascent of Lady Fame which none could spy	403	Inigo Jones 1	35
The Eloquence of Masques! What need of prose	403	Inigo Jones 1	40
You are the Spectacles of State! Tis true	403	Inigo Jones 1	42
In the mere perspective of an Inch board!	404	Inigo Jones 1	44
Of many Coulors! read them! & reveale	404	Inigo Jones 1	47
Painting & Carpentry are the Soule of Masque.	404	Inigo Jones 1	50
Terme of the Architects is called Designe!	404	Inigo Jones 1	56
Of any Art, besyde what he calls his!	404	Inigo Jones 1	58
The maker of the Propertyes! in summe	404	Inigo Jones 1	61
Of Lanterne-lerry: with fuliginous heat	405	Inigo Jones 1	72
Suckt from the Veynes of shop-philosophy.	405	Inigo Jones 1	74

OF (cont.)

	Page	Title	Line
In presentacion of some puppet play!	405	Inigo Jones 1	76
In setting forth of such a solemne Toye!	405	Inigo Jones 1	78
In setting forth of such a serious Toye!	405	Inigo Jones 1	V 78
On the new priming of thy old Signe postes	405	Inigo Jones 1	87
Of thy dead Standards: or (with miracle) see	405	Inigo Jones 1	89
Of all the Worthyes hope t'outlast thy one,	406	Inigo Jones 1	99
Soe the Materialls be of Purbeck stone!	406	Inigo Jones 1	100
But cause thou hearst the mighty k. of Spaine	406	Inigo Jones 2	1
From the fam'd pillars of old Hercules!	407	Inigo Jones 2	14
An Earle of show: for all thy worke is showe:	407	Inigo Jones 2	21
An Earle of show: for all thy worth is showe:	407	Inigo Jones 2	V 21
Or canst of truth the least intrenchment pitch,	407	Inigo Jones 2	23
Wee'll have thee styld the Marquess of New-Ditch.	407	Inigo Jones 2	24
Wee'll have thee styld the Marquess of Town-Ditch.	407	Inigo Jones 2	V 24
To a Freind an Epigram Of him.	407	Inigo Jones 3	Ttl
(And labours to seem worthy of that feare)	407	Inigo Jones 3	2
The Marrow! Wretch, I quitt thee of thy paine	408	Inigo Jones 3	5
Will well designe thee, to be viewd of all	408	Inigo Jones 3	12
Th'envy'd returne, of forty pound in gold.	408	Detractor	4
Thy Dirty braines, Men smell thy want of worth.	409	Detractor	22
. . . the Author of this Work, M. Rich. Brome.	409	Brome	Ttl
Of Fellowship, professing my old Arts.	409	Brome	4
By observation of those Comick Lawes	409	Brome	7
It was not so of old: Men tooke up trades	410	Brome	13
Shall the prosperity of a Pardon still	410	Gill	1
Pillory nor Whip, nor want of Ears,	410	Gill	4
To be the Denis of thy Father's School,	410	Gill	7
A Tune to drown the Ballads of thy Father:	411	Gill	12
But Tune and Noise the Eccho of thy Shame.	411	Gill	14
And in them view'd th'uncertainty of Life,	411	Sutcliffe	3
The Peace of Conscience, and the Godly's strife,	411	Sutcliffe	7
The Danger of delaying to Repent,	411	Sutcliffe	9
And the deceipt of pleasures, by Consent.	411	Sutcliffe	11
The comfort of weake Christians, with their warning,	411	Sutcliffe	13
I sayd, who'had supp'd so deepe of this sweet Chalice,	412	Sutcliffe	21
Must Celia bee, the Anagram of Alice.	412	Sutcliffe	23
The Ghyrlond of the blessed Virgin Marie.	412	Ghyrlond	Ttl
The Eye of flowers, worthy, for his scent,	413	Ghyrlond	14
Preserved, in her antique bed of Vert,	413	Ghyrlond	19
Which, of the field is clep'd the sweetest brier,	413	Ghyrlond	22
On the reverse of this your circling crowne,	413	Ghyrlond	30
All, pouring their full showre of graces downe,	413	Ghyrlond	31
Daughter, and Mother, and the Spouse of God,	413	Ghyrlond	33
Alike of kin, to that most blessed Trine,	413	Ghyrlond	34
Of Persons, yet in Union (One) divine.	413	Ghyrlond	35
Sweet Tree of Life, King Davids Strength and Tower,	413	Ghyrlond	38
The House of gold, the Gate of heavens power,	413	Ghyrlond	39
Great Queen of Queens, most mild, most meek, most wise,	414	Ghyrlond	41
Most venerable. Cause of all our joy.	414	Ghyrlond	42
The Seat of Sapience, the most lovely Mother,	414	Ghyrlond	45
And most to be admired of thy Sexe,	414	Ghyrlond	46
Thou Throne of glory, beauteous as the Moone,	414	Ghyrlond	49
Till he hath reach'd his two-fold point of Noone.	414	Ghyrlond	52
Through all the lines of this circumference,	414	Ghyrlond	54
Of being Daughter, Mother, Spouse of God!	414	Ghyrlond	56
Unto the world, in praise of your first Play:	414	Rutter	2
You know, I never was of Truth afeard,	414	Rutter	4
Office of Wit, a Mint, and (this is true)	415	Rutter	20
Cry'd up of late: Whereto there must be first	415	Rutter	21
Of wit, and a new made: a Warden then,	415	Rutter	23
Of Finenesse, and alloy: follow his hint,	415	Rutter	27
Yo'have all the Mysteries of Wits new Mint,	415	Rutter	28
. . . on his great Instauration of his Hunting, . . .	415	Dover	Ttl
Renew the Glories of our blessed Jeames:	415	Dover	4
In spite of Hipocrites, who are the worst	416	Dover	9
Of Subjects; Let such envie, till they burst.	416	Dover	10
Our first of fruits, that is the prime of flowers	416	Welcome	2
Bred by your breath, on this low bancke of ours;	416	Welcome	3
And you, with them, as Father of our spring.	416	Welcome	8
To the wonders of the Peake,	416	Moon	1
she desires of every birth	417	Moon	19
Specially the newes of Darby;	417	Moon	21
and of Circle be as free,	417	Moon	30
This was Mr Ben: Johnsons Answer of the suddayne.	418	Answer	Ttl
God blesse the Councell of Estate,	419	Grace	5
Of that true Face	419	Ode:If Men	2
That were the happie subject of my songe.	419	Ode:If Men	9
Of Civill virtue, that hee now is not	420	Ode:If Men	12
nor cann be of desert,	420	Ode:If Men	13
Whilest lyke a blaze of strawe,	420	Ode:If Men	15
And once more stryke the eare of tyme with those fresh straynes:	420	Ode:If Men	32
And Cunninge of their grownde	420	Ode:If Men	34
Give cause to some of wonnder, some despite,	420	Ode:If Men	35
I have, with strict advantage of free tyme	421	Censure	6
It is an Act of Tyranye, not Love,	422	Censure	18
in Course of Frindshipp, wholie to reprove:	422	Censure	19
From each of which, I labor to be free,	422	Censure	21
For noe Man Lyves, soe out of passions swaye,	422	Censure	24
A speech out of Lucane.	422	Lucan	Ttl
The mayne comaund of scepters, soone doth perishe	422	Lucan	9
To the Oracle of Apollo.	657	Door Apollo	2
Here he speaks out of his Pottle,	657	Door Apollo	3

```
                                              Page    Title      Line
OF  (cont.)
   Cries Old Sym, the King of Skinkers;      .    .    .  657  Door Apollo    8
   He the half of Life abuses,         .    .    .    .  657  Door Apollo    9
   Wine it is the Milk of Venus,       .    .    .    .  657  Door Apollo   12
   To the Oracle of Apollo.      .    .    .    .    .  657  Door Apollo   20
   Lucy of Bedford; she, that Bounty        .    .    .  662  Bedford        3
   of her white Hand; or she can spare it.  .    .    .  662  Bedford       10
   As the token of my Love       .    .    .    .    .  666  Glover         3
   And to the perpetuating of our freindship     .    .  666  Glover         4
   Till I, at much expense of Time, and Taper    .    .  666  Glover         7
OFF
   But then, fist-fill'd, to put me off the sent.  .    .  154  U13 Sacvile   52
   Or was she gracious a-farre off? but neere     .    .  169  U18 Elegy Can  5
   Then com'st thou off with Victorie and Palme,  .    .  187  U33 Councellour 35
   We cut not off, till all Cures else doe faile:  .    .  192  U38 Elegy 'Tis 46
   Streight puts off all his Anger, and doth kisse  .   .  193  U38 Elegy 'Tis 88
   Or slipper was left off, and kisse it too,     .    .  201  U42 Elegy Let  56
   Yet are got off thence, with cleare mind, and hands  .  234  U61 Epigram    7
   To keepe him off; and how-so-e're he gleanes   .    .  242  U69 Friend Son 16
   As it slid moulded off from Heaven.      .    .    .  280  U84 Mind      56
   From off her pillow, and deluded bed;    .    .    .  283  U84 Muse      43
   And with his hooke lops off the fruitlesse race,  .  .  290  U85 Country   11
   That I bright Chloe off should shake;    .    .    .  294  U87 Hor.3:9   19
   Shall perish: so farre off it is, the state,   .    .  309  Horace        99
   'Tis cleare, this way I have got off from blame,  .  .  323  Horace       395
   But you, Pompilius off-spring, spare you not   .    .  325  Horace       415
   As some the farther off: This loves the darke;  .    .  331  Horace       541
   Cut off superfluous ornaments; and when  .    .    .  335  Horace       636
   Till he drop off, a Horse-leech, full of blood.  .   .  337  Horace       680
   Till, horse-leech-like, he drop off, full of blood.  .  355  Horace      V680
   If, maymed, she come off, 'tis not of men  .  .    .  401  Beaumont      16
   As it were spun by nature, off the fleece:     .    .  415  Rutter        18
OFFALL
   To put the skins, and offall in a pastie?  .   .    .   88  E133 Voyage  148
OFFENCE
   But, when they heard it tax'd, tooke more offence.  .   60  E94 Bedford 3  10
   Be nor put on you, nor you take offence.  .   .    .   69  E108 Soldiers  4
   So of uncleannesse, or offence,     .    .    .    .  152  U12 Corbet    17
   Where only a mans birth is his offence,  .    .    .  177  U25 Desmond   32
   When only a mans birth is his offence,   .    .    .  177  U25 Desmond  V 32
   And drives it in to eat on my offence,   .    .    .  191  U38 Elegy 'Tis  6
   God lightens not at mans each fraile offence,  .    .  193  U38 Elegy 'Tis 68
   As all defence, or offence, were a chime!  .   .    .  232  U59 Newcastle  6
   Will take offence, at this: Nor, though it strike   .  321  Horace       361
   Take just offence at this: nor, though it strike    .  347  Horace    V353/361
OFFEND
   Ile not offend thee with a vaine teare more,   .    .   37  E33 Roe 3      1
   Would not be fearefull to offend a dame  .    .    .  112  F11 Epode    109
   Where weaknesse doth offend, and vertue grieve,  .  .  192  U38 Elegy 'Tis 33
   And let your mercie make me asham'd t'offend.  .    .  194  U38 Elegy 'Tis 106
   The angry, and love those that feare t'offend.  .    .  317  Horace       282
   How then? Why, as a Scrivener, if h'offend     .    .  329  Horace       529
   Or thick grosse ointment, but offend the Guests:  .  .  331  Horace       558
OFFENDED
   Offended Mistris, you are yet so faire,   .   .    .  191  U38 Elegy 'Tis  9
   Offended with the dazeling flame,    .    .    .    .  234  U60 La-ware    9
   Had not our every Poet like offended.    .    .    .  325  Horace       414
   Offended with few spots, which negligence .    .    .  329  Horace       527
OFFENDERS
   Wherewith, against thy bloud, they'offenders bee.   .   60  E93 Radcliffe 16
OFFENDING
   Or appetite of offending, but a skill,   .    .    .  156  U13 Sacvile  107
OFFER
   For your most noble offer had supply'd me.     .    .   54  E84 Bedford 2  4
   And offer your just service on these plaines;  .    .  263  U79 New-yeares 12
   Yet, who dares offer a redoubt to reare?  .   .    .  401  Beaumont      11
   We offer as a Circle the most fit   .    .    .    .  416  Welcome        6
OFFER'D
   Not offer'd, as it made sute to be bought;     .    .   28  E3 Bookseller  6
   Were the Rack offer'd them, how they came so;  .    .  157  U13 Sacvile  130
OFFERING
   In offering this thy worke to no great Name,   .    .  161  U14 Selden    69
OFFERS
   Yet he that offers at it, may sweat much,  .   .    .  321  Horace       351
OFFICE
   Nor office in the towne, nor place in court,   .    .   63  E97 Motion    11
   Yet is the office not to be despis'd,    .    .    .   78  E121 Rudyerd 1  5
   Rather then Office, when it doth or may  .    .    .  158  U14 Selden     9
   And as within your Office, you doe take  .    .    .  216  U45 Squib     13
   Hee's Master of the Office; yet no more  .    .    .  258  U75 Epithalam. 187
   Never at Law; seldome in office gown'd;  .    .    .  295  U90 Mart.10:47  5
   Lay that aside, the Epicks office is.    .    .    .  307  Horace        64
   An Actors parts, and Office too, the Quire     .    .  317  Horace       276
   Their Charge, and Office, whence their wealth to fet, .  325  Horace      436
   And office of a Judge are, what the parts .    .    .  325  Horace       450
   Office of Wit, a Mint, and (this is true) .    .    .  415  Rutter        20
OFFICER
   An Officer there, did make most solemne love,  .    .  201  U42 Elegy Let  53
OFFICERS
   Them, and all their officers.     .    .    .    .    .  105  F8 Sicknesse  35
   Them, or their officers: and no man know, .    .    .  118  F13 Aubigny   79
OFFICES
   Whose Offices, and honours did surprize, .    .    .  185  U30 Burleigh  15
```

OFFICES (cont.)
All Offices were done . . . . 244 U70 Ode 48
To doe their Offices in Natures Chime, . . . 253 U75 Epithalam. 27
OFFICIOUS
Haste, haste, officious Sun, and send them Night . . 257 U75 Epithalam. 145
OFFICIOUSLY
Officiously, at first, themselves betray. . . . 94 F2 Penshurst 36
OFF'RING
Who as an off'ring at your shrine, ... 174 U22 Elegy Tho 29
OFFRING
For offring, with thy smiles, my wit to grace, . . 45 E58 Groome 3
With you, I know, my offring will find grace. . . 114 F12 Rutland 30
An offring meet . . . . 127 U1 Trinitie 12
By offring not more sureties, then inow, . . . 386 Browne 12
OFF-SPRING
But you, Pompilius off-spring, spare you not . . 325 Horace 415
OFT
And so is Jone. Oft-times, when Giles doth find . 40 E42 Giles 9
That quit'st the cause so oft, and ray'st at men? . 44 E54 Chev'ril 2 4
I oft looke on false coyne, to know't from true: . 68 E107 Hungry 3
That both for wit, and sense, so oft dost plucke, . 73 E112 Gamster 18
And thence, the ruddy Satyres oft provoke . . 94 F2 Penshurst 17
In spring, oft roused for thy masters sport, . . 97 F3 Wroth 23
Moodes, which the god-like Sydney oft did prove, . 116 F12 Rutland 91
Boast, but how oft they have gone wrong to man: . 119 F13 Aubigny 84
Such as oft I wanton in! . . . . . 136 U2 Cupid 23
As the Downe, and shew it oft; . . . . 141 U2 Her man 26
And mine not least) I have too oft preferr'd . . 159 U14 Selden 20
When oft the Bearer, is borne out of dore? . . 166 U15 Friend-Wars 120
Oft scape an Imputation, more through luck, then wit. 179 U25 Desmond 52
Oft scape theyr Imputation, more through luck, then wit. 179 U25 Desmond V 52
Though Envie oft his shadow be, ... 189 U36 Song 3
Fit for a Bishops knees! O bow them oft, . . 234 U61 Epigram 13
Ye have oft-times, that may ore-shine the rest, . 305 Horace 18
Ye have oft-times, that may out-shine the rest, . 338 Horace V 18
With swelling throat: and, oft, the tragick wight . 311 Horace 134
Oft-times a Sharpe, when we require a Flat: . . 329 Horace 523
Or builders of Story have oft imputation . . 380 Coryat 3 30
Though shee chainge as oft as shee, . . . 417 Moon 29
OFTEN
His often change of clime (though not of mind) . . 37 E32 Roe 2 6
And is t'a body, often, ill inclin'd, . . . 82 E130 Ferrab. 1 7
That had, so often, shew'd 'hem merry prankes. . 89 E133 Voyage 184
The jolly wassall walkes the often round, . . 98 F3 Wroth 59
Doe change, though man, and often fight, . . 146 U6 Defence 8
But as 'tis often vext and tri'd. . . . 146 U6 Defence 18
On th'often comming of this Holy-day: . . . 249 U72 King 16
How well, and how often his shoes too were mended, . 380 Coryat 3 39
OFTNER
And change possessions, oftner with his breath, . . 99 F3 Wroth 75
OFT-TIMES
And so is Jone. Oft-times, when Giles doth find . 40 E42 Giles 9
Ye have oft-times, that may ore-shine the rest, . 305 Horace 18
Ye have oft-times, that may out-shine the rest, . 338 Horace V 18
Oft-times a Sharpe, when we require a Flat: . . 329 Horace 523
OGLE
. . . eldest Daughter, to Cuthbert Lord Ogle: . . . 394 Jane Ogle Ttl
For this did Katherine, Ladie Ogle, die . . . 400 Lady Ogle 33
OH
What should the cause be? Oh, you live at court: . 46 E62 Would-bee 9
Oh doe not wanton with those eyes, . . . 144 U4 Song 1
Oh, but my conscious feares, ... 149 U9 Picture 11
Oh how a Lover may mistake! to thinke, . . . 170 U18 Elegy Can 15
But, why, oh why, my Ligurine, ... 293 U86 Hor.4:1 33
Oh, to make Boardes to speake! There is a taske . 404 Inigo Jones 1 49
Whither? oh whither will this Tire-man growe? . . 404 Inigo Jones 1 59
Oh wise Surveyor! wyser Architect! . . . 405 Inigo Jones 1 85
OIL (See OYLE)
OINTMENT
Or thick grosse ointment, but offend the Guests: . 331 Horace 558
OKE
The lighter Faunes, to reach thy Ladies oke. . . 94 F2 Penshurst 18
Then now beneath some ancient Oke he may, . . 290 U85 Country 23
OLBYON
Of all that reade thy Poly-Olbyon. . . . 397 Drayton 52
OLD
But see! th'old baud hath serv'd him in his trim, . 31 E12 Shift 23
Of old, they gave a cock to Aesculape; . . . 31 E13 Empirick 2
When both it is the old way, and the true. . . 32 E18 Censurer 2
On Old Colt. . . . . 39 E39 Colt Ttl
To Old-end Gatherer. . . . . . . 43 E53 Old-end Ttl
Long-gathering Old-end, I did feare thee wise, . . 43 E53 Old-end 1
Buy the reversion of old playes; now growne . . 45 E56 Poet-Ape 6
Nor glad as those, that old dependents bee, . . 47 E64 Salisbury 3 5
On the true causes, ere they grow too old. . . 50 E70 Wm Roe 1 4
Surly's old whore in her new silkes doth swim: . 54 E82 Surly 1
See you yond' Motion? Not the old Fa-ding, . . 62 E97 Motion 1
A new Susanna, equall to that old? . . . 67 E104 Montgomery 4
Acts old Iniquitie, and in the fit . . . 74 E115 Honest Man 27
Old men so duely, ... 77 E120 S. P. 14
Of old, even by her practise, to be fam'd; . . 82 E130 Ferrab. 1 10
Hung stench, diseases, and old filth, their mother, . 86 E133 Voyage 70
Whereof old Democrite, and Hill Nicholas, . . 87 E133 Voyage 128

OLD (cont.)
    Old Bankes the juggler, our Pythagoras,   .   .   .   88   E133 Voyage   156
    When Love is fled, and I grow old.   .   .   .   93   F1 Why write no   12
    Such, and no other was that age, of old,   .   .   .   98   F3 Wroth   63
    Yet art thou both shrunke up, and old,   .   .   .   100   F4 To the World   14
    With his old earthly labours. T'exact more,   .   .   .   107   F10 Proludium   5
    Let the old boy, your sonne, ply his old taske, .   .   .   107   F10 Proludium   19
    Will prove old Orpheus act no tale to be: .   .   .   115   F12 Rutland   77
    Will prove old Orpheus Arts no tale to be: .   .   .   115   F12 Rutland   V 77
    Some have lov'd as old agen.   .   .   .   131   U2 Excuse   6
    She shall make the old man young,   .   .   .   131   U2 Excuse   20
    His new Cassandra, 'bove the old;   .   .   .   181   U27 Ode Helen   23
    As Horace fat; or as Anacreon old;   .   .   .   199   U42 Elegy Let   2
    Under that cover; an old Mid-wives hat!   .   .   .   202   U42 Elegy Let   83
    Was it because thou wert of old denied   .   .   .   203   U43 Vulcan   11
    Wast not hee: thou wert of old denied   .   .   .   203   U43 Vulcan   V 11
    All the old Venusine, in Poetrie,   .   .   .   207   U43 Vulcan   89
    What the old Venusine, in Poetrie,   .   .   .   207   U43 Vulcan   V 89
    With the old Venusine, in Poetrie,   .   .   .   207   U43 Vulcan   V 89
    Old Aesope Gundomar: the French can tell,   .   .   .   213   U44 Speach   5
    What a strong Fort old Pimblicoe had bin!   .   .   .   213   U44 Speach   21
    Beauchamps, and Nevills, Cliffords, Audleys old; .   .   .   214   U44 Speach   52
    They cannot last. No lie grew ever old.   .   .   .   216   U45 Squib   20
    As new rewards of her old secrecie?   .   .   .   223   U49 Pucell   20
    As makes Penelopes old fable true,   .   .   .   224   U50 Countesse   20
    Unprofitable Chattell, fat and old,   .   .   .   230   U56 Covell   8
    As the old Bard, should no Canary lack.   .   .   .   241   U68 House-hold   11
    That when you both are old,   .   .   .   258   U75 Epithalam.   165
    The old Greek-hands in picture, or in stone.   .   .   .   260   U77 Treasurer   9
    To day old Janus opens the new yeare,   .   .   .   263   U79 New-yeares   9
    And shuts the old. Haste, haste, all loyall Swaines, . .   263   U79 New-yeares   10
    Spun out in name of some of the old Nine!   .   .   .   282   U84 Muse   6
    As the old race of Mankind were,   .   .   .   289   U85 Country   2
    As the old stock of Mankind were,   .   .   .   289   U85 Country   V 2
    To deck the hallow'd Harth with old wood fir'd   .   .   .   291   U85 Country   43
    But, say old Love returne should make,   .   .   .   294   U87 Hor.3:9   17
    Darke thy cleare glasse with old Falernian Wine; .   .   .   295   U89 Mart.8:77   5
    Or an Heroe; if a ripe old man,   .   .   .   313   Horace   162
    The old man many evils doe girt round;   .   .   .   315   Horace   241
    Or old Silenus, Bacchus guard, and Nurse.   .   .   .   321   Horace   348
    To these succeeded the old Comoedie,   .   .   .   321   Horace   365
    Your Ancestors, old Plautus numbers prais'd,   .   .   .   348   Horace   V385/399
    This was the wisdome, that they had of old,   .   .   .   327   Horace   486
    Salute old Mone,   .   .   .   367   Ode Who saith   38
    In heav'n the Signe of old Eridanus: .   .   .   369   Ode Who saith   109
    Old Hat here, torne Hose, with Shoes full of gravell, . .   375   Coryat 1   26
    Yet neyther of you seeme to th'other old.   .   .   .   384   Somerset   24
    When the old words doe strike on the new times, .   .   .   389   Aleman   4
    Which made me thinke, the old Theocritus,   .   .   .   397   Drayton   27
    Thou hadst brought Lapland, or old Cobalus,   .   .   .   398   Drayton   86
    On the new priming of thy old Signe postes   .   .   .   405   Inigo Jones 1   87
    From the fam'd pillars of old Hercules!   .   .   .   407   Inigo Jones 2   14
    To my old Faithfull Servant: And   409   Brome   Ttl
    Of Fellowship, professing my old Arts.   .   .   .   409   Brome   4
    It was not so of old: Men tooke up trades   .   .   .   410   Brome   13
    A Master-worker call'd, th'old standerd burst   .   .   .   415   Rutter   22
    Cries Old Sym, the King of Skinkers;   .   .   .   657   Door Apollo   8
OLDE
    Olde Hesiods Ore, and give it us; but thine,   .   .   .   388   Chapman   2
OLD-END
    To Old-end Gatherer.   .   .   .   43   E53 Old-end   Ttl
    Long-gathering Old-end, I did feare thee wise,   .   .   .   43   E53 Old-end   1
OLIMPICKE
    Twixt Cotswold, and the Olimpicke exercise: .   .   .   415   Dover   2
OLIVE
    An olive, capers, or some better sallade   .   .   .   64   E101 Supper   10
    Shoot up an Olive fruitfull, faire,   .   .   .   251   U74 Weston   28
OLIVEERS
    All the madde Rolands, and sweet Oliveers;   .   .   .   206   U43 Vulcan   70
OLIVES
    More sweet then Olives, that new gather'd be   .   .   .   291   U85 Country   55
OMEN
    Good Omen to him, in the note thou sing'st,   .   .   .   263   U78 Digby   22
OMINOUS
    A vow as new, and ominous as the yeare,   .   .   .   116   F12 Rutland   98
OMITTED
    Much, that mought now be spoke: omitted here   .   .   .   307   Horace   62
    . . . omitted, and now communicated to the World .   .   .   379   Coryat 3   Ttl
OMNIPOTENT
    Aymd at in thy omnipotent Designe!   .   .   .   406   Inigo Jones 1   96
ON'
    Yet who could have hit on't but the wise noddell .   .   .   379   Coryat 3   6
    Pies on't, you have his historicall faith.   .   .   .   380   Coryat 3   22
    I shall think on't ere't be day.   .   .   .   417   Moon   11
ON (OF)
    Lesse must not be thought on then Mistresse: or, .   .   .   165   U15 Friend-Wars   95
ON
    Nor have my title-leafe on posts, or walls,   .   .   .   28   E3 Bookseller   7
    On the Union.   .   .   .   28   E5 Union   Ttl
    On the new Hot-house.   .   .   .   28   E7 Hot-house   Ttl
    On a robbery.   .   .   .   29   E8 Robbery   Ttl
    On some-thing, that walkes some-where.   .   .   .   30   E11 Something   Ttl
    On lieutenant Shift.   .   .   .   30   E12 Shift   Ttl

	Page	Title	Line
ON (cont.)			
On Court-worme.	31	E15 Court-worm	Ttl
On Sir Cod the perfumed.	33	E19 Cod 1	Ttl
On reformed Gam'ster.	33	E21 Gam'ster	Ttl
On my first Daughter.	33	E22 Daughter	Ttl
On Sir Voluptuous Beast.	34	E25 Beast 1	Ttl
On the same Beast.	35	E26 Beast 2	Ttl
On Sir John Roe.	35	E27 Roe 1	Ttl
On Don Surly.	35	E28 Surly	Ttl
On Banck the Usurer.	36	E31 Banck	Ttl
On Sir John Roe.	37	E32 Roe 2	Ttl
On Chev'rill the Lawyer.	38	E37 Chev'ril	Ttl
But as they come, on both sides he takes fees,	38	E37 Chev'ril	2
On Old Colt.	39	E39 Colt	Ttl
On Margaret Ratcliffe.	39	E40 Ratcliffe	Ttl
All the gazers on the skies	39	E40 Ratcliffe	5
On Gypsee.	39	E41 Gypsee	Ttl
On Giles and Jone.	40	E42 Giles	Ttl
On Chuffe, Bancks the Usurer's Kinsman.	41	E44 Chuff	Ttl
On my First Sonne.	41	E45 First Son	Ttl
Exacted by thy fate, on the just day.	41	E45 First Son	4
'Tis Lucklesse he, that tooke up one on band	42	E46 Luckless 1	3
On Mungril Esquire.	42	E48 Mungril	Ttl
On Chev'ril.	44	E54 Chev'ril 2	Ttl
On Poet-Ape.	44	E56 Poet-Ape	Ttl
On Baudes, and Usurers.	45	E57 Bawds	Ttl
On Spies.	45	E59 Spies	Ttl
In a great belly. Write, then on thy wombe,	46	E62 Would-bee	11
With what thy vertue on the times hath won,	47	E63 Salisbury 2	2
To see thy fathers rites new laid on thee.	47	E64 Salisbury 3	6
On Play-wright.	49	E68 Playwrt 2	Ttl
On the true causes, ere they grow too old.	50	E70 Wm Roe 1	4
On Court-Parrat.	50	E71 Parrat	Ttl
I lent you, on meere acquaintance, at a feast.	51	E73 Fine Grand	6
Item, an epitaph on my lords cock,	51	E73 Fine Grand	18
On Lippe, the Teacher.	52	E75 Lippe	Ttl
On Lucy Countesse of Bedford.	52	E76 Bedford 1	Ttl
On whom, if he were living now, to looke,	53	E79 Rutland	10
On Cashierd Capt. Surly.	54	E82 Surly	Ttl
On Captaine Hazard the Cheater.	56	E87 Hazard	Ttl
On English Mounsieur.	56	E88 Monsieur	Ttl
And land on one, whose face durst never bee	56	E88 Monsieur	5
Or hung some Mounsieurs picture on the wall,	56	E88 Monsieur	12
On Mill my Ladies Woman.	57	E90 Mill	Ttl
Went on: and proving him still, day by day,	57	E90 Mill	7
When on thy trumpet shee did sound a blast,	58	E91 Vere	7
With ignorance on us, as they have done	59	E92 New Crie	37
On them: And therefore doe not onely shunne	59	E92 New Crie	38
On the new Motion.	62	E97 Motion	Ttl
On Play-wright.	64	E100 Playwrt 3	Ttl
It is an Epigramme, on all man-kind;	66	E102 Pembroke	2
Were leading forth the Graces on the greene:	68	E105 L Wroth 2	12
That saw you put on Pallas plumed caske:	68	E105 L Wroth 2	16
All-vertuous Herbert! on whose every part	68	E106 E Herbert	3
I oft looke on false coyne, to know't from true:	68	E107 Hungry	3
Be nor put on you, nor you take offence.	69	E108 Soldiers	4
Who now calls on thee, Nevil, is a Muse,	70	E109 Nevil	1
Goe on, and doubt not, what posteritie,	70	E109 Nevil	15
To Clement Edmonds, on his Caesars . . .	71	E110 Edmonds 1	Ttl
To the same; On the same.	72	E111 Edmonds 2	Ttl
On the Townes honest Man.	74	E115 Honest Man	Ttl
And him it layes on; if he be not there.	74	E115 Honest Man	16
'Twas not entayl'd on title. That some word	75	E116 Jephson	7
On Groyne.	75	E117 Groyne	Ttl
On Gut.	76	E118 Gut	Ttl
Epitaph on S. P. a Child of Q. El. Chappel.	77	E120 S. P.	Ttl
Epitaph on Elizabeth, L. H.	79	E124 Elizabeth	Ttl
Into the debt; and reckon on her head,	80	E127 Aubigny	5
Or (mounted on a stoole) thy face doth hit	81	E129 Mime	13
On some new gesture, that's imputed wit?	81	E129 Mime	14
To Alphonso Ferrabosco, on his Booke.	82	E130 Ferrab. 1	Ttl
I, yet, had utter'd nothing on thy part,	82	E130 Ferrab. 1	15
They were not to be nam'd on the same day.	83	E131 Ferrab. 2	12
On the famous Voyage.	84	E133 Voyage	Ttl
Of those, that put out moneyes, on returne	85	E133 Voyage	32
Betweene two walls; where, on one side, to scar men,	86	E133 Voyage	67
Gorgonian scolds, and Harpyes: on the other	86	E133 Voyage	69
And, on they went, like Castor brave, and Pollux:	86	E133 Voyage	77
No going backe; on still you rogues, and row.	86	E133 Voyage	88
Poore Mercury, crying out on Paracelsus,	86	E133 Voyage	96
By which the Masters sweare, when, on the stoole	87	E133 Voyage	122
Behold where Cerberus, rear'd on the wall	89	E133 Voyage	176
Bright eeles, that emulate them, and leape on land,	94	F2 Penshurst	37
Hang on thy walls, that every child may reach.	94	F2 Penshurst	44
Shine bright on every harth as the desires	95	F2 Penshurst	78
Of thy Penates had beene set on flame,	95	F2 Penshurst	79
On thy good lady, then! who, therein, reap'd	95	F2 Penshurst	84
God wisheth, none should wracke on a strange shelfe.	99	F3 Wroth	95
My part is ended on thy stage.	100	F4 To the World	4
On my lips, thus hardly sundred,	103	F6 Celia 2	7
Sicknesse; onely on us men.	105	F8 Sicknesse	14
Lying on the spirit of amber.	105	F8 Sicknesse	V 32
Dare entayle their loves on any,	105	F8 Sicknesse	39

ON (cont.)

	Page	Title	Line
On their beds, most prostitute,	106	F8 Sicknesse	45
Pallas, nor thee I call on, mankinde maid,	107	F10 Proludium	13
Pallas, nor thee we call on, mankinde maid,	107	F10 Proludium	V 13
With whom who sailes, rides on the surge of feare,	110	F11 Epode	41
That falls like sleepe on lovers, and combines	110	F11 Epode	49
The wealthy treasure of her love on him;	112	F11 Epode	105
Were yet unfound, and better plac'd on earth,	114	F12 Rutland	V 25
Who, wheresoere he be, on what dear coast,	116	F12 Rutland	93
Now thincking on you, though to England lost,	116	F12 Rutland	94
On the close groome, and page, on new-yeeres day,	118	F13 Aubigny	74
Let 'hem on poulders, oyles, and paintings, spend,	118	F13 Aubigny	77
Eate on her clients, and some one devoure.	119	F13 Aubigny	88
You are depending on his word, and will;	119	F13 Aubigny	114
Ode. To Sir William Sydney, on his Birth-day.	120	F14 Sydney	Ttl
And he may thinke on that	120	F14 Sydney	15
On what's deceast.	121	F14 Sydney	38
And take compassion on my grievous plight.	127	U1 Trinitie	14
3. A Hymne On the Nativitie of my Saviour.	130	U1 Nativitie	Ttl
And tooke on him our Nature.	130	U1 Nativitie	18
I Beheld her, on a day,	132	U2 How he saw	1
For I ran and call'd on Cupid;	132	U2 How he saw	6
And would on Conditions, be	133	U2 Suffered	5
Doe but looke on her eyes, they doe light	134	U2 Triumph	11
Doe but looke on her Haire, it is bright	134	U2 Triumph	13
7. Begging another, on colour of mending the former.	139	U2 Another	Ttl
And that promise set on fire	139	U2 Promise	5
On what they viewing know.	144	U3 Musicall	20
On which they see or know.	144	U3 Musicall	V 20
Nor looke too kind on my desires,	144	U4 Song	7
We were not bred to sit on stooles,	146	U6 Defence	3
on a lovers dust, made sand for ane Houre Glasse	148	U8 Houre-glasse	VTtl
Verses on his Picture	149	U9 Picture	VTtl
On all mens Fruit, and flowers, as well as mine.	150	U10 Jealousie	8
Or Scorne, or pittie on me take,	150	U11 Dreame	1
An Epitaph on Master Vincent Corbet.	151	U12 Corbet	Ttl
Well knowne, and practiz'd borrowers on their word,	154	U13 Sacvile	48
Or on the sudden. It were strange that he	156	U13 Sacvile	125
Yet we must more then move still, or goe on,	157	U13 Sacvile	135
But I on yours farre otherwise shall doe,	159	U14 Selden	17
On whom I could take up, and ne're abuse	161	U14 Selden	83
Looke on th'ambitious man, and see him nurse	162	U15 Friend-Wars	11
Looke on the false, and cunning man, that loves	162	U15 Friend-Wars	15
And then, leape mad on a neat Pickardill,	164	U15 Friend-Wars	70
For man to spend his money on? his wit?	165	U15 Friend-Wars	102
Those thousands on his back, shall after blow	165	U15 Friend-Wars	104
Coach'd, or on foot-cloth, thrice chang'd every day,	165	U15 Friend-Wars	107
Is it that man pulls on himselfe Disease?	165	U15 Friend-Wars	114
Brought on us, and will every hour increase.	166	U15 Friend-Wars	122
Light thee from hell on earth: where flatterers, spies,	167	U15 Friend-Wars	163
That whatsoever face thy fate puts on,	168	U15 Friend-Wars	185
An Epitaph on Master Philip Gray.	168	U16 Gray	Ttl
Did her perfections call me on to gaze,	169	U18 Elegy Can	3
But which shall lead me on? both these are blind:	170	U18 Elegy Can	11
I'le lead you on; or if my fate will so,	170	U18 Elegy Can	22
Put on for fashion, and take up on trust:	171	U20 Shrub	8
And on them burne so chaste a flame,	173	U22 Elegy Tho	21
That eats on wits, and Arts, and destroyes them both.	174	U23 Himselfe	6
Should not on fortune pause,	174	U23 Himselfe	17
Wake, and put on the wings of Pindars Muse,	176	U25 Desmond	3
On these darke rymes; that my affection	177	U25 Desmond	15
On these darke rymes; that our affection	177	U25 Desmond	V 15
Did Sappho on her seven-tongu'd Lute,	181	U27 Ode Helen	3
An Epigram On William Lord Burl:	185	U30 Burleigh	Ttl
As though the Court pursues them on the sent,	186	U32 Elsmere	13
On which with profit, I shall never looke,	189	U37 Friend-Book	5
And drives it in to eat on my offence,	191	U38 Elegy 'Tis	6
Would live his glory that could keepe it on;	192	U38 Elegy 'Tis	48
On every wall, and sung where e're I walke.	193	U38 Elegy 'Tis	98
Like the dull wearied Crane that (come on land)	198	U40 Elegy That	35
Put on my Ivy Garland, let me see	200	U42 Elegy Let	9
Whose like I have knowne the Taylors Wife put on	201	U42 Elegy Let	39
When by thy sordid bountie she hath on	201	U42 Elegy Let	45
Wrung on the Withers, by Lord Loves despight,	201	U42 Elegy Let	63
That chanc'd the lace, laid on a Smock, to see,	201	U42 Elegy Let	66
Varietie of Silkes were on th'Exchange!	202	U42 Elegy Let	72
What had I done that might call on thine ire?	202	U43 Vulcan	2
What have I done that might call on thine ire?	202	U43 Vulcan	V 2
But, on thy malice, tell me, didst thou spie	203	U43 Vulcan	19
Acrostichs, and Telestichs, on jumpe names,	204	U43 Vulcan	39
Acrostichs, and Telestichs, on fine names,	204	U43 Vulcan	V 39
On such my serious follies; But, thou'lt say,	204	U43 Vulcan	41
Or Captaine Pamphletts, which on foote doe sally	206	U43 Vulcan	V 79
Well fare the wise-men yet, on the Banckside,	208	U43 Vulcan	123
Bred on the Banck, in time of Poperie,	209	U43 Vulcan	143
Pox on your flameship, Vulcan; if it be	211	U43 Vulcan	191
Pox on your fire workes, Vulcan; if it be	211	U43 Vulcan	V191
On both sides doe your mischiefes with delight;	212	U43 Vulcan	204
Pox on thee, Vulcan, thy Pandora's pox,	212	U43 Vulcan	213
Light on thee: Or if those plagues will not doo,	212	U43 Vulcan	215
Thy Wives pox on thee, and B.B.'s too.	212	U43 Vulcan	216
Thy Wives pox on thee, and Bess Broughtons too.	212	U43 Vulcan	V216
But on thy practise, and the Posture booke:	213	U44 Speach	28

		Page	Title	Line
ON (cont.)				
Goe on, increase in vertue; and in fame:	. . . .	214	U44 Speach	49
Our Ancestors impos'd on Prince and State.	.	215	U44 Speach	78
I may no longer on these pictures stay,	.	216	U44 Speach	98
Those are poore Ties, depend on those false ends,	. .	216	U45 Squib	11
An Epigram on Sir Edward Coke, when . . .	.	217	U46 Coke	Ttl
Or th'other on their borders, that will jeast	.	218	U47 Tribe	16
On all Soules that are absent; even the dead;	.	218	U47 Tribe	17
And set us all on skipping,	. . .	222	U48 Bacchus	51
An Epigram on The Court Pucell.	.	222	U49 Pucell	Ttl
What though she ride two mile on Holy-dayes	.	222	U49 Pucell	15
What though she hath won on Trust, as many doe,	.	223	U49 Pucell	21
To conquer rumour, and triumph on spight;	.	224	U50 Countesse	4
. . . On his Horsemanship, and Stable.	.	228	U53 Newcastle	VTtl
Or Castor mounted on his Cyllarus:	.	228	U53 Newcastle	8
And then to be return'd; on protestation	.	229	U54 Squib	18
To make you merry on the Dressing stoole	.	230	U56 Covell	21
If they goe on, and that thou lov'st a-life	.	232	U58 Book-seller	13
An Epitaph, on Henry L. La-ware. To the Passer-by.	.	233	U60 La-ware	Ttl
. . . On the Universary day of his Raigne. 1629.	.	236	U64 Charles 3	VTtl
. . . On his Anniversary Day. 1629.	.	236	U64 Charles 3	Ttl
An Epigram on the Princes birth. 1630.	.	237	U65 Prince	Ttl
An Epigram on Prince Charles his Birth: May. 29th. 1630	.	237	U65 Prince	VTtl
On the Princes Birth-day. An Epigram	. . .	237	U65 Prince	VTtl
To the Queene on her Birth-day	. . .	239	U67 Muses	VTtl
Had got the Ceston on!	. . .	240	U67 Muses	36
Had put the Ceston on!	. . .	240	U67 Muses	V 36
Wise-crafts, on which the flatterer ventures not.	.	241	U69 Friend Son	6
To Sir Lucius Carey, on the death of his Brother Morison	.	242	U70 Ode	VTtl
Lay trampled on; the deeds of death, and night,	.	243	U70 Ode	14
And all on utmost ruine set;	.	243	U70 Ode	18
Produce thy masse of miseries on the Stage,	.	244	U70 Ode	55
Accept this garland, plant it on thy head,	.	245	U70 Ode	77
Whilst that in heav'n, this light on earth must shine.	.	246	U70 Ode	96
Who, e're the first downe bloomed on the chin,	.	247	U70 Ode	127
To the King. On his Birth-day . . .	.	249	U72 King	Ttl
On th'often comming of this Holy-day:	.	249	U72 King	16
On the Right Honourable, and vertuous Lord Weston, L. . . .	.	250	U73 Weston	Ttl
Feed on thy selfe for spight, and shew thy Kind:	.	250	U73 Weston	9
Thou canst not meet more Glory, on the way,	.	252	U75 Epithalam.	3
On all that come her Simplesse to rebuke!	.	253	U75 Epithalam.	44
On the same floore,	. . .	254	U75 Epithalam.	70
Like Swine, or other Cattell here on earth:	.	257	U75 Epithalam.	154
Their names are not recorded on the File	.	257	U75 Epithalam.	155
Hath drawne on me, from the times,	.	259	U76 Petition	17
Hath drawne on him, from the times,	.	259	U76 Petition	V 17
Then goe on, and doe its worst;	.	260	U76 Petition	29
. . . on her Husband, Sir Kenelme Digby.	.	262	U78 Digby	Ttl
And offer your just service on these plaines;	.	263	U79 New-yeares	12
Who walkes on Earth as May still went along,	.	264	U79 New-yeares	26
Still waited on 'hem where they were.	.	264	U79 New-yeares	39
To My L. the King, On the Christning His second Sonne James.	.	268	U80 Christning	Ttl
An Elegie On the Lady Jane Pawlet, Marchion: of Winton.	.	268	U81 Pawlet	Ttl
Stick on your Cupping-glasses, feare not, put	.	270	U81 Pawlet	53
On Natures secrets, there, as her owne bookes:	.	271	U81 Pawlet	70
On naturall secret, there, as her owne bookes:	.	271	U81 Pawlet	V 70
On every Stall.	. . .	273	U84 Cradle	28
As you goe on, by what brave way	. . .	278	U84 Mind	18
9. Elegie on my Muse. The truly honoured Lady, . . .	.	282	U84 Muse	Ttl
By Death, on Earth, I should have had remorse	.	282	U84 Muse	12
On Nature, for her: who did let her lie,	.	282	U84 Muse	13
Looke on thy sloth, and give thy selfe undone,	.	283	U84 Muse	21
And on her Innocence, a garment fresh	.	285	U84 Muse	94
And white, as that, put on: and in her hand,	.	285	U84 Muse	95
Put black, and mourning on? and say you misse	.	285	U84 Muse	98
Accumulated on her, by the Lord	.	285	U84 Muse	111
Poring, as on a Map, to find the wayes	.	288	U84 Muse	196
On all the world! She saw him on the Crosse	.	288	U84 Muse	201
The kind of Man, on whom his doome should fall!	.	288	U84 Muse	208
Or straines on his small forke his subtill nets	.	290	U85 Country	33
Or straines on his small forke his subtler nets	.	290	U85 Country	V 33
And I, am mutually on fire	. . .	293	U87 Hor.3:9	13
Let us not then rush blindly on unto it,	.	294	U88 Petronius	3
On every limbe, ta'en from a severall creature,	.	305	Horace	3
Creepes on the ground; too safe, too afraid of storme.	.	307	Horace	39
On popular noise with, and doe businesse in.	.	311	Horace	120
To every state of fortune; she helpes on,	.	311	Horace	153
To every Fortunes habit; she helps on,	.	342	Horace	V153
The businesse either on the Stage is done,	.	317	Horace	255
On steele, though 't selfe be dull, and cannot cut.	.	325	Horace	434
On life, and manners, and make those his booke,	.	325	Horace	454
On edge the Masculine spirits, and did whet	.	327	Horace	494
Is laugh'd at, that still jarreth on one string:	.	329	Horace	532
Lest the throng'd heapes should on a laughter take:	.	331	Horace	569
On artlesse Verse; the hard ones he will blame;	.	335	Horace	634
Looke here on Bretons worke, the master print:	.	362	Author	5
Now must we plie our ayme; our Swan's on wing.	.	368	Ode Who saith	64
Their hornes, and Germany pukes on his head.	.	375	Coryat 1	31
hee freely bringes; and on this Alter layes	.	383	Rich	9
shall looke, & on hyme soe, then arte's a lyer	.	383	Rich	15
To rise with eyther of you, on the morrow.	.	384	Somerset	16
To the worthy Author on the Husband.	. . .	385	Husband	Ttl
To my truly-belov'd Freind, Mr Browne: on his Pastorals.	.	386	Browne	Ttl

	Page	Title	Line

ON (cont.)

	Page	Title	Line
And, where the most reade bookes, on Authors fames,	386	Browne	9
On credit, and are cossen'd; see, that thou	386	Browne	11
. . . on his Translation of Hesiods Works, & Dayes.	388	Chapman	Ttl
On the Author, Worke, and Translator.	389	Aleman	Ttl
When the old words doe strike on the new times,	389	Aleman	4
Not on his Picture, but his Booke.	390	Reader	10
To draw no envy (Shakespeare) on thy name,	390	Shakespeare	1
For seeliest Ignorance on these may light,	390	Shakespeare	7
And shake a Stage: Or, when thy Sockes were on,	391	Shakespeare	37
To call on Sicknes still, to be her Guest,	394	Jane Ogle	19
The Vision Of Ben. Jonson, On The . . .	396	Drayton	Ttl
That all Earth look'd on; and that earth, all Eyes!	396	Drayton	16
So shall our English Youth urge on, and cry	398	Drayton	69
I looke on Cynthia, and Sirenas sport,	398	Drayton	80
As, on two flowry Carpets, that did rise,	398	Drayton	81
On the honor'd Poems of his honored Friend, . . .	400	Beaumont	Ttl
That Art, or Ingine, on the strength can raise.	400	Beaumont	10
. . . on his Worke published.	401	Filmer	Ttl
Drawne Aristotle on us! & thence showne	402	Inigo Jones 1	9
Mythology there painted on slit deale!	404	Inigo Jones 1	48
Hee's warme on his feet now he sayes, & can	405	Inigo Jones 1	67
On the new priming of thy old Signe postes	405	Inigo Jones 1	87
What Poesy ere was painted on a wall	406	Inigo Jones 1	97
But bawle thou on; I pitty thee, poore Curre,	408	Detractor	7
I now would write on thee? No, wretch; thy name	409	Detractor	11
To Mrs. Alice Sutcliffe, on her divine Meditations.	411	Sutcliffe	Ttl
With wonder on the thorny regiment.	413	Ghyrlond	16
But lowlie laid, as on the earth asleep,	413	Ghyrlond	18
The Reverse on the backe side.	413	Ghyrlond	Ttl
On the reverse of this your circling crowne,	413	Ghyrlond	30
. . . on his great Instauration of his Hunting, . . .	415	Dover	Ttl
Bred by your breath, on this low bancke of ours;	416	Welcome	3

ONCE (See also ONES)

	Page	Title	Line
Which conquers all, be once over-come by thee.	31	E14 Camden	12
At once thou mak'st me happie, and unmak'st;	44	E55 Beaumont	5
Whil'st thou art certaine to thy words, once gone,	52	E74 Chancelor	7
Not though that haire grew browne, which once was amber,	57	E90 Mill	9
That thou at once, then, nobly maist defend	63	E98 Th Roe 1	7
Your great profession; which I once, did prove:	70	E108 Soldiers	6
Or his to Antwerpe. Therefore, once more, list ho'.	85	E133 Voyage	40
Still, with thy former labours; yet, once more,	85	E133 Voyage	56
Ycleped Mud, which, when their oares did once stirre,	85	E133 Voyage	62
It is enough, they once did get	93	F1 Why write no	5
Doe not once hope, that thou canst tempt	100	F4 To the World	5
But if once we loose this light,	102	F5 Celia 1	7
But when once wee lose the light,	102	F5 Celia 1	V 7
The truth of times) was once of more esteeme,	114	F12 Rutland	21
For he, that once is good, is ever great.	118	F13 Aubigny	52
Could be brought once back to looke.	132	U2 How he saw	19
For Loves-sake, kisse me once againe,	139	U2 Another	1
Once more, and (faith) I will be gone,	139	U2 Another	7
What w'are but once to doe, we should doe long.	139	U2 Another	12
Honour'd at once, and envi'd (if it can	162	U15 Friend-Wars	24
Then once to number, or bring forth to hand,	167	U15 Friend-Wars	173
And Fortune once, t'assist the spirits that dare.	170	U18 Elegy Can	10
Where men at once may plant, and gather blisses:	170	U19 Elegy By	10
In whom Anacreon once did joy,	181	U27 Ode Helen	6
Thinke that I once was yours, or may be now;	192	U38 Elegy 'Tis	35
And then with pause; for sever'd once, that's gone,	192	U38 Elegy 'Tis	47
But to exact againe what once is given,	192	U38 Elegy 'Tis	63
Rather then once displease you more, to die,	193	U38 Elegy 'Tis	92
That have good places: therefore once agen,	212	U43 Vulcan	212
That have good fortunes: therefore once agen,	212	U43 Vulcan	V212
That have good places: wherefore once agen,	212	U43 Vulcan	V212
What though she talke, and cannot once with them,	222	U49 Pucell	11
The wits will leave you, if they once perceive	223	U49 Pucell	37
Haile Mary, full of grace, it once was said,	238	U66 Queene	1
You once enjoy'd: A short space severs yee,	285	U84 Muse	105
Once rowable, but now doth nourish men	309	Horace	94
Th'unbearded Youth, his Guardian once being gone,	315	Horace	229
Once seene, to be againe call'd for, and plaid,	317	Horace	271
Sixe ounces. O, when once the canker'd rust,	327	Horace	472
Angry, if once I heare good Homer snore,	351	Horace	V512/536
Will in the light be view'd: This, once, the sight	331	Horace	543
The Writ, once out, never returned yet.	331	Horace	580
The word, once out, never returned yet.	352	Horace	V556/580
Did learne them first, and once a Master fear'd.	333	Horace	592
Once say I'me ignorant. Just as a Cryer,	353	Horace	V597
The man once mock'd, and suffer'd wrong to tread.	335	Horace	642
Nor did he doe this once; for if you can	335	Horace	667
Nor did he do this once; if yet you can,	355	Horace	V667
Learn'd and unlearn'd; holding, whom once he takes;	337	Horace	677
Learn'd, and unlearn'd; holdeth whom once he takes;	355	Horace	V677
Were Cycnus, once high flying	369	Ode Who saith	99
Doth he once dissemble, but tels he did ride	380	Coryat 3	52
I had you for a Servant, once, Dick Brome;	409	Brome	1
And once more stryke the eare of tyme with those fresh straynes:	420	Ode:If Men	32
And by their takeinge, lett it once appeare	421	Ode:If Men	44
And at once three Senses pleases.	657	Door Apollo	18

ONE'

	Page	Title	Line
Our great, our good. Where one's so drest	265	U79 New-yeares	44

			Page	Title	Line

ONE   (OWN?)
Of all the Worthyes hope t'outlast thy one, ... 406 Inigo Jones 1   99
ONE
By that one spell he lives, eates, drinkes, arrayes . . . 30 E12 Shift   5
Scarse thy weekes swearing brings thee of, of one. . . . 32 E16 Brain-hardy   4
Who, to thy one, all other braines refuse; . . . . 34 E23 Donne 1   2
Nay more, for greatnesse sake, he will be one . . . 36 E28 Surly   19
'Tis Lucklesse he, that tooke up one on band . . . . 42 E46 Luckless 1   3
Sir Lucklesse, troth, for lucks sake passe by one: . . . 42 E47 Luckless 2   1
Baudrie', and usurie were one kind of game. . . . . 45 E57 Bawds   2
So have I seene at Christ-masse sports one lost, . . . 45 E58 Groome   7
One doth not stroke me, nor the other strike. . . . 46 E61 Foole   2
Yet by thy weapon liv'st! Th'hast one good part. . . . 50 E69 Cob   2
Your partie-per-pale picture, one halfe drawne . . . 51 E73 Fine Grand   13
And know thee, then, a judge, not of one yeare; . . . 51 E74 Chancelor   2
As is thy conscience, which is alwayes one: . . . . 52 E74 Chancelor   8
To one that desired me not to name him. . . . . 53 E77 Not name   Ttl
And here, it should be one of our first strifes, . . . 54 E80 Life/Death   6
And land on one, whose face durst never bee . . . 56 E88 Monsieur   5
So many Poets life, by one should live. . . . . 57 E89 Allen   14
To any one, were envie: which would live . . . . 58 E91 Vere   11
Unto the cryes of London Ile adde one; . . . . 58 E92 New Crie   2
Or, every day, some one at Rimee's looks, ... 59 E92 New Crie   23
It is the next deed, and a great one too. . . . . 61 E95 Savile   26
Reade all I send: and, if I find but one . . . . 62 E96 Donne 2   7
But one more rare, and in the case so new: . . . . 62 E97 Motion   3
Since he was gone, more then the one he weares. . . . 63 E97 Motion   17
Almost, is exercis'd: and scarse one knowes, . . . 66 E102 Pembroke   7
But thou, whose noblesse keeps one stature still, . . . 66 E102 Pembroke   13
And one true posture, though besieg'd with ill . . . 66 E102 Pembroke   14
Of former age, or glorie of our one, ... 67 E104 Montgomery   10
If men get name, for some one vertue: Then, . . . 68 E106 E Herbert   1
Thou are not one, seek'st miseries with hope, . . . 70 E109 Nevil   5
For, where his person liv'd scarce one just age, . . . 71 E110 Edmonds 1   13
Naming so many, too! But, this is one, ... 74 E115 Honest Man   3
Give every one his dose of mirth: and watches . . . 74 E115 Honest Man   14
With such a one. And therein keepes it's word. . . . 74 E115 Honest Man   21
As, sooth, the Parcae thought him one, ... 77 E120 S. P.   15
And heare her speake with one, and her first tongue; . . 78 E122 Rudyerd 2   6
One name was Elizabeth, ... 79 E124 Elizabeth   9
But the first question is, when one saw thee? . . . 81 E129 Mime   2
To Braynford, Hackney, Bow, but thou mak'st one; . . . 81 E129 Mime   4
Cocytus, Phlegeton, our have prov'd in one; . . . 84 E133 Voyage   8
And for one Cerberus, the whole coast was dogs. . . . 84 E133 Voyage   14
One was; and he, for brawne, and braine, right able . . 84 E133 Voyage   23
His three for one. Now, lordings, listen well. . . . 84 E133 Voyage   28
Betweene two walls: where, on one side, to scar men, . . 86 E133 Voyage   67
One said, it was bold Briareus, or the beadle, . . . 86 E133 Voyage   81
Yet, one day in the yeere, for sweet 'tis voyc't, . . . 87 E133 Voyage   119
One said, the other swore, the world consists. . . . 87 E133 Voyage   129
Being, beyond sea, burned for one witch: . . . . 88 E133 Voyage   158
And no one empty-handed, to salute . . . . 95 F2 Penshurst   49
(Though they were crusht into one forme) could make . . 108 F10 Proludium   26
Peace, Luxurie, thou art like one of those . . . 111 F11 Epode   69
All her best symmetrie in that one feature! . . . 112 F11 Epode   101
And some one apteth to be trusted, then, ... 113 F12 Rutland   10
And this shall be no false one, but as much . . . 117 F13 Aubigny   27
Eate on her clients, and some one devoure. . . . 119 F13 Aubigny   88
How you love one, and him you should; how still . . 119 F13 Aubigny   113
Each into other, and had now made one. . . . . 120 F13 Aubigny   120
Live that one, still; and as long yeeres doe passe, . . 120 F13 Aubigny   121
First, midst, and last, converted one, and three; . . 122 F15 Heaven   10
Of persons, still one God, in Unitie, ... 127 U1 Trinitie   2
Of persons, still one God in Unitie; . . . . 128 U1 Trinitie   30
Beholding one in three, and three in one, . . . 128 U1 Trinitie   33
One God to see, ... 128 U1 Trinitie   40
Both wills were in one stature; . . . . . 130 U1 Nativitie   15
Mock'd of all: and call'd of one . . . . . 132 U2 How he saw   28
Or else one that plaid his Ape, ... 132 U2 How he saw   31
Make in one, the same were shee. . . . . . 137 U2 Cupid   48
Can he that loves, aske lesse then one? . . . . 139 U2 Another   8
Charis one day in discourse . . . . . . 139 U2 Promise   1
As, untill she tell her one, ... 140 U2 Promise   11
But of one, if short he came, ... 142 U2 Her man   55
'Tis one good part I'ld lie withall. . . . . . 142 U2 Exception   8
Find some one good, in some one man; . . . . 145 U5 Woman-kind   9
One good enough for a songs sake. . . . . . 145 U5 Woman-kind   12
To love one man, hee'd leave her first. . . . . 146 U6 Defence   24
One un-becomming thought doth move . . . . 148 U7 Nymph   31
Of one that lov'd? . . . . 148 U8 Houre-glasse   6
Who makes the one, so't be first, makes both. . . . 152 U12 Corbet   40
Of pressure, like one taken in a streight? . . . 154 U13 Sacvile   32
No! Gifts and thankes should have one cheerefull face, . . 154 U13 Sacvile   39
But one is bitten by the Dog he fed, ... 155 U13 Sacvile   67
Many a pound, and piece, will place one well; . . . 155 U13 Sacvile   78
But like to be, that every day mends one, . . . 156 U13 Sacvile   116
Who was this Morning such a one, should be . . . 157 U13 Sacvile   126
And like a Compasse keeping one foot still . . . 159 U14 Selden   31
And manly elocution, not one while . . . . . 160 U14 Selden   56
And masculine elocution, not one while . . . . 160 U14 Selden V 56
Hee's one of blood, and fashion! and with these . . . 164 U15 Friend-Wars   55
How they may make some one that day an Asse . . . 164 U15 Friend-Wars   64
Ready to cast, at one, whose band sits ill, . . . 164 U15 Friend-Wars   69

481

	Page	Title	Line

ONE (cont.)

	Page	Title	Line
What reputation to beare one Glasse more?	166	U15 Friend-Wars	119
Tilt one upon another, and now beare	166	U15 Friend-Wars	125
till one upon another, and now beare	166	U15 Friend-Wars	V125
Thou shrinke or start not, but be alwayes one;	168	U15 Friend-Wars	186
That I must send one first, my Choyce assignes,	170	U18 Elegy Can	23
(Though they may number bodyes) or but one.	171	U19 Elegy By	14
Of all that can be done him; Such a one	171	U19 Elegy By	23
Forgive me this one foolish deadly sin,	171	U20 Shrub	2
Then all Ingredients made into one curse,	172	U20 Shrub	18
This subjects you to love of one.	173	U22 Elegy Tho	8
One sparke of your Diviner heat	174	U22 Elegy Tho	31
In one full Action; nor have you now more	180	U26 Ode High	17
Read here in one, what thou in all canst find,	185	U30 Burleigh	2
Lawes; and no change e're come to one decree:	185	U31 Elsmere	2
One beautie in an Age, and free from thee?	188	U34 Small Poxe	2
All lights into his one doth run;	189	U36 Song	6
There is no Father that for one demerit,	192	U38 Elegy 'Tis	41
Is fix'd upon one leg, and dares not come	198	U40 Elegy That	33
Due to that one, that doth believe him just.	198	U40 Elegy That	40
Lift up some one, and doe, I tell not what.	201	U42 Elegy Let	58
Or in Moore-fields, this other night! sings one,	202	U42 Elegy Let	73
A cause before; or leave me more behind.	203	U43 Vulcan	28
Not snatcht them hence in one poor minutes rage.	205	U43 Vulcan	V 56
Kindled the fire! But then, did one returne,	209	U43 Vulcan	149
Will be remembred by Six Clerkes, to one.	210	U43 Vulcan	172
One lesson we have both learn'd, and well read;	216	U45 Squib	4
I neither am, nor art thou one of those	216	U45 Squib	5
An Epistle answering to one that asked . . .	218	U47 Tribe	Ttl
I studie other friendships, and more one,	219	U47 Tribe	29
Of Spaine or France; or were not prick'd downe one	219	U47 Tribe	47
For Sermoneeres: of which now one, now other,	223	U49 Pucell	39
For when they find so many meet in one,	225	U50 Countesse	35
With one great blot, yo'had form'd me as I am.	227	U52 Answer	12
With one great blot, you had drawne me as I am.	227	U52 Answer	V 12
It doe not come: One piece I have in store,	229	U54 Squib	15
Marrie the Muse is one, can tread the Aire,	230	U56 Covell	13
Marrie his Muse is one, can tread the Aire,	230	U56 Covell	V 13
One Poet, then of other folke ten score.	235	U62 Charles 1	10
Her one and twenty yeare!	240	U67 Muses	V 48
Here's one out-liv'd his Peeres,	243	U70 Ode	25
And keepe the one halfe from his Harry.	246	U70 Ode	94
Two names of friendship, but one Starre:	246	U70 Ode	98
That liking; and approach so one the tother,	247	U70 Ode	109
The Muse not peepes out, one of hundred dayes;	248	U71 Treasurer	9
One in the others hand,	256	U75 Epithalam.	125
These two, now holy Church hath made them one,	257	U75 Epithalam.	139
One to the other, long e're these to light were brought.	257	U75 Epithalam.	144
How each one playes his part, of the large Pedigree.	258	U75 Epithalam.	176
And never may there want one of the Stem,	258	U75 Epithalam.	177
This I would doe, could I know Weston, one	260	U77 Treasurer	10
This I would doe, if I could thinke you one	260	U77 Treasurer	V 10
Being sent to one, they will be read of all.	263	U78 Digby	32
You seeme a faire one! O that you had breath,	269	U81 Pawlet	6
You seeme a faire one! O that I had breath,	269	U81 Pawlet	V 6
Stiffe! starke! my joynts 'gainst one another knock!	269	U81 Pawlet	9
With what injustice should one soule pretend	271	U81 Pawlet	92
With what injustice can one soule pretend	271	U81 Pawlet	V 92
And give you reasons more then one.	277	U84 Mind	4
Hang all your roomes, with one large Pedigree:	282	U84 Kenelme	20
Thou hast no more blowes, Fate, to drive at one:	283	U84 Muse	27
One corporall, only; th'other spirituall,	284	U84 Muse	52
Shall meet with gladnesse in one Theatre;	285	U84 Muse	114
And each shall know, there, one anothers face,	285	U84 Muse	115
To one she said, Doe this, he did it; So	287	U84 Muse	169
She was, in one, a many parts of life;	287	U84 Muse	173
As her whole life was now become one note	287	U84 Muse	178
As neither head, nor foot, one forme retaine.	305	Horace	10
Be simple quite throughout, and wholly one.	307	Horace	32
Be simple quite throughout, and alwayes one.	339	Horace	V 32
One thing prodigiously, paints in the woods	307	Horace	41
To be that Smith; then live, mark'd one of those,	307	Horace	51
Loves Dogges, and Horses; and is ever one	315	Horace	230
These studies alter now, in one, growne man;	315	Horace	237
Is laugh'd at, that still jarreth on one string:	329	Horace	532
So doth the one, the others helpe require,	333	Horace	585
And friendly should unto one end conspire.	333	Horace	586
You doe not bring, to judge your Verses, one,	333	Horace	609
For, if one should, and with a rope make haste	335	Horace	655
Here's one makes verses, but there's none knows why:	355	Horace	V670
Not one but thrives; in spite of stormes & thunder,	361	Palmer	7
till th'one hath drownd the other in our sightes,	361	Palmer	20
For, as one comming with a laterall viewe,	362	Author	9
Behold, where one doth swim;	366	Ode Who saith	3
Nor let one River boast	367	Ode Who saith	35
It covers, first, a Virgin; and then, one	371	Epitaph	3
I meane that one paire, wherewith he so hobled	380	Coryat 3	41
Jest, he saies. Item one sute of blacke taffata	380	Coryat 3	48
What can one witnesse, and a weake one, add	385	Brooke	4
Was worthy of a Good one; And this, here,	386	Husband	10
To say but one, were single. Then it chimes,	389	Aleman	3
But in one tongue, was form'd with the worlds wit:	389	Aleman	6
And this hath met that one, that may be stil'd	389	Aleman	13

ONE (cont.)

Triumph, my Britaine, thou hast one to showe,	391	Shakespeare	41
But of one Husband; and since he left life,	394	Jane Ogle	16
Like him, to make the ayre, one volary:	397	Drayton	36
Under one title. Thou hast made thy way	397	Drayton	48
Of Persons, yet in Union (One) divine.	413	Ghyrlond	35

ONELY

His onely answere is to all, god payes.	31	E12 Shift	20
In onely thee, might be both great, and glad.	48	E66 Cary	4
As, to be rais'd by her, is onely fame.	49	E67 Suffolk	4
Onely a learned, and a manly soule	52	E76 Bedford 1	13
As others speake, but onely thou dost act.	57	E89 Allen	12
Which of thy names I take, not onely beares	58	E91 Vere	1
On them: And therefore doe not onely shunne	59	E92 New Crie	38
Onely to boast thy merit in supply.	61	E95 Savile	12
Onely his clothes have over-leaven'd him.	63	E97 Motion	20
T'all future time, not onely doth restore	71	E110 Edmonds 1	21
He hath not onely gain'd himselfe his eyes,	74	E114 Sydney	7
If onely love should make the action pris'd:	78	E121 Rudyerd 1	6
That onely fooles make thee a saint,	100	F4 To the World	15
Sicknesse; onely on us men.	105	F8 Sicknesse	14
Drinke to me, onely, with thine eyes,	106	F9 Celia 3	1
But thou thereon did'st onely breath,	106	F9 Celia 3	13
Such spirits as are onely continent,	111	F11 Epode	77
How onely shee bestowes	112	F11 Epode	104
Well, or ill, onely, all the following yeere,	113	F12 Rutland	7
But Poets, rapt with rage divine?	115	F12 Rutland	63
'Tis onely that can time, and chance defeat:	118	F13 Aubigny	51
That doe sinne onely for the infamie:	119	F13 Aubigny	86
Onely, thus much, out of a ravish'd zeale,	119	F13 Aubigny	108
As farre as sense, and onely by the eyes.	261	U77 Treasurer	12
As farre as sense, and onely by his eyes.	261	U77 Treasurer	V 12
Jesus, the onely-gotten Christ! who can	288	U84 Muse	212
Like lustfull beasts, that onely know to doe it:	294	U88 Petronius	4
This Swanne is onely his,	366	Ode Who saith	15
I writ he onely his taile there did wave;	380	Coryat 3	56
Who cannot reade, but onely doth desire	383	Author	9
It fits not onely him that makes a Booke,	385	Husband	1
To the Greeke coast thine onely knew the way.	388	Chapman	9
That would have done, that, which you onely can.	389	Aleman	24
Onely my losse is, that I am not there:	398	Drayton	91
As it, alone, (and onely it) had roome,	412	Ghyrlond	11
By bringing forth God's onely Son, no other.	414	Ghyrlond	48

ONELY-GOTTEN

Jesus, the onely-gotten Christ! who can	288	U84 Muse	212

ONE'S

Our great, our good. Where one's so drest	265	U79 New-yeares	44

ONES (ONCE)

Two kindes of valour he doth shew, at ones;	49	E68 Playwrt 2	3
By all your Titles, & whole style at ones	402	Inigo Jones 1	15

ONES

Well, though thy name lesse then our great ones bee,	64	E99 Th Roe 2	11
Rudyerd, as lesser dames, to great ones use,	78	E121 Rudyerd 1	1
Wish, you had fowle ones, and deformed got;	200	U42 Elegy Let	22
If such a ones applause thou dost require,	315	Horace	220
On artlesse Verse; the hard ones he will blame;	335	Horace	634
Nay they will venter ones Descent to hitt,	394	Jane Ogle	11

ONIONS

With juyce of limons, onions, pisse, to write.	59	E92 New Crie	28

ONLY

Surly, use other arts, these only can	36	E28 Surly	21
Thy person only, Courtling, is the vice.	50	E72 Court-ling	6
Since they can only judge, that can conferre.	83	E132 Sylvester	6
The filth, stench, noyse: save only what was there	84	E133 Voyage	9
only pursewinge Constancy, in Chainge;	108	F10 Proludium	10
Thou sai'st, thou only cam'st to prove	150	U10 Jealousie	10
You then, whose will not only, but desire	153	U13 Sacvile	7
Carryed and wrapt, I only am alow'd	155	U13 Sacvile	88
It true respects. He will not only love,	161	U14 Selden	73
That kept man living! Pleasures only sought!	163	U15 Friend-Wars	41
And only pitious scorne, upon their folly waites.	175	U23 Himselfe	24
Where only a mans birth is his offence,	177	U25 Desmond	32
When only a mans birth is his offence,	177	U25 Desmond	V 32
The only faithfull Watchman for the Realme,	185	U30 Burleigh	9
In will and power, only to defeat.	191	U38 Elegy 'Tis	18
Which thou hast only vented, not enjoy'd.	210	U43 Vulcan	168
Subject to quarrell only; or else such	218	U47 Tribe	11
Not only shunning by your act, to doe	224	U50 Countesse	5
Only your time you better entertaine,	224	U50 Countesse	23
I only can the Paper staine;	230	U55 Burges	6
And only, his great Soule envy'd,	234	U60 La-ware	17
But whisper'd Counsells, and those only thrive;	234	U61 Epigram	6
Who seldome sleepes! whom bad men only hate!	250	U73 Weston	6
Through which not only we, but all our Species are.	253	U75 Epithalam.	32
Pan only our great Shep'ard is,	265	U79 New-yeares	43
This only the great Shep'ard is.	265	U79 New-yeares	65
One corporall, only; th'other spirituall,	284	U84 Muse	52
Know'st only well to paint a Cipresse tree.	305	Horace	25
For so, they shall not only gaine the worth,	325	Horace	425
The Muse not only gave the Greek's a wit,	327	Horace	461
In these pide times, only to shewe their braines,	362	Author	4
And clothes, and guifts, that only do thee grace	384	Somerset	2
Not only this, but every day of thine,	384	Somerset	9

ONLY (cont.)
```
    these only hide part of my flesh, and bones:       .    .    .  387   Cavendish        2
    and the immortall gods; love only those       .     .    .    .  422   Lucan            5
ON'T
    Yet who could have hit on't but the wise noddell     .   .    .  379   Coryat 3         6
    Pies on't, you have his historicall faith.     .     .    .    .  380   Coryat 3        22
    I shall think on't ere't be day.     .    .    .     .    .    .  417   Moon            11
OPE'
    To ope' the character.  They'have found the sleight  .   .    .   59   E92 New Crie    27
    Of that eternall Port kept ope'     .    .    .  .    .    .    .  274   U84 Cradle      39
OPE
    Then ope thy wardrobe, thinke me that poore Groome   .   .    .  201   U42 Elegy Let   51
    And to left-Lydia, now the gate stood ope.    .     .    .    .  294   U87 Hor.3:9     20
OPEN
    But open, and un-armed encounter'd all:    .    .    .    .    .   87   E133 Voyage    135
    To crowne thy open table, doth provide     .    .    .    .    .   94   F2 Penshurst    27
    And fills thy open hall with mirth, and cheere,  .   .    .    .   98   F3 Wroth        49
    No, Mistris, no, the open merrie Man     .    .    .    .    .    .  198   U40 Elegy That  25
    All mouthes are open, and all stomacks free:     .   .    .    .  232   U58 Book-seller  2
    I'the open field; is Waxe like to be wrought    .    .    .    .  315   Horace         231
    Peace, and the open ports, that peace doth cause.    .   .    .  317   Horace         284
    The open ports, and sports that peace doth cause,    .   .    .  345   Horace        V284
    A good and wise man will crye open shame   .    .    .    .    .  354   Horace        V633
    Thou mad'st in open Feild     .    .    .   .    .    .    .    .  421   Ode:If Men      40
OPENS
    See, now the Chappell opens; where the King     .   .    .    .  256   U75 Epithalam. 121
    To day old Janus opens the new yeare,    .    .    .    .    .    .  263   U79 New-yeares   9
OPINION
    Of miming, gets th'opinion of a wit.     .    .  .    .    .    .   74   E115 Honest Man 28
    And though Opinion stampe them not, are gold.    .   .    .    .  218   U47 Tribe        4
OPINIONS
    Antiquities search'd! Opinions dis-esteem'd!     .   .    .    .  160   U14 Selden      40
OPPOSE
    Both arm'd with wealth, and slander to oppose,   .   .    .    .  186   U32 Elsmere      8
OPPRESSOR
    Thy just defénces made th' oppressor afraid.     .   .    .    .  217   U46 Coke         8
OPPREST
    That they have more opprest me, then my want?    .   .    .    .  153   U13 Sacvile     28
OR
    To catch the worlds loose laughter, or vaine gaze.   .   .    .   27   E2 My Booke     12
    Call'st a booke good, or bad, as it doth sell,   .   .    .    .   27   E3 Bookseller    2
    Nor have my title-leafe on posts, or walls,  .  .    .    .    .   28   E3 Bookseller    7
    Or in cleft-sticks, advanced to make calls   .  .    .    .    .   28   E3 Bookseller    8
    For termers, or some clarke-like serving-man,    .   .    .    .   28   E3 Bookseller    9
    Or celebrated with more truth of state?    .    .    .    .    .   28   E5 Union         2
    For strict degrees of ranke, or title looke:    .   .    .    .   29   E9 To All        2
    Or else by water goes, and so to playes;   .    .    .    .    .   30   E12 Shift       17
    Blaspheme god, greatly.  Or some poore hinde beat,   .   .    .   36   E28 Surly       17
    He that feares death, or mournes it, in the just,   .   .    .   37   E34 Death        1
    Expresser truth, or truer glorie;    .    .    .     .    .    .   39   E40 Ratcliffe    7
    All this doth Jone.  Or that his long yearn'd life   .   .    .   40   E42 Giles       11
    What need hast thou of me? or of my Muse?    .   .    .    .    .   40   E43 Salisbury 1  1
    Or fumie clysters, thy moist lungs to bake:  .  .    .    .    .   42   E50 Cod 3        2
    From locks of wooll, or shreds from the whole peece? .   .    .   45   E56 Poet-Ape    14
    An obeliske, or columne to thy name,     .    .     .    .    .   46   E60 Mounteagle   2
    Or, if shee would but modestly have prais'd  .  .    .    .    .   46   E60 Mounteagle   3
    Thy fact, in brasse or marble writ the same)     .   .    .    .   46   E60 Mounteagle   4
    To Foole, or Knave.     .    .    .    .     .     .    .    .    .   46   E61 Foole      Ttl
    Thy praise, or dispraise is to me alike,   .    .    .    .    .   46   E61 Foole        1
    Or your complexions losse? you have a pot,   .  .    .    .    .   46   E62 Would-bee    6
    Curst be his Muse, that could lye dumbe, or hid  .   .    .    .   47   E63 Salisbury 2 11
    Curst be my voyce if it lye dumbe, or hid    .   .    .    .    .   47   E63 Salisbury 2 V 11
    Not glad, like those that have new hopes, or sutes,  .   .    .   47   E64 Salisbury 3  1
    Or thou more happie, it to justifie   .    .    .    .    .    .   49   E66 Cary         8
    It may be much, or little, in the cause.   .    .    .    .    .   49   E66 Cary        16
    Goe high, or low, as thou wilt value it.   .    .    .    .    .   50   E72 Court-ling   4
    Or take an Epigramme so fearefully:    .   .    .    .    .    .   51   E73 Fine Grand   2
    As't were a challenge, or a borrowers letter?    .   .    .    .   51   E73 Fine Grand   3
    Item, a tale or two, some fortnight after;   .  .    .    .    .   51   E73 Fine Grand   7
    For which, or pay me quickly', or Ile pay you.   .   .    .    .   51   E73 Fine Grand  22
    Or then, or since, about our Muses springs,  .  .    .    .    .   53   E79 Rutland      3
    As he would burne, or better farre his booke.   .   .    .    .   53   E79 Rutland     12
    Or that I'have by, two good sufficient men,  .  .    .    .    .   54   E81 Proule       3
    Or had his father, when he did him get,    .    .    .    .    .   56   E88 Monsieur     9
    Or hung some Mounsieurs picture on the wall,     .   .    .    .   56   E88 Monsieur    12
    Or is it some french statue? No: 'T doth move,   .   .    .    .   56   E88 Monsieur    13
    Discern'd no difference of his yeeres, or play,  .   .    .    .   57   E90 Mill         8
    Illustrous Vere, or Horace; fit to be  .  .    .     .    .    .   58   E91 Vere         3
    Sung by a Horace, or a Muse as free;   .   .    .    .    .    .   58   E91 Vere         4
    And the Gazetti, or Gallo-Belgicus:    .   .    .    .    .    .   59   E92 New Crie    16
    Or, every day, some one at Rimee's looks,  .    .    .    .    .   59   E92 New Crie    23
    Or Bils, and there he buyes the names of books.  .   .    .    .   59   E92 New Crie    24
    Or 'gainst the Bishops, for the Brethren, raile,     .   .    .   59   E92 New Crie    35
    Thou yet remayn'st, un-hurt in peace, or warre,  .   .    .    .   60   E93 Radcliffe  13
    Or, better worke! were thy glad countrey blest,  .   .    .    .   61   E95 Savile     14
    Where ere he met me; now hee's dumbe, or proud.  .   .    .    .   62   E97 Motion      8
    From place, or fortune, are made high, or low,   .   .    .    .   64   E99 Th Roe 2    9
    An olive, capers, or some better sallade   .    .    .    .    .   64   E101 Supper    10
    Livie, or of some better booke to us,    .    .     .    .    .   65   E101 Supper    22
    Of which had Horace, or Anacreon tasted,   .    .    .    .    .   65   E101 Supper    31
    Tabacco, Nectar, or the Thespian spring,   .    .    .    .    .   65   E101 Supper    33
    And we will have no Pooly', or Parrot by;  .    .    .    .    .   65   E101 Supper    36
    Shall make us sad next morning: or affright  .  .    .    .    .   65   E101 Supper    41
```

		Page	Title	Line

OR (cont.)

	Page	Title	Line
As nothing else discernes the vertue' or vice.	66	E102 Pembroke	12
Or did our times require it, to behold	67	E104 Montgomery	3
Or, because some scarce thinke that storie true,	67	E104 Montgomery	5
Or, more then borne for the comparison	67	E104 Montgomery	9
Of former age, or glorie of our one,	67	E104 Montgomery	10
You were the bright Oenone, Flora, or May?	68	E105 L Wroth 2	10
Or, keeping your due state, that would not cry,	68	E105 L Wroth 2	17
Whether thy learning they would take, or wit,	68	E106 E Herbert	5
Or valour, or thy judgement seasoning it,	68	E106 E Herbert	6
Wrestlest with dignities, or fain'st a scope	70	E109 Nevil	6
Not all these, Edmonds, or what else put too,	71	E110 Edmonds 1	11
Action, or engine, worth a note of thine,	71	E110 Edmonds 1	20
Or thy ranke setting? that thou dar'st put in	72	E112 Gamster	4
Tragick, or Comick; but thou writ'st the play.	72	E112 Gamster	8
When Sydnyes name I heare, or face I see:	73	E114 Sydney	2
At every meale, where it doth dine, or sup,	74	E115 Honest Man	23
Them in, if not, from thee; or must commit	75	E116 Jephson	15
Writing thy selfe, or judging others writ,	78	E123 Rudyerd 3	1
I know not which th'hast most, candor, or wit:	78	E123 Rudyerd 3	2
Made for what Nature could, or Vertue can;	79	E125 Uvedale	2
So, all reward, or name, that growes to mee	80	E127 Aubigny	9
That there's no journey set, or thought upon,	81	E129 Mime	3
Think'st thou, Mime, this is great? or, that they strive	81	E129 Mime	9
Out-dance the Babion, or out-boast the Brave;	81	E129 Mime	12
Or (mounted on a stoole) thy face doth hit	81	E129 Mime	13
Which Musick had; or speake her knowne effects,	82	E130 Ferrab. 1	3
Say, this, or that man they to thee preferre;	83	E131 Ferrab. 2	9
Of Hercules, or Theseus going to hell,	84	E133 Voyage	2
Orpheus, Ulysses: or the Latine Muse,	84	E133 Voyage	3
From Venice, Paris, or some in-land passage	85	E133 Voyage	33
Or him that backward went to Berwicke, or which	85	E133 Voyage	35
Or his to Antwerpe. Therefore, once more, list ho'.	85	E133 Voyage	40
Or goddesse to invoke, to stuffe my verse;	85	E133 Voyage	45
Sans helpe of Sybil, or a golden bough,	85	E133 Voyage	48
Or magick sacrifice, they past along!	85	E133 Voyage	49
One said, it was bold Briareus, or the beadle,	86	E133 Voyage	81
The other thought it Hydra, or the rock	86	E133 Voyage	83
Or were precipitated downe the jakes,	87	E133 Voyage	137
Or, that it lay, heap'd like an usurers masse,	88	E133 Voyage	139
Were you Jove's sonnes, or had Alcides might.	89	E133 Voyage	182
Of touch, or marble; nor canst boast a row	93	F2 Penshurst	2
Of polish'd pillars, or a roofe of gold:	93	F2 Penshurst	3
Or stayre, or courts; but stand'st an ancient pile,	93	F2 Penshurst	5
When thou would'st feast, or exercise thy friends.	94	F2 Penshurst	21
As loth, the second draught, or cast to stay,	94	F2 Penshurst	35
Before the fisher, or into his hand.	94	F2 Penshurst	38
The better cheeses, bring 'hem; or else send	95	F2 Penshurst	53
An embleme of themselves, in plum, or peare.	95	F2 Penshurst	56
For fire, or lights, or livorie: all is there;	95	F2 Penshurst	73
As if thou, then, wert mine, or I raign'd here:	95	F2 Penshurst	74
To entertayne them; or the countrey came,	95	F2 Penshurst	80
Whether by choice, or fate, or both;	96	F3 Wroth	2
Of Sheriffes dinner, or Majors feast.	96	F3 Wroth	6
Of Sergeants dinner, or sheriffes feast.	96	F3 Wroth	V 6
The richer hangings, or crowne-plate;	96	F3 Wroth	8
Free from proud porches, or their guilded roofes,	97	F3 Wroth	15
Or, if thou list the night in watch to breake,	97	F3 Wroth	21
Or with thy friends; the heart of all the yeere,	97	F3 Wroth	25
Or with thy friends; the heate of all the yeere,	97	F3 Wroth	V 25
Or in the winter, hunt'st the flying hare,	97	F3 Wroth	V 29
Or hauking at the river, or the bush,	97	F3 Wroth	33
Or shooting at the greedie thrush,	97	F3 Wroth	34
Or shooting at the hungrie thrush,	97	F3 Wroth	V 34
Sit mixt with losse of state, or reverence.	98	F3 Wroth	57
Then either money, warre, or death:	99	F3 Wroth	76
To take the weake, or make them stop:	100	F4 To the World	19
Or, having scap'd, shall I returne,	101	F4 To the World	25
What bird, or beast, is knowne so dull,	101	F4 To the World	29
That fled his cage, or broke his chaine,	101	F4 To the World	30
And every goodnesse tax'd, or griev'd.	101	F4 To the World	52
Or his easier eares beguile,	102	F5 Celia 1	13
Or hir easier eares beguile,	102	F5 Celia 1	V 13
Or the sands in Chelsey fields,	103	F6 Celia 2	14
Or the drops in silver Thames,	103	F6 Celia 2	15
Or the starres, that guild thy streames,	103	F6 Celia 2	16
At noone, they are or short, or none:	104	F7 Women but	8
Or if needs thy lust will tast	105	F8 Sicknesse	15
Bald, or blinde, or nere so many:	105	F8 Sicknesse	40
Or leave a kisse but in the cup,	106	F9 Celia 3	3
Or whose great name in Poets heaven use,	107	F10 Proludium	2
Or, with thy Tribade trine, invent new sports,	107	F10 Proludium	17
And riffle him: or pawne his Petasus.	107	F10 Proludium	24
Or safe, but shee'll procure	109	F11 Epode	6
That no strange, or unkinde	109	F11 Epode	10
Or else the sentinell	109	F11 Epode	22
Or some great thought doth keepe	109	F11 Epode	24
Or those, who doubt the common mouth of fame,	111	F11 Epode	79
Or those, which doubt the common mouth of fame,	111	F11 Epode	V 79
Much more a noble, or a generous mind	112	F11 Epode	V111
To every squire, or groome, that will report	113	F12 Rutland	6
To every squire, or groome, that can report	113	F12 Rutland	V 6
Well, or ill, onely, all the following yeere,	113	F12 Rutland	7

485

OR (cont.)

	Page	Title	Line
Or perhaps lesse: whil'st gold beares all this sway,	113	F12 Rutland	18
Or put to flight Astrea, when her ingots	114	F12 Rutland	24
Then, now give pride fame, or peasants birth.	114	F12 Rutland	V 26
Almost you have, or may have, when you will?	114	F12 Rutland	34
Inscrib'd in touch or marble, or the cotes	114	F12 Rutland	44
Painted, or carv'd upon our great-mens tombs,	114	F12 Rutland	45
Or in their windowes; doe but prove the wombs,	114	F12 Rutland	46
Or, in an armies head, that, lockt in brasse,	114	F12 Rutland	52
Ajax, or Idomen, or all the store,	114	F12 Rutland	54
Unto the starres? or the Tyndarides?	115	F12 Rutland	58
Or set bright Ariadnes crowne so high?	115	F12 Rutland	60
Or lifted Cassiopea in her chayre?	115	F12 Rutland	62
And such, or my hopes faile, shall make you shine.	115	F12 Rutland	64
(Or Poet, in the court account) then I,	115	F12 Rutland	69
Or common places, filch'd, that take these times,	116	F12 Rutland	88
Or so my selfe abandon'd, as because	117	F13 Aubigny	17
Men are not just, or keepe no holy lawes	117	F13 Aubigny	18
Or feare to draw true lines, 'cause others paint:	117	F13 Aubigny	20
Or cos'ning farmer of the customes so,	117	F13 Aubigny	39
Without which, all the rest were sounds, or lost.	118	F13 Aubigny	50
Not looking by, or back (like those, that waite	118	F13 Aubigny	62
Them, or their officers: and no man know,	118	F13 Aubigny	79
Whether it be a face they weare, or no.	118	F13 Aubigny	80
'Gainst stormes, or pyrats, that might charge your peace;	119	F13 Aubigny	93
Not fashion'd for the court, or strangers eyes;	119	F13 Aubigny	115
Doth urge him to runne wrong, or to stand still.	121	F14 Sydney	30
To ought but grace, or ayme at other end.	122	F15 Heaven	8
Yet dare I not complaine, or wish for death	122	F15 Heaven	23
Of discontent; or that these prayers bee	122	F15 Heaven	25
But 'bove the fat of rammes, or bulls, to prize	127	U1 Trinitie	11
Clothes, or Fortune gives the grace;	131	U2 Excuse	8
Or the feature, or the youth:	131	U2 Excuse	9
Either whom to love, or how:	131	U2 Excuse	16
Or his courage; for away	132	U2 How he saw	15
Nor for any threat, or call,	132	U2 How he saw	18
Or else one that plaid his Ape,	132	U2 How he saw	31
And in either Prose, or Song,	133	U2 Suffered	23
Each that drawes, is a Swan, or a Dove,	134	U2 Triumph	3
Or Swans Downe ever?	135	U2 Triumph	26
Or have smelt o'the bud o'the Brier?	135	U2 Triumph	27
Or the Nard i' the fire?	135	U2 Triumph	28
Or have tasted the bag o'the Bee?	135	U2 Triumph	29
Or Saturnias gate	136	U2 Triumph	V 44
Whether we have lost, or wonne,	138	U2 Kisse	6
Or, that did you sit, or walke,	138	U2 Kisse	13
Or, if you did move to night	138	U2 Kisse	21
Or if you would yet have stay'd,	138	U2 Kisse	29
Or have charg'd his sight of Crime,	138	U2 Kisse	32
Here's none to spie, or see;	139	U2 Another	3
Why doe you doubt, or stay?	139	U2 Another	4
Let who will thinke us dead, or wish our death.	139	U2 Another	18
And pronounce, which band, or lace,	140	U2 Promise	19
There; or to reforme a curle;	140	U2 Promise	24
Or with Secretarie Sis	140	U2 Promise	25
Noble; or of greater Blood:	140	U2 Her man	4
Noble; or of greatest Blood:	140	U2 Her man	V 4
Chestnut colour, or more slack	141	U2 Her man	13
And make Love or me afeard.	141	U2 Her man	24
Or were set up in a Brake.	142	U2 Her man	40
Or were pent up in a Brake.	142	U2 Her man	V 40
At such a Call, what beast or fowle,	143	U3 Musicall	5
What Tree or stone doth want a soule?	143	U3 Musicall	7
On which they see or know.	144	U3 Musicall	V 20
The fooles, or Tyrants with your friends,	145	U5 Woman-kind	2
For what is better, or to make	146	U6 Defence	14
As Summers sky, or purged Ayre,	147	U7 Nymph	17
If Love, or feare, would let me tell his name.	148	U7 Nymph	35
or else it could not be,	149	U9 Picture	V 2
Or Scorne, or pittie on me take,	150	U11 Dreame	1
Or Spight,	151	U11 Dreame	9
So of uncleannesse, or offence,	152	U12 Corbet	17
Nor wants it here through penurie, or sloth,	152	U12 Corbet	39
Lesse list of proud, hard, or ingratefull Men.	153	U13 Sacvile	4
Excuses, or Delayes? or done 'hem scant,	153	U13 Sacvile	27
Or if he did it not to succour me,	154	U13 Sacvile	29
But by meere Chance? for interest? or to free	154	U13 Sacvile	30
Himselfe of farther trouble, or the weight	154	U13 Sacvile	31
Or that doth sound a Trumpet, and doth call	154	U13 Sacvile	35
His Groomes to witnesse; or else lets it fall	154	U13 Sacvile	36
He neither gives, or do's, that doth delay	154	U13 Sacvile	41
A Benefit; or that doth throw't away:	154	U13 Sacvile	42
Lest Ayre, or Print, but flies it: Such men would	154	U13 Sacvile	45
Or stands to be'n Commission o' the blade?	155	U13 Sacvile	64
Or robbing the poore Market-folkes should nurse	155	U13 Sacvile	90
Of our Towne Gallantry! or why there rests	155	U13 Sacvile	92
Or swaggering with the Watch, or Drawer, drunke;	156	U13 Sacvile	94
Or feats of darknesse acted in Mid-Sun,	156	U13 Sacvile	95
Or appetite of offending, but a skill,	156	U13 Sacvile	107
Or Science of discerning Good and Ill.	156	U13 Sacvile	108
Or growne; by height or lowenesse of the Sunne?	156	U13 Sacvile	119
And my minds motion not? or have I none?	156	U13 Sacvile	122
Or on the sudden. It were strange that he	156	U13 Sacvile	125

	Page	Title	Line

OR (cont.)

	Page	Title	Line
Sydney e're night! or that did goe to bed	157	U13 Sacvile	127
Yet we must more then move still, or goe on,	157	U13 Sacvile	135
(As their true rule or lesson) either men,	158	U13 Sacvile	162
Donnor's or Donnee's, to their practise shall	158	U13 Sacvile	163
Lesse shall I for the Art or dressing care,	158	U14 Selden	3
Rather then Office, when it doth or may	158	U14 Selden	9
Or faith in things? or is't your wealth and will	159	U14 Selden	36
T'instruct and teach? or your unweary'd paine	159	U14 Selden	37
To informe and teach? or your unweary'd paine	159	U14 Selden	V 37
Where is that nominall marke, or reall rite,	160	U14 Selden	47
Forme, Art or Ensigne, that hath scap'd your sight?	160	U14 Selden	48
Forme, Act or Ensigne, that hath scap'd your sight?	160	U14 Selden	V 48
All that dare rowse: or are not loth to quit	162	U15 Friend-Wars	3
His unjust hopes, with praises begg'd, or (worse)	162	U15 Friend-Wars	12
Or Feathers: lay his fortune out to show,	162	U15 Friend-Wars	21
Till envie wound, or maime it at a blow!	162	U15 Friend-Wars	22
No part or corner man can looke upon,	163	U15 Friend-Wars	27
As farre as he can flie, or follow day,	163	U15 Friend-Wars	29
As farre as he can flee, or follow day,	163	U15 Friend-Wars V	29
Not to be checkt, or frighted now with fate,	163	U15 Friend-Wars	35
In bravery, or gluttony, or coyne,	163	U15 Friend-Wars	45
To do't with Cloth, or Stuffes, lusts name might merit;	164	U15 Friend-Wars	57
Not make a verse; Anger; or laughter would,	164	U15 Friend-Wars	62
That payes, or what he will: The Dame is steele.	164	U15 Friend-Wars	78
Where Pittes, or Wright, or Modet would not venter,	164	U15 Friend-Wars	80
Adulteries, now, are not so hid, or strange,	165	U15 Friend-Wars	85
The Husband now's call'd churlish, or a poore	165	U15 Friend-Wars	89
Or use all arts, or haunt all Companies	165	U15 Friend-Wars	91
Lesse must not be thought on then Mistresse: or,	165	U15 Friend-Wars	95
His body to the Counters, or the Fleete?	165	U15 Friend-Wars	105
His body to the compters, or the Fleete?	165	U15 Friend-Wars V	105
Coach'd, or on foot-cloth, thrice chang'd every day,	165	U15 Friend-Wars	107
Or by Damnation voids it? or by stealth?	166	U15 Friend-Wars	116
But being in Motion still (or rather in race)	166	U15 Friend-Wars	124
More then themselves, or then our lives could take,	166	U15 Friend-Wars	127
Or side, but threatens Ruine. The whole Day	166	U15 Friend-Wars	131
Can we not leave this worme? or will we not?	166	U15 Friend-Wars	141
Is that the truer excuse? or have we got	166	U15 Friend-Wars	142
In Sugar Candide, or in butter'd beere,	167	U15 Friend-Wars	153
Then once to number, or bring forth to hand,	167	U15 Friend-Wars	173
Thou shrinke or start not, but be alwayes one;	168	U15 Friend-Wars	186
So, 'live or dead, thou wilt preserve a fame	168	U15 Friend-Wars	189
Or was she gracious a-farre off? but neere	169	U18 Elegy Can	5
A terror? or is all this but my feare?	169	U18 Elegy Can	6
Or Love, or Fortune blind, when they but winke	170	U18 Elegy Can	16
To see feare: or else for truth, and State,	170	U18 Elegy Can	17
I'le lead you on; or if my fate will so,	170	U18 Elegy Can	22
Tell me (my lov'd Friend) doe you love, or no,	170	U19 Elegy By	11
(Though they may number bodyes) or but one.	171	U19 Elegy By	14
Or have the least of Good, but what it must	171	U20 Shrub	7
were such as I will now relate, or worse?	172	U20 Shrub	14
How penitent I am, or I should be!	172	U20 Shrub	16
Against or Faith, or honours lawes.	173	U22 Elegy Tho	12
Or droop they as disgrac't,	174	U23 Himselfe	11
Raising the World to good or evill fame,	175	U24 Frontispice	3
Or the times envie:	176	U25 Desmond	7
Or the dis-favour	177	U25 Desmond	33
Of Phaos forme? or doth the Boy	181	U27 Ode Helen	5
Or Delia's Graces, by Tibullus?	181	U27 Ode Helen	10
Or hath Corynna, by the name	181	U27 Ode Helen	17
Equall with her? or Ronsart prais'd	181	U27 Ode Helen	22
Or Constables Ambrosiack Muse	182	U27 Ode Helen	27
Nor is my Muse, or I asham'd to owe it	182	U28 Worth	5
Without the pompe of Counsell; or more Aide,	186	U32 Elsmere	3
Or the great Hall at Westminster, the field	186	U33 Councellour	3
But when I read or heare the names so rife	187	U33 Councellour	7
To the Wolves studie, or Dogs eloquence;	187	U33 Councellour	12
Or skill, to carry out an evill cause!	187	U33 Councellour	18
Quarrell with Nature, or in ballance brought	188	U34 Small Poxe	6
Or Turners oyle of Talck. Nor ever got	188	U34 Small Poxe	11
That heaven should make no more; or should amisse,	188	U34 Small Poxe	15
Or doe upon my selfe some desperate ill;	191	U38 Elegy 'Tis	3
Or there to sterve it. Helpe, O you that may	191	U38 Elegy 'Tis	7
There may some face or menace of a storme	191	U38 Elegy 'Tis	13
Of Graces, or your mercie here in me,	191	U38 Elegy 'Tis	16
Or lay the excuse upon the Vintners vault;	191	U38 Elegy 'Tis	22
Or in confessing of the Crime be nice,	191	U38 Elegy 'Tis	23
Or goe about to countenance the vice,	191	U38 Elegy 'Tis	24
Thinke that I once was yours, or may be now;	192	U38 Elegy 'Tis	35
Or two, or three, a Sonne will dis-inherit,	192	U38 Elegy 'Tis	42
Or winds the Spirit, by which the flower so grew?	192	U38 Elegy 'Tis	58
Can pumpe for; or a Libell without salt	193	U38 Elegy 'Tis	96
Produce; though threatning with a coale, or chalke	193	U38 Elegy 'Tis	97
Then sword, or fire, or what is of the race	193	U38 Elegy 'Tis	101
There is not any punishment, or paine,	194	U38 Elegy 'Tis	103
Absence, or Distance, shall not breed decay.	194	U38 Elegy 'Tis	116
I give, or owe my friends, into your Rites,	197	U40 Elegy That	12
But ever without blazon, or least shade	197	U40 Elegy That	13
As neither wine doe rack it out, or mirth.	197	U40 Elegy That	18
Can lock the Sense up, or the heart a thought,	198	U40 Elegy That	43
And never be by time, or folly brought,	198	U40 Elegy That	44
Weaknesse of braine, or any charme of Wine,	198	U40 Elegy That	45

OR (cont.)

	Page	Title	Line
The sinne of Boast, or other countermine	198	U40 Elegy That	46
Or that the Sun was here, but forc't away;	199	U41 Elegy Since	6
Or like a Ghost walke silent amongst men,	199	U41 Elegy Since	21
As Horace fat; or as Anacreon old;	199	U42 Elegy Let	2
No face, no hand, proportion, line, or Ayre	200	U42 Elegy Let	14
There is not worne that lace, purle, knot or pin,	200	U42 Elegy Let	16
Made longer by our praises. Or, if not,	200	U42 Elegy Let	21
Curst in their Cradles, or there chang'd by Elves,	200	U42 Elegy Let	23
Yet keepe those up in sackcloth too, or lether,	200	U42 Elegy Let	25
As any Mercer; or the whale-bone man	200	U42 Elegy Let	31
Whether their faces were their owne, or no:	200	U42 Elegy Let	36
Upon a Velvet Petticote, or a Gowne,	200	U42 Elegy Let	38
Her presently? Or leape thy Wife of force,	201	U42 Elegy Let	44
Or slipper was left off, and kisse it too,	201	U42 Elegy Let	56
Or in Moore-fields, this other night! sings one,	202	U42 Elegy Let	73
A Goat in Velvet; or some block could move	202	U42 Elegy Let	82
Or a Close-stoole so cas'd; or any fat	202	U42 Elegy Let	84
Thou art jealous of thy Wifes, or Daughters Case:	202	U42 Elegy Let	87
More then of eithers manners, wit, or face!	202	U42 Elegy Let	88
Or urge thy Greedie flame, thus to devoure	202	U43 Vulcan	3
Or beg thy Greedie flame, thus to devoure	202	U43 Vulcan	V 3
Or in remembrance of thy afront, and scorne,	203	U43 Vulcan	7
Had I wrote treason there, or heresie,	203	U43 Vulcan	15
Imposture, witchcraft, charmes, or blasphemie,	203	U43 Vulcan	16
Any, least loose, or scurrile paper, lie	203	U43 Vulcan	20
Conceal'd, or kept there, that was fit to be,	203	U43 Vulcan	21
Or taxe the Glories of the Church, and Gowne?	203	U43 Vulcan	24
Or taxe the Glories of the Church, or Gowne?	203	U43 Vulcan	V 24
Itch to defame the State? or brand the Times?	203	U43 Vulcan	25
If none of these, then why this fire? Or find	203	U43 Vulcan	27
A cause before; or leave me one behind.	203	U43 Vulcan	28
Or spun out Riddles, and weav'd fiftie tomes	204	U43 Vulcan	33
Or spun or weav'd in Riddles 50 tomes	204	U43 Vulcan	V 33
or spent my wretched paper or my tyme	204	U43 Vulcan	V 33
Or pomp'd for those hard trifles, Anagrams,	204	U43 Vulcan	35
Or pomp'd for those fine trifles, Anagrams,	204	U43 Vulcan	V 35
Or Eteostichs, or those finer flammes	204	U43 Vulcan	36
Or else Acrosticks, or those finer flammes	204	U43 Vulcan	V 36
Acrostichs, and Telestichs, or jumpe names,	204	U43 Vulcan	V 39
Or such my serious follies; But, thou'lt say,	204	U43 Vulcan	V 41
Or if thou needs would'st trench upon her power,	204	U43 Vulcan	48
or if thou wouldst enforce the power from her,	204	U43 Vulcan	V 48
To light Tobacco, or save roasted Geese,	205	U43 Vulcan	52
To light Tobacco, or have roasted Geese,	205	U43 Vulcan	V 52
Sindge Capons, or poore Pigges, dropping their eyes;	205	U43 Vulcan	53
Cloth Spices, or guard sweet meates from the flies;	205	U43 Vulcan	V 53
Sindge capons, or crispe Pigges, dropping their eyes;	205	U43 Vulcan	V 53
T'have held a Triumph, or a feast of fire,	205	U43 Vulcan	60
Or Captaine Pamphlets horse, and foot, that sallie	206	U43 Vulcan	79
Or Captaine Pamphletts, which on foote doe sally	206	U43 Vulcan	V 79
These, had'st thou pleas'd either to dine, or sup,	206	U43 Vulcan	83
These, had'st thou been pleas'd either to dine, or sup,	206	U43 Vulcan	V 83
Or Goddesse, could be raptent of thy face.	207	U43 Vulcan	108
Thou woo Minerva! or to wit aspire!	208	U43 Vulcan	109
Some Alchimist there may be yet, or odde	208	U43 Vulcan	118
No Foole would his owne harvest spoile, or burne!	209	U43 Vulcan	150
Or lest that vapour might the Citie choake,	211	U43 Vulcan	182
Or lest that vapour should the Citie choake,	211	U43 Vulcan	V182
Condemne him to the Brick-kills, or some Hill-/foot	211	U43 Vulcan	183
Condemne him to some Brick-hills, or some Hill-/foot	211	U43 Vulcan	V183
Condemne him to the Brick-kills, or a forge	211	U43 Vulcan	V183
Or in small Fagots have him blaze about	211	U43 Vulcan	185
Or else in penny Fagots blaze about	211	U43 Vulcan	V185
Or in the Bell-Mans Lanthorne, like a spie,	211	U43 Vulcan	187
Or Alexandria; and though a Divine	211	U43 Vulcan	195
Maintain'd the trade at Bilbo, or else-where;	212	U43 Vulcan	199
Maintain'd the trade of Bilbo, or else-where;	212	U43 Vulcan	V199
Or stay'd but where the Fryar, and you first met,	212	U43 Vulcan	201
Or fixt in the Low-Countrey's, where you might	212	U43 Vulcan	203
Light on thee: Or if those plagues will not doo,	212	U43 Vulcan	215
Light upon thee: Or if those plagues will not doo,	212	U43 Vulcan	V215
Powder, or paper, to bring up the youth	213	U44 Speach	25
Would thinke no more of Vlushing, or the Brill:	213	U44 Speach	30
The Cittie-Question, whether Tilly, or he,	214	U44 Speach	38
Why are we rich, or great, except to show	215	U44 Speach	69
More then to praise a Dog? or Horse? or speake	215	U44 Speach	71
The Hawking language? or our Day to breake	215	U44 Speach	72
In so much land a yeare, or such a Banke,	215	U44 Speach	76
From Guy, or Bevis, Arthur, or from whom	215	U44 Speach	81
Was issue of the Taverne, or the Spit:	216	U45 Squib	8
Much lesse a name would we bring up, or nurse,	216	U45 Squib	9
'Tis vertue alone, or nothing, that knits friends:	216	U45 Squib	12
No piece of money, but you know, or make	216	U45 Squib	14
Whom Fortune aided lesse, or vertue more.	217	U46 Coke	4
None Fortune aided lesse, or Vertue more.	217	U46 Coke	22
Or if Chance must, to each man that doth rise,	217	U46 Coke	23
Subject to quarrell only; or else such	218	U47 Tribe	11
That never yet did friend, or friendship seeke	218	U47 Tribe	14
Or th'other on their borders, that will jeast	218	U47 Tribe	16
Like flies, or wormes, with mans corrupt parts fed:	218	U47 Tribe	18
Then these can ever be; or else wish none.	219	U47 Tribe	30

	Page	Title	Line
OR (cont.)			
Be, or be not, to get the Val-telline?	219	U47 Tribe	32
Or the States Ships sent forth belike to meet	219	U47 Tribe	33
Or that the Match from Spaine was ever meant?	219	U47 Tribe	36
To live, or fall a Carkasse in the cause.	219	U47 Tribe	42
Of Spaine or France; or were not prick'd downe one	219	U47 Tribe	47
Lest it be justled, crack'd, made nought, or lesse:	219	U47 Tribe	58
Oylie Expansions, or shrunke durtie folds,	220	U47 Tribe	68
Or gratulates the passage	221	U48 Bacchus	45
Or else a health advances,	222	U48 Bacchus	49
Or if it would, the Court is the worst place,	223	U49 Pucell	43
And when you want those friends, or neere in blood,	224	U50 Countesse	26
Or your Allies, you make your bookes your friends,	224	U50 Countesse	27
Ne knowes he flatt'ring Colours, or false light.	227	U52 Answer	21
Or Castor mounted on his Cyllarus:	228	U53 Newcastle	8
Or what we heare our home-borne Legend tell,	228	U53 Newcastle	9
His friends, but to breake Chaires, or cracke a Coach.	230	U56 Covell	10
Widow or Wife, without the jealousie	230	U56 Covell	17
Of either Suitor, or a Servant by.	230	U56 Covell	18
Of suitor, or of servant standing by.	230	U56 Covell	V 18
Of gambol, or sport	231	U57 Burges	19
No Plover, or Coney	231	U57 Burges	22
Or Wine to enable	232	U57 Burges	24
The Muse, or the Poet,	232	U57 Burges	25
Like a rung Beare, or Swine: grunting out wit	232	U58 Book-seller	11
As all defence, or offence, were a chime!	232	U59 Newcastle	6
To bend, to breake, provoke, or suffer it!	233	U59 Newcastle	18
To bend, or breake, provoke, or suffer it!	233	U59 Newcastle	V 18
Of fortune! when, or death appear'd, or bands!	233	U59 Newcastle	23
And valiant were, with, or without their hands.	233	U59 Newcastle	24
No aime at glorie, or, in warre,	234	U60 La-ware	13
Then now, to love the Soveraigne, or his Lawes?	236	U64 Charles 3	V 8
How is she barren growne of love! or broke!	237	U64 Charles 3	15
How is she barren growne in love! or broke!	237	U64 Charles 3	V 15
An Ode, or Song, by all the Muses. . . .	239	U67 Muses	Ttl
This Citie, or to shake	239	U67 Muses	11
Are they so scanted in their store? or driven	241	U68 House-hold	3
To mee; or beene the same to you; if show,	241	U69 Friend Son	2
Profit, or Chance had made us: But I know	241	U69 Friend Son	3
His is more safe commoditie, or none:	241	U69 Friend Son	7
Or masked man, if valu'd by his face,	243	U70 Ode	23
How well at twentie had he falne, or stood!	243	U70 Ode	31
Or standing long an Oake, three hundred yeare,	245	U70 Ode	67
Or taste a part of that full joy he meant	246	U70 Ode	87
Made, or indentur'd, or leas'd out t'advance	246	U70 Ode	100
Of rimes, or ryots, at your feasts,	246	U70 Ode	103
Orgies of drinke, or fain'd protests:	246	U70 Ode	104
But as a Cary, or a Morison.	247	U70 Ode	116
Of Princes aides, or good mens Charities.	248	U71 Treasurer	3
Health, or scarce breath, as she had never bin,	248	U71 Treasurer	12
What Drums or Trumpets, or great Ord'nance can,	249	U72 King	9
Why doe I irritate, or stirre up thee,	250	U73 Weston	7
Epithalamion; Or, A Song: Celebrating The nuptials of . . .	252	U75 Epithalam.	Ttl
Or were Affaires in tune,	253	U75 Epithalam.	15
Or so did shine,	253	U75 Epithalam.	22
Or canker'd Jealousie,	257	U75 Epithalam.	135
Like Swine, or other Cattell here on earth:	257	U75 Epithalam.	154
Upon a Thomas, or a Francis call;	258	U75 Epithalam.	171
Upon a Thomas, or a Sister call;	258	U75 Epithalam.	V171
Strifes, murmures, or delay,	258	U75 Epithalam.	189
For done service, or to come:	259	U76 Petition	V 13
Or dispenc'd in bookes, or bread,	259	U76 Petition	15
Well dispenc'd in bookes, or bread,	259	U76 Petition	V 15
Of Noremberg, or Turkie; hang your roomes	260	U77 Treasurer	3
I would, if price, or prayer could them get,	260	U77 Treasurer	5
Send in, what or Romano, Tintoret,	260	U77 Treasurer	6
Send what Romano or what Tintoret,	260	U77 Treasurer	V 6
Titian, or Raphael, Michael Angelo,	260	U77 Treasurer	7
Have left in fame to equall, or out-goe	260	U77 Treasurer	8
The old Greek-hands in picture, and in stone.	260	U77 Treasurer	9
And act the businesse, which they paint, or carve.	261	U77 Treasurer	16
And act the businesse, which these paint, or carve.	261	U77 Treasurer	V 16
In glorious Piles, or Pyramids erect	261	U77 Treasurer	26
Court can call hers, or Man could call his Arts.	262	U78 Digby	4
Court can call hers, or Man would call the Arts.	262	U78 Digby	V 4
Busie, or frowne at first; when he sees thee,	262	U78 Digby	20
That have a Flock, or Herd, upon these plaines;	265	U79 New-yeares	47
Then ever Pales could, or Pan;	265	U79 New-yeares	61
To pluck a Garland, for her selfe, or mee?	268	U81 Pawlet	4
Their Carract was! I, or my trump must breake,	269	U81 Pawlet	27
Your hottest Causticks to, burne, lance, or cut:	270	U81 Pawlet	54
Your hotter Causticks to, burne, lance, or cut:	270	U81 Pawlet	V 54
And see all dead here, or about to dye!	271	U81 Pawlet	86
Eupheme; Or, The Faire Fame Left To Posteritie . . .	272	U84 Eupheme	Ttl
With Gold, or Claspes, which might be bought	273	U84 Cradle	27
That ever Nature, or the later Ayre	274	U84 Descent	4
Some Forme defective, or decay'd;	275	U84 Body	6
With all that Youth, or it can bring:	276	U84 Body	22
The Sunne, a Sea, or soundlesse Pit;	278	U84 Mind	11
Or hath she here, upon the ground,	280	U84 Mind	49
Some Paradise, or Palace found	280	U84 Mind	50
Upon a banke, or field of flowers,	280	U84 Mind	67
. . . apotheosis, or Relation to the Saints.	282	U84 Muse	Ttl

		Page	Title	Line

OR (cont.)

	Page	Title	Line
All that was good, or great in me she weav'd,	282	U84 Muse	4
To hang a window, or make darke the roome,	282	U84 Muse	7
Nothing, that could remaine, or yet can stirre	282	U84 Muse	9
Sleepie, or stupid Nature, couldst thou part	282	U84 Muse	15
To 'greet, or grieve her soft Euthanasee?	283	U84 Muse	40
Those other two; which must be judg'd, or crown'd:	284	U84 Muse	55
This as it guilty is, or guiltlesse found,	284	U84 Muse	56
T'accuse, or quit all Parties to be heard!	284	U84 Muse	60
This being thus: why should my tongue, or pen	284	U84 Muse	69
That she is in, or, make it more compleat?	284	U84 Muse	72
A Wife, a Friend, a Lady, or a Love;	285	U84 Muse	99
Wine, or delicious fruits, unto the Taste;	286	U84 Muse	123
Unto the Sent, a Spicerie, or Balme;	286	U84 Muse	125
Not tost or troubled with light Lady-aire;	287	U84 Muse	164
Her solemne houres she spent, or giving Almes,	288	U84 Muse	192
Or doing other deeds of Charitie,	288	U84 Muse	193
There, or the tall witch-hazill hee doth twine	290	U85 Country	V 9
Or in the bending Vale beholds a-farre	290	U85 Country	13
Or in the bending Vale beholds from far	290	U85 Country	V 13
Or the prest honey in pure pots doth keepe	290	U85 Country	15
Or when that Autumne, through the fields, lifts round	290	U85 Country	17
Or hence, or thence, he drives with many a Hound	290	U85 Country	31
Or straines on his small forke his subtill nets	290	U85 Country	33
Or straines on his small forke his subtler nets	290	U85 Country	V 33
For th'eating Thrush, or Pit-falls sets:	290	U85 Country	34
Such as the Sabines, or a Sun-burnt-blowse,	291	U85 Country	41
Or the herb Sorrell, that loves Meadows still,	291	U85 Country	57
Or Mallowes loosing bodyes ill:	291	U85 Country	58
Or Mallowes good for bodyes ill:	291	U85 Country	V 58
Or at the Feast of Bounds, the Lambe then slaine,	291	U85 Country	59
Or Kid forc't from the Wolfe againe.	291	U85 Country	60
Or with fresh flowers to girt my temple round.	293	U86 Hor.4:1	32
Or why, my well-grac'd words among,	293	U86 Hor.4:1	35
Or Tybers winding streames, I follow thee.	293	U86 Hor.4:1	40
No sowre, or sollen bed-mate, yet a Chast;	295	U90 Mart.10:47	10
With Doves; or Lambes, with Tygres coupled be.	305	Horace	16
A Scarlet peece, or two, stitch'd in: when or	305	Horace	19
A purple piece, or two stitch'd in: when either	338	Horace	V 19
Diana's Grove, or Altar, with the bor-/Dring	305	Horace	20
Diana's Grove, or Altar, with the nether	338	Horace	V 20
The pleasant grounds, or when the River Rhine,	305	Horace	22
Or Rainbow is describ'd. But here was now	305	Horace	23
Prove what your shoulders will, or will not beare.	339	Horace	V 57/ 55
The vertue and grace of which, or I mistake,	339	Horace	V 60/ 59
Or I am much deceiv'd, shall be to place	307	Horace	60
Or Plautus, and in Virgil disavow,	309	Horace	78
Or Varius? Why am I now envi'd so,	309	Horace	79
A kingly worke; or that long barren fen	309	Horace	93
Or the wilde river, who hath changed now	309	Horace	96
Or grace of speech, should hope a lasting date.	309	Horace	100
To ignorance still, then either learne, or know?	311	Horace	131
To ignorance still, then yet to learne, or know?	341	Horace	V126/131
Peleus, or Telephus. If you speake vile	311	Horace	147
And ill-penn'd things, I shall, or sleepe, or smile.	311	Horace	148
Or urgeth us to anger; and anon	311	Horace	154
Or an Heroe; if a ripe old man,	311	Horace	162
Or some hot youth, yet in his flourishing course;	313	Horace	163
Where some great Lady, or her diligent Nourse;	313	Horace	164
A ventring Merchant, or the Farmer free	313	Horace	165
A ventring Merchant, or the husband free	342	Horace	V165
Of Colchis borne; or in Assyria bred;	313	Horace	167
Or, with the milke of Thebes; or Argus, fed.	313	Horace	168
Or follow fame, thou that dost write, or faine	313	Horace	169
From whence thy Modestie, or Poemes law	313	Horace	193
Who nought assaies unaptly, or amisse?	315	Horace	200
Where the midst differs from the first: or where	315	Horace	217
And sits, till th'Epilogue saies Clap, or Crowne;	315	Horace	222
Soone angry, and soone pleas'd, is sweet, or sowre,	315	Horace	227
Or do's all businesse coldly, and with feare;	317	Horace	244
The parts of age to youth be given; or men	317	Horace	252
Or acted told. But, ever, things that run	317	Horace	256
Have more or lesse then just five Acts: nor laid,	317	Horace	272
The Idiot, keeping holy-day, or drudge,	319	Horace	301
Or Semi-god, that late was seene to weare	321	Horace	332
Or, whilst he shuns the Earth, to catch at Aire	321	Horace	335
Or old Silenus, Bacchus guard, and Nurse.	321	Horace	348
Or play young tricks in over-wanton verse;	347	Horace	V350/358
Or crack out bawdie speeches, and uncleane.	321	Horace	359
Or cracke out shamefull speeches, and uncleane.	347	Horace	V351/359
Him that buyes chiches blanch't, or chance to like	321	Horace	362
Him that buyes Pulse there, or perhaps may like	347	Horace	V354/362
Receive, or give it an applause, the more.	321	Horace	364
Receive, or give it any Crowne the more.	347	Horace	V356/364
Of fellowship, the fourth, or second place.	323	Horace	380
Or a worse Crime, the ignorance of art.	323	Horace	386
Or rather, thinking all my faults may spie,	323	Horace	392
If either you, or I, know the right way	323	Horace	402
If either you, or I know any way	348	Horace	V388/402
To part scurrilitie from wit: or can	323	Horace	403
A lawfull Verse, by th'eare, or finger scan.	323	Horace	404
Or 'twere the gowned Comoedy they taught.	323	Horace	410
A pound, or piece, by their long compting arts:	327	Horace	466

OR (cont.)

	Page	Title	Line
Thinke wee, or hope, there can be Verses fain'd	327	Horace	474
Poets would either profit, or delight,	327	Horace	477
Or mixing sweet, and fit, teach life the right.	327	Horace	478
Or Muse, upon the Lyre, thou chance b'asham'd.	329	Horace	502
Hath shed, or humane frailtie not kept thence.	329	Horace	528
Deserves no pardon; or who'd play, and sing	329	Horace	531
Twice, or thrice good, I wonder: but am more	329	Horace	535
Or Pleader at the Barre, that may come short	331	Horace	551
Or knowes not what Cassellius Aulus can;	331	Horace	553
Or thick grosse ointment, but offend the Guests:	331	Horace	558
So, any Poeme, fancied, or forth-brought	331	Horace	561
Or, who's unskilfull at the Coit, or Ball,	331	Horace	567
Or trundling Wheele, he can sit still, from all;	331	Horace	568
Wilt nothing against nature speake, or doe:	331	Horace	574
Nature, or Art. My Judgement will not pierce	331	Horace	582
Can; or all toile, without a wealthie veine:	331	Horace	584
Or, of the things, that ne're came in my mind,	333	Horace	596
Or great in money's out at use, command	333	Horace	600
Or wealthy in money's out at use, command	353	Horace	V600
Make a great Supper; or for some poore man	333	Horace	602
Will be a suretie; or can helpe him out	333	Horace	603
Whether his soothing friend speake truth, or no.	333	Horace	606
(Whether yo'are given to, or giver are.)	333	Horace	608
If of their friendship he be worthy, or no:	333	Horace	619
And twice, or thrice had 'ssayd it, still in vaine:	333	Horace	626
And twice, or thrice assay'd it, but in vain;	354	Horace	V626
Then change; no word, or worke, more would he spend	335	Horace	630
Infected with the leprosie, or had	335	Horace	645
The yellow Jaundies, or were furious mad	335	Horace	646
The yellow jaundis, or were truely mad,	354	Horace	V646
Into a pit, or hole; although he call,	335	Horace	652
Himselfe there purposely, or no; and would	335	Horace	657
Or love of this so famous death lay by.	335	Horace	669
Or love of this his famous death lay by.	355	Horace	V669
Or the sad thunder-stroken thing he have	335	Horace	672
Unseason'd frostes, or the most envyous weather.	361	Palmer	8
Or (by our Turtles Augure)	364	Phoenix	5
Or alter kinde.	367	Ode Who saith	30
Humber, or Owse, decline;	368	Ode Who saith	74
Or thought they, Leda's white Adult'rers place	369	Ode Who saith	104
Or Tames be rap't from us	369	Ode Who saith	107
Set out a like, or second to our Swan.	369	Ode Who saith	120
Lady, or Pusil, that weares maske, or fan,	370	Fletcher	4
Velvet, or Taffata cap, rank'd in the darke	371	Fletcher	5
With the shops Foreman, or some such brave sparke,	371	Fletcher	6
Or moathes shall eate, what all these Fooles admire.	371	Fletcher	16
Or builders of Story have oft imputation	380	Coryat 3	30
Of his foote, or his penne, his braine or his hoofe,	380	Coryat 3	32
Yes. And thanks God in his Pistle or his Booke	380	Coryat 3	43
So that not them, his scabbes, lice, or the stewes,	380	Coryat 3	50
Or any thing else that another should hide,	380	Coryat 3	51
With the same looke, or with a better, shine.	384	Somerset	10
So, be there never discontent, or sorrow,	384	Somerset	15
Or, to so many, and so Broad-seales had,	385	Brooke	3
Or skill of making matches in my life:	386	Husband	7
Some men, of Bookes or Freinds not speaking right,	386	Browne	1
Or, like our Money-Brokers, take up names	386	Browne	10
which, did they neere so neate, or proudly dwell,	387	Cavendish	3
And who make thither else, rob, or invade.	389	Chapman.	12
Who tracks this Authors, or Translators Pen,	389	Aleman	1
Upon it, but will loath, or let it passe,	389	Aleman	9
Or blinde Affection, which doth ne're advance	391	Shakespeare	9
Or crafty Malice, might pretend this praise,	391	Shakespeare	11
These are, as some infamous Baud, or Whore,	391	Shakespeare	13
Above th'ill fortune of them, or the need.	391	Shakespeare	16
Chaucer, or Spenser, or bid Beaumont lye	391	Shakespeare	20
Or sporting Kid, or Marlowes mighty line.	391	Shakespeare	30
And shake a Stage: Or, when thy Sockes were on,	391	Shakespeare	37
Of all, that insolent Greece, or haughtie Rome	391	Shakespeare	39
Sent forth, or since did from their ashes come.	391	Shakespeare	40
Our eares, or like a Mercury to charme!	392	Shakespeare	46
Or for the lawrell, he may gaine a scorne,	392	Shakespeare	63
Or influence, chide, or cheere the drooping Stage;	392	Shakespeare	78
What Muse, or rather God of harmony	395	May	14
Phoebus, and Hermes? They whose tongue, or pen	395	May	17
As not the smallest joint, or gentlest word	395	May	21
In the great masse, or machine there is stirr'd?	395	May	22
The Sunne translated, or the Sonne of May.	395	May	24
A Friend at all; or, if at all, to thee:	396	Drayton	2
Hanch against Hanch, or raise a riming Club	396	Drayton	8
Or Rurall Virgil come, to pipe to us!	397	Drayton	28
Or universall circumduction	397	Drayton	51
An Agincourt, an Agincourt, or dye.	398	Drayton	70
Thou hadst brought Lapland, or old Cobalus,	398	Drayton	86
Empusa, Lamia, or some Monster, more	398	Drayton	87
Then Affricke knew, or the full Grecian store!	398	Drayton	88
Or of a parent! or a freind!	399	Lady Ogle	13
Or without angles, it was shee!	399	Lady Ogle	16
Or else Magnetique in the force,	399	Lady Ogle	19
Or sweet, or various, in the course!	399	Lady Ogle	20
What was proportion, or could bee	399	Lady Ogle	21
In number, measure, or degree	399	Lady Ogle	23

```
                                                    Page      Title      Line
OR  (cont.)
   Of weight, or fashion, it was shee.          .    .    .    399   Lady Ogle        24
   Above his Reader, or his Prayser, is.        .    .    .    400   Beaumont          2
   That Art, or Ingine, on the strength can raise.   .    .    400   Beaumont         10
   To cut a Dike? or sticke a Stake up, here,   .    .    .    401   Beaumont         12
   Defies, what's crosse to Piety, or good Fame.  .   .   .    401   Beaumont         20
   Whether the buylding of the Stage or Scene!    .   .   .    402   Inigo Jones 1    11
   Or making of the Propertyes it meane?   .    .    .    .    402   Inigo Jones 1    12
   Vizors or Anticks? or it comprehend          .    .    .    402   Inigo Jones 1    13
   Will any of these express your place? or witt?   .   .     402   Inigo Jones 1    18
   Or are you soe ambitious 'bove your peers?   .    .    .    402   Inigo Jones 1    19
   Though gold or Ivory haftes would make it good.   .   .    403   Inigo Jones 1    28
   Though gold or Ivory haftes cant make it good.   .   .     403   Inigo Jones 1  V 28
   Or Verse, or Sense t'express Immortall you?    .   .   .    403   Inigo Jones 1    41
   He is, or would be the mayne Dominus doe     .    .    .    404   Inigo Jones 1    64
   Moulded or stroakt up to survey a State!     .    .    .    405   Inigo Jones 1    84
   Of thy dead Standards: or (with miracle) see   .   .   .    405   Inigo Jones 1    89
   Vermilion, Lake, or Cinnopar affoards        .    .    .    406   Inigo Jones 1    94
   Or Ale! He build a pallace! Thou a shopp     .    .    .    407   Inigo Jones 2     9
   Or Dowgate Torrent falling into Thames,      .    .    .    407   Inigo Jones 2    16
   Or canst of truth the least intrenchment pitch,  .   .     407   Inigo Jones 2    23
   With rotten chalk, or Cole upon a wall,      .    .    .    408   Inigo Jones 3    11
   That sit upon the Comon Draught: or Strand!    .   .   .    408   Inigo Jones 3    13
   If such a Tyke as thou, er'e wer't, or noe?    .   .   .    409   Detractor        14
   And the Physician teach men spue, or shite;    .   .   .    410   Brome            16
   No faith's more firme, or flat, then where't doth creep. . 413   Ghyrlond         20
   The rosie Morning, or the rising Sun,        .    .    .    414   Ghyrlond         50
   Or why to like; they found, it all was new,    .   .   .    415   Rutter            9
   or as some would say to breake               .    .    .    416   Moon              3
   Tough, foule, or Tender.          .    .    .    .    .    417   Moon             16
   And as either newes or mirth      .    .    .    .    .    417   Moon             17
   rise or fall upon the earth,      .    .    .    .    .    417   Moon             18
   for if there, or peace or warr be,     .    .    .    .    417   Moon             22
   or hir quarters lighter bee,      .    .    .    .    .    417   Moon             31
   Or if any strife bety'de          .    .    .    .    .    417   Moon             33
   Or if't be the Gossipps happ      .    .    .    .    .    417   Moon             37
   Or by chance if in their grease   .    .    .    .    .    418   Moon             41
   or theire Ale, they break the peace,   .    .    .    .    418   Moon             42
   And come forth worthie Ivye, or the Bayes,     .   .   .    420   Ode:If Men       26
   Hee that soe Censureth, or adviseth synns,     .   .   .    421   Censure           4
   or Malyce to make Faultes, which nowe is skill.  .   .     421   Censure          11
   Looke how the starres from earth, or seas from flames  .   422   Lucan             7
   Welcome all, who lead or follow,       .    .    .    .    657   Door Apollo       1
   Or the Tripos, his Tower Bottle:       .    .    .    .    657   Door Apollo       4
   Welcome all, who lead or follow,       .    .    .    .    657   Door Apollo      19
   of her white Hand; so she can spare it.  .   .   .    .    662   Bedford          10
ORACLE
   To the Oracle of Apollo.          .    .    .    .    .    657   Door Apollo       2
   To the Oracle of Apollo.          .    .    .    .    .    657   Door Apollo      20
ORACLES
   The Oracles, too, were given out in Verse;     .   .   .    329   Horace          496
ORBE
   Closde in an orbe of Christall.        .    .    .    .    365   Ode Splendor     12
   And fill'd an Orbe as circular, as heaven!     .   .   .    396   Drayton          19
   The Orbe was cut forth into Regions seaven.    .   .   .    396   Drayton          20
ORCADES
   The scatter'd Orcades;       .    .    .    .    .    .    368   Ode Who saith    67
ORCHARD
   Then hath thy orchard fruit, thy garden flowers,   .   .    94   F2 Penshurst     39
ORDAIN'D
   Faire Fame, who art ordain'd to crowne   .   .    .    .    272   U84 Cradle        1
ORDER
   Mov'd by her order, and the ninth more high,   .   .   .     82   E130 Ferrab. 1   13
   All order, and Disposure, still.       .    .    .    .    151   U12 Corbet       14
   Her order is to cherish, and preserve,   .   .   .    .    192   U38 Elegy 'Tis   61
   No order? no Decree? Though we be gone   .   .   .    .    211   U43 Vulcan      176
   Because the order of the whole is faire!   .   .   .   .    251   U74 Weston       12
   To every Order, ev'ry Hierarchie!      .    .    .    .    271   U81 Pawlet       72
   Nor language, nor cleere order ere forsakes.   .   .   .    307   Horace           58
   Nor language, nor cleere order will forsake.   .   .   .    339   Horace     V 59/ 58
   The vertue of which order, and true grace,     .   .   .    307   Horace           59
   Of Order, and Connexion; so much grace   .   .   .    .    321   Horace          353
   For order, and for governing the pixe,   .   .   .    .    415   Rutter           25
ORDERS
   The councells, actions, orders, and events     .   .   .     62   E95 Savile       32
ORDINANCE
   Who with the Divell did Ordinance beget;   .   .   .   .    212   U43 Vulcan     V202
ORDINARIES
   He steales to ordinaries; there he playes  .   .   .   .     30   E12 Shift        11
ORD'NANCE
   And Ord'nance too: so much as from the Tower   .   .   .    213   U44 Speach        3
   What Drums or Trumpets, or great Ord'nance can,  .   .     249   U72 King          9
ORD'RING
   Of ord'ring all.        .    .    .    .    .    .    .    273   U84 Cradle       32
O'RE
   Lookes o're the bill, likes it: and say's, god payes.  .    30   E12 Shift        10
   And brooding o're it sit, with broadest eyes,  .   .   .     99   F3 Wroth         83
   To make us still sing o're, and o're,    .   .   .    .    145   U5 Woman-kind     3
   That spread his body o're, to kill:    .    .    .    .    234   U60 La-ware      16
   Not, ten times o're, corrected to the naile.   .   .   .    325   Horace          418
   O're read, examin'd, try'd, and prov'd your Ryme  .   .    421   Censure           7
ORE  (NOUN)
   Olde Hesiods Ore, and give it us; but thine,   .   .   .    388   Chapman           2
```

		Page	Title	Line

ORE
His rosie tyes and garters so ore-blowne,   •   •   •   •   62   E97 Motion   5
Pr'y thee, yet save thy rest; give ore in time: •   •   •   73   E112 Gamster   21
Of Hol'borne (three sergeants heads) lookes ore,   •   89   E133 Voyage   177
T'advance his doubtfull issue, and ore-flow   •   •   117   F13 Aubigny   40
Nor o're-praise, nor yet condemne;   •   •   •   142   U2 Her man   47
Thou didst tell me; and wert o're-joy'd to peepe   201   U42 Elegy Let   59
A horse neck joyn, & sundry plumes ore-fold   •   338   Horace   V 2
Ye have oft-times, that may ore-shine the rest,   •   305   Horace   18
But flowes out, that ore-swelleth in full brests.   •   329   Horace   506
Who (see) already hath ore-flowne   •   •   368   Ode Who saith   65
And howrely brooding ore the same,   •   •   •   400   Lady Ogle   29
ORE-BLOWNE
His rosie tyes and garters so ore-blowne,   •   •   62   E97 Motion   5
ORE-FLOW
T'advance his doubtfull issue, and ore-flow   •   •   117   F13 Aubigny   40
ORE-FLOWNE
Who (see) already hath ore-flowne   •   •   368   Ode Who saith   65
ORE-FOLD
A horse neck joyn, & sundry plumes ore-fold   •   •   338   Horace   V 2
O'RE-JOY'D
Thou didst tell me; and wert o're-joy'd to peepe   •   201   U42 Elegy Let   59
O'RE-PRAISE
Nor o're-praise, nor yet condemne;   •   •   •   142   U2 Her man   47
ORE-SHINE
Ye have oft-times, that may ore-shine the rest,   •   •   305   Horace   18
ORESTES
Poore Io wandring; wild Orestes mad: •   •   •   313   Horace   177
Io still wandring; griev'd Orestes sad: •   •   342   Horace   V177
ORE-SWELLETH
But flowes out, that ore-swelleth in full brests.   •   329   Horace   506
O'REWHELM'D
Their vitious ease, and be o'rewhelm'd with it.   •   •   162   U15 Friend-Wars   4
ORGANES
By being organes to great sinne,   •   •   •   •   99   F3 Wroth   86
ORGIES
Orgies of drinke, or fain'd protests: •   •   •   246   U70 Ode   104
ORIENT
His cloke with orient velvet quite lin'd through,   •   •   62   E97 Motion   4
ORIGINALL
Thine the originall; and France shall boast,   •   •   83   E132 Sylvester   13
And all the originall riots of the place: •   •   202   U42 Elegy Let   80
As hath thy James; cleans'd from originall drosse,   •   268   U80 Christning   9
Her spirit home, to her originall!   •   •   •   270   U81 Pawlet   64
ORNAMENT
In gracefull Ornament of Garland, Gemmes, and Haire.   •   253   U75 Epithalam.   40
ORNAMENTS
Take better ornaments, my teares, and verse.   •   •   35   E27 Roe 1   2
Above your under-carved ornaments,   •   •   •   115   F12 Rutland   85
Cut off superfluous ornaments; and when   •   •   335   Horace   636
ORNITHS
With gentle Calais, Thurine Orniths Sonne;   •   •   •   293   U87 Hor.3:9   14
ORPHANES
To blow up orphanes, widdowes, and their states;   •   •   99   F3 Wroth   79
ORPHANS
The Orphans Pillar, the true Subjects shield,   •   •   185   U30 Burleigh   7
ORPHEUS
Orpheus, Ulysses: or the Latine Muse,   •   •   84   E133 Voyage   3
Will prove old Orpheus act no tale to be: •   •   115   F12 Rutland   77
Will prove old Orpheus Arts no tale to be: •   •   115   F12 Rutland   V 77
Orpheus, a priest, and speaker for the Gods   •   •   327   Horace   479
I thought thee then our Orpheus, that wouldst try   •   397   Drayton   35
And I had stil'd thee, Orpheus, but before   •   •   397   Drayton   37
O'TH'
They say you weekly invite with fits o'th' Mother,   •   223   U49 Pucell   40
O'THE
Have you mark'd but the fall o'the Snow   •   •   134   U2 Triumph   23
Have you seene the fall o'the Snow   •   •   •   135   U2 Triumph   V 23
Or have smelt o'the bud o'the Brier?   •   •   •   135   U2 Triumph   27
Or have tasted the bag o'the Bee?   •   •   •   135   U2 Triumph   29
OTHER   (See also T'OTHER)
Who, to thy one, all other braines refuse;   •   •   34   E23 Donne 1   2
Surly, use other arts, these only can   •   •   •   36   E28 Surly   21
And, if no other miserie, yet age?   •   •   •   41   E45 First Son   8
This but thy judgement fooles: the other way   •   •   43   E52 Courtling   5
One doth not stroke me, nor the other strike.   •   •   46   E61 Foole   2
Whose house, if it no other honor had,   •   •   48   E66 Cary   3
In solemne cypres, the other cob-web-lawne.   •   •   51   E73 Fine Grand   14
This world deaths region is, the other lifes: •   •   54   E80 Life/Death   5
I speake thy other graces, not lesse showne,   •   •   58   E91 Vere   13
Need seeke no other strength, no other height;   •   •   63   E98 Th Roe 1   4
I need no other arts, but studie thee: •   •   78   E122 Rudyerd 2   9
Th'other let it sleepe with death: •   •   •   79   E124 Elizabeth   10
We each to other may this voyce enspire;   •   •   81   E128 Wm Roe 2   11
That, not a paire of friends each other see,   •   •   81   E129 Mime   1
The other was a squire, of faire degree;   •   •   84   E133 Voyage   25
Gorgonian scolds, and Harpyes: on the other   •   •   86   E133 Voyage   69
The other thought it Hydra, or the rock   •   •   86   E133 Voyage   83
One said, the other swore, the world consists.   •   •   87   E133 Voyage   129
With other edifices, when they see   •   •   •   96   F2 Penshurst   100
Such, and no other was that age, of old,   •   •   98   F3 Wroth   63
The soules, shee loves. Those other glorious notes,   114   F12 Rutland   43
You, and that other starre, that purest light,   •   •   115   F12 Rutland   65

OTHER   (cont.)

Other great wives may blush at: when they see . . . . . 119 F13 Aubigny   111
Each into other, and had now made one. . . . . 120 F13 Aubigny   120
To ought but grace, or ayme at other end. . . . . 122 F15 Heaven   8
This here sung, can be no other . . . . . 136 U2 Cupid   11
To no other Grace but you! . . . . . 138 U2 Kisse   20
All other Acts of Worldlings, are but toyle . . . . . 162 U15 Friend-Wars   9
All other Acts of Worldlings, are meere toyle . . . . . 162 U15 Friend-Wars V 9
And jealous each of other, yet thinke long . . . . . 164 U15 Friend-Wars   73
Unto the other; and live patternes, how . . . . . 171 U19 Elegy By   17
Amongst my many other, that I may . . . . . 171 U20 Shrub   3
Other ceasure. . . . . . 184 U29 Fit of Rime   48
Was drawne to practise other hue, then that . . . . . 188 U34 Small Poxe   8
Out with the other, for hee's still at home; . . . . . 198 U40 Elegy That   34
The sinne of Boast, or other countermine . . . . . 198 U40 Elegy That   46
And straight-way spent a Sonnet; with that other . . . . . 201 U42 Elegy Let   67
Or in Moore-fields, this other night! sings one, ... 202 U42 Elegy Let   73
As th'other may his braines with Quicksilver. . . . . 208 U43 Vulcan   122
This other for his eye-browes; hence, away, ... 215 U44 Speach   97
Or th'other on their borders, that will jeast . . . . . 218 U47 Tribe   16
I studie other friendships, and more one, ... 219 U47 Tribe   29
And not a Song be other . . . . . 221 U48 Bacchus   35
For Sermoneeres: of which now one, now other, ... 223 U49 Pucell   39
And can for other Graces her commend, ... 230 U56 Covell   20
Thanke him: if other, hee can give no Bayes. . . . . 232 U58 Book-seller   6
One Poet, then of other folke ten score. . . . . 235 U62 Charles 1   10
What, by that name, wee each to other owe, ... 241 U69 Friend Son   4
Till either grew a portion of the other: . . . . . 247 U70 Ode   110
Like Eccho playing from the other shore. . . . . 249 U72 King   8
One to the other, long e're these to light were brought. . . . . 257 U75 Epithalam.   144
Like Swine, or other Cattell here on earth: . . . . . 257 U75 Epithalam.   154
As other soules, to his, dwell in a Lane: . . . . . 262 U78 Digby   12
Wee know no other power then his, ... 265 U79 New-yeares   42
Pan knowes no other power then his, ... 265 U79 New-yeares   64
One corporall, only; th'other spirituall, ... 284 U84 Muse   52
Those other two; which must be judg'd, or crown'd: . . . . . 284 U84 Muse   55
All other gladnesse, with the thought is barr'd; . . . . . 284 U84 Muse   67
Or doing other deeds of Charitie, ... 288 U84 Muse   193
Downe close by shore, this other creeping steales, ... 339 Horace   V 40/ 39
Betweene the Acts, a quite cleane other thing . . . . . 317 Horace   278
Whilst other soules convert to base abuse . . . . . 361 Palmer   11
till th'one hath drownd the other in our sightes, ... 361 Palmer   20
For other formes come short all . . . . . 364 Ode Splendor   2
Besides the other Swannes admiring him, ... 366 Ode Who saith   5
. . . Which should Have beene Printed with the other . . . . . . 379 Coryat 3   Ttl
Since he treads in no other Mans steps but his owne. . . . . 379 Coryat 3   12
Yet neyther of you seeme to th'other old. . . . . 384 Somerset   24
As, since, she will vouchsafe no other Wit. . . . . 392 Shakespeare   50
But Sorrow, she desir'd no other Friend: . . . . . 394 Jane Ogle   17
By bringing forth God's onely Son, no other. . . . . 414 Ghyrlond   48
And in this Age, canst hope no other grace. . . . . 420 Ode:If Men   27

OTHERS

May others feare, flie, and traduce thy name, ... 32 E17 Critic   1
For all night-sinnes, with others wives, unknowne, ... 39 E39 Colt   1
As others speake, but onely thou dost act. . . . . 57 E89 Allen   12
Others more modest, but contemne us too, ... 59 E92 New Crie   39
Whil'st others toyle for titles to their tombes. . . . . 70 E109 Nevil   18
Where, what makes others great, doth keepe thee good! . . . . . 73 E113 Overbury   4
Writing thy selfe, or judging others writ, ... 78 E123 Rudyerd 3   1
The very call, to make all others come: . . . . . 81 E129 Mime   8
Let others watch in guiltie armes, and stand . . . . . 98 F3 Wroth   67
For others ill, ought none their good forget. . . . . 116 F13 Aubigny   6
Or feare to draw true lines, 'cause others paint: . . . . . 117 F13 Aubigny   20
Each suck others breath. . . . . . 139 U2 Another   16
That others should not warme them at my fire, ... 150 U10 Jealousie   6
The way to meet, what others would upbraid; . . . . . 153 U13 Sacvile   10
Of others honours, thus, enjoy thine owne. . . . . 160 U14 Selden   66
Of others honours, thus, enjoy thine owne. . . . . 160 U14 Selden   V 66
Others, in time may love, as we doe now. . . . . 171 U19 Elegy By   18
But charme the Senses, others over-come . . . . . 182 U28 Worth   7
Others by common Stars their courses run, ... 194 U38 Elegy 'Tis   119
To others, as he will deserve the Trust . . . . . 198 U40 Elegy That   39
But, others fell with that conceipt by the eares, ... 209 U43 Vulcan   145
But, others fell by that conceipt by the eares, ... 209 U43 Vulcan   V145
In others-evill best is understood: . . . . . 217 U46 Coke   6
To Church, as others doe to Feasts and Playes, ... 222 U49 Pucell   16
One in the others hand, ... 256 U75 Epithalam.   125
Am turned with an others powers. My Passion . . . . . 283 U84 Muse   31
So doth the one, the others helpe require, ... 333 Horace   585

OTHERS-EVILL

In others-evill best was understood: . . . . . 217 U46 Coke   6

OTHERWISE

But I on yours farre otherwise shall doe, ... 159 U14 Selden   17

OTHES

At hunting railes, having no guift in othes, ... 76 E119 Shelton   2

OUGHT   (VERB)

We ought not give them taste, we had an eare. . . . . 83 E131 Ferrab. 2   6
For others ill, ought none their good forget. . . . . 116 F13 Aubigny   6

OUGHT

To this, if ought appeare, which I not know of, ... 65 E101 Supper   25
By me, their priest (if they can ought divine) . . . . . 119 F13 Aubigny   101
To ought but grace, or ayme at other end. . . . . 122 F15 Heaven   8
Profit in ought: each day some little adde, ... 157 U13 Sacvile   132

OUGHT (cont.)

I ne're attempted ought against thy life; · · · 202 U43 Vulcan V 5
Ought that is ill, but the suspition too, · · 224 U50 Countesse 6
Of daring ought, hath still beene given; we know it: · 338 Horace V 12
To bettring of the mind of man, in ought, · · · 331 Horace 562
If to Quintilius, you recited ought: · · · 333 Horace 623

OUNCE

There's Albin's sonne will say, Substract an ounce · · 327 Horace 467
An ounce, what makes it then? The halfe pound just; · · 327 Horace 471

OUNCES

From the five ounces; what remaines? pronounce · · 327 Horace 468
A third of twelve, you may: foure ounces. Glad, · · 327 Horace 469
Sixe ounces. O, when once the canker'd rust, · · 327 Horace 472

OUR

For then, our water-conduits doe runne wine; · · 36 E29 Tilter 5
Was his blest fate, but our hard lot to find. · · 37 E32 Roe 2 8
Left us of feare, but first our crimes, then lawes. · 38 E35 James 2 6
First thou preserved wert, our king to bee, · · 38 E35 James 2 9
And hath no honor lost, our Due'llists say. · · 42 E48 Mungril 3
That we thy losse might know, and thou our love, · · 43 E51 James 3 1
For we, that have our eyes still in our eares, · · 43 E51 James 3 9
Looke not upon thy dangers, but our feares. · · 43 E51 James 3 10
Poore Poet-Ape, that would be thought our chiefe, · 44 E56 Poet-Ape 1
I'have sung the greater fortunes of our state. · · 48 E64 Salisbury 3 18
Who, to upbraid the sloth of this our time, · · 48 E66 Cary 5
Each best day of our life escapes us, first. · · 50 E70 Wm Roe 1 6
T'our times return'd, hath made her heaven in thee. · 52 E74 Chancelor 10
Or then, or since, about our Muses springs, · · 53 E79 Rutland 3
Through which, our merit leads us to our meeds. · · 53 E80 Life/Death 2
And here, it should be one of our first strifes, · 54 E80 Life/Death 6
Lucy, you brightnesse of our spheare, who are · · 60 E94 Bedford 3 1
Lucy, you brightnesse of our spheare, who are · · 61 E94 Bedford 3 15
Well, though thy name lesse then our great ones bee, · 64 E99 Th Roe 2 11
But that your worth will dignifie our feast, · · 64 E101 Supper 4
Is not to be despair'd of, for our money; · · 65 E101 Supper 14
Of which wee'll speake our minds, amidst our meate; · 65 E101 Supper 23
Nor shall our cups make any guiltie men: · · 65 E101 Supper 37
But, at our parting, we will be, as when · · 65 E101 Supper 38
That shall be utter'd at our mirthfull boord, · · 65 E101 Supper 40
Or did our times require it, to behold · · 67 E104 Montgomery 3
Of former age, or glorie of our one, · · 67 E104 Montgomery 10
More, then to varie what our elders knew: · · 72 E111 Edmonds 2 6
A worke of ours, we part with our owne right; · 82 E131 Ferrab. 2 2
With tales of Troyes just knight, our faiths abuse: · 84 E133 Voyage 4
Cocytus, Phlegeton, our have prov'd in one; · · 84 E133 Voyage 8
Old Bankes the juggler, our Pythagoras, · · 88 E133 Voyage 156
Our brave Heroes with a milder glare, · · 88 E133 Voyage 163
Our fraile condition it is such, · · · 101 F4 To the World 54
He, at length, our good will sever. · · 102 F5 Celia 1 4
He, at length, our blisse will sever. · · 102 F5 Celia 1 V 4
Why should we deferre our joyes? · · 102 F5 Celia 1 9
So removed by our wile? · · · 102 F5 Celia 1 14
Scarce will take our present store? · · 105 F8 Sicknesse 11
Scarce will take our present score? · · 105 F8 Sicknesse V 11
For the more countenance to our active Muse? · 107 F10 Proludium V 3
And foundred thy hot teame, to tune our lay. · 107 F10 Proludium V 9
To raise our spirits with thy conjuring wine, · 107 F10 Proludium V 11
Thou, nor their loosenesse with our making sorts. · 107 F10 Proludium V 18
His absence in our verse, is all I aske. · · 107 F10 Proludium V 21
Our muse up by commission: No, we bring · · 108 F10 Proludium V 28
Our owne true fire. Now our thought takes wing, · 108 F10 Proludium V 29
the glories of yt. Now our muse takes winge, · 108 F10 Proludium 15
Object arrive there, but the heart (our spie) · 109 F11 Epode 11
To wakefull reason, our affections king: · · 109 F11 Epode 13
To make our sense our slave. · · · 109 F11 Epode 18
For either our affections doe rebell, · · 109 F11 Epode 21
And strike our reason blinde. · · · 110 F11 Epode 30
In our enflamed brests: · · · 110 F11 Epode 34
And yet (in this t'expresse our selves more cleare) · 111 F11 Epode 75
But we propose a person like our Dove, · · 112 F11 Epode 91
Then this, our guilt, nor golden age can deeme, · 114 F12 Rutland 22
Painted, or carv'd upon our great-mens tombs, · 114 F12 Rutland 45
To take our nature; became'st man, and dyd'st, · 128 U1 Trinitie 22
To pay our debts, upon thy Crosse, and cryd'st, · 128 U1 Trinitie 23
And tooke on him our Nature. · · · 130 U1 Nativitie 18
A Martyr borne in our defence; · · 130 U1 Nativitie 23
And whilst our tongues perplexed lie, · · 139 U2 Another 17
Let who will thinke us dead, or wish our death. · 139 U2 Another 18
Come, with our Voyces, let us warre, · · 143 U3 Musicall 1
Nay, rather both our soules bee strayn'd · · 144 U3 Musicall 25
Our owne false praises, for your ends: · · 145 U5 Woman-kind 4
And having pleas'd our art, wee'll try · · 145 U5 Woman-kind 17
Our proper vertue is to range: · · · 146 U6 Defence 4
Take that away, you take our lives, · · 146 U6 Defence 5
Our pleasure; but preserves us more · · 146 U6 Defence 21
For that's a narrow joy is but our owne. · · 147 U7 Nymph 7
Of our Towne Gallantry! or why there rests · 155 U13 Sacvile 92
Our Delicacies are growne capitall, · · 163 U15 Friend-Wars 37
And even our sports are dangers! what we call · 163 U15 Friend-Wars 38
Nor is the title question'd with our proud, · 164 U15 Friend-Wars 83
What furie of late is crept into our Feasts? · 166 U15 Friend-Wars 117
This hath our ill-us'd freedome, and soft peace · 166 U15 Friend-Wars 121
Our vices doe not tarry in a place, · · 166 U15 Friend-Wars 123

OUR (cont.)

	Page	Title	Line
More then themselves, or then our lives could take,	166	U15 Friend-Wars	127
And whilst our states, strength, body, and mind we waste,	166	U15 Friend-Wars	133
Goe make our selves the Usurers at a cast.	166	U15 Friend-Wars	134
That scratching now's our best Felicitie?	166	U15 Friend-Wars	144
Be brought by us to meet our Destinie.	170	U18 Elegy Can	20
And since our Daintie age,	175	U23 Himselfe	31
On these darke rymes; that our affection	177	U25 Desmond	V 15
Then shall our Verses, like strong Charmes,	177	U25 Desmond	V 18
(As my hope tells) that our faire Phoebe's shine,	179	U25 Desmond	58
(As my hope tells) that our drad Cynthia's shine,	179	U25 Desmond	V 58
O then (our best-best lov'd) let me importune,	180	U25 Desmond	V 63
Hath our great Sidney, Stella set,	181	U27 Ode Helen	25
Shortly againe: and make our absence sweet.	197	U40 Elegy That	8
That Article, may not become our lover:	198	U40 Elegy That	48
Made longer by our praises. Or, if not,	200	U42 Elegy Let	21
To our owne Ladyes; and in storie there	207	U43 Vulcan	97
for our owne Ladyes; and in storie there	207	U43 Vulcan	V 97
Of our fift Henry, eight of his nine yeare;	207	U43 Vulcan	98
Of our fift Henry, right of his nine yeare;	207	U43 Vulcan	V 98
Our friends, the Watermen! They could provide	208	U43 Vulcan	V124
In those Records, which, were our Chroniclers gone,	210	U43 Vulcan	V171
'Bove all our Fire-workes, had at Ephesus,	211	U43 Vulcan	V194
Nor markes of wealth so from our Nation fled,	213	U44 Speech	12
And could (if our great men would let their Sonnes	214	U44 Speech	57
For education of our Lordings; Soone	214	U44 Speech	62
Us, in our bearing, that are thus, and thus,	215	U44 Speech	65
All licence in our lives? What need we know,	215	U44 Speech	70
The Hawking language? or our Day to breake	215	U44 Speech	72
We will beleeve, like men of our owne Ranke,	215	U44 Speech	75
Our Ancestors impos'd on Prince and State.	215	U44 Speech	78
The Herald will. Our blood is now become	215	U44 Speech	82
Or what we heare our home-borne Legend tell,	228	U53 Newcastle	9
My Lord, till felt griefe make our stone hearts soft,	234	U61 Epigram	14
And wee doe weepe, to water, for our sinne.	234	U61 Epigram	15
As thou dost cure our Evill, at thy charge.	235	U62 Charles 1	8
An Epigram. To our great and good K. Charles . . .	236	U64 Charles 3	Ttl
And as it turnes our joyfull yeare about,	236	U64 Charles 3	5
That so hath crown'd our hopes, our spring, and earth,	237	U65 Prince	2
which thus hast crown'd our hopes, our spring, and earth,	237	U65 Prince	V 2
That so hath crown'd our hopes, our spring, our earth,	237	U65 Prince	V 2
That thus hath crown'd our hopes, with thee, our Spring & May,	237	U65 Prince	V 2
And long in changing. Let our Nephewes see	238	U65 Prince	7
In changing, let our Nephewes joyfull see	238	U65 Prince	V 7
In changing. Let our after Nephewes see	238	U65 Prince	V 7
The Mother of our Lord: why may not I	238	U66 Queene	3
The Mother of our Prince? When was there seene	238	U66 Queene	6
Our thanks to God. Then, Haile to Mary! spring	238	U66 Queene	V 13
Of so much health, both to our Land, and King.	238	U66 Queene	V 14
Yet, let our Trumpets sound;	239	U67 Muses	13
With beating of our Drums;	239	U67 Muses	15
See, see our active King	240	U67 Muses	37
O how will then our Court be pleas'd,	251	U74 Weston	25
A-while with us bright Sun, and helpe our light;	252	U75 Epithalam.	2
A-while with us bright Sun, and mend our light;	252	U75 Epithalam.	V 2
Through which not only we, but all our Species are.	253	U75 Epithalam.	32
Although that thou, O Sun, at our intreaty stay!	254	U75 Epithalam.	56
With all the pompe of Youth, and all our Court beside.	254	U75 Epithalam.	72
Our Court, and all the Grandees; now, Sun, looke,	254	U75 Epithalam.	73
But dare not aske our wish in Language fescennine:	257	U75 Epithalam.	160
(After the last child borne;) This is our wedding day.	258	U75 Epithalam.	168
Unto our yeare doth give the longest light.	262	U78 Digby	16
To fit the softnesse of our Yeares-gift: when	263	U79 New-yeares	6
Pan is the great Preserver of our bounds.	264	U79 New-yeares	14
To him we owe all profits of our grounds.	264	U79 New-yeares	15
Our milke. Our fells. Our fleeces. and first Lambs.	264	U79 New-yeares	16
Our teeming Ewes, and lustie-mounting Rammes.	264	U79 New-yeares	17
Of brightest Mira, doe we raise our Song,	264	U79 New-yeares	24
That leades our flocks and us, and calls both forth	264	U79 New-yeares	29
Of brightest Mira, is our Song; the grace	264	U79 New-yeares	32
Hee is the Father of our peace;	264	U79 New-yeares	40
Pan only our great Shep'ard is,	265	U79 New-yeares	43
Our great, our good. Where one's so drest	265	U79 New-yeares	44
This is the great Preserver of our bounds,	265	U79 New-yeares	48
Hee is the author of our peace.	265	U79 New-yeares	57
Hee drives diseases from our Folds,	265	U79 New-yeares	62
Hee is the author of our peace.	265	U79 New-yeares	69
Our sense you doe with knowledge fill,	278	U84 Mind	19
And yet remaine our wonder still.	278	U84 Mind	20
our grossnesse; There's the how, and why.	279	U84 Mind	V 44
The vision of our Saviour, face to face,	286	U84 Muse	132
The price of our Redemption, and to teach	286	U84 Muse	134
The safetie of our soules, and forfeit breath!	286	U84 Muse	136
Had lost our selves? and prodigally spent	286	U84 Muse	141
Our native portions, and possessed rent;	286	U84 Muse	142
He that shall be our supreme Judge, should leave	286	U84 Muse	148
The smallest Fibre of our flesh; he can	286	U84 Muse	151
Find all our Atomes from a point t' a span!	287	U84 Muse	152
Our closest Creekes, and Corners, and can trace	287	U84 Muse	153
Suffring, and dying to redeeme our losse!	288	U84 Muse	202
Into our Seas send any such:	291	U85 Country	52
And wealth unto our language; and brought forth	309	Horace	82
Our selves, and all that's ours, to death we owe:	309	Horace	90

	Page	Title	Line

OUR (cont.)

	Page	Title	Line
And so to turne our earnest into jest,	346	Horace	V322/330
Our Ancestors did Plautus numbers praise,	323	Horace	399
Our Poets, too, left nought unproved here;	323	Horace	405
And celebrating our owne home-borne facts;	323	Horace	408
Nor had our Italie more glorious bin	325	Horace	411
Had not our every Poet like offended.	325	Horace	414
Our Roman Youths they learne the subtle wayes	327	Horace	464
Our Roman Youths they learne more thriving wayes	350	Horace	V464
And care of getting, thus, our minds hath stain'd,	327	Horace	473
The Poems void of profit, our grave men	329	Horace	511
Our Gallants give them none, but passe them by:	329	Horace	513
till th'one hath drownd the other in our sightes,	361	Palmer	20
Or (by our Turtles Augure)	364	Phoenix	5
Who saith our Times nor have, nor can	366	Ode Who saith	1
Now must we plie our ayme; our Swan's on wing.	368	Ode Who saith	64
Set out a like, or second to our Swan.	369	Ode Who saith	120
Here, like Arion, our Coryate doth draw	374	Coryat 1	10
Of our Odcombian, that literate Elfe?	379	Coryat 3	7
There nam'd to be travell'd? For this our Tom saith:	380	Coryat 3	21
Or, like our Money-Brokers, take up names	386	Browne	10
More of our writers would like thee, not swell	386	Browne	15
Still, still, dost thou arrive with, at our shore,	388	Chapman	5
To make thy honour, and our wealth the more!	388	Chapman	6
The applause! delight! the wonder of our Stage!	391	Shakespeare	18
And tell, how farre thou didst our Lily out-shine,	391	Shakespeare	29
Our eares, or like a Mercury to charme!	392	Shakespeare	46
To see thee in our waters yet appeare,	392	Shakespeare	72
That so did take Eliza, and our James!	392	Shakespeare	74
Heard the soft ayres, between our Swaynes & thee,	397	Drayton	26
I thought thee then our Orpheus, that wouldst try	397	Drayton	35
Our right in France! if ritely understood.	397	Drayton	58
So shall our English Youth urge on, and cry	398	Drayton	69
The Bound, and Frontire of our Poetrie;	400	Beaumont	8
Our Charles should make thee such? 'Twill not become	406	Inigo Jones 2	3
To follow Goodnesse, by our owne discerning	412	Sutcliffe	17
Our great reward, th'aeternall Crown to win.	412	Sutcliffe	19
The Morning-star, whose light our Fal hath stay'd.	413	Ghyrlond	40
Most venerable. Cause of all our joy.	414	Ghyrlond	42
Whose chearfull look our sadnesse doth destroy,	414	Ghyrlond	43
Renew the Glories of our blessed Jeames:	415	Dover	4
Our first of fruits, that is the prime of flowers	416	Welcome	2
And you, with them, as Father of our spring.	416	Welcome	8
Our King and Queen the Lord-God blesse,	418	Grace	1
Our King and Queen the Prince God blesse,	418	Grace	V 1
Wee'l rip our Richest veynes	420	Ode:If Men	31
And to the perpetuating of our freindship	666	Glover	4

OURE

	Page	Title	Line
Oure Captaine Pamphlets horse, and foot, that sallie	206	U43 Vulcan	V 79

OURS

	Page	Title	Line
May judge it to be his, as well as ours.	45	E56 Poet-Ape	12
Nor to give Caesar this, makes ours the lesse.	72	E111 Edmonds 2	8
A worke of ours, we part with our owne right;	82	E131 Ferrab. 2	2
Their wherry had no saile, too; ours had none:	84	E133 Voyage	11
Shee brought the Poets forth, but ours th'adventer.	84	E133 Voyage	20
And that ours did. For, yet, no nare was tainted,	87	E133 Voyage	133
Time will not be ours, for ever:	102	F5 Celia 1	3
Heard what times past have said, seene what ours doe:	159	U14 Selden	34
Our selves, and all that's ours, to death we owe:	309	Horace	90
Bred by your breath, on this low bancke of ours;	416	Welcome	3

OUT

	Page	Title	Line
Shall out-live gyrlands, stolne from the chast tree.	32	E17 Critic	6
If any Muse out-live their spight, his can;	35	E27 Roe 1	4
His monyes travaile for him, in and out:	36	E31 Banck	2
Life, whose griefe was out of fashion,	39	E40 Ratcliffe	13
And having got him out of doores is glad.	40	E42 Giles	7
Were quite out-spun. The like wish hath his wife.	40	E42 Giles	12
For, but thy selfe, where, out of motly, 's hee	44	E53 Old-end	9
Chev'ril cryes out, my verses libells are;	44	E54 Chev'ril 2	1
And proud, my worke shall out-last common deeds,	46	E60 Mounteagle	6
To put out the word, whore, thou do'st me woo,	54	E83 Friend	1
Throughout my booke. 'Troth put out woman too.	54	E83 Friend	4
Out-strip't, then they did all that went before:	57	E89 Allen	10
O, (thou cry'st out) that is thy proper game.	73	E112 Gamster	16
In meere out-formes, untill he lost his sight,	73	E114 Sydney	4
Of newes, and noyse, to strow out a long meale.	74	E115 Honest Man	10
Of newes, and noyse, to sow out a long meale.	74	E115 Honest Man	V 10
Might be found out as good, and not my Lord.	75	E116 Jephson	8
Groyne, come of age, his state sold out of hand	75	E117 Groyne	1
Lust it comes out, that gluttony went in.	76	E118 Gut	6
Cryes out 'gainst cocking, since he cannot bet,	76	E119 Shelton	3
But dost it out of judgement, not disease;	76	E119 Shelton	8
Out-dance the Babion, or out-boast the Brave;	81	E129 Mime	12
Thou dost out-zany Cokely, Pod; nay, Gue:	81	E129 Mime	16
For fame, with breath soone kindled, soone blowne out.	83	E131 Ferrab. 2	14
Of those, that put out moneyes, on returne	85	E133 Voyage	32
And many a sinke pour'd out her rage anenst 'hem;	86	E133 Voyage	75
Poore Mercury, crying out on Paracelsus,	86	E133 Voyage	96
White, black, blew, greene, and in more formes out-started,	87	E133 Voyage	126
And out-cryes of the damned in the Fleet?	88	E133 Voyage	172
They cry'd out Pusse. He told them he was Bankes,	89	E133 Voyage	183
Thou dost with some delight the day out-weare,	97	F3 Wroth	35
Thou canst with some delight the day out-weare,	97	F3 Wroth	V 35

OUT (cont.)

The trees cut out in log; and those boughes made   .   .   98   F3 Wroth   45
Shall not give out, that I have made thee stay,   .   .   107   F10 Proludium   8
Shall not give out, that we have made thee stay,   .   .   107   F10 Proludium   V 8
Let these in wanton feete daunce out their soules.   .   108   F10 Proludium   11
And, in this name, am given out dangerous   .   .   117   F13 Aubigny   11
Onely, thus much, out of a ravish'd zeale,   .   .   119   F13 Aubigny   108
When her looke out-flourisht May: .   .   132   U2 How he saw   2
And her dressing did out-brave   .   .   132   U2 How he saw   3
Nor out-praise, nor yet condemne;   .   .   142   U2 Her man   V 47
Nor out-valew, nor contemne;   .   .   142   U2 Her man   48
And out of inward pleasure feed   .   .   144   U3 Musicall   19
And out of inward passion feed   .   .   144   U3 Musicall   V 19
Though hate had put them out;   .   .   147   U7 Nymph   25
Man out their Boates to th' Temple, and not shift   .   155   U13 Sacvile   83
That with these mixtures we put out her light.   .   156   U13 Sacvile   110
And last, goe out in nothing: You that see   .   .   157   U13 Sacvile   153
Of Gathering? Bountie' in pouring out againe?   .   .   159   U14 Selden   38
Sought out the Fountaines, Sources, Creekes, paths, wayes,   .   160   U14 Selden   45
Or Feathers: lay his fortune out to show,   .   .   162   U15 Friend-Wars   21
And being a thing, blowne out of nought, rebells   .   163   U15 Friend-Wars   32
Is lov'd, though he let out his owne for life: .   165   U15 Friend-Wars   88
When oft the Bearer, is borne out of dore?   .   .   166   U15 Friend-Wars   120
And that pour'd out upon Man-kind can be!   .   .   172   U20 Shrub   19
Out of his Grave, and poyson every eare.   .   .   172   U21 Ltl Shrub   4
Gold, that is perfect, will out-live the fire.   .   .   179   U25 Desmond   45
And now are out of sight.   .   .   180   U26 Ode High   8
Or skill, to carry out an evill cause!   .   .   187   U33 Councellour   18
For no man lives so out of passions sway,   .   .   190   U37 Friend-Book   31
Out of your eyes, and be awhile away;   .   .   194   U38 Elegy 'Tis   115
As neither wine doe rack it out, or mirth.   .   .   197   U40 Elegy That   18
Out with the other, for hee's still at home;   .   198   U40 Elegy That   34
Or spun out Riddles, and weav'd fiftie tomes   .   .   204   U43 Vulcan   33
Upon th'Exchange, still, out of Popes-head-Alley.   .   206   U43 Vulcan   80
Flanck'd with a Ditch, and forc'd out of a Marish,   .   209   U43 Vulcan   134
Fenced with a Ditch, and forc'd out of a Marish,   .   209   U43 Vulcan   V134
The Brethren, they streight nois'd it out for Newes,   .   209   U43 Vulcan   139
There were, that streight did nose it out for newes,   .   209   U43 Vulcan   V139
The brethren they streight ways noisd out for newes,   .   209   U43 Vulcan   V139
Lyes there no Writ, out of the Chancerie   .   .   210   U43 Vulcan   174
To live in Sea-coale, and goe out in smoake;   .   211   U43 Vulcan   V181
Hill-/foot (out in Sussex) to an iron Mill;   .   .   211   U43 Vulcan   184
Hill-/foot (out in Sussex) to some iron Mill;   .   211   U43 Vulcan   V184
Vile Tavernes, and the Drunkards pisse him out;   .   211   U43 Vulcan   186
Vile Tavernes, and have Drunkards pisse him out;   .   211   U43 Vulcan   V186
Burne to a snuffe, and then stinke out, and die: .   211   U43 Vulcan   188
wast to a snuffe, and then stinke out, and die: .   211   U43 Vulcan   V188
And all the Evils that flew out of her box   .   .   212   U43 Vulcan   214
And all Those ills that flew out of her box   .   212   U43 Vulcan   V214
How it held out! how (last) 'twas taken in!   .   .   212   U43 Vulcan   V214
To speake my selfe out too ambitiously,   .   .   213   U44 Speach   22
They'ave glutted in, and letcher'd out that weeke,   .   218   U47 Tribe   6
Of newes they get, to strew out the long meale,   .   218   U47 Tribe   13
New in their stead, out of the Candidates?   .   .   218   U47 Tribe   28
To his poore Instrument, now out of grace.   .   .   222   U49 Pucell   6
Out of their Choysest, and their whitest wooll.   .   223   U49 Pucell   34
To goe out after—till when take this letter   .   .   225   U51 Bacon   16
Verse, that should thee, and me out-live.   .   .   229   U54 Squib   19
But Scarlet-like out-lasts the Cloth.   .   .   229   U55 Burges   4
Like a rung Beare, or Swine: grunting out wit   .   230   U55 Burges   8
Their weapons shot out, with that flame, and force,   .   232   U58 Book-seller   11
As they out-did the lightning in the course;   .   233   U59 Newcastle   11
For safetie of such Majestie, cry out?   .   .   233   U59 Newcastle   12
Their noises out in Thunder;   .   .   236   U64 Charles 3   6
E're thou wert halfe got out,   .   .   239   U67 Muses   V 9
From out the horrour of that sack?   .   .   242   U70 Ode   6
Here's one out-liv'd his Peeres,   .   .   243   U70 Ode   12
Goe now, and tell out dayes summ'd up with feares,   .   243   U70 Ode   25
Made, or indentur'd, or leas'd out t'advance   .   244   U70 Ode   53
The Muse not peepes out, one of hundred dayes;   .   246   U70 Ode   100
Let Ireland meet it out at Sea, halfe way,   .   .   248   U71 Treasurer   9
But we last out, still unlay'd.   .   .   249   U72 King   5
Have left in fame to equall, or out-goe   .   .   259   U76 Petition   24
And, out of that, make Day to breake;   .   .   260   U77 Treasurer   8
Spun out in name of some of the old Nine!   .   276   U84 Body   14
O! had I seene her laid out a faire Corse,   .   282   U84 Muse   6
Out of her noble body, to this Feast,   .   .   282   U84 Muse   11
And she doth know, out of the shade of Death,   .   284   U84 Muse   82
To turne mere farmer, had spoke out,   .   .   285   U84 Muse   91
At th'Calends, puts all out againe.   .   .   291   U85 Country   68
Ye have oft-times, that may out-shine the rest,   .   291   U85 Country   70
Thy labouring wheele, comes scarce a Pitcher out?   .   338   Horace   V 18
Th'Aemilian Schoole, in brasse can fashion out   .   307   Horace   30
To be that fellow, then to be markt out   .   .   307   Horace   46
Her voyce, and angry Chremes chafes out-right   .   339   Horace   V 53/ 51
And Roman Gentrie, jearing, will laugh out.   .   311   Horace   133
That found out profit, and foretold each thing,   .   313   Horace   160
Thespis is said to be the first found out   .   .   319   Horace   309
And farre unworthy to blurt out light rimes;   .   319   Horace   311
I can out of knowne geare, a fable frame,   .   .   321   Horace   337
I can, out of knowne stuff, a Fable frame,   .   321   Horace   349
Or crack out bawdie speeches, and uncleane.   .   347   Horace   V341/349
    .   321   Horace   359

	Page	Title	Line

OUT (cont.)

	Page	Title	Line
Or cracke out shamefull speeches, or uncleane.	347	Horace	V351/359
Out better Poems? But I cannot buy	325	Horace	431
The Oracles, too, were given out in Verse;	329	Horace	496
Playes were found out; and rest, the end, and crowne	329	Horace	499
But flowes out, that ore-swelleth in full brests.	329	Horace	506
The Child, when Lamia'has din'd, out of her maw.	329	Horace	510
Cast out by voyces; want they pleasure, then	329	Horace	512
These, the free meale might have beene well drawne out:	331	Horace	560
The Writ, once out, never returned yet.	331	Horace	580
The word, once out, never returned yet.	352	Horace	V556/580
Or great in money's out at use, command	333	Horace	600
Or wealthy in money's out at use, command	353	Horace	V600
Will be a suretie; or can helpe him out	333	Horace	603
Out at his friendly eyes, leape, beat the groun'.	333	Horace	613
The Scoffer, the true Praiser doth out-goe.	333	Horace	616
A wise, and honest man will cry out shame	335	Horace	633
Blot out the carelesse, with his turned pen;	335	Horace	635
The while he belcheth loftie Verses out,	335	Horace	649
That late were out.	367	Ode Who saith	46
Set out a like, or second to our Swan.	369	Ode Who saith	120
Marry he sets it out at his owne charge;	378	Coryat 2	83
Yes thou wert borne out of his travelling thigh	378	Coryat 2	89
To his strength, hath measur'd it out with his feet.	379	Coryat 3	4
To line out no stride, but pas'd by himselfe?	379	Coryat 3	8
He went out at each place, and at what he came in,	380	Coryat 3	25
Out-bee that Wife, in worth, thy freind did make:	384	Somerset	12
Let such as justly have out-liv'd all prayse,	387	Cavendish	5
With Nature, to out-doo the life:	390	Reader	4
And tell, how farre thou didst our Lily out-shine,	391	Shakespeare	29
With mistooke Names out of Vitruvius!	402	Inigo Jones 1	8
yearly set out there, to sayle downe the Street,	407	Inigo Jones 2	18
Seek out some hungry painter, that for bread	408	Inigo Jones 3	10
Shall not worke out unto it, such a fame.	409	Detractor	12
Out in the Dog-daies, least the killer meete	409	Detractor	20
Breake then thie quills, blott out	420	Ode:If Men	19
For noe Man Lyves, soe out of passions swaye,	422	Censure	24
A speech out of Lucane.	422	Lucan	Ttl
Here he speaks out of his Pottle,	657	Door Apollo	3

OUT-BEE

	Page	Title	Line
Out-bee that Wife, in worth, thy freind did make:	384	Somerset	12

OUT-BOAST

| Out-dance the Babion, or out-boast the Brave; | 81 | E129 Mime | 12 |

OUT-BRAVE

| And her dressing did out-brave | 132 | U2 How he saw | 3 |

OUT-CRYES

| And out-cryes of the damned in the Fleet? | 88 | E133 Voyage | 172 |

OUT-DANCE

| Out-dance the Babion, or out-boast the Brave; | 81 | E129 Mime | 12 |

OUT-DID

| As they out-did the lightning in the course; | 233 | U59 Newcastle | 12 |

OUT-DOO

| With Nature, to out-doo the life: | 390 | Reader | 4 |

OUT-FLOURISHT

| When her looke out-flourisht May: | 132 | U2 How he saw | 2 |

OUT-FORMES

| In meere out-formes, untill he lost his sight, | 73 | E114 Sydney | 4 |

OUT-GOE

| Have left in fame to equall, or out-goe | 260 | U77 Treasurer | 8 |
| The Scoffer, the true Praiser doth out-goe. | 333 | Horace | 616 |

OUT-LAST

| And proud, my worke shall out-last common deeds, | 46 | E60 Mounteagle | 6 |

OUTLAST

| Of all the Worthyes hope t'outlast thy one, | 406 | Inigo Jones 1 | 99 |

OUT-LASTS

| But Scarlet-like out-lasts the Cloth. | 230 | U55 Burges | 8 |

OUT-LIVE

Shall out-live gyrlands, stolne from the chast tree.	32	E17 Critic	6
If any Muse out-live their spight, his can;	35	E27 Roe 1	4
Gold, that is perfect, will out-live the fire.	179	U25 Desmond	45
Verse, that should thee, and me out-live.	229	U55 Burges	4

OUT-LIV'D

| Here's one out-liv'd his Peeres, | 243 | U70 Ode | 25 |
| Let such as justly have out-liv'd all prayse, | 387 | Cavendish | 5 |

OUT-PRAISE

| Nor out-praise, nor yet condemne; | 142 | U2 Her man | V 47 |

OUT-RIGHT

| Her voyce, and angry Chremes chafes out-right | 311 | Horace | 133 |

OUT-SHINE

| Ye have oft-times, that may out-shine the rest, | 338 | Horace | V 18 |
| And tell, how farre thou didst our Lily out-shine, | 391 | Shakespeare | 29 |

OUT-SPUN

| Were quite out-spun. The like wish hath his wife. | 40 | E42 Giles | 12 |

OUT-STARTED

| White, black, blew, greene, and in more formes out-started, | 87 | E133 Voyage | 126 |

OUT-STRIP

| T'out-strip your peeres: | 121 | F14 Sydney | 26 |

OUT-STRIPT

| Out-stript, then they did all that went before: | 57 | E89 Allen | 10 |

OUT-VALEW

| Nor out-valew, nor contemne; | 142 | U2 Her man | 48 |

OUTWARD

| And, in those outward formes, all fooles are wise. | 117 | F13 Aubigny | 36 |

```
                                             Page      Title         Line

OUTWARD   (cont.)
    Outward Grace weake love beguiles:     .   .   .   .   137   U2 Cupid        51
    In outward face, but inward, light as Furre, .  .   .   162   U15 Friend-Wars 20
    Of many Colours; outward fresh, from spots, .   .   .   171   U20 Shrub       11
OUT-WEARE
    Thou dost with some delight the day out-weare, . .   .    97   F3 Wroth        35
    Thou canst with some delight the day out-weare, .  .     97   F3 Wroth      V 35
OUT-ZANY
    Thou dost out-zany Cokely, Pod; nay, Gue: .  .   .   .    81   E129 Mime       16
OVENS
    Condemn'd me to the Ovens with the pies;  .  .   .   .   205   U43 Vulcan      54
    Condemn'd them to the Ovens with the pies;  .   .   .    205   U43 Vulcan    V 54
OVER    (See also O'RE, ORE)
    Which conquers all, be once over-come by thee.  .   .     31   E14 Camden      12
    Onely his clothes have over-leaven'd him.  .   .   .      63   E97 Motion      20
    So all his meate he tasteth over, twise: .   .   .   .    76   E118 Gut         2
    Over your heads: Well, row.  At this a loud  .   .   .    86   E133 Voyage     93
    Which thus we over-blow.   .   .   .   .   .   .   .     110   F11 Epode       36
    To say over every purle  .   .   .   .   .   .   .      140   U2 Promise      23
    But charme the Senses, others over-come  .   .   .      182   U28 Worth        7
    But give them over to the common eare  .   .   .   .    214   U44 Speach      31
    Of cares, and over-seer  .   .   .   .   .   .   .      221   U48 Bacchus     14
    Shee saw him rise, triumphing over Death  .   .   .     288   U84 Muse       203
    Being over-safe, and fearing of the flaw:  .   .   .    339   Horace     V 41/ 39
    So over-thick, but, where the people met,  .   .   .    319   Horace         292
    Their youthfull tricks in over-wanton verse:  .   .     321   Horace         358
    Or play young tricks in over-wanton verse;  .   .   .   347   Horace     V350/358
    In hand, and turne them over, day, and night.  .   .    323   Horace         398
    Doth please; this, ten times over, will delight. .  .   331   Horace         544
    With joy of what is given him, over-gone:  .   .   .    333   Horace         610
    Over Ierna maine,  .   .   .   .   .   .   .   .        367   Ode Who saith   42
    And over Grampius mountaine,   .   .   .   .   .   .    368   Ode Who saith   71
    But over Land to Trent:  .   .   .   .   .   .   .      368   Ode Who saith   75
    Pearch'd over head, the wise Athenian Owle: .  .   .    397   Drayton         34
    I feele it by mine owne, that over flow,  .   .   .     398   Drayton         77
    Over the Door at the Entrance into the Apollo.  .   .   657   Door Apollo    Ttl
OVERBEARING
    Controll Ctesibius: overbearing us  .   .   .   .   .   402   Inigo Jones 1    7
OVER-BLOW
    Which thus we over-blow.   .   .   .   .   .   .   .     110   F11 Epode       36
OVERBURY
    To Sir Thomas Overbury.   .   .   .   .   .   .   .      73   E113 Overbury   Ttl
    As but to speake thee, Overbury, is praise:  .   .      73   E113 Overbury    2
OVERCAME
    Quite overcame,   .   .   .   .   .   .   .   .         129   U1 Father       25
OVER-COME
    Which conquers all, be once over-come by thee.  .  .     31   E14 Camden      12
    But charme the Senses, others over-come  .   .   .     182   U28 Worth        7
OVERDOOE
    How would he firke? lyke Adam overdooe  .   .   .      405   Inigo Jones 1   79
OVER-GONE
    With joy of what is given him, over-gone:  .   .   .    333   Horace         610
OVER-LEAVEN'D
    Onely his clothes have over-leaven'd him.  .   .   .     63   E97 Motion      20
OVER-SAFE
    Being over-safe, and fearing of the flaw:  .   .   .    339   Horace     V 41/ 39
OVER-SEER
    Of cares, and over-seer  .   .   .   .   .   .   .      221   U48 Bacchus     14
OVER-THICK
    So over-thick, but, where the people met,  .   .   .    319   Horace         292
OVERTHROW
    His very eyes are yours to overthrow.  .   .   .   .    182   U28 Worth       11
OVER-WANTON
    Their youthfull tricks in over-wanton verse:  .   .     321   Horace         358
    Or play young tricks in over-wanton verse;  .   .   .   347   Horace     V350/358
OVID
    Her Ovid gave her, dimn'd the fame  .   .   .   .   .   181   U27 Ode Helen   18
OWE
    Camden, most reverend head, to whom I owe  .   .   .     31   E14 Camden       1
    In-primis, Grand, you owe me for a jest,  .   .   .      51   E73 Fine Grand   5
    And what each prince doth for intelligence owe,  .      59   E92 New Crie    12
    If time to facts, as unto men would owe?  .   .   .      64   E99 Th Roe 2     6
    All gentrie, yet, owe part of their best flame!  .      75   E116 Jephson     2
    I ne're will owe my health to a disease.  .   .   .     150   U10 Jealousie   16
    This Good from you, as freely will it owe;  .   .      153   U13 Sacvile     14
    Can I owe thankes, for Curtesies receiv'd  .   .   .    153   U13 Sacvile     25
    Find you to reckon nothing, me owe all.  .   .   .      158   U13 Sacvile    164
    Nor is my Muse, or I asham'd to owe it  .   .   .   .   182   U28 Worth        5
    I give, or owe my friends, into your Rites,  .   .     197   U40 Elegy That  12
    How much to heaven for thee, great Charles, they owe!  237   U64 Charles 3   22
    To compare small with great, as still we owe  .   .    238   U66 Queene      12
    What, by that name, wee each to other owe,  .   .      241   U69 Friend Son   4
    Of Nuptiall Sweets, at such a season, owe,  .   .   .   257   U75 Epithalam. 148
    What worlds of blessings to good Kings they owe:  .    261   U77 Treasurer   20
    To him we owe all profits of our grounds.  .   .   .    264   U79 New-yeares  15
    To whom you owe all duties of your grounds;  .   .     265   U79 New-yeares  49
    Our selves, and all that's ours, to death we owe:  .   309   Horace          90
    Perversly modest, had I rather owe  .   .   .   .   .   311   Horace         130
    To whom all Scenes of Europe homage owe.  .   .   .    391   Shakespeare     42
OW'D
    For benefits are ow'd with the same mind  .   .   .    153   U13 Sacvile      5
OWERS
    They are not, Sir, worst Owers, that doe pay  .   .    169   U17 Friend-Debt  1
```

		Page	Title	Line
OWES				
(How nothing's that?) to whom my countrey owes	. . . .	31	E14 Camden	3
To which, yet, of the sides himselfe he owes.	. . .	66	E102 Pembroke	8
What to his Countrey, what his friends he owes,	. . .	325	Horace	446
OWING				
By her attempt, shall still be owing thee.	. . .	80	E127 Aubigny	10
OWLE				
Pearch'd over head, the wise Athenian Owle:	. . .	397	Drayton	34
OWN (See ONE)				
OWNE				
He that departs with his owne honesty	. . .	27	E2 My Booke	13
And now, her (hourely) her owne cucqueane makes,	. .	34	E25 Beast 1	5
That's greater, yet: to crie his owne up neate.	. .	35	E28 Surly	11
Be thine, I taxe, yet doe not owne my rimes:	. .	36	E30 Guiltie	2
Colt, now, doth daily penance in his owne.	. .	39	E39 Colt	2
Ere blacks were bought for his owne funerall,	. .	41	E44 Chuff	3
In my chast booke: professe them in thine owne.	. .	42	E49 Playwrt	6
He takes up all, makes each mans wit his owne.	. .	45	E56 Poet-Ape	8
As her owne conscience, still, the same reward.	. .	48	E64 Salisbury 3	14
Item, your owne, sew'd in your mistris smock.	. .	51	E73 Fine Grand	17
Of destinie, and spin her owne free houres.	. .	52	E76 Bedford 1	16
And thine owne goodnesse to encrease thy merit,	. .	60	E93 Radcliffe	10
If workes (not th'authors) their owne grace should looke,	.	60	E94 Bedford 3	3
Crowne with their owne. Rare poemes aske rare friends.	.	60	E94 Bedford 3	6
To thine owne proper I ascribe then more;	. .	61	E95 Savile	9
With thine owne course the judgement of thy friend,	.	63	E98 Th Roe 1	8
And first to know thine owne state, then the States.	.	70	E109 Nevil	12
To have engrav'd these acts, with his owne stile,	.	71	E110 Edmonds 1	6
From friendship, is it's owne fames architect.	.	75	E115 Honest Man	30
And, in their errors maze, thine owne way know:	.	76	E119 Shelton	13
And those to turne to bloud, and make thine owne:	.	80	E128 Wm Roe 2	4
And thine owne Coriat too. But (would'st thou see)	.	81	E129 Mime	17
A worke of ours, we part with our owne right;	.	82	E131 Ferrab. 2	2
For, then, all mouthes will judge, and their owne way:	.	82	E131 Ferrab. 2	3
They should be fooles, for me, at their owne charge.	.	83	E131 Ferrab. 2	8
In it' owne hall; when these (in worthy scorne	.	85	E133 Voyage	31
And pikes, now weary their owne kinde to eat,	.	94	F2 Penshurst	34
Without his feare, and of thy lords owne meate:	.	95	F2 Penshurst	62
His children thy great lord may call his owne:	.	96	F2 Penshurst	91
And such since thou canst make thine owne content,	.	98	F3 Wroth	65
My owne true fire. Now my thought takes wing,	.	108	F10 Proludium	29
Our owne true fire. Now our thought takes wing,	.	108	F10 Proludium	V 29
For their owne cap'tall crimes, t'indite my wit;	.	117	F13 Aubigny	14
When their owne Parasites laugh at their fall,	.	118	F13 Aubigny	82
9. Her man described by her owne Dictamen.	.	140	U2 Her man	Ttl
Mine owne enough betray me.	. . .	145	U4 Song	12
Our owne false praises, for your ends:	. .	145	U5 Woman-kind	4
For that's a narrow joy is but our owne.	. .	147	U7 Nymph	7
I have the lyst of mine owne faults to know,	.	156	U13 Sacvile	114
Of others honours, thus, enjoy thine owne.	.	160	U14 Selden	66
Of others honours, thus, enjoy their owne.	.	160	U14 Selden	V 66
Till he becomes both their, and his owne curse!	.	162	U15 Friend-Wars	14
Is lov'd, though he let out his owne for life:	.	165	U15 Friend-Wars	88
Vaile their owne eyes, and would impartially	.	170	U18 Elegy Can	19
'Tis crowne enough to vertue still, her owne applause.	.	174	U23 Himselfe	18
Assisted by no strengths, but are her owne,	.	176	U24 Frontispice	14
True valour doth her owne renowne command	.	180	U26 Ode High	16
Her owne bloud gave her: Shee ne're had, nor hath	.	188	U34 Small Poxe	9
Spare your owne goodnesse yet; and be not great	.	191	U38 Elegy 'Tis	17
Whether their faces were their owne, or no:	.	200	U42 Elegy Let	36
By thy owne vote, a sacrifice to thee?	.	203	U43 Vulcan	22
To our owne Ladyes; and in storie there	.	207	U43 Vulcan	97
for our owne Ladyes; and in storie there	.	207	U43 Vulcan	V 97
No Foole would his owne harvest spoile, or burne!	.	209	U43 Vulcan	150
We will beleeve, like men of our owne Ranke,	.	215	U44 Speach	75
For that is first requir'd, A man be his owne.	.	216	U45 Squib	23
Well, with mine owne fraile Pitcher, what to doe	.	219	U47 Tribe	56
From whence they fall, cast downe with their owne weight.	.	224	U50 Countesse	12
As they are hard, for them to make their owne,	.	225	U50 Countesse	33
For 't were a narrow gladnesse, kept thine owne.	.	225	U51 Bacon	18
Most pious King, but his owne good in you!	.	236	U64 Charles 3	2
And what are bounds to her, you make your owne?	.	236	U64 Charles 3	10
Adding her owne glad accents, to this Day,	.	249	U72 King	7
Adding her owne greate accents, to this Day,	.	249	U72 King	V 7
T'effect it, feele, thou'ast made thine owne heart ake.	.	250	U73 Weston	12
When he beholds a graft of his owne hand,	.	251	U74 Weston	27
To give a greater Name, and Title to! Their owne!	.	255	U75 Epithalam.	96
On Natures secrets, there, as her owne bookes:	.	271	U81 Pawlet	70
On naturall secret, there, as her owne bookes:	.	271	U81 Pawlet	V 70
If you can envie your owne Daughters blisse,	.	271	U81 Pawlet	83
If you can enjoy your owne Daughters blisse,	.	271	U81 Pawlet	V 83
Worke with my fancie, his owne hand.	.	276	U84 Body	12
Up to her owne sublimed hight?	.	279	U84 Mind	48
When your owne Vertues, equall'd have their Names,	.	281	U84 Kenelme	12
Which all men doe, that urge not their owne deeds	.	281	U84 Kenelme	17
I summe up mine owne breaking, and wish all.	.	283	U84 Muse	26
With his owne Oxen tills his Sires left lands,	.	289	U85 Country	3
How plucking Peares, his owne hand grafted had,	.	290	U85 Country	19
Of Homers, forth in acts, then of thine owne.	.	313	Horace	185
Yet common matter thou thine owne maist make,	.	313	Horace	187
For his owne good, a carelesse letter-goe	. .	315	Horace	234
And celebrating our owne home-borne facts;	.	323	Horace	408
He cries, Good boy, thou'lt keepe thine owne. Now, adde	.	327	Horace	470

OWNE   (cont.)
    Marry he sets it out at his owne charge;   378   Coryat 2   83
    Since he treads in no other Mans steps but his owne. 379   Coryat 3   12
    It must be thine owne judgment, yet, that sends 386   Browne   7
    Hold thyne owne worth unbroke: which is so good 386   Browne   13
    I feele it by mine owne, that over flow,   398   Drayton   77
    To veiw the truth and owne it. Doe but looke   399   Lady Ogle   5
    How much Architectonice is your owne!   402   Inigo Jones 1 10
    To follow Goodnesse, by our owne discerning   412   Sutcliffe   17
    Now, for mine owne part, and it is but due,   415   Rutter   12
    Is her owne scourge, when it sustaines their states 422   Lucan   3
OWN'D
    Which own'd the creature.   77   E120 S. P.   8
OWSE
    Humber, or Owse, decline;   368   Ode Who saith 74
OXE
    Spake to 'hem louder, then the oxe in Livie: 86   E133 Voyage   74
OXEN
    With his owne Oxen tills his Sires left lands,   289   U85 Country   3
    To view the weary Oxen draw, with bare   291   U85 Country   63
OYLE
    The milke, nor oyle, did ever flowe soe free   98   F3 Wroth   V 60
    That for th'oyle of Talke, dare spend   105   F8 Sicknesse 33
    Or Turners oyle of Talck. Nor ever got   188   U34 Small Poxe 11
    Wherein was oyle, beside the succour spent,   207   U43 Vulcan   99
    By Carew, Cotton, Selden, oyle was spent   207   U43 Vulcan V100
    By Carew, Cotton, Seldens oyle was spent   207   U43 Vulcan V100
    As smooth as Oyle pour'd forth, and calme   280   U84 Mind   59
    Her fellowes, with the oyle of gladnesse, bright 285   U84 Muse   101
    If thou be'st wise, with 'Syrian Oyle let shine 294   U89 Mart.8:77 3
OYLES
    Let 'hem on poulders, oyles, and paintings, spend, 118   F13 Aubigny 77
    Of Carew, Cotton, Selden, oyles were spent   207   U43 Vulcan V100
OYLIE
    Oylie Expansions, or shrunke durtie folds,   220   U47 Tribe   68
OYSTERS
    Not Lucrine Oysters I could then more prize,   291   U85 Country   49
P
    Epitaph on S. P. a Child of Q. El. Chappel.   77   E120 S. P.   Ttl
PACCUVIUS
    Paccuvius, Accius, him of Cordova dead,   391   Shakespeare   35
PAC'D
    Of Trimeter, when yet it was sixe-pac'd,   323   Horace   373
PACETH
    See, how she paceth forth in Virgin-white,   253   U75 Epithalam. 41
PACK
    Pack with your pedling Poetry to the Stage,   404   Inigo Jones 1 51
PAC'T
    Sleepe, that will make the darkest howres swift-pac't; 295   U90 Mart.10:47 11
PAGAN
    May to thy name a Pagan prayer say;   208   U43 Vulcan V120
PAGE   (BOOK)
    With pause upon it; make this page your booke;   399   Lady Ogle   6
PAGE
    The nicer thing to tast her ladies page;   57   E90 Mill   5
    On the close groome, and page, on new-yeeres day, 118   F13 Aubigny   74
    Make not thy selfe a Page,   175   U23 Himselfe 33
PAGEANT
    And vouches both the Pageant, and the Day,   202   U42 Elegy Let 77
    Squire of the Squibs, against the Pageant day,   208   U43 Vulcan   119
    Squire of the Squibs, upon the Pageant day,   208   U43 Vulcan V119
PAID
    Lent him a pockie whore. Shee hath paid him.   31   E12 Shift   24
    There wasted, some not paid for yet!   97   F3 Wroth   12
    And it is paid 'hem with a trembling zeale,   155   U13 Sacvile   85
    For a just wager, and that wager paid   229   U54 Squib   2
    T' have paid againe a blessing was but lent,   271   U81 Pawlet   80
PAINE   (See also PAYNE)
    Is it the paine affrights? that's soone forgot.   46   E62 Would-bee 5
    In most vile verses, and cost me more paine,   51   E73 Fine Grand 19
    I answer'd, Daphne now no paine can prove.   80   E126 Mrs Cary 6
    If wee would search with care, and paine,   145   U5 Woman-kind 8
    T'instruct and teach? or your unweary'd paine   159   U14 Selden   37
    To informe and teach? or your unweary'd paine   159   U14 Selden V 37
    No man inflicts that paine, till hope be spent: 192   U38 Elegy 'Tis 44
    There is not any punishment, or paine,   194   U38 Elegy 'Tis 103
    That since thou tak'st all envious care and paine, 203   U43 Vulcan   13
    Shee lies deliver'd, without paine,   251   U74 Weston   5
    'Gainst th'Ides, his moneys he gets in with paine, 291   U85 Country 69
    'Gainst th'Ides, his gott moneyes he gets in with paine, 291   U85 Country V 69
    The Marrow! Wretch, I quitt thee of thy paine   408   Inigo Jones 3 5
PAINES
    How can I speake of thy great paines, but erre?   83   E132 Sylvester 5
    'Tis but light paines: Indeede this Dock's no rose. 85   E133 Voyage 60
    To view the jewells, stuffes, the paines, the wit 97   F3 Wroth   11
    Any paines; yea, thinke it price,   105   F8 Sicknesse 27
    And estimate thy Paines; as having wrought   161   U14 Selden   75
    Withall, the dirtie paines those Citizens take, 213   U44 Speach   15
PAINT
    I know too, though thou strut, and paint,   100   F4 To the World 13
    Or feare to draw true lines, 'cause others paint: 117   F13 Aubigny 20
    But, you are he can paint; I can but write: 227   U52 Answer   19
    And act the businesse, which they paint, or carve. 261   U77 Treasurer 16

	Page	Title	Line

PAINT (cont.)
```
And act the businesse, which these paint, or carve.   .   .   . 261  U77 Treasurer    V 16
You could make shift to paint an Eye,        .   .   .   . 278  U84 Mind            9
Know'st only well to paint a Cipresse tree.  .   .   .   . 305  Horace             25
To paint him, hath by swimming, hopelesse, scap'd,   .   . 305  Horace             27
Thou paint a Lane, where Thumb the Pygmy meets!      .   . 407  Inigo Jones 2      12
Thou paint a Lane, where Thumb with Geffry meets!    .   . 407  Inigo Jones 2    V 12
```
PAINTED
```
The painted partrich lyes in every field,   .   .   .   .  94  F2 Penshurst       29
Along'st the curled woods, and painted meades,   .   .   .  97  F3 Wroth           17
Turne the stale prologue to some painted maske,  .   .   . 107  F10 Proludium      20
Painted, or carv'd upon our great-mens tombs,    .   .   . 114  F12 Rutland        45
Perjur'd! and painted! if she were no more--,    .   .   . 172  U20 Shrub          22
Painted a Dog, that now his subtler skill    .   .   .   . 241  U69 Friend Son     10
Their painted Maskes, their paper Boates,    .   .   .   . 273  U84 Cradle         22
And thou hast painted beauties world.        .   .   .   . 277  U84 Body           28
Mythology there painted on slit deale!       .   .   .   . 404  Inigo Jones 1      48
What Poesy ere was painted on a wall   .   .   .   .   .   . 406  Inigo Jones 1      97
```
PAINTER
```
And as a cunning Painter takes      .   .   .   .   .   .   . 145  U5 Woman-kind      13
My Answer.  The Poet to the Painter.     .   .   .   .   . 226  U52 Answer        Ttl
But as the wretched Painter, who so ill  .   .   .   .   . 241  U69 Friend Son      9
But, Painter, see thou doe not sell    .   .   .   .   .   . 277  U84 Body           29
Painter yo' are come, but may be gone,   .   .   .   .   . 277  U84 Mind            1
If to a Womans head a Painter would    .   .   .   .   .   . 305  Horace             1
But equall power, to Painter, and to Poet,   .   .   .   . 305  Horace             11
No place for these.  And, Painter, hap'ly, thou  .   .   . 305  Horace             24
Seek out some hungry painter, that for bread     .   .   . 408  Inigo Jones 3      10
```
PAINTERS
```
You were not tied, by any Painters Law,  .   .   .   .   . 227  U52 Answer          7
Yet something, to the Painters view,     .   .   .   .   . 275  U84 Body            9
```
PAINTING
```
All is but web, and painting; be the strife      .   .   . 242  U69 Friend Son     24
As Painting, so is Poesie.  Some mans hand   .   .   .   . 329  Horace            539
Painting & Carpentry are the Soule of Masque.    .   .   . 404  Inigo Jones 1      50
```
PAINTINGS
```
Let 'hem on poulders, oyles, and paintings, spend,   .   . 118  F13 Aubigny        77
```
PAINTS
```
One thing prodigiously, paints in the woods      .   .   . 307  Horace             41
```
PAIRE   (See also PAYRE)
```
The spoused paire two realmes, the sea the ring.     .   .  28  E5 Union            4
That, not a paire of friends each other see,     .   .   .  81  E129 Mime           1
A paire of Scisars, and a Combe in verse;    .   .   .   . 204  U43 Vulcan         38
A quick, and dazeling motion! when a paire   .   .   .   . 233  U59 Newcastle       9
. . . paire, Sir Lucius Cary, and Sir H. Morison.    .   . 242  U70 Ode           Ttl
To welcome home a Paire, and deck the nuptiall bower?    . 253  U75 Epithalam.     24
With light of love, this Paire doth intertexe!   .   .   . 254  U75 Epithalam.     60
Saw'st thou that Paire, became these Rites so well,  .   . 254  U75 Epithalam.     76
They are th'exampled Paire, and mirrour of their kind.   . 255  U75 Epithalam.     80
I meane that one paire, wherewith he so hobled   .   .   . 380  Coryat 3           41
When, Rome, I reade thee in thy mighty paire,    .   .   . 395  May                 1
Of two, the choicest Paire of Mans delights, .   .   .   . 401  Filmer              4
```
PALACE
```
His brest is a brave Palace, a broad Street, .   .   .   . 262  U78 Digby           9
Some Paradise, or Palace found    .   .   .   .   .   .   . 280  U84 Mind           50
```
PALATE
```
Yet shall you have, to rectifie your palate, .   .   .   .  64  E101 Supper         9
```
PALE   (NOUN)
```
Your partie-per-pale picture, one halfe drawne   .   .   .  51  E73 Fine Grand     13
With thy soft notes, and hold them within Pale   .   .   . 367  Ode Who saith      45
```
PALE
```
Flow my thin teares, downe these pale cheeks of mine?    . 293  U86 Hor.4:1        34
Looke pale, distill a showre (was never meant)   .   .   . 333  Horace            612
Look pale, distill a dew was never meant     .   .   .   . 353  Horace           V612
The pale Pyrene, and the forked Mount:   .   .   .   .   . 366  Ode Who saith      21
Reviving with fresh coulors the pale Ghosts  .   .   .   . 405  Inigo Jones 1      88
```
PALES
```
To better Pastures then great Pales can:     .   .   .   . 264  U79 New-yeares     30
Then ever Pales could, or Pan;    .   .   .   .   .   .   . 265  U79 New-yeares     61
```
PALINDROMES
```
Of Logogriphes, and curious Palindromes, .   .   .   .   . 204  U43 Vulcan         34
```
PALLACE
```
Or Ale! He build a pallace! Thou a shopp .   .   .   .   . 407  Inigo Jones 2       9
```
PALLAS
```
That saw you put on Pallas plumed caske: .   .   .   .   .  68  E105 L Wroth 2     16
Pallas, nor thee I call on, mankinde maid,   .   .   .   . 107  F10 Proludium      13
Pallas, nor thee we call on, mankinde maid,  .   .   .   . 107  F10 Proludium    V 13
Pallas frowning.   .   .   .   .   .   .   .   .   .   .   . 183  U29 Fit of Rime    30
Taught Pallas language; Cynthia modesty; .   .   .   .   . 371  Epitaph             7
To be his Bacchus as his Pallas: bee     .   .   .   .   . 378  Coryat 2           91
Whoe worthie wine, whoe not, to bee wyse Pallas guests.  . 421  Ode:If Men         45
```
PALLAT
```
What should, yet, thy pallat please?     .   .   .   .   . 105  F8 Sicknesse       21
```
PALME
```
Have you seen the Palme-trees state  .   .   .   .   .   . 136  U2 Triumph       V 43
True noblesse.  Palme groves straight, though handled ne're so rude. 177  U25 Desmond  26
Then com'st thou off with Victorie and Palme,    .   .   . 187  U33 Councellour    35
With boughs of Palme, a crowned Victrice stand!  .   .   . 285  U84 Muse           96
And to the Touch, a Flower, like soft as Palme.  .   .   . 286  U84 Muse          126
It carries Palme with it, (where e're it goes)   .   .   . 363  Riches              6
```
PALMER
```
When late (grave Palmer) these thy graffs and flowers    . 361  Palmer              1
Palmer thy travayles well becum thy name,    .   .   .   . 362  Palmer             30
```

503

	Page	Title	Line
PALMERINS			
Th'Esplandians, Arthurs, Palmerins, and all	203	U43 Vulcan	30
PALME-TREES			
Have you seen the Palme-trees state	136	U2 Triumph	V 43
PALSIES			
He that no more for Age, Cramps, Palsies, can	166	U15 Friend-Wars	135
PALTZGRAVE			
The Paltzgrave, and the Lady Besse,	418	Grace	2
PAMPHLETS			
Or Captaine Pamphlets horse, and foot, that sallie	206	U43 Vulcan	79
Oure Captaine Pamphlets horse, and foot, that sallie	206	U43 Vulcan	V 79
PAMPHLETTS			
Or Captaine Pamphletts, which on foote doe sally	206	U43 Vulcan	V 79
PAN (DISH)			
Nor any quick-warming-pan helpe him to bed,	232	U57 Burges	27
PAN			
Where Pan, and Bacchus their high feasts have made,	93	F2 Penshurst	11
Thus Pan, and Sylvane, having had their rites,	98	F3 Wroth	47
When Pan, and Sylvane, having had their rites,	98	F3 Wroth	V 47
Pan is the great Preserver of our bounds.	264	U79 New-yeares	14
Of Pan wee sing, the best of Hunters, Pan,	264	U79 New-yeares	20
Sister of Pan, and glory of the Spring:	264	U79 New-yeares	25
Of Pan wee sing, the Chiefe of Leaders, Pan,	264	U79 New-yeares	28
Pan only our great Shep'ard is,	265	U79 New-yeares	43
And hunting, Pan, exceedeth thee.	265	U79 New-yeares	55
Then ever Pales could, or Pan;	265	U79 New-yeares	61
Pan knowes no other power then his,	265	U79 New-yeares	64
And hunting, Pan, exceedeth thee.	265	U79 New-yeares	67
PANCHARIS			
The Swan that so relish'd Pancharis)	182	U27 Ode Helen	30
Who warbleth Pancharis,	369	Ode Who saith	98
PANCRIDGE			
Content thee to be Pancridge Earle the whyle;	407	Inigo Jones 2	20
PANDECTS			
Code, Digests, Pandects of all faemale glory!	399	Lady Ogle	8
PANDORA'S			
Pox on thee, Vulcan, thy Pandora's pox,	212	U43 Vulcan	213
PANEGYRICKE			
. . . Panegyricke lines, but then were upon some occasions . . .	379	Coryat 3	Ttl
PANICK			
Which though it did but panick terror prove,	43	E51 James 3	3
PANTON			
Supplant bold Panton; and brought there to view	214	U44 Speach	34
PAPER			
That will the pastrie, not my paper, show of.	65	E101 Supper	26
You will not from the paper slightly passe:	117	F13 Aubigny	25
Wrapt in this paper lie,	180	U26 Ode High	10
Any, least loose, or scurrile paper, lie	203	U43 Vulcan	20
or spent my wretched paper or my tyme	204	U43 Vulcan	V 33
Especially in paper; that, that steame	205	U43 Vulcan	61
Especially in paper; many a Reame	205	U43 Vulcan	V 61
Powder, or paper, to bring up the youth	213	U44 Speach	25
Not built with Canvasse, paper, and false lights,	220	U47 Tribe	65
I only can the Paper staine;	230	U55 Burges	6
Their painted Maskes, their paper Boates,	273	U84 Cradle	22
And stradling shews the Boyes Brown paper fleet,	407	Inigo Jones 2	17
With Chequer Inke, upon his guift, my paper,	666	Glover	8
PAPERS			
Takes physick, teares the papers: still god payes.	30	E12 Shift	16
Nine yeares kept in, your papers by, yo'are free	331	Horace	578
Nine yeares kept by, your papers in, y'are free	352	Horace	V554/578
PARACELSUS			
Poore Mercury, crying out on Paracelsus,	86	E133 Voyage	96
PARADISE			
And Paradise confining these.	276	U84 Body	24
Some Paradise, or Palace found	280	U84 Mind	50
PARASITE			
Things manly, and not smelling parasite.	48	E65 Muse	14
PARASITES			
When their owne Parasites laugh at their fall,	118	F13 Aubigny	82
What Fooles, and all their Parasites can apply;	193	U38 Elegy 'Tis	94
PARCAE			
As, sooth, the Parcae thought him one,	77	E120 S. P.	15
PARCELL			
By his each glorious parcell to be knowne!	62	E97 Motion	6
A parcell of Court-durt, a heape, and masse	172	U21 Ltl Shrub	5
PARCELLS			
Wee shall, at last, of parcells make	145	U5 Woman-kind	11
PARCELS			
And as false stampe there; parcels of a Play,	204	U43 Vulcan	43
PARDON			
Beg'd Ridwayes pardon: Duncote, now, doth crye;	29	E8 Robbery	4
Pardon free truth, and let thy modestie,	31	E14 Camden	11
Pardon, sayes he, that were a way to see	155	U13 Sacvile	71
Pardon his Lordship. Flattry's growne so cheape	167	U15 Friend-Wars	155
Pardon, I read it in thy face, the day	225	U51 Bacon	5
Who reades, will pardon my Intelligence,	289	U84 Muse	226
Deserves no pardon; or who'd play, and sing	329	Horace	531
Shall the prosperity of a Pardon still	410	Gill	1
PARDON'D			
A Nations sinne got pardon'd! 'twere a taske	234	U61 Epigram	12
PARDONING			
The Subject of your Grace in pardoning me,	191	U38 Elegy 'Tis	28

		Page	Title	Line
PARDONS				
He pardons slips, goes by a world of ills,		193	U38 Elegy 'Tis	69
PARE				
In Helicon; a great sort will not pare		325	Horace	422
PARENT				
What height of love, a Parent will fit best,		325	Horace	447
Or of a parent! or a freind!		399	Lady Ogle	13
PARENTS				
Here lyes to each her parents ruth,		33	E22 Daughter	1
My countries parents I have many knowne;		46	E60 Mounteagle	9
Reade, in their vertuous parents noble parts,		96	F2 Penshurst	97
Of your compassion; Parents should be mild:		192	U38 Elegy 'Tis	40
Which their glad Parents taught		257	U75 Epithalam.	143
To pious parents, who would have their blood		268	U80 Christning	7
With gladnesse temper'd her sad Parents teares!		270	U81 Pawlet	59
Which gladnesse temper'd her sad Parents teares!		270	U81 Pawlet	V 59
Goe now, her happy Parents, and be sad,		271	U81 Pawlet	77
And Sons, and Daughters, with their Parents talke;		285	U84 Muse	118
PARIS				
From Venice, Paris, or some in-land passage		85	E133 Voyage	33
The meate-boate of Beares colledge, Paris-garden,		87	E133 Voyage	117
Her armes when Paris wonne her		135	U2 Triumph	V 34
PARIS-GARDEN				
The meate-boate of Beares colledge, Paris-garden,		87	E133 Voyage	117
PARISH (NAME)				
And that accursed ground, the Parish-Garden:		209	U43 Vulcan	147
And that prophaner ground, the Parish-Garden:		209	U43 Vulcan	V147
PARISH				
Which, though it were the Fort of the whole Parish,		209	U43 Vulcan	133
The Parish will know it.		232	U57 Burges	26
And though the Parish-steeple		239	U67 Muses	4
PARISH-GARDEN				
And that accursed ground, the Parish-Garden:		209	U43 Vulcan	147
And that prophaner ground, the Parish-Garden:		209	U43 Vulcan	V147
PARISH-STEEPLE				
And though the Parish-steeple		239	U67 Muses	4
PARITIE				
The king of Creatures, take his paritie		255	U75 Epithalam.	83
PARKE				
From Hide-Parke to the Stage, where at the last		165	U15 Friend-Wars	109
PARLIAMENT				
To the Parliament.		34	E24 Parliament	Ttl
Of the grave fart, late let in parliament,		87	E133 Voyage	108
And Call to the high Parliament		273	U84 Cradle	30
PARLYAMENT				
Whom not ten fyres, nor a Parlyament can		406	Inigo Jones 1	103
PARNASSUS				
All Parnassus Greene did wither,		183	U29 Fit of Rime	17
PARRAT				
On Court-Parrat.		50	E71 Parrat	Ttl
PARROT				
And we will have no Pooly', or Parrot by;		65	E101 Supper	36
PART				
Yet by thy weapon liv'st! Th'hast one good part.		50	E69 Cob	2
For every part a character assign'd.		67	E103 L Wroth 1	12
All-vertuous Herbert! on whose every part		68	E106 E Herbert	3
Will you part with them, here, unthriftely?		69	E107 Hungry	28
(As if a new creation) part by part,		71	E110 Edmonds 1	18
All gentrie, yet, owe part of their best flame!		75	E116 Jephson	2
I, yet, had utter'd nothing on thy part,		82	E130 Ferrab. 1	15
A worke of ours, we part with our owne right;		82	E131 Ferrab. 2	2
My part is ended on thy stage.		100	F4 To the World	4
Is my best part:		129	U1 Father	3
Such a man, with every part,		142	U2 Her man	53
'Tis one good part I'ld lie withall.		142	U2 Exception	8
No part or corner man can looke upon,		163	U15 Friend-Wars	27
Nothing is vile, that is a part of you:		192	U38 Elegy 'Tis	36
How much you are the better part of me;		194	U38 Elegy 'Tis	110
And didst invade part of the Common-wealth,		210	U43 Vulcan	170
As if that part lay for a < > most fit!		232	U58 Book-seller	12
Or taste a part of that full joy he meant		246	U70 Ode	87
How each one playes his part, of the large Pedigree.		258	U75 Epithalam.	176
But rather I, should I of that part speake!		269	U81 Pawlet	28
Sleepie, or stupid Nature, couldst thou part		282	U84 Muse	15
The greater part, that boast the Muses fire,		339	Horace	V 33
Of too much haste, and negligence in part,		323	Horace	385
To part scurrilitie from wit: or can		323	Horace	403
That part nor Winde,		366	Ode Who saith	28
these only hide part of my flesh, and bones:		387	Cavendish	2
My gentle Shakespeare, must enjoy a part.		392	Shakespeare	56
Now, for mine owne part, and it is but due,		415	Rutter	12
PARTAKES				
This grave partakes the fleshly birth.		34	E22 Daughter	11
PARTED				
At sixe moneths end, shee parted hence		33	E22 Daughter	5
And, though the sound were parted thence,		279	U84 Mind	39
PARTES				
unto thee, king of men; their noblest partes		382	Rich	3
PARTICULAR				
And allow you for each particular mile,		379	Coryat 3	9
PARTIE				
Your partie-per-pale picture, one halfe drawne		51	E73 Fine Grand	13

	Page	Title	Line

PARTIE-PER-PALE
Your partie-per-pale picture, one halfe drawne . . . 51 E73 Fine Grand 13
PARTIES
T'accuse, or quit all Parties to be heard! . . . 284 U84 Muse 60
PARTING
But, at our parting, we will be, as when . . . 65 E101 Supper 38
Of parting, drowne it in the hope to meet . . . 197 U40 Elegy That 7
Be idle words, though of a parting Man; . . . 199 U41 Elegy Since 4
PARTRICH
Of partrich, pheasant, wood-cock, of which some . . . 65 E101 Supper 18
The painted partrich lyes in every field, . . . 94 F2 Penshurst 29
In autumne, at the Partrich makes a flight, . . . 97 F3 Wroth 27
PARTS
For who can master those great parts like thee, . . . 61 E95 Savile 17
Tell them, what parts yo'have tane, whence run away, . . . 69 E107 Hungry 9
In these west-parts, nor when that warre was done, . . . 71 E110 Edmonds 1 2
And that, midst envy' and parts; then fell by rage: . . . 71 E110 Edmonds 1 14
Parts, then th'Italian could doe, with his dore. . . . 74 E115 Honest Man 26
Reade, in their vertuous parents noble parts, . . . 96 F2 Penshurst 97
What you please, you parts may call, . . . 142 U2 Exception 7
I dare not say a body, but some parts . . . 206 U43 Vulcan 87
Like flies, or wormes, with mans corrupt parts fed: . . . 218 U47 Tribe 18
No noble furniture of parts, . . . 234 U60 La-ware 11
Hee entred well, by vertuous parts, . . . 244 U70 Ode 33
Parts of me (they judg'd) decay'd, . . . 259 U76 Petition 23
Parts of him, the Judge decay'd, . . . 259 U76 Petition V 23
In honour, courtesie, and all the parts . . . 262 U78 Digby 3
She was, in one, a many parts of life; . . . 287 U84 Muse 173
And most his Justice, in the fitting parts, . . . 289 U84 Muse 223
The parts of age to youth be given; or men . . . 317 Horace 252
An Actors parts, and Office too, the Quire . . . 317 Horace 276
And office of a Judge are, what the parts . . . 325 Horace 450
How to divide, into a hundred parts, . . . 327 Horace 465
All which are parts commend the cunning hand; . . . 370 Author 4
But when againe I veiw the parts so peiz'd, . . . 395 May 7
And those so sweet, and well proportion'd parts, . . . 396 Drayton 21
And you perform'd a Servants faithfull parts: . . . 409 Brome 2
PAS'D
To line out no stride, but pas'd by himselfe? . . . 379 Coryat 3 8
PASQUILL'S
With Nicholas Pasquill's, Meddle with your match, . . . 206 U43 Vulcan 77
PASSAGE
From Venice, Paris, or some in-land passage . . . 85 E133 Voyage 33
To this dire passage. Say, thou stop thy nose: . . . 85 E133 Voyage 59
Tempte such a passage? when each privies seate . . . 88 E133 Voyage 168
Into your harbor, and all passage shut . . . 119 F13 Aubigny 92
Or gratulates the passage . . . 221 U48 Bacchus 45
Who reads may roave, and call the passage darke, . . . 383 Author 5
Such Passage hast thou found, such Returnes made, . . . 389 Chapman 10
PASSE
But in my royall subject I passe thee, . . . 38 E36 Martial 3
Sir Lucklesse, troth, for lucks sake passe by one: . . . 42 E47 Luckless 2 1
I passe to Elegies; Thou meet'st me there: . . . 73 E112 Gamster 13
But they unfrighted passe, though many a privie . . . 86 E133 Voyage 73
All was to them the same, they were to passe, . . . 88 E133 Voyage 140
You will not from the paper slightly passe: . . . 117 F13 Aubigny 25
Live that one, still; and as long yeeres doe passe, . . . 120 F13 Aubigny 121
Sweet bags, sweet Powders, nor sweet words will passe . . . 165 U15 Friend-Wars 112
They may say Grace, and for Loves Chaplaines passe; . . . 198 U40 Elegy That 31
Your Joane to passe her melancholie time. . . . 231 U56 Covell 24
Cary to passe her melancholie time. . . . 231 U56 Covell V 24
Our Gallants give them none, but passe them by: . . . 329 Horace 513
Will passe the Seas, and long as nature is, . . . 329 Horace 518
made prospective, behould hym, hee must passe . . . 383 Rich 12
Upon it, but will loath, or let it passe, . . . 389 Aleman 9
Those ambling visits, passe in verse, betweene . . . 396 Drayton 4
PASS'D
The Lady Mayresse pass'd through the Towne, . . . 201 U42 Elegy Let 70
PASSENGER
If, Passenger, thou canst but reade: . . . 233 U60 La-ware 1
PASSER
An Epitaph, on Henry L. La-ware. To the Passer-by. . . . 233 U60 La-ware Ttl
PASSER-BY
An Epitaph, on Henry L. La-ware. To the Passer-by. . . . 233 U60 La-ware Ttl
PASSION
For wit, feature, and true passion, . . . 39 E40 Ratcliffe 16
With the Ardor, and the Passion, . . . 131 U2 Excuse 11
And out of inward passion feed . . . 144 U3 Musicall V 19
A Nymphs Passion. . . . 147 U7 Nymph Ttl
Of race accompted, that no passion have . . . 201 U42 Elegy Let 49
Am turned with an others powers. My Passion . . . 283 U84 Muse 31
I struggled with this passion that did drowne . . . 362 Palmer 28
Thou, that wouldst finde the habit of true passion, . . . 362 Author 1
Each subt'lest Passion, with her source, and spring, . . . 370 Author 7
Each subject Passion, with her source, and spring, . . . 370 Author V 7
PASSION'S
To judge which Passion's false, and which is true, . . . 370 Author 11
PASSIONS
Doe severall passions invade the minde, . . . 110 F11 Epode 29
For no man lives so out of passions sway, . . . 190 U37 Friend-Book 31
For noe Man Lyves, soe out of passions swaye, . . . 422 Censure 24
PASSIVE
Active in's braine, and passive in his bones. . . . 49 E68 Playwrt 2 4

506

PAST
In the past pleasures of his sensuall life,   · · · ·   34 E25 Beast 1   2
So to front death, as men might judge us past it.   · ·   54 E80 Life/Death   7
Five of my jests, then stolne, past him a play.   · ·   64 E100 Playwrt 3   4
Were you advanced, past those times, to be   · · · ·   67 E104 Montgomery 11
This is that good Aeneas, past through fire,   · · ·   81 E128 Wm Roe 2   12
Or magick sacrifice, they past along!   · · · ·   85 E133 Voyage   49
They laugh't, at his laugh-worthy fate. And past   ·   89 E133 Voyage 185
All your sweet of life is past,   · · · ·   140 U2 Promise   28
Men past their termes, and prais'd some names too much,   159 U14 Selden   21
Heard what times past have said, seene what ours doe: 159 U14 Selden   34
Crush'd in the snakie brakes, that he had past!   · ·   162 U15 Friend-Wars 18
Past any need of vertue. Let them care,   · ·   215 U44 Speach   83
And saw a Centaure, past those tales of Greece;   ·   228 U53 Newcastle   5
Though thou hast past thy Summer standing, stay   ·   252 U75 Epithalam.   1
Though thou art past thy Summer standing, stay   ·   252 U75 Epithalam. V 1
Of the times past, when he was a young lad;   · ·   317 Horace 248
Thy Richard, rais'd in song, past pulling downe.   ·   385 Brooke   8
PASTIE
To put the skins, and offall in a pastie?   · · ·   88 E133 Voyage 148
PASTORALL
The Musicall Strife; In a Pastorall Dialogue.   · ·   143 U3 Musicall Ttl
PASTORALS
To my truly-belov'd Freind, Mr Browne: on his Pastorals.   ·   386 Browne Ttl
PASTRIE
That will the pastrie, not my paper, show of.   · ·   65 E101 Supper   26
PASTURES
To better Pastures then great Pales can: · · ·   264 U79 New-yeares 30
To sweeter Pastures lead hee can,   · · · ·   265 U79 New-yeares 60
PAT
And the ratling pit-pat-noyse,   · · · ·   259 U76 Petition   19
PATE
Under the Morall? shewe he had a pate   · · ·   405 Inigo Jones 1   83
PATH
Treading a better path, not contrary;   · · ·   76 E119 Shelton   12
If in th'escape an artlesse path we tread.   · ·   339 Horace V 46/ 44
PATHES
For, though but early in these pathes thou tread,   ·   386 Browne   5
PATHS
In single paths, dangers with ease are watch'd: ·   118 F13 Aubigny   57
Sought out the Fountaines, Sources, Creekes, paths, wayes,   160 U14 Selden   45
The bright Brides paths, embelish'd more then thine   ·   254 U75 Epithalam.   59
Their nailes, nor shave their beards, but to by-paths   325 Horace 423
Their nails, nor shave their beards, but seek by-paths   349 Horace V423
Were not the paths I meant unto thy praise: · ·   390 Shakespeare   6
PATIENCE
It might thy patience richly pay: · · · ·   168 U16 Gray   5
As patience lasteth.   · · · ·   179 U25 Desmond   47
Nor is't long since, they did with patience take   ·   323 Horace 375
PATIENT
Or Goddesse, could be patient of thy face.   · ·   207 U43 Vulcan 108
PATIENTLY
Too patiently, that I not fondly say;   · · ·   323 Horace 401
PATRIOT
A perfect Patriot, and a noble friend,   · · ·   244 U70 Ode   46
PATRONAGE
More for thy Patronage, then for their Cause,   · ·   217 U46 Coke   12
PATRONS
But when (in place) thou didst the patrons choose,   ·   43 E53 Old-end   4
When his proud patrons favours are asleepe;   · ·   113 F12 Rutland   14
PATTERNES
Unto the other; and live patternes, how   · · ·   171 U19 Elegy By   17
PAUL
With holy Paul, lest it be thought the breath   ·   122 F15 Heaven   24
PAULES
Shewes he dares more then Paules Church-yard durst do.   ·   378 Coryat 2   85
PAULS
Though Lippe, at Pauls, ranne from his text away,   ·   52 E75 Lippe   3
Daily to turne in Pauls, and helpe the trade.   · ·   56 E88 Monsieur   16
The weekly Corrants, with Pauls Seale; and all   ·   206 U43 Vulcan   81
And to Pauls-Steeple; which was unto us   · · ·   211 U43 Vulcan 193
PAULS-STEEPLE
And to Pauls-Steeple; which was unto us   · · ·   211 U43 Vulcan 193
PAULUS
With thy bright Swans, of Paulus Maximus: · ·   292 U86 Hor.4:1   10
PAUSE
And farre beneath least pause of such a king,   · ·   43 E51 James 3   4
That, Allen, I should pause to publish thee?   · ·   57 E89 Allen   8
Should not on fortune pause,   · · · ·   174 U23 Himselfe   17
And then with pause; for sever'd once, that's gone,   ·   192 U38 Elegy 'Tis   47
With pause upon it; make this page your booke;   ·   399 Lady Ogle   6
PAWLET
An Elegie On the Lady Jane Pawlet, Marchion: of Winton.   ·   268 U81 Pawlet Ttl
PAWNE
And riffle him: or pawne his Petasus.   · · ·   107 F10 Proludium   24
each to pawne hir husbands capp,   · · · ·   417 Moon   38
PAY
Seven yeeres tho'wert lent to me, and I thee pay,   ·   41 E45 First Son   3
To pay at's day of marriage. By my hand   · ·   42 E46 Luckless 1   4
The knight-wright's cheated then: Hee'll never pay.   ·   42 E46 Luckless 1   5
Hee's valiant'st, that dares fight, and not for pay;   ·   49 E66 Cary   17
For which, or pay me quickly', or Ile pay you.   ·   51 E73 Fine Grand   22
To morrow vice, if shee give better pay: · ·   66 E102 Pembroke   10

PAY (cont.)

		Page	Title	Line
What States yo'have gull'd, and which yet keepes yo'in pay.	.	69	E107 Hungry	10
To thanke thy benefits: which is, to pay.	.	80	E127 Aubigny	12
Thou hast thy ponds, that pay thee tribute fish,	.	94	F2 Penshurst	32
Wherewith, then, Madame, can you better pay	.	118	F13 Aubigny	53
To pay your lord the pledges of chast love:	.	119	F13 Aubigny	96
To pay our debts, upon thy Crosse, and cryd'st,	.	128	U1 Trinitie	23
It might thy patience richly pay:	.	168	U16 Gray	5
They are not, Sir, worst Owers, that doe pay	.	169	U17 Friend-Debt	1
And should grow rich, I much more to pay.	.	231	U56 Covell	30
And should grow rich, if I had more to pay.	.	231	U56 Covell	V 30
Hee can, he will, and with large int'rest pay,	.	236	U63 Charles 2	5
His Poet Sack, the House-hold will not pay?	.	241	U68 House-hold	2
The cries, the gladnesse, which their hearts would pay,	.	249	U72 King	V 14
To pay, with honours, to his noble Sonne	.	256	U75 Epithalam.	106
Exacts then she is pleas'd to pay: no suits,	.	258	U75 Epithalam.	188
gentlie hee asketh, shee will pay: no suits,	.	258	U75 Epithalam.	V188
About the towne: this reck'ning I will pay,	.	396	Drayton	9

PAYD

Thy twice conceyvd, thrice payd for Imagery?	.	405	Inigo Jones 1	90

PAYES

The charge of that state, with this charme, god payes.	.	30	E12 Shift	4
Himselfe: his whole revennue is, god payes.	.	30	E12 Shift	6
Shee must have money: he returnes, god payes.	.	30	E12 Shift	8
Lookes o're the bill, likes it: and say's, god payes.	.	30	E12 Shift	10
At dice his borrow'd money: which, god payes.	.	30	E12 Shift	12
Signes to new bond, forfeits: and cryes, god payes.	.	30	E12 Shift	14
Takes physick, teares the papers: still god payes.	.	30	E12 Shift	16
Calls for his stoole, adornes the stage: god payes.	.	30	E12 Shift	18
His onely answere is to all, god payes.	.	30	E12 Shift	20
Thus: and for his letcherie, scores, god payes.	.	31	E12 Shift	22
That payes, or what he will: The Dame is steele.	.	164	U15 Friend-Wars	78

PAYNE

for when the profitt with the payne doth meete,	.	418	Answer	6

PAYNTED

A Goddess is, then paynted Cloth, Deal-boards,	.	406	Inigo Jones 1	93

PAYRE

Sure, this glad payre were married, but this day.	.	384	Somerset	26

PAYS

Pays all Debts, cures all Diseases,	.	657	Door Apollo	17

PEACE

For this: that winnes, for whom he holds his peace.	.	38	E37 Chev'ril	4
Rest in soft peace, and, ask'd, say here doth lye	.	41	E45 First Son	9
If the States make peace, how it will goe	.	59	E92 New Crie	30
Thou yet remayn'st, un-hurt in peace, or warre,	.	60	E93 Radcliffe	13
Thy peace is made; and, when man's state is well,	.	99	F3 Wroth	93
Nor for my peace will I goe farre,	.	102	F4 To the World	65
O, who is he, that (in this peace) enjoyes	.	110	F11 Epode	55
Peace, Luxurie, thou art like one of those	.	111	F11 Epode	69
'Gainst stormes, or pyrats, that might charge your peace;	.	119	F13 Aubigny	93
This hath our ill-us'd freedome, and soft peace	.	166	U15 Friend-Wars	121
That may stand by, and hold my peace? will he,	.	167	U15 Friend-Wars	150
These take, and now goe seeke thy peace in Warre,	.	168	U15 Friend-Wars	195
Clos'd to their peace, he saw his branches shoot,	.	185	U30 Burleigh	17
We aske your absence here, we all love peace,	.	212	U43 Vulcan	209
We crave your absence here, we all love peace,	.	212	U43 Vulcan	V209
The wished Peace of Europe:	.	222	U48 Bacchus	48
Of sweets, and safeties, they possesse by Peace.	.	261	U77 Treasurer	22
Fame and Honour you, they possesse by Peace.	.	261	U77 Treasurer	V 22
Hee is the Father of our peace;	.	264	U79 New-yeares	40
Hee is the author of our peace.	.	265	U79 New-yeares	57
Hee is the author of our peace.	.	265	U79 New-yeares	69
Peace, and the open ports, that peace doth cause.	.	317	Horace	284
The open ports, and sports that peace doth cause,	.	345	Horace	V284
Which law receiv'd, the Chorus held his peace,	.	323	Horace	369
Peace.	.	363	Peace	Ttl
Flowes from the surfets which we take in peace.	.	363	Peace	4
presentes a Royall Alter of fayre peace,	.	382	Rich	6
The Peace of Conscience, and the Godly's strife,	.	411	Sutcliffe	7
for if there, or peace or warr be,	.	417	Moon	22
or theire Ale, they break the peace,	.	418	Moon	42

PEACH

The blushing apricot, and woolly peach	.	94	F2 Penshurst	43
Chin, as woolly as the Peach;	.	141	U2 Her man	21

PEACOCK

There Juno sate, and yet no Peacock by.	.	68	E105 L Wroth 2	18

PEAKE

To the wonders of the Peake,	.	416	Moon	1
to the Peake it is so hard-by,	.	417	Moon	23

PEALES

What charming Peales are these,	.	401	Filmer	1

PEARCH'D

Pearch'd over head, the wise Athenian Owle:	.	397	Drayton	34

PEARE

An embleme of themselves, in plum, or peare.	.	95	F2 Penshurst	56

PEARES

How plucking Peares, his owne hand grafted had,	.	290	U85 Country	19

PEARLE (See also PURLE)

But they may see Gold-Chaines, and Pearle worne then,	.	213	U44 Speach	13

PEASANTS

Then, here, to give pride fame, and peasants birth.	.	114	F12 Rutland	26
Then, now give pride fame, or peasants birth.	.	114	F12 Rutland	V 26

```
                                                              Page     Title        Line
PEASON
    When every clerke eates artichokes, and peason,    .    .    .    88   E133 Voyage       166
PEDICULOUS
    How scabbed, how ragged, and how pediculous    .    .    .    380   Coryat 3          34
PEDIGREE  (See also 'GREE)
    Where all is faire, beside thy pedigree.    .    .    .    .    70   E109 Nevil         4
    How each one playes his part, of the large Pedigree.    .    .    258   U75 Epithalam.    176
    Hang all your roomes, with one large Pedigree:    .    .    .    282   U84 Kenelme        20
PEDLING
    Pack with your pedling Poetry to the Stage,    .    .    .    404   Inigo Jones 1      51
PEECE
    From locks of wooll, or shreds from the whole peece?    .    .    45   E56 Poet-Ape       14
    In any curious peece you see    .    .    .    .    .    145   U5 Woman-kind      14
    So seem'd your horse and you, both of a peece!    .    .    .    228   U53 Newcastle       6
    A Copie of this peece; nor tell    .    .    .    .    .    277   U84 Body           30
    This peece, my Piso's, and that booke agree,    .    .    .    305   Horace              8
    A Scarlet peece, or two, stitch'd in: when or    .    .    .    305   Horace             19
PEECES
    As my heart lies in peeces, all confus'd,    .    .    .    127   U1 Trinitie         7
    A Celebration of Charis in ten Lyrick Peeces.    .    .    .    131   U2 Charis         Ttl
    Arm'd at all peeces, as to keepe a Fort    .    .    .    .    187   U33 Councellour    30
    Get broken peeces, and fight well by those.    .    .    .    398   Drayton            74
PEEPE
    No, nor forth your window peepe,    .    .    .    .    .    140   U2 Promise         16
    Thou didst tell me; and wert o're-joy'd to peepe    .    .    201   U42 Elegy Let      59
    Peepe forth a Gemme; to see    .    .    .    .    .    258   U75 Epithalam.    175
PEEPES
    The Muse not peepes out, one of hundred dayes;    .    .    248   U71 Treasurer       9
PEERE
    Of some grand peere, whose ayre doth make rejoyce    .    .    113   F12 Rutland        12
PEERES
    T'out-strip your peeres:    .    .    .    .    .    .    121   F14 Sydney         26
    I have had, and have my Peeres;    .    .    .    .    .    131   U2 Excuse           4
    Of your Peeres, you were beheld,    .    .    .    .    .    138   U2 Kisse           23
    Here's one out-liv'd his Peeres,    .    .    .    .    .    243   U70 Ode            25
    Amongst her Peeres, those Princes of all good!    .    .    .    284   U84 Muse           84
    I should commit thee surely with thy peeres,    .    .    .    391   Shakespeare        28
PEERING
    And peering forth of Iris in the Shrowdes!    .    .    .    403   Inigo Jones 1      34
PEERS
    The Tristrams, Lanc'lots, Turpins, and the Peers,    .    .    206   U43 Vulcan         69
    Or are you soe ambitious 'bove your peers!    .    .    .    403   Inigo Jones 1      19
    At libelling? Shall no Star-Chamber Peers,    .    .    .    410   Gill                3
PEGASUS
    Though he would steale his sisters Pegasus,    .    .    .    107   F10 Proludium      23
    Pegasus did flie away,    .    .    .    .    .    .    183   U29 Fit of Rime    19
    You shew'd like Perseus upon Pegasus;    .    .    .    .    228   U53 Newcastle       7
PEIRCE
    Whose ayre will sooner Hell, then their dull senses peirce,    .    420   Ode:If Men         23
PEIZ'D
    But when againe I veiw the parts so peiz'd,    .    .    .    395   May                 7
PELEUS
    And Peleus, if they seeke to heart-strike us    .    .    .    311   Horace            136
    Peleus, or Telephus.  If you speake vile    .    .    .    311   Horace            147
PELFE
    And turning all he toucheth into pelfe,    .    .    .    197   U40 Elegy That     22
PELLETS
    With their pellets of small wit,    .    .    .    .    .    259   U76 Petition       22
PELTS
    A Punke here pelts him with egs.  How so?    .    .    .    375   Coryat 1           18
PEM
    at Pem Wakers good ale Tapp,    .    .    .    .    .    417   Moon               39
PEMBROKE
    To William Earle of Pembroke.    .    .    .    .    .    66   E102 Pembroke     Ttl
    I Doe but name thee Pembroke, and I find    .    .    .    66   E102 Pembroke       1
PEN
    The least indulgent thought thy pen drops forth!    .    .    44   E55 Beaumont        4
    To be the wealthy witnesse of my pen:    .    .    .    .    54   E81 Proule          4
    Of state, and censure them: we need his pen    .    .    .    62   E95 Savile         33
    Hast taught thy selfe worthy thy pen to tread,    .    .    63   E99 Th Roe 2        3
    No more, then I dare now doe, with my pen.    .    .    .    70   E108 Soldiers       8
    Because they lack'd the sacred pen, could give    .    .    115   F12 Rutland        56
    And with the heart, not pen,    .    .    .    .    .    247   U70 Ode           124
    This being thus: why should my tongue, or pen    .    .    284   U84 Muse           69
    Blot out the carelesse, with his turned pen;    .    .    .    335   Horace            635
    Who tracks this Authors, or Translators Pen,    .    .    .    389   Aleman              1
    Phoebus, and Hermes? They whose tongue, or pen    .    .    395   May                17
PENALTIE
    Then he, which for sinnes penaltie forbeares.    .    .    112   F11 Epode          89
    Then he, that for sinnes penaltie forbeares.    .    .    .    112   F11 Epode        V 89
PENANCE
    Colt, now, doth daily penance in his owne.    .    .    .    39   E39 Colt            2
    And doe their penance, to avert Gods rod,    .    .    .    235   U61 Epigram        19
PENATES
    Of thy Penates had beene set on flame,    .    .    .    .    95   F2 Penshurst       79
    Speake it, you bold Penates, you that stand    .    .    .    274   U84 Descent         7
PENCE
    That may judge for his six-pence) had, before    .    .    .    371   Fletcher            7
PEND
    In five monthes he went it, in five monthes he pend it.    .    379   Coryat 3           16
PENELOPES
    As makes Penelopes old fable true,    .    .    .    .    224   U50 Countesse      20
```

	Page	Title	Line

PENITENT
How penitent I am, or I should be! . . . . . 172 U20 Shrub 16
PENITENTS
As I the penitents here emulate: . . . . 193 U38 Elegy 'Tis 86
PENNANCE
A pennance, where a man may not be free, ... 158 U14 Selden 8
PENN'D
And ill-penn'd things, I shall, or sleepe, or smile. . . 311 Horace 148
PENNE
Of his foote, or his penne, his braine or his hoofe, . . 380 Coryat 3 32
PENNING
That penning the glad flock in hurdles by, . . . 291 U85 Country 45
PENNY
Or else in penny Fagots blaze about . . . . . 211 U43 Vulcan V185
PENSHURST
To Penshurst. . . . . . . 93 F2 Penshurst Ttl
Thou art not, Penshurst, built to envious show, . . . 93 F2 Penshurst 1
These, Penshurst, are thy praise, and yet not all. . . . 96 F2 Penshurst 89
Now, Penshurst, they that will proportion thee . . . 96 F2 Penshurst 99
PENSION
Of a yeares Pension, ... 231 U57 Burges 12
Of a free Poetique Pension, ... 259 U76 Petition 10
To his Poet of a Pension, ... 259 U76 Petition V 10
PENT
Or were pent up in a Brake. . . . . . 142 U2 Her man V 40
PENURIE
Nor wants it here through penurie, or sloth, . . . 152 U12 Corbet 39
PEOPLE
To teach the people, how to fast, and pray, . . . 235 U61 Epigram 18
Be silent, to the people . . . . 239 U67 Muses 5
The People her doe call! . . . . 240 U67 Muses 50
What prayers (People) can you thinke too much? . . . 249 U72 King 20
And by thy blessing, may thy People see . . . 268 U80 Christning 3
Heare, what it is the People, and I desire: . . 315 Horace 219
Her Sonnes before the people; nor the ill-/Natur'd . . 317 Horace 264
So over-thick, but, where the people met, . . . 319 Horace 292
More strongly takes the people with delight. . . . 327 Horace 458
PEOPLES
Proves, that is gods, which was the peoples voice. . . 49 E67 Suffolk 12
But, that he cure the Peoples Evill too? . . . 235 U62 Charles 1 14
PER
Your partie-per-pale picture, one halfe drawne . . . 51 E73 Fine Grand 13
PERCEIVE
The wits will leave you, if they once perceive . . 223 U49 Pucell 37
PERCEIV'D
Knew I all this afore? had I perceiv'd, ... 171 U20 Shrub 9
PERFECT
The entertaynment perfect: not the cates. . . . 64 E101 Supper 8
And perfect in a circle alwayes meet. . . . 81 E128 Wm Roe 2 8
But grant us perfect, they're not knowne. . . . 104 F7 Women but 10
Pure, perfect, nay divine; . . . . 110 F11 Epode 46
It perfect, proper, pure, and naturall, . . . 117 F13 Aubigny 32
Gold, that is perfect, will out-live the fire. . . 179 U25 Desmond 45
What wonder perfect, all were fil'd, . . . U35 Chute 3
A perfect Patriot, and a noble friend, . . . 244 U70 Ode 46
And in short measures, life may perfect bee. . . 245 U70 Ode 74
Unto the Vertue. Nothing perfect done, . . . 247 U70 Ode 115
A Mind so pure, so perfect fine, . . . 278 U84 Mind 25
So polish't, perfect, round, and even, . . . 280 U84 Mind 55
For his designed worke, the perfect end . . . 288 U84 Muse 206
And see a minde attir'd in perfect straines; . . 362 Author 2
I found it pure, and perfect Poesy, . . . 397 Drayton 24
In her! and what could perfect bee, . . . 399 Lady Ogle 15
PERFECTION
In the full floud of her admir'd perfection? . . 112 F11 Epode 107
Is that which doth perfection breed. . . . 146 U6 Defence 12
And celebrate (perfection at the worth) . . . 253 U75 Epithalam. 28
Could summe to a perfection, was her Act! . . . 270 U81 Pawlet 46
Could heap to a perfection, was her Act! . . . 270 U81 Pawlet V 46
Hee will all Glory, all Perfection be, . . . 286 U84 Muse 127
Have not kept in; and (lest perfection faile) . . 325 Horace 417
PERFECTIONS
Did her perfections call me on to gaze, . . . 169 U18 Elegy Can 3
Where, such perfections to the life doe rise. . . 362 Author 6
PERFORME
This worke I can performe alone; . . . . 277 U84 Mind 3
PERFORM'D
And you perform'd a Servants faithfull parts: . . 409 Brome 2
PERFUM'D
Their perfum'd judgements, let them kisse thy Wife. . 232 U58 Book-seller 14
PERFUMED
On Sir Cod the perfumed. . . . . . 33 E19 Cod 1 Ttl
PERFUMES
(The holy perfumes of the Mariage bed.) . . . 257 U75 Epithalam. 162
For, Prayer is the Incense most perfumes . . . 288 U84 Muse 187
PERHAPS
As lowdest praisers, who perhaps would find . . 67 E103 L Wroth 1 11
Yet thou, perhaps, shalt meet some tongues will grutch, . 72 E111 Edmonds 2 9
Or perhaps lesse: whil'st gold beares all this sway, . 113 F12 Rutland 18
That would, perhaps, have prais'd, and thank'd the same, . 161 U14 Selden 70
Although, perhaps it has, what's that to me, . . 167 U15 Friend-Wars 149
Perhaps, to have beene burned with my bookes. . . 203 U43 Vulcan 18
Him that buyes Pulse there, or perhaps may like . 347 Horace V354/362

510

PERIEGESIS
  In thy admired Periegesis, ...   397   Drayton   50
PERILL
  No lesse than if from perill; and devout,   .   .   .   43   E51 James 3   7
PERILLS
  What two brave perills of the private sword   .   .   .   37   E32 Roe 2   1
  The many perills of this Port, and how   85   E133 Voyage   47
PERIOD
  Of joy the Circle, and sole Period!   284   U84 Muse   66
PERISH
  Thou mightst have had me perish, piece, by piece,   .   . 205   U43 Vulcan   51
  Thou mightst have had them perish, piece, by piece,   .   . 205   U43 Vulcan   V 51
  Shall perish: so farre off it is, the state,   .   .   . 309   Horace   99
  Let Poets perish, that will not be kept.   335   Horace   664
PERISHE
  The mayne comaund of scepters, soone doth perishe   .   . 422   Lucan   9
PERJURE
  In Contract twice, what can shee perjure more?   .   .   . 223   U49 Pucell   30
PERJUR'D
  Boasters, and perjur'd, with the infinite more   .   .   . 167   U15 Friend-Wars 169
  Perjur'd! and painted! if she were no more--,   .   .   . 172   U20 Shrub   22
PERJURIE
  Who, though their guilt, and perjurie they know,   .   .   . 186   U32 Elsmere   11
PERMANENT
  Such as are square, wel-tagde, and permanent,   .   .   . 220   U47 Tribe   64
PERNITIOUS
  Pernitious enemie; we see, before   158   U14 Selden   14
PERPETUALL
  'Tis, with us, perpetuall night.   102   F5 Celia 1   8
PERPETUATING
  And to the perpetuating of our freindship   666   Glover   4
PERPLEXED
  And whilst our tongues perplexed lie, ... 139   U2 Another   17
PERSEUS
  You shew'd like Perseus upon Pegasus;   228   U53 Newcastle   7
PERSIAN
  Not with the Arras, but the Persian Loomes.   260   U77 Treasurer   4
  Not from the Arras, but the Persian Loomes.   260   U77 Treasurer   V 4
  I thought me richer then the Persian King.   293   U87 Hor.3:9   4
PERSON
  To Person Guiltie.   36   E30 Guiltie   Ttl
  And person to the world; ere I thy name.   36   E30 Guiltie   4
  To Person Guiltie.   38   E38 Guiltie 2   Ttl
  Thy person only, Courtling, is the vice.   50   E72 Court-ling   6
  For, where his person liv'd scarce one just age,   .   .   71   E110 Edmonds 1   13
  Being no vitious person, but the vice   74   E115 Honest Man   5
  But we propose a person like our Dove, ... 112   F11 Epode   91
  But I Conceive a person like my Dove, ... 112   F11 Epode   V 91
  In the person of Woman-kind. A Song Apologetique.   .   . 145   U5 Woman-kind   Ttl
  That I may love your Person (as I doe)   157   U13 Sacvile   157
  No person, nor is lov'd: what wayes he proves   .   .   . 162   U15 Friend-Wars 16
  Thy person fit for any charge thou tak'st;   168   U15 Friend-Wars 182
  Annexed to thy Person, and thy place, ... 235   U62 Charles 1   2
  Else, who doth praise a person by a new, ... 270   U81 Pawlet   37
  A meere new person, looke he keepe his state   .   .   . 313   Horace   180
PERSONS
  Of persons, still one God, in Unitie, ... 127   U1 Trinitie   2
  Of persons, still one God in Unitie;   128   U1 Trinitie   30
  Distinct in persons, yet in Unitie   128   U1 Trinitie   39
  Attyre the Persons as noe thought can teach   404   Inigo Jones 1   54
  Of Persons, yet in Union (One) divine.   413   Ghyrlond   35
PERSPECTIVE
  Unto a cunning piece wrought perspective, ... 362   Author   10
  In the mere perspective of an Inch board!   404   Inigo Jones 1   44
PERSWADE
  An Epistle to a Friend, to perswade him to the Warres.   . 162   U15 Friend-Wars Ttl
  But he that should perswade, to have this done   .   .   . 214   U44 Speach   61
PERSWADES
  Declineth anger, perswades clemencie, ...   82   E130 Ferrab. 1   5
PERSWADING
  And fills my powers with perswading joy, ... 191   U38 Elegy 'Tis   11
PERTINAX
  To Pertinax Cob.   50   E69 Cob   Ttl
PERVERSLY
  Perversly modest, had I rather owe   311   Horace   130
PERVERTS
  And crie good! good! This quite perverts my sense,   .   .   38   E38 Guiltie 2   5
PEST
  Spittles, pest-house, hospitalls, ... 104   F8 Sicknesse   10
  But fly thee, like the Pest! Walke not the street   .   . 409   Detractor   19
PEST-HOUSE
  Spittles, pest-house, hospitalls, ... 104   F8 Sicknesse   10
PETARDS
  Make your Petards, and Granats, all your fine   .   .   . 212   U43 Vulcan   206
PETASUS
  And riffle him: or pawne his Petasus.   107   F10 Proludium   24
PETITE
  In all her petite actions, so devote, ... 287   U84 Muse   177
PETITION
  The Humble Petition of Poore Ben.   259   U76 Petition   Ttl
PETRARCH
  Hath Petrarch since his Laura rais'd   181   U27 Ode Helen   21

PETTICOTE
Telling the motions of each petticote, ... 34 E25 Beast 1 3
Upon a Velvet Petticote, or a Gowne, ... 200 U42 Elegy Let 38
To ev'ry Petticote he brush'd, and Glove . . . . 201 U42 Elegy Let 54

PETTICOTES
And spangled Petticotes brought forth to eye, ... 223 U49 Pucell 19

PETTIE
And what hast thou done in these pettie spights, . . . 210 U43 Vulcan 163

PETULANT
Become a petulant thing, hurle inke, and wit, . . . 27 E2 My Booke 5
What are thy petulant pleadings, Chev'ril, then, . . . 44 E54 Chev'ril 2 3
From what th'obscene, and petulant Satyres are. . . . 321 Horace 340

PEWTER
For, here they were throwne in wi'the melted pewter, . . 88 E133 Voyage 153

PHAOS
Of Phaos forme? or doth the Boy . . . . . . 181 U27 Ode Helen 5

PHEASANT
He doth, at meales, alone, his pheasant eate, . . . 35 E28 Surly 12
Of partrich, pheasant, wood-cock, of which some . . . 65 E101 Supper 18
The purpled pheasant, with the speckled side: . . . 94 F2 Penshurst 28

PHILIP
To Mrs. Philip Sydney. . . . . 73 E114 Sydney Ttl
An Epitaph on Master Philip Gray. . . . . . 168 U16 Gray Ttl
All that is left of Philip Gray, ... 168 U16 Gray 4

PHILOSOPHERS
And that, say Philosophers, is the best modell. . . . 379 Coryat 3 5

PHILOSOPHY
Suckt from the Veynes of shop-philosophy. . . . . 405 Inigo Jones 1 74

PHLEBOTOMIE
Is but a Statists theame, to read Phlebotomie. . . . 179 U25 Desmond 39

PHLEGETON
Cocytus, Phlegeton, our have prov'd in one; . . . 84 E133 Voyage 8

PHOEBEIAN
Tis the true Phoebeian Liquor, ... 657 Door Apollo 15

PHOEBE'S
(As my hope tells) that our faire Phoebe's shine, . . 179 U25 Desmond 58

PHOEBUS
Donne, the delight of Phoebus, and each Muse, . . . 34 E23 Donne 1 1
And Phoebus-selfe should be at eating it. . . . . 55 E84 Bedford 2 8
So Phoebus makes me worthy of his bayes, ... 73 E113 Overbury 1
'Mongst Hampton shades, and Phoebus grove of bayes, . . 80 E126 Mrs Cary 2
Phoebus replyed. Bold head, it is not shee: . . . 80 E126 Mrs Cary 7
Phoebus. No? tend thy cart still. Envious day . . 107 F10 Proludium 7
Phoebus to his Crowne againe; . . . . . . 184 U29 Fit of Rime 40
Then Phoebus; and much stronger . . . . . . 221 U48 Bacchus 22
And Phoebus love cause of his blackenesse is. . . . 366 Ode Who saith 16
Phoebus, and Hermes? They whose tongue, or pen . . 395 May 17

PHOEBUS-SELFE
And Phoebus-selfe should be at eating it. . . . . 55 E84 Bedford 2 8

PHOENIX
Grac'd with a Phoenix love; . . . . . . 112 F11 Epode 92
Force from the Phoenix, then, no raritie . . . . 255 U75 Epithalam. 81
Thou wouldst have lost the Phoenix, had the kind . . 283 U84 Muse 19
The Phoenix Analysde. . . . . 364 Phoenix Ttl
The Phoenix place of breeding, ... 365 Ode Splendor 14
Into a Phoenix, which is shee. . . . . . . 400 Lady Ogle 32

PHRASE
Much lesse with lewd, prophane, and beastly phrase, . . 27 E2 My Booke 11
And with both bombard-stile, and phrase, rehearse . . 85 E133 Voyage 46
Doth labour with the Phrase more then the sense? . . 222 U49 Pucell 14
Much phrase that now is dead, shall be reviv'd; . . 309 Horace 101
Complaines in humble phrase. Both Telephus, . . . 311 Horace 135
Their bombard-phrase, and foot-and-halfe-foot words. . . 311 Horace 139
If now the phrase of him that speakes, shall flow, . . 313 Horace 158
Plaine phrase, my Piso's, as alone, t'approve . . . 321 Horace 342

PHRASES
Of words decay, and phrases borne but late . . . 309 Horace 88

PHRYGIAN
And Phrygian Hau'boy, not without the Flute. . . . 292 U86 Hor.4:1 24

PHYSICIAN
And the Physician teach men spue, or shite: . . . 410 Brome 16

PHYSICK
Takes physick, teares the papers: still god payes. . . 30 E12 Shift 16
Yet doth some wholsome Physick for the mind, . . . 180 U26 Ode High 9

PHISITIAN
Gypsee, new baud, is turn'd physitian, ... 39 E41 Gypsee 1

PICKARDILL
And then, leape mad on a neat Pickardill, ... 164 U15 Friend-Wars 70

PICKE
At first he made low shifts, would picke and gleane, . 45 E56 Poet-Ape 5

PICKT
That haunt Pickt-hatch, Mersh-Lambeth, and White-fryers, . 30 E12 Shift 2

PICKT-HATCH
That haunt Pickt-hatch, Mersh-Lambeth, and White-fryers, . 30 E12 Shift 2

PICTURE
Your partie-per-pale picture, one halfe drawne . . . 51 E73 Fine Grand 13
Or hung some Mounsieurs picture on the wall, . . . 56 E88 Monsieur 12
A picture, which the world for yours must know, . . 67 E104 Montgomery 14
Executes men in picture. By defect, ... 75 E115 Honest Man 29
My Picture left in Scotland. . . . . . . 149 U9 Picture Ttl
Verses on his Picture . . . . 149 U9 Picture VTtl
Though now of flattery, as of picture, are . . . 242 U69 Friend Son 21
The old Greek-hands in picture, or in stone. . . . 260 U77 Treasurer 9

	Page	Title	Line
PICTURE (cont.)			
3. The Picture of the Body.	275	U84 Body	Ttl
This is no Picture, but the same.	278	U84 Mind	24
In Picture, they which truly understand,	370	Author	1
Not on his Picture, but his Booke.	390	Reader	10
PICTURES			
I may no longer on these pictures stay,	216	U44 Speach	98
PIDE			
In these pide times, only to shewe their braines,	362	Author	4
PIE			
To Sir Robert Pie:	231	U57 Burges	4
PIECE (See also PEECE)			
Ben. Jonson his best piece of poetrie.	41	E45 First Son	10
But when I read that speciall piece, restor'd,	61	E95 Savile	7
Shall reade a piece of Virgil, Tacitus,	65	E101 Supper	21
Uv'dale, thou piece of the first times, a man	79	E125 Uvedale	1
Many a pound, and piece, will plague one well;	155	U13 Sacvile	78
Thou mightst have had me perish, piece, by piece,	205	U43 Vulcan	51
Thou mightst have had them perish, piece, by piece,	205	U43 Vulcan	V 51
No piece of money, but you know, or make	216	U45 Squib	14
You made it a brave piece, but not like me.	227	U52 Answer	15
It doe not come: One piece I have in store,	229	U54 Squib	15
Till he had sold his Piece, drawne so unlike:	242	U69 Friend Son	15
That Book, my Piso's, and this piece agree,	338	Horace	V 8
A purple piece, or two stitch'd in: when either	338	Horace	V 19
A pound, or piece, by their long compting arts:	327	Horace	466
Unto a cunning piece wrought perspective,	362	Author	10
So soft, and smooth it handles, the whole piece,	415	Rutter	17
PIECES			
There were some pieces of as base allay,	204	U43 Vulcan	42
With pieces of the Legend; The whole summe	205	U43 Vulcan	66
More subtle workes, and finer pieces farre,	242	U69 Friend Son	22
PIERCE			
Nature, or Art. My Judgement will not pierce	331	Horace	582
Eyes that can pierce into the Misteryes	404	Inigo Jones 1	46
Able to eat into his bones & pierce	407	Inigo Jones 3	4
PIES			
To see their Seats and Bowers by chattring Pies defac't?	174	U23 Himselfe	12
Condemn'd me to the Ovens with the pies;	205	U43 Vulcan	54
Condemn'd them to the Ovens with the pies;	205	U43 Vulcan	V 54
Pies on't, you have his historicall faith.	380	Coryat 3	22
PIETIE			
But for their powers, accept my pietie.	31	E14 Camden	14
Humanitie, and pietie, which are	58	E91 Vere	15
Like straight, thy pietie to God, and friends:	68	E106 E Herbert	8
Doth sweeten mirth, and heighten pietie,	82	E130 Ferrab. 1	6
I Have my Pietie too, which could	151	U12 Corbet	1
'T is not enough (thy pietie is such)	235	U62 Charles 1	3
O pietie! so to weigh the poores estates!	235	U62 Charles 1	11
And pietie the Center, where all met.	270	U81 Pawlet	42
Of Pietie, and private holinesse.	287	U84 Muse	179
PIETY			
Defies, what's crosse to Piety, or good Fame.	401	Beaumont	20
PIGGES			
Singde Capons, or poore Pigges, dropping their eyes;	205	U43 Vulcan	53
Singde capons, or crispe Pigges, dropping their eyes;	205	U43 Vulcan	V 53
PIKES			
And pikes, now weary their owne kinde to eat,	94	F2 Penshurst	34
PILE			
Or stayre, or courts; but stand'st an ancient pile,	93	F2 Penshurst	5
Haile, happie Genius of this antient pile!	225	U51 Bacon	1
PILES			
See the worlds Ruines! nothing but the piles	209	U43 Vulcan	137
In glorious Piles, or Pyramids erect	261	U77 Treasurer	26
In stately Piles, and Pyramids erect	261	U77 Treasurer	V 26
PILLAR			
Some note of which each varied Pillar beares,	176	U24 Frontispice	15
The Orphans Pillar, the true Subjects shield,	185	U30 Burleigh	7
PILLARS			
Of polish'd pillars, or a roofe of gold:	93	F2 Penshurst	3
But neither, Men, nor Gods, nor Pillars meant,	331	Horace	555
From the fam'd pillars of old Hercules!	407	Inigo Jones 2	14
PILL'D			
When having pill'd a booke, which no man buyes,	43	E53 Old-end	2
PILLER			
Which was a cater-piller. So 'twill dye.	31	E15 Court-worm	4
PILLORY			
Pillory nor Whip, nor want of Ears,	410	Gill	4
PILLOW			
From off her pillow, and deluded bed;	283	U84 Muse	43
PILLS			
His spirits, now, in pills, and eeke in potions,	86	E133 Voyage	101
PILOT			
Hee'll be a Pilot, scarce can guide a Plough.	410	Brome	18
PIMBLICOE			
What a strong Fort old Pimblicoe had bin!	213	U44 Speach	21
PIN			
There is not worne that lace, purle, knot or pin,	200	U42 Elegy Let	16
PINDAR			
Where Pindar swamme;	366	Ode Who saith	20
PINDARS			
Wake, and put on the wings of Pindars Muse,	176	U25 Desmond	3

```
                                                   Page      Title        Line

PIN'D
    What their number is, be pin'd.     .    .    .    .    .    .   103   F6 Celia 2        22
PINN
    At every line some pinn thereof should slacke       .    .    .   395   May                5
PIONERS
    Such, as the creeping common Pioners use       .    .    .    .   400   Beaumont           5
PIOUS
    If any pious life ere lifted man          .    .    .    .    .    35   E27 Roe 1          6
    Most pious King, but his owne good in you!      .    .    .    .   236   U64 Charles 3      2
    To pious parents, who would have their blood     .    .    .    .   268   U80 Christning     7
    In frequent speaking by the pious Psalmes   .    .    .    .    .   288   U84 Muse         191
PIPE
    Or Rurall Virgil come, to pipe to us!     .    .    .    .    .   397   Drayton           28
PIPER
    Thus, to his antient Art the Piper lent    .    .    .    .    .   319   Horace           303
PIPKINS
    From thirty pound in pipkins, to the Man    .    .    .    .    .   402   Inigo Jones 1      2
PISO
    But you, my Piso, carefully beware,     .    .    .    .    .    333   Horace           607
PISO'S
    .  .  . the Art of Poetry to the Piso's.     .    .    .    .    338   Horace          VTtl
    This peece, my Piso's, and that booke agree,   .    .    .    .   305   Horace             8
    That Book, my Piso's, and this piece agree,   .    .    .    .   338   Horace           V  8
    Plaine phrase, my Piso's, as alone, t'approve   .    .    .    .   321   Horace           342
PISSE
    With juyce of limons, onions, pisse, to write.    .    .    .    .    59   E92 New Crie      28
    Vile Tavernes, and the Drunkards pisse him out;   .    .    .    .   211   U43 Vulcan       186
    Vile Tavernes, and have Drunkards pisse him out;   .    .    .    .   211   U43 Vulcan       V186
PISS'D
    Whether he piss'd upon his Fathers grave;     .    .    .    .    335   Horace           671
PISTLE
    Yes.  And thanks God in his Pistle or his Booke    .    .    .   380   Coryat 3          43
PIT    (SOUND)
    And the ratling pit-pat-noyse,     .    .    .    .    .    .   259   U76 Petition       19
PIT
    What though her Chamber be the very pit     .    .    .    .    .   222   U49 Pucell         3
    The Sunne, a Sea, or soundlesse Pit;     .    .    .    .    .    278   U84 Mind          11
    For th'eating Thrush, or Pit-falls sets:    .    .    .    .    .   290   U85 Country       34
    Into a pit, or hole; although he call,    .    .    .    .    .    335   Horace           652
PITCH
    Or canst of truth the least intrenchment pitch,    .    .    .   407   Inigo Jones 2     23
PITCH'D
    Wild Bores into his toyles pitch'd round:    .    .    .    .    290   U85 Country       32
PITCHER
    Well, with mine owne fraile Pitcher, what to doe    .    .    .   219   U47 Tribe         56
    Thy labouring wheele, comes scarce a Pitcher out?    .    .    .   307   Horace            30
PITFALL
    And every Dressing for a Pitfall set     .    .    .    .    .    164   U15 Friend-Wars   66
PIT-FALLS
    For th'eating Thrush, or Pit-falls sets:    .    .    .    .    .   290   U85 Country       34
PITIOUS
    And only pitious scorne, upon their folly waites.    .    .    .   175   U23 Himselfe      24
PIT-PAT-NOYSE
    And the ratling pit-pat-noyse,     .    .    .    .    .    .   259   U76 Petition       19
PITTES
    Where Pittes, or Wright, or Modet would not venter,    .    .    .   164   U15 Friend-Wars   80
PITTIE
    As we, the rob'd, leave rage, and pittie it.    .    .    .    .    44   E56 Poet-Ape       4
    But the Pittie comes too late.     .    .    .    .    .    .   133   U2 Suffered       20
    Or Scorne, or pittie on me take,     .    .    .    .    .    150   U11 Dreame         1
    The ignorant, and fooles, no pittie have.    .    .    .    .    191   U38 Elegy 'Tis    20
PITTIED
    And of them pittied be,     .    .    .    .    .    .    .   147   U7 Nymph          11
PITTIOUS
    And, in a pittious tune, began.  How dare    .    .    .    .    88   E133 Voyage      164
PITTY
    Troth, if it be, I pitty thy ill lucke;    .    .    .    .    .    73   E112 Gamster      17
    And pitty 'tis, I cannot call 'hem knights:    .    .    .    .    84   E133 Voyage       22
    To pitty him, as smiling at his Feat    .    .    .    .    .    405   Inigo Jones 1     71
    But bawle thou on; I pitty thee, poore Curre,    .    .    .    .   408   Detractor          7
PIXE
    For order, and for governing the pixe,     .    .    .    .    .   415   Rutter            25
PLACE
    In place of scutcheons, that should decke thy herse,    .    .    .    35   E27 Roe 1          1
    But when (in place) thou didst the patrons choose,    .    .    .    43   E53 Old-end        4
    Thy ignorance still laughs in the wrong place.    .    .    .    .    45   E58 Groome         4
    With thy new place, bring I these early fruits    .    .    .    .    47   E64 Salisbury 3    2
    High in thy bloud, thy place, but highest then,    .    .    .    49   E67 Suffolk        6
    Blowne up; and he (too'unwieldie for that place)    .    .    .    57   E90 Mill          14
    Nor office in the towne, nor place in court,    .    .    .    .    63   E97 Motion        11
    From place, or fortune, are made high, or low,    .    .    .    .    64   E99 Th Roe 2       9
    That we had left us, nor by time, nor place,    .    .    .    .    67   E105 L Wroth 2     3
    Could make such men, and such a place repent:    .    .    .    .    73   E113 Overbury     10
    How hight the place? a voyce was heard, Cocytus.    .    .    .    86   E133 Voyage       89
    Airising in that place, through which, who goes,    .    .    .    87   E133 Voyage      131
    That, with still-scalding steemes, make the place hell.    .    .    88   E133 Voyage      144
    Thy noblest spouse affords them welcome place;    .    .    .    .    98   F3 Wroth         V 55
    Get place, and honor, and be glad to keepe    .    .    .    .    99   F3 Wroth          87
    Get place, and honor, and be proud to keepe    .    .    .    .    99   F3 Wroth         V 87
    And for their place, and name,     .    .    .    .    .    .   111   F11 Epode         80
    Shall thronging come, and boast the happy place    .    .    .   115   F12 Rutland       80
    Many a pound, and piece, will place one well;    .    .    .    .   155   U13 Sacvile       78
    But here's no time, nor place, my wealth to tell,    .    .    .   161   U14 Selden        85
```

	Page	Title	Line
PLACE (cont.)			
Our vices doe not tarry in a place,	166	U15 Friend-Wars	123
As in his place, because he would not varie,	171	U19 Elegy By	27
You may so place me, and in such an ayre,	192	U38 Elegy 'Tis	51
And all the originall riots of the place:	202	U42 Elegy Let	80
The place, that was thy Wives inheritance.	209	U43 Vulcan	152
I never stood for any place: my wit	223	U49 Pucell	23
Or if it would, the Court is the worst place,	223	U49 Pucell	43
A letter'd mind, and a large heart would place	227	U52 Answer	23
Annexed to thy Person, and thy place,	235	U62 Charles 1	2
O happy bands! and thou more happy place,	256	U75 Epithalam.	129
And were shee lost, could best supply her place,	264	U79 New-yeares	34
The glorie, and gaine of rest, which the place gives!	283	U84 Muse	38
And give her place, according to her blood,	284	U84 Muse	83
By beatifick vertue of the Place.	285	U84 Muse	116
To that eternall Rest, where now sh'hath place	288	U84 Muse	197
And sets more happy in the place:	290	U85 Country	12
And graftes more happy in the place:	290	U85 Country	V 12
With thee 'bove all his Rivals gifts take place,	292	U86 Hor.4:1	18
No place for these. And, Painter, hap'ly, thou	305	Horace	24
Or I am much deceiv'd, shall be to place	307	Horace	60
The place allotted it, with decent thewes.	311	Horace	125
The place allotted it, with decent praise.	341	Horace	V131/125
There comes sometimes to things of meanest place.	321	Horace	354
Like men Town-born, and neere the place, reherse	347	Horace	V349/357
Of fellowship, the fourth, or second place.	323	Horace	380
The Phoenix place of breeding,	365	Ode Splendor	14
And (in the place) envie	369	Ode Who saith	95
Or thought they, Leda's white Adult'rers place	369	Ode Who saith	104
He went out at each place, and at what he came in,	380	Coryat 3	25
What place is for my testimony void?	385	Brooke	2
Will any of these express your place? or witt?	402	Inigo Jones 1	18
PLAC'D			
Hath plac'd amongst her virgin-traine:	34	E22 Daughter	9
Were yet unfound, and better plac'd in earth,	114	F12 Rutland	25
Were yet unfound, and better plac'd on earth,	114	F12 Rutland	V 25
Have you plac'd the banke of kisses,	136	U2 Cupid	25
He had so highly plac'd; and, in what Barbican.	256	U75 Epithalam.	V112
Of Body and Spirit together, plac'd betwixt	284	U84 Muse	54
PLACED			
Who placed Jasons Argo in the skie?	115	F12 Rutland	59
And with thy Angels, placed side, by side,	128	U1 Trinitie	46
PLACES			
They know the states of Christendome, not the places:	59	E92 New Crie	8
Of historie, and how to apt their places;	61	E95 Savile	28
Or common places, filch'd, that take these times,	116	F12 Rutland	88
Shall light those places	179	U25 Desmond	59
That have good places: therefore once agen,	212	U43 Vulcan	212
That have good places: wherefore once agen,	212	U43 Vulcan	V212
Pursue thee in all places,	221	U48 Bacchus	34
In secret places, flee the public baths.	349	Horace	V424
With specious places, and being humour'd right,	327	Horace	457
PLACING			
Are, by thy cunning placing, made meere new.	307	Horace	68
PLAÇ'T			
A Trench against it, nor a Battry plac't?	401	Beaumont	14
PLAGIARY			
To Proule the Plagiary.	54	E81 Proule	Ttl
PLAGUE			
Laden with plague-sores, and their sinnes, were heard,	84	E133 Voyage	17
The least of which was to the plague a cosen.	86	E133 Voyage	72
Cannot the Plague-bill keepe you backe? nor bells	88	E133 Voyage	173
It were a plague 'bove scorne,	147	U7 Nymph	12
Two letters were enough the plague to teare	172	U21 Ltl Shrub	3
PLAGUE-BILL			
Cannot the Plague-bill keepe you backe? nor bells	88	E133 Voyage	173
PLAGUES			
Light on thee: Or if those plagues will not doo,	212	U43 Vulcan	215
Light upon thee: Or if those plagues will not doo,	212	U43 Vulcan	V215
PLAGUE-SORES			
Laden with plague-sores, and their sinnes, were heard,	84	E133 Voyage	17
PLAID			
Who, with his axe, thy fathers mid-wife plaid.	107	F10 Proludium	15
Or else one that plaid his Ape,	132	U2 How he saw	31
And all the games of Fortune, plaid at Court;	234	U61 Epigram	2
Once seene, to be againe call'd for, and plaid,	317	Horace	271
PLAI'D			
He plai'd so truely.	77	E120 S. P.	16
PLAIES			
Who sings so sweet, and with such cunning plaies,	293	U87 Hor.3:9	10
PLAINE			
My praise is plaine, and where so ere profest,	67	E103 L Wroth 1	13
Plaine phrase, my Piso's, as alone, t'approve	321	Horace	342
Here, up the Alpes (not so plaine as to Dunstable)	374	Coryat 1	16
PLAINES			
And offer your just service on these plaines;	263	U79 New-yeares	12
That have a Flock, or Herd, upon these plaines;	265	U79 New-yeares	47
PLAISTERS			
Urine, and plaisters? when the noise doth beate	88	E133 Voyage	170
PLANETS			
That the eight spheare, no lesse, then planets seaven,	82	E130 Ferrab. 1	12
PLANT			
Some way of entrance) we must plant a guard	109	F11 Epode	7

	Page	Title	Line

PLANT (cont.)
Where men at once may plant, and gather blisses: . . . 170 U19 Elegy By 10
It was the Plant, and flowre of light. . . . 245 U70 Ode 72
Accept this garland, plant it on thy head, . . . 245 U70 Ode 77
And ev'ry Plant the sense surprize, . . . 251 U74 Weston 11
To plant the Musick where noe eare can reach! . . . 404 Inigo Jones 1 53
PLANTED
Then, in a soile hast planted me, . . . 101 F4 To the World 45
As what it spoke, it planted there. . . . 279 U84 Mind 36
By which yo'are planted, shew's your fruit shall bide. . . . 281 U84 Kenelme 19
That, planted round, there sing before the Lamb, . . . 285 U84 Muse 89
PLANTING
Planting their Purles, and Curles spread forth like Net, . . . 164 U15 Friend-Wars 65
PLANTS
Rare Plants from ev'ry banke doe rise, . . . 251 U74 Weston 10
that mongst so manie plants transplanted hether, . . . 361 Palmer 6
PLAT
Art, her false servant; Nor, for Sir Hugh Plat, . . . 188 U34 Small Poxe 7
PLATE
To have her linnen, plate, and all things nigh, . . . 96 F2 Penshurst 86
The richer hangings, or crowne-plate; . . . 96 F3 Wroth 8
And, so they ride in purple, eate in plate, . . . 99 F3 Wroth 89
I would present you now with curious plate . . . 260 U77 Treasurer 2
I would present you with some curious plate . . . 260 U77 Treasurer V 2
PLAUTUS
Or Plautus, and in Virgil disavow, . . . 309 Horace 78
Our Ancestors did Plautus numbers praise, . . . 323 Horace 399
Your Ancestors, old Plautus numbers prais'd, . . . 348 Horace V385/399
Neat Terence, witty Plautus, now not please; . . . 392 Shakespeare 52
PLAY'
Since when, hee's sober againe, and all play's made. . . . 56 E87 Hazard 6
PLAY
To Play-wright. . . . 42 E49 Playwrt 1 Ttl
Play-wright me reades, and still my verses damnes, . . . 42 E49 Playwrt 1 1
Play-wright, I loath to have thy manners knowne . . . 42 E49 Playwrt 1 5
On Play-wright. . . . 49 E68 Playwrt 2 Ttl
Play-wright convict of publike wrongs to men, . . . 49 E68 Playwrt 2 1
T'inveigh 'gainst playes: what did he then but play? . . . 52 E75 Lippe 4
Touch'd with the sinne of false play, in his punque, . . . 56 E87 Hazard 1
Discern'd no difference of his yeeres, or play, . . . 57 E90 Mill 8
On Play-wright. . . . 64 E100 Playwrt 3 Ttl
Play-wright, by chance, hearing some toyes I'had writ, . . . 64 E100 Playwrt 3 1
Five of my jests, then stolne, past him a play. . . . 64 E100 Playwrt 3 4
Tragick, or Comick; but thou writ'st the play. . . . 72 E112 Gamster 8
And, shifting of it's faces, doth play more . . . 74 E115 Honest Man 25
Play away, health, wealth, and fame. . . . 105 F8 Sicknesse 42
Men, if you love us, play no more . . . 145 U5 Woman-kind 1
Is not enough now, but the Nights to play: . . . 166 U15 Friend-Wars 132
Is not enough now, but the Nights we play: . . . 166 U15 Friend-Wars V132
And as false stampe there; parcels of a Play, . . . 204 U43 Vulcan 43
Is, she will play Dame Justice, too severe; . . . 229 U54 Squib 8
When you would play so nobly, and so free. . . . 230 U56 Covell 2
The Revells, and the Play, . . . 240 U67 Muses 46
Harke how the Bells upon the waters play . . . 253 U75 Epithalam. 33
And can tread firme, longs with like lads to play; . . . 315 Horace 226
Or play young tricks in over-wanton verse; . . . 347 Horace V350/358
Deserves no pardon; or who'd play, and sing . . . 329 Horace 531
They saw it halfe, damd thy whole play, and more; . . . 371 Fletcher 8
In presentacion of some puppet play! . . . 405 Inigo Jones 1 76
Unto the world, in praise of your first Play: . . . 414 Rutter 2
And weigh'd your Play: untwisted ev'ry thread, . . . 415 Rutter 14
PLAY'D
From the poore wretch, which though he play'd in prose, . . . 201 U42 Elegy Let 61
PLAYER
Whil'st thou dost rayse some Player, from the grave, . . . 81 E129 Mime 11
PLAYERS
'Twixt puritanes, and players, as some cry; . . . 52 E75 Lippe 2
Let pui'nees, porters, players praise delight, . . . 62 E96 Donne 2 10
PLAYES
He steales to ordinaries; there he playes . . . 30 E12 Shift 11
Or else to playes; and so to playes: . . . 30 E12 Shift 17
Buy the reversion of old playes; now growne . . . 45 E56 Poet-Ape 6
T'inveigh 'gainst playes: what did he then but play? . . . 52 E75 Lippe 4
All that they doe at Playes. O, but first here . . . 215 U44 Speach 91
To Church, as others doe to Feasts and Playes, . . . 222 U49 Pucell 16
How each one playes his part, of the large Pedigree. . . . 258 U75 Epithalam. 176
And they uncensur'd might at Feasts, and Playes . . . 319 Horace 297
Playes were found out; and rest, the end, and crowne . . . 329 Horace 499
Upon the Life, and Death of Playes, and Wits, . . . 370 Fletcher 2
Both learned, and unlearned, all write Playes. . . . 410 Brome 12
That sit to censure Playes, yet know not when, . . . 414 Rutter 8
PLAYING
And in his Mrs. flame, playing like a flye, . . . 149 U8 Houre-glasse 7
And in his Mrs. flaming, playing like a flye, . . . 149 U8 Houre-glasse V 7
Like Eccho playing from the other shore. . . . 249 U72 King 8
Like Eccho playing from another shore. . . . 249 U72 King V 8
PLAY'S
Since when, hee's sober againe, and all play's made. . . . 56 E87 Hazard 6
PLAY'ST
At this so subtile sport: and play'st so ill? . . . 72 E112 Gamster 2
PLAY-WRIGHT
To Play-wright. . . . 42 E49 Playwrt 1 Ttl
Play-wright me reades, and still my verses damnes, . . . 42 E49 Playwrt 1 1

		Page	Title	Line
PLAY-WRIGHT (cont.)				
Play-wright, I loath to have thy manners knowne	. . .	42	E49 Playwrt 1	5
On Play-wright.	. . .	49	E68 Playwrt 2	Ttl
Play-wright convict of publike wrongs to men,	. . .	49	E68 Playwrt 2	1
On Play-wright.	. . .	64	E100 Playwrt 3	Ttl
Play-wright, by chance, hearing some toyes I'had writ,	. .	64	E100 Playwrt 3	1
PLEA				
All this by Faith she saw, and fram'd a Plea,	. . . .	288	U84 Muse	209
PLEAD				
And thou, right guiltlesse, may'st plead to it, why?	. . .	36	E29 Tilter	2
PLEADED				
An Epigram to the Councellour that pleaded, . . .	. . .	186	U33 Councellour	Ttl
PLEADER				
Or Pleader at the Barre, that may come short	. . .	331	Horace	551
PLEADERS				
Upon the reverend Pleaders; doe now shut	. . .	187	U33 Councellour	10
PLEADINGS				
What are thy petulant pleadings, Chev'ril, then,	. .	44	E54 Chev'ril 2	3
PLEASANT				
Most pleasant Martial; Substance got with ease,	. . .	295	U90 Mart.10:47	2
The pleasant grounds, or when the River Rhine,	. . .	305	Horace	22
PLEASE				
Which shewes, where ever death doth please t'appeare,	. .	37	E32 Roe 2	9
What should, yet, thy pallat please?	.	105	F8 Sicknesse	21
But to please him, who is the dearer prise	. . .	119	F13 Aubigny	116
Which the prouder Beauties please, ...	.	133	U2 Suffered	2
I will tell what Man would please me.	. . .	140	U2 Her man	2
What you please, you parts may call, . . .	.	142	U2 Exception	7
Seeke doubting Men to please, ...	.	150	U10 Jealousie	15
Please your Majestie to make	.	260	U76 Petition	25
This hath pleas'd, doth please, and long will please; never	.	294	U88 Petronius	9
If custome please; at whose disposing will	. . .	309	Horace	103
If custome please, with whom both choyse, and will,	. .	341	Horace	V103
Doth please; this, ten times over, will delight.	. .	331	Horace	544
Neat Terence, witty Plautus, now not please;	. .	392	Shakespeare	52
That, while they bind the senses, doe so please?	. .	401	Filmer	2
And newer, then could please them, by-cause trew.	. .	415	Rutter	10
PLEAS'D				
And having pleas'd our art, wee'll try	. .	145	U5 Woman-kind	17
These, had'st thou pleas'd either to dine, or sup,	. .	206	U43 Vulcan	83
These, had'st thou been pleas'd either to dine, or sup,	. .	206	U43 Vulcan	V 83
(Which, some are pleas'd to stile but thy madde pranck)	. .	208	U43 Vulcan	131
O how will then our Court be pleas'd, . . .	.	251	U74 Weston	25
Exacts then she is pleas'd to pay: no suits,	. .	258	U75 Epithalam.	188
James the blessed, pleas'd the rather, . . .	.	259	U76 Petition	6
This hath pleas'd, doth please, and long will please; never	.	294	U88 Petronius	9
Soone angry, and soone pleas'd, is sweet, or sowre,	. .	315	Horace	227
Whil'st pleas'd Apollo	.	366	Ode Who saith	12
PLEASED				
and she is pleased.	.	417	Moon	36
PLEASES				
And at once three Senses pleases. . . .	.	657	Door Apollo	18
PLEASETH				
And pleaseth both. For while he melts his greace	. .	38	E37 Chev'ril	3
PLEASURE				
For none ere tooke that pleasure in sinnes sense,	. .	60	E94 Bedford 3	9
That, to make all pleasure theirs, . . .	.	105	F8 Sicknesse	36
And out of inward pleasure feed . . .	.	144	U3 Musicall	19
More pleasure while the thing he makes	. .	145	U5 Woman-kind	15
Our pleasure; but preserves us more	. .	146	U6 Defence	21
The pleasure is as good as none,	. .	147	U7 Nymph	6
Her joy in state, and pleasure;	. .	240	U67 Muses	44
Such pleasure as the teeming Earth,	. .	250	U74 Weston	1
At pleasure, to be call'd for, every day!	. .	271	U81 Pawlet	82
Doing, a filthy pleasure is, and short;	. .	294	U88 Petronius	1
Cast out by voyces; want they pleasure, then	. .	329	Horace	512
Those that in blood such violent pleasure have,	. .	363	Murder	1
PLEASURES				
In the past pleasures of his sensuall life,	. .	34	E25 Beast 1	2
Now, in whose pleasures I have this discerned,	. .	55	E85 Goodyere 1	11
That kept man living! Pleasures only sought!	. .	163	U15 Friend-Wars	44
None of their pleasures! nor will aske thee, why	. .	202	U42 Elegy Let	86
Are growne so fruitfull, and false pleasures climbe,	. .	224	U50 Countesse	10
No pleasures vaine did chime, . . .	.	246	U70 Ode	102
Let what thou fain'st for pleasures sake, be neere	. .	329	Horace	507
And the deceipt of pleasures, by Consent.	. .	411	Sutcliffe	11
PLEDGE				
And I will pledge with mine; . . .	.	106	F9 Celia 3	2
PLEDGES				
To pay your lord the pledges of chast love:	. .	119	F13 Aubigny	96
So, may those Mariage-Pledges, comforts prove:	. .	384	Somerset	19
PLENTEOUS				
Ne're came to taste the plenteous Mariage-horne.	. .	165	U15 Friend-Wars	100
With what full hands, and in how plenteous showers	. .	254	U75 Epithalam.	65
PLENTIE				
He knowes, below, he shall finde plentie of meate,	. .	95	F2 Penshurst	70
Hee gives all plentie, and encrease, . . .	.	265	U79 New-yeares	56
Hee gives all plentie, and encrease, . . .	.	265	U79 New-yeares	68
PLIE				
Rich men are said with many cups to plie,	. .	333	Horace	617
Now must we plie our ayme; our Swan's on wing.	. .	368	Ode Who saith	64
PLIGHT				
And take compassion on my grievous plight.	. .	127	U1 Trinitie	14

517

	Page	Title	Line

PLIGHT (cont.)
To worke the hearers minds, still, to their plight. . . 311 Horace 142

PLIGHTS
Askes first, Who gives her (I Charles) then he plights . . 256 U75 Epithalam. 124

PLOT
And of the poulder-plot, they will talke yet. . . . 59 E92 New Crie 32
The Plot, that was thy Wives inheritance. . . . . 209 U43 Vulcan V152
Thou Seed-plot of the warre, that hast not spar'd . . 213 U44 Speach 24

PLOUED
The apple-harvest and ploued land up cast; . . . . 98 F3 Wroth V 43

PLOUGH
In neighbour-townes, and feeles the weightie plough: . . 309 Horace 95
Hee'll be a Pilot, scarce can guide a Plough. . . . 410 Brome 18

PLOUGH'D
My Muse had plough'd with his, that sung A-jax. . . 89 E133 Voyage 196

PLOUGHING
Ploughing the mayne. When, see (the worst of all lucks) . 86 E133 Voyage 78

PLOVER
No Plover, or Coney . . . . 231 U57 Burges 22

PLUCK
To pluck a Garland, for her selfe, or mee? . . . 268 U81 Pawlet 4

PLUCKE
To plucke downe mine, Poll sets up new wits still, . . 50 E71 Parrat 1
That both for wit, and sense, so oft dost plucke, . . 73 E112 Gamster 18

PLUCK'D
I pluck'd a branch; the jealous god did frowne, . . 80 E126 Mrs Cary 3

PLUCKING
How plucking Peares, his owne hand grafted had, . . 290 U85 Country 19

PLUM
The earely cherry, with the later plum, ... 94 F2 Penshurst 41
An embleme of themselves, in plum, or peare. . . . 95 F2 Penshurst 56

PLUMED
That saw you put on Pallas plumed caske: . . . . 68 E105 L Wroth 2 16

PLUMES
A horse neck joyn, & sundry plumes ore-fold . . . 338 Horace V 2
There coole thy Plumes, ... 368 Ode Who saith 76

PLUSH
With Velvet, Plush, and Tissues, it is spirit. . . . 164 U15 Friend-Wars 58

PLUSHES
The Stuffes, the Velvets, Plushes, Fringes, Lace, . . 202 U42 Elegy Let 79

PLUTO
Tempt not his furie, Pluto is away: . . . . 89 E133 Voyage 179

PLUTO'S
But you will visit grisly Pluto's hall? . . . . 89 E133 Voyage 175

PLY
When youths ply their stolne delights. . . . . 103 F6 Celia 2 18
Let the old boy, your sonne, ply his old taske, . . 107 F10 Proludium 19
Ply it, and you all are mounted. . . . . . 657 Door Apollo 14

PLYE
Great men are said with many cups to plye, . . . 354 Horace V617

PO
At their returne, nor Po, ... 369 Ode Who saith 114

POCKET
Stinketh my credit, if into the Pocket . . . . 229 U54 Squib 14

POCKETS
They carry in their pockets Tacitus, ... 59 E92 New Crie 15

POCKETT
Made up still as the pockett doth abound. . . . 230 U56 Covell V 12

POCKIE
Lent him a pockie whore. Shee hath paid him. . . 31 E12 Shift 24

POD
Nor Captayne Pod, nor yet the Eltham-thing; . . . 62 E97 Motion 2
Thou dost out-zany Cokely, Pod; nay, Gue: . . . 81 E129 Mime 16

POEME
An Epick poeme; thou hast the same end. . . . 72 E112 Gamster 10
A Poeme, of no grace, weight, art, in rimes, . . . 327 Horace 456
Much in the Poeme shine, I will not bee . . . 329 Horace 526
So, any Poeme, fancied, or forth-brought . . . 331 Horace 561
Do crowne thy murdred Poeme: which shall rise . . 371 Fletcher 14

POEMES
That wish my poemes a legitimate fame, ... 32 E17 Critic 3
Whose poemes would not wish to be your booke? . . 60 E94 Bedford 3 4
Crowne with their owne. Rare poemes aske rare friends. . 60 E94 Bedford 3 6
Dare for these poemes, yet, both aske, and read, . . 60 E94 Bedford 3 12
From whence thy Modestie, or Poemes law . . . 313 Horace 193
To note in Poemes, breach of harmonie; . . . 323 Horace 388

POEM'S
Her Poem's beautie, but a sweet delight . . . . 311 Horace 141

POEMS
They hold in my strange poems, which, as yet, . . 115 F12 Rutland 81
Under-woods. Consisting Of Divers Poems. . . . 125 Under-wood Ttl
I. Poems Of Devotion. . . . . . . 127 Under-wood Ttl
Of Poems here describ'd, I can, nor use, . . . 311 Horace 127
Out better Poems? But I cannot buy . . . . 325 Horace 431
The Poems void of profit, our grave men . . . 329 Horace 511
On the honor'd Poems of his honored Friend, . . . 400 Beaumont Ttl

POESIE
Item, a faire greeke poesie for a ring: . . . . 51 E73 Fine Grand 10
And thinke it Poesie? . . . . 175 U23 Himselfe 22
As Painting, so is Poesie. Some mans hand . . . 329 Horace 539
Musique and Poesie: . . . . 401 Filmer 5

POESY
I found it pure, and perfect Poesy, ... 397 Drayton 24

	Page	Title	Line

POESY (cont.)
What Poesy ere was painted on a wall . . . . . . 406 Inigo Jones 1 97
POET'
For a good Poet's made, as well as borne. . . . . 392 Shakespeare 64
POET
For such a Poet, while thy dayes were greene, . . . 28 E4 James 1 5
And, I a Poet here, no Herald am. . . . . 29 E9 To All 4
Thou call'st me Poet, as a terme of shame: . . . 29 E10 Ignorant 1
On Poet-Ape. . . . . 44 E56 Poet-Ape Ttl
Poore Poet-Ape, that would be thought our chiefe, . 44 E56 Poet-Ape 1
Straight went I home; and there most like a Poet, . 55 E84 Bedford 2 5
Who shall doubt, Donne, where I a Poet bee, . . 62 E96 Donne 2 1
(Or Poet, in the court account) then I, ... 115 F12 Rutland 69
A better lover, and much better Poet. . . . . 182 U28 Worth 4
Not a Poet in an Age, ... 183 U29 Fit of Rime 26
And thou make many a Poet, ... 221 U48 Bacchus 29
My Answer. The Poet to the Painter. . . . . 226 U52 Answer Ttl
A Poet hath no more but black and white, . . . 227 U52 Answer 20
The Muse, or the Poet, ... 232 U57 Burges 25
One Poet, then of other folke ten score. . . . 235 U62 Charles 1 10
What can the Poet wish his King may doe, . . . 235 U62 Charles 1 13
(Without prophanenesse) yet, a Poet, cry, . . . 238 U66 Queene 4
(Without prophanenesse) as, a Poet, cry, . . . 238 U66 Queene V 4
His Poet Sack, the House-hold will not pay? . . . 241 U68 House-hold 2
For want of knowing the Poet, to say him nay? . . 241 U68 House-hold 4
His Poet leave to sing his House-hold true; . . . 241 U68 House-hold 6
To your Majestie your Poet: . . . . . . 259 U76 Petition 4
To his Poet of a Pension, ... 259 U76 Petition V 4
When I, who would her Poet have become, . . . 269 U81 Pawlet 17
What's left a Poet, when his Muse is gone? . . . 283 U84 Muse 28
But equall power, to Painter, and to Poet, . . . 305 Horace 11
Am I call'd Poet? wherefore with wrong shame, . . 311 Horace 129
For, being a Poet, thou maist feigne, create, . . 313 Horace 189
Had not our every Poet like offended. . . . . 325 Horace 414
The Poet, what becommeth, and what not: . . . 325 Horace 438
So doth the Poet, who is rich in land, ... 333 Horace 599
So doth the Poet, that is rich in Land, ... 353 Horace V599
Wise, sober folke, a frantick Poet feare, . . . 335 Horace 643
Those that are wise, a furious Poet feare, . . . 354 Horace V643
Of the Sicilian Poet Empedocles, ... 335 Horace 660
POET-APE
On Poet-Ape. . . . . 44 E56 Poet-Ape Ttl
Poore Poet-Ape, that would be thought our chiefe, . 44 E56 Poet-Ape 1
POETIQUE
Of a free Poetique Pension, ... 259 U76 Petition 10
Of the lesse-Poetique boyes; . . . . . 259 U76 Petition 20
Of the brave Poetique boyes; . . . . . 259 U76 Petition V 20
POETRIE
Ben. Jonson his best piece of poetrie. . . . . 41 E45 First Son 10
All good Poetrie hence was flowne, ... 183 U29 Fit of Rime 14
All the old Venusine, in Poetrie, ... 207 U43 Vulcan 89
What the old Venusine, in Poetrie, ... 207 U43 Vulcan V 89
With the old Venusine, in Poetrie, ... 207 U43 Vulcan V 89
The Poetrie of Steeples, with the Bells, . . . 249 U72 King 10
The Poetrie of Steeples, with their Bells, . . . 249 U72 King V 10
Horace, His Art of Poetrie Made English . . . 303 Horace Ttl
Horace, of The Art of Poetrie. . . . . . 305 Horace Ttl
The Bound, and Frontire of our Poetrie; . . . 400 Beaumont 8
POETRY
To a weake Gamster in Poetry. . . . . . 72 E112 Gamster Ttl
. . . the Art of Poetry to the Piso's. . . . 338 Horace VTtl
Not they that sided her, Dame Poetry, ... 403 Inigo Jones 1 36
Pack with your pedling Poetry to the Stage, . . 404 Inigo Jones 1 51
POET'S
For a good Poet's made, as well as borne. . . . 392 Shakespeare 64
POETS
How, best of Poets, do'st thou laurell weare! . . 28 E4 James 1 2
Of Kings for grace; of Poets for my test? . . . 28 E4 James 1 10
'Tofore, great men were glad of Poets: Now, . . 40 E43 Salisbury 1 5
From servile flatterie (common Poets shame) . . 41 E43 Salisbury 1 11
To honor, serve, and love; as Poets use. . . . 52 E76 Bedford 1 4
That Poets are far rarer births then kings, . . 53 E79 Rutland 1
So many Poets life, by one should live. . . . 57 E89 Allen 14
Shee brought the Poets forth, but ours th'adventer. 84 E133 Voyage 20
Can Poets hope to fetter mee? . . . . . 93 F1 Why write no 5
Or whose great name in Poets heaven use, . . . 107 F10 Proludium 2
But onely Poets, rapt with rage divine? . . . 115 F12 Rutland 63
But holie Poets, rapt with sence divine? . . . 115 F12 Rutland V 63
Poets, though divine, are men: . . . . . 131 U2 Excuse 5
No Poets verses yet did ever move, ... 199 U42 Elegy Let 3
His lynes, and hourely sits the Poets horse? . . 200 U42 Elegy Let 8
But is the Poets matter: And he must, . . . 200 U42 Elegy Let 17
To cure the Poets Evill, Povertie: . . . . 235 U62 Charles 1 6
For in the Genius of a Poets Verse, ... 241 U68 House-hold 13
Of which we Priests, and Poets say . . . . 245 U70 Ode 82
And so warme the Poets tongue . . . . . 260 U76 Petition 31
To Roman Poets. Shall I therefore weave . . . 323 Horace 390
Our Poets, too, left nought unproved here; . . 323 Horace 405
Exclude all sober Poets, from their share . . . 325 Horace 421
But fame of Poets, they thinke, if they come forth, 325 Horace 426
Poets would either profit, or delight, . . . 327 Horace 477
To divine Poets, and their Verses came. . . . 327 Horace 492

	Page	Title	Line
POETS (cont.)			
Poets should ever be indifferent.	331	Horace	556
Let Poets perish, that will not be kept.	335	Horace	664
For though the Poets matter, Nature be,	392	Shakespeare	57
Shine forth, thou Starre of Poets, and with rage,	392	Shakespeare	77
The Poets act! and for his Country's sake	398	Drayton	63
And the Poets' Horse accounted.	657	Door Apollo	13
POINT (See also POYNTE)			
Live to that point I will, for which I am man,	219	U47 Tribe	59
So that upon the point, my corporall feare	229	U54 Squib	7
Find all our Atomes from a point t' a span!	287	U84 Muse	152
These Mysteries do point to three more great,	413	Ghyrlond	29
Till he hath reach'd his two-fold point of Noone.	414	Ghyrlond	52
POINTED			
Upon his pointed Lance:	240	U67 Muses	39
POINTS			
Then thou did'st late my sense, loosing my points.	45	E58 Groome	6
Feed those, at whom the Table points at still?	155	U13 Sacvile	74
POISON (See POYSON)			
POLAND			
In Hungary, and Poland, Turkie too;	69	E107 Hungry	13
POLICIE			
'Tis the securest policie we have,	109	F11 Epode	17
POLISH'D			
Of polish'd pillars, or a roofe of gold:	93	F2 Penshurst	3
Nay, her white and polish'd neck,	137	U2 Cupid	29
Sonnes, seeke not me amonge these polish'd stones:	387	Cavendish	1
POLISHT			
So polisht, perfect, round, and even,	280	U84 Mind	55
POLITIQUE			
Of politique pretext, that wryes a State,	177	U25 Desmond	29
Of politique pretext, that swayes a State,	177	U25 Desmond	V 29
In Politique, and Militar Affaires.	214	U44 Speach	60
You aske noe more then certeyne politique Eyes,	404	Inigo Jones 1	45
POLL			
To plucke downe mine, Poll sets up new wits still,	50	E71 Parrat	1
POLLUTED'			
Polluted, touch't: but certainly he's mad:	355	Horace	V673
POLLUX			
And, on they went, like Castor brave, and Pollux:	86	E133 Voyage	77
POLY			
Of all that reade thy Poly-Olbyon.	397	Drayton	52
POLY-OLBYON			
Of all that reade thy Poly-Olbyon.	397	Drayton	52
POLYPHEME			
Of the hulke touch'd, and, as by Polypheme	87	E133 Voyage	112
Scylla, Charybdis, Polypheme, with these.	315	Horace	206
POMPE			
Without the pompe of Counsell; or more Aide,	186	U32 Elsmere	3
Comes in the pompe, and glorie	240	U67 Muses	28
With all the pompe of Youth, and all our Court beside.	254	U75 Epithalam.	72
Of sorrow, then all pompe of gaudy daies:	287	U84 Muse	182
What is the cause you pompe it soe? I aske,	403	Inigo Jones 1	29
POMP'D			
Or pomp'd for those hard trifles, Anagrams,	204	U43 Vulcan	35
Or pomp'd for those fine trifles, Anagrams,	204	U43 Vulcan	V 35
POMPEY			
The name of Pompey for an enemie,	71	E110 Edmonds 1	3
POMPEY'S			
As neither Pompey's popularitie,	395	May	9
POMPILIUS			
But you, Pompilius off-spring, spare you not	325	Horace	415
POMPOUS			
In Ireland, Holland, Sweden, pompous lies,	69	E107 Hungry	12
PONDEROUS			
thus, as a ponderous thinge in water cast	361	Palmer	17
PONDS			
Thou hast thy ponds, that pay thee tribute fish,	94	F2 Penshurst	32
POOLE			
By this time had they reach'd the Stygian poole,	87	E133 Voyage	121
And, now, above the poole, a face right fat	88	E133 Voyage	160
POOLY'			
And we will have no Pooly', or Parrot by;	65	E101 Supper	36
POOR			
Not snatch them hence in one poor minutes rage.	205	U43 Vulcan	V 56
I'll laugh at thee poor wretched Tike, go send	410	Gill	10
Hang up all the poor Hop-Drinkers,	657	Door Apollo	7
POORE			
Not his poore cocatrice but he betrayes	31	E12 Shift	21
His clothes two fashions of, and poore! his sword	33	E21 Gam'ster	3
Blaspheme god, greatly. Or some poore hinde beat,	36	E28 Surly	17
Indeed, poore Giles he married ever.	40	E42 Giles	3
Poore Poet-Ape, that would be thought our chiefe,	44	E56 Poet-Ape	1
To night, grave sir, both my poore house, and I	64	E101 Supper	1
Twirle the poore chaine you run a feasting in.	69	E107 Hungry	30
Makes the poore Banck-side creature wet it' shoone,	84	E133 Voyage	30
Poore Mercury, crying out on Paracelsus,	86	E133 Voyage	96
Of a few poore houshold spyes?	102	F5 Celia 1	12
That, at thy birth, mad'st the poore Smith affraid,	107	F10 Proludium	14
While thus it buyes great grace, and hunts poore fame;	113	F12 Rutland	15
While thus it gets grace, and hunts poore fame;	113	F12 Rutland	V 15
To vent that poore desire,	150	U10 Jealousie	5
My Sword ('tis but a poore Sword, understand)	154	U13 Sacvile	54
As farre as any poore Sword i' the Land.	154	U13 Sacvile	55

	Page	Title	Line
POORE (cont.)			
Or robbing the poore Market-folkes should nurse	155	U13 Sacvile	90
Honour and honestie, as poore things thought	163	U15 Friend-Wars	42
The Husband now's call'd churlish, or a poore	165	U15 Friend-Wars	89
As a poore single flatterer, without Baud,	167	U15 Friend-Wars	158
Of the poore sufferers) where the envious, proud,	167	U15 Friend-Wars	167
Then ope thy wardrobe, thinke me that poore Groome	201	U42 Elegy Let	51
From the poore wretch, which though he play'd in prose,	201	U42 Elegy Let	61
Let the poore fooles enjoy their follies, love	202	U42 Elegy Let	81
Sindge Capons, or poore Pigges, dropping their eyes;	205	U43 Vulcan	53
I saw with two poore Chambers taken in,	209	U43 Vulcan	135
Let poore Nobilitie be vertuous: Wee,	215	U44 Speach	79
Those are poore Ties, depend on those false ends,	216	U45 Squib	11
When, being the Strangers helpe, the poore mans aide,	217	U46 Coke	7
To his poore Instrument, now out of grace.	223	U49 Pucell	34
Poore wretched states, prest by extremities,	248	U71 Treasurer	1
The Humble Petition of Poore Ben.	259	U76 Petition	Ttl
When they are poore, and banish'd, must throw by	311	Horace	138
Poore Io wandring; wild Orestes mad:	313	Horace	177
Fortune would love the poore, and leave the proud.	319	Horace	286
With poore base termes, through every baser shop:	321	Horace	334
Make a great Supper; or for some poore man	333	Horace	602
Poore Tom have we cause to suspect just thee?	381	Coryat 3	58
But bawle thou on; I pitty thee, poore Curre,	408	Detractor	7
POORES			
The poores full Store-house, and just servants field.	185	U30 Burleigh	8
O pietie! so to weigh the poores estates!	235	U62 Charles 1	11
POPE			
And at the Pope, and Spaine slight faces make.	59	E92 New Crie	34
POPENHEIM			
Of Hannow, Shieter-huissen, Popenheim,	69	E107 Hungry	25
POPERIE			
Bred on the Banck, in time of Poperie,	209	U43 Vulcan	143
POPES			
Upon th'Exchange, still, out of Popes-head-Alley;	206	U43 Vulcan	80
POPES-HEAD-ALLEY			
Upon th'Exchange, still, out of Popes-head-Alley;	206	U43 Vulcan	80
POPLAR			
The Poplar tall, he then doth marrying twine	290	U85 Country	9
POPPIE			
As Poppie, and Sardane honey; 'cause without	331	Horace	559
POPPY			
Poppy, with hony of Sardus; 'cause without	351	Horace	V535/559
POPULAR			
On popular noise with, and doe businesse in.	311	Horace	120
Of popular noyses, borne to actuate things.	341	Horace	V120
POPULARITIE			
As neither Pompey's popularitie,	395	May	9
PORCHES			
Free from proud porches, or their guilded roofes,	97	F3 Wroth	15
PORC'LANE			
And animated Porc'lane of the Court,	219	U47 Tribe	53
PORING			
Poring, as on a Map, to find the wayes	288	U84 Muse	196
PORT			
The many perills of this Port, and how	85	E133 Voyage	47
Hath rais'd to be the Port unto his Land!	250	U73 Weston	4
Of that eternall Port kept ope'	274	U84 Cradle	39
PORTA			
They all get Porta, for the sundrie wayes	59	E92 New Crie	25
PORTERS			
Let pui'nees, porters, players praise delight,	62	E96 Donne 2	10
PORTING			
Porting the Ensignes of united Two,	254	U75 Epithalam.	51
PORTION			
I have no portion in them, nor their deale	218	U47 Tribe	27
Till either grew a portion of the other:	247	U70 Ode	110
And saw that portion of her selfe to die.	282	U84 Muse	14
PORTIONS			
Our native portions, and possessed rent;	286	U84 Muse	142
PORTLAND			
. . . made Earle of Portland. 17. Febr. 1632. To the Envious.	250	U73 Weston	Ttl
PORTS			
The ports of death are sinnes; of life, good deeds:	53	E80 Life/Death	1
At th'eye and eare (the ports unto the minde)	109	F11 Epode	9
Peace, and the open ports, that peace doth cause.	317	Horace	284
The open ports, and sports that peace doth cause,	345	Horace	V284
POSSESSE			
Thou rather striv'st the matter to possesse,	70	E109 Nevil	9
That though they did possesse each limbe,	151	U12 Corbet	9
Of sweets, and safeties, they possesse by Peace.	261	U77 Treasurer	22
Fame and Honour you, they possesse by Peace.	261	U77 Treasurer	V 22
POSSESSED			
Our native portions, and possessed rent;	286	U84 Muse	142
POSSESSIONS			
And change possessions, oftner with his breath,	99	F3 Wroth	75
(Brave Youths) th'are their possessions, none of yours:	281	U84 Kenelme	11
POSSEST			
And not being borrow'd by thee, but possest.	187	U33 Councellour	28
Possest with holy rage,	245	U70 Ode	80
Yet know, with what thou art possest,	281	U84 Mind	70
Her soule possest her fleshes state	399	Lady Ogle	25

	Page	Title	Line

POST   (VERB)
Now, Sun, and post away the rest of day: . . . . . 257 U75 Epithalam. 138

POST
And, hood-wink'd, for a man, embrace a post. . . . . 45 E58 Groome 8

POSTERITIE
The light, and marke unto posteritie? . . . . 67 E104 Montgomery 12
Goe on, and doubt not, what posteritie, ... 70 E109 Nevil 15
No, I doe, therefore, call Posteritie . . . . 80 E127 Aubigny 4
To all posteritie; I will write Burlase. . . . . 227 U52 Answer 24
With a long, large, and blest posteritie! . . . . 236 U63 Charles 2 12
It brings Friends Joy, Foes Griefe, Posteritie Fame; . . 256 U75 Epithalam. 114
For Fame keepes Vertue up, and it Posteritie. . . . 257 U75 Epithalam. 152
Which I have vow'd posteritie to give. . . . 262 U78 Digby 18
T' inlive posteritie, her Fame may tell! . . . . 269 U81 Pawlet 34
Eupheme; Or, The Faire Fame Left To Posteritie . . . . 272 U84 Eupheme Ttl
That all Posteritie, as wee, ... 273 U84 Cradle 13
Charles Cavendish to his posteritie. . . . . 387 Cavendish Ttl
With the Glad Countrey, and Posteritie: . . . . 416 Dover 6

POSTES
On the new priming of thy old Signe postes . . . 405 Inigo Jones 1 87

POSTS
Nor have my title-leafe on posts, or walls, . . . 28 E3 Bookseller 7

POSTURE
And one true posture, though besieg'd with ill . . 66 E102 Pembroke 14
But on thy practise, and the Posture booke: . . . 213 U44 Speach 28
Light, Posture, Height'ning, Shadow, Culloring, . . 370 Author 3

POT
Or your complexions losse? you have a pot, . . . 46 E62 Would-bee 6
When their pot-guns ayme to hit, ... 259 U76 Petition 21
When their pot-guns thinke to fitt, ... 259 U76 Petition V 21

POT-GUNS
When their pot-guns ayme to hit, ... 259 U76 Petition 21
When their pot-guns thinke to fitt, ... 259 U76 Petition V 21

'POTHECARIE
Your 'pothecarie, and his drug sayes no. . . . . 46 E62 Would-bee 4

POTIONS
His spirits, now, in pills, and eeke in potions, . . 86 E133 Voyage 101

POTS
Or the prest honey in pure pots doth keepe . . . 290 U85 Country 15

POTTLE
Here he speaks out of his Pottle, ... 657 Door Apollo 3

POULDER
And of the poulder-plot, they will talke yet. . . 59 E92 New Crie 32

POULDER-PLOT
And of the poulder-plot, they will talke yet. . . 59 E92 New Crie 32

POULDERS
Let 'hem on poulders, oyles, and paintings, spend, . 118 F13 Aubigny 77

POULES
The weekly Corrants, with Poules stall; and all . . 206 U43 Vulcan V 81

POUND
Ridway rob'd Duncote of three hundred pound, . . 29 E8 Robbery 1
Many a pound, and piece, will place one well; . . 155 U13 Sacvile 78
To catch the flesh in, and to pound a Prick. . . 164 U15 Friend-Wars 67
For t'other pound of sweet-meats, he shall feele . 164 U15 Friend-Wars 77
Full twentie stone; of which I lack two pound: . 229 U54 Squib 12
His weight is twenty Stone within two pound; . . 230 U56 Covell 11
A pound, or piece, by their long compting arts: . 327 Horace 466
An ounce, what makes it then? The halfe pound just; . 327 Horace 471
From thirty pound in pipkins, to the Man . . . 402 Inigo Jones 1 2
Th'envy'd returne, of forty pound in gold. . . . 408 Detractor 4

POUNDS
An Epigram. To K. Charles for a 100. Pounds . . . . 235 U62 Charles 1 Ttl
Those your Fathers Markes, your Pounds; . . . 260 U76 Petition 27

POURE
Melt downe their husbands land, to poure away . . 118 F13 Aubigny 73
And Gunnes there, spare to poure . . . . 239 U67 Muses 8

POUR'D
And many a sinke pour'd out her rage anenst 'hem; . 86 E133 Voyage 75
And that pour'd out upon Man-kind can be! . . 172 U20 Shrub 19
As smooth as Oyle pour'd forth, and calme . . 280 U84 Mind 59

POURING
Of Gathering? Bountie' in pouring out againe? . 159 U14 Selden 38
All, pouring their full showre of graces downe, . 413 Ghyrlond 31

POVERTIE
Sure, willing povertie lives most in you. . . . 29 E6 Alchymists 2
And which thou brought'st me, welcome povertie. . 48 E65 Muse 12
To cure the Poets Evill, Povertie: . . . . 235 U62 Charles 1 6

POWDER
And for it lose his eyes with Gun-powder, . . . 208 U43 Vulcan 121
But we have Powder still for the Kings Day, . . 213 U44 Speach 2
Powder, or paper, to bring up the youth . . . 213 U44 Speach 25

POWDERS
Sweet bags, sweet Powders, nor sweet words will passe . 165 U15 Friend-Wars 112

POWER
Had power to act, what they to faine had not. . . 84 E133 Voyage 6
And thinke his power doth equall Fates. . . . 99 F3 Wroth 80
Doe I reflect. Some alderman has power, . . . 117 F13 Aubigny 38
If, Sackvile, all that have the power to doe . . 153 U13 Sacvile 1
In will and power, only to defeat. . . . . 191 U38 Elegy 'Tis 18
Or if thou needs would'st trench upon her power, . 204 U43 Vulcan 48
or if thou wouldst enforce the power from her, . 204 U43 Vulcan V 48
Though but in daunces, it shall know his power; . 210 U43 Vulcan 157
Though but in daunces, it shall know high power; . 210 U43 Vulcan V157

	Page	Title	Line
POWER (cont.)			
Though but in daunger, it snall know thy power;	210	U43 Vulcan	V157
Your Power of handling shadow, ayre, and spright,	227	U52 Answer	17
Wee know no other power then his,	265	U79 New-yeares	42
Pan knowes no other power then his,	265	U79 New-yeares	64
As being the Sonne of Man) to shew his Power,	288	U84 Muse	217
Where first his Power will appeare, by call	289	U84 Muse	220
But equall power, to Painter, and to Poet,	305	Horace	11
His choise, who's matter to his power doth reare,	339	Horace	V 58/ 56
His matter to his power, in all he makes,	307	Horace	57
The power, and rule of speaking resteth still.	309	Horace	104
His power of foulely hurting made to cease.	323	Horace	370
Of eloquent Messalla's power in Court,	331	Horace	552
"Musicke hath power to draw,	367	Ode Who saith	47
But higher power, as spight could not make lesse,	401	Beaumont	18
The House of gold, the Gate of heavens power,	413	Ghyrlond	39
deignes myne the power to find, yett want I will	421	Censure	10
POWERFULL			
It was the day, what time the powerfull Moone	84	E133 Voyage	29
POWERS			
But for their powers, accept my pietie.	31	E14 Camden	14
Whose manners draw, more than thy powers constraine.	37	E35 James 2	3
I purpos'd her; that should, with even powers,	52	E76 Bedford 1	14
And hath it, in his powers, to make his way!	53	E80 Life/Death	4
With all my powers, my selfe to loose?	101	F4 To the World	28
My gratefull soule, the subject of her powers,	115	F12 Rutland	73
To be beholders, when their powers are spent.	166	U15 Friend-Wars	140
Such are his powers, whom time hath stil'd,	189	U36 Song	13
And fills my powers with perswading joy,	191	U38 Elegy 'Tis	11
To shift their seasons, and destroy their powers!	199	U41 Elegy Since	10
Have multipli'd their arts, and powers,	251	U74 Weston	17
Am turned with an others powers. My Passion	283	U84 Muse	31
The Dominations, Vertues, and the Powers,	285	U84 Muse	87
A quiet mind; free powers; and body sound;	295	U90 Mart.10:47	6
Was said to move the stones, by his Lutes powers,	327	Horace	484
weare made the objects to my weaker powers;	361	Palmer	3
POWRE			
Shall powre forth many a line, drop many a letter,	666	Glover	9
POX			
Pox on your flameship, Vulcan; if it be	211	U43 Vulcan	191
Pox on your fire workes, Vulcan; if it be	211	U43 Vulcan	V191
Pox on thee, Vulcan, thy Pandora's pox,	212	U43 Vulcan	213
Thy Wives pox on thee, and B.B.'s too.	212	U43 Vulcan	216
Thy Wives pox on thee, and Bess Broughtons too.	212	U43 Vulcan	V216
POXE			
Shuns prease, for two maine causes, poxe, and debt,	76	E119 Shelton	4
An Epigram. To the small Poxe.	188	U34 Small Poxe	Ttl
POYNTE			
still that same little poynte hee was; but when	383	Rich	13
POYNTES			
hath armde att all poyntes; charge mee humblye kneele	382	Rich	2
POYSON			
Though poyson, thinke it a great fate.	99	F3 Wroth	90
Out of his Grave, and poyson every eare.	172	U21 Ltl Shrub	4
PRACTICE			
Nor lesse in practice; but lesse mark'd, lesse knowne:	58	E91 Vere	14
PRACIISD			
But in the practisd truth Destruction is	404	Inigo Jones 1	57
PRACTISE			
Such her quaint practise is, so it allures,	39	E41 Gypsee	3
Vertuously practise must at least allow	75	E116 Jephson	14
Of old, even by her practise, to be fam'd;	82	E130 Ferrab. 1	10
By arts, and practise of the vicious,	117	F13 Aubigny	12
Donnor's or Donnee's, to their practise shall	158	U13 Sacvile	163
Nothing, but practise upon honours thrall.	179	U25 Desmond	35
Thy sincere practise, breeds not thee a fame	187	U33 Councellour	39
Was drawne to practise other hue, then that	188	U34 Small Poxe	8
But on thy practise, and the Posture booke:	213	U44 Speach	28
They learne and studie; and then practise there.	215	U44 Speach	92
And practise for a Miracle; take heed,	223	U49 Pucell	41
When your assiduous practise doth secure	236	U64 Charles 3	11
The good, and durst not practise it, were glad	247	U70 Ode	119
PRACTIS'D			
Not boasted in your life, but practis'd true,	225	U50 Countesse	32
PRACTISES			
The councels, projects, practises they know,	59	E92 New Crie	11
PRACTIZ'D			
Well knowne, and practiz'd borrowers on their word,	154	U13 Sacvile	48
In practiz'd friendship wholly to reprove,	190	U37 Friend-Book	26
PRAECIPICE			
This Praecipice, and Rocks that have no end,	166	U15 Friend-Wars	130
PRAEOCCUPIE			
Being, the best clothes still to praeoccupie.	201	U42 Elegy Let	42
PRAEVARICATORS			
Praevaricators swarme. Of which the store,	167	U15 Friend-Wars	170
PRAISE (See also PRAYSE)			
For vulgar praise, doth it too dearely buy.	27	E2 My Booke	14
And which no' affection praise enough can give!	34	E23 Donne 1	6
All which I meant to praise, and, yet, I would;	34	E23 Donne 1	9
Dispraise my worke, then praise it frostily:	43	E52 Courtling	2
Thy praise, or dispraise is to me alike,	46	E61 Foole	1
Since men have left to doe praise-worthy things,	49	E67 Suffolk	1
Still, 'tis his lucke to praise me 'gainst his will.	50	E71 Parrat	2

	Page	Title	Line
PRAISE (cont.)			
Where, though 't be love, that to thy praise doth move	55	E86 Goodyere 2	7
Let pui'nees, porters, players praise delight,	62	E96 Donne 2	10
Whose life, ev'n they, that envie it, must praise;	66	E102 Pembroke	16
Need any Muses praise to give it fame?	66	E103 L Wroth 1	6
My praise is plaine, and where so ere profest,	67	E103 L Wroth 1	13
Their latter praise would still the greatest bee,	68	E106 E Herbert	9
As but to speake thee, Overbury, is praise:	73	E113 Overbury	2
Retyr'd, with purpose your faire worth to praise,	80	E126 Mrs Cary	1
If to admire were to commend, my praise	83	E132 Sylvester	1
Did'st thou, then, make 'hem! and what praise was heap'd	95	F2 Penshurst	83
These, Penshurst, are thy praise, and yet not all.	96	F2 Penshurst	89
To Sir Robert Wroth in praise of a Country life. Epode.	96	F3 Wroth	VTtl
Nor o're-praise, nor yet condemne;	142	U2 Her man	47
Nor out-praise, nor yet condemne;	142	U2 Her man	V 47
Unto their praise, in certaine swearing rites!	156	U13 Sacvile	102
Before men get a verse: much lesse a Praise;	159	U14 Selden	26
I yeeld, I yeeld, the matter of your praise	160	U14 Selden	61
Though Beautie be the Marke of praise,	173	U22 Elegy Tho	1
As not the World can praise too much,	173	U22 Elegy Tho	3
Nor a lyne deserving praise,	183	U29 Fit of Rime	29
Engines of Murder, and receive the praise	212	U43 Vulcan	207
Engines of Murder, and enjoy with praise	212	U43 Vulcan	V207
More then to praise a Dog? or Horse? or speake	215	U44 Speach	71
No lesse of praise, then readers in all kinds	217	U46 Coke	19
And though all praise bring nothing to your name,	224	U50 Countesse	13
His judgement is; If he be wise, and praise,	232	U58 Book-seller	5
And praise them too. O! what a fame 't will be?	263	U78 Digby	25
Heare, o you Groves, and, Hills, resound his praise.	264	U79 New-yeares	23
Else, who doth praise a person by a new,	270	U81 Pawlet	37
A new Song to his praise, and great I Am:	285	U84 Muse	90
The Youths and tender Maids shall sing thy praise:	292	U86 Hor.4:1	26
Most worthie praise, when words that common grew,	307	Horace	67
Most worthie praise, when words that vulgar grew,	340	Horace	V 67
The place allotted it, with decent praise.	341	Horace	V131/125
Praise the spare diet, wholsome justice, lawes,	317	Horace	283
And not without much praise; till libertie	321	Horace	366
Our Ancestors did Plautus numbers praise,	323	Horace	399
Being men were covetous of nought, but praise.	327	Horace	463
His proofe their praise, will meete, as in this line.	362	Author	14
In thought to praise this Ladie,	365	Ode Splendor	18
Least a false praise do make theyr dotage his.	385	Husband	4
May hurt them more with praise, then Foes with spight.	386	Browne	2
As neither Man, nor Muse, can praise too much.	390	Shakespeare	4
Were not the paths I meant unto thy praise:	390	Shakespeare	6
Or crafty Malice, might pretend this praise,	391	Shakespeare	11
Should praise a Matron. What could hurt her more?	391	Shakespeare	14
And we have wits to read, and praise to give.	391	Shakespeare	24
And doth deserve all muniments of praise,	400	Beaumont	9
Unto the world, in praise of your first Play:	414	Rutter	2
PRAIS'D			
Or, if shee would but modestly have prais'd	46	E60 Mounteagle	3
For worth he has not, He is tax'd, not prais'd.	48	E65 Muse	16
So both the prais'd, and praisers suffer: Yet,	116	F13 Aubigny	5
So hath Homer prais'd her haire:	136	U2 Cupid	13
Men past their termes, and prais'd some names too much,	159	U14 Selden	21
That would, perhaps, have prais'd, and thank'd the same,	161	U14 Selden	70
Equall with her? or Ronsart prais'd	181	U27 Ode Helen	10
In him the times, no lesse then Prince, are prais'd,	256	U75 Epithalam.	115
Your Ancestors, old Plautus numbers prais'd,	348	Horace	V385/399
PRAISER			
I, Madame, am become your praiser. Where,	117	F13 Aubigny	21
The Scoffer, the true Praiser doth out-goe.	333	Horace	616
PRAISERS			
And even the praisers judgement suffers so.	64	E99 Th Roe 2	10
As lowdest praisers, who perhaps would find	67	E103 L Wroth 1	11
So both the prais'd, and praisers suffer: Yet,	116	F13 Aubigny	5
His praisers to their gaine: but say he can	353	Horace	V601
PRAISES			
Most thinke all praises flatteries. But truth brings	49	E67 Suffolk	2
When these were but the praises of the Art.	82	E130 Ferrab. 1	16
Our owne false praises, for your ends:	145	U5 Woman-kind	4
His unjust hopes, with praises begg'd, or (worse)	162	U15 Friend-Wars	12
Made longer by our praises. Or, if not,	200	U42 Elegy Let	21
Sound, sound his praises loud, and with his, hers divide.	264	U79 New-yeares	19
Whose praises let's report unto the Woods,	265	U79 New-yeares	52
The praises of a Countrie life.	289	U85 Country	Ttl
For praises, where the mind conceales a foxe.	333	Horace	622
For praises, where the mind harbours a foxe.	354	Horace	V622
If Praises, when th'are full, heaping admit,	385	Brooke	6
PRAISE-WORTHY			
Since men have left to doe praise-worthy things,	49	E67 Suffolk	1
PRAISEWORTHY			
Is more praiseworthy still,	112	F11 Epode	V 88
PRAISING			
When I am hoarse, with praising his each cast,	167	U15 Friend-Wars	151
PRANCK			
(Which, some are pleas'd to stile but thy madde pranck)	208	U43 Vulcan	131
PRANKES			
That had, so often, shew'd 'hem merry prankes.	89	E133 Voyage	184
PRATING			
And so their prating to present was best,	321	Horace	329

PRATLING
And so their pratling to present were best, ... 346 Horace V321/329
'PRAY
'Pray thee, feed contented, then, ... 105 F8 Sicknesse 13
PRAY   (See also PR'Y)
Pray thee, take care, that tak'st my booke in hand, . . . 27 E1 Reader 1
Nor, when I take my lodging, need I pray . . . . . 95 F2 Penshurst 72
Each morne, and even, they are taught to pray, ... 96 F2 Penshurst 95
And pray who shall my sorrowes read, ... 152 U12 Corbet 33
And pray the fruites thereof, and the increase; . . . 212 U43 Vulcan 210
I wish all well, and pray high heaven conspire . . . . 219 U47 Tribe 37
For whose returnes, and many, all these pray: . . . . 225 U51 Bacon 6
To teach the people, how to fast, and pray, ... 235 U61 Epigram 18
That cry that gladnesse, which their hearts would pray, . . 249 U72 King 14
We pray may grace . . . . . 257 U75 Epithalam. 158
Long intermitted, pray thee, pray thee spare: 292 U86 Hor.4:1 2
Hide faults, pray to the Gods, and wish aloud . . . . 319 Horace 285
Hide faults, and pray to th'gods, and wish aloud . . . 345 Horace V285
And pray, thy joyes as lasting bee, as great. . . . . 384 Somerset 8
And pray thee Reader, bring thy weeping Eyes . . . . 394 Jane Ogle 2
There, thou art Homer! Pray thee, use the stile . . . 398 Drayton 59
PRAY'D
Ideot, last night, I pray'd thee but forbeare . . . . 45 E58 Groome 1
PRAYER
Be thankes to him, and earnest prayer, to finde . . . 99 F3 Wroth 101
Is thankes to him, and earnest prayer, to finde . . . 99 F3 Wroth V101
May to thy name a Pagan prayer say; . . . . . 208 U43 Vulcan V120
I would, if price, or prayer could them get, ... 260 U77 Treasurer 5
For, Prayer is the Incense most perfumes . . . . 288 U84 Muse 187
PRAYERS
Of discontent; or that these prayers bee . . . . 122 F15 Heaven 25
Not at my prayers, but your sense; which laid . . . . 153 U13 Sacvile 9
What prayers (People) can you thinke too much? . . . 249 U72 King 20
PRAYES
The holy Prelate prayes, then takes the Ring, ... 256 U75 Epithalam. 123
PRAYSE
Of adding to thy prayse; thine may to me, ... 41 E43 Salisbury 1 V 8
An Ode in Horace in prayse of a Countrye lyfe, Translated. . 289 U85 Country VTtl
Let such as justly have out-liv'd all prayse, ... 387 Cavendish 5
A list of Epithites: And prayse this way. . . . . 394 Jane Ogle 8
PRAYSED
make many, hurt themselves; a praysed faith . . . . 422 Lucan 2
make many, hurt himselfe; a praysed faith . . . . 422 Lucan V 2
PRAYSER
Above his Reader, or his Prayser, is. . . . . 400 Beaumont 2
PRAYSES
That seeming prayses, are, yet accusations. . . . . 75 E115 Honest Man 32
PRAYSEST
When even there, where most thou praysest mee, . . . 44 E55 Beaumont 9
PREACH
In his humanitie! To heare him preach . . . . 286 U84 Muse 133
PREASE
Shuns prease, for two maine causes, poxe, and debt, . . 76 E119 Shelton 4
Contagion in the prease is soonest catch'd. . . . . 118 F13 Aubigny 58
PRECEDE
That strives, his manners should precede his wit. . . . 78 E121 Rudyerd 1 8
PRECEDENT
Repent thee not of thy faire precedent, ... 73 E113 Overbury 9
PRECEDING
Save the preceding Two? . . . . . 255 U75 Epithalam. 77
PRECEPTS
The docile mind may soone thy precepts know, ... 329 Horace 504
PRECIOUS   (See PRETIOUS)
PRECIPICE   (See PRAECIPICE)
PRECIPITATED
Or were precipitated downe the jakes, ... 87 E133 Voyage 137
PREDESTIN'D
That day, which I predestin'd am to sing, ... 262 U78 Digby V 17
By sure Election, and predestin'd grace! . . . . 288 U84 Muse 198
PREFERRE
Say, this, or that man they to thee preferre; . . . . 83 E131 Ferrab. 2 9
'Tis not your fault, if they shall sense preferre, . . . 370 Author 13
PREFERR'D
And mine not least) I have too oft preferr'd . . . . 159 U14 Selden 20
PREJUDICE
'Tis not thy judgement breeds the prejudice, ... 50 E72 Court-ling 5
PRELATE
The holy Prelate prayes, then takes the Ring, ... 256 U75 Epithalam. 123
PRENTISE
A Prentise-ship: which few doe now a dayes. . . . . 410 Brome 10
PRENTISE-SHIP
A Prentise-ship: which few doe now a dayes. . . . . 410 Brome 10
PREOCCUPY   (See PRAEOCCUPIE)
PREPARE
First, prepare you to be sorie, ... 131 U2 Excuse 14
PREPAR'D
I, that am gratefull for him, have prepar'd . . . . 116 F12 Rutland 96
As comming with his Harpe, prepar'd . . . . 274 U84 Cradle 35
Who will be there, against that day prepar'd, ... 284 U84 Muse 59
PRESCIOUS
Then I admir'd, the rare and prescious use . . . . 361 Palmer 9
PRESCRIBE
Wild raging lusts; prescribe the mariage good; . . . 327 Horace 489

PRESENCE
But in thy presence, truly glorified, ... 128 U1 Trinitie 47
The theefe from spoyle, his presence holds. . . . . 265 U79 New-yeares 63
PRESENT   (See also PRAESENTATION)
That still th'art present to the better cause; . . . 52 E74 Chancelor 5
And present worth in all dost so contract, ... 57 E89 Allen 11
That hast thy brest so cleere of present crimes, . . . 61 E95 Savile 19
Whose name's un-welcome to the present eare, ... 74 E115 Honest Man 15
Scarce will take our present store? . . . . . 105 F8 Sicknesse 11
Scarce will take our present score? . . . . . 105 F8 Sicknesse V 11
A present, which (if elder writs reherse . . . . 113 F12 Rutland 20
10. Another Ladyes exception present at the hearing. . . 142 U2 Exception Ttl
To use the present, then, is not abuse, ... 171 U19 Elegy By 21
Thy present Aide: Arise Invention, ... 176 U25 Desmond 2
Thy present Aide: Spirit Invention, ... 176 U25 Desmond V 2
Hee leap'd the present age, ... 245 U70 Ode 79
I would present you now with curious plate . . . . 260 U77 Treasurer 2
I would present you with some curious plate . . . . 260 U77 Treasurer V 2
Present anone: Medea must not kill . . . . . 317 Horace 263
And so their prating to present was best, ... 321 Horace 329
And so their pratling to present were best, . . . 346 Horace V321/329
They are not those, are present with theyre face, . . . 384 Somerset 1
PRESENTACION
In presentacion of some puppet play! . . . . . 405 Inigo Jones 1 76
PRESENTED
A Speach Presented unto King James at a tylting . . . 382 Rich Ttl
PRESENTES
presentes a Royall Alter of fayre peace, ... 382 Rich 6
PRESENTING
Presenting upwards, a faire female feature, ... 305 Horace 4
Will well confesse; presenting, limiting, ... 370 Author 6
PRESENTLY
Her presently? Or leape thy Wife of force, ... 201 U42 Elegy Let 44
PRESENTS
Just to the waight their this dayes-presents beare; . . . 113 F12 Rutland 8
And show, how, to the life, my soule presents . . . 115 F12 Rutland 86
PRESERVE
So, 'live or dead, thou wilt preserve a fame . . . 168 U15 Friend-Wars 189
Her order is to cherish, and preserve, ... 192 U38 Elegy 'Tis 61
And free it from all question to preserve. . . . . 220 U47 Tribe 72
PRESERV'D
And since, the whole land was preserv'd for thee. . . . 38 E35 James 2 10
PRESERVED
First thou preserved wert, our king to bee, . . . 38 E35 James 2 9
Preserved, in her antique bed of Vert, ... 413 Ghyrlond 19
PRESERVER
Pan is the great Preserver of our bounds. . . . . 264 U79 New-yeares 14
This is the great Preserver of our bounds, ... 265 U79 New-yeares 48
PRESERVES
Preserves communitie. . . . . . 110 F11 Epode 54
Our pleasure; but preserves us more . . . . . 146 U6 Defence 21
Hee that preserves a man, against his will, ... 335 Horace 665
PRESIDENT
When all your life's a president of dayes, ... 237 U64 Charles 3 13
PRESIDENTS
Of Bookes, of Presidents, hast thou at hand! . . . 187 U33 Councellour 25
PRESSE   (See also PREASE)
I have decreed; keepe it from waves, and presse; . . . 219 U47 Tribe 57
PRESSURE
Of pressure, like one taken in a streight? . . . . 154 U13 Sacvile 32
PREST
But both fell prest under the load they make. . . . 166 U15 Friend-Wars 128
Poore wretched states, prest by extremities, ... 248 U71 Treasurer 1
Or the prest honey in pure pots doth keepe . . . . 290 U85 Country 15
prest in to se you. . . . . . 416 Moon 8
PRESUME
Vanish'd away: as you must all presume . . . . 87 E133 Voyage 110
Presume to interpell that fulnesse, when . . . . 284 U84 Muse 70
PRESUMES
The holy Altars, when it least presumes. . . . . 288 U84 Muse 188
PRETEND
And judge me after: if I dare pretend . . . . 122 F15 Heaven 7
With what injustice should one soule pretend . . . . 271 U81 Pawlet 92
With what injustice can one soule pretend . . . . 271 U81 Pawlet V 92
Or crafty Malice, might pretend this praise, ... 391 Shakespeare 11
PRETEXT
Of politique pretext, that wryes a State, ... 177 U25 Desmond 29
Of politique pretext, that swayes a State, ... 177 U25 Desmond V 29
PRETIOUS
Still pretious, with the odour of thy name. . . . . 168 U15 Friend-Wars 190
That pure, that pretious, and exalted mind . . . . 285 U84 Muse 104
Of vertue, pretious in the frame: . . . . . 399 Lady Ogle 18
PRETTIE
What manners prettie, Nature milde, ... 188 U35 Chute 2
PRETTY
Like pretty Spies, ... 258 U75 Epithalam. 174
PREVAILE
Much like those Brethren; thinking to prevaile . . . 59 E92 New Crie 36
PREVAIL'D
I, that thy Ayme was; but her fate prevail'd: . . . 188 U34 Small Poxe 17
PREVARICATOR   (See PRAEVARICATORS)
PREVENT
And in the Act did so my blush prevent, ... 153 U13 Sacvile 11

			Page	Title	Line

PREVENTED
And, ere I could aske you, I was prevented: . . . . 54 E84 Bedford 2 3

PRIAM'S
I sing a noble Warre, and Priam's Fate. . . . . 313 Horace 196

PRIAPUS
With which, Priapus, he may thanke thy hands, . . . 290 U85 Country 21
With which, Priapus, he may greet thy hands, . . . 290 U85 Country V 21

PRICE
And are so good, and bad, just at a price, . . . 66 E102 Pembroke 11
About the towne; and knowne too, at that price. . . 74 E115 Honest Man 6
For every price, in every jarre, ... 99 F3 Wroth 74
Any paines; yea, thinke it price, ... 105 F8 Sicknesse 27
But let this drosse carry what price it will . . . 114 F12 Rutland 27
Who made himselfe the price of sinne, ... 130 U1 Nativitie 20
I would, if price, or prayer could them get, . . . 260 U77 Treasurer 5
The price of our Redemption, and to teach . . . 286 U84 Muse 134
Is to make cheape, the Lord, the lines, the price. . . 408 Detractor 6

PRICK
To catch the flesh in, and to pound a Prick. . . . 164 U15 Friend-Wars 67

PRICK'D
Of Spaine or France; or were not prick'd downe one . . 219 U47 Tribe 47

PRIDE
Hating that solemne vice of greatnesse, pride; . . 52 E76 Bedford 1 10
Upbraiding rebells armes, and barbarous pride: . . 60 E93 Radcliffe 6
Of what ambition, faction, pride can raise; . . . 66 E102 Pembroke 15
For since, what ignorance, what pride is fled! . . 73 E113 Overbury 7
And pride, and ignorance the schooles, . . . 101 F4 To the World 48
Then, here, to give pride fame, and peasants birth. . 114 F12 Rutland 26
Then, now give pride fame, or peasants birth. . . 114 F12 Rutland V 26
All the Pride the fields than have: . . . . 132 U2 How he saw 4
As they are made! Pride, and stiffe Clownage mixt . 163 U15 Friend-Wars 43
To see the Pride at Court, their Wives doe make: . . 213 U44 Speach 16
That you have seene the pride, beheld the sport, . . 234 U61 Epigram 1
(But pride, that schisme of incivilitie) . . . 287 U84 Muse 160
Nor takes she pride to know them. . . . . 365 Ode Splendor 24
The choise of Europes pride; . . . . 368 Ode Who saith 83
Butt, Clownishe pride hath gott . . . . 420 Ode:If Men 10

PRIEST
The world the temple was, the priest a king, . . . 28 E5 Union 3
By me, their priest (if they can ought divine) . . 119 F13 Aubigny 101
Thy Priest in this strange rapture; heat my braine . 177 U25 Desmond 11
Orpheus, a priest, and speaker for the Gods . . . 327 Horace 479

PRIESTS
Of which we Priests, and Poets say . . . . 245 U70 Ode 82

PRIME
There's no vexation, that can make thee prime. . . 73 E112 Gamster 22
Alas I ha' lost my heat, my blood, my prime, . . . 199 U41 Elegy Since 11
Where fight the prime Cocks of the Game, for wit? . . 222 U49 Pucell 4
Of the prime beautie of the yeare, the Spring. . . 251 U74 Weston 6
doth his prime Carract, and just Standard keepe . . 255 U75 Epithalam. V100
Their Corrals, Whistles, and prime Coates, . . . 273 U84 Cradle 21
The conqu'ring Champion, the prime Horse in course, . 311 Horace 115
And all the Muses still were in their prime, . . . 391 Shakespeare 44
Our first of fruits, that is the prime of flowers . . 416 Welcome 2

PRIMING
On the new priming of thy old Signe postes . . . 405 Inigo Jones 1 87

PRIMIS
In-primis, Grand, you owe me for a jest, . . . 51 E73 Fine Grand 5

PRINCE
And such a Prince thou art, wee daily see, . . . 28 E4 James 1 7
A Prince, that rules by'example, more than sway? . . 37 E35 James 2 2
And what each prince doth for intelligence owe, . . 59 E92 New Crie 12
With his brave sonne, the Prince, they saw thy fires . 95 F2 Penshurst 77
Our Ancestors impos'd on Prince and State. . . . 215 U44 Speach 78
At which there are, would sell the Prince, and State: . 234 U61 Epigram 78
An Epigram on Prince Charles his Birth: May. 29th. 1630 . 237 U65 Prince VTtl
This Prince of flowers? Soone shoot thou up, and grow . 237 U65 Prince 5
The Mother of our Prince? When was there seene . . 238 U66 Queene 6
As in this Prince? Let it be lawfull, so . . . 238 U66 Queene 11
The wish is great; but where the Prince is such, . . 249 U72 King 19
In him the times, no lesse then Prince, are prais'd, . 256 U75 Epithalam. 115
And Day, deceasing! with the Prince of light, . . 271 U81 Pawlet 88
Our King and Queen the Prince God blesse, . . . 418 Grace V 1
That prince that shames a tyrants name to beare, . . 423 Lucan 19

PRINCES
And yet are with their Princes: Fill them full . . 69 E107 Hungry 7
A Princes fortune: These are gifts of chance, . . 117 F13 Aubigny 41
My Princes safetie, and my Kings desire, . . . 219 U47 Tribe 38
An Epigram on the Princes birth. 1630. . . . 237 U65 Prince Ttl
On the Princes Birth-day. An Epigram . . . 237 U65 Prince VTtl
Of Princes aides, or good mens Charities. . . . 248 U71 Treasurer 3
Would they would understand it! Princes are . . . 268 U80 Christning 5
Amongst her Peeres, those Princes of all good! . . 284 U84 Muse 84

PRINCIPALITIES
Angels, Arch-angels, Principalities, . . . 285 U84 Muse 86

PRINT
Lest Ayre, or Print, but flies it: Such men would . . 154 U13 Sacvile 45
Looke here on Bretons worke, the master print: . . 362 Author 5
His face; the Print would then surpasse . . . 390 Reader 7

PRINTED
It was as if thou printed had'st an oath, . . . 43 E53 Old-end 5
. . . Which should Have beene Printed with the other . . . 379 Coryat 3 Ttl

PRISE
But to please him, who is the dearer prise   .   .   .   119 F13 Aubigny   116
PRIS'D
If onely love should make the action pris'd: .   .   78 E121 Rudyerd 1   6
PRIVATE
What two brave perills of the private sword   .   37 E32 Roe 2   1
Not from the publike voyce, but private fact;   .   47 E63 Salisbury 2   6
Takes private beatings, and begins againe.   .   49 E68 Playwrt 2   2
Is private gaine, which hath long guilt to friend.   .   70 E109 Nevil   8
The Wisdome, Madam, of your private Life,   .   224 U50 Countesse   1
Of Pietie, and private holinesse.   287 U84 Muse   179
Abhorres low numbers, and the private straine   311 Horace   123
The publike, from the private; to abate   .   327 Horace   488
PRIVIE
But they unfrighted passe, though many a privie   .   86 E133 Voyage   73
PRIVIES
Tempte such a passage? when each privies seate   .   88 E133 Voyage   168
PRIVILEDGE
The learn'd have no more priviledge, then the lay.   .   82 E131 Ferrab. 2   4
PRIZE (See also PRISE)
Could ne'er make prize of thy white Chastetye.   .   108 F10 Proludium   6
But 'bove the fat of rammes, or bulls, to prize   127 U1 Trinitie   11
All as their prize, turne Pyrats here at Land,   155 U13 Sacvile   81
Not Lucrine Oysters I could then more prize,   291 U85 Country   49
He makes the Camell & dull Ass his prize.   .   408 Inigo Jones 3   8
PROCEEDES
The thirst, that from the soule proceedes,   106 F9 Celia 3   V 5
PROCEEDING
Eternall Spirit, God from both proceeding,   .   128 U1 Trinitie   25
PROCESSE
Such was thy Processe, when Integritie,   .   217 U46 Coke   9
PROCESSION
See, the Procession! what a Holy day   .   .   252 U75 Epithalam.   9
PROCLAIME
By thy great helpe: and doth proclaime by mee,   72 E111 Edmonds 2   13
By thy great Art: and doth proclaime by mee,   72 E111 Edmonds 2   V 13
So, may the King proclaime your Conscience is   185 U31 Elsmere   3
Though you sometimes proclaime me too severe,   190 U37 Friend-Book   16
PROCLAMATION
And whisper what a Proclamation sayes.   .   59 E92 New Crie   20
PROCURE
Or safe, but shee'll procure   .   .   109 F11 Epode   6
PRODIGALLY
Had lost our selves? and prodigally spent   .   286 U84 Muse   141
PRODIGIE
They met the second Prodigie, would feare a   .   86 E133 Voyage   79
PRODIGIOUS
Why? though I seeme of a prodigious wast,   .   226 U52 Answer   1
When the Prodigious Hannibal did crowne   .   242 U70 Ode   3
PRODIGIOUSLY
One thing prodigiously, paints in the woods   .   307 Horace   41
PRODUCE
Produce; though threatning with a coale, or chalke   193 U38 Elegy 'Tis   97
Produce thy masse of miseries on the Stage,   .   244 U70 Ode   55
Produce us a blacke Swan?   .   .   .   366 Ode Who saith   2
PROFANE (See also PROPHANE)
Things sacred, from profane to separate;   .   327 Horace   487
PROFESSE
In my chast booke: professe them in thine owne.   .   42 E49 Playwrt 1   6
And Ile professe no verses to repeate: .   65 E101 Supper   24
I, therefore, who professe my selfe in love   116 F13 Aubigny   7
Much from him I professe I wonne,   .   .   152 U12 Corbet   29
Little know they, that professe Amitie,   .   190 U37 Friend-Book   19
PROFESSED
Where envious arts professed be,   .   .   101 F4 To the World   47
PROFESSETH
That Faith, which she professeth to be pure?   .   236 U64 Charles 3   12
PROFESSING
Professing greatnesse, swells: That, low by lee   307 Horace   38
His Muse professing height, and greatnesse, swells;   339 Horace   V 39/ 38
Of Fellowship, professing my old Arts.   .   409 Brome   4
PROFESSION
Your great profession; which I once, did prove: 70 E108 Soldiers   6
And this profession of a store   .   .   146 U6 Defence   19
PROFEST
My praise is plaine, and where so ere profest,   67 E103 L Wroth 1   13
In grave beginnings, and great things profest,   305 Horace   17
PROFFESSE
Little knowne they that proffesse Amitye   421 Censure   12
PROFFITT
are distant, so is proffitt from just aymes.   422 Lucan   8
PROFICIENCIE
As make it their proficiencie, how much   .   218 U47 Tribe   12
PROFIT
Profit in ought: each day some little adde,   .   157 U13 Sacvile   132
On which with profit, I shall never looke,   .   189 U37 Friend-Book   5
Th'admir'd discourses of the Profit Ball: .   206 U43 Vulcan   V 82
Profit, or Chance had made us: But I know   241 U69 Friend Son   3
That found out profit, and foretold each thing,   319 Horace   309
Poets would either profit, or delight,   .   327 Horace   477
The Poems void of profit, our grave men   .   329 Horace   511
PROFITABLE
So are they profitable to be knowne: .   .   225 U50 Countesse   34

		Page	Title	Line

PROFITS
The profits for a time. . . . . 246 U70 Ode 101
To him we owe all profits of our grounds. . . . . 264 U79 New-yeares 15
Into the Profits, what a meere rude braine . . . 331 Horace 583

PROFITT
for when the profitt with the payne doth meete, . . . 418 Answer 6

PROGNE
His Nephews entrailes; nor must Progne flie . . . 317 Horace 266

PROJECT
So large; his Body then, not boughs, project his shade. . . 258 U75 Epithalam. V184

PROJECTS
The councels, projects, practises they know, . . . 59 E92 New Crie 11
So great; his Body now alone projects the shade. . . 258 U75 Epithalam. 184

PROLOGUE
Turne the stale prologue to some painted maske, . . 107 F10 Proludium 20

PROLUDIUM
Proludium. . . . . . . 108 F10 Proludium Ttl

PROMETHEAN
Thy learned hand, and true Promethean art . . . 71 E110 Edmonds 1 17

PROMISE
As chiefe of those still promise they will bee. . . 28 E4 James 1 8
8. Urging her of a promise. . . . 139 U2 Promise Ttl
And that promise set on fire . . . 139 U2 Promise 5
Then would I promise here to give . . . 229 U55 Burges 3
Doth by his doubt, distrust his promise more. . . 235 U63 Charles 2 4
(Bearing the promise of some better fate) . . 252 U75 Epithalam. 10

PROMIS'D
Lightly promis'd, she would tell . . . 139 U2 Promise 3
The same that thou art promis'd, but be slow, . . 237 U65 Prince 6
The same that thou hast promis'd, but be slow, . . 237 U65 Prince V 6

PROMISER
What doth this Promiser such gaping worth . . 313 Horace 197
What doth this Promiser such great gaping worth . . 343 Horace V197

PROMPT
prompt me that she hath seene . . 149 U9 Picture V 13
Can Beautie that did prompt me first to write, . . 169 U18 Elegy Can 1

PRONE
The first; as prone to move . . . 110 F11 Epode 32
Mens faces, still, with such as laugh, are prone . . 311 Horace 143
Mens count'nances, with such as laugh, are prone . 342 Horace V143

PRONOUNCE
And pronounce, which band, or lace, . . . 140 U2 Promise 19
From the five ounces; what remaines? pronounce . . 327 Horace 468

PROOFE
His proofe their praise, will meete, as in this line. . 362 Author 14
Be proofe, the glory of his hand, . . . 367 Ode Who saith 49
But thou art proofe against them, and indeed . . 391 Shakespeare 15

PROOFES
But when I have said, The proofes of all these bee . 82 E130 Ferrab. 1 17

PROPAGATE
To propagate their Names, ... 257 U75 Epithalam. 149

PROPER
To thine owne proper I ascribe then more; . . 61 E95 Savile 9
O, (thou cry'st out) that is thy proper game. . . 73 E112 Gamster 16
It perfect, proper, pure, and naturall, . . 117 F13 Aubigny 32
Our proper vertue is to range: . . . 146 U6 Defence 4
Strike in thy proper straine, . . . 175 U23 Himselfe 26
stryke him in thy proper straine, . . . 175 U23 Himselfe V 26
By which as proper titles, she is knowne . . 176 U24 Frontispice 16
Thou should'st have cry'd, and all beene proper stuffe. . 205 U43 Vulcan 64
Thou should'st have cry'd, and all fine proper stuffe. . 205 U43 Vulcan V 64
In fitting proper adjuncts to each day. . . 317 Horace 254

PROPERLY
'Tis hard, to speake things common, properly: . . 313 Horace 183

PROPERTIE
How much they lame her in her propertie. . . 190 U37 Friend-Book 21

PROPERTIUS
Doth Cynthia, in Propertius song . . . 181 U27 Ode Helen 11

PROPERTYE
Howe much they lame hir, in hir propertye: . . 421 Censure 14

PROPERTYES
Or making of the Propertyes it meane? . . 402 Inigo Jones 1 12
The maker of the Propertyes! in summe . . 404 Inigo Jones 1 61

PROPHANE
Much lesse with lewd, prophane, and beastly phrase, . . 27 E2 My Booke 11
Dare I prophane, so irreligious bee . . . 283 U84 Muse 39
Dull, and prophane, weake, and imperfect eyes, . . 284 U84 Muse 79
Hence, then, prophane: Here needs no words expense . 400 Beaumont 3

PROPHANENESSE
(Without prophanenesse) yet, a Poet, cry, . . 238 U66 Queene 4
(Without prophanenesse) as, a Poet, cry, . . 238 U66 Queene V 4

PROPHANER
And that prophaner ground, the Parish-Garden: . . 209 U43 Vulcan V147

PROPHET'
Will cal't a Bastard, when a Prophet's borne. . . 223 U49 Pucell 46

PROPHET
Th'admir'd discourses of the Prophet Ball: . . 206 U43 Vulcan 82
Th'admir'd discourses of the Prophet Baal: . . 206 U43 Vulcan V 82

PROPHETICKE
Conceal'd from all but cleare Propheticke eyes. . . 369 Ode Who saith 112

PROPHET'S
Will cal't a Bastard, when a Prophet's borne. . . 223 U49 Pucell 46

<table>
<thead>
<tr><th></th><th>Page</th><th>Title</th><th>Line</th></tr>
</thead>
<tbody>
<tr><td>PROPHETS</td><td></td><td></td><td></td></tr>
<tr><td>Were they that nam'd you, prophets? Did they see,</td><td>67</td><td>E104 Montgomery</td><td>1</td></tr>
<tr><td>Saints, Martyrs, Prophets, with those Hierarchies,</td><td>285</td><td>U84 Muse</td><td>85</td></tr>
<tr><td>PROPORTION</td><td></td><td></td><td></td></tr>
<tr><td>Now, Penshurst, they that will proportion thee</td><td>96</td><td>F2 Penshurst</td><td>99</td></tr>
<tr><td>No face, no hand, proportion, line, or Ayre</td><td>200</td><td>U42 Elegy Let</td><td>14</td></tr>
<tr><td>Keepe due proportion in the ample song,</td><td>395</td><td>May</td><td>12</td></tr>
<tr><td>What was proportion, or could bee</td><td>399</td><td>Lady Ogle</td><td>21</td></tr>
<tr><td>PROPORTION'D</td><td></td><td></td><td></td></tr>
<tr><td>And those so sweet, and well proportion'd parts,</td><td>396</td><td>Drayton</td><td>21</td></tr>
<tr><td>PROPORTIONS</td><td></td><td></td><td></td></tr>
<tr><td>In small proportions, we just beautie see:</td><td>245</td><td>U70 Ode</td><td>73</td></tr>
<tr><td>PROPOSE</td><td></td><td></td><td></td></tr>
<tr><td>But we propose a person like our Dove,</td><td>112</td><td>F11 Epode</td><td>91</td></tr>
<tr><td>PROPOS'D</td><td></td><td></td><td></td></tr>
<tr><td>Propos'd to goe to Hol'borne in a wherry:</td><td>85</td><td>E133 Voyage</td><td>38</td></tr>
<tr><td>PROPOUND</td><td></td><td></td><td></td></tr>
<tr><td>Nor care I now healths to propound;</td><td>293</td><td>U86 Hor.4:1</td><td>31</td></tr>
<tr><td>PROPPING</td><td></td><td></td><td></td></tr>
<tr><td>Propping Verse, for feare of falling</td><td>183</td><td>U29 Fit of Rime</td><td>8</td></tr>
<tr><td>PROP'REST</td><td></td><td></td><td></td></tr>
<tr><td>As prop'rest gifts, to Girles, and Boyes,</td><td>273</td><td>U84 Cradle</td><td>19</td></tr>
<tr><td>PROPTER</td><td></td><td></td><td></td></tr>
<tr><td>To make propter viam, ever, where thou go'st;</td><td>205</td><td>U43 Vulcan</td><td>V 58</td></tr>
<tr><td>PROSE</td><td></td><td></td><td></td></tr>
<tr><td>And in either Prose, or Song,</td><td>133</td><td>U2 Suffered</td><td>23</td></tr>
<tr><td>From the poore wretch, which though he play'd in prose,</td><td>201</td><td>U42 Elegy Let</td><td>61</td></tr>
<tr><td>That can but reade; who cannot, may in prose</td><td>398</td><td>Drayton</td><td>73</td></tr>
<tr><td>The Eloquence of Masques! What need of prose</td><td>403</td><td>Inigo Jones 1</td><td>40</td></tr>
<tr><td>PROSEQUUTE</td><td></td><td></td><td></td></tr>
<tr><td>I leave thy acts, which should I prosequute</td><td>58</td><td>E91 Vere</td><td>9</td></tr>
<tr><td>I leave, then, acts, which should I prosequute</td><td>58</td><td>E91 Vere</td><td>V 9</td></tr>
<tr><td>PROSERPINA</td><td></td><td></td><td></td></tr>
<tr><td>And Madame Caesar, great Proserpina,</td><td>89</td><td>E133 Voyage</td><td>180</td></tr>
<tr><td>PROSPECTIVE</td><td></td><td></td><td></td></tr>
<tr><td>made prospective, behould hym, hee must passe</td><td>383</td><td>Rich</td><td>12</td></tr>
<tr><td>PROSPERITIE</td><td></td><td></td><td></td></tr>
<tr><td>A right by the prosperitie of their Crimes;</td><td>186</td><td>U32 Elsmere</td><td>10</td></tr>
<tr><td>Cover'd with Tissue, whose prosperitie mocks</td><td>216</td><td>U44 Speach</td><td>100</td></tr>
<tr><td>PROSPERITY</td><td></td><td></td><td></td></tr>
<tr><td>Shall the prosperity of a Pardon still</td><td>410</td><td>Gill</td><td>1</td></tr>
<tr><td>PROSTITUTE</td><td></td><td></td><td></td></tr>
<tr><td>On their beds, most prostitute,</td><td>106</td><td>F8 Sicknesse</td><td>45</td></tr>
<tr><td>PROTECTES</td><td></td><td></td><td></td></tr>
<tr><td>It is a lycense to doe ill, protectes,</td><td>423</td><td>Lucan</td><td>12</td></tr>
<tr><td>PROTECTION</td><td></td><td></td><td></td></tr>
<tr><td>Happy Greeke, by this protection,</td><td>184</td><td>U29 Fit of Rime</td><td>32</td></tr>
<tr><td>PROTEST</td><td></td><td></td><td></td></tr>
<tr><td>But for a Sealing: let these men protest.</td><td>218</td><td>U47 Tribe</td><td>15</td></tr>
<tr><td>He there doth protest he saw of the eleven.</td><td>380</td><td>Coryat 3</td><td>46</td></tr>
<tr><td>PROTESTATION</td><td></td><td></td><td></td></tr>
<tr><td>And then to be return'd; on protestation</td><td>229</td><td>U54 Squib</td><td>18</td></tr>
<tr><td>PROTESTED</td><td></td><td></td><td></td></tr>
<tr><td>Nor should I at this time protested be,</td><td>169</td><td>U17 Friend-Debt</td><td>7</td></tr>
<tr><td>PROTESTS</td><td></td><td></td><td></td></tr>
<tr><td>Orgies of drinke, or fain'd protests:</td><td>246</td><td>U70 Ode</td><td>104</td></tr>
<tr><td>PROTEUS</td><td></td><td></td><td></td></tr>
<tr><td>As in this Spanish Proteus; who, though writ</td><td>389</td><td>Aleman</td><td>5</td></tr>
<tr><td>PROTRACTION</td><td></td><td></td><td></td></tr>
<tr><td>And so went bravely backe, without protraction.</td><td>89</td><td>E133 Voyage</td><td>192</td></tr>
<tr><td>PROUD (See also PROWDE)</td><td></td><td></td><td></td></tr>
<tr><td>And proud, my worke shall out-last common deeds,</td><td>46</td><td>E60 Mounteagle</td><td>6</td></tr>
<tr><td>Where ere he met me; now hee's dumbe, or proud.</td><td>62</td><td>E97 Motion</td><td>8</td></tr>
<tr><td>O, runne not proud of this. Yet, take thy due.</td><td>81</td><td>E129 Mime</td><td>15</td></tr>
<tr><td>Those proud, ambitious heaps, and nothing else,</td><td>96</td><td>F2 Penshurst</td><td>101</td></tr>
<tr><td>Free from proud porches, or their guilded roofes,</td><td>97</td><td>F3 Wroth</td><td>15</td></tr>
<tr><td>Get place, and honor, and be proud to keepe</td><td>99</td><td>F3 Wroth</td><td>V 87</td></tr>
<tr><td>When his proud patrons favours are asleepe;</td><td>113</td><td>F12 Rutland</td><td>14</td></tr>
<tr><td>Lesse list of proud, hard, or ingratefull Men.</td><td>153</td><td>U13 Sacvile</td><td>4</td></tr>
<tr><td>In that proud manner, as a good so gain'd,</td><td>154</td><td>U13 Sacvile</td><td>37</td></tr>
<tr><td>O, these so ignorant Monsters! light, as proud,</td><td>164</td><td>U15 Friend-Wars</td><td>59</td></tr>
<tr><td>Nor is the title question'd with our proud,</td><td>164</td><td>U15 Friend-Wars</td><td>83</td></tr>
<tr><td>Of the poore sufferers) where the envious, proud,</td><td>167</td><td>U15 Friend-Wars</td><td>167</td></tr>
<tr><td>I could forgive her being proud! a whore!</td><td>172</td><td>U20 Shrub</td><td>21</td></tr>
<tr><td>Proud, false, and trecherous, vindictive, all</td><td>172</td><td>U21 Ltl Shrub</td><td>7</td></tr>
<tr><td>Not swelling like the Ocean proud,</td><td>280</td><td>U84 Mind</td><td>57</td></tr>
<tr><td>But flees the Barre and Courts, with the proud bords,</td><td>289</td><td>U85 Country</td><td>7</td></tr>
<tr><td>Fortune would love the poore, and leave the proud.</td><td>319</td><td>Horace</td><td>286</td></tr>
<tr><td>Nature her selfe was proud of his designes,</td><td>392</td><td>Shakespeare</td><td>47</td></tr>
<tr><td>In Towne & Court? Are you growne rich? & proud?</td><td>403</td><td>Inigo Jones 1</td><td>24</td></tr>
<tr><td>PROUDER</td><td></td><td></td><td></td></tr>
<tr><td>Which the prouder Beauties please,</td><td>133</td><td>U2 Suffered</td><td>2</td></tr>
<tr><td>PROUDLY</td><td></td><td></td><td></td></tr>
<tr><td>which, did they neere so neate, or proudly dwell,</td><td>387</td><td>Cavendish</td><td>3</td></tr>
<tr><td>PROULE</td><td></td><td></td><td></td></tr>
<tr><td>To Proule the Plagiary.</td><td>54</td><td>E81 Proule</td><td>Ttl</td></tr>
<tr><td>Forbeare to tempt me, Proule, I will not show</td><td>54</td><td>E81 Proule</td><td>1</td></tr>
<tr><td>Thy wit lives by it, Proule, and belly too.</td><td>54</td><td>E81 Proule</td><td>6</td></tr>
<tr><td>PROVE</td><td></td><td></td><td></td></tr>
<tr><td>Which though it did but panick terror prove,</td><td>43</td><td>E51 James 3</td><td>3</td></tr>
<tr><td>And stoupe, and cringe. O then, it needs must prove</td><td>56</td><td>E88 Monsieur</td><td>14</td></tr>
<tr><td>Your great profession; which I once, did prove:</td><td>70</td><td>E108 Soldiers</td><td>6</td></tr>
<tr><td>Thy deedes, unto thy name, will prove new wombes,</td><td>70</td><td>E109 Nevil</td><td>17</td></tr>
</tbody>
</table>

PROVE (cont.)
  I answer'd, Daphne now no paine can prove.   80   E126 Mrs Cary   6
  As the beginnings here, prove purely sweet,   .   .   .   81   E128 Wm Roe 2   7
  Come my Celia, let us prove, ...   102   F5 Celia 1   1
  Come sweet Celia, let us prove, ...   102   F5 Celia 1   V   1
  No such effects doth prove;   110   F11 Epode   44
  Or in their windowes; doe but prove the wombs,   .   .   114   F12 Rutland   46
  Will prove old Orpheus act no tale to be: .   .   115   F12 Rutland   77
  Will prove old Orpheus Arts no tale to be: .   .   115   F12 Rutland   V 77
  Moodes, which the god-like Sydney oft did prove,   .   .   116   F12 Rutland   91
  That I may prove   129   U1 Father   5
  Mixe then your Notes, that we may prove   .   .   143   U3 Musicall   9
  Thou sai'st, thou only cam'st to prove   .   .   150   U10 Jealousie   10
  And so that either may example prove   171   U19 Elegy By   16
  Before you prove a medicine, is unjust.   .   .   .   192   U38 Elegy 'Tis   50
  Upon your shoulders. Prove what they will beare,   .   .   307   Horace   55
  Prove what your shoulders will, or will not beare.   .   .   339   Horace   V 57/ 55
  Prove of his Mistris Feature,   .   .   .   364   Phoenix   7
  But prove the Aire, and saile from Coast to Coast: .   .   367   Ode Who saith   37
  So, may those Mariage-Pledges, comforts prove: .   .   384   Somerset   19
PROV'D
  Your noblest father prov'd: like whom, before,   .   .   53   E79 Rutland   2
  Cocytus, Phlegeton, our have prov'd in one;   .   .   84   E133 Voyage   8
  (As prov'd in you)   177   U25 Desmond   24
  In all the prov'd assayes, ...   255   U75 Epithalam.   101
  O're read, examin'd, try'd, and prov'd your Ryme   .   .   421   Censure   7
PROVES
  Proves, that is gods, which was the peoples voice.   .   .   49   E67 Suffolk   12
  Chance that the Friends affection proves Allay   .   .   .   158   U14 Selden   10
  No person, nor is lov'd: what wayes he proves   .   .   .   162   U15 Friend-Wars   16
  At a Friends freedome, proves all circling meanes   .   .   242   U69 Friend Son   15
PROVIDE
  To crowne thy open table, doth provide   .   .   .   94   F2 Penshurst   27
  My friends, the Watermen! They could provide   .   .   208   U43 Vulcan   124
  Our friends, the Watermen! They could provide   .   .   208   U43 Vulcan   V124
PROVIDED
  Provided, ne're to yeeld, in any case   323   Horace   379
  And, where the matter is provided still,   .   .   .   325   Horace   443
PROVIDENCE
  Wise Providence would so; that nor the good   .   .   .   176   U24 Frontispice   5
  high Providence would so; that nor the good   .   .   .   176   U24 Frontispice V   5
PROVIDER
  To endure counsell: a Provider slow   315   Horace   233
PROVING
  Went on: and proving him still, day by day,   .   .   57   E90 Mill   7
PROVISION
  Live, with un-bought provision blest;   .   .   97   F3 Wroth   14
PROVISIONS
  Adde to thy free provisions, farre above   .   .   .   95   F2 Penshurst   58
PROVOKE
  And thence, the ruddy Satyres oft provoke   .   .   .   94   F2 Penshurst   17
  Provoke his mettall, and command his force   .   .   228   U53 Newcastle   2
  To bend, to breake, provoke, or suffer it!   .   .   233   U59 Newcastle   18
  To bend, to breake, provoke, or suffer it!   .   .   233   U59 Newcastle   V 18
  That nothing can her gratitude provoke!   .   .   .   237   U64 Charles 3   16
  That nothing will her gratitude provoke!   .   .   .   237   U64 Charles 3   V 16
  It rages, runs, flies, stands, and would provoke   .   .   283   U84 Muse   24
PROV'ST
  Who prov'st, all these were, and againe may bee.   .   .   .   78   E122 Rudyerd 2   10
  Thou prov'st the gentler wayes, to clense the wound,   .   .   187   U33 Councellour   20
PROWDE
  From whose prowde bosome, thou began'st thy flight.   .   .   368   Ode Who saith   80
  Tames, prowde of thee, and of his Fate   368   Ode Who saith   81
PROWESSE
  And of her Fathers prowesse!   240   U67 Muses   30
  And of her Brothers prowesse!   240   U67 Muses   V 30
PROYNE
  Where I sit and proyne my wings   137   U2 Cupid   35
PRUDENT
  Hee's prudent, valiant, just, and temperate;   .   .   262   U78 Digby   5
PR'Y
  Pr'y thee beleeve still, and not judge so fast,   .   .   32   E18 Censurer   9
  Pr'y thee, yet save thy rest; give ore in time: .   .   73   E112 Gamster   21
PSALMES
  In frequent speaking by the pious Psalmes   .   .   .   288   U84 Muse   191
PTOLEMEY
  Just and fit actions Ptolemey (he saith)   .   .   .   422   Lucan   1
PUBLIC
  In secret places, flee the public baths.   .   .   .   349   Horace   V424
PUBLIKE
  Not from the publike voyce, but private fact;   .   .   47   E63 Salisbury 2   6
  Play-wright convict of publike wrongs to men,   .   .   49   E68 Playwrt 2   1
  Her ends are honestie, and publike good!   .   .   .   156   U13 Sacvile   111
  The Care, and wish still of the publike wealth: .   .   186   U31 Elsmere   6
  Publike affaires command me now to goe   194   U38 Elegy 'Tis   114
  Thou should'st have stay'd, till publike fame said so. .   .   204   U43 Vulcan   46
  That scarce you heare a publike voyce alive,   .   .   234   U61 Epigram   5
  Up publike joy, remember   239   U67 Muses   1
  Retire themselves, avoid the publike baths;   .   .   325   Horace   424
  The publike, from the private; to abate   .   .   .   327   Horace   488
PUBLIQUE
  Of service to the publique, when the end   .   .   .   70   E109 Nevil   7
  Desired Justice to the publique Weale,   .   .   .   217   U46 Coke   16

	Page	Title	Line
PUBLIQUE (cont.)			
Should take first Seisin of the publique good,	268	U80 Christning	8
PUBLISH			
That, Allen, I should pause to publish thee?	57	E89 Allen	8
That to the world I publish, for him, this;	83	E132 Sylvester	9
To publish her a Saint. My Muse is gone.	289	U84 Muse	228
First publish things unspoken, and unknowne.	313	Horace	186
With entheate rage, to publish their bright tracts?	368	Ode Who saith	61
PUBLISHED			
- - - on his Worke published.	401	Filmer	Ttl
PUCELL (See also PUSIL)			
An Epigram on The Court Pucell.	222	U49 Pucell	Ttl
Do's the Court-Pucell then so censure me,	222	U49 Pucell	1
Shall I advise thee, Pucell? steale away	223	U49 Pucell	35
PUFFE			
Nay, now you puffe, tuske, and draw up your chin,	69	E107 Hungry	29
PUI'NEES			
Let pui'nees, porters, players praise delight,	62	E96 Donne 2	10
PUKES			
Their hornes, and Germany pukes on his head.	375	Coryat 1	31
PULL			
Ha's Feathers, and will serve a man to pull.	154	U13 Sacvile	58
The Harmony may pull	239	U67 Muses	20
And stuck in clay here, it would pull	279	U84 Mind	46
PULLING			
Thy Richard, rais'd in song, past pulling downe.	385	Brooke	8
PULLS			
Is it that man pulls on himselfe Disease?	165	U15 Friend-Wars	114
PULPIT			
Whose dice not doing well, to'a pulpit ran.	76	E119 Shelton	6
PULSE (PEAS)			
Him that buyes Pulse there, or perhaps may like	347	Horace	V354/362
PULSE			
That hearkens to a Jacks-pulse, when it goes.	216	U45 Squib	6
PUMPE			
Can pumpe for; or a Libell without salt	193	U38 Elegy 'Tis	96
PUNCK			
Such worship due to kicking of a Punck!	155	U13 Sacvile	93
PUNISHMENT			
Their punishment.	129	U1 Father	16
And the reward, and punishment assur'd,	176	U24 Frontispice V	8
They will come of, and scape the Punishment.	186	U32 Elsmere	14
There is not any punishment, or paine,	194	U38 Elegy 'Tis	103
A meere upbraiding Griefe, and tort'ring punishment.	256	U75 Epithalam.	120
PUNISHMENTS			
That as the last of punishments is meant;	192	U38 Elegy 'Tis	43
PUNKE			
A Punke here pelts him with egs. How so?	375	Coryat 1	18
Here, finer then comming from his Punke you him see,	375	Coryat 1	28
PUNQUE			
Touch'd with the sinne of false play, in his punque,	56	E87 Hazard	1
And then lye with you, closer, then a punque,	69	E107 Hungry	20
PUPPET			
In presentacion of some puppet play!	405	Inigo Jones 1	76
PUR			
An ancient pur-blinde fletcher, with a high nose;	89	E133 Voyage	190
PURBECK			
Soe the Materialls be of Purbeck stone!	406	Inigo Jones 1	100
PUR-BLINDE			
An ancient pur-blinde fletcher, with a high nose;	89	E133 Voyage	190
PURCHASE			
It is a richer Purchase then of land.	216	U45 Squib	26
Her right, by gift, and purchase of the Lambe:	400	Lady Ogle	36
PURCHAS'D			
Purchas'd by rapine, worse then stealth,	99	F3 Wroth	82
He purchas'd friends, and fame, and honours then,	244	U70 Ode	35
PURE			
Is a pure cup of rich Canary-wine,	65	E101 Supper	29
The world's pure gold, and wise simplicitie;	78	E122 Rudyerd 2	4
Pure, perfect, nay divine;	110	F11 Epode	46
It perfect, proper, pure, and naturall,	117	F13 Aubigny	32
Pure thoughts in man: with fiery zeale them feeding	128	U1 Trinitie	27
His Mind as pure, and neatly kept,	151	U12 Corbet	15
By those pure bathes your either cheeke discloses,	170	U19 Elegy By	7
That (in pure Madrigall) unto his Mother	201	U42 Elegy Let	68
That Faith, which she professeth to be pure?	236	U64 Charles 3	12
A Mind so pure, so perfect fine,	278	U84 Mind	25
So swift, so pure, should yet apply	279	U84 Mind	42
That pure, that pretious, and exalted mind	285	U84 Muse	104
Or the prest honey in pure pots doth keepe	290	U85 Country	15
The Vale, that bred thee pure, as her Hills Snow.	367	Ode Who saith	40
I found it pure, and perfect Poesy,	397	Drayton	24
Most holy, & pure Virgin, blessed Mayd,	413	Ghyrlond	37
PURELY			
As the beginnings here, prove purely sweet,	81	E128 Wm Roe 2	7
PUREST			
Whil'st I behold thee live with purest hands;	51	E74 Chancelor	3
You, and that other starre, that purest light,	115	F12 Rutland	65
PURGE			
O I left-witted, that purge every spring	325	Horace	429
PURG'D			
Hast purg'd thy realmes, as we have now no cause	38	E35 James 2	5
What blots and errours, have you watch'd and purg'd	160	U14 Selden	42

532

PURG'D (cont.)
　　T'imprint in all purg'd hearts this virgin sence, · · · 414 Ghyrlond 55
PURGED
　　As Summers sky, or purged Ayre, · · · · · 147 U7 Nymph 17
PURGING
　　A purging bill, now fix'd upon the dore, · · · · 29 E7 Hot-house 2
PURITANES
　　And that, as puritanes at baptisme doo, · · · 44 E53 Old-end 7
　　'Twixt puritanes, and players, as some cry; · · · 52 E75 Lippe 2
PURITIE
　　The puritie of Language; and among · · · · · 207 U43 Vulcan 93
PURLE
　　To say over every purle · · · · · · · 140 U2 Promise 23
　　There is not worne that lace, purle, knot or pin, · · 200 U42 Elegy Let 16
PURLES
　　Planting their Purles, and Curles spread forth like Net, · 164 U15 Friend-Wars 65
PURPLE
　　And, so they ride in purple, eate in plate, · · · 99 F3 Wroth 89
　　And purple-matching Grapes, hee's glad! · · · 290 U85 Country 20
　　A purple piece, or two stitch'd in: when either · · 338 Horace V 19
　　A royall Crowne, and purple, be made hop, · · · 321 Horace 333
PURPLED
　　The purpled pheasant, with the speckled side: · · 94 F2 Penshurst 28
PURPLE-MATCHING
　　And purple-matching Grapes, hee's glad! · · · 290 U85 Country 20
PURPOSE
　　Retyr'd, with purpose your faire worth to praise, · · 80 E126 Mrs Cary 1
　　But 'twas with purpose to have made them such. · · 159 U14 Selden 22
　　Then to the purpose leades, and fitly 'grees. · · 317 Horace 279
PURPOS'D
　　I purpos'd her; that should, with even powers, · · 52 E76 Bedford 1 14
PURPOSELY
　　Himselfe there purposely, or no; and would · · · 335 Horace 657
PURSE
　　My wonder, why the taking a Clownes purse, · · 155 U13 Sacvile 89
　　Bought Flatteries, the issue of his purse, · · · 162 U15 Friend-Wars 13
　　That could but claime a kindred from the purse. · · 216 U45 Squib 10
　　And that's made up as doth the purse abound. · · 230 U56 Covell 12
　　Simo; and, of a talent wip'd his purse; · · · 321 Horace 347
　　Simo, and of a talent cleans'd his purse; · · · 346 Horace V339/347
PURSEWINGE
　　only pursewinge Constancy, in Chainge; · · · 108 F10 Proludium 10
PURSUE
　　To Satyres; and thou dost pursue me. Where, · · 73 E112 Gamster 14
　　Seeme to flye it, it will pursue: · · · · 104 F7 Women but 2
　　Pursue thee in all places, · · · · · 221 U48 Bacchus 34
　　Up so much truth, as could I it pursue · · · 372 Epitaph 13
PURSUES
　　To take the box up for him; and pursues · · · 166 U15 Friend-Wars 137
　　As though the Court pursues them on the sent, · · 186 U32 Elsmere 13
PUSIL
　　Lady, or Pusil, that weares maske, or fan, · · · 370 Fletcher 4
PUSSE
　　They cry'd out Pusse. He told them he was Bankes, · 89 E133 Voyage 183
PUT
　　But that's put in, thou'lt say. Why, so is thine. · · 36 E29 Tilter 6
　　To put out the word, whore, thou do'st me woo, · · 54 E83 Friend 1
　　Throughout my booke. 'Troth put out woman too. · · 54 E83 Friend 2
　　That saw you put on Pallas plumed caske: · · · 68 E105 L Wroth 2 16
　　Be nor put on you, nor you take offence. · · · 69 E108 Soldiers 4
　　Not all these, Edmonds, or what else put too, · · 71 E110 Edmonds 1 11
　　Or thy ranke setting? that thou dar'st put in · · 72 E112 Gamster 4
　　Of those, that put out moneyes, on returne · · 85 E133 Voyage 32
　　To put the skins, and offall in a pastie? · · · 88 E133 Voyage 148
　　Or put to flight Astrea, when her ingots · · · 114 F12 Rutland 24
　　And, keeping a just course, have earely put · · 119 F13 Aubigny 91
　　After flight; and put new stings · · · · 137 U2 Cupid 36
　　Though hate had put them out; · · · · 147 U7 Nymph 25
　　But then, fist-fill'd, to put me off the sent. · · 154 U13 Sacvile 52
　　That with these mixtures we put out her light. · · 156 U13 Sacvile 110
　　That makes the Arch. The rest that there were put · 157 U13 Sacvile 137
　　That as the water makes things, put in't streight, · · 170 U18 Elegy Can 7
　　Put on for fashion, and take up on trust: · · · 171 U20 Shrub 8
　　Wake, and put on the wings of Pindars Muse, · · 176 U25 Desmond 3
　　Hook-handed Harpies, gowned Vultures, put · · 187 U33 Councellour 9
　　Thou hast the brave scorne, to put back the fee! · · 187 U33 Councellour 22
　　To put all relish from my memorie · · · · 197 U40 Elegy That 6
　　Put on my Ivy Garland, let me see · · · · 200 U42 Elegy Let 9
　　Whose like I have knowne the Taylors Wife put on. · 201 U42 Elegy Let 39
　　Put a Coach-mare in Tissue, must I horse · · · 201 U42 Elegy Let 43
　　Care not what trials they are put unto; · · · 218 U47 Tribe 2
　　Put conscience and my right to compromise. · · 218 U47 Tribe 8
　　To put his Court in dances, · · · · · 222 U48 Bacchus 50
　　Put him in mind · · · · · · · 231 U57 Burges 14
　　Had put the Ceston on! · · · · · · 240 U67 Muses V 36
　　Stick on your Cupping-glasses, fear not, put · · 270 U81 Pawlet 53
　　And white, as that, put on: and in her hand, · · 285 U84 Muse 95
　　Put black, and mourning on? and say you misse · · 285 U84 Muse 98
　　Be like a Whet-stone, that an edge can put · · 325 Horace 433
　　This Figure, that thou here seest put, · · · 390 Reader 1
PUTRID
　　Of putrid flesh alive! of blood, the sinke! · · · 172 U21 Ltl Shrub 9

PUTS
  Comus puts in, for new delights; . . .   98   F3 Wroth   48
  That puts it in his Debt-booke e're 't be done; . . 154   U13 Sacvile   34
  That whatsoever face thy fate puts on, . . 168   U15 Friend-Wars 185
  Streight puts off all his Anger, and doth kisse . 193   U38 Elegy 'Tis 88
  When shee puts forth the life of ev'ry thing; . 250   U74 Weston   3
  At th'Calends, puts all out againe. . . 291   U85 Country   70
  All; So this grievous Writer puts to flight . 337   Horace   676
  Honest Tom Tell-Troth puts downe Roger, How? . 378   Coryat 2   81
PYGMY
  Thou paint a Lane, where Thumb the Pygmy meets! . 407   Inigo Jones 2 12
PYRACMON'S
  Pyracmon's houre will come to give them ease, . 179   U25 Desmond   42
PYRAMEDE
  There like a rich, and golden pyramede, . . 115   F12 Rutland   83
PYRAMIDE
  The citie since hath rais'd a Pyramide. . .   89   E133 Voyage   194
PYRAMIDS
  In glorious Piles, or Pyramids erect . . 261   U77 Treasurer   26
  In stately Piles, and Pyramids erect . . 261   U77 Treasurer V 26
PYRATS
  'Gainst stormes, or pyrats, that might charge your peace; 119   F13 Aubigny   93
  All as their prize, turne Pyrats here at Land, . 155   U13 Sacvile   81
PYRENE
  The pale Pyrene, and the forked Mount: . . 366   Ode Who saith 21
PYTHAGORAS
  That stranger doctrine of Pythagoras, . .   61   E95 Savile   2
  Old Bankes the juggler, our Pythagoras, . .   88   E133 Voyage   156
PYTHIAN
  Who, since, to sing the Pythian rites is heard, . 333   Horace   591
  Who now to sing the Pythian Rites is heard, . 353   Horace   V591
PYTHIAS
  And the bold Pythias, having cheated weake . 321   Horace   346
PYTHIUS
  Pythius, I applie 176   U25 Desmond   V 8
Q
  Epitaph on S. P. a Child of Q. El. Chappel. .   77   E120 S. P.   Ttl
  To K. Charles, and Q. Mary. For the losse of their . 235   U63 Charles 2 Ttl
QUADRIVIALL
  He draw a Forum, with quadriviall Streets! . 407   Inigo Jones 2 11
QUAINT
  Such her quaint practise is, so it allures, .   39   E41 Gypsee   3
QUAKE
  He cannot angrie be, but all must quake, . 193   U38 Elegy 'Tis 71
QUALITIE
  So blacke a Bird, so bright a Qualitie. . 369   Ode Who saith 96
QUALITIES
  Their Qualities, and races, . . . 220   U48 Bacchus   10
QUARREL
  Surfet? and Quarrel? drinkes the tother health? . 166   U15 Friend-Wars 115
QUARRELL
  Quarrell with Nature, or in ballance brought . 188   U34 Small Poxe 6
  Subject to quarrell only; or else such . . 218   U47 Tribe   11
  So may there never Quarrell . . . 221   U48 Bacchus   31
  And murmure cannot quarrell at your wayes? . 237   U64 Charles 3 14
  If you dare Quarrell Heaven, and repent . 271   U81 Pawlet   V 79
  The soft birds quarrell in the Woods, . . 290   U85 Country   26
QUARRELLS
  Some hundred quarrells, yet dost thou fight none; .   32   E16 Brain-hardy 6
QUARRELS
  Their loves, their quarrels, jealousies, and wrongs, . 397   Drayton   30
QUARRIE
  Till they be sure to make the foole their quarrie. .   55   E85 Goodyere 1 10
QUARRIES
  To make the Mountaine Quarries move, . . 143   U3 Musicall   11
QUARTER
  The quarter day is come; the hostesse sayes, .   30   E12 Shift   7
  Turne, upon scorned verse, their quarter-face: . 114   F12 Rutland   29
  Winter is come a Quarter e're his Time, . 199   U41 Elegy Since 12
QUARTER-FACE
  Turne, upon scorned verse, their quarter-face: . 114   F12 Rutland   29
QUARTERS
  or hir quarters lighter bee, . . . 417   Moon   31
QUEEN
  Swim without Corke! Why, thank the good Queen Anne. . 405   Inigo Jones 1 68
  Great Queen of Queens, most mild, most meek, most wise, . 414   Ghyrlond   41
  Our King and Queen the Lord-God blesse, . 418   Grace   1
  Our King and Queen the Prince God blesse, . 418   Grace   V 1
QUEENE
  Whose soule heavens Queene, (whose name shee beares) .   33   E22 Daughter   7
  If dancing, all would cry th'Idalian Queene, .   68   E105 L Wroth 2 11
  How many equall with the Argive Queene, . 114   F12 Rutland   49
  To be envi'd of the Queene. . . . 138   U2 Kisse   28
  . . . in Queene Elizabeths Time, since lost, and recovered. 176   U25 Desmond   Ttl
  Whilst the Latin, Queene of Tongues, . . 184   U29 Fit of Rime 34
  An Epigram to the Queene, then lying in. 1630. . 238   U66 Queene   Ttl
  Haile Mary, full of honours, to my Queene, . 238   U66 Queene   5
  To the Queene on her Birth-day . . 239   U67 Muses   VTtl
  The fained Queene of Love, . . . 240   U67 Muses   32
  The bountie of a King, and beautie of his Queene! . 252   U75 Epithalam. 8
  Nought of a Maiden Queene, . . . 254   U75 Epithalam. 47
  All is a story of the King and Queene! . 255   U75 Epithalam. 91
  The miseries of Margaret the Queene . . 398   Drayton   75

		Page	Title	Line

QUEENES
Nor are the Queenes most honor'd maides by th'eares — 63 E97 Motion 18
Have you seene Love-Queenes embraces — 135 U2 Triumph V 35

QUEENS
An Epigram to the Queens Health. — 238 U66 Queene VTtl
Great Queen of Queens, most mild, most meek, most wise, — 414 Ghyrlond 41

QUESTION
But the first question is, when one saw thee? — 81 E129 Mime 2
The Cittie-Question, whether Tilly, or he, — 214 U44 Speach 38
That Clients strove, in Question of the Lawes, — 217 U46 Coke 11
And free it from all question to preserve. — 220 U47 Tribe 72
Because, who have the question, have not seene — 396 Drayton 3

QUESTION'D
But, if it shall be question'd, undertakes, — 74 E115 Honest Man 18
Nor is the title question'd with our proud, — 164 U15 Friend-Wars 83
It hath beene question'd, Michael, if I bee — 396 Drayton 1

QUICK
Quick in his lips! who hath this wonder wrought? — 33 E21 Gam'ster 5
Nor any quick-warming-pan helpe him to bed, — 232 U57 Burges 27
A quick, and dazeling motion! when a paire — 233 U59 Newcastle 9
Some lustie quick Apulians spouse, — 291 U85 Country 42

QUICKE
Her wit as quicke, and sprightfull — 365 Ode Splendor 5

QUICKEN
Let this thought quicken thee, — 174 U23 Himselfe 15
To justifie, and quicken us in breath! — 288 U84 Muse 204

QUICKER
Upon th'accompt, hers grew the quicker trade. — 56 E87 Hazard 5
And thinke thy streame more quicker — 221 U48 Bacchus 27
Clears the Brains, makes Wit the Quicker: — 657 Door Apollo 16

QUICKEST
And strikes the quickest-sighted Judgement blinde. — 363 Riches 16

QUICKEST-SIGHTED
And strikes the quickest-sighted Judgement blinde. — 363 Riches 16

QUICKLY'
For which, or pay me quickly', or Ile pay you. — 51 E73 Fine Grand 22

QUICKLY
Will quickly taste the treason, and commit — 109 F11 Epode 15
(And that quickly) speake your Man. — 140 U2 Promise 30
Quickly fir'd, as in beginners — 141 U2 Her man 31
Goe, get thee quickly forth, — 150 U10 Jealousie 13
Thee quickly come the gardens eye to bee, — 238 U65 Prince 8

QUICKNING
Quickning dead Nature, to her noblest strife. — 162 U15 Friend-Wars 8

QUICKSILVER
As th'other may his braines with Quicksilver. — 208 U43 Vulcan 122

QUICK-WARMING-PAN
Nor any quick-warming-pan helpe him to bed, — 232 U57 Burges 27

QUIET
A quiet mind; free powers; and body sound; — 295 U90 Mart.10:47 6

QUILLS
Breake then thie quills, blott out — 420 Ode:If Men 19

QUILTS
That quilts those bodies, I have leave to span: — 200 U42 Elegy Let 32

QUINCE
Fig, grape, and quince, each in his time doth come: — 94 F2 Penshurst 42

QUINTILIUS
If to Quintilius, you recited ought: — 333 Horace 623

QUINTUS
Quintus Horatius Flaccus his book of . . . — 338 Horace VTtl

QUIRE
May wish us of their Quire. — 144 U3 Musicall 28
That when the Quire is full, — 239 U67 Muses 19
The Solemne Quire cryes, Joy; and they returne, Amen. — 256 U75 Epithalam. 128
An Actors parts, and Office too, the Quire — 317 Horace 276

QUIT
I modestly quit that, and thinke to write, — 72 E112 Gamster 11
Hence-forth I quit thee from my thought, — 100 F4 To the World 3
Both the Arrow he had quit, — 132 U2 How he saw 21
All that dare rowse: or are not loth to quit — 162 U15 Friend-Wars 3
Goe, quit 'hem all. And take along with thee, — 167 U15 Friend-Wars 175
That in all tempests, never quit the helme, — 185 U30 Burleigh 10
T'accuse, or quit all Parties to be heard! — 284 U84 Muse 60

QUITE   (AVOID)
So huge, it seem'd, they could by no meanes quite her. — 86 E133 Voyage 86

QUITE
And crie good! good! This quite perverts my sense, — 38 E38 Guiltie 2 5
Were quite out-spun. The like wish hath his wife. — 40 E42 Giles 12
His cloke with orient velvet quite lin'd through, — 62 E97 Motion 4
Is now from home. You lose your labours quite, — 89 E133 Voyage 181
Quite overcame, — 129 U1 Father 25
And my motion from me quite; — 132 U2 How he saw 26
And spunge-like with it dry up the blood quite: — 155 U13 Sacvile 69
Be simple quite throughout, and wholly one. — 307 Horace 32
Be simple quite throughout, and alwayes one. — 339 Horace V 32
In sound, quite from his fortune; both the rout, — 313 Horace 159
Betweene the Acts, a quite cleane other thing — 317 Horace 278
Quite from all face of Tragedie to goe, — 321 Horace 344
And sworne, that he will quite discard thee — 662 Bedford 7

QUIT'ST
That quit'st the cause so oft, and rayl'st at men? — 44 E54 Chev'ril 2 4

QUITT
The Marrow! Wretch, I quitt thee of thy paine — 408 Inigo Jones 3 5

QUITT (cont.)
  he that will honest be, may quitt the Court, . . . 423 Lucan 17
QUIVER
  Where's thy Quiver? bend thy Bow: . . . 132 U2 How he saw 9
  His flames, his shafts, his Quiver, and his Bow, . . . 182 U28 Worth 10
QUIXOTE
  The learned Librarie of Don Quixote; . . . 204 U43 Vulcan 31
QUOIT (See COIT, COYT)
QUOTH
  But many Moones there shall not wane (quoth hee) . . 87 E133 Voyage 103
  Which when he felt, Away (quoth hee) . . . 93 F1 Why write no 3
R
  R. Rose, I. Ivy, E. sweet Eglantine. . . . 412 Ghyrlond 4
RABBIN
  A Rabbin confutes him with the Bastinado. . . . 375 Coryat 1 23
RACE (RUN)
  Before his swift and circled race be run, . . . 116 F12 Rutland 99
  Before his swift and fetherd race be run, . . . 116 F12 Rutland V 99
  But being in Motion still (or rather in race) . . . 166 U15 Friend-Wars 124
  To all the uses of the field, and race, . . . 228 U53 Newcastle 3
  Chear'd her faire Sisters in her race to runne! . . . 270 U81 Pawlet 58
  Faine words, unheard of to the girded race . . . 340 Horace V 71
  Hee, that's ambitious in the race to touch . . . 333 Horace 587
RACE
  Saw all his race approch the blacker floods: . . . 41 E44 Chuff 4
  And the great Heroes, of her race, . . . 98 F3 Wroth 56
  Then sword, or fire, or what is of the race . . . 193 U38 Elegy 'Tis 101
  Of race accompted, that no passion have . . . 201 U42 Elegy Let 49
  Alone, and such a race, . . . 257 U75 Epithalam. 157
  Till you behold a race to fill your Hall, . . . 258 U75 Epithalam. 169
  Hee were the wretched'st of the race of men: . . . 272 U81 Pawlet 97
  As the old race of Mankind were, . . . 289 U85 Country 2
  And with his hooke lops off the fruitlesse race, . . . 290 U85 Country 11
  Faine words, unheard of to the well-truss'd race . . . 309 Horace 71
  To chant the Gods, and all their God-like race, . . . 311 Horace 114
  With all the race . . . 369 Ode Who saith 118
  Lives in his issue, even so, the race . . . 392 Shakespeare 66
RACES
  Their Qualities, and races, . . . 220 U48 Bacchus 10
RACK (DRIVE)
  As neither wine doe rack it out, or mirth. . . . 197 U40 Elegy That 18
RACK
  Were the Rack offer'd them, how they came so; . . . 157 U13 Sacvile 130
  In admiration, stretch'd upon the rack . . . 163 U15 Friend-Wars 50
  Rime, the rack of finest wits, . . . 183 U29 Fit of Rime 1
  The Clowdes rack cleare before the Sun, . . . 251 U74 Weston 8
  And rack, with Wine, the man whom they would try, . . . 333 Horace 618
RADAMANTHUS
  Calling for Radamanthus, that dwelt by, . . . 89 E133 Voyage 187
RADCLIFFE
  To Sir John Radcliffe. . . . 60 E93 Radcliffe Ttl
  How like a columne, Radcliffe, left alone . . . 60 E93 Radcliffe 1
RADIANT
  As 'tis not radiant, but divine: . . . 278 U84 Mind 26
RAGE
  To have so soone scap'd worlds, and fleshes rage, . . . 41 E45 First Son 7
  As we, the rob'd, leave rage, and pittie it. . . . 44 E56 Poet-Ape 4
  And that, midst envy' and parts; then fell by rage: . . . 71 E110 Edmonds 1 14
  And many a sinke pour'd out her rage anenst 'hem; . . . 86 E133 Voyage 75
  Goe enter breaches, meet the cannons rage, . . . 98 F3 Wroth 69
  But onely Poets, rapt with rage divine? . . . 115 F12 Rutland 63
  Not ravish'd all hence in a minutes rage. . . . 205 U43 Vulcan 56
  Not snatch them hence in one poor minutes rage. . . . 205 U43 Vulcan V 56
  His rage, with razing your immortall Towne. . . . 242 U70 Ode 4
  Possest with holy rage, . . . 245 U70 Ode 80
  With entheate rage, to publish their bright tracts? . . . 368 Ode Who saith 61
  Shine forth, thou Starre of Poets, and with rage, . . . 392 Shakespeare 77
RAGES
  It rages, runs, flies, stands, and would provoke . . . 283 U84 Muse 24
RAGGED
  How scabbed, how ragged, and how pediculous . . . 380 Coryat 3 34
RAGING
  About in Cloudes, and wrapt in raging weather, . . . 193 U38 Elegy 'Tis 75
  Wild raging lusts; prescribe the mariage good; . . . 327 Horace 489
RAIGNE
  And in this short time of thy happiest raigne, . . . 37 E35 James 2 4
  As if in Saturnes raigne it were; . . . 98 F3 Wroth 50
  . . . On the Universary day of his Raigne. 1629. . . . 236 U64 Charles 3 VTtl
  When you that raigne, are her Example growne, . . . 236 U64 Charles 3 9
RAIGN'D
  As if thou, then, wert mine, or I raign'd here: . . . 95 F2 Penshurst 74
RAIGNES
  in whom the flame of every beauty raignes, . . . 108 F10 Proludium 8
RAIGNING
  But, that shee raigning here, . . . 240 U67 Muses 35
  Meere raigning words: nor will I labour so . . . 321 Horace 343
RAILE (BIRD)
  Knat, raile, and ruffe too. How so ere, my man . . . 65 E101 Supper 20
RAILE (See also RAYL'ST)
  Or 'gainst the Bishops, for the Brethren, raile, . . . 59 E92 New Crie 35
  And firke, and jerke, and for the Coach-man raile, . . . 164 U15 Friend-Wars 72
RAILES
  At hunting railes, having no guift in othes, . . . 76 E119 Shelton 2

	Page	Title	Line
RAILING			
Secure thy railing Rhymes, infamous Gill,	410	Gill	2
RAINBOW			
Or Rainbow is describ'd. But here was now	305	Horace	23
RAINE			
Why was't? did e're the Cloudes aske back their raine?	192	U38 Elegy 'Tis	56
The name of Cruell weather, storme, and raine?	193	U38 Elegy 'Tis	82
And in a dew of sweetest Raine,	251	U74 Weston	4
RAINGE			
Such, as in lustes wilde forrest love to rainge,	108	F10 Proludium	9
RAISE (See also RAYSE)			
Of what ambition, faction, pride can raise;	66	E102 Pembroke	15
Might then both thee, thy worke and merit raise:	83	E132 Sylvester	2
To raise my spirits with thy conjuring wine,	107	F10 Proludium	11
To raise our spirits with thy conjuring wine,	107	F10 Proludium	V 11
It is the Muse, alone, can raise to heaven,	114	F12 Rutland	41
And raise not vertue; they may vice enhance.	117	F13 Aubigny	42
And raise a noble stemme, to give the fame,	119	F13 Aubigny	97
Flowes in upon me, and I cannot raise	160	U14 Selden	62
Yet is't your vertue now I raise.	173	U22 Elegy Tho	4
Of brightest Mira, doe we raise our Song,	264	U79 New-yeares	24
And voyce to raise them from my brazen Lungs,	269	U81 Pawlet	24
Yet sometime both the Comoedy doth raise	341	Horace	V132
And jests; and both to admiration raise	323	Horace	400
And thinke to ruine, where it seem'd to raise.	391	Shakespeare	12
Hanch against Hanch, or raise a riming Club	396	Drayton	8
That Art, or Ingine, on the strength can raise.	400	Beaumont	10
RAIS'D			
Loe, what my countrey should have done (have rais'd	46	E60 Mounteagle	1
But I repent me: Stay. Who e're is rais'd,	48	E65 Muse	15
As, to be rais'd by her, is onely fame.	49	E67 Suffolk	4
Judge they, that can: here I have rais'd to show	67	E104 Montgomery	13
The citie since hath rais'd a Pyramide.	89	E133 Voyage	194
Hath Petrarch since his Laura rais'd	181	U27 Ode Helen	21
And steps of all rais'd servants of the Crowne,	217	U46 Coke	2
Hath rais'd to be the Port unto his Land!	250	U73 Weston	4
Stand there; for when a noble Nature's rais'd,	256	U75 Epithalam.	113
And jests; and both to admiration rais'd,	348	Horace	V386/400
Thy Richard, rais'd in song, past pulling downe.	385	Brooke	8
And those in number so, and measure rais'd,	395	May	8
RAISING			
Raising the World to good or evill fame,	175	U24 Frontispice	3
Of raising, judging, and rewarding all	288	U84 Muse	207
RAK'D			
That was rak'd up in the Winchestrian Goose	209	U43 Vulcan	142
Which was rak'd up in the Winchestrian Goose	209	U43 Vulcan	V142
RAM'D			
Were they as strong ram'd up as Aetna gates.	363	Riches	10
RAMMES			
But 'bove the fat of rammes, or bulls, to prize	127	U1 Trinitie	11
Our teeming Ewes, and lustie-mounting Rammes.	264	U79 New-yeares	17
Your teeming Ewes, aswell as mounting Rammes.	265	U79 New-yeares	51
RAMPARTS			
In Bulwarkes, Rav'lins, Ramparts, for defense,	400	Beaumont	4
RAN			
Whose dice not doing well, to'a pulpit ran.	76	E119 Shelton	6
The sinkes ran grease, and haire of meazled hogs,	88	E133 Voyage	145
For I ran and call'd on Cupid;	132	U2 How he saw	6
Strait hee ran, and durst not stay,	132	U2 How he saw	16
As all with storme and tempest ran together.	193	U38 Elegy 'Tis	76
RANCK			
Thy skill hath made of ranck dispised weedes;	361	Palmer	10
RANCKE			
Of which usurping rancke, some have thought love	110	F11 Epode	31
RANCK'D			
For, if thou shame, ranck'd with my friends, to goe,	53	E77 Not name	3
RANDOME			
My Verse at randome, and licentiously?	323	Horace	391
RANGE			
Our proper vertue is to range:	146	U6 Defence	4
RANKE (ADJECTIVE)			
Or thy ranke setting? that thou dar'st put in	72	E112 Gamster	4
RANKE			
For strict degrees of ranke, or title looke:	29	E9 To All	2
Alone, but all thy ranke a reverend Name.	187	U33 Councellour	40
We will beleeve, like men of our owne Ranke,	215	U44 Speach	75
RANK'D			
Velvet, or Taffata cap, rank'd in the darke	371	Fletcher	5
RANKNESSE			
But still, it seem'd, the ranknesse did convince 'hem.	88	E133 Voyage	152
And impious ranknesse of all Sects and seeds:	163	U15 Friend-Wars	34
RANNE			
Though Lippe, at Pauls, ranne from his text away,	52	E75 Lippe	3
RANULPH			
By Ranulph———	274	U84 Descent	18
RAPE			
From Zephyr's rape would close him with his beames.	366	Ode Who saith	24
RAP'D			
And whither rap'd, now thou but stoup'st to mee?	122	F15 Heaven	14
RAPH			
To Sir Raph Shelton	76	E119 Shelton	Ttl
And God blesse me, and God blesse Raph.	419	Grace	8

		Page	Title	Line
RAPHAEL				
Titian, or Raphael, Michael Angelo,	• • • • •	260	U77 Treasurer	7
RAPINE				
Purchas'd by rapine, worse then stealth,	• • • •	99	F3 Wroth	82
RAPPS				
(As if he knew it) rapps his hearer to	• • • •	315	Horace	212
RAP'S				
which rap's mee up to the true heav'en of love;	• •	108	F10 Proludium	13
RAP'T				
Rap't from the Earth, as not to die?	• • • •	181	U27 Ode Helen	14
And is not rap't	• • • • • •	367	Ode Who saith	60
Or Tames be rap't from us	• • • • •	369	Ode Who saith	107
RAPT				
This morning, timely rapt with holy fire,	• • •	52	E76 Bedford 1	1
But onely Poets, rapt with rage divine?	• • •	115	F12 Rutland	63
But holie Poets, rapt with sence divine?	• • •	115	F12 Rutland	V 63
But, that a Mind so rapt, so high,	• • • •	279	U84 Mind	41
In this sweet Extasie, she was rapt hence.	• •	289	U84 Muse	225
Next, that which rapt mee, was: I might behold	• •	361	Palmer	13
RAPTURE				
Thy Priest in this strange rapture; heat my braine	• •	177	U25 Desmond	11
RARE				
But two things, rare, the Fates had in their store,	• •	28	E4 James 1	3
Rare, as wonder, was her wit;	• • • •	39	E40 Ratcliffe	9
He should those rare, and absolute numbers view,	• •	53	E79 Rutland	11
As noble in great chiefes, as they are rare.	• •	58	E91 Vere	16
Crowne with their owne. Rare poemes aske rare friends.	•	60	E94 Bedford 3	6
But one more rare, and in the case so new:	• •	62	E97 Motion	3
Richer then Time, and as Time's vertue, rare.	• •	111	F11 Epode	59
They speake; since you are truly that rare wife,	• •	119	F13 Aubigny	110
Rather to boast rich hangings, then rare friends.	• •	242	U69 Friend Son	26
Rare Plants from ev'ry banke doe rise,	• • •	251	U74 Weston	10
Of Accius, and Ennius, rare appeares:	• • •	323	Horace	382
So rare, as with some taxe it doth ingage	• •	323	Horace	383
Then I admir'd, the rare and prescious use	• •	361	Palmer	9
Be then both Rare, and Good; and long	• • •	367	Ode Who saith	33
RARELY				
A fortune, in this age, but rarely knowne.	• •	96	F2 Penshurst	92
Rarely repent,	• • • • • •	129	U1 Father	14
RARENESSE				
"For stile of rarenesse, to degenerate.	• • •	367	Ode Who saith	32
RARER				
That Poets are far rarer births then kings,	• •	53	E79 Rutland	1
RARIFIED				
In all his Actions rarified to spright;	• • •	197	U40 Elegy That	20
Of bodies, meet like rarified ayre!	• • •	233	U59 Newcastle	10
RARITIE				
Force from the Phoenix, then, no raritie	• • •	255	U75 Epithalam.	81
With such a Raritie, and not rowse Art	• •	282	U84 Muse	16
RASH				
The furie of a rash command,	• • • •	98	F3 Wroth	68
The furie of some rash command,	• • • •	98	F3 Wroth	V 68
The rash, and head-long eloquence brought forth	•	319	Horace	307
RASHNESSE				
'Twixt feare and rashnesse: not a lust obscene,	• •	156	U13 Sacvile	106
RATCLIFFE				
On Margaret Ratcliffe.	• • • • •	39	E40 Ratcliffe	Ttl
RATE (CHIDE)				
Foole, doe not rate my Rymes; I'have found thy Vice	• •	408	Detractor	5
RATE				
Of Valour, but at this Idolatrous rate?	• •	156	U13 Sacvile	104
Without your gift, though I can rate that too,	• •	157	U13 Sacvile	158
Of all the Land. Who now at such a Rate,	• •	185	U30 Burleigh	19
That turnes us so much moneys, at which rate	• •	215	U44 Speach	77
View'd there the mercat, read the wretched rate	•	234	U61 Epigram	3
My title, at their rate, I'ad rather, I,	• • •	325	Horace	432
RATED				
Thy table without art, and easy-rated:	• • •	295	U90 Mart.10:47	8
RATES				
O bountie! so to difference the rates!	• • •	235	U62 Charles 1	12
RATHER				
Courtling, I rather thou should'st utterly	• • •	43	E52 Courtling	1
Thou rather striv'st the matter to possesse,	• •	70	E109 Nevil	9
Nay, rather both our soules bee strayn'd	• •	144	U3 Musicall	25
I Now thinke, Love is rather deafe, then blind,	•	149	U9 Picture	1
I Doubt that, Love is rather deafe, then blind,	•	149	U9 Picture	V 1
I feele, I'm rather dead then he!	• • •	152	U12 Corbet	36
Rather then Office, when it doth or may	• •	158	U14 Selden	9
Rather then here so bogg'd in vices stay.	• •	163	U15 Friend-Wars	30
But being in Motion still (or rather in race)	•	166	U15 Friend-Wars	124
Rather than meet him: And, before his eyes	•	185	U30 Burleigh	16
Rather then once displease you more, to die,	•	193	U38 Elegy 'Tis	92
Rather then want your light, I wish a grave.	•	194	U38 Elegy 'Tis	122
O, keepe it still; for it had rather be	• •	199	U41 Elegy Since	17
If that were so, thou rather would'st advance	•	209	U43 Vulcan	151
Of Wines, to thee the rather	• • • •	220	U48 Bacchus	2
The rather when the vices of the Time	• •	224	U50 Countesse	9
But rather with advantage to be found	• •	224	U50 Squib	11
And rather wish, in their expence of Sack,	• •	229	U54 Squib	11
Rather to boast rich hangings, then rare friends.	• •	241	U68 House-hold	9
James the blessed, pleas'd the rather,	• •	242	U69 Friend Son	26
But rather I, should I of that part speake!	•	259	U76 Petition	6
May rather yet adore, then spy.	• • •	269	U81 Pawlet	28
		276	U84 Body	20

		Page	Title	Line

RATHER   (cont.)
     Hath given wholly to the Sonne (the rather   288   U84 Muse   216
     Perversly modest, had I rather owe   311   Horace   130
     Or rather, thinking all my faults may spie,   .   .   . 323   Horace   392
     My title, at their rate, I'ad rather, I, ... 325   Horace   432
     Then: If your fault you rather had defend   .   .   . 335   Horace   629
     It should rather have bene Tom that a horse did lack.   . 374   Coryat 1   15
     Rather his sonne, I should have cal'd thee, why?   .   . 378   Coryat 2   88
     What Muse, or rather God of harmony   395   May   14
     Thy blatant Muse abroad, and teach it rather   .   .   . 411   Gill   11
     And rather to the Fyre, then to the Rowte   .   .   . 420   Ode:If Men   21
RATLING
     And the ratling pit-pat-noyse, ... 259   U76 Petition   19
RATTLES
     For, though that Rattles, Timbrels, Toyes,   .   .   . 273   U84 Cradle   17
RATTLING
     'Bove rattling Rime.   273   U84 Cradle   16
RAVE
     Th'Iambick arm'd Archilochus to rave, ... 311   Horace   117
RAVENOUS
     So ravenous, and vast an appetite?   206   U43 Vulcan   86
RAVISH'D
     Onely, thus much, out of a ravish'd zeale,   .   .   . 119   F13 Aubigny   108
     And like the ravish'd Sheep'erds said, ... 130   U1 Nativitie   4
     Not ravish'd all hence in a minutes rage.   .   .   . 205   U43 Vulcan   56
     Whilst all the ravish'd rout   240   U67 Muses   40
     It makes me ravish'd with just wonder, cry   .   .   . 395   May   13
     That reade it? that are ravish'd! such was I   .   .   . 397   Drayton   53
RAVISHED
     The Belgick fever ravished away.   60   E93 Radcliffe   8
RAV'LINS
     In Bulwarkes, Rav'lins, Ramparts, for defense,   .   . 400   Beaumont   4
RAYL'ST
     That quit'st the cause so oft, and rayl'st at men?   .   . 44   E54 Chev'ril 2   4
RAYN'D
     Must now be rayn'd.   180   U26 Ode High   15
RAY'SD
     A farther fury my ray'sd spirit Controules,   .   .   . 108   F10 Proludium   12
RAYSE
     Whil'st thou dost rayse some Player, from the grave,   . 81   E129 Mime   11
     trust in the tombes, their care-full freinds do rayse;   . 387   Cavendish   6
     I then could rayse my notes   419   Ode:If Men   6
RAYSING
     In raysing him the wisdome of my King.   225   U51 Bacon   20
RAZ'D
     And raz'd, e're thought could urge, This might have bin!   . 209   U43 Vulcan   136
RAZING
     His rage, with razing your immortall Towne.   .   .   . 242   U70 Ode   4
RE
     Which if they misse, they yet should re-advance   .   . 55   E85 Goodyere 1   8
     Sol will re-shine. If not, Charles hath a Sonne.   .   . 238   U65 Prince   12
     That shall re-joyne yee. Was she, then, so deare,   .   . 285   U84 Muse   107
REACH
     The lighter Faunes, to reach thy Ladies oke.   .   .   . 94   F2 Penshurst   18
     Hang on thy walls, that every child may reach.   .   . 94   F2 Penshurst   44
     Her upright head, above the reach of Chance,   .   .   . 176   U25 Desmond   6
     If his wit reach no higher, but to spring   232   U58 Book-seller   7
     To plant the Musick where noe eare can reach!   .   . 404   Inigo Jones 1   53
REACH'D
     What not the envie of the seas reach'd too,   .   .   . 37   E32 Roe 2   4
     By this time had they reach'd the Stygian poole,   .   . 87   E133 Voyage   121
     Till he hath reach'd his two-fold point of Noone.   .   . 414   Ghyrlond   52
REACHING
     Extend a reaching vertue, early and late: 258   U75 Epithalam. 180
READ   (See also REED)
     Read not in faire heavens storie, ... 39   E40 Ratcliffe   6
     When I am read, thou fain'st a weake applause,   .   . 43   E52 Courtling   3
     Dare for these poemes, yet, both aske, and read,   .   . 60   E94 Bedford 3   12
     But when I read that speciall piece, restor'd,   .   .   . 61   E95 Savile   7
     And that to write things worthy to be read: .   .   . 63   E99 Th Roe 2   4
     How few have read! how fewer understood!)   .   .   . 71   E110 Edmonds 1   16
     Weepe with me all you that read   77   E120 S. P.   1
     If you then will read the Storie, ... 131   U2 Excuse   13
     Read so much wast, as she cannot imbrace   .   .   . 150   U9 Picture   16
     And pray who shall my sorrowes read, ... 152   U12 Corbet   33
     Your Booke, my Selden, I have read, and much   .   . 158   U14 Selden   5
     Is but a Statists theame, to read Phlebotomie.   .   . 179   U25 Desmond   39
     Read here in one, what thou in all canst find,   .   . 185   U30 Burleigh   2
     But when I read or heare the names so rife   .   .   . 187   U33 Councellour   7
     Translated Aelian tatickes to be read, ... 214   U44 Speach   35
     One lesson we have both learn'd, and well read;   .   . 216   U45 Squib   4
     So short you read my Character, and theirs   .   .   . 220   U47 Tribe   73
     Pardon, I read it in thy face, the day   225   U51 Bacon   5
     Me thought I read the ancient Art of Thrace,   .   .   . 228   U53 Newcastle   4
     View'd there the mercat, read the wretched rate   .   . 234   U61 Epigram   3
     Where they might read, and find   247   U70 Ode   122
     Yet read him in these lines: He doth excell   .   .   . 262   U78 Digby   2
     When hee shall read them at the Treasurers bord,   . 263   U78 Digby   27
     When hee doth read them at the Treasurers bord,   . 263   U78 Digby   V 27
     Being sent to one, they will be read of all.   .   .   . 263   U78 Digby   32
     Who read what the Crepundia bee, ... 273   U84 Cradle   14
     Read here a little, that thou mayst know much.   .   . 371   Epitaph   2
     I find thee write most worthy to be read.   .   .   . 386   Browne   6

READ (cont.)

	Page	Title	Line
Shall finde, that either hath read Bookes, and Men:	389	Aleman	2
And we have wits to read, and praise to give.	391	Shakespeare	24
There read I, streight, thy learned Legends three,	397	Drayton	25
I saw, and read, it was thy Barons Warres!	397	Drayton	42
Looke, how we read the Spartans were inflam'd	398	Drayton	67
Of many Coulors! read them! & reveale	404	Inigo Jones 1	47
If thou be soe desyrous to be read,	408	Inigo Jones 3	9
When I had read your holy Meditations,	411	Sutcliffe	1
(You have deserv'd it from me) I have read,	415	Rutter	13
O're read, examin'd, try'd, and prov'd your Ryme	421	Censure	7

READE

	Page	Title	Line
To reade it well: that is, to understand.	27	E1 Reader	2
When, in my booke, men reade but Cecill's name,	41	E43 Salisbury 1	9
When, in my Verse, men reade but Sarum's name,	41	E43 Salisbury 1 V	9
To reade my verses; now I must to heare:	45	E58 Groome	2
Reade all I send: and, if I find but one	62	E96 Donne 2	7
Shall reade a piece of Virgil, Tacitus,	65	E101 Supper	21
Reade, in their vertuous parents noble parts,	96	F2 Penshurst	97
Had he had the facultie to reade, and write!	201	U42 Elegy Let	64
If, Passenger, thou canst but reade:	233	U60 La-ware	1
Thy faint, and narrow eyes, to reade the King	250	U73 Weston	2
You'ld reade a Snake, in his next Song.	260	U76 Petition	32
Who cannot reade, but onely doth desire	383	Author	9
And, where the most reade bookes, on Authors fames,	386	Browne	9
When, Rome, I reade thee in thy mighty paire,	395	May	1
Of all that reade thy Poly-olbyon.	397	Drayton	52
That reade it? that are ravish'd! such was I	397	Drayton	53
Thou hast deserv'd: And let me reade the while	398	Drayton	60
That can but reade; who cannot, may in prose	398	Drayton	73

READER

	Page	Title	Line
To the Reader.	27	E1 Reader	Ttl
In a little? Reader, stay.	79	E124 Elizabeth	2
Reader, whose life, and name, did e're become	152	U12 Corbet	37
So that my Reader is assur'd, I now	159	U14 Selden	27
Reader stay,	168	U16 Gray	1
Sweet mix'd with sowre, to his Reader, so	329	Horace	515
To the Reader.	390	Reader	Ttl
But, since he cannot, Reader, looke	390	Reader	9
And pray thee Reader, bring thy weepinge Eyes	394	Jane Ogle	2
Above his Reader, or his Prayser, is.	400	Beaumont	2

READERS

	Page	Title	Line
All, that are readers: but, me thinkes 'tis od,	85	E133 Voyage	43
Her joyes, her smiles, her loves, as readers take	182	U28 Worth	13
Whose Readers did not thinke he was in love.	199	U42 Elegy Let	4
No lesse of praise, then readers in all kinds	217	U46 Coke	19
So with this Authors Readers will it thrive:	362	Author	12

READES

	Page	Title	Line
That lost, he keepes his chamber, reades Essayes,	30	E12 Shift	15
Which hee thinkes great; and so reades verses, too:	35	E28 Surly	5
Play-wright me reades, and still my verses damnes,	42	E49 Playwrt 1	1
Who Edmonds, reades thy booke, and doth not see	72	E111 Edmonds 2	1
Who reades, will pardon my Intelligence,	289	U84 Muse	226

READING

	Page	Title	Line
And there an end of him with reading makes:	355	Horace	V678

READS

	Page	Title	Line
Who reads may roave, and call the passage darke,	383	Author	5
Who reads, who roaves, who hopes to understand,	383	Author	7

RE-ADVANCE

	Page	Title	Line
Which if they misse, they yet should re-advance	55	E85 Goodyere 1	8

READY

	Page	Title	Line
Ready to cast, at one, whose band sits ill,	164	U15 Friend-Wars	69
To teach each suit he has, the ready way	165	U15 Friend-Wars	108
Sitting, and ready to be drawne,	275	U84 Body	1
And unbought viands ready makes:	291	U85 Country	48

REALL

	Page	Title	Line
Where is that nominall marke, or reall rite,	160	U14 Selden	47
But when thou turnst a Reall Inigo;	407	Inigo Jones 2	22

REALME

	Page	Title	Line
The only faithfull Watchman for the Realme,	185	U30 Burleigh	9
Of so much safetie to the Realme, and King.	238	U66 Queene	14

REALMES

	Page	Title	Line
The spoused paire two realmes, the sea the ring.	28	E5 Union	4
Hast purg'd thy realmes, as we have now no cause	38	E35 James 2	5

REAME

	Page	Title	Line
Especially in paper; many a Reame	205	U43 Vulcan	V 61
Had tickled your large Nosthrill: many a Reame	205	U43 Vulcan	62

REAP'D

	Page	Title	Line
On thy good lady, then! who, therein, reap'd	95	F2 Penshurst	84

REARE

	Page	Title	Line
Borne up by statues, shall I reare your head,	115	F12 Rutland	84
besett with statues, shall I reare your head,	115	F12 Rutland	V 84
This hasty sacrifice, wherein I reare	116	F12 Rutland	97
Reare-Suppers in their Names! and spend whole nights	156	U13 Sacvile	101
And what they will not. Him, whose choice doth reare	307	Horace	56
His choise, who's matter to his power doth reare,	339	Horace	V 58/ 56
Yet, who dares offer a redoubt to reare?	401	Beaumont	11

REAR'D

	Page	Title	Line
Behold where Cerberus, rear'd on the wall	89	E133 Voyage	176
They'are rear'd with no mans ruine, no mans grone,	94	F2 Penshurst	46
His falling Temples you have rear'd,	173	U22 Elegy Tho	17

REARES

	Page	Title	Line
Shee chearfully supporteth what she reares,	176	U24 Frontispice	13

	Page	Title	Line

REARE-SUPPERS
Reare-Suppers in their Names! and spend whole nights . . 156 U13 Sacvile 101
REARING
That in rearing such a Schoole, ... 184 U29 Fit of Rime 59
REASON'
Betweene the doubtfull sway of Reason', and sense; . . . 370 Author 12
REASON
There's reason good, that you good lawes should make: . . 34 E24 Parliament 1
Little, for me, had reason done, ... 101 F4 To the World 35
To wakefull reason, our affections king: . . 109 F11 Epode 13
And strike our reason blinde. . . . . . 110 F11 Epode 30
Till she be the reason why, ... 131 U2 Excuse 23
Of reason emptie is?! . . . . 143 U3 Musicall 6
Stil may reason warre with rime, ... 184 U29 Fit of Rime 53
What use, what strength of reason! and how much . . 187 U33 Councellour 24
Being tould there, Reason cannot, Sense may erre. . . 370 Author 14
REASONS
But all so cleare, and led by reasons flame, . . 220 U47 Tribe 69
And give you reasons more then one. . . . . 277 U84 Mind 4
REBELL
For either our affections doe rebell, . . 109 F11 Epode 21
Yet I rebell, ... 129 U1 Father 26
The Rebell Gyants stoope, and Gorgon Envye yeild, . . 421 Ode:If Men 41
REBELLS
Upbraiding rebells armes, and barbarous pride: . . 60 E93 Radcliffe 6
And being a thing, blowne out of nought, rebells . . 163 U15 Friend-Wars 32
That Rebells actions, are but valiant crimes! . . 397 Drayton 44
REBUKE
On all that come her Simplesse to rebuke! . . . 253 U75 Epithalam. 44
RECALL
Recall him yet, hee'ld be no more a man: . . . 335 Horace 668
RECEAVE
Nor doe wrongs, nor wrongs receave; . . . 142 U2 Her man 49
But, as a friend, which name your selfe receave, . . 190 U37 Friend-Book 10
RECEIPT
Spanish receipt, to make her teeth to rot. . . . 188 U34 Small Poxe 12
Thrice happy house, that hast receipt . . . 280 U84 Mind 53
RECEIVE
No more then he doth thanke, that will receive . . 154 U13 Sacvile 43
Engines of Murder, and receive the praise . . 212 U43 Vulcan 207
And those thy new, and late-coyn'd words receive, . . 309 Horace 74
Receive, or give it an applause, the more. . . 321 Horace 364
Receive, or give it any Crowne the more. . . 347 Horace V356/364
Receive it for a Fable, ... 364 Phoenix 2
RECEIV'D
Then what he hath receiv'd. Gifts stinke from some, . 153 U13 Sacvile 22
Can I owe thankes, for Curtesies receiv'd . . 153 U13 Sacvile 25
Whether the Sea receiv'd into the shore, . . 309 Horace 91
Which law receiv'd, the Chorus held his peace, . . 323 Horace 369
Will bee receiv'd in Court; If not, would I . . 389 Aleman 19
RECEIVED
And are received for the Covey of Witts; . . . 218 U47 Tribe 22
RECELEBRATES
Recelebrates the joyfull Match with France. . . 401 Filmer 10
RECEPTION
Of the late Mysterie of reception, . . . 219 U47 Tribe 48
RECITED
If to Quintilius, you recited ought: . . . 333 Horace 623
RECITING
And, there an end of him, reciting makes: . . 337 Horace 678
RECK'NED
Cannot a man be reck'ned in the State . . 156 U13 Sacvile 103
RECK'NING
About the towne: this reck'ning I will pay, . . 396 Drayton 9
RECKON
Into the debt; and reckon on her head, . . 80 E127 Aubigny 5
Find you to reckon nothing, me owe all. . . 158 U13 Sacvile 164
RECONCIL'D
And, reconcil'd, keepe him suspected still. . . 48 E65 Muse 8
Reconcil'd to Love, and me. . . . . 133 U2 Suffered 6
RECORD
Upon record, in this blest child. . . 188 U35 Chute 4
T'Is a Record in heaven. You, that were . . 399 Lady Ogle 1
And this a coppie is of the Record. . . 400 Lady Ogle 40
RECORDED
Their names are not recorded on the File . . 257 U75 Epithalam. 155
RECORDS
Records, and Authors of! how rectified . . 160 U14 Selden 43
In those Records, which, were all Chroniclers gone, . . 210 U43 Vulcan 171
In those Records, which, were our Chroniclers gone, . . 210 U43 Vulcan V171
Whose lines her rowles were, and records. . . 247 U70 Ode 126
Whose lives her rowles were, and records. . . 247 U70 Ode V126
RECOVERED
. . . in Queene Elizabeths Time, since lost, and recovered. . 176 U25 Desmond Ttl
RECOVERY
For the recovery of my voyce? No, there . . . 167 U15 Friend-Wars 154
RECTIFIE
Yet shall you have, to rectifie your palate, . . 64 E101 Supper 9
RECTIFIED
Records, and Authors of! how rectified . . . 160 U14 Selden 43
REDEEME
And never will redeeme a day, ... 100 F4 To the World 23
To redeeme mine, I had sent in; Enough, . . 205 U43 Vulcan 63

REDEEME (cont.)
Suffring, and dying to redeeme our losse! . . . . 288 U84 Muse 202
REDEEM'D
What fables have you vext! what truth redeem'd! . . 159 U14 Selden 39
REDEEMER
Whom her Redeemer, honour'd hath above . . . . 285 U84 Muse 100
(As being Redeemer, and Repairer too . . . . 288 U84 Muse 213
REDEMPTION
The price of our Redemption, and to teach . . . 286 U84 Muse 134
REDOUBT
Yet, who dares offer a redoubt to reare? . . . . 401 Beaumont 11
REDUICTS
Reduicts, Halfe-moones, Horne-workes, and such close wayes, . 248 U71 Treasurer 8
REED (VERB)
Her Children, and Grand-children, reed it heere! . . 399 Lady Ogle 2
REED
They had, but were a Reed unto thy Sword. . . . 187 U33 Councellour 34
REEDES
They made a Vulcan of a sheafe of Reedes, . . . 208 U43 Vulcan 126
It is a wretched thing to trust to reedes; . . . 281 U84 Kenelme 16
REEDS
But, O those Reeds! thy meere disdaine of them, . . 208 U43 Vulcan 129
REEKING
Their reeking fumes; . . . . 368 Ode Who saith 78
REFINE
Whose worke could this be, Chapman, to refine . . 388 Chapman 1
REFIN'D
My mirror is more subtile, cleere, refin'd, . . . 117 F13 Aubigny 43
The same it was inspir'd, rich, and refin'd. . . . 225 U50 Countesse 30
REFLECT
Doe I reflect. Some alderman has power, . . . 117 F13 Aubigny 38
But wisest Inigo! who can reflect . . . . 405 Inigo Jones 1 86
REFLECTION
Graced by your Reflection! . . . . . 177 U25 Desmond 17
REFLEXE
Shee was the light (without reflexe . . . . 399 Lady Ogle 9
Who mad'st us happy all, in thy reflexe, . . . 414 Ghyrlond 47
REFORME
There; or to reforme a curle; . . . . . 140 U2 Promise 24
REFORMED
On reformed Gam'ster. . . . . . 33 E21 Gam'ster Ttl
REFRAINE
Though I acknowledge, who can so refraine, . . 112 F11 Epode V 85
That knowes the waight of guilt: He will refraine . . 112 F11 Epode 113
Of the good Cynara I was: Refraine, . . . 292 U86 Hor.4:1 4
REFRESHED
But then refreshed, with thy Fayerie Court, . . 398 Drayton 79
REFUSE
Who, to thy one, all other braines refuse; . . . 34 E23 Donne 1 2
Which should thy countries love to speake refuse, . . 40 E43 Salisbury 1 3
Made Dian, not his notes refuse? . . . 182 U27 Ode Helen 28
The first of which, I feare, you will refuse; . . . 230 U56 Covell 6
The first of which, I doubt, you will refuse; . . . 230 U56 Covell V 6
Not, that your Art I doe refuse: . . . 277 U84 Mind 5
His armes in Mars his field, he doth refuse; . . . 331 Horace 566
REFUSED
That they long since have refused . . . . 184 U29 Fit of Rime 47
REFUSES
Though now he refuses, ... 231 U57 Burges 10
REGARD
Contends t'have worth enjoy, from his regard, . . 48 E64 Salisbury 3 13
For that firme grace he holdes in your regard, . . 116 F12 Rutland 95
Where shame, faith, honour, and regard of right . . 243 U70 Ode 13
REGENERATE
I am regenerate now, become the child . . . 192 U38 Elegy 'Tis 39
REGENT
A Merchants Wife is Regent of the Scale. . . . 229 U54 Squib 4
REGIMENT
With wonder on the thorny regiment. . . . 413 Ghyrlond 16
REGION
This world deaths region is, the other lifes: . . 54 E80 Life/Death 5
REGIONS
The Orbe was cut forth into Regions seaven. . . 396 Drayton 20
REHEARSE
And with both bombard-stile, and phrase, rehearse . . 85 E133 Voyage 46
As he whom Maro did rehearse? . . . . 181 U27 Ode Helen 8
Their minds to Warres, with rimes they did rehearse; . 329 Horace 495
REHERSE
Some act of Love's bound to reherse. . . . 93 F1 Why write no 1
A present, which (if elder writs reherse . . 113 F12 Rutland 20
Like men street-borne, and neere the Hall, reherse . 321 Horace 357
Like men Town-born, and neere the place, reherse . . 347 Horace V349/357
Their labour'd tunes reherse, ... 420 Ode:If Men 22
REIGNE (See also RAIGNE)
I am not such, as in the Reigne 292 U86 Hor.4:1 3
REIN (See RAYN'D)
REJECT
Though it reject not those of Fortune: such . . 117 F13 Aubigny 45
REJOYCE
Of some grand peere, whose ayre doth make rejoyce . 113 F12 Rutland 12
RE-JOYNE
That shall re-joyne yee. Was she, then, so deare, . . 285 U84 Muse 107

```
                                                      Page      Title        Line

RELATE
   were such as I will now relate, or worse?      .    .    .    .    .    172  U20 Shrub        14
   With love, to heare your modestie relate,      .    .    .    .    251  U74 Weston       21
RELATION
   I must the true Relation make,      .    .    .    .    .    150  U11 Dreame        2
   . . . apotheosis, or Relation to the Saints.    .    .    .    .    282  U84 Muse        Ttl
RELEAST
   Nor need'st thou: for those few, by oath releast,    .    .    .    32  E16 Brain-hardy    7
RELENTLESSE
   Of Vulture death, and those relentlesse cleies?    .    .    .    283  U84 Muse        18
RELIEFE
   Rob'd both of money, and the lawes reliefe,    .    .    .    .    29  E8 Robbery        5
   As shall not need thy false reliefe.    .    .    .    .    .    102  F4 To the World    64
RELIEVE
   There greatnesse takes a glorie to relieve.    .    .    .    192  U38 Elegy 'Tis    34
   Dare thinke it, to relieve, no lesse renowne,    .    .    .    248  U71 Treasurer    14
RELIGION
   That unto me dost such religion use!    .    .    .    .    .    44  E55 Beaumont        2
   If, my religion safe, I durst embrace    .    .    .    .    61  E95 Savile        1
   They are, and have beene taught religion: Thence    .    .    96  F2 Penshurst    93
   Mak'st it religion to grow rich by Crimes!    .    .    .    187  U33 Councellour    16
   Make State, Religion, Bawdrie, all a theame?    .    .    222  U49 Pucell        12
   And strike Religion in the standers-by;    .    .    .    261  U77 Treasurer    24
RELIGIOUS
   Such a religious horrour in the brests    .    .    .    .    155  U13 Sacvile        91
   So charitable, to religious end,    .    .    .    .    .    287  U84 Muse        176
   The sole Religious house, and Votary,    .    .    .    .    372  Epitaph        10
   Religious, wise, chast, loving, gratious, good,    .    .    394  Jane Ogle        5
   if it begyn religious thoughts to cherish;    .    .    .    422  Lucan        10
RELIGIOUSLY
   Religiously here he bids, row from the stewes,    .    .    375  Coryat 1        20
RELIQUE
   'Twas verily some Relique of the Stewes:    .    .    .    209  U43 Vulcan        140
RELISH
   To put all relish from my memorie    .    .    .    .    197  U40 Elegy That        6
   And relish merry make him.    .    .    .    .    .    220  U48 Bacchus        12
RELISH'D
   Where, how it would have relish'd well;    .    .    .    139  U2 Another        14
   The Swan that so relish'd Pancharis)    .    .    .    .    182  U27 Ode Helen        30
RELLISH
   Whose rellish to eternitie shall last.    .    .    .    .    58  E91 Vere        8
   Whose rellish to eternitie will last.    .    .    .    .    58  E91 Vere        V  8
REMAINE
   Where, while that sever'd doth remaine,    .    .    .    34  E22 Daughter        10
   Your sacrifice, then here remaine with me.    .    .    .    199  U41 Elegy Since    18
   That thou remaine here taster    .    .    .    .    .    220  U48 Bacchus        7
   And yet remaine our wonder still.    .    .    .    .    278  U84 Mind        20
   Nothing, that could remaine, or yet can stirre    .    .    282  U84 Muse        9
REMAINES
   Came forth example, and remaines so, yet:    .    .    .    34  E23 Donne 1        4
   Losse, remaines yet, as unrepair'd as mine.    .    .    .    211  U43 Vulcan        196
   Losse, remaines yet, as much despair'd as mine.    .    .    211  U43 Vulcan        V196
   From the five ounces; what remaines? pronounce    .    .    327  Horace        468
REMAYNE
   that it remayne with him    .    .    .    .    .    666  Glover        6
REMAYN'ST
   Thou yet remayn'st, un-hurt in peace, or warre,    .    .    60  E93 Radcliffe        13
REMEMBER
   Up publike joy, remember    .    .    .    .    .    239  U67 Muses        1
REMEMBRANCE
   To her remembrance; which when time shall bring    .    .    115  F12 Rutland        75
   Or in remembrance of thy afront, and scorne,    .    .    203  U43 Vulcan        7
REMEMBRED
   Will be remembred by Six Clerkes, to one.    .    .    .    210  U43 Vulcan        172
REMONSTRANCE
   With all Remonstrance make an honest man.    .    .    406  Inigo Jones 1    104
REMORSE
   By Death, on Earth, I should have had remorse    .    .    282  U84 Muse        12
REMOVE
   Grant then, no rude hand remove her.    .    .    .    .    39  E40 Ratcliffe        4
REMOV'D
   And he remov'd to gent'man of the horse,    .    .    .    57  E90 Mill        12
   Remov'd, as you from need to have it such.    .    .    .    117  F13 Aubigny        28
REMOVED
   So removed by our wile?    .    .    .    .    .    102  F5 Celia 1        14
   Thus removed by many a mile?    .    .    .    .    102  F5 Celia 1        V 14
REMOVETH
   That shee removeth cares, sadnesse ejects,    .    .    .    82  E130 Ferrab. 1        4
RENDER
   Render his head in there againe?    .    .    .    .    101  F4 To the World    32
   To render word for word: nor with thy sleight    .    .    313  Horace        191
   And the beholder to himselfe doth render.    .    .    .    317  Horace        259
RENDRED
   So hast thou rendred him in all his bounds,    .    .    .    61  E95 Savile        5
RENEW
   Renew the Glories of our blessed Jeames:    .    .    .    415  Dover        4
RENEWED
   There; but, renewed, say,    .    .    .    .    .    258  U75 Epithalam.    167
RENEWING
   As in renewing thy good Grandsires fame;    .    .    .    268  U80 Christning        12
RENOWNE
   The great renowne, and name wherewith shee goes.    .    .    31  E14 Camden        4
   Love thy great losse, which a renowne hath wonne,    .    .    49  E66 Cary        11
```

		Page	Title	Line
RENOWNE (cont.)				
Weare this renowne. 'Tis just, that who did give · · ·		57	E89 Allen	13
True valour doth her owne renowne command · · ·		180	U26 Ode High	16
Dare thinke it, to relieve, no lesse renowne, · · ·		248	U71 Treasurer	14
With ever-greene, and great renowne, · · ·		272	U84 Cradle	2
In vertue, and renowne of armes, then in · · ·		325	Horace	412
RENOWN'D				
The Roman Ilia was not more renown'd. · · ·		293	U87 Hor.3:9	8
RENOWNING				
When seeking her renowning, · · · ·		365	Ode Splendor	19
RENT				
Our native portions, and possessed rent; · · ·		286	U84 Muse	142
REPAIRE (RESTORE)				
This, and that box his Beautie to repaire; · · ·		215	U44 Speach	96
REPAIRE				
What could not worke; at home in his repaire · · ·		37	E32 Roe 2	7
He meant they thither should make swift repaire, · · ·		41	E44 Chuff	5
REPAIRER				
(As being Redeemer, and Repairer too · · ·		288	U84 Muse	213
REPEAT				
Repeat of things a throng, · · · · ·		245	U70 Ode	57
REPEATE				
And Ile professe no verses to repeate: · · ·		65	E101 Supper	24
And glorie of them all, but to repeate! · · ·		66	E103 L Wroth 1	8
REPEATING				
Repeating all Great Britain's joy, and more, · · ·		249	U72 King	6
REPENT				
But I repent me: Stay. Who e're is rais'd, · · ·		48	E65 Muse	15
Repent thee not of thy faire precedent, · · ·		73	E113 Overbury	9
Could make such men, and such a place repent: · · ·		73	E113 Overbury	10
Rarely repent, · · · · · ·		129	U1 Father	14
If you dare grudge at Heaven, and repent · · ·		271	U81 Pawlet	79
If you dare Quarrell Heaven, and repent · · ·		271	U81 Pawlet	V 79
And done, we straight repent us of the sport: · · ·		294	U88 Petronius	2
The Danger of delaying to Repent, · · ·		411	Sutcliffe	9
REPENTED				
Madame, I told you late how I repented, · · ·		54	E84 Bedford 2	1
They have repented. · · · · ·		77	E120 S. P.	20
She repented of the deed, · · · ·		133	U2 Suffered	18
REPENTS				
Indeed, poore Giles repents he married ever. · · ·		40	E42 Giles	3
REPLIDE				
I confesse all, I replide, · · · ·		137	U2 Cupid	39
REPLYED				
Phoebus replyed. Bold head, it is not shee: · · ·		80	E126 Mrs Cary	7
REPLYES				
Taught Lucan these true moodes! Replyes my sence · · ·		395	May	15
REPORT				
Goodyere, I'am glad, and gratefull to report, · · ·		55	E85 Goodyere 1	1
Crack did report it selfe, as if a cloud · · ·		86	E133 Voyage	94
To every squire, or groome, that will report · · ·		113	F12 Rutland	6
To every squire, or groome, that can report · · ·		113	F12 Rutland	V 6
Whose praises let's report unto the Woods, · · ·		265	U79 New-yeares	52
Since nothing can report that flame, · · ·		278	U84 Mind	15
Since nothing can report her flame, · · ·		278	U84 Mind	V 15
Before the Judge, it hangs, and waites report. · · ·		309	Horace	112
Much from the sight, which faire report will make · · ·		317	Horace	262
REPORTS				
Her truch-man, she reports the minds each throw. · · ·		313	Horace	157
REPREHEND				
'Tis true, he could not reprehend; · · ·		152	U12 Corbet	21
REPROOFE				
Cannot indure reproofe, · · · ·		175	U23 Himselfe	32
Of lying, he feares so much the reproofe · · ·		380	Coryat 3	31
REPROVE				
In practiz'd friendship wholly to reprove, · · ·		190	U37 Friend-Book	26
Reprove; and, what is to be changed, note: · · ·		335	Horace	638
in Course of Frindshipp, wholie to reprove: · · ·		422	Censure	19
REPULSE				
Gold is a sutor, never tooke repulse, · · ·		363	Riches	5
REPUTATION				
What reputation to beare one Glasse more? · · ·		166	U15 Friend-Wars	119
What reputation to my lines, and me, · · ·		263	U78 Digby	26
REPUTES				
The world reputes you barren: but I know · · ·		46	E62 Would-bee	3
REQUIRE				
Or did our times require it, to behold · · ·		67	E104 Montgomery	3
If such a ones applause thou dost require, · · ·		315	Horace	220
Oft-times a Sharpe, when we require a Flat: · · ·		329	Horace	523
So doth the one, the others helpe require, · · ·		333	Horace	585
Require (besides the likenesse of the thing) · · ·		370	Author	2
REQUIR'D				
Where sweetnesse is requir'd, and where weight; · · ·		62	E95 Savile	30
For that is first requir'd, A man be his owne. · · ·		216	U45 Squib	23
REQUITE				
Cannot but heape that grace, he will requite. · · ·		236	U63 Charles 2	14
RESERV'D				
And talke reserv'd, lock'd up, and full of feare, · · ·		59	E92 New Crie	17
Keepe in reserv'd in his Dark-lanterne face, · · ·		198	U40 Elegy That	23
RE-SHINE				
Sol will re-shine. If not, Charles hath a Sonne. · · ·		238	U65 Prince	12
RESIDE				
Fit in that softer bosome to reside. · · · ·		52	E76 Bedford 1	12

		Page	Title	Line

RESIGN'D
Among the starres should be resign'd . . . . . . 369 Ode Who saith 105

RESIST
Even states most hated, when no lawes resist . . . 423 Lucan 13

RESOLV'D
A spirit so resolv'd to tread . . . . . 100 F4 To the World 6

RESORT
Thy Mount, to which the Dryads doe resort, . . . 93 F2 Penshurst 10

RESOUND
Apollo's harpe, and Hermes lyre resound, . . 98 F3 Wroth 51
Heare, o you Groves, and, Hills, resound his praise. . . 264 U79 New-yeares 23
Heare, O you Groves, and, Hills, resound his worth. . . 264 U79 New-yeares 31
The hand, and mind would, but it will resound . . 329 Horace 522

RESPECT
But I, no child, no foole, respect the kinde, . . . 79 E125 Uvedale 7
That all respect; She must lie downe: Nay more, . . 163 U15 Friend-Wars 53
Respect, and observation; it uncovers . . . 363 Riches 7

RESPECTS
It true respects. He will not only love, . . . 161 U14 Selden 73
whole armyes fall, swayd by those nyce respects. . . 423 Lucan 11

REST   (VERB)
Rest in soft peace, and, ask'd, say here doth lye . . 41 E45 First Son 9
But canst, at home, in thy securer rest, . . . 97 F3 Wroth 13
Not weary, rest . . . . . . 121 F14 Sydney 37
Shall I there rest! . . . . . 128 U1 Trinitie 48
I can rest me where I am. . . . 142 U2 Her man 56
Even ashes of lovers find no rest. . . . 149 U8 Houre-glasse 11
Then rest, and a friends value understand, . . . 216 U45 Squib 25
Himselfe to rest . . . . . 246 U70 Ode 86
In rest, like spirits left behind . . . 280 U84 Mind 66
In thee, faire Mansion, let it rest, . . . 281 U84 Mind 69
The glorie, and gaine of rest, which the place gives! . . 283 U84 Muse 38
That great eternall Holy-day of rest, . . . 284 U84 Muse 63
To that eternall Rest, where now sh'hath place . . 288 U84 Muse 197
Playes were found out; and rest, the end, and crowne . 329 Horace 499

REST
Make good what thou dar'st doe in all the rest. . . 32 E16 Brain-hardy 8
O, would'st thou adde like hand, to all the rest! . . 61 E95 Savile 13
Pr'y thee, yet save thy rest; give ore in time: . . 73 E112 Gamster 21
None but them, and leave the rest. . . . 106 F8 Sicknesse 48
Without which, all the rest were sounds, or lost. . . 118 F13 Aubigny 50
With the rest, I long expected, . . . 140 U2 Promise 7
That makes the Arch. The rest that there were put . 157 U13 Sacvile 137
Some grounds are made the richer, for the Rest; . . 169 U17 Friend-Debt 17
So much my Subject drownes the rest. . . . 182 U27 Ode Helen 36
The rest, my journey into Scotland song, . . . 207 U43 Vulcan 94
The rest, my journey into Scotland sung . . . 207 U43 Vulcan V 94
These Graces, when the rest of Ladyes view . . ?225 U50 Countesse 31
To see you set apart, thus, from the rest, . . 234 U61 Epigram 10
Want, with the rest of his conceal'd compeeres, . . 248 U71 Treasurer 5
Above the rest . . . . . 253 U75 Epithalam. 38
Now, Sun, and post away the rest of day: . . . 257 U75 Epithalam. 138
Alas, I am all Marble! write the rest . . . 269 U81 Pawlet 13
And set it forth; the rest were Cobwebs fine, . . 282 U84 Muse 5
Ye have oft-times, that may ore-shine the rest, . . 305 Horace 18
Ye have oft-times, that may out-shine the rest, . . 338 Horace V 18
did sparcle foorth in Center of the rest: . . . 361 Palmer 16
Smiles in his Sphaere, to see the rest affect, . . 366 Ode Who saith 13
Nor Sunne could make to vary from the rest, . . 367 Ode Who saith 29
To knit thy Crowne, and glorifie the rest. . . 412 Ghyrlond 12

RESTETH
The power, and rule of speaking resteth still. . . 309 Horace 104

RESTING
Resting never. . . . . . 184 U29 Fit of Rime 54

RESTITUTION
Expected with the fleshes restitution. . . . 283 U84 Muse 50

RESTORE
If any friends teares could restore, his would; . . 35 E27 Roe 1 5
That can restore that. Will it hurt your feature? . . 46 E62 Would-bee 7
So are you Natures Index, and restore, . . . 68 E105 L Wroth 2 19
T'all future time, not onely doth restore . . . 71 E110 Edmonds 1 21
I would restore, and keepe it ever such; . . . 78 E122 Rudyerd 2 8
She content was to restore . . . 133 U2 Suffered 3
To restore . . . . . 184 U29 Fit of Rime 39
You would restore it? No, that's worth a feare, . . 199 U41 Elegy Since 15
Who doubts, those fruits God can with gaine restore, . 235 U63 Charles 2 3

RESTOR'D
But when I read that speciall piece, restor'd, . . 61 E95 Savile 7
By whom he is restor'd to men: . . . 173 U22 Elegy Tho 15
And force back that, which will not be restor'd, . . 219 U47 Tribe 40
And with their grassie greene restor'd mine eyes. . 398 Drayton 82

RESTORED
Restored in thy body, and thy minde! . . . 79 E125 Uvedale 4

RESTRAIN'D
Her licence fit to be restrain'd by law: . . . 321 Horace 368
Her force was fit to be restrain'd by law: . . 348 Horace V402/368

RESTS   (REMAINS)
But rests foiled. . . . . . 184 U29 Fit of Rime 36

RESTS
Of our Towne Gallantry! or why there rests . . . 155 U13 Sacvile 92
Two rests, a short and long, th'Iambick frame; . . 323 Horace 371
And hold them faithfully; For nothing rests, . . 329 Horace 505

	Page	Title	Line
RESURRECTION			
Shewes of the resurrection little trust.	37	E34 Death	2
Who in that feast of Resurrection trust!	284	U84 Muse	62
RETAINE			
As neither head, nor foot, one forme retaine.	305	Horace	10
Fit for the sock: Each subject should retaine	311	Horace	124
RETAIN'D			
So they in state of Grace retain'd,	144	U3 Musicall	27
RETIRE			
Retire themselves, avoid the publike baths;	325	Horace	424
Retire, and say; Her Graces	365	Ode Splendor	21
RETORNED			
Untill the dust retorned bee	400	Lady Ogle	31
RETRACT			
What straight-way he must labour to retract.	315	Horace	240
RETRIBUTION			
To have that finall retribution,	283	U84 Muse	49
RETRIV'D			
Conjectures retriv'd! And a Storie now	160	U14 Selden	50
RETURNE			
So, when we, blest with thy returne, shall see	81	E128 Wm Roe 2	9
Who gave, to take at his returne from Hell,	84	E133 Voyage	27
Of those, that put out moneyes, on returne	85	E133 Voyage	32
Or, having scap'd, shall I returne,	101	F4 To the World	25
Kindled the fire! But then, did one returne,	209	U43 Vulcan	149
And the returne those thankfull Courtiers yeeld,	213	U44 Speach	17
Wise child, did'st hastily returne,	242	U70 Ode	7
No doubt all Infants would returne like thee.	243	U70 Ode	20
. . . gratulatorie For his Returne from his Embassie. 1632.	250	U74 Weston	Ttl
Such joyes, such sweet's doth your Returne	251	U74 Weston	19
The Soleme Quire cryes, Joy; and they returne, Amen.	256	U75 Epithalam.	128
But, say old Love returne should make,	294	U87 Hor.3:9	17
Of Meleager, brings he the returne	315	Horace	208
At their returne, nor Po,	315	Horace	...
Th'envy'd returne, of forty pound in gold.	408	Detractor	4
RETURN'D			
T'our times return'd, hath made her heaven in thee.	52	E74 Chancelor	10
The hogs return'd home fat from mast;	98	F3 Wroth	44
The hogs return'd home fat with mast;	98	F3 Wroth	V 44
And then to be return'd; on protestation	229	U54 Squib	18
RETURNED			
The Writ, once out, never returned yet.	331	Horace	580
The word, once out, never returned yet.	352	Horace	V556/580
RETURNES			
Shee must have money: he returnes, god payes.	30	E12 Shift	8
As they are done, and such returnes they find:	153	U13 Sacvile	6
For whose returnes, and many, all these pray:	225	U51 Bacon	6
Such Passage hast thou found, such Returnes made,	389	Chapman	10
RETYR'D			
Retyr'd, with purpose your faire worth to praise,	80	E126 Mrs Cary	1
REVEALD			
Reveald (if some can judge) of Argenis,	207	U43 Vulcan	V 96
Reveald (if some do judge) of Argenis,	207	U43 Vulcan	V 96
REVEALE			
That to the world thou should'st reveale so much,	72	E111 Edmonds 2	10
But the sweet theft to reveale:	102	F5 Celia 1	16
But which the Fates forbid me to reveale.	119	F13 Aubigny	107
And superstition I dare scarce reveale,	155	U13 Sacvile	86
Of many Coulors! read them! & reveale	404	Inigo Jones 1	47
REVEALED			
Will there revealed be in Majestie!	286	U84 Muse	130
REVELLS			
The Revells, and the Play,	240	U67 Muses	46
REVELS			
He burnt that Idoll of the Revels too:	210	U43 Vulcan	155
Nay, let White-Hall with Revels have to doe,	210	U43 Vulcan	156
Scarce let White-Hall with Revels have to doe,	210	U43 Vulcan	V156
REVENGE			
But I have my revenge made, in thy name.	29	E10 Ignorant	2
To revenge me with my Tongue,	133	U2 Suffered	24
REVENNUE			
Himselfe: his whole revennue is, god payes.	30	E12 Shift	6
REVERENCE			
Who more should seeke mens reverence, then feare.	58	E91 Vere	18
Sit mixt with losse of state, or reverence.	98	F3 Wroth	57
That men such reverence to such actions show!	156	U13 Sacvile	98
With reverence using all the gifts thence given.	219	U47 Tribe	62
Who claimes (of reverence) to be heard,	274	U84 Cradle	34
Cause Reverence, yf not Feare,	421	Ode:If Men	42
REVERENC'D			
That art so reverenc'd, as thy comming in,	66	E102 Pembroke	17
And these grudg'd at, art reverenc'd the while.	93	F2 Penshurst	6
REVEREND			
Camden, most reverend head, to whom I owe	31	E14 Camden	1
Behold! the reverend shade of Bartas stands	83	E132 Sylvester	7
Upon the reverend Pleaders; doe now shut	187	U33 Councellour	10
Alone, but all thy ranke a reverend Name.	187	U33 Councellour	40
And with a reverend feare,	240	U67 Muses	45
A reverend State she had, an awfull Eye,	270	U81 Pawlet	43
REVERENT			
These I looke up at, with a reverent eye,	261	U77 Treasurer	23
REVERENTLY			
For men to use their fortune reverently,	181	U26 Ode High	23

```
REVERSE
  The Reverse on the backe side.    .    .    .   413  Ghyrlond       Ttl
  On the reverse of this your circling crowne,   .    .    .   413  Ghyrlond        30
REVERSION
  Buy the reversion of old playes; now growne    .    .    .    45  E56 Poet-Ape     6
REVIVE
  That gaspe for action, and would yet revive    ..   .    .   162  U15 Friend-Wars  6
REVIV'D
  Much phrase that now is dead, shall be reviv'd;    .    .   309  Horace         101
REVIVING
  Reviving with fresh coulors the pale Ghosts    .    .    .   405  Inigo Jones 1   88
REVOLT
  As farre from all revolt, as you are now from Fortune.  .   180  U25 Desmond     65
REWARD'
  That vertuous is, when the reward's away.    .    .    .    49  E66 Cary        18
REWARD
  And that thou seek'st reward of thy each act,    .    .    .    47  E63 Salisbury 2  5
  As her owne conscience, still, the same reward.    .    .    48  E64 Salisbury 3 14
  They follow vertue, for reward, to day;    .    .    .    66  E102 Pembroke    9
  So, all reward, or name, that growes to mee    .    .    .    80  E127 Aubigny     9
  The just reward of her high huswifery;    .    .    .    96  F2 Penshurst    85
  And the reward, and punishment assur'd,    .    .    .   176  U24 Frontispice V 8
  Upon reward, till the reward him sought.    .    .    .   185  U30 Burleigh    14
  Will be reward enough: to weare like those,    .    .    .   232  U58 Book-seller  9
  Hope, hath her end! and Faith hath her reward!    .    .   284  U84 Muse        68
  Our great reward, th'aeternall Crown to win.    .    .   412  Sutcliffe       19
REWARDE
  if any way she do rewarde thee    .    .    .    .   662  Bedford          8
REWARDED
  Are in your selfe rewarded; yet 'twill be    .    .    .   224  U50 Countesse   15
REWARDING
  Of raising, judging, and rewarding all    .    .    .   288  U84 Muse       207
REWARD'S
  That vertuous is, when the reward's away.    .    .    .    49  E66 Cary        18
REWARDS
  As new rewards of her old secrecie?    .    .    .    .   223  U49 Pucell      20
  And 'counts them sweet rewards so ta'en:    .    .    .   290  U85 Country     36
REYNES
  O, be thou witnesse, that the reynes dost know,    .    .   122  F15 Heaven       5
RHAPSODY
  And thou maist better bring a Rhapsody    .    .    .   313  Horace         184
RHEINE
  Iberus, Tagus, Rheine,    .    .    .    .    .    .   369  Ode Who saith  115
RHETIA
  The Low-countries, Germany and Rhetia    .    .    .   379  Coryat 3        20
RHINE
  The pleasant grounds, or when the River Rhine,    .    .   305  Horace          22
RHINOCEROTES
  He speakes to men with a Rhinocerotes nose,    .    .    .    35  E28 Surly        4
RHONE
  Slow Arar, nor swift Rhone; the Loyre, nor Seine,    .    .   369  Ode Who saith  117
RHYMES    (See also RIME, RYME)
  Secure thy railing Rhymes, infamous Gill,    .    .    .   410  Gill             2
RHYTHM    (See RITHME)
RICH    (NAME)
  . . .  & sir Henrye Rich, now Earles of warwick and Hollande.  .   382  Rich        Ttl
  . . .  the Author of this Work, M. Rich. Brome.    .    .    .   409  Brome        Ttl
RICH
  Rich, as nature could bequeath thee:    .    .    .    .    39  E40 Ratcliffe    3
  Chuffe, lately rich in name, in chattels, goods,    .    .    41  E44 Chuff       1
  And rich in issue to inherit all,    .    .    .    .    41  E44 Chuff       2
  Is a pure cup of rich Canary-wine,    .    .    .    .    65  E101 Supper     29
  There like a rich, and golden pyramede,    .    .    .   115  F12 Rutland     83
  His Clothes rich, and band sit neat,    .    .    .    .   142  U2 Exception     4
  In the rich Mines of knowledge; and thence brought    .   161  U14 Selden    V 76
  Of lust, to his rich Suit and Title, Lord?    .    .    .   163  U15 Friend-Wars 51
  Rich beame of honour, shed your light    .    .    .   177  U25 Desmond     14
  Mak'st it religion to grow rich by Crimes!    .    .    .   187  U33 Councellour 16
  Why are we rich, or great, except to show    .    .    .   215  U44 Speach      69
  The same it was inspir'd, rich, and refin'd.    .    .    .   225  U50 Countesse   30
  And should grow rich, had I much more to pay.    .    .   231  U56 Covell      30
  And should grow rich, if I had more to pay.    .    .    .   231  U56 Covell    V 30
  Rather to boast rich hangings, then rare friends.    .    .   242  U69 Friend Son  26
  So doth the Poet, who is rich in Land,    .    .    .   333  Horace         599
  So doth the Poet, that is rich in Land,    .    .    .   353  Horace        V599
  Rich men are said with many cups to plie,    .    .    .   333  Horace         617
  The seaven-fold flower of Arte (more rich then gold)    .   361  Palmer          15
  of thy rich labors worlds of thoughts created,    .    .   361  Palmer          22
  Who hadst before wrought in rich Homers Mine?    .    .   388  Chapman          3
  In Towne & Court? Are you growne rich? & proud?    .    .   403  Inigo Jones 1   24
RICHARD
  A Richard, and a Hierome, by their names    .    .    .   258  U75 Epithalam. 170
  To his friend the Author upon his Richard.    .    .    .   385  Brooke         Ttl
  Thy Richard, rais'd in song, past pulling downe.    .    .   385  Brooke           8
RICHE
  The elder of these two, riche hopes Increase,    .    .    .   382  Rich             5
RICHER
  Minervaes loome was never richer spred.    .    .    .    61  E95 Savile      16
  The richer hangings, or crowne-plate;    .    .    .    96  F3 Wroth         8
  Richer then Time, and as Time's vertue, rare.    .    .   111  F11 Epode       59
  Some grounds are made the richer, for the Rest;    .    .   169  U17 Friend-Debt 17
  It is a richer Purchase then of land.    .    .    .    .   216  U45 Squib       26
  I thought me richer then the Persian King.    .    .    .   293  U87 Hor.3:9       4
```

	Page	Title	Line

RICHES
Yet crown'd with honors, as with riches, then; . . . 56 E89 Allen 4
Riches thought most: But, Madame, thinke what store . . . 114 F12 Rutland 38
Their Jemme of Riches, and bright Stone, that brings . . . 206 U43 Vulcan 74
Riches. . . . . 363 Riches Ttl
RICHEST (See also RITCHEST)
That hang their richest jewells i'their nose; . . . 232 U58 Book-seller 10
Wee'l rip our Richest veynes . . . . 420 Ode:If Men 31
RICHLY
It might thy patience richly pay: . . . 168 U16 Gray 5
Wherein she sits so richly drest, . . . 251 U74 Weston 14
Which were so richly spun, and woven so fit, . . . 392 Shakespeare 49
RICHNESSE
I wonder'd at the richnesse, but am lost, . . . 160 U14 Selden 53
RID
A Bed-rid Wit, then a besieged Towne. . . . 248 U71 Treasurer 15
RIDDLES
Or spun out Riddles, and weav'd fiftie tomes . . . 204 U43 Vulcan 33
Or spun or weav'd in Riddles 50 tomes . . . 204 U43 Vulcan V 33
in weaving Riddles in more wretched ryme, . . . 204 U43 Vulcan V 34
RIDDLING
Now differ'd not from Delphick riddling. . . . 319 Horace 310
RIDE
And, so they ride in purple, eate in plate, . . . 99 F3 Wroth 89
Through Swords, through Seas, whether she would ride. . 134 U2 Triumph 10
Ride, saile, am coach'd, know I how farre I have gone, . 156 U13 Sacvile 121
What though she ride two mile on Holy-dayes . . . 222 U49 Pucell 15
Till then unknowne, in Carts, wherein did ride . . . 319 Horace 313
Doth he once dissemble, but tels he did ride . . . 380 Coryat 3 52
'tis but the next neighbour ride . . . . 417 Moon 35
RIDES
With whom who sailes, rides on the surge of feare, . . 110 F11 Epode 41
And, sure of Heaven, rides triumphing in. . . . 272 U81 Pawlet 100
RIDETH
Wherein my Lady rideth! . . . . 134 U2 Triumph 2
RIDICULOUS
Then all those Atomi ridiculous, . . . 87 E133 Voyage 127
RIDWAY
Ridway rob'd Duncote of three hundred pound, . . . 29 E8 Robbery 1
Ridway was tane, arraign'd, condemn'd to dye; . . . 29 E8 Robbery 2
RIDWAYES
Beg'd Ridwayes pardon: Duncote, now, doth crye; . . . 29 E8 Robbery 4
RIFE
But when I read or heare the names so rife . . . 187 U33 Councellour 7
RIFFLE
And riffle him: or pawne his Petasus. . . . 107 F10 Proludium 24
RIGHT (See also RITELY)
Keepe thy selfe there, and thinke thy valure right, . . 32 E16 Brain-hardy 9
And thou, right guiltlesse, may'st plead to it, why? . . 36 E29 Tilter 2
Farewell, thou child of my right hand, and joy; . . . 41 E45 First Son 1
Who can consider thy right courses run, . . . 47 E63 Salisbury 2 1
A worke of ours, we part with our owne right; . . . 82 E131 Ferrab. 2 2
Before my thought, and (in thy right) commands . . . 83 E132 Sylvester 8
One was; and he, for brawne, and braine, right able . . 84 E133 Voyage 23
And, now, above the poole, a face right fat . . . 88 E133 Voyage 160
And giv'st thy welcome guests the right; . . . 97 F3 Wroth V 28
To doe thy countrey service, thy selfe right; . . . 100 F3 Wroth 103
Much more a noble, and right generous mind . . . 112 F11 Epode 111
Right, the right way: yet must your comfort bee . . . 118 F13 Aubigny 68
Strive all right wayes it can, . . . 121 F14 Sydney 25
For thy acceptance. O, behold me right, . . . 127 U1 Trinitie 13
A right by the prosperitie of their Crimes; . . . 186 U32 Elsmere 10
He do's you wrong, that craves you to doe right. . . . 186 U32 Elsmere 16
Fathers, and Husbands, I doe claime a right . . . 200 U42 Elegy Let 11
Of our fift Henry, right of his nine yeare; . . . 207 U43 Vulcan V 98
He was right Vulcan still! He did not spare . . . 210 U43 Vulcan V159
A Court of Equitie should doe us right, . . . 211 U43 Vulcan 178
Put conscience and my right to compromise. . . . 218 U47 Tribe 8
And the right wayes you take unto the right, . . . 224 U50 Countesse 3
To the Right Honorable William Viscount Mansfield: . . . 228 U53 Newcastle VTtl
To the Right Honorable William Earle of Newcastle. . . . 232 U59 Newcastle VTtl
Where shame, faith, honour, and regard of right . . . 243 U70 Ode 13
Hee stood, a Souldier to the last right end, . . . 244 U70 Ode 45
To the Right Honourable, the Lord high Treasurer of . . . 248 U71 Treasurer Ttl
On the Right Honourable, and vertuous Lord Weston, L. . . . 250 U73 Weston Ttl
To the Right Hon'ble Hieromee, L. Weston. An Ode . . . 250 U74 Weston Ttl
To the right Honourable, the Lord Treasurer of England. . . . 260 U77 Treasurer Ttl
B'imputed right to an inheritance . . . 286 U84 Muse 144
Father, and sons right worthy of your Sire, . . . 339 Horace V 34
Right spare, and warie: then thou speak'st to mee . . . 307 Horace 66
If now the turnes, the colours, and right hues . . . 311 Horace 126
Her voyce, and angry Chremes chafes out-right. . . . 311 Horace 133
Into their birth-right, and for fitnesse sake, . . . 323 Horace 376
If either you, or I, know the right way . . . 323 Horace 402
With specious places, and being humour'd right, . . . 327 Horace 457
Or mixing sweet, and fit, teach life the right. . . . 327 Horace 478
May, with some right, upon an Author creepe. . . . 329 Horace 538
To the Right Noble Tom, Tell-Troth of his travailes, . . . 378 Coryat 2 Ttl
Some men, of Bookes or Freinds not speaking right, . . . 386 Browne 1
Which, when it sounds at best, but eccho's right; . . . 390 Shakespeare 8
Our right in France! if ritely understood. . . . 397 Drayton 58
Her right, by gift, and purchase of the Lambe: . . . 400 Lady Ogle 36

548

	Page	Title	Line
RIGHT (cont.)			
That knew the Crafts they had bin bred in, right:	410	Brome	14
To my Deare Sonne, and right-learned Friend, . . .	414	Rutter	Ttl
RIGHTEOUSNESSE			
Through his inherent righteousnesse, in death,	286	U84 Muse	135
RIGHT-LEARNED			
To my Deare Sonne, and right-learned Friend, . . .	414	Rutter	Ttl
RIGHTLY			
Informed rightly, by your Fathers care,	331	Horace	546
RIGID			
Rigid, and harsh, which is a Drug austere	190	U37 Friend-Book	17
And a Comptroller, two most rigid men	415	Rutter	24
RIGOUR			
Then Mistris, here, here let your rigour end,	194	U38 Elegy 'Tis	105
RIME			
A Fit of Rime against Rime.	183	U29 Fit of Rime	Ttl
Rime, the rack of finest wits,	183	U29 Fit of Rime	1
Tyran Rime hath so abused,	184	U29 Fit of Rime	46
Stil may reason warre with rime,	184	U29 Fit of Rime	53
Away ill company, and helpe in rime	231	U56 Covell	23
'Bove rattling Rime.	273	U84 Cradle	16
And tune too, fitted to the Chorus rime,	319	Horace	290
Now each Court-Hobby-horse will wince in rime;	410	Brome	11
RIMEE'S			
Or, every day, some one at Rimee's looks,	59	E92 New Crie	23
RI'MES			
Into my ri'mes could ne're be got	93	F1 Why write no	9
RIMES			
Be thine, I taxe, yet doe not owne my rimes:	36	E30 Guiltie	2
Your forme imprest there: not with tickling rimes,	116	F12 Rutland	87
Your forme imprest there: not with tinckling rimes,	116	F12 Rutland	V 87
Friend, flie from hence; and let these kindled rimes	167	U15 Friend-Wars	162
Starveling rimes did fill the Stage,	183	U29 Fit of Rime	25
Greeke was free from Rimes infection,	184	U29 Fit of Rime	31
Is not yet free from Rimes wrongs,	184	U29 Fit of Rime	35
And my selfe most, in some selfe-boasting Rimes?	203	U43 Vulcan	26
And my selfe most, in lewd selfe-boasting Rimes?	203	U43 Vulcan	V 26
To vent their Libels, and to issue rimes,	218	U47 Tribe	26
Of rimes, or ryots, at your feasts,	246	U70 Ode	103
And farre unworthy to blurt out light rimes;	321	Horace	337
A Poeme, of no grace, weight, art, in rimes,	327	Horace	456
Their minds to Warres, with rimes they did rehearse;	329	Horace	495
RIMING			
Hanch against Hanch, or raise a riming Club	396	Drayton	8
RING (SOUND)			
(That should ring larum to the heart) doth sleepe,	109	F11 Epode	23
(That shal ring larum to the heart) doth sleepe,	109	F11 Epode	V 23
Some ring,	120	F14 Sydney	3
Ring thou it Holy-day.	239	U67 Muses	6
And all did ring th'approches of the Bride;	253	U75 Epithalam.	36
RING			
The spoused paire two realmes, the sea the ring.	28	E5 Union	4
Item, a faire greeke poesie for a ring:	51	E73 Fine Grand	10
Thy Wife a fit of laughter; a Cramp-ring	232	U58 Book-seller	8
Hath taken twice the Ring	240	U67 Muses	38
The holy Prelate prayes, then takes the Ring,	256	U75 Epithalam.	123
Were like a ring of Vertues, 'bout her set,	270	U81 Pawlet	41
If thou the vile, broad-troden ring forsake.	313	Horace	188
RINGS			
Cast in thousand snares, and rings	141	U2 Her man	11
By that tall Grove, your haire; whose globy rings	170	U19 Elegy By	5
Their Seales, their Characters, Hermetique rings,	206	U43 Vulcan	73
Their Charmes, their Characters, Hermetique rings,	206	U43 Vulcan	V 73
Lest the throng'd rings should a free laughter take:	352	Horace	V545/569
RIOT			
Of riot, and consumption, knowes the way	235	U61 Epigram	17
Gesture, and riot, whilst he swooping went	319	Horace	304
Gesture, and riot, whilst he wandring went	346	Horace	V304
RIOTING			
With horrour rough, then rioting with wit!	160	U14 Selden	57
RIOTS (See also RYOTS)			
And all the originall riots of the place:	202	U42 Elegy Let	80
RIP			
Wee'l rip our Richest veynes	420	Ode:If Men	31
RIPE			
Ere cherries ripe, and straw-berries be gone,	58	E92 New Crie	1
Ripe statesmen, ripe: They grow in every street.	58	E92 New Crie	3
At sixe and twentie, ripe. You shall 'hem meet,	58	E92 New Crie	4
Ripe are their ruffes, their cuffes, their beards, their gate,	58	E92 New Crie	6
And grave as ripe, like mellow as their faces,	59	E92 New Crie	7
By their ripe daughters, whom they would commend	95	F2 Penshurst	54
It shall a ripe and timely issue fall,	119	F13 Aubigny	104
Which Vertue from your Father, ripe, will fall;	282	U84 Kenelme	22
Or an Heroe; if a ripe old man,	313	Horace	162
RIPENED			
The ripened eares, yet humble in their height,	98	F3 Wroth	41
RIP'NED			
Rip'ned with a breath more sweet,	137	U2 Cupid	27
RISE			
I meant the day-starre should not brighter rise,	52	E76 Bedford 1	7
Sunnes, that set, may rise againe:	102	F5 Celia 1	6
The thirst, that from the soule doth rise,	106	F9 Celia 3	5
Of her face, and made to rise,	136	U2 Cupid	15

RISE (cont.)
Nor cast them downe, but let them rise,	144	U4 Song	3
Coriat, should rise the most sufficient head	157	U13 Sacvile	128
They need no stilts, nor rise upon their toes,	157	U13 Sacvile	145
'Tis like light Canes, that first rise big and brave,	157	U13 Sacvile	149
Who falls for love of God, shall rise a Starre.	168	U15 Friend-Wars	196
So, from all sicknesse, may you rise to health,	186	U31 Elsmere	5
Or if Chance must, to each man that doth rise,	217	U46 Coke	23
Rare Plants from ev'ry banke doe rise,	251	U74 Weston	10
And by his Rise, in active men, his Name	256	U75 Epithalam.	116
Shee saw him rise, triumphing over Death	288	U84 Muse	203
Where, such perfections to the life doe rise.	362	Author	6
Do crowne thy murdred Poeme: which shall rise	371	Fletcher	14
yf from a little sparke hee rise not fier.	383	Rich	16
To rise with eyther of you, on the morrow.	384	Somerset	16
And when your yeares rise more, then would be told,	384	Somerset	23
My Shakespeare, rise; I will not lodge thee by	391	Shakespeare	19
I saw a Beauty from the Sea to rise,	396	Drayton	15
As, on two flowry Carpets, that did rise,	398	Drayton	81
rise or fall uppon the earth,	417	Moon	18

RISETH
No more would Jone he should. Giles riseth early,	40	E42 Giles	6
As Loves starre when it riseth!	134	U2 Triumph	14

RISING
And betweene each rising breast,	137	U2 Cupid	33
Rising through it e're it came;	141	U2 Her..man	29
The rosie Morning, or the rising Sun,	414	Ghyrlond	50

RITE
Where is that nominall marke, or reall rite,	160	U14 Selden	47

RITELY
Our right in France! if ritely understood.	397	Drayton	58

RITES
To see thy fathers rites new laid on thee.	47	E64 Salisbury 3	6
The aged Saturne's age, and rites to know;	78	E122 Rudyerd 2	2
Thus Pan, and Sylvane, having had their rites,	98	F3 Wroth	47
When Pan, and Sylvane, having had their rites,	98	F3 Wroth	V 47
Doe not men, ynow of rites	104	F8 Sicknesse	3
And greater rites, yet writ in mysterie,	119	F13 Aubigny	106
And did think, such Rites were due	138	U2 Kisse	19
Unto their praise, in certaine swearing rites!	156	U13 Sacvile	102
I give, or owe my friends, into your Rites,	197	U40 Elegy That	12
To doe her Husbands rites in, e're 'twere gone	201	U42 Elegy Let	40
But that's a marke, wherof thy Rites doe boast,	205	U43 Vulcan	57
More then advanc'd the houses, and their rites?	210	U43 Vulcan	164
Stay, thou wilt see what rites the Virgins doe!	254	U75 Epithalam.	49
Saw'st thou that Paire, became these Rites so well,	254	U75 Epithalam.	76
And Bishop stay, to consummate the Rites:	256	U75 Epithalam.	122
To shew the rites, and t'usher forth the way	263	U79 New-yeares	4
Fit rites. The Child, that now knowes how to say,	315	Horace	225
Having well eat, and drunke (the rites being done)	319	Horace	325
Who, since, to sing the Pythian rites is heard,	333	Horace	591
Who now to sing the Pythian Rites is heard,	353	Horace	V591
With Rites not bound, but conscience. Wouldst thou All?	372	Epitaph	11
They are the Mariage-rites	401	Filmer	3

RITHME
Who shall forbid me then in Rithme to bee	200	U42 Elegy Let	5

RITHMES
Though not in these, in rithmes not wholly dumbe,	182	U28 Worth	2

RIVALL
Will be my Rivall, though she have but eares.	148	U7 Nymph	28
And rivall with the Trumpet for his sound,	319	Horace	288
Alone, without a rivall, by his will.	335	Horace	632
Alone, without a rivall, at your will.	354	Horace	V632

RIVALS
With thee 'bove all his Rivals gifts take place,	292	U86 Hor.4:1	18

RIVER
The lower land, that to the river bends,	94	F2 Penshurst	22
Through which a serpent river leades	97	F3 Wroth	18
Or hauking at the river, or the bush,	97	F3 Wroth	33
Moves like a sprightly River, and yet can	198	U40 Elegy That	26
The pleasant grounds, or when the River Rhine,	305	Horace	22
Or the wilde river, who hath changed now	309	Horace	96
Nor let one River boast	367	Ode Who saith	35
Who ever sipt at Baphyre river,	367	Ode Who saith	57

RIVERS
The Rivers in their shores doe run,	251	U74 Weston	7
Rivers, and Vallies, Eccho what wee sing.	264	U79 New-yeares	27
Rivers, and Valleys, Eccho what wee sing.	264	U79 New-yeares	35
Earle Rivers Grand-Child--serve not formes, good Fame,	269	U81 Pawlet	21
Earle Rivers Grand-Child--serve not titles Fame,	269	U81 Pawlet	V 21
Foure Rivers branching forth like Seas,	276	U84 Body	23
Up to their Ancestors; the rivers side,	281	U84 Kenelme	18

ROAD
Thorough her wombe they make their famous road,	85	E133 Voyage	66

ROAR (See RORE)

ROASTED (See also ROSTED)
To light Tobacco, or save roasted Geese,	205	U43 Vulcan	52
To light Tobacco, or have roasted Geese,	205	U43 Vulcan	V 52

ROAVE
Who reads may roave, and call the passage darke,	383	Author	5

ROAVES
Who reads, who roaves, who hopes to understand,	383	Author	7

	Page	Title	Line

ROB
Of Sex, to rob the Creature; but from Man . . . . . 255 U75 Epithalam. 82
But a fain'd way, doth rob it of the true. . . . . 270 U81 Pawlet 38
And who make thither else, rob, or invade. . . . . 389 Chapman 12
ROBBERY
On a robbery. . . . . 29 E8 Robbery Ttl
ROBBING
Or robbing the poore Market-folkes should nurse . . . 155 U13 Sacvile 90
ROBD
Beeing in feare to be robd, he most learnedly begs. . . . 375 Coryat 1 35
ROBE
Is Banke-rupt turn'd! Cloak, Cassock, Robe, & Gowne, . . 237 U64 Charles 3 V 20
And let there be a starry Robe . . . . . 276 U84 Body 26
In heaven Empyre, and with a robe of light? . . . 285 U84 Muse 102
Brought in the Visor, and the robe of State, . . . 319 Horace 316
ROB'D
Ridway rob'd Duncote of three hundred pound, . . . 29 E8 Robbery 1
Rob'd both of money, and the lawes reliefe, . . . 29 E8 Robbery 5
As we, the rob'd, leave rage, and pittie it. . . . 44 E56 Poet-Ape 4
ROBERT
To Robert Earle of Salisburie. . . . . . 40 E43 Salisburie 1 Ttl
To the most Worthy of his Honors. Robert, ... 40 E43 Salisburie 1 VTtl
To Robert Earle of Salisburie. . . . . . 47 E63 Salisburie 2 Ttl
To Sir Robert Wroth. . . . . . . 96 F3 Wroth Ttl
To Sir Robert Wroth in praise of a Country life. Epode. . 96 F3 Wroth VTtl
To Sir Robert Pie: . . . . 231 U57 Burges 4
. . . in the Behalfe of the two Noble Brothers sir Robert . . 382 Rich Ttl
. . . Robert, Earle of Somerset. . . . . 384 Somerset Ttl
An Epigram To My Joviall Good Freind Mr. Robert Dover, . . 415 Dover Ttl
ROBES
Such weare true wedding robes, and are true freindes, . . 384 Somerset 5
ROCK
The rock, the spindle, and the sheeres controule . . . 52 E76 Bedford 1 15
The other thought it Hydra, or the rock . . . . 86 E133 Voyage 83
Whose Daughter? ha? Great Savage of the Rock? . . . 269 U81 Pawlet 10
ROCKETS
At Bonefires, Rockets, Fire-workes, with the Shoutes . . 249 U72 King 13
ROCKIE
My mountaine belly, and my rockie face, ... 150 U9 Picture 17
ROCKS
This Praecipice, and Rocks that have no end, . . . 166 U15 Friend-Wars 130
ROD
Use still thy rod, ... 129 U1 Father 4
And doe their penance, to avert Gods rod, . . . 235 U61 Epigram 19
And came forth ever cheered, with the rod . . . 287 U84 Muse 183
ROE
On Sir John Roe. . . . . 35 E27 Roe 1 Ttl
On Sir John Roe. . . . . 37 E32 Roe 2 Ttl
Glad-mention'd Roe: thou art but gone before, . . . 37 E33 Roe 3 2
To William Roe. . . . . 50 E70 Wm Roe 1 Ttl
Then to begin, my Roe: He makes a state . . . 50 E70 Wm Roe 1 2
To Sir Thomas Roe. . . . . 63 E98 Th Roe 1 Ttl
Thou hast begun well, Roe, which stand well too, . . 63 E98 Th Roe 1 1
How much of great example wert thou, Roe, . . . 64 E99 Th Roe 2 5
To William Roe. . . . . 80 E128 Wm Roe 2 Ttl
Roe (and my joy to name) th'art now, to goe . . . 80 E128 Wm Roe 2 1
ROE'S
If any sword could save from Fates, Roe's could; . . 35 E27 Roe 1 3
ROGER
Trie and trust Roger, was the word, but now . . . 378 Coryat 2 80
Honest Tom Tell-Troth puts downe Roger, How? . . . 378 Coryat 2 81
ROGUE
He would be call'd, henceforth, the English-Rogue, . . 389 Aleman 16
A Rogue by Statute, censur'd to be whipt, . . . 411 Gill 15
ROGUES
No going backe; on still you rogues, and row. . . . 86 E133 Voyage 88
ROLANDS
All the madde Rolands, and sweet Oliveers; . . . 206 U43 Vulcan 70
ROLLS (See also ROWLES, ROULE)
So would'st th'have run upon the Rolls by stealth, . . 210 U43 Vulcan 169
ROMAN
The Roman Ilia was not more renown'd. 293 U87 Hor.3:9 8
A Roman to Caecilius will allow, ... 309 Horace 77
And Roman Gentrie, jearing, will laugh out. . . . 313 Horace 160
And Roman Gentrie, will with laughter shout. . . . 342 Horace V160
The Roman Gentrie, men of birth, and meane, . . . 321 Horace 360
To Roman Poets. Shall I therefore weave . . . 323 Horace 390
Our Roman Youths they learne the subtle wayes . . . 327 Horace 464
Our Roman Youths they learne more thriving wayes . . 350 Horace V464
ROMANE
A romane sound, but romane vertue weares, . . . 58 E91 Vere 2
No more then Salust in the Romane state! . . . 61 E95 Savile 23
ROMANO
Send in, what or Romano, Tintoret, ... 260 U77 Treasurer 6
Send what Romano or what Tintoret, ... 260 U77 Treasurer V 6
ROMANS
Send in, what Romans famous, Tintoret, ... 260 U77 Treasurer V 6
ROME
If Rome so great, and in her wisest age, . . . 56 E89 Allen 1
What at Ligorne, Rome, Florence you did doe: . . . 69 E107 Hungry 14
Cato's to boote, Rome, and her libertie, . . . 71 E110 Edmonds 1 4
As wandrers doe, that still doe rome, . . . 102 F4 To the World 66
Did not she save from thence, to build a Rome? . . 210 U43 Vulcan 162

551

	Page	Title	Line

ROME (cont.)
Of all, that insolent Greece, or haughtie Rome . . . . 391 Shakespeare 39
When, Rome, I reade thee in thy mighty paire, . . . 395 May 1
RONSART
Equall with her? or Ronsart prais'd . . . . 181 U27 Ode Helen 22
ROOFE
Of polish'd pillars, or a roofe of gold: . . . 93 F2 Penshurst 3
Beneath a Sweet-wood Roofe, neere Alba Lake: . . . 292 U86 Hor.4:1 20
ROOFES
Free from proud porches, or their guilded roofes, . . . 97 F3 Wroth 15
ROOME
When shee was farre: and not a roome, but drest, . . . 96 F2 Penshurst 87
So well! as when I saw the floore, and Roome, . . . 228 U53 Newcastle 17
So well! as when I view'd the floore, and Roome, . . . 228 U53 Newcastle V 17
And he is built like some imperiall roome . . . . 262 U78 Digby 7
To hang a window, or make darke the roome, . . . 282 U84 Muse 7
A little further, to make thee a roome: . . . 391 Shakespeare 21
Lyve long the Feasting Roome. And ere thou burne . 406 Inigo Jones 1 101
Now, you are got into a nearer roome, . . . 409 Brome 3
As it, alone, (and onely it) had roome, . . . 412 Ghyrlond 11
ROOMES
Of Noremberg, or Turkie; hang your roomes . . . 260 U77 Treasurer 3
Hang all your roomes, with one large Pedigree: . . . 282 U84 Kenelme 20
ROOR
To live when Broeck not stands, nor Roor doth runne. . 49 E66 Cary 12
ROOT
And in the noblest Families tooke root . . . 185 U30 Burleigh 18
The very root of writing well, and spring . . . 325 Horace 440
ROOTE
To be the same in roote, thou art in height; . . . 70 E109 Nevil 13
Heare, what the Muses sing about thy roote, . . . 119 F13 Aubigny 100
ROOTED
As they are high; are rooted, and will last. . . . 157 U13 Sacvile 144
Now in the rooted Grasse him lay, ... 290 U85 Country 24
ROOTES
Run from your rootes; Tell, testifie the grand . . . 274 U84 Descent 9
ROPE
Descended in a rope of Titles, be . . . 215 U44 Speach 80
For, if one should, and with a rope make haste . . 335 Horace 655
RORE
Any man else, you clap your hands, and rore, . . . 38 E38 Guiltie 2 4
My lippes could forme the voyce, I heard that Rore, . . 397 Drayton 38
ROSCIUS
As skilfull Roscius, and grave Aesope, men, . . . 56 E89 Allen 3
ROSE (VERB)
Caesar stands up, as from his urne late rose, . . . 72 E111 Edmonds 2 12
And Men may thinke, all light rose there. . . . 276 U84 Body 16
ROSE
'Tis but light paines: Indeede this Dock's no rose. . . 85 E133 Voyage 60
Have you seene a faire Damaske-rose . . . 135 U2 Triumph V 31
The bed of the chast Lilly, and the Rose! . . . 237 U65 Prince 3
Her Rose, and Lilly, intertwind, have made. . . . 268 U80 Christning 16
Againe hath brought the Lillie to the Rose; . . . 401 Filmer 8
R. Rose, I. Ivy, E. sweet Eglantine. . . . 412 Ghyrlond 4
The third, is from the garden cull'd, the Rose, . . . 413 Ghyrlond 13
ROSES
In her cheekes, of Milke, and Roses; . . . 136 U2 Cupid 22
Where he doth steepe himselfe in Milke and Roses; . . 170 U19 Elegy By 8
See, how with Roses, and with Lillies shine, . . . 254 U75 Epithalam. 57
(Lillies and Roses, Flowers of either Sexe) . . . 254 U75 Epithalam. 58
ROSIE
His rosie tyes and garters so ore-blowne, . . . 62 E97 Motion 5
I sent thee, late, a rosie wreath, . . . 106 F9 Celia 3 9
I sent to thee a rosie wreath, . . . 106 F9 Celia 3 V 9
With the Chimaera of the Rosie-Crosse, . . . 206 U43 Vulcan 72
Thy locks, and rosie garlands crowne thy head; . . . 294 U89 Mart.8:77 4
The rosie Morning, or the rising Sun, . . . 414 Ghyrlond 50
ROSIE-CROSSE
With the Chimaera of the Rosie-Crosse, . . . 206 U43 Vulcan 72
ROSTED
Cats there lay divers had beene flead, and rosted, . . 88 E133 Voyage 149
ROT
Spanish receipt, to make her teeth to rot. . . . 188 U34 Small Poxe 12
ROTTEINBERG
Hans-spiegle, Rotteinberg, and Boutersheim, . . . 69 E107 Hungry 26
ROTTEN
With rotten chalk, or Cole upon a wall, . . . 408 Inigo Jones 3 11
ROUGH
Rough, swelling, like a storme: . . . 110 F11 Epode 40
With horrour rough, then rioting with wit! . . . 160 U14 Selden 57
Nor Souldier-like started with rough alarmes, . . . 289 U85 Country 5
And then rough Adria, angrier, farre; . . . 294 U87 Hor.3:9 23
The rough rude Satyres naked; and would try, . . . 319 Horace 321
ROULE
Nor could I, had I seene all Natures roule, . . . 60 E93 Radcliffe 12
ROUND
His neck fenc'd round with ruffe! his eyes halfe shut! . 33 E21 Gam'ster 2
He that is round within himselfe, and streight, . . . 63 E98 Th Roe 1 3
The jolly wassall walkes the often round, . . . 98 F3 Wroth 59
Livers, round about the towne. . . . 105 F8 Sicknesse 17
But he hath eyes so round, and bright, . . . 147 U7 Nymph 22
A banke against it. Nothing but the round . . . 160 U14 Selden 63
His double Bow, and round his Arrowes sends; . . . 170 U19 Elegy By 4

		Page	Title	Line

ROUND (cont.)
Whose even Thred the Fates spinne round, and full, . . . 225 U51 Bacon 15
And the whole lumpe growes round, deform'd, and droupes, . . 227 U52 Answer 5
By him, so ample, full, and round, . . . 244 U70 Ode 49
So polisht, perfect, round, and even, . . . 260 U84 Mind 55
That, planted round, there sing before the Lamb, . . . 285 U84 Muse 89
Or when that Autumne, through the fields, lifts round . 290 U85 Country 17
Wild Bores into his toyles pitch'd round: . . . 290 U85 Country 32
Or with fresh flowers to girt my temple round. . . . 293 U86 Hor.4:1 32
The old man many evils doe girt round; . . . 315 Horace 241
That wider Walls embrac'd their Citie round, . . . 319 Horace 296
And stalketh, like a Fowler, round about, . . . 335 Horace 650
Hot from thy trumpet, round, about the world. . . . 396 Drayton 14
Where it runs round, and even: where so well, . . . 415 Rutter 16

ROUNDE
Aboute this Isle, and Charme the rounde, as when . . . 421 Ode:If Men 39

ROUNDS
Thy Circuits, and thy Rounds free, ... 221 U48 Bacchus 41
Run all the Rounds in a soft Ladyes eare, ... 230 U56 Covell 16

ROUSED
In spring, oft roused for thy masters sport, . . . 97 F3 Wroth 23
In spring tyme roused for their masters sport, . . . 97 F3 Wroth V 23

ROUT
The rout of rurall folke come thronging in, . . . 98 F3 Wroth 53
Whilst all the ravish'd rout . . . . . 240 U67 Muses 40
In sound, quite from his fortune; both the rout, . . . 313 Horace 159
There charme the rout . . . . . . 367 Ode Who saith 44

ROUTES
Had they but grace, of thinking, at these routes, . . . 249 U72 King 15

ROUTS
If they had leisure, at these lawfull routs, . . . 249 U72 King V 15

ROUZE
And Rouze, the Marching of a mighty force, . . . 397 Drayton 39

ROVE (See ROAVE)

ROVINGE
The skilfull mischife of a rovinge Eye . . . 108 F10 Proludium 5

ROW (LINE)
Of touch, or marble; nor canst boast a row . . . 93 F2 Penshurst 2

ROW (NAME)
From Greenwich, hither, to Row-hampton gate! . . . 252 U75 Epithalam. 12

ROW
No going backe; on still you rogues, and row. . . . 86 E133 Voyage 88
Row close then, slaves. Alas, they will beshite us. . . 86 E133 Voyage 90
No matter, stinkards, row. What croaking sound . . 86 E133 Voyage 91
Over your heads: Well, row. At this a loud . . . 86 E133 Voyage 93
Religiously here he bids, row from the stewes, . . . 375 Coryat 1 20

ROWABLE
Once rowable, but now doth nourish men . . . 309 Horace 94

ROW-HAMPTON
From Greenwich, hither, to Row-hampton gate! . . . 252 U75 Epithalam. 12

ROWLE
To fetch the flesh, we keepe the Rowle. . . . 188 U35 Chute 6

ROWLES
Whose lines her rowles were, and records. . . . 247 U70 Ode 126
Whose lives her rowles were, and records. . . . 247 U70 Ode V126

ROWSE
All that dare rowse: or are not loth to quit . . . 162 U15 Friend-Wars 3
With such a Raritie, and not rowse Art . . . 282 U84 Muse 16

ROWTE
And rather to the Fyre, then to the Rowte . . . 420 Ode:If Men 21

ROYAL
your Royal Eye which still creates new men . . . 383 Rich 14

ROYALL
But in my royall subject I passe thee, . . . 38 E36 Martial 3
When with his royall shipping . . . 222 U48 Bacchus 52
Then, Royall Charles, and Mary, doe not grutch . . 236 U63 Charles 2 7
Behold the royall Mary, ... 240 U67 Muses 25
That whereas your royall Father . . . 259 U76 Petition 5
Whereas late your royall Father . . . 259 U76 Petition V 5
A royall Crowne, and purple, be made hop, . . . 321 Horace 333
A royall Crowne, and Scarlet; be made hop, . . . 346 Horace V325/333
presentes a Royall Alter of fayre peace, . . . 382 Rich 6

ROYES
For newes) your Ville-royes, and Silleries, . . . 69 E107 Hungry 21

RUB
And, though I now begin, 'tis not to rub . . . 396 Drayton 7

RUDDY
And thence, the ruddy Satyres oft provoke . . . 94 F2 Penshurst 17

RUDE
Grant then, no rude hand remove her. . . . 39 E40 Ratcliffe 4
Before rude hands have touch'd it? . . . 134 U2 Triumph 22
True noblesse. Palme growes straight, though handled ne're so rude. 177 U25 Desmond 26
With silence, and amazement! not with rude, . . . 284 U84 Muse 78
The rough rude Satyres naked; and would try, . . 319 Horace 321
Into the Profits, what a meere rude braine . . . 331 Horace 583

RUDENESSE
(Their rudenesse then is thought no sinne) . . . 98 F3 Wroth 54

RUDEST
The rudest Winds obey the calmest Ayre: . . . 251 U74 Weston 9

RUDYERD
To Benjamin Rudyerd. . . . . . 78 E121 Rudyerd 1 Ttl
Rudyerd, as lesser dames, to great ones use, . . . 78 E121 Rudyerd 1 1

	Page	Title	Line

RUE
It makes the father, lesse, to rue. — 33 E22 Daughter 4
RU'DE
In these times. Few so have ru'de — 39 E40 Ratcliffe 14
RUFFE
His neck fenc'd round with ruffe! his eyes halfe shut! — 33 E21 Gam'ster 2
Knat, raile, and ruffe too. How so ere, my man — 65 E101 Supper 20
RUFFES
Ripe are their ruffes, their cuffes, their beards, their gate, 58 E92 New Crie 6
RUINE
They'are rear'd with no mans ruine, no mans grone, — 94 F2 Penshurst 46
Or side, but threatens Ruine. The whole Day — 166 U15 Friend-Wars 131
To ruine any issue of the braine? — 203 U43 Vulcan 14
To ruine every issue of her braine? — 203 U43 Vulcan V 14
Blow up, and ruine, myne, and countermyne, — 212 U43 Vulcan 205
And all on utmost ruine set; — 243 U70 Ode 18
The world to ruine with it; in her Fall, — 283 U84 Muse 25
And thinke to ruine, where it seem'd to raise. — 391 Shakespeare 12
RUIN'D
Make all hereafter, had'st thou ruin'd this? — 188 U34 Small Poxe 16
RUINES
How in these ruines, Vulcan, thou dost lurke, — 207 U43 Vulcan 105
How in these ruines, Vulcan, durst thou lurke, — 207 U43 Vulcan V105
See the worlds Ruines! nothing but the piles — 209 U43 Vulcan 137
Among the daily Ruines that fall foule, — 224 U50 Countesse 17
RULE
(As their true rule or lesson) either men, — 158 U13 Sacvile 162
The power, and rule of speaking resteth still. — 309 Horace 104
RULES
A Prince, that rules by'example, more than sway? — 37 E35 James 2 2
RUL'ST
When thou that rul'st, are her Example growne, — 236 U64 Charles 3 V 9
RUMNEY
All the grasse that Rumney yeelds, — 103 F6 Celia 2 13
RUMOR
Fame, and rumor are but toyes. — 102 F5 Celia 1 10
RUMOR'D
But, as 'tis rumor'd, so beleev'd: — 101 F4 To the World 50
RUMOUR
To King James. Upon the happy false rumour of his death, — 43 E51 James 3 Ttl
Who this thy scape from rumour gratulate, — 43 E51 James 3 6
To conquer rumour, and triumph on spight; — 224 U50 Countesse 4
RUN
Who can consider thy right courses run, — 47 E63 Salisbury 2 1
Tell them, what parts yo'have tane, whence run away, — 69 E107 Hungry 9
Twirle the poore chaine you run a feasting in. — 69 E107 Hungry 30
Before his swift and circled race be run, — 116 F12 Rutland 99
Before his swift and fetherd race be run, — 116 F12 Rutland V 99
That they still were to run by her side, — 134 U2 Triumph 9
Run from the Conscience of it, if they could. — 154 U13 Sacvile 46
All lights into his one doth run; — 189 U36 Song 6
Of Credit lost. And I am now run madde: — 191 U38 Elegy 'Tis 2
Others by common Stars their courses run, — 194 U38 Elegy 'Tis 119
So would'st th'have run upon the Rolls by stealth, — 210 U43 Vulcan 169
Run all the Rounds in a soft Ladyes eare, — 230 U56 Covell 16
The Rivers in their shores doe run, — 251 U74 Weston 7
Run from your rootes; Tell, testifie the grand — 274 U84 Descent 9
Where it may run to any good; — 280 U84 Mind 62
He run; and all did strive with diligence — 287 U84 Muse 171
So Fates would have let the Boy a long thred run. — 293 U87 Hor.3:9 16
Obscure. This, striving to run smooth, and flow, — 307 Horace 36
Or acted told. But, ever, things that run — 317 Horace 256
Who like a Giant hasts his course to run, — 414 Ghyrlond 51
RUNG
Like a rung Beare, or Swine: grunting out wit — 232 U58 Book-seller 11
RUNNE
All braines, at times of triumph, should runne wit. — 36 E29 Tilter 4
For then, our water-conduits doe runne wine; — 36 E29 Tilter 5
To live when Broeck not stands, nor Roor doth runne. — 49 E66 Cary 12
O, runne not proud of this. Yet, take thy due. — 81 E129 Mime 15
Fat, aged carps, that runne into thy net. — 94 F2 Penshurst 33
Doth urge him to runne wrong, or to stand still. — 121 F14 Sydney 30
And can I lesse of substance? When I runne, — 156 U13 Sacvile 120
And threat' the great Eclipse. Two houres but runne, — 238 U65 Prince 11
And thereat the great Eclipse. Two houres but runne, — 238 U65 Prince V 11
Chear'd her faire Sisters in her race to runne! — 270 U81 Pawlet 58
Obscure. Another striving smooth to runne, — 339 Horace V 37/ 36
RUNNING
To stay the running floods, — 143 U3 Musicall 10
Here running in the Glasse, — 148 U8 Houre-glasse 2
RUNS
Runs betweene man, and man; 'tweene dame, and dame; — 113 F12 Rutland 16
Runs sweetly, as it had his Lordships Soule; — 167 U15 Friend-Wars 148
It rages, runs, flies, stands, and would provoke — 283 U84 Muse 24
Where it runs round, and even: where so well, — 415 Rutter 16
RUPT
Is Banke-rupt turn'd! the Cassock, Cloake, and Gowne, — 237 U64 Charles 3 20
Is Banke-rupt turn'd! Cloak, Cassock, Robe, & Gowne, — 237 U64 Charles 3 V 20
RURALL
Some bring a capon, some a rurall cake, — 95 F2 Penshurst 51
The rout of rurall folke come thronging in, — 98 F3 Wroth 53
Or Rurall Virgil come, to pipe to us! — 397 Drayton 28

RUSH (REED)
Skin as smooth as any rush, ... 141 U2 Her man 27
RUSH
Let us not then rush blindly on unto it, ... 294 U88 Petronius 3
RUST
Sixe ounces. O, when once the canker'd rust, . . . 327 Horace 472
RUTH
Here lyes to each her parents ruth, ... 33 E22 Daughter 1
RUTLAND
To Elizabeth Countesse of Rutland. . . . . 53 E79 Rutland Ttl
Epistle To Elizabeth Countesse of Rutland. . . . 113 F12 Rutland Ttl
To the Countesse of Rutland: An Elegie. . . . . 113 F12 Rutland VTtl
RUTTER
. . . Master Joseph Rutter. . . . . . . 414 Rutter Ttl
RYME
in weaving Riddles in more wretched ryme, . . . 204 U43 Vulcan V 34
O're read, examin'd, try'd, and prov'd your Ryme . . . 421 Censure 7
RYMES
On these darke rymes; that my affection . . . 177 U25 Desmond 15
On these darke rymes; that our affection . . . 177 U25 Desmond V 15
All the envie of the Rymes, ... 259 U76 Petition 18
All there envie of the Rymes, ... 259 U76 Petition V 18
Foole, doe not rate my Rymes; I'have found thy Vice . . 408 Detractor 5
RYMING
It is a ryming Age, and Verses swarme . . . . 200 U42 Elegy Let 27
RYOTS
Of rimes, or ryots, at your feasts, ... 246 U70 Ode 103
S
Epitaph on S. P. a Child of Q. El. Chappel. . . . 77 E120 S. P. Ttl
SABINES
Such as the Sabines, or a Sun-burnt-blowse, . . . 291 U85 Country 41
SACK (PLUNDER)
From out the horrour of that sack? . . . . . 243 U70 Ode 12
SACK
His Poet Sack, the House-hold will not pay? . . . 241 U68 House-hold 2
And rather wish, in their expence of Sack, . . . 241 U68 House-hold 9
SACKCLOTH
Yet keepe those up in sackcloth too, or lether, . . 200 U42 Elegy Let 25
SACK'T
Speake to me, Muse, the Man, who, after Troy was sack't, . 315 Horace 201
SACKVILE
If, Sackvile, all that have the power to doe . . . 153 U13 Sacvile 1
SACRED
And why that bird was sacred to Apollo, . . . 55 E85 Goodyere 1 4
Because they lack'd the sacred pen, could give . . . 115 F12 Rutland 56
Which, how most sacred I will ever keepe, . . . 190 U37 Friend-Book 13
Of vowes so sacred, and in silence made; . . . 197 U40 Elegy That 14
Be kept alive those Sweet, and Sacred fires . . . 257 U75 Epithalam. 163
There twice a day in sacred Laies, ... 292 U86 Hor.4:1 25
Things sacred, from profane to separate; . . . 327 Horace 487
That sacred to Odcombe are there now suspended, . . 380 Coryat 3 40
SACRIFICE
Or magick sacrifice, they past along! . . . 85 E133 Voyage 49
To become thy sacrifice. . . . . . . 105 F8 Sicknesse 28
This hasty sacrifice, wherein I reare . . . . 116 F12 Rutland 97
1. The Sinners Sacrifice. To the Holy Trinitie. . . 127 U1 Trinitie Ttl
All-gracious God, the Sinners sacrifice, . . . 127 U1 Trinitie 9
Lowd sacrifice of drinke, for their health-sake! . . 156 U13 Sacvile 100
Your sacrifice, then here remaine with me. . . . 199 U41 Elegy Since 18
By thy owne vote, a sacrifice to thee? . . . 203 U43 Vulcan 22
And as an ever-lasting Sacrifice . . . . . 382 Rich 7
SACVILE
An Epistle to Sir Edward Sacvile, now Earle of Dorset. . 153 U13 Sacvile Ttl
SAD
Wee, sad for him, may glorie, and not sinne. . . . 35 E27 Roe 1 8
The like is Jone. But turning home, is sad. . . . 40 E42 Giles 8
Shall make us sad next morning: or affright . . . 65 E101 Supper 41
And hearts of all, if I be sad for show, . . . 122 F15 Heaven 6
Must make me sad for what I have obtain'd. . . . 154 U13 Sacvile 38
With gladnesse temper'd her sad Parents teares! . . 270 U81 Pawlet 59
Which gladnesse temper'd her sad Parents teares! . . 270 U81 Pawlet V 59
Goe now, her happy Parents, and be sad, . . . 271 U81 Pawlet 77
For her devotions, and those sad essayes . . . 287 U84 Muse 181
The gests of Kings, great Captaines, and sad Warres, . 309 Horace 105
The deeds of Kings, great Captaines, and sad Warres, . 341 Horace V105
Sad language fits sad lookes; stuff'd menacings, . . 311 Horace 149
Io still wandring, griev'd Orestes sad: . . . 342 Horace V177
Of Diomede; nor Troyes sad Warre begins . . . 315 Horace 209
Or the sad thunder-stroken thing he have . . . 335 Horace 672
SADDEST
Sober, as saddest care: . . . . 111 F11 Epode 60
SADLED
A Horse here is sadled, but no Tom him to backe, . . 374 Coryat 1 14
SADNESSE
That shee removeth cares, sadnesse ejects, . . . 82 E130 Ferrab. 1 4
This sadnesse makes no approaches, but to kill. . . 191 U38 Elegy 'Tis 4
From any thought like sadnesse. . . . . . 221 U48 Bacchus 20
Whose chearfull look our sadnesse doth destroy, . . 414 Ghyrlond 43
SAFE
Be safe, nor feare thy selfe so good a fame, . . . 53 E77 Not name 1
If, my religion safe, I durst embrace . . . . 61 E95 Savile 1
The common-wealth still safe, must studie thee. . . 66 E102 Pembroke 20
Dar'st breath in any ayre; and with safe skill, . . 76 E119 Shelton 9

SAFE (cont.)
Or safe, but shee'll procure . . . . . 109 F11 Epode 6
Without companions? 'Tis safe to have none. . . . 118 F13 Aubigny 56
(They finde it both so wittie, and safe to give.) . . . 118 F13 Aubigny 76
Safe from the wolves black jaw, and the dull Asses hoofe. . 175 U23 Himselfe 36
Who thus long safe, would gaine upon the times . . . 186 U32 Elsmere 9
Men that are safe, and sure, in all they doe, . . . 218 U47 Tribe 1
His is more safe commoditie, or none: . . . . 241 U69 Friend Son 7
Sate safe enough, but now secured more. . . . . 268 U80 Christning 14
Creepes on the ground; too safe, too afraid of storme. . . 307 Horace 39
Being over-safe, and fearing of the flaw: . . . 339 Horace V 41/ 39
That from the North, the Navie safe doth store, . . . 309 Horace 92
Grow a safe Writer, and be warie-driven . . . 323 Horace 393
God blesse them all, and keepe them safe: . . . 419 Grace 7
God blesse us all, Bedford keepe safe: . . . 419 Grace V 7
not safe; but when thou dost them thoroughlie: . . . 423 Lucan 16
SAFELY
Cannot so safely sinne. Their chastitie . . . 111 F11 Epode 81
Man may securely sinne, but safely never. . . . 113 F11 Epode 116
A man may safely sinne, securely never. . . . 113 F11 Epode V116
And safely trust to dresse, not burne their Boates. . . 208 U43 Vulcan 128
SAFETIE
With safetie of her innocence; . . . . . 33 E22 Daughter 6
As with the safetie, and honour of the Lawes, . . . 186 U31 Elsmere 9
My Princes safetie, and my Kings desire, . . . 219 U47 Tribe 38
For safetie of such Majestie, cry out? . . . 236 U64 Charles 3 6
Whereby the safetie of Man-kind was wrought) . . . 238 U66 Queene 8
Whereby the safetie of the world was wrought) . . . 238 U66 Queene V 8
Of so much safetie to the Realme, and King. . . . 238 U66 Queene 14
The safetie of our soules, and forfeit breath! . . . 286 U84 Muse 136
Though sower, with safetie of his gravitie, . . . 319 Horace 322
SAFETIES
Of sweets, and safeties, they possesse by Peace. . . 261 U77 Treasurer 22
SAGUNTUM
Brave Infant of Saguntum, cleare . . . 242 U70 Ode 1
SAID
Thou wert, as chiefe of them are said t'have beene. . . 28 E4 James 1 6
Said I wrong'd him, and (which was more) his love. . . 80 E126 Mrs Cary 5
But when I have said, The proofes of all these bee . . 82 E130 Ferrab. 1 17
One said, it was bold Briareus, or the beadle, . . . 86 E133 Voyage 81
One said, the other swore, the world consists. . . . 87 E133 Voyage 129
And like the ravish'd Sheep'erds said, . . . 130 U1 Nativitie 4
Sure, said he, if I have Braine, ... 136 U2 Cupid 10
Heard what times past have said, seene what ours doe: . . 159 U14 Selden 34
Thou should'st have stay'd, till publike fame said so. . 204 U43 Vulcan 46
My gentle Arthur; that it might be said . . . 216 U45 Squib 3
Haile Mary, full of grace, it once was said, . . . 238 U66 Queene 1
For, had we here said lesse, we had sung nothing then. . . 263 U79 New-yeares 8
To one she said, Doe this, he did it; So . . . 287 U84 Muse 169
Thespis is said to be the first found out . . . 319 Horace 311
Was Tigers, said, and Lyons fierce, to tame. . . . 327 Horace 482
Was said to move the stones, by his Lutes powers, . . 327 Horace 484
Rich men are said with many cups to plie, . . . 333 Horace 617
Great men are said with many cups to plye, . . . 354 Horace V617
No: as I first said, who would write a story at . . 381 Coryat 3 59
SAIES
And sits, till th'Epilogue saies Clap, or Crowne: . . 315 Horace 222
Jest, he saies. Item one sute of blacke taffata . . 380 Coryat 3 48
SAILE (See also SAYLE)
Their wherry had no saile, too; ours had none: . . . 84 E133 Voyage 11
Ride, saile, am coach'd, know I how farre I have gone, . . 156 U13 Sacvile 121
But prove the Aire, and saile from Coast to Coast: . . 367 Ode Who saith 37
SAILES
With whom who sailes, rides on the surge of feare, . . 110 F11 Epode 41
SAINT
That onely fooles make thee a saint, . . . 100 F4 To the World 15
If they stay here, but till Saint Georges Day. . . 213 U44 Speach 10
In great Saint Georges Union; . . . . 221 U48 Bacchus 44
To publish her a Saint. My Muse is gone. . . . 289 U84 Muse 228
Of Ethnicisme, makes his Muse a Saint. . . . 401 Beaumont 22
SAINTS
Among thy Saints elected to abide, . . . 128 U1 Trinitie 45
. . . apotheosis, or Relation to the Saints. . . 282 U84 Muse Ttl
The joy of Saints! the Crowne for which it lives, . . 283 U84 Muse 37
Saints, Martyrs, Prophets, with those Hierarchies, . . 285 U84 Muse 85
Both Saints, and Martyrs, by her loved Lord. . . . 400 Lady Ogle 39
SAI'ST
Thou sai'st, thou only cam'st to prove . . . 150 U10 Jealousie 10
SAIST
Thou saist, that cannot be: for thou hast seene . . 32 E18 Censurer 3
SAITH
Who saith our Times nor have, nor can . . . 366 Ode Who saith 1
There nam'd to be travell'd? For this our Tom saith: . . 380 Coryat 3 21
Just and fit actions Ptolemey (he saith) . . . 422 Lucan 1
SAKE
For the lucks sake, it thus much favour have, . . . 27 E3 Bookseller 4
Mens manners ne're were viler, for your sake. . . 34 E24 Parliament 2
Nay more, for greatnesse sake, he will be one . . . 36 E28 Surly 19
For whose sake, hence-forth, all his vowes be such, . . 41 E45 First Son 11
Sir Lucklesse, troth, for lucks sake passe by one: . . 42 E47 Luckless 2 1
From all my kinde: that, for my sake, . . . 101 F4 To the World 59
There are those, that, for thy sake, . . . 105 F8 Sicknesse 25
For Loves-sake, kisse me once againe, . . . 139 U2 Another 1

	Page	Title	Line
SAKE (cont.)			
One good enough for a songs sake.	145	U5 Woman-kind	12
Familiar, for the uses sake;	146	U6 Defence	16
Nor will he tell me for whose sake	151	U11 Dreame	7
Lowd sacrifice of drinke, for their health-sake!	156	U13 Sacvile	100
That still was good for goodnesse sake, nor thought	185	U30 Burleigh	13
Of your grace, for goodnesse sake,	260	U76 Petition	26
This Cradle, and for Goodnesse sake,	273	U84 Cradle	10
In many a Gumme, and for thy soft eares sake	292	U86 Hor.4:1	22
Into their birth-right, and for fitnesse sake,	323	Horace	376
Let what thou fain'st for pleasures sake, be neere	329	Horace	507
Where spight of Death, next Life, for her Loves sake	394	Jane Ogle	25
The Poets act! and for his Country's sake	398	Drayton	63
SAKES			
And I could wish for their eterniz'd sakes,	89	E133 Voyage	195
SALE			
That to the sale of Wares calls every Buyer;	333	Horace	598
SALIAN			
And in the Salian manner meet	292	U86 Hor.4:1	27
SALISBURIE			
To Robert Earle of Salisburie.	40	E43 Salisbury 1	Ttl
To Robert Earle of Salisburie.	47	E63 Salisbury 2	Ttl
And can to these be silent, Salisburie,	47	E63 Salisbury 2	9
SALISBURY			
. . . Earle of Salisbury. Epigramme.	40	E43 Salisbury 1	VTtl
SALLADE			
An olive, capers, or some better sallade	64	E101 Supper	10
SALLIE			
Or Captaine Pamphlets horse, and foot, that sallie	206	U43 Vulcan	79
Oure Captaine Pamphlets horse, and foot, that sallie	206	U43 Vulcan	V 79
SALLY			
Or Captaine Pamphletts, which on foote doe sally	206	U43 Vulcan	V 79
SALT			
I have no salt: no bawdrie he doth meane.	42	E49 Playwrt 1	3
Can pumpe for; or a Libell without salt	193	U38 Elegy 'Tis	96
SALUST			
No more then Salust in the Romane state!	61	E95 Savile	23
SALUTE			
Nor did the king of Denmarke him salute,	63	E97 Motion	15
And no one empty-handed, to salute	95	F2 Penshurst	49
I first salute thee so; and gratulate,	161	U14 Selden	67
Goe, Muse, in, and salute him. Say he be	262	U78 Digby	19
Goe, Muse, in, and salute him thoughe he be	262	U78 Digby	V 19
Salute old Mone,	367	Ode Who saith	38
I doe salute you! Are you fitted yet?	402	Inigo Jones 1	17
SALVATION			
That did us all salvation bring,	130	U1 Nativitie	8
SAME			
To the same Sir Cod.	33	E20 Cod 2	Ttl
On the same Beast.	35	E26 Beast 2	Ttl
Of a great man, and to be thought the same,	35	E28 Surly	2
To the same.	37	E33 Roe 3	Ttl
The selfe-same things, a note of concord be:	40	E42 Giles	17
To the same.	42	E47 Luckless	Ttl
If, as their ends, their fruits were so, the same,	45	E57 Bawds	1
Thy fact, in brasse or marble writ the same)	46	E60 Mounteagle	4
To the same.	47	E64 Salisbury 3	Ttl
As her owne conscience, still, the same reward.	48	E64 Salisbury 3	14
And thou design'd to be the same thou art,	49	E67 Suffolk	9
To the Same.	55	E86 Goodyere 2	Ttl
Mill was the same. Since, both his body and face	57	E90 Mill	13
Be alwayes to thy gather'd selfe the same:	63	E98 Th Roe 1	9
To the same.	63	E99 Th Roe 2	Ttl
The selfe-same deeds, as diversly they come,	64	E99 Th Roe 2	8
To be the same in roote, thou art in height;	70	E109 Nevil	13
He wrote, with the same spirit that he fought,	71	E110 Edmonds 1	8
To the same; On the same.	72	E111 Edmonds 2	Ttl
An Epick poeme; thou hast the same end.	72	E112 Gamster	10
To the same.	78	E122 Rudyerd 2	Ttl
To the same.	78	E123 Rudyerd 3	Ttl
And, than this same, I know no abler way	80	E127 Aubigny	11
To the same.	82	E131 Ferrab. 2	Ttl
They were not to be nam'd on the same day.	83	E131 Ferrab. 2	12
All was to them the same, they were to passe,	88	E133 Voyage	140
Where the same beere, and bread, and selfe-same wine,	95	F2 Penshurst	63
To the same.	103	F6 Celia 2	Ttl
Wherein, your forme, you still the same shall finde;	120	F13 Aubigny	123
And slight the same.	129	U1 Father	27
Aymed with that selfe-same shaft.	133	U2 Suffered	12
With my Mothers is the same.	137	U2 Cupid	38
Make in one, the same were shee.	137	U2 Cupid	48
For benefits are ow'd with the same mind	153	U13 Sacvile	5
That would, perhaps, have prais'd, and thank'd the same,	161	U14 Selden	70
In the same Mines of knowledge; and thence brought	161	U14 Selden	76
From Death, and darke oblivion, neere the same,	175	U24 Frontispice	1
This same which you have caught,	180	U26 Ode High	20
That this sparke of the same fire let loose	209	U43 Vulcan	V141
Alive yet, in the noise; and still the same;	214	U44 Speach	56
The same it was inspir'd, rich, and refin'd.	225	U50 Countesse	30
The same that thou art promis'd, but be slow,	237	U65 Prince	6
The same that thou hast promis'd, but be slow,	237	U65 Prince	V 6
To mee; or beene the same to you; if show,	241	U69 Friend Son	2
. . . Surviving Duke of the same name.	252	U75 Epithalam.	Ttl

SAME (cont.)

	Page	Title	Line
On the same floore,			
Him up, to doe the same himselfe had done.	254	U75 Epithalam.	70
This is no Picture, but the same.	256	U75 Epithalam.	108
The same translated.	278	U84 Mind	24
The same translated.	294	U88 Petronius	Ttl
And so, as every man may hope the same;	294	U89 Mart.8:77	Ttl
From slaughters, and foule life; and for the same	321	Horace	350
Still in the same, and warned will not mend,	327	Horace	481
Doth the same thing with him, that would him kill.	329	Horace	530
To write it with the selfe same spirit he went,	335	Horace	666
still that same little poynte hee was; but when	379	Coryat 3	14
Who bluntly doth but looke upon the same,	383	Rich	13
With the same looke, or with a better, shine.	383	Author	3
Upon the Muses anvile: turne the same,	384	Somerset	10
The selfe same Genius! so the worke will say.	392	Shakespeare	61
And howrely brooding ore the same,	395	May	23
All kings to doe the self same deeds with some!	400	Lady Ogle	29
The valuations, mixtures, and the same	406	Inigo Jones 2	4

SANCTIFIER

	Page	Title	Line
My Maker, Saviour, and my Sanctifier:	415	Rutter	29

SAND

	Page	Title	Line
	128	U1 Trinitie	41
Nor death; but when thy latest sand is spent,	100	F3 Wroth	105
on a lovers dust, made sand for ane Houre Glasse	148	U8 Houre-glasse	VTtl

SANDS

	Page	Title	Line
Or the sands in Chelsey fields,	103	F6 Celia 2	14
All the sands in Chelsey fields,	103	F6 Celia 2	V 14

SANGUINE

	Page	Title	Line
To my lesse sanguine Muse, wherein she'hath wonne	115	F12 Rutland	72

SANS

	Page	Title	Line
Sans helpe of Sybil, or a golden bough,	85	E133 Voyage	48

SAPIENCE

	Page	Title	Line
The Seat of Sapience, the most lovely Mother,	414	Ghyrlond	45

SAPPHO

	Page	Title	Line
Did Sappho on her seven-tongu'd Lute,	181	U27 Ode Helen	3

SARDANE

	Page	Title	Line
As Poppie, and Sardane honey; 'cause without	331	Horace	559

SARDUS

	Page	Title	Line
Poppy, with hony of Sardus; 'cause without	351	Horace	V535/559

SARUM'S

	Page	Title	Line
When, in my Verse, men reade but Sarum's name,	41	E43 Salisbury 1	V 9

SATE

	Page	Title	Line
There Juno sate, and yet no Peacock by.	68	E105 L Wroth 2	18
. . . the last Terme he sate Chancellor.	185	U31 Elsmere	Ttl
Sate safe enough, but now secured more.	268	U80 Christning	14

SATHAN

	Page	Title	Line
By sinne, and Sathan; and my flesh misus'd,	127	U1 Trinitie	6

SATURNE'S

	Page	Title	Line
The aged Saturne's age, and rites to know;	78	E122 Rudyerd 2	2

SATURNES

	Page	Title	Line
As if in Saturnes raigne it were;	98	F3 Wroth	50

SATURNIAS

	Page	Title	Line
Or Saturnias gate	136	U2 Triumph	V 44

SATYRES

	Page	Title	Line
To Lucy, Countesse of Bedford, with Mr. Donnes Satyres.	60	E94 Bedford 3	Ttl
Yet, Satyres, since the most of mankind bee	60	E94 Bedford 3	7
To Satyres; and thou dost pursue me. Where,	73	E112 Gamster	14
And thence, the ruddy Satyres oft provoke	94	F2 Penshurst	17
The rough rude Satyres naked; and would try,	319	Horace	321
Yet so the scoffing Satyres to mens view,	321	Horace	328
From what th'obscene, and petulant Satyres are.	321	Horace	340
Nor I, when I write Satyres, will so love	321	Horace	341

SATYRICALL

	Page	Title	Line
A Satyricall Shrub.	171	U20 Shrub	Ttl

SAUCE

	Page	Title	Line
Limons, and wine for sauce: to these, a coney	65	E101 Supper	13

SAUT

	Page	Title	Line
Doe all the tricks of a saut Lady Bitch;	164	U15 Friend-Wars	76

SAVAGE

	Page	Title	Line
What savage, brute affection,	112	F11 Epode	108
Whose Daughter? ha? Great Savage of the Rock?	269	U81 Pawlet	10

SAVE (EXCEPT)

	Page	Title	Line
(Save that most masculine issue of his braine)	53	E79 Rutland	6
His deedes too dying, save in bookes (whose good	71	E110 Edmonds 1	V 15
The filth, stench, noyse: save only what was there	84	E133 Voyage	9
All is Venus: save unchaste.	137	U2 Cupid	42
Save the preceding Two?	255	U75 Epithalam.	77
Draw first a Cloud: all save her neck;	276	U84 Body	13

SAVE

	Page	Title	Line
The bodies stripes, I see, the soule may save.	33	E21 Gam'ster	8
If any sword could save from Fates, Roe's could;	35	E27 Roe 1	3
Could save that line to dedicate to thee?	44	E53 Old-end	10
Pr'y thee, yet save thy rest; give ore in time:	73	E112 Gamster	21
God, and the good, know to forgive, and save.	191	U38 Elegy 'Tis	19
To light Tobacco, or save roasted Geese.	205	U43 Vulcan	52
Did not she save from thence, to build a Rome?	210	U43 Vulcan	162
With all her aydes, to save her from the seize	283	U84 Muse	17

SAV'D

	Page	Title	Line
That the wit there, and manners might be sav'd:	73	E113 Overbury	6
Not thence be sav'd, although indeed he could?	335	Horace	658

SAVER

	Page	Title	Line
But saver of my countrey thee alone.	46	E60 Mounteagle	10

```
                                                        Page     Title          Line
SAVILE
   To Sir Henrie Savile.      .       .       .     .     .     61   E95 Savile     Ttl
   In thee, most weighty Savile, liv'd to us:        .     .     61   E95 Savile     4
SAVING
   Unlesse some saving-Honour of the Crowne,         .     .    248   U71 Treasurer  13
SAVING-HONOUR
   Unlesse some saving-Honour of the Crowne,         .     .    248   U71 Treasurer  13
SAVIOUR
   My Maker, Saviour, and my Sanctifier:             .     .    128   U1 Trinitie    41
   3. A Hymne On the Nativitie of my Saviour.        .     .    130   U1 Nativitie   Ttl
   The vision of our Saviour, face to face,          .     .    286   U84 Muse       132
   Shee saw her Saviour, by an early light,          .     .    288   U84 Muse       199
SAVIOURS
   This day, by Baptisme, and his Saviours crosse:   .     .    268   U80 Christning 10
SAVOUR
   And have'hem yeeld no savour, but of state.       .     .     58   E92 New Crie   5
   Of such as savour      .       .       .     .     .    177   U25 Desmond    34
SAVOY
   France, Savoy, Italy, and Helvetia,       .       .     .    379   Coryat 3       19
SAW
   And, that is done, as he saw great men doe.       .     .     35   E28 Surly      6
   Saw all his race approch the blacker floods:      .     .     41   E44 Chuff      4
   He, that but saw you weare the wheaten hat,       .     .     68   E105 L Wroth 2 7
   That saw you put on Pallas plumed caske:    .     .     .     68   E105 L Wroth 2 16
   But the first question is, when one saw thee?     .     .     81   E129 Mime      2
   With his brave sonne, the Prince, they saw thy fires   .     95   F2 Penshurst   77
   Who saw the light, and were afraid,       .       .     .    130   U1 Nativitie   5
   2. How he saw her.                                .     .    132   U2 How he saw  Ttl
   Clos'd to their peace, he saw his branches shoot, .     .    185   U30 Burleigh   17
   I saw with two poore Chambers taken in,     .     .     .    209   U43 Vulcan     135
   They saw too store of feathers, and more may,     .     .    213   U44 Speach     9
   He that but saw thy curious Captaines drill,      .     .    213   U44 Speach     29
   Were now the greater Captaine? for they saw       .     .    214   U44 Speach     39
   My Superficies: that was all you saw.       .     .     .    227   U52 Answer     9
   When first, my Lord, I saw you backe your horse,  .     .    228   U53 Newcastle  1
   And saw a Centaure, past those tales of Greece;   .     .    228   U53 Newcastle  5
   For never saw I yet the Muses dwell,        .     .     .    228   U53 Newcastle  15
   So well! as when I saw the floore, and Roome,     .     .    228   U53 Newcastle  17
   As they that saw      .       .       .     .     .    247   U70 Ode        118
   Who saw the way was made it! and were sent        .     .    270   U81 Pawlet     65
   That saw the way was made it! and were sent       .     .    270   U81 Pawlet     V 65
   And saw that portion of her selfe to die.   .     .     .    282   U84 Muse       14
   Shee saw her Saviour, by an early light,          .     .    288   U84 Muse       199
   On all the world! She saw him on the Crosse       .     .    288   U84 Muse       201
   Shee saw him rise, triumphing over Death    .     .     .    288   U84 Muse       203
   Shee saw him too, in glory to ascend        .     .     .    288   U84 Muse       205
   All this by Faith she saw, and fram'd a Plea,     .     .    288   U84 Muse       209
   Saw many Townes, and Men, and could their manners tract.     315   Horace         202
   How he could jest, because he mark'd and saw,     .     .    319   Horace         323
   Fell into fault so farre, as now they saw   .     .     .    321   Horace         367
   They saw it halfe, damd thy whole play, and more; .     .    371   Fletcher       8
   He there doth protest he saw of the eleven.       .     .    380   Coryat 3       46
   It was no Dreame! I was awake, and saw!     .     .     .    396   Drayton        11
   I saw a Beauty from the Sea to rise,      .       .     .    396   Drayton        15
   And looking up, I saw Minervas fowle,     .       .     .    397   Drayton        33
   I saw, and read, it was thy Barons Warres!        .     .    397   Drayton        42
SAWE
   To every sence, and scorne to those that sawe     .     .    420   Ode:If Men     17
SAW'ST
   Saw'st thou that Paire, became these Rites so well,    .    254   U75 Epithalam. 76
SAY     (ASSAY)
   Great Say-Master of State, who cannot erre,       .     .    255   U75 Epithalam. 99
   Great Say-Master of State, who not to erre,       .     .    255   U75 Epithalam. V 99
SAY     (See also SAIES, SEY'D)
   What doth he say, but say, leave to be chast,     .     .     34   E25 Beast 1    7
   For thy late sharpe device.  I say 'tis fit       .     .     36   E29 Tilter     3
   But that's put in, thou'lt say.  Why, so is thine. .     .     36   E29 Tilter     6
   Rest in soft peace, and, ask'd, say here doth lye .     .     41   E45 First Son  9
   And hath no honor lost, our Due'llists say.       .     .     42   E48 Mungril    3
   Forgive me then, if mine but say you are    .     .     .     67   E103 L Wroth 1 9
   And, drest in shepheards tyre, who would not say: .     .     68   E105 L Wroth 2 9
   Would'st thou heare, what man can say        .     .     .     79   E124 Elizabeth 1
   To say, indeed, shee were the soule of heaven,    .     .     82   E130 Ferrab. 1 11
   Say, this, or that man they to thee preferre;     .     .     83   E131 Ferrab. 2 9
   And would (being ask'd the truth) ashamed say,    .     .     83   E131 Ferrab. 2 11
   Thou hast seene hell (some say) and know'st all nookes there, 85   E133 Voyage    51
   To this dire passage.  Say, thou stop thy nose:   .     .     85   E133 Voyage    59
   For, to say truth, what scullion is so nastie,    .     .     88   E133 Voyage    147
   What (great, I will not say, but) sodayne cheare  .     .     95   F2 Penshurst   82
   May say, their lords have built, but thy lord dwells.   .     96   F2 Penshurst   102
   Say, are not women truely, then,          .       .     .    104   F7 Women but   5
   Say, are not women truely, then,          .       .     .    104   F7 Women but   11
   Looke then, and see your selfe.  I will not say    .     .    117   F13 Aubigny    29
   As I, can say, and see it doth excell.      .     .     .    117   F13 Aubigny    34
   Doth say,    .       .       .       .     .     .    120   F14 Sydney      14
   Say you have follow'd farre,        .       .     .     .    121   F14 Sydney      45
   Where, you say, men gather blisses,       .       .     .    136   U2 Cupid       26
   To say over every purle        .       .     .     .    140   U2 Promise      23
   They say the Angells marke each deed,     .       .     .    144   U3 Musicall    17
   Would say as much, as both have done      .       .     .    151   U12 Corbet     3
   And if I had no more to say,        .       .     .     .    168   U16 Gray       2
   No more, I am sorry for so fond cause, say,       .     .    171   U20 Shrub      4
   In darke, and sullen mornes, doe we not say,      .     .    193   U38 Elegy 'Tis 79
```

	Page	Title	Line
SAY (cont.)			
They may say Grace, and for Loves Chaplaines passe;	198	U40 Elegy That	31
On such my serious follies; But, thou'lt say,	204	U43 Vulcan	41
Or such my serious follies; But, thou'lt say,	204	U43 Vulcan	V 41
I dare not say a body, but some parts	206	U43 Vulcan	87
May to thy name a Vulcanale say;	208	U43 Vulcan	120
May to thy name a Pagan prayer say;	208	U43 Vulcan	V120
But say, all sixe good men, what answer yee?	210	U43 Vulcan	173
Why yet, my noble hearts, they cannot say,	213	U44 Speach	1
Well, I say, thrive, thrive brave Artillerie yard,	213	U44 Speach	23
I could say more of such, but that I flie	218	U47 Tribe	5
They say you weekly invite with fits o'th' Mother,	223	U49 Pucell	40
How many times, Live long, Charles, would he say,	236	U64 Charles 3	3
For want of knowing the Poet, to say him nay?	241	U68 House-hold	4
Of which we Priests, and Poets say	245	U70 Ode	82
There; but, renewed, say,	258	U75 Epithalam.	167
Goe, Muse, in, and salute him. Say he be	262	U78 Digby	19
And to the Torturers (her Doctors) say,	270	U81 Pawlet	52
Sweet Mind, then speake your selfe, and say,	278	U84 Mind	17
That all may say, that see the frame,	278	U84 Mind	23
Put black, and mourning on? and say you misse	285	U84 Muse	98
But all of God: They still shall have to say,	286	U84 Muse	119
But, say old Love returne should make,	294	U87 Hor.3:9	17
Fit rites. The Child, that now knowes how to say,	315	Horace	225
Fit dues. The Child, that now knowes how to say,	344	Horace	V225
Too patiently, that I not fondly say;	323	Horace	401
There's Albin's sonne will say, Substract an ounce	327	Horace	467
But, now, it is enough to say; I make	333	Horace	593
To say, I'm ignorant. Just as a Crier	333	Horace	597
Once say I'me ignorant. Just as a Cryer,	333	Horace	V597
His flatterers to their gaine. But say, he can	333	Horace	601
His praisers to their gaine: but say he can	353	Horace	V601
Hee'd say, Mend this, good friend, and this; 'tis naught.	333	Horace	624
He'd say, mend this my friend, and this, 'tis nought.	354	Horace	V624
Become an Aristarchus. And, not say,	335	Horace	639
Retire, and say; Her Graces	365	Ode Splendor	21
And that, say Philosophers, is the best modell.	379	Coryat 3	5
Some want, they say in a sort he did crave:	380	Coryat 3	55
That all, that view you then, and late; may say,	384	Somerset	25
Were askt of thy Discoveries; They must say,	388	Chapman	8
To say but one, were single. Then it chimes,	389	Aleman	3
But every Table in this Church can say,	394	Jane Ogle	7
The selfe same Genius! so the worke will say.	395	May	23
My verses were commended, thou dar'st say,	408	Detractor	1
You looke, my Joseph, I should something say	414	Rutter	1
A Say-master, hath studied all the tricks	415	Rutter	26
or as some would say to breake	416	Moon	3
I had somwhat else to say,	417	Moon	9
SAYD			
And sayd twas sure a threatning to the beares;	209	U43 Vulcan	V146
you'l be as Langley sayd, an Inigo still.	403	Inigo Jones 1	22
I sayd, who'had supp'd so deepe of this sweet Chalice,	412	Sutcliffe	21
SAYES			
The quarter day is come; the hostesse sayes,	30	E12 Shift	7
Who sayes that Giles and Jone at discord be?	40	E42 Giles	1
He sayes, I want the tongue of Epigrammes;	42	E49 Playwrt 1	2
Your 'pothecarie, and his drug sayes no.	46	E62 Would-bee	4
And whisper what a Proclamation sayes.	59	E92 New Crie	20
This day sayes, then, the number of glad yeeres	120	F14 Sydney	21
Pardon, sayes he, that were a way to see	155	U13 Sacvile	71
What each man sayes of it, and of what coat	232	U58 Book-seller	4
He sayes to the world; let any man mend it,	379	Coryat 3	15
As true oblations; his Brothers Embleme sayes,	383	Rich	10
Hee's warme on his feet now he sayes, & can	405	Inigo Jones 1	67
SAYING			
This saying: To some things there is assign'd	331	Horace	548
SAYLE			
yearly set out there, to sayle downe the Street,	407	Inigo Jones 2	18
SAYLES			
With Sayles of silke, as the first notes	273	U84 Cradle	23
SAY-MASTER			
Great Say-Master of State, who cannot erre,	255	U75 Epithalam.	99
Great Say-Master of State, who not to erre,	255	U75 Epithalam.	V 99
A Say-master, hath studied all the tricks	415	Rutter	26
SAY'S			
Lookes o're the bill, likes it: and say's, god payes.	30	E12 Shift	10
SAYST			
Sayst thou so, Lucan? But thou scornst to stay	397	Drayton	47
SAYTH			
Nay, sayth a sister, Venus Nun, Kate Arden,	209	U43 Vulcan	V148
SCAB			
An admirable verse: the great Scab take	353	Horace	V594
SCABBED			
How scabbed, how ragged, and how pediculous	380	Coryat 3	34
SCABBERD			
Bawd, in a Velvet scabberd! I envy	202	U42 Elegy Let	85
SCABBES			
So that not them, his scabbes, lice, or the stewes,	380	Coryat 3	50
SCALDING			
That, with still-scalding steemes, make the place hell.	88	E133 Voyage	144
SCALE			
Live by their Scale, that dare doe nothing free?	215	U44 Speach	68
A Merchants Wife is Regent of the Scale.	229	U54 Squib	4

		Page	Title	Line

SCALE (cont.)
By the scale of his booke, a yard of his stile? • • • 379 Coryat 3 10
SCAN
A lawfull Verse, by th'eare, or finger scan. • • • 323 Horace 404
SCANDERONE
Witnesse his Action done at Scanderone; • • • 262 U78 Digby 13
SCANDEROONE
And his great Action done at Scanderoone; • • • 262 U78 Digby V 13
SCAN'D
And all your Booke (when it is throughly scan'd) • • • 370 Author 5
SCANT
But that I understood him scant. • • • 152 U12 Corbet 31
Excuses, or Delayes? or done 'hem scant, • • • 153 U13 Sacvile 27
Which if it kindle not, but scant • • • 174 U22 Elegy Tho 33
Words, and sweetnesse, and be scant • • • 184 U29 Fit of Rime 44
And seeke to scant her comelie libertie, • • • 190 U37 Friend-Book 20
and seeke to scant her comelye Libertye, • • • 421 Censure 13
SCANTED
Are they so scanted in their store? or driven • • • 241 U68 House-hold 3
SCAPE
When men a dangerous disease did scape, • • • 31 E13 Empirick 1
Who this thy scape from rumour gratulate, • • • 43 E51 James 3 6
Where shall I scape thee? in an Epigramme? • • • 73 E112 Gamster 15
Oft scape an Imputation, more through luck, then wit. • • 179 U25 Desmond 52
Oft scape theyr Imputation, more through luck, then wit. • 179 U25 Desmond V 52
They will come of, and scape the Punishment. • • • 186 U32 Elsmere 14
SCAP'D
To have so soone scap'd worlds, and fleshes rage, • • 41 E45 First Son 7
Or, having scap'd, shall I returne, • • • 101 F4 To the World 25
Forme, Art or Ensigne, that hath scap'd your sight? • • 160 U14 Selden 48
Forme, Act or Ensigne, that hath scap'd your sight? • • 160 U14 Selden V 48
Scap'd not his Justice any jot the more: • • • 210 U43 Vulcan 154
Scap'd not this Justice any jot the more: • • • 210 U43 Vulcan V154
Scap'd not thy Justice any whitt the more: • • • 210 U43 Vulcan V154
To paint him, hath by swimming, hopelesse, scap'd, • • 305 Horace 27
SCAR
Betweene two walls; where, on one side, to scar men, • • 86 E133 Voyage 67
SCARCE
And, though fowle, now, be scarce, yet there are clarkes, • 65 E101 Supper 15
Or, because some scarce thinke that storie true, • • 67 E104 Montgomery 5
For, where his person liv'd scarce one just age, • • 71 E110 Edmonds 1 13
Nor scarce dost colour for it, which is lesse. • • 73 E112 Gamster 20
Not doing good, scarce when he dyes. • • • 99 F3 Wroth 84
Scarce will take our present store? • • • 105 F8 Sicknesse 11
Scarce will take our present score? • • • 105 F8 Sicknesse V 11
I feele my griefes too, and there scarce is ground, • • 122 F15 Heaven 21
And superstition I dare scarce reveale, • • • 155 U13 Sacvile 86
Is nothing, such scarce meat and drinke he'le give, • • 167 U15 Friend-Wars 159
Scarce the Hill againe doth flourish, • • • 184 U29 Fit of Rime 37
Scarce the world a Wit doth nourish, • • • 184 U29 Fit of Rime 38
Scarce let White-Hall with Revels have to doe, • • 210 U43 Vulcan V156
That scarce you heare a publike voyce alive, • • 234 U61 Epigram 5
Health, or scarce breath, as she had never bin, • • 248 U71 Treasurer 12
Thy labouring wheele, comes scarce a Pitcher out? • • 307 Horace 30
Hee'll be a Pilot, scarce can guide a Plough. • • 410 Brome 18
How well I lov'd Truth: I was scarce allow'd • • 414 Rutter 6
SCARF (See SKARFE)
SCARLET
Commended the French-hood, and Scarlet gowne • • 201 U42 Elegy Let 69
But Scarlet-like out-lasts the Cloth. • • • 230 U55 Burges 8
A Scarlet peece, or two, stitch'd in: when or • • 305 Horace 19
A royall Crowne, and Scarlet; be made hop • • 346 Horace V325/333
SCARLET-LIKE
But Scarlet-like out-lasts the Cloth. • • • 230 U55 Burges 8
SCARRE
And make the Scarre faire; If that will not be, • • 187 U33 Councellour 21
As not alone the Cure, but scarre be faire. • • 192 U38 Elegy 'Tis 52
SCARRES
That they may sleepe with scarres in age. • • • 98 F3 Wroth 70
SCARSE
Who scarse can spell th'hard names: whose knight lesse can. • 28 E3 Bookseller 10
Man scarse can make that doubt, but thou canst teach. • 31 E14 Camden 10
Scarse thy weekes swearing brings thee of, of one. • 32 E16 Brain-hardy 4
Almost, is exercis'd: and scarse one knowes, • • 66 E102 Pembroke 7
Yeeres he numbred scarse thirteene • • • 77 E120 S. P. 9
That scarse the Towne designeth any feast • • 81 E129 Mime 5
By many? scarse by any. • • • 109 F11 Epode 20
SCATTER'D
May none, whose scatter'd names honor my booke, • • 29 E9 To All 1
The scatter'd Orcades; • • • 368 Ode Who saith 67
SCENE
To'a little wealth, and credit in the scene, • • 45 E56 Poet-Ape 7
And to your Scene lent no lesse dignitie • • 67 E104 Montgomery 7
Unto the Scene thou bringst, and dar'st create • • 313 Horace 179
Whether the buylding of the Stage or Scene! • • 402 Inigo Jones 1 11
The Scene! the Engyne! but he now is come • • 404 Inigo Jones 1 62
SCENES
As are the Glorious Scenes, at the great sights; • • 220 U47 Tribe 66
To whom all Scenes of Europe homage owe. • • 391 Shakespeare 42
SCENT (See also SENT)
The Eye of flowers, worthy, for his scent, • • 413 Ghyrlond 14
SCEPTER
How, best of Kings, do'st thou a scepter beare! • • 28 E4 James 1 1

		Page	Title	Line

SCEPTERS
The mayne comaund of scepters, soone doth perishe   422   Lucan   9
SCEPTRED
Where darknesse with her gloomie-sceptred hand,   180   U25 Desmond   61
SCHELDT
Scheldt, nor the Maas,   369   Ode Who saith   116
SCHISME
Where it were friendships schisme,   246   U70 Ode   90
(But pride, that schisme of incivilitie)   287   U84 Muse   160
SCHOOL
To be the Denis of thy Father's School,   410   Gill   7
SCHOOLE
Unworthy such a mistris, such a schoole,   57   E90 Mill   2
In loves schoole, and yet no sinners.   141   U2 Her man   32
That in rearing such a Schoole,   184   U29 Fit of Rime   59
Th'Aemilian Schoole, in brasse can fashion out   307   Horace   46
They are a Schoole to win   402   Filmer   11
SCHOOLEMEN
For, as there are three Natures, Schoolemen call   284   U84 Muse   51
SCHOOLES
And pride, and ignorance the schooles,   101   F4 To the World   48
Come to their Schooles,) show 'hem the use of Guns;   214   U44 Speach   58
SCIENCE
Or Science of discerning Good and Ill.   156   U13 Sacvile   108
The noble Science, and the maistring skill   232   U59 Newcastle   3
SCISARS
A paire of Scisars, and a Combe in verse;   204   U43 Vulcan   38
SCOFFER
The Scoffer, the true Praiser doth out-goe.   333   Horace   616
SCOFFING
Yet so the scoffing Satyres to mens view,   321   Horace   328
SCOLD
Furies there wanted not: each scold was ten.   84   E133 Voyage   15
SCOLDS
Gorgonian scolds, and Harpyes: on the other   86   E133 Voyage   69
SCOPE
Wrestlest with dignities, or fain'st a scope   70   E109 Nevil   6
Mee, the scope of his next draught,   133   U2 Suffered   11
SCORE
Kisse, and score up wealthy summes   103   F6 Celia 2   6
Scarce will take our present score?   105   F8 Sicknesse   V 11
One Poet, then of other folke ten score.   235   U62 Charles 1   10
For three of his foure-score, he did no good.   243   U70 Ode   32
SCORES
Thus: and for his letcherie, scores, god payes.   31   E12 Shift   22
SCORNE
In it' owne hall; when these (in worthy scorne   85   E133 Voyage   31
But I will beare these, with that scorne,   102   F4 To the World   63
I know my state, both full of shame, and scorne,   122   F15 Heaven   17
It were a plague 'bove scorne,   147   U7 Nymph   12
Or Scorne, or pittie on me take,   150   U11 Dreame   1
The Servant of the Serving-woman, in scorne,   165   U15 Friend-Wars   99
And only pitious scorne, upon their folly waites.   175   U23 Himselfe   24
Thou hast the brave scorne, to put back the fee!   187   U33 Councellour   22
To suffer tortures, scorne, and Infamie,   193   U38 Elegy 'Tis   93
Or in remembrance of thy afront, and scorne,   203   U43 Vulcan   7
For there the wicked in the Chaire of scorne,   223   U49 Pucell   45
Medea make brave with impetuous scorne: 313   Horace   175
Him that is last, I scorne to come behind,   333   Horace   595
Him that is last, I scorne to be behind,   353   Horace   V595
Or for the lawrell, he may gaine a scorne,   392   Shakespeare   63
To every sence, and scorne to those that sawe   420   Ode:If Men   17
The emptye Carper, scorne, not Creditt wynns.   421   Censure   5
SCORN'D
And scorn'd, thou'ast showne thy malice, but hast fail'd.   188   U34 Small Poxe   18
SCORNED
Turne, upon scorned verse, their quarter-face: 114   F12 Rutland   29
A scorned Mouse! O, how much better this,   315   Horace   199
SCORNES
After many scornes like these,   133   U2 Suffered   1
SCORNST
Sayst thou so, Lucan? But thou scornst to stay   397   Drayton   47
SCOTLAND
My Picture left in Scotland.   149   U9 Picture   Ttl
The rest, my journey into Scotland song.   207   U43 Vulcan   94
The rest, my journey into Scotland sung   207   U43 Vulcan   V 94
SCOURGE
Is her owne scourge, when it sustaines their states   422   Lucan   3
SCRATCHING
That scratching now's our best Felicitie?   166   U15 Friend-Wars   144
SCRIVENER
How then? Why, as a Scrivener, if h'offend   329   Horace   529
SCULLION
For, to say truth, what scullion is so nastie,   88   E133 Voyage   147
SCULPTURE
And Goody Sculpture, brought with much adoe   403   Inigo Jones 1   38
SCURFE
An admirable Verse. The great Scurfe take   333   Horace   594
SCURRILE
Any, least loose, or scurrile paper, lie   203   U43 Vulcan   20
SCURRILITIE
To part scurrilitie from wit: or can   323   Horace   403

		Page	Title	Line
SCUTCHEONS				
In place of scutcheons, that should decke thy herse,		35	E27 Roe 1	1
SCYLLA				
Scylla, Charybdis, Polypheme, with these.		315	Horace	206
SE				
prest in to se you.		416	Moon	8
SEA				
The spoused paire two realmes, the sea the ring.		28	E5 Union	4
Toward the sea, farther then halfe-way tree?		56	E88 Monsieur	6
For which there must more sea, and land be leap'd,		69	E107 Hungry	16
Being, beyond sea, burned for one witch:		88	E133 Voyage	158
Inconstant, like the sea, of whence 'tis borne,		110	F11 Epode	39
Inconstant, as the sea, of whence 'tis borne,		110	F11 Epode	V 39
Who, being at sea, suppose,		111	F11 Epode	70
That, being at sea, suppose,		111	F11 Epode	V 70
To live in Sea-coale, and goe forth in smoake;		211	U43 Vulcan	181
To live in Sea-coale, and goe out in smoake;		211	U43 Vulcan	V181
This sea-girt Isle upon:		240	U67 Muses	33
This sea-girt ground upon:		240	U67 Muses	V 33
And sunke in that dead sea of life		244	U70 Ode	40
Let Ireland meet it out at Sea, halfe way,		249	U72 King	5
Me thought, Great Britaine in her Sea, before,		268	U80 Christning	13
The Sunne, a Sea, or soundlesse Pit;		278	U84 Mind	11
Whether the Sea receiv'd into the shore,		309	Horace	91
I saw a Beauty from the Sea to rise,		396	Drayton	15
SEA-COALE				
To live in Sea-coale, and goe forth in smoake;		211	U43 Vulcan	181
To live in Sea-coale, and goe out in smoake;		211	U43 Vulcan	V181
SEA-GIRT				
This sea-girt Isle upon:		240	U67 Muses	33
This sea-girt ground upon:		240	U67 Muses	V 33
SEALE				
The weekly Corrants, with Pauls Seale; and all		206	U43 Vulcan	81
And seale thee thy Commission:		220	U48 Bacchus	5
Sonne to the grave wise Keeper of the Seale,		225	U51 Bacon	9
SEAL'D				
My title's seal'd. Those that for claps doe write,		62	E96 Donne 2	9
All historie seal'd up, and fables crost;		67	E105 L Wroth 2	2
Seal'd and deliver'd to her, in the sight		400	Lady Ogle	37
SEALED				
. . . to be Sealed of the Tribe of Ben.		218	U47 Tribe	Ttl
Sir, you are Sealed of the Tribe of Ben.		220	U47 Tribe	78
SEALES				
To breake up seales, and close 'hem. And they know,		59	E92 New Crie	29
Their Seales, their Characters, Hermetique rings,		206	U43 Vulcan	73
Or, to so many, and so Broad-seales had,		385	Brooke	3
SEALING				
But for a Sealing: let these men protest.		218	U47 Tribe	15
SEARCH				
If wee would search with care, and paine,		145	U5 Woman-kind	8
In sharpnesse of all Search, wisdome of Choise,		160	U14 Selden	59
Who would with judgement search, searching conclude		177	U25 Desmond	25
But first dost vexe, and search it! If not sound,		187	U33 Councellour	19
There were of search, and mastry in the Arts.		206	U43 Vulcan	88
There were of search, and mastry of the Arts.		206	U43 Vulcan	V 88
He that should search all Glories of the Gowne,		217	U46 Coke	1
Search, Sun, and thou wilt find,		255	U75 Epithalam.	79
Search, Sun, and thou shalt find,		255	U75 Epithalam.	V 79
Have busie search made in his mysteries!		284	U84 Muse	80
SEARCH'D				
Yet search'd, and true they found it.		130	U1 Nativitie	6
Antiquities search'd! Opinions dis-esteem'd!		160	U14 Selden	40
SEARCHETH				
Of Truth that searcheth the most hidden Springs,		176	U24 Frontispice	10
Of Truth which searcheth the most hidden Springs,		176	U24 Frontispice V	10
SEARCHING				
What sight in searching the most antique springs!		31	E14 Camden	8
(By searching) what before was strange,		146	U6 Defence	15
Who would with judgement search, searching conclude		177	U25 Desmond	25
Searching for knowledge, and to keepe your mind		225	U50 Countesse	29
SEARE				
To fall a logge at last, dry, bald, and seare:		245	U70 Ode	68
SEAS				
What not the envie of the seas reach'd too,		37	E32 Roe 2	4
Seas, serenes, swords, shot, sicknesse, all are there.		37	E32 Roe 2	10
Through seas, stormes, tempests: and imbarqu'd for hell,		81	E128 Wm Roe 2	13
Through Swords, through Seas, whether she would ride.		134	U2 Triumph	10
The narrow Seas are shadie,		222	U48 Bacchus	53
Foure Rivers branching forth like Seas,		276	U84 Body	23
Nor dreads the Seas inraged harmes:		289	U85 Country	6
Nor treades the Seas inraged harmes:		289	U85 Country	V 6
Into our Seas send any such:		291	U85 Country	52
Will passe the Seas, and long as nature is,		329	Horace	518
To utmost Thule: whence, he backes the Seas		368	Ode Who saith	69
He some Colossus to bestryde the Seas,		407	Inigo Jones 2	13
Looke how the starres from earth, or seas from flames		422	Lucan	7
SEAS'NING				
To marke the excellent seas'ning of your Stile!		160	U14 Selden	55
SEASON				
Your daintie nostrills (in so hot a season,		88	E133 Voyage	165
In season, and so brought		245	U70 Ode	61
As all the wealth of Season, there was spread;		251	U74 Weston	15
It is the kindly Season of the time,		253	U75 Epithalam.	25

	Page	Title	Line

SEASON (cont.)
Of Nuptiall Sweets, at such a season, owe, ... 257 U75 Epithalam. 148
Till fitter season. Now, to like of this, ... 307 Horace 63
SEASON'D
That never failes to serve thee season'd deere, . . . 94 F2 Penshurst 20
SEASONING
Or valour, or thy judgement seasoning it, ... 68 E106 E Herbert 6
SEASONS
The whil'st, the severall seasons thou hast seene . . . 97 F3 Wroth 37
To shift their seasons, and destroy their powers! . . . 199 U41 Elegy Since 10
That know the times, and seasons when t'appeare, . . . 263 U79 New-yeares 11
SEAT
Nor lend like influence from his lucent seat. . . . 52 E76 Bedford 1 8
The Seat made of a more then civill warre; . . . . 186 U33 Councellour 2
Nothing can more adorne it, then the seat . . . . 284 U84 Muse 71
The doore of Grace, and found the Mercy-Seat. . . . 288 U84 Muse 190
The Seat of Sapience, the most lovely Mother, . . . 414 Ghyrlond 45
SEATE
Tempte such a passage? when each privies seate . . . 88 E133 Voyage 168
Nay, so your Seate his beauties did endorse, . . . 228 U53 Newcastle 11
In blood, in birth, by match, and by her seate; . . . 394 Jane Ogle 4
SEATES
As loud enough to fill the seates, not yet . . . 319 Horace 291
SEATS
To see their Seats and Bowers by chattring Pies defac't? . . 174 U23 Himselfe 12
SEAVEN
That the eight spheare, no lesse, then planets seaven, . . 82 E130 Ferrab. 1 12
The seaven-fold flower of Arte (more rich then gold) . . 361 Palmer 15
The Orbe was cut forth into Regions seaven. . . . 396 Drayton 20
SEAVEN-FOLD
The seaven-fold flower of Arte (more rich then gold) . . 361 Palmer 15
SECOND
They met the second Prodigie, would feare a . . . 86 E133 Voyage 79
As loth, the second draught, or cast to stay, . . . 94 F2 Penshurst 35
6. Clayming a second kisse by Desert. . . . 137 U2 Kisse Ttl
To My L. the King, On the Christning His second Sonne James. . 268 U80 Christning Ttl
Great King, thy having of a second Sonne: . . . 268 U80 Christning 2
Of fellowship, the fourth, or second place. . . . 323 Horace 380
Set out a like, or second to our Swan. . . . 369 Ode Who saith 120
(Such as thine are) and strike the second heat . . . 392 Shakespeare 60
To lay her here, inclos'd, his second Bride. . . . 394 Jane Ogle 24
This second marriage, will aeternall make. . . . 394 Jane Ogle 26
The second string is the sweet Almond bloome . . . 412 Ghyrlond 9
SECONDED
Had it beene seconded, and not in fume . . . 87 E133 Voyage 109
SECRECIE
As new rewards of her old secrecie? . . . . 223 U49 Pucell 20
SECRET
Keepe secret in his Channels what he breedes, . . . 198 U40 Elegy That 27
On naturall secret, there, as her owne bookes: . . . 271 U81 Pawlet V 70
In secret places, flee the public baths. . . . 349 Horace V424
SECRETARIE
Or with Secretarie Sis . . . . . 140 U2 Promise 25
SECRETS
The secrets, that shall breake their sleepe: . . . 99 F3 Wroth 88
(Made to blow up loves secrets) to discover . . . 198 U40 Elegy That 47
On Natures secrets, there, as her owne bookes: . . . 271 U81 Pawlet 70
SECTS
And impious ranknesse of all Sects and seeds: . . . 163 U15 Friend-Wars 34
SECURE
When your assiduous practise doth secure . . . 236 U64 Charles 3 11
Secure thy railing Rhymes, infamous Gill, . . . 410 Gill 2
SECUR'D
Might be defrauded, nor the great secur'd; . . . 176 U24 Frontispice 6
Nor flatt'ry! but secur'd, by the Authors Name, . . 401 Beaumont 19
SECURED
Sate safe enough, but now secured more. . . . 268 U80 Christning 14
SECURELY
Man may securely sinne, but safely never. . . . 113 F11 Epode 116
A man may safely sinne, securely never. . . . 113 F11 Epode V116
That an ill man dares not securely looke . . . 389 Aleman 8
SECURER
But canst, at home, in thy securer rest, . . . 97 F3 Wroth 13
SECUREST
'Tis the securest policie we have, . . . 109 F11 Epode 17
SECURITIE
And, finding good securitie in his age, . . . 57 E90 Mill 6
For lesse Securitie? O for these . . . 165 U15 Friend-Wars 113
For less Securitie? O Freind, for these . . . 165 U15 Friend-Wars V113
And this Securitie, ... 174 U23 Himselfe 4
For your securitie. I can no better. . . . 229 U54 Squib 20
SEE (See also SE)
It will be look'd for, booke, when some but see . . 27 E2 My Booke 1
And such a Prince thou art, wee daily see, . . . 28 E4 James 1 7
But see! th'old baud hath serv'd him in his trim, . . . 31 E12 Shift 23
The bodies stripes, I see, the soule may save. . . . 33 E21 Gam'ster 8
Th'observing neighbours no such mood can see. . . . 40 E42 Giles 2
And not thy fortune; who can cleerely see . . . 47 E63 Salisbury 2 3
To see thy fathers rites new laid on thee. . . . 47 E64 Salisbury 3 6
But I am glad to see that time survive, . . . 47 E64 Salisbury 3 9
Wherein what wonder thy name hath wrought? . . . 48 E64 Salisbury 3 16
The Virgin, long-since fled from earth, I see, . . . 52 E74 Chancelor 9
Such when I meant to faine, and wish'd to see, . . . 52 E76 Bedford 1 17

SEE (cont.)

For good men but see death, the wicked tast it.   .   .   .   54   E80 Life/Death   8
Make it your gift. See whither that will beare mee.   .   .   55   E84 Bedford 2   10
Would you beleeve, when you this Mounsieur see,   .   .   56   E88 Monsieur   1
Their un-avoided subject, fewest see: .   .   .   60   E94 Bedford 3   8
See you yond' Motion? Not the old Fa-ding,   .   .   62   E97 Motion   1
Thou must draw more: and they, that hope to see   .   .   66   E102 Pembroke   19
That but the twi-light of your sprite did see,   .   .   66   E103 L Wroth 1   2
Were they that nam'd you, prophets? Did they see,   .   .   67   E104 Montgomery   1
Who Edmonds, reades thy booke, and doth not see   .   .   72   E111 Edmonds 2   1
When Sydneys name I heare, or face I see: .   .   .   73   E114 Sydney   2
'Twill see it's sister naked, and see a sword.   .   .   74   E115 Honest Man   22
So, when we, blest with thy returne, shall see   .   .   81   E128 Wm Roe 2   9
That, not a paire of friends each other see,   .   .   81   E129 Mime   1
And thine owne Coriat too. But (would'st thou see)   .   .   81   E129 Mime   17
Ploughing the mayne. When, wee (the worst of all lucks)   .   86   E133 Voyage   78
With other edifices, when they see   .   .   .   96   F2 Penshurst   100
Your selfe but told unto your selfe, and see   .   .   117   F13 Aubigny   23
Looke then, and see your selfe. I will not say   .   .   117   F13 Aubigny   29
Your beautie; for you see that every day: .   .   117   F13 Aubigny   30
As I, can say, and see it doth excell.   .   .   .   117   F13 Aubigny   34
Giddie with change, and therefore cannot see   .   .   118   F13 Aubigny   67
Other great wives may blush at: when they see   .   .   119   F13 Aubigny   111
One God to see, ...   128   U1 Trinitie   40
To see this Babe, all innocence;   130   U1 Nativitie   22
Love, if thou wilt ever see   132   U2 How he saw   7
See the Chariot at hand here of Love,   .   .   .   134   U2 Triumph   1
Where he chanc't your name to see   .   .   .   136   U2 Cupid   8
Which you call my Shafts. And see!   .   .   .   136   U2 Cupid   19
So to see a Lady tread, ...   138   U2 Kisse   25
Here's none to spie, or see;   139   U2 Another   3
And so thin, to see a blush   141   U2 Her man   28
On which they see or know.   144   U3 Musicall   V 20
In any curious peece you see   145   U5 Woman-kind   14
Pardon, sayes he, that were a way to see   .   .   155   U13 Sacvile   71
And last, goe out in nothing: You that see   .   .   157   U13 Sacvile   153
Pernitious enemie; we see, before   .   .   .   158   U14 Selden   14
To see the workmanship so'xceed the cost!   .   .   160   U14 Selden   54
Among my commings in, and see it mount,   .   .   161   U14 Selden   80
Looke on th'ambitious man, and see him nurse   .   .   162   U15 Friend-Wars   11
See the grave, sower, and supercilious Sir   .   .   162   U15 Friend-Wars   19
See him, that's call'd, and thought the happiest man,   .   162   U15 Friend-Wars   23
To see 'hem aye discoursing with their Glasse,   .   .   164   U15 Friend-Wars   63
Be at their Visits, see 'hem squeamish, sick,   .   .   164   U15 Friend-Wars   68
Now use the bones, we see doth hire a man   .   .   166   U15 Friend-Wars   136
Now use the bales, we see doth hire a man   .   .   166   U15 Friend-Wars V136
To see men feare: or else for truth, and State,   .   170   U18 Elegy Can   17
Knew I this Woman? yes; And you doe see,   .   .   172   U20 Shrub   15
To see their Seats and Bowers by chattring Pies defac't?   .   174   U23 Himselfe   12
So fooles, we see, ...   179   U25 Desmond   51
Helen, did Homer never see   181   U27 Ode Helen   1
Where men may see whom I doe sing?   .   .   .   182   U27 Ode Helen   32
So to see the Fountaine drie, ...   183   U29 Fit of Rime   22
And have their being, their waste to see;   .   .   189   U36 Song   11
If there be nothing worthy you can see   .   .   191   U38 Elegy 'Tis   15
O, that you could but by dissection see   .   .   194   U38 Elegy 'Tis   109
When I see you, then I doe see my Sun,   .   .   194   U38 Elegy 'Tis   120
Till I may see both it and you agen.   .   .   .   199   U41 Elegy Since   22
Put on my Ivy Garland, let me see   .   .   .   200   U42 Elegy Let   9
In at a hole, and see these Actions creepe   .   .   201   U42 Elegy Let   60
That chanc'd the lace, laid on a Smock, to see,   .   201   U42 Elegy Let   66
Fitter to see the fire-light, then the day;   .   .   204   U43 Vulcan   44
See the worlds Ruines! nothing but the piles   .   .   209   U43 Vulcan   137
For they did see it the last tilting well,   .   .   213   U44 Speach   6
But they may see Gold-Chaines, and Pearle worne then,   .   213   U44 Speach   13
To see the Pride at Court, their Wives doe make: .   213   U44 Speach   16
Turne him, and see his Threds: looke, if he be   .   .   216   U45 Squib   21
See then thou dost attend him,   .   .   .   221   U48 Bacchus   17
And thinkes I dare not her? let the world see.   .   222   U49 Pucell   2
A cheerefull worke to all good eyes, to see   .   .   224   U50 Countesse   16
An Archetype, for all the world to see,   .   .   227   U52 Answer   14
To see you set apart, thus, from the rest,   .   .   234   U61 Epigram   10
And long in changing. Let our Nephewes see   .   238   U65 Prince   7
In changing, let our Nephewes joyfull see   .   .   238   U65 Prince   V 7
In changing. Let our after Nephewes see   .   .   238   U65 Prince   V 7
See, see our active King   240   U67 Muses   37
As, could they but lifes miseries fore-see,   .   .   243   U70 Ode   19
In small proportions, we just beautie see: .   .   245   U70 Ode   73
To see that bright eternall Day: .   .   .   245   U70 Ode   81
Thou sluggish spawne, that canst, but wilt not see?   .   250   U73 Weston   8
To see great Charles of Travaile eas'd,   .   .   251   U74 Weston   26
Then thou shalt see to day: 252   U75 Epithalam.   5
And see, what can be seene, ...   252   U75 Epithalam.   7
See, the Procession! what a Holy day   .   .   .   252   U75 Epithalam.   9
As they came all to see, and to be seene!   .   .   253   U75 Epithalam.   20
See, how she paceth forth in Virgin-white,   .   .   253   U75 Epithalam.   41
Stay, thou wilt see what rites the Virgins doe!   .   254   U75 Epithalam.   49
See, how with Roses, and with Lillies shine,   .   .   254   U75 Epithalam.   57
Stay, see the Virgins sow, ...   254   U75 Epithalam.   61
See, at another doore, ...   254   U75 Epithalam.   69
All else we see beside, are Shadowes, and goe lesse.   .   255   U75 Epithalam.   88
See, now the Chappell opens; where the King   .   256   U75 Epithalam.   121
Peepe forth a Gemme; to see   258   U75 Epithalam.   175

SEE (cont.)

	Page	Title	Line
See where he walkes with Mira by his side.	264	U79 New-yeares	18
And by thy blessing, may thy People see	268	U80 Christning	3
Beholds her Maker! and, in him, doth see	271	U81 Pawlet	73
And see all dead here, or about to dye!	271	U81 Pawlet	86
May something by that twilight see	273	U84 Cradle	15
But, Painter, see thou doe not sell	277	U84 Body	29
That all may say, that see the frame,	278	U84 Mind	23
That happy Day, that never shall see night!	286	U84 Muse	121
Together: not that we should Serpents see	305	Horace	15
To gentle: not that we should Serpents see	338	Horace	V 15
Which it doth threaten. Therefore, where I see	329	Horace	525
A Choerilus, in whom if I but see	329	Horace	534
And see a minde attir'd in perfect straines;	362	Author	2
Smiles in his Sphaere, to see the rest affect,	366	Ode Who saith	13
Who (see) already hath ore-flowne	368	Ode Who saith	65
Here, finer then comming from his Punke you him see,	375	Coryat 1	28
And that you may see he most luckily ment	379	Coryat 3	13
So, in theyr number, may you never see	384	Somerset	21
To see his worke be good; but that he looke	385	Husband	2
On credit, and are cossen'd; see, that thou	386	Browne	11
To see thee in our waters yet appeare,	392	Shakespeare	72
But stay, I see thee in the Hemisphere	392	Shakespeare	75
To see (who'it is?) A noble Countesse, greate,	394	Jane Ogle	3
And see both climing up the slippery staire	395	May	2
I call the world, that envies mee, to see	398	Drayton	93
Of thy dead Standards: or (with miracle) see	405	Inigo Jones 1	89

SEED

	Page	Title	Line
Thou Seed-plot of the warre, that hast not spar'd	213	U44 Speach	24
Looke up, thou seed of envie, and still bring	250	U73 Weston	1

SEEDES

	Page	Title	Line
His course so hurtfull both to graine, and seedes,	309	Horace	97
the sweetest simples, and most soveraigne seedes.	361	Palmer	12

SEED-PLOT

	Page	Title	Line
Thou Seed-plot of the warre, that hast not spar'd	213	U44 Speach	24

SEEDS

	Page	Title	Line
And impious ranknesse of all Sects and seeds:	163	U15 Friend-Wars	34

SEEING

	Page	Title	Line
of seeing your face.	128	U1 Trinitie	32
Lest I be sick with seeing;	144	U4 Song	2
That farre-all-seeing Eye	256	U75 Epithalam.	109

SEEK

	Page	Title	Line
Their nails, nor shave their beards, but seek by-paths	349	Horace	V423
Seek out some hungry painter, that for bread	408	Inigo Jones 3	10

SEEKE

	Page	Title	Line
Who more should seeke mens reverence, then feare.	58	E91 Vere	18
A man should seeke great glorie, and not broad.	62	E96 Donne 2	12
Need seeke no other strength, no other height;	63	E98 Th Roe 1	4
Then stand unto thy selfe, not seeke without	83	E131 Ferrab. 2	13
And great, must seeke for new,	121	F14 Sydney	35
That, laden with my sinnes, I seeke for ease?	122	F15 Heaven	4
Seeke doubting Men to please,	150	U10 Jealousie	15
And seeke not wants to succour: but enquire,	155	U13 Sacvile	61
These take, and now goe seeke thy peace in Warre,	168	U15 Friend-Wars	195
And seeke to scant her comelie libertie,	190	U37 Friend-Book	20
That never yet did friend, or friendship seeke	218	U47 Tribe	14
Are faine to seeke for succours, and supplies	248	U71 Treasurer	2
That drives the Hart to seeke unused wayes,	264	U79 New-yeares	21
If a fit livor thou dost seeke to toast;	292	U86 Hor.4:1	12
And Peleus, if they seeke to heart-strike us	311	Horace	136
Sonnes, seeke not me amonge these polish'd stones:	387	Cavendish	1
From thence to honour thee, I would not seeke	391	Shakespeare	32
and seeke to scant her comelye Libertye,	421	Censure	13

SEEKES

	Page	Title	Line
His better'd mind seekes wealth, and friendship: than	315	Horace	238
Either because he seekes, and, having found,	317	Horace	242

SEEKING

	Page	Title	Line
This, seeking, in a various kind, to forme	307	Horace	40
When seeking her renowning,	365	Ode Splendor	19

SEEKS

	Page	Title	Line
And hurt seeks Cure, the Surgeon bids take bread,	155	U13 Sacvile	68

SEEK'ST

	Page	Title	Line
And that thou seek'st reward of thy each act,	47	E63 Salisbury 2	5
Thou are not one, seek'st miseries with hope,	70	E109 Nevil	5

SEELIEST

	Page	Title	Line
For seeliest Ignorance on these may light,	390	Shakespeare	7

SEEM

	Page	Title	Line
(And labours to seem worthy of that feare)	407	Inigo Jones 3	2

SEEME

	Page	Title	Line
To seeme a statesman: as I neere it came,	30	E11 Something	3
As french-men in his companie, should seeme dutch?	56	E88 Monsieur	8
Throughout, might flatt'rie seeme; and to be mute	58	E91 Vere	10
With those that come; whose grace may make that seeme	64	E101 Supper	5
Seeme to flye it, it will pursue:	104	F7 Women but	2
Times, and occasions, to start forth, and seeme)	118	F13 Aubigny	63
Why? though I seeme of a prodigious wast,	226	U52 Answer	1
You seeme a faire one! O that you had breath,	269	U81 Pawlet	6
You seeme a faire one! O that I had breath,	269	U81 Pawlet	V 6
If they seeme wry, to such as looke asquint,	362	Author	7
Yet neyther of you seeme to th'other old.	384	Somerset	24

SEEM'D

	Page	Title	Line
As Heaven and Nature seem'd to strive	77	E120 S. P.	7
So huge, it seem'd, they could by no meanes quite her.	86	E133 Voyage	86

SEEM'D (cont.)
But still, it seem'd, the ranknesse did convince 'hem. . . . 88 E133 Voyage 152
So seem'd your horse and you, both of a peece! . . . 228 U53 Newcastle 6
And thinke to ruine, where it seem'd to raise. . . . 391 Shakespeare 12
SEEMES
To thee, my way in Epigrammes seemes new, . . . 32 E18 Censurer 1
Which Fate (it seemes) caus'd in the historie, . . . 61 E95 Savile 11
In each of which, he seemes to shake a Lance, . . . 392 Shakespeare 69
SEEMING
That seeming prayses, are, yet accusations. . . . 75 E115 Honest Man 32
SEEN
Have you seen the Palme-trees state . . . . 136 U2 Triumph V 43
SEENE
Thou saist, that cannot be: for thou hast seene . . . 32 E18 Censurer 3
So have I seene at Christ-masse sports one lost, . . . 45 E58 Groome 7
Yet have they seene the maps, and bought 'hem too, . . . 59 E92 New Crie 9
Nor could I, had I seene all Natures roule, . . . 60 E93 Radcliffe 12
Thou hast seene hell (some say) and know'st all nookes there, . . 85 E133 Voyage 51
Were seene your ugly Centaures, yee call Car-men, . . . 86 E133 Voyage 68
The whil'st, the severall seasons thou hast seene . . . 97 F3 Wroth 37
To be taken, to be seene, ... 102 F5 Celia 1 17
The world hath seene, which all these had in trust, . . . 114 F12 Rutland 39
Have beautie knowne, yet none so famous seene? . . . 114 F12 Rutland 50
Have you seene but a bright Lillie grow, . . . 134 U2 Triumph 21
Have you seene the white Lillie grow, . . . 134 U2 Triumph V 21
Have you seene the fall o'the Snow . . . . 135 U2 Triumph V 23
Have you seene a faire Damaske-rose . . . 135 U2 Triumph V 31
Have you seene faire Helen disclose . . . 135 U2 Triumph V 33
Have you seene Love-Queenes embraces . . . 135 U2 Triumph V 35
Have you seene the boy from the Chace . . . 135 U2 Triumph V 39
Have you seene faire Ledas face . . . . . 135 U2 Triumph V 41
And was worthy (being so seene) . . . . . 138 U2 Kisse 27
Tell me that she hath seene . . . . 149 U9 Picture 13
prompt me that she hath seene . . . . 149 U9 Picture V 13
As I have seene some Infants of the Sword, . . . 154 U13 Sacvile 47
Ever at home: yet, have all Countries seene: . . . 159 U14 Selden 30
Heard what times past have said, seene what ours doe: . . 159 U14 Selden 34
And surely had I but your Stable seene . . . 228 U53 Newcastle 13
That you have seene the pride, beheld the sport, . . . 234 U61 Epigram 1
The Mother of our Prince? When was there seene . . . 238 U66 Queene 6
And see, what can be seene, ... 252 U75 Epithalam. 7
As they came all to see, and to be seene! . . . 253 U75 Epithalam. 20
With Modestie so crown'd, and Adoration seene. . . . 254 U75 Epithalam. 48
It is their Grace, and favour, that makes seene, . . . 255 U75 Epithalam. 89
O! had I seene her laid out a faire Corse, . . . 282 U84 Muse 11
Once seene, to be againe call'd for, and plaid, . . . 317 Horace 271
Or Semi-god, that late was seene to weare . . . 321 Horace 332
But I have seene thy worke, and I know thee: . . . 386 Browne 3
Because, who make the question, have not seene . . . 396 Drayton 3
Of tender eyes will more be wept, then seene: . . . 398 Drayton 76
SEER
Of cares, and over-seer . . . . . 221 U48 Bacchus 14
SEES
Then thee the age sees not that thing more grave, . . . 31 E14 Camden 5
Who sees a soule, in such a body set, . . . 79 E125 Uvedale 5
He when he sees a sorrow such as this, . . . 193 U38 Elegy 'Tis 87
Busie, or frowne at first; when he sees thee, . . . 262 U78 Digby 20
Is it because it sees us dull, ... 279 U84 Mind 45
The Mappe of his journey, and sees in his booke, . . 379 Coryat 3 18
SEEST
But alas, thou seest the least . . . . 137 U2 Cupid 43
This Figure, that thou here seest put, . . . 390 Reader 1
whom thou seest happy; wretches flee as foes: . . . 422 Lucan 6
whom thou seest happy; wretches, shun, as foes: . . . 422 Lucan V 6
SEINE
Slow Arar, nor swift Rhone; the Loyre, nor Seine, . . . 369 Ode Who saith 117
SEISE
shee will not seise it. . . . . . 418 Moon 44
SEISIN
Should take first Seisin of the publique good, . . . 268 U80 Christning 8
SEIZE
With all her aydes, to save her from the seize . . . 283 U84 Muse 17
SEIZ'D
Honour'd Achilles chance by thee be seiz'd, . . . 313 Horace 171
SELDEN
An Epistle to Master John Selden. . . . 158 U14 Selden Ttl
Ben: Jonson To His Honord Friend Mr John Selden Health. . . 158 U14 Selden VTtl
Your Booke, my Selden, I have read, and much . . . 158 U14 Selden 5
Selden! two Names that so much understand! . . . 161 U14 Selden 82
Which noble Carew, Cotton, Selden lent: . . . 207 U43 Vulcan 100
By Carew, Cotton, Selden, oyle was spent . . . 207 U43 Vulcan V100
Of Carew, Cotton, Selden, oyles were spent . . . 207 U43 Vulcan V100
SELDENS
By Carew, Cotton, Seldens oyle was spent . . . 207 U43 Vulcan V100
SELDOME
Who seldome sleepes! whom bad men only hate! . . . 250 U73 Weston 6
Never at Law; seldome in office gown'd; . . . 295 U90 Mart.10:47 5
Seldome descend but bleeding to their grave. . . . 363 Murder 2
SELF
And yet (in this t'expresse my self more cleare) . . . 111 F11 Epode V 75
Wake, friend, and finde thy self; awake, the Drum . . . 162 U15 Friend-Wars V 1
All kings to doe the self same deeds with some! . . . 406 Inigo Jones 2 4

Page   Title   Line

SELFE
Thou are not covetous of least selfe-fame,   27 E2 My Booke   9
Thy selfe into fresh braules: when, call'd upon,   32 E16 Brain-hardy   3
Keepe thy selfe there, and thinke thy valure right,   32 E16 Brain-hardy   9
That selfe-divided Belgia did afford;   37 E32 Roe 2   3
The selfe-same things, a note of concord be: 40 E42 Giles   17
For, but thy selfe, where, out of motly, 's hee   44 E53 Old-end   9
How I doe feare my selfe, that am not worth   44 E55 Beaumont   3
What fate is mine, that so it selfe bereaves?   44 E55 Beaumont   7
To so true worth, though thou thy selfe forbid.   47 E63 Salisbury 2   12
To such true worth, though thou thy selfe forbid.   47 E63 Salisbury 2 V 12
Be safe, nor feare thy selfe so good a fame,   53 E77 Not name   1
To draw thee custome: but her selfe gets all.   53 E78 Hornet   2
For all thou hear'st, thou swear'st thy selfe didst doo.   54 E81 Proule   5
I fancied to my selfe, what wine, what wit   55 E84 Bedford 2   6
And Phoebus-selfe should be at eating it.   55 E84 Bedford 2   8
My selfe a witnesse of thy few dayes sport: 55 E85 Goodyere 1   2
Who both their graces in thy selfe hast more   57 E89 Allen   9
Which thou art to thy selfe: whose fame was wonne   58 E91 Vere   5
Fortune upon him breakes her selfe, if ill,   63 E98 Th Roe 1   5
Be alwayes to thy gather'd selfe the same: 63 E98 Th Roe 1   9
Hast taught thy selfe worthy thy pen to tread,   63 E99 Th Roe 2   3
The selfe-same deeds, as diversly they come,   64 E99 Th Roe 2   8
Which is, it selfe, the imprese of the great,   66 E103 L Wroth 1   7
I' your selfe, all treasure lost of th'age before.   68 E105 L Wroth 2   20
Thy standing upright to thy selfe, thy ends   68 E106 E Herbert   7
Tell's of him, all the tales, it selfe then makes;   74 E115 Honest Man   17
That to the vulgar canst thy selfe apply,   76 E119 Shelton   11
Death's selfe is sorry.   77 E120 S. P.   4
Writing thy selfe, or judging others writ,   78 E123 Rudyerd 3   1
Thy selfe, with thy first thoughts, brought home by thee,   81 E128 Wm Roe 2   10
Then stand unto thy selfe, not seeke without   83 E131 Ferrab. 2   13
Crack did report it selfe, as if a cloud   86 E133 Voyage   94
The Voyage it selfe.   84 E134 Voyage   Ttl
Where the same beere, and bread, and selfe-same wine,   95 F2 Penshurst   63
To doe thy countrey service, thy selfe right;   100 F3 Wroth   103
With all my powers, my selfe to loose?   101 F4 To the World   28
Not of it selfe, but thee.   106 F9 Celia 3   16
Not like it selfe, but thee.   106 F9 Celia 3   V 16
Then which, a nobler heaven it selfe knowes not.   115 F12 Rutland   67
I, therefore, who professe my selfe in love   116 F13 Aubigny   7
Or so my selfe abandon'd, as because   117 F13 Aubigny   17
Your selfe but told unto your selfe, and see   117 F13 Aubigny   23
Looke then, and see your selfe. I will not say   117 F13 Aubigny   29
My selfe up to thee, harrow'd, torne, and bruis'd   127 U1 Trinitie   5
My selfe and thee.   129 U1 Father   11
Aymed with that selfe-same shaft.   133 U2 Suffered   12
Sheds it selfe through the face,   134 U2 Triumph   18
It vent it selfe, but as it would,   151 U12 Corbet   2
Upon my selfe, and aske to whom? and why?   159 U14 Selden   24
That by commanding first thy selfe, thou mak'st   168 U15 Friend-Wars   181
'Tis of your selfe, and that you use   173 U22 Elegy Tho   10
Make not thy selfe a Page,   175 U23 Himselfe   33
Nor thinke your selfe unfortunate,   177 U25 Desmond   27
But to your selfe, most loyal Lord,   179 U25 Desmond   53
Next to your selfe, for making your love true: 189 U37 Friend-Book   2
But, as a friend, which name your selfe receave,   190 U37 Friend-Book   10
Or doe upon my selfe some desperate ill;   191 U38 Elegy 'Tis   3
Thinke that your selfe like heaven forgive me can: 192 U38 Elegy 'Tis   32
I may dilate my selfe, but not depart.   194 U38 Elegy 'Tis   118
And my selfe most, in some selfe-boasting Rimes?   203 U43 Vulcan   26
And my selfe most, in lewd selfe-boasting Rimes?   203 U43 Vulcan   V 26
Whilst I informe my selfe, I would teach thee,   216 U45 Squib   2
Like Solons selfe; explat'st the knottie Lawes   217 U46 Coke   17
To speake my selfe out too ambitiously,   218 U47 Tribe   6
My selfe a little. I will take you so,   220 U47 Tribe   76
As you have writ your selfe. Now stand, and then,   220 U47 Tribe   77
Thinkes it selfe nought, though she should valew it.   223 U49 Pucell   24
Are in your selfe rewarded; yet 'twill be   224 U50 Countesse   15
As I began to wish my selfe a horse.   228 U53 Newcastle   12
And, in these Cures, do'st so thy selfe enlarge,   235 U62 Charles 1   7
And interpose thy selfe, ('care not how soone.)   238 U65 Prince   10
May wish it selfe a sense,   239 U67 Muses   23
Feed on thy selfe for spight, and shew thy Kind: 250 U73 Weston   9
To pluck a Garland, for her selfe, or mee?   268 U81 Pawlet   4
Sweet Mind, then speake your selfe, and say,   278 U84 Mind   17
It selfe to us, and come so nigh   279 U84 Mind   43
And saw that portion of her selfe to die.   282 U84 Muse   14
Beene trusted to thee: not to't selfe assign'd.   283 U84 Muse   20
Locke on thy sloth, and give thy selfe undone,   283 U84 Muse   21
She spent more time in teares her selfe to dresse   287 U84 Muse   180
My selfe for shortnesse labour; and I grow   307 Horace   35
My selfe for shortnesse labour, and am stil'd   339 Horace   V 36/ 35
Thy selfe in teares, then me thy losse will wound,   311 Horace   146
Thy selfe in tears, then me thy harms will wound,   342 Horace   V146
On steele, though 't selfe be dull, and cannot cut.   325 Horace   434
I, writing nought my selfe, will teach them yet   325 Horace   435
And, of your selfe too, understand; yet mind   331 Horace   547
My selfe am so neare drowning?   365 Ode Splendor   20
And conquers all things, yea it selfe, at length.   367 Ode Who saith   56
To write it with the selfe same spirit he went,   379 Coryat 3   14
And, if thou list thy selfe, what thou canst bee.   386 Browne   4
When you behold me wish my selfe, the man   389 Aleman   23

568

SELFE (cont.)
  Nature her selfe was proud of his designes, ... 392 Shakespeare   47
  The selfe same Genius! so the worke will say.   .   .   .   . 395 May   23
  Upon her selfe) to all her sexe!   .   .   .   . 399 Lady Ogle   10
  howe soone with a selfe ticklinge hee was spent.   .   .   . 420 Ode:If Men   18
SELFE-BOASTING
  And my selfe most, in some selfe-boasting Rimes?   .   .   . 203 U43 Vulcan   26
  And my selfe most, in lewd selfe-boasting Rimes?   .   .   . 203 U43 Vulcan   V 26
SELFE-DIVIDED
  That selfe-divided Belgia did afford;   .   .   .   .   37 E32 Roe 2   3
SELFE-FAME
  Thou are not covetous of least selfe-fame, ...   27 E2 My Booke   9
SELFE-SAME
  The selfe-same things, a note of concord be: .   .   .   40 E42 Giles   17
  The selfe-same deeds, as diversly they come, ...   64 E99 Th Foe 2   8
  Where the same beere, and bread, and selfe-same wine, .   .   .   95 F2 Penshurst   63
  Aymed with that selfe-same shaft.   .   .   .   .   .   . 133 U2 Suffered   12
SELINIS
  Ymounted high upon Selinis crest: .   .   .   .   .   . 412 Ghyrlond   10
'SELL
  She was 'Sell Boulstred. In which name, I call   .   .   . 372 Epitaph   12
SELL
  Call'st a booke good, or bad, as it doth sell,   .   .   .   27 E3 Bookseller   2
  If, without these vile arts, it will not sell,   .   .   .   28 E3 Bookseller   11
  At which there are, would sell the Prince, and State: .   . 234 U61 Epigram   4
  But, Painter, see thou doe not sell   .   .   .   .   .   . 277 U84 Body   29
SELLER
  To my Booke-seller.   .   .   .   .   27 E3 Bookseller   Ttl
  Epigram, to my Book-seller.   .   .   .   . 232 U58 Book-seller Ttl
SELLING
  Then, selling not, a dish was tane to mince 'hem,   .   .   .   88 E133 Voyage   151
SELVES
  Who, when you'have burnt your selves downe to the snuffe,   .   45 E59 Spies   2
  And yet (in this t'expresse our selves more cleare)   .   . 111 F11 Epode   75
  Such as suspect them-selves, and thinke it fit .   .   . 117 F13 Aubigny   13
  Goe make our selves the Usurers at a cast.   .   .   . 166 U15 Friend-Wars 134
  So to be sure you doe injoy your selves.   .   .   . 200 U42 Elegy Let   24
  Had lost our selves? and prodigally spent .   .   .   . 286 U84 Muse   141
  Our selves, and all that's ours, to death we owe: .   . 309 Horace   90
SEMI
  Or Semi-god, that late was seene to weare   .   .   . 321 Horace   332
SEMI-GOD
  Or Semi-god, that late was seene to weare   .   .   . 321 Horace   332
SENCE
  But holie Poets, rapt with sence divine?   .   .   . 115 F12 Rutland   V 63
  First: thy successe did strike my sence with wonder; .   . 361 Palmer   15
  Taught Lucan these true moodes! Replyes my sence   .   . 395 May   15
  T'imprint in all purg'd hearts this virgin sence,   .   . 414 Ghyrlond   55
  To every sence, and scorne to those that sawe   .   .   . 420 Ode:If Men   17
SEND
  Send it to Bucklers-bury, there 'twill, well.   .   .   .   28 E3 Bookseller   12
  When I dare send my Epigrammes to thee?   .   .   .   62 E96 Donne 2   2
  Reade all I send: and, if I find but one   .   .   .   62 E96 Donne 2   7
  To make those faithfull, did the Fates send you?   .   .   67 E104 Montgomery   6
  The better cheeses, bring 'hem; or else send   .   .   .   95 F2 Penshurst   53
  I, that have none (to send you) send you verse.   .   . 113 F12 Rutland   19
  That I must send one first, my Choyce assignes,   .   . 170 U18 Elegy Can   23
  I send nor Balmes, nor Cor'sives to your wound,   .   . 180 U26 Ode High   2
  Such, (if her manners like you) I doe send: .   .   . 230 U56 Covell   19
  To send my Debentur. .   .   .   . 231 U57 Burges   6
  Haste, haste, officious Sun, and send them Night   .   . 257 U75 Epithalam.   145
  Send in, what or Romano, Tintoret, ... 260 U77 Treasurer   6
  Send what Romano or what Tintoret, ... 260 U77 Treasurer   V 6
  Send these suspected helpes, to aide .   .   .   .   . 275 U84 Body   5
  Into our Seas send any such: .   .   .   .   . 291 U85 Country   52
  For the vile Goat, soone after, forth did send .   .   . 319 Horace   320
  To send it to be judg'd by Metius eare,   .   .   . 331 Horace   576
  I'll laugh at thee poor wretched Tike, go send .   .   . 410 Gill   10
  some tast to send hir.   .   .   .   . 417 Moon   20
  I send this small, but hearty testimony: and with charge, . 666 Glover   5
SENDS
  His double Bow, and round his Arrowes sends;   .   .   . 170 U19 Elegy By   4
  It must be thine owne judgment, yet, that sends .   .   . 386 Browne   7
SENSE
  And crie good! good! This quite perverts my sense, .   .   38 E38 Guiltie 2   5
  Then thou did'st late my sense, loosing my points. .   .   45 E58 Groome   6
  For none ere tooke that pleasure in sinnes sense,   .   .   60 E94 Bedford 3   9
  And all his numbers, both of sense, and sounds. .   .   .   61 E95 Savile   6
  That both for wit, and sense, so oft dost plucke,   .   .   73 E112 Gamster   18
  If these, who have but sense, can shun   .   .   . 101 F4 To the World   33
  To make our sense our slave.   .   .   .   .   . 109 F11 Epode   18
  And to his sense object this sentence ever,   .   .   . 113 F11 Epode   115
  Not at my prayers, but your sense; which laid   .   .   . 153 U13 Sacvile   9
  Newnesse of Sense, Antiquitie of voyce!   .   .   . 160 U14 Selden   60
  May his Sense, when it would meet   .   .   .   .   . 184 U29 Fit of Rime   55
  It is a Darknesse hath blockt up my sense,   .   .   . 191 U38 Elegy 'Tis   5
  Can lock the Sense up, or the heart a thought, .   .   . 198 U40 Elegy That   43
  Doth labour with the Phrase more then the sense?   .   . 222 U49 Pucell   14
  May wish it selfe a sense, ... 239 U67 Muses   23
  And ev'ry Plant the sense surprize, ... 251 U74 Weston   11
  As farre as sense, and onely by the eyes.   .   .   . 261 U77 Treasurer   12
  As farre as sense, and onely by his eyes.   .   .   . 261 U77 Treasurer   V 12
  Surprize their sense: .   .   .   . 273 U84 Cradle   24

	Page	Title	Line

SENSE (cont.)
No, to express a Mind to sense, • • • • • 278 U84 Mind 13
No, to express this Mind to sense, • • • • 278 U84 Mind V 13
Our sense you doe with knowledge fill, • • • • 278 U84 Mind 19
Still left an Eccho in the sense. • • • • 278 U84 Mind 40
Must come to take a sentence, by the sense • • • 279 U84 Mind 57
Her broken sighes did never misse whole sense: • • 284 U84 Muse 57
Unwonted language; and that sense of worth • • • 288 U84 Muse 185
Betweene the doubtfull sway of Reason'', and sense; • 319 Horace 308
'Tis not your fault, if they shall sense preferre; • • 370 Author 12
Being tould there, Reason cannot, Sense may erre. • • 370 Author 13
Or Verse, or Sense t'express Immortall you? • • • 370 Author 14
Sense, what they are! which by a specious fyne • • 403 Inigo Jones 1 41
SENSES • • • • 404 Inigo Jones 1 55
But charme the Senses, others over-come • • • 182 U28 Worth 7
Spoyling Senses of their Treasure, • • • • 183 U29 Fit of Rime 4
That, while they bind the senses, doe so please? • • 401 Filmer 2
Whose ayre will sooner Hell, then their dull senses peirce, • 420 Ode:If Men 23
And at once three Senses pleases. • • • • 657 Door Apollo 18
SENSUALL
In the past pleasures of his sensuall life, • • • 34 E25 Beast 1 2
SENT (SCENT)
I sent the cause: Hee wooes with an ill sprite. • • 33 E19 Cod 1 2
But then, fist-fill'd, to put me off the sent. • • 154 U13 Sacvile 52
As though the Court pursues them on the sent, • • 186 U32 Elsmere 13
Unto the Sent, a Spicerie, or Balme; • • • 286 U84 Muse 125
Hee dyes with an Ill sent, • • • • • 420 Ode:If Men 16
SENT
I sent thee, late, a rosie wreath, • • • • 106 F9 Celia 3 9
I sent to thee a rosie wreath, • • • • 106 F9 Celia 3 V 9
To redeeme mine, I had sent in; Enough, • • • 205 U43 Vulcan 63
Wherin (besides the noble aydes were sent, • • • 207 U43 Vulcan V 99
Or the States Ships sent forth belike to meet • • 219 U47 Tribe 33
Whether the Dispensation yet be sent, • • • 219 U47 Tribe 35
'Mongst which, if I have any friendships sent, • • 220 U47 Tribe 63
- - - he sent me in my Sicknesse. 1629. • • • 235 U62 Charles 1 Ttl
Being sent to one, they will be read of all. • • 263 U78 Digby 32
And I, into the world, all Soule, was sent! • • 270 U81 Pawlet 56
And I, into the world with my Soule, was sent! • • 270 U81 Pawlet V 56
Who saw the way was made it! and were sent • • 270 U81 Pawlet 65
That saw the way was made it! and were sent • • 270 U81 Pawlet V 65
That first sent forth the dapper Elegie, • • • 270 U81 Pawlet
Those heavie Verses, sent so to the Stage, • • • 309 Horace 110
Of a brave Chiefe sent to the warres: He can, • • 323 Horace 384
Hath sent her Mermaides in, • • • • • 325 Horace 451
Sent forth, or since did from their ashes come. • • 368 Ode Who saith 91
to Cynthias fayrest Nymph hath sent thee, • • • 391 Shakespeare 40
SENTENCE • • 662 Bedford 6
Keepe a starre-chamber sentence close, twelve dayes: • 59 E92 New Crie 19
And to his sense object this sentence ever, • • 113 F11 Epode 115
In sentence, of as subtile feet, • • • • 149 U9 Picture 8
I could invent a sentence, yet were worse; • • • 211 U43 Vulcan 189
I could invent a sentence, yet more worse; • • • 211 U43 Vulcan V189
Must come to take a sentence, by the sense • • 284 U84 Muse 57
SENTINELL
Or else the sentinell • • • • • 109 F11 Epode 22
SENT'ST
And sent'st it backe to mee: • • • • • 106 F9 Celia 3 14
SEPARATE
To separate these twi-/Lights • • • • 246 U70 Ode 92
Things sacred, from profane to separate; • • • 327 Horace 487
SEPULCHER'D
Where merit is not sepulcher'd alive. • • • 47 E64 Salisbury 3 10
SEPULCHRES
Of loud Sepulchres with their hourely knells, • • 89 E133 Voyage 174
SERAPHICK
The Thrones, the Cherube, and Seraphick bowers, • • 285 U84 Muse 88
SERAPHIM
Of Heaven; where Seraphim take tent • • • 273 U84 Cradle 31
SERENES
Seas, serenes, swords, shot, sicknesse, all are there. • 37 E32 Roe 2 10
SERENITIE
O imitate that sweet Serenitie • • • • 193 U38 Elegy 'Tis 77
SERGEANTS
Of Hol'borne (three sergeants heads) lookes ore, • • 89 E133 Voyage 177
Of Sergeants dinner, or sheriffes feast. • • • 96 F3 Wroth V 6
SERIOUS
Makes serious use of all great trade he knowes. • • 35 E28 Surly 3
What would his serious actions me have learned? • • 55 E85 Goodyere 1 12
On such my serious follies; But, thou'lt say, • • 204 U43 Vulcan 41
Or such my serious follies; But, thou'lt say, • • 204 U43 Vulcan V 41
And the severe, speech ever serious. • • • 311 Horace 151
These trifles into serious mischiefes lead • • • 335 Horace 641
In setting forth of such a serious Toye! • • • 405 Inigo Jones 1 V 78
SERMON
Unto the Spittle Sermon. O, what strange • • • 201 U42 Elegy Let 71
SERMONEERES
For Sermoneeres: of which now one, now other, • • 223 U49 Pucell 39
SERPENT
Through which a serpent river leades • • • 97 F3 Wroth 18
SERPENTS
The Serpents head: Gets above Death, and Sinne, • • 272 U81 Pawlet 99
Together: not that we should Serpents see • • • 305 Horace 15

                                                              Page   Title   Line

SERPENTS (cont.)
    To gentle: not that we should Serpents see   338   Horace   V 15
SERVANT
    The Servant of the Serving-woman, in scorne,   .   .   . 165   U15 Friend-Wars   99
    Art, her false servant; Nor, for Sir Hugh Plat,   .   .   . 188   U34 Small Poxe   7
    And such your Servant is, who vowes to keepe   .   .   . 196   U40 Elegy That   41
    Heare, Mistris, your departing servant tell   .   .   . 199   U41 Elegy Since   2
    So have you gain'd a Servant, and a Muse: 230   U56 Covell   5
    Of either Suitor, or a Servant by.   230   U56 Covell   18
    Of suitor, or of servant standing by.   230   U56 Covell   V 18
    To be a watchfull Servant for this State;   .   .   . 258   U75 Epithalam.   178
    To my old Faithfull Servant: And 409   Brome   Ttl
    I had you for a Servant, once, Dick Brome;   .   .   . 409   Brome   1
SERVANTS
    But, in your love, made all his servants wise.   .   .   . 74   E114 Sydney   8
    All which he makes the servants of the Groine, ... 163   U15 Friend-Wars   46
    The poores full Store-house, and just servants field.   .   . 185   U30 Burleigh   8
    And steps of all rais'd servants of the Crowne,   .   .   . 217   U46 Coke   2
    Tenants, and Servants, have they harts, and eyes,   .   .   . 399   Lady Ogle   4
    And you perform'd a Servants faithfull parts: 409   Brome   2
SERVE
    To honor, serve, and love; as Poets use.   .   .   . 52   E76 Bedford 1   4
    That never failes to serve thee season'd deere,   .   .   . 94   F2 Penshurst   20
    Ha's Feathers, and will serve a man to pull.   .   .   . 154   U13 Sacvile   58
    Of divine blessing, would not serve a State?   .   .   . 185   U30 Burleigh   20
    Against thy furie, when to serve their needs,   .   .   . 208   U43 Vulcan   125
    To serve the State by Councels, and by Armes: .   .   . 215   U44 Speach   85
    These I will honour, love, embrace, and serve: 220   U47 Tribe   71
    Earle Rivers Grand-Child--serve not formes, good Fame,   .   . 269   U81 Pawlet   21
    Earle Rivers Grand-Child--serve not titles Fame,   .   .   . 269   U81 Pawlet   V 21
    T'obey, and serve her sweet Commandements.   287   U84 Muse   172
SERV'D
    But see! th'old baud hath serv'd him in his trim,   .   .   . 31   E12 Shift   23
    You learn'd it well; and for it, serv'd your time   .   .   . 410   Brome   9
SERVES
    That serves nor fame, nor titles; but doth chuse   .   .   . 70   E109 Nevil   2
SERVICE
    Of service to the publique, when the end   .   .   . 70   E109 Nevil   7
    To doe thy countrey service, thy selfe right;   .   .   . 100   F3 Wroth   103
    To day, the Fathers service; who could bring   .   .   . 256   U75 Epithalam.   107
    For done service, and to come: 259   U76 Petition   13
    For done service, or to come: 259   U76 Petition   V 13
    And offer your just service on these plaines;   .   .   . 263   U79 New-yeares   12
SERVICEABLE
    While it makes huishers serviceable men, ... 113   F12 Rutland   9
SERVICES
    Give them your services, and embassies   69   E107 Hungry   11
SERVILE
    From servile flatterie (common Poets shame)   .   .   . 41   E43 Salisbury 1   11
SERVING
    For termers, or some clarke-like serving-man,   .   .   . 28   E3 Bookseller   9
    The Servant of the Serving-woman, in scorne,   .   .   . 165   U15 Friend-Wars   99
SERVING-MAN
    For termers, or some clarke-like serving-man,   .   .   . 28   E3 Bookseller   9
SERVING-WOMAN
    The Servant of the Serving-woman, in scorne,   .   .   . 165   U15 Friend-Wars   99
SET
    If I would vertue set, as shee was yong, ... 78   E122 Rudyerd 2   5
    Who sees a soule, in such a body set, ... 79   E125 Uvedale   5
    That there's no journey set, or thought upon,   .   .   . 81   E129 Mime   3
    That taller tree, which of a nut was set, ... 94   F2 Penshurst   13
    Of thy Penates had beene set on flame, ... 95   F2 Penshurst   79
    Sunnes, that set, may rise againe: 102   F5 Celia 1   6
    Or set bright Ariadnes crowne so high?   115   F12 Rutland   60
    Set, and to this softer straine;   136   U2 Cupid   9
    And that promise set on fire   139   U2 Promise   5
    Or were set up in a Brake.   142   U2 Her man   40
    And every Dressing for a Pitfall set   164   U15 Friend-Wars   66
    Hath our great Sidney, Stella set, ... 181   U27 Ode Helen   25
    Of those that set by their false faces more   .   .   . 188   U34 Small Poxe   4
    A Sparke to set whole worlds a-fire, ... 189   U36 Song   9
    And set us all on skipping, ... 222   U48 Bacchus   51
    To see you set apart, thus, from the rest,   .   .   . 234   U61 Epigram   10
    And all on utmost ruine set;   243   U70 Ode   18
    And set the marke upon, ... 255   U75 Epithalam.   95
    And set their marke upon, ... 255   U75 Epithalam.   V 95
    He had so highly set; and, in what Barbican.   .   .   . 256   U75 Epithalam.   112
    Were like a ring of Vertues, 'bout her set,   .   .   . 270   U81 Pawlet   41
    And set it forth; the rest were Cobwebs fine,   .   .   . 282   U84 Muse   5
    And 'bout the steeming Chimney set!   291   U85 Country   66
    And 'bout the shining Chimney set!   291   U85 Country   V 66
    Shall Verse be set to Harpe and Lute,   .   .   . 292   U86 Hor.4:1   23
    Set a Horse-neck, and divers feathers fold   .   .   . 305   Horace   2
    Next these great Homer and Tyrtaeus set   327   Horace   493
    Of their long labours, was in Verse set downe: .   .   . 329   Horace   500
    To change, and mend, what you not forth doe set.   .   .   . 331   Horace   579
    Set out a like, or second to our Swan.   .   .   . 369   Ode Who saith   120
    With the how much they set forth, but th'how well.   .   .   . 386   Browne   16
    yearly set out there, to sayle downe the Street,   .   .   . 407   Inigo Jones 2   18
SETS
    To plucke downe mine, Poll sets up new wits still,   .   .   . 50   E71 Parrat   1
    And sets more happy in the place: 290   U85 Country   12
    For th'eating Thrush, or Pit-falls sets: .   .   . 290   U85 Country   34

                                   571

		Page	Title	Line
SETS (cont.)				
Marry he sets it out at his owne charge;		378	Coryat 2	83
SETTING				
Or thy ranke setting? that thou dar'st put in		72	E112 Gamster	4
In setting forth of such a solemne Toye!		405	Inigo Jones 1	78
In setting forth of such a serious Toye!		405	Inigo Jones 1	V 78
SEVEN (See also SEAVEN)				
Seven yeeres tho'wert lent to me, and I thee pay,		41	E45 First Son	3
Told seven and fortie yeares,		150	U9 Picture	15
Did Sappho on her seven-tongu'd Lute,		181	U27 Ode Helen	3
Of Latine and Greeke, to his friendship. And seven		380	Coryat 3	45
SEVEN-TONGU'D				
Did Sappho on her seven-tongu'd Lute,		181	U27 Ode Helen	3
SEVER				
He, at length, our good will sever.		102	F5 Celia 1	4
He, at length, our blisse will sever.		102	F5 Celia 1	V 4
SEVERALL				
What severall wayes men to their calling have!		33	E21 Gam'ster	7
To write in cypher, and the severall keyes,		59	E92 New Crie	26
We need a man that knowes the severall graces		61	E95 Savile	27
The whil'st, the severall seasons thou hast seene		97	F3 Wroth	37
Doe severall passions invade the minde,		110	F11 Epode	29
Of severall makings? helps, helps, t'attire		215	U44 Speach	94
On every limbe, ta'en from a severall creature,		305	Horace	3
If now the changes, and the severall hues		341	Horace	V121/126
The severall figures, languish in suspence,		370	Author	10
SEVERE				
Though you sometimes proclaime me too severe,		190	U37 Friend-Book	16
Is, she will play Dame Justice, too severe;		229	U54 Squib	8
And the severe, speech ever serious.		311	Horace	151
SEVER'D				
Where, while that sever'd doth remaine,		34	E22 Daughter	10
And then with pause; for sever'd once, that's gone,		192	U38 Elegy 'Tis	47
SEVERS				
You once enjoy'd: A short space severs yee,		285	U84 Muse	105
SEV'RALL				
Against their breasts. Here, sev'rall ghosts did flit		87	E133 Voyage	124
SEW'D				
Item, your owne, sew'd in your mistris smock.		51	E73 Fine Grand	17
SEX				
Of her Sex; But could'st thou, Love,		137	U2 Cupid	45
Thinke but the Sin of all her sex, 'tis she!		172	U20 Shrub	20
Of Sex, to rob the Creature; but from Man		255	U75 Epithalam.	82
SEXE				
How well, faire crowne of your faire sexe, might hee,		66	E103 L Wroth 1	1
(Lillies and Roses, Flowers of either Sexe)		254	U75 Epithalam.	58
The wonder of her Sexe, and of your Blood.		274	U84 Descent	12
Upon her selfe) to all her sexe!		399	Lady Ogle	10
And most to be admired of thy Sexe,		414	Ghyrlond	46
SEY'D				
Who was my Muse, and life of all I sey'd,		282	U84 Muse	2
SHADDOW				
Follow a shaddow, it still flies you;		104	F7 Women but	1
SHADDOWES				
Song. That Women are but Mens shaddowes.		104	F7 Women but	Ttl
Stil'd but the shaddowes of us men?		104	F7 Women but	6
Stil'd but the shaddowes of us men?		104	F7 Women but	12
SHADE				
Behold! the reverend shade of Bartas stands		83	E132 Sylvester	7
Beneath the broad beech, and the chest-nut shade;		93	F2 Penshurst	12
To some coole, courteous shade, which he calls his,		97	F3 Wroth	19
A fire now, that lent a shade!		98	F3 Wroth	46
Come, let us here enjoy the shade;		189	U36 Song	1
But ever without blazon, or least shade		197	U40 Elegy That	13
It is as if a night should shade noone-day,		199	U41 Elegy Since	5
So great; his Body now alone projects the shade.		258	U75 Epithalam.	184
So large; his Body then, not boughs, project his shade.		258	U75 Epithalam.	V184
At land she triumphs in the triple shade,		268	U80 Christning	15
To give your shade a name! Stay, stay, I feele		269	U81 Pawlet	7
To give your shade a lasting name! Stay, stay, I feele		269	U81 Pawlet	V 7
With her, in shade		272	U84 Cradle	4
And she doth know, out of the shade of Death,		285	U84 Muse	91
SHADES				
'Mongst Hampton shades, and Phoebus grove of bayes,		80	E126 Mrs Cary	2
At morne, and even, shades are longest;		104	F7 Women but	7
SHADIE				
The narrow Seas are shadie,		222	U48 Bacchus	53
SHADOW				
That sits in shadow of Apollo's tree.		149	U9 Picture	10
For Love in shadow best is made.		189	U36 Song	2
Though Envie oft his shadow be,		189	U36 Song	3
Your Power of handling shadow, ayre, and spright,		227	U52 Answer	17
To be a shadow to his Heire,		251	U74 Weston	29
Light, Posture, Height'ning, Shadow, Culloring,		370	Author	3
SHADOWES				
Can I discerne how shadowes are decreast,		156	U13 Sacvile	118
All else we see beside, are Shadowes, and goe lesse.		255	U75 Epithalam.	88
SHAFT				
Here's a shaft, thou art to slow!		132	U2 How he saw	10
Both the Bow, and shaft I held,		133	U2 Suffered	8
Aymed with that selfe-same shaft.		133	U2 Suffered	12
SHAFTS				
Arm'd with bow, shafts, and fire;		110	F11 Epode	38

			Page	Title	Line

SHAFTS (cont.)
Which you call my Shafts. And see!   . . . . .   136 U2 Cupid   19
To my shafts! Her very Name, ...   137 U2 Cupid   37
His flames, his shafts, his Quiver, and his Bow, . . . 182 U28 Worth   10
SHAKE
At naming the French King, their heads they shake, . . . 59 E92 New Crie 33
It shakes even him, that all things else doth shake. . . . 193 U38 Elegy 'Tis 72
This Citie, or to shake   . . . . 239 U67 Muses   11
The Citie, as to shake   . . . . 239 U67 Muses   V 11
And shake both ayre and ground, ... 239 U67 Muses   V 14
That I bright Chloe off should shake; 294 U87 Hor.3:9   19
And shake a Stage: Or, when thy Sockes were on, . . . 391 Shakespeare   37
In each of which, he seemes to shake a Lance, . . . 392 Shakespeare   69
SHAKES
It shakes even him, that all things else doth shake. . . 193 U38 Elegy 'Tis 72
SHAKESPEARE
It was for gentle Shakespeare cut;   . . . . . 390 Reader   2
. . . Mr. William Shakespeare: And what he hath left us. . . 390 Shakespeare   Ttl
To draw no envy (Shakespeare) on thy name, ... 390 Shakespeare   1
My Shakespeare, rise; I will not lodge thee by . . . 391 Shakespeare   19
My gentle Shakespeare, must enjoy a part. . . . . 392 Shakespeare   56
SHAKESPEARES
Of Shakespeares minde, and manners brightly shines . . 392 Shakespeare   67
SHAL
(That shal ring larum to the heart) doth sleepe, . . . 109 F11 Epode   V 23
SHALL
Shall out-live gyrlands, stolne from the chast tree. . . 32 E17 Critic   6
And proud, my worke shall out-last common deeds, . . 46 E60 Mounteagle 6
Shee shall instruct my after-thoughts to write . . . 48 E65 Muse   13
Whose rellish to eternitie shall last. . . . . . 58 E91 Vere   8
At sixe and twentie, ripe. You shall 'hem meet, . . 58 E92 New Crie   4
Who shall doubt, Donne, where I a Poet bee, . . . 62 E96 Donne 2   1
Yet shall you have, to rectifie your palate, . . . 64 E101 Supper   9
Shall reade a piece of Virgil, Tacitus, ... 65 E101 Supper   21
Which is the Mermaids, now, but shall be mine: . . 65 E101 Supper   30
Nor shall our cups make any guiltie men: . . . 65 E101 Supper   37
That shall be utter'd at our mirthfull boord, . . . 65 E101 Supper   40
Shall make us sad next morning: or affright . . . 65 E101 Supper   41
Now I have sung thee thus, shall judge of thee. . . 70 E109 Nevil   16
Where shall I scape thee? in an Epigramme? . . . 73 E112 Gamster   15
But, if it shall be question'd, undertakes, . . . 74 E115 Honest Man 18
By her attempt, shall still be owing thee. . . . 80 E127 Aubigny   10
So, when we, blest with thy returne, shall see . . . 81 E128 Wm Roe 2   9
Whose noyse shall keepe thy miming most alive, . . 81 E129 Mime   10
Thine the originall; and France shall boast, . . . 83 E132 Sylvester 13
Who shall discharge first his merd-urinous load: . . 85 E133 Voyage   65
But many Moones there shall not wane (quoth hee) . . 87 E133 Voyage   103
But I will speake (and know I shall be heard) . . . 87 E133 Voyage   105
That is his Lordships, shall be also mine. . . . 95 F2 Penshurst   64
He knowes, below, he shall finde plentie of meate, . . 95 F2 Penshurst   70
They thinke not, then, which side the cause shall leese, . . 98 F3 Wroth   61
The secrets, that shall breake their sleepe: . . . 99 F3 Wroth   88
Or, having scap'd, shall I returne, ... 101 F4 To the World 25
As shall not need thy false reliefe. . . . . . 102 F4 To the World 64
I shall feare, you'll surfet too. . . . . . 104 F8 Sicknesse   8
And must I sing? what subject shall I chuse? . . . 107 F10 Proludium   1
We must sing too? what subject shall we chuse? . . 107 F10 Proludium V 1
Shall not give out, that I have made thee stay, . . 107 F10 Proludium   8
Shall not give out, that we have made thee stay, . . 107 F10 Proludium V 8
Hermes, the cheater, shall not mixe with us, . . . 107 F10 Proludium   22
And such, or my hopes faile, shall make you shine. . 115 F12 Rutland   64
To her remembrance; which when time shall bring . . 115 F12 Rutland   75
To curious light, the notes, I then shall sing, . . 115 F12 Rutland   76
To curious light, to notes, I then shall sing, . . 115 F12 Rutland   V 76
For I shall move stocks, stones, no lesse then he. . 115 F12 Rutland   78
Shall thronging come, and boast the happy place . . 115 F12 Rutland   80
Borne up by statues, shall I reare your head, . . 115 F12 Rutland   84
besett with statues, shall I reare your head, . . 115 F12 Rutland   V 84
And this shall be no false one, but as much . . . 117 F13 Aubigny   27
It shall a ripe and timely issue fall, ... 119 F13 Aubigny   104
Wherein, your forme, you still the same shall finde; . 120 F13 Aubigny   123
Shall I there rest!   . . . . 128 U1 Trinitie   48
She shall make the old man young, ... 131 U2 Excuse   20
You shall neither eat, nor sleepe, ... 140 U2 Promise   15
Wee shall, at last, of parcells make . . . . . 145 U5 Woman-kind 11
And pray who shall my sorrowes read, ... 152 U12 Corbet   33
Now dam'mee, Sir, if you shall not command . . . 154 U13 Sacvile   53
Donnor's or Donnee's, to their practise shall . . 158 U13 Sacvile   163
Lesse shall I for the Art or dressing care, . . . 158 U14 Selden   3
But I on yours farre otherwise shall doe, . . . 159 U14 Selden   17
But I to yours, farre from this fault, shall doo; . 159 U14 Selden   V 17
Which Grace shall I make love to first? your skill, . 159 U14 Selden   35
For t'other pound of sweet-meats, he shall feele . 164 U15 Friend-Wars 77
Those thousands on his back, shall after blow . . 165 U15 Friend-Wars 104
But he that's both, and slave to boote, shall live, . 167 U15 Friend-Wars 160
But he that's both, and slave to both, shall live, . 167 U15 Friend-Wars V160
Thy true friends wishes, Colby, which shall be, . . 167 U15 Friend-Wars 176
Thy true friends wishes, which shall ever be, . . 167 U15 Friend-Wars V176
Who falls for love of God, shall rise a Starre. . . 168 U15 Friend-Wars 196
But which shall lead me on? both these are blind: . 170 U18 Elegy Can   11
Then shall my Verses, like strong Charmes, . . . 177 U25 Desmond   18
Then shall our Verses, like strong Charmes, . . . 177 U25 Desmond   V 18
Shall light those places   . . . . 179 U25 Desmond   59

SHALL (cont.)
And shall not I my Celia bring,   182   U27 Ode Helen   31
Such shall you heare to day, and find great foes,   186   U32 Elsmere   7
On which with profit, I shall never looke,   189   U37 Friend-Book   5
But shall sometimes be tempted to obey   190   U37 Friend-Book   32
Absence, or Distance, shall not breed decay.   194   U38 Elegy 'Tis   116
Shall find their depth: they're sounded with a spoone.   198   U40 Elegy That   30
How shall I doe, sweet Mistris, for my heart?   199   U41 Elegy Since   14
Who shall forbid me then in Rithme to bee   200   U42 Elegy Let   5
Though but in daunces, it shall know his power;   210   U43 Vulcan   157
Though but in daunces, it shall know high power;   210   U43 Vulcan   V157
Though but in daunger, it shall know thy power;   210   U43 Vulcan   V157
Shall carry me at Call; and I'le be well,   219   U47 Tribe   45
Shall feast it, thou maist love there   221   U48 Bacchus   38
As shall the feasts faire grounds be.   221   U48 Bacchus   42
Shall I advise thee, Pucell? steale away   223   U49 Pucell   35
And you shall make me good, in weight, and fashion,   229   U54 Squib   17
That thought shall make, he will this losse supply   236   U63 Charles 2   11
With all the fruit shall follow it,   251   U74 Weston   23
(Where we shall goe)   254   U75 Epithalam.   62
Which Time shall not,   257   U75 Epithalam.   134
When hee shall read them at the Treasurers bord,   263   U78 Digby   27
Allowes them? Then, what copies shall be had,   263   U78 Digby   29
Wilt thou be, Muse, when this shall them befall?   263   U78 Digby   31
Wilt thou be, Muse, when this shall then befall?   263   U78 Digby   V 31
Hee shall, if he can understand,   276   U84 Body   11
By which yo'are planted, shew's your fruit shall bide.   281   U84 Kenelme   19
That shall re-joyne yee. Was she, then, so deare,   285   U84 Muse   107
Shall meet with gladnesse in one Theatre;   285   U84 Muse   114
And each shall know, there, one anothers face,   285   U84 Muse   115
There shall the Brother, with the Sister walke,   285   U84 Muse   117
But all of God; They still shall have to say,   286   U84 Muse   119
That happy Day, that never shall see night!   286   U84 Muse   121
He that shall be our supreme Judge, should leave   286   U84 Muse   148
There shall thy dainty Nostrill take   292   U86 Hor.4:1   21
Shall Verse be set to Harpe and Lute,   292   U86 Hor.4:1   23
The Youths and tender Maids shall sing thy praise: 292   U86 Hor.4:1   26
Or I am much deceiv'd, shall be to place   307   Horace   60
Shall perish: so farre off it is, the state,   309   Horace   99
Much phrase that now is dead, shall be reviv'd;   309   Horace   101
And much shall dye, that now is nobly liv'd,   309   Horace   102
And ill-penn'd things, I shall, or sleepe, or smile.   311   Horace   148
If now the phrase of him that speakes, shall flow,   313   Horace   158
To Roman Poets. Shall I therefore weave   323   Horace   390
For so, they shall not only gaine the worth,   325   Horace   425
Of thine, shall thinke the Maine   368   Ode Who saith   90
Yet, looking in thy face, they shall begin   369   Ode Who saith   93
It is inough, their griefe shall know   369   Ode Who saith   113
'Tis not your fault, if they shall sense preferre,   370   Author   13
Do crowne thy murdred Poeme: which shall rise   371   Fletcher   14
Or moathes shall eate, what all these Fooles admire.   371   Fletcher   16
shall looke, & on hyme soe, then arte's a lyer   383   Rich   15
Shall finde, that either hath read Bookes, and Men: 389   Aleman   2
So shall our English Youth urge on, and cry   398   Drayton   69
All in the Worke! And soe shall still for Ben: 404   Inigo Jones 1   65
That might compare with thee? what story shall   406   Inigo Jones 1   98
Shall not worke out unto it, such a fame.   409   Detractor   12
Shall the prosperity of a Pardon still   410   Gill   1
At libelling? Shall no Star-Chamber Peers,   410   Gill   3
I shall think on't ere't be day.   417   Moon   11
as the standerd shall engage hir,   417   Moon   27
As shall besides delyght   420   Ode:If Men   33
But sometymes shall bee tempted to obaye   422   Censure   25
shall never dare do any thing but feare.   423   Lucan   20
Shall powre forth many a line, drop many a letter,   666   Glover   9
SHALT
Yet thou, perhaps, shalt meet some tongues will grutch,   72   E111 Edmonds 2   9
Shalt neither that, nor this envy: 99   F3 Wroth   92
Then thou shalt see to day: 252   U75 Epithalam.   5
Search, Sun, and thou shalt find,   255   U75 Epithalam. V 79
But, if hereafter thou shalt write, not feare   331   Horace   575
And thou in them shalt live as longe as Fame.   362   Palmer   31
SHAME
Made from the hazard of anothers shame: 27   E2 My Booke   10
Thou call'st me Poet, as a terme of shame: 29   E10 Ignorant   1
Beleeve it, Guiltie, if you loose your shame,   38   E38 Guiltie 2   7
From servile flatterie (Common Poets shame)   41   E43 Salisbury 1 11
For, if thou shame, ranck'd with my friends, to goe,   53   E77 Not name   3
And did not shame it with my actions, then,   70   E108 Soldiers   7
I know my state, both full of shame, and scorne,   122   F15 Heaven   17
Lest shame destroy their being.   144   U4 Song   4
Yet choyce from whom I take them; and would shame   153   U13 Sacvile   17
As but to stumble in her sight were shame;   220   U47 Tribe   70
It will be shame for them, if they have none.   225   U50 Countesse   36
Where shame, faith, honour, and regard of right   243   U70 Ode   13
There is no labour, nor no shame in this: 294   U88 Petronius   8
Am I call'd Poet? wherefore with wrong shame,   311   Horace   129
A wise, and honest man will cry out shame   335   Horace   633
A good and wise man will crye open shame   354   Horace   V633
But Tune and Noise the Eccho of thy Shame.   411   Gill   14
SHAMEFAC'D
To Dance, so she should, shamefac'd, differ farre   321   Horace   339

	Page	Title	Line

SHAMEFAC'DNESSE
And shamefac'dnesse together! All lawes dead, ... 163 U15 Friend-Wars V 40
SHAMEFASTNESSE
And shamefastnesse together! All lawes dead, . . . 163 U15 Friend-Wars 40
SHAMEFULL
Or cracke out shamefull speeches, or uncleane. . . . 347 Horace V351/359
SHAMES
That prince that shames a tyrants name to beare, . . 423 Lucan 19
SHAPE
In a Hercules-his shape. . . . . . . 132 U2 How he saw 32
SHAP'D
The whole fleet wreck'd? a great jarre to be shap'd, . . 305 Horace 28
SHAPES
In varied shapes, which for his lust shee takes: . . 34 E25 Beast 1 6
Whose shapes, like sick-mens dreames, are fain'd so vaine, . 305 Horace 9
Whose shapes, like sick-mens dreames, are form'd so vaine, . 338 Horace V 9
SHARE
And fainting necks, the turned Share! . . . . 291 U85 Country 64
Exclude all sober Poets, from their share . . . . 325 Horace 421
SHARP
When this appeares, just Lord, to your sharp sight, . . 186 U32 Elsmere 15
That I should wryte upon him some sharp verse, . . . 407 Inigo Jones 3 3
SHARPE
Wormewood, and sulphure, sharpe, and tooth'd withall; . . 27 E2 My Booke 4
For thy late sharpe device. I say 'tis fit . . . 36 E29 Tilter 3
Your change of Notes, the flat, the meane, the sharpe, . . 263 U79 New-yeares 3
Sharpe, and contemning lawes, at him should aime, . . 313 Horace 173
Oft-times a Sharpe, when we require a Flat: . . . 329 Horace 523
SHARPER
Since, being deceiv'd, I turne a sharper eye . . . 159 U14 Selden 23
SHARPLYE
Censure, not sharplye then, but mee advise . . . . 421 Censure 1
SHARPNESSE
And so my sharpnesse thou no lesse dis-joynts, . . . 45 E58 Groome 5
In sharpnesse of all Search, wisdome of Choise, . . . 160 U14 Selden 59
SHAVE
Their nailes, nor shave their beards, but to by-paths . . 325 Horace 423
Their nails, nor shave their beards, but seek by-paths . . 349 Horace V423
SH'
Of divine Comfort, when sh'had talk'd with God. . . . 287 U84 Muse 184
To that eternall Rest, where now sh hath place . . . 288 U84 Muse 197
SHE'
To my lesse sanguine Muse, wherein she'hath wonne . . 115 F12 Rutland 72
SHE
When you know, that this is she, ... 131 U2 Excuse 18
She shall make the old man young, ... 131 U2 Excuse 20
Till she be the reason why, ... 131 U2 Excuse 23
This my object. But she threw . . . . . 132 U2 How he saw 23
She content was to restore . . . . . . 133 U2 Suffered 3
Which when she beheld to bleed, ... 133 U2 Suffered 17
She repented of the deed, ... 133 U2 Suffered 18
As she goes, all hearts doe duty . . . . . 134 U2 Triumph 5
Through Swords, through Seas, whether she would ride. . 134 U2 Triumph 10
O so white! O so soft! O so sweet is she! . . . 135 U2 Triumph 30
O so faire! O so soft! O so sweet is she! . . . 135 U2 Triumph V 30
When with Joves swans she sported . . . . 135 U2 Triumph V 42
Shee is Venus, when she smiles, ... 137 U2 Cupid 52
But shee's Juno, when she walkes, ... 137 U2 Cupid 53
And Minerva, when she talkes. . . . . . 137 U2 Cupid 54
Lightly promis'd, she would tell . . . . . 139 U2 Promise 3
What a man she could love well: . . . . . 139 U2 Promise 4
As, untill she tell her one, ... 140 U2 Promise 11
We all feare, she loveth none. . . . . . 140 U2 Promise 12
Will be my Rivall, though she have but eares. . . . 148 U7 Nymph 28
That she, ... 149 U9 Picture 3
Tell me that she hath seene . . . . . 149 U9 Picture 13
prompt me that she hath seene . . . . . 149 U9 Picture V 13
Read so much wast, as she cannot imbrace . . . 150 U9 Picture 16
And where they want, she is not understood. . . . 156 U13 Sacvile 112
I, that's a Charme and halfe! She must afford . . . 163 U15 Friend-Wars 52
That all respect; She must lie downe: Nay more, . . 163 U15 Friend-Wars 53
The bravery makes, she can no honour leese: . . . 164 U15 Friend-Wars 56
But what she gives, thou dar'st give her againe; . . 168 U15 Friend-Wars 184
Now threaten, with those meanes she did invite? . . 169 U18 Elegy Can 2
Or was she gracious a-farre off? but neere . . . 169 U18 Elegy Can 5
Doe not you aske to know her, she is worse . . . 172 U20 Shrub 17
Thinke but the Sin of all her sex, 'tis she! . . . 172 U20 Shrub 20
Perjur'd! and painted! if she were no more--, . . . 172 U20 Shrub 22
But she is such, as she might, yet, forestall . . . 172 U20 Shrub 23
Shee chearfully supporteth what she reares, . . . 176 U24 Frontispice 13
By which as proper titles, she is knowne . . . 176 U24 Frontispice 16
Shine more, then she, the Stars among? . . . 181 U27 Ode Helen 12
What did she worth thy spight? were there not store . 188 U34 Small Poxe 3
Then this did by her true? She never sought . . . 188 U34 Small Poxe 5
When by thy sordid bountie she hath on . . . 201 U42 Elegy Let 45
She durst not kisse, but flung thee from her brest. . . 208 U43 Vulcan 114
Did not she save from thence, to build a Rome? . . 210 U43 Vulcan 162
Needs lend an aide, to thine she had her eyes. . . . 217 U46 Coke 24
What though with Tribade lust she force a Muse, . . 222 U49 Pucell 7
What though she talke, and cannot once with them, . . 222 U49 Pucell 11
What though she ride two mile on Holy-dayes . . . 222 U49 Pucell 15
What though she be with Velvet gownes indu'd, . . 222 U49 Pucell 18
What though she hath won on Trust, as many doe, . . 223 U49 Pucell 21

SHE (cont.)

	Page	Title	Line
Thinkes it selfe nought, though she should valew it.	223	U49 Pucell	24
Is, she will play Dame Justice, too severe;	229	U54 Squib	8
That Faith, which she professeth to be pure?	236	U64 Charles 3	12
How is she barren growne of love! or broke!	237	U64 Charles 3	15
How is she barren growne in love! or broke!	237	U64 Charles 3	V 15
Health, or scarce breath, as she had never bin,	248	U71 Treasurer	12
Wherein she sits so richly drest,	251	U74 Weston	14
See, how she paceth forth in Virgin-white,	253	U75 Epithalam.	41
Like what she is, the Daughter of a Duke,	253	U75 Epithalam.	42
As she did lack	254	U75 Epithalam.	46
(Where she shall goe)	254	U75 Epithalam.	62
Have they bedew'd the Earth, where she doth tread,	254	U75 Epithalam.	66
Have they bedew'd the Earth, where she did tread,	254	U75 Epithalam.	V 66
And all the Ground were Garden, where she led!	254	U75 Epithalam.	68
Exacts then she is pleas'd to pay: no suits,	258	U75 Epithalam.	188
At land she triumphs in the triple shade,	268	U80 Christning	15
What she did here, by great example, well,	269	U81 Pawlet	33
What she did by a great example, well,	269	U81 Pawlet	V 33
A reverend State she had, an awfull Eye,	270	U81 Pawlet	43
How did she leave the world? with what contempt?	270	U81 Pawlet	47
Just as she in it liv'd! and so exempt	270	U81 Pawlet	48
And now, through circumfused light, she lookes	271	U81 Pawlet	69
Or hath she here, upon the ground,	280	U84 Mind	49
All that was good, or great in me she weav'd,	282	U84 Muse	4
Indeed, she is not dead! but laid to sleepe	283	U84 Muse	45
That she is in, or, make it more compleat?	284	U84 Muse	72
And she doth know, out of the shade of Death,	285	U84 Muse	91
That shall re-joyne yee. Was she, then, so deare,	285	U84 Muse	107
She had, and it became her! she was fit	287	U84 Muse	161
She had a mind as calme, as she was faire;	287	U84 Muse	163
Mov'd by the wind, so comely moved she.	287	U84 Muse	166
She swaid all bus'nesse in the Familie!	287	U84 Muse	168
To one she said, Doe this, he did it; So	287	U84 Muse	169
She was, in one, a many parts of life;	287	U84 Muse	173
She spent more time in teares her selfe to dresse	287	U84 Muse	180
Her solemne houres she spent, or giving Almes,	288	U84 Muse	192
On all the world! She saw him on the Crosse	288	U84 Muse	201
All this by Faith she saw, and fram'd a Plea,	288	U84 Muse	209
In this sweet Extasie, she was rapt hence.	289	U84 Muse	225
To every state of fortune; she helpes on,	311	Horace	153
To every Fortunes habit; she helps on,	342	Horace	V153
With weightie woes she hurles us all along	342	Horace	V155
Her truch-man, she reports the minds each throw.	313	Horace	157
To Dance, so she should, shamefac'd, differ farre	321	Horace	339
Nor takes she pride to know them.	365	Ode Splendor	24
To fill an Epitaph. But she had more.	371	Epitaph	5
She might have claym'd t'have made the Graces foure;	371	Epitaph	6
Of Spheares, as light of starres; She was earthes Eye:	372	Epitaph	9
She was 'Sell Boulstred. In which name, I call	372	Epitaph	12
May she, whome thou for spouse, to day, dost take,	384	Somerset	11
As, since, she will vouchsafe no other Wit.	392	Shakespeare	50
At least so great a Lady. She was wife	394	Jane Ogle	15
But Sorrow, she desir'd no other Friend:	394	Jane Ogle	17
And her, she made her Inmate, to the End,	394	Jane Ogle	18
Stay, till she make her vaine Approches. Then	401	Beaumont	15
If, maymed, she come off, 'tis not of men	401	Beaumont	16
she desires of every birth	417	Moon	19
and she is pleased.	417	Moon	36
Lucy of Bedford; she, that Bounty	662	Bedford	3
if any way she do rewarde thee	662	Bedford	8
of her white Hand; or she can spare it.	662	Bedford	10

SHEAFE

	Page	Title	Line
They made a Vulcan of a sheafe of Reedes,	208	U43 Vulcan	126

SHEARERS

	Page	Title	Line
And feasts, that either shearers keepe;	97	F3 Wroth	40
And feasts, which either shearers keepe;	97	F3 Wroth	V 40

SHEARES   (See also SHEERES)

	Page	Title	Line
Of Earth, and sheares the tender Sheepe:	290	U85 Country	16

SHEATH

	Page	Title	Line
Noe velvet Sheath you weare, will alter kynde.	403	Inigo Jones 1	26

SHED

	Page	Title	Line
And know, for whom a teare you shed,	77	E120 S. P.	3
Shed in thy Songs; 'tis true: but short of thee.	82	E130 Ferrab. 1	18
That they for me their teares will shed;	152	U12 Corbet	34
Rich beame of honour, shed your light	177	U25 Desmond	14
And the Greeke Discipline (with the moderne) shed	214	U44 Speach	36
Hath shed, or humane frailtie not kept thence.	329	Horace	528
Here France, and Italy both to him shed	375	Coryat 1	30

SHEDS

	Page	Title	Line
Sheds it selfe through the face,	134	U2 Triumph	18

SHEE'

	Page	Title	Line
Or safe, but shee'll procure	109	F11 Epode	6
But shee's Juno, when she walkes,	137	U2 Cupid	53
For these with her young Companie shee'll enter,	164	U15 Friend-Wars	79
And e're I can aske more of her, shee's gone!	269	U81 Pawlet	12
Yet shee's nor nice to shew them,	365	Ode Splendor	23

SHEE

	Page	Title	Line
Shee must have money: he returnes, god payes.	30	E12 Shift	8
Lent him a pockie whore. Shee hath paid him.	31	E12 Shift	24
The great renowne, and name wherewith shee goes.	31	E14 Camden	4
More high, more holy, that shee more would crave.	31	E14 Camden	6
At sixe moneths end, shee parted hence	33	E22 Daughter	5

```
                                                        Page      Title        Line

SHEE  (cont.)
  Whose soule heavens Queene, (whose name shee beares)  .  .  .   33   E22 Daughter     7
  In varied shapes, which for his lust shee takes:      .  .  .   34   E25 Beast 1      6
  For what shee gave, a whore; a baud, shee cures.      .  .  .   39   E41 Gypsee       4
  In all affections shee concurreth still.     .     .  .  .      40   E42 Giles       15
  Or, if shee would but modestly have prais'd     .     .  .  .   46   E60 Mounteagle   3
  Shee shall instruct my after-thoughts to write   .     .  .  .  48   E65 Muse        13
  I meant shee should be curteous, facile, sweet,    .     .  .   52   E76 Bedford 1    9
  My Muse bad, Bedford write, and that was shee.    .     .  .    52   E76 Bedford 1   18
  At which, shee happily displeas'd, made you:     .     .  .     53   E79 Rutland      9
  He cast, yet keeps her well! No, shee keeps him.    .     .  .  54   E82 Surly        2
  Shee doth instruct men by her gallant flight,    .     .  .     55   E85 Goodyere 1   5
  Of what shee had wrought came in, and wak'd his braine,  .  .   56   E87 Hazard       4
  Was dull, and long, ere shee would goe to man:    .     .  .    57   E90 Mill         3
  And it is hop'd, that shee, like Milo, wull       .     .  .    57   E90 Mill        17
  When on thy trumpet shee did sound a blast,     .     .  .      58   E91 Vere         7
  To morrow vice, if shee give better pay:     .     .  .  .      66   E102 Pembroke   10
  Whose better studies while shee emulates,     .     .  .  .     78   E121 Rudyerd 1   3
  Shee learnes to know long difference of their states.  .  .  .  78   E121 Rudyerd 1   4
  If I would vertue set, as shee was yong,     .     .  .  .      78   E122 Rudyerd 2   5
  If, at all, shee had a fault,     .     .     .  .  .  .        79   E124 Elizabeth   7
  Phoebus replyed.  Bold head, it is not shee:     .     .  .     80   E126 Mrs Cary    7
  That shee removeth cares, sadnesse ejects,     .     .  .  .    82   E130 Ferrab. 1   4
  To say, indeed, shee were the soule of heaven,    .     .  .    82   E130 Ferrab. 1  11
  No more, those mayden glories shee hath lost.    .     .  .     83   E132 Sylvester  14
  Shee brought the Poets forth, but ours th'adventer.  .  .  .    84   E133 Voyage     20
  Stunke not so ill; nor, when shee kist, Kate Arden.  .  .  .    87   E133 Voyage    118
  When shee was farre: and not a roome, but drest,   .     .  .   96   F2 Penshurst    87
  So court a mistris, shee denyes you;     .     .  .  .  .       104  F7 Women but     3
  Let her alone, shee will court you.     .     .  .  .  .        104  F7 Women but     4
  As sweet, as shee is fayre.     .     .     .  .  .  .          112  F11 Epode       98
  How onely shee bestowes     .     .     .     .  .  .  .        112  F11 Epode      104
  The soules, shee loves.  Those other glorious notes,  .  .  .   114  F12 Rutland     43
  Who, though shee have a better verser got,     .     .  .  .    115  F12 Rutland     68
  Yet, for the timely favours shee hath done,    .     .  .  .    115  F12 Rutland     71
  O so faire O so kind o so sweet so sweet is shee   .     .  .   135  U2 Triumph    V 38
  O so yong o so streight O so chast so chast is shee  .  .  .    136  U2 Triumph    V 46
  Make in one, the same were shee.     .     .  .  .  .           137  U2 Cupid        48
  Shee is Venus, when she smiles,     .     .  .  .  .  .         137  U2 Cupid        52
  Shee chearfully supporteth what she reares,    .     .  .  .    176  U24 Frontispice  13
  Her owne bloud gave her: Shee ne're had, nor hath  .  .  .      188  U34 Small Poxe    9
  Shee is the Judge, Thou Executioner:     .     .  .  .  .       204  U43 Vulcan       47
  In Contract twice, what can shee perjure more?   .     .  .  .  223  U49 Pucell       30
  Who, when shee heard the match, concluded streight,  .  .  .    229  U54 Squib         5
  Shee showes so farre above     .     .     .  .  .  .           240  U67 Muses        31
  But, that shee raigning here,     .     .     .  .  .  .        240  U67 Muses        35
  When shee puts forth the life of ev'ry thing:    .     .  .     250  U74 Weston        3
  Shee lies deliver'd, without paine,     .     .  .  .  .        251  U74 Weston        5
  gentle hee asketh, shee will pay: no suits,    .     .  .  .    258  U75 Epithalam.  V188
  And were shee lost, could best supply her place,   .     .  .   264  U79 New-yeares   34
  Shee, to the Crowne, hath brought encrease.    .     .  .  .    264  U79 New-yeares   41
  Shee was the Lady Jane, and Marchionisse     .     .  .  .      269  U81 Pawlet       19
  For such as Shee.     .     .     .     .     .  .  .  .        274  U84 Cradle       40
  And Stanley, to the which shee was Co-heire.     .     .  .     274  U84 Descent       6
  Of vertues in her, as, in short, shee grew     .     .  .  .    274  U84 Descent      11
  'Twere time that I dy'd too, now shee is dead,   .     .  .     282  U84 Muse          1
  (For so thou art with me) now shee is gone.    .     .  .  .    283  U84 Muse         22
  When shee departed? you will meet her there,   .     .  .  .    285  U84 Muse        108
  To cloath the naked, feed the hungry.  Shee    .     .  .  .    288  U84 Muse        194
  Shee saw her Saviour, by an early light,     .     .  .  .      288  U84 Muse        199
  Shee saw him rise, triumphing over Death     .     .  .  .      288  U84 Muse        203
  Shee saw him too, in glory to ascend     .     .  .  .  .       288  U84 Muse        205
  Ever his thighes Male then, and his braines Shee.  .  .  .      378  Coryat 2       92
  That went before, a Husband.  Shee, Ile sweare,   .     .  .    386  Husband         9
  Shee need not blush upon the Mariage-Day.    .     .  .  .      386  Husband        12
  Whom shee, with Sorrow first did lodge, then feast,  .  .  .    394  Jane Ogle      20
  Shee was the light (without reflexe     .     .  .  .  .        399  Lady Ogle       9
  Or without angles, it was shee!     .     .  .  .  .  .         399  Lady Ogle      16
  Of weight, or fashion, it was shee.     .     .  .  .  .        399  Lady Ogle      24
  Into a Phoenix, which is shee.     .     .  .  .  .  .          400  Lady Ogle      32
  shee soone will heare it.     .     .     .  .  .  .  .         417  Moon           24
  Though shee chainge as oft as shee,     .     .  .  .  .        417  Moon           29
  shee will not seise it.     .     .     .  .  .  .  .           418  Moon           44
SHEE'LL
  Or safe, but shee'll procure     .     .  .  .  .  .  .         109  F11 Epode        6
  For these with her young Companie shee'll enter,  .  .  .  .    164  U15 Friend-Wars  79
SHEEPE
  Thy sheepe, thy bullocks, kine, and calves doe feed:  .  .  .   94   F2 Penshurst    23
  The mowed meddowes, with the fleeced sheepe,   .     .  .  .    97   F3 Wroth        39
  In earth, till the last Trumpe awake the Sheepe    .     .  .   283  U84 Muse        46
  Of Earth, and sheares the tender Sheepe:     .     .  .  .      290  U85 Country     16
SHEEP'ERDS
  And like the ravish'd Sheep'erds said,     .  .  .  .  .  .     130  U1 Nativitie     4
SHEEPES
  The slie Ulysses stole in a sheepes-skin,    .     .  .  .  .   87   E133 Voyage    113
SHEEPES-SKIN
  The slie Ulysses stole in a sheepes-skin,    .     .  .  .  .   87   E133 Voyage    113
SHEERES
  The rock, the spindle, and the sheeres controule   .     .  .   52   E76 Bedford 1   15
SHEE'S
  But shee's Juno, when she walkes,     .     .  .  .  .  .       137  U2 Cupid        53
  And e're I can aske more of her, shee's gone!    .     .  .     269  U81 Pawlet       12
  Yet shee's nor nice to shew them,     .     .  .  .  .  .       365  Ode Splendor   23
```

		Page	Title	Line

SHEETES
  Night, and the sheetes will show   ·   ·   ·   258   U75 Epithalam.   191
SHE'HATH
  To my lesse sanguine Muse, wherein she'hath wonne   ·   ·   115   F12 Rutland   72
SHEILD
  Thie Chrystall sheild   ·   ·   ·   ·   ·   ·   421   Ode:If Men   38
SHELFE
  God wisheth, none should wracke on a strange shelfe.   ·   ·   99   F3 Wroth   95
SHELTON
  To Sir Raph Shelton   ·   ·   ·   ·   76   E119 Shelton   Ttl
  No, Shelton, give me thee, canst want all these,   ·   ·   76   E119 Shelton   7
  We have a Shelton, and a Heyden got,   ·   ·   ·   84   E133 Voyage   5
SHELVES
  You, Madame, yong have learn'd to shunne these shelves,   ·   ·   119   F13 Aubigny   89
SHEP'ARD
  Pan only our great Shep'ard is,   ·   ·   ·   265   U79 New-yeares   43
  This only the great Shep'ard is.   ·   ·   ·   265   U79 New-yeares   65
SHEPHEARDS
  And, drest in shepheards tyre, who would not say: ·   ·   68   E105 L Wroth 2   9
SHERIFFES
  Of Sheriffes dinner, or Majors feast.   ·   ·   96   F3 Wroth   6
  Of Sergeants dinner, or sheriffes feast.   ·   ·   96   F3 Wroth   V 6
SHEW
  And gave thee both, to shew they could no more.   ·   ·   28   E4 James 1   4
  Nor glad for fashion. Nor to shew a fit   ·   ·   47   E64 Salisbury 3   7
  Two kindes of valour he doth shew, at ones;   ·   ·   49   E68 Playwrt 2   3
  Stand'st thou, to shew the times what you all were?   ·   ·   60   E93 Radcliffe   4
  And shew their feathers shot, and cullors torne,   ·   ·   98   F3 Wroth   71
  I know thou canst nor shew, nor beare   ·   ·   ·   101   F4 To the World   39
  Of nobles vertue, shew in you;   ·   ·   ·   121   F14 Sydney   32
  As the Downe, and shew it oft;   ·   ·   ·   141   U2 Her man   26
  I That have beene a lover, and could shew it,   ·   ·   182   U28 Worth   1
  To shew their Tires? to view, and to be view'd?   ·   ·   222   U49 Pucell   17
  To shew thou hast beene long,   ·   ·   ·   245   U70 Ode   58
  Feed on thy selfe for spight, and shew thy Kind: ·   ·   245   U70 Ode   58
  To shew the rites, and t'usher forth the way   ·   ·   250   U73 Weston   9
  As being the Sonne of Man) to shew his Power,   ·   ·   263   U79 New-yeares   4
  Yet shee's nor nice to shew them,   ·   ·   ·   288   U84 Muse   217
SHEWE
  In these pide times, only to shewe their braines,   ·   ·   365   Ode Splendor   23
  Under the Morall? shewe he had a pate   ·   ·   362   Author   4
SHEW'D
  That had, so often, shew'd 'hem merry prankes.   ·   ·   405   Inigo Jones 1   83
  You shew'd like Perseus upon Pegasus;   ·   ·   89   E133 Voyage   184
  He shew'd him first the hoofe-cleft Spring,   ·   ·   228   U53 Newcastle   7
SHEWEN
  All way of life was shewen; the grace of Kings   ·   ·   366   Ode Who saith   17
SHEWES
  Which shewes, where ever death doth please t'appeare,   ·   ·   329   Horace   497
  Shewes of the resurrection little trust.   ·   ·   37   E32 Roe 2   9
  Though not unprov'd: which shewes, thy fortunes are   ·   ·   37   E34 Death   2
  So bold, as shewes your Art you can command.   ·   ·   60   E93 Radcliffe   14
  F.   shewes what he was, K. what he will bee.   ·   ·   370   Author   8
  Shewes he dares more then Paules Church-yard durst do.   ·   375   Coryat 1   29
SHEWING
  Shewing danger more then ire.   ·   ·   ·   378   Coryat 2   85
  And shewing so weake an Act to vulgar eyes,   ·   ·   142   U2 Her man   42
SHEW'N
  There was a Judgement shew'n too in an houre.   ·   ·   218   U47 Tribe   7
SHEW'S
  By which yo'are planted, shew's your fruit shall bide.   ·   ·   210   U43 Vulcan   158
SHEWS
  And stradling shews the Boyes Brown paper fleet,   ·   ·   281   U84 Kenelme   19
SHEW'ST
  Wherein thou shew'st, how much the latter are   ·   ·   407   Inigo Jones 2   17
SH'HATH
  To that eternall Rest, where now sh'hath place   ·   ·   72   E111 Edmonds 2   3
SHIELD
  The Orphans Pillar, the true Subjects shield,   ·   ·   288   U84 Muse   197
SHIETER
  Of Hannow, Shieter-huissen, Popenheim,   ·   ·   185   U30 Burleigh   7
SHIETER-HUISSEN
  Of Hannow, Shieter-huissen, Popenheim,   ·   ·   69   E107 Hungry   25
SHIFT
  On lieutenant Shift.   ·   ·   ·   ·   ·   69   E107 Hungry   25
  Shift, here, in towne, not meanest among squires,   ·   ·   30   E12 Shift   Ttl
  Man out their Boates to th' Temple, and not shift   ·   ·   30   E12 Shift   1
  As would make shift, to make himselfe alone,   ·   ·   155   U13 Sacvile   83
  To shift their seasons, and destroy their powers!   ·   ·   171   U19 Elegy By   24
  You could make shift to paint an Eye,   ·   ·   199   U41 Elegy Since   10
SHIFTING
  And, shifting of it's faces, doth play more   ·   ·   278   U84 Mind   9
SHIFTS
  At first he made low shifts, would picke and gleane,   ·   ·   74   E115 Honest Man   25
SHINE
  The judgement of the king so shine in thee;   ·   ·   45   E56 Poet-Ape   5
  Shine bright on every harth as the desires   ·   ·   47   E63 Salisbury 2   4
  And such, or my hopes faile, shall make you shine.   ·   ·   95   F2 Penshurst   78
  A Trinitie, to shine in Union;   ·   ·   ·   115   F12 Rutland   64
  I wish the Sun should shine   ·   ·   ·   128   U1 Trinitie   34
  May shine (through every chincke) to every sight   ·   ·   150   U10 Jealousie   7
  (As my hope tells) that our faire Phoebe's shine,   ·   ·   177   U25 Desmond   16
  (As my hope tells) that our drad Cynthia's shine,   ·   ·   179   U25 Desmond   58
                          ·   ·   179   U25 Desmond   V 58

SHINE (cont.)
  Shine more, then she, the Stars among?   .   .   .   181   U27 Ode Helen   12
  Where Love doth shine, there needs no Sunne,   .   .   .   189   U36 Song   5
  Sol will re-shine. If not, Charles hath a Sonne.   .   .   238   U65 Prince   12
  And Sol will shine. If not, Charles hath a Sonne.   .   .   238   U65 Prince   V 12
  And let thy lookes with gladnesse shine: .   .   .   245   U70 Ode   76
  Whilst that in heav'n, this light on earth must shine. .   .   246   U70 Ode   96
  And shine as you exalted are;   .   .   .   246   U70 Ode   97
  Or so did shine,   .   .   .   253   U75 Epithalam.   22
  See, how with Roses, and with Lillies shine,   .   .   .   254   U75 Epithalam.   57
  If thou be'st wise, with 'Syrian Oyle let shine   .   .   294   U89 Mart.8:77   3
  Ye have oft-times, that may ore-shine the rest,   .   .   .   305   Horace   18
  Ye have oft-times, that may out-shine the rest,   .   .   .   338   Horace   V 18
  Much in the Poeme shine, I will not bee   .   .   .   329   Horace   526
  Doth shine in her discerning,   .   .   .   365   Ode Splendor   10
  With the same looke, or with a better, shine.   .   .   .   384   Somerset   10
  And tell, how farre thou didst our Lily out-shine,   .   .   391   Shakespeare   29
  Shine forth, thou Starre of Poets, and with rage,   .   .   392   Shakespeare   77
  Inflam'd with ardor to that mystick Shine,   .   .   .   413   Ghyrlond   23
SHINES
  The Birth-day shines, when logs not burne, but men.   .   .   121   F14 Sydney   60
  Your forme shines here, here fixed in my heart: .   .   194   U38 Elegy 'Tis   117
  Of Shakespeares minde, and manners brightly shines   .   .   392   Shakespeare   67
SHINING
  Incarnate in the Manger, shining bright   .   .   .   288   U84 Muse   200
  And 'bout the shining Chimney set!   .   .   .   291   U85 Country   V 66
SHIN'ST
  O, now thou smil'st, faire Sun, and shin'st, as thou wouldst stay! 254   U75 Epithalam.   64
SHIP
  If holiest friend-ship, naked to the touch,   .   .   78   E122 Rudyerd 2   7
  Besides he tried Ship, Cart, Waggon, and Chayre, .   .   .   380   Coryat 3   27
  A Prentise-ship: which few doe now a dayes.   .   .   .   410   Brome   10
SHIPPING
  When with his royall shipping   222   U48 Bacchus   52
SHIPS
  Or the States Ships sent forth belike to meet   .   .   .   219   U47 Tribe   33
  Unto the Ships, and they from tier, to tier,   .   .   .   249   U72 King   2
  Thy Catalogue of Ships, exceeding his, ...   398   Drayton   61
  And when he ships them where to use their Armes, .   .   .   398   Drayton   65
SHITE
  And the Physician teach men spue, or shite;   .   .   .   410   Brome   16
SHITTEN
  And, in so shitten sort, so long had us'd him: .   .   .   86   E133 Voyage   98
SHOES
  Old Hat here, torne Hose, with Shoes full of gravell, .   .   375   Coryat 1   26
  How well, and how often his shoes too were mended,   .   .   380   Coryat 3   39
SHONE
  Where never Star shone brighter yet?   181   U27 Ode Helen   26
SHOOE
  And shooe, and tye, and garter should come hether,   .   .   56   E88 Monsieur   4
  He did lay up, and would adore the shooe,   .   .   .   201   U42 Elegy Let   55
SHOONE
  Makes the poore Banck-side creature wet it' shoone,   .   .   84   E133 Voyage   30
SHOOT
  Shoot forth in smooth and comely spaces; have   .   .   .   157   U13 Sacvile   150
  Clos'd to their peace, he saw his branches shoot,   .   .   185   U30 Burleigh   17
  This Prince of flowers? Soone shoot thou up, and grow   .   237   U65 Prince   5
  Shoot up an Olive fruitfull, faire, ...   251   U74 Weston   28
  Like tender buds shoot up, and freshly grow.   .   .   .   309   Horace   89
SHOOTE
  Grow, grow, faire tree, and as thy branches shoote,   .   .   119   F13 Aubigny   99
SHOOTING
  Or shooting at the greedie thrush, ...   97   F3 Wroth   34
  Or shooting at the hungrie thrush, ...   97   F3 Wroth   V 34
SHOP
  I know thou whole art but a shop   100   F4 To the World   17
  With poore base termes, through every baser shop: .   .   321   Horace   334
  Suckt from the Veynes of shop-philosophy.   .   .   .   405   Inigo Jones 1   74
SHOPP
  Or Ale! He build a pallace! Thou a shopp   .   .   .   407   Inigo Jones 2   9
SHOP-PHILOSOPHY
  Suckt from the Veynes of shop-philosophy.   .   .   .   405   Inigo Jones 1   74
SHOPS
  When not the Shops, but windowes doe display   .   .   .   202   U42 Elegy Let   78
  All live dogs from the lane, and his shops sight,   .   .   241   U69 Friend Son   12
  With the shops Foreman, or some such brave sparke,   .   .   371   Fletcher   6
SHORE
  About the shore, of farts, but late departed,   .   .   .   87   E133 Voyage   125
  Like Eccho playing from the other shore.   .   .   .   249   U72 King   8
  Like Eccho playing from another shore.   .   .   .   249   U72 King   V 8
  Downe close by shore, this other creeping steales,   .   .   339   Horace   V 40/ 39
  Whether the Sea receiv'd into the shore,   .   .   .   309   Horace   91
  Still, still, dost thou arrive with, at our shore,   .   .   388   Chapman   5
SHORES
  The Rivers in their shores doe run, ...   251   U74 Weston   7
SHORT
  So, in short time, th'art in arrerage growne   .   .   .   32   E16 Brain-hardy   5
  And in this short time of thy happiest raigne,   .   .   .   37   E35 James 2   4
  Though life be short, let us not make it so.   .   .   .   50   E70 Wm Roe 1   8
  Ushring the mutton; with a short-leg'd hen, .   .   .   64   E101 Supper   11
  Shed in thy Songs; 'tis true: but short of thee. .   .   .   82   E130 Ferrab. 1   18
  Of the short braverie of the night;   96   F3 Wroth   10
  At noone, they are or short, or none: 104   F7 Women but   8

SHORT (cont.)

	Page	Title	Line
But of one, if short he came,	142	U2 Her man	55
Though I am short, I cannot be obscure:	158	U14 Selden	2
Come short of all this learned throng,	182	U27 Ode Helen	34
So short you read my Character, and theirs	220	U47 Tribe	73
And in short measures, life may perfect bee.	245	U70 Ode	74
Of vertues in her, as, in short, shee grew	274	U84 Descent	11
You once enjoy'd: A short space severs yee,	285	U84 Muse	105
Doing, a filthy pleasure is, and short;	294	U88 Petronius	1
In short; I bid, Let what thou work'st upon,	307	Horace	31
Two rests, a short and long, th'Iambick frame;	323	Horace	371
Or Pleader at the Barre, that may come short	331	Horace	551
For other formes come short all	364	Ode Splendor	2

SHORTEST
| Appear, and that to shortest view, | 174 | U22 Elegy Tho | 34 |

SHORT-LEG'D
| Ushring the mutton; with a short-leg'd hen, | 64 | E101 Supper | 11 |

SHORTLY
| Shortly againe: and make our absence sweet. | 197 | U40 Elegy That | 8 |

SHORTNESSE
| My selfe for shortnesse labour; and I grow | 307 | Horace | 35 |
| My selfe for shortnesse labour, and am stil'd | 339 | Horace V 36/ | 35 |

SHOT
Seas, serenes, swords, shot, sicknesse, all are there.	37	E32 Roe 2	10
And shew their feathers shot, and cullors torne,	98	F3 Wroth	71
No Armour to the mind! he is shot-free	179	U25 Desmond	48
Their weapons shot out, with that flame, and force,	233	U59 Newcastle	11

SHOT-FREE
| No Armour to the mind! he is shot-free | 179 | U25 Desmond | 48 |

SHOULD
Whom should my Muse then flie to, but the best	28	E4 James 1	9
But leave, because I cannot as I should!	34	E23 Donne 1	10
There's reason good, that you good lawes should make:	34	E24 Parliament	1
In place of scutcheons, that should decke thy herse,	35	E27 Roe 1	1
All braines, at times of triumph, should runne wit.	36	E29 Tilter	4
No more would Jone he should. Giles riseth early,	40	E42 Giles	6
Which should thy countries love to speake refuse,	40	E43 Salisbury 1	3
He meant they thither should make swift repaire,	41	E44 Chuff	5
Will man lament the state he should envie?	41	E45 First Son	6
Loe, what my countrey should have done (have rais'd	46	E60 Mounteagle	1
Fine Madame Would-Bee, wherefore should you feare,	46	E62 Would-bee	1
What should the cause be? Oh, you live at court?	46	E62 Would-bee	9
I meant the day-starre should not brighter rise,	52	E76 Bedford 1	7
I meant shee should be curteous, facile, sweet,	52	E76 Bedford 1	9
I meant each softest vertue, there should meet,	52	E76 Bedford 1	11
I purpos'd her; that should, with even powers,	52	E76 Bedford 1	14
That, any way, my booke should speake thy name:	53	E77 Not name	2
He should those rare, and absolute numbers view,	53	E79 Rutland	11
And here, it should be one of our first strifes,	54	E80 Life/Death	6
I would have spent: how every Muse should know it,	55	E84 Bedford 2	7
And Phoebus-selfe should be at eating it.	55	E84 Bedford 2	8
That they to knowledge so should toure upright,	55	E85 Goodyere 1	6
Which if they misse, they yet should re-advance	55	E85 Goodyere 1	8
That his whole body should speake french, not he?	56	E88 Monsieur	2
And shooe, and tye, and garter should come hether,	56	E88 Monsieur	4
That he, untravell'd, should be french so much,	56	E88 Monsieur	7
As french-men in his companie, should seeme dutch?	56	E88 Monsieur	8
That, Allen, I should pause to publish thee?	57	E89 Allen	8
So many Poets life, by one should live.	57	E89 Allen	14
I leave thy acts, which should I prosequute	58	E91 Vere	9
I leave, then, acts, which should I prosequute	58	E91 Vere V	9
Who more should seeke mens reverence, then feare.	58	E91 Vere	18
If workes (not th'authors) their owne grace should looke,	60	E94 Bedford 3	3
I should beleeve, the soule of Tacitus	61	E95 Savile	3
A man should seeke great glorie, and not broad.	62	E96 Donne 2	12
If not, 'tis fit for you, some should envy.	67	E104 Montgomery	16
And that thy soule should give thy flesh her weight.	70	E109 evil	14
If onely love should make the action pris'd:	78	E12 Rudyerd 1	6
That strives, his manners should precede his wit.	78	E121 Rudyerd 1	8
Of the best writer, and judge, should emulate.	78	E123 Rudyerd 3	4
If I should faile, in gratitude, to thee,	80	E127 Aubigny	2
They should be fooles, for me, at their owne charge.	83	E131 Ferrab. 2	8
God wisheth, none should wracke on a strange shelfe.	99	F3 Wroth	95
That neither want should thee affright,	100	F3 Wroth	V104
And, knowing this, should I yet stay,	100	F4 To the World	21
Else, I my state should much mistake,	101	F4 To the World	57
There shoulda miracle be wrought.	101	F4 To the World	60
Why should we deferre our joyes?	102	F5 Celia 1	9
What should, yet, thy pallat please?	105	F8 Sicknesse	21
A beautie of that merit, that should take	108	F10 Proludium	27
(That should ring larum to the heart) doth sleepe,	109	F11 Epode	23
Were it to thinke, that you should not inherit	114	F12 Rutland	32
Of nature, and societie, I should faint;	117	F13 Aubigny	19
What your try'd manners are, what theirs should bee.	119	F13 Aubigny	112
How you love one, and him you should; how still	119	F13 Aubigny	113
Wherefore should I	120	F14 Sydney	7
I long, and should not beg in vaine,	139	U2 Another	7
What w'are but once to doe, we should doe long.	139	U2 Another	12
And his lip should kissing teach,	141	U2 Her man	22
He should have a hand as soft	141	U2 Her man V	25
All his blood should be a flame	141	U2 Her man	30
In a body, should be there.	141	U2 Her man	35
Well he should his clothes to weare;	141	U2 Her man	36

	Page	Title	Line
SHOULD (cont.)			
Drest, you still for man should take him;	141	U2 Her man	38
Valiant he should be as fire,	142	U2 Her man	41
Of Angels should be driven	144	U3 Musicall	22
For if the Nymphs should know my Swaine,	147	U7 Nymph	3
Whom I adore so much, should so slight me,	149	U9 Picture	4
That others should not warme them at my fire,	150	U10 Jealousie	6
I wish the Sun should shine	150	U10 Jealousie	7
And more, and more, I should have done,	152	U12 Corbet	30
And knew their how, and where: we should have, then,	153	U13 Sacvile	3
No! Gifts and thankes should have one cheerefull face,	154	U13 Sacvile	39
Or robbing the poore Market-folkes should nurse	155	U13 Sacvile	90
Who was this Morning such a one, should be	157	U13 Sacvile	126
Coriat, should rise the most sufficient head	157	U13 Sacvile	128
No more, then we should thinke a Lord had had	168	U15 Friend-Wars	193
Nor should I at this time protested be,	169	U17 Friend-Debt	7
How penitent I am, or I should be!	172	U20 Shrub	16
Aske not to know this Man. If fame should speake	172	U21 Ltl Shrub	1
But who should lesse expect from you,	173	U22 Elegy Tho	13
Should not on fortune pause,	174	U23 Himselfe	17
Where art thou, Genius? I should use	176	U25 Desmond	1
Genius, where art thou? I should use	176	U25 Desmond	V 1
That heaven should make no more; or should amisse,	188	U34 Small Poxe	15
That you should be too noble to destroy.	191	U38 Elegy 'Tis	12
Of your compassion; Parents should be mild:	192	U38 Elegy 'Tis	40
Should aske the blood, and spirits he hath infus'd	192	U38 Elegy 'Tis	65
A man should flie from, as he would disdaine.	194	U38 Elegy 'Tis	104
Yet should the Lover still be ayrie and light,	197	U40 Elegy That	19
It is as if a night should shade noone-day,	199	U41 Elegy Since	5
It is not likely I should now looke downe	200	U42 Elegy Let	37
A Court of Equitie should doe us right,	211	U43 Vulcan	178
Or lest that vapour should the Citie choake,	211	U43 Vulcan	V182
But he that should perswade, to have this done	214	U44 Speach	61
Should he heare of billow, wind, and storme,	214	U44 Speach	63
He that should search all Glories of the Gowne,	217	U46 Coke	1
Thinkes it selfe nought, though she should valew it.	223	U49 Pucell	24
Not he, that should the body have, for Case	223	U49 Pucell	33
Verse, that should thee, and me out-live.	229	U55 Burges	4
And should grow rich, had I much more to pay.	231	U56 Covell	30
And should grow rich, if I had more to pay.	231	U56 Covell	V 30
T'obtaine of God, what all the Land should aske?	234	U61 Epigram	11
Well, they should know him, would the K. but grant	241	U68 House-hold	5
As the old Bard, should no Canary lack.	241	U68 House-hold	11
Some houres before it should, that these may know	257	U75 Epithalam.	146
Should take first Seisin of the publique good,	268	U80 Christning	8
But rather I, should I of that part speake!	269	U81 Pawlet	28
With what injustice should one soule pretend	271	U81 Pawlet	92
So swift, so pure, should yet apply	279	U84 Mind	42
By Death, on Earth, I should have had remorse	282	U84 Muse	12
This being thus: why should my tongue, or pen	284	U84 Muse	69
He that shall be our supreme Judge, should leave	286	U84 Muse	148
The kind of Man, on whom his doome should fall!	288	U84 Muse	208
To him should be her Judge, true God, true Man,	288	U84 Muse	211
But, say old Love returne should make,	294	U87 Hor.3:9	17
That I bright Chloe off should shake;	294	U87 Hor.3:9	19
Yet, not as therefore wild, and tame should cleave	305	Horace	14
Yet not as therefore cruell things should cleave	338	Horace	V 14
Together: not that we should Serpents see	305	Horace	15
To gentle: not that we should Serpents see	338	Horace	V 15
Not to designe the whole. Should I aspire	307	Horace	49
Or grace of speech, should hope a lasting date.	309	Horace	100
Were also clos'd: But, who the man should be,	309	Horace	109
Fit for the sock: Each subject should retaine	311	Horace	124
Sharpe, and contemning lawes, at him should aime,	313	Horace	173
To Dance, so she should, shamefac'd, differ farre	321	Horace	339
Poets should ever be indifferent.	331	Horace	556
Lest the throng'd heapes should on a laughter take:	331	Horace	569
Lest the throng'd rings should a free laughter take:	352	Horace	V545/569
And friendly should unto one end conspire.	333	Horace	586
And friendly should unto their end conspire.	353	Horace	V586
I wonder how this happie man should know,	333	Horace	605
In vaine, but you, and yours, you should love still	335	Horace	631
Why should I grieve my friend, this trifling way?	335	Horace	640
For, if one should, and with a rope make haste	335	Horace	655
Then why should we dispaire? Dispaire, away:	363	Riches	17
But should they know (as I) that this,	369	Ode Who saith	97
Among the starres should be resign'd	369	Ode Who saith	105
It should rather have bene Tom that a horse did lack.	374	Coryat 1	15
Rather his sonne, I should have cal'd thee, why?	378	Coryat 2	88
. . . Which should have beene Printed with the other . . .	379	Coryat 3	Ttl
Who, because his matter in all should be meete,	379	Coryat 3	3
Or any thing else that another should hide,	380	Coryat 3	51
Should praise a Matron. What could hurt her more?	391	Shakespeare	14
I should commit thee surely with thy peeres,	391	Shakespeare	28
At every line some pinn thereof should slacke	395	May	5
Should but the king his Justice-hood employ	405	Inigo Jones 1	77
Our Charles should make thee such? 'Twill not become	406	Inigo Jones 2	3
That I should wryte upon him some sharp verse,	407	Inigo Jones 3	3
You looke, my Joseph, I should something say	414	Rutter	1
SHOULDERS			
Upon your shoulders. Prove what they will beare,	307	Horace	55
Prove what your shoulders will, or will not beare.	339	Horace	V 57/ 55

```
                                                    Page      Title      Line

SHOULD'ST
    Thou should'st be bold, licentious, full of gall,        27   E2 My Booke      3
    Courtling, I rather thou should'st utterly   .    .    .   43   E52 Courtling    1
    That to the world thou should'st reveale so much,    .    .   72   E111 Edmonds 2  10
    And will, long ere thou should'st starve,    .    .    .  106   F8 Sicknesse    44
    Thou should'st have stay'd, till publike fame said so.   204   U43 Vulcan      46
    Thou should'st have cry'd, and all beene proper stuffe.  205   U43 Vulcan      64
    Thou should'st have cry'd, and all fine proper stuffe.   205   U43 Vulcan    V 64
    A Mungrel Curre?  Thou should'st stinck forth, and dye   409   Detractor       15
SHOUT
    Doe mingle in a shout,      .    .    .    .    .    .  240   U67 Muses       41
    And Roman Gentrie, will with laughter shout.   .    .   342   Horace        V160
SHOUTE
    And caried, though with shoute, and noyse, confesse    .   397   Drayton         45
SHOUTES
    At Bonefires, Rockets, Fire-workes, with the Shoutes   .   249   U72 King        13
    At Bonefires, squibs, and mirth, with all their Shoutes   249   U72 King      V 13
SHOUTS
    They vexe, and follow him with shouts, and noise,    .    335   Horace         648
SHOW    (See also SHEW)
    Forbeare to tempt me, Proule, I will not show    .    .   54   E81 Proule       1
    That will the pastrie, not my paper, show of.    .    .   65   E101 Supper     26
    Judge they, that can: here I have rais'd to show    .    67   E104 Montgomery 13
    Which is to live to conscience, not to show.   .    .   76   E119 Shelton    14
    If I would wish, for truth, and not for show,    .    .   78   E122 Rudyerd 2   1
    Thou art not, Penshurst, built to envious show,    .    93   F2 Penshurst     1
    And show, how, to the life, my soule presents   .    .  115   F12 Rutland     86
    And hearts of all, if I be sad for show,    .    .    .  122   F15 Heaven       6
    That men such reverence to such actions show!    .    .  156   U13 Sacvile     98
    Or Feathers: lay his fortune out to show,    .    .    .  162   U15 Friend-Wars 21
    Come to their Schooles,) show 'hem the use of Guns;    .  214   U44 Speach      58
    Why are we rich, or great, except to show    .    .    .  215   U44 Speach      69
    To mee; or beene the same to you; if show,    .    .    .  241   U69 Friend Son   2
    Doth show, the Graces, and the Houres    .    .    .    .  251   U74 Weston      16
    Night, and the sheetes will show    .    .    .    .    .  258   U75 Epithalam. 191
    —Doth most humbly show it,    .    .    .    .    .    .  259   U76 Petition     3
    The Cloud, and show the Universe;    .    .    .    .    .  276   U84 Body        18
    Of all are dead to life! His Wisdome show    .    .    .  289   U84 Muse       221
    What he despaires, being handled, might not show.    .    315   Horace         214
    Then those the faithfull eyes take in by show,   .    .  317   Horace         258
    Which the Socratick writings best can show:   .    .    325   Horace         442
    An Earle of show: for all thy worke is showe:    .    .  407   Inigo Jones 2   21
    An Earle of show: for all thy worth is showe:    .    .  407   Inigo Jones 2 V 21
SHOWE
    Triumph, my Britaine, thou hast one to showe,    .    .  391   Shakespeare     41
    An Earle of show: for all thy worke is showe:    .    .  407   Inigo Jones 2   21
    An Earle of show: for all thy worth is showe:    .    .  407   Inigo Jones 2 V 21
SHOWERS
    With what full hands, and in how plenteous showers    .  254   U75 Epithalam.  65
    As showers; and sweet as drops of Balme.    .    .    .  280   U84 Mind        60
    Begotten by that wind, and showers.    .    .    .    .  280   U84 Mind        68
SHOWES
    Because that studies spectacles, and showes,    .    .  118   F13 Aubigny     65
    Shee showes so farre above    .    .    .    .    .    .  240   U67 Muses       31
    That doe cry up the Machine, & the Showes!    .    .    403   Inigo Jones 1   32
    To hold her up.  O Showes! Showes! Mighty Showes!    .  403   Inigo Jones 1   39
SHOWNE
    I speake thy other graces, not lesse showne,    .    .   58   E91 Vere        13
    And feare much more, that more of him be showne.    .  147   U7 Nymph        21
    Monarch in Letters! 'Mongst thy Titles showne    .    .  160   U14 Selden      65
    And scorn'd, thou'ast showne thy malice, but hast fail'd.  188   U34 Small Poxe  18
    What so is showne, I not beleeve, and hate.   .    .    317   Horace         269
    Drawne Aristotle on us! & thence showne    .    .    .  402   Inigo Jones 1    9
SHOWRE
    Looke pale, distill a showre (was never meant)   .    .  333   Horace         612
    All, pouring their full showre of graces downe,    .    413   Ghyrlond        31
SHOWRES
    Then when the thundring Jove his Snow and showres    .  290   U85 Country     29
SHOW'ST
    Nay, and in this, thou show'st to value more    .    .  235   U62 Charles 1    9
SHREDS
    From locks of wooll, or shreds from the whole peece?    .   45   E56 Poet-Ape    14
SHREWSBURY
    . . . and Countesse of Shrewsbury:--    .    .    .    .  394   Jane Ogle      Ttl
SHRINE
    Who as an off'ring at your shrine,    .    .    .    .  174   U22 Elegy Tho    29
SHRIN'D
    To him, and he there shrin'd;    .    .    .    .    .  369   Ode Who saith  106
SHRINKE
    Thou need'st not shrinke at voyce of after-times;    .   61   E95 Savile      20
    Thou shrinke or start not, but be alwayes one;   .    .  168   U15 Friend-Wars 186
SHROWDES
    And peering forth of Iris in the Shrowdes!   .    .    .  403   Inigo Jones 1   34
SHRUB
    A Satyricall Shrub.    .    .    .    .    .    .    .  171   U20 Shrub      Ttl
    A little Shrub growing by.   .    .    .    .    .    .  172   U21 Ltl Shrub  Ttl
SHRUNKE
    Yet art thou both shrunke up, and old,    .    .    .  100   F4 To the World 14
    Oylie Expansions, or shrunke durtie folds,   .    .    .  220   U47 Tribe       68
SHUN
    If these, who have but sense, can shun    .    .    .  101   F4 To the World 33
    And shun to touch him, as a man that were    .    .    335   Horace         644
    whom thou seest happy; wretches, shun, as foes:    .    422   Lucan          V 6
```

SHUNNE
  On them: And therefore doe not onely shunne   59   E92 New Crie   38
  You, Madame, yong have learn'd to shunne these shelves,   .   .   119   F13 Aubigny   89
SHUNNES
  Yet Comick matter shunnes to be exprest   341   Horace   V127/121
SHUNNING
  Not only shunning by your act, to doe   224   U50 Countesse   5
  So, shunning faults, to greater fault doth lead,   .   .   .   307   Horace   43
  The shunning vice, to greater vice doth lead,   .   .   .   339   Horace   V 45/ 43
SHUNS
  Shuns prease, for two maine causes, poxe, and debt,   .   .   76   E119 Shelton   4
  Or, whilst he shuns the Earth, to catch at Aire   .   .   321   Horace   335
SHUT
  His neck fenc'd round with ruffe! his eyes halfe shut!   .   .   33   E21 Gam'ster   2
  Into your harbor, and all passage shut.   119   F13 Aubigny   92
  Are nothing till that comes to bind and shut.   .   .   .   157   U13 Sacvile   138
  Upon the reverend Pleaders; doe now shut   187   U33 Councellour   10
  Not, like a Midas, shut up in himselfe, ...   197   U40 Elegy That   21
  They both are slip'd to Bed; Shut fast the Doore,   .   .   258   U75 Epithalam.   185
  And when the flesh, here, shut up day, ...   400   Lady Ogle   27
SHUTS
  And shuts the old. Haste, haste, all loyall Swaines,   .   263   U79 New-yeares   10
SHUTTER
  The last of houres, and shutter up of all;   289   U84 Muse   219
SICILIAN
  To speake the fate of the Sicilian Maid   207   U43 Vulcan   96
  Of the Sicilian Poet Empedocles, ...   335   Horace   660
SICK
  Lest I be sick with seeing;   144   U4 Song   2
  Be at their Visits, see 'hem squemish, sick, ...   164   U15 Friend-Wars   68
  Whose shapes, like sick-mens dreames, are fain'd so vaine,   .   305   Horace   9
  Whose shapes, like sick-mens dreames, are form'd so vaine,   .   338   Horace   V   9
SICK-MENS
  Whose shapes, like sick-mens dreames, are fain'd so vaine,   .   305   Horace   9
  Whose shapes, like sick-mens dreames, are form'd so vaine,   .   338   Horace   V   9
SICKNES
  To call on Sicknes still, to be her Guest, ...   394   Jane Ogle   19
SICKNESSE
  Seas, serenes, swords, shot, sicknesse, all are there.   .   .   37   E32 Roe 2   10
  To age, misfortune, sicknesse, griefe: 102   F4 To the World   62
  To Sicknesse.   104   F8 Sicknesse   Ttl
  To Sicknesse. Ode Anacreon: 104   F8 Sicknesse   VTtl
  Take heed, Sicknesse, what you doe, ...   104   F8 Sicknesse   7
  Sicknesse; onely on us men.   105   F8 Sicknesse   14
  Loves sicknesse, and his noted want of worth,   .   .   .   150   U10 Jealousie   14
  So, from all sicknesse, may you rise to health,   .   .   .   186   U31 Elsmere   5
  . . . he sent me in my Sicknesse. 1629.   235   U62 Charles 1   Ttl
SIDE
  Forbidd' his side! and nothing, but the word   33   E21 Gam'ster   4
  Makes the poore Banck-side creature wet it' shoone,   .   .   84   E133 Voyage   30
  Betweene two walls; where, on one side, to scar men,   .   .   86   E133 Voyage   67
  The purpled pheasant, with the speckled side: .   .   .   94   F2 Penshurst   28
  They thinke not, then, which side the cause shall leese,   .   98   F3 Wroth   61
  And with thy Angels, placed side, by side, ...   128   U1 Trinitie   46
  That they still were to run by her side, ...   134   U2 Triumph   9
  And the Glasse hangs by her side, ...   137   U2 Cupid   40
  Or side, but threatens Ruine. The whole Day   .   .   .   166   U15 Friend-Wars   131
  Where mutuall frauds are fought, and no side yeild;   .   .   186   U33 Councellour   4
  Any Comparison had with his Cheap-side.   202   U42 Elegy Let   76
  Their Sister-tunes, from Thames his either side,   .   .   .   253   U75 Epithalam.   34
  See where he walkes with Mira by his side.   264   U79 New-yeares   18
  Up to their Ancestors; the rivers side, ...   281   U84 Kenelme   18
  Importune wish; and by her lov'd Lords side   394   Jane Ogle   23
  The Reverse on the backe side.   413   Ghyrlond   Ttl
SIDED
  Not they that sided her, Dame Poetry, ...   403   Inigo Jones 1   36
SIDES
  But as they come, on both sides he takes fees,   .   .   .   38   E37 Chev'ril   2
  To which, yet, of the sides himselfe he owes.   66   E102 Pembroke   8
  Whom Faction had not drawne to studie sides.   207   U43 Vulcan   104
  Whom fashion had not drawne to studie sides.   207   U43 Vulcan   V104
  Whom Faction had not taught to studie sides.   207   U43 Vulcan   V104
  On both sides doe your mischiefes with delight;   .   .   .   212   U43 Vulcan   204
SIDNEY
  Hath our great Sidney, Stella set, ...   181   U27 Ode Helen   25
SIEGE
  The Berghen siege, and taking in Breda, ...   214   U44 Speach   40
SIGH'D
  Nay, sigh'd a Sister, 'twas the Nun, Kate Arden,   .   .   .   209   U43 Vulcan   148
SIGHES
  Her broken sighes did never misse whole sense: .   .   .   288   U84 Muse   185
SIGHT
  What sight in searching the most antique springs! .   .   .   31   E14 Camden   8
  In meere out-formes, untill he lost his sight,   .   .   .   73   E114 Sydney   4
  Nor throng'st (when masquing is) to have a sight   .   .   .   96   F3 Wroth   9
  Nor throng'st (where masquing is) to have a sight .   .   .   96   F3 Wroth   V   9
  And giv'st thy gladder guests the sight;   97   F3 Wroth   28
  A beautie of that cleere, and sparkling sight,   .   .   .   112   F11 Epode   V 93
  But, he had not gain'd his sight   132   U2 How he saw   13
  At my face, that tooke my sight, ...   132   U2 How he saw   25
  But enjoy such a sight, ...   134   U2 Triumph   8
  So, as those that had your sight, ...   138   U2 Kisse   17
  Or have charg'd his sight of Crime, ...   138   U2 Kisse   32

	Page	Title	Line

SIGHT (cont.)

To have left all sight for you:	138	U2 Kisse	33
As since he dares not come within my sight.	151	U11 Dreame	14
As twice to trespasse in his sight,	152	U12 Corbet	26
Forme, Art or Ensigne, that hath scap'd your sight?	160	U14 Selden	48
Forme, Act or Ensigne, that hath scap'd your sight?	160	U14 Selden	V 48
May shine (through every chincke) to every sight	177	U25 Desmond	16
And now are out of sight.	180	U26 Ode High	8
When this appeares, just Lord, to your sharp sight,	186	U32 Elsmere	15
In all that is call'd lovely: take my sight	200	U42 Elegy Let	12
And Spinola have blushed at the sight.	214	U44 Speach	42
As but to stumble in her sight were shame,	220	U47 Tribe	70
This were a spectacle! A sight to draw	233	U59 Newcastle	13
All live dogs from the lane, and his shops sight,	241	U69 Friend Son	12
Hee stoop'd in all mens sight	244	U70 Ode	38
Betweene thy Tropicks, to arrest thy sight,	252	U75 Epithalam.	4
And the whole Banquet is full sight of God!	284	U84 Muse	65
Where Hee will be, all Beautie to the Sight;	286	U84 Muse	122
Among these Cates how glad the sight doth come	291	U85 Country	61
Admitted to the sight, although his friends	305	Horace	6
Much from the sight, which faire report will make	317	Horace	262
Will in the light be view'd: This, once, the sight	331	Horace	543
As the whole heard in sight,	366	Ode Who saith	26
Sweet Swan of Avon! what a sight it were	392	Shakespeare	71
And stop my sight, in every line I goe.	398	Drayton	78
Seal'd and deliver'd to her, in the sight	400	Lady Ogle	37

SIGHTED

| And strikes the quickest-sighted Judgement blinde. | 363 | Riches | 16 |

SIGHTES

| till th'one hath drownd the other in our sightes, | 361 | Palmer | 20 |

SIGHTS

| Harsh sights at home, Giles wisheth he were blind. | 40 | E42 Giles | 10 |
| As are the Glorious Scenes, at the great sights; | 220 | U47 Tribe | 66 |

SIGNE

In signe the Subject, and the Song will live,	262	U78 Digby	17
In heav'n the Signe of old Eridanus:	369	Ode Who saith	109
How long he did stay, at what signe he did Inne.	380	Coryat 3	26
On the new priming of thy old Signe postes	405	Inigo Jones 1	87

SIGNES

| Signes to new bond, forfeits: and cryes, god payes. | 30 | E12 Shift | 14 |

SILENCE

If hence thy silence be,	174	U23 Himselfe	13
Of vowes so sacred, and in silence made;	197	U40 Elegy That	14
With silence, and amazement! not with rude,	284	U84 Muse	78
With an uncomely silence failes my tongue?	293	U86 Hor.4:1	36

SILENT

And can to these be silent, Salisburie,	47	E63 Salisbury 2	9
In the silent sommer-nights,	103	F6 Celia 2	17
Stand silent by,	120	F14 Sydney	8
If hence they silent be,	174	U23 Himselfe	V 13
Or like a Ghost walke silent amongst men,	199	U41 Elegy Since	21
No friend to vertue, could be silent here.	224	U50 Countesse	8
Be silent, to the people	239	U67 Muses	5

SILENUS

| Or old Silenus, Bacchus guard, and Nurse. | 321 | Horace | 348 |

SILKE

All men are wormes: But this no man. In silke	31	E15 Court-worm	1
For Silke will draw some sneaking Songster thither.	200	U42 Elegy Let	26
Where I may handle Silke, as free, and neere,	200	U42 Elegy Let	30
With Sayles of silke, as the first notes	273	U84 Cradle	23

SILKEN

| Of the New Yeare, in a new silken warpe, | 263 | U79 New-yeares | 5 |

SILKES

Surly's old whore in her new silkes doth swim:	54	E82 Surly	1
Varietie of Silkes were on th'Exchange!	202	U42 Elegy Let	72
Another answers, 'Lasse, those Silkes are none,	202	U42 Elegy Let	74
What makes these Velvets, Silkes, and Lawne,	275	U84 Body	2

SILLERIES

| For newes) your Ville-royes, and Silleries, | 69 | E107 Hungry | 21 |

SILVER

| Or the drops in silver Thames, | 103 | F6 Celia 2 | 15 |
| That's six in silver; now within the Socket | 229 | U54 Squib | 13 |

SIMO

| Simo; and, of a talent wip'd his purse; | 321 | Horace | 347 |
| Simo, and of a talent cleans'd his purse; | 346 | Horace | V339/347 |

SIMPLE

We innocently met. No simple word,	65	E101 Supper	39
My tender, first, and simple yeeres	101	F4 To the World	41
But simple love of greatnesse, and of good;	246	U70 Ode	105
Be simple quite throughout, and wholly one.	307	Horace	32
Be simple quite throughout, and alwayes one.	339	Horace	V 32
But soft, and simple, at few holes breath'd time	319	Horace	289

SIMPLES

| the sweetest simples, and most soveraigne seedes. | 361 | Palmer | 12 |

SIMPLESSE

| On all that come her Simplesse to rebuke! | 253 | U75 Epithalam. | 44 |

SIMPLICITIE

As free simplicitie, to dis-avow,	62	E96 Donne 2	5
The world's pure gold, and wise simplicitie;	78	E122 Rudyerd 2	4
Her wary guardes, her wise simplicitie,	270	U81 Pawlet	40
Will honour'd be in all simplicitie!	284	U84 Muse	76

SIMPLICITY

| A wise simplicity; freindes alike-stated; | 295 | U90 Mart.10:47 | 7 |

		Page	Title	Line

SIMPLY
Simply my Band, his trust in me forsakes, ... 169 U17 Friend-Debt 12
SIN'
For, sin's so sweet, ... 129 U1 Father 12
SIN (See also SYNNS)
Thus, in his belly, can he change a sin, ... 76 E118 Gut 5
Forgive me this one foolish deadly sin, ... 171 U20 Shrub 2
Thinke but the Sin of all her sex, 'tis she! . . . 172 U20 Shrub 20
Upon the hope to have another sin . . . . . 193 U38 Elegy 'Tis 90
SINCE
And since, the whole land was preserv'd for thee. . . . 38 E35 James 2 10
Since men have left to doe praise-worthy things, . . . 49 E67 Suffolk 1
Then, since we (more then many) these truths know: . . 50 E70 Wm Roe 1 7
The Virgin, long-since fled from earth, I see, . . . 52 E74 Chancelor 9
Or then, or since, about our Muses springs, . . . 53 E79 Rutland 3
Since when, hee's sober againe, and all play's made. . . 56 E87 Hazard 6
Mill was the same. Since, both his body and face . . 57 E90 Mill 13
Yet, Satyrs, since the most of mankind bee . . . 60 E94 Bedford 3 7
Since he was gone, more then the one he weares. . . . 63 E97 Motion 17
For since, what ignorance, what pride is fled! . . . 73 E113 Overbury 7
Cryes out 'gainst cocking, since he cannot bet, . . . 76 E119 Shelton 3
But viewing him since (alas, too late) . . . . 77 E120 S. P. 19
Since they can only judge, that can conferre. . . . 83 E132 Sylvester 6
The citie since hath rais'd a Pyramide. . . . . 89 E133 Voyage 194
That since, my numbers are so cold, ... 93 F1 Why write no 11
And such since thou canst make thine owne content, . . 98 F3 Wroth 65
False world, good-night: since thou hast brought . . 100 F4 To the World 1
Since stird'st up jealousies and feares, . . . 101 F4 To the World 43
Since when it growes, and smells, I sweare, . . . 106 F9 Celia 3 15
Since when it lives, and smells, I sweare, . . . 106 F9 Celia 3 V 15
Which to effect (since no brest is so sure, . . . 109 F11 Epode 5
They speake; since you are truly that rare wife, . . 119 F13 Aubigny 110
Since he doth lacke . . . . 121 F14 Sydney 27
With all since bought. . . . . . . 129 U1 Father 22
Since I drew a Morning kisse . . . . . 137 U2 Kisse 2
As since he dares not come within my sight. . . . 151 U11 Dreame 14
For truly, since he left to be, ... 152 U12 Corbet 35
Since, naked, best Truth, and the Graces are. . . . 158 U14 Selden V 4
Since, being deceiv'd, I turne a sharper eye . . . 159 U14 Selden 23
And since our Daintie age, ... 175 U23 Himselfe 31
. . . in Queene Elizabeths Time, since lost, and recovered. . 176 U25 Desmond Ttl
Hath Petrarch since his Laura rais'd . . . . 181 U27 Ode Helen 21
Since I exscribe your Sonnets, am become . . . 182 U28 Worth 3
That they long since have refused . . . . . 184 U29 Fit of Rime 47
Thou art my Cause: whose manners since I knew, . . . 187 U33 Councellour 13
Since you must goe, and I must bid farewell, . . . 199 U41 Elegy Since 1
That since thou tak'st all envious care and paine, . . 203 U43 Vulcan 13
Left! and wit since to cover it with Tiles. . . . 209 U43 Vulcan 138
Since, Bacchus, thou art father . . . . . 220 U48 Bacchus 1
Since Bacon, and thy Lord was borne, and here; . . . 225 U51 Bacon 8
What then his Father was, that since is hee; . . . 225 U51 Bacon 11
But since the Wine hath steep'd my braine, . . . 230 U55 Burges 5
Since nothing can report that flame, ... 278 U84 Mind 15
Since nothing can report her flame, ... 278 U84 Mind V 15
But in the maine worke haplesse: since he knowes . . 307 Horace 48
Nor is't long since, they did with patience take . . 323 Horace 375
Who, since, to sing the Pythian rites is heard, . . 333 Horace 591
Their motives were, since it had not to do . . . 371 Fletcher 9
Since he treads in no other Mans steps but his owne. . . 379 Coryat 3 12
But, since he cannot, Reader, looke . . . . 390 Reader 9
Sent forth, or since did from their ashes come. . . 391 Shakespeare 40
As, since, she will vouchsafe no other Wit. . . . 392 Shakespeare 50
Which, since thy flight from hence, hath mourn'd like night, . 392 Shakespeare 79
But of one Husband; and since he left life, . . . 394 Jane Ogle 16
Yett: since the bright, and wyse, ... 420 Ode:If Men 28
SINCERE
Is done for gaine: If't be, 'tis not sincere. . . . 169 U17 Friend-Debt 6
Thy sincere practise, breeds not thee a fame . . . 187 U33 Councellour 39
SINDGE
Sindge Capons, or poore Pigges, dropping their eyes; . . 205 U43 Vulcan 53
Sindge Capons, or crispe Pigges, dropping their eyes; . . 205 U43 Vulcan V 53
SINEWES
Hath neither soule, nor sinewes. Loftie he . . . 307 Horace 37
Wants strength, and sinewes, as his spirits were done; . . 339 Horace V 38/ 37
SING
To greatnesse, Cary, I sing that, and thee. . . . 48 E66 Cary 2
Item, the babylonian song you sing; . . . . 51 E73 Fine Grand 9
Are all but Luthers beere, to this I sing. . . . 65 E101 Supper 34
Except the duell. Can sing songs, and catches; . . 74 E115 Honest Man 13
I Sing the brave adventure of two wights, . . . 84 E133 Voyage 21
And must I sing? what subject shall I chuse? . . . 107 F10 Proludium 1
We must sing too? what subject shall we chuse? . . . 107 F10 Proludium V 1
And now an Epode to deepe eares I sing. . . . 108 F10 Proludium 30
And now an Epode to deepe eares we sing. . . . 108 F10 Proludium V 30
As this chaste love we sing. . . . . . 111 F11 Epode 68
As this chaste love I sing. . . . . . 111 F11 Epode V 68
To curious light, the notes, I then shall sing, . . 115 F12 Rutland 76
To curious light, to notes, I then shall sing, . . 115 F12 Rutland V 76
Heare, what the Muses sing about thy roote, . . . 119 F13 Aubigny 100
Some sing, ... 120 F14 Sydney 4
I Sing the birth, was borne to night, ... 130 U1 Nativitie 1
What need of mee? doe you but sing, ... 143 U3 Musicall 13
O sing not you then, lest the best . . . . 144 U3 Musicall 21

```
                                                      Page      Title        Line

SING   (cont.)
    Sing you no more then, lest the best     .    .     .      144   U3 Musicall      V 21
    To make us still sing o're, and o're,    .    .     .      145   U5 Woman-kind       3
    And if wee must, let's sing of you.   .    .     .     .   145   U5 Woman-kind       6
    And yours of whom I sing be such      .    .     .     .   173   U22 Elegy Tho       2
    But sing high and aloofe,          .     .     .     .     175   U23 Himselfe       35
    That I may sing my thoughts, in some unvulgar straine.    177   U25 Desmond        13
    Where men may see whom I doe sing?         .    .     .    182   U27 Ode Helen      32
    Give me a deep-crown'd-Bowle, that I may sing    .    .    225   U51 Bacon          19
    His Poet leave to sing his House-hold true;   .    .     . 241   U68 House-hold      6
    That day, which I predestin'd am to sing,  .    .     .    262   U78 Digby        V 17
    We sing the best of Monarchs, Masters, Men;   .    .      263   U79 New-yeares      7
    Of Pan wee sing, the best of Hunters, Pan,    .    .      264   U79 New-yeares     20
    Rivers, and Vallies, Eccho what wee sing.   .    .     .   264   U79 New-yeares     27
    Of Pan wee sing, the Chiefe of Leaders, Pan,   .    .     264   U79 New-yeares     28
    Rivers, and Valleys, Eccho what wee sing.  .    .     .    264   U79 New-yeares     35
    Let Angels sing her glories, who did call   .    .     .   270   U81 Pawlet         63
    I Sing the just, and uncontrol'd Descent    .    .     .   274   U84 Descent         1
    That, planted round, there sing before the Lamb,    .     285   U84 Muse           89
    The Youths and tender Maids shall sing thy praise:   .    292   U86 Hor.4:1        26
    I sing a noble Warre, and Priam's Fate.   .    .     .     313   Horace            196
    Must maintaine manly; not be heard to sing,   .    .      317   Horace            277
    Must manly keep, and not be heard to sing   .    .     .   345   Horace           V277
    Those that did sing, and act: their faces dy'd   .    .    319   Horace            314
    Deserves no pardon; or who'd play, and sing    .    .     329   Horace            531
    Who, since, to sing the Pythian rites is heard,    .      333   Horace            591
    Who now to sing the Pythian Rites is heard,  .    .     .  353   Horace           V591
    Neere which, the Thespiad's sing;   .    .     .     .     366   Ode Who saith      18
    When him alone we sing)         .     .     .     .     .   368   Ode Who saith      63
    (Which makes him sing    .    .     .     .     .     .    369   Ode Who saith     102
SINGE
    and now an Epode, to deepe Eares, wee singe.    .    .    108   F10 Proludium      16
SINGER
    Lest of the singer Apollo, and Muses fam'd   .    .     .  353   Horace        V579/501
    Haste, Haste, sweete Singer: Nor to Tine,   .    .     .   368   Ode Who saith      73
SINGING
    'Tis hee, 'tis hee, in singing hee,    .    .     .     .  265   U79 New-yeares     54
    'Tis hee, 'tis hee, in singing hee,    .    .     .     .  265   U79 New-yeares     66
SINGLE
    In single paths, dangers with ease are watch'd:   .     . 118   F13 Aubigny        57
    As a poore single flatterer, without Baud,   .    .     . 167   U15 Friend-Wars   158
    Like single; so, there is a third, commixt,   .    .     . 284   U84 Muse           53
    To say but one, were single.  Then it chimes,    .    .   389   Aleman              3
SINGS
    That not a Nymph now sings?     .     .     .     .     .  174   U23 Himselfe       10
    Or in Moore-fields, this other night! sings one,   .     202   U42 Elegy Let      73
    Who sings so sweet, and with such cunning plaies,   .    293   U87 Hor.3:9        10
SING'ST
    Good Omen to him, in the note thou sing'st,   .    .     . 263   U78 Digby          22
    Good fortune to him, in the note thou sing'st,    .    .  263   U78 Digby        V 22
SINKE
    And many a sinke pour'd out her rage anenst 'hem;   .    . 86   E133 Voyage        75
    They are the Noblest benefits, and sinke   .    .     .   153   U13 Sacvile        19
    Of putrid flesh alive! of blood, the sinke!   .    .     . 172   U21 Ltl Shrub       9
    Sinke not beneath these terrors:    .     .     .     .    177   U25 Desmond        30
SINKES
    The sinkes ran grease, and haire of meazled hogs,    .    88   E133 Voyage       145
SINKETH
    And highest; sinketh to the lowest, and worst.   .    .   331   Horace            564
SINNE'
    As farre as Sinne's from lightnesse.   .    .     .     .  364   Ode Splendor        4
SINNE
    Th'expence in odours is a most vaine sinne,   .    .     . 33    E20 Cod 2           1
    Wee, sad for him, may glorie, and not sinne.   .    .     35    E27 Roe 1           8
    My sinne was too much hope of thee, lov'd boy,    .    .   41    E45 First Son       2
    Touch'd with the sinne of false play, in his punque,   .  56    E87 Hazard          1
    But in the view, doth interrupt their sinne;    .    .     66    E102 Pembroke      18
    (Their rudenesse then is thought no sinne)   .    .     .  98    F3 Wroth           54
    By being organes to great sinne,    .     .     .     .    99    F3 Wroth           86
    'Tis no sinne, loves fruit to steale,   .    .     .     . 102   F5 Celia 1         15
    Of his dull god-head, were sinne.  Ile implore    .    .  107   F10 Proludium       6
    Of his dull god-head, were sinne.  Lets implore   .    .  107   F10 Proludium     V  6
    Cannot so safely sinne.  Their chastitie   .    .     .   111   F11 Epode          81
    Man may securely sinne, but safely never.   .    .     .  113   F11 Epode         116
    A man may safely sinne, securely never.   .    .     .    113   F11 Epode        V116
    For what a sinne 'gainst your great fathers spirit,   .   114   F12 Rutland        31
    With sinne and vice, though with a throne endew'd;   .    116   F13 Aubigny        10
    And call it their brave sinne.  For such there be    .    119   F13 Aubigny        85
    That doe sinne onely for the infamie:   .    .     .     . 119   F13 Aubigny        86
    Conceiv'd in sinne, and unto labour borne,   .    .     .  122   F15 Heaven         18
    By sinne, and Sathan; and my flesh misus'd,   .    .     . 127   U1 Trinitie         6
    Sinne, Death, and Hell,      .     .     .     .     .     129   U1 Father          23
    Who made himselfe the price of sinne,   .    .     .     . 130   U1 Nativitie       20
    As I would urge Authoritie for sinne.   .    .     .     . 191   U38 Elegy 'Tis     26
    The sinne of Boast, or other countermine    .    .     .  198   U40 Elegy That     46
    That to speake well, thinke it above all sinne,   .    .  218   U47 Tribe          19
    A Nations sinne got pardon'd! 'twere a taske    .    .     234   U61 Epigram        12
    And wee doe weepe, to water, for our sinne.   .    .     . 234   U61 Epigram        15
    The Serpents head: Gets above Death, and Sinne,    .     . 272   U81 Pawlet         99
    He will expiate this sinne with converting the Jewes.   . 375   Coryat 1           21
SINNERS
    1. The Sinners Sacrifice. To the Holy Trinitie.    .    . 127   U1 Trinitie       Ttl
    All-gracious God, the Sinners sacrifice,   .    .     .   127   U1 Trinitie         9
```

		Page	Title	Line

SINNERS (cont.)
In loves schoole, and yet no sinners. . . . . . 141 U2 Her man 32
In loves art, and yet no sinners. . . . . . 141 U2 Her man V 32
SINNE'S
As farre as Sinne's from lightnesse. . . . . 364 Ode Splendor 4
SINNES
For all night-sinnes, with others wives, unknowne, . . 39 E39 Colt 1
The ports of death are sinnes; of life, good deeds: . . 53 E80 Life/Death 1
For none ere tooke that pleasure in sinnes sense, . . 60 E94 Bedford 3 9
Laden with plague-sores, and their sinnes, were heard, . 84 E133 Voyage 17
Then he, which for sinnes penaltie forbeares. . . . 112 F11 Epode 89
Then he, that for sinnes penaltie forbeares. . . . 112 F11 Epode V 89
His heart sinnes, though he feares. . . . . 112 F11 Epode 90
That, laden with my sinnes, I seeke for ease? . . 122 F15 Heaven 4
SIN'S
For, sin's so sweet, ... 129 U1 Father 12
SIPP
But might I of love's Nectar sipp, ... 106 F9 Celia 3 V 7
SIPT
Who ever sipt at Baphyre river, ... 367 Ode Who saith 57
SIR (See also SURSHIP)
On Sir Cod the perfumed. . . . . . . 33 E19 Cod 1 Ttl
To the same Sir Cod. . . . . . . 33 E20 Cod 2 Ttl
Except thou could'st, Sir Cod, weare them within. . . 33 E20 Cod 2 2
On Sir Voluptuous Beast. . . . . . . 34 E25 Beast 1 Ttl
On Sir John Roe. . . . . 35 E27 Roe 1 Ttl
To Sir Annual Tilter. . . . . . . 36 E29 Tilter Ttl
On Sir John Roe. . . . . 37 E32 Roe 2 Ttl
To Sir Lucklesse Woo-all. . . . . . . 42 E46 Luckless 1 Ttl
Is this the Sir, who, some wast wife to winne, . . 42 E46 Luckless 1 1
Sir Lucklesse, troth, for lucks sake passe by one: . . 42 E47 Luckless 2 1
To Sir Cod. . . . . 42 E50 Cod 3 Ttl
To Sir Henrie Cary. . . . . 48 E66 Cary Ttl
To Sir Henry Goodyere. . . . . . . 55 E85 Goodyere 1 Ttl
To Sir Horace Vere. . . . . 58 E91 Vere Ttl
To the worthy Sir Horace Vere. . . . . . 58 E91 Vere VTtl
To Sir John Radcliffe. . . . . . . 60 E93 Radcliffe Ttl
To Sir Henrie Savile. . . . . . . 61 E95 Savile Ttl
To Sir Thomas Roe. . . . . 63 E98 Th Roe 1 Ttl
To night, grave sir, both my poore house, and I . . 64 E101 Supper 1
It is the faire acceptance, Sir, creates . . . . 64 E101 Supper 7
To Sir Edward Herbert. . . . . . . 68 E106 E Herbert Ttl
To Sir Henry Nevil. . . . . 70 E109 Nevil Ttl
To Sir Thomas Overbury. . . . . . . 73 E113 Overbury Ttl
To Sir William Jephson. . . . . . . 75 E116 Jephson Ttl
To Sir Raph Shelton. . . . . . . 76 E119 Shelton Ttl
To Sir William Uvedale. . . . . . . 79 E125 Uvedale Ttl
To Sir Robert Wroth. . . . . . . 96 F3 Wroth Ttl
To Sir Robert Wroth in praise of a Country life. Epode. . 96 F3 Wroth VTtl
Ode. To Sir William Sydney, on his Birth-day. . . 120 F14 Sydney Ttl
An Epistle to Sir Edward Sacvile, now Earle of Dorset. . 153 U13 Sacvile Ttl
Now dam'mee, Sir, if you shall not command . . . 154 U13 Sacvile 53
And you, Sir, know it well, to whom I write, . . . 156 U13 Sacvile 109
See the grave, sower, and supercilious Sir . . . 162 U15 Friend-Wars 19
They are not, Sir, worst Owers, that doe pay . . . 169 U17 Friend-Debt 1
Art, her false servant; Nor, for Sir Hugh Plat, . . 188 U34 Small Poxe 7
Sir, I am thankfull, first, to heaven, for you; . . 189 U37 Friend-Book 1
Well did thy craftie Clerke, and Knight, Sir Hugh, . . 214 U44 Speach 33
An Epigram on Sir Edward Coke, when . . . . . 217 U46 Coke Ttl
Sir, you are Sealed of the Tribe of Ben. . . . 220 U47 Tribe 78
Of bold Sir Bevis, and his Arundell: . . . . 228 U53 Newcastle 10
To Sir Robert Pie: . . . . 231 U57 Burges 4
To Sir Lucius Carey, on the death of his Brother Morison . 242 U70 Ode VTtl
. . . paire, Sir Lucius Cary, and Sir H. Morison. . . 242 U70 Ode Ttl
To Sir Kenelme Digby. An Epigram . . . . . 262 U78 Digby VTtl
. . . on her Husband, Sir Kenelme Digby. . . . 262 U78 Digby Ttl
. . . late Wife of Sir Kenelme Digby, Knight: . . . 272 U84 Eupheme Ttl
And will you, worthy Sonne, Sir, knowing this, . . 285 U84 Muse 97
You Sir, the elder brother, though you are . . . 331 Horace 545
. . . in the Behalfe of the two Noble Brothers sir Robert . . 382 Rich Ttl
. . . Sir John Beaumont, Baronet. . . . . 400 Beaumont Ttl
Sir Inigo doth feare it as I heare . . . . . 407 Inigo Jones 3 1
SIRE
Not labour'd for, but left thee by thy Sire, . . . 295 U90 Mart.10:47 3
Most Writers, noble Sire, and either Sonne, . . . 307 Horace 33
Father, and sons right worthy of your Sire, . . . 339 Horace V 34
SIRENAS
I looke on Cynthia, and Sirenas sport, ... 398 Drayton 80
SIRES
Let him, then hardest sires, more disinherit, . . . 99 F3 Wroth 77
With his owne Oxen tills his Sires left lands, . . . 289 U85 Country 3
SIRRUP
And take some sirrup after; so doe I, ... 197 U40 Elegy That 5
SIS
Or with Secretarie Sis . . . . . . 140 U2 Promise 25
SISTER
'Twill see it's sister naked, ere a sword. . . . 74 E115 Honest Man 22
The brother trades a sister; and the friend . . . 165 U15 Friend-Wars 93
Nay, sigh'd a Sister, 'twas the Nun, Kate Arden, . . 209 U43 Vulcan 148
Nay, sayth a sister, Venus Nun, Kate Arden, . . . 209 U43 Vulcan V148
And Sister to just Lewis! . . . . . . 240 U67 Muses 27
. . . Esme D. of Lenox deceased, and Sister of the . . . 252 U75 Epithalam. Ttl
Their Sister-tunes, from Thames his either side, . . 253 U75 Epithalam. 34

SISTER   (cont.)
And Sister: darting forth a dazling light . . . . 253 U75 Epithalam.   43
Upon a Thomas, or a Sister call; . . . . 258 U75 Epithalam. V171
New yeares, expect new gifts: Sister, your Harpe, . . . 263 U79 New-yeares   1
Sister of Pan, and glory of the Spring: . . . . 264 U79 New-yeares 25
There shall the Brother, with the Sister walke, . . . 285 U84 Muse 117
SISTERS
Though he would steale his sisters Pegasus, ... 107 F10 Proludium 23
Chear'd her faire Sisters in her race to runne! . . . 270 U81 Pawlet 58
SISTER-TUNES
Their Sister-tunes, from Thames his either side, . . . 253 U75 Epithalam. 34
SIT
That's, sit, and eate: doe not my eares abuse. . . . 68 E107 Hungry   2
And I not faine to sit (as some, this day, ... 95 F2 Penshurst 65
Sit mixt with losse of state, or reverence. . . . . 98 F3 Wroth 57
And brooding o're it sit, with broadest eyes, . . . 99 F3 Wroth 83
Where I sit and proyne my wings . . . . . 137 U2 Cupid 35
Or, that did you sit, or walke, ... 138 U2 Kisse 13
Nay, I will not let you sit . . . . . 140 U2 Promise 21
His Clothes rich, and band sit neat, ... 142 U2 Exception   4
We were not bred to sit on stooles, ... 146 U6 Defence   3
To draw a thing that cannot sit. . . . . 277 U84 Mind   8
In his eternall Kingdome, where we sit . . . . 286 U84 Muse 145
Would sit in an Infirmery, whole dayes . . . . 288 U84 Muse 195
Or trundling Wheele, he can sit still, from all; . . . 331 Horace 568
That sit upon the Comon Draught: or Strand! . . . 408 Inigo Jones 3 13
That sit to censure Playes, yet know not when, . . . 414 Rutter   8
SITS
That sits in shadow of Apollo's tree. . . . . 149 U9 Picture 10
Ready to cast, at one, whose band sits ill, . . . 164 U15 Friend-Wars 69
His lynes, and hourely sits the Poets horse? . . . 200 U42 Elegy Let   8
Wherein she sits so richly drest, ... 251 U74 Weston 14
And sits, till th'Epilogue saies Clap, or Crowne: . . . 315 Horace 222
The wise, and many-headed Bench, that sits . . . 370 Fletcher   1
That sits watering with the Muses. . . . . 657 Door Apollo 10
SITTING
Sitting, and ready to be drawne, ... 275 U84 Body   1
Next sitting we will draw her mind. . . . . 277 U84 Body 32
SIX
Told six and fortie yeares, ... 150 U9 Picture V 15
Will be remembred by Six Clerkes, to one. . . . 210 U43 Vulcan 172
That's six in silver; now within the Socket . . . 229 U54 Squib 13
That may judge for his six-pence) had, before . . . 371 Fletcher   7
SIXE
At sixe moneths end, shee parted hence . . . . 33 E22 Daughter   5
At sixe and twentie, ripe. You shall 'hem meet, . . . 58 E92 New Crie   4
Of sixe times to, and fro, without embassage, . . . 85 E133 Voyage 34
But say, all sixe good men, what answer yee? . . . 210 U43 Vulcan 173
Of Trimeter, when yet it was sixe-pac'd, . . . 323 Horace 373
Sixe ounces. O, when once the canker'd rust, . . . 327 Horace 472
SIXE-PAC'D
Of Trimeter, when yet it was sixe-pac'd, . . . 323 Horace 373
SIXES
They meet in sixes, and at every mart, ... 59 E92 New Crie 21
SIX-PENCE
That may judge for his six-pence) had, before . . . 371 Fletcher   7
SIXTEENTH
This sixteenth of November, ... 239 U67 Muses   2
SIXTIETH
And so doe I. This is the sixtieth yeare . . . 225 U51 Bacon   7
SKARFE
That so much skarfe of France, and hat, and fether, . . . 56 E88 Monsieur   3
SKEUOPOIOS
His name is Skeuopoios wee all knowe, ... 404 Inigo Jones 1 60
SKIE
The skie not falling, thinke we may have larkes. . . . 65 E101 Supper 16
Who placed Jasons Argo in the skie? . . . . 115 F12 Rutland 59
In a calme skie, then when the heaven is horl'd . . . 193 U38 Elegy 'Tis 74
SKIES
All the gazers on the skies . . . . . 39 E40 Ratcliffe   5
And up againe, in skies, and aire to vent . . . 368 Ode Who saith 77
SKILFULL
And no lesse wise, then skilfull in the lawes; . . . 52 E74 Chancelor   6
As skilfull Roscius, and grave Aesope, men, . . . 56 E89 Allen   3
The skilfull mischife of a rovinge Eye . . . 108 F10 Proludium   5
SKILL
What name, what skill, what faith hast thou in things! . . . 31 E14 Camden   7
Better'd thy trust to letters; that thy skill; . . . 63 E99 Th Roe 2   2
Dar'st breath in any ayre; and with safe skill, . . . 76 E119 Shelton   9
His love unto the Muses, when his skill . . . 114 F12 Rutland 33
Or appetite of offending, but a skill, . . . 156 U13 Sacvile 107
Which Grace shall I make love to first? your skill, . . . 159 U14 Selden 35
Or skill, to carry out an evill cause! . . . 187 U33 Councellour 18
And skill in thee, now, grew Authoritie; . . . 217 U46 Coke 10
The noble Science, and the maistring skill . . . 232 U59 Newcastle   3
Painted a Dog, that now his subtler skill . . . 241 U69 Friend Son 10
Thy skill hath made of ranck dispised weedes; . . . 361 Palmer 10
Or skill of making matches in my life: . . . 386 Husband   7
He may have skill & judgment to designe . . . 406 Inigo Jones 2   7
or Malyce to make Faultes, which nowe is skill. . . . 421 Censure 11
SKIN
The slie Ulysses stole in a sheepes-skin, . . . 87 E133 Voyage 113
Skin as smooth as any rush, ... 141 U2 Her man 27

SKIN (cont.)
   Not letting goe the skin, where he drawes food, . . . 355 Horace V679
SKINKERS
   Cries Old Sym, the King of Skinkers; . . . . . 657 Door Apollo 8
SKINS
   To put the skins, and offall in a pastie? . . . . 88 E133 Voyage 148
SKIP
   Then can a flea at twise skip i'the Map. . . . . 69 E107 Hungry 18
SKIPPING
   And set us all on skipping, ... 222 U48 Bacchus 51
SKY
   As Summers sky, or purged Ayre, ... 147 U7 Nymph 17
SKYE
   An Eagle towring in the skye, ... 278 U84 Mind 10
SLACK
   Chestnut colour, or more slack . . . . . 141 U2 Her man 13
   Too stubborne for Commands so slack: 292 U86 Hor.4:1 7
SLACKE
   At every line some pinn thereof should slacke . . . 395 May 5
SLAINE
   Is my Mothers! Hearts of slaine . . . . 137 U2 Cupid 31
   Or at the Feast of Bounds, the Lambe then slaine, . . 291 U85 Country 59
SLANDER
   Both arm'd with wealth, and slander to oppose, . . 186 U32 Elsmere 8
   Il may Ben Johnson slander so his feete, . . . 418 Answer 5
SLANDERERS
   Lewd slanderers, soft whisperers that let blood . . 167 U15 Friend-Wars 165
SLANDERS
   An inginer, in slanders, of all fashions, ... 75 E115 Honest Man 31
SLAUGHTERS
   From slaughters, and foule life; and for the same . . 327 Horace 481
SLAVE
   To make our sense our slave. . . . . . 109 F11 Epode 18
   To free a slave, ... 129 U1 Father 20
   But he that's both, and slave to boote, shall live, . . 167 U15 Friend-Wars 160
   But he that's both, and slave to both, shall live, . . 167 U15 Friend-Wars V160
SLAVES
   Row close then, slaves. Alas, they will beshite us. . . 86 E133 Voyage 90
SLAY
   For so will sorrow slay me; . . . . . 145 U4 Song 10
SLEEKED
   Sleeked limmes, and finest blood? . . . . 105 F8 Sicknesse 23
   Sleeked limmes, and fyned blood? . . . . 105 F8 Sicknesse V 23
SLEEPE
   Th'other let it sleepe with death: . . . . 79 E124 Elizabeth 10
   And makes sleepe softer then it is! . . . . 97 F3 Wroth 20
   That they may sleepe with scarres in age. . . . 98 F3 Wroth 70
   The secrets, that shall breake their sleepe: . . . 99 F3 Wroth 88
   (That should ring larum to the heart) doth sleepe, . . 109 F11 Epode 23
   (That shal ring larum to the heart) doth sleepe, . . 109 F11 Epode V 23
   That falls like sleepe on lovers, and combines . . 110 F11 Epode 49
   You shall neither eat, nor sleepe, ... 140 U2 Promise 15
   Sleepe, and the Grave will wake. . . . . 143 U3 Musicall 14
   Of sleepe againe, who was his Aid; . . . . 151 U11 Dreame 12
   And sleepe so guiltie and afraid, ... 151 U11 Dreame 13
   And Fame wake for me, when I yeeld to sleepe. . . 190 U37 Friend-Book 15
   The Jewell of your name, as close as sleepe . . . 198 U40 Elegy That 42
   Sleepe in a Virgins bosome without feare, . . . 230 U56 Covell 15
   Indeed, she is not dead! but laid to sleepe . . . 283 U84 Muse 45
   And all invite to easie sleepe. . . . . 290 U85 Country 28
   Sleepe, that will make the darkest howres swift-pac't; . . 295 U90 Mart.10:47 7
   And ill-penn'd things, I shall, or sleepe, or smile. . . 311 Horace 148
   But, I confesse, that, in a long worke, sleepe . . . 329 Horace 537
   Though I confesse, that, in a long worke, sleepe . . 351 Horace V513/537
SLEEPES
   Knowledge, that sleepes, doth die; . . . . 174 U23 Himselfe 3
   Who seldome sleepes! whom bad men only hate! . . 250 U73 Weston 6
SLEEPIE
   Mans buried honour, in his sleepie life: . . . 162 U15 Friend-Wars 7
   Sleepie, or stupid Nature, couldst thou part . . . 282 U84 Muse 15
SLEEPING
   T'have wak'd, if sleeping, Spaines Ambassadour, . . 213 U44 Speach 4
SLEIGHT (DISDAIN)
   Valour! to sleight it, being done to you! . . . 233 U59 Newcastle 16
SLEIGHT
   To ope' the character. They'have found the sleight . . 59 E92 New Crie 27
   To render word for word: nor with thy sleight . . 313 Horace 191
SLID
   As it slid moulded off from Heaven. . . . 280 U84 Mind 56
SLIDE
   Whilst from the higher Bankes doe slide the floods; . . 290 U85 Country 25
SLIDES
   From fearefull back-slides; And the debt we'are in, . . 412 Sutcliffe 15
SLIDING
   Still in their leaves, throughout the sliding yeares, . . 309 Horace 86
SLIE
   The slie Ulysses stole in a sheepes-skin, . . . 87 E133 Voyage 113
SLIGHT
   And at the Pope, and Spaine slight faces make. . . 59 E92 New Crie 34
   And slight the same. . . . . . 129 U1 Father 27
   Whom I adore so much, should so slight me, . . 149 U9 Picture 4
   Us forth, by some Celestiall slight . . . . 279 U84 Mind 47

		Page	Title	Line
SLIGHTLY				
You will not from the paper slightly passe:		117	F13 Aubigny	25
SLIGHTS				
And, told of this, he slights it. Tut, such crimes		45	E56 Poet-Ape	9
SLIP				
Slip no occasion; As time stands not still,		171	U19 Elegy By	19
SLIP'D				
They both are slip'd to Bed; Shut fast the Doore,		258	U75 Epithalam.	185
SLIPPER				
Or slipper was left off, and kisse it too,		201	U42 Elegy Let	56
SLIPPERY				
And see both climing up the slippery staire		395	May	2
SLIPS (COINS)				
For there are many slips, and Counterfeits.		216	U45 Squib	17
SLIPS				
He pardons slips, goes by a world of ills,		193	U38 Elegy 'Tis	69
SLIT				
Mythology there painted on slit deale!		404	Inigo Jones 1	48
Cropt, branded, slit, neck-stockt; go, you are stript.		411	Gill	16
SLOTH				
Who, to upbraid the sloth of this our time,		48	E66 Cary	5
Nor wants it here through penurie, or sloth,		152	U12 Corbet	39
Buried in ease and sloth?		174	U23 Himselfe	2
Looke on thy sloth, and give thy selfe undone,		283	U84 Muse	21
With sloth, yet greedy still of what's to come:		317	Horace	246
SLOW				
Here's a shaft, thou art to slow!		132	U2 How he saw	10
Now swift, now slow, now tame, now wild;		189	U36 Song	14
The same that thou art promis'd, but be slow,		237	U65 Prince	6
The same that thou hast promis'd, but be slow,		237	U65 Prince	V 6
To endure counsell: a Provider slow		315	Horace	233
In at the eare, doe stirre the mind more slow		317	Horace	257
More slow, and come more weightie to the eare:		323	Horace	378
Slow Arar, nor swift Rhone; the Loyre, nor Seine,		369	Ode Who saith	117
SLOWER				
Though slower Spaine; and Italy mature.		368	Ode Who saith	88
SLUGGISH				
The sluggish gaping auditor devoures;		45	E56 Poet-Ape	10
Thou sluggish spawne, that canst, but wilt not see?		250	U73 Weston	8
SLYDING				
With slyding windowes, & false Lights a top!		407	Inigo Jones 2	10
SMALL				
With thy small stocke, why art thou ventring still,		72	E112 Gamster	1
Doe but consider this small dust,		148	U8 Houre-glasse	1
An Epigram. To the small Poxe.		188	U34 Small Poxe	Ttl
Or in small Fagots have him blaze about		211	U43 Vulcan	185
From Court, while yet thy fame hath some small day;		223	U49 Pucell	36
To compare small with great, as still we owe		238	U66 Queene	12
In small proportions, we just beautie see:		245	U70 Ode	73
With their pellets of small wit,		259	U76 Petition	22
Or straines on his small forke his subtill nets		290	U85 Country	33
Or straines on his small forke his subtler nets		290	U85 Country	V 33
If I can give some small increase? when, loe,		309	Horace	80
Of some small thankfull land: whether he bee		313	Horace	166
Built a small-timbred Stage, and taught them talke		319	Horace	317
And though thou hadst small Latine, and lesse Greeke,		391	Shakespeare	31
I send this small, but hearty testimony: and with charge,		666	Glover	5
SMALLEST				
The smallest courtesies with thankes, I make		153	U13 Sacvile	16
The smallest Fibre of our flesh; he can		286	U84 Muse	151
As not the smallest joint, or gentlest word		395	May	21
SMALL-TIMBRED				
Built a small-timbred Stage, and taught them talke		319	Horace	317
SMELL				
What, to make legs? yes, and to smell most sweet,		215	U44 Speach	90
Thy Dirty braines, Men smell thy want of worth.		409	Detractor	22
SMELLING				
Things manly, and not smelling parasite.		48	E65 Muse	14
SMELLS				
Since when it growes, and smells, I sweare,		106	F9 Celia 3	15
Since when it lives, and smells, I sweare,		106	F9 Celia 3	V 15
SMELT				
Or have smelt o'the bud o'the Brier?		135	U2 Triumph	27
SMILE				
How comes it all things so about thee smile?		225	U51 Bacon	2
To make the hearts of a whole Nation smile,		238	U66 Queene	10
And ill-penn'd things, I shall, or sleepe, or smile.		311	Horace	148
SMILES				
For offring, with thy smiles, my wit to grace,		45	E58 Groome	3
Shee is Venus, when she smiles,		137	U2 Cupid	52
Her joyes, her smiles, her loves, as readers take		182	U28 Worth	13
Smiles in his Sphaere, to see the rest affect,		366	Ode Who saith	13
SMILING				
Now that the harth is crown'd with smiling fire,		120	F14 Sydney	1
In smiling L'envoye, as he would deride		202	U42 Elegy Let	75
And when he smiling finds his Grace		292	U86 Hor.4:1	17
To pitty him, as smiling at his Feat		405	Inigo Jones 1	71
SMIL'ST				
O, now thou smil'st, faire Sun, and shin'st, as thou wouldst stay!		254	U75 Epithalam.	64
SMITH				
That, at thy birth, mad'st the poore Smith affraid,		107	F10 Proludium	14
To be that Smith; then live, mark'd one of those,		307	Horace	51
An honest Bilbo-Smith would make good blades,		410	Brome	15

		Page	Title	Line
SMITHS				
For none but Smiths would have made thee a God.		208	U43 Vulcan	117
SMOAKE				
To live in Sea-coale, and goe forth in smoake;		211	U43 Vulcan	181
To live in Sea-coale, and goe out in smoake;		211	U43 Vulcan	V181
Hee thinkes not, how to give you smoake from light,		315	Horace	203
But light from smoake; that he may draw his bright		315	Horace	204
SMOCK				
Item, your owne, sew'd in your mistris smock.		51	E73 Fine Grand	17
That chanc'd the lace, laid on a Smock, to see,		201	U42 Elegy Let	66
SMOOTH				
Smooth as is the Billiard Ball:		141	U2 Her man	20
Skin as smooth as any rush,		141	U2 Her man	27
Shoot forth in smooth and comely spaces; have		157	U13 Sacvile	150
As smooth as Oyle pour'd forth, and calme		280	U84 Mind	59
Smooth, soft, and sweet, in all a floud		280	U84 Mind	61
Obscure. This, striving to run smooth, and flow,		307	Horace	36
Obscure. Another striving smooth to runne,		339	Horace	V 37/ 36
And in smooth Cypresse boxes to be keep'd?		327	Horace	476
So soft, and smooth it handles, the whole piece,		415	Rutter	17
SMOOTHER				
Doe but marke, her forehead's smoother		134	U2 Triumph	15
SMUTCH'D				
Before the soyle hath smutch'd it?		134	U2 Triumph	24
SNAKE				
You'ld reade a Snake, in his next Song.		260	U76 Petition	32
To eate a Snake, in his next Song.		260	U76 Petition	V 32
Upon the Stage, the figure of a Snake.		317	Horace	268
SNAKIE				
Crush'd in the snakie brakes, that he had past!		162	U15 Friend-Wars	18
SNARES				
Of toyes, and trifles, traps, and snares,		100	F4 To the World	18
Cast in thousand snares, and rings		141	U2 Her man	11
And snares the fearfull Hare, and new-come Crane,		290	U85 Country	35
SNATCH				
All the Towne-curs take each their snatch at me.		155	U13 Sacvile	72
SNATCHT				
Not snatcht them hence in one poor minutes rage.		205	U43 Vulcan	V 56
SNEAKING				
For Silke will draw some sneaking Songster thither.		200	U42 Elegy Let	26
SNORE				
Angry. Sometimes, I heare good Homer snore.		329	Horace	536
Angry, if once I heare good Homer snore.		351	Horace	V512/536
SNORTS				
Goe, crampe dull Mars, light Venus, when he snorts,		107	F10 Proludium	16
SNOUT				
With faire black eyes, and hair, and some vile snout.		339	Horace	V 54/ 52
SNOW				
Have you mark'd but the fall o'the Snow		134	U2 Triumph	23
Have you seene the fall o'the Snow		135	U2 Triumph	V 23
Front, an ample field of snow;		141	U2 Her man	18
Forehead large, and white as snow;		141	U2 Her man	V 18
Then when the thundring Jove his Snow and showres		290	U85 Country	29
The Vale, that bred thee pure, as her Hills Snow.		367	Ode Who saith	40
SNUFFE				
Who, when you'have burnt your selves downe to the snuffe,		45	E59 Spies	2
Burne to a snuffe, and then stinke out, and die:		211	U43 Vulcan	188
wast to a snuffe, and then stinke out, and die:		211	U43 Vulcan	V188
SO'				
That so alone canst judge, so'alone dost make:		62	E96 Donne 2	3
Who makes the one, so't be first, makes both.		152	U12 Corbet	40
To see the workmanship so'xceed the cost!		160	U14 Selden	54
Be nought so'bove him but his sword let claime.		313	Horace	174
Be nought so'bove him, but his bold sword claime.		342	Horace	V174
SO				
Deceive their malice, who could wish it so.		27	E2 My Booke	7
Use mine so, too: I give thee leave. But crave		27	E3 Bookseller	3
Tells you it is a hot-house: So it ma',		29	E7 Hot-house	3
Or else by water goes, and so to playes;		30	E12 Shift	17
Which was a cater-piller. So 'twill dye.		31	E15 Court-worm	4
So, in short time, th'art in arrearage growne		32	E16 Brain-hardy	5
And mine come nothing like. I hope so. Yet,		32	E18 Censurer	5
Pr'y thee beleeve still, and not judge so fast,		32	E18 Censurer	9
The late tane bastinado. So I thought.		33	E21 Gam'ster	6
Came forth example, and remaines so, yet:		34	E23 Donne 1	4
Which hee thinkes great; and so reades verses, too:		35	E28 Surly	5
But that's put in, thou'lt say. Why, so is thine.		36	E29 Tilter	6
And lyes so farre from wit, 'tis impudence.		38	E38 Guiltie 2	6
In these times. Few so have ru'de		39	E40 Ratcliffe	14
Such her quaint practise is, so it allures,		39	E41 Gypsee	3
And so is Jone. Oft-times, when Giles doth find		40	E42 Giles	9
Of his begetting. And so sweares his Jone.		40	E42 Giles	14
Whose actions so themselves doe celebrate;		40	E43 Salisbury 1	2
To have so soone scap'd worlds, and fleshes rage,		41	E45 First Son	7
That quit'st the cause so oft, and rayl'st at men?		44	E54 Chev'ril 2	4
What fate is mine, that so it selfe bereaves?		44	E55 Beaumont	7
What art is thine, that so thy friend deceives?		44	E55 Beaumont	8
From brocage is become so bold a thiefe,		44	E56 Poet-Ape	3
If, as their ends, their fruits were so, the same,		45	E57 Bawds	1
And so my sharpnesse thou no lesse dis-joynts,		45	E58 Groome	5
So have I seene at Christ-masse sports one lost,		45	E58 Groome	7
But thine, for which I doo't, so much exceeds!		46	E60 Mounteagle	8
That love to make so well, a child to beare?		46	E62 Would-bee	2

SO (cont.)

	Page	Title	Line
The judgement of the king so shine in thee;	47	E63 Salisbury 2	4
Who can behold all envie so declin'd	47	E63 Salisbury 2	7
To so true worth, though thou thy selfe forbid.	47	E63 Salisbury 2	12
And not to dangers. When so wise a king	47	E64 Salisbury 3	12
When, in mens wishes, so thy vertues wrought,	49	E67 Suffolk	7
Though life be short, let us not make it so.	50	E70 Wm Roe 1	8
Or take an Epigramme so fearefully:	51	E73 Fine Grand	2
Be safe, nor feare thy selfe so good a fame,	53	E77 Not name	1
Came not that soule exhausted so their store.	53	E79 Rutland	4
No male unto him: who could so exceed	53	E79 Rutland	7
So to front death, as men might judge us past it.	54	E80 Life/Death	7
That they to knowledge so should toure upright,	55	E85 Goodyere 1	6
That so much skarfe of France, and hat, and fether,	56	E88 Monsieur	5
That he, untravell'd, should be french so much,	56	E88 Monsieur	7
If Rome so great, and in her wisest age,	56	E89 Allen	1
How can so great example dye in mee,	57	E89 Allen	7
And present worth in all dost so contract,	57	E89 Allen	11
So many Poets life, by one should live.	57	E89 Allen	14
That know not so much state, wrong, as they doo.	59	E92 New Crie	40
So hast thou rendred him in all his bounds,	61	E95 Savile	5
That thy brest so cleere of present crimes,	61	E95 Savile	19
That so alone canst judge, so'alone dost make:	62	E96 Donne 2	3
But one more rare, and in the case so new:	62	E97 Motion	3
His rosie tyes and garters so ore-blowne,	62	E97 Motion	5
About his forme. What then so swells each lim?	63	E97 Motion	19
And even the praisers judgement suffers so.	64	E99 Th Roe 2	10
Ile tell you of more, and lye, so you will come:	65	E101 Supper	17
Knat, raile, and ruffe too. How so ere, my man	65	E101 Supper	20
And are so good, and bad, just at a price,	66	E102 Pembroke	11
That art so reverenc'd, as thy comming in,	66	E102 Pembroke	17
My praise is plaine, and where so ere profest,	67	E103 L Wroth 1	13
And, armed to the chase, so bare her bow	68	E105 L Wroth 2	13
Diana'alone, so hit, and hunted so.	68	E105 L Wroth 2	14
There's none so dull, that for your stile would aske,	68	E105 L Wroth 2	15
So are you Natures Index, and restore,	68	E105 L Wroth 2	19
What man art thou, that art so many men,	68	E106 E Herbert	2
And that so strong and deepe, as 't might be thought,	71	E110 Edmonds 1	7
Can so speake Caesar, so thy labours doe.	71	E110 Edmonds 1	12
That to the world thou should'st reveale so much,	72	E111 Edmonds 2	10
At this so subtile sport: and play'st so ill?	72	E112 Gamster	2
Thy all, at all: and what so ere I doe,	72	E112 Gamster	5
That both for wit, and sense, so oft dost plucke,	73	E112 Gamster	18
So Phoebus makes me worthy of his bayes,	73	E113 Overbury	1
So, where thou liv'st, thou mak'st life understood!	73	E113 Overbury	3
Where finding so much beautie met with vertue,	74	E114 Sydney	6
Him not, aloud, that boasts so good a fame:	74	E115 Honest Man	2
Naming so many, too! But, this is one,	74	E115 Honest Man	3
So did thy vertue'enforme, thy wit sustaine	75	E116 Jephson	3
So all his meate he tasteth over, twise:	76	E118 Gut	2
And, striving so to double his delight,	76	E118 Gut	3
'Twas a child, that so did thrive	77	E120 S. P.	5
Old men so duely,	77	E120 S. P.	14
He plai'd so truely.	77	E120 S. P.	16
So, by error, to his fate	77	E120 S. P.	17
But, being so much too good for earth,	77	E120 S. P.	23
But both th'hast so, as who affects the state	78	E123 Rudyerd 3	3
To whom I am so bound, lov'd Aubigny?	80	E127 Aubigny	3
So, all reward, or name, that growes to mee	80	E127 Aubigny	9
So, when we, blest with thy returne, shall see	81	E128 Wm Roe 2	9
So well in that are his inventions wrought,	83	E132 Sylvester	11
So huge, it seem'd, they could by no meanes quite her.	86	E133 Voyage	86
And all his followers, that had so abus'd him:	86	E133 Voyage	97
And, in so shitten sort, so long had us'd him:	86	E133 Voyage	98
Stunke not so ill; nor, when shee kist, Kate Arden.	87	E133 Voyage	118
And so they did, from Styx, to Acheron:	88	E133 Voyage	141
For, to say truth, what scullion is so nastie,	88	E133 Voyage	147
Your daintie nostrills (in so hot a season,	88	E133 Voyage	165
Upon your eares, of discords so un-sweet?	88	E133 Voyage	171
That had, so often, shew'd 'hem merry prankes.	89	E133 Voyage	184
And so went bravely backe, without protraction.	89	E133 Voyage	192
That since, my numbers are so cold,	93	F1 Why write no	11
And, though so neere the citie, and the court,	96	F3 Wroth	3
And, so they ride in purple, eate in plate,	99	F3 Wroth	89
A spirit so resolv'd to tread	100	F4 To the World	6
From whence, so lately, I did burne,	101	F4 To the World	27
What bird, or beast, is knowne so dull,	101	F4 To the World	29
But, as 'tis rumor'd, so beleev'd:	101	F4 To the World	50
So removed by our wile?	102	F5 Celia 1	14
Adde a thousand, and so more:	103	F6 Celia 2	11
So court a mistris, shee denyes you;	104	F7 Women but	3
So men at weakest, they are strongest,	104	F7 Women but	9
Bald, or blinde, or nere so many:	105	F8 Sicknesse	40
Not so much honoring thee,	106	F9 Celia 3	
Not so to honor thee,	106	F9 Celia 3	V 10
Which to effect (since no brest is so sure,	109	F11 Epode	5
Whereof the loyall conscience so complaines.	110	F11 Epode	27
Because they move, the continent doth so:	111	F11 Epode	71
Cannot so safely sinne. Their chastitie	111	F11 Epode	81
Though we acknowledge, who can so abstayne,	112	F11 Epode	85
Though I acknowledge, who can so refraine,	112	F11 Epode	V 85
A body so harmoniously compos'd,	112	F11 Epode	99
O, so divine a creature	112	F11 Epode	102

SO (cont.)

	Page	Title		Line
Have beautie knowne, yet none so famous seene?	114	F12	Rutland	50
That Homer brought to Troy; yet none so live:	115	F12	Rutland	55
Or set bright Ariadnes crowne so high?	115	F12	Rutland	60
And your brave friend, and mine so well did love.	116	F12	Rutland	92
Of any good minde, now: There are so few.	116	F13	Aubigny	2
The bad, by number, are so fortified,	116	F13	Aubigny	3
So both the prais'd, and praisers suffer: Yet,	116	F13	Aubigny	5
Or so my selfe abandon'd, as because	117	F13	Aubigny	17
And so doe many more. All which can call	117	F13	Aubigny	31
Or cos'ning farmer of the customes so,	117	F13	Aubigny	39
Of so great title, birth, but vertue most,	118	F13	Aubigny	49
(They finde it both so wittie, and safe to give.)	118	F13	Aubigny	76
Unto himselfe, by being so deare to you.	119	F13	Aubigny	117
So good	121	F14	Sydney	34
So may you live in honor, as in name,	121	F14	Sydney	51
So may	121	F14	Sydney	53
As thou art all, so be thou all to mee,	122	F15	Heaven	9
For, sin's so sweet,	129	U1	Father	12
The Angels so did sound it,	130	U1	Nativitie	3
The Fathers wisedome will'd it so,	130	U1	Nativitie	13
So that, there, I stood a stone,	132	U2	How he saw	27
And enamour'd, doe wish, so they might	134	U2	Triumph	7
O so white! O so soft! O so sweet is she!	135	U2	Triumph	30
O so faire! O so soft! O so sweet is she!	135	U2	Triumph V	30
O so faire O so kind o so sweet so sweet is shee	135	U2	Triumph V	38
O so yong o so streight O so chast so chast is shee	136	U2	Triumph V	46
So hath Homer prais'd her haire;	136	U2	Cupid	13
So, Anacreon drawne the Ayre	136	U2	Cupid	14
Look'd not halfe so fresh, and faire,	138	U2	Kisse	9
So, as those that had your sight,	138	U2	Kisse	17
So to see a Lady tread,	138	U2	Kisse	25
And was worthy (being so seene)	138	U2	Kisse	27
For I will so urge you to't,	140	U2	Promise	14
And so thin, to see a blush	141	U2	Her man	28
No voice so sweet, nor words have sting,	143	U3	Musicall V	15
So they in state of Grace retain'd,	144	U3	Musicall	27
For so will sorrow slay me;	145	U4	Song	10
So going thorow all your straine,	145	U5	Woman-kind	10
Then when 'tis made, why so will wee.	145	U5	Woman-kind	16
But he hath eyes so round, and bright,	147	U7	Nymph	22
What Nymph so e're his voyce but heares,	148	U7	Nymph	27
But so exempt from blame,	148	U7	Nymph	33
Whom I adore so much, should so slight me,	149	U9	Picture	4
Read so much wast, as she cannot imbrace	150	U9	Picture	16
And sleepe so guiltie and afraid,	151	U11	Dreame	13
Deare Vincent Corbet who so long	151	U12	Corbet	7
But was by sweetning so his will,	151	U12	Corbet	13
So of uncleannesse, or offence,	152	U12	Corbet	17
They were so even, grave, and holy;	152	U12	Corbet	23
No stubbornnesse so stiffe, nor folly	152	U12	Corbet	24
To license ever was so light,	152	U12	Corbet	25
His lookes would so correct it, when	152	U12	Corbet	27
And in the Act did so my blush prevent,	153	U13	Sacvile	11
They are so long a comming, and so hard;	153	U13	Sacvile	23
In that proud manner, as a good so gain'd,	154	U13	Sacvile	37
So each, that's done, and tane, becomes a Brace.	154	U13	Sacvile	40
Are they not worthy to be answer'd so,	154	U13	Sacvile	59
O, is it so? knowes he so much? and will	155	U13	Sacvile	73
If it were cleare, but being so in cloud	155	U13	Sacvile	87
Were the Rack offer'd them, how they came so;	157	U13	Sacvile	130
May grow so great to be example, when	158	U13	Sacvile	161
Of this so vitious Humanitie.	158	U14	Selden	12
So that my Reader is assur'd, I now	159	U14	Selden	27
I first salute thee so; and gratulate,	161	U14	Selden	67
Selden! two Names that so much understand!	161	U14	Selden	82
You both are modest. So am I. Farewell.	161	U14	Selden	86
Be honour is so mixt) by such as would,	162	U15	Friend-Wars	25
Rather then here so bogg'd in vices stay.	163	U15	Friend-Wars	30
O, these so ignorant Monsters! light, as proud,	164	U15	Friend-Wars	59
Adulteries, now, are not so hid, or strange,	165	U15	Friend-Wars	85
Pardon his Lordship. Flattry's growne so cheape	167	U15	Friend-Wars	155
So, 'live or dead, thou wilt preserve a fame	168	U15	Friend-Wars	189
Now so much friend, as you would trust in me,	169	U17	Friend-Debt	14
Crooked appeare; so that doth my conceipt:	170	U18	Elegy Can	8
I'le lead you on; or if my fate will so,	170	U18	Elegy Can	22
So well as I may tell in verse, 'tis so?	170	U19	Elegy By	12
And so that either may example prove	171	U19	Elegy By	16
No more, I am sorry for so fond cause, say,	171	U20	Shrub	4
And so I leave to stirre him, lest he stinke.	172	U21	Ltl Shrub	10
A vertue, like Allay, so gone	173	U22	Elegy Tho	5
And on them burne so chaste a flame,	173	U22	Elegy Tho	21
With so much Loyalties expence,	173	U22	Elegy Tho	22
Wise Providence would so; that nor the good	176	U24	Frontispice	5
high Providence would so; that nor the good	176	U24	Frontispice V	5
True noblesse. Palme growes straight, though handled ne're so rude.	177	U25	Desmond	26
So fooles, we see,	179	U25	Desmond	51
So speake (as yet it is not mute)	181	U27	Ode Helen	4
Is Horace his each love so high	181	U27	Ode Helen	13
The Swan that so relish'd Pancharis)	182	U27	Ode Helen	30
So much my Subject drownes the rest.	182	U27	Ode Helen	36
But then his Mothers sweets you so apply,	182	U28	Worth	12
So to see the Fountaine drie,	183	U29	Fit of Rime	22

SO (cont.)

	Page	Title	Line
Tyran Rime hath so abused,	184	U29 Fit of Rime	46
So, justest Lord, may all your Judgements be	185	U31 Elsmere	1
So, may the King proclaime your Conscience is	185	U31 Elsmere	3
So, from all sicknesse, may you rise to health,	186	U31 Elsmere	5
So may the gentler Muses, and good fame	186	U31 Elsmere	7
Thinke, yea and boast, that they have done it so	186	U32 Elsmere	12
But when I read or heare the names so rife	187	U33 Councellour	7
So dost thou studie matter, men, and times,	187	U33 Councellour	15
So comm'st thou like a Chiefe into the Court,	187	U33 Councellour	29
So brightly brandish'd) wound'st, defend'st! the while	187	U33 Councellour	32
Of Beautie, so to nullifie a face,	188	U34 Small Poxe	14
So may the fruitfull Vine my temples steepe,	190	U37 Friend-Book	14
For no man lives so out of passions sway,	190	U37 Friend-Book	31
Offended Mistris, you are yet so faire,	191	U38 Elegy 'Tis	9
You may so place me, and in such an ayre,	192	U38 Elegy 'Tis	51
Or winds the Spirit, by which the flower so grew?	192	U38 Elegy 'Tis	58
And take some sirrup after; so doe I,	197	U40 Elegy That	5
Of vowes so sacred, and in silence made;	197	U40 Elegy That	14
And must be bred, so to conceale his birth,	197	U40 Elegy That	17
Farre from the Nest, and so himselfe belie	198	U40 Elegy That	38
And so I spare it. Come what can become	199	U41 Elegy Since	19
So to be sure you doe injoy your selves.	200	U42 Elegy Let	24
Of love, and hate: and came so nigh to know	200	U42 Elegy Let	35
So I might dote upon thy Chaires and Stooles	201	U42 Elegy Let	47
Or a Close-stoole so cas'd; or any fat	202	U42 Elegy Let	84
So many my Yeares-labours in an houre?	202	U43 Vulcan	4
And so some goodlier monster had begot:	204	U43 Vulcan	32
Thou should'st have stay'd, till publike fame said so.	204	U43 Vulcan	46
And so, have kept me dying a whole age,	205	U43 Vulcan	55
And so, have kept them dying a whole age,	205	U43 Vulcan	V 55
And the strong lines, that so the time doe catch:	206	U43 Vulcan	78
And the strong lines, which so the time doe catch:	206	U43 Vulcan	V 78
So ravenous, and vast an appetite?	206	U43 Vulcan	86
Sonne of the Wind! for so thy mother gone	208	U43 Vulcan	111
And so did Jove, who ne're meant thee his Cup:	208	U43 Vulcan	115
If that were so, thou rather would'st advance	209	U43 Vulcan	151
Troy, though it were so much his Venus care.	210	U43 Vulcan	160
Troy, though it were so much thy Venus joycare.	210	U43 Vulcan	V160
So would'st th'have run upon the Rolls by stealth,	210	U43 Vulcan	169
Of massacring Man-kind so many wayes.	212	U43 Vulcan	208
So doth the King, and most of the Kings men	212	U43 Vulcan	211
And Ord'nance too: so much as from the Tower	213	U44 Speach	3
Nor markes of wealth so from our Nation fled,	213	U44 Speach	12
So, in that ground, as soone it grew to be	214	U44 Speach	37
So acted to the life, as Maurice might,	214	U44 Speach	41
In so much land a yeare, or such a Banke,	215	U44 Speach	76
That turnes us so much moneys, at which rate	215	U44 Speach	77
Inquirie of the worth: So must we doe,	216	U45 Squib	15
And shewing so weake an Act to vulgar eyes,	218	U47 Tribe	7
So farre without inquirie what the States,	219	U47 Tribe	43
But all so cleare, and led by reasons flame,	220	U47 Tribe	69
So short you read my Character, and theirs	220	U47 Tribe	73
My selfe a little. I will take you so,	220	U47 Tribe	76
So mayst thou still be younger	221	U48 Bacchus	21
So may the Muses follow	221	U48 Bacchus	25
So may there never Quarrell	221	U48 Bacchus	31
Do's the Court-Pucell then so censure me,	222	U49 Pucell	1
Is of so brave example, as he were	224	U50 Countesse	7
Are growne so fruitfull, and false pleasures climbe,	224	U50 Countesse	10
So great a Vertue stand upright to view,	224	U50 Countesse	19
So are they profitable to be knowne:	225	U50 Countesse	34
For when they find so many meet in one,	225	U50 Countesse	35
How comes it all things so about thee smile?	225	U51 Bacon	2
And so doe I. This is the sixtieth yeare	225	U51 Bacon	7
I am not so voluminous, and vast,	226	U52 Answer	2
'Tis true, as my wombe swells, so my backe stoupes,	227	U52 Answer	4
So seem'd your horse and you, both of a peece!	228	U53 Newcastle	6
Nay, so your Seate his beauties did endorse,	228	U53 Newcastle	11
Nor any of their houshold, halfe so well.	228	U53 Newcastle	16
So well! as when I saw the floore, and Roome,	228	U53 Newcastle	17
So well! as when I view'd the floore, and Roome,	228	U53 Newcastle	V 17
So that upon the point, my corporall feare	229	U54 Squib	7
When you would play so nobly, and so free.	230	U56 Covell	2
So have you gain'd a Servant, and a Muse:	230	U56 Covell	5
If the 'Chequer be emptie, so will be his Head.	232	U57 Burges	28
And, in these Cures, do'st so thy selfe enlarge,	235	U62 Charles 1	7
O pietie! so to weigh the poores estates!	235	U62 Charles 1	11
O bountie! so to difference the rates!	235	U62 Charles 1	12
For God, whose essence is so infinite,	236	U63 Charles 2	13
That so hath crown'd our hopes, and spring, and earth,	237	U65 Prince	2
That so hath crown'd our hopes, our spring, our earth,	237	U65 Prince	V 2
And there to stand so. Hast now envious Moone,	238	U65 Prince	9
And still to stand so. Hast thou envious Moone,	238	U65 Prince	V 9
So generall a gladnesse to an Isle,	238	U66 Queene	9
As in this Prince? Let it be lawfull, so	238	U66 Queene	11
Of so much safetie to the Realme, and King.	238	U66 Queene	14
Of so much health, both to our Land, and King.	238	U66 Queene	V 14
Shee showes so farre above	240	U67 Muses	31
So fruitfull, and so faire,	240	U67 Muses	52
Are they so scanted in their store? or driven	241	U68 House-hold	3
So, the allowance from the King to use,	241	U68 House-hold	10
Sonne, and my Friend, I had not call'd you so	241	U69 Friend Son	1

SO (cont.)

	Page	Title	Line
But as the wretched Painter, who so ill	241	U69 Friend Son	9
Till he had sold his Piece, drawne so unlike:	242	U69 Friend Son	13
So doth the flatt'rer with faire cunning strike	242	U69 Friend Son	14
To keepe him off; and how-so-e're he gleanes	242	U69 Friend Son	16
To judge; So all men comming neere can spie,	242	U69 Friend Son	20
Never so great to get them: and the ends,	242	U69 Friend Son	25
So deep, as he did then death's waters sup;	244	U70 Ode	41
By him, so ample, full, and round,	244	U70 Ode	49
In season, and so brought	245	U70 Ode	61
But fate doth so alternate the designe,	246	U70 Ode	95
That liking; and approach so one the tother,	247	U70 Ode	109
Of two so early men,	247	U70 Ode	125
Wherein she sits so richly drest,	251	U74 Weston	14
So like a feast?	253	U75 Epithalam.	14
By all the Spheares consent, so in the heart of June?	253	U75 Epithalam.	16
Doe boast their Loves, and Brav'ries so at large,	253	U75 Epithalam.	19
When look'd the Earth so fine,	253	U75 Epithalam.	21
Or so did shine,	253	U75 Epithalam.	22
With Modestie so crown'd, and Adoration seene.	254	U75 Epithalam.	48
Saw'st thou that Paire, became these Rites so well,	254	U75 Epithalam.	76
He had so highly set; and, in what Barbican.	256	U75 Epithalam.	112
He had so highly plac'd; and, in what Barbican.	256	U75 Epithalam.	V112
Doe long to make themselves, so, another way:	257	U75 Epithalam.	140
Of Life, that fall so; Christians know their birth	257	U75 Epithalam.	156
So great; his Body now alone projects the shade.	258	U75 Epithalam.	184
So large; his Body then, not boughs, project his shade.	258	U75 Epithalam.	V184
And that this so accepted summe,	259	U76 Petition	14
And that this so thriftye summe,	259	U76 Petition	V 14
And so warme the Poets tongue	260	U76 Petition	31
Our great, our good. Where one's so drest	265	U79 New-yeares	44
Hayles me, so solemnly, to yonder Yewgh?	268	U81 Pawlet	2
Just as she in it liv'd! and so exempt	270	U81 Pawlet	48
And trusted so, as it deposited lay	271	U81 Pawlet	81
Meeting of Graces, that so swell'd the flood	274	U84 Descent	10
Were fitly interpos'd; so new:	275	U84 Body	10
A Mind so pure, so perfect fine,	278	U84 Mind	25
And so disdaining any tryer;	278	U84 Mind	27
The Voyce so sweet, the words so faire,	279	U84 Mind	37
But, that a Mind so rapt, so high,	279	U84 Mind	41
So swift, so pure, should yet apply	279	U84 Mind	42
It selfe to us, and come so nigh	279	U84 Mind	43
For this so loftie forme, so streight,	280	U84 Mind	54
So polish't, perfect, round, and even,	280	U84 Mind	55
. . . gave me leave to call her so. Being Her . . .	282	U84 Muse	Ttl
(For so thou art with me) now shee is gone.	283	U84 Muse	22
Dare I prophane, so irreligious bee	283	U84 Muse	39
So sweetly taken to the Court of blisse,	283	U84 Muse	41
Like single; so, there is a third, commixt,	284	U84 Muse	53
That shall re-joyne yee. Was she, then, so deare,	285	U84 Muse	107
Himselfe so un-inform'd of his elect,	286	U84 Muse	149
Mov'd by the wind, so comely moved she.	287	U84 Muse	166
To one she said, Doe this, he did it; So	287	U84 Muse	169
A solemne Mistresse, and so good a Friend,	287	U84 Muse	175
So charitable, to religious end,	287	U84 Muse	176
In all her petite actions, so devote,	287	U84 Muse	177
In the discerning of each conscience, so!	289	U84 Muse	222
And 'counts them sweet rewards so ta'en:	290	U85 Country	36
Loves cares so evill, and so great?	290	U85 Country	38
Too stubborne for Commands so slack:	292	U86 Hor.4:1	7
Who sings so sweet, and with such cunning plaies,	293	U87 Hor.3:9	10
So Fate would give her life, and longer daies.	293	U87 Hor.3:9	12
So Fates would let the Boy a long thred run.	293	U87 Hor.3:9	16
Whose shapes, like sick-mens dreames, are fain'd so vaine,	305	Horace	9
Whose shapes, like sick-mens dreames, are form'd so vaine,	338	Horace	V 9
So he that varying still affects to draw	339	Horace	V 42/ 40
So, shunning faults, to greater fault doth lead,	307	Horace	43
So they fall gently from the Grecian spring,	309	Horace	75
Or Varius? Why am I now envi'd so,	309	Horace	79
The first-borne dying; so the aged state	309	Horace	87
The first-borne dying; so the aged Fate	340	Horace	V 87
His course so hurtfull both to graine, and seedes,	309	Horace	97
Shall perish: so farre off it is, the state,	309	Horace	99
To laughter; so they grieve with those that mone.	311	Horace	144
Nor so begin, as did that Circler late,	313	Horace	195
He ever hastens to the end, and so	315	Horace	211
And so well faines, so mixeth cunningly	315	Horace	215
What so is showne, I not beleeve, and hate.	317	Horace	269
So over-thick, but, where the people met,	319	Horace	292
In his train'd Gowne about the Stage: So grew	319	Horace	305
Yet so the scoffing Satyres to mens view,	321	Horace	328
And so their prating to present was best,	321	Horace	329
And so their pratling to present were best,	346	Horace	V321/329
And so to turne all earnest into jest,	321	Horace	330
And so to turne our earnest into jest,	346	Horace	V322/330
To Dance, so she should, shamefac'd, differ farre	321	Horace	339
Nor I, when I write Satyres, will so love	321	Horace	341
Meere raigning words: nor will I labour so	321	Horace	343
And so, as every man may hope the same;	321	Horace	350
Of Order, and Connexion; so much grace	321	Horace	353
Fell into fault so farre, as now they saw	321	Horace	367
The steadie Spondaees; so themselves to beare	323	Horace	377
The steadie Spondaees; so themselves doe beare	347	Horace	V363/377

SO (cont.)

	Page	Title	Line
So rare, as with some taxe it doth ingage	323	Horace	383
Those heavie Verses, sent so to the Stage,	323	Horace	384
For so, they shall not only gaine the worth,	323	Horace	384
Be briefe, in what thou wouldst command, that so	325	Horace	425
Sweet mix'd with sowre, to his Reader, so	329	Horace	503
So he that flaggeth much, becomes to me	329	Horace	515
As Painting, so is Poesie. Some mans hand	329	Horace	533
So, any Poeme, fancied, or forth-brought	329	Horace	539
If ne're so little it depart the first,	331	Horace	561
So doth the one, the others helpe require,	331	Horace	563
So doth the Poet, who is rich in land,	333	Horace	585
So doth the Poet, that is rich in Land,	333	Horace	599
Cry, and doe more then the true Mourners: so	353	Horace	V599
When you write Verses, with your judge do so:	333	Horace	615
When you make verses, with your judge doe so:	333	Horace	620
Or love of this so famous death lay by.	354	Horace	V620
All; So this grievous Writer puts to flight	335	Horace	669
(so well dispos'd by thy auspicious hand)	337	Horace	676
that mongst so manie plants transplanted hether,	361	Palmer	2
So in my braine; the stronge impression	361	Palmer	6
So with this Authors Readers will it thrive:	361	Palmer	21
If a Bird so amiable,	362	Author	12
My selfe am so neare drowning?	364	Phoenix	3
"So much doth Virtue hate,	365	Ode Splendor	20
So blacke a Bird, so bright a Qualitie.	367	Ode Who saith	31
So bold, as shewes your Art you can command.	369	Ode Who saith	96
Up so much truth, as could I it pursue	370	Author	8
Here, up the Alpes (not so plaine as to Dunstable)	372	Epitaph	13
A Punke here pelts him with egs. How so?	374	Coryat 1	16
For he did but kisse her, and so let her go.	375	Coryat 1	18
Of travell he discourseth so at large,	375	Coryat 1	19
Of lying, he feares so much the reproofe	378	Coryat 2	82
I meane that one paire, wherewith he so hobled	380	Coryat 3	31
So that not them, his scabbes, lice, or the stewes,	380	Coryat 3	41
Which he not denies. Now being so free,	380	Coryat 3	50
So, be there never discontent, or sorrow,	381	Coryat 3	57
So, be your Concord, still, as deepe, as mute;	384	Somerset	15
So, may those Mariage-Pledges, comforts prove:	384	Somerset	17
So, in theyr number, may you never see	384	Somerset	19
Or, to so many, and so Broad-seales had,	384	Somerset	21
Hold thyne owne worth unbroke: which is so good	385	Brooke	3
which, did they neere so neate, or proudly dwell,	386	Browne	13
Had cloath'd him so. Here's all I can supply	387	Cavendish	3
That I not mixe thee so, my braine excuses;	389	Aleman	20
Which were so richly spun, and woven so fit,	391	Shakespeare	25
Lives in his issue, even so, the race	392	Shakespeare	49
That so did take Eliza, and our James!	392	Shakespeare	66
At least so great a Lady. She was wife	392	Shakespeare	74
So wood at last, that he was wonne to her	394	Jane Ogle	15
But when againe I veiw the parts so peiz'd,	394	Jane Ogle	22
And those in number so, and measure rais'd,	395	May	7
Lucans whole frame unto us, and so wrought,	395	May	8
The selfe same Genius! so the worke will say.	395	May	20
And those so sweet, and well proportion'd parts,	395	May	23
Did all so strike me, as I cry'd, who can	396	Drayton	21
Sayst thou so, Lucan? But thou scornst to stay	397	Drayton	31
With every song, I sweare, and so would dye:	397	Drayton	47
Thy list of aydes, and force, for so it is:	397	Drayton	54
So shall our English Youth urge on, and cry	398	Drayton	62
This Fort of so impregnable accesse,	398	Drayton	69
That, while they bind the senses, doe so please?	401	Beaumont	17
It was not so of old: Men tooke up trades	401	Filmer	2
I sayd, who'had supp'd so deepe of this sweet Chalice,	410	Brome	13
Is so implexed, and laid in, between,	412	Sutcliffe	21
(Divinest graces) are so entermixt,	412	Ghyrlond	7
And truely, so I would, could I be heard.	413	Ghyrlond	26
Such men I met withall, and so have you.	414	Rutter	3
Where it runs round, and even: where so well,	415	Rutter	11
So soft, and smooth it handles, the whole piece,	415	Rutter	16
to the Peake it is so hard-by,	415	Rutter	17
Il may Ben Johnson slander so his feete,	417	Moon	23
are distant, so is proffitt from just aymes.	418	Answer	5

SO'ALONE
| That so alone canst judge, so'alone dost make: | 422 | Lucan | 8 |

SOAP   (See SOPE)

SOARES
| But as he soares at that, he bruiseth then | 62 | E96 Donne 2 | 3 |

SOBER
Since when, hee's sober againe, and all play's made.	272	U81 Pawlet	98
Sober, as saddest care:	56	E87 Hazard	6
Exclude all sober Poets, from their share	111	F11 Epode	60
Wise, sober folke, a frantick Poet feare,	325	Horace	421

SO'BOVE
Be nought so'bove him but his sword let claime.	335	Horace	643
Be nought so'bove him, but his bold sword claime.	313	Horace	174
	342	Horace	V174

SOCIETIE
Arsenike would thee fit for societie make.	42	E50 Cod 3	3
Of nature, and societie, I should faint;	117	F13 Aubigny	19
And free societie, hee's borne else-where,	197	U40 Elegy That	16

SOCK
| Fit for the sock: Each subject should retaine | 311 | Horace | 124 |

	Page	Title	Line
SOCKES			
And shake a Stage: Or, when thy Sockes were on,	391	Shakespeare	37
SOCKET			
That's six in silver; now within the Socket	229	U54 Squib	13
SOCKS			
This foot the socks tooke up, and buskins grave,	311	Horace	118
SOCRATICK			
Which the Socratick writings best can show:	325	Horace	442
SODAINE			
Thy curtesie but sodaine starts,	100	F4 To the World	11
SODAYNE			
What (great, I will not say, but) sodayne cheare	95	F2 Penshurst	82
SOE			
The milke, nor oyle, did ever flowe soe free	98	F3 Wroth	V 60
shall looke, & on hyme soe, then arte's a lyer	383	Rich	15
Or are you soe ambitious 'bove your peers!	403	Inigo Jones 1	19
What makes your Wretchednes to bray soe loud	403	Inigo Jones 1	23
What is the cause you pompe it soe? I aske,	403	Inigo Jones 1	29
All in the Worke! And soe shall still for Ben:	404	Inigo Jones 1	65
Soe the Materialls be of Purbeck stone!	406	Inigo Jones 1	100
your workes thus differing, troth let soe your style:	407	Inigo Jones 2	19
If thou be soe desyrous to be read,	408	Inigo Jones 3	9
soe much the starte	420	Ode:If Men	11
Uppon soe humbled earth to cast hir eyes:	420	Ode:If Men	30
Soe ended your Epistle, myne beginns	421	Censure	3
Hee that soe Censureth, or adviseth synns,	421	Censure	4
For noe Man Lyves, soe out of passions swaye,	422	Censure	24
SOFT			
Rest in soft peace, and, ask'd, say here doth lye	41	E45 First Son	9
May windes as soft as breath of kissing friends,	81	E128 Wm Roe 2	5
The soft, and sweetest mindes	110	F11 Epode	50
Of all his happinesse? But soft: I heare	111	F11 Epode	65
If it may stand with your soft blush to heare	117	F13 Aubigny	22
O so white! O so soft! O so sweet is she!	135	U2 Triumph	30
O so faire! O so soft! O so sweet is she!	135	U2 Triumph	V 30
He would have a hand as soft	141	U2 Her man	25
He should have a hand as soft	141	U2 Her man	V 25
This hath our ill-us'd freedome, and soft peace	166	U15 Friend-Wars	121
Lewd slanderers, soft whisperers that let blood	167	U15 Friend-Wars	165
Lewd standers, soft whisperers that let blood	167	U15 Friend-Wars	V165
Lie drawne to life, in his soft Verse,	181	U27 Ode Helen	7
In his soft Cradle to his Fathers Chaire,	225	U51 Bacon	14
Run all the Rounds in a soft Ladyes eare,	230	U56 Covell	16
My Lord, till felt griefe make our stone hearts soft,	234	U61 Epigram	14
In making soft her aromatique bed.	251	U74 Weston	18
As some soft chime had stroak'd the ayre;	279	U84 Mind	38
Smooth, soft, and sweet, in all a floud	280	U84 Mind	61
To 'greet, or grieve her soft Euthanasee?	283	U84 Muse	40
And to the Touch, a Flower, like soft as Palme.	286	U84 Muse	126
The soft birds quarrell in the Woods,	290	U85 Country	26
Goe where Youths soft intreaties call thee back.	292	U86 Hor.4:1	8
In many a Gumme, and for thy soft eares sake	292	U86 Hor.4:1	22
But soft, and simple, at few holes breath'd time	319	Horace	289
And lead them with soft songs, where that he would.	327	Horace	485
With thy soft notes, and hold them within Pale	367	Ode Who saith	45
Heard the soft ayres, between our Swaynes & thee,	397	Drayton	26
With od'rous sweets and soft humilitie,	413	Ghyrlond	27
So soft, and smooth it handles, the whole piece,	415	Rutter	17
SOFTER			
Fit in that softer bosome to reside.	52	E76 Bedford 1	12
And makes sleepe softer then it is!	97	F3 Wroth	20
Daintinesse, and softer ease,	105	F8 Sicknesse	22
Set, and to this softer straine;	136	U2 Cupid	9
And heat, with softest love, thy softer bed.	295	U89 Mart.8:77	6
SOFTEST			
I meant each softest vertue, there should meet,	52	E76 Bedford 1	11
And heat, with softest love, thy softer bed.	295	U89 Mart.8:77	6
SOFTLY			
Of me, I'le softly tread unto my Tombe;	199	U41 Elegy Since	20
SOFTNESSE			
To fit the softnesse of our Yeares-gift: when	263	U79 New-yeares	6
Her Sweetnesse, Softnesse, her faire Courtesie,	270	U81 Pawlet	39
SOFTNESSES			
Were to be staid with softnesses, and wonne	321	Horace	326
SOILE (See also SOYLE)			
Then, in a soile hast planted me,	101	F4 To the World	45
SOL			
Sol will re-shine. If not, Charles hath a Sonne.	238	U65 Prince	12
And Sol will shine. If not, Charles hath a Sonne.	238	U65 Prince	V 12
SOLD			
Groyne, come of age, his state sold out of hand	75	E117 Groyne	1
And all thy good is to be sold.	100	F4 To the World	16
Whil'st that, for which, all vertue now is sold,	113	F12 Rutland	1
Till he had sold his Piece, drawne so unlike:	242	U69 Friend Son	13
SOLDERS			
Solders crackt friendship; makes love last a day;	113	F12 Rutland	17
SOLDIER (See SOULDIER)			
SOLDIERIE			
Of bearing Armes! most civill Soldierie!	214	U44 Speach	44
SOLE			
Charge them, for crowne, to thy sole censure hye.	32	E17 Critic	4
Of joy the Circle, and sole Period!	284	U84 Muse	66
The sole Religious house, and Votary,	372	Epitaph	10

	Page	Title	Line
SOLEMNE			
Of solemne greatnesse. And he dares, at dice,	36	E28 Surly	16
In solemne cypres, the other cob-web-lawne.	51	E73 Fine Grand	14
Hating that solemne vice of greatnesse, pride;	52	E76 Bedford 1	10
An Officer there, did make most solemne love,	201	U42 Elegy Let	53
The Solemne Quire cryes, Joy; and they returne, Amen.	256	U75 Epithalam.	128
A solemne Mistresse, and so good a Friend,	287	U84 Muse	175
Her solemne houres she spent, or giving Almes,	288	U84 Muse	192
But, as a Matrone drawne at solemne times	321	Horace	338
In setting forth of such a solemne Toye!	405	Inigo Jones 1	78
SOLEMNLY			
Hayles me, so solemnly, to yonder Yewgh?	268	U81 Pawlet	2
SOLID			
All that was solid, in the name	399	Lady Ogle	17
SOLIDE			
'Mongst loughing heards, and solide hoofes:	97	F3 Wroth	16
SOLLEN			
No sowre, or sollen bed-mate, yet a Chast;	295	U90 Mart.10:47	10
SOLOECISME			
A desperate soloecisme in truth and wit.	75	E116 Jephson	16
SOLONS			
Like Solons selfe; explat'st the knottie Lawes	217	U46 Coke	17
SOLS			
Sols Chariot for new fire,	175	U23 Himselfe	28
SOME			
It will be look'd for, booke, when some but see	27	E2 My Booke	1
For termers, or some clarke-like serving-man,	28	E3 Bookseller	9
On some-thing, that walkes some-where.	30	E11 Something	Ttl
Some hundred quarrells, yet dost thou fight none;	32	E16 Brain-hardy	6
Blaspheme god, greatly. Or some poore hinde beat,	36	E28 Surly	17
Is this the Sir, who, some wast wife to winne,	42	E46 Luckless 1	1
Item, a tale or two, some fortnight after;	51	E73 Fine Grand	7
'Twixt puritanes, and players, as some cry;	52	E75 Lippe	2
Or hung some Mounsieurs picture on the wall,	56	E88 Monsieur	12
Or is it some french statue? No: 'T doth move,	56	E88 Monsieur	13
Or, every day, some one at Rimee's looks,	59	E92 New Crie	23
Play-wright, by chance, hearing some toyes I'had writ,	64	E100 Playwrt 3	1
An olive, capers, or some better sallade	64	E101 Supper	10
Of partrich, pheasant, wood-cock, of which some	65	E101 Supper	18
Livie, or of some better booke to us,	65	E101 Supper	22
Or, because some scarce thinke that storie true,	67	E104 Montgomery	5
If not, 'tis fit for you, some should envy.	67	E104 Montgomery	16
If men get name, for some one vertue: Then,	68	E106 E Herbert	1
And, in some yeere, all these together heap'd,	69	E107 Hungry	15
Yet thou, perhaps, shalt meet some tongues will grutch,	72	E111 Edmonds 2	9
I Must beleeve some miracles still bee,	73	E114 Sydney	1
'Twas not entayl'd on title. That some word	75	E116 Jephson	7
Whil'st thou dost rayse some Player, from the grave,	81	E129 Mime	11
On some new gesture, that's imputed wit?	81	E129 Mime	14
From Venice, Paris, or some in-land passage	85	E133 Voyage	33
Of some Bride-well, and may, in time, concerne us	85	E133 Voyage	42
That all this while I have forgot some god,	85	E133 Voyage	44
Thou hast seene hell (some say) and know'st all nookes there,	85	E133 Voyage	51
Some act of Love's bound to reherse,	93	F1 Why write no	1
Some bring a capon, some a rurall cake,	95	F2 Penshurst	51
Some nuts, some apples; some that thinke they make	95	F2 Penshurst	52
And I not faine to sit (as some, this day,	95	F2 Penshurst	65
There wasted, some not paid for yet!	97	F3 Wroth	12
To some coole, courteous shade, which he calls his,	97	F3 Wroth	19
Thou dost with some delight the day out-weare,	97	F3 Wroth	35
Thou canst with some delight the day out-weare,	97	F3 Wroth	V 35
The furie of some rash command,	98	F3 Wroth	V 68
Turne the stale prologue to some painted maske,	107	F10 Proludium	20
Some way of entrance) we must plant a guard	109	F11 Epode	7
Or some great thought doth keepe	109	F11 Epode	24
Of which usurping rancke, some have thought love	110	F11 Epode	31
Some vicious foole draw neare,	111	F11 Epode	66
And some one apteth to be trusted, then,	113	F12 Rutland	10
Of some grand peere, whose ayre doth make rejoyce	113	F12 Rutland	12
I have already us'd some happy houres,	115	F12 Rutland	74
No lady, but, at some time, loves her glasse.	117	F13 Aubigny	26
Doe I reflect. Some alderman has power,	117	F13 Aubigny	38
Eate on her clients, and some one devoure.	119	F13 Aubigny	88
And some doe drinke, and some doe dance,	120	F14 Sydney	2
Some ring,	120	F14 Sydney	3
Some sing,	120	F14 Sydney	4
Some have lov'd as old agen.	131	U2 Excuse	6
Find some one good, in some one man;	145	U5 Woman-kind	9
Then what he hath receiv'd. Gifts stinke from some,	153	U13 Sacvile	22
As I have seene some Infants of the Sword,	154	U13 Sacvile	47
Profit in ought: each day some little adde,	157	U13 Sacvile	132
Meet some new matter to looke up and wonder!	157	U13 Sacvile	142
Men past their termes, and prais'd some names too much,	159	U14 Selden	21
How they may make some one that day an Asse	164	U15 Friend-Wars	64
To be abroad chanting some baudie song,	164	U15 Friend-Wars	74
But that some greater names have broke with me,	169	U17 Friend-Debt	8
Some grounds are made the richer, for the Rest;	169	U17 Friend-Debt	17
Some one of which each varied Pillar beares,	176	U24 Frontispice	15
That I may sing my thoughts, in some unvulgar straine.	177	U25 Desmond	13
Yet doth some wholsome Physick for the mind,	180	U26 Ode High	9
To those true numerous Graces; whereof some,	182	U28 Worth	6
Or doe upon my selfe some desperate ill;	191	U38 Elegy 'Tis	3
There may some face or menace of a storme	191	U38 Elegy 'Tis	13

	Page	Title	Line

SOME (cont.)

	Page	Title ·	Line
And take some sirrup after; so doe I,	197	U40 Elegy That	5
For Silke will draw some sneaking Songster thither.	200	U42 Elegy Let	26
Lift up some one, and doe, I tell not what.	201	U42 Elegy Let	58
A Goat in Velvet; or some block could move	202	U42 Elegy Let	82
And my selfe most, in some selfe-boasting Rimes?	203	U43 Vulcan	26
And so some goodlier monster had begot:	204	U43 Vulcan	32
Thou then hadst had some colour for thy flames,	204	U43 Vulcan	40
There were some pieces of as base allay,	204	U43 Vulcan	42
With some more thrift, and more varietie:	205	U43 Vulcan	50
With some more change, and tast of tyranny:	205	U43 Vulcan	V 50
With some more thrift, and yet varietie:	205	U43 Vulcan	V 50
I dare not say a body, but some parts	206	U43 Vulcan	87
To teach some that, their Nurses could not doe,	207	U43 Vulcan	92
To teach some what, their Nurses could not doe,	207	U43 Vulcan	V 92
Reveald (if some can judge) of Argenis,	207	U43 Vulcan	V 96
Reveald (if some do judge) of Argenis,	207	U43 Vulcan	V 96
Some Alchimist there may be yet, or odde	208	U43 Vulcan	118
(Which, some are pleas'd to stile but thy madde pranck)	208	U43 Vulcan	131
'Twas verily some Relique of the Stewes:	209	U43 Vulcan	140
Condemne him to the Brick-kills, or some Hill-/foot	211	U43 Vulcan	183
Condemne him to some Brick-hills, or some Hill-/foot	211	U43 Vulcan	V183
Hill-/foot (out in Sussex) to some iron Mill;	211	U43 Vulcan	V184
some 4 myles hence and have him there disgorge	211	U43 Vulcan	V184
Launces, and men, and some a breaking force.	213	U44 Speach	8
Some hopes of Spaine in their West-Indian Fleet?	219	U47 Tribe	34
Of some wel-wrought Embassage:	221	U48 Bacchus	46
Indeed, her Dressing some man might delight,	223	U49 Pucell	31
From Court, while yet thy fame hath some small day;	223	U49 Pucell	36
Thou stand'st as if some Mysterie thou did'st!	225	U51 Bacon	4
Some brave un-common way:	239	U67 Muses	3
Some of his formes, he lets him not come neere	242	U69 Friend Son	17
Unlesse some saving-Honour of the Crowne,	248	U71 Treasurer	13
(Bearing the promise of some better fate)	252	U75 Epithalam.	10
Some houres before it should, that these may know	257	U75 Epithalam.	146
I would present you with some curious plate	260	U77 Treasurer	V 2
And he is built like some imperiall roome	262	U78 Digby	7
Some Forme defective, or decay'd;	275	U84 Body	6
As some soft chime had stroak'd the ayre;	279	U84 Mind	38
Us forth, by some Celestiall slight	279	U84 Mind	47
Some Paradise, or Palace found	280	U84 Mind	50
Spun out in name of some of the old Nine!	282	U84 Muse	6
But, kept an even gate, as some streight tree	287	U84 Muse	165
Then now beneath some ancient Oke he may,	290	U85 Country	23
Some lustie quick Apulians spouse,	291	U85 Country	42
Which in some swarthie fish uncomely ends:	305	Horace	5
With faire black eyes, and hair, and some vile snout.	339	Horace	V 54/ 52
If I can give some small increase? when, loe,	309	Horace	80
Or some hot youth, yet in his flourishing course;	313	Horace	163
Where some great Lady, or her diligent Nourse;	313	Horace	164
Of some small thankfull land: whether he bee	313	Horace	166
So rare, as with some taxe it doth ingage	323	Horace	383
May, with some right, upon an Author creepe.	329	Horace	538
As Painting, so is Poesie. Some mans hand	329	Horace	539
As some the farther off: This loves the darke;	331	Horace	541
This saying: To some things there is assign'd	331	Horace	548
Make a great Supper; or for some poore man	333	Horace	602
With the shops Foreman, or some such brave sparke,	371	Fletcher	6
. . . Panegyricke lines, but then were upon some occasions . . .	379	Coryat 3	Ttl
Some want, they say in a sort he did crave:	380	Coryat 3	55
Some men, of Bookes or Freinds not speaking right,	386	Browne	1
These are, as some infamous Baud, or Whore,	391	Shakespeare	13
At every line some pinn thereof should slacke	395	May	5
Is fayre got up, and day some houres begun!	396	Drayton	18
Empusa, Lamia, or some Monster, more	398	Drayton	87
In presentacion of some puppet play!	405	Inigo Jones 1	76
All kings to doe the self same deeds with some!	406	Inigo Jones 2	4
He some Colossus to bestryde the Seas,	407	Inigo Jones 2	13
Thy Canvas Gyant, at some Channell aymes,	407	Inigo Jones 2	15
That I should wryte upon him some sharp verse,	407	Inigo Jones 3	3
Seek out some hungry painter, that for bread	408	Inigo Jones 3	10
or as some would say to breake	416	Moon	3
some tast to send hir.	417	Moon	20
Give cause to some of wonnder, some despite,	420	Ode:If Men	35

SOMERSET

	Page	Title	Line
. . . Robert, Earle of Somerset.	384	Somerset	Ttl
Which I do, early, vertuous Somerset,	384	Somerset	7

SOME-THING

	Page	Title	Line
On some-thing, that walkes some-where.	30	E11 Something	Ttl

SOMETHING

	Page	Title	Line
Something, which, else, could hope for no esteeme.	64	E101 Supper	6
Something more then thou hast spi'd.	137	U2 Cupid	50
And the disposure will be something new,	269	U81 Pawlet	16
May something by that twilight see	273	U84 Cradle	15
Yet something, to the Painters view,	275	U84 Body	9
If something strange, that never yet was had	313	Horace	178
If something fresh, that never yet was had	342	Horace	V178
With something that was acceptably new.	321	Horace	327
But, I would have, thee, to know something new,	394	Jane Ogle	13
Something your Surship doth not yet intend!	402	Inigo Jones 1	14
You looke, my Joseph, I should something say	414	Rutter	1

SOMETIME

	Page	Title	Line
This makes me, Mrs. that sometime by stealth,	197	U40 Elegy That	9

599

		Page	Title	Line

SOMETIME (cont.)
Yet, sometime, doth the Comedie excite . . . . . 311 Horace 132
Yet sometime both the Comoedy doth raise . . . . 341 Horace V132
SOMETIMES
Though you sometimes proclaime me too severe, . . 190 U37 Friend-Book 16
But shall sometimes be tempted to obey . . . . 190 U37 Friend-Book 32
There comes sometimes to things of meanest place. . 321 Horace 354
Thence draw forth true expressions. For, sometimes, . 327 Horace 455
Angry. Sometimes, I heare good Homer snore. . . 329 Horace 536
Yet may as blind men sometimes hit the marke. . . 383 Author 6
SOMETYMES
But sometymes shall bee tempted to obaye . . . 422 Censure 25
SOMEWHAT
And the disposure will be somewhat new, ... 269 U81 Pawlet V 16
That he dares to informe you, but somewhat meticulous, . 380 Coryat 3 33
SOME-WHERE
On some-thing, that walkes some-where. . . . . 30 E11 Something Ttl
SOMMER
In the silent sommer-nights, ... 103 F6 Celia 2 17
SOMMER-NIGHTS
In the silent sommer-nights, ... 103 F6 Celia 2 17
SOMWHAT
I had somwhat else to say, ... 417 Moon 9
SON
. . . that Noble Gentleman, Mr. Hierome Weston, Son, and . . . 252 U75 Epithalam. Ttl
By bringing forth God's onely Son, no other. . . 414 Ghyrlond 48
SONG
Item, the babylonian song you sing; . . . . 51 E73 Fine Grand 9
Next morne, an Ode: Thou mak'st a song ere night. . 72 E112 Gamster 12
Alcides, be thou succouring to my song. . . . 85 E133 Voyage 50
Song. To Celia. . . . . 102 F5 Celia 1 Ttl
Song. That Women are but Mens shaddowes. . . . 104 F7 Women but Ttl
Song. To Celia. . . . . 106 F9 Celia 3 Ttl
And in either Prose, or Song, ... 133 U2 Suffered 23
A Song. . . . . 144 U4 Song Ttl
In the person of Woman-kind. A Song Apologetique. . 145 U5 Woman-kind Ttl
Another. In defence of their Inconstancie. A Song. . 146 U6 Defence Ttl
To be abroad chanting some baudie song, . . . 164 U15 Friend-Wars 74
Doth Cynthia, in Propertius song . . . . . 181 U27 Ode Helen 11
Though I, in working of my song, ... 182 U27 Ode Helen 33
A Song. . . . . 189 U36 Song Ttl
The rest, my journey into Scotland song, . . . 207 U43 Vulcan 94
And not a Song be other . . . . . . 221 U48 Bacchus 35
An Ode, or Song, by all the Muses. . . . . . 239 U67 Muses Ttl
And ever close the burden of the Song, . . . 249 U72 King 17
And then noyse forth the burden of their Song, . . 249 U72 King V 17
Epithalamion; Or, A Song: Celebrating The nuptials of . . . 252 U75 Epithalam. Ttl
You'ld reade a Snake, in his next Song. . . . 260 U76 Petition 32
To eate a Snake, in his next Song. . . . . 260 U76 Petition V 32
Unto your honour: I can tune in song . . . . 261 U77 Treasurer 27
Unto your honour: I can voyce in song . . . . 261 U77 Treasurer V 27
In signe the Subject, and the Song will live, . . 262 U78 Digby 17
Of brightest Mira, doe we raise our Song, . . . 264 U79 New-yeares 24
Of brightest Mira, is our Song; the grace . . . 264 U79 New-yeares 32
But, here's a Song of her Descent; . . . . 273 U84 Cradle 29
2. The Song of her Descent. . . . . . . 274 U84 Descent Ttl
A new Song to his praise, and great I Am: . . . 285 U84 Muse 90
Continue thy sweete Song. . . . . . . 367 Ode Who saith 34
Thy Richard, rais'd in song, past pulling downe. . 385 Brooke 8
Keepe due proportion in the ample song, . . . 395 May 12
With every song, I sweare, and so would dye: . . 397 Drayton 54
And, graced with her song, ... 402 Filmer 13
SONGE
That were the happie subject of my songe. . . . 419 Ode:If Men 9
SONGS
Except the duell. Can sing songs, and catches; . 74 E115 Honest Man 13
Shed in thy Songs; 'tis true: but short of thee. . 82 E130 Ferrab. 1 18
One good enough for a songs sake. . . . . 145 U5 Woman-kind 12
And lead them with soft songs, where that he would. . 327 Horace 485
But then, thy'epistolar Heroick Songs, . .` . . 397 Drayton 29
SONGSTER
For Silke will draw some sneaking Songster thither. . 200 U42 Elegy Let 26
SONGSTERS
Such Songsters there are store of; witnesse he . . 201 U42 Elegy Let 65
SONNE
On my First Sonne. . . . . 41 E45 First Son Ttl
With his brave sonne, the Prince, they saw thy fires . 95 F2 Penshurst 77
Let the old boy, your sonne, ply his old taske, . . 107 F10 Proludium 19
My best of wishes, may you beare a sonne. . . . 116 F12 Rutland 100
'T will be exacted of your name, whose sonne, . . 121 F14 Sydney 41
Eternall God the Sonne, who not denyd'st . . . 128 U1 Trinitie 21
Father and Sonne; the Comforter, in breeding . . 128 U1 Trinitie 26
Father, and Sonne, and Holy Ghost, you three . . 128 U1 Trinitie 37
That gav'st a Sonne, ... 129 U1 Father 19
The Sonne of God, th'Eternall King, ... 130 U1 Nativitie 7
Before me here, the Friend and Sonne: . . . . 151 U12 Corbet 4
Or two, or three, a Sonne will dis-inherit, . . 192 U38 Elegy 'Tis 42
Sonne of the Wind! for so thy mother gone . . . 208 U43 Vulcan 111
Sonne to the grave wise Keeper of the Seale, . . 225 U51 Bacon 9
Sol will re-shine. If not, Charles hath a Sonne. . 238 U65 Prince 12
And Sol will shine. If not, Charles hath a Sonne. . 238 U65 Prince V 12
Epigram. To a Friend, and Sonne. . . . . 241 U69 Friend Son Ttl
Sonne, and my Friend, I had not call'd you so . . 241 U69 Friend Son 1

600

			Page	Title	Line

SONNE (cont.)
But most, a vertuous Sonne. . . . . 244 U70 Ode 47
To pay, with honours, to his noble Sonne . . . 256 U75 Epithalam. 106
To My L. the King, On the Christning His second Sonne James. . 268 U80 Christning Ttl
Great King, thy having of a second Sonne: . . . 268 U80 Christning 2
Then comforted her Lord! and blest her Sonne! . . 270 U81 Pawlet 57
And will you, worthy Sonne, Sir, knowing this, . . 285 U84 Muse 97
Of life, and light, the Sonne of God, the Word! . . 285 U84 Muse 112
Hath given wholly to the Sonne (the rather . . 288 U84 Muse 216
As being the Sonne of Man) to shew his Power, . . 288 U84 Muse 217
With gentle Calais, Thurine Orniths Sonne; . . 293 U87 Hor.3:9 14
Most Writers, noble Sire, and either Sonne, . . 307 Horace 33
There's Albin's sonne will say, Substract an ounce . 327 Horace 467
Rather his sonne, I should have cal'd thee, why? . 378 Coryat 2 88
The Sunne translated, or the Sonne of May. . . . 395 May 24
To my Deare Sonne, and right-learned Friend, ... 414 Rutter Ttl
SONNES
Were you Jove's sonnes, or had Alcides might. . . . 89 E133 Voyage 182
The Sonnes obedience knew no No, . . 130 U1 Nativitie 14
And could (if our great men would let their Sonnes . 214 U44 Speach 57
Their Sonnes to studie Arts, the Lawes, the Creed: . 215 U44 Speach 74
Her Sonnes before the people; nor the ill-/Natur'd . 317 Horace 264
Sonnes, seeke not me amonge these polish'd stones: . 387 Cavendish 1
SONNET
A Sonnet, to the noble Lady, the Lady Mary Worth. . . 182 U28 Worth Ttl
And straight-way spent a Sonnet; with that other . . 201 U42 Elegy Let 67
SONNETS
Since I exscribe your Sonnets, am become . . . . 182 U28 Worth 3
SONS
And Sons, and Daughters, with their Parents talke; . 285 U84 Muse 118
Father, and sons right worthy of your Sire, . . . 339 Horace V 34
SOON
Of money, haughtie, to desire soon mov'd, . . . 315 Horace 235
SOONE
He toyles to be at hell, as soone as they. . . 36 E31 Banck 4
To have so soone scap'd worlds, and fleshes rage, . 41 E45 First Son 7
Is it the paine affrights? that's soone forgot. . 46 E62 Would-bee 5
Which, if thou leave not soone (though I am loth) . 54 E81 Proule 7
For fame, with breath soone kindled, soone blowne out. 83 E131 Ferrab. 2 14
But be glad, as soone with me, ... 131 U2 Excuse 17
As I did feele it done, as soone as meant: . . 153 U13 Sacvile 12
Soone as lazie thou wert knowne, . . . 183 U29 Fit of Rime 13
They looke at best like Creame-bowles, and you soone . 198 U40 Elegy That 29
So, in that ground, as soone it grew to be . . 214 U44 Speach 37
For education of our Lordings; Soone . . . 214 U44 Speach 62
This Prince of flowers? Soone shoot thou up, and grow 237 U65 Prince 5
And interpose thy selfe, ('care not how soone.) . 238 U65 Prince 10
Could soone espie . . . . . . 256 U75 Epithalam. 110
Soone angry, and soone pleas'd, is sweet, or sowre, . 315 Horace 227
For the vile Goat, soone after, forth did send . 319 Horace 320
The docile mind may soone thy precepts know, . 329 Horace 504
shee soone will heare it. . . . 417 Moon 24
howe soone with a selfe ticklinge hee was spent. . 420 Ode:If Men 18
The mayne comaund of scepters, soone doth perishe . 422 Lucan 9
SOONER
The cloth's no sooner gone, but it gets up . . 74 E115 Honest Man 24
Sooner, then he lost his might, . . . 132 U2 How he saw 14
He no sooner heard the Law, ... 133 U2 Suffered 13
Sooner then my affection from the faire. . . 200 U42 Elegy Let 13
Whose ayre will sooner Hell, then their dull senses peirce, . 420 Ode:If Men 23
SOONEST
Contagion in the prease is soonest catch'd. . . . 118 F13 Aubigny 58
SOOTE
All soote, and embers! odious, as thy worke! . . 207 U43 Vulcan 106
SOOTH (VERB)
Then words that sooth her! . . . 134 U2 Triumph 16
SOOTH
As, sooth, the Parcae thought him one, . . . 77 E120 S. P. 15
SOOTHING
Whether his soothing friend speake truth, or no. . 333 Horace 606
SOP
The tripple head without a sop. At last, . . 89 E133 Voyage 186
SOPE
A sope-boyler; and Aeacus him nigh, . . . 89 E133 Voyage 188
SOPE-BOYLER
A sope-boyler; and Aeacus him nigh, . . . 89 E133 Voyage 188
SOPHOCLES
Euripides, and Sophocles to us, ... 391 Shakespeare 34
SORDID
When by thy sordid bountie she hath on . . . 201 U42 Elegy Let 45
To sordid flatteries, acts of strife, . . . 244 U70 Ode 39
SORE
Great Club-fist, though thy backe, and bones be sore, . 85 E133 Voyage 55
Hercules? alas his bones are yet sore, . . . 107 F10 Proludium 4
SORES
Laden with plague-sores, and their sinnes, were heard, . 84 E133 Voyage 17
SORIE
First, prepare you to be sorie, ... 131 U2 Excuse 14
SORRELL
Or the herb Sorrell, that loves Meadows still, . . 291 U85 Country 57
SORROW
For so will sorrow slay me; . . . . 145 U4 Song 10
He when he sees a sorrow such as this, . . 193 U38 Elegy 'Tis 87

	Page	Title	Line

SORROW (cont.)
A sorrow in me, fit to wait to her!   .   .   .   .   .   282 U84 Muse   10
Of sorrow, then all pompe of gaudy daies: .   .   .   287 U84 Muse   182
With weightie sorrow hurles us all along,   .   .   .   311 Horace   155
So, be there never discontent, or sorrow,   .   .   .   384 Somerset   15
But Sorrow, she desir'd no other Friend: .   .   .   394 Jane Ogle   17
Whom shee, with Sorrow first did lodge, then feast,   .   394 Jane Ogle   20
SORROWES
With famine, wants, and sorrowes many a dosen,   .   .   86   E133 Voyage   71
And turne the blackest sorrowes to bright joyes: .   . 112   F11 Epode   95
And pray who shall my sorrowes read, ...   152 U12 Corbet   33
SORRY
Death's selfe is sorry.   77   E120 S. P.   4
No more, I am sorry for so fond cause, say,   .   .   . 171   U20 Shrub   4
SORT
And, in so shitten sort, so long had us'd him: .   .   86   E133 Voyage   98
I, and for this neglect, the courser sort   .   .   . 219   U47 Tribe   54
In Helicon; a great sort will not pare   .   .   .   325 Horace   422
Some want, they say in a sort he did crave: .   .   . 380 Coryat 3   55
SORTS (VERB)
Thou, nor thy loosenesse with my making sorts.   .   . 107   F10 Proludium   18
SORTS
Thou, nor their loosenesse with our making sorts.   . 107   F10 Proludium V 18
All sorts of fish with Musicke of his maw.   .   .   . 374 Coryat 1   11
SORY
And never but for doing wrong be sory;   .   .   .   . 168 U15 Friend-Wars 180
SOSII
This booke will get the Sosii money; This   .   .   . 329 Horace   517
SO'T
Who makes the one, so't be first, makes both.   .   . 152   U12 Corbet   40
SOUGH
And bad her fare-well sough, unto the lurden: .   .   87   E133 Voyage   115
SOUGHT
To lye upon thy stall, till it be sought;   .   .   .   28   E3 Bookseller   5
As all thy honors were by them first sought: .   .   49   E67 Suffolk   8
And have sought (to give new birth)   77   E120 S. P.   21
Sought out the Fountaines, Sources, Creekes, paths, wayes,   .   160   U14 Selden   45
That kept man living! Pleasures only sought!   .   . 163 U15 Friend-Wars 41
Upon reward, till the reward him sought.   .   .   . 185 U30 Burleigh   14
Then this did by her true? She never sought   .   . 188 U34 Small Poxe   5
SOULDIER
Cob, thou nor souldier, thiefe, nor fencer art,   .   50   E69 Cob   1
Hee stood, a Souldier to the last right end,   .   . 244 U70 Ode   45
Nor Souldier-like started with rough alarmes,   .   . 289 U85 Country   5
SOULDIER-LIKE
Nor Souldier-like started with rough alarmes,   .   . 289 U85 Country   5
SOULDIERS
To true Souldiers.   69   E108 Soldiers   Ttl
What th'antique souldiers were, the moderne bee?   .   72   E111 Edmonds 2   2
SOULE
The bodies stripes, I see, the soule may save.   .   .   33   E21 Gam'ster   8
Whose soule heavens Queene, (whose name shee beares)   .   33   E22 Daughter   7
Onely a learned, and a manly soule   52   E76 Bedford 1   13
Came not that soule exhausted so their store.   .   .   53   E79 Rutland   4
Then whose I doe not know a whiter soule,   .   .   .   60   E93 Radcliffe   11
I should beleeve, the soule of Tacitus   .   .   .   61   E95 Savile   3
And that thy soule should give thy flesh her weight.   .   70   E109 Nevil   14
Hath chang'd his soule, and made his object you: .   74   E114 Sydney   5
Who sees a soule, in such a body set,   .   .   .   79   E125 Uvedale   5
To say, indeed, shee were the soule of heaven,   .   82   E130 Ferrab. 1   11
The thirst, that from the soule doth rise,   .   . 106   F9 Celia 3   5
The thirst, that from the soule proceedes,   .   . 106   F9 Celia 3   V 5
My gratefull soule, the subject of her powers,   . 115   F12 Rutland   73
And show, how, to the life, my soule presents   . 115   F12 Rutland   86
And freed the soule from danger;   130   U1 Nativitie   9
What Tree or stone doth want a soule?   .   .   . 143   U3 Musicall   7
His time? health? soule? will he for these goe throw   . 165 U15 Friend-Wars 103
Runs sweetly, as it had his Lordships Soule;   .   . 167 U15 Friend-Wars 148
And, till the coming of the Soule   .   .   .   . 188 U35 Chute   5
The contrite Soule, who hath no thought to win   . 193 U38 Elegy 'Tis   89
Of State, of fame, of body, and of soule,   .   . 224 U50 Countesse   18
And only, his great Soule envy'd, ... 234 U60 La-ware   17
Sound thou her Vertues, give her soule a Name.   . 269 U81 Pawlet   22
It is too neere of kin to Heaven, the Soule,   .   . 269 U81 Pawlet   29
It is too neere of kin to God, the Soule,   .   . 269 U81 Pawlet   V 29
Of her disease, how did her soule assure   .   . 270 U81 Pawlet   50
And I, into the world, all Soule, was sent!   .   . 270 U81 Pawlet   56
And I, into the world with my Soule, was sent!   . 270 U81 Pawlet   V 56
With what injustice should one soule pretend   . 271 U81 Pawlet   92
With what injustice can one soule pretend   .   . 271 U81 Pawlet   V 92
Her blessed Soule, hence, forth this valley vane   . 283 U84 Muse   34
To Body, and Soule! where Love is all the guest!   . 284 U84 Muse   64
Hath neither soule, nor sinewes. Loftie he   .   . 307 Horace   37
I, therefore will begin. Soule of the Age!   .   . 391 Shakespeare   17
Her soule possest her fleshes state   .   .   . 399 Lady Ogle   25
Painting & Carpentry are the Soule of Masque.   . 404 Inigo Jones 1   50
A Noble honest Soule! what's this to thee?   .   . 406 Inigo Jones 2   6
SOULES
And noted for what flesh such soules were fram'd,   .   66   E103 L Wroth 1   3
Let these in wanton feete daunce out their soules.   . 108   F10 Proludium   11
And, for it, life, conscience, yea, soules are given,   . 113   F12 Rutland   4
The soules, shee loves. Those other glorious notes,   . 114   F12 Rutland   43
And that your soules conspire, as they were gone   . 119   F13 Aubigny   119

		Page	Title	Line

SOULES (cont.)
Nay, rather both our soules bee strayn'd . . . . . 144 U3 Musicall 25
On all Soules that are absent; even the dead; . . . . 218 U47 Tribe 17
As other soules, to his, dwell in a Lane: . . . . 262 U78 Digby 12
There, all the happy soules, that ever were, ... 285 U84 Muse 113
The safetie of our soules, and forfeit breath! . . . 286 U84 Muse 136
Whilst other soules convert to base abuse . . . . 361 Palmer 11
SOUND (SWOON)
Doth mete, whose lyne doth sound the depth of things:) . . 176 U24 Frontispice 12
SOUND (HEALTHY)
A body sound, with sounder minde; . . . . . 99 F3 Wroth 102
But first dost vexe, and search it! If not sound, . . . 187 U33 Councellour 19
Upright and sound, ... 258 U75 Epithalam. 182
A quiet mind; free powers; and body sound; 295 U90 Mart.10:47 6
SOUND
That sound, and that authoritie with her name, ... 49 E67 Suffolk 3
A romane sound, but romane vertue weares, ... 58 E91 Vere 2
When on thy trumpet shee did sound a blast, ... 58 E91 Vere 7
No matter, stinkards, row. What croaking sound . . . 86 E133 Voyage 91
The Angels so did sound it, ... 130 U1 Nativitie 3
Or that doth sound a Trumpet, and doth call . . . . 154 U13 Sacvile 35
Yet, let our Trumpets sound; . . . . . 239 U67 Muses 13
In weight, in measure, number, sound, ... 244 U70 Ode 50
Sound, sound his praises loud, and with his, hers divide. . . 264 U79 New-yeares 19
Sound thou her Vertues, give her soule a Name. . . . 269 U81 Pawlet 22
And, though the sound were parted thence, ... 279 U84 Mind 39
Nor after Chloe did his Lydia sound; 293 U87 Hor.3:9 6
In sound, quite from his fortune; both the rout, . . . 313 Horace 159
And rivall with the Trumpet for his sound, ... 319 Horace 288
For, neither doth the String still yeeld that sound . . . 329 Horace 521
But mixt with sound, transcending . . . . . 365 Ode Splendor 15
SOUNDE
But unto more dispayre to Imitate their sounde. . . . 420 Ode:If Men 36
SOUNDED
Shall find their depth: they're sounded with a spoone. . . 198 U40 Elegy That 30
SOUNDER
A body sound, with sounder minde; . . . . . 99 F3 Wroth 102
SOUNDEST
And though the soundest legs goe every day, ... 36 E31 Banck 3
SOUNDLESSE
The Sunne, a Sea, or soundlesse Pit; . . . . . 278 U84 Mind 11
SOUNDS
And all his numbers, both of sense, and sounds. . . . 61 E95 Savile 6
Without which, all the rest were sounds, or lost. . . . 118 F13 Aubigny 50
Which, when it sounds at best, but eccho's right; . . . 390 Shakespeare 8
SOURCE
Fresh Lovers businesse, and the Wines free source. . . . 311 Horace 116
Each subt'lest Passion, with her source, and spring, . . 370 Author 7
Each subject Passion, with her source, and spring, . . . 370 Author V 7
SOURCES
Sought out the Fountaines, Sources, Creekes, paths, wayes, . 160 U14 Selden 45
SOVERAIGNE
Then now, to love the Soveraigne, and the Lawes? . . . 236 U64 Charles 3 8
Then now, to love the Soveraigne, or his Lawes? . . . 236 U64 Charles 3 V 8
the sweetest simples, and most soveraigne seedes. . . . 361 Palmer 12
SOVERAIGNTIE
Virtue, and Soveraigntie, they not consort. . . . . 423 Lucan 18
SOV'RAIGNE
No lesse a sov'raigne cure, then to the mind; . . . . 82 E130 Ferrab. 1 8
SOW
Of newes, and noyse, to sow out a long meale. . . . 74 E115 Honest Man V 10
To sow consumption, every where thou go'st; . . . 205 U43 Vulcan V 58
Stay, see the Virgins sow, ... 254 U75 Epithalam. 61
SOW'D
Had sow'd these fruits, and got the harvest in. . . . 247 U70 Ode 128
SOWER
See the grave, sower, and supercilious Sir . . . . 162 U15 Friend-Wars 19
Till the sower Minute comes of taking leave, . . . 197 U40 Elegy That 2
Sower Mother of sweet Loves, forbeare 292 U86 Hor.4:1 5
Though sower, with safetie of his gravitie, ... 319 Horace 322
SOWRE
No sowre, or sollen bed-mate, yet a Chast; 295 U90 Mart.10:47 10
In Verse unequall match'd, first sowre Laments, . . . 309 Horace 107
Soone angry, and soone pleas'd, is sweet, or sowre, . . . 315 Horace 227
Sweet mix'd with sowre, to his Reader, so . . . . 329 Horace 515
SO'XCEED
To see the workmanship so'xceed the cost! . . . . 160 U14 Selden 54
SOYLE
Thou joy'st in better markes, of soyle, of ayre, . . . 93 F2 Penshurst 7
Before the soyle hath smutch'd it? . . . . . 134 U2 Triumph 24
A Soyle, not barren; a continewall fire; 295 U90 Mart.10:47 4
SPACE
For, what is life, if measur'd by the space, ... 243 U70 Ode 21
You once enjoy'd: A short space severs yee, ... 285 U84 Muse 105
SPACES
Shoot forth in smooth and comely spaces; have . . . 157 U13 Sacvile 150
SPAINE
And at the Pope, and Spaine slight faces make. . . . 59 E92 New Crie 34
Some hopes of Spaine in their West-Indian Fleet? . . . 219 U47 Tribe 34
Or that the Match from Spaine was ever meant? . . . 219 U47 Tribe 36
Of Spaine or France; or were not prick'd downe one . . . 219 U47 Tribe 47
Though slower Spaine; and Italy mature. . . . . 368 Ode Who saith 88
For though Spaine gave him his first ayre and Vogue, . . 389 Aleman 15

	Page	Title	Line
SPAINE (cont.)			
But cause thou hearst the mighty k. of Spaine	406	Inigo Jones 2	1
SPAINES			
T'have wak'd, if sleeping, Spaines Ambassadour,	213	U44 Speach	4
SPAKE			
Spake to 'hem louder, then the oxe in Livie:	86	E133 Voyage	74
SPAN			
That quilts those bodies, I have leave to span:	200	U42 Elegy Let	32
Find all our Atomes from a point t' a span!	287	U84 Muse	152
SPANGLED			
And spangled Petticotes brought forth to eye,	223	U49 Pucell	19
SPANISH			
Spanish receipt, to make her teeth to rot.	188	U34 Small Poxe	12
As in this Spanish Proteus; who, though writ	389	Aleman	5
Finer then was his Spanish, if my Oath	389	Aleman	18
SPARCLE			
did sparcle foorth in Center of the rest:	361	Palmer	16
SPARE			
That's a Toy, that I could spare:	142	U2 Exception	2
Spare your owne goodnesse yet; and be not great	191	U38 Elegy 'Tis	17
And so I spare it. Come what can become	199	U41 Elegy Since	19
Hee is true Vulcan still! He did not spare	210	U43 Vulcan	159
Thou art true Vulcan still! Thou durst not spare	210	U43 Vulcan	V159
He was right Vulcan still! He did not spare	210	U43 Vulcan	V159
And Gunnes there, spare to poure	239	U67 Muses	8
'T were better spare a Butt, then spill his Muse.	241	U68 House-hold	12
Long intermitted, pray thee, pray thee spare:	292	U86 Hor.4:1	2
Right spare, and warie: then thou speak'st to mee	307	Horace	66
Praise the spare diet, wholsome justice, lawes,	317	Horace	283
But you, Pompilius off-spring, spare you not	325	Horace	415
of her white Hand; or she can spare it.	662	Bedford	10
SPAR'D			
Thou Seed-plot of the warre, that hast not spar'd	213	U44 Speach	24
SPARKE			
One sparke of your Diviner heat	174	U22 Elegy Tho	31
Yet he himselfe is but a sparke.	189	U36 Song	8
A Sparke to set whole worlds a-fire,	189	U36 Song	9
That this sparke of the same fire let loose	209	U43 Vulcan	V141
With the shops Foreman, or some such brave sparke,	371	Fletcher	6
yf from a little sparke hee rise not fier.	383	Rich	16
SPARKLE			
And this a Sparkle of that fire let loose	209	U43 Vulcan	141
SPARKLING			
A beautie of that cleere, and sparkling light,	112	F11 Epode	93
A beautie of that cleere, and sparkling sight,	112	F11 Epode	V 93
Just above her sparkling eyes,	136	U2 Cupid	16
SPARROWES			
Though thy wild thoughts with sparrowes wings doe flye,	111	F11 Epode	73
SPARTANS			
Looke, how we read the Spartans were inflam'd	398	Drayton	67
SPAWNE			
Thou sluggish spawne, that canst, but wilt not see?	250	U73 Weston	8
SPEACH			
A speach according to Horace.	213	U44 Speach	Ttl
A Speach Presented unto King James at a tylting . . .	382	Rich	Ttl
SPEAK			
Is now to speak, and even now to differ	339	Horace	V 61
It much will sway whether a god speak, than;	342	Horace	V161
SPEAKE			
Which should thy countries love to speake refuse,	40	E43 Salisbury 1	3
That, any way, my booke should speake thy name:	53	E77 Not name	2
That his whole body should speake french, not he?	56	E88 Monsieur	2
As others speake, but onely thou dost act.	57	E89 Allen	12
I speake thy other graces, not lesse showne,	58	E91 Vere	13
We need a man, can speake of the intents,	62	E95 Savile	31
Of which wee'll speake our minds, amidst our meate;	65	E101 Supper	23
Can so speake Caesar, as thy labours doe.	71	E110 Edmonds 1	12
As but to speake thee, Overbury, is praise:	73	E113 Overbury	2
And heare her speake with one, and her first tongue;	78	E122 Rudyerd 2	6
Which Musick had; or speake her knowne effects,	82	E130 Ferrab. 1	3
How can I speake of thy great paines, but erre?	83	E132 Sylvester	2
But I will speake (and know I shall be heard)	87	E133 Voyage	105
A-bed canst heare the loud stag speake,	97	F3 Wroth	22
'Tis growne almost a danger to speake true	116	F13 Aubigny	1
They speake; since you are truly that rare wife,	119	F13 Aubigny	110
Is, that I have leave to speake,	133	U2 Suffered	22
(And that quickly) speake your Man.	140	U2 Promise	30
'Twere to long, to speake of all:	141	U2 Her man	33
Meane what I speake: and still will keepe that Vow.	159	U14 Selden	28
Aske not to know this Man. If fame should speake	172	U21 Ltl Shrub	1
So speake (as yet it is not mute)	181	U27 Ode Helen	4
To speake the fate of the Sicilian Maid	207	U43 Vulcan	96
More then to praise a Dog? or Horse? or speake	215	U44 Speach	71
To speake my selfe out too ambitiously,	218	U47 Tribe	6
That to speake well, thinke it above all sinne,	218	U47 Tribe	19
Your happinesse, and doth not speake you blest,	234	U61 Epigram	9
This is King Charles his Day. Speake it, thou Towre,	249	U72 King	1
This is King Charles his birth day. Speake it, thou Towre,	249	U72 King	V 1
With Angels, Muse, to speake these: Nothing can	255	U75 Epithalam.	84
But rather I, should I of that part speake!	269	U81 Pawlet	28
Speake it, you bold Penates, you that stand	274	U84 Descent	7
Sweet Mind, then speake your selfe, and say,	278	U84 Mind	17
Invention. Now, to speake; and then differ	307	Horace	61

604

		Page	Title	Line
SPEAKE (cont.)				
Peleus, or Telephus. If you speake vile	. . . .	311	Horace	147
It much will differ, if a God speake, than,	. . .	313	Horace	161
'Tis hard, to speake things common, properly:	. . .	313	Horace	183
Speake to me, Muse, the Man, who, after Troy was sack't,	.	315	Horace	201
Any fourth man, to speake at all, aspire. .	. . .	317	Horace	275
As not make difference, whether Davus speake,	. . .	321	Horace	345
Wilt nothing against nature speake, or doe:	. . .	331	Horace	574
Whether his soothing friend speake truth, or no.	. .	333	Horace	606
If all the vulgar Tongues, that speake this day,	. .	388	Chapman	7
Oh, to make Boardes to speake! There is a taske	. .	404	Inigo Jones 1	49
I am come to Add, and speake, ...	.	416	Moon	2
SPEAKER				
Orpheus, a priest, and speaker for the Gods	. . .	327	Horace	479
SPEAKES				
He speakes to men with a Rhinocerotes nose,	. . .	35	E28 Surly	4
Speakes Heavens Language! and discourseth free	. . .	271	U81 Pawlet	71
Speakes Heavens Language! and discovereth free	. . .	271	U81 Pawlet	V 71
If now the phrase of him that speakes, shall flow,	. .	313	Horace	158
SPEAKING				
By speaking well o' the company' it 's in.	. . .	74	E115 Honest Man	8
And speaking worst of those, from whom they went	. .	154	U13 Sacvile	51
In frequent speaking by the pious Psalmes .	. . .	288	U84 Muse	191
The power, and rule of speaking resteth still.	. . .	309	Horace	104
Some men, of Bookes or Freinds not speaking right,	. .	386	Browne	1
SPEAKS				
Here he speaks out of his Pottle, ...	.	657	Door Apollo	3
SPEAK'ST				
Right spare, and warie: then thou speak'st to mee	. .	307	Horace	66
SPECIALL				
But when I read that speciall piece, restor'd,	. . .	61	E95 Savile	7
Of his speciall grace to Letters, ...	.	259	U76 Petition	7
SPECIALLY				
Specially the newes of Darby;	.	417	Moon	21
SPECIES				
Through which not only we, but all our Species are.	. .	253	U75 Epithalam.	32
SPECIOUS				
They were as specious as his Trees. .	. . .	152	U12 Corbet	20
With specious places, and being humour'd right,	. . .	327	Horace	457
Sense, what they are! which by a specious fyne	. . .	404	Inigo Jones 1	55
SPECKLED				
The purpled pheasant, with the speckled side:	. . .	94	F2 Penshurst	28
SPECTACLE				
This were a spectacle! A sight to draw	. . .	233	U59 Newcastle	13
SPECTACLES				
Because that studies spectacles, and showes,	. . .	118	F13 Aubigny	65
You are the Spectacles of State! Tis true	. . .	403	Inigo Jones 1	42
SPECTATORS				
That are Spectators, with their miserie,	. . .	311	Horace	137
The free spectators, subject to no Law,	. . .	319	Horace	324
SPEECH				
What weight, and what authoritie in thy speech!	. .	31	E14 Camden	9
In speech; it is with that excesse . . .	.	279	U84 Mind	34
Or grace of speech, should hope a lasting date.	. .	309	Horace	100
And the severe, speech ever serious. . .	.	311	Horace	151
A speech out of Lucane.	.	422	Lucan	Ttl
SPEECHES				
Or crack out bawdie speeches, and uncleane.	. . .	321	Horace	359
Or cracke out shamefull speeches, or uncleane.	. . .	347	Horace	V351/359
SPELL (NOUN)				
By that one spell he lives, eates, drinkes, arrayes	.	30	E12 Shift	5
SPELL				
Who scarse can spell th'hard names: whose knight lesse can.		28	E3 Bookseller	10
Not liv'd; for Life doth her great actions spell,	. .	245	U70 Ode	59
SPEND				
Truth might spend all her voyce, Fame all her art.	. .	68	E106 E Herbert	4
Spend not then his quifts in vaine. . . .	.	102	F5 Celia 1	5
That for th'oyle of Talke, dare spend . .	.	105	F8 Sicknesse	33
Let 'hem on poulders, oyles, and paintings, spend,	. .	118	F13 Aubigny	77
Reare-Suppers in their Names! and spend whole nights	.	156	U13 Sacvile	101
Thither it flowes. How much did Stallion spend	. .	163	U15 Friend-Wars	47
For man to spend his money on? his wit? .	. .	165	U15 Friend-Wars	102
Then change; no word, or worke, more would he spend	. .	335	Horace	630
Thou that doest spend thie dayes . . .	.	420	Ode:If Men	24
SPENSER				
Chaucer, or Spenser, or bid Beaumont lye	. . .	391	Shakespeare	20
SPENSER'S				
Upon them, (next to Spenser's noble booke,)	. . .	263	U78 Digby	24
SPENT				
I would have spent: how every Muse should know it,	. .	55	E84 Bedford 2	7
Nor death; but when thy latest sand is spent,	. . .	100	F3 Wroth	105
Spent in surfets: and their dayes, . . .	.	104	F8 Sicknesse	5
Because lust's meanes are spent:	.	111	F11 Epode	78
To be beholders, when their powers are spent.	. . .	166	U15 Friend-Wars	140
No man inflicts that paine, till hope be spent:	. .	192	U38 Elegy 'Tis	44
And straight-way spent a Sonnet; with that other	. .	201	U42 Elegy Let	67
or spent my wretched paper or my tyme	. . .	204	U43 Vulcan	V 33
Wherein was oyle, beside the succour spent,	. . .	207	U43 Vulcan	99
Wherin (besides the noble Aydes were spent,	. . .	207	U43 Vulcan	V 99
By Carew, Cotton, Selden, oyle was spent	. . .	207	U43 Vulcan	V100
By Carew, Cotton, Seldens oyle was spent	. . .	207	U43 Vulcan	V100
Of Carew, Cotton, Selden, oyles were spent	. . .	207	U43 Vulcan	V100
Had lost our selves? and prodigally spent	. . .	286	U84 Muse	141

```
                                                      Page      Title        Line
SPENT  (cont.)
    She spent more time in teares her selfe to dresse   .   287  U84 Muse        180
    Her solemne houres she spent, or giving Almes,  .   .   288  U84 Muse        192
    wear spent with wonder as they weare delated,   .   .   361  Palmer           24
    howe soone with a selfe ticklinge hee was spent.   .   420  Ode:If Men       18
SPHAERE
    Smiles in his Sphaere, to see the rest affect,    .   .   366  Ode Who saith    13
SPHEARE
    Lucy, you brightnesse of our spheare, who are    .   .    60  E94 Bedford 3     1
    Lucy, you brightnesse of our spheare, who are   .   .    61  E94 Bedford 3    15
    That the eight sphere, no lesse, then planets seaven, .   82  E110 Ferrab. 1   12
    His life was of Humanitie the Spheare.    .   .   .   244  U70 Ode          52
    There, high exalted in the Spheare,  .   .   .   .   279  U84 Mind         29
SPHEARES
    And challenge all the Spheares,   .   .   .   .   .   143  U3 Musicall       2
    The Angels from their Spheares:   .   .   .   .   .   239  U67 Muses        21
    By all the Spheares consent, so in the heart of June?  .   253  U75 Epithalam.   16
    Of Spheares, as light of starres; She was earthes Eye:  .   372  Epitaph          9
SPHERE
    (Whose heart in that bright Sphere flames clearest,  .   .   179  U25 Desmond      54
SPICE
    He keepes anothers wife, which is a spice    .   .    36  E28 Surly        15
    A nest of odorous spice, and gummes.   .   .   .   280  U84 Mind         64
    Keeps warme the spice of her good name,   .   .   .   400  Lady Ogle        30
SPICERIE
    Unto the Sent, a Spicerie, or Balme;   .   .   .   286  U84 Muse        125
SPICES
    Cloth Spices, or guard sweet meates from the flies;  .   205  U43 Vulcan     V 53
    A nest of Spices, Odors, Gummes.   .   .   .   .   280  U84 Mind       V 64
SPIDE
    Times, manners, customes! Innovations spide!   .   .   160  U14 Selden       44
SPIE
    Object arrive there, but the heart (our spie)   .   .   109  F11 Epode        11
    Here's none to spie, or see;   .   .   .   .   .   139  U2 Another        3
    But, on thy malice, tell me, didst thou spie   .   .   203  U43 Vulcan       19
    and lighted by the Stagirite, could spie,   .   .   207  U43 Vulcan       90
    Or in the Bell-Mans Lanthorne, like a spie,   .   .   211  U43 Vulcan      187
    To judge; So all men comming neere can spie,   .   .   242  U69 Friend Son   20
    Or rather, thinking all my faults may spie,   .   .   323  Horace          392
SPI'D
    Something more then thou hast spi'd.   .   .   .   137  U2 Cupid         50
SPIEGLE
    Hans-spiegle, Rotteinberg, and Boutersheim,   .   .    69  E107 Hungry      26
SPIES
    On Spies.   .   .   .   .   .   .   .   .    45  E59 Spies       Ttl
    Spies, you are lights in state, but of base stuffe,  .    45  E59 Spies         1
    Light thee from hell on earth: where flatterers, spies, .   167  U15 Friend-Wars 163
    Like pretty Spies,   .   .   .   .   .   .   258  U75 Epithalam.  174
SPIGHT
    If any Muse out-live their spight, his can;   .   .    35  E27 Roe 1         4
    And her blacke spight expell.   .   .   .   .   109  F11 Epode         4
    In the Daunces, with what spight   .   .   .   .   138  U2 Kisse         22
    Or Spight,   .   .   .   .   .   .   .   151  U11 Dreame        9
    For all their spight, be like him if they could:   .   162  U15 Friend-Wars  26
    What did she worth thy spight? were there not store  .   188  U34 Small Poxe    3
    To conquer rumour, and triumph on spight;   .   .   224  U50 Countesse     4
    What could their care doe 'gainst the spight   .   .   234  U60 La-ware       5
    Feed on thy selfe for spight, and shew thy Kind:   .   250  U73 Weston        9
    That heard but Spight deliver   .   .   .   .   367  Ode Who saith    58
    May hurt them more with praise, then Foes with spight.  .   386  Browne            2
    Where spight of Death, next Life, for her Loves sake  .   394  Jane Ogle        25
    But higher power, as spight could not make lesse,  .   401  Beaumont         18
SPIGHTS
    And what hast thou done in these pettie spights,  .   .   210  U43 Vulcan      163
SPILL
    For then my hopes will spill me.   .   .   .   .   144  U4 Song           8
    'T were better spare a Butt, then spill his Muse.  .   241  U68 House-hold   12
SPILT
    And wish that all the Muses blood were spilt,   .   .   371  Fletcher         12
SPIN
    Of destinie, and spin her owne free houres.   .   .    52  E76 Bedford 1    16
SPINDLE
    The rock, the spindle, and the sheeres controule  .   .    52  E76 Bedford 1    15
SPINNE
    Whose even Thred the Fates spinne round, and full,  .   225  U51 Bacon        15
SPINOLA
    And Spinola have blushed at the sight.   .   .   .   214  U44 Speach       42
SPIRE
    Cast himselfe from the spire   .   .   .   .   .   111  F11 Epode        64
SPIRIT
    Thou, that art all their valour, all their spirit,  .   .    60  E93 Radcliffe     9
    He wrote, with the same spirit that he fought,  .   .    71  E110 Edmonds 1    8
    A spirit so resolv'd to tread   .   .   .   .   100  F4 To the World   6
    Lying for the spirit of amber.   .   .   .   .   105  F8 Sicknesse     32
    Lying on the spirit of amber.   .   .   .   .   105  F8 Sicknesse    V 32
    A farther fury my ray'sd spirit Controules,   .   .   108  F10 Proludium    12
    For what a sinne 'gainst your great fathers spirit,  .   114  F12 Rutland      31
    Eternall Spirit, God from both proceeding,   .   .   128  U1 Trinitie      25
    With Velvet, Plush, and Tissues, it is spirit.   .   .   164  U15 Friend-Wars  58
    Of woman of fashion, and a Lady of spirit:   .   .   164  U15 Friend-Wars  82
    Thy present Aide: Spirit Invention,   .   .   .   176  U25 Desmond     V  2
    That hold your spirit:   .   .   .   .   .   .   177  U25 Desmond      20
    That curbes your spirit:   .   .   .   .   .   .   177  U25 Desmond     V 20
```

				Page	Title	Line

SPIRIT (cont.)
Or winds the Spirit, by which the flower so grew? . . . 192 U38 Elegy 'Tis 58
How all my Fibres by your Spirit doe move, ... 194 U38 Elegy 'Tis 111
I have a body, yet, that spirit drawes . . . . 219 U47 Tribe 41
Her spirit home, to her originall! . . . . 270 U81 Pawlet 64
The Spirit that I wrote with, and conceiv'd; . . . 282 U84 Muse 3
As spirits had stolne her Spirit, in a kisse, . . . 283 U84 Muse 42
Of Body and Spirit together, plac'd betwixt . . . 284 U84 Muse 54
To have her captiv'd spirit freed from flesh, . . . 285 U84 Muse 93
To write it with the selfe same spirit he went, . . . 379 Coryat 3 14
SPIRITED
High-spirited friend, ... 180 U26 Ode High 1
SPIRITS
His spirits, now, in pills, and eeke in potions, . . . 86 E133 Voyage 101
Their spirits transmigrated to a cat: . . . 88 E133 Voyage 159
Their gentler spirits have suck'd innocence. . . . 96 F2 Penshurst 94
To raise my spirits with thy conjuring wine, . . . 107 F10 Proludium 11
To raise our spirits with thy conjuring wine, . . . 107 F10 Proludium V 11
Such spirits as are onely continent, ... 111 F11 Epode 77
It is a call to keepe the spirits alive . . . 162 U15 Friend-Wars 5
And Fortune once, t'assist the spirits that dare. . . 170 U18 Elegy Can 10
In letters, that mixe spirits, thus to weave. . . . 190 U37 Friend-Book 12
Should aske the blood, and spirits he hath infus'd . . 192 U38 Elegy 'Tis 65
In rest, like spirits left behind . . . . 280 U84 Mind 66
As spirits had stolne her Spirit, in a kisse, . . . 283 U84 Muse 42
Wants strength, and sinewes, as his spirits were done; . 339 Horace V 38/ 37
On edge the Masculine spirits, and did whet . . . 327 Horace 494
SPIRITUALL
One corporall, only; th'other spirituall, . . . 284 U84 Muse 52
By light, and comfort of spirituall Grace; . . . 286 U84 Muse 131
SPIRRITS
By Cherissheinge the Spirrits that gave their greatnesse grace: 419 Ode:If Men 5
SPIT (VERB)
Thrise did it spit: thrise div'd. At last, it view'd . . 88 E133 Voyage 162
SPIT
Which is indeed but friendship of the spit: . . 190 U37 Friend-Book 9
Was issue of the Taverne, or the Spit: . . . 216 U45 Squib 8
SPITE
Would both thy folly, and thy spite betray. . . . 43 E52 Courtling 6
Let their spite (which now abounds) . . . 260 U76 Petition 28
Not one but thrives; in spite of stormes & thunder, . . 361 Palmer 7
In spite of Hipocrites, who are the worst . . . 416 Dover 9
SPITTLE
Unto the Spittle Sermon. O, what strange . . . 201 U42 Elegy Let 71
SPITTLES
Spittles, pest-house, hospitalls, ... 104 F8 Sicknesse 10
SPLENDOR
Where brevitie, where splendor, and where height, . . 62 E95 Savile 29
The blaze, and splendor, but not handle fire! . . 269 U81 Pawlet 32
The heat, and splendor, but not handle fire! . . 269 U81 Pawlet V 32
Splendor! O more then mortall, ... 364 Ode Splendor 1
SPOILE (See also SPOYLE)
In dreames, begun in hope, and end in spoile. . . 162 U15 Friend-Wars 10
No Foole would his owne harvest spoile, or burne! . . 209 U43 Vulcan 150
SPOKE
As what it spoke, it planted there. . . . 279 U84 Mind 36
To turne mere farmer, had spoke out, . . . 291 U85 Country 68
Much, that mought now be spoke: omitted here . . 307 Horace 62
SPONDAEES
The steadie Spondaees; so themselves to beare . . 323 Horace 377
The steadie Spondaees; so themselves doe beare . . 347 Horace V363/377
SPONGE (See SPUNGE)
SPOONE
Shall find their depth: they're sounded with a spoone. . 198 U40 Elegy That 30
SPORT
And there's both losse of time, and losse of sport . . 46 E62 Would-bee 10
My selfe a witnesse of thy few dayes sport: . . 55 E85 Goodyere 1 2
Nor 'bout the beares, nor noyse to make lords sport. . 63 E97 Motion 12
At this so subtile sport: and play'st so ill? . . 72 E112 Gamster 2
Thou hast thy walkes for health, as well as sport: . . 93 F2 Penshurst 9
Art tane with neithers vice, nor sport: . . . 96 F3 Wroth 4
In spring, oft roused for thy masters sport, . . 97 F3 Wroth 23
In spring tyme roused for their masters sport, . . 97 F3 Wroth V 23
Of gambol, or sport . . . . . 231 U57 Burges 19
That you have seene the pride, beheld the sport, . . 234 U61 Epigram 1
And done, we straight repent us of the sport: . . 294 U88 Petronius 2
I looke on Cynthia, and Sirenas sport, . . . 398 Drayton 80
SPORTED
When with Joves swans she sported . . . 135 U2 Triumph V 42
SPORTING
Or sporting Kid, or Marlowes mighty line. . . . 391 Shakespeare 30
SPORTIVE
The angry brow; the sportive, wanton things; . . 311 Horace 150
SPORTS
So have I seene at Christ-masse sports one lost, . . 45 E58 Groome 7
While we may, the sports of love; . . . 102 F5 Celia 1 2
While we can, the sports of love; . . . 102 F5 Celia 1 V 2
Or, with thy Tribade trine, invent new sports, . . 107 F10 Proludium 17
And even our sports are dangers! what we call . . 163 U15 Friend-Wars 38
The open ports, and sports that peace doth cause, . . 345 Horace V284
Then the stolne sports of Lovers, . . . 365 Ode Splendor 7
SPOTLESSE
And art the spotlesse Mirrour to Mans eyes. . . 414 Ghyrlond 44

	Page	Title	Line

SPOTS
Of many Colours; outward fresh, from spots, ... 171 U20 Shrub 11
Offended with few spots, which negligence . . . . 329 Horace 527

SPOUSE
Thy noblest spouse affords them welcome grace; . . . 98 F3 Wroth 55
Thy noblest spouse affords them welcome place; . . . 98 F3 Wroth V 55
Some lustie quick Apulians spouse, ... 291 U85 Country 42
May she, whome thou for spouse, to day, dost take, . . 384 Somerset 11
Daughter, and Mother, and the Spouse of God, . . . 413 Ghyrlond 33
Of being Daughter, Mother, Spouse of God! . . . 414 Ghyrlond 56

SPOUSED
The spoused paire two realmes, the sea the ring. . . 28 E5 Union 4

SPOYLE
The theefe from spoyle, his presence holds. . . . 265 U79 New-yeares 63
But a fain'd way, doth spoyle it of the true. . . 270 U81 Pawlet V 38

SPOYLED
Was not spoyled. . . . . . . 184 U29 Fit of Rime 33

SPOYLING
Spoyling Senses of their Treasure, ... 183 U29 Fit of Rime 4

SPREAD
From all the nets that thou canst spread. . . . 100 F4 To the World 8
Nor spread them as distract with feares, . . . 145 U4 Song 11
Planting their Purles, and Curles spread forth like Net, . 164 U15 Friend-Wars 65
Spread through the World) is easier farre to find, . . 167 U15 Friend-Wars 172
That spread his body o're, to kill: . . . 234 U60 La-ware 16
As all the wealth of Season, there was spread; . . 251 U74 Weston 15

SPREADING
Your fruitfull spreading Vine, ... 257 U75 Epithalam. 159

SPRED
Minervaes loome was never richer spred. . . . 61 E95 Savile 16

SPRIGGE
And, but a sprigge of bayes, given by thee, . . . 32 E17 Critic 5

SPRIGHT
In all his Actions rarified to spright; . . . 197 U40 Elegy That 20
Your Power of handling shadow, ayre, and spright, . . 227 U52 Answer 17
at my back, I am no spright, ... 416 Moon 6

SPRIGHTFULL
Her wit as quicke, and sprightfull . . . 365 Ode Splendor 5

SPRIGHTLY
Moves like a sprightly River, and yet can . . . 198 U40 Elegy That 26

SPRING
Tabacco, Nectar, or the Thespian spring, . . . 65 E101 Supper 33
In spring, oft roused for thy masters sport, . . . 97 F3 Wroth 23
In spring tyme roused for thy masters sport, . . . 97 F3 Wroth V 23
And laugh, and measure thighes, then squeake, spring, itch, . 164 U15 Friend-Wars 75
If his wit reach no higher, but to spring . . . 232 U58 Book-seller 7
That so hath crown'd our hopes, our spring, and earth, . 237 U65 Prince 2
which thus hast crown'd our hopes, our spring, and earth, . 237 U65 Prince V 2
That so hath crown'd our hopes, our spring, and earth, . 237 U65 Prince V 2
That thus hath crown'd our hopes, with thee, our Spring & May, 237 U65 Prince V 2
Glorie to God. Then, Haile to Mary! spring . . 238 U66 Queene 13
Our thanks to God. Then, Haile to Mary! spring . . 238 U66 Queene V 13
Of the prime beautie of the yeare, the Spring. . . 251 U74 Weston 6
As if her ayrie steps did spring the flowers, . . 254 U75 Epithalam. 67
Sister of Pan, and glory of the Spring: . . . 264 U79 New-yeares 25
The Heaven design'd, draw next a Spring, . . . 276 U84 Body 21
So they fall gently from the Grecian spring, . . 309 Horace 75
But you, Pompilius off-spring, spare you not . . . 325 Horace 415
O I left-witted, that purge every spring . . . 325 Horace 429
The very root of writing well, and spring . . . 325 Horace 440
He shew'd him first the hoofe-cleft Spring, . . . 366 Ode Who saith 17
Each subt'lest Passion, with her source, and spring, . . 370 Author 7
Each subject Passion, with her source, and spring, . . 370 Author V 7
All Circles had their spring and end . . . 399 Lady Ogle 14
And you, with them, as Father of our spring. . . 416 Welcome 8

SPRINGING
To Loumond lake, and Twedes blacke-springing fountaine. . . 368 Ode Who saith 72

SPRINGS
What sight in searching the most antique springs! . . 31 E14 Camden 8
Or then, or since, about our Muses springs, . . 53 E79 Rutland 3
Are all th'Aonian springs . . . . 174 U23 Himselfe 7
Of Truth that searcheth the most hidden Springs, . . 176 U24 Frontispice 10
Of Truth which searcheth the most hidden Springs, . . 176 U24 Frontispice V 10

SPRITE
I sent the cause: Hee wooes with an ill sprite. . . 33 E19 Cod 1 2
That but the twi-light of your sprite did see, . . 66 E103 L Wroth 1 2

SPROUTINGE
With sproutinge tendrells of the Vine; . . . 290 U85 Country V 10

SPRUNG
Harpe, Lute, Theorbo sprung, ... 239 U67 Muses 17

SPUE
And the Physician teach men spue, or shite; . . . 410 Brome 16

SPUN
Were quite out-spun. The like wish hath his wife. . . 40 E42 Giles 12
And excuse spun every day, ... 140 U2 Promise 10
Or spun out Riddles, and weav'd fiftie tomes . . 204 U43 Vulcan 33
Or spun or weav'd in Riddles 50 tomes . . . 204 U43 Vulcan V 33
Spun out in name of some of the old Nine! . . . 282 U84 Muse 6
Which were so richly spun, and woven so fit, . . 392 Shakespeare 49
As it were spun by nature, off the fleece: . . . 415 Rutter 18

SPUNGE
And spunge-like with it dry up the blood quite: . . 155 U13 Sacvile 69

SPUNGE-LIKE
  And spunge-like with it dry up the blood quite: · · · 155 U13 Sacvile   69
SPUR
  To th' dull, a Spur   · · · 256 U75 Epithalam. 118
SPURRES
  The motives, and true Spurres to all good Nations.   · · 411 Sutcliffe   5
SPY   (See also SPIE)
  May rather yet adore, then spy.   · · · · 276 U84 Body   20
  Th'ascent of Lady Fame which none could spy   · · 403 Inigo Jones 1 35
SPYES
  Of a few poore houshold spyes?   · · · · 102 F5 Celia 1   12
SQUARE
  Such as are square, wel-tagde, and permanent,   · · · 220 U47 Tribe   64
  To square my Circle, I confesse; but draw   · · · 227 U52 Answer   8
SQUEAKE
  And laugh, and measure thighes, then squeake, spring, itch,   · 164 U15 Friend-Wars 75
SQUEMISH
  Be at their Visits, see 'hem squemish, sick,   · · · 164 U15 Friend-Wars 68
SQUIB
  An Epistle to Master Arth: Squib.   · · · · 216 U45 Squib   Ttl
  Epistle To Mr. Arthur Squib.   · · · · 229 U54 Squib   Ttl
SQUIBS
  Squire of the Squibs, against the Pageant day,   · · 208 U43 Vulcan   119
  Squire of the Squibs, upon the Pageant day,   · · 208 U43 Vulcan   V119
  Squire of the Squibs, against the next Maiors day,   · 208 U43 Vulcan   V119
  At Bonefires, squibs, and mirth, with all their Shoutes   · 249 U72 King   V 13
SQUIRE
  The other was a squire, of faire degree;   · · · 84 E133 Voyage   25
  To every squire, or groome, that will report   · · · 113 F12 Rutland   6
  To every squire, or groome, that can report   · · · 113 F12 Rutland   V 6
  Squire of the Squibs, against the Pageant day,   · · 208 U43 Vulcan   119
  Squire of the Squibs, upon the Pageant day,   · · 208 U43 Vulcan   V119
  Squire of the Squibs, against the next Maiors day,   · 208 U43 Vulcan   V119
SQUIRES
  Shift, here, in towne, not meanest among squires,   · · 30 E12 Shift   1
  Of any Madames, hath neadd squires, and must.   · · · 63 E97 Motion   14
'SSAYD
  And twice, or thrice had 'ssayd it, still in vaine: · · 333 Horace   626
'SSAYES
  The taylor brings a suite home; he it 'ssayes,   · · · 30 E12 Shift   9
STABLE
  . . . On his Horsemanship, and Stable.   · · · 228 U53 Newcastle   VTtl
  And surely had I but your Stable seene   · · · · 228 U53 Newcastle   13
STAG
  A-bed canst heare the loud stag speake,   · · · 97 F3 Wroth   22
STAGE
  Calls for his stoole, adornes the stage: god payes.   · · 30 E12 Shift   18
  Fear'd not to boast the glories of her stage,   · · · 56 E89 Allen   2
  I cannot for the stage a Drama lay,   · · · · 72 E112 Gamster   7
  My part is ended on thy stage.   · · · · 100 F4 To the World   4
  From Hide-Parke to the Stage, where at the last   · · 165 U15 Friend-Wars 109
  To that strumpet the Stage,   · · · · · 175 U23 Himselfe   34
  Starveling rimes did fill the Stage,   · · · · 183 U29 Fit of Rime   25
  Produce thy masse of miseries on the Stage,   · · 244 U70 Ode   55
  Unto the Stage thou bringst, and dar'st create   · · 342 Horace   V179
  The businesse either on the Stage is done,   · · · 317 Horace   255
  Yet, to the Stage, at all thou maist not tender   · · 317 Horace   260
  Upon the Stage, the figure of a Snake.   · · · 317 Horace   268
  In his train'd Gowne about the Stage: So grew   · · 319 Horace   305
  In his train'd Gowne about the Stage: thus grew   · · 346 Horace   V305
  Built a small-timbred Stage, and taught them talke   · 319 Horace   317
  Those heavie Verses, sent so to the Stage,   · · · 323 Horace   384
  The applause! delight! the wonder of our Stage!   · · 391 Shakespeare   18
  And shake a Stage: Or, when thy Sockes were on,   · · 391 Shakespeare   37
  Or influence, chide, or cheere the drooping Stage;   · · 392 Shakespeare   78
  Whether the buylding of the Stage or Scene!   · · 402 Inigo Jones 1   11
  Pack with your pedling Poetry to the Stage,   · · 404 Inigo Jones 1   51
  Which you have justly gained from the Stage,   · · 409 Brome   6
STAGES
  The stages jewell;   · · · · · · 77 E120 S. P.   12
STAGIRITE
  and lighted by the Stagirite, could spie,   · · · 207 U43 Vulcan   90
STAID
  Were to be staid with softnesses, and wonne   · · 321 Horace   326
STAINE
  I only can the Paper staine;   · · · · · 230 U55 Burges   6
STAIN'D
  And care of getting, thus, our minds hath stain'd,   · · 327 Horace   473
STAIRE   (See also STAYRE)
  And see both climing up the slippery staire   · · · 395 May   2
STAIRES
  I would call mine, to which not many Staires   · · · 220 U47 Tribe   74
STAKE
  And not thinke h'had eat a stake,   · · · · 142 U2 Her man   39
  To cut a Dike? or sticke a Stake up, here,   · · · 401 Beaumont   12
STALE
  Turne the stale prologue to some painted maske,   · · 107 F10 Proludium   20
STALKE
  Loftie, and grave; and in the buskin stalke.   · · · 319 Horace   318
STALKETH
  And stalketh, like a Fowler, round about,   · · · 335 Horace   650
STALL
  To lye upon thy stall, till it be sought;   · · · · 28 E3 Bookseller   5

		Page	Title	Line

STALL (cont.)
   Hornet, thou hast thy wife drest, for the stall,   53   E78 Hornet   1
   That thought can adde, unthankfull, the lay-stall   172   U21 Ltl Shrub   8
   At every stall; The Cittie Cap's a charme.   200   U42 Elegy Let   28
   The weekly Corrants, with Poules stall; and all   206   U43 Vulcan   V 81
   On every Stall.   273   U84 Cradle   28
STALLION
   Thither it flowes. How much did Stallion spend   163   U15 Friend-Wars   47
STALLS
   Live not we, as, all thy stalls,   104   F8 Sicknesse   9
STAMPE
   And as false stampe there; parcels of a Play,   204   U43 Vulcan   43
   And though Opinion stampe them not, are gold.   218   U47 Tribe   4
STAMP'D
   Stamp'd to the time. As woods whose change appeares   309   Horace   85
STAND
   Stand high, then, Howard, high in eyes of men,   49   E67 Suffolk   5
   Whose knowledge claymeth at the helme to stand;   61   E95 Savile   21
   Thou hast begun well, Roe, which stand well too,   63   E98 Th Roe 1   1
   Then stand unto thy selfe, not seeke without   83   E131 Ferrab. 2   13
   Let others watch in guiltie armes, and stand   98   F3 Wroth   67
   If it may stand with your soft blush to heare   117   F13 Aubigny   22
   Stand silent by,   120   F14 Sydney   8
   Doth urge him to runne wrong, or to stand still.   121   F14 Sydney   30
   Stand forth my Object, then, you that have beene   159   U14 Selden   29
   That may stand by, and hold my peace? will he,   167   U15 Friend-Wars   150
   By that faire Stand, your forehead, whence he bends   170   U19 Elegy By   3
   That you will stand   180   U25 Desmond   64
   I will not stand to justifie my fault,   191   U38 Elegy 'Tis   21
   No, I will stand arraign'd, and cast, to be   191   U38 Elegy 'Tis   27
   Forgiven him; And in that lyne stand I,   193   U38 Elegy 'Tis   91
   Doth, while he keepes his watch, betray his stand.   198   U40 Elegy That   36
   And now such is thy stand; while thou dost deale   217   U46 Coke   15
   As you have writ your selfe. Now stand, and then,   220   U47 Tribe   77
   So great a Vertue stand upright to view,   224   U50 Countesse   19
   And hold me to it close; to stand upright   229   U54 Squib   9
   And there to stand so. Hast now envious Moone,   238   U65 Prince   9
   And still to stand so. Hast thou envious Moone,   238   U65 Prince   V 9
   Was, t'have a Boy stand with a Club, and fright   241   U69 Friend Son   11
   Stand there; for when a noble Nature's rais'd,   256   U75 Epithalam.   113
   Whilst they both stand,   256   U75 Epithalam.   126
   Speake it, you bold Penates, you that stand   274   U84 Descent   7
   With boughs of Palme, a crowned Victrice stand!   285   U84 Muse   96
   Will take you more, the neerer that you stand;   331   Horace   540
   I could not but in admiracion stand.   361   Palmer   4
   To lie at Livory, while the Horses did stand.   375   Coryat 1   33
STANDARD
   But doth his Carract, and just Standard keepe   255   U75 Epithalam.   100
   doth his prime Carract, and just Standard keepe   255   U75 Epithalam.   V100
STANDARDS
   Of thy dead Standards: or (with miracle) see   405   Inigo Jones 1   89
STANDERD
   A Master-worker call'd, th'old standerd burst   415   Rutter   22
   as the standerd shall engage hir,   417   Moon   27
STANDERS
   Lewd standers, soft whisperers that let blood   167   U15 Friend-Wars   V165
   And strike Religion in the standers-by;   261   U77 Treasurer   24
   And, in her last act, taught the Standers-by,   270   U81 Pawlet   61
STANDERS-BY
   And strike Religion in the standers-by;   261   U77 Treasurer   24
   And, in her last act, taught the Standers-by,   270   U81 Pawlet   61
STANDING
   Thy standing upright to thy selfe, thy ends   68   E106 E Herbert   7
   Here no man tells my cups; nor, standing by,   95   F2 Penshurst   67
   Standing with feare, and must with horror fall,   122   F15 Heaven   19
   'Bove all your standing waters, choak'd with weedes.   198   U40 Elegy That   28
   Of suitor, or of servant standing by.   230   U56 Covell   V 18
   Or standing long an Oake, three hundred yeare,   245   U70 Ode   67
   Though thou hast past thy Summer standing, stay   252   U75 Epithalam.   1
   Though thou art past thy Summer standing, stay   252   U75 Epithalam.   V 1
   When, by thy bright Ideas standing by,   397   Drayton   23
STANDS
   To live when Broeck not stands, nor Roor doth runne.   49   E66 Cary   12
   Caesar stands up, as from his urne late rose,   72   E111 Edmonds 2   12
   Behold! the reverend shade of Bartas stands   83   E132 Sylvester   7
   Or stands to be'n Commission o' the blade?   155   U13 Sacvile   64
   Then stands it a triumphall marke! then Men   157   U13 Sacvile   139
   Slip no occasion; As time stands not still,   171   U19 Elegy By   19
   It rages, runs, flies, stands, and would provoke   283   U84 Muse   24
STAND'ST
   As thou stand'st cleere of the necessitie.   41   E43 Salisbury 1   12
   Stand'st thou, to shew the times what you all were?   60   E93 Radcliffe   4
   Or stayre, or courts; but stand'st an ancient pile,   93   F2 Penshurst   5
   Thou stand'st as if some Mysterie thou did'st!   225   U51 Bacon   4
STANLEY
   And Stanley, to the which shee was Co-heire.   274   U84 Descent   6
STAR
   Where never Star shone brighter yet?   181   U27 Ode Helen   26
   At libelling? Shall no Star-Chamber Peers,   410   Gill   3
   The Morning-star, whose light our Fal hath stay'd.   413   Ghyrlond   40
STARCH
   His Lace and Starch; And fall upon her back   163   U15 Friend-Wars   49

STAR-CHAMBER
At libelling? Shall no Star-Chamber Peers, ... 410 Gill 3
STARKE
Stiffe! starke! my joynts 'gainst one another knock! . . 269 U81 Pawlet 9
STARRE
And threatens the starre-chamber, and the barre: . . . 44 E54 Chev'ril 2 2
I meant the day-starre should not brighter rise, . . . 52 E76 Bedford 1 7
Keepe a starre-chamber sentence close, twelve dayes: . . 59 E92 New Crie 19
Life of the Muses day, their morning-starre! . . . 60 E94 Bedford 3 2
The Muses evening, as their morning-starre. . . . . 61 E94 Bedford 3 16
You, and that other starre, that purest light, . . . 115 F12 Rutland 65
As Loves starre when it riseth! . . . . . 134 U2 Triumph 14
Both my fortune, and my Starre! . . . . . 136 U2 Cupid 2
Till each of us be made a Starre, ... 143 U3 Musicall 3
Till each of us is made a Starre, ... 143 U3 Musicall V 3
Who falls for love of God, shall rise a Starre. . . 168 U15 Friend-Wars 196
Ambition to become a Starre, ... 234 U60 La-ware 14
Two names of friendship, but one Starre: . . . 246 U70 Ode 98
Though he be fairer then a Starre; 294 U87 Hor.3:9 21
Shine forth, thou Starre of Poets, and with rage, . . 392 Shakespeare 77
STARRE-CHAMBER
And threatens the starre-chamber, and the barre: . . . 44 E54 Chev'ril 2 2
Keepe a starre-chamber sentence close, twelve dayes: . . 59 E92 New Crie 19
STARRES
Or the starres, that guild his streames, ... 103 F6 Celia 2 16
Unto the starres? or the Tyndarides? . . . . 115 F12 Rutland 58
This blessing of your starres, then by that way . . . 118 F13 Aubigny 54
The Starres, that are the Jewels of the Night, . . . 271 U81 Pawlet 87
Among the starres should be resign'd . . . . 369 Ode Who saith 105
Of Spheares, as light of starres; She was earthes Eye: . 372 Epitaph 9
Looke how the starres from earth, or seas from flames . 422 Lucan 7
STARRY
And let there be a starry Robe . . . . . 276 U84 Body 26
STARS
Shine more, then she, the Stars among? . . . . 181 U27 Ode Helen 12
Others by common Stars their courses run, ... 194 U38 Elegy 'Tis 119
START
Times, and occasions, to start forth, and seeme) . . . 118 F13 Aubigny 63
Thou shrinke or start not, but be alwayes one; . . . 168 U15 Friend-Wars 186
Calme Brutus tenor start; but all along . . . 395 May 11
STARTE
soe much the starte . . . . . . 420 Ode:If Men 11
STARTED
I Grieve not, Courtling, thou are started up . . . 50 E72 Court-ling 1
White, black, blew, greene, and in more formes out-started, . 87 E133 Voyage 126
Not souldier-like started with rough alarmes, . . . 289 U85 Country 5
STARTS
Thy curtesie but sodaine starts, ... 100 F4 To the World 11
STARVE (See also STERVE)
And will, long ere thou should'st starve, ... 106 F8 Sicknesse 44
STARVELING
Starveling rimes did fill the Stage, ... 183 U29 Fit of Rime 25
STATE
Or celebrated with more truth of state? . . . . 28 E5 Union 2
The charge of that state, with this charme, god payes. . . 30 E12 Shift 4
To heaven; his hath: O happy state! wherein . . . 35 E27 Roe 1 7
Will man lament the state he should envie? . . . 41 E45 First Son 6
Doe beg thy care unto thy after-state. . . . . 43 E51 James 3 8
Spies, you are lights in state, but of base stuffe, . . 45 E59 Spies 1
I'have sung the greater fortunes of our state. . . . 48 E64 Salisbury 3 18
Then to begin, my Roe: He makes a state . . . 50 E70 Wm Roe 1 2
And have'hem yeeld no savour, but of state. . . . 58 E92 New Crie 5
For twelve yeeres yet to come, what each state lacks. . . 59 E92 New Crie 14
That know not so much state, wrong, as they doo. . . 59 E92 New Crie 40
No more then Salust in the Romane state! . . . . 61 E95 Savile 23
Of state, and censure them: we need his pen . . . 62 E95 Savile 33
Or, keeping your due state, that would not cry, . . . 68 E105 L Wroth 2 17
And first to know thine owne state, then the States. . . 70 E109 Nevil 12
Groyne, come of age, his state sold out of hand . . 75 E117 Groyne 1
But both th'hast so, as who affects the state . . . 78 E123 Rudyerd 3 3
Nor com'st to view the better cloth of state; . . . 96 F3 Wroth 7
Sit mixt with losse of state, or reverence. . . . 98 F3 Wroth 57
Thy peace is made; and, when man's state is well, . . 99 F3 Wroth 93
Else, I my state should much mistake, ... 101 F4 To the World 57
Not to know vice at all, and keepe true state, . . . 109 F11 Epode 1
For such a lot! that mixt you with a state . . . 118 F13 Aubigny 48
Let 'hem waste body, and state; and after all, . . . 118 F13 Aubigny 81
My faith, my hope, my love: and in this state, . . . 122 F15 Heaven 11
I know my state, both full of shame, and scorne, . . 122 F15 Heaven 17
And breath'st into it, life, and light, with state . . 127 U1 Trinitie 19
Have you seen the Palme-trees state . . . . 136 U2 Triumph V 43
So they in state of Grace retain'd, ... 144 U3 Musicall 27
Cannot a man be reck'ned in the State . . . . 156 U13 Sacvile 103
With that thy Stile, thy keeping of thy State, . . . 161 U14 Selden 68
To see men feare: or else for truth, and State, . . . 170 U18 Elegy Can 17
Of politique pretext, that wryes a State, . . . 177 U25 Desmond 29
Of politique pretext, that swayes a State, . . . 177 U25 Desmond V 29
Of divine blessing, would not serve a State? . . . 185 U30 Burleigh 20
But view the mildnesse of your Makers state, . . . 193 U38 Elegy 'Tis 85
Itch to defame the State? or brand the Times? . . . 203 U43 Vulcan 25
Our Ancestors impos'd on Prince and State. . . . 215 U44 Speach 78
To serve the State by Councels, and by Armes: . . . 215 U44 Speach 85
Make State, Religion, Bawdrie, all a theame? . . . 222 U49 Pucell 12

				Page	Title	Line
STATE (cont.)						
Of State, of fame, of body, and of soule,	.	.	.	224	U50 Countesse	18
At which there are, would sell the Prince, and State:		.	.	234	U61 Epigram	4
Her joy in state, and pleasure;	.	.	.	240	U67 Muses	44
He vexed time, and busied the whole State;	.	.	.	243	U70 Ode	27
Weston! That waking man! that Eye of State!	.	.	.	250	U73 Weston	5
Both to the honour of the King and State.	.	.	.	251	U74 Weston	24
Great Say-Master of State, who cannot erre,	.	.	.	255	U75 Epithalam.	99
Great Say-Master of State, who not to erre,	.	.	.	255	U75 Epithalam.	V 99
To be a watchfull Servant for this State;	.	.	.	258	U75 Epithalam.	178
If to my mind, great Lord, I had a state,	.	.	.	260	U77 Treasurer	1
In him all vertue is beheld in State:	.	.	.	262	U78 Digby	6
In him all action is beheld in State:	.	.	.	262	U78 Digby	V 6
A reverend State she had, an awfull Eye,	.	.	.	270	U81 Pawlet	43
And wish her state lesse happie then it is!	.	.	.	271	U81 Pawlet	84
The first-borne dying; so the aged state	.	.	.	309	Horace	87
Shall perish: so farre off it is, the state,	.	.	.	309	Horace	99
To every state of fortune; she helpes on,	.	.	.	311	Horace	153
A meere new person, looke he keepe his state	.	.	.	313	Horace	180
Brought in the Visor, and the robe of State,	.	.	.	319	Horace	316
Your booke? your volume! Nay, the state, and story!	.	.	.	399	Lady Ogle	7
Her soule possest her fleshes state	.	.	.	399	Lady Ogle	25
You are the Spectacles of State! Tis true	.	.	.	403	Inigo Jones 1	42
Moulded or stroakt up to survey a State!	.	.	.	405	Inigo Jones 1	84
God blesse the Councell and the State,	.	.	.	419	Grace	V 5
STATED						
A wise simplicity; freindes alike-stated;	.	.	.	295	U90 Mart.10:47	7
STATELY						
In stately Piles, and Pyramids erect	.	.	.	261	U77 Treasurer	V 26
STATES						
They know the states of Christendome, not the places:	.	.	59	E92 New Crie	8
If the States make peace, how it will goe	.	.	.	59	E92 New Crie	30
What States yo'have gull'd, and which yet keepes yo'in pay.	.	69	E107 Hungry	10
Give your yong States-men, (that first make you drunke,	.	69	E107 Hungry	19
And first to know thine owne state, then the States.	.	.	70	E109 Nevil	12
Shee learnes to know long difference of their states.	.	.	78	E121 Rudyerd 1	4
To blow up orphanes, widdowes, and their states;	.	.	99	F3 Wroth	79
And whilst our states, strength, body, and mind we waste,	.	166	U15 Friend-Wars	133
Or the States Ships sent forth belike to meet	.	.	.	219	U47 Tribe	33
So farre without inquirie what the States,	.	.	.	219	U47 Tribe	43
I am no States-man, and much lesse Divine,	.	.	.	223	U49 Pucell	25
Poore wretched states, prest by extremities,	.	.	.	248	U71 Treasurer	1
Can tell a States-mans dutie, what the arts	.	.	.	325	Horace	449
Is her owne scourge, when it sustaines their states	.	.	422	Lucan	3
Even states most hated, when no lawes resist	.	.	.	423	Lucan	13
STATES-MAN						
I am no States-man, and much lesse Divine,	.	.	.	223	U49 Pucell	25
STATESMAN						
To seeme a statesman: as I neere it came,	.	.	.	30	E11 Something	3
STATES-MANS						
Can tell a States-mans dutie, what the arts	.	.	.	325	Horace	449
STATES-MEN						
Give your yong States-men, (that first make you drunke,	.	69	E107 Hungry	19
STATESMEN						
Ripe statesmen, ripe: They grow in every street.	.	.	58	E92 New Crie	3
STATISTS						
Is but a Statists theame, to read Phlebotomie.	.	.	.	179	U25 Desmond	39
STATUARIES						
The worst of Statuaries, here about	.	.	.	307	Horace	45
STATUE						
Or is it some french statue? No: 'T doth move,	.	.	56	E88 Monsieur	13
Cupids Statue with a Beard,	.	.	.	132	U2 How he saw	30
Discerne betweene a Statue, and a Man;	.	.	.	261	U77 Treasurer	14
He'll thee a Marble Statue make	.	.	.	292	U86 Hor.4:1	19
STATUES						
Borne up by statues, shall I reare your head,	.	.	.	115	F12 Rutland	84
besett with statues, shall I reare your head,	.	.	.	115	F12 Rutland	V 84
Can doe the things that Statues doe deserve,	.	.	.	261	U77 Treasurer	15
STATURE						
But thou, whose noblesse keeps one stature still,	.	.	66	E102 Pembroke	13
Both wills were in one stature;	.	.	.	130	U1 Nativitie	15
As if they would belie their stature; those	.	.	.	157	U13 Sacvile	146
STATUTE						
A Rogue by Statute, censur'd to be whipt,	.	.	.	411	Gill	15
STAY (SUPPORT)						
Her language, if the Stay, and Care t'have mended,	.	.	325	Horace	413
STAY (See also STAID)						
But I repent me: Stay. Who e're is rais'd,	.	.	.	48	E65 Muse	15
In a little? Reader, stay.	.	.	.	79	E124 Elizabeth	2
As loth, the second draught, or cast to stay,	.	.	.	94	F2 Penshurst	35
There's nothing I can wish, for which I stay.	.	.	.	95	F2 Penshurst	75
And, knowing this, should I yet stay,	.	.	.	100	F4 To the World	21
Shall not give out, that I have made thee stay,	.	.	107	F10 Proludium	8
Shall not give out, that we have made thee stay,	.	.	107	F10 Proludium	V 8
Keepe the middle age at stay,	.	.	.	131	U2 Excuse	21
Strait hee ran, and durst not stay,	.	.	.	132	U2 How he saw	16
Why doe you doubt, or stay?	.	.	.	139	U2 Another	4
To stay the running floods,	.	.	.	143	U3 Musicall	10
Rather then here so bogg'd in vices stay.	.	.	.	163	U15 Friend-Wars	30
Reader stay,	.	.	.	168	U16 Gray	1
At the Well no Muse did stay,	.	.	.	183	U29 Fit of Rime	20
Alone lend succours, and this furie stay,	.	.	.	191	U38 Elegy 'Tis	8
If they stay here, but till Saint Georges Day.	.	.	213	U44 Speach	10

	Page	Title	Line

STAY (cont.)

I may no longer on these pictures stay,	216	U44 Speach	98
Stay, drop a teare for him that's dead,	233	U60 La-ware	2
Though thou hast past thy Summer standing, stay	252	U75 Epithalam.	1
Though thou art past thy Summer standing, stay	252	U75 Epithalam. V	1
We wooe thee, stay	252	U75 Epithalam.	6
Stay, thou wilt see what rites the Virgins doe!	254	U75 Epithalam.	49
Although that thou, O Sun, at our intreaty stay!	254	U75 Epithalam.	56
Stay, see the Virgins sow,	254	U75 Epithalam.	61
O, now thou smil'st, faire Sun, and shin'st, as thou wouldst stay!	254	U75 Epithalam.	64
And Bishop stay, to consummate the Rites:	256	U75 Epithalam.	122
To give your shade a name! Stay, stay, I feele	269	U81 Pawlet	7
To give your shade a lasting name! Stay, stay, I feele	269	U81 Pawlet	V 7
To children; we must alwayes dwell, and stay	317	Horace	253
Stay, view this stone: And, if thou beest not such,	371	Epitaph	1
How long he did stay, at what signe he did Inne.	380	Coryat 3	26
But stay, I see thee in the Hemisphere	392	Shakespeare	75
Sayst thou so, Lucan? But thou scornst to stay	397	Drayton	47
Fames heate upon the grave did stay;	400	Lady Ogle	28
Stay, till she make her vaine Approches. Then	401	Beaumont	15

STAY'D

Or if you would yet have stay'd,	138	U2 Kisse	29
Thou should'st have stay'd, till publike fame said so.	204	U43 Vulcan	46
Or stay'd but where the Fryar, and you first met,	212	U43 Vulcan	201
The Morning-star, whose light our Fal hath stay'd.	413	Ghyrlond	40

STAYES

And stayes but till you come unto the dore!	89	E133 Voyage	178
And he that stayes	121	F14 Sydney	49
And where it stayes, it there becomes	280	U84 Mind	63
And better stayes them there, then all fine noise	327	Horace	459

STAYRE

Or stayre, or courts; but stand'st an ancient pile,	93	F2 Penshurst	5

STEAD

And letters, and humanitie in the stead!	73	E113 Overbury	8
Arses were heard to croake, in stead of frogs;	84	E133 Voyage	13
Up among Nations. In the stead of bold	214	U44 Speach	51
New in their stead, out of the Candidates?	222	U49 Pucell	6

STEADIE

The steadie Spondaees; so themselves to beare	323	Horace	377
The steadie Spondaees; so themselves doe beare	347	Horace	V363/377

STEALE

'Tis no sinne, loves fruit to steale,	102	F5 Celia 1	15
Though he would steale his sisters Pegasus,	107	F10 Proludium	23
Shall I advise thee, Pucell? steale away	223	U49 Pucell	35

STEALES

He steales to ordinaries; there he playes	30	E12 Shift	11
Downe close by shore, this other creeping steales,	339	Horace	V 40/ 39

STEALTH

Purchas'd by rapine, worse then stealth,	99	F3 Wroth	82
Give thankes by stealth, and whispering in the eare,	154	U13 Sacvile	49
Or by Damnation voids it? or by stealth?	166	U15 Friend-Wars	116
This makes me, Mrs. that sometime by stealth,	197	U40 Elegy That	9
So would'st th'have run upon the Rolls by stealth,	210	U43 Vulcan	169

STEAME

Especially in paper; that, that steame	205	U43 Vulcan	61
Had filled your large nostrills with the steame:	205	U43 Vulcan	V 62

STED'S

By this Sun's Noone-sted's made	258	U75 Epithalam.	183

STEELE

That payes, or what he will: The Dame is steele.	164	U15 Friend-Wars	78
A horrour in mee! all my blood is steele!	269	U81 Pawlet	8
On steele, though 't selfe be dull, and cannot cut.	325	Horace	434

STEEMES

That, with still-scalding steemes, make the place hell.	88	E133 Voyage	144

STEEMING

And 'bout the steeming Chimney set!	291	U85 Country	66

STEEPE (ADJECTIVE)

Would, at suggestion of a steepe desire,	111	F11 Epode	63
Here, not up Holdborne, but downe a steepe hill,	374	Coryat 1	12

STEEPE

In bathes to steepe him;	77	E120 S. P.	22
O, doe not steepe them in thy Teares,	145	U4 Song	9
Where he doth steepe himselfe in Milke and Roses;	170	U19 Elegy By	8
So may the fruitfull Vine my temples steepe,	190	U37 Friend-Book	14
Steepe the glad Genius in the Wine, whole dayes,	319	Horace	298

STEEP'D

But since the Wine hath steep'd my braine,	230	U55 Burges	5
In juyce of Cedar worthy to be steep'd,	327	Horace	475

STEEPLE

And to Pauls-Steeple; which was unto us	211	U43 Vulcan	193
And though the Parish-steeple	239	U67 Muses	4

STEEPLES

The Poetrie of Steeples, with the Bells,	249	U72 King	10
The Poetrie of Steeples, with their Bells,	249	U72 King	V 10

STELLA

Hath our great Sidney, Stella set,	181	U27 Ode Helen	25

STEM

And never may there want one of the Stem,	258	U75 Epithalam.	177

STEMME

Their Mercury did now. By this, the stemme	87	E133 Voyage	111
And raise a noble stemme, to give the fame,	119	F13 Aubigny	97
At either Stemme, and know the veines of good	274	U84 Descent	8

		Page	Title	Line

STENCH
The filth, stench, noyse: save only what was there   .   .   84   E133 Voyage   9
Hung stench, diseases, and old filth, their mother,   .   .   86   E133 Voyage   70
STEPS
And steps of all rais'd servants of the Crowne,   .   .   217   U46 Coke   2
As if her ayrie steps did spring the flowers,   .   .   .   254   U75 Epithalam.   67
Since he treads in no other Mans steps but his owne.   .   379   Coryat 3   12
STERNE
Beene sterne to mee, ...   129   U1 Father   8
STEROPES
Let Brontes, and black Steropes,   .   .   .   179   U25 Desmond   40
STERVE
Or there to sterve it. Helpe, O you that may   .   .   191   U38 Elegy 'Tis   7
Consumptions nature to destroy, and sterve.   .   .   192   U38 Elegy 'Tis   62
STEW
Every stew in towne to know;   .   .   .   105   F8 Sicknesse   38
STEWARDS
Hath got the stewards chaire; he will not tarry   .   57   E90 Mill   15
STEWES
'Twas verily some Relique of the Stewes: .   .   209   U43 Vulcan   140
Religiously here he bids, row from the stewes,   .   375   Coryat 1   20
So that not them, his scabbes, lice, or the stewes,   .   380   Coryat 3   50
STICK
Stick on your Cupping-glasses, fear not, put   .   270   U81 Pawlet   53
STICKE
To cut a Dike? or sticke a Stake up, here,   .   .   401   Beaumont   12
STICKING
Left it sticking in my heart: .   .   .   133   U2 Suffered   16
STICKS
Or in cleft-sticks, advanced to make calls   .   28   E3 Bookseller   8
STIFFE
No stubbornnesse so stiffe, nor folly   .   .   152   U12 Corbet   24
As they are made! Pride, and stiffe Clownage mixt   .   163   U15 Friend-Wars   43
Stiffe! starke! my joynts 'gainst one another knock!   .   269   U81 Pawlet   9
It thawes the frostiest, and most stiffe disdaine: .   363   Riches   13
STIL
Stil may reason warre with rime,   .   .   184   U29 Fit of Rime   53
STILDE
What Beautie would have lovely stilde,   .   188   U35 Chute   1
STILE
Stile thee a most great foole, but no great man.   .   36   E28 Surly   22
There's none so dull, that for your stile would aske,   .   68   E105 L Wroth 2   15
To have engrav'd these acts, with his owne stile,   .   71   E110 Edmonds 1   6
And with both bombard-stile, and phrase, rehearse   .   85   E133 Voyage   46
To marke the excellent seas'ning of your Stile!   .   160   U14 Selden   55
With that thy Stile, thy keeping of thy State,   .   161   U14 Selden   68
And comes by these Degrees, the Stile t'inherit   .   164   U15 Friend-Wars   81
Against a multitude: and (with thy Stile   .   187   U33 Councellour   31
(Which, some are pleas'd to stile but thy madde pranck)   .   208   U43 Vulcan   131
"For stile of rarenesse, to degenerate.   .   367   Ode Who saith   32
By the scale of his booke, a yard of his stile?   .   379   Coryat 3   10
There, thou art Homer! Pray thee, use the stile   .   398   Drayton   59
STIL'D
Stil'd but the shaddowes of us men?   .   104   F7 Women but   6
Stil'd but the shaddowes of us men?   .   104   F7 Women but   12
Such are his powers, whom time hath stil'd,   .   189   U36 Song   13
And (stil'd your mercies Creature) will live more   .   191   U38 Elegy 'Tis   29
My selfe for shortnesse labour, and am stil'd   .   339   Horace   V 36/   35
And this hath met that one, that may be stil'd   .   389   Aleman   13
And I had stil'd thee, Orpheus, but before   .   397   Drayton   37
STILED
To have beene stiled of King Arthurs table.   .   84   E133 Voyage   24
Each stiled, by his end,   .   247   U70 Ode   111
STILES
As Stiles, Dike, Ditchfield, Millar, Crips, and Fen: .   214   U44 Speach   54
STILL
As chiefe of those still promise they will bee.   .   28   E4 James 1   8
And still be a whore-house. Th'are Synonima.   .   29   E7 Hot-house   4
For I will dare none. Good Lord, walke dead still.   .   30   E11 Something   8
Takes physick, teares the papers: still god payes.   .   30   E12 Shift   16
Pr'y thee beleeve still, and not judge so fast,   .   32   E18 Censurer   9
He'adulters still: his thoughts lye with a whore.   .   35   E26 Beast 2   2
Which is maine greatnesse. And, at his still boord,   .   35   E28 Surly   13
In all affections shee concurreth still.   .   40   E42 Giles   15
Play-wright me reades, and still my verses damnes,   .   42   E49 Playwrt 1   1
For we, that have our eyes still in our eares,   .   43   E51 James 3   9
Thy ignorance still laughs in the wrong place.   .   45   E58 Groome   4
As her owne conscience, still, the same reward.   .   48   E64 Salisbury 3   14
And, reconcil'd, keepe him suspected still.   .   48   E65 Muse   8
To plucke downe mine, Poll sets up new wits still,   .   50   E71 Parrat   1
Still, 'tis his lucke to praise me 'gainst his will.   .   50   E71 Parrat   2
That still th'art present to the better cause;   .   52   E74 Chancelor   5
Went on: and proving him still, day by day,   .   57   E90 Mill   7
Still Mill continu'd: Nay, his face growing worse,   .   57   E90 Mill   11
And what would hurt his vertue makes it still.   .   63   E98 Th Roe 1   6
But thou, whose noblesse keeps one stature still,   .   66   E102 Pembroke   13
The common-wealth still safe, must studie thee.   .   66   E102 Pembroke   20
Their latter praise would still the greatest bee,   .   68   E106 E Herbert   9
But 's angry for the Captayne, still: is such.   .   70   E108 Soldiers   10
With thy small stocke, why art thou ventring still,   .   72   E112 Gamster   1
Art still at that, and still'st to blow me'up too?   .   72   E112 Gamster   6
I Must beleeve some miracles still bee,   .   73   E114 Sydney   1
For'his whore: Groyne doth still occupy his land.   .   75   E117 Groyne   2

STILL (cont.)

	Page	Title	Line
By her attempt, shall still be owing thee.	80	E127 Aubigny	10
That still th'art made the suppers flagge, the drum,	81	E129 Mime	7
Still, with thy former labours; yet, once more,	85	E133 Voyage	56
But still their valour, and their vertue fenc't 'hem,	86	E133 Voyage	76
No going backe; on still you rogues, and row.	86	E133 Voyage	88
That, with still-scalding steemes, make the place hell.	88	E133 Voyage	144
But still, it seem'd, the ranknesse did convince 'hem.	88	E133 Voyage	152
As wandrers doe, that still doe rome,	102	F4 To the World	66
Follow a shadow, it still flies you;	104	F7 Women but	1
Phoebus. No? tend thy cart still. Envious day	107	F10 Proludium	7
Is more crowne-worthy still,	112	F11 Epode	88
Is more praiseworthy still,	112	F11 Epode	V 88
With noble ignorants, and let them still,	114	F12 Rutland	28
How you love one, and him you should; how still	119	F13 Aubigny	113
This makes, that your affections still be new,	119	F13 Aubigny	118
Live that one, still; and as long yeeres doe passe,	120	F13 Aubigny	121
Wherein, your forme, you still the same shall finde;	120	F13 Aubigny	123
Doth urge him to runne wrong, or to stand still.	121	F14 Sydney	30
Dwell, dwell here still: O, being every-where,	122	F15 Heaven	15
Of persons, still one God, in Unitie;	127	U1 Trinitie	2
Of persons, still one God in Unitie;	128	U1 Trinitie	30
Use still thy rod,	129	U1 Father	4
That they still were to run by her side,	134	U2 Triumph	9
Drest, you still for man should take him;	141	U2 Her man	38
To make us still sing o're, and o're,	145	U5 Woman-kind	3
All order, and Disposure, still.	151	U12 Corbet	14
Still, still, the hunters of false fame apply	155	U13 Sacvile	65
Feed those, at whom the Table points at still?	155	U13 Sacvile	74
Yet we must more then move still, or goe on,	157	U13 Sacvile	135
It was erected; and still walking under	157	U13 Sacvile	141
Meane what I speake: and still will keepe that Vow.	159	U14 Selden	28
And like a Compasse keeping one foot still	159	U14 Selden	31
But to the Subject, still the Colours fit	160	U14 Selden	58
But being in Motion still (or rather in race)	166	U15 Friend-Wars	124
Still pretious, with the odour of thy name.	168	U15 Friend-Wars	190
And then the best are, still, the blindest friends!	170	U18 Elegy Can	14
Slip no occasion; As time stands not still,	171	U19 Elegy By	19
'Tis crowne enough to vertue still, her owne applause.	174	U23 Himselfe	18
Still may Syllabes jarre with time,	184	U29 Fit of Rime	52
That still was good for goodnesse sake, nor thought	185	U30 Burleigh	13
The Care, and wish still of the publike wealth:	186	U31 Elsmere	6
Still flie about the Odour of your Name;	186	U31 Elsmere	8
Of Argument, still drawing forth the best,	187	U33 Councellour	27
And waste still, that they still might bee.	189	U36 Song	12
The eldest God, yet still a Child.	189	U36 Song	16
As flatt'ry with friends humours still to move.	190	U37 Friend-Book	27
That is, if still your Favours you apply,	192	U38 Elegy 'Tis	53
Yet should the Lover still be ayrie and light,	197	U40 Elegy That	19
Out with the other, for hee's still at home;	198	U40 Elegy That	34
O, keepe it still; for it had rather be	199	U41 Elegy Since	17
Being, the best clothes still to praeoccupie.	201	U42 Elegy Let	42
Upon th'Exchange, still, out of Popes-head-Alley;	206	U43 Vulcan	80
Hee is true Vulcan still! He did not spare	210	U43 Vulcan	159
Thou art true Vulcan still! Thou durst not spare	210	U43 Vulcan	V159
He was right Vulcan still! He did not spare	210	U43 Vulcan	V159
Would you had kept your Forge at Aetna still,	212	U43 Vulcan	197
But we have Powder still for the Kings Day,	213	U44 Speach	2
Alive yet, in the noise; and still the same;	214	U44 Speach	56
Still looking to, and ever loving heaven;	219	U47 Tribe	61
And still begin'st the greeting:	221	U48 Bacchus	16
So mayst thou still be younger	221	U48 Bacchus	21
Thee still, and leave Apollo,	221	U48 Bacchus	26
Made up still as the pockett doth abound.	230	U56 Covell	V 12
And thinke all still the best, that he will doe.	236	U63 Charles 2	10
And still to stand so. Hast thou envious Moone,	238	U65 Prince	V 9
To compare small with great, as still we owe	238	U66 Queene	12
Still to have such a Charles, but this Charles long.	249	U72 King	18
Looke up, thou seed of envie, and still bring	250	U73 Weston	1
Whilst the maine tree, still found	258	U75 Epithalam.	181
But we last out, still unlay'd.	259	U76 Petition	24
For that to dwell in, and be still at home.	262	U78 Digby	8
For those to dwell in, and be still at home.	262	U78 Digby	V 8
Who walkes on Earth as May still went along,	264	U79 New-yeares	26
Still waited on 'hem where they were.	264	U79 New-yeares	39
Of Goodnesse still: Vouchsafe to take	273	U84 Cradle	9
And yet remaine our wonder still.	278	U84 Mind	20
Still left an Eccho in the sense.	279	U84 Mind	40
But all of God; They still shall have to say,	286	U84 Muse	119
Or the herb Sorrell, that loves Meadows still,	291	U85 Country	57
Of daring all, hath still beene given; we know it:	305	Horace	12
Of daring ought, hath still beene given; we know it:	338	Horace	V 12
Was meant at first. Why, forcing still about	307	Horace	29
So he that varying still affects to draw	339	Horace	V 42/ 40
Take, therefore, you that write, still, matter fit	307	Horace	53
Still in their leaves, throughout the sliding yeares,	309	Horace	86
The power, and rule of speaking resteth still.	309	Horace	104
To ignorance still, then either learne, or know?	311	Horace	131
To ignorance still, then yet to learne, or know?	341	Horace	V126/131
To worke the hearers minds, still, to their plight.	311	Horace	142
Mens faces, still, with such as laugh, are prone	311	Horace	143
Keepe him still active, angry, un-appeas'd,	313	Horace	172
Io still wandring; griev'd Orestes sad:	342	Horace	V177

		Page	Title	Line

STILL   (cont.)
```
    Still to be like himselfe, and hold his worth.      .    .    .    .   313   Horace          182
    With sloth, yet greedy still of what's to come:      .    .    .   317   Horace          246
    And still correcting youth, and censuring.           .    .    .   317   Horace          249
    It still must favour good men, and to these          .    .    .   317   Horace          280
    And, where the matter is provided still,      .      .    .    .   325   Horace          443
    And I still bid the learned Maker looke              .    .    .   325   Horace          453
    For, neither doth the String still yeeld that sound  .    .    .   329   Horace          521
    Still in the same, and warned will not mend,    .    .    .    .   329   Horace          530
    Is laugh'd at, that still jarreth on one string:     .    .    .   329   Horace          532
    Or trundling Wheele, he can sit still, from all;     .    .    .   331   Horace          568
    And twice, or thrice had 'ssayd it, still in vaine:  .    .    .   333   Horace          626
    In vaine, but you, and yours, you should love still  .    .    .   335   Horace          631
    still making that the greatest that is last     .    .    .    .   361   Palmer           19
    And still is in the Brest:      .    .    .    .    .   366   Ode Who saith    27
    still that same little poynte hee was; but when      .    .    .   383   Rich             13
    your Royal Eye which still creates new men      .    .    .    .   383   Rich             14
    Must be intended still to understand:           .    .    .    .   383   Author            2
    So, be your Concord, still, as deepe, as mute;       .    .    .   384   Somerset         17
    Still, still, dost thou arrive with, at our shore,   .    .    .   388   Chapman           5
    And art alive still, while thy Booke doth live,      .    .    .   391   Shakespeare      23
    And all the Muses still were in their prime,    .    .    .    .   391   Shakespeare      44
    To call on Sicknes still, to be her Guest,      .    .    .    .   394   Jane Ogle        19
    Are still th'interpreters twixt godds, and men!      .    .    .   395   May              18
    you'l be as Langley sayd, an Inigo still.            .    .    .   403   Inigo Jones 1    22
    All in the Worke! And soe shall still for Ben:       .    .    .   404   Inigo Jones 1    65
    Shall the prosperity of a Pardon still          .    .    .    .   410   Gill              1
    And though your virtue (as becomes it) still         .    .    .   421   Censure           9
    And Flatterye, with Frindes humors: still to move.   .    .    .   422   Censure          20
    appropriates still unto that County:      .    .    .    .    .   662   Bedford           4
STILL-SCALDING
    That, with still-scalding steemes, make the place hell.   .    .    88   E133 Voyage     144
STILTS
    They need no stilts, nor rise upon their toes,   .    .    .    .   157   U13 Sacvile     145
STINCK
    A Mungrel Curre?  Thou should'st stinck forth, and dye    .    .   409   Detractor        15
STING
    No tunes are sweet, nor words have sting,        .    .    .    .   143   U3 Musicall      15
    No voice so sweet, nor words have sting,         .    .    .    .   143   U3 Musicall     V 15
STINGS
    After flight; and put new stings      .    .    .    .    .   137   U2 Cupid         36
STINKARDS
    No matter, stinkards, row.  What croaking sound      .    .    .    86   E133 Voyage      91
STINKE   (See also STUNKE)
    Stinke, and are throwne away.  End faire enough.     .    .    .    45   E59 Spies         3
    Then what he hath receiv'd.  Gifts stinke from some, .    .    .   153   U13 Sacvile      22
    And so I leave to stirre him, lest he stinke.   .    .    .    .   172   U21 Ltl Shrub    10
    Burne to a snuffe, and then stinke out, and die:     .    .    .   211   U43 Vulcan      188
    wast to a snuffe, and then stinke out, and die:      .    .    .   211   U43 Vulcan      V188
STINKETH
    Stinketh my credit, if into the Pocket     .    .    .    .    .   229   U54 Squib        14
STINT
    To compose men, and manners; stint the strife        .    .    .   261   U77 Treasurer    18
    To Compasse men, and manners; stint the strife       .    .    .   261   U77 Treasurer   V 18
STIR
    Thinking to stir me, thou hast lost thy End,    .    .    .    .   410   Gill              9
STIRD'ST
    Since stird'st up jealousies and feares,      .    .    .    .   101   F4 To the World  43
STIRRE
    Ycleped Mud, which, when their oares did once stirre,     .    .    85   E133 Voyage      62
    And so I leave to stirre him, lest he stinke.        .    .    .   172   U21 Ltl Shrub    10
    Why doe I irritate, or stirre up thee,      .    .    .    .    .   250   U73 Weston        7
    Doth Emulation stirre;      .    .    .    .    .    .   256   U75 Epithalam.  117
    Nothing, that could remaine, or yet can stirre       .    .    .   282   U84 Muse          9
    In the eare, doe stirre the mind more slow      .    .    .    .   317   Horace          257
    That thou hast lost thy noyse, thy foame, thy stirre, .   .    .   408   Detractor         8
STIRR'D
    In the great masse, or machine there is stirr'd?     .    .    .   395   May              22
STIRRER
    What did this Stirrer, but die late?       .    .    .    .    .   243   U70 Ode          30
STITCH'D
    A Scarlet peece, or two, stitch'd in: when or        .    .    .   305   Horace           19
    A purple piece, or two stitch'd in: when either      .    .    .   338   Horace          V 19
STITCHERS
    Of hirelings, wranglers, stitchers-to of strife,     .    .    .   187   U33 Councellour   8
STITCHERS-TO
    Of hirelings, wranglers, stitchers-to of strife,     .    .    .   187   U33 Councellour   8
STOCK
    Nor baudie stock, that travells for encrease,        .    .    .    63   E97 Motion       10
    As the old stock of Mankind were,      .    .    .    .    .   289   U85 Country      V  2
STOCKE
    With thy small stocke, why art thou ventring still,  .    .    .    72   E112 Gamster      1
STOCKS
    For I shall move stocks, stones, no lesse then he.   .    .    .   115   F12 Rutland      78
STOCKT
    Cropt, branded, slit, neck-stockt; go, you are stript. .  .    .   411   Gill             16
STOLE
    The slie Ulysses stole in a sheepes-skin,       .    .    .    .    87   E133 Voyage     113
STOLNE
    Shall out-live gyrlands, stolne from the chast tree.      .    .    32   E17 Critic        6
    Five of my jests, then stolne, past him a play.      .    .    .    64   E100 Playwrt 3    4
    When youths ply their stolne delights.          .    .    .    .   103   F6 Celia 2       18
    As spirits had stolne her Spirit, in a kisse,        .    .    .   283   U84 Muse         42
```

	Page	Title	Line

STOLNE (cont.)
Then the stolne sports of Lovers, ... 365 Ode Splendor 7
STOMACKS
All mouthes are open, and all stomacks free: . . . . 232 U58 Book-seller 2
STONE
Mark'd by thy hand, and with the better stone, . . . 62 E96 Donne 2 8
Under-neath this stone doth lye . . . . . . 79 E124 Elizabeth 3
And though thy walls be of the countrey stone, . . . 94 F2 Penshurst 45
So that, there, I stood a stone, ... 132 U2 How he saw 27
What Tree or stone doth want a soule? . . . . 143 U3 Musicall 7
We must accomplish; 'Tis the last Key-stone . . . 157 U13 Sacvile 136
Their Jemme of Riches, and bright Stone, that brings . 206 U43 Vulcan 74
Full twentie stone; of which I lack two pound: . . . 229 U54 Squib 12
His weight is twenty Stone within two pound; . . . 230 U56 Covell 11
My Lord, till felt griefe make our stone hearts soft, . 234 U61 Epigram 14
The old Greek-hands in picture, or in stone. . . . 260 U77 Treasurer 9
Hee's good, as great. I am almost a stone! . . . 269 U81 Pawlet 11
Be like a Whet-stone, that an edge can put . . . 325 Horace 433
Stay, view this stone: And, if thou beest not such, . 371 Epitaph 1
No stone in any wall here, but can tell . . . 394 Jane Ogle 9
Soe the Materialls be of Purbeck stone! . . . . 406 Inigo Jones 1 100
STONES
As mad-men stones: not caring whom they hit. . . . 27 E2 My Booke 6
For I shall move stocks, stones, no lesse then he. . . 115 F12 Rutland 78
Was said to move the stones, by his Lutes powers, . . 327 Horace 484
Sonnes, seeke not me amonge these polish'd stones: . 387 Cavendish 1
STONIE
Breake the knit Circle of her Stonie Armes, . . . 177 U25 Desmond 19
STOOD
So that, there, I stood a stone, ... 132 U2 How he saw 27
But stood unshaken in his Deeds, and Name, . . . 185 U30 Burleigh 11
More then the surfets, in thee, that day stood. . . 214 U44 Speach 48
Stood up thy Nations fame, her Crownes defence. . . 217 U46 Coke 14
I never stood for any place: my wit . . . . 223 U49 Pucell 23
How well at twentie had he falne, or stood! . . . 243 U70 Ode 31
Hee stood, a Souldier to the last right end! . . . 244 U70 Ode 45
And to left-Lydia, now the gate stood ope. . . . 294 U87 Hor.3:9 20
STOOD'ST
That age, when thou stood'st up the master-braine: . 75 E116 Jephson 4
STOOLE
Calls for his stoole, adornes the stage: god payes. . 30 E12 Shift 18
Or (mounted on a stoole) thy face doth hit . . . 81 E129 Mime 13
By which the Masters sweare, when, on the stoole . . 87 E133 Voyage 122
Or a Close-stoole so cas'd; or any fat . . . 202 U42 Elegy Let 84
To make you merry on the Dressing stoole . . . 230 U56 Covell 21
STOOLES
Can come from Tripoly, leape stooles, and winke, . . 74 E115 Honest Man 11
We were not bred to sit on stooles, ... 146 U6 Defence 3
So I might dote upon thy Chaires and Stooles . . . 201 U42 Elegy Let 47
STOOPE
But first to Cluid stoope low, ... 367 Ode Who saith 39
The Rebell Gyants stoope, and Gorgon Envye yeild, . 421 Ode:If Men 41
STOOP'D
Hee stoop'd in all mens sight . . . . . 244 U70 Ode 38
STOOPING
But stooping gently, as a Cloud, ... 280 U84 Mind 58
STOP
To this dire passage. Say, thou stop thy nose: . . 85 E133 Voyage 59
Nor thumbe, nor finger to the stop acquainted, . . 87 E133 Voyage 134
To take the weake, or make them stop: . . . 100 F4 To the World 19
Could stop the malice of this ill, ... 234 U60 La-ware 15
And stop my sight, in every line I goe. . . . 398 Drayton 78
STOPT
And all these through her eyes, have stopt her eares. . 150 U9 Picture 18
Is borrowing; that but stopt, they doe invade . . 155 U13 Sacvile 80
STORE
But two things, rare, the Fates had in their store, . 28 E4 James 1 3
Came not that soule exhausted so their store. . . 53 E79 Rutland 4
Till you equall with the store, ... 103 F6 Celia 2 12
Scarce will take our present store? . . . . 105 F8 Sicknesse 11
Riches thought most: But, Madame, thinke what store . 114 F12 Rutland 38
Ajax, or Idomen, or all the store, ... 114 F12 Rutland 54
Nor can a little of the common store, ... 121 F14 Sydney 31
And this profession of a store . . . . . 146 U6 Defence 19
Praevaricators swarme. Of which the store, . . . 167 U15 Friend-Wars 170
To doe, then be a husband of that store. . . . 180 U26 Ode High 18
The poores full Store-house, and just servants field. . 185 U30 Burleigh 8
As if the generall store thou didst command . . . 187 U33 Councellour 26
What did she worth thy spight? were there not store . 188 U34 Small Poxe 3
You have unto my Store added a booke, . . . 189 U37 Friend-Book 4
Such Songsters there are store of; witnesse he . . 201 U42 Elegy Let 65
They saw too store of feathers, and more may, . . 213 U44 Speach 9
He could not find, then thee, of all that store . . 217 U46 Coke 3
It doe not come: One piece I have in store, . . . 229 U54 Squib 15
Are they so scanted in their store? or driven . . 241 U68 House-hold 3
Hee'ld frame such ditties of their store, and want, . 241 U68 House-hold 7
By all the wealth of blessings, and the store . . 285 U84 Muse 110
That from the North, the Navie safe doth store, . . 309 Horace 92
What treasure hast thou brought us! and what store . 388 Chapman 4
Then Affricke knew, or the full Grecian store! . . 398 Drayton 88
STOR'D
Though many Gems be in your bosome stor'd, . . . 179 U25 Desmond 55
And twice-twelve-yeares stor'd up humanitie, . . . 207 U43 Vulcan 101

	Page	Title	Line

STOR'D (cont.)
With twice-twelve-yeares stor'd up humanitie, — · · 207 U43 Vulcan V101

STORE-HOUSE
The poores full Store-house, and just servants field. · 185 U30 Burleigh 8

STORIE
Read not in faire heavens storie, · · · · 39 E40 Ratcliffe 6
To have her storie woven in thy thred; · · · 61 E95 Savile 15
Or, because some scarce thinke that storie true, · 67 E104 Montgomery 5
This little storie: · · · · · 77 E120 S. P. 2
Can man forget this Storie? · · · · 130 U1 Nativitie 24
If you then will read the Storie, · · · 131 U2 Excuse 13
Conjectures retriv'd! And a Storie now · · 160 U14 Selden 50
To our owne Ladyes; and in storie there · · 207 U43 Vulcan 97
for our owne Ladyes; and in storie there · · 207 U43 Vulcan V 97
Of all her Brothers storie, · · · 240 U67 Muses 29
Of all her Fathers storie, · · · 240 U67 Muses V 29

STORME
Had burst with storme, and downe fell, ab excelsis, · 86 E133 Voyage 95
Rough, swelling, like a storme: · · · 110 F11 Epode 40
There may some face or menace of a storme · · 191 U38 Elegy 'Tis 13
As all with storme and tempest ran together. · · 193 U38 Elegy 'Tis 76
The name of Cruell weather, storme, and raine? · 193 U38 Elegy 'Tis 82
Should he heare of billow, wind, and storme, · · 214 U44 Speach 63
Creepes on the ground; too safe, too afraid of storme. · 307 Horace 39

STORMES
Through seas, stormes, tempests: and imbarqu'd for hell, · 81 E128 Wm Roe 2 13
'Gainst stormes, or pyrats, that might charge your peace; · 119 F13 Aubigny 93
Not one but thrives; in spite of stormes & thunder, · 361 Palmer 7

STORY
All is a story of the King and Queene! · · 255 U75 Epithalam. 91
Who ever he be, would write a Story at · · 379 Coryat 3 1
Or builders of Story have oft imputation · · 380 Coryat 3 30
No: as I first said, who would write a story at · 381 Coryat 3 59
Your booke? your volume! Nay, the state, and story! · 399 Lady Ogle 7
That might compare with thee? what story shall · 406 Inigo Jones 1 98

STOUPE
And never stoupe, but to strike ignorance; · · 55 E85 Goodyere 1 7
And stoupe, and cringe. O then, it needs must prove · 56 E88 Monsieur 14

STOUPES
'Tis true, as my wombe swells, so my backe stoupes, · 227 U52 Answer 4

STOUP'ST
And whither rap'd, now thou but stoup'st to mee? · 122 F15 Heaven 14

STRADLING
And stradling shews the Boyes Brown paper fleet, · 407 Inigo Jones 2 17

STRAIGHT
Straight went I home; and there most like a Poet, · 55 E84 Bedford 2 5
Like straight, thy pietie to God, and friends; · · 68 E106 E Herbert 8
But it must, straight, my melancholy bee? · · 122 F15 Heaven 2
True noblesse. Palme growes straight, though handled ne're so rude. 177 U25 Desmond 26
And straight-way spent a Sonnet; with that other · 201 U42 Elegy Let 67
And done, we straight repent us of the sport: · · 294 U88 Petronius 2
What straight-way he must labour to retract. · · 315 Horace 240

STRAIGHTNED
But lyes block'd up, and straightned, narrow'd in, · 248 U71 Treasurer 10

STRAIGHT-WAY
And straight-way spent a Sonnet; with that other · 201 U42 Elegy Let 67
What straight-way he must labour to retract. · · 315 Horace 240

STRAINE
An elegie? no, muse; yt askes a straine · · 108 F10 Proludium 1
From thoughts of such a straine. · · · 112 F11 Epode 114
Set, and to this softer straine; · · · 136 U2 Cupid 9
So going thorow all your straine, · · · 145 U5 Woman-kind 10
Strike in thy proper straine, · · · 175 U23 Himselfe 26
stryke him in thy proper straine, · · · 175 U23 Himselfe V 26
That I may sing my thoughts, in some unvulgar straine. · 177 U25 Desmond 13
Abhorres low numbers, and the private straine · · 311 Horace 123
If you denied, you had no better straine, · · 333 Horace 625
All which, when they but heare a straine · · 368 Ode Who saith 89
Of thy strange Moon-Calfe, both thy straine of mirth, · 398 Drayton 84

STRAINES
That thus have ventur'd these true straines upon; · 289 U84 Muse 227
Or straines on his small forke his subtill nets · · 290 U85 Country 33
Or straines on his small forke his subtler nets · · 290 U85 Country V 33
And see a minde attir'd in perfect straines; · · 362 Author 2
Straines fancie unto foule Apostacie, · · · 363 Riches 15

STRAIT
Strait hee ran, and durst not stay, · · · 132 U2 How he saw 16

STRAITE
And guided by Experience, whose straite wand · · 176 U24 Frontispice 11

STRAITS
Thy subtle wayes, be narrow straits; · · · 100 F4 To the World 10

STRAND
Ha' their Bermudas, and their streights i'th' Strand: · 155 U13 Sacvile 82
That sit upon the Comon Draught: or Strand! · · 408 Inigo Jones 3 13

STRANGE
God wisheth, none should wracke on a strange shelfe. · 99 F3 Wroth 95
That no strange, or unkinde · · · · 109 F11 Epode 10
They hold in my strange poems, which, as yet, · · 115 F12 Rutland 81
(By searching) what before was strange, · · 146 U6 Defence 15
Or on the sudden. It were strange that he · · 156 U13 Sacvile 125
Adulteries, now, are not so hid, or strange, · · 165 U15 Friend-Wars 85
Thy Priest in this strange rapture; heat my braine · 177 U25 Desmond 11
Unto the Spittle Sermon. O, what strange · · 201 U42 Elegy Let 71

STRANGE (cont.)
  If something strange, that never yet was had • • • 313 Horace 178
  Of thy strange Moon-Calfe, both thy straine of mirth, • • 398 Drayton 84
STRANGER
  That stranger doctrine of Pythagoras, • • • • 61 E95 Savile 2
  And utter stranger to all ayre of France) • • • 83 E132 Sylvester 4
  What brethren, what a stranger, and his quest, • • • 325 Horace 448
STRANGERS
  Nor are the Muses strangers found: • • • • 98 F3 Wroth 52
  Not fashion'd for the court, or strangers eyes; • • 119 F13 Aubigny 115
  When, being the Strangers helpe, the poore mans aide, • 217 U46 Coke 7
STRATAGEM
  Made thee beget that cruell Stratagem, • • • • 208 U43 Vulcan 130
STRATAGEME
  In every counsell, stratageme, designe, • • • 71 E110 Edmonds 1 19
STRAW
  Ere cherries ripe, and straw-berries be gone, • • 58 E92 New Crie 1
  And lay in straw with the horses at Bergamo, • • 380 Coryat 3 38
STRAW-BERRIES
  Ere cherries ripe, and straw-berries be gone, • • 58 E92 New Crie 1
STRAWE
  Whilest lyke a blaze of strawe, • • • • • 420 Ode:If Men 15
STRAY
  How wilfull blind is he then, that would stray, • • 53 E80 Life/Death 3
STRAYN'D
  Nay, rather both our soules bee strayn'd • • • 144 U3 Musicall 25
STRAYNES
  And once more stryke the eare of tyme with those fresh straynes: 420 Ode:If Men 32
STREAME
  And thinke thy streame more quicker • • • • 221 U48 Bacchus 27
STREAMES
  Or the starres, that guild his streames, • • • 103 F6 Celia 2 16
  The Fountaines murmure as the streames doe creepe, • 290 U85 Country 27
  Or Tybers winding streames, I follow thee. • • 293 U86 Hor.4:1 40
  To brookes, and broader streames, • • • • 366 Ode Who saith 23
STREET
  Ripe statesmen, ripe: They grow in every street. • 58 E92 New Crie 3
  Is it for these that Fine-man meets the street • • 165 U15 Friend-Wars 106
  His brest is a brave Palace, a broad Street, • • 262 U78 Digby 9
  Like men street-borne, and neere the Hall, reherse • 321 Horace 357
  yearly set out there, to sayle downe the Street, • 407 Inigo Jones 2 18
  But fly thee, like the Pest! Walke not the street • 409 Detractor 19
STREET-BORNE
  Like men street-borne, and neere the Hall, reherse • 321 Horace 357
STREETS
  At Bread-streets Mermaid, having din'd, and merry, • 85 E133 Voyage 37
  He draw a Forum, with quadriviall Streets! • • 407 Inigo Jones 2 11
STREIGHT (NARROW)
  Of pressure, like one taken in a streight? • • 154 U13 Sacvile 32
  Of imitation, leape into a streight, • • • 313 Horace 192
STREIGHT
  He that is round within himselfe, and streight, • 63 E98 Th Roe 1 3
  O so yong o so streight O so chast so chast is shee 136 U2 Triumph V 46
  For what they streight would to the world forsweare; 154 U13 Sacvile 50
  That as the water makes things, put in't streight, 170 U18 Elegy Can 7
  Streight puts off all his Anger, and doth kisse 193 U38 Elegy 'Tis 88
  The Brethren, they streight nois'd it out for Newes, 209 U43 Vulcan 139
  There were, that streight did nose it out for newes, 209 U43 Vulcan V139
  The brethren they streight ways noisd out for newes, 209 U43 Vulcan V139
  Who, when shee heard the match, concluded streight, 229 U54 Squib 5
  For this so loftie forme, so streight, • • • 280 U84 Mind 54
  But, kept an even gate, as some streight tree • 287 U84 Muse 165
  There read I, streight, thy learned Legends three, • 397 Drayton 25
STREIGHTNED
  Aloft, grow lesse and streightned, full of knot; • 157 U13 Sacvile 152
STREIGHTS
  Ha' their Bermudas, and their streights i'th' Strand: 155 U13 Sacvile 82
STRENGTH
  Need seeke no other strength, no other height; • 63 E98 Th Roe 1 4
  Strength of my Countrey, whilst I bring to view • 69 E108 Soldiers 1
  Thou wert the first, mad'st merit know her strength, 75 E116 Jephson 5
  Observe the strength, the height, the why, and when, 157 U13 Sacvile 140
  And strength to be a Champion, and defend • • 161 U14 Selden 78
  And whilst our states, strength, body, and mind we waste, 166 U15 Friend-Wars 133
  What use, what strength of reason! and how much • 187 U33 Councellour 24
  Invisibilitie, and strength, and tongues: • • 206 U43 Vulcan 75
  And both a strength, and Beautie to his Land! • 251 U74 Weston 30
  Wants strength, and sinewes, as his spirits were done; 339 Horace V 38/ 37
  Unto your strength, and long examine it, • • 307 Horace 54
  Unto your strength, and long be turning it: • 339 Horace V 56/ 54
  And, as a Beare, if he the strength but had • • 337 Horace 674
  Whose strength is above strength; • • • 367 Ode Who saith 55
  To his strength, hath measur'd it out with his feet. • 379 Coryat 3 4
  That Art, or Ingine, on the strength can raise. • 400 Beaumont 10
  Sweet Tree of Life, King Davids Strength and Tower, • 413 Ghyrlond 38
STRENGTHS
  But make my strengths, such as they are, • • 102 F4 To the World 67
  Assisted by no strengths, but are her owne, • • 176 U24 Frontispice 14
STRETCH'D
  In admiration, stretch'd upon the rack • • • 163 U15 Friend-Wars 50
STREW (See also STROW)
  Of newes they get, to strew out the long meale, • 218 U47 Tribe 28

		Page	Title	Line
STRICT				
For strict degrees of ranke, or title looke:	· · · ·	29	E9 To All	2
I have, with strict advantage of free tyme	· · ·	421	Censure	6
STRICTER				
to loose, and Cap'ring, for thy stricter veyne.	· ·	108	F10 Proludium	2
STRIDE				
To line out no stride, but pas'd by himselfe?	· ·	379	Coryat 3	8
STRIFE				
Which might with halfe mankind maintayne a strife.	·	34	E23 Donne 1	8
Nor could the age have mist thee, in this strife	·	66	E102 Pembroke	5
Farre from the maze of custome, error, strife,	·	118	F13 Aubigny	60
All the Gaine, all the Good, of the Elements strife.	·	134	U2 Triumph	20
The Musicall Strife; In a Pastorall Dialogue.	·	143	U3 Musicall	Ttl
A life that knew nor noise, nor strife:	· ·	151	U12 Corbet	12
Which you will bury; but therein, the strife	·	158	U13 Sacvile	160
Quickning dead Nature, to her noblest strife.	·	162	U15 Friend-Wars	8
Of hirelings, wranglers, stitchers-to of strife,	·	187	U33 Councellour	8
All is but web, and painting; be the strife	·	242	U69 Friend Son	24
To sordid flatteries, acts of strife,	·	244	U70 Ode	39
That holy strife,	· ·	253	U75 Epithalam.	30
To compose men, and manners; stint the strife	·	261	U77 Treasurer	18
To Compasse men, and manners; stint the strife	·	261	U77 Treasurer	V 18
And, but for that Contention, and brave strife	·	271	U81 Pawlet	95
Wherein the Graver had a strife	· · · ·	390	Reader	3
The Peace of Conscience, and the Godly's strife,	·	411	Sutcliffe	7
Or if any strife bety'de	· · · ·	417	Moon	33
STRIFES				
And here, it should be one of our first strifes,	·	54	E80 Life/Death	6
Strifes, murmures, or delay,	· · ·	258	U75 Epithalam.	189
STRIKE (See also STRYKE)				
One doth not stroke me, nor the other strike.	·	46	E61 Foole	2
And never stoupe, but to strike ignorance:	·	55	E85 Goodyere 1	7
And strike our reason blinde.	· · ·	110	F11 Epode	30
Strike in thy proper straine,	· ·	175	U23 Himselfe	26
So doth the flatt'rer with faire cunning strike	·	242	U69 Friend Son	14
And strike Religion in the standers-by;	·	261	U77 Treasurer	24
And Peleus, if they seeke to heart-strike us	·	311	Horace	136
Will take offence, at this: Nor, though it strike	·	321	Horace	361
Take just offence at this: nor, though it strike	·	347	Horace	V353/361
First: thy successe did strike my sence with wonder;	·	361	Palmer	5
When the old words doe strike on the new times,	·	389	Aleman	4
(Such as thine are) and strike the second heat	·	392	Shakespeare	60
Did all so strike me, as I cry'd, who can	·	397	Drayton	31
A better cause, and strike the bravest heate	·	397	Drayton	56
STRIKES				
And strikes the quickest-sighted Judgement blinde.	· ·	363	Riches	16
STRING				
For, neither doth the String still yeeld that sound	· ·	329	Horace	521
Is laugh'd at, that still jarreth on one string:	· ·	329	Horace	532
The second string is the sweet Almond bloome	· ·	412	Ghyrlond	9
STRINGS				
Doth Clarius Harp want strings,	· · · ·	174	U23 Himselfe	9
Unto the Lyrick Strings, the Muse gave grace	· ·	309	Horace	113
Attempted by the Muses tunes, and strings;	· ·	329	Horace	498
STRIP				
T'out-strip your peeres:	· · · ·	121	F14 Sydney	26
STRIPES				
The bodies stripes, I see, the soule may save.	·	33	E21 Gam'ster	8
STRIPT (RUN)				
Out-stript, then they did all that went before:	· ·	57	E89 Allen	10
STRIPT				
Cropt, branded, slit, neck-stockt; go, you are stript.	· ·	411	Gill	16
STRIVE				
As Heaven and Nature seem'd to strive	· · ·	77	E120 S. P.	7
If I would strive to bring backe times, and trie	·	78	E122 Rudyerd 2	3
Think'st thou, Mime, this is great? or, that they strive	·	81	E129 Mime	9
Strive, Wroth, to live long innocent.	· ·	98	F3 Wroth	66
Strive, Wroth, to be long innocent.	· ·	98	F3 Wroth	V 66
And all doe strive t'advance	· · ·	120	F14 Sydney	5
Strive all right wayes it can,	· · ·	121	F14 Sydney	25
And from that thought strive to be understood.	·	168	U15 Friend-Wars	188
He run; and all did strive with diligence	·	287	U84 Muse	171
All the Grammarians strive; and yet in Court	·	309	Horace	111
STRIVES				
That strives, his manners should precede his wit.	·	78	E121 Rudyerd 1	8
STRIVING				
And, striving so to double his delight,	·	76	E118 Gut	3
Obscure. This, striving to run smooth, and flow,	·	307	Horace	36
Obscure. Another striving smooth to runne,	·	339	Horace	V 37/ 36
STRIV'ST				
Thou rather striv'st the matter to possesse,	·	70	E109 Nevil	9
STROAK'D				
As some soft chime had stroak'd the ayre;	· ·	279	U84 Mind	38
STROAKT				
Moulded or stroakt up to survey a State!	·	405	Inigo Jones 1	84
STROKE (BLOW)				
My wounded mind cannot sustaine this stroke,	·	283	U84 Muse	23
STROKE				
One doth not stroke me, nor the other strike.	·	46	E61 Foole	2
And stroke the water, nimble, chast, and faire,	·	230	U56 Covell	14
STROKEN				
Or the sad thunder-stroken thing he have	·	335	Horace	672

		Page	Title	Line

STROKES
    Gave killing strokes. There were brave men, before   • • • 114 F12 Rutland   53
STRONG
    Till time, strong by her bestowing,   • • • • 39 E40 Ratcliffe   11
    And that so strong and deepe, as 't might be thought,   • • 71 E110 Edmonds 1   7
    And, at her strong armes end, hold up, and even,   • • 114 F12 Rutland   42
    And, at her strong armes end, there hold up even,   • • 114 F12 Rutland V 42
    Had wrestled with Diseases strong,   • • • • 151 U12 Corbet   8
    Then shall my Verses, like strong Charmes,   • • 177 U25 Desmond   18
    Then shall our Verses, like strong Charmes,   • • 177 U25 Desmond V 18
    And the strong lines, that so the time doe catch: • • 206 U43 Vulcan   78
    And the strong lines, which so the time doe catch: • • 206 U43 Vulcan V 78
    What a strong Fort old Pimblicoe had bin!   • • • 213 U44 Speach   21
    And that thy strong and manly Eloquence   • • • 217 U46 Coke   13
    And made those strong approaches, by False braies,   • • 248 U71 Treasurer   7
    For they are strong Supporters: But, till then,   • • 281 U84 Kenelme   14
    Were they as strong ram'd up as Aetna gates.   • • 363 Riches   10
STRONGE
    So in my braine; the stronge impression   • • • 361 Palmer   21
STRONGER
    Then Phoebus; and much stronger   • • • 221 U48 Bacchus   22
STRONGEST
    So men at weakest, they are strongest,   • • • 104 F7 Women but   9
STRONGLY
    More strongly takes the people with delight,   • • 327 Horace   458
STROOKE
    Strooke in at Millan with the Cutlers there;   • • 212 U43 Vulcan   200
    Strooke in at Millan with the villors there;   • • 212 U43 Vulcan V200
    And that as any are strooke, her breath creates   • • 222 U49 Pucell   5
STROVE
    Call to mind the formes, that strove   • • • 137 U2 Cupid   46
    That Clients strove, in Question of the Lawes,   • • 217 U46 Coke   11
STROW
    Of newes, and noyse, to strow out a long meale.   • • 74 E115 Honest Man   10
STRUGGLED
    I struggled with this passion that did drowne   • • 362 Palmer   28
STRUMPET
    To that strumpet the Stage,   • • • • 175 U23 Himselfe   34
STRUNG
    Let every Lyre be strung,   • • • • 239 U67 Muses   16
STRUT
    I know too, though thou strut, and paint,   • • • 100 F4 To the World   13
STRYKE
    stryke him in thy proper straine,   • • • • 175 U23 Himselfe V 26
    And once more stryke the eare of tyme with those fresh straynes: 420 Ode:If Men   32
STUART
    . . . England, with the Lady Frances Stuart, Daughter of . . . 252 U75 Epithalam. Ttl
STUBBORNE
    Too stubborne for Commands so slack: • • • 292 U86 Hor.4:1   7
STUBBORNNESSE
    No stubbornnesse so stiffe, nor folly   • • • 152 U12 Corbet   24
STUCK
    And stuck in clay here, it would pull   • • • 279 U84 Mind   46
STUCKE
    Whether it languishing stucke upon the wall,   • • • 87 E133 Voyage   136
STUDIE'
    Then which there is not unto Studie'a more   • • 158 U14 Selden   13
STUDIE
    Attending such a studie, such a choice.   • • • 55 E86 Goodyere 2   6
    And studie conscience, more then thou would'st fame.   • 63 E98 Th Roe 1   10
    The common-wealth still safe, must studie thee.   • • 66 E102 Pembroke   20
    I need no other arts, but studie thee: • • • 78 E122 Rudyerd 2   9
    And studie more: • • • • • 121 F14 Sydney   36
    To the Wolves studie, or Dogs eloquence;   • • • 187 U33 Councellour   12
    So dost thou studie matter, men, and times,   • • 187 U33 Councellour   15
    Then I will studie falshood, to be true.   • • • 194 U38 Elegy 'Tis   108
    Whom Faction had not drawne to studie sides.   • • 207 U43 Vulcan   104
    Whom fashion had not drawne to studie sides.   • • 207 U43 Vulcan V104
    Whom Faction had not taught to studie sides.   • • 207 U43 Vulcan V104
    Their Sonnes to studie Arts, the Lawes, the Creed: • 215 U44 Speach   74
    They learne and studie; and then practise there.   • 215 U44 Speach   92
    I studie other friendships, and more one,   • • • 219 U47 Tribe   29
    And studie them unto the noblest ends,   • • • 224 U50 Countesse   28
STUDIE'A
    Then which there is not unto Studie'a more   • • 158 U14 Selden   13
STUDIED
    What you have studied are the arts of life;   • • 261 U77 Treasurer   17
    Hee, that hath studied well the debt, and knowes   • 325 Horace   445
    As Love, here studied to keep Grace alive.   • • 412 Ghyrlond   8
    A Say-master, hath studied all the tricks   • • 415 Rutter   26
STUDIES
    Whose better studies while shee emulates,   • • 78 E121 Rudyerd 1   3
    Because that studies spectacles, and showes,   • • 118 F13 Aubigny   65
    These studies alter now, in one, growne man;   • • 315 Horace   237
STUDY
    Ben: Jonson upon the burning of his study and bookes   • 202 U43 Vulcan VTtl
    What love you then? your whore. what study? gate,   • 215 U44 Speach   87
    Study illustrious Him, and you have all.   • • 282 U84 Kenelme   23
STUDYED
    I know thy formes are studyed arts,   • • • 100 F4 To the World   9
STUDYING
    Who (herein studying conscience, and not fame)   • • 224 U50 Countesse   14

		Page	Title	Line

STUFF
I can, out of knowne stuff, a Fable frame, ... 347 Horace V341/349

STUFFE
Spies, you are lights in state, but of base stuffe, . . . 45 E59 Spies 1
Or goddesse to invoke, to stuffe my verse; . . . 85 E133 Voyage 45
Thou should'st have cry'd, and all beene proper stuffe. . . 205 U43 Vulcan 64
Thou should'st have cry'd, and all fine proper stuffe. . . 205 U43 Vulcan V 64

STUFF'D
Sad language fits sad lookes; stuff'd menacings, . . . 311 Horace 149

STUFFES
To view the jewells, stuffes, the paines, the wit . . 97 F3 Wroth 11
To do't with Cloth, or Stuffes, lusts name might merit; . . 164 U15 Friend-Wars 57
The Stuffes, the Velvets, Plushes, Fringes, Lace, . . . 202 U42 Elegy Let 79
To stuffes and Laces, those my Man can buy. . . . 223 U49 Pucell 28

STUMBLE
As but to stumble in her sight were shame; . . . 220 U47 Tribe 70

STUNKE
Stunke not so ill; nor, when shee kist, Kate Arden. . . 87 E133 Voyage 118

STUPID
Farre I was from being stupid, ... 132 U2 How he saw 5
Sleepie, or stupid Nature, couldst thou part . . . 282 U84 Muse 15

STYGIAN
By this time had they reach'd the Stygian poole, . . . 87 E133 Voyage 121

STYLD
Wee'll have thee styld the Marquess of New-Ditch. . . 407 Inigo Jones 2 24
Wee'll have thee styld the Marquess of Town-Ditch. . . 407 Inigo Jones 2 V 24

STYLE (See also STILE)
To style us Friends, who were, by Nature, Foes? . . . 286 U84 Muse 139
By all your Titles, & whole style at ones . . . 402 Inigo Jones 1 15
your workes thus differing, troth let soe your style: . . 407 Inigo Jones 2 19

STYL'D
Which all the world then styl'd divine? . . . . 181 U27 Ode Helen 20
Of Dame Venetia Digby, styl'd The Faire: . . . 274 U84 Descent 2

STYX (See also STIX)
All, that they boast of Styx, of Acheron, . . . 84 E133 Voyage 7
And so they did, from Styx, to Acheron: . . . 88 E133 Voyage 141

SUBJECT
Who would not be thy subject, James, t'obay . . . 37 E35 James 2 1
But in my royall subject I passe thee, . . . 38 E36 Martial 3
Their un-avoided subject, fewest see: . . . 60 E94 Bedford 3 8
And must I sing? what subject shall I chuse? . . . 107 F10 Proludium 1
We must sing too? what subject shall we chuse? . . 107 F10 Proludium V 1
My gratefull soule, the subject of her powers, . . . 115 F12 Rutland 73
But to the Subject, still the Colours fit . . . 160 U14 Selden 58
If subject to the jealous errors . . . . . 177 U25 Desmond 28
So much my Subject drownes the rest. . . . . 182 U27 Ode Helen 36
The Subject of your Grace in pardoning me, . . . 191 U38 Elegy 'Tis 28
Subject to quarrell only; or else such . . . 218 U47 Tribe 11
How happy were the Subject, if he knew . . . 236 U64 Charles 3 1
In signe the Subject, and the Song will live, . . . 262 U78 Digby 17
Take therefore, you that write, a subject fit . . . 339 Horace V 55/ 53
Fit for the sock: Each subject should retaine . . . 311 Horace 124
The free spectators, subject to no Law, . . . 319 Horace 324
Each subject Passion, with her source, and spring, . . 370 Author V 7
That were the happie subject of my songe. . . . 419 Ode:If Men 9

SUBJECTS
Yet give thy jealous subjects leave to doubt: . . . 43 E51 James 3 5
This subjects you to love of one. . . . . 173 U22 Elegy Tho 8
The Orphans Pillar, the true Subjects shield, . . . 185 U30 Burleigh 7
Of murmuring Subjects; make the Nations know . . 261 U77 Treasurer 19
Of Subjects; Let such envie, till they burst. . . . 416 Dover 10

SUBLIMED
Up to her owne sublimed hight? . . . . . 279 U84 Mind 48

SUBSTANCE
And can I lesse of substance? When I runne, . . . 156 U13 Sacvile 120
Most pleasant Martial; Substance got with ease, . . 295 U90 Mart.10:47 2

SUBSTRACT
There's Albin's sonne will say, Substract an ounce . . 327 Horace 467

SUBTILE
At this so subtile sport: and play'st so ill? . . . 72 E112 Gamster 2
My mirror is more subtile, cleere, refin'd, . . . 117 F13 Aubigny 43
In sentence, of as subtile feet, ... 149 U9 Picture 8
In numbers, of as subtile feet, ... 149 U9 Picture V 8
Love in a subtile Dreame disguis'd, ... 151 U11 Dreame 4

SUBTILL
Or straines on his small forke his subtill nets . . . 290 U85 Country 33

SUBTILTIE
And subtiltie of mettalls) they dispense . . . . 86 E133 Voyage 100

SUBTILTY
Whirling his Whymseys, by a subtilty . . . . 405 Inigo Jones 1 73

SUBTLE
A subtle thing, that doth affections win . . . 74 E115 Honest Man 7
Thy subtle wayes, be narrow straits; . . . . 100 F4 To the World 10
Thus, by these subtle traines, ... 110 F11 Epode 28
More subtle workes, and finer pieces farre, . . . 242 U69 Friend Son 22
Our Roman Youths they learne the subtle wayes . . 327 Horace 464

SUBTLER
Painted a Dog, that now his subtler skill . . . 241 U69 Friend Son 10
Or straines on his small forke his subtler nets . . . 290 U85 Country V 33

SUBT'LEST
Each subt'lest Passion, with her source, and spring, . . 370 Author 7

SUBTLEST
This, fearing not the subtlest Judges marke, . . . 331 Horace 542

		Page	Title	Line

SUBTLY
Subtly distinguish'd, was confused here. . . . . 84 E133 Voyage 10
SUCCEEDED
To these succeeded the old Comoedie, ... 321 Horace 365
SUCCESSE
First: thy successe did strike my sence with wonder; . . 361 Palmer 5
SUCCOUR
To succour my necessities, tooke fire, ... 153 U13 Sacvile 8
Or if he did it not to succour me, ... 154 U13 Sacvile 29
And seeke not wants to succour: but enquire, . . . 155 U13 Sacvile 61
Wherein was oyle, beside the succour spent, . . . 207 U43 Vulcan 99
SUCCOURING
Alcides, be thou succouring to my song. . . . . 85 E133 Voyage 50
SUCCOURS
Lent timely succours, and new life begot: . . . 80 E127 Aubigny 8
Alone lend succours, and this furie stay, . . . 191 U38 Elegy 'Tis 8
Are faine to seeke for succours, and supplies . . . 248 U71 Treasurer 2
SUCH
For such a Poet, while thy dayes were greene, . . . 28 E4 James 1 5
And such a Prince thou art, wee daily see, . . . 28 E4 James 1 7
And such from whom let no man hope least good, . . 30 E11 Something 6
Earth, thou hast not such another. . . . . 39 E40 Ratcliffe 17
Such her quaint practise is, so it allures, . . . 39 E41 Gypsee 3
Th'observing neighbours no such mood can see. . . 40 E42 Giles 2
For whose sake, hence-forth, all his vowes be such, . . 41 E45 First Son 11
And farre beneath least pause of such a king, . . . 43 E51 James 3 4
That unto me dost such religion use! . . . . 44 E55 Beaumont 2
And, told of this, he slights it. Tut, such crimes . . 45 E56 Poet-Ape 9
To such true worth, though thou thy selfe forbid. . . 47 E63 Salisbury 2 V 12
Such when I meant to faine, and wish'd to see, . . 52 E76 Bedford 1 17
Attending such a studie, such a choice. . . . . 55 E86 Goodyere 2 6
Unworthy such a mistris, such a schoole, . . . 57 E90 Mill 2
Not that we thinke us worthy such a ghest, . . . 64 E101 Supper 3
And noted for what flesh such soules were fram'd, . . 66 E103 L Wroth 1 3
Such as are misse-call'd Captaynes, and wrong you; . . 69 E108 Soldiers 2
But 's angry for the Captayne, still: is such. . . 70 E108 Soldiers 10
Could make such men, and such a place repent: . . 73 E113 Overbury 10
Who in such ambition can but follow thee. . . . 73 E113 Overbury 12
With such a one. And therein keepes it's word. . . 74 E115 Honest Man 21
That Nature no such difference had imprest . . . 75 E116 Jephson 9
He, that, but living halfe his age, dyes such; . . 76 E119 Shelton 15
I would restore, and keepe it ever such; . . . 78 E122 Rudyerd 2 8
Who sees a soule, in such a body set, ... 79 E125 Uvedale 5
Laxative lettuce, and such windie meate) . . . 88 E133 Voyage 167
Tempte such a passage? when each privies seate . . 88 E133 Voyage 168
The neede of such? whose liberall board doth flow, . . 95 F2 Penshurst 59
As if it had expected such a guest; . . . . 96 F2 Penshurst 88
Such, and no other was that age, of old, . . . 98 F3 Wroth 63
And such since thou canst make thine owne content, . . 98 F3 Wroth 65
Which who can use is happy: Such be thou. . . . 99 F3 Wroth 99
Which who can use is happy: Such art thou. . . . 99 F3 Wroth V 99
Like such as blow away their lives, ... 100 F4 To the World 22
Our fraile condition it is such, ... 101 F4 To the World 54
But make my strengths, such as they are, . . . 102 F4 To the World 67
If thy leanenesse love such food, ... 105 F8 Sicknesse 24
Such, as in lustes wilde forrest love to rainge, . . 108 F10 Proludium 9
No such effects doth prove; . . . . . . 110 F11 Epode 44
Who (blest with such high chance) . . . . . 111 F11 Epode 62
That cryes, we dreame, and sweares, there's no such thing, . 111 F11 Epode 67
That cryes, I dreame, and sweares, there's no such thing, . 111 F11 Epode V 67
Such spirits as are onely continent, ... 111 F11 Epode 77
From thoughts of such a straine. . . . . . 112 F11 Epode 114
And such, or my hopes faile, shall make you shine. . . 115 F12 Rutland 64
But high, and noble matter, such as flies . . . 116 F12 Rutland 89
Such as suspect them-selves, and thinke it fit . . 117 F13 Aubigny 13
Remov'd, as you from need to have it such. . . . 117 F13 Aubigny 28
Though it reject not those of Fortune: such . . . 117 F13 Aubigny 45
For such a lot! that mixt you with a state . . . 118 F13 Aubigny 48
And call it their brave sinne. For such there be . . 119 F13 Aubigny 85
Because nor it can change, nor such a minde. . . . 120 F13 Aubigny 124
Such a Lightning (as I drew) . . . . . . 132 U2 How he saw 24
But enjoy such a sight, ... 134 U2 Triumph 8
And from her arched browes, such a grace . . . 134 U2 Triumph 17
Such my Mothers blushes be, ... 136 U2 Cupid 20
Such as oft I wanton in! . . . . . . 136 U2 Cupid 23
And did think, such Rites were due . . . . . 138 U2 Kisse 19
And, if such a verse as this, ... 138 U2 Kisse 35
All his actions to be such, ... 142 U2 Her man 45
Such a man, with every part, ... 142 U2 Her man 53
At such a Call, what beast or fowle, ... 143 U3 Musicall 5
To fall againe; at such a feast, ... 144 U3 Musicall 23
Such as in valour would excell, ... 146 U6 Defence 7
As they are done, and such returnes they find: . . 153 U13 Sacvile 6
To have such doe me good, I durst not name: . . . 153 U13 Sacvile 18
Lest Ayre, or Print, but flies it: Such men would . . 154 U13 Sacvile 45
That to such Natures let their full hands flow, . . 154 U13 Sacvile 60
Such a religious horrour in the brests . . . . 155 U13 Sacvile 91
Such worship due to kicking of a Punck! . . . 155 U13 Sacvile 93
That men such reverence to such actions show! . . 156 U13 Sacvile 98
Who was this Morning such a one, should be . . . 157 U13 Sacvile 126
Such Notes are vertuous men! they live as fast . . 157 U13 Sacvile 143
For me to be your Indice. Keep you such, . . . 157 U13 Sacvile 156
Was trusted, that you thought my judgement such . . 158 U14 Selden 6

SUCH (cont.)

	Page	Title	Line
But 'twas with purpose to have made them such.	159	U14 Selden	22
Large claspe of Nature, such a wit can bound.	160	U14 Selden	64
Be honour is so mixt) by such as would,	162	U15 Friend-Wars	25
Is nothing, such scarce meat and drinke he'le give,	167	U15 Friend-Wars	159
For, if such men as he could die,	168	U16 Gray	6
Such Guides men use not, who their way would find,	170	U18 Elegy Can	12
Of all that can be done him; Such a one	171	U19 Elegy By	23
were such as I will now relate, or worse?	172	U20 Shrub	14
But she is such, as she might, yet, forestall	172	U20 Shrub	23
And yours of whom I sing be such	173	U22 Elegy Tho	2
As Love, t'aquit such excellence,	173	U22 Elegy Tho	23
Of such as savour	177	U25 Desmond	34
Such thoughts wil make you more in love with truth.	181	U26 Ode High	21
That in rearing such a Schoole,	184	U29 Fit of Rime	59
Of all the Land. Who now at such a Rate,	185	U30 Burleigh	19
Such shall you heare to day, and find great foes,	186	U32 Elsmere	7
Such are his powers, whom time hath stil'd,	189	U36 Song	13
Looke forth, but cannot last in such a forme.	191	U38 Elegy 'Tis	14
You may so place me, and in such an ayre,	192	U38 Elegy 'Tis	51
Of crueltie, lest they doe make you such.	193	U38 Elegy 'Tis	84
He when he sees a sorrow such as this,	193	U38 Elegy 'Tis	87
And such your Servant is, who vowes to keepe	198	U40 Elegy That	41
Such Songsters there are store of; witnesse he	201	U42 Elegy Let	65
On such my serious follies; But, thou'lt say,	204	U43 Vulcan	41
Or such my serious follies; But, thou'lt say,	204	U43 Vulcan	V 41
Adulterate moneys, such as might not goe:	204	U43 Vulcan	45
Adulterate maskings, such as might not goe:	204	U43 Vulcan	V 45
In so much land a yeare, or such a Banke,	215	U44 Speach	76
Such, Coke, were thy beginnings, when thy good	217	U46 Coke	5
Such was thy Processe, when Integritie,	217	U46 Coke	9
And now such is thy stand; while thou dost deale	217	U46 Coke	15
Such is thy All; that (as I sung before)	217	U46 Coke	21
I could say more of such, but that I flie	218	U47 Tribe	5
Subject to quarrell only; or else such	218	U47 Tribe	11
Such as are square, wel-tagde, and permanent,	220	U47 Tribe	64
Such, (if her manners like you) I doe send:	230	U56 Covell	19
I hate such measur'd, give me mettall'd fire	233	U59 Newcastle	7
He, that in such a flood, as we are in	234	U61 Epigram	16
'T is not enough (thy pietie is such)	235	U62 Charles 1	3
That the Almighties will to you is such:	236	U63 Charles 2	8
For safetie of such Majestie, cry out?	236	U64 Charles 3	6
hee'ld frame such ditties of their store, and want,	241	U68 House-hold	7
Such truths, as we expect for happy men,	246	U70 Ode	83
And such a force the faire example had,	247	U70 Ode	117
That such a Law	247	U70 Ode	120
Reducts, Halfe-moones, Horne-workes, and such close wayes,	248	U71 Treasurer	8
Still to have such a Charles, but this Charles long.	249	U72 King	18
The wish is great; but where the Prince is such,	249	U72 King	19
Such pleasure as the teeming Earth,	250	U74 Weston	1
Such joyes, such sweet's doth your Returne	251	U74 Weston	19
Of Nuptiall Sweets, at such a season, owe,	257	U75 Epithalam.	148
Alone, and such a race,	257	U75 Epithalam.	157
Where Nature such a large survey hath ta'en,	262	U78 Digby	11
I durst not aime at that: The dotes were such	269	U81 Pawlet	25
I durst not aime at, the dotes thereof were such	269	U81 Pawlet	V 25
Yet, here are no such Trifles brought,	273	U84 Cradle	25
For such as Shee.	274	U84 Cradle	40
Gave two such Houses as Northumberland,	274	U84 Descent	5
But at such distance, as the eye	276	U84 Body	19
But at such distance, all the eye	276	U84 Body	V 19
But such a Mind, mak'st God thy Guest.	281	U84 Mind	72
With such a Raritie, and not rowse Art	282	U84 Muse	16
And to that forme, lent two such veines of blood	287	U84 Muse	157
Such as the Sabines, or a Sun-burnt-blowse,	291	U85 Country	41
Into our Seas send any such:	291	U85 Country	52
I am not such, as in the Reigne	292	U86 Hor.4:1	3
Who sings so sweet, and with such cunning plaies,	293	U87 Hor.3:9	10
hee, that but living halfe his dayes, dies such,	295	U89 Mart.8:77	7
Mens faces, still, with such as laugh, are prone	311	Horace	143
Mens count'nances, with such as laugh, are prone	342	Horace	V143
What doth this Promiser such great gaping worth	313	Horace	197
What doth this Promiser such great gaping worth	343	Horace	V197
If such a ones applause thou dost require,	315	Horace	220
And toile in vaine: the excellence is such	321	Horace	352
Thou, such thy judgement is, thy knowledge too,	331	Horace	573
Where, such perfections to the life doe rise.	362	Author	6
If they seeme wry, to such as looke asquint,	362	Author	7
Those that in blood such violent pleasure have,	363	Murder	1
With the shops Foreman, or some such brave sparke,	371	Fletcher	6
In such a Martirdome; To vexe their eyes,	371	Fletcher	13
Stay, view this stone: And, if thou beest not such,	371	Epitaph	1
Such weare true wedding robes, and are true freindes,	384	Somerset	5
When these, and such, their voices have employd;	385	Brooke	1
To such a worke, as could not need theirs? Yet	385	Brooke	5
I know for such, as (if my word will waigh)	386	Husband	11
Let such as justly have out-liv'd all prayse,	387	Cavendish	5
Such Passage hast thou found, such Returnes made,	389	Chapman	10
Such Bookes deserve Translators, of like coate	389	Aleman	11
While I confesse thy writings to be such,	390	Shakespeare	3
(Such as thine are) and strike the second heat	392	Shakespeare	60
And such wert thou. Looke how the fathers face	392	Shakespeare	65
Such things, of every body, and as well.	394	Jane Ogle	10

	Page	Title	Line

SUCH (cont.)
That reade it? that are ravish'd! such was I — 397 Drayton 53
Such, as the creeping common Pioners use — 400 Beaumont 5
In setting forth of such a solemne Toye! — 405 Inigo Jones 1 78
In setting forth of such a serious Toye! — 405 Inigo Jones 1 V 78
Our Charles should make thee such? 'Twill not become — 406 Inigo Jones 2 3
Shall not worke out unto it, such a fame. — 409 Detractor 12
If such a Tyke as thou, er'e wer't, or noe? — 409 Detractor 14
Such men I met withall, and so have you. — 415 Rutter 11
Of Subjects; Let such envie, till they burst. — 416 Dover 10

SUCK
Each suck others breath. — 139 U2 Another 16

SUCK'D
Their gentler spirits have suck'd innocence. — 96 F2 Penshurst 94
From your lips, and suck'd an ayre — 137 U2 Kisse 3

SUCKT
Suckt from the Veynes of shop-philosophy. — 405 Inigo Jones 1 74

SUDDAYNE
This was Mr Ben: Johnsons Answer of the suddayne. — 418 Answer Ttl

SUDDEN (See also SODAINE)
Or on the sudden. It were strange that he — 156 U13 Sacvile 125

SUFFER
So both the prais'd, and praisers suffer: Yet, — 116 F13 Aubigny 5
To suffer tortures, scorne, and Infamie, — 193 U38 Elegy 'Tis 93
To bend, to breake, provoke, or suffer it! — 233 U59 Newcastle 18
To bend, or breake, provoke, or suffer it! — 233 U59 Newcastle V 18

SUFFER'D
I, that have suffer'd this; and, though forsooke — 117 F13 Aubigny 15
The wished goale, both did, and suffer'd much — 333 Horace 588
The man once mock'd, and suffer'd wrong to tread. — 335 Horace 642

SUFFERED
3. What hee suffered. — 133 U2 Suffered Ttl

SUFFERERS
Of the poore sufferers) where the envious, proud, — 167 U15 Friend-Wars 167

SUFFERS
And even the praisers judgement suffers so. — 64 E99 Th Roe 2 10
Suffers no name, but a description: — 74 E115 Honest Man 4

SUFFICIENT
Or that I'have by, two good sufficient men, — 54 E81 Proule 3
Coriat, should rise the most sufficient head — 157 U13 Sacvile 128

SUFFOLKE
To Thomas Earle of Suffolke. — 49 E67 Suffolk Ttl

SUFFRAGE
But he hath every suffrage, can apply — 329 Horace 514
My suffrage brings thee all increase, to crowne — 385 Brooke 7
'Tis true, and all mens suffrage. But these wayes — 390 Shakespeare 5

SUFFRING
By constant suffring of thy equall mind; — 47 E63 Salisbury 2 8
T' have knowne no envy, but by suffring it! — 287 U84 Muse 162
Suffring, and dying to redeeme our losse! — 288 U84 Muse 202

SUFFRINGS
Her suffrings, as the body had beene away! — 270 U81 Pawlet 51

SUGAR
In Sugar Candide, or in butter'd beere, — 167 U15 Friend-Wars 153

SUGGESTION
Would, at suggestion of a steepe desire, — 111 F11 Epode 63

SUIT (See also SUTE)
Of lust, to his rich Suit and Title, Lord? — 163 U15 Friend-Wars 51
To teach each suit he has, the ready way — 165 U15 Friend-Wars 108
Of an entangling suit; and bring 't about: — 333 Horace 604

SUITE
The taylor brings a suite home; he it 'ssayes, — 30 E12 Shift 9
And cast my suite behind: — 149 U9 Picture V 5

SUITOR (See also SUTOR)
Of either Suitor, or a Servant by. — 230 U56 Covell 18
Of suitor, or of servant standing by. — 230 U56 Covell V 18

SUITS
Exacts then she is pleas'd to pay: no suits, — 258 U75 Epithalam. 188
gentlie hee asketh, shee will pay: no suits, — 258 U75 Epithalam. V188

SULLEN (See also SOLLEN)
In darke, and sullen mornes, doe we not say, — 193 U38 Elegy 'Tis 79

SULPHURE
Wormewood, and sulphure, sharpe, and tooth'd withall; — 27 E2 My Booke 4

SUMME
With pieces of the Legend; The whole summe — 205 U43 Vulcan 66
Summe up this crowned day, — 240 U67 Muses 47
And that this so accepted summe, — 259 U76 Petition 14
And that this so thriftye summe, — 259 U76 Petition V 14
Could summe to a perfection, was her Act! — 270 U81 Pawlet 46
I summe up mine owne breaking, and wish all. — 283 U84 Muse 26
The maker of the Propertyes! in summe — 404 Inigo Jones 1 61

SUMM'D
Are justly summ'd, that make you man; — 120 F14 Sydney 22
How summ'd a circle didst thou leave man-kind — 243 U70 Ode 9
Goe now, and tell out dayes summ'd up with feares, — 244 U70 Ode 53

SUMMER (See also SOMMER)
Though thou hast past thy Summer standing, stay — 252 U75 Epithalam. 1
Though thou art past thy Summer standing, stay — 252 U75 Epithalam. V 1

SUMMERS
As Summers sky, or purged Ayre, — 147 U7 Nymph 17
Of Summers Liveries, and gladding greene; — 253 U75 Epithalam. 18

SUMMES
Kisse, and score up wealthy summes — 103 F6 Celia 2 6

SUMMES (cont.)
     But, that which summes all, is the Eglantine,   .   .   .   413 Ghyrlond   21
SUN
     I wish the Sun should shine   .   .   .   .   150 U10 Jealousie   7
     Or feats of darknesse acted in Mid-Sun, ...   156 U13 Sacvile   95
     None brookes the Sun-light worse then he. .   .   .   .   189 U36 Song   4
     When I see you, then I doe see my Sun, ...   194 U38 Elegy 'Tis   120
     Or that the Sun was here, but forc't away;   .   .   .   199 U41 Elegy Since   6
     The Clowdes rack cleare before the Sun, ...   251 U74 Weston   8
     A-while with us bright Sun, and helpe our light;   .   .   252 U75 Epithalam.   2
     A-while with us bright Sun, and mend our light;   .   .   252 U75 Epithalam.   V 2
     Although that thou, O Sun, at our intreaty stay!   .   .   254 U75 Epithalam.   56
     O, now thou smil'st, faire Sun, and shin'st, as thou wouldst stay! 254 U75 Epithalam.   64
     Our Court, and all the Grandees; now, Sun, looke,   .   .   254 U75 Epithalam.   73
     Search, Sun, and thou wilt find, ...   254 U75 Epithalam.   79
     Search, Sun, and thou shalt find;   .   .   .   .   255 U75 Epithalam.   79
     Now, Sun, and post away the rest of day; .   .   .   .   255 U75 Epithalam.   V 79
     Haste, haste, officious Sun, and send them Night   .   .   257 U75 Epithalam.   138
     Such as the Sabines, or a Sun-burnt-blowse,   .   .   .   257 U75 Epithalam.   145
     It cast a beame as when the chear-full Sun   .   .   .   291 U85 Country   41
     The rosie Morning, or the rising Sun, ...   396 Drayton   17
SUN-BURNT-BLOWSE   .   414 Ghyrlond   50
     Such as the Sabines, or a Sun-burnt-blowse,   .   .   .   291 U85 Country   41
SUNDRED
     On my lips, thus hardly sundred, ...   103 F6 Celia 2   7
SUNDRIE
     They all get Porta, for the sundrie wayes .   .   .   .   59 E92 New Crie   25
SUNDRY
     A horse neck joyn, & sundry plumes ore-fold   .   .   .   338 Horace   V 2
SUNG
     I'have sung the greater fortunes of our state. .   .   .   48 E64 Salisbury 3   18
     Sung by a Horace, or a Muse as free;   .   .   .   .   58 E91 Vere   4
     Now I have sung thee thus, shall judge of thee.   .   .   70 E109 Nevil   16
     My Muse had plough'd with his, that sung A-jax.   .   .   89 E133 Voyage   196
     Of whose Beautie it was sung, ...   131 U2 Excuse   19
     This here sung, can be no other   .   .   .   .   136 U2 Cupid   11
     Have sung this Hymne, and here intreat   .   .   .   .   174 U22 Elegy Tho   30
     Was Lesbia sung by learn'd Catullus?   .   .   .   .   181 U27 Ode Helen   9
     On every wall, and sung where e're I walke.   .   .   .   193 U38 Elegy 'Tis   98
     The rest, my journey into Scotland sung   .   .   .   .   207 U43 Vulcan   V 94
     Such is thy All; that (as I sung before) .   .   .   .   217 U46 Coke   21
     Jonson, who sung this of him, e're he went   .   .   .   246 U70 Ode   85
     A New-yeares gift Sung to King Charles, 1635. .   .   .   263 U79 New-yeares   Ttl
     For, had we here said lesse, we had sung nothing then.   .   263 U79 New-yeares   8
     Is sung: as als' her getting up   .   .   .   .   274 U84 Cradle   37
SUNKE
     And sunke in that dead sea of life   .   .   .   .   244 U70 Ode   40
SUN-LIGHT
     None brookes the Sun-light worse then he. .   .   .   .   189 U36 Song   4
SUNNE
     In cheifest glory Sunne-her   .   .   .   .   135 U2 Triumph   V 32
     Or growne; by height or lowenesse of the Sunne?   .   .   156 U13 Sacvile   119
     Where Love doth shine, there needs no Sunne,   .   .   .   189 U36 Song   5
     The Sunne his heat, and light, the ayre his dew?   .   .   192 U38 Elegy 'Tis   57
     The Sunne! great Kings, and mightiest Kingdomes fall!   .   271 U81 Pawlet   89
     The Sunne! great Kings, and mighty Kingdomes fall! .   .   271 U81 Pawlet   V 89
     The Sunne, a Sea, or soundlesse Pit;   .   .   .   .   278 U84 Mind   11
     Nor Sunne could make to vary from the rest,   .   .   .   367 Ode Who saith   29
     The Sunne translated, or the Sonne of May.   .   .   .   395 May   24
SUNNE-HER
     In cheifest glory Sunne-her   .   .   .   .   135 U2 Triumph   V 32
SUNNES
     Sunnes, that set, may rise againe: .   .   .   .   102 F5 Celia 1   6
SUN'S
     By this Sun's Noone-sted's made   .   .   .   .   258 U75 Epithalam.   183
SUP
     A chamber-critick, and dost dine, and sup .   .   .   .   50 E72 Court-ling   2
     Of this we will sup free, but moderately, ...   65 E101 Supper   35
     At every meale, where it doth dine, or sup,   .   .   .   74 E115 Honest Man   23
     But might I of Jove's Nectar sup, ...   106 F9 Celia 3   7
     These, had'st thou pleas'd either to dine, or sup, .   .   206 U43 Vulcan   83
     These, had'st thou been pleas'd either to dine, or sup, .   206 U43 Vulcan   V 83
     So deep, as he did then death's waters sup;   .   .   .   244 U70 Ode   41
SUPERCILIOUS
     See the grave, sower, and supercilious Sir   .   .   .   162 U15 Friend-Wars   19
SUPERFICIES
     My Superficies: that was all you saw.   .   .   .   .   227 U52 Answer   9
SUPERFLUOUS
     Cut off superfluous ornaments; and when .   .   .   .   335 Horace   636
SUPERSTITION
     And superstition I dare scarce reveale, ...   155 U13 Sacvile   86
SUPERSTITIOUS
     Ambitious, factious, superstitious, lowd .   .   .   .   167 U15 Friend-Wars 168
     Better be dumbe, then superstitious!   .   .   .   .   284 U84 Muse   73
SUPP'D
     I sayd, who'had supp'd so deepe of this sweet Chalice,   .   412 Sutcliffe   21
SUPPER
     Inviting a friend to supper.   .   .   .   .   64 E101 Supper   Ttl
     Call every night to Supper in these fitts,   .   .   .   218 U47 Tribe   21
     Make a great Supper; or for some poore man   .   .   .   333 Horace   602
SUPPERS
     That still th'art made the suppers flagge, the drum,   .   81 E129 Mime   7
     Beare-Suppers in their Names! and spend whole nights   .   156 U13 Sacvile   101

	Page	Title	Line
SUPPLANT			
Supplant bold Panton; and brought there to view	214	U44 Speach	34
SUPPLE			
And makes her supple feete, as swift as winde.	363	Riches	12
SUPPLIES			
Are faine to seeke for succours, and supplies	248	U71 Treasurer	2
SUPPLY			
Onely to boast thy merit in supply.	61	F95 Savile	12
That thought shall make, he will this losse supply	236	U63 Charles 2	11
And were shee lost, could best supply her place,	264	U79 New-yeares	34
Had cloath'd him so. Here's all I can supply	389	Aleman	20
SUPPLY'D			
For your most noble offer had supply'd me.	54	E84 Bedford 2	4
SUPPORTERS			
For they are strong Supporters: But, till then,	281	U84 Kenelme	14
SUPPORTETH			
Shee chearfully supporteth what she reares,	176	U24 Frontispice	13
SUPPOSE			
Who, being at sea, suppose,	111	F11 Epode	70
That, being at sea, suppose,	111	F11 Epode	V 70
SUPPOSITORIES			
Suppositories, cataplasmes, and lotions.	86	E133 Voyage	102
SUPREME			
He that shall be our supreme Judge, should leave	286	U84 Muse	148
SURCOATES			
No cobweb Call's; no Surcoates wrought	273	U84 Cradle	26
SURE			
Sure, willing povertie lives most in you.	29	E6 Alchymists	2
Till they be sure to make the foole their quarrie.	55	E85 Goodyere 1	10
Are sure to con the catalogue by hart;	59	E92 New Crie	22
Digestive cheese, and fruit there sure will bee;	65	E101 Supper	27
For your next meale: this you are sure of. Why	69	E107 Hungry	27
To answere me. And sure, it was th'intent	87	E133 Voyage	107
Which to effect (since no brest is so sure,	109	F11 Epode	5
As sure to win	130	U1 Father	31
Sure, said he, if I have Braine,	136	U2 Cupid	10
I'm sure my language to her, was as sweet,	149	U9 Picture	6
I'm sure my language to her, is as sweet,	149	U9 Picture	V 6
Sure there is Misterie in it, I not know,	156	U13 Sacvile	97
I Know to whom I write. Here, I am sure,	158	U14 Selden	1
Yet sure my tunes will be the best,	182	U27 Ode Helen	35
So to be sure you doe injoy your selves.	200	U42 Elegy Let	24
And sayd twas sure a threatning to the beares;	209	U43 Vulcan	V146
Men that are safe, and sure, in all they doe,	218	U47 Tribe	1
Whereby he may knit sure up	222	U48 Bacchus	47
Which they that have the Crowne are sure to know!	271	U81 Pawlet	76
Which the Elect of God are sure to know!	271	U81 Pawlet	V 76
And, sure of Heaven, rides triumphing in.	272	U81 Pawlet	100
Sure, I am dead, and know it not! I feele	283	U84 Muse	29
By sure Election, and predestin'd grace!	288	U84 Muse	198
Looke through him, and be sure, you take not mocks	333	Horace	621
Their cares in wine; with sure	368	Ode Who saith	87
Sure, this glad payre were married, but this day.	384	Somerset	26
SURELY			
And surely had I but your Stable seene	228	U53 Newcastle	13
I should commit thee surely with thy peeres,	391	Shakespeare	28
SURETIE			
What suretie of life have thou, and I?	168	U16 Gray	7
O Day of joy, and suretie to the just!	284	U84 Muse	61
Will be a suretie; or can helpe him out	333	Horace	603
SURETIES			
By offring not more sureties, then inow,	386	Browne	12
SURFET			
I shall feare, you'll surfet too.	104	F8 Sicknesse	8
I doe feare, you'll surfet too.	104	F8 Sicknesse	V 8
Surfet? and Quarrel? drinkes the tother health?	166	U15 Friend-Wars	115
O Times! O Manners! Surfet bred of ease,	237	U64 Charles 3	17
SURFETS			
Spent in surfets: and their dayes,	104	F8 Sicknesse	5
More then the surfets, in thee, that day stood.	214	U44 Speach	48
Flowes from the surfets which we take in peace.	363	Peace	4
SURGE			
With whom who sailes, rides on the surge of feare,	110	F11 Epode	41
SURGEON			
And hurt seeks Cure, the Surgeon bids take bread,	155	U13 Sacvile	68
SURGEONS			
In Surgeons hall)	179	U25 Desmond	38
SURLY (ADJECTIVE)			
The knottie heads of the most surly Groomes,	363	Riches	8
SURLY			
On Don Surly.	35	E28 Surly	Ttl
Don Surly, to aspire the glorious name	35	E28 Surly	1
Surly, use other arts, these only can	36	E28 Surly	21
On Cashierd Capt. Surly.	54	E82 Surly	Ttl
SURLY'S			
Surly's old whore in her new silkes doth swim:	54	E82 Surly	1
SURNAMES			
You liv'd to be the great surnames,	247	U70 Ode	113
SURPASSE			
His face; the Print would then surpasse	390	Reader	7
SURPRIZE			
Whose Offices, and honours did surprize,	185	U30 Burleigh	15
And ev'ry Plant the sense surprize,	251	U74 Weston	11

		Page	Title	Line

SURPRIZE (cont.)
Surprize their sense: 273   U84 Cradle   24
SURPRIZ'D
Hath both my heart and me surpriz'd, ...   151   U11 Dreame   5
SURROUNDING
Item, a charme surrounding fearefully   51   E73 Fine Grand   12
SURSHIP
Something your Surship doth not yet intend!   .   .   .   402   Inigo Jones 1   14
SURVEY
Where Nature such a large survey hath ta'en,   .   .   .   262   U78 Digby   11
Moulded or stroakt up to survey a State!   405   Inigo Jones 1   84
SURVEYOR
Mr Surveyor, you that first begann   402   Inigo Jones 1   1
Oh wise Surveyor! wyser Architect!   405   Inigo Jones 1   85
SURVIVE
But I am glad to see that time survive, ...   47   E64 Salisbury 3   9
SURVIVING
. . . Surviving Duke of the same name.   252   U75 Epithalam.   Ttl
SUSAN
To Susan Countesse of Montgomery.   67   E104 Montgomery   Ttl
SUSANNA
A new Susanna, equall to that old?   67   E104 Montgomery   4
SUSPECT
And those that lack'd it, to suspect at length,   .   .   75   E116 Jephson   6
Such as suspect them-selves, and thinke it fit   .   .   117   F13 Aubigny   13
Poore Tom have we cause to suspect just thee?   .   .   381   Coryat 3   58
SUSPECTED
And, reconcil'd, keepe him suspected still.   .   .   .   48   E65 Muse   8
Send these suspected helpes, to aide   275   U84 Body   5
SUSPENCE
The severall figures, languish in suspence,   .   .   .   370   Author   10
SUSPENDED
That sacred to Odcombe are there now suspended,   .   .   380   Coryat 3   40
SUSPITION
Not flie the Crime, but the Suspition too;   .   .   .   159   U14 Selden   18
Ought that is ill, but the suspition too,   .   .   .   224   U50 Countesse   6
SUSSEX
Hill-/foot (out in Sussex) to an iron Mill;   .   .   .   211   U43 Vulcan   184
Hill-/foot (out in Sussex) to some iron Mill;   .   .   .   211   U43 Vulcan   V184
SUSTAINE
So did thy vertue'enforme, thy wit sustaine   .   .   .   75   E116 Jephson   3
My wounded mind cannot sustaine this stroke,   .   .   283   U84 Muse   23
SUSTAINES
Is her owne scourge, when it sustaines their states   .   .   422   Lucan   3
SUTCLIFFE
To Mrs. Alice Sutcliffe, on her divine Meditations.   .   .   411   Sutcliffe   Ttl
SUTE
Not offer'd, as it made sute to be bought;   .   .   .   28   E3 Bookseller   6
When he was here. Nor hath he got a sute,   .   .   .   63   E97 Motion   16
Thy lord, and lady, though they have no sute.   .   .   95   F2 Penshurst   50
Move it, as their humblest sute, ...   106   F8 Sicknesse   46
Move it, as their humble sute, ...   106   F8 Sicknesse   V 46
Jest, he saies. Item one sute of blacke taffata   .   .   380   Coryat 3   48
SUTED
But that hee's too well suted, in a cloth,   .   .   .   389   Aleman   17
SUTES
Not glad, like those that have new hopes, or sutes,   .   .   47   E64 Salisbury 3   1
SUTOR
Gold is a sutor, never tooke repulse, ...   363   Riches   5
SWAGGERING
Or swaggering with the Watch, or Drawer, drunke;   .   .   156   U13 Sacvile   94
SWAID
She swaid all bus'nesse in the Familie!   287   U84 Muse   168
SWAINE
For if the Nymphs should know my Swaine,   .   .   .   147   U7 Nymph   3
SWAINES
And shuts the old. Haste, haste, all loyall Swaines,   .   .   263   U79 New-yeares   10
Haste, haste you hither, all you gentler Swaines,   .   .   265   U79 New-yeares   46
SWALLOW
Into a Swallow there; Nor Cadmus take,   .   .   .   317   Horace   267
SWALLOW'D
How full of want, how swallow'd up, how dead   .   .   80   E127 Aubigny   6
SWAMME
Where Pindar swamme;   366   Ode Who saith   20
SWAN'
Now must we plie our ayme; our Swan's on wing.   .   .   368   Ode Who saith   64
SWAN
Each that drawes, is a Swan, or a Dove,   .   .   .   134   U2 Triumph   3
The Swan that so relish'd Pancharis)   182   U27 Ode Helen   30
Produce us a blacke Swan?   366   Ode Who saith   2
Set out a like, or second to our Swan.   .   .   .   369   Ode Who saith   120
Sweet Swan of Avon! what a sight it were   .   .   .   392   Shakespeare   71
SWANNE
This Swanne is onely his, ...   366   Ode Who saith   15
SWANNES
Besides the other Swannes admiring him,   .   .   .   366   Ode Who saith   5
SWAN'S
Now must we plie our ayme; our Swan's on wing.   .   .   368   Ode Who saith   64
SWANS
Or Swans Downe ever?   135   U2 Triumph   26
When with Joves swans she sported   135   U2 Triumph   V 42
With thy bright Swans, of Paulus Maximus: .   .   .   292   U86 Hor.4:1   10

SWARE
    I can helpe that with boldnesse; And Love sware,   .   .   .   170   U18 Elegy Can   9
SWARME
    Praevaricators swarme. Of which the store,   .   .   .   167   U15 Friend-Wars   170
    It is a ryming Age, and Verses swarme   200   U42 Elegy Let   27
    The wealthy houshold swarme of bondmen met,   .   .   .   291   U85 Country   65
SWARTHIE
    Which in some swarthie fish uncomely ends: .   .   .   305   Horace   5
SWAY
    A Prince, that rules by'example, more than sway?   .   .   37   E35 James 2   2
    Or perhaps lesse: whil'st gold beares all this sway,   .   .   113   F12 Rutland   18
    For no man lives so out of passions sway,   .   .   .   190   U37 Friend-Book   31
    It much will sway whether a god speak, than;   .   .   342   Horace   V161
    Be wonne a friend; it must both sway, and bend   .   .   317   Horace   281
    Betweene the doubtfull sway of Reason', and sense.   .   .   370   Author   12
SWAYD
    whole armyes fall, swayd by those nyce respects.   .   .   423   Lucan   11
SWAYE
    For noe Man Lyves, soe out of passions swaye,   .   .   422   Censure   24
SWAYES
    Of politique pretext, that swayes a State,   .   .   .   177   U25 Desmond   V 29
SWAYNES
    Heard the soft ayres, between our Swaynes & thee,   .   .   397   Drayton   26
SWEARE
    I sweare by your true friend, my Muse, I love   .   .   70   E108 Soldiers   5
    By which the Masters sweare, when, on the stoole   .   .   87   E133 Voyage   122
    Since when it growes, and smells, I sweare,   .   .   106   F9 Celia 3   15
    Since when it lives, and smells, I sweare,   .   .   .   106   F9 Celia 3   V 15
    Man thought the valianter, 'cause he durst sweare,   .   .   168   U15 Friend-Wars 192
    These ten yeares day; As all may sweare that looke   .   .   213   U44 Speach   27
    That went before, a Husband. Shee, Ile sweare,   .   .   386   Husband   9
    With every song, I sweare, and so would dye: .   .   397   Drayton   54
    And I sweare by all the light   416   Moon   5
SWEARES
    The children, that he keepes, Giles sweares are none   .   .   40   E42 Giles   13
    Of his begetting. And so sweares his Jone.   .   .   .   40   E42 Giles   14
    Backe the intelligence, and falsely sweares,   .   .   109   F11 Epode   25
    That cryes, we dreame, and sweares, there's no such thing,   .   111   F11 Epode   67
    That cryes, I dreame, and sweares, there's no such thing,   .   111   F11 Epode   V 67
SWEARING
    Scarse thy weekes swearing brings thee of, of one.   .   .   32   E16 Brain-hardy   4
    Unto their praise, in certaine swearing rites!   .   .   156   U13 Sacvile   102
SWEAR'ST
    For all thou hear'st, thou swear'st thy selfe didst doo.   .   54   E81 Proule   5
SWEAT
    Let this man sweat, and wrangle at the barre,   .   .   99   F3 Wroth   73
    Sweat at the forge, their hammers beating;   .   .   179   U25 Desmond   41
    Yet he that offers at it, may sweat much,   .   .   .   321   Horace   351
    While he was young; he sweat; and freez'd againe: .   .   333   Horace   589
    Who casts to write a living line, must sweat,   .   .   392   Shakespeare   59
    When they doe sweat to fortifie a Muse.   .   .   .   400   Beaumont   6
SWEATE
    Is fill'd with buttock? And the walls doe sweate   .   .   88   E133 Voyage   169
SWEATES
    Of humane life! as all the frosts, and sweates   .   .   233   U59 Newcastle   22
SWEDEN
    In Ireland, Holland, Sweden, pompous lies,   .   .   .   69   E107 Hungry   12
SWEET
    I meant shee should be curteous, facile, sweet,   .   .   52   E76 Bedford 1   9
    As the beginnings here, prove purely sweet,   .   .   81   E128 Wm Roe 2   7
    Yet, one day in the yeere, for sweet 'tis voyc't,   .   .   87   E133 Voyage   119
    Upon your eares, of discords so un-sweet?   .   .   .   88   E133 Voyage   171
    And, howsoever we may thinke things sweet,   .   .   99   F3 Wroth   97
    Come sweet Celia, let us prove, ...   102   F5 Celia 1   V 1
    But the sweet theft to reveale: 102   F5 Celia 1   16
    Kisse me, sweet: The warie lover   103   F6 Celia 2   1
    As sweet, as shee is fayre.   112   F11 Epode   98
    To thee more sweet?   127   U1 Trinitie   16
    For, sin's so sweet, ...   129   U1 Father   12
    O so white! O so soft! O so sweet is she!   .   .   .   135   U2 Triumph   30
    O so faire! O so soft! O so sweet is she!   .   .   .   135   U2 Triumph   V 30
    O so faire O so kind o so sweet so sweet is shee   .   .   135   U2 Triumph   V 38
    Rip'ned with a breath more sweet, ...   137   U2 Cupid   27
    Thence, as sweet, as you are faire, ...   137   U2 Kisse   4
    All your sweet of life is past, ...   140   U2 Promise   28
    No tunes are sweet, nor words have sting,   .   .   143   U3 Musicall   15
    No voice so sweet, nor words have sting,   .   .   143   U3 Musicall   V 15
    I'm sure my language to her, was as sweet,   .   .   149   U9 Picture   6
    I'm sure my language to her, is as sweet,   .   .   149   U9 Picture   V 6
    For t'other pound of sweet-meats, he shall feele   .   .   164   U15 Friend-Wars   77
    Sweet bags, sweet Powders, nor sweet words will passe   .   165   U15 Friend-Wars   112
    O imitate that sweet Serenitie   193   U38 Elegy 'Tis   77
    That Love's a bitter sweet, I ne're conceive   .   .   197   U40 Elegy That   1
    Shortly againe: and make our absence sweet.   .   .   197   U40 Elegy That   8
    How shall I doe, sweet Mistris, for my heart?   .   .   199   U41 Elegy Since   14
    Cloth Spices, or guard sweet meates from the flies;   .   .   205   U43 Vulcan   V 53
    All the madde Rolands, and sweet Oliveers;   .   .   206   U43 Vulcan   70
    What, to make legs? yes, and to smell most sweet,   .   .   215   U44 Speach   90
    Sweet! happy Mary! All   240   U67 Muses   49
    Be kept alive those Sweet, and Sacred fires   .   .   .   257   U75 Epithalam.   163
    Grow up, sweet Babe, as blessed, in thy Name,   .   .   268   U80 Christning   11
    Sweet Mind, then speake your selfe, and say,   .   .   278   U84 Mind   17
    The Voyce so sweet, the words so faire,   .   .   .   279   U84 Mind   37

SWEET (cont.)
As showers; and sweet as drops of Balme. . . . . . 280 U84 Mind 60
Smooth, soft, and sweet, in all a floud . . . . . 280 U84 Mind 61
T'obey, and serve her sweet Commandements. . . . . . 287 U84 Muse 172
In this sweet Extasie, she was rapt hence. . . . . 289 U84 Muse 225
And 'counts them sweet rewards so ta'en: . . . . . 290 U85 Country 36
For houshold aid, and Children sweet; . . . . . 291 U85 Country 40
And from the sweet Tub Wine of this yeare takes, ... 291 U85 Country 47
More sweet then Olives, that new gather'd be . . . . . 291 U85 Country 55
Sower Mother of sweet Loves, forbeare 292 U86 Hor.4:1 5
Beneath a Sweet-wood Roofe, neere Alba Lake: 292 U86 Hor.4:1 20
Who sings so sweet, and with such cunning plaies, ... 293 U87 Hor.3:9 10
Her Poem's beautie, but a sweet delight . . . . . 311 Horace 141
Soone angry, and soone pleas'd, is sweet, or sowre, . . . 315 Horace 227
Or mixing sweet, and fit, teach life the right. . . . . 327 Horace 478
Sweet mix'd with sowre, to his Reader, so . . . . . 329 Horace 515
Sweet Swan of Avon! what a sight it were . . . . . 392 Shakespeare 71
And those so sweet, and well proportion'd parts, ... 396 Drayton 21
Or sweet, or various, in the course! . . . . . 399 Lady Ogle 20
To make the Language sweet upon her tongue. . . . . . 402 Inigo Jones 1 14
I sayd, who'had supp'd so deepe of this sweet Chalice, . . . 412 Sutcliffe 21
R. Rose, I. Ivy, E. sweet Eglantine. . . . . . 412 Ghyrlond 4
The second string is the sweet Almond bloome . . . . . 412 Ghyrlond 9
Sweet Tree of Life, King Davids Strength and Tower, ... 413 Ghyrlond 38
SWEETE
Her breath for sweete exceeding . . . . . 365 Ode Splendor 13
Her breath farre sweete exceeding . . . . . 365 Ode Splendor V 13
Continue thy sweete Song. . . . . . 367 Ode Who saith 34
Haste, Haste, sweete Singer: Nor to Tine, ... 368 Ode Who saith 73
Although the gate were hard, the gayne is sweete. . . . . 418 Answer 7
SWEETEN
Doth sweeten mirth, and heighten pietie, ... 82 E130 Ferrab. 1 6
To heare, to mediate, sweeten my desire, ... 128 U1 Trinitie 42
SWEETER
To sweeter Pastures lead hee can, ... 265 U79 New-yeares 60
SWEETEST
The soft, and sweetest mindes . . . . . 110 F11 Epode 50
And in a dew of sweetest Raine, ... 251 U74 Weston 4
Liber, of all thy friends, thou sweetest care, ... 294 U89 Mart.8:77 1
the sweetest simples, and most soveraigne seedes. . . . . 361 Palmer 12
Which, of the field is clep'd the sweetest brier, ... 413 Ghyrlond 22
SWEETLY
Runs sweetly, as it had his Lordships Soule; . . . . . 167 U15 Friend-Wars 148
So sweetly taken to the Court of blisse, ... 283 U84 Muse 41
SWEET-MEATS
For t'other pound of sweet-meats, he shall feele . . . . 164 U15 Friend-Wars 77
SWEETNESSE
Where sweetnesse is requir'd, and where weight; . . . . 62 E95 Savile 30
Words, and sweetnesse, and be scant . . . . . 184 U29 Fit of Rime 44
her Sweetnesse, Softnesse, her faire Courtesie, ... 270 U81 Pawlet 39
SWEETNING
But was by sweetning so his will, ... 151 U12 Corbet 13
SWEET'S
Such joyes, such sweet's doth your Returne . . . . . 251 U74 Weston 19
SWEETS
But then his Mothers sweets you so apply, ... 182 U28 Worth 12
Of Nuptiall Sweets, at such a season, owe, ... 257 U75 Epithalam. 148
Of sweets, and safeties, they possesse by Peace. . . . . 261 U77 Treasurer 22
With od'rous sweets and soft humilitie, ... 413 Ghyrlond 27
SWEET-WOOD
Beneath a Sweet-wood Roofe, neere Alba Lake: 292 U86 Hor.4:1 20
SWELD
That at every motion sweld . . . . . 138 U2 Kisse 24
SWELL
For they, that swell . . . . . 121 F14 Sydney 39
To swell thine age; . . . . . 244 U70 Ode 56
More of our writers would like thee, not swell . . . . 386 Browne 15
will all turne dust, & may not make me swell. . . . . 387 Cavendish 4
Will all be dust, & may not make me swell. . . . . . 387 Cavendish V 4
SWELL'D
Meeting of Graces, that so swell'd the flood . . . . . 274 U84 Descent 10
SWELLETH
But flowes out, that ore-swelleth in full brests. . . . . 329 Horace 506
SWELLING
Rough, swelling, like a storme: . . . . . 110 F11 Epode 40
Not swelling like the Ocean proud, ... 280 U84 Mind 57
Their swelling udders doth draw dry: . . . . . 291 U85 Country 46
With swelling throat: and, oft, the tragick wight . . . . 311 Horace 134
SWELLS
About his forme. What then so swells each lim? . . . . 63 E97 Motion 19
The whole world here leaven'd with madnesse swells; . . . 163 U15 Friend-Wars 31
'Tis true, as my wombe swells, so my backe stoupes, . . . 227 U52 Answer 4
Professing greatnesse, swells: That, low by lee . . . . 307 Horace 38
His Muse professing height, and greatnesse, swells; . . . 339 Horace V 39/ 38
SWEPT
As were his Nourceries; and swept . . . . . 151 U12 Corbet 16
Till swept away, th'were cancell'd with a broome! . . . . 282 U84 Muse 8
SWERVE
And give their yeares, and natures, as they swerve, . . . 315 Horace 224
SWIFT
He meant they thither should make swift repaire, ... 41 E44 Chuff 5
Before his swift and circled race be run, ... 116 F12 Rutland 99
Before his swift and fetherd race be run, ... 116 F12 Putland V 99

	Page	Title	Line

SWIFT (cont.)

Now swift, now slow, now tame, now wild;	189	U36 Song	14
As lowd as Thunder, and as swift as fire.	249	U72 King	4
So swift, so pure, should yet apply	279	U84 Mind	42
Sleepe, that will make the darkest howres swift-pac't;	295	U90 Mart.10:47	11
bor-/Dring Circles of swift waters that intwine	305	Horace	21
And then as swift to leave what he hath lov'd.	315	Horace	236
And makes her supple feete, as swift as winde.	363	Riches	12
Slow Arar, nor swift Rhone; the Loyre, nor Seine,	369	Ode Who saith	117

SWIFTNESSE

A foot, whose swiftnesse gave the Verse the name	323	Horace	372

SWIFT-PAC'T

Sleepe, that will make the darkest howres swift-pac't;	295	U90 Mart.10:47	11

SWIM

Surly's old whore in her new silkes doth swim:	54	E82 Surly	1
Making his fortunes swim	112	F11 Epode	106
Behold, where one doth swim;	366	Ode Who saith	3
Swim without Corke! Why, thank the good Queen Anne.	405	Inigo Jones 1	68

SWIMMING

To paint him, hath by swimming, hopelesse, scap'd,	305	Horace	27

SWINE

Like a rung Beare, or Swine: grunting out wit	232	U58 Book-seller	11
Like Swine, or other Cattell here on earth:	257	U75 Epithalam.	154

SWOLNE

And if the high-swolne Medway faile thy dish,	94	F2 Penshurst	31

SWOM

And, after, swom abroad in ample flakes,	87	E133 Voyage	138

SWOOPING

Gesture, and riot, whilst he swooping went	319	Horace	304

SWORD

His clothes two fashions of, and poore! his sword	33	E21 Gam'ster	3
If any sword could save from Fates, Roe's could;	35	E27 Roe 1	3
What two brave perills of the private sword	37	E32 Roe 2	1
'Twill see it's sister naked, ere a sword.	74	E115 Honest Man	22
As I have seene some Infants of the Sword,	154	U13 Sacvile	47
My Sword ('tis but a poore Sword, understand)	154	U13 Sacvile	54
As farre as any poore Sword i' the Land.	154	U13 Sacvile	55
They had, but were a Reed unto thy Sword.	187	U33 Councellour	34
Then sword, or fire, or what is of the race	193	U38 Elegy 'Tis	101
But if, for honour, we must draw the Sword,	219	U47 Tribe	39
Sword, fire, and famine, with fell fury met;	243	U70 Ode	17
Be nought so'bove him but his sword let claime.	313	Horace	174
Be nought so'bove him, but his bold sword claime.	342	Horace	V174
the sword, but that it acteth what it list.	423	Lucan	14

SWORDS

Seas, serenes, swords, shot, sicknesse, all are there.	37	E32 Roe 2	10
Through Swords, through Seas, whether she would ride.	134	U2 Triumph	10
And there made Swords, Bills, Glaves, and Armes your fill;	212	U43 Vulcan	198

SWORE

One said, the other swore, the world consists.	87	E133 Voyage	129

SWORNE

And sworne, that he will quite discard thee	662	Bedford	7

SWOUNE

As those that hir'd to weepe at Funeralls, swoune,	333	Horace	614

SWYNNERTON

Under the Auspice of young Swynnerton.	213	U44 Speach	20

SYBIL

Sans helpe of Sybil, or a golden bough,	85	E133 Voyage	48

SYDNEY

Know you to be a Sydney, though un-named?	66	E103 L Wroth 1	4
A Sydney: but in that extend as farre	67	E103 L Wroth 1	10
To Mrs. Philip Sydney.	73	E114 Sydney	Ttl
Moodes, which the god-like Sydney oft did prove,	116	F12 Rutland	91
Ode. To Sir William Sydney, on his Birth-day.	120	F14 Sydney	Ttl
That I may tell to Sydney, what	120	F14 Sydney	12
Sydney e're night! or that did goe to bed	157	U13 Sacvile	127

SYDNEY'S

Fertile of wood, Ashore, and Sydney's copp's,	94	F2 Penshurst	26

SYDNYES

When Sydnyes name I heare, or face I see:	73	E114 Sydney	2

SYLLAB'E

Each syllab'e answer'd, and was form'd, how faire;	245	U70 Ode	63

SYLLABES

Joynting Syllabes, drowning Letters,	183	U29 Fit of Rime	10
Still may Syllabes jarre with time,	184	U29 Fit of Rime	52

SYLVANE

Of many a Sylvane, taken with his flames.	94	F2 Penshurst	16
Thus Pan, and Sylvane, having had their rites,	98	F3 Wroth	47
When Pan, and Sylvane, having had their rites,	98	F3 Wroth	V 47
And, Sylvane, thine that keptst his Lands!	290	U85 Country	22
And, Sylvane, thine that keep'st his Lands!	290	U85 Country	V 22

SYLVANUS

And in the chase, more then Sylvanus can,	264	U79 New-yeares	22

SYLVESTER

To Mr. Josuah Sylvester.	83	E132 Sylvester	Ttl

SYM

Cries Old Sym, the King of Skinkers;	657	Door Apollo	8

SYMBOLES

Without conferring symboles. This's my day.	396	Drayton	10

SYMETRY

By warrant call'd just Symetry,	399	Lady Ogle	22

SYMMETRIE

All her best symmetrie in that one feature!	112	F11 Epode	101

SYNNS
   Hee that soe Censureth, or adviseth synns, · · · · 421 Censure 4
SYNONIMA
   And still be a whore-house. Th'are Synonima. · · · · 29 E7 Hot-house 4
'SYRIAN
   If thou be'st wise, with 'Syrian Oyle let shine · · 294 U89 Mart.8:77 3
SYRUP   (See SIRRUP)
T'A
   And is t'a body, often, ill inclin'd, · · · · 82 E130 Ferrab. 1 7
TABACCO
   Leave Cod, tabacco-like, burnt gummes to take, · · · 42 E50 Cod 3 1
   Tabacco, Nectar, or the Thespian spring, · · · · 65 E101 Supper 33
TABACCO-LIKE
   Leave Cod, tabacco-like, burnt gummes to take, · · · 42 E50 Cod 3 1
TABLE
   At Madames table, where thou mak'st all wit · · · 50 E72 Court-ling 3
   To have beene stiled of King Arthurs table. · · · 84 E133 Voyage 24
   To crowne thy open table, doth provide · · · · 94 F2 Penshurst 27
   Feed those, at whom the Table points at still? · · · 155 U13 Sacvile 74
   Will come to the Table, · · · · 232 U57 Burges 23
   It is a large faire table, and a true, · · · · 269 U81 Pawlet 15
   Thy table without art, and easy-rated: · · · · 295 U90 Mart.10:47 8
   But every Table in this Church can say, · · · · 394 Jane Ogle 7
TABLES
   At great mens tables) and yet dine away. · · · · 95 F2 Penshurst 66
   Thy tables hoord not up for the next day, · · · · 95 F2 Penshurst 71
   With Merlins Marvailes, and his tables losse, · · · 206 U43 Vulcan V 71
T'ACCUSE
   T'accuse, or quit all Parties to be heard! · · · 284 U84 Muse 60
TACITUS
   They carry in their pockets Tacitus, · · · · 59 E92 New Crie 15
   I should beleeve, the soule of Tacitus · · · · 61 E95 Savile 3
   Shall reade a piece of Virgil, Tacitus, · · · · 65 E101 Supper 21
TACTICKES
   Translated Aelian tactickes to be read, · · · · 214 U44 Speach 35
T'ADMIRE
   When thou wert wont t'admire, not censure men. · · · 32 E18 Censurer 8
T'ADORE
   Yet give me leave t'adore in you · · · · 174 U22 Elegy Tho 35
T'ADVANCE
   T'advance his doubtfull issue, and ore-flow · · · 117 F13 Aubigny 40
   And all doe strive t'advance · · · · 120 F14 Sydney 5
   Made, or indentur'd, or leas'd out t'advance · · · 246 U70 Ode 100
TA'EN
   Where Nature such a large survey hath ta'en, · · · 262 U78 Digby 11
   I murmure against God, for having ta'en · · · 283 U84 Muse 33
   And 'counts them sweet rewards so ta'en: · · · 290 U85 Country 36
   On every limbe, ta'en from a severall creature, · · 305 Horace 3
   That tarries till the hangings be ta'en downe, · · 315 Horace 221
TAFFATA
   Velvet, or Taffata cap, rank'd in the darke · · · 371 Fletcher 5
   Jest, he saies. Item one sute of blacke taffata · · 380 Coryat 3 48
TAGDE
   Such as are square, wel-tagde, and permanent, · · 220 U47 Tribe 64
TAGUS
   Iberus, Tagus, Rheine, · · · · 369 Ode Who saith 115
TAILE
   I writ he onely his taile there did wave; · · · 380 Coryat 3 56
TAILOR   (See TAYLOR)
TAINT
   And like a hallow'd Temple, free from taint · · · 401 Beaumont 21
TAINTED   (See also TEYNTED)
   And that ours did. For, yet, no nare was tainted, · · 87 E133 Voyage 133
   yett, yf with eythers vyce, I tainted bee, · · · 422 Censure 22
TAKE
   Pray thee, take care, that tak'st my booke in hand, · 27 E1 Reader 1
   Take better ornaments, my teares, and verse. · · · 35 E27 Roe 1 2
   Leave Cod, tabacco-like, burnt gummes to take, · · 42 E50 Cod 3 1
   Or take an Epigramme so fearefully: · · · · 51 E73 Fine Grand 2
   Which of thy names I take, not onely beares · · · 58 E91 Vere 1
   And, in thy censures, evenly, dost take · · · 62 E96 Donne 2 4
   But that, which most doth take my Muse, and mee, · 65 E101 Supper 28
   Whether thy learning they would take, or wit, · · 68 E106 E Herbert 5
   Be nor put on you, nor you take offence. · · · 69 E108 Soldiers 4
   O, runne not proud of this. Yet, take thy due. · · 81 E129 Mime 15
   Who gave, to take at his returne from Hell, · · 84 E133 Voyage 27
   Nor, when I take my lodging, need I pray · · · 95 F2 Penshurst 72
   To take the weake, or make them stop: · · · 100 F4 To the World 19
   Take heed, Sicknesse, what you doe, · · · 104 F8 Sicknesse 7
   Scarce will take our present store? · · · 105 F8 Sicknesse 11
   Scarce will take our present score? · · · 105 F8 Sicknesse V 11
   Doe enough; and who would take · · · 105 F8 Sicknesse 26
   A beautie of that merit, that should take · · · 108 F10 Proludium 27
   Or common places, filch'd, that take these times, · 116 F12 Rutland 88
   O take my gift. · · · · 127 U1 Trinitie 8
   And take compassion on my grievous plight. · · 127 U1 Trinitie 14
   To take our nature; becam'st man, and dyd'st, · · 128 U1 Trinitie 22
   Hee whom the whole world could not take, · · 130 U1 Nativitie 10
   Unto her; which love might take · · · 133 U2 Suffered 9
   Titles, I confesse, doe take me; · · · 140 U2 Her man 5
   Drest, you still for man should take him; · · 141 U2 Her man 38
   Take that away, you take our lives, · · · 146 U6 Defence 5
   Or Scorne, or pittie on me take, · · · 150 U11 Dreame 1

TAKE (cont.)
And though my fortune humble me, to take . . . . 153 U13 Sacvile 15
Yet choyce from whom I take them; and would shame . . . 153 U13 Sacvile 17
And hurt seeks Cure, the Surgeon bids take bread, . . . 155 U13 Sacvile 68
All the Towne-curs take each their snatch at me. . . . 155 U13 Sacvile 72
On whom I could take up, and ne're abuse . . . . 161 U14 Selden 83
More then themselves, or then our lives could take, . . . 166 U15 Friend-Wars 127
To take the box up for him; and pursues . . . . 166 U15 Friend-Wars 137
Goe, quit 'hem all. And take along with them, . . . 167 U15 Friend-Wars 175
These take, and now goe seeke thy peace in Warre, . . . 168 U15 Friend-Wars 195
Put on for fashion, and take up on trust: . . . . 171 U20 Shrub 8
Then take in hand thy Lyre, ... 175 U23 Himselfe 25
Her joyes, her smiles, her loves, as readers take . . . 182 U28 Worth 13
O may your wisdome take example hence, ... 193 U38 Elegy 'Tis 67
And take some sirrup after; so doe I, ... 197 U40 Elegy That 5
Under another Name, I take your health; . . . . 197 U40 Elegy That 10
In all that is call'd lovely: take my sight . . . 200 U42 Elegy Let 12
Withall, the dirtie paines those Citizens take, . . . 213 U44 Speach 15
And as within your Office, you doe take . . . . 216 U45 Squib 13
Of worthiest knowledge, that can take mens minds. . . . 217 U46 Coke 20
Let these men have their wayes, and take their times . . 218 U47 Tribe 25
My selfe a little. I will take you so, ... 220 U47 Tribe 76
That both, their odour take him, ... 220 U48 Bacchus 11
And practise for a Miracle; take heed, ... 223 U49 Pucell 41
And the right wayes you take unto the right, . . . 224 U50 Countesse 3
How I would draw, and take hold and delight. . . . 227 U52 Answer 18
To goe out after—till when take this letter . . . 229 U54 Squib 19
To take Apprehension . . . . . 231 U57 Burges 11
What (at his liking) he will take away. . . . . 236 U63 Charles 2 6
Doth take in easie Natures birth, ... 250 U74 Weston 2
The king of Creatures, take his paritie . . . . 255 U75 Epithalam. 83
Yet take him in these lines: He doth excell . . . 262 U78 Digby V 2
That they may take it eccho'd by the Floods. . . . 265 U79 New-yeares 53
Should take first Seisin of the publique good, . . . 268 U80 Christning 8
Of Goodnesse still: Vouchsafe to take . . . . 273 U84 Cradle 9
Take little Infants with their noyse, ... 273 U84 Cradle 18
Of Heaven; where Seraphim take tent . . . . 273 U84 Cradle 31
Must come to take a sentence, by the sense . . . 284 U84 Muse 57
With the make 'bove all his Rivals gifts take place, . . 292 U86 Hor.4:1 18
There shall thy dainty Nostrill take 292 U86 Hor.4:1 21
Take, therefore, you that write, still, matter fit . . 307 Horace 53
Take therefore, you that write, a subject fit . . . 339 Horace V 55/ 53
As his departing take much thence: lest, then, . . . 317 Horace 251
Then those the faithfull eyes take in by show, . . . 317 Horace 258
Things worthy to be done within, but take . . . 317 Horace 261
Into a Swallow there; Nor Cadmus take, ... 317 Horace 267
Will take offence, at this: Nor, though it strike . . 321 Horace 361
Take just offence at this: nor, though it strike . . 347 Horace V353/361
Nor is't long since, they did with patience take . . 323 Horace 375
Take you the Greeke Examples, for your light, . . . 323 Horace 397
Will take you more, the neerer that you stand; . . . 331 Horace 540
Lest the throng'd heapes should on a laughter take: . . 331 Horace 569
Lest the throng'd rings should a free laughter take: . . 352 Horace V545/569
An admirable Verse. The great Scurfe take . . . 333 Horace 594
An admirable verse: the great Scab take . . . . 353 Horace V594
Looke through him, and be sure, you take not mocks . . 333 Horace 621
There's none will take the care, to helpe him then; . . 335 Horace 654
Flowes from the surfets which we take in peace. . . . 363 Peace 4
May take thy volume to his vertuous hand. . . . 383 Author 8
May she, whome thou for spouse, to day, dost take, . . 384 Somerset 11
Or, like our Money-Brokers, take up names . . . 386 Browne 10
That so did take Eliza, and our James! . . . . 392 Shakespeare 74
TAKEINGE
And by their takeinge, lett it once appeare . . . 421 Ode:If Men 44
TAKEN (See also TA'EN, TA'NE)
Of many a Sylvane, taken with his flames. . . . 94 F2 Penshurst 16
To be taken, to be seene, ... 102 F5 Celia 1 17
Not taken up o' th' doctors, but as well . . . 117 F13 Aubigny 33
Of pressure, like one taken in a streight? . . . 154 U13 Sacvile 32
Be taken with false Baytes . . . . . 175 U23 Himselfe 20
I saw with two poore Chambers taken in, . . . 209 U43 Vulcan 135
How it held out! how (last) 'twas taken in! . . . 213 U44 Speach 22
Hath taken twice the Ring . . . . . 240 U67 Muses 38
So sweetly taken to the Court of blisse, . . . 283 U84 Muse 41
And give, being taken modestly, this leave, . . . 309 Horace 73
TAKES
Then takes up fresh commoditie, for dayes; . . . 30 E12 Shift 13
Takes physick, teares the papers: still god payes. . . 30 E12 Shift 16
In varied shapes, which for his lust shee takes: . . 34 E25 Beast 1 6
But as they come, on both sides he takes fees, . . . 38 E37 Chev'ril 2
He takes up all, makes each mans wit his owne. . . . 45 E56 Poet-Ape 8
Takes private beatings, and begins againe. . . . 49 E68 Playwrt 2 2
In life, that can employ it; and takes hold . . . 50 E70 Wm Roe 1 3
My owne true fire. Now my thought takes wing, . . . 108 F10 Proludium 29
Our owne true fire. Now our thought takes wing, . . 108 F10 Proludium V 29
the glories of yt. Now our muse takes winge, . . . 108 F10 Proludium 15
And takes, and gives the beauties of the mind. . . . 117 F13 Aubigny 44
And as a cunning Painter takes . . . . . 145 U5 Woman-kind 13
That as the lesser breach: for he that takes . . . 169 U17 Friend-Debt 11
There greatnesse takes a glorie to relieve. . . . 192 U38 Elegy 'Tis 34
The holy Prelate prayes, then takes the Ring, . . . 256 U75 Epithalam. 123
Where every lim takes like a face? . . . . 275 U84 Body 4
And from the sweet Tub Wine of this yeare takes, . . 291 U85 Country 47

		Page	Title	Line
TAKES (cont.)				
More strongly takes the people with delight,		327	Horace	458
Learn'd and unlearn'd; holding, whom once he takes;		337	Horace	677
Learn'd, and unlearn'd; holdeth whom once he takes;		355	Horace	V677
Nor takes she pride to know them.		355	Horace	V677
Marke, marke, but when his wing he takes,		365	Ode Splendor	24
Who takes thy volume to his vertuous hand,		366	Ode Who saith	9
		383	Author	1
TAKING				
My wonder, why the taking a Clownes purse,		155	U13 Sacvile	89
Which in the taking if you mis-apply,		180	U26 Ode High	11
Till the sower Minute comes of taking leave,		197	U40 Elegy That	2
The Berghen siege, and taking in Breda.		214	U44 Speach	40
TAK'ST				
Pray thee, take care, that tak'st my booke in hand,		27	E1 Reader	1
And giving largely to me, more thou tak'st.		44	E55 Beaumont	6
Thy person fit for any charge thou tak'st;		168	U15 Friend-Wars	182
That since thou tak'st all envious care and paine,		203	U43 Vulcan	13
TALCK				
Or Turners oyle of Talck. Nor ever got		188	U34 Small Poxe	11
TALE				
Item, a tale or two, some fortnight after;		51	E73 Fine Grand	7
Will prove old Orpheus act no tale to be:		115	F12 Rutland	77
Will prove old Orpheus Arts no tale to be:		115	F12 Rutland	V 77
If I doe lose it: And, without a Tale,		229	U54 Squib	3
TALENT				
Simo; and, of a talent wip'd his purse;		321	Horace	347
Simo, and of a talent cleans'd his purse;		346	Horace	V339/347
TALES				
Tell the grosse Dutch those grosser tales of yours,		68	E107 Hungry	5
Tell's of him, all the tales, it selfe then makes;		74	E115 Honest Man	17
With tales of Troyes just knight, our faiths abuse:		84	E133 Voyage	4
Thou hast no lantherne, whereof tales are told;		93	F2 Penshurst	4
And have thy tales and jests too,		221	U48 Bacchus	40
And saw a Centaure, past those tales of Greece;		228	U53 Newcastle	5
TALK				
Able to talk of Euclide, and correct		402	Inigo Jones 1	4
TALKE (TALC)				
That for th'oyle of Talke, dare spend		105	F8 Sicknesse	33
TALKE				
And talke reserv'd, lock'd up, and full of feare,		59	E92 New Crie	17
And of the poulder-plot, they will talke yet.		59	E92 New Crie	32
For, if the hum'rous world will talke at large,		83	E131 Ferrab. 2	7
You were more the eye, and talke		138	U2 Kisse	14
That talke abroad of Womans change,		146	U6 Defence	2
Thus they doe talke. And are these objects fit		165	U15 Friend-Wars	101
Let those that meerely talke, and never thinke,		218	U47 Tribe	9
What though she talke, and cannot once with them,		222	U49 Pucell	11
They talke of Fencing, and the use of Armes,		232	U59 Newcastle	1
And Sons, and Daughters, with their Parents talke;		285	U84 Muse	118
Built a small-timbred Stage, and taught them talke		319	Horace	317
TALK'D				
Of divine Comfort, when sh' had talk'd with God.		287	U84 Muse	184
TALKES				
Talkes loud, and baudy, has a gather'd deale		74	E115 Honest Man	9
And Minerva, when she talkes.		137	U2 Cupid	54
T'ALL				
T'all future time, not onely doth restore		71	E110 Edmonds 1	21
TALL				
By that tall Grove, your haire; whose globy rings		170	U19 Elegy By	5
The Poplar tall, he then doth marrying twine		290	U85 Country	9
There, or the tall witch-hazill hee doth twine		290	U85 Country	V 9
T'ALLEDGE				
T'alledge, that greatest men were not asham'd,		82	E130 Ferrab. 1	9
TALLER				
That taller tree, which of a nut was set,		94	F2 Penshurst	13
T'ALLOW				
As thou hast best authoritie, t'allow.		62	E96 Donne 2	6
TALMUD				
The Talmud, and the Alcoran had come,		205	U43 Vulcan	65
TAME				
Of building townes, and making wilde beasts tame,		82	E130 Ferrab. 1	2
Now swift, now slow, now tame, now wild;		189	U36 Song	14
That keepe the warre, though now't be growne more tame,		214	U44 Speach	55
Yet, not as therefore wild, and tame should cleave		305	Horace	14
Was Tigers, said, and Lyons fierce, to tame.		327	Horace	482
T'AMEND				
His very Manners taught t'amend,		152	U12 Corbet	22
TAMES				
Till thou at Tames alight,		368	Ode Who saith	79
Tames, prowde of thee, and of his Fate		368	Ode Who saith	81
Or Tames be rap't from us		369	Ode Who saith	107
TAMISIS				
Did never dint the breast of Tamisis.		366	Ode Who saith	8
TA'NE				
Whilst your Ulisses hath ta'ne leave to goe,		224	U50 Countesse	21
TANE				
Ridway was tane, arraign'd, condemn'd to dye;		29	E8 Robbery	2
The late tane bastinado. So I thought.		33	E21 Gam'ster	6
Tell them, what parts yo'have tane, whence run away,		69	E107 Hungry	9
Then, selling not, a dish was tane to mince 'hem,		88	E133 Voyage	151
Art tane with neithers vice, nor sport:		96	F3 Wroth	4
So each, that's done, and tane, becomes a Brace.		154	U13 Sacvile	40
The withered Garlands tane away;		173	U22 Elegy Tho	18

	Page	Title	Line
TAPER			
Till I, at much expense of Time, and Taper	666	Glover	7
TAPP			
at Pem Wakers good ale Tapp,	417	Moon	39
T'APPEARE			
Which shewes, where ever death doth please t'appeare,	37	E32 Roe 2	9
That know the times, and seasons when t'appeare,	263	U79 New-yeares	11
T'APPROVE			
and Conjures all my faculties t'approve	108	F10 Proludium	14
Plaine phrase, my Piso's, as alone, t'approve	321	Horace	342
T'AQUIT			
As Love, t'aquit such excellence,	173	U22 Elegy Tho	23
TARDIE			
And you may justly, being a tardie, cold,	230	U56 Covell	7
TARRIE			
To former height, and there in circle tarrie,	55	E85 Goodyere 1	9
TARRIES			
And feeles it; Else he tarries by the Beast.	156	U13 Sacvile	117
That tarries till the hangings be ta'en downe,	315	Horace	221
TARRY			
Hath got the stewards chaire; he will not tarry	57	E90 Mill	15
Our vices doe not tarry in a place,	166	U15 Friend-Wars	123
(Were not his Lucius long with us to tarry)	246	U70 Ode	91
No man will tarry by thee, as hee goes,	409	Detractor	17
TART			
The merry Greeke, tart Aristophanes,	392	Shakespeare	51
TASKE			
Let the old boy, your sonne, ply his old taske,	107	F10 Proludium	19
A Nations sinne got pardon'd! 'twere a taske	234	U61 Epigram	12
Oh, to make Boardes to speake! There is a taske	404	Inigo Jones 1	49
TASQUE			
A harder tasque, then either his to Bristo',	85	E133 Voyage	39
T'ASSIST			
And Fortune once, t'assist the spirits that dare.	170	U18 Elegy Can	10
TAST			
For good men but see death, the wicked tast it.	54	E80 Life/Death	8
The nicer thing to tast her ladies page;	57	E90 Mill	5
Or if needs thy lust will tast	105	F8 Sicknesse	15
With some more change, and tast of tyranny:	205	U43 Vulcan	V 50
some tast to send hir.	417	Moon	20
TASTE			
We ought not give them taste, we had an eare.	83	E131 Ferrab. 2	6
Will quickly taste the treason, and commit	109	F11 Epode	15
All taste of bitternesse, and makes the ayre	112	F11 Epode	97
I'le taste as lightly as the Bee,	139	U2 Another	5
Ne're came to taste the plenteous Mariage-horne.	165	U15 Friend-Wars	100
And then I taste it. But as men drinke up	197	U40 Elegy That	3
Or taste a part of that full joy he meant	246	U70 Ode	87
Wine, or delicious fruits, unto the Taste;	286	U84 Muse	123
TASTED			
Of which had Horace, or Anacreon tasted,	65	E101 Supper	31
Or have tasted the bag o'the Bee?	135	U2 Triumph	29
Have you tasted the Cinnamon-tree	135	U2 Triumph	V 37
Have you tasted virginitye	136	U2 Triumph	V 45
TASTER			
That thou remaine here taster	220	U48 Bacchus	7
TASTETH			
So all his meate he tasteth over, twise:	76	E118 Gut	2
TASTING			
And tasting ayre, and freedome, wull	101	F4 To the World	31
T'ATTIRE			
Of severall makings? helps, helps, t'attire	215	U44 Speach	94
TAUGHT			
Hast taught thy selfe worthy thy pen to tread,	63	E99 Th Roe 2	3
They are, and have beene taught religion: Thence	96	F2 Penshurst	93
Each morne, and even, they are taught to pray,	96	F2 Penshurst	95
A fixed thought, an eye un-taught to glance;	111	F11 Epode	61
His very Manners taught t'amend,	152	U12 Corbet	22
Whom Faction had not taught to studie sides.	207	U43 Vulcan	V104
Which their glad Parents taught	257	U75 Epithalam.	143
And, in her last act, taught the Standers-by,	270	U81 Pawlet	61
Being taught a better way. All mortall deeds	309	Horace	98
Built a small-timbred Stage, and taught them talke	319	Horace	317
Or 'twere the gowned Comoedy they taught.	323	Horace	410
Taught Pallas language; Cynthia modesty;	371	Epitaph	7
Taught Lucan these true moodes! Replyes my sence	395	May	15
TAVERNE			
Was issue of the Taverne, or the Spit:	216	U45 Squib	8
TAVERNES			
Vile Tavernes, and the Drunkards pisse him out;	211	U43 Vulcan	186
Vile Tavernes, and have Drunkards pisse him out;	211	U43 Vulcan	V186
TAXE			
Be thine, I taxe, yet doe not owne my rimes:	36	E30 Guiltie	2
Or taxe the Glories of the Church, and Gowne?	203	U43 Vulcan	24
Or taxe the Glories of the Church, or Gowne?	203	U43 Vulcan	V 24
So rare, as with some taxe it doth ingage	323	Horace	383
To taxe that Verse, which many a day, and blot	325	Horace	416
TAX'D			
For worth he has not, He is tax'd, or prais'd.	48	E65 Muse	16
But, when they heard it tax'd, tooke more offence.	60	E94 Bedford 3	10
And every goodnesse tax'd, or griev'd.	101	F4 To the World	52
TAXETH			
Who frownes, who jealous is, who taxeth me.	200	U42 Elegy Let	10

TAYLE
    As if a Brize were gotten i' their tayle;   164   U15 Friend-Wars   71
TAYLOR
    The taylor brings a suite home; he it 'ssayes,   30   E12 Shift   9
    Yet no Taylor help to make him;   141   U2 Her man   37
TAYLORS
    The new french-taylors motion, monthly made,   56   E88 Monsieur   15
    Whose like I have knowne the Taylors Wife put on   201   U42 Elegy Let   39
    These Carkasses of honour; Taylors blocks,   216   U44 Speach   99
TEACH
    Man scarse can make that doubt, but thou canst teach.   31   E14 Camden   10
    They teach you, how.   121   F14 Sydney   48
    And his lip should kissing teach,   141   U2 Her man   22
    T'instruct and teach? or your unweary'd paine   159   U14 Selden   37
    To informe and teach? or your unweary'd paine   159   U14 Selden   V 37
    To teach each suit he has, the ready way   165   U15 Friend-Wars   108
    To teach some that, their Nurses could not doe,   207   U43 Vulcan   92
    To teach some what, their Nurses could not doe,   207   U43 Vulcan   V 92
    Whilst I informe my selfe, I would teach thee,   216   U45 Squib   2
    To teach the people, how to fast, and pray,   235   U61 Epigram   18
    The price of our Redemption, and to teach   286   U84 Muse   134
    I, writing nought my selfe, will teach them yet   325   Horace   435
    Or mixing sweet, and fit, teach life the right.   327   Horace   478
    And teach your nephewes it to aemulate: 387   Cavendish   10
    Attyre the Persons as noe thought can teach   404   Inigo Jones 1   54
    Which I, your Master, first did teach the Age.   409   Brome   8
    And the Physician teach men spue, or shite;   410   Brome   16
    Thy blatant Muse abroad, and teach it rather   411   Gill   11
TEACHER
    On Lippe, the Teacher.   52   E75 Lippe   Ttl
TEAME
    And foundred thy hot teame, to tune my lay.   107   F10 Proludium   9
    And foundred thy hot teame, to tune our lay.   107   F10 Proludium   V 9
TEARE   (VERB)
    Two letters were enough the plague to teare   172   U21 Ltl Shrub   3
TEARE
    Ile not offend thee with a vaine teare more,   37   E33 Roe 3   1
    And know, for whom a teare you shed,   77   E120 S. P.   3
    Stay, drop a teare for him that's dead,   233   U60 La-ware   2
TEARES   (VERB)
    Takes physick, teares the papers: still god payes.   30   E12 Shift   16
TEARES
    In comfort of her mothers teares,   33   E22 Daughter   8
    Take better ornaments, my teares, and verse.   35   E27 Roe 1   2
    If any friends teares could restore, his would;   35   E27 Roe 1   5
    O, doe not steepe them in thy Teares,   145   U4 Song   9
    That they for me their teares will shed,   152   U12 Corbet   34
    With gladnesse temper'd her sad Parents teares!   270   U81 Pawlet   59
    Which gladnesse temper'd her sad Parents teares!   270   U81 Pawlet   V 59
    Of teares, and dungeon of calamitie!   283   U84 Muse   35
    She spent more time in teares her selfe to dresse   287   U84 Muse   180
    Flow my thin teares, downe these pale cheeks of mine?   293   U86 Hor.4:1   34
    Thy selfe in teares, then me thy losse will wound,   311   Horace   146
TEARS
    Thy selfe in tears, then me thy harms will wound,   342   Horace   V146
TEEMING
    Such pleasure as the teeming Earth,   250   U74 Weston   1
    Our teeming Ewes, and lustie-mounting Rammes.   264   U79 New-yeares   17
    Your teeming Ewes, aswell as mounting Rammes.   265   U79 New-yeares   51
TEETH
    Spanish receipt, to make her teeth to rot.   188   U34 Small Poxe   12
T'EFFECT
    T'effect it, feele, thou'ast made thine owne heart ake.   250   U73 Weston   12
TEIRCE
    The Kings fame lives. Go now, denie his Teirce.   241   U68 House-hold   14
TELEPHUS
    Complaines in humble phrase. Both Telephus,   311   Horace   135
    Peleus, or Telephus. If you speake vile   311   Horace   147
TELESTICHS
    Acrostichs, and Telestichs, on jumpe names,   204   U43 Vulcan   39
    Acrostichs, and Telestichs, or jumpe names,   204   U43 Vulcan   V 39
    Acrostichs, and Telestichs, on fine names,   204   U43 Vulcan   V 39
TELL'
    How to tell' hem, as they flow,   103   F6 Celia 2   20
TELL
    I'le loose my modestie, and tell your name.   38   E38 Guiltie 2   8
    Ile tell you of more, and lye, so you will come: 65   E101 Supper   17
    Tell the grosse Dutch those grosser tales of yours,   68   E107 Hungry   5
    Tell them, what parts yo'have tane, whence run away,   69   E107 Hungry   9
    Fitter, where it dyed, to tell,   79   E124 Elizabeth   11
    No more let Greece her bolder fables tell   84   E133 Voyage   1
    Canst tell me best, how every Furie lookes there,   85   E133 Voyage   52
    That I may tell to Sydney, what   120   F14 Sydney   12
    Which I doe tell: 120   F14 Sydney   16
    I will but mend the last, and tell   139   U2 Another   13
    Lightly promis'd, she would tell   139   U2 Promise   3
    As, untill she tell her one,   140   U2 Promise   11
    I will tell what Man would please me.   140   U2 Her man   2
    Yet dare I not tell who;   147   U7 Nymph   2
    I'le tell, that if they be not glad,   147   U7 Nymph   8
    I'le tell no more, and yet I love,   148   U7 Nymph   29
    If Love, or feare, would let me tell his name.   148   U7 Nymph   35
    Tell me that she hath seene   149   U9 Picture   13

	Page	Title	Line
TELL (cont.)			
Nor will he tell me for whose sake	151	U11 Dreame	7
Yea, of th'ingratefull: and he forth must tell	155	U13 Sacvile	77
But here's no time, nor place, my wealth to tell,	161	U14 Selden	85
Tell me (my lov'd Friend) doe you love, or no,	170	U19 Elegy By	11
So well as I may tell in verse, 'tis so?	170	U19 Elegy By	12
Which in assurance to your brest I tell,	198	U40 Elegy That	49
Heare, Mistris, your departing servant tell	199	U41 Elegy Since	2
Lift up some one, and doe, I tell not what.	201	U42 Elegy Let	58
Thou didst tell me; and wert o're-joy'd to peepe	201	U42 Elegy Let	59
But, on thy malice, tell me, didst thou spie	203	U43 Vulcan	19
Old Aesope Gundomar: the French can tell,	213	U44 Speach	5
And comming home, to tell what acts were done	213	U44 Speach	19
Though I doe neither heare these newes, nor tell	219	U47 Tribe	46
Or what we heare our home-borne Legend tell,	228	U53 Newcastle	9
Accept his Muse; and tell, I know you can,	231	U56 Covell	26
Tell him his Ben	231	U57 Burges	7
Goe now, and tell out dayes summ'd up with feares,	244	U70 Ode	53
And looking with thy best Inquirie, tell,	254	U75 Epithalam.	74
Of Winchester; the Heralds can tell this:	269	U81 Pawlet	20
Of Winchester; the Heralds could tell this:	269	U81 Pawlet	V 20
T' inlive posteritie, her Fame may tell!	269	U81 Pawlet	34
Run from your rootes; Tell, testifie the grand	274	U84 Descent	9
And tell thou, Alde-Legh, None can tell more true	274	U84 Descent	13
A Copie of this peece; nor tell	277	U84 Body	30
Can tell a States-mans dutie, what the arts	325	Horace	449
All which I tell, lest when Apollo's nam'd,	329	Horace	501
I'le tell you but the death, and the disease	335	Horace	659
To the Right Noble Tom, Tell-Troth of his travailes,	378	Coryat 2	Ttl
Honest Tom Tell-Troth puts downe Roger, How?	378	Coryat 2	81
it will be matter lowd inoughe to tell	387	Cavendish	11
And tell, how farre thou didst our Lily out-shine,	391	Shakespeare	29
No stone in any wall here, but can tell	394	Jane Ogle	9
And know the woofe, and warpe thereof; can tell	415	Rutter	15
But I can tell thee, Dover, how thy Games	415	Dover	3
Tell her, his Muse that did invent thee	662	Bedford	5
TELLINE			
Be, or be not, to get the Val-telline?	219	U47 Tribe	32
TELLING			
Telling the motions of each petticote,	34	E25 Beast 1	3
TELL'S			
Tell's of him, all the tales, it selfe then makes;	74	E115 Honest Man	17
The truth of his heart there, and tell's what a clocke	380	Coryat 3	24
TELLS			
Tells you it is a hot-house: So it ma',	29	E7 Hot-house	3
Here no man tells my cups; nor, standing by,	95	F2 Penshurst	67
Of what it tells us) weav'd in to instruct.	160	U14 Selden	52
(As my hope tells) that our faire Phoebe's shine,	179	U25 Desmond	58
(As my hope tells) that our drad Cynthia's shine,	179	U25 Desmond	V 58
TELL-TROTH			
To the Right Noble Tom, Tell-Troth of his travailes,	378	Coryat 2	Ttl
Honest Tom Tell-Troth puts downe Roger, How?	378	Coryat 2	81
TELS			
Doth he once dissemble, but tels he did ride	380	Coryat 3	52
TEMPER			
And by thy wiser temper, let men know	27	E2 My Booke	8
TEMPERATE			
Hee's prudent, valiant, just, and temperate;	262	U78 Digby	5
TEMPER'D			
With gladnesse temper'd her sad Parents teares!	270	U81 Pawlet	59
Which gladnesse temper'd her sad Parents teares!	270	U81 Pawlet	V 59
TEMPEST			
In a continuall tempest. Now, true Love	110	F11 Epode	43
As all with storme and tempest ran together.	193	U38 Elegy 'Tis	76
TEMPESTS			
Through seas, stormes, tempests: and imbarqu'd for hell,	81	E128 Wm Roe 2	13
That in all tempests, never quit the helme,	185	U30 Burleigh	10
TEMPESTUOUS			
From the Tempestuous Grandlings, Who'll informe	215	U44 Speach	64
TEMPLE (PLACENAME)			
Man out their Boates to th' Temple, and not shift	155	U13 Sacvile	83
TEMPLE (HEAD)			
Or with fresh flowers to girt my temple round.	293	U86 Hor.4:1	32
TEMPLE			
The world the temple was, the priest a king,	28	E5 Union	3
And like a hallow'd Temple, free from taint	401	Beaumont	21
TEMPLES (HEAD)			
So may the fruitfull Vine my temples steepe,	190	U37 Friend-Book	14
TEMPLES			
His falling Temples you have rear'd,	173	U22 Elegy Tho	17
Cittyes & Temples! thou a Cave for Wyne,	406	Inigo Jones 2	8
TEMPT			
Forbeare to tempt me, Proule, I will not show	54	E81 Proule	1
Tempt not his furie, Pluto is away:	89	E133 Voyage	179
Doe not once hope, that thou canst tempt	100	F4 To the World	5
TEMPTE			
Tempte such a passage? when each privies seate	88	E133 Voyage	168
TEMPTED			
But shall sometimes be tempted to obey	190	U37 Friend-Book	32
But sometymes shall bee tempted to obaye	422	Censure	25
TEN			
Furies there wanted not: each scold was ten.	84	E133 Voyage	15
With ten Emp'ricks, in their chamber,	105	F8 Sicknesse	31

		Page	Title	Line
TEN (cont.)				
A Celebration of Charis in ten Lyrick Peeces.	• • •	131	U2 Charis	Ttl
These ten yeares day; As all may sweare that looke	• •	213	U44 Speach	27
One Poet, then of other folke ten score.	• • •	235	U62 Charles 1	10
Not, ten times o're, corrected to the naile.	•	325	Horace	418
Doth please; this, ten times over, will delight.	•	331	Horace	544
Whom not ten fyres, nor a Parlyament can	•	406	Inigo Jones 1	103
TENANTS				
Tenants, and Servants, have they harts, and eyes,	• •	399	Lady Ogle	4
TEND				
Phoebus. No? tend thy cart still. Envious day	•	107	F10 Proludium	7
A gentler, and more agile hand, to tend	•	180	U26 Ode High	4
TENDER (VERB)				
Yet, to the Stage, at all thou maist not tender	•	317	Horace	260
to tender thus, their lives, their loves, their hartes!	•	382	Rich	4
TENDER				
My tender, first, and simple yeeres	• • • •	101	F4 To the World	41
A tender Mother, a discreeter Wife,	• • •	287	U84 Muse	174
Of Earth, and sheares the tender Sheepe:	• •	290	U85 Country	16
The Youths and tender Maids shall sing thy praise:	•	292	U86 Hor.4:1	26
Like tender buds shoot up, and freshly grow.	•	309	Horace	89
Of tender eyes will more be wept, then seene:	•	398	Drayton	76
Tough, foule, or Tender.	• • • • •	417	Moon	16
TENDRELLS				
With sproutinge tendrells of the Vine;	• • •	290	U85 Country	V 10
TENDRING				
I can lose none in tendring these to you.	• • •	231	U56 Covell	28
T'ENJOY				
The Christian hath t'enjoy the future life,	• •	271	U81 Pawlet	96
What 'tis t'enjoy, an everlasting breath!	• •	285	U84 Muse	92
TENOR				
Calme Brutus tenor start; but all along	• •	395	May	11
TENT				
Of Heaven; where Seraphim take tent	• • •	273	U84 Cradle	31
TENTH				
The Credit, what would furnish a tenth Muse!	• •	161	U14 Selden	84
T'ENVY				
I am too fat t'envy him. He too leane	•	405	Inigo Jones 1	69
TERENCE				
Neat Terence, witty Plautus, now not please;	• •	392	Shakespeare	52
TERGUM				
How faine for his venery he was to crie (Tergum o)	• •	380	Coryat 3	37
TERME				
Thou call'st me Poet, as a terme of shame:	•	29	E10 Ignorant	1
. . . the last Terme he sate Chancellor.	•	185	U31 Elsmere	Ttl
Terme of the Architects is called Designe!	• •	404	Inigo Jones 1	56
TERMERS				
For termers, or some clarke-like serving-man,	• •	28	E3 Bookseller	9
TERMES				
Men past their termes, and prais'd some names too much,	•	159	U14 Selden	21
Thou need new termes; thou maist, without excuse,	•	307	Horace	70
And ever will, to utter termes that bee	•	309	Horace	84
With poore base termes, through every baser shop:	•	321	Horace	334
TERROR				
Which though it did but panick terror prove,	•	43	E51 James 3	3
A terror? or is all this but my feare?	• •	169	U18 Elegy Can	6
TERRORS				
Sinke not beneath these terrors:	• • •	177	U25 Desmond	30
T'ESCAPE				
T'escape this common knowne necessitie,	• •	271	U81 Pawlet	93
TEST				
Of Kings for grace; of Poets for my test?	•	28	E4 James 1	10
They meet the fire, the Test, as Martyrs would;	•	218	U47 Tribe	3
Who are his Test, and what their judgement is:	•	385	Husband	3
TESTIFIE				
Run from your rootes; Tell, testifie the grand	•	274	U84 Descent	9
TESTIMONY				
What place is for my testimony void?	• • •	385	Brooke	2
I send this small, but hearty testimony: and with charge,	•	666	Glover	5
T'EXACT				
With his old earthly labours. T'exact more,	•	107	F10 Proludium	5
T'EXCHANGE				
As fit t'exchange discourse; a Verse to win	•	311	Horace	119
T'EXPECT				
As what th'have lost t'expect, they dare deride.	•	116	F13 Aubigny	4
T'expect the honors of great 'Aubigny:	•	119	F13 Aubigny	105
T'EXPRESS				
Or Verse, or Sense t'express Immortall you?	•	403	Inigo Jones 1	41
T'EXPRESSE				
And yet (in this t'expresse our selves more cleare)	•	111	F11 Epode	75
And yet (in this t'expresse my self more cleare)	•	111	F11 Epode	V 75
TEXT				
Though Lippe, at Pauls, ranne from his text away,	•	52	E75 Lippe	3
T'EXTRACT				
T'extract, and choose the best of all these knowne,	•	80	E128 Wm Roe 2	3
TEYNTED				
Yet if with eithers vice I teynted be,	• •	190	U37 Friend-Book	29
TH'ACCOMPT				
Upon th'accompt, hers grew the quicker trade.	•	56	E87 Hazard	5
TH'ADMIR'D				
Th'admir'd discourses of the Prophet Ball:	• •	206	U43 Vulcan	82
Th'admir'd discourses of the Profit Ball:	•	206	U43 Vulcan	V 82
Th'admir'd discourses of the Prophet Baal:	•	206	U43 Vulcan	V 82

		Page	Title	Line
TH'ADVANTAGE				
With th'advantage of her haire,		138	U2 Kisse	10
TH'ADVENTER				
Shee brought the Poets forth, but ours th'adventer.		84	E133 Voyage	20
TH'ADVENTURES				
With all th'adventures; Three bookes not afraid		207	U43 Vulcan	95
With all th'adventures; Three bookes not amisse		207	U43 Vulcan	V 95
TH'AEMILIAN				
Th'Aemilian Schoole, in brasse can fashion out		307	Horace	46
TH'AETERNALL				
Our great reward, th'aeternall Crown to win.		412	Sutcliffe	19
TH'AFFAIRES				
That censure all the Towne, and all th'affaires,		218	U47 Tribe	23
TH'AFFRIGHTED				
Upon th'affrighted world:		243	U70 Ode	16
TH'AGE				
A treasure, art: contemn'd in th'age of gold.		47	E64 Salisbury 3	4
I' your selfe, all treasure lost of th'age before.		68	E105 L Wroth 2	20
TH'AMBITIOUS				
Looke on th'ambitious man, and see him nurse		162	U15 Friend-Wars	11
THAMES				
Or the drops in silver Thames,		103	F6 Celia 2	15
Their Sister-tunes, from Thames his either side,		253	U75 Epithalam.	34
And make those flights upon the bankes of Thames,		392	Shakespeare	73
Or Dowgate Torrent falling into Thames,		407	Inigo Jones 2	16
THAN (THEN)				
All the Pride the fields than have:		132	U2 How he saw	4
It much will differ, if a God speake, than,		313	Horace	161
It much will sway whether a god speak, than;		342	Horace	V161
His better'd mind seekes wealth, and friendship: than		315	Horace	238
THAN				
A Prince, that rules by'example, more than sway?		37	E35 James 2	2
Whose manners draw, more than thy powers constraine.		37	E35 James 2	3
And than in them, how could we know god more?		38	E35 James 2	8
To thy Domitian, than I can my James:		38	E36 Martial	2
No lesse than if from perill; and devout,		43	E51 James 3	7
And, than this same, I know no abler way		80	E127 Aubigny	11
Rather than meet him: And, before his eyes		185	U30 Burleigh	16
THANK				
Swim without Corke! Why, thank the good Queen Anne.		405	Inigo Jones 1	68
THANKE				
To thanke thy benefits: which is, to pay.		80	E127 Aubigny	12
No more then he doth thanke, that will receive		154	U13 Sacvile	43
Thanke him: if other, hee can give no Bayes.		232	U58 Book-seller	6
But thanke his greatnesse, and his goodnesse too;		236	U63 Charles 2	9
With which, Priapus, he may thanke thy hands,		290	U85 Country	21
THANK'D				
That would, perhaps, have prais'd, and thank'd the same,		161	U14 Selden	70
THANKEFULL				
Is there a hope, that Man would thankefull bee,		80	E127 Aubigny	1
THANKES				
Be thankes to him, and earnest prayer, to finde		99	F3 Wroth	101
Is thankes to him, and earnest prayer, to finde		99	F3 Wroth	V101
The smallest courtesies with thankes, I make		153	U13 Sacvile	16
Can I owe thankes, for Curtesies receiv'd		153	U13 Sacvile	25
All this corrupts the thankes; lesse hath he wonne,		154	U13 Sacvile	33
No! Gifts and thankes should have one cheerefull face,		154	U13 Sacvile	39
Give thankes by stealth, and whispering in the eare,		154	U13 Sacvile	49
THANKFULL				
Sir, I am thankfull, first, to heaven, for you;		189	U37 Friend-Book	1
And the returne those thankfull Courtiers yeeld,		213	U44 Speach	17
Of some small thankfull land: whether he bee		313	Horace	166
THANKING				
By thanking thus the curtesie to life,		158	U13 Sacvile	159
THANKS				
Our thanks to God. Then, Haile to Mary! spring		238	U66 Queene	V 13
Yes. And thanks God in his Pistle or his Booke		380	Coryat 3	43
TH'ANTIQUE				
What th'antique souldiers were, the moderne bee?		72	E111 Edmonds 2	2
TH'AONIAN				
Are all th'Aonian springs		174	U23 Himselfe	7
TH'APPROCHES				
And all did ring th'approches of the Bride;		253	U75 Epithalam.	36
TH'ARE				
And still be a whore-house. Th'are Synonima.		29	E7 Hot-house	4
Th'are base, and idle feares		109	F11 Epode	26
(Because th'are every where amongst Man-kind		167	U15 Friend-Wars	171
(Brave Youths) th'are their possessions, none of yours:		281	U84 Kenelme	11
If Praises, when th'are full, heaping admit,		385	Brooke	6
As if they' ador'd the Head, wheron th'are fixt.		413	Ghyrlond	28
TH'ART				
So, in short time, th'art in arrerage growne		32	E16 Brain-hardy	5
That still th'art present to the better cause;		52	E74 Chancelor	5
Roe (and my joy to name) th'art now, to goe		80	E128 Wm Roe 2	1
That still th'art made the suppers flagge, the drum,		81	E129 Mime	7
TH'ASCENT				
Th'ascent of Lady Fame which none could spy		403	Inigo Jones 1	35
TH'ASSEMBLY				
Of th'Assembly, as did you!		138	U2 Kisse	12
THAT'				
That's greater, yet: to crie his owne up neate.		35	E28 Surly	11
He drinkes to no man: that's, too, like a lord.		35	E28 Surly	14
But that's put in, thou'lt say. Why, so is thine.		36	E29 Tilter	6

THAT' (cont.)

	Page	Title	Line
Is it the paine affrights? that's soone forgot.	46	E62 Would-bee	5
That's, sit, and eate: doe not my eares abuse.	68	E107 Hungry	2
Where vertue makes them both, and that's in thee:	70	E109 Nevil	3
On some new gesture, that's imputed wit?	81	E129 Mime	14
That's a Toy, that I could spare:	142	U2 Exception	2
For that's a narrow joy is but our owne.	147	U7 Nymph	7
So each, that's done, and tane, becomes a Brace.	154	U13 Sacvile	40
See him, that's call'd, and thought the happiest man,	162	U15 Friend-Wars	23
I, that's a Charme, and halfe! She must afford	163	U15 Friend-Wars	52
But he that's both, and slave to boote, shall live,	167	U15 Friend-Wars	160
But he that's both, and slave to both, shall live,	167	U15 Friend-Wars V160	
And then with pause; for sever'd once, that's gone,	192	U38 Elegy 'Tis	47
You would restore it? No, that's worth a feare,	199	U41 Elegy Since	15
But that's a marke, wherof thy Rites doe boast,	205	U43 Vulcan	57
But he that's too-much that, is friend of none.	216	U45 Squib	24
But that's a blow, by which in time I may	219	U47 Tribe	51
That's six in silver; now within the Socket	229	U54 Squib	13
And that's made up as doth the purse abound.	230	U56 Covell	12
Stay, drop a teare for him that's dead,	233	U60 La-ware	2
These make the lines of life, and that's her ayre.	245	U70 Ode	64
Our selves, and all that's ours, to death we owe:	309	Horace	90
Hee, that's ambitious in the race to touch	333	Horace	587
They're darke, bid cleare this: all that's doubtfull wrote	335	Horace	637
They're dark, bid cleare 'hem; al that's doubtful wrote	354	Horace	V637

THAT

	Page	Title	Line
Pray thee, take care, that tak'st my booke in hand,	27	E1 Reader	1
To reade it well: that is, to understand.	27	E1 Reader	2
He that departs with his owne honesty	27	E2 My Booke	13
Thou, that mak'st gaine thy end, and wisely well,	27	E3 Bookseller	1
On some-thing, that walkes some-where.	30	E11 Something	Ttl
That haunt Pickt-hatch, Mersh-Lambeth, and White-fryers,	30	E12 Shift	2
The charge of that state, with this charme, god payes.	30	E12 Shift	4
By that one spell he lives, eates, drinkes, arrayes	30	E12 Shift	5
That lost, he keepes his chamber, reades Essayes,	30	E12 Shift	15
Let me give two: that doubly am got free,	31	E13 Empirick	3
All that I am in arts, all that I know,	31	E14 Camden	2
(How nothing's that?) to whom my countrey owes	31	E14 Camden	3
Then thee the age sees not that thing more grave,	31	E14 Camden	5
More high, more holy, that shee more would crave.	31	E14 Camden	6
Man scarse can make that doubt, but thou canst teach.	31	E14 Camden	10
Thou more; that with it every day, dar'st jest	32	E16 Brain-hardy	2
He that dares damne himselfe, dares more then fight.	32	E16 Brain-hardy	10
That wish my poemes a legitimate fame,	32	E17 Critic	3
Thou saist, that cannot be: for thou hast seene	32	E18 Censurer	3
Thy faith is all the knowledge that thou hast.	32	E18 Censurer	10
That Cod can get no widdow, yet a knight,	33	E19 Cod 1	1
Where, while that sever'd doth remaine,	34	E22 Daughter	10
There's reason good, that you good lawes should make:	34	E24 Parliament	1
In place of scutcheons, that should decke thy herse,	35	E27 Roe 1	1
And, that is done, as he saw great men doe.	35	E28 Surly	6
That breathes in his dogs way: and this is great.	36	E28 Surly	18
That selfe-divided Belgia did afford;	37	E32 Roe 2	3
He that feares death, or mournes it, in the just,	37	E34 Death	1
A Prince, that rules by'example, more than sway?	37	E35 James 2	2
For this: that winnes, for whom he holds his peace.	38	E37 Chev'ril	4
Who sayes that Giles and Jone at discord be?	40	E42 Giles	1
But that his Jone doth too. And Giles would never,	40	E42 Giles	4
All this doth Jone. Or that his long yearn'd life	40	E42 Giles	11
The children, that he keepes, Giles sweares are none	40	E42 Giles	13
'Tis Lucklesse he, that tooke up one on band	42	E46 Luckless 1	3
Hee that wooes every widdow, will get none.	42	E47 Luckless 2	2
That we thy losse might know, and thou our love,	43	E51 James 3	1
For we, that have our eyes still in our eares,	43	E51 James 3	9
And that, as puritanes at baptisme doo,	44	E53 Old-end	7
Could save that line to dedicate to thee?	44	E53 Old-end	10
That quit'st the cause so oft, and rayl'st at men?	44	E54 Chev'ril 2	4
That unto me dost such religion use!	44	E55 Beaumont	2
How I doe feare my selfe, that am not worth	44	E55 Beaumont	3
What fate is mine, that so it selfe bereaves?	44	E55 Beaumont	7
What art is thine, that so thy friend deceives?	44	E55 Beaumont	8
Poore Poet-Ape, that would be thought our chiefe,	44	E56 Poet-Ape	1
I, that am glad of thy great chance, here doo!	46	E60 Mounteagle	5
That love to make so well, a child to beare?	46	E62 Would-bee	2
That can restore that. Will it hurt your feature?	46	E62 Would-bee	7
And that thou seek'st reward of thy each act,	47	E63 Salisbury 2	5
Curst be his Muse, that could lye dumbe, or hid	47	E63 Salisbury 2	11
Not glad, like those that have new hopes, or sutes,	47	E64 Salisbury 3	1
Nor glad as those, that old dependents bee,	47	E64 Salisbury 3	5
But I am glad to see that time survive,	47	E64 Salisbury 3	9
That whil'st I meant but thine to gratulate,	48	E64 Salisbury 3	17
That hast betray'd me to a worthlesse lord;	48	E65 Muse	2
That neither fame, nor love might wanting be	48	E66 Cary	1
To greatnesse, Cary, I sing that, and thee.	48	E66 Cary	2
Against thy fortune: when no foe, that day,	49	E66 Cary	9
Hee's valiant'st, that dares fight, and not for pay;	49	E66 Cary	17
That vertuous is, when the reward's away.	49	E66 Cary	18
That sound, and that authoritie with her name,	49	E67 Suffolk	3
Proves, that is gods, which was the peoples voice.	49	E67 Suffolk	12
In life, that can employ it; and takes hold	50	E70 Wm Roe 1	3
That yet maintaynes you, and your house in laughter.	51	E73 Fine Grand	8
That no affection in thy voyce commands;	51	E74 Chancelor	4
That still th'art present to the better cause;	52	E74 Chancelor	5

		Page	Title	Line
THAT (cont.)				
I Cannot thinke there's that antipathy	. . . .	52	E75 Lippe	1
Hating that solemne vice of greatnesse, pride;	. . .	52	E76 Bedford 1	10
Fit in that softer bosome to reside.	. . . .	52	E76 Bedford 1	12
I purpos'd her; that should, with even powers,	. . .	52	E76 Bedford 1	14
My Muse bad, Bedford write, and that was shee.	. . .	52	E76 Bedford 1	18
To one that desired me not to name him.	. . .	53	E77 Not name	Ttl
That, any way, my booke should speake thy name:	. . .	53	E77 Not name	2
That Poets are far rarer births then kings,	. . .	53	E79 Rutland	1
Came not that soule exhausted so their store.	. . .	53	E79 Rutland	4
Hence was it, that the destinies decreed	. . .	53	E79 Rutland	5
(Save that most masculine issue of his braine)	. . .	53	E79 Rutland	6
Nature, they thought, in all, that he would faine.	. . .	53	E79 Rutland	8
How wilfull blind is he then, that would stray,	. . .	53	E80 Life/Death	3
Or that I'have by, two good sufficient men,	. . .	54	E81 Proule	3
Make it your gift. See whither that will beare mee.	. .	55	E84 Bedford 2	10
And why that bird was sacred to Apollo,	. . .	55	E85 Goodyere 1	4
That they to knowledge so should toure upright,	. . .	55	E85 Goodyere 1	6
Where, though 't be love, that to thy praise doth move	. .	55	E86 Goodyere 2	7
It was a knowledge, that begat that love.	. . .	55	E86 Goodyere 2	8
That his whole body should speake french, not he?	. .	56	E88 Monsieur	2
That so much skarfe of France, and hat, and fether,	. .	56	E88 Monsieur	3
That he, untravell'd, should be french so much,	. .	56	E88 Monsieur	7
That, Allen, I should pause to publish thee?	. . .	57	E89 Allen	8
Out-strip, then they did all that went before:	. . .	57	E89 Allen	10
Weare this renowne. 'Tis just, that who did give	. .	57	E89 Allen	13
Not though that haire grew browne, which once was amber,	.	57	E90 Mill	9
Blowne up; and he (too'unwieldie for that place)	. .	57	E90 Mill	14
And it is hop'd, that shee, like Milo, wull	. .	57	E90 Mill	17
That know not so much state, wrong, as they doo.	. .	59	E92 New Crie	40
And two, that would have falne as great, as they,	. .	60	E93 Radcliffe	7
Thou, that art all their valour, all their spirit,	. .	60	E93 Radcliffe	9
For none ere tooke that pleasure in sinnes sense,	. .	60	E94 Bedford 3	9
They, then, that living where the matter is bred,	. .	60	E94 Bedford 3	11
That stranger doctrine of Pythagoras,	. . .	61	E95 Savile	2
But when I read that speciall piece, restor'd,	. .	61	E95 Savile	7
That liv'st from hope, from feare, from faction free;	.	61	E95 Savile	18
That hast thy brest so cleere of present crimes,	. .	61	E95 Savile	19
We need a man that knowes the severall graces	. .	61	E95 Savile	27
That dares nor write things false, nor hide things true.	.	62	E95 Savile	36
That so alone canst judge, so'alone dost make:	. .	62	E96 Donne 2	3
My title's seal'd. Those that for claps doe write,	. .	62	E96 Donne 2	9
Nor baudie stock, that travells for encrease,	. .	63	E97 Motion	10
He that is round within himselfe, and streight,	. .	63	E98 Th Roe 1	3
That thou at once, then, nobly maist defend	. .	63	E98 Th Roe 1	7
That thou hast kept thy love, encreast thy will,	. .	63	E99 Th Roe 2	1
Better'd thy trust to letters; that thy skill;	. .	63	E99 Th Roe 2	2
And that to write things worthy to be read,	. .	63	E99 Th Roe 2	4
Not that we thinke us worthy such a ghest,	. .	64	E101 Supper	3
But that your worth will dignifie our feast,	. .	64	E101 Supper	4
With those that come; whose grace may make that seeme	.	64	E101 Supper	5
That will the pastrie, not my paper, show of.	. .	65	E101 Supper	26
But that, which most doth take my Muse, and mee,	. .	65	E101 Supper	28
That shall be utter'd at our mirthfull boord,	. .	65	E101 Supper	40
The libertie, that wee'll enjoy to night.	. . .	65	E101 Supper	42
Whose praise, ev'n they, that envie it, must praise;	.	66	E102 Pembroke	16
That art so reverenc'd, as thy comming in,	. .	66	E102 Pembroke	17
Thou must draw more: and they, that hope to see	. .	66	E102 Pembroke	19
That but the twi-light of your sprite did see,	. .	66	E103 L Wroth 1	2
And, being nam'd, how little doth that name	. .	66	E103 L Wroth 1	5
A Sydney: but in that extend as farre	. . .	67	E103 L Wroth 1	10
Were they that nam'd you, prophets? Did they see,	.	67	E104 Montgomery	1
A new Susanna, equall to that old?	. . .	67	E104 Montgomery	4
Or, because some scarce thinke that storie true,	. .	67	E104 Montgomery	5
Judge they, that can: here I have rais'd to show	. .	67	E104 Montgomery	13
That we had left us, nor by time, nor place,	. .	67	E105 L Wroth 2	3
He, that but saw you weare the wheaten hat,	. .	68	E105 L Wroth 2	7
Would call you more then Ceres, if not that:	. .	68	E105 L Wroth 2	8
There's none so dull, that for your stile would aske,	.	68	E105 L Wroth 2	15
That saw you put on Pallas plumed caske:	. .	68	E105 L Wroth 2	16
Or, keeping your due state, that would not cry,	. .	68	E105 L Wroth 2	17
What man art thou, that art so many men,	. . .	68	E106 E Herbert	2
Not that I love it, more, then I will you.	. .	68	E107 Hungry	4
Give your yong States-men, (that first make you drunke,		69	E107 Hungry	19
That are your wordes of credit. Keepe your Names	.	69	E107 Hungry	24
And your high names: I doe desire, that thence	. .	69	E108 Soldiers	3
He that not trusts me, having vow'd thus much,	. .	70	E108 Soldiers	9
That serves nor fame, nor titles; but doth chuse	. .	70	E109 Nevil	2
And that thy soule should give thy flesh her weight.	.	70	E109 Nevil	14
In these west-parts, nor when that warre was done,	.	71	E110 Edmonds 1	2
And that so strong and deepe, as 't might be thought,	.	71	E110 Edmonds 1	7
He wrote, with the same spirit that he fought,	. .	71	E110 Edmonds 1	8
Nor that his worke liv'd in the hands of foes,	. .	71	E110 Edmonds 1	9
And that, midst envy' and parts; then fell by rage:	.	71	E110 Edmonds 1	14
His life, but makes, that he can dye no more.	. .	71	E110 Edmonds 1	22
And that, in action, there is nothing new,	. .	72	E111 Edmonds 2	5
That to the world thou should'st reveale so much,	.	72	E111 Edmonds 2	10
They murder him againe, that envie thee.	. .	72	E111 Edmonds 2	14
Think'st thou it is meere fortune, that can win?	. .	72	E112 Gamster	3
Or thy ranke setting? that thou dar'st put in	. .	72	E112 Gamster	4
Art still at that, and think'st to blow me'up too?	.	72	E112 Gamster	6
I modestly quit that, and thinke to write,	. .	72	E112 Gamster	11
O, (thou cry'st out) that is thy proper game.	. .	73	E112 Gamster	16

641

THAT (cont.)

	Page	Title		Line
That both for wit, and sense, so oft dost plucke,	73	E112	Gamster	18
There's no vexation, that can make thee prime.	73	E112	Gamster	22
That the wit there, and manners might be sav'd:	73	E113	Overbury	6
Him not, aloud, that boasts so good a fame:	74	E115	Honest Man	2
About the towne; and knowne too, at that price.	74	E115	Honest Man	6
A subtle thing, that doth affections win	74	E115	Honest Man	7
Doe all, that longs to the anarchy of drinke,	74	E115	Honest Man	12
Not that it feares, but will not have to doo	74	E115	Honest Man	20
That seeming prayses, are, yet accusations.	75	E115	Honest Man	32
That age, when thou stood'st up the master-braine:	75	E116	Jephson	4
And those that lack'd it, to suspect at length,	75	E116	Jephson	6
'Twas not entayl'd on title. That some word	75	E116	Jephson	7
That Nature no such difference had imprest	75	E116	Jephson	9
That bloud not mindes, but mindes did bloud adorne:	75	E116	Jephson	11
Lust it comes out, that gluttony went in.	76	E118	Gut	6
Not he that flies the court for want of clothes,	76	E119	Shelton	1
With me can merit more, then that good man,	76	E119	Shelton	5
That to the vulgar canst thy selfe apply,	76	E119	Shelton	11
He, that, but living halfe his age, dyes such;	76	E119	Shelton	15
Weepe with me all you that read	77	E120	S. P.	1
'Twas a child, that so did thrive	77	E120	S. P.	5
That strives, his manners should precede his wit.	78	E121	Rudyerd 1	8
Then that it liv'd at all. Farewell.	79	E124	Elizabeth	12
Is there a hope, that Man would thankefull bee,	80	E127	Aubigny	1
So, all reward, or name, that growes to mee	80	E127	Aubigny	9
This is that good Aeneas, past through fire,	81	E128	Wm Roe 2	12
That, not a paire of friends each other see,	81	E129	Mime	1
That there's no journey set, or thought upon,	81	E129	Mime	3
That scarse the Towne designeth any feast	81	E129	Mime	5
That still th'art made the suppers flagge, the drum,	81	E129	Mime	7
Think'st thou, Mime, this is great? or, that they strive	81	E129	Mime	9
To urge, my lov'd Alphonso, that bold fame	82	E130	Ferrab. 1	1
That shee removeth cares, sadnesse ejects,	82	E130	Ferrab. 1	4
T'alledge, that greatest men were not asham'd,	82	E130	Ferrab. 1	9
That the eight spheare, no lesse, then planets seaven,	82	E130	Ferrab. 1	12
Say, this, or that man they to thee preferre;	83	E131	Ferrab. 2	9
Since they can only judge, that can conferre.	83	E132	Sylvester	6
That to the world I publish, for him, this;	83	E132	Sylvester	9
So well in that are his inventions wrought,	83	E132	Sylvester	11
All, that they boast of Styx, of Acheron,	84	E133	Voyage	7
Of those, that put out moneyes, on returne	85	E133	Voyage	32
Or him that backward went to Berwicke, or which	85	E133	Voyage	35
A Docke there is, that called is Avernus,	85	E133	Voyage	41
All, that are readers: but, me thinkes 'tis od,	85	E133	Voyage	43
That all this while I have forgot some god,	85	E133	Voyage	44
In the first jawes appear'd that ugly monster,	85	E133	Voyage	61
Man, that had never heard of a Chimaera.	86	E133	Voyage	80
Made of the trull, that cut her fathers lock:	86	E133	Voyage	84
And all his followers, that had so abus'd him:	86	E133	Voyage	97
And that is when it is the Lord Maiors foist.	87	E133	Voyage	120
Airising in that place, through which, who goes,	87	E133	Voyage	131
And that ours did. For, yet, no nare was tainted,	87	E133	Voyage	133
Or, that it lay, heap'd like an usurers masse,	88	E133	Voyage	139
That, with still-scalding steemes, make the place hell.	88	E133	Voyage	144
That had, so often, shew'd 'hem merry prankes.	89	E133	Voyage	184
Calling for Radamanthus, that dwelt by,	89	E133	Voyage	187
My Muse had plough'd with his, that sung A-jax.	89	E133	Voyage	196
That since, my numbers are so cold,	93	F1	Why write no	11
That taller tree, which of a nut was set,	94	F2	Penshurst	13
That never failes to serve thee season'd deere,	94	F2	Penshurst	20
The lower land, that to the river bends,	94	F2	Penshurst	22
Thou hast thy ponds, that pay thee tribute fish,	94	F2	Penshurst	32
Fat, aged carps, that runne into thy net.	94	F2	Penshurst	33
Bright eeles, that emulate them, and leape on land,	94	F2	Penshurst	37
Hang on thy walls, that every child may reach.	94	F2	Penshurst	44
There's none, that dwell about them, wish them downe;	94	F2	Penshurst	47
Some nuts, some apples; some that thinke they make	95	F2	Penshurst	52
With all, that hospitalitie doth know!	95	F2	Penshurst	60
That is his Lordships, shall be also mine.	95	F2	Penshurst	64
That found King James, when hunting late, this way,	95	F2	Penshurst	76
Now, Penshurst, they that will proportion thee	96	F2	Penshurst	99
That at great times, art no ambitious guest	96	F3	Wroth	5
While all, that follow, their glad eares apply	97	F3	Wroth	31
And feasts, that either shearers keepe;	97	F3	Wroth	40
The apple-harvest, that doth longer last;	98	F3	Wroth	43
A fire now, that lent a shade!	98	F3	Wroth	46
Such, and no other was that age, of old,	98	F3	Wroth	63
That they may sleepe with scarres in age.	98	F3	Wroth	70
And brag, that they were therefore borne.	99	F3	Wroth	72
Let that goe heape a masse of wretched wealth,	99	F3	Wroth	81
The secrets, that shall breake their sleepe:	99	F3	Wroth	88
Shalt neither that, nor this envy:	99	F3	Wroth	92
That neither want doe thee affright,	100	F3	Wroth	104
That neither want should thee affright,	100	F3	Wroth	V104
That houre upon my morne of age,	100	F4	To the World	2
Doe not once hope, that thou canst tempt	100	F4	To the World	5
From all the nets that thou canst spread.	100	F4	To the World	8
That onely fooles make thee a saint,	100	F4	To the World	15
That fled his cage, or broke his chaine,	101	F4	To the World	30
The engines, that have them annoy'd;	101	F4	To the World	34
That, what to all may happen here,	101	F4	To the World	55
From all my kinde: that, for my sake,	101	F4	To the World	59

THAT (cont.)

	Page	Title	Line
No, I doe know, that I was borne	101	F4 To the World	61
But I will beare these, with that scorne,	102	F4 To the World	63
As wandrers doe, that still doe rome,	102	F4 To the World	66
Sunnes, that set, may rise againe:	102	F5 Celia 1	6
All the grasse that Rumney yeelds,	103	F6 Celia 2	13
Or the starres, that guild his streames,	103	F6 Celia 2	16
That the curious may not know	103	F6 Celia 2	19
Song. That Women are but Mens shaddowes.	104	F7 Women but	Ttl
There are those, that, for thy sake,	105	F8 Sicknesse	25
That distill their husbands land	105	F8 Sicknesse	29
That for th'oyle of Talke, dare spend	105	F8 Sicknesse	33
That, to make all pleasure theirs,	105	F8 Sicknesse	36
And, for that, at common game,	105	F8 Sicknesse	V 41
The thirst, that from the soule doth rise,	106	F9 Celia 3	5
The thirst, that from the soule proceedes,	106	F9 Celia 3	V 5
As giving it a hope, that there	106	F9 Celia 3	11
but being well assured that there	106	F9 Celia 3	V 11
Shall not give out, that I have made thee stay,	107	F10 Proludium	8
Shall not give out, that we have made thee stay,	107	F10 Proludium	V 8
That, at thy birth, mad'st the poore Smith affraid,	107	F10 Proludium	14
A beautie of that merit, that should take	108	F10 Proludium	27
Next, to that vertue, is to know vice well,	109	F11 Epode	3
That no strange, or unkinde	109	F11 Epode	10
(That should ring larum to the heart) doth sleepe,	109	F11 Epode	23
(That shal ring larum to the heart) doth sleepe,	109	F11 Epode	V 23
That is an essence, farre more gentle, fine,	110	F11 Epode	45
That is an essence, most gentile and fine,	110	F11 Epode	V 45
That falls like sleepe on lovers, and combines	110	F11 Epode	49
O, who is he, that (in this peace) enjoyes	110	F11 Epode	55
That cryes, we dreame, and sweares, there's no such thing,	111	F11 Epode	67
That cryes, I dreame, and sweares, there's no such thing,	111	F11 Epode	V 67
That, being at sea, suppose,	111	F11 Epode	V 70
He that for love of goodnesse hateth ill,	112	F11 Epode	87
Then he, that for sinnes penaltie forbeares.	112	F11 Epode	V 89
A beautie of that cleere, and sparkling light,	112	F11 Epode	93
A beautie of that cleere, and sparkling sight,	112	F11 Epode	V 93
All her best symmetrie in that one feature!	112	F11 Epode	101
That knowes the waight of guilt: He will refraine	112	F11 Epode	113
Whil'st that, for which, all vertue now is sold,	113	F12 Rutland	1
That which, to boote with hell, is thought worth heaven,	113	F12 Rutland	3
To every squire, or groome, that will report	113	F12 Rutland	6
To every squire, or groome, that can report	113	F12 Rutland	V 6
The foole that gave it; who will want, and weepe,	113	F12 Rutland	13
The foole that gave it; that will want, and weepe,	113	F12 Rutland	V 13
I, that have none (to send you) send you verse.	113	F12 Rutland	19
Were it to thinke, that you should not inherit	114	F12 Rutland	32
Worth an estate, treble to that you have.	114	F12 Rutland	36
That bred them, graves: when they were borne, they di'd,	114	F12 Rutland	47
That had no Muse to make their fame abide.	114	F12 Rutland	48
Achilles was not first, that valiant was,	114	F12 Rutland	51
Or, in an armies head, that, lockt in brasse,	114	F12 Rutland	52
That Homer brought to Troy; yet none so live:	115	F12 Rutland	55
You, and that other starre, that purest light,	115	F12 Rutland	65
Then all, that have but done my Muse least grace,	115	F12 Rutland	79
Then all, that have but done my verse lesse grace,	115	F12 Rutland	V 79
Or common places, filch'd, that take these times,	116	F12 Rutland	88
For that firme grace he holdes in your regard,	116	F12 Rutland	95
I, that am gratefull for him, have prepar'd	116	F12 Rutland	96
I, that have suffer'd this; and, though forsooke	117	F13 Aubigny	15
Your beautie; for you see that every day:	117	F13 Aubigny	30
That askes but to be censur'd by the eyes:	117	F13 Aubigny	35
Nor that your beautie wanted not a dower,	117	F13 Aubigny	37
For such a lot! that mixt you with a state	118	F13 Aubigny	48
'Tis onely that can time, and chance defeat:	118	F13 Aubigny	51
For he, that once is good, is ever great.	118	F13 Aubigny	52
This blessing of your starres, then by that way	118	F13 Aubigny	54
This makes, that wisely you decline your life,	118	F13 Aubigny	59
Not looking by, or back (like those, that waite	118	F13 Aubigny	62
Because that studies spectacles, and showes,	118	F13 Aubigny	65
Till that no usurer, nor his bawds dare lend	118	F13 Aubigny	78
That doe sinne onely for the infamie:	119	F13 Aubigny	86
'Gainst stormes, or pyrats, that might charge your peace;	119	F13 Aubigny	93
To Clifton's bloud, that is deny'd their name.	119	F13 Aubigny	98
They speake; since you are truly that rare wife,	119	F13 Aubigny	110
This makes, that your affections still be new,	119	F13 Aubigny	118
And that your soules conspire, as they were gone	119	F13 Aubigny	119
Live that one, still; and as long yeeres doe passe,	120	F13 Aubigny	121
Now that the harth is crown'd with smiling fire,	120	F14 Sydney	1
That I may tell to Sydney, what	120	F14 Sydney	12
And he may thinke on that	120	F14 Sydney	15
Are justly summ'd, that make you man;	120	F14 Sydney	22
For they, that swell	121	F14 Sydney	39
And he that stayes	121	F14 Sydney	49
That, laden with my sinnes, I seeke for ease?	122	F15 Heaven	4
O, be thou witnesse, that the reynes dost know,	122	F15 Heaven	5
Of discontent; or that these prayers bee	122	F15 Heaven	25
That I may prove	129	U1 Father	5
That gav'st a Sonne,	129	U1 Father	19
That did us all salvation bring,	130	U1 Nativitie	8
And as that wisedome had decreed,	130	U1 Nativitie	16
Lesse your laughter; that I love.	131	U2 Excuse	2
That you never knew till now,	131	U2 Excuse	15

THAT (cont.)

	Page	Title	Line
When you know, that this is she,	131	U2 Excuse	18
At my face, that tooke my sight,	132	U2 How he saw	25
So that, there, I stood a stone,	132	U2 How he saw	27
Or else one that plaid his Ape,	132	U2 How he saw	31
First, that I must kneeling yeeld	133	U2 Suffered	7
Aymed with that selfe-same shaft.	133	U2 Suffered	12
Is, that I have leave to speake,	133	U2 Suffered	22
Each that drawes, is a Swan, or a Dove,	134	U2 Triumph	3
That they still were to run by her side,	134	U2 Triumph	9
All that Loves world compriseth!	134	U2 Triumph	12
Then words that sooth her!	134	U2 Triumph	16
Noblest Charis, you that are	136	U2 Cupid	1
With the Lace that doth it deck,	137	U2 Cupid	30
Call to mind the formes, that strove	137	U2 Cupid	46
That the Bride (allow'd a Maid)	138	U2 Kisse	8
Or, that did you sit, or walke,	138	U2 Kisse	13
Else that glister'd in White-hall;	138	U2 Kisse	16
So, as those that had your sight,	138	U2 Kisse	17
That at every motion sweld	138	U2 Kisse	24
That doth but touch his flower, and flies away.	139	U2 Another	6
Can he that loves, aske lesse then one?	139	U2 Another	8
And that promise set on fire	139	U2 Promise	5
All that heard her, with desire.	139	U2 Promise	6
But we find that cold delay,	140	U2 Promise	9
(And that quickly) speake your Man.	140	U2 Promise	30
And his Manners of that Nation.	141	U2 Her man	8
That's a Toy, that I could spare:	142	U2 Exception	2
Mixe then your Notes, that we may prove	143	U3 Musicall	9
Nor doe we doubt, but that we can,	145	U5 Woman-kind	7
To make a new, and hang that by.	145	U5 Woman-kind	18
That talke abroad of Womans change,	146	U6 Defence	2
Take that away, you take our lives,	146	U6 Defence	5
Is that which doth perfection breed.	146	U6 Defence	12
I'le tell, that if they be not glad,	147	U7 Nymph	8
That were this morning blowne;	147	U7 Nymph	19
And feare much more, that more of him be showne.	147	U7 Nymph	21
Could you beleeve, that this,	148	U8 Houre-glasse	4
Of one that lov'd?	148	U8 Houre-glasse	6
I Doubt that, Love is rather deafe, then blind,	149	U9 Picture	V 1
That she,	149	U9 Picture	3
That sits in shadow of Apollo's tree.	149	U9 Picture	10
That flie my thoughts betweene,	149	U9 Picture	12
Tell me that she hath seene	149	U9 Picture	13
prompt me that she hath seene	149	U9 Picture	V 13
To vent that poore desire,	150	U10 Jealousie	5
That others should not warme them at my fire,	150	U10 Jealousie	6
Think'st thou that love is help'd by feare?	150	U10 Jealousie	12
That though they did possesse each limbe,	151	U12 Corbet	9
A life that knew nor noise, nor strife:	151	U12 Corbet	12
That never came ill odour thence:	152	U12 Corbet	18
But that I understood him scant.	152	U12 Corbet	31
That they for me their teares will shed;	152	U12 Corbet	34
If, Sackvile, all that have the power to doe	153	U13 Sacvile	1
Against his will that do's 'hem? that hath weav'd	153	U13 Sacvile	26
That they have more opprest me, then my want?	153	U13 Sacvile	28
That puts it in his Debt-booke e're 't be done;	154	U13 Sacvile	34
Or that doth sound a Trumpet, and doth call	154	U13 Sacvile	35
In that proud manner, as a good so gain'd,	154	U13 Sacvile	37
He neither gives, or do's, that doth delay	154	U13 Sacvile	41
A Benefit; or that doth throw't away:	154	U13 Sacvile	42
No more then he doth thanke, that will receive	154	U13 Sacvile	43
That to such Natures let their full hands flow,	154	U13 Sacvile	60
Their bounties forth, to him that last was made,	155	U13 Sacvile	63
Then give it to the Hound that did him bite;	155	U13 Sacvile	70
Pardon, sayes he, that were a way to see	155	U13 Sacvile	71
Is borrowing; that but stopt, they doe invade	155	U13 Sacvile	80
That men such reverence to such actions show!	156	U13 Sacvile	98
I thought that Fortitude had beene a meane	156	U13 Sacvile	105
That with these mixtures we put out her light.	156	U13 Sacvile	110
But like to be, that every day mends one,	156	U13 Sacvile	116
No! he must feele and know, that will advance.	156	U13 Sacvile	123
Or on the sudden. It were strange that he	156	U13 Sacvile	125
Sydney e're night! or that did goe to bed	157	U13 Sacvile	127
'Tis by degrees that men arrive at glad	157	U13 Sacvile	131
That makes the Arch. The rest that there were put	157	U13 Sacvile	137
Are nothing till that comes to bind and shut.	157	U13 Sacvile	138
'Tis like light Canes, that first rise big and brave,	157	U13 Sacvile	149
And last, goe out in nothing: You that see	157	U13 Sacvile	153
That I may love your Person (as I doe)	157	U13 Sacvile	157
Without your gift, though I can rate that too,	157	U13 Sacvile	158
Was trusted, that you thought my judgement such	158	U14 Selden	6
Chance that the Friends affection proves Allay	158	U14 Selden	10
Themselves through favouring that is there not found:	159	U14 Selden	V 16
So that my Reader is assur'd, I now	159	U14 Selden	27
Meane what I speake: and still will keepe that Vow.	159	U14 Selden	28
Stand forth my Object, then, you that have beene	159	U14 Selden	29
Where is that nominall marke, or reall rite,	160	U14 Selden	47
Forme, Art or Ensigne, that hath scap'd your sight?	160	U14 Selden	48
Forme, Act or Ensigne, that hath scap'd your sight?	160	U14 Selden	V 48
With that thy Stile, thy keeping of thy State,	161	U14 Selden	68
That would, perhaps, have prais'd, and thank'd the same,	161	U14 Selden	70
Selden! two Names that so much understand!	161	U14 Selden	82

	Page	Title	Line
THAT (cont.)			
All that dare rowse: or are not loth to quit	162	U15 Friend-Wars	3
That gaspe for action, and would yet revive	162	U15 Friend-Wars	6
Looke on the false, and cunning man, that loves	162	U15 Friend-Wars	15
Crush'd in the snakie brakes, that he had past!	162	U15 Friend-Wars	18
That kept man living! Pleasures only sought!	163	U15 Friend-Wars	41
That all respect; She must lie downe: Nay more,	163	U15 Friend-Wars	53
How they may make some one that day an Asse	164	U15 Friend-Wars	64
That payes, or what he will: The Dame is steele.	164	U15 Friend-Wars	78
He that will follow but anothers wife,	165	U15 Friend-Wars	87
Nature, that will not let his Wife be a whore;	165	U15 Friend-Wars	90
That may corrupt her, even in his eyes.	165	U15 Friend-Wars	92
Is it for these that Fine-man meets the street	165	U15 Friend-Wars	106
Is it that man pulls on himselfe Disease?	165	U15 Friend-Wars	114
This way, now that, as if their number were	166	U15 Friend-Wars	126
This Praecipice, and Rocks that have no end,	166	U15 Friend-Wars	130
He that no more for Age, Cramps, Palsies, can	166	U15 Friend-Wars	135
Is that the truer excuse? or have we got	166	U15 Friend-Wars	142
That scratching now's our best Felicitie?	166	U15 Friend-Wars	144
Although, perhaps it has, what's that to me,	167	U15 Friend-Wars	149
That may stand by, and hold my peace? will he,	167	U15 Friend-Wars	150
Give me but that, that I must wast	167	U15 Friend-Wars	152
Give me but that againe, which I must wast	167	U15 Friend-Wars	V152
With him, for he is follow'd with that heape	167	U15 Friend-Wars	156
That watch, and catch, at what they may applaud,	167	U15 Friend-Wars	157
Lewd slanderers, soft whisperers that let blood	167	U15 Friend-Wars	165
Lewd standers, soft whisperers that let blood	167	U15 Friend-Wars	V165
That thine be just, and honest; that thy Deeds	167	U15 Friend-Wars	177
That thou dost all things more for truth, then glory,	168	U15 Friend-Wars	179
That by commanding first thy selfe, thou mak'st	168	U15 Friend-Wars	181
That fortune never make thee to complaine,	168	U15 Friend-Wars	183
That whatsoever face thy fate puts on,	168	U15 Friend-Wars	185
That thou thinke nothing great, but what is good,	168	U15 Friend-Wars	187
And from that thought strive to be understood.	168	U15 Friend-Wars	188
All that is left of Philip Gray,	168	U16 Gray	4
They are not, Sir, worst Owers, that doe pay	169	U17 Friend-Debt	1
But that some greater names have broke with me,	169	U17 Friend-Debt	8
I adde that (but) because I understand	169	U17 Friend-Debt	10
That as the lesser breach: for he that takes	169	U17 Friend-Debt	11
Can Beautie that did prompt me first to write,	169	U18 Elegy Can	1
That as the water makes things, put in't streight,	170	U18 Elegy Can	7
Crooked appeare; so that doth my conceipt:	170	U18 Elegy Can	8
I can helpe that with boldnesse; And Love sware,	170	U18 Elegy Can	9
And Fortune once, t'assist the spirits that dare.	170	U18 Elegy Can	10
That I must send one first, my Choyce assignes,	170	U18 Elegy Can	23
By that faire Stand, your forehead, whence he bends	170	U19 Elegy By	3
By that tall Grove, your haire; whose globy rings	170	U19 Elegy By	5
And so that either may example prove	171	U19 Elegy By	16
I know no beautie, nor no youth that will.	171	U19 Elegy By	20
Of all that can be done him; Such a one	171	U19 Elegy By	23
That which we can, who both in you, his Wife,	171	U19 Elegy By	25
Amongst my many other, that I may	171	U20 Shrub	3
That ne're was knowne to last above a fit!	171	U20 Shrub	6
That their whole life was wickednesse, though weav'd	171	U20 Shrub	10
Knew I, that all their Dialogues, and discourse,	172	U20 Shrub	13
And that pour'd out upon Man-kind can be!	172	U20 Shrub	19
That thought can adde, unthankfull, the lay-stall	172	U21 Ltl Shrub	8
Throughout your forme; as though that move,	173	U22 Elegy Tho	6
'Tis of your selfe, and that you use	173	U22 Elegy Tho	10
That envie wish'd, and Nature fear'd.	173	U22 Elegy Tho	20
That would their better objects find:	173	U22 Elegy Tho	27
Appeare, and that to shortest view,	174	U22 Elegy Tho	34
Knowledge, that sleepes, doth die;	174	U23 Himselfe	3
That eats on wits, and Arts, and destroyes them both.	174	U23 Himselfe	6
That not a Nymph now sings?	174	U23 Himselfe	10
Minds that are great and free,	174	U23 Himselfe	16
To that strumpet the Stage,	175	U23 Himselfe	34
Wise Providence would so; that nor the good	176	U24 Frontispice	5
high Providence would so; that nor the good	176	U24 Frontispice	V 5
Which makes that (lighted by the beamie hand	176	U24 Frontispice	9
This makes, that lighted by the beamie hand	176	U24 Frontispice	V 9
Of Truth that searcheth the most hidden Springs,	176	U24 Frontispice	10
High, as his mind, that doth advance	176	U25 Desmond	5
That I may sing my thoughts, in some unvulgar straine.	177	U25 Desmond	13
On these darke rymes; that my affection	177	U25 Desmond	15
On these darke rymes; that our affection	177	U25 Desmond	V 15
That hold your spirit:	177	U25 Desmond	20
That curbes your spirit:	177	U25 Desmond	V 20
Of politique pretext, that wryes a State,	177	U25 Desmond	29
Of politique pretext, that swayes a State,	177	U25 Desmond	V 29
Gold, that is perfect, will out-live the fire.	179	U25 Desmond	45
That is not hurt; not he, that is not hit;	179	U25 Desmond	50
(Whose heart in that bright Sphere flames clearest,	179	U25 Desmond	54
(As my hope tells) that our faire Phoebe's shine,	179	U25 Desmond	58
(As my hope tells) that our drad Cynthia's shine,	179	U25 Desmond	V 58
That you will stand	180	U25 Desmond	64
The Cure of that, which is but corporall,	180	U26 Ode High	5
Happy in that faire honour it hath gain'd,	180	U26 Ode High	14
To doe, then be a husband of that store.	180	U26 Ode High	18
'Tis wisdome, and that high,	181	U26 Ode High	22
The Swan that so relish'd Pancharis)	182	U27 Ode Helen	30
I That have beene a lover, and could shew it,	182	U28 Worth	1
That expresseth but by fits,	183	U29 Fit of Rime	2

645

THAT (cont.)

		Page	Title	Line
Vulgar Languages that want	. . .	184	U29 Fit of Rime	43
That they long since have refused	. . .	184	U29 Fit of Rime	47
He that first invented thee,	. . .	184	U29 Fit of Rime	49
That in rearing such a Schoole,	. . .	184	U29 Fit of Rime	59
What is there more that can ennoble blood?	. .	185	U30 Burleigh	6
That in all tempests, never quit the helme,	. .	185	U30 Burleigh	10
That still was good for goodnesse sake, nor thought	.	185	U30 Burleigh	13
When those good few, that her Defenders be,	. .	186	U32 Elsmere	5
Thinke, yea and boast, that they have done it so	.	186	U32 Elsmere	12
He do's you wrong, that craves you to doe right.	.	186	U32 Elsmere	16
An Epigram to the Councellour that pleaded, . . .	.	186	U33 Councellour	Ttl
That I, hereafter, doe not thinke the Barre,	.	186	U33 Councellour	1
That, henceforth, I beleeve nor bookes, nor men,	.	187	U33 Councellour	5
All mouthes, that dare entitle them (from hence)	.	187	U33 Councellour	11
And make the Scarre faire; If that will not be,	.	187	U33 Councellour	21
But in a businesse, that will bide the Touch,	.	187	U33 Councellour	23
Of those that set by their false faces more	.	188	U34 Small Poxe	4
Was drawne to practise other hue, then that	.	188	U34 Small Poxe	8
That heaven should make no more; or should amisse,	.	188	U34 Small Poxe	15
I, that thy Ayme was; but her fate prevail'd:	.	188	U34 Small Poxe	17
And waste still, that they still might bee.	.	189	U36 Song	12
Not like your Countrie-neighbours, that commit	.	190	U37 Friend-Book	7
In letters, that mixe spirits, thus to weave.	.	190	U37 Friend-Book	12
Little know they, that professe Amitie,	.	190	U37 Friend-Book	19
That friendship which no chance but love did chuse,	.	190	U37 Friend-Book	23
Will unto Licence that faire leave abuse.	.	190	U37 Friend-Book	24
Or there to sterve it. Helpe, O you that may	.	191	U38 Elegy 'Tis	7
As light breakes from you, that affrights despaire,	.	191	U38 Elegy 'Tis	10
That you should be too noble to destroy.	.	191	U38 Elegy 'Tis	12
Thinke that your selfe like heaven forgive me can:	.	192	U38 Elegy 'Tis	32
Thinke that I once was yours, or may be now;	.	192	U38 Elegy 'Tis	35
Nothing is vile, that is a part of you:	.	192	U38 Elegy 'Tis	36
There is no Father that for one demerit,	.	192	U38 Elegy 'Tis	41
That as the last of punishments is meant;	.	192	U38 Elegy 'Tis	43
No man inflicts that paine, till hope be spent:	.	192	U38 Elegy 'Tis	44
Would live his glory that could keepe it on;	.	192	U38 Elegy 'Tis	48
That is, if still your Favours you apply,	.	192	U38 Elegy 'Tis	53
That were to wither all, and make a Grave	.	192	U38 Elegy 'Tis	59
Of that wise Nature would a Cradle have.	.	192	U38 Elegy 'Tis	60
It shakes even him, that all things else doth shake.	.	193	U38 Elegy 'Tis	72
O imitate that sweet Serenitie	. .	193	U38 Elegy 'Tis	77
That makes us live, not that which calls to die.	.	193	U38 Elegy 'Tis	78
Forgiven him; And in that lyne stand I,	.	193	U38 Elegy 'Tis	91
O, that you could but by dissection see	.	194	U38 Elegy 'Tis	109
And that there is no life in me, but love.	.	194	U38 Elegy 'Tis	112
You would be then most confident, that tho	.	194	U38 Elegy 'Tis	113
Till then 'tis all but darknesse, that I have;	.	194	U38 Elegy 'Tis	121
That Love's a bitter sweet, I ne're conceive	.	197	U40 Elegy That	1
This makes me, Mrs. that sometime by stealth,	.	197	U40 Elegy That	9
As if that ex'lent Dulnesse were Loves grace;	.	198	U40 Elegy That	24
Like the dull wearied Crane that (come on land)	.	198	U40 Elegy That	35
Where he that knowes will, like a Lapwing, flie	.	198	U40 Elegy That	37
Due to that one, that doth believe him just.	.	198	U40 Elegy That	40
That Article, may not become our lover:	.	198	U40 Elegy That	48
Or that the Sun was here, but forc't away;	.	199	U41 Elegy Since	6
And we were left under that Hemisphere,	.	199	U41 Elegy Since	7
That from the Muses fountaines doth indorse	.	200	U42 Elegy Let	7
In all that is call'd lovely: take my sight	.	200	U42 Elegy Let	12
There is not worne that lace, purle, knot or pin,	.	200	U42 Elegy Let	16
That quilts those bodies, I have leave to span:	.	200	U42 Elegy Let	32
A Gowne of that, was the Caparison?	. .	201	U42 Elegy Let	46
That are like cloath'd: must I be of those fooles	.	201	U42 Elegy Let	48
Of race accompted, that no passion have	.	201	U42 Elegy Let	49
Then ope thy wardrobe, thinke me that poore Groome	.	201	U42 Elegy Let	51
that from the Foot-man, when he was become	.	201	U42 Elegy Let	52
Court every hanging Gowne, and after that,	.	201	U42 Elegy Let	57
That chanc'd the lace, laid on a Smock, to see,	.	201	U42 Elegy Let	66
And straight-way spent a Sonnet; with that other	.	201	U42 Elegy Let	67
That (in pure Madrigall) unto his Mother	.	201	U42 Elegy Let	68
Under that cover; an old Mid-wives hat!	.	202	U42 Elegy Let	83
What had I done that might call on thine ire?	.	202	U43 Vulcan	2
What have I done that might call on thine ire?	.	202	U43 Vulcan	V 2
'Twas Jupiter that hurl'd thee headlong downe,	.	203	U43 Vulcan	9
'Twas Jupiter that cast thee headlong downe,	.	203	U43 Vulcan	V 9
And Mars, that gave thee a Lanthorne for a Crowne.	.	203	U43 Vulcan	10
That since thou tak'st all envious care and paine,	.	203	U43 Vulcan	13
Conceal'd, or kept there, that was fit to be,	.	203	U43 Vulcan	21
Especially in paper; that, that steame	.	205	U43 Vulcan	61
Their Jemme of Riches, and bright Stone, that brings	.	206	U43 Vulcan	74
And the strong lines, that so the time doe catch:	.	206	U43 Vulcan	78
Or Captaine Pamphlets horse, and foot, that sallie	.	206	U43 Vulcan	79
Oure Captaine Pamphlets horse, and foot, that sallie	.	206	U43 Vulcan	V 79
To teach some that, their Nurses could not doe,	.	207	U43 Vulcan	92
When thou wert borne, and that thou look'st at best,	.	208	U43 Vulcan	113
Made thee beget that cruell Stratagem,	.	208	U43 Vulcan	130
There were, that streight did nose it out for newes,	.	209	U43 Vulcan	V139
And this a Sparkle of that fire let loose	.	209	U43 Vulcan	141
That this sparke of the same fire let loose	.	209	U43 Vulcan	V141
That rak'd up in the Winchestrian Goose	.	209	U43 Vulcan	142
That was lock'd up in the Winchestrian Goose	.	209	U43 Vulcan	V142
But, others fell with that conceipt by the eares,	.	209	U43 Vulcan	145
But, others fell by that conceipt by the eares,	.	209	U43 Vulcan	V145

646

THAT (cont.)

And that accursed ground, the Parish-Garden:	209	U43 Vulcan	147
And that prophaner ground, the Parish-Garden:	209	U43 Vulcan	V147
If that were so, thou rather would'st advance	209	U43 Vulcan	151
The place, that was thy Wives inheritance.	209	U43 Vulcan	152
The Plot, that was thy Wives inheritance.	209	U43 Vulcan	V152
He burnt that Idoll of the Revels too:	210	U43 Vulcan	155
Foole, wilt thou let that in example come?	210	U43 Vulcan	161
'Tis true, that in thy wish they were destroy'd,	210	U43 Vulcan	167
Or lest that vapour might the Citie choake,	211	U43 Vulcan	182
Or lest that vapour should the Citie choake,	211	U43 Vulcan	V182
That from the Divels-Arse did Guns beget;	212	U43 Vulcan	V202
That have good places: therefore once agen;	212	U43 Vulcan	212
That have good fortunes: therefore once agen,	212	U43 Vulcan	V212
That have good places: wherefore once agen,	212	U43 Vulcan	V212
And all the Evils that flew out of her box	212	U43 Vulcan	214
And all Those ills that flew out of her box	212	U43 Vulcan	V214
That we have Trumpets, Armour, and great Horse,	213	U44 Speach	7
Thou Seed-plot of the warre, that hast not spar'd	213	U44 Speach	24
These ten yeares day; As all may sweare that looke	213	U44 Speach	27
He that but saw thy curious Captaines drill,	213	U44 Speach	29
For that unnecessarie Charge they were.	214	U44 Speach	32
So, in that ground, as soone it grew to be	214	U44 Speach	37
More then the surfets, in thee, that day stood.	214	U44 Speach	48
That keepe the warre, though now't be growne more tame,	214	U44 Speach	55
But he that should perswade, to have this done	214	U44 Speach	61
Us, in our bearing, that are thus, and thus,	215	U44 Speach	65
Live by their Scale, that dare doe nothing free?	215	U44 Speach	68
That turnes us so much moneys, at which rate	215	U44 Speach	77
That in the Cradle of their Gentrie are;	215	U44 Speach	84
All that they doe at Playes. O, but first here	215	U44 Speach	91
His Lordship. That is for his Band, his haire	215	U44 Speach	95
This, and that box his Beautie to repaire;	215	U44 Speach	96
My gentle Arthur; that it might be said	216	U45 Squib	3
That hearkens to a Jacks-pulse, when it goes.	216	U45 Squib	6
Nor ever trusted to that friendship yet,	216	U45 Squib	7
That could but claime a kindred from the purse.	216	U45 Squib	10
'Tis vertue alone, or nothing, that knits friends:	216	U45 Squib	12
Friend to himselfe, that would be friend to thee.	216	U45 Squib	22
For that is first requir'd, A man be his owne.	216	U45 Squib	23
But he that's too-much that; is friend of none.	216	U45 Squib	24
He that should search all Glories of the Gowne,	217	U46 Coke	1
He could not find, then thee, of all that store	217	U46 Coke	3
That Clients strove, in Question of the Lawes,	217	U46 Coke	11
And that thy strong and manly Eloquence	217	U46 Coke	13
Of worthiest knowledge, that can take mens minds.	217	U46 Coke	20
Such is thy All; that (as I sung before)	217	U46 Coke	21
Or if Chance must, to each man that doth rise,	217	U46 Coke	23
An Epistle answering to one that asked . . .	218	U47 Tribe	Ttl
Men that are safe, and sure, in all they doe,	218	U47 Tribe	1
I could say more of such, but that I flie	218	U47 Tribe	5
Let those that meerely talke, and never thinke,	218	U47 Tribe	9
That live in the wild Anarchie of Drinke,	218	U47 Tribe	10
They'ave glutted in, and letcher'd out that weeke,	218	U47 Tribe	13
That never yet did friend, or friendship seeke	218	U47 Tribe	14
Or th'other on their borders, that will jeast	218	U47 Tribe	16
On all Soules that are absent; even the dead;	218	U47 Tribe	17
That to speake well, thinke it above all sinne,	218	U47 Tribe	19
Of any Companie but that they are in,	218	U47 Tribe	20
That censure all the Towne, and all th'affaires,	218	U47 Tribe	23
Or that the Match from Spaine was ever meant?	219	U47 Tribe	36
And force back that, which will not be restor'd,	219	U47 Tribe	40
I have a body, yet, that spirit drawes	219	U47 Tribe	41
That guides the Motions, and directs the beares.	219	U47 Tribe	50
Live to that point I will, for which I am man,	219	U47 Tribe	59
And that there be no fev'ry heats, nor colds,	220	U47 Tribe	67
That thou remaine here taster	220	U48 Bacchus	7
That both, their odour take him,	220	U48 Bacchus	11
That when King James, above here,	221	U48 Bacchus	37
And that as any are strooke, her breath creates	222	U49 Pucell	5
Equall with that, which for the best newes goes,	222	U49 Pucell	9
And that her truster feares her? Must I too?	223	U49 Pucell	22
And trust her I would least, that hath forswore	223	U49 Pucell	29
Not he, that should the body have, for Case	223	U49 Pucell	33
Ought that is ill, but the suspition too,	224	U50 Countesse	6
By all oblique Degrees, that killing height	224	U50 Countesse	11
Among the daily Ruines that fall foule,	224	U50 Countesse	17
What then his Father was, that since is hee,	225	U51 Bacon	11
Give me a deep-crown'd-Bowle, that I may sing	225	U51 Bacon	19
My Superficies: that was all you saw.	227	U52 Answer	9
For a just wager, and that wager paid	229	U54 Squib	2
So that upon the point, my corporall feare	229	U54 Squib	7
Verse, that should thee, and me out-live.	229	U55 Burges	4
Yet with a Dye, that feares no Moth,	230	U55 Burges	7
And that he will venter	231	U57 Burges	5
That hang their richest jewells i'their nose;	232	U58 Book-seller	10
As if that part lay for a < > most fit!	232	U58 Book-seller	12
If they goe on, and that thou lov'st a-life	232	U58 Book-seller	13
That trembles in the blaze, but (then) mounts higher!	233	U59 Newcastle	8
Their weapons shot out, with that flame, and force,	233	U59 Newcastle	11
Their weapons darted, with that flame, and force,	233	U59 Newcastle	V 11
Of a Disease, that lov'd no light	234	U60 La-ware	6
That spread his body o're, to kill:	234	U60 La-ware	16

	Page	Title	Line
THAT (cont.)			
That you have seene the pride, beheld the sport,	234	U61 Epigram	1
That scarce you heare a publike voyce alive,	234	U61 Epigram	5
He, that in such a flood, as we are in	234	U61 Epigram	16
But, that he cure the Peoples Evill too?	235	U62 Charles 1	14
Who dares denie, that all first-fruits are due	235	U63 Charles 2	1
That the Almighties will to you is such:	236	U63 Charles 2	8
And thinke all still the best, that he will doe.	236	U63 Charles 2	10
That thought shall make, he will this losse supply	236	U63 Charles 2	11
Cannot but heape that grace, he will requite.	236	U63 Charles 2	14
When you that raigne, are her Example growne,	236	U64 Charles 3	9
When thou that rul'st, are her Example growne,	236	U64 Charles 3	V 9
That Faith, which she professeth to be pure?	236	U64 Charles 3	12
That nothing can her gratitude provoke!	237	U64 Charles 3	16
That nothing will her gratitude provoke!	237	U64 Charles 3	V 16
That so hath crown'd our hopes, our spring, and earth,	237	U65 Prince	2
That so hath crown'd our hopes, our spring, our earth,	237	U65 Prince	V 2
That thus hath crown'd our hopes, with thee, our Spring & May,	237	U65 Prince	V 2
The same that thou art promis'd, but be slow,	237	U65 Prince	6
The same that thou hast promis'd, but be slow,	237	U65 Prince	V 6
(Except the joy that the first Mary brought,	238	U66 Queene	7
(And leave the joy that the first Mary brought,	238	U66 Queene	V 7
That when the Quire is full,	239	U67 Muses	19
But, that shee raigning here,	240	U67 Muses	35
What, by that name, wee each to other owe,	241	U69 Friend Son	4
Painted a Dog, that now his subtler skill	241	U69 Friend Son	10
To the immortall memorie, and friendship of that noble . . .	242	U70 Ode	Ttl
Thy coming forth in that great yeare,	242	U70 Ode	2
From out the horrour of that sack?	243	U70 Ode	12
But weary of that flight,	244	U70 Ode	37
And sunke in that dead sea of life	244	U70 Ode	40
But that the Corke of Title boy'd him up.	244	U70 Ode	42
Although it fall, and die that night;	245	U70 Ode	71
To see that bright eternall Day:	245	U70 Ode	81
Or taste a part of that full joy he meant	246	U70 Ode	87
Whilst that in heav'n, this light on earth must shine.	246	U70 Ode	96
That knits brave minds, and manners, more then blood.	246	U70 Ode	106
That liking; and approach so one the tother,	247	U70 Ode	109
As they that saw	247	U70 Ode	118
That such a Law	247	U70 Ode	120
That cry that gladnesse, which their hearts would pray,	249	U72 King	14
Weston! That waking man! that Eye of State!	250	U73 Weston	5
Thou sluggish spawne, that canst, but wilt not see?	250	U73 Weston	8
Bring all your friends, (faire Lord) that burne	251	U74 Weston	20
. . . that Noble Gentleman, Mr. Hierome Weston, Son, and . . .	252	U75 Epithalam.	Ttl
That holy strife,	253	U75 Epithalam.	30
On all that come her Simplesse to rebuke!	253	U75 Epithalam.	44
Although that thou, O Sun, at our intreaty stay!	254	U75 Epithalam.	56
Saw'st thou that Paire, became these Rites so well,	254	U75 Epithalam.	76
It is their Grace, and favour, that makes seene,	255	U75 Epithalam.	89
That Mine of Wisdome, and of Counsells deep,	255	U75 Epithalam.	98
That farre-all-seeing Eye	256	U75 Epithalam.	109
Some houres before it should, that these may know	257	U75 Epithalam.	146
All that their Fathers, and their Mothers might	257	U75 Epithalam.	147
Of Life, that fall so; Christians know their birth	257	U75 Epithalam.	156
That when you both are old,	258	U75 Epithalam.	165
The longing Couple, all that elder Lovers know.	258	U75 Epithalam.	192
That whereas your royall Father	259	U76 Petition	5
And that this so accepted summe,	259	U76 Petition	14
And that this so thriftye summe,	259	U76 Petition	V 14
That would all their envie burst:	260	U76 Petition	V 30
Can doe the things that Statues doe deserve,	261	U77 Treasurer	15
For that to dwell in, and be still at home.	262	U78 Digby	8
That day, which I predestin'd am to sing,	262	U78 Digby	V 17
The knowing Weston, and that learned Lord	263	U78 Digby	28
That know the times, and seasons when t'appeare,	263	U79 New-yeares	11
That drives the Hart to seeke unused wayes,	264	U79 New-yeares	21
That leades our flocks and us, and calls both forth	264	U79 New-yeares	29
Of all that Nature, yet, to life did bring;	264	U79 New-yeares	33
That have a Flock, or Herd, upon these plaines;	265	U79 New-yeares	47
That they may take it eccho'd by the Floods.	265	U79 New-yeares	53
That thou art lov'd of God, this worke is done,	268	U80 Christning	1
You seeme a faire one! O that you had breath,	269	U81 Pawlet	6
You seeme a faire one! O that I had breath,	269	U81 Pawlet	V 6
I durst not aime at that: The dotes were such	269	U81 Pawlet	25
But rather I, should I of that part speake!	269	U81 Pawlet	28
And, calling truth to witnesse, make that good	270	U81 Pawlet	35
That saw the way was made it! and were sent	270	U81 Pawlet	V 65
And all beatitudes, that thence doe flow:	271	U81 Pawlet	75
Which they that have the Crowne are sure to know!	271	U81 Pawlet	76
The Starres, that are the Jewels of the Night,	271	U81 Pawlet	87
That ever had beginning there, to'ave end!	271	U81 Pawlet	91
And, but for that Contention, and brave strife	271	U81 Pawlet	95
But as he soares at that, he bruiseth then	272	U81 Pawlet	98
. . . Of that truly-noble Lady, the Lady Venetia Digby, . . .	272	U84 Eupheme	Ttl
Their Heads, that Envy would hold downe	272	U84 Cradle	3
That all Posteritie, as wee,	273	U84 Cradle	13
May something by that twilight see	273	U84 Cradle	15
For, though that Rattles, Timbrels, Toyes,	273	U84 Cradle	17
Of that eternall Port kept ope'	274	U84 Cradle	39
That ever Nature, or the later Ayre	274	U84 Descent	4
Speake it, you bold Penates, you that stand	274	U84 Descent	7
Meeting of Graces, that so swell'd the flood	274	U84 Descent	10

	Page	Title	Line
THAT (cont.)			
Thy Neeces line, then thou that gav'st thy Name . . .	274	U84 Descent	14
And, out of that, make Day to breake;	276	U84 Body	14
Then let the beames of that, disperse	276	U84 Body	17
With all that Youth, or it can bring:	276	U84 Body	22
Not, that your Art I doe refuse:	277	U84 Mind	5
To draw a thing that cannot sit.	277	U84 Mind	8
Since nothing can report that flame, ...	278	U84 Mind	15
That all may say, that see the frame, ...	278	U84 Mind	23
In speech; it is with that excesse	279	U84 Mind	34
But, that a Mind so rapt, so high, ...	279	U84 Mind	41
Thrice happy house, that hast receipt	280	U84 Mind	53
Begotten by that wind, and showers.	280	U84 Mind	68
Which all men doe, that urge not their owne deeds . . .	281	U84 Kenelme	17
'Twere time that I dy'd too, now shee is dead, . . .	282	U84 Muse	1
The Spirit that I wrote with, and conceiv'd; . . .	282	U84 Muse	3
All that was good, or great in me she weav'd, . . .	282	U84 Muse	4
Nothing, that could remaine, or yet can stirre . . .	282	U84 Muse	9
And saw that portion of her selfe to die. . . .	282	U84 Muse	14
To have that finall retribution, ...	283	U84 Muse	49
Of that great Evidence, the Conscience! . . .	284	U84 Muse	58
Who will be there, against that day prepar'd, . . .	284	U84 Muse	59
Who in that feast of Resurrection trust! . . .	284	U84 Muse	62
That great eternall Holy-day of rest, . . .	284	U84 Muse	63
Presume to interpell that fulnesse, when . . .	284	U84 Muse	70
That she is in, or, make it more compleat? . . .	284	U84 Muse	72
That, planted round, there sing before the Lamb, . .	285	U84 Muse	89
And white, as that, put on: and in her hand, . . .	285	U84 Muse	95
That pure, that pretious, and exalted mind . . .	285	U84 Muse	104
Compar'd unto that long eternitie, . . .	285	U84 Muse	106
That shall re-joyne yee. Was she, then, so deare, .	285	U84 Muse	107
There, all the happy soules, that ever were, . . .	285	U84 Muse	113
But make him All in All, their Theme, that Day: . .	286	U84 Muse	120
That happy Day, that never shall see night! . . .	286	U84 Muse	121
That holy, great, and glorious Mysterie, . . .	286	U84 Muse	129
He that shall be our supreme Judge, should leave . .	286	U84 Muse	148
And to that forme, lent two such veines of blood . .	287	U84 Muse	157
(But pride, that schisme of incivilitie) . . .	287	U84 Muse	160
To that eternall Rest, where now sh'hath place . .	288	U84 Muse	197
In that great Act of judgement: which the Father . .	288	U84 Muse	215
His Wisdome, and his Justice, in that houre, . . .	288	U84 Muse	218
That thus have ventur'd these true straines upon; . .	289	U84 Muse	227
Happie is he, that from all Businesse cleere, . . .	289	U85 Country	1
Or when that Autumne, through the fields, lifts round .	290	U85 Country	17
And, Sylvane, thine that keptst his Lands! . . .	290	U85 Country	22
And, Sylvane, thine that keep'st his Lands! . . .	290	U85 Country	V 22
That penning the glad flock in hurdles by, . . .	291	U85 Country	45
More sweet then Olives, that new gather'd be . . .	291	U85 Country	55
Or the herb Sorrell, that loves Meadows still, . . .	291	U85 Country	57
That I bright Chloe off should shake; . . .	294	U87 Hor.3:9	19
Like lustfull beasts, that onely know to doe it: . .	294	U88 Petronius	4
For lust will languish, and that heat decay. . . .	294	U88 Petronius	5
Hee, that but living halfe his dayes, dies such, . .	295	U89 Mart.8:77	7
The Things that make the happier life, are these, . .	295	U90 Mart.10:47	1
Sleepe, that will make the darkest howres swift-pac't; .	295	U90 Mart.10:47	11
This peece, my Piso's, and that booke agree, . . .	305	Horace	8
That Book, my Piso's, and this piece agree, . . .	338	Horace	V 8
Together: not that we should Serpents see . . .	305	Horace	15
To gentle: not that we should Serpents see . . .	338	Horace	V 15
Ye have oft-times, that may ore-shine the rest, . .	305	Horace	18
Ye have oft-times, that may out-shine the rest, . .	338	Horace	V 18
bor-/Dring Circles of swift waters that intwine . .	305	Horace	21
Bouts of fleet waters, that doe intertwine . . .	338	Horace	V 21
The greater part, that boast the Muses fire, . . .	339	Horace	V 33
Professing greatnesse, swells: That, low by lee . .	307	Horace	38
So he that varying still affects to draw . . .	339	Horace	V 42/ 40
To be that Smith; then live, mark'd one of those, . .	307	Horace	51
To be that fellow, then to be markt out . . .	339	Horace	V 53/ 51
Take, therefore, you that write, still, matter fit . .	307	Horace	53
Take therefore, you that write, a subject fit . . .	339	Horace	V 55/ 53
Much, that mought now be spoke: omitted here . . .	307	Horace	62
Lay that aside, the Epicks office is. . . .	307	Horace	64
Most worthie praise, when words that common grew, . .	307	Horace	67
Most worthie praise, when words that vulgar grew, . .	340	Horace	V 67
And come not too much wrested. What's that thing, . .	309	Horace	76
And ever will, to utter termes that bee . . .	309	Horace	84
That from the North, the Navie safe doth store, . .	309	Horace	92
A kingly worke; or that long barren fen . . .	309	Horace	93
Much phrase that now is dead, shall be reviv'd; . .	309	Horace	101
And much shall dye, that now is nobly liv'd, . . .	309	Horace	102
That first sent forth the dapper Elegie, . . .	309	Horace	110
That are Spectators, with their miserie, . . .	311	Horace	137
To laughter; so they grieve with those that mone. . .	311	Horace	144
If now the phrase of him that speakes, shall flow, . .	313	Horace	158
Or follow fame, thou that dost write, or faine . .	313	Horace	169
If something strange, that never yet was had . . .	313	Horace	178
If something fresh, that never yet was had . . .	342	Horace	V178
Nor so begin, as did that Circler late, . . .	313	Horace	195
But light from smoake; that he may draw his bright . .	315	Horace	204
From the two Egges, that did disclose the twins, . .	315	Horace	210
That tarries till the hangings be ta'en downe, . .	315	Horace	221
Fit rites. The Child, that now knowes how to say, .	315	Horace	225
Fit dues. The Child, that now knowes how to say, .	344	Horace	V225

	Page	Title	Line
THAT (cont.)			
Or acted told. But, ever, things that run	317	Horace	256
Nor must the Fable, that would hope the Fate,	317	Horace	270
The angry, and love those that feare t'offend.	317	Horace	282
Peace, and the open ports, that peace doth cause.	317	Horace	284
The open ports, and sports that peace doth cause,	345	Horace	V284
Chaste, thriftie, modest folke, that came to view.	319	Horace	294
That wider Walls embrac'd their Citie round,	319	Horace	296
Unwonted language; and that sense of worth	319	Horace	308
That found out profit, and foretold each thing,	319	Horace	309
Those that did sing, and act: their faces dy'd	319	Horace	314
Hee too, that did in Tragick Verse contend	319	Horace	319
With something that was acceptably new.	321	Horace	327
Or Semi-god, that late was seene to weare	321	Horace	332
Yet he that offers at it, may sweat much,	321	Horace	351
Him that buyes chiches blanch't, or chance to like	321	Horace	362
Him that buyes Pulse there, or perhaps may like	347	Horace	V354/362
Too patiently, that I not fondly say;	323	Horace	401
To taxe that Verse, which many a day, and blot	325	Horace	416
The head that three Anticira's cannot heale.	349	Horace	V428
O I left-witted, that purge every spring	325	Horace	429
Be like a Whet-stone, that an edge can put	325	Horace	433
Hee, that hath studied well the debt, and knowes	325	Horace	445
First frighted men, that wildly liv'd, at ods,	327	Horace	480
Amphion, too, that built the Theban towres,	327	Horace	483
And lead them with soft songs, where that he would.	327	Horace	485
This was the wisdome, that they had of old,	327	Horace	486
Be briefe, in what thou wouldst command, that so	329	Horace	503
But flowes out, that ore-swelleth in full brests.	329	Horace	506
For, neither doth the String still yeeld that sound	329	Horace	521
Nor alwayes doth the loosed Bow, hit that	329	Horace	524
Is laugh'd at, that still jarreth on one string:	329	Horace	532
So he that flaggeth much, becomes to me	329	Horace	533
But, I confesse, that, in a long worke, sleepe	329	Horace	537
Though I confesse, that, in a long worke, sleepe	351	Horace	V513/537
Will take you more, the neerer that you stand;	331	Horace	540
Or Pleader at the Barre, that may come short	331	Horace	551
Hee, that not knowes the games, nor how to use	331	Horace	565
Him that is last, I scorne to come behind,	333	Horace	595
Him that is last, I scorne to be behind,	353	Horace	V595
Or, of the things, that ne're came in my mind,	333	Horace	596
That to the sale of Wares calls every Buyer;	333	Horace	598
So doth the Poet, that is rich in Land,	353	Horace	V599
As those that hir'd to weepe at Funeralls, swoune,	333	Horace	614
Those that are wise, a furious Poet feare	354	Horace	V643
And shun to touch him, as a man that were	335	Horace	644
And flye to touch him, as a man that were	354	Horace	V644
Let Poets perish, that will not be kept.	335	Horace	664
Hee that preserves a man, against his will,	335	Horace	665
Doth the same thing with him, that would him kill.	335	Horace	666
To force the grates, that hold him in, would fright	337	Horace	675
that mongst so manie plants transplanted hether,	361	Palmer	6
Next, that which rapt mee, was: I might behold	361	Palmer	13
still making that the greatest that is last	361	Palmer	19
I struggled with this passion that did drowne	362	Palmer	28
Thou, that wouldst finde the habit of true passion,	362	Author	1
Those that in blood such violent pleasure have,	363	Murder	1
That Natures fairest Creature,	364	Phoenix	6
That part nor Winde,	366	Ode Who saith	28
The Vale, that bred thee pure, as her Hills Snow.	367	Ode Who saith	40
That late were out.	367	Ode Who saith	46
That heard but Spight deliver	367	Ode Who saith	58
The Danes that drench	368	Ode Who saith	86
To loose that feare;	369	Ode Who saith	94
But should they know (as I) that this,	369	Ode Who saith	97
But now, your Worke is done, if they that view	370	Author	9
The wise, and many-headed Bench, that sits	370	Fletcher	1
Lady, or Pusil, that weares maske, or fan,	370	Fletcher	4
That may judge for his six-pence) had, before	371	Fletcher	7
I, that am glad, thy Innocence was thy Guilt,	371	Fletcher	11
And wish that all the Muses blood were spilt,	371	Fletcher	12
Read here a little, that thou mayst know much.	371	Epitaph	2
That durst be that in Court: a vertu' alone	371	Epitaph	4
It should rather have bene Tom that a horse did lack.	374	Coryat 1	15
Of Tom of Odcombe that odde Joviall Author,	378	Coryat 2	87
And that, say Philosophers, is the best modell.	379	Coryat 3	5
Of our Odcombian, that literate Elfe?	379	Coryat 3	7
And that you may see he most luckily ment	379	Coryat 3	13
But who will beleeve this, that chanceth to looke	379	Coryat 3	17
That he dares to informe you, but somewhat meticulous,	380	Coryat 3	33
That sacred to Odcombe are there now suspended,	380	Coryat 3	40
I meane that one paire, wherewith he so hobled	380	Coryat 3	41
So not them, his scabbes, lice, or the stewes,	380	Coryat 3	50
Or any thing else that another should hide,	380	Coryat 3	51
still that same little poynte hee was; but when	383	Rich	13
And clothes, and guifts, that only do thee grace	384	Somerset	2
That bid, God give thee joy, and have no endes.	384	Somerset	6
Out-bee that Wife, in worth, thy freind did make:	384	Somerset	12
And thou to her, that Husband, may exalt	384	Somerset	13
That all, that view you then, and late; may say,	384	Somerset	25
It fits not onely him that makes a Booke,	385	Husband	1
To see his worke be good; but that he looke	385	Husband	2
I do not feele that ever yet I had	385	Husband	5

	Page	Title	Line
THAT (cont.)			
That went before, a Husband. Shee, Ile sweare,	386	Husband	9
It must be thine owne judgment, yet, that sends	386	Browne	7
This thy worke forth: that judgment mine commends.	386	Browne	8
On credit, and are cossen'd; see, that thou	386	Browne	11
to which there's no materiall that endures;	387	Cavendish	8
nor yet inscription like it. Write but that;	387	Cavendish	9
nor yet inscription like it writt but that	387	Cavendish V	9
If all the vulgar Tongues, that speake this day,	388	Chapman	7
Shall finde, that either hath read Bookes, and Men:	389	Aleman	2
That an ill man dares not securely looke	389	Aleman	8
And this hath met that one, that may be stil'd	389	Aleman	13
But that hee's too well suted, in a cloth,	389	Aleman	17
That would have done, that, which you onely can.	389	Aleman	24
This Figure, that thou here seest put,	390	Reader	1
All, that was ever writ in brasse.	390	Reader	8
That I not mixe thee so, my braine excuses;	391	Shakespeare	25
Of all, that insolent Greece, or haughtie Rome	391	Shakespeare	39
His Art doth give the fashion. And, that he,	392	Shakespeare	58
(And himselfe with it) that he thinkes to frame;	392	Shakespeare	62
That so did take Eliza, and our James!	392	Shakespeare	74
To the memorye of that most Honoured Ladie Jane,	394	Jane Ogle	Ttl
I Could begin with that grave forme, Here lies,	394	Jane Ogle	1
So wood at last, that he was wonne to her	394	Jane Ogle	22
Lend me thy voyce, O Fame, that I may draw	396	Drayton	12
That all Earth look'd on; and that earth, all Eyes!	396	Drayton	16
I thought thee then our Orpheus, that wouldst try	397	Drayton	35
My lippes could forme the voyce, I heard that Rore,	397	Drayton	38
That Rebells actions, are but valiant crimes!	397	Drayton	44
Of all that reade thy Poly-Olbyon.	397	Drayton	52
That reade it? that are ravish'd! such was I	397	Drayton	53
But that I heare, againe, thy Drum to beate	397	Drayton	55
That ever yet did fire the English blood!	397	Drayton	57
Brave are the Musters, that the Muse will make.	398	Drayton	64
That can but reade; who cannot, may in prose	398	Drayton	73
I feele it by mine owne, that over flow,	398	Drayton	77
As, on two flowry Carpets, that did rise,	398	Drayton	81
Onely my losse is, that I am not there:	398	Drayton	91
I call the world, that envies mee, to see	398	Drayton	93
T'Is a Record in heaven. You, that were	399	Lady Ogle	1
All that was solid, in the name	399	Lady Ogle	17
That Art, or Ingine, on the strength can raise.	400	Beaumont	10
That, while they bind the senses, doe so please?	401	Filmer	2
Mr Surveyor, you that first begann	402	Inigo Jones 1	1
The noblest Ingenyre that ever was!	402	Inigo Jones 1	6
I chyme that too: And I have mett with those	403	Inigo Jones 1	31
That doe cry up the Machine, & the Showes!	403	Inigo Jones 1	32
Not they that sided her, Dame Poetry,	403	Inigo Jones 1	36
Eyes that can pierce into the Misteryes	404	Inigo Jones 1	46
What would he doe now, gi'ng his mynde that waye	405	Inigo Jones 1	75
Expression for! with that unbounded lyne	406	Inigo Jones 1	95
That might compare with thee? what story shall	406	Inigo Jones 1	98
(And labours to seem worthy of that feare)	407	Inigo Jones 3	2
That I should wryte upon him some sharp verse,	407	Inigo Jones 3	3
Seek out some hungry painter, that for bread	408	Inigo Jones 3	10
That sit upon the Comon Draught: or Strand!	408	Inigo Jones 3	13
That thou hast lost thy noyse, thy foame, thy stirre,	408	Detractor	8
That knew the Crafts they had bin bred in, right:	410	Brome	14
To top the fairest Lillie, now, that growes,	413	Ghyrlond	15
But, that which summes all, is the Eglantine,	413	Ghyrlond	21
Inflam'd with ardor to that mystick Shine,	413	Ghyrlond	23
Alike of kin, to that most blessed Trine,	413	Ghyrlond	34
That sit to censure Playes, yet know not when,	414	Rutter	8
Our first of fruits, that is the prime of flowers	416	Welcome	2
those turnd up, and those that fall,	417	Moon	14
morts, and mirkins that wagg all,	417	Moon	15
that the wife heades for a wager	417	Moon	26
That lives, and breath's, and loves the King.	418	Grace	4
That the King loves, and loves the King.	418	Grace V	4
Of that true Face	419	Ode:If Men	2
that Fortune to imbrace,	419	Ode:If Men	4
By Cherissheinge the Spirrits that gave their greatnesse grace:	419	Ode:If Men	5
That were the happie subject of my songe.	419	Ode:If Men	9
Of Civill virtue, that hee now is not	420	Ode:If Men	12
That hath not Countrye impudence enough to laughe att Arte,	420	Ode:If Men	14
To every sence, and scorne to those that sawe	420	Ode:If Men	17
Thou that doest spend thie dayes	420	Ode:If Men	24
Hee that soe Censureth, or adviseth synns,	421	Censure	4
Little knowne they that proffesse Amitye	421	Censure	12
And lesse they knowe, that being free to use	422	Censure	15
That Frindshipp, which noe Chaunce, but Love did Chuse,	422	Censure	16
Will unto Lycence, that free Leave Abuse;	422	Censure	17
the sword, but that it acteth what it list.	423	Lucan	14
he that will honest be, may quitt the Court,	423	Lucan	17
That prince that shames a tyrants name to beare,	423	Lucan	19
That sits watering with the Muses.	657	Door Apollo	10
Lucy of Bedford; she, that Bounty	662	Bedford	3
appropriates still unto that County:	662	Bedford	4
Tell her, his Muse that did invent thee	662	Bedford	5
And sworne, that he will quite discard thee	662	Bedford	7
that it remayne with him	666	Glover	6
THAT'S			
That's greater, yet: to crie his owne up neate.	35	E28 Surly	11

	Page	Title	Line
THAT'S (cont.)			
He drinkes to no man: that's, too, like a lord.	35	E28 Surly	14
But that's put in, thou'lt say. Why, so is thine.	36	E29 Tilter	6
Is it the paine affrights? that's soone forgot.	46	E62 Would-bee	5
That's, sit, and eate: doe not my eares abuse.	68	E107 Hungry	2
Where vertue makes them both, and that's in thee:	70	E109 Nevil	3
On some new gesture, that's imputed wit?	81	E129 Mime	14
That's a Toy, that I could spare:	142	U2 Exception	2
For that's a narrow joy is but our owne.	147	U7 Nymph	7
So each, that's done, and tane, becomes a Brace.	154	U13 Sacvile	40
See him, that's call'd, and thought the happiest man,	162	U15 Friend-Wars	23
I, that's a Charme and halfe! She must afford	163	U15 Friend-Wars	52
But he that's both, and slave to boote, shall live,	167	U15 Friend-Wars	160
But he that's both, and slave to both, shall live,	167	U15 Friend-Wars	V160
And then with pause; for sever'd once, that's gone,	192	U38 Elegy 'Tis	47
You would restore it? No, that's worth a feare,	199	U41 Elegy Since	15
But that's a marke, wherof thy Rites doe boast,	205	U43 Vulcan	57
But he that's too-much that, is friend of none.	216	U45 Squib	24
But that's a blow, by which in time I may	219	U47 Tribe	51
That's six in silver; now within the Socket	229	U54 Squib	13
And that's made up as doth the purse abound.	230	U56 Covell	12
Stay, drop a teare for him that's dead,	233	U60 La-ware	2
These make the lines of life, and that's her ayre.	245	U70 Ode	64
Our selves, and all that's ours, to death we owe:	309	Horace	90
Hee, that's ambitious in the race to touch	333	Horace	587
They're darke, bid cleare this: all that's doubtfull wrote	335	Horace	637
They're dark, bid cleare 'hem; al that's doubtful wrote	354	Horace	V637
TH'AUTHORS			
If workes (not th'authors) their owne grace should looke,	60	E94 Bedford 3	3
T'HAVE			
Thou wert, as chiefe of them are said t'have beene.	28	E4 James 1	6
Contends t'have worth enjoy, from his regard,	48	E64 Salisbury 3	13
Which boasts t'have had the head of gold.	98	F3 Wroth	64
T'have held a Triumph, or a feast of fire,	205	U43 Vulcan	60
T'have wak'd, if sleeping, Spaines Ambassadour,	213	U44 Speach	4
Was, t'have a Boy stand with a Club, and fright	241	U69 Friend Son	11
Her language, if the Stay, and Care t'have mended,	325	Horace	413
She might have claym'd t'have made the Graces foure;	371	Epitaph	6
THAWES			
It thawes the frostiest, and most stiffe disdaine:	363	Riches	13
TH'BEST			
To Th'Best Of Monarchs, Masters, Men, King Charles	259	U76 Petition	2
TH'CALENDS			
At th'Calends, puts all out againe.	291	U85 Country	70
TH'			
Who scarse can spell th'hard names: whose knight lesse can.	28	E3 Bookseller	10
But see! th'old baud hath serv'd him in his trim,	31	E12 Shift	23
Th'expence in odours is a most vaine sinne,	33	E20 Cod 2	1
Th'observing neighbours no such mood can see.	40	E42 Giles	2
A treasure, art: contemn'd in th'age of gold.	47	E64 Salisbury 3	4
Upon th'accompt, hers grew the quicker trade.	56	E87 Hazard	5
In th'eye of Europe, where thy deeds were done,	58	E91 Vere	6
If workes (not th'authors) their owne grace should looke,	60	E94 Bedford 3	3
Nor are the Queenes most honor'd maides by th'eares	63	E97 Motion	18
Cry'd to my face, they were th'elixir of wit:	64	E100 Playwrt 3	2
If dancing, all would cry th'Idalian Queene,	68	E105 L Wroth 2	11
I' your selfe, all treasure lost of th'age before.	68	E105 L Wroth 2	20
What th'antique souldiers were, the moderne bee?	72	E111 Edmonds 2	2
Parts, then th'Italian could doe, with his dore.	74	E115 Honest Man	26
Of miming, gets th'opinion of a wit.	74	E115 Honest Man	28
Th'other let it sleepe with death:	79	E124 Elizabeth	10
And bad me lay th'usurped laurell downe:	80	E126 Mrs Cary	4
Shee brought the Poets forth, but ours th'adventer.	84	E133 Voyage	20
To answere me. And sure, it was th'intent	87	E133 Voyage	107
That for th'oyle of Talke, dare spend	105	F8 Sicknesse	33
At th'eye and eare (the ports unto the minde)	109	F11 Epode	9
Who (in th'examining)	109	F11 Epode	14
Not taken up o' th' doctors, but as well	117	F13 Aubigny	33
The Sonne of God, th'Eternall King,	130	U1 Nativitie	7
With th'advantage of her haire,	138	U2 Kisse	10
Of th'Assembly, as did you!	138	U2 Kisse	12
Yea, of th'ingratefull: and he forth must tell	155	U13 Sacvile	77
Man out their Boates to th' Temple, and not shift	155	U13 Sacvile	83
Looke on th'ambitious man, and see him nurse	162	U15 Friend-Wars	11
Are all th'Aonian springs	174	U23 Himselfe	7
Varietie of Silkes were on th'Exchange!	202	U42 Elegy Let	72
Th'Esplandians, Arthurs, Palmerins, and all	203	U43 Vulcan	30
Upon th'Exchange, still, out of Popes-head-Alley;	206	U43 Vulcan	80
Th'admir'd discourses of the Prophet Ball:	206	U43 Vulcan	82
Th'admir'd discourses of the Profit Ball:	206	U43 Vulcan	V 82
Th'admir'd discourses of the Prophet Baal:	206	U43 Vulcan	V 82
With all th'adventures; Three bookes not afraid	207	U43 Vulcan	95
With all th'adventures; Three bookes not amisse	207	U43 Vulcan	V 95
As th'other may his braines with Quicksilver.	208	U43 Vulcan	122
Thy just defences made th' oppressor afraid.	217	U46 Coke	8
Or th'other on their borders, that will jeast	218	U47 Tribe	16
That censure all the Towne, and all th'affaires	218	U47 Tribe	23
Upon th'affrighted world:	243	U70 Ode	16
On th'often comming of this Holy-day:	249	U72 King	16
And all did ring th'approches of the Bride;	253	U75 Epithalam.	36
They are th'exampled Paire, and mirrour of their kind.	255	U75 Epithalam.	80
To th' dull, a Spur	256	U75 Epithalam.	118
It is: to th' envious meant,	256	U75 Epithalam.	119

TH' (cont.)
    Th'Ignoble never liv'd, they were a-while   .   .   .   257 U75 Epithalam.   153
    To Th'Best Of Monarchs, Masters, Men, King Charles   .   259 U76 Petition   2
    Where ere they tread th'enamour'd ground,   .   .   .   264 U79 New-yeares   36
    At least may beare th'inscription to her Tombe.   .   .   269 U81 Pawlet   18
    Till swept away, th'were cancell'd with a broome!   .   282 U84 Muse   8
    One corporall, only; th'other spirituall,   .   .   .   284 U84 Muse   52
    For th'eating Thrush, or Pit-falls sets: .   .   .   290 U85 Country   34
    Th'Ionian God-wit, nor the Ginny hen   .   .   .   .   291 U85 Country   53
    'Gainst th'Ides, his moneys he gets in with paine,   .   291 U85 Country   69
    'Gainst th'Ides, his gott moneyes he gets in with paine,   291 U85 Country   V 69
    At th'Calends, puts all out againe.   .   .   .   .   291 U85 Country   70
    If in th'escape an artlesse path we tread.   .   .   .   339 Horace   V 46/ 44
    Th'Aemilian Schoole, in brasse can fashion out   .   .   307 Horace   46
    Th'Iambick arm'd Archilochus to rave, ...   311 Horace   117
    'Tis not enough, th'elaborate Muse affords   .   .   .   311 Horace   140
    And sits, till th'Epilogue saies Clap, or Crowne;   .   315 Horace   222
    Th'unbearded Youth, his Guardian once being gone,   .   315 Horace   229
    ill-/Natur'd, and wicked Atreus cooke, to th'eye,   .   317 Horace   265
    Hide faults, and pray to th'gods, and wish aloud   .   345 Horace   V285
    From what th'obscene, and petulant Satyres are.   .   321 Horace   340
    Two rests, a short and long, th'Iambick frame;   .   .   323 Horace   371
    A lawfull Verse, by th'eare, or finger scan.   .   .   323 Horace   404
    till th'one hath drownd the other in our sightes,   .   361 Palmer   20
    Yet neyther of you seeme to th'other old.   .   .   .   384 Somerset   24
    If Praises, when th'are full, heaping admit,   .   .   385 Brooke   6
    Upon th'Exchange of Letters, as I wou'd   .   .   .   386 Browne   14
    With the how much they set forth, but th'how well.   .   386 Browne   16
    Above th'ill fortune of them, or the need.   .   .   .   391 Shakespeare   16
    Are still th'interpreters twixt godds, and men!   .   395 May   18
    Th'ascent of Lady Fame which none could spy   .   .   403 Inigo Jones 1   35
    Th'envy'd returne, of forty pound in gold.   .   .   .   408 Detractor   4
    And in them view'd th'uncertainty of Life,   .   .   .   411 Sutcliffe   3
    Our great reward, th'aeternall Crown to win.   .   .   412 Sutcliffe   19
    A Master-worker call'd, th'old standerd burst   .   .   415 Rutter   22
THE'
    Must trie the'un-used valour of a nose: .   .   .   87 E133 Voyage   132
    The'Elixir of all joyes?   .   .   .   .   110 F11 Epode   56
THEAME
    Is but a Statists theame, to read Phlebotomie.   .   .   179 U25 Desmond   39
    Make State, Religion, Bawdrie, all a theame?   .   .   222 U49 Pucell   12
TH'EARE
    A lawfull Verse, by th'eare, or finger scan.   .   .   323 Horace   404
TH'EARES
    Nor are the Queenes most honor'd maides by th'eares   .   63 E97 Motion   18
TH'EATING
    For th'eating Thrush, or Pit-falls sets: .   .   .   290 U85 Country   34
THEATRE
    Shall meet with gladnesse in one Theatre;   .   .   .   285 U84 Muse   114
THEBAN
    Amphion, too, that built the Theban towres,   .   .   327 Horace   483
THEBES
    Or, with the milke of Thebes; or Argus, fed.   .   .   313 Horace   168
THEE
    Pray thee, take care, that tak'st my booke in hand,   .   27 E1 Reader   1
    Use mine so, too: I give thee leave. But crave   .   27 E3 Bookseller   3
    And gave thee both, to shew they could no more.   .   28 E4 James 1   4
    From my diseases danger, and from thee.   .   .   .   31 E13 Empirick   4
    Then the the age sees not that thing more grave,   .   31 E14 Camden   5
    Which conquers all, be once over-come by thee.   .   .   31 E14 Camden   12
    Scarse thy weekes swearing brings thee of, of one.   .   32 E16 Brain-hardy   4
    And, but a sprigge of bayes, given by thee,   .   .   32 E17 Critic   5
    To thee, my way in Epigrammes seemes new,   .   .   .   32 E18 Censurer   1
    As theirs did with thee, mine might credit get: .   32 E18 Censurer   6
    Pr'y thee beleeve still, and not judge so fast,   .   32 E18 Censurer   9
    Stile thee a most great foole, but no great man.   .   36 E28 Surly   22
    Tilter, the most may'admire thee, though not I: .   36 E29 Tilter   1
    'Twere madnesse in thee, to betray thy fame,   .   .   36 E30 Guiltie   3
    Ile not offend thee with a vaine teare more,   .   .   37 E33 Roe 3   1
    And since, the whole land was preserv'd for thee.   .   38 E35 James 2   10
    But in my royall subject I passe thee,   .   .   .   38 E36 Martial   3
    A dead beautie under-neath thee, ...   39 E40 Ratcliffe   2
    Rich, as nature could bequeath thee: .   .   .   .   39 E40 Ratcliffe   3
    Her foes enough would fame thee in their hate.   .   .   40 E43 Salisbury 1   4
    I, not the worst, am covetous of thee.   .   .   .   40 E43 Salisbury 1   6
    My sinne was too much hope of thee, lov'd boy,   .   41 E45 First Son   2
    Seven yeeres tho'wert lent to me, and I thee pay,   .   41 E45 First Son   3
    Arsenike would thee fit for societie make.   .   .   42 E50 Cod 3   3
    Long-gathering Old-end, I did feare thee wise,   .   43 E53 Old-end   1
    Could save that line to dedicate to thee?   .   .   .   44 E53 Old-end   10
    How I doe love thee Beaumont, and thy Muse,   .   .   44 E55 Beaumont   1
    For writing better, I must envie thee.   .   .   .   44 E55 Beaumont   10
    Ideot, last night, I pray'd thee but forbeare   .   .   45 E58 Groome   1
    But saver of my countrey thee alone.   .   .   .   .   46 E60 Mounteagle   10
    The judgement of the king so shine in thee;   .   .   47 E63 Salisbury 2   4
    To see thy fathers rites new laid on thee.   .   .   .   47 E64 Salisbury 3   6
    With me thou leav'st an happier Muse then thee,   .   48 E65 Muse   11
    To greatnesse, Cary, I sing that, and thee.   .   .   48 E66 Cary   2
    In onely thee, might be both great, and glad.   .   .   48 E66 Cary   4
    Could conquer thee, but chance, who did betray.   .   49 E66 Cary   10
    What is't, fine Grand, makes thee my friendship flye,   51 E73 Fine Grand   1
    And know thee, then, a judge, not of one yeare;   .   51 E74 Chancelor   2
    Whil'st I behold thee live with purest hands;   .   .   51 E74 Chancelor   3

THEE (cont.)

	Page	Title	Line
T'our times return'd, hath made her heaven in thee.	52	E74 Chancelor	10
I'am more asham'd to have thee thought my foe.	53	E77 Not name	4
To draw thee custome: but her selfe gets all.	53	E78 Hornet	2
A line unto thee, till the world it know;	54	E81 Proule	2
When I would know thee Goodyere, my thought lookes	55	E86 Goodyere 2	1
Then doe I love thee, and behold thy ends	55	E86 Goodyere 2	3
That, Allen, I should pause to publish thee?	57	E89 Allen	8
Who did, alike with thee, thy house up-beare,	60	E93 Radcliffe	3
Willing to expiate the fault in thee,	60	E93 Radcliffe	15
In thee, most weighty Savile, liv'd to us:	61	E95 Savile	4
For who can master those great parts like thee,	61	E95 Savile	17
When I dare send my Epigrammes to thee?	62	E96 Donne 2	2
Thy fact is more: let truth encourage thee.	64	E99 Th Roe 2	12
I Doe but name thee Pembroke, and I find	66	E102 Pembroke	1
Both which are ask'd, to have thee understood.	66	E102 Pembroke	4
Nor could the age have mist thee, in this strife	66	E102 Pembroke	5
The common-wealth still safe, must studie thee.	66	E102 Pembroke	20
And yet, they, all together, lesse then thee.	68	E106 E Herbert	10
Who now calls on thee, Nevil, is a Muse,	70	E109 Nevil	1
Where vertue makes them both, and that's in thee:	70	E109 Nevil	3
Now I have sung thee thus, shall judge of thee.	70	E109 Nevil	16
And thence, deprave thee, and thy worke. To those	72	E111 Edmonds 2	11
They murder him againe, that envie thee.	72	E111 Edmonds 2	14
I leave thee there, and giving way, entend	72	E112 Gamster	9
Where shall I scape thee? in an Epigramme?	73	E112 Gamster	15
Pr'y thee, yet save thy rest; give ore in time:	73	E112 Gamster	21
There's no vexation, that can make thee prime.	73	E112 Gamster	22
As but to speake thee, Overbury, is praise:	73	E113 Overbury	2
Where, what makes others great, doth keepe thee good!	73	E113 Overbury	4
Repent thee not of thy faire precedent,	73	E113 Overbury	9
Who'in such ambition can but follow thee.	73	E113 Overbury	12
Them in, if not, from thee; or must commit	75	E116 Jephson	15
No, Shelton, give me thee, canst want all these,	76	E119 Shelton	7
I need no other arts, but studie thee:	78	E122 Rudyerd 2	9
If I should faile, in gratitude, to thee,	80	E127 Aubigny	2
By her attempt, shall still be owing thee.	80	E127 Aubigny	10
Attend thee hence; and there, may all thy ends,	81	E128 Wm Roe 2	6
Thy selfe, with thy first thoughts, brought home by thee,	81	E128 Wm Roe 2	10
But the first question is, when one saw thee?	81	E129 Mime	2
Men love thee not for this: They laugh at thee.	81	E129 Mime	18
Shed in thy Songs; 'tis true: but short of thee.	82	E130 Ferrab. 1	18
Say, this, or that man they to thee preferre;	83	E131 Ferrab. 2	9
Might then both thee, thy worke and merit raise:	83	E132 Sylvester	2
And art a god, if Fame thee not abuses,	85	E133 Voyage	53
That never failes to serve thee season'd deere,	94	F2 Penshurst	20
Each banke doth yeeld thee coneyes; and the topps	94	F2 Penshurst	25
Thou hast thy ponds, that pay thee tribute fish,	94	F2 Penshurst	32
Now, Penshurst, they that will proportion thee	96	F2 Penshurst	99
That neither want doe thee affright,	100	F3 Wroth	104
That neither want should thee affright,	100	F3 Wroth	V104
Hence-forth I quit thee from my thought,	100	F4 To the World	3
That onely fooles make thee a saint,	100	F4 To the World	15
As little, as I hope from thee:	101	F4 To the World	38
'Pray thee, feed contented, then,	105	F8 Sicknesse	13
And, for thee, at common game,	105	F8 Sicknesse	41
These, disease, will thee deserve:	106	F8 Sicknesse	43
I sent thee, late, a rosie wreath,	106	F9 Celia 3	9
I sent to thee a rosie wreath,	106	F9 Celia 3	V 9
Not so much honoring thee,	106	F9 Celia 3	10
Not so to honor thee,	106	F9 Celia 3	V 10
Not of it selfe, but thee.	106	F9 Celia 3	16
Not like it selfe, but thee.	106	F9 Celia 3	V 16
Shall not give out, that I have made thee stay,	107	F10 Proludium	8
Shall not give out, that we have made thee stay,	107	F10 Proludium	V 8
Nor will I beg of thee, Lord of the vine,	107	F10 Proludium	10
Nor will we beg of thee, Lord of the vine,	107	F10 Proludium	V 10
Pallas, nor thee I call on, mankinde maid,	107	F10 Proludium	13
Pallas, nor thee we call on, mankinde maid,	107	F10 Proludium	V 13
No, vice, we let thee know,	111	F11 Epode	72
No, vice, I let thee know,	111	F11 Epode	V 72
Good, and great God, can I not thinke of thee,	122	F15 Heaven	1
Where have I beene this while exil'd from thee?	122	F15 Heaven	13
How can I doubt to finde thee ever, here?	122	F15 Heaven	16
For wearinesse of life, not love of thee.	122	F15 Heaven	26
My selfe up to thee, harrow'd, torne, and bruis'd	127	U1 Trinitie	5
To thee more sweet?	127	U1 Trinitie	16
To worship thee.	127	U1 Trinitie	20
My selfe and thee.	129	U1 Father	11
Goe, get thee quickly forth,	150	U10 Jealousie	13
I first salute thee so; and gratulate,	161	U14 Selden	67
I'le bid thee looke no more, but flee, flee friend,	166	U15 Friend-Wars	129
Light thee from hell on earth: where flatterers, spies,	167	U15 Friend-Wars	163
Goe, quit 'hem all. And take along with thee,	167	U15 Friend-Wars	175
That fortune never make thee to complaine,	168	U15 Friend-Wars	183
Let this thought quicken thee,	174	U23 Himselfe	15
Who aided him, will thee, the issue of Joves braine.	175	U23 Himselfe	30
Who aided them, will thee, the issue of Joves braine.	175	U23 Himselfe	V 30
Thy beauties, yet could write of thee?	181	U27 Ode Helen	2
He that first invented thee,	184	U29 Fit of Rime	49
And not being borrow'd by thee, but possest.	187	U33 Councellour	28
Thy sincere practise, breeds not thee a fame	187	U33 Councellour	39
One beautie in an Age, and free from thee?	188	U34 Small Poxe	2

THEE (cont.)

	Page	Title		Line
None of their pleasures! nor will aske thee, why	202	U42	Elegy Let	86
With Clownes, and Tradesmen, kept thee clos'd in horne.	203	U43	Vulcan	8
'Twas Jupiter that hurl'd thee headlong downe,	203	U43	Vulcan	9
'Twas Jupiter that cast thee headlong downe,	203	U43	Vulcan	V 9
And Mars, that gave thee a Lanthorne for a Crowne.	203	U43	Vulcan	10
By thy owne vote, a sacrifice to thee?	203	U43	Vulcan	22
With lust conceiv'd thee; Father thou hadst none.	208	U43	Vulcan	112
She durst not kisse, but flung thee from her brest.	208	U43	Vulcan	114
And so did Jove, who ne're meant thee his Cup:	208	U43	Vulcan	115
No mar'le the Clownes of Lemnos tooke thee up,	208	U43	Vulcan	116
For none but Smiths would have made thee a God.	208	U43	Vulcan	117
Made thee beget that cruell Stratagem,	208	U43	Vulcan	130
I will not argue thee, from those, of guilt,	210	U43	Vulcan	165
I will not argue thee, from them, of guilt,	210	U43	Vulcan	V165
I will not argue thee Iron. Them of guilt	210	U43	Vulcan	V165
Pox on thee, Vulcan, thy Pandora's pox,	212	U43	Vulcan	213
Light on thee: Or if those plagues will not doo,	212	U43	Vulcan	215
Light upon thee: Or if those plagues will not doo,	212	U43	Vulcan	V215
Thy Wives pox on thee, and B.B.'s too.	212	U43	Vulcan	216
Thy Wives pox on thee, and Bess Broughtons too.	212	U43	Vulcan	V216
More then the surfets, in thee, that day stood.	214	U44	Speach	48
Whilst I informe my selfe, I would teach thee,	216	U45	Squib	2
Friend to himselfe, that would be friend to thee.	216	U45	Squib	22
He could not find, then thee, of all that store	217	U46	Coke	3
And skill in thee, now, grew Authoritie;	217	U46	Coke	10
Of Wines, to thee the rather	220	U48	Bacchus	2
And seale thee thy Commission	220	U48	Bacchus	5
Thee still, and leave Apollo,	221	U48	Bacchus	26
Pursue thee in all places,	221	U48	Bacchus	34
Shall I advise thee, Pucell? steale away	223	U49	Pucell	35
How comes it all things so about thee smile?	225	U51	Bacon	2
Verse, that should thee, and me out-live.	229	U55	Burges	4
Thou, Friend, wilt heare all censures; unto thee	232	U58	Book-seller	1
How much to heaven for thee, great Charles, they owe!	237	U64	Charles 3	22
That thus hath crown'd our hopes, with thee, our Spring & May,	237	U65	Prince	V 2
Thee quickly come the gardens eye to bee,	238	U65	Prince	8
Did wiser Nature draw thee back,	243	U70	Ode	11
Did wisest Nature draw thee back,	243	U70	Ode	V 11
No doubt all Infants would returne like thee.	243	U70	Ode	20
Why doe I irritate, or stirre up thee,	250	U73	Weston	7
We wooe thee, stay	252	U75	Epithalam.	6
Busie, or frowne at first; when he sees thee,	262	U78	Digby	20
And hunting, Pan, exceedeth thee.	265	U79	New-yeares	55
And hunting, Pan, exceedeth thee.	265	U79	New-yeares	67
How much they are belov'd of God, in thee;	268	U80	Christning	4
By Thee, and Conscience, both who thrive	273	U84	Cradle	7
In thee, faire Mansion, let it rest,	281	U84	Mind	69
Beene trusted to thee: not to't selfe assign'd.	283	U84	Muse	20
Long intermitted, pray thee, pray thee spare:	292	U86	Hor.4:1	2
Goe where Youths soft intreaties call thee back.	292	U86	Hor.4:1	8
More timely hie thee to the house,	292	U86	Hor.4:1	9
With thee 'bove all his Rivals gifts take place,	292	U86	Hor.4:1	18
He'll thee a Marble Statue make	292	U86	Hor.4:1	19
I hold thee fast! but fled hence, with the Light,	293	U86	Hor.4:1	38
Or Tybers winding streames, I follow thee.	293	U86	Hor.4:1	40
Whilst, Lydia, I was lov'd of thee,	293	U87	Hor.3:9	1
Yet would I wish to love, live, die with thee.	294	U87	Hor.3:9	24
Not labour'd for, but left thee by thy Sire;	295	U90	Mart.10:47	3
What's this? if he whose money hireth thee	305		Horace	26
Honour'd Achilles chance by thee be seiz'd,	313		Horace	171
Forbids thee forth againe thy foot to draw.	313		Horace	194
The Vale, that bred thee pure, as her Hills Snow.	367		Ode Who saith	40
Tames, prowde of thee, and of his Fate	368		Ode Who saith	81
Rather his sonne, I should have cal'd thee, why?	378		Coryat 2	88
Poore Tom have we cause to suspect just thee?	381		Coryat 3	58
unto thee, king of men; their noblest partes	382		Rich	3
And clothes, and guifts, that only do thee grace	384		Somerset	2
Do wayte upon thee: and theyre Love not bought.	384		Somerset	4
That bid, God give thee joy, and have no endes.	384		Somerset	6
My suffrage brings thee all increase, to crowne	385		Brooke	7
But I have seene thy worke, and I know thee:	386		Browne	3
I find thee write most worthy to be read.	386		Browne	6
More of our writers would like thee, not swell	386		Browne	15
My Shakespeare, rise; I will not lodge thee by	391		Shakespeare	19
A little further, to make thee a roome:	391		Shakespeare	21
That I not mixe thee so, my braine excuses;	391		Shakespeare	25
I should commit thee surely with thy peeres,	391		Shakespeare	28
From thence to honour thee, I would not seeke	391		Shakespeare	32
Leave thee alone, for the comparison	391		Shakespeare	38
To see thee in our waters yet appeare,	392		Shakespeare	72
But stay, I see thee in the Hemisphere	392		Shakespeare	75
And pray thee Reader, bring thy weepinge Eyes	394		Jane Ogle	2
But, I would have, thee, to know something new,	394		Jane Ogle	13
When, Rome, I reade thee in thy mighty paire,	395		May	1
A Friend at all; or, if at all, to thee:	396		Drayton	2
Heard the soft ayres, between our Swaynes & thee,	397		Drayton	26
I thought thee then our Orpheus, that wouldst try	397		Drayton	35
And I had stil'd thee, Orpheus, but before	397		Drayton	37
There, thou art Homer! Pray thee, use the stile	398		Drayton	59
I gratulate it to thee, and thy Ends,	398		Drayton	89
If I can be a Friend, and Friend to thee.	398		Drayton	94
That might compare with thee? what story shall	406		Inigo Jones 1	98

THEE (cont.)

	Page	Title	Line
Our Charles should make thee such? 'Twill not become	406	Inigo Jones 2	3
A Noble honest Soule! what's this to thee?	406	Inigo Jones 2	6
Content thee to be Pancridge Earle the whyle;	407	Inigo Jones 2	20
Wee'll have thee styld the Marquess of New-Ditch.	407	Inigo Jones 2	24
Wee'll have thee styld the Marquess of Town-Ditch.	407	Inigo Jones 2	V 24
The Marrow! Wretch, I quitt thee of thy paine	408	Inigo Jones 3	5
Will well designe thee, to be viewd of all	408	Inigo Jones 3	12
But bawle thou on; I pitty thee, poore Curre,	408	Detractor	7
I now would write on thee? No, wretch; thy name	409	Detractor	11
No man will tarry by thee, as hee goes,	409	Detractor	17
But fly thee, like the Pest! Walke not the street	409	Detractor	19
I'll laugh at thee poor wretched Tike, go send	410	Gill	10
For thou hast nought in thee to cure his Fame,	411	Gill	13
But I can tell thee, Dover, how thy Games	415	Dover	3
to gett thee a leane Face,	420	Ode:If Men	25
Tell her, his Muse that did invent thee	662	Bedford	5
to Cynthias fayrest Nymph hath sent thee,	662	Bedford	6
And sworne, that he will quite discard thee	662	Bedford	7
if any way she do rewarde thee	662	Bedford	8

THEEFE

	Page	Title	Line
The theefe from spoyle, his presence holds.	265	U79 New-yeares	63

THE'ELIXIR

	Page	Title	Line
The'Elixir of all joyes?	110	F11 Epode	56

THEFT

	Page	Title	Line
But the sweet theft to reveale:	102	F5 Celia 1	16

THEIR (See also THERE, THEYR)

	Page	Title	Line
Deceive their malice, who could wish it so.	27	E2 My Booke	7
But two things, rare, the Fates had in their store,	28	E4 James 1	3
But for their powers, accept my pietie.	31	E14 Camden	14
What severall wayes men to their calling have!	33	E21 Gam'ster	7
Mary, the daughter of their youth:	33	E22 Daughter	2
If any Muse out-live their spight, his can;	35	E27 Roe 1	4
Her foes enough would fame thee in their hate.	40	E43 Salisbury 1	4
If, as their ends, their fruits were so, the same,	45	E57 Bawds	1
Came not that soule exhausted so their store.	53	E79 Rutland	4
Till they be sure to make the foole their quarrie.	55	E85 Goodyere 1	10
Who had no lesse a trumpet of their name,	57	E89 Allen	5
Who both their graces in thy selfe hast more	57	E89 Allen	9
Ripe are their ruffes, their cuffes, their beards, their gate,	58	E92 New Crie	6
And grave as ripe, like mellow as their faces.	59	E92 New Crie	7
They carry in their pockets Tacitus,	59	E92 New Crie	15
At naming the French King, their heads they shake,	59	E92 New Crie	33
Thou, that art all their valour, all their spirit,	60	E93 Radcliffe	9
Life of the Muses day, their morning-starre!	60	E94 Bedford 3	2
If workes (not th'authors) their owne grace should looke,	60	E94 Bedford 3	3
Crowne with their owne. Rare poemes aske rare friends.	60	E94 Bedford 3	6
Their un-avoided subject, fewest see:	60	E94 Bedford 3	8
The Muses evening, as their morning-starre.	61	E94 Bedford 3	16
Of historie, and how to apt their places;	61	E95 Savile	28
And, till they burst, their backs, like asses load:	62	E96 Donne 2	11
Their lives, as doe their lines, till now had lasted.	65	E101 Supper	32
But in the view, doth interrupt their sinne:	66	E102 Pembroke	18
But even their names were to be made a-new,	67	E105 L Wroth 2	5
Their latter praise would still the greatest bee,	68	E106 E Herbert	9
How great you were with their two Emperours;	68	E107 Hungry	6
And yet are with their Princes: Fill them full	69	E107 Hungry	7
Whil'st others toyle for titles to their tombes.	70	E109 Nevil	18
Nor may'any feare, to loose of their degree,	73	E113 Overbury	11
All gentrie, yet, owe part of their best flame!	75	E116 Jephson	2
And, in their errors maze, thine owne way know:	76	E119 Shelton	13
Shee should to know long difference of their states.	78	E121 Rudyerd 1	4
For, then, all mouthes will judge, and their owne way:	82	E131 Ferrab. 2	3
They should be fooles, for me, at their owne charge.	83	E131 Ferrab. 2	8
Their wherry had no saile, too; ours had none:	84	E133 Voyage	11
Laden with plague-sores, and their sinnes, were heard,	84	E133 Voyage	17
Lash'd by their consciences, to die, affeard.	84	E133 Voyage	18
Ycleped Mud, which, when their oares did once stirre,	85	E133 Voyage	62
Thorough her wombe they make their famous road,	85	E133 Voyage	66
Hung stench, diseases, and old filth, their mother,	86	E133 Voyage	70
But still their valour, and their vertue fenc't 'hem,	86	E133 Voyage	76
Backe, cry'd their brace of Charons: they cry'd, no,	86	E133 Voyage	87
Their Mercury did now. By this, the stemme	87	E133 Voyage	111
Of worship, they their nodding chinnes doe hit	87	E133 Voyage	123
Against their breasts. Here, sev'rall ghosts did flit	87	E133 Voyage	124
Their spirits transmigrated to a cat:	88	E133 Voyage	159
Of loud Sepulchres with their hourely knells,	89	E133 Voyage	174
They tooke 'hem all to witnesse of their action:	89	E133 Voyage	191
And I could wish for their eterniz'd sakes,	89	E133 Voyage	195
Mars, and my Mother, in their net:	93	F1 Why write no	6
Where Pan, and Bacchus their high feasts have made,	93	F2 Penshurst	11
And pikes, now weary their owne kinde to eat,	94	F2 Penshurst	34
By their ripe daughters, whom they would commend	95	F2 Penshurst	54
But what can this (more then expresse their love)	95	F2 Penshurst	57
With all their zeale, to warme their welcome here.	95	F2 Penshurst	81
Their gentler spirits have suck'd innocence.	96	F2 Penshurst	94
Reade, in their vertuous parents noble parts,	96	F2 Penshurst	97
May say, their lords have built, but thy lord dwells.	96	F2 Penshurst	102
Free from proud porches, or their guilded roofes,	97	F3 Wroth	15
In spring tyme roused for their masters sport,	97	F3 Wroth	V 23
While all, that follow, their glad eares apply	97	F3 Wroth	31
The ripened eares, yet humble in their height,	98	F3 Wroth	41
The eares cut downe in their most height,	98	F3 Wroth	V 41

	Page	Title	Line
THEIR (cont.)			
And furrowes laden with their weight;	98	F3 Wroth	42
Thus Pan, and Sylvane, having had their rites,	98	F3 Wroth	47
When Pan, and Sylvane, having had their rites,	98	F3 Wroth	V 47
(Their rudenesse then is thought no sinne)	98	F3 Wroth	54
And in their cups, their cares are drown'd:	98	F3 Wroth	60
And shew their feathers shot, and cullors torne,	98	F3 Wroth	71
To blow up orphanes, widdowes, and their states;	99	F3 Wroth	79
The secrets, that shall breake their sleepe:	99	F3 Wroth	88
Like such as blow away their lives,	100	F4 To the World	22
Enamor'd of their golden gyves?	100	F4 To the World	24
When youths ply their stolne delights.	103	F6 Celia 2	18
What their number is, be pin'd.	103	F6 Celia 2	22
To thy altars, by their nights	104	F8 Sicknesse	4
Spent in surfets: and their dayes,	104	F8 Sicknesse	5
That distill their husbands land	105	F8 Sicknesse	29
With ten Emp'ricks, in their chamber,	105	F8 Sicknesse	31
Them, and all their officers.	105	F8 Sicknesse	35
Dare entayle their loves on any,	105	F8 Sicknesse	39
Dare entayle their loves to any,	105	F8 Sicknesse	V 39
On their beds, most prostitute,	106	F8 Sicknesse	45
Move it, as their humblest sute,	106	F8 Sicknesse	46
Move it, as their humble sute,	106	F8 Sicknesse	V 46
Thou, nor their loosenesse with our making sorts.	107	F10 Proludium	V 18
Let these in wanton feete daunce out their soules.	108	F10 Proludium	11
And for their place, and name,	111	F11 Epode	80
Cannot so safely sinne. Their chastitie	111	F11 Epode	81
Just to the waight their this dayes-presents beare;	113	F12 Rutland	8
Turne, upon scorned verse, their quarter-face:	114	F12 Rutland	29
And now lye lost in their forgotten dust.	114	F12 Rutland	40
Or in their windowes; doe but prove the wombs,	114	F12 Rutland	46
That had no Muse to make their fame abide.	114	F12 Rutland	48
Had not their forme touch'd by an English wit.	115	F12 Rutland	82
For others ill, ought none their good forget.	116	F13 Aubigny	6
For their owne cap'tall crimes, t'indite my wit;	117	F13 Aubigny	14
Maintayne their liedgers forth, for forraine wyres,	118	F13 Aubigny	72
Melt downe their husbands land, to poure away	118	F13 Aubigny	73
Them, or their officers: and no man know,	118	F13 Aubigny	79
When their owne Parasites laugh at their fall,	118	F13 Aubigny	82
And call it their brave sinne. For such there be	119	F13 Aubigny	85
To Clifton's bloud, that is deny'd their name.	119	F13 Aubigny	98
By me, their priest (if they can ought divine)	119	F13 Aubigny	101
Before the moones have fill'd their tripple trine,	119	F13 Aubigny	102
Their punishment.	129	U1 Father	16
To meet their high desire;	144	U3 Musicall	26
May wish us of their Quire.	144	U3 Musicall	28
Lest shame destroy their being.	144	U4 Song	4
For then their threats will kill me;	144	U4 Song	6
Another. In defence of their Inconstancie. A Song.	146	U6 Defence	Ttl
That they for me their teares will shed,	152	U12 Corbet	34
And knew their how, and where: we should have, then,	153	U13 Sacvile	3
Well knowne, and practiz'd borrowers on their word,	154	U13 Sacvile	48
That to such Natures let their full hands flow,	154	U13 Sacvile	60
Their bounties forth, to him that last was made,	155	U13 Sacvile	63
Their thoughts and meanes to making loude the cry;	155	U13 Sacvile	66
All the Towne-curs take each their snatch at me.	155	U13 Sacvile	72
But these men ever want: their very trade	155	U13 Sacvile	79
All as their prize, turne Pyrats here at Land,	155	U13 Sacvile	81
Ha' their Bermudas, and their streights i'th' Strand:	155	U13 Sacvile	82
Man out their Boates to th' Temple, and not shift	155	U13 Sacvile	83
Lowd sacrifice of drinke, for their health-sake!	156	U13 Sacvile	100
Reare-Suppers in their Names! and spend whole nights	156	U13 Sacvile	101
Unto their praise, in certaine swearing rites!	156	U13 Sacvile	102
They need no stilts, nor rise upon their toes,	157	U13 Sacvile	145
As if they would belie their stature; those	157	U13 Sacvile	146
Their difference, cannot choose which you will be.	157	U13 Sacvile	154
(As their true rule or lesson) either men,	158	U13 Sacvile	162
Donnor's or Donnee's, to their practise shall	158	U13 Sacvile	163
Men past their termes, and prais'd some names too much,	159	U14 Selden	21
Of others honours, thus, enjoy their owne.	160	U14 Selden	V 66
Their vitious ease, and be o'rewhelm'd with it.	162	U15 Friend-Wars	4
Till he becomes both their, and his owne curse!	162	U15 Friend-Wars	14
For all their spight, be like him if they could:	162	U15 Friend-Wars	26
Who can behold their Manners, and not clowd-/Like	164	U15 Friend-Wars	60
To see 'hem aye discoursing with their Glasse,	164	U15 Friend-Wars	63
Planting their Purles, and Curles spread forth like Net,	164	U15 Friend-Wars	65
Be at their Visits, see 'hem squeamish, sick,	164	U15 Friend-Wars	68
As if a Brize were gotten i' their tayle;	164	U15 Friend-Wars	71
This way, now that, as if their number were	166	U15 Friend-Wars	126
To be beholders, when their powers are spent.	166	U15 Friend-Wars	140
Debts when they can: good men may breake their day,	169	U17 Friend-Debt	2
And their words too; where I but breake my Band.	169	U17 Friend-Debt	9
Such Guides men use not, who their way would find,	170	U18 Elegy Can	12
Vaile their owne eyes, and would impartially	170	U18 Elegy Can	19
That their whole life was wickednesse, though weav'd	171	U20 Shrub	10
But their whole inside full of ends, and knots?	171	U20 Shrub	12
Knew I, that all their Dialogues, and discourse,	172	U20 Shrub	13
That would their better objects find:	173	U22 Elegy Tho	27
To see their Seats and Bowers by chattring Pies defac't?	174	U23 Himselfe	12
They die with their conceits,	175	U23 Himselfe	21
They drincke with their conceits,	175	U23 Himselfe	V 23
And only pitious scorne, upon their folly waites.	175	U23 Himselfe	24
But both might know their wayes were understood,	176	U24 Frontispice	7

		Page	Title	Line

THEIR (cont.)

	Page	Title	Line
But both might know their wayes are understood,	176	U24 Frontispice	V 7
Sweat at the forge, their hammers beating;	179	U25 Desmond	41
Have made their fairest flight,	180	U26 Ode High	7
For men to use their fortune reverently,	181	U26 Ode High	23
Spoyling Senses of their Treasure,	183	U29 Fit of Rime	4
Wresting words, from their true calling;	183	U29 Fit of Rime	7
And the Muses to their braine;	184	U29 Fit of Rime	41
Clos'd to their peace, he saw his branches shoot,	185	U30 Burleigh	17
A right by the prosperitie of their Crimes;	186	U32 Elsmere	10
Who, though their guilt, and perjurie they know,	186	U32 Elsmere	11
Of those that set by their false faces more	188	U34 Small Poxe	4
And have their being, their waste to see;	189	U36 Song	11
Their vice of loving for a Christmasse fit;	190	U37 Friend-Book	8
Why was't? did e're the Cloudes aske back their raine?	192	U38 Elegy 'Tis	56
What Fooles, and all their Parasites can apply;	193	U38 Elegy 'Tis	94
Others by common Stars their courses run,	194	U38 Elegy 'Tis	119
Shall find their depth: they're sounded with a spoone.	198	U40 Elegy That	30
To shift their seasons, and destroy their powers!	199	U41 Elegy Since	10
(If they be faire and worth it) have their lives	200	U42 Elegy Let	20
Curst in their Cradles, or there chang'd by Elves,	200	U42 Elegy Let	23
And braveries of Court, and felt their fits	200	U42 Elegy Let	34
Whether their faces were their owne, or no:	200	U42 Elegy Let	36
Let the poore fooles enjoy their follies, love	202	U42 Elegy Let	81
None of their pleasures! nor will aske thee, why	202	U42 Elegy Let	86
Sindge Capons, or poore Pigges, dropping their eyes;	205	U43 Vulcan	53
Sindge capons, or crispe Pigges, dropping their eyes;	205	U43 Vulcan	V 53
Their Seales, their Characters, Hermetique rings,	206	U43 Vulcan	73
Their Charmes, their Characters, Hermetique rings,	206	U43 Vulcan	V 73
Their Jemme of Riches, and bright Stone, that brings	206	U43 Vulcan	74
To teach some that, their Nurses could not doe,	207	U43 Vulcan	92
To teach some what, their Nurses could not doe,	207	U43 Vulcan	V 92
Against thy furie, when to serve their needs,	208	U43 Vulcan	125
Whom they durst handle in their holy-day coates,	208	U43 Vulcan	127
Whom they durst handle in their high day coates,	208	U43 Vulcan	V127
And safely trust to dresse, not burne their Boates.	208	U43 Vulcan	128
More then advanc'd the houses, and their rites?	210	U43 Vulcan	164
The Glasse-house, Dye-fats, and their Fornaces;	211	U43 Vulcan	180
To see the Pride at Court, their Wives doe make:	213	U44 Speach	16
To have their Husbands drawne forth to the field,	213	U44 Speach	18
And could (if our great men would let their Sonnes	214	U44 Speach	57
Come to their Schooles,) show 'hem the use of Guns;	214	U44 Speach	58
Live by their Scale, that dare doe nothing free?	215	U44 Speach	68
Their Sonnes to studie Arts, the Lawes, the Creed:	215	U44 Speach	74
That in the Cradle of their Gentrie are;	215	U44 Speach	84
Her broken Armes up, to their emptie moulds.	216	U44 Speach	102
More for thy Patronage, then for their Cause,	217	U46 Coke	12
As make it their proficiencie, how much	218	U47 Tribe	12
Or th'other on their borders, that will jeast	218	U47 Tribe	16
Let these men have their wayes, and take their times	218	U47 Tribe	25
To vent their Libels, and to issue rimes,	218	U47 Tribe	26
I have no portion in them, nor their deale	218	U47 Tribe	27
Some hopes of Spaine in their West-Indian Fleet?	219	U47 Tribe	34
And looke unto their faces,	220	U48 Bacchus	9
Their Qualities, and races,	220	U48 Bacchus	10
That both, their odour take him,	220	U48 Bacchus	11
To give mankind their eases,	220	U48 Bacchus	21
New in their stead, out of the Candidates?	221	U48 Bacchus	23
To shew their Tires? to view, and to be view'd?	222	U49 Pucell	6
From whence they fall, cast downe with their owne weight.	222	U49 Pucell	17
As they are hard, for them to make their owne,	224	U50 Countesse	12
Out of their Choysest, and their whitest wooll.	225	U50 Countesse	33
Nor any of their houshold, halfe so well.	225	U51 Bacon	16
That hang their richest jewells i'their nose;	228	U53 Newcastle	16
Their perfum'd judgements, let them kisse thy Wife.	232	U58 Book-seller	10
Their weapons shot out, with that flame, and force,	232	U58 Book-seller	14
Their weapons darted, with that flame, and force,	233	U59 Newcastle	11
And valiant were, with, or without their hands.	233	U59 Newcastle	V 11
What could their care doe 'gainst the spight	233	U59 Newcastle	24
And doe their penance, to avert Gods rod,	234	U60 La-ware	5
To K. Charles, and Q. Mary. For the losse of their . . .	235	U61 Epigram	19
Their noises forth in Thunder:	235	U63 Charles 2	Ttl
Their noises out in Thunder:	239	U67 Muses	9
Their guarded gates asunder?	239	U67 Muses	V 9
With beating of their Drums:	239	U67 Muses	12
The Angels from their Spheares:	239	U67 Muses	V 15
Are they so scanted in their store? or driven	239	U67 Muses	21
Hee'ld frame such ditties of their store, and want,	241	U68 House-hold	3
And rather wish, in their expence of Sack,	241	U68 House-hold	7
The Poetrie of Steeples, with their Bells,	241	U68 House-hold	9
At Bonefires, squibs, and mirth, with all their Shoutes	249	U72 King	V 10
That cry that gladnesse, which their hearts would pray,	249	U72 King	V 13
The cries, the gladnesse, which their hearts would pay,	249	U72 King	14
And then noyse forth the burden of their Song,	249	U72 King	V 14
The Rivers in their shores doe run,	249	U72 King	V 17
Have multipli'd their arts, and powers,	251	U74 Weston	7
Doe boast their Loves, and Brav'ries so at large,	251	U74 Weston	17
To doe their Offices in Natures Chime,	253	U75 Epithalam.	19
Their Sister-tunes, from Thames his either side,	253	U75 Epithalam.	27
Both Crownes, and Kingdomes in their either hand;	253	U75 Epithalam.	34
The Emblemes of their way.	254	U75 Epithalam.	52
They are th'exampled Paire, and mirrour of their kind.	254	U75 Epithalam.	63
It is their Grace, and favour, that makes seene,	255	U75 Epithalam.	80
	255	U75 Epithalam.	89

	Page	Title	Line
THEIR (cont.)			
And set their marke upon,	255	U75 Epithalam.	V 95
To give a greater Name, and Title to! Their owne!	255	U75 Epithalam.	96
Weston, their Treasure, as their Treasurer,	255	U75 Epithalam.	97
Hearing their charge, and then	256	U75 Epithalam.	127
And this their chosen Bishop celebrate,	256	U75 Epithalam.	132
Which their glad Parents taught	257	U75 Epithalam.	143
All that their Fathers, and their Mothers might	257	U75 Epithalam.	147
To propagate their Names,	257	U75 Epithalam.	149
And keepe their Fames	257	U75 Epithalam.	150
Their names are not recorded on the File	257	U75 Epithalam.	155
Of Life, that fall so; Christians know their birth	257	U75 Epithalam.	156
A Richard, and a Hierome, by their names	258	U75 Epithalam.	170
A Kate, a Frank, to honour their Grand-dames,	258	U75 Epithalam.	172
And 'tweene their Grandsires thighes,	258	U75 Epithalam.	173
When their pot-guns ayme to hit,	259	U76 Petition	21
When their pot-guns thinke to fitt,	259	U76 Petition	V 21
With their pellets of small wit,	259	U76 Petition	22
Let their spite (which now abounds)	260	U76 Petition	28
This would all their envie burst:	260	U76 Petition	30
That would all their envie burst:	260	U76 Petition	V 30
To pious parents, who would have their blood	268	U80 Christning	7
Their Carract was! I, or my trump must breake,	269	U81 Pawlet	27
Their Carract was! for my trump must breake,	269	U81 Pawlet	V 27
Made her friends joyes to get above their feares!	270	U81 Pawlet	60
Their Heads, that Envy would hold downe	272	U84 Cradle	3
Their names of being kept alive,	273	U84 Cradle	6
Take little Infants with their noyse,	273	U84 Cradle	18
Their Corrals, Whistles, and prime Coates,	273	U84 Cradle	21
Their painted Maskes, their paper Boates,	273	U84 Cradle	22
Surprize their sense:	273	U84 Cradle	24
(Brave Youths) th'are their possessions, none of yours:	281	U84 Kenelme	11
When your owne Vertues, equall'd have their Names,	281	U84 Kenelme	12
'Twill be but faire, to leane upon their Fames:	281	U84 Kenelme	13
Which all men doe, that urge not their owne deeds	281	U84 Kenelme	17
Up to their Ancestors; the rivers side,	281	U84 Kenelme	18
To heare their Judge, and his eternall doome;	283	U84 Muse	48
And Sons, and Daughters, with their Parents talke;	285	U84 Muse	118
But make him All in All, their Theme, that Day:	286	U84 Muse	120
Their swelling udders doth draw dry:	291	U85 Country	46
Thrice 'bout thy Altar with their Ivory feet.	292	U86 Hor.4:1	28
Still in their leaves, throughout the sliding yeares,	309	Horace	86
After, mens Wishes, crown'd in their events,	309	Horace	108
To chant the Gods, and all their God-like race,	311	Horace	114
That are Spectators, with their miserie,	311	Horace	137
Their bombard-phrase, and foot-and-halfe-foot words.	311	Horace	139
To worke the hearers minds, still, to their plight.	311	Horace	142
Saw many Townes, and Men, and could their manners tract.	315	Horace	202
And give their yeares, and natures, as they swerve,	315	Horace	224
But, as they conquer'd, and enlarg'd their bound,	319	Horace	295
That wider Walls embrac'd their Citie round,	319	Horace	296
Both in their tunes, the licence greater grew,	319	Horace	299
And in their numbers; For, alas, what knew	319	Horace	300
Those that did sing, and act: their faces dy'd	319	Horace	314
And so their prating to present was best,	321	Horace	329
And so their pratling to present were best,	346	Horace	V321/329
But, let the Faunes, drawne from their Groves, beware,	321	Horace	355
Be I their Judge, they doe at no time dare	321	Horace	356
Their youthfull tricks in over-wanton verse:	321	Horace	358
Into their birth-right, and for fitnesse sake,	323	Horace	376
Exclude all sober Poets, from their share	325	Horace	421
Their nailes, nor shave their beards, but to by-paths	325	Horace	423
Their nails, nor shave their beards, but seek by-paths	349	Horace	V423
Their heads, which three Anticyra's cannot heale.	325	Horace	428
My title, at their rate, I'ad rather, I,	325	Horace	432
Their Charge, and Office, whence their wealth to fet,	325	Horace	436
There words will follow, not against their will.	325	Horace	444
There words will never follow 'gainst their will.	349	Horace	V444
A pound, or piece, by their long compting arts:	327	Horace	466
To divine Poets, and their Verses came.	327	Horace	492
Their minds to Warres, with rimes they did rehearse;	329	Horace	495
Of their long labours, was in Verse set downe:	329	Horace	500
And friendly should unto their end conspire.	353	Horace	V586
His flatterers to their gaine. But say, he can	333	Horace	601
His praisers to their gaine: but say he can	353	Horace	V601
If of their friendship he be worthy, or no:	333	Horace	619
In these pide times, only to shewe their braines,	362	Author	4
The fault's not in the object, but their eyes.	362	Author	8
His proofe their praise, will meete, as in this line.	362	Author	14
Seldome descend but bleeding to their grave.	363	Murder	2
When night their meeting covers.	365	Ode Splendor	8
Are deeper then their Faces:	365	Ode Splendor	22
With entheate rage, to publish their bright tracts?	368	Ode Who saith	61
Their reeking fumes;	368	Ode Who saith	78
Their cares in wine; with sure	368	Ode Who saith	87
It is inough, their griefe shall know	369	Ode Who saith	113
At their returne, nor Po,	369	Ode Who saith	114
Their motives were, since it had not to do	371	Fletcher	9
In such a Martirdome; To vexe their eyes,	371	Fletcher	13
Their hornes, and Germany pukes on his head.	375	Coryat 1	31
unto thee, king of men; their noblest partes	382	Rich	3
to tender thus, their lives, their loves, their hartes!	382	Rich	4
When these, and such, their voices have employd;	385	Brooke	1

	Page	Title	Line
THEIR (cont.)			
Who are his Test, and what their judgement is:	385	Husband	3
trust in the tombes, their care-full freinds do rayse;	387	Cavendish	6
Sent forth, or since did from their ashes come.	391	Shakespeare	40
And all the Muses still were in their prime,	391	Shakespeare	44
Their loves, their quarrels, jealousies, and wrongs,	397	Drayton	30
And when he ships them where to use their Armes,	398	Drayton	65
And with their grassie greene restor'd mine eyes.	398	Drayton	82
All Circles had their spring and end	399	Lady Ogle	14
And, with their Chained dance,	401	Filmer	9
The comfort of weake Christians, with their warning,	411	Sutcliffe	13
All, pouring their full showre of graces downe,	413	Ghyrlond	31
Or by chance if in their grease	418	Moon	41
forfeitinge their drinking lease,	418	Moon	43
By Cherissheinge the Spirrits that gave their greatnesse grace:	419	Ode:If Men	5
And better Blason them, then all their Coates,	419	Ode:If Men	8
Their labour'd tunes reherse,	420	Ode:If Men	22
Whose ayre will sooner Hell, then their dull senses peirce,	420	Ode:If Men	23
And Cunninge of their grownde	420	Ode:If Men	34
But unto more dispayre to Imitate their sounde.	420	Ode:If Men	36
Throughout their generall breasts,	421	Ode:If Men	43
And by their takeinge, lett it once appeare	421	Ode:If Men	44
Is her owne scourge, when it sustaines their states	422	Lucan	3
THEIRE			
or theire Ale, they break the peace,	418	Moon	42
THEIRS			
As theirs did with thee, mine might credit get:	32	E18 Censurer	6
That, to make all pleasure theirs,	105	F8 Sicknesse	36
What your try'd manners are, what theirs should bee.	119	F13 Aubigny	112
And know whose ignorance is more then theirs;	218	U47 Tribe	24
So short you read my Character, and theirs	220	U47 Tribe	73
To such a worke, as could not need theirs? Yet	385	Brooke	5
TH'ELABORATE			
'Tis not enough, th'elaborate Muse affords	311	Horace	140
TH'ELIXIR			
Cry'd to my face, they were th'elixir of wit:	64	E100 Playwrt 3	2
'HEM			
Of bearing them in field, he threw 'hem away:	42	E48 Mungril	2
Then had I made 'hem good, to fit your vaine.	51	E73 Fine Grand	20
At sixe and twentie, ripe. You shall 'hem meet,	58	E92 New Crie	4
And have'hem yeeld no savour, but of state.	58	E92 New Crie	5
Yet have they seene the maps, and bought 'hem too,	59	E92 New Crie	9
And understand 'hem, as most chapmen doe.	59	E92 New Crie	10
To breake up seales, and close 'hem. And they know,	59	E92 New Crie	29
And pitty 'tis, I cannot call 'hem knights:	84	E133 Voyage	22
Spake to 'hem louder, then the oxe in Livie:	86	E133 Voyage	74
And many a sinke pour'd out her rage anenst 'hem;	86	E133 Voyage	75
But still their valour, and their vertue fenc't 'hem,	86	E133 Voyage	76
(In the meane time, let 'hem imprison mee)	87	E133 Voyage	104
Then, selling not, a dish was tane to mince 'hem,	88	E133 Voyage	151
But still, it seem'd, the ranknesse did convince 'hem.	88	E133 Voyage	152
That had, so often, shew'd 'hem merry prankes.	89	E133 Voyage	184
They tooke 'hem all to witnesse of their action:	89	E133 Voyage	191
The better cheeses, bring 'hem; or else send	95	F2 Penshurst	53
Did'st thou, then, make 'hem! and what praise was heap'd	95	F2 Penshurst	83
How to tell' hem, as they flow,	103	F6 Celia 2	20
Like life unto 'hem. Who heav'd Hercules	115	F12 Rutland	57
Let 'hem on poulders, oyles, and paintings, spend,	118	F13 Aubigny	77
Let 'hem waste body, and state; and after all,	118	F13 Aubigny	81
Against his will that do's 'hem? that hath weav'd	153	U13 Sacvile	26
Excuses, or Delayes? or done 'hem scant,	153	U13 Sacvile	27
And it is paid 'hem with a trembling zeale,	155	U13 Sacvile	85
To see 'hem aye discoursing with their Glasse,	164	U15 Friend-Wars	63
Be at their Visits, see 'hem squemish, sick,	164	U15 Friend-Wars	68
Goe, quit 'hem all. And take along with thee,	167	U15 Friend-Wars	175
Come to their Schooles,) show 'hem the use of Guns;	214	U44 Speach	58
Still waited on 'hem where they were.	264	U79 New-yeares	39
They're dark, bid cleare 'hem; al that's doubtful wrote	354	Horace	V637
THEM			
Thou wert, as chiefe of them are said t'have beene.	28	E4 James 1	6
Charge them, for crowne, to thy sole censure hye.	32	E17 Critic	4
Except thou could'st, Sir Cod, weare them within.	33	E20 Cod 2	2
And than in them, how could we know god more?	38	E35 James 2	8
Of bearing them in field, he threw 'hem away:	42	E48 Mungril	2
In my chast booke: professe them in thine owne.	42	E49 Playwrt 1	6
Where good mens vertues them to honors bring,	47	E64 Salisbury 3	11
As all thy honors were by them first sought:	49	E67 Suffolk	8
On them: And therefore doe not onely shunne	59	E92 New Crie	38
And like them too; must needfully, though few,	61	E94 Bedford 3	13
Of state, and censure them: we need his pen	62	E95 Savile	33
And glorie of them all, but to repeate!	66	E103 L Wroth 1	8
Who could not but create them all, from you?	67	E105 L Wroth 2	6
And yet are with their Princes: Fill them full	69	E107 Hungry	7
Tell them, what parts yo'have tane, whence run away,	69	E107 Hungry	9
Give them your services, and embassies	69	E107 Hungry	11
Will you part with them, here, unthriftely?	69	E107 Hungry	28
Where vertue makes them both, and that's in thee:	70	E109 Nevil	3
Them in, if not, from thee; or must commit	75	E116 Jephson	15
We ought not give them taste, we had an eare.	83	E131 Ferrab. 2	6
All was to them the same, they were to passe,	88	E133 Voyage	140
They cry'd out Pusse. He told them he was Bankes,	89	E133 Voyage	183
Bright eeles, that emulate them, and leape on land,	94	F2 Penshurst	37
There's none, that dwell about them, wish them downe;	94	F2 Penshurst	47

THEM (cont.)

	Page	Title	Line
To entertayne them; or the countrey came,	95	F2 Penshurst	80
Thy noblest spouse affords them welcome grace;	98	F3 Wroth	55
Thy noblest spouse affords them welcome place;	98	F3 Wroth	V 55
To take the weake, or make them stop:	100	F4 To the World	19
The engines, that have them annoy'd;	101	F4 To the World	34
Ladies? and of them the best?	104	F8 Sicknesse	2
Them, and all their officers.	105	F8 Sicknesse	35
None but them, and leave the rest.	106	F8 Sicknesse	48
None but them, and leave the best.	106	F8 Sicknesse	V 48
With noble ignorants, and let them still,	114	F12 Rutland	28
That bred them, graves: when they were borne, they di'd,	114	F12 Rutland	47
Such as suspect them-selves, and thinke it fit	117	F13 Aubigny	13
Them, or their officers: and no man know,	118	F13 Aubigny	79
Pure thoughts in man: with fiery zeale them feeding	128	U1 Trinitie	27
Nor cast them downe, but let them rise,	144	U4 Song	3
O, doe not steepe them in thy Teares,	145	U4 Song	9
Nor spread them as distract with feares,	145	U4 Song	11
And of them pittied be,	147	U7 Nymph	11
Though hate had put them out;	147	U7 Nymph	25
That others should not warme them at my fire,	150	U10 Jealousie	6
Yet he broke them, e're they could him,	151	U12 Corbet	10
Great and good turns, as wel could time them too,	153	U13 Sacvile	2
Yet choyce from whom I take them; and would shame	153	U13 Sacvile	17
No more are these of us, let them then goe,	156	U13 Sacvile	113
Were the Rack offer'd them, how they came so;	157	U13 Sacvile	130
But 'twas with purpose to have made them such.	159	U14 Selden	22
clowd-/Like upon them lighten? If nature could	164	U15 Friend-Wars	61
And on them burne so chaste a flame,	173	U22 Elegy Tho	21
That eats on wits, and Arts, and destroyes them both.	174	U23 Himselfe	6
Who aided them, will thee, the taste of Joves braine.	175	U23 Himselfe	V 30
Pyracmon's houre will come to give them ease,	179	U25 Desmond	42
As though the Court pursues them on the sent,	186	U32 Elsmere	13
All mouthes, that dare entitle them (from hence)	187	U33 Councellour	11
Thou mightst have had them perish, piece, by piece,	205	U43 Vulcan	V 51
Condemn'd them to the Ovens with the pies;	205	U43 Vulcan	V 54
And so, have kept them dying a whole age,	205	U43 Vulcan	V 55
Not snatcht them hence in one poor minutes rage.	205	U43 Vulcan	V 56
But, O those Reeds! thy meere disdaine of them,	208	U43 Vulcan	129
But, O those weedes; thy meere disdaine of them,	208	U43 Vulcan	V129
I will not argue thee, from them, of guilt,	210	U43 Vulcan	V165
I will not argue thee Iron. Them of guilt	210	U43 Vulcan	V165
But give them over to the common eare	214	U44 Speach	31
Past any need of vertue. Let them care,	215	U44 Speach	83
And though Opinion stampe them not, are gold.	218	U47 Tribe	4
I have no portion in them, nor their deale	218	U47 Tribe	27
What though she talke, and cannot once with them,	222	U49 Pucell	11
You cling to Lords, and Lords, if them you leave	223	U49 Pucell	38
And studie them unto the noblest ends,	224	U50 Countesse	28
As they are hard, for them to make their owne,	225	U50 Countesse	33
It will be shame for them, if they have none.	225	U50 Countesse	36
You won them too, your oddes did merit it.	230	U56 Covell	4
Their perfum'd judgements, let them kisse thy Wife.	232	U58 Book-seller	14
Fit for a Bishops knees! O bow them oft.	234	U61 Epigram	13
Never so great to get them: and the ends,	242	U69 Friend Son	25
And make them yeares;	244	U70 Ode	54
These two, now holy Church hath made them one,	257	U75 Epithalam.	139
To them of kind,	257	U75 Epithalam.	142
Haste, haste, officious Sun, and send them Night	257	U75 Epithalam.	145
But like an Arme of Eminence 'mongst them,	258	U75 Epithalam.	179
I would, if price, or prayer could them get,	260	U77 Treasurer	5
Caught them these Arts, wherein the Judge is wise	261	U77 Treasurer	V 11
Upon them, (next to Spenser's noble booke,)	263	U78 Digby	24
And praise them too. O! what a fame 't will be?	263	U78 Digby	25
When hee shall read them at the Treasurers bord,	263	U78 Digby	27
When hee doth read them at the Treasurers bord,	263	U78 Digby	V 27
Allowes them? Then, what copies shall be had,	263	U78 Digby	29
Allowes them? Then, what copies will be had,	263	U78 Digby	V 29
Wilt thou be, Muse, when this shall them befall?	263	U78 Digby	31
And voyce to raise them from my brazen Lungs,	269	U81 Pawlet	24
And 'counts them sweet rewards so ta'en:	290	U85 Country	36
Mans comming yeares much good with them doe bring:	317	Horace	250
Built a small-timbred Stage, and taught them talke	319	Horace	317
In hand, and turne them over, day, and night.	323	Horace	398
I, writing nought my selfe, will teach them yet	325	Horace	435
And better stayes them there, then all fine noise	327	Horace	459
And lead them with soft songs, where that he would.	327	Horace	485
And hold them faithfully; For nothing rests,	329	Horace	505
Our Gallants give them none, but passe them by:	329	Horace	513
Did learne them first, and once a Master fear'd.	333	Horace	592
And thou in them shalt live as longe as Fame.	362	Palmer	31
Yet shee's nor nice to shew them,	365	Ode Splendor	23
Nor takes she pride to know them.	365	Ode Splendor	24
With thy soft notes, and hold them within Pale	367	Ode Who saith	45
To hold them here:	368	Ode Who saith	92
So that not them, his scabbes, lice, or the stewes,	380	Coryat 3	50
May hurt them more with praise, then Foes with spight.	386	Browne	2
But thou art proofe against them, and indeed	391	Shakespeare	15
Above th'ill fortune of them, or the need.	391	Shakespeare	16
But who hath them interpreted, and brought	395	May	19
And when he ships them where to use their Armes,	398	Drayton	65
you are; from them leapt forth an Architect,	402	Inigo Jones 1	3
Of many Coulors! read them! & reveale	404	Inigo Jones 1	47

THEM (cont.)
```
And you doe doe them well, with good applause,        409  Brome             5
And in them view'd th'uncertainty of Life,            411  Sutcliffe         3
And newer, then could please them, by-cause trew.     415  Rutter           10
And you, with them, as Father of our spring.          416  Welcome           8
God blesse them all, and keepe them safe:             419  Grace             7
And better Blason them, then all their Coates,        419  Ode:If Men        8
not safe; but when thou dost them thoroughlie:        423  Lucan            16
```
THEME   (See also THEAME)
```
But make him All in All, their Theme, that Day:       286  U84 Muse        120
```
THEM-SELVES
```
Such as suspect them-selves, and thinke it fit        117  F13 Aubigny      13
```
THEMSELVES
```
Whose actions so themselves doe celebrate;             40  E43 Salisbury 1   2
Officiously, at first, themselves betray.              94  F2 Penshurst     36
An embleme of themselves, in plum, or peare.          95  F2 Penshurst     56
Whereon the most of mankinde wracke themselves,      119  F13 Aubigny      90
Themselves through favouring what is there not found: 159  U14 Selden       16
Themselves through favouring that is there not found: 159  U14 Selden      V 16
More then themselves, or then our lives could take,  166  U15 Friend-Wars 127
But these with wearing will themselves unfold:       216  U45 Squib        19
Themselves to day,                                   255  U75 Epithalam.   86
Doe long to make themselves, so, another way:        257  U75 Epithalam.  140
Things in themselves agreeing: If againe             313  Horace          170
The steadie Spondaees; so themselves to beare        323  Horace          377
The steadie Spondaees; so themselves doe beare       347  Horace      V363/377
Retire themselves, avoid the publike baths;          325  Horace          424
make many, hurt themselves; a praysed faith          422  Lucan             2
```
THEN   (THAN)
```
Then thee the age sees not that thing more grave,     31  E14 Camden        5
Many of thine this better could, then I,              31  E14 Camden       13
He that dares damne himselfe, dares more then fight.  32  E16 Brain-hardy  10
Longer a knowing, then most wits doe live.            34  E23 Donne 1       5
Then his chast wife, though Beast now know no more,   35  E26 Beast 2       1
Then they might in her bright eyes.                   39  E40 Ratcliffe     8
And get more gold, then all the colledge can:         39  E41 Gypsee        2
Then thou did'st late my sense, loosing my points.    45  E58 Groome        6
With me thou leav'st an happier Muse then thee,       48  E65 Muse         11
Which, by no lesse confirm'd, then thy kings choice,  49  E67 Suffolk      11
Then had I made 'hem good, to fit your vaine.         51  E73 Fine Grand   20
And no lesse wise, then skilfull in the lawes;        52  E74 Chancelor     6
Of greatest bloud, and yet more good then great;     52  E76 Bedford 1      6
That Poets are far rarer births then kings,          53  E79 Rutland        1
Toward the sea, farther then halfe-way tree?         56  E88 Monsieur       6
Then Cicero, whose every breath was fame:            57  E89 Allen          6
Out-strip't, then they did all that went before:     57  E89 Allen         10
Who more should seeke mens reverence, then feare.    58  E91 Vere          18
Then whose I doe not know a whiter soule,            60  E93 Radcliffe     11
No more then Salust in the Romane state!             61  E95 Savile        23
Although to write be lesser then to doo,             61  E95 Savile        25
Since he was gone, more then the one he weares.      63  E97 Motion        17
And studie conscience, more then thou would'st fame. 63  E98 Th Roe 1      10
Well, though thy name lesse then our great ones bee, 64  E99 Th Roe 2      11
Becomes none more then you, who need it least.       67  E103 L Wroth 1    14
Or, more then borne for the comparison               67  E104 Montgomery    9
Would call you more then Ceres, if not that:         68  E105 L Wroth 2     8
And yet, they, all together, lesse then thee.        68  E106 E Herbert    10
Not that I love it, more, then I will you.           68  E107 Hungry        4
Then can a flea at twise skip i'the Map.             69  E107 Hungry       18
And then lye with you, closer, then a punque,        69  E107 Hungry       20
No more, then I dare now doe, with my pen.           70  E108 Soldiers      8
And elements of honor, then the dresse:              70  E109 Nevil        10
More, then to varie what our elders knew:            72  E111 Edmonds 2     6
Parts, then th'Italian could doe, with his dore.     74  E115 Honest Man   26
And to live great, was better, then great borne.     75  E116 Jephson      12
With me can merit more, then that good man,          76  E119 Shelton       5
Makes, the whole longer, then 'twas given him, much. 76  E119 Shelton      16
To more vertue, then doth live.                      79  E124 Elizabeth     6
Then that it liv'd at all.  Farewell.                79  E124 Elizabeth    12
No lesse a sov'raigne cure, then to the mind;        82  E130 Ferrab. 1     8
That the eight sphaere, no lesse, then planets seaven, 82 E130 Ferrab. 1   12
The learn'd have no more priviledge, then the lay.   82  E131 Ferrab. 2     4
And in it, two more horride knaves, then Charon.     84  E133 Voyage       12
But, in the action, greater man then hee:            84  E133 Voyage       26
A harder tasque, then either his to Bristo',         85  E133 Voyage       39
Spake to 'hem louder, then the oxe in Livie:         86  E133 Voyage       74
Then all those Atomi ridiculous,                     87  E133 Voyage      127
But what can this (more then expresse their love)    95  F2 Penshurst      57
And makes sleepe softer then it is!                  97  F3 Wroth          20
More for thy exercise, then fare;                    97  F3 Wroth          30
Then either money, warre, or death:                  99  F3 Wroth          76
Let him, then hardest sires, more disinherit,        99  F3 Wroth          77
Then hardest let him more disherrit,                 99  F3 Wroth         V 77
Purchas'd by rapine, worse then stealth,             99  F3 Wroth          82
To him, man's dearer, then t'himselfe.               99  F3 Wroth          96
Yet art thou falser then thy wares.                 100  F4 To the World   20
More hatred, then thou hast to mee.                 101  F4 To the World   40
More then citizens dare lend                        105  F8 Sicknesse      34
A forme more fresh, then are the Eden bowers,       111  F11 Epode         57
Richer then Time, and as Time's vertue, rare.       111  F11 Epode         59
Then he, which for sinnes penaltie forbeares.       112  F11 Epode         89
Then he, that for sinnes penaltie forbeares.        112  F11 Epode        V 89
Then this, our guilt, nor golden age can deeme,     114  F12 Rutland       22
```

THEN (cont.)

	Page	Title	Line
Then, here, to give pride fame, and peasants birth.	114	F12 Rutland	26
Then, now give pride fame, or peasants birth.	114	F12 Rutland	V 26
Then which, a nobler heaven it selfe knowes not.	115	F12 Rutland	67
(Or Poet, in the court account) then I,	115	F12 Rutland	69
For I shall move stocks, stones, no lesse then he.	115	F12 Rutland	78
As bloud, and match. Wherein, how more then much	117	F13 Aubigny	46
This blessing of your starres, then by that way	118	F13 Aubigny	54
O, then how blest,	128	U1 Trinitie	44
Then thou hast done?	129	U1 Father	18
Sooner, then he lost his might,	132	U2 How he saw	14
Then words that sooth her!	134	U2 Triumph	16
Then the various Moone the flood!	136	U2 Cupid	4
Then when flowers, and West-winds meet	137	U2 Cupid	28
Something more then thou hast spi'd.	137	U2 Cupid	50
Of the Court, to day, then all	138	U2 Kisse	15
Can he that loves, aske lesse then one?	139	U2 Another	8
Better fits him, then his face;	140	U2 Promise	20
Shewing danger more then ire.	142	U2 Her man	42
Then when 'tis made, why so will wee.	145	U5 Woman-kind	16
From being forsaken, then doth worth:	146	U6 Defence	22
I Now thinke, Love is rather deafe, then blind,	149	U9 Picture	1
I Doubt that, Love is rather deafe, then blind,	149	U9 Picture	V 1
I feele, I'm rather dead then he!	152	U12 Corbet	36
Then what he hath receiv'd. Gifts stinke from some,	153	U13 Sacvile	22
That they have more opprest me, then my want?	153	U13 Sacvile	28
No more then he doth thanke, that will receive	154	U13 Sacvile	43
And told of with more License then th'were done!	156	U13 Sacvile	96
Yet we must more then move still, or goe on,	157	U13 Sacvile	135
Rather then Office, when it doth or may	158	U14 Selden	9
Then which there is not unto Studie'a more	158	U14 Selden	13
Rather then here so bogg'd in vices stay.	163	U15 Friend-Wars	30
Lesse must not be thought on then Mistresse: or,	165	U15 Friend-Wars	95
More then themselves, or then our lives could take,	166	U15 Friend-Wars	127
Well, let it goe. Yet this is better, then	166	U15 Friend-Wars	145
Then once to number, or bring forth to hand,	167	U15 Friend-Wars	173
That thou dost all things more for truth, then glory,	168	U15 Friend-Wars	179
No more, then we should thinke a Lord had had	168	U15 Friend-Wars	193
Then all Ingredients made into one curse,	172	U20 Shrub	18
Oft scape an Imputation, more through luck, then wit.	179	U25 Desmond	52
Oft scape theyr Imputation, more through luck, then wit.	179	U25 Desmond	V 52
To doe, then be a husband of that store.	180	U26 Ode High	18
Shine more, then she, the Stars among?	181	U27 Ode Helen	12
Then to make falshood blush, and fraud afraid:	186	U32 Elsmere	4
The Seat made of a more then civill warre;	186	U33 Councellour	2
Then this did by her true? She never sought	188	U34 Small Poxe	5
Was drawne to practise other hue, then that	188	U34 Small Poxe	8
None brookes the Sun-light worse then he.	189	U36 Song	4
Your honour now, then your disgrace before.	191	U38 Elegy 'Tis	30
And then his thunder frights more, then it kills.	193	U38 Elegy 'Tis	70
In a calme skie, then when the heaven is horl'd	193	U38 Elegy 'Tis	74
Rather then once displease you more, to die,	193	U38 Elegy 'Tis	92
Then sword, or fire, or what is of the race	193	U38 Elegy 'Tis	101
Then I will studie falshood, to be true.	194	U38 Elegy 'Tis	108
Rather then want your light, I wish a grave.	194	U38 Elegy 'Tis	122
Your sacrifice, then here remaine with me.	199	U41 Elegy Since	18
Sooner then my affection from the faire.	200	U42 Elegy Let	13
More then of eithers manners, wit, or face!	202	U42 Elegy Let	88
Fitter to see the fire-light, then the day;	204	U43 Vulcan	44
More then advanc'd the houses, and their rites?	210	U43 Vulcan	164
More then the surfets, in thee, that day stood.	214	U44 Speach	48
More then to praise a Dog? or Horse? or speake	215	U44 Speach	71
It is a richer Purchase then of land.	216	U45 Squib	26
He could not find, then thee, of all that store	217	U46 Coke	3
More for thy Patronage, then for their Cause,	217	U46 Coke	12
No lesse of praise, then readers in all kinds	217	U46 Coke	19
And know whose ignorance is more then theirs;	218	U47 Tribe	24
Then these can ever be; or else wish none.	219	U47 Tribe	30
Then Phoebus; and much stronger	221	U48 Bacchus	22
Then Hippocrenes liquor:	221	U48 Bacchus	28
Then Cupid, and his Mother.	221	U48 Bacchus	36
Doth labour with the Phrase more then the sense?	222	U49 Pucell	14
Then the great Homers wit, for her, could faine;	224	U50 Countesse	24
One Poet, then of other folke ten score.	235	U62 Charles 1	10
Then now, to love the Soveraigne, and the Lawes?	236	U64 Charles 3	8
Then now, to love the Soveraigne, or his Lawes?	236	U64 Charles 3	V 8
What Month then May, was fitter to disclose	237	U65 Prince	4
'T were better spare a Butt, then spill his Muse.	241	U68 House-hold	12
Then knew the former ages: yet to life,	242	U69 Friend Son	23
Rather to boast rich hangings, then rare friends.	242	U69 Friend Son	26
That knits brave minds, and manners, more then blood.	246	U70 Ode	106
Which knits brave minds, and manners, more then blood.	246	U70 Ode	V106
A Bed-rid Wit, then a besieged Towne.	248	U71 Treasurer	15
Then thou shalt see to day:	252	U75 Epithalam.	5
This Feast, then can the Day,	254	U75 Epithalam.	55
The bright Brides paths, embelish'd more then thine	254	U75 Epithalam.	59
In him the times, no lesse then Prince, are prais'd,	256	U75 Epithalam.	115
Exacts then she is pleas'd to pay: no suits,	258	U75 Epithalam.	188
And in the chase, more then Sylvanus can,	264	U79 New-yeares	22
To better Pastures then great Pales can:	264	U79 New-yeares	30
Wee know no other power then his,	265	U79 New-yeares	42
Then ever Pales could, or Pan;	265	U79 New-yeares	61
Pan knowes no other power then his,	265	U79 New-yeares	64

	Page	Title	Line
THEN (cont.)			
And wish her state lesse happie then it is!	271	U81 Pawlet	84
Thy Neeces line, then thou that gav'st thy Name	274	U84 Descent	14
May rather yet adore, then spy.	276	U84 Body	20
And give you reasons more then one.	277	U84 Mind	4
Nothing can more adorne it, then the seat	284	U84 Muse	71
Better be dumbe, then superstitious!	284	U84 Muse	73
Much more desir'd, and dearer then before,	285	U84 Muse	109
Of sorrow, then all pompe of gaudy daies:	287	U84 Muse	182
More sweet then Olives, that new gather'd be	291	U85 Country	55
I thought me richer then the Persian King.	293	U87 Hor.3:9	4
Though he be fairer then a Starre;	294	U87 Hor.3:9	21
Thou lighter then the barke of any tree,	294	U87 Hor.3:9	22
And then rough Adria, angrier, farre;	294	U87 Hor.3:9	23
Makes his life longer then 'twas given him, much.	295	U89 Mart.8:77	8
To be that Smith; then live, mark'd one of those,	307	Horace	51
To be that fellow, then to be markt out	339	Horace V 53/ 51
To ignorance still, then either learne, or know?	311	Horace	131
To ignorance still, then yet to learne, or know?	341	Horace V126/131
Of Homers, forth in acts, then of thine owne,	313	Horace	185
Then those the faithfull eyes take in by show,	317	Horace	258
Have more or lesse then just five Acts: nor laid,	317	Horace	272
Then to the purpose leades, and fitly 'grees.	317	Horace	279
In vertue, and renowne of armes, then in	325	Horace	412
Happier then wretched art, and doth, by it,	325	Horace	420
And better stayes them there, then all fine noise	327	Horace	459
Cry, and doe more then the true Mourners: so	333	Horace	615
Then change; no word, or worke, more would he spend	335	Horace	630
The seaven-fold flower of Arte (more rich then gold)	361	Palmer	15
Splendor! O more then mortall,	364	Ode Splendor	1
Beautye, more then mortall,	364	Ode Splendor V 1
Then the stolne sports of Lovers,	365	Ode Splendor	7
Are deeper then their Faces:	365	Ode Splendor	22
A gentler Bird, then this,	366	Ode Who saith	7
Then Time hath donne,	367	Ode Who saith	54
Here, finer then comming from his Punke you him see,	375	Coryat 1	28
Shewes he dares more then Paules Church-yard durst do.	378	Coryat 2	85
And when your yeares rise more, then would be told,	384	Somerset	23
May hurt thee more with praise, then Foes with spight.	386	Browne	2
By offring not more sureties, then inow,	386	Browne	12
More then the Foster-father of this Child;	389	Aleman	14
Finer then was his Spanish, if my Oath	389	Aleman	18
Of tender eyes will more be wept, then seene:	398	Drayton	76
Then Affricke knew, or the full Grecian store!	398	Drayton	88
You aske noe more then certeyne politique Eyes,	404	Inigo Jones 1	45
A Goddess is, then paynted Cloth, Deal-boards,	406	Inigo Jones 1	93
No faith's more firme, or flat, then where't doth creep.	413	Ghyrlond	20
And newer, then could please them, by-cause trew.	415	Rutter	10
Of wit, and a new made: a Warden then,	415	Rutter	23
And better Blason them, then all their Coates,	419	Ode:If Men	8
And rather to the Fyre, then to the Rowte	420	Ode:If Men	21
Whose ayre will sooner Hell, then their dull senses peirce,	420	Ode:If Men	23
THEN			
Whom should my Muse then flie to, but the best	28	E4 James 1	9
Then takes up fresh commoditie, for dayes;	30	E12 Shift	13
If thou'ldst but use thy faith, as thou didst then,	32	E18 Censurer	7
For then, our water-conduits doe runne wine;	36	E29 Tilter	5
Left us of feare, but first our crimes, then lawes.	38	E35 James 2	6
Grant then, no rude hand remove her.	39	E40 Ratcliffe	4
The knight-wright's cheated then: Hee'll never pay.	42	E46 Luckless 1	5
Dispraise my worke, then praise it frostily;	43	E52 Courtling	2
What are thy petulant pleadings, Chev'ril, then,	44	E54 Chev'ril 2	3
In a great belly. Write, then on thy wombe,	46	E62 Would-bee	11
Stand high, then, Howard, high in eyes of men,	49	E67 Suffolk	5
High in thy bloud, thy place, but highest then,	49	E67 Suffolk	6
Then to begin, my Roe: He makes a state	50	E70 Wm Roe 1	2
Then, since we (more then many) these truths know:	50	E70 Wm Roe 1	7
And know thee, then, a judge, not of one yeare;	51	E74 Chancelor	2
T'inveigh 'gainst playes: what did he then but play?	52	E75 Lippe	4
Or then, or since, about our Muses springs,	53	E79 Rutland	3
How wilfull blind is he then, that would stray,	53	E80 Life/Death	3
Then doe I love thee, and behold thy ends	55	E86 Goodyere 2	3
And stoupe, and cringe. O then, it needs must prove	56	E88 Monsieur	14
Yet crown'd with honors, as with riches, then;	56	E89 Allen	4
I leave, then, acts, which should I prosequute	58	E91 Vere V 9
They, then, that living where the matter is bred,	60	E94 Bedford 3	11
To thine owne proper I ascribe then more;	61	E95 Savile	9
As, then, his cause, his glorie emulate.	61	E95 Savile	24
About his forme. What then so swells each lim?	63	E97 Motion	19
That thou at once, then, nobly maist defend	63	E98 Th Roe 1	7
Five of my jests, then stolne, past him a play.	64	E100 Playwrt 3	4
If we can get her, full of egs, and then,	64	E101 Supper	12
Forgive me then, if mine but say you are	67	E103 L Wroth 1	9
If men get name, for some one vertue: Then,	68	E106 E Herbert	1
And then lye with you, closer, then a punque,	69	E107 Hungry	20
And did not shame it with my actions, then,	70	E108 Soldiers	7
And first to know thine owne state, then the States.	70	E109 Nevil	12
Un-argued then, and yet hath fame from those;	71	E110 Edmonds 1	10
And that, midst envy' and parts; then fell by rage:	71	E110 Edmonds 1	14
Tell's of him, all the tales, it selfe then makes;	74	E115 Honest Man	17
Then, The townes honest Man's her errant'st knave.	75	E115 Honest Man	34
To his Lady, then Mrs. Cary.	80	E126 Mrs Cary	Ttl
For, then, all mouthes will judge, and their owne way:	82	E131 Ferrab. 2	3

664

THEN (cont.)

	Page	Title	Line
Then stand unto thy selfe, not seeke without	83	E131 Ferrab. 2	13
Might then both thee, thy worke and merit raise:	83	E132 Sylvester	2
Then let the former age, with this content her,	84	E133 Voyage	19
How close then, slaves. Alas, they will beshite us.	86	E133 Voyage	90
Then, selling not, a dish was tane to mince 'hem,	88	E133 Voyage	151
By any arte. Then wonder not,	93	F1 Why write no	10
Then hath thy orchard fruit, thy garden flowers,	94	F2 Penshurst	39
As if thou, then, wert mine, or I raign'd here:	95	F2 Penshurst	74
Did'st thou, then, make 'hem! and what praise was heap'd	95	F2 Penshurst	83
On thy good lady, then! who, therein, reap'd	95	F2 Penshurst	84
(Their rudenesse then is thought no sinne)	98	F3 Wroth	54
They thinke not, then, which side the cause shall leese,	98	F3 Wroth	61
'Tis better, if he then can dwell.	99	F3 Wroth	V 94
Thou did'st abuse, and then betray;	101	F4 To the World	42
Then, in a soile hast planted me,	101	F4 To the World	45
Spend not then his guifts in vaine.	102	F5 Celia 1	5
Then a thousand, then another	103	F6 Celia 2	9
Hundred, then unto the tother	103	F6 Celia 2	10
Say, are not women truely, then,	104	F7 Women but	5
Say, are not women truely, then,	104	F7 Women but	11
'Pray thee, feed contented, then,	105	F8 Sicknesse	13
Then, leave these lighter numbers, to light braines	108	F10 Proludium	7
And some one apteth to be trusted, then,	113	F12 Rutland	10
To curious light, the notes, I then shall sing,	115	F12 Rutland	76
To curious light, to notes, I then shall sing,	115	F12 Rutland	V 76
Then all, that have but done my Muse least grace,	115	F12 Rutland	79
Then all, that have but done my verse lesse grace,	115	F12 Rutland	V 79
Looke then, and see your selfe. I will not say	117	F13 Aubigny	29
Wherewith, then, Madame, can you better pay	118	F13 Aubigny	53
This day sayes, then, the number of glad yeeres	120	F14 Sydney	21
Will, then,	121	F14 Sydney	44
Of bone-fires. Then	121	F14 Sydney	59
What odour can be, then a heart contrite,	127	U1 Trinitie	15
If you then will read the Storie,	131	U2 Excuse	13
Mixe then your Notes, that we may prove	143	U3 Musicall	9
O sing not you then, lest the best	144	U3 Musicall	21
Sing you no more then, lest the best	144	U3 Musicall	V 21
For then their threats will kill me;	144	U4 Song	6
For then my hopes will spill me.	144	U4 Song	8
We are no women then, but wives.	146	U6 Defence	6
But then if I grow jealous madde,	147	U7 Nymph	10
But then t'increase my feares,	148	U7 Nymph	26
And knew their how, and where: we should have, then,	153	U13 Sacvile	3
You then, whose will not only, but desire	153	U13 Sacvile	7
But then, fist-fill'd, to put me off the sent.	154	U13 Sacvile	52
Then turning unto him is next at hand,	154	U13 Sacvile	56
Then give it to the Hound that did him bite;	155	U13 Sacvile	70
No more are these of us, let them then goe,	156	U13 Sacvile	113
Then stands it a triumphall marke! then Men	157	U13 Sacvile	139
Stand forth my Object, then, you that have beene	159	U14 Selden	29
And then of times (besides the bare Conduct	160	U14 Selden	51
With horrour rough, then rioting with wit!	160	U14 Selden	57
And then, leape mad on a neat Pickardill,	164	U15 Friend-Wars	70
And laugh, and measure thighes, then squeake, spring, itch,	164	U15 Friend-Wars	75
'Tis then a crime, when the Usurer is Judge.	169	U17 Friend-Debt	4
Then like, then love; and now would they amaze?	169	U18 Elegy Can	4
And then the best are, still, the blindest friends!	170	U18 Elegy Can	14
To use the present, then, is not abuse,	171	U19 Elegy By	21
Then take in hand thy Lyre,	175	U23 Himselfe	25
O, then inspire	177	U25 Desmond	10
Then shall my Verses, like strong Charmes,	177	U25 Desmond	18
Then shall our Verses, like strong Charmes,	177	U25 Desmond	V 18
O then (my best-best lov'd) let me importune,	180	U25 Desmond	63
O then (our best-best lov'd) let me importune,	180	U25 Desmond	V 63
Which all the world then styl'd divine?	181	U27 Ode Helen	20
But then his Mothers sweets you so apply,	182	U28 Worth	12
The Judge his favour timely then extends,	186	U32 Elsmere	1
Then com'st thou off with Victorie and Palme,	187	U33 Councellour	35
What was the cause then? Thought'st thou in disgrace	188	U34 Small Poxe	13
Then to your love, and gift. And all's but due.	189	U37 Friend-Book	3
And then with pause; for sever'd once, that's gone,	192	U38 Elegy 'Tis	47
And then his thunder frights more, then it kills.	193	U38 Elegy 'Tis	70
Then Mistris, here, here let your rigour end,	194	U38 Elegy 'Tis	105
You would be then most confident, that tho	194	U38 Elegy 'Tis	113
When I see you, then I doe see my Sun,	194	U38 Elegy 'Tis	120
Till then 'tis all but darknesse, that I have;	194	U38 Elegy 'Tis	121
And then I taste it. But as men drinke up	197	U40 Elegy That	3
Who shall forbid me then in Rithme to bee	200	U42 Elegy Let	5
But then consent, your Daughters and your Wives,	200	U42 Elegy Let	19
Then ope thy wardrobe, thinke me that poore Groome	201	U42 Elegy Let	51
I had deserv'd, then, thy consuming lookes,	203	U43 Vulcan	17
If none of these, then why this fire? Or find	203	U43 Vulcan	27
Thou hadst had some colour for thy flames,	204	U43 Vulcan	40
Kindled the fire! But then, did one returne,	209	U43 Vulcan	149
Burne to a snuffe, and then stinke out, and die:	211	U43 Vulcan	188
wast to a snuffe, and then stinke out, and die:	211	U43 Vulcan	V188
But they may see Gold-Chaines, and Pearle worne then,	213	U44 Speach	13
What love you then? your whore. what study? gate,	215	U44 Speach	87
They learne and studie; and then practise there.	215	U44 Speach	92
First weigh a friend, then touch, and trie him too:	216	U45 Squib	16
Then rest, and a friends value understand,	216	U45 Squib	25
As you have writ your selfe. Now stand, and then,	220	U47 Tribe	77

THEN (cont.)

	Page	Title	Line
See then thou dost attend him,	221	U48 Bacchus	17
Do's the Court-Pucell then so censure me,	222	U49 Pucell	1
What then his Father was, that since is hee,	225	U51 Bacon	11
And then to be return'd; on protestation	229	U54 Squib	18
Then would I promise here to give	229	U55 Burges	3
That trembles in the blaze, but (then) mounts higher!	233	U59 Newcastle	8
Then, Royall Charles, and Mary, doe not grutch	236	U63 Charles 2	7
An Epigram to the Queene, then lying in. 1630.	238	U66 Queene	Ttl
Glorie to God. Then, Haile to Mary! spring	238	U66 Queene	13
Our thanks to God. Then, Haile to Mary! spring	238	U66 Queene	V 13
Thou, looking then about,	242	U70 Ode	5
He purchas'd friends, and fame, and honours then,	244	U70 Ode	35
So deep, as he did then death's waters sup;	244	U70 Ode	41
Call, noble Lucius, then for Wine,	245	U70 Ode	75
You lik'd, then after, to apply	247	U70 Ode	108
And then noyse forth the burden of their Song,	249	U72 King	V 17
O how will then our Court be pleas'd,	251	U74 Weston	25
Force from the Phoenix, then, no raritie	255	U75 Epithalam.	81
The holy Prelate prayes, then takes the Ring,	256	U75 Epithalam.	123
Askes first, Who gives her (I Charles) then he plights	256	U75 Epithalam.	124
Hearing their charge, and then	256	U75 Epithalam.	127
So large; his Body then, not boughs, project his shade.	258	U75 Epithalam.	V184
Then goe on, and doe its worst;	260	U76 Petition	29
Allowes them? Then, what copies shall be had,	263	U78 Digby	29
Allowes them? Then, what copies will be had,	263	U78 Digby	V 29
Wilt thou be, Muse, when this shall then befall?	263	U78 Digby	V 31
For, had we here said lesse, we had sung nothing then.	263	U79 New-yeares	8
Then comforted her Lord! and blest her Sonne!	270	U81 Pawlet	57
But as he soares at that, he bruiseth then	272	U81 Pawlet	98
Then let the beames of that, disperse	276	U84 Body	17
Sweet Mind, then speake your selfe, and say,	278	U84 Mind	17
For they are strong Supporters: But, till then,	281	U84 Kenelme	14
That shall re-joyne yee. Was she, then, so deare,	285	U84 Muse	107
The Poplar tall, he then doth marrying twine	290	U85 Country	9
Then now beneath some ancient Oke he may,	290	U85 Country	23
Then when the thundring Jove his Snow and showres	290	U85 Country	29
Not Lucrine Oysters I could then more prize,	291	U85 Country	49
Could not goe downe my belly then	291	U85 Country	54
Or at the Feast of Bounds, the Lambe then slaine,	291	U85 Country	59
Let us not then rush blindly on unto it,	294	U88 Petronius	3
Invention. Now, to speake; and then differ	307	Horace	61
Right spare, and warie: then thou speak'st to mee	307	Horace	66
Thy selfe in teares, then me thy losse will wound,	311	Horace	146
Thy selfe in tears, then me thy harms will wound,	342	Horace	V146
And then as swift to leave what he hath lov'd.	315	Horace	236
As his departing take much thence: lest, then,	317	Horace	251
Till then unknowne, in Carts, wherein did ride	319	Horace	313
An ounce, what makes it then? The halfe pound just;	327	Horace	471
Cast out by voyces; want they pleasure, then	329	Horace	512
How then? Why, as a Scrivener, if h'offend	329	Horace	529
Then: If your fault you rather had defend	335	Horace	629
According to the Moone. But, then the boyes	335	Horace	647
Under the angry Moon. But then the boys	354	Horace	V647
There's none will take the care, to helpe him then;	335	Horace	654
Then I admir'd, the rare and prescious use	361	Palmer	9
Then why should we dispaire? Dispaire, away:	363	Riches	17
Alas: then whither wade I,	365	Ode Splendor	17
Alas: then whither trade I,	365	Ode Splendor	V 17
Be then both Rare, and Good; and long	367	Ode Who saith	33
It covers, first, a Virgin; and then, one	371	Epitaph	3
Come forth thou bonnie bouncing booke then, daughter	378	Coryat 2	86
Ever his thighes Male then, and his braines Shee.	378	Coryat 2	92
. . . Panegyricke lines, but then were upon some occasions	379	Coryat 3	Ttl
shall looke, & on hyme soe, then arte's a lyer	383	Rich	15
That all, that view you then, and late; may say,	384	Somerset	25
To say but one, were single. Then it chimes,	389	Aleman	3
His face; the Print would then surpasse	390	Reader	7
Whom shee, with Sorrow first did lodge, then feast,	394	Jane Ogle	20
Then entertaine, and as Deaths Harbinger;	394	Jane Ogle	21
But then, thy'epistolar Heroick Songs,	397	Drayton	29
I thought thee then our Orpheus, that wouldst try	397	Drayton	35
But then refreshed, with thy Fayerie Court,	398	Drayton	79
Hence, then, prophane: Here needs no words expense	400	Beaumont	3
Stay, till she make her vaine Approches. Then	401	Beaumont	15
I then could rayse my notes	419	Ode:If Men	6
Breake then thie quills, blott out	420	Ode:If Men	19
Throwe, Holye Virgin, then	421	Ode:If Men	37
Censure, not sharplye then, but mee advise	421	Censure	1

TH'ENAMOUR'D

	Page	Title	Line
Where ere they tread th'enamour'd ground,	264	U79 New-yeares	36

THENCE

	Page	Title	Line
And your high names: I doe desire, that thence	69	E108 Soldiers	3
And thence, deprave thee, and thy worke. To those	72	E111 Edmonds 2	11
Including all, were thence call'd harmonie:	82	E130 Ferrab. 1	14
And thence, the ruddy Satyres oft provoke	94	F2 Penshurst	17
They are, and have beene taught religion: Thence	96	F2 Penshurst	93
Thence, as sweet, as you are faire,	137	U2 Kisse	4
That never came ill odour thence:	152	U12 Corbet	18
In the same Mines of knowledge; and thence brought	161	U14 Selden	76
In the rich Mines of knowledge; and thence brought	161	U14 Selden	V 76
Did not she save from thence, to build a Rome?	210	U43 Vulcan	162
With reverence using all the gifts thence given.	219	U47 Tribe	62

	Page	Title	Line
THENCE (cont.)			
Yet are got off thence, with cleare mind, and hands	234	U61 Epigram	7
And all beatitudes, that thence doe flow:	271	U81 Pawlet	75
And, though the sound were parted thence,	279	U84 Mind	39
Or hence, or thence, he drives with many a Hound	290	U85 Country	31
As his departing take much thence: lest, then,	317	Horace	251
Thence draw forth true expressions. For, sometimes,	327	Horace	455
Hath shed, or humane frailtie not kept thence.	329	Horace	528
Not thence be sav'd, although indeed he could?	335	Horace	658
From thence, display thy wing againe	367	Ode Who saith	41
From thence is gon	368	Ode Who saith	68
From thence to honour thee, I would not seeke	391	Shakespeare	32
Drawne Aristotle on us! & thence showne	402	Inigo Jones 1	9
Disguis'd? and thence drag forth Enormity?	405	Inigo Jones 1	81
TH'ENVY'D			
Th'envy'd returne, of forty pound in gold.	408	Detractor	4
THEOCRITUS			
Which made me thinke, the old Theocritus,	397	Drayton	27
THEORBO			
Harpe, Lute, Theorbo sprung,	239	U67 Muses	17
Lute, Lyre, Theorbo, all are call'd to day.	263	U79 New-yeares	2
TH'EPILOGUE			
And sits, till th'Epilogue saies Clap, or Crowne:	315	Horace	222
THERE'			
There's reason good, that you good lawes should make:	34	E24 Parliament	1
And there's both losse of time, and losse of sport	46	E62 Would-bee	10
I Cannot thinke there's that antipathy	52	E75 Lippe	1
There's none so dull, that for your stile would aske,	68	E105 L Wroth 2	15
Doe what you come for, Captayne, There's your meate.	69	E107 Hungry	32
There's no vexation, that can make thee prime.	73	E112 Gamster	22
That there's no journey set, or thought upon,	81	E129 Mime	3
There's none, that dwell about them, wish them downe;	94	F2 Penshurst	47
There's nothing I can wish, for which I stay.	95	F2 Penshurst	75
That cryes, we dreame, and sweares, there's no such thing,	111	F11 Epode	67
That cryes, I dreame, and sweares, there's no such thing,	111	F11 Epode	V 67
Her face there's none can like by Candle light.	223	U49 Pucell	32
Earths grossnesse; There's the how, and why.	279	U84 Mind	44
our grossnesse; There's the how, and why.	279	U84 Mind	V 44
There's Albin's sonne will say, Substract an ounce	327	Horace	467
Yet, there's a value given to this man.	331	Horace	554
There's none will take the care, to helpe him then;	335	Horace	654
Here's one makes verses, but there's none knows why:	355	Horace	V670
to which there's no materiall that endures;	387	Cavendish	8
THERE			
Send it to Bucklers-bury, there 'twill, well.	28	E3 Bookseller	12
When was there contract better driven by Fate?	28	E5 Union	1
He steales to ordinaries; there he playes	30	E12 Shift	11
Keepe thy selfe there, and thinke thy valure right,	32	E16 Brain-hardy	9
Seas, serenes, swords, shot, sicknesse, all are there.	37	E32 Roe 2	10
When even there, where most thou praysest mee,	44	E55 Beaumont	9
I meant each softest vertue, there should meet,	52	E76 Bedford 1	11
Straight went I home; and there not like a Poet,	55	E84 Bedford 2	5
To former height, and there in circle tarrie,	55	E85 Goodyere 1	9
Or Bils, and there he buyes the names of books.	59	E92 New Crie	24
And, though fowle, now, be scarce, yet there are clarkes,	65	E101 Supper	15
May ye be there; and godwit, if we can:	65	E101 Supper	19
Digestive cheese, and fruit there sure will bee;	65	E101 Supper	27
There Juno sate, and yet no Peacock by.	68	E105 L Wroth 2	18
For which there must more sea, and land be leap'd,	69	E107 Hungry	16
And that, in action, there is nothing new,	72	E111 Edmonds 2	5
I leave thee there, and giving way, entend	72	E112 Gamster	9
I passe to Elegies; Thou meet'st me there:	73	E112 Gamster	13
That the wit there, and manners might be sav'd:	73	E113 Overbury	6
And him it layes on; if he be not there.	74	E115 Honest Man	16
The full, the flowing graces there enshrin'd;	79	E125 Uvedale	8
Is there a hope, that Man would thankefull bee,	80	E127 Aubigny	1
Attend thee hence; and there, may all thy ends,	81	E128 Wm Roe 2	6
The filth, stench, noyse: save only what was there	84	E133 Voyage	9
Furies there wanted not: each scold was ten.	84	E133 Voyage	15
A Docke there is, that called is Avernus,	85	E133 Voyage	41
Thou hast seene hell (some say) and know'st all nookes there,	85	E133 Voyage	51
Canst tell me best, how every Furie lookes there,	85	E133 Voyage	52
But many Moones there shall not wane (quoth hee)	87	E133 Voyage	103
Cats there lay divers had beene flead, and rosted,	88	E133 Voyage	149
But 'mong'st these Tiberts, who do'you thinke there was?	88	E133 Voyage	155
There, in the writhed barke, are cut the names	94	F2 Penshurst	15
Thy copp's, too, nam'd of Gamage, thou hast there,	94	F2 Penshurst	19
For fire, or lights, or livorie: all is there;	95	F2 Penshurst	73
There wasted, some not paid for yet!	97	F3 Wroth	12
'Tis better, if there can dwell.	99	F3 Wroth	94
Render his head in there againe?	101	F4 To the World	32
There should a miracle be wrought.	101	F4 To the World	60
There are those, that, for thy sake,	105	F8 Sicknesse	25
As giving it a hope, that there	106	F9 Celia 3	11
but being well assured that there	106	F9 Celia 3	V 11
Object arrive there, but the heart (our spie)	109	F11 Epode	11
And, at her strong armes end, there hold up even,	114	F12 Rutland	V 42
Gave killing strokes. There were brave men, before	114	F12 Rutland	53
There like a rich, and golden pyramede,	115	F12 Rutland	83
Your forme imprest there: not with tickling rimes,	116	F12 Rutland	87
Your forme imprest there: not with tinckling rimes,	116	F12 Rutland	V 87
Of any good minde, now: There are so few.	116	F13 Aubigny	2
And call it their brave sinne. For such there be	119	F13 Aubigny	85

THERE (cont.)

	Page	Title	Line
I feele my griefes too, and there scarce is ground,	122	F15 Heaven	21
Shall I there rest!	128	U1 Trinitie	48
I foole-hardie, there up-tooke	132	U2 How he saw	20
So that, there, I stood a stone,	132	U2 How he saw	27
As alone there triumphs to the life	134	U2 Triumph	19
There; or to reforme a curle;	140	U2 Promise	24
In a body, should be there.	141	U2 Her man	35
Of our Towne Gallantry! or why there rests	155	U13 Sacvile	92
Sure there is Misterie in it, I not know,	156	U13 Sacvile	97
That makes the Arch. The rest that there were put	157	U13 Sacvile	137
Then which there is not unto Studie'a more	158	U14 Selden	13
Themselves through favouring what is there not found:	159	U14 Selden	16
Themselves through favouring that is there not found:	159	U14 Selden	V 16
How are Traditions there examin'd: how	160	U14 Selden	49
But there are objects, bid him to be gone	163	U15 Friend-Wars	28
To have his Court-bred-fillie there commend	163	U15 Friend-Wars	48
'Tis there civilitie to be a whore;	163	U15 Friend-Wars	54
For the recovery of my voyce? No, there	167	U15 Friend-Wars	154
And he is not in friendship. Nothing there	169	U17 Friend-Debt	5
Of all vice hurld together, there he was,	172	U21 Ltl Shrub	6
What is there more that can ennoble blood?	185	U30 Burleigh	6
Are there for Charitie, and not for fee.	186	U32 Elsmere	6
Envious and foule Disease, could there not be	188	U34 Small Poxe	1
What did she worth thy spight? were there not store	188	U34 Small Poxe	3
Where Love doth shine, there needs no Sunne,	189	U36 Song	5
Or there to sterve it. Helpe, O you that may	191	U38 Elegy 'Tis	7
There may some face or menace of a storme	191	U38 Elegy 'Tis	13
If there be nothing worthy you can see	191	U38 Elegy 'Tis	15
There greatnesse takes a glorie to relieve.	192	U38 Elegy 'Tis	34
There is no Father that for one demerit,	192	U38 Elegy 'Tis	41
There is not any punishment, or paine,	194	U38 Elegy 'Tis	103
And that there is no life in me, but love.	194	U38 Elegy 'Tis	112
As if it were not worthy to be there:	199	U41 Elegy Since	16
There is not worne that lace, purle, knot or pin,	200	U42 Elegy Let	16
Curst in their Cradles, or there chang'd by Elves,	200	U42 Elegy Let	23
An Officer there, did make most solemne love,	201	U42 Elegy Let	53
Such Songsters there are store of; witnesse he	201	U42 Elegy Let	65
Had I wrote treason there, or heresie,	203	U43 Vulcan	15
Conceal'd, or kept there, that was fit to be,	203	U43 Vulcan	21
Did I there wound the honours of the Crowne?	203	U43 Vulcan	23
There were some pieces of as base allay,	204	U43 Vulcan	42
And as false stampe there; parcels of a Play,	204	U43 Vulcan	43
But in my Deske, what was there to accite	206	U43 Vulcan	85
But in my Deske, what was there to envite	206	U43 Vulcan	V 85
There were of search, and mastry in the Arts.	206	U43 Vulcan	88
There were of search, and mastry of the Arts.	206	U43 Vulcan	V 88
Was there made English: with the Grammar too,	207	U43 Vulcan	91
To our owne Ladyes; and in storie there	207	U43 Vulcan	97
for our owne Ladyes; and in storie there	207	U43 Vulcan	V 97
Some Alchimist there may be yet, or odde	208	U43 Vulcan	118
There were, that streight did nose it out for newes,	209	U43 Vulcan	V139
When Venus there maintain'd the Misterie.	209	U43 Vulcan	144
There was a Judgement shew'n too in an houre.	210	U43 Vulcan	158
Lyes there no Writ, out of the Chancerie	210	U43 Vulcan	174
some 4 myles hence and have him there disgorge	211	U43 Vulcan	V184
And there made Swords, Bills, Glaves, and Armes your fill;	212	U43 Vulcan	198
Strooke in at Millan with the Cutlers there;	212	U43 Vulcan	200
Strooke in at Millan with the villors there;	212	U43 Vulcan	V200
Supplant bold Panton; and brought there to view	214	U44 Speach	34
And there instruct the noble English heires	214	U44 Speach	59
Carriage, and dressing. There is up of late	215	U44 Speach	88
They learne and studie, and then practise there.	215	U44 Speach	92
For there are many slips, and Counterfeits.	216	U45 Squib	17
Of earthen Jarres, there may molest me too:	219	U47 Tribe	55
And that there be no fev'ry heats, nor colds,	220	U47 Tribe	67
So may there never Quarrell	221	U48 Bacchus	31
Shall feast it, thou maist love there	221	U48 Bacchus	38
For there the wicked in the Chaire of scorne,	223	U49 Pucell	45
But there are lines, wherewith I might b'embrac'd.	226	U52 Answer	3
If there be no money;	231	U57 Burges	21
View'd there the mercat, read the wretched rate	234	U61 Epigram	3
At which there are, would sell the Prince, and State:	234	U61 Epigram	4
And there to stand so. Hast now envious Moone,	238	U65 Prince	9
The Mother of our Prince? When was there seene	238	U66 Queene	6
And Gunnes there, spare to poure	239	U67 Muses	8
And there he lives with memorie; and Ben	246	U70 Ode	84
As all the wealth of Season, there was spread;	251	U74 Weston	15
Stand there; for when a noble Nature's rais'd,	256	U75 Epithalam.	113
There is a Feast behind,	257	U75 Epithalam.	141
There; but, renewed, say,	258	U75 Epithalam.	167
And never may there want one of the Stem,	258	U75 Epithalam.	177
All there envie of the Rymes,	259	U76 Petition	V 18
On Natures secrets, there, as her owne bookes:	271	U81 Pawlet	70
On naturall secret, there, as her owne bookes:	271	U81 Pawlet	V 70
That ever had beginning there, to'ave end!	271	U81 Pawlet	91
And Men may thinke, all light rose there.	276	U84 Body	16
And let there be a starry Robe	276	U84 Body	26
There, high exalted in the Spheare,	279	U84 Mind	29
As what it spoke, it planted there.	279	U84 Mind	36
For her t'inhabit? There is it.	280	U84 Mind	52
And where it stayes, it there becomes	280	U84 Mind	63
For, as there are three Natures, Schoolemen call	284	U84 Muse	51

	Page	Title	Line

THERE (cont.)
Like single; so, there is a third, commixt,	284	U84 Muse	53
Who will be there, against that day prepar'd,	284	U84 Muse	59
That, planted round, there sing before the Lamb,	285	U84 Muse	89
Thither, you hope to come; and there to find	285	U84 Muse	103
When shee departed? you will meet her there,	285	U84 Muse	108
There, all the happy soules, that ever were,	285	U64 Muse	113
And each shall know, there, one anothers face,	285	U84 Muse	115
There shall the Brother, with the Sister walke,	285	U84 Muse	117
Will there revealed be in Majestie!	286	U84 Muse	130
There, or the tall witch-hazill hee doth twine	290	U85 Country	V 9
The lowing herds there grazing are:	290	U85 Country	14
There jest, and feast, make him thine host,	292	U86 Hor.4:1	11
There shall thy dainty Nostrill take	292	U86 Hor.4:1	21
There twice a day in sacred Laies,	292	U86 Hor.4:1	25
There is no labour, nor no shame in this;	294	U88 Petronius	8
Into a Swallow there; Nor Cadmus take	317	Horace	267
Worth his untying happen there: And not	317	Horace	274
As neither any God, were brought in there,	321	Horace	331
As neither any God, be brought in there,	346	Horace	V323/331
There comes sometimes to things of meanest place.	321	Horace	354
Him that buyes Pulse there, or perhaps may like	347	Horace	V354/362
And there is given too unworthy leave	323	Horace	389
There words will follow, not against their will.	325	Horace	444
There words will never follow 'gainst their will.	349	Horace	V444
And better stayes them there, then all fine noise	327	Horace	459
Thinke wee, or hope, there can be Verses fain'd	327	Horace	474
There are yet faults, which we would well forgive,	329	Horace	520
This saying: To some things there is assign'd	331	Horace	548
There may a Lawyer be, may not excell;	331	Horace	550
Himselfe there purposely, or no; and would	335	Horace	657
And, there an end of him, reciting makes:	337	Horace	678
And there an end of him with reading makes:	355	Horace	V678
There charme the rout	367	Ode Who saith	44
There coole thy Plumes,	368	Ode Who saith	76
To him, and he there shrin'd;	369	Ode Who saith	106
Being tould there, Reason cannot, Sense may erre.	370	Author	14
And there, while he gives the zealous Bravado,	375	Coryat 1	22
There nam'd to be travell'd? For this our Tom saith:	380	Coryat 3	21
The truth of his heart there, and tell's what a clocke	380	Coryat 3	24
That sacred to Odcombe are there now suspended,	380	Coryat 3	40
He there doth protest he saw of the eleven.	380	Coryat 3	46
I writ he onely his taile there did wave;	380	Coryat 3	56
So, be there never discontent, or sorrow,	384	Somerset	15
Advanc'd, and made a Constellation there!	392	Shakespeare	76
In the great masse, or machine there is stirr'd?	395	May	22
There read I, streight, thy learned Legends three,	397	Drayton	25
There, thou art Homer! Pray thee, use the stile	398	Drayton	59
Onely my losse is, that I am not there:	398	Drayton	91
Mythology there painted on slit deale!	404	Inigo Jones 1	48
Oh, to make Boardes to speake! There is a taske	404	Inigo Jones 1	49
yearly set out there, to sayle downe the Street,	407	Inigo Jones 2	18
This is my censure. Now there is a new	415	Rutter	19
Cry'd up of late: Whereto there must be first	415	Rutter	21
for if there, or peace or warr be,	417	Moon	22
If there be a Coockold Major,	417	Moon	25

THEREAT
| And thereat the great Eclipse. Two houres but runne, | 238 | U65 Prince | V 11 |

THEREBY
| As well as from his braines, and claimest thereby | 378 | Coryat 2 | 90 |

THEREFORE
On them: And therefore doe not onely shunne	59	E92 New Crie	38
No, I doe, therefore, call Posteritie	80	E127 Aubigny	4
Or his to Antwerpe. Therefore, once more, list ho'.	85	E133 Voyage	40
And brag, that they were therefore borne.	99	F3 Wroth	72
I, therefore, who professe my selfe in love	116	F13 Aubigny	7
Giddie with change, and therefore cannot see	118	F13 Aubigny	67
Therefore, Charis, you must do't,	140	U2 Promise	13
I'le therefore aske no more, but bid you love;	171	U19 Elegy By	15
That have good places: therefore once agen,	212	U43 Vulcan	212
That have good fortunes: therefore once agen,	212	U43 Vulcan	V212
Yet, not as therefore wild, and tame should cleave	305	Horace	14
Yet not as therefore cruell things should cleave	338	Horace	V 14
Take, therefore, you that write, still, matter fit	307	Horace	53
Take therefore, you that write, a subject fit	339	Horace	V 55/ 53
The nut-crackers throughout, will they therefore	321	Horace	363
To Roman Poets. Shall I therefore weave	323	Horace	390
Which it doth threaten. Therefore, where I see	329	Horace	525
And therefore how ever the travelling nation,	380	Coryat 3	29
And therefore I commend unto the Wife,	386	Husband	8
I, therefore will begin. Soule of the Age!	391	Shakespeare	17

THEREIN
With such a one. And therein keepes it's word.	74	E115 Honest Man	21
Of wood, of water: therein thou art faire.	93	F2 Penshurst	8
On thy good lady, then! who, therein, reap'd	95	F2 Penshurst	84
Therein, thy Love.	129	U1 Father	6
Which you will bury; but therein, the strife	158	U13 Sacvile	160
And therein (which is worth his valour too)	378	Coryat 2	84

THEREOF
And what I write thereof find farre, and free	41	E43 Salisbury 1	10
And pray the fruites thereof, and the increase;	212	U43 Vulcan	210
I durst not aime at, the dotes thereof were such	269	U81 Pawlet	V 25
Thereof, no notion can expresse how much	269	U81 Pawlet	26

THEREOF (cont.)
Thereof, to Time. . . . 273 U84 Cradle 12
At every line some pinn thereof should slacke . . . 395 May 5
And know the woofe, and warpe thereof; can tell . . . 415 Rutter 15
THEREON
But thou thereon did'st onely breath, . . . 106 F9 Celia 3 13
Now I have better thought thereon, . . . 277 U84 Mind 2
THERE'S
There's reason good, that you good lawes should make: . . 34 E24 Parliament 1
And there's both losse of time, and losse of sport . . 46 E62 Would-bee 10
I Cannot thinke there's that antipathy . . . 52 E75 Lippe 1
There's none so dull, that for your stile would aske, . . 68 E105 L Wroth 2 15
Doe what you come for, Captayne, There's your meate. . . 69 E107 Hungry 32
There's no vexation, that can make thee prime. . . 73 E112 Gamster 22
That there's no journey set, or thought upon, . . . 81 E129 Mime 3
There's none, that dwell about them, wish them downe; . . 94 F2 Penshurst 47
There's nothing I can wish, for which I stay. . . . 95 F2 Penshurst 75
That cryes, we dreame, and sweares, there's no such thing, . 111 F11 Epode 67
That cryes, I dreame, and sweares, there's no such thing, . 111 F11 Epode V 67
Her face there's none can like by Candle light. . . 223 U49 Pucell 32
Earths grossnesse; There's the how, and why. . . 279 U84 Mind 44
our grossnesse; There's the how, and why. . . . 279 U84 Mind V 44
There's Albin's sonne will say, Substract an ounce . . 327 Horace 467
Yet, there's a value given to this man. . . . 331 Horace 554
There's none will take the care, to helpe him then; . . 335 Horace 654
Here's one makes verses, but there's none knows why: . . 355 Horace V670
to which there's no materiall that endures; . . . 387 Cavendish 8
THERFORE
Nor feare thy latest day, nor wish therfore. . . . 295 U90 Mart.10:47 13
TH'ESCAPE
If in th'escape an artlesse path we tread. . . . 339 Horace V 46/44
THESE
If, without these vile arts, it will not sell, . . 28 E3 Bookseller 11
Surly, use other arts, these only can . . . 36 E28 Surly 21
In these times. Few so have ru'de . . . 39 E40 Ratcliffe 14
And can to these be silent, Salisburie, . . . 47 E63 Salisbury 2 9
With thy new place, bring I these early fruits . . 47 E64 Salisbury 3 2
These (noblest Cecil) labour'd in my thought, . . 48 E64 Salisbury 3 15
Then, since we (more than many) these truths know: . . 50 E70 Wm Roe 1 7
But these, desir'd by you, the makers ends . . . 60 E94 Bedford 3 5
Dare for these poemes, yet, both aske, and read, . . 60 E94 Bedford 3 12
Limons, and wine for sauce: to these, a coney . . 65 E101 Supper 13
And, in some yeere, all these together heap'd, . . 69 E107 Hungry 15
In these west-parts, nor when that warre was done, . . 71 E110 Edmonds 1 2
To have engrav'd these acts, with his owne stile, . . 71 E110 Edmonds 1 6
Not all these, Edmonds, or what else put too, . . 71 E110 Edmonds 1 11
These were thy knowing arts: which who doth now . . 75 E116 Jephson 13
No, Shelton, give me thee, canst want all these, . . 76 E119 Shelton 7
Who prov'st, all these were, and againe may bee. . . 78 E122 Rudyerd 2 10
I'extract, and choose the best of all these knowne, . . 80 E128 Wm Roe 2 3
When these were but the praises of the Art. . . 82 E130 Ferrab. 1 16
But when I have said, The proofes of all these bee . . 82 E130 Ferrab. 1 17
In it' owne hall; when these (in worthy scorne . . 85 E133 Voyage 31
These be the cause of those thicke frequent mists . . 87 E133 Voyage 130
But 'mong'st these Tiberts, who do'you thinke there was? . 88 E133 Voyage 155
I weare not these my wings in vaine. . . . 93 F1 Why write no 7
And these grudg'd at, art reverenc'd the while. . . 93 F2 Penshurst 6
These, Penshurst, are thy praise, and yet not all. . . 96 F2 Penshurst 89
If these, who have but sense, can shun . . . 101 F4 To the World 33
But I will beare these, with that scorne, . . . 102 F4 To the World 63
These have crimes accounted beene. . . . 102 F5 Celia 1 18
These, disease, will thee deserve: . . . 106 F8 Sicknesse 43
These, disease, will they deserve: . . . 106 F8 Sicknesse V 43
Then, leave these lighter numbers, to light braines . . 108 F10 Proludium 7
Let these in wanton feete daunce out their soules. . . 108 F10 Proludium 11
Thus, by these subtle traines, . . . 110 F11 Epode 28
The world hath seene, which all these had in trust, . . 114 F12 Rutland 39
Or common places, filch'd, that take these times, . . 116 F12 Rutland 88
A Princes fortune: These are gifts of chance, . . 117 F13 Aubigny 41
You, Madame, yong have learn'd to shunne these shelves, . 119 F13 Aubigny 89
Of these forc'd joyes, . . . 120 F14 Sydney 18
Of discontent; or that these prayers bee . . . 122 F15 Heaven 25
After many scornes like these, . . . 133 U2 Suffered 1
Guesse of these, which is the true; . . . 138 U2 Kisse 34
And all these through her eyes, have stopt her eares. . . 150 U9 Picture 18
And adde his Actions unto these, . . . 152 U12 Corbet 19
But these men ever want: their very trade . . . 155 U13 Sacvile 79
That with these mixtures we put out her light. . . 156 U13 Sacvile 110
No more are these of us, let them then goe, . . . 156 U13 Sacvile 113
Of Christendome! And neither of these know, . . . 157 U13 Sacvile 129
Hee's one of blood, and fashion! and with these . . 164 U15 Friend-Wars 55
O, these so ignorant Monsters! light, as proud, . . 164 U15 Friend-Wars 59
For these with her young Companie shee'll enter, . . 164 U15 Friend-Wars 79
And comes by these Degrees, the Stile t'inherit . . 164 U15 Friend-Wars 81
Great, brave, and fashion'd folke, these are allow'd . . 164 U15 Friend-Wars 84
Thus these doe talke. And are these objects fit . . 165 U15 Friend-Wars 101
His time? health? soule? will he for these goe throw . . 165 U15 Friend-Wars 103
Is it for these that Fine-man meets the street . . 165 U15 Friend-Wars 106
For lesse Securitie? O for these . . . 165 U15 Friend-Wars 113
For less Securitie? O Freind, for these . . . 165 U15 Friend-Wars V113
Friend, flie from hence; and let these kindled rimes . . 167 U15 Friend-Wars 162
These take, and now goe seeke thy peace in Warre, . . 168 U15 Friend-Wars 195
But which shall lead me on? both these are blind: . . 170 U18 Elegy Can 11

THESE (cont.)

	Page	Title	Line
On these darke rymes; that my affection	177	U25 Desmond	15
On these darke rymes; that our affection	177	U25 Desmond	V 15
Sinke not beneath these terrors:	177	U25 Desmond	30
Have all these done (and yet I misse	182	U27 Ode Helen	29
Though not in these, in rithmes not wholly dumbe,	182	U28 Worth	2
Be not affected with these markes too much	193	U38 Elegy 'Tis	83
I number these as being of the Chore	193	U38 Elegy 'Tis	99
In at a hole, and see these Actions creepe	201	U42 Elegy Let	60
If none of these, then why this fire? Or find	203	U43 Vulcan	27
These, had'st thou pleas'd either to dine, or sup,	206	U43 Vulcan	83
These, had'st thou been pleas'd either to dine, or sup,	206	U43 Vulcan	V 83
How in these ruines, Vulcan, thou dost lurke,	207	U43 Vulcan	105
How in these ruines, Vulcan, durst thou lurke,	207	U43 Vulcan	V105
Cause thou canst doe these halting tricks in fire?	208	U43 Vulcan	V110
And what hast thou done in these pettie spights,	210	U43 Vulcan	163
These ten yeares day; As all may sweare that looke	213	U44 Speach	27
But why are all these Irons i'the fire	215	U44 Speach	93
I may no longer on these pictures stay,	216	U44 Speach	98
These Carkasses of honour; Taylors blocks,	216	U44 Speach	99
But these with wearing will themselves unfold:	216	U45 Squib	19
But for a Sealing: let these men protest.	218	U47 Tribe	15
Call every night to Supper in these fitts,	218	U47 Tribe	21
Let these men have their wayes, and take their times	218	U47 Tribe	25
Then these can ever be; or else wish none.	219	U47 Tribe	30
Though I doe neither heare these newes, nor tell	219	U47 Tribe	46
These I will honour, love, embrace, and serve:	220	U47 Tribe	71
These Graces, when the rest of Ladyes view	225	U50 Countesse	31
For whose returnes, and many, all these pray:	225	U51 Bacon	6
At these Immortall Mangers Virgil fed.	228	U53 Newcastle	20
I can lose none in tendring these to you.	231	U56 Covell	28
And, in these Cures, do'st so thy selfe enlarge,	235	U62 Charles 1	7
These make the lines of life, and that's her ayre.	245	U70 Ode	64
To separate these twi-/Lights	246	U70 Ode	92
Had sow'd these fruits, and got the harvest in.	247	U70 Ode	128
Had they but grace, of thinking, at these routes,	249	U72 King	15
If they had leisure, at these lawfull routs,	249	U72 King	V 15
Saw'st thou that Paire, became these Rites so well,	254	U75 Epithalam.	76
With Angels, Muse, to speake these: Nothing can	255	U75 Epithalam.	84
Illustrate these, but they	255	U75 Epithalam.	85
These two, now holy Church hath made them one,	257	U75 Epithalam.	139
One to the other, long e're these to light were brought.	257	U75 Epithalam.	144
Some houres before it should, that these may know	257	U75 Epithalam.	146
Catch'd with these Arts, wherein the Judge is wise	261	U77 Treasurer	11
Caught them thus, wherein the Judge is wise	261	U77 Treasurer	V 11
And act the businesse, which these paint, or carve.	261	U77 Treasurer	V 16
These I looke up at, with a reverent eye,	261	U77 Treasurer	23
These looke you up at, with a measuring eye,	261	U77 Treasurer	V 23
Yet read him in these lines: He doth excell	262	U78 Digby	2
Yet take him in these lines: He doth excell	262	U78 Digby	V 2
And offer your just service on these plaines;	263	U79 New-yeares	12
That have a Flock, or Herd, upon these plaines;	265	U79 New-yeares	47
To touch these Mysteries! We may admire	269	U81 Pawlet	31
What makes these Velvets, Silkes, and Lawne,	275	U84 Body	2
Send these suspected helpes, to aide	275	U84 Body	5
And Paradise confining these.	276	U84 Body	24
But these are like a Mind, not it.	278	U84 Mind	12
Boast not these Titles of your Ancestors;	281	U84 Kenelme	10
That thus have ventur'd these true straines upon;	289	U84 Muse	227
Who (amongst these delights) would not forget	290	U85 Country	37
But if, to boot with these, a chaste Wife meet	291	U85 Country	39
Among these Cates how glad the sight doth come	291	U85 Country	61
These thoughts when Usurer Alphius, now about	291	U85 Country	67
These thinges when Usurer Alphius, now about	291	U85 Country	V 67
Flow my thin teares, downe these pale cheeks of mine?	293	U86 Hor.4:1	34
The Things that make the happier life, are these,	295	U90 Mart.10:47	1
No place for these. And, Painter, hap'ly, thou	305	Horace	24
Scylla, Charybdis, Polypheme, with these.	315	Horace	206
These studies alter now, in one, growne man;	315	Horace	237
It still must favour good men, and to these	317	Horace	280
To these succeeded the old Comoedie,	321	Horace	365
Next these great Homer and Tyrtaeus set	327	Horace	493
These, the free meale might have beene well drawne out:	331	Horace	560
These trifles into serious mischiefes lead	335	Horace	641
When late (grave Palmer) these thy graffs and flowers	361	Palmer	1
In these pide times, only to shewe their braines,	362	Author	4
But these are Mysteries	369	Ode Who saith	111
Or moathes shall eate, what all these Fooles admire.	371	Fletcher	16
The elder of these two, riche hopes Increase,	382	Rich	5
At these thy Nuptials; but, whose heart, and thought	384	Somerset	3
When these, and such, their voices have employd;	385	Brooke	1
For, though but early in these pathes thou tread,	386	Browne	5
Sonnes, seeke not me amonge these polish'd stones:	387	Cavendish	1
these only hide part of my flesh, and bones:	387	Cavendish	2
'Tis true, and all mens suffrage. But these wayes	390	Shakespeare	5
For seeliest Ignorance on these may light,	390	Shakespeare	7
These are, as some infamous Baud, or Whore,	391	Shakespeare	13
Taught Lucan these true moodes! Replyes my sence	395	May	15
O, how in those, dost thou instruct these times,	397	Drayton	43
What charming Peales are these,	401	Filmer	1
Will any of these express your place? or witt?	402	Inigo Jones 1	18
These forme thy Ghyrlond. Wherof Myrtle green,	412	Ghyrlond	5
These Mysteries do point to three more great,	413	Ghyrlond	29

		Page	Title	Line
THESE (cont.)				
To make these good, and what comes after, better.	. .	666	Glover	10
THESEUS				
Of Hercules, or Theseus going to hell,	. .	84	E133 Voyage	2
THESPIA				
Dri'd up? lyes Thespia wast?	. .	174	U23 Himselfe	8
THESPIAD'S				
Neere which, the Thespiad's sing;	. .	366	Ode Who saith	18
THESPIAN				
Tabacco, Nectar, or the Thespian spring,	. .	65	E101 Supper	33
Nor all the ladies of the Thespian lake,	. .	108	F10 Proludium	25
Give me my cup, but from the Thespian well,	. .	120	F14 Sydney	11
THESPIS				
Thespis is said to be the first found out	. .	319	Horace	311
TH'ESPLANDIANS				
Th'Esplandians, Arthurs, Palmerins, and all	. .	203	U43 Vulcan	30
TH'ETERNALL				
The Sonne of God, th'Eternall King,	. .	130	U1 Nativitie	7
THE'UN				
Must trie the'un-used valour of a nose:	. .	87	E133 Voyage	132
THE'UN-USED				
Must trie the'un-used valour of a nose:	. .	87	E133 Voyage	132
THEWES				
The place allotted it, with decent thewes.	. .	311	Horace	125
TH'EXAMINING				
Who (in th'examining)	. .	109	F11 Epode	14
TH'EXAMPLED				
They are th'exampled Paire, and mirrour of their kind.	.	255	U75 Epithalam.	80
TH'EXCHANGE				
Varietie of Silkes were on th'Exchange!	.	202	U42 Elegy Let	72
Upon th'Exchange, still, out of Popes-head-Alley;	.	206	U43 Vulcan	80
Upon th'Exchange of Letters, as I wou'd	.	386	Browne	14
TH'EXPENCE				
Th'expence in odours is a most vaine sinne,	.	33	E20 Cod 2	1
TH'				
And still be a whore-house. Th'are Synonima.	.	29	E7 Hot-house	4
Th'are base, and idle feares	.	109	F11 Epode	26
As what th'have lost t'expect, they dare deride.	.	116	F13 Aubigny	4
And told of with more License then th'were done!	.	156	U13 Sacvile	96
(Because th'are every where amongst Man-kind	.	167	U15 Friend-Wars	171
(Brave Youths) th'are their possessions, none of yours:	.	281	U84 Kenelme	11
As if they' ador'd the Head, wheron th'are fixt.	.	413	Ghyrlond	28
THEY'				
To ope' the character. They'have found the sleight	.	59	E92 New Crie	27
Wherewith, against thy bloud, they'offenders bee.	.	60	E93 Radcliffe	16
They'are rear'd with no mans ruine, no mans grone,	.	94	F2 Penshurst	46
But grant us perfect, they're not knowne.	.	104	F7 Women but	10
I feare they'd love him too;	.	147	U7 Nymph	4
Shall find their depth: they're sounded with a spoone.	.	198	U40 Elegy That	30
They'ave glutted in, and letcher'd out that weeke,	.	218	U47 Tribe	13
They're darke, bid cleare this: all that's doubtfull wrote	.	335	Horace	637
They're dark, bid cleare 'hem; al that's doubtful wrote	.	354	Horace	V637
As if they' ador'd the Head, wheron th'are fixt.	.	413	Ghyrlond	28
THEY				
As mad-men stones: not caring whom they hit.	.	27	E2 My Booke	6
And gave thee both, to shew they could no more.	.	28	E4 James 1	4
As chiefe of those still promise they will bee.	.	28	E4 James 1	8
Of old, they gave a cock to Aesculape;	.	31	E13 Empirick	2
He toyles to be at hell, as soone as they.	.	36	E31 Banck	4
But as they come, on both sides he takes fees,	.	38	E37 Chev'ril	2
Then they might in her bright eyes.	.	39	E40 Ratcliffe	8
He meant they thither should make swift repaire,	.	41	E44 Chuff	5
When they cost dearest, and are done most free,	.	49	E66 Cary	14
On the true causes, ere they grow too old.	.	50	E70 Wm Roe 1	4
Nature, they thought, in all, that he would faine.	.	53	E79 Rutland	8
That they to knowledge so should toure upright,	.	55	E85 Goodyere 1	6
Which if they misse, they yet should re-advance	.	55	E85 Goodyere 1	8
Till they be sure to make the foole their quarrie.	.	55	E85 Goodyere 1	10
Out-strip, then they did all that went before:	.	57	E89 Allen	10
As noble in great chiefes, as they are rare.	.	58	E91 Vere	16
Ripe statesmen, ripe: They grow in every street.	.	58	E92 New Crie	3
They know the states of Christendome, not the places:	.	59	E92 New Crie	8
Yet have they seene the maps, and bought 'hem too,	.	59	E92 New Crie	9
The councels, projects, practises they know,	.	59	E92 New Crie	11
And unto whom: They are the almanacks	.	59	E92 New Crie	13
They carry in their pockets Tacitus,	.	59	E92 New Crie	15
They meet in sixes, and at every mart,	.	59	E92 New Crie	21
They all get Porta, for the sundrie wayes	.	59	E92 New Crie	25
To breake up seales, and close 'hem. And they know,	.	59	E92 New Crie	29
With England. All forbidden bookes they get.	.	59	E92 New Crie	31
And of the poulder-plot, they will talke yet.	.	59	E92 New Crie	32
At naming the French King, their heads they shake,	.	59	E92 New Crie	33
With ignorance on us, as they have done	.	59	E92 New Crie	37
That know not so much state, wrong, as they doo.	.	59	E92 New Crie	40
And two, that would have falne as great, as they,	.	60	E93 Radcliffe	7
But, when they heard it tax'd, tooke more offence.	.	60	E94 Bedford 3	10
They, then, that living where the matter is bred,	.	60	E94 Bedford 3	11
And, till they burst, their backs, like asses load:	.	62	E96 Donne 2	11
The selfe-same deeds, as diversly they come,	.	64	E99 Th Roe 2	8
Cry'd to my face, they were th'elixir of wit:	.	64	E100 Playwrt 3	2
They follow vertue, for reward, to day;	.	66	E102 Pembroke	9
Whose life, ev'n they, that envie it, must praise;	.	66	E102 Pembroke	16
Thou must draw more: and they, that hope to see	.	66	E102 Pembroke	19

	Page	Title	Line
THEY (cont.)			
Were they that nam'd you, prophets? Did they see,	67	E104 Montgomery	1
Judge they, that can: here I have rais'd to show	67	E104 Montgomery	13
And like it too; if they looke equally:	67	E104 Montgomery	15
Whether thy learning they would take, or wit,	68	E106 E Herbert	5
And yet, they, all together, lesse then thee.	68	E106 E Herbert	10
They murder him againe, that envie thee.	72	E111 Edmonds 2	14
They all consented;	77	E120 S. P.	18
They have repented.	77	E120 S. P.	20
Think'st thou, Mime, this is great? or, that they strive	81	E129 Mime	9
Men love thee not for this: They laugh at thee.	81	E129 Mime	18
They should be fooles, for me, at their owne charge.	83	E131 Ferrab. 2	8
Say, this, or that man they to thee preferre;	83	E131 Ferrab. 2	9
Even those for whom they doe this, know they erre:	83	E131 Ferrab. 2	10
They were not to be nam'd on the same day.	83	E131 Ferrab. 2	12
Since they can only judge, that can conferre.	83	E132 Sylvester	6
Had power to act, what they to faine had not.	84	E133 Voyage	6
All, that they boast of Styx, of Acheron,	84	E133 Voyage	7
Or magick sacrifice, they past along!	85	E133 Voyage	49
Thorough her wombe they make their famous road,	85	E133 Voyage	66
But they unfrighted passe, though many a privie	86	E133 Voyage	73
And, on they went, like Castor brave, and Pollux:	86	E133 Voyage	77
They met the second Prodigie, would feare a	86	E133 Voyage	79
But, comming neere, they found it but a liter,	86	E133 Voyage	85
So huge, it seem'd, they could by no meanes quite her.	86	E133 Voyage	86
Backe, cry'd their brace of Charons: they cry'd, no,	86	E133 Voyage	87
Row close then, slaves. Alas, they will beshite us.	86	E133 Voyage	90
And subtiltie of mettalls) they dispense	86	E133 Voyage	100
Touching this cause, where they will be affeard	87	E133 Voyage	106
By this time had they reach'd the Stygian poole,	87	E133 Voyage	121
Of worship, they their nodding chinnes doe hit	87	E133 Voyage	123
All was to them the same, they were to passe,	88	E133 Voyage	140
And so they did, from Styx, to Acheron:	88	E133 Voyage	141
For, here they were throwne in wi'the melted pewter,	88	E133 Voyage	153
Yet drown'd they not. They had five lives in future.	88	E133 Voyage	154
They cry'd out Pusse. He told them he was Bankes,	89	E133 Voyage	183
They laugh't, at his laugh-worthy fate. And past	89	E133 Voyage	185
They tooke 'hem all to witnesse of their action:	89	E133 Voyage	191
It is enough, they once did get	93	F1 Why write no	5
Thy lord, and lady, though they have no sute.	95	F2 Penshurst	50
Some nuts, some apples; some that thinke they make	95	F2 Penshurst	52
By their ripe daughters, whom they would commend	95	F2 Penshurst	54
With his brave sonne, the Prince, they saw thy fires	95	F2 Penshurst	77
They are, and have beene taught religion: Thence	96	F2 Penshurst	93
Each morne, and even, they are taught to pray,	96	F2 Penshurst	95
Now, Penshurst, they that will proportion thee	96	F2 Penshurst	99
With other edifices, when they see	96	F2 Penshurst	100
They thinke not, then, which side the cause shall leese,	98	F3 Wroth	61
That they may sleepe with scarres in age.	98	F3 Wroth	70
And brag, that they were therefore borne.	99	F3 Wroth	72
And, so they ride in purple, eate in plate,	99	F3 Wroth	89
But make my strengths, such as they are,	102	F4 To the World	67
How to tell' hem, as they flow,	103	F6 Celia 2	20
And the envious, when they find	103	F6 Celia 2	21
At noone, they are or short, or none:	104	F7 Women but	8
So men at weakest, they are strongest,	104	F7 Women but	9
They maintayne the truest trade,	105	F8 Sicknesse	19
These, disease, will they deserve:	106	F8 Sicknesse	V 43
(Though they were crusht into one forme) could make	108	F10 Proludium	26
The thing, they here call Love, is blinde Desire,	110	F11 Epode	37
Because they move, the continent doth so:	111	F11 Epode	71
That bred them, graves: when they were borne, they di'd,	114	F12 Rutland	47
Because they lack'd the sacred pen, could give	115	F12 Rutland	56
They hold in my strange poems, which, as yet,	115	F12 Rutland	81
As what th'have lost t'expect, they dare deride.	116	F13 Aubigny	4
And raise not vertue; they may vice enhance.	117	F13 Aubigny	42
For truthes complexion, where they all weare maskes.	118	F13 Aubigny	70
And almost, all dayes after, while they live;	118	F13 Aubigny	75
(They finde it both so wittie, and safe to give.)	118	F13 Aubigny	76
Whether it be a face they weare, or no.	118	F13 Aubigny	80
May they have nothing left, whereof they can	118	F13 Aubigny	83
Boast, but how oft they have gone wrong to man:	119	F13 Aubigny	84
By me, their priest (if they can ought divine)	119	F13 Aubigny	101
They speake; since you are truly that rare wife,	119	F13 Aubigny	110
Other great wives may blush at: when they see	119	F13 Aubigny	111
And that your soules conspire, as they were gone	119	F13 Aubigny	119
For they, that swell	121	F14 Sydney	39
They teach you, how.	121	F14 Sydney	48
Untill they meet	129	U1 Father	15
Yet search'd, and true they found it.	130	U1 Nativitie	6
And enamour'd, doe wish, so they might	134	U2 Triumph	7
That they still were to run by her side,	134	U2 Triumph	9
Doe but looke on her eyes, they doe light	134	U2 Triumph	11
They say the Angells marke each deed,	144	U3 Musicall	17
On what they viewing know.	144	U3 Musicall	20
On which they see or know.	144	U3 Musicall	V 20
So they in state of Grace retain'd,	144	U3 Musicall	27
I'le tell, that if they be not glad,	147	U7 Nymph	8
They yet may envie me:	147	U7 Nymph	9
He is, if they can find him, faire,	147	U7 Nymph	15
That though they did possesse each limbe,	151	U12 Corbet	9
Yet he broke them, e're they could him,	151	U12 Corbet	10
They were as specious as his Trees.	152	U12 Corbet	20

THEY (cont.)

	Page	Title	Line
They were so even, grave, and holy;	152	U12 Corbet	23
That they for me their teares will shed;	152	U12 Corbet	34
As they are done, and such returnes they find:	153	U13 Sacvile	6
They are the Noblest benefits, and sinke	153	U13 Sacvile	19
They are so long a comming, and so hard;	153	U13 Sacvile	23
That they have more opprest me, then my want?	153	U13 Sacvile	28
Run from the Conscience of it, if they could.	154	U13 Sacvile	46
For what they streight would to the world forsweare;	154	U13 Sacvile	50
And speaking worst of those, from whom they went	154	U13 Sacvile	51
Are they not worthy to be answer'd so,	154	U13 Sacvile	59
Is borrowing; that but stopt, they doe invade	155	U13 Sacvile	80
And where they want, she is not understood.	156	U13 Sacvile	112
Were the Rack offer'd them, how they came so;	157	U13 Sacvile	130
Such Notes are vertuous men! they live as fast	157	U13 Sacvile	143
As they are high; are rooted, and will last.	157	U13 Sacvile	144
They need no stilts, nor rise upon their toes,	157	U13 Sacvile	145
As if they would belie their stature; those	157	U13 Sacvile	146
Nor fashion; if they chance aspire to height,	157	U13 Sacvile	148
For all their spight, be like him if they could:	162	U15 Friend-Wars	26
As they are made! Pride, and stiffe Clownage mixt	163	U15 Friend-Wars	43
How they may make some one that day an Asse	164	U15 Friend-Wars	64
Thus they doe talke. And are these objects fit	165	U15 Friend-Wars	101
But both fell prest under the load they make.	166	U15 Friend-Wars	128
That watch, and catch, at what they may applaud,	167	U15 Friend-Wars	157
They are not, Sir, that doe pay	169	U17 Friend-Debt	1
Debts when they can: good men may breake their day,	169	U17 Friend-Debt	2
Then like, then love; and now would they amaze?	169	U18 Elegy Can	4
Or Love, or Fortune blind, when they but winke	170	U18 Elegy Can	16
Because they would free Justice imitate,	170	U18 Elegy Can	18
(Though they may number bodyes) or but one.	171	U19 Elegy By	14
Or droop they as disgrac't,	174	U23 Himselfe	11
If hence they silent be,	174	U23 Himselfe	V 13
They die with their conceits,	175	U23 Himselfe	23
They drincke with their conceits,	175	U23 Himselfe	V 23
An hower will come they must affect theyr Ease,	179	U25 Desmond	V 42
They were bound!	183	U29 Fit of Rime	12
That they long since have refused	184	U29 Fit of Rime	47
Who, though their guilt, and perjurie they know,	186	U32 Elsmere	11
Thinke, yea and boast, that they have done it so	186	U32 Elsmere	12
They will come of, and scape the Punishment.	186	U32 Elsmere	14
They had, but were a Reed unto thy Sword.	187	U33 Councellour	34
Who more they burne, they more desire,	189	U36 Song	10
And waste still, that they still might bee.	189	U36 Song	12
Little know they, that professe Amitie.	190	U37 Friend-Book	19
How much they lame her in her propertie.	190	U37 Friend-Book	21
And lesse they know, who being free to use	190	U37 Friend-Book	22
Of crueltie, lest they doe make you such.	193	U38 Elegy 'Tis	84
They looke at best like Creame-bowles, and you soone	198	U40 Elegy That	29
They may say Grace, and for Loves Chaplaines passe;	198	U40 Elegy That	31
What it is like: And doe not thinke they can	199	U41 Elegy Since	3
(If they be faire and worth it) have their lives	200	U42 Elegy Let	20
My friends, the Watermen! They could provide	208	U43 Vulcan	124
Our friends, the Watermen! They could provide	208	U43 Vulcan	V124
They made a Vulcan of a sheafe of Reedes,	208	U43 Vulcan	126
Whom they durst handle in their holy-day coates,	208	U43 Vulcan	127
Whom they durst handle in their high day coates,	208	U43 Vulcan	V127
The Brethren, they streight nois'd it out for Newes,	209	U43 Vulcan	139
The brethren they streight ways noisd out for newes,	209	U43 Vulcan	V139
For they were burnt, but to be better built.	210	U43 Vulcan	166
'Tis true, that in thy wish they were destroy'd,	210	U43 Vulcan	167
To all as chargefull as they have beene to me,	211	U43 Vulcan	V192
Why yet, my noble hearts, they cannot say,	213	U44 Speach	1
For they did see it the last tilting well,	213	U44 Speach	6
They saw too store of feathers, and more may,	213	U44 Speach	9
If they stay here, but till Saint Georges Day.	213	U44 Speach	10
But they may see Gold-Chaines, and Pearle worne then,	213	U44 Speach	13
For that unnecessarie Charge they were.	214	U44 Speach	32
Were now the greater Captaine? for they saw	214	U44 Speach	39
All that they doe at Playes. O, but first here	215	U44 Speach	91
They learne and studie; and then practise there.	215	U44 Speach	92
They cannot last. No lie grew ever old.	216	U45 Squib	20
Men that are safe, and sure, in all they doe,	218	U47 Tribe	1
Care not what trials they are put unto;	218	U47 Tribe	2
They meet the fire, the Test, as Martyrs would;	218	U47 Tribe	3
Of any Companie but that they are in,	218	U47 Tribe	20
Of newes they get, to strew out the long meale,	218	U47 Tribe	28
The wits will leave you, if they once perceive	223	U49 Pucell	37
They say you weekly invite with fits o'th' Mother,	223	U49 Pucell	40
From whence they fall, cast downe with their owne weight.	224	U50 Countesse	12
As they are hard, for them to make their owne,	225	U50 Countesse	33
So are they profitable to be knowne:	225	U50 Countesse	34
For when they find so many meet in one,	225	U50 Countesse	35
It will be shame for them, if they have none.	225	U50 Countesse	36
If they goe on, and that thou lov'st a-life	232	U58 Book-seller	13
They talke of Fencing, and the use of Armes,	232	U59 Newcastle	1
As they out-did the lightning in the course;	233	U59 Newcastle	12
How much to heaven for thee, great Charles, they owe!	237	U64 Charles 3	22
Are they so scanted in their store? or driven	241	U68 House-hold	3
Well, they should know him, would the K. but grant	241	U68 House-hold	5
As, could they but lifes miseries fore-see,	243	U70 Ode	19
As they that saw	247	U70 Ode	118
Where they might read, and find	247	U70 Ode	122

	Page	Title	Line
THEY (cont.)			
Unto the Ships, and they from tier, to tier,	249	U72 King	2
Had they but grace, of thinking, at these routes,	249	U72 King	15
If they had leisure, at these lawfull routs,	249	U72 King	V 15
As they came all to see, and to be seene!	253	U75 Epithalam.	20
As they had learn'd new changes, for the day,	253	U75 Epithalam.	35
As they did lack	254	U75 Epithalam.	V 46
Have they bedew'd the Earth, where she doth tread,	254	U75 Epithalam.	66
Have they bedew'd the Earth, where she did tread,	254	U75 Epithalam.	V 66
Who, in all they doe,	255	U75 Epithalam.	78
They are th'exampled Paire, and mirrour of their kind.	255	U75 Epithalam.	80
Illustrate these, but they	255	U75 Epithalam.	85
Whom they have chose,	255	U75 Epithalam.	94
Whilst they both stand,	256	U75 Epithalam.	126
The Solemne Quire cryes, Joy; and they returne, Amen.	256	U75 Epithalam.	128
Th'Ignoble never liv'd, they were a-while	257	U75 Epithalam.	153
They both are slip'd to Bed; Shut fast the Doore,	258	U75 Epithalam.	185
Parts of me (they judg'd) decay'd,	259	U76 Petition	23
And act the businesse, which they paint, or carve.	261	U77 Treasurer	16
What worlds of blessings to good Kings they owe!	261	U77 Treasurer	20
Of sweets, and safeties, they possesse by Peace.	261	U77 Treasurer	22
Fame and Honour you, they possesse by Peace.	261	U77 Treasurer	V 22
Being sent to one, they will be read of all.	263	U78 Digby	32
Where ere they tread th'enamour'd ground,	264	U79 New-yeares	36
Still waited on 'hem where they were.	264	U79 New-yeares	39
That they may take it eccho'd by the Floods.	265	U79 New-yeares	53
How much they are belov'd of God, in thee;	268	U80 Christning	4
Would they would understand it! Princes are	268	U80 Christning	5
Great aides to Empire, as they are great care	268	U80 Christning	6
From all affection! when they urg'd the Cure	270	U81 Pawlet	49
Which they that have the Crowne are sure to know!	271	U81 Pawlet	76
For they are strong Supporters: But, till then,	281	U84 Kenelme	14
And Goates together, whither they must come	283	U84 Muse	47
But all of God; They still shall have to say,	286	U84 Muse	119
And hers were all Humilitie! they beat	288	U84 Muse	189
Upon your shoulders. Prove what they will beare,	307	Horace	55
And what they will not. Him, whose choice doth reare	307	Horace	56
So they fall gently from the Grecian spring,	309	Horace	75
And Peleus, if they seeke to heart-strike us	311	Horace	136
When they are poore, and banish'd, must throw by	311	Horace	138
To laughter; so they grieve with those that mone.	311	Horace	144
And give their yeares, and natures, as they swerve,	315	Horace	224
They might with ease be numbred, being a few	319	Horace	293
But, as they conquer'd, and enlarg'd their bound,	319	Horace	295
And they uncensur'd might at Feasts, and Playes	319	Horace	297
Be I their Judge, they doe at no time dare	321	Horace	356
The nut-crackers throughout, will they therefore	321	Horace	363
Fell into fault so farre, as now they saw	321	Horace	367
Nor is't long since, they did with patience take	323	Horace	375
Nor did they merit the lesse Crowne to weare,	323	Horace	406
Whether the guarded Tragedie they wrought,	323	Horace	409
Or 'twere the gowned Comoedy they taught.	323	Horace	410
For so, they shall not only gaine the worth,	325	Horace	425
But fame of Poets, they thinke, if they come forth,	325	Horace	426
Our Roman Youths they learne the subtle wayes	327	Horace	464
Our Roman Youths they learne more thriving wayes	350	Horace	V464
This was the wisdome, that they had of old,	327	Horace	486
Their minds to Warres, with rimes they did rehearse;	329	Horace	495
Cast out by voyces; want they pleasure, then	329	Horace	512
And rack, with Wine, the man whom they would try,	333	Horace	618
They vexe, and follow him with shouts, and noise,	335	Horace	648
They vexe, and carelesse follow him with noise.	354	Horace	V648
wear spent with wonder as they weare delated,	361	Palmer	24
If they seeme wry, to such as looke asquint,	362	Author	7
Were they as strong ram'd up as Aetna gates.	363	Riches	10
And, when they came	366	Ode Who saith	22
All which, when they but heare a straine	368	Ode Who saith	89
Yet, looking in thy face, they shall begin	369	Ode Who saith	93
But should they know (as I) that this,	369	Ode Who saith	97
Or thought they, Leda's white Adult'rers place	369	Ode Who saith	104
How they would frowne!	369	Ode Who saith	110
In Picture, they which truly understand,	370	Author	1
But now, your Worke is done, if they that view	370	Author	9
'Tis not your fault, if they shall sense preferre,	370	Author	13
They saw it halfe, damd thy whole play, and more;	371	Fletcher	8
With vices, which they look'd for, and came to.	371	Fletcher	10
For Grapes he had gather'd before they were eaten.	375	Coryat 1	25
For grapes he had gather'd, before they were eaten,	380	Coryat 3	36
From Venice to Flushing, were not they well cobled?	380	Coryat 3	42
Some want, they say in a sort he did crave:	380	Coryat 3	55
They are not those, are present with theyre face,	384	Somerset	1
The art of uttring wares, if they were bad;	385	Husband	6
With the how much they set forth, but th'how well.	386	Browne	16
which, did they neere so neate, or proudly dwell,	387	Cavendish	3
Were askt of thy Discoveries; They must say,	388	Chapman	8
As was the Genius wherewith they were wrote;	389	Aleman	12
As they were not of Natures family.	392	Shakespeare	54
Nay they will venter ones Descent to hitt,	394	Jane Ogle	11
Phoebus, and Hermes? They whose tongue, or pen	395	May	17
Thy Muse, and mine, as they expect. 'Tis true:	396	Drayton	5
Tenants, and Servants, have they harts, and eyes,	399	Lady Ogle	4
When they doe sweat to fortifie a Muse.	400	Beaumont	6
That, while they bind the senses, doe so please?	401	Filmer	2

THEY (cont.)

They are the Mariage-rites	401	Filmer	3
They are a Schoole to win	402	Filmer	11
Not they that sided her, Dame Poetry,	403	Inigo Jones 1	36
Sense, what they are! which by a specious fyne	404	Inigo Jones 1	55
And they were very good: yet thou think'st nay.	408	Detractor	2
That knew the Crafts they had bin bred in, right:	410	Brome	14
Or why to like; they found, it all was new,	415	Rutter	9
How they doe keepe alive his memorie;	416	Dover	5
How they advance true Love, and neighbourhood,	416	Dover	7
Of Subjects; Let such envie, till they burst.	416	Dover	10
or theire Ale, they break the peace,	418	Moon	42
As when they both were greate, and both knewe howe	419	Ode:If Men	3
Little knowne they that proffesse Amitye	421	Censure	12
Howe much they lame hir, in hir propertye:	421	Censure	14
And lesse they knowe, that being free to use	422	Censure	15
Virtue, and Soveraigntie, they not consort.	423	Lucan	18
THEY'ARE
They'are rear'd with no mans ruine, no mans grone,	94	F2 Penshurst	46
THEY'AVE
They'ave glutted in, and letcher'd out that weeke,	218	U47 Tribe	13
THEY'D
I feare they'd love him too;	147	U7 Nymph	4
TH'EYE
In th'eye of Europe, where thy deeds were done,	58	E91 Vere	6
At th'eye and eare (the ports unto the minde)	109	F11 Epode	9
ill-/Natur'd, and wicked Atreus cooke, to th'eye,	317	Horace	265
THEY'HAVE
To ope' the character. They'have found the sleight	59	E92 New Crie	27
THEY'OFFENDERS
Wherewith, against thy bloud, they'offenders bee.	60	E93 Radcliffe	16
THEYR
An hower will come they must affect theyr Ease,	179	U25 Desmond	V 42
And, after all theyr Aetnean Ire,	179	U25 Desmond	44
Oft scape theyr Imputation, more through luck, then wit.	179	U25 Desmond	V 52
So, in theyr number, may you never see	384	Somerset	21
Least a false praise do make theyr dotage his.	385	Husband	4
THEY'RE
But grant us perfect, they're not knowne.	104	F7 Women but	10
They're growne Commoditie upon Exchange;	165	U15 Friend-Wars	86
Shall find their depth: they're sounded with a spoone.	198	U40 Elegy That	30
They're darke, bid cleare this: all that's doubtfull wrote	335	Horace	637
They're dark, bid cleare 'hem; al that's doubtful wrote	354	Horace	V637
THEYRE
They are not those, are present with theyre face,	384	Somerset	1
Do wayte upon thee: and theyre Love not bought.	384	Somerset	4
TH'GODS
Hide faults, and pray to th'gods, and wish aloud	345	Horace	V285
TH'HARD
Who scarse can spell th'hard names: whose knight lesse can.	28	E3 Bookseller	10
TH'HAST
Yet by thy weapon liv'st! Th'hast one good part.	50	E69 Cob	2
I know not which th'hast most, candor, or wit:	78	E123 Rudyerd 3	2
But both th'hast so, as who affects the state	78	E123 Rudyerd 3	3
TH'HAVE
As what th'have lost t'expect, they dare deride.	116	F13 Aubigny	4
So would'st th'have run upon the Rolls by stealth,	210	U43 Vulcan	169
TH'HOW
With the how much they set forth, but th'how well.	386	Browne	16
TH'IAMBICK
Th'Iambick arm'd Archilochus to rave,	311	Horace	117
Two rests, a short and long, th'Iambick frame;	323	Horace	371
THICK
So over-thick, but, where the people met,	319	Horace	292
Or thick grosse ointment, but offend the Guests:	331	Horace	558
THICKE
These be the cause of those thicke frequent mists	87	E133 Voyage	130
TH'IDALIAN
If dancing, all would cry th'Idalian Queene,	68	E105 L Wroth 2	11
TH'IDES
'Gainst th'Ides, his moneys he gets in with paine,	291	U85 Country	69
'Gainst th'Ides, his gott moneyes he gets in with paine,	291	U85 Country	V 69
THIE
Breake then thie quills, blott out	420	Ode:If Men	19
Thie long watch'd verse	420	Ode:If Men	20
Thou that doest spend thie dayes	420	Ode:If Men	24
Thie Chrystall sheild	421	Ode:If Men	38
THIEFE (See also THEEFE)
The courtier is become the greater thiefe.	29	E8 Robbery	6
From brocage so bold a thiefe,	44	E56 Poet-Ape	3
Cob, thou nor souldier, thiefe, nor fencer art,	50	E69 Cob	1
THIGH
Yes thou wert borne out of his travelling thigh	378	Coryat 2	89
THIGhES
And laugh, and measure thighes, then squeake, spring, itch,	164	U15 Friend-Wars	75
And 'tweene their Grandsires thighes,	258	U75 Epithalam.	173
Ever his thighes Male then, and his braines Shee.	378	Coryat 2	92
TH'IGNOBLE
Th'Ignoble never liv'd, they were a-while	257	U75 Epithalam.	153
Td'ILL
Above th'ill fortune of them, or the need.	391	Shakespeare	16
T'HIMSELFE
To him, man's dearer, then t'himselfe.	99	F3 Wroth	96

	Page	Title	Line
THIN			
And so thin, to see a blush	141	U2 Her man	28
Flow my thin teares, downe these pale cheeks of mine?	293	U86 Hor.4:1	34
THiNCKING			
Now thinckking on you, though to England lost,	116	F12 Rutland	94
THINE (See also THYNE)			
Many of thine this better could, then I,	31	E14 Camden	13
But that's put in, thou'lt say. Why, so is thine.	36	E29 Tilter	6
Be thine, I taxe, yet doe not owne my rimes:	36	E30 Guiltie	2
Which if most gracious heaven grant like thine,	37	E33 Roe 3	5
Thou flattered'st thine, mine cannot flatter'd bee.	38	E36 Martial	4
Of adding to thy fame; thine may to me,	41	E43 Salisbury 1	8
Of adding to thy prayse; thine may to me,	41	E43 Salisbury 1 V	8
In my chast booke: professe them in thine owne.	42	E49 Playwrt 1	6
What art is thine, that so thy friend deceives?	44	E55 Beaumont	8
But thine, for which I doo't, so much exceeds!	46	E60 Mounteagle	8
Without his, thine, and all times injurie?	47	E63 Salisbury 2	10
That whil'st I meant but thine to gratulate,	48	E64 Salisbury 3	17
And thine owne goodnesse to encrease thy merit,	60	E93 Radcliffe	10
To thine owne proper I ascribe then more;	61	E95 Savile	9
With thine owne course the judgement of thy friend,	63	E98 Th Roe 1	8
And first to know thine owne state, then the States.	70	E109 Nevil	12
Action, or engine, worth a note of thine,	71	E110 Edmonds 1	20
And, in their errors maze, thine owne way know:	76	E119 Shelton	13
And those to turne to bloud, and make thine owne:	80	E128 Wm Roe 2	4
And thine owne Coriat too. But (would'st thou see)	81	E129 Mime	17
Thine the originall; and France shall boast,	83	E132 Sylvester	13
And such since thou canst make thine owne content,	98	F3 Wroth	65
Drinke to me, onely, with thine eyes,	106	F9 Celia 3	1
Drinke to me, Coelia, with thine eyes,	106	F9 Celia 3 V	1
I would not change for thine.	106	F9 Celia 3	8
Of others honours, thus, enjoy thine owne.	160	U14 Selden	66
That thine be just, and honest; that thy Deeds	167	U15 Friend-Wars	177
What had I done that might call on thine ire?	202	U43 Vulcan	2
What have I done that might call on thine ire?	202	U43 Vulcan V	2
Needs lend an aide, to thine she had her eyes.	217	U46 Coke	24
For 't were a narrow gladnesse, kept thine owne.	225	U51 Bacon	18
And mad'st thy Mothers wombe thine urne.	242	U70 Ode	8
To swell thine age;	244	U70 Ode	56
T'effect it, feele, thou'ast made thine owne heart ake.	250	U73 Weston	12
The bright Brides paths, embelish'd more then thine	254	U75 Epithalam.	59
And, Sylvane, thine that keptst his Lands!	290	U85 Country	22
And, Sylvane, thine that keep'st his Lands!	290	U85 Country V	22
There jest, and feast, make him thine host,	292	U86 Hor.4:1	11
Of Homers, forth in acts, then of thine owne,	313	Horace	185
Yet common matter thou thine owne maist make,	313	Horace	187
He cries, Good boy, thou'lt keepe thine owne. Now, adde	327	Horace	470
Of thine, shall thinke the Maine	368	Ode Who saith	90
Not only this, but every day of thine,	384	Somerset	9
It must be thine owne judgment, yet, that sends	386	Browne	7
Olde Hesiods Ore, and give it us; but thine,	388	Chapman	2
To the Greeke coast thine onely knew the way.	388	Chapman	9
(Such as thine are) and strike the second heat	392	Shakespeare	60
THING			
Become a petulant thing, hurle inke, and wit,	27	E2 My Booke	5
On some-thing, that walkes some-where.	30	E11 Something	Ttl
Then thee the age sees not that thing more grave,	31	E14 Camden	5
Away, and leave me, thou thing most abhord,	48	E65 Muse	1
The nicer thing to tast her ladies page;	57	E90 Mill	5
Nor Captayne Pod, nor yet the Eltham-thing;	62	E97 Motion	2
A subtle thing, that doth affections win	74	E115 Honest Man	7
Thou maist thinke life, a thing but lent.	100	F3 Wroth	106
The thing, they here call Love, is blinde Desire,	110	F11 Epode	37
That cryes, we dreame, and sweares, there's no such thing,	111	F11 Epode	67
That cryes, I dreame, and sweares, there's no such thing,	111	F11 Epode V	67
As to doe no thing too much.	142	U2 Her man	46
More pleasure while the thing he makes	145	U5 Woman-kind	15
And being a thing, blowne out of nought, rebells	163	U15 Friend-Wars	32
When shee puts forth the life of ev'ry thing:	250	U74 Weston	3
To draw a thing that cannot sit.	277	U84 Mind	8
It is a wretched thing to trust to reedes;	281	U84 Kenelme	16
One thing prodigiously, paints in the woods	307	Horace	41
And come not too much wrested. What's that thing,	309	Horace	76
Betweene the Acts, a quite cleane other thing	317	Horace	278
That found out profit, and foretold each thing,	319	Horace	309
Doth the same thing with him, that would him kill.	335	Horace	666
Or the sad thunder-stroken thing he have	335	Horace	672
Require (besides the likenesse of the thing)	370	Author	2
Or any thing else that another should hide,	380	Coryat 3	51
And God blesse every living thing,	418	Grace	3
shall never dare do any thing but feare.	423	Lucan	20
THINGE			
thus, as a ponderous thinge in water cast	361	Palmer	17
THINGES			
These thinges when Usurer Alphius, now about	291	U85 Country V	67
TH'INGRATEFULL			
Yea, of th'ingratefull: and he forth must tell	155	U13 Sacvile	77
THINGS			
But two things, rare, the Fates had in their store,	28	E4 James 1	3
What name, what skill, what faith hast thou in things!	31	E14 Camden	7
The selfe-same things, a note of concord be:	40	E42 Giles	17
Things manly, and not smelling parasite.	48	E65 Muse	14
Since men have left to doe praise-worthy things,	49	E67 Suffolk	1

677

THINGS (cont.)

Fortie things more, deare Grand, which you know true,   •   51   E73 Fine Grand   21
Can write the things, the causes, and the men.   •   •   62   E95 Savile   34
That dares nor write things false, nor hide things true.   •   62   E95 Savile   36
And that to write things worthy to be read: •   •   63   E99 Th Roe 2   4
To have her linnen, plate, and all things nigh,   •   •   96   F2 Penshurst   86
And, howsoever we may thinke things sweet,   •   •   99   F3 Wroth   97
Or faith in things? or is't your wealth and will   •   •   159   U14 Selden   36
Honour and honestie, as poore things thought   •   •   163   U15 Friend-Wars   42
That thou dost all things more for truth, then glory,   •   168   U15 Friend-Wars   179
That as the water makes things, put in't streight,   •   170   U18 Elegy Can   7
Doth mete, whose lyne doth sound the depth of things:)   •   176   U24 Frontispice   12
It shakes even him, that all things else doth shake.   •   193   U38 Elegy 'Tis   72
The fate of things: whilst totter'd vertue holds   •   216   U44 Speach   101
How comes it all things so about thee smile?   •   •   225   U51 Bacon   2
Repeat of things a throng,   •   •   •   •   245   U70 Ode   57
Can doe the things that Statues doe deserve,   •   •   261   U77 Treasurer   15
The Things that make the happier life, are these,   •   295   U90 Mart.10:47   1
Yet not as therefore cruell things should cleave   •   338   Horace   V 14
In grave beginnings, and great things profest,   •   •   305   Horace   17
Yet, if by chance, in utt'ring things abstruse,   •   •   307   Horace   69
New names of things. It hath beene ever free,   •   •   309   Horace   83
Of popular noyses, borne to actuate things.   •   •   341   Horace   V120
And ill-penn'd things, I shall, or sleepe, or smile.   •   311   Horace   148
The angry brow; the sportive, wanton things;   •   •   311   Horace   150
Things in themselves agreeing: If againe   •   •   313   Horace   170
'Tis hard, to speake things common, properly.   •   •   313   Horace   183
First publish things unspoken, and unknowne.   •   •   313   Horace   186
Doth wretchedly the use of things forbeare,   •   •   317   Horace   243
Or acted told. But, ever, things that run   •   •   317   Horace   256
Things worthy to be done within, but take   •   •   317   Horace   261
There comes sometimes to things of meanest place.   •   321   Horace   354
Things sacred, from profane to separate;   •   •   327   Horace   487
This saying: To some things there is assign'd   •   •   331   Horace   548
Or, of the things, that ne're came in my mind,   •   •   333   Horace   596
And conquers all things, yea it selfe, at length.   •   367   Ode Who saith   56
Such things, of every body, and as well.   •   •   394   Jane Ogle   10
Yet ware; thou mayst do all things cruellie: •   •   423   Lucan   15

THINK   (See also THINCKING)

And did think, such Rites were due   •   •   •   138   U2 Kisse   19
I shall think on't ere't be day.   •   •   •   417   Moon   11

THINKE

Keepe thy selfe there, and thinke thy valure right,   •   32   E16 Brain-hardy   9
Durst thinke it great, and worthy wonder too,   •   •   46   E60 Mounteagle   7
Most thinke all praises flatteries. But truth brings   •   49   E67 Suffolk   2
I Cannot thinke there's that antipathy   •   •   •   52   E75 Lippe   1
Not that we thinke us worthy such a ghest,   •   •   64   E101 Supper   3
The skie not falling, thinke we may have larkes.   •   65   E101 Supper   16
Or, because some scarce thinke that storie true,   •   67   E104 Montgomery   5
I modestly quit that, and thinke to write,   •   •   72   E112 Gamster   11
I thinke, the Fate of court thy comming crav'd,   •   73   E113 Overbury   5
But 'mong'st these Tiberts, who do'you thinke there was?   88   E133 Voyage   155
Some nuts, some apples; some that thinke they make   95   F2 Penshurst   52
They thinke not, then, which side the cause shall leese,   98   F3 Wroth   61
And thinke his power doth equall Fates.   •   •   99   F3 Wroth   80
Though poyson, thinke it a great fate.   •   •   99   F3 Wroth   90
And, howsoever we may thinke things sweet,   •   •   99   F3 Wroth   97
Thou maist thinke life, a thing but lent.   •   •   100   F3 Wroth   106
Any paines; yea, thinke it price,   •   •   •   105   F8 Sicknesse   27
Were it to thinke, that you should not inherit   •   114   F12 Rutland   32
Riches thought most: But, Madame, thinke what store   114   F12 Rutland   38
Such as suspect them-selves, and thinke it fit   •   117   F13 Aubigny   13
And never thinke, how vice doth every houre,   •   119   F13 Aubigny   87
And he may thinke on that   •   •   •   •   120   F14 Sydney   15
Good, and great God, can I not thinke of thee,   •   122   F15 Heaven   1
The gladdest light, darke man can thinke upon;   •   128   U1 Trinitie   35
Let who will thinke us dead, or wish our death.   •   139   U2 Another   18
And not thinke h'had eat a stake,   •   •   •   142   U2 Her man   39
I Now thinke, Love is rather deafe, then blind,   •   149   U9 Picture   1
Deepest in Man, of which when he doth thinke,   •   153   U13 Sacvile   20
And jealous each of other, yet thinke long   •   •   164   U15 Friend-Wars   73
That thou thinke nothing great, but what is good,   168   U15 Friend-Wars   187
No more, then we should thinke a Lord had had   •   168   U15 Friend-Wars   193
Oh how a Lover may mistake! to thinke,   •   •   170   U18 Elegy Can   15
Thinke but the Sin of all her sex, 'tis she!   •   172   U20 Shrub   20
And thinke it Poesie?   •   •   •   •   •   175   U23 Himselfe   22
Nor thinke your selfe unfortunate,   •   •   •   177   U25 Desmond   27
Thinke but how deare you bought   •   •   •   180   U26 Ode High   19
Law, to his Law; and thinke your enemies his: •   185   U31 Elsmere   4
Thinke, yea and boast, that they have done it so   186   U32 Elsmere   12
That I, hereafter, doe not thinke the Barre,   •   186   U33 Councellour   1
Thinke it was frailtie, Mistris, thinke me man,   •   192   U38 Elegy 'Tis   31
Thinke that your selfe like heaven forgive me can: 192   U38 Elegy 'Tis   32
Thinke that I once was yours, or may be now;   •   192   U38 Elegy 'Tis   35
What it is like: And doe not thinke they can   •   199   U41 Elegy Since   3
Whose Readers did not thinke he was in love.   •   199   U42 Elegy Let   4
Then ope thy wardrobe, thinke me that poore Groome   201   U42 Elegy Let   51
Would thinke no more of Vlushing, or the Brill: •   213   U44 Speach   30
Let those that meerely talke, and never thinke,   •   218   U47 Tribe   9
That to speake well, thinke it above all sinne,   •   218   U47 Tribe   19
And thinke thy streame more quicker   •   •   221   U48 Bacchus   27
Before, I thinke my wish absolv'd had beene.   •   228   U53 Newcastle   14
Would God, my Burges, I could thinke   •   •   229   U55 Burges   1

THINKE   (cont.)
  And thinke all still the best, that he will doe. . . . 236 U63 Charles 2 10
  And thinke, nay know, thy Morison's not dead. . . . 245 U70 Ode 78
  Dare thinke it, to relieve, no lesse renowne, . . . 248 U71 Treasurer 14
  What prayers (People) can you thinke too much? . . . 249 U72 King 20
  When their pot-guns thinke to fitt, ... 259 U76 Petition V 21
  This 1 would doe, if I could thinke you one . . . 260 U77 Treasurer V 10
  He will cleare up his forehead, thinke thou bring'st . . 263 U78 Digby 21
  He will cheare up his forehead, thinke thou bring'st . . 263 U78 Digby V 21
  And Men may thinke, all light rose there. . . . 276 U84 Body 16
  But fame of Poets, they thinke, if they come forth, . . 325 Horace 426
  Thinke wee, or hope, there can be Verses fain'd . . 327 Horace 474
  The truth; nor let thy Fable thinke, what e're . . . 329 Horace 508
  Of thine, shall thinke the Maine . . . . 368 Ode Who saith 90
  And thinke to ruine, where it seem'd to raise. . . . 391 Shakespeare 12
  Which made me thinke, the old Theocritus, . . . 397 Drayton 27
THINKES
  Which hee thinkes great; and so reades verses, too: . . 35 E28 Surly 5
  All, that are readers: but, me thinkes 'tis od, . . 85 E133 Voyage 43
  At Common-Law: me thinkes in his despight . . . 211 U43 Vulcan 177
  At Common-Law: me thinkes in this despight . . . 211 U43 Vulcan V177
  And thinkes I dare not her? let the world see. . . 222 U49 Pucell 2
  Thinkes it selfe nought, though shee should valew it. . 223 U49 Pucell 24
  Hee thinkes not, how to give you smoake from light, . . 315 Horace 203
  (And himselfe with it) that he thinkes to frame; . . 392 Shakespeare 62
THINKING
  Much like those Brethren; thinking to prevaile . . . 59 E92 New Crie 36
  Had they but grace, of thinking, at these routes, . . 249 U72 King 15
  Or rather, thinking all my faults may spie . . . 323 Horace 392
  Thinking to stir me, thou hast lost thy End, . . . 410 Gill 9
THINKS
  He always gives what he thinks meet; . . . . 99 F3 Wroth V 98
THINK'ST
  Think'st thou it is meere fortune, that can win? . . 72 E112 Gamster 3
  Art still at that, and think'st to blow me'up too? . . 72 E112 Gamster 6
  Think'st thou, Mime, this is great? or, that they strive . 81 E129 Mime 9
  Think'st thou that love is help'd by feare? . . . 150 U10 Jealousie 12
  And they were very good: yet thou think'st nay. . . 408 Detractor 2
TH'INSCRIPTION
  At least may beare th'inscription to her Tombe. . . 269 U81 Pawlet 18
TH'INTENT
  To answere me. And sure, it was th'intent . . . 87 E133 Voyage 107
TH'INTERPRETERS
  Are still th'interpreters twixt godds, and men! . . . 395 May 18
TH'IONIAN
  Th'Ionian God-wit, nor the Ginny hen . . . . 291 U85 Country 53
THIRD
  Like single; so, there is a third, commixt, . . . 284 U84 Muse 53
  To another, Move; he went; To a third, Go, . . . 287 U84 Muse 170
  A third of twelve, you may: foure ounces. Glad, . . 327 Horace 469
  The third, is from the garden cull'd, the Rose, . . . 413 Ghyrlond 13
THIRST
  The thirst, that from the soule doth rise, . . . 106 F9 Celia 3 5
  The thirst, that from the soule proceeds, . . . 106 F9 Celia 3 V 5
THIRSTIE
  And as lip-thirstie, in each words expence, . . . 222 U49 Pucell 13
THIRSTY
  What, though the thirsty Tower . . . . 239 U67 Muses V 7
THIRTEENE
  Yeeres he numbred scarse thirteene . . . . 77 E120 S. P. 9
THIRTY
  From thirty pound in pipkins, to the Man . . . 402 Inigo Jones 1 2
THIS'
  Without conferring symboles. This's my day. . . . 396 Drayton 10
THIS   (See also THYS)
  But, for this money was a courtier found, . . . 29 E8 Robbery 3
  The charge of that state, with this charme, god payes. . 30 E12 Shift 4
  To every cause he meets, this voyce he brayes: . . 31 E12 Shift 19
  Many of thine this better could, then I, . . . 31 E14 Camden 13
  All men are wormes: But this no man. In silke . . 31 E15 Court-worm 1
  Quick in his lips! who hath this wonder wrought? . . 33 E21 Gam'ster 5
  This grave partakes the fleshly birth. . . . 34 E22 Daughter 11
  That breathes in his dogs way: and this is great. . . 36 E28 Surly 18
  And in this short time of thy happiest raigne, . . 37 E35 James 2 4
  For this: that winnes, for whom he holds his peace. . 38 E37 Chev'ril 4
  And crie good! good! This quite perverts my sense, . . 38 E38 Guiltie 2 5
  All this doth Jone. Or that his long yearn'd life . . 40 E42 Giles 11
  Is this the Sir, who, some wast wife to winne, . . 42 E46 Luckless 1 1
  Who this thy scape from rumour gratulate, . . . 43 E51 James 3 6
  This but thy judgement fooles: the other way . . . 43 E52 Courtling 5
  And, told of this, he slights it. Tut, such crimes . . 45 E56 Poet-Ape 9
  Who, to upbraid the sloth of this our time, . . . 48 E66 Cary 5
  This morning, timely rapt with holy fire, . . . 52 E76 Bedford 1 1
  This world deaths region is, the other lifes: . . . 54 E80 Life/Death 5
  Now, in whose pleasures I have this discerned, . . . 55 E85 Goodyere 1 11
  Would you beleeve, when you this Mounsieur see, . . 56 E88 Monsieur 1
  Weare this renowne. 'Tis just, that who did give . . 57 E89 Allen 13
  To this, if ought appeare, which I not know of, . . 65 E101 Supper 25
  Are all but Luthers beere, to this I sing. . . . 65 E101 Supper 34
  Of this we will sup free, but moderately, . . . 65 E101 Supper 35
  Nor could the age have mist thee, in this strife . . 66 E102 Pembroke 5
  For your next meale: this you are sure of. Why . . 69 E107 Hungry 27
  Beholding, to this master of the warre; . . . 72 E111 Edmonds 2 4

THIS (cont.)

	Page	Title	Line
Beholden, to this master of the warre;	72	E111 Edmonds 2	V 4
Nor to give Caesar this, makes ours the lesse.	72	E111 Edmonds 2	8
At this so subtile sport: and play'st so ill?	72	E112 Gamster	2
You wonder, who this is! and, why I name	74	E115 Honest Man	1
Naming so many, too! But, this is one,	74	E115 Honest Man	3
This little storie:	77	E120 S. P.	2
Under-neath this stone doth lye	79	E124 Elizabeth	3
Leave it buryed in this vault.	79	E124 Elizabeth	8
I, and this Muse had beene, if thou hadst not	80	E127 Aubigny	7
And, than this same, I know no abler way	80	E127 Aubigny	11
We each to other may this voyce enspire;	81	E128 Wm Roe 2	11
This is that good Aeneas, past through fire,	81	E128 Wm Roe 2	12
Came backe untouch'd. This man hath travail'd well.	81	E128 Wm Roe 2	14
Think'st thou, Mime, this is great? or, that they strive	81	E129 Mime	9
O, runne not proud of this. Yet, take thy due.	81	E129 Mime	15
Men love thee not for this: They laugh at thee.	81	E129 Mime	18
Say, this, or that man they to thee preferre:	83	E131 Ferrab. 2	9
Even those for whom they doe this, know they erre:	83	E131 Ferrab. 2	10
That to the world I publish, for him, this;	83	E132 Sylvester	9
Then let the former age, with this content her,	84	E133 Voyage	19
That all this while I have forgot some god,	85	E133 Voyage	44
The many perills of this Port, and how	85	E133 Voyage	47
To this dire passage. Say, thou stop thy nose:	85	E133 Voyage	59
'Tis but light paines: Indeede this Dock's no rose.	85	E133 Voyage	60
Is this we heare? of frogs? No, guts wind-bound,	86	E133 Voyage	92
Over your heads: Well, row. At this a loud	86	E133 Voyage	93
Touching this cause, where they will be affeard	87	E133 Voyage	106
Their Mercury did now. By this, the stemme	87	E133 Voyage	111
By this time had they reach'd the Stygian poole,	87	E133 Voyage	121
This way to husbands; and whose baskets beare	95	F2 Penshurst	55
But what can this (more then expresse their love)	95	F2 Penshurst	57
And I not faine to sit (as some, this day,	95	F2 Penshurst	65
That found King James, when hunting late, this way,	95	F2 Penshurst	76
A fortune, in this age, but rarely knowne.	96	F2 Penshurst	92
Let this man sweat, and wrangle at the barre,	99	F3 Wroth	73
Shalt neither thet, nor this envy:	99	F3 Wroth	92
And, knowing this, should I yet stay,	100	F4 To the World	21
But if once we loose this light,	102	F5 Celia 1	7
And this age will build no more:	105	F8 Sicknesse	12
But this true course is not embrac'd by many:	109	F11 Epode	19
But this faire course is not embrac'd by many:	109	F11 Epode	V 19
But this doth from the cloud of error grow,	110	F11 Epode	35
In equall knots: This beares no brands, nor darts,	110	F11 Epode	51
O, who is he, that (in this peace) enjoyes	110	F11 Epode	55
As this chaste love we sing.	111	F11 Epode	68
As this chaste love I sing.	111	F11 Epode	V 68
And yet (in this t'expresse our selves more cleare)	111	F11 Epode	75
And yet (in this t'expresse my self more cleare)	111	F11 Epode	V 75
Of this excelling frame?	112	F11 Epode	110
And to his sense object this sentence ever,	113	F11 Epode	115
Just to the waight their this dayes-presents beare;	113	F12 Rutland	8
Or perhaps lesse: whil'st gold beares all this sway,	113	F12 Rutland	18
Then this, our guilt, nor golden age can deeme,	114	F12 Rutland	22
But let this drosse carry what price it will	114	F12 Rutland	27
This hasty sacrifice, wherein I reare	116	F12 Rutland	97
And, in this name, am given out dangerous	117	F13 Aubigny	11
I, that have suffer'd this; and, though forsooke	117	F13 Aubigny	15
And this shall be no false one, but as much	117	F13 Aubigny	27
This blessing of your starres, then by that way	118	F13 Aubigny	54
This makes, that wisely you decline your life,	118	F13 Aubigny	59
This makes, that your affections still be new,	119	F13 Aubigny	118
Madame, be bold to use this truest glasse:	120	F13 Aubigny	122
This day	120	F14 Sydney	13
This day sayes, then, the number of glad yeeres	120	F14 Sydney	21
If with this truth you be inspir'd,	121	F14 Sydney	52
This day	121	F14 Sydney	54
My faith, my hope, my love: and in this state,	122	F15 Heaven	11
Where have I beene this while exil'd from thee?	122	F15 Heaven	13
This All of nothing, gavest it forme, and fate,	127	U1 Trinitie	18
To see this Babe, all innocence;	130	U1 Nativitie	22
Can man forget this Storie?	130	U1 Nativitie	24
When you know, that this is she,	131	U2 Excuse	18
This my object. But she threw	132	U2 How he saw	23
Set, and to this softer straine:	136	U2 Cupid	9
This here sung, can be no other	136	U2 Cupid	11
For this Beauty yet doth hide	137	U2 Cupid	49
And, if such a verse as this,	138	U2 Kisse	35
Nay, you may erre in this,	139	U2 Another	9
This could be call'd but halfe a kisse.	139	U2 Another	11
To consult, if Fucus this	140	U2 Promise	26
And this profession of a store	146	U6 Defence	19
That were this morning blowne;	147	U7 Nymph	19
Doe but consider this small dust,	148	U8 Houre-glasse	1
Could you beleeve, that this,	148	U8 Houre-glasse	4
Of him whose bones this Grave doth gather:	151	U12 Corbet	6
This Good from you, as freely will it owe;	153	U13 Sacvile	14
All this corrupts the thankes; lesse hath he wonne,	154	U13 Sacvile	33
Of Valour, but at this Idolatrous rate?	156	U13 Sacvile	104
Who was this Morning such a one, should be	157	U13 Sacvile	126
In time 'twill be a heape; This is not true	157	U13 Sacvile	133
Of this so vitious Humanitie.	158	U14 Selden	12
But I to yours, farre from this fault, shall doo;	159	U14 Selden	V 17

	Page	Title	Line

THIS (cont.)

	Page	Title		Line
In offering this thy worke to no great Name,	161	U14 Selden		69
This hath our ill-us'd freedome, and soft peace	166	U15 Friend-Wars		121
This way, now that, as if their number were	166	U15 Friend-Wars		126
This Praecipice, and Rocks that have no end,	166	U15 Friend-Wars		130
Can we not leave this worme? or will we not?	166	U15 Friend-Wars		141
In this, and like, an itch of Vanitie,	166	U15 Friend-Wars		143
Well, let it goe. Yet this is better, then	166	U15 Friend-Wars		145
Nor should I at this time protested be,	169	U17 Friend-Debt		7
A terror? or is all this but my feare?	169	U18 Elegy Can		6
Forgive me this one foolish deadly sin,	171	U20 Shrub		2
Knew I all this afore? had I perceiv'd,	171	U20 Shrub		9
Knew I this Woman? yes; And you doe see,	172	U20 Shrub		15
Aske not to know this Man. If fame should speake	172	U21 Ltl Shrub		1
This subjects you to love of one.	173	U22 Elegy Tho		8
Have sung this Hymne, and here intreat	174	U22 Elegy Tho		30
And this Securitie,	174	U23 Himselfe		4
Let this thought quicken thee,	174	U23 Himselfe		15
This makes, that lighted by the beamie hand	176	U24 Frontispice V		9
Thy Priest in this strange rapture; heat my braine	177	U25 Desmond		11
Wrapt in this paper lie,	180	U26 Ode High		10
This same which you have caught,	180	U26 Ode High		20
Come short of all this learned throng,	182	U27 Ode Helen		34
Happy Greeke, by this protection,	184	U29 Fit of Rime		32
And goe no farther: let this Circle be	185	U30 Burleigh		3
You favour Truth, and me, in this mans Cause.	186	U31 Elsmere		10
When this appeares, just Lord, to your sharp sight,	186	U32 Elsmere		15
Then this did by her true? She never sought	188	U34 Small Poxe		5
Make all hereafter, had'st thou ruin'd this?	188	U34 Small Poxe		16
Upon record, in this blest child.	188	U35 Chute		4
This sadnesse makes no approaches, but to kill.	191	U38 Elegy 'Tis		4
Alone lend succours, and this furie stay,	191	U38 Elegy 'Tis		8
This looketh like an Execution day?	193	U38 Elegy 'Tis		80
He when he sees a sorrow such as this,	193	U38 Elegy 'Tis		87
This makes me, Mrs. that sometime by stealth,	197	U40 Elegy That		9
What fate is this, to change mens dayes and houres,	199	U41 Elegy Since		9
Or in Moore-fields, this other night! sings one,	202	U42 Elegy Let		73
And why to me this, thou lame Lord of fire,	202	U43 Vulcan		1
And why to me this, thou lame god of fire,	202	U43 Vulcan	V	1
If none of these, then why this fire? Or find	203	U43 Vulcan		27
Had I fore-knowne of this thy least desire	205	U43 Vulcan		59
And raz'd, e're thought could urge, This might have bin!	209	U43 Vulcan		136
And this a Sparkle of that fire let loose	209	U43 Vulcan		141
That this sparke of the same fire let loose	209	U43 Vulcan	V	141
Scap'd not this Justice any jot the more:	210	U43 Vulcan	V	154
Against this Vulcan? No Injunction?	210	U43 Vulcan		175
At Common-Law: me thinkes in this despight	211	U43 Vulcan	V	177
But he that should perswade, to have this done	214	U44 Speach		61
This, and that box his Beautie to repaire;	215	U44 Speach		96
This other for his eye-browes; hence, away,	215	U44 Speach		97
Brunsfield, and Mansfield doe this yeare, my fates	219	U47 Tribe		44
I, and for this neglect, the courser sort	219	U47 Tribe		54
We dedicate this Cellar,	220	U48 Bacchus		3
This Age would faine no faith to Dorrels Deed;	223	U49 Pucell		42
Wherewith this while you live a widow'd wife,	224	U50 Countesse		2
Haile, happie Genius of this antient pile!	225	U51 Bacon		1
And so doe I. This is the sixtieth yeare	225	U51 Bacon		7
To goe out after—till when take this letter	229	U54 Squib		19
Thoughts worthy of thy gift, this Inke,	229	U55 Burges		2
By this, although you fancie not the man,	231	U56 Covell		25
This were a spectacle! A sight to draw	233	U59 Newcastle		13
All this (my Lord) is Valour! This is yours!	233	U59 Newcastle		19
Could stop the malice of this ill,	234	U60 La-ware		15
Nay, and in this, thou show'st to value more	235	U62 Charles 1		9
That thought shall make, he will this losse supply	236	U63 Charles 2		11
If he but weigh'd the blessings of this day?	236	U64 Charles 3		4
This Prince of flowers? Soone shoot thou up, and grow	237	U65 Prince		5
As in this Prince? Let it be lawfull, so	238	U66 Queene		11
This sixteenth of November,	239	U67 Muses		2
This Citie, or to shake	239	U67 Muses		11
This sea-girt Isle upon:	240	U67 Muses		33
This sea-girt ground upon:	240	U67 Muses	V	33
This day the Court doth measure	240	U67 Muses		43
Summe up this crowned day,	240	U67 Muses		47
Make up this crowned day,	240	U67 Muses	V	47
And this the wombe divine.	240	U67 Muses		51
What did this Stirrer, but die late?	243	U70 Ode		30
Accept this garland, plant it on thy head,	245	U70 Ode		77
Jonson, who sung this of him, e're he went	246	U70 Ode		85
In this bright Asterisme:	246	U70 Ode		89
Whilst that in heav'n, this light on earth must shine.	246	U70 Ode		96
This made you first to know the Why	247	U70 Ode		107
This is King Charles his Day. Speake it, thou Towre,	249	U72 King		1
This is King Charles his birth day. Speake it, thou Towre,	249	U72 King	V	1
Adding her owne glad accents, to this Day,	249	U72 King		7
Adding her owne greate accents, to this Day,	249	U72 King	V	7
On th'often comming of this Holy-day:	249	U72 King		16
Still to have such a Charles, but this Charles long.	249	U72 King		18
This Feast, then can the Day,	254	U75 Epithalam.		55
With light of love, this Paire doth intertexe!	254	U75 Epithalam.		60
And wonder'd at the bounties of this day:	255	U75 Epithalam.		90
And this well mov'd the Judgement of the King	256	U75 Epithalam.		105
Which to this use, wert built and consecrate!	256	U75 Epithalam.		130

THIS (cont.)

	Page	Title	Line
And this their chosen Bishop celebrate,	256	U75 Epithalam.	132
(After the last child borne;) This is our wedding day.	258	U75 Epithalam.	168
To be a watchfull Servant for this State;	258	U75 Epithalam.	178
By this Sun's Noone-sted's made	258	U75 Epithalam.	183
And that this so accepted summe,	259	U76 Petition	14
And that this so thriftye summe,	259	U76 Petition	V 14
This would all their envie burst:	260	U76 Petition	30
This I would doe, could I know Weston, one	260	U77 Treasurer	10
This I would doe, if I could thinke you one	260	U77 Treasurer	V 10
Wilt thou be, Muse, when this shall them befall?	263	U78 Digby	31
Wilt thou be, Muse, when this shall then befall?	263	U78 Digby	V 31
This is the great Preserver of our bounds,	265	U79 New-yeares	48
This only the great Shep'ard is.	265	U79 New-yeares	65
That thou art lov'd of God, this worke is done,	268	U80 Christning	1
This day, by Baptisme, and his Saviours crosse:	268	U80 Christning	10
Of Winchester; the Heralds can tell this:	269	U81 Pawlet	20
Of Winchester; the Heralds could tell this:	269	U81 Pawlet	V 20
T'escape this common knowne necessitie,	271	U81 Pawlet	93
This Cradle, and for Goodnesse sake,	273	U84 Cradle	10
This, utter'd by an antient Bard,	274	U84 Cradle	33
This beautie without falshood fayre,	275	U84 Body	7
Last, draw the circles of this Globe,	276	U84 Body	25
A Copie of this peece; nor tell	277	U84 Body	30
This worke I can performe alone;	277	U84 Mind	3
No, to expresse this Mind to sense,	278	U84 Mind	V 13
This is no Picture, but the same.	278	U84 Mind	24
For this so loftie forme, so streight,	280	U84 Mind	54
My wounded mind cannot sustaine this stroke,	283	U84 Muse	23
Her blessed Soule, hence, forth this valley vane	283	U84 Muse	34
This as it guilty is, or guiltlesse found,	284	U84 Muse	56
This being thus: why should my tongue, or pen	284	U84 Muse	69
Hee knowes, what worke h'hath done, to call this Guest,	284	U84 Muse	81
Out of her noble body, to this Feast:	284	U84 Muse	82
And will you, worthy Sonne, Sir, knowing this,	285	U84 Muse	97
To one she said, Doe this, he did it; So	287	U84 Muse	169
All this by Faith she saw, and fram'd a Plea,	288	U84 Muse	209
In this sweet Extasie, she was rapt hence.	289	U84 Muse	225
And from the sweet Tub Wine of this yeare takes,	291	U85 Country	47
There is no labour, nor no shame in this;	294	U88 Petronius	8
This hath pleas'd, doth please, and long will please; never	294	U88 Petronius	9
Can this decay, but is beginning ever.	294	U88 Petronius	10
This peece, my Piso's, and that booke agree,	305	Horace	8
That Book, my Piso's, and this piece agree,	338	Horace	V 8
And both doe crave, and give againe, this leave.	305	Horace	13
What's this? if he whose money hireth thee	305	Horace	26
Obscure. This, striving to run smooth, and flow,	307	Horace	36
Downe close by shore, this other creeping steales,	339	Horace	V 40/ 39
This, seeking, in a various kind, to forme	307	Horace	40
Till fitter season. Now, to like of this,	307	Horace	63
And give, being taken modestly, this leave,	309	Horace	73
This foot the socks tooke up, and buskins grave,	311	Horace	118
What doth this Promiser such gaping worth	313	Horace	197
What doth this Promiser such great gaping worth	343	Horace	V197
A scorned Mouse! O, how much better this,	315	Horace	199
A trifling Mouse! O, how much better this,	343	Horace	V199
Will take offence, at this: Nor, though it strike	321	Horace	361
Take just offence at this: nor, though it strike	347	Horace	V353/361
This foot yet, in the famous Trimeters	323	Horace	381
'Tis cleare, this way I have got off from blame,	323	Horace	395
This was the wisdome, that they had of old,	327	Horace	486
This booke will get the Sosii money; This	329	Horace	517
As some the farther off: This loves the darke;	331	Horace	541
This, fearing not the subtlest Judges marke,	331	Horace	542
Will in the light be view'd: This, once, the sight	331	Horace	543
Doth please; this, ten times over, will delight.	331	Horace	544
This saying: To some things there is assign'd	331	Horace	548
Yet, there's a value given to this man.	331	Horace	554
I wonder how this happie man should know,	333	Horace	605
Hee'd say, Mend this, good friend, and this; 'tis naught.	333	Horace	624
He'd say, mend this my friend, and this, 'tis nought.	354	Horace	V624
They're darke, bid cleare this: all that's doubtfull wrote	335	Horace	637
Why should I grieve my friend, this trifling way?	335	Horace	640
Nor did he doe this once; for if you can	335	Horace	667
Nor did he do this, once; if yet you can,	355	Horace	V667
Or love of this so famous death lay by.	335	Horace	669
Or love of this his famous death lay by.	355	Horace	V669
All; So this grievous Writer puts to flight	337	Horace	676
I struggled with this passion that did drowne	362	Palmer	28
So with this Authors Readers will it thrive:	362	Author	12
His proofe their praise, will meete, as in this line.	362	Author	14
In thought to praise this Ladie;	365	Ode Splendor	18
A gentler Bird, then this,	366	Ode Who saith	7
This Swanne is onely his,	366	Ode Who saith	15
This change'd his Downe; till this, as white	366	Ode Who saith	25
(But this more apt	368	Ode Who saith	62
But should they know (as I) that this,	369	Ode Who saith	97
Stay, view this stone: And, if thou beest not such,	371	Epitaph	1
He will expiate this sinne with converting the Jewes.	375	Coryat 1	21
But who will beleeve this, that chanceth to looke	379	Coryat 3	17
There nam'd to be travell'd? For this our Tom saith:	380	Coryat 3	21
hee freely bringes; and on this Alter layes	383	Rich	9
Not only this, but every day of thine,	384	Somerset	9

682

		Page	Title	Line

THIS (cont.)

	Page	Title	Line
Sure, this glad payre were married, but this day.	384	Somerset	26
Was worthy of a Good one; And this, here,	386	Husband	10
This thy worke forth: that judgment mine commends.	386	Browne	8
Whose worke could this be, Chapman, to refine	388	Chapman	1
If all the vulgar Tongues, that speake this day,	388	Chapman	7
Who tracks this Authors, or Translators Pen,	389	Aleman	1
As in this Spanish Proteus; who, though writ	389	Aleman	5
And this hath met that one, that may be stil'd	389	Aleman	13
More then the Foster-father of this Child;	389	Aleman	14
To your desert, who'have done it, Friend. And this	389	Aleman	21
This Figure, that thou here seest put,	390	Reader	1
Or crafty Malice, might pretend this praise,	391	Shakespeare	11
But every Table in this Church can say,	394	Jane Ogle	7
A list of Epithites: And prayse this way.	394	Jane Ogle	8
This second marriage, will aeternall make.	394	Jane Ogle	26
About the towne: this reck'ning I will pay,	396	Drayton	9
With us be call'd, the Naso, but this man?	397	Drayton	32
And flight about the Ile, well neare, by this,	397	Drayton	49
This booke! it is a Catechisme to fight,	398	Drayton	71
With pause upon it; make this page your booke;	399	Lady Ogle	6
For this did Katherine, Ladie Ogle, die	400	Lady Ogle	33
And this a coppie is of the Record.	400	Lady Ogle	40
This Booke will live; It hath a Genius: This	400	Beaumont	1
Before this worke? where Envy hath not cast	401	Beaumont	13
This Fort of so impregnable accesse,	401	Beaumont	17
Who did this Knot compose,	401	Filmer	7
This is the money-gett, Mechanick Age!	404	Inigo Jones 1	52
Whither? oh whither will this Tire-man growe?	404	Inigo Jones 1	59
A Noble honest Soule! what's this to thee?	406	Inigo Jones 2	6
- - - the Author of this Work, M. Rich. Brome.	409	Brome	Ttl
I sayd, who'had supp'd so deepe of this sweet Chalice,	412	Sutcliffe	21
Here, are five letters in this blessed Name,	412	Ghyrlond	1
On the reverse of this your circling crowne,	413	Ghyrlond	30
Through all the lines of this circumference,	414	Ghyrlond	54
T'imprint in all purg'd hearts this virgin sence,	414	Ghyrlond	55
This is my censure. Now there is a new	415	Rutter	19
Office of Wit, a Mint, and (this is true)	415	Rutter	20
Bred by your breath, on this low bancke of ours;	416	Welcome	3
Upon this obeliske, advanc'd for it,	416	Welcome	5
This was Mr Ben: Johnsons Answer of the suddayne.	418	Answer	Ttl
And in this Age, canst hope no other grace.	420	Ode:If Men	27
Aboute this Isle, and Charme the rounde, as when	421	Ode:If Men	39
I send this small, but hearty testimony: and with charge,	666	Glover	5

THIS'S

	Page	Title	Line
Without conferring symboles. This's my day.	396	Drayton	10

TH'ITALIAN

	Page	Title	Line
Parts, then th'Italian could doe, with his dore.	74	E115 Honest Man	26

THITHER

	Page	Title	Line
He meant they thither should make swift repaire,	41	E44 Chuff	5
Thither it flowes. How much did Stallion spend	163	U15 Friend-Wars	47
For Silke will draw some sneaking Songster thither.	200	U42 Elegy Let	26
Thither, you hope to come; and there to find	285	U84 Muse	103
And who make thither else, rob, or invade.	389	Chapman	12

THO'

	Page	Title	Line
Tho', happy Muse, thou know my Digby well;	262	U78 Digby	1

THO

	Page	Title	Line
You would be then most confident, that tho	194	U38 Elegy 'Tis	113

TH'OBSCENE

	Page	Title	Line
From what th'obscene, and petulant Satyres are.	321	Horace	340

TH'OBSERVING

	Page	Title	Line
Th'observing neighbours no such mood can see.	40	E42 Giles	2

TH'OFTEN

	Page	Title	Line
On th'often comming of this Holy-day:	249	U72 King	16

TH'OLD

	Page	Title	Line
But see! th'old baud hath serv'd him in his trim,	31	E12 Shift	23
A Master-worker call'd, th'old standerd burst	415	Rutter	22

THOMAS

	Page	Title	Line
To Thomas Earle of Suffolke.	49	E67 Suffolk	Ttl
To Thomas Lord Chancelor.	51	E74 Chancelor	Ttl
To Sir Thomas Roe.	63	E98 Th Roe 1	Ttl
To Sir Thomas Overbury.	73	E113 Overbury	Ttl
An Epigram. To Thomas Lo: Elsmere, - - -	185	U31 Elsmere	Ttl
Upon a Thomas, or a Francis call;	258	U75 Epithalam.	171
Upon a Thomas, or a Sister call;	258	U75 Epithalam.	V171
- - - Thomas May, Esquire.	395	May	Ttl

TH'ONE

	Page	Title	Line
till th'one hath drownd the other in our sightes,	361	Palmer	20

TH'OPINION

	Page	Title	Line
Of miming, gets th'opinion of a wit.	74	E115 Honest Man	28

THORNY

	Page	Title	Line
With wonder on the thorny regiment.	413	Ghyrlond	16

THOROUGH

	Page	Title	Line
He makes himselfe a thorough-fare of vice.	76	E118 Gut	4
Thorough her wombe they make their famous road,	85	E133 Voyage	66

THOROUGH-FARE

	Page	Title	Line
He makes himselfe a thorough-fare of vice.	76	E118 Gut	4

THOROUGHLIE

	Page	Title	Line
not safe; but when thou dost them thoroughlie:	423	Lucan	16

THOROW

	Page	Title	Line
So going thorow all your straine,	145	U5 Woman-kind	10

THOSE

	Page	Title	Line
As chiefe of those still promise they will bee.	28	E4 James 1	8

THOSE (cont.)

	Page	Title	Line
Nor need'st thou: for those few, by oath releast,	32	E16 Brain-hardy	7
Not glad, like those that have new hopes, or sutes,	47	E64 Salisbury 3	1
Nor glad as those, that old dependents bee,	47	E64 Salisbury 3	5
He should those rare, and absolute numbers view,	53	E79 Rutland	11
Much like those Brethren: thinking to prevaile	59	E92 New Crie	36
For the great marke of vertue, those being gone	60	E93 Radcliffe	2
Be of the best: and 'mongst those, best are you.	61	E94 Bedford 3	14
For who can master those great parts like thee,	61	E95 Savile	17
My title's seal'd. Those that for claps doe write,	62	E96 Donne 2	9
With those that come; whose grace may make that seeme	64	E101 Supper	5
To make those faithfull, did the Fates send you?	67	E104 Montgomery	6
Were you advanced, past those times, to be	67	E104 Montgomery	11
Tell the grosse Dutch those grosser tales of yours,	68	E107 Hungry	5
Un-argued then, and yet hath fame from those;	71	E110 Edmonds 1	10
And thence, deprave thee, and thy worke. To those	72	E111 Edmonds 2	11
And those that lack'd it, to suspect at length,	75	E116 Jephson	6
And those to turne to bloud, and make thine owne:	80	E128 Wm Roe 2	4
Even those for whom they doe this, know they erre:	83	E131 Ferrab. 2	10
No more, those mayden glories shee hath lost.	83	E132 Sylvester	14
Of those, that put out moneyes, on returne	85	E133 Voyage	32
Then all those Atomi ridiculous,	87	E133 Voyage	127
These be the cause of those thicke frequent mists	87	E133 Voyage	130
Those proud, ambitious heaps, and nothing else,	96	F2 Penshurst	101
The trees cut out in log; and those boughes made	98	F3 Wroth	45
There are those, that, for thy sake,	105	F8 Sicknesse	25
Peace, Luxurie, thou art like one of those	111	F11 Epode	69
Or those, who doubt the common mouth of fame,	111	F11 Epode	79
Or those, which doubt the common mouth of fame,	111	F11 Epode	V 79
Nor meane we those, whom vowes and conscience	111	F11 Epode	83
Nor meane I those, whose vowes and conscience	111	F11 Epode	V 83
The soules, shee loves. Those other glorious notes,	114	F12 Rutland	43
And, in those outward formes, all fooles are wise.	117	F13 Aubigny	36
Though it reject not those of Fortune: such	117	F13 Aubigny	45
Not looking by, or back (like those, that waite	118	F13 Aubigny	62
Increase those acts, o glorious Trinitie	128	U1 Trinitie	29
For the Apple, and those three	137	U2 Cupid	47
So, as those that had your sight,	138	U2 Kisse	17
But what those lips doe make.	143	U3 Musicall	16
Oh doe not wanton with those eyes,	144	U4 Song	1
O, be not angry with those fires,	144	U4 Song	5
Hang up those dull, and envious fooles,	146	U6 Defence	1
And speaking worst of those, from whom they went	154	U13 Sacvile	51
Feed those, at whom the Table points at still?	155	U13 Sacvile	74
As if they would belie their stature; those	157	U13 Sacvile	146
Those thousands on his back, shall after blow	165	U15 Friend-Wars	104
Now threaten, with those meanes she did invite?	169	U18 Elegy Can	2
Except the way be errour to those ends:	170	U18 Elegy Can	13
By those bright Eyes, at whose immortall fires	170	U19 Elegy By	1
By those pure bathes your either cheeke discloses,	170	U19 Elegy By	7
Shall light those places	179	U25 Desmond	59
To those true numerous Graces; whereof some,	182	U28 Worth	6
When those good few, that her Defenders be,	186	U32 Elsmere	5
Of those that set by their false faces more	188	U34 Small Poxe	4
Your just commands; yet those, not I, be lost.	192	U38 Elegy 'Tis	38
And turne the Ceremonies of those Nights	197	U40 Elegy That	11
Yet keepe those up in sackcloth too, or lether,	200	U42 Elegy Let	25
That quilts those bodies, I have leave to span:	200	U42 Elegy Let	32
That are like cloath'd: must I be of those fooles	201	U42 Elegy Let	48
He would have done in verse, with any of those	201	U42 Elegy Let	62
Another answers, 'Lasse, those Silkes are none,	202	U42 Elegy Let	74
Or pomp'd for those hard trifles, Anagrams,	204	U43 Vulcan	35
Or pomp'd for those fine trifles, Anagrams,	204	U43 Vulcan	V 35
Or Eteostichs, or those finer flammes	204	U43 Vulcan	36
Or else Acrostichs, or those finer flammes	204	U43 Vulcan	V 36
After the Fathers, and those wiser Guides	207	U43 Vulcan	103
But, O those Reeds! thy meere disdaine of them,	208	U43 Vulcan	129
But, O those weedes! thy meere disdaine of them,	208	U43 Vulcan	V129
I will not argue thee, from those, of guilt,	210	U43 Vulcan	165
In those Records, which, were all Chroniclers gone,	210	U43 Vulcan	171
In those Records, which, were our Chroniclers gone,	210	U43 Vulcan	V171
And all Those ills that flew out of her box	212	U43 Vulcan	214
Light on thee: Or if those plagues will not doo,	212	U43 Vulcan	215
Light upon thee: Or if those plagues will not doo,	212	U43 Vulcan	V215
Withall, the dirtie paines those Citizens take,	213	U44 Speach	15
And the returne those thankfull Courtiers yeeld,	213	U44 Speach	17
Insert thy Hodges, and those newer men,	214	U44 Speach	53
I neither am, nor art thou one of those	216	U45 Squib	5
Those are poore Ties, depend on those false ends,	216	U45 Squib	11
Let those that meerely talke, and never thinke,	218	U47 Tribe	9
As aerie light, and as like wit as those?	222	U49 Pucell	10
To stuffes and Laces, those my Man can buy.	223	U49 Pucell	28
And when you want those friends, or neere in blood,	224	U50 Countesse	26
And saw a Centaure, past those tales of Greece;	228	U53 Newcastle	5
Will be reward enough: to weare like those,	232	U58 Book-seller	9
But whisper'd Counsells, and those only thrive;	234	U61 Epigram	6
Who doubts, those fruits God can with gaine restore,	235	U63 Charles 2	3
Freedome, and Truth; with love from those begot:	241	U69 Friend Son	5
Of hearts the union. And those not by chance	246	U70 Ode	99
And made those strong approaches, by False braies,	248	U71 Treasurer	7
Be duly done to those	255	U75 Epithalam.	93
Be kept alive those Sweet, and Sacred fires	257	U75 Epithalam.	163
Those your Fathers Markes, your Pounds;	260	U76 Petition	27

	Page	Title	Line
THOSE (cont.)			
For those to dwell in, and be still at home.	262	U78 Digby	V 8
To touch those Mysteries! We may admire	269	U81 Pawlet	V 31
Of Vulture death, and those relentlesse cleies?	283	U84 Muse	18
Those other two; which must be judg'd, or crown'd:	284	U84 Muse	55
Amongst her Peeres, those Princes of all good!	284	U84 Muse	84
Saints, Martyrs, Prophets, with those Hierarchies,	285	U84 Muse	85
Adopt us Heires, by grace, who were of those	286	U84 Muse	140
For her devotions, and those sad essayes	287	U84 Muse	181
To be that Smith; then live, mark'd one of those,	307	Horace	51
And those thy new, and late-coyn'd words receive,	309	Horace	74
To laughter; so they grieve with those that mone.	311	Horace	144
Then those the faithfull eyes take in by show,	317	Horace	258
The angry, and love those that feare t'offend.	317	Horace	282
Those that did sing, and act: their faces dy'd	319	Horace	314
Those heavie Verses, sent so to the Stage,	323	Horace	384
On life, and manners, and make those his booke,	325	Horace	454
As those that hir'd to weepe at Funeralls, swoune,	333	Horace	614
Those ill-torn'd Verses, to new hammering.	333	Horace	628
Those that are wise, a furious Poet feare,	354	Horace	V643
Those that in blood such violent pleasure have,	363	Murder	1
They are not those, are present with theyre face,	384	Somerset	1
So, may those Mariage-Pledges, comforts prove;	384	Somerset	19
And make those flights upon the bankes of Thames,	392	Shakespeare	73
And those in number so, and measure rais'd,	395	May	8
What godds but those of arts, and eloquence?	395	May	16
Those ambling visits, passe in verse, betweene	396	Drayton	4
And those so sweet, and well proportion'd parts,	396	Drayton	21
O, how in those, dost thou instruct these times,	397	Drayton	43
Get broken peeces, and fight well by those.	398	Drayton	74
I chyme that too: And I have mett with those	403	Inigo Jones 1	31
By observation of those Comick Lawes	409	Brome	7
By those deepe-grounded, understanding men,	414	Rutter	7
those turnd up, and those that fall,	417	Moon	14
To every sence, and scorne to those that sawe	420	Ode:If Men	17
And once more stryke the eare of tyme with those fresh straynes:	420	Ode:If Men	32
and the immortall gods; love only those	422	Lucan	5
whole armyes fall, swayd by those nyce respects.	423	Lucan	11
Those dull Girls, no good can mean us,	657	Door Apollo	11
TH'OTHER			
Th'other let it sleepe with death:	79	E124 Elizabeth	10
As th'other may his braines with Quicksilver.	208	U43 Vulcan	122
Or th'other on their borders, that will jeast	218	U47 Tribe	16
One corporall, only; th'other spirituall,	284	U84 Muse	52
Yet neyther of you seeme to th'other old.	384	Somerset	24
TH'			
So, in short time, th'art in arrerage growne	32	E16 Brain-hardy	5
Yet by thy weapon liv'st! Th'hast one good part.	50	E69 Cob	2
That still th'art present to the better cause;	52	E74 Chancelor	5
I know not which th'hast most, candor, or wit:	78	E123 Rudyerd 3	2
But both th'hast so, as who affects the state	78	E123 Rudyerd 3	3
Roe (and my joy to name) th'art now, to goe	80	E128 Wm Roe 2	1
That still th'art made the suppers flagge, the drum,	81	E129 Mime	7
So would'st th'have run upon the Rolls by stealth,	210	U43 Vulcan	169
THO'			
Seven yeeres tho'wert lent to me, and I thee pay,	41	E45 First Son	3
THOU'			
If thou'ldst but use thy faith, as thou didst then,	32	E18 Censurer	7
But that's put in, thou'lt say. Why, so is thine.	36	E29 Tilter	6
And, as thou'hast mine, his houres, and youth abuse.	48	E65 Muse	6
To which thou'rt not a weeke, bespoke a guest;	81	E129 Mime	6
And scorn'd, thou'ast showne thy malice, but hast fail'd.	188	U34 Small Poxe	18
On such my serious follies; But, thou'lt say,	204	U43 Vulcan	41
Or such my serious follies; But, thou'lt say,	204	U43 Vulcan	V 41
T'effect it, feele, thou'ast made thine owne heart ake.	250	U73 Weston	12
He cries, Good boy, thou'lt keepe thine owne. Now, adde	327	Horace	470
Thou'rt too ambitious: and dost fear in vaine!	408	Inigo Jones 3	6
THOU			
Thou should'st be bold, licentious, full of gall,	27	E2 My Booke	3
Thou are not covetous of least selfe-fame,	27	E2 My Booke	9
Thou, that mak'st gaine thy end, and wisely well,	27	E3 Bookseller	1
How, best of Kings, do'st thou a scepter beare!	28	E4 James 1	1
How, best of Poets, do'st thou laurell weare!	28	E4 James 1	2
Thou wert, as chiefe of them are said t'have beene.	28	E4 James 1	6
And such a Prince thou art, wee daily see,	28	E4 James 1	7
Thou call'st me Poet, as a terme of shame:	29	E10 Ignorant	1
What name, what skill, what faith hast thou in things!	31	E14 Camden	7
Man scarse can make that doubt, but thou canst teach.	31	E14 Camden	10
Thou more; that with it every day, dar'st jest	32	E16 Brain-hardy	2
Some hundred quarrells, yet dost thou fight none;	32	E16 Brain-hardy	6
Nor need'st thou: for those few, by oath releast,	32	E16 Brain-hardy	7
Make good what thou dar'st doe in all the rest.	32	E16 Brain-hardy	8
Thou saist, that cannot be: for thou hast seene	32	E18 Censurer	3
If thou'ldst but use thy faith, as thou didst then,	32	E18 Censurer	7
When thou wert wont t'admire, not censure men.	32	E18 Censurer	8
Thy faith is all the knowledge that thou hast.	32	E18 Censurer	10
Except thou could'st, Sir Cod, weare them within.	33	E20 Cod 2	2
And thou, right guiltlesse, may'st plead to it, why?	36	E29 Tilter	2
Guiltie, be wise; and though thou know'st the crimes	36	E30 Guiltie	1
Glad-mention'd Roe: thou art but gone before,	37	E33 Roe 3	2
First thou preserved wert, our king to bee,	38	E35 James 2	9
Martial, thou gav'st farre nobler Epigrammes	38	E36 Martial	1
Thou flattered'st thine, mine cannot flatter'd bee.	38	E36 Martial	4

685

THOU (cont.)

	Page	Title	Line
Marble, weepe, for thou dost cover	39	E40 Ratcliffe	1
Earth, thou hast not such another.	39	E40 Ratcliffe	17
What need hast thou of me? or of my Muse?	40	E43 Salisbury 1	1
As thou stand'st cleere of the necessitie.	41	E43 Salisbury 1	12
Farewell, thou child of my right hand, and joy;	41	E45 First Son	1
That we thy losse might know, and thou our love,	43	E51 James 3	1
Courtling, I rather thou should'st utterly	43	E52 Courtling	1
When I am read, thou fain'st a weake applause,	43	E52 Courtling	3
As if thou wert my friend, but lack'dst a cause.	43	E52 Courtling	4
Thou wert content the authors name to loose,	43	E53 Old-end	3
But when (in place) thou didst the patrons choose,	43	E53 Old-end	4
It was as if thou printed had'st an oath,	43	E53 Old-end	5
To give the world assurance thou wert both;	43	E53 Old-end	6
Thou art the father, and the witnesse too.	44	E53 Old-end	8
At once thou mak'st me happie, and unmak'st;	44	E55 Beaumont	5
And giving largely to me, more thou tak'st.	44	E55 Beaumont	6
When even there, where most thou praysest mee,	44	E55 Beaumont	9
And so my sharpnesse thou no lesse dis-joynts,	45	E58 Groome	5
Then thou did'st late my sense, loosing my points.	45	E58 Groome	6
And that thou seek'st reward of thy each act,	47	E63 Salisbury 2	5
To so true worth, though thou thy selfe forbid.	47	E63 Salisbury 2	12
To such true worth, though thou thy selfe forbid.	47	E63 Salisbury 2 V	12
Away, and leave me, thou thing most abhord,	48	E65 Muse	1
With me thou leav'st an happier Muse then thee,	48	E65 Muse	11
And which thou brought'st me, welcome povertie.	48	E65 Muse	12
Or thou more happie, it to justifie	49	E66 Cary	8
And thou design'd to be the same thou art,	49	E67 Suffolk	9
Before thou wert it, in each good mans heart.	49	E67 Suffolk	10
Cob, thou nor souldier, thiefe, nor fencer art,	50	E69 Cob	1
I Grieve not, Courtling, thou are started up	50	E72 Court-ling	1
At Madames table, where thou mak'st all wit	50	E72 Court-ling	3
Goe high, or low, as thou wilt value it.	50	E72 Court-ling	4
Whil'st thou art certaine to thy words, once gone,	52	E74 Chancelor	1
For, if thou shame, ranck'd with my friends, to goe,	53	E77 Not name	3
Hornet, thou hast thy wife drest, for the stall,	53	E78 Hornet	1
For all thou hear'st, thou swear'st thy selfe didst doo.	54	E81 Proule	5
Which, if thou leave not soone (though I am loth)	54	E81 Proule	7
To put out the word, whore, thou do'st me woo,	54	E83 Friend	1
As others speake, but onely thou dost act.	57	E89 Allen	12
Which thou art to thy selfe: whose fame was wonne	58	E91 Vere	5
Stand'st thou, to shew the times what you all were?	60	E93 Radcliffe	4
Thou, that art all their valour, all their spirit,	60	E93 Radcliffe	9
Thou yet remayn'st, un-hurt in peace, or warre,	60	E93 Radcliffe	13
So hast thou rendred him in all his bounds,	61	E95 Savile	5
O, would'st thou adde like hand, to all the rest!	61	E95 Savile	13
Thou need'st not shrinke at voyce of after-times;	61	E95 Savile	20
As thou hast best authoritie, t'allow.	62	E96 Donne 2	6
Thou hast begun well, Roe, which stand well too,	63	E98 Th Roe 1	1
And I know nothing more thou hast to doo.	63	E98 Th Roe 1	2
That thou at once, then, nobly maist defend	63	E98 Th Roe 1	7
And studie conscience, more then thou would'st fame.	63	E98 Th Roe 1	10
That thou hast kept thy love, encrease thy will,	63	E99 Th Roe 2	1
How much of great example wert thou, Roe,	64	E99 Th Roe 2	5
But thou, whose noblesse keeps one stature still,	66	E102 Pembroke	13
Thou must draw more: and they, that hope to see	66	E102 Pembroke	19
What man art thou, that art so many men,	68	E106 E Herbert	2
Thou are not one, seek'st miseries with hope,	70	E109 Nevil	5
Thou rather striv'st the matter to possesse,	70	E109 Nevil	9
To be the same in roote, thou art in height;	70	E109 Nevil	13
Wherein thou shew'st, how much the latter are	72	E111 Edmonds 2	3
Yet thou, perhaps, shalt meet some tongues will grutch,	72	E111 Edmonds 2	9
That to the world thou should'st reveale so much,	72	E111 Edmonds 2	10
With thy small stocke, why art thou ventring still,	72	E112 Gamster	1
Think'st thou it is meere fortune, that can win?	72	E112 Gamster	3
Or thy ranke setting? that thou dar'st put in	72	E112 Gamster	4
Tragick, or Comick; but thou writ'st the play.	72	E112 Gamster	8
An Epick poeme; thou hast the same end.	72	E112 Gamster	10
Next morne, an Ode: Thou mak'st a song ere night.	72	E112 Gamster	12
I passe to Elegies; Thou meet'st me there:	73	E112 Gamster	13
To Satyres; and thou dost pursue me. Where,	73	E112 Gamster	14
O, (thou cry'st out) that is thy proper game.	73	E112 Gamster	16
So, where thou liv'st, thou mak'st life understood!	73	E113 Overbury	3
Jephson, thou man of men, to whose lov'd name	75	E116 Jephson	1
That age, when thou stood'st up the master-braine:	75	E116 Jephson	4
Thou wert the first, mad'st merit know her strength,	75	E116 Jephson	5
Till thou canst finde the best, choose the least ill.	76	E119 Shelton	10
Would'st thou heare, what man can say	79	E124 Elizabeth	1
Uv'dale, thou piece of the first times, a man	79	E125 Uvedale	1
I, and this Muse had beene, if thou hadst not	80	E127 Aubigny	7
To Braynford, Hackney, Bow, but thou mak'st one;	81	E129 Mime	4
Think'st thou, Mime, this is great? or, that they strive	81	E129 Mime	9
Whil'st thou dost rayse some Player, from the grave,	81	E129 Mime	11
Thou dost out-zany Cokely, Pod; nay, Gue:	81	E129 Mime	16
And thine owne Coriat too. But (would'st thou see)	81	E129 Mime	17
Alcides, be thou succouring to my song.	85	E133 Voyage	50
Thou hast seene hell (some say) and know'st all nookes there,	85	E133 Voyage	51
To this dire passage. Say, thou stop thy nose:	85	E133 Voyage	59
Thou art not, Penshurst, built to envious show,	93	F2 Penshurst	1
Thou hast no lanterne, whereof tales are told;	93	F2 Penshurst	4
Thou joy'st in better markes, of soyle, of ayre,	93	F2 Penshurst	7
Of wood, of water: therein thou art faire.	93	F2 Penshurst	8
Thou hast thy walkes for health, as well as sport:	93	F2 Penshurst	9

THOU (cont.)

	Page	Title	Line
Thy copp's, too, nam'd of Gamage, thou hast there,	94	F2 Penshurst	19
When thou would'st feast, or exercise thy friends.	94	F2 Penshurst	21
Thou hast thy ponds, that pay thee tribute fish,	94	F2 Penshurst	32
As if thou, then, wert mine, or I raign'd here:	95	F2 Penshurst	74
Did'st thou, then, make 'hem! and what praise was heap'd	95	F2 Penshurst	83
How blest art thou, canst love the countrey, Wroth,	96	F3 Wroth	1
Or, if thou list the night in watch to breake,	97	F3 Wroth	21
Thou dost with some delight the day out-weare,	97	F3 Wroth	35
Thou canst with some delight the day out-weare,	97	F3 Wroth	V 35
The whil'st, the severall seasons thou hast seene	97	F3 Wroth	37
And such since thou canst make thine owne content,	98	F3 Wroth	65
But thou, my Wroth, if I can truth apply,	99	F3 Wroth	91
But thou, my Wroth, if I may truth apply,	99	F3 Wroth	V 91
Which who can use is happy: Such be thou.	99	F3 Wroth	99
Which who can use is happy: Such art thou.	99	F3 Wroth	V 99
Thou maist thinke life, a thing but lent.	100	F3 Wroth	106
False world, good-night: since thou hast brought	100	F4 To the World	1
Doe not once hope, that thou canst tempt	100	F4 To the World	5
From all the nets that thou canst spread.	100	F4 To the World	8
And what thou call'st thy gifts are baits.	100	F4 To the World	12
I know too, though thou strut, and paint,	100	F4 To the World	13
Yet art thou both shrunke up, and old,	100	F4 To the World	14
I know thou whole art but a shop	100	F4 To the World	17
Yet art thou falser then thy wares.	100	F4 To the World	20
I know thou canst nor shew, nor beare	101	F4 To the World	39
More hatred, then thou hast to mee.	101	F4 To the World	40
Thou did'st abuse, and then betray;	101	F4 To the World	42
Why, Disease, dost thou molest	104	F8 Sicknesse	1
And will, long ere thou should'st starve,	106	F8 Sicknesse	44
But thou thereon did'st onely breath,	106	F9 Celia 3	13
Thou, nor thy loosenesse with my making sorts.	107	F10 Proludium	18
Thou, nor their loosenesse with our making sorts.	107	F10 Proludium	V 18
Peace, Luxurie, thou art like one of those	111	F11 Epode	69
O, be thou witnesse, that the reynes dost know,	122	F15 Heaven	5
As thou art all, so be thou all to mee,	122	F15 Heaven	9
And whither rap'd, now thou but stoup'st to mee?	122	F15 Heaven	14
A broken heart thou wert not wont despise,	127	U1 Trinitie	10
If thou hadst not	129	U1 Father	7
Then thou hast done?	129	U1 Father	18
Love, if thou wilt ever see	132	U2 How he saw	7
Here's a shaft, thou art to slow!	132	U2 How he saw	10
But alas, thou seest the least	137	U2 Cupid	43
Of her Sex; But could'st thou, Love,	137	U2 Cupid	45
Something more then thou hast spi'd.	137	U2 Cupid	50
How cam'st thou thus to enter me?	150	U10 Jealousie	2
Thou sai'st, thou only cam'st to prove	150	U10 Jealousie	10
Think'st thou that love is help'd by feare?	150	U10 Jealousie	12
But nought beyond. He thou hast given it to,	161	U14 Selden	71
Though thou wert Muster-master of the Land.	167	U15 Friend-Wars	174
That thou dost all things more for truth, then glory,	168	U15 Friend-Wars	179
That by commanding first thy selfe, thou mak'st	168	U15 Friend-Wars	181
Thy person fit for any charge thou tak'st;	168	U15 Friend-Wars	182
But what she gives, thou dar'st give her againe;	168	U15 Friend-Wars	184
Thou shrinke or start not, but be alwayes one;	168	U15 Friend-Wars	186
That thou thinke nothing great, but what is good,	168	U15 Friend-Wars	187
So, 'live or dead, thou wilt preserve a fame	168	U15 Friend-Wars	189
What suretie of life have thou, and I?	168	U16 Gray	7
Where do'st thou carelesse lie,	174	U23 Himselfe	1
Where art thou, Genius? I should use	176	U25 Desmond	1
Genius, where art thou? I should use	176	U25 Desmond	V 1
O, thou inspire	177	U25 Desmond	V 10
Soone as lazie thou wert knowne,	183	U29 Fit of Rime	13
If thou wouldst know the vertues of Man-kind,	185	U30 Burleigh	1
Read here in one, what thou in all canst find,	185	U30 Burleigh	2
Thou art my Cause: whose manners since I knew,	187	U33 Councellour	13
So dost thou studie matter, men, and times,	187	U33 Councellour	15
Thou prov'st the gentler wayes, to clense the wound,	187	U33 Councellour	20
Thou hast the brave scorne, to put back the fee!	187	U33 Councellour	22
Of Bookes, of Presidents, hast thou at hand!	187	U33 Councellour	25
As if the generall store thou didst command	187	U33 Councellour	26
So comm'st thou like a Chiefe into the Court,	187	U33 Councellour	29
Then com'st thou off with Victorie and Palme,	187	U33 Councellour	35
What was the cause then? Thought'st thou in disgrace	188	U34 Small Poxe	13
Make all hereafter, had'st thou ruin'd this?	188	U34 Small Poxe	16
But when thy Wife (as thou conceiv'st) is brave?	201	U42 Elegy Let	50
Thou didst tell me; and wert o're-joy'd to peepe	201	U42 Elegy Let	59
Thou art jealous of thy Wifes, or Daughters Case:	202	U42 Elegy Let	87
And why to me this, thou lame Lord of fire,	202	U43 Vulcan	1
And why to me this, thou lame god of fire,	202	U43 Vulcan	V 1
Was it because thou wert of old denied	203	U43 Vulcan	11
Wast not hee: thou wert of old denied	203	U43 Vulcan	V 11
That since thou tak'st all envious care and paine,	203	U43 Vulcan	13
But, on thy malice, tell me, didst thou spie	203	U43 Vulcan	19
Thou then hadst had some colour for thy flames,	204	U43 Vulcan	40
Thou should'st have stay'd, till publike fame said so.	204	U43 Vulcan	46
Shee is the Judge, Thou Executioner:	204	U43 Vulcan	47
Or if thou needs would'st trench upon her power,	204	U43 Vulcan	48
or if thou wouldst enforce the power from her,	204	U43 Vulcan	V 48
Thou mightst have yet enjoy'd thy crueltie	204	U43 Vulcan	49
Thou mightst have had me perish, piece, by piece,	205	U43 Vulcan	51
Thou mightst have had them perish, piece, by piece,	205	U43 Vulcan	V 51
To make consumption, ever, where thou go'st;	205	U43 Vulcan	58

THOU (cont.)

Text	Page	Title	Line
To make consumption, every where thou go'st;	205	U43 Vulćan	V 58
To sow consumption, every where thou go'st;	205	U43 Vulcan	V 58
To make propter viam, ever, where thou go'st;	205	U43 Vulcan	V 58
Thou should'st have cry'd, and all beene proper stuffe.	205	U43 Vulcan	64
Thou should'st have cry'd, and all fine proper stuffe.	205	U43 Vulcan	V 64
These, had'st thou pleas'd either to dine, or sup,	206	U43 Vulcan	83
These, had'st thou been pleas'd either to dine, or sup,	206	U43 Vulcan	V 83
How in these ruines, Vulcan, thou dost lurke,	207	U43 Vulcan	105
How in these ruines, Vulcan, durst thou lurke,	207	U43 Vulcan	V105
Thou woo Minerva! or to wit aspire!	208	U43 Vulcan	109
'Cause thou canst halt, with us, in Arts, and Fire!	208	U43 Vulcan	110
Cause thou canst doe these halting tricks in fire?	208	U43 Vulcan	V110
With lust conceiv'd thee; Father thou hadst none.	208	U43 Vulcan	112
When thou wert borne, and that thou look'st at best,	208	U43 Vulcan	113
When thou wert borne, and when thou look'st at best,	208	U43 Vulcan	V113
If that were so, thou rather would'st advance	209	U43 Vulcan	151
Thou art true Vulcan still! Thou durst not spare	210	U43 Vulcan	V159
Foole, wilt thou let that in example come?	210	U43 Vulcan	161
And what hast thou done in these pettie spights,	210	U43 Vulcan	163
Which thou hast only vented, not enjoy'd.	210	U43 Vulcan	168
Thou Seed-plot of the warre, that hast not spar'd	213	U44 Speach	24
Thou canst draw forth thy forces, and fight drie	214	U44 Speach	45
I neither am, nor art thou one of those	216	U45 Squib	5
And now such is thy stand; while thou dost deale	217	U46 Coke	15
Since, Bacchus, thou art father	220	U48 Bacchus	1
Where now, thou art made Dweller;	220	U48 Bacchus	4
That thou remaine here taster	220	U48 Bacchus	7
For, Bacchus, thou art freer	221	U48 Bacchus	13
See then thou dost attend him,	221	U48 Bacchus	17
So mayst thou still be younger	221	U48 Bacchus	21
And thou make many a Poet,	221	U48 Bacchus	29
Shall feast it, thou maist love there	221	U48 Bacchus	38
Thou stand'st as if some Mysterie thou did'st!	225	U51 Bacon	4
Thou, Friend, wilt heare all censures; unto thee	232	U58 Book-seller	1
Bee thou my Bookes intelligencer, note	232	U58 Book-seller	3
If they goe on, and that thou lov'st a-life	232	U58 Book-seller	13
If, Passenger, thou canst but reade:	233	U60 La-ware	1
But thou wilt yet a Kinglier mastrie trie,	235	U62 Charles 1	5
As thou dost cure our Evill, at thy charge.	235	U62 Charles 1	8
Nay, and in this, thou show'st to value more	235	U62 Charles 1	9
When thou that rul'st, are her Example growne,	236	U64 Charles 3	V 9
And art thou borne, brave Babe? Blest be thy birth,	237	U65 Prince	1
And art thou borne, brave Babe? Blest be the day,	237	U65 Prince	V 1
This Prince of flowers? Soone shoot thou up, and grow	237	U65 Prince	5
The same that thou art promis'd, but be slow,	237	U65 Prince	6
The same that thou hast promis'd, but be slow,	237	U65 Prince	V 6
And still to stand so. Hast thou envious Moone,	238	U65 Prince	V 9
Ring thou it Holy-day.	239	U67 Muses	6
Thou, looking then about,	242	U70 Ode	5
E're thou wert halfe got out,	242	U70 Ode	6
How summ'd a circle didst thou leave man-kind	243	U70 Ode	9
Hee never fell, thou fall'st, my tongue.	244	U70 Ode	44
Hee never fell, thou tripst, my tongue.	244	U70 Ode	V 44
To shew thou hast beene long,	245	U70 Ode	58
This is King Charles his Day. Speake it, thou Towre,	249	U72 King	1
This is King Charles his birth day. Speake it, thou Towre,	249	U72 King	V 1
Looke up, thou seed of envie, and still bring	250	U73 Weston	1
Thou sluggish spawne, that canst, but wilt not see?	250	U73 Weston	5
Dreame thou could'st hurt it; but before thou wake	250	U73 Weston	11
Though thou hast past thy Summer standing, stay	252	U75 Epithalam.	1
Though thou art past thy Summer standing, stay	252	U75 Epithalam.	V 1
Thou canst not meet more Glory, on the way,	252	U75 Epithalam.	3
Then thou shalt see to day:	252	U75 Epithalam.	5
Stay, thou wilt see what rites the Virgins doe!	254	U75 Epithalam.	49
Although that thou, O Sun, at our intreaty stay!	254	U75 Epithalam.	56
O, now thou smil'st, faire Sun, and shin'st, as thou wouldst stay!	254	U75 Epithalam.	64
In all thy age of Journals thou hast tooke,	254	U75 Epithalam.	75
Saw'st thou that Paire, became these Rites so well,	254	U75 Epithalam.	76
Search, Sun, and thou wilt find,	255	U75 Epithalam.	79
Search, Sun, and thou shalt find,	255	U75 Epithalam.	V 79
O happy bands! and thou more happy place,	256	U75 Epithalam.	129
The Chappell empties, and thou may'st be gone	257	U75 Epithalam.	137
Tho', happy Muse, thou know my Digby well;	262	U78 Digby	1
He will cleare up his forehead, thinke thou bring'st	263	U78 Digby	21
He will cheare up his forehead, thinke thou bring'st	263	U78 Digby	V 21
Good Omen to him, in the note thou sing'st,	263	U78 Digby	22
Good fortune to him, in the note thou sing'st,	263	U78 Digby	V 22
Wilt thou be, Muse, when this shall them befall?	263	U78 Digby	31
Wilt thou be, Muse, when this shall befall?	263	U78 Digby	V 31
That thou art lov'd of God, this worke is done,	268	U80 Christning	1
Thou wouldst have written, Fame, upon my brest:	269	U81 Pawlet	14
Sound thou her Vertues, give her soule a Name.	269	U81 Pawlet	22
And tell thou, Alde-Legh, None can tell more true	274	U84 Descent	13
Thy Neeces line, then thou that gav'st thy Name	274	U84 Descent	14
And thou hast painted beauties world.	277	U84 Body	28
But, Painter, see thou doe not sell	277	U84 Body	29
Yet know, with what thou art possest,	281	U84 Mind	70
Thou entertaining in thy brest,	281	U84 Mind	71
Sleepie, or stupid Nature, couldst thou part	282	U84 Muse	15
Thou wouldst have lost the Phoenix, had the kind	283	U84 Muse	19
(For so thou art with me) now shee is gone.	283	U84 Muse	22
Thou hast no more blowes, Fate, to drive at one:	283	U84 Muse	27

THOU (cont.)

	Page	Title	Line
Venus, againe thou mov'st a warre	292	U86 Hor.4:1	1
If a fit livor thou dost seeke to toast;	292	U86 Hor.4:1	12
Whether in Mars his field thou bee,	293	U86 Hor.4:1	39
Thou lighter then the barke of any tree,	294	U87 Hor.3:9	22
Liber, of all thy friends, thou sweetest care,	294	U89 Mart.8:77	1
Thou worthy in eternall Flower to fare,	294	U89 Mart.8:77	2
If thou be'st wise, with 'Syrian Oyle let shine	294	U89 Mart.8:77	3
Will to bee, what thou art; and nothing more:	295	U90 Mart.10:47	12
No place for these. And, Painter, hap'ly, thou	305	Horace	24
In short; I bid, Let what thou work'st upon,	307	Horace	31
Heare me conclude; let what thou workst upon	339	Horace	V 31
Right spare, and warie: then thou speak'st to mee	307	Horace	66
Thou need new termes; thou maist, without excuse,	307	Horace	70
If thou would'st have me weepe, be thou first drown'd	311	Horace	145
Or follow fame, thou that dost write, or faine	313	Horace	169
Unto the Scene thou bringst, and dar'st create	313	Horace	179
Unto the Stage thou bringst, and dar'st create	342	Horace	V179
And thou maist better bring a Rhapsody	313	Horace	184
Yet common matter thou thine owne maist make,	313	Horace	187
If thou the vile, broad-troden ring forsake.	313	Horace	188
For, being a Poet, thou maist feigne, create,	313	Horace	189
Not care, as thou wouldst faithfully translate,	313	Horace	190
If such a ones applause thou dost require,	315	Horace	220
The customes of each age thou must observe,	315	Horace	223
Yet, to the Stage, at all thou maist not tender	317	Horace	260
Or Muse, upon the Lyre, thou chance b'asham'd.	329	Horace	502
Upon the Lyre, thou chance to be asham'd.	353	Horace	V580/502
Be briefe, in what thou wouldst command, that so	329	Horace	503
Let what thou fain'st for pleasures sake, be neere	329	Horace	507
Thou, such thy judgement is, thy knowledge too,	331	Horace	573
But, if hereafter thou shalt write, not feare	331	Horace	575
And thou in them shalt live as longe as Fame.	362	Palmer	31
Thou, that wouldst finde the habit of true passion,	362	Author	1
Till thou at Tames alight,	368	Ode Who saith	79
From whose prowde bosome, thou began'st thy flight.	368	Ode Who saith	80
Stay, view this stone: And, if thou beest not such,	371	Epitaph	1
Read here a little, that thou mayst know much.	371	Epitaph	2
With Rites not bound, but conscience. Wouldst thou All?	372	Epitaph	11
Come forth thou bonnie bouncing booke then, daughter	378	Coryat 2	86
Yes thou wert borne out of his travelling thigh	378	Coryat 2	89
May she, whome thou for spouse, to day, dost take,	384	Somerset	11
And thou to her, that Husband, may exalt	384	Somerset	13
And, if thou list thy selfe, what thou canst bee.	386	Browne	4
For, though but early in these pathes thou tread,	386	Browne	5
On credit, and are cossen'd; see, that thou	386	Browne	11
What treasure hast thou brought us! and what store	388	Chapman	4
Still, still, dost thou arrive with, at our shore,	388	Chapman	5
Such Passage hast thou found, such Returnes made,	389	Chapman	10
This Figure, that thou here seest put,	390	Reader	1
But thou art proofe against them, and indeed	391	Shakespeare	15
Thou art a Moniment, without a tombe,	391	Shakespeare	22
And tell, how farre thou didst our Lily out-shine,	391	Shakespeare	29
And though thou hadst small Latine, and lesse Greeke,	391	Shakespeare	31
Triumph, my Britaine, thou hast one to showe,	391	Shakespeare	41
And such wert thou. Looke how the fathers face	392	Shakespeare	65
Shine forth, thou Starre of Poets, and with rage,	392	Shakespeare	77
O, how in those, dost thou instruct these times,	397	Drayton	43
Sayst thou so, Lucan? But thou scornst to stay	397	Drayton	47
Under one title. Thou hast made thy way	397	Drayton	48
There, thou art Homer! Pray thee, use the stile	398	Drayton	59
Thou hast deserv'd: And let me reade the while	398	Drayton	60
With bold Tyrtaeus verse, when thou art nam'd,	398	Drayton	68
Thou hadst brought Lapland, or old Cobalus,	398	Drayton	86
Lyve long the Feasting Roome. And ere thou burne	406	Inigo Jones 1	101
But cause thou hearst the mighty k. of Spaine	406	Inigo Jones 2	1
Hath made his Inigo Marquess, wouldst thou fayne	406	Inigo Jones 2	2
Cittyes & Temples! thou a Cave for Wyne,	406	Inigo Jones 2	8
Or Ale! He build a pallace! Thou a shopp	407	Inigo Jones 2	9
Thou paint a Lane, where Thumb the Pygmy meets!	407	Inigo Jones 2	12
Thou paint a Lane, where Thumb with Geffry meets!	407	Inigo Jones 2	V 12
But when thou turnst a Reall Inigo;	407	Inigo Jones 2	22
If thou be soe desyrous to be read,	408	Inigo Jones 3	9
My verses were commended, thou dar'st say,	408	Detractor	1
And they were very good: yet thou think'st nay.	408	Detractor	2
For thou objectest (as thou hast been told)	408	Detractor	3
But bawle thou on; I pitty thee, poore Curre,	408	Detractor	7
That thou hast lost thy noyse, thy foame, thy stirre,	408	Detractor	8
To be knowne what thou art, a blatant beast,	408	Detractor	9
By barking against mee. Thou look'st at least,	408	Detractor	10
Thou art not worth it. Who will care to knowe	409	Detractor	13
If such a Tyke as thou, er'e wer't, or noe?	409	Detractor	14
A Mungrel Curre? Thou should'st stinck forth, and dye	409	Detractor	15
All which thou hast incurr'd deservedly:	410	Gill	5
Keep in thy barking Wit, thou bawling Fool?	410	Gill	8
Thinking to stir me, thou hast lost thy End,	410	Gill	11
For thou hast nought in thee to cure his Fame,	411	Gill	13
Thou Throne of glory, beauteous as the Moone,	414	Ghyrlond	49
Thou that doest spend thie dayes	420	Ode:If Men	24
Thou mad'st in open Feild	421	Ode:If Men	40
whom thou seest happy; wretches flee as foes:	422	Lucan	6
whom thou seest happy; wretches, shun, as foes:	422	Lucan	V 6
Yet ware; thou mayst do all things cruellie:	423	Lucan	15

THOU (cont.)

	Page	Title	Line
not safe; but when thou dost them thoroughlie:	423	Lucan	16
But with a Kisse, (if thou canst dare it)	662	Bedford	9

THOU'AST

	Page	Title	Line
And scorn'd, thou'ast showne thy malice, but hast fail'd.	188	U34 Small Poxe	18
T'effect it, feele, thou'ast made thine owne heart ake.	250	U73 Weston	12

THOUGH (See also THO')

	Page	Title	Line
Then his chast wife, though Beast now know no more,	35	E26 Beast 2	1
Tilter, the most may'admire thee, though not I:	36	E29 Tilter	1
Guiltie, be wise; and though thou know'st the crimes	36	E30 Guiltie	1
And though the soundest legs goe every day,	36	E31 Banck	3
His often change of clime (though not of mind)	37	E32 Roe 2	6
Which though it did but panick terror prove,	43	E51 James 3	3
To so true worth, though thou thy selfe forbid.	47	E63 Salisbury 2	12
To such true worth, though thou thy selfe forbid.	47	E63 Salisbury 2 V	12
Though every fortitude deserves applause,	49	E66 Cary	15
Though life be short, let us not make it so.	50	E70 Wm Roe 1	8
Though Lippe, at Pauls, ranne from his text away,	52	E75 Lippe	3
Which, if thou leave not soone (though I am loth)	54	E81 Proule	7
Where, though 't be love, that to thy praise doth move	55	E86 Goodyere 2	7
Not though that haire grew browne, which once was amber,	57	E90 Mill	9
Though not unprov'd: which shewes, thy fortunes are	60	E93 Radcliffe	14
And like them too; must needfully, though few,	61	E94 Bedford 3	13
Though both be good, the latter yet is worst,	63	E98 Th Roe 1	11
Well, though thy name lesse then our great ones bee,	64	E99 Th Roe 2	11
And, though fowle, now, be scarce, yet there are clarkes,	65	E101 Supper	15
And one true posture, though besieg'd with ill	66	E102 Pembroke	14
Know you to be a Sydney, though un-named?	66	E103 L Wroth 1	4
And though we could all men, all censures heare,	83	E131 Ferrab. 2	5
Great Club-fist, though thy backe, and bones be sore,	85	E133 Voyage	55
But thy unfrighted passe, though many a privie	86	E133 Voyage	73
And though thy walls be of the countrey stone,	94	F2 Penshurst	45
Thy lord, and lady, though they have no sute.	95	F2 Penshurst	50
And, though so neere the citie, and the court,	96	F3 Wroth	3
Though poyson, thinke it a great fate.	99	F3 Wroth	90
I know too, though thou strut, and paint,	100	F4 To the World	13
Though he would steale his sisters Pegasus,	107	F10 Proludium	23
(Though they were crusht into one forme) could make	108	F10 Proludium	26
Though thy wild thoughts with sparrowes wings doe flye,	111	F11 Epode	73
Though we acknowledge, who can so abstayne,	112	F11 Epode	85
Though I acknowledge, who can so refraine,	112	F11 Epode	V 85
His heart sinnes, though he feares.	112	F11 Epode	90
Though never after; whiles it gaynes the voyce	113	F12 Rutland	11
Though never after; whiles it gaynes the will	113	F12 Rutland	V 11
Who, though shee have a better verser got,	115	F12 Rutland	68
And, who doth me (though I not him) envy,	115	F12 Rutland	70
Now thincking on you, though to England lost,	116	F12 Rutland	94
With sinne and vice, though with a throne endew'd;	116	F13 Aubigny	10
I, that have suffer'd this; and, though forsooke	117	F13 Aubigny	15
Though it reject not those of Fortune: such	117	F13 Aubigny	45
Which though the turning world may dis-esteeme,	118	F13 Aubigny	64
Though I now write fiftie yeares,	131	U2 Excuse	3
Poets, though divine, are men:	131	U2 Excuse	5
Doe change, though man, and often fight,	146	U6 Defence	8
Though hate had put them out;	147	U7 Nymph	25
Will be my Rivall, though shee have but eares.	148	U7 Nymph	28
That though they did possesse each limbe,	151	U12 Corbet	9
And humble my fortune humble me, to take	153	U13 Sacvile	15
Without your gift, though I can rate that too,	157	U13 Sacvile	158
Though I am short, I cannot be obscure:	158	U14 Selden	2
To aske it: though in most of workes it be	158	U14 Selden	7
Though I confesse (as every Muse hath err'd,	159	U14 Selden	19
Is lov'd, though he let out his owne for life:	165	U15 Friend-Wars	88
Though thou wert Muster-master of the Land.	167	U15 Friend-Wars	174
(Though they may number bodyes) or but one.	171	U19 Elegy By	14
That their whole life was wickednesse, though weav'd	171	U20 Shrub	10
Though Beautie be the Marke of praise,	173	U22 Elegy Tho	1
Throughout your forme; as though they move,	173	U22 Elegy Tho	6
What though the greedie Frie	175	U23 Himselfe	19
True noblesse. Palme growes straight, though handled ne're so rude.	177	U25 Desmond	26
Though but while mettal's heating:	179	U25 Desmond	43
Though many Gems be in your bosome stor'd,	179	U25 Desmond	55
Though I, in working of my song,	182	U27 Ode Helen	33
Though not in these, in rithmes not wholly dumbe,	182	U28 Worth	2
Thy Universe, though his Epitome.	185	U30 Burleigh	4
Who, though their guilt, and perjurie they know,	186	U32 Elsmere	11
As though the Court pursues them on the sent,	186	U32 Elsmere	13
Though Envie oft his shadow be,	189	U36 Song	3
Though you sometimes proclaime me too severe,	190	U37 Friend-Book	16
Produce; though threatning with a coale, or chalke	193	U38 Elegy 'Tis	97
For though Love thrive, and may grow up with cheare,	197	U40 Elegy That	15
Be idle words, though of a parting Man;	199	U41 Elegy Since	4
From the poore wretch, which though he play'd in prose,	201	U42 Elegy Let	61
Which, though it were the Fort of the whole Parish,	209	U43 Vulcan	133
Though but in daunces, it shall know his power;	210	U43 Vulcan	157
Though but in daunces, it shall know high power;	210	U43 Vulcan	V157
Though but in daunger, it shall know his power;	210	U43 Vulcan	V157
Troy, though it were so much his Venus care.	210	U43 Vulcan	160
Troy, though it were so much thy Venus joycare.	210	U43 Vulcan	V160
No order? no Decree? Though we be gone	211	U43 Vulcan	176
Or Alexandria; and though a Divine	211	U43 Vulcan	195
That keepe the warre, though now't be growne more tame,	214	U44 Speach	55
And though Opinion stampe them not, are gold.	218	U47 Tribe	4

		Page	Title	Line
THOUGH (cont.)				
Though I doe neither heare these newes, nor tell	• •	219	U47 Tribe	46
What though her Chamber be the very pit		222	U49 Pucell	3
What though with Tribade lust she force a Muse,		222	U49 Pucell	7
What though she talke, and cannot once with them,		222	U49 Pucell	11
What though she ride two mile on Holy-dayes	•	222	U49 Pucell	15
What though she be with Velvet gownes indu'd,	•	222	U49 Pucell	18
What though she hath won on Trust, as many doe,		223	U49 Pucell	21
Thinkes it selfe nought, though she should valew it.		223	U49 Pucell	24
And though all praise bring nothing to your name,		224	U50 Countesse	13
Why? though I seeme of a prodigious wast,	•	226	U52 Answer	1
By thys Tyme, though you fancie not the man,		231	U56 Covell	V 25
Though now he refuses,	•	231	U57 Burges	10
And though the Parish-steeple	•	239	U67 Muses	4
What, though the thriftie Tower	• •	239	U67 Muses	7
What, though the thirsty Tower	• •	239	U67 Muses	V 7
Though now of flattery, as of picture, are		242	U69 Friend Son	21
As though his age imperfect might appeare,	•	244	U70 Ode	51
Though thou hast past thy Summer standing, stay		252	U75 Epithalam.	1
Though thou art past thy Summer standing, stay		252	U75 Epithalam.	V 1
Which, though I cannot as an Architect		261	U77 Treasurer	25
Which, though I cannot like as an Architect		261	U77 Treasurer	V 25
For, though that Rattles, Timbrels, Toyes,		273	U84 Cradle	17
And, though the sound were parted thence,	•	279	U84 Mind	39
Though he be fairer then a Starre;		294	U87 Hor.3:9	21
Though sower, with safetie of his gravitie,		319	Horace	322
Will take offence, at this: Nor, though it strike		321	Horace	361
Take just offence at this: nor, though it strike		347	Horace	V353/361
On steele, though 't selfe be dull, and cannot cut.		325	Horace	434
Though I confesse, that, in a long worke, sleepe		351	Horace	V513/537
You Sir, the elder brother, though you are		331	Horace	545
And, to your Fathers, and to mine; though 't be		331	Horace	577
Though slower Spaine; and Italy mature.	•	368	Ode Who saith	88
Though, now by Love transform'd, & dayly dying:		369	Ode Who saith	101
For, though but early in these pathes thou tread,		386	Browne	5
As in this Spanish Proteus; who, though writ	•	389	Aleman	5
For though Spaine gave him his first ayre and Vogue,		389	Aleman	15
And though thou hadst small Latine, and lesse Greeke,		391	Shakespeare	31
For though the Poets matter, Nature be,		392	Shakespeare	57
And, though I now begin, 'tis not to rub		396	Drayton	7
And caried, though with shoute, and noyse, confesse		397	Drayton	45
Though I confesse a Beaumonts Booke to bee	•	400	Beaumont	7
Though gold or Ivory haftes would make it good.		403	Inigo Jones 1	28
Though gold or Ivory haftes cant make it good.		403	Inigo Jones 1	V 28
Though shee chainge as oft as shee,	•	417	Moon	29
And though your virtue (as becomes it) still		421	Censure	9
hir Furye, though though noe Frindshipp hee betraye.		422	Censure	26
THOUGHE				
Goe, Muse, in, and salute him thoughe he be	• •	262	U78 Digby	V 19
THOUGHT				
The late tane bastinado. So I thought.	•	33	E21 Gam'ster	6
Of a great man, and to be thought the same,	•	35	E28 Surly	2
Yet dare not, to my thought, lest hope allow		41	E43 Salisbury 1	7
The least indulgent thought thy pen drops forth!		44	E55 Beaumont	4
Poore Poet-Ape, that would be thought our chiefe,		44	E56 Poet-Ape	1
To make amends, yo'are thought a wholesome creature.		46	E62 Would-bee	8
These (noblest Cecil) labour'd in my thought,	•	48	E64 Salisbury 3	15
I thought to forme unto my zealous Muse,	•	52	E76 Bedford 1	2
I'am more asham'd to have thee thought my foe.		53	E77 Not name	4
Nature, they thought, in all, that he would faine.		53	E79 Rutland	8
When I would know thee Goodyere, my thought lookes		55	E86 Goodyere 2	1
And that so strong and deepe, as 't might be thought,		71	E110 Edmonds 1	7
As, sooth, the Parcae thought him one,	•	77	E120 S. P.	15
Nor he, for friendship, to be thought unfit,	•	78	E121 Rudyerd 1	7
That there's no journey set, or thought upon,	•	81	E129 Mime	3
Before my thought, and (in thy right) commands		83	E132 Sylvester	8
As his will now be the translation thought,		83	E132 Sylvester	12
The other thought it Hydra, or the rock	•	86	E133 Voyage	83
I thought to binde him, in my verse:	•	93	F1 Why write no	2
(Their rudenesse then is thought no sinne)	•	98	F3 Wroth	54
Hence-forth I quit thee from my thought,	•	100	F4 To the World	3
To harbour a divided thought	• •	101	F4 To the World	58
My owne true fire. Now my thought takes wing,		108	F10 Proludium	29
Our owne true fire. Now our thought takes wing,		108	F10 Proludium	V 29
Or some great thought doth keepe	•	109	F11 Epode	24
Of which usurping rancke, some have thought love		110	F11 Epode	31
A fixed thought, an eye un-taught to glance;		111	F11 Epode	61
That which, to boote with hell, is thought worth heaven,		113	F12 Rutland	3
Riches thought most: But, Madame, thinke what store		114	F12 Rutland	38
With holy Paul, lest it be thought the breath		122	F15 Heaven	24
And the Bow: with thought to hit	•	132	U2 How he saw	22
Unlesse my heart would as my thought be torne.		147	U7 Nymph	14
One un-becoming thought doth move	•	148	U7 Nymph	31
I thought that Fortitude had beene a meane		156	U13 Sacvile	105
Was trusted, that you thought my judgement such		158	U14 Selden	6
See him, that's call'd, and thought the happiest man,		162	U15 Friend-Wars	23
Honour and honestie, as poore things thought	•	163	U15 Friend-Wars	42
Lesse must not be thought on then Mistresse: or,		165	U15 Friend-Wars	95
If it be thought kild like her Embrions; for,		165	U15 Friend-Wars	96
And from that thought strive to be understood.		168	U15 Friend-Wars	188
Man thought the valianter, 'cause he durst sweare,		168	U15 Friend-Wars	192
That thought can adde, unthankfull, the lay-stall		172	U21 Ltl Shrub	8
Let this thought quicken thee,	• •	174	U23 Himselfe	15

	Page	Title	Line

THOUGHT (cont.)
That still was good for goodnesse sake, nor thought . . . 185 U30 Burleigh 13
The contrite Soule, who hath no thought to win . . . 193 U38 Elegy 'Tis 89
Can lock the Sense up, or the heart a thought, . . . 198 U40 Elegy That 43
And raz'd, e're thought could urge, This might have bin! . . . 209 U43 Vulcan 136
From any thought like sadnesse. . . . 221 U48 Bacchus 20
Me thought I read the ancient Art of Thrace, . . . 228 U53 Newcastle 4
That thought shall make, he will this losse supply . . . 236 U63 Charles 2 11
Me thought, Great Britaine in her Sea, before, . . . 268 U80 Christning 13
Now I have better thought thereon, . . . 277 U84 Mind 2
All other gladnesse, with the thought is barr'd; . . . 284 U84 Muse 67
I thought me richer then the Persian King. . . . 293 U87 Hor.3:9 4
Hee, while he labour'd to be thought a God . . . 335 Horace 661
In thought to praise this Ladie; . . . 365 Ode Splendor 18
Or thought they, Leda's white Adult'rers place . . . 369 Ode Who saith 104
At these thy Nuptials: but, whose heart, and thought . . . 384 Somerset 3
For, if I thought my judgement were of yeeres, . . . 391 Shakespeare 27
I thought thee then our Orpheus, that wouldst try . . . 397 Drayton 35
Attyre the Persons as noe thought can teach . . . 404 Inigo Jones 1 54
THOUGHTS
He'adulters still: his thoughts lye with a whore. . . . 35 E26 Beast 2 2
Shee shall instruct my after-thoughts to write . . . 48 E65 Muse 13
Thy selfe, with thy first thoughts, brought home by thee, . . . 81 E128 Wm Roe 2 10
Thy thoughts did never melt in amorous fire, . . . 108 F10 Proludium 3
Of thoughts to watch, and ward . . . 109 F11 Epode 8
Though thy wild thoughts with sparrowes wings doe flye, . . . 111 F11 Epode 73
From thoughts of such a straine. . . . 112 F11 Epode 114
Pure thoughts in man: with fiery zeale them feeding . . . 128 U1 Trinitie 27
That flie my thoughts betweene, . . . 149 U9 Picture 12
Their thoughts and meanes to making loude the cry; . . . 155 U13 Sacvile 66
That I may sing my thoughts, in some unvulgar straine. . . . 177 U25 Desmond 13
Such thoughts wil make you more in love with truth. . . . 181 U26 Ode High 21
Thoughts worthy of thy gift, this Inke, . . . 229 U55 Burges 2
Where all heroique ample thoughts doe meet: . . . 262 U78 Digby 10
These thoughts when Usurer Alphius, now about . . . 291 U85 Country 67
of thy rich labors worlds of thoughts created, . . . 361 Palmer 22
which thoughts being circumvolvd in gyerlyk mocion . . . 361 Palmer 23
if it begyn religious thoughts to cherish; . . . 422 Lucan 10
THOUGHT'ST
What was the cause then? Thought'st thou in disgrace . . . 188 U34 Small Poxe 13
THOU'HAST
And, as thou'hast mine, his houres, and youth abuse. . . . 48 E65 Muse 6
THOU'LDST
If thou'ldst but use thy faith, as thou didst then, . . . 32 E18 Censurer 7
THOU'LT
But that's put in, thou'lt say. Why, so is thine. . . . 36 E29 Tilter 6
On such my serious follies; But, thou'lt say, . . . 204 U43 Vulcan 41
Or such my serious follies; But, thou'lt say, . . . 204 U43 Vulcan V 41
He cries, Good boy, thou'lt keepe thine owne. Now, adde . . . 327 Horace 470
THOU'RT
To which thou'rt not a weeke, bespoke a guest; . . . 81 E129 Mime 6
Thou'rt too ambitious: and dost fear in vaine! . . . 408 Inigo Jones 3 6
THOUSAND
Then a thousand, then another . . . 103 F6 Celia 2 9
Adde a thousand, and so more: . . . 103 F6 Celia 2 11
Cast in thousand snares, and rings . . . 141 U2 Her man 11
For a thousand yeares together, . . . 183 U29 Fit of Rime 16
Had I a thousand Mouthes, as many Tongues, . . . 269 U81 Pawlet 23
THOUSANDS
Let thousands more goe flatter vice, and winne, . . . 99 F3 Wroth 85
Those thousands on his back, shall after blow . . . 165 U15 Friend-Wars 104
THO'WERT
Seven yeeres tho'wert lent to me, and I thee pay, . . . 41 E45 First Son 3
TH'OYLE
That for th'oyle of Talke, dare spend . . . 105 F8 Sicknesse 33
THRACE
Me thought I read the ancient Art of Thrace, . . . 228 U53 Newcastle 4
THRACIAN
'Tis true, I'am Thracian Chloes, I, . . . 293 U87 Hor.3:9 9
THRALL
Nothing, but practise upon honours thrall. . . . 179 U25 Desmond 35
THREAD
And weigh'd your Play: untwisted ev'ry thread, . . . 415 Rutter 14
THREAT'
And threat' the great Eclipse. Two houres but runne, . . . 238 U65 Prince 11
THREAT
Nor for any threat, or call, . . . 132 U2 How he saw 18
THREATEN
Yes, threaten, doe. Alas I feare . . . 101 F4 To the World 37
Now threaten, with those meanes she did invite? . . . 169 U18 Elegy Can 2
Which it doth threaten. Therefore, where I see . . . 329 Horace 525
THREATENS
And threatens the starre-chamber, and the barre: . . . 44 E54 Chev'ril 2 2
Or side, but threatens Ruine. The whole Day . . . 166 U15 Friend-Wars 131
THREATNING
Produce; though threatning with a coale, or chalke . . . 193 U38 Elegy 'Tis 97
And cry'd, it was a threatning to the beares; . . . 209 U43 Vulcan 146
And sayd twas sure a threatning to the beares; . . . 209 U43 Vulcan V146
And cry'd 'Twas verily a threatning to the beares; . . . 209 U43 Vulcan V146
THREATS
For then their threats will kill me; . . . 144 U4 Song 6
THRED
To have her storie woven in thy thred; . . . 61 E95 Savile 15

THRED (cont.)
Whose even Thred the Fates spinne round, and full, • • • 225 U51 Bacon   15
So Fates would let the Boy a long thred run. • • • • 293 U87 Hor.3:9 16
THREDS
Turne him, and see his Threds: looke, if he be • • 216 U45 Squib   21
THREE
Ridway rob'd Duncote of three hundred pound, • • • 29 E8 Robbery   1
Yet three fill'd Zodiackes had he beene • • • • 77 E120 S. P.   11
His three for one. Now, lordings, listen well. • • 84 E133 Voyage 28
Of Hol'borne (three sergeants heads) lookes ore, • • 89 E133 Voyage 177
First, midst, and last, converted one, and three; • • 122 F15 Heaven   10
Beholding one in three, and three in one, • • • 128 U1 Trinitie   33
Father, and Sonne, and Holy Ghost, you three • • 128 U1 Trinitie   37
For the Apple, and those three • • • • 137 U2 Cupid   47
Or two, or three, a Sonne will dis-inherit, • • 192 U38 Elegy 'Tis 42
With all th'adventures; Three bookes not afraid • • 207 U43 Vulcan   95
With all th'adventures; Three bookes not amisse • • 207 U43 Vulcan V 95
For three of his foure-score, he did no good. • • 243 U70 Ode   32
Or standing long an Oake, three hundred yeare, • • 245 U70 Ode   67
Three Kingdomes Mirth, in light, and aerie man, • • 249 U72 King   11
For, as there are three Natures, Schoolemen call • • 284 U84 Muse   51
Their heads, which three Anticyra's cannot heale. • • 325 Horace   428
The head that three Anticira's cannot heale. • • 349 Horace   V428
There read I, streight, thy learned Legends three, • • 397 Drayton   25
These Mysteries do point to three more great, • • 413 Ghyrlond   29
And at once three Senses pleases. • • • • 657 Door Apollo   18
THREW
Of bearing them in field, he threw 'hem away: • • 42 E48 Mungril   2
This my object. But she threw • • • 132 U2 How he saw 23
THRICE
Coach'd, or on foot-cloth, thrice chang'd every day, • 165 U15 Friend-Wars 107
Thrice happy house, that hast receipt • • • 280 U84 Mind   53
Thrice 'bout thy Altar with their Ivory feet. • • 292 U86 Hor.4:1 28
Twice, or thrice good, I wonder: but am more • • 329 Horace   535
And twice, or thrice had 'ssayd it, still in vaine: • 333 Horace   626
And twice, or thrice assay'd it, but in vain; • • 354 Horace   V626
Thy twice conceyvd, thrice payd for Imagery? • • 405 Inigo Jones 1 90
THRIFT
With some more thrift, and more varietie: • • • 205 U43 Vulcan   50
With some more thrift, and yet varietie: • • • 205 U43 Vulcan V 50
THRIFTIE
What, though the thriftie Tower • • • • 239 U67 Muses   7
Chaste, thriftie, modest folke, that came to view. • 319 Horace   294
THRIFTYE
And that this so thriftye summe, • • • • 259 U76 Petition V 14
THRISE
Thrise did it spit: thrise div'd. At last, it view'd • 88 E133 Voyage 162
THRIVE
'Twas a child, that so did thrive • • • • 77 E120 S. P.   5
For though Love thrive, and may grow up with cheare, • 197 U40 Elegy That 15
Well, I say, thrive, thrive brave Artillerie yard, • • 213 U44 Speach   23
But whisper'd Counsells, and those only thrive; • • 234 U61 Epigram   6
By Thee, and Conscience, both who thrive • • • 273 U84 Cradle   7
So with this Authors Readers will it thrive: • • 362 Author   12
THRIV'D
Got up and thriv'd with honest arts: • • • • 244 U70 Ode   34
THRIVES
Not one but thrives; in spite of stormes & thunder, • 361 Palmer   7
THRIVING
Our Roman Youths they learne more thriving wayes • • 350 Horace   V464
THROAT
With swelling throat: and, oft, the tragick wight • • 311 Horace   134
THROATE
Upon thy throate, and live exempt • • • • 100 F4 To the World 7
THRONE
With sinne and vice, though with a throne endew'd; • 116 F13 Aubigny   10
Thou Throne of glory, beauteous as the Moone, • • 414 Ghyrlond   49
THRONES
The Thrones, the Cherube, and Seraphick bowers, • • 285 U84 Muse   88
THRONG
Come short of all this learned throng, • • • 182 U27 Ode Helen 34
Repeat of things a throng, • • • • • 245 U70 Ode   57
THRONGE
Lowd to the wondringe thronge • • • • 419 Ode:If Men   7
THRONG'D
Lest the throng'd heapes should on a laughter take: • 331 Horace   569
Lest the throng'd rings should a free laughter take: • 352 Horace V545/569
THRONGING
The rout of rurall folke come thronging in, • • • 98 F3 Wroth   53
Shall thronging come, and boast the happy place • • 115 F12 Rutland 80
THRONG'ST
Nor throng'st (when masquing is) to have a sight • • 96 F3 Wroth   9
Nor throng'st (where masquing is) to have a sight • • 96 F3 Wroth V 9
THROTES
When gold was made no weapon to cut throtes, • • 114 F12 Rutland 23
THROUGH (See also THOROW)
To a great image through thy luxurie. • • • • 48 E65 Muse   4
Through which, our merit leads us to our meeds. • • 53 E80 Life/Death 2
His cloke with orient velvet quite lin'd through, • • 62 E97 Motion   4
This is that good Aeneas, past through fire, • • • 81 E128 Wm Roe 2 12
Through seas, stormes, tempests: and imbarqu'd for hell, • 81 E128 Wm Roe 2 13
Airising in that place, through which, who goes, • • 87 E133 Voyage 131
Through which a serpent river leades • • • • 97 F3 Wroth   18

THROUGH (cont.)
      Through Swords, through Seas, whether she would ride.   .   . 134 U2 Triumph   10
      Sheds it selfe through the face, ... 134 U2 Triumph   18
      Rising through it e're it came;   .   .   .   .   . 141 U2 Her man   29
      And all these through her eyes, have stopt her eares.   .   . 150 U9 Picture   18
      Nor wants it here through penurie, or sloth,   .   .   . 152 U12 Corbet   39
      Themselves through favouring what is there not found: .   . 159 U14 Selden   16
      Themselves through favouring that is there not found: .   . 159 U14 Selden   V 16
      Spread through the World) is easier farre to find,   .   . 167 U15 Friend-Wars   172
      May shine (through every chincke) to every sight   .   . 177 U25 Desmond   16
      Oft scape an Imputation, more through luck, then wit.   .   . 179 U25 Desmond   52
      Oft scape theyr Imputation, more through luck, then wit.   . 179 U25 Desmond   V 52
      The Lady Mayresse pass'd through the Towne,   .   .   . 201 U42 Elegy Let   70
      But crept like darknesse through his blood?   .   .   . 234 U60 La-ware   8
      Through which not only we, but all our Species are.   .   . 253 U75 Epithalam.   32
      And now, through circumfused light, she lookes   .   . 271 U81 Pawlet   69
      Through his inherent righteousnesse, in death,   .   . 286 U84 Muse   135
      Or when that Autumne, through the fields, lifts round   . 290 U85 Country   17
      With poore base termes, through every baser shop: .   . 321 Horace   334
      Looke through him, and be sure, you take not mocks   .   . 333 Horace   621
      Except your Gratious Eye as through a Glass   .   .   . 383 Rich   11
      Through all the lines of this circumference,   .   .   . 414 Ghyrlond   54
THROUGHLY
      And all your Booke (when it is throughly scan'd)   .   . 370 Author   5
THROUGHOUT
      Throughout my booke. 'Troth put out woman too.   .   .   . 54 E83 Friend   2
      Throughout, might flatt'rie seeme; and to be mute   .   .   . 58 E91 Vere   10
      Throughout your forme; as though that move,   .   .   . 173 U22 Elegy Tho   6
      Be simple quite throughout, and wholly one.   .   .   . 307 Horace   32
      Be simple quite throughout, and alwayes one.   .   .   . 339 Horace   V 32
      Still in their leaves, throughout the sliding yeares,   .   . 309 Horace   86
      The nut-crackers throughout, will they therefore   .   . 321 Horace   363
      Throughout their generall breasts, ... 421 Ode:If Men   43
THROW'
      A Benefit; or that doth throw't away: .   .   .   . 154 U13 Sacvile   42
THROW
      His time? health? soule? will he for these goe throw   . 165 U15 Friend-Wars   103
      When they are poore, and banish'd, must throw by   .   . 311 Horace   138
      Her truch-man, she reports the minds each throw.   .   . 313 Horace   157
THROWE
      Throwe, Holye Virgin, then   .   .   .   .   .   . 421 Ode:If Men   37
THROWES
      Of what he throwes: Like letchers growne content   .   . 166 U15 Friend-Wars   139
THROWNE
      Stinke, and are throwne away. End faire enough.   .   .   . 45 E59 Spies   3
      For, here they were throwne in wi'the melted pewter,   .   . 88 E133 Voyage   153
THROW'T
      A Benefit; or that doth throw't away: .   .   .   . 154 U13 Sacvile   42
THRUSH
      Or shooting at the greedie thrush, ... 97 F3 Wroth   34
      Or shooting at the hungrie thrush, ... 97 F3 Wroth   V 34
      For th'eating Thrush, or Pit-falls sets: .   .   . 290 U85 Country   34
THRUST
      And thrust my necke into the noose, ... 101 F4 To the World   26
THRUSTS
      But, wisely, thrusts not forth a forward hand,   .   .   . 61 E95 Savile   22
THULE
      To utmost Thule: whence, he backes the Seas   .   .   . 368 Ode Who saith   69
THUMB
      Thou paint a Lane, where Thumb the Pygmy meets!   .   . 407 Inigo Jones 2   12
      Thou paint a Lane, where Thumb with Geffry meets!   .   . 407 Inigo Jones 2   V 12
THUMBE
      Nor thumbe, nor finger to the stop acquainted,   .   .   . 87 E133 Voyage   134
THUM'S
      With touch of daintie thum's!   .   .   .   .   . 239 U67 Muses   18
TH'UNBEARDED
      Th'unbearded Youth, his Guardian once being gone,   .   . 315 Horace   229
TH'UNCERTAINTY
      And in them view'd th'uncertainty of Life,   .   .   . 411 Sutcliffe   3
THUNDER
      And then his thunder frights more, then it kills.   .   . 193 U38 Elegy 'Tis   70
      Their noises forth in Thunder: .   .   .   .   . 239 U67 Muses   9
      Their noises out in Thunder: .   .   .   .   . 239 U67 Muses   V 9
      As lowd as Thunder, and as swift as fire.   .   .   . 249 U72 King   4
      Or the sad thunder-stroken thing he have   .   .   . 335 Horace   672
      Not one but thrives; in spite of stormes & thunder,   .   . 361 Palmer   7
THUNDER-STROKEN
      Or the sad thunder-stroken thing he have   .   .   . 335 Horace   672
THUND'RING
      For names; but call forth thund'ring Aeschilus,   .   . 391 Shakespeare   33
THUNDRING
      Then when the thundring Jove his Snow and showres   .   . 290 U85 Country   29
THURINE
      With gentle Calais, Thurine Orniths Sonne;   .   .   . 293 U87 Hor.3:9   14
THUS
      For the lucks sake, it thus much favour have,   .   .   . 27 E3 Bookseller   4
      Thus: and for his letcherie, scores, god payes.   .   .   . 31 E12 Shift   22
      O Madame, if your grant did thus transferre mee,   .   .   . 55 E84 Bedford 2   9
      He that not trusts me, having vow'd thus much,   .   .   . 70 E108 Soldiers   9
      Now I have sung thee thus, shall judge of thee.   .   .   . 70 E109 Nevil   16
      Describ'd, it 's thus: Defin'd would you it have?   .   .   . 75 E115 Honest Man   33
      Thus, in his belly, can he change a sin, ... 76 E118 Gut   5
      Thus Pan, and Sylvane, having had their rites,   .   .   . 98 F3 Wroth   47

	Page	Title	Line

THUS (cont.)

Thus removed by many a mile?	102	F5 Celia 1	V 14
On my lips, thus hardly sundred,	103	F6 Celia 2	7
Thus, by these subtle traines,	110	F11 Epode	28
Which thus we over-blow.	110	F11 Epode	36
While thus it buyes great grace, and hunts poore fame;	113	F12 Rutland	15
While thus it gets grace, and hunts poore fame;	113	F12 Rutland	V 15
Onely, thus much, out of a ravish'd zeale,	119	F13 Aubigny	108
How cam'st thou thus to enter me?	150	U10 Jealousie	2
By thanking thus the curtesie to life,	158	U13 Sacvile	159
Of others honours, thus, enjoy thine owne.	160	U14 Selden	66
Of others honours, thus, enjoy their owne.	160	U14 Selden	V 66
Thus they doe talke. And are these objects fit	165	U15 Friend-Wars	101
If it be thus; Come Love, and Fortune goe,	170	U18 Elegy Can	21
Who thus long safe, would gaine upon the times	186	U32 Elsmere	9
In letters, that mixe spirits, thus to weave.	190	U37 Friend-Book	12
Or urge thy Greedie flame, thus to devoure	202	U43 Vulcan	3
Or beg thy Greedie flame, thus to devoure	202	U43 Vulcan	V 3
Us, in our bearing, that are thus, and thus,	215	U44 Speach	65
To see you set apart, thus, from the rest,	234	U61 Epigram	10
which thus hast crown'd our hopes, our spring, and earth,	237	U65 Prince	V 2
That thus hath crown'd our hopes, with thee, our Spring & May,	237	U65 Prince	V 2
This being thus: why should my tongue, or pen	284	U84 Muse	69
That thus have ventur'd these true straines upon;	289	U84 Muse	227
But thus, thus, keeping endlesse Holy-day,	294	U88 Petronius	6
Thus, to his antient Art the Piper lent	319	Horace	303
In his train'd Gowne about the Stage: thus grew	346	Horace	V305
And care of getting, thus, our minds hath stain'd,	327	Horace	473
And thus, at first, an honour, and a name	327	Horace	491
thus, as a ponderous thinge in water cast	361	Palmer	17
my abler faculties; and thus brake foorth	362	Palmer	29
to tender thus, their lives, their loves, their hartes!	382	Rich	4
Am I thus ample to thy Booke, and Fame:	390	Shakespeare	2
your workes thus differing, troth let soe your style:	407	Inigo Jones 2	19
Thus, Love, and Hope, and burning Charitie,	413	Ghyrlond	25

TH'USURPED

| And bad me lay th'usurped laurell downe: | 80 | E126 Mrs Cary | 4 |

TH'WERE

| And told of with more License then th'were done! | 156 | U13 Sacvile | 96 |
| Till swept away, th'were cancell'd with a broome! | 282 | U84 Muse | 8 |

THY'

| But then, thy'epistolar Heroick Songs, | 397 | Drayton | 29 |

THY (See also THIE)

Thy title, Epigrammes, and nam'd of mee,	27	E2 My Booke	2
And by thy wiser temper, let men know	27	E2 My Booke	8
Thou, that mak'st gaine thy end, and wisely well,	27	E3 Bookseller	1
To lye upon thy stall, till it be sought;	28	E3 Bookseller	5
For such a Poet, while thy dayes were greene,	28	E4 James 1	5
But I have my revenge made, in thy name.	29	E10 Ignorant	2
What weight, and what authoritie in thy speech!	31	E14 Camden	9
Pardon free truth, and let thy modestie,	31	E14 Camden	11
Hardie, thy braine is valiant, 'tis confest,	32	E16 Brain-hardy	1
Thy selfe into fresh braules: when, call'd upon,	32	E16 Brain-hardy	3
Scarse thy weekes swearing brings thee of, of one.	32	E16 Brain-hardy	4
Keepe thy selfe there, and thinke thy valure right,	32	E16 Brain-hardy	9
May others feare, flie, and traduce thy name,	32	E17 Critic	1
Charge them, for crowne, to thy sole censure hye.	32	E17 Critic	4
If thou'ldst but use thy faith, as thou didst then,	32	E18 Censurer	7
Thy faith is all the knowledge that thou hast.	32	E18 Censurer	10
Who, to thy one, all other braines refuse;	34	E23 Donne 1	2
Whose every worke, of thy most earely wit,	34	E23 Donne 1	3
To it, thy language, letters, arts, best life,	34	E23 Donne 1	7
In place of scutcheons, that should decke thy herse,	35	E27 Roe 1	1
For thy late sharpe device. I say 'tis fit	36	E29 Tilter	3
'Twere madnesse in thee, to betray thy fame,	36	E30 Guiltie	3
And person to the world; ere I thy name.	36	E30 Guiltie	4
Who would not be thy subject, James, t'obay	37	E35 James 2	1
Whose manners draw, more then thy powers constraine.	37	E35 James 2	3
And in this short time of thy happiest raigne,	37	E35 James 2	4
Hast purg'd thy realmes, as we have now no cause	38	E35 James 2	5
To thy Domitian, than I can my James:	38	E36 Martial	2
Which should thy countries love to speake refuse,	40	E43 Salisbury 1	3
Of adding to thy fame; thine may to me,	41	E43 Salisbury 1	8
Of adding to thy prayse; thine may to me,	41	E43 Salisbury 1 V	8
Exacted by thy fate, on the just day.	41	E45 First Son	4
Play-wright, I loath to have thy manners knowne	42	E49 Playwrt 1	5
Or fumie clysters, thy moist lungs to bake:	42	E50 Cod 3	2
That we thy losse might know, and thou our love,	43	E51 James 3	1
Yet give thy jealous subjects leave to doubt:	43	E51 James 3	5
Who this thy scape from rumour gratulate,	43	E51 James 3	6
Doe beg thy care unto thy after-state.	43	E51 James 3	8
Looke not upon thy dangers, but our feares.	43	E51 James 3	10
This but thy judgement fooles: the other way	43	E52 Courtling	5
Would both thy folly, and thy spite betray.	43	E52 Courtling	6
For, but thy selfe, where, out of motly, 's hee	44	E53 Old-end	9
What are thy petulant pleadings, Chev'ril, then,	44	E54 Chev'ril 2	3
How I doe love thee Beaumont, and thy Muse,	44	E55 Beaumont	1
The least indulgent thought thy pen drops forth!	44	E55 Beaumont	4
What art is thine, that so thy friend deceives?	44	E55 Beaumont	8
For offring, with thy smiles, my wit to grace,	45	E58 Groome	3
Thy ignorance still laughs in the wrong place.	45	E58 Groome	4
An obeliske, or columne to thy name,	46	E60 Mounteagle	2
Thy fact, in brasse or marble writ the same)	46	E60 Mounteagle	4

THY (cont.)

I, that am glad of thy great chance, here doo!   .   .   .   46 E60 Mounteagle   5
Thy praise, or dispraise is to me alike,   .   .   .   46 E61 Foole   1
In a great belly. Write, then on thy wombe,   .   .   .   46 E62 Would-bee   11
Who can consider thy right courses run,   .   .   .   47 E63 Salisbury 2   1
With what thy vertue on the times hath won,   .   .   .   47 E63 Salisbury 2   2
And not thy fortune; who can cleerely see   .   .   .   47 E63 Salisbury 2   3
And that thou seek'st reward of thy each act,   .   .   .   47 E63 Salisbury 2   4
By constant suffring of thy equall mind;   .   .   .   47 E63 Salisbury 2   8
To so true worth, though thou thy selfe forbid.   .   .   .   47 E63 Salisbury 2 12
To such true worth, though thou thy selfe forbid.   .   .   .   47 E63 Salisbury 2 V 12
With thy new place, bring I these early fruits   .   .   .   47 E64 Salisbury 3   2
To see thy fathers rites new laid on thee.   .   .   .   47 E64 Salisbury 3   6
Of flatterie to thy titles. Nor of wit.   .   .   .   47 E64 Salisbury 3   8
Wherein what wonder see thy name hath wrought?   .   .   .   48 E64 Salisbury 3 16
To a great image through thy luxurie.   .   .   .   48 E65 Muse   4
Be thy next masters more unluckie Muse,   .   .   .   48 E65 Muse   5
Against thy fortune: when no foe, that day,   .   .   .   49 E66 Cary   9
Love thy great losse, which a renowne hath wonne,   .   .   .   49 E66 Cary   11
High in thy bloud, thy place, but highest then,   .   .   .   49 E67 Suffolk   6
When, in mens wishes, thy vertues wrought,   .   .   .   49 E67 Suffolk   7
As all thy honors were by them first sought: .   .   .   49 E67 Suffolk   8
Which, by no lesse confirm'd, then thy kings choice, .   .   .   49 E67 Suffolk   11
Yet by thy weapon liv'st! Th'hast one good part.   .   .   .   50 E69 Cob   2
'Tis not thy judgement breeds the prejudice,   .   .   .   50 E72 Court-ling   5
Thy person only, Courtling, is the vice.   .   .   .   50 E72 Court-ling   6
Whil'st thy weigh'd judgements, Egerton, I heare,   .   .   .   51 E74 Chancelor   1
That no affection in thy voyce commands;   .   .   .   51 E74 Chancelor   4
Whil'st thou art certaine to thy words, once gone,   .   .   .   52 E74 Chancelor   7
As is thy conscience, which is alwayes one: .   .   .   52 E74 Chancelor   8
Be safe, nor feare thy selfe so good a fame,   .   .   .   53 E77 Not name   1
That, any way, my booke should speake thy name: .   .   .   53 E77 Not name   2
Hornet, thou hast thy wife drest, for the stall,   .   .   .   53 E78 Hornet   1
For all thou hear'st, thou swear'st thy selfe didst doo. . . .   54 E81 Proule   5
Thy wit lives by it, Proule, and belly too.   .   .   .   54 E81 Proule   6
My selfe a witnesse of thy few dayes sport: .   .   .   55 E85 Goodyere 1   2
Upon thy wel-made choise of friends, and bookes;   .   .   .   55 E86 Goodyere 2   2
Then doe I love thee, and behold thy ends   .   .   .   55 E86 Goodyere 2   3
In making thy friends bookes, and thy bookes friends: . . .   55 E86 Goodyere 2   4
Now, I must give thy life, and deed, the voice   .   .   .   55 E86 Goodyere 2   5
Where, though 't be love, that to thy praise doth move . . .   55 E86 Goodyere 2   7
Who both their graces in thy selfe hast more   .   .   .   57 E89 Allen   9
Which of thy names I take, not onely beares   .   .   .   58 E91 Vere   1
Which thou art to thy selfe: whose fame was wonne   .   .   .   58 E91 Vere   5
In th'eye of Europe, where thy deeds were done,   .   .   .   58 E91 Vere   6
When on thy trumpet shee did sound a blast,   .   .   .   58 E91 Vere   7
I leave thy acts, which should I prosecute   .   .   .   58 E91 Vere   9
I speake thy other graces, not lesse showne,   .   .   .   58 E91 Vere   13
Who did, alike with thee, thy house up-beare,   .   .   .   60 E93 Radcliffe   3
And thine owne goodnesse to encrease thy merit,   .   .   .   60 E93 Radcliffe   10
Though not unprov'd: which shewes, thy fortunes are .   .   .   60 E93 Radcliffe   14
Wherewith, against thy bloud, they'offenders bee.   .   .   .   60 E93 Radcliffe   16
Onely to boast thy merit in supply.   .   .   .   .   .   61 E95 Savile   12
Or, better worke! were thy glad countrey blest,   .   .   .   61 E95 Savile   14
To have her storie woven in thy thred;   .   .   .   61 E95 Savile   15
That hast thy brest so cleere of present crimes,   .   .   .   61 E95 Savile   19
And, in thy censures, evenly, dost take   .   .   .   62 E96 Donne 2   4
Mark'd by thy hand, and with the better stone,   .   .   .   62 E96 Donne 2   8
With thine owne course the judgement of thy friend, .   .   .   63 E98 Th Roe 1   8
Be alwayes to thy gather'd selfe the same: .   .   .   63 E98 Th Roe 1   9
That thou hast kept thy love, encreast thy will,   .   .   .   63 E99 Th Roe 2   1
Better'd thy trust to letters; that thy skill;   .   .   .   63 E99 Th Roe 2   2
Hast taught thy selfe worthy thy pen to tread,   .   .   .   63 E99 Th Roe 2   3
Well, though thy name lesse then our great ones bee, .   .   .   64 E99 Th Roe 2   11
Thy fact is more: let truth encourage thee.   .   .   .   64 E99 Th Roe 2   12
That art so reverenc'd, as thy comming in,   .   .   .   66 E102 Pembroke   17
Whether thy learning they would take, or wit,   .   .   .   68 E106 E Herbert   5
Or valour, or thy judgement seasoning it,   .   .   .   68 E106 E Herbert   6
Thy standing upright to thy selfe, thy ends   .   .   .   68 E106 E Herbert   7
Like straight, thy pietie to God, and friends: .   .   .   68 E106 E Herbert   8
Where all is faire, beside thy pedigree.   .   .   .   70 E109 Nevil   4
To make thy lent life, good against the Fates: .   .   .   70 E109 Nevil   11
And that thy soule should give thy flesh her weight. .   .   .   70 E109 Nevil   14
Thy deedes, unto thy name, will prove new wombes,   .   .   .   70 E109 Nevil   17
Can so speake Caesar, as thy labours doe.   .   .   .   71 E110 Edmonds 1   12
Thy learned hand, and true Promethean art   .   .   .   71 E110 Edmonds 1   17
Who Edmonds, reades thy booke, and doth not see   .   .   .   72 E111 Edmonds 2   1
And thence, deprave thee, and thy worke. To those   .   .   .   72 E111 Edmonds 2   13
By thy great helpe: and doth proclaime by mee,   .   .   .   72 E111 Edmonds 2   13
By thy great Art: and doth proclaime by mee,   .   .   .   72 E111 Edmonds 2 V 13
With thy small stocke, why art thou ventring still, .   .   .   72 E112 Gamster   1
Or thy ranke setting? that thou dar'st put in   .   .   .   72 E112 Gamster   4
Thy all, at all: and what so ere I doe,   .   .   .   72 E112 Gamster   5
O, (thou cry'st out) that is thy proper game.   .   .   .   73 E112 Gamster   16
Troth, if it be, I pitty thy ill lucke;   .   .   .   73 E112 Gamster   17
Pr'y thee, yet save thy rest; give ore in time: .   .   .   73 E112 Gamster   21
I thinke, the Fate of court thy comming crav'd,   .   .   .   73 E113 Overbury   5
Repent thee not of thy faire precedent,   .   .   .   73 E113 Overbury   9
So did thy vertue'enforme, thy wit sustaine   .   .   .   75 E116 Jephson   3
These were thy knowing arts: which who doth now   .   .   .   75 E116 Jephson   13
That to the vulgar canst thy selfe apply, ...   76 E119 Shelton   11
My lighter comes, to kisse thy learned Muse;   .   .   .   78 E121 Rudyerd 1   2
Writing thy selfe, or judging others writ,   .   .   .   78 E123 Rudyerd 3   1

	Page	Title	Line
THY (cont.)			
Restored in thy body, and thy minde!	79	E125 Uvedale	4
To thanke thy benefits: which is, to pay.	80	E127 Aubigny	12
Attend thee hence; and there, may all thy ends,	81	E128 Wm Roe 2	6
So, when we, blest with thy returne, shall see	81	E128 Wm Roe 2	9
Thy selfe, with thy first thoughts, brought home by thee,	81	E128 Wm Roe 2	10
Whose noyse shall keepe thy miming most alive,	81	E129 Mime	10
Or (mounted on a stoole) thy face doth hit	81	E129 Mime	13
O, runne not proud of this. Yet, take thy due.	81	E129 Mime	15
I, yet, had utter'd nothing on thy part,	82	E130 Ferrab. 1	15
Shed in thy Songs; 'tis true: but short of thee.	82	E130 Ferrab. 1	18
Then stand unto thy selfe, not seeke without	83	E131 Ferrab. 2	13
Might then both thee, thy worke and merit raise:	83	E132 Sylvester	2
How can I speake of thy great paines, but erre?	83	E132 Sylvester	5
Before my thought, and (in thy right) commands	83	E132 Sylvester	8
Bartas doth wish thy English now were his.	83	E132 Sylvester	10
Great Club-fist, though thy backe, and bones be sore,	85	E133 Voyage	55
Still, with thy former labours; yet, once more,	85	E133 Voyage	56
Act a brave worke, call it thy last adventry:	85	E133 Voyage	57
To this dire passage. Say, thou stop thy nose:	85	E133 Voyage	59
Thou hast thy walkes for health, as well as sport:	93	F2 Penshurst	9
Thy Mount, to which the Dryads doe resort,	93	F2 Penshurst	10
The lighter Faunes, to reach thy Ladies oke.	94	F2 Penshurst	18
Thy copp's, too, nam'd of Gamage, thou hast there,	94	F2 Penshurst	19
When thou would'st feast, or exercise thy friends.	94	F2 Penshurst	21
Thy sheepe, thy bullocks, kine, and calves doe feed:	94	F2 Penshurst	23
The middle grounds thy mares, and horses breed.	94	F2 Penshurst	24
To crowne thy open table, doth provide	94	F2 Penshurst	27
And, for thy messe, is willing to be kill'd.	94	F2 Penshurst	30
And if the high-swolne Medway faile thy dish,	94	F2 Penshurst	31
Thou hast thy ponds, that pay thee tribute fish,	94	F2 Penshurst	32
Fat, aged carps, that runne into thy net.	94	F2 Penshurst	33
Then hath thy orchard fruit, thy garden flowers,	94	F2 Penshurst	39
Hang on thy walls, that every child may reach.	94	F2 Penshurst	44
And though thy walls be of the countrey stone,	94	F2 Penshurst	45
Thy lord, and lady, though they have no sute.	95	F2 Penshurst	50
Adde to thy free provisions, farre above	95	F2 Penshurst	58
Without his feare, and of thy lords owne meate:	95	F2 Penshurst	62
Thy tables hoord not up for the next day,	95	F2 Penshurst	71
With his brave sonne, the Prince, they saw thy fires	95	F2 Penshurst	77
Of thy Penates had beene set on flame,	95	F2 Penshurst	79
On thy good lady, then! who, therein, reap'd	95	F2 Penshurst	84
These, Penshurst, are thy praise, and yet not all.	96	F2 Penshurst	89
Thy lady's noble, fruitfull, chaste withall.	96	F2 Penshurst	90
His children thy great lord may call his owne:	96	F2 Penshurst	91
May say, their lords have built, but thy lord dwells.	96	F2 Penshurst	102
But canst, at home, in thy securer rest,	97	F3 Wroth	13
In spring, oft roused for thy masters sport,	97	F3 Wroth	23
Who, for it, makes thy house his court;	97	F3 Wroth	24
Who, for it, makes thy lodge his court;	97	F3 Wroth	V 24
Or with thy friends; the heart of all the yeere,	97	F3 Wroth	25
Or with thy friends; the heate of all the yeere,	97	F3 Wroth	V 25
And giv'st thy gladder guests the sight;	97	F3 Wroth	28
And giv'st thy welcome guests the right;	97	F3 Wroth	V 28
More for thy exercise, then fare;	97	F3 Wroth	30
And fills thy open hall with mirth, and cheere,	98	F3 Wroth	49
Thy noblest spouse affords them welcome grace;	98	F3 Wroth	55
Thy noblest spouse affords them welcome place;	98	F3 Wroth	V 55
Thy peace is made; and, when man's state is well,	99	F3 Wroth	93
Thy morning's, and thy evening's vow	99	F3 Wroth	100
To doe thy countrey service, thy selfe right;	100	F3 Wroth	103
Nor death; but when thy latest sand is spent,	100	F3 Wroth	105
My part is ended on thy stage.	100	F4 To the World	4
Upon thy throate, and live exempt	100	F4 To the World	7
I know thy formes are studyed arts,	100	F4 To the World	9
Thy subtle wayes, be narrow straits;	100	F4 To the World	10
Thy curtesie but sodaine starts,	100	F4 To the World	11
And what thou call'st thy gifts are baits.	100	F4 To the World	12
And all thy good is to be sold.	100	F4 To the World	16
Yet art thou falser then thy wares.	100	F4 To the World	20
If I could not thy ginnes avoyd.	101	F4 To the World	36
Where breathe the basest of thy fooles;	101	F4 To the World	46
As shall not need thy false reliefe.	102	F4 To the World	64
To thy altars, by their nights	104	F8 Sicknesse	4
Live not we, as, all thy stalls,	104	F8 Sicknesse	9
Or if needs thy lust will tast	105	F8 Sicknesse	15
But, forgive me, with thy crowne	105	F8 Sicknesse	18
What should, yet, thy pallat please?	105	F8 Sicknesse	21
If thy leanenesse love such food,	105	F8 Sicknesse	24
There are those, that, for thy sake,	105	F8 Sicknesse	25
To become thy sacrifice.	105	F8 Sicknesse	28
In thy justice to molest	106	F8 Sicknesse	47
Phoebus. No? tend thy cart still. Envious day	107	F10 Proludium	7
And foundred thy hot teame, to tune my lay.	107	F10 Proludium	9
And foundred thy hot teame, to tune our lay.	107	F10 Proludium	V 9
To raise my spirits with thy conjuring wine,	107	F10 Proludium	11
To raise our spirits with thy conjuring wine,	107	F10 Proludium	V 11
In the greene circle of thy Ivy twine.	107	F10 Proludium	12
That, at thy birth, mad'st the poore Smith affraid,	107	F10 Proludium	14
Who, with his axe, thy fathers mid-wife plaid.	107	F10 Proludium	15
Or, with thy Tribade trine, invent new sports,	107	F10 Proludium	17
Thou, nor thy loosenesse with my making sorts.	107	F10 Proludium	18
to loose, and Cap'ring, for thy stricter veyne.	108	F10 Proludium	2

THY (cont.)

	Page	Title	Line
Thy thoughts did never melt in amorous fire,	108	F10 Proludium	3
Could ne'er make prize of thy white Chastetye.	108	F10 Proludium	6
Though thy wild thoughts with sparrowes wings doe flye,	111	F11 Epode	73
Grow, grow, faire tree, and as thy branches shoote,	119	F13 Aubigny	99
Heare, what the Muses sing about thy roote,	119	F13 Aubigny	100
For thy acceptance. O, behold me right,	127	U1 Trinitie	13
To pay our debts, upon thy Crosse, and cryd'st,	128	U1 Trinitie	23
Among thy Saints elected to abide,	128	U1 Trinitie	45
And with thy Angels, placed side, by side,	128	U1 Trinitie	46
But in thy presence, truly glorified,	128	U1 Trinitie	47
Use still thy rod,	129	U1 Father	4
Therein, thy Love.	129	U1 Father	6
Where's thy Quiver? bend thy Bow:	132	U2 How he saw	9
O, doe not steepe them in thy Teares,	145	U4 Song	9
I ne're was of thy kind;	150	U10 Jealousie	3
Monarch in Letters! 'Mongst thy Titles showne	160	U14 Selden	65
With that thy Stile, thy keeping of thy State,	161	U14 Selden	68
In offering this thy worke to no great Name,	161	U14 Selden	69
Thy learned Chamber-fellow, knowes to doe	161	U14 Selden	72
And estimate thy Paines; as having wrought	161	U14 Selden	75
Thy gift 'gainst envie. O how I doe count	161	U14 Selden	79
Wake, friend, from forth thy Lethargie: the Drum	162	U15 Friend-Wars	1
Wake, friend, and finde thy self; awake, the Drum	162	U15 Friend-Wars V	1
Thy true friends wishes, Colby, which shall be,	167	U15 Friend-Wars	176
Thy true friends wishes, which shall ever be,	167	U15 Friend-Wars V176	
That thine be just, and honest; that thy Deeds	167	U15 Friend-Wars	177
Not wound thy conscience, when thy body bleeds;	168	U15 Friend-Wars	178
That by commanding first thy selfe, thou mak'st	168	U15 Friend-Wars	181
Thy person fit for any charge thou tak'st;	168	U15 Friend-Wars	182
That whatsoever face thy fate puts on,	168	U15 Friend-Wars	185
Still pretious, with the odour of thy name.	168	U15 Friend-Wars	190
These take, and now goe seeke thy peace in Warre,	168	U15 Friend-Wars	195
It might thy patience richly pay:	168	U16 Gray	5
If hence thy silence be,	174	U23 Himselfe	13
Then take in hand thy Lyre,	175	U23 Himselfe	25
Strike in thy proper straine,	175	U23 Himselfe	26
stryke him in thy proper straine,	175	U23 Himselfe V 26	
Make not thy selfe a Page,	175	U23 Himselfe	33
Thy present Aide: Arise Invention,	176	U25 Desmond	2
Thy present Aide: Spirit Invention,	176	U25 Desmond V 2	
My bolder numbers to thy golden Lyre:	177	U25 Desmond	9
My flowing numbers to thy golden Lyre:	177	U25 Desmond V 9	
Thy Priest in this strange rapture; heat my braine	177	U25 Desmond	11
Thy beauties, yet could write of thee?	181	U27 Ode Helen	2
Thy Universe, though his Epitome.	185	U30 Burleigh	4
Dar'st not abuse thy wisdome, in the Lawes,	187	U33 Councellour	17
Against a multitude; and (with thy Stile	187	U33 Councellour	31
Thy Adversaries fall, as not a word	187	U33 Councellour	33
They had, but were a Reed unto thy Sword.	187	U33 Councellour	34
Thy Hearers Nectar, and thy Clients Balme,	187	U33 Councellour	36
The Courts just honour, and thy Judges love.	187	U33 Councellour	37
Thy sincere practise, breeds not thee a fame	187	U33 Councellour	39
Alone, but all thy ranke a reverend Name.	187	U33 Councellour	40
What did she worth thy spight? were there not store	188	U34 Small Poxe	3
I, that thy Ayme was; but her fate prevail'd:	188	U34 Small Poxe	17
And scorn'd, thou'ast showne thy malice, but hast fail'd.	188	U34 Small Poxe	18
Her presently? Or leape thy Wife of force,	201	U42 Elegy Let	44
When by thy sordid bountie she hath on	201	U42 Elegy Let	45
So I might dote upon thy Chaires and Stooles	201	U42 Elegy Let	47
But when thy Wife (as thou conceiv'st) is brave?	201	U42 Elegy Let	50
Then ope thy wardrobe, thinke me that poore Groome	201	U42 Elegy Let	51
Thou art jealous of thy Wifes, or Daughters Case:	202	U42 Elegy Let	87
Or urge thy Greedie flame, thus to devoure	202	U43 Vulcan	3
Or beg thy Greedie flame, thus to devoure	202	U43 Vulcan V 3	
I ne're attempted, Vulcan, 'gainst thy life;	202	U43 Vulcan	5
I ne're attempted ought against thy life;	202	U43 Vulcan V 5	
Nor made least line of love to thy loose Wife;	203	U43 Vulcan	6
Or in remembrance of thy afront, and scorne,	203	U43 Vulcan	7
By Jove to have Minerva for thy Bride,	203	U43 Vulcan	12
I had deserv'd, then, thy consuming lookes,	203	U43 Vulcan	17
But, on thy malice, tell me, didst thou spie	203	U43 Vulcan	19
By thy owne vote, a sacrifice to thee?	203	U43 Vulcan	22
Thou then hadst had some colour for thy flames,	204	U43 Vulcan	40
Thou mightst have yet enjoy'd thy crueltie	204	U43 Vulcan	49
But that's a marke, wherof thy Rites doe boast,	205	U43 Vulcan	57
Had I fore-knowne of this thy least desire	205	U43 Vulcan	59
Had I fore-knowne but of thy least desire	205	U43 Vulcan V 59	
All soote, and embers! odious, as thy worke!	207	U43 Vulcan	106
Or Goddesse, could be patient of thy face.	207	U43 Vulcan	108
Sonne of the Wind! for so thy mother gone	208	U43 Vulcan	111
May to thy name a Vulcanale say;	208	U43 Vulcan	120
May to thy name a Pagan prayer say;	208	U43 Vulcan V120	
Against thy furie, when to serve their needs,	208	U43 Vulcan	125
But, O those Reeds! thy meere disdaine of them,	208	U43 Vulcan	129
But, O those weedes: thy meere disdaine of them,	208	U43 Vulcan V129	
(Which, some are pleas'd to stile but thy madde pranck)	208	U43 Vulcan	131
The place, that was thy Wives inheritance.	209	U43 Vulcan	152
The Plot, that was thy Wives inheritance.	209	U43 Vulcan V152	
Scap'd not thy Justice any whitt the more:	210	U43 Vulcan V154	
Though but in daunger, it shall know thy power;	210	U43 Vulcan V157	
Troy, though it were so much thy Venus joycare.	210	U43 Vulcan V160	
'Tis true, that in thy wish they were destroy'd,	210	U43 Vulcan	167

THY (cont.)

	Page	Title	Line
Pox on thee, Vulcan, thy Pandora's pox,	212	U43 Vulcan	213
Thy Wives pox on thee, and B.B.'s too.	212	U43 Vulcan	216
Thy Wives pox on thee, and Bess Broughtons too.	212	U43 Vulcan	V216
But on thy practise, and the Posture booke:	213	U44 Speach	28
He that but saw thy curious Captaines drill,	213	U44 Speach	29
Well did thy craftie Clerke, and Knight, Sir Hugh,	214	U44 Speach	33
Thou canst draw forth thy forces, and fight drie	214	U44 Speach	45
The Battells of thy Aldermanitie;	214	U44 Speach	46
Insert thy Hodges, and those newer men,	214	U44 Speach	53
Such, Coke, were thy beginnings, when thy good	217	U46 Coke	5
Thy just defences made th' oppressor afraid.	217	U46 Coke	8
Such was thy Processe, when Integritie,	217	U46 Coke	9
More for thy Patronage, then for their Cause,	217	U46 Coke	12
And that thy strong and manly Eloquence	217	U46 Coke	13
Stood up thy Nations fame, her Crownes defence.	217	U46 Coke	14
And now such is thy stand; while thou dost deale	217	U46 Coke	15
With endlesse labours, whilst thy learning drawes	217	U46 Coke	18
Such is thy All; that (as I sung before)	217	U46 Coke	21
And seale thee thy Commission:	220	U48 Bacchus	5
And thinke thy streame more quicker	221	U48 Bacchus	27
And have thy tales and jests too,	221	U48 Bacchus	40
Thy Circuits, and thy Rounds free,	221	U48 Bacchus	41
From Court, while yet thy fame hath some small day;	223	U49 Pucell	36
Pardon, I read it in thy face, the day	225	U51 Bacon	5
Since Bacon, and thy Lord was borne, and here;	225	U51 Bacon	8
Thoughts worthy of thy gift, this Inke;	229	U55 Burges	2
Thy Wife a fit of laughter; a Cramp-ring	232	U58 Book-seller	8
Their perfum'd judgements, let them kisse thy Wife.	232	U58 Book-seller	14
Annexed to thy Person, and thy place,	235	U62 Charles 1	2
'T is not enough (thy pietie is such)	235	U62 Charles 1	3
To cure the call'd Kings Evill with thy touch;	235	U62 Charles 1	4
And, in these Cures, do'st so thy selfe enlarge,	235	U62 Charles 1	7
As thou dost cure our Evill, at thy charge.	235	U62 Charles 1	8
And art thou borne, brave Babe? Blest be thy birth,	237	U65 Prince	1
And interpose thy selfe, ('care not how soone.)	238	U65 Prince	10
Thy comming forth in that great yeare,	242	U70 Ode	2
And mad'st thy Mothers wombe thine urne.	242	U70 Ode	8
Produce thy masse of miseries on the Stage,	244	U70 Ode	55
And let thy lookes with gladnesse shine:	245	U70 Ode	76
Accept this garland, plant it on thy head,	245	U70 Ode	77
And thinke, nay know, thy Morison's not dead.	245	U70 Ode	78
Thy faint, and narrow eyes, to reade the King	250	U73 Weston	2
Feed on thy selfe for spight, and shew thy Kind:	250	U73 Weston	9
Though thou hast past thy Summer standing, stay	252	U75 Epithalam.	1
Though thou art past thy Summer standing, stay	252	U75 Epithalam.	V 1
Betweene thy Tropicks, to arrest thy sight,	252	U75 Epithalam.	4
And looking with thy best Inquirie, tell,	254	U75 Epithalam.	74
In all thy age of Journals thou hast tooke,	254	U75 Epithalam.	75
To have thy God to blesse, thy King to grace,	256	U75 Epithalam.	131
Great King, thy having of a second Sonne:	268	U80 Christning	2
And by thy blessing, may thy People see	268	U80 Christning	3
As hath thy James; cleans'd from originall drosse,	268	U80 Christning	9
Grow up, sweet Babe, as blessed, in thy Name,	268	U80 Christning	11
As in renewing thy good Grandsires fame;	268	U80 Christning	12
Thy Neeces line, then thou that gav'st thy Name	274	U84 Descent	14
Into the Kindred, whence thy Adam drew	274	U84 Descent	15
Thou entertaining in thy brest,	281	U84 Mind	71
But such a Mind, mak'st God thy Guest.	281	U84 Mind	72
Looke on thy sloth, and give thy selfe undone,	283	U84 Muse	21
With which, Priapus, he may thanke thy hands,	290	U85 Country	21
With which, Priapus, he may greet thy hands,	290	U85 Country	V 21
With thy bright Swans, of Paulus Maximus:	292	U86 Hor.4:1	10
Will he display the Ensignes of thy warre.	292	U86 Hor.4:1	16
There shall thy dainty Nostrill take	292	U86 Hor.4:1	21
In many a Gumme, and for thy soft eares sake	292	U86 Hor.4:1	22
The Youths and tender Maids shall sing thy praise:	292	U86 Hor.4:1	26
Thrice 'bout thy Ivory neck,) no youth did fling	292	U86 Hor.4:1	28
And ('bout thy Ivory neck,) no youth did fling	293	U87 Hor.3:9	2
Liber, of all thy friends, thou sweetest care,	294	U89 Mart.8:77	1
Thy locks, and rosie garlands crowne thy head;	294	U89 Mart.8:77	4
Darke thy cleare glasse with old Falernian Wine;	295	U89 Mart.8:77	5
And heat, with softest love, thy softer bed.	295	U89 Mart.8:77	6
Not labour'd for, but left thee by thy Sire;	295	U90 Mart.10:47	3
Thy table without art, and easy-rated:	295	U90 Mart.10:47	8
Thy night not dronken, but from cares layd wast;	295	U90 Mart.10:47	9
Nor feare thy latest day, nor wish therfore.	295	U90 Mart.10:47	13
Thy labouring wheele, comes scarce a Pitcher out?	307	Horace	30
Are, by thy cunning placing, made meere new.	307	Horace	68
And those thy new, and late-coyn'd words receive,	309	Horace	74
Thy selfe in teares, then me thy losse will wound,	311	Horace	146
Thy selfe in tears, then me thy harms will wound,	342	Horace	V146
To render word for word: nor with thy sleight	313	Horace	191
From whence thy Modestie, or Poemes law	313	Horace	193
Forbids thee forth againe thy foot to draw.	313	Horace	194
Is to be wise; thy matter first to know;	325	Horace	441
The docile mind may soone thy precepts know,	329	Horace	504
The truth; nor let thy Fable thinke, what e're	329	Horace	508
Thou, such thy judgement is, thy knowledge too,	331	Horace	573
When late (grave Palmer) these thy graffs and flowers	361	Palmer	1
(so well dispos'd by thy auspicious hand)	361	Palmer	2
First: thy successe did strike my sence with wonder;	361	Palmer	5
Thy skill hath made of ranck dispised weedes;	361	Palmer	10

THY (cont.)

	Page	Title	Line
of thy rich labors worlds of thoughts created,	361	Palmer	22
* * * * When loe to crowne thy worth	361	Palmer	27
Palmer thy travayles well becum thy name,	362	Palmer	30
Continue thy sweete Song.	367	Ode Who saith	34
Thy tunes alone;	367	Ode Who saith	36
From thence, display thy wing againe	367	Ode Who saith	41
With thy soft notes, and hold them within Pale	367	Ode Who saith	45
There coole thy Plumes,	368	Ode Who saith	76
From whose prowde bosome, thou began'st thy flight.	368	Ode Who saith	80
Yet, looking in thy face, they shall begin	369	Ode Who saith	93
They saw it halfe, damd thy whole play, and more;	371	Fletcher	8
I, that am glad, thy Innocence was thy Guilt,	371	Fletcher	11
Do crowne thy murdred Poeme: which shall rise	371	Fletcher	14
Who takes thy volume to his vertuous hand,	383	Author	1
May take thy volume to his vertuous hand.	383	Author	8
At these thy Nuptials; but, whose heart, and thought	384	Somerset	5
And pray, thy joyes as lasting bee, as great.	384	Somerset	8
Out-bee that Wife, in worth, thy freind did make:	384	Somerset	12
Thy Richard, rais'd in song, past pulling downe.	385	Brooke	8
But I have seene thy worke, and I know thee:	386	Browne	3
And, if thou list thy selfe, what thou canst bee.	386	Browne	4
This thy worke forth: that judgment mine commends.	386	Browne	8
To make thy honour, and our wealth the more!	388	Chapman	6
Were askt of thy Discoveries; They must say,	388	Chapman	8
As, now, of all men, it is call'd thy Trade:	389	Chapman	11
To draw no envy (Shakespeare) on thy name,	390	Shakespeare	1
Am I thus ample to thy Booke, and Fame:	390	Shakespeare	2
While I confesse thy writings to be such,	390	Shakespeare	3
Were not the paths I meant unto thy praise:	390	Shakespeare	6
And art alive still, while thy Booke doth live,	391	Shakespeare	23
I should commit thee surely with thy peeres,	391	Shakespeare	28
To life againe, to heare thy Buskin tread,	391	Shakespeare	36
And shake a Stage: Or, when thy Sockes were on,	391	Shakespeare	37
Yet must I not give Nature all: Thy Art,	391	Shakespeare	55
Which, since thy flight from hence, hath mourn'd like night,	392	Shakespeare	79
And despaires day, but for thy Volumes light.	392	Shakespeare	80
And pray thee Reader, bring thy weepinge Eyes	394	Jane Ogle	2
When, Rome, I reade thee in thy mighty paire,	395	May	1
Thy Muse, and mine, as they expect. 'Tis true:	396	Drayton	5
lend me thy voyce, O Fame, that I may draw	396	Drayton	12
Hot from thy trumpet, round, about the world.	396	Drayton	14
When, by thy bright Ideas standing by,	397	Drayton	23
There read I, streight, thy learned Legends three,	397	Drayton	25
I saw, and read, it was thy Barons Warres!	397	Drayton	42
Under one title. Thou hast made thy way	397	Drayton	48
In thy admired Periegesis,	397	Drayton	50
Of all that reade thy Poly-Olbyon.	397	Drayton	52
But that I heare, againe, thy Drum to beate	397	Drayton	55
Thy Catalogue of Ships, exceeding his,	398	Drayton	61
Thy list of aydes, and force, for so it is:	398	Drayton	62
But then refreshed, with thy Fayerie Court,	398	Drayton	79
Of thy strange Moon-Calfe, both thy straine of mirth,	398	Drayton	84
I gratulate it to thee, and thy Ends,	398	Drayton	89
To all thy vertuous, and well chosen Friends,	398	Drayton	90
On the new priming of thy old Signe postes	405	Inigo Jones 1	87
Of thy dead Standards: or (with miracle) see	405	Inigo Jones 1	89
Thy twice conceyvd, thrice payd for Imagery?	405	Inigo Jones 1	90
Aymd at in thy omnipotent Designe!	406	Inigo Jones 1	96
Of all the Worthyes hope t'outlast thy one,	406	Inigo Jones 1	99
Again, thy Architect to ashes turne!	406	Inigo Jones 1	102
Thy Canvas Gyant, at some Channell aymes,	407	Inigo Jones 2	15
An Earle of show: for all thy worke is showe:	407	Inigo Jones 2	21
An Earle of show: for all thy worth is showe:	407	Inigo Jones 2	V 21
The Marrow! Wretch, I quitt thee of thy paine	408	Inigo Jones 3	5
Thy Forehead is too narrow for my Brand.	408	Inigo Jones 3	14
Foole, doe not rate my Rymes; I'have found thy Vice	408	Detractor	5
That hast lost thy noyse, thy foame, thy stirre,	408	Detractor	8
I now would write on thee? No, wretch; thy name	409	Detractor	11
Nameless, and noysome, as thy infamy!	409	Detractor	16
To aske thy name, if he have half his Nose!	409	Detractor	18
Thy Noddle, with his clubb; and dashing forth	409	Detractor	21
Thy Dirty braines, Men smell thy want of worth.	409	Detractor	22
Secure thy railing Rhymes, infamous Gill,	410	Gill	2
To be the Denis of thy Father's School,	410	Gill	7
Keep in thy barking Wit, thou bawling Fool?	410	Gill	8
Thinking to stir me, thou hast lost thy End,	410	Gill	9
Thy blatant Muse abroad, and teach it rather	411	Gill	11
A Tune to drown the Ballads of thy Father:	411	Gill	12
But Tune and Noise the Eccho of thy Shame.	411	Gill	14
These forme thy Ghyrlond. Wherof Myrtle green,	412	Ghyrlond	5
To knit thy Crowne, and glorifie the rest.	412	Ghyrlond	12
How are thy gifts, and graces blaz'd abroad!	413	Ghyrlond	36
And most to be admired of thy Sexe,	414	Ghyrlond	46
Who mad'st us happy all, in thy reflexe,	414	Ghyrlond	47
How are thy gifts and graces blaz'd abro'd,	414	Ghyrlond	53
But I can tell thee, Dover, how thy Games	415	Dover	3

THY'EPISTOLAR

	Page	Title	Line
But then, thy'epistolar Heroick Songs,	397	Drayton	29

THYESTES

	Page	Title	Line
In tragick Verse; no lesse Thyestes feast	311	Horace	122

THYNE

	Page	Title	Line
Hold thyne owne worth unbroke: which is so good	386	Browne	13

	Page	Title	Line
THYS			
By thys Tyme, though you fancie not the man,	231	U56 Covell	V 25
TIBER (See TYBERS)			
TIBERTS			
But 'mong'st these Tiberts, who do'you thinke there was?	88	E133 Voyage	155
TIBULLUS			
Or Delia's Graces, by Tibullus?	181	U27 Ode Helen	10
TICKLED			
Had tickled your large Nosthrill: many a Reame	205	U43 Vulcan	62
TICKLING			
Your forme imprest there: not with tickling rimes,	116	F12 Rutland	87
TICKLINGE			
howe soone with a selfe ticklinge hee was spent.	420	Ode:If Men	18
T'IDOLATRIE			
I could adore, almost t'idolatrie.	79	E125 Uvedale	10
TIE (See also TYE)			
Nor tie knots, nor knots unweave;	142	U2 Her man	50
TIED			
You were not tied, by any Painters Law,	227	U52 Answer	7
TIER			
Unto the Ships, and they from tier, to tier,	249	U72 King	2
TIES			
Those are poore Ties, depend on those false ends,	216	U45 Squib	11
TIGERS (See also TYGERS)			
Was Tigers, said, and Lyons fierce, to tame.	327	Horace	482
TIKE			
I'll laugh at thee poor wretched Tike, go send	410	Gill	10
TILES			
Left! and wit since to cover it with Tiles.	209	U43 Vulcan	138
TILL			
To lye upon thy stall, till it be sought;	28	E3 Bookseller	5
Till time, strong by her bestowing,	39	E40 Ratcliffe	11
A line unto thee, till the world it know;	54	E81 Proule	2
Till they be sure to make the foole their quarrie.	55	E85 Goodyere 1	10
And, till they burst, their backs, like asses load:	62	E96 Donne 2	11
Their lives, as doe their lines, till now had lasted.	65	E101 Supper	32
Till thou canst finde the best, choose the least ill.	76	E119 Shelton	10
And stayes but till you come unto the dore!	89	E133 Voyage	178
Till you equall with the store,	103	F6 Celia 2	12
Till that no usurer, nor his bawds dare lend	118	F13 Aubigny	78
Till I attaine the long'd-for mysterie	128	U1 Trinitie	31
That you never knew till now,	131	U2 Excuse	15
Till she be the reason why,	131	U2 Excuse	23
Till he cherish'd too much beard,	141	U2 Her man	23
Till each of us be made a Starre,	143	U3 Musicall	3
Till each of us is made a Starre,	143	U3 Musicall	V 3
Are nothing till that comes to bind and shut.	157	U13 Sacvile	138
Till he becomes both their, and his owne curse!	162	U15 Friend-Wars	14
Till envie wound, or maime it at a blow!	162	U15 Friend-Wars	22
till one upon another, and now beare	166	U15 Friend-Wars	V125
But here doth lie, till the last Day,	168	U16 Gray	3
Upon reward, till the reward him sought.	185	U30 Burleigh	14
And, till the comming of the Soule	188	U35 Chute	5
No man inflicts that paine, till hope be spent:	192	U38 Elegy 'Tis	44
We cut not off, till all Cures else doe faile:	192	U38 Elegy 'Tis	46
Till then 'tis all but darknesse, that I have;	194	U38 Elegy 'Tis	121
Till the sower Minute comes of taking leave,	197	U40 Elegy That	2
Till I may see both it and you agen.	199	U41 Elegy Since	22
Thou should'st have stay'd, till publike fame said so.	204	U43 Vulcan	46
If they stay here, but till Saint Georges Day.	213	U44 Speach	10
To goe out after__till when take this letter	229	U54 Squib	19
My Lord, till griefe felt younge make our stone hearts soft,	234	U61 Epigram	14
Till he had sold his Piece, drawne so unlike:	242	U69 Friend Son	13
Till either grew a portion of the other:	247	U70 Ode	110
Till you behold a race to fill your Hall,	258	U75 Epithalam.	169
Will last till day;	258	U75 Epithalam.	190
Till, like her face, it doe appeare,	276	U84 Body	15
For they are strong Supporters: But, till then,	281	U84 Kenelme	14
Till swept away, th'were cancell'd with a broome!	282	U84 Muse	8
In earth, till the last Trumpe awake the Sheepe	283	U84 Muse	46
Till fitter season. Now, to like of this,	307	Horace	63
That tarries till the hangings be ta'en downe,	315	Horace	221
And sits, till th'Epilogue saies Clap, or Crowne:	315	Horace	222
Till then unknowne, in Carts, wherein did ride	319	Horace	313
And not without much praise; till libertie	321	Horace	366
Till he drop off, a Horse-leech, full of blood.	337	Horace	680
Till, horse-leech-like, he drop off, full of blood.	355	Horace	V680
till th'one hath drownd the other in our sightes,	361	Palmer	20
till giddie with amazement I fell downe	361	Palmer	25
This change'd his Downe; till this, as white	366	Ode Who saith	25
Till thou at Tames alight,	368	Ode Who saith	79
Mortality, till you immortall bee.	384	Somerset	22
And, till I worthy am to wish I were,	398	Drayton	92
Stay, till she make her vaine Approches. Then	401	Beaumont	15
Till he hath reach'd his two-fold point of Noone.	414	Ghyrlond	52
Of Subjects; Let such envie, till they burst.	416	Dover	10
Till I, at much expense of Time, and Taper.	666	Glover	7
TILLS			
With his owne Oxen tills his Sires left lands,	289	U85 Country	3
TILLY			
The Cittie-Question, whether Tilly, or he,	214	U44 Speach	38
TILT (See also TYLTING)			
Item, a gulling imprese for you, at tilt.	51	E73 Fine Grand	15

	Page	Title	Line

TILT (cont.)
Tilt one upon another, and now beare · · · · 166 U15 Friend-Wars 125
TILTER
To Sir Annual Tilter. · · · · · 36 E29 Tilter Ttl
Tilter, the most may'admire thee, though not I: · · · 36 E29 Tilter 1
TILTING
For they did see it the last tilting well, · · · · 213 U44 Speach 6
TIMBRED
Built a small-timbred Stage, and taught them talke · · · 319 Horace 317
TIMBRELS
For, though that Rattles, Timbrels, Toyes, · · · 273 U84 Cradle 17
TIME (See also TYME)
So, in short time, th'art in arrerage growne · · · 32 E16 Brain-hardy 5
And in this short time of thy happiest raigne, · · · 37 E35 James 2 4
Till time, strong by her bestowing, · · · · 39 E40 Ratcliffe 11
And there's both losse of time, and losse of sport · · 46 E62 Would-bee 10
But I am glad to see that time survive, · · · 47 E64 Salisbury 3 9
Who, to upbraid the sloth of this our time, · · · 48 E66 Cary 5
Against my grave, and time could not forgive. · · · 58 E91 Vere 12
If time to facts, as unto men would owe? · · · · 64 E99 Th Roe 2 6
That we had left us, nor by time, nor place, · · · 67 E105 L Wroth 2 3
T'all future time, not onely doth restore · · · 71 E110 Edmonds 1 21
Pr'y thee, yet save thy rest; give ore in time: · · · 73 E112 Gamster 21
It was the day, what time the powerfull Moone · · · 84 E133 Voyage 29
Of some Bride-well, and may, in time, concerne us · · 85 E133 Voyage 42
(In the meane time, let 'hem imprison mee) · · · 87 E133 Voyage 104
By this time had they reach'd the Stygian poole, · · · 87 E133 Voyage 121
Fig, grape, and quince, each in his time doth come: · · 94 F2 Penshurst 42
Time will not be ours, for ever. · · · · 102 F5 Celia 1 3
Richer then Time, and as Time's vertue, rare. · · · 111 F11 Epode 59
To her remembrance; which when time shall bring · · 115 F12 Rutland 75
No lady, but, at some time, loves her glasse. · · · 117 F13 Aubigny 26
'Tis onely that can time, and chance defeat: · · · 118 F13 Aubigny 51
To himselfe his losse of Time; · · · · 138 U2 Kisse 31
Great and good turns, as wel could time them too, · · 153 U13 Sacvile 2
In time 'twill be a heape; This is not true · · · 157 U13 Sacvile 133
But here's no time, nor place, my wealth to tell, · · · 161 U14 Selden 85
His time? health? soule? will he for these goe throw · · 165 U15 Friend-Wars 103
Nor should I at this time protested be, · · · · 169 U17 Friend-Debt 7
Venter a longer time, and willingly: · · · · 169 U17 Friend-Debt 15
Others, in time may love, as we doe now. · · · 171 U19 Elegy By 18
Slip no occasion; As time stands not still, · · · 171 U19 Elegy By 19
When Vice alike in time with vertue dur'd. · · · 176 U24 Frontispice 8
· · · in Queene Elizabeths Time, since lost, and recovered. · · 176 U25 Desmond Ttl
Still may Syllabes jarre with time, · · · · 184 U29 Fit of Rime 52
Such are his powers, whom time hath stil'd, · · · 189 U36 Song 13
And never be by time, or folly brought, · · · 198 U40 Elegy That 44
Winter is come a Quarter e're his Time, · · · 199 U41 Elegy Since 12
And the strong lines, that so the time doe catch: · · 206 U43 Vulcan 78
And the strong lines, which so the time doe catch: · · 206 U43 Vulcan V 78
Bred on the Banck, in time of Poperie, · · · 209 U43 Vulcan 143
But that's a blow, by which in time I may · · · 219 U47 Tribe 51
The rather when the vices of the Time · · · 224 U50 Countesse 9
Only your time you better entertaine, · · · · 224 U50 Countesse 23
Your Joane to passe her melancholie time. · · · 231 U56 Covell 24
Cary to passe her melancholie time. · · · · 231 U56 Covell V 24
Knew the time, when · · · · · 231 U57 Burges 8
To hit in angles, and to clash with time: · · · 232 U59 Newcastle 5
He vexed time, and busied the whole State; · · · 243 U70 Ode 27
The profits for a time. · · · · · 246 U70 Ode 101
It is the kindly Season of the time, · · · · 253 U75 Epithalam. 25
Which Time shall not, · · · · · 257 U75 Epithalam. 134
Thereof, to Time. · · · · · 273 U84 Cradle 12
'Twere time that I dy'd too, now shee is dead, · · · 282 U84 Muse 1
She spent more time in teares her selfe to dresse · · 287 U84 Muse 180
Stamp'd to the time. As woods whose change appeares · · 309 Horace 85
But soft, and simple, at few holes breath'd time · · 319 Horace 289
In time to Tragedie, a Musicke new. · · · 319 Horace 306
Be I their Judge, they doe at no time dare · · · 321 Horace 356
Then Time hath donne, · · · · · 367 Ode Who saith 54
A glorified worke to Time, when Fire, · · · 371 Fletcher 15
He was not of an age, but for all time! · · · 391 Shakespeare 43
You learn'd it well; and for it, serv'd your time · · 410 Brome 9
Till I, at much expense of Time, and Taper · · · 666 Glover 7
TIMELY
This morning, timely rapt with holy fire, · · · 52 E76 Bedford 1 1
Lent timely succours, and new life begot: · · · 80 E127 Aubigny 8
Yet, for the timely favours shee hath done, · · · 115 F12 Rutland 71
It shall a ripe and timely issue fall, · · · 119 F13 Aubigny 104
The Judge his favour timely then extends, · · · 186 U32 Elsmere 1
More timely hie thee to the house, · · · 292 U86 Hor.4:1 9
TIME'S
Richer then Time, and as Time's vertue, rare. · · · 111 F11 Epode 59
TIMES
All braines, at times of triumph, should runne wit. · · 36 E29 Tilter 4
In these times. Few so have ru'de · · · 39 E40 Ratcliffe 14
And so is Jone. Oft-times, when Giles doth find · · 40 E42 Giles 9
He markes not whose 'twas first: and after-times · · 45 E56 Poet-Ape 11
With what thy vertue on the times hath won, · · · 47 E63 Salisbury 2 2
Without his, thine, and all times injurie? · · · 47 E63 Salisbury 2 10
Get him the times long grudge, the courts ill will; · · 48 E65 Muse 7
T'our times return'd, hath made her heaven in thee. · · 52 E74 Chancelor 10
Stand'st thou, to shew the times what you all were? · · 60 E93 Radcliffe 4

702

TIMES (cont.)

Entry	Page	Title	Line
Thou need'st not shrinke at voyce of after-times;	61	E95 Savile	20
Or did our times require it, to behold	67	E104 Montgomery	3
Were you advanced, past those times, to be	67	E104 Montgomery	11
If I would strive to bring backe times, and trie	78	E122 Rudyerd 2	3
Uv'dale, thou piece of the first times, a man	79	E125 Uvedale	1
Of sixe times to, and fro, without embassage,	85	E133 Voyage	34
That at great times, art no ambitious guest	96	F3 Wroth	5
The truth of times) was once of more esteeme,	114	F12 Rutland	21
Or common places, filch'd, that take these times,	116	F12 Rutland	88
Times, and occasions, to start forth, and seeme)	118	F13 Aubigny	63
Heard what times past have said, seene what ours doe:	159	U14 Selden	34
Times, manners, customes! Innovations spide!	160	U14 Selden	44
And then of times (besides the bare Conduct	160	U14 Selden	51
And be belov'd, while the Whores last. O times,	167	U15 Friend-Wars	161
Times witnesse, herald of Antiquitie,	176	U24 Frontispice	17
Or the times envie:	176	U25 Desmond	7
Who thus long safe, would gaine upon the times	186	U32 Elsmere	9
So dost thou studie matter, men, and times,	187	U33 Councellour	15
Itch to defame the State? or brand the Times?	203	U43 Vulcan	25
Let these men have their wayes, and take their times	218	U47 Tribe	25
How many times, Live long, Charles, would he say,	236	U64 Charles 3	3
O Times! O Manners! Surfet bred of ease,	237	U64 Charles 3	17
In him the times, no lesse then Prince, are prais'd,	256	U75 Epithalam.	115
Hath drawne on me, from the times,	259	U76 Petition	17
Hath drawne on him, from the times,	259	U76 Petition	V 17
That know the times, and seasons when t'appeare,	263	U79 New-yeares	11
Ye have oft-times, that may ore-shine the rest,	305	Horace	18
Ye have oft-times, that may out-shine the rest,	338	Horace	V 18
Of the times past, when he was a young lad;	317	Horace	248
But, as a Matrone drawne at solemne times	321	Horace	338
Not, ten times o're, corrected to the naile.	325	Horace	418
Oft-times a Sharpe, when we require a Flat:	329	Horace	523
Doth please; this, ten times over, will delight.	331	Horace	544
In these pide times, only to shewe their braines,	362	Author	4
Who saith our Times nor have, nor can	366	Ode Who saith	1
When the old words doe strike on the new times,	389	Aleman	4
O, how in those, dost thou instruct these times,	397	Drayton	43

T'IMPRINT

Entry	Page	Title	Line
T'imprint in all purg'd hearts this virgin sence,	414	Ghyrlond	55

TINCKLING

Entry	Page	Title	Line
Your forme imprest there: not with tinckling rimes,	116	F12 Rutland	V 87
Of verse meere-matter-lesse, and tinckling toies.	327	Horace	460

T'INCREASE

Entry	Page	Title	Line
But then t'increase my feares,	148	U7 Nymph	26

T'INDITE

Entry	Page	Title	Line
For their owne cap'tall crimes, t'indite my wit;	117	F13 Aubigny	14

TINE

Entry	Page	Title	Line
Haste, Haste, sweete.Singer: Nor to Tine,	368	Ode Who saith	73

T'INFLICT

Entry	Page	Title	Line
Upon my flesh t'inflict another wound.	122	F15 Heaven	22

T'INHABIT

Entry	Page	Title	Line
For her t'inhabit? There is it.	280	U84 Mind	52

T'INHERIT

Entry	Page	Title	Line
And comes by these Degrees, the Stile t'inherit	164	U15 Friend-Wars	81

T'INSTRUCT

Entry	Page	Title	Line
T'instruct and teach? or your unweary'd paine	159	U14 Selden	37

TINTORET

Entry	Page	Title	Line
Send in, what or Romano, Tintoret,	260	U77 Treasurer	6
Send in, what Romans famous, Tintoret,	260	U77 Treasurer	V 6

T'INVEIGH

Entry	Page	Title	Line
T'inveigh 'gainst playes: what did he then but play?	52	E75 Lippe	4

TIRE (ATTIRE)

Entry	Page	Title	Line
Whither? oh whither will this Tire-man growe?	404	Inigo Jones 1	59

TIR'D

Entry	Page	Title	Line
Against the Husband comes home tir'd;	291	U85 Country	44

TIRE-MAN

Entry	Page	Title	Line
Whither? oh whither will this Tire-man growe?	404	Inigo Jones 1	59

TIRES

Entry	Page	Title	Line
To shew their Tires? to view, and to be view'd?	222	U49 Pucell	17

'TIS

Entry	Page	Title	Line
'Tis 'gainst the manners of an Epigram:	29	E9 To All	3
Hardie, thy braine is valiant, 'tis confest,	32	E16 Brain-hardy	1
For thy late sharpe device. I say 'tis fit	36	E29 Tilter	3
And lyes so farre from wit, 'tis impudence.	38	E38 Guiltie 2	6
'Tis Lucklesse he, that tooke up one on band	42	E46 Luckless 1	3
When Nature bids us leave to live, 'tis late	50	E70 Wm Roe 1	1
Still, 'tis his lucke to praise me 'gainst his will.	50	E71 Parrat	2
'Tis not thy judgement breeds the prejudice,	50	E72 Court-ling	5
Weare this renowne. 'Tis just, that who did give	57	E89 Allen	13
If not, 'tis fit for you, some should envy.	67	E104 Montgomery	16
Shed in thy Songs; 'tis true: but short of thee.	82	E130 Ferrab. 1	18
And pitty 'tis, I cannot call 'hem knights:	84	E133 Voyage	22
All, that are readers: but, me thinkes 'tis od,	85	E133 Voyage	43
'Tis but light paines: Indeede this Dock's no rose.	85	E133 Voyage	60
Yet, one day in the yeere, for sweet 'tis voyc't,	87	E133 Voyage	119
'Tis better, if he there can dwell.	99	F3 Wroth	94
'Tis better, if he then can dwell.	99	F3 Wroth	V 94
But, as 'tis rumor'd, so beleev'd?	101	F4 To the World	50
'Tis, with us, perpetuall night.	102	F5 Celia 1	8
'Tis no sinne, loves fruit to steale,	102	F5 Celia 1	15
'Tis the securest policie we have,	109	F11 Epode	17
Inconstant, like the sea, of whence 'tis borne,	110	F11 Epode	39

		Page	Title	Line
'TIS (cont.)				
Inconstant, as the sea, of whence 'tis borne,		110	F11 Epode	V 39
'Tis growne almost a danger to speake true		116	F13 Aubigny	1
'Tis onely that can time, and chance defeat:		118	F13 Aubigny	51
Without companions? 'Tis safe to have none.		118	F13 Aubigny	56
'Tis one good part I'ld lie withall.		142	U2 Exception	8
Then when 'tis made, why so will wee.		145	U5 Woman-kind	16
But as 'tis often vext and tri'd.		146	U6 Defence	18
'Tis true, he could not reprehend;		152	U12 Corbet	21
My Sword ('tis but a poore Sword, understand)		154	U13 Sacvile	54
'Tis by degrees that men arrive at glad		157	U13 Sacvile	131
We must accomplish; 'Tis the last Key-stone		157	U13 Sacvile	136
'Tis like light Canes, that first rise big and brave,		157	U13 Sacvile	149
'Tis there civilitie to bee a whore;		163	U15 Friend-Wars	54
'Tis then a crime, when the Usurer is Judge.		169	U17 Friend-Debt	4
Is done for gaine: If't be, 'tis not sincere.		169	U17 Friend-Debt	6
So well as I may tell in verse, 'tis so?		170	U19 Elegy By	12
Thinke but the Sin of all her sex, 'tis she!		172	U20 Shrub	20
'Tis of your selfe, and that you use		173	U22 Elegy Tho	10
As 'tis too just a cause;		174	U23 Himselfe	14
'Tis crowne enough to vertue still, her owne applause.		174	U23 Himselfe	18
'Tis wisdome, and that high,		181	U26 Ode High	22
'Tis true, I'm broke! Vowes, Oathes, and all I had		191	U38 Elegy 'Tis	1
Till then 'tis all but darknesse, that I have;		194	U38 Elegy 'Tis	121
'Tis true, that in thy wish they were destroy'd,		210	U43 Vulcan	167
'Tis vertue alone, or nothing, that knits friends:		216	U45 Squib	12
But 'tis with a condition,		220	U48 Bacchus	6
For bawdry, 'tis her language, not mine.		223	U49 Pucell	26
'Tis a brave cause of joy, let it be knowne,		225	U51 Bacon	17
'Tis true, as my wombe swells, so my backe stoupes,		227	U52 Answer	4
To know the heads of danger! where 'tis fit		233	U59 Newcastle	17
'Tis hee, 'tis hee, in singing hee,		265	U79 New-yeares	54
'Tis hee, 'tis hee, in singing hee,		265	U79 New-yeares	66
'Tis but a body which you can torment,		270	U81 Pawlet	55
Whose 'tis: but if it favour find,		277	U84 Body	31
As 'tis not radiant, but divine:		278	U84 Mind	26
'Tis got where it can try the fire.		278	U84 Mind	28
'Tis Vertue alone, is true Nobilitie.		282	U84 Kenelme	21
What 'tis t'enjoy, an everlasting breath!		285	U84 Muse	92
'Tis true, I'am Thracian Chloes, I,		293	U87 Hor.3:9	9
'Tis not enough, th'elaborate Muse affords		311	Horace	140
'Tis not enough, the labouring Muse affords		341	Horace	V140
'Tis hard, to speake things common, properly:		313	Horace	183
'Tis cleare, this way I have got off from blame,		323	Horace	395
'Tis now inquir'd, which makes the nobler Verse,		331	Horace	581
Hee'd say, Mend this, good friend, and this; 'tis naught.		333	Horace	624
He'd say, mend this my friend, and this, 'tis nought.		354	Horace	V624
'Tis not your fault, if they shall sense preferre,		370	Author	13
'Tis true, and all mens suffrage. But these wayes		390	Shakespeare	5
Thy Muse, and mine, as they expect. 'Tis true:		396	Drayton	5
And, though I now begin, 'tis not to rub		396	Drayton	7
T'Is a Record in heaven. You, that were		399	Lady Ogle	1
If, maymed, she come off, 'tis not of men		401	Beaumont	16
'tis but the next neighbour ride		417	Moon	35
TIS				
You are the Spectacles of State! Tis true		403	Inigo Jones 1	42
Tis the true Phoebeian Liquor,		657	Door Apollo	15
TISSUE				
Put a Coach-mare in Tissue, must I horse		201	U42 Elegy Let	43
Cover'd with Tissue, whose prosperitie mocks		216	U44 Speach	100
TISSUES				
With Velvet, Plush, and Tissues, it is spirit.		164	U15 Friend-Wars	58
TITIAN				
Titian, or Raphael, Michael Angelo,		260	U77 Treasurer	7
TITLE'				
My title's seal'd. Those that for claps doe write,		62	E96 Donne 2	9
TITLE				
Thy title, Epigrammes, and nam'd of mee,		27	E2 My Booke	2
Nor have my title-leafe on posts, or walls,		28	E3 Bookseller	7
For strict degrees of ranke, or title looke:		29	E9 To All	2
'Twas not entayl'd on title. That some word		75	E116 Jephson	7
Of so great title, birth, but vertue most,		118	F13 Aubigny	49
Let his Title be but great,		142	U2 Exception	3
Of lust, to his rich Suit and Title, Lord?		163	U15 Friend-Wars	51
Nor is the title question'd with our proud,		164	U15 Friend-Wars	83
And his Title be long foole:		184	U29 Fit of Rime	58
Now with a Title more to the Degree:		225	U51 Bacon	12
But that the Corke of Title boy'd him up.		244	U70 Ode	42
To give a greater Name, and Title to! Their owne!		255	U75 Epithalam.	96
Of title in her! All Nobilitie		287	U84 Muse	159
My title, at their rate, I'ad rather, I,		325	Horace	432
Under one title. Thou hast made thy way		397	Drayton	48
TITLE-LEAFE				
Nor have my title-leafe on posts, or walls,		28	E3 Bookseller	7
TITLE'S				
My title's seal'd. Those that for claps doe write,		62	E96 Donne 2	9
TITLES				
Of flatterie to thy titles. Nor of wit.		47	E64 Salisbury 3	8
That serves nor fame, nor titles; but doth chuse		70	E109 Nevil	2
Whil'st others toyle for titles to their tombes.		70	E109 Nevil	18
Titles, I confesse, doe take me;		140	U2 Her man	5
Monarch in Letters! 'Mongst thy Titles showne		160	U14 Selden	65
By which as proper titles, she is knowne		176	U24 Frontispice	16

TITLES (cont.)

	Page	Title	Line
Descended in a rope of Titles, be	215	U44 Speach	80
And titles, by which all made claimes	247	U70 Ode	114
Earle Rivers Grand-Child--serve not titles Fame,	269	U81 Pawlet	V 21
Boast not these Titles of your Ancestors;	281	U84 Kenelme	10
To the most noble, and above his Titles, . . .	384	Somerset	Ttl
By all your Titles, & whole style at ones	402	Inigo Jones 1	15

T'

	Page	Title	Line
Thou wert, as chiefe of them are said t'have beene.	28	E4 James 1	6
When thou wert wont t'admire, not censure men.	32	E18 Censurer	8
Which shewes, where ever death doth please t'appeare,	37	E32 Roe 2	9
Who would not be thy subject, James, t'obay	37	E35 James 2	1
Contends t'have worth enjoy, from his regard,	48	E64 Salisbury 3	13
T'our times return'd, hath made her heaven in thee.	52	E74 Chancelor	10
T'inveigh 'gainst playes: what did he then but play?	52	E75 Lippe	4
As thou hast best authoritie, t'allow.	62	E96 Donne 2	6
T'all future time, not onely doth restore	71	E110 Edmonds 1	21
I could adore, almost t'idolatrie.	79	E125 Uvedale	10
T'extract, and choose the best of all these knowne,	80	E128 Wm Roe 2	3
And is t'a body, often, ill inclin'd,	82	E130 Ferrab. 1	7
T'alledge, that greatest men were not asham'd,	82	E130 Ferrab. 1	9
Which boasts t'have had the head of gold.	98	F3 Wroth	64
To him, man's dearer, then t'himselfe.	99	F3 Wroth	96
With his old earthly labours. T'exact more,	107	F10 Proludium	5
and Conjures all my faculties t'approve	108	F10 Proludium	14
And yet (in this t'expresse our selves more cleare)	111	F11 Epode	75
And yet (in this t'expresse my self more cleare)	111	F11 Epode	V 75
As what th'have lost t'expect, they dare deride.	116	F13 Aubigny	4
For their owne cap'tall crimes, t'indite my wit;	117	F13 Aubigny	14
T'advance his doubtfull issue, and ore-flow	117	F13 Aubigny	40
T'expect the honors of great 'Aubigny:	119	F13 Aubigny	105
And all doe strive t'advance	120	F14 Sydney	5
T'out-strip your peeres:	121	F14 Sydney	26
Upon my flesh t'inflict another wound.	122	F15 Heaven	22
But then t'increase my feares,	148	U7 Nymph	26
His very Manners taught t'amend,	152	U12 Corbet	22
T'instruct and teach? or your unweary'd paine	159	U14 Selden	37
And comes by these Degrees, the Stile t'inherit	164	U15 Friend-Wars	81
And Fortune once, t'assist the spirits that dare.	170	U18 Elegy Can	10
As Love, t'aquit such excellence,	173	U22 Elegy Tho	23
Yet give me leave t'adore in you	174	U22 Elegy Tho	35
And let your mercie make me asham'd t'offend.	194	U38 Elegy 'Tis	106
T'have held a Triumph, or a feast of fire,	205	U43 Vulcan	60
T'have wak'd, if sleeping, Spaines Ambassadour,	213	U44 Speach	4
Of severall makings? helps, helps, t'attire	215	U44 Speach	94
T'obtaine of God, what all the Land should aske?	234	U61 Epigram	11
Was, t'have a Boy stand with a Club, and fright	241	U69 Friend Son	11
Made, or indentur'd, or leas'd out t'advance	246	U70 Ode	100
T'effect it, feele, thou'ast made thine owne heart ake.	250	U73 Weston	12
To shew the rites, and t'usher forth the way	263	U79 New-yeares	4
That know the times, and seasons when t'appeare,	263	U79 New-yeares	11
T' inlive posteritie, her Fame may tell!	269	U81 Pawlet	34
T' have paid againe a blessing was but lent,	271	U81 Pawlet	80
T'escape this common knowne necessitie,	271	U81 Pawlet	93
The Christian hath t'enjoy the future life,	271	U81 Pawlet	96
For her t'inhabit? There is it.	280	U84 Mind	52
T'accuse, or quit all Parties to be heard!	284	U84 Muse	60
What 'tis t'enjoy, an everlasting breath!	285	U84 Muse	92
Find all our Atomes from a point t' a span!	287	U84 Muse	152
T' have knowne no envy, but by suffring it!	287	U84 Muse	162
T'obey, and serve her sweet Commandements.	287	U84 Muse	172
As fit t'exchange discourse; a Verse to win	311	Horace	119
Nor know t'observe: why (i'the Muses name)	311	Horace	128
The angry, and love those that feare t'offend.	317	Horace	282
Plaine phrase, my Piso's, as alone, t'approve	321	Horace	342
Her language, if the Stay, and Care t'have mended,	325	Horace	413
She might have claym'd t'have made the Graces foure;	371	Epitaph	6
Or Verse, or Sense t'express Immortall you?	403	Inigo Jones 1	41
I am too fat t'envy him. He too leane	405	Inigo Jones 1	69
Of all the Worthyes hope t'outlast thy one,	406	Inigo Jones 1	99
T'imprint in all purg'd hearts this virgin sence,	414	Ghyrlond	55

TO'

	Page	Title	Line
To'a little wealth, and credit in the scene,	45	E56 Poet-Ape	7
Whose dice not doing well, to'a pulpit ran.	76	E119 Shelton	6
For I will so urge you to't,	140	U2 Promise	14
That ever had beginning there, to'ave end!	271	U81 Pawlet	91
Beene trusted to thee: not to't selfe assign'd.	283	U84 Muse	20

TO

	Page	Title	Line
To the Reader.	27	E1 Reader	Ttl
To reade it well: that is, to understand.	27	E1 Reader	2
To my Booke.	27	E2 My Booke	Ttl
To catch the worlds loose laughter, or vaine gaze.	27	E2 My Booke	12
To my Booke-seller.	27	E3 Bookseller	Ttl
To lye upon thy stall, till it be sought;	28	E3 Bookseller	5
Not offer'd, as it made sute to be bought;	28	E3 Bookseller	6
Or in cleft-sticks, advanced to Bookseller	28	E3 Bookseller	8
Send it to Bucklers-bury, there 'twill, well.	28	E3 Bookseller	12
To King James.	28	E4 James 1	Ttl
And gave thee both, to shew they could no more.	28	E4 James 1	4
Whom should my Muse then flie to, but the best	28	E4 James 1	9
To Alchymists.	29	E6 Alchymists	Ttl
Ridway was tane, arraign'd, condemn'd to dye;	29	E8 Robbery	2
To all, to whom I write.	29	E9 To All	Ttl

TO (cont.)

	Page	Title		Line
To my lord Ignorant.	29	E10	Ignorant	Ttl
To be a courtier; and lookes grave enough,	30	E11	Something	2
To seeme a statesman: as I neere it came,	30	E11	Something	3
He steales to ordinaries; there he playes	30	E12	Shift	11
Signes to new bond, forfeits: and cryes, god payes.	30	E12	Shift	14
Or else by water goes, and so to playes:	30	E12	Shift	17
To every cause he meets, this voyce he brayes:	31	E12	Shift	19
His onely answere is to all, god payes.	31	E12	Shift	20
To doctor Empirick.	31	E13	Empirick	Ttl
Of old, they gave a cock to Aesculape;	31	E13	Empirick	2
To William Camden.	31	E14	Camden	Ttl
Camden, most reverend head, to whom I owe	31	E14	Camden	1
(How nothing's that?) to whom my countrey owes	31	E14	Camden	3
'Twas brought to court first wrapt, and white as milke;	31	E15	Court-worm	2
To Brayne-hardie.	32	E16	Brain-hardy	Ttl
To the learned Critick.	32	E17	Critic	Ttl
Charge them, for crowne, to thy sole censure hye.	32	E17	Critic	4
To my meere English Censurer.	32	E18	Censurer	Ttl
To thee, my way in Epigrammes seemes new,	32	E18	Censurer	1
To the same Sir Cod.	33	E20	Cod 2	Ttl
What severall wayes men to their calling have!	33	E21	Gam'ster	7
Here lyes to each her parents ruth,	33	E22	Daughter	1
It makes the father, lesse, to rue.	33	E22	Daughter	4
To John Donne.	34	E23	Donne 1	Ttl
Who, to thy one, all other braines refuse;	34	E23	Donne 1	2
To it, thy language, letters, arts, best life,	34	E23	Donne 1	7
All which I meant to praise, and, yet, I would;	34	E23	Donne 1	9
To the Parliament.	34	E24	Parliament	Ttl
What doth he else, but say, leave to be chast,	34	E25	Beast 1	1
Just wife, and, to change me, make womans hast?	34	E25	Beast 1	8
To heaven; his hath: O happy state! wherein	35	E27	Roe 1	7
Don Surly, to aspire the glorious name	35	E28	Surly	1
Of a great man, and to be thought the same,	35	E28	Surly	2
He speakes to men with a Rhinocerotes nose,	35	E28	Surly	4
That's greater, yet: to crie his owne up neate.	35	E28	Surly	11
He drinkes to no man: that's, too, like a lord.	35	E28	Surly	14
To Sir Annual Tilter.	36	E29	Tilter	Ttl
And thou, right guiltlesse, may'st plead to it, why?	36	E29	Tilter	2
To Person Guiltie.	36	E30	Guiltie	Ttl
'Twere madnesse in thee, to betray thy fame,	36	E30	Guiltie	3
And person to the world; ere I thy name.	36	E30	Guiltie	4
He toyles to be at hell, as soone as they.	36	E31	Banck	4
Was his blest fate, but our hard lot to find.	37	E32	Roe 2	8
To the same.	37	E33	Roe 3	Ttl
Breathe to expect my when, and make my how.	37	E33	Roe 3	4
To King James.	37	E35	James 2	Ttl
First thou preserved wert, our king to bee,	38	E35	James 2	9
To the Ghost of Martial.	38	E36	Martial	Ttl
To thy Domitian, than I can my James:	38	E36	Martial	2
To Person Guiltie.	38	E38	Guiltie 2	Ttl
And to conceale your ulcers, did advise,	38	E38	Guiltie 2	2
Fate, in a brother. To conclude,	39	E40	Ratcliffe	15
If, now, with man and wife, to will, and nill	40	E42	Giles	16
To Robert Earle of Salisburie.	40	E43	Salisbury 1	Ttl
To the most Worthy of his Honors. Robert, . . .	40	E43	Salisbury 1	VTtl
Which should thy countries love to speake refuse,	40	E43	Salisbury 1	3
Yet dare not, to my thought, lest hope allow	41	E43	Salisbury 1	7
Of adding to thy fame; thine may to me,	41	E43	Salisbury 1	8
Of adding to thy prayse; thine may to me,	41	E43	Salisbury 1 V	8
And rich in issue to inherit all,	41	E44	Chuff	2
Seven yeeres tho'wert lent to me, and I thee pay,	41	E45	First Son	3
To have so soone scap'd worlds, and fleshes rage,	41	E45	First Son	7
To Sir Lucklesse Woo-all.	42	E46	Luckless 1	Ttl
Is this the Sir, who, some wast wife to winne,	42	E46	Luckless 1	1
A knight-hood bought, to goe a wooing in?	42	E46	Luckless 1	2
To pay at's day of marriage. By my hand	42	E46	Luckless 1	4
To the same.	42	E47	Luckless 2	Ttl
To Play-wright.	42	E49	Playwrt 1	Ttl
Play-wright, I loath to have thy manners knowne	42	E49	Playwrt 1	5
To Sir Cod.	42	E50	Cod 3	Ttl
Leave Cod, tabacco-like, burnt gummes to take,	42	E50	Cod 3	1
Or fumie clysters, thy moist lungs to bake:	42	E50	Cod 3	2
To King James. Upon the happy false rumour of his death, . . .	43	E51	James 3	Ttl
Great heav'n did well, to give ill fame free wing;	43	E51	James 3	2
Yet give thy jealous subjects leave to doubt:	43	E51	James 3	5
To Censorious Courtling.	43	E52	Courtling	Ttl
To Old-end Gatherer.	43	E53	Old-end	Ttl
Thou wert content the authors name to loose:	43	E53	Old-end	3
To give the world assurance thou wert both;	43	E53	Old-end	6
Could save that line to dedicate to thee?	44	E53	Old-end	10
To Francis Beaumont.	44	E55	Beaumont	Ttl
And giving largely to me, more thou tak'st.	44	E55	Beaumont	6
May judge it to be his, as well as ours.	45	E56	Poet-Ape	12
To Groome Ideot.	45	E58	Groome	Ttl
To reade my verses; now I must to heare:	45	E58	Groome	2
For offring, with thy smiles, my wit to grace,	45	E58	Groome	3
Who, when you'have burnt your selves downe to the snuffe,	45	E59	Spies	2
To William Lord Mounteagle.	46	E60	Mounteagle	Ttl
An obeliske, or columne to thy name,	46	E60	Mounteagle	2
To Foole, or Knave.	46	E61	Foole	Ttl
Thy praise, or dispraise is to me alike,	46	E61	Foole	1
To Fine Lady Would-bee.	46	E62	Would-bee	Ttl

TO (cont.)

	Page	Title	Line
That love to make so well, a child to beare?	46	E62 Would-bee	2
To make amends, yo'are thought a wholesome creature.	46	E62 Would-bee	8
To Robert Earle of Salisburie.	47	E63 Salisbury 2	Ttl
And can to these be silent, Salisburie,	47	E63 Salisbury 2	9
To so true worth, though thou thy selfe forbid.	47	E63 Salisbury 2	12
To such true worth, though thou thy selfe forbid.	47	E63 Salisbury 2	V 12
To the same.	47	E64 Salisbury 3	Ttl
To see thy fathers rites new laid on thee.	47	E64 Salisbury 3	6
Nor glad for fashion. Nor to shew a fit	47	E64 Salisbury 3	7
Of flatterie to thy titles. Nor of wit.	47	E64 Salisbury 3	8
But I am glad to see that time survive,	47	E64 Salisbury 3	9
Where good mens vertues them to honors bring,	47	E64 Salisbury 3	11
And not to dangers. When so wise a king	47	E64 Salisbury 3	12
That whil'st I meant but thine to gratulate,	48	E64 Salisbury 3	17
To my Muse.	48	E65 Muse	Ttl
That hast betray'd me to a worthlesse lord;	48	E65 Muse	2
To a great image through thy luxurie.	48	E65 Muse	4
Almost all wayes, to any better course.	48	E65 Muse	10
Shee shall instruct my after-thoughts to write	48	E65 Muse	13
To Sir Henrie Cary.	48	E66 Cary	Ttl
To greatnesse, Cary, I sing that, and thee.	48	E66 Cary	2
Who, to upbraid the sloth of this our time,	48	E66 Cary	5
Or thou more happie, it to justifie	49	E66 Cary	8
To live when Broeck not stands, nor Roor doth runne.	49	E66 Cary	12
To Thomas Earle of Suffolke.	49	E67 Suffolk	Ttl
Since men have left to doe praise-worthy things,	49	E67 Suffolk	1
As, to be rais'd by her, is onely fame.	49	E67 Suffolk	4
And thou design'd to be the same thou art,	49	E67 Suffolk	9
Play-wright convict of publike wrongs to men,	49	E68 Playwrt 2	1
To Pertinax Cob.	50	E69 Cob	Ttl
To William Roe.	50	E70 Wm Roe 1	Ttl
When Nature bids us leave to live, 'tis late	50	E70 Wm Roe 1	1
Then to begin, my Roe: He makes a state	50	E70 Wm Roe 1	2
To plucke downe mine, Poll sets up new wits still,	50	E71 Parrat	1
Still, 'tis his lucke to praise me 'gainst his will.	50	E71 Parrat	2
To Court-ling.	50	E72 Court-ling	Ttl
To Fine Grand.	51	E73 Fine Grand	Ttl
Then had I made 'hem good, to fit your vaine.	51	E73 Fine Grand	20
To Thomas Lord Chancelor.	51	E74 Chancelor	Ttl
That still th'art present to the better cause;	52	E74 Chancelor	5
Whil'st thou art certaine to thy words, once gone,	52	E74 Chancelor	7
I thought to forme unto my zealous Muse,	52	E76 Bedford 1	2
To honor, serve, and love; as Poets use.	52	E76 Bedford 1	4
I meant to make her faire, and free, and wise,	52	E76 Bedford 1	5
Fit in that softer bosome to reside.	52	E76 Bedford 1	12
Such when I meant to faine, and wish'd to see,	52	E76 Bedford 1	17
To one that desired me not to name him.	53	E77 Not name	Ttl
For, if thou shame, ranck'd with my friends, to goe,	53	E77 Not name	3
I'am more asham'd to have thee thought my foe.	53	E77 Not name	4
To Hornet.	53	E78 Hornet	Ttl
To draw thee custome: but her selfe gets all.	53	E78 Hornet	2
To Elizabeth Countesse of Rutland.	53	E79 Rutland	Ttl
On whom, if he were living now, to looke,	53	E79 Rutland	10
Through which, our merit leads us to our meeds.	53	E80 Life/Death	2
And hath it, in his powers, to make his way!	53	E80 Life/Death	4
So to front death, as men might judge us past it.	54	E80 Life/Death	7
To Proule the Plagiary.	54	E81 Proule	Ttl
Forbeare to tempt me, Proule, I will not show	54	E81 Proule	1
To be the wealthy witnesse of my pen:	54	E81 Proule	4
To a Friend.	54	E83 Friend	Ttl
To put out the word, whore, thou do'st me woo,	54	E83 Friend	1
To Lucy Countesse of Bedford.	54	E84 Bedford 2	Ttl
I fancied to my selfe, what wine, what wit	55	E84 Bedford 2	6
To Sir Henry Goodyere.	55	E85 Goodyere 1	Ttl
Goodyere, I'am glad, and gratefull to report,	55	E85 Goodyere 1	1
And why that bird was sacred to Apollo,	55	E85 Goodyere 1	4
That they to knowledge so should toure upright,	55	E85 Goodyere 1	6
And never stoupe, but to strike ignorance:	55	E85 Goodyere 1	7
To former height, and there in circle tarrie,	55	E85 Goodyere 1	9
Till they be sure to make the foole their quarrie.	55	E85 Goodyere 1	10
To the Same.	55	E86 Goodyere 2	Ttl
Where, though 't be love, that to thy praise doth move	55	E86 Goodyere 2	7
Each night, to drowne his cares: But when the gaine	56	E87 Hazard	3
Daily to turne in Pauls, and helpe the trade.	56	E88 Monsieur	16
To Edward Allen.	56	E89 Allen	Ttl
Fear'd not to boast the glories of her stage,	56	E89 Allen	2
That, Allen, I should pause to publish thee?	57	E89 Allen	8
When Mill first came to court, the unprofiting foole,	57	E90 Mill	1
Was dull, and long, ere shee would goe to man:	57	E90 Mill	3
The nicer thing to tast her ladies page;	57	E90 Mill	5
And he growne youth, was call'd to his ladies chamber.	57	E90 Mill	10
And he remov'd to gent'man of the horse,	57	E90 Mill	12
To Sir Horace Vere.	58	E91 Vere	Ttl
To the worthy Sir Horace Vere.	58	E91 Vere	VTtl
Illustrous Vere, or Horace; fit to be	58	E91 Vere	3
Which thou art to thy selfe: whose fame was wonne	58	E91 Vere	5
Whose rellish to eternitie shall last.	58	E91 Vere	8
Whose rellish to eternitie will last.	58	E91 Vere	V 8
Throughout, might flatt'rie seeme; and to be mute	58	E91 Vere	10
To any one, were envie: which would live	58	E91 Vere	11
And best become the valiant man to weare,	58	E91 Vere	17
For twelve yeeres yet to come, what each state lacks.	59	E92 New Crie	14

TO (cont.)

	Page	Title		Line
Are sure to con the catalogue by hart;	59	E92 New Crie		22
To write in cypher, and the severall keyes,	59	E92 New Crie		26
To ope' the character. They'have found the sleight	59	E92 New Crie		27
With juyce of limons, onions, pisse, to write.	59	E92 New Crie		28
To breake up seales, and close 'hem. And they know,	59	E92 New Crie		29
Much like those Brethren; thinking to prevaile	59	E92 New Crie		36
To Sir John Radcliffe	60	E93 Radcliffe		Ttl
Stand'st thou, to shew the times what you all were?	60	E93 Radcliffe		4
And thine owne goodnesse to encrease thy merit,	60	E93 Radcliffe		10
Willing to expiate the fault in thee,	60	E93 Radcliffe		15
To Lucy, Countesse of Bedford, with Mr. Donnes Satyres.	60	E94 Bedford 3		Ttl
Whose poemes would not wish to be your booke?	60	E94 Bedford 3		4
To Sir Henrie Savile.	61	E95 Savile		Ttl
In thee, most weighty Savile, liv'd to us:	61	E95 Savile		4
To thine owne proper I ascribe then more;	61	E95 Savile		9
Onely to boast thy merit in supply.	61	E95 Savile		12
O, would'st thou adde like hand, to all the rest!	61	E95 Savile		13
To have her storie woven in thy thred;	61	E95 Savile		15
Whose knowledge claymeth at the helme to stand;	61	E95 Savile		21
Although to write be lesser then to doo,	61	E95 Savile		25
Of historie, and how to apt their places;	61	E95 Savile		28
To John Donne.	62	E96 Donne 2		Ttl
When I dare send my Epigrammes to thee?	62	E96 Donne 2		2
As free simplicitie, to dis-avow,	62	E96 Donne 2		5
By his each glorious parcell to be knowne!	62	E97 Motion		6
He wont was to encounter me, aloud,	62	E97 Motion		7
Nor 'bout the beares, nor noyse to make lords sport.	63	E97 Motion		12
To Sir Thomas Roe.	63	E98 Th Roe 1		Ttl
And I know nothing more thou hast to doo.	63	E98 Th Roe 1		2
Be alwayes to thy gather'd selfe the same:	63	E98 Th Roe 1		9
To the same.	63	E99 Th Roe 2		Ttl
Better'd thy trust to letters; that thy skill;	63	E99 Th Roe 2		2
Hast taught thy selfe worthy thy pen to tread,	63	E99 Th Roe 2		3
And that to write things worthy to be read:	63	E99 Th Roe 2		4
If time to facts, as unto men would owe?	64	E99 Th Roe 2		6
Cry'd to my face, they were th'elixir of wit:	64	E100 Playwrt 3		2
And I must now beleeve him: for, to day,	64	E100 Playwrt 3		3
Inviting a friend to supper.	64	E101 Supper		Ttl
To night, grave sir, both my poore house, and I	64	E101 Supper		1
Yet shall you have, to rectifie your palate,	64	E101 Supper		9
Limons, and wine for sauce: to these, a coney	65	E101 Supper		13
Is not to be despair'd of, for our money;	65	E101 Supper		14
Livie, or of some better booke to us,	65	E101 Supper		22
And Ile professe no verses to repeate:	65	E101 Supper		24
To this, if ought appeare, which I not know of,	65	E101 Supper		25
Are all but Luthers beere, to this I sing.	65	E101 Supper		34
The libertie, that wee'll enjoy to night.	65	E101 Supper		42
To William Earle of Pembroke.	66	E102 Pembroke		Ttl
Against the bad, but of, and to the good:	66	E102 Pembroke		3
Both which are ask'd, to have thee understood.	66	E102 Pembroke		4
To which, yet, of the sides himselfe he owes.	66	E102 Pembroke		8
They follow vertue, for reward, to day;	66	E102 Pembroke		9
To morrow vice, if shee give better pay:	66	E102 Pembroke		10
Thou must draw more: and they, that hope to see	66	E102 Pembroke		19
To Mary Lady Wroth.	66	E103 L Wroth 1		Ttl
Know you to be a Sydney, though un-named?	66	E103 L Wroth 1		1
Need any Muses praise to give it fame?	66	E103 L Wroth 1		6
And glorie of them all, but to repeate!	66	E103 L Wroth 1		8
To Susan Countesse of Montgomery.	67	E104 Montgomery		Ttl
Or did our times require it, to behold	67	E104 Montgomery		3
A new Susanna, equall to that old?	67	E104 Montgomery		4
To make those faithfull, did the Fates send you?	67	E104 Montgomery		6
And to your Scene lent no lesse dignitie	67	E104 Montgomery		7
Were you advanced, past those times, to be	67	E104 Montgomery		11
Judge they, that can: here I have rais'd to show	67	E104 Montgomery		13
To Mary Lady Wroth.	67	E105 L Wroth 2		Ttl
But even their names were to be made a-new,	67	E105 L Wroth 2		5
And, armed to the chase, so bare her bow	68	E105 L Wroth 2		13
To Sir Edward Herbert.	68	E106 E Herbert		Ttl
Thy standing upright to thy selfe, thy ends	68	E106 E Herbert		7
Like straight, thy pietie to God, and friends:	68	E106 E Herbert		8
To Captayne Hungry.	68	E107 Hungry		Ttl
I oft looke on false coyne, to know't from true:	68	E107 Hungry		3
If but to be beleev'd you have the hap,	69	E107 Hungry		17
To true Souldiers.	69	E108 Soldiers		Ttl
Strength of my Countrey, whilst I bring to view	69	E108 Soldiers		1
To Sir Henry Nevil.	70	E109 Nevil		Ttl
Of service to the publique, when the end	70	E109 Nevil		7
Is private gaine, which hath long guilt to friend.	70	E109 Nevil		8
Thou rather striv'st the matter to possesse,	70	E109 Nevil		9
To make thy lent life, good against the Fates:	70	E109 Nevil		11
And first to know thine owne state, then the States.	70	E109 Nevil		12
To be the same in roote, thou art in height;	70	E109 Nevil		13
Whil'st others toyle for titles to their tombes.	70	E109 Nevil		18
To Clement Edmonds, on his Caesars . . .	71	E110 Edmonds 1		Ttl
Cato's to boote, Rome, and her libertie,	71	E110 Edmonds 1		4
All yeelding to his fortune, nor, the while,	71	E110 Edmonds 1		5
To have engrav'd these acts, with his owne stile,	71	E110 Edmonds 1		6
To the same; On the same.	72	E111 Edmonds 2		Ttl
Beholding, to this master of the warre;	72	E111 Edmonds 2		4
Beholden, to this master of the warre;	72	E111 Edmonds 2	V	4
More, then to varie what our elders knew:	72	E111 Edmonds 2		6

	Page	Title	Line
TO (cont.)			
Nor to give Caesar this, makes ours the lesse.	72	E111 Edmonds 2	8
That to the world thou should'st reveale so much,	72	E111 Edmonds 2	10
And thence, deprave thee, and thy worke. To those	72	E111 Edmonds 2	11
To a weake Gamster in Poetry.	72	E112 Gamster	Ttl
Art still at that, and think'st to blow me'up too?	72	E112 Gamster	6
I modestly quit that, and thinke to write,	72	E112 Gamster	11
I passe to Elegies; Thou meet'st me there:	73	E112 Gamster	13
To Satyres; and thou dost pursue me. Where,	73	E112 Gamster	14
To Sir Thomas Overbury.	73	E113 Overbury	Ttl
As but to speake thee, Overbury, is praise:	73	E113 Overbury	2
Nor may'any feare, to loose of their degree,	73	E113 Overbury	11
To Mrs. Philip Sydney.	73	E114 Sydney	Ttl
Of newes, and noyse, to strow out a long meale.	74	E115 Honest Man	10
Of newes, and noyse, to sow out a long meale.	74	E115 Honest Man V	10
Doe all, that longs to the anarchy of drinke,	74	E115 Honest Man	12
Whose name's un-welcome to the present eare,	74	E115 Honest Man	15
Not that it feares, but will not have to doo	74	E115 Honest Man	20
To Sir William Jephson.	75	E116 Jephson	Ttl
Jephson, thou man of men, to whose lov'd name	75	E116 Jephson	1
And those that lack'd it, to suspect at length,	75	E116 Jephson	6
And to live great, was better, then great borne.	75	E116 Jephson	12
And, striving so to double his delight,	76	E118 Gut	3
To Sir Raph Shelton	76	E119 Shelton	Ttl
That to the vulgar canst thy selfe apply,	76	E119 Shelton	11
Which is to live to conscience, not to show.	76	E119 Shelton	14
As Heaven and Nature seem'd to strive	77	E120 S. P.	7
So, by error, to his fate	77	E120 S. P.	17
And have sought (to give new birth)	77	E120 S. P.	21
In bathes to steepe him;	77	E120 S. P.	22
Heaven vowes to keepe him.	77	E120 S. P.	24
To Benjamin Rudyerd.	78	E121 Rudyerd 1	Ttl
Rudyerd, as lesser dames, to great ones use,	78	E121 Rudyerd 1	1
My lighter comes, to kisse thy learned Muse;	78	E121 Rudyerd 1	2
Shee learnes to know long difference of their states.	78	E121 Rudyerd 1	4
Yet is the office not to be despis'd,	78	E121 Rudyerd 1	5
Nor he, for friendship, to be thought unfit,	78	E121 Rudyerd 1	7
To the same.	78	E122 Rudyerd 2	Ttl
The aged Saturne's age, and rites to know;	78	E122 Rudyerd 2	2
If I would strive to bring backe times, and trie	78	E122 Rudyerd 2	3
If holiest friend-ship, naked to the touch,	78	E122 Rudyerd 2	7
To the same.	78	E123 Rudyerd 3	Ttl
To more vertue, then doth live.	79	E124 Elizabeth	6
Fitter, where it dyed, to tell,	79	E124 Elizabeth	11
To Sir William Uvedale.	79	E125 Uvedale	Ttl
To his Lady, then Mrs. Cary.	80	E126 Mrs Cary	Ttl
Retyr'd, with purpose your faire worth to praise,	80	E126 Mrs Cary	1
To Esme, Lord 'Aubigny.	80	E127 Aubigny	Ttl
If I should faile, in gratitude, to thee,	80	E127 Aubigny	2
To whom I am so bound, lov'd Aubigny?	80	E127 Aubigny	3
So, all reward, or name, that growes to mee	80	E127 Aubigny	9
To thanke thy benefits: which is, to pay.	80	E127 Aubigny	12
To William Roe.	80	E128 Wm Roe 2	Ttl
Roe (and my joy to name) th'art now, to goe	80	E128 Wm Roe 2	1
Countries, and climes, manners, and men to know,	80	E128 Wm Roe 2	2
And those to turne to bloud, and make thine owne:	80	E128 Wm Roe 2	4
We each to other may this voyce enspire;	81	E128 Wm Roe 2	11
To Mime.	81	E129 Mime	Ttl
To Braynford, Hackney, Bow, but thou mak'st one;	81	E129 Mime	4
To which thou'rt not a weeke, bespoke a guest;	81	E129 Mime	6
The very call, to make all others come:	81	E129 Mime	8
To Alphonso Ferrabosco, on his Booke.	82	E130 Ferrab. 1	Ttl
To urge, my lov'd Alphonso, that bold fame	82	E130 Ferrab. 1	1
No lesse a sov'raigne cure, then to the mind;	82	E130 Ferrab. 1	8
Of old, even by her practise, to be fam'd;	82	E130 Ferrab. 1	10
To say, indeed, shee were the soule of heaven,	82	E130 Ferrab. 1	11
To the same.	82	E131 Ferrab. 2	Ttl
When we doe give, Alphonso, to the light,	82	E131 Ferrab. 2	1
Say, this, or that man they to thee preferre;	83	E131 Ferrab. 2	9
They were not to be nam'd on the same day.	83	E131 Ferrab. 2	12
To Mr. Josuah Sylvester.	83	E132 Sylvester	Ttl
If to admire were to commend, my praise	83	E132 Sylvester	1
And utter stranger to all ayre of France)	83	E132 Sylvester	4
That to the world I publish, for him, this;	83	E132 Sylvester	9
Of Hercules, or Theseus going to hell,	84	E133 Voyage	2
Had power to act, what they to faine had not.	84	E133 Voyage	6
Arses were heard to croake, in stead of frogs;	84	E133 Voyage	13
Lash'd by their consciences, to die, affeard.	84	E133 Voyage	18
To have beene stiled of King Arthurs table.	84	E133 Voyage	24
Who gave, to take at his returne from Hell,	84	E133 Voyage	27
Of sixe times to, and fro, without embassage,	85	E133 Voyage	34
Or him that backward went to Berwicke, or which	85	E133 Voyage	35
Propos'd to goe to Hol'borne in a wherry:	85	E133 Voyage	38
A harder tasque, then either his to Bristo',	85	E133 Voyage	39
Or his to Antwerpe. Therefore, once more, list ho'.	85	E133 Voyage	40
Or goddesse to invoke, to stuffe my verse;	85	E133 Voyage	45
Alcides, be thou succouring to my song.	85	E133 Voyage	50
Alwayes at hand, to aide the merry Muses.	85	E133 Voyage	54
To this dire passage. Say, thou stop thy nose:	85	E133 Voyage	59
Betweene two walls: where, on one side, to scar men,	86	E133 Voyage	67
The least of which was to the plague a cosen.	86	E133 Voyage	72
Spake to 'hem louder, then the oxe in Livie:	86	E133 Voyage	74
To answere me. And sure, it was th'intent	87	E133 Voyage	107

	Page	Title	Line
TO (cont.)			
Nor thumbe, nor finger to the stop acquainted,	87	E133 Voyage	134
All was to them the same, they were to passe,	88	E133 Voyage	140
And so they did, from Styx, to Acheron;	88	E133 Voyage	141
For, to say truth, what scullion is so nastie,	88	E133 Voyage	147
To put the skins, and offall in a pastie?	88	E133 Voyage	148
Then, selling not, a dish was tane to mince 'hem,	88	E133 Voyage	151
Grave tutor to the learned horse. Both which,	88	E133 Voyage	157
Their spirits transmigrated to a cat:	88	E133 Voyage	159
They tooke 'hem all to witnesse of their action:	89	E133 Voyage	191
Some act of Love's bound to reherse,	93	F1 Why write no	1
I thought to binde him, in my verse:	93	F1 Why write no	2
Can Poets hope to fetter mee?	93	F1 Why write no	4
To Penshurst.	93	F2 Penshurst	Ttl
Thou art not, Penshurst, built to envious show,	93	F2 Penshurst	1
Thy Mount, to which the Dryads doe resort,	93	F2 Penshurst	10
The lighter Faunes, to reach thy Ladies oke.	94	F2 Penshurst	18
That never failes to serve thee season'd deere,	94	F2 Penshurst	20
The lower land, that to the river bends,	94	F2 Penshurst	22
To crowne thy open table, doth provide	94	F2 Penshurst	27
And, for thy messe, is willing to be kill'd.	94	F2 Penshurst	30
And pikes, now weary their owne kinde to eat,	94	F2 Penshurst	34
As loth, the second draught, or cast to stay,	94	F2 Penshurst	35
And no one empty-handed, to salute	95	F2 Penshurst	49
This way to husbands; and whose baskets beare	95	F2 Penshurst	55
Adde to thy free provisions, farre above	95	F2 Penshurst	58
Where comes no guest, but is allow'd to eate,	95	F2 Penshurst	61
And I not faine to sit (as some, this day,	95	F2 Penshurst	65
To entertayne them; or the countrey came,	95	F2 Penshurst	80
With all their zeale, to warme their welcome here.	95	F2 Penshurst	81
To have her linnen, plate, and all things nigh,	96	F2 Penshurst	86
Each morne, and even, they are taught to pray,	96	F2 Penshurst	95
To Sir Robert Wroth.	96	F3 Wroth	Ttl
To Sir Robert Wroth in praise of a Country life. Epode.	96	F3 Wroth	VTtl
Nor com'st to view the better cloth of state;	96	F3 Wroth	7
Nor throng'st (when masquing is) to have a sight	96	F3 Wroth	9
Nor throng'st (where masquing is) to have a sight	96	F3 Wroth	V 9
To view the jewells, stuffes, the paines, the wit	97	F3 Wroth	11
To some coole, courteous shade, which he calls his,	97	F3 Wroth	19
Or, if thou list the night in watch to breake,	97	F3 Wroth	21
To the full greatnesse of the cry:	97	F3 Wroth	32
Nor how to get the lawyer fees.	98	F3 Wroth	62
Strive, Wroth, to live long innocent.	98	F3 Wroth	66
Strive, Wroth, to be long innocent.	98	F3 Wroth	V 66
To blow up orphanes, widdowes, and their states;	99	F3 Wroth	79
By being organes to great sinne,	99	F3 Wroth	86
Get place, and honor, and be glad to keepe	99	F3 Wroth	87
Get place, and honor, and be proud to keepe	99	F3 Wroth	V 87
To him, man's dearer, then t'himselfe.	99	F3 Wroth	96
Be thankes to him, and earnest prayer, to finde	99	F3 Wroth	101
Is thankes to him, and earnest prayer, to finde	99	F3 Wroth	V101
To doe thy countrey service, thy selfe right;	100	F3 Wroth	103
To the World. A farewell for a Gentle-woman, ...	100	F4 To the World	Ttl
A spirit so resolv'd to tread	100	F4 To the World	6
And all thy good is to be sold.	100	F4 To the World	16
To take the weake, or make them stop:	100	F4 To the World	19
With all my powers, my selfe to loose?	101	F4 To the World	28
More hatred, then thou hast to love.	101	F4 To the World	40
That, what to all may happen here,	101	F4 To the World	55
If't chance to me, I must not grutch.	101	F4 To the World	56
To harbour a divided thought	101	F4 To the World	58
To age, misfortune, sicknesse, griefe:	102	F4 To the World	62
Song. To Celia.	102	F5 Celia 1	Ttl
'Tis no sinne, loves fruit to steale,	102	F5 Celia 1	15
But the sweet theft to reveale:	102	F5 Celia 1	16
To be taken, to be seene,	102	F5 Celia 1	17
To the same.	103	F6 Celia 2	Ttl
How to tell' hem, as they flow,	103	F6 Celia 2	20
Seeme to flye it, it will pursue:	104	F7 Women but	2
To Sicknesse.	104	F8 Sicknesse	Ttl
To Sicknesse. Ode Anacreon:	104	F8 Sicknesse	VTtl
To thy altars, by their nights	104	F8 Sicknesse	4
To become thy sacrifice.	105	F8 Sicknesse	28
That, to make all pleasure theirs,	105	F8 Sicknesse	36
Every stew in towne to know;	105	F8 Sicknesse	38
Every Cranck in towne to know;	105	F8 Sicknesse	V 38
Dare entayle their loves to any,	105	F8 Sicknesse	V 39
In thy justice to molest	106	F8 Sicknesse	47
Song. To Celia.	106	F9 Celia 3	Ttl
To his Mistress	106	F9 Celia 3	VTtl
Drinke to me, onely, with thine eyes,	106	F9 Celia 3	1
Drinke to me, Coelia, with thine eyes,	106	F9 Celia 3	V 1
I sent to thee a rosie wreath,	106	F9 Celia 3	V 9
Not so to honor thee,	106	F9 Celia 3	V 10
And sent'st it backe to mee:	106	F9 Celia 3	14
For the more countenance to my active Muse?	107	F10 Proludium	3
For the more countenance to our active Muse?	107	F10 Proludium	V 3
And foundred thy hot teame, to tune my lay.	107	F10 Proludium	9
And foundred thy hot teame, to tune our lay.	107	F10 Proludium	V 9
To raise my spirits with thy conjuring wine,	107	F10 Proludium	11
To raise our spirits with thy conjuring wine,	107	F10 Proludium	V 11
Turne the stale prologue to some painted maske,	107	F10 Proludium	20
And now an Epode to deepe eares I sing.	108	F10 Proludium	30

	Page	Title	Line
TO (cont.)			
And now an Epode to deepe eares we sing.	108	F10 Proludium	V 30
to loose, and Cap'ring, for thy stricter veyne.	108	F10 Proludium	2
Then, leave these lighter numbers, to light braines	108	F10 Proludium	7
Such, as in lustes wilde forrest love to rainge,	108	F10 Proludium	9
which rap's mee up to the true heav'en of love;	108	F10 Proludium	13
and now an Epode, to deepe Eares, wee singe.	108	F10 Proludium	16
Not to know vice at all, and keepe true state,	109	F11 Epode	1
Next, to that vertue, is to know vice well,	109	F11 Epode	3
Which to effect (since no brest is so sure,	109	F11 Epode	5
Of thoughts to watch, and ward	109	F11 Epode	8
To wakefull reason, our affections king:	109	F11 Epode	13
To make our sense our slave.	109	F11 Epode	18
(That should ring larum to the heart) doth sleepe,	109	F11 Epode	23
(That shal ring larum to the heart) doth sleepe,	109	F11 Epode	V 23
The first; as prone to move	110	F11 Epode	32
To murther different hearts,	110	F11 Epode	52
A fixed thought, an eye un-taught to glance;	111	F11 Epode	61
And turne the blackest sorrowes to bright joyes:	112	F11 Epode	95
Who could be false to? chiefly, when he knowes	112	F11 Epode	103
Who would be false to? chiefly, when he knowes	112	F11 Epode	V103
Would not be fearefull to offend a dame	112	F11 Epode	109
(To vertuous moods inclin'd)	112	F11 Epode	112
And to his sense object this sentence ever,	113	F11 Epode	115
Epistle To Elizabeth Countesse of Rutland.	113	F12 Rutland	Ttl
To the Countesse of Rutland: An Elegie.	113	F12 Rutland	VTtl
That which, to boote with hell, is thought worth heaven,	113	F12 Rutland	3
To every squire, or groome, that will report	113	F12 Rutland	6
To every squire, or groome, that can report	113	F12 Rutland	V 6
Just to the waight their this dayes-presents beare;	113	F12 Rutland	8
And some one apteth to be trusted, then,	113	F12 Rutland	10
I, that have none (to send you) send you verse.	113	F12 Rutland	19
When gold was made no weapon to cut throtes,	114	F12 Rutland	23
Or put to flight Astrea, when her ingots	114	F12 Rutland	24
Then, here, to give pride fame, and peasants birth.	114	F12 Rutland	26
Were it to thinke, that you should not inherit	114	F12 Rutland	32
Worth an estate, treble to that you have.	114	F12 Rutland	36
It is the Muse, alone, can raise to heaven,	114	F12 Rutland	41
That had no Muse to make their fame abide.	114	F12 Rutland	48
That Homer brought to Troy; yet none so live:	115	F12 Rutland	55
To my lesse sanguine Muse, wherein she'hath wonne	115	F12 Rutland	72
To her remembrance; which when time shall bring	115	F12 Rutland	75
To curious light, the notes, I then shall sing,	115	F12 Rutland	76
To curious light, to notes, I then shall sing,	115	F12 Rutland	V 76
Will prove old Orpheus act no tale to be:	115	F12 Rutland	77
Will prove old Orpheus Arts no tale to be:	115	F12 Rutland	V 77
And show, how, to the life, my soule presents	115	F12 Rutland	86
And your brave friend, and mine to well did love.	116	F12 Rutland	V 92
Now thinking on you, though to England lost,	116	F12 Rutland	94
Epistle. To Katherine, Lady Aubigny.	116	F13 Aubigny	Ttl
'Tis growne almost a danger to speake true	116	F13 Aubigny	1
Or feare to draw true lines, 'cause others paint:	117	F13 Aubigny	20
If it may stand with your soft blush to heare	117	F13 Aubigny	22
Remov'd, as you from need to have it such.	117	F13 Aubigny	28
That askes but to be censur'd by the eyes:	117	F13 Aubigny	35
Are you engaged to your happy fate,	118	F13 Aubigny	47
Without companions? 'Tis safe to have none.	118	F13 Aubigny	56
Times, and occasions, to start forth, and seeme)	118	F13 Aubigny	63
Melt downe their husbands land, to poure away	118	F13 Aubigny	73
(They finde it both so wittie, and safe to give.)	118	F13 Aubigny	76
Boast, but how oft they have gone wrong to man:	119	F13 Aubigny	84
You, Madame, yong have learn'd to shunne these shelves,	119	F13 Aubigny	89
To pay your lord the pledges of chast love:	119	F13 Aubigny	96
And raise a noble stemme, to give the fame,	119	F13 Aubigny	97
To Clifton's bloud, that is deny'd their name.	119	F13 Aubigny	98
To crowne the burthen which you goe withall,	119	F13 Aubigny	103
But which the Fates forbid me to reveale.	119	F13 Aubigny	107
But to please him, who is the dearer prise	119	F13 Aubigny	116
Unto himselfe, by being so deare to you.	119	F13 Aubigny	117
Madame, be bold to use this truest glasse:	120	F13 Aubigny	122
Ode. To Sir William Sydney, on his Birth-day.	120	F14 Sydney	Ttl
That I may tell to Sydney, what	120	F14 Sydney	12
Doth urge him to runne wrong, or to stand still.	121	F14 Sydney	30
To live untill to morrow' hath lost two dayes.	121	F14 Sydney	50
To Heaven.	122	F15 Heaven	Ttl
To ought but grace, or ayme at other end.	122	F15 Heaven	8
As thou art all, so be thou all to mee,	122	F15 Heaven	9
And whither rap'd, now thou but stoup'st to mee?	122	F15 Heaven	14
How can I doubt to finde thee ever, here?	122	F15 Heaven	16
1. The Sinners Sacrifice. To the Holy Trinitie.	127	U1 Trinitie	Ttl
Helpe, helpe to lift	127	U1 Trinitie	4
My selfe up to thee, harrow'd, torne, and bruis'd	127	U1 Trinitie	5
But 'bove the fat of rammes, or bulls, to prize	127	U1 Trinitie	11
To thee more sweet?	127	U1 Trinitie	16
To worship thee.	127	U1 Trinitie	20
To take our nature; becam'st man, and dyd'st,	128	U1 Trinitie	22
To pay our debts, upon thy Crosse, and cryd'st,	128	U1 Trinitie	23
A Trinitie, to shine in Union;	128	U1 Trinitie	34
One God to see,	128	U1 Trinitie	40
To heare, to mediate, sweeten my desire,	128	U1 Trinitie	42
Among thy Saints elected to abide,	128	U1 Trinitie	45
2. A Hymne to God the Father.	129	U1 Father	Ttl
Beene sterne to mee,	129	U1 Father	8

			Page	Title		Line
TO (cont.)						
To free a slave,			129	U1 Father		20
As sure to win			130	U1 Father		31
I Sing the birth, was borne to night,			130	U1 Nativitie		1
To make us heires of glory!			130	U1 Nativitie		21
To see this Babe, all innocence;			130	U1 Nativitie		22
First, prepare you to be sorie,			131	U2 Excuse		14
Either whom to love, or how:			131	U2 Excuse		16
Here's a shaft, thou art to slow!			132	U2 How he saw		10
Could be brought once back to looke.			132	U2 How he saw		19
And the Bow: with thought to hit			132	U2 How he saw		22
She content was to restore			133	U2 Suffered		3
Eyes and limbes; to hurt me more.			133	U2 Suffered		4
Reconcil'd to Love, and me.			133	U2 Suffered		6
At her hand, with oath, to make			133	U2 Suffered		10
And (to gaine her by his Art)			133	U2 Suffered		15
Which when she beheld to bleed,			133	U2 Suffered		17
Is, that I have leave to speake,			133	U2 Suffered		22
To revenge me with my Tongue,			133	U2 Suffered		24
That they still were to run by her side,			134	U2 Triumph		9
As alone there triumphs to the life			134	U2 Triumph		19
Where he chanc't your name to see			136	U2 Cupid		8
Set, and to this softer straine;			136	U2 Cupid		9
Of her face, and made to rise,			136	U2 Cupid		15
To my shafts! Her very Name,			137	U2 Cupid		37
Call to mind the formes, that strove			137	U2 Cupid		46
And her Jewels, to the view			138	U2 Kisse		11
Of the Court, to day, then all			138	U2 Kisse		15
Wisht the Bride were chang'd to night,			138	U2 Kisse		18
To no other Grace but you!			138	U2 Kisse		20
Or, if you did move to night			138	U2 Kisse		21
So to see a Lady tread,			138	U2 Kisse		25
To be envi'd of the Queene.			138	U2 Kisse		28
To himselfe his losse of Time;			138	U2 Kisse		31
To have left all sight for you:			138	U2 Kisse		33
Here's none to spie, or see;			139	U2 Another		3
What w'are but once to doe, we should doe long.			139	U2 Another		12
Joyne lip to lip, and try:			139	U2 Another		15
To fetch in the Formes goe by:			140	U2 Promise		18
To say over every purle			140	U2 Promise		23
There; or to reforme a curle;			140	U2 Promise		24
To consult, if Fucus this			140	U2 Promise		26
Of your Trouble, Ben, to ease me,			140	U2 Her man		1
French to boote, at least in fashion,			141	U2 Her man		7
Young Il'd have him to, and faire,			141	U2 Her man		9
And so thin, to see a blush			141	U2 Her man		28
'Twere to long, to speake of all:			141	U2 Her man		33
Well he should his clothes to weare;			141	U2 Her man		36
Yet no Taylor help to make him;			141	U2 Her man		37
Bounteous as the clouds to earth;			142	U2 Her man		43
All his actions to be such,			142	U2 Her man		45
As to doe no thing too much.			142	U2 Her man		46
And from basenesse to be free,			142	U2 Her man		51
To stay the running floods,			143	U3 Musicall		10
To make the Mountaine Quarries move,			143	U3 Musicall		11
To fall againe; at such a feast,			144	U3 Musicall		23
To meet their high desire;			144	U3 Musicall		26
To make us still sing o're, and o're,			145	U5 Woman-kind		3
To make a new, and hang that by.			145	U5 Woman-kind		18
We were not bred to sit on stooles,			146	U6 Defence		3
Our proper vertue is to range;			146	U6 Defence		4
Nor is't inconstancie to change			146	U6 Defence		13
For what is better, or to make			146	U6 Defence		14
To love one man, hee'd leave her first.			146	U6 Defence		24
As it would be to each a fame:			148	U7 Nymph		34
Turn'd to cinders by her eye?			149	U8 Houre-glasse		8
To have't exprest,			149	U8 Houre-glasse		10
I'm sure my language to her, was as sweet,			149	U9 Picture		6
I'm sure my language to her, is as sweet,			149	U9 Picture	V	6
How cam'st thou thus to enter me?			150	U10 Jealousie		2
To vent that poore desire,			150	U10 Jealousie		5
Thou sai'st, thou only cam'st to prove			150	U10 Jealousie		10
Seeke doubting Men to please,			150	U10 Jealousie		15
I ne're will owe my health to a disease.			150	U10 Jealousie		16
I am undone to night;			150	U11 Dreame		3
But leaves me to inquire,			151	U11 Dreame		10
To license ever was so light,			152	U12 Corbet		25
As twice to trespasse in his sight,			152	U12 Corbet		26
For truly, since he left to be,			152	U12 Corbet		35
An Epistle to Sir Edward Sacvile, now Earle of Dorset.			153	U13 Sacvile		Ttl
If, Sackvile, all that have the power to doe			153	U13 Sacvile		1
To succour my necessities, tooke fire,			153	U13 Sacvile		8
The way to meet, what others would upbraid;			153	U13 Sacvile		10
And though my fortune humble me, to take			153	U13 Sacvile		15
To have such doe me good, I durst not name:			153	U13 Sacvile		18
Or if he did it not to succour me,			154	U13 Sacvile		29
But by meere Chance? for interest? or to free			154	U13 Sacvile		30
His Groomes to witnesse; or else lets it fall			154	U13 Sacvile		36
Nought but in corners; and is loath to leave,			154	U13 Sacvile		44
For what they streight would to the world forsweare;			154	U13 Sacvile		50
But then, fist-fill'd, to put me off the sent.			154	U13 Sacvile		52
Dam's whom he damn'd to, as the veriest Gull.			154	U13 Sacvile		57
Ha's Feathers, and will serve a man to pull.			154	U13 Sacvile		58

TO (cont.)
  Are they not worthy to be answer'd so, ...   154   U13 Sacvile   59
  That to such Natures let their full hands flow,   .   .   .   154   U13 Sacvile   60
  And seeke not wants to succour: but enquire,   .   .   .   155   U13 Sacvile   61
  Their bounties forth, to him that last was made,   .   .   .   155   U13 Sacvile   63
  Or stands to be'n Commission o' the blade?   .   .   .   155   U13 Sacvile   64
  Their thoughts and meanes to making loude the cry; .   .   .   155   U13 Sacvile   66
  Then give it to the hound that did him bite;   .   .   .   155   U13 Sacvile   70
  Pardon, sayes he, that were a way to see   155   U13 Sacvile   71
  I not deny it, but to helpe the need   155   U13 Sacvile   75
  Man out their Boates to th' Temple, and not shift   .   .   .   155   U13 Sacvile   83
  Such worship due to kicking of a Punck!   .   .   .   155   U13 Sacvile   93
  That men such reverence to such actions show!   156   U13 Sacvile   98
  And you, Sir, know it well, to whom I write,   .   .   .   156   U13 Sacvile   109
  I have the lyst of mine owne faults to know,   .   .   .   156   U13 Sacvile   114
  Looke to and cure; Hee's not a man hath none,   .   .   .   156   U13 Sacvile   115
  But like to be, that every day mends one, ...   156   U13 Sacvile   116
  Sydney e're night! or that did goe to bed   .   .   .   157   U13 Sacvile   127
  Are nothing till that comes to bind and shut.   .   .   .   157   U13 Sacvile   138
  Meet some new matter to looke up and wonder!   .   .   .   157   U13 Sacvile   142
  Nor fashion; if they chance aspire to height,   .   .   .   157   U13 Sacvile   148
  For me to be your Indice. Keep you such,   .   .   .   157   U13 Sacvile   156
  By thanking thus the curtesie to life,   .   .   .   158   U13 Sacvile   159
  May grow so great to be example, when   .   .   .   158   U13 Sacvile   161
  Donnor's or Donnee's, to their practise shall   .   .   .   158   U13 Sacvile   163
  Find you to reckon nothing, me owe all.   158   U13 Sacvile   164
  An Epistle to Master John Selden.   158   U14 Selden   Ttl
  Ben: Jonson To His Honord Friend Mr John Selden Health.   . .   158   U14 Selden   VTtl
  I Know to whom I write. Here, I am sure, ...   158   U14 Selden   1
  To aske it: though in most of workes it be   158   U14 Selden   7
  But I to yours, farre from this fault, shall doo;   .   .   .   159   U14 Selden   V 17
  But 'twas with purpose to have made them such.   .   .   .   159   U14 Selden   22
  Upon my selfe, and aske to whom? and why?   .   .   .   159   U14 Selden   24
  Which Grace shall I make love to first? your skill, .   .   .   159   U14 Selden   35
  To informe and teach? or your unweary'd paine   .   .   .   159   U14 Selden   V 37
  Of what it tells us) weav'd in to instruct.   .   .   .   160   U14 Selden   52
  To see the workmanship so'xceed the cost!   160   U14 Selden   54
  To marke the excellent seas'ning of your Stile!   .   .   .   160   U14 Selden   55
  But to the Subject, still the Colours fit   160   U14 Selden   58
  In offering this thy worke to no great Name,   .   .   .   161   U14 Selden   69
  But nought beyond. He thou hast given it to,   .   .   .   161   U14 Selden   71
  Thy learned Chamber-fellow, knowes to doe   .   .   .   161   U14 Selden   72
  Humanitie enough to be a friend,   .   .   .   161   U14 Selden   77
  And strength to be a Champion, and defend   161   U14 Selden   78
  But here's no time, nor place, my wealth to tell,   .   .   .   161   U14 Selden   85
  An Epistle to a Friend, to perswade him to the Warres.   . .   162   U15 Friend-Wars Ttl
  All that dare rowse: or are not loth to quit   .   .   .   162   U15 Friend-Wars   3
  It is a call to keepe the spirits alive   162   U15 Friend-Wars   5
  Quickning dead Nature, to her noblest strife.   .   .   .   162   U15 Friend-Wars   8
  To gaine upon his belly; and at last   .   .   .   162   U15 Friend-Wars   17
  Or Feathers: lay his fortune out to show,   .   .   .   162   U15 Friend-Wars   21
  But there are objects, bid him to be gone   .   .   .   163   U15 Friend-Wars   28
  Not to be checkt, or frighted now with fate,   .   .   .   163   U15 Friend-Wars   35
  To make up Greatnesse! and mans whole good fix'd   .   .   .   163   U15 Friend-Wars   44
  To have his Court-bred-fillie there commend   .   .   .   163   U15 Friend-Wars   48
  Of lust, to his rich Suit and Title, Lord?   .   .   .   163   U15 Friend-Wars   51
  'Tis there civilitie to be a whore;   163   U15 Friend-Wars   54
  To do't with Cloth, or Stuffes, lusts name might merit; . .   164   U15 Friend-Wars   57
  To see 'hem aye discoursing with their Glasse,   .   .   .   164   U15 Friend-Wars   63
  To catch the flesh in, and to pound a Prick.   .   .   .   164   U15 Friend-Wars   67
  Ready to cast, at one, whose band sits ill,   .   .   .   164   U15 Friend-Wars   69
  To be abroad chanting some baudie song, ...   164   U15 Friend-Wars   74
  Lives to the Lord, but to the Ladies end.   .   .   .   165   U15 Friend-Wars   94
  Lives for the Lord, but to the Ladies end.   .   .   .   165   U15 Friend-Wars V 94
  Ne're came to taste the plenteous Mariage-horne.   .   .   .   165   U15 Friend-Wars 100
  For man to spend his money on? his wit?   .   .   .   165   U15 Friend-Wars 102
  His body to the Counters, or the Fleete?   .   .   .   165   U15 Friend-Wars 105
  His body to the compters, or the Fleete?   .   .   .   165   U15 Friend-Wars V105
  To teach each suit he has, the ready way   165   U15 Friend-Wars 108
  From Hide-Parke, to the Stage, where at the last   .   .   .   165   U15 Friend-Wars 109
  What honour given to the drunkennest Guests?   .   .   .   166   U15 Friend-Wars 118
  What reputation to beare one Glasse more?   166   U15 Friend-Wars 119
  Is not enough now, but the Nights to play: .   .   .   166   U15 Friend-Wars 132
  To take the box up for him; and pursues   166   U15 Friend-Wars 137
  The Dice with glassen eyes, to the glad viewes   .   .   .   166   U15 Friend-Wars 138
  The Dice with glassen eyes, to the glad Viewers   .   .   .   166   U15 Friend-Wars V138
  To be beholders, when their powers are spent.   .   .   .   166   U15 Friend-Wars 140
  To lose the formes, and dignities of men,   .   .   .   166   U15 Friend-Wars 146
  To flatter my good Lord, and cry his Bowle   .   .   .   167   U15 Friend-Wars 147
  Although, perhaps it has, what's that to me,   .   .   .   167   U15 Friend-Wars 149
  But he that's both, and slave to boote, shall live, .   .   .   167   U15 Friend-Wars 160
  But he that's both, and slave to both, shall live, .   .   .   167   U15 Friend-Wars V160
  Spread through the World) is easier farre to find, .   .   .   167   U15 Friend-Wars 172
  Then once to number, or bring forth to hand,   .   .   .   167   U15 Friend-Wars 173
  That fortune never make thee to complaine,   .   .   .   168   U15 Friend-Wars 183
  And from that thought strive to be understood.   .   .   .   168   U15 Friend-Wars 188
  And if I had no more to say, ...   168   U16 Gray   2
  Epistle To a Friend.   169   U17 Friend-Debt Ttl
  Can Beautie that did prompt me first to write,   .   .   .   169   U18 Elegy Can   1
  Did her perfections call me on to gaze,   .   .   .   169   U18 Elegy Can   3
  Except the way be errour to those ends: .   .   .   170   U18 Elegy Can   13
  Oh how a Lover may mistake! to thinke, ...   170   U18 Elegy Can   15
  To see men feare: or else for truth, and State,   .   .   .   170   U18 Elegy Can   17

TO (cont.)
Be brought by us to meet our Destinie.   170   U18 Elegy Can   20
Love to my heart, and Fortune to my lines.   170   U18 Elegy Can   24
Love lights his torches to inflame desires;   170   U19 Elegy By   2
To use the present, then, is not abuse,   171   U19 Elegy By   21
As would make shift, to make himselfe alone,   171   U19 Elegy By   24
Is constant to be extraordinarie.   171   U19 Elegy By   28
At fifty yeares, almost, to value it,   171   U20 Shrub   5
That ne're was knowne to last above a fit!   171   U20 Shrub   6
Doe not you aske to know her, she is worse   172   U20 Shrub   17
Aske not to know this Man. If fame should speake   172   U21 Ltl Shrub   1
Two letters were enough the plague to teare   172   U21 Ltl Shrub   3
And so I leave to stirre him, lest he stinke.   172   U21 Ltl Shrub   10
This subjects you to love of one.   173   U22 Elegy Tho   8
The noblest freedome, not to chuse   173   U22 Elegy Tho   11
By whom he is restor'd to men: 173   U22 Elegy Tho   15
To whom all Lovers are design'd,   173   U22 Elegy Tho   26
To light upon a Love of mine.   173   U22 Elegy Tho   32
Appeare, and that to shortest view,   174   U22 Elegy Tho   32
What I, in her, am griev'd to want.   174   U22 Elegy Tho   34
An Ode. To himselfe.   174   U23 Himselfe   Ttl
To see their Seats and Bowers by chattring Pies defac't?   174   U23 Himselfe   12
'Tis crowne enough to vertue still, her owne applause.   174   U23 Himselfe   18
To give the world againe: 175   U23 Himselfe   29
To that strumpet the Stage,   175   U23 Himselfe   34
The mind of the Frontispice to a Booke.   175   U24 Frontispice Ttl
Raising the World to good or evill fame,   175   U24 Frontispice   3
Doth vindicate it to eternitie.   175   U24 Frontispice   4
An Ode to James Earle of Desmond, writ . . .   176   U25 Desmond   Ttl
To towre with my intention   176   U25 Desmond   4
My bolder numbers to thy golden Lyre: 177   U25 Desmond   9
My flowing numbers to thy golden Lyre: 177   U25 Desmond   V 9
May shine (through every chincke) to every sight   177   U25 Desmond   16
If subject to the jealous errors   177   U25 Desmond   28
Is but a Statists theame, to read Phlebotomie.   179   U25 Desmond   39
Pyracmon's houre will come to give them ease,   179   U25 Desmond   42
No Armour to the mind! he is shot-free   179   U25 Desmond   48
But to your selfe, most loyal Lord,   179   U25 Desmond   53
I send nor Balmes, nor Cor'sives to your wound,   180   U26 Ode High   2
A gentler, and more agile hand, to tend   180   U26 Ode High   4
To doe, then be a husband of that store.   180   U26 Ode High   18
For men to use their fortune reverently,   181   U26 Ode High   23
Lie drawne to life, in his soft Verse,   181   U27 Ode Helen   7
Rap't from the Earth, as not to die?   181   U27 Ode Helen   14
A Sonnet, to the noble Lady, the Lady Mary Worth.   182   U28 Worth   Ttl
Nor is my Muse, or I asham'd to owe it   182   U28 Worth   5
To those true numerous Graces; whereof some,   182   U28 Worth   6
His very eyes are yours to overthrow.   182   U28 Worth   11
To the ground.   183   U29 Fit of Rime   9
So to see the Fountaine drie,   183   U29 Fit of Rime 22
To restore   184   U29 Fit of Rime 39
Phoebus to his Crowne againe;   184   U29 Fit of Rime 40
And the Muses to their braine;   184   U29 Fit of Rime 41
Clos'd to their peace, he saw his branches shoot,   185   U30 Burleigh   9
An Epigram. To Thomas Lo: Elsmere, . . .   185   U31 Elsmere   Ttl
Lawes; and no change e're come to one decree: 185   U31 Elsmere   2
Law, to his Law; and thinke your enemies his: 185   U31 Elsmere   4
So, from all sicknesse, may you rise to health,   186   U31 Elsmere   5
Another to him.   186   U32 Elsmere   Ttl
Then to make falshood blush, and fraud afraid: 186   U32 Elsmere   4
Such shall you heare to day, and find great foes,   186   U32 Elsmere   7
Both arm'd with wealth, and slander to oppose,   186   U32 Elsmere   8
When this appeares, just Lord, to your sharp sight,   186   U32 Elsmere   15
He do's you wrong, that craves you to doe right.   186   U32 Elsmere   16
An Epigram to the Councellour that pleaded, . . .   186   U33 Councellour Ttl
Of hirelings, wranglers, stitchers-to of strife,   187   U33 Councellour   8
To the Wolves studie, or Dogs eloquence;   187   U33 Councellour 12
Have made me to conceive a Lawyer new.   187   U33 Councellour 14
Mak'st it religion to grow rich by Crimes!   187   U33 Councellour 16
Or skill, to carry out an evill cause!   187   U33 Councellour 18
Thou prov'st the gentler wayes, to clense the wound,   187   U33 Councellour 20
Thou hast the brave scorne, to put back the fee!   187   U33 Councellour 22
Arm'd at all peeces, as to keepe a Fort   187   U33 Councellour 30
An Epigram. To the small Poxe.   188   U34 Small Poxe Ttl
Was drawne to practise other hue, then that   188   U34 Small Poxe   8
Spanish receipt, to make her teeth to rot.   188   U34 Small Poxe   12
Of Beautie, so to nullifie a face,   188   U34 Small Poxe   14
To fetch the flesh, we keepe the Rowle.   188   U35 Chute   6
A Sparke to set whole worlds a-fire,   189   U36 Song   9
And have their being, their waste to see;   189   U36 Song   11
An Epistle to a friend.   189   U37 Friend-Book Ttl
Sir, I am thankfull, first, to heaven, for you;   189   U37 Friend-Book   1
Next to your selfe, for making your love true: 189   U37 Friend-Book   2
Then to your love, and gift. And all's but due.   189   U37 Friend-Book   3
In letters, that mixe spirits, thus to weave.   190   U37 Friend-Book   12
And Fame wake for me, when I yeeld to sleepe.   190   U37 Friend-Book   15
And seeke to scant her comelie libertie,   190   U37 Friend-Book   20
And lesse they know, who being free to use   190   U37 Friend-Book   22
In practiz'd friendship wholly to reprove,   190   U37 Friend-Book   26
As flatt'ry with friends humours still to move.   190   U37 Friend-Book   27
From each of which I labour to be free,   190   U37 Friend-Book   28
But shall sometimes be tempted to obey   190   U37 Friend-Book   32
Her furie, yet no friendship to betray.   190   U37 Friend-Book   33

TO (cont.)

	Page	Title	Line
This sadnesse makes no approaches, but to kill.	191	U38 Elegy 'Tis	4
And drives it in to eat on my offence,	191	U38 Elegy 'Tis	6
Or there to sterve it. Helpe, O you that may	191	U38 Elegy 'Tis	7
That you should be too noble to destroy.	191	U38 Elegy 'Tis	12
In will and power, only to defeat.	191	U38 Elegy 'Tis	18
God, and the good, know to forgive, and save.	191	U38 Elegy 'Tis	19
I will not stand to justifie my fault,	191	U38 Elegy 'Tis	21
Or goe about to countenance the vice,	191	U38 Elegy 'Tis	24
No, I will stand arraign'd, and cast, to be	191	U38 Elegy 'Tis	27
There greatnesse takes a glorie to relieve.	192	U38 Elegy 'Tis	34
Doe not despaire my mending; to distrust	192	U38 Elegy 'Tis	49
That were to wither all, and make a Grave	192	U38 Elegy 'Tis	59
Her order is to cherish, and preserve,	192	U38 Elegy 'Tis	61
Consumptions nature to destroy, and sterve.	192	U38 Elegy 'Tis	62
But to exact againe what once is given,	192	U38 Elegy 'Tis	63
That makes us live, not that which calls to die.	193	U38 Elegy 'Tis	78
The contrite Soule, who hath no thought to win	193	U38 Elegy 'Tis	89
Upon the hope to have another sin	193	U38 Elegy 'Tis	90
Rather then once displease you more, to die,	193	U38 Elegy 'Tis	92
To suffer tortures, scorne, and Infamie,	193	U38 Elegy 'Tis	93
To carry noble danger in the face:	194	U38 Elegy 'Tis	102
I will no more abuse my vowes to you,	194	U38 Elegy 'Tis	107
Then I will studie falshood, to be true.	194	U38 Elegy 'Tis	108
Publike affaires command me now to goe	194	U38 Elegy 'Tis	114
To put all relish from my memorie	197	U40 Elegy That	6
Of parting, drowne it in the hope to meet	197	U40 Elegy That	7
And must be bred, so to conceale his birth,	197	U40 Elegy That	17
In all his Actions rarified to spright;	197	U40 Elegy That	20
To others, as he will deserve the Trust	198	U40 Elegy That	39
Due to that one, that doth believe him just.	198	U40 Elegy That	40
And such your Servant is, who vowes to keepe	198	U40 Elegy That	41
(Made to blow up loves secrets) to discover	198	U40 Elegy That	47
Which in assurance to your brest I tell,	198	U40 Elegy That	49
What fate is this, to change mens dayes and houres,	199	U41 Elegy Since	9
To shift their seasons, and destroy their powers!	199	U41 Elegy Since	10
As if it were not worthy to be there:	199	U41 Elegy Since	16
Who shall forbid me then in Rithme to bee	200	U42 Elegy Let	5
So to be sure you doe injoy your selves.	200	U42 Elegy Let	24
That quilts those bodies, I have leave to span:	200	U42 Elegy Let	32
Of love, and hate: and came so nigh to know	200	U42 Elegy Let	35
To doe her Husbands rites in, e're 'twere gone	201	U42 Elegy Let	40
Home to the Customer: his Letcherie	201	U42 Elegy Let	41
Being, the best clothes still to praeoccupie.	201	U42 Elegy Let	42
To ev'ry Petticote he brush'd, and Glove	201	U42 Elegy Let	54
Thou didst tell me; and wert o're-joy'd to peepe	201	U42 Elegy Let	59
Had he had the facultie to reade, and write!	201	U42 Elegy Let	64
That chanc'd the lace, laid on a Smock, to see,	201	U42 Elegy Let	66
And why to me this, thou lame Lord of fire,	202	U43 Vulcan	1
And why to me this, thou lame god of fire,	202	U43 Vulcan V	1
Or urge thy Greedie flame, thus to devoure	202	U43 Vulcan	3
Or beg thy Greedie flame, thus to devoure	202	U43 Vulcan V	3
Nor made least line of love to thy loose Wife;	203	U43 Vulcan	6
By Jove to have Minerva for thy Bride,	203	U43 Vulcan	12
To ruine any issue of the braine?	203	U43 Vulcan	14
To ruine every issue of her braine?	203	U43 Vulcan V	14
Perhaps, to have beene burned with my bookes.	203	U43 Vulcan	18
Conceal'd, or kept there, that was fit to be,	203	U43 Vulcan	21
By thy owne vote, a sacrifice to thee?	203	U43 Vulcan	22
Itch to defame the State? or brand the Times?	203	U43 Vulcan	25
Fitter to see the fire-light, then the day;	204	U43 Vulcan	44
To light Tobacco, or save roasted Geese,	205	U43 Vulcan	52
To light Tobacco, or have roasted Geese,	205	U43 Vulcan V	52
Condemn'd me to the Ovens with the pies;	205	U43 Vulcan	54
Condemn'd them to the Ovens with the pies;	205	U43 Vulcan V	54
To make consumption, ever, where thou go'st;	205	U43 Vulcan	58
To make consumption, every where thou go'st;	205	U43 Vulcan V	58
To sow consumption, every where thou go'st;	205	U43 Vulcan V	58
To make propter viam, ever, where thou go'st;	205	U43 Vulcan V	58
To redeeme mine, I had sent in; Enough,	205	U43 Vulcan	63
To Merlins Marvailes, and his Caballs losse,	206	U43 Vulcan	71
To Martins Marvailes, and his Caballs losse,	206	U43 Vulcan V	71
These, had'st thou pleas'd either to dine, or sup,	206	U43 Vulcan	83
These, had'st thou been pleas'd either to dine, or sup,	206	U43 Vulcan V	83
Had made a meale for Vulcan to lick up.	206	U43 Vulcan	84
Had bin fitt meate for Vulcan to lick up.	206	U43 Vulcan V	84
But in my Deske, what was there to accite	206	U43 Vulcan	85
But in my Deske, what was there to envite	206	U43 Vulcan V	85
To teach some that, their Nurses could not doe,	207	U43 Vulcan	92
To teach some what, their Nurses could not doe,	207	U43 Vulcan V	92
To speake the fate of the Sicilian Maid	207	U43 Vulcan	96
To our owne Ladyes; and in storie there	207	U43 Vulcan	97
Whom Faction had not drawne to studie sides.	207	U43 Vulcan	104
Whom fashion had not drawne to studie sides.	207	U43 Vulcan V104	
Whom Faction had not taught to studie sides.	207	U43 Vulcan V104	
I now begin to doubt, if ever Grace,	207	U43 Vulcan	107
Thou woo Minerva! or to wit aspire!	208	U43 Vulcan	109
May to thy name a Vulcanale say;	208	U43 Vulcan	120
May to thy name a Pagan prayer say;	208	U43 Vulcan V120	
Against thy furie, when to serve their needs,	208	U43 Vulcan	125
And safely trust to dresse, not burne their Boates.	208	U43 Vulcan	128
(Which, some are pleas'd to stile but thy madde pranck)	208	U43 Vulcan	131
Left! and wit since to cover it with Tiles.	209	U43 Vulcan	138

715

	Page	Title	Line
TO (cont.)			
And cry'd, it was a threatning to the beares;	209	U43 Vulcan	146
And sayd twas sure a threatning to the beares;	209	U43 Vulcan	V146
And cry'd 'Twas verily a threatning to the beares;	209	U43 Vulcan	V146
Nay, let White-Hall with Revels have to doe,	210	U43 Vulcan	156
Scarce let White-Hall with Revels have to doe,	210	U43 Vulcan	V156
Did not she save from thence, to build a Rome?	210	U43 Vulcan	162
For they were burnt, but to be better built.	210	U43 Vulcan	166
Will be remembred by Six Clerkes, to one.	210	U43 Vulcan	172
But to confine him to the Brew-houses,	211	U43 Vulcan	179
To live in Sea-coale, and goe forth in smoake;	211	U43 Vulcan	181
To live in Sea-coale, and goe out in smoake;	211	U43 Vulcan	V181
Condemne him to the Brick-kills, or some Hill-/foot	211	U43 Vulcan	183
Condemne him to the Brick-hills, or some Hill-/foot	211	U43 Vulcan	V183
Condemne him to the Brick-kills, or a forge	211	U43 Vulcan	V183
Hill-/foot (out in Sussex) to an iron Mill;	211	U43 Vulcan	184
Hill-/foot (out in Sussex) to some iron Mill;	211	U43 Vulcan	V184
Burne to a snuffe, and then stinke out, and die:	211	U43 Vulcan	188
wast to a snuffe, and then stinke out, and die:	211	U43 Vulcan	V188
To all as fatall as't hath beene to me,	211	U43 Vulcan	192
To all as chargefull as they have beene to me,	211	U43 Vulcan	V192
And to Pauls-Steeple; which was unto us	211	U43 Vulcan	193
A speach according to Horace.	213	U44 Speach	Ttl
Lent by the London Dames, to the Lords men;	213	U44 Speach	14
To see the Pride at Court, their Wives doe make:	213	U44 Speach	16
To have their Husbands drawne forth to the field,	213	U44 Speach	18
And comming home, to tell what acts were done	213	U44 Speach	19
Powder, or paper, to bring up the youth	213	U44 Speach	25
But give them over to the common eare	214	U44 Speach	31
Supplant bold Panton; and brought there to view	214	U44 Speach	34
Translated Aelian tactickes to be read,	214	U44 Speach	35
So, in that ground, as soone it grew to be	214	U44 Speach	37
So acted to the life, as Maurice might,	214	U44 Speach	41
Come to their Schooles,) show 'hem the use of Guns;	214	U44 Speach	58
But he that should perswade, to have this done	214	U44 Speach	61
Are we by Booke-wormes to be awde? must we	215	U44 Speach	67
Why aré we rich, or great, except to show	215	U44 Speach	69
More then to praise a Dog? or Horse? or speake	215	U44 Speach	71
The Hawking language? or our Day to breake	215	U44 Speach	72
Their Sonnes to studie Arts, the Lawes, the Creed:	215	U44 Speach	74
To serve the State by Councels, and by Armes:	215	U44 Speach	85
What, to make legs? yes, and to smell most sweet,	215	U44 Speach	90
This, and that box his Beautie to repaire;	215	U44 Speach	96
Her broken Armes up, to their emptie moulds.	216	U44 Speach	102
An Epistle to Master Arth: Squib.	216	U45 Squib	Ttl
That hearkens to a Jacks-pulse, when it goes.	216	U45 Squib	6
Nor ever trusted to that friendship yet,	216	U45 Squib	7
Friend to himselfe, that would be friend to thee.	216	U45 Squib	22
Desired Justice to the publique Weale,	217	U46 Coke	16
Or if Chance must, to each man that doth rise,	217	U46 Coke	23
Needs lend an aide, to thine she had her eyes.	217	U46 Coke	24
An Epistle answering to one that asked . . .	218	U47 Tribe	Ttl
To speake my selfe too ambitiously,	218	U47 Tribe	6
And shewing so weake an Act to vulgar eyes,	218	U47 Tribe	7
Put conscience and my right to compromise.	218	U47 Tribe	8
Subject to quarrell only; or else such	218	U47 Tribe	11
That to speake well, thinke it above all sinne,	218	U47 Tribe	19
Call every night to Supper in these fitts,	218	U47 Tribe	21
To vent their Libels, and to issue rimes,	218	U47 Tribe	26
Of newes they get, to strew out the long meale,	218	U47 Tribe	28
What is't to me whether the French Designe	219	U47 Tribe	31
Be, or be not, to get the Val-telline?	219	U47 Tribe	32
Or the States Ships sent forth belike to meet	219	U47 Tribe	33
To live, or fall a Carkasse in the cause.	219	U47 Tribe	42
Although my Fame, to his, not under-heares,	219	U47 Tribe	49
Well, with mine owne fraile Pitcher, what to doe	219	U47 Tribe	56
Live to that point I will, for which I am man,	219	U47 Tribe	59
Still looking to, and ever loving heaven;	219	U47 Tribe	61
As but to stumble in her sight were shame;	220	U47 Tribe	70
And free it from all question to preserve.	220	U47 Tribe	72
I would call mine, to which not many Staires	220	U47 Tribe	74
Are asked to climbe. First give me faith, who know	220	U47 Tribe	75
The Dedication of the Kings new Cellar. to Bacchus.	220	U48 Bacchus	Ttl
Of Wines, to thee the rather	220	U48 Bacchus	2
Of all to the great Master.	220	U48 Bacchus	8
To give mankind their eases,	221	U48 Bacchus	23
To put his Court in dances,	222	U48 Bacchus	50
To Church, as others doe to Feasts and Playes,	222	U49 Pucell	16
To shew their Tires? to view, and to be view'd?	222	U49 Pucell	17
And spangled Petticotes brought forth to eye,	223	U49 Pucell	19
To stuffes and Laces, those my Man can buy.	223	U49 Pucell	28
To his poore Instrument, now out of grace.	223	U49 Pucell	34
You cling to Lords, and Lords, if them you leave	223	U49 Pucell	38
This Age would lend no faith to Dorrels Deed;	223	U49 Pucell	42
An Epigram. To the honour'd ——— Countesse of ———	224	U50 Countesse	Ttl
To conquer rumour, and triumph on spight;	224	U50 Countesse	4
Not only shunning by your act, to doe	224	U50 Countesse	5
No friend to vertue, could be silent here.	224	U50 Countesse	8
And though all praise bring nothing to your name,	224	U50 Countesse	13
A cheerefull worke to all good eyes, to see	224	U50 Countesse	16
So great a Vertue stand upright to view,	224	U50 Countesse	19
Whilst your Ulisses hath ta'ne leave to goe,	224	U50 Countesse	21
Countries, and Climes, manners, and men to know.	224	U50 Countesse	22

		Page	Title	Line

TO   (cont.)

	Page	Title	Line
Searching for knowledge, and to keepe your mind	225	U50 Countesse	29
As they are hard, for them to make their owne,	225	U50 Countesse	33
So are they profitable to be knowne:	225	U50 Countesse	34
Sonne to the grave wise Keeper of the Seale,	225	U51 Bacon	9
Now with a Title more to the Degree;	225	U51 Bacon	12
In his soft Cradle to his Fathers Chaire,	225	U51 Bacon	14
My Answer. The Poet to the Painter.	226	U52 Answer	Ttl
To square my Circle, I confesse; but draw	227	U52 Answer	8
To be describ'd by a Monogram,	227	U52 Answer	11
But whilst you curious were to have it be	227	U52 Answer	13
An Archetype, for all the world to see,	227	U52 Answer	14
To all posteritie; I will write Burlase.	227	U52 Answer	24
An Epigram. To William, Earle of Newcastle.	228	U53 Newcastle	Ttl
To the Right Honorable William Viscount Mansfield:	228	U53 Newcastle	VTtl
To all the uses of the field, and race,	228	U53 Newcastle	3
As I began to wish my selfe a horse,	228	U53 Newcastle	12
I look'd for Hercules to be the Groome:	228	U53 Newcastle	18
Epistle To Mr. Arthur Squib.	229	U54 Squib	Ttl
I Am to dine, Friend, where I must be weigh'd	229	U54 Squib	1
And hold me to it close; to stand upright	229	U54 Squib	9
But rather with advantage to be found	229	U54 Squib	11
And then to be return'd; on protestation	229	U54 Squib	18
To goe out after—till when take this letter	229	U54 Squib	19
To Mr. John Burges.	229	U55 Burges	Ttl
Then would I promise here to give	229	U55 Burges	3
Epistle. To my Lady Covell.	230	U56 Covell	Ttl
A booke to a few lynes: but, it was fit	230	U56 Covell	3
His friends, but to breake Chaires, or cracke a Coach.	230	U56 Covell	10
To make you merry on the Dressing stoole	230	U56 Covell	21
A mornings, and at afternoones, to foole	230	U56 Covell	22
Your Joane to passe her melancholie time.	231	U56 Covell	24
Cary to passe her melancholie time.	231	U56 Covell	V 24
I can lose none in tendring these to you.	231	U56 Covell	28
I gaine, in having leave to keepe my Day,	231	U56 Covell	29
And should grow rich, had I much more to pay.	231	U56 Covell	30
And should grow rich, if I had more to pay.	231	U56 Covell	V 30
To Master John Burges.	231	U57 Burges	Ttl
To Sir Robert Pie:	231	U57 Burges	4
To send my Debentur.	231	U57 Burges	6
To take Apprehension	231	U57 Burges	11
Will come to the Table,	232	U57 Burges	23
Or Wine to enable	232	U57 Burges	24
Nor any quick-warming-pan helpe him to bed,	232	U57 Burges	27
Epigram, to my Book-seller.	232	U58 Book-seller	Ttl
If his wit reach no higher, but to spring	232	U58 Book-seller	7
Will be reward enough: to weare like those,	232	U58 Book-seller	9
An Epigram. To William Earle of Newcastle.	232	U59 Newcastle	Ttl
To the Right Honorable William Earle of Newcastle.	232	U59 Newcastle	VTtl
Of making just approaches, how to kill,	232	U59 Newcastle	4
To hit in angles, and to clash with time:	232	U59 Newcastle	5
This were a spectacle! A sight to draw	233	U59 Newcastle	13
Wonder to Valour! No, it is the Law	233	U59 Newcastle	14
Of daring, not to doe a wrong, is true	233	U59 Newcastle	15
Valour! to sleight it, being done to you!	233	U59 Newcastle	16
To know the heads of danger! where 'tis fit	233	U59 Newcastle	17
To bend, to breake, provoke, or suffer it!	233	U59 Newcastle	18
To bend, or breake, provoke, or suffer it!	233	U59 Newcastle	V 18
An Epitaph, on Henry L. La-ware. To the Passer-by.	233	U60 La-ware	Ttl
Ambition to become a Starre,	234	U60 La-ware	14
That spread his body o're, to kill:	234	U60 La-ware	16
To lift to heaven: who is't not understands	234	U61 Epigram	8
To see you set apart, thus, from the rest,	234	U61 Epigram	10
And wee doe weepe, to water, for our sinne.	234	U61 Epigram	15
To teach the people, how to fast, and pray,	235	U61 Epigram	18
And doe their penance, to avert Gods rod,	235	U61 Epigram	19
An Epigram. To K. Charles for a 100. Pounds	235	U62 Charles 1	Ttl
Annexed to thy Person, and thy place,	235	U62 Charles 1	2
To cure the call'd Kings Evill with thy touch;	235	U62 Charles 1	4
To cure the Poets Evill, Povertie:	235	U62 Charles 1	6
Nay, and in this, thou show'st to value more	235	U62 Charles 1	9
O pietie! so to weigh the poores estates!	235	U62 Charles 1	11
O bountie! so to difference the rates!	235	U62 Charles 1	12
To K. Charles, and Q. Mary. For the losse of their	235	U63 Charles 2	Ttl
To God, denies the God-head to be true:	235	U63 Charles 2	2
That the Almighties will to you is such:	236	U63 Charles 2	8
An Epigram. To our great and good K. Charles	236	U64 Charles 3	Ttl
To the great and Gratious King Charles.	236	U64 Charles 3	VTtl
Then now, to love the Soveraigne, and the Lawes?	236	U64 Charles 3	8
Then now, to love the Soveraigne, or his Lawes?	236	U64 Charles 3	V 8
And what are bounds to her, you make your owne?	236	U64 Charles 3	10
That Faith, which she professeth to be pure?	236	U64 Charles 3	12
How much to heaven for thee, great Charles, they owe!	237	U64 Charles 3	22
What Month then May, was fitter to disclose	237	U65 Prince	4
Thee quickly come the gardens eye to bee,	238	U65 Prince	8
And there to stand so. Hast now envious Moone,	238	U65 Prince	9
And still to stand so. Hast thou envious Moone,	238	U65 Prince	V 9
An Epigram to the Queene, then lying in. 1630.	238	U66 Queene	Ttl
An Epigram to the Queens Health.	238	U66 Queene	VTtl
And by an Angell, to the blessed'st Maid,	238	U66 Queene	2
Haile Mary, full of honours, to my Queene,	238	U66 Queene	5
So generall a gladnesse to an Isle,	238	U66 Queene	9
To make the hearts of a whole Nation smile,	238	U66 Queene	10

	Page	Title	Line

TO (cont.)

	Page	Title	Line
To compare small with great, as still we owe	238	U66 Queene	12
Glorie to God. Then, Haile to Mary! spring	238	U66 Queene	13
Our thanks to God. Then, Haile to Mary! spring	238	U66 Queene	V 13
Of so much safetie to the Realme, and King.	238	U66 Queene	14
Of so much health, both to our Land, and King.	238	U66 Queene	V 14
To the Queene on her Birth-day	239	U67 Muses	VTtl
Be silent, to the people	239	U67 Muses	5
And Gunnes there, spare to poure	239	U67 Muses	8
As fearfull to awake	239	U67 Muses	10
This Citie, or to shake	239	U67 Muses	11
The Citie, as to shake	239	U67 Muses	V 11
And Sister to just Lewis!	240	U67 Muses	27
An Epigram, To the House-hold. 1630.	241	U68 House-hold	Ttl
For want of knowing the Poet, to say him nay?	241	U68 House-hold	4
His Poet leave to sing his House-hold true;	241	U68 House-hold	6
Would make the very Greene-cloth to looke blew:	241	U68 House-hold	8
So, the allowance from the King to use,	241	U68 House-hold	10
Epigram. To a Friend, and Sonne.	241	U69 Friend Son	Ttl
To mee; or beene the same to you; if show,	241	U69 Friend Son	2
What, by that name, wee each to other owe,	241	U69 Friend Son	4
To keepe him off; and how-so-e're he gleanes	242	U69 Friend Son	16
To judge; So all men comming neere can spie,	242	U69 Friend Son	20
Then knew the former ages: yet to life,	242	U69 Friend Son	23
Never so great to get them: and the ends,	242	U69 Friend Son	25
Rather to boast rich hangings, then rare friends.	242	U69 Friend Son	26
To the immortall memorie, and friendship of that noble	242	U70 Ode	Ttl
To Sir Lucius Carey, on the death of his Brother Morison	242	U70 Ode	VTtl
But ever to no ends:	243	U70 Ode	29
To sordid flatteries, acts of strife,	244	U70 Ode	39
Hee stood, a Souldier to the last right end,	244	U70 Ode	45
To swell thine age;	244	U70 Ode	56
To shew thou hast beene long,	245	U70 Ode	58
To light: her measures are, how well	245	U70 Ode	62
To fall a logge at last, dry, bald, and seare:	245	U70 Ode	68
To see that bright eternall Day:	245	U70 Ode	81
Himselfe to rest,	246	U70 Ode	86
To have exprest,	246	U70 Ode	88
(Were not his Lucius long with us to tarry)	246	U70 Ode	91
To separate these twi-/Lights	246	U70 Ode	92
This made you first to know the Why	247	U70 Ode	107
You lik'd, then after, to apply	247	U70 Ode	108
You liv'd to be the great surnames,	247	U70 Ode	113
Was left yet to Man-kind;	247	U70 Ode	121
To the Right Honourable, the Lord high Treasurer of	248	U71 Treasurer	Ttl
To my Lord Weston, Lo: Treasurer. A Letter	248	U71 Treasurer	VTtl
Are faine to seeke for succours, and supplies	248	U71 Treasurer	2
Fix'd to the bed, and boords, unlike to win	248	U71 Treasurer	11
Fix'd to the bed, and borde, and like to win	248	U71 Treasurer	V 11
Dare thinke it, to relieve, no lesse renowne,	248	U71 Treasurer	14
To the King. On his Birth-day	249	U72 King	Ttl
Unto the Ships, and they from tier, to tier,	249	U72 King	2
Adding her owne glad accents, to this Day,	249	U72 King	7
Adding her owne greate accents, to this Day,	249	U72 King	V 7
Still to have such a Charles, but this Charles long.	249	U72 King	18
. . . made Earle of Portland. 17. Febr. 1632. To the Envious.	250	U73 Weston	Ttl
Thy faint, and narrow eyes, to reade the King	250	U73 Weston	2
Hath rais'd to be the Port unto his Land!	250	U73 Weston	4
To vertue, and true worth, be ever blind.	250	U73 Weston	10
To the Right Hon'ble Hierome, L. Weston. An Ode	250	U74 Weston	Ttl
With love, to heare your modestie relate,	251	U74 Weston	21
Both to the honour of the King and State.	251	U74 Weston	24
To see great Charles of Travaile eas'd,	251	U74 Weston	26
To be a shadow to his Heire,	251	U74 Weston	29
And both a strength, and Beautie to his Land!	251	U74 Weston	30
Betweene thy Tropicks, to arrest thy sight,	252	U75 Epithalam.	4
Then thou shalt see to day:	252	U75 Epithalam.	5
From Greenwich, hither, to Row-hampton gate!	252	U75 Epithalam.	12
As they came all to see, and to be seene!	253	U75 Epithalam.	20
To welcome home a Paire, and deck the nuptiall bower?	253	U75 Epithalam.	24
To doe their Offices in Natures Chime,	253	U75 Epithalam.	27
On all that come her Simplesse to rebuke!	253	U75 Epithalam.	44
To make more cleare	254	U75 Epithalam.	54
Of Sex, to rob the Creature; but from Man	255	U75 Epithalam.	82
With Angels, Muse, to speake these: Nothing can	255	U75 Epithalam.	84
Themselves to day,	255	U75 Epithalam.	86
Be duly done to those	255	U75 Epithalam.	93
To give a greater Name, and Title to! Their owne!	255	U75 Epithalam.	96
Great Say-Master of State, who not to erre,	255	U75 Epithalam.	V 99
Of Tryals, to worke downe	255	U75 Epithalam.	103
Mens Loves unto the Lawes, and Lawes to love the Crowne.	255	U75 Epithalam.	104
To pay, with honours, to his noble Sonne	256	U75 Epithalam.	106
To day, the Fathers service; who could bring	256	U75 Epithalam.	107
Him up, to doe the same himselfe had done.	256	U75 Epithalam.	108
To th' dull, a Spur	256	U75 Epithalam.	118
It is: to th' envious meant,	256	U75 Epithalam.	119
And Bishop stay, to consummate the Rites:	256	U75 Epithalam.	122
Which to this use, wert built and consecrate!	256	U75 Epithalam.	130
To have thy God to blesse, thy King to grace,	256	U75 Epithalam.	131
With all corroding Arts, be able to untie!	257	U75 Epithalam.	136
Doe long to make themselves, so, another way:	257	U75 Epithalam.	140
To them of kind,	257	U75 Epithalam.	142
One to the other, long e're these to light were brought.	257	U75 Epithalam.	144

718

10 (cont.)

	Page	Title		Line
To propagate their Names,	257	U75	Epithalam.	149
Till you behold a race to fill your Hall,	258	U75	Epithalam.	169
A Kate, a Frank, to honour their Grand-dames,	258	U75	Epithalam.	172
Peepe forth a Gemme; to see	258	U75	Epithalam.	175
To be a watchfull Servant for this State;	258	U75	Epithalam.	178
They both are slip'd to Bed; Shut fast the Doore,	258	U75	Epithalam.	185
Exacts then she is pleas'd to pay: no suits,	258	U75	Epithalam.	188
To the Kings Most Excellent Majesty	259	U76	Petition	VTtl
To Th'Best Of Monarchs, Masters, Men, King Charles	259	U76	Petition	2
To your Majestie your Poet:	259	U76	Petition	4
Of his speciall grace to Letters,	259	U76	Petition	7
To make all the Muses debters	259	U76	Petition	8
To his bountie; by extension	259	U76	Petition	9
To his bountie; by dimension	259	U76	Petition	V 9
To his Poet of a Pension,	259	U76	Petition	V 10
To be given me in gratuitie	259	U76	Petition	12
For done service, and to come:	259	U76	Petition	13
For done service, or to come:	259	U76	Petition	V 13
When their pot-guns ayme to hit,	259	U76	Petition	21
When their pot-guns thinke to fitt,	259	U76	Petition	V 21
Please your Majestie to make	260	U76	Petition	25
To eate a Snake, in his next Song.	260	U76	Petition	V 32
To the right Honourable, the Lord Treasurer of England.	260	U77	Treasurer	Ttl
If to my mind, great Lord, I had a state,	260	U77	Treasurer	1
Have left in fame to equall, or out-goe	260	U77	Treasurer	8
To compose men, and manners; stint the strife	261	U77	Treasurer	18
To Compasse men, and manners; stint the strife	261	U77	Treasurer	V 18
What worlds of blessings to good Kings they owe:	261	U77	Treasurer	20
An Epigram To my Muse, the Lady Digby,	262	U78	Digby	Ttl
To Sir Kenelme Digby. An Epigram	262	U78	Digby	VTtl
For that to dwell in, and be still at home.	262	U78	Digby	8
For those to dwell in, and be still at home.	262	U78	Digby	V 8
As other soules, to his, dwell in a Lane:	262	U78	Digby	12
That day, which I predestin'd am to sing,	262	U78	Digby	V 17
Which I have vow'd posteritie to give.	262	U78	Digby	18
For Brittains honour, and to Charles my King:	262	U78	Digby	V 18
Good Omen to him, in the note thou sing'st,	263	U78	Digby	22
Good fortune to him, in the note thou sing'st,	263	U78	Digby	V 22
Upon them, (next to Spenser's noble booke,)	263	U78	Digby	24
What reputation to my lines, and me,	263	U78	Digby	26
Being sent to one, they will be read of all.	263	U78	Digby	32
A New-yeares gift Sung to King Charles, 1635.	263	U79	New-yeares	Ttl
Lute, Lyre, Theorbo, all are call'd to day.	263	U79	New-yeares	2
To shew the rites, and t'usher forth the way	263	U79	New-yeares	4
To fit the softnesse of our Yeares-gift: when	263	U79	New-yeares	6
To day old Janus opens the new yeare,	263	U79	New-yeares	9
To him we owe all profits of our grounds.	264	U79	New-yeares	15
That drives the Hart to seeke unused wayes,	264	U79	New-yeares	21
To better Pastures then great Pales can:	264	U79	New-yeares	30
Of all that Nature, yet, to life did bring;	264	U79	New-yeares	33
Shee, to the Crowne, hath brought encrease.	264	U79	New-yeares	41
To whom you owe all duties of your grounds;	265	U79	New-yeares	49
To sweeter Pastures lead hee can,	265	U79	New-yeares	60
To My L. the King, On the Christning His second Sonne James.	268	U80	Christning	Ttl
Great aides to Empire, as they are great care	268	U80	Christning	6
To pious parents, who would have their blood	268	U80	Christning	7
Hayles me, so solemnly, to yonder Yewgh?	268	U81	Pawlet	2
To pluck a Garland, for her selfe, or mee?	268	U81	Pawlet	4
To give your shade a name! Stay, stay, I feele	269	U81	Pawlet	7
To give your shade a lasting name! Stay, stay, I feele	269	U81	Pawlet	V 7
At least may beare th'inscription to her Tombe.	269	U81	Pawlet	18
And voyce to raise them from my brazen Lungs,	269	U81	Pawlet	24
It is too neere of kin to Heaven, the Soule,	269	U81	Pawlet	29
It is too neere of kin to God, the Soule,	269	U81	Pawlet	V 29
To be describ'd! Fames fingers are too foule	269	U81	Pawlet	30
To touch these Mysteries! We may admire	269	U81	Pawlet	31
To touch those Mysteries! We may admire	269	U81	Pawlet	V 31
And, calling truth to witnesse, make that good	270	U81	Pawlet	35
And, calling truth to witnesse, make it good	270	U81	Pawlet	V 35
Could summe to a perfection, was her Act!	270	U81	Pawlet	46
Could heap to a perfection, was her Act!	270	U81	Pawlet	V 46
And to the Torturers (her Doctors) say,	270	U81	Pawlet	52
Your hottest Causticks to, burne, lance, or cut:	270	U81	Pawlet	54
Your hotter Causticks to, burne, lance, or cut:	270	U81	Pawlet	V 54
Chear'd her faire Sisters in her race to runne!	270	U81	Pawlet	58
Made her friends joyes to get above their feares!	270	U81	Pawlet	60
With admiration, and applause to die!	270	U81	Pawlet	62
Her spirit home, to her originall!	270	U81	Pawlet	64
To carry, and conduct the Complement	270	U81	Pawlet	66
Became her Birth-day to Eternitie!	271	U81	Pawlet	68
To every Order, ev'ry Hierarchie!	271	U81	Pawlet	72
Which they that have the Crowne are sure to know!	271	U81	Pawlet	76
Which the Elect of God are sure to know!	271	U81	Pawlet	V 76
At pleasure, to be call'd for, every day!	271	U81	Pawlet	82
And see all dead here, or about to dye!	271	U81	Pawlet	86
When we were all borne, we began to die;	271	U81	Pawlet	94
Eupheme; Or, The Faire Fame Left To Posteritie	272	U84	Eupheme	Ttl
Faire Fame, who art ordain'd to crowne	272	U84	Cradle	1
Of Goodnesse still: Vouchsafe to take	273	U84	Cradle	9
Thereof, to Time.	273	U84	Cradle	12
As prop'rest gifts, to Girles, and Boyes,	273	U84	Cradle	19
And Call to the high Parliament	273	U84	Cradle	30

	Page	Title	Line

TO (cont.)

	Page	Title	Line
Who claimes (of reverence) to be heard,	274	U84 Cradle	34
To chant her 'gree,	274	U84 Cradle	36
By Jacobs Ladder, to the top	274	U84 Cradle	38
And Stanley, to the which shee was Co-heire.	274	U84 Cradle	38
Of the first Lupus, to the Familie	274	U84 Descent	6
Sitting, and ready to be drawne,	274	U84 Descent	17
Send these suspected helpes, to aide	275	U84 Body	1
Needs nought to cloath it but the ayre.	275	U84 Body	5
Yet something, to the Painters view,	275	U84 Body	8
And, out of that, make Day to breake;	275	U84 Body	9
To draw a thing that cannot sit.	276	U84 Body	14
You could make shift to paint an Eye,	277	U84 Mind	8
No, to expresse a Mind to sense,	278	U84 Mind	9
No, to expresse this Mind to sense,	278	U84 Mind	13
But what's of kinne to whence it came.	278	U84 Mind	V 13
Of grace, and Musique to the eare,	278	U84 Mind	16
It selfe to us, and come so nigh	279	U84 Mind	35
Up to her owne sublimed hight?	279	U84 Mind	43
Where it may run to any good?	279	U84 Mind	48
To Kenelme, John, George.	280	U84 Mind	62
'Twill be but faire, to leane upon their Fames;	281	U84 Kenelme	Ttl
It is a wretched thing to trust to reedes;	281	U84 Kenelme	13
Up to their Ancestors; the rivers side,	281	U84 Kenelme	16
. . . gave me leave to call her so. Being Her . . .	281	U84 Kenelme	18
To hang a window, or make darke the roome,	282	U84 Muse	Ttl
A sorrow in me, fit to wait to her!	282	U84 Muse	7
And saw that portion of her selfe to die.	282	U84 Muse	10
With all her aydes, to save her from the seize	282	U84 Muse	14
Beene trusted to thee: not to't selfe assign'd.	283	U84 Muse	17
The world to ruine with it; in her Fall,	283	U84 Muse	20
Thou hast no more blowes, Fate, to drive at one:	283	U84 Muse	25
Whoorles me about, and to blaspheme in fashion!	283	U84 Muse	27
To 'greet, or grieve her soft Euthanasee?	283	U84 Muse	32
So sweetly taken to the Court of blisse,	283	U84 Muse	40
Indeed, she is not dead! but laid to sleepe	283	U84 Muse	41
To heare their Judge, and his eternall doome;	283	U84 Muse	45
To have that finall retribution,	283	U84 Muse	48
Must come to take a sentence, by the sense	283	U84 Muse	49
T'accuse, or quit all Parties to be heard!	284	U84 Muse	57
O Day of joy, and suretie to the just!	284	U84 Muse	60
To Body, and Soule! where Love is all the guest!	284	U84 Muse	61
Presume to interpell that fulnesse, when	284	U84 Muse	64
Hee knowes, what worke h'hath done, to call this Guest,	284	U84 Muse	70
Out of her noble body, to this Feast:	284	U84 Muse	81
And give her place, according to her blood,	284	U84 Muse	82
A new Song to his praise, and great I Am:	284	U84 Muse	83
To have her captiv'd spirit freed from flesh,	285	U84 Muse	90
Thither, you hope to come; and there to find	285	U84 Muse	93
But all of God; They still shall have to say,	285	U84 Muse	103
Where Hee will be, all Beautie to the Sight;	286	U84 Muse	119
And to the Touch, a Flower, like soft as Palme.	286	U84 Muse	122
The vision of our Saviour, face to face,	286	U84 Muse	126
In his humanitie! To heare him preach	286	U84 Muse	132
The price of our Redemption, and to teach	286	U84 Muse	133
To style us Friends, who were, by Nature, Foes?	286	U84 Muse	134
B'imputed right to an inheritance	286	U84 Muse	139
And to that forme, lent two such veines of blood	286	U84 Muse	144
To one she said, Doe this, he did it; So	287	U84 Muse	157
To another, Move; he went; To a third, Go,	287	U84 Muse	169
So charitable, to religious end,	287	U84 Muse	170
She spent more time in teares her selfe to dresse	287	U84 Muse	176
To cloath the naked, feed the hungry. Shee	287	U84 Muse	180
Poring, as on a Map, to find the wayes	288	U84 Muse	194
To that eternall Rest, where now sh'hath place	288	U84 Muse	196
Suffring, and dying to redeeme our losse!	288	U84 Muse	197
To justifie, and quicken us in breath!	288	U84 Muse	202
Shee saw him too, in glory to ascend	288	U84 Muse	204
To him should be her Judge, true God, true Man,	288	U84 Muse	205
Of lapsed Nature) best know what to doe,	288	U84 Muse	211
Hath given wholly to the Sonne (the rather	288	U84 Muse	214
As being the Sonne of Man) to shew his Power,	288	U84 Muse	216
Of all are dead to life! His Wisdome show	288	U84 Muse	217
And giving dues to all Mankinds deserts!	289	U84 Muse	221
To publish her a Saint. My Muse is gone.	289	U84 Muse	224
And all invite to easie sleepe.	289	U84 Muse	228
But if, to boot with these, a chaste Wife meet	290	U85 Country	28
To deck the hallow'd Harth with old wood fir'd	291	U85 Country	39
To view the weary Oxen draw, with bare	291	U85 Country	43
To turne mere farmer, had spoke out,	291	U85 Country	63
Ode the first. The fourth Booke. To Venus.	291	U85 Country	68
To bend a man, now at his fiftieth yeare	292	U86 Hor.4:1	Ttl
More timely hie thee to the house,	292	U86 Hor.4:1	6
If a fit livor thou dost seeke to toast;	292	U86 Hor.4:1	9
Shall Verse be set to Harpe and Lute,	292	U86 Hor.4:1	12
Nor care I now healths to propound;	292	U86 Hor.4:1	23
Or with fresh flowers to girt my temple round.	293	U86 Hor.4:1	31
Ode IX. 3 Booke, to Lydia. Dialogue of Horace, and Lydia.	293	U86 Hor.4:1	32
As, for her, I'ld not feare to die,	293	U87 Hor.3:9	Ttl
And us dis-joyn'd force to her brazen yoke,	293	U87 Hor.3:9	11
And to left-Lydia, now the gate stood ope.	294	U87 Hor.3:9	18
Yet would I wish to love, live, die with thee.	294	U87 Hor.3:9	20
Like lustfull beasts, that onely know to doe it:	294	U87 Hor.3:9	24
	294	U88 Petronius	4

```
                                                    Page    Title         Line
TO  (cont.)
  Thou worthy in eternall Flower to fare,      .   .   .   294   U89 Mart.8:77     2
  Will to bee, what thou art; and nothing more: .  .   .   295   U90 Mart.10:47   12
  . . . the Art of Poetry to the Piso's.       .   .   .   338   Horace          VTtl
  If to a Womans head a Painter would          .   .   .   305   Horace             1
  Admitted to the sight, although his friends, "   .   .   305   Horace             6
  But equall power, to Painter, and to Poet,   .   .   .   305   Horace            11
  To gentle: not that we should Serpents see   .   .   .   338   Horace          V 15
  Know'st only well to paint a Cipresse tree.  .   .   .   305   Horace            25
  To paint him, hath by swimming, hopelesse, scap'd, .  305   Horace            27
  The whole fleet wreck'd? a great jarre to be shap'd,  305   Horace            28
  Obscure.  This, striving to run smooth, and flow, .   307   Horace            36
  Obscure. Another striving smooth to runne,   .   .   .   339   Horace      V 37/ 36
  This, seeking, in a various kind, to forme   .   .   .   307   Horace            40
  So he that varying still affects to draw     .   .   .   339   Horace      V 42/ 40
  So, shunning faults, to greater fault doth lead, .    307   Horace            43
  The shunning vice, to greater vice doth lead, .   .   339   Horace      V 45/ 43
  Not to designe the whole.  Should I aspire   .   .   .   307   Horace            49
  To forme a worke, I would no more desire     .   .   .   307   Horace            50
  To frame a worke, I would no more desire     .   .   .   339   Horace      V 52/ 50
  To be that Smith; then live, mark'd one of those, .   307   Horace            51
  To be that fellow, then to be markt out      .   .   .   339   Horace      V 53/ 51
  His choise, who's matter to his power doth reare,  .   339   Horace      V 58/ 56
  His matter to his power, in all he makes,    .   .   .   307   Horace            57
  Or I am much deceiv'd, shall be to place     .   .   .   307   Horace            60
  Invention.  Now, to speake; and then differ  .   .   .   307   Horace            61
  Is now to speak, and even now to differ      .   .   .   339   Horace      V 61
  Till fitter season.  Now, to like of this,   .   .   .   307   Horace            63
  In using also of new words, to be            .   .   .   307   Horace            65
  Right spare, and warie: then thou speak'st to mee .   307   Horace            66
  Faine words, unheard of to the well-truss'd race .    309   Horace            71
  Faine words, unheard of to the girded race   .   .   .   340   Horace      V 71
  A Roman to Caecilius will allow,             .   .   .   309   Horace            77
  And ever will, to utter termes that bee      .   .   .   309   Horace            84
  Stamp'd to the time.  As woods whose change appeares  309   Horace            85
  Our selves, and all that's ours, to death we owe:  .   309   Horace            90
  His course so hurtfull both to graine, and seedes, .   309   Horace            97
  To chant the Gods, and all their God-like race,  .    311   Horace           114
  Th'Iambick arm'd Archilochus to rave,        .   .   .   311   Horace           117
  As fit t'exchange discourse; a Verse to win  .   .   .   311   Horace           119
  Of popular noyses, borne to actuate things.  .   .   .   341   Horace          V120
  Yet Comick matter shunnes to be exprest      .   .   .   341   Horace      V127/121
  To ignorance still, then either learne, or know?  .   311   Horace           131
  To ignorance still, then yet to learne, or know?  .   341   Horace      V126/131
  And Peleus, if they seeke to heart-strike us  .   .   .   311   Horace           136
  To worke the hearers minds, still, to their plight.   311   Horace           142
  To laughter; so they grieve with those that mone.  .   311   Horace           144
  To every state of fortune; she helpes on,    .   .   .   311   Horace           153
  To every Fortunes habit; she helps on,       .   .   .   342   Horace          V153
  Or urgeth us to anger; and anon              .   .   .   311   Horace           154
  Still to be like himselfe, and hold his worth.   .    313   Horace           182
  'Tis hard, to speake things common, properly:   .    313   Horace           183
  To render word for word: nor with thy sleight   .    313   Horace           191
  Forbids thee forth againe thy foot to draw.  .   .   .   313   Horace           194
  Speake to me, Muse, the Man, who, after Troy was sack't, 315  Horace           201
  Hee thinkes not, how to give you smoake from light, .  315   Horace           203
  He ever hastens to the end, and so           .   .   .   315   Horace           211
  (As if he knew it) rapps his hearer to       .   .   .   315   Horace           212
  Fit rites.  The Child, that now knowes how to say,    315   Horace           225
  Fit dues. The Child, that now knowes how to say,  .   344   Horace          V225
  And can tread firme, longs with like lads to play;    315   Horace           226
  I'the open field; is Waxe like to be wrought  .   .   .   315   Horace           231
  To every vice, as hardly to be brought       "   .   .   315   Horace           232
  To endure counsell: a Provider slow          .   .   .   315   Horace           233
  Of money, haughtie, to desire soon mov'd,    .   .   .   315   Horace           235
  And then as swift to leave what he hath lov'd. .   .   315   Horace           236
  Lookes after honours, and bewares to act     .   .   .   315   Horace           239
  What straight-way he must labour to retract. .   .   .   315   Horace           240
  With sloth, yet greedy still of what's to come:   .    317   Horace           246
  The parts of age to youth be given; or men   .   .   .   317   Horace           252
  To children; we must alwayes dwell, and stay .   .   .   317   Horace           253
  In fitting proper adjuncts to each day.      .   .   .   317   Horace           254
  And the beholder to himselfe doth render.    .   "   .   317   Horace           259
  Yet, to the Stage, at all thou maist not tender  .    317   Horace           260
  Things worthy to be done within, but take    .   .   .   317   Horace           261
  ill-/Natur'd, and wicked Atreus cooke, to th'eye, .    317   Horace           265
  Once seene, to be againe call'd for, and plaid, .   .   317   Horace           271
  To have a God come in; except a knot         .   .   .   317   Horace           273
  Any fourth man, to speake at all, aspire.    .   .   .   317   Horace           275
  Must maintaine manly; not be heard to sing,  .   .   .   317   Horace           277
  Must manly keep, and not be heard to sing    .   .   .   345   Horace          V277
  Then to the purpose leades, and fitly 'grees. .   .   317   Horace           279
  It still must favour good men, and to these  .   .   .   317   Horace           280
  Hide faults, pray to the Gods, and wish aloud .   .   319   Horace           285
  Hide faults, and pray to th'gods, and wish aloud .    345   Horace          V285
  And tune too, fitted to the Chorus rime,     .   .   .   319   Horace           290
  As loud enough to fill the seates, not yet   .   .   .   319   Horace           291
  Chaste, thriftie, modest folke, that came to view.    319   Horace           294
  Clowne, Towns-man, base, and noble, mix'd, to judge?  319   Horace           302
  Thus, to his antient Art the Piper lent      .   .   .   319   Horace           303
  In time to Tragedie, a Musicke new.          .   .   .   319   Horace           306
  To the grave Harp, and Violl voyces new;     .   .   .   346   Horace          V306
  Thespis is said to be the first found out    .   .   .   319   Horace           311
```

TO (cont.)

	Page	Title	Line
The free spectators, subject to no Law,	319	Horace	324
Were to be staid with softnesses, and wonne	321	Horace	326
Yet so the scoffing Satyres to mens view,	321	Horace	328
And so their prating to present was best,	321	Horace	329
And so their pratling to present were best,	346	Horace	V321/329
And so to turne all earnest into jest,	321	Horace	330
And so to turne our earnest into jest,	346	Horace	V322/330
Or Semi-god, that late was seene to weare	321	Horace	332
Or, whilst he shuns the Earth, to catch at Aire	321	Horace	335
And farre unworthy to blurt out light rimes;	321	Horace	337
To Dance, so she should, shamefac'd, differ farre	321	Horace	339
Quite from all face of Tragedie to goe,	321	Horace	344
There comes sometimes to things of meanest place.	321	Horace	354
Him that buyes chiches blanch't, or chance to like	321	Horace	362
To these succeeded the old Comoedie,	321	Horace	365
Her licence fit to be restrain'd by law:	321	Horace	368
Her force was fit to be restrain'd by law:	348	Horace	V402/368
His power of foulely hurting made to cease.	323	Horace	370
But meere Iambicks all, from first to last.	323	Horace	374
The steadie Spondaees; so themselves to beare	323	Horace	377
More slow, and come more weightie to the eare:	323	Horace	378
Provided, ne're to yeeld, in any case	323	Horace	379
Those heavie Verses, sent so to the Stage,	323	Horace	384
To note in Poemes, breach of harmonie:	323	Horace	388
To Roman Poets. Shall I therefore weave	323	Horace	390
And jests; and both to admiration raise	323	Horace	400
And jests; and both to admiration rais'd,	348	Horace	V386/400
To part scurrilitie from wit: or can	323	Horace	403
Nor did they merit the lesse Crowne to weare,	323	Horace	406
In daring to forsake the Grecian tracts,	323	Horace	407
To taxe that Verse, which many a day, and blot	325	Horace	416
Not, ten times o're, corrected to the naile.	325	Horace	418
Their nailes, nor shave their beards, but to by-paths	325	Horace	423
Their Charge, and Office, whence their wealth to fet,	325	Horace	436
Is to be wise; thy matter first to know;	325	Horace	441
What to his Countrey, what his friends he owes,	325	Horace	446
Of a brave Chiefe sent to the warres: He can,	325	Horace	451
Indeed, give fitting dues to every man.	325	Horace	452
But a well-compass'd mouth to utter it;	327	Horace	462
How to divide, into a hundred parts,	327	Horace	465
In juyce of Cedar worthy to be steep'd,	327	Horace	475
And in smooth Cypresse boxes to be keep'd?	327	Horace	476
Was Tigers, said, and Lyons fierce, to tame.	327	Horace	482
Was said to move the stones, by his Lutes powers,	327	Horace	484
Things sacred, from profane to separate;	327	Horace	487
The publike, from the private; to abate	327	Horace	488
To divine Poets, and their Verses came.	327	Horace	492
Their minds to Warres, with rimes they did rehearse;	329	Horace	495
Upon the Lyre, thou chance to be asham'd.	353	Horace	V580/502
Sweet mix'd with sowre, to his Reader, so	329	Horace	515
So he that flaggeth much, becomes to me	329	Horace	533
This saying: To some things there is assign'd	331	Horace	548
Yet, there's a value given to this man.	331	Horace	554
To bettring of the mind of man, in ought,	331	Horace	562
And highest; sinketh to the lowest, and worst.	331	Horace	564
Hee, that not knowes the games, nor how to use	331	Horace	565
Vice, and, am knowne to have a Knights estate.	331	Horace	572
Vice, and is knowne to have a Knights estate.	352	Horace	V548/572
To send it to be judg'd by Metius eare,	331	Horace	576
And, to your Fathers, and to mine; though 't be	331	Horace	577
To change, and mend, what you not forth doe set.	331	Horace	579
Hee, that's ambitious in the race to touch	333	Horace	587
Who, since, to sing the Pythian rites is heard,	333	Horace	591
Who now to sing the Pythian Rites is heard,	353	Horace	V591
But, now, it is enough to say; I make	333	Horace	593
Him that is last, I scorne to come behind,	333	Horace	595
Him that is last, I scorne to be behind,	353	Horace	V595
To say, I'm ignorant. Just as a Crier	333	Horace	597
That to the sale of Wares calls every Buyer;	333	Horace	598
His flatterers to their gaine. But say, he can	333	Horace	601
His praisers to their gaine: but say he can	353	Horace	V601
(Whether yo'are given to, or giver are.)	333	Horace	608
You doe not bring, to judge your Verses, one,	333	Horace	609
As those that hir'd to weepe at Funeralls, swoune,	333	Horace	614
Rich men are said with many cups to plie,	333	Horace	617
Great men are said with many cups to plye,	354	Horace	V617
If to Quintilius, you recited ought:	333	Horace	623
Hee'd bid, blot all: and to the anvile bring	333	Horace	627
Those ill-torn'd Verses, to new hammering.	333	Horace	628
Reprove; and, what is to be changed, note:	335	Horace	638
Dispute; and what is to be changed, note:	354	Horace	V638
The man once mock'd, and suffer'd wrong to tread.	335	Horace	642
And shun to touch him, as a man that were	335	Horace	644
And flye to touch him, as a man that were	354	Horace	V644
According to the Moone. But, then the boyes	335	Horace	647
Busie to catch a Black-bird; if he fall	335	Horace	651
There's none will take the care, to helpe him then;	335	Horace	654
To let it downe, who knowes, if he did cast	335	Horace	656
Hee, while he labour'd to be thought a God	335	Horace	661
To force the grates, that hold him in, would fright	337	Horace	675
All; So this grievous Writer puts to flight	337	Horace	676
weare made the objects to my weaker powers;	361	Palmer	3

TO (cont.)

Whilst other soules convert to base abuse	361	Palmer	11
* * * * When loe to crowne thy worth	361	Palmer	27
In these pide times, only to shewe their braines,	362	Author	4
Where, such perfections to the life doe rise.	362	Author	6
If they seeme wry, to such as looke asquint,	362	Author	7
Wants facultie to make a censure true:	362	Author	11
Seldome descend but bleeding to their grave.	363	Murder	2
Enforcing yron doores to yeeld it way,	363	Riches	9
In thought to praise this Ladie;	365	Ode Splendor	18
Yet shee's nor nice to shew them,	365	Ode Splendor	23
Nor takes she pride to know them.	365	Ode Splendor	24
Smiles in his Sphaere, to see the rest affect,	366	Ode Who saith	13
In vaine to follow:	366	Ode Who saith	14
To brookes, and broader streames,	366	Ode Who saith	23
Nor Sunne could make to vary from the rest,	367	Ode Who saith	29
"For stile of rarenesse, to degenerate.	367	Ode Who saith	32
But prove the Aire, and saile from Coast to Coast:	367	Ode Who saith	37
But first to Cluid stoope low,	367	Ode Who saith	39
To the Eugenian dale;	367	Ode Who saith	43
"Musicke hath power to draw,	367	Ode Who saith	47
With entheate rage, to publish their bright tracts?	368	Ode Who saith	61
To utmost Thule: whence, he backes the Seas	368	Ode Who saith	69
To Caledon,	368	Ode Who saith	70
To Loumond lake, and Twedes blacke-springing fountaine.	368	Ode Who saith	72
Haste, Haste, sweete Singer: Nor to Tine,	368	Ode Who saith	73
But over Land to Trent:	368	Ode Who saith	75
And up againe, in skies, and aire to vent	368	Ode Who saith	77
To hold them here:	368	Ode Who saith	92
To loose that feare;	369	Ode Who saith	94
To him, and he there shrin'd;	369	Ode Who saith	106
To dimme and drowne	369	Ode Who saith	108
Set out a like, or second to our Swan.	369	Ode Who saith	120
To the Author.	370	Author	Ttl
To judge which Passion's false, and which is true,	370	Author	11
To the worthy Author M. John Fletcher.	370	Fletcher	Ttl
Their motives were, since it had not to do	371	Fletcher	9
With vices, which they look'd for, and came to.	371	Fletcher	10
In such a Martirdome; To vexe their eyes,	371	Fletcher	13
A glorified worke to Time, when Fire,	371	Fletcher	15
To fill an Epitaph. But she had more.	371	Epitaph	5
As fit to have encreas'd the harmony	371	Epitaph	8
A Horse here is sadled, but no Tom him to backe,	374	Coryat 1	14
Here, up the Alpes (not so plaine as to Dunstable)	374	Coryat 1	16
Hee's carried like a Cripple, from Constable to Constable.	374	Coryat 1	17
Here, by a Boore too, hee's like to be beaten	375	Coryat 1	24
Here France, and Italy both to him shed	375	Coryat 1	30
To lie at Livory, while the Horses did stand.	375	Coryat 1	33
Beeing in feare to be robd, he most learnedly begs.	375	Coryat 1	35
To the Right Noble Tom, Tell-Troth of his travailes, . . .	378	Coryat 2	Ttl
To be his Bacchus as his Pallas: bee	378	Coryat 2	91
. . . omitted, and now communicated to the World	379	Coryat 3	Ttl
To his strength, hath measur'd it out with his feet.	379	Coryat 3	4
To line out no stride, but pas'd by himselfe?	379	Coryat 3	8
To write it with the selfe same spirit he went,	379	Coryat 3	14
He sayes to the world, let any man mend it,	379	Coryat 3	15
But who will beleeve this, that chanceth to looke	379	Coryat 3	17
There nam'd to be travell'd? For this our Tom saith:	380	Coryat 3	21
That he dares to informe you, but somewhat meticulous,	380	Coryat 3	33
He was in his travaile, how like to be beaten,	380	Coryat 3	35
How faine for his venery he was to crie (Tergum o)	380	Coryat 3	37
That sacred to Odcombe are there now suspended,	380	Coryat 3	40
From Venice to Flushing, were not they well cobled?	380	Coryat 3	42
Of Latine and Greeke, to his friendship. And seven	380	Coryat 3	45
And being at Flushing enforced to feele	380	Coryat 3	54
Poore Tom have we cause to suspect just thee?	381	Coryat 3	58
to tender thus, their lives, their loves, their hartes!	382	Rich	4
To his much and worthily esteemed friend the Author.	383	Author	Ttl
Who takes thy volume to his vertuous hand,	383	Author	1
Must be intended still to understand:	383	Author	2
Who reads, who roaves, who hopes to understand,	383	Author	7
May take thy volume to his vertuous hand.	383	Author	8
To understand, hee may at length admire.	383	Author	10
To the most noble, and above his Titles, . . .	384	Somerset	Ttl
May she, whome thou for spouse, to day, dost take,	384	Somerset	11
And thou to her, that Husband, may exalt	384	Somerset	13
Hymens amends, to make it worth his fault.	384	Somerset	14
To rise with eyther of you, on the morrow.	384	Somerset	16
Yet neyther of you seeme to th'other old.	384	Somerset	24
To his friend the Author upon his Richard.	385	Brooke	Ttl
Or, to so many, and so Broad-seales had,	385	Brooke	3
To such a worke, as could not need theirs? Yet	385	Brooke	5
My suffrage brings thee all increase, to crowne	385	Brooke	7
To the worthy Author on the Husband.	385	Husband	Ttl
To see his worke be good; but that he looke	385	Husband	2
To my truly-belov'd Freind, Mr Browne: on his Pastorals.	386	Browne	Ttl
I find thee write most worthy to be read.	386	Browne	6
Charles Cavendish to his posteritie.	387	Cavendish	Ttl
to which there's no materiall that endures;	387	Cavendish	8
And teach your nephewes it to aemulate:	387	Cavendish	10
it will be matter lowd inoughe to tell	387	Cavendish	11
To my worthy and honour'd Friend, Mr George Chapman, . . .	388	Chapman	Ttl
Whose worke could this be, Chapman, to refine	388	Chapman	1

TO (cont.)

	Page	Title	Line
To make thy honour, and our wealth the more!	388	Chapman	6
To the Greeke coast thine onely knew the way.	388	Chapman	9
To say but one, were single. Then it chimes,	389	Aleman	3
To your desert, who'have done it, Friend. And this	389	Aleman	21
To the Reader.	390	Reader	Ttl
With Nature, to out-doo the life:	390	Reader	4
To the memory of my beloved, the Author . . .	390	Shakespeare	Ttl
To draw no envy (Shakespeare) on thy name,	390	Shakespeare	1
Am I thus ample to thy Booke, and Fame:	390	Shakespeare	2
While I confesse thy writings to be such,	390	Shakespeare	3
And thinke to ruine, where it seem'd to raise.	391	Shakespeare	12
A little further, to make thee a roome:	391	Shakespeare	21
And we have wits to read, and praise to give.	391	Shakespeare	24
From thence to honour thee, I would not seeke	391	Shakespeare	32
Euripides, and Sophocles to us,	391	Shakespeare	34
To life againe, to heare thy Buskin tread,	391	Shakespeare	36
Triumph, my Britaine, thou hast one to showe,	391	Shakespeare	41
To whom all Scenes of Europe homage owe.	391	Shakespeare	42
When like Apollo he came forth to warme	392	Shakespeare	45
Our eares, or like a Mercury to charme!	392	Shakespeare	46
And joy'd to weare the dressing of his lines!	392	Shakespeare	48
Who casts to write a living line, must sweat,	392	Shakespeare	59
(And himselfe with it) that he thinkes to frame;	392	Shakespeare	62
In each of which, he seemes to shake a Lance,	392	Shakespeare	69
To see thee in our waters yet appeare,	392	Shakespeare	72
To the memorye of that most Honoured Ladie Jane, . . .	394	Jane Ogle	Ttl
To see (who'it is?) A noble Countesse, greate,	394	Jane Ogle	3
Nay they will venter ones Descent to hitt,	394	Jane Ogle	11
But, I would have, thee, to know something new,	394	Jane Ogle	13
And her, she made her Inmate, to the End,	394	Jane Ogle	18
To call on Sicknes still, to be her Guest,	394	Jane Ogle	19
So wood at last, that he was wonne to her	394	Jane Ogle	22
To lay her here, inclos'd, his second Bride.	394	Jane Ogle	24
To my chosen Friend, the learned Translator of Lucan, . . .	395	May	Ttl
And the world in it, I begin to doubt,	395	May	4
A Friend at all; or, if at all, to thee:	396	Drayton	2
You have not writ to me, nor I to you;	396	Drayton	6
And, though I now begin, 'tis not to rub	396	Drayton	7
Wonder to truth! and have my Vision hoorld,	396	Drayton	13
I saw a Beauty from the Sea to rise,	396	Drayton	15
Or Rurall Virgil come, to pipe to us!	397	Drayton	28
Like him, to make the ayre, one volary:	397	Drayton	36
Sayst thou so, Lucan? But thou scornst to stay	397	Drayton	47
But that I heare, againe, thy Drum to beate	397	Drayton	55
And when he ships them where to use their Armes,	398	Drayton	65
This booke! it is a Catechisme to fight,	398	Drayton	71
Yet give mee leave, to wonder at the birth	398	Drayton	83
And Gossip-got acquaintance, as, to us	398	Drayton	85
I gratulate it to thee, and thy Ends,	398	Drayton	89
To all thy vertuous, and well chosen Friends,	398	Drayton	90
And, till I worthy am to wish I were,	398	Drayton	92
I call the world, that envies mee, to see	398	Drayton	93
If I can be a Friend, and Friend to thee.	398	Drayton	94
Transmitt it to your Nephewes, Freinds, Allies,	399	Lady Ogle	3
To veiw the truth and owne it. Doe but looke	399	Lady Ogle	5
Upon her selfe) to all her sexe!	399	Lady Ogle	10
To gaine the Crowne of immortalitye,	400	Lady Ogle	34
Seal'd and deliver'd to her, in the sight	400	Lady Ogle	37
When they doe sweat to fortifie a Muse.	400	Beaumont	6
Though I confesse a Beaumonts Booke to bee	400	Beaumont	7
Yet, who dares offer a redoubt to reare?	401	Beaumont	11
To cut a Dike? or sticke a Stake up, here,	401	Beaumont	12
Defies, what's crosse to Piety, or good Fame.	401	Beaumont	20
To my worthy Friend, Master Edward Filmer, . . .	401	Filmer	Ttl
Againe hath brought the Lillie to the Rose;	401	Filmer	8
They are a Schoole to win	402	Filmer	11
The faire French Daughter to learne English in;	402	Filmer	12
From thirty pound in pipkins, to the Man	402	Inigo Jones 1	2
Able to talk of Euclide, and correct	402	Inigo Jones 1	4
To make the Language sweet upon her tongue.	402	Inigo Jones 1	14
What makes your Wretchednes to bray soe loud	403	Inigo Jones 1	23
To hold her up. O Showes! Showes! Mighty Showes!	403	Inigo Jones 1	39
Oh, to make Boardes to speake! There is a taske	404	Inigo Jones 1	49
Pack with your pedling Poetry to the Stage,	404	Inigo Jones 1	51
To plant the Musick where noe eare can reach!	404	Inigo Jones 1	53
To be the Musick Master! Fabler too!	404	Inigo Jones 1	63
To be worth Envy. Henceforth I doe meane	405	Inigo Jones 1	70
To pitty him, as smiling at his Feat	405	Inigo Jones 1	71
Moulded or stroakt up to survey a State!	405	Inigo Jones 1	84
Again, thy Architect to ashes turne!	406	Inigo Jones 1	102
To Inigo Marquess Would Be A Corollary	406	Inigo Jones 2	Ttl
All kings to doe the self same deeds with some!	406	Inigo Jones 2	4
A Noble honest Soule! what's this to thee?	406	Inigo Jones 2	6
He may have skill & judgment to designe	406	Inigo Jones 2	7
He some Colossus to bestryde the Seas,	407	Inigo Jones 2	13
yearly set out there, to sayle downe the Street,	407	Inigo Jones 2	18
Content thee to be Pancridge Earle the whyle;	407	Inigo Jones 2	20
To a Freind an Epigram Of him.	407	Inigo Jones 3	Ttl
(And labours to seem worthy of that feare)	407	Inigo Jones 3	2
Able to eat into his bones & pierce	407	Inigo Jones 3	4
If thou be soe desyrous to be read,	408	Inigo Jones 3	9
Will well designe thee, to be viewd of all	408	Inigo Jones 3	12

724

	Page	Title	Line
TO (cont.)			
To my Detractor.	408	Detractor	Ttl
Is to make cheape, the Lord, the lines, the price.	408	Detractor	6
To be knowne what thou art, a blatant beast,	408	Detractor	9
Thou art not worth it. Who will care to knowe	409	Detractor	13
To aske thy name, if he have half his Nose!	409	Detractor	18
To my old Faithfull Servant: And . . .	409	Brome	Ttl
The Cobler kept him to his nall; but, now	410	Brome	17
To be the Denis of thy Father's School,	410	Gill	7
Thinking to stir me, thou hast lost thy End,	410	Gill	9
A Tune to drown the Ballads of thy Father:	411	Gill	12
For thou hast nought in thee to cure his Fame,	411	Gill	13
A Rogue by Statute, censur'd to be whipt,	411	Gill	15
To Mrs. Alice Sutcliffe, on her divine Meditations.	411	Sutcliffe	Ttl
The motives, and true Spurres to all good Nations.	411	Sutcliffe	5
The Danger of delaying to Repent,	411	Sutcliffe	9
To follow Goodnesse, by our owne discerning	412	Sutcliffe	17
Our great reward, th'aeternall Crown to win.	412	Sutcliffe	19
The gladdest ground to all the numbred-five,	412	Ghyrlond	6
As Love, here studied to keep Grace alive.	412	Ghyrlond	8
To knit thy Crowne, and glorifie the rest.	412	Ghyrlond	12
To top the fairest Lillie, now, that growes,	413	Ghyrlond	15
Inflam'd with ardor to that mystick Shine,	413	Ghyrlond	23
These Mysteries do point to three more great,	413	Ghyrlond	29
Alike of kin, to that most blessed Trine,	413	Ghyrlond	34
And art the spotlesse Mirrour to Mans eyes.	414	Ghyrlond	44
And most to be admired of thy Sexe,	414	Ghyrlond	46
Who like a Giant hasts his course to run,	414	Ghyrlond	51
To my Deare Sonne, and right-learned Friend, . . .	414	Rutter	Ttl
That sit to censure Playes, yet know not when,	414	Rutter	8
Or why to like; they found, it all was new,	415	Rutter	9
Concluded from a Carract to a dramme.	415	Rutter	30
An Epigram To My Joviall Good Freind Mr. Robert Dover,	415	Dover	Ttl
I Cannot bring my Muse to dropp her Vies	415	Dover	1
To Crowne the years, which you begin, great king,	416	Welcome	7
To the wonders of the Peake,	416	Moon	1
I am come to Add, and speake,	416	Moon	2
or as some would say to breake	416	Moon	3
prest in to se you.	416	Moon	8
I had somwhat else to say,	417	Moon	9
To the merry beards in Hall,	417	Moon	13
some tast to send hir.	417	Moon	20
to the Peake it is so hard-by,	417	Moon	23
each to pawne hir husbands capp,	417	Moon	38
that Fortune to imbrace,	419	Ode:If Men	4
Lowd to the wondringe thronge	419	Ode:If Men	7
That hath not Countrye impudence enough to laughe att Arte,	420	Ode:If Men	14
To every sence, and scorne to those that sawe	420	Ode:If Men	17
And rather to the Fyre, then to the Rowte	420	Ode:If Men	21
to gett thee a leane Face,	420	Ode:If Men	25
Uppon soe humbled earth to cast hir eyes:	420	Ode:If Men	30
Give cause to some of wonnder, some despite,	420	Ode:If Men	35
But unto more dispayre to Imitate their sounde.	420	Ode:If Men	36
Whoe worthie wine, whoe not, to bee wyse Pallas guests.	421	Ode:If Men	45
before, I wryte more verse, to bee more wyse.	421	Censure	2
deignes myne the power to find, yett want I will	421	Censure	10
or Malyce to make Faultes, which nowe is skill.	421	Censure	11
and seeke to scant her comelye Libertye,	421	Censure	13
And lesse they knowe, that being free to use	422	Censure	15
in Course of Frindshipp, wholie to reprove:	422	Censure	19
And Flatterye, with Frindes humors: still to move.	422	Censure	20
From each of which, I labor to be free,	422	Censure	21
But sometymes shall bee tempted to obaye	422	Censure	25
if it begyn religious thoughts to cherish;	422	Lucan	10
It is a lycense to doe ill, protectes,	423	Lucan	12
That prince that shames a tyrants name to beare,	423	Lucan	19
To the Oracle of Apollo.	657	Door Apollo	2
To the Oracle of Apollo.	657	Door Apollo	20
to Cynthias fayrest Nymph hath sent thee,	662	Bedford	6
To my worthy, and deserving Brother	666	Glover	1
And to the perpetuating of our freindship	666	Glover	4
To make these good, and what comes after, better.	666	Glover	10
TO'A			
To'a little wealth, and credit in the scene,	45	E56 Poet-Ape	7
Whose dice not doing well, to'a pulpit ran.	76	E119 Shelton	6
TOAST (See also TOSTED)			
If a fit livor thou dost seeke to toast;	292	U86 Hor.4:1	12
TO'AVE			
That ever had beginning there, to'ave end!	271	U81 Pawlet	91
TOBACCO (See also TABACCO)			
To light Tobacco, or save roasted Geese,	205	U43 Vulcan	52
To light Tobacco, or have roasted Geese,	205	U43 Vulcan	V 52
T'OBAY			
Who would not be thy subject, James, t'obay	37	E35 James 2	1
T'OBEY			
T'obey, and serve her sweet Commandements.	287	U84 Muse	172
T'OBSERVE			
Nor know t'observe: why (i'the Muses name)	311	Horace	128
T'OBTAINE			
T'obtaine of God, what all the Land should aske?	234	U61 Epigram	11
TOES			
They need no stilts, nor rise upon their toes,	157	U13 Sacvile	145

	Page	Title	Line
T'OFFEND			
And let your mercie make me asham'd t'offend.	194	U38 Elegy 'Tis	106
The angry, and love those that feare t'offend.	317	Horace	282
'TOFORE			
'Tofore, great men were glad of Poets: Now,	40	E43 Salisbury 1	5
TOGETHER			
And, yet, they, all together, lesse then thee.	68	E106 E Herbert	10
And, in some yeere, all these together heap'd,	69	E107 Hungry	15
And shamefastnesse together! All lawes dead,	163	U15 Friend-Wars	40
And shamefac'dnesse together! All lawes dead,	163	U15 Friend-Wars V	40
Of all vice hurld together, there he was,	172	U21 Ltl Shrub	6
For a thousand yeares together,	183	U29 Fit of Rime	16
As all with storme and tempest ran together.	193	U38 Elegy 'Tis	76
And Goates together, whither they must come	283	U84 Muse	47
Of Body and Spirit together, plac'd betwixt	284	U84 Muse	54
Let us together closely lie, and kisse,	294	U88 Petronius	7
Together: not that we should Serpents see	305	Horace	15
As doctrine, and delight together go.	329	Horace	516
TOIES			
Of verse meere-matter-lesse, and tinckling toies.	327	Horace	460
TOILE (See also TOYLE)			
And toile in vaine: the excellence is such	321	Horace	352
Can; or all toile, without a wealthie veine:	331	Horace	584
TOKEN			
As the token of my Love	666	Glover	3
TOLD (See also TOULD)			
And, told of this, he slights it. Tut, such crimes	45	E56 Poet-Ape	9
Madame, I told you late how I repented,	54	E84 Bedford 2	1
They cry'd out Pusse. He told them he was Bankes,	89	E133 Voyage	183
Thou hast no lantherne, whereof tales are told;	93	F2 Penshurst	4
Your selfe but told unto your selfe, and see	117	F13 Aubigny	23
Told seven and fortie yeares,	150	U9 Picture	15
Told six and fortie yeares,	150	U9 Picture V	15
And told of with more License then th'were done!	156	U13 Sacvile	96
And told forth fourescore yeares:	243	U70 Ode	26
Or acted told. But, ever, things that run	317	Horace	256
And when your yeares rise more, then would be told,	384	Somerset	23
For thou objectest (as thou hast been told)	408	Detractor	3
And lesse asham'd; not when I told the crowd	414	Rutter	5
TOLERATION			
A meane, and toleration, which does well:	331	Horace	549
TOM			
A Horse here is sadled, but no Tom him to backe,	374	Coryat 1	14
It should rather have bene Tom that a horse did lack.	374	Coryat 1	15
To the Right Noble Tom, Tell-Troth of his travailes,	378	Coryat 2	Ttl
Honest Tom Tell-Troth puts downe Roger, How?	378	Coryat 2	81
Of Tom of Odcombe that odde Joviall Author,	378	Coryat 2	87
The height, let him learne of Mr. Tom. Coryate;	379	Coryat 3	2
There nam'd to be travell'd? For this our Tom saith:	380	Coryat 3	21
Poore Tom have we cause to suspect just thee?	381	Coryat 3	58
The height, let him learne of Mr. Tom Coryate.	381	Coryat 3	60
TOMBE			
Of the not borne, yet buried, here's the tombe.	46	E62 Would-bee	12
An Epitaph, deserv'd a Tombe:	152	U12 Corbet	38
Of me, I'le softly tread unto my Tombe;	199	U41 Elegy Since	20
At least may beare th'inscription to her Tombe.	269	U81 Pawlet	18
Thou art a Moniment, without a tombe,	391	Shakespeare	22
TOMBES			
Whil'st others toyle for titles to their tombes.	70	E109 Nevil	18
trust in the tombes, their care-full freinds do rayse;	387	Cavendish	6
TOMBS			
Painted, or carv'd upon our great-mens tombs,	114	F12 Rutland	45
TOMES			
Or spun out Riddles, and weav'd fiftie tomes	204	U43 Vulcan	33
Or spun or weav'd in Riddles 50 tomes	204	U43 Vulcan V	33
TONGU'D			
Did Sappho on her seven-tongu'd Lute,	181	U27 Ode Helen	3
TONGUE			
He sayes, I want the tongue of Epigrammes;	42	E49 Playwrt 1	2
And heare her speake with one, and her first tongue;	78	E122 Rudyerd 2	6
To revenge me with my Tongue,	133	U2 Suffered	24
Hee never fell, thou fall'st, my tongue.	244	U70 Ode	44
Hee never fell, thou tripst, my tongue.	244	U70 Ode V	44
And so warme the Poets tongue	260	U76 Petition	31
This being thus: why should my tongue, or pen	284	U84 Muse	69
And for the troubled Clyent fyl's his tongue,	292	U86 Hor.4:1	14
With an uncomely silence failes my tongue?	293	U86 Hor.4:1	36
And tortures us: and, after, by the tongue	311	Horace	156
But in one tongue, was form'd with the worlds wit:	389	Aleman	6
Phoebus, and Hermes? They whose tongue, or pen	395	May	17
To make the Language sweet upon her tongue.	402	Inigo Jones 1	14
TONGUES			
Yet thou, perhaps, shalt meet some tongues will grutch,	72	E111 Edmonds 2	9
And whilst our tongues perplexed lie,	139	U2 Another	17
Whilst the Latin, Queene of Tongues,	184	U29 Fit of Rime	34
Invisibilitie, and strength, and tongues:	206	U43 Vulcan	75
Had I a thousand Mouthes, as many Tongues,	269	U81 Pawlet	23
Cato's and Ennius tongues have lent much worth,	309	Horace	81
If all the vulgar Tongues, that speake this day,	388	Chapman	7
TOO'			
Blowne up; and he (too'unwieldie for that place)	57	E90 Mill	14

726

TOO

	Page	Title	Line
For vulgar praise, doth it too dearely buy.	27	E2 My Booke	14
Use mine so, too: I give thee leave. But crave	27	E3 Bookseller	3
Which hee thinkes great; and so reades verses, too:	35	E28 Surly	5
He drinkes to no man: that's, too, like a lord.	35	E28 Surly	14
What not the envie of the seas reach'd too,	37	E32 Roe 2	4
But that his Jone doth too. And Giles would never,	40	E42 Giles	4
My sinne was too much hope of thee, lov'd boy,	41	E45 First Son	2
As what he loves may never like too much.	41	E45 First Son	12
Thou art the father, and the witnesse too.	44	E53 Old-end	8
Durst thinke it great, and worthy wonder too,	46	E60 Mounteagle	7
On the true causes, ere they grow too old.	50	E70 Wm Roe 1	4
Thy wit lives by it, Proule, and belly too.	54	E81 Proule	6
Throughout my booke. 'Troth put out woman too.	54	E83 Friend	2
Yet have they seene the maps, and bought 'hem too,	59	E92 New Crie	9
Others more modest, but contemne us too,	59	E92 New Crie	39
And like them too; must needfully, though few,	61	E94 Bedford 3	13
It is the next deed, and a great one too.	61	E95 Savile	26
Thou hast begun well, Roe, which stand well too,	63	E98 Th Roe 1	1
Knat, raile, and ruffe too. How so ere, my man	65	E101 Supper	20
And like it too; if they looke equally:	67	E104 Montgomery	15
In Hungary, and Poland, Turkie too;	69	E107 Hungry	13
Not all these, Edmonds, or what else put too,	71	E110 Edmonds 1	11
His deedes too dying, but in bookes (whose good	71	E110 Edmonds 1	15
His deedes too dying, save in bookes (whose good	71	E110 Edmonds 1	V 15
Art still at that, and think'st to blow me'up too?	72	E112 Gamster	6
Naming so many, too! But, this is one,	74	E115 Honest Man	3
About the towne; and knowne too, at that price.	74	E115 Honest Man	6
It will deny all; and forsweare it too:	74	E115 Honest Man	19
But viewing him since (alas, too late)	77	E120 S. P.	19
But, being so much too good for earth,	77	E120 S. P.	23
And thine owne Coriat too. But (would'st thou see)	81	E129 Mime	17
Their wherry had no saile, too; ours had none:	84	E133 Voyage	11
Thy copp's, too, nam'd of Gamage, thou hast there,	94	F2 Penshurst	19
I know too, though thou strut, and paint,	100	F4 To the World	13
And nights too, in worser wayes?	104	F8 Sicknesse	6
I shall feare, you'll surfet too.	104	F8 Sicknesse	8
I doe feare, you'll surfet too.	104	F8 Sicknesse	V 8
We must sing too? what subject shall we chuse?	107	F10 Proludium	V 1
I feele my griefes too, and there scarce is ground,	122	F15 Heaven	21
But the Pittie comes too late.	133	U2 Suffered	20
Heare and make Example too.	133	U2 Suffered	26
Till he cherish'd too much beard,	141	U2 Her man	23
As to doe no thing too much.	142	U2 Her man	46
Nor looke too kind on my desires,	144	U4 Song	7
Wee have both wits, and fancies too,	145	U5 Woman-kind	5
I feare they'd love him too;	147	U7 Nymph	4
And fresh and fragrant too,	147	U7 Nymph	16
I have my Pietie too, which could	151	U12 Corbet	1
Great and good turns, as wel could time them too,	153	U13 Sacvile	2
Alone in money, but in manners too.	157	U13 Sacvile	134
You know (without my flatt'ring you) too much	157	U13 Sacvile	155
Without your gift, though I can rate that too,	157	U13 Sacvile	158
Not flie the Crime, but the Suspition too:	159	U14 Selden	18
And mine not least) I have too oft preferr'd	159	U14 Selden	20
Men past their termes, and prais'd some names too much,	159	U14 Selden	21
Of generall knowledge; watch'd men, manners too,	159	U14 Selden	33
And their words too; where I but breake my Band.	169	U17 Friend-Debt	9
As not the World can praise too much,	173	U22 Elegy Tho	3
As 'tis too just a cause;	174	U23 Himselfe	14
Though you sometimes proclaime me too severe,	190	U37 Friend-Book	16
That you should be too noble to destroy.	191	U38 Elegy 'Tis	12
Be not affected with these markes too much	193	U38 Elegy 'Tis	83
Yet keepe those up in sackcloth too, or lether,	200	U42 Elegy Let	25
Or slipper was left off, and kisse it too,	201	U42 Elegy Let	56
Was there made English: with the Grammar too,	207	U43 Vulcan	91
He burnt that Idoll of the Revels too:	210	U43 Vulcan	155
There was a Judgement shew'n too in an houre.	210	U43 Vulcan	158
Thy Wives pox on thee, and B.B.'s too.	212	U43 Vulcan	216
Thy Wives pox on thee, and Bess Broughtons too..	212	U43 Vulcan	V216
And Ord'nance too: so much as from the Tower	213	U44 Speach	3
They saw too store of feathers, and more may,	213	U44 Speach	9
First weigh a friend, then touch, and trie him too;	216	U45 Squib	16
But he that's too-much that, is friend of none.	216	U45 Squib	24
To speake my selfe out too ambitiously,	218	U47 Tribe	6
Of earthen Jarres, there may molest me too:	219	U47 Tribe	55
The causes and the Guests too,	221	U48 Bacchus	39
And have thy tales and jests too,	221	U48 Bacchus	40
And that her truster feares her? Must I too?	223	U49 Pucell	22
Ought that is ill, but the suspition too,	224	U50 Countesse	6
Is, she will play Dame Justice, too severe;	229	U54 Squib	8
You won them too, your oddes did merit it.	230	U56 Covell	4
But, that he cure the Peoples Evill too?	235	U62 Charles 1	14
But thanke his greatnesse, and his goodnesse too;	236	U63 Charles 2	9
What prayers (People) can you thinke too much?	249	U72 King	20
And praise them too. O! what a fame 't will be?	263	U78 Digby	25
It is too neere of kin to Heaven, the Soule,	269	U81 Pawlet	29
It is too neere of kin to God, the Soule,	269	U81 Pawlet	V 29
To be describ'd! Fames fingers are too foule	269	U81 Pawlet	30
'Twere time that I dy'd too, now shee is dead,	282	U84 Muse	1
Shee saw him too, in glory to ascend	288	U84 Muse	205
(As being Redeemer, and Repairer too	288	U84 Muse	213
Too stubborne for Commands so slack:	292	U86 Hor.4:1	7

TOO (cont.)

	Page	Title	Line
Creepes on the ground; too safe, too afraid of storme.	307	Horace	39
And come not too much wrested. What's that thing,	309	Horace	76
An Actors parts, and Office too, the Quire	317	Horace	276
And tune too, fitted to the Chorus rime,	319	Horace	290
Hee too, that did in Tragick Verse contend	319	Horace	319
Of too much haste, and negligence in part,	323	Horace	385
And there is given too unworthy leave	323	Horace	389
Too patiently, that I not fondly say;	323	Horace	401
Our Poets, too, left nought unproved here;	323	Horace	405
Amphion, too, that built the Theban towres,	327	Horace	483
The Oracles, too, were given out in Verse;	329	Horace	496
And, of your selfe too, understand; yet mind	331	Horace	547
Thou, such thy judgement is, thy knowledge too,	331	Horace	573
Here, by a Boore too, hee's like to be beaten	375	Coryat 1	24
And therein (which is worth his valour too)	378	Coryat 2	84
How well, and how often his shoes too were mended,	380	Coryat 3	39
But that hee's too well suted, in a cloth,	389	Aleman	17
As neither Man, nor Muse, can praise too much.	390	Shakespeare	4
And Christian name too, with a Heralds witt.	394	Jane Ogle	12
I chyme that too: And I have mett with those	403	Inigo Jones 1	31
Dame History, Dame Architecture too,	403	Inigo Jones 1	37
To be the Musick Master! Fabler too!	404	Inigo Jones 1	63
I am too fat t'envy him. He too leane	405	Inigo Jones 1	69
Up & about? Dyve into Cellars too	405	Inigo Jones 1	80
Thou'rt too ambitious: and dost fear in vaine!	408	Inigo Jones 3	6
Thy Forehead is too narrow for my Brand.	408	Inigo Jones 3	14

TOOKE

	Page	Title	Line
'Tis Lucklesse he, that tooke up one on band	42	E46 Luckless 1	3
For none ere tooke that pleasure in sinnes sense,	60	E94 Bedford 3	9
But, when they heard it tax'd, tooke more offence.	60	E94 Bedford 3	10
For Cupid, who (at first) tooke vaine delight,	73	E114 Sydney	3
They tooke 'hem all to witnesse of their action:	89	E133 Voyage	191
And tooke on him our Nature.	130	U1 Nativitie	18
I foole-hardie, there up-tooke	132	U2 How he saw	20
At my face, that tooke my sight,	132	U2 How he saw	25
To succour my necessities, tooke fire,	153	U13 Sacvile	8
And in the noblest Families tooke root	185	U30 Burleigh	18
But must confesse from whom what gift I tooke.	189	U37 Friend-Book	6
No mar'le the Clownes of Lemnos tooke thee up,	208	U43 Vulcan	116
In all thy age of Journals thou hast tooke,	208	U43 Vulcan	116
This foot the socks tooke up, and buskins grave,	311	Horace	118
Immortall, tooke a melancholique, odde	335	Horace	662
Gold is a sutor, never tooke repulse,	363	Riches	5
It was not so of old: Men tooke up trades	410	Brome	13

TOO-MUCH

	Page	Title	Line
But he that's too-much that, is friend of none.	216	U45 Squib	24

TOOTH'D

	Page	Title	Line
Wormewood, and sulphure, sharpe, and tooth'd withall;	27	E2 My Booke	4

TOO'UNWIELDIE

	Page	Title	Line
Blowne up; and he (too'unwieldie for that place)	57	E90 Mill	14

TOP

	Page	Title	Line
By Jacobs Ladder, to the top	274	U84 Cradle	38
With slyding windowes, & false Lights a top!	407	Inigo Jones 2	10
To top the fairest Lillie, now, that growes,	413	Ghyrlond	15

TOPPS

	Page	Title	Line
Each banke doth yeeld thee coneyes; and the topps	94	F2 Penshurst	25

TORCH

	Page	Title	Line
But hold my torch, while I describe the entry	85	E133 Voyage	58

TORCHES

	Page	Title	Line
Where Love may all his Torches light,	147	U7 Nymph	24
Love lights his torches to inflame desires;	170	U19 Elegy By	2

TORMENT

	Page	Title	Line
'Tis but a body which you can torment,	270	U81 Pawlet	55

TORMENTED

	Page	Title	Line
May his joynts tormented bee,	184	U29 Fit of Rime	50

TORN'D

	Page	Title	Line
Those ill-torn'd Verses, to new hammering.	333	Horace	628

TORNE

	Page	Title	Line
And shew their feathers shot, and cullors torne,	98	F3 Wroth	71
My selfe up to thee, harrow'd, torne, and bruis'd	127	U1 Trinitie	5
Unlesse my heart would as my thought be torne.	147	U7 Nymph	14
Old Hat here, torne Hose, with Shoes full of gravell,	375	Coryat 1	26

TORNED

	Page	Title	Line
In his well torned, and true-filed lines:	392	Shakespeare	68

TORRENT

	Page	Title	Line
Or Dowgate Torrent falling into Thames,	407	Inigo Jones 2	16

TORT'RING

	Page	Title	Line
A meere upbraiding Griefe, and tort'ring punishment.	256	U75 Epithalam.	120

TORTURERS

	Page	Title	Line
And to the Torturers (her Doctors) say,	270	U81 Pawlet	52

TORTURES

	Page	Title	Line
To suffer tortures, scorne, and Infamie,	193	U38 Elegy 'Tis	93
And tortures us: and, after, by the tongue	311	Horace	156

TOSSE

	Page	Title	Line
Me farther tosse,	130	U1 Father	30

TOST

	Page	Title	Line
Not tost or troubled with light Lady-aire;	287	U84 Muse	164

TOSTED

	Page	Title	Line
And, after mouldie growne, againe were tosted,	88	E133 Voyage	150

TO'T

	Page	Title	Line
For I will so urge you to't,	140	U2 Promise	14
Beene trusted to thee: not to't selfe assign'd.	283	U84 Muse	20

T'OTHER
   For t'other pound of sweet-meats, he shall feele . . . 164   U15 Friend-Wars   77
TOTHER
   Hundred, then unto the tother 103   F6 Celia 2   10
   Surfet? and Quarrel? drinkes the tother health? . . . 166   U15 Friend-Wars   115
   That liking; and approach so one the tother, . . . 247   U70 Ode   109
TOTTER'D
   The fate of things: whilst totter'd vertue holds . . . 216   U44 Speach   101
TOUCH
   If holiest friend-ship, naked to the touch,   ,, . . 78   E122 Rudyerd 2   7
   Of touch, or marble; nor canst boast a row   ,, . . 93   F2 Penshurst   2
   Inscrib'd in touch or marble, or the cotes . . . 114   F12 Rutland   44
   That doth but touch his flower, and flies away. . . . 139   U2 Another   6
   But in a businesse, that will bide the Touch,   ,, . . 187   U33 Councellour   23
   First weigh a friend, then touch, and trie him too: . . 216   U45 Squib   16
   To cure the call'd Kings Evill with thy touch; . . . 235   U62 Charles 1   4
   With touch of learned thum's! 239   U67 Muses   18
   To touch these Mysteries! We may admire . . . 269   U81 Pawlet   31
   To touch those Mysteries! We may admire . . . 269   U81 Pawlet   V 31
   And to the Touch, a Flower, like soft as Palme. . . 286   U84 Muse   126
   Hee, that's ambitious in the race to touch . . . 333   Horace   587
   And shun to touch him, as a man that were . . . 335   Horace   644
   And flye to touch him, as a man that were . . . 354   Horace   V644
TOUCH'D
   You laugh when you are touch'd, and long before . . 38   E38 Guiltie 2   3
   Touch'd with the sinne of false play, in his punque, . . 56   E87 Hazard   1
   Of the hulke touch'd, and, as by Polypheme . . . 87   E133 Voyage   112
   Had not their forme touch'd by an English wit. . . 115   F12 Rutland   82
   Before rude hands have touch'd it? 134   U2 Triumph   22
   (Defiled) touch'd; but certaine he was mad, . . . 337   Horace   673
TOUCHETH
   And turning all he toucheth into pelfe, . . . 197   U40 Elegy That   22
TOUCHING
   Touching this cause, where they will be affeard . . 87   E133 Voyage   106
TOUCH'T
   Polluted, touch't: but certainly he's mad: . . . 355   Horace   V673
TOUGH
   Tough, foule, or Tender. 417   Moon   16
TOULD
   Being tould there, Reason cannot, Sense may erre. . . 370   Author   14
T'OUR
   T'our times return'd, hath made her heaven in thee. . . 52   E74 Chancelor   10
TOURE
   That they to knowledge so should toure upright, . . 55   E85 Goodyere 1   6
T'OUT
   T'out-strip your peeres: 121   F14 Sydney   26
T'OUTLAST
   Of all the Worthyes hope t'outlast thy one, . . 406   Inigo Jones 1   99
T'OUT-STRIP
   T'out-strip your peeres: 121   F14 Sydney   26
TOWARD
   Toward the sea, farther then halfe-way tree? . . 56   E88 Monsieur   6
TOWER
   And Ord'nance too: so much as from the Tower . . 213   U44 Speach   3
   What, though the thriftie Tower 239   U67 Muses   7
   What, though the thirsty Tower 239   U67 Muses   V 7
   Sweet Tree of Life, King Davids Strength and Tower, . . 413   Ghyrlond   38
   Or the Tripos, his Tower Bottle: 657   Door Apollo   4
TOWN
   Like men Town-born, and neere the place, reherse . . 347   Horace   V349/357
   Wee'll have thee styld the Marquess of Town-Ditch. . . 407   Inigo Jones 2   V 24
TOWN-BORN
   Like men Town-born, and neere the place, reherse . . 347   Horace   V349/357
TOWN-DITCH
   Wee'll have thee styld the Marquess of Town-Ditch. . . 407   Inigo Jones 2   V 24
TOWNE
   Shift, here, in towne, not meanest among squires, . . 30   E12 Shift   1
   Nor office in the towne, nor place in court, . . 63   E97 Motion   11
   About the towne; and knowne too, at that price. . . 74   E115 Honest Man   6
   That scarse the Towne designeth any feast . . . 81   E129 Mime   5
   Livers, round about the towne. 105   F8 Sicknesse   17
   Every stew in towne to know; 105   F8 Sicknesse   38
   Every Cranck in towne to know; 105   F8 Sicknesse   V 38
   All the Towne-curs take each their snatch at me. . . 155   U13 Sacvile   72
   Of our Towne Gallantry! or why there rests . . . 155   U13 Sacvile   92
   The Lady Mayresse pass'd through the Towne, . . 201   U42 Elegy Let   70
   That censure all the Towne, and all th'affaires, . . 218   U47 Tribe   23
   His rage, with razing your immortall Towne. . . . 242   U70 Ode   4
   A Bed-rid Wit, then a besieged Towne. . . . 248   U71 Treasurer   15
   About the towne: this reck'ning I will pay, . . 396   Drayton   9
   In Towne & Court? Are you growne rich? & proud? . . 403   Inigo Jones 1   24
TOWNE-CURS
   All the Towne-curs take each their snatch at me. . . 155   U13 Sacvile   72
TOWNES
   On the Townes honest Man. 74   E115 Honest Man   Ttl
   Then, The townes honest Man's her errant'st knave. . . 75   E115 Honest Man   34
   Of building townes, and making wilde beasts tame, . . 82   E130 Ferrab. 1   2
   In neighbour-townes, and feeles the weightie plough: . . 309   Horace   95
   Saw many Townes, and Men, and could their manners tract. . 315   Horace   202
   Build Townes, and carve the Lawes in leaves of wood. . 327   Horace   490
TOWNS
   Clowne, Towns-man, base, and noble, mix'd, to judge? . . 319   Horace   302

	Page	Title	Line
TOWNS-MAN			
Clowne, Towns-man, base, and noble, mix'd, to judge?	319	Horace	302
TOWRE			
To towre with my intention	176	U25 Desmond	4
This is King Charles his Day. Speake it, thou Towre,	249	U72 King	1
This is King Charles his birth day. Speake it, thou Towre,	249	U72 King	V 1
TOWRES			
Amphion, too, that built the Theban towres,	327	Horace	483
TOWRING			
An Eagle towring in the skye,	278	U84 Mind	10
TOY (See also TOIES)			
That's a Toy, that I could spare:	142	U2 Exception	2
TOYE			
In setting forth of such a solemne Toye!	405	Inigo Jones 1	78
In setting forth of such a serious Toye!	405	Inigo Jones 1	V 78
TOYES			
Play-wright, by chance, hearing some toyes I'had writ,	64	E100 Playwrt 3	1
Of toyes, and trifles, traps, and snares,	100	F4 To the World	18
Fame, and rumor are but toyes.	102	F5 Celia 1	10
For, though that Rattles, Timbrels, Toyes,	273	U84 Cradle	17
TOYLE			
Whil'st others toyle for titles to their tombes.	70	E109 Nevil	18
All other Acts of Worldlings, are but toyle	162	U15 Friend-Wars	9
All other Acts of Worldlings, are meere toyle	162	U15 Friend-Wars V	9
TOYLES (NETS)			
Wild Bores into his toyles pitch'd round:	290	U85 Country	32
TOYLES			
He toyles to be at hell, as soone as they.	36	E31 Banck	4
Toyles, by grave custome, up and downe the court,	113	F12 Rutland	5
TRACE			
Our closest Creekes, and Corners, and can trace	287	U84 Muse	153
TRACKS			
Who tracks this Authors, or Translators Pen,	389	Aleman	1
TRACT			
Saw many Townes, and Men, and could their manners tract.	315	Horace	202
TRACTS			
In daring to forsake the Grecian tracts,	323	Horace	407
With entheate rage, to publish their bright tracts?	368	Ode Who saith	61
TRADE			
Makes serious use of all great trade he knowes.	35	E28 Surly	3
Upon th'accompt, hers grew the quicker trade.	56	E87 Hazard	5
Daily to turne in Pauls, and helpe the trade.	56	E88 Monsieur	16
They maintayne the truest trade,	105	F8 Sicknesse	19
But these men ever want: their very trade	155	U13 Sacvile	79
Maintain'd the trade at Bilbo, or else-where;	212	U43 Vulcan	199
Maintain'd the trade of Bilbo, or else-where;	212	U43 Vulcan	V199
By the just trade	273	U84 Cradle	8
Alas: then whither trade I,	365	Ode Splendor	V 17
As, now, of all men, it is call'd thy Trade:	389	Chapman	11
TRADES			
The brother trades a sister; and the friend	165	U15 Friend-Wars	93
It was not so of old: Men tooke up trades	410	Brome	13
TRADESMEN			
With Clownes, and Tradesmen, kept thee clos'd in horne.	203	U43 Vulcan	8
With Citizens? let Clownes, and Tradesmen breed	215	U44 Speach	73
TRADITIONS			
How are Traditions there examin'd: how	160	U14 Selden	49
TRADUCE			
May others feare, flie, and traduce thy name,	32	E17 Critic	1
TRAGEDIE			
In time to Tragedie, a Musicke new.	319	Horace	306
The Tragedie, and carried it about,	319	Horace	312
And emptie Clowdes. For Tragedie is faire,	321	Horace	336
Quite from all face of Tragedie to goe,	321	Horace	344
Whether the guarded Tragedie they wrought,	323	Horace	409
TRAGICK			
Tragick, or Comick; but thou writ'st the play.	72	E112 Gamster	8
In tragick Verse; no lesse Thyestes feast	311	Horace	122
With swelling throat: and, oft, the tragick wight	311	Horace	134
Hee too, that did in Tragick Verse contend	319	Horace	319
TRAINE			
Hath plac'd amongst her virgin-traine:	34	E22 Daughter	9
Of all Lucina's traine; Lucy the bright,	115	F12 Rutland	66
TRAIN'D			
In his train'd Gowne about the Stage: So grew	319	Horace	305
In his train'd Gowne about the Stage: thus grew	346	Horace	V305
TRAINES			
Thus, by these subtle traines,	110	F11 Epode	28
TRAMPLED			
Lay trampled on; the deeds of death, and night,	243	U70 Ode	14
TRANCE			
in a deepe trance; * * * * *	361	Palmer	26
TRANSCENDING			
But mixt with sound, transcending	365	Ode Splendor	15
TRANSCRIPTS			
What transcripts begg'd? how cry'd up, and how glad,	263	U78 Digby	30
What transcripts made? how cry'd up, and how glad,	263	U78 Digby	V 30
TRANSFERRE			
O Madame, if your grant did thus transferre mee,	55	E84 Bedford 2	9
TRANSFORM'D			
Though, now by Love transform'd, & dayly dying:	369	Ode Who saith	101
TRANSLATE			
Not care, as thou wouldst faithfully translate,	313	Horace	190

	Page	Title	Line

TRANSLATED
```
. . . Commentaries observed, and translated.            71   E110 Edmonds 1   Ttl
Translated Aelian tactickes to be read,                214   U44 Speach       35
An Ode in Horace in prayse of a Countrye lyfe, Translated.  289  U85 Country  VTtl
The same translated.                                   294   U88 Petronius    Ttl
The same translated.                                   294   U89 Mart.8:77    Ttl
The Sunne translated, or the Sonne of May.             395   May              24
```
TRANSLATION
```
As his will now be the translation thought,            83   E132 Sylvester   12
. . . on his Translation of Hesiods Works, & Dayes.   388   Chapman          Ttl
```
TRANSLATOR
```
On the Author, Worke, and Translator.                 389   Aleman           Ttl
To my chosen Friend, the learned Translator of Lucan, . . .  395  May         Ttl
```
TRANSLATORS
```
Who tracks this Authors, or Translators Pen,          389   Aleman            1
Such Bookes deserve Translators, of like coate        389   Aleman           11
```
TRANSMIGRATED
```
Their spirits transmigrated to a cat:                  88   E133 Voyage      159
```
TRANSMITT
```
Transmitt it to your Nephewes, Freinds, Allies,       399   Lady Ogle         3
```
TRANSPLANTED
```
that mongst so manie plants transplanted hether,      361   Palmer            6
```
TRAPPINGS
```
your Trappings will not change you.  Change your mynd.  403  Inigo Jones 1   25
```
TRAPS
```
Of toyes, and trifles, traps, and snares,             100   F4 To the World  18
```
TRAVAILE
```
His monyes travaile for him, in and out:               36   E31 Banck         2
To see great Charles of Travaile eas'd,               251   U74 Weston       26
He was in his travaile, how like to be beaten,        380   Coryat 3         35
```
TRAVAIL'D
```
Came backe untouch'd.  This man hath travail'd well.   81   E128 Wm Roe 2    14
Afford? The Mountaines travail'd, and brought forth   315   Horace          198
```
TRAVAILES
```
To the Right Noble Tom, Tell-Troth of his travailes, . . .  378  Coryat 2    Ttl
```
TRAVAYLES
```
Palmer thy travayles well becum thy name,             362   Palmer           30
```
TRAVELL
```
And louse-dropping Case, are the Armes of his travell.  375  Coryat 1        27
. . . the Coryate of Odcombe, and his Booke now going to travell  378  Coryat 2  Ttl
Of travell he discourseth so at large,                378   Coryat 2         82
```
TRAVELL'D
```
There nam'd to be travell'd? For this our Tom saith:  380   Coryat 3         21
```
TRAVELLING
```
Yes thou wert borne out of his travelling thigh       378   Coryat 2         89
And therefore how ever the travelling nation,         380   Coryat 3         29
```
TRAVELLS
```
Nor baudie stock, that travells for encrease,          63   E97 Motion       10
```
TREAD
```
Hast taught thy selfe worthy thy pen to tread,         63   E99 Th Roe 2      3
A spirit so resolv'd to tread                         100   F4 To the World   6
Of vertue, which you tread? what if alone?            118   F13 Aubigny      55
So to see a Lady tread,                               138   U2 Kisse         25
Of me, I'le softly tread unto my Tombe;               199   U41 Elegy Since  20
Marrie the Muse is one, can tread the Aire,           230   U56 Covell       13
Marrie the Muse is one, can tread the Aire,           230   U56 Covell     V 13
Have they bedew'd the Earth, where she doth tread,    254   U75 Epithalam.   66
Have they bedew'd the Earth, where she did tread,     254   U75 Epithalam.  V 66
Where ere they tread th'enamour'd ground,             264   U79 New-yeares   36
When in a wrong, and artlesse way we tread.           307   Horace           44
If in th'escape an artlesse path we tread.            339   Horace      V 46/ 44
And can tread firme, longs with like lads to play;    315   Horace          226
The man once mock'd, and suffer'd wrong to tread.     335   Horace          642
For, though but early in these pathes thou tread,     386   Browne            5
To life againe, to heare thy Buskin tread,            391   Shakespeare      36
```
TREADES
```
Nor treades the Seas inraged harmes:                  289   U85 Country     V 6
```
TREADING
```
Treading a better path, not contrary;                 76   E119 Shelton     12
```
TREADS
```
Since he treads in no other Mans steps but his owne.  379   Coryat 3         12
```
TREASON
```
Will quickly taste the treason, and commit            109   F11 Epode        15
Had I wrote treason there, or heresie,                203   U43 Vulcan       15
```
TREASONS
```
Like aydes 'gainst treasons who hath found before?     38   E35 James 2       7
```
TREASURE
```
A treasure, art: contemn'd in th'age of gold.         47   E64 Salisbury 3    4
I' your selfe, all treasure lost of th'age before.    68   E105 L Wroth 2    20
Might love the treasure for the cabinet.              79   E125 Uvedale       6
The wealthy treasure of her love on him;             112   F11 Epode        105
The wealthy treasure of her love in him;             112   F11 Epode       V105
Spoyling Senses of their Treasure,                   183   U29 Fit of Rime    4
Weston, their Treasure, as their Treasurer,          255   U75 Epithalam.    97
What treasure hast thou brought us! and what store   388   Chapman            4
```
TREASURER
```
. . . Lo: high Treasurer of England.                185   U30 Burleigh     Ttl
To the Right Honourable, the Lord high Treasurer of . . .  248  U71 Treasurer  Ttl
To my Lord Weston, Lo: Treasurer. A Letter           248   U71 Treasurer    VTtl
. . . high Treasurer of England, Upon the Day, Hee was . . .  250  U73 Weston  Ttl
. . . Heire, of the Lord Weston, Lord high Treasurer of . . .  252  U75 Epithalam.  Ttl
Weston, their Treasure, as their Treasurer,          255   U75 Epithalam.    97
To the right Honourable, the Lord Treasurer of England. . . .  260  U77 Treasurer  Ttl
```

TREASURERS
When hee shall read them at the Treasurers bord,   .   .   . 263 U78 Digby   27
When hee doth read them at the Treasurers bord,   .   .   . 263 U78 Digby   V 27
TREBLE
Worth an estate, treble to that you have.   .   .   .   . 114 F12 Rutland   36
TRECHEROUS
Proud, false, and trecherous, vindictive, all   .   .   . 172 U21 Ltl Shrub   7
TREE
Shall out-live gyrlands, stolne from the chast tree.   .   . 32 E17 Critic   6
Toward the sea, farther then halfe-way tree?   .   .   . 56 E88 Monsieur   6
Cary my love is, Daphne but my tree.   .   .   .   . 80 E126 Mrs Cary   8
That taller tree, which of a nut was set,   .   .   . 94 F2 Penshurst   13
Nor yellow honie from the tree   .   .   .   .   . 98 F3 Wroth   V 60
Grow, grow, faire tree, and as thy branches shoote,   .   . 119 F13 Aubigny   99
Have you tasted the Cinnamon-tree   .   .   .   .   . 135 U2 Triumph   V 37
What Tree or stone doth want a soule?   .   .   .   . 143 U3 Musicall   7
That sits in shadow of Apollo's tree.   .   .   .   . 149 U9 Picture   10
It is not growing like a tree   .   .   .   .   . 245 U70 Ode   65
Whilst the maine tree, still found   .   .   .   . 258 U75 Epithalam.   181
And beckning wooes me, from the fatall tree   .   .   . 268 U81 Pawlet   3
But, kept an even gate, as some streight tree   .   .   . 287 U84 Muse   165
From fattest branches of the Tree: .   .   .   . 291 U85 Country   56
Thou lighter then the barke of any tree, ... 294 U87 Hor.3:9   22
Know'st only well to paint a Cipresse tree.   .   .   . 305 Horace   25
Sweet Tree of Life, King Davids Strength and Tower,   .   . 413 Ghyrlond   38
TREES
The trees cut out in log; and those boughes made   .   . 98 F3 Wroth   45
Have you seen the Palme-trees state   .   .   .   . 136 U2 Triumph   V 43
They were as specious as his Trees.   .   .   .   . 152 U12 Corbet   20
TREMBLES
That trembles in the blaze, but (then) mounts higher!   . 233 U59 Newcastle   8
TREMBLING
And it is paid 'hem with a trembling zeale,   .   .   . 155 U13 Sacvile   85
TRENCH
Or if thou needs would'st trench upon her power,   .   . 204 U43 Vulcan   48
Have cast a trench about mee, now, five yeares;   .   . 248 U71 Treasurer   6
A Trench against it, nor a Battry plac't?   .   .   . 401 Beaumont   14
TRENT
But over Land to Trent: .   .   .   .   .   . 368 Ode Who saith   75
TRESPASSE
As twice to trespasse in his sight, ... 152 U12 Corbet   26
TRESSES
Her tresses trim her back, ... 254 U75 Epithalam.   45
TREW
And newer, then could please them, by-cause trew.   .   . 415 Rutter   10
TRIALL   (See TRYALS)
TRIALS
Care not what trials they are put unto;   .   .   .   . 218 U47 Tribe   2
TRIBADE
Or, with thy Tribade trine, invent new sports,   .   . 107 F10 Proludium   17
What though with Tribade lust she force a Muse,   .   . 222 U49 Pucell   7
TRIBE
- - - to be Sealed of the Tribe of Ben.   .   .   . 218 U47 Tribe   Ttl
Sir, you are Sealed of the Tribe of Ben.   .   .   . 220 U47 Tribe   78
TRIBUTE
Thou hast thy ponds, that pay thee tribute fish,   .   . 94 F2 Penshurst   32
Now, but command; make tribute, what was gift;   .   . 155 U13 Sacvile   84
TRICKS
Doe all the tricks of a saut Lady Bitch;   .   .   . 164 U15 Friend-Wars   76
Cause thou canst doe these halting tricks in fire?   .   . 208 U43 Vulcan   V110
Their youthfull tricks in over-wanton verse;   .   .   . 321 Horace   358
Or play young tricks in over-wanton verse;   .   .   . 347 Horace   V350/358
A Say-master, hath studied all the tricks   .   .   . 415 Rutter   26
TRIE
If I would strive to bring backe times, and trie   .   . 78 E122 Rudyerd 2   3
Must trie the'un-used valour of a nose: .   .   . 87 E133 Voyage   132
First weigh a friend, then touch, and trie him too: .   . 216 U45 Squib   16
But thou wilt yet a Kinglier mastrie trie,   .   .   . 235 U62 Charles 1   5
Trie and trust Roger, was the word, but now   .   .   . 378 Coryat 2   80
TRI'D
But as 'tis often vext and tri'd.   .   .   .   . 146 U6 Defence   18
TRIED
Besides he tried Ship, Cart, Waggon, and Chayre,   .   . 380 Coryat 3   27
TRIFLES
Of toyes, and trifles, traps, and snares,   .   .   . 100 F4 To the World   18
Or pomp'd for those hard trifles, Anagrams,   .   .   . 204 U43 Vulcan   35
Or pomp'd for those fine trifles, Anagrams,   .   .   . 204 U43 Vulcan   V 35
Yet, here are no such Trifles brought,   .   .   . 273 U84 Cradle   25
These trifles into serious mischiefes lead   .   .   . 335 Horace   641
TRIFLING
A trifling Mouse! O, how much better this,   .   .   . 343 Horace   V199
Why should I grieve my friend, this trifling way?   .   . 335 Horace   640
TRIM
But see! th'old baud hath serv'd him in his trim,   .   . 31 E12 Shift   23
Her tresses trim her back, ... 254 U75 Epithalam.   45
TRIMETER
Of Trimeter, when yet it was six-pac'd,   .   .   . 323 Horace   373
TRIMETERS
This foot yet, in the famous Trimeters   .   .   .   . 323 Horace   381
TRINE
Or, with thy Tribade trine, invent new sports,   .   . 107 F10 Proludium   17
Before the moones have fill'd their tripple trine,   .   . 119 F13 Aubigny   102
Alike of kin, to that most blessed Trine,   .   .   . 413 Ghyrlond   34

		Page	Title	Line

TRINITIE
 1. The Sinners Sacrifice. To the Holy Trinitie. . . . 127 U1 Trinitie Ttl
 O Holy, blessed, glorious Trinitie . . .. . . 127 U1 Trinitie 1
 Increase those acts, o glorious Trinitie . . . . 128 U1 Trinitie 29
 A Trinitie, to shine in Union; . . . . . 128 U1 Trinitie 34
 God, in the Union, and the Trinitie! . . . . . 286 U84 Muse 128
TRINITY
 The glorious Trinity in Union met. . . . . . 413 Ghyrlond 32
TRIPLE
 At land she triumphs in the triple shade, ... 268 U80 Christning 15
TRIPOLY
 Can come from Tripoly, leape stooles, and winke, . . . 74 E115 Honest Man 11
TRIPOS
 Or the Tripos, his Tower Bottle: . . . . . 657 Door Apollo 4
TRIPPLE
 The tripple head without a sop. At last, ... 89 E133 Voyage 186
 Before the moones have fill'd their tripple trine, . . . 119 F13 Aubigny 102
TRIPST
 Hee never fell, thou tripst, my tongue. . . . . 244 U70 Ode V 44
TRISTRAMS
 The Tristrams, Lanc'lots, Turpins, and the Peers, . . . 206 U43 Vulcan 69
TRIUMPH
 All braines, at times of triumph, should runne wit. . . . 36 E29 Tilter 4
 4. Her Triumph. . . . . 134 U2 Triumph Ttl
 Wherein you triumph yet: because . . . . . 173 U22 Elegy Tho 9
 T'have held a Triumph, or a feast of fire, ... 205 U43 Vulcan 60
 To conquer rumour, and triumph on spight; . . . . 224 U50 Countesse 4
 Triumph, my Britaine, thou hast one to showe, ... 391 Shakespeare 41
TRIUMPHALL
 Then stands it a triumphall marke! then Men . . . . 157 U13 Sacvile 139
TRIUMPHING
 And, sure of Heaven, rides triumphing in. . . . . 272 U81 Pawlet 100
 Shee saw him rise, triumphing over Death . . . . 288 U84 Muse 203
TRIUMPHS
 As alone there triumphs to the life . . . . . 134 U2 Triumph 19
 At land she triumphs in the triple shade, ... 268 U80 Christning 15
TRODEN
 If thou the vile, broad-troden ring forsake. . . . . 313 Horace 188
TROOPE
 Among which faithfull troope am I. . . . . . 173 U22 Elegy Tho 28
TROPICKS
 Betweene thy Tropicks, to arrest thy sight, ... 252 U75 Epithalam. 4
'TROTH
 Throughout my booke. 'Troth put out woman too. . . . 54 E83 Friend 2
TROTH   (NAME)
 Sir Lucklesse, troth, for lucks sake passe by one: . . . 42 E47 Luckless 2 1
 To the Right Noble Tom, Tell-Troth of his travailes, . . . 378 Coryat 2 Ttl
 Honest Tom Tell-Troth puts downe Roger, How? . . . 378 Coryat 2 81
TROTH
 Troth, if it be, I pitty thy ill lucke; . . . . 73 E112 Gamster 17
 your workes thus differing, troth let soe your style: . . 407 Inigo Jones 2 19
TROUBLE
 Of your Trouble, Ben, to ease me, ... 140 U2 Her man 1
 Himselfe of farther trouble, or the weight . . . . 154 U13 Sacvile 31
TROUBLED
 Troubled both foes, and friends; . . . . . 243 U70 Ode 28
 Not tost or troubled with light Lady-aire; . . . . 287 U84 Muse 164
 If with bright floods, the Winter troubled much, . . . 291 U85 Country 51
 If with East floods, the Winter troubled much, . . . 291 U85 Country V 51
 And for the troubled Clyent fyl's his tongue, . . . 292 U86 Hor.4:1 14
TROUBLES
 We neither love the Troubles, nor the harmes. . . . 215 U44 Speach 86
TROUP
 The choisest Virgin-troup of all the Land! . . . . 254 U75 Epithalam. 50
TROY
 That Homer brought to Troy; yet none so live: . . . 115 F12 Rutland 55
 Which all the Fate of Troy foretold? . . . . 181 U27 Ode Helen 24
 Troy, though it were so much his Venus care. . . . 210 U43 Vulcan 160
 Troy, though it were so much thy Venus joycare. . . . 210 U43 Vulcan V160
 Speake to me, Muse, the Man, who, after Troy was sack't, . . 315 Horace 201
TROYES
 With tales of Troyes just knight, our faiths abuse: . . . 84 E133 Voyage 4
 Of Diomede; nor Troyes sad Warre begins . . . . 315 Horace 209
TRUCH
 Her truch-man, she reports the minds each throw. . . . 313 Horace 157
TRUCH-MAN
 Her truch-man, she reports the minds each throw. . . . 313 Horace 157
TRUE   (See also TREW)
 If all you boast of your great art be true; . . . 29 E6 Alchymists 1
 When both it is the old way, and the true. . . . 32 E18 Censurer 2
 For wit, feature, and true passion, ... 39 E40 Ratcliffe 16
 To so true worth, though thou thy selfe forbid. . . . 47 E63 Salisbury 2 12
 To such true worth, though thou thy selfe forbid. . . . 47 E63 Salisbury 2 V 12
 On the true causes, ere they grow too old. . . . 50 E70 Wm Roe 1 4
 Fortie things more, deare Grand, which you know true, . . 51 E73 Fine Grand 21
 That dares nor write things false, nor hide things true. . . 62 E95 Savile 36
 And one true posture, though besieg'd with ill . . . 66 E102 Pembroke 14
 Or, because some scarce thinke that storie true, . . . 67 E104 Montgomery 5
 I oft looke on false coyne, to know't from true: . . . 68 E107 Hungry 5
 To true Souldiers. . . . . . 69 E108 Soldiers Ttl
 I sweare by your true friend, my Muse, I love . . . 70 E108 Soldiers 5
 Thy learned hand, and true Promethean art . . . 71 E110 Edmonds 1 17
 Shed in thy Songs; 'tis true: but short of thee. . . . 82 E130 Ferrab. 1 18

TRUE (cont.)

	Page	Title	Line
My owne true fire. Now my thought takes wing,	108	F10 Proludium	29
Our owne true fire. Now our thought takes wing,	108	F10 Proludium	V 29
which rap's mee up to the true heav'en of love;	108	F10 Proludium	13
Not to know vice at all, and keepe true state,	109	F11 Epode	1
But this true course is not embrac'd by many:	109	F11 Epode	19
In a continuall tempest. Now, true Love	110	F11 Epode	43
'Tis growne almost a danger to speake true	116	F13 Aubigny	1
Or feare to draw true lines, 'cause others paint:	117	F13 Aubigny	20
Yet search'd, and true they found it.	130	U1 Nativitie	6
Love, and I have had; and true.	136	U2 Cupid	6
Guesse of these, which is the true;	138	U2 Kisse	34
I must the true Relation make,	150	U11 Dreame	2
'Tis true, he could not reprehend:	152	U12 Corbet	21
In time 'twill be a heape; This is not true	157	U13 Sacvile	133
(As their true rule or lesson) either men,	158	U13 Sacvile	162
It true respects. He will not only love,	161	U14 Selden	73
Thy true friends wishes, Colby, which shall be,	167	U15 Friend-Wars	176
Thy true friends wishes, which shall ever be,	167	U15 Friend-Wars	V176
And kept, and bred, and brought up true.	173	U22 Elegy Tho	16
Of eyes more true,	177	U25 Desmond	23
True noblesse. Palme growes straight, though handled ne're so rude.	177	U25 Desmond	26
True valour doth her owne renowne command	180	U26 Ode High	16
To those true numerous Graces; whereof some,	182	U28 Worth	6
True Conceipt,	183	U29 Fit of Rime	3
Wresting words, from their true calling;	183	U29 Fit of Rime	7
Of true measure,	184	U29 Fit of Rime	45
The Orphans Pillar, the true Subjects shield,	185	U30 Burleigh	7
Then this did by her true? She never sought	188	U34 Small Poxe	5
Next to your selfe, for making your love true:	189	U37 Friend-Book	2
'Tis true, I'm broke! Vowes, Oathes, and all I had	191	U38 Elegy 'Tis	1
Then I will studie falshood, to be true.	194	U38 Elegy 'Tis	108
The art of kindling the true Coale, by Lungs;	206	U43 Vulcan	76
The art of kindling the true Coale, of Lungs:	206	U43 Vulcan	V 76
Hee is true Vulcan still! He did not spare	210	U43 Vulcan	159
Thou art true Vulcan still! Thou durst not spare	210	U43 Vulcan	V159
'Tis true, that in thy wish they were destroy'd,	210	U43 Vulcan	167
As makes Penelopes old fable true,	224	U50 Countesse	20
Not boasted in your life, but practis'd true,	225	U50 Countesse	32
'Tis true, as my wombe swells, so my backe stoupes,	227	U52 Answer	4
Of daring, not to doe a wrong, is true	233	U59 Newcastle	15
To God, denies the God-head to be true:	235	U63 Charles 2	2
His Poet leave to sing his House-hold true;	241	U68 House-hold	6
To vertue, and true worth, be ever blind.	250	U73 Weston	10
It is a large faire table, and a true,	269	U81 Pawlet	15
But a fain'd way, doth rob it of the true.	270	U81 Pawlet	38
But a fain'd way, doth spoyle it of the true.	270	U81 Pawlet	V 38
And tell thou, Alde-Legh, None can tell more true	274	U84 Descent	13
I call you Muse: now make it true:	278	U84 Mind	21
'Tis Vertue alone, is true Nobilitie.	282	U84 Keuelme	21
To him should be her Judge, true God, true Man,	288	U84 Muse	211
That thus have ventur'd these true straines upon;	289	U84 Muse	227
'Tis true, I'am Thracian Chloes, I,	293	U87 Hor.3:9	9
The vertue of which order, and true grace,	307	Horace	59
Thence draw forth true expressions. For, sometimes,	327	Horace	455
Cry, and doe more then the true Mourners: so	333	Horace	615
The Scoffer, the true Praiser doth out-goe.	333	Horace	616
Thou, that wouldst finde the habit of true passion,	362	Author	1
Wants facultie to make a censure true:	362	Author	11
Betray it true:	366	Ode Who saith	6
To judge which Passion's false, and which is true,	370	Author	11
Might make the Fable of Good Women true.	372	Epitaph	14
Two noble knightes, whome true desire and zeale,	382	Rich	1
As true oblations; his Brothers Embleme sayes,	383	Rich	10
Such weare true wedding robes, and are true freindes,	384	Somerset	5
As a deformed face doth a true glasse.	389	Aleman	10
'Tis true, and all mens suffrage. But these wayes	390	Shakespeare	5
In his well torned, and true-filed lines:	392	Shakespeare	68
Not usuall in a Lady; and yet true:	394	Jane Ogle	14
Taught Lucan these true moodes! Replyes my sence	395	May	15
Your true freind in Judgement and Choise	395	May	25
Thy Muse, and mine, as they expect. 'Tis true:	396	Drayton	5
You are the Spectacles of State! Tis true	403	Inigo Jones 1	42
The motives, and true Spurres to all good Nations.	411	Sutcliffe	5
Office of Wit, a Mint, and (this is true)	415	Rutter	20
How they advance true Love, and neighbourhood,	416	Dover	7
Of that true Face	419	Ode:If Men	2
Tis the true Phoebeian Liquor,	657	Door Apollo	15

TRUE-FILED

	Page	Title	Line
In his well torned, and true-filed lines:	392	Shakespeare	68

TRUELY

	Page	Title	Line
He plai'd so truely.	77	E120 S. P.	16
Say, are not women truely, then,	104	F7 Women but	5
Say, are not women truely, then,	104	F7 Women but	11
The yellow jaundis, or were truely mad,	354	Horace	V646
And truely, so I would, could I be heard.	414	Rutter	3

TRUER

	Page	Title	Line
Expresser truth, or truer glorie,	39	E40 Ratcliffe	7
Is that the truer excuse? or have we got	166	U15 Friend-Wars	142

TRUEST

	Page	Title	Line
They maintayne the truest trade,	105	F8 Sicknesse	19
Madame, be bold to use this truest glasse:	120	F13 Aubigny	122

	Page	Title	Line

TRULL
Made of the trull, that cut her fathers lock: — — — — 86 E133 Voyage 84

TRULY
They speake; since you are truly that rare wife, — — — 119 F13 Aubigny 110
But in thy presence, truly glorified, — — — 128 U1 Trinitie 47
For truly, since he left to be, — — — — — 152 U12 Corbet 35
The truly Epidemicall disease! — — — 237 U64 Charles 3 18
. . . Of that truly-noble Lady, the Lady Venetia Digby, . . . 272 U84 Eupheme Ttl
9. Elegie on my Muse. The truly honoured Lady, . . . — 282 U84 Muse Ttl
In Picture, they which truly understand, — — — 370 Author 1
To my truly-belov'd Freind, Mr Browne: on his Pastorals. — 386 Browne Ttl

TRULY-BELOV'D
To my truly-belov'd Freind, Mr Browne: on his Pastorals. — — 386 Browne Ttl

TRULY-NOBLE
. . . Of that truly-noble Lady, the Lady Venetia Digby, . . . 272 U84 Eupheme Ttl

TRUMP
Their Carract was! I, or my trump must breake, — — — 269 U81 Pawlet 27
Their Carract was! for my trump must breake, — — — 269 U81 Pawlet V 27

TRUMPE
In earth, till the last Trumpe awake the Sheepe — — 283 U84 Muse 46

TRUMPET
Who had no lesse a trumpet of their name, — — — — 57 E89 Allen 5
When on thy trumpet shee did sound a blast, — — — 58 E91 Vere 7
Or that doth sound a Trumpet, and doth call — — — 154 U13 Sacvile 35
And rivall with the Trumpet for his sound, — — — 319 Horace 288
Hot from thy trumpet, round, about the world. — — — 396 Drayton 14

TRUMPETS
That we have Trumpets, Armour, and great Horse, — — 213 U44 Speach 7
Yet, let our Trumpets sound; — — — — 239 U67 Muses 13
What Drums or Trumpets, or great Ord'nance can, — — 249 U72 King 9
How do his trumpets breath! What loud alarmes! — — 398 Drayton 66

TRUNDLING
Or trundling Wheele, he can sit still, from all; — — — 331 Horace 568

TRUSS'D
Faine words, unheard of to the well-truss'd race — — 309 Horace 71

TRUST
Shewes of the resurrection little trust. — — — — 37 E34 Death 2
He is no favourites favourite, no deare trust — — — 63 E97 Motion 13
Better'd thy trust to letters; that thy skill; — — — 63 E99 Th Roe 2 2
The world hath seene, which all these had in trust, — — 114 F12 Rutland 39
Simply my Band, his trust in me forsakes, — — — 169 U17 Friend-Debt 12
Now so much friend, as you would trust in me, — — — 169 U17 Friend-Debt 14
A Womans friendship! God whom I trust in, — — — 171 U20 Shrub 1
Put on for fashion, and take up on trust: — — — 171 U20 Shrub 8
To others, as he will deserve the Trust — — — 198 U40 Elegy That 39
And safely trust to dresse, not burne their Boates. — — 208 U43 Vulcan 128
What though she hath won on Trust, as many doe, — — 223 U49 Pucell 21
And trust her I would least, that hath forswore — — 223 U49 Pucell 29
It is a wretched thing to trust to reedes; — — — 281 U84 Kenelme 16
Who in that feast of Resurrection trust! — — — 284 U84 Muse 62
Trie and trust Roger, was the word, but now — — — 378 Coryat 2 80
trust in the tombes, their care-full freinds do rayse; — 387 Cavendish 6

TRUSTED
And some one apteth to be trusted, then, — — — 113 F12 Rutland 10
Was trusted, that you thought my judgement such — — 158 U14 Selden 6
Nor ever trusted to that friendship yet, — — — 216 U45 Squib 7
And trusted so, as it deposited lay — — — 271 U81 Pawlet 81
Beene trusted to thee: not to't selfe assign'd. — — 283 U84 Muse 20

TRUSTER
And that her truster feares her? Must I too? — — — 223 U49 Pucell 22

TRUSTING
But here, neither trusting his hands, nor his legs, — — 375 Coryat 1 34

TRUSTS
He that not trusts me, having vow'd thus much, — — 70 E108 Soldiers 9

TRUTH
Or celebrated with more truth of state? — — — 28 E5 Union 2
Pardon free truth, and let thy modestie, — — — 31 E14 Camden 11
Expresser truth, or truer glorie, — — — 39 E40 Ratcliffe 7
Most thinke all praises flatteries. But truth brings — 49 E67 Suffolk 2
Thy fact is more: let truth encourage thee. — — — 64 E99 Th Roe 2 12
Truth might spend all her voyce, Fame all her art. — 68 E106 E Herbert 4
A desperate soloecisme in truth and wit. — — — 75 E116 Jephson 16
If I would wish, for truth, and not for show, — — 78 E122 Rudyerd 2 1
And would (being ask'd the truth) ashamed say, — — 83 E131 Ferrab. 2 11
For, to say truth, what scullion is so nastie, — — 88 E133 Voyage 147
But thou, my Wroth, if I can truth apply, — — — 99 F3 Wroth 91
But thou, my Wroth, if I may truth apply, — — — 99 F3 Wroth V 91
The truth of times) was of more esteeme, — — — 114 F12 Rutland 21
If with this truth you be inspir'd, — — — 121 F14 Sydney 52
But the Language, and the Truth, — — — 131 U2 Excuse 10
As he durst love Truth and me. — — — — 142 U2 Her man 52
Truth, and the Graces best, when naked are. — — 158 U14 Selden 4
Since, naked, best Truth, and the Graces are. — — 158 U14 Selden V 4
What fables have you vext! what truth redeem'd! — 159 U14 Selden 39
That thou dost all things more for truth, then glory, — 168 U15 Friend-Wars 179
To see men feare: or else for truth, and State, — — 170 U18 Elegy Can 17
Of Truth that searcheth the most hidden Springs, — 176 U24 Frontispice 10
Of Truth which searcheth the most hidden Springs, — 176 U24 Frontispice V 10
The light of Truth, and life of Memorie. — — — 176 U24 Frontispice 18
Such thoughts wil make you more in love with truth. — 181 U26 Ode High 21
You favour Truth, and me, in this mans Cause. — — 186 U31 Elsmere 10
Of London, in the Militarie truth, — — — 213 U44 Speach 26
Freedome, and Truth; with love from those begot: — 241 U69 Friend Son 5

		Page	Title	Line
TRUTH (cont.)				
In truth of colours, both are best.		265	U79 New-yeares	45
And, calling truth to witnesse, make that good		270	U81 Pawlet	35
And, calling truth to witnesse, make it good		270	U81 Pawlet	V 35
Are, with the likenesse of the truth, undone.		307	Horace	34
Are with the likeness of the truth beguil'd:		339	Horace	V 35/ 34
Falshood with truth, as no man can espie		315	Horace	216
Falsehood and truth, as no man can espy		343	Horace	V216
Whether truth may, and whether error bring.		325	Horace	439
The truth; nor let thy Fable thinke, what e're		329	Horace	508
Whether his soothing friend speake truth, or no.		333	Horace	606
Up so much truth, as could I it pursue		372	Epitaph	13
The truth of his heart there, and tell's what a clocke		380	Coryat 3	24
The truth, but gropes, and urgeth all by chance;		391	Shakespeare	10
Wonder to truth! and have my Vision hoorld,		396	Drayton	13
To veiw the truth and owne it. Doe but looke		399	Lady Ogle	5
But in the practisd truth Destruction is		404	Inigo Jones 1	57
Or canst of truth the least intrenchment pitch,		407	Inigo Jones 2	23
You know, I never was of Truth afeard,		414	Rutter	4
How well I lov'd Truth: I was scarce allow'd		414	Rutter	6
Truth itself doth flow in Wine.		657	Door Apollo	6
TRUTHES				
For truthes complexion, where they all weare maskes.		118	F13 Aubigny	70
TRUTHS				
Then, since we (more then many) these truths know:		50	E70 Wm Roe 1	7
Such truths, as we expect for happy men,		246	U70 Ode	83
TRY (See also TRIE)				
Joyne lip to lip, and try:		139	U2 Another	15
And having pleas'd our art, wee'll try		145	U5 Woman-kind	17
'Tis got where it can try the fire.		278	U84 Mind	28
The rough rude Satyres naked; and would try,		319	Horace	321
And rack, with Wine, the man whom they would try,		333	Horace	618
I thought thee then our Orpheus, that wouldst try		397	Drayton	35
TRYALS				
Of Tryals, to worke downe		255	U75 Epithalam.	103
TRY'D				
What your try'd manners are, what theirs should bee.		119	F13 Aubigny	112
O're read, examin'd, try'd, and prov'd your Ryme		421	Censure	7
TRYER				
And so disdaining any tryer;		278	U84 Mind	27
TUB				
And from the sweet Tub Wine of this yeare takes,		291	U85 Country	47
TUBS				
Of all your night-tubs, when the carts doe cluster,		85	E133 Voyage	64
TUILLERIES				
Janin's, your Nuncio's, and your Tuilleries,		69	E107 Hungry	22
TUMOR				
The cold tumor in his feet,		184	U29 Fit of Rime	56
TUMULTS				
Most frequent tumults, horrors, and unrests,		110	F11 Epode	33
TUN				
But yet the Tun at Heidelberg had houpes.		227	U52 Answer	6
TUNE				
And, in a pittious tune, began. How dare		88	E133 Voyage	164
And foundred thy hot teame, to tune my lay.		107	F10 Proludium	9
And foundred thy hot teame, to tune our lay.		107	F10 Proludium	V 9
Or were Affaires in tune,		253	U75 Epithalam.	15
Unto your honour: I can tune in song		261	U77 Treasurer	27
And tune too, fitted to the Chorus rime,		319	Horace	290
A Tune to drown the Ballads of thy Father:		411	Gill	12
But Tune and Noise the Eccho of thy Shame.		411	Gill	14
TUNES				
No tunes are sweet, nor words have sting,		143	U3 Musicall	15
Yet sure my tunes will be the best,		182	U27 Ode Helen	35
Their Sister-tunes, from Thames his either side,		253	U75 Epithalam.	34
Both in their tunes, the licence greater grew,		319	Horace	299
Attempted by the Muses tunes, and strings;		329	Horace	498
Thy tunes alone;		367	Ode Who saith	36
Their labour'd tunes reherse,		420	Ode:If Men	22
TURBOT				
Nor Turbot, nor bright Golden-eyes:		291	U85 Country	50
TURKIE				
In Hungary, and Poland, Turkie too;		69	E107 Hungry	13
Of Noremberg, or Turkie; hang your roomes		260	U77 Treasurer	3
TURND				
those turnd up, and those that fall,		417	Moon	14
TURNE (See also TORN'D)				
Daily to turne in Pauls, and helpe the trade.		56	E88 Monsieur	16
And those to turne to bloud, and make thine owne:		80	E128 Wm Roe 2	4
Turne the stale prologue to some painted maske,		107	F10 Proludium	20
And turne the blackest sorrowes to bright joyes:		112	F11 Epode	95
Turne, upon scorned verse, their quarter-face:		114	F12 Rutland	29
And all the world turne Eares.		143	U3 Musicall	4
All as their prize, turne Pyrats here at Land,		155	U13 Sacvile	81
Since, being deceiv'd, I turne a sharper eye		159	U14 Selden	23
And turne the Ceremonies of those Nights		197	U40 Elegy That	11
Turne him, and see his Threds: looke, if he be		216	U45 Squib	21
To turne mere farmer, had spoke out,		291	U85 Country	68
And so to turne all earnest into jest,		321	Horace	330
And so to turne our earnest into jest,		346	Horace	V322/330
In hand, and turne them over, day, and night.		323	Horace	398
Do turne into a Woman.		364	Phoenix	4
And eve'ry joy, in mariage, turne a fruite.		384	Somerset	18

TURNE (cont.)
will all turne dust, & may not make me swell. . . . 387 Cavendish 4
Upon the Muses anvile: turne the same, . . . 392 Shakespeare 61
Again, thy Architect to ashes turne! . . . 406 Inigo Jones 1 102
TURN'D
Gypsee, new baud, is turn'd physitian, . . . 39 E41 Gypsee 1
When Fates turn'd cruell, . . . 77 E120 S. P. 10
Turn'd to cinders by her eye? . . . 149 U8 Houre-glasse 8
Is Banke-rupt turn'd! the Cassock, Cloake, and Gowne, . . 237 U64 Charles 3 20
Is Banke-rupt turn'd! Cloak, Cassock, Robe, & Gowne, . . 237 U64 Charles 3 V 20
TURNED
Am turned with an others powers. My Passion . . 283 U84 Muse 31
And fainting necks, the turned Share! . . . 291 U85 Country 64
Blot out the carelesse, with his turned pen; . . . 335 Horace 635
TURNERS
Or Turners oyle of Talck. Nor ever got . . . 188 U34 Small Poxe 11
TURNES
That turnes us so much moneys, at which rate . . . 215 U44 Speach 77
And as it turnes our joyfull yeare about, . . . 236 U64 Charles 3 5
If now the turnes, the colours, and right hues . . . 311 Horace 126
TURNING
The like is Jone. But turning home, is sad. . . . 40 E42 Giles 8
Which though the turning world may dis-esteeme, . . . 118 F13 Aubigny 64
Then turning unto him is next at hand, . . . 154 U13 Sacvile 56
And turning all he toucheth into pelfe, . . . 197 U40 Elegy That 22
Unto your strength, and long be turning it: . . . 339 Horace V 56/ 54
TURNS
Great and good turns, as wel could time them too, . . 153 U13 Sacvile 2
TURNST
But when thou turnst a Reall Inigo; . . . 407 Inigo Jones 2 22
TURPINS
The Tristrams, Lanc'lots, Turpins, and the Peers, . . 206 U43 Vulcan 69
TURTLES
Turtles can chastly dye; . . . 111 F11 Epode 74
Turtles will chastly dye; . . . 111 F11 Epode V 74
Or (by our Turtles Augure) . . . 364 Phoenix 5
T'USHER
To shew the rites, and t'usher forth the way . . . 263 U79 New-yeares 4
TUSKE
Nay, now you puffe, tuske, and draw up your chin, . . 69 E107 Hungry 29
TUT
And, told of this, he slights it. Tut, such crimes . . 45 E56 Poet-Ape 9
TUTOR
Grave tutor to the learned horse. Both which, . . . 88 E133 Voyage 157
Borne, bred, allied? what's he dare tutor us? . . . 215 U44 Speach 66
'TWAS
'Twas brought to court first wrapt, and white as milke; . 31 E15 Court-worm 2
He markes not whose 'twas first: and after-times . . 45 E56 Poet-Ape 11
'Twas not entayl'd on title. That some word . . . 75 E116 Jephson 7
Makes, the whole longer, then 'twas given him, much. . 76 E119 Shelton 16
'Twas a child, that so did thrive . . . 77 E120 S. P. 5
But 'twas with purpose to have made them such. . . 159 U14 Selden 22
By naming in what companie 'twas in, . . . 191 U38 Elegy 'Tis 25
'Twas Jupiter that hurl'd thee headlong downe, . . . 203 U43 Vulcan 9
'Twas Jupiter that cast thee headlong downe, . . . 203 U43 Vulcan V 9
'Twas verily some Relique of the Stewes; . . . 209 U43 Vulcan 140
And cry'd 'Twas verily a threatning to the beares; . . 209 U43 Vulcan V146
Nay, sigh'd a Sister, 'twas the Nun, Kate Arden, . . 209 U43 Vulcan 148
How it held out! how (last) 'twas taken in! . . . 213 U44 Speach 22
For 'twas himselfe who form'd, and gave it her. . . 287 U84 Muse 156
Makes his life longer then 'twas given him, much. . . 295 U89 Mart.8:77 8
TWAS
And sayd twas sure a threatning to the beares; . . . 209 U43 Vulcan V146
TWEDES
To Loumond lake, and Twedes blacke-springing fountaine. . 368 Ode Who saith 72
'TWEENE
Runs betweene man, and man; 'tweene dame, and dame; . . 113 F12 Rutland 16
And 'tweene their Grandsires thighes, . . . 258 U75 Epithalam. 173
TWELVE
For twelve yeeres yet to come, what each state lacks, . 59 E92 New Crie 14
Keepe a starre-chamber sentence close, twelve dayes: . 59 E92 New Crie 19
And twice-twelve-yeares stor'd up humanitie, . . . 207 U43 Vulcan 101
With twice-twelve-yeares stor'd up humanitie, . . . 207 U43 Vulcan V101
A third of twelve, you may: foure ounces. Glad, . . 327 Horace 469
TWENTIE
At sixe and twentie, ripe. You shall 'hem meet, . . 58 E92 New Crie 4
But I who live, and have liv'd twentie yeare . . . 200 U42 Elegy Let 29
Full twentie stone; of which I lack two pound: . . 229 U54 Squib 12
How well at twentie had he falne, or stood! . . . 243 U70 Ode 31
TWENTIETH
. . . the two and twentieth day of March, 1607. . . 43 E51 James 3 Ttl
TWENTI'TH
Her two and twenti'th yeare! . . . 240 U67 Muses 48
TWENTY
His weight is twenty Stone within two pound; . . . 230 U56 Covell 11
Her one and twenty yeare! . . . 240 U67 Muses V 48
'TWERE
'Twere madnesse in thee, to betray thy fame, . . . 36 E30 Guiltie 3
'Twere to long, to speake of all: . . . 141 U2 Her man 33
To doe her Husbands rites in, e're 'twere gone . . . 201 U42 Elegy Let 40
A Nations sinne got pardon'd! 'twere a taske . . . 234 U61 Epigram 12
'Twere time that I dy'd too, now shee is dead, . . . 282 U84 Muse 1
Or 'twere the gowned Comoedy they taught. . . . 323 Horace 410

		Page	Title	Line
TWI				
That but the twi-light of your sprite did see,		66	E103 L Wroth 1	2
To separate these twi-/Lights		246	U70 Ode	92
twi-/Lights, the Dioscuri;		246	U70 Ode	93
TWICE				
As twice to trespasse in his sight,		152	U12 Corbet	26
And twice-twelve-yeares stor'd up humanitie,		207	U43 Vulcan	101
With twice-twelve-yeares stor'd up humanitie,		207	U43 Vulcan	V101
In Contract twice, what can shee perjure more?		223	U49 Pucell	30
Hath taken twice the Ring		240	U67 Muses	38
There twice a day in sacred Laies,		292	U86 Hor.4:1	25
Twice, or thrice good, I wonder: but am more		329	Horace	535
And twice, or thrice had 'ssayd it, still in vaine:		333	Horace	626
And twice, or thrice assay'd it, but in vain;		354	Horace	V626
Thy twice conceyvd, thrice payd for Imagery?		405	Inigo Jones 1	90
TWICE-TWELVE-YEARES				
And twice-twelve-yeares stor'd up humanitie,		207	U43 Vulcan	101
With twice-twelve-yeares stor'd up humanitie,		207	U43 Vulcan	V101
TWI-LIGHT				
That but the twi-light of your sprite did see,		66	E103 L Wroth 1	2
TWILIGHT				
May something by that twilight see		273	U84 Cradle	15
TWI-LIGHTS				
To separate these twi-/Lights		246	U70 Ode	92
twi-/Lights, the Dioscuri;		246	U70 Ode	93
'TWILL				
Send it to Bucklers-bury, there 'twill, well.		28	E3 Bookseller	12
Which was a cater-piller. So 'twill dye.		31	E15 Court-worm	4
'Twill see it's sister naked, ere a sword.		74	E115 Honest Man	22
In time 'twill be a heape; This is not true		157	U13 Sacvile	133
Are in your selfe rewarded; yet 'twill be		224	U50 Countesse	15
'Twill be but faire, to leane upon their Fames;		281	U84 Kenelme	13
Our Charles should make thee such? 'Twill not become		406	Inigo Jones 2	3
TWINE				
In the greene circle of thy Ivy twine.		107	F10 Proludium	12
The Poplar tall, he then doth marrying twine		290	U85 Country	9
There, or the tall witch-hazill hee doth twine		290	U85 Country	V 9
TWINS				
From the two Egges, that did disclose the twins.		315	Horace	210
TWIRLE				
Twirle the poore chaine you run a feasting in.		69	E107 Hungry	30
TWISE				
Then can a flea at twise skip i'the Map.		69	E107 Hungry	18
So all his meate he tasteth over, twise:		76	E118 Gut	2
'TWIXT				
'Twixt puritanes, and players, as some cry;		52	E75 Lippe	2
'Twixt feare and rashnesse: not a lust obscene,		156	U13 Sacvile	106
'Twixt death and life! Where her mortalitie		271	U81 Pawlet	67
Hee's carried 'twixt Montrell and Abbevile.		374	Coryat 1	13
TWIXT				
In a Cart twixt Montrell and Abbevile.		380	Coryat 3	53
Are still th'interpreters twixt godds, and men!		395	May	18
Twixt Cotswold, and the Olimpicke exercise:		415	Dover	2
TWO				
But two things, rare, the Fates had in their store,		28	E4 James 1	3
The spoused paire two realmes, the sea the ring.		28	E5 Union	4
Let me give two: that doubly am got free,		31	E13 Empirick	3
His clothes two fashions of, and poore! his sword		33	E21 Gam'ster	3
What two brave perills of the private sword		37	E32 Roe 2	1
- - - the two and twentieth day of March, 1607.		43	E51 James 3	Ttl
Two kindes of valour he doth shew, at ones;		49	E68 Playwrt 2	3
Item, a tale or two, some fortnight after;		51	E73 Fine Grand	7
Or that I'have by, two good sufficient men,		54	E81 Proule	3
Two bravely in the battaile fell, and dy'd,		60	E93 Radcliffe	5
And two, that would have falne as great, as they,		60	E93 Radcliffe	7
How great you were with their two Emperours;		68	E107 Hungry	6
Shuns prease, for two maine causes, poxe, and debt,		76	E119 Shelton	4
And in it, two more horride knaves, then Charon.		84	E133 Voyage	12
I Sing the brave adventure of two wights,		84	E133 Voyage	21
Betweene two walls; where, on one side, to scar men,		86	E133 Voyage	67
To live untill to morrow' hath lost two dayes.		121	F14 Sydney	50
The Gaine of your two friendships! Hayward and		161	U14 Selden	81
The Graine of your two friendships! Hayward and		161	U14 Selden	V 81
Selden! two Names that so much understand!		161	U14 Selden	82
Two letters were enough the plague to teare		172	U21 Ltl Shrub	3
Or two, or three, a Sonne will dis-inherit,		192	U38 Elegy 'Tis	42
I saw with two poore Chambers taken in,		209	U43 Vulcan	135
What though she ride two mile on Holy-dayes,		222	U49 Pucell	15
Full twentie stone; of which I lack two pound:		229	U54 Squib	12
His weight is twenty Stone within two pound.		230	U56 Covell	11
And threat' the great Eclipse. Two houres but runne,		238	U65 Prince	11
And thereat the great Eclipse. Two houres but runne,		238	U65 Prince	V 11
Her two and twenti'th yeare!		240	U67 Muses	48
Two names of friendship, but one Starre:		246	U70 Ode	98
Of two so early men,		247	U70 Ode	125
Porting the Ensignes of united Two,		254	U75 Epithalam.	51
Save the preceding Two?		255	U75 Epithalam.	77
These two, now holy Church hath made them one,		257	U75 Epithalam.	139
Gave two such Houses as Northumberland,		274	U84 Descent	5
Those other two; which must be judg'd, or crown'd:		284	U84 Muse	55
And to that forme, lent two such veines of blood		287	U84 Muse	157
A Scarlet peece, or two, stitch'd in: when or		305	Horace	19
A purple piece, or two stitch'd in: when either		338	Horace	V 19

738

	Page	Title	Line
TWO (cont.)			
From the two Egges, that did disclose the twins.	315	Horace	210
Two rests, a short and long, th'Iambick frame;	323	Horace	371
. . . in the Behalfe of the two Noble Brothers sir Robert	382	Rich	Ttl
Two noble knightes, whome true desire and zeale,	382	Rich	1
The elder of these two, riche hopes Increase,	382	Rich	5
As, on two flowry Carpets, that did rise,	398	Drayton	81
Of two, the choicest Paire of Mans delights,	401	Filmer	4
Till he hath reach'd his two-fold point of Noone.	414	Ghyrlond	52
And a Comptroller, two most rigid men	415	Rutter	24
TWO-FOLD			
Till he hath reach'd his two-fold point of Noone.	414	Ghyrlond	52
TYBERS			
Or Tybers winding streames, I follow thee.	293	U86 Hor.4:1	40
TYE			
And shooe, and tye, and garter should come hether,	56	E88 Monsieur	4
TYES			
His rosie tyes and garters so ore-blowne,	62	E97 Motion	5
TYGRES			
With Doves: or Lambes, with Tygres coupled be.	305	Horace	16
TYKE (See also TIKE)			
If such a Tyke as thou, er'e wer't, or noe?	409	Detractor	14
TYLTING			
A Speach Presented unto King James at a tylting . . .	382	Rich	Ttl
TYME			
In spring tyme roused for their masters sport,	97	F3 Wroth	V 23
or spent my wretched paper or my tyme	204	U43 Vulcan	V 33
By thys Tyme, though you fancie not the man,	231	U56 Covell	V 25
And once more stryke the eare of tyme with those fresh straynes:	420	Ode:If Men	32
I have, with strict advantage of free tyme	421	Censure	6
TYMES			
Yff Men, and tymes were nowe	419	Ode:If Men	1
TYMPANIES			
H'has tympanies of businesse, in his face,	35	E28 Surly	7
TYNDARIDES			
Unto the starres? or the Tyndarides?	115	F12 Rutland	58
TYPE			
But a bare Type and Figure.	364	Phoenix	8
TYRAN			
Tyran Rime hath so abused,	184	U29 Fit of Rime	46
TYRANNIE			
It is an Act of tyrannie, not love,	190	U37 Friend-Book	25
TYRANNY			
With some more change, and tast of tyranny:	205	U43 Vulcan	V 50
TYRANTS			
The fooles, or Tyrants with your friends,	145	U5 Woman-kind	2
That prince that shames a tyrants name to beare,	423	Lucan	19
TYRANYE			
It is an Act of Tyranye, not Love,	422	Censure	18
TYRE			
And, drest in shepheards tyre, who would not say:	68	E105 L Wroth 2	9
Of Tyre-man, Mounte-bank & Justice Jones,	402	Inigo Jones 1	16
TYRE-MAN			
Of Tyre-man, Mounte-bank & Justice Jones,	402	Inigo Jones 1	16
TYRTAEUS			
Next these great Homer and Tyrtaeus set	327	Horace	493
With bold Tyrtaeus verse, when thou art nam'd,	398	Drayton	68
UDDERS			
Their swelling udders doth draw dry:	291	U85 Country	46
UGLY			
In the first jawes appear'd that ugly monster,	85	E133 Voyage	61
Were seene your ugly Centaures, yee call Car-men,	86	E133 Voyage	68
ULCERS			
And to conceale your ulcers, did advise,	38	E38 Guiltie 2	2
ULISSES			
Whilst your Ulisses hath ta'ne leave to goe,	224	U50 Countesse	21
ULYSSES			
Orpheus, Ulysses: or the Latine Muse,	84	E133 Voyage	3
The slie Ulysses stole in a sheepes-skin,	87	E133 Voyage	113
UN			
Thou yet remayn'st, un-hurt in peace, or warre,	60	E93 Radcliffe	13
Their un-avoided subject, fewest see:	60	E94 Bedford 3	8
Know you to be a Sydney, though un-named?	66	E103 L Wroth 1	4
Un-argued then, and yet hath fame from those;	71	E110 Edmonds 1	10
Whose name's un-welcome to the present eare,	74	E115 Honest Man	15
But open, and un-armed encounter'd all:	87	E133 Voyage	135
Upon your eares, of discords so un-sweet?	88	E133 Voyage	171
Live, with un-bought provision blest;	97	F3 Wroth	14
A fixed thought, an eye un-taught to glance;	111	F11 Epode	61
One un-becomming thought doth move	148	U7 Nymph	31
Some brave un-common way:	239	U67 Muses	3
Himselfe so un-inform'd of his elect,	286	U84 Muse	149
Keepe him still active, angry, un-appeas'd,	313	Horace	172
In Moses bush, un-wasted in the fire.	413	Ghyrlond	24
UNALTER'D			
And keepe an even, and unalter'd gaite;	118	F13 Aubigny	61
UN-APPEAS'D			
Keepe him still active, angry, un-appeas'd,	313	Horace	172
UNAPTLY			
Who nought assaies unaptly, or amisse?	315	Horace	200
UN-ARGUED			
Un-argued then, and yet hath fame from those;	71	E110 Edmonds 1	10

		Page	Title	Line
UN-ARMED				
But open, and un-armed encounter'd all:	• • • •	87	E133 Voyage	135
UN-AVOIDED				
Their un-avoided subject, fewest see:	• • • •	60	E94 Bedford 3	8
UNBEARDED				
Th'unbearded Youth, his Guardian once being gone,	• •	315	Horace	229
UN-BECOMMING				
One un-becomming thought doth move	• • • •	148	U7 Nymph	31
UNBLEST				
Yes; and in death, as life, unblest,	• • •	149	U8 Houre-glasse	9
UN-BOUGHT				
Live, with un-bought provision blest;	• • •	97	F3 Wroth	14
UNBOUGHT				
And unbought viands ready makes:	• • • •	291	U85 Country	48
UNBOUNDED				
Expression for! with that unbounded lyne	• •	406	Inigo Jones 1	95
UNBROKE				
Hold thyne owne worth unbroke: which is so good	• •	386	Browne	13
UNCENSUR'D				
And they uncensur'd might at Feasts, and Playes	• •	319	Horace	297
UNCERTAINTY				
And in them view'd th'uncertainty of Life,	• •	411	Sutcliffe	3
UNCHASTE				
All is Venus: save unchaste.	• • • •	137	U2 Cupid	42
UNCLEANE				
Or crack out bawdie speeches, and uncleane.	• •	321	Horace	359
Or cracke out shamefull speeches, or uncleane.	• •	347	Horace	V351/359
UNCLEANNESSE				
So of uncleannesse, or offence,	• • •	152	U12 Corbet	17
UNCOMELY				
With an uncomely silence failes my tongue?	• •	293	U86 Hor.4:1	36
Which in some swarthie fish uncomely ends:	• •	305	Horace	5
Which in a blacke foule fish uncomely ends:	• •	338	Horace	V 5
UN-COMMON				
Some brave un-common way:	• • • •	239	U67 Muses	3
UNCONTROL'D				
I Sing the just, and uncontrol'd Descent	• •	274	U84 Descent	1
UNCOVERS				
Respect, and observation; it uncovers	• • •	363	Riches	7
UNDER				
A dead beautie under-neath thee,	• • •	39	E40 Ratcliffe	2
Under-neath this stone doth lye	• • •	79	E124 Elizabeth	3
Above your under-carved ornaments,	• • •	115	F12 Rutland	85
Under-woods. Consisting Of Divers Poems.	• • •	125	Under-wood	Ttl
Under-wood.	• • •	127	Under-wood	Ttl
Under his Crosse.	• • •	130	U1 Father	32
But under the Disguise of love,	• • •	150	U10 Jealousie	9
It was erected; and still walking under	• • •	157	U13 Sacvile	141
But both fell prest under the load they make.	• •	166	U15 Friend-Wars	128
Under another Name, I take your health:	• •	197	U40 Elegy That	10
And we were left under that Hemisphere,	• •	199	U41 Elegy Since	7
Under that cover; an old Mid-wives hat!	• •	202	U42 Elegy Let	83
Under the Auspice of young Swynnerton.	• •	213	U44 Speach	20
Although my Fame, to his, not under-heares,	• •	219	U47 Tribe	49
Nor dare we under blasphemy conceive	• •	286	U84 Muse	147
Under the angry Moon. But then the boys	• •	354	Horace	V647
Under one title. Thou hast made thy way	• •	397	Drayton	48
Under the Morall? shewe he had a pate	• •	405	Inigo Jones 1	83
UNDER-CARVED				
Above your under-carved ornaments,	• •	115	F12 Rutland	85
UNDER-HEARES				
Although my Fame, to his, not under-heares,	• •	219	U47 Tribe	49
UNDER-NEATH				
A dead beautie under-neath thee,	• • •	39	E40 Ratcliffe	2
Under-neath this stone doth lye	• • •	79	E124 Elizabeth	3
UNDERSTAND				
To reade it well: that is, to understand.	• •	27	E1 Reader	2
And understand 'hem, as most chapmen doe.	• •	59	E92 New Crie	10
My Sword ('tis but a poore Sword, understand)	• •	154	U13 Sacvile	54
Selden! two Names that so much understand!	• •	161	U14 Selden	82
I adde that (but) because I understand	• •	169	U17 Friend-Debt	10
Then rest, and a friends value understand,	• •	216	U45 Squib	25
Would they would understand it! Princes are	• •	268	U80 Christning	5
If you not understand, what Child you had.	• •	271	U81 Pawlet	78
Hee shall, if he can understand,	• •	276	U84 Body	11
And, of your selfe too, understand; yet mind	• •	331	Horace	547
In Picture, they which truly understand,	• •	370	Author	1
Must be intended still to understand:	• •	383	Author	2
Who reads, who roaves, who hopes to understand,	• •	383	Author	7
To understand, hee may at length admire.	• •	383	Author	10
UNDERSTANDING				
By those deepe-grounded, understanding men,	• •	414	Rutter	7
UNDERSTANDS				
To lift to heaven: who is't not understands	• •	234	U61 Epigram	8
UNDERSTOOD				
Both which are ask'd, to have thee understood.	• •	66	E102 Pembroke	4
How few have read! how fewer understood!)	• •	71	E110 Edmonds 1	16
So, where thou liv'st, thou mak'st life understood!	• •	73	E113 Overbury	3
All I wish is understood.	• •	142	U2 Exception	6
But that I understood him scant.	• •	152	U12 Corbet	31
And where they want, she is not understood.	• •	156	U13 Sacvile	112
The life, and fame-vaynes (yet not understood	• •	167	U15 Friend-Wars	166
And from that thought strive to be understood.	• •	168	U15 Friend-Wars	188

			Page	Title	Line
UNDERSTOOD (cont.)					
But both might know their wayes were understood,	.	.	176	U24 Frontispice	7
But both might know their wayes are understood,	.	.	176	U24 Frontispice V	7
In others-evill best was understood:	.	.	217	U46 Coke	6
Our right in France! if ritely understood.	.	.	397	Drayton	58
UNDERTAKES					
But, if it shall be question'd, undertakes,	.	.	74	E115 Honest Man	18
UNDER-WOOD					
Under-wood.	.	.	127	Under-wood	Ttl
UNDER-WOODS					
Under-woods. Consisting Of Divers Poems.	.	.	125	Under-wood	Ttl
UNDONE					
I am undone to night;	.	.	150	U11 Dreame	3
Looke on thy sloth, and give thy selfe undone,	.	.	283	U84 Muse	21
Are, with the likenesse of the truth, undone.	.	.	307	Horace	34
UNEQUALL					
In Verse unequall match'd, first sowre Laments,	.	.	309	Horace	107
UNFIT					
Nor he, for friendship, to be thought unfit,	.	.	78	E121 Rudyerd 1	7
UNFOLD					
But these with wearing will themselves unfold:	.	.	216	U45 Squib	19
UNFORTUNATE					
Nor thinke your selfe unfortunate,	.	.	177	U25 Desmond	27
UNFOUND					
Were yet unfound, and better plac'd in earth,	.	.	114	F12 Rutland	25
Were yet unfound, and better plac'd on earth,	.	.	114	F12 Rutland	V 25
UNFRIGHTED					
But they unfrighted passe, though many a privie	.	.	86	E133 Voyage	73
UNGRATEFULL (See INGRATEFULL)					
UNHEARD					
Faine words, unheard of to the well-truss'd race	.	.	309	Horace	71
Faine words, unheard of to the girded race	.	.	340	Horace	V 71
UN-HURT					
Thou yet remayn'st, un-hurt in peace, or warre,	.	.	60	E93 Radcliffe	13
UN-INFORM'D					
Himselfe so un-inform'd of his elect,	.	.	286	U84 Muse	149
UNION					
On the Union.	.	.	28	E5 Union	Ttl
A Trinitie, to shine in Union;	.	.	128	U1 Trinitie	34
In great Saint Georges Union;	.	.	221	U48 Bacchus	44
Of hearts the union. And those not by chance	.	.	246	U70 Ode	99
God, in the Union, and the Trinitie!	.	.	286	U84 Muse	128
The glorious Trinity in Union met.	.	.	413	Ghyrlond	32
Of Persons, yet in Union (One) divine.	.	.	413	Ghyrlond	35
UNITED					
Porting the Ensignes of united Two,	.	.	254	U75 Epithalam.	51
UNITIE					
But, in a calme, and god-like unitie,	.	.	110	F11 Epode	53
Of persons, still one God, in Unitie,	.	.	127	U1 Trinitie	2
Of persons, still one God in Unitie;	.	.	128	U1 Trinitie	30
Distinct in persons, yet in Unitie	.	.	128	U1 Trinitie	39
UNIVERSALL					
Or universall circumduction	.	.	397	Drayton	51
UNIVERSARY					
- - - On the Universary day of his Raigne. 1629.	.	.	236	U64 Charles 3	VTtl
UNIVERSE					
Thy Universe, though his Epitome.	.	.	185	U30 Burleigh	4
The Cloud, and show the Universe;	.	.	276	U84 Body	18
UNJUST					
His unjust hopes, with praises begg'd, or (worse)	.	.	162	U15 Friend-Wars	12
Before you prove a medicine, is unjust.	.	.	192	U38 Elegy 'Tis	50
UNKIND					
You are unkind.	.	.	180	U26 Ode High	12
UNKINDE					
That no strange, or unkinde	.	.	109	F11 Epode	10
UNKNOWNE					
For all night-sinnes, with others wives, unknowne,	.	.	39	E39 Colt	1
Unknowne which is the Dearest)	.	.	179	U25 Desmond	56
First publish things unspoken, and unknowne.	..	.	313	Horace	186
Till then unknowne, in Carts, wherein did ride	.	.	319	Horace	313
UNLAY'D					
But we last out, still unlay'd.	.	.	259	U76 Petition	24
But hee lasteth and unlay'd.	.	.	259	U76 Petition	V 24
UNLEARN'D					
Learn'd and unlearn'd; holding, whom once he takes;	.	.	337	Horace	677
Learn'd, and unlearn'd; holdeth whom once he takes;	.	.	355	Horace	V677
UNLEARNED					
Both learned, and unlearned, all write Playes.	.	.	410	Brome	12
UNLESSE					
Make accompt, unlesse you can,	.	.	140	U2 Promise	29
Unlesse my heart would as my thought be torne.	.	.	147	U7 Nymph	14
Unlesse some saving-Honour of the Crowne,	.	.	248	U71 Treasurer	13
UNLIKE					
Till he had sold his Piece, drawne so unlike:	.	.	242	U69 Friend Son	13
Fix'd to the bed, and boords, unlike to win	.	.	248	U71 Treasurer	11
UNLOCKE					
Each leafe of his journall, and line doth unlocke	.	.	380	Coryat 3	23
UNLUCKIE					
Be thy next masters more unluckie Muse,	.	.	48	E65 Muse	5
UNMAK'ST					
At once thou mak'st me happie, and unmak'st;	.	.	44	E55 Beaumont	5
UN-NAMED					
Know you to be a Sydney, though un-named?	.	.	66	E103 L Wroth 1	4

741

	Page	Title	Line

UNNECESSARIE
For that unnecessarie Charge they were. . . . . 214 U44 Speach 32
UNPROFITABLE
Unprofitable Chattell, fat and old, ... 230 U56 Covell 8
UNPROFITING
When Mill first came to court, the unprofiting foole, . . 57 E90 Mill 1
UNPROV'D
Though not unprov'd: which shewes, thy fortunes are . . . 60 E93 Radcliffe 14
UNPROVED
Our Poets, too, left nought unproved here; . . . 323 Horace 405
UNREPAIR'D
Losse, remaines yet, as unrepair'd as mine. . . . 211 U43 Vulcan 196
UNRESTS
Most frequent tumults, horrors, and unrests, . . . 110 F11 Epode 33
UNSEASON'D
Unseason'd frostes, or the most envyous weather. . . . 361 Palmer 8
UNSHAKEN
But stood unshaken in his Deeds, and Name, . . . 185 U30 Burleigh 11
UNSKILFULL
Or, who's unskilfull at the Coit, or Ball, . . . 331 Horace 567
UNSOUNDER
Grow unsounder. . . . . 184 U29 Fit of Rime 57
UNSPOKEN
First publish things unspoken, and unknowne. . . . 313 Horace 186
UN-SWEET
Upon your eares, of discords so un-sweet? . . . . 88 E133 Voyage 171
UN-TAUGHT
A fixed thought, an eye un-taught to glance; . . . 111 F11 Epode 61
UNTHANKFULL
That thought can adde, unthankfull, the lay-stall . . 172 U21 Ltl Shrub 8
UNTHOUGHT
And left her lovely body unthought dead! . . . 283 U84 Muse 44
UNTHRIFTELY
Will you part with them, here, unthriftely? . . . 69 E107 Hungry 28
UNTIE
And (withall) I did untie . . . . . 132 U2 How he saw 11
With all corroding Arts, be able to untie! . . . 257 U75 Epithalam. 136
UNTILL
In meere out-formes, untill he lost his sight, . . 73 E114 Sydney 4
To live untill to morrow' hath lost two dayes. . . 121 F14 Sydney 50
Untill they meet . . . . 129 U1 Father 15
As, untill she tell her one, ... 140 U2 Promise 11
Untill the dust retorned bee . . . . . 400 Lady Ogle 31
UNTO
Doe beg thy care unto thy after-state. . . . 43 E51 James 3 8
That unto me dost such religion use! . . . 44 E55 Beaumont 2
I thought to forme unto my zealous Muse, . . . 52 E76 Bedford 1 2
No male unto him: who could so exceed . . . 53 E79 Rutland 7
A line unto thee, till the world it know; . . . 54 E81 Proule 2
Unto the cryes of London Ile adde one; . . . 58 E92 New Crie 2
And unto whom: They are the almanacks . . . 59 E92 New Crie 13
If time to facts, as unto men would owe? . . . 64 E99 Th Roe 2 6
The light, and marke unto posteritie? . . . 67 E104 Montgomery 12
Thy deedes, unto thy name, will prove new wombes, . . 70 E109 Nevil 17
Then stand unto thy selfe, not seeke without . . 83 E131 Ferrab. 2 13
Did dance the famous Morrisse, unto Norwich) . . 85 E133 Voyage 36
And bad her fare-well sough, unto the lurden: . . 87 E133 Voyage 115
And stayes but till you come unto the dore! . . 89 E133 Voyage 178
Hundred, then unto the tother . . . . 103 F6 Celia 2 10
At th'eye and eare (the ports unto the minde) . . 109 F11 Epode 9
His love unto the Muses, when his skill . . 114 F12 Rutland 33
Like life unto 'hem. Who heav'd Hercules . . 115 F12 Rutland 57
Unto the starres? or the Tyndarides? . . . 115 F12 Rutland 58
Your selfe but told unto your selfe, and see . . 117 F13 Aubigny 23
Unto your name, and goodnesse of your life, . . 119 F13 Aubigny 109
Unto himselfe, by being so deare to you. . . 119 F13 Aubigny 117
Conceiv'd in sinne, and unto labour borne, . . 122 F15 Heaven 18
And destin'd unto judgement, after all. . . 122 F15 Heaven 20
Unto her; which Love might take . . . 133 U2 Suffered 9
Unto her beauty; . . . . . 134 U2 Triumph 6
And adde his Actions unto these, . . . 152 U12 Corbet 19
Then turning unto him is next at hand, . . 154 U13 Sacvile 56
Unto their praise, in certaine swearing rites! . . 156 U13 Sacvile 102
Unto the Censure. Yours all need doth flie . . 158 U14 Selden 11
Then which there is not unto Studie'a more . . 158 U14 Selden 13
And lookes unto the forfeit. If you be . . 169 U17 Friend-Debt 13
Unto the other; and live patternes, how . . 171 U19 Elegy By 17
They had, but were a Reed unto thy Sword. . . 187 U33 Councellour 34
You have unto my Store added a booke, . . 189 U37 Friend-Book 4
Will unto Licence that faire leave abuse. . . 190 U37 Friend-Book 24
Of me, I'le softly tread unto my Tombe; . . 199 U41 Elegy Since 20
That (in pure Madrigall) unto his Mother . . 201 U42 Elegy Let 68
Unto the Spittle Sermon. O, what strange . . 201 U42 Elegy Let 71
And to Pauls-Steeple; which was unto us . . 211 U43 Vulcan 193
Care not what trials they are put unto; . . 218 U47 Tribe 2
And looke unto their faces, . . . 220 U48 Bacchus 9
And the right wayes you take unto the right, . . 224 U50 Countesse 3
And studie them unto the noblest ends, . . 224 U50 Countesse 28
Thou, Friend, wilt heare all censures; unto thee . . 232 U58 Book-seller 1
Unto the Vertue. Nothing perfect done, . . 247 U70 Ode 115
Unto the Ships, and they from tier, to tier, . . 249 U72 King 2
Hath rais'd to be the Port unto his Land! . . 250 U73 Weston 4
Mens Loves unto the Lawes, and Lawes to love the Crowne. . . 255 U75 Epithalam. 104

```
                                              Page      Title          Line

UNTO  (cont.)
  Unto your honour: I can tune in song        261   U77 Treasurer      27
  Unto your honour: I can voyce in song       261   U77 Treasurer    V 27
  Unto our yeare doth give the longest light. 262   U78 Digby          16
  Whose praises let's report unto the Woods,  265   U79 New-yeares     52
  Compar'd unto that long eternitie,          285   U84 Muse          106
  Wine, or delicious fruits, unto the Taste;  286   U84 Muse          123
  Unto the Sent, a Spicerie, or Balme;        286   U84 Muse          125
  Let us not then rush blindly on unto it,    294   U88 Petronius       3
  Unto your strength, and long examine it,    307   Horace             54
  Unto your strength, and long be turning it: 339   Horace        V 56/ 54
  And wealth unto our language; and brought forth  309  Horace        82
  Unto the Lyrick Strings, the Muse gave grace 309  Horace           113
  Unto the Scene thou bringst, and dar'st create  313  Horace        179
  Unto the Stage thou bringst, and dar'st create  342  Horace       V179
  Unto the last, as when he first went forth, 313   Horace           181
  And friendly should unto one end conspire.  333   Horace           586
  And friendly should unto their end conspire. 353  Horace          V586
  Unto a cunning piece wrought perspective,   362   Author            10
  Straines fancie unto foule Apostacie,       363   Riches            15
  Which, unto all Ages, for his will be knowne, 379  Coryat 3         11
  A Speach Presented unto King James at a tylting  382  Rich         Ttl
  unto thee, king of men; their noblest partes 382  Rich              3
  And therefore I commend unto the Wife,      386   Husband            8
  Were not the paths I meant unto thy praise: 390   Shakespeare        6
  And number Attributes unto a flood:         394   Jane Ogle          6
  Lucans whole frame unto us, and so wrought, 395   May               20
  Shall not worke out unto it, such a fame.   409   Detractor         12
  Unto the world, in praise of your first Play: 414  Rutter           2
  my mind unto you,                           416   Moon               4
  But unto more dispayre to Imitate their sounde. 420  Ode:If Men     36
  Will unto Lycence, that free Leave Abuse:   422   Censure           17
  unto the bright, and amiable               662   Bedford            2
  appropriates still unto that County:        662   Bedford            4
UNTOUCH'D
  Came backe untouch'd.  This man hath travail'd well.  81  E128 Wm Roe 2  14
UNTRAVELL'D
  That he, untravell'd, should be french so much,  56  E88 Monsieur    7
UNTWISTED
  And weigh'd your Play: untwisted ev'ry thread,  415  Rutter         14
UNTYING
  Worth his untying happen there: And not     317   Horace           274
UN-USED
  Must trie the'un-used valour of a nose:      87   E133 Voyage      132
  That drives the Hart to seeke unused wayes, 264   U79 New-yeares    21
UNVULGAR
  That I may sing my thoughts, in some unvulgar straine.  177  U25 Desmond  13
UN-WASTED
  In Moses bush, un-wasted in the fire.       413   Ghyrlond          24
UNWEARY'D
  T'instruct and teach? or your unweary'd paine  159  U14 Selden      37
  To informe and teach? or your unweary'd paine  159  U14 Selden    V 37
UNWEAVE
  Nor tie knots, nor knots unweave;           142   U2 Her man        50
UN-WELCOME
  Whose name's un-welcome to the present eare,  74  E115 Honest Man   15
UNWIELDIE
  Blowne up; and he (too'unwieldie for that place)  57  E90 Mill      14
UNWONTED
  Unwonted language; and that sense of worth  319   Horace           308
UNWORTHY
  Unworthy such a mistris, such a schoole,     57   E90 Mill           2
  And farre unworthy to blurt out light rimes; 321  Horace          337
  And there is given too unworthy leave       323   Horace           389
UP
  Then takes up fresh commoditie, for dayes;   30   E12 Shift         13
  That's greater, yet: to crie his owne up neate.  35  E28 Surly      11
  'Tis Lucklesse he, that tooke up one on band  42  E46 Luckless 1     3
  He takes up all, makes each mans wit his owne.  45  E56 Poet-Ape     8
  To plucke downe mine, Poll sets up new wits still,  50  E71 Parrat   1
  I Grieve not, Courtling, thou are started up  50  E72 Court-ling     1
  Blowne up; and he (too'unwieldie for that place)  57  E90 Mill      14
  And talke reserv'd, lock'd up, and full of feare,  59  E92 New Crie  17
  To breake up seales, and close 'hem.  And they know,  59  E92 New Crie  29
  Who did, alike with thee, thy house up-beare,  60  E93 Radcliffe     2
  All historie seal'd up, and fables crost;    67   E105 L Wroth 2     2
  Nay, now you puffe, tuske, and draw up your chin,  69  E107 Hungry  29
  Caesar stands up, as from his urne late rose,  72  E111 Edmonds 2   12
  Art still at that, and think'st to blow me'up too?  72  E112 Gamster  6
  The cloth's no sooner gone, but it gets up   74   E115 Honest Man   24
  That age, when thou stood'st up the master-braine:  75  E116 Jephson  4
  How full of want, how swallow'd up, how dead  80  E127 Aubigny       6
  With great gray eyes, are lifted up, and mew'd;  88  E133 Voyage   161
  Thy tables hoord not up for the next day,    95   F2 Penshurst      71
  The apple-harvest and ploued land up cast;   98   F3 Wroth        V 43
  To blow up orphanes, widdowes, and their states;  99  F3 Wroth      79
  Yet art thou both shrunke up, and old,      100   F4 To the World   14
  Since stird'st up jealousies and feares,    101   F4 To the World   43
  Kisse, and score up wealthy summes          103   F6 Celia 2         6
  My Muse up by commission: No, I bring       108   F10 Proludium     28
  Our muse up by commission: No, we bring     108   F10 Proludium   V 28
  like glasse, blowne up, and fashion'd by desire.  108  F10 Proludium  4
  which rap's mee up to the true heav'en of love;  108  F10 Proludium  13
```

                                    743

UP (cont.)

Toyles, by grave custome, up and downe the court,   .   .   .   113 F12 Rutland   5
And, at her strong armes end, hold up, and even,   .   .   .   114 F12 Rutland   42
And, at her strong armes end, there hold up even,   .   .   .   114 F12 Rutland   ⅴ 42
Borne up by statues, shall I reare your head,   .   .   .   115 F12 Rutland   84
Not taken up o' th' doctors, but as well   .   .   .   .   117 F13 Aubigny   33
My selfe up to thee, harrow'd, torne, and bruis'd   .   .   .   127 U1 Trinitie   5
I foole-hardie, there up-tooke   .   .   .   .   .   132 U2 How he saw   20
Whether any would up-braid   .   .   .   .   .   .   138 U2 Kisse   30
Or were set up in a Brake.   .   .   .   .   .   .   142 U2 Her man   40
Or were pent up in a Brake.   .   .   .   .   .   142 U2 Her man   ⅴ 40
Hang up those dull, and envious fooles, ...   146 U6 Defence   1
And spunge-like with it dry up the blood quite: .   .   .   155 U13 Sacvile   69
Meet some new matter to looke up and wonder!   .   .   .   157 U13 Sacvile   142
On whom I could take up, and ne're abuse   .   .   .   .   161 U14 Selden   83
To make up Greatnesse! and mans whole good fix'd   .   .   .   163 U15 Friend-Wars 44
To take the box up for him; and pursues   .   .   .   .   166 U15 Friend-Wars 137
Put on for fashion, and take up on trust: .   .   .   171 U20 Shrub   8
And kept, and bred, and brought up true.   .   .   .   .   173 U22 Elegy Tho   16
Dri'd up? lyes Thespia wast?   .   .   .   .   .   .   174 U23 Himselfe   8
It is a Darknesse hath blockt up my sense,   .   .   .   191 U38 Elegy 'Tis   5
And then I taste it. But as men drinke up   .   .   .   197 U40 Elegy That   3
For though Love thrive, and may grow up with cheare, .   .   .   197 U40 Elegy That   15
Not, like a Midas, shut up in himselfe, ...   197 U40 Elegy That   21
Can lock the Sense up, or the heart a thought,   .   .   .   198 U40 Elegy That   43
(Made to blow up loves secrets) to discover   .   .   .   198 U40 Elegy That   47
Yet keepe those up in sackcloth too, or lether,   .   .   .   200 U42 Elegy Let   25
He did lay up, and would adore the shooe,   .   .   .   201 U42 Elegy Let   55
Lift up some one, and doe, I tell not what.   .   .   .   201 U42 Elegy Let   58
Had made a meale for Vulcan to lick up.   .   .   .   .   206 U43 Vulcan   84
Had bin fitt meate for Vulcan to lick up.   .   .   .   206 U43 Vulcan   ⅴ 84
And twice-twelve-yeares stor'd up humanitie,   .   .   .   207 U43 Vulcan   101
With twice-twelve-yeares stor'd up humanitie,   .   .   .   207 U43 Vulcan   ⅴ101
No mar'le the Clownes of Lemnos tooke thee up,   .   .   .   208 U43 Vulcan   116
That was rak'd up in the Winchestrian Goose   .   .   .   209 U43 Vulcan   142
Which was rak'd up in the Winchestrian Goose   .   .   .   209 U43 Vulcan   ⅴ142
That was lock'd up in the Winchestrian Goose   .   .   .   209 U43 Vulcan   ⅴ142
Blow up, and ruine, myne, and countermyne,   .   .   .   212 U43 Vulcan   205
Powder, or paper, to bring up the youth   .   .   .   .   213 U44 Speach   25
Up among Nations. In the stead of bold   .   .   .   .   214 U44 Speach   51
Carriage, and dressing. There is up of late   .   .   .   215 U44 Speach   88
Her broken Armes up, to their emptie moulds.   .   .   .   216 U44 Speach   102
Much lesse a name would we bring up, or nurse,   .   .   .   216 U45 Squib   9
Stood up thy Nations fame, her Crownes defence.   .   .   .   217 U46 Coke   14
Whereby he may knit sure up   .   .   .   .   .   .   222 U48 Bacchus   47
And that's made up as doth the purse abound.   .   .   .   230 U56 Covell   12
Made up still as the pockett doth abound.   .   .   .   230 U56 Covell   ⅴ 12
This Prince of flowers? Soone shoot thou up, and grow .   .   .   237 U65 Prince   5
Up publike joy, remember   .   .   .   .   .   .   239 U67 Muses   1
Summe up this crowned day, ...   240 U67 Muses   47
Make up this crowned day, ...   240 U67 Muses   ⅴ 47
Got up and thriv'd with honest arts: .   .   .   .   244 U70 Ode   34
But that the Corke of Title boy'd him up.   .   .   .   244 U70 Ode   42
Goe now, and tell out dayes summ'd up with feares,   .   .   .   244 U70 Ode   53
But lyes block'd up, and straightned, narrow'd in,   .   .   .   248 U71 Treasurer   10
Looke up, thou seed of envie, and still bring   .   .   .   250 U73 Weston   1
Why doe I irritate, or stirre up thee, ...   250 U73 Weston   7
Shoot up an Olive fruitfull, faire, ...   251 U74 Weston   28
Him up, to doe the same himselfe had done.   .   .   .   256 U75 Epithalam.   108
For Fame keepes Vertue up, and it Posteritie.   .   .   .   257 U75 Epithalam.   152
These I looke up at, with a reverent eye,   .   .   .   261 U77 Treasurer   23
These looke you up at, with a measuring eye,   .   .   .   261 U77 Treasurer   ⅴ 23
He will cleare up his forehead, thinke thou bring'st .   .   .   263 U78 Digby   21
He will cheare up his forehead, thinke thou bring'st .   .   .   263 U78 Digby   ⅴ 21
What transcripts begg'd? how cry'd up, and how glad, .   .   .   263 U78 Digby   30
What transcripts made? how cry'd up, and how glad,   .   .   .   263 U78 Digby   ⅴ 30
Grow up, sweet Babe, as blessed, in thy Name,   .   .   .   268 U80 Christning   11
Is sung: as als' her getting up   .   .   .   .   .   274 U84 Cradle   37
Up to her owne sublimed hight?   .   .   .   .   .   279 U84 Mind   48
Up to their Ancestors; the rivers side, `   .   .   .   281 U84 Kenelme   18
I summe up mine owne breaking, and wish all.   .   .   .   283 U84 Muse   26
The last of houres, and shutter up of all;   .   .   .   289 U84 Muse   219
Like tender buds shoot up, and freshly grow.   .   .   .   309 Horace   89
This foot the socks tooke up, and buskins grave,   .   .   .   311 Horace   118
Were they as strong ram'd up as Aetna gates.   .   .   .   363 Riches   10
And up againe, in skies, and aire to vent   .   .   .   368 Ode Who saith   77
Up so much truth, as could I pursue   .   .   .   .   372 Epitaph   13
Here, not up Holdborne, but downe a steepe hill,   .   .   .   374 Coryat 1   12
Here, up the Alpes (not so plaine as to Dunstable)   .   .   .   374 Coryat 1   16
Or, like our Money-Brokers, take up names   .   .   .   386 Browne   10
And see both climing up the slippery staire   .   .   .   395 May   2
Is fayre got up, and day some houres begun!   .   .   .   396 Drayton   18
And looking up, I saw Minervas fowle, ...   397 Drayton   33
And when the flesh, here, shut up day,   .   .   .   400 Lady Ogle   27
To cut a Dike? or sticke a Stake up, here,   .   .   .   401 Beaumont   12
That doe cry up the Machine, & the Showes!   .   .   .   403 Inigo Jones 1   32
To hold her up. O Showes! Showes! Mighty Showes!   .   .   .   403 Inigo Jones 1   39
Up & about? Dyve into Cellars too   .   .   .   .   .   405 Inigo Jones 1   80
Moulded or stroakt up to survey a State!   .   .   .   405 Inigo Jones 1   84
It was not so of old: Men tooke up trades   .   .   .   410 Brome   13
Cry'd up of late: Whereto there must be first   .   .   .   415 Rutter   21
those turnd up, and those that fall, ...   417 Moon   14
Hang up all the poor Hop-Drinkers, ...   657 Door Apollo   7

UP-BEARE
Who did, alike with thee, thy house up-beare,   60   E93 Radcliffe   3
UP-BRAID
Whether any would up-braid   138   U2 Kisse   30
UPBRAID
Who, to upbraid the sloth of this our time,   48   E66 Cary   5
The way to meet, what others would upbraid;   153   U13 Sacvile   10
UPBRAIDING
Upbraiding rebells armes, and barbarous pride: 60   E93 Radcliffe   6
A meere upbraiding Griefe, and tort'ring punishment.   256   U75 Epithalam.   120
UPON
To lye upon thy stall, till it be sought;   28   E3 Bookseller   5
A purging bill, now fix'd upon the dore,   29   E7 Hot-house   2
Thy selfe into fresh braules: when, call'd upon,   32   E16 Brain-hardy   4
To King James. Upon the happy false rumour of his death,   43   E51 James 3   Ttl
Looke not upon thy dangers, but our feares.   43   E51 James 3   10
Upon thy wel-made choise of friends, and bookes;   55   E86 Goodyere 2   2
Upon th'accompt, hers grew the quicker trade.   56   E87 Hazard   5
Fortune upon him breakes her selfe, if ill,   63   E98 Th Roe 1   5
That there's no journey set, or thought upon,   81   E129 Mime   3
Whether it languishing stucke upon the wall,   87   E133 Voyage   136
The ever-boyling floud. Whose bankes upon   88   E133 Voyage   142
Upon your eares, of discords so un-sweet?   88   E133 Voyage   171
Divid'st, upon the lesser Deere;   97   F3 Wroth   26
Dispend'st, upon the lesser Deere;   97   F3 Wroth   V 26
That houre upon my morne of age,   100   F4 To the World   2
Upon thy throate, and live exempt   100   F4 To the World   7
Turne, upon scorned verse, their quarter-face: 114   F12 Rutland   29
Painted, or carv'd upon our great-mens tombs,   114   F12 Rutland   45
Upon my flesh t'inflict another wound.   122   F15 Heaven   22
To pay our debts, upon thy Crosse, and cryd'st,   128   U1 Trinitie   23
The gladdest light, darke man can thinke upon;   128   U1 Trinitie   35
Gold, upon a ground of black.   141   U2 Her man   14
They need no stilts, nor rise upon their toes,   157   U13 Sacvile   145
Upon my selfe, and aske to whom? and why?   159   U14 Selden   24
Upon your Center, doe your Circle fill   159   U14 Selden   32
Flowes in upon me, and I cannot raise   160   U14 Selden   62
To gaine upon his belly; and at last   162   U15 Friend-Wars   17
No part or corner man can looke upon,   163   U15 Friend-Wars   27
His Lace and Starch; And fall upon her back   163   U15 Friend-Wars   49
In admiration, stretch'd upon the rack   163   U15 Friend-Wars   50
clowd-/Like upon them lighten? If nature could   164   U15 Friend-Wars   61
They're growne Commoditie upon Exchange;   165   U15 Friend-Wars   86
Tilt one upon another, and now beare   166   U15 Friend-Wars   125
till one upon another, and now beare   166   U15 Friend-Wars   V125
And that pour'd out upon Man-kind can be!   172   U20 Shrub   19
To light upon a Love of mine.   174   U22 Elegy Tho   32
And only pitious scorne, upon their folly waites.   175   U23 Himselfe   24
Nothing, but practise upon honours thrall.   179   U25 Desmond   35
Upon reward, till the reward him sought.   185   U30 Burleigh   14
Who thus long safe, would gaine upon the times   186   U32 Elsmere   9
Upon the reverend Pleaders; doe now shut   187   U33 Councellour   10
Upon record, in this blest child.   188   U35 Chute   4
Or doe upon my selfe some desperate ill;   191   U38 Elegy 'Tis   3
Or lay the excuse upon the Vintners vault;   191   U38 Elegy 'Tis   22
Upon the hope to have another sin   193   U38 Elegy 'Tis   90
Is fix'd upon one leg, and dares not come   198   U40 Elegy That   33
Upon a Velvet Petticote, or a Gowne,   200   U42 Elegy Let   38
So I might dote upon thy Chaires and Stooles   201   U42 Elegy Let   47
An Execration upon Vulcan.   202   U43 Vulcan   Ttl
Ben: Jonson upon the burning of his study and bookes   202   U43 Vulcan   VTtl
Or if thou needs would'st trench upon her power,   204   U43 Vulcan   48
Upon th'Exchange, still, out of Popes-head-Alley;   206   U43 Vulcan   80
Squire of the Squibs, upon the Pageant day,   208   U43 Vulcan   V119
So would'st th'have run upon the Rolls by stealth,   210   U43 Vulcan   169
Light upon thee: Or if those plagues will not doo,   212   U43 Vulcan   V215
You shew'd like Perseus upon Pegasus;   228   U53 Newcastle   7
So that upon the point, my corporall feare   229   U54 Squib   7
Are lost upon accompt! And none will know   237   U64 Charles 3   21
Are lost upon accompt! And none doe know   237   U64 Charles 3   V 21
This sea-girt Isle upon: 240   U67 Muses   33
This sea-girt ground upon: 240   U67 Muses   V 33
Upon his pointed Lance: 240   U67 Muses   39
Upon th'affrighted world: 243   U70 Ode   16
Upon King Charles his Birth-day.   249   U72 King   VTtl
. . . high Treasurer of England, Upon the Day, Hee was   250   U73 Weston   Ttl
Harke how the Bells upon the waters play   253   U75 Epithalam.   33
And set the marke upon,   255   U75 Epithalam.   95
And set their marke upon,   255   U75 Epithalam.   V 95
Upon a Thomas, or a Francis call;   258   U75 Epithalam.   171
Upon a Thomas, or a Sister call;   258   U75 Epithalam.   V171
Upon my Birth-day the eleventh of June;   262   U78 Digby   14
Upon them, (next to Spenser's noble booke,)   263   U78 Digby   24
That have a Flock, or Herd, upon these plaines;   265   U79 New-yeares   47
Where e're he goes upon the ground,   265   U79 New-yeares   58
Thou wouldst have written, Fame, upon my brest: 269   U81 Pawlet   14
Or hath she here, upon the ground,   280   U84 Mind   49
Upon a banke, or field of flowers,   280   U84 Mind   67
'Twill be but faire, to leane upon their Fames;   281   U84 Kenelme   13
That thus have ventur'd these true straines upon;   289   U84 Muse   227
In short; I bid, Let what thou work'st upon,   307   Horace   31
Heare me conclude; let what thou workst upon   339   Horace   V 31
Upon your shoulders. Prove what they will beare,   307   Horace   55

	Page	Title	Line
UPON (cont.)			
Upon the Stage, the figure of a Snake.	317	Horace	268
Or Muse, upon the Lyre, thou chance b'asham'd.	329	Horace	502
Upon the Lyre, thou chance to be asham'd.	353	Horace	V580/502
May, with some right, upon an Author creepe.	329	Horace	538
Whether he piss'd upon his Fathers grave;	335	Horace	671
Upon the Kerne, and wildest Irishry,	367	Ode Who saith	53
Upon the Life, and Death of Playes, and Wits,	370	Fletcher	2
Certaine Verses Written Upon Coryats Crudities,	379	Coryat 3	Ttl
Who bluntly doth but looke upon the same,	383	Author	3
Do wayte upon thee: and theyre Love not bought.	384	Somerset	4
To his friend the Author upon his Richard.	385	Brooke	Ttl
Shee need not blush upon the Mariage-Day.	386	Husband	12
Upon th'Exchange of Letters, as I wou'd	386	Browne	14
Upon it, but will loath, or let it passe,	389	Aleman	9
Upon the Muses anvile: turne the same,	392	Shakespeare	61
And make those flights upon the bankes of Thames,	392	Shakespeare	73
With pause upon it; make this page your booke;	399	Lady Ogle	6
Upon her selfe) to all her sexe!	399	Lady Ogle	10
Fames heate upon the grave did stay;	400	Lady Ogle	28
To make the Language sweet upon her tongue.	402	Inigo Jones 1	14
That I should wryte upon him some sharp verse,	407	Inigo Jones 3	3
With rotten chalk, or Cole upon a wall,	408	Inigo Jones 3	11
That sit upon the Comon Draught: or Strand!	408	Inigo Jones 3	13
Ymounted high upon Selinis crest:	412	Ghyrlond	10
Upon this obeliske, advanc'd for it,	416	Welcome	5
With Chequer Inke, upon his guift, my paper,	666	Glover	8
UPPON			
rise or fall uppon the earth,	417	Moon	18
Uppon soe humbled earth to cast hir eyes:	420	Ode:If Men	30
UPRIGHT			
That they to knowledge so should toure upright,	55	E85 Goodyere 1	6
Thy standing upright to thy selfe, thy ends	68	E106 E Herbert	7
Her upright head, above the reach of Chance,	176	U25 Desmond	6
So great a Vertue stand upright to view,	224	U50 Countesse	19
And hold me to it close; to stand upright	229	U54 Squib	9
Upright and sound,	258	U75 Epithalam.	182
UP-TOOKE			
I foole-hardie, there up-tooke	132	U2 How he saw	20
UPWARD			
How upward, and direct!	366	Ode Who saith	11
UPWARDS			
Presenting upwards, a faire female feature,	305	Horace	4
URGE			
To urge, my lov'd Alphonso, that bold fame	82	E130 Ferrab. 1	1
Doth urge him to runne wrong, or to stand still.	121	F14 Sydney	30
For I will so urge you to't,	140	U2 Promise	14
As I would urge Authoritie for sinne.	191	U38 Elegy 'Tis	26
Of Contumelie, and urge a good man more	193	U38 Elegy 'Tis	100
Or urge thy Greedie flame, thus to devoure	202	U43 Vulcan	3
And raz'd, e're thought could urge, This might have bin!	209	U43 Vulcan	136
Which all men doe, that urge not their owne deeds	281	U84 Kenelme	17
So shall our English Youth urge on, and cry	398	Drayton	69
URG'D			
Impostures branded! And Authorities urg'd!	160	U14 Selden	41
Urg'd, hurried forth, and horld	243	U70 Ode	15
From all affection! when they urg'd the Cure	270	U81 Pawlet	49
URGES			
Necessitie urges	231	U57 Burges	2
URGETH			
Or urgeth us to anger; and anon	311	Horace	154
The truth, but gropes, and urgeth all by chance;	391	Shakespeare	10
URGING			
8. Urging her of a promise.	139	U2 Promise	Ttl
The art of urging, and avoyding harmes,	232	U59 Newcastle	2
URINE			
Urine, and plaisters? when the noise doth beate	88	E133 Voyage	170
URINOUS			
Who shall discharge first his merd-urinous load:	85	E133 Voyage	65
URNE			
Caesar stands up, as from his urne late rose,	72	E111 Edmonds 2	12
And mad'st thy Mothers wombe thine urne.	242	U70 Ode	8
'S			
And if wee must, let's sing of you.	145	U5 Woman-kind	6
Whose praises let's report unto the Woods,	265	U79 New-yeares	52
US			
Left us of feare, but first our crimes, then lawes.	38	E35 James 2	6
When Nature bids us leave to live, 'tis late	50	E70 Wm Roe 1	1
Each best day of our life escapes us, first.	50	E70 Wm Roe 1	6
Though life be short, let us not make it so.	50	E70 Wm Roe 1	8
Through which, our merit leads us to our meeds.	53	E80 Life/Death	2
So to front death, as men might judge us past it.	54	E80 Life/Death	7
With ignorance on us, as they have done	59	E92 New Crie	37
Others more modest, but contemne us too,	59	E92 New Crie	39
In thee, most weighty Savile, liv'd to us:	61	E95 Savile	4
Not that we thinke us worthy such a ghest,	64	E101 Supper	3
Livie, or of some better booke to us,	65	E101 Supper	22
Shall make us sad next morning: or affright	65	E101 Supper	41
That we had left us, nor by time, nor place,	67	E105 L Wroth 2	3
Of some Bride-well, and may, in time, concerne us	85	E133 Voyage	42
Row close then, slaves. Alas, they will beshite us.	86	E133 Voyage	90
Come my Celia, let us prove,	102	F5 Celia 1	1
Come sweet Celia, let us prove,	102	F5 Celia 1	V 1

		Page	Title	Line
US (cont.)				
'Tis, with us, perpetuall night.	. . . . .	102	F5 Celia 1	8
Stil'd but the shaddowes of us men?	. . . . .	104	F7 Women but	6
But grant us perfect, they're not knowne.	. . . .	104	F7 Women but	10
Stil'd but the shaddowes of us men?	. . . . .	104	F7 Women but	12
Sicknesse; onely on us men.	. . . . .	105	F8 Sicknesse	14
Hermes, the cheater, shall not mixe with us,	. . .	107	F10 Proludium	22
Hermes, the cheater, cannot mixe with us,	. . .	107	F10 Proludium	V 22
That did us all salvation bring,	. . . . .	130	U1 Nativitie	8
To make us heires of glory!	. . . . .	130	U1 Nativitie	21
If by us, the oddes were laid,	. . . .	138	U2 Kisse	7
Let who will thinke us dead, or wish our death.	. .	139	U2 Another	18
Come, with our Voyces, let us warre,	. . . .	143	U3 Musicall	1
Till each of us be made a Starre,	. . . .	143	U3 Musicall	3
Till each of us is made a Starre,	. . . .	143	U3 Musicall	V 3
May wish us of their Quire.	. . . . .	144	U3 Musicall	28
Men, if you love us, play no more	. . . .	145	U5 Woman-kind	1
To make us still sing o're, and o're,	. . . .	145	U5 Woman-kind	3
Our pleasure; but preserves us more	. . . .	146	U6 Defence	21
No more are these of us, let them then goe,	. . .	156	U13 Sacvile	113
Of what it tells us) weav'd in to instruct.	. . .	160	U14 Selden	52
Brought on us, and will every hour increase.	. .	166	U15 Friend-Wars	122
Be brought by us to meet our Destinie.	. . .	170	U18 Elegy Can	20
The Divell; and be the damning of us all.	. . .	172	U20 Shrub	24
Come, let us here enjoy the shade;	. . . .	189	U36 Song	1
That makes us live, not that which calls to die.	. .	193	U38 Elegy 'Tis	78
'Cause thou canst halt, with us, in Arts, and Fire!	.	208	U43 Vulcan	110
A Court of Equitie should doe us right,	. . .	211	U43 Vulcan	178
And to Pauls-Steeple; which was unto us	. . .	211	U43 Vulcan	193
Us, in our bearing, that are thus, and thus,	. . .	215	U44 Speach	65
Borne, bred, allied? what's he dare tutor us?	. .	215	U44 Speach	66
That turnes us so much moneys, at which rate	. .	215	U44 Speach	77
And set us all on skipping,	. . . .	222	U48 Bacchus	51
Profit, or Chance had made us: But I know	. . .	241	U69 Friend Son	3
(Were not his Lucius long with us to tarry)	. .	246	U70 Ode	91
A-while with us bright Sun, and helpe our light;	.	252	U75 Epithalam.	2
A-while with us bright Sun, and mend our light,	.	252	U75 Epithalam.	V 2
That leades our flocks and us, and calls both forth	.	264	U79 New-yeares	29
It selfe to us, and come so nigh	. . . .	279	U84 Mind	43
Is it because it sees us dull,	. . . .	279	U84 Mind	45
Us forth, by some Celestiall slight	. . .	279	U84 Mind	47
To style us Friends, who were, by Nature, Foes?	.	286	U84 Muse	139
Adopt us Heires, by grace, who were of those	. .	286	U84 Muse	140
Yet have all debts forgiven us, and advance	. .	286	U84 Muse	143
To justifie, and quicken us in breath!	. . .	288	U84 Muse	204
And us dis-joyn'd force to her brazen yoke,	. .	294	U87 Hor.3:9	18
And done, we straight repent us of the sport:	. .	294	U88 Petronius	2
Let us not then rush blindly on unto it,	. . .	294	U88 Petronius	3
Let us together closely lie, and kisse,	. . .	294	U88 Petronius	7
And Peleus, if they seeke to heart-strike us	. .	311	Horace	136
For Nature, first, within doth fashion us	. . .	311	Horace	152
Or urgeth us to anger; and anon	. . . .	311	Horace	154
With weightie sorrow hurles us all along,	. . .	311	Horace	155
With weightie woes she hurles us all along	. .	342	Horace	V155
And tortures us: and, after, by the tongue	. . .	311	Horace	156
Produce us a blacke Swan?	. . . .	366	Ode Who saith	2
Or Tames be rap't from us	. . . .	369	Ode Who saith	107
Olde Hesiods Ore, and give it us; but thine,	. .	388	Chapman	2
What treasure hast thou brought us! and what store	.	388	Chapman	4
. . . Mr. William Shakespeare: And what he hath left us.		390	Shakespeare	Ttl
Euripides, and Sophocles to us,	. . . .	391	Shakespeare	34
Lucans whole frame unto us, and so wrought,	. .	395	May	20
Or Rurall Virgil come, to pipe to us!	. . .	397	Drayton	28
With us be call'd, the Naso, but this man?	. .	397	Drayton	32
And Gossip-got acquaintance, as, to us	. . .	398	Drayton	85
Controll Ctesibius: overbearing us	. . .	402	Inigo Jones 1	7
Drawne Aristotle on us! & thence showne	. .	402	Inigo Jones 1	9
Who mad'st us happy all, in thy reflexe,	. . .	414	Ghyrlond	47
God blesse us all, Bedford keepe safe:	. . .	419	Grace	V 7
Those dull Girls, no good can mean us,	. . .	657	Door Apollo	11
USE				
Use mine so, too: I give thee leave. But crave	. .	27	E3 Bookseller	3
If thou'ldst but use thy faith, as thou didst then,	.	32	E18 Censurer	7
Makes serious use of all great trade he knowes.	. .	35	E28 Surly	3
Surly, use other arts, these only can	. . .	36	E28 Surly	21
That unto me dost such religion use!	. . .	44	E55 Beaumont	2
To honor, serve, and love; as Poets use.	. . .	52	E76 Bedford 1	4
Rudyerd, as lesser dames, to great ones use,	. .	78	E121 Rudyerd 1	1
Which who can use is happy: Such be thou.	. .	99	F3 Wroth	99
Which who can use is happy: Such art thou.	. .	99	F3 Wroth	V 99
Or whose great name in Poets heaven use,	. .	107	F10 Proludium	2
Madame, be bold to use this truest glasse:	. .	120	F13 Aubigny	122
Use still thy rod,	. . . . .	129	U1 Father	4
Or use all arts, or haunt all Companies	. . .	165	U15 Friend-Wars	91
Now use the bones, we see doth hire a man	. .	166	U15 Friend-Wars	136
Now use the bales, we see doth hire a man	. .	166	U15 Friend-Wars	V136
Such Guides men use not, who their way would find,	.	170	U18 Elegy Can	12
To use the present, then, is not abuse,	. . .	171	U19 Elegy By	21
'Tis of your selfe, and that you use	. . .	173	U22 Elegy Tho	10
Where art thou, Genius? I should use	. . .	176	U25 Desmond	1
Genius, where art thou? I should use	. . .	176	U25 Desmond	V 1

USE (cont.)

	Page	Title	Line
For men to use their fortune reverently,	181	U26 Ode High	23
What use, what strength of reason! and how much	187	U33 Councellour	24
And lesse they know, who being free to use	190	U37 Friend-Book	22
Come to their Schooles,) show 'hem the use of Guns;	214	U44 Speach	58
They talke of Fencing, and the use of Armes,	232	U59 Newcastle	1
So, the allowance from the King to use,	241	U68 House-hold	10
Which to this use, wert built and consecrate!	256	U75 Epithalam.	130
But here I may no colours use.	277	U84 Mind	6
But here we may no colours use.	277	U84 Mind	V 6
Of Poems here describ'd, I can, nor use,	311	Horace	127
Doth wretchedly the use of things forbeare,	317	Horace	243
Hee, that not knowes the games, nor how to use	331	Horace	565
Or great in money's out at use, command	333	Horace	600
Or wealthy in money's out at use, command	353	Horace	V600
Then I admir'd, the rare and prescious use	361	Palmer	9
There, thou art Homer! Pray thee, use the stile	398	Drayton	59
And when he ships them where to use their Armes,	398	Drayton	65
Such, as the creeping common Pioners use	400	Beaumont	5
And lesse they knowe, that being free to use	422	Censure	15

US'D

	Page	Title	Line
And, in so shitten sort, so long had us'd him:	86	E133 Voyage	98
I have already us'd some happy houres,	115	F12 Rutland	74
This hath our ill-us'd freedome, and soft peace	166	U15 Friend-Wars	121

USED

	Page	Title	Line
Must trie the'un-used valour of a nose:	87	E133 Voyage	132

USES

	Page	Title	Line
Familiar, for the uses sake;	146	U6 Defence	16
To all the uses of the field, and race,	228	U53 Newcastle	3

USHER (See also HUISHERS)

	Page	Title	Line
To shew the rites, and t'usher forth the way	263	U79 New-yeares	4

USHRING

	Page	Title	Line
Ushring the mutton; with a short-leg'd hen,	64	E101 Supper	11

USING

	Page	Title	Line
With reverence using all the gifts thence given.	219	U47 Tribe	62
In using also of new words, to be	307	Horace	65

USUALL

	Page	Title	Line
Not usuall in a Lady; and yet true:	394	Jane Ogle	14

USURER

	Page	Title	Line
On Banck the Usurer.	36	E31 Banck	Ttl
Till that no usurer, nor his bawds dare lend	118	F13 Aubigny	78
'Tis then a crime, when the Usurer is Judge.	169	U17 Friend-Debt	4
These thoughts when Usurer Alphius, now about	291	U85 Country	67
These thinges when Usurer Alphius, now about	291	U85 Country	V 67

USURER'S

	Page	Title	Line
On Chuffe, Bancks the Usurer's Kinsman.	41	E44 Chuff	Ttl

USURERS

	Page	Title	Line
On Baudes, and Usurers.	45	E57 Bawds	Ttl
Or, that it lay, heap'd like an usurers masse,	88	E133 Voyage	139
Goe make our selves the Usurers at a cast.	166	U15 Friend-Wars	134
And is not in the Usurers bands:	289	U85 Country	4

USURIE

	Page	Title	Line
Baudrie', and usurie were one kind of game.	45	E57 Bawds	2

USURPED

	Page	Title	Line
And bad me lay th'usurped laurell downe:	80	E126 Mrs Cary	4

USURPING

	Page	Title	Line
Of which usurping rancke, some have thought love	110	F11 Epode	31

UTMOST

	Page	Title	Line
And all on utmost ruine set;	243	U70 Ode	18
To utmost Thule: whence, he backes the Seas	368	Ode Who saith	69

UTTER (ADJECTIVE)

	Page	Title	Line
And utter stranger to all ayre of France)	83	E132 Sylvester	4

UTTER

	Page	Title	Line
And ever will, to utter termes that bee	309	Horace	84
But a well-compass'd mouth to utter it;	327	Horace	462

UTTER'D

	Page	Title	Line
That shall be utter'd at our mirthfull boord,	65	E101 Supper	40
I, yet, had utter'd nothing on thy part,	82	E130 Ferrab. 1	15
This, utter'd by an antient Bard,	274	U84 Cradle	33

UTTERLY

	Page	Title	Line
Courtling, I rather thou should'st utterly	43	E52 Courtling	1

UTT'RING

	Page	Title	Line
Yet, if by chance, in utt'ring things abstruse,	307	Horace	69

UTTRING

	Page	Title	Line
The art of uttring wares, if they were bad;	385	Husband	6

UV'DALE

	Page	Title	Line
Uv'dale, thou piece of the first times, a man	79	E125 Uvedale	1

UVEDALE

	Page	Title	Line
To Sir William Uvedale.	79	E125 Uvedale	Ttl

VAILE

	Page	Title	Line
Vaile their owne eyes, and would impartially	170	U18 Elegy Can	19

VAIN

	Page	Title	Line
And twice, or thrice assay'd it, but in vain;	354	Horace	V626

VAINE (VEIN)

	Page	Title	Line
Then I made 'hem good, to fit your vaine.	51	E73 Fine Grand	20

VAINE

	Page	Title	Line
To catch the worlds loose laughter, or vaine gaze.	27	E2 My Booke	12
Th'expence in odours is a most vaine sinne,	33	E20 Cod 2	1
Ile not offend thee with a vaine teare more,	37	E33 Roe 3	1
For Cupid, who (at first) tooke vaine delight,	73	F114 Sydney	3
I weare not these my wings in vaine.	93	F1 Why write no	7
Spend not then his guifts in vaine,	102	F5 Celia 1	5
I long, and should not beg in vaine,	139	U2 Another	2
No pleasures vaine did chime,	246	U70 Ode	102

VAINE (cont.)
Whose shapes, like sick-mens dreames, are fain'd so vaine, . 305 Horace   9
Whose shapes, like sick-mens dreames, are form'd so vaine, . 338 Horace   V 9
And toile in vaine: the excellence is such   .   .   .   . 321 Horace   352
And twice, or thrice had 'ssayd it, still in vaine: .   .   . 333 Horace   626
In vaine, but you, and yours, you should love still .   -   . 335 Horace   631
In vaine to follow: .   .   .   . 366 Ode Who saith   14
Stay, till she make her vaine Approches. Then   .   .   . 401 Beaumont   15
Thou'rt too ambitious: and dost fear in vaine!   .   .   . 408 Inigo Jones 3   6
VAL
Be, or be not, to get the Val-telline?   .   .   .   . 219 U47 Tribe   32
VALE
Or in the bending Vale beholds a-farre   .   .   .   . 290 U85 Country   13
Or in the bending Vale beholds from far   .   .   .   . 290 U85 Country   V 13
The Vale, that bred thee pure, as her Hills Snow. .   .   . 367 Ode Who saith   40
VALEW
Nor out-valew, nor contemne;   .   .   .   .   .   . 142 U2 Her man   48
Thinkes it selfe nought, though she should valew it.   .   . 223 U49 Pucell   24
VALIANT
Hardie, thy braine is valiant, 'tis confest, ... 32 E16 Brain-hardy   1
And best become the valiant man to weare, ... 58 E91 Vere   17
Achilles was not first, that valiant was, ... 114 F12 Rutland   51
Valiant he should be as fire, ... 142 U2 Her man   41
And valiant were, with, or without their hands.   .   .   . 233 U59 Newcastle   24
Hee's prudent, valiant, just, and temperate;   .   .   . 262 U78 Digby   5
That Rebells actions, are but valiant crimes!   .   .   . 397 Drayton   44
VALIANTER
Man thought the valianter, 'cause he durst sweare,   .   . 168 U15 Friend-Wars   192
VALIANT'ST
Hee's valiant'st, that dares fight, and not for pay;   .   . 49 E66 Cary   17
VALLEY
Lyes the Valley, cal'd my nest, ... 137 U2 Cupid   34
Her blessed Soule, hence, forth this valley vane   .   .   . 283 U84 Muse   34
VALLEYS
Rivers, and Valleys, Eccho what wee sing. .   .   .   . 264 U79 New-yeares   35
VALLIES
Rivers, and Vallies, Eccho what wee sing. .   .   .   . 264 U79 New-yeares   27
VALOUR
Durst valour make, almost, but not a crime.   .   .   . 48 E66 Cary   6
Two kindes of valour he doth shew, at ones;   .   .   . 49 E68 Playwrt 2   3
Thou, that art all their valour, all their spirit,   .   .   . 60 E93 Radcliffe   9
Or valour, or thy judgement seasoning it, ... 68 E106 E Herbert   6
But still their valour, and their vertue fenc't 'hem,   .   . 86 E133 Voyage   76
Must trie the'un-used valour of a nose: .   .   .   . 87 E133 Voyage   132
Such as in valour would excell, ... 146 U6 Defence   7
Of Valour, but at this Idolatrous rate?   .   .   .   . 156 U13 Sacvile   104
True valour doth her owne renowne command .   .   . 180 U26 Ode High   16
Wonder to Valour! No, it is the Law   .   .   .   . 233 U59 Newcastle   14
Valour! to sleight it, being done to you! .   .   .   . 233 U59 Newcastle   16
All this (my Lord) is Valour! This is yours!   .   .   . 233 U59 Newcastle   19
And therein (which is worth his valour too)   .   .   . 378 Coryat 2   84
VAL-TELLINE
Be, or be not, to get the Val-telline?   .   .   .   . 219 U47 Tribe   32
VALUATIONS
The valuations, mixtures, and the same   .   .   .   . 415 Rutter   29
VALUE
Goe high, or low, as thou wilt value it.   .   .   .   . 50 E72 Court-ling   4
At fifty yeares, almost, to value it, ... 171 U20 Shrub   5
Then rest, and a friends value understand, ... 216 U45 Squib   25
Nay, and in this, thou show'st to value more   .   .   . 235 U62 Charles 1   9
Yet, there's a value given to this man.   .   .   .   . 331 Horace   554
VALU'D
Or masked man, if valu'd by his face, ... 243 U70 Ode   23
VALURE
Keepe thy selfe there, and thinke thy valure right, .   .   . 32 E16 Brain-hardy   9
VANE
Her blessed Soule, hence, forth this valley vane   .   .   . 283 U84 Muse   34
VANISH'D
Vanish'd away: as you must all presume   .   .   . 87 E133 Voyage   110
And wit vanish'd.   .   .   .   . 183 U29 Fit of Rime   18
VANITIE
In this, and like, an itch of Vanitie, ... 166 U15 Friend-Wars   143
VAPOUR
Or lest that vapour might the Citie choake, .   .   . 211 U43 Vulcan   182
Or lest that vapour should the Citie choake,   .   .   . 211 U43 Vulcan   V182
VARIE
More, then to varie what our elders knew: .   .   . 72 E111 Edmonds 2   6
As in his place, because he would not varie,   .   .   . 171 U19 Elegy By   27
VARIED
In varied shapes, which for his lust shee takes: .   . 34 E25 Beast 1   6
Some note of which each varied Pillar beares,   .   .   . 176 U24 Frontispice   15
VARIETIE
Varietie of Silkes were on th'Exchange!   .   .   . 202 U42 Elegy Let   72
With some more thrift, and more varietie: .   .   . 205 U43 Vulcan   50
With some more thrift, and yet varietie: .   .   . 205 U43 Vulcan   V 50
VARIOUS
Then the various Moone the flood!   .   .   .   . 136 U2 Cupid   4
This, seeking, in a various kind, to forme .   .   .   . 307 Horace   40
Or sweet, or various, in the course!   .   .   . 399 Lady Ogle   20
VARIUS
Or Varius? Why am I now envi'd so, ... 309 Horace   79
VARY
Nor Sunne could make to vary from the rest,   .   .   . 367 Ode Who saith   29

VARYED
    And after varyed, as fresh objects goes, ...   118   F13 Aubigny   66
VARYING
    The frequent varying of the deed, ...   146   U6 Defence   11
    So he that varying still affects to draw   339   Horace   V 42/ 40
VAST
    So ravenous, and vast an appetite?   206   U43 Vulcan   86
    I am not so voluminous, and vast, ...   226   U52 Answer   2
VAULT
    Leave it buryed in this vault.   79   E124 Elizabeth   8
    Or lay the excuse upon the Vintners vault;   191   U38 Elegy 'Tis   22
VAYNES
    The life, and fame-vaynes (yet not understood   167   U15 Friend-Wars   166
VEIL   (See VAILE)
VEINE   (See also VEYNE, VAINE)
    Can; or all toile, without a wealthie veine: 331   Horace   584
VEINES
    At either Stemme, and know the veines of good   274   U84 Descent   8
    And to that forme, lent two such veines of blood   287   U84 Muse   157
VEIW
    But when againe I veiw the parts so peiz'd, ...   395   May   7
    To veiw the truth and owne it. Doe but looke   399   Lady Ogle   5
VELVET
    His cloke with orient velvet quite lin'd through, ...   62   E97 Motion   4
    With Velvet, Plush, and Tissues, it is spirit.   164   U15 Friend-Wars   58
    Upon a Velvet Petticote, or a Gowne, ...   200   U42 Elegy Let   38
    A Goat in Velvet; or some block could move   202   U42 Elegy Let   82
    Bawd, in a Velvet scabberd! I envy   202   U42 Elegy Let   85
    What though she be with Velvet gownes indu'd, ...   222   U49 Pucell   18
    Velvet, or Taffata cap, rank'd in the darke   371   Fletcher   5
    Noe velvet Sheath you weare, will alter kynde.   403   Inigo Jones 1   26
VELVETS
    The Stuffes, the Velvets, Plushes, Fringes, Lace, ...   202   U42 Elegy Let   79
    What makes these Velvets, Silkes, and Lawne, ...   275   U84 Body   2
VENERABLE
    Most venerable. Cause of all our joy.   414   Ghyrlond   42
VENERY
    How faine for his venery he was to crie (Tergum o) .   .   .   380   Coryat 3   37
VENETIA
    . . . Of that truly-noble Lady, the Lady Venetia Digby, . . .   272   U84 Eupheme   Ttl
    Of Dame Venetia Digby, styl'd The Faire: 274   U84 Descent   2
    . . . the Lady Venetia Digby; who living, ...   282   U84 Muse   Ttl
VENETIAN
    Of your Moravian horse, Venetian bull.   69   E107 Hungry   8
VENICE
    From Venice, Paris, or some in-land passage   85   E133 Voyage   33
    From Venice to Flushing, were not they well cobled? .   .   .   380   Coryat 3   42
VENT
    To vent that poore desire, ...   150   U10 Jealousie   5
    It vent it selfe, but as it would, ...   151   U12 Corbet   2
    To vent their Libels, and to issue rimes, ...   218   U47 Tribe   26
    And up againe, in skies, and aire to vent   368   Ode Who saith   77
VENTED
    Which thou hast only vented, not enjoy'd.   210   U43 Vulcan   168
VENTER
    Where Pittes, or Wright, or Modet would not venter, .   .   .   164   U15 Friend-Wars   80
    Venter a longer time, and willingly: 169   U17 Friend-Debt   15
    And that he will venter   231   U57 Burges   5
    Nay they will venter ones Descent to hitt, ...   394   Jane Ogle   11
VENTRING
    With thy small stocke, why art thou ventring still, .   .   .   72   E112 Gamster   1
    A ventring Merchant, or the Farmer free   313   Horace   165
    A ventring Merchant, or the husband free   342   Horace   V165
VENTUR'D
    That thus have ventur'd these true straines upon;   289   U84 Muse   227
VENTURES
    Wise-crafts, on which the flatterer ventures not. .   .   .   241   U69 Friend Son   6
VENUS
    Goe, crampe dull Mars, light Venus, when he snorts, .   .   .   107   F10 Proludium   16
    All is Venus: save unchaste.   137   U2 Cupid   42
    Shee is Venus, when she smiles, ...   137   U2 Cupid   52
    Venus, and Minerva's eyes, ...   141   U2 Her man   15
    For Venus Ceston, every line you make.   182   U28 Worth   14
    When Venus there maintain'd the Misterie.   209   U43 Vulcan   144
    Nay, sayth a sister, Venus Nun, Kate Arden, ...   209   U43 Vulcan   V148
    Troy, though it were so much his Venus care.   210   U43 Vulcan   160
    Troy, though it were so much thy Venus joycare.   210   U43 Vulcan   V160
    But Venus and the Graces   221   U48 Bacchus   33
    As here no Venus were;   240   U67 Muses   34
    Ode the first.   The fourth Booke.   To Venus.   292   U86 Hor.4:1   Ttl
    Venus, againe thou mov'st a warre   292   U86 Hor.4:1   1
    Wine it is the Milk of Venus, ...   657   Door Apollo   12
VENUSINE
    All the old Venusine, in Poetrie, ...   207   U43 Vulcan   89
    What the old Venusine, in Poetrie, ...   207   U43 Vulcan   V 89
    With the old Venusine, in Poetrie, ...   207   U43 Vulcan   V 89
VERDURE
    The very verdure of her nest, ...   251   U74 Weston   13
VERE
    To Sir Horace Vere.   58   E91 Vere   Ttl
    To the worthy Sir Horace Vere.   58   E91 Vere   VTtl
    Illustrous Vere, or Horace; fit to be   58   E91 Vere   3

	Page	Title	Line

VERIEST
Dam's whom he damn'd to, as the veriest Gull, ... 154 U13 Sacvile 57
VERILY
'Twas verily some Relique of the Stewes: . . . 209 U43 Vulcan 140
And cry'd 'Twas verily a threatning to the beares; . . 209 U43 Vulcan V146
VERMILION
Vermilion, Lake, or Cinnopar affoards . . . . 406 Inigo Jones 1 94
VERSE
Take better ornaments, my teares, and verse. . . 35 E27 Roe 1 2
When, in my Verse, men reade but Sarum's name, . . . 41 E43 Salisbury 1 V 9
Or goddesse to invoke, to stuffe my verse; . . . 85 E133 Voyage 45
I thought to binde him, in my verse: . . . 93 F1 Why write no 2
His absence in my verse, is all I aske. . . 107 F10 Proludium 21
His absence in our verse, is all I aske. . . 107 F10 Proludium V 21
I, that have none (to send you) send you verse. . . 113 F12 Rutland 19
Turne, upon scorned verse, their quarter-face: . . 114 F12 Rutland 29
Then all, that have but done my verse lesse grace, . . 115 F12 Rutland V 79
As the Bath your verse discloses . . . . 136 U2 Cupid 21
And, if such a verse as this, ... 138 U2 Kisse 35
Before men get a verse: much lesse a Praise; . . 159 U14 Selden 26
Not make a verse; or Anger; or laughter would, . . 164 U15 Friend-Wars 62
So well as I may tell in verse, 'tis so? . . 170 U19 Elegy By 12
Lie drawne to life, in his soft Verse, . . . 181 U27 Ode Helen 7
For in your verse all Cupids Armorie, . . . 182 U28 Worth 9
Propping Verse, for feare of falling . . . 183 U29 Fit of Rime 8
He would have done in verse, with any of those . . 201 U42 Elegy Let 62
A paire of Scisars, and a Combe in verse; . . 204 U43 Vulcan 38
Verse, that should thee, and me out-live. . . . 229 U55 Burges 4
For in the Genius of a Poets Verse, . . . 241 U68 House-hold 13
Shall Verse be set to Harpe and Lute, . . . 292 U86 Hor.4:1 23
In Verse unequall match'd, first sowre Laments, . . 309 Horace 107
As fit t'exchange discourse; a Verse to win . . 311 Horace 119
In tragick Verse; no lesse Thyestes feast . . . 311 Horace 122
Hee too, that did in Tragick Verse contend . . 319 Horace 319
Their youthfull tricks in over-wanton verse: . . 321 Horace 358
Or play young tricks in over-wanton verse; . . 347 Horace V350/358
A foot, whose swiftnesse gave the Verse the name . . 323 Horace 372
My Verse at randome, and licentiously? . . 323 Horace 391
A lawfull Verse, by th'eare, or finger scan. . . 323 Horace 404
To taxe that Verse, which many a day, and blot . . 325 Horace 416
Of verse meere-matter-lesse, and tinckling toies. . . 327 Horace 460
The Oracles, too, were given out in Verse: . . 329 Horace 496
Of their long labours, was in Verse set downe: . . 329 Horace 500
'Tis now inquir'd, which makes the nobler Verse, . . 331 Horace 581
An admirable Verse. The great Scurfe take . . 333 Horace 594
An admirable Verse: the great Scab take . . 353 Horace V594
On artlesse Verse; the hard ones he will blame; . . 335 Horace 634
Those ambling visits, passe in verse, betweene . . 396 Drayton 4
With bold Tyrtaeus verse, when thou art nam'd, . . 398 Drayton 68
French Aire and English Verse here Wedded lie. . . 401 Filmer 6
Or Verse, or Sense t'express Immortall you? . . 403 Inigo Jones 1 41
That I should wryte upon him some sharp verse, . . 407 Inigo Jones 3 3
Thie long watch'd verse . . . . 420 Ode:If Men 20
before, I wryte more verse, to bee more wyse. . . 421 Censure 2
VERSER
Who, though shee have a better verser got, . . 115 F12 Rutland 68
VERSES
Which hee thinkes great; and so reades verses, too: . . 35 E28 Surly 5
Play-wright me reades, and still my verses damnes, . . 42 E49 Playwrt 1 1
Chev'ril cryes out, my verses libells are; . . 44 E54 Chev'ril 2 1
To reade my verses; now I must to heare: . . . 45 E58 Groome 2
In most vile verses, and cost me more paine, . . 51 E73 Fine Grand 19
And Ile professe no verses to repeate: . . . 65 E101 Supper 24
Verses on his Picture . . . . . 149 U9 Picture VTtl
Then shall my Verses, like strong Charmes, . . 177 U25 Desmond 18
Then shall our Verses, like strong Charmes, . . 177 U25 Desmond V 18
No Poets verses yet did ever move, . . . 199 U42 Elegy Let 3
It is a ryming Age, and Verses swarme . . . 200 U42 Elegy Let 27
You won not Verses, Madam, you won mee, . . 230 U56 Covell 1
How many verses, Madam, are your Due! . . 231 U56 Covell 27
For he doth love my Verses, and will looke . . 263 U78 Digby 23
Those heavie Verses, sent so to the Stage, . . 323 Horace 384
Thinke wee, or hope, there can be Verses fain'd . . 327 Horace 474
To divine Poets, and their Verses came. . . 327 Horace 492
Yet who's most ignorant, dares Verses make. . . 331 Horace 570
You doe not bring, to judge your Verses, one, . . 333 Horace 609
When you write Verses, with your judge do so: . . 333 Horace 620
When you make verses, with your judge doe so: . . 354 Horace V620
Those ill-torn'd Verses, to new nammering. . . 333 Horace 628
The while he belcheth loftie Verses out, . . 335 Horace 649
His cause of making Verses none knowes why: . . 335 Horace 670
Here's one makes verses, but there's none knows why: . . 355 Horace V670
Certaine Verses Written Upon Coryats Crudities, . . . 379 Coryat 3 Ttl
My verses were commended, thou dar'st say, . . 408 Detractor 1
VERT
Preserved, in her antique bed of Vert, . . . 413 Ghyrlond 19
VERTU'
That durst be that in Court: a vertu' alone . . 371 Epitaph 4
VERTUE'
As nothing else discernes the vertue' or vice. . . 66 E102 Pembroke 12
So did thy vertue'enforme, thy wit sustaine . . 75 E116 Jephson 3
VERTUE
With what thy vertue on the times hath won, . . 47 E63 Salisbury 2 2

			Page	Title	Line

VERTUE (cont.)
I meant each softest vertue, there should meet, . . . 52 E76 Bedford 1 11
A romane sound, but romane vertue weares, . . . 58 E91 Vere 2
For the great marke of vertue, those being gone . . . 60 E93 Radcliffe 2
And what would hurt his vertue makes it still. . . . 63 E98 Th Roe 1 6
Of vice, and vertue; wherein all great life . . . 66 E102 Pembroke 6
They follow vertue, for reward, to day; . . . 66 E102 Pembroke 9
If men get name, for some one vertue: Then, . . . 68 E106 E Herbert 1
Where vertue makes them both, and that's in thee: . . . 70 E109 Nevil 3
Where finding so much beautie met with vertue, . . . 74 E114 Sydney 6
If I would vertue set, as shee was yong, . . . 78 E122 Rudyerd 2 5
To more vertue, then doth live. . . . 79 E124 Elizabeth 6
Made for what Nature could, or Vertue can: . . . 79 E125 Uvedale 2
But still their valour, and their vertue fenc't 'hem, . . . 86 E133 Voyage 76
Is vertue, and not Fate: . . . 109 F11 Epode 2
Next, to that vertue, is to know vice well, . . . 109 F11 Epode 3
Richer then Time, and as Time's vertue, rare. . . . 111 F11 Epode 59
Whil'st that, for which, all vertue now is sold, . . . 113 F12 Rutland 1
With every vertue, wheresoere it move, . . . 116 F13 Aubigny 8
And raise not vertue; they may vice enhance. . . . 117 F13 Aubigny 42
Of so great title, birth, but vertue most, . . . 118 F13 Aubigny 49
Of vertue, which you tread? what if alone? . . . 118 F13 Aubigny 55
Of nobles vertue, shew in you: . . . 121 F14 Sydney 32
Our proper vertue is to range: . . . 146 U6 Defence 4
Yet is't your vertue now I raise. . . . 173 U22 Elegy Tho 4
A vertue, like Allay, so gone . . . 173 U22 Elegy Tho 5
'Tis crowne enough to vertue still, her owne applause. . . . 174 U23 Himselfe 18
When Vice alike in time with vertue dur'd. . . . 176 U24 Frontispice 8
Where weaknesse doth offend, and vertue grieve, . . . 192 U38 Elegy 'Tis 33
Goe on, increase in vertue; and in fame: . . . 214 U44 Speach 49
Past any need of vertue. Let them care, . . . 215 U44 Speach 83
The fate of things: whilst totter'd vertue holds . . . 216 U44 Speach 101
'Tis vertue alone, or nothing, that knits friends: . . . 216 U45 Squib 12
Whom Fortune aided lesse, or vertue more. . . . 217 U46 Coke 4
None Fortune aided lesse, or Vertue more. . . . 217 U46 Coke 22
No friend to vertue, could be silent here. . . . 224 U50 Countesse 8
So great a Vertue stand upright to view, . . . 224 U50 Countesse 19
Of Vertue, got above his name? . . . 234 U60 La-ware 10
Unto the Vertue. Nothing perfect done, . . . 247 U70 Ode 115
To vertue, and true worth, be ever blind. . . . 250 U73 Weston 10
For Fame keepes Vertue up, and it Posteritie. . . . 257 U75 Epithalam. 152
Extend a reaching vertue, early and late: . . . 258 U75 Epithalam. 180
In him all vertue is beheld in State: . . . 262 U78 Digby 6
'Tis Vertue alone, is true Nobilitie. . . . 282 U84 Kenelme 21
Which Vertue from your Father, ripe, will fall; . . . 282 U84 Kenelme 22
By beatifick vertue of the Place. . . . 285 U84 Muse 116
The vertue of which order, and true grace, . . . 307 Horace 59
The vertue and grace of which, or I mistake, . . . 339 Horace V 60/ 59
In vertue, and renowne of armes, then in . . . 325 Horace 412
Of vertue, pretious in the frame: . . . 399 Lady Ogle 18
. . . (by his continu'd Vertue) my loving friend: . . . . 409 Brome Ttl
VERTUE'ENFORME
So did thy vertue'enforme, thy wit sustaine . . . 75 E116 Jephson 3
VERTUES
Where good mens vertues them to honors bring, . . . 47 E64 Salisbury 3 11
When, in mens wishes, so thy vertues wrought, . . . 49 E67 Suffolk 7
O vertues fall, . . . 179 U25 Desmond 36
If thou wouldst know the vertues of Man-kind, . . . 185 U30 Burleigh 1
Sound thou her Vertues, give her soule a Name. . . . 269 U81 Pawlet 22
Were like a ring of Vertues, 'bout her set, . . . 270 U81 Pawlet 41
Of vertues in her, as, in short, shee grew . . . 274 U84 Descent 11
When your owne Vertues, equall'd have their Names, . . . 281 U84 Kenelme 12
The Dominations, Vertues, and the Powers, . . . 285 U84 Muse 87
VERTUOUS
That vertuous is, when the reward's away. . . . 49 E66 Cary 18
All-vertuous Herbert! on whose every part . . . 68 E106 E Herbert 3
Reade, in their vertuous parents noble parts, . . . 96 F2 Penshurst 97
. . . vertuous and Noble. . . . 100 F4 To the World Ttl
(To vertuous moods inclin'd) . . . 112 F11 Epode 112
Such Notes are vertuous men! they live as fast . . . 157 U13 Sacvile 143
Let poore Nobilitie be vertuous: Wee, . . . 215 U44 Speach 79
Hee entred well, by vertuous parts, . . . 244 U70 Ode 33
But most, a vertuous Sonne. . . . 244 U70 Ode 47
On the Right Honourable, and vertuous Lord Weston, L. . . . . 250 U73 Weston Ttl
Who takes thy volume to his vertuous hand, . . . 383 Author 1
May take thy volume to his vertuous hand. . . . 383 Author 8
Which I do, early, vertuous Somerset, . . . 384 Somerset 7
To all thy vertuous, and well chosen Friends, . . . 398 Drayton 90
VERTUOUSLY
Vertuously practise must at least allow . . . 75 E116 Jephson 14
VERY
The very call, to make all others come: . . . 81 E129 Mime 8
To my shafts! Her very Name, . . . 137 U2 Cupid 37
I could give my very heart; . . . 142 U2 Her man 54
His very Manners taught t'amend, . . . 152 U12 Corbet 22
But these men ever want: their very trade . . . 155 U13 Sacvile 79
His very eyes are yours to overthrow. . . . 182 U28 Worth 11
What though her Chamber be the very pit . . . 222 U49 Pucell 3
Would make the very Greene-cloth to looke blew: . . . 241 U68 House-hold 8
The very verdure of her nest. . . . 251 U74 Weston 13
The very root of writing well, and spring . . . 325 Horace 440
And they were very good: yet thou think'st nay. . . . 408 Detractor 2
But a very merry wight . . . 416 Moon 7

		Page	Title	Line

VESTALL
  Cleare as a naked vestall . . . . . 365 Ode Splendor 11
VEXATION
  There's no vexation, that can make thee prime. . . 73 E112 Gamster 22
VEXE
  And what I write? and vexe it many dayes . 159 U14 Selden 25
  But first dost vexe, and search it! If not sound, . 187 U33 Councellour 19
  They vexe, and follow him with shouts, and noise, . 335 Horace 648
  They vexe, and carelesse follow him with noise. . 354 Horace V648
  In such a Martirdome; To vexe their eyes, . . 371 Fletcher 13
VEXED
  He vexed time, and busied the whole State; . 243 U70 Ode 27
VEXT
  But as 'tis often vext and tri'd. . 146 U6 Defence 18
  What fables have you vext! what truth redeem'd! . 159 U14 Selden 39
VEYNE
  to loose, and Cap'ring, for thy stricter veyne. . 108 F10 Proiudium 2
VEYNES
  Suckt from the Veynes of shop-philosophy. . 405 Inigo Jones 1 74
  Wee'l rip our Richest veynes . . . . 420 Ode:If Men 31
VIAM
  To make propter viam, ever, where thou go'st; . 205 U43 Vulcan V 58
VIANDS
  And unbought viands ready makes: . . 291 U85 Country 48
VICE (See also VYCE)
  Thy person only, Courtling, is the vice. . 50 E72 Court-ling 6
  Hating that solemne vice of greatnesse, pride; . 52 E76 Bedford 1 10
  Of vice, and vertue; wherein all great life . 66 E102 Pembroke 6
  To morrow vice, if shee give better pay: . 66 E102 Pembroke 10
  As nothing else discernes the vertue' or vice. . 66 E102 Pembroke 12
  Being no vitious person, but the vice . 74 E115 Honest Man 5
  He makes himselfe a thorough-fare of vice. . 76 E118 Gut 4
  Art tane with neithers vice, nor sport: . 96 F3 Wroth 4
  Let thousands more goe flatter vice, and winne, . 99 F3 Wroth 85
  Not to know vice at all, and keepe true state, . 109 F11 Epode 1
  Next, to that vertue, is to know vice well, . 109 F11 Epode 3
  No, vice, we let thee know, . . . 111 F11 Epode 72
  No, vice, I let thee know, . . . 111 F11 Epode V 72
  And almost every vice, almightie gold, . 113 F12 Rutland 2
  With sinne and vice, though with a throne endew'd; . 116 F13 Aubigny 10
  And raise not vertue; they may vice enhance. . 117 F13 Aubigny 42
  And never thinke, how vice doth every houre, . 119 F13 Aubigny 87
  It chid the vice, yet not the Men. . 152 U12 Corbet 28
  Of all vice hurld together, there he was, . 172 U21 Ltl Shrub 6
  When Vice alike in time with vertue dur'd. . 176 U24 Frontispice 8
  Their vice of loving for a Christmasse fit; . 190 U37 Friend-Book 8
  Yet if with eithers vice I teynted be, . 190 U37 Friend-Book 29
  Or goe about to countenance the vice, . 191 U38 Elegy 'Tis 24
  The shunning vice, to greater vice doth lead, . 339 Horace V 45/ 43
  To every vice, as hardly to be brought . 315 Horace 232
  Vice, and, am knowne to have a Knights estate. . 331 Horace 572
  Vice, and is knowne to have a Knights estate. . 352 Horace V548/572
  Discover Vice? Commit Absurdity? . . 405 Inigo Jones 1 82
  Foole, doe not rate my Rymes; I'have found thy Vice . 408 Detractor 5
VICES
  Rather then here so bogg'd in vices stay. . 163 U15 Friend-Wars 30
  Our vices doe not tarry in a place, . 166 U15 Friend-Wars 123
  The rather when the vices of the Time . 224 U50 Countesse 9
  With vices, which they look'd for, and came to. . 371 Fletcher 10
VICIOUS (See also VITIOUS)
  Some vicious foole draw neare, . . 111 F11 Epode 66
  By arts, and practise of the vicious, . 117 F13 Aubigny 12
VICTORIE
  Then com'st thou off with Victorie and Palme, . 187 U33 Councellour 35
VICTRICE
  With boughs of Palme, a crowned Victrice stand! . 285 U84 Muse 96
VIES
  I Cannot bring my Muse to dropp her Vies . 415 Dover 1
VIEW (See also VEIW)
  He should those rare, and absolute numbers view, . 53 E79 Rutland 11
  But in the view, doth interrupt their sinne; . 66 E102 Pembroke 18
  Strength of my Countrey, whilst I bring to view . 69 E108 Soldiers 1
  Nor com'st to view the better cloth of state; . 96 F3 Wroth 7
  To view the jewells, stuffes, the paines, the wit . 97 F3 Wroth 11
  And her Jewels, to the view . 138 U2 Kisse 11
  Appeare, and that to shortest view, . 174 U22 Elegy Tho 34
  Lock't in her cold embraces, from the view . 177 U25 Desmond 22
  But view the mildnesse of your Makers state, . 193 U38 Elegy 'Tis 85
  Supplant bold Panton; and brought there to view . 214 U44 Speach 34
  To shew their Tires? to view, and to be view'd? . 222 U49 Pucell 17
  So great a Vertue stand upright to view, . 224 U50 Countesse 19
  These Graces, when the rest of Ladyes view . 225 U50 Countesse 31
  In his great Actions: view whom his large hand . 250 U73 Weston 3
  Yet something, to the Painters view, . 275 U84 Body 9
  To view the weary Oxen draw, with bare . 291 U85 Country 63
  Chaste, thriftie, modest folke, that came to view. . 319 Horace 294
  Yet so the scoffing Satyres to mens view, . 321 Horace 328
  But now, your Worke is done, if they that view . 370 Author 9
  Stay, view this stone: And, if thou beest not such, . 371 Epitaph 1
  That all, that view you then, and late; may say, . 384 Somerset 25
VIEWD
  Will well designe thee, to be viewd of all . . 408 Inigo Jones 3 12

	Page	Title	Line
VIEWE			
For, as one comming with a laterall viewe,	362	Author	9
VIEW'D			
Thrise did it spit: thrise div'd. At last, it view'd	88	E133 Voyage	162
To shew their Tires? to view, and to be view'd?	222	U49 Pucell	17
So well! as when I view'd the floore, and Roome,	228	U53 Newcastle	V 17
View'd there the mercat, read the wretched rate	234	U61 Epigram	3
Have all his actions wondred at, and view'd	284	U84 Muse	77
Will in the light be view'd: This, once, the sight	331	Horace	543
And in them view'd th'uncertainty of Life,	411	Sutcliffe	3
VIEWERS			
The Dice with glassen eyes, to the glad Viewers	166	U15 Friend-Wars	V138
VIEWES			
The Dice with glassen eyes, to the glad viewes	166	U15 Friend-Wars	138
VIEWING			
But viewing him since (alas, too late)	77	E120 S. P.	19
On what they viewing know.	144	U3 Musicall	20
VIGILANCE			
It bends the hams of Gossip Vigilance,	363	Riches	11
VILE			
If, without these vile arts, it will not sell,	28	E3 Bookseller	11
In most vile verses, and cost me more paine,	51	E73 Fine Grand	19
Nothing is vile, that is a part of you:	192	U38 Elegy 'Tis	36
Vile Tavernes, and the Drunkards pisse him out;	211	U43 Vulcan	186
Vile Tavernes, and have Drunkards pisse him out;	211	U43 Vulcan	V186
With faire black eyes, and hair, and some vile snout.	339	Horace	V 54/ 52
Peleus, or Telephus. If you speake vile	311	Horace	147
If thou the vile, broad-troden ring forsake.	313	Horace	188
For the vile Goat, soone after, forth did send	319	Horace	320
VILER			
Mens manners ne're were viler, for your sake.	34	E24 Parliament	2
VILLE			
For newes) your Ville-royes, and Silleries,	69	E107 Hungry	21
VILLE-ROYES			
For newes) your Ville-royes, and Silleries,	69	E107 Hungry	21
VILLORS			
Strooke in at Millan with the villors there;	212	U43 Vulcan	V200
VINCENT			
An Epitaph on Master Vincent Corbet.	151	U12 Corbet	Ttl
Deare Vincent Corbet who so long	151	U12 Corbet	7
VINDICATE			
Doth vindicate it to eternitie.	175	U24 Frontispice	4
VINDICTIVE			
Proud, false, and trecherous, vindictive, all	172	U21 Ltl Shrub	7
VINE			
Nor will I beg of thee, Lord of the vine,	107	F10 Proludium	10
Nor will we beg of thee, Lord of the vine,	107	F10 Proludium	V 10
So may the fruitfull Vine my temples steepe,	190	U37 Friend-Book	14
Your fruitfull spreading Vine,	257	U75 Epithalam.	159
With the growne issue of the Vine;	290	U85 Country	10
With sproutinge tendrells of the Vine;	290	U85 Country	V 10
VINTNERS			
Or lay the excuse upon the Vintners vault;	191	U38 Elegy 'Tis	22
VIOLATES			
Who violates the God-head, is most vitious	284	U84 Muse	74
VIOLENT			
Those that in blood such violent pleasure have,	363	Murder	1
VIOLL			
To the grave Harp, and Violl voyces new;	346	Horace	V306
VIRGIL			
Shall reade a piece of Virgil, Tacitus,	65	E101 Supper	21
Let me be what I am, as Virgil cold;	199	U42 Elegy Let	1
At these Immortall Mangers Virgil fed.	228	U53 Newcastle	20
Or Plautus, and in Virgil disavow,	309	Horace	78
Or Rurall Virgil come, to pipe to us!	397	Drayton	28
VIRGIN			
Hath plac'd amongst her virgin-traine:	34	E22 Daughter	9
The Virgin, long-since fled from earth, I see,	52	E74 Chancelor	9
See, how she paceth forth in Virgin-white,	253	U75 Epithalam.	41
The choisest Virgin-troup of all the Land!	254	U75 Epithalam.	50
It covers, first, a Virgin; and then, one	254	U75 Epithalam.	50
The Ghyrlond of the blessed Virgin Marie.	371	Epitaph	3
Most holy, & pure Virgin, blessed Mayd,	412	Ghyrlond	Ttl
T'imprint in all purg'd hearts this virgin sence,	413	Ghyrlond	37
Throwe, Holye Virgin, then	414	Ghyrlond	55
VIRGINITYE	421	Ode:If Men	37
Have you tasted virginitye	136	U2 Triumph	V 45
VIRGINS			
Sleepe in a Virgins bosome without feare,	230	U56 Covell	15
Stay, thou wilt see what rites the Virgins doe!	254	U75 Epithalam.	49
Stay, see the Virgins sow,	254	U75 Epithalam.	61
VIRGIN-TRAINE			
Hath plac'd amongst her virgin-traine:	34	E22 Daughter	9
VIRGIN-TROUP			
The choisest Virgin-troup of all the Land!	254	U75 Epithalam.	50
VIRGIN-WHITE			
See, how she paceth forth in Virgin-white,	253	U75 Epithalam.	41
VIRTUE			
"So much doth Virtue hate,	367	Ode Who saith	31
Of Civill virtue, that hee now is not	420	Ode:If Men	12
And though your virtue (as becomes it) still	421	Censure	9
Virtue, and Soveraigntie, they not consort.	423	Lucan	18

	Page	Title	Line
VISCOUNT			
To the Right Honorable William Viscount Mansfield: . . .	228	U53 Newcastle	VTtl
VISION			
The vision of our Saviour, face to face,	286	U84 Muse	132
The Vision Of Ben. Jonson, On The . . .	396	Drayton	Ttl
Wonder to truth! and have my Vision hoorld,	396	Drayton	13
VISIT			
But you will visit grisly Pluto's hall?	89	E133 Voyage	175
VISITS			
Be at their Visits, see 'hem squemish, sick,	164	U15 Friend-Wars	68
Those ambling visits, passe in verse, betweene	396	Drayton	4
VISOR			
Brought in the Visor, and the robe of State,	319	Horace	316
VITIOUS			
Being no vitious person, but the vice	74	E115 Honest Man	5
Of this so vitious Humanitie.	158	U14 Selden	12
Their vitious ease, and be o'rewhelm'd with it.	162	U15 Friend-Wars	4
Who violates the God-head, is most vitious	284	U84 Muse	74
VITRUVIUS			
With mistooke Names out of Vitruvius!	402	Inigo Jones 1	8
VIZORS			
Vizors or Anticks? or it comprehend	402	Inigo Jones 1	13
VLUSHING			
Would thinke no more of Vlushing, or the Brill:	213	U44 Speach	30
VOGUE			
For though Spaine gave him his first ayre and Vogue,	389	Aleman	15
VOICE			
Proves, that is gods, which was the peoples voice.	49	E67 Suffolk	12
Now, I must give thy life, and deed, the voice	55	E86 Goodyere 2	5
No voice so sweet, nor words have sting,	143	U3 Musicall	V 15
Whose fame hath an eternall voice?	181	U27 Ode Helen	16
VOICES			
When these, and such, their voices have employd;	385	Brooke	1
VOID (See also VOYD)			
The Poems void of profit, our grave men	329	Horace	511
What place is for my testimony void?	385	Brooke	2
VOIDS			
Or by Damnation voids it? or by stealth?	166	U15 Friend-Wars	116
VOLARY			
Like him, to make the ayre, one volary:	397	Drayton	36
VOLUME			
Who takes thy volume to his vertuous hand,	383	Author	1
May take thy volume to his vertuous hand.	383	Author	8
Your booke? your volume! Nay, the state, and story!	399	Lady Ogle	7
VOLUMES			
And despaires day, but for thy Volumes light.	392	Shakespeare	80
VOLUMINOUS			
I am not so voluminous, and vast,	226	U52 Answer	2
VOLUPTUOUS			
On Sir Voluptuous Beast.	34	E25 Beast 1	Ttl
VOTARY			
The sole Religious house, and Votary,	372	Epitaph	10
VOTE			
By thy owne vote, a sacrifice to thee?	203	U43 Vulcan	22
VOUCHES			
And vouches both the Pageant, and the Day,	202	U42 Elegy Let	77
VOUCHSAFE			
Of Goodnesse still: Vouchsafe to take	273	U84 Cradle	9
As, since, she will vouchsafe no other Wit.	392	Shakespeare	50
VOW			
Thy morning's, and thy evening's vow	99	F3 Wroth	100
Whose morning, and whose evening vow	99	F3 Wroth	V100
A vow as new, and ominous as the yeare,	116	F12 Rutland	98
Your vow	120	F14 Sydney	23
Meane what I speake: and still will keepe that Vow.	159	U14 Selden	28
VOW'D			
He that not trusts me, having vow'd thus much,	70	E108 Soldiers	9
Which I have vow'd posteritie to give.	262	U78 Digby	18
VOWELLS			
Fastning Vowells, as with fetters	183	U29 Fit of Rime	11
VOWES			
For whose sake, hence-forth, all his vowes be such,	41	E45 First Son	11
Heaven vowes to keepe him.	77	E120 S. P.	24
Nor meane we those, whom vowes and conscience	111	F11 Epode	83
Nor meane I those, whose vowes and conscience	111	F11 Epode	V 83
'Tis true, I'm broke! Vowes, Oathes, and all I had	191	U38 Elegy 'Tis	1
I will no more abuse my vowes to you,	194	U38 Elegy 'Tis	107
Of vowes so sacred, and in silence made;	197	U40 Elegy That	14
And such your Servant is, who vowes to keepe	198	U40 Elegy That	41
VOYAGE			
On the famous Voyage.	84	E133 Voyage	Ttl
The Voyage it selfe.	84	E134 Voyage	Ttl
VOYCE			
To every cause he meets, this voyce he brayes:	31	E12 Shift	19
Not from the publike voyce, but private fact;	47	E63 Salisbury 2	6
Curst be my voyce if it lye dumbe, or hid	47	E63 Salisbury 2	V 11
That no affection in thy voyce commands;	51	E74 Chancelor	4
Thou need'st not shrinke at voyce of after-times;	61	E95 Savile	20
Truth might spend all her voyce, Fame all her art.	68	E106 E Herbert	4
We each to other may this voyce enspire;	81	E128 Wm Roe 2	11
How hight the place? a voyce was heard, Cocytus.	86	E133 Voyage	89
Though never after; whiles it gaynes the voyce	113	F12 Rutland	11
What Nymph so e're his voyce but heares,	148	U7 Nymph	27

	Page	Title	Line

VOYCE (cont.)

Newnesse of Sense, Antiquitie of voyce! . . . 160 U14 Selden 60
For the recovery of my voyce? No, there . . . 167 U15 Friend-Wars 154
That scarce you heare a publike voyce alive, . . . 234 U61 Epigram 5
Unto your honour: I can voyce in song . . . 261 U77 Treasurer V 27
And voyce to raise them from my brazen Lungs, . . . 269 U81 Pawlet 24
The Voyce so sweet, the words so faire, . . . 279 U84 Mind 37
Her voyce, and angry Chremes chafes out-right . . . 311 Horace 133
Lend me thy voyce, O Fame, that I may draw . . . 396 Drayton 12
My lippes could forme the voyce, I heard that Rore, . . . 397 Drayton 38

VOYCES

Come, with our Voyces, let us warre, . . . 143 U3 Musicall 1
To the grave Harp, and Violl voyces new; . . . 346 Horace V306
Cast out by voyces; want they pleasure, then . . . 329 Horace 512

VOYC'T

Yet, one day in the yeere, for sweet 'tis voyc't, . . . 87 E133 Voyage 119

VULCAN

An Execration upon Vulcan. . . . 202 U43 Vulcan Ttl
I ne're attempted, Vulcan, 'gainst thy life; . . . 202 U43 Vulcan 5
Had made a meale for Vulcan to lick up. . . . 206 U43 Vulcan 84
Had bin fitt meate for Vulcan to lick up. . . . 206 U43 Vulcan V 84
How in these ruines, Vulcan, thou dost lurke, . . . 207 U43 Vulcan 105
How in these ruines, Vulcan, durst thou lurke, . . . 207 U43 Vulcan V105
They made a Vulcan of a sheafe of Reedes, . . . 208 U43 Vulcan 126
Hee is true Vulcan still! He did not spare . . . 210 U43 Vulcan 159
Thou art true Vulcan still! Thou durst not spare . . . 210 U43 Vulcan V159
He was right Vulcan still! He did not spare . . . 210 U43 Vulcan V159
Against this Vulcan? No Injunction? . . . 210 U43 Vulcan 175
Pox on your flameship, Vulcan; if it be . . . 211 U43 Vulcan 191
Pox on your fire workes, Vulcan; if it be . . . 211 U43 Vulcan V191
Pox on thee, Vulcan, thy Pandora's pox, . . . 212 U43 Vulcan 213

VULCANALE

May to thy name a Vulcanale say; . . . 208 U43 Vulcan 120

VULGAR

For vulgar praise, doth it too dearely buy. . . . 27 E2 My Booke 14
That to the vulgar canst thy selfe apply, . . . 76 E119 Shelton 11
Vulgar Languages that want . . . 184 U29 Fit of Rime 43
And with the vulgar doth it not obtaine . . . 193 U38 Elegy 'Tis 81
And shewing so weake an Act to vulgar eyes, . . . 218 U47 Tribe 7
Most worthie praise, when words that vulgar grew, . . . 340 Horace V 67
If all the vulgar Tongues, that speake this day, . . . 388 Chapman 7

VULTURE

Of Vulture death, and those relentlesse cleies? . . . 283 U84 Muse 18

VULTURES

Hook-handed Harpies, gowned Vultures, put . . . 187 U33 Councellour 9

VYCE

yett, yf with eythers vyce, I tainted bee, . . . 422 Censure 22

WADE

Alas: then whither wade I, . . . 365 Ode Splendor 17

WAGER

For a just wager, and that wager paid . . . 229 U54 Squib 2
that the wife heades for a wager . . . 417 Moon 26

WAGG

morts, and mirkins that wagg all, . . . 417 Moon 15

WAGGON

Besides he tried Ship, Cart, Waggon, and Chayre, . . . 380 Coryat 3 27

WAIGH

I know for such, as (if my word will waigh) . . . 386 Husband 11

WAIGHT

That knowes the waight of guilt: He will refraine . . . 112 F11 Epode 113
Just to the waight their this dayes-presents beare; . . . 113 F12 Rutland 8

WAIST (See WASTE)
WAIT (See also WAYTE)

A sorrow in me, fit to wait to her! . . . 282 U84 Muse 10

WAITE

Not looking by, or back (like those, that waite . . . 118 F13 Aubigny 62

WAITED

Still waited on 'hem where they were. . . . 264 U79 New-yeares 39

WAITER

A waiter, doth my gluttony envy: . . . 95 F2 Penshurst 68

WAITES

And only pitious scorne, upon their folly waites. . . . 175 U23 Himselfe 24
Before the Judge, it hangs, and waites report. . . . 309 Horace 112

WAITING

And waiting Chambers of great Lords. . . . 289 U85 Country 8

WAKE

Sleepe, and the Grave will wake. . . . 143 U3 Musicall 14
Wake, friend, from forth thy Lethargie: the Drum . . . 162 U15 Friend-Wars 1
Wake, friend, and finde thy self; awake, the Drum . . . 162 U15 Friend-Wars V 1
Wake, and put on the wings of Pindars Muse, . . . 176 U25 Desmond 3
And Fame wake for me, when I yeeld to sleepe. . . . 190 U37 Friend-Book 15
Dreame thou could'st hurt it; but before thou wake . . . 250 U73 Weston 11

WAK'D

Of what shee had wrought came in, and wak'd his braine, . . . 56 E87 Hazard 4
T'have wak'd, if sleeping, Spaines Ambassadour, . . . 213 U44 Speach 4

WAKEFULL

To wakefull reason, our affections king: . . . 109 F11 Epode 13

WAKERS

at Pem Wakers good ale Tapp, . . . 417 Moon 39

WAKING

Weston! That waking man! that Eye of State! . . . 250 U73 Weston 5
What kind of waking Man . . . 256 U75 Epithalam. 111

		Page	Title	Line

WALK
Loftie, and great; and in the buskin walk. — • • . 348 Horace V398/318
WALKE
For I will dare none. Good Lord, walke dead still. — • — 30 E11 Something 8
Or, that did you sit, or walke, • . • . • 138 U2 Kisse 13
On every wall, and sung where e're I walke. • • . 193 U38 Elegy 'Tis 98
Or like a Ghost walke silent amongst men, • • . 199 U41 Elegy Since 21
There shall the Brother, with the Sister walke, • . 285 U84 Muse 117
But fly thee, like the Pest! Walke not the street • . . 409 Detractor 19
WALKES
On some-thing, that walkes some-where. . • • . 30 E11 Something Ttl
Thou hast thy walkes for health, as well as sport: • . 93 F2 Penshurst 9
The jolly wassall walkes the often round, • • . 98 F3 Wroth 59
But shee's Juno, when she walkes, . • . • 137 U2 Cupid 53
See where he walkes with Mira by his side. • . 264 U79 New-yeares 18
Who walkes on Earth as May still went along, • • . 264 U79 New-yeares 26
WALKING
And call the walking woods? . • • . . 143 U3 Musicall 12
It was erected; and still walking under • • . 157 U13 Sacvile 141
WALL
Or hung some Mounsiers picture on the wall, • . . 56 E88 Monsieur 12
Whether it languishing stucke upon the wall, • . . 87 E133 Voyage 136
Behold where Cerberus, rear'd on the wall • • . 89 E133 Voyage 176
On every wall, and sung where e're I walke. • . . 193 U38 Elegy 'Tis 98
No stone in any wall here, but can tell • . . 394 Jane Ogle 9
What Poesy ere was painted on a wall • • . 406 Inigo Jones 1 97
With rotten chalk, or Cole upon a wall, • . . 408 Inigo Jones 3 11
WALLS
Nor have my title-leafe on posts, or walls, • . 28 E3 Bookseller 7
Betweene two walls; where, on one side, to scar men, • . 86 E133 Voyage 67
Is fill'd with buttock? And the walls doe sweate • . 88 E133 Voyage 169
Hang on thy walls, that every child may reach. . . 94 F2 Penshurst 44
And though thy walls be of the countrey stone, • • . 94 F2 Penshurst 45
That wider Walls embrac'd their Citie round, • . 319 Horace 296
WAN
At last, ease, appetite, and example wan • • . 57 E90 Mill 4
WAND
And guided by Experience, whose straite wand • . 176 U24 Frontispice 11
WANDRERS
As wandrers doe, that still doe rome, • • . 102 F4 To the World 66
WANDRING
Poore Io wandring; wild Orestes mad: • • • . 313 Horace 177
Io still wandring; griev'd Orestes sad: • • . 342 Horace V177
Gesture, and riot, whilst he wandring went • • . 346 Horace V304
WANE
But many Moones there shall not wane (quoth hee) • . 87 E133 Voyage 103
WANT
He sayes, I want the tongue of Epigrammes; • • . 42 E49 Playwrt 1 2
Not he that flies the court for want of clothes, • . 76 E119 Shelton 1
No, Shelton, give me thee, canst want all these, • . 76 E119 Shelton 7
How full of want, how swallow'd up, how dead • • . 80 E127 Aubigny 6
That neither want doe thee affright, • • . 100 F3 Wroth 104
That neither want should thee affright, • — • . 100 F3 Wroth V104
The foole that gave it; who will want, and weepe, • . 113 F12 Rutland 13
The foole that gave it; that will want, and weepe, • . 113 F12 Rutland V 13
What Tree or stone doth want a soule? • . . 143 U3 Musicall 7
Loves sicknesse, and his noted want of worth, • . 150 U10 Jealousie 14
Now I conceive him by my want, . • • . 152 U12 Corbet 32
That they have more opprest me, then my want? • . 153 U13 Sacvile 28
But these men ever want: their very trade • . 155 U13 Sacvile 79
And where they want, she is not understood. • . 156 U13 Sacvile 112
What I, in her, am griev'd to want. • — • . 174 U22 Elegy Tho 36
Doth Clarius Harp want strings, • • . . 174 U23 Himselfe 9
Vulgar Languages that want • • . • 184 U29 Fit of Rime 43
Rather then want your light, I wish a grave. • . 194 U38 Elegy 'Tis 122
And when you want those friends, or neere in blood, • . 224 U50 Countesse 26
Within the ballance; and not want a mite; • • . 229 U54 Squib 10
For want of knowing the Poet, to say him nay? • . 241 U68 House-hold 4
Hee'ld frame such ditties of their store, and want, • . 241 U68 House-hold 7
Want, with the rest of his conceal'd compeeres, • . 248 U71 Treasurer 5
And never may there want one of the Stem, • . 258 U75 Epithalam. 177
Nor can the bruised heart want eloquence: • . 288 U84 Muse 186
Cast out by voyces; want they pleasure, then • . 329 Horace 512
Some want, they say in a sort he did crave: • . 380 Coryat 3 55
Thy Dirty braines, Men smell thy want of worth. • . 409 Detractor 22
Pillory nor Whip, nor want of Ears, • . . 410 Gill 4
deignes myne the power to find, yett want I will • . 421 Censure 10
WANTED
Furies there wanted not: each scold was ten. • . 84 E133 Voyage 15
Nor that your beautie wanted not a dower, • . 117 F13 Aubigny 37
WANTING
That neither fame, nor love might wanting be • . 48 E66 Cary 1
WANTON
Let these in wanton feete daunce out their soules. • . 108 F10 Proludium 11
Such as oft I wanton in! • • • • . 136 U2 Cupid 23
For he must looke wanton-wise. • • . 141 U2 Her man 16
Oh doe not wanton with those eyes, • . . 144 U4 Song 1
Me now, nor Wench, nor wanton Boy, • . . 293 U86 Hor.4:1 29
The angry brow; the sportive, wanton things; • . 311 Horace 150
Their youthfull tricks in over-wanton verse: • . 321 Horace 358
Or play young tricks in over-wanton verse; • . 347 Horace V350/358
WANTON-WISE
For he must looke wanton-wise. • • • • . 141 U2 Her man 16

WANTS
<pre>
  With famine, wants, and sorrowes many a dosen,   .   .   .   86   E133 Voyage   71
  Nor wants it here through penurie, or sloth,   .   .   .   152   U12 Corbet   39
  And seeke not wants to succour: but enquire,   .   .   .   155   U13 Sacvile   61
  Wants strength, and sinewes, as his spirits were done;   .   .   339   Horace   V 38/ 37
  Wants facultie to make a censure true: 362   Author   11
</pre>
WARBLETH
<pre>
  Who warbleth Pancharis, ...   369   Ode Who saith   98
</pre>
WARD
<pre>
  Of thoughts to watch, and ward   109   F11 Epode   8
</pre>
WARDEN
<pre>
  Of wit, and a new made: a Warden then,   .   .   .   415   Rutter   23
</pre>
WARDROBE
<pre>
  Then ope thy wardrobe, thinke me that poore Groome   .   .   201   U42 Elegy Let   51
  Nay more in his wardrobe, if you will laugh at a   .   .   380   Coryat 3   47
</pre>
W'ARE
<pre>
  What w'are but once to doe, we should doe long.   .   .   139   U2 Another   12
</pre>
WARE   (NAME)
<pre>
  An Epitaph, on Henry L. La-ware. To the Passer-by.   .   .   233   U60 La-ware   Ttl
  Henry, the brave young Lord La-ware,   .   .   .   233   U60 La-ware   3
</pre>
WARE
<pre>
  Yet ware; thou mayst do all things cruellie: .   .   423   Lucan   15
</pre>
WARES
<pre>
  Yet art thou falser then thy wares.   100   F4 To the World   20
  That to the sale of Wares calls every Buyer;   .   .   333   Horace   598
  The art of uttring wares, if they were bad;   .   .   385   Husband   6
</pre>
WARIE
<pre>
  Kisse me, sweet: The warie lover   103   F6 Celia 2   1
  Right spare, and warie: then thou speak'st to mee   .   .   307   Horace   66
  Grow a safe Writer, and be warie-driven   .   .   .   323   Horace   393
</pre>
WARIE-DRIVEN
<pre>
  Grow a safe Writer, and be warie-driven   .   .   .   323   Horace   393
</pre>
WARME
<pre>
  With all their zeale, to warme their welcome here.   .   .   95   F2 Penshurst   81
  That others should not warme them at my fire,   .   .   150   U10 Jealousie   6
  And so warme the Poets tongue   260   U76 Petition   31
  When like Apollo he came forth to warme   .   .   .   392   Shakespeare   45
  Keeps warme the spice of her good name,   .   .   .   400   Lady Ogle   30
  Hee's warme on his feet now he sayes, & can   .   .   405   Inigo Jones 1   67
</pre>
WARMING
<pre>
  Nor any quick-warming-pan helpe him to bed,   .   .   232   U57 Burges   27
</pre>
WARNED
<pre>
  Still in the same, and warned will not mend,   .   .   329   Horace   530
</pre>
WARNING
<pre>
  The comfort of weake Christians, with their warning,   .   411   Sutcliffe   13
</pre>
WARPE
<pre>
  Of the New Yeare, in a new silken warpe,   .   .   .   263   U79 New-yeares   5
  And know the woofe, and warpe thereof; can tell   .   .   415   Rutter   15
</pre>
WARR
<pre>
  for if there, or peace or warr be, ...   417   Moon   22
</pre>
WARRANT
<pre>
  By warrant call'd just Symetry, ...   399   Lady Ogle   22
</pre>
WARRE
<pre>
  Thou yet remayn'st, un-hurt in peace, or warre,   .   .   60   E93 Radcliffe   13
  In these west-parts, nor when that warre was done,   .   .   71   E110 Edmonds 1   2
  Beholding, to this master of the warre;   .   .   .   72   E111 Edmonds 2   4
  Beholden, to this master of the warre;   .   .   .   72   E111 Edmonds 2   V 4
  Then either money, warre, or death: 99   F3 Wroth   76
  Come, with our Voyces, let us warre,   .   .   .   143   U3 Musicall   1
  These take, and now goe seeke thy peace in Warre,   .   .   168   U15 Friend-Wars 195
  Stil may reason warre with rime, ...   184   U29 Fit of Rime   53
  The Seat made of a more then civill warre;   .   .   186   U33 Councellour   2
  All Ensignes of a Warre, are not yet dead,   .   .   213   U44 Speach   11
  Thou Seed-plot of the warre, that hast not spar'd   .   .   213   U44 Speach   24
  That keepe the warre, though now't be growne more tame,   .   214   U44 Speach   55
  No aime at glorie, or, in warre, ...   234   U60 La-ware   13
  And the allowed warre: 253   U75 Epithalam.   31
  Venus, againe thou mov'st a warre   292   U86 Hor.4:1   1
  Will he display the Ensignes of thy warre.   .   .   292   U86 Hor.4:1   16
  I sing a noble Warre, and Priam's Fate.   .   .   .   313   Horace   196
  Of Diomede; nor Troyes sad Warre begins   .   .   .   315   Horace   209
</pre>
WARRES
<pre>
  An Epistle to a Friend, to perswade him to the Warres.   .   162   U15 Friend-Wars   Ttl
  The gests of Kings, great Captaines, and sad Warres,   .   .   309   Horace   105
  The deeds of Kings, great Captaines, and sad Warres,   .   .   341   Horace   V105
  Of a brave Chiefe sent to the warres: He can,   .   .   325   Horace   451
  Their minds to Warres, with rimes they did rehearse;   .   .   329   Horace   495
  Warres greatest woes, and miseries increase,   .   .   363   Peace   3
  I saw, and read, it was thy Barons Warres!   .   .   397   Drayton   42
</pre>
WARWICK
<pre>
  . . . & sir Henrye Rich, now Earles of Warwick and Hollande.   .   382   Rich   Ttl
</pre>
WARY   (See also WARIE)
<pre>
  Her wary guardes, her wise simplicitie,   .   .   .   270   U81 Pawlet   40
</pre>
WAS'
<pre>
  Why was't? did e're the Cloudes aske back their raine?   .   192   U38 Elegy 'Tis   56
</pre>
WAS   (See also 'TWAS)
<pre>
  When was there contract better driven by Fate?   .   .   28   E5 Union   1
  The world the temple was, the priest a king,   .   .   28   E5 Union   3
  Ridway was tane, arraign'd, condemn'd to dye;   .   .   29   E8 Robbery   2
  But, for this money was a courtier found,   .   .   29   E8 Robbery   3
  Which was a cater-piller. So 'twill dye.   .   .   .   31   E15 Court-worm   4
  Was his blest fate, but our hard lot to find.   .   .   37   E32 Roe 2   8
  And since, the whole land was preserv'd for thee.   .   38   E35 James 2   10
</pre>

WAS (cont.)
  Rare, as wonder, was her wit;   .   .   .   .   .   .   39 E40 Ratcliffe   9
  Life, whose griefe was out of fashion, ...   39 E40 Ratcliffe 13
  My sinne was too much hope of thee, lov'd boy,   .   .   41 E45 First Son   2
  It was as if thou printed had'st an oath,   .   .   .   43 E53 Old-end   5
  Proves, that is gods, which was the peoples voice.   .   49 E67 Suffolk 12
  My Muse bad, Bedford write, and that was shee.   .   .   52 E76 Bedford 1 18
  Hence was it, that the destinies decreed   .   .   .   53 E79 Rutland   5
  And, ere I could aske you, I was prevented: .   .   54 E84 Bedford 2   3
  And why that bird was sacred to Apollo,   .   .   .   55 E85 Goodyere 1   4
  It was a knowledge, that begat that love.   .   .   .   55 E86 Goodyere 2   8
  Then Cicero, whose every breath was fame: .   .   57 E89 Allen   6
  Was dull, and long, ere shee would goe to man: .   .   57 E90 Mill   3
  Not though that haire grew browne, which once was amber,   .   57 E90 Mill   9
  And he growne youth, was call'd to his ladies chamber.   .   57 E90 Mill 10
  Mill was the same. Since, both his body and face   .   57 E90 Mill 13
  Which thou art to thy selfe: whose fame was wonne   .   58 E91 Vere   5
  Minervaes loome was never richer spred.   .   .   .   61 E95 Savile 16
  He wont to encounter me, aloud, ...   62 E97 Motion   7
  When he was here. Nor hath he got a sute,   .   .   .   63 E97 Motion 16
  Since he was gone, more then the one he weares.   .   63 E97 Motion 17
  In these west-parts, nor when that warre was done,   .   71 E110 Edmonds 1   2
  In men, but every bravest was the best: .   .   .   75 E116 Jephson 10
  And to live great, was better, then great borne.   .   75 E116 Jephson 12
  If I would vertue set, as shee was yong,   .   .   .   78 E122 Rudyerd 2   5
  One name was Elizabeth, ...   79 E124 Elizabeth   9
  Said I wrong'd him, and (which was more) his love.   .   80 E126 Mrs Cary   5
  The filth, stench, noyse: save only what was there   .   84 E133 Voyage   9
  Subtly distinguish'd, was confused here.   .   .   .   84 E133 Voyage 10
  And for one Cerberus, the whole coast was dogs.   .   84 E133 Voyage 14
  Furies there wanted not: each scold was ten.   .   .   84 E133 Voyage 15
  One was; and he, for brawne, and braine, right able   .   84 E133 Voyage 23
  The other was a squire, of faire degree;   .   .   .   84 E133 Voyage 25
  It was the day, what time the powerfull Moone   .   84 E133 Voyage 29
  The least of which was to the plague a cosen.   .   .   86 E133 Voyage 72
  One said, it was bold Briareus, or the beadle,   .   .   86 E133 Voyage 81
  How hight the place? a voyce was heard, Cocytus.   .   86 E133 Voyage 89
  For (where he was the god of eloquence,   .   .   .   86 E133 Voyage 99
  To answere me. And sure, it was th'intent   .   .   87 E133 Voyage 107
  And that ours did. For, yet, no nare was tainted,   .   87 E133 Voyage 133
  All was to them the same, they were to passe,   .   .   88 E133 Voyage 140
  Then, selling nose, a dish was tane to mince 'hem,   .   88 E133 Voyage 151
  But 'mong'st these Tiberts, who do'you thinke there was?   88 E133 Voyage 155
  They cry'd out Pusse. He told them he was Bankes,   .   89 E133 Voyage 183
  That taller tree, which of a nut was set,   .   .   .   94 F2 Penshurst 13
  Did'st thou, then, make 'hem! and what praise was heap'd   95 F2 Penshurst 83
  When shee was farre: and not a roome, but drest,   .   96 F2 Penshurst 87
  Such, and no other was that age, of old,   .   .   .   98 F3 Wroth 63
  No, I doe know, that I was borne   .   .   .   .   101 F4 To the World 61
  The truth of times) was once of more esteeme,   .   .   114 F12 Rutland 21
  When gold was made no weapon to cut throtes,   .   .   114 F12 Rutland 23
  Achilles was not first, that valiant was,   .   .   .   114 F12 Rutland 51
  I Sing the birth, was borne to night,   .   .   .   130 U1 Nativitie   1
  Was now laid in a Manger.   .   .   .   .   .   130 U1 Nativitie 12
  The Word was now made Flesh indeed,   .   .   .   130 U1 Nativitie 17
  Of whose Beautie it was sung, ...   131 U2 Excuse 19
  Farre I was from being stupid, ...   132 U2 How he saw   5
  She content was to restore   .   .   .   .   .   133 U2 Suffered   3
  And was worthy (being so seene)   .   .   .   .   138 U2 Kisse 27
  Be as good, as was the last: .   .   .   .   140 U2 Promise 27
  (By searching) what before was strange,   .   .   .   146 U6 Defence 15
  The body was   .   .   .   .   148 U8 Houre-glasse   5
  I'm sure my language to her, was as sweet,   .   .   149 U9 Picture   6
  I ne're was of thy kind;   .   .   .   .   .   150 U10 Jealousie   3
  Of sleepe againe, who was his Aid;   .   .   .   151 U11 Dreame 12
  But was by sweetning so his will, ...   151 U12 Corbet 13
  To license ever was so light, ...   152 U12 Corbet 25
  Their bounties forth, to him that last was made,   .   155 U13 Sacvile 63
  Now, but command; make tribute, what was gift;   .   155 U13 Sacvile 84
  Who was this Morning such a one, should be   .   .   157 U13 Sacvile 126
  It was erected; and still walking under   .   .   .   157 U13 Sacvile 141
  Was trusted, that you thought my judgement such   .   158 U14 Selden   6
  Or was she gracious a-farre off? but neere   .   .   169 U18 Elegy Can   5
  That ne're was knowne to last above a fit!   .   .   171 U20 Shrub   6
  That their whole life was wickednesse, though weav'd   171 U20 Shrub 10
  Of all vice hurld together, there he was,   .   .   172 U21 Ltl Shrub   6
  Was Lesbia sung by learn'd Catullus?   .   .   .   181 U27 Ode Helen   9
  All good Poetrie hence was flowne,   .   .   .   183 U29 Fit of Rime 14
  Greeke was free from Rimes infection,   .   .   .   184 U29 Fit of Rime 31
  Was not spoyled.   .   .   .   .   184 U29 Fit of Rime 33
  Was the founder.   .   .   .   .   184 U29 Fit of Rime 60
  That still was good for goodnesse sake, nor thought   185 U30 Burleigh 13
  Was drawne to practise other hue, then that   .   .   188 U34 Small Poxe   8
  What was the cause then? Thought'st thou in disgrace   188 U34 Small Poxe 13
  I, that thy Ayme was; but her fate prevail'd: .   188 U34 Small Poxe 17
  Thinke it was frailtie, Mistris, thinke me man,   .   192 U38 Elegy 'Tis 31
  Thinke that I once was yours, or may be now;   .   192 U38 Elegy 'Tis 35
  But the grave Lover ever was an Asse;   .   .   .   198 U40 Elegy That 32
  Or that the Sun was here, but forc't away;   .   .   199 U41 Elegy Since   6
  Whose Readers did not thinke he was in love.   .   .   199 U42 Elegy Let   4
  A Gowne of that, was the Caparison?   .   .   .   201 U42 Elegy Let 46
  that from the Foot-man, when he was become   .   .   201 U42 Elegy Let 52
  Or slipper was left off, and kisse it too,   .   .   201 U42 Elegy Let 56

	Page	Title	Line

WAS (cont.)

Text	Page	Title	Line
Was it because thou wert of old denied	203	U43 Vulcan	11
Conceal'd, or kept there, that was fit to be,	203	U43 Vulcan	21
But in my Deske, what was there to accite	206	U43 Vulcan	85
But in my Deske, what was there to envite	206	U43 Vulcan	V 85
Was there made English: with the Grammar too,	207	U43 Vulcan	91
Wherein was oyle, beside the succour spent,	207	U43 Vulcan	99
By Carew, Cotton, Selden, oyle was spent	207	U43 Vulcan	V100
By Carew, Cotton, Seldens oyle was spent	207	U43 Vulcan	V100
That was rak'd up in the Winchestrian Goose	209	U43 Vulcan	142
Which was rak'd up in the Winchestrian Goose	209	U43 Vulcan	V142
That was lock'd up in the Winchestrian Goose	209	U43 Vulcan	V142
And cry'd, it was a threatning to the beares;	209	U43 Vulcan	146
The place, that was thy Wives inheritance.	209	U43 Vulcan	152
The Plot, that was thy Wives inheritance.	209	U43 Vulcan	V152
There was a Judgement shew'n too in an houre.	210	U43 Vulcan	158
He was right Vulcan still! He did not spare	210	U43 Vulcan	V159
And to Pauls-Steeple; which was unto us	211	U43 Vulcan	193
Was issue of the Taverne, too to a wit;	216	U45 Squib	8
. . . he was Lord chiefe Justice of England.	217	U46 Coke	Ttl
In others-evill best was understood:	217	U46 Coke	6
Such was thy Processe, when Integritie,	217	U46 Coke	9
Or that the Match from Spaine was ever meant?	219	U47 Tribe	36
The same it was inspir'd, rich, and refin'd.	225	U50 Countesse	30
Since Bacon, and thy Lord was borne, and here;	225	U51 Bacon	8
What then his Father was, that since is hee,	225	U51 Bacon	11
My Superficies: that was all you saw.	227	U52 Answer	9
A booke to a few lynes: but, it was fit	230	U56 Covell	3
And was your Fathers! All your Ancestours!	233	U59 Newcastle	20
What Month then May, was fitter to disclose	237	U65 Prince	4
Haile Mary, full of grace, it once was said,	238	U66 Queene	1
The Mother of our Prince? When was there seene	238	U66 Queene	6
Whereby the safetie of Man-kind was wrought)	238	U66 Queene	8
Whereby the safetie of the world was wrought)	238	U66 Queene	V 8
Was, t'have a Boy stand with a Club, and fright	241	U69 Friend Son	11
His life was of Humanitie the Spheare.	244	U70 Ode	52
By what was done and wrought	245	U70 Ode	60
Each syllab'e answer'd, and was form'd, how faire;	245	U70 Ode	63
It was the Plant, and flowre of light.	245	U70 Ode	72
Was left yet to Man-kind;	247	U70 Ode	121
Friendship, in deed, was written, not in words:	247	U70 Ode	123
. . . high Treasurer of England, Upon the Day, Hee was	250	U73 Weston	Ttl
As all the wealth of Season, there was spread;	251	U74 Weston	15
(For with both the Muse was fed)	259	U76 Petition	16
Shee was the Lady Jane, and Marchionisse	269	U81 Pawlet	19
Their Carract was! I, or my trump must breake,	269	U81 Pawlet	27
Their Carract was! I, or my trump must breake,	269	U81 Pawlet	V 27
Could summe to a perfection, was her Act!	270	U81 Pawlet	46
Could heap to a perfection, was her Act!	270	U81 Pawlet	V 46
And I, into the world, all Soule, was sent!	270	U81 Pawlet	56
And I, into the world with my Soule, was sent!	270	U81 Pawlet	V 56
Who saw the way was made it! and were sent	270	U81 Pawlet	65
That saw the way was made it! and were sent	270	U81 Pawlet	V 65
T' have paid againe a blessing was but lent,	271	U81 Pawlet	80
And Stanley, to the which shee was Co-heire.	274	U84 Descent	6
Who was my Muse, and life of all I sey'd,	282	U84 Muse	2
All that was good, or great in me she weav'd,	282	U84 Muse	4
That shall re-joyne yee. Was she, then, so deare,	285	U84 Muse	107
She had, and it became her! she was fit	287	U84 Muse	161
She had a mind as calme, as she was faire;	287	U84 Muse	163
She was, in one, a many parts of life;	287	U84 Muse	173
As her whole life was now become one note	287	U84 Muse	178
In this sweet Extasie, she was rapt hence.	289	U84 Muse	225
Of the good Cynara I was: Refraine,	292	U86 Hor.4:1	4
Whilst, Lydia, I was lov'd of thee,	293	U87 Hor.3:9	1
The Roman Ilia was not more renown'd.	293	U87 Hor.3:9	8
Or Rainbow is describ'd. But here was now	305	Horace	23
Was meant at first. Why, forcing still about	307	Horace	29
If something strange, that never yet was had	313	Horace	178
If something fresh, that never yet was had	342	Horace	V178
Speake to me, Muse, the Man, who, after Troy was sack't,	315	Horace	201
Of the times past, when he was a young lad;	317	Horace	248
With something that was acceptably new.	321	Horace	327
And so their prating to present was best,	321	Horace	329
Or Semi-god, that late was seene to weare	321	Horace	332
Her force was fit to be restrain'd by law:	348	Horace	V402/368
Of Trimeter, when yet it was sixe-pac'd,	323	Horace	373
Was Tigers, said, and Lyons fierce, to tame.	327	Horace	482
Was said to move the stones, by his Lutes powers,	327	Horace	484
This was the wisdome, that they had of old,	327	Horace	486
All way of life was shewen; the grace of Kings	329	Horace	497
Of their long labours, was in Verse set downe:	329	Horace	500
While he was young; he sweat; and freez'd againe:	333	Horace	589
Looke pale, distill a showre (was never meant)	333	Horace	612
Look pale, distill a dew was never meant	353	Horace	V612
(Defiled) touch'd; but certaine he was mad,	337	Horace	673
Next, that which rapt mee, was: I might behold	361	Palmer	13
I, that am glad, thy Innocence was thy Guilt,	371	Fletcher	11
Of Spheares, as light of starres; She was earthes Eye:	372	Epitaph	9
She was 'Sell Boulstred. In which name, I call	372	Epitaph	12
F. shewes what he was, K. what he will bee.	375	Coryat 1	29
Trie and trust Roger, was the word, but now	378	Coryat 2	80
He was in his travaile, how like to be beaten,	380	Coryat 3	35

WAS (cont.)
  How faine for his venery he was to crie (Tergum o) .   .   . 380 Coryat 3   37
  still that same little poynte hee was; but when   .   .   . 383 Rich   13
  Was worthy of a Good one; And this, here, .   .   . 386 Husband   10
  But in one tongue, was form'd with the worlds wit: .   . 389 Aleman   6
  As was the Genius wherewith they were wrote; .   . 389 Aleman   12
  Finer then was his Spanish, if my Oath .   .   . 389 Aleman   18
  It was for gentle Shakespeare cut; .   .   . 390 Reader   2
  All, that was ever writ in brasse. .   .   . 390 Reader   8
  He was not of an age, but for all time! .   . 391 Shakespeare 43
  Nature her selfe was proud of his designes, .   . 392 Shakespeare 47
  At least so great a Lady. She was wife .   .   . 394 Jane Ogle   15
  So wood at last, that he was wonne to her .   . 394 Jane Ogle   22
  It was no Dreame! I was awake, and saw! .   . 396 Drayton   11
  The Orbe was cut forth into Regions seaven. .   . 396 Drayton   20
  I saw, and read, it was thy Barons Warres! .   . 397 Drayton   42
  That reade it? that are ravish'd! such was I .   . 397 Drayton   53
  Shee was the light (without reflexe .   .   . 399 Lady Ogle   9
  Was the example of a wife! .   .   . 399 Lady Ogle   12
  Or without angles, it was shee! .   .   . 399 Lady Ogle   16
  All that was solid, in the name .   .   . 399 Lady Ogle   17
  What was proportion, or could bee .   .   . 399 Lady Ogle   21
  Of weight, or fashion, it was shee. .   .   . 399 Lady Ogle   24
  The noblest Ingenyre that ever was! .   .   . 402 Inigo Jones 1 6
  What Poesy ere was painted on a wall .   .   . 406 Inigo Jones 1 97
  It was not so of old: Men tooke up trades .   . 410 Brome   13
  You know, I never was of Truth afeard, .   .   . 414 Rutter   4
  How well I lov'd Truth: I was scarce allow'd .   . 414 Rutter   6
  Or why to like; they found, it all was new, .   . 415 Rutter   9
  This was Mr Ben: Johnsons Answer of the suddayne. . 418 Answer   Ttl
  howe soone with a selfe ticklinge hee was spent. .   . 420 Ode:If Men 18
WASSALL
  The jolly wassall walkes the often round, .   .   .   98 F3 Wroth   59
WAS'T
  Why was't? did e're the Cloudes aske back their raine? . 192 U38 Elegy 'Tis 56
WAST (WAIST)
  Read so much wast, as she cannot imbrace .   .   . 150 U9 Picture   16
  Why? though I seeme of a prodigious wast, .   .   . 226 U52 Answer   1
WAST
  Is this the Sir, who, some wast wife to winne, .   .   42 E46 Luckless 1   1
  Woman-kinde; devoure the wast .   .   .   . 105 F8 Sicknesse 16
  Give me but that againe, that I must wast .   . 167 U15 Friend-Wars 152
  Give me but that againe, which I must wast .   . 167 U15 Friend-Wars V152
  Dri'd up? lyes Thespia wast? .   .   .   . 174 U23 Himselfe   8
  Wast not hee: thou wert of old denied .   .   . 203 U43 Vulcan   V 11
  wast to a snuffe, and then stinke out, and die: .   . 211 U43 Vulcan   V188
  Thy night not dronken, but from cares layd wast; .   . 295 U90 Mart.10:47 9
WASTE (WAIST)
  And the Girdle 'bout her waste, ... 137 U2 Cupid   41
WASTE
  Let 'hem waste body, and state; and after all, .   . 118 F13 Aubigny   81
  And whilst our states, strength, body, and mind we waste, . 166 U15 Friend-Wars 133
  And have their being, their waste to see; .   .   . 189 U36 Song   11
  And waste still, that they still might bee. .   .   . 189 U36 Song   12
WASTED
  There wasted, some not paid for yet! .   .   .   97 F3 Wroth   12
  In Moses bush, un-wasted in the fire. .   .   . 413 Ghyrlond   24
WASTETH
  For fury wasteth, ... 179 U25 Desmond 46
WATCH
  Or, if thou list the night in watch to breake, .   .   97 F3 Wroth   21
  Let others watch in guiltie armes, and stand .   .   98 F3 Wroth   67
  Of thoughts to watch, and ward .   .   .   . 109 F11 Epode   8
  Or swaggering with the Watch, or Drawer, drunke; . 156 U13 Sacvile   94
  That watch, and catch, at what they may applaud, . 167 U15 Friend-Wars 157
  Doth, while he keepes his watch, betray his stand. . 198 U40 Elegy That 36
WATCH'D
  In single paths, dangers with ease are watch'd: .   . 118 F13 Aubigny   57
  Of generall knowledge; watch'd men, manners too, . 159 U14 Selden   33
  What blots and errours, have you watch'd and purg'd . 160 U14 Selden   42
  Thie long watch'd verse .   .   .   .   . 420 Ode:If Men 20
WATCHES
  Give every one his dose of mirth: and watches .   .   74 E115 Honest Man 14
WATCHFULL
  To be a watchfull Servant for this State; .   .   . 258 U75 Epithalam. 178
WATCHMAN
  The only faithfull Watchman for the Realme, .   . 185 U30 Burleigh   9
WATER
  Or else by water goes, and so to playes; .   .   .   30 E12 Shift   17
  For then, our water-conduits doe runne wine; .   .   36 E29 Tilter   5
  Of wood, of water: therein thou art faire. .   .   93 F2 Penshurst   8
  Will by coach, and water goe. .   .   .   . 105 F8 Sicknesse 37
  That as the water makes things, put in't streight, . 170 U18 Elegy Can   7
  And stroke the water, nimble, chast, and faire, . 230 U56 Covell   14
  And wee doe weepe, to water, for our sinne. .   . 234 U61 Epigram 15
  thus, as a ponderous thinge in water cast .   . 361 Palmer   17
WATER-CONDUITS
  For then, our water-conduits doe runne wine; .   .   36 E29 Tilter   5
WATERING
  That sits watering with the Muses. .   .   . 657 Door Apollo 10
WATERMEN
  My friends, the Watermen! They could provide .   . 208 U43 Vulcan   124
  Our friends, the Watermen! They could provide .   . 208 U43 Vulcan   V124

		Page	Title	Line
WATERS				
'Bove all your standing waters, choak'd with weedes.		198	U40 Elegy That	28
So deep, as he did then death's waters sup;		244	U70 Ode	41
Harke how the Bells upon the waters play		253	U75 Epithalam.	33
bor-/Dring Circles of swift waters that intwine		305	Horace	21
Bouts of fleet waters, that doe intertwine		338	Horace	V 21
Of Europes waters can		369	Ode Who saith	119
To see thee in our waters yet appeare,		392	Shakespeare	72
WAVE				
I writ he onely his taile there did wave;		380	Coryat 3	56
WAVES				
I have decreed; keepe it from waves, and presse;		219	U47 Tribe	57
WAXE				
I'the open field; is Waxe like to be wrought		315	Horace	231
WAY				
To thee, my way in Epigrammes seemes new,		32	E18 Censurer	1
When both it is the old way, and the true.		32	E18 Censurer	2
That breathes in his dogs way: and this is great.		36	E28 Surly	18
This but thy judgement fooles: the other way		43	E52 Courtling	5
That, any way, my booke should speake thy name:		53	E77 Not name	2
And hath it, in his powers, to make his way!		53	E80 Life/Death	4
Toward the sea, farther then halfe-way tree?		56	E88 Monsieur	6
I leave thee there, and giving way, entend		72	E112 Gamster	9
And, in their errors maze, thine owne way know:		76	E119 Shelton	13
And, than this same, I know no abler way		80	E127 Aubigny	11
For, then, all mouthes will judge, and their owne way:		82	E131 Ferrab. 2	3
This way to husbands; and whose baskets beare		95	F2 Penshurst	55
That found King James, when hunting late, this way,		95	F2 Penshurst	76
Some way of entrance) we must plant a guard		109	F11 Epode	7
This blessing of your starres, then by that way		118	F13 Aubigny	54
Right, the right way: yet must your comfort bee		118	F13 Aubigny	68
The way to meet, what others would upbraid;		153	U13 Sacvile	10
Pardon, sayes he, that were a way to see		155	U13 Sacvile	71
To teach each suit he has, the ready way		165	U15 Friend-Wars	108
This way, now that, as if their number were		166	U15 Friend-Wars	126
Such Guides men use not, who their way would find,		170	U18 Elegy Can	12
Except the way be errour to their eyes,		170	U18 Elegy Can	13
And straight-way spent a Sonnet; with that other		201	U42 Elegy Let	67
Of riot, and consumption, knowes the way		235	U61 Epigram	17
Some brave un-common way:		239	U67 Muses	3
Let Ireland meet it out at Sea, halfe way,		249	U72 King	5
Thou canst not meet more Glory, on the way,		252	U75 Epithalam.	3
Hath filled, with Caroches, all the way,		252	U75 Epithalam.	11
The Emblemes of their way.		254	U75 Epithalam.	63
Doe long to make themselves, so, another way:		257	U75 Epithalam.	140
To shew the rites, and t'usher forth the way		263	U79 New-yeares	4
But a fain'd way, doth rob it of the true.		270	U81 Pawlet	38
But a fain'd way, doth spoyle it of the true.		270	U81 Pawlet	V 38
Who saw the way was made it! and were sent		270	U81 Pawlet	65
That saw the way was made it! and were sent		270	U81 Pawlet	V 65
As you goe on, by what brave way		278	U84 Mind	18
When in a wrong, and artlesse way we tread.		307	Horace	44
Being taught a better way. All mortall deeds		309	Horace	98
What straight-way he must labour to retract.		315	Horace	240
'Tis cleare, this way I have got off from blame,		323	Horace	395
If either you, or I, know the right way		323	Horace	402
If either you, or I know any way		348	Horace	V388/402
All way of life was shewen; the grace of Kings		329	Horace	497
Why should I grieve my friend, this trifling way?		335	Horace	640
Enforcing yron doores to yeeld it way,		363	Riches	9
To the Greeke coast thine onely knew the way.		388	Chapman	9
A list of Epithites: And prayse this way.		394	Jane Ogle	8
Under one title. Thou hast made thy way		397	Drayton	48
but have lost it by the way,		417	Moon	10
if any way she do rewarde thee		662	Bedford	8
WAYE				
What would he doe now, gi'ng his mynde that waye		405	Inigo Jones 1	75
WAYES				
What severall wayes men to their calling have!		33	E21 Gam'ster	7
Almost all wayes, to any better course.		48	E65 Muse	10
They all get Porta, for the sundrie wayes		59	E92 New Crie	25
Thy subtle wayes, be narrow straits;		100	F4 To the World	10
And nights too, in worser wayes?		104	F8 Sicknesse	6
Strive all right wayes it can,		121	F14 Sydney	25
Sought out the Fountaines, Sources, Creekes, paths, wayes,		160	U14 Selden	45
No person, nor is lov'd: what wayes he proves		162	U15 Friend-Wars	16
But both might know their wayes were understood,		176	U24 Frontispice	7
But both might know their wayes are understood,		176	U24 Frontispice V	7
Thou prov'st the gentler wayes, to clense the wound,		187	U33 Councellour	20
Of massacring Man-kind so many wayes.		212	U43 Vulcan	208
Of murthering of mankind many wayes.		212	U43 Vulcan	V208
Let these men have their wayes, and take their times		218	U47 Tribe	25
And the right wayes you take unto the right,		224	U50 Countesse	3
And murmure cannot quarrell at your wayes?		237	U64 Charles 3	14
Reducts, Halfe-moones, Horne-workes, and such close wayes,		248	U71 Treasurer	8
And legall wayes		255	U75 Epithalam.	102
That drives the Hart to seeke unused wayes,		264	U79 New-yeares	21
Poring, as on a Map, to find the wayes		288	U84 Muse	196
Our Roman Youths they learne the subtle wayes		327	Horace	464
Our Roman Youths they learne more thriving wayes		350	Horace	V464
'Tis true, and all mens suffrage. But these wayes		390	Shakespeare	5
WAYS				
The brethren they streight ways noisd out for newes,		209	U43 Vulcan	V139

                                                               Page   Title   Line

WAYTE
    Do wayte upon thee: and theyre Love not bought.   .   .   .   384   Somerset   4
W'
    What w'are but once to doe, we should doe long.   .   .   .   139   U2 Another   12
WE'
    But, what we'are borne for, we must beare: .   .   .   101   F4 To the World   53
    More honour in him, 'cause we'ave knowne him mad: .   .   168   U15 Friend-Wars 194
    From fearefull back-slides; And the debt we'are in,   .   .   412   Sutcliffe   15
WE   (See also WEE)
    Hast purg'd thy realmes, as we have now no cause   .   .   38   E35 James 2   5
    And than in them, how could we know god more?   .   .   .   38   E35 James 2   8
    That we thy losse might know, and thou our love,   .   .   43   E51 James 3   1
    For we, that have our eyes still in our eares,   .   .   .   43   E51 James 3   9
    As we, the rob'd, leave rage, and pittie it.   .   .   .   44   E56 Poet-Ape   4
    Then, since we (more then many) these truths know: .   .   50   E70 Wm Roe 1   7
    We need a man that knowes the severall graces   .   .   .   61   E95 Savile   27
    We need a man, can speake of the intents,   .   .   .   62   E95 Savile   31
    Of state, and censure them: we need his pen   .   .   .   62   E95 Savile   33
    But most we need his faith (and all have you)   .   .   .   62   E95 Savile   35
    Not that we thinke us worthy such a ghest,   .   .   .   64   E101 Supper   3
    If we can get her, full of egs, and then,   .   .   .   64   E101 Supper   12
    The skie not falling, thinke we may have larkes.   .   .   65   E101 Supper   16
    May yet be there; and godwit, if we can: .   .   .   65   E101 Supper   19
    Of this we will sup free, but moderately,   .   .   .   65   E101 Supper   35
    And we will have no Pooly', or Parrot by;   .   .   .   65   E101 Supper   36
    But, at our parting, we will be, as when   .   .   .   65   E101 Supper   38
    We innocently met. No simple word,   .   .   .   65   E101 Supper   39
    That we had left us, nor by time, nor place,   .   .   .   67   E105 L Wroth 2   3
    And did act (what now we mone)   .   .   .   77   E120 S. P.   13
    So, when we, blest with thy returne, shall see   .   .   81   E128 Wm Roe 2   9
    We each to other may this voyce enspire;   .   .   .   81   E128 Wm Roe 2   11
    When we doe give, Alphonso, to the light,   .   .   .   82   E131 Ferrab. 2   1
    A worke of ours, we part with our owne right;   .   .   82   E131 Ferrab. 2   2
    And though we could all men, all censures heare,   .   .   83   E131 Ferrab. 2   5
    We ought not give them taste, we had an eare.   .   .   83   E131 Ferrab. 2   6
    We have a Shelton, and a Heyden got,   .   .   .   84   E133 Voyage   5
    Is this we heare? of frogs? No, guts wind-bound,   .   .   86   E133 Voyage   92
    And, howsoever we may thinke things sweet,   .   .   .   99   F3 Wroth   97
    But, what we'are borne for, we must beare: .   .   .   101   F4 To the World   53
    While we may, the sports of love;   .   .   .   102   F5 Celia 1   2
    While we can, the sports of love;   .   .   .   102   F5 Celia 1   V 2
    But if once we loose this light,   .   .   .   102   F5 Celia 1   7
    Why should we deferre our joyes?   .   .   .   102   F5 Celia 1   9
    Cannot we delude the eyes   .   .   .   102   F5 Celia 1   11
    Live not we, as, all thy stalls,   .   .   .   104   F8 Sicknesse   9
    We must sing too? what subject shall we chuse?   .   .   107   F10 Proludium V 1
    Shall not give out, that we have made thee stay,   .   .   107   F10 Proludium V 8
    Nor will we beg of thee, Lord of the vine,   .   .   107   F10 Proludium V 10
    Pallas, nor thee we call on, mankinde maid,   .   .   107   F10 Proludium V 13
    Our muse up by commission: No, we bring   .   .   .   108   F10 Proludium V 28
    And now an Epode to deepe eares we sing.   .   .   .   108   F10 Proludium V 30
    Some way of entrance) we must plant a guard   .   .   109   F11 Epode   7
    'Tis the securest policie we have,   .   .   .   109   F11 Epode   17
    Which thus we over-blow.   .   .   .   110   F11 Epode   36
    That cryes, we dreame, and sweares, there's no such thing,   .   111   F11 Epode   67
    As this chaste love we sing.   .   .   .   111   F11 Epode   68
    No, vice, we let thee know,   .   .   .   111   F11 Epode   72
    We doe not number, here,   .   .   .   111   F11 Epode   76
    Nor meane we those, whom vowes and conscience   .   .   111   F11 Epode   83
    Though we acknowledge, who can so abstayne,   .   .   112   F11 Epode   85
    But we propose a person like our Dove,   .   .   .   112   F11 Epode   91
    Whether we have lost, or wonne,   .   .   .   138   U2 Kisse   6
    What w'are but once to doe, we should doe long.   .   .   139   U2 Another   12
    But we find that cold delay,   .   .   .   140   U2 Promise   9
    We all feare, she loveth none.   .   .   .   140   U2 Promise   12
    What we harmonie doe call   .   .   .   141   U2 Her man   34
    Mixe then your Notes, that we may prove   .   .   143   U3 Musicall   9
    Nor doe we doubt, but that we can,   .   .   .   145   U5 Woman-kind   7
    We were not bred to sit on stooles,   .   .   .   146   U6 Defence   3
    We are women then, but wives.   .   .   .   146   U6 Defence   6
    Which we in love must doe aswell,   .   .   .   146   U6 Defence   9
    If ever we will love aright.   .   .   .   146   U6 Defence   10
    And knew their how, and where: we should have, then,   .   153   U13 Sacvile   3
    That with these mixtures we put out her light.   .   .   156   U13 Sacvile   110
    Yet we must more then move still, or goe on,   .   .   157   U13 Sacvile   135
    We must accomplish; 'Tis the last Key-stone   .   .   157   U13 Sacvile   136
    Pernitious enemie; we see, before   .   .   .   158   U14 Selden   14
    And even our sports are dangers! what we call   .   .   163   U15 Friend-Wars 38
    Is not enough now, but the Nights we play: .   .   166   U15 Friend-Wars V132
    And whilst our states, strength, body, and mind we waste,   .   166   U15 Friend-Wars 133
    Now use the bones, we see doth hire a man   .   .   166   U15 Friend-Wars 136
    Now use the bales, we see doth hire a man   .   .   166   U15 Friend-Wars V136
    Can we not leave this worme? or will we not?   .   .   166   U15 Friend-Wars 141
    Is that the truer excuse? or have we got   .   .   166   U15 Friend-Wars 142
    And last, blaspheme not, we did never heare   .   .   168   U15 Friend-Wars 191
    No more, then we should thinke a Lord had had   .   .   168   U15 Friend-Wars 193
    Others, in time may love, as we doe now.   .   .   171   U19 Elegy By   18
    That which we can, who both in you, his Wife,   .   .   171   U19 Elegy By   25
    So fooles, we see,   .   .   .   179   U25 Desmond   51
    To fetch the flesh, we keepe the Rowle.   .   .   188   U35 Chute   6
    We cut not off, till all Cures else doe faile: .   .   192   U38 Elegy 'Tis   46
    In darke, and sullen mornes, doe we not say,   .   .   193   U38 Elegy 'Tis   79
    And we were left under that Hemisphere,   .   .   199   U41 Elegy Since   7

                                  763

	Page	Title	Line

WE (cont.)

	Page	Title	Line
Where we must feele it Darke for halfe a yeare.	199	U41 Elegy Since	8
No order? no Decree? Though we be gone	211	U43 Vulcan	176
We aske your absence here, we all love peace,	212	U43 Vulcan	209
We crave your absence here, we all love peace,	212	U43 Vulcan	V209
But we have Powder still for the Kings Day,	213	U44 Speach	2
That we have Trumpets, Armour, and great Horse,	213	U44 Speach	7
Are we by Booke-wormes to be awde? must we	215	U44 Speach	67
Why are we rich, or great, except to show	215	U44 Speach	69
All licence in our lives? What need we know,	215	U44 Speach	70
We will beleeve, like men of our owne Ranke,	215	U44 Speach	75
We neither love the Troubles, nor the harmes.	215	U44 Speach	86
One lesson we have both learn'd, and well read;	216	U45 Squib	4
Much lesse a name would we bring up, or nurse,	216	U45 Squib	9
Inquirie of the worth: So must we doe,	216	U45 Squib	15
But if, for honour, we must draw the Sword,	219	U47 Tribe	39
We dedicate this Cellar,	220	U48 Bacchus	3
Or what we heare our home-borne Legend tell,	228	U53 Newcastle	9
He, that in such a flood, as we are in	234	U61 Epigram	16
To compare small with great, as still we owe	238	U66 Queene	12
Of deepest lore, could we the Center find!	243	U70 Ode	10
In small proportions, we just beautie see:	245	U70 Ode	73
Of which we Priests, and Poets say	245	U70 Ode	82
Such truths, as we expect for happy men,	246	U70 Ode	83
We wooe thee, stay	252	U75 Epithalam.	6
Through which not only we, but all our Species are.	253	U75 Epithalam.	32
All else we see beside, are Shadowes, and goe lesse.	255	U75 Epithalam.	88
We pray may grace	257	U75 Epithalam.	158
Yet, as we may, we will, with chast desires,	257	U75 Epithalam.	161
But we last out, still unlay'd.	259	U76 Petition	24
We sing the best of Monarchs, Masters, Men;	263	U79 New-yeares	7
For, had we here said lesse, we had sung nothing then.	263	U79 New-yeares	8
To him we owe all profits of our grounds.	264	U79 New-yeares	15
Of brightest Mira, doe we raise our Song,	264	U79 New-yeares	24
To touch these Mysteries! We may admire	269	U81 Pawlet	31
To touch those Mysteries! We may admire	269	U81 Pawlet	V 31
When we were all borne, we began to die;	271	U81 Pawlet	94
Next sitting we will draw her mind.	277	U84 Body	32
But here we may no colours use.	277	U84 Mind	V 6
In his eternall Kingdome, where we sit	286	U84 Muse	145
Nor dare we under blasphemy conceive	286	U84 Muse	147
And done, we straight repent us of the sport:	294	U88 Petronius	2
Of daring all, hath still beene given; we know it:	305	Horace	12
Of daring ought, hath still beene given; we know it:	338	Horace	V 12
Together: not that we should Serpents see	305	Horace	15
To gentle: not that we should Serpents see	338	Horace	V 15
When in a wrong, and artlesse way we tread.	307	Horace	44
If in th'escape an artlesse path we tread.	339	Horace	V 46/ 44
Our selves, and all that's ours, to death we owe:	309	Horace	90
To children; we must alwayes dwell, and stay	317	Horace	253
There are yet faults, which we would well forgive,	329	Horace	520
Oft-times a Sharpe, when we require a Flat:	329	Horace	523
Flowes from the surfets which we take in peace.	363	Peace	4
Then why should we dispaire? Dispaire, away:	363	Riches	17
When him alone we sing)	368	Ode Who saith	63
Now must we plie our ayme; our Swan's on wing.	368	Ode Who saith	64
Poore Tom have we cause to suspect just there?	381	Coryat 3	58
And we have wits to read, and praise to give.	391	Shakespeare	24
Looke, how we read the Spartans were inflam'd	398	Drayton	67
We offer as a Circle the most fit	416	Welcome	6

WEAKE

	Page	Title	Line
When I am read, thou fain'st a weake applause,	43	E52 Courtling	3
To a weake Gamster in Poetry.	72	E112 Gamster	Ttl
To take the weake, or make them stop:	100	F4 To the World	19
Outward Grace weake love beguiles:	137	U2 Cupid	51
And shewing so weake an Act to vulgar eyes,	218	U47 Tribe	7
Dull, and prophane, weake, and imperfect eyes,	284	U84 Muse	79
And the bold Pythias, having cheated weake	321	Horace	346
What can one witnesse, and a weake one, add	385	Brooke	4
The comfort of weake Christians, with their warning,	411	Sutcliffe	13

WEAKER

	Page	Title	Line
weare made the objects to my weaker powers;	361	Palmer	3

WEAKEST

	Page	Title	Line
So men at weakest, they are strongest,	104	F7 Women but	9

WEAKNESSE

	Page	Title	Line
Where weaknesse doth offend, and vertue grieve,	192	U38 Elegy 'Tis	33
Weakenesse of braine, or any charme of Wine,	198	U40 Elegy That	45

WEALE

	Page	Title	Line
Desired Justice to the publique Weale,	217	U46 Coke	16
Fame, and foundation of the English Weale.	225	U51 Bacon	10

WEALTH

	Page	Title	Line
To'a little wealth, and credit in the scene,	45	E56 Poet-Ape	7
The common-wealth still safe, must studie thee.	66	E102 Pembroke	20
Let that goe heape a masse of wretched wealth,	99	F3 Wroth	81
Play away, health, wealth, and fame.	105	F8 Sicknesse	42
Or faith in things? or is't your wealth and will	159	U14 Selden	36
But here's no time, nor place, my wealth to tell,	161	U14 Selden	85
The Care, and wish still of the publike wealth:	186	U31 Elsmere	6
Both arm'd with wealth, and slander to oppose,	186	U32 Elsmere	8
And didst invade part of the Common-wealth,	210	U43 Vulcan	170
Nor markes of wealth so from our Nation fled,	213	U44 Speach	12
As all the wealth of Season, there was spread;	251	U74 Weston	15
By all the wealth of blessings, and the store	285	U84 Muse	110

WEALTH (cont.)
And wealth unto our language; and brought forth . . . 309 Horace 82
His better'd mind seekes wealth, and friendship: than . 315 Horace 238
Their Charge, and Office, whence their wealth to fet, . 325 Horace 436
The Dutch whom Wealth (not Hatred) doth divide; . . 368 Ode Who saith 85
To make thy honour, and our wealth the more! . . 388 Chapman 6
And doe both Church, and Common-wealth the good, . . 416 Dover 8
WEALTHIE
Can; or all toile, without a wealthie veine: . . 331 Horace 584
WEALTHY
To be the wealthy witnesse of my pen: . . . . 54 E81 Proule 4
Kisse, and score up wealthy summes . . . . 103 F6 Celia 2 6
The wealthy treasure of her love on him; . . . 112 F11 Epode 105
The wealthy treasure of her love in him; . . . 112 F11 Epode V105
The wealthy houshold swarme of bondmen met, . . 291 U85 Country 65
Or wealthy in money's out at use, command . . . 353 Horace V600
WEAPON
Yet by thy weapon liv'st! Th'hast one good part. . . 50 E69 Cob 2
When gold was made no weapon to cut throtes, . . 114 F12 Rutland 23
WEAPONS
Their weapons shot out, with that flame, and force, . 233 U59 Newcastle 11
Their weapons darted, with that flame, and force, . 233 U59 Newcastle V 11
WEAR
wear spent with wonder as they weare delated, . . 361 Palmer 24
WE'ARE
But, what we'are borne for, we must beare: . . . 101 F4 To the World 53
From fearefull back-slides; And the debt we'are in, . 412 Sutcliffe 15
WEARE (WERE)
weare made the objects to my weaker powers; . . 361 Palmer 3
wear spent with wonder as they weare delated, . . 361 Palmer 24
WEARE
How, best of Poets, do'st thou laurell weare! . . 28 E4 James 1 2
Except thou could'st, Sir Cod, weare them within. . 33 E20 Cod 2 2
Weare this renowne. 'Tis just, that who did give . 57 E89 Allen 13
And best become the valiant man to weare, . . . 58 E91 Vere 17
He, that but saw you weare the wheaten hat, . . 68 E105 L Wroth 2 7
I weare not these my wings in vaine. . . . . 93 F1 Why write no 7
Thou dost with some delight the day out-weare, . . 97 F3 Wroth 35
Thou canst with some delight the day out-weare, . . 97 F3 Wroth V 35
For truthes complexion, where they all weare maskes. . 118 F13 Aubigny 70
Whether it be a face they weare, or no. . . . 118 F13 Aubigny 80
Well he should his clothes to weare; . . . 141 U2 Her man 36
Will be reward enough: to weare like those, . . 232 U58 Book-seller 9
Or Semi-god, that late was seene to weare . . 321 Horace 332
Nor did they merit the lesse Crowne to weare, . . 323 Horace 406
Such weare true wedding robes, and are true freindes, . 384 Somerset 5
And joy'd to weare the dressing of his lines! . . 392 Shakespeare 48
Noe velvet Sheath you weare, will alter kynde. . . 403 Inigo Jones 1 26
WEARES
Yes, now he weares his knight-hood every day. . . 42 E46 Luckless 1 6
A romane sound, but romane vertue weares, . . . 58 E91 Vere 2
Since he was gone, more then the one he weares. . 63 E97 Motion 17
Lady, or Pusil, that weares maske, or fan, . . 370 Fletcher 4
WEARIED
Like the dull wearied Crane that (come on land) . . 198 U40 Elegy That 35
WEARINESSE
For wearinesse of life, not love of thee. . . . 122 F15 Heaven 26
WEARING
But these with wearing will themselves unfold: . . 216 U45 Squib 19
Not wearing moodes, as gallants doe a fashion, . . 362 Author 3
WEARY
And pikes, now weary their owne kinde to eat, . . 94 F2 Penshurst 34
Not weary, rest . . . . 121 F14 Sydney 37
But weary of that flight, ... 244 U70 Ode 37
To view the weary Oxen draw, with bare . . . 291 U85 Country 63
WEATHER
About in Cloudes, and wrapt in raging weather, . . 193 U38 Elegy 'Tis 75
The name of Cruell weather, storme, and raine? . . 193 U38 Elegy 'Tis 82
Unseason'd frostes, or the most envyous weather. . . 361 Palmer 8
WE'AVE
More honour in him, 'cause we'ave knowne him mad: . . 168 U15 Friend-Wars 194
WEAVE
Who 'gainst the Law, weave Calumnies, my ——: . . 187 U33 Councellour 6
In letters, that mixe spirits, thus to weave. . . 190 U37 Friend-Book 12
To Roman Poets. Shall I therefore weave . . . 323 Horace 390
WEAV'D
Against his will that do's 'hem? that hath weav'd . . 153 U13 Sacvile 26
Of what it tells us) weav'd in to instruct. . . 160 U14 Selden 52
That their whole life was wickednesse, though weav'd . 171 U20 Shrub 10
Or spun out Riddles, and weav'd fiftie tomes . . 204 U43 Vulcan 33
Or spun or weav'd in Riddles 50 tomes . . . 204 U43 Vulcan V 33
All that was good, or great in me she weav'd, . . 282 U84 Muse 4
WEAVING
in weaving Riddles in more wretched ryme, . . . 204 U43 Vulcan V 34
WEB
In solemne cypres, the other cob-web-lawne. . . 51 E73 Fine Grand 14
All is but web, and painting; be the strife . . 242 U69 Friend Son 24
WEDDED
French Aire and English Verse here Wedded lie. . . 401 Filmer 6
WEDDING
(After the last child borne;) This is our wedding day. . 258 U75 Epithalam. 168
Such weare true wedding robes, and are true freindes, . 384 Somerset 5

				Page	Title	Line

WEE'
Of which wee'll speake our minds, amidst our meate;   .   .   .   65   E101 Supper   23
The libertie, that wee'll enjoy to night.   65   E101 Supper   42
And having pleas'd our art, wee'll try   145   U5 Woman-kind   17
Wee'll have thee styld the Marquess of New-Ditch.   .   .   407   Inigo Jones 2   24
Wee'll have thee styld the Marquess of Town-Ditch.   .   .   407   Inigo Jones 2   V 24

WEE
And such a Prince thou art, wee daily see,   .   .   .   28   E4 James 1   7
Wee, sad for him, may glorie, and not sinne.   .   .   .   35   E27 Roe 1   8
But when once wee lose the light,   .   .   .   102   F5 Celia 1   V 7
and now an Epode, to deepe Eares, wee singe.   .   .   108   F10 Proludium   16
What comfort by him doe wee winne,   .   .   .   130   U1 Nativitie   19
Wee exercise below, ...   144   U3 Musicall   V 18
Wee have both wits, and fancies too,   .   .   .   144   U3 Musicall   V 18
And if wee must, let's sing of you.   145   U5 Woman-kind   5
If wee would search with care, and paine,   .   .   145   U5 Woman-kind   6
Wee shall, at last, of parcells make   .   .   .   145   U5 Woman-kind   8
Then when 'tis made, why so will wee.   .   .   .   145   U5 Woman-kind   11
Let poore Nobilitie be vertuous: Wee,   .   .   .   145   U5 Woman-kind   16
And wee doe weepe, to water, for our sinne.   .   .   215   U44 Speach   79
What, by that name, wee each to other owe,   .   .   234   U61 Epigram   15
Of Pan wee sing, the best of Hunters, Pan,   .   .   241   U69 Friend Son   4
Rivers, and Vallies, Eccho what wee sing.   .   .   264   U79 New-yeares   20
Of Pan wee sing, the Chiefe of Leaders, Pan,   .   .   264   U79 New-yeares   27
Rivers, and Valleys, Eccho what wee sing.   .   .   264   U79 New-yeares   28
Wee know no other power then his,   .   .   .   264   U79 New-yeares   35
That all Posteritie, as wee, ...   265   U79 New-yeares   42
Thinke wee, or hope, there can be Verses fain'd   .   .   273   U84 Cradle   13
His name is Skeuopoios wee all knowe,   .   .   .   327   Horace   474
And such a Prince thou art, wee daily see,   .   .   .   404   Inigo Jones 1   60

WEEDES
'Bove all your standing waters, choak'd with weedes.   .   198   U40 Elegy That   28
But, O those weedes; thy meere disdaine of them,   .   208   U43 Vulcan   V129
Thy skill hath made of ranck dispised weedes;   .   .   361   Palmer   10

WEEDS
Against his Maker; high alone with weeds,   .   .   .   163   U15 Friend-Wars   33

WEEKE
To which thou'rt not a weeke, bespoke a guest;   .   .   81   E129 Mime   6
They'ave glutted in, and letcher'd out that weeke,   .   218   U47 Tribe   13
Lend me, deare Arthur, for a weeke five more,   .   .   229   U54 Squib   16

WEEKES
Scarse thy weekes swearing brings thee of, of one.   .   32   E16 Brain-hardy   4

WEEKLY
The weekly Corrants, with Pauls Seale; and all   .   .   206   U43 Vulcan   81
The weekly Corrants, with Poules stall; and all   .   206   U43 Vulcan   V 81
They say you weekly invite with fits o'th' Mother,   .   223   U49 Pucell   40

WEE'L
Wee'l rip our Richest veynes   420   Ode:If Men   31

WEE'LL
Of which wee'll speake our minds, amidst our meate;   .   65   E101 Supper   23
The libertie, that wee'll enjoy to night.   .   .   .   65   E101 Supper   42
And having pleas'd our art, wee'll try   .   .   .   145   U5 Woman-kind   17
Wee'll have thee styld the Marquess of New-Ditch.   .   407   Inigo Jones 2   24
Wee'll have thee styld the Marquess of Town-Ditch.   .   407   Inigo Jones 2   V 24

WEEPE
Marble, weepe, for thou dost cover   39   E40 Ratcliffe   1
Weepe with me all you that read   77   E120 S. P.   1
The foole that gave it; who will want, and weepe,   .   113   F12 Rutland   13
The foole that gave it; that will want, and weepe,   .   113   F12 Rutland   V 13
And wee doe weepe, to water, for our sinne.   .   .   234   U61 Epigram   15
If thou would'st have me weepe, be thou first drown'd   .   311   Horace   145
As those that hir'd to weepe at Funeralls, swoune,   .   333   Horace   614

WEEPINGE
And pray thee Reader, bring thy weepinge Eyes   .   .   394   Jane Ogle   2

WEEVER
Davis, and Weever, and the best have beene,   .   .   32   E18 Censurer   4

WEIGH (See also WAIGH)
First weigh a friend, then touch, and trie him too: .   216   U45 Squib   16
O pietie! so to weigh the poores estates!   .   .   235   U62 Charles 1   11

WEIGH'D
Whil'st thy weigh'd judgements, Egerton, I heare,   .   51   E74 Chancelor   1
Where nothing is examin'd, weigh'd,   .   .   .   101   F4 To the World   49
I Am to dine, Friend, where I must be weigh'd   .   229   U54 Squib   1
If he but weigh'd the blessings of this day?   .   .   236   U64 Charles 3   4
And weigh'd your Play: untwisted ev'ry thread,   .   .   415   Rutter   14

WEIGHT
What weight, and what authoritie in speech!   .   .   31   E14 Camden   9
Where sweetnesse is requir'd, and where weight;   .   62   E95 Savile   30
And that thy soule should give thy flesh her weight.   .   70   E109 Nevil   14
And furrowes laden with their weight;   .   .   .   98   F3 Wroth   42
Gives the Lover weight, and fashion.   .   .   .   131   U2 Excuse   12
Himselfe of farther trouble, or the weight   .   .   154   U13 Sacvile   31
Are Dwarfes of Honour, and have neither weight   .   157   U13 Sacvile   147
But false weight.   183   U29 Fit of Rime   6
From whence they fall, cast downe with their owne weight.   .   224   U50 Countesse   12
An ill commoditie! 'T must make good weight.   .   .   229   U54 Squib   6
And you shall make me good, in weight, and fashion,   .   229   U54 Squib   17
His weight is twenty Stone within two pound;   .   .   230   U56 Covell   11
In weight, in measure, number, sound,   .   .   .   244   U70 Ode   50
A Poeme, of no grace, weight, art, in rimes,   .   .   327   Horace   456
Of weight, or fashion, it was shee.   .   .   .   399   Lady Ogle   24

WEIGHTIE
In neighbour-townes, and feeles the weightie plough: .   309   Horace   95
With weightie sorrow hurles us all along,   .   .   311   Horace   155

				Page	Title	Line

WEIGHTIE (cont.)
| With weightie woes she hurles us all along | . | . | . | . | 342 | Horace | V155 |
| More slow, and come more weightie to the eare: | . | . | . | . | 323 | Horace | 378 |

WEIGHTY
| In thee, most weighty Savile, liv'd to us: | . | . | . | . | 61 | E95 Savile | 4 |

WEL
Upon thy wel-made choise of friends, and bookes;	.	.	.	.	55	E86 Goodyere 2	2
Great and good turns, as wel could time them too,	.	.	.	.	153	U13 Sacvile	2
Such as are square, wel-tagde, and permanent,	.	.	.	.	220	U47 Tribe	64
Of some wel-wrought Embassage:	.	.	.	.	221	U48 Bacchus	46

WELCOME
And which thou brought'st me, welcome povertie.	.	.	.	.	48	E65 Muse	12
Whose name's un-welcome to the present eare,	.	.	.	.	74	E115 Honest Man	15
With all their zeale, to warme their welcome here.	.	.	.	.	95	F2 Penshurst	81
And giv'st thy welcome guests the right;	.	.	.	.	97	F3 Wroth	V 28
Thy noblest spouse affords them welcome grace;	.	.	.	.	98	F3 Wroth	55
Thy noblest spouse affords them welcome place;	.	.	.	.	98	F3 Wroth	V 55
To welcome home a Paire, and deck the nuptiall bower?	.	.	.	.	253	U75 Epithalam.	24
Welcome all, who lead or follow,	.	.	.	.	657	Door Apollo	1
Welcome all, who lead or follow,	.	.	.	.	657	Door Apollo	19

WELL   (NAME)
| Of some Bride-well, and may, in time, concerne us | . | . | . | 85 | E133 Voyage | 42 |

WELL
To reade it well: that is, to understand.	.	.	.	.	27	E1 Reader	2
Thou, that mak'st gaine thy end, and wisely well,	.	.	.	.	27	E3 Bookseller	1
Send it to Bucklers-bury, there 'twill, well.	.	.	.	.	28	E3 Bookseller	12
Great heav'n did well, to give ill fame free wing;	.	.	.	.	43	E51 James 3	2
May judge it to be his, as well as ours.	.	.	.	.	45	E56 Poet-Ape	12
That love to make so well, a child to beare?	.	.	.	.	46	E62 Would-bee	2
He cast, yet keeps her well! No, shee keeps him.	.	.	.	.	54	E82 Surly	2
Thou hast begun well, Roe, which stand well too,	.	.	.	.	63	E98 Th Roe 1	1
Well, though thy name lesse then our great ones bee,	.	.	.	.	64	E99 Th Roe 2	11
How well, faire crowne of your faire sexe, might hee,	.	.	.	.	66	E103 L Wroth 1	1
By speaking well o' the company' it 's in.	.	.	.	.	74	E115 Honest Man	8
Whose dice not doing well, to'a pulpit ran.	.	.	.	.	76	E119 Shelton	6
Came backe untouch'd. This man hath travail'd well.	.	.	.	.	81	E128 Wm Roe 2	14
So well in that are his inventions wrought,	.	.	.	.	83	E132 Sylvester	11
His three for one. Now, lordings, listen well.	.	.	.	.	84	E133 Voyage	28
Over your heads: Well, row. At this a loud	.	.	.	.	86	E133 Voyage	93
The well-greas'd wherry now had got betweene,	.	.	.	.	87	E133 Voyage	114
And bad her fare-well sough, unto the lurden:	.	.	.	.	87	E133 Voyage	115
Thou hast thy walkes for health, as well as sport:	.	.	.	.	93	F2 Penshurst	9
Thy peace is made; and, when man's state is well,	.	.	.	.	99	F3 Wroth	93
but being well assured that there	.	.	.	.	106	F9 Celia 3	V 11
Next, to that vertue, is to know vice well,	.	.	.	.	109	F11 Epode	3
Well, or ill, onely, all the following yeere,	.	.	.	.	113	F12 Rutland	7
And your brave friend, and mine so well did love.	.	.	.	.	116	F12 Rutland	92
And your brave friend, and mine to well did love.	.	.	.	.	116	F12 Rutland	V 92
Not taken up o' th' doctors, but as well	.	.	.	.	117	F13 Aubigny	33
Give me my cup, but from the Thespian well,	.	.	.	.	120	F14 Sydney	11
When well begunne:	.	.	.	.	121	F14 Sydney	46
And well the Carre Love guideth.	.	.	.	.	134	U2 Triumph	4
Where, how it would have relish'd well;	.	.	.	.	139	U2 Another	14
What a man she could love well:	.	.	.	.	139	U2 Promise	4
Well he should his clothes to weare;	.	.	.	.	141	U2 Her man	36
On all mens Fruit, and flowers, as well as mine.	.	.	.	.	150	U10 Jealousie	8
Well knowne, and practiz'd borrowers on their word,	.	.	.	.	154	U13 Sacvile	48
Many a pound, and piece, will place one well;	.	.	.	.	155	U13 Sacvile	78
And you, Sir, know it well, to whom I write,	.	.	.	.	156	U13 Sacvile	109
Well, let it goe. Yet this is better, then	.	.	.	.	166	U15 Friend-Wars	145
So well as I may tell in verse, 'tis so?	.	.	.	.	170	U19 Elegy By	12
At the Well no Muse did stay,	.	.	.	.	183	U29 Fit of Rime	20
Well fare the wise-men yet, on the Banckside,	.	.	.	.	208	U43 Vulcan	123
For they did see it the last tilting well,	.	.	.	.	213	U44 Speach	6
Well, I say, thrive, thrive brave Artillerie yard,	.	.	.	.	213	U44 Speach	23
Well did thy craftie Clerke, and Knight, Sir Hugh,	.	.	.	.	214	U44 Speach	33
One lesson we have both learn'd, and well read;	.	.	.	.	216	U45 Squib	4
That to speake well, thinke it above all sinne,	.	.	.	.	218	U47 Tribe	19
I wish all well, and pray high heaven conspire	.	.	.	.	219	U47 Tribe	37
Shall carry me at Call; and I'le be well,	.	.	.	.	219	U47 Tribe	45
Well, with mine owne fraile Pitcher, what to doe	.	.	.	.	219	U47 Tribe	56
Nor any of their houshold, halfe so well.	.	.	.	.	228	U53 Newcastle	16
So well! as when I saw the floore, and Roome,	.	.	.	.	228	U53 Newcastle	17
So well! as when I view'd the floore, and Roome,	.	.	.	.	228	U53 Newcastle	V 17
Well, they should know him, would the K. but grant	.	.	.	.	241	U68 House-hold	5
How well at twentie had he falne, or stood!	.	.	.	.	243	U70 Ode	31
Hee entred well, by vertuous parts,	.	.	.	.	244	U70 Ode	33
To light: her measures are, how well	.	.	.	.	245	U70 Ode	62
Saw'st thou that Paire, became these Rites so well,	.	.	.	.	254	U75 Epithalam.	76
And this well mov'd the Judgement of the King	.	.	.	.	256	U75 Epithalam.	105
Well dispenc'd in bookes, or bread,	.	.	.	.	259	U76 Petition	V 15
Tho', happy Muse, thou know my Digby well;	.	.	.	.	262	U78 Digby	1
What she did here, by great example, well,	.	.	.	.	269	U81 Pawlet	33
What she did by a great example, well,	.	.	.	.	269	U81 Pawlet	V 33
Or why, my well-grac'd words among,	.	.	.	.	293	U86 Hor.4:1	35
Know'st only well to paint a Cipresse tree.	.	.	.	.	305	Horace	25
Faine words, unheard of to the well-truss'd race	.	.	.	.	309	Horace	71
And so well faines, so mixeth cunningly	.	.	.	.	315	Horace	215
Having well eat, and drunke (the rites being done)	.	.	.	.	319	Horace	325
The very root of writing well, and spring	.	.	.	.	325	Horace	440
Hee, that hath studied well the debt, and knowes	.	.	.	.	325	Horace	445
But a well-compass'd mouth to utter it;	.	.	.	.	327	Horace	462
There are yet faults, which we would well forgive,	.	.	.	.	329	Horace	520

WELL   (cont.)

	Page	Title	Line
A meane, and toleration, which does well:	331	Horace	549
These, the free meale might have beene well drawne out:	331	Horace	560
(so well dispos'd by thy auspicious hand)	361	Palmer	2
Palmer thy travayles well becum thy name,	362	Palmer	30
Will well confesse; presenting, limiting,	370	Author	6
As well as from his braines, and claimest thereby	378	Coryat 2	90
How well, and how often his shoes too were mended,	380	Coryat 3	39
From Venice to Flushing, were not they well cobled?	380	Coryat 3	42
With the how much they set forth, but th'how well.	386	Browne	16
But that hee's too well suted, in a cloth,	389	Aleman	17
As well in brasse, as he hath hit	390	Reader	6
For a good Poet's made, as well as borne.	392	Shakespeare	64
In his well torned, and true-filed lines:	392	Shakespeare	68
Such things, of every body, and as well.	394	Jane Ogle	10
And those so sweet, and well proportion'd parts,	396	Drayton	21
And flight about the Ile, well neare, by this,	397	Drayton	49
Get broken peeces, and fight well by those.	398	Drayton	74
To all thy vertuous, and well chosen Friends,	398	Drayton	90
Will well designe thee, to be viewd of all	408	Inigo Jones 3	12
And you doe doe them well, with good applause,	409	Brome	5
You learn'd it well; and for it, serv'd your time	410	Brome	9
How well I lov'd Truth: I was scarce allow'd	414	Rutter	6
Where it runs round, and even: where so well,	415	Rutter	16

WELL-COMPASS'D

	Page	Title	Line
But a well-compass'd mouth to utter it;	327	Horace	462

WELL-GRAC'D

	Page	Title	Line
Or why, my well-grac'd words among,	293	U86 Hor.4:1	35

WELL-GREAS'D

	Page	Title	Line
The well-greas'd wherry now had got betweene,	87	E133 Voyage	114

WELL-TRUSS'D

	Page	Title	Line
Faine words, unheard of to the well-truss'd race	309	Horace	71

WEL-MADE

	Page	Title	Line
Upon thy wel-made choise of friends, and bookes;	55	E86 Goodyere 2	2

WEL-TAGDE

	Page	Title	Line
Such as are square, wel-tagde, and permanent,	220	U47 Tribe	64

WEL-WROUGHT

	Page	Title	Line
Of some wel-wrought Embassage:	221	U48 Bacchus	46

WENCH

	Page	Title	Line
Me now, nor Wench, nor wanton Boy,	293	U86 Hor.4:1	29

WENT

	Page	Title	Line
Straight went I home; and there most like a Poet,	55	E84 Bedford 2	5
Out-stript, then they did all that went before:	57	E89 Allen	10
Went on: and proving him still, day by day,	57	E90 Mill	7
Lust it comes out, that gluttony went in.	76	E118 Gut	6
Or him that backward went to Berwicke, or which	85	E133 Voyage	35
And, on they went, like Castor brave, and Pollux.	86	E133 Voyage	77
And so went bravely backe, without protraction.	89	E133 Voyage	192
And speaking worst of those, from whom they went	154	U13 Sacvile	51
Jonson, who sung this of him, e're he went	246	U70 Ode	85
Who walkes on Earth as May still went along,	264	U79 New-yeares	26
To another, Move; he went; To a third, Go,	287	U84 Muse	170
In name, I went all names before,	293	U87 Hor.3:9	7
Unto the last, as when he first went forth,	313	Horace	181
Gesture, and riot, whilst he swooping went	319	Horace	304
Gesture, and riot, whilst he wandring went	346	Horace	V304
To write it with the selfe same spirit he went,	379	Coryat 3	14
In five monthes he went it, in five monthes he pend it.	379	Coryat 3	16
He went out at each place, and at what he came in,	380	Coryat 3	25
That went before, a Husband. Shee, Ile sweare,	386	Husband	9

WEPT

	Page	Title	Line
Of tender eyes will more be wept, then seene:	398	Drayton	76

WERE   (See also 'TWERE)

	Page	Title	Line
For such a Poet, while thy dayes were greene,	28	E4 James 1	5
Mens manners ne're were viler, for your sake.	34	E24 Parliament	2
Harsh sights at home, Giles wisheth he were blind.	40	E42 Giles	10
Were quite out-spun. The like wish hath his wife.	40	E42 Giles	12
'Tofore, great men were glad of Poets: Now,	40	E43 Salisbury 1	5
Ere blacks were bought for his owne funerall,	41	E44 Chuff	3
If, as their ends, their fruits were so, the same,	45	E57 Bawds	1
Baudrie', and usurie were one kind of game.	45	E57 Bawds	2
Which deed I know not, whether were more high,	49	E66 Cary	7
As all thy honors were by them first sought:	49	E67 Suffolk	8
As't were a challenge, or a borrowers letter?	51	E73 Fine Grand	3
On whom, if he were living now, to looke,	53	E79 Rutland	10
In th'eye of Europe, where thy deeds were done,	58	E91 Vere	6
To any one, were envie: which would live	58	E91 Vere	11
Stand'st thou, to shew the times what you all were?	60	E93 Radcliffe	4
Or, better worke! were thy glad countrey blest,	61	E95 Savile	14
Cry'd to my face, they were th'elixir of wit:	64	E100 Playwrt 3	2
And noted for what flesh such soules were fram'd,	66	E103 L Wroth 1	3
Were they that nam'd you, prophets? Did they see,	67	E104 Montgomery	1
Were you advanced, past those times, to be	67	E104 Montgomery	11
But even their names were to be made a-new,	67	E105 L Wroth 2	5
You were the bright Oenone, Flora, or May?	68	E105 L Wroth 2	10
Were leading forth the Graces on the greene:	68	E105 L Wroth 2	12
How great you were with their two Emperours;	68	E107 Hungry	6
What th'antique souldiers were, the moderne bee?	72	E111 Edmonds 2	2
These were thy knowing arts: which who doth now	75	E116 Jephson	13
Who prov'st, all these were, and againe may bee.	78	E122 Rudyerd 2	10
T'alledge, that greatest men were not asham'd,	82	E130 Ferrab. 1	9
To say, indeed, shee were the soule of heaven,	82	E130 Ferrab. 1	11
Including all, were thence call'd harmonie:	82	E130 Ferrab. 1	14

WERE (cont.)
	Page	Title	Line
When these were but the praises of the Art.	82	E130 Ferrab. 1	16
They were not to be nam'd on the same day.	83	E131 Ferrab. 2	12
If to admire were to commend, my praise	83	E132 Sylvester	1
Bartas doth wish thy English now were his.	83	E132 Sylvester	10
Arses were heard to croake, in stead of frogs;	84	E133 Voyage	13
Laden with plague-sores, and their sinnes, were heard,	84	E133 Voyage	17
Were seene your ugly Centaures, yee call Car-men,	86	E133 Voyage	68
Or were precipitated downe the jakes,	87	E133 Voyage	137
All was to them the same, they were to passe,	88	E133 Voyage	140
And, after mouldie growne, againe were tosted,	88	E133 Voyage	150
For, here they were throwne in wi'the melted pewter,	88	E133 Voyage	153
Were you Jove's sonnes, or had Alcides might.	89	E133 Voyage	182
As if in Saturnes raigne it were;	98	F3 Wroth	50
And brag, that they were therefore borne.	99	F3 Wroth	72
When all the causes were away.	101	F4 To the World	44
Of his dull god-head, were sinne. Ile implore	107	F10 Proludium	6
Of his dull god-head, were sinne. Lets implore	107	F10 Proludium V	6
(Though they were crusht into one forme) could make	108	F10 Proludium	26
And boyles, as if he were	110	F11 Epode	42
Were yet unfound, and better plac'd in earth,	114	F12 Rutland	25
Were yet unfound, and better plac'd on earth,	114	F12 Rutland V	25
Were it to thinke, that you should not inherit	114	F12 Rutland	32
That bred them, graves: when they were borne, they di'd,	114	F12 Rutland	47
Gave killing strokes. There were brave men, before	114	F12 Rutland	53
Without which, all the rest were sounds, or lost.	118	F13 Aubigny	50
And that your soules conspire, as they were gone	119	F13 Aubigny	119
Who saw the light, and were afraid,	130	U1 Nativitie	5
Both wills were in one stature;	130	U1 Nativitie	15
That they still were to run by her side,	134	U2 Triumph	9
Make in one, the same were shee.	137	U2 Cupid	48
If by us, the oddes were laid,	138	U2 Kisse	7
You were more the eye, and talke	138	U2 Kisse	14
Wisht the Bride were chang'd to night,	138	U2 Kisse	18
And did think, such Rites were due	138	U2 Kisse	19
Of your Peeres, you were beheld,	138	U2 Kisse	23
Or were set up in a Brake.	142	U2 Her man	40
Or were pent up in a Brake.	142	U2 Her man V	40
We were not bred to sit on stooles,	146	U6 Defence	3
For were the worthiest woman curst	146	U6 Defence	23
It were a plague 'bove scorne,	147	U7 Nymph	12
That were this morning blowne;	147	U7 Nymph	19
What my Affections were.	150	U10 Jealousie	11
As were his Nourceries; and swept	151	U12 Corbet	16
They were as specious as his Trees.	152	U12 Corbet	20
They were so even, grave, and holy;	152	U12 Corbet	23
Pardon, sayes he, that were a way to see	155	U13 Sacvile	71
If it were cleare, but being so in cloud	155	U13 Sacvile	87
And told of with more License then th'were done!	156	U13 Sacvile	96
Or on the sudden. It were strange that he	156	U13 Sacvile	125
Were the Rack offer'd them, how they came so;	157	U13 Sacvile	130
That makes the Arch. The rest that there were put	157	U13 Sacvile	137
As if a Brize were gotten i' their tayle;	164	U15 Friend-Wars	71
This way, now that, as if their number were	166	U15 Friend-Wars	126
were such as I will now relate, or worse?	172	U20 Shrub	14
Perjur'd! and painted! if she were no more--,	172	U20 Shrub	22
Two letters were enough the plague to teare	172	U21 Ltl Shrub	3
But both might know their wayes were understood,	176	U24 Frontispice	7
And doubtfull Dayes (which were nam'd Criticall,)	180	U26 Ode High	6
They were bound!	183	U29 Pit of Rime	12
They had, but were a Reed unto thy Sword.	187	U33 Councellour	34
What did she worth thy spight? were there not store	188	U34 Small Poxe	3
What wonder perfect, all were fil'd,	188	U35 Chute	3
Without which all the world were darke;	189	U36 Song	7
That were to wither all, and make a Grave	192	U38 Elegy 'Tis	59
As if that ex'lent Dulnesse were Loves grace;	198	U40 Elegy That	24
And we were left under that Hemisphere,	199	U41 Elegy Since	7
As if it were not worthy to be there:	199	U41 Elegy Since	16
Whether their faces were their owne, or no:	200	U42 Elegy Let	36
Varietie of Silkes were on th'Exchange!	202	U42 Elegy Let	72
There were some pieces of as base allay,	204	U43 Vulcan	42
There were of search, and mastry in the Arts.	206	U43 Vulcan	88
There were of search, and mastry of the Arts.	206	U43 Vulcan V	88
Wherin (besides the noble aydes were lent,	207	U43 Vulcan V	99
Wherin (besides the noble Aydes were spent,	207	U43 Vulcan V	99
Wherin (besides the noble aydes were sent,	207	U43 Vulcan V	99
Of Carew, Cotton, Selden, oyles were spent	207	U43 Vulcan	V100
Which, though it were the Fort of the whole Parish,	209	U43 Vulcan	133
There were, that streight did nose it out for newes,	209	U43 Vulcan	V139
If that were so, thou rather would'st advance	209	U43 Vulcan	151
Troy, though it were so much his Venus care.	210	U43 Vulcan	160
Troy, though it were so much thy Venus joycare.	210	U43 Vulcan	V160
For they were burnt, but to be better built.	210	U43 Vulcan	166
'Tis true, that in thy wish they were destroy'd,	210	U43 Vulcan	167
In those Records, which, were all Chroniclers gone,	210	U43 Vulcan	171
In those Records, which, were our Chroniclers gone,	210	U43 Vulcan	V171
I could invent a sentence, yet were worse;	211	U43 Vulcan	189
And comming home, to tell what acts were done	213	U44 Speach	19
For that unnecessarie Charge they were.	214	U44 Speach	32
Were now the greater Captaine? for they saw	214	U44 Speach	39
Such, Coke, were thy beginnings, why thy good	217	U46 Coke	5
Of Spaine or France; or were not prick'd downe one	219	U47 Tribe	47
As but to stumble in her sight were shame;	220	U47 Tribe	70

	Page	Title	Line
WERE (cont.)			
Is of so brave example, as he were	224	U50 Countesse	7
For 't were a narrow gladnesse, kept thine owne.	225	U51 Bacon	18
You were not tied, by any Painters Law,	227	U52 Answer	7
But whilst you curious were to have it be	227	U52 Answer	13
As all defence, or offence, were a chime!	232	U59 Newcastle	6
This were a spectacle! A sight to draw	233	U59 Newcastle	13
And valiant were, with, or without their hands.	233	U59 Newcastle	24
How happy were the Subject, if he knew	236	U64 Charles 3	1
As here no Venus were;	240	U67 Muses	34
'T were better spare a Butt, then spill his Muse.	241	U68 House-hold	12
All Offices were done	244	U70 Ode	48
Where it were friendships schisme,	246	U70 Ode	90
(Were not his Lucius long with us to tarry)	246	U70 Ode	91
The good, and durst not practise it, were glad	247	U70 Ode	119
Whose lines her rowles were, and records.	247	U70 Ode	126
Whose lives her rowles were, and records.	247	U70 Ode	V126
Or were Affaires in tune,	253	U75 Epithalam.	15
And all the Ground were Garden, where she led!	254	U75 Epithalam.	68
One to the other, long e're these to light were brought.	257	U75 Epithalam.	144
Th'Ignoble never liv'd, they were a-while	257	U75 Epithalam.	153
And were shee lost, could best supply her place,	264	U79 New-yeares	34
Still waited on 'hem where they were.	264	U79 New-yeares	39
I durst not aime at that: The dotes were such	269	U81 Pawlet	25
I durst not aime at, the dotes thereof were such	269	U81 Pawlet	V 25
Were like a ring of Vertues, 'bout her set,	270	U81 Pawlet	41
Who saw the way was made it! and were sent	270	U81 Pawlet	65
That saw the way was made it! and were sent	270	U81 Pawlet	V 65
When we were all borne, we began to die;	271	U81 Pawlet	94
Hee were the wretched'st of the race of men:	272	U81 Pawlet	97
Were fitly interpos'd; so new:	275	U84 Body	10
As it another Nature were,	279	U84 Mind	30
And, though the sound were parted thence,	279	U84 Mind	39
And set it forth; the rest were Cobwebs fine,	282	U84 Muse	5
Till swept away, th'were cancell'd with a broome!	282	U84 Muse	8
There, all the happy soules, that ever were,	285	U84 Muse	113
To style us Friends, who were, by Nature, Foes?	286	U84 Muse	139
Adopt us Heires, by grace, who were of those	286	U84 Muse	140
Each line, as it were graphick, in the face!	287	U84 Muse	154
And hers were all Humilitie! they beat	288	U84 Muse	189
As the old race of Mankind were,	289	U85 Country	2
As the old stock of Mankind were,	289	U85 Country	V 2
Wants strength, and sinewes, as his spirits were done;	339	Horace	V 38/ 37
Were also clos'd: But, who the man should be,	309	Horace	109
Were to be staid with softnesses, and wonne	321	Horace	326
And so their pratling to present were best,	346	Horace	V321/329
As neither any God, were brought in there,	321	Horace	331
Being men were covetous of nought, but praise.	327	Horace	463
The Oracles, too, were given out in Verse;	329	Horace	496
Playes were found out; and rest, the end, and crowne	329	Horace	499
And shun to touch him, as a man that were	335	Horace	644
And flye to touch him, as a man that were	354	Horace	V644
The yellow Jaundies, or were furious mad	335	Horace	646
The yellow jaundis, or were truely mad,	354	Horace	V646
Were they as strong ram'd up as Aetna gates.	363	Riches	10
That late were out.	367	Cynic	46
Were Cycnus, once high flying	367	Ode Who saith	46
Their motives were, since it had not to do	369	Ode Who saith	99
And wish that all the Muses blood were spilt,	371	Fletcher	9
For Grapes he had gather'd before they were eaten.	371	Fletcher	12
- - - Panegyricke lines, but then were upon some occasions . . .	375	Coryat 1	25
For grapes he had gather'd, before they were eaten.	379	Coryat 3	Ttl
How well, and how often his shoes too were mended,	380	Coryat 3	36
From Venice to Flushing, were not they well cobled?	380	Coryat 3	39
Sure, this glad payre were married, but this day.	380	Coryat 3	42
The art of uttring wares, if they were bad;	384	Somerset	26
Were askt of thy Discoveries; They must say,	385	Husband	6
To say but one, were single. Then it chimes,	388	Chapman	8
As was the Genius wherewith they were wrote;	389	Aleman	3
Were not the paths I meant unto thy praise:	389	Aleman	12
For, if I thought my judgement were of yeeres,	390	Shakespeare	6
And shake a Stage: Or, when thy Sockes were on,	391	Shakespeare	27
And all the Muses still were in their prime,	391	Shakespeare	37
Which were so richly spun, and woven so fit,	391	Shakespeare	44
As they were not of Natures family.	392	Shakespeare	49
Sweet Swan of Avon! what a sight it were	392	Shakespeare	54
Looke, how we read the Spartans were inflam'd	392	Shakespeare	71
And, till I worthy am to wish I were,	398	Drayton	67
T'Is a Record in heaven. You, that were	398	Drayton	92
My verses were commended, thou dar'st say,	399	Lady Ogle	1
And they were very good: yet thou think'st nay.	408	Detractor	1
As it were spun by nature, off the fleece;	408	Detractor	2
Although the gate were hard, the gayne is sweete.	415	Rutter	18
Yff Men, and tymes were nowe	418	Answer	7
As when they both were greate, and both knewe howe	419	Ode:If Men	1
That were the happie subject of my songe.	419	Ode:If Men	3
WER'T	419	Ode:If Men	9
If such a Tyke as thou, er'e wer't, or noe?	409	Detractor	14
WERT			
Thou wert, as chiefe of them are said t'have beene.	28	E4 James 1	6
When thou wert wont t'admire, not censure men.	32	E18 Censurer	8
First thou preserved wert, our king to bee,	38	E35 James 2	9
Seven yeeres tho'wert lent to me, and I thee pay,	41	E45 First Son	3

770

		Page	Title	Line
WERT (cont.)				
As if thou wert my friend, but lack'dst a cause.	. . .	43	E52 Courtling	4
Thou wert content the authors name to loose:	. . .	43	E53 Old-end	3
To give the world assurance thou wert both;	. . .	43	E53 Old-end	6
Before thou wert it, in each good mans heart.	. . .	49	E67 Suffolk	10
How much of great example wert thou, Roe,	. . .	64	E99 Th Roe 2	5
Thou wert the first, mad'st merit know her strength,	. . .	75	E116 Jephson	5
As if thou, then, wert mine, or I raign'd here:	. . .	95	F2 Penshurst	74
A broken heart thou wert not wont despise,	. . .	127	U1 Trinitie	10
Though thou wert Muster-master of the Land.	. . .	167	U15 Friend-Wars	174
Soone as lazie thou wert knowne,	. . .	183	U29 Fit of Rime	13
Thou didst tell me; and wert o're-joy'd to peepe	. . .	201	U42 Elegy Let	59
Was it because thou wert of old denied	. . .	203	U43 Vulcan	11
Wast not hee: thou wert of old denied	. . .	203	U43 Vulcan	V 11
When thou wert borne, and that thou look'st at best,	. . .	208	U43 Vulcan	113
When thou wert borne, and when thou look'st at best,	. . .	208	U43 Vulcan	V113
E're thou wert halfe got out,	. . . .	242	U70 Ode	6
Which to this use, wert built and consecrate!	. . .	256	U75 Epithalam.	130
Yes thou wert borne out of his travelling thigh	. . .	378	Coryat 2	89
And such wert thou. Looke how the fathers face	. . .	392	Shakespeare	65
WEST				
In these west-parts, nor when that warre was done,	. . .	71	E110 Edmonds 1	2
Then when flowers, and West-winds meet,	. . .	137	U2 Cupid	28
Some hopes of Spaine in their West-Indian Fleet?	. . .	219	U47 Tribe	34
WEST-INDIAN				
Some hopes of Spaine in their West-Indian Fleet?	. . .	219	U47 Tribe	34
WESTMINSTER				
Or the great Hall at Westminster, the field	. . .	186	U33 Councellour	3
WESTON				
To my Lord Weston, Lo: Treasurer. A Letter	. . .	248	U71 Treasurer	VTtl
On the Right Honourable, and vertuous Lord Weston, L.	. . .	250	U73 Weston	Ttl
Weston! That waking man! that Eye of State!	. . .	250	U73 Weston	5
To the Right Hon'ble Hierome, L. Weston. An Ode . . .	. . .	250	U74 Weston	Ttl
. . . that Noble Gentleman, Mr. Hierome Weston, Son, and . . .	. . .	252	U75 Epithalam.	Ttl
Weston, their Treasure, as their Treasurer,	. . .	255	U75 Epithalam.	97
This I would doe, could I know Weston, one	. . .	260	U77 Treasurer	10
The knowing Weston, and that learned Lord	. . .	263	U78 Digby	28
WEST-PARTS				
In these west-parts, nor when that warre was done,	. . .	71	E110 Edmonds 1	2
WEST-WINDS				
Then when flowers, and West-winds meet,	. . .	137	U2 Cupid	28
WET				
Makes the poore Banck-side creature wet it' shoone,	. . .	84	E133 Voyage	30
WETS				
Who wets my grave, can be no friend of mine.	. . .	37	E33 Roe 3	6
WHALE				
As any Mercer; or the whale-bone man	. . . .	200	U42 Elegy Let	31
WHALE-BONE				
As any Mercer; or the whale-bone man	. . . .	200	U42 Elegy Let	31
WHARFES				
The charmed Boates, and the inchanted Wharfes;	. . .	205	U43 Vulcan	68
The charmed beauty and the inchanted Wharfes;	. . .	205	U43 Vulcan	V 68
WHAT'				
But much it now availes, what's done, of whom:	. . .	64	E99 Th Roe 2	7
On what's deceast.	. . . . .	121	F14 Sydney	38
Although, perhaps it has, what's that to me,	. . .	167	U15 Friend-Wars	149
Borne, bred, allied? what's he dare tutor us?	. . .	215	U44 Speach	66
But what's of kinne to whence it came.	. . .	278	U84 Mind	16
What's left a Poet, when his Muse is gone?	. . .	283	U84 Muse	28
What's this? if he whose money hireth thee	. . .	305	Horace	26
And come not too much wrested. What's that thing,	. . .	309	Horace	76
With sloth, yet greedy still of what's to come:	. . .	317	Horace	246
Defies, what's crosse to Piety, or good Fame.	. . .	401	Beaumont	20
A Noble honest Soule! what's this to thee?	. . .	406	Inigo Jones 2	6
WHAT				
What name, what skill, what faith hast thou in things!	. . .	31	E14 Camden	7
What sight in searching the most antique springs!	. . .	31	E14 Camden	8
What weight, and what authoritie in thy speech!	. . .	31	E14 Camden	9
Make good what thou dar'st doe in all the rest.	. . .	32	E16 Brain-hardy	8
What severall wayes men to their calling have!	. . .	33	E21 Gam'ster	7
What doth he else, but say, leave to be chast,	. . .	34	E25 Beast 1	7
What two brave perills of the private sword	. . .	37	E32 Roe 2	1
What not the envie of the seas reach'd too,	. . .	37	E32 Roe 2	4
What could not worke; at home in his repaire	. . .	37	E32 Roe 2	7
For what shee gave, a whore; a baud, shee cures.	. . .	39	E41 Gypsee	4
What need hast thou of me? or of my Muse?	. . .	40	E43 Salisbury 1	1
And what I write thereof find farre, and free	. . .	41	E43 Salisbury 1	10
As what he loves may never like too much.	. . .	41	E45 First Son	12
What are thy petulant pleadings, Chev'ril, then,	. . .	44	E54 Chev'ril 2	3
What fate is mine, that so it selfe bereaves?	. . .	44	E55 Beaumont	7
What art is thine, that so thy friend deceives?	. . .	44	E55 Beaumont	8
Loe, what my countrey should have done (have rais'd	. . .	46	E60 Mounteagle	1
What should the cause be? Oh, you live at court:	. . .	46	E62 Would-bee	9
With what thy vertue on the times hath won,	. . .	47	E63 Salisbury 2	2
Of love, and what the golden age did hold	. . .	47	E64 Salisbury 3	3
Wherein what wonder see thy name hath wrought?	. . .	48	E64 Salisbury 3	16
What is't, fine Grand, makes thee my friendship flye,	. . .	51	E73 Fine Grand	1
T'inveigh 'gainst playes: what did he then but play?	. . .	52	E75 Lippe	4
What kinde of creature I could most desire,	. . .	52	E76 Bedford 1	3
I fancied to my selfe, what wine, what wit	. . .	55	E84 Bedford 2	6
What would his serious actions me have learned?	. . .	55	E85 Goodyere 1	12
Of what shee had wrought came in, and wak'd his braine,	. . .	56	E87 Hazard	4
And what each prince doth for intelligence owe,	. . .	59	E92 New Crie	12

	Page	Title	Line
WHAT (cont.)			
For twelve yeeres yet to come, what each state lacks.	59	E92 New Crie	14
And whisper what a Proclamation sayes.	59	E92 New Crie	20
Stand'st thou, to shew the times what you all were?	60	E93 Radcliffe	4
About his forme. What then so swells each lim?	63	E97 Motion	19
And what would hurt his vertue makes it still.	63	E98 Th Roe 1	6
Of what ambition, faction, pride can raise;	66	E102 Pembroke	15
And noted for what flesh such soules were fram'd,	66	E103 L Wroth 1	3
Even in the dew of grace, what you would bee?	67	E104 Montgomery	2
What man art thou, that art so many men,	68	E106 E Herbert	2
Doe what you come for, Captayne, with your newes;	68	E107 Hungry	1
Tell them, what parts yo'have tane, whence run away,	69	E107 Hungry	9
What States yo'have gull'd, and which yet keepes yo'in pay.	69	E107 Hungry	10
What at Ligorne, Rome, Florence you did doe:	69	E107 Hungry	14
Doe what you come for, Captayne, There's your meate.	69	E107 Hungry	32
Goe on, and doubt not, what posteritie,	70	E109 Nevil	15
Not all these, Edmonds, or what else put too,	71	E110 Edmonds 1	11
What th'antique souldiers were, the moderne bee?	72	E111 Edmonds 2	2
More, then to varie what our elders knew:	72	E111 Edmonds 2	6
Thy all, at all: and what so ere I doe,	72	E112 Gamster	5
Where, what makes others great, doth keepe thee good!	73	E113 Overbury	4
For since, what ignorance, what pride is fled!	73	E113 Overbury	7
And did act (what now we mone)	77	E120 S. P.	13
Would'st thou heare, what man can say	79	E124 Elizabeth	1
Made for what Nature could, or Vertue can;	79	E125 Uvedale	2
Had power to act, what they to faine had not.	84	E133 Voyage	6
The filth, stench, noyse: save only what was there	84	E133 Voyage	9
It was the day, what time the powerfull Moone	84	E133 Voyage	29
No matter, stinkards, row. What croaking sound	86	E133 Voyage	91
For, to say truth, what scullion is so nastie,	88	E133 Voyage	147
But what can this (more then expresse their love)	95	F2 Penshurst	57
But gives me what I call, and lets me eate,	95	F2 Penshurst	69
What (great, I will not say, but) sodayne cheare	95	F2 Penshurst	82
Did'st thou, then, make 'hem! and what praise was heap'd	95	F2 Penshurst	83
He alwayes gives what he knowes meet;	99	F3 Wroth	98
He alwayes gives what he thinks meet;	99	F3 Wroth	V 98
And what thou call'st thy gifts are baits.	100	F4 To the World	12
What bird, or beast, is knowne so dull,	101	F4 To the World	29
But, what we'are borne for, we must beare:	101	F4 To the World	53
That, what to all may happen here,	101	F4 To the World	55
What thy number is, be pin'd.	103	F6 Celia 2	22
Take heed, Sicknesse, what you doe,	104	F8 Sicknesse	7
What should, yet, thy pallat please?	105	F8 Sicknesse	21
And must I sing? what subject shall I chuse?	107	F10 Proludium	1
We must sing too? what subject shall we chuse?	107	F10 Proludium	V 1
What savage, brute affection,	112	F11 Epode	108
But let this drosse carry what price it will	114	F12 Rutland	27
For what a sinne 'gainst your great fathers spirit,	114	F12 Rutland	31
Riches thought most: But, Madame, thinke what store	114	F12 Rutland	38
Who, wheresoere he be, on what dear coast,	116	F12 Rutland	93
As what th'have lost t'expect, they dare deride.	116	F13 Aubigny	4
In my character, what your features bee,	117	F13 Aubigny	24
Of vertue, which you tread? what if alone?	118	F13 Aubigny	55
Heare, what the Muses sing about thy roote,	119	F13 Aubigny	100
What your try'd manners are, what theirs should bee.	119	F13 Aubigny	112
That I may tell to Sydney, what	120	F14 Sydney	12
What odour can be, then a heart contrite,	127	U1 Trinitie	15
What comfort by him doe wee winne,	130	U1 Nativitie	19
3. What hee suffered.	133	U2 Suffered	Ttl
Heare, what late Discourse of you,	136	U2 Cupid	5
What my Muse and I have done:	138	U2 Kisse	5
In the Daunces, with what spight	138	U2 Kisse	22
What w'are but once to doe, we should doe long.	139	U2 Another	12
What a man she could love well:	139	U2 Promise	4
I will tell what Man would please me.	140	U2 Her man	2
What we harmonie doe call	141	U2 Her man	34
What you please, you parts may call,	142	U2 Exception	7
At such a Call, what beast or fowle,	143	U3 Musicall	5
What Tree or stone doth want a soule?	143	U3 Musicall	7
What man but must lose his?	143	U3 Musicall	8
What need of mee? doe you but sing,	143	U3 Musicall	13
But what those lips doe make.	143	U3 Musicall	16
But what your lips doe make.	143	U3 Musicall	V 16
On what they viewing move.	144	U3 Musicall	20
For what is better, or to make	146	U6 Defence	14
(By searching) what before was strange,	146	U6 Defence	15
What Nymph so e're his voyce but heares,	148	U7 Nymph	27
What my Affections were.	150	U10 Jealousie	11
The way to meet, what others would upbraid;	153	U13 Sacvile	10
Then what he hath receiv'd. Gifts stinke from some,	153	U13 Sacvile	22
Must make me sad for what I have obtain'd.	154	U13 Sacvile	38
For what they streight would to the world forsweare;	154	U13 Sacvile	50
Now, but command; make tribute, what was gift;	155	U13 Sacvile	84
Themselves through favouring what is there not found:	159	U14 Selden	16
And what I write? and vexe it many dayes	159	U14 Selden	25
Meane what I speake: and still will keepe that Vow.	159	U14 Selden	28
Heard what times past have said, seene what ours doe:	159	U14 Selden	34
What fables have you vext! what truth redeem'd!	159	U14 Selden	39
What blots and errours, have you watch'd and purg'd	160	U14 Selden	42
Of what it tells us) weav'd in to instruct.	160	U14 Selden	52
The Credit, what would furnish a tenth Muse!	161	U14 Selden	84
No person, nor is lov'd: what wayes he proves	162	U15 Friend-Wars	16
And even our sports are dangers! what we call	163	U15 Friend-Wars	38

	Page	Title	Line

WHAT (cont.)

	Page	Title	Line
That payes, or what he will: The Dame is steele.	164	U15 Friend-Wars	78
What furie of late is crept into our Feasts?	166	U15 Friend-Wars	117
What honour given to the drunkennest Guests?	166	U15 Friend-Wars	118
What reputation to beare one Glasse more?	166	U15 Friend-Wars	119
Of what he throwes: Like letchers growne content	166	U15 Friend-Wars	139
That watch, and catch, at what they may applaud,	167	U15 Friend-Wars	157
But what she gives, thou dar'st give her againe;	168	U15 Friend-Wars	184
That thou thinke nothing great, but what is good,	168	U15 Friend-Wars	187
What suretie of life have thou, and I?	168	U16 Gray	7
Or have the least of Good, but what it must	171	U20 Shrub	7
What I, in her, am griev'd to want.	174	U22 Elegy Tho	36
What though the greedie Frie	175	U23 Himselfe	19
Shee chearfully supporteth what she reares,	176	U24 Frontispice	13
Read here in one, what thou in all canst find,	185	U30 Burleigh	2
What is there more that can ennoble blood?	185	U30 Burleigh	6
What use, what strength of reason! and how much	187	U33 Councellour	24
What did she worth thy spight? were there not store	188	U34 Small Poxe	3
What was the cause then? Thought'st thou in disgrace	188	U34 Small Poxe	13
What Beautie would have lovely stilde,	188	U35 Chute	1
What manners prettie, Nature milde,	188	U35 Chute	2
What wonder perfect, all were fil'd,	188	U35 Chute	3
But must confesse from whom what gift I tooke.	189	U37 Friend-Book	6
By naming in what companie 'twas in,	191	U38 Elegy 'Tis	25
An ill-affected limbe (what e're it aile)	192	U38 Elegy 'Tis	45
But to exact againe what once is given,	192	U38 Elegy 'Tis	63
What Fooles, and all their Parasites can apply;	193	U38 Elegy 'Tis	94
Then sword, or fire, or what is of the race	193	U38 Elegy 'Tis	101
Keepe secret in his Channels what he breedes,	198	U40 Elegy That	27
What it is like: And doe not thinke they can	199	U41 Elegy Since	3
What fate is this, to change mens dayes and houres,	199	U41 Elegy Since	9
And so I spare it. Come what can become	199	U41 Elegy Since	19
Let me be what I am, as Virgil cold;	199	U42 Elegy Let	1
Lift up some one, and doe, I tell not what.	201	U42 Elegy Let	58
Unto the Spittle Sermon. O, what strange	201	U42 Elegy Let	71
What had I done that might call on thine ire?	202	U43 Vulcan	2
What have I done that might call on thine ire?	202	U43 Vulcan	V 2
But in my Deske, what was there to accite	206	U43 Vulcan	85
But in my Deske, what was there to envite	206	U43 Vulcan	V 85
What the old Venusine, in Poetrie,	207	U43 Vulcan	V 89
To teach some what, their Nurses could not doe,	207	U43 Vulcan	V 92
And what hast thou done in these pettie spights,	210	U43 Vulcan	163
But say, all sixe good men, what answer yee?	210	U43 Vulcan	173
And comming home, to tell what acts were done	213	U44 Speach	19
What a strong Fort old Pimblicoe had bin!	213	U44 Speach	21
All licence in our lives? What need we know,	215	U44 Speach	70
What love you then? your whore. what study? gate,	215	U44 Speach	87
What, to make legs? yes, and to smell most sweet,	215	U44 Speach	90
What I am not, and what I faine would be,	216	U45 Squib	1
Care not what trials they are put unto;	218	U47 Tribe	2
What is't to me whether the French Designe	219	U47 Tribe	31
So farre without inquirie what the States,	219	U47 Tribe	43
Well, with mine owne fraile Pitcher, what to doe	219	U47 Tribe	56
What though her Chamber be the very pit	222	U49 Pucell	3
What though with Tribade lust she force a Muse,	222	U49 Pucell	7
What though she talke, and cannot once with them,	222	U49 Pucell	11
What though she ride two mile on Holy-dayes	222	U49 Pucell	15
What though she be with Velvet gownes indu'd,	222	U49 Pucell	18
What though she hath won on Trust, as many doe,	223	U49 Pucell	21
In Contract twice, what can shee perjure more?	223	U49 Pucell	30
What then his Father was, that since is hee,	225	U51 Bacon	11
Or what we heare our home-borne Legend tell,	228	U53 Newcastle	9
What each man sayes of it, and of what coat	232	U58 Book-seller	4
What could their care doe 'gainst the spight	234	U60 La-ware	5
T'obtaine of God, what all the Land should aske?	234	U61 Epigram	11
What can the Poet wish his King may doe,	235	U62 Charles 1	13
What (at his liking) he will take away.	236	U63 Charles 2	6
And what are bounds to her, you make your owne?	236	U64 Charles 3	10
What Month then May, was fitter to disclose	237	U65 Prince	4
What, though the thriftie Tower	239	U67 Muses	7
What, though the thirsty Tower	239	U67 Muses	V 7
What can the cause be, when the K. hath given	241	U68 House-hold	1
What, by that name, wee each to other owe,	241	U69 Friend Son	4
For, what is life, if measur'd by the space,	243	U70 Ode	21
What did this Stirrer, but die late?	243	U70 Ode	30
By what was done and wrought	245	U70 Ode	60
What Drums or Trumpets, or great Ord'nance can,	249	U72 King	9
What prayers (People) can you thinke too much?	249	U72 King	20
And see, what can be seene,	252	U75 Epithalam.	7
See, the Procession! what a Holy day	252	U75 Epithalam.	9
What Beavie of beauties, and bright youths at charge	253	U75 Epithalam.	17
Like what she is, the Daughter of a Duke,	253	U75 Epithalam.	42
Stay, thou wilt see what rites the Virgins doe!	254	U75 Epithalam.	49
With what full hands, and in how plenteous showers	254	U75 Epithalam.	65
And what of Dignitie, and Honour may	255	U75 Epithalam.	92
What kind of waking Man	256	U75 Epithalam.	111
He had so highly set; and, in what Barbican.	256	U75 Epithalam.	112
He had so highly plac'd; and, in what Barbican.	256	U75 Epithalam.	V112
Send in, what or Romano, Tintoret,	260	U77 Treasurer	6
Send in Romano or what Tintoret,	260	U77 Treasurer	V 6
What you have studied are the arts of life;	261	U77 Treasurer	17
What worlds of blessings to good Kings they owe:	261	U77 Treasurer	20
And mightiest Monarchs feele what large increase	261	U77 Treasurer	21

WHAT (cont.)

And praise them too. O! what a fame 't will be?	.	.	263	U78 Digby	25
What reputation to my lines, and me,	.	.	263	U78 Digby	26
Allowes them? Then, what copies shall be had,	.	.	263	U78 Digby	29
Allowes them? Then, what copies will be had,	.	.	263	U78 Digby	V 29
What transcripts begg'd? how cry'd up, and how glad,	.	.	263	U78 Digby	30
What transcripts made? how cry'd up, and how glad,	.	.	263	U78 Digby	V 30
Rivers, and Vallies, Eccho what wee sing.	.	.	264	U79 New-yeares	27
Rivers, and Valleys, Eccho what wee sing.	.	.	264	U79 New-yeares	35
What gentle Ghost, besprent with April deaw,	.	.	268	U81 Pawlet	1
What goodly Ghost, besprent with April deaw,	.	.	268	U81 Pawlet	V 1
What she did here, by great example, well,	.	.	269	U81 Pawlet	33
What she did by a great example, well,	.	.	269	U81 Pawlet	V 33
What Nature, Fortune, Institution, Fact	.	.	270	U81 Pawlet	45
How did she leave the world? with what contempt?	.	.	270	U81 Pawlet	47
What the beginnings of all beauties be;	.	.	271	U81 Pawlet	74
If you not understand, what Child you had.	.	.	271	U81 Pawlet	78
With what injustice should one soule pretend	.	.	271	U81 Pawlet	92
With what injustice can one soule pretend	.	.	271	U81 Pawlet	V 92
Who read what the Crepundia bee,	.	.	273	U84 Cradle	14
What makes these Velvets, Silkes, and Lawne,	.	.	275	U84 Body	2
As you goe on, by what brave way	.	.	278	U84 Mind	18
As what it spoke, it planted there.	.	.	279	U84 Mind	36
Yet know, with what thou art possest,	.	.	281	U84 Mind	70
Hee knowes, what worke h'hath done, to call this Guest,	.	.	284	U84 Muse	81
What 'tis t'enjoy, an everlasting breath!	.	.	285	U84 Muse	92
What fulnesse of beatitude is here?	.	.	286	U84 Muse	137
What love with mercy mixed doth appeare?	.	.	286	U84 Muse	138
Of lapsed Nature) best know what to doe,	.	.	288	U84 Muse	214
Will to bee, what thou art; and nothing more:	.	.	295	U90 Mart.10:47	12
In short; I bid, Let what thou work'st upon,	.	.	307	Horace	31
Heare me conclude; let what thou workst upon	.	.	339	Horace	V 31
Upon your shoulders. Prove what they will beare,	.	.	307	Horace	55
Prove what your shoulders will, or will not beare.	.	.	339	Horace	V 57/ 55
And what they will not. Him, whose choice doth reare	.	.	307	Horace	56
What number best can fit, Homer declares.	.	.	309	Horace	106
What doth this Promiser such gaping worth	.	.	313	Horace	197
What doth this Promiser such great gaping worth	.	.	343	Horace	V197
What he despaires, being handled, might not show.	.	.	315	Horace	214
Heare, what it is the People, and I desire:	.	.	315	Horace	219
And then as swift to leave what he hath lov'd.	.	.	315	Horace	236
What straight-way he must labour to retract.	.	.	315	Horace	240
What so is showne, I not beleeve, and hate.	.	.	317	Horace	269
And in their numbers; For, alas, what knew	.	.	319	Horace	300
From what th'obscene, and petulant Satyres are.	.	.	321	Horace	340
What nourisheth, what formed, what begot	.	.	325	Horace	437
The Poet, what becommeth, and what not:	.	.	325	Horace	438
What to his Countrey, what his friends he owes,	.	.	325	Horace	446
What height of love, a Parent will fit best,	.	.	325	Horace	447
What brethren, what a stranger, and his guest,	.	.	325	Horace	448
Can tell a States-mans dutie, what the arts	.	.	325	Horace	449
And office of a Judge are, what the parts	.	.	325	Horace	450
From the five ounces; what remaines? pronounce	.	.	327	Horace	468
An ounce, what makes it then? The halfe pound just;	.	.	327	Horace	471
Be briefe, in what thou wouldst command, that so	.	.	329	Horace	503
Let what thou fain'st for pleasures sake, be neere	.	.	329	Horace	507
The truth; nor let thy Fable thinke, what e're	.	.	329	Horace	508
Or knowes not what Cassellius Aulus can;	.	.	331	Horace	553
To change, and mend, what you not forth doe set.	.	.	331	Horace	579
Into the Profits, what a meere rude braine	.	.	331	Horace	583
With joy of what is given him, over-gone:	.	.	333	Horace	610
Reprove; and, what is to be changed, note:	.	.	335	Horace	638
Dispute; and what is to be changed, note;	.	.	354	Horace	V638
Or moathes shall eate, what all these Fooles admire.	.	.	371	Fletcher	16
F. shewes what he was, K. what he will bee.	.	.	375	Coryat 1	29
The truth of his heart there, and tell's what a clocke	.	.	380	Coryat 3	24
He went out at each place, and at what he came in,	.	.	380	Coryat 3	25
How long he did stay, at what signe he did Inne.	.	.	380	Coryat 3	26
May aske, what Author would conceale his name?	.	.	383	Author	4
What place is for my testimony void?	.	.	385	Brooke	2
What can one witnesse, and a weake one, add	.	.	385	Brooke	4
Who are his Test, and what their judgement is:	.	.	385	Husband	3
And, if thou list thy selfe, what thou canst bee.	.	.	386	Browne	4
What treasure hast thou brought us! and what store	.	.	388	Chapman	4
. . . Mr. William Shakespeare: And what he hath left us.	.	.	390	Shakespeare	Ttl
Should praise a Matron. What could hurt her more?	.	.	391	Shakespeare	14
Sweet Swan of Avon! what a sight it were	.	.	392	Shakespeare	71
What Muse, or rather God of harmony	.	.	395	May	14
What godds but those of arts, and eloquence?	.	.	395	May	16
How do his trumpets breath! What loud alarmes!	.	.	398	Drayton	66
In her! and what could perfect bee,	.	.	399	Lady Ogle	15
What was proportion, or could bee	.	.	399	Lady Ogle	21
What charming Peales are these,	.	.	401	Filmer	1
Why much good doo't you! Be what beast you will,	.	.	403	Inigo Jones 1	21
What makes your Wretchednes to bray soe loud	.	.	403	Inigo Jones 1	23
What is the cause you pompe it soe? I aske,	.	.	403	Inigo Jones 1	29
The Eloquence of Masques! What need of prose	.	.	403	Inigo Jones 1	40
Sense, what they are! which by a specious fyne	.	.	404	Inigo Jones 1	55
Of any Art, besyde what he calls his!	.	.	404	Inigo Jones 1	58
What would he doe now, gi'ng his mynde that waye	.	.	405	Inigo Jones 1	75
What Poesy ere was painted on a wall	.	.	406	Inigo Jones 1	97
That might compare with thee? what story shall	.	.	406	Inigo Jones 1	98
To be knowne what thou art, a blatant beast,	.	.	408	Detractor	9

WHAT (cont.)
    the sword, but that it acteth what it list.   .   .   .   423   Lucan   14
    To make these good, and what comes after, better.   .   .   666   Glover   10
WHAT'S
    But much it now availes, what's done, of whom: .   .   .   64   E99 Th Roe 2   7
    On what's deceast.   121   F14 Sydney   38
    Although, perhaps it has, what's that to me,   .   .   .   167   U15 Friend-Wars 149
    Borne, bred, allied? what's he dare tutor us?   .   .   .   215   U44 Speach   66
    But what's of kinne to whence it came.   .   .   .   278   U84 Mind   16
    What's left a Poet, when his Muse is gone?   .   .   .   283   U84 Muse   28
    What's this? if he whose money hireth thee   .   .   .   305   Horace   26
    And come not too much wrested. What's that thing,   .   .   309   Horace   76
    With sloth, yet greedy still of what's to come: .   .   317   Horace   246
    Defies, what's crosse to Piety, or good Fame.   .   .   .   401   Beaumont   20
    A Noble honest Soule! what's this to thee?   .   .   .   406   Inigo Jones 2   6
WHATSOEVER
    That whatsoever face thy fate puts on, ...   168   U15 Friend-Wars 185
WHEATEN
    He, that but saw you weare the wheaten hat,   .   .   .   68   E105 L Wroth 2 7
WHEELE
    Nothing I doe; but, like a heavie wheele,   .   .   .   283   U84 Muse   30
    Thy labouring wheele, comes scarce a Pitcher out?   .   .   307   Horace   30
    Or trundling Wheele, he can sit still, from all;   .   .   331   Horace   568
    Of Fortunes wheele by Lucan driv'n about,   .   .   .   395   May   3
WHEN
    It will be look'd for, booke, when some but see   .   .   27   E2 My Booke   1
    When was there contract better driven by Fate?   .   .   28   E5 Union   1
    When men a dangerous disease did scape,   .   .   .   31   E13 Empirick   1
    Thy selfe into fresh braules: when, call'd upon,   .   .   32   E16 Brain-hardy 3
    When both it is the old way, and the true.   .   .   .   32   E18 Censurer   2
    When thou wert wont t'admire, not censure men.   .   .   32   E18 Censurer   8
    Breathe to expect my when, and make my how.   .   .   37   E33 Roe 3   4
    You laugh when you are touch'd, and long before   .   .   38   E38 Guiltie 2   3
    And so is Jone. Oft-times, when Giles doth find   .   .   40   E42 Giles   9
    When, in my booke, men reade but Cecill's name,   .   .   41   E43 Salisbury 1 9
    When, in my Verse, men reade but Sarum's name,   .   .   41   E43 Salisbury 1 V 9
    When he made him executor, might be heire.   .   .   .   41   E44 Chuff   6
    When I am read, thou fain'st a weake applause,   .   .   43   E52 Courtling   3
    When having pill'd a booke, which no man buyes,   .   .   43   E53 Old-end   2
    But when (in place) thou didst the patrons choose,   .   .   43   E53 Old-end   4
    When even there, where most thou praysest mee,   .   .   44   E55 Beaumont   9
    Who, when you'have burnt your selves downe to the snuffe,   .   45   E59 Spies   2
    And not to dangers. When so wise a king   .   .   .   47   E64 Salisbury 3 12
    Against thy fortune: when no foe, that day,   .   .   .   49   E66 Cary   9
    To live when Broeck not stands, nor Roor doth runne.   .   49   E66 Cary   12
    When they cost dearest, and are done most free,   .   .   49   E66 Cary   14
    That vertuous is, when the reward's away.   .   .   .   49   E66 Cary   18
    When, in mens wishes, so thy vertues wrought,   .   .   49   E67 Suffolk   7
    When Nature bids us leave to live, 'tis late   .   .   50   E70 Wm Roe 1   1
    Such when I meant to faine, and wish'd to see,   .   .   52   E76 Bedford 1 17
    When I would know thee Goodyere, my thought lookes   .   55   E86 Goodyere 2 1
    Each night, to drowne his cares: But when the gaine   .   56   E87 Hazard   3
    Since when, hee's sober againe, and all play's made.   .   56   E87 Hazard   6
    Would you beleeve, when you this Monsieur see,   .   .   56   E88 Monsieur   1
    Or had his father, when he did him get,   .   .   .   56   E88 Monsieur   9
    When Mill first came to court, the unprofiting foole,   .   57   E90 Mill   1
    When on thy trumpet shee did sound a blast,   .   .   58   E91 Vere   7
    But, when they heard it tax'd, tooke more offence.   .   60   E94 Bedford 3 10
    But when I read that speciall piece, restor'd,   .   .   61   E95 Savile   7
    When I dare send my Epigrammes to thee?   .   .   .   62   E96 Donne 2   2
    When he was here. Nor hath he got a sute,   .   .   63   E97 Motion   16
    But, at our parting, we will be, as when   .   .   .   65   E101 Supper   38
    Of service to the publique, when the end   .   .   .   70   E109 Nevil   7
    In these west-parts, nor when that warre was done,   .   71   E110 Edmonds 1 2
    When Sydnyes name I heare, or face I see: .   .   .   73   E114 Sydney   2
    That age, when thou stood'st up the master-braine: .   75   E116 Jephson   4
    When Fates turn'd cruell, ...   77   E120 S. P.   10
    So, when we, blest with thy returne, shall see   .   .   81   E128 Wm Roe 2   9
    But the first question is, when one saw thee?   .   .   81   E129 Mime   2
    When these were but the praises of the Art.   .   .   82   E130 Ferrab. 1 16
    But when I have said, The proofes of all these bee   .   82   E130 Ferrab. 1 17
    When we doe give, Alphonso, to the light,   .   .   .   82   E131 Ferrab. 2   1
    In it' owne hall; when these (in worthy scorne   .   .   85   E133 Voyage   31
    Ycleped Mud, which, when their oares did once stirre,   .   85   E133 Voyage   62
    Of all your night-tubs, when the carts doe cluster,   .   85   E133 Voyage   64
    Ploughing the mayne. When, see (the worst of all lucks)   .   86   E133 Voyage   78
    (Who hath the hundred hands when he doth meddle)   .   86   E133 Voyage   82
    Stunke not so ill; nor, when shee kist, Kate Arden.   .   87   E133 Voyage   118
    And that is when it is the Lord Maiors foist.   .   .   87   E133 Voyage   120
    By which the Masters sweare, when, on the stoole   .   87   E133 Voyage   122
    When every clerke eates artichokes, and peason,   .   .   88   E133 Voyage   166
    Tempte such a passage? when each privies seate   .   .   88   E133 Voyage   168
    Urine, and plaisters? when the noise doth beate   .   .   88   E133 Voyage   170
    Which when he felt, Away (quoth hee)   .   .   .   93   F1 Why write no 3
    When Love is fled, and I grow old.   93   F1 Why write no 12
    When thou would'st feast, or exercise thy friends.   .   94   F2 Penshurst   21
    Nor, when I take my lodging, need I pray   .   .   .   95   F2 Penshurst   72
    That found King James, when hunting late, this way,   .   95   F2 Penshurst   76
    When shee was farre: and not a roome, but drest,   .   96   F2 Penshurst   87
    With other edifices, when they see   96   F2 Penshurst   100
    Nor throng'st (when masquing is) to have a sight   .   96   F3 Wroth   9
    When Pan, and Sylvane, having had their rites,   .   .   98   F3 Wroth   V 47
    Not doing good, scarce when he dyes.   .   .   .   99   F3 Wroth   84

WHEN (cont.)

	Page	Title	Line
Thy peace is made; and, when man's state is well,	99	F3 Wroth	93
Nor death; but when thy latest sand is spent,	100	F3 Wroth	105
When all the causes were away.	101	F4 To the World	44
But when once wee lose the light,	102	F5 Celia 1	V 7
When the common courting jay	103	F6 Celia 2	3
When youths ply their stolne delights.	103	F6 Celia 2	18
And the envious, when they find	103	F6 Celia 2	21
Since when it growes, and smells, I sweare,	106	F9 Celia 3	15
Since when it lives, and smells, I sweare,	106	F9 Celia 3	V 15
Goe, crampe dull Mars, light Venus, when he snorts,	107	F10 Proludium	16
Who could be false to? chiefly, when he knowes	112	F11 Epode	103
Who would be false to? chiefly, when he knowes	112	F11 Epode	V103
When his proud patrons favours are asleepe;	113	F12 Rutland	14
When gold was made no weapon to cut throtes,	114	F12 Rutland	23
Or put to flight Astrea, when her ingots	114	F12 Rutland	24
His love unto the Muses, when his skill	114	F12 Rutland	33
Almost you have, or may have, when you will?	114	F12 Rutland	34
That bred them, graves: when they were borne, they di'd,	114	F12 Rutland	47
To her remembrance; which when time shall bring	115	F12 Rutland	75
When their owne Parasites laugh at their fall,	118	F13 Aubigny	82
Other great wives may blush at: when they see	119	F13 Aubigny	111
When all the noyse	120	F14 Sydney	17
When well begunne:	121	F14 Sydney	46
The Birth-day shines, when logs not burne, but men.	121	F14 Sydney	60
When you know, that this is she,	131	U2 Excuse	18
When her looke out-flourisht May:	132	U2 How he saw	2
Which when she beheld to bleed,	133	U2 Suffered	17
As Loves starre when it riseth!	134	U2 Triumph	14
Her armes when Paris wonne her	135	U2 Triumph	V 34
When with Joves swans she sported	135	U2 Triumph	V 42
Then when flowers, and West-winds meet,	137	U2 Cupid	28
Shee is Venus, when she smiles,	137	U2 Cupid	52
But shee's Juno, when she walkes,	137	U2 Cupid	53
And Minerva, when she talkes,	137	U2 Cupid	54
When the worke would be effected:	140	U2 Promise	8
Then when 'tis made, why so will wee.	145	U5 Woman-kind	16
His lookes would so correct it, when	152	U12 Corbet	27
Deepest in Man, of which when he doth thinke,	153	U13 Sacvile	20
And can I lesse of substance? When I runne,	156	U13 Sacvile	120
Observe the strength, the height, the why, and when,	157	U13 Sacvile	140
May grow so great to be example, when	158	U13 Sacvile	161
Truth, and the Graces best, when naked are.	158	U14 Selden	4
Rather then Office, when it doth or may	158	U14 Selden	9
When not his Combes, his Curling-irons, his Glasse,	165	U15 Friend-Wars	111
When oft the Bearer, is borne out of dore?	166	U15 Friend-Wars	120
To be beholders, when their powers are spent.	166	U15 Friend-Wars	140
When I am hoarse, with praising his each cast,	167	U15 Friend-Wars	151
Not wound thy conscience, when thy body bleeds:	168	U15 Friend-Wars	178
Debts when they can: good men may breake their day,	169	U17 Friend-Debt	2
'Tis then a crime, when the Usurer is Judge.	169	U17 Friend-Debt	4
Or Love, or Fortune blind, when they but winke	170	U18 Elegy Can	16
When Vice alike in time with vertue dur'd.	176	U24 Frontispice	8
When only a mans birth is his offence,	177	U25 Desmond	V 32
When her dead essence (like the Anatomie	179	U25 Desmond	37
May his Sense, when it would meet	184	U29 Fit of Rime	55
When a good Cause is destitute of friends,	186	U32 Elsmere	2
When those good few, that her Defenders be,	186	U32 Elsmere	5
When this appeares, just Lord, to your sharp sight,	186	U32 Elsmere	15
But when I read or heare the names so rife	187	U33 Councellour	7
And Fame wake for me, when I yeeld to sleepe.	190	U37 Friend-Book	15
In a calme skie, then when the heaven is horl'd	193	U38 Elegy 'Tis	74
He when he sees a sorrow such as this,	193	U38 Elegy 'Tis	87
When I see you, then I doe see my Sun,	194	U38 Elegy 'Tis	120
My health will leave me; and when you depart,	199	U41 Elegy Since	13
When he is furious, love, although not lust.	200	U42 Elegy Let	18
When by thy sordid bountie she hath on	201	U42 Elegy Let	45
But when thy Wife (as thou conceiv'st) is brave?	201	U42 Elegy Let	50
that from the Foot-man, when he was become	201	U42 Elegy Let	52
When not the Shops, but windowes doe display	202	U42 Elegy Let	78
When thou wert borne, and that thou look'st at best,	208	U43 Vulcan	113
When thou wert borne, and when thou look'st at best,	208	U43 Vulcan	V113
Against thy furie, when to serve their needs,	208	U43 Vulcan	125
When Venus there maintain'd the Misterie.	209	U43 Vulcan	144
That hearkens to a Jacks-pulse, when it goes.	216	U45 Squib	6
An Epigram on Sir Edward Coke, when . . .	217	U46 Coke	Ttl
Such, Coke, were thy beginnings, when thy good	217	U46 Coke	5
When, being the Strangers helpe, the poore mans aide,	217	U46 Coke	7
Such was thy Processe, when Integritie,	217	U46 Coke	9
That when King James, above here,	221	U48 Bacchus	37
When with his royall shipping	222	U48 Bacchus	52
Will cal't a Bastard, when a Prophet's borne.	223	U49 Pucell	46
The rather when the vices of the Time	224	U50 Countesse	9
And when you want those friends, or neere in blood,	224	U50 Countesse	26
These Graces, when the rest of Ladyes view	225	U50 Countesse	31
For when they find so many meet in one,	225	U50 Countesse	35
Yet when of friendship I would draw the face,	227	U52 Answer	22
When first, my Lord, I saw you backe your horse,	228	U53 Newcastle	1
So well! as when I saw the floore, and Roome,	228	U53 Newcastle	17
So well! as when I view'd the floore, and Roome,	228	U53 Newcastle	V 17
Who, when shee heard the match, concluded streight,	229	U54 Squib	5
To goe out after—till when take this letter	229	U54 Squib	19
When you would play so nobly, and so free.	230	U56 Covell	2

	Page	Title	Line

WHEN (cont.)

	Page	Title	Line
Knew the time, when	231	U57 Burges	8
A quick, and dazeling motion! when a paire	233	U59 Newcastle	9
Of fortune! when, or death appear'd, or bands!	233	U59 Newcastle	23
Indeed, when had great Britaine greater cause	236	U64 Charles 3	7
When you that raigne, are her Example growne,	236	U64 Charles 3	9
When thou that rul'st, are her Example growne,	236	U64 Charles 3	V 9
When your assiduous practise doth secure	236	U64 Charles 3	11
When all your life's a president of dayes,	237	U64 Charles 3	13
The Mother of our Prince? When was there seene	238	U66 Queene	6
That when the Quire is full,	239	U67 Muses	19
What can the cause be, when the K. hath given	241	U68 House-hold	1
When the Prodigious Hannibal did crowne	242	U70 Ode	3
When shee puts forth the life of ev'ry thing:	250	U74 Weston	3
When he beholds a graft of his owne hand,	251	U74 Weston	27
When look'd the yeare, at best,	253	U75 Epithalam.	13
When look'd the Earth so fine,	253	U75 Epithalam.	21
Stand there; for when a noble Nature's rais'd,	256	U75 Epithalam.	113
That when you both are old,	258	U75 Epithalam.	165
When their pot-guns ayme to hit,	259	U76 Petition	21
When their pot-guns thinke to fitt,	259	U76 Petition	V 21
When the Apostle Barnabee the bright	262	U78 Digby	15
Busie, or frowne at first; when he sees thee,	262	U78 Digby	20
When hee shall read them at the Treasurers bord,	263	U78 Digby	27
When hee doth read them at the Treasurers bord,	263	U78 Digby	V 27
Wilt thou be, Muse, when this shall then befall?	263	U78 Digby	31
Wilt thou be, Muse, when this shall then befall?	263	U78 Digby	V 31
To fit the softnesse of our Yeares-gift: when	263	U79 New-yeares	6
That know the times, and seasons when t'appeare,	263	U79 New-yeares	11
When I, who would her Poet have become,	269	U81 Pawlet	17
From all affection! when they urg'd the Cure	270	U81 Pawlet	49
When we were all borne, we began to die;	271	U81 Pawlet	94
Whose Notions when it will expresse	279	U84 Mind	33
When your owne Vertues, equall'd have their Names,	281	U84 Kenelme	12
What's left a Poet, when his Muse is gone?	283	U84 Muse	28
Presume to interpell that fulnesse, when	284	U84 Muse	70
When shee departed? you will meet her there,	285	U84 Muse	108
Of divine Comfort, when sh' had talk'd with God.	287	U84 Muse	184
The holy Altars, when it least presumes,	288	U84 Muse	188
Or when that Autumne, through the fields, lifts round	290	U85 Country	17
Then when the thundring Jove his Snow and showres	290	U85 Country	29
These thoughts when Usurer Alphius, now about	291	U85 Country	67
These thinges when Usurer Alphius, now about	291	U85 Country	V 67
And when he smiling finds his Grace	292	U86 Hor.4:1	17
A Scarlet peece, or two, stitch'd in: when or	305	Horace	19
A purple piece, or two stitch'd in: when either	338	Horace	V 19
The pleasant grounds, or when the River Rhine,	305	Horace	22
When in a wrong, and artlesse way we tread.	307	Horace	44
Most worthie praise, when words that common grew,	307	Horace	67
Most worthie praise, when words that vulgar grew,	340	Horace	V 67
If I can give some small increase? when, loe,	309	Horace	80
When they are poore, and banish'd, must throw by	311	Horace	138
Unto the last, as when he first went forth,	313	Horace	181
Of the times past, when he was a young lad;	317	Horace	248
Nor I, when I write Satyres, will so love	321	Horace	341
Of Trimeter, when yet it was sixe-pac'd,	323	Horace	373
Sixe ounces. O, when once the canker'd rust,	327	Horace	472
All which I tell, lest when Apollo's nam'd,	329	Horace	501
The Child, when Lamia'has din'd, out of her maw.	329	Horace	510
Oft-times a Sharpe, when we require a Flat:	329	Horace	523
When you write Verses, with your judge doe so:	333	Horace	620
When you make verses, with your judge doe so:	354	Horace	V620
Cut off superfluous ornaments; and when	335	Horace	636
When late (grave Palmer) these thy graffs and flowers	361	Palmer	1
* * * * When loe to crowne thy worth	361	Palmer	27
When night their meeting covers.	365	Ode Splendor	8
When seeking her renowning,	365	Ode Splendor	19
Marke, marke, but when his wing he takes,	366	Ode Who saith	9
And, when they came	366	Ode Who saith	22
When him alone we sing)	368	Ode Who saith	63
All which, when they but heare a straine	368	Ode Who saith	89
And all your Booke (when it is throughly scan'd)	370	Author	5
A glorified worke to Time, when Fire,	371	Fletcher	15
still that same little poynte hee was; but when	383	Rich	13
And when your yeares rise more, then would be told,	384	Somerset	23
When these, and such, their voices have employd;	385	Brooke	1
If Praises, when th'are full, heaping admit,	385	Brooke	6
not when I die'd, but how I livd. Farewell.	387	Cavendish	12
When the old words doe strike on the new times,	389	Aleman	4
When you behold me wish my selfe, the man	389	Aleman	23
Which, when it sounds at best, but eccho's right;	390	Shakespeare	8
And shake a Stage: Or, when thy Sockes were on,	391	Shakespeare	37
When like Apollo he came forth to warme	392	Shakespeare	45
When, Rome, I reade thee in thy mighty paire,	395	May	1
But when againe I veiw the parts so peiz'd,	395	May	7
It cast a beame as when the chear-full Sun	396	Drayton	17
When, by thy bright Ideas standing by,	397	Drayton	23
And when he ships them where to use their Armes,	398	Drayton	65
With bold Tyrtaeus verse, when thou art nam'd,	398	Drayton	68
And when the flesh, here, shut up day,	400	Lady Ogle	27
When they doe sweat to fortifie a Muse.	400	Beaumont	6
But when thou turnst a Reall Inigo;	407	Inigo Jones 2	22
When I had read your holy Meditations,	411	Sutcliffe	1

WHEN (cont.)
And lesse asham'd; not when I told the crowd ⸱ ⸱ ⸱ ⸱ 414 Rutter 5
That sit to censure Playes, yet know not when, ⸱ ⸱ ⸱ 414 Rutter 8
for when the profitt with the payne doth meete, ⸱ ⸱ ⸱ 418 Answer 6
As when they both were greate, and both knewe howe ⸱ ⸱ 419 Ode:If Men 3
Aboute this Isle, and Charme the rounde, as when ⸱ ⸱ 421 Ode:If Men 39
Is her owne scourge, when it sustaines their states ⸱ 422 Lucan 3
Even states most hated, when no lawes resist ⸱ ⸱ ⸱ 423 Lucan 13
not safe; but when thou dost them thoroughlie: ⸱ ⸱ ⸱ 423 Lucan 16
WHENCE
Tell them, what parts yo'have tane, whence run away, ⸱ ⸱ 69 E107 Hungry 9
From whence, so lately, I did burne, ⸱ ⸱ ⸱ ⸱ ⸱ 101 F4 To the World 27
Inconstant, like the sea, of whence 'tis borne, ⸱ ⸱ 110 F11 Epode 39
Inconstant, as the sea, of whence 'tis borne, ⸱ ⸱ 110 F11 Epode V 39
By that faire Stand, your forehead, whence he bends ⸱ ⸱ 170 U19 Elegy By 3
From whence they fall, cast downe with their owne weight. ⸱ 224 U50 Countesse 12
Into the Kindred, whence my Adam drew ⸱ ⸱ ⸱ ⸱ 274 U84 Descent 15
But what's of kinne to whence it came. ⸱ ⸱ ⸱ ⸱ 278 U84 Mind 16
From whence thy Modestie, or Poemes law ⸱ ⸱ ⸱ ⸱ 313 Horace 193
Their Charge, and Office, whence their wealth to fet, ⸱ 325 Horace 436
To utmost Thule: whence, he backes the Seas ⸱ ⸱ ⸱ 368 Ode Who saith 69
WHERE'
Where's thy Quiver? bend thy Bow: ⸱ ⸱ ⸱ ⸱ ⸱ 132 U2 How he saw 9
No faith's more firme, or flat, then where't doth creep. ⸱ 413 Ghyrlond 20
WHERE
Where lately harbour'd many a famous whore, ⸱ ⸱ ⸱ 29 E7 Hot-house 1
On some-thing, that walkes some-where. ⸱ ⸱ ⸱ ⸱ 30 E11 Something Ttl
Where, afterwards, it grew a butter-flye: ⸱ ⸱ ⸱ 31 E15 Court-worm 3
Where, while that sever'd doth remaine, ⸱ ⸱ ⸱ ⸱ 34 E22 Daughter 10
Which shewes, where ever death doth please t'appeare, ⸱ 37 E32 Roe 2 9
For, but thy selfe, where, out of motly, 's hee ⸱ ⸱ 44 E53 Gld-end 9
When even there, where most thou praysest mee, ⸱ ⸱ ⸱ 44 E55 Beaumont 9
Where merit is not sepulcher'd alive. ⸱ ⸱ ⸱ ⸱ 47 E64 Salisbury 3 10
Where good mens vertues them to honors bring, ⸱ ⸱ ⸱ 47 E64 Salisbury 3 11
At Madames table, where thou mak'st all wit ⸱ ⸱ ⸱ 50 E72 Court-ling 3
Where I both learn'd, why wise-men hawking follow, ⸱ ⸱ 55 E85 Goodyere 1 3
Where, though 't be love, that to thy praise doth move ⸱ 55 E86 Goodyere 2 7
In th'eye of Europe, where thy deeds were done, ⸱ ⸱ 58 E91 Vere 6
They, then, that living where the matter is bred, ⸱ ⸱ 60 E94 Bedford 3 11
Where Nero falls, and Galba is ador'd, ⸱ ⸱ ⸱ ⸱ 61 E95 Savile 8
Where brevitie, where splendor, and where height, ⸱ ⸱ 62 E95 Savile 29
Where sweetnesse is requir'd, and where weight; ⸱ ⸱ 62 E95 Savile 30
Who shall doubt, Donne, where I a Poet bee, ⸱ ⸱ ⸱ 62 E96 Donne 2 1
Where ere he met me; now hee's dumbe, or proud. ⸱ ⸱ 62 E97 Motion 8
My praise is plaine, and where so ere profest, ⸱ ⸱ 67 E103 L Wroth 1 13
Where vertue makes them both, and that's in thee: ⸱ ⸱ 70 E109 Nevil 3
Where all is faire, beside thy pedigree. ⸱ ⸱ ⸱ 70 E109 Nevil 4
For, where his person liv'd scarce one just age, ⸱ ⸱ 71 E110 Edmonds 1 13
To Satyres; and thou dost pursue me. Where, ⸱ ⸱ ⸱ 73 E112 Gamster 14
Where shall I scape thee? in an Epigramme? ⸱ ⸱ ⸱ 73 E112 Gamster 15
So, where thou liv'st, thou mak'st life understood! ⸱ ⸱ 73 E113 Overbury 3
Where, what makes others great, doth keepe thee good! ⸱ 73 E113 Overbury 4
Where finding so much beautie met with vertue, ⸱ ⸱ ⸱ 74 E114 Sydney 6
At every meale, where it doth dine, or sup, ⸱ ⸱ ⸱ 74 E115 Honest Man 23
Fitter, where it dyed, to tell, ⸱ ⸱ ⸱ ⸱ ⸱ 79 E124 Elizabeth 11
Betweene two walls: where, on one side, to scar men, ⸱ 86 E133 Voyage 67
For (where he was the god of eloquence, ⸱ ⸱ ⸱ ⸱ 86 E133 Voyage 99
Touching this cause, where they will be affeard ⸱ ⸱ 87 E133 Voyage 106
Behold where Cerberus, rear'd on the wall ⸱ ⸱ ⸱ 89 E133 Voyage 176
Where Pan, and Bacchus their high feasts have made, ⸱ ⸱ 93 F2 Penshurst 11
At his great birth, where all the Muses met. ⸱ ⸱ ⸱ 94 F2 Penshurst 14
Where comes no guest, but is allow'd to eate, ⸱ ⸱ ⸱ 95 F2 Penshurst 61
Where the same beere, and bread, and selfe-same wine, ⸱ 95 F2 Penshurst 63
Nor throng'st (where masquing is) to have a sight ⸱ ⸱ 96 F3 Wroth V 9
And each where boast it as his merit. ⸱ ⸱ ⸱ ⸱ 99 F3 Wroth 78
Where breathe the basest of thy fooles; ⸱ ⸱ ⸱ ⸱ 101 F4 To the World 46
Where envious arts professed be, ⸱ ⸱ ⸱ ⸱ ⸱ 101 F4 To the World 47
Where nothing is examin'd, weigh'd, ⸱ ⸱ ⸱ ⸱ 101 F4 To the World 49
Where every freedome is betray'd, ⸱ ⸱ ⸱ ⸱ ⸱ 101 F4 To the World 51
I, Madame, am become your praiser. Where, ⸱ ⸱ ⸱ 117 F13 Aubigny 21
For truthes complexion, where they all weare maskes. ⸱ 118 F13 Aubigny 70
Where have I beene this while exil'd from thee? ⸱ ⸱ 122 F15 Heaven 13
Dwell, dwell here still: O, being every-where, ⸱ ⸱ ⸱ 122 F15 Heaven 15
Where he chanc't your name to see ⸱ ⸱ ⸱ ⸱ ⸱ 136 U2 Cupid 8
Where, you say, men gather blisses, ⸱ ⸱ ⸱ ⸱ 136 U2 Cupid 26
Where I sit and proyne my wings ⸱ ⸱ ⸱ ⸱ ⸱ 137 U2 Cupid 35
Where, how it would have relish'd well; ⸱ ⸱ ⸱ ⸱ 139 U2 Another 14
I can rest me where I am. ⸱ ⸱ ⸱ ⸱ ⸱ 142 U2 Her man 56
Where Love may all his Torches light, ⸱ ⸱ ⸱ ⸱ 147 U7 Nymph 24
And knew their how, and where: we should have, then, ⸱ 153 U13 Sacvile 3
Where any Deed is forc't, the Grace is mard. ⸱ ⸱ ⸱ 153 U13 Sacvile 24
And where they want, she is not understood. ⸱ ⸱ ⸱ 156 U13 Sacvile 112
A pennance, where a man may not be free, ⸱ ⸱ ⸱ 158 U14 Selden 8
Where is that nominall marke, or reall rite, ⸱ ⸱ ⸱ 160 U14 Selden 47
Where Pittes, or Wright, or Modet would not venter, ⸱ ⸱ 164 U15 Friend-Wars 80
From Hide-Parke to the Stage, where at the last ⸱ ⸱ 165 U15 Friend-Wars 109
Light thee from hell on earth: where flatterers, spies, ⸱ 167 U15 Friend-Wars 163
Of the poore sufferers) where the envious, proud, ⸱ ⸱ 167 U15 Friend-Wars 167
(Because th'are every where amongst Man-kind ⸱ ⸱ ⸱ 167 U15 Friend-Wars 171
And their words too; whil'st I but breake my Band. ⸱ ⸱ 169 U17 Friend-Debt 9
Where he doth steepe himselfe in Milke and Roses; ⸱ ⸱ 170 U19 Elegy By 8
Where men at once may plant, and gather blisses: ⸱ ⸱ 170 U19 Elegy By 10
Where do'st thou carelesse lie, ⸱ ⸱ ⸱ ⸱ ⸱ 174 U23 Himselfe 1

		Page	Title	Line

WHERE (cont.)

Where art thou, Genius? I should use	176	U25 Desmond	1
Genius, where art thou? I should use	176	U25 Desmond	V 1
Where only a mans birth is his offence.	177	U25 Desmond	32
Where darknesse with her gloomie-sceptred hand,	180	U25 Desmond	61
Where never Star shone brighter yet?	181	U27 Ode Helen	26
Where men may see whom I doe sing?	182	U27 Ode Helen	32
Where mutuall frauds are fought, and no side yeild;	186	U33 Councellour	4
Where Love doth shine, there needs no Sunne,	189	U36 Song	5
Where weaknesse doth offend, and vertue grieve,	192	U38 Elegy 'Tis	33
On every wall, and sung where e're I walke.	193	U38 Elegy 'Tis	98
And free societie, hee's borne else-where,	197	U40 Elegy That	16
Where he that knowes will, like a Lapwing, flie	198	U40 Elegy That	37
Where we must feele it Darke for halfe a yeare.	199	U41 Elegy Since	8
Where I may handle Silke, as free, and neere,	200	U42 Elegy Let	30
To make consumption, ever, where thou go'st;	205	U43 Vulcan	58
To make consumption, every where thou go'st;	205	U43 Vulcan	V 58
To sow consumption, every where thou go'st;	205	U43 Vulcan	V 58
To make propter viam, ever, where thou go'st;	205	U43 Vulcan	V 58
Maintain'd the trade at Bilbo, or else-where;	212	U43 Vulcan	199
Maintain'd the trade of Bilbo, or else-where;	212	U43 Vulcan	V199
Or stay'd but where the Fryar, and you first met,	212	U43 Vulcan	201
Or fixt in the Low-Countrey's, where you might	212	U43 Vulcan	203
The Academie, where the Gallants meet--	215	U44 Speach	89
Where now, thou art made Dweller;	220	U48 Bacchus	4
Where fight the prime Cocks of the Game, for wit?	222	U49 Pucell	4
I Am to dine, Friend, where I must be weigh'd	229	U54 Squib	1
To know the heads of danger! where 'tis fit	233	U59 Newcastle	17
Where he would fixe, for the distinctions feare.	242	U69 Friend Son	18
Where shame, faith, honour, and regard of right	243	U70 Ode	13
Where it were friendships schisme,	246	U70 Ode	90
Where they might read, and find	247	U70 Ode	122
The wish is great; but where the Prince is such,	249	U72 King	19
(Where she shall goe)	254	U75 Epithalam.	62
Have they bedew'd the Earth, where she doth tread,	254	U75 Epithalam.	66
Have they bedew'd the Earth, where she did tread,	254	U75 Epithalam.	V 66
And all the Ground were Garden, where she led!	254	U75 Epithalam.	68
See, now the Chappell opens; where the King	256	U75 Epithalam.	121
Where all heroique ample thoughts doe meet:	262	U78 Digby	10
Where Nature such a large survey hath ta'en;	262	U78 Digby	11
See where he walkes with Mira by his side.	264	U79 New-yeares	18
Where ere they tread th'enamour'd ground,	264	U79 New-yeares	36
Still waited on 'hem where they were.	264	U79 New-yeares	39
Our great, our good. Where one's so drest	265	U79 New-yeares	44
Where e're he goes upon the ground,	265	U79 New-yeares	58
And pietie the Center, where all met.	270	U81 Pawlet	42
'Twixt death and life! Where her mortalitie	271	U81 Pawlet	67
Of Heaven; where Seraphim take tent	273	U84 Cradle	31
Where every lim takes like a face?	275	U84 Body	4
'Tis got where it can try the fire.	278	U84 Mind	28
Where it may run to any good;	280	U84 Mind	62
And where it stayes, it there becomes	280	U84 Mind	63
To Body, and Soule! where Love is all the guest!	284	U84 Muse	64
Where Hee will be, all Beautie to the Sight;	286	U84 Muse	122
In his eternall Kingdomé, where we sit	286	U84 Muse	145
To that eternall Rest, where now sh'hath place	288	U84 Muse	197
Where first his Power will appeare, by call	289	U84 Muse	220
Goe where Youths soft intreaties call thee back.	292	U86 Hor.4:1	8
Where some great Lady, or her diligent Nourse;	313	Horace	164
Where the midst differs from the first: or where	315	Horace	217
So over-thick, but, where the people met,	319	Horace	292
And, where the matter is provided still,	325	Horace	443
And lead them with soft songs, where that he would.	327	Horace	485
Which it doth threaten. Therefore, where I see	329	Horace	525
For praises, where the mind conceales a foxe.	333	Horace	622
For praises, where the mind harbours a foxe.	354	Horace	V622
Not letting goe his hold, where he drawes food,	337	Horace	679
Not letting goe the skin, where he drawes food,	355	Horace	V679
Where, such perfections to the life doe rise.	362	Author	6
It carries Palme with it, (where e're it goes)	363	Riches	6
Where Gold's the Motive, women have no Nay.	363	Riches	18
Behold, where one doth swim;	366	Ode Who saith	3
Where Pindar swamme;	366	Ode Who saith	20
"Where neither Force can bend, nor Feare can awe.	367	Ode Who saith	48
And, where the most reade bookes, on Authors fames,	386	Browne	9
And thinke to ruine, where it seem'd to raise.	391	Shakespeare	12
Where spight of Death, next Life, for her Armes sake	394	Jane Ogle	25
And when he ships them where to use their Armes,	398	Drayton	65
Before this worke? where Envy hath not cast	401	Beaumont	13
To plant the Musick where noe eare can reach!	404	Inigo Jones 1	53
Thou paint a Lane, where Thumb the Pygmy meets!	407	Inigo Jones 2	12
Thou paint a Lane, where Thumb with Geffry meets!	407	Inigo Jones 2	V 12
Where it runs round, and even: where so well,	415	Rutter	16

WHEREAS

| That whereas your royall Father | 259 | U76 Petition | 5 |
| Whereas late your royall Father | 259 | U76 Petition | V 5 |

WHEREBY

Whereby he may knit sure up	222	U48 Bacchus	47
Whereby the safetie of Man-kind was wrought)	238	U66 Queene	8
Whereby the safetie of the world was wrought)	238	U66 Queene	V 8

WHEREFORE

| Fine Madame Would-Bee, wherefore should you feare, | 46 | E62 Would-bee | 1 |
| Wherefore should I | 120 | F14 Sydney | 7 |

WHEREFORE (cont.)
```
    That have good places: wherefore once agen,        . . . .   212   U43 Vulcan       V212
    Am I call'd Poet? wherefore with wrong shame,      . . .     311   Horace           129
```
WHEREIN
```
    To heaven; his hath: O happy state! wherein
    Wherein what wonder see thy name hath wrought?     . . . .    35   E27 Roe 1          7
    Of vice, and vertue; wherein all great life        . . . .    48   E64 Salisbury 3   16
    Wherein thou shew'st, how much the latter are      . . .      66   E102 Pembroke      6
    Wherein wise Nature you a dowrie gave,             . . . .    72   E111 Edmonds 2     3
    To my lesse sanguine Muse, wherein she'hath wonne  . . . .   114   F12 Rutland       35
    This hasty sacrifice, wherein I reare              . . . .   115   F12 Rutland       72
    As bloud, and match. Wherein, how more then much             116   F12 Rutland       97
    Wherein, your forme, you still the same shall finde;  . .    117   F13 Aubigny       46
    Wherein my Lady rideth!   .    .    .    .    .    .          120   F13 Aubigny      123
    Wherein you triumph yet: because                   .  .      134   U2 Triumph         2
    Wherein was oyle, beside the succour spent,        . .       173   U22 Elegy Tho      9
    Wherein she sits so richly drest,                  . . . .   207   U43 Vulcan        99
    Catch'd with these Arts, wherein the Judge is wise . .      251   U74 Weston        14
    Caught them these arts, wherein the Judge is wise           261   U77 Treasurer     11
    Till then unknowne, in Carts, wherein did ride     . . .    261   U77 Treasurer   V 11
    Wherein the Graver had a strife  .  .  .  .        .        319   Horace           313
```
WHEREOF
```
    Whereof old Democrite, and Hill Nicholas,    .              390   Reader             3
    Thou hast no lantherne, whereof tales are told;   . .       87   E133 Voyage       128
    Whereof the loyall conscience so complaines.      . .       93   F2 Penshurst        4
    May they have nothing left, whereof they can      . .      110   F11 Epode         27
    To those true numerous Graces; whereof some,      . . . .  118   F13 Aubigny       83
```
WHEREON
```
    Whereon the most of mankinde wracke themselves,   . . .    119   F13 Aubigny       90
```
WHERE'S
```
    Where's thy Quiver? bend thy Bow:    .    .    .    .       132   U2 How he saw      9
```
WHERESOERE
```
    Who, wheresoere he be, on what dear coast,        . .  .   116   F12 Rutland       93
    With every vertue, wheresoere it move,            .  .  .  116   F13 Aubigny        8
```
WHERE'T
```
    No faith's more firme, or flat, then where't doth creep.  . .  413   Ghyrlond       20
```
WHERETO
```
    Cry'd up of late: Whereto there must be first     .  .  .  415   Rutter           21
```
WHEREWITH
```
    The great renowne, and name wherewith shee goes.  . .      31   E14 Camden         4
    Wherewith, against thy bloud, they'offenders bee.  . .     60   E93 Radcliffe     16
    Wherewith, then, Madame, can you better pay       . .  .  118   F13 Aubigny       53
    Wherewith this while you live a widow'd wife,     . .     224   U50 Countesse      2
    But there are lines, wherewith I might b'embrac'd. .      226   U52 Answer         3
    I meane that one paire, wherewith he so hobled    . .  .  380   Coryat 3          41
    As was the Genius wherewith they were wrote;      .  .  . 389   Aleman            12
```
WHERIN
```
    Wherin (besides the noble aydes were lent,        .  .    207   U43 Vulcan      V 99
    Wherin (besides the noble Aydes were spent,       .  .    207   U43 Vulcan      V 99
    Wherin (besides the noble aydes were sent,        .  .    207   U43 Vulcan      V 99
```
WHEROF
```
    But that's a marke, wherof thy Rites doe boast,   .  .    205   U43 Vulcan        57
    These forme thy Ghyrlond. Wherof Myrtle green,    .  .    412   Ghyrlond           5
```
WHERON
```
    As if they' ador'd the Head, wheron th'are fixt.  .  .    413   Ghyrlond          28
```
WHERRY
```
    Their wherry had no saile, too; ours had none:    . .     84   E133 Voyage       11
    Propos'd to goe to Hol'borne in a wherry:         .  .    85   E133 Voyage       38
    The well-greas'd wherry now had got betweene,     .  .    87   E133 Voyage      114
```
WHET
```
    Be like a Whet-stone, that an edge can put        .  .   325   Horace           433
    On edge the Masculine spirits, and did whet       . . .  327   Horace           494
```
WHETHER (WHITHER)
```
    Through Swords, through Seas, whether she would ride.  .  134   U2 Triumph       10
```
WHETHER (See also WHE'R)
```
    Which deed I know not, whether were more high,    . . .   49   E66 Cary           7
    Whether their learning they would take, or wit,   . . .   68   E106 E Herbert     5
    Whether it languishing stucke upon the wall,      . . .   87   E133 Voyage      136
    Whether by choice, or fate, or both;  .    .    .  .      96   F3 Wroth           2
    Whether it be a face they weare, or no.           . . .  118   F13 Aubigny       80
    Whether we have lost, or wonne,   .    .    .     . .    138   U2 Kisse           6
    Whether any would up-braid                        . . .  138   U2 Kisse          30
    Whether their faces were their owne, or no:       . .    200   U42 Elegy Let     36
    The Cittie-Question, whether Tilly, or he,        . .    214   U44 Speach        38
    What is't to me whether the French Designe        .     219   U47 Tribe         31
    Whether the Dispensation yet be sent,             . .   219   U47 Tribe         35
    Whether in Mars his field thou bee,    .    .     .     293   U86 Hor.4:1       39
    Whether the Sea receiv'd into the shore,          . .   309   Horace            91
    It much will sway whether a god speak, than;      . .   342   Horace          V161
    Of some small thankfull land: whether he bee      . .   313   Horace           166
    As not make difference, whether Davus speake,     .     321   Horace           345
    Whether the guarded Tragedie they wrought,        . .   323   Horace           409
    Whether truth may, and whether error bring.       .     325   Horace           439
    Whether his soothing friend speake truth, or no.  . .   333   Horace           606
    (Whether yo'are given to, or giver are.)    .     . .   333   Horace           608
    Whether he piss'd upon his Fathers grave;         . .   335   Horace           671
    Whether the buylding of the Stage or Scene!       . .   402   Inigo Jones 1     11
```
WHET-STONE
```
    Be like a Whet-stone, that an edge can put        .  .   325   Horace           433
```
WHICH
```
    At dice his borrow'd money: which, god payes.     . . .   30   E12 Shift         12
    Which conquers all, be once over-come by thee.    . . .   31   E14 Camdon        12
    Which was a cater-piller. So 'twill dye.          . . .   31   E15 Court-worm     4
```

		Page	Title	Line

WHICH (cont.)

	Page	Title	Line
Or those, which doubt the common mouth of fame,	111	F11 Epode	V 79
Then he, which for sinnes penaltie forbeares.	112	F11 Epode	89
Whil'st that, for which, all vertue now is sold,	113	F12 Rutland	1
That which, to boote with hell, is thought worth heaven,	113	F12 Rutland	3
A present, which (if elder writs reherse	113	F12 Rutland	20
The world hath seene, which all these had in trust,	114	F12 Rutland	39
Then which, a nobler heaven it selfe knowes not.	115	F12 Rutland	67
To her remembrance; which when time shall bring	115	F12 Rutland	75
They hold in my strange poems, which, as yet,	115	F12 Rutland	81
Moodes, which the god-like Sydney oft did prove,	116	F12 Rutland	91
And so doe many more. All which can call	117	F13 Aubigny	31
Without which, all the rest were sounds, or lost.	118	F13 Aubigny	50
Of vertue, which you tread? what if alone?	118	F13 Aubigny	55
Which though the turning world may dis-esteeme,	118	F13 Aubigny	64
For which you worthy are the glad encrease	119	F13 Aubigny	94
To crowne the burthen which you goe withall,	119	F13 Aubigny	103
But which the Fates forbid me to reveale.	119	F13 Aubigny	107
Which I doe tell:	120	F14 Sydney	16
Which must be now,	121	F14 Sydney	47
The Word, which heaven, and earth did make;	130	U1 Nativitie	11
(Which with griefe and wrath I heard)	132	U2 How he saw	29
Which the prouder Beauties please,	133	U2 Suffered	2
Unto her; which Love might take	133	U2 Suffered	9
Which when she beheld to bleed,	133	U2 Suffered	17
Which how Dexterously I doe,	133	U2 Suffered	25
Which you call my Shafts. And see!	136	U2 Cupid	19
Guesse of these, which is the true;	138	U2 Kisse	34
And pronounce, which band, or lace,	140	U2 Promise	19
On which they see or know.	144	U3 Musicall	V 20
Which we in love must doe aswell,	146	U6 Defence	9
Is that which doth perfection breed.	146	U6 Defence	12
I Have my Pietie too, which could	151	U12 Corbet	1
Not at my prayers, but your sense; which laid	153	U13 Sacvile	9
Deepest in Man, of which when he doth thinke,	153	U13 Sacvile	20
Their difference, cannot choose which you will be.	157	U13 Sacvile	154
Which you will bury; but therein, the strife	158	U13 Sacvile	160
Then which there is not unto Studie'a more	158	U14 Selden	13
Which Grace shall I make love to first? your skill,	159	U14 Selden	35
All which he makes the servants of the Groine,	163	U15 Friend-Wars	46
Give me but that againe, which I must wast	167	U15 Friend-Wars	V152
Praevaricators swarme. Of which the store,	167	U15 Friend-Wars	170
Thy true friends wishes, Colby, which shall be,	167	U15 Friend-Wars	176
Thy true friends wishes, which shall ever be,	167	U15 Friend-Wars	V176
But which shall lead me on? both these are blind:	170	U18 Elegy Can	11
That which we can, who both in you, his Wife,	171	U19 Elegy By	25
Among which faithfull troope am I.	173	U22 Elegy Tho	28
Which if it kindle not, but scant	174	U22 Elegy Tho	33
Which makes that (lighted by the beamie hand	176	U24 Frontispice	9
Of Truth which searcheth the most hidden Springs,	176	U24 Frontispice	V 10
Some note of which each varied Pillar beares,	176	U24 Frontispice	15
By which as proper titles, she is knowne	176	U24 Frontispice	16
Unknowne which is the Dearest)	179	U25 Desmond	56
The Cure of that, which is but corporall,	180	U26 Ode High	5
And doubtfull Dayes (which were nam'd Criticall,)	180	U26 Ode High	6
Which in the taking if you mis-apply,	180	U26 Ode High	11
This same which you have caught,	180	U26 Ode High	20
Which all the world then styl'd divine?	181	U27 Ode Helen	20
Which all the Fate of Troy foretold?	181	U27 Ode Helen	24
And (which doth all Atchievements get above)	187	U33 Councellour	38
Without which all the world were darke;	189	U36 Song	7
On which with profit, I shall never looke,	189	U37 Friend-Book	5
Which is indeed but friendship of the spit:	190	U37 Friend-Book	9
But, as a friend, which name your selfe receave,	190	U37 Friend-Book	10
And which you (being the worthier) gave me leave	190	U37 Friend-Book	11
Which, how most sacred I will ever keepe,	190	U37 Friend-Book	13
Rigid, and harsh, which is a Drug austere	190	U37 Friend-Book	17
That friendship which no chance but love did chuse,	190	U37 Friend-Book	23
From each of which I labour to be free,	190	U37 Friend-Book	28
Or winds the Spirit, by which the flower so grew?	192	U38 Elegy 'Tis	58
That makes us live, not that which calls to die.	193	U38 Elegy 'Tis	78
Which in assurance to your brest I tell,	198	U40 Elegy That	49
From the poore wretch, which though he play'd in prose,	201	U42 Elegy Let	61
And the strong lines, which so the time doe catch:	206	U43 Vulcan	V 78
Or Captaine Pamphletts, which on foote doe sally	206	U43 Vulcan	V 79
Which noble Carew, Cotton, Selden lent:	207	U43 Vulcan	100
(Which, some are pleas'd to stile but thy madde pranck)	208	U43 Vulcan	131
Which, though it were the Fort of the whole Parish,	209	U43 Vulcan	133
Which was rak'd up in the Winchestrian Goose	209	U43 Vulcan	V142
Which thou hast only vented, not enjoy'd.	210	U43 Vulcan	168
In those Records, which, were all Chroniclers gone,	210	U43 Vulcan	171
In those Records, which, were our Chroniclers gone,	210	U43 Vulcan	V171
And to Pauls-Steeple; which was unto us	211	U43 Vulcan	193
That turnes us so much moneys, at which rate	215	U44 Speach	77
And force back that, which will not be restor'd,	219	U47 Tribe	40
But that's a blow, by which in time I may	219	U47 Tribe	51
Live to that point I will, for which I am man,	219	U47 Tribe	59
'Mongst which, if I have any friendships sent,	220	U47 Tribe	63
I would call mine, to which not many Staires	220	U47 Tribe	74
Equall with that, which for the best newes goes,	222	U49 Pucell	9
For Sermoneeres: of which now one, now other,	223	U49 Pucell	39
Which if in compasse of no Art it came	227	U52 Answer	10
Full twentie stone; of which I lack two pound:	229	U54 Squib	12

```
                                                          Page      Title       Line

WHICH  (cont.)
   The first of which, I feare, you will refuse;      .   .   .   230   U56 Covell         6
   The first of which, I doubt, you will refuse;      .   .   .   230   U56 Covell     V   6
   At which there are, would sell the Prince, and State: .   .   234   U61 Epigram        4
   That Faith, which she professeth to be pure?       .   .   .   236   U64 Charles 3     12
   which thus hast crown'd our hopes, our spring, and earth, .   237   U65 Prince     V   2
   Wise-crafts, on which the flatterer ventures not.  .   .   .   241   U69 Friend Son     6
   Of which we Priests, and Poets say       .    .   .   .   .   245   U70 Ode           82
   Which knits brave minds, and manners, more then blood. .   .   246   U70 Ode        V106
   And titles, by which all made claimes    .    .   .   .   .   247   U70 Ode          114
   That cry that gladnesse, which their hearts would pray, .   .   249   U72 King          14
   The cries, the gladnesse, which their hearts would pay, .   .   249   J72 King       V  14
   The Month of youth, which calls all Creatures forth .  .   .   253   U75 Epithalam.    26
   Through which not only we, but all our Species are. .   .   .   253   U75 Epithalam.    32
   Which to this use, wert built and consecrate!     .   .   .   256   U75 Epithalam.   130
   Which Time shall not,    .    .    .    .    .    .    .    .   257   U75 Epithalam.   134
   Which their glad Parents taught          .    .   .   .   .   257   U75 Epithalam.   143
   Alive, which else would die,             .    .   .   .   .   257   U75 Epithalam.   151
   Let their spite (which now abounds)      .    .   .   .   .   260   U76 Petition      28
   And act the businesse, which they paint, or carve.     .   .   261   U77 Treasurer     16
   And act the businesse, which these paint, or carve.    .   .   261   U77 Treasurer  V  16
   Which, though I cannot as an Architect    .   .   .   .   .   261   U77 Treasurer     25
   Which, though I cannot like as an Architect   .   .   .   .   261   U77 Treasurer  V  25
   That day, which I predestin'd am to sing,     .   .   .   .   262   U78 Digby      V  17
   Which I have vow'd posteritie to give.    .   .   .   .   .   262   U78 Digby         18
   'Tis but a body which you can torment,    .   .   .   .   .   270   U81 Pawlet        55
   Which gladnesse temper'd her sad Parents teares!  .   .   .   270   U81 Pawlet     V  59
   Which they that have the Crowne are sure to know!  .   .   .   271   U81 Pawlet        76
   Which the Elect of God are sure to know!  .   .   .   .   .   271   U81 Pawlet     V  76
   With Gold, or Claspes, which might be bought  .   .   .   .   273   U84 Cradle        27
   And Stanley, to the which shee was Co-heire.  .   .   .   .   274   U84 Descent        6
   Which all men doe, that urge not their owne deeds  .   .   .   281   U84 Kenelme       17
   By which yo'are planted, shew's your fruit shall bide. .   .   281   U84 Kenelme       19
   Which Vertue from your Father, ripe, will fall;   .   .   .   282   U84 Kenelme       22
   The joy of Saints! the Crowne for which it lives,  .   .   .   283   U84 Muse          37
   The glorie, and gaine of rest, which the place gives!  .   .   283   U84 Muse          38
   Those other two; which must be judg'd, or crown'd:     .   .   284   U84 Muse          55
   In that great Act of judgement: which the Father  .   .   .   288   U84 Muse         215
   With which, Priapus, he may thanke thy hands,     .   .   .   290   U85 Country       21
   With which, Priapus, he may greet thy hands,      .   .   .   290   U85 Country    V  21
   Which in some swarthie fish uncomely ends:    .   .   .   .   305   Horace             5
   Which in a blacke foule fish uncomely ends:   .   .   .   .   338   Horace         V   5
   The vertue of which order, and true grace,    .   .   .   .   307   Horace            59
   The vertue and grace of which, or I mistake,  .   .   .   .   339   Horace    V 60/ 59
   Nor from the brand, with which the life did burne  .   .   .   315   Horace           207
   Much from the sight, which faire report will make  .   .   .   317   Horace           262
   Which law receiv'd, the Chorus held his peace,    .   .   .   323   Horace           369
   To taxe that Verse, which many a day, and blot    .   .   .   325   Horace           416
   Their heads, which three Anticyra's cannot heale. .   .   .   325   Horace           428
   Which the Socratick writings best can show:   .   .   .   .   325   Horace           442
   All which I tell, lest when Apollo's nam'd,   .   .   .   .   329   Horace           501
   There are yet faults, which we would well forgive, .   .   .   329   Horace           520
   Which it doth threaten.  Therefore, where I see    .   .   .   329   Horace           525
   Offended with few spots, which negligence     .   .   .   .   329   Horace           527
   A meane, and toleration, which does well:     .   .   .   .   331   Horace           549
   'Tis now inquir'd, which makes the nobler Verse,  .   .   .   331   Horace           581
   Next, that which rapt mee, was: I might behold    .   .   .   361   Palmer            13
   which thoughts being circumvolvd in gyerlyk mocion .   .   .   361   Palmer            23
   Which being eyed directly, I divine,     .    .   .   .   .   362   Author            13
   Flowes from the surfets which we take in peace.   .   .   .   363   Peace              4
   Neere which, the Thespiad's sing;        .    .   .   .   .   366   Ode Who saith     18
   All which, when they but heare a straine  .   .   .   .   .   368   Ode Who saith     89
   (Which makes him sing      .    .    .    .   .   .   .   .   369   Ode Who saith    102
   In Picture, they which truly understand,  .   .   .   .   .   370   Author             1
   All which are parts commend the cunning hand; .   .   .   .   370   Author             4
   To judge which Passion's false, and which is true, .   .   .   370   Author            11
   With vices, which they look'd for, and came to.   .   .   .   371   Fletcher          10
   Do crowne thy murdred Poeme: which shall rise .   .   .   .   371   Fletcner          14
   She was 'Sell Boulstred.  In which name, I call   .   .   .   372   Epitaph           12
   And therein (which is worth his valour too)   .   .   .   .   378   Coryat 2          84
   - - - Which should Have beene Printed with the other . . .   379   Coryat 3         Ttl
   Which, unto all Ages, for his will be knowne, .   .   .   .   379   Coryat 3          11
   Which he not denies.  Now being so free,  .   .   .   .   .   381   Coryat 3          57
   his life, his love, his honour, which ne'r dyes,  .   .   .   382   Rich               8
   your Royal Eye which still creates new men    .   .   .   .   383   Rich              14
   Which I do, early, vertuous Somerset,    .    .   .   .   .   384   Somerset           7
   Hold thyne owne worth unbroke: which is so good   .   .   .   386   Browne            13
   which, did they neere so neate, or proudly dwell, .   .   .   387   Cavendish          3
   to which there's no materiall that endures;   .   .   .   .   387   Cavendish          8
   That would have done, that, which you onely can.  .   .   .   389   Aleman            24
   Which, when it sounds at best, but eccho's right; .   .   .   390   Shakespeare        8
   Or blinde Affection, which doth ne're advance .   .   .   .   391   Shakespeare        9
   Which were so richly spun, and woven so fit,  .   .   .   .   392   Shakespeare       49
   In each of which, he seemes to shake a Lance, .   .   .   .   392   Shakespeare       69
   Which, since thy flight from hence, hath mourn'd like night, . 392   Shakespeare       79
   Which made me thinke, the old Theocritus, .   .   .   .   .   397   Drayton           27
   Into a Phoenix, which is shee.           .    .   .   .   .   400   Lady Ogle         32
   Aeternities great charter; which became   .   .   .   .   .   400   Lady Ogle         35
   Th'ascent of Lady Fame which none could spy   .   .   .   .   403   Inigo Jones 1     35
   Sense, what they are! which by a specious fyne    .   .   .   404   Inigo Jones 1     55
   Which you have justly gained from the Stage,  .   .   .   .   409   Brome              6
   Which I, your Master, first did teach the Age.    .   .   .   409   Brome              8
   A Prentise-ship: which few doe now a dayes.   .   .   .   .   410   Brome             10
```

WHICH (cont.)

All which thou hast incurr'd deservedly:	410	Gill	5
Which, chang'd, a five-fold mysterie designe,	412	Ghyrlond	2
But, that which summes all, is the Eglantine,	413	Ghyrlond	21
Which, of the field is clep'd the sweetest brier,	413	Ghyrlond	22
To Crowne the years, which you begin, great king,	416	Welcome	7
or Malyce to make Faultes, which nowe is skill.	421	Censure	11
That Frindshipp, which noe Chaunce, but Love did Chuse,	422	Censure	16
From each of which, I labor to be free,	422	Censure	21

WHILE (See also WHYLE)

For such a Poet, while thy dayes were greene,	28	E4 James 1	5
Where, while that sever'd doth remaine,	34	E22 Daughter	10
While Beast instructs his faire, and innocent wife,	34	E25 Beast 1	1
And pleaseth both. For while he melts his greace	38	E37 Chev'ril	3
All yeelding to his fortune, nor, the while,	71	E110 Edmonds 1	5
Whose better studies while shee emulates,	78	E121 Rudyerd 1	3
That all this while I have forgot some god,	85	E133 Voyage	44
But hold my torch, while I describe the entry	85	E133 Voyage	58
And these grudg'd at, art reverenc'd the while.	93	F2 Penshurst	6
While all, that follow, their glad eares apply	97	F3 Wroth	31
While we may, the sports of love:	102	F5 Celia 1	2
While we can, the sports of love;	102	F5 Celia 1	V 2
While you breath. First give a hundred,	103	F6 Celia 2	8
While it makes huishers serviceable men,	113	F12 Rutland	9
While thus it buyes great grace, and hunts poore fame;	113	F12 Rutland	15
While thus it gets grace, and hunts poore fame;	113	F12 Rutland	V 15
And almost, all dayes after, while they live;	118	F13 Aubigny	75
Where have I beene this while exil'd from thee?	122	F15 Heaven	13
More pleasure while the thing he makes	145	U5 Woman-kind	15
And manly elocution, not one while	160	U14 Selden	56
And masculine elocution, not one while	160	U14 Selden	V 56
And be belov'd, while the Whores last. O times,	167	U15 Friend-Wars	161
Though but while mettal's heating:	179	U25 Desmond	43
So brightly brandish'd) wound'st, defend'st! the while	187	U33 Councellour	32
Doth, while he keepes his watch, betray his stand.	198	U40 Elegy That	36
And now such is thy stand; while thou dost deale	217	U46 Coke	15
From Court, while yet thy fame hath some small day;	223	U49 Pucell	36
Wherewith this while you live a widow'd wife,	224	U50 Countesse	2
A-while with us bright Sun, and helpe our light!	252	U75 Epithalam.	2
A-while with us bright Sun, and mend our light;	252	U75 Epithalam.	V 2
Th'Ignoble never liv'd, they were a-while	257	U75 Epithalam.	153
While he was young; he sweat; and freez'd againe:	333	Horace	589
The while he belcheth loftie Verses out,	335	Horace	649
Hee, while he labour'd to be thought a God	335	Horace	661
And there, while he gives the zealous Bravado,	375	Coryat 1	22
To lie at Livory, while the Horses did stand.	375	Coryat 1	33
While I confesse thy writings to be such,	390	Shakespeare	3
And art alive still, while thy Booke doth live,	391	Shakespeare	23
Thou hast deserv'd: And let me reade the while	398	Drayton	60
That, while they bind the senses, doe so please?	401	Filmer	2

WHILES

Though never after; whiles it gaynes the voyce	113	F12 Rutland	11
Though never after; whiles it gaynes the will	113	F12 Rutland	V 11

WHILEST

Whilest lyke a blaze of strawe,	420	Ode:If Men	15

WHIL'ST

That whil'st I meant but thine to gratulate,	48	E64 Salisbury 3	17
Whil'st thy weigh'd judgements, Egerton, I heare,	51	E74 Chancelor	1
Whil'st I behold thee live with purest hands;	51	E74 Chancelor	3
Whil'st thou art certaine to thy words, once gone,	52	E74 Chancelor	7
Whil'st others toyle for titles to their tombes.	70	E109 Nevil	18
Whil'st thou dost rayse some Player, from the grave,	81	E129 Mime	11
The whil'st, the severall seasons thou hast seene	97	F3 Wroth	37
Whil'st that, for which, all vertue now is sold,	113	F12 Rutland	1
Or perhaps lesse: whil'st gold beares all this sway,	113	F12 Rutland	18
Whil'st pleas'd Apollo	366	Ode Who saith	12

WHILST

Strength of my Countrey, whilst I bring to view	69	E108 Soldiers	1
And whilst our tonques perplexed lie,	139	U2 Another	17
And whilst our states, strength, body, and mind we waste,	166	U15 Friend-Wars	133
Whilst the Latin, Queene of Tongues,	184	U29 Fit of Rime	34
The fate of things: whilst totter'd vertue holds	216	U44 Speach	101
Whilst I informe my selfe, I would teach thee,	216	U45 Squib	2
With endlesse labours, whilst thy learning drawes	217	U46 Coke	18
Whilst your Ulisses hath ta'ne leave to goe,	224	U50 Countesse	21
But whilst you curious were to have it be	227	U52 Answer	13
Whilst it the Dittie heares.	239	U67 Muses	24
Whilst all the ravish'd rout	240	U67 Muses	40
Whilst that in heav'n, this light on earth must shine.	246	U70 Ode	96
Whilst they both stand,	256	U75 Epithalam.	126
Whilst the maine tree, still found	258	U75 Epithalam.	181
Whilst from the higher Bankes doe slide the floods;	290	U85 Country	25
Whilst, Lydia, I was lov'd of thee,	293	U87 Hor.3:9	1
Whilst Horace lov'd no Mistres more,	293	U87 Hor.3:9	5
Gesture, and riot, whilst he swooping went	319	Horace	304
Gesture, and riot, whilst he wandring went	346	Horace	V304
Or, whilst he shuns the Earth, to catch at Aire	321	Horace	335
Whilst other soules convert to base abuse	361	Palmer	11

WHIMSY (See WHYMSEYS)

WHIP

Pillory nor Whip, nor want of Ears,	410	Gill	4

WHIPT

A Rogue by Statute, censur'd to be whipt,	411	Gill	15

WHIRLING   (See also WHOORLES)
  Whirling his Whymseys, by a subtilty   405   Inigo Jones 1   73
WHISPER
  And whisper what a Proclamation sayes.   59   E92 New Crie   20
  But whisper; O glad Innocence, ...   177   U25 Desmond   31
WHISPER'D
  But whisper'd Counsells, and those only thrive;   .   .   234   U61 Epigram   6
WHISPERERS
  Lewd slanderers, soft whisperers that let blood   .   .   167   U15 Friend-Wars   165
  Lewd standers, soft whisperers that let blood   167   U15 Friend-Wars V165
WHISPERING
  Give thankes by stealth, and whispering in the eare,   .   154   U13 Sacvile   49
WHISTLE
  Be Inigo, the Whistle, & his men!   405   Inigo Jones 1   66
WHISTLES
  Their Corrals, Whistles, and prime Coates,   .   .   .   273   U84 Cradle   21
WHIT
  'Fore your Idoll Glasse a whit, ...   140   U2 Promise   22
WHITE   (NAME)
  That haunt Pickt-hatch, Mersh-Lambeth, and White-fryers,   .   30   E12 Shift   2
  Else that glister'd in White-hall;   138   U2 Kisse   16
  Nay, let White-Hall with Revels have to doe,   .   .   .   210   U43 Vulcan   156
  Scarce let White-Hall with Revels have to doe,   .   .   .   210   U43 Vulcan   V156
WHITE
  'Twas brought to court first wrapt, and white as milke;   .   31   E15 Court-worm   2
  White, black, blew, greene, and in more formes out-started,   .   87   E133 Voyage   126
  Could ne'er make prize of thy white Chastetye.   .   .   .   108   F10 Proludium   6
  Have you seene the white Lillie grow, ...   134   U2 Triumph   V 21
  O so white! O so soft! O so sweet is she!   .   .   .   135   U2 Triumph   30
  Nay, her white and polish'd neck, ...   137   U2 Cupid   29
  Forehead large, and white as snow;   141   U2 Her man   V 18
  A Poet hath no more but black and white, ...   227   U52 Answer   20
  See, how she paceth forth in Virgin-white,   .   .   .   253   U75 Epithalam.   41
  And white, as that, put on: and in her hand,   .   .   .   285   U84 Muse   95
  This change'd his Downe; till this, as white   .   .   .   366   Ode Who saith   25
  Or thought they, Leda's white Adult'rers place   .   .   .   369   Ode Who saith   104
  of her white Hand; or she can spare it.   662   Bedford   10
WHITE-FRYERS
  That haunt Pickt-hatch, Mersh-Lambeth, and White-fryers,   .   30   E12 Shift   2
WHITE-HALL
  Else that glister'd in White-hall;   138   U2 Kisse   16
  Nay, let White-Hall with Revels have to doe,   .   .   .   210   U43 Vulcan   156
  Scarce let White-Hall with Revels have to doe,   .   .   .   210   U43 Vulcan   V156
WHITER
  Then whose I doe not know a whiter soule, ...   60   E93 Radcliffe   11
WHITEST
  Out of their Choysest, and their whitest wooll.   .   .   225   U51 Bacon   16
WHITHER   (See also WHETHER)
  Whither the world must follow. And I, now,   .   .   .   37   E33 Roe 3   3
  Make it your gift. See whither that will beare mee.   .   55   E84 Bedford 2   10
  And whither rap'd, now thou but stoup'st to mee?   .   .   122   F15 Heaven   14
  And Goates together, whither they must come   .   .   .   283   U84 Muse   47
  Alas: then whither wade I, ...   365   Ode Splendor   17
  Alas: then whither trade I, ...   365   Ode Splendor   V 17
  Whither? oh whither will this Tire-man growe?   .   .   .   404   Inigo Jones 1   59
WHITT
  Scap'd not thy Justice any whitt the more: .   .   .   210   U43 Vulcan   V154
WHO'
  Who'in such ambition can but follow thee.   73   E113 Overbury   12
  From the Tempestuous Grandlings, Who'll informe   .   .   215   U44 Speach   64
  Or, who's unskilfull at the Coit, or Ball,   .   .   .   331   Horace   567
  Yet who's most ignorant, dares Verses make.   .   .   .   331   Horace   570
  To your desert, who'have done it, Friend. And this   .   389   Aleman   21
  To see (who'it is?) A noble Countesse, greate,   .   .   394   Jane Ogle   3
  I sayd, who'had supp'd so deepe of this sweet Chalice,   .   412   Sutcliffe   21
WHO
  Deceive their malice, who could wish it so.   .   .   .   27   E2 My Booke   7
  Who scarse can spell th'hard names: whose knight lesse can.   .   28   E3 Bookseller   10
  Quick in his lips! who hath this wonder wrought?   .   .   33   E21 Gam'ster   5
  Who, to thy one, all other braines refuse;   .   .   .   34   E23 Donne 1   2
  Who wets my grave, can be no friend of mine.   .   .   .   37   E33 Roe 3   6
  Who would not be thy subject, James, t'obay   .   .   .   37   E35 James 2   1
  Like aydes 'gainst treasons who hath found before?   .   .   38   E35 James 2   7
  Who sayes that Giles and Jone at discord be?   .   .   .   40   E42 Giles   1
  Is this the Sir, who, some wast wife to winne,   .   .   .   42   E46 Luckless 1   1
  Who this thy scape from rumour gratulate, ...   43   E51 James 3   6
  Who, when you'have burnt your selves downe to the snuffe,   .   45   E59 Spies   2
  Who can consider thy right courses run, ...   47   E63 Salisbury 2   1
  And not thy fortune; who can cleerely see   47   E63 Salisbury 2   3
  Who can behold all envie so declin'd   47   E63 Salisbury 2   7
  But I repent me: Stay. Who e're is rais'd,   .   .   .   48   E65 Muse   15
  Who, to upbraid the sloth of this our time,   .   .   .   48   E66 Cary   5
  Could conquer thee, but chance, who did betray.   .   .   49   E66 Cary   10
  No male unto him: who could so exceed   53   E79 Rutland   7
  Who had no lesse a trumpet of their name, ...   57   E89 Allen   5
  Who both their graces in thy selfe hast more   .   .   .   57   E89 Allen   9
  Weare this renowne. 'Tis just, that who did give   .   .   57   E89 Allen   13
  Who more should seeke mens reverence, then feare.   .   .   58   E91 Vere   18
  Who did, alike with thee, thy house up-beare,   .   .   .   60   E93 Radcliffe   3
  Lucy, you brightnesse of our sphaere, who are   .   .   .   60   E94 Bedford 3   1
  Lucy, you brightnesse of our sphaere, who are   .   .   .   61   E94 Bedford 3   15
  For who can master those great parts like thee,   .   .   61   E95 Savile   17
  Who shall doubt, Donne, where I a Poet bee,   .   .   .   62   E96 Donne 2   1

WHO (cont.)

	Page	Title	Line
As lowdest praisers, who perhaps would find	67	E103 L Wroth 1	11
Becomes none more then you, who need it least.	67	E103 L Wroth 1	14
Who could not but create them all, from you?	67	E105 L Wroth 2	6
And, drest in shepheards tyre, who would not say:	68	E105 L Wroth 2	9
Who now calls on thee, Nevil, is a Muse,	70	E109 Nevil	1
Who Edmonds, reades thy booke, and doth not see	72	E111 Edmonds 2	1
For Cupid, who (at first) tooke vaine delight,	73	E114 Sydney	3
You wonder, who this is! and, why I name	74	E115 Honest Man	1
These were thy knowing arts: which who doth now	75	E116 Jephson	13
Who prov'st, all these were, and againe may bee.	78	E122 Rudyerd 2	10
But both th'hast so, as who affects the state	78	E123 Rudyerd 3	3
Who sees a soule, in such a body set,	79	E125 Uvedale	5
Who gave, to take at his returne from Hell,	84	E133 Voyage	27
Who shall discharge first his merd-urinous load:	85	E133 Voyage	65
(Who hath the hundred hands when he doth meddle)	86	E133 Voyage	82
Airising in that place, through which, who goes,	87	E133 Voyage	131
But 'mong'st these Tiberts, who do'you thinke there was?	88	E133 Voyage	155
Who kept an ale-house; with my little Minos,	89	E133 Voyage	189
On thy good lady, then! who, therein, reap'd	95	F2 Penshurst	84
Who, for it, makes thy house his court;	97	F3 Wroth	24
Who, for it, makes thy lodge his court;	97	F3 Wroth	V 24
Which who can use is happy: Such be thou.	99	F3 Wroth	99
Which who can use is happy: Such art thou.	99	F3 Wroth	V 99
If these, who have but sense, can shun	101	F4 To the World	33
Doe enough; and who would take	105	F8 Sicknesse	26
Who, with his axe, thy fathers mid-wife plaid.	107	F10 Proludium	15
Who (in th'examining)	109	F11 Epode	14
With whom who sailes, rides on the surge of feare,	110	F11 Epode	41
O, who is he, that (in this peace) enjoyes	110	F11 Epode	55
Who (blest with such high chance)	111	F11 Epode	62
Who, being at sea, suppose,	111	F11 Epode	70
Or those, who doubt the common mouth of fame,	111	F11 Epode	79
Though we acknowledge, who can so abstayne,	112	F11 Epode	85
Though I acknowledge, who can so refraine,	112	F11 Epode	V 85
Who could be false to? chiefly, when he knowes	112	F11 Epode	103
Who would be false to? chiefly, when he knowes	112	F11 Epode	V103
The foole that gave it; who will want, and weepe,	113	F12 Rutland	13
Like life unto 'hem. Who heav'd Hercules	115	F12 Rutland	57
Who placed Jasons Argo in the skie?	115	F12 Rutland	59
Who made a lampe of Berenices hayre?	115	F12 Rutland	61
Who, though shee have a better verser got,	115	F12 Rutland	68
And, who doth me (though I not him) envy,	115	F12 Rutland	70
Who, wheresoere he be, on what dear coast,	116	F12 Rutland	93
I, therefore, who professe my selfe in love	116	F13 Aubigny	7
Let who will follow fashions, and attyres,	118	F13 Aubigny	71
But to please him, who is the dearer prise	119	F13 Aubigny	116
Who not the least,	120	F14 Sydney	9
Eternall Father, God, who did'st create	127	U1 Trinitie	17
Eternall God the Sonne, who not denyd'st	128	U1 Trinitie	21
Who more can crave	129	U1 Father	17
Who saw the light, and were afraid,	130	U1 Nativitie	5
Who made himselfe the price of sinne,	130	U1 Nativitie	20
Of her good, who is the best	137	U2 Cupid	44
Let who will thinke us dead, or wish our death.	139	U2 Another	18
Yet dare I not tell who;	147	U7 Nymph	2
Of sleepe againe, who was his Aid;	151	U11 Dreame	12
Deare Vincent Corbet who so long	151	U12 Corbet	7
And pray who shall my sorrowes read,	152	U12 Corbet	33
Who makes the one, so't be first, makes both.	152	U12 Corbet	40
You cannot doubt, but I, who freely know	153	U13 Sacvile	13
Who was this Morning such a one, should be	157	U13 Sacvile	126
Who can behold their Manners, and not clowd-/Like	164	U15 Friend-Wars	60
Who falls for love of God, shall rise a Starre.	168	U15 Friend-Wars	196
Such Guides men use not, who their way would find,	170	U18 Elegy Can	12
That which we can, who both in you, his Wife,	171	U19 Elegy By	25
But who should lesse expect from you,	173	U22 Elegy Tho	13
Who as an off'ring at your shrine,	174	U22 Elegy Tho	29
Who aided him, will thee, the issue of Joves braine.	175	U23 Himselfe	30
Who aided them, will thee, the issue of Joves braine.	175	U23 Himself	V 30
Who would with judgement search, searching conclude	177	U25 Desmond	25
Of all the Land. Who now at such a Rate,	185	U30 Burleigh	19
Who thus long safe, would gaine upon the times	186	U32 Elsmere	9
Who, though their guilt, and perjurie they know,	186	U32 Elsmere	11
Who 'gainst the Law, weave Calumnies, my — ;	187	U33 Councellour	6
Who more they burne, they more desire,	189	U36 Song	10
And lesse they know, who being free to use	190	U37 Friend-Book	22
The contrite Soule, who hath no thought to win	193	U38 Elegy 'Tis	89
And such your Servant is, who vowes to keepe	198	U40 Elegy That	41
Who shall forbid me then in Rithme to bee	200	U42 Elegy Let	5
Who frownes, who jealous is, who taxeth me.	200	U42 Elegy Let	10
But I who live, and have liv'd twentie yeare	200	U42 Elegy Let	29
And so did Jove, who ne're meant thee his Cup:	208	U43 Vulcan	115
Who from the Divels-Arse did Guns beget;	212	U43 Vulcan	202
Who with the Divell did Ordinance beget;	212	U43 Vulcan	V202
Are asked to climbe. First give me faith, who know	220	U47 Tribe	75
Who (herein studying conscience, and not fame)	224	U50 Countesse	14
Who, when shee heard the match, concluded streight,	229	U54 Squib	5
Who durst live great, 'mongst all the colds, and heates,	233	U59 Newcastle	21
To lift to heaven: who is't not understands	234	U61 Epigram	8
Who dares denie, that all first-fruits are due	235	U63 Charles 2	1
Who doubts, those fruits God can with gaine restore,	235	U63 Charles 2	3
But as the wretched Painter, who so ill	241	U69 Friend Son	9

		Page	Title	Line
WHO (cont.)				
Jonson, who sung this of him, e're he went		246	U70 Ode	85
Who, e're the first downe bloomed on the chin,		247	U70 Ode	127
Who seldome sleepes! whom bad men only hate!		250	U73 Weston	6
Who, in all they doe,		255	U75 Epithalam.	78
Who the whole Act expresse;		255	U75 Epithalam.	87
Great Say-Master of State, who cannot erre,		255	U75 Epithalam.	99
Great Say-Master of State, who not to erre,		255	U75 Epithalam.	V 99
To day, the Fathers service; who could bring		256	U75 Epithalam.	107
Askes first, Who gives her (I Charles) then he plights		256	U75 Epithalam.	124
Who walkes on Earth as May still went along,		264	U79 New-yeares	26
To pious parents, who would have their blood		268	U80 Christning	7
When I, who would her Poet have become,		269	U81 Pawlet	17
Else, who doth praise a person by a new,		270	U81 Pawlet	37
Let Angels sing her glories, who did call		270	U81 Pawlet	63
Who saw the way was made it! and were sent		270	U81 Pawlet	65
Faire Fame, who art ordain'd to crowne		272	U84 Cradle	1
By Thee, and Conscience, both who thrive		273	U84 Cradle	7
Who read what the Crepundia bee,		273	U84 Cradle	14
Who claimes (of reverence) to be heard,		274	U84 Cradle	34
. . . . the Lady Venetia Digby; who living, . . .		282	U84 Muse	Ttl
Who was my Muse, and life of all I sey'd,		282	U84 Muse	2
On Nature, for her: who did let her lie,		282	U84 Muse	13
Who will be there, against that day prepar'd,		284	U84 Muse	59
Who in that feast of Resurrection trust!		284	U84 Muse	62
Who violates the God-head, is most vitious		284	U84 Muse	74
To style us Friends, who were, by Nature, Foes?		286	U84 Muse	139
Adopt us Heires, by grace, who were of those		286	U84 Muse	140
Who knowes the hearts of all, and can dissect		286	U84 Muse	150
For 'twas himselfe who form'd, and gave it her.		287	U84 Muse	156
Jesus, the onely-gotten Christ! who can		288	U84 Muse	212
Who reades, will pardon my Intelligence,		289	U84 Muse	226
Who (amongst these delights) would not forget		290	U85 Country	37
Who sings so sweet, and with such cunning plaies,		293	U87 Hor.3:9	10
Or the wilde river, who hath changed now		309	Horace	96
Were also clos'd: But, who the man should be,		309	Horace	109
Who nought assaies unaptly, or amisse?		315	Horace	200
Speake to me, Muse, the Man, who, after Troy was sack't,		315	Horace	201
For choller! If I did not, who could bring		325	Horace	430
Who, since, to sing the Pythian rites is heard,		333	Horace	591
Who now to sing the Pythian Rites is heard,		353	Horace	V591
So doth the Poet, who is rich in land,		333	Horace	599
To let it downe, who knowes, if he did cast		335	Horace	656
Who saith our Times nor have, nor can		366	Ode Who saith	1
Who ever sipt at Baphyre river,		367	Ode Who saith	57
Who (see) already hath ore-flowne		368	Ode Who saith	65
Who warbleth Pancharis,		369	Ode Who saith	98
Who ever he be, would write a Story at		379	Coryat 3	1
Who, because his matter in all should be meete,		379	Coryat 3	3
Yet who could have hit on't but the wise noddell		379	Coryat 3	6
But who will beleeve this, that chanceth to looke		379	Coryat 3	17
No: as I first said, who would write a story at		381	Coryat 3	59
Who takes thy volume to his vertuous hand,		383	Author	1
Who bluntly doth but looke upon the same,		383	Author	3
Who reads may roave, and call the passage darke,		383	Author	5
Who reads, who roaves, who hopes to understand,		383	Author	7
Who cannot reade, but onely doth desire		383	Author	9
Who are his Test, and what their judgement is:		385	Husband	3
Who hadst before wrought in rich Homers Mine?		388	Chapman	3
And who make thither else, rob, or invade.		389	Chapman	12
Who tracks this Authors, or Translators Pen,		389	Aleman	1
As in this Spanish Proteus; who, though writ		389	Aleman	5
Who casts to write a living line, must sweat,		392	Shakespeare	59
But who hath them interpreted, and brought		395	May	19
Because, who make the question, have not seene		396	Drayton	3
Did all so strike me, as I cry'd, who can		397	Drayton	31
That can but reade; who cannot, may in prose		398	Drayton	73
Yet, who dares offer a redoubt to reare?		401	Beaumont	11
Who did this Knot compose,		401	Filmer	7
But wisest Inigo! who can reflect		405	Inigo Jones 1	86
Allmighty Architecture? who noe less		406	Inigo Jones 1	92
Thou art not worth it. Who will care to knowe		409	Detractor	13
Who mad'st us happy all, in thy reflexe,		414	Ghyrlond	47
Who like a Giant hasts his course to run,		414	Ghyrlond	51
In spite of Hipocrites, who are the worst		416	Dover	9
Welcome all, who lead or follow,		657	Door Apollo	1
Welcome all, who lead or follow,		657	Door Apollo	19
WHOE				
Whoe worthie wine, whoe not, to bee wyse Pallas guests.		421	Ode:If Men	45
WHO'D				
Deserves no pardon; or who'd play, and sing		329	Horace	531
WHO'HAD				
I sayd, who'had supp'd so deepe of this sweet Chalice,		412	Sutcliffe	21
WHO'HAVE				
To your desert, who'have done it, Friend. And this		389	Aleman	21
WHO'IN				
Who'in such ambition can but follow thee.		73	E113 Overbury	12
WHO'IT				
To see (who'it is?) A noble Countesse, greate,		394	Jane Ogle	3
WHOLE				
Himselfe: his whole revennue is, god payes.		30	E12 Shift	6
And since, the whole land was preserv'd for thee.		38	E35 James 2	10
From locks of wooll, or shreds from the whole peece?		45	E56 Poet-Ape	14

	Page	Title	Line

WHOLE (cont.)

	Page	Title	Line
That his whole body should speake french, not he?	56	E88 Monsieur	2
Makes, the whole longer, then 'twas given him, much.	76	E119 Shelton	16
And for one Cerberus, the whole coast was dogs.	84	E133 Voyage	14
With the whole houshold, and may, every day,	96	F2 Penshurst	96
I know thou whole art but a shop	100	F4 To the World	17
Hee whom the whole world could not take,	130	U1 Nativitie	10
Reare-Suppers in their Names! and spend whole nights	156	U13 Sacvile	101
The whole world here leaven'd with madnesse swells;	163	U15 Friend-Wars	31
To make up Greatnesse! and mans whole good fix'd	163	U15 Friend-Wars	44
Or side, but threatens Ruine. The whole Day	166	U15 Friend-Wars	131
That their whole life was wickednesse, though weav'd	171	U20 Shrub	10
But their whole inside full of ends, and knots?	171	U20 Shrub	12
A Sparke to set whole worlds a-fire,	189	U36 Song	9
And so, have kept me dying a whole age,	205	U43 Vulcan	55
And so, have kept them dying a whole age,	205	U43 Vulcan	V 55
With pieces of the Legend; The whole summe	205	U43 Vulcan	66
Which, though it were the Fort of the whole Parish,	209	U43 Vulcan	133
And the whole lumpe growes round, deform'd, and droupes,	227	U52 Answer	5
To make the hearts of a whole Nation smile,	238	U66 Queene	10
He vexed time, and busied the whole State;	243	U70 Ode	27
Because the order of the whole is faire!	251	U74 Weston	12
Who the whole Act expresse;	255	U75 Epithalam.	87
Whole Nations! nay, Mankind! the World, with all	271	U81 Pawlet	90
And the whole Banquet is full sight of God!	284	U84 Muse	65
As her whole life was now become one note	287	U84 Muse	178
Her broken sighes did never misse whole sense:	288	U84 Muse	185
Would sit in an Infirmery, whole dayes	288	U84 Muse	195
The whole fleet wreck'd? a great jarre to be shap'd,	305	Horace	28
Not to designe the whole. Should I aspire	307	Horace	49
Steepe the glad Genius in the Wine, whole dayes,	319	Horace	298
As the whole heard in sight,	366	Ode Who saith	26
They saw it halfe, damd thy whole play, and more;	371	Fletcher	8
Lucans whole frame unto us, and so wrought,	395	May	20
The best of Woemen! her whole life	399	Lady Ogle	11
By all your Titles, & whole style at ones	402	Inigo Jones 1	15
So soft, and smooth it handles, the whole piece,	415	Rutter	17
whole armyes fall, swayd by those nyce respects.	423	Lucan	11

WHOLESOME

	Page	Title	Line
To make amends, yo'are thought a wholesome creature.	46	E62 Would-bee	8

WHOLIE

	Page	Title	Line
in Course of Frindshipp, wholie to reprove:	422	Censure	19

WHO'LL

	Page	Title	Line
From the Tempestuous Grandlings, Who'll informe	215	U44 Speach	64

WHOLLY

	Page	Title	Line
Though not in these, in rithmes not wholly dumbe,	182	U28 Worth	2
In practiz'd friendship wholly to reprove,	190	U37 Friend-Book	26
Hath given wholly to the Sonne (the rather	288	U84 Muse	216
Be simple quite throughout, and wholly one.	307	Horace	32

WHOLSOME

	Page	Title	Line
Yet doth some wholsome Physick for the mind,	180	U26 Ode High	9
Praise the spare diet, wholsome justice, lawes,	317	Horace	283

WHOM

	Page	Title	Line
As mad-men stones: not caring whom they hit.	27	E2 My Booke	6
Whom should my Muse then flie to, but the best	28	E4 James 1	9
To all, to whom I write.	29	E9 To All	Ttl
And such from whom let no man hope least good,	30	E11 Something	6
Camden, most reverend head, to whom I owe	31	E14 Camden	1
(How nothing's that?) to whom my countrey owes	31	E14 Camden	3
For this: that winnes, for whom he holds his peace.	38	E37 Chev'ril	4
Your noblest father prov'd: like whom, before,	53	E79 Rutland	2
On whom, if he were living now, to looke,	53	E79 Rutland	10
And unto whom: They are the almanacks	59	E92 New Crie	13
But much it now availes, what's done, of whom:	64	E99 Th Roe 2	7
And know, for whom a teare you shed,	77	E120 S. P.	3
To whom I am so bound, lov'd Aubigny?	80	E127 Aubigny	3
Even those for whom they doe this, know they erre:	83	E131 Ferrab. 2	10
By their ripe daughters, whom they would commend	95	F2 Penshurst	54
in whom the flame of every beauty raignes,	108	F10 Proludium	8
With whom who sailes, rides on the surge of feare,	110	F11 Epode	41
Nor meane we those, whom vowes and conscience	111	F11 Epode	83
Hee whom the whole world could not take,	130	U1 Nativitie	10
Either whom to love, or how?	131	U2 Excuse	16
Whom I adore so much, should so slight me,	149	U9 Picture	4
Whom never yet he durst attempt awake;	151	U11 Dreame	6
Yet choyce from whom I take them; and would shame	153	U13 Sacvile	17
The memorie delights him more, from whom	153	U13 Sacvile	21
And speaking worst of those, from whom they went	154	U13 Sacvile	51
Dam's whom he damn'd to, as the veriest Gull,	154	U13 Sacvile	57
Feed those, at whom the Table points at still?	155	U13 Sacvile	74
And you, Sir, know it well, to whom I write,	156	U13 Sacvile	109
I Know to whom I write. Here, I am sure,	158	U14 Selden	1
Upon my selfe, and aske to whom? and why?	159	U14 Selden	24
On whom I could take up, and ne're abuse	161	U14 Selden	83
Whom no great Mistresse hath as yet infam'd,	165	U15 Friend-Wars	97
A Womans friendship! God whom I trust in,	171	U20 Shrub	1
And yours of whom I sing be such	173	U22 Elegy Tho	2
In whom alone Love lives agen?	173	U22 Elegy Tho	14
By whom he is restor'd to men:	173	U22 Elegy Tho	15
To whom all Lovers are design'd,	173	U22 Elegy Tho	26
In whom Anacreon once did joy,	181	U27 Ode Helen	6
As he whom Maro did rehearse?	181	U27 Ode Helen	8
Where men may see whom I doe sing?	182	U27 Ode Helen	32

	Page	Title	Line
WHOM (cont.)			
Such are his powers, whom time hath stil'd,	189	U36 Song	13
But must confesse from whom what gift I tooke.	189	U37 Friend-Book	6
Whom Faction had not drawne to studie sides.	207	U43 Vulcan	104
Whom fashion had not drawne to studie sides.	207	U43 Vulcan	V104
Whom fashion had not taught to studie sides.	207	U43 Vulcan	V104
Whom they durst handle in their holy-day coates,	208	U43 Vulcan	127
Whom they durst handle in their high day coates,	208	U43 Vulcan	V127
From Guy, or Bevis, Arthur, or from whom	215	U44 Speach	81
Whom Fortune aided lesse, or vertue more.	217	U46 Coke	4
In his great Actions: view whom his large hand	250	U73 Weston	3
Who seldome sleepes! whom bad men only hate!	250	U73 Weston	6
Whom they have chose,	255	U75 Epithalam.	94
To whom you owe all duties of your grounds;	265	U79 New-yeares	49
Whom her Redeemer, honour'd hath above	285	U84 Muse	100
The kind of Man, on whom his doome should fall!	288	U84 Muse	208
For whom I doubly would expire,	293	U87 Hor.3:9	15
If custome please, with whom both choyse, and will,	341	Horace	V103
A Choerilus, in whom if I but see	329	Horace	534
And rack, with Wine, the man whom they would try,	333	Horace	618
Learn'd and unlearn'd; holding, whom once he takes;	337	Horace	677
Learn'd, and unlearn'd; holdeth whom once he takes;	355	Horace	V677
The Dutch whom Wealth (not Hatred) doth divide;	368	Ode Who saith	85
To whom all Scenes of Europe homage owe.	391	Shakespeare	42
Whom shee, with Sorrow first did lodge, then feast,	394	Jane Ogle	20
Whom not ten fyres, nor a Parlyament can	406	Inigo Jones 1	103
whom fortune hath deprest; come nere the fates	422	Lucan	4
whom, yf fortune hath deprest; come nere the fates	422	Lucan	V 4
whom thou seest happy; wretches flee as foes	422	Lucan	6
whom thou seest happy; wretches, shun, as foes:	422	Lucan	V 6
WHOME			
Two noble knightes, whome true desire and zeale,	382	Rich	1
May she, whome thou for spouse, to day, dost take,	384	Somerset	11
WHOORLES			
Whoorles me about, and to blaspheme in fashion!	283	U84 Muse	32
WHORE			
Where lately harbour'd many a famous whore,	29	E7 Hot-house	1
And still be a whore-house. Th'are Synonima.	29	E7 Hot-house	4
Lent him a pockie whore. Shee hath paid him.	31	E12 Shift	24
He'adulters still: his thoughts lye with a whore.	35	E26 Beast 2	2
For what shee gave, a whore; a baud, shee cures.	39	E41 Gypsee	4
Surly's old whore in her new silkes doth swim:	54	E82 Surly	1
To put out the word, whore, thou do'st me woo,	54	E83 Friend	1
For'his whore: Groyne doth still occupy his land.	75	E117 Groyne	2
'Tis there civilitie to be a whore;	163	U15 Friend-Wars	54
Nature, that will not let his Wife be a whore;	165	U15 Friend-Wars	90
I could forgive her being proud! a whore!	172	U20 Shrub	21
O no, cry'd all, Fortune, for being a whore,	209	U43 Vulcan	153
What love you then? your whore. what study? gate,	215	U44 Speach	87
These are, as some infamous Baud, or Whore,	391	Shakespeare	13
WHORE-HOUSE			
And still be a whore-house. Th'are Synonima.	29	E7 Hot-house	4
WHORES			
And be belov'd, while the Whores last. O times,	167	U15 Friend-Wars	161
WHO'S			
His choise, who's matter to his power doth reare,	339	Horace	V 58/ 56
Or, who's unskilfull at the Coit, or Ball,	331	Horace	567
Yet who's most ignorant, dares Verses make.	331	Horace	570
WHOSE			
Who scarse can spell th'hard names: whose knight lesse can.	28	E3 Bookseller	10
May none, whose scatter'd names honor my booke,	29	E9 To All	1
Whose soule heavens Queene, (whose name shee beares)	33	E22 Daughter	7
Whose every worke, of thy most earely wit,	34	E23 Donne 1	3
Whose manners draw, more than thy powers constraine.	37	E35 James 2	3
Life, whose griefe was out of fashion,	39	E40 Ratcliffe	13
Whose actions so themselves doe celebrate;	40	E43 Salisbury 1	2
For whose sake, hence-forth, all his vowes be such,	41	E45 First Son	11
Whose workes are eene the fripperie of wit,	44	E56 Poet-Ape	2
He markes not whose 'twas first: and after-times	45	E56 Poet-Ape	11
Whose house, if it no other honor had,	48	E66 Cary	3
Now, in whose pleasures I have this discerned,	55	E85 Goodyere 1	11
And land on one, whose face durst never bee	56	E88 Monsieur	5
Then Cicero, whose every breath was fame:	57	E89 Allen	6
Which thou art to thy selfe: whose fame was wonne	58	E91 Vere	5
Whose rellish to eternitie shall last.	58	E91 Vere	8
Whose rellish to eternitie will last.	58	E91 Vere	V 8
Then whose I doe not know a whiter soule,	60	E93 Radcliffe	11
Whose poemes would not wish to be your booke?	60	E94 Bedford 3	4
Whose knowledge claymeth at the helme to stand;	61	E95 Savile	21
With those that come; whose grace may make that seeme	64	E101 Supper	5
But thou, whose noblesse keeps one stature still,	66	E102 Pembroke	13
Whose life, ev'n they, that envie it, must praise;	66	E102 Pembroke	16
All-vertuous Herbert! on whose every part	68	E106 E Herbert	3
His deedes too dying, but in bookes (whose good	71	E110 Edmonds 1	15
His deedes too dying, save in bookes (whose good	71	E110 Edmonds 1	V 15
Whose name's un-welcome to the present eare,	74	E115 Honest Man	15
Jephson, thou man of men, to whose lov'd name	75	E116 Jephson	1
Whose dice not doing well, to'a pulpit ran.	76	E119 Shelton	6
Whose better studies while shee emulates,	78	E121 Rudyerd 1	3
Both whose dimensions, lost, the world might finde	79	E125 Uvedale	3
Whose noyse shall keepe thy miming most alive,	81	E129 Mime	10
The ever-boyling floud. Whose bankes upon	88	E133 Voyage	142
This way to husbands; and whose baskets beare	95	F2 Penshurst	55

		Page	Title	Line
WHOSE (cont.)				
The neede of such? whose liberall boord doth flow,		95	F2 Penshurst	59
Whose morning, and whose evening vow		99	F3 Wroth	V100
Or whose great name in Poets heaven use,		107	F10 Proludium	2
Whose linkes are bright, and even,		110	F11 Epode	48
Nor meane I those, whose vowes and conscience		111	F11 Epode	V 83
Whose od'rous breath destroyes		112	F11 Epode	96
Of some grand peere, whose ayre doth make rejoyce		113	F12 Rutland	12
Little, whose will		121	F14 Sydney	29
'T will be exacted of your name, whose sonne,		121	F14 Sydney	41
Whose nephew, whose grand-child you are;		121	F14 Sydney	42
Of whose Beautie it was sung,		131	U2 Excuse	19
Nor will he tell me for whose sake		151	U11 Dreame	7
Of him whose bones this Grave doth gather:		151	U12 Corbet	6
Reader, whose life, and name, did e're become		152	U12 Corbet	37
You then, whose will not only, but desire		153	U13 Sacvile	7
Ready to cast, at one, whose band sits ill,		164	U15 Friend-Wars	69
By those bright Eyes, at whose immortall fires		170	U19 Elegy By	1
By that tall Grove, your haire; whose globy rings		170	U19 Elegy By	5
And guided by Experience, whose straite wand		176	U24 Frontispice	11
Doth mete, whose lyne doth sound the depth of things:)		176	U24 Frontispice	12
(Whose heart in that bright Sphere flames clearest,		179	U25 Desmond	54
Whose fame hath an eternall voice?		181	U27 Ode Helen	16
Whose Offices, and honours did surprize,		185	U30 Burleigh	15
Thou art my Cause: whose manners since I knew,		187	U33 Councellour	13
Whose Readers did not thinke he was in love.		199	U42 Elegy Let	4
Whose like I have knowne the Taylors Wife put on		201	U42 Elegy Let	39
Cover'd with Tissue, whose prosperitie mocks		216	U44 Speach	100
And know whose ignorance is more then theirs;		218	U47 Tribe	24
For whose returnes, and many, all these pray:		225	U51 Bacon	6
Whose even Thred the Fates spinne round, and full,		225	U51 Bacon	15
For God, whose essence is so infinite,		236	U63 Charles 2	13
Whose lines her rowles were, and records.		247	U70 Ode	126
Whose lives her rowles were, and records.		247	U70 Ode	V126
Whose Majesties appeare,		254	U75 Epithalam.	53
Whose praises let's report unto the Woods,		265	U79 New-yeares	52
Whose Daughter? ha? Great Savage of the Rock?		269	U81 Pawlet	10
Whose 'tis: but if it favour find,		277	U84 Body	31
Whose Notions when it will expresse		279	U84 Mind	33
Whose shapes, like sick-mens dreames, are fain'd so vaine,		305	Horace	9
Whose shapes, like sick-mens dreames, are form'd so vaine,		338	Horace	V 9
What's this? if he whose money hireth thee		305	Horace	26
And what they will not. Him, whose choice doth reare		307	Horace	56
Stamp'd to the time. As woods whose change appeares		309	Horace	85
If Custome please; at whose disposing will		309	Horace	103
A foot, whose swiftnesse gave the Verse the name		323	Horace	372
Whose Note, and Hue,		366	Ode Who saith	4
(Charles Montjoy) whose command		367	Ode Who saith	50
Whose strength is above strength;		367	Ode Who saith	55
From whose prowde bosome, thou began'st thy flight.		368	Ode Who saith	80
At these thy Nuptials; but, whose heart, and thought		384	Somerset	3
Whose worke could this be, Chapman, to refine		388	Chapman	1
Phoebus, and Hermes? They whose tongue, or pen		395	May	17
The Morning-star, whose light our Fal hath stay'd.		413	Ghyrlond	40
Whose chearfull look our sadnesse doth destroy,		414	Ghyrlond	43
Whose ayre will sooner Hell, then their dull senses peirce,		420	Ode:If Men	23
WHY				
And thou, right guiltlesse, may'st plead to it, why?		36	E29 Tilter	2
But that's put in, thou'lt say. Why, so is thine.		36	E29 Tilter	6
O, could I loose all father, now. For why		41	E45 First Son	5
Where I both learn'd, why wise-men hawking follow,		55	E85 Goodyere 1	3
And why that bird was sacred to Apollo,		55	E85 Goodyere 1	4
For your next meale: this you are sure of. Why		69	E107 Hungry	27
With thy small stocke, why art thou ventring still,		72	E112 Gamster	1
You wonder, who this is! and, why I name		74	E115 Honest Man	1
Why I write not of Love.		93	F1 Why write no	Ttl
Why should we deferre our joyes?		102	F5 Celia 1	9
Why, Disease, dost thou molest		104	F8 Sicknesse	1
Till she be the reason why,		131	U2 Excuse	23
Why doe you doubt, or stay?		139	U2 Another	4
Then when 'tis made, why so will wee.		145	U5 Woman-kind	16
My wonder, why the taking a Clownes purse,		155	U13 Sacvile	89
Of our Towne Gallantry! or why there rests		155	U13 Sacvile	92
Observe the strength, the height, the why, and when,		157	U13 Sacvile	140
Upon my selfe, and aske to whom? and why?		159	U14 Selden	24
Why was't? did e're the Cloudes aske back their raine?		192	U38 Elegy 'Tis	56
None of their pleasures! nor will aske thee, why		202	U42 Elegy Let	86
And why to me this, thou lame Lord of fire,		202	U43 Vulcan	1
And why to me this, thou lame god of fire,		202	U43 Vulcan	V 1
If none of these, then why this fire? Or find		203	U43 Vulcan	27
Why yet, my noble hearts, they cannot say,		213	U44 Speach	1
Why are we rich, or great, except to show		215	U44 Speach	69
But why are all these Irons i'the fire		215	U44 Speach	93
Why? though I seeme of a prodigious wast,		226	U52 Answer	1
The Mother of our Lord: why may not I		238	U66 Queene	3
This made you first to know the Why		247	U70 Ode	107
Why doe I irritate, or stirre up thee,		250	U73 Weston	7
Earths grossenesse; There's the how, and why.		279	U84 Mind	44
our grossnesse; There's the how, and why.		279	U84 Mind	V 44
This being thus: why should my tongue, or pen		284	U84 Muse	69
But, why, oh why, my Ligurine,		293	U86 Hor.4:1	33
Or why, my well-grac'd words among,		293	U86 Hor.4:1	35
Was meant at first. Why, forcing still about		307	Horace	29

	Page	Title	Line
WHY (cont.)			
Or Varius? Why am I now envi'd so,	309	Horace	79
Nor know t'observe: why (i'the Muses name)	311	Horace	128
He knowes not why, and changeth every houre.	315	Horace	228
How then? Why, as a Scrivener, if h'offend	329	Horace	529
Why not? I'm gentle, and free-borne, doe hate	331	Horace	571
Why not? being honest, and free-borne, doth hate	352	Horace	V547/571
Why should I grieve my friend, this trifling way?	335	Horace	640
His cause of making Verses none knowes why:	335	Horace	670
Here's one makes verses, but there's none knows why:	355	Horace	V670
Then why should we dispaire? Dispaire, away:	363	Riches	17
Rather his sonne, I should have cal'd thee, why?	378	Coryat 2	88
Why much good doo't you! Be what beast you will,	403	Inigo Jones 1	21
Swim without Corke! Why, thank the good Queen Anne.	405	Inigo Jones 1	68
Or why to like; they found, it all was new,	415	Rutter	9
WHYLE			
Content thee to be Pancridge Earle the whyle;	407	Inigo Jones 2	20
WHYMSEYS			
Whirling his Whymseys, by a subtilty	405	Inigo Jones 1	73
WI'			
For, here they were throwne in wi'the melted pewter,	88	E133 Voyage	153
WICKED			
For good men but see death, the wicked tast it.	54	E80 Life/Death	8
For there the wicked in the Chaire of scorne,	223	U49 Pucell	45
ill-/Natur'd, and wicked Atreus cooke, to th'eye,	317	Horace	265
WICKEDNESSE			
That their whole life was wickednesse, though weav'd	171	U20 Shrub	10
A wild, and an authoriz'd wickednesse!	397	Drayton	46
WIDDOW			
That Cod can get no widdow, yet a knight,	33	E19 Cod 1	1
Hee that wooes every widdow, will get none.	42	E47 Luckless 2	2
WIDDOWES			
To blow up orphanes, widdowes, and their states;	99	F3 Wroth	79
WIDER			
That wider Walls embrac'd their Citie round,	319	Horace	296
WIDOW			
Widow or Wife, without the jealousie	230	U56 Covell	17
WIDOW'D			
Wherewith this while you live a widow'd wife,	224	U50 Countesse	2
WIFE			
While Beast instructs his faire, and innocent wife,	34	E25 Beast 1	1
Just wife, and, to change me, make womans hast?	34	E25 Beast 1	8
Then his chast wife, though Beast now know no more,	35	E26 Beast 2	1
He keepes anothers wife, which is a spice	36	E28 Surly	15
Were quite out-spun. The like wish hath his wife.	40	E42 Giles	12
If, now, with man and wife, to will, and nill	40	E42 Giles	16
Is this the Sir, who, some wast wife to winne,	42	E46 Luckless 1	1
Hornet, thou hast thy wife drest, for the stall,	53	E78 Hornet	1
Who, with his axe, thy fathers mid-wife plaid.	107	F10 Proludium	15
They speake; since you are truly that rare wife,	119	F13 Aubigny	110
He that will follow but anothers wife,	165	U15 Friend-Wars	87
Nature, that will not let his Wife be a whore;	165	U15 Friend-Wars	90
That which we can, who both in you, his Wife,	171	U19 Elegy By	25
Whose like I have knowne the Taylors Wife put on	201	U42 Elegy Let	39
Her presently? Or leape thy Wife of force,	201	U42 Elegy Let	44
But when thy Wife (as thou conceiv'st) is brave?	201	U42 Elegy Let	50
Nor make least line of love to thy loose Wife;	203	U43 Vulcan	6
Wherewith this while you live a widow'd wife,	224	U50 Countesse	2
A Merchants Wife is Regent of the Scale.	229	U54 Squib	4
Widow or Wife, without the jealousie	230	U56 Covell	17
Thy Wife a fit of laughter; a Cramp-ring	232	U58 Book-seller	8
Their perfum'd judgements, let them kisse thy Wife.	232	U58 Book-seller	14
. . . late Wife of Sir Kenelme Digby, Knight: . . .	272	U84 Eupheme	Ttl
A Wife, a Friend, a Lady, or a Love;	285	U84 Muse	99
A tender Mother, a discreeter Wife,	287	U84 Muse	174
But if, to boot with these, a chaste Wife meet	291	U85 Country	39
Out-bee that Wife, in worth, thy freind did make:	384	Somerset	12
And therefore I commend unto the Wife,	386	Husband	8
At least so great a Lady. She was wife	394	Jane Ogle	15
Was the example of a wife!	399	Lady Ogle	12
that the wife heades for a wager	417	Moon	26
WIFES			
Thou art jealous of thy Wifes, or Daughters Case:	202	U42 Elegy Let	87
WIGHT			
With swelling throat: and, oft, the tragick wight	311	Horace	134
But a very merry wight	416	Moon	7
WIGHTS			
I Sing the brave adventure of two wights,	84	E133 Voyage	21
WIL			
Such thoughts wil make you more in love with truth.	181	U26 Ode High	21
WILD			
Though thy wild thoughts with sparrowes wings doe flye,	111	F11 Epode	73
In all my wild desire,	151	U11 Dreame	11
Now swift, now slow, now tame, now wild;	189	U36 Song	14
That live in the wild Anarchie of Drinke,	218	U47 Tribe	10
Wild Bores into his toyles pitch'd round:	290	U85 Country	32
Yet, not as therefore wild, and tame should cleave	305	Horace	14
Medea make wild, fierce, impetuous;	342	Horace	V175
Poore Io wandring; wild Orestes mad:	313	Horace	177
Wild raging lusts; prescribe the mariage good;	327	Horace	489
A wild, and an authoriz'd wickednesse!	397	Drayton	46
WILDE			
Of building townes, and making wilde beasts tame,	82	E130 Ferrab. 1	2

791

		Page	Title	Line

WILDE (cont.)
Such, as in lustes wilde forrest love to rainge,   •   •   •   108   F10 Proludium   9
Or the wilde river, who hath changed now   •   •   •   •   309   Horace   96
WILDEST
Upon the Kerne, and wildest Irishry,   •   •   •   •   367   Ode Who saith   53
WILDLY
First frighted men, that wildly liv'd, at ods,   •   •   •   327   Horace   480
WILE
So removed by our wile?   •   •   •   •   102   F5 Celia 1   14
WILFULL
How wilfull blind is he then, that would stray,   •   •   •   53   E80 Life/Death   3
WILL   (VOLITION)
It will be look'd for, booke, when some but see   •   •   •   27   E2 My Booke   1
As chiefe of those still promise they will bee.   •   •   •   28   E4 James 1   8
For I will doe none: and as little ill,   •   •   •   30   E11 Something   7
For I will dare none. Good Lord, walke dead still.   •   •   •   30   E11 Something   8
He will both argue, and discourse in oathes,   •   •   •   35   E28 Surly   9
Nay more, for greatnesse sake, he will be one   •   •   •   36   E28 Surly   19
By his free will, be in Jones company.   •   •   •   •   40   E42 Giles   5
If, now, with man and wife, to will, and nill   •   •   •   40   E42 Giles   16
Will man lament the state he should envie?   •   •   •   41   E45 First Son   6
Hee that wooes every widdow, will get none.   •   •   •   42   E47 Luckless 2   2
Get him the times long grudge, the courts ill will;   •   •   •   48   E65 Muse   7
Still, 'tis his lucke to praise me 'gainst his will.   •   •   •   50   E71 Parrat   2
Forbeare to tempt me, Proule, I will not show   •   •   •   54   E81 Proule   1
Longer a day, but with his Mill will marry.   •   •   •   57   E90 Mill   16
That thou hast kept thy love, encreast thy will,   •   •   •   63   E99 Th Roe 2   1
For, if the hum'rous world will talke at large,   •   •   •   83   E131 Ferrab. 2   7
But I will speake (and know I shall be heard)   •   •   •   87   E133 Voyage   105
But you will visit grisly Pluto's hall?   •   •   •   89   E133 Voyage   175
But I will beare these, with that scorne,   •   •   •   102   F4 To the World   63
Let her alone, shee will court you.   •   •   •   104   F7 Women but   4
Or if needs thy lust will tast   •   •   •   •   105   F8 Sicknesse   15
Will by coach, and water goe,   •   •   •   •   105   F8 Sicknesse   37
Though never after; whiles it gaynes the will   •   •   •   113   F12 Rutland   V 11
But let this drosse carry what price it will   •   •   •   114   F12 Rutland   27
Almost you have, or may have, when you will?   •   •   •   114   F12 Rutland   34
Let who will follow fashions, and attyres,   •   •   •   118   F13 Aubigny   71
You are depending on his word, and will;   •   •   •   119   F13 Aubigny   114
Little, whose will   •   •   •   •   121   F14 Sydney   29
If you then will read the Storie,   •   •   •   131   U2 Excuse   13
Let who will thinke us dead, or wish our death.   •   •   •   139   U2 Another   18
Nor will he tell me for whose sake   •   •   •   151   U11 Dreame   7
But was by sweetning so his will,   •   •   •   151   U12 Corbet   13
That they for me their teares will shed;   •   •   •   152   U12 Corbet   34
You then, whose will not only, but desire   •   •   •   153   U13 Sacvile   7
Against his will that do's 'hem? that hath weav'd   •   •   •   153   U13 Sacvile   26
O, is it so? knowes he so much? and will   •   •   •   155   U13 Sacvile   73
No! he must feele and know, that will advance.   •   •   •   156   U13 Sacvile   123
Their difference, cannot choose which you will be.   •   •   •   157   U13 Sacvile   154
Meane what I speake: and still will keepe that Vow.   •   •   •   159   U14 Selden   28
Or faith in things? or is't your wealth and will   •   •   •   159   U14 Selden   36
That payes, or what he will: The Dame is steele.   •   •   •   164   U15 Friend-Wars   78
He that will follow but anothers wife,   •   •   •   165   U15 Friend-Wars   87
Nature, that will not let his Wife be a whore;   •   •   •   165   U15 Friend-Wars   90
Can we not leave this worme? or will we not?   •   •   •   166   U15 Friend-Wars   141
I'le lead you on; or if my fate will so,   •   •   •   170   U18 Elegy Can   22
Who aided him, will thee, the issue of Joves braine.   •   •   •   175   U23 Himselfe   30
Who aided them, will thee, the issue of Joves braine.   •   •   •   175   U23 Himselfe   V 30
In will and power, only to defeate.   •   •   •   191   U38 Elegy 'Tis   18
The Herald will. Our blood is now become   •   •   •   215   U44 Speach   82
And force back that, which will not be restor'd,   •   •   •   219   U47 Tribe   40
Live to that point I will, for which I am man,   •   •   •   219   U47 Tribe   59
And that he will venter   •   •   •   •   231   U57 Burges   5
Hee can, he will, and with large int'rest pay,   •   •   •   236   U63 Charles 2   5
What (at his liking) he will take away.   •   •   •   236   U63 Charles 2   6
That the Almighties will to you is such: •   •   •   236   U63 Charles 2   8
And thinke all still the best, that he will doe.   •   •   •   236   U63 Charles 2   10
That thought shall make, he will this losse supply   •   •   •   236   U63 Charles 2   11
Cannot but heape that grace, he will requite.   •   •   •   236   U63 Charles 2   14
His Poet Sack, the House-hold will not pay?   •   •   •   241   U68 House-hold   2
Yet, as we may, we will, with chast desires,   •   •   •   257   U75 Epithalam.   161
Whose Notions when it will expresse   •   •   •   279   U84 Mind   33
And will you, worthy Sonne, Sir, knowing this,   •   •   •   285   U84 Muse   97
Who reades, will pardon my Intelligence,   •   •   •   289   U84 Muse   226
Will to bee, what thou art; and nothing more: •   •   •   295   U90 Mart.10:47   12
Upon your shoulders. Prove what they will beare,   •   •   •   307   Horace   55
Prove what your shoulders will, or will not beare.   •   •   •   339   Horace   V 57/ 55
And what they will not. Him, whose choice doth reare   •   •   •   307   Horace   56
If Custome please; at whose disposing will   •   •   •   309   Horace   103
If custome please, with whom both choyse, and will,   •   •   •   341   Horace   V103
The Comick matter will not be exprest   •   •   •   311   Horace   121
In Helicon; a great sort will not pare   •   •   •   325   Horace   422
There words will follow, not against their will.   •   •   •   325   Horace   444
There words will never follow 'gainst their will.   •   •   •   349   Horace   V444
Will in the light be view'd: This, once, the sight   •   •   •   331   Horace   543
Alone, without a rivall, by his will.   •   •   •   335   Horace   632
Alone, without a rivall, at your will.   •   •   •   354   Horace   V632
Let Poets perish, that will not be kept.   •   •   •   335   Horace   664
Hee that preserves a man, against his will,   •   •   •   335   Horace   665
But who will beleeve this, that chanceth to looke   •   •   •   379   Coryat 3   17
Why much good doo't you! Be what beast you will,   •   •   •   403   Inigo Jones 1   21
Whither? oh whither will this Tire-man growe?   •   •   •   404   Inigo Jones 1   59

WILL (cont.)

	Page	Title	Line
Thou art not worth it. Who will care to knowe	409	Detractor	13
deignes myne the power to find, yett want I will	421	Censure	10
he that will honest be, may quitt the Court,	423	Lucan	17
And sworne, that he will quite discard thee	662	Bedford	7

WILL (See also 'LE, 'LL, 'LT, 'TWIL)

	Page	Title	Line
If, without these vile arts, it will not sell,	28	E3 Bookseller	11
No cause, nor client fat, will Chev'rill leese,	38	E37 Chev'ril	1
Foole, as if halfe eyes will not know a fleece	45	E56 Poet-Ape	13
That can restore that. Will it hurt your feature?	46	E62 Would-bee	7
Make it your gift. See whither that will beare mee.	55	E84 Redford 2	10
Hath got the stewards chaire; he will not tarry	57	E90 Mill	15
Whose rellish to eternitie will last.	58	E91 Vere	V 8
If the States make peace, how it will goe	59	E92 New Crie	30
And of the poulder-plot, they will talke yet.	59	E92 New Crie	32
But that your worth will dignifie our feast,	64	E101 Supper	4
Ile tell you of more, and lye, so you will come:	65	E101 Supper	17
That will the pastrie, not my paper, show of.	65	E101 Supper	26
Digestive cheese, and fruit there sure will bee;	65	E101 Supper	27
Of this we will sup free, but moderately,	65	E101 Supper	35
And we will have no Pooly', or Parrot by;	65	E101 Supper	36
But, at our parting, we will be, as when	65	E101 Supper	38
Not that I love it, more, then I will you.	68	E107 Hungry	4
Will you part with them, here, unthriftely?	69	E107 Hungry	28
Thy deedes, unto thy name, will prove new wombes,	70	E109 Nevil	17
Which all, but ignorant Captaynes, will confesse:	72	E111 Edmonds 2	7
Yet thou, perhaps, shalt meet some tongues will grutch,	72	E111 Edmonds 2	9
It will deny all; and forsweare it too:	74	E115 Honest Man	19
Not that it feares, but will not have to doo	74	E115 Honest Man	20
For, then, all mouthes will judge, and their owne way:	82	E131 Ferrab. 2	3
As his will now be the translation thought,	83	E132 Sylvester	12
Row close then, slaves. Alas, they will beshite us.	86	E133 Voyage	90
Touching this cause, where they will be affeard	87	E133 Voyage	106
What (great, I will not say, but) sodayne cheare	95	F2 Penshurst	82
Now, Penshurst, they that will proportion thee	96	F2 Penshurst	99
And never will redeeme a day,	100	F4 To the World	23
Nor for my peace will I goe farre,	102	F4 To the World	65
Time will not be ours, for ever:	102	F5 Celia 1	3
He, at length, our good will sever.	102	F5 Celia 1	4
He, at length, our blisse will sever.	102	F5 Celia 1	V 4
All your bounties will betray.	103	F6 Celia 2	4
Seeme to flye it, it will pursue:	104	F7 Women but	2
Scarce will take our present store?	105	F8 Sicknesse	11
Scarce will take our present score?	105	F8 Sicknesse	V 11
And this age will build no more:	105	F8 Sicknesse	12
These, disease, will thee deserve:	106	F8 Sicknesse	43
These, disease, will they deserve:	106	F8 Sicknesse	V 43
And will, long ere thou should'st starve,	106	F8 Sicknesse	44
And I will pledge with mine;	106	F9 Celia 3	2
Nor will I beg of thee, Lord of the vine,	107	F10 Proludium	10
Nor will we beg of thee, Lord of the vine,	107	F10 Proludium	V 10
Will quickly taste the treason, and commit	109	F11 Epode	15
Turtles will chastly dye;	111	F11 Epode	V 74
That knowes the waight of guilt: He will refraine	112	F11 Epode	113
To every squire, or groome, that will report	113	F12 Rutland	6
The foole that gave it; who will want, and weepe,	113	F12 Rutland	13
The foole that gave it; that will want, and weepe,	113	F12 Rutland	V 13
With you, I know, my offring will find grace.	114	F12 Rutland	30
Will prove old Orpheus act no tale to be:	115	F12 Rutland	77
Will prove old Orpheus Arts no tale to be:	115	F12 Rutland	V 77
You will not from the paper slightly passe:	117	F13 Aubigny	25
Looke then, and see your selfe. I will not say	117	F13 Aubigny	29
'T will be exacted of your name, whose sonne,	121	F14 Sydney	41
Will, then,	121	F14 Sydney	44
Once more, and (faith) I will be gone,	139	U2 Another	7
I will but mend the last, and tell	139	U2 Another	13
For I will so urge you to't,	140	U2 Promise	14
Nay, I will not let you sit	140	U2 Promise	21
I will tell what Man would please me.	140	U2 Her man	2
Sleepe, and the Grave will wake.	143	U3 Musicall	14
For then their threats will kill me;	144	U4 Song	6
For then my hopes will spill me.	144	U4 Song	8
For so will sorrow slay me;	145	U4 Song	10
Then when 'tis made, why so will wee.	145	U5 Woman-kind	16
If ever we will love aright.	146	U6 Defence	10
Will be my Rivall, though she have but eares.	148	U7 Nymph	28
I ne're will owe my health to a disease.	150	U10 Jealousie	16
This Good from you, as freely will it owe;	153	U13 Sacvile	14
No more then he doth thanke, that will receive	154	U13 Sacvile	43
Ha's Feathers, and will serve a man to pull.	154	U13 Sacvile	58
Many a pound, and piece, will place one well;	155	U13 Sacvile	78
As they are high; are rooted, and will last.	157	U13 Sacvile	144
Which you will bury; but therein, the strife	158	U13 Sacvile	160
It true respects. He will not only love,	161	U14 Selden	73
His time? health? soule? will he for these goe throw	165	U15 Friend-Wars	103
Sweet bags, sweet Powders, nor sweet words will passe	165	U15 Friend-Wars	112
Brought on us, and will every hour increase.	166	U15 Friend-Wars	122
That may stand by, and hold my peace? will he,	167	U15 Friend-Wars	150
And I will bring a Crop, if not the best.	169	U17 Friend-Debt	18
I know no beautie, nor no youth that will.	171	U19 Elegy By	20
were such as I will now relate, or worse?	172	U20 Shrub	14
Pyracmon's houre will come to give them ease,	179	U25 Desmond	42
An hower will come they must affect theyr Ease,	179	U25 Desmond	V 42

```
WILL (cont.)
   Gold, that is perfect, will out-live the fire.    .    .    .  179  U25 Desmond      45
   That you will stand        .     .     .     .    .    .    .  180  U25 Desmond      64
   Yet sure my tunes will be the best,               .    .    .  182  U27 Ode Helen    35
   They will come of, and scape the Punishment.      .    .    .  186  U32 Elsmere      14
   And make the Scarre faire; If that will not be,   .    .    .  187  U33 Councellour  21
   But in a businesse, that will bide the Touch,     .    .    .  187  U33 Councellour  23
   Which, how most sacred I will ever keepe,         .    .    .  190  U37 Friend-Book  13
   Will unto Licence that faire leave abuse.         .    .    .  190  U37 Friend-Book  24
   I will not stand to justifie my fault,            .    .    .  191  U38 Elegy 'Tis   21
   No, I will stand arraign'd, and cast, to be       .    .    .  191  U38 Elegy 'Tis   27
   And (stil'd your mercies Creature) will live more .    .    .  191  U38 Elegy 'Tis   29
   Or two, or three, a Sonne will dis-inherit,       .    .    .  192  U38 Elegy 'Tis   42
   I will no more abuse my vowes to you,             .    .    .  194  U38 Elegy 'Tis  107
   Then I will studie falshood, to be true.          .    .    .  194  U38 Elegy 'Tis  108
   Where he that knowes will, like a Lapwing, flie   .    .    .  198  U40 Elegy That   37
   To others, as he will deserve the Trust           .    .    .  198  U40 Elegy That   39
   My health will leave me; and when you depart,     .    .    .  199  U41 Elegy Since  13
   For Silke will draw some sneaking Songster thither..    .    .  200  U42 Elegy Let    26
   None of their pleasures! nor will aske thee, why  .    .    .  202  U42 Elegy Let    86
   I will not argue thee, from those, of guilt,      .    .    .  210  U43 Vulcan      165
   I will not argue thee, from them, of guilt,       .    .    .  210  U43 Vulcan     V165
   I will not argue thee Iron. Them of guilt         .    .    .  210  U43 Vulcan     V165
   Will be remembred by Six Clerkes, to one.         .    .    .  210  U43 Vulcan      172
   Light on thee: Or if those plagues will not doo,  .    .    .  212  U43 Vulcan      215
   Light upon thee: Or if those plagues will not doo,.    .    .  212  U43 Vulcan     V215
   We will beleeve, like men of our owne Ranke,      .    .    .  215  U44 Speach       75
   But these with wearing will themselves unfold:    .    .    .  216  U45 Squib        19
   Or th'other on their borders, that will jeast     .    .    .  218  U47 Tribe        16
   These I will honour, love, embrace, and serve:    .    .    .  220  U47 Tribe        71
   My selfe a little.  I will take you so,           .    .    .  220  U47 Tribe        76
   The wits will leave you, if they once perceive    .    .    .  223  U49 Pucell       37
   Will cal't a Bastard, when a Prophet's borne.     .    .    .  223  U49 Pucell       46
   It will be shame for them, if they have none.     .    .    .  225  U50 Countesse    36
   To all posteritie; I will write Burlase.          .    .    .  227  U52 Answer       24
   Is, she will play Dame Justice, too severe;       .    .    .  229  U54 Squib         8
   The first of which, I feare, you will refuse;     .    .    .  230  U56 Covell        6
   The first of which, I doubt, you will refuse;     .    .    .  230  U56 Covell      V  6
   Will come at the Court,     .     .     .     .    .    .    .  231  U57 Burges       20
   Will come to the Table,     .     .     .     .    .    .    .  232  U57 Burges       23
   The Parish will know it.    .     .     .     .    .    .    .  232  U57 Burges       26
   If the 'Chequer be emptie, so will be his Head.   .    .    .  232  U57 Burges       28
   Will be reward enough: to weare like those,       .    .    .  232  U58 Book-seller   9
   That nothing will her gratitude provoke.          .    .    .  237  U64 Charles 3  V 16
   Are lost upon accompt! And none will know         .    .    .  237  U64 Charles 3    21
   Sol will re-shine.  If not, Charles hath a Sonne. .    .    .  238  U65 Prince       12
   And Sol will shine.  If not, Charles hath a Sonne..    .    .  238  U65 Prince     V 12
   O how will then our Court be pleas'd,             .    .    .  251  U74 Weston       25
   gentlie hee asketh, shee will pay: no suits,      .    .    .  258  U75 Epithalam. V188
   Will last till day;         .     .     .     .    .    .    .  258  U75 Epithalam.  190
   Night, and the sheetes will show                  .    .    .  258  U75 Epithalam.  191
   In signe the Subject, and the Song will live,     .    .    .  262  U78 Digby       17
   He will cleare up his forehead, thinke thou bring'st   .    .  263  U78 Digby       21
   He will cheare up his forehead, thinke thou bring'st   .    .  263  U78 Digby     V 21
   For hee doth love my Verses, and will looke       .    .    .  263  U78 Digby       23
   And praise them too.  O! what a fame 't will be?  .    .    .  263  U78 Digby       25
   Allowes them? Then, what copies will be had,      .    .    .  263  U78 Digby     V 29
   Being sent to one, they will be read of all.      .    .    .  263  U78 Digby       32
   And the disposure will be something new,          .    .    .  269  U81 Pawlet      16
   And the disposure will be somewhat new,           .    .    .  269  U81 Pawlet    V 16
   Next sitting we will draw her mind.               .    .    .  277  U84 Body        32
   Beside, your hand will never hit,                 .    .    .  277  U84 Mind         7
   Which Vertue from your Father, ripe, will fall;   .    .    .  282  U84 Kenelme     22
   Who will be there, against that day prepar'd,     .    .    .  284  U84 Muse        59
   Will honour'd be in all simplicitie!              .    .    .  284  U84 Muse        76
   When shee departed? you will meet her there,      .    .    .  285  U84 Muse       108
   Where Hee will be, all Beautie to the Sight;      .    .    .  286  U84 Muse       122
   A Musique in the Eares, will ever last;           .    .    .  286  U84 Muse       124
   Hee will all Glory, all Perfection be,            .    .    .  286  U84 Muse       127
   Will there revealed be in Majestie!               .    .    .  286  U84 Muse       130
   Where first his Power will appeare, by call       .    .    .  286  U84 Muse       220
   Will he display the Ensignes of thy warre.        .    .    .  289  U84 Muse       220
   For lust will languish, and that heat decay.      .    .    .  292  U86 Hor.4:1     16
   This hath pleas'd, doth please, and long will please; never  .  294  U88 Petronius    5
   Sleepe, that will make the darkest howres swift-pac't;   .    .  294  U88 Petronius    9
   Nor language, nor cleere order will forsake.      .    .    .  295  U90 Mart.10:47   11
   Of the Cethegi; And all men will grace,           .    .    .  339  Horace     V 59/ 58
   A Roman to Caecilius will allow,                  .    .    .  309  Horace           72
   And ever will, to utter termes that bee           .    .    .  309  Horace           77
   Thy selfe in teares, then me thy losse will wound,.    .    .  309  Horace           84
   Thy selfe in tears, then me thy harms will wound, .    .    .  311  Horace          146
   And Roman Gentrie, jearing, will laugh out.       .    .    .  342  Horace         V146
   And Roman Gentrie, will with laughter shout.      .    .    .  313  Horace          160
   It much will differ, if a God speake, than,       .    .    .  342  Horace         V160
   It much will sway whether a god speak, than;      .    .    .  313  Horace          161
   Much from the sight, which faire report will make .    .    .  342  Horace         V161
   Nor I, when I write Satyres, will so love         .    .    .  317  Horace          262
   Meere raigning words: nor will I labour so        .    .    .  321  Horace          341
   Will take offence, at this: Nor, though it strike .    .    .  321  Horace          343
   The nut-crackers throughout, will they therefore  .    .    .  321  Horace          361
   I, writing nought my selfe, will teach them yet   .    .    .  321  Horace          363
   There words will follow, not against their will.  .    .    .  325  Horace          435
   There words will never follow 'gainst their will. .    .    .  325  Horace          444
                                                     .    .    .  349  Horace         V444

                                   794
```

WILL (cont.)

What height of love, a Parent will fit best,   . . . 325 Horace 447
There's Albin's sonne will say, Substract an ounce . . . 327 Horace 467
This booke will get the Sosii money; This . . . . 329 Horace 517
Will passe the Seas, and long as nature is, . . . 329 Horace 518
The hand, and mind would, but it will resound . . . 329 Horace 522
Much in the Poeme shine, I will not bee . . . 329 Horace 526
Still in the same, and warned will not mend, . . . 329 Horace 530
Will take you more, the neerer that you stand; . . . 331 Horace 540
Doth please; this, ten times over, will delight. . . . 331 Horace 544
Nature, or Art. My Judgement will not pierce . . . 331 Horace 582
Will be a suretie; or can helpe him out . . . 333 Horace 603
A wise, and honest man will cry out shame . . . 335 Horace 633
A good and wise man will crye open shame . . . 354 Horace V633
On artlesse Verse; the hard ones he will blame; . . . 335 Horace 634
There's none will take the care, to helpe him then; . . . 335 Horace 654
So with this Authors Readers will it thrive: . . . 362 Author 12
His proofe their praise, will meete, as in this line. . . . 362 Author 14
Will well confesse; presenting, limiting, . . . 370 Author 6
He will expiate this sinne with converting the Jewes. . . . 375 Coryat 1 21
F. shewes what he was, K. what he will bee. . . . 375 Coryat 1 29
Which, unto all Ages, for his will be knowne, . . . 379 Coryat 3 11
Nay more in his wardrobe, if you will laugh at a . . . 380 Coryat 3 47
I know for such, as (if my word will waigh) . . . 386 Husband 11
will all turne dust, & may not make me swell. . . . 387 Cavendish 4
Will all be dust, & may not make me swell. . . . 387 Cavendish V 4
it will be matter lowd inoughe to tell . . . 387 Cavendish 11
Upon it, but will loath, or let it passe, . . . 389 Aleman 9
Will bee receiv'd in Court; If not, would I . . . 389 Aleman 19
I, therefore will begin. Soule of the Age! . . . 391 Shakespeare 17
My Shakespeare, rise; I will not lodge thee by . . . 391 Shakespeare 19
As, since, she will vouchsafe no other Wit. . . . 392 Shakespeare 50
Nay they will venter ones Descent to hitt, . . . 394 Jane Ogle 11
This second marriage, will aeternall make. . . . 394 Jane Ogle 26
The selfe same Genius! so the worke will say. . . . 395 May 23
About the towne: this reck'ning I will pay, . . . 396 Drayton 9
Brave are the Musters, that the Muse will make. . . . 398 Drayton 64
And will be bought of every Lord, and Knight, . . . 398 Drayton 72
Of tender eyes will more be wept, then seene: . . . 398 Drayton 76
This Booke will live; It hath a Genius: This . . . 400 Beaumont 1
Will any of these express your place? or witt? . . . 402 Inigo Jones 1 18
your Trappings will not change you. Change your mynd. . . . 403 Inigo Jones 1 25
Noe velvet Sheath you weare, will alter kynde. . . . 403 Inigo Jones 1 26
Will well designe thee, to be viewd of all . . . 408 Inigo Jones 3 12
No man will tarry by thee, as hee goes, . . . 409 Detractor 17
Now each Court-Hobby-horse will wince in rime; . . . 410 Brome 11
shee soone will heare it. . . . 417 Moon 24
the Moone will beare it. . . . 417 Moon 28
shee will not seise it. . . . 418 Moon 44
Whose ayre will sooner Hell, then their dull senses peirce, . . . 420 Ode:If Men 23
Will unto Lycence, that free Leave Abuse: . . . 422 Censure 17

WILL'D

The Fathers wisedome will'd it so, . . . 130 U1 Nativitie 13

WILLIAM

To William Camden. . . . 31 E14 Camden Ttl
To William Lord Mounteagle. . . . 46 E60 Mounteagle Ttl
To William Roe. . . . 50 E70 Wm Roe 1 Ttl
To William Earle of Pembroke. . . . 66 E102 Pembroke Ttl
To Sir William Jephson. . . . 75 E116 Jephson Ttl
To Sir William Uvedale. . . . 79 E125 Uvedale Ttl
To William Roe. . . . 80 E128 Wm Roe 2 Ttl
Ode. To Sir William Sydney, on his Birth-day. . . . 120 F14 Sydney Ttl
An Epigram On William Lord Burl: . . . . 185 U30 Burleigh Ttl
An Epigram. To William, Earle of Newcastle. . . . 228 U53 Newcastle Ttl
To the Right Honorable William Viscount Mansfield: . . . 228 U53 Newcastle VTtl
An Epigram. To William Earle of Newcastle. . . . 232 U59 Newcastle Ttl
To the Right Honorable William Earle of Newcastle. . . . 232 U59 Newcastle VTtl
. . . Mr. William Shakespeare: And what he hath left us. . . . 390 Shakespeare Ttl

WILLING

Sure, willing povertie lives most in you. . . . 29 E6 Alchymists 2
Willing to expiate the fault in thee, . . . 60 E93 Radcliffe 15
And, for thy messe, is willing to be kill'd. . . . 94 F2 Penshurst 30

WILLINGLY

Venter a longer time, and willingly: . . . 169 U17 Friend-Debt 15

WILLS

Both wills were in one stature; . . . 130 U1 Nativitie 15

WILT (VOLITION)

Goe high, or low, as thou wilt value it. . . . 50 E72 Court-ling 4
But thou wilt yet a Kinglier mastrie trie, . . . 235 U62 Charles 1 5
Thou sluggish spawne, that canst, but wilt not see? . . . 250 U73 Weston 8

WILT

Love, if thou wilt ever see . . . 132 U2 How he saw 7
So, 'live or dead, thou wilt preserve a fame . . . 168 U15 Friend-Wars 189
Foole, wilt thou let that in example come? . . . 210 U43 Vulcan 161
Thou, Friend, wilt heare all censures; unto thee . . . 232 U58 Book-seller 1
Stay, thou wilt see what rites the Virgins doe! . . . 254 U75 Epithalam. 49
Search, Sun, and thou wilt find, . . . 255 U75 Epithalam. 79
Wilt thou be, Muse, when this shall them befall? . . . 263 U78 Digby 31
Wilt thou be, Muse, when this shall them befall? . . . 263 U78 Digby V 31
Wilt nothing against nature speake, or doe: . . . 331 Horace 574

WIN (See also WYNNS)

Think'st thou it is meere fortune, that can win? . . . 72 E112 Gamster 3
A subtle thing, that doth affections win . . . 74 E115 Honest Man 7

			Page	Title	Line
WIN (cont.)					
As sure to win			130	U1 Father	31
The contrite Soule, who hath no thought to win			193	U38 Elegy 'Tis	89
Fix'd to the bed, and boords, unlike to win			248	U71 Treasurer	11
Fix'd to the bed, and borde, and like to win			248	U71 Treasurer	V 11
As fit t'exchange discourse; a Verse to win			311	Horace	119
They are a Schoole to win			402	Filmer	11
Our great reward, th'aeternall Crown to win.			412	Sutcliffe	19
WINCE					
Now each Court-Hobby-horse will wince in rime;			410	Brome	11
WINCHESTER					
Of Winchester; the Heralds can tell this:			269	U81 Pawlet	20
Of Winchester; the Heralds could tell this:			269	U81 Pawlet	V 20
WINCHESTRIAN					
That was rak'd up in the Winchestrian Goose			209	U43 Vulcan	142
Which was rak'd up in the Winchestrian Goose			209	U43 Vulcan	V142
That was lock'd up in the Winchestrian Goose			209	U43 Vulcan	V142
WIND					
Is this we heare? of frogs? No, guts wind-bound,			86	E133 Voyage	92
Sonne of the Wind! for so thy mother gone			208	U43 Vulcan	111
Should he heare of billow, wind, and storme,			214	U44 Speach	63
In action, winged as the wind,			280	U84 Mind	65
Begotten by that wind, and showers.			280	U84 Mind	68
Mov'd by the wind, so comely moved she.			287	U84 Muse	166
WIND-BOUND					
Is this we heare? of frogs? No, guts wind-bound,			86	E133 Voyage	92
WINDE					
And makes her supple feete, as swift as winde.			363	Riches	12
That part nor Winde,			366	Ode Who saith	28
WINDES					
May windes as soft as breath of kissing friends,			81	E128 Wm Roe 2	5
WINDIE					
Laxative lettuce, and such windie meate)			88	E133 Voyage	167
WINDING					
Or Tybers winding streames, I follow thee.			293	U86 Hor.4:1	40
WINDOW					
No, nor forth your window peepe,			140	U2 Promise	16
To hang a window, or make darke the roome,			282	U84 Muse	7
WINDOWES					
Or in their windowes; doe but prove the wombs,			114	F12 Rutland	46
When not the Shops, but windowes doe display			202	U42 Elegy Let	78
With slyding windowes, & false Lights a top!			407	Inigo Jones 2	10
WINDS					
Then when flowers, and West-winds meet,			137	U2 Cupid	28
Or winds the Spirit, by which the flower so grew?			192	U38 Elegy 'Tis	58
Made loftier by the Winds all noises else,			249	U72 King	V 12
The rudest Winds obey the calmest Ayre:			251	U74 Weston	9
WINE (See also WYNE)					
For then, our water-conduits doe runne wine;			36	E29 Tilter	5
I fancied to my selfe, what wine, what wit			55	E84 Bedford 2	6
Limons, and wine for sauce: to these, a coney			65	E101 Supper	13
Is a pure cup of rich Canary-wine,			65	E101 Supper	29
Where the same beere, and bread, and selfe-same wine,			95	F2 Penshurst	63
And Ile not looke for wine.			106	F9 Celia 3	4
And Ile expect no wine.			106	F9 Celia 3	V 4
To raise my spirits with thy conjuring wine,			107	F10 Proludium	11
To raise our spirits with thy conjuring wine,			107	F10 Proludium	V 11
As neither wine doe rack it out, or mirth.			197	U40 Elegy That	18
Weaknesse of braine, or any charme of Wine,			198	U40 Elegy That	45
The fire, the wine, the men! and in the midst,			225	U51 Bacon	3
But since the Wine hath steep'd my braine,			230	U55 Burges	5
Or Wine to enable			232	U57 Burges	24
Call, noble Lucius, then for Wine,			245	U70 Ode	75
Made lighter with the Wine. All noises else,			249	U72 King	12
Wine, or delicious fruits, unto the Taste;			286	U84 Muse	123
And from the sweet Tub Wine of this yeare takes,			291	U85 Country	47
Darke thy cleare glasse with old Falernian Wine;			295	U89 Mart.8:77	5
Steepe the glad Genius in the Wine, whole dayes,			319	Horace	298
With lees of Wine. Next Eschylus, more late,			319	Horace	315
And both from Wine, and Women did abstaine.			333	Horace	590
And rack, with Wine, the man whom they would try,			333	Horace	618
Their cares in wine; with sure			368	Ode Who saith	87
Whoe worthie wine, whoe not, to bee wyse Pallas guests.			421	Ode:If Men	45
Truth itself doth flow in Wine.			657	Door Apollo	6
Wine it is the Milk of Venus,			657	Door Apollo	12
WINES					
Of Wines, to thee the rather			220	U48 Bacchus	2
Fresh Lovers businesse, and the Wines free source.			311	Horace	116
WING					
Great heav'n did well, to give ill fame free wing;			43	E51 James 3	2
My owne true fire. Now my thought takes wing,			108	F10 Proludium	29
Our owne true fire. Now our thought takes wing,			108	F10 Proludium	V 29
Marke, marke, but when his wing he takes,			366	Ode Who saith	9
From thence, display thy wing againe			367	Ode Who saith	41
Now must we plie our ayme; our Swan's on wing.			368	Ode Who saith	64
With Cupids wing;			369	Ode Who saith	100
WINGE					
the glories of yt. Now our muse takes winge,			108	F10 Proludium	15
WINGED					
In action, winged as the wind,			280	U84 Mind	65
WINGS					
I weare not these my wings in vaine.			93	F1 Why write no	7
Though thy wild thoughts with sparrowes wings doe flye,			111	F11 Epode	73

		Page	Title	Line

WINGS (cont.)
Where I sit and proyne my wings . . . . . 137 U2 Cupid 35
For Loves fingers, and his wings: . . . . 141 U2 Her man 12
He flying curles, and crispeth, with his wings; . . 170 U19 Elegy By 6
Wake, and put on the wings of Pindars Muse, . . 176 U25 Desmond 3
WINK'D
And, hood-wink'd, for a man, embrace a post. . . 45 E58 Groome 8
WINKE
Can come from Tripoly, leape stooles, and winke, . . 74 F115 Honest Man 11
Or Love, or Fortune blind, when they but winke . . 170 U18 Elegy Can 16
WINNE
Is this the Sir, who, some wast wife to winne, . . 42 F46 Luckless 1 1
Let thousands more goe flatter vice, and winne, . . 99 F3 Wroth 85
What comfort by him doe wee winne, ... 130 U1 Nativitie 19
WINNES
For this: that winnes, for whom he holds his peace. . . 38 E37 Chev'ril 4
WINTER
And, in the winter, hunt'st the flying hare, . . 97 F3 Wroth 29
Or in the winter, hunt'st the flying hare, . . 97 F3 Wroth V 29
Winter is come a Quarter e're his Time, . . . 199 U41 Elegy Since 12
If with bright floods, the Winter troubled much, . . 291 U85 Country 51
If with East floods, the Winter troubled much, . . 291 U85 Country V 51
WINTON
An Elegie On the Lady Jane Pawlet, Marchion: of Winton. . 268 U81 Pawlet Ttl
WINTRY
Are gathering by the Wintry houres; . . . . 290 U85 Country 30
WIP'D
Simo; and, of a talent wip'd his purse; . . . 321 Horace 347
WIRE (See WYRES)
WISDOME
In sharpnesse of all Search, wisdome of Choise, . . 160 U14 Selden 59
'Tis wisdome, and that high, ... 181 U26 Ode High 22
Dar'st not abuse thy wisdome, in the Lawes, . . 187 U33 Councellour 17
O may your wisdome take example hence, . . . 193 U38 Elegy 'Tis 67
The Wisdome, Madam, of your private Life, . . . 224 U50 Countesse 1
In raysing him the wisdome of my King. . . . 225 U51 Bacon 20
That Mine of Wisdome, and of Counsells deep, . . 255 U75 Epithalam. 98
His Wisdome, and his Justice, in that houre, . . 288 U84 Muse 218
Of all are dead to life! His Wisdome show . . . 289 U84 Muse 221
This was the wisdome, that they had of old, . . 327 Horace 486
WISE (See also WYSE)
Guiltie, be wise; and though thou know'st the crimes . 36 E30 Guiltie 1
Guiltie, because I bad you late be wise, . . . 38 E38 Guiltie 2 1
Long-gathering Old-end, I did feare thee wise, . . 43 E53 Old-end 1
And not to dangers. When so wise a king . . . 47 E64 Salisbury 3 12
And no lesse wise, then skilfull in the lawes; . . 52 E74 Chancelor 6
I meant to make her faire, and free, and wise, . . 52 E76 Bedford 5
Where I both learn'd, why wise-men hawking follow, . . 55 E85 Goodyere 1 3
But, in your love, made all his servants wise. . . 74 E114 Sydney 8
The world's pure gold, and wise simplicitie; . . 78 E122 Rudyerd 2 4
Wherein wise Nature you a dowrie gave, . . . 114 F12 Rutland 35
And, in those outward formes, all fooles are wise. . . 117 F13 Aubigny 36
For he must looke wanton-wise. . . . . . 141 U2 Her man 16
Wise Providence would so; that nor the good . . 176 U24 Frontispice 5
Cecill, the grave, the wise, the great, the good, . . 185 U30 Burleigh 5
Of that wise Nature would a Cradle have. . . . 192 U38 Elegy 'Tis 60
Well fare the wise-men yet, on the Banckside, . . 208 U43 Vulcan 123
O happy Art! and wise Epitome . . . . . 214 U44 Speach 43
Sonne to the grave wise Keeper of the Seale, . . 225 U51 Bacon 9
His judgement is; If he be wise, and praise, . . 232 U58 Book-seller 5
Wise-crafts, on which the flatterer ventures not. . . 241 U69 Friend Son 6
Wise child, did'st hastily returne, ... 242 U70 Ode 7
Catch'd with these Arts, wherein the Judge is wise . . 261 U77 Treasurer 11
Caught them these Arts, wherein the Judge is wise . . 261 U77 Treasurer V 11
Her wary guardes, her wise simplicitie, . . . 270 U81 Pawlet 40
If thou be'st wise, with 'Syrian Oyle let shine . . 294 U89 Mart.8:77 3
A wise simplicity; freindes alike-stated; . . . 295 U90 Mart.10:47 7
Is to be wise; thy matter first to know; . . . 325 Horace 441
A wise, and honest man will cry out shame . . . 335 Horace 633
A good and wise man will crye open shame . . . 354 Horace V633
Wise, sober folke, a frantick Poet feare, . . . 335 Horace 643
Those that are wise, a furious Poet feare, . . . 354 Horace V643
The wise, and many-headed Bench, that sits . . . 370 Fletcher 1
Yet who could have hit on't but the wise noddell . . 379 Coryat 3 6
Religious, wise, chast, loving, gratious, good, . . 394 Jane Ogle 5
Pearch'd over head, the wise Athenian Owle: . . 397 Drayton 34
Oh wise Surveyor! wyser Architect! . . . . 405 Inigo Jones 1 85
Great Queen of Queens, most mild, most meek, most wise, . 414 Ghyrlond 41
WISE-CRAFTS
Wise-crafts, on which the flatterer ventures not. . . 241 U69 Friend Son 6
WISEDOME
The Fathers wisedome will'd it so, ... 130 U1 Nativitie 13
And as that wisedome had decreed, ... 130 U1 Nativitie 16
WISELY
Thou, that mak'st gaine thy end, and wisely well, . . 27 E3 Bookseller 1
But, wisely, thrusts not forth a forward hand, . . 61 E95 Savile 22
This makes, that wisely you decline your life, . . 118 F13 Aubigny 59
WISE-MEN
Where I both learn'd, why wise-men hawking follow, . . 55 E85 Goodyere 1 3
Well fare the wise-men yet, on the Banckside, . . 208 U43 Vulcan 123
WISER
And by thy wiser temper, let men know . . . 27 E2 My Booke 8
After the Fathers, and those wiser Guides . . . 207 U43 Vulcan 103

WISER (cont.)
Did wiser Nature draw thee back, ... 243 U70 Ode 11
WISEST
If Rome so great, and in her wisest age, ... 56 E89 Allen 1
Did wisest Nature draw thee back, ... 243 U70 Ode V 11
But wisest Inigo! who can reflect . . . . 405 Inigo Jones 1 86
WISH
Deceive their malice, who could wish it so. . . . 27 E2 My Booke 7
That wish my poemes a legitimate fame, ... 32 E17 Critic 3
Were quite out-spun. The like wish hath his wife. . . 40 E42 Giles 12
Whose poemes would not wish to be your booke? . . . 60 E94 Bedford 3 4
If I would wish, for truth, and not for show, . . . 78 E122 Rudyerd 2 1
Bartas doth wish thy English now were his. . . . 83 E132 Sylvester 10
And I could wish for their eterniz'd sakes, . . . 89 E133 Voyage 195
There's none, that dwell about them, wish them downe; . . 94 F2 Penshurst 47
There's nothing I can wish, for which I stay. . . . 95 F2 Penshurst 75
Yet dare I not complaine, or wish for death . . . 122 F15 Heaven 23
And enamour'd, doe wish, so they might . . . . 134 U2 Triumph 7
Let who will thinke us dead, or wish our death. . . 139 U2 Another 18
All I wish is understood. . . . . . 142 U2 Exception 6
May wish us of their Quire. . . . . . 144 U3 Musicall 28
I wish the Sun should shine . . . . . 150 U10 Jealousie 7
The Care, and wish still of the publike wealth: . . 186 U31 Elsmere 6
Rather then want your light, I wish a grave. . . . 194 U38 Elegy 'Tis 122
Wish, you had fowle ones, and deformed got; . . . 200 U42 Elegy Let 22
'Tis true, that in thy wish they were destroy'd, . . 210 U43 Vulcan 167
Then these can ever be; or else wish none. . . . 219 U47 Tribe 30
I wish all well, and pray high heaven conspire . . 219 U47 Tribe 37
As I began to wish my selfe a horse. . . . . 228 U53 Newcastle 12
Before, I thinke my wish absolv'd had beene. . . . 228 U53 Newcastle 14
What can the Poet wish his King may doe, . . . 235 U62 Charles 1 13
May wish it selfe a sense, ... 239 U67 Muses 23
And rather wish, in their expence of Sack, . . . 241 U68 House-hold 9
The wish is great; but where the Prince is such, . . 249 U72 King 19
But dare not aske our wish in Language fescennine: . . 257 U75 Epithalam. 160
And wish her state lesse happie then it is! . . . 271 U81 Pawlet 84
I summe up mine owne breaking, and wish all. . . . 283 U84 Muse 26
Yet would I wish to love, live, die with thee. . . 294 U87 Hor.3:9 24
Nor feare thy latest day, nor wish therfore. . . . 295 U90 Mart.10:47 13
Hide faults, pray to the Gods, and wish aloud . . 319 Horace 285
Hide faults, and pray to th'gods, and wish aloud . . 345 Horace V285
And wish that all the Muses blood were spilt, . . 371 Fletcher 12
When you behold me wish my selfe, the man . . . 389 Aleman 23
Importune wish; and by her lov'd Lords side . . . 394 Jane Ogle 23
And, till I worthy am to wish I were, . . . 398 Drayton 92
WISH'D
Such when I meant to faine, and wish'd to see, . . 52 E76 Bedford 1 17
That envie wish'd, and Nature fear'd. . . . . 173 U22 Elegy Tho 20
WISHED
The wished Peace of Europe: . . . . . 222 U48 Bacchus 48
The wished goale, both did, and suffer'd much . . 333 Horace 588
WISHES
When, in mens wishes, so thy vertues wrought, . . 49 E67 Suffolk 7
My best of wishes, may you beare a sonne. . . . 116 F12 Rutland 100
Thy true friends wishes, Colby, which shall be, . . 167 U15 Friend-Wars 176
Thy true friends wishes, which shall ever be, . . 167 U15 Friend-Wars V176
After, mens Wishes, crown'd in their events, . . . 309 Horace 108
WISHETH
Harsh sights at home, Giles wisheth he were blind. . . 40 E42 Giles 10
God wisheth, none should wracke on a strange shelfe. . 99 F3 Wroth 95
WISHT
Wisht the Bride were chang'd to night, . . . 138 U2 Kisse 18
WIT (BIRD)
Th'Ionian God-wit, nor the Ginny hen . . . . 291 U85 Country 53
WIT
Become a petulant thing, hurle inke, and wit, . . 27 E2 My Booke 5
Whose every worke, of thy most earely wit, . . . 34 E23 Donne 1 3
All braines, at times of triumph, should runne wit. . 36 E29 Tilter 4
And lyes so farre from wit, 'tis impudence. . . . 38 E38 Guiltie 2 6
Rare, as wonder, was her wit; . . . . . 39 E40 Ratcliffe 9
For wit, feature, and true passion, ... 39 E40 Ratcliffe 16
Whose workes are eene the fripperie of wit, . . . 44 E56 Poet-Ape 2
He takes up all, makes each mans wit his owne. . . 45 E56 Poet-Ape 5
For offring, with thy smiles, my wit to grace, . . 45 E58 Groome 3
Of flatterie to thy titles. Nor of wit. . . . 47 E64 Salisbury 3 3
At Madames table, where thou mak'st all wit . . . 50 E72 Court-ling 3
Thy wit lives by it, Proule, and belly too. . . . 54 E81 Proule 6
I fancied to my selfe, what wine, what wit . . . 55 E84 Bedford 2 6
Cry'd to my face, they were th'elixir of wit: . . 64 E100 Playwrt 3 2
Whether thy learning they would take, or wit, . . 68 E106 E Herbert 5
That both for wit, and sense, so oft dost plucke, . . 73 E112 Gamster 18
That the wit there, and manners might be sav'd: . . 73 E113 Overbury 6
Of miming, gets th'opinion of a wit. . . . . 74 E115 Honest Man 28
So did thy vertue'enforme, thy wit sustaine . . . 75 E116 Jephson 3
A desperate soloecisme in truth and wit. . . . 75 E116 Jephson 16
That strives, his manners should precede his wit. . . 78 E121 Rudyerd 1 8
I know not which th'hast most, candor, or wit: . . 78 E123 Rudyerd 3 2
On some new gesture, that's imputed wit? . . . 81 E129 Mime 14
To view the jewells, stuffes, the paines, the wit . . 97 F3 Wroth 11
Had not their forme touch'd by an English wit. . . 115 F12 Rutland 82
For their owne cap'tall times, t'indite my wit; . . 117 F13 Aubigny 14
With horrour rough, then rioting with wit! . . . 160 U14 Selden 57
Large claspe of Nature, such a wit can bound. . . 160 U14 Selden 64

			Page	Title		Line

WIT (cont.)

	Page		Title	Line
For man to spend his money on? his wit?	165	U15	Friend-Wars	102
Oft scape an Imputation, more through luck, then wit.	179	U25	Desmond	52
Oft scape theyr Imputation, more through luck, then wit.	179	U25	Desmond	V 52
And wit vanish'd.	183	U29	Fit of Rime	18
Scarce the world a Wit doth nourish,	184	U29	Fit of Rime	38
The wit of Ale, and Genius of the Malt	193	U38	Elegy 'Tis	95
More then of eithers manners, wit, or face!	202	U42	Elegy Let	88
Thou woo Minerva! or to wit aspire!	208	U43	Vulcan	109
Left! and wit since to cover it with Tiles.	209	U43	Vulcan	138
Where fight the prime Cocks of the Game, for wit?	222	U49	Pucell	4
As aerie light, and as like wit as those?	222	U49	Pucell	10
I never stood for any place: my wit	223	U49	Pucell	23
Then the great Homers wit, for her, could faine;	224	U50	Countesse	24
Mirth, fooling, nor wit,	231	U57	Burges	17
If his wit reach no higher, but to spring	232	U58	Book-seller	7
Like a rung Beare, or Swine: grunting out wit	232	U58	Book-seller	11
A Bed-rid Wit, then a besieged Towne.	248	U71	Treasurer	15
The bus'nesse of your blooming wit,	251	U74	Weston	22
With their pellets of small wit,	259	U76	Petition	22
To part scurrilitie from wit: or can	323		Horace	403
Because Democritus beleeves a wit	325		Horace	419
The Muse not only gave the Greek's a wit,	327		Horace	461
Her wit as quicke, and sprightfull	365		Ode Splendor	5
But in one tongue, was form'd with the worlds wit:	389		Aleman	6
O, could he but have drawne his wit	390		Reader	5
As, since, she will vouchsafe no other Wit.	392		Shakespeare	50
Keep in thy barking Wit, thou bawling Fool?	410		Gill	8
Office of Wit, a Mint, and (this is true)	415		Rutter	20
Of wit, and a new made: a Warden then,	415		Rutter	23
Clears the Brains, makes Wit the Quicker:	657		Door Apollo	16

WITCH

	Page		Title	Line
Being, beyond sea, burned for one witch:	88	E133	Voyage	158
There, or the tall witch-hazill hee doth twine	290	U85	Country	V 9

WITCHCRAFT

	Page		Title	Line
Imposture, witchcraft, charmes, or blasphemie,	203	U43	Vulcan	16

WITCH-HAZILL

	Page		Title	Line
There, or the tall witch-hazill hee doth twine	290	U85	Country	V 9

WITH

	Page		Title	Line
Much lesse with lewd, prophane, and beastly phrase,	27	E2	My Booke	11
He that departs with his owne honesty	27	E2	My Booke	13
Or celebrated with more truth of state?	28	E5	Union	2
Keepes himselfe, with halfe a man, and defrayes	30	E12	Shift	3
The charge of that state, with this charme, god payes.	30	E12	Shift	4
Thou more; that with it every day, dar'st jest	32	E16	Brain-hardy	2
As theirs did with thee, mine might credit get:	32	E18	Censurer	6
I sent the cause: Hee wooes with an ill sprite.	33	E19	Cod 1	2
His neck fenc'd round with ruffe! his eyes halfe shut!	33	E21	Gam'ster	2
With safetie of her innocence;	33	E22	Daughter	6
Which might with halfe mankind maintayne a strife.	34	E23	Donne 1	8
He'adulters still: his thoughts lye with a whore.	35	E26	Beast 2	2
He speakes to men with a Rhinocerotes nose,	35	E28	Surly	4
And, can forget mens names, with a great grace.	35	E28	Surly	8
Ile not offend thee with a vaine teare more,	37	E33	Roe 3	1
For all night-sinnes, with others wives, unknowne,	39	E39	Colt	1
If, now, with man and Wife, to will, and nill	40	E42	Giles	16
For offring, with thy smiles, my wit to grace,	45	E58	Groome	3
With what thy vertue on the times hath won,	47	E63	Salisbury 2	2
With thy new place, bring I these early fruits	47	E63	Salisbury 3	2
With me thou leav'st an happier Muse then thee,	48	E65	Muse	11
That sound, and that authoritie with her name,	49	E67	Suffolk	3
With which a learned Madame you belye.	51	E73	Fine Grand	11
Whil'st I behold thee live with purest hands;	51	E74	Chancelor	3
This morning, timely rapt with holy fire,	52	E76	Bedford 1	1
I purpos'd her; that should, with even powers,	52	E76	Bedford 1	14
For, if thou shame, ranck'd with my friends, to goe,	53	E77	Not name	3
Touch'd with the sinne of false play, in his punque.	56	E87	Hazard	1
The french disease, with which he labours yet?	56	E88	Monsieur	10
Yet crown'd with honors, as with riches, then;	56	E89	Allen	4
Longer a day, but with his Mill will marry.	57	E90	Mill	16
With juyce of limons, onions, pisse, to write.	59	E92	New Crie	28
With England. All forbidden bookes they get.	59	E92	New Crie	31
With ignorance on us, as they have done	59	E92	New Crie	37
Who did, alike with thee, thy house up-beare,	60	E93	Radcliffe	3
To Lucy, Countesse of Bedford, with Mr. Donnes Satyres.	60	E94	Bedford 3	Ttl
Crowne with their owne. Rare poemes aske rare friends.	60	E94	Bedford 3	8
Mark'd by thy hand, and with the better stone,	62	E96	Donne 2	8
His cloke with orient velvet quite lin'd through,	62	E97	Motion	4
With thine owne course the judgement of thy friend,	63	E98	Th Roe 1	8
With those that come; whose grace may make that seeme	64	E101	Supper	8
Ushring the mutton; with a short-leg'd hen,	64	E101	Supper	11
And one true posture, though besieg'd with ill	66	E102	Pembroke	14
Doe what you come for, Captayne, with your newes;	68	E107	Hungry	1
How great you were with their two Emperours;	68	E107	Hungry	6
And yet are with their Princes: Fill them full	69	E107	Hungry	7
And then lye with you, closer, then a punque.	69	E107	Hungry	20
Will you part with them, here, unthriftely?	69	E107	Hungry	28
And did not shame it with my actions, then,	70	E108	Soldiers	7
No more, then I dare now doe, with my pen.	70	E108	Soldiers	8
Thou are not one, seek'st miseries with hope,	70	E109	Nevil	5
Wrestlest with dignities, or fain'st a scope	70	E109	Nevil	6
To have engrav'd these acts, with his owne stile,	71	E110	Edmonds 1	6
He wrote, with the same spirit that he fought,	71	E110	Edmonds 1	8

                                                        Page   Title   Line

WITH (cont.)
   With thy small stocke, why art thou ventring still,   .   .   . 72   E112 Gamster   1
   Where finding so much beautie met with vertue,   .   .   . 74   E114 Sydney   6
   With such a one. And therein keepes it's word.   .   .   . 74   E115 Honest Man   21
   Parts, then th'Italian could doe, with his dore.   .   .   . 74   E115 Honest Man   26
   With me can merit more, then that good man,   .   .   . 76   E119 Shelton   5
   Dar'st breath in any ayre; and with safe skill,   .   .   . 76   E119 Shelton   9
   Weepe with me all you that read   .   .   . 77   E120 S. P.   1
   And heare her speake with one, and her first tongue; .   .   . 78   E122 Rudyerd 2   6
   Th'other let it sleepe with death: .   .   . 79   E124 Elizabeth   10
   Retyr'd, with purpose your faire worth to praise,   .   .   . 80   E126 Mrs Cary   1
   So, when we, blest with thy returne, shall see   .   .   . 81   E128 Wm Roe 2   9
   Thy selfe, with thy first thoughts, brought home by thee, . . 81   E128 Wm Roe 2   10
   A worke of ours, we part with our owne right;   .   .   . 82   E131 Ferrab. 2   2
   For fame, with breath soone kindled, soone blowne out. .   .   . 83   E131 Ferrab. 2   14
   With tales of Troyes just knight, our faiths abuse: .   .   . 84   E133 Voyage   4
   Laden with plague-sores, and their sinnes, were heard, .   .   . 84   E133 Voyage   17
   Then let the former age, with this content her,   .   .   . 84   E133 Voyage   19
   And with both bombard-stile, and phrase, rehearse   .   .   . 85   E133 Voyage   46
   Still, with thy former labours; yet, once more,   .   .   . 85   E133 Voyage   56
   With famine, wants, and sorrowes many a dosen,   .   .   . 86   E133 Voyage   71
   Had burst with storme, and downe fell, ab excelsis,   .   .   . 86   E133 Voyage   95
   That, with still-scalding steemes, make the place hell. . .   . 88   E133 Voyage   144
   With great gray eyes, are lifted up, and mew'd;   .   .   . 88   E133 Voyage   161
   Our brave Heroes with a milder glare,   .   .   . 88   E133 Voyage   163
   Is fill'd with buttock? And the walls doe sweate   .   .   . 88   E133 Voyage   169
   Of loud Sepulchres with their hourely knells,   .   .   . 89   E133 Voyage   174
   Who kept an ale-house; with my little Minos,   .   .   . 89   E133 Voyage   189
   An ancient pur-blinde fletcher, with a high nose;   .   .   . 89   E133 Voyage   190
   My Muse had plough'd with his, that sung A-jax.   .   .   . 89   E133 Voyage   196
   With which he fled me: and againe,   .   .   . 93   F1 Why write no   8
   Of many a Sylvane, taken with his flames.   .   .   . 94   F2 Penshurst   16
   The purpled pheasant, with the speckled side: .   .   . 94   F2 Penshurst   28
   The earely cherry, with the later plum,   .   .   . 94   F2 Penshurst   41
   They'are rear'd with no mans ruine, no mans grone,   .   .   . 94   F2 Penshurst   46
   With all, that hospitalitie doth know!   .   .   . 95   F2 Penshurst   60
   With his brave sonne, the Prince, they saw thy fires .   .   . 95   F2 Penshurst   77
   With all their zeale, to warme their welcome here.   .   .   . 95   F2 Penshurst   81
   With the whole houshold, and may, every day,   .   .   . 96   F2 Penshurst   96
   With other edifices, when they see   .   .   . 96   F2 Penshurst   100
   Art tane with neithers vice, nor sport: .   .   . 96   F3 Wroth   4
   Live, with un-bought provision blest;   .   .   . 97   F3 Wroth   14
   Or with thy friends; the heart of all the yeere,   .   .   . 97   F3 Wroth   25
   Or with thy friends; the heate of all the yeere,   .   .   . 97   F3 Wroth   V 25
   Thou dost with some delight the day out-weare,   .   .   . 97   F3 Wroth   35
   Thou canst with some delight the day out-weare,   .   .   . 97   F3 Wroth   V 35
   The mowed meddowes, with the fleeced sheepe,   .   .   . 97   F3 Wroth   39
   And furrowes laden with their weight;   .   .   . 98   F3 Wroth   42
   The hogs return'd home fat with mast;   .   .   . 98   F3 Wroth   V 44
   And fills thy open hall with mirth, and cheere,   .   .   . 98   F3 Wroth   49
   Sit mixt with losse of state, or reverence.   .   .   . 98   F3 Wroth   57
   Freedome doth with degree dispense.   .   .   . 98   F3 Wroth   58
   That they may sleepe with scarres in age.   .   .   . 98   F3 Wroth   70
   And change possessions, oftner with his breath,   .   .   . 99   F3 Wroth   75
   And brooding o're it sit, with broadest eyes,   .   .   . 99   F3 Wroth   83
   A body sound, with sounder minde.   .   .   . 99   F3 Wroth   102
   With all my powers, my selfe to loose?   .   .   . 101   F4 To the World   28
   But I will beare these, with that scorne,   .   .   . 102   F4 To the World   63
   'Tis, with us, perpetuall night.   .   .   . 102   F5 Celia 1   8
   Till you equall with the store,   .   .   . 103   F6 Celia 2   12
   But, forgive me, with thy crowne   .   .   . 105   F8 Sicknesse   18
   With ten Emp'ricks, in their chamber,   .   .   . 105   F8 Sicknesse   31
   Drinke to me, onely, with thine eyes,   .   .   . 106   F9 Celia 3   1
   Drinke to me, Coelia, with thine eyes,   .   .   . 106   F9 Celia 3   V 1
   And I will pledge with mine;   .   .   . 106   F9 Celia 3   2
   With his old earthly labours. T'exact more,   .   .   . 107   F10 Proludium   5
   To raise my spirits with thy conjuring wine,   .   .   . 107   F10 Proludium   11
   To raise our spirits with thy conjuring wine,   .   .   . 107   F10 Proludium   V 11
   Who, with his axe, thy fathers mid-wife plaid.   .   .   . 107   F10 Proludium   15
   Or, with thy Tribade trine, invent new sports,   .   .   . 107   F10 Proludium   17
   Thou, nor thy loosenesse with my making sorts.   .   .   . 107   F10 Proludium   18
   Thou, nor their loosenesse with our making sorts.   .   .   . 107   F10 Proludium   V 18
   Hermes, the cheater, shall not mixe with us,   .   .   . 107   F10 Proludium   22
   Hermes, the cheater, cannot mixe with us,   .   .   . 107   F10 Proludium   V 22
   Arm'd with bow, shafts, and fire;   .   .   . 110   F11 Epode   38
   With whom who sailes, rides on the surge of feare,   .   .   . 110   F11 Epode   41
   Who (blest with such high chance)   .   .   . 111   F11 Epode   62
   Though thy wild thoughts with sparrowes wings doe flye, . .   . 111   F11 Epode   73
   Have fill'd with abstinence: .   .   . 111   F11 Epode   84
   Have grac'd with abstinence: .   .   . 111   F11 Epode   V 84
   Grac'd with a Phoenix love;   .   .   . 112   F11 Epode   92
   That which, to boote with hell, is thought worth heaven, . .   . 113   F12 Rutland   3
   With noble ignorants, and let them still,   .   .   . 114   F12 Rutland   28
   With you, I know, my offring will find grace.   .   .   . 114   F12 Rutland   30
   How many equall with the Argive Queene,   .   .   . 114   F12 Rutland   49
   But onely Poets, rapt with rage divine?   .   .   . 115   F12 Rutland   63
   But holie Poets, rapt with sence divine?   .   .   . 115   F12 Rutland   V 63
   besett with statues, shall I reare your head,   .   .   . 115   F12 Rutland   V 84
   Your forme imprest there: not with tickling rimes,   .   .   . 116   F12 Rutland   87
   Your forme imprest there: not with tinckling rimes,   .   .   . 116   F12 Rutland   V 87
   From braines entranc'd, and fill'd with extasies;   .   .   . 116   F12 Rutland   90
   With every vertue, wheresoere it move,   .   .   . 116   F13 Aubigny   8
   With sinne and vice, though with a throne endew'd;   .   .   . 116   F13 Aubigny   10

WITH (cont.)

If it may stand with your soft blush to heare	117	F13 Aubigny	22
For such a lot! that mixt you with a state	118	F13 Aubigny	48
In single paths, dangers with ease are watch'd:	118	F13 Aubigny	57
Giddie with change, and therefore cannot see	118	F13 Aubigny	67
Now that the harth is crown'd with smiling fire,	120	F14 Sydney	1
And he, with his best Genius left alone.	120	F14 Sydney	20
With dust of ancestors, in graves but dwell.	121	F14 Sydney	40
If with this truth you be inspir'd,	121	F14 Sydney	52
And with the flame	121	F14 Sydney	56
As with the light	121	F14 Sydney	58
That, laden with my sinnes, I seeke for ease?	122	F15 Heaven	4
Standing with feare, and must with horror fall,	122	F15 Heaven	19
With holy Paul, lest it be thought the breath	122	F15 Heaven	24
And breath'st into it, life, and light, with state	127	U1 Trinitie	19
Pure thoughts in man: with fiery zeale them feeding	128	U1 Trinitie	27
With grace, with love, with cherishing intire:	128	U1 Trinitie	43
And with thy Angels, placed side, by side,	128	U1 Trinitie	46
With all since bought.	129	U1 Father	22
With the Ardor, and the Passion,	131	U2 Excuse	11
But be glad, as soone with me,	131	U2 Excuse	17
Marke of glorie, come with me;	132	U2 How he saw	8
And the Bow: with thought to hit	132	U2 How he saw	22
(Which with griefe and wrath I heard)	132	U2 How he saw	29
Cupids Statue with a Beard,	132	U2 How he saw	30
At her hand, with oath, to make	133	U2 Suffered	10
Aymed with that selfe-same shaft.	133	U2 Suffered	12
To revenge me with my Tongue,	133	U2 Suffered	24
With lovely Graces	135	U2 Triumph	V 36
When with Joves swans she sported	135	U2 Triumph	V 42
5. His discourse with Cupid.	136	U2 Cupid	Ttl
Rip'ned with a breath more sweet,	137	U2 Cupid	27
With the Lace that doth it deck,	137	U2 Cupid	30
With my Mothers is the same.	137	U2 Cupid	38
With th'advantage of her haire,	138	U2 Kisse	10
In the Daunces, with what spight	138	U2 Kisse	22
All that heard her, with desire.	139	U2 Promise	6
With the rest, I long expected,	140	U2 Promise	7
With your emissarie eye,	140	U2 Promise	17
Or with Secretarie Sis	140	U2 Promise	25
Yet a man; with crisped haire	141	U2 Her man	10
Such a man, with every part,	142	U2 Her man	53
Come, with our Voyces, let us warre,	143	U3 Musicall	1
Oh doe not wanton with those eyes,	144	U4 Song	1
Lest I be sick with seeing;	144	U4 Song	2
O, be not angry with those fires,	144	U4 Song	5
Nor spread them as distract with feares,	145	U4 Song	11
The fooles, or Tyrants with your friends,	145	U5 Woman-kind	2
If wee would search with care, and paine,	145	U5 Woman-kind	8
Had wrestled with Diseases strong,	151	U12 Corbet	8
With the just Canon of his life,	151	U12 Corbet	11
For benefits are ow'd with the same mind	153	U13 Sacvile	5
The smallest courtesies with thankes, I make	153	U13 Sacvile	16
And spunge-like with it dry up the blood quite:	155	U13 Sacvile	69
And it is paid 'hem with a trembling zeale,	155	U13 Sacvile	85
Or swaggering with the Watch, or Drawer, drunke;	156	U13 Sacvile	94
And told of with more License then th'were done!	156	U13 Sacvile	96
That with these mixtures we put out her light.	156	U13 Sacvile	110
But 'twas with purpose to have made them such.	159	U14 Selden	22
With horrour rough, then rioting with wit!	160	U14 Selden	57
With that thy Stile, thy keeping of thy State,	161	U14 Selden	68
Their vitious ease, and be o'rewhelm'd with it.	162	U15 Friend-Wars	4
His unjust hopes, with praises begg'd, or (worse)	162	U15 Friend-Wars	12
The whole world here leaven'd with madnesse swells;	163	U15 Friend-Wars	31
Against his Maker; high alone with weeds,	163	U15 Friend-Wars	33
Not to be checkt, or frighted now with fate,	163	U15 Friend-Wars	35
Hee's one of blood, and fashion! and with these	164	U15 Friend-Wars	55
To do't with Cloth, or Stuffes, lusts name might merit;	164	U15 Friend-Wars	57
With Velvet, Plush, and Tissues, it is spirit.	164	U15 Friend-Wars	58
To see 'hem aye discoursing with their Glasse,	164	U15 Friend-Wars	63
For these with her young Companie shee'll enter,	164	U15 Friend-Wars	79
Nor is the title question'd with our proud,	164	U15 Friend-Wars	83
The Dice with glassen eyes, to the glad viewes	166	U15 Friend-Wars	138
The Dice with glassen eyes, to the glad Viewers	166	U15 Friend-Wars	V138
When I am hoarse, with praising his each cast,	167	U15 Friend-Wars	151
With him, for he is follow'd with that heape	167	U15 Friend-Wars	156
Boasters, and perjur'd, with the infinite more	167	U15 Friend-Wars	169
Goe, quit 'hem all. And take along with thee,	167	U15 Friend-Wars	175
Still pretious, with the odour of thy name.	168	U15 Friend-Wars	190
But that some greater names have broke with me,	169	U17 Friend-Debt	8
Now threaten, with those meanes she did invite?	169	U18 Elegy Can	2
I can helpe that with boldnesse: And Love sware,	170	U18 Elegy Can	9
He flying curles, and crispeth, with his wings;	170	U19 Elegy By	6
With so much Loyalties expence,	173	U22 Elegy Tho	22
Be taken with false Baytes,	175	U23 Himselfe	20
They die with their conceits,	175	U23 Himselfe	23
They drincke with their conceits,	175	U23 Himselfe	V 23
With Japhets lyne, aspire	175	U23 Himselfe	27
When Vice alike in time with vertue dur'd.	176	U24 Frontispice	8
To towre with my intention	176	U25 Desmond	4
With Delphick fire:	177	U25 Desmond	12
Who would with judgement search, searching conclude	177	U25 Desmond	25
With lustrous Graces,	179	U25 Desmond	60

WITH (cont.)

	Page	Title	Line
Where darknesse with her gloomie-sceptred hand,	180	U25 Desmond	61
Such thoughts wil make you more in love with truth.	181	U26 Ode High	21
With bright Lycoris, Gallus choice,	181	U27 Ode Helen	15
Equall with her? or Ronsart prais'd	181	U27 Ode Helen	22
Cosening Judgement with a measure,	183	U29 Fit of Rime	5
Fastning Vowells, as with fetters	183	U29 Fit of Rime	11
Still may Syllabes jarre with time,	184	U29 Fit of Rime	52
Stil may reason warre with rime,	184	U29 Fit of Rime	53
And labour'd in the worke; not with the fame:	185	U30 Burleigh	12
As with the safetie, and honour of the Lawes,	186	U31 Elsmere	9
Both arm'd with wealth, and slander to oppose,	186	U32 Elsmere	8
Against a multitude; and (with thy Stile	187	U33 Councellour	31
Then com'st thou off with Victorie and Palme,	187	U33 Councellour	35
Quarrell with Nature, or in ballance brought	188	U34 Small Poxe	6
On which with profit, I shall never looke,	189	U37 Friend-Book	5
As flatt'ry with friends humours still to move.	190	U37 Friend-Book	27
Yet if with eithers vice I teynted be,	190	U37 Friend-Book	29
And fills my powers with perswading joy,	191	U38 Elegy 'Tis	11
And then with pause; for sever'd once, that's gone,	192	U38 Elegy 'Tis	47
As all with storme and tempest ran together.	193	U38 Elegy 'Tis	76
And with the vulgar doth it not obtaine	193	U38 Elegy 'Tis	81
Be not affected with these markes too much	193	U38 Elegy 'Tis	83
Produce; though threatning with a coale, or chalke	193	U38 Elegy 'Tis	97
For though Love thrive, and may grow up with cheare,	197	U40 Elegy That	15
'Bove all your standing waters, choak'd with weedes.	198	U40 Elegy That	28
Shall find their depth: they're sounded with a spoone.	198	U40 Elegy That	30
Out with the other, for hee's still at home;	198	U40 Elegy That	34
Your sacrifice, then here remaine with me.	199	U41 Elegy Since	18
Have eaten with the Beauties, and the wits,	200	U42 Elegy Let	33
He would have done in verse, with any of those	201	U42 Elegy Let	62
And straight-way spent a Sonnet; with that other	201	U42 Elegy Let	67
Any Comparison had with his Cheap-side.	202	U42 Elegy Let	76
With Clownes, and Tradesmen, kept thee clos'd in horne.	203	U43 Vulcan	8
Perhaps, to have beene burned with my bookes.	203	U43 Vulcan	18
With some more thrift, and more varietie:	205	U43 Vulcan	50
With some more change, and tast of tyranny:	205	U43 Vulcan	50
With some more thrift, and yet varietie:	205	U43 Vulcan	V 50
Condemn'd me to the Ovens with the pies;	205	U43 Vulcan	54
Condemn'd them to the Ovens with the pies;	205	U43 Vulcan	V 54
Had filled your large nostrills with the steame:	205	U43 Vulcan	V 62
With pieces of the Legend; The whole summe	205	U43 Vulcan	66
Of errant Knight-hood, with the Dames, and Dwarfes;	205	U43 Vulcan	67
With Merlins Marvailes, and his tables losse,	206	U43 Vulcan	V 71
With the Chimaera of the Rosie-Crosse,	206	U43 Vulcan	72
With Nicholas Pasquill's, Meddle with your match,	206	U43 Vulcan	77
With Nicholas Bretons Meddle with your match,	206	U43 Vulcan	V 77
The weekly Corrants, with Pauls Seale; and all	206	U43 Vulcan	81
The weekly Corrants, with Poules stall; and all	206	U43 Vulcan	V 81
With the old Venusine, in Poetrie,	207	U43 Vulcan	V 89
Was there made English: with the Grammar too,	207	U43 Vulcan	91
With all th'adventures; Three bookes not afraid	207	U43 Vulcan	95
With all th'adventures; Three bookes not amisse	207	U43 Vulcan	V 95
With twice-twelve-yeares stor'd up humanitie,	207	U43 Vulcan	V101
With humble Gleanings in Divinitie,	207	U43 Vulcan	102
'Cause thou canst halt, with us, in Arts, and Fire!	208	U43 Vulcan	110
With lust conceiv'd thee; Father thou hadst none.	208	U43 Vulcan	112
And for it lose his eyes with Gun-powder,	208	U43 Vulcan	121
As th'other may his braines with Quicksilver.	208	U43 Vulcan	122
Flanck'd with a Ditch, and forc'd out of a Marish,	209	U43 Vulcan	134
Fenced with a Ditch, and forc'd out of a Marish,	209	U43 Vulcan	V134
I saw with two poore Chambers taken in,	209	U43 Vulcan	135
Left! and wit since to cover it with Tiles.	209	U43 Vulcan	138
But, others fell with that conceipt by the eares,	209	U43 Vulcan	145
Nay, let White-Hall with Revels have to doe,	210	U43 Vulcan	156
Scarce let White-Hall with Revels have to doe,	210	U43 Vulcan	V156
Strooke in at Millan with the Cutlers there;	212	U43 Vulcan	200
Strooke in at Millan with the villors there;	212	U43 Vulcan	V200
Who with the Divell did Ordinance beget;	212	U43 Vulcan	V202
On both sides doe your mischiefes with delight;	212	U43 Vulcan	204
Engines of Murder, and enjoy with praise	212	U43 Vulcan	V207
And the Greeke Discipline (with the moderne) shed	214	U44 Speach	36
With Citizens? let Clownes, and Tradesmen breed	215	U44 Speach	73
Cover'd with Tissue, whose prosperitie mocks	216	U44 Speach	100
But these with wearing will themselves unfold:	216	U45 Squib	19
With endlesse labours, whilst thy learning drawes	217	U46 Coke	18
Like flies, or wormes, with mans corrupt parts fed:	218	U47 Tribe	18
Lose all my credit with my Christmas Clay,	219	U47 Tribe	52
Well, with mine owne fraile Pitcher, what to doe	219	U47 Tribe	56
With reverence using all the gifts thence given.	219	U47 Tribe	62
Not built with Canvasse, paper, and false lights,	220	U47 Tribe	65
But 'tis with a condition,	220	U48 Bacchus	6
When with his royall shipping	222	U48 Bacchus	52
What though with Tribade lust she force a Muse,	222	U49 Pucell	7
Equall with that, which for the best newes goes,	222	U49 Pucell	9
What though she talke, and cannot once with them,	222	U49 Pucell	11
Doth labour with the Phrase more then the sense?	222	U49 Pucell	14
What though she be with Velvet gownes indu'd,	222	U49 Pucell	18
They say you weekly invite with fits o'th' Mother,	223	U49 Pucell	40
From whence they fall, cast downe with their owne weight.	224	U50 Countesse	12
Now with a Title more to the Degree;	225	U51 Bacon	12
With one great blot, yo'had form'd me as I am.	227	U52 Answer	12
With one great blot, you had drawne me as I am.	227	U52 Answer	V 12

		Page	Title	Line

WITH (cont.)

	Page	Title	Line
And cri'd, Away with the Caesarian bread,	228	U53 Newcastle	19
But rather with advantage to be found	229	U54 Squib	11
Yet with a Dye, that feares no Moth,	230	U55 Burges	7
Laden with Bellie, and doth hardly approach	230	U56 Covell	9
To hit in angles, and to clash with time:	232	U59 Newcastle	5
Their weapons shot out, with that flame, and force,	233	U59 Newcastle	11
Their weapons darted, with that flame, and force,	233	U59 Newcastle	V 11
And valiant were, with, or without their hands.	233	U59 Newcastle	24
Offended with the dazeling flame	234	U60 La-ware	9
Yet are got off thence, with cleare mind, and hands	234	U61 Epigram	7
To cure the call'd Kings Evill with thy touch;	235	U62 Charles 1	4
Who doubts, those fruits God can with gaine restore,	235	U63 Charles 2	3
Hee can, he will, and with large int'rest pay,	236	U63 Charles 2	5
With a long, large, and blest posteritie!	236	U63 Charles 2	12
That thus hath crown'd our hopes, with thee, our Spring & May,	237	U65 Prince	V 2
To compare small with great, as still we owe	238	U66 Queene	12
With beating of our Drums:	239	U67 Muses	15
With beating of their Drums:	239	U67 Muses	V 15
With touch of learned thum's!	239	U67 Muses	18
And with a reverend feare,	240	U67 Muses	45
Freedome, and Truth; with love from those begot:	241	U69 Friend Son	5
Was, t'have a Boy stand with a Club, and fright	241	U69 Friend Son	11
So doth the flatt'rer with faire cunning strike	242	U69 Friend Son	14
His rage, with razing your immortall Towne.	242	U70 Ode	4
Sword, fire, and famine, with fell fury met;	243	U70 Ode	17
Got up and thriv'd with honest arts:	244	U70 Ode	34
And had his noble name advanc'd with men:	244	U70 Ode	36
Goe now, and tell out dayes summ'd up with feares,	244	U70 Ode	53
And let thy lookes with gladnesse shine:	245	U70 Ode	76
Possest with holy rage,	245	U70 Ode	80
And there he lives with memorie; and Ben	246	U70 Ode	84
(Were not his Lucius long with us to tarry)	246	U70 Ode	91
And with the heart, not pen,	247	U70 Ode	124
Want, with the rest of his conceal'd compeeres,	248	U71 Treasurer	5
The Poetrie of Steeples, with the Bells,	249	U72 King	10
The Poetrie of Steeples, with their Bells,	249	U72 King	V 10
Made lighter with the Wine. All noises else,	249	U72 King	12
At Bonefires, Rockets, Fire-workes, with the Shoutes	249	U72 King	13
At Bonefires, squibs, and mirth, with all their Shoutes	249	U72 King	V 13
With love, to heare your modestie relate,	251	U74 Weston	21
With all the fruit shall follow it,	251	U74 Weston	23
. . . England, with the Lady Frances Stuart, Daughter of . . .	252	U75 Epithalam.	Ttl
A-while with us bright Sun, and helpe our light;	252	U75 Epithalam.	2
A-while with us bright Sun, and mend our light;	252	U75 Epithalam.	V 2
Hath filled, with Caroches, all the way,	252	U75 Epithalam.	11
With Modestie so crown'd, and Adoration seene.	254	U75 Epithalam.	48
See, how with Roses, and with Lillies shine,	254	U75 Epithalam.	57
With light of love, this Paire doth intertexe!	254	U75 Epithalam.	60
With what full hands, and in how plenteous showers	254	U75 Epithalam.	65
With all the pompe of Youth, and all our Court beside.	254	U75 Epithalam.	72
And looking with thy best Inquirie, tell,	254	U75 Epithalam.	74
With Angels, Muse, to speake these: Nothing can	255	U75 Epithalam.	84
To pay, with honours, to his noble Sonne	256	U75 Epithalam.	106
With all corroding Arts, be able to untie!	257	U75 Epithalam.	136
Yet, as we may, we will, with chast desires,	257	U75 Epithalam.	161
(For with both the Muse was fed)	259	U76 Petition	16
(For with both the Muse it fed)	259	U76 Petition	V 16
With their pellets of small wit,	259	U76 Petition	22
I would present you now with curious plate	260	U77 Treasurer	2
I would present you with some curious plate	260	U77 Treasurer	V 2
Not with the Arras, but the Persian Loomes.	260	U77 Treasurer	4
Catch'd with these Arts, wherein the Judge is wise	261	U77 Treasurer	11
These I looke up at, with a reverent eye,	261	U77 Treasurer	23
These looke you up at, with a measuring eye,	261	U77 Treasurer	V 23
See where he walkes with Mira by his side.	264	U79 New-yeares	18
Sound, sound his praises loud, and with his, hers divide.	264	U79 New-yeares	19
What gentle Ghost, besprent with April deaw,	268	U81 Pawlet	1
What goodly Ghost, besprent with April deaw,	268	U81 Pawlet	V 1
How did she leave the world? with what contempt?	270	U81 Pawlet	47
And I, into the world with my Soule, was sent!	270	U81 Pawlet	V 56
With gladnesse temper'd her sad Parents teares!	270	U81 Pawlet	59
With admiration, and applause to die!	270	U81 Pawlet	62
And Day, deceasing! with the Prince of light,	271	U81 Pawlet	88
Whole Nations! nay, Mankind! the World, with all	271	U81 Pawlet	90
With what injustice should one soule pretend	271	U81 Pawlet	92
With what injustice can one soule pretend	271	U81 Pawlet	V 92
With ever-greene, and great renowne,	272	U84 Cradle	2
With her, in shade	272	U84 Cradle	4
Take little Infants with their noyse,	273	U84 Cradle	18
With Sayles of silke, as the first notes	273	U84 Cradle	23
With Gold, or Claspes, which might be bought	273	U84 Cradle	27
As comming with his Harpe, prepar'd	274	U84 Cradle	35
Meschines honour with the Cestrian fame	274	U84 Descent	16
Worke with my fancie, his owne hand.	276	U84 Body	12
With all that Youth, or it can bring:	276	U84 Body	22
Our sense you doe with knowledge fill,	278	U84 Mind	19
In speech; it is with that excesse	279	U84 Mind	34
Yet know, with what thou art possest,	281	U84 Mind	70
Hang all your roomes, with one large Pedigree:	282	U84 Kenelme	20
The Spirit that I wrote with, and conceiv'd;	282	U84 Muse	3
Till swept away, th'were cancell'd with a broome!	282	U84 Muse	8
With such a Raritie, and not rowse Art	282	U84 Muse	16

WITH (cont.)

	Page	Title		Line
With all her aydes, to save her from the seize · · · ·	283	U84 Muse		17
(For so thou art with me) now shee is gone. · · · ·	283	U84 Muse		22
The world to ruine with it; in her Fall, · · · ·	283	U84 Muse		25
Am turned with an others powers. My Passion · · ·	283	U84 Muse		31
Expected with the fleshes restitution. · · · ·	283	U84 Muse		50
All other gladnesse, with the thought is barr'd; · · ·	284	U84 Muse		67
With silence, and amazement! not with rude, · · · ·	284	U84 Muse		78
Saints, Martyrs, Prophets, with those Hierarchies, · ·	285	U84 Muse		85
With boughs of Palme, a crowned Victrice stand! · · ·	285	U84 Muse		96
Her fellowes, with the oyle of gladnesse, bright · · ·	285	U84 Muse		101
In heaven Empyre, and with a robe of light? · · · ·	285	U84 Muse		102
Shall meet with gladnesse in one Theatre; · · · ·	285	U84 Muse		114
There shall the Brother, with the Sister walke, · · ·	285	U84 Muse		117
And Sons, and Daughters, with their Parents talke; · ·	285	U84 Muse		117
What love with mercy mixed doth appeare? · · · ·	285	U84 Muse		118
Equall with Angels, and Co-heires of it? · · · ·	286	U84 Muse		138
Not tost or troubled with light Lady-aire; · · · ·	286	U84 Muse		146
He run; and all did strive with diligence · · · ·	287	U84 Muse		164
And came forth ever cheered, with the rod · · · ·	287	U84 Muse		171
Of divine Comfort, when sh' had talk'd with God. · · ·	287	U84 Muse		183
With his owne Oxen tills his Sires left lands, · · ·	287	U84 Muse		184
Nor Souldier-like started with rough alarmes, · · ·	289	U85 Country		3
But flees the Barre and Courts, with the proud bords, ·	289	U85 Country		5
With the growne issue of the Vine; · · · ·	289	U85 Country		7
With sproutinge tendrells of the Vine; · · · ·	290	U85 Country		10
And with his hooke lops off the fruitlesse race, · · ·	290	U85 Country	V	10
His head, with mellow Apples crown'd, · · · ·	290	U85 Country		11
With which, Priapus, he may thanke thy hands, · · ·	290	U85 Country		18
With which, Priapus, he may greet thy hands, · · ·	290	U85 Country		21
Or hence, or thence, he drives with many a Hound · · ·	290	U85 Country	V	21
But if, to boot with these, a chaste Wife meet · · ·	290	U85 Country		31
To deck the hallow'd Harth with old wood fir'd · · ·	291	U85 Country		39
If with bright floods, the Winter troubled much, · · ·	291	U85 Country		43
If with East floods, the Winter troubled much, · · ·	291	U85 Country		51
To view the weary Oxen draw, with bare · · · ·	291	U85 Country	V	51
'Gainst th'Ides, his moneys he gets in with paine, · ·	291	U85 Country		63
'Gainst th'Ides, his gott moneyes he gets in with paine,	291	U85 Country		69
With thy bright Swans, of Paulus Maximus: · · ·	291	U85 Country	V	69
With the 'bove all his Rivals gifts take place, · · ·	292	U86 Hor.4:1		10
Thrice 'bout thy Altar with their Ivory feet. · · ·	292	U86 Hor.4:1		18
Or with fresh flowers to girt my temple round. · · ·	292	U86 Hor.4:1		28
With an uncomely silence failes my tongue? · · ·	293	U86 Hor.4:1		32
I hold thee fast! but fled hence, with the Light, · · ·	293	U86 Hor.4:1		36
Who sings so sweet, and with such cunning plaies, · · ·	293	U86 Hor.4:1		38
With gentle Calais, Thurine Orniths Sonne; · · ·	293	U87 Hor.3:9		10
Yet would I wish to love, live, die with thee. · · ·	293	U87 Hor.3:9		14
If thou be'st wise, with 'Syrian Oyle let shine · · ·	294	U87 Hor.3:9		24
Darke thy cleare glasse with old Falernian Wine; · · ·	294	U89 Mart.8:77		3
And heat, with softest love, thy softer bed. · · ·	295	U89 Mart.8:77		5
Most pleasant Martial; Substance got with ease, · · ·	295	U89 Mart.8:77		6
With Doves; or Lambes, with Tygres coupled be. · · ·	295	U90 Mart.10:47		2
Diana's Grove, or Altar, with the bor-/Dring · · ·	305	Horace		16
Diana's Grove, or Altar, with the nether · · ·	305	Horace		20
Are, with the likenesse of the truth, undone. · · ·	338	Horace	V	20
Are with the likeness of the truth beguil'd: · · ·	307	Horace		34
With faire black eyes, and haire; and a wry nose. · · ·	339	Horace	V 35/	34
With faire black eyes, and hair, and some vile snout. ·	307	Horace		52
If custome please, with whom both choyse, and will, · ·	339	Horace	V 54/	52
On popular noise with, and doe businesse in. · · ·	341	Horace		V103
The place allotted it, with decent thewes. · · ·	311	Horace		120
The place allotted it, with decent praise. · · ·	311	Horace		125
Am I call'd Poet? wherefore with wrong shame, · · ·	341	Horace		V131/125
With swelling throat: and, oft, the tragick wight · · ·	311	Horace		129
That are Spectators, with their miserie, · · ·	311	Horace		134
Mens faces, still, with such as laugh, are prone · · ·	311	Horace		137
Mens count'nances, with such as laugh, are prone · · ·	342	Horace		143
To laughter; so they grieve with those that mone. · · ·	311	Horace		V143
With weightie sorrow hurles us all along, · · ·	311	Horace		144
With weightie woes she hurles us all along · · ·	342	Horace		155
And Roman Gentrie, will with laughter shout. · · ·	342	Horace		V155
Or, with the milke of Thebes; or Argus, fed. · · ·	313	Horace		V160
Medea make brave with impetuous scorne; · · ·	313	Horace		168
To render word for word: nor with thy sleight · · ·	313	Horace		175
Scylla, Charybdis, Polypheme, with these. · · ·	315	Horace		191
Nor from the brand, with which the life did burne · · ·	315	Horace		206
Falshood with truth, as no man can espie · · ·	315	Horace		207
And can tread firme, longs with like lads to play; · · ·	315	Horace		216
Or do's all businesse coldly, and with feare; · · ·	317	Horace		226
With sloth, yet greedy still of what's to come: · · ·	317	Horace		244
Mans comming yeares much good with them doe bring: · ·	317	Horace		246
The Hau'-boy, not as now with latten bound, · · ·	319	Horace		250
And rivall with the Trumpet for his sound, · · ·	319	Horace		287
They might with ease be numbred, being a few · · ·	319	Horace		288
With lees of Wine. Next Eschylus, more late, · · ·	319	Horace		293
Though sower, with safetie of his gravitie, · · ·	319	Horace		315
Were to be staid with softnesses, and wonne · · ·	321	Horace		322
With something that was acceptably new. · · ·	321	Horace		326
With poore base termes, through every baser shop: · ·	321	Horace		327
Nor is't long since, they did with patience take · · ·	323	Horace		334
So rare, as with some taxe it doth ingage · · ·	323	Horace		375
With specious places, and being humour'd right, · · ·	327	Horace		383
More strongly takes the people with delight, · · ·	327	Horace		457
				458

	Page	Title	Line

IITH (cont.)

And lead them with soft songs, where that he would..	327	Horace	485
Their minds to Warres, with rimes they did rehearse;	329	Horace	495
Sweet mix'd with sowre, to his Reader, so	329	Horace	515
With honour make the farre-knowne Author live.	329	Horace	519
Offended with few spots, which negligence	329	Horace	527
May, with some right, upon an Author creepe..	329	Horace	538
Poppy, with hony of Sardus; 'cause without	351	Horace	V535/559
With joy of what is given him, over-gone:	333	Horace	610
Rich men are said with many cups to plie,	333	Horace	617
Great men are said with many cups to plye,	354	Horace	V617
And rack, with Wine, the man whom they would try,	333	Horace	618
When you write Verses, with your judge do so:	333	Horace	620
When you make verses, with your judge doe so:	354	Horace	V620
Blot out the carelesse, with his turned pen;	335	Horace	635
Infected with the leprosie, or had	335	Horace	645
They vexe, and follow him with shouts, and noise,	335	Horace	648
They vexe, and carelesse follow him with noise.	354	Horace	V648
For, if one should, and with a rope make haste	335	Horace	655
Doth the same thing with him, that would him kill.	335	Horace	666
And there an end of him with reading makes:	355	Horace	V678
First: thy successe did strike my sence with wonder;	361	Palmer	5
wear spent with wonder as they weare delated,	361	Palmer	24
till giddie with amazement I fell downe	361	Palmer	25
I struggled with this passion that did drowne	362	Palmer	28
For, as one comming with a laterall viewe,	362	Author	9
So with this Authors Readers will it thrive:	362	Author	12
It carries Palme with it, (where e're it goes)	363	Riches	6
Judgement (adornd with Learning)	365	Ode Splendor	9
But mixt with sound, transcending	365	Ode Splendor	15
From Zephyr's rape would close him with his beames.	366	Ode Who saith	24
With thy soft notes, and hold them within Pale	367	Ode Who saith	45
With entheate rage, to publish their bright tracts?	368	Ode Who saith	61
Their cares in wine; with sure	368	Ode Who saith	87
With Cupids wing;	369	Ode Who saith	100
With more delight, and grace)	369	Ode Who saith	103
With all the race	369	Ode Who saith	118
Each subt'lest Passion, with her source, and spring,	370	Author	7
Each subject Passion, with her source, and spring,	370	Author	V 7
With the shops Foreman, or some such brave sparke,	371	Fletcher	6
With vices, which they look'd for, and came to.	371	Fletcher	11
With Rites not bound, but conscience. Wouldst thou All?	372	Epitaph	11
All sorts of fish with Musicke of his maw.	374	Coryat 1	11
A Punke here pelts him with egs. How so?	375	Coryat 1	16
He will expiate this sinne with converting the Jewes.	375	Coryat 1	21
A Rabbin confutes him with the Bastinado.	375	Coryat 1	23
Old Hat here, torne Hose, with Shoes full of gravell,	375	Coryat 1	26
. . . Which should Have beene Printed with the other . . .	379	Coryat 3	Ttl
To his strength, hath measur'd it out with his feet.	379	Coryat 3	4
To write it with the selfe same spirit he went,	379	Coryat 3	14
And lay in straw with the horses at Bergamo,	380	Coryat 3	38
How many learned men he have drawne with his hooke	380	Coryat 3	44
They are not those, are present with theyre face,	384	Somerset	1
With the same looke, or with a better, shine.	384	Somerset	10
To rise with eyther of you, on the morrow.	384	Somerset	16
May hurt them more with praise, then Foes with spight.	386	Browne	2
With the how much they set forth, but th'how well.	386	Browne	16
Still, still, dost thou arrive with, at our shore,	388	Chapman	5
But in one tongue, was form'd with the worlds wit:	389	Aleman	6
With Nature, to out-doo the life:	390	Reader	4
I meane with great, but disproportion'd Muses:	391	Shakespeare	26
I should commit thee surely with thy peeres,	391	Shakespeare	28
(And himselfe with it) that he thinkes to frame;	392	Shakespeare	62
Shine forth, thou Starre of Poets, and with rage,	392	Shakespeare	77
I Could begin with that grave forme, Here lies,	394	Jane Ogle	1
And Christian name too, with a Heralds witt.	394	Jane Ogle	12
Whom shee, with Sorrow first did lodge, then feast,	394	Jane Ogle	20
It makes me ravish'd with just wonder, cry	395	May	13
With us be call'd, the Naso, but this man?	397	Drayton	32
And caried, though with shoute, and noyse, confesse	397	Drayton	45
With every song, I sweare, and so would dye:	397	Drayton	54
With bold Tyrtaeus verse, when thou art nam'd,	398	Drayton	68
But then refreshed, with thy Fayerie Court,	398	Drayton	79
And with their grassie greene restor'd mine eyes.	398	Drayton	82
With pause upon it; make this page your booke;	399	Lady Ogle	6
And, with their Chained dance,	401	Filmer	9
Recelebrates the joyfull Match with France.	401	Filmer	10
And, graced with her song,	402	Filmer	13
An Expostulacion with Inigo Jones.	402	Inigo Jones 1	Ttl
With mistooke Names out of Vitruvius!	402	Inigo Jones 1	8
I chyme that too: And I have mett with those	403	Inigo Jones 1	31
And Goody Sculpture, brought with much adoe	403	Inigo Jones 1	38
Pack with your pedling Poetry to the Stage,	404	Inigo Jones 1	51
Of Lanterne-lerry: with fuliginous heat	405	Inigo Jones 1	72
Reviving with fresh coulors the pale Ghosts	405	Inigo Jones 1	88
Of thy dead Standards: or (with miracle) see	405	Inigo Jones 1	89
Expression for! with that unbounded lyne	406	Inigo Jones 1	95
That might compare with thee? what story shall	406	Inigo Jones 1	98
With all Remonstrance make an honest man.	406	Inigo Jones 1	104
All kings to doe the self same deeds with some!	406	Inigo Jones 2	4
With slyding windowes, & false Lights a top!	407	Inigo Jones 2	10
He draw a Forum, with quadriviall Streets!	407	Inigo Jones 2	11
Thou paint a Lane, where Thumb with Geffry meets!	407	Inigo Jones 2	V 12

	Page	Title	Line

WITH (cont.)

With rotten chalk, or Cole upon a wall,	408	Inigo Jones 3	11
Thy Noddle, with his clubb; and dashing forth	409	Detractor	21
And you doe doe them well, with good applause,	409	Brome	5
The comfort of weake Christians, with their warning,	411	Sutcliffe	13
With wonder on the thorny regiment.	413	Ghyrlond	16
Inflam'd with ardor to that mystick Shine,	413	Ghyrlond	23
With od'rous sweets and soft humilitie,	413	Ghyrlond	27
With the Glad Countrey, and Posteritie:	416	Dover	6
And you, with them, as Father of our spring.	416	Welcome	8
for the breeches with the bride,	417	Moon	34
for when the profitt with the payne doth meete,	418	Answer	6
Hee dyes with an Ill sent,	420	Ode:If Men	16
howe soone with a selfe ticklinge hee was spent.	420	Ode:If Men	18
And once more stryke the eare of tyme with those fresh straynes:	420	Ode:If Men	32
I have, with strict advantage of free tyme	421	Censure	6
And Flatterye, with Frindes humors: still to move.	422	Censure	20
yett, yf with eythers vyce, I tainted bee,	422	Censure	22
That sits watering with the Muses.	657	Door Apollo	10
But with a Kisse, (if thou canst dare it)	662	Bedford	9
I send this small, but hearty testimony: and with charge,	666	Glover	5
that it remayne with him	666	Glover	6
With Chequer Inke, upon his guift, my paper,	666	Glover	8

WITHALL

Wormewood, and sulphure, sharpe, and tooth'd withall;	27	E2 My Booke	4
Thy lady's noble, fruitfull, chaste withall.	96	F2 Penshurst	90
To crowne the burthen which you goe withall,	119	F13 Aubigny	103
And (withall) I did untie	132	U2 How he saw	11
Even nose, and cheeke (withall)	141	U2 Her man	19
'Tis one good part I'ld lie withall.	142	U2 Exception	8
Withall, the dirtie paines those Citizens take,	213	U44 Speach	15
Such men I met withall, and so have you.	415	Rutter	11

WI'THE

| For, here they were throwne in wi'the melted pewter, | 88 | E133 Voyage | 153 |

WITHER

| All Parnassus Greene did wither, | 183 | U29 Fit of Rime | 17 |
| That were to wither all, and make a Grave | 192 | U38 Elegy 'Tis | 59 |

WITHERED

It could not withered bee.	106	F9 Celia 3	12
It would not withered bee.	106	F9 Celia 3	V 12
The withered Garlands tane away;	173	U22 Elegy Tho	18

WITHERS

| Wrung on the Withers, by Lord Loves despight, | 201 | U42 Elegy Let | 63 |

WITHIN

Except thou could'st, Sir Cod, weare them within.	33	E20 Cod 2	2
He that is round within himselfe, and streight,	63	E98 Th Roe 1	3
Leave but a kisse within the cup,	106	F9 Celia 3	V 3
As since he dares not come within my sight.	151	U11 Dreame	14
And as within your Office, you doe take	216	U45 Squib	13
Within the ballance; and not want a mite.	229	U54 Squib	10
That's six in silver; now within the Socket	229	U54 Squib	13
His weight is twenty Stone within two pound;	230	U56 Covell	11
For Nature, first, within doth fashion us	311	Horace	152
Things worthy to be done within, but take	317	Horace	261
Within the hope of having all forgiven?	323	Horace	394
With thy soft notes, and hold them within Pale	367	Ode Who saith	45

WITHOUT

If, without these vile arts, it will not sell,	28	E3 Bookseller	11
Without his, thine, and all times injurie?	47	E63 Salisbury 2	10
And ever is ill got without the first.	63	E98 Th Roe 1	12
Then stand unto thy selfe, not seeke without	83	E131 Ferrab. 2	13
Of sixe times to, and fro, without embassage,	85	E133 Voyage	34
The tripple head without a sop. At last,	89	E133 Voyage	186
And so went bravely backe, without protraction.	89	E133 Voyage	192
Without his feare, and of thy lords owne meate:	95	F2 Penshurst	62
Without which, all the rest were sounds, or lost.	118	F13 Aubigny	50
Without companions? 'Tis safe to have none.	118	F13 Aubigny	56
You know (without my flatt'ring you) too much	157	U13 Sacvile	155
Without your gift, though I can rate that too,	157	U13 Sacvile	158
As a poore single flatterer, without Baud,	167	U15 Friend-Wars	158
Without the pompe of Counsell; or more Aide,	186	U32 Elsmere	3
Without which all the world were darke;	189	U36 Song	7
Can pumpe for; or a Libell without salt	193	U38 Elegy 'Tis	96
But ever without blazon, or least shade	197	U40 Elegy That	13
Without the hazard of a drop of blood,	214	U44 Speach	47
So farre without inquirie what the States,	219	U47 Tribe	43
If I doe lose it: And, without a Tale,	229	U54 Squib	3
Sleepe in a Virgins bosome without feare,	230	U56 Covell	15
Widow or Wife, without the jealousie	230	U56 Covell	17
And valiant were, with, or without their hands.	233	U59 Newcastle	24
(Without prophanenesse) yet, a Poet, cry,	238	U66 Queene	4
(Without prophanenesse) as, a Poet, cry,	238	U66 Queene	V 4
Shee lies deliver'd, without paine,	251	U74 Weston	5
This beautie without falshood fayre,	275	U84 Body	7
And Phrygian Hau'boy, not without the Flute.	292	U86 Hor.4:1	24
Thy table without art, and easy-rated:	295	U90 Mart.10:47	8
Thou need new termes; thou maist, without excuse,	307	Horace	70
And not without much praise; till libertie	321	Horace	366
As Poppie, and Sardane honey; 'cause without	331	Horace	559
Poppy, with hony of Sardus; 'cause without	351	Horace	V535/559
Can; or all toile, without a wealthie veine:	331	Horace	584
Alone, without a rivall, by his will.	335	Horace	632
Alone, without a rivall, at your will.	354	Horace	V632

		Page	Title	Line
WITHOUT (cont.)				
Thou art a Moniment, without a tombe,		391	Shakespeare	22
Without conferring symboles. This's my day.		396	Drayton	10
Shee was the light (without reflexe		399	Lady Ogle	9
Or without angles, it was shee!		399	Lady Ogle	16
Swim without Corke! Why, thank the good Queen Anne.		405	Inigo Jones 1	68
WITNESSE				
Thou art the father, and the witnesse too.		44	E53 Old-end	8
To be the wealthy witnesse of my pen:		54	E81 Proule	4
My selfe a witnesse of thy few dayes sport:		55	E85 Goodyere 1	2
They tooke 'hem all to witnesse of their action:		89	E133 Voyage	191
O, be thou witnesse, that the reynes dost know,		122	F15 Heaven	5
My judge, my witnesse, and my advocate.		122	F15 Heaven	12
His Groomes to witnesse; or else lets it fall		154	U13 Sacvile	36
Times witnesse, herald of Antiquitie,		176	U24 Frontispice	17
Such Songsters there are store of; witnesse he		201	U42 Elegy Let	65
Witnesse his Action done at Scanderone;		262	U78 Digby	13
Witnesse my Birth-day the eleventh of June;		262	U78 Digby	V 14
And, calling truth to witnesse, make that good		270	U81 Pawlet	35
And, calling truth to witnesse, make it good		270	U81 Pawlet	V 35
What can one witnesse, and a weake one, add		385	Brooke	4
WITNESSES				
Of Angells, and all witnesses of light,		400	Lady Ogle	38
WITS				
Longer a knowing, then most wits doe live.		34	E23 Donne 1	5
To plucke downe mine, Poll sets up new wits still,		50	E71 Parrat	1
Wee have both wits, and fancies too,		145	U5 Woman-kind	5
That eats on wits, and Arts, and destroyes them both.		174	U23 Himselfe	6
Rime, the rack of finest wits,		183	U29 Fit of Rime	1
Have eaten with the Beauties, and the wits,		200	U42 Elegy Let	33
The wits will leave you, if they once perceive		223	U49 Pucell	37
Upon the Life, and Death of Playes, and Wits,		370	Fletcher	2
And we have wits to read, and praise to give.		391	Shakespeare	24
Yo'have all the Mysteries of Wits new Mint,		415	Rutter	28
WITT				
And Christian name too, with a Heralds witt.		394	Jane Ogle	12
Will any of these express your place? or witt?		402	Inigo Jones 1	18
WITTED				
O I left-witted, that purge every spring		325	Horace	429
WITTIE				
For wittie, in his language, is obscene.		42	E49 Playwrt 1	4
(They finde it both so wittie, and safe to give.)		118	F13 Aubigny	76
WITTS				
And are received for the Covey of Witts;		218	U47 Tribe	22
WITTY				
Neat Terence, witty Plautus, now not please;		392	Shakespeare	52
WIVES				
For all night-sinnes, with others wives, unknowne,		39	E39 Colt	1
Other great wives may blush at: when they see		119	F13 Aubigny	111
We are no women then, but wives.		146	U6 Defence	6
But then consent, your Daughters and your Wives,		200	U42 Elegy Let	19
Under that cover; an old Mid-wives hat!		202	U42 Elegy Let	83
The place, that was thy Wives inheritance.		209	U43 Vulcan	152
The Plot, that was thy Wives inheritance.		209	U43 Vulcan	V152
Thy Wives pox on thee, and B.B.'s too.		212	U43 Vulcan	216
Thy Wives pox on thee, and Bess Broughtons too.		212	U43 Vulcan	V216
To see the Pride at Court, their Wives doe make:		213	U44 Speach	16
WODDEN				
A wodden Dagger, is a Dagger of wood		403	Inigo Jones 1	27
WOEMEN				
The best of Woemen! her whole life		399	Lady Ogle	11
WOES				
With weightie woes she hurles us all along		342	Horace	V155
Warres greatest woes, and miseries increase,		363	Peace	3
WOFULL				
My wofull crie,		231	U57 Burges	3
WOLFE				
Or Kid forc't from the Wolfe againe.		291	U85 Country	60
WOLVES				
Safe from the wolves black jaw, and the dull Asses hoofe.		175	U23 Himselfe	36
To the Wolves studie, or Dogs eloquence;		187	U33 Councellour	12
WOMAN				
Throughout my booke. 'Troth put out woman too.		54	E83 Friend	2
On Mill my Ladies Woman.		57	E90 Mill	Ttl
To the World. A farewell for a Gentle-woman, . . .		100	F4 To the World	Ttl
Woman-kinde; devoure the wast		105	F8 Sicknesse	16
And a woman God did make me:		140	U2 Her man	6
In the person of Woman-kind. A Song Apologetique.		145	U5 Woman-kind	Ttl
For were the worthiest woman curst		146	U6 Defence	23
Of woman of fashion, and a Lady of spirit:		164	U15 Friend-Wars	82
The Servant of the Serving-woman, in scorne,		165	U15 Friend-Wars	99
Knew I this Woman? yes; And you doe see,		172	U20 Shrub	15
Do turne into a Woman.		364	Phoenix	4
WOMAN-KIND				
In the person of Woman-kind. A Song Apologetique.		145	U5 Woman-kind	Ttl
WOMAN-KINDE				
Woman-kinde; devoure the wast		105	F8 Sicknesse	16
WOMANS				
Just wife, and, to change me, make womans hast?		34	E25 Beast 1	8
That talke abroad of Womans change,		146	U6 Defence	2
A Womans friendship! God whom I trust in,		171	U20 Shrub	1
If to a Womans head a Painter would		305	Horace	1

WOMBE
   In a great belly. Write, then on thy wombe, ...   46   E62 Would-bee   11
   Thorough her wombe they make their famous road,   .   .   .   85   E133 Voyage   66
   Of your blest wombe, made fruitfull from above,   .   .   .   119   F13 Aubigny   95
   'Tis true, as my wombe swells, so my backe stoupes,   .   .   .   227   U52 Answer   4
   And this the wombe divine.   240   U67 Muses   51
   And mad'st thy Mothers wombe thine urne.   242   U70 Ode   8
WOMBES
   Thy deedes, unto thy name, will prove new wombes,   .   .   .   70   E109 Nevil   17
WOMBS
   Or in their windowes; doe but prove the wombs,   .   .   .   114   F12 Rutland   46
WOMEN
   And, for the cryes of Ghosts, women, and men,   .   .   .   84   E133 Voyage   16
   Song. That Women are but Mens shaddowes.   104   F7 Women but   Ttl
   Say, are not women truely, then, ...   104   F7 Women but   5
   Say, are not women truely, then, ...   104   F7 Women but   11
   We are no women then, but wives.   146   U6 Defence   6
   And both from Wine, and Women did abstaine.   333   Horace   590
   Where Gold's the Motive, women have no Nay.   .   .   .   363   Riches   18
   Might make the Fable of Good Women true.   372   Epitaph   14
WON
   With what thy vertue on the times hath won,   .   .   .   47   E63 Salisbury 2   2
   What though she hath won on Trust, as many doe,   .   .   .   223   U49 Pucell   21
   You won not Verses, Madam, you won mee, ...   230   U56 Covell   1
   You won them too, your oddes did merit it.   .   .   .   230   U56 Covell   4
WONDER
   Quick in his lips! who hath this wonder wrought?   .   .   .   33   E21 Gam'ster   5
   Rare, as wonder, was her wit;   39   E40 Ratcliffe   9
   Durst thinke it great, and worthy wonder too,   .   .   .   46   E60 Mounteagle   7
   Wherein what wonder see thy name hath wrought?   .   .   .   48   E64 Salisbury 3   16
   You wonder, who this is! and, why I name   74   E115 Honest Man   1
   By any arte. Then wonder not, ...   93   F1 Why write no   10
   Your conscience, and not wonder, if none askes   .   .   .   118   F13 Aubigny   69
   Let it not your wonder move, ...   131   U2 Excuse   1
   My wonder, why the taking a Clownes purse,   .   .   .   155   U13 Sacvile   89
   Meet some new matter to looke up and wonder!   .   .   .   157   U13 Sacvile   142
   What wonder perfect, all were fil'd, ...   188   U35 Chute   3
   Wonder to Valour! No, it is the Law   233   U59 Newcastle   14
   The wonder of her Sexe, and of your Blood.   .   .   .   274   U84 Descent   12
   And yet remaine our wonder still.   278   U84 Mind   20
   Twice, or thrice good, I wonder: but am more   .   .   .   329   Horace   535
   I wonder how this happie man should know, ...   333   Horace   605
   First: thy successe did strike my sence with wonder;   .   .   .   361   Palmer   5
   wear spent with wonder as they weare delated,   .   .   .   361   Palmer   24
   The applause! delight! the wonder of our Stage!   .   .   .   391   Shakespeare   18
   It makes me ravish'd with just wonder, cry   .   .   .   395   May   13
   Wonder to truth! and have my Vision hoorld,   .   .   .   396   Drayton   13
   Yet give mee leave, to wonder at the birth   .   .   .   398   Drayton   83
   With wonder on the thorny regiment.   413   Ghyrlond   16
WONDER'D
   I wonder'd at the richnesse, but am lost, ...   160   U14 Selden   53
   And wonder'd at the bounties of this day: 255   U75 Epithalam.   90
WONDERS
   Wonders forth after: As Antiphates, ...   315   Horace   205
   To the wonders of the Peake, ...   416   Moon   1
WONDRED
   Have all his actions wondred at, and view'd   .   .   .   284   U84 Muse   77
WONDRING
   The Fights, the Cryes, and wondring at the Jarres   .   .   .   397   Drayton   41
WONDRINGE
   Lowd to the wondringe thronge   419   Ode:If Men   7
WONNDER
   Give cause to some of wonnder, some despite,   .   .   .   420   Ode:If Men   35
WONNE
   Love thy great losse, which a renowne hath wonne,   .   .   .   49   E66 Cary   11
   Which thou art to thy selfe: whose fame was wonne   .   .   .   58   E91 Vere   5
   Not Caesars deeds, nor all his honors wonne,   .   .   .   71   E110 Edmonds 1   1
   To my lesse sanguine Muse, wherein she'hath wonne   .   .   .   115   F12 Rutland   72
   Her armes when Paris wonne her   135   U2 Triumph   V 34
   Whether we have lost, or wonne, ...   138   U2 Kisse   6
   Much from him I professe I wonne, ...   152   U12 Corbet   29
   All this corrupts the thankes; lesse hath he wonne,   .   .   .   154   U13 Sacvile   33
   Be wonne a friend; it must both sway, and bend   .   .   .   317   Horace   281
   Were to be staid with softnesses, and wonne   .   .   .   321   Horace   326
   And more hath wonne   367   Ode Who saith   52
   So wood at last, that he was wonne to her   .   .   .   394   Jane Ogle   22
WONT
   When thou wert wont t'admire, not censure men.   .   .   .   32   E18 Censurer   8
   He wont was to encounter me, aloud, ...   62   E97 Motion   7
   A broken heart thou wert not wont despise,   .   .   .   127   U1 Trinitie   10
WOO
   To Sir Lucklesse Woo-all.   42   E46 Luckless 1   Ttl
   To put out the word, whore, thou do'st me woo,   .   .   .   54   E83 Friend   1
   Thou woo Minerva! or to wit aspire!   208   U43 Vulcan   109
WOO-ALL
   To Sir Lucklesse Woo-all.   42   E46 Luckless 1   Ttl
WOOD   (See also WODDEN)
   Of partrich, pheasant, wood-cock, of which some   .   .   .   65   E101 Supper   18
   Of wood, of water: therein thou art faire.   .   .   .   93   F2 Penshurst   8
   Fertile of wood, Ashore, and Sydney's copp's,   .   .   .   94   F2 Penshurst   26
   Under-wood.   127   Under-wood   Ttl
   To deck the hallow'd Harth with old wood fir'd   .   .   .   291   U85 Country   43
   Beneath a Sweet-wood Roofe, neere Alba Lake: .   .   .   292   U86 Hor.4:1   20

WOOD   (cont.)
  Build Townes, and carve the Lawes in leaves of wood.   .   .   327   Horace   490
  So wood at last, that he was wonne to her   394   Jane Ogle   22
  A wodden Dagger, is a Dagger of wood   403   Inigo Jones 1   27
WOOD-COCK
  Of partrich, pheasant, wood-cock, of which some   .   .   65   E101 Supper   18
WOODS
  Along'st the curled woods, and painted meades,   .   .   97   F3 Wroth   17
  Under-woods. Consisting Of Divers Poems.   .   .   .   125   Under-wood   Ttl
  And call the walking woods?   143   U3 Musicall   12
  Whose praises let's report unto the Woods,   .   .   .   265   U79 New-yeares   52
  The soft birds quarrell in the Woods,   .   .   .   290   U85 Country   26
  One thing prodigiously, paints in the woods   .   .   307   Horace   41
  Stamp'd to the time. As woods whose change appeares   .   309   Horace   85
WOOE
  We wooe thee, stay   252   U75 Epithalam.   6
WOOES
  I sent the cause: Hee wooes with an ill sprite.   .   .   33   E19 Cod 1   2
  Hee that wooes every widdow, will get none.   .   .   .   42   E47 Luckless 2   2
  And beckning wooes me, from the fatall tree   .   .   268   U81 Pawlet   3
WOOFE
  And know the woofe, and warpe thereof; can tell   .   415   Rutter   15
WOOING
  A knight-hood bought, to goe a wooing in?   .   .   .   42   E46 Luckless 1   2
WOOLL
  From locks of wooll, or shreds from the whole peece?   .   45   E56 Poet-Ape   14
  Have you felt the wooll o' the Bever?   .   .   .   135   U2 Triumph   25
  Out of their Choysest, and their whitest wooll.   .   .   225   U51 Bacon   16
WOOLLY
  The blushing apricot, and woolly peach   .   .   .   94   F2 Penshurst   43
  Chin, as woolly as the Peach;   141   U2 Her man   21
WORD
  Forbidd' his side! and nothing, but the word   .   .   33   E21 Gam'ster   4
  To put out the word, whore, thou do'st me woo,   .   .   54   E83 Friend   1
  We innocently met. No simple word, ...   65   E101 Supper   39
  With such a one. And therein keepes it's word.   .   .   74   E115 Honest Man   21
  'Twas not entayl'd on title. That some word   .   .   75   E116 Jephson   7
  You are depending on his word, and will;   .   .   .   119   F13 Aubigny   114
  The Word, which heaven, and earth did make;   .   .   130   U1 Nativitie   11
  The Word was now made Flesh indeed,   .   .   .   130   U1 Nativitie   17
  Well knowne, and practiz'd borrowers on their word,   .   154   U13 Sacvile   48
  Thy Adversaries fall, as not a word   .   .   .   187   U33 Councellour   33
  If I had writ no word, but Deare, farewell.   .   .   198   U40 Elegy That   50
  Of life, and light, the Sonne of God, the Word!   .   .   285   U84 Muse   112
  To render word for word: nor with thy sleight   .   .   313   Horace   191
  The word, once out, never returned yet.   .   .   352   Horace   V556/580
  Then change; no word, or worke, more would he spend   .   335   Horace   630
  Trie and trust Roger, was the word, but now   .   .   378   Coryat 2   80
  I know for such, as (if my word will waigh)   .   .   386   Husband   11
  As not the smallest joint, or gentlest word   .   .   395   May   21
WORDED
  Of worded Balladrie, ...   175   U23 Himselfe   21
WORDES
  That are your wordes of credit. Keepe your Names   .   69   E107 Hungry   24
WORDS
  Whil'st thou art certaine to thy words, once gone,   .   52   E74 Chancelor   7
  Then words that sooth her!   134   U2 Triumph   16
  No tunes are sweet, nor words have sting,   .   .   143   U3 Musicall   15
  No voice so sweet, nor words have sting,   .   .   143   U3 Musicall   V 15
  Sweet bags, sweet Powders, nor sweet words will passe   165   U15 Friend-Wars 112
  And their words too; where I but breake my Band.   .   169   U17 Friend-Debt   9
  Wresting words, from their true calling;   .   .   183   U29 Fit of Rime   7
  Words, and sweetnesse, and be scant   .   .   .   184   U29 Fit of Rime   44
  Be idle words, though of a parting Man;   .   .   199   U41 Elegy Since   4
  And as lip-thirstie, in each words expence,   .   .   222   U49 Pucell   13
  Friendship, in deed, was written, not in words: .   247   U70 Ode   123
  The Voyce so sweet, the words so faire,   .   .   279   U84 Mind   37
  Or why, my well-grac'd words among,   .   .   .   293   U86 Hor.4:1   35
  In using also of new words, to be   .   .   .   307   Horace   65
  Most worthie praise, when words that common grew,   .   307   Horace   67
  Most worthie praise, when words that vulgar grew,   .   340   Horace   V 67
  Faine words, unheard of to the well-truss'd race   .   309   Horace   71
  Faine words, unheard of to the girded race   .   340   Horace   V 71
  And those thy new, and late-coyn'd words receive,   .   309   Horace   74
  Of words decay, and phrases borne but late   .   .   309   Horace   88
  Their bombard-phrase, and foot-and-halfe-foot words.   .   311   Horace   139
  Meere raigning words: nor will I labour so   .   .   321   Horace   343
  There words will follow, not against their will.   .   325   Horace   444
  There words will never follow 'gainst their will.   .   349   Horace   V444
  When the old words doe strike on the new times,   .   389   Aleman   4
  Hence, then, prophane: Here needs no words expense   .   400   Beaumont   3
WORK
  . . . the Author of this Work, M. Rich. Brome.   .   .   409   Brome   Ttl
WORKE
  Whose every worke, of thy most earely wit,   .   .   34   E23 Donne 1   3
  What could not worke; at home in his repaire   .   .   37   E32 Roe 2   7
  Dispraise my worke, then praise it frostily: .   .   43   E52 Courtling   2
  And proud, my worke shall out-last common deeds,   .   46   E60 Mounteagle   6
  Or, better worke! were thy glad countrey blest,   .   61   E95 Savile   14
  Nor that his worke liv'd in the hands of foes,   .   71   E110 Edmonds 1   9
  And thence, deprave thee, and thy worke. To those   .   72   E111 Edmonds 2   11
  A worke of ours, we part with our owne right;   .   .   82   E131 Ferrab. 2   2
  Might then both thee, thy worke and merit raise: .   83   E132 Sylvester   2

		Page	Title	Line
WORKE (cont.)				
Act a brave worke, call it thy last adventry:	. . . .	85	E133 :Voyage	57
When the worke would be effected:	. . . .	140	U2 Promise	8
In offering this thy worke to no great Name,	. . . .	161	U14 Selden	69
Not a worke deserving Baies,	. . . .	183	U29 Fit of Rime	28
And labour'd in the worke; not with the fame:	. . . .	185	U30 Burleigh	12
All soote, and embers! odious, as thy worke!	. . .	207	U43 Vulcan	106
A cheerefull worke to all good eyes, to see	. . .	224	U50 Countesse	16
Of Tryals, to worke downe	. . .	255	U75 Epithalam.	103
That thou art lov'd of God, this worke is done,	. . .	268	U80 Christning	1
Worke with my fancie, his owne hand.	. . . .	276	U84 Body	12
This worke I can performe alone;	. . . .	277	U84 Mind	3
Hee knowes, what worke h'hath done, to call this Guest,	. . .	284	U84 Muse	81
For his designed worke, the perfect end	. . .	288	U84 Muse	206
But in the maine worke haplesse: since he knowes	. .	307	Horace	48
To forme a worke, I would no more desire	. . . .	307	Horace	50
To frame a worke, I would no more desire	. . .	339	Horace	V 52/ 50
A kingly worke; or that long barren fen	. . .	309	Horace	93
To worke the hearers minds, still, to their plight.	. .	311	Horace	142
But, I confesse, that, in a long worke, sleepe	. .	329	Horace	537
Though I confesse, that, in a long worke, sleepe	. .	351	Horace	V513/537
Then change; no word, or worke, more would he spend	.	335	Horace	630
Looke here on Bretons worke, the master print:	. .	362	Author	5
But now, your Worke is done, if they that view	. .	370	Author	9
A glorified worke to Time, when Fire,	. . .	371	Fletcher	15
To such a worke, as could not need theirs? Yet	. .	385	Brooke	5
To see his worke be good; but that he looke	. .	385	Husband	2
But I have seene thy worke, and I know thee:	. .	386	Browne	3
This thy worke forth: that judgment mine commends.	.	386	Browne	8
Whose worke could this be, Chapman, to refine	. .	388	Chapman	1
On the Author, Worke, and Translator.	. .	389	Aleman	Ttl
The selfe same Genius! so the worke will say.	. .	395	May	23
Before this worke? where Envy hath not cast	. .	401	Beaumont	13
. . . on his Worke published.	. . .	401	Filmer	Ttl
All in the Worke! And soe shall still for Ben:	. .	404	Inigo Jones 1	65
An Earle of show: for all thy worke is showe:	. .	407	Inigo Jones 2	21
Shall not worke out unto it, such a fame.	. . .	409	Detractor	12
IORKER				
A Master-worker call'd, th'old standerd burst	. .	415	Rutter	22
IORKES				
Whose workes are eene the fripperie of wit,	. . .	44	E56 Poet-Ape	2
If workes (not th'authors) their owne grace should looke,	.	60	E94 Bedford 3	3
To aske it: though in most of workes it be	. .	158	U14 Selden	7
Pox on your fire workes, Vulcan; if it be	. .	211	U43 Vulcan	V191
'Bove all your Fire-workes, had at Ephesus,	. .	211	U43 Vulcan	194
Beyond your Fire-workes, had at Ephesus,	. .	211	U43 Vulcan	V194
'Bove all our Fire-workes, had at Ephesus,	. .	211	U43 Vulcan	V194
More subtle workes, and finer pieces farre,	. .	242	U69 Friend Son	22
Reducts, Halfe-moones, Horne-workes, and such close wayes,	.	248	U71 Treasurer	8
At Bonefires, Rockets, Fire-workes, with the Shoutes	.	249	U72 King	13
your workes thus differing, troth let soe your style:	.	407	Inigo Jones 2	19
IORKING				
Though I, in working of my song,	. . . .	182	U27 Ode Helen	33
IORKMANSHIP				
To see the workmanship so'xceed the cost!	. . .	160	U14 Selden	54
IORKS				
. . . on his Translation of Hesiods Works, & Dayes.	.	388	Chapman	Ttl
IORK'ST				
In short; I bid, Let what thou work'st upon,	. .	307	Horace	31
IORKST				
Heare me conclude; let what thou workst upon	. .	339	Horace	V 31
IORLD				
The world the temple was, the priest a king,	. .	28	E5 Union	3
And person to the world; ere I thy name.	. . .	36	E30 Guiltie	4
Whither the world must follow. And I, now,	. . .	37	E33 Roe 3	3
To give the world assurance thou wert both;	. .	43	E53 Old-end	6
The world reputes you barren: but I know	. . .	46	E62 Would-bee	3
The world must know your greatnesse is my debter.	.	51	E73 Fine Grand	4
This world deaths region is, the other lifes:	. .	54	E80 Life/Death	5
A line unto thee, till the world it know;	. .	54	E81 Proule	2
A picture, which the world for yours must know,	. .	67	E104 Montgomery	14
That to the world thou should'st reveale so much,	.	72	E111 Edmonds 2	10
Both whose dimensions, lost, the world might finde	.	79	E125 Uvedale	3
Which (would the world not mis-call't flatterie)	.	79	E125 Uvedale	9
For, if the hum'rous world will talke at large,	.	83	E131 Ferrab. 2	7
That to the world I publish, for him, this;	. .	83	E132 Sylvester	9
One said, the other swore, the world consists.	.	87	E133 Voyage	129
To the World. A farewell for a Gentle-woman, . . .		100	F4 To the World	Ttl
False world, good-night: since thou hast brought	.	100	F4 To the World	1
The world hath seene, which all these had in trust,	.	114	F12 Rutland	39
Which though the turning world may dis-esteeme,	.	118	F13 Aubigny	64
Hee whom the whole world could not take,	. .	130	U1 Nativitie	10
All the world for love may die.	. . .	131	U2 Excuse	24
All that Loves world compriseth!	. . .	134	U2 Triumph	12
And all the world turne Eares.	. . .	143	U3 Musicall	4
For what they streight would to the world forsweare;	.	154	U13 Sacvile	50
The whole world here leaven'd with madnesse swells;	.	163	U15 Friend-Wars	4
Spread through the World) is easier farre to find,	.	167	U15 Friend-Wars	172
As not the World can praise too much,	. .	173	U22 Elegy Tho	3
To give the world againe:	. . .	175	U23 Himselfe	29
Raising the World to good or evill fame,	. .	175	U24 Frontispice	3
Which all the world then styl'd divine?	. .	181	U27 Ode Helen	20
Scarce the world a Wit doth nourish,	. . .	184	U29 Fit of Rime	38

```
                                                              Page      Title        Line
WORLD  (cont.)
     Without which all the world were darke;        .     .     .     .     . 189   U36 Song          7
     He pardons slips, goes by a world of ills,     .     .     .     .     . 193   U38 Elegy 'Tis   69
     And how more faire, and lovely lookes the world   .     .     .     . 193   U38 Elegy 'Tis   73
     And thinkes I dare not her? let the world see.   .     .     .     . 222   U49 Pucell        2
     An Archetype, for all the world to see,        .     .     .     .     . 227   U52 Answer       14
     Whereby the safetie of the world was wrought)   .     .     .     . 238   U66 Queene      V 8
     Upon th'affrighted world:                      .     .     .     .     . 243   U70 Ode          16
     How did she leave the world? with what contempt?   .     .     . 270   U81 Pawlet       47
     And I, into the world, all Soule, was sent!     .     .     .     . 270   U81 Pawlet       56
     And I, into the world with my Soule, was sent!   .     .     . 270   U81 Pawlet     V 56
     Whole Nations! nay, Mankind! the World, with all   .     .     . 271   U81 Pawlet       90
     And thou hast painted beauties world.          .     .     .     .     . 277   U84 Body         28
     The world to ruine with it; in her Fall,       .     .     .     .     . 283   U84 Muse         25
     On all the world! She saw him on the Crosse    .     .     .     . 288   U84 Muse        201
     . . . omitted, and now communicated to the World   .     .     . 379   Coryat 3        Ttl
     He sayes to the world, let any man mend it,    .     .     .     . 379   Coryat 3         15
     And the world in it, I begin to doubt,         .     .     .     .     . 395   May               4
     Hot from thy trumpet, round, about the world.   .     .     .     . 396   Drayton          14
     I call the world, that envies mee, to see      .     .     .     . 398   Drayton          93
     Unto the world, in praise of your first Play:   .     .     .     . 414   Rutter            2
WORLDLINGS
     All other Acts of Worldlings, are but toyle    .     .     .     . 162   U15 Friend-Wars   9
     All other Acts of Worldlings, are meere toyle   .     .     .     . 162   U15 Friend-Wars V 9
WORLD'S
     The world's pure gold, and wise simplicitie;   .     .     .     . 78    E122 Rudyerd 2    4
WORLDS
     To catch the worlds loose laughter, or vaine gaze.   .     .     . 27    E2 My Booke      12
     To have so soone scap'd worlds, and fleshes rage,   .     .     . 41    E45 First Son     7
     A Sparke to set whole worlds a-fire,           .     .     .     .     . 189   U36 Song          9
     See the worlds Ruines! nothing but the piles   .     .     .     . 209   U43 Vulcan      137
     And cure the Worlds diseases:                  .     .     .     .     . 221   U48 Bacchus      24
     What worlds of blessings to good Kings they owe:   .     .     . 261   U77 Treasurer    20
     of thy rich labors worlds of thoughts created,   .     .     .     . 361   Palmer           22
     But in one tongue, was form'd with the worlds wit:   .     .     . 389   Aleman            6
WORME
     On Court-worme.        .     .     .     .     .     .     .     . 31    E15 Court-worm  Ttl
     Can we not leave this worme? or will we not?   .     .     .     . 166   U15 Friend-Wars 141
WORMES
     All men are wormes: But this no man.  In silke   .     .     . 31    E15 Court-worm    1
     Are we by Booke-wormes to be awde? must we     .     .     .     . 215   U44 Speach       67
     Like flies, or wormes, with mans corrupt parts fed:   .     . 218   U47 Tribe        18
WORMEWOOD
     Wormewood, and sulphure, sharpe, and tooth'd withall;   .     . 27    E2 My Booke       4
WORNE
     There is not worne that lace, purle, knot or pin,   .     .     . 200   U42 Elegy Let    16
     But they may see Gold-Chaines, and Pearle worne then,   .     . 213   U44 Speach       13
WORSE
     Make him loose all his friends; and, which is worse,   .     . 48    E65 Muse          9
     Delay is bad, doubt worse, depending worst;    .     .     .     . 50    E70 Wm Roe 1      5
     Still Mill continu'd: Nay, his face growing worse,   .     .     . 57    E90 Mill         11
     Purchas'd by rapine, worse then stealth,       .     .     .     . 99    F3 Wroth         82
     His unjust hopes, with praises begg'd, or (worse)   .     .     . 162   U15 Friend-Wars  12
     were such as I will now relate, or worse?      .     .     .     . 172   U20 Shrub        14
     Doe not you aske to know her, she is worse     .     .     .     . 172   U20 Shrub        17
     None brookes the Sun-light worse then he.      .     .     .     . 189   U36 Song          4
     I could invent a sentence, yet were worse;     .     .     .     . 211   U43 Vulcan      189
     I could invent a sentence, yet more worse;     .     .     .     . 211   U43 Vulcan     V189
     Or a worse Crime, the ignorance of art.        .     .     .     . 323   Horace          386
WORSER
     And nights too, in worser wayes?               .     .     .     . 104   F8 Sicknesse      6
WORSHIP
     Of worship, they their nodding chinnes doe hit   .     .     . 87    E133 Voyage     123
     To worship thee.        .     .     .     .     .     .     .     . 127   U1 Trinitie      20
     Such worship due to kicking of a Punck!        .     .     .     . 155   U13 Sacvile      93
     Against the Nature he would worship.  Hee      .     .     .     . 284   U84 Muse         75
WORST
     I, not the worst, am covetous of thee.         .     .     .     . 40    E43 Salisbury 1   6
     Delay is bad, doubt worse, depending worst;    .     .     .     . 50    E70 Wm Roe 1      5
     Though both be good, the latter yet is worst,   .     .     .     . 63    E98 Th Roe 1     11
     Ploughing the mayne.  When, see (the worst of all lucks)   . 86    E133 Voyage      78
     And speaking worst of those, from whom they went   .     . 154   U13 Sacvile      51
     They are not, Sir, worst Owers, that doe pay   .     .     .     . 169   U17 Friend-Debt   1
     Or if it would, the Court is the worst place,   .     .     .     . 223   U49 Pucell       43
     Then goe on, and doe its worst;                .     .     .     . 260   U76 Petition     29
     The worst of Statuaries, here about            .     .     .     . 307   Horace           45
     And highest; sinketh to the lowest, and worst.   .     .     . 331   Horace          564
     In spite of Hipocrites, who are the worst      .     .     .     . 416   Dover             9
WORTH  (NAME)
     A Sonnet, to the noble Lady, the Lady Mary Worth.   .     .     . 182   U28 Worth       Ttl
WORTH
     How I doe feare my selfe, that am not worth    .     .     .     . 44    E55 Beaumont      3
     To so true worth, though thou thy selfe forbid.   .     .     . 47    E63 Salisbury 2  12
     To such true worth, though thou thy selfe forbid.   .     . 47    E63 Salisbury 2 V 12
     Contends t'have worth enjoy, from his regard,   .     .     .     . 48    E64 Salisbury 3  13
     For worth he has not, He is tax'd, not prais'd.   .     .     . 48    E65 Muse         16
     And present worth in all dost so contract,     .     .     .     . 57    E89 Allen        11
     But that your worth will dignifie our feast,   .     .     .     . 64    E101 Supper       4
     Action, or engine, worth a note of thine,      .     .     .     . 71    E110 Edmonds 1   20
     Retyr'd, with purpose your faire worth to praise,   .     .     . 80    E126 Mrs Cary     1
     That which, to boote with hell, is thought worth heaven,   . 113   F12 Rutland        3
     Worth an estate, treble to that you have.      .     .     .     . 114   F12 Rutland      36
     From being forsaken, then doth worth:          .     .     .     . 146   U6 Defence       22
```

WORTH (cont.)
Loves sicknesse, and his noted want of worth, ... 150 U10 Jealousie 14
Worth a crowning. . . . . 183 U29 Fit of Rime 27
What did she worth thy spight? were there not store . . 188 U34 Small Poxe 3
You would restore it? No, that's worth a feare, . . 199 U41 Elegy Since 15
(If they be faire and worth it) have their lives . . 200 U42 Elegy Let 20
Inquirie of the worth: So must we doe, ... 216 U45 Squib 15
To vertue, and true worth, be ever blind. . . . 250 U73 Weston 10
And celebrate (perfection at the worth) . . . 253 U75 Epithalam. 28
Heare, O you Groves, and, Hills, resound his worth. . . 264 U79 New-yeares 31
Cato's and Ennius tongues have lent much worth, . . 309 Horace 81
Still to be like himselfe, and hold his worth. . . 313 Horace 182
What doth this Promiser such gaping worth . . . 313 Horace 197
What doth this Promiser such great gaping worth . . 343 Horace V197
Worth his untying happen there: And not . . . 317 Horace 274
Unwonted language; and that sense of worth . . . 319 Horace 308
For so, they shall not only gaine the worth, . . . 325 Horace 425
* * * * * When loe to crowne thy worth . . . 361 Palmer 27
And therein (which is worth his valour too) . . . 378 Coryat 2 84
Out-bee that Wife, in worth, thy freind did make: . . 384 Somerset 12
Hymens amends, to make it worth his fault. . . . 384 Somerset 14
Hold thyne owne worth unbroke: which is so good . . 386 Browne 13
To be worth Envy. Henceforth I doe meane . . . 405 Inigo Jones 1 70
An Earle of show: for all thy worth is showe: . . 407 Inigo Jones 2 V 21
Thou art not worth it. Who will care to knowe . . 409 Detractor 13
Thy Dirty braines, Men smell thy want of worth. . . 409 Detractor 22
WORTHIE
Most worthie praise, when words that common grew, . . 307 Horace 67
Most worthie praise, when words that vulgar grew, . . 340 Horace V 67
And come forth worthie Ivye, or the Bayes, . . . 420 Ode:If Men 26
Whoe worthie wine, whoe not, to bee wyse Pallas guests. . 421 Ode:If Men 45
WORTHIER
And which you (being the worthier) gave me leave . . 190 U37 Friend-Book 11
WORTHIEST
For were the worthiest woman curst . . . . 146 U6 Defence 23
Of worthiest knowledge, that can take mens minds. . . 217 U46 Coke 20
WORTHILY
To his much and worthily esteemed friend the Author. . 383 Author Ttl
WORTHLESSE
That hast betray'd me to a worthlesse lord; . . . 48 E65 Muse 2
WORTHY
To the most Worthy of his Honors. Robert, . . . 40 E43 Salisbury 1 VTtl
Durst thinke it great, and worthy wonder too, . . 46 E60 Mounteagle 7
Since men have left to doe praise-worthy things, . . 49 E67 Suffolk 1
To the worthy Sir Horace Vere. . . . . 58 E91 Vere VTtl
Hast taught thy selfe worthy thy pen to tread, . . 63 E99 Th Roe 2 3
And that to write things worthy to be read: . . . 63 E99 Th Roe 2 4
Not that we thinke us worthy such a ghest, . . . 64 E101 Supper 3
So Phoebus makes me worthy of his bayes, . . . 73 E113 Overbury 1
In it' owne hall; when these (in worthy scorne . . 85 E133 Voyage 31
They laugh't, at his laugh-worthy fate. And past . . 89 E133 Voyage 185
Is more crowne-worthy still, ... 112 F11 Epode 88
For which you worthy are the glad encrease . . . 119 F13 Aubigny 94
And was worthy (being so seene) . . . . 138 U2 Kisse 27
Are they not worthy to be answer'd so, . . . 154 U13 Sacvile 59
If there be nothing worthy you can see . . . 191 U38 Elegy 'Tis 15
As if it were not worthy to be there: . . . 199 U41 Elegy Since 16
Thoughts worthy of thy gift, this Inke, . . . 229 U55 Burges 2
And will you, worthy Sonne, Sir, knowing this, . . 285 U84 Muse 97
Thou worthy in eternall Flower to fare, . . . 294 U89 Mart.8:77 2
Father, and sons right worthy of your Sire, . . . 339 Horace V 34
Things worthy to be done within, but take . . . 317 Horace 261
In juyce of Cedar worthy to be steep'd; . . . 327 Horace 475
If of their friendship he be worthy, or no: . . . 333 Horace 619
To the worthy Author M. John Fletcher. . . . 370 Fletcher Ttl
To the worthy Author on the Husband. . . . 385 Husband Ttl
Was worthy of a Good one; And this, here, . . . 386 Husband 10
I find thee write most worthy to be read. . . . 386 Browne 6
To my worthy and honour'd Friend, Mr George Chapman, . . . 388 Chapman Ttl
And, till I worthy am to wish I were, . . . 398 Drayton 92
To my worthy Friend, Master Edward Filmer, . . . 401 Filmer Ttl
(And labours to seem worthy of that feare) . . . 407 Inigo Jones 3 2
The Eye of flowers, worthy, for his scent, . . . 413 Ghyrlond 14
To my worthy, and deserving Brother . . . 666 Glover 1
WORTHYES
Of all the Worthyes hope t'outlast thy one, . . . 406 Inigo Jones 1 99
WOU'D
Upon th'Exchange of Letters, as I wou'd . . . 386 Browne 14
WOULD (See also 'D, 'LD)
More high, more holy, that shee more would crave. . . 31 E14 Camden 6
All which I meant to praise, and, yet, I would; . . 34 E23 Donne 1 9
If any friends teares could restore, his would; . . 35 E27 Roe 1 5
Who would not be thy subject, James, t'obay . . . 37 E35 James 2 1
But that his Jone doth too. And Giles would never, . . 40 E42 Giles 4
No more would Jone he should. Giles riseth early, . . 40 E42 Giles 6
Her foes enough would fame thee in their hate. . . 40 E43 Salisbury 1 4
Arsenike would thee fit for societie make. . . . 42 E50 Cod 3 3
Would both thy folly, and thy spite betray. . . . 43 E52 Courtling 6
Poore Poet-Ape, that would be thought our chiefe, . . 44 E56 Poet-Ape 1
At first he made low shifts, would picke and gleane, . . 45 E56 Poet-Ape 5
Or, if shee would but modestly have prais'd . . . 46 E60 Mounteagle 3
To Fine Lady Would-bee. . . . . . . 46 E62 Would-bee Ttl
Fine Madame Would-Bee, wherefore should you feare, . . 46 E62 Would-bee 1

WOULD (cont.)

	Page	Title	Line
Nature, they thought, in all, that he would faine.	53	E79 Rutland	8
As he would burne, or better farre his booke.	53	E79 Rutland	12
How wilfull blind is he then, that would stray,	53	E80 Life/Death	3
I would have spent: how every Muse should know it,	55	E84 Bedford 2	7
What would his serious actions me have learned?	55	E85 Goodyere 1	12
When I would know thee Goodyere, my thought lookes	55	E86 Goodyere 2	1
Would you beleeve, when you this Mounsieur see,	56	E88 Monsieur	1
Was dull, and long, ere shee would goe to man:	57	E90 Mill	3
To any one, were envie: which would live	58	E91 Vere	11
And two, that would have falne as great, as they,	60	E93 Radcliffe	7
Whose poemes would not wish to be your booke?	60	E94 Bedford 3	4
And what would hurt his vertue makes it still.	63	E98 Th Roe 1	6
If time to facts, as unto men would owe?	64	E99 Th Roe 2	6
As lowdest praisers, who perhaps would find	67	E103 L Wroth 1	11
Even in the dew of grace, what you would bee?	67	E104 Montgomery	2
Would call you more then Ceres, if not that:	68	E105 L Wroth 2	8
And, drest in shepheards tyre, who would not say:	68	E105 L Wroth 2	9
If dancing, all would cry th'Idalian Queene,	68	E105 L Wroth 2	11
There's none so dull, that for your stile would aske,	68	E105 L Wroth 2	15
Or, keeping your due state, that would not cry,	68	E105 L Wroth 2	17
Whether thy learning they would take, or wit,	68	E106 E Herbert	5
Their latter praise would still the greatest bee,	68	E106 E Herbert	9
Describ'd, it 's thus: Defin'd would you it have?	75	E115 Honest Man	33
If I would wish, for truth, and not for show,	78	E122 Rudyerd 2	1
If I would strive to bring backe times, and trie	78	E122 Rudyerd 2	3
If I would vertue set, as shee was yong,	78	E122 Rudyerd 2	5
I would restore, and keepe it ever such;	78	E122 Rudyerd 2	8
Which (would the world not mis-call't flatterie)	79	E125 Uvedale	9
Is there a hope, that Man would thankefull bee,	80	E127 Aubigny	1
And would (being ask'd the truth) ashamed say,	83	E131 Ferrab. 2	11
They met the second Prodigie, would feare a	86	E133 Voyage	79
By their ripe daughters, whom they would commend	95	F2 Penshurst	54
Doe enough; and who would take	105	F8 Sicknesse	26
I would not change for thine.	106	F9 Celia 3	8
It would not withered bee.	106	F9 Celia 3	V 12
Though he would steale his sisters Pegasus,	107	F10 Proludium	23
Would, at suggestion of a steepe desire,	111	F11 Epode	63
Would make a day of night,	112	F11 Epode	94
Who would be false to? chiefly, when he knowes	112	F11 Epode	V103
Would not be fearefull to offend a dame	112	F11 Epode	109
And would on Conditions, be	133	U2 Suffered	5
And would faine have chang'd the fate,	133	U2 Suffered	19
Through Swords, through Seas, whether she would ride.	134	U2 Triumph	10
Or if you would yet have stay'd,	138	U2 Kisse	29
Whether any would up-braid	138	U2 Kisse	30
Where, how it would have relish'd well;	139	U2 Another	14
Lightly promis'd, she would tell	139	U2 Promise	3
When the worke would be effected:	140	U2 Promise	8
I will tell what Man would please me.	140	U2 Her man	2
I would have him, if I could,	140	U2 Her man	3
He would have a hand as soft	141	U2 Her man	25
If wee would search with care, and paine,	145	U5 Woman-kind	8
Such in valour would excell,	146	U6 Defence	7
Unlesse my heart would as my thought be torne.	147	U7 Nymph	14
As it would be to each a fame:	148	U7 Nymph	34
If Love, or feare, would let me tell his name.	148	U7 Nymph	35
It vent it selfe, but as it would,	151	U12 Corbet	2
Would say as much, as both have done	151	U12 Corbet	3
His lookes would so correct it, when	152	U12 Corbet	27
The way to meet, what others would upbraid;	153	U13 Sacvile	10
Yet choyce from whom I take them; and would shame	153	U13 Sacvile	17
Lest Ayre, or Print, but flies it: Such men would	154	U13 Sacvile	45
For what they streight would to the world forsweare;	154	U13 Sacvile	50
As if they would belie their stature; those	157	U13 Sacvile	146
That would, perhaps, have prais'd, and thank'd the same,	161	U14 Selden	70
The Credit, what would furnish a tenth Muse!	161	U14 Selden	84
That gaspe for action, and would yet revive	162	U15 Friend-Wars	6
Be honour is so mixt) by such as would,	162	U15 Friend-Wars	25
Not make a verse; Anger; or laughter would,	164	U15 Friend-Wars	62
Where Pittes, or Wright, or Modet would not venter,	164	U15 Friend-Wars	80
Now so much friend, as you would trust in me,	169	U17 Friend-Debt	14
Then like, then love; and now would they amaze?	169	U18 Elegy Can	4
Such Guides men use not, who their way would find,	170	U18 Elegy Can	12
Because they would free Justice imitate,	170	U18 Elegy Can	18
Vaile their owne eyes, and would impartially	170	U18 Elegy Can	19
As would make shift, to make himselfe alone,	171	U19 Elegy By	24
As in his place, because he would not varie,	171	U19 Elegy By	27
His name in any mettall, it would breake.	172	U21 Ltl Shrub	2
That would their better objects find:	173	U22 Elegy Tho	27
Wise Providence would so; that nor the good	176	U24 Frontispice	5
high Providence would so; that nor the good	176	U24 Frontispice V	5
Who would with judgement search, searching conclude	177	U25 Desmond	25
May his Sense, when it would meet	184	U29 Fit of Rime	55
Of divine blessing, would not serve a State?	185	U30 Burleigh	20
Who thus long safe, would gaine up the times	186	U32 Elsmere	9
What Beautie would have lovely stilde,	188	U35 Chute	1
As I would urge Authoritie for sinne.	191	U38 Elegy 'Tis	26
Would live his glory that could keepe it on;	192	U38 Elegy 'Tis	48
Of that wise Nature would a Cradle have.	192	U38 Elegy 'Tis	60
A man should flie from, as he would disdaine.	194	U38 Elegy 'Tis	104
You would be then most confident, that tho	194	U38 Elegy 'Tis	113
You would restore it? No, that's worth a feare,	199	U41 Elegy Since	15

		Page	Title	Line

WOULD (cont.)

	Page	Title	Line
He did lay up, and would adore the shooe,	201	U42 Elegy Let	55
He would have done in verse, with any of those	201	U42 Elegy Let	62
In smiling L'envoye, as he would deride	202	U42 Elegy Let	75
For none but Smiths would have made thee a God.	208	U43 Vulcan	117
No Foole would his owne harvest spoile, or burne!	209	U43 Vulcan	150
Would you had kept your Forge at Aetna still,	212	U43 Vulcan	197
Would thinke no more of Vlushing, or the Brill:	213	U44 Speach	30
And could (if our great men would let their Sonnes	214	U44 Speach	57
What I am not, and what I faine would be,	216	U45 Squib	1
Whilst I informe my selfe, I would teach thee,	216	U45 Squib	2
Much lesse a name would we bring up, or nurse,	216	U45 Squib	9
Friend to himselfe, that would be friend to thee.	216	U45 Squib	22
They meet the fire, the Test, as Martyrs would;	218	U47 Tribe	3
I would call mine, to which not many Staires	220	U47 Tribe	74
And trust her I would least, that hath forswore	223	U49 Pucell	29
This Age would lend no faith to Dorrels Deed:	223	U49 Pucell	42
Or if it would, the Court is the worst place,	223	U49 Pucell	43
How I would draw, and take hold and delight.	227	U52 Answer	18
Yet when of friendship I would draw the face,	227	U52 Answer	22
A letter'd mind, and a large heart would place	227	U52 Answer	23
Would God, my Burges, I could thinke	229	U55 Burges	1
Then would I promise here to give	229	U55 Burges	3
When you would play so nobly, and so free.	230	U56 Covell	2
At which there are, would sell the Prince, and State:	234	U61 Epigram	4
How many times, Live long, Charles, would he say,	236	U64 Charles 3	3
Well, they should know him, would the K. but grant	241	U68 House-hold	5
Would make the very Greene-cloth to looke blew:	241	U68 House-hold	8
Where he would fixe, for the distinctions feare.	242	U69 Friend Son	18
No doubt all Infants would returne like thee.	243	U70 Ode	20
That cry that gladnesse, which their hearts would pray,	249	U72 King	14
The cries, the gladnesse, which their hearts would pay,	249	U72 King	V 14
Alive, which else would die,	257	U75 Epithalam.	151
This would all their envie burst:	260	U76 Petition	30
That would all their envie burst:	260	U76 Petition	V 30
I would present you now with curious plate	260	U77 Treasurer	2
I would present you with some curious plate	260	U77 Treasurer	V 2
I would, if price, or prayer could them get,	260	U77 Treasurer	5
This I would doe, could I know Weston, one	260	U77 Treasurer	10
This I would doe, if I could thinke you one	260	U77 Treasurer	V 10
Court can call hers, or Man would call the Arts.	262	U78 Digby	V 4
Would they would understand it! Princes are	268	U80 Christning	5
To pious parents, who would have their blood	268	U80 Christning	7
When I, who would her Poet have become,	269	U81 Pawlet	17
Their Heads, that Envy would hold downe	272	U84 Cradle	3
Would aske a Heavens Intelligence;	278	U84 Mind	14
And stuck in clay here, it would pull	279	U84 Mind	46
It rages, runs, flies, stands, and would provoke	283	U84 Muse	24
Against the Nature he would worship. Hee	284	U84 Muse	75
Would sit in an Infirmery, whole dayes	288	U84 Muse	195
Who (amongst these delights) would not forget	290	U85 Country	37
So Fate would give her life, and longer daies.	293	U87 Hor.3:9	12
For whom I doubly would expire,	293	U87 Hor.3:9	15
So Fates would let the Boy a long thred run.	293	U87 Hor.3:9	16
Yet would I wish to love, live, die with thee.	294	U87 Hor.3:9	24
If to a Womans head a Painter would	305	Horace	1
To forme a worke, I would no more desire	307	Horace	50
To frame a worke, I would no more desire	339	Horace	V 52/ 50
Nor must the Fable, that would hope the Fate,	317	Horace	270
Fortune would love the poore, and leave the proud.	319	Horace	286
The rough rude Satyres naked; and would try,	319	Horace	321
Poets would either profit, or delight,	327	Horace	477
And lead them with soft songs, where that he would.	327	Horace	485
It would, must be: lest it alive would draw	329	Horace	509
There are yet faults, which we would well forgive,	329	Horace	520
The hand, and mind would, but it will resound	329	Horace	522
And rack, with Wine, the man whom they would try,	333	Horace	618
Then change; no word, or worke, more would he spend	335	Horace	630
Himselfe there purposely, or no; and would	335	Horace	657
Doth the same thing with him, that would him kill.	335	Horace	666
To force the grates, that hold him in, would fright	337	Horace	675
From Zephyr's rape would close him with his beames.	366	Ode Who saith	24
How they would frowne!	369	Ode Who saith	110
Who ever he be, would write a Story at	379	Coryat 3	1
No: as I first said, who would write a story at	381	Coryat 3	59
May aske, what Author would conceale his name?	383	Author	4
And when your yeares rise more, then would be told,	384	Somerset	23
More of our writers would like thee, not swell	386	Browne	15
He would be call'd, henceforth, the English-Rogue,	389	Aleman	16
Will bee receiv'd in Court; If not, would I	389	Aleman	19
That would have done, that, which you onely can.	389	Aleman	24
His face; the Print would then surpasse	390	Reader	7
From thence to honour thee, I would not seeke	391	Shakespeare	32
But, I would have, thee, to know something new,	394	Jane Ogle	13
With every song, I sweare, and so would dye:	397	Drayton	54
you would be an Asinigo, by your eares?	403	Inigo Jones 1	20
Though gold or Ivory haftes would make it good.	403	Inigo Jones 1	28
He is, or would be the mayne Dominus doe	404	Inigo Jones 1	64
What would he doe now, gi'ng his mynde that waye	405	Inigo Jones 1	75
How would he firke? lyke Adam overdooe	405	Inigo Jones 1	79
To Inigo Marquess Would Be A Corollary	406	Inigo Jones 2	Ttl
I now would write on thee? No, wretch; thy name	409	Detractor	11
An honest Bilbo-Smith would make good blades,	410	Brome	15

WOULD (cont.)
    And truely, so I would, could I be heard.   414   Rutter   3
    or as some would say to breake   416   Moon   3
WOULD-BEE
    To Fine Lady Would-bee.   .   . 46   E62 Would-bee   Ttl
    Fine Madame Would-Bee, wherefore should you feare,   .   . 46   E62 Would-bee   1
WOULD'ST
    O, would'st thou adde like hand, to all the rest!   .   . 61   E95 Savile   13
    And studie conscience, more then thou would'st fame.   .   . 63   E98 Th Roe 1   10
    Would'st thou heare, what man can say   .   . 79   E124 Elizabeth   1
    And thine owne Coriat too. But (would'st thou see)   .   . 81   E129 Mime   17
    When thou would'st feast, or exercise thy friends.   .   . 94   F2 Penshurst   21
    Or if thou needs would'st trench upon her power,   .   . 204 U43 Vulcan   48
    If that were so, thou rather would'st advance   .   . 209 U43 Vulcan   151
    So would'st th'have run upon the Rolls by stealth,   .   . 210 U43 Vulcan   169
    If thou would'st have me weepe, be thou first drown'd   .   . 311 Horace   145
WOULDST
    If thou wouldst know the vertues of Man-kind,   .   . 185 U30 Burleigh   1
    or if thou wouldst enforce the power from her,   .   . 204 U43 Vulcan   V 48
    O, now thou smil'st, faire Sun, and shin'st, as thou wouldst stay! 254 U75 Epithalam.   64
    Thou wouldst have written, Fame, upon my brest: .   . 269 U81 Pawlet   14
    Thou wouldst have lost the Phoenix, had the kind   .   . 283 U84 Muse   19
    Not care, as thou wouldst faithfully translate,   .   . 313 Horace   190
    Be briefe, in what thou wouldst command, that so   .   . 329 Horace   503
    Thou, that wouldst finde the habit of true passion,   .   . 362 Author   1
    With Rites not bound, but conscience. Wouldst thou All?   .   . 372 Epitaph   11
    I thought thee then our Orpheus, that wouldst try   .   . 397 Drayton   35
    Hath made his Inigo Marquess, wouldst thou fayne   .   . 406 Inigo Jones 2   2
WOUND
    Upon my flesh t'inflict another wound.   .   .   . 122 F15 Heaven   22
    A many of bookes, even good judgements wound   .   . 159 U14 Selden   15
    Till envie wound, or maime it at a blow!   .   .   . 162 U15 Friend-Wars   22
    Not wound thy conscience, when thy body bleeds;   .   . 168 U15 Friend-Wars   178
    I send nor Balmes, nor Cor'sives to your wound,   .   . 180 U26 Ode High   2
    Thou prov'st the gentler wayes, to clense the wound,   .   . 187 U33 Councellour   20
    Did I there wound the honours of the Crowne?   .   . 203 U43 Vulcan   23
    Thy selfe in teares, then me thy losse will wound,   .   . 311 Horace   146
    Thy selfe in tears, then me thy harms will wound,   .   . 342 Horace   V146
WOUNDED
    My wounded mind cannot sustaine this stroke,   .   . 283 U84 Muse   23
WOUND'ST
    So brightly brandish'd) wound'st, defend'st! the while   .   . 187 U33 Councellour   32
WOVEN
    To have her storie woven in thy thred;   .   .   . 61   E95 Savile   15
    Which were so richly spun, and woven so fit,   .   . 392 Shakespeare   49
WRACKE
    God wisheth, none should wracke on a strange shelfe.   .   . 99   F3 Wroth   95
    Whereon the most of mankinde wracke themselves,   .   . 119 F13 Aubigny   90
WRANGLE
    Let this man sweat, and wrangle at the barre,   .   . 99   F3 Wroth   73
WRANGLERS
    Of hirelings, wranglers, stitchers-to of strife,   .   . 187 U33 Councellour   8
WRAPT
    'Twas brought to court first wrapt, and white as milke;   .   . 31   E15 Court-worm   2
    Carryed and wrapt, I only am alow'd   .   .   . 155 U13 Sacvile   88
    Wrapt in this paper lie, ... 180 U26 Ode High   10
    About in Cloudes, and wrapt in raging weather,   .   . 193 U38 Elegy 'Tis   75
WRATH
    (Which with griefe and wrath I heard)   .   .   . 132 U2 How he saw   29
WREAKE
    Looser-like, now, all my wreake   .   .   .   . 133 U2 Suffered   21
WREATH
    I sent thee, late, a rosie wreath, ... 106 F9 Celia 3   9
    I sent to thee a rosie wreath, ... 106 F9 Celia 3   V 9
WRECK'D
    The whole fleet wreck'd? a great jarre to be shap'd,   .   . 305 Horace   28
WRESTED
    And come not too much wrested. What's that thing,   .   . 309 Horace   76
WRESTING
    Wresting words, from their true calling;   .   .   . 183 U29 Fit of Rime   7
WRESTLED
    Had wrestled with Diseases strong, ... 151 U12 Corbet   8
WRESTLEST
    Wrestlest with dignities, or fain'st a scope   .   .   . 70   E109 Nevil   6
WRETCH
    From the poore wretch, which though he play'd in prose,   .   . 201 U42 Elegy Let   61
    The Marrow! Wretch, I guitt thee of thy paine   .   . 408 Inigo Jones 3   5
    I now would write on thee? No, wretch; thy name   .   . 409 Detractor   11
WRETCHED
    Let that goe heape a masse of wretched wealth,   .   . 99   F3 Wroth   81
    Wretched and foolish Jealousie, ... 150 U10 Jealousie   1
    or spent my wretched paper or my tyme   .   .   . 204 U43 Vulcan   V 33
    in weaving Riddles in more wretched ryme,   .   . 204 U43 Vulcan   V 34
    View'd there the mercat, read the wretched rate   .   . 234 U61 Epigram   3
    But as the wretched Painter, who so ill   .   .   . 241 U69 Friend Son   9
    Poore wretched states, prest by extremities,   .   . 248 U71 Treasurer   1
    It is a wretched thing to trust to reedes;   .   . 281 U84 Kenelme   16
    Happier then wretched art, and doth, by it,   .   . 325 Horace   420
    I'll laugh at thee poor wretched Tike, go send   .   . 410 Gill   10
WRETCHEDLY
    Doth wretchedly the use of things forbeare,   .   . 317 Horace   243
WRETCHEDNES
    What makes your Wretchednes to bray soe loud   .   . 403 Inigo Jones 1   23

WRETCHED'ST
Hee were the wretched'st of the race of men: . . . . 272 U81 Pawlet 97
WRETCHES
whom thou seest happy; wretches flee as foes: . . . 422 Lucan 6
whom thou seest happy; wretches, shun, as foes: . . . 422 Lucan V 6
WRIGHT (NAME)
Where Pittes, or Wright, or Modet would not venter, . . 164 U15 Friend-Wars 80
WRIGHT
To Play-wright. . . . . 42 E49 Playwrt 1 Ttl
Play-wright me reades, and still my verses damnes, . . . 42 E49 Playwrt 1 1
Play-wright, I loath to have thy manners knowne . . . 42 E49 Playwrt 1 5
On Play-wright. . . . . 49 E68 Playwrt 2 Ttl
Play-wright convict of publike wrongs to men, . . . 49 E68 Playwrt 2 1
On Play-wright. . . . . 64 E100 Playwrt 3 Ttl
Play-wright, by chance, hearing some toyes I'had writ, . . 64 E100 Playwrt 3 1
WRIGHT'S
The knight-wright's cheated then: Hee'll never pay. . . 42 E46 Luckless 1 5
WRIT
Thy fact, in brasse or marble writ the same) . . . 46 E60 Mounteagle 4
Play-wright, by chance, hearing some toyes I'had writ, . . 64 E100 Playwrt 3 1
Writing thy selfe, or judging others writ, . . . 78 E123 Rudyerd 3 1
And greater rites, yet writ in mysterie, . . . 119 F13 Aubigny 106
An Ode to James Earle of Desmond, writ . . . . . 176 U25 Desmond Ttl
If I had writ no word, but Deare, farewell. . . . 198 U40 Elegy That 50
Lyes there no Writ, out of the Chancerie . . . 210 U43 Vulcan 174
As you have writ your selfe. Now stand, and then, . . 220 U47 Tribe 77
The Writ, once out, never returned yet. . . . 331 Horace 580
I writ he onely his taile there did wave; . . . 380 Coryat 3 56
As in this Spanish Proteus; who, though writ . . . 389 Aleman 5
All, that was ever writ in brasse. . . . . 390 Reader 8
You have not writ to me, nor I to you; . . . 396 Drayton 6
WRITE (See also WRYTE)
To all, to whom I write. . . . . . 29 E9 To All Ttl
And what I write thereof find farre, and free . . . 41 E43 Salisbury 1 10
In a great belly. Write, then on thy wombe, . . . 46 E62 Would-bee 11
Shee shall instruct my after-thoughts to write . . . 48 E65 Muse 13
My Muse bad, Bedford write, and that was shee. . . . 52 E76 Bedford 1 18
To write in cypher, and the severall keyes, . . . 59 E92 New Crie 26
With juyce of limons, onions, pisse, to write. . . . 59 E92 New Crie 28
Although to write be lesser then to doo, . . . 61 E95 Savile 25
Can write the things, the causes, and the men. . . . 62 E95 Savile 34
That dares nor write things false, nor hide things true. . . 62 E95 Savile 36
My title's seal'd. Those that for claps doe write, . . 62 E96 Donne 2 9
And that to write things worthy to be read: . . . 63 E99 Th Roe 2 4
I modestly quit that, and thinke to write, . . . 72 E112 Gamster 11
Why I write not of Love. . . . . . 93 F1 Why write no Ttl
Though I now write fiftie yeares, ... 131 U2 Excuse 3
And you, Sir, know it well, to whom I write, . . . 156 U13 Sacvile 109
I Know to whom I write. Here, I am sure, . . . 158 U14 Selden 1
And what I write? and vexe it many dayes . . . 159 U14 Selden 25
Can Beautie that did prompt mee first to write, . . . 169 U18 Elegy Can 1
Thy beauties, yet could write of thee? . . . 181 U27 Ode Helen 2
Had he had the facultie to reade, and write! . . . 201 U42 Elegy Let 64
And in an Epicoene fury can write newes . . . 222 U49 Pucell 8
But, you are he can paint; I can but write: . . . 227 U52 Answer 19
To all posteritie; I will write Burlase. . . . 227 U52 Answer 24
Alas, I am all Marble! write the rest . . . 269 U81 Pawlet 13
Take, therefore, you that write, still, matter fit . . 307 Horace 53
Take therefore, you that write, a subject fit . . . 339 Horace V 55/ 53
Or follow fame, thou that dost write, or faine . . . 313 Horace 169
Nor I, when I write Satyres, will so love . . . 321 Horace 341
But, if hereafter thou shalt write, not feare . . . 331 Horace 575
When you write Verses, with your judge do so: . . 333 Horace 620
Who ever he be, would write a Story at . . . 379 Coryat 3 1
To write it with the selfe same spirit he went, . . 379 Coryat 3 14
No: as I first said, who would write a story at . . 381 Coryat 3 59
I find thee write most worthy to be read. . . . 386 Browne 6
nor yet inscription like it. Write but that; . . . 387 Cavendish 9
Who casts to write a living line, must sweat, . . . 392 Shakespeare 59
I now would write on thee? No, wretch; thy name . . 409 Detractor 11
Both learned, and unlearned, all write Playes. . . . 410 Brome 12
WRITER
Of the best writer, and judge, should emulate. . . . 78 E123 Rudyerd 3 4
Grow a safe Writer, and be warie-driven . . . 323 Horace 393
All; So this grievous Writer puts to flight . . . 337 Horace 676
WRITERS
Most Writers, noble Sire, and either Sonne, . . . 307 Horace 33
More of our writers would like thee, not swell . . . 386 Browne 15
WRITHED
There, in the writhed barke, are cut the names . . . 94 F2 Penshurst 15
WRITING
For writing better, I must envie thee. . . . 44 E55 Beaumont 10
Writing thy selfe, or judging others writ, . . . 78 E123 Rudyerd 3 1
I, writing nought my selfe, will teach them yet . . 325 Horace 435
The very root of writing well, and spring . . . 325 Horace 440
WRITINGS
Which the Socratick writings best can show: . . . 325 Horace 442
While I confesse thy writings to be such, . . . 390 Shakespeare 3
WRITS
A present, which (if elder writs reherse . . . 113 F12 Rutland 20
WRIT'ST
Tragick, or Comick; but thou writ'st the play. . . . 72 E112 Gamster 8

		Page	Title	Line

WRITT
nor yet inscription like it writt but that   .   .   .   387 Cavendish   V 9

WRITTEN
Friendship, in deed, was written, not in words: .   .   .   247 U70 Ode   123
Thou wouldst have written, Fame, upon my brest: .   .   269 U81 Pawlet   14
Certaine Verses Written Upon Coryats Crudities, ...   379 Coryat 3   Ttl

WRONG
Thy ignorance still laughs in the wrong place.   .   .   45 E58 Groome   4
That know not so much state, wrong, as they doo.   .   .   59 E92 New Crie   40
Such as are misse-call'd Captaynes, and wrong you;   .   .   69 E108 Soldiers   2
Boast, but how oft they have gone wrong to man: .   .   119 F13 Aubigny   84
Doth urge him to runne wrong, or to stand still.   .   .   121 F14 Sydney   30
And all your bountie wrong: .   .   139 U2 Another   10
And never but for doing wrong be sory;   .   .   168 U15 Friend-Wars   180
He do's you wrong, that craves you to doe right.   .   .   186 U32 Elsmere   16
Of daring, not to doe a wrong, is true   .   .   233 U59 Newcastle   15
When in a wrong, and artlesse way we tread.   .   .   307 Horace   44
Am I call'd Poet? wherefore with wrong shame,   .   .   311 Horace   129
The man once mock'd, and suffer'd wrong to tread.   .   .   335 Horace   642

WRONG'D
Said I wrong'd him, and (which was more) his love.   .   .   80 E126 Mrs Cary   5

WRONGS
Play-wright convict of publike wrongs to men,   .   .   49 E68 Playwrt 2   1
Nor doe wrongs, nor wrongs receeve;   .   .   .   142 U2 Her man   49
Is not yet free from Rimes wrongs,   .   .   .   184 U29 Fit of Rime   35
Their loves, their quarrels, jealousies, and wrongs,   .   397 Drayton   30

WROTE
He wrote, with the same spirit that he fought,   .   .   71 E110 Edmonds 1   8
Had I wrote treason there, or heresie,   .   .   203 U43 Vulcan   15
The Spirit that I wrote with, and conceiv'd;   .   .   282 U84 Muse   3
They're darke, bid cleare this: all that's doubtfull wrote   .   335 Horace   637
They're dark, bid cleare 'hem; al that's doubtful wrote   .   354 Horace   V637
As was the Genius wherewith they were wrote;   .   .   389 Aleman   12

WROTH   (See also WORTH)
To Mary Lady Wroth.   .   .   .   .   .   66 E103 L Wroth 1   Ttl
To Mary Lady Wroth.   .   .   .   .   .   67 E105 L Wroth 2   Ttl
To Sir Robert Wroth.   .   .   .   .   96 F3 Wroth   Ttl
To Sir Robert Wroth in praise of a Country life. Epode.   96 F3 Wroth   VTtl
How blest art thou, canst love the countrey, Wroth,   .   96 F3 Wroth   1
Strive, Wroth, to live long innocent.   .   .   98 F3 Wroth   66
Strive, Wroth, to be long innocent.   .   .   98 F3 Wroth   V 66
But thou, my Wroth, if I can truth apply,   .   .   99 F3 Wroth   91
But thou, my Wroth, if I may truth apply,   .   .   99 F3 Wroth   V 91

WROUGHT
Quick in his lips! who hath this wonder wrought?   .   .   33 E21 Gam'ster   5
Wherein what wonder see thy name hath wrought?   .   .   48 E64 Salisbury 3   16
When, in mens wishes, so thy vertues wrought,   .   .   49 E67 Suffolk   7
Of what shee had wrought came in, and wak'd his braine,   .   56 E87 Hazard   4
So well in that are his inventions wrought,   .   .   83 E132 Sylvester   11
There should a miracle be wrought.   .   .   101 F4 To the World   60
And estimate thy Paines; as having wrought   .   .   161 U14 Selden   75
Of some wel-wrought Embassage: .   .   .   221 U48 Bacchus   46
Whereby the safetie of Man-kind was wrought)   .   .   238 U66 Queene   8
Whereby the safetie of the world was wrought)   .   .   238 U66 Queene   V 8
By what was done and wrought   .   .   .   245 U70 Ode   60
No cobweb Call's; no Surcoates wrought   .   .   273 U84 Cradle   26
I'the open field; is Waxe like to be wrought   .   .   315 Horace   231
Whether the guarded Tragedie they wrought,   .   .   323 Horace   409
Unto a cunning piece wrought perspective,   .   .   362 Author   10
Who hadst before wrought in rich Homers Mine?   .   .   388 Chapman   3
Lucans whole frame unto us, and so wrought,   .   .   395 May   20

WRUNG
Wrung on the Withers, by Lord Loves despight,   .   .   201 U42 Elegy Let   63

WRY
With faire black eyes, and haire; and a wry nose.   .   .   307 Horace   52
If they seeme wry, to such as looke asquint,   .   .   362 Author   7

WRYES
Of politique pretext, that wryes a State,   .   .   177 U25 Desmond   29

WRYTE
That I should wryte upon him some sharp verse,   .   .   407 Inigo Jones 3   3
before, I wryte more verse, to bee more wyse.   .   .   421 Censure   2

WULL
And it is hop'd, that shee, like Milo, wull   .   .   57 E90 Mill   17
And tasting ayre, and freedome, wull   .   .   .   101 F4 To the World   31

WYNE
Cittyes & Temples! thou a Cave for Wyne,   .   .   406 Inigo Jones 2   8

WYNNS
The emptye Carper, scorne, not Creditt wynns.   .   .   421 Censure   5

WYRES
Maintayne their liedgers forth, for forraine wyres,   .   118 F13 Aubigny   72

WYSE
Yett: since the bright, and wyse,   .   .   .   420 Ode:If Men   28
Whoe worthie wine, whoe not, to bee wyse Pallas guests.   421 Ode:If Men   45
before, I wryte more verse, to bee more wyse.   .   .   421 Censure   2

WYSER
Oh wise Surveyor! wyser Architect!   .   .   405 Inigo Jones 1   85

XCEED
To see the workmanship so'xceed the cost!   .   .   160 U14 Selden   54

Y'
Nine yeares kept by, your papers in, y'are free   .   .   352 Horace   V554/578

YARD   (MEASURE)
By the scale of his booke, a yard of his stile?   .   .   379 Coryat 3   10

		Page	Title	Line

YARD
Well, I say, thrive, thrive brave Artillerie yard, . . 213 U44 Speach 23
Shewes he dares more then Paules Church-yard durst do. . . 378 Coryat 2 85

Y'ARE
Nine yeares kept by, your papers in, y'are free . . 352 Horace V554/578

YCLEPED
Ycleped Mud, which, when their oares did once stirre, . . 85 E133 Voyage 62

YE
Ye have oft-times, that may ore-shine the rest, . . 305 Horace 18
Ye have oft-times, that may out-shine the rest, . . 338 Horace V 18

YEA
Any paines; yea, thinke it price, . . . 105 F8 Sicknesse 27
And, for it, life, conscience, yea, soules are given, . . 113 F12 Rutland 4
Yea, of th'ingratefull: and he forth must tell . . 155 U13 Sacvile 77
Thinke, yea and boast, that they have done it so . . 186 U32 Elsmere 12
And conquers all things, yea it selfe, at length. . . 367 Ode Who saith 56

YEARE
And know thee, then, a judge, not of one yeare; . . 51 E74 Chancelor 2
A vow as new, and ouinous as the yeare, . . 116 F12 Rutland 98
Where we must feele it Darke for halfe a yeare. . . 199 U41 Elegy Since 8
But I who live, and have liv'd twentie yeare . . 200 U42 Elegy Let 29
Of our fift Henry, eight of his nine yeare; . . 207 U43 Vulcan 98
Of our fift Henry, right of his nine yeare; . . 207 U43 Vulcan V 98
In so much land a yeare, or such a Banke, . . 215 U44 Speach 76
Brunsfield, and Mansfield doe this yeare, my fates . . 219 U47 Tribe 44
And so doe I. This is the sixtieth yeare . . 225 U51 Bacon 7
And as it turnes our joyfull yeare about, . . 236 U64 Charles 3 5
Her two and twenti'th yeare! . . 240 U67 Muses 48
Her one and twenty yeare! . . . 240 U67 Muses V 48
Thy comming forth in that great yeare, . . 242 U70 Ode 2
Or standing long an Oake, three hundred yeare, . . 245 U70 Ode 67
Of the prime beautie of the yeare, the Spring. . . 251 U74 Weston 6
When look'd the yeare, at best, . . 253 U75 Epithalam. 13
Unto our yeare doth give the longest light. . . 262 U78 Digby 16
Of the New Yeare, in a new silken warpe, . . 263 U79 New-yeares 5
To day old Janus opens the new yeare, . . 263 U79 New-yeares 9
As if the beauties of the yeare, . . 264 U79 New-yeares 38
And from the sweet Tub Wine of this yeare takes, . . 291 U85 Country 47
To bend a man, now at his fiftieth yeare . . 292 U86 Hor.4:1 6

YEARES
Though I now write fiftie yeares, . . 131 U2 Excuse 3
Told seven and fortie yeares, . . 150 U9 Picture 15
Told six and fortie yeares, . . 150 U9 Picture V 15
At fifty yeares, almost, to value it, . . 171 U20 Shrub 5
For a thousand yeares together, . . 183 U29 Fit of Rime 16
So many my Yeares-labours in an houre? . . 202 U43 Vulcan 4
And twice-twelve-yeares stor'd up humanitie, . . 207 U43 Vulcan 101
With twice-twelve-yeares stor'd up humanitie, . . 207 U43 Vulcan V101
These ten yeares day; As all may sweare that looke . . 213 U44 Speach 27
Of a yeares Pension, . . 231 U57 Burges 12
And told forth fourescore yeares; . . 243 U70 Ode 26
And make them yeares; . . 244 U70 Ode 54
Have cast a trench about mee, now, five yeares; . . 248 U71 Treasurer 6
A New-yeares gift Sung to King Charles, 1635. . . 263 U79 New-yeares Ttl
New yeares, expect new gifts: Sister, your Harpe, . . 263 U79 New-yeares 1
To fit the softnesse of our Yeares-gift: when . . 263 U79 New-yeares 6
Still in their leaves, throughout the sliding yeares, . . 309 Horace 86
And give their yeares, and natures, as they swerve, . . 315 Horace 224
Mans comming yeares much good with them doe bring: . . 317 Horace 250
Nine yeares kept in, your papers by, yo'are free . . 331 Horace 578
Nine yeares kept by, your papers in, y'are free . . 352 Horace V554/578
And when your yeares rise more, then would be told, . . 384 Somerset 23

YEARES-GIFT
To fit the softnesse of our Yeares-gift: when . . 263 U79 New-yeares 6

YEARES-LABOURS
So many my Yeares-labours in an houre? . . 202 U43 Vulcan 4

YEARLY
yearly set out there, to sayle downe the Street, . . 407 Inigo Jones 2 18

YEARN'D
All this doth Jone. Or that his long yearn'd life . . 40 E42 Giles 11

YEARS
To Crowne the years, which you begin, great king, . . 416 Welcome 7

YEE
Were seene your ugly Centaures, yee call Car-men, . . 86 E133 Voyage 68
But say, all sixe good men, what answer yee? . . 210 U43 Vulcan 173
You once enjoy'd: A short space severs yee, . . 285 U84 Muse 105
That shall re-joyne yee. Was she, then, so deare, . . 285 U84 Muse 107

YEELD
And have'hem yeeld no savour, but of state. . . 58 E92 New Crie 5
Each banke doth yeeld thee coneyes; and the topps . . 94 F2 Penshurst 25
First, that I must kneeling yeeld . . 133 U2 Suffered 7
I yeeld, I yeeld, the matter of your praise . . 160 U14 Selden 61
And Fame wake for me, when I yeeld to sleepe. . . 190 U37 Friend-Book 15
And the returne those thankfull Courtiers yeeld, . . 213 U44 Speach 17
Provided, ne're to yeeld, in any case . . 323 Horace 379
For, neither doth the String still yeeld that sound . . 329 Horace 521
Enforcing yron doores to yeeld it way, . . 363 Riches 9

YEELDING
All yeelding to his fortune, nor, the while, . . 71 E110 Edmonds 1 5

YEELDS
All the grasse that Rumney yeelds, . . 103 F6 Celia 2 13

YEERE
And, in some yeere, all these together heap'd, . . 69 E107 Hungry 15

	Page	Title	Line

YEERE (cont.)
```
Yet, one day in the yeere, for sweet 'tis voyc't,        .   .   .    87   E133 Voyage       119
Or with thy friends; the heart of all the yeere,         .   .   .    97   F3 Wroth          25
Or with thy friends; the heate of all the yeere,         .   .   .    97   F3 Wroth        V 25
Although the coldest of the yeere!       .   .   .   .   .   .   .    97   F3 Wroth          36
Well, or ill, onely, all the following yeere,            .   .   .   113   F12 Rutland        7
```
YEERES
```
Seven yeeres tho'wert lent to me, and I thee pay,        .   .   .    41   E45 First Son      3
Discern'd no difference of his yeeres, or play,          .   .   .    57   E90 Mill           8
For twelve yeeres yet to come, what each state lacks.    .   .   .    59   E92 New Crie      14
Yeeres he numbred scarse thirteene       .   .   .   .   .   .   .    77   E120 S. P.         9
My tender, first, and simple yeeres      .   .   .   .   .   .   .   101   F4 To the World   41
On the close groome, and page, on new-yeeres day,        .   .   .   118   F13 Aubigny       74
Live that one, still; and as long yeeres doe passe,      .   .   .   120   F13 Aubigny      121
This day sayes, then, the number of glad yeeres          .   .   .   120   F14 Sydney        21
For, if I thought my judgement were of yeeres,           .   .   .   391   Shakespeare       27
```
YEILD
```
Where mutuall frauds are fought, and no side yeild;      .   .   .   186   U33 Councellour    4
The Rebell Gyants stoope, and Gorgon Envye yeild,        .   .   .   421   Ode:If Men        41
```
YELLOW
```
Nor yellow honie from the tree       .   .   .   .   .   .   .   .    98   F3 Wroth        V 60
The yellow Jaundies, or were furious mad     .   .   .   .   .   .   335   Horace           646
The yellow jaundis, or were truely mad,      .   .   .   .   .   .   354   Horace          V646
```
YES
```
Yes, now he weares his knight-hood every day.        .   .   .   .    42   E46 Luckless 1     6
Yes, threaten, doe. Alas I feare     .   .   .   .   .   .   .   .   101   F4 To the World   37
Yes; and in death, as life, unblest,     .   .   .   .   .   .   .   149   U8 Houre-glasse    9
Knew I this Woman? yes; And you doe see,      .   .   .   .   .   .   172   U20 Shrub         15
What, to make legs? yes, and to smell most sweet,    .   .   .   .   215   U44 Speach        90
Yes thou wert borne out of his travelling thigh      .   .   .   .   378   Coryat 2          89
Yes. And thanks God in his Pistle or his Booke       .   .   .   .   380   Coryat 3          43
```
YET
```
Some hundred quarrells, yet dost thou fight none;        .   .   .    32   E16 Brain-hardy    6
And mine come nothing like. I hope so. Yet,      .   .   .   .   .    32   E18 Censurer       5
That Cod can get no widdow, yet a knight,        .   .   .   .   .    33   E19 Cod 1          1
Yet, all heavens gifts, being heavens due,       .   .   .   .   .    33   E22 Daughter       3
Came forth example, and remaines so, yet:        .   .   .   .   .    34   E23 Donne 1        4
All which I meant to praise, and, yet, I would;      .   .   .   .    34   E23 Donne 1        9
That's greater, yet: to crie his owne up neate.      .   .   .   .    35   E28 Surly         11
Be thine, I taxe, yet doe not owne my rimes:         .   .   .   .    36   E30 Guiltie        2
Yet dare not, to my thought, lest hope allow         .   .   .   .    41   E43 Salisbury 1    7
And, if no other miserie, yet age?       .   .   .   .   .   .   .    41   E45 First Son      8
Yet give thy jealous subjects leave to doubt:        .   .   .   .    43   E51 James 3        5
Of the not borne, yet buried, here's the tombe.      .   .   .   .    46   E62 Would-bee     12
Yet by thy weapon liv'st! Th'hast one good part.     .   .   .   .    50   E69 Cob            2
That yet maintaynes you, and your house in laughter.     .   .   .    51   E73 Fine Grand     8
Of greatest bloud, and yet more good then great;     .   .   .   .    52   E76 Bedford 1      6
He cast, yet keeps her well! No, shee keeps him.     .   .   .   .    54   E82 Surly          2
Which if they misse, they yet should re-advance      .   .   .   .    55   E85 Goodyere 1     8
The french disease, with which he labours yet?       .   .   .   .    56   E88 Monsieur      10
Yet crown'd with honors, as with riches, then;      .   .   .   .    56   E89 Allen          4
Yet have they seene the maps, and bought 'hem too,   .   .   .   .    59   E92 New Crie       9
For twelve yeeres yet to come, what each state lacks.    .   .   .    59   E92 New Crie      14
And of the poulder-plot, they will talke yet.        .   .   .   .    59   E92 New Crie      32
Thou yet remayn'st, un-hurt in peace, or warre,      .   .   .   .    60   E93 Radcliffe     13
Yet, Satyres, since the most of mankind bee      .   .   .   .   .    60   E94 Bedford 3      7
Dare for these poemes, yet, both aske, and read,     .   .   .   .    60   E94 Bedford 3     12
Nor Captayne Pod, nor yet the Eltham-thing,      .   .   .   .   .    62   E97 Motion         2
Though both be good, the latter yet is worst,        .   .   .   .    63   E98 Th Roe 1      11
Yet shall you have, to rectifie your palate,         .   .   .   .    64   E101 Supper        9
And, though fowle, now, be scarce, yet there are clarkes,    .   .    65   E101 Supper       15
May yet be there; and godwit, if we can:         .   .   .   .   .    65   E101 Supper       19
To which, yet, of the sides himselfe he owes.        .   .   .   .    66   E102 Pembroke      8
There Juno sate, and yet no Peacock by.      .   .   .   .   .   .    68   E105 L Wroth 2    18
And yet, they, all together, lesse then thee.        .   .   .   .    68   E106 E Herbert    10
And yet are with their Princes: Fill them full       .   .   .   .    69   E107 Hungry        7
What States yo'have gull'd, and which yet keepes yo'in pay.   .   .    69   E107 Hungry       10
Un-argued then, and yet hath fame from those;        .   .   .   .    71   E110 Edmonds 1    10
Yet thou, perhaps, shalt meet some tongues will grutch,   .   .   .    72   E111 Edmonds 2     9
Pr'y thee, yet save thy rest; give ore in time:      .   .   .   .    73   E112 Gamster      21
That seeming prayses, are, yet accusations.      .   .   .   .   .    75   E115 Honest Man   32
All gentrie, yet, owe part of their best flame!      .   .   .   .    75   E116 Jephson       2
Yet three fill'd Zodiackes had he beene      .   .   .   .   .   .    77   E120 S. P.        11
Yet is the office not to be despis'd,        .   .   .   .   .   .    78   E121 Rudyerd 1     5
O, runne not proud of this. Yet, take thy due.       .   .   .   .    81   E129 Mime         15
I, yet, had utter'd nothing on thy part,         .   .   .   .   .    82   E130 Ferrab. 1    15
Still, with thy former labours; yet, once more,      .   .   .   .    85   E133 Voyage       56
Yet, one day in the yeere, for sweet 'tis voyc't,    .   .   .   .    87   E133 Voyage      119
And that ours did. For, yet, no nare was tainted,    .   .   .   .    87   E133 Voyage      133
Yet drown'd they not. They had five lives in future.     .   .   .    88   E133 Voyage      154
At great mens tables) and yet dine away.         .   .   .   .   .    95   F2 Penshurst      66
These, Penshurst, are thy praise, and yet not all.   .   .   .   .    96   F2 Penshurst      89
There wasted, some not paid for yet!         .   .   .   .   .   .    97   F3 Wroth          12
The ripened eares, yet humble in their height,       .   .   .   .    98   F3 Wroth          41
Yet art thou both shrunke up, and old,       .   .   .   .   .   .   100   F4 To the World   14
Yet art thou falser then thy wares.      .   .   .   .   .   .   .   100   F4 To the World   20
And, knowing this, should I yet stay,        .   .   .   .   .   .   100   F4 To the World   21
What should, yet, thy pallat please?         .   .   .   .   .   .   105   F8 Sicknesse      21
Hercules? alas his bones are yet sore,       .   .   .   .   .   .   107   F10 Proludium      4
And yet (in this t'expresse our selves more cleare)      .   .   .   111   F11 Epode         75
And yet (in this t'expresse my self more cleare)     .   .   .   .   111   F11 Epode       V 75
Were yet unfound, and better plac'd in earth,        .   .   .   .   114   F12 Rutland       25
Were yet unfound, and better plac'd on earth,        .   .   .   .   114   F12 Rutland     V 25
```

YET (cont.)

	Page	Title	Line
Have beautie knowne, yet none so famous seene?	114	F12 Rutland	50
That Homer brought to Troy; yet none so live:	115	F12 Rutland	55
Yet, for the timely favours shee hath done,	115	F12 Rutland	71
They hold in my strange poems, which, as yet,	115	F12 Rutland	81
So both the prais'd, and praisers suffer: Yet,	116	F13 Aubigny	5
Of Fortune, have not alter'd yet my looke,	117	F13 Aubigny	16
Right, the right way: yet must your comfort bee	118	F13 Aubigny	68
And greater rites, yet writ in mysterie,	119	F13 Aubigny	106
Yet dare I not complaine, or wish for death	122	F15 Heaven	23
Distinct in persons, yet in Unitie	128	U1 Trinitie	39
Yet I rebell,	129	U1 Father	26
Yet search'd, and true they found it.	130	U1 Nativitie	6
For this Beauty yet doth hide	137	U2 Cupid	49
Or if you would yet have stay'd,	138	U2 Kisse	29
Yet a man; with crisped haire	141	U2 Her man	10
In loves schoole, and yet no sinners.	141	U2 Her man	32
In loves art, and yet no sinners.	141	U2 Her man	V 32
Yet no Taylor help to make him;	141	U2 Her man	37
Nor o're-praise, nor yet condemne;	142	U2 Her man	47
Nor out-praise, nor yet condemne;	142	U2 Her man	V 47
Yet dare I not tell who;	147	U7 Nymph	2
Yet if it be not knowne,	147	U7 Nymph	5
They yet may envie me:	147	U7 Nymph	9
And yet it cannot be foreborne,	147	U7 Nymph	13
Yet, yet I doubt he is not knowne,	147	U7 Nymph	20
I'le tell no more, and yet I love,	148	U7 Nymph	29
And he loves me; yet no	148	U7 Nymph	30
Nor have I yet the narrow mind	150	U10 Jealousie	4
Whom never yet he durst attempt awake;	151	U11 Dreame	6
Yet he broke them, e're they could him,	151	U12 Corbet	10
It chid the vice, yet not the Men.	152	U12 Corbet	28
Yet choyce from whom I take them; and would shame	153	U13 Sacvile	17
Yet we must more then move still, or goe on,	157	U13 Sacvile	135
Ever at home: yet, have all Countries seene:	159	U14 Selden	30
That gaspe for action, and would yet revive	162	U15 Friend-Wars	6
And jealous each of other, yet thinke long	164	U15 Friend-Wars	73
Whom no great Mistresse hath as yet infam'd,	165	U15 Friend-Wars	97
Well, let it goe. Yet this is better, then	166	U15 Friend-Wars	145
The life, and fame-vaynes (yet not understood	167	U15 Friend-Wars	166
And yet the noble Nature never grudge;	169	U17 Friend-Debt	3
But she is such, as she might, yet, forestall	172	U20 Shrub	23
Yet is't your vertue now I raise.	173	U22 Elegy Tho	4
Wherein you triumph yet: because	173	U22 Elegy Tho	9
Yet give me leave t'adore in you	174	U22 Elegy Tho	35
Yet doth some wholsome Physick for the mind,	180	U26 Ode High	9
Thy beauties, yet could write of thee?	181	U27 Ode Helen	2
So speake (as yet it is not mute)	181	U27 Ode Helen	4
Where never Star shone brighter yet?	181	U27 Ode Helen	26
Have all these done (and yet I misse	182	U27 Ode Helen	29
Yet sure my tunes will be the best,	182	U27 Ode Helen	35
Is not yet free from Rimes wrongs,	184	U29 Fit of Rime	35
Yet he himselfe is but a sparke.	189	U36 Song	8
The eldest God, yet still a Child.	189	U36 Song	16
Yet if with eithers vice I teynted be,	190	U37 Friend-Book	29
Her furie, yet no friendship to betray.	190	U37 Friend-Book	33
Offended Mistris, you are yet so faire,	191	U38 Elegy 'Tis	9
Spare your owne goodnesse yet; and be not great	191	U38 Elegy 'Tis	17
Your just commands; yet those, not I, be lost.	192	U38 Elegy 'Tis	38
Yet should the Lover still be ayrie and light,	197	U40 Elegy That	19
Moves like a sprightly River, and yet can	198	U40 Elegy That	26
No Poets verses yet did ever move,	199	U42 Elegy Let	3
Yet keepe those up in sackcloth too, or lether,	200	U42 Elegy Let	25
Thou mightst never yet enjoy'd thy crueltie	204	U43 Vulcan	49
With some more thrift, and yet varietie:	205	U43 Vulcan	V 50
Some Alchimist there may be yet, or odde	208	U43 Vulcan	118
Well fare the wise-men yet, on the Banckside,	208	U43 Vulcan	123
I could invent a sentence, yet were worse;	211	U43 Vulcan	189
I could invent a sentence, yet more worse;	211	U43 Vulcan	V189
Losse, remaines yet, as unrepair'd as mine.	211	U43 Vulcan	196
Losse, remaines yet, as much despair'd as mine.	211	U43 Vulcan	V196
Why yet, my noble hearts, they cannot say,	213	U44 Speach	1
All Ensignes of a Warre, are not yet dead,	213	U44 Speach	11
Alive yet, in the noise; and still the same;	214	U44 Speach	56
Nor ever trusted to that friendship yet,	216	U45 Squib	7
That never yet did friend, or friendship seeke	218	U47 Tribe	14
Whether the Dispensation yet be sent,	219	U47 Tribe	35
I have a body, yet, that spirit drawes	219	U47 Tribe	41
From Court, while yet thy fame hath some small day;	223	U49 Pucell	36
Are in your selfe rewarded; yet 'twill be	224	U50 Countesse	15
But yet the Tun at Heidelberg had houpes.	227	U52 Answer	6
Yet when of friendship I would draw the face,	227	U52 Answer	22
For never saw I yet the Muses dwell,	228	U53 Newcastle	15
Yet with a Dye, that feares no Moth,	230	U55 Burges	7
Yet are got off thence, with cleare mind, and hands	234	U61 Epigram	7
But thou wilt yet a Kinglier mastrie trie,	235	U62 Charles 1	5
(Without prophanenesse) yet, a Poet, cry,	238	U66 Queene	4
Yet, let our Trumpets sound;	239	U67 Muses	13
Then knew the former ages: yet to life,	242	U69 Friend Son	23
Was left yet to Man-kind;	247	U70 Ode	121
Yet, as we may, we will, with chast desires,	257	U75 Epithalam.	161
Hee's Master of the Office; yet no more	258	U75 Epithalam.	187
Yet read him in these lines: He doth excell	262	U78 Digby	2

YET (cont.)

	Page	Title	Line
Yet take him in these lines: He doth excell	262	U78 Digby	V 2
Of all that Nature, yet, to life did bring;	264	U79 New-yeares	33
A dazling, yet inviting, Majestie:	270	U81 Pawlet	44
A darling, yet inviting, Majestie:	270	U81 Pawlet	V 44
Yet, here are no such Trifles brought,	273	U84 Cradle	25
Yet something, to the Painters view,	275	U84 Body	9
May rather yet adore, then spy.	276	U84 Body	20
And yet remaine our wonder still.	278	U84 Mind	20
So swift, so pure, should yet apply	279	U84 Mind	42
Yet know, with what thou art possest,	281	U84 Mind	70
Nothing, that could remaine, or yet can stirre	282	U84 Muse	9
Yet have all debts forgiven us, and advance	286	U84 Muse	143
Yet would I wish to love, live, die with thee.	294	U87 Hor.3:9	24
No sowre, or sollen bed-mate, yet a Chast;	295	U90 Mart.10:47	10
Yet, not as therefore wild, and tame should cleave	305	Horace	14
Yet not as therefore cruell things should cleave	338	Horace	V 14
Yet, if by chance, in utt'ring things abstruse,	307	Horace	69
All the Grammarians strive; and yet in Court	309	Horace	111
Yet Comick matter shunnes to be exprest	341	Horace	V127/121
To ignorance still, then yet to learne, or know?	341	Horace	V126/131
Yet, sometime, doth the Comedie excite	311	Horace	132
Yet sometime both the Comoedy doth raise	341	Horace	V132
Or some hot youth, yet in his flourishing course;	313	Horace	163
If something strange, that never yet was had	313	Horace	178
If something fresh, that never yet was had	342	Horace	V178
Yet common matter thou thine owne maist make,	313	Horace	187
With sloth, yet greedy still of what's to come:	317	Horace	246
Yet, to the Stage, at all thou maist not tender	317	Horace	260
As loud enough to fill the seates, not yet	319	Horace	291
Yet so the scoffing Satyres to mens view,	321	Horace	328
Yet he that offers at it, may sweat much,	321	Horace	351
Of Trimeter, when yet it was sixe-pac'd,	323	Horace	373
This foot yet, in the famous Trimeters	323	Horace	381
I, writing nought my selfe, will teach them yet	325	Horace	435
There are yet faults, which we would well forgive,	329	Horace	520
And, of your selfe too, understand; yet mind	331	Horace	547
Yet, there's a value given to this man.	331	Horace	554
Yet who's most ignorant, dares Verses make.	331	Horace	570
The Writ, once out, never returned yet.	331	Horace	580
The word, once out, never returned yet.	352	Horace	V556/580
Nor did he do this, once; if yet you can,	355	Horace	V667
Recall him yet, hee'ld be no more a man:	335	Horace	668
Yet shee's nor nice to shew them,	365	Ode Splendor	23
Yet, looking in thy face, they shall begin	369	Ode Who saith	93
Yet who could have hit on't but the wise noddell	379	Coryat 3	6
Yet may as blind men sometimes hit the marke.	383	Author	6
Yet neyther of you seeme to th'other old.	384	Somerset	24
To such a worke, as could not need theirs? Yet	385	Brooke	5
I do not feele that ever yet I had	385	Husband	5
It must be thine owne judgment, yet, that sends	386	Browne	7
nor yet inscription like it. Write but that;	387	Cavendish	9
nor yet inscription like it writt but that	387	Cavendish	V 9
Yet must I not give Nature all: Thy Art,	392	Shakespeare	55
To see thee in our waters yet appeare,	392	Shakespeare	72
Not usuall in a Lady; and yet true:	394	Jane Ogle	14
That ever yet did fire the English blood!	397	Drayton	57
Yet give mee leave, to wonder at the birth	398	Drayton	83
Yet, who dares offer a redoubt to reare?	401	Beaumont	11
Something your Surship doth not yet intend!	402	Inigo Jones 1	14
I doe salute you! Are you fitted yet?	402	Inigo Jones 1	17
And they were very good: yet thou think'st nay.	408	Detractor	2
Of Persons, yet in Union (One) divine.	413	Ghyrlond	35
That sit to censure Playes, yet know not when,	414	Rutter	8
yet doe not feare it.	417	Moon	32
Yet ware; thou mayst do all things cruellie:	423	Lucan	15

YETT

	Page	Title	Line
Yett: since the bright, and wyse,	420	Ode:If Men	28
deignes myne the power to find, yett want I will	421	Censure	10
yett, yf with eythers vyce, I tainted bee,	422	Censure	22

YEWGH

	Page	Title	Line
Hayles me, so solemnly, to yonder Yewgh?	268	U81 Pawlet	2

YF

	Page	Title	Line
yf from a little sparke hee rise not fier.	383	Rich	16
Cause Reverence, yf not Feare,	421	Ode:If Men	42
yett, yf with eythers vyce, I tainted bee,	422	Censure	22
whom, yf fortune hath deprest; come nere the fates	422	Lucan	V 4

YFF

	Page	Title	Line
Yff Men, and tymes were nowe	419	Ode:If Men	1

YIELD (See YEELD)

YMOUNTED

	Page	Title	Line
Ymounted high upon Selinis crest:	412	Ghyrlond	10

YNOW

	Page	Title	Line
Doe not men, ynow of rites	104	F8 Sicknesse	3

YO'ARE

	Page	Title	Line
To make amends, yo'are thought a wholesome creature.	46	E62 Would-bee	8
By which yo'are planted, shew's your fruit shall bide.	281	U84 Kenelme	19
Nine yeares kept in, your papers by, yo'are free	331	Horace	578
(Whether yo'are given to, or giver are.)	333	Horace	608

YO'HAD

	Page	Title	Line
With one great blot, yo'had form'd me as I am.	227	U52 Answer	12

YO'HAVE

	Page	Title	Line
Tell them, what parts yo'have tane, whence run away,	69	E107 Hungry	9

YO'HAVE (cont.)
What States yo'have gull'd, and which yet keepes yo'in pay. . 69 E107 Hungry 10
Yo'have all the Mysteries of Wits new Mint, . . . 415 Rutter 28
YO'IN
What States yo'have gull'd, and which yet keepes yo'in pay. . 69 E107 Hungry 10
YOKE
And us dis-joyn'd force to her brazen yoke, . . . 294 U87 Hor.3:9 18
YOND'
See you yond' Motion? Not the old Fa-ding, . . . 62 E97 Motion 1
YONDER
Hayles me, so solemnly, to yonder Yewgh? . . . 268 U81 Pawlet 2
YONG
Give your yong States-men, (that first make you drunke, . 69 E107 Hungry 19
If I would vertue set, as shee was yong, . . . 78 E122 Rudyerd 2 5
You, Madame, yong have learn'd to shunne these shelves, . 119 F13 Aubigny 89
O so yong o so streight O so chast so chast is shee . 136 U2 Triumph V 46
YO'
To make amends, yo'are thought a wholesome creature. . 46 E62 Would-bee 8
Tell them, what parts yo'have tane, whence run away, . 69 E107 Hungry 9
What States yo'have gull'd, and which yet keepes yo'in pay. . 69 E107 Hungry 10
With one great blot, yo'had form'd me as I am. . . 227 U52 Answer 12
Painter yo' are come, but may be gone, . . . 277 U84 Mind 1
By which yo'are planted, shew's your fruit shall bide. . 281 U84 Kenelme 19
Nine yeares kept in, your papers by, yo'are free . . 331 Horace 578
(Whether yo'are given to, or giver are.) . . . 333 Horace 608
Yo'have all the Mysteries of Wits new Mint, . . . 415 Rutter 28
YOU'
Who, when you'have burnt your selves downe to the snuffe, . 45 E59 Spies 2
I shall feare, you'll surfet too. . . . . 104 F8 Sicknesse 8
I doe feare, you'll surfet too. . . . . 104 F8 Sicknesse V 8
You'ld reade a Snake, in his next Song. . . . 260 U76 Petition 32
YOU (See also Y')
If all you boast of your great art be true; . . . 29 E6 Alchymists 1
Sure, willing povertie lives most in you. . . . 29 E6 Alchymists 2
Tells you it is a hot-house: So it ma', . . . 29 E7 Hot-house 3
There's reason good, that you good lawes should make: . 34 E24 Parliament 1
Guiltie, because I bad you late be wise, . . . 38 E38 Guiltie 2 1
You laugh when you are touch'd, and long before . . 38 E38 Guiltie 2 3
Any man else, you clap your hands, and rore, . . . 38 E38 Guiltie 2 4
Beleeve it, Guiltie, if you loose your shame, . . . 38 E38 Guiltie 2 7
Spies, you are lights in state, but of base stuffe, . . 45 E59 Spies 1
Fine Madame Would-Bee, wherefore should you feare, . 46 E62 Would-bee 1
The world reputes you barren: but I know . . . 46 E62 Would-bee 3
Or your complexions losse? you have a pot, . . . 46 E62 Would-bee 6
What should the cause be? Oh, you live at court: . . 46 E62 Would-bee 9
In-primis, Grand, you owe me for a jest, . . . 51 E73 Fine Grand 5
I lent you, on meere acquaintance, at a feast. . . 51 E73 Fine Grand 6
That yet maintaynes you, and your house in laughter. . 51 E73 Fine Grand 8
Item, the babylonian song you sing; . . . 51 E73 Fine Grand 9
With which a learned Madame you belye. . . . 51 E73 Fine Grand 11
Item, a gulling imprese for you, at tilt. . . . 51 E73 Fine Grand 15
Fortie things more, deare Grand, which you know true, . 51 E73 Fine Grand 21
For which, or pay me quickly', or Ile pay you. . . 51 E73 Fine Grand 22
At which, shee happily displeas'd, made you: . . . 53 E79 Rutland 9
Madame, I told you late how I repented, . . . 54 E84 Bedford 2 1
And, ere I could aske you, I was prevented: . . . 54 E84 Bedford 2 3
Would you beleeve, when you this Mounsieur see, . . 56 E88 Monsieur 1
At sixe and twentie, ripe. You shall 'hem meet, . . 58 E92 New Crie 4
Nay, aske you, how the day goes, in your eare. . . 59 E92 New Crie 18
Stand'st thou, to shew the times what you all were? . 60 E93 Radcliffe 4
Lucy, you brightnesse of our spheare, who are . . 60 E94 Bedford 3 1
But these, desir'd by you, the makers ends . . . 60 E94 Bedford 3 5
Be of the best: and 'mongst those, best are you. . . 61 E94 Bedford 3 14
Lucy, you brightnesse of our spheare, who are . . 61 E94 Bedford 3 15
But most we need his faith (and all have you) . . 62 E95 Savile 35
See you yond' Motion? Not the old Fa-ding, . . . 62 E97 Motion 1
Know you the cause? H'has neither land, nor lease, . . 63 E97 Motion 9
Yet shall you have, to rectifie your palate, . . . 64 E101 Supper 9
Ile tell you of more, and lye, so you will come: . . 65 E101 Supper 17
Know you to be a Sydney, though un-named? . . . 66 E103 L Wroth 1 4
Forgive me then, if mine but say you are . . . 67 E103 L Wroth 1 9
Becomes none more then you, who need it least. . . 67 E103 L Wroth 1 14
Were they that nam'd you, prophets? Did they see, . 67 E104 Montgomery 1
Even in the dew of grace, what you would bee? . . 67 E104 Montgomery 2
To make those faithfull, did the Fates send you? . . 67 E104 Montgomery 6
Were you advanced, past those times, to be . . . 67 E104 Montgomery 11
If not, 'tis fit for you, some should envy. . . . 67 E104 Montgomery 16
Who could not but create them all, from you? . . 67 E105 L Wroth 2 6
He, that but saw you weare the wheaten hat, . . . 68 E105 L Wroth 2 7
Would call you more then Ceres, if not that: . . . 68 E105 L Wroth 2 8
You were the bright Oenone, Flora, or May? . . . 68 E105 L Wroth 2 10
That saw you put on Pallas plumed caske: . . . 68 E105 L Wroth 2 16
So are you Natures Index, and restore, . . . 68 E105 L Wroth 2 19
Doe what you come for, Captayne, with your newes; . 68 E107 Hungry 1
Not that I love it, more, then I will you. . . . 68 E107 Hungry 4
How great you were with their two Emperours; . . 68 E107 Hungry 6
What at Ligorne, Rome, Florence you did doe: . . . 69 E107 Hungry 14
If but to beleev'd you have the hap, . . . 69 E107 Hungry 17
Give your yong States-men, (that first make you drunke, . 69 E107 Hungry 19
And then lye with you, closer, then a punque, . . 69 E107 Hungry 20
For your next meale: this you are sure of. Why . . 69 E107 Hungry 27
Will you part with them, here, unthriftely? . . . 69 E107 Hungry 28
Nay, now you puffe, tuske, and draw up your chin, . 69 E107 Hungry 29

	Page	Title	Line
YOU (cont.)			
Twirle the poore chaine you run a feasting in.	69	E107 Hungry	30
Come, be not angrie, you are Hungry; eate;	69	E107 Hungry	31
Doe what you come for, Captayne, There's your meate.	69	E107 Hungry	32
Such as are misse-call'd Captaynes, and wrong you;	69	E108 Soldiers	2
Be nor put on you, nor you take offence.	69	E108 Soldiers	4
Hath chang'd his soule, and made his object you:	74	E114 Sydney	5
You wonder, who this is! and, why I name	74	E115 Honest Man	1
Describ'd, it 's thus: Defin'd would you it have?	75	E115 Honest Man	33
Weepe with me all you that read	77	E120 S. P.	1
And know, for whom a teare you shed,	77	E120 S. P.	3
No going backe; on still you rogues, and row.	86	E133 Voyage	88
Vanish'd away: as you must all presume	87	E133 Voyage	110
But 'mong'st these Tiberts, who do'you thinke there was?	88	E133 Voyage	155
Cannot the Plague-bill keepe you backe? nor bells	88	E133 Voyage	173
But you will visit grisly Pluto's hall?	89	E133 Voyage	175
And stayes but till you come unto the dore!	89	E133 Voyage	178
Is now from home. You lose your labours quite,	89	E133 Voyage	181
Were you Jove's sonnes, or had Alcides might.	89	E133 Voyage	182
While you breath. First give a hundred,	103	F6 Celia 2	8
Till you equall with the store,	103	F6 Celia 2	12
Follow a shadow, it still flies you;	104	F7 Women but	1
So court a mistris, shee denyes you;	104	F7 Women but	3
Let her alone, shee will court you.	104	F7 Women but	4
Take heed, Sicknesse, what you doe,	104	F8 Sicknesse	7
I, that have none (to send you) send you verse.	113	F12 Rutland	19
With you, I know, my offring will find grace.	114	F12 Rutland	30
Were it to thinke, that you should not inherit	114	F12 Rutland	32
Almost you have, or may have, when you will?	114	F12 Rutland	34
Wherein wise Nature you a dowrie gave,	114	F12 Rutland	35
Worth an estate, treble to that you have.	114	F12 Rutland	36
And such, or my hopes faile, shall make you shine.	115	F12 Rutland	64
You, and that other starre, that purest light,	115	F12 Rutland	65
Now thincking on you, though to England lost,	116	F12 Rutland	94
My best of wishes, may you beare a sonne.	116	F12 Rutland	100
You will not from the paper slightly passe:	117	F13 Aubigny	25
Remov'd, as you from need to have it such.	117	F13 Aubigny	28
Your beautie; for you see that every day:	117	F13 Aubigny	30
Are you engaged to your happy fate,	118	F13 Aubigny	47
For such a lot! that mixt you with a state	118	F13 Aubigny	48
Wherewith, then, Madame, can you better pay	118	F13 Aubigny	53
Of vertue, which you tread? what if alone?	118	F13 Aubigny	55
This makes, that wisely you decline your life,	118	F13 Aubigny	59
You, Madame, yong have learn'd to shunne these shelves,	119	F13 Aubigny	89
For which you worthy are the glad encrease	119	F13 Aubigny	94
To crowne the burthen which you goe withall,	119	F13 Aubigny	103
They speake; since you are truly that rare wife,	119	F13 Aubigny	110
How you love one, and him you should; how still	119	F13 Aubigny	113
You are depending on his word, and will;	119	F13 Aubigny	114
Unto himselfe, by being so deare to you.	119	F13 Aubigny	117
Wherein, your forme, you still the same shall finde;	120	F13 Aubigny	123
Are justly summ'd, that make you man;	120	F14 Sydney	22
Of nobles vertue, shew in you;	121	F14 Sydney	32
Whose nephew, whose grand-child you are;	121	F14 Sydney	42
Say you have follow'd farre,	121	F14 Sydney	45
They teach you, how.	121	F14 Sydney	48
So may you live in honor, as in name,	121	F14 Sydney	51
If with this truth you be inspir'd,	121	F14 Sydney	52
Father, and Sonne, and Holy Ghost, you three	128	U1 Trinitie	37
If you then will read the Storie,	131	U2 Excuse	13
First, prepare you to be sorie,	131	U2 Excuse	14
That you never knew till now,	131	U2 Excuse	15
When you know, that this is she,	131	U2 Excuse	18
Have you seene but a bright Lillie grow,	134	U2 Triumph	21
Have you seene the white Lillie grow,	134	U2 Triumph	V 21
have you mark'd but the fall o'the Snow	134	U2 Triumph	23
Have you seene the fall o'the Snow	135	U2 Triumph	V 23
Have you felt the wooll o' the Bever?	135	U2 Triumph	25
Have you seene a faire Damaske-rose	135	U2 Triumph	V 31
Have you seene faire Helen disclose	135	U2 Triumph	V 33
Have you seene Love-Queenes embraces	135	U2 Triumph	V 35
Have you tasted the Cinnamon-tree	135	U2 Triumph	V 37
Have you seene the boy from the Chace	135	U2 Triumph	V 39
Have you seene faire Ledas face	135	U2 Triumph	V 41
Have you seen the Palme-trees state	136	U2 Triumph	V 43
Have you tasted virginitye	136	U2 Triumph	V 45
Noblest Charis, you that are	136	U2 Cupid	1
Heare, what late Discourse of you,	136	U2 Cupid	5
Which you call my Shafts. And see!	136	U2 Cupid	19
Have you plac'd the banke of kisses,	136	U2 Cupid	25
Where, you say, men gather blisses,	136	U2 Cupid	26
Thence, as sweet, as you are faire,	137	U2 Kisse	4
Of th'Assembly, as did you!	138	U2 Kisse	12
Or, that did you sit, or walke,	138	U2 Kisse	13
You were more the eye, and talke	138	U2 Kisse	14
To no other Grace but you!	138	U2 Kisse	20
Or, if you did move to night	138	U2 Kisse	21
Of your Peeres, you were beheld,	138	U2 Kisse	23
Or if you would yet have stay'd,	138	U2 Kisse	29
To have left all sight for you:	138	U2 Kisse	33
Why doe you doubt, or stay?	139	U2 Another	4
Nay, you may erre in this,	139	U2 Another	9
Therefore, Charis, you must do't,	140	U2 Promise	13

823

YOU (cont.)

	Page	Title	Line
For I will so urge you to't,	140	U2 Promise	14
You shall neither eat, nor sleepe,	140	U2 Promise	15
Nay, I will not let you sit	140	U2 Promise	21
Make accompt, unlesse you can,	140	U2 Promise	29
Drest, you still for man should take him;	141	U2 Her man	38
What you please, you parts may call,	142	U2 Exception	7
What need of mee? doe you but sing,	143	U3 Musicall	13
O sing not you then, lest the best	144	U3 Musicall	21
Sing you no more then, lest the best	144	U3 Musicall	V 21
Men, if you love us, play no more	145	U5 Woman-kind	1
And if wee must, let's sing of you.	145	U5 Woman-kind	6
In any curious peece you see	145	U5 Woman-kind	14
Take that away, you take our lives,	146	U6 Defence	5
Could you beleeve, that this,	148	U8 Houre-glasse	4
You then, whose will not only, but desire	153	U13 Sacvile	7
You cannot doubt, but I, who freely know	153	U13 Sacvile	13
This Good from you, as freely will it owe;	153	U13 Sacvile	14
Now dam'mee, Sir, if you shall not command	154	U13 Sacvile	53
And you, Sir, know it well, to whom I write,	156	U13 Sacvile	109
And last, goe out in nothing: You that see	157	U13 Sacvile	153
Their difference, cannot choose which you will be.	157	U13 Sacvile	154
You know (without my flatt'ring you) too much	157	U13 Sacvile	155
For me to be your Indice. Keep you such,	157	U13 Sacvile	156
Which you will bury; but therein, the strife	158	U13 Sacvile	160
Find you to reckon nothing, me owe all.	158	U13 Sacvile	164
Was trusted, that you thought my judgement such	158	U14 Selden	6
Stand forth my Object, then, you that have beene	159	U14 Selden	29
What fables have you vext! what truth redeem'd!	159	U14 Selden	39
What blots and errours, have you watch'd and purg'd	160	U14 Selden	42
You both are modest. So am I. Farewell.	161	U14 Selden	86
And lookes unto the forfeit. If you be	169	U17 Friend-Debt	13
Now so much friend, as you would trust in me,	169	U17 Friend-Debt	14
I'le lead you on; or if my fate will so,	170	U18 Elegy Can	22
Tell me (my lov'd Friend) doe you love, or no,	170	U19 Elegy By	11
You blush, but doe not: friends are either none,	171	U19 Elegy By	13
I'le therefore aske no more, but bid you love;	171	U19 Elegy By	15
You have a Husband is the just excuse	171	U19 Elegy By	22
That which we can, who both in you, his Wife,	171	U19 Elegy By	25
Knew I this Woman? yes; And you doe see,	172	U20 Shrub	15
Doe not you aske to know her, she is worse	172	U20 Shrub	17
This subjects you to love of one.	173	U22 Elegy Tho	8
Wherein you triumph yet: because	173	U22 Elegy Tho	9
'Tis of your selfe, and that you use	173	U22 Elegy Tho	10
But who should lesse expect from you,	173	U22 Elegy Tho	13
His falling Temples you have rear'd,	173	U22 Elegy Tho	17
And you are he: the Dietie	173	U22 Elegy Tho	25
Yet give me leave t'adore in you	174	U22 Elegy Tho	35
(As prov'd in you)	177	U25 Desmond	24
That you will stand	180	U25 Desmond	64
As farre from all revolt, as you are now from Fortune.	180	U25 Desmond	65
Which in the taking if you mis-apply,	180	U26 Ode High	11
You are unkind.	180	U26 Ode High	12
In one full Action; nor have you now more	180	U26 Ode High	17
Thinke but how deare you bought	180	U26 Ode High	19
This same which you have caught,	180	U26 Ode High	20
Such thoughts wil make you more in love with truth.	181	U26 Ode High	21
But then his Mothers sweets you so apply,	182	U28 Worth	12
For Venus Ceston, every line you make.	182	U28 Worth	14
So, from all sicknesse, may you rise to health,	186	U31 Elsmere	5
You favour Truth, and mee, in this mans Cause.	186	U31 Elsmere	10
Such shall you heare to day, and find great foes,	186	U32 Elsmere	7
He do's you wrong, that craves you to doe right.	186	U32 Elsmere	16
Sir, I am thankfull, first, to heaven, for you;	189	U37 Friend-Book	1
You have unto my Store added a booke,	189	U37 Friend-Book	4
And which you (being the worthier) gave me leave	190	U37 Friend-Book	11
Though you sometimes proclaime me too severe,	190	U37 Friend-Book	16
Or there to sterve it. Helpe, O you that may	191	U38 Elegy 'Tis	7
Offended Mistris, you are yet so faire,	191	U38 Elegy 'Tis	9
As light breakes from you, that affrights despaire,	191	U38 Elegy 'Tis	10
That you should be too noble to destroy.	191	U38 Elegy 'Tis	12
If there be nothing worthy you can see	191	U38 Elegy 'Tis	15
Nothing is vile, that is a part of you:	192	U38 Elegy 'Tis	36
Before you prove a medicine, is unjust.	192	U38 Elegy 'Tis	50
You may so place me, and in such an ayre,	192	U38 Elegy 'Tis	51
That is, if still your Favours you apply,	192	U38 Elegy 'Tis	53
And not the bounties you ha' done, deny.	192	U38 Elegy 'Tis	54
Could you demand the gifts you gave, againe?	192	U38 Elegy 'Tis	55
Of crueltie, lest they doe make you such.	193	U38 Elegy 'Tis	84
Rather then once displease you more, to die,	193	U38 Elegy 'Tis	92
I will no more abuse my vowes to you,	194	U38 Elegy 'Tis	107
O, that you could but by dissection see	194	U38 Elegy 'Tis	109
How much you are the better part of me;	194	U38 Elegy 'Tis	110
You would be then most confident, that tho	194	U38 Elegy 'Tis	113
When I see you, then I doe see my Sun,	194	U38 Elegy 'Tis	120
They looke at best like Creame-bowles, and you soone	198	U40 Elegy That	29
Since you must goe, and I must bid farewell,	199	U41 Elegy Since	1
My health will leave me; and when you depart,	199	U41 Elegy Since	13
You would restore it? No, that's worth a feare,	199	U41 Elegy Since	15
Till I may see both it and you agen.	199	U41 Elegy Since	22
Wish, you had fowle ones, and deformed got;	200	U42 Elegy Let	22
So to be sure you doe injoy your selves.	200	U42 Elegy Let	24
Would you had kept your Forge at Aetna still,	212	U43 Vulcan	197

YOU (cont.)

Or stay'd but where the Fryar, and you first met, . . .   212   U43 Vulcan   201
Or fixt in the Low-Countrey's, where you might . . .   212   U43 Vulcan   203
What love you then? your whore. what study? gate, . .   215   U44 Speach   87
And as within your Office, you doe take . . .   216   U45 Squib   13
No piece of money, but you know, or make . . .   216   U45 Squib   14
So short you read my Character, and theirs . . .   220   U47 Tribe   73
My selfe a little. I will take you so, . . .   220   U47 Tribe   76
As you have writ your selfe. Now stand, and then, . .   220   U47 Tribe   77
Sir, you are Sealed of the Tribe of Ben. . . .   220   U47 Tribe   78
The wits will leave you, if they once perceive . .   223   U49 Pucell   37
You cling to Lords, and Lords, if them you leave . .   223   U49 Pucell   38
They say you weekly invite with fits o'th' Mother, . .   223   U49 Pucell   40
Wherewith this while you live a widow'd wife, . . .   224   U50 Countesse   2
And the right wayes you take unto the right, . . .   224   U50 Countesse   3
Only your time you better entertaine, . . .   224   U50 Countesse   23
For you admit no companie, but good, . . .   224   U50 Countesse   25
And when you want those friends, or neere in blood, . .   224   U50 Countesse   26
Or your Allies, you make your bookes your friends, . .   224   U50 Countesse   27
You were not tied, by any Painters Law, . . .   227   U52 Answer   7
My Superficies: that was all you saw. . . .   227   U52 Answer   9
With one great blot, you had drawne me as I am. . .   227   U52 Answer   V 12
But whilst you curious were to have it be . . .   227   U52 Answer   13
You made it a brave piece, but not like me. . . .   227   U52 Answer   15
But, you are he can paint; I can but write: . . .   227   U52 Answer   19
When first, my Lord, I saw backe your horse, . . .   228   U53 Newcastle   1
So seem'd your horse and you, both of a peece! . .   228   U53 Newcastle   6
You shew'd like Perseus upon Pegasus; . . .   228   U53 Newcastle   7
And you shall make me good, in weight, and fashion, . .   229   U54 Squib   17
You won not Verses, Madam, you won mee, . . .   230   U56 Covell   1
When you would play so nobly, and so free. . . .   230   U56 Covell   2
You won them too, your oddes did merit it. . . .   230   U56 Covell   4
So have you gain'd a Servant, and a Muse: . . .   230   U56 Covell   5
The first of which, I feare, you will refuse; . . .   230   U56 Covell   6
The first of which, I doubt, you will refuse; . . .   230   U56 Covell   V 6
And you may justly, being a tardie, cold, . . .   230   U56 Covell   7
Such, (if her manners like you) I doe send: . . .   230   U56 Covell   19
To make you merry on the Dressing stoole . . .   230   U56 Covell   21
By this, although you fancie not the man, . . .   231   U56 Covell   25
By thys Tyme, though you fancie not the man, . .   231   U56 Covell   V 25
Accept his Muse; and tell, I know you can, . . .   231   U56 Covell   26
I can lose none in tendring these to you. . . .   231   U56 Covell   28
Valour! to sleight it, being done to you! . . .   233   U59 Newcastle   16
That you have seene the pride, beheld the sport, . .   234   U61 Epigram   1
That scarce you heare a publike voyce alive, . . .   234   U61 Epigram   5
Your happinesse, and doth not speake you blest, . .   234   U61 Epigram   9
To see you set apart, thus, from the rest, . . .   234   U61 Epigram   10
That the Almighties will to you is such: . . .   236   U63 Charles 2   8
Most pious King, but his owne good in you! . . .   236   U64 Charles 3   2
When you that raigne, are her Example growne, . .   236   U64 Charles 3   9
And what are bounds to her, you make your owne? . .   236   U64 Charles 3   10
Sonne, and my Friend, I had not call'd you so . .   241   U69 Friend Son   1
To mee; or beene the same to you; if show, . . .   241   U69 Friend Son   2
And shine as you exalted are; . . .   246   U70 Ode   97
This made you first to know the Why . . .   247   U70 Ode   107
You lik'd, then after, to apply . . .   247   U70 Ode   108
You liv'd to be the great surnames, . . .   247   U70 Ode   113
What prayers (People) can you thinke too much? . .   249   U72 King   20
Of Love betweene you, and your Lovely-head: . . .   257   U75 Epithalam.   164
That when you both are old, . . .   258   U75 Epithalam.   165
You find no cold . . .   258   U75 Epithalam.   166
You feele no cold . . .   258   U75 Epithalam.   V166
Till you behold a race to fill your Hall, . . .   258   U75 Epithalam.   169
I would present you now with curious plate . . .   260   U77 Treasurer   2
I would present you with some curious plate . . .   260   U77 Treasurer   V 2
This I would doe, if I could thinke you one . . .   260   U77 Treasurer   V 10
But you I know, my Lord; and know you can . . .   261   U77 Treasurer   13
What you have studied are the arts of life; . . .   261   U77 Treasurer   17
Fame and Honour you, they possesse by Peace. . .   261   U77 Treasurer   V 22
These looke you up at, with a measuring eye, . .   261   U77 Treasurer   V 23
Heare, o you Groves, and, Hills, resound his praise. .   264   U79 New-yeares   23
Heare, O you Groves, and, Hills, resound his worth. .   264   U79 New-yeares   31
Haste, haste you hither, all you gentler Swaines, . .   265   U79 New-yeares   46
To whom you owe all duties of your grounds; . . .   265   U79 New-yeares   49
I doe obey you, Beauty! for in death, . . .   269   U81 Pawlet   5
You seeme a faire one! O that you had breath, . .   269   U81 Pawlet   6
You seeme a faire one! O that I had breath, . . .   269   U81 Pawlet   V 6
'Tis but a body which you can torment, . . .   270   U81 Pawlet   55
If you not understand, what Child you had. . . .   271   U81 Pawlet   78
If you dare grudge at Heaven, and repent . . .   271   U81 Pawlet   79
If you dare Quarrell Heaven, and repent . . .   271   U81 Pawlet   V 79
If you can envie your owne Daughters blisse, . .   271   U81 Pawlet   83
If you can enjoy your owne Daughters blisse, . .   271   U81 Pawlet   V 83
If you can cast about your either eye, . . .   271   U81 Pawlet   85
Speake it, you bold Penates, you that stand . . .   274   U84 Descent   7
And give you reasons more then one. . . .   277   U84 Mind   4
You could make shift to paint an Eye, . . .   278   U84 Mind   9
As you goe on, by what brave way . . .   278   U84 Mind   18
Our sense you doe with knowledge fill, . . .   278   U84 Mind   19
I call you Muse; now make it true: . . .   278   U84 Mind   21
Hence-forth may every line be you; . . .   278   U84 Mind   22
Study illustrious Him, and you have all. . . .   282   U84 Kenelme   23
And will you, worthy Sonne, Sir, knowing this, . .   285   U84 Muse   97

	Page	Title	Line

YOU (cont.)

Put black, and mourning on? and say you misse . . . . 285 U84 Muse 98
Thither, you hope to come; and there to find . . . . 285 U84 Muse 103
You once enjoy'd: A short space severs yee, ... 285 U84 Muse 105
When shee departed? you will meet her there, ... 285 U84 Muse 108
Could you containe your laughter? Credit mee, ... 305 Horace 7
Take, therefore, you that write, still, matter fit . . . . 307 Horace 53
Take therefore, you that write, a subject fit . . . . 339 Horace V 55/ 53
Peleus, or Telephus. If you speake vile . . . . 311 Horace 147
Hee thinkes not, how to give you smoake from light, ... 315 Horace 203
Take you the Greeke Examples, for your light, ... 323 Horace 397
If either you, or I, know the right way . . . . 323 Horace 402
If either you, or I know any way . . . . 348 Horace V388/402
But you, Pompilius off-spring, spare you not . . . . 325 Horace 415
A third of twelve, you may: foure ounces. Glad, ... 327 Horace 469
Will take you more, the neerer that you stand; . . . . 331 Horace 540
You Sir, the elder brother, though you are . . . . 331 Horace 545
To change, and mend, what you not forth doe set. . . . . 331 Horace 579
But you, my Piso, carefully beware, ... 333 Horace 607
You doe not bring, to judge your Verses, one, ... 333 Horace 609
When you write Verses, with your judge do so: . . . . 333 Horace 620
When you make verses, with your judge doe so: . . . . 354 Horace V620
Looke through him, and be sure, you take not mocks . . . . 333 Horace 621
If to Quintilius, you recited ought: . . . . 333 Horace 623
If you denied, you had no better straine, ... 333 Horace 625
Then: If your fault you rather had defend . . . . 335 Horace 629
In vaine, but you, and yours, you should love still . . . . 335 Horace 631
I'le tell you but the death, and the disease . . . . 335 Horace 659
Nor did he doe this once; for if you can . . . . 335 Horace 667
Nor did he do this once; if yet you can, ... 355 Horace V667
So bold, as shewes your Art you can command. . . . . 370 Author 8
Here, finer then comming from his Punke you him see, ... 375 Coryat 1 28
And allow you for each particular mile, ... 379 Coryat 3 9
And that you may see he most luckily ment . . . . 379 Coryat 3 13
Pies on't, you have his historicall faith. . . . . 380 Coryat 3 22
That he dares to informe you, but somewhat meticulous, ... 380 Coryat 3 33
Nay more in his wardrobe, if you will laugh at a . . . . 380 Coryat 3 47
To rise with eyther of you, on the morrow. . . . . 384 Somerset 16
So, in theyr number, may you never see . . . . 384 Somerset 21
Mortality, till you immortall bee. . . . . 384 Somerset 22
Yet neyther of you seeme to th'other old. . . . . 384 Somerset 24
That all, that view you then, and late; may say, ... 384 Somerset 25
When you behold me wish my selfe, the man . . . . 389 Aleman 23
That would have done, that, which you onely can. . . . . 389 Aleman 24
You have not writ to me, nor I to you; . . . . 396 Drayton 6
T'is a Record in heaven. You, that were . . . . 399 Lady Ogle 1
Mr Surveyor, you that first begann . . . . 402 Inigo Jones 1 1
you are; from them leapt forth an Architect, ... 402 Inigo Jones 1 3
I doe salute you! Are you fitted yet? . . . . 402 Inigo Jones 1 17
Or are you soe ambitious 'bove your peers! . . . . 403 Inigo Jones 1 19
you would be an Asinigo, by your ears? . . . . 403 Inigo Jones 1 20
Why much good doo't you! Be what beast you will, ... 403 Inigo Jones 1 21
In Towne & Court? Are you growne rich? & proud? . . . . 403 Inigo Jones 1 24
your Trappings will not change you. Change your mynd. . . . . 403 Inigo Jones 1 25
Noe velvet Sheath you weare, will alter kynde. . . . . 403 Inigo Jones 1 26
What is the cause you pompe it soe? I aske, ... 403 Inigo Jones 1 29
And all men eccho you have made a Masque, ... 403 Inigo Jones 1 30
Or Verse, or Sense t'express Immortall you? . . . . 403 Inigo Jones 1 41
You are the Spectacles of State! Tis true . . . . 403 Inigo Jones 1 42
You aske noe more then certeyne politique Eyes, ... 404 Inigo Jones 1 45
I had you for a Servant, once, Dick Brome; . . . . 409 Brome 1
And you perform'd a Servants faithfull parts: . . . . 409 Brome 2
Now, you are got into a nearer roome, ... 409 Brome 3
And you doe doe them well, with good applause, ... 409 Brome 5
Which you have justly gained from the Stage, ... 409 Brome 6
You learn'd it well; and for it, serv'd your time . . . . 410 Brome 9
Cropt, branded, slit, neck-stockt; go, you are stript. . . . . 411 Gill 16
You looke, my Joseph, I should something say . . . . 414 Rutter 1
You know, I never was of Truth afeard, ... 414 Rutter 4
Such men I met withall, and so have you. . . . . 415 Rutter 11
(You have deserv'd it from me) I have read, ... 415 Rutter 13
To Crowne the years, which you begin, great king, ... 416 Welcome 7
And you, with them, as Father of our spring. . . . . 416 Welcome 8
my mind unto you, ... 416 Moon 4
prest in to se you. . . . . 416 Moon 8
Ply it, and you all are mounted. . . . . 657 Door Apollo 14

YOU'HAVE

Who, when you'have burnt your selves downe to the snuffe, . . 45 E59 Spies 2

YOU'L

you'l be as Langley sayd, an Inigo still. . . . . 403 Inigo Jones 1 22

YOU'LD

You'ld reade a Snake, in his next Song. . . . . 260 U76 Petition 32

YOU'LL

I shall feare, you'll surfet too. . . . . 104 F8 Sicknesse 8
I doe feare, you'll surfet too. . . . . 104 F8 Sicknesse V 8

YOUNG (See also YONG)

She shall make the old man young, ... 131 U2 Excuse 20
The young Adonis courted . . . . 135 U2 Triumph V 40
Young Il'd have him to, and faire, ... 141 U2 Her man 9
Himselfe young, and face be good, ... 142 U2 Exception 5
For these with her young Companie shee'll enter, ... 164 U15 Friend-Wars 79
Under the Auspice of young Swynnerton. . . . . 213 U44 Speach 20
Henry, the brave young Lord La-ware, ... 233 U60 La-ware 3

	Page	Title	Line
YOUNG (cont.)			
Alas, but Morison fell young:	244	U70 Ode	43
For he's both noble, lovely, young,	292	U86 Hor.4:1	13
Of the times past, when he was a young lad;	317	Horace	248
Or play young tricks in over-wanton verse;	347	Horace	V350/358
While he was young; he sweat; and freez'd againe:	333	Horace	589
YOUNGER			
So mayst thou still be younger	221	U48 Bacchus	21
YOUNGEST			
As hath the youngest Hee,	149	U9 Picture	9
As makes the youngest Hee,	149	U9 Picture	V 9
As light, and active as the youngest hee	200	U42 Elegy Let	6
YOUR			
If all you boast of your great art be true;	29	E6 Alchymists	1
Mens manners ne're were viler, for your sake.	34	E24 Parliament	2
And to conceale your ulcers, did advise,	38	E38 Guiltie 2	2
Any man else, you clap your hands, and rore,	38	E38 Guiltie 2	4
Beleeve it, Guiltie, if you loose your shame,	38	E38 Guiltie 2	7
I'le loose my modestie, and tell your name.	38	E38 Guiltie 2	8
Who, when you'have burnt your selves downe to the snuffe,	45	E59 Spies	2
Your 'pothecarie, and his drug sayes no.	46	E62 Would-bee	4
Or your complexions losse? you have a pot,	46	E62 Would-bee	6
That can restore that. Will it hurt your feature?	46	E62 Would-bee	7
The world must know your greatnesse is my debter.	51	E73 Fine Grand	4
That yet maintaynes you, and your house in laughter.	51	E73 Fine Grand	8
Your partie-per-pale picture, one halfe drawne	51	E73 Fine Grand	13
Item, your mistris anagram, i' your hilt.	51	E73 Fine Grand	16
Item, your owne, sew'd in your mistris smock.	51	E73 Fine Grand	17
Then had I made 'hem good, to fit your vaine.	51	E73 Fine Grand	20
Your noblest father prov'd: like whom, before,	53	E79 Rutland	2
For your most noble offer had supply'd me.	54	E84 Bedford 2	4
O Madame, if your grant did thus transferre mee,	55	E84 Bedford 2	9
Make it your gift. See whither that will beare mee.	55	E84 Bedford 2	10
Nay, aske you, how the day goes, in your eare.	59	E92 New Crie	18
Whose poemes would not wish to be your booke?	60	E94 Bedford 3	4
Doe equally desire your companie:	64	E101 Supper	2
But that your worth will dignifie our feast,	64	E101 Supper	4
Yet shall you have, to rectifie your palate,	64	E101 Supper	9
How well, faire crowne of your faire sexe, might hee,	66	E103 L Wroth 1	1
That but the twi-light of your sprite did see,	66	E103 L Wroth 1	2
And to your Scene lent no lesse dignitie	67	E104 Montgomery	7
There's none so dull, that for your stile would aske,	68	E105 L Wroth 2	15
Or, keeping your due state, that would not cry,	68	E105 L Wroth 2	17
I' your selfe, all treasure lost of th'age before.	68	E105 L Wroth 2	20
Doe what you come for, Captayne, with your newes;	68	E107 Hungry	1
Of your Moravian horse, Venetian bull.	69	E107 Hungry	8
Give them your services, and embassies	69	E107 Hungry	11
Give your yong States-men, (that first make you drunke,	69	E107 Hungry	19
For newes) your Ville-royes, and Silleries,	69	E107 Hungry	21
Janin's, your Nuncio's, and your Tuilleries,	69	E107 Hungry	22
Your Arch-Dukes Agents, and your Beringhams,	69	E107 Hungry	23
That are your wordes of credit. Keepe your Names	69	E107 Hungry	24
For your next meale: this you are sure of. Why	69	E107 Hungry	27
Nay, now you puffe, tuske, and draw up your chin,	69	E107 Hungry	29
Doe what you come for, Captayne, There's your meate.	69	E107 Hungry	32
And your high names: I doe desire, that thence	69	E108 Soldiers	3
I sweare by your true friend, my Muse, I love	70	E108 Soldiers	5
Your great profession; which I once, did prove:	70	E108 Soldiers	6
But, in your love, made all his servants wise.	74	E114 Sydney	8
Retyr'd, with purpose your faire worth to praise,	80	E126 Mrs Cary	1
Of all your night-tubs, when the carts doe cluster,	85	E133 Voyage	64
Were seene your ugly Centaures, yee call Car-men,	86	E133 Voyage	68
Over your heads: Well, row. At this a loud	36	E133 Voyage	93
Your Fleet-lane Furies; and hot cookes doe dwell,	88	E133 Voyage	143
Your daintie nostrills (in so hot a season,	88	E133 Voyage	165
Upon your eares, of discords so un-sweet?	88	E133 Voyage	171
Is now from home. You lose your labours quite,	89	E133 Voyage	181
Can your favours keepe, and cover,	103	F6 Celia 2	2
All your bounties will betray.	103	F6 Celia 2	4
Let the old boy, your sonne, ply his old taske,	107	F10 Proludium	19
For what a sinne 'gainst your great fathers spirit,	114	F12 Rutland	31
Borne up by statues, shall I reare your head,	115	F12 Rutland	84
besett with statues, shall I reare your head,	115	F12 Rutland	V 84
Above your under-carved ornaments,	115	F12 Rutland	85
Your forme imprest there: not with tickling rimes,	116	F12 Rutland	87
Your forme imprest there: not with tinckling rimes,	116	F12 Rutland	V 87
And your brave friend, and mine so well did love.	116	F12 Rutland	92
And your brave friend, and mine to well did love.	116	F12 Rutland	V 92
For that firme grace he holdes in your regard,	116	F12 Rutland	95
I, Madame, am become your praiser. Where,	117	F13 Aubigny	21
If it may stand with your soft blush to heare	117	F13 Aubigny	22
Your selfe but told unto your selfe, and see	117	F13 Aubigny	23
In my character, what your features bee,	117	F13 Aubigny	24
Looke then, and see your selfe. I will not say	117	F13 Aubigny	29
Your beautie; for you see that every day:	117	F13 Aubigny	30
Nor that your beautie wanted not a dower,	117	F13 Aubigny	37
Are you engaged to your happy fate,	118	F13 Aubigny	47
This blessing of your starres, then by that way	118	F13 Aubigny	54
This makes, that wisely you decline your life,	118	F13 Aubigny	59
Right, the right way: yet must your comfort bee	118	F13 Aubigny	68
Your conscience, and not wonder, if none askes	118	F13 Aubigny	69
Into your harbor, and all passage shut	119	F13 Aubigny	92
'Gainst stormes, or pyrats, that might charge your peace;	119	F13 Aubigny	93

	Page	Title	Line
YOUR (cont.)			
Of your blest wombe, made fruitfull from above,	119	F13 Aubigny	95
To pay your lord the pledges of chast love:	119	F13 Aubigny	96
Unto your name, and goodnesse of your life,	119	F13 Aubigny	109
What your try'd manners are, what theirs should bee.	119	F13 Aubigny	112
This makes, that your affections still be new,	119	F13 Aubigny	118
And that your soules conspire, as they were gone	119	F13 Aubigny	119
Wherein, your forme, you still the same shall finde;	120	F13 Aubigny	123
Your vow	120	F14 Sydney	23
T'out-strip your peeres:	121	F14 Sydney	26
Your blood	121	F14 Sydney	33
'T will be exacted of your name, whose sonne,	121	F14 Sydney	41
of seeing your face.	128	U1 Trinitie	32
All coeternall in your Majestie,	128	U1 Trinitie	38
Let it not your wonder move,	131	U2 Excuse	1
Lesse your laughter; that I love.	131	U2 Excuse	2
Where he chanc't your name to see	136	U2 Cupid	8
As the Bath your verse discloses	136	U2 Cupid	21
From your lips, and suck'd an ayre	137	U2 Kisse	3
So, as those that had your sight,	138	U2 Kisse	17
Of your Peeres, you were beheld,	138	U2 Kisse	23
And all your bountie wrong:	139	U2 Another	10
No, nor forth your window peepe,	140	U2 Promise	16
With your emissarie eye,	140	U2 Promise	17
'Fore your Idoll Glasse a whit,	140	U2 Promise	22
All your sweet of life is past,	140	U2 Promise	28
(And that quickly) speake your Man.	140	U2 Promise	30
Of your Trouble, Ben, to ease me,	140	U2 Her man	1
Mixe then your Notes, that we may prove	143	U3 Musicall	9
But what your lips doe make.	143	U3 Musicall	V 16
The fooles, or Tyrants with your friends,	145	U5 Woman-kind	2
Our owne false praises, for your ends:	145	U5 Woman-kind	4
So going thorow all your straine,	145	U5 Woman-kind	10
Not at my prayers, but your sense; which laid	153	U13 Sacvile	9
For me to be your Indice. Keep you such,	157	U13 Sacvile	156
That I may love your Person (as I doe)	157	U13 Sacvile	157
Without your gift, though I can rate that too,	157	U13 Sacvile	158
Your Booke, my Selden, I have read, and much	158	U14 Selden	5
Upon your Center, doe your Circle fill	159	U14 Selden	32
Which Grace shall I make love to first? your skill,	159	U14 Selden	35
Or faith in things? or is't your wealth and will	159	U14 Selden	36
T'instruct and teach? or your unweary'd paine	159	U14 Selden	37
To informe and teach? or your unweary'd paine	159	U14 Selden	V 37
Forme, Art or Ensigne, that hath scap'd your sight?	160	U14 Selden	48
Forme, Act or Ensigne, that hath scap'd your sight?	160	U14 Selden	V 48
To marke the excellent seas'ning of your Stile!	160	U14 Selden	55
I yeeld, I yeeld, the matter of your praise	160	U14 Selden	61
The Gaine of your two friendships! Hayward and	161	U14 Selden	81
The Graine of your two friendships! Hayward and	161	U14 Selden	V 81
By that faire Stand, your forehead, whence he bends	170	U19 Elegy By	3
By that tall Grove, your haire: whose globy rings	170	U19 Elegy By	5
By those pure bathes your either cheeke discloses,	170	U19 Elegy By	7
And lastly by your lips, the banke of kisses,	170	U19 Elegy By	9
Yet is't your vertue now I raise.	173	U22 Elegy Tho	4
Throughout your forme; as though that move,	173	U22 Elegy Tho	6
'Tis of your selfe, and that you use	173	U22 Elegy Tho	10
Is gone himselfe into your Name.	173	U22 Elegy Tho	24
Who as an off'ring at your shrine,	174	U22 Elegy Tho	29
One sparke of your Diviner heat	174	U22 Elegy Tho	31
Rich beame of honour, shed your light	177	U25 Desmond	14
Graced by your Reflection!	177	U25 Desmond	17
That hold your spirit:	177	U25 Desmond	20
That curbes your spirit:	177	U25 Desmond	V 20
And keepes your merit	177	U25 Desmond	21
Nor thinke your selfe unfortunate,	177	U25 Desmond	27
But to your selfe, most loyal Lord,	179	U25 Desmond	53
Though many Gems be in your bosome stor'd,	179	U25 Desmond	55
I send nor Balmes, nor Cor'sives to your wound,	180	U26 Ode High	2
Your fate hath found,	180	U26 Ode High	3
Your covetous hand,	180	U26 Ode High	13
Since I exscribe your Sonnets, am become	182	U28 Worth	3
For in your verse all Cupids Armorie,	182	U28 Worth	9
So, justest Lord, may all your Judgements be	185	U31 Elsmere	1
So, may the King proclaime your Conscience is	185	U31 Elsmere	3
Law, to his Law; and thinke your enemies his:	185	U31 Elsmere	4
Still flie about the Odour of your Name;	186	U31 Elsmere	8
When this appeares, just Lord, to your sharp sight,	186	U32 Elsmere	15
Next to your selfe, for making your love true:	189	U37 Friend-Book	2
Then to your love, and gift. And all's but due.	189	U37 Friend-Book	3
Not like your Countrie-neighbours, that commit	190	U37 Friend-Book	7
But, as a friend, which name your selfe receave,	190	U37 Friend-Book	10
Of Graces, or your mercie here in me,	191	U38 Elegy 'Tis	16
Spare your owne goodnesse yet; and be not great	191	U38 Elegy 'Tis	17
The Subject of your Grace in pardoning me,	191	U38 Elegy 'Tis	28
And (stil'd your mercies Creature) will live more	191	U38 Elegy 'Tis	29
Your honour now, then your disgrace before.	191	U38 Elegy 'Tis	30
Thinke that your selfe like heaven forgive me can:	192	U38 Elegy 'Tis	32
Your just commands; yet those, not I, be lost.	192	U38 Elegy 'Tis	38
Of your compassion; Parents should be mild:	192	U38 Elegy 'Tis	40
That is, if still your Favours you apply,	192	U38 Elegy 'Tis	53
O may your wisdome take example hence,	193	U38 Elegy 'Tis	67
But view the mildnesse of your Makers state,	193	U38 Elegy 'Tis	85
Then Mistris, here, here let your rigour end,	194	U38 Elegy 'Tis	105

YOUR (cont.)
  And let your mercie make me asham'd t'offend.   .   .   .   194 U38 Elegy 'Tis 106
  How all my Fibres by your Spirit doe move,   .   .   .   194 U38 Elegy 'Tis 111
  Out of your eyes, and be awhile away;   .   .   .   .   194 U38 Elegy 'Tis 115
  Your forme shines here, here fixed in my heart: .   .   194 U38 Elegy 'Tis 117
  Rather then want your light, I wish a grave.   .   .   .   194 U38 Elegy 'Tis 122
  Under another Name, I take your health;   .   .   .   .   197 U40 Elegy That   10
  I give, or owe my friends, into your Rites,   .   .   .   197 U40 Elegy That   12
  'Bove all your standing waters, choak'd with weedes. .   .   198 U40 Elegy That   28
  And such your Servant is, who vowes to keepe   .   .   .   198 U40 Elegy That   41
  The Jewell of your name, as close as sleepe   .   .   .   198 U40 Elegy That   42
  Which in assurance to your brest I tell, ...   198 U40 Elegy That   49
  Heare, Mistris, your departing servant tell   .   .   .   199 U41 Elegy Since   2
  Your sacrifice, then here remaine with me.   .   .   .   199 U41 Elegy Since 18
  But then consent, your Daughters and your Wives,   .   .   200 U42 Elegy Let   19
  So to be sure you doe injoy your selves.   .   .   .   .   200 U42 Elegy Let   24
  Had tickled your large Nosthrill: many a Reame .   .   .   205 U43 Vulcan   62
  Had filled your large nostrills with the steame: .   .   205 U43 Vulcan   V 62
  With Nicholas Pasquill's, Meddle with your match,   .   .   206 U43 Vulcan   77
  With Nicholas Bretons Meddle with your match,   .   .   .   206 U43 Vulcan   V 77
  Pox on your flameship, Vulcan; if it be   .   .   .   .   211 U43 Vulcan   191
  Pox on your fire workes, Vulcan; if it be .   .   .   .   211 U43 Vulcan   V191
  'Bove all your Fire-workes, had at Ephesus,   .   .   .   211 U43 Vulcan   194
  Beyond your Fire-workes, had at Ephesus, ...   211 U43 Vulcan   V194
  Would you had kept your Forge at Aetna still,   .   .   .   212 U43 Vulcan   197
  And there made Swords, Bills, Glaves, and Armes your fill;   .   212 U43 Vulcan   198
  On both sides doe your mischiefes with delight; .   .   .   212 U43 Vulcan   204
  Make your Petards, and Granats, all your fine   .   .   .   212 U43 Vulcan   206
  We aske your absence here, we all love peace,   .   .   .   212 U43 Vulcan   209
  We crave your absence here, we all love peace, .   .   .   212 U43 Vulcan   V209
  What love you then? your whore. what study? gate,   .   .   215 U44 Speach   87
  And as within your Office, you doe take   .   .   .   .   216 U45 Squib   13
  As you have writ your selfe. Now stand, and then,   .   .   220 U47 Tribe   77
  The Wisdome, Madam, of your private Life, ...   224 U50 Countesse   1
  Not only shunning by your act, to doe   .   .   .   .   224 U50 Countesse   5
  And though all praise bring nothing to your name,   .   .   224 U50 Countesse   13
  Are in your selfe rewarded; yet 'twill be .   .   .   .   224 U50 Countesse   15
  Whilst your Ulisses hath ta'ne leave to goe,   .   .   .   224 U50 Countesse   21
  Only your time you better entertaine, ...   224 U50 Countesse   23
  Or your Allies, you make your bookes your friends,   .   .   224 U50 Countesse   27
  Searching for knowledge, and to keepe your mind   .   .   225 U50 Countesse   29
  Not boasted in your life, but practis'd true,   .   .   .   225 U50 Countesse   32
  O, had I now your manner, maistry, might, ...   227 U52 Answer   16
  Your Power of handling shadow, ayre, and spright,   .   .   227 U52 Answer   17
  When first, my Lord, I saw you backe your horse,   .   .   228 U53 Newcastle   1
  So seem'd your horse and you, both of a peece! .   .   .   228 U53 Newcastle   6
  Nay, so your Seate his beauties did endorse,   .   .   .   228 U53 Newcastle   11
  And surely had I but your Stable seene   .   .   .   .   228 U53 Newcastle   13
  For your securitie. I can no better.   .   .   .   .   229 U54 Squib   20
  You won them too, your oddes did merit it.   .   .   .   230 U56 Covell   4
  Your Joane to passe her melancholie time. .   .   .   .   231 U56 Covell   24
  How many verses, Madam, are your Due!   .   .   .   .   231 U56 Covell   27
  And was your Fathers! All your Ancestours!   .   .   .   233 U59 Newcastle   20
  Your happinesse, and doth not speake you blest, .   .   .   234 U61 Epigram   9
  And what are bounds to her, you make your owne? .   .   .   236 U64 Charles 3   10
  When your assiduous practise doth secure   .   .   .   .   236 U64 Charles 3   11
  When all your life's a president of dayes, ...   237 U64 Charles 3   13
  And murmure cannot quarrell at your wayes?   .   .   .   237 U64 Charles 3   14
  His rage, with razing your immortall Towne.   .   .   .   242 U70 Ode   4
  Of rimes, or ryots, at your feasts, ...   246 U70 Ode   103
  Such joyes, such sweet's doth your Returne   .   .   .   251 U74 Weston   19
  Bring all your friends, (faire Lord) that burne .   .   .   251 U74 Weston   20
  With love, to heare your modestie relate, ...   251 U74 Weston   21
  The bus'nesse of your blooming wit, ...   251 U74 Weston   22
  Your fruitfull spreading Vine, ...   257 U75 Epithalam. 159
  Of Love betweene you, and your Lovely-head: .   .   .   257 U75 Epithalam. 164
  Till you behold a race to fill your Hall, ...   258 U75 Epithalam. 169
  To your Majestie your Poet: .   .   .   .   .   .   259 U76 Petition   4
  That whereas your royall Father   .   .   .   .   .   259 U76 Petition   5
  Whereas late your royall Father   .   .   .   .   .   259 U76 Petition   V 5
  Please your Majestie to make   .   .   .   .   .   .   260 U76 Petition   25
  Of your grace, for goodnesse sake, ...   260 U76 Petition   26
  Those your Fathers Markes, your Pounds;   .   .   .   .   260 U76 Petition   27
  Of Noremberg, or Turkie; hang your roomes .   .   .   .   260 U77 Treasurer   3
  Unto your honour: I can tune in song   .   .   .   .   261 U77 Treasurer   27
  Unto your honour: I can voyce in song   .   .   .   .   261 U77 Treasurer V 27
  New yeares, expect new gifts: Sister, your Harpe,   .   .   263 U79 New-yeares   1
  Your change of Notes, the flat, the meane, the sharpe,   .   263 U79 New-yeares   3
  And offer your just service on these plaines;   .   .   .   263 U79 New-yeares   12
  Best Kings expect first-fruits of your glad gaines.   .   .   263 U79 New-yeares   13
  To whom you owe all duties of your grounds;   .   .   .   265 U79 New-yeares   49
  Your Milkes, your Fells, your Fleeces, and first Lambes,   .   265 U79 New-yeares   50
  Your teeming Ewes, aswell as mounting Rammes,   .   .   .   265 U79 New-yeares   51
  To give your shade a name! Stay, stay, I feele .   .   .   269 U81 Pawlet   7
  To give your shade a lasting name! Stay, stay, I feele   .   269 U81 Pawlet   V 7
  Stick on your Cupping-glasses, fear not, put   .   .   .   270 U81 Pawlet   53
  Your hottest Causticks to, burne, lance, or cut: .   .   270 U81 Pawlet   54
  Your hotter Causticks to, burne, lance, or cut: .   .   .   270 U81 Pawlet   V 54
  If you can envie your owne Daughters blisse,   .   .   .   271 U81 Pawlet   83
  If you can enjoy your owne Daughters blisse,   .   .   .   271 U81 Pawlet   V 83
  If you can cast about your either eye, ...   271 U81 Pawlet   85
  Run from your rootes; Tell, testifie the grand .   .   .   274 U84 Descent   9
  The wonder of her Sexe, and of your Blood.   .   .   .   274 U84 Descent   12

```
                                                           Page    Title      Line

YOUR  (cont.)
   Not, that your Art I doe refuse:        .   .   .   .   .   277   U84 Mind        5
   Beside, your hand will never hit,       .   .   .   .   .   277   U84 Mind        7
   Sweet Mind, then speake your selfe, and say,    .   .   .   278   U84 Mind       17
   Boast not these Titles of your Ancestors,   .   .   .   .   281   U84 Kenelme    10
   When your owne Vertues, equall'd have their Names,  .   .   281   U84 Kenelme    12
   By which yo'are planted, shew's your fruit shall bide.  .   281   U84 Kenelme    19
   Hang all your roomes, with one large Pedigree:  .   .   .   282   U84 Kenelme    20
   Which Vertue from your Father, ripe, will fall;  .   .   .  282   U84 Kenelme    22
   Could you containe your laughter? Credit mee,   .   .   .   305   Horace          7
   Father, and sons right worthy of your Sire,  .   .   .   .   339   Horace       V 34
   Unto your strength, and long examine it,   .   .   .   .   307   Horace         54
   Unto your strength, and long be turning it:  .   .   .   .   339   Horace     V 56/ 54
   Upon your shoulders.  Prove what they will beare,  .   .   307   Horace         55
   Prove what your shoulders will, or will not beare.  .   .   339   Horace     V 57/ 55
   Take you the Greeke Examples, for your light,  .   .   .   323   Horace        397
   Your Ancestors, old Plautus numbers prais'd,  .   .   .   348   Horace     V385/399
   Informed rightly, by your Fathers care,   .   .   .   .   331   Horace        546
   And, of your selfe too, understand: yet mind   .   .   .   331   Horace        547
   And, to your Fathers, and to mine; though 't be  .   .   331   Horace        577
   Nine yeares kept in, your papers by, yo'are free  .   .   331   Horace        578
   Nine yeares kept by, your papers in, y'are free  .   .   352   Horace     V554/578
   You doe not bring, to judge your Verses, one,  .   .   .   333   Horace        609
   When you write Verses, with your judge do so:  .   .   .   333   Horace        620
   When you make verses, with your judge doe so:  .   .   354   Horace       V620
   Then: If your fault you rather had defend   .   .   .   .   335   Horace        629
   Alone, without a rivall, at your will.   .   .   .   .   354   Horace       V632
   And all your Booke (when it is throughly scan'd)  .   .   370   Author          5
   So bold, as shewes your Art you can command.  .   .   .   370   Author          8
   But now, your Worke is done, if they that view  .   .   370   Author          9
   'Tis not your fault, if they shall sense preferre,  .   .  370   Author         13
   Except your Gratious Eye as through a Glass  .   .   .   383   Rich           11
   your Royal Eye which still creates new men  .   .   .   .   383   Rich           14
   So, be your Concord, still, as deepe, as mute;  .   .   .   384   Somerset       17
   And when your yeares rise more, then would be told,  .   384   Somerset       23
   And teach your nephewes it to aemulate:   .   .   .   .   387   Cavendish      10
   To your desert, who'have done it, Friend.  And this  .   389   Aleman         21
   Your true freind in Judgement and Choise   .   .   .   .   395   May            25
   Transmitt it to your Nephewes, Freinds, Allies,  .   .   399   Lady Ogle       3
   With pause upon it; make this page your booke;  .   .   399   Lady Ogle       6
   Your booke? your volume! Nay, the state, and story!  .   399   Lady Ogle       7
   How much Architectonice is your owne!   .   .   .   .   402   Inigo Jones 1  10
   Something your Surship doth not yet intend!  .   .   .   402   Inigo Jones 1  14
   By all your Titles, & whole style at ones   .   .   .   402   Inigo Jones 1  15
   Will any of these express your place? or witt?  .   .   402   Inigo Jones 1  18
   Or are you soe ambitious 'bove your peers!  .   .   .   403   Inigo Jones 1  19
   you would be an Asinigo, by your ears?   .   .   .   .   403   Inigo Jones 1  20
   What makes your Wretchednes to bray soe loud  .   .   403   Inigo Jones 1  23
   your Trappings will not change you.  Change your mynd.  403   Inigo Jones 1  25
   Pack with your pedling Poetry to the Stage,  .   .   .   404   Inigo Jones 1  51
   your workes thus differing, troth see your style:  .   .  407   Inigo Jones 2  19
   Which I, your Master, first did teach the Age.  .   .   409   Brome           8
   You learn'd it well; and for it, serv'd your time  .   .   410   Brome           9
   When I had read your holy Meditations,   .   .   .   .   411   Sutcliffe       1
   On the reverse of this your circling crowne,  .   .   .   413   Ghyrlond       30
   Unto the world, in praise of your first Play:  .   .   .   414   Rutter          2
   And weigh'd your Play: untwisted ev'ry thread,  .   .   415   Rutter         14
   Bred by your breath, on this low bancke of ours;  .   .   416   Welcome         3
   Soe ended your Epistle, myne beginns   .   .   .   .   421   Censure         3
   O're read, examin'd, try'd, and prov'd your Ryme  .   .   421   Censure         7
   And though your virtue (as becomes it) still  .   .   .   421   Censure         9
YOURS
   A picture, which the world for yours must know,  .   .   67   E104 Montgomery 14
   Tell the grosse Dutch those grosser tales of yours,  .   68   E107 Hungry     5
   Unto the Censure.  Yours all need doth flie  .   .   .   158   U14 Selden     11
   But I on yours farre otherwise shall doe,   .   .   .   159   U14 Selden     17
   But I to yours, farre from this fault, shall doo;  .   .  159   U14 Selden    V 17
   And yours of whom I sing be such   .   .   .   .   173   U22 Elegy Tho   2
   His very eyes are yours to overthrow.   .   .   .   .   182   U28 Worth      11
   Thinke that I once was yours, or may be now;  .   .   192   U38 Elegy 'Tis 35
   All this (my Lord) is Valour! This is yours!  .   .   .   233   U59 Newcastle  19
   (Brave Youths) th'are their possessions, none of yours:  281   U84 Kenelme    11
   In vaine, but you, and yours, you should love still  .   335   Horace        631
   I made my lyfe my monument, & yours:   .   .   .   .   387   Cavendish       7
YOURSELFE
   As Cleare, and distant, as yourselfe from Cryme;  .   .   421   Censure         8
YOUTH
   Mary, the daughter of their youth:   .   .   .   .   33   E22 Daughter    2
   And, as thou'hast mine, his houres, and youth abuse.  .   48   E65 Muse        6
   And he growne youth, was call'd to his ladies chamber.  .   57   E90 Mill      10
   Or the feature, or the youth:   .   .   .   .   .   131   U2 Excuse       9
   I know no beautie, nor no youth that will.   .   .   .   171   U19 Elegy Bv   20
   Even in youth.   .   .   .   .   .   .   .   181   U26 Ode High   24
   Powder, or paper, to bring up the youth   .   .   .   213   U44 Speach     25
   The Month of youth, which calls all Creatures forth  .   253   U75 Epithalam. 26
   With all the pompe of Youth, and all our Court beside.  .   254   U75 Epithalam. 72
   With all that Youth, or it can bring:   .   .   .   .   276   U84 Body       22
   And ('bout thy Ivory neck,) no youth did fling  .   .   293   U87 Hor.3:9     2
   Or some hot youth, yet in his flourishing course;  .   .   313   Horace        163
   Th'unbearded Youth, his Guardian once being gone,  .   315   Horace        229
   And still correcting youth, and censuring.  .   .   .   317   Horace        249
   The parts of age to youth be given; or men   .   .   .   317   Horace        252
   So shall our English Youth urge on, and cry  .   .   .   398   Drayton        69
```

		Page	Title	Line

YOUTHFULL
Their youthfull tricks in over-wanton verse: . . . . 321 Horace 358
YOUTHS
When youths ply their stolne delights. . . . . 103 F6 Celia 2 18
What Beavie of beauties, and bright youths at charge . . 253 U75 Epithalam. 17
(Brave Youths) th'are their possessions, none of yours: . . 281 U84 Kenelme 11
Goe where Youths soft intreaties call thee back. . . 292 U86 Hor.4:1 8
The Youths and tender Maids shall sing thy praise: . . 292 U86 Hor.4:1 26
Our Roman Youths they learne the subtle wayes . . . 327 Horace 464
Our Roman Youths they learne more thriving wayes . . 350 Horace V464
YRON
Enforcing yron doores to yeeld it way, ... 363 Riches 9
YT
An elegie? no, muse; yt askes a straine . . . 108 F10 Proludium 1
the glories of yt. Now our muse takes winge, . . . 108 F10 Proludium 15
ZANY
Thou dost out-zany Cokely, Pod; nay, Gue: . . . . 81 E129 Mime 16
ZEALE
With all their zeale, to warme their welcome here. . . 95 F2 Penshurst 81
Onely, thus much, out of a ravish'd zeale, . . . 119 F13 Aubigny 108
Pure thoughts in man: with fiery zeale them feeding . . 128 U1 Trinitie 27
And it is paid 'hem with a trembling zeale, . . . 155 U13 Sacvile 85
Two noble knightes, whome true desire and zeale, . . . 382 Rich 1
ZEALOUS
I thought to forme unto my zealous Muse, ... 52 E76 Bedford 1 2
And there, while he gives the zealous Bravado, . . . 375 Coryat 1 22
ZEPHYR'S
From Zephyr's rape would close him with his beames. . . 366 Ode Who saith 24
ZODIACKES
Yet three fill'd Zodiackes had he beene . . . . 77 E120 S. P. 11

APPENDIXES

-2610-
AND

-2581-
THE

-1834-
TO

-1527-
OF

-1097-
A

-1077-
THAT

-1012-
IN

-743-
OR

-701-
BUT

-628-
WITH

-614-
HIS

-595-
NOT

-569-
ALL

-559-
AS

-549-
IT

-504-
THY

-491-
FOR

-485-
BE

-474-
IS

-468-
SO

-438-
HE

-423-
MY

-412-
YOU

-395-
THOU

-364-
THEIR

-347-
THIS

-341-
HER

-331-
THEY

-327-
HAVE

-324-
YOUR

-306-
WHAT

-287-
WHICH

-280-
ARE

-279-
NO

-278-
IF

-274-
AT

-260-
WHEN

-247-
MORE

-242-
THEE

-230-
DOE

-226-
FROM

-221-
CAN
WAS

-218-
YET

-217-
OUR

-209-
ME

-207-
THEN
WERE

-202-
DOTH

-200-
NOW
WOULD

-196-
THERE

-195-
WHO

-191-
NOR

-190-
HIM

-182-
MAKE

-176-
SUCH

-175-
DID

-171-
AN
HAD

-163-
GREAT
LOVE

-162-
OUT

-154-
MAN
THESE

-151-
SHOULD

-150-
WHERE

-148-
STILL

-144-
HOW

-143-
WE

-141-
MEN
SOME

-140-
GOOD

-139-
KNOW

-134-
DAY
HATH

-132-
THOUGH

-131-
SHALL
THOSE

-129-
SEE

-126-
'S

-123-
COULD
THEM

-120-
UP

-118-
TOO

-111-
LET

-110-
SHE

-108-
UPON

-105-
MUCH

-104-
BOTH

-103-
MADE

-99-
FIRST

-97-
MUST

-96-
HERE
SELFE

-95-
LIFE

-93-
OWNE

-92-
NAME
TRUE

-91-
EVERY

-89-
TAKE
WHOSE

-86-
US

-85-
GOD
WILL

-83-
MOST

-82-
TH'
UNTO

-77-
FORTH
MUSE
SHEE

-75-
COME
FAME
GIVE
'TIS

-74-
O

-73-
OLD

-72-
OTHER

-70-
ANY

-69-
NEW
WHOM

-67-
FAIRE

-66-
AM
THINKE

-65-
EACH
HEE

-64-
STATE

-63-
SAME
T'

-62-
BEST
TIME

-61-
GRACE
NEVER
THOUGHT

-59-
EVER
FRIEND
GOE
MAKES

-58-
FREE
SWEET

-57-
BEING
EYES
TILL

-56-
MANY
ONCE
PRAISE

-55-
SINCE

-54-
KING
LOOKE

-53-
BETTER
DONE
LESSE
LORD
TELL

-51-
COURT
NONE
PLACE
SIR
VERTUE
WORLD

-50-
FIRE
WAY
WHY

-49-
CALL

-48-
BEFORE
FEARE
INTO
KEEPE
LIVE
TRUTH
TWO

-47-
BOOKE
FACE
RIGHT
SING
THINE

-46-
TIMES
VERSE

-45-
'T
MIND
NOBLE
SPEAKE
WORKE

-44-
JUST
NATURE

-43-
CAUSE

-42-
AGE
FARRE
HAND
THINGS
THUS

-41-
CANNOT
WITHOUT

-40-
FRIENDS
HEARE
WHILE
WHOLE

-39-
BRAVE
HIGH
NOTHING
POORE
USE
WRITE

-38-
AGAINE
ILL
READ
WISH

-37-
GLAD
SEENE
SOULE
WISE

-36-
BIRTH
ELSE
FORTUNE
ONELY
SAW
SIGHT

-35-
AFTER
BRIGHT
BROUGHT
CROWNE
LOVES
MEE
ONLY
POET
PUT
SONG

-34-
ABOUT
ARTS
BEENE
BLOOD
DEATH
DRAW
FIND
JUDGE
KNOWNE

-33-
AWAY
FULL
HEAVEN
HIMSELFE
SONNE
WORTHY

-32-
ALONE
BRING
DARE
DOST
FATE
HONOUR
HOPE
NIGHT
RATHER
SET

-31-
AGAINST
BODY
EITHER
END
I'
LAND
LATE
POETS
SENSE
'HEM
WIFE

-30-
&
ART
EARTH
LADY
PEACE
SOFT
STAND
WANT

-29-
HEAD
LOST
MUSES
NAMES
PLAY
VICE

-28-
EPIGRAM
EYE
FALL
GONE
HEART
MANNERS
PART
SINNE
THROUGH

-27-
BEAUTIE
FALSE
OTHERS
THAT'
THAT'S
THING
VERSES
WINE

-26-
ASKE
CANST
FOUND
GOT
HOLY
KNOWES
SHINE

SURE
WORDS

-25-
CHARLES
FORME
HOME
POWER

-24-
ACT
BECAUSE
CAME
DEAD
ERE'
FATHER
GET
HAPPY
HEE'
HOLD
LITTLE
NAY
NEITHER
PARTS
SPRING
STORE
THENCE

-23-
CARE
CAST
CHANCE
COMMON
ENOUGH
FOLLOW
HORSE
NEED
OVER
PAY
PROVE
RISE
SHOW
TAKES
WAYES
WERT
WONDER

-22-
ABOVE
BOOKES
BREATH
DESIRE
ENVIE
HENCE
JOY
JUDGEMENT
KEPT
LAWES
LIVES
MASTER
MENS
OFT
RITES
SPIRIT
STAGE
WEE
YEARE
YEARES

-21-
ANOTHER
CHILD
DAYES
DURST
FRIENDSHIP
GAVE
GRAVE
MATTER
MOVE
NEXT
OFF
OWE
VIEW

-20-

BRAINE
DIE
DIVINE
ERE
FEAST
GIVEN
GROW
GROWNE
HALFE
KIND
MANS
ROUND
RUN
SAKE
SEND
SLEEPE
SOONE
THEREFORE
THREE

-19-

CONSCIENCE
DOUBT
GOLD
HOUSE
KINGS
KISSE
LANGUAGE
LOV'D
MEANT
PROUD
SAFE
SAID
SHORT
THERE'
THERE'S
TURNE
VOYCE
WENT

-18-

BECOME
BOAST
CHANGE
DO
DRAWNE
EXAMPLE
FATHERS
KNEW
LARGE
LEARNED
PRESENT
READE
SEA
SEEKE
SPENT
STRIFE
SUBJECT
SUN
TEACH
THOUGHTS
UNDER
WARRE
WEALTH
WORD

-17-

CLEARE
CRY
DELIGHT
EARLE
FAITH
FORCE
GAINE
HAVING
LEAVE
LINE
LOSSE
MEERE
NE'RE
PAST
SCORNE
SHAME
STRENGTH
TOOKE
TREE
WHEREIN

WROUGHT

-16-

'GAINST
AUTHOR
BREAKE
DULL
ENDS
FASHION
HEE'S
LINES
MARKE
MONEY
NOUGHT
PASSE
PERFECT
PIECE
POWERS
PRAY
PURE
RAISE
SIDE
STONE
TREAD
TRUST
YOUTH

-15-

ACTIONS
BACKE
DISEASE
EARE
FEELE
FEW
FINE
FLAME
FOOLE
FOOT
FRESH
GREW
GROUND
HELPE
ISSUE
LAST
LENT
'LL
LOOKES
MR
NUMBER
ODE
PERSON
PLEASE
PRIDE
PRINCE
RETURNE
SAD
SHEW
SIT
SMALL
STARRE
STATES
STUDIE
SUNG
THEMSELVES
TITLE
TOWNE
'TWAS
WEIGHT

-14-

ACTS
BED
BEN
BLEST
BOLD
CLOSE
COMES
COMMAND
CONFESSE
CUT
ENGLISH
FEARES
FLESH
FLOWERS
FRENCH
GLASSE
GREATER
GREATNESSE
HEALTH

HEIGHT
JAMES
JUSTICE
LAW
'LE
MARY
MERIT
MET
MOTHER
QUEENE
RARE
REST
RIMES
SHADE
SKILL
SOE
SPIRITS
STRIKE
STRONG
SWORD
TOUCH
UN
UNDERSTAND
VENUS
VERTUOUS
VULCAN
WHORE
WILLIAM
WITNESSE

-13-

ALIVE
APPEARE
BACK
BEHOLD
BOUGHT
BRED
BURNE
CHARGE
COMMING
DARES
DARKE
DEEDS
DWELL
EPISTLE
FLIE
FOOLES
GIVES
GLORIE
HAIRE
HANDS
HEARTS
HIT
HORACE
HOURES
JOHN
KNOWLEDGE
MAKING
NEWES
NOBLEST
PAINE
PAPER
POSTERITIE
PRACTISE
SEAS
SPARE
SPIGHT
TAUGHT
TOLD
TONGUE
VALOUR
WRIT

-12-

ACTION
ALTHOUGH
ALWAYES
AMONG
APPLY
CIRCLE
COUNTREY
CRY'D
CURE
DAUGHTER
EASE
ELEGIE
ENJOY
ENVIOUS
ENVY
ETERNALL
FATES

FIELD
FLIGHT
GENTLE
GLADNESSE
GLORY
GOES
HONEST
HUNDRED
IGNORANCE
I'LE
NUMBERS
PAIRE
PICTURE
PLAYES
PLEASURE
RAGE
RAIS'D
SISTER
SPORT
STILE
TITLES
TOGETHER
UNDERSTOOD
VERY
WITHIN
WONNE
WRONG
YOUNG
YOURS

-11-

'BOVE
ABUSE
ALAS
ALMOST
BELEEVE
BETRAY
BETWEENE
BID
BIRTH-DAY
CHAST
CLOTHES
DEARE
DEED
DOO
DUE
EQUALL
FAT
FINDE
GIFT
GLORIOUS
GOODNESSE
GOWNE
GRAND
HALL
HARD
HOPES
HOURE
HURT
INCREASE
KNIGHT
LAUGH
LIKE
LIV'D
MADAME
MINDS
MISTRIS
NATURES
NOTE
NOYSE
OFFICE
ORDER
PAYES
PEN
PRAISES
RUNNE
SAYES
SECOND
SEEME
SOMETHING
SOULES
STORIE
STRAINE
SWIFT
WHAT'
WHAT'S
WHENCE
WOMAN
WORKES
WORSE
WORST
WOULDST

-10-

'BOUT
ADVANCE
ANGRY
BLESSED
BOY
BRAINES
CENSURE
COLD
CREATURE
CROWN'D
CRYES
DRINKE
EPITAPH
FIVE
FLOW
FORGIVE
FORMES
FRAME
GENIUS
GREENE
HELL
HIR
HONOURS
HOT
HUSBAND
INDEED
LAID
LAUGHTER
LEAD
LETTERS
MINDE
MORNING
NAM'D
NOE
NOTES
OFFENCE
OPEN
OURS
PAINT
PAINTED
PARENTS
PASSION
PHOEBUS
PLEAS'D
POETRIE
POUND
PROPER
PUBLIKE
READER
REWARD
ROE
SEARCH
SERVANT
SERVE
STRANGE
STRIVE
TAKEN
THEY'
THOU'
TRADE
TWICE
WHIL'ST
WILD
WISDOME
WITS
WIVES
WRETCHED

-9-

ADDE
AFFECTION
ANGELS
AUTHORS
BEAST
BEAUTIES
BEGIN
BLACK
BLESSE
BLOUD
BREST
BUSINESSE
CALLS
CHAMBER
CHARME
CREDIT
CRIMES
CURIOUS
DAR'ST
DESIGNE
DIDST
EATE

SIDES
SIMPLE
SIXE
SNOW
SOMETIMES
SONNES
SPARKE
SPOUSE
SPREAD
SQUIRE
STALL
STORY
STREET
SUTE
SWAY
SWEAT
TALES
TH'ARE
THEIRS
THEREIN
THRIVE
THUNDER
TIMELY
TOUCH'D
TOWNES
TRANSLATED
TRIUMPH
TRY
'TWERE
UPRIGHT
VINE
WAKE
WALKE
WALKES
WALLS
WARME
WATCH
WEALTHY
WIND
WINGS
WOMBE
WROTE
YEERE

-5-

ABROAD
ADORE
ALE
ALIKE
ALLOW
ANACREON
ASK'D
AUTHORITIE
AWAKE
BARRE
BAYES
BEARING
BEG
BEGINNINGS
BENEATH
BESIDE
BLAZE
BLOT
BOSOME
BOYES
BRASSE
BRETHREN
BROAD
BROKEN
BURNT
BUYES
CALLING
CALME
CAPTAYNE
CARRACT
CAUSES
CENTER
CHARACTER
CHARIS
CHILDREN
CHOICE
CHOISE
CLAIME
CONCEIPT
CONCEIVE
CONDEMNE
COVER
CRADLE
CREATE

CRIE
CUPS
CUSTOME
DAILY
DANCE
DEBT
DEGREE
DESCRIB'D
DESIRES
DESTROY
DICE
DISCLOSE
DOGS
DOING
DO'S
DO'ST
DRAWES
DROP
DUMBE
EDWARD
EPODE
ETERNITIE
EXCELL
EXERCISE
EXPENCE
FACT
FAILE
FAIN'D
FARE
FINER
FIRES
FIT
FIX'D
FLAMES
FLOOD
FLYING
FOLD
FOLKE
FOLLY
FOREHEAD
FORM'D
FRIENDSHIPS
GAIN'D
GAME
GARLAND
GATHER'D
GENERALL
GENTRIE
GHOST
GIVING
GOING
GRATULATE
GRIEVE
GROWES
GUNS
HAILE
HANDLE
HARPE
H'
HEAPE
HERS
HIGHER
HOUSHOLD
HUNTING
INTELLIGENCE
JONSON
KNIT
KNOT
L
LABOUR'D
LACK
LADYES
LANE
LASTING
'LD
LENGTH
LESSER
LETTER
LIBERTIE
LILLIE
LOFTIE
LOVING
LOWD
LYNE
MAD'ST
MAID
MAKER
MALICE
MARK'D
MARS
MEANES
MEETS
MIDST
MILL
MISERIES

MIXE
MIXT
MODESTIE
MUSIQUE
NATION
NECTAR
NEPHEWES
NEST
NINE
OBJECTS
ODOUR
PAID
PAUSE
PERSONS
PLAGUE
PLATE
POEME
POINT
POMPE
POX
PRAYER
PRIZE
PROFESSE
PROV'D
PUBLISH
PUNISHMENT
QUESTION
QUICKLY
RAN
REACH
READERS
READES
RECEIV'D
RECORDS
REHERSE
RELIGIOUS
REMAINE
REQUIRE
REVEALE
RING
RINGS
ROUGH
RYMES
SAINT
SAINTS
SCENE
SCHOOLE
SEAT
SECURITIE
SEEM'D
SENCE
SENSES
SENT
SEXE
SHAKESPEARE
SHARPE
SHEE'
SHOOT
SLOTH
SO'
SOFTER
SONGS
SOONER
SPEAKING
SPEECH
SPHEARE
SPRINGS
STEALTH
STINKE
STOLNE
STOOLE
STOP
STRAINES
SUBJECTS
SUBTILE
SUBTLE
SWAN
SWEARES
SWEETE
SWEETEST
SWELL
SWELLS
SYLVANE
TA'EN
TAME
TAST
TAXE
TELLS
THANKE
THEYR
THEY'RE
THINK'ST
THITHER
TH'OTHER
THOUSAND

TO'
TOMBE
TOWER
TRAGEDIE
TRICKS
TRIE
TRIFLES
TRINITIE
TROUBLED
TROY
TRUELY
TRUMPET
TRUSTED
TURN'D
TURNING
TWELVE
TYME
UNTILL
USURER
VALUE
VEXE
VIRGIL
VOW
WANTS
WEE'
WEE'LL
WEIGH'D
WHEREOF
WINTER
WISHES
YEA
ZEALE

-4-

ABLE
ACCOMPT
ADDING
ADMIRATION
ADVANC'D
AFFAIRES
AFFORDS
AGED
AIDED
AIME
ALLOW'D
AMBITION
ANCIENT
ANGER
ANOTHERS
APOLLO'S
'RE
ARGUE
ARM'D
ARMES
ARTHUR
ASKES
AYME
BABE
BAD
BALL
BEARDS
BEAUMONT
BECAME
BEGET
BEGOT
BEHOLDS
BELLS
BIDS
BLESSING
BLISSE
BOATES
BOOTE
BOUNTIES
BOX
BREED
BRIGHTNESSE
BROTHERS
BUILD
BURGES
BURIED
BUY
CAESAR
CARELESSE
CAREW
CARRIED
CERTAINE
CHAINE
CHARMES
CHEARE
CHIME
CHIN
CHOOSE

CIRCLES
CITIZENS
CIVILL
CLOWNES
COACH
COAST
COATES
COLOUR
COMICK
COMMANDS
COMMISSION
COMMODITIE
COMPARISON
CONCEALE
CONCEIV'D
CONCLUDE
CONSPIRE
CONSUMPTION
CORYATE
COTTON
COURTLING
COURTS
COVETOUS
CRUELL
CUPID
CUPIDS
CURES
CURST
DAMES
DANGERS
DARING
DEBTS
DEFENCE
DEFEND
DEGREES
DELAY
DESCENT
DESERV'D
DESIR'D
DEVOURE
DEW
DIFFER
DISCERNING
DISDAINE
DISTANCE
DITCH
DOG
DORE
DOUBTFULL
DOWNE
DRIVEN
DRIVES
DROWNE
DRUM
DRUMS
DRUNKE
DYES
EARNEST
ELDER
ELIZABETH
EMBRACE
EMPTIE
EMULATE
EPIGRAMME
ERROR
ESSENCE
ESTATE
EUROPE
EXCELLENT
EXPREST
FACTION
FACULTIE
FALLING
FALLS
FALSHOOD
FANCIE
FARMER
FAVOURS
FAYRE
FELT
FIERCE
FIRE-WORKES
FISH
FITTER
FLEE
FLOWES
FORBEARE
FORBID
FORGET
FORT
FOURE
FOURTH
FREELY
FREQUENT
FURY

FRAILTIE
FREINDS
FRIENDLY
FRINDSHIPP
FRONT
FROWNE
FURIES
FUTURE
GALLANTS
GAMES
GAPING
GATHERING
GAV'ST
GENEROUS
GESTURE
GHOSTS
GOD-LIKE
GOODYERE
GOOSE
GRACIOUS
GRAND-CHILD
GRAPES
GRASSE
GRATEFULL
GRATIOUS
GRATITUDE
GREATE
GRECIAN
GREECE
GROVES
GROYNE
GRUDGE
GRUTCH
GUARD
GUIDES
GUMMES
HANGINGS
HAPPIER
HARDLY
HARE
HARMONIE
HARTH
HAST
HATRED
HA'
'AVE
HEAP'D
HEARES
HEARING
HEAV'N
HEE'D
HEE'LL
HENCEFORTH
HENCE-FORTH
HERALD
HERALDS
HEREAFTER
HID
HIEROME
HIRE
HOGS
HOLDS
HOMERS
HONOURABLE
HOOFE
HOP
HORNE
HOURELY
HOUSE-HOLD
HOUSES
HOWE
HUNTS
I
I'AM
IDOLATRIE
IF'
IF'T
I'HAVE
IMITATE
IMFORTUNE
IMPREST
IMPUTATION
INFANTS
INFINITE
INHERITANCE
INKE
INNOCENT
INQUIRIE
INSCRIPTION
INVENTION
INVITE
INVITING

INWARD
IRON
ISLE
ITALY
ITCH
JANE
JONES
JOVE
JOVES
JOYFULL
JOYNTS
JUDG'D
JUDGMENT
JUNE
JUNO
JUSTIFIE
KEEPS
KIN
KINDLED
KNIGHT-HOOD
KNIGHTS
KNITS
KNOTS
KNOTTIE
KNOWE
KNOW'ST
LANDS
LATELY
LATINE
LATTER
LAWFULL
LEADES
LEAP'D
LEARNING
LEESE
LEGS
LETCHERIE
LIFT
LIFTED
LIGHTED
LIGHTLY
LILLIES
LIMBE
LIP
LIVD
LIV'ST
LO
LOAD
LOATH
LODGE
LOE
LONDON
LOOK'ST
LOTH
LOUDE
LOVE'S
LUCKLESSE
LUCKS
LYKE
MAINTAIN'D
MAINTAYNE
MANKINDE
MAN'S
MARKES
MARTYRS
MARVAILES
MASCULINE
MAYST
MEASUR'D
MEDDLE
MEDEA
MEET
MEETING
MERCHANT
MERCURY
MID
MIDDLE
MIGHTST
MILD
MILE
MINERVA
MIRA
MIRACLE
MISTAKE
MODESTLY
MOLEST
MONARCHS
MONEYS
MONSTER
MONTH
MOODES
MOONES
MORTALL
MOUNTAINE
MOUNTED

MOUTH
MURMURE
MUSICK
MUSICKE
MUTE
NAILES
NAMING
NEARE
NEAT
NET
NEWCASTLE
NOBILITIE
NOBLER
NOBLY
NOTED
NOW'
NUMBRED
NUPTIALL
NUT
OBSCENE
OBSCURE
OBSERVE
ODCOMBE
ODDE
OFFICES
ON'
ON'T
ORBE
ORNAMENTS
OUNCES
OWES
PAGEANT
PAINTING
PAPERS
PARIS
PARLIAMENT
PARTING
PARTRICH
PASSIONS
PATIENCE
PEDIGREE
PEEPE
PEERS
PEGASUS
PENSION
PERSIAN
PETTICOTE
PETULANT
PHEASANT
PHILIP
PIECES
PIERCE
PILES
PILLARS
PISSE
PLAINE
PLENTIE
PLOT
PLY
POETIQUE
POLISH'D
POOR
PORT
PORTION
POSTURE
POT
POUR'D
POVERTIE
POWDER
PRAYERS
PREPAR'D
PRESERVE
PRESERVES
PRETIOUS
PRINT
PRODUCE
PROFESSING
PROFITS
PROMIS'D
PRONE
PROOFE
PROULE
PROVIDE
PUBLIQUE
PUCELL
PULL
PURG'D
PURPOSE
QUARTER
QUESTION'D
QUICKER
RAINE
RAMMES
RAP'T
RASH

RAYSE
RE
REACH'D
REAR'D
REBELL
REBELLS
RECORD
REDEEME
REFRAINE
REGARD
REHEARSE
RENDER
REPENTED
REPROVE
RESPECT
REVELS
RICHARD
RICHLY
RIOT
RISING
ROB
ROB'D
ROCK
ROD
RUMOUR
RURALL
RUTLAND
SAILE
SAITH
SALISBURIE
SATE
SAYD
SAY-MASTER
SCALE
SCOTLAND
SEALE
SEAL'D
SEALES
SEASONS
SEATE
SEAVEN
SECRET
SECRETS
SECURELY
SEEING
SEEMES
SELDOME
SELF
SERPENTS
SETTING
SEVERE
SEX
SHADDOWES
SHAFT
SHAPES
SHEE'S
SHELTON
SHEW'D
SHINES
SHIP
SHOP
SHOPS
SHOWE
SHOWERS
SHUN
SHUNNING
SINGS
SIRE
SKIE
SKILFULL
SKIN
SMALLEST
SMILE
SMITH
SNAKE
SNARES
SNUFFE
SOCIETIE
SOLE
SOMETIME
SORROWES
SOULDIER
SOUNDS
SOURCE
SOVERAIGNE
SOW
SOYLE
SPANISH
SPARKLING
SPECIOUS
SPICE
SPOKE
SPRIGHT
STANDERS
STAR

START
STARTED
STATUES
STATURE
STEELE
STEELE
STEMME
STEPS
STEWES
STOOLES
STOR'D
STORMES
STRANGER
STRANGERS
STRING
STRINGS
STRIVING
STROOKE
STUDIES
STUDY
STYLE
SUCCOURS
SUFFER'D
SUFFRAGE
SUFFRING
SUIT
SUMM'D
SUPPER
SURETIE
SURFETS
SURPRIZE
SUSPECT
SWANS
SWARME
SWEETNESSE
SWORDS
TABLES
TACITUS
T'ADVANCE
TALL
TAMES
TASKE
TAX'D
TAYLORS
TEEMING
TELESTICHS
TEMPT
TERME
TEST
TH'ADMIR'D
THANKFULL
THESPIAN
TH'EXCHANGE
TH'EYE
TH'HAST
THIEFE
THIGHES
THREATEN
THRED
THROW
THRUSH
TOMES
TOP
TOTHER
TOWRE
TOYLE
TRAVAILE
TRAVELL
TREES
TRENCH
TRINE
TROTH
TURNED
TURNES
TURTLES
TWI
TWINE
TWIXT
UNCOMELY
UNDONE
UNLESSE
UNWORTHY
URG'D
UTTER'D
VALE
VARIETIE
VARIOUS
VENETIA
VENTRING
VENUSINE
VERE
VIRGINS
VISION
VOLUME
VOYCES

WANDRING
WARES
WARIE
WE'
WEATHER
WEAVE
WEEDES
WEEKE
WEEKLY
WEST
WHEREBY
WHERIN
WHERRY
WHITE-HALL
WHO'S
WICKED
WILDE
WILLING
WILT
WINCHESTRIAN
WINDOWES
WINNE
WISELY
WISER
WISEST
WITHERED
WONT
WOO
WOOES
WOOLI
WORMES
WRETCH
WRITER
WRITTEN
WYSE
YELLOW
YETT
YO'HAVE
YOUNGEST

-2-

ABBEVILE
ABIDE
ABLER
ABOUND
ABSOLUTE
ABSTINENCE
ABUS'D
ABUSES
ACCENTS
ACCEPTANCE
ACCIUS
ACHILLES
ACKNOWLEDGE
ACQUAINTANCE
ADAM
ADD
ADMIRABLE
ADMIR'D
ADMIT
ADOR'D
ADORNE
ADULTERATE
ADVANCED
ADVENTURES
AERIE
AESOPE
AETERNALL
A-FARRE
AFEARD
AFFEARD
AFFECT
AFFECTED
AFFECTS
AFFRIGHTS
AFTER-TIMES
AGES
AID
AIDES
ALCIDES
ALICE
ALL'
ALLEN
ALLIES
ALLOTTED
ALLOWES
ALL'S
ALPHIUS
ALREADY

ALTER
AMAZEMENT
AMENDS
AMIABLE
AMITIE
ANAGRAM
ANAGRAMS
ANGELLS
ANGLES
ANGRIE
ANNULTIE
ANSWERE
ANSWERS
ANVILE
APPEAR'D
APPLE-HARVEST
APPLES
APPLIE
APPROACH
APPROCHES
APRIL
APT
ARCHITECTURE
ARDOR
ARGENIS
ARMED
ARMOUR
ARRAIGN'D
ARRAS
ARSE
'RT
ARTHURS
AS'
ASKED
ASSE
ASSES
ASSURANCE
ASSUR'D
AS'T
ASWELL
ATOMES
ATT
ATTEMPT
ATTEND
AUBIGNY
'AUBIGNY
AUTUMNE
AWFULL
AYMES
AYRIE
BALD
BALLANCE
BANISH'D
BANKE-RUPT
BANKES
BARBICAN
BARD
BARKE
BARKING
BARTAS
BASTINADO
BATH
BATHES
BATHS
BAUDIE
BAWDRIE
BEAME
BEAMES
BEAMIE
BEARD
BEARE
BEASTS
BEATE
BEATEN
BEDEW'D
BEE
BEEN
BEFALL
BEGG'D
BEGINNING
BEGINS
BEGUILE
BEHOLDING
BELEEV'D
BELIE
BENDING
BESPRENT
BEST-BEST
BETRAY'D
BETTER'D
BETWEEN
BEWARE
BIDE
BIND
BISHOP

BISHOPS
BLATANT
BLAZ'D
BLEW
BLISSES
BLOOME
BLOW
BLOWNE
BOASTING
BOASTS
BOLDER
BOMBARD
BONE
BONEFIRES
BOR
BORD
BOR-DRING
BORNE
BORROWERS
BOUGHS
BRACE
BRAKE
BRANDED
BRAVELY
BRAVEST
BRAZEN
BREAKES
BREAKING
BREAST
BREASTS
BREATHE
BREEDING
BREEDS
BRETONS
BRICK-KILLS
BRIER
BRIGHTER
BRIGHTEST
BRIGHTLY
BRINGST
BRING'ST
BROKERS
BROME
BROODING
BULL
BURDEN
BURNED
BUSH
BUS'NESSE
BUTT
BUTTER
BY-PATHS
CABALLS
CAL'D
CALFE
CALLED
CAMDEN
CAM'ST
CANARY
CANKER'D
CAPONS
CAPTAYNES
CARTS
CASE
CASSOCK
CASTOR
CATALOGUE
CATCH'D
CATES
CAUGHT
CAUSTICKS
CELEBRATING
CELEBRATION
CELLAR
CENSUR'D
CERBERUS
CHAINGE
CHAIRES
CHALLENGE
CHAMBERS
CHAMPION
CHANCELLOR
CHANGES
CHANT
CHAPMAN
CHAPPELL
CHARACTERS
CHARIOT
CHARMED
CHASE
CHASTITIE
CHASTLY
CHAYRE
CHEAPE
CHEATED

CHEEKE
CHEERE
CHEEREFULL
CHELSEY
CHEV'RILL
CHIEFLY
CHIMAERA
CHIMNEY
CHLOE
CHOAKE
CHORUS
CHOYCE
CHRIST
CHRISTENDOME
CHRISTIAN
CHRISTIANS
CHRISTMAS
CHRONICLERS
CHUFFE
CIRCLING
CIRCULAR
CITTIE
CLAIMES
CLAP
CLAY
CLEANS'D
CLEFT
CLERKE
CLIMBE
CLIMES
CLOATH
CLOATH'D
CLOWD
CLOWDES
CLOWD-LIKE
CO
COACH'D
COB
COCYTUS
COKE
COLDS
COLLEDGE
COLT
COLUMNE
COMELY
COMMENDED
COMMON-LAW
COMODY
COMPANY
COMPARE
COMPASSION
COMPLAINE
COMPLAINES
COMPOSE
COMPOS'D
COM'ST
CONCEITS
CONCLUDED
CONCORD
CONDITION
CONDUCT
CONEY
CONJURING
CONQUER'D
CONQUERS
CONSIDER
CONSTANT
CONTEMNE
CONTINENT
CONTINU'D
CONTRITE
COOLE
COPIE
COPIES
COPP'S
CORBET
CORIAT
CORKE
CORNERS
CORRANTS
CORRECT
CORRUPT
COTSWOLD
COULORS
COUNCELL
COUNCELS
COUNSELLS
COUNTRIE
COUNTRYE
COUPLE
COURSES
COURTESIE
COVERS
COYNE
CRACK

CRADLES
CRAFTS
CRANE
CREATURES
CREEKES
CREEPING
CREPT
CRITICK
CROST
CROWNES
CRUELTIE
CRYE
CURLED
CURLES
CURRE
CURTESIE
DAMNE
DANGEROUS
DAPHNE
DARK
DAZELING
DAZLING
DEAFE
DEAREST
DEATH'S
DEATHS
DEAW
DECEIV'D
DECENT
DECLINE
DECREE
DEDICATE
DEDICATION
DEEPEST
DEFEAT
DEFORMED
DELIVER'D
DELPHICK
DENIE
DENIES
DEPARTED
DEPARTING
DEPENDING
DEPREST
DEPTH
DERIDE
DESCRIPTION
DESERVES
DESIRED
DESKE
DESPAIRE
DESPAIR'D
DESPAIRES
DESTIN'D
DESTINIE
DESTROYES
DIALOGUE
DIANA'S
DIGNITIE
DIGNITIES
DIKE
DIN'D
DINNER
DISCERNE
DISCHARGE
DISCLOSES
DISCONTENT
DISCOURSETH
DISCOVER
DISGRACE
DISH
DIS-JOYN'D
DISPENC'D
DISPENSE
DISPRAISE
DISTANT
DISTRUST
DIVELL
DIVELS
DIVELS-ARSE
DIVIDED
DOCTORS
DOCTRINE
DOO'
DOOME
DOORES
DOO'T
DO'T
DOTES
DOUBLE
DOUBLY
DOVER
DRIE
DRING
DROSSE

DROWNING	FILLED	GRAY	I'LD	LIKENESSE
DRUG	FILLS	GREASE	ILL-NATUR'D	LIKING
DRUNKARDS	FILTH	GRIEVOUS	ILLS	LILLY
DUKE	FINEST	GROOMES	ILLUSTRATE	LIM
DUNCOTE	FINGER	GROSSE	IMBRACE	LIMMES
DWARFES	FINGERS	GROSSNESSE	IMPERFECT	LIMONS
DYE	FIR'D	GUARDED	IMPETUOUS	LIPPE
EARES	FIRKE	GUESSE	IMPLORE	LIQUOR
EARS	FIST	GUIFT	IMPRESE	LIVIE
EASIE	FITLY	GUIFTS	IMPUDENCE	LOCK'D
EATING	FITT	GUILTLESSE	IMPUTED	LOCKS
EDGE	FITTED	GUT	IN'	LONG
EFFECTS	FIXED	GYPSEE	INCHANTED	LONGEST
EGGES	FIXT	H	INCLIN'D	LOOK
EGLANTINE	FLAMMES	HABIT	INCONSTANCIE	LOOMES
EGS	FLATTER	HAFTES	INCONSTANT	LOOSENESSE
EIGHT	FLATTERER	HALF	INFAMIE	LOOSING
EITHERS	FLATTERERS	HALLOW'D	INFAMOUS	LORDINGS
ELDEST	FLATT'RING	HAMPTON	INFLAM'D	LORDSHIP
ELECT	FLEECE	HANDED	INFLUENCE	LORDSHIPS
ELECTION	FLEECES	HANDLED	INGRATEFULL	LOT
ELEMENTS	FLEETE	HANGS	INHERENT	LOYALL
ELEVENTH	FLETCHER	HAPPEN	INJURIE	LUCK
ELIXIR	FLEW	HAPPIEST	INJUSTICE	LUCKE
ELOCUTION	FLIES	HAPPINESSE	INMATE	LURKE
EMBASSAGE	FLOCK	HAPP'LY	INRAGED	LUSTIE
EMBLEME	FLOCKS	HARBOUR	INSPIRE	LUSTS
EMBRACES	FLOWNE	HARDEST	INSPIR'D	LUXURIE
EMPLOY	FLOWRE	HARDIE	INTEREST	LYFE
ENCOUNTER'D	FLUSHING	HARP	INTERPRETED	LYNES
ENDED	FOE	HARRY	IO	LYRICK
ENDLESSE	FOLDS	HARSH	IRELAND	MACHINE
ENGINE	FOLLOW'D	'AST	IRONS	MADAMES
ENNIUS	FOOLISH	HAUGHTIE	IT'	MADNESSE
ENTAYLE	FOORTH	HAUNT	JEALOUSIES	MAIORS
ENTERTAINE	FORBEARES	HAVE'	JEPHSON	MAJESTIES
ENTERTAINING	FORE-KNOWNE	HAWKING	JEWELL	MAJESTY
ENTRAILES	FORETOLD	HAYWARD	JEWELLS	MAKERS
ENTRANCE	FORFEIT	HEADLONG	JEWELS	MALE
EPITOME	FORKE	HEALE	JEWES	MALLOWES
EQUALLY	FORRAINE	HEARERS	JOHNSON	MAN'
ERECT	FORREST	HEAVIE	JOLLY	MANGER
ERRORS	FORSAKES	HEED	JOSEPH	MANSFIELD
ERROUR	FORSWEARE	HEE'LD	JOT	MAP
ESCAPE	FORTITUDE	HE'LE	JOVE'S	MARGARET
ESME	FOUGHT	HELEN	JOVIALL	MARISH
ESPECIALLY	FOUNDRED	HELME	JOYN'D	MARRIAGE
ESPIE	FOUNTAINE	HELP	JOYNE	MARRIE
ESSAYES	FOXE	HELPES	JUDGES	MARRIED
EUROPES	FRAM'D	HELPS	JUDGING	MASKE
EVEN	FRANCES	HEMISPHERE	JUMPE	MASKES
EVENING	FRANCIS	HEN	JUPITER	MASQUE
EVENTS	FREE-BORNE	HENRIE	JUYCE	MASQUES
EVILS	FREED	HERBERT	KATHERINE	MASQUING
EWES	FREINDES	HERMETIQUE	KILLING	MAST
EXACT	FRIGHT	HEROES	KILLS	MASTRY
EXACTED	FRIGHTED	HERSE	KINDLING	MAW
EXCEEDETH	FRINGES	HE'S	KINDRED	MAY'
EXCELLENCE	FROGS	HESIODS	KISSES	MAY'ST
EXCUSES	FROWARD	HETHER	KISSING	MAZE
EXPENSE	FULNESSE	H'HAS	KNAVE	MEANEST
EXPIATE	GAM'STER	HIDDEN	LA	MEASURES
EXPRESS	GARLANDS	HIGHEST	LABOURING	MEDITATIONS
EXTEND	GATE	HIGHLY	LACK'D	MELANCHOLIE
FACTS	GATES	'S	LAMBE	MELLOW
FACULTIES	GAYNE	HITHER	LAMBES	MELT
FAGOTS	GAYNES	HOL'BORNE	LANGUISH	MENDED
FAILES	GAZE	HOLE	LANTERNE	MENDING
FAINT	GEESE	HOME-BORNE	LANTHORNE	MERCIE
FAIRER	GENTLEMAN	HONESTIE	LARUM	MERCY
FAITHFULLY	GENTLY	HONEY	LASTETH	MERE
FALNE	GEORGE	HONORABLE	LATER	MERLINS
FAMILIE	GEORGES	HONOR'D	LATEST	MICHAEL
FAMINE	GERMANY	HONOURED	LAURELL	MIGHTIEST
FANCIED	GETT	HOOKE	LA-WARE	MILLAN
FAR	GETTING	HORLD	LAWNE	MIME
FATALL	GHYRLOND	HORNET	LAYES	MIMING
FAUNES	GIDDIE	HOT-HOUSE	LEAPE	MINDES
FAVOURING	GIV'ST	HOUND	LEASE	MINE
FEAR	GLADDEST	HOWSOEVER	LED	MINERVA'S
FEAREFULL	GLASSEN	HUE	LEECH	MINES
FEAREFULLY	GLOBE	HUES	LEGEND	MINT
FEARFULL	GLORIFIED	HUGH	LESS	MINUTES
FEARING	GOAT	HUMANE	LESSON	MIRROUR
FEASTING	GODDESSE	HUMILITIE	LEST	MIS
FEE	GODDS	HUNG	LET'	MISCHIEFES
FEES	GOSSIP	HUNTERS	LET'S	MISERIE
FELLOWSHIP	GOTT	HUNT'ST	LIBELL	MISTERIE
FELLS	GOTTEN	HURLES	LICENSE	MIX'D
FEN	GOWNED	IAMBICK	LICENTIOUS	MOCK'D
FETCH	GRACED	IDEOT	LICK	MOCKS
FIFT	GRAC'D	IDES	LIES	MODERNE
	GRAINE	IDLE	LIFES	MONEY-BROKERS
	GRANDSIRES	IDOLL	LIGHTNING	MONEYES
	GRAVES	ILAND	LIK'D	MONEY'S

MONTRELL	PENALTIE	QUEENS	SCARRE	SORRY
MOON	PENANCE	QUICKEN	SCATTER'D	SOULDIERS
MORNING-STARRE	PENATES	QUITT	SCENES	SPACE
MORROW	PEOPLES	QUIVER	SCHISME	SPAN
MOTIONS	PERFECTIONS	QUOTH	SCHOOLES	SPEACH
MOTIVES	PERFUMES	RADCLIFFE	SCIENCE	SPEAK
MOULDED	PERILLS	RAGING	SCOPE	SPECIALL
MOUNSIEUR	PERJUR'D	RAIGNING	SCORNED	SPECTACLES
MOUNTING	PERSPECTIVE	RAISING	SEA-COALE	SPECTATORS
MOUSE	PERSWADE	RAK'D	SEA-GIRT	SPEECHES
MUSTER	PEST	RANKNESSE	SEALED	SPICES
MUTUALL	PHYSICK	RAPH	SEARCH'D	SPILL
MYNE	PIGGES	RARELY	SEARCHETH	SPIRITUALL
MYRTLE	PILE	RARIFIED	SECURE	SPOILE
NATURALL	PILLAR	RARITIE	SECUR'D	SPOTS
NATUR'D	PITCHER	READS	SEED	SPOYLE
NEATE	PLACED	REALL	SEEDES	SPRITE
NEATH	PLAGUES	REALME	SEEK	SPY
NEED'ST	PLAINES	REALMES	SEEKES	SQUARE
NEGLIGENCE	PLANTS	REAME	SEEKING	SQUIB
NEIGHBOUR	PLAYERS	REASONS	SEEK'ST	SQUIRES
NEIGHBOURS	PLEASANT	RECEAVE	SELFE-BOASTING	STABLE
NEVIL	PLEDGES	RECEIPT	SELLER	STAKE
NEWER	PLENTEOUS	RECKON	SENDS	STAMPE
NICE	PLIE	RECONCIL'D	SEPARATE	STANDARD
NIMBLE	PLIGHT	REDEEMER	SERGEANTS	STANDERD
NOBLESSE	PLOUGH	REEDES	SERV'D	STANDERS-BY
NOSTRILLS	PLUCKE	REFIN'D	SERVING	STARRE-CHAMBER
NOURISH	PLUM	REFLECT	SEVER	STARS
NOWE	PLUMES	REFLEXE	SEVER'D	STEADIE
NOW'S	POD	RELATE	SHADES	STEALES
NUN	POESY	RELATION	SHADOWES	STEAME
NUPTIALS	POET-APE	RELIEFE	SHARE	STEEPE
NURSES	POETS'	RELIEVE	SHARP	STEEP'D
NYMPHS	POLYPHEME	RELISH	SHARPNESSE	STEEPLE
OATHES	POMP'D	RELISH'D	SHAVE	STEEPLES
OBELISKE	POOLE	RELLISH	SH'	STENCH
OBSERVATION	POORES	REMEMBRANCE	SHEARERS	STERVE
OBTAINE	POPULAR	REMOVED	SHEE'LL	STILED
OCCASIONS	POSSESSIONS	REMOV'D	SHEP'ARD	STING
ODDES	POT-GUNS	REPEATE	SHERIFFES	STINT
OD'ROUS	POUNDS	REPROOFE	SHEWE	STITCH'D
OFFER'D	POURE	REPUTATION	SHEWING	STOCK
OFFICERS	POURING	REQUIR'D	SHINING	STOOPE
OGLE	POXE	RESERV'D	SHOES	STOPT
OKE	POYSON	RESPECTS	SHOOE	STOUPE
OLD-END	PRACTIZ'D	RESTRAIN'D	SHOOTING	STRAIGHT-WAY
OLIVE	PRAISER	RESURRECTION	SHORTNESSE	STRAND
OMITTED	PRAYSED	RETAINE	SHOULDERS	STRAW
ONES	PREASE	RETIRE	SHOUT	STREETS
OPE'	PREDESTIN'D	RETURNED	SHOUTES	STREIGHT
OPE	PREFERRE	REVEALD	SHOWRE	STRENGTHS
OPENS	PRESENCE	REVENGE	SHRINKE	STRICT
OPINION	PRESENTING	REVERENC'D	SHRUB	STRIFES
ORACLE	PRESENTS	REVERSE	SHRUNKE	STROVE
ORD'NANCE	PRESERVED	REWARDS	SHUNNE	STRYKE
ORESTES	PRESERVER	RICH	SHUNS	STUPID
OUGHT	PRESUME	RICHEST	SICILIAN	STYLD
OUNCE	PRETEXT	RIDES	SICK-MENS	STYL'D
OUT-GOE	PRIAPUS	RIDWAY	SIGHTS	STYX
OUT-LIV'D	PRINTED	RIGID	SILVER	SUBSTANCE
OUT-SHINE	PRODIGIOUS	RISETH	SIMO	SUBTLER
OUT-WEARE	PROFESSION	ROASTED	SINCERE	SUCK'D
OVENS	PROFEST	ROGER	SINDGE	SUFFERS
OVERBURY	PROJECTS	ROGUE	SINEWES	SUFFICIENT
OVER-COME	PROMISER	ROMANE	SINGER	SUITE
OVER-WANTON	PROMPT	ROMANO	SINGING	SUITOR
OXEN	PRONOUNCE	ROOFE	SING'ST	SUITS
OYLES	PROPERTYES	ROOMES	SIRES	SUMMER
PAINTERS	PROPHANENESSE	ROOT	SISTERS	SUMMERS
PALACE	PROPHET	ROOTE	SITTING	SUMMES
PALE	PROPHETS	ROOTED	SKIES	SUPERSTITIOUS
PALES	PROSEQUUTE	ROPE	SLACK	SUPPERS
PALMER	PROSPERITIE	RORE	SLAINE	SUPPOSE
PAMPHLETS	PROTEST	ROSE	SLANDER	SURELY
PANCHARIS	PROVIDED	ROUNDS	SLEEKED	SURVEY
PARADISE	PROVIDENCE	ROUSED	SLEEPES	SURVEYOR
PARASITES	PROV'ST	ROWLES	SLEEPIE	SUSPECTED
PARCELL	PROWDE	ROWSE	SLIT	SUSPITION
PARENT	PROWESSE	RUDYERD	SLUGGISH	SUSSEX
PARISH	PR'Y	RUFFE	SMELL	SUSTAINE
PARISH-GARDEN	PUNKE	RULE	SMELLS	SWAINES
PARTED	PUNQUE	RUNNING	SMOCK	SWEARING
PASTURES	PURCHASE	RUPT	SNORE	SWEETEN
PATH	PURCHAS'D	RYME	SO'BOVE	SWEETLY
PATRONS	PUREST	SAIES	SOFTEST	SWEPT
PAWNE	PURITANES	SALLIE	SOFTNESSE	SWINE
PEACH	PURLE	SALT	SOL	SYLLABES
PEAKE	PURSUES	SAND	SOMERSET	TABACCO
PEASANTS	PYRAMIDS	SANDS	SOMEWHAT	TAFFATA
PELEUS	PYRATS	SAVAGE	SON	TAINTED
	PYTHAGORAS	SAV'D	SONNET	TALENT
	PYTHIAN	SAVILE	SONS	TALKES
	Q	SAVOUR	SORDID	T'APPEARE
PEMBROKE	QUEENES	SAY	SORE	T'APPROVE

TARRIES
TAVERNES
TAYLOR
TEAME
TELEPHUS
TELL'S
TELL-TROTH
TEMPER'D
TEMPEST
TEMPESTS
TEMPTED
TEND
TENDER
T'ENJOY
TERROR
TESTIMONY
T'EXPECT
T'EXPRESSE
TH'ADVENTURES
TH'AGE
THANKS
THE'
THEAME
THEORBO
THEREON
THEYRE
TH'HAVE
TH'IAMBICK
THICK
TH'IDES
THIN
THINK
THIRST
TH'OLD
THOROUGH
THOU'AST
THOU'RT
THOUSANDS
THREATENS
THREW
THRIFT
THRIFTIE
THRONE
THRONG
THRONG'D
THRONGING
THRONG'ST
THROWNE
THUMB
TH'WERE
TILT
TILTER
TINCKLING
TINTORET
TIS
TISSUE
TO'A
TOBACCO
T'OFFEND
TOILE
TOMBES
TORCHES
TORTURES
TO'T
TOWN
TOYE
TRACTS
TRADES
TRADESMEN
TRAINE
TRAIN'D
TRANSCRIPTS
TRANSLATION
TRANSLATOR
TRANSLATORS
TRAVAIL'D
TRAVELLING
TREASON
TREASURERS
TRIBADE
TRIBE
TRIBUTE
TRIFLING
TRIM
TRIPPLE
TRIUMPHING
TRIUMPHS
TROUBLE
TROYES
TRUER
TRUEST
TRUMP

TRUTHS
TRY'D
TURKIE
TUTOR
'TWEENE
TWENTY
TWICE-TWELVE-YEARES
TWI-LIGHTS
TWISE
TYRANTS
TYRE
TYRTAEUS
UGLY
ULYSSES
UNCLEANE
UNDER-NEATH
UNFOUND
UNHEARD
UNIVERSE
UNJUST
UNLAY'D
UNLEARN'D
UNLIKE
UNTIE
UNUSED
UNWEARY'D
UPBRAID
UPBRAIDING
UPPON
URGETH
URGING
URNE
'S
US'D
USES
USING
UTMOST
VALEW
VALLEY
VANISH'D
VAPOUR
VARIE
VARIED
VARYING
VAST
VAULT
VEINES
VEIW
VELVETS
VENICE
VERILY
VERTUE'
VEXT
VEYNES
VICIOUS
VIEWING
VINCENT
VISITS
VOID
VOUCHSAFE
VOW'D
VOYAGE
WAGER
WAITES
WAK'D
WAKING
WALKING
WANTED
WARDROBE
WARE
WARPE
WAST
WASTED
WATERMEN
WEAKNESSE
WEALE
WEAPON
WEAPONS
WE'ARE
WEARE
WEARING
WEB
WEDDING
WEIGH
WHARFES
WHERE'
WHEREAS
WHERESOERE
WHEROF
WHET
WHILES
WHISPER
WHISPERERS
WHOLSOME
WHOME

WICKEDNESSE
WIDDOW
WIGHT
WINCHESTER
WINDE
WINDOW
WINES
WINKE
WISEDOME
WISE-MEN
WISHED
WISH'D
WISHETH
WITCH
WITHER
WITT
WITTIE
WOES
WOLVES
WONDER'D
WONDERS
WOOLLY
WORLDLINGS
WORME
WORNE
WORTHIEST
WOULD-BEE
WOVEN
WRACKE
WREATH
WRETCHES
WRITERS
WRITINGS
WRY
WRYTE
WULL
YE
YEILD
YOU'LL
YT
ZEALOUS

AARONS
AB
ABANDON'D
ABATE
A-BED
ABHORD
ABHORRES
ABOUNDS
ABOUTE
ABRO'D
ABSENT
ABSOLV'D
ABSTAINE
ABSTAYNE
ABSTRUSE
ABSURDITY
ABUSED
ACADEMIE
ACCEPTABLE
ACCEPTABLY
ACCEPTED
ACCESSE
ACCITE
ACCOMPLISH
ACCOMPTED
ACCOUNT
ACCOUNTS
ACCUMULATED
ACCURSED
ACCUSATIONS
ACHE
ACHIEVEMENT
ACQUAINTED
ACROSTICKS
ACTETH
ACTORS
ACTUATE
AD
ADDED
ADJUNCTS
ADMIRACION
ADMIRING
ADMITTED
ADMYRED
ADOE
ADONIS
ADOPT
ADORATION
ADORND

ADORNES
ADRIA
ADULTERIES
ADULTERS
ADULT'RERS
ADVANCES
ADVENTER
ADVENTRY
ADVENTURE
ADVERSARIES
ADVISETH
ADVOCATE
AEACUS
AELIAN
AEMILIAN
AEMULATE
AEMULATION
AENEAS
AESCHILUS
AESCULAPE
AETERNITIES
AETNEAN
AFFOARDS
AFFOORD
AFFRAID
AFFRICKE
AFFRIGHTED
A-FIRE
AFORE
AFRONT
AFTERNOONES
AFTER-STATE
AFTER-THOUGHTS
AFTERWARDS
AGAIN
AGENTS
AGILE
AGINCOURT
AGREEING
'GREES
AILE
AIRE
AIRISING
A-JAX
AJAX
AKE
AL
ALARUM
ALBA
ALBIN'S
ALCHIMIST
ALCHYMISTS
ALCORAN
ALDE
ALDE-LEGH
ALDERMAN
ALDERMANITIE
ALE-HOUSE
ALEXANDER
ALEXANDRIA
A-LIFE
ALIGHT
ALIKE-STATED
ALLEDGE
ALLEGORIC
ALLEY
ALL-GRACIOUS
ALLIED
ALLMIGHTY
ALLOWANCE
ALLOWED
ALLOY
ALLURES
ALL-VERTUOUS
ALMANACKS
ALMES
ALMIGHTIE
ALMIGHTIES
ALMOND
ALMONDS
ALOFT
ALONG'ST
ALOOFE
ALOW'D
ALPES
ALS'
ALTER'D
ALTERNATE
'ME
AMADIS
AMAZE
AMBASSADOUR
AMBITIOUSLY
AMBLING
AMBROSIACK

AMEN
AMEND
AMID'
AMIDST
AMITYE
AMONGE
'MONG'ST
AMOROUS
AMPHION
ANALYSDE
ANARCHIE
ANARCHY
ANATOMIE
ANCESTOURS
ANE
ANENST
A-NEW
ANGELL
ANGELO
ANGRIER
ANIMATED
ANNE
ANNEXED
ANNIVERSARIE
ANNIVERSARY
ANNOY'D
ANNUAL
ANON
ANONE
ANSWERING
ANTICIRA'S
ANTICKS
ANTICYRA'S
ANTIPATHY
ANTIPHATES
ANTIQUATED
ANTIQUITIES
ANTWERPE
AONIAN
APART
APOLLO'
APOLOGETIQUE
APOSTACIE
APOSTLE
APOTHECARY
APOTHEOSIS
APPEAS'D
APPLAUD
APPREHENSION
APPROACHING
APPROCH
APPROPRIATES
APRICOT
APTETH
APULIANS
AQUIT
ARAR
ARCH
ARCH-ANGELS
ARCH-DUKES
ARCHED
ARCHETYPE
ARCHILOCHUS
ARCHIMEDE
ARCHITAS
ARCHITECTONICE
ARCHITECTS
ARGIVE
ARGO
ARGUED
ARGUMENT
ARGUS
ARIADNES
ARIGHT
ARION
ARISE
ARISTARCHUS
ARISTOPHANES
ARISTOTLE
ARMDE
ARME
ARMIES
ARMORIE
ARMYES
AROMATIQUE
ARRAYES
ARRERAGE
ARREST
ARROWES
ARSENIKE
ARSES
ARTE'
ARTE'S
ARTES
ARTH

-1- (CONT.)

ARTICHOKES
ARTICLE
ARTILLERIE
ARUNDELL
ASCEND
ASCENT
ASCRIBE
ASHAMED
ASHORE
ASIDE
ASINIGO
ASKETH
ASKT
ASLEEP
ASLEEPE
ASQUINT
ASS
ASSAIES
ASSAY'D
ASSAYES
ASSEMBLY
ASSIDUOUS
ASSIGNES
ASSIST
ASSISTED
ASSURE
ASSURED
ASSYRIA
ASTERISME
ASTREA
ASUNDER
AT'
ATCHIEVEMENTS
ATHENIAN
ATOMI
ATREUS
AT'S
ATTAINE
ATTENDING
ATTIRE
ATTIR'D
ATTRIBUTES
ATTYRE
ATTYRES
AUDITOR
AUGHT
AUGURE
AULUS
AUSPICE
AUSPICIOUS
AUSPITIOUSLY
AUSTERE
AUTHOREM
AUTHORITIES
AUTHORIZ'D
AVAILES
AVERNUS
AVERT
AVOID
AVOIDED
AVON
AVOW
AVOYD
AVOYDING
AWDE
AWE
AWL
AXE
AYE
AYMD
AYMED
AYRE
AYRES
BAAL
BABES
BABION
BABYLONIAN
BACKES
BACKS
BACK-SLIDES
BACKWARD
BACON
BACONS
BAG
BAGS
BAIES
BAITS
BAKE
BALES
BALLADRIE
BALLADS
BALMES

BANCK
BANCKE
BANCKS
BANCK-SIDE
BANCKSIDE
BANQUET
BAPHYRE
BAR
BARBAROUS
BARBER
BARE
BARNABEE
BARONET
BARONS
BARK'D
BARRELL
BASENESSE
BASER
BASEST
B'ASHAM'D
BASKETS
BASTARD
BATTAILE
BATTELLS
BATTRY
BAUD-BEES
BAUDES
BAUDRIE'
BAUDY
BAWD
BAWDIE
BAWDRY
BAWDS
BAWLE
BAWLING
BAYTES
BB'S
BE'
BEADLE
BEARER
BEASTLY
BEATES
BEATIFICK
BEATINGS
BEATITUDE
BEATITUDES
BEAUCHAMPS
BEAUMONIS
BEAUTEOUS
BEAUTYE
BEAVIE
BECAM'ST
BECKNING
BECOMMETH
BECOMMING
BECUM
BED-MATE
BED-RID
BEDS
BEECH
BEEING
BEES
BEEST
BEGANN
BEGAN'ST
BEGAT
BEG'D
BEGETTING
BEGGING
BEGINNERS
BEGINNS
BEGIN'ST
BEGOTTEN
BEGS
BEGUIL'D
BEGUILES
BEGUNNE
BEGYN
BEHALFE
BEHOLDEN
BEHOLDER
BEHOLDERS
BEHOULD
BELCH'D
BELCHETH
BELEEVED
BELEEVES
BELGIA
BELGICK
BELGICUS
BELIEFE
BELIEVE
BELIKE
BELL
BELLIE

BELL-MANS
BELONG
BELOV'D
BELOVED
BELYE
B'EMBRAC'D
BE'N
BENCH
BENE
BENEFIT
BENJAMIN
BEQUEATH
BEREAVES
BERENICES
BERGAMO
BERGHEN
BERINGHAMS
BERMUDAS
BERRIES
BERWICKE
BESETT
BESHITE
BESIEGED
BESIEG'D
BESPOKE
BESS
BESSE
BE'ST
BESTOWES
BESTOWING
BESTRYDE
BESYDE
BESYDES
BETIDE
BETRAYE
BETRAYES
BETTRING
BETWIXT
BETY'DE
BEVER
BEVY
BEWAILD
BEWAIL'D
BEWARES
BIG
BILBO-SMITH
BILLIARD
BILLOW
BILLS
BILS
B'IMPUTED
BINDE
BIRDS
BIRTH-RIGHT
BIRTHS
BITCH
BITE
BITTEN
BITTER
BITTERNESSE
BLACK-BIRD
BLACKENESSE
BLACKER
BLACKE-SPRINGING
BLACKEST
BLACKS
BLADE
BLADES
BLANCH'T
BLASON
BLASPHEMIE
BLASPHEMY
BLAST
BLAZON
BLEED
BLEEDING
BLEEDS
BLESSED'ST
BLINDEST
BLINDLY
BLOCK
BLOCK'D
BLOCKS
BLOCKT
BLOOMED
BLOOMING
BLOTS
BLOTT
BLOWES
BLUE
BLUNTLY
BLURT
BLUSHED
BLUSHES
BLUSHING

BOARD
BOARDES
BOARDS
BOARE
BOASTED
BOASTERS
BOATE
BOIL
BOLDNESSE
BOMBARD-PHRASE
BOMBARD-STILE
BOND
BONDMEN
BONE-FIRES
BONNIE
BOOKE-SELLER
BOOKE-WORMES
BOOKS
BOOK-SELLER
BOORDS
BOORE
BOOT
BORDE
BORDERS
BORDS
BORES
BORN
BORROWING
BOTTLE
BOTTOM
BOTTOME
BOUGH
BOUGHES
BOULSTRED
BOUNCING
BOUNTEOUS
BOUNTIE'
BOUNTY
BOUTERSHEIM
BOUTS
BOW
BOWER
BOWLE
BOWLES
BOXES
BOY'D
BOYLER
BOYLES
BOYLING
BOYS
BRAG
BRAID
BRAIES
BRAINS
BRAKES
BRANCH
BRANCHING
BRANDISH'D
BRANDISH'T
BRANDS
BRAULES
BRAVADO
BRAVERIE
BRAVERIES
BRAWL
BRAWNE
BRAY
BRAYES
BRAYNE
BRAYNE-HARDIE
BRAYNFORD
BREACHES
BREAD-STREETS
BREAK
BREATH'D
BREATHES
BREATH'S
BREATH'ST
BREDA
BREECHES
BREEDES
BREVITIE
BREW
BREW-HOUSES
BRIAREUS
BRICK-HILLS
BRIDEGROOME
BRIDES
BRIDE-WELL
BRIEFE
BRILL
BRINGES
BRINGING
BRISTO'
BRITAIN'S

BRITTAINS
BRIZE
BROADER
BROADEST
BROAD-SEALES
BROAD-TRODEN
BROCAGE
BROECK
BRONTES
BROOKES
BROOME
BROUGHTONS
BROUGHT'ST
BROW
BROWN
BROWNE
BROWS
BRUISED
BRUIS'D
BRUISETH
BRUNSFIELD
BRUSH'D
BRUTE
BRUTUS
BUCK
BUCKINGHAM
BUCKLERS
BUCKLERS-BURY
BUD
BUDS
BUILDERS
BUILDING
BULKE
BULLOCKS
BULLS
BUOY
BURL
BUPLASE
BURTHEN
BURY
BURYED
BUSIED
BUSKINS
BUTTER'D
BUTTER-FLYE
BUTTOCK
BUYER
BUYLDING
BY
BY'
BY-CAUSE
BY'EXAMPLE
CABINET
CADMUS
CAECILIUS
CAESARIAN
CAESAR'S
CAESURA
CAGE
CAKE
CAL'
CALAIS
CALAMITIE
CALEDON
CALENDS
CALL'D
CALL'S
CALL'T
CALMEST
CAL'T
CALUMNIES
CALVES
CAMELL
CANARY-WINE
CANCELL'D
CANDIDATES
CANDIDE
CANDLE
CANDOR
CANES
CANN
CANNONS
CANON
CANT
CANTILENA
CANVAS
CANVASSE
CAP
CAPARISON
CAPERS
CAPITALL
CAPON
CAPP
CAP'RING
CAP'S

CAPT
CAP'TALL
CAPTIV'D
CAR
CARBUNCLE
'CARE
CARE-FULL
CAREFULLY
CAREY
CARIED
CARING
CARKASSE
CARKASSES
CAR-MEN
CAROCHES
CAROLINE
CARPENTRY
CARPER
CARPETS
CARPS
CARRE
CARRIAGE
CARRIES
CARRYED
CARVED
CARV'D
CAS'D
CASHIERD
CASKE
CASSANDRA
CASSELLIUS
CASSIOPEA
CASTS
CAT
CATAPLASMES
CATCHES
CATECHISME
CATER
CATER-PILLER
CATS
CATTELL
CATULLUS
CAUS'D
CAVE
CAVENDISH
CEASE
CEASURE
CECILIA
CECILL
CECILL'S
CEDAR
CELEBRATED
CELESTIALL
CELLARS
CENSORIOUS
CENSURER
CENSURETH
CENSURING
CENTAURE
CENTAURES
CEREMONIES
CERES
CERTAINLY
CERTEYNE
CESTRIAN
CETHEGI
CHACE
CHAFES
CHAINED
CHAINES
CHALICE
CHALK
CHALKE
CHAMBER-CRITICK
CHAMBER-FELLOW
CHANC'D
CHANCELOR
CHANCERIE
CHANCETH
CHANC'T
CHANGE'D
CHANGETH
CHANNELL
CHANNELS
CHANTING
CHAPLAINES
CHAPMEN
CHAPPEL
CHARG'D
CHANGEFULL
CHARITABLE
CHARITIES

CHARMING
CHARON
CHARONS
CHARTER
CHARYBDIS
CHASTETYE
CHATTELL
CHATTELS
CHATTRING
CHAUCER
CHAUNCE
CHEAP
CHEAP-SIDE
CHEAR
CHEAR'D
CHEAR-FULL
CHEARFULL
CHEARFULLY
CHECKT
CHEEKES
CHEEKS
CHEERED
CHEESE
CHEESES
CHEIFEST
'CHEQUER
CHEQUER
CHERISH'D
CHERISHING
CHERISSHEINGE
CHERRIES
CHERRY
CHERUBE
CHEST
CHEST-NUT
CHESTNUT
CHICHES
CHID
CHIDE
CHIEFES
CHIMES
CHINCKE
CHINNES
CHLOES
CHOAK'D
CHOERILUS
CHOIR
CHOISEST
CHOLER
CHOLLER
CHORE
CHOYSE
CHOYSEST
CHREMES
CHRISTALL
CHRISTMASSE
CHRIST-MASSE
CHRISTNING
CHRYSTALL
CHURCH-YARD
CHURLISH
CHYME
CICERO
CINDERS
CINNAMON
CINNAMON-TREE
CINNOPAR
CIPRESSE
CIRCLED
CIRCLER
CIRCUITS
CIRCUMDUCTION
CIRCUMFERENCE
CIRCUMFUSED
CIRCUMSTANCE
CIRCUMVOLVD
CITTIE-QUESTION
CITTYES
CIVILITIE
CLAIMEST
CLAME
CLAPS
CLARIUS
CLARKE
CLARKE-LIKE
CLARKES
CLASH
CLASPE
CLAW
CLAYM'D
CLAYMETH
CLAYMING
CLEANE
CLEAREST

CLEARNESSE
CLEARS
CLEERELY
CLEFT-STICKS
CLEIES
CLEMENCIE
CLEMENT
CLENSE
CLEP'D
CLERKES
CLIENT
CLIFFORDS
CLIFTON'S
CLIME
CLIMING
CLING
CLOAK
CLOAKE
CLOCKE
CLOKE
CLOSDE
CLOSELY
CLOSER
CLOSES
CLOSEST
CLOSE-STOOLE
CLOTH'
CLOTH'S
CLOUDS
CLOWNAGE
CLOWNISHE
CLUBB
CLUB-FIST
CLUID
CLUSTER
CLYENT
CLYSTERS
COACH-MAN
COACH-MARE
COARSE
COAT
COATE
COBALUS
COBLED
COBLER
COBWEB
COB-WEB-LAWNE
COBWEBS
COCATRICE
COCKING
COCKS
CODE
COELIA
COETERNALL
CO-HEIRE
COIN
COIT
COKELY
COLBY
COLCHIS
COLDEST
COLDLY
COLE
COLOSSUS
COMAUND
COMBE
COMBES
COMBINES
COMEDIE
COMELIE
COMELYE
COMENDS
COMFORTED
COMFORTER
COMFORTS
COMMANDEMENTS
COMMANDING
COMMENDER
COMMENDING
COMMENDS
COMMENTARIES
COMMINGS
COMMIXT
COMM'ST
COMMUNICATED
COMMUNION
COMMUNITIE
COMOEDIE
COMON
COMPANIES
COMPANIONS
COMPANY'
COMPAR'D
COMPASS'D
COMPEERES

COMPIL'D
COMPLAINING
COMPLEAT
COMPLEMENT
COMPLEXION
COMPLEXIONS
COMPREHEND
COMPRISETH
COMPROMISE
COMPTERS
COMPTING
COMPTROLLER
COMUS
CON
CONCEALES
CONCEIV'ST
CONCERNE
CONCEYVD
CONCLUSION
CONCURRETH
CONDITIONS
CONDUITS
CONEYES
CONFERRE
CONFERRING
CONFESS
CONFESSING
CONFEST
CONFIDENT
CONFINE
CONFINING
CONFIRM'D
CONFUS'D
CONFUSED
CONFUTES
CONJECTURES
CONJURES
CONNEXION
CONQU'RING
CONSCIENCES
CONSCIOUS
CONSECRATE
CONSENTED
CONSISTING
CONSISTS
CONSOLATORIE
CONSORT
CONSTABLE
CONSTABLES
CONSTANCY
CONSTELLATION
CONSTELLATIONS
CONSTRAINE
CONSULT
CONSUMING
CONSUMMATE
CONSUMPTIONS
CONTAGION
CONTAINE
CONTEMN'D
CONTEMNING
CONTEMPT
CONTEND
CONTENDS
CONTENTED
CONTENTION
CONTINEWALL
CONTINUALL
CONTINUE
CONTRARY
CONTROLL
CONTROULE
CONTROULES
CONTUMELIE
CONVERT
CONVERTED
CONVERTING
CONVICT
CONVINCE
COOCKOLD
COOKE
COOKES
COP'CES
COPPIE
CORDOVA
CORNER
COROLLARY
CORRALS
CORRECTED
CORRECTING
CORRODING
CORRUPTS
CORSE
COR'SIVES
CORYATS

CORYNNA
COSEN
COSENING
COS'NING
COSSEN'D
COTES
COULDST
COUNCELLOUR
COUNCELLS
COUNT
COUNTERFEITS
COUNTERMINE
COUNTERMYNE
COUNTERS
COUNTING
COUNT'NANCES
COUNTREY-MEN
COUNTREY'S
COUNTRIE-NEIGHBOURS
COUNTRY
COUNTRY'S
'COUNTS
COUNTY
COUPLED
COURAGE
COURSE
COURSER
COURT-BRED-FILLIE
COURT-DURT
COURTED
COURTEOUS
COURTESIES
COURT-HOBBY-HORSE
COURTIERS
COURTING
COURT-LING
COURT-PARRAT
COURT-PUCELL
COUSIN
COVELL
COVER'D
COVEY
COYN'D
CRACK'D
CRACKERS
CRACKT
CRAFTIE
CRAFTY
CRAMP
CRAMPE
CRAMP'D
CRAMP-RING
CRAMPS
CRANCK
CRAV'D
CRAVES
CREAME
CREAME-BOWLES
CREATED
CREATION
CREDITT
CREDULOUS
CREED
CREEP
CREEPES
CREPUNDIA
CREST
CRI'D
CRIER
CRINGE
CRIPPLE
CRIPS
CRISPE
CRISPED
CRISPETH
CRITICALL
CROAKE
CROAKING
CROOKED
CROP
CROPT
CROSSE
CROWD
CROWN
CROWN'D
CROWNE-PLATE
CROWNE-WORTHY
CROWNING
CRUDITIES
CRUELLIE
CRUSH'D
CRUSHT
CRYD'ST
CRYED
CRYER

CRYING
CRYME
CRYSTAL
CUCKOLD
CUCQUEANE
CUFFES
CULL'D
CULLORING
CULLORS
CUNNINGE
CUNNINGLY
CUPPING
CUPPING-GLASSES
CURBES
CURLE
CURLING
CURLING-IRONS
CURS
CURTEOUS
CURTESIES
CUSTOMER
CUTHBERT
CUTLERS
CYCNUS
CYLLARUS
CYNARA
CYNTHIAS
CYNTHIA'S
CYNTHIUS
CYPHER
CYPRES
CYPRESSE
DAGGER
DAINTINESSE
DAINTY
DALE
DAM'
DAMASKE
DAMASKE-ROSE
DAMD
DAMME
DAM'MEE
DAMNATION
DAMN'D
DAMNED
DAMNES
DAMNING
DAM'S
DANCES
DANCING
DANES
DAPPER
DARBY
DARKEST
DARK-LANTERNE
DARLING
DARTED
DARTING
DARTS
DASHING
DATE
DAUNCE
DAUNCING
DAUNGER
DAVIDS
DAVIS
DAVUS
DAYES-PRESENTS
DAYLY
DAY-STARRE
DE
DEADLY
DEAL
DEAL-BOARDS
DEALE
DEAR
DEARELY
DEBENTUR
DEBT-BOOKE
DEBTER
DEBTERS
DECAYES
DECEASED
DECEASING
DECEAST
DECEIPT
DECEIT
DECEIVE
DECEIVES
DECKE
DECLARES
DECLIN'D

DECLINETH
DECOCTIONS
DECREAST
DEDICATED
DEEME
DEEP-CROWN'D-BOWLE
DEEPE-GROUNDED
DEEPER
DEFAC'T
DEFAME
DEFECT
DEFECTIVE
DEFENCES
DEFENDERS
DEFEND'ST
DEFENSE
DEFERRE
DEFERRER
DEFIES
DEFILED
DEFIN'D
DEFORM'D
DEFRAUDED
DEFRAYES
DEGENERATE
DEGRADATION
DEIFIE
DEITY
DELATED
DELAYES
DELAYING
DELIA'S
DELICACIES
DELICIOUS
DELIGHTFULL
DELIVER
DELUDE
DELUDED
DELYGHT
DEMAND
DEMERIT
DEMOCRITE
DEMOCRITUS
DENIS
DENMARKE
DENYD'ST
DENYED
DENY'D
DENYES
DEPARTS
DEPEND
DEPENDENTS
DEPOSITED
DEPRAVE
DEPRIVE
DESCEND
DESCENDED
DESCRIBE
DESCRIBED
DESCRIDE
DESERTED
DESERTS
DESERVEDLY
DESIGNED
DESIGNES
DESIGNETH
DESMOND
DESPISE
DESPIS'D
DESPITE
DESTINIES
DESTITUTE
DESTROY'D
DESTRUCTION
DESYROUS
DETRACTOR
DEVIL
DEVOTE
DEVOTION
DEVOTIONS
DEVOURES
DEVOUT
DEXTEROUSLY
DIALOGUES
DIAN
DIANA'
DIANA'ALONE
DICK
DICTAMEN
DI'D
DIE'D
DIES
DIET
DIETIE
DIFFER'D

DIFFERENT
DIFFERING
DIFFERS
DIGESTIVE
DIGESTS
DIGNIFIE
DILATE
DILIGENCE
DILIGENT
DIMENSION
DIMENSIONS
DIMME
DIMN'D
DING
DINT
DIOMEDE
DIOSCURI
DIRCAEAN
DIRE
DIRECT
DIRECTLY
DIRECTS
DIRTIE
DIRTY
DISAVOW
DIS-AVOW
DISCARD
DISCERNED
DISCERN'D
DISCERNES
DISCHARGING
DISCIPLINE
DISCLOS'D
DISCORD
DISCORDS
DISCOURSING
DISCOVERETH
DISCOVERIES
DISCREETER
DISDAINED
DISDAINING
DIS-ESTEEME
DIS-ESTEEM'D
DIS-FAVOUR
DISGORGE
DISGRAC'T
DISGUISD
DISGUISE
DISGUIS'D
DISHERRIT
DIS-INHERIT
DISINHERIT
DIS-JOYNTS
DISPAIRE
DISPAYRE
DISPEND'ST
DISPENSATION
DISPERSE
DISPISED
DISPLEASE
DISPLEAS'D
DISPOS'D
DISPOSING
DISPROPORTION'D
DISPUTE
DISSECT
DISSECTION
DISSEMBLE
DISTINCT
DISTINCTIONS
DISTINGUISH'D
DISTRACT
DITCHFIELD
DITTIE
DITTIES
DIV'D
DIVERSLY
DIVID'ST
DIVINER
DIVINEST
DIVISION
DIVISIONS
DOCILE
DOCK'
DOCKE
DOCK'S
DOCTOR
DOES
DOEST
DOG-DAIES
DOGGES
DOLPHIN
DOMINATIONS
DOMINUS
DOMITIAN

DONNE
DONNE'S
DONNES
DONNOR'S
DOOR
DORRELS
DORSET
DOSE
DOSEN
DOTAGE
DOTE
DOUBTFUL
DOUBTING
DOUBTS
DOVES
DOWER
DOWGATE
DOWRIE
DOZEN
DRAD
DRAG
DRAMA
DRAMME
DRAWER
DRAWING
DRAYTON
DREADS
DRENCH
DRI'D
DRILL
DRINCKE
DRINKERS
DRINKING
DRIVE
DRIV'N
DRONKEN
DROOP
DROOPING
DROPP
DROUPES
DROWN
DROWND
DROWNES
DRUDGE
DRUNKENNEST
DRYADS
DUBLET
DUELI
DUE'LLISTS
DUELY
DUKES
DULNESSE
DULY
DUNGEON
DUNSTABLE
DUR'D
DURT
DURTIE
DUTIE
DUTIES
DUTY
DWELLER
DWELLS
DWELT
DYD'ST
DYED
DYE-FATS
DYERS
DYVE
E
EAGLE
EARLES
EARTHEN
EARTHES
EARTHLY
EARTHS
EAS'D
EASED
EASES
EAST
EASY
EASY-RATED
EATS
ECCHO'D
ECCHO'S
ECSTASY
EDEN
EDIFICES
EDUCATION
EEKE
EELES
EENE
EFFECTED
EGERTON
EJECTS

EL
ELABORATE
ELDERS
ELECTED
ELEGIES
ELFE
ELIZA
ELIZABETHS
ELOQUENT
ELSMERE
ELTHAM
ELTHAM-THING
EMBARK
EMBASSIE
EMBASSIES
EMBELISH'D
EMBERS
EMBLEMES
EMBRIONS
EMBRODERIES
EMINENCE
EMISSARIE
EMPEDOCLES
EMPEROURS
EMPIRE
EMPIRICK
EMPLOYD
EMP'RICKS
EMPTIES
EMPTY
EMPTYE
EMPTY-HANDED
EMPUSA
EMPYRE
EMULATES
EMULATION
ENABLE
ENAMOR'D
ENCLOSE
ENCOUNTER
ENCOURAGE
ENCREAS'D
ENCREAST
ENDES
ENDEW'D
ENDORSE
ENDURE
ENDURES
ENEMIES
ENFLAMED
ENFORCE
ENFORCED
ENFORCING
ENFORME
ENGAGE
ENGAGED
ENGLANDS
ENGLISH-ROGUE
ENGRAV'D
ENGYNE
ENHANCE
ENJOYES
ENLARGE
ENLIVEN
ENNOBLE
ENORMITY
ENRAGE
ENSHRIN'D
ENSPIRE
ENTANGLING
ENTAYL'D
ENTEND
ENTERMIXT
ENTERTAYNE
ENTERTAYNMENT
ENTHEATE
ENTIRE
ENTITLE
ENTREAT
ENTRED
ENTWINE
ENVIES
ENVITE
ENVOYE
ENVY'
ENVYE
ENVY'D
ENVYOUS
EPICK
EPICKS
EPICOENE
EPIDEMICALL
EPILOGUE
EPISTOLAR

EPITHALAMION
EPITHITES
EQUALL'D
EQUITIE
ERECTED
ERE'T
ERIDANUS
ERRANT
ERRANT'ST
ERR'D
ERROURS
ESCAPES
ESCHYLUS
ESPLANDIANS
ESPY
ESSAY
ESTATES
ESTEEM'D
ESTEEMED
ESTIMATE
ETEOSTICHS
ETERNIZ'D
ETHNICISME
EUCLIDE
EUGENIAN
EUPHEME
EURIPIDES
EUTHANASEE
EVENING'S
EVENLY
EVER-BOYLING
EVER-GREENE
EVER-LASTING
EVERLASTING
EVE'RY
EVERY-WHERE
EVIDENCE
EV'N
EXACTS
EXALT
EXAMINE
EXAMINING
EXAMPLED
EXAMPLES
EXCEED
EXCEEDS
EXCELLING
EXCELSIS
EXCEPTION
EXCESSE
EXCHEQUER
EXCITE
EXCLUDE
EXECRATION
EXECUTES
EXECUTION
EXECUTIONER
EXECUTOR
EXERCIS'D
EXHAUSTED
EXIL'D
EX'LENT
EXPANSIONS
EXPELL
EXPERIENCE
EXPIRE
EXPLAT'ST
EXPOSTULACION
EXPRESSER
EXPRESSETH
EXPRESSION
EXPRESSIONS
EXSCRIBE
EXTASIE
EXTASIES
EXTEMPORE
EXTENDETH
EXTENDS
EXTENSION
EXTRACT
EXTRAORDINARIE
EXTREMITIES
EYE-BROWES
EYE-BROWS
EYED
EYTHER
EYTHERS
F
FA
FABLER
FACILE
FACTIOUS

FA-DING
FAEMALE
FAILED
FAIL'D
FAINED
FAINES
FAINTING
FAIRY
FAITH'
FAITHS
FAITH'S
FAL
FALERNIAN
FALLOW
FALL'ST
FALSEHOOD
FALSELY
FALSER
FAME-VAYNES
FAMILIAR
FAMILIES
FAMILY
FAN
FANCIES
FARE-WELL
FARRE-ADMIRED
FARRE-ALL-SEEING
FARRE-KNOWNE
FART
FARTHEST
FARTS
FAST
FASTNING
FATHER'S
FATS
FATTEST
FAULT'
FAULTES
FAULT'S
FAVORITE
FAVOURITE
FAVOURITES
FAYERIE
FAYNE
FAYREST
FEAT
FEATS
FEATURES
FEBR
FEEDING
FEIGNE
FEILD
FELICITIE
FELL
FELLOWES
FEMALE
FENCED
FENC'D
FENCER
FENCING
FENC'T
FERRABOSCO
FERTILE
FESCENNINE
FET
FETHER
FETHERD
FETTER
FETTERS
FEVER
FEV'RY
FEWD
FEWER
FEWEST
FIBRE
FIBRES
FIER
FIERY
FIFTIETH
FIFTY
FIG
FIGHTS
FIGURES
FILCH'D
FILE
FIL'D
FILED
FILL'D
FILLIE
FILMER
FILTHY
FINALL
FINDS
FINE-MAN
FINENESSE

FIRE-LIGHT
FISHER
FIST-FILL'D
FITNESSE
FITTS
FIVE-FOLD
FIXE
FLACCUS
FLAGGE
FLAGGETH
FLAKES
FLAMESHIP
FLAMING
FLANCK'D
FLATTER'D
FLATTERED'ST
FLATTERY
FLATTERYE
FLATT'RER
FLATT'RIE
FLATTRY'S
FLAW
FLEA
FLEAD
FLEECED
FLEES
FLEET
FLEET-LANE
FLESHLY
FLIGHTS
FLING
FLIT
FLORA
FLORENCE
FLOURISH
FLOURISHING
FLOURISHT
FLOWE
FLOWRIE
FLOWRY
FLUNG
FLUTE
FLY
FLYES
FOAME
FOILED
FOIST
FOLKES
FOLLOWERS
FOLLOWING
FOND
FONDLY
FOOL
FOOLE-HARDIE
FOOLING
FOOT-AND-HALFE-FOOT
FOOT-CLOTH
FOOT-MAN
FOR'
FORBIDD'
FORBIDDEN
FORBIDS
FORCES
FORCING
'FORE
FOREBORNE
FOREHEAD'
FOREHEAD'S
FOREMAN
FORE-SEE
FORESTALL
FORFEITINGE
FORFEITS
FORGOTTEN
FOR'HIS
FORKED
FORMED
FORNACES
FORSAKEN
FORSOOKE
FORSWARE
FORSWORE
FORSWORNE
FORTH-BROUGHT
FORTIFIE
FORTIFIED
FORTNIGHT
FORTUNATE
FORTY
FORUM
FORWARD
FOSTER
FOSTER-FATHER
FOULELY
FOUNDATION

FOUNDER
FOUNT
FOURESCORE
FOURE-SCORE
FOWLE
FOWLER
FRAGRANT
FRANK
FRANTICK
FRAUD
FRAUDS
FRAYLTIE
FREEHOULD
FREER
FREEZ'D
FREINDSHIP
FRENCH-HOOD
FRENCH-MEN
FRENCH-TAYLORS
FRIAR
FRIE
FRIEND-SHIP
FRIGHTS
FRINDES
FRIPPERIE
FRO
FRONTIRE
FRONTISPICE
FROSTES
FROSTIEST
FROSTILY
FROSTS
FROWNES
FROWNING
FRUITE
FRUITES
FRUITLESSE
FRY
FRYAR
FRYERS
FUCUS
FULIGINOUS
FUME
FUMES
FUMIE
FUNERALL
FUNERALLS
FURNACE
FURNACES
FURNISH
FURNITURE
FURRE
FURROWES
FURTHER
FURYE
FYL'S
FYNE
FYNED
FYRE
FYRES
GAINED
GAINES
GAITE
GALBA
GALL
GALLANT
GALLANTRY
GALLO
GALLO-BELGICUS
GALLUS
GAMAGE
GAMBOL
GAMESTER
GAMSTER
GANIMEDE
GARDENS
GARMENT
GARTER
GARTERS
GASPE
GATHERER
GAUDY
GAULE
GAVEST
GAZERS
GAZETTI
GEARE
GEFFRY
GEMME
GEMMES
GEMS
GENTILE
GENTLEMEN
GENTLEST
GENTLE-WOMAN

GENTLIE
GENT'MAN
GESTS
GHEST
GIANT
GILD
GILL
GI'NG
GINNES
GINNY
GIRDED
GIRDLE
GIRLES
GIRLS
GIVER
GLADDER
GLADDING
GLAD-MENTION'D
GLANCE
GLARE
GLASS
GLASSE-HOUSE
GLASSES
GLASSHOUSE
GLAVES
GLEANE
GLEANES
GLEANINGS
GLISTER'D
GLOBY
GLOOMIE
GLOOMIE-SCEPTRED
GLORIFIE
GLOVE
GLOVER
GLUTTED
GNAT
GOALE
GOATE
GOATES
GODDESS
GODLY'S
GOD'S
GODWIT
GOD-WIT
GOLD'
GOLD-CHAINES
GOLDEN-EYES
GOLD'S
GON
GOODLIER
GOODLY
GOOD-NIGHT
GOODS
GOODY
GORGON
GORGONIAN
GOSSIP-GOT
GOSSIPPS
GOUT
GOVERNE
GOVERNING
GOWN'D
GOWNES
GRAC'D
GRACEFULL
GRAFFS
GRAFT
GRAFTED
GRAFTES
GRAMMAR
GRAMMARIANS
GRAMPIUS
GRANATS
GRAND-CHILDREN
GRAND-DAMES
GRANDEES
GRANDLINGS
GRAPE
GRAPHICK
GRASSIE
GRATES
GRATUITIE
GRATULATES
GRATULATORIE
GRAVELL
GRAVER
GRAVITIE
GRAZING
GREACE
GREAS'D
GREATLY
GREAT-MENS
'GREE
GREEDY

-1- (CONT.)

GREEK
GREEK-HANDS
GREEK'S
GREEN
GREENE-CLOTH
GREENWICH
'GREET
GREET
GREETING
GRIEFES
GRISLY
GROINE
GRONE
GROPES
GROSSER
GROUN'
GROUNDED
GROWE
GROWNDE
GRUDG'D
GRUNTING
GUARDES
GUARDIAN
GUE
GUIDE
GUIDED
GUIDETH
GUILD
GUILDED
GUILT
GUILTY
GULL
GULL'D
GULLING
GUMME
GUN
GUNDOMAR
GUNNES
GUN-POWDER
GUIS
GUY
GYANT
GYANTS
GYERLYK
GYRLANDS
GYVES
HA
HACKNEY
'AD
HAIR
HAIRES
HALBERDS
HALFE-MOONES
HALFE-WAY
HALT
HALTING
HAMMERING
HAMMERS
HAMS
HANCH
HANDLES
HANDLING
HANGING
HANNIBAL
HANNOW
HANS
HANS-SPIEGLE
HAP
HAPLESSE
HAP'LY
HAPP
HAPPILY
HARBINGER
HARBOR
HARBOUR'D
HARBOURS
HARD-BY
HARDER
HARD-HEARTED
HARKE
HARMONIOUSLY
HARMS
HARPIES
HARPYES
HARROW'D
HART
HARTES
HARTS
HA'S
HASTENS
HASTILY
HASTS

HASTY
HATCH
HATED
HATETH
HATING
HAU'
HAU'-BOY
HAU'BOY
HAUNCH
HAVE'HEM
HAVE'T
HAY
HAYLES
HAYRE
HAZILL
HEADED
HEADES
HEAD-LONG
HE'ADULTERS
HEALTHS
HEALTH-SAKE
HEAP
HEAPES
HEAPING
HEAPS
HEARD
HEARDS
HEARER
HEARSE
HEARST
HEAR'ST
HEARTH
HEART-STRIKE
HEARTY
HEATES
HEATING
HEATS
HEAV'D
HEAV'EN
HEBRID
HE'D
HEERE
HEIDELBERG
HEIGHTEN
HEIGHT'NING
HELICON
HE'LL
HELP'D
HELVETIA
HENRYE
HERB
HERCULES-HIS
HERD
HERDS
HEREIN
HERETOFORE
HEROE
HEROICK
HEROIQUE
HEYDEN
H'HAD
H'HATH
HIDE
HIDE-PARKE
HIDES
HIE
HIERARCHIE
HIERARCHIES
HIEROGLYPHICKS
HIGH-SPIRITED
HIGH-SWOLNE
HIGHT
HILT
HINDE
HINT
HIPOCRITES
HIPPOCRENES
HIR'D
HIRELINGS
HIRETH
HISTORICALL
HISTORY
HITT
HOARD
HOARSE
HOBBY
HOBLED
HODGES
H'OFFEND
HOLDBORNE
HOLDES
HOLDETH
HOLDING
HOLES
HOLIE

HOLIEST
HOLINESSE
HOLLAND
HOLLANDE
HOLY-DAYES
HOLYE
HOMAGE
HON'BLE
HONESTY
HONIE
HONORD
HONORED
HONORING
HONY
HOOD
HOOD-WINK'D
HOOFE-CLEFT
HOOFES
HOOK
HOOP
HOORD
HOORLD
HOP-DRINKERS
HOP'D
HOPELESSE
HORATIUS
HORL'D
HORNES
HORNE-WORKES
HORRIDE
HORROR
HORRORS
HORSE-LEECH
HORSE-LEECH-LIKE
HORSEMANSHIP
HORSE-NECK
HOSE
HOSPITALITIE
HOSPITALLS
HOST
HOSTESSE
HOTTER
HOTTEST
HOUGHS
HOUPES
HOUR
HOURE-GLASSE
HOWARD
HOWER
HOWERS
HOWRELY
HOWRES
HOW-SO-E'RE
HUGE
HUISHERS
HUISSEN
HULKE
HUMBER
HUMBLED
HUMBLEST
HUMBLY
HUMBLYE
HUMORS
HUMOUR'D
HUMOURS
HUM'ROUS
HUNGARY
HUNGRIE
HUNTED
HURDLES
HURLD
HURLED
HURL'D
HURRIED
HURTFULL
HURTING
HUSWIFERY
HYDRA
HYE
HYM
HYME
HYMENS
HYPOCRITE
I'AD
IAMBICKS
IBERUS
IDALIAN
IDEAS
IDIOT
IDOLATROUS
IDOMEN
IERNA
IGNOBLE
IGNORANTS
I'HAD

IL
ILE
IL'D
ILIA
I'LL
ILL-AFFECTED
ILL-MADE
ILL-FENN'D
ILL-TORN'D
ILL-US'D
ILLUSTRIOUS
ILLUSTROUS
IMAGE
IMAGERY
IMBARQU'D
I'ME
IMITATION
IMMORTALITYE
IMPARTIALLY
IMPERIALL
IMPIOUS
IMPLEXED
IMPOS'D
IMPOSTURE
IMPOSTURES
IMPREGNABLE
IMPRESSION
IMPRINT
IMPRISON
'N
INCARNATE
INCENSE
INCH
INCIVILITIE
INCLOS'D
INCLUDING
INCURR'D
INDEEDE
INDENTUR'D
INDEX
INDIAN
INDICE
INDIFFERENT
INDITE
INDORSE
INDU'D
INDULGENT
INDURE
INFAM'D
INFAMY
INFANT
INFECTED
INFECTION
INFINITS
INFIRMERY
INFLAME
INFLICT
INFLICTS
INFORM'D
INFORMED
INFORMERS
INFUS'D
INGAGE
INGENYRE
INGINE
INGINEERES
INGINER
INGOTS
INGREDIENTS
INHABIT
INIQUITIE
INJOY
INJUNCTION
IN-LAND
INLIVE
INNE
INNOCENTLY
INNOVATIONS
INO
INOUGH
INOUGHE
INOW
IN-PRIMIS
INQUIRE
INQUIR'D
IN'S
INSCRIB'D
INSERT
INSIDE
INSOLENT
INSTANTLY
INSTAURATION
INSTITUTION
INSTRUCTS
INSTRUMENT

IN'T
INTEGRITIE
INTELLIGENCER
INTEND
INTENDED
INTENT
INTENTION
INTENTS
INTERMIX
INTERPELL
INTERPOSE
INTERPOS'D
INTERPRETERS
INTERRUPT
INTERSERT
INTERTEXE
INTERTWIND
INTERTWINE
INTIRE
INTREAT
INTREATIES
INTREATY
INTRENCHMENT
INT'REST
INTWINE
INVEIGH
INVENTED
INVENTIONS
INVISIBILITIE
INVOKE
IONIAN
IRIS
IRISH
IRISHRY
IRRELIGIOUS
IRRITATE
ISLES
ITALIAN
ITALIE
I'TH'
I'THEIR
ITS
ITSELF
IVYE
IXION
JACKS
JACKS-PULSE
JACOBS
JAKES
JANIN'S
JANUS
JAPHETS
JARRE
JARRES
JARRETH
JARRING
JASONS
JAUNDIES
JAUNDIS
JAW
JAWES
JAX
JAY
JEAMES
JEARING
JEAST
JEMME
JERKE
JESUS
JOANE
JOIN
JOINT
JOSUAH
JOURNALL
JOURNALS
JOYCARE
JOY'D
JOYN
JOYNTING
JOY'ST
JUICE
JUSTEST
JUSTICE-HOOD
JUSTLED
KEEP'D
KEEPER
KEEP'ST
KEPTST
KERNE
KEY
KEYES
KEY-STONE
KICKING
KID
KILD

KILL'D
KILLER
KILN
KINDES
KINDLE
KINDLY
KINDS
KINE
KINGDOME
KINGLIER
KINGLY
KINNE
KINSMAN
KIST
KNAT
KNAVES
KNEELE
KNEELING
KNEES
KNELLS
KNEWE
KNIGHTES
KNIGHT'S
KNIGHT-WRIGHT'
KNIGHT-WRIGHT'S
KNOCK
KNOW'
KNOWS
KYD
KYNDE
L'
LABOR
LABORS
LACES
LACKE
LACK'DST
LACKS
LAD
LADDER
LADS
LADY'
LADY-AIRE
LADY'S
LAIES
LAMB
LAMBETH
LAMBS
LAMENESSE
LAMENT
LAMENTS
LAMIA'
LAMIA
LAMIA'HAS
LAMPE
LANC'LOTS
LANGLEY
LANGUAGES
LANGUISHING
LANTERNE-LERRY
LANTHERNE
LAPLAND
LAPSED
LAPWING
LARGELY
LARKES
LASH'D
'LASSE
LASTED
LASTLY
LASTS
LATE-COYN'D
LATERALL
LATIN
LATTEN
LAUGHE
LAUGH'D
LAUGHS
LAUGH'T
LAUGH-WORTHY
LAUNCES
LAURA
LAWRELL
LAXATIVE
LAY
LAYD
LAY-STALL
LAZIE
LDST
LEADERS
LEADING
LEADS
LEANE

LEANENESSE
LEAPT
LEARNEDLY
LEARNES
LEAS'D
LEATHER
LEAVEN'D
LEAVES
LEAV'ST
LECHERS
LEDA'S
LEDGER
LEE
LEES
LEFT
LEFT-LYDIA
LEFT-WITTED
LEG
LEGALL
LEG'D
LEGENDS
LEGH
LEGITIMATE
LEISURE
LEMON
LENOX
L'ENVOYE
LEPROSIE
LERRY
LESBIA
LESSE-POETIQUE
LETCHER'D
LETCHERS
LETHARGIE
LETHER
LETT
LETTER'D
LETTER-GOE
LETTUCE
LEWIS
LIBELLING
LIBELLS
LIBELS
LIBER
LIBERALL
LIBERTYE
LIBRARIE
LIBRUM
LICE
LICENTIOUSLY
LICINUS
LIE
LIEDGERS
LIEUTENANT
LIFE'
LIFE'S
LIFTS
LIGHTEN
LIGHTENS
LIGHTNESSE
LIGORNE
LIGURINE
LIKELY
LIKENESS
LIKES
LILY
LIMBES
LIMITING
LIN'D
LING
LINKES
LINNEN
LION
LIPPES
LIP-THIRSTIE
LIQUID
LIST
LISTEN
LITER
LITERATE
'LIVE
LIVERIES
LIVERS
LIVOR
LIVORIE
LIVORY
LOCK
LOCKT
LOCK'T
LODGING
LOFTIER
LOG
LOGGE
LOGOGRIPHES
LOIRE

LONG'D
LONGE
LONG'D-FOR
LONG-GATHERING
LONGING
LONGS
LONG-SINCE
LOOKETH
LOOKS
LOOME
LOOSED
LOOSER
LOOSER-LIKE
LOPS
LORD-GOD
LORE
LOTIONS
LOUDER
LOUGHING
LOUMOND
LOUSE
LOUSE-DROPPING
LOVE'
LOVED
LOVELY-HEAD
LOVE-QUEENES
LOVES-SAKE
LOVETH
LOV'ST
LOW-COUNTREY'S
LOW-COUNTRIES
LOWDEST
LOWENESSE
LOWER
LOWEST
LOWING
LOWLIE
LOYAL
LOYALTIES
LOYRE
LUCANE
LUCANS
LUCENT
LUCINA'S
LUCKILY
LUCRINE
LUMPE
LUPUS
LURDEN
LUSTES
LUSTFULL
LUSTIE-MOUNTING
LUSTROUS
LUST'S
LUTES
LUTHERS
LYAEUS
LYBIAN
LYCENCE
LYCENSE
LYCORIS
LYE
LYER
LYING
LYONS
LYST
LYVE
LYVES
MAAS
MAD-MEN
MADRIGALL
MAGICK
MAGISTRATES
MAGNETIQUE
MAIDEN
MAIDENS
MAIDES
MAIDS
MAIME
MAINTAINE
MAINTAYNES
MAISTRING
MAISTRY
MAJOR
MAJORS
MAKINGS
MALT
MALYCE
MANAGE
MANGERS
MANIE
MANKINDS
MANN'D
MANSION
MANY-HEADED

MAPPE
MAPS
MARCH
MARCHING
MARCHION
MARCHIONISSE
MARD
MARE
MARES
MARIAGE-DAY
MARIAGE-HORNE
MARIAGE-PLEDGES
MARIAGE-RITES
MARIE
MARKET
MARKET-FOLKES
MARKT
MAR'LE
MARLOWES
MARO
MARROW
MARRY
MARRYING
MART
MARTINS
MARTIRDOME
MARTYR
MASK'D
MASKED
MASKINGS
MASSACRING
MASSE
MASTER-BRAINE
MASTER-WORKER
MASTRIE
MATCH'D
MATCHES
MATCHING
MATE
MATERIALL
MATERIALLS
MATRON
MATRONE
MATURE
MAURICE
MAXIMUS
MA'
MAY'ADMIRE
MAY'ANY
MAYD
MAYDEN
MAYMED
MAYOR
MAYRESSE
ME'
MEADES
MEADOWS
MEALES
MEAN
MEANE
MEASURING
MEAT
MEATE-BOATE
MEATES
MEATS
MEAZLED
MECHANICK
MED'CIN'D
MEDDOWES
MEDIATE
MEDICINE
MEDWAY
MEEDS
MEEK
MEERELY
MEERE-MATTER-LESSE
MEETE
MEET'ST
MELANCHOLIQUE
MELANCHOLY
MELEAGER
MELTED
MELTS
MEMORY
MEMORYE
MENACE
MENACINGS
MENDICANT
MENDS
MENT
MENTION
MENTION'D
MERCAT
MERCER
MERCHANTS

MERCIES
MERCY-SEAT
MERD
MERD-URINOUS
MERITED
MERMAID
MERMAIDES
MERMAIDS
MERRIE
MERSH
MERSH-LAMBETH
MESCHINES
MESSALLA'S
MESSE
METE
METICULOUS
METIUS
METT
METTAL'
METTALL
METTALL'D
METTALLS
METTAL'S
ME'UP
MEW'D
MIDAS
MID-SUN
MID-WIFE
MID-WIVES
MIGHT
MILDE
MILDER
MILDNESSE
MILITAR
MILITARIE
MILK
MILKES
MILLAR
MILO
MINCE
MINERVAES
MINERVAS
MINGLE
MINISTRY
MINOS
MINUTE
MIRACLES
MIRKINS
MIRROR
MIRTHFULL
MIS-APPLY
MIS-CALL'
MIS-CALL'T
MISCHIFE
MISFORTUNE
MISSE-CALL'D
MIST
MISTAKING
MISTERYES
MISTOOKE
MISTRES
MISTRESS
MISTS
MISUS'D
MITE
MIXED
MIXETH
MIXING
MOAN
MOATH
MOATHES
MOCION
MODELL
MODERATELY
MODESTY
MODET
MOIST
MONARCH
MONE
MONETHS
MONEY-GETT
MONGST
MONIMENT
MONSIEUR
MONSTERS
MONTGOMERY
MONTHES
MONTHLY
MONTJOY
MONUMENT
MONYES
MOOD
MOODS
MOON-CALFE
MOORE

MOORE-FIELDS
MORALL
MORAVIAN
MORISON'
MORISON'S
MORNES
MORNING'S
MORNINGS
MORNING-STAR
MORRISSE
MORROW'
MORTALITIE
MORTALITY
MORTS
MOSCO
MOSES
MOTH
MOTIVE
MOTLY
MOUGHT
MOULDIE
MOULDS
MOUNSIEURS
MOUNT
MOUNTAINES
MOUNTE
MOUNTEAGLE
MOUNTE-BANCK
MOUNTS
MOURN'D
MOURNERS
MOURNES
MOURNING
MOVED
MOVES
MOVETH
MOV'ST
MOWED
MUD
MUFFLES
MULTIPLI'D
MULTITUDE
MUNG'
MUNGREL
MUNGRIL
MUNIMENTS
MURDERED
MURMURES
MURMURING
MURTHER
MURTHERING
MUSICALL
MUSTER-MASTER
MUSTERS
MUTTON
MUTUALLY
MYLES
MYND
MYNDE
MYNERVA
MYSTICK
MYTHOLOGY
NAILE
NAILS
NALL
NAME'
NAMED
NAMELESS
NAME'S
NARD
NARE
NARROW'D
NASO
NASTIE
NATIVE
NATIVITIE
NATURE'
NATURE'S
NAUGHT
NAVIE
NE
NEADD
NEARER
NEATLY
NECESSITIES
NECKE
NECKS
NECK-STOCKT
NEECES
NEEDE
NEEDFULLY
NE'ER

NEERE
NEERER
NEGLECT
NEIGHBOURHOOD
NEIGHBOUR-TOWNES
NEIGHING
NEITHERS
NEPHEW
NEPHEWS
NE'R
NERE
NERO
NETHER
NEVILLS
NEW-COME
NEW-DITCH
NEWNESSE
NEW-YEARES
NEW-YEERES
NEYTHER
NICER
NIECE
NIGHT-SINNES
NIGHT-TUBS
NILL
NINTH
NO'
NOBLES
NOBLIER
NODDELL
NODDING
NODDLE
NOISD
NOIS'D
NOISOME
NOMINALL
NOOKES
NOONE-DAY
NOONE-STED'
NOONE-STED'S
NOOSE
NOREMBERG
NORTH
NORTHUMBERLAND
NORWICH
NOSTHRILL
NOSTRILL
NOTHING'
NOTHING'S
NOTION
NOTIONS
NOURCERIES
NOURISHETH
NOURSE
NOVEMB
NOVEMBER
NOW'T
NOYSES
NOYSOME
NULLIFIE
NUMBE
NUMBRED-FIVE
NUMEROUS
NUNCIO'S
NURSERY
NUT-CRACKERS
NUTS
NYCE
OAKE
OARES
OBAY
OBAYE
OBEDIENCE
OBJECTEST
OBLATIONS
OBLIQUE
OBLIQUITIE
OBLIVION
OBSERVED
OBSERVING
OBTAIN'D
OCCASION
OCCUPY
OCEAN
OD
ODCOMBIAN
ODIOUS
ODOROUS
ODORS
ODOURS
ODS
OENONE
OFFALL
OFFENDERS
OFFENDING

OFFERING
OFFERS
OFFICER
OFFICIOUS
OFFICIOUSLY
OFF'RING
OFF-SPRING
OFTNER
OIL
OINTMENT
OLBYON
OLDE
OLIMPICKE
OLIVEERS
OLIVES
OMEN
OMINOUS
OMNIPOTENT
ON
ONE'
ONE
ONELY-GOTTEN
ONE'S
ONIONS
OPINIONS
OPPOSE
OPPRESSOR
OPPREST
ORACLES
ORCADES
ORCHARD
ORDAIN'D
ORDERS
ORDINANCE
ORDINARIES
ORD'RING
ORE
ORE-BLOWNE
ORE-FLOW
ORE-FLOWNE
ORE-FOLD
O'RE-JOY'D
O'RE-PRAISE
ORE-SHINE
ORE-SWELLETH
O'REWHELM'D
ORGANES
ORGIES
ORIENT
ORNAMENT
ORNITHS
ORPHANES
ORPHANS
O'TH'
OTHERS-EVILL
OTHERWISE
OTHES
OURE
OUT-BEE
OUT-BOAST
OUT-BRAVE
OUT-CRYES
OUT-DANCE
OUT-DID
OUT-DOO
OUT-FLOURISHT
OUT-FORMES
OUT-LAST
OUTLAST
OUT-LASTS
OUT-PRAISE
OUT-RIGHT
OUT-SPUN
OUT-STARTED
OUT-STRIP
OUT-STRIPT
OUT-VALEW
OUT-ZANY
OVERBEARING
OVER-BLOW
OVERCAME
OVERDOOE
OVER-GONE
OVER-LEAVEN'D
OVER-SAFE
OVER-SEER
OVER-THICK
OVERTHROW
OVID
OW'D
OWERS
OWING
OWN
OWN'D
OWSE

OXE
OYLIE
OYSTERS
P
PACCUVIUS
PAC'D
PACETH
PACK
PAC'T
PAGAN
PAGE
PAINTINGS
PAINTS
PALATE
PALINDROMES
PALLACE
PALLAT
PALMERINS
PALME-TREES
PALSIES
PALTZGRAVE
PAMPHLETTS
PAN
PANCRIDGE
PANDECTS
PANDORA'S
PANEGYRICKE
PANICK
PANTON
PARACELSUS
PARASITE
PARCAE
PARCELLS
PARCELS
PARDON'D
PARDONING
PARDONS
PARE
PARIS-GARDEN
PARISH-STEEPLE
PARITIE
PARKE
PARLYAMENT
PARNASSUS
PARRAT
PARROT
PARTAKES
PARTES
PARTICULAR
PARTIE
PARTIE-PER-PALE
PARTIES
PAS'D
PASQUILL'S
PASS'D
PASSENGER
PASSER
PASSER-BY
PASSION'S
PASSIVE
PASTIE
PASTORALL
PASTORALS
PASTRIE
PAT
PATE
PATHES
PATIENT
PATIENTLY
PATRIOT
PATRONAGE
PATTERNES
PAUL
PAULES
PAULS-STEEPLE
PAULUS
PAWLET
PAYD
PAYNE
PAYNTED
PAYRE
PAYS
PEACOCK
PEALES
PEARCH'D
PEARE
PEARES
PEARIE
PEASON
PEDICULOUS
PEDLING
PEEPES
PEERE
PEERING
PEIRCE

PEIZ'D
PELFE
PELLETS
PELTS
PEM
PENCE
PEND
PENELOPES
PENITENT
PENITENTS
PENNANCE
PENN'D
PENNE
PENNING
PENNY
PENT
PENURIE
PER
PERCEIVE
PERCEIV'D
PERFORME
PERFORM'D
PERFUM'D
PERFUMED
PERIEGESIS
PERILL
PERIOD
PERISHE
PERJURE
PERJURIE
PERMANENT
PERNITIOUS
PERPETUALL
PERPETUATING
PERPLEXED
PERSEUS
PERSWADES
PERSWADING
PERTINAX
PERVERSLY
PERVERTS
PEST-HOUSE
PETARDS
PETASUS
PETITE
PETITION
PETRARCH
PETTICOTES
PETTIE
PEWTER
PHAOS
PHILOSOPHERS
PHILOSOPHY
PHLEBOTOMIE
PHLEGETON
PHOEBEIAN
PHOEBE'S
PHOEBUS-SELFE
PHRASES
PHRYGIAN
PHYSICIAN
PHYSITIAN
PICKARDILL
PICKE
PICKT
PICKT-HATCH
PICTURES
PIDE
PIE
PIETY
PIKES
PILL'D
PILLER
PILLORY
PILLOW
PILLS
PILOT
PIMBLICOE
PIN
PINDAR
PINDARS
PIN'D
PINN
PIONERS
PIPE
PIPER
PIPKINS
PISO
PISS'D
PISTLE
PIT
PITCH
PITCH'D
PITFALL
PIT-FALLS

PITIOUS	POTIONS	PROMETHEAN	QUICK-WARMING-PAN	REFORMED
PIT-PAT-NOYSE	POTS	PROOFES	QUIET	REFRESHED
PITIES	POTTLE	PROPAGATE	QUILLS	REFUSED
PITTIED	POULDER	PROPERLY	QUILTS	REFUSES
PITTIOUS	POULDER-PLOT	PROPERTIE	QUINCE	REGENERATE
PIXE	POULDERS	PROPERTIUS	QUINTILIUS	REGENT
PLACING	POULES	PROPERTYE	QUINTUS	REGIMENT
PLAC'T	POWDERS	PROPHANER	QUITE	REGION
PLAGIARY	POWERFULL	PROPHET'	QUIT'ST	REGIONS
PLAGUE-BILL	POWRE	PROPHETICKE	QUOIT	REIN
PLAGUE-SORES	POYNTE	PROPHET'S	R	REJECT
PLAI'D	POYNTES	PROPORTION'D	RABBIN	REJOYCE
PLAIES	PRACTICE	PROPORTIONS	RACES	RE-JOYNE
PLAISTERS	PRACTISD	PROPOSE	RACK	RELEAST
PLANETS	PRACTIS'D	PROPOS'D	RADAMANTHUS	RELENTLESSE
PLANTING	PRACTISES	PROPOUND	RADIANT	RELIGIOUSLY
PLAT	PRAECIPICE	PROPPING	RAGES	RELIQUE
PLAY'	PRAEOCCUPIE	PROP'REST	RAGGED	REMAYNE
PLAY'D	PRAEVARICATORS	PROPTER	RAIGN'D	REMAYN'ST
PLAYER	PRAISE-WORTHY	PROSERPINA	RAIGNES	REMEMBER
PLAY'S	PRAISEWORTHY	PROSPECTIVE	RAILE	REMEMBRED
PLAY'ST	PRAISING	PROSPERITY	RAILES	REMONSTRANCE
PLEA	PRANCK	PROSTITUTE	RAILING	REMORSE
PLEAD	PRANKES	PROTECTES	RAINBOW	REMOVE
PLEADED	PRATING	PROTECTION	RAINGE	REMOVETH
PLEADER	PRATLING	PROTESTATION	RAM'D	RENDRED
PLEADERS	'PRAY	PROTESTED	RAMPARTS	RENEW
PLEADINGS	PRAY'D	PROTESTS	RANCK	RENEWED
PLEASED	PRAYES	PROTEUS	RANCKE	RENEWING
PLEASES	PRAYSER	PROTRACTION	RANCK'D	RENOWN'D
PLEASETH	PRAYSES	PROUDER	RANDOME	RENOWNING
PLEDGE	PRAYSEST	PROUDLY	RANGE	RENT
PLIGHTS	PREACH	PROVIDER	RANKE	REPAIRE
PLOUED	PRECEDE	PROVING	RANK'D	REPAIRER
PLOUGH'D	PRECEDENT	PROVISION	RANNE	REPEAT
PLOUGHING	PRECEDING	PROVISIONS	RANUIPH	REPEATING
PLOVER	PRECIPICE	PROYNE	RAPE	REPENTS
PLUCK	PRECIPITATED	PRUDENT	RAP'D	REPLIDE
PLUCK'D	PREFERR'D	PSALMES	RAPHAEL	REPLYED
PLUCKING	PREJUDICE	PTOLEMEY	RAPINE	REPLYES
PLUMED	PRELATE	PUBLIC	RAPPS	REPORTS
PLUSH	PRENTISE	PUBLISHED	RAP'S	REPREHEND
PLUSHES	PREOCCUPY	PUFFE	RAPTURE	REPULSE
PLUTO	PREPARE	PUI'NEES	RARENESSE	REPUTES
PLUTO'S	PRESCIOUS	PUKES	RARER	REQUITE
PLYE	PRESCRIBE	PULLING	RASHNESSE	RE-SHINE
PO	PRESENTACION	PULLS	RATCLIFFE	RESIDE
POCKET	PRESENTED	PULPIT	RATE	RESIGN'D
POCKETS	PRESENTES	PULSE	RATED	RESIST
POCKETT	PRESENTLY	PUMPE	RATES	RESOLV'D
POCKIE	PRESERV'D	PUNCK	RATLING	RESORT
POEM'S	PRESIDENT	PUNISHMENTS	RATTLES	RESTETH
POET'	PRESIDENTS	PUPPET	RATTLING	RESTING
POINTED	PRESSE	PUR	RAVE	RESTITUTION
POISON	PRESSURE	PURBECK	RAVENOUS	RESTORED
POLAND	PRESUMES	PUR-BLINDE	RAVISHED	RESTS
POLICIE	PRETTIE	PURELY	RAV'LINS	RETAIN'D
POLISHT	PRETTY	PURGE	RAYL'ST	RETORNED
POLL	PREVAILE	PURGED	RAYN'D	RETRACT
POLLUTED	PREVARICATOR	PURGING	RAY'SD	RETRIBUTION
POLLUX	PREVENT	PURITIE	RAYSING	RETRIV'D
POLY	PREVENTED	PURLES	RAZ'D	RETYR'D
POLY-OLBYON	PRIAM'S	PURPLED	RAZING	REVEALED
POMPEY	PRICK	PURPLE-MATCHING	REACHING	REVELLS
POMPEY'S	PRICK'D	PURPOS'D	READING	REVENNUE
POMPILIUS	PRIESTS	PURPOSELY	RE-ADVANCE	REVERENT
POMPOUS	PRIMING	PURSEWINGE	REAP'D	REVERENTLY
PONDEROUS	PRIMIS	PUSIL	REARES	REVERSION
PONDS	PRINCIPALITIES	PUSSE	REARE-SUPPERS	REVIVE
POOLY'	PRISE	PUTRID	REARING	REVIV'D
POPE	PRIS'D	PYGMY	REASON'	REVIVING
POPENHEIM	PRIVIE	PYRACMON'S	REBUKE	REVOLT
POPERIE	PRIVIES	PYRAMEDE	RECALL	REWARD'
POPES	PRIVILEDGE	PYRAMIDE	RECEIVED	REWARDE
POPES-HEAD-ALLEY	PROCEEDES	PYRENE	RECELEBRATES	REWARDED
POPLAR	PROCEEDING	PYTHIAS	RECEPTION	REWARDING
POPPIE	PROCESSE	PYTHIUS	RECITED	REWARD'S
POPPY	PROCESSION	QUADRIVIALL	RECITING	REYNES
POPULARITIE	PROCLAMATION	QUAINT	RECK'NED	RHAPSODY
PORCHES	PROCURE	QUAKE	RECK'NING	RHEINE
PORC'LANE	PRODIGALLY	QUALITIE	RECORDED	RHETIA
PORING	PRODIGIE	QUALITIES	RECOVERED	RHINE
PORTA	PRODIGIOUSLY	QUARREL	RECOVERY	RHINOCEROTES
PORTERS	PROFANE	QUARRELLS	RECTIFIE	RHONE
PORTING	PROFESSED	QUARRELS	RECTIFIED	RHYTHM
PORTIONS	PROFESSETH	QUARRIE	REDEEM'D	RICHE
PORTLAND	PROFFESSE	QUARRIES	REDEMPTION	RICHNESSE
POSSESSED	PROFFITT	QUARTER-FACE	REDOUBT	RID
POST	PROFICIENCIE	QUARTERS	REDUICTS	RIDDLING
POSTES	PROFITABLE	QUICKE	REED	RIDETH
POSTS	PROFITT	QUICKEST	REEDS	RIDICULOUS
'POTHECARIE	PROGNE	QUICKEST-SIGHTED	REEKING	RIDWAYES
	PROJECT	QUICKLY'	REFINE	RIFE
	PROLOGUE	QUICKNING	REFLECTION	RIFFLE
	PROLUDIUM	QUICKSILVER	REFORME	RIGHTEOUSNESSE

RIGHT-LEARNED	SALLADE	SEER	SHREDS	SOFTNESSES
RIGHTLY	SALLY	SEINE	SHREWSBURY	SOILE
RIGOUR	SALUST	SEISE	SHRINE	SOLDIER
RIMEE'S	SALVATION	SEISIN	SHRIN'D	SOLDIERIE
RI'MES	SANCTIFIER	SEIZE	SHROWDES	SOLEMNLY
RIMING	SANGUINE	SEIZ'D	SHUNNES	SOLID
RIOTING	SANS	SELDENS	SHUTS	SOLIDE
RIOTS	SAPIENCE	SELFE-DIVIDED	SHUTTER	SOLLEN
RIP	SAPPHO	SELFE-FAME	SICKNES	SOLOECISME
RIPENED	SARDANE	SELINIS	SIDED	SOLONS
RIP'NED	SARDUS	'SELL	SIDNEY	SOLS
RITE	SARUM'S	SELLING	SIEGE	SOME-THING
RITELY	SATHAN	SEMI	SIGH'D	SOMETYMES
RITHME	SATURNE'S	SEMI-GOD	SIGHES	SOME-WHERE
RITHMES	SATURNES	SENSUALL	SIGHTED	SOMMER
RIVALS	SATURNIAS	SENTINELL	SIGHTES	SOMMER-NIGHTS
ROAR	SATYRICALL	SENT'ST	SIGNES	SOMWHAT
ROAVE	SAUCE	SEPULCHER'D	SILENUS	SONGE
ROAVES	SAUT	SEPULCHRES	SILKEN	SONGSTER
ROBBERY	SAVER	SERAPHICK	SILLERIES	SONGSTERS
ROBBING	SAVING	SERAPHIM	SIMPLES	SONNETS
ROED	SAVING-HONOUR	SERENES	SIMPIESSE	SOON
ROBES	SAVIOURS	SERENITIE	SIMPLICITY	SOONEST
ROCKETS	SAVOY	SERMON	SIMPLY	SOOTE
ROCKIE	SAWE	SERMONEERES	SIN'	SOOTH
ROCKS	SAW'ST	SERPENT	SINGE	SOOTHING
ROE'S	SAYING	SERVES	SINKES	SOP
ROGUES	SAYLE	SERVICEABLE	SINKETH	SOPE
ROLANDS	SAYLES	SERVICES	SINNE'	SOPE-BOYLER
ROLLS	SAY'S	SERVILE	SINNE'S	SOPHOCLES
ROMANS	SAYST	SERVING-MAN	SIN'S	SORES
RONSART	SAYTH	SERVING-WOMAN	SIPP	SORIE
ROOFES	SCAB	SEVEN-TONGU'D	SIPT	SORRELL
ROOB	SCABBED	SEVERS	SIRENAS	SORTS
ROCIES	SCABBERD	SEV'RALL	SIRRUP	SORY
ROSCIUS	SCABBES	SEW'D	SIS	SOSII
ROSIE-CROSSE	SCALDING	SEY'D	SISTER-TUNES	SO'T
ROSTED	SCAN	SHADDOW	SIXE-PAC'D	SOUGH
ROT	SCANDERONE	SHADIE	SIXES	SOULDIER-LIKE
ROTTEINBERG	SCANDERCONE	SHAKES	SIX-PENCE	SOUND
ROTTEN	SCAN'D	SHAKESPEARES	SIXTEENTH	SOUNDE
ROULE	SCANTED	SHAL	SIXTIETH	SOUNDED
ROUNDE	SCAR	SHAMEFAC'D	SKARFE	SOUNDER
ROUTES	SCARF	SHAMEFAC'DNESSE	SKEUOPOIOS	SOUNDEST
ROUTS	SCARLET-LIKE	SHAMEFASTNESSE	SKINKERS	SOUNDLESSE
ROVE	SCARRES	SHAMEFULL	SKINS	SOURCES
ROVINGE	SCENT	SHAMES	SKIP	SOVERAIGNTIE
ROW	SCEPTER	SHAPE	SKIPPING	SOV'RAIGNE
ROWAELE	SCEPTERS	SHAP'D	SKY	SOW'D
ROW-HAMPTON	SCEPTRED	SHARPER	SKYE	SO'XCEED
ROWLE	SCHELDT	SHARPLYE	SLACKE	SPACES
ROWTE	SCHOOL	SHE'	SLANDERERS	SPAINES
ROYAL	SCHOOLEMEN	SHEAFE	SLANDERS	SPAKE
ROYES	SCISARS	SHEARES	SLAUGHTERS	SPANGLED
RUB	SCOFFER	SHEATH	SLAVES	SPARCLE
RUDDY	SCOFFING	SHEDS	SLAY	SPAR'D
RUDENESSE	SCOLD	SHEEP'ERDS	SLEEPING	SPARKLE
RUDEST	SCOLDS	SHEEPES	SLEIGHT	SPARROWES
RUE	SCORES	SHEEPES-SKIN	SLID	SPARTANS
RU'DE	SCORN'D	SHEERES	SLIDE	SPAWNE
RUFFES	SCORNES	SHEETES	SLIDES	SPEAKER
RUIN'D	SCORNST	SHE'HATH	SLIDING	SPEAKS
RULES	SCOURGE	SHEILD	SLIE	SPEAK'ST
RUL'ST	SCRATCHING	SHELFE	SLIGHTLY	SPECIALLY
RUMNEY	SCRIVENER	SHELVES	SLIGHTS	SPECIES
RUMOR	SCULLION	SHEPHEARDS	SLIP	SPECKLED
RUMOR'D	SCULPTURE	SHEWEN	SLIP'D	SPECTACLE
RUNG	SCURFE	SHEW'N	SLIPPER	SPELL
RUSH	SCURRILE	SHEW'S	SLIPPERY	SPENSER
RUST	SCURRILITIE	SHEWS	SLIPS	SPENSER'S
RUTH	SCUTCHEONS	SHEW'ST	SLOWER	SPHAERE
RUTTER	SCYLLA	SH'HATH	SLYDING	SPHERE
RYMING	SE	SHIELD	SMALL-TIMBRED	SPICERIE
RYOTS	SEALING	SHILTER	SMELLING	SPIDE
S	SEARE	SHIETER-HUISSEN	SMELT	SPI'D
SABINES	SEAS'NING	SHIFTING	SMIL'ST	SPIEGLE
SACK	SEASON'D	SHIFTS	SMITHS	SPIGHTS
SACKCLOTH	SEASONING	SHIN'ST	SMOOTHER	SPILT
SACK'T	SEATES	SHIPPING	SMUTCH'D	SPIN
SACKVILE	SEATS	SHITE	SNAKIE	SPINDLE
SACVILE	SEAVEN-FOLD	SHITTEN	SNATCH	SPINNE
SADDEST	SECONDED	SHONE	SNATCHT	SPINOLA
SADLED	SECRECIE	SHOONE	SNEAKING	SPIRE
SAFETIES	SECRETARIE	SHOOTE	SNORTS	SPIRITED
SAGUNTUM	SECTS	SHOPP	SNOUT	SPIRRITS
SAILES	SECURED	SHOP-PHILOSOPHY	SOAP	SPIT
SAIST	SECURER	SHORES	SOARES	SPITTLE
SAI'ST	SECUREST	SHORTEST	SOCK	SPITTLES
SAKES	SEED-PLOT	SHORT-LEG'D	SOCKES	SPONGE
SALE	SEEDS	SHORTLY	SOCKET	SPOONE
SALIAN	SEEKS	SHOT-FREE	SOCKS	SPORTED
SALISBURY	SEELIEST	SHOUTE	SOCRATICK	SPORTING
	SEEM	SHOUTS	SODAINE	SPORTIVE
	SEEMING	SHOWRES	SODAYNE	SPOTLESSE
	SEEN	SHOW'ST	SOFTLY	SPOUSED

SPOYLED
SPOYLING
SPREADING
SPRED
SPRIGGE
SPRIGHTFULL
SPRIGHTLY
SPRINGING
SPROUTINGE
SPRUNG
SPUE
SPUNGE
SPUNGE-LIKE
SPUR
SPURRES
SPYES
SQUEAKE
SQUEMISH
'SSAYD
'SSAYES
STAG
STAGES
STAGIRITE
STAID
STAINE
STAIN'D
STAIRE
STAIRES
STALE
STALKE
STALKETH
STALLION
STALLS
STAMP'D
STANDARDS
STANLEY
STARCH
STAR-CHAMBER
STARKE
STARRY
STARTE
STARTS
STARVE
STARVELING
STATED
STATELY
STATESMAN
STATES-MAN
STATES-MANS
STATES-MEN
STATESMEN
STATISTS
STATUARIES
STATUTE
STAY
STAYRE
STED'S
STEEMES
STEEMING
STELLA
STEM
STERNE
STEROPES
STEW
STEWARDS
STICK
STICKE
STICKING
STICKS
STIL
STILDE
STILES
STILL-SCALDING
STILTS
STINCK
STINGS
STINKARDS
STINKETH
STIR
STIRD'ST
STIRR'D
STIRRER
STITCHERS
STITCHERS-TO
STOCKE
STOCKS
STOCKT
STOLE
STOMACKS
STONIE
STOOD'ST
STOOP'D

STOOPING
STORE-HOUSE
STOUPES
STOUP'ST
STRADLING
STRAIGHTNED
STRAIT
STRAITE
STRAITS
STRATAGEM
STRATAGEME
STRAW-BERRIES
STRAWE
STRAY
STRAYN'D
STRAYNES
STREAME
STREET-BORNE
STREIGHTNED
STREIGHTS
STRETCH'D
STREW
STRICTER
STRIDE
STRIKES
STRIP
STRIPES
STRIPT
STRIVES
STRIV'ST
STROAK'D
STROAKT
STROKE
STROKEN
STROKES
STRONGE
STRONGER
STRONGEST
STRONGLY
STROW
STRUGGLED
STRUMPET
STRUNG
STRUT
STUART
STUBBORNE
STUBBORNNESSE
STUCK
STUCKE
STUDIE'
STUDIE'A
STUDYED
STUDYING
STUFF
STUFF'D
STUMBLE
STUNKE
STYGIAN
SUBLIMED
SUBSTRACT
SUBTILL
SUBTILTIE
SUBTILTY
SUBT'LEST
SUBTILEST
SUBTLY
SUCCEEDED
SUCCESSE
SUCCOURING
SUCK
SUCKT
SUDDAYNE
SUDDEN
SUFFERED
SUFFERERS
SUFFOLKE
SUFFRINGS
SUGAR
SUGGESTION
SULLEN
SULPHURE
SUN-BURNT-BLOWSE
SUNDRED
SUNDRIE
SUNDRY
SUNKE
SUN-LIGHT
SUNNE-HER
SUNNES
SUN'S
SUPERCILIOUS
SUPERFICIES
SUPERFLUOUS
SUPERSTITION
SUPP'D

SUPPLANT
SUPPLE
SUPPLIES
SUPPLY'D
SUPPORTERS
SUPPORTETH
SUPPOSITORIES
SUPREME
SURCOATES
SURETIES
SURGE
SURGEON
SURGEONS
SURLY
SURLY'S
SURNAMES
SURPASSE
SURPRIZ'D
SURROUNDING
SURSHIP
SURVIVE
SURVIVING
SUSAN
SUSANNA
SUSPENCE
SUSPENDED
SUSTAINES
SUTCLIFFE
SUTED
SUTES
SUTOR
SWAGGERING
SWAID
SWAINE
SWALLOW
SWALLOW'D
SWAMME
SWAN'
SWANNE
SWANNES
SWAN'S
SWARE
SWARTHIE
SWAYD
SWAYE
SWAYES
SWAYNES
SWEAR'ST
SWEATE
SWEATES
SWEDEN
SWEETER
SWEET-MEATS
SWEETNING
SWEET'S
SWEET-WOOD
SWELD
SWELL'D
SWELLETH
SWERVE
SWIFTNESSE
SWIFT-PAC'T
SWIMMING
SWOLNE
SWOM
SWOOPING
SWORE
SWORNE
SWOUNE
SWYNNERTON
SYBIL
SYDNEY'S
SYDNYES
SYLLAB'E
SYLVANUS
SYLVESTER
SYM
SYMBOLES
SYMETRY
SYMMETRIE
SYNNS
SYNONIMA
SYRUP
T'A
TABACCO-LIKE
T'ACCUSE
TACTICKES
T'ADMIRE
T'ADORE
TAGDE
TAGUS
TAILOR
TAINT
TAKEINGE
TALCK

TALK
TALKE
TALK'D
T'ALL
T'ALLEDGE
TALLER
T'ALLOW
TALMUD
T'AMEND
TAMISIS
TA'NE
TAPER
TAPP
T'AQUIT
TARDIE
TARRIE
TART
TASQUE
T'ASSIST
TASTER
TASTETH
TASTING
T'ATTIRE
TAVERNE
TAXETH
TAYLE
TEACHER
TEARE
TEARES
TEARS
TEETH
T'EFFECT
TEIRCE
TELL'
TELLINE
TELLING
TELS
TEMPER
TEMPERATE
TEMPESTUOUS
TEMPLE
TEMPIES
TEMPTE
TENANTS
TENDRELLS
TENDRING
TENOR
TENT
TENTH
T'ENVY
TERENCE
TERGUM
TERMERS
TERRORS
T'ESCAPE
TESTIFIE
T'EXACT
T'EXCHANGE
T'EXPRESS
TEXT
T'EXTRACT
TEYNTED
TH'ACCOMPT
TH'ADVANTAGE
TH'ADVENTER
TH'AEMILIAN
TH'AETERNALL
TH'AFFAIRES
TH'AFFRIGHTED
TH'AMBITIOUS
THANK
THANK'D
THANKEFULL
THANKING
TH'ANTIQUE
TH'AONIAN
TH'APPROCHES
TH'ASCENT
TH'ASSEMBLY
TH'AUTHORS
THAWES
TH'BEST
TH'CALENDS
TH'EARE
TH'EARES
TH'EATING
THEATRE
THEBAN
THEBES
THEEFE
THE'ELIXIR
THEFT
THEIRE
TH'ELABORATE
TH'ELIXIR

THEME
THEM-SELVES
TH'ENAMOUR'D
TH'ENVY'D
THEOCRITUS
TH'EPILOGUE
THEREAT
THEREBY
THERFORE
TH'ESCAPE
THESEUS
THESPIA
THESPIAD'S
THESPIS
TH'ESPLANDIANS
TH'ETERNALL
THE'UN
THE'UN-USED
THEWES
TH'EXAMINING
TH'EXAMPLED
TH'EXPENCE
THEY'ARE
THEY'AVE
THEY'D
THEY'HAVE
THEY'OFFENDERS
TH'GODS
TH'HARD
TH'HOW
THICKE
TH'IDALIAN
THIGH
TH'IGNOBLE
TH'ILL
T'HIMSELFE
THINCKING
THINGE
THINGES
TH'INGRATEFULL
THINKS
TH'INSCRIPTION
TH'INTENT
TH'INTERPRETERS
TH'IONIAN
THIRSTIE
THIRSTY
THIRTEENE
THIRTY
THIS'
THIS'S
TH'ITALIAN
THO'
THO
TH'OBSCENE
TH'OBSERVING
TH'OFTEN
TH'ONE
TH'OPINION
THORNY
THOROUGH-FARE
THOROUGHLIE
THOROW
THO'
THOUGHE
THOUGHT'ST
THOU'HAST
THOU'LDST
THO'WERT
TH'OYLE
THRACE
THRACIAN
THRALL
THREAD
THREAT'
THREAT
THREATS
THREDS
THRIFTYE
THRISE
THRIV'D
THRIVES
THRIVING
THROAT
THROATE
THRONES
THRONGE
THROTES
THROUGHLY
THROW'
THROWE
THROWES
THROW'T
THRUST
THRUSTS

-1- (CONT.)

THULE
THUMBE
THUM'S
TH'UNBEARDED
TH'UNCERTAINTY
THUNDER-STROKEN
THUND'RING
THUNDRING
THURINE
TH'USURPED
THY'
THY'EPISTOLAR
THYESTES
THYNE
TIBER
TIBERTS
TIBULLUS
TICKLED
TICKLING
TICKLINGE
T'IDOLATRIE
TIE
TIED
TIER
TIES
TIGERS
TIKE
TILES
TILLS
TILLY
TILTING
TIMBRED
TIMBRELS
TIME'S
T'IMPRINT
T'INCREASE
T'INDITE
TINE
T'INFLICT
T'INHABIT
T'INHERIT
T'INSTRUCT
T'INVEIGH
TIRE
TIR'D
TIRE-MAN
TIRES
TISSUES
TITIAN
TITLE'
TITLE-LEAFE
TITLE'S
TOAST
TO'AVE
T'OBAY
T'OBEY
T'OBSERVE
T'OBTAINE
TOES
'TOFORE
TOIES
TOKEN
TOLERATION
TOMBS
TONGU'D
TOO'
TOO-MUCH
TOOTH'D
TOO'UNWIELDIE
TOPPS
TORCH
TORMENT
TORMENTED
TORN'D
TORNED
TORRENT
TORT'RING
TORTURERS
TOSSE
TOST
TOSTED
T'OTHER
TOTTER'D
TOUCHETH
TOUCHING
TOUCH'T
TOUGH
TOULD
T'OUR
TOURE
T'OUT
T'OUTLAST

T'OUT-STRIP
TOWARD
TOWN-BORN
TOWN-DITCH
TOWNE-CURS
TOWNS
TOWNS-MAN
TOWKES
TOWRING
TOY
TOYLES
TRACE
TRACKS
TRACT
TRADITIONS
TRADUCE
TRAINES
TRAMPLED
TRANCE
TRANSCENDING
TRANSFERRE
TRANSFORM'D
TRANSLATE
TRANSMIGRATED
TRANSMITT
TRANSPLANTED
TRAPPINGS
TRAPS
TRAVAILES
TRAVAYLES
TRAVELL'D
TRAVELLS
TREADES
TREADING
TREADS
TREASONS
TREBLE
TRECHEROUS
TREMBLES
TREMBLING
TRENT
TRESPASSE
TRESSES
TRIALL
TRIALS
TRI'D
TRIED
TRIMETER
TRIMETERS
TRINITY
TRIPLE
TRIPOLY
TRIPOS
TRIPST
TRISTRAMS
TRIUMPHALL
TRODEN
TROOPE
TROPICKS
'TROTH
TROUBLES
TROUP
TRUCH
TRUCH-MAN
TRUE-FILED
TRULL
TRULY-BELOV'D
TRULY-NOBLE
TRUMPE
TRUNDLING
TRUSS'D
TRUSTER
TRUSTING
TRUSTS
TRUTHES
TRYALS
TRYER
TUB
TUBS
TUILLERIES
TUMOR
TUMULTS
TUN
TURBOT
TURND
TURNERS
TURNS
TURNST
TURPINS
T'USHER
TUSKE
TUT
TWAS
TWEDES
TWENTIETH

TWENTI'TH
TWILIGHT
TWI-LIGHT
TWINS
TWIRLE
TWO-FOLD
TYBERS
TYE
TYES
TYGRES
TYKE
TYLTING
TYMES
TYMPANIES
TYNDARIDES
TYPE
TYRAN
TYRANNIE
TYRANNY
TYRANYE
TYRE-MAN
UDDERS
ULCERS
ULISSES
UNALTER'D
UN-APPEAS'D
UNAPTLY
UN-ARGUED
UN-ARMED
UN-AVOIDED
UNBEARDED
UN-BECOMING
UNBLEST
UN-BOUGHT
UNBOUGHT
UNBOUNDED
UNBROKE
UNCENSUR'D
UNCERTAINTY
UNCHASTE
UNCLEANNESSE
UN-COMMON
UNCONTROL'D
UNCOVERS
UNDER-CARVED
UNDER-HEARES
UNDERSTANDING
UNDERSTANDS
UNDERTAKES
UNDER-WOOD
UNDER-WOODS
UNEQUALL
UNFIT
UNFOLD
UNFORTUNATE
UNGRATEFULL
UN-HURT
UN-INFORM'D
UNITED
UNIVERSALL
UNIVERSARY
UNKIND
UNKINDE
UNLEARNED
UNLOCKE
UNLUCKIE
UNMAK'ST
UN-NAMED
UNNECESSARIE
UNPROFITABLE
UNPROFITING
UNPROV'D
UNPROVED
UNREPAIR'D
UNRESTS
UNSEASON'D
UNSHAKEN
UNSKILFULL
UNSOUNDER
UNSPOKEN
UN-SWEET
UN-TAUGHT
UNTHANKFULL
UNTHOUGHT
UNTHRIFTELY
UNTOUCH'D
UNTRAVELL'D
UNTWISTED
UNTYING
UNVULGAR
UN-WASTED
UNWEAVE
UN-WELCOME
UNWIELDIE
UNWONTED

UP-BEARE
UP-BRAID
UP-TOOKE
UPWARD
UPWARDS
URGES
URINE
URINOUS
US'D
USED
USHER
USHRING
USUALL
USURER'S
USURIE
USURPED
USURFING
UTTER
UTTERLY
UTTRING
UTT'RING
UVEDALE
UV'DALE
VAILE
VAIN
VAINE
VAL
VALIANTER
VALIANT'ST
VALLEYS
VALLIES
VAL-TELLINE
VALUATIONS
VALU'D
VALURE
VANE
VANITIE
VARIUS
VARY
VARYED
VEIL
VEINE
VENERABLE
VENERY
VENETIAN
VENTED
VENTUR'D
VENTURES
VERDURE
VERIEST
VERMILION
VERSER
VERT
VERTU'
VERTUE'ENFORME
VERTUOUSLY
VESTALL
VEXATION
VEXED
VEYNE
VIAM
VIANDS
VICTORIE
VICTRICE
VIES
VIEWD
VIEWE
VIEWERS
VIEWES
VIGILANCE
VILER
VILLE
VILLE-ROYES
VILLORS
VINDICATE
VINDICTIVE
VINTNERS
VIOLATES
VIOLENT
VIOLL
VIRGINITYE
VIRGIN-TRAINE
VIRGIN-TROUP
VIRGIN-WHITE
VISCOUNT
VISIT
VISOR
VITRUVIUS
VIZORS
VLUSHING
VOGUE
VOICES
VOIDS
VOLARY
VOLUMES

VOLUMINOUS
VOLUPTUOUS
VOTARY
VOTE
VOUCHES
VOWELLS
VOYC'T
VULCANALE
VULTURE
VULTURES
VYCE
WADE
WAGG
WAGGON
WAIGH
WAIST
WAIT
WAITE
WAITED
WAITER
WAITING
WAKEFULL
WAKERS
WALK
WAN
WAND
WANDRERS
WANE
WANTING
WANTON-WISE
WARBLETH
WARD
WARDEN
W'ARE
WARIE-DRIVEN
WARMING
WARNED
WARNING
WARR
WARRANT
WARWICK
WARY
WAS'
WASSALL
WAS'T
WASTE
WASTETH
WATCHES
WATCHFULL
WATCHMAN
WATER-CONDUITS
WATERING
WAVE
WAVES
WAXE
WAYE
WAYS
WAYTE
W'
WEAKER
WEAKEST
WEALTHIE
WEAR
WEARIED
WEARINESSE
WE'AVE
WEAVING
WEDDED
WEEDS
WEEKES
WEE'L
WEEPINGE
WEEVER
WEIGHTY
WELL
WELL-COMPASS'D
WELL-GRAC'D
WELL-GREAS'D
WELL-TRUSS'D
WEL-MADE
WEL-TAGDE
WEL-WROUGHT
WENCH
WEPT
WER'T
WEST-INDIAN
WESTMINSTER
WEST-PARTS
WEST-WINDS
WET
WETS
WHALE
WHALE-BONE
WHATSOEVER
WHEATEN

857

1097	A	4	APOLLO'S	5	BENEATH	5	BURNT
4	ABLE	13	APPEARE	3	BENEFITS	6	BURST
10	'BOUT	3	APPEARES	3	BENT	3	BUSIE
34	ABOUT	3	APPETITE	5	BESIDE	9	BUSINESSE
11	'BOVE	8	APPLAUSE	8	BESIDES	3	BUSKIN
22	ABOVE	3	APPLE	62	BEST	701	BUT
5	ABROAD	12	APPLY	11	BETRAY	4	BUY
6	ABSENCE	3	APPROACHES	53	BETTER	5	BUYES
11	ABUSE	3	APPROVE	11	BETWEENE	4	CAESAR
3	ACCEPT	6	ARCHITECT	3	BEYOND	49	CALL
4	ACCOMPT	3	ARDEN	11	BID	5	CALLING
3	ACCORDING	4	'RE	4	BIDS	9	CALLS
3	ACROSTICHS	280	ARE	3	BILBO	3	CALL'ST
24	ACT	4	ARGUE	3	BILL	5	CALME
3	ACTED	4	ARM'D	6	BIN	24	CAME
12	ACTION	4	ARMES	6	BIRD	221	CAN
15	ACTIONS	3	ARRIVE	36	BIRTH	41	CANNOT
7	ACTIVE	3	ARROW	11	BIRTH-DAY	26	CANST
14	ACTS	30	ART	9	BLACK	6	CAPTAINE
9	ADDE	3	ARTE	6	BLACKE	3	CAPTAINES
4	ADDING	4	ARTHUR	3	BLAME	5	CAPTAYNE
4	ADMIRATION	3	ARTLESSE	3	BLASPHEME	23	CARE
7	ADMIRE	34	ARTS	5	BLAZE	4	CARELESSE
3	ADMIRED	559	AS	9	BLESSE	7	CARES
5	ADORE	6	ASHAM'D	10	BLESSED	4	CAREW
10	ADVANCE	3	ASHES	4	BLESSING	5	CARRACT
4	ADVANC'D	26	ASKE	3	BLESSINGS	4	CARRIED
3	ADVANTAGE	5	ASK'D	14	BLEST	6	CARRY
3	ADVISE	4	ASKES	8	BLIND	3	CART
3	AETNA	6	ASPIRE	6	BLINDE	3	CARVE
4	AFFAIRES	3	ASSIGN'D	4	BLISSE	7	CARY
9	AFFECTION	274	AT	34	BLOOD	23	CAST
6	AFFECTIONS	3	ATTEMPTED	5	BLOT	7	CATCH
3	AFFORD	16	AUTHOR	9	BLOUD	3	CATO'S
4	AFFORDS	5	AUTHORITIE	7	BLUSH	6	'CAUSE
3	AFFRIGHT	9	AUTHORS	18	BOAST	43	CAUSE
6	AFRAID	5	AWAKE	4	BOATES	5	CAUSES
35	AFTER	33	AWAY	3	BODIES	3	CELEBRATE
38	AGAINE	3	A-WHILE	31	BODY	6	CELIA
16	'GAINST	6	AYDES	3	BODYES	10	CENSURE
31	AGAINST	4	AYME	14	BOLD	3	CENSURES
42	AGE	3	B'	7	BONES	5	CENTER
4	AGED	4	BABE	3	BOOK	4	CERTAINE
6	AGEN	6	BACCHUS	47	BOOKE	3	CESTON
3	AGREE	13	BACK	22	BOOKES	4	CHAINE
7	AIDE	15	BACKE	3	BOORD	3	CHAIRE
4	AIDED	4	BAD	4	BOOTE	9	CHAMBER
4	AIME	4	BALL	3	BORROW'D	23	CHANCE
11	ALAS	3	BALME	5	BOSOME	18	CHANGE
5	ALE	7	BAND	104	BOTH	7	CHANG'D
5	ALIKE	3	BANDS	13	BOUGHT	3	CHANGED
13	ALIVE	3	BANKE	3	BOUND	3	CHANGING
569	ALL	5	BARRE	6	BOUNDS	5	CHARACTER
3	ALLAY	6	BARREN	6	BOUNTIE	13	CHARGE
5	ALLOW	6	BASE	4	BOUNTIES	5	CHARIS
4	ALLOW'D	6	BAUD	3	BOWERS	3	CHARITIE
11	ALMOST	5	BAYES	4	BOX	25	CHARLES
32	ALONE	485	BE	10	BOY	9	CHARME
6	ALONG	4	BEARDS	5	BOYES	4	CHARMES
6	ALOUD	6	BEARES	20	BRAINE	11	CHAST
3	ALPHONSO	5	BEARING	10	BRAINES	6	CHASTE
3	ALSO	9	BEAST	3	BRANCHES	4	CHEARE
3	ALTAR	3	BEAT	3	BRAND	3	CHEATER
3	ALTARS	3	BEATING	5	BRASSE	3	CHERISH
12	ALTHOUGH	4	BEAUMONT	39	BRAVE	3	CHEV'RIL
12	ALWAYES	27	BEAUTIE	3	BRAVERY	7	CHIEFE
6	'M	9	BEAUTIES	3	BREACH	21	CHILD
66	AM	6	BEAUTY	7	BREAD	5	CHILDREN
3	AMBER	4	BECAME	16	BREAKE	4	CHIME
4	AMBITION	24	BECAUSE	22	BREATH	4	CHIN
7	AMBITIOUS	18	BECOME	13	BRED	5	CHOICE
3	AMISSE	6	BECOMES	4	BREED	5	CHOISE
12	AMONG	14	BED	9	BREST	4	CHOOSE
8	'MONGST	6	BEDFORD	3	BRESTS	3	CHOSEN
6	AMONGST	34	BEENE	5	BRETHREN	7	CHURCH
6	AMPLE	3	BEERE	3	BRICK	6	CHUSE
171	AN	48	BEFORE	8	BRIDE	12	CIRCLE
5	ANACREON	5	BEG	35	BRIGHT	4	CIRCLES
6	ANCESTORS	3	BEGAN	4	BRIGHTNESSE	7	CITIE
4	ANCIENT	4	BEGET	32	BRING	4	CITIZENS
30	&	9	BEGIN	8	BRINGS	4	CIVILL
2610	AND	5	BEGINNINGS	3	BRITAINE	5	CLAIME
9	ANGELS	4	BEGOT	5	BROAD	17	CLEARE
4	ANGER	3	BEGUN	6	BROKE	3	CLEAVE
10	ANGRY	6	BEHELD	5	BROKEN	4	CLEERE
21	ANOTHER	8	BEHIND	6	BROTHER	3	CLIENTS
4	ANOTHERS	13	BEHOLD	4	BROTHERS	14	CLOSE
3	ANSWER	4	BEHOLDS	35	BROUGHT	3	CLOS'D
3	ANSWER'D	57	BEING	3	BROWES	8	CLOTH
3	ANTIENT	11	BELEEVE	4	BUILD	11	CLOTHES
3	ANTIQUE	4	BELLS	8	BUILT	7	CLOUD
3	ANTIQUITIE	3	BELOW	4	BURGES	3	CLOUDES
70	ANY	14	BEN	4	BURIED	3	CLOWNE
3	APE	6	BEND	13	BURNE	4	CLOWNES
8	APOLLO	3	BENDS	3	BURNING	3	CLUB

Count	Word	Count	Word	Count	Word	Count	Word
4	COACH	5	DANCE	202	DOTH	4	ERROR
4	COAST	7	DANGER	19	DOUBT	4	ESSENCE
4	COATES	4	DANGERS	4	DOUBTFULL	4	ESTATE
3	COCK	32	DARE	3	DOVE	3	ESTEEME
6	COD	13	DARES	4	DOWNE	12	ETERNALL
10	COLD	4	DARING	3	DRAUGHT	5	ETERNITIE
4	COLOUR	13	DARKE	34	DRAW	4	EUROPE
7	COLOURS	6	DARKNESSE	5	DRAWES	59	EVER
75	COME	9	DAR'ST	18	DRAWNE	91	EVERY
14	COMES	12	DAUGHTER	7	DREAME	8	EVILL
6	COMFORT	6	DAUGHTERS	3	DREAMES	7	EV'RY
4	COMICK	3	DAUNCES	3	DRESSE	3	EXALTED
14	COMMAND	134	DAY	7	DRESSING	3	EXAMIN'D
4	COMMANDS	21	DAYES	7	DREST	18	EXAMPLE
6	COMMEND	24	DEAD	3	DREW	3	EXCEEDING
13	COMMING	11	DEARE	10	DRINKE	5	EXCELL
4	COMMISSION	3	DEARER	3	DRINKES	4	EXCELLENT
6	COMMIT	34	DEATH	4	DRIVEN	8	EXCEPT
4	COMMODITIE	5	DEBT	4	DRIVES	4	EXCUSE
23	COMMON	4	DEBTS	5	DROP	3	EXEMPT
3	COMMON-WEALTH	6	DECAY	3	DROPPING	5	EXERCISE
6	COMPANIE	3	DECAY'D	3	DROPS	9	EXPECT
4	COMPARISON	3	DECK	4	DROWNE	3	EXPECTED
3	COMPASSE	3	DECREED	3	DROWN'D	5	EXPENCE
4	CONCEALE	11	DEED	4	DRUM	9	EXPRESSE
3	CONCEAL'D	3	DEEDES	4	DRUMS	4	EXPREST
5	CONCEIPT	13	DEEDS	4	DRUNKE	28	EYE
5	CONCEIVE	3	DEEP	3	DRY	57	EYES
4	CONCEIV'D	8	DEEPE	11	DUE	8	FABLE
4	CONCLUDE	3	DEERE	3	DUES	3	FABLES
5	CONDEMNE	4	DEFENCE	16	DULL	47	FACE
3	CONDEMN'D	4	DEFEND	5	DUMBE	9	FACES
14	CONFESSE	5	DEGREE	21	DURST	5	FACT
3	CONQUER	4	DEGREES	7	DUST	4	FACTION
19	CONSCIENCE	4	DELAY	3	DUTCH	4	FACULTIE
3	CONSENT	17	DELIGHT	13	DWELL	5	FAILE
4	CONSPIRE	6	DELIGHTS	3	DY'D	7	FAINE
4	CONSUMPTION	3	DENIED	4	DYES	5	FAIN'D
6	CONTENT	3	DENY	8	DYING	3	FAIN'ST
3	CONTRACT	3	DEPART	65	EACH	67	FAIRE
3	CORPORALL	4	DESCENT	15	EARE	17	FAITH
4	CORYATE	5	DESCRIB'D	3	EARELY	7	FAITHFULL
3	COST	3	DESERT	17	EARLE	28	FALL
4	COTTON	6	DESERVE	7	EARLY	4	FALLING
123	COULD	4	DESERV'D	4	EARNEST	4	FALLS
3	COULD'ST	3	DESERVING	30	EARTH	27	FALSE
3	COUNSELL	9	DESIGNE	12	EASE	4	FALSHOOD
3	COUNTENANCE	3	DESIGN'D	3	EASIER	75	FAME
12	COUNTREY	22	DESIRE	6	EAT	3	FAM'D
6	COUNTRIES	4	DESIR'D	9	EATE	6	FAMES
51	COURT	5	DESIRES	3	EATEN	9	FAMOUS
3	COURTIER	3	DESPERATE	3	EATES	4	FANCIE
4	COURTLING	3	DESPIGHT	7	ECCHO	5	FARE
4	COURTS	5	DESTROY	3	EDMONDS	7	FAREWELL
5	COVER	4	DEVOURE	5	EDWARD	4	FARMER
4	COVETOUS	4	DEW	3	EFFECT	42	FARRE
3	CRACKE	5	DICE	31	EITHER	6	FARTHER
5	CRADLE	175	DID	4	ELDER	16	FASHION
6	CRAVE	7	DID'ST	12	ELEGIE	3	FASHION'D
5	CREATE	9	DIDST	4	ELIZABETH	3	FASHIONS
3	CREATES	20	DIE	7	ELOQUENCE	11	FAT
10	CREATURE	4	DIFFER	36	ELSE	32	FATE
9	CREDIT	6	DIFFERENCE	3	ELSE-WHERE	12	FATES
3	CREEPE	7	DIGBY	4	EMBRACE	24	FATHER
5	CRIE	6	DINE	3	EMBRAC'D	18	FATHERS
3	CRIES	8	DIS	4	EMPTIE	9	FAULT
6	CRIME	4	DISCERNING	4	EMULATE	6	FAULTS
9	CRIMES	5	DISCLOSE	7	ENCREASE	7	FAVOUR
35	CROWNE	6	DISCOURSE	31	END	4	FAVOURS
10	CROWN'D	3	DISCOURSES	16	ENDS	4	FAYRE
3	CROWNED	4	DISDAINE	3	ENEMIE	48	FEARE
4	CRUELL	15	DISEASE	2	ENGINES	3	FEAR'D
17	CRY	7	DISEASES	8	ENGLAND	14	FEARES
12	CRY'D	3	DISPLAY	14	ENGLISH	20	FEAST
10	CRYES	3	DISPOSURE	12	ENJOY	5	FEASTS
7	CUNNING	4	DISTANCE	3	ENJOY'D	6	FEATHERS
6	CUP	3	DISTILL	23	ENOUGH	7	FEATURE
4	CUPID	4	DITCH	3	ENSIGNE	7	FED
4	CUPIDS	3	DIVERS	3	ENSIGNES	7	FEED
5	CUPS	3	DIVIDE	3	ENTER	15	FEELE
12	CURE	20	DIVINE	22	ENVIE	3	FEELES
4	CURES	3	DO'	3	ENVI'D	3	FEET
9	CURIOUS	18	DO	12	ENVIOUS	3	FEETE
3	CURSE	230	DOE	12	ENVY	3	FELLOW
4	CURST	4	DOG	3	EPHESUS	4	FELT
5	CUSTOME	5	DOGS	28	EPIGRAM	15	FEW
3	CUSTOMES	5	DOING	4	EPIGRAMME	12	FIELD
14	CUT	3	DON	7	EPIGRAMMES	6	FIELDS
3	CYNTHIA	53	DONE	13	EPISTLE	4	FIERCE
6	'D	11	DOO	10	EPITAPH	3	FIFTIE
3	DAIES	3	DOORE	5	EPODE	8	FIGHT
5	DAILY	4	DORE	11	EQUALL	3	FIGURE
3	DAINTIE	5	DO'S	24	ERE'	8	FILL
7	DAME	5	DO'ST	20	ERE	34	FIND
4	DAMES	32	DOST	6	ERRE	11	FINDE

#	Word	#	Word	#	Word	#	Word
3	FINDING	5	FRIENDSHIPS	6	GROOME	8	HERE'S
15	FINE	3	FRINDSHIPP	15	GROUND	4	HERMES
5	FINER	226	FROM	6	GROUNDS	5	HERS
50	FIRE	6	FRONT	4	GROVE	3	HID
5	FIRES	3	FROWNE	3	GROVES	3	HIEROME
4	FIRE-WORKES	6	FRUIT	20	GROW	39	HIGH
3	FIRME	8	FRUITFULL	5	GROWES	5	HIGHER
99	FIRST	33	FULL	4	GROWING	7	HILL
3	FIRST-BORNE	8	FURIE	20	GROWNE	4	HILL-FOOT
3	FIRST-FRUITS	3	FURIES	3	GROYNE	4	HILLS
4	FISH	4	FURY	3	GRUDGE	190	HIM
5	FIT	3	FUTURE	3	GRUTCH	33	HIMSELFE
3	FITS	17	GAINE	3	GUARD	10	HIR
4	FITTER	5	GAIN'D	9	GUEST	3	HIRE
3	FITTING	3	GALLANTS	6	GUESTS	614	HIS
10	FIVE	5	GAME	3	GUIDES	4	HISTORIE
5	FIX'D	3	GAMES	9	GUILTIE	13	HIT
15	FLAME	3	GAPING	3	GUMMES	3	HOGS
5	FLAMES	6	GARDEN	5	GUNS	24	HOLD
3	FLAT	5	GARLAND	171	HAD	3	HOLDS
3	FLATTERIE	4	GATHER	4	HAD'ST	26	HOLY
3	FLATTERIES	5	GATHER'D	7	HADST	6	HOLY-DAY
3	FLATT'RY	3	GATHERING	5	HAILE	25	HOME
9	FLED	21	GAVE	13	HAIRE	8	HOMER
4	FLEE	3	GAV'ST	20	HALFE	3	HOMERS
14	FLESH	5	GENERALL	11	HALL	12	HONEST
3	FLESHES	3	GENEROUS	42	HAND	9	HONOR
13	FLIE	10	GENIUS	5	HANDLE	7	HONORS
12	FLIGHT	12	GENTLE	13	HANDS	32	HONOUR
5	FLOOD	6	GENTLER	8	HANG	3	HONOURABLE
7	FLOODS	5	GENTRIE	3	HANGINGS	6	HONOUR'D
3	FLOORE	3	GESTURE	7	HAPPIE	10	HONOURS
3	FLOUD	24	GET	3	HAPPIER	3	HOOFE
10	FLOW	7	GETS	24	HAPPY	3	HOP
6	FLOWER	5	GHOST	11	HARD	32	HOPE
14	FLOWERS	3	GHOSTS	3	HARDLY	11	HOPES
4	FLOWES	11	GIFT	3	HARE	13	HORACE
3	FLOWING	8	GILES	4	HARMES	3	HORNE
3	FLYE	4	GIRT	3	HARMONIE	4	HORROUR
5	FLYING	75	GIVE	4	HARMONY	23	HORSE
9	FOES	20	GIVEN	5	HARPE	4	HORSES
5	FOLD	13	GIVES	3	HARTH	10	HOT
5	FOLKE	5	GIVING	4	HARVEST	11	HOURE
3	FOLLIES	37	GLAD	8	HAS	3	HOURELY
23	FOLLOW	12	GLADNESSE	3	HAST	13	HOURES
5	FOLLY	14	GLASSE	6	HASTE	19	HOUSE
3	FOOD	13	GLORIE	4	HAT	3	HOUSE-HOLD
15	FOOLE	8	GLORIES	9	HATE	3	HOUSES
13	FOOLES	11	GLORIOUS	134	HATH	5	HOUSHOLD
15	FOOT	12	GLORY	3	HATRED	144	HOW
3	FOOTE	6	GO	3	'AVE	3	HOWE
491	FOR	85	GOD	3	HA'	8	HUMANITIE
4	FORBEARE	4	GOD-HEAD	327	HAVE	7	HUMBLE
4	FORBID	3	GOD-LIKE	17	HAVING	12	HUNDRED
17	FORCE	8	GODS	4	HAZARD	4	HUNGRY
3	FORC'D	59	GOE	5	H'	5	HUNTING
3	FORC'T	12	GOES	7	HE'	3	HUNTS
3	FORE	5	GOING	438	HE	11	HURT
5	FOREHEAD	19	GOLD	29	HEAD	10	HUSBAND
3	FORGE	9	GOLDEN	8	HEADS	7	HUSBANDS
4	FORGET	28	GONE	14	HEALTH	31	I'
10	FORGIVE	140	GOOD	5	HEAPE	3	I
3	FORGIVEN	11	GOODNESSE	3	HEAP'D	3	I'AM
3	FORGOT	3	GOODYERE	40	HEARE	3	IDOLATRIE
25	FORME	3	GOOSE	3	HEARES	3	IF'
5	FORM'D	4	GO'ST	3	HEARING	278	IF
6	FORMER	26	GOT	28	HEART	3	IF'T
10	FORMES	11	GOWNE	13	HEARTS	12	IGNORANCE
3	FORSAKE	61	GRACE	9	HEAT	7	IGNORANT
4	FORT	8	GRACES	4	HEATE	3	I'HAVE
77	FORTH	3	GRACIOUS	33	HEAVEN	12	I'LE
3	FORTIE	11	GRAND	7	HEAVENS	38	ILL
36	FORTUNE	3	GRAND-CHILD	3	HEAV'N	6	I'M
6	FORTUNES	6	GRANT	24	HEE'	3	IMITATE
7	FOULE	3	GRAPES	65	HEE	8	IMMORTALL
26	FOUND	3	GRASSE	3	HEE'D	3	IMPORTUNE
3	FOUNTAINES	3	GRATEFULL	3	HEE'LL	3	IMPREST
4	FOURE	3	GRATIOUS	16	HEE'S	3	IMPUTATION
4	FOURTH	3	GRATITUDE	14	HEIGHT	9	I'
3	FRAILE	5	GRATULATE	6	HEIRE	1012	IN
3	FRAILTIE	21	GRAVE	4	HEIRES	11	INCREASE
10	FRAME	163	GREAT	4	HELD	10	INDEED
9	FRANCE	3	GREATE	10	HELL	3	INFANTS
58	FREE	14	GREATER	15	HELPE	3	INFINITE
7	FREEDOME	7	GREATEST	22	HENCE	4	INFORME
4	FREELY	14	GREATNESSE	3	HENCE-FORTH	4	INHERIT
7	FREIND	3	GRECIAN	3	HENCEFORTH	3	INHERITANCE
3	FREINDS	3	GREECE	6	HENRY	8	INIGO
14	FRENCH	4	GREEDIE	341	HER	3	INKE
4	FREQUENT	9	GREEKE	3	HERALD	6	INNOCENCE
15	FRESH	10	GREENE	3	HERALDS	3	INNOCENT
59	FRIEND	15	GREW	6	HERCULES	3	INQUIRIE
3	FRIENDLY	7	GRIEFE	8	HERE'	3	INSCRIPTION
40	FRIENDS	5	GRIEVE	96	HERE	6	INSTRUCT
21	FRIENDSHIP	4	GRIEV'D	3	HEREAFTER	5	INTELLIGENCE

48	INTO	30	LADY	3	LOUDE	3	MID
4	INVADE	5	LADYES	163	LOVE	3	MIDDLE
4	INVENT	10	LAID	19	LOV'D	5	MIDST
3	INVENTION	4	LAKE	8	LOVELY	3	MIGHTST
3	INVITE	4	LAME	8	LOVER	6	MIGHTY
3	INVITING	4	LANCE	8	LOVERS	3	MILD
3	INWARD	31	LAND	3	LOVE'S	3	MILE
4	IRE	3	LANDS	35	LOVES	6	MILKE
3	IRON	5	LANE	5	LOVING	5	MILL
126	'S	19	LANGUAGE	9	LOW	45	MIND
7	IS'	18	LARGE	5	LOWD	10	MINDE
474	IS	15	LAST	4	'LT	11	MINDS
3	ISLE	5	LASTING	4	LUCAN	3	MINERVA
15	ISSUE	31	LATE	4	LUCIUS	3	MIRA
7	IS'T	3	LATELY	3	LUCKLESSE	3	MIRACLE
45	'T	3	LATINE	3	LUCKS	9	MIRTH
549	IT	3	LATTER	7	LUCY	5	MISERIES
3	ITALY	11	LAUGH	4	LUNGS	6	MISSE
3	ITCH	10	LAUGHTER	9	LUST	3	MISTAKE
9	ITEM	14	LAW	4	LUTE	4	MISTRESSE
4	I'THE	22	LAWES	4	LYDIA	11	MISTRIS
4	IT'S	3	LAWFULL	7	LYES	5	MIXE
4	IVORY	4	LAWYER	3	LYKE	5	MIXT
4	IVY	5	'LD	5	LYNE	4	MODEST
14	JAMES	14	'LE	8	LYRE	5	MODESTIE
3	JANE	10	LEAD	4	M	3	MODESTLY
7	JEALOUS	3	LEADES	8	MAD	3	MOLEST
4	JEALOUSIE	6	LEAPE	4	MADAM	3	MONARCHS
7	JEST	3	LEAP'D	11	MADAME	16	MONEY
4	JESTS	9	LEARNE	4	MADDE	3	MONEYS
13	JOHN	9	LEARN'D	103	MADE	3	MONSTER
8	JONE	18	LEARNED	5	MAD'ST	3	MONTH
3	JONES	3	LEARNING	5	MAID	3	MOODES
5	JONSON	17	LEAVE	6	MAINE	8	MOONE
4	JOURNEY	3	LEESE	3	MAINTAIN'D	3	MOONES
3	JOVE	3	LEGS	3	MAINTAYNE	247	MORE
3	JOVES	8	LEND	8	MAIST	4	MORISON
22	JOY	5	LENGTH	7	MAJESTIE	4	MORNE
8	JOYES	15	LENT	182	MAKE	10	MORNING
3	JOYFULL	53	LESSE	5	MAKER	3	MORTALL
3	JOYNTS	5	LESSER	59	MAKES	83	MOST
34	JUDGE	111	LET	13	MAKING	14	MOTHER
3	JUDG'D	3	LETCHERIE	9	MAK'ST	8	MOTHERS
22	JUDGEMENT	4	LETS	5	MALICE	8	MOTION
4	JUDGEMENTS	5	LETTER	154	MAN	3	MOUNTAINE
3	JUDGMENT	10	LETTERS	8	MAN-KIND	3	MOUNTED
3	JUNE	4	LETTING	7	MANKIND	3	MOUTH
3	JUNO	4	LEWD	3	MANKINDE	4	MOUTHES
44	JUST	5	LIBERTIE	6	MANLY	21	MOVE
14	JUSTICE	4	LICENCE	4	MANNER	6	MOV'D
3	JUSTIFIE	95	LIFE	28	MANNERS	15	MR
4	JUSTLY	3	LIFT	3	MAN'S	6	MRS
7	K	3	LIFTED	20	MANS	105	MUCH
4	KATE	4	LIGHT	56	MANY	4	MURDER
4	KEEP	3	LIGHTED	6	MARBLE	3	MURMURE
48	KEEPE	6	LIGHTER	8	MARIAGE	77	MUSE
9	KEEPES	3	LIGHTLY	16	MARKE	29	MUSES
6	KEEPING	8	LIGHTS	5	MARK'D	3	MUSICK
3	KEEPS	11	LIKE	3	MARKES	3	MUSICKE
4	KENELME	5	LILLIE	4	MARQUESS	5	MUSIQUE
22	KEPT	3	LILLIES	5	MARS	97	MUST
6	KILL	3	LIMBE	4	MARTIAL	3	MUTE
3	KIN	17	LINE	3	MARTYRS	423	MY
20	KIND	16	LINES	3	MARVAILES	7	MYSTERIE
6	KINDE	3	LIP	14	MARY	7	MYSTERIES
3	KINDLED	6	LIPS	3	MASCULINE	3	NAILES
54	KING	24	LITTLE	22	MASTER	7	NAKED
4	KINGDOMES	3	LIVD	7	MASTERS	92	NAME
19	KINGS	48	LIVE	8	MATCH	10	NAM'D
19	KISSE	11	LIV'D	21	MATTER	29	NAMES
18	KNEW	22	LIVES	9	MAY	3	NAMING
11	KNIGHT	8	LIVING	3	MAYST	7	NARROW
3	KNIGHT-HOOD	3	LIV'ST	209	ME	5	NATION
3	KNIGHTS	15	'LL	7	MEALE	7	NATIONS
5	KNIT	3	LO	5	MEANES	44	NATURE
3	KNITS	3	LOAD	19	MEANT	11	NATURES
5	KNOT	3	LOATH	7	MEASURE	24	NAY
3	KNOTS	3	LODGE	3	MEASUR'D	3	NEARE
3	KNOTTIE	3	LOE	8	MEATE	3	NEAT
139	KNOW	5	LOFTIE	3	MEDDLE	4	NECESSITIE
3	KNOWE	3	LONDON	3	MEDEA	7	NECK
26	KNOWES	9	LONGER	35	MEE	5	NECTAR
6	KNOWING	54	LOOKE	17	MEERE	23	NEED
13	KNOWLEDGE	7	LOOK'D	3	MEET	8	NEEDS
34	KNOWNE	15	LOOKES	3	MEETING	24	NEITHER
3	KNOW'ST	6	LOOKING	5	MEETS	5	NEPHEWES
5	L	3	LOOK'ST	7	MEMORIE	17	NE'RE
8	LABOUR	6	LOOSE	141	MEN	5	NEST
5	LABOUR'D	53	LORD	7	MEND	3	NET
9	LABOURS	8	LORDS	22	MENS	4	NETS
7	LACE	8	LOSE	3	MERCHANT	61	NEVER
5	LACK	17	LOSSE	3	MERCURY	69	NEW
4	LADEN	29	LOST	14	MERIT	3	NEWCASTLE
4	LADIE	3	LOTH	9	MERRY	13	NEWES
8	LADIES	8	LOUD	14	MET	21	NEXT

4 NIGH
32 NIGHT
7 NIGHTS
5 NINE
279 NO
3 NOBILITIE
45 NOBLE
3 NOBLER
13 NOBLEST
3 NOBLY
10 NOE
8 NOISE
51 NONE
4 NOONE
191 NOR
9 NOSE
595 NOT
11 NOTE
3 NOTED
10 NOTES
39 NOTHING
16 NOUGHT
3 NOW'
200 NOW
11 NOYSE
15 NUMBER
12 NUMBERS
3 NUMBRED
3 NUPTIALL
3 NUT
4 NYMPH
74 O
4 OATH
4 OBEY
6 OBJECT
5 OBJECTS
3 OBSCENE
3 OBSCURE
3 OBSERVE
3 ODCOMBE
3 ODDE
15 ODE
5 ODOUR
8 O'
1527 OF
21 OFF
10 OFFENCE
7 OFFEND
4 OFFENDED
4 OFFER
11 OFFICE
3 OFFICES
4 OFFRING
22 OFT
8 OFTEN
4 OFT-TIMES
73 OLD
3 ON'
56 ONCE
36 ONELY
35 ONLY
3 ON'T
10 OPEN
743 OR
3 ORBE
11 ORDER
6 O'RE
4 ORIGINALL
3 ORNAMENTS
6 ORPHEUS
4 O'THE
72 OTHER
27 OTHERS
3 OUNCES
217 OUR
10 OURS
162 OUT
4 OUT-LIVE
4 OUTWARD
23 OVER
21 OWE
3 OWES
93 OWNE
9 OYLE
3 PAGEANT
5 PAID
13 PAINE
6 PAINES
10 PAINT
10 PAINTED
9 PAINTER
3 PAINTING
12 PAIRE
7 PALLAS
6 PALME

13 PAPER
3 PAPERS
8 PARDON
10 PARENTS
3 PARIS
3 PARLIAMENT
28 PART
3 PARTING
3 PARTRICH
24 PARTS
7 PASSAGE
16 PASSE
10 PASSION
3 PASSIONS
17 PAST
6 PATHS
3 PATIENCE
4 PAULS
5 PAUSE
23 PAY
11 PAYES
30 PEACE
3 PEDIGREE
6 PEECE
4 PEECES
3 PEEPE
6 PEERES
3 PEERS
3 PEGASUS
11 PEN
4 PENSHURST
3 PENSION
9 PEOPLE
16 PERFECT
7 PERFECTION
7 PERHAPS
4 PERISH
3 PERSIAN
15 PERSON
5 PERSONS
3 PETTICOTE
3 PETULANT
3 PHEASANT
3 PHILIP
10 PHOEBUS
6 PHOENIX
8 PHRASE
12 PICTURE
16 PIECE
3 PIECES
3 PIERCE
4 PIES
9 PIETIE
3 PILES
3 PILLARS
4 PIOUS
4 PISO'S
3 PISSE
4 PITTIE
4 PITTY
51 PLACE
6 PLAC'D
9 PLACES
5 PLAGUE
4 PLAID
3 PLAINE
6 PLANT
4 PLANTED
5 PLATE
4 PLAUTUS
29 PLAY
12 PLAYES
4 PLAYING
7 PLAY-WRIGHT
15 PLEASE
10 PLEAS'D
12 PLEASURE
8 PLEASURES
3 PLENTIE
3 PLOT
3 PLY
5 POEME
6 POEMES
7 POEMS
4 POESIE
35 POET
3 POETIQUE
10 POETRIE
4 POETRY
31 POETS
5 POINT
3 POLISH'D
4 POLITIQUE
5 POMPE
3 POOR

39 POORE
3 PORT
3 PORTION
4 PORTS
4 POSSESSE
4 POSSEST
13 POSTERITIE
3 POSTURE
3 POT
10 POUND
3 POUR'D
3 POVERTIE
3 POWDER
25 POWER
16 POWERS
5 POX
13 PRACTISE
56 PRAISE
9 PRAIS'D
4 PRAISERS
11 PRAISES
16 PRAY
5 PRAYER
3 PRAYERS
4 PRAYSE
3 PREPAR'D
18 PRESENT
3 PRESERVE
3 PRESERVES
4 PREST
4 PRETEND
3 PRETIOUS
9 PRICE
15 PRIDE
4 PRIEST
9 PRIME
15 PRINCE
8 PRINCES
3 PRINT
8 PRIVATE
5 PRIZE
4 PROCLAIME
3 PRODUCE
5 PROFESSE
3 PROFESSING
7 PROFIT
3 PROFITS
6 PROMISE
3 PROMIS'D
3 PRONE
3 PROOFE
10 PROPER
4 PROPHANE
4 PROPORTION
4 PROSE
19 PROUD
3 PROULE
23 PROVE
5 PROV'D
4 PROVES
3 PROVIDE
7 PROVOKE
10 PUBLIKE
3 PUBLIQUE
5 PUBLISH
3 PUCELL
3 PULL
5 PUNISHMENT
16 PURE
3 PURG'D
4 PURPLE
3 PURPOSE
6 PURSE
4 PURSUE
35 PUT
8 PUTS
6 QUARRELL
3 QUARTER
4 QUEEN
14 QUEENE
5 QUESTION
3 QUESTION'D
4 QUICK
3 QUICKER
5 QUICKLY
4 QUIRE
7 QUIT
7 RACE
12 RAGE
4 RAIGNE
3 RAINE
16 RAISE
12 RAIS'D
3 RAMMES
5 RAN

3 RAP'T
6 RAPT
14 RARE
3 RASH
32 RATHER
6 RAVISH'D
3 RAYSE
3 RE
5 REACH
3 REACH'D
38 READ
18 READE
10 READER
5 READERS
5 READES
4 READY
7 REARE
3 REAR'D
9 REASON
3 REBELL
3 REBELLS
6 RECEIVE
5 RECEIV'D
3 RECORD
5 RECORDS
3 REDEEME
3 REFRAINE
7 REFUSE
3 REGARD
3 REHEARSE
5 REHERSE
6 RELIGION
5 RELIGIOUS
5 REMAINE
4 REMAINES
3 RENDER
7 RENOWNE
8 REPENT
3 REPENTED
9 REPORT
3 REPROVE
5 REQUIRE
4 RESOUND
3 RESPECT
14 REST
9 RESTORE
4 RESTOR'D
15 RETURNE
4 RETURN'D
4 RETURNES
5 REVEALE
3 REVELS
6 REVERENCE
6 REVEREND
10 REWARD
3 RICHARD
6 RICHER
4 RICHES
3 RICHLY
4 RIDDLES
7 RIDE
47 RIGHT
8 RIME
14 RIMES
5 RING
5 RINGS
3 RIOT
9 RIPE
23 RISE
3 RISING
22 RITES
4 RIVALL
8 RIVER
7 RIVERS
3 ROB
4 ROBE
3 ROB'D
9 ROBERT
3 ROCK
3 ROD
10 ROE
8 ROMAN
7 ROME
9 ROOME
4 ROSES
6 ROSIE
5 ROUGH
20 ROUND
4 ROUT
9 ROYALL
6 RUDE
8 RUINE
4 RUINES
3 RUMOUR
20 RUN

11	RUNNE	6	SHADOW	30	SOFT	16	STONE
4	RUNS	3	SHAFT	5	SOFTER	4	STONES
3	RURALL	4	SHAFTS	4	SOLD	8	STOOD
3	RUTLAND	8	SHAKE	3	SOLE	5	STOOLE
5	RYMES	5	SHAKESPEARE	9	SOLEMNE	3	STOOLES
8	SACRED	131	SHALL	141	SOME	5	STOP
9	SACRIFICE	6	SHALT	11	SOMETHING	24	STORE
15	SAD	17	SHAME	3	SOMETIME	3	STOR'D
4	SADNESSE	3	SHAPES	6	SOMETIMES	11	STORIE
19	SAFE	5	SHARPE	35	SONG	7	STORME
4	SAFELY	110	SHE	5	SONGS	3	STORMES
9	SAFETIE	7	SHED	33	SONNE	6	STORY
19	SAID	5	SHEE'	6	SONNES	7	STRAIGHT
3	SAILE	77	SHEE	20	SOONE	11	STRAINE
5	SAINT	4	SHEEPE	5	SOONER	5	STRAINES
5	SAINTS	3	SHEE'S	8	SORROW	10	STRANGE
3	SAITH	3	SHELTON	3	SORROWES	3	STRANGER
20	SAKE	15	SHEW	4	SORT	3	STRANGERS
3	SALISBURIE	3	SHEW'D	7	SOUGHT	4	STREAMES
7	SALUTE	6	SHEWES	3	SOULDIER	6	STREET
63	SAME	6	SHIFT	37	SOULE	17	STRENGTH
3	SATE	26	SHINE	11	SOULES	18	STRIFE
8	SATYRES	3	SHINES	3	SOUNDS	14	STRIKE
6	SAVE	3	SHIP	3	SOURCE	3	STRING
4	SAVIOUR	4	SHIPS	3	SOVERAIGNE	3	STRINGS
36	SAW	5	SHOOT	3	SOW	10	STRIVE
3	SAYD	3	SHOP	4	SOWER	3	STRIVING
11	SAYES	3	SHOPS	4	SOWRE	14	STRONG
3	SAY-MASTER	6	SHORE	3	SOYLE	3	STROOKE
3	SCALE	19	SHORT	7	SPAINE	15	STUDIE
6	SCANT	4	SHOT	3	SPANISH	4	STUDIED
6	SCAPE	151	SHOULD	13	SPARE	3	STUDIES
8	SCAP'D	8	SHOULD'ST	6	SPARKE	3	STUDY
4	SCARLET	23	SHOW	3	SPARKLING	4	STUFFE
7	SCARSE	3	SHOWE	45	SPEAKE	4	STUFFES
5	SCENE	3	SHOWERS	4	SPEAKES	4	STYLE
5	SCHOOLE	4	SHOWES	5	SPEAKING	18	SUBJECT
4	SCORE	6	SHOWNE	3	SPECIOUS	5	SUBJECTS
17	SCORNE	3	SHUN	5	SPEECH	5	SUBTILE
3	SCOTLAND	3	SHUNNING	9	SPEND	5	SUBTLE
18	SEA	7	SHUT	18	SPENT	4	SUCCOUR
3	SEALE	4	SICK	5	SPHEARE	3	SUCCOURS
3	SEAL'D	9	SICKNESSE	4	SPHEARES	176	SUCH
3	SEALES	16	SIDE	3	SPICE	4	SUFFER
10	SEARCH	6	SIDES	7	SPIE	3	SUFFER'D
4	SEARCHING	36	SIGHT	4	SPIES	3	SUFFRAGE
13	SEAS	4	SIGNE	13	SPIGHT	3	SUFFRING
6	SEASON	4	SILENCE	22	SPIRIT	3	SUIT
3	SEASONS	7	SILENT	14	SPIRITS	7	SUMME
5	SEAT	4	SILKE	4	SPITE	3	SUMM'D
3	SEATE	4	SILKES	4	SPLENDOR	18	SUN
3	SEAVEN	6	SIMPLE	3	SPOKE	15	SUNG
11	SECOND	4	SIMPLICITIE	12	SPORT	9	SUNNE
3	SECRET	4	SIN	7	SPORTS	7	SUP
3	SECRETS	55	SINCE	6	SPOUSE	3	SUPPER
3	SECURELY	47	SING	6	SPREAD	4	SUPPLY
5	SECURITIE	4	SINGLE	3	SPRIGHT	26	SURE
129	SEE	3	SINGS	24	SPRING	3	SURETIE
3	SEEING	4	SINKE	5	SPRINGS	4	SURFET
18	SEEKE	28	SINNE	8	SPUN	3	SURFETS
11	SEEME	4	SINNERS	4	SQUIBS	3	SURPRIZE
5	SEEM'D	8	SINNES	6	SQUIRE	3	SUSPECT
3	SEEMES	51	SIR	22	STAGE	6	SUTE
37	SEENE	3	SIRE	6	STALL	5	SWAN
6	SEES	12	SISTER	30	STAND	3	SWANS
4	SEEST	15	SIT	3	STANDERS	3	SWARME
7	SELDEN	7	SITS	9	STANDING	6	SWAY
3	SELDOME	4	SIX	7	STANDS	9	SWEARE
3	SELF	6	SIXE	4	STAND'ST	5	SWEARES
96	SELFE	3	SKIE	3	STAR	6	SWEAT
4	SELFE-SAME	3	SKILFULL	15	STARRE	58	SWEET
4	SELL	14	SKILL	7	STARRES	5	SWEETE
7	SELVES	3	SKIN	3	START	5	SWEETEST
5	SENCE	4	SLAVE	3	STARTED	3	SWEETNESSE
20	SEND	20	SLEEPE	64	STATE	4	SWEETS
31	SENSE	4	SLIGHT	15	STATES	5	SWELL
5	SENSES	5	SLOTH	4	STATUE	4	SWELLING
5	SENT	8	SLOW	3	STATUES	5	SWELLS
6	SENTENCE	15	SMALL	3	STATURE	11	SWIFT
7	SERIOUS	3	SMALLEST	4	STAY'D	4	SWIM
3	SERPENTS	3	SMILE	4	STAYES	14	SWORD
10	SERVANT	4	SMILES	4	STEAD	3	SWORDS
6	SERVANTS	4	SMILING	3	STEALE	7	SYDNEY
10	SERVE	3	SMITH	5	STEALTH	5	SYLVANE
6	SERVICE	4	SMOAKE	3	STEELE	8	TABLE
32	SET	9	SMOOTH	3	STEMME	3	TABLES
4	SETS	3	SNAKE	3	STEPS	3	TACITUS
3	SETTING	3	SNARES	3	STEWES	3	T'ADVANCE
4	SEVEN	6	SNOW	4	STIFFE	5	TA'EN
9	SEVERALL	3	SNUFFE	12	STILE	89	TAKE
3	SEVERE	5	SO'	7	STIL'D	10	TAKEN
3	SEX	468	SO	148	STILL	23	TAKES
5	SEXE	4	SOBER	5	STINKE	4	TAKING
3	SHADDOWES	3	SOCIETIE	7	STIRRE	4	TAK'ST
14	SHADE	14	SOE	5	STOLNE	4	TALE

6 TALES	3 THRUSH	82 UNTO	9 WELCOME
3 TALL	6 THUNDER	3 UNWORTHY	19 WENT
5 TAME	42 THUS	120 UP	207 WERE
3 TAMES	504 THY	108 UPON	23 WERT
7 TANE	57 TILL	6 UPRIGHT	3 WEST
4 TARRY	62 TIME	9 URGE	8 WESTON
3 TASKE	6 TIMELY	3 URG'D	11 WHAT'
5 TAST	46 TIMES	86 US	306 WHAT
8 TASTE	75 'TIS	39 USE	11 WHAT'S
4 TASTED	15 TITLE	5 USURER	4 WHEELE
13 TAUGHT	12 TITLES	4 USURERS	260 WHEN
5 TAXE	63 T'	3 UTTER'D	11 WHENCE
3 TAX'D	5 TO'	3 VALE	150 WHERE
3 TAYLORS	1834 TO	7 VALIANT	3 WHEREBY
18 TEACH	12 TOGETHER	13 VALOUR	4 WHERFORE
3 TEEMING	13 TOLD	5 VALUE	17 WHEREIN
3 TELESTICHS	9 TOM	3 VARIETIE	5 WHEROF
53 TELL	5 TOMBE	3 VARIOUS	7 WHEREWITH
5 TELLS	3 TOMES	8 VELVET	3 WHERIN
3 TEMPT	13 TONGUE	3 VENETIA	3 WHERRY
8 TEN	7 TONGUES	4 VENT	287 WHICH
3 TERME	118 TOO	4 VENTER	40 WHILE
4 TERMES	17 TOOKE	3 VENTRING	10 WHIL'ST
3 TEST	3 TOP	14 VENUS	4 WHITE
3 TH'ADMIR'D	4 TORNE	3 VENUSINE	3 WHITE-HALL
4 THAMES	3 TOTHER	3 VERE	7 WHITHER
4 THAN	14 TOUCH	46 VERSE	7 WHO'
5 THANKE	6 TOUCH'D	27 VERSES	195 WHO
7 THANKES	5 TOWER	51 VERTUE	40 WHOLE
3 THANKFULL	15 TOWNE	9 VERTUES	4 WHOLLY
6 TH'ARE	6 TOWNES	14 VERTUOUS	69 WHOM
4 TH'ART	3 TOWRE	12 VERY	14 WHORE
27 THAT'	4 TOYES	5 VEXE	3 WHO'S
1077 THAT	3 TOYLE	29 VICE	89 WHOSE
27 THAT'S	10 TRADE	4 VICES	50 WHY
8 T'HAVE	5 TRAGEDIE	21 VIEW	3 WICKED
82 TH'	4 TRAGICK	7 VIEW'D	31 WIFE
2581 THE	6 TRANSLATED	9 VILE	10 WILD
242 THEE	3 TRAVAILE	6 VINE	3 WILDE
364 THEIR	3 TRAVELL	5 VIRGIL	85 WILL
6 THEIRS	16 TREAD	9 VIRGIN	14 WILLIAM
31 'HEM	8 TREASURE	3 VIRGINS	3 WILLING
123 THEM	7 TREASURER	4 VIRTUE	3 WILT
15 THEMSELVES	17 TREE	3 VISION	9 WIN
207 THEN	3 TREES	4 VITIOUS	3 WINCHESTRIAN
24 THENCE	3 TRENCH	4 VOICE	6 WIND
19 THERE'	5 TRICKS	3 VOLUME	3 WINDOWES
196 THERE	5 TRIE	5 VOW	4 WINDS
20 THEREFORE	5 TRIFLES	8 VOWES	27 WINE
6 THEREIN	3 TRINE	19 VOYCE	7 WING
7 THEREOF	5 TRINITIE	3 VOYCES	6 WINGS
19 THERE'S	6 TRIUMPH	14 VULCAN	3 WINNE
154 THESE	3 TROTH	7 VULGAR	5 WINTER
3 THESPIAN	5 TROUBLED	6 WAKE	10 WISDOME
3 TH'EXCHANGE	5 TROY	6 WALKE	37 WISE
7 TH'	92 TRUE	6 WALKES	3 WISELY
10 THEY'	5 TRUELY	7 WALL	3 WISER
331 THEY	8 TRULY	6 WALLS	3 WISEST
3 TH'EYE	5 TRUMPET	3 WANDRING	38 WISH
5 THEYR	4 TRUMPETS	30 WANT	5 WISHES
5 THEY'RE	16 TRUST	8 WANTON	628 WITH
3 TH'HAST	5 TRUSTED	5 WANTS	8 WITHALL
4 THIE	48 TRUTH	3 WARES	3 WITHERED
3 THIEFE	6 TRY	3 WARIE	12 WITHIN
3 THIGHES	8 TUNE	6 WARME	41 WITHOUT
47 THINE	7 TUNES	18 WARRE	14 WITNESSE
27 THING	19 TURNE	7 WARRES	10 WITS
42 THINGS	5 TURN'D	221 WAS	10 WIVES
66 THINKE	3 TURNED	6 WATCH	11 WOMAN
8 THINKES	3 TURNES	4 WATCH'D	4 WOMANS
4 THINKING	5 TURNING	8 WATER	6 WOMBE
5 THINK'ST	3 TURTLES	7 WATERS	8 WOMEN
4 THIRD	15 'TWAS	50 WAY	4 WON
347 THIS	5 TWELVE	23 WAYES	23 WONDER
5 THITHER	4 TWENTIE	3 WE'	12 WONNE
8 THOMAS	6 'TWERE	143 WE	3 WONT
131 THOSE	3 TWI	9 WEAKE	3 WOO
5 TH'OTHER	10 TWICE	18 WEALTH	9 WOOD
8 TH'	7 'TWILL	6 WEALTHY	7 WOODS
10 THOU'	3 TWINE	4 WEARES	3 WOOES
395 THOU	4 'TWIXT	4 WEARY	3 WOOLL
132 THOUGH	3 TWIXT	3 WEATHER	18 WORD
61 THOUGHT	48 TWO	3 WEAVE	26 WORDS
18 THOUGHTS	5 TYME	7 WEAV'D	45 WORKE
4 THOU'LT	14 UN	5 WEE'	11 WORKES
5 THOUSAND	3 UNCOMELY	22 WEE	51 WORLD
3 THREATEN	18 UNDER	3 WEEDES	8 WORLDS
4 THREATNING	14 UNDERSTAND	3 WEEKE	3 WORMES
3 THRED	12 UNDERSTOOD	3 WEEKLY	11 WORSE
20 THREE	3 UNDONE	5 WEE'LL	4 WORSHIP
7 THRICE	7 UNION	7 WEEPE	11 WORST
6 THRIVE	4 UNITIE	5 WEIGH'D	4 WORTHIE
28 THROUGH	4 UNKNOWNE	15 WEIGHT	33 WORTHY
8 THROUGHOUT	3 UNLESSE	4 WEIGHTIE	200 WOULD
3 THROW	5 UNTILL	4 WEL	9 WOULD'ST

```
    9   WOUND
    4   WRAPT
    3   WRETCH
   10   WRETCHED
   13   WRIT
   39   WRITE
    3   WRITER
    4   WRITING
    3   WRITTEN
   12   WRONG
    4   WRONGS
    6   WROTE
    9   WROTH
   17   WROUGHT
    3   WYSE
    5   YEA
   22   YEARE
   22   YEARES
    4   YEE
    9   YEELD
    6   YEERE
    9   YEERES
    3   YELLOW
    7   YES
  218   YET
    3   YETT
    4   YF
    4   YO'ARE
    3   YO'HAVE
    4   YONG
    9   YO'
    4   YOU'
  412   YOU
   12   YOUNG
    3   YOUNGEST
  324   YOUR
   12   YOURS
   16   YOUTH
    7   YOUTHS
    5   ZEALE
```

A-BED
A-FARRE
A-FIRE
AFTER-STATE
AFTER-THOUGHTS
AFTER-TIMES
A-JAX
ALDE-LEGH
ALE-HOUSE
A-LIFE
ALIKE-STATED
ALL-GRACIOUS
ALL-VERTUOUS
A-NEW
APPLE-HARVEST
ARCH-ANGELS
ARCH-DUKES
A-WHILE
BACK-SLIDES
BANCK-SIDE
BANKE-RUPT
BAUD-BEES
BED-MATE
BED-RID
BELL-MANS
BEST-BEST
BILBO-SMITH
BIRTH-DAY
BIRTH-RIGHT
BLACK-BIRD
BLACKE-SPRINGING
BOMBARD-PHRASE
BOMBARD-STILE
BONE-FIRES
BOOKE-SELLER
BOOKE-WORMES
BOOK-SELLER
BOR-DRING
BRAYNE-HARDIE
BREAD-STREETS
BREW-HOUSES
BRICK-HILLS
BRICK-KILLS
BRIDE-WELL
BROAD-SEALES
BROAD-TRODEN
BUCKLERS-BURY
BUTTER-FLYE
BY-CAUSE
BY-PATHS
CANARY-WINE
CARE-FULL
CAR-MEN
CATER-FILLER
CHAMBER-CRITICK
CHAMBER-FELLOW
CHEAP-SIDE
CHEAR-FULL
CHEST-NUT
CHRIST-MASSE
CHURCH-YARD
CINNAMON-TREE
CITTIE-QUESTION
CLARKE-LIKE
CLEFT-STICKS
CLOSE-STOOLE
CLOWD-LIKE
CLUB-FIST
COACH-MAN
COACH-MARE
COB-WEB-LAWNE
CO-HEIRE
COMMON-LAW
COMMON-WEALTH
COUNTREY-MEN
COUNTRIE-NEIGHBOURS
COURT-BRED-FILLIE
COURT-DURT
COURT-HOBBY-HORSE
COURT-LING
COURT-PARRAT
COURT-PUCELL
COURT-WORME
CRAMP-RING
CREAME-BOWLES
CROWNE-PLATE
CROWNE-WORTHY
CUPPING-GLASSES
CURLING-IRONS
DAMASKE-ROSE
DARK-LANTERNE
DAYES-PRESENTS
DAY-STARRE

DEAL-BOARDS
DEBT-BOOKE
DEEP-CROWN'D-BOWLE
DEEPE-GROUNDED
DIS-AVOW
DIS-ESTEEM'D
DIS-ESTEEME
DIS-FAVOUR
DIS-INHERIT
DIS-JOYN'D
DIS-JOYNTS
DIVELS-ARSE
DOG-DAIES
DYE-FATS
EASY-RATED
ELSE-WHERE
ELTHAM-THING
EMPTY-HANDED
ENGLISH-ROGUE
EVER-BOYLING
EVER-GREENE
EVER-LASTING
EVERY-WHERE
EYE-BROWES
EYE-BROWS
FA-DING
FAME-VAYNES
FARE-WELL
FARRE-ADMIRED
FARRE-ALL-SEEING
FARRE-KNOWNE
FINE-MAN
FIRE-LIGHT
FIRE-WORKES
FIRST-BORNE
FIRST-FRUITS
FIST-FILL'D
FIVE-FOLD
FLEET-LANE
FOOLE-HARDIE
FOOT-AND-HALFE-FOOT
FOOT-CLOTH
FOOT-MAN
FORE-KNOWNE
FORE-SEE
FORTH-BROUGHT
FOSTER-FATHER
FOURE-SCORE
FREE-BORNE
FRENCH-HOOD
FRENCH-MEN
FRENCH-TAYLORS
FRIEND-SHIP
GALLO-BELGICUS
GENTLE-WOMAN
GLAD-MENTION'D
GLASSE-HOUSE
GLOOMIE-SCEPTRED
GOD-HEAD
GOD-LIKE
GOD-WIT
GOLD-CHAINES
GOLDEN-EYES
GOOD-NIGHT
GOSSIP-GOT
GRAND-CHILD
GRAND-CHILDREN
GRAND-DAMES
GREAT-MENS
GREEK-HANDS
GREENE-CLOTH
GUN-POWDER
HALFE-MOONES
HALFE-WAY
HANS-SPIEGLE
HARD-BY
HARD-HEARTED
HAU'-BOY
HEAD-LONG
HEALTH-SAKE
HEART-STRIKE
HENCE-FORTH
HERCULES-HIS
HIDE-PARKE
HIGH-SPIRITED
HIGH-SWOLNE
HILL-FOOT
HOLY-DAY
HOLY-DAYES
HOME-BORNE
HOOD-WINK'D
HOOFE-CLEFT
HOOK-HANDED

HOP-DRINKERS
HORNE-WORKES
HORSE-LEECH
HORSE-LEECH-LIKE
HORSE-NECK
HOT-HOUSE
HOURE-GLASSE
HOUSE-HOLD
HOW-SO-E'RE
ILL-AFFECTED
ILL-MADE
ILL-NATUR'D
ILL-PENN'D
ILL-TORN'D
ILL-US'D
IN-LAND
IN-PRIMIS
JACKS-PULSE
JUSTICE-HOOD
KEY-STONE
KNIGHT-HOOD
KNIGHT-WRIGHT'S
LADY-AIRE
LANTERNE-LERRY
LATE-COYN'D
LAUGH-WORTHY
LA-WARE
LAY-STALL
LEFT-LYDIA
LEFT-WITTED
LESSE-POETIQUE
LETTER-GOE
LIP-THIRSTIE
LONG'D-FOR
LONG-GATHERING
LONG-SINCE
LOOSER-LIKE
LORD-GOD
LOUSE-DROPPING
LOVELY-HEAD
LOVE-QUEENES
LOVES-SAKE
LOW-COUNTREY'S
LOW-COUNTRIES
LUSTIE-MOUNTING
MAD-MEN
MAN-KIND
MANY-HEADED
MARIAGE-DAY
MARIAGE-HORNE
MARIAGE-PLEDGES
MARIAGE-RITES
MARKET-FOLKES
MASTER-BRAINE
MASTER-WORKER
MEATE-BOATE
MEERE-MATTER-LESSE
MERCY-SEAT
MERD-URINOUS
MERSH-LAMBETH
MID-SUN
MID-WIFE
MID-WIVES
MIS-APPLY
MIS-CALL'T
MISSE-CALL'D
MONEY-BROKERS
MONEY-GETT
MOON-CALFE
MOORE-FIELDS
MORNING-STAR
MORNING-STARRE
MOUNTE-BANCK
MUSTER-MASTER
NECK-STOCKT
NEIGHBOUR-TOWNES
NEW-COME
NEW-DITCH
NEW-YEARES
NEW-YEERES
NIGHT-SINNES
NIGHT-TUBS
NOONE-DAY
NOONE-STED'S
NUMBRED-FIVE
NUT-CRACKERS
OFF-SPRING
OFT-TIMES
OLD-END
ONELY-GOTTEN
ORE-BLOWNE
ORE-FLOW
ORE-FLOWNE

ORE-FOLD
O'RE-JOY'D
O'RE-PRAISE
ORE-SHINE
ORE-SWELLETH
OTHERS-EVILL
OUT-BEE
OUT-BOAST
OUT-BRAVE
OUT-CRYES
OUT-DANCE
OUT-DID
OUT-DOO
OUT-FLOURISHT
OUT-FORMES
OUT-GOE
OUT-LAST
OUT-LASTS
OUT-LIV'D
OUT-LIVE
OUT-PRAISE
OUT-RIGHT
OUT-SHINE
OUT-SPUN
OUT-STARTED
OUT-STRIPT
OUT-VALEW
OUT-WEARE
OUT-ZANY
OVER-BLOW
OVER-COME
OVER-GONE
OVER-LEAVEN'D
OVER-SAFE
OVER-SEER
OVER-THICK
OVER-WANTON
PALME-TREES
PARIS-GARDEN
PARISH-GARDEN
PARISH-STEEPLE
PARTIE-PER-PALE
PASSER-BY
PAULS-STEEPLE
PEST-HOUSE
PHOEBUS-SELFE
PICKT-HATCH
PIT-FALLS
PIT-PAT-NOYSE
PLAGUE-BILL
PLAGUE-SORES
PLAY-WRIGHT
POET-APE
POLY-OLBYON
POPES-HEAD-ALLEY
POT-GUNS
POULDER-PLOT
PRAISE-WORTHY
PRENTISE-SHIP
PUR-BLINDE
PURPLE-MATCHING
QUARTER-FACE
QUICKEST-SIGHTED
QUICK-WARMING-PAN
RE-ADVANCE
REARE-SUPPERS
RE-JOYNE
RE-SHINE
RIGHT-LEARNED
ROSIE-CROSSE
ROW-HAMPTON
SAVING-HONOUR
SAY-MASTER
SCARLET-LIKE
SEA-COALE
SEA-GIRT
SEAVEN-FOLD
SEED-PLOT
SELFE-BOASTING
SELFE-DIVIDED
SELFE-FAME
SELFE-SAME
SEMI-GOD
SERVING-MAN
SERVING-WOMAN
SEVEN-TONGU'D
SHEEPES-SKIN
SHIETER-HUISSEN
SHOP-PHILOSOPHY
SHORT-LEG'D
SHOT-FREE
SICK-MENS
SISTER-TUNES

SIXE-PAC'D
SIX-PENCE
SMALL-TIMBRED
SOME-THING
SOME-WHERE
SOMMER-NIGHTS
SOPE-BOYLER
SOULDIER-LIKE
SPUNGE-LIKE
STANDERS-BY
STAR-CHAMBER
STARRE-CHAMBER
STATES-MAN
STATES-MANS
STATES-MEN
STILL-SCALDING
STITCHERS-TO
STORE-HOUSE
STRAIGHT-WAY
STRAW-BERRIES
STREET-BORNE
SUN-BURNT-BLOWSE
SUN-LIGHT
SUNNE-HER
SWEET-MEATS
SWEET-WOOD
SWIFT-PAC'T
TABACCO-LIKE
TELL-TROTH
THEM-SELVES
THE'UN-USED
THOROUGH-FARE
THUNDER-STROKEN
TIRE-MAN
TITLE-LEAFE
TOO-MUCH
T'OUT-STRIP
TOWN-BORN
TOWN-DITCH
TOWNE-CURS
TOWNS-MAN
TRUCH-MAN
TRUE-FILED
TRULY-BELOV'D
TRULY-NOBLE
TWICE-TWELVE-YEARES
TWI-LIGHT
TWI-LIGHTS
TWO-FOLD
TYRE-MAN
UN-APPEAS'D
UN-ARGUED
UN-ARMED
UN-AVOIDED
UN-BECOMMING
UN-BOUGHT
UN-COMMON
UNDER-CARVED
UNDER-HEARES
UNDER-NEATH
UNDER-WOOD
UNDER-WOODS
UN-HURT
UN-INFORM'D
UN-NAMED
UN-SWEET
UN-TAUGHT
UN-WASTED
UN-WELCOME
UP-BEARE
UP-BRAID
UP-TOOKE
VAL-TELLINE
VILLE-ROYES
VIRGIN-TRAINE
VIRGIN-TROUP
VIRGIN-WHITE
WANTON-WISE
WARIE-DRIVEN
WATER-CONDUITS
WELL-COMPASS'D
WELL-GRAC'D
WELL-GREAS'D
WELL-TRUSS'D
WEL-MADE
WEL-TAGDE
WEL-WROUGHT
WEST-INDIAN
WEST-PARTS
WEST-WINDS
WHALE-BONE
WHET-STONE
WHITE-FRYERS

WHITE-HALL
WHORE-HOUSE
WIND-BOUND
WISE-CRAFTS
WISE-MEN
WITCH-HAZILL
WOMAN-KIND
WOMAN-KINDE
WOO-ALL
WOOD-COCK
WOULD-BEE
YEARES-GIFT
YEARES-LABOURS

FARRE-ADMIRED
RE-ADVANCE
ILL-AFFECTED
LADY-AIRE
FARRE-ALL-SEEING
WOO-ALL
FOOT-AND-HALFE-FOOT
ARCH-ANGELS
POET-APE
UN-APPEAS'D
MIS-APPLY
UN-ARGUED
UN-ARMED
DIVELS-ARSE
UN-AVOIDED
DIS-AVOW
MOUNTE-BANCK
UP-BEARE
UN-BECOMMING
A-BED
OUT-BEE
WOULD-BEE
BAUD-BEES
GALLO-BELGICUS
TRULY-BELOV'D
STRAW-BERRIES
BEST-BEST
PLAGUE-BILL
BLACK-BIRD
PUR-BLINDE
OVER-BLOW
ORE-BLOWNE
DEAL-BOARDS
OUT-BOAST
SELFE-BOASTING
MEATE-BOATE
WHALE-BONE
DEBT-BOOKE
TOWN-BORN
FIRST-BORNE
FREE-BORNE
HOME-BORNE
STREET-BORNE
UN-BOUGHT
WIND-BOUND
CREAME-BOWLES
HAU'-BOY
SOPE-BOYLER
EVER-BOYLING
UP-BRAID
MASTER-BRAINE
OUT-BRAVE
COURT-BRED-FILLIE
MONEY-BROKERS
FORTH-BROUGHT
EYE-BROWES
EYE-BROWS
SUN-BURNT-BLOWSE
BUCKLERS-BURY
HARD-BY
PASSER-BY
STANDERS-BY
MOON-CALFE
MISSE-CALL'D
MIS-CALL'T
UNDER-CARVED
BY-CAUSE
GOLD-CHAINES
STAR-CHAMBER
STARRE-CHAMBER
GRAND-CHILD
GRAND-CHILDREN
HOOFE-CLEFT
FOOT-CLOTH
GREENE-CLOTH
SEA-COALE
WOOD-COCK
NEW-COME
OVER-COME
UN-COMMON
WELL-COMPASS'D
WATER-CONDUITS
LOW-COUNTREY'S
LOW-COUNTRIES
LATE-COYN'D
NUT-CRACKERS
WISE-CRAFTS
CHAMBER-CRITICK
ROSIE-CROSSE
DEEP-CROWN'D-BOWLE
OUT-CRYES
TOWNE-CURS
DOG-DAIES

GRAND-DAMES
OUT-DANCE
BIRTH-DAY
HOLY-DAY
MARIAGE-DAY
NOONE-DAY
HOLY-DAYES
OUT-DID
FA-DING
NEW-DITCH
TOWN-DITCH
SELFE-DIVIDED
OUT-DOO
BOR-DRING
HOP-DRINKERS
WARIE-DRIVEN
LOUSE-DROPPING
ARCH-DUKES
COURT-DURT
OLD-END
DIS-ESTEEM'D
DIS-ESTEEME
OTHERS-EVILL
GOLDEN-EYES
QUARTER-FACE
PIT-FALLS
SELFE-FAME
THOROUGH-FARE
A-FARRE
FOSTER-FATHER
DYE-FATS
DIS-FAVOUR
CHAMBER-FELLOW
MOORE-FIELDS
TRUE-FILED
FIST-FILL'D
A-FIRE
BONE-FIRES
CLUB-FIST
NUMBRED-FIVE
OUT-FLOURISHT
ORE-FLOW
ORE-FLOWNE
BUTTER-FLYE
FIVE-FOLD
ORE-FOLD
SEAVEN-FOLD
TWO-FOLD
MARKET-FOLKES
HILL-FOOT
LONG'D-FOR
OUT-FORMES
HENCE-FORTH
SHOT-FREE
FIRST-FRUITS
WHITE-FRYERS
CARE-FULL
CHEAR-FULL
PARIS-GARDEN
PARISH-GARDEN
LONG-GATHERING
MONEY-GETT
YEARES-GIFT
SEA-GIRT
HOURE-GLASSE
CUPPING-GLASSES
LORD-GOD
SEMI-GOD
LETTER-GOE
OUT-GOE
OVER-GONE
GOSSIP-GOT
ONELY-GOTTEN
WELL-GRAC'D
ALL-GRACIOUS
WELL-GREAS'D
EVER-GREENE
DEEPE-GROUNDED
POT-GUNS
WHITE-HALL
ROW-HAMPTON
EMPTY-HANDED
HOOK-HANDED
GREEK-HANDS
BRAYNE-HARDIE
FOOLE-HARDIE
APPLE-HARVEST
PICKT-HATCH
WITCH-HAZILL
GOD-HEAD
LOVELY-HEAD
POPES-HEAD-ALLEY
MANY-HEADED

UNDER-HEARES
HARD-HEARTED
CO-HEIRE
SUNNE-HER
BRICK-HILLS
HERCULES-HIS
COURT-HOBBY-HORSE
HOUSE-HOLD
SAVING-HONOUR
FRENCH-HOOD
JUSTICE-HOOD
KNIGHT-HOOD
MARIAGE-HORNE
ALE-HOUSE
GLASSE-HOUSE
HOT-HOUSE
PEST-HOUSE
STORE-HOUSE
WHORE-HOUSE
BREW-HOUSES
SHIETER-HUISSEN
UN-HURT
WEST-INDIAN
UN-INFORM'D
DIS-INHERIT
CURLING-IRONS
A-JAX
O'RE-JOY'D
DIS-JOYN'D
RE-JOYNE
DIS-JOYNTS
BRICK-KILLS
MAN-KIND
WOMAN-KIND
WOMAN-KINDE
FARRE-KNOWNE
FORE-KNOWNE
YEARES-LABOURS
MERSH-LAMBETH
IN-LAND
FLEET-LANE
DARK-LANTERNE
OUT-LAST
EVER-LASTING
OUT-LASTS
COMMON-LAW
TITLE-LEAFE
RIGHT-LEARNED
OVER-LEAVEN'D
HORSE-LEECH-LIKE
HORSE-LEECH
SHORT-LEG'D
ALDE-LEGH
LANTERNE-LERRY
A-LIFE
FIRE-LIGHT
SUN-LIGHT
TWI-LIGHT
TWI-LIGHTS
CLARKE-LIKE
CLOWD-LIKE
GOD-LIKE
LOOSER-LIKE
SCARLET-LIKE
SOULDIER-LIKE
SPUNGE-LIKE
TABACCO-LIKE
COURT-LING
OUT-LIV'D
OUT-LIVE
HEAD-LONG
LEFT-LYDIA
ILL-MADE
WEL-MADE
COACH-MAN
FINE-MAN
FOOT-MAN
SERVING-MAN
STATES-MAN
TIRE-MAN
TOWNS-MAN
TRUCH-MAN
TYRE-MAN
BELL-MANS
STATES-MANS
COACH-MARE
CHRIST-MASSE
MUSTER-MASTER
SAY-MASTER
PURPLE-MATCHING
BED-MATE
MEERE-MATTER-LESSE
SWEET-MEATS

CAR-MEN
COUNTREY-MEN
FRENCH-MEN
MAD-MEN
STATES-MEN
WISE-MEN
GREAT-MENS
SICK-MENS
GLAD-MENTION'D
HALFE-MOONES
LUSTIE-MOUNTING
TOO-MUCH
UN-NAMED
ILL-NATUR'D
UNDER-NEATH
HORSE-NECK
COUNTRIE-NEIGHBOURS
A-NEW
GOOD-NIGHT
SOMMER-NIGHTS
TRULY-NOBLE
CHEST-NUT
POLY-OLBYON
SIXE-PAC'D
SWIFT-PAC'T
HIDE-PARKE
COURT-PARRAT
WEST-PARTS
PIT-PAT-NOYSE
BY-PATHS
SIX-PENCE
ILL-PENN'D
PARTIE-PER-PALE
SHOP-PHILOSOPHY
BOMBARD-PHRASE
CATER-PILLER
CROWNE-PLATE
MARIAGE-PLEDGES
POULDER-PLOT
SEED-PLOT
LESSE-POETIQUE
GUN-POWDER
O'RE-PRAISE
OUT-PRAISE
DAYES-PRESENTS
IN-PRIMIS
COURT-PUCELL
JACKS-PULSE
LOVE-QUEENES
CITTIE-QUESTION
EASY-RATED
BEE-RID
BIRTH-RIGHT
OUT-RIGHT
CRAMP-RING
MARIAGE-RITES
ENGLISH-ROGUE
DAMASKE-ROSE
VILLE-ROYES
BANKE-RUPT
OVER-SAFE
HEALTH-SAKE
LOVES-SAKE
SELFE-SAME
STILL-SCALDING
GLOOMIE-SCEPTRED
FOURE-SCORE
BROAD-SEALES
MERCY-SEAT
FORE-SEE
OVER-SEER
PHOEBUS-SELFE
BOOK-SELLER
BOOKE-SELLER
THEM-SELVES
ORE-SHINE
OUT-SHINE
RE-SHINE
FRIEND-SHIP
PRENTISE-SHIP
BANCK-SIDE
CHEAP-SIDE
QUICKEST-SIGHTED
LONG-SINCE
NIGHT-SINNES
SHEEPES-SKIN
BACK-SLIDES
BILBO-SMITH
HOW-SO-E'RE
PLAGUE-SORES
HANS-SPIEGLE
HIGH-SPIRITED
OFF-SPRING

BLACKE-SPRINGING
OUT-SPUN
LAY-STALL
MORNING-STAR
DAY-STARRE
MORNING-STARRE
OUT-STARTED
AFTER-STATE
ALIKE-STATED
NOONE-STED'S
PARISH-STEEPLE
PAULS-STEEPLE
CLEFT-STICKS
BOMBARD-STILE
NECK-STOCKT
KEY-STONE
WHET-STONE
CLOSE-STOOLE
BREAD-STREETS
HEART-STRIKE
T'OUT-STRIP
OUT-STRIPT
THUNDER-STROKEN
MID-SUN
REARE-SUPPERS
UN-SWEET
ORE-SWELLETH
HIGH-SWOLNE
WEL-TAGDE
UN-TAUGHT
FRENCH-TAYLORS
VAL-TELLINE
OVER-THICK
ELTHAM-THING
SOME-THING
LIP-THIRSTIE
AFTER-THOUGHTS
SMALL-TIMBRED
AFTER-TIMES
OFT-TIMES
STITCHERS-TO
SEVEN-TONGU'D
UP-TOOKE
ILL-TORN'D
NEIGHBOUR-TOWNES
VIRGIN-TRAINE
CINNAMON-TREE
PALME-TREES
BROAD-TRODEN
TELL-TROTH
VIRGIN-TROUP
WELL-TRUSS'D
NIGHT-TUBS
SISTER-TUNES
TWICE-TWELVE-YEARES
MERD-URINOUS
ILL-US'D
THE'UN-USED
OUT-VALEW
FAME-VAYNES
ALL-VERTUOUS
OVER-WANTON
LA-WARE
QUICK-WARMING-PAN
UN-WASTED
HALFE-WAY
STRAIGHT-WAY
COMMON-WEALTH
OUT-WEARE
COB-WEB-LAWNE
UN-WELCOME
BRIDE-WELL
FARE-WELL
ELSE-WHERE
EVERY-WHERE
SOME-WHERE
A-WHILE
VIRGIN-WHITE
MID-WIFE
WEST-WINDS
CANARY-WINE
HOOD-WINK'D
WANTON-WISE
GOD-WIT
LEFT-WITTED
MID-WIVES
GENTLE-WOMAN
SERVING-WOMAN
SWEET-WOOD
UNDER-WOOD
UNDER-WOODS
MASTER-WORKER
FIRE-WORKES

HORNE-WORKES
COURT-WORME
BOOKE-WORMES
CROWNE-WORTHY
LAUGH-WORTHY
PRAISE-WORTHY
PLAY-WRIGHT
KNIGHT-WRIGHT'S
WEL-WROUGHT
CHURCH-YARD
NEW-YEARES
NEW-YEERES
OUT-ZANY

POPES-HEAD-ALLEY
SUN-BURNT-BLOWSE
DEEP-CROWN'D-BOWLE
HOW-SO-E'RE
COURT-BRED-FILLIE
FOOT-AND-HALFE-FOOT
COURT-HOBBY-HORSE
COB-WEB-LAWNE
MEERE-MATTER-LESSE
HORSE-LEECH-LIKE
PIT-PAT-NOYSE
PARTIE-PER-PALE
QUICK-WARMING-PAN
FARRE-ALL-SEEING
TWICE-TWELVE-YEARES

ABANDON'D	CAP'S	DIANA'S	FLATTRY'S	ILL-NATUR'D
ABBO'D	CAP'TALL	DI'D	FOLLOW'D	ILL-PENN'D
ABSOLV'D	CAPTIV'D	DID'ST	FORBIDD'	ILL-TORN'D
ABUS'D	'CARE	DIE'D	FORC'D	ILL-US'D
ADMIR'D	CARV'D	DIFFER'D	FORC'T	I'M
ADOR'D	CAS'D	DIMN'D	'FORE	IMBARQU'D
ADULT'RERS	CATCH'D	DIN'D	FOREHEAD'S	I'ME
ADVANC'D	CATO'S	DISCERN'D	FOR'HIS	IMPOS'D
ALBIN'S	CAUS'D	DISCLOS'D	FORM'D	INCLIN'D
ALLOW'D	'CAUSE	DIS-ESTEEM'D	FRAM'D	INCLOS'D
ALL'S	CECILL'S	DISGRAC'T	FREEZ'D	INCURR'D
ALONG'ST	CENSUR'D	DISGUIS'D	FYL'S	INDENTUR'D
ALOW'D	CHANC'D	DIS-JOYN'D	GAIN'D	INDU'D
ALS'	CHANC'T	DISPENC'D	'GAINST	INFAM'D
ALTER'D	CHANG'D	DISPEND'ST	GAM'STER	INFLAM'D
AMID'	CHANGE'D	DISPLEAS'D	GATHER'D	INFUS'D
ANNOY'D	CHARG'D	DISPOS'D	GAV'ST	INQUIR'D
ANSWER'D	CHEAR'D	DISPROPORTION'D	GENT'MAN	IN'S
ANTICIBRA'S	'CHEQUER	DISTINGUISH'D	GI'NG	INSCRIB'D
ANTICYRA'S	CHERISH'D	DIV'D	GIV'ST	INSPIR'D
APOLLO'S	CHEV'RIL	DIVID'ST	GLAD-MENTION'D	IN'T
APOLLO'S	CHEV'RILL	DOCK'S	GLISTER'D	INTERPOS'D
APPEAR'D	CHOAK'D	DONNEE'S	GODLY'S	INT'REST
ARM'E	CLAYM'D	DONNOR'S	GOD'S	IS'T
ARRAIGN'D	CLEANS'D	DOO'T	GOLD'S	IT'
ARTE'S	CLEP'D	DO'S	GO'ST	I'TH'
ASHAM'D	CLIFTON'S	DO'ST	GOWN'D	I'THE
ASK'D	CLOATH'D	DO'T	GRAC'D	I'THEIR
ASSAY'D	CLOS'D	DO'YOU	'GREE	IT'S
ASSIGN'D	CLOTH'S	DRI'D	GREEK'S	JANIN'S
ASSUR'D	COACH'D	DRIV'N	'GREES	JOVE'S
AS'T	COMM'ST	DROWN'D	'GREET	JOY'D
AT'S	COMPANY'	DUE'LLISTS	GRIEV'D	JOY'ST
ATTIR'D	COMPAR'D	DUR'D	GROUN'	JUDG'D
'AUBIGNY	COMPIL'D	DY'D	GRUDG'D	KEEP'D
AUTHORIZ'D	COMPOS'D	DYD'ST	GULL'D	KEEP'ST
BANISH'D	COM'ST	EAS'D	HA'	KILL'D
BARR'D	CONCEAL'D	ECCHO'D	HAD'ST	KNIGHT'S
B'ASHAM'D	CONCEIV'D	ECCHO'S	HALLOW'D	KNIGHT-WRIGHT'S
BAUDRIE'	CONCEIV'ST	EMBELISH'D	HAP'LY	KNOW'ST
BB'S	CONDEMN'D	EMBRAC'D	HAPP'LY	KNOW'T
BECAM'ST	CONFIRM'D	EMP'RICKS	HARBOUR'D	LABOUR'D
BEDEW'D	CONFUS'D	ENAMOR'D	HARROW'D	LACK'D
BEGAN'ST	CONQUER'D	ENCOUNTER'D	HA'S	LACK'DST
BEG'D	CONQU'RING	ENCREAS'D	HAU'-BOY	LADY'S
BEGG'D	CONTEMN'D	ENDEW'D	HAU'BOY	LAMIA'HAS
BEGIN'ST	CONTINU'D	ENGRAV'D	HAVE'HEM	LANC'LOTS
BEGUIL'D	COP'CES	ENJOY'D	HAVE'T	LASH'D
BELCH'D	COPP'S	ENSHRIN'D	HE'ADULTERS	'LASSE
BELEEV'D	COR'SIVES	ENTAYL'D	HEAP'D	LATE-COYN'D
BELOV'D	COS'NING	ENVI'D	HEAR'ST	LAUGH'D
E'EMBRAC'D	COSSEN'D	ENVY'	HEAV'D	LAUGH'T
BE'N	COULD'ST	ENVY'D	HEAV'EN	LEAP'D
BESIEG'D	COUNT'NANCES	EQUALL'D	HEAV'N	LEARN'D
BE'ST	COUNTRY'S	E'RE	HE'D	LEAS'D
BETRAY'D	'COUNTS	ERE'T	HEE'D	LEAVEN'D
BETTER'D	COVER'D	ERRANT'ST	HEE'LD	LEAV'ST
BETY'DE	CRACK'D	ERR'D	HEE'LL	LEDA'S
BEWAIL'D	CRAMP'D	ETERNIZ'D	HEE'S	L'ENVOYE
B'IMPUTED	CRAV'D	EVENING'S	HEIGHT'NING	LETCHER'D
BLANCH'T	CRI'D	EVE'RY	HE'LE	LET'S
BLAZ'D	CROWN'D	EV'N	HE'LL	LETTER'D
BLESSED'ST	CRUSH'D	EV'RY	HELP'D	LIFE'S
BLOCK'D	CRY'D	EXAMIN'D	'HEM	LIK'D
BORROW'D	CRYD'ST	EXERCIS'D	HERE'S	LIN'D
BOUNTIE'	CULL'D	EXIL'D	HE'S	LIV'D
'BOUT	CYNTHIA'S	EX'LENT	H'HAD	'LIVE
'BOVE	DAM'MEE	EXPLAT'ST	H'HAS	LIV'ST
BOY'D	DAMN'D	FAIL'D	H'HATH	LOCK'D
BRANDISH'D	DAM'S	FAIN'D	HIR'D	LOCK'T
BRANDISH'T	DAR'ST	FAIN'ST	H'OFFEND	LONG'D-FOR
BREATH'D	DEATH'S	FAITH'S	HOL'BORNE	LOOK'D
BREATH'S	DECAY'D	FALL'ST	HON'BLE	LOOK'ST
BREATH'ST	DECEIV'D	FAM'D	HONOR'D	LOV'D
BRING'ST	DECLIN'D	FASHION'D	HONOUR'D	LOVE'S
BRISTO'	DEEP-CROWN'D-BOWLE	FATHER'S	HOOD-WINK'D	LOVE'S
BRITAIN'S	DEFAC'T	FAULT'S	HOP'D	LOV'ST
BROUGHT'ST	DEFEND'ST	FEAR'D	HORL'D	LOW-COUNTREY'S
BRUIS'D	DEFIN'D	FENC'D	HOW-SO-E'RE	LUCINA'S
BRUSH'D	DEFORM'D	FENC'T	HUMOUR'D	LUST'S
BUS'NESSE	DELIA'S	FEV'RY	HUM'ROUS	MA'
BUTTER'D	DELIVER'D	FILCH'D	HUNT'ST	MAD'ST
BY'EXAMPLE	DENY'D	FIL'D	HURL'D	MAINTAIN'D
CAESAR'S	DENYD'ST	FILL'D	I'	MAK'ST
CAL'D	DESCRIB'D	FIR'D	I'AD	MANN'D
CALL'D	DESERV'D	FIST-FILL'D	I'AM	MAN'S
CALL'S	DESIGN'D	FIX'D	IF'T	MARK'D
CALL'ST	DESIR'D	FLANCK'D	I'HAD	MAR'LE
CAL'T	DESPAIR'D	FLATTER'D	I'HAVE	MASK'D
CAM'ST	DESPIS'D	FLATTERED'ST	I'LD	MATCH'D
CANCELL'D	DESTIN'D	FLATT'RER	IL'D	MAY'ADMIRE
CANKER'D	DESTROY'D	FLATT'RIE	I'LE	MAY'ANY
CAP'RING	DIANA'ALONE	FLATT'RING	I'LL	MAY'ST

MEASUR'D	POMPEY'S	SCATTER'D	SYDNEY'S	TH'ILL
MED'CIN'D	POOLY'	SCORN'D	SYLLAB'E	T'HIMSELFE
MEET'ST	PORC'LANE	SEAL'D	T'A	TH'INGRATEFULL
MESSALLA'S	'POTHECARIE	SEARCH'D	T'ACCUSE	THINK'ST
METTALL'D	POUR'D	SEAS'NING	T'ADMIRE	TH'INSCRIPTION
METTAL'S	PRACTIS'D	SEASON'D	T'ADORE	TH'INTENT
ME'UP	PRACTIZ'D	SECUR'D	T'ADVANCE	TH'INTERPRETERS
MEW'D	PRAIS'D	SEEK'ST	TA'EN	TH'IONIAN
MINERVA'S	'PRAY	SEEM'D	TAK'ST	THIS'S
MIS-CALL'T	PRAY'D	SEIZ'D	TALK'D	TH'ITALIAN
MISSE-CALL'D	PREDESTIN'D	'SELL	T'ALL	THO'
MISUS'D	PREFERR'D	SENT'ST	T'ALLEDGE	TH'OBSCENE
MIX'D	PREPAR'D	SEPULCHER'D	T'ALLOW	TH'OBSERVING
MOCK'D	PRESERV'D	SERV'D	T'AMEND	TH'OFTEN
MONEY'S	PRIAM'S	SEVEN-TONGU'D	TA'NE	TH'OLD
'MONGST	PRICK'D	SEVER'D	T'APPEARE	TH'ONE
'MONG'ST	PRIS'D	SEV'RALL	T'APPROVE	TH'OPINION
MORISON'S	PROMIS'D	SEW'D	T'AQUIT	TH'OTHER
MORNING'S	PROPHET'S	SEY'D	T'ASSIST	THOU'AST
MORROW'	PROPORTION'D	SH'	T'ATTIRE	THOUGHT'ST
MOURN'D	PROPOS'D	SHAMEFAC'D	TAX'D	THOU'HAST
MOV'D	PROP'REST	SHAMEFAC'DNESSE	T'EFFECT	THOU'LDST
MOV'ST	PROV'D	SHAP'D	TELL'	THOU'LT
MULTIPLI'D	PROV'ST	SHEE'LL	TELL'S	THOU'RT
MUNG'	PR'Y	SHEEP'ERDS	TEMPER'D	THO'WERT
NAM'D	PUI'NEES	SHEE'S	T'ENJOY	TH'OYLE
NAME'S	PURCHAS'D	SHE'HATH	T'ENVY	THREAT'
NARROW'D	PURG'D	SHEP'ARD	T'ESCAPE	THRIV'D
NATURE'S	PURPOS'D	SHEW'D	T'EXACT	THRONG'D
NEED'ST	PYRACMON'S	SHEW'N	T'EXCHANGE	THRONG'ST
NE'ER	QUESTION'D	SHEW'S	T'EXPECT	THROW'T
NE'R	QUICKLY'	SHEW'ST	T'EXPRESS	THUM'S
NE'RE	QUIT'ST	SH'HATH	T'EXPRESSE	TH'UNBEARDED
NO'	RAIGN'D	SHIN'ST	T'EXTRACT	TH'UNCERTAINTY
NOIS'D	RAIS'D	SHORT-LEG'D	TH'ACCOMPT	THUND'RING
NOONE-STED'S	RAK'D	SHOULD'ST	TH'ADMIR'D	TH'USURPED
NOTHING'S	RAM'D	SHOW'ST	TH'ADVANTAGE	TH'WERE
NOW'S	RANCK'D	SHRIN'D	TH'ADVENTER	THY'EPISTOLAR
NOW'T	RANK'D	SIGH'D	TH'ADVENTURES	T'IDOLATRIE
NUNCIO'S	RAP'D	SING'ST	TH'AEMILIAN	TIME'S
O'	RAP'S	SINNE'S	TH'AETERNALL	T'IMPRINT
OBTAIN'D	RAP'T	SIN'S	TH'AFFAIRES	T'INCREASE
OD'ROUS	RAVISH'D	SIXE-PAC'D	TH'AFFRIGHTED	T'INDITE
OFFER'D	RAV'LINS	SLIP'D	TH'AGE	T'INFLICT
OFF'RING	RAYL'ST	SMIL'ST	TH'AMBITIOUS	T'INHABIT
ONE'S	RAYN'D	SMUTCH'D	THANK'D	T'INHERIT
ON'T	RAY'SD	SO'ALONE	TH'ANTIQUE	T'INSTRUCT
OPE'	RAZ'D	SO'BOVE	TH'AONIAN	T'INVEIGH
ORDAIN'D	REACH'D	SO'T	TH'APPROCHES	TIR'D
ORD'NANCE	REAP'D	SOV'RAIGNE	TH'ARE	'TIS
ORD'RING	REAR'D	SOW'D	TH'ART	TITLE'S
O'RE	REASON'	SO'XCEED	TH'ASCENT	TO'A
O'RE-JOY'D	RECEIV'D	SPAR'D	TH'ASSEMBLY	TO'AVE
O'RE-PRAISE	RECK'NED	SPEAK'ST	THAT'S	T'OBAY
O'REWHELM'D	RECK'NING	SPENSER'S	TH'AUTHORS	T'OBEY
O'TH'	RECONCIL'D	SPI'D	TH'AVE	T'OBSERVE
O'THE	REDEEM'D	'SSAYD	TH'BEST	T'OBTAINE
OUT-LIV'D	REFIN'D	'SSAYES	TH'CALENDS	T'OFFEND
OVER-LEAVEN'D	RELISH'D	STAIN'D	TH'EARE	'TOFORE
OW'D	REMAYN'ST	STAMP'D	TH'EARES	TOOTH'D
OWN'D	REMOV'D	STAND'ST	TH'EATING	TOO'UNWIELDIE
PANDORA'S	RENOWN'D	STAY'D	THE'ELIXIR	TORT'RING
PARDON'D	REQUIR'D	STEEP'D	TH'ELABORATE	TO'T
PAS'D	RESERV'D	STIL'D	TH'ELIXIR	T'OTHER
PASQUILL'S	RESIGN'D	STIRD'ST	TH'ENAMOUR'D	TOTTER'D
PASS'D	RESOLV'D	STIRR'D	TH'ENVY'D	TOUCH'D
PASSION'S	RESTOR'D	STITCH'D	TH'EPILOGUE	TOUCH'T
PEARCH'D	RESTRAIN'D	STOOD'ST	THERE'S	T'OUR
PEIZ'D	RETAIN'D	STOOP'D	TH'ESCAPE	T'OUTLAST
PERCEIV'D	RETRIV'D	STOR'D	THESPIAD'S	T'OUT-STRIP
PERFORM'D	RETURN'D	STOUP'ST	TH'ESPLANDIANS	TRAIN'D
PERFUM'D	RETYR'D	STRAYN'D	TH'ETERNALL	TRANSFORM'D
PERJUR'D	REVERENC'D	STRETCH'D	THE'UN-USED	TRAVAIL'D
PHOEBE'S	REVIV'D	STRIV'ST	TH'EXAMINING	TRAVELL'D
PILL'D	REWARD'S	STROAK'D	TH'EXAMPLED	TRI'D
PIN'D	RIMEE'S	STUDIE'A	TH'EXCHANGE	'TROTH
PISO'S	RI'MES	STUFF'D	TH'EXPENCE	TRULY-BELOV'D
PISS'D	RIP'NED	STYL'D	THEY'ARE	TRY'D
PITCH'D	ROB'D	SUBT'LEST	THEY'AVE	TURN'D
PLAC'D	ROE'S	SUCK'D	THEY'D	T'USHER
PLAC'T	RU'DE	SUFFER'D	TH'EYE	'TWAS
PLAI'D	RUIN'D	SUMM'D	THEY'HAVE	'TWEENE
PLAY'D	RUL'ST	SUN'S	THEY'OFFENDERS	TWENTI'TH
PLAY'S	RUMOR'D	SUPP'D	THEY'RE	'TWERE
PLAY'ST	SACK'T	SUPPLY'D	TH'GODS	'TWILL
PLEAS'D	SAI'ST	SURLY'S	TH'HARD	'TWIXT
PLOUGH'D	SARUM'S	SURPRIZ'D	TH'HAST	UNALTER'D
PLUCK'D	SATURNE'S	SWALLOW'D	TH'HAVE	UN-APPEAS'D
PLUTO'S	SAV'D	SWAN'S	TH'HOW	UNCENSUR'D
POEM'S	SAW'ST	SWEAR'ST	TH'IAMBICK	UNCONTROL'D
POET'S	SAY'S	SWEET'S	TH'IDALIAN	UN-INFORM'D
POLISH'D	SCAN'D	SWELL'D	TH'IDES	UNLAY'D
POMP'D	SCAP'D	SWIFT-PAC'T	TH'IGNOBLE	UNLEARN'D

UNMAK'ST
UNPROV'D
UNREPAIR'D
UNSEASON'D
UNTOUCH'D
UNTRAVELL'D
UNWEARY'D
URG'D
US'D
USURER'S
UTTER'D
UTT'RING
UV'DALE
VALIANT'ST
VALU'D
VANISH'D
VENTUR'D
VERTU'
VERTUE'
VERTUE'ENFORME
VIEW'D
VOW'D
VOYC'T
WAK'D
W'ARE
WAS'T
WATCH'D
WE'ARE
WEAV'D
WE'AVE
WEE'L
WEE'LL
WEIGH'D
WELL-COMPASS'D
WELL-GRAC'D
WELL-GREAS'D
WELL-TRUSS'D
WER'T
WHAT'S
WHERE'S
WHERE'T
WHIL'ST
WHISPER'D
WHO'D
WHO'HAD
WHO'HAVE
WHO'IN
WHO'IT
WHO'LL
WHO'S
WIDOW'D
WILL'D
WISH'D
WI'THE
WONDER'D
WORK'ST
WORLD'S
WOU'D
WOULD'ST
WOUND'ST
WRECK'D
WRETCHED'ST
WRIT'ST
WRONG'D
Y'ARE
YEARN'D
YO'ARE
YO'HAD
YO'HAVE
YO'IN
YOND'
YOU'HAVE
YOU'L
YOU'LD
YOU'LL
ZEPHYR'S

STUDIE'A
T'A
TO'A
TH'ACCOMPT
T'ACCUSE
I'AD
TH'ADMIR'D
MAY'ADMIRE
T'ADMIRE
T'ADORE
HE'ADULTERS
T'ADVANCE
TH'ADVANTAGE
TH'ADVENTER
TH'ADVENTURES
TH'AEMILIAN
TH'AETERNALL
TH'AFFAIRES
TH'AFFRIGHTED
TH'AGE
T'ALL
T'ALLEDGE
T'ALLOW
DIANA'ALONE
SO'ALONE
I'AM
TH'AMBITIOUS
T'AMEND
TH'ANTIQUE
MAY'ANY
TH'AONIAN
T'APPEARE
TH'APPROCHES
T'APPROVE
T'AQUIT
SHEP'ARD
TH'ARE
THEY'ARE'
W'ARE
WE'ARE
Y'ARE
YO'ARE
TH'ART
TH'ASCENT
B'ASHAM'D
TH'ASSEMBLY
T'ASSIST
THOU'AST
T'ATTIRE
TH'AUTHORS
THEY'AVE
TO'AVE
WE'AVE
TH'BEST
HON'ELE
HOL'BORNE
SO'BOVE
HAU'BOY
HAU'-BOY
TH'CALENDS
COP'CES
MED'CIN'D
ABANDON'D
ABRO'D
ABSOLV'D
ABUS'D
ADMIR'D
ADOR'D
ADVANC'D
ALLOW'D
ALOW'D
ALTER'D
ANNOY'D
ANSWER'D
APPEAR'D
ARM'D
ARRAIGN'D
ASHAM'D
ASK'D
ASSAY'D
ASSIGN'D
ASSUR'D
ATTIR'D
AUTHORIZ'D
BANISH'D
BARR'D
BEDEW'D
BEG'D
BEGG'D
BEGUIL'D
BELCH'D
BELEEV'D
BELOV'D

BESIEG'D
BETRAY'D
BETTER'D
BEWAIL'D
BLAZ'D
BLOCK'D
BORROW'D
BOY'D
BRANDISH'D
BREATH'D
BRUIS'D
BRUSH'D
BUTTER'D
CAL'D
CALL'D
CANCELL'D
CANKER'D
CAPTIV'D
CARV'D
CAS'D
CATCH'D
CAUS'D
CENSUR'D
CHANC'D
CHANG'D
CHANGE'D
CHARG'D
CHEAR'D
CHERISH'D
CHOAK'D
CLAYM'D
CLEANS'D
CLEP'D
CLOATH'D
CLOS'D
COACH'D
COMPAR'D
COMPIL'D
COMPOS'D
CONCEAL'D
CONCEIV'D
CONDEMN'D
CONFIRM'D
CONFUS'D
CONQUER'D
CONTEMN'D
CONTINU'D
COSSEN'D
COVER'D
CRACK'D
CRAMP'D
CRAV'D
CRI'D
CROWN'D
CRUSH'D
CRY'D
CULL'D
DAMN'D
DECAY'D
DECEIV'D
DECLIN'D
DEFIN'D
DEFORM'D
DELIVER'D
DENY'D
DESCRIB'D
DESERV'D
DESIGN'D
DESIR'D
DESPAIR'D
DESPIS'D
DESTIN'D
DESTROY'D
DI'D
DIE'D
DIFFER'D
DIMN'D
DIN'D
DISCERN'D
DISCLOS'D
DIS-ESTEEM'D
DISGUIS'D
DIS-JOYN'D
DISPENC'D
DISPLEAS'D
DISPOS'D
DISPROPORTION'D
DISTINGUISH'D
DIV'D
DRI'D
DROWN'D
DUR'D
DY'D

EAS'D
ECCHO'D
EMBELLISH'D
EMBRAC'D
ENAMOR'D
ENCOUNTER'D
ENCREAS'D
ENDEW'D
ENGRAV'D
ENJOY'D
ENSHRIN'D
ENTAYL'D
ENVI'D
ENVY'D
EQUALL'D
ERR'D
ETERNIZ'D
EXAMIN'D
EXERCIS'D
EXIL'D
FAIL'D
FAIN'D
FAM'D
FASHION'D
FEAR'D
FENC'D
FIL'D
FILCH'D
FILL'D
FIR'D
FIST-FILL'D
FIX'D
FLANCK'D
FLATTER'D
FOLLOW'D
FORC'D
FORM'D
FRAM'D
FREEZ'D
GAIN'D
GATHER'D
GLAD-MENTION'D
GLISTER'D
GOWN'D
GRAC'D
GRIEV'D
GRUDG'D
GULL'D
HALLOW'D
HARBOUR'D
HARROW'D
HE'D
HEAP'D
HEAV'D
HEE'D
HELP'D
HIR'D
HONOR'D
HONOUR'D
HOOD-WINK'D
HOP'D
HORL'D
HUMOUR'D
HURL'D
IL'D
ILL-NATUR'D
ILL-PENN'D
ILL-TORN'D
ILL-US'D
IMBARQU'D
IMPOS'D
INCLIN'D
INCLOS'D
INCURR'D
INDENTUR'D
INDU'D
INFAM'D
INFLAM'D
INFUS'D
INQUIR'D
INSCRIB'D
INSPIR'D
INTERPOS'D
JOY'D
JUDG'D
KEEP'D
KILL'D
LABOUR'D
LACK'D
LASH'D
LATE-COYN'D
LAUGH'D
LEAP'D

LEARN'D
LEAS'D
LEAVEN'D
LETCHER'D
LETTER'D
IIK'D
LIN'D
LIV'D
LOCK'D
LOOK'D
LOV'D
MAINTAIN'D
MANN'D
MARK'D
MASK'D
MATCH'D
MEASUR'D
METTALL'D
MEW'D
MISSE-CALL'D
MISUS'D
MIX'D
MOCK'D
MOURN'D
MOV'D
MULTIPLI'D
NAM'D
NARROW'D
NOIS'D
OBTAIN'D
OFFER'D
ORDAIN'D
OUT-LIV'D
OVER-LEAVEN'D
OW'D
OWN'D
PARDON'D
PAS'D
PASS'D
PEARCH'D
PEIZ'D
PERCEIV'D
PERFORM'D
PERFUM'D
PERJUR'D
PILL'D
PIN'D
PISS'D
PITCH'D
PLAC'D
PLAI'D
PLAY'D
PLEAS'D
PLOUGH'D
PLUCK'D
POLISH'D
POMP'D
POUR'D
PRACTIS'D
PRACTIZ'D
PRAIS'D
PRAY'D
PREDESTIN'D
PREFERR'D
PREPAR'D
PRESERV'D
PRICK'D
PRIS'D
PROMIS'D
PROPORTION'D
PROPOS'D
PROV'D
PURCHAS'D
PURG'D
PURPOS'D
QUESTION'D
RAIGN'D
RAIS'D
RAK'D
RAM'D
RANCK'D
RANK'D
RAP'D
RAVISH'D
RAYN'D
RAZ'D
REACH'D
REAP'D
REAR'D
RECEIV'D
RECONCIL'D
REDEEM'D
REFIN'D

RELISH'D
REMOV'D
RENOWN'D
REQUIR'D
RESERV'D
RESIGN'D
RESOLV'D
RESTOR'D
RESTRAIN'D
RETAIN'D
RETRIV'D
RETURN'D
RETYR'D
REVERENC'D
REVIV'D
ROB'D
RUIN'D
RUMOR'D
SAV'D
SCAN'D
SCAP'D
SCATTER'D
SCORN'D
SEAL'D
SEARCH'D
SEASON'D
SECUR'D
SEEM'D
SEIZ'D
SEPULCHER'D
SERV'D
SEVEN-TONGU'D
SEVER'D
SEW'D
SEY'D
SHAMEFAC'D
SHAP'D
SHEW'D
SHORT-LEG'D
SHRIN'D
SIGH'D
SIXE-PAC'D
SLIP'D
SMUTCH'D
SOW'D
SPAR'D
SPI'D
STAIN'D
STAMP'D
STAY'D
STEEP'D
STIL'D
STIRR'D
STITCH'D
STOOP'D
STOR'D
STRAYN'D
STRETCH'D
STROAK'D
STUFF'D
STYL'D
SUCK'D
SUFFER'D
SUMM'D
SUPP'D
SUPPLY'D
SURPRIZ'D
SWALLOW'D
SWELL'D
TALK'D
TAX'D
TEMPER'D
THANK'D
THEY'D
THRIV'D
THRONG'D
TIR'D
TOOTH'D
TOTTER'D
TOUCH'D
TRAIN'D
TRANSFORM'D
TRAVAIL'D
TRAVELL'D
TRI'D
TRULY-BELOV'D
TRY'D
TURN'D
UNALTER'D
UN-APPEAS'D
UNCENSUR'D
UNCONTROL'D
UN-INFORM'D

UNLAY'D
UNLEARN'D
UNPROV'D
UNREPAIR'D
UNSEASON'D
UNTOUCH'D
UNTRAVELL'D
UNWEARY'D
URG'D
US'D
UTTER'D
VALU'D
VANISH'D
VENTUR'D
VIEW'D
VOW'D
WAK'D
WATCH'D
WEAV'D
WEIGH'D
WELL-COMPASS'D
WELL-GRAC'D
WELL-GREAS'D
WELL-TRUSS'D
WHISPER'D
WHO'D
WIDOW'D
WILL'D
WISH'D
WONDER'D
WOU'D
WRECK'D
WRONG'D
YEARN'D
UV'DALE
DEEP-CROWN'D-BOWLE
BETY'DE
RU'DE
LONG'D-FOR
SHAMEFAC'DNESSE
LACK'DST
SYLLAB'E
TH'EARE
TH'EARES
TH'EATING
T'EFFECT
TH'ELABORATE
TH'ELIXIR
THE'ELIXIR
B'EMBRAC'D
HEAV'EN
TA'EN
TH'ENAMOUR'D
VERTUE'ENFORME
T'ENJOY
L'ENVOYE
T'ENVY
TH'ENVY'D
TH'EPILOGUE
THY'EPISTOLAR
NE'ER
SHEEP'ERDS
T'ESCAPE
TH'ESCAPE
TH'ESPLANDIANS
TH'ETERNALL
T'EXACT
TH'EXAMINING
BY'EXAMPLE
TH'EXAMPLED
T'EXCHANGE
TH'EXCHANGE
T'EXPECT
TH'EXPENCE
T'EXPRESS
T'EXPRESSE
T'EXTRACT
TH'EYE
TH'GODS
H'HAD
I'HAD
WHO'HAD
YO'HAD
TH'HARD
H'HAS
LAMIA'HAS
TH'HAST
THOU'HAST
H'HATH
SH'HATH
SHE'HATH
I'HAVE
T'HAVE

TH'HAVE
THEY'HAVE
WHO'HAVE
YO'HAVE
YOU'HAVE
HAVE'HEM
T'HIMSELFE
FOR'HIS
TH'HOW
TH'IAMBICK
TH'IDALIAN
TH'IDES
T'IDOLATRIE
TH'IGNOBLE
TH'ILL
T'IMPRINT
B'IMPUTED
WHO'IN
YO'IN
T'INCREASE
T'INDITE
T'INFLICT
TH'INGRATEFULL
T'INHABIT
T'INHERIT
TH'INSCRIPTION
T'INSTRUCT
TH'INTENT
TH'INTERPRETERS
T'INVEIGH
TH'IONIAN
WHO'IT
TH'ITALIAN
WEE'L
YOU'L
PORC'LANE
HEE'LD
I'LD
YOU'LD
THOU'IDST
HE'LE
I'LE
MAR'LE
EX'LENT
SUBT'LEST
RAV'LINS
HE'LL
HEE'LL
I'LL
SHEE'LL
WEE'LL
WHO'LL
YOU'LL
DUE'LLISTS
LANC'LOIS
THOU'LT
HAP'LY
HAPP'LY
I'M
GENT'MAN
I'ME
DAM'MEE
RI'MES
BE'N
DRIV'N
EV'N
HEAV'N
SHEW'N
ORD'NANCE
COUNT'NANCES
TA'NE
RECK'NED
RIP'NED
PUI'NEES
BUS'NESSE
GI'NG
COS'NING
HEIGHT'NING
RECK'NING
SEAS'NING
T'OBAY
T'OBEY
TH'OBSCENE
T'OBSERVE
TH'OBSERVING
T'OBTAINE
H'OFFEND
T'OFFEND
THEY'OFFENDERS
TH'OFTEN
TH'OLD
TH'ONE
TH'OPINION

T'OTHER
TH'OTHER
T'OUR
T'OUTLAST
T'OUT-STRIP
TH'OYLE
NE'R
SOV'RAIGNE
SEV'RALL
E'RE
HOW-SO-E'RE
NE'RE
O'RE
THEY'RE
O'RE-JOY'D
O'RE-PRAISE
FLATT'RER
ADULT'RERS
INT'REST
PROP'REST
O'REWHELM'D
EMP'RICKS
FLATT'RIE
CHEV'RIL
CHEV'RILL
CAP'RING
CONQU'RING
FLATT'RING
OFF'RING
ORD'RING
THUND'RING
TORT'RING
UTT'RING
HUM'ROUS
OD'ROUS
THOU'RT
EV'RY
EVE'RY
FEV'RY
ALBIN'S
ALL'S
ANTICIRA'S
ANTICYRA'S
APOLLO'S
APOLLO'S
ARTE'S
AT'S
BB'S
BREATH'S
BRITAIN'S
CAESAR'S
CALL'S
CAP'S
CATO'S
CECILL'S
CLIFTON'S
CLOTH'S
COPP'S
COUNTRY'S
CYNTHIA'S
DAM'S
DEATH'S
DELIA'S
DIANA'S
DO'S
DOCK'S
DONNEE'S
DONNOR'S
ECCHO'S
EVENING'S
FAITH'S
FATHER'S
FAULT'S
FLATTRY'S
FOREHEAD'S
FYL'S
GOD'S
GODLY'S
GOLD'S
GREEK'S
HA'S
HE'S
HEE'S
HERE'S
IN'S
IT'S
JANIN'S
JOVE'S
KNIGHT'S
KNIGHT-WRIGHT'S
LADY'S
LEDA'S
LET'S

LIFE'S
LOVE'S
LOVE'S
LOW-COUNTREY'S
LUCINA'S
LUST'S
MAN'S
MESSALLA'S
METTAL'S
MINERVA'S
MONEY'S
MORISON'S
MORNING'S
NAME'S
NATURE'S
NOONE-STED'S
NOTHING'S
NOW'S
NUNCIO'S
ONE'S
PANDORA'S
PASQUILL'S
PASSION'S
PHOEBE'S
PISO'S
PLAY'S
PLUTO'S
POEM'S
POET'S
POMPEY'S
PRIAM'S
PROPHET'S
PYRACMON'S
RAP'S
REWARD'S
RIMEE'S
ROE'S
SARUM'S
SATURNE'S
SAY'S
SHEE'S
SHEW'S
SIN'S
SINNE'S
SPENSER'S
SUN'S
SURLY'S
SWAN'S
SWEET'S
SYDNEY'S
TELL'S
THAT'S
THERE'S
THESPIAD'S
THIS'S
THUM'S
TIME'S
TITLE'S
USURER'S
WHAT'S
WHERE'S
WHO'S
WORLD'S
ZEPHYR'S
RAY'SD
COR'SIVES
ALONG'ST
BE'ST
BECAM'ST
BEGAN'ST
BEGIN'ST
BLESSED'ST
BREATH'ST
BRING'ST
BROUGHT'ST
CALL'ST
CAM'ST
COM'ST
COMM'ST
CONCEIV'ST
COULD'ST
CRYD'ST
DAR'ST
DEFEND'ST
DENYD'ST
DID'ST
DISPEND'ST
DIVID'ST
DO'ST
DYD'ST
ERRANT'ST
EXPLAT'ST
FAIN'ST

FALL'ST
FLATTERED'ST
GAV'ST
GIV'ST
GO'ST
HAD'ST
HEAR'ST
HUNT'ST
JOY'ST
KEEP'ST
KNOW'ST
LEAV'ST
LIV'ST
LOOK'ST
LOV'ST
MAD'ST
MAK'ST
MAY'ST
MEET'ST
MOV'ST
NEED'ST
PLAY'ST
PROV'ST
QUIT'ST
RAYL'ST
REMAYN'ST
RUL'ST
SAI'ST
SAW'ST
SEEK'ST
SENT'ST
SHEW'ST
SHIN'ST
SHOULD'ST
SHOW'ST
SING'ST
SMIL'ST
SPEAK'ST
STAND'ST
STIRD'ST
STOOD'ST
STOUP'ST
STRIV'ST
SWEAR'ST
TAK'ST
THINK'ST
THOUGHT'ST
THRONG'ST
UNMAK'ST
VALIANT'ST
WHIL'ST
WORK'ST
WOULD'ST
WOUND'ST
WRETCHED'ST
WRIT'ST
GAM'STER
AS'T
BLANCH'T
BRANDISH'T
CAL'T
CHANC'T
DEFAC'T
DISGRAC'T
DO'T
DOO'T
ERE'T
FENC'T
FORC'T
HAVE'T
IF'T
IN'T
IS'T
KNOW'T
LAUGH'T
LOCK'T
MIS-CALL'T
NOW'T
ON'T
PLAC'T
RAP'T
SACK'T
SO'T
SWIFT-PAC'T
THROW'T
TO'T
TOUCH'T
VOYC'T
WAS'T
WER'T
WHERE'T
CAP'TALL
I'TH'

```
O'TH'
TWENTI'TH
I'THE
O'THE
WI'THE
I'THEIR
TH'UNBEARDED
TH'UNCERTAINTY
THE'UN-USED
TOO'UNWIELDIE
ME'UP
T'USHER
TH'USURPED
TH'WERE
THO'WERT
SO'XCEED
PR'Y
DO'YOU
```

HOMOGRAPHS

AIRE
ALTER
ARCH
ARMES
ART
AYRE
BAD
BANCK
BANKE
BANKES
BARE
BEARE
BEARES
BEE
BLOW
BLOWNE
BORNE
BOUND
BOW
BOWLE
BRAKE
BROOKES
BROWNE
BURDEN
BURY
BY
CASE
COB
COSEN
COURSE
CROSSE
DEALE
DONNE
DOWNE
DYE
DY'D
EARES
EVEN
FAINE
FAST
FELL
FIT
FITS
FLEET
FLIES
FLYE
FOWLE
GATE
GRACES
GRAVE
GRAY
GUILT
HARDIE
HART
HAST
HEARD
HIDE
HIGHT
HOOD
I
ILE
JARRE
JARRES
KID
KILLS
LAST
LAY
LEANE
LEAVE
LEAVES
LEFT
LEST
LIE
LIES
LIGHT
LIKE
LIST
LOCK
LONG
LONGS
LOOSE
LYE
LYING
MARKES
MARRY
MASSE
MAY
MEANE
MEET
MEETE
METTALL
MIGHT
MILL

MINE
MONE
MOUNT
MYNE
NEERE
NERE
ON
ONE
ONES
ORE
OUGHT
PAGE
PALE
PAN
PARISH
PIT
POST
PULSE
QUITE
RACE
RACK
RAILE
RANKE
RATE
REED
REPAIRE
REST
RESTS
RICH
RING
ROSE
ROW
RUSH
SACK
SAVE
SENT
SLEIGHT
SLIPS
SOOTH
SORTS
SOUND
SPELL
SPIT
STAY
STEEPE
STREIGHT
STRIPT
STROKE
SURLY
TALKE
TEARE
TEARES
TEMPLE
TEMPLES
TENDER
THAN
THEN
TIRE
TOYLES
TROTH
UTTER
VAINE
WARE
WAST
WASTE
WEARE
WELL
WHETHER
WHITE
WILL
WILT
WIT
WORTH
WRIGHT
YARD

Library of Congress Cataloging in Publication Data
(For library cataloging purposes only)

Di Cesare, Mario A
    A concordance to the poems of Ben Jonson.

    (The Cornell concordances)
    Basic text is the 1925–1952 ed. of Jonson's complete works by C. H. Herford
and Percy and Evelyn Simpson.
    Includes index.
    1. Jonson, Ben, 1573?–1637—Concordances. 2. Jonson, Ben, 1573?–1637—
Poetic works. I. Fogel, Ephim, joint author. II. Title. III. Series.
PR2645.D   821'.3   78–59630
ISBN 0–8014–1217–X